P I ...

Ann Wroe is the American editor of *The Economist*, and was formerly its literary editor. She is the author of *Lives, Lies and the Iran-Contra Affair* and *A Fool and His Money: Life in a Partitioned Medieval Town.*

ALSO BY ANN WROE

Lives, Lies and the Iran-Contra Affair
A Fool and His Money: Life in a Partitioned Medieval Town

'There are far too many "spiritual books" around which are problem-raising or problem-solving. Far too few are aware of the need to find a poetry and an imagination to equip us for the spiritual quest. This book has some of that rare quality. It is free from moralising clichés about wishy-washy leadership, and understands that our need is not so much to solve as to deepen the mysteries of faith. Christian people above all should know the Truth is not the same as erasing ambiguity'

Robert Runcie, *Sunday Times*

'An outstandingly accomplished book...Her erudition is extraordinary. She seems to have complete command of every relevant source for the past two millennia. Most brilliant is her showing of two cultures, Graeco-Roman and Jewish...What makes this book so magnificent is the writing...Wroe manages to create vivid word-pictures in just a few lines'

Kathryn Hughes, *Literary Review*

'A splendid biography...meticulous and eloquent...The reader discovers in a new way that evil and good are often deeply and mysteriously complementary; that religion has little to do with history as we understand it today; and that Christianity's success as a world faith is due to the *mythos* of Jesus's death and resurrection depicting a timeless truth, which each generation has been able to apply to its own circumstances'

Karen Armstrong, *The Good Book Guide*

Ann Wroe

PILATE

The Biography of
an Invented Man

VINTAGE

Published by Vintage 2000

2 4 6 8 10 9 7 5 3 1

Copyright © Ann Wroe 1999

The right of Ann Wroe to be identified as the author of this work
has been asserted by her in accordance with the Copyright,
Designs and Patents Act, 1988

First published in Great Britain in 1999
by Jonathan Cape

Vintage
Random House, 20 Vauxhall Bridge Road,
London SW1V 2SA

Random House Australia (Pty) Limited
20 Alfred Street, Milsons Point, Sydney
New South Wales 2061, Australia

Random House New Zealand Limited
18 Poland Road, Glenfield,
Auckland 10, New Zealand

Random House (Pty) Limited
Endulini, 5A Jubilee Road, Parktown 2193,
South Africa

The Random House Group Limited Reg. No. 954009
www.randomhouse.co.uk

A CIP catalogue record for this book
is available from the British Library

ISBN 0 09 928793 5

Papers used by Random House are natural, recyclable
products made from wood grown in sustainable forests.
The manufacturing processes conform to the environ-
mental regulations of the country of origin

Printed and bound in Great Britain by
Cox & Wyman Limited, Reading, Berkshire

For my husband

Contents

Introduction

'Why Pontius Pilate? Couldn't you choose a different subject?' cries the demon Woland to the Master in Bulgakov's *The Master and Margarita*. And well may the Master wish he had chosen something else. His novel about the fifth governor of Judea, the man who crucified Christ, has been rejected by his editor and savaged by the editorial board; so he has burned it in the stove, and now he finds himself in Doctor Stravinsky's hospital for the insane.

The Master tells his story to Ivan Nikolayich Poniryov, also in the asylum for Pilate-related reasons. The demon has sown thoughts of Pilate in Ivan's head. Because he cannot stop talking about him, he is being regularly injected with ether and subjected to reflex therapy with hammers. He is told that it is hazardous to his health to think about Pilate at all. Of course, he is not put off. He wants to struggle free and report everything to the police. The head of the asylum tells him, kindly, that if he were to turn up at the police station dressed as he is, in his underpants, saying he has met a man who has met Pontius Pilate, he would rapidly be recommitted.

'Because of my underpants?' Ivan asks.

'Chiefly because of Pontius Pilate.'

When I first read Bulgakov, I laughed at this exchange. Once Pilate was under my skin, I began to worry. How had he got there? Could he be made to go away? Did I really want to pursue this and, if I did, how much charred ash would my manuscript produce?

There were other difficulties too, beyond failure and scorn and madness. Pilate would bring me up against two redoubtable tribes, biblical scholars and classical experts, both of whom would pick holes in whatever I wrote, no matter how careful I was. I would be plunged into dark waters of anti-Semitism – for Pilate's reputation has often, though not always, risen and fallen with attitudes towards the Jews – and would be drawn into impossible controversies about the resurrection. I would find myself arguing over obscure dates and personalities I didn't want to spend time on, while Pilate – that strange amalgam of human struggling and human failing – would somehow slip away from me.

Friends were no help. 'Pilate? But surely we know nothing about him!' they'd say. Their next question, invariably, was either 'Are you going to do a whitewash job?' or 'So, was he a goodie or a baddie, then?' When I mumbled some response (I still do; how many flaws and failings, how often repeated, make up a bad man?), they would leap in with details they felt sure I would appreciate. One friend told me she had heard that Pilate was Hungarian (Hungarians, I'm sure, think he was Romanian). Another exclaimed: 'Ah! Fortingall!' His story was that Pilate was born in this village, seven miles west of Aberfeldy on Tayside, the son of a Roman ambassador and a daughter of the clan MacClaren. On the site of the earthworks there, known locally as the Praetorium, the Roman dignitary and his Scottish lass had somehow come together under the northern rain to produce a typically dour interrogator of Christ.

For three years or so I did research on him. My friends were right; there was almost nothing to go on. We do not even know his *praenomen*, the name his mother and wife and friends called him by. The only direct evidence we have for this man is one inscribed stone and a few small coins. All the records he kept, as he was bound to keep them, have disappeared, and so have two chapters of Tacitus, covering 30 and 31, that might have mentioned him. The only documentary sources for Pilate are a few paragraphs in the writings of Josephus, a Romanised Jew who wrote forty years after the governor was recalled from Judea; two or three pages from Philo of Alexandria, a defiantly non-Romanised Jew and one of Pilate's contemporaries; one neutral sentence in Tacitus, looking back from the time of Hadrian; and those almost too-familiar scenes from the New Testament. All these have their biases. They give versions of Pilate's character, but so wrapped in propaganda or agendas that it is difficult to detect what, if anything, may be true in them.

Plenty of people have tried to fill in the gaps, though. They have fallen over themselves to make Pilate up. Early Christian apocryphal writers scrambled to embroider his conduct before, during and after the trial of Jesus – especially after, when they imagined he began to feel Christian sympathies. Medieval writers invented his origins, which they took to be German, and built up his disreputable childhood and youth. Tremendous myths were created to account for the lost last years of Pilate's life. As a result, although the real Pilate is frustratingly hard to uncover, the mythological Pilate emerges ten feet tall.

This was the next stage of my research. I ransacked the London Library for the apocrypha and hagiographies of Pilate, written by obscure clerics centuries ago and translated with nineteenth-century enthusiasm into huge octavo volumes. I read fairy tales, legends, travelogues, guide books, to follow where his ghost had walked round Europe. With (almost) unflagging ardour, and usually in dusty solitude, I checked every life of Christ on the fifth-floor Theology shelves to track how Pilate had been seen by commentators in Europe and America for the past two centuries. Then, as an antidote, and to try to get close to some shadow of the Roman Pilate, I read whatever literature I could find from his lifetime or from shortly before or after. I did this not just to find out the duties of governors or the monstrosities of emperors, but to try to ascertain the view of the world someone in his position might have had. This would always have to be an approximation; however vivid, this Pilate-shadow would never be the real one. But it was better than nothing.

Friends sometimes suggested that I should just give up struggling, and write a novel about Pilate. But I always concluded that nonfiction – in the shape of a voyage through the various accounts of his life – would be much more challenging, more satisfying and often more fantastic. It would be the story of a man seen from dozens of different angles, in dozens of different colours. So that is how this book proceeds, as a collage of biographical scenes that move sequentially through the life: but some are Roman, some Victorian, some medieval, some early Christian, some even modern. Centuries may shift at the turn of a page, and so may the styles in which the scenes are written. But the constant thread, which readers should hold on to, is the life and character of Pilate from his birth to his death, and then some.

This is not a search for the 'real' Pilate. He can't be found. At best, all we have are glints and hypotheses. Nothing here – save that stone and those coins – is 'real' in the sense a biography can be when we have journals, letters, photographs, diaries or the memories of friends. Even the Roman reconstructions, though as plausible as I can make them, rely on the accounts of contemporary historians and writers with their own agendas, or on the experiences of other people. Everything is the surmise of different centuries, including the late twentieth century looking back at the first. We are all grasping at shadows.

Perhaps this striving to make Pilate up should just be dismissed as fiction. But then again, it isn't fiction at all: it's an attempt, made in different ways in every age, to express what the character of Pilate means and why he is important. The Pilate we think we know is a mixture of dozens of invented men, each symbolic of something: the State facing the individual, the pagan world opposing the Christian one, scepticism versus truth, ourselves facing God. He represents either man's free will, or his hopelessness before fate, or his struggle to distinguish good and evil, or the tyranny of hard choices. People ceaselessly project their own ideas and anxieties on him. They use him, and have always used him, exactly as they want to, often revealing in the process as much about themselves as they reveal about him.

Yet somewhere behind all this philosophy and fantasy lurks a flesh-and-blood Roman. And this world – this real world in which Pilate moved – is every bit as strange as the mythological one. It's tempting to feel we understand the Romans: that they were men and women much like ourselves, civilised, sophisticated, worldly, rational, only wearing different clothes. Pilate is often treated this way, as some modern man (of any age) distinguished only by his toga and his haircut. Yet there is of course another side, one of utter distance and difference. I was sometimes made startlingly aware of it: not just in the grand arcana of Roman myths and gods, or their revolting quack medicine, or their sensual appreciation of blood; but in the details.

Marcus Aurelius in his *Meditations* tries to describe at one point the beauty of small, almost unexpected, effects in nature. He mentions 'the cracks and little breaks in the surface of a loaf . . . figs, which, when they are ripe, open and gape; and olives, which when they fall by themselves and are near decaying, are particularly pretty to look at.' This image of putrescence as beauty brought me up short: these really were different eyes looking at the world.

This was the real reason I couldn't shake Pilate off. There was too thrilling a tension between the man and the symbols, between Pilate as he probably was and Pilate as we have imagined him. He saw the world in his way, but we all want him to see it in ours. And he was never really important in that provincial job of his; but he has become hugely important since.

This, then, is a book about all our Pilates. Some of these are familiar characters, but more are surprising. They have depths and contrasts that are unexpected. They do extraordinary things. Among these surprises, perhaps, are the hints we can occasionally get of a man actually walking on a marble floor in Caesarea, feeling his shoes pinch, clicking his fingers for a slave, while clouds of lasting infamy gather over his head.

Prologue: Pilate on the beach

On the seventeenth of September 1870, a gale of extraordinary force swept ashore in Blackpool. By eight in the evening, it was impossible to walk along the beach. Men in stovepipe hats and newsboys in caps struggled, bent horizontal, across the sandflats. The tide ran fast with unaccustomed foam; towards Ireland, the night sky towered like a bruised fist.

All night the wind blew. Behind the Manchester Hotel the sea destroyed the embankment of the Lytham and Blackpool railway; the rail bent and sagged over gaping air. In two places the waves crashed through the promenade, sweeping away field walls and pouring in a torrent across the Lytham Road. John Knowles, a local farmer, lost four fields of oats, reduced to a mass of blackened straw floating with the scum of the sea.

In the morning, bleary walkers found the water knee-deep inside the Blackpool gasworks. Bathing vans had been blown all over town, tipped on their sides in the middle of roads, or upended in fields far from the water's edge. Their spars stuck up like the horns of giant cattle. Oddest of all was the fate of the wooden confectioner's kiosk that had stood at the corner of the Foxhall Hotel. It was found upside down in the middle of the bowling green, as if challenging customers to exchange their woods for gobstoppers, jaw-breakers and fizzing sherbet balls.

Two days earlier, Her Majesty's Ship *Captain* was caught in the same gale off the coast of Finistère. The *Captain* was an ironclad battleship of a new and unusual design. She carried cannon on turrets at stem and stern; she boasted the tallest masts in the Royal Navy, and the greatest area of sail. The ship was 857 tons heavier than she should have been, and her sides were a mere six and a half feet above the water. During previous voyages to Vigo and back, water had often washed over the decks in relatively calm seas. The former Secretary of the Navy had condemned earlier ships of this design as 'wretched low-lying, ill-ventilated, wave-washed, unworthy abortions'. Even the *Captain*'s captain recognised her liabilities: that at an angle of more than 21 degrees, for example, she could not right herself. His advice was trenchant: 'Don't hesitate if you get into bad weather to furl all sails, use steam and get her bow to the sea.'

The *Captain* had been out with the rest of the squadron that afternoon, all flying their ensigns about twenty miles west of Cape Finistère. Admiral Milne, on board the *Lord Warden*, admired the *Captain*'s speed but noticed that, even in a moderate wind, the sea was washing over the lee side of her decks. By midnight the barometer had fallen and the wind had increased. Milne saw the *Captain* 'heeling over a good deal to starboard, with the wind on her port side'. At about 1.30 a.m. he noticed that he could not see the *Captain*'s red bow light; but by then it was 'thick with rain' and the *Lord Warden* herself was labouring in a heavy cross-sea. Milne never saw the *Captain* again.

On board the *Captain* herself Robert Hirst, an able seaman, was stationed on the fore-deck for the starboard watch. Like most of the officers and crew, he was a west countryman. His frightened burr still sounds in the account he gave later to the man from *The Times*.

There was a strong wind, and the ship was then under her three top sails, double reefs in each, and the foretopmast staysail. The yards were braced sharp up, and the ship did not seem to have much way upon her. As the watch was mustered, I heard Captain Burgoyne give the order, 'Let go the fore-top sail halliards', followed by, 'Let go fore and main topsail sheets.' By the time the men got to the topsail sheets the ship was heeling over to starboard so much that the men were washed away off the deck, the ship lying down on her side as she was gradually turning over, and trembling with every blow which the short jumping seas (the sea was now white all round with the squall) struck her, and the roar of the steam from the funnels roaring horribly above everything, and continuing to do so even when under water.

Hirst and two of his companions rushed to the fore-deck netting and jumped overboard. Almost at once, they found themselves washed scrambling and sliding on to the ship's bottom; and then the ship went down, taking them with her.

The next thing Hirst knew he banged against a floating spar, to which he tied himself with his black silk handkerchief. It kept him buoyant for a while, until the tie broke. Tossed here and there on the foaming seas, he managed to catch hold of the stern of one of the *Captain*'s launches, still with its canvas cover lashed round it. Clinging to the cover were half a dozen other men. One produced a knife, hacked away the canvas, and set the launch floating. Hirst and his colleagues then tried to row back to the *Captain* to rescue Captain Burgoyne, but the boat was immediately swamped by the sea, and two men were washed out of her. Back went Hirst a second time, bailing out the boat with a cap, but so many oars had been washed away that the craft was barely manoeuverable in the raging seas. 'Nothing could be done,' he concluded; 'Captain Burgoyne was away to starboard, clinging to the bottom of a boat, in all that storm of broken water.'

All this time, they had not been alone. They had been able to make out the red and green bow lights of the other members of the squadron, but could not attract their attention. Their companions never knew they were in trouble. After the squall, as the weather moderated, the heavy bank of clouds rolled away to the east; the stars came out, and the moon shone down on an apparently empty sea.

At last, at around five in the morning, the drifting remnants of the *Captain*'s crew saw another light, that of the Finistère lighthouse. Day was breaking. The men struggled to the shore and collapsed. By good fortune, they had found the only place on that rock-bound coast where a safe landing was possible.

Five hundred men had been on board the ship. Eighteen survived. Captain Cowper Coles, who had designed the *Captain* despite his complete lack of training in naval architecture, was drowned in his own invention. In the morning, as the disconsolate squadron regrouped, there seemed to be no trace of the missing vessel. But by sunset the *Psyche*, coming up from Vigo, reported having passed 'two cutters, painted white, bottom up, with a large amount of wreck'. Among the wreckage floated the body of a seaman with 'Rose' marked on his flannel underwear.

There was one more survivor. Before the *Captain* sailed the second lieutenant, John Trevithick, had cut a parchment page from an Ethiopian manuscript and given it to a friend, a sailor on HMS *Malibu*. It is doubtful whether Trevithick could read the Coptic in which the manuscript was written. He had been on attachment to Lord Napier's expedition of 1858, helping to chart a course for ships through the Hormuz Strait at the entrance to the Persian Gulf. Boxes of such manuscripts had come home with him as plunder. The page in question was attractive, with well-spaced, looping Ethiopian script traced in black ink and scattered with red ornamental crosses, which formed the points of punctuation. One column was almost filled with a painting of a group, one man and five women, placing a body in a tomb. It made a decent present. The rest of the manuscript, no doubt pretty too, went with Trevithick's luggage in his cabin on the *Captain*.

A few months later, Trevithick's friend handed in the page to the Ashmolean Museum in Oxford as a curiosity. And it is curious enough. Beneath the scene of the burial stands a man in priest's vestments, his arms outstretched. He is praying in the manner of ancient and modern Christians, palms uplifted and fingers spread. Unlike the swarthy figures at the tomb, this man is white-faced: a European. It is Pilate at the tomb of Jesus, making a profession of repentance.

To the Victorians who saw it and translated it, this relic was unbearably poignant. The only written remnant of the wreck of the *Captain*, beyond poor Rose's nametapes sewn in his flannel vest, was Pilate's prayer for forgiveness from the man he had sentenced to death: a prayer which, in its short Coptic cadences, also reads like the words of a man gasping for air.

> I believe
> that you have risen
> and have appeared to me, and
> you will not judge me,
> oh my Lord, because I acted
> for you,
> fearing this
> from the Jews.
> And it is not that I
> deny your resurrection, oh
> my
> Lord. I believe
> in your word and in the
> mighty
> works you wrought
> among them when you

4

> were alive, you raised
> many
> dead. Therefore, oh my God,
> be not angry with me
> because of what

A whole fantastical story was originally wrapped around this prayer. Most of it has since become part of the silt and sand at the bottom of the Bay of Biscay, or perhaps has been cut out of fish on the kitchen slab, as rings and jewels were cut out of cod in the fables of old Europe. Trevithick's page itself turned out to be missing its bottom half, so that the columns of script broke off in the middle; even this tiny part of the story was in inconsequential pieces. Yet it remained disturbing and strange.

On the page that survives, the Jews and Pilate have quarrelled after the burial of Jesus. The governor has gone to the tomb; it is not 'proper' or 'desirable', the Jews tell him, that a high Roman official should do that. Besides, the body laid in the tomb is not even Christ's; disquietingly, it belongs to someone else. Why should Pilate cause such horror among the Jews on account of some corpse of no importance? But Pilate is disconsolate, thinking of the evil that has been done by the 'injustice' of the crucifixion of Christ. He begins to pray for the resurrection. As he stretches his hands over the tomb, a voice comes from inside, from the mouth of the dead: 'Roll away the stone, my Lord Pilate, that I may come out in the power of my lord Jesus Christ.'

The next section is lost, but it is clear that a miracle occurs. Pilate cries out in joy, and is next found standing at a distance in a state of rapture and enchantment. He himself has raised the dead; and besides, the cloths that are left are heavy with the sweetness of Christ. He had noticed that before, begun to tremble before, even as he had approached the tomb.

> he said,
> 'Oh my brother, don't you see
> how
> it smells and is beautiful, the
> fragrance
> of that linen cloth, and it is not like
> the smell of the dead, but like
> the fine purple of kings'
> wrappings?'

The Jews therefore said
to Pilate,
'You know yourself how Joseph
put spice on him,
and incense, and rubbed him with
myrrh and aloes, and this is why
they smell fragrant.' And Pilate said,
'Although they put ointment on the
linen cloth,
why is the whole sepulchre
like a chamber, which has in it
musk and sweet spices, and is warm
and smells fragrant?' And they said,
'The perfume you smell, Pilate,
is the smell of the garden
which the winds blow into it.'

So the wind blew. The wind of God that had upended the *Captain*
and had whirled the little sweet stall across the close-cropped green
beside the promenade, scattering humbugs and toffees and sticks of
coloured rock, now blew out sweetness from the sepulchre of Christ.
The Jews said it was no miracle, no reversal of corruption; only the
wind in the garden. But as he stood beneath the lifting branches, with
the breeze in his hair, the pagan governor began to believe. Or so the
Ethiopians said.

It was only a fragment, after all. Like so many other scraps of Pilate's
story, it survived only by chance. Yet it is still worth laying these
fragments out, as on that desk in the Ashmolean (if the daylight is dim,
you can adjust the lamp) to see if they approximate the outline of a life.

I

The Forum and the forest

The most plausible account runs as follows: that he was born a few years before Christ, somewhere in Italy, most probably in Rome. But this was not, in the deepest sense, his country. His ancestors were mountain men from Samnium, south of Rome. There in the brutal hills the men scratched at stony plots, the women spun wool; they worshipped oak-groves and springs and woodpeckers, and their talk was of war. From time to time the Samnites would descend to the poppy-strewn fields of Campania, which they devastated. For years they fought the Romans, but in 290 BC Rome defeated them. The struggle had always been unequal.

After that defeat – much of their territory gone, and their power broken – the Samnites slowly and sourly picked up Roman ways. Some even became citizens. But they were still mostly peasant-fighters, as intractable as their mountains; and when civil war broke out between Marius and Sulla in 86 BC, the Samnites tried to wrestle free again. This time Sulla defeated them just outside Rome itself, right by the Colline Gate, and the reprisals were brutal. Those Samnite leaders that survived were executed; their mountain villages were burned like torches; the people were killed or scattered, and soft-skinned Roman colonists were sent to take their places.

Cicero, writing about it later, described this as the milder sort of war. The Romans were not fighting the Samnites as enemies, only as rivals for supremacy. They thought them rough and brave as Spartans; they respected them. But the difference in treatment was sometimes hard to perceive. Cicero himself described how, after the 'respected' people of Marseilles had forfeited their supremacy, a wooden model of the city

9

was carried through Rome in triumphal procession 'to show the world that they had been defeated'. In the case of the Samnites, though the names of their various families were scattered all over northern and central Italy, the polity was destroyed. There would never again be a mountain redoubt where people dreamed of liberty in quite the same way.

That is why we do not know where Pilate was born. His tribe, the Pontii of Samnium, was dispersed and broken. The Samnites were known in Rome as rustic buffoons, gallumphing creatures who were wild and clumsy as horses; Horace described one he met on the road, with such a scar on his face from the removal of warts 'that he could dance the Cyclops-shepherd dance without a mask.' The older ones spoke not Latin but Oscan, primitive country words that Pilate may have heard from his grandfather: 'sollo' for *totus*, 'abzet' for *habet*, 'pipas' for *clamas*; 'Petis pipas?', addressed to a child, meant: 'What are you chirping for?' Even in the gladiator's ring these men were comic turns. It was traditional to deck them out in parti-coloured plate and helmets with huge bobbing crests, in mockery of the gorgeous new armour they had once worn proudly, according to Livy, to one of their defeats by the Romans. They would go into the ring heavily but ludicrously armed, with wooden swords and quarter-staffs, and simply belabour each other for hours, until darkness fell and the audience went home.

Yet the tribe of the Pontii was of the Samnite nobility, and it was not without heroes. The Pontii were even slightly larger than life, numinous with legends and fame. If Pilate's father ever aspired to an *atrium*, an entrance hall decorated with painted wax masks of the family ancestors (in which a small boy could slide on the tiles in his slippers), it might well have contained a mask of Gavius Pontius, who had defeated the Roman army in 321 BC in a high mountain pass called the Caudine Forks. Under those walls of rock, loud with the sound of water, the Romans had fallen on their faces. But Gavius Pontius did not kill them. He simply took their weapons, made them strip to their tunics and sent them under a triumphal yoke of three spears lashed together. Thirty years later, he met the Romans again; they took him prisoner, sent his own men under the yoke and killed him, showing him no shred of the mercy he had shown them. The defeated Samnites, too, were made to strip to their tunics, giving up to the Romans the marvellous leather belts, studded with bronze clasps, that were the symbols of their liberty. Only the buffoon-gladiators wore such belts after that.

Next in the parade of family heroes came two brothers, both of whom had been caught up in the fighting in 82 BC after the Social War. Many of the Pontii were Roman citizens now, but they had been weaned on the legend of Gavius. The first brother, Pontius Telesinus, commanded the Samnite contingent for Marius against Sulla; he died beside the Colline Gate as the battle raged in the dark, cut down on the point of entering Rome. Those Samnites who survived were slaughtered by Sulla in the Campus Martius, where Pilate might later have wrestled or played hand-ball in the dust.

The brother of Telesinus was besieged with Marius' son in Praeneste, outside the city. Heartlessly, Sulla sent them the severed heads of Telesinus and his men. At the sight of those gagging faces, with white eyes and bloodied hair, they resolved to die by one another's hands. The younger Marius drew his sword and offered it to the breast of his friend, who fell on it. He then drew it out, shining with Samnite blood, and fell on it himself. 'And so perished,' wrote a modern Italian historian, 'the noblest and last of the sons of Italy, the soul of resistance to Rome.'

These were the stories: a collection, thrilling as a Boys' Annual, of desperate battles, struggles for liberty, magnanimous gestures, heroic sacrifices. The boy Pilate could glean from them that mercy shown to your enemies was both noble and futile: had Gavius Pontius killed those Romans, he might not have died by public execution. From the scene in the cell in Praeneste, where the two friends embraced each other and the cold blade in the dripping darkness, he could deduce that suicide for the honour of one's nation was the ultimate act; and that death was all the nobler for being premeditated, sealed by mutual resolution and carried out with quiet efficiency. There were many such deaths to admire, from Socrates onwards.

There were lives to admire, too: for many of the Pontii had struggled after the dispersal, and their sense of illustriousness was difficult to recover. They had lost a generation of young men in the 80s BC, the generation of Pilate's great-grandfather, and for fifty years afterwards the Samnites scarcely appeared in any public capacity in Rome. Still, they tried. Within two generations the most thriving members could be classed as just below patrician rank, respectable but decidedly second class. Julius Caesar recruited Samnites for their valour; they became *equites illustriores*, then special administrators, prefects and private imperial trouble-shooters. Yet not all could escape their origins. Titus Pontius became one of Caesar's centurions in the civil war; when he refused to abandon his leader he became a hero of sorts, but only of sorts. 'The great lights of our country,' wrote Valerius Maximus, 'will not be offended to see big-hearted centurions [like Titus] beside their own glorious and resplendent names . . . Nobility should encourage, not scorn, a natural goodness that springs from the breast of obscurity.' A little later on, gracious Valerius summed up Titus again: *Sine ullis imaginibus nobilem animum!* 'What a noble soul, even with no masks of the ancestors in the hall!'

It may have been during these years – if Pilate did not earn the name himself later – that the cognomen *Pilatus*, skilled with the javelin, became attached to his family. Javelin-throwing was thought to have come from the Samnites anyway, and the Oscan version of *Pilatus*, *ehpeilatus,* has been found on an inscription from Capua. It was another clue to Pilate's origins: an indication of the violent past that beat, however faintly, behind him.

So his father, if not Pilate himself, held and balanced the javelin, which quivered in his hand like something living. This was the second skill of the Roman soldier, after he had been trained in the use of sword and shield. The *pilum* was five feet of wooden shaft and two feet of tapered iron, of which the bottom half was left soft and untempered. When the point lodged in a shield the shaft would bend and hang down, making it impossible to throw back. A trained javelin-thrower could tilt his heavy weapon skywards, flex his body, hurl the javelin thirty yards, and hit the mark. His training had consisted precisely in aiming at a fixed target, aiming again, aiming again, until his arm, bruised from the effort, could smoothly direct the missile anywhere he wanted. If you were called *pilatus*, it meant you excelled at doing that: that you showed decisiveness, strength, straightness of aim. But not all qualities could be transferred from the field of battle to public life.

His army service done, Pilate's father probably settled down as a member of the Roman knightly class. We assume this because prefect-governors in the early empire were knights and sons of knights; it was not yet done to open the postings to freedmen. His father, then, had his own large house, with an atrium and colonnaded garden and piped water; several slaves would wait on him. He had a patron to whom he would present his morning greetings, but also a few men dependent on himself. Perhaps, like so many of the knights lampooned by contemporary writers, his aspirations ran ahead of his taste in furnishings, tableware and statues; perhaps, like them, he needed to impress and feel secure. And the vital element of his security was his children, the next generation. These would be given every piece of ceremonial, training and education, in order eventually to clamber back to the noble rank the *gens* had held before. By the time Pilate was born, the clan of the Pontii was on the point of producing Roman consuls and Roman millionaires, and the expectations had grown accordingly: the official's *toga praetexta* with its purple border; a private bath, with windows overlooking a view; a litter for the streets; a villa by the sea. Wordlessly, these ambitions were laid on the shoulders of the next male child in line.

No one knows what Pilate's first name was. As a child, whether he was called Marcus or Gaius or Lucius would have mattered; but as he grew older his friends and even his lovers would have used his cognomen, *Pilate* with three syllables in the vocative, when they talked or wrote to him. *Mi Pilate*, my Pilate, would have been a term of endearment or a nickname for the man; but his mother bending over his cradle would have whispered a name that history has rubbed away.

As a baby he would have been presented to the gods and given a *bulla*, a little golden pouch containing a lucky charm, which was hung around his neck. As a child he sat through several years of rote-learning in school, scratching with a metal stylus on a wax slate over which his long curls fell, absorbing the rudiments of mathematics, reading, rhetoric and writing. In order to write, he would put his small hand inside the strong hand of an adult; together they would trace the wobbly characters, until he was ready to draw them on his own. A rich boy would have slaves to carry his book-rolls; perhaps Pilate had one, or perhaps he carried the rolls himself, 'slate and satchel slung over his left arm', as the poets described it. At Saturnalia in December he was given presents: sweets, nuts and little terracotta figures you could fight with, at least until they broke. Richer boys got ponies and parrots.

In the last years of school he learned, like a little lawyer, to unpick the multiple sides of every question. The questions were well-worn: 'Should Alexander have sailed the ocean, or not?' 'Should the Spartans have fled when they were sent against Xerxes?' 'Should Cicero have begged Antony's pardon?' Each had its series of set opposing answers, the different 'colours' of the schoolman, and these he would have learned too, declaiming them as well as he could with the right hand-movements and the right pitch of his breaking voice. This may have been most of his training in the practice of the law.

At the age of seventeen he would have been given his first ceremonial shave in front of the family shrine. The down was consigned to a tiny decorated box; then, dressed in the white toga of a new adult, the *toga virilis*, he was taken through the Forum to pray in the temple of Jupiter. The *bulla* was left behind at the family shrine, among the statuettes and fading flowers; and there may have been times in the years ahead when he regretted the leaving of that little piece of luck.

His days now had to be spent preparing for a career in public service. This usually meant trying for a commission in the army as a junior officer, for which he would need a recommendation to the commander. He would begin, therefore, the routine Roman round of getting himself known and noticed by the powerful. In the morning he would pay his respects, arriving at dawn at the entrance hall of the man he hoped would be his patron. He would have to wait until the *nomenclator* (only a slave, but the sort of slave who revelled in his authority) noticed him in the throng of hopefuls and passed on his name to his master. The nervous greetings were passed on too: *Quid agis? Quid commode vales?* 'How are you? I hope you're well?' and in exchange might come a commission, a recommendation, or a little money. By these means he learned the essential etiquette of Roman life: all paths to advancement lay through politeness, persistence, and the favour of richer and nobler men.

Horace described the ritual in painful detail. As soon as he aspired to any rank or any noble friendship, he wrote, 'people start asking, "Who is this fellow? What was his father?"' Approaching the would-be patron was agony:

On coming into your presence, I said a few faltering words, for speechless shame stopped me from saying more. My tale was not that I was a famous father's son, nor that I rode about my estate on a Saturian steed; I told you what I was. As is your way, you answered little and I withdrew; then, nine months later, you sent for me again and bade me join your friends. I count it as a great favour that I pleased you . . .

Part of Horace's social disadvantage, though he did not say so, was that he was a provincial, from Venusia in Apulia. Those 'few faltering words' showed that he was still rough-cut, without polish, and with a country accent that could be heard; he still needed to learn the soft urbanity of Roman speech and manners, as perhaps Pilate did.

At last, somehow, the right impression was given. Having found a patron, Pilate would do whatever tasks he was assigned. He would run errands, take messages, whirl between the rich man's house and the Janus Arcade where the bankers were. Sometimes he would ride in his patron's carriage as his companion, where (by Horace's account) he would be favoured with such conversation as 'What's the time?' or: 'Do you think Thraex is a match for Syro the Chicken?' But on his free afternoons he would enjoy himself. At the games he and his friends would sit for hours on the hard benches, discussing the muscles and stamina of fighters and the blows they had endured. There was no greater thrill than to see a man still fighting, still struggling out of the dust, when he was painted like an actor with the streams of his own blood. At that point the nameless criminal or captive, oiled and caged and conveyed to the circus in a cart, acquired a name and a reputation; he acquired the dignity of a man. And he died with that dignity on him, his own scarlet cloak.

Young men would build up their bodies in conscious imitation of their heroes. To be strong in every way, *vir fortis ac strenuus,* the steely character in the steel-hard body, was the Roman ideal. Together Pilate and his friends would attack the baths in style, leaping in off the side, splashing all and sundry with their ferocious strokes, wrestling one another like dolphins, belting out songs in the wonderful echo of the changing rooms. In the exercise yard they ran, lifted weights, did the long-jump and played ball until their bodies were pink with effort; then, exhausted, they made for the wineseller and the hot-sausage man. They were oiled and rubbed on adjacent tables, hung their clothes on adjacent pegs, used the same cold sponge in the latrines, fainted for the same mistresses.

Possibly Pilate was treated to a repetition of the famous lecture on sex once given (the story ran) by the philosopher Archytas to Herennius Pontius, the father of Gavius. Cicero related this story in his treatise 'On Old Age', recording too that Herennius was so deeply studious and intellectual that he had debated with Plato. 'No more deadly curse than sensual pleasure,' Archytas told Herennius, 'has been inflicted on mankind by nature. It is a fruitful source of treasons, revolutions, secret communications with the enemy. In fact, there is no crime, no evil deed, to which the appetite for sensual pleasure does not impel us . . . Intellect is the best gift of nature or the gods. To this divine gift and endowment there is nothing so inimical as pleasure . . . since, when more than ordinarily violent and lasting, it darkens all the light of the soul.' But perhaps your soul was not too much darkened if, during the Floral games in April, you watched the actresses take their clothes off.

In any case, sex took second stage when the call to the army came through. It probably took Pilate away from Rome for years. There seems not much doubt, from the record of his actions in office, that he was a soldier first and a diplomat second. Some have imagined he fought as a legionary, acquiring a taste for blood he never lost. Yet his class dictated against it; and if he had really been a foot-soldier, the sort of blunt and thick-headed strongman who is sometimes pictured, he would hardly have risen to become the governor of Judea. Legionaries spent their careers in the army, but Pilate clearly joined in the military tribune class that would lead, eventually, to a foreign posting as the governor of a province.

In the late Republic there was no longer an obligatory five-year stint of service before a man became a military tribune, or legionary staff officer; the minimum age for the office was eighteen, when a boy had scarcely shaved and might have been a soldier for only a year or so. His duties could be rigorous; but the experience could also be as much a shambles as military service in France in the 1970s. 'Although our early manhood was spent in camp,' wrote Pliny, 'it was at a time when merit was under suspicion and apathy an asset, when officers lacked influence and soldiers respect, when there was neither authority nor obedience, and the whole system was slack, disorganised and chaotic, better forgotten than remembered.'

Pliny, bound for the civil service, would leave in a couple of years; but Pilate seemed to take the harder path. He probably did several tours of military service, both as a military tribune and as a prefect of cavalry or auxiliaries. Since he was a commanding officer, even of a relatively lowly sort and barely out of his teens, he wore lighter armour and had few encumbering weapons. The mark of his office was the *parazonium,* a waist-band that carried the sword on his left side, where ordinary soldiers wore it on the right. When he drew his sword the action was statelier and slower, crossing his chest like a half-salute; and he was not required to do it so often. The hardest marching, too, was not required of him. Slaves carried his gear; lowlier soldiers dug the ditches and put up the camp palisades. Superior commanding officers included him in their meetings, and sometimes offered him dinner in their tents.

Pilate was less a fighter than an administrator, keeping things straight behind the lines. For this he was paid 50,000 *sesterces* a year: about as much, the elder Pliny noted, as some connoisseurs would pay for a nice chandelier. He was in charge of the pay, food and floggings for his unit; he had to keep his men motivated and see they did not desert. Modern soldiers would call it a soft billet. Yet it was still active military service. He took the same oath as any foot-soldier, every third of January and on the anniversary of the emperor's accession, to obey the emperor and his superior officers. Inside the camp palisade he would sleep as the others did, wrapped in his regulation red cloak under the cold stars, and in the morning he too woke to the long summoning blast of the army bugle. He ate the same porridge, drank the same sour wine – the wine that was offered to Jesus on the cross – and sang the same bawdy songs, like the mocking soldiers' tribute to Julius Caesar known as 'The Triumph over Gaul':

> Watch your wives, everyone, here we've got a man
> Who may be bald but fucks the girls in any way he can.
> Guess who's spent your money on many a Gallic
> whore?
> He's used up every penny, and he's coming to borrow
> more.

Not least, he took part in the same wars of conquest. Some suppose he fought in the German campaigns of Tiberius in AD 9 or Germanicus in 14, where it was sometimes cold enough to wear trousers and ride along muffled in a cloak. These were campaigns of victory, fought by legions nicknamed 'The Triumphant' and 'The Indomitable' to impose the peace of Rome on bearded and foul-smelling barbarians. Whether or not he was fighting, Pilate would have ridden out most mornings, his bridle heavy with his service medals, to see the standards with their silver medallions and wreaths and eagles flashing in the sun; and most evenings, tired, hungry, aching, he would relive his part in the day's engagements. He was not constantly in the thick of things, but he was sometimes close enough to be in danger of enemy spears and to dread that his horse would be cut down under him; close enough to see the dilated eyes of the enemy and hear again the screams of the dying as he lay in the dark.

This was unlikely to have bothered him. The war he was fighting was generally considered a good one, a war for the future of civilisation, protected by the gods. Military discipline, wrote Valerius Maximus at about the time Pilate left for Judea, was 'the principal glory of the Roman empire and its most secure foundation'; it was the one ancestral virtue that had been preserved intact by the soft and corrupted Romans of his day. Others among the prefects and tribunes, more languid young men doing their part-time service only because they had to, may have taken a more cynical view; like Catullus, they may have called it 'playing billiards with our world'. But even military-tribune Pliny, not much of a soldier, could recall with emotion 'life under arms, the camps, bugles and trumpets, sweat and dust and heat of the sun'; and Pilate probably took his soldiering seriously.

He could have gone to Judea straight from his military postings, and never become a civil servant in Rome. Yet he was not without position there. He was possibly a knight, an *eques,* by virtue of successive tours of military service; and it is likely that by inheritance he was also an *eques* in the civilian sense, with a minimum net worth of 400,000 *sesterces.* That would buy him two medium-sized houses in the city. He was entitled to wear a gold ring and to sit in the first fourteen rows at the theatre, where he would not be 'elbowed or besmirched by the mob', as Martial put it; although he was not so elevated that, naked at the baths, he could not be gently but firmly moved aside by the slave of an equally naked man of praetorian rank.

As a professional soldier, he did not have to stay abroad to qualify for governorship of a province. Although many governors-to-be passed through the same junior ranks, ending up as a military prefect on some difficult frontier, what was important was to catch the attention of the powerful at the right moment. For that, it was useful to linger in the city for a while. His family was known there; another of the Pontii, C. Petronius Pontius Nigrinus ('the black-haired one') was a consul when Tiberius died in 37, and there were other rich and influential relations. But Pilate's own reputation still rested on exploits performed far away, and he would need to burnish it somehow at home.

If he stayed for a time in Rome, he may have become a member of the Praetorian Guard, the 1,000 strong personal bodyguard of the emperor himself. Tiberius, obsessed with security, had reorganised the guard, taking them out of their scattered lodgings round the city and giving them a permanent camp in which to nourish their *esprit de corps.* If Pilate was among them, this would explain (since Praetorians were famous for it) his well-attested public devotion to the emperor, his cult and his welfare. And it might have produced an association that was to make, as well as almost break, him.

Many scholars suppose that Pilate was taken under the wing of Lucius Aelius Sejanus, the brutal commander of the Praetorian Guard who, from 23 to 31, held sway over the emperor's affections. Tacitus wrote that Tiberius, 'always dark and mysterious with others, was carefree and outspoken only with him.' Sejanus was hardy, daring and spirited, but he could affect humility when he needed to; he was a strange combination of the energetic and the watchful. In his military duties he ingratiated himself with the troops, perhaps with Pilate too, by mixing with them and learning everybody's names. Some of those names he would then put forward to advance his own designs.

Sejanus commended himself to Tiberius by his efforts, in 22, to put out the fire that almost destroyed Pompey's theatre. When the theatre was rebuilt, a bronze statue of Sejanus was placed in it. Others were put up round Rome and in the shrines of the legions, and his birthday was publicly celebrated with the burning of incense and candles before them. But he was deeply unpopular. Like Pilate, he was a knight, not a noble; he was something of an upstart and, worse, an ambitious one. This made him anathema to Roman historians, even without his misdeeds. According to them, Sejanus wished to destroy the older heirs of the imperial house in order to gain control over the younger ones, and he was not scrupulous about how he achieved his end. He was said to have murdered Tiberius' son Drusus by slow poison in 23 with the connivance of the victim's wife; and it is possible that Pilate glimpsed Tiberius, already greying and withdrawn, on the day when, as Tacitus recorded, he came to the Senate to rebuke the senators for weeping for his son. He made a speech of perfect, indeed chilling, composure until the very end, when he suddenly appealed to the consuls 'or anyone else' to relieve him of his power. Tacitus thought these remarks were stupid; they may have been merely tactical, to shore up his authority. But what might Pilate have made of this show of humanity and despair on the part of his emperor?

Sejanus then began to work towards the downfall of the rival house of Germanicus, headed by his widow Agrippina. He sowed fears in the emperor's mind about the threat of civil war, and succeeded in getting two of the widow's close friends charged with extortion and treason. Other charges followed against other enemies of Sejanus; all of them fell, as the favourite wormed himself still deeper into Tiberius' affections. But in 25 Sejanus overplayed his hand by asking to marry Livia Julia, the widow of Drusus. His letter to Tiberius and the emperor's reply, included by Tacitus in the *Annals*, are possibly both forgeries. But, genuine or not, they give a vivid impression of the social handicaps of an *eques* such as both Sejanus and Pilate were.

Sejanus said he was deeply grateful for the favours he had received. He insisted that he had never sought high office, because it was an honour merely to serve such a master as Tiberius, to whose ear he brought his hopes and desires 'as readily as to the gods'. He could think of no honour higher than marriage to a member of the imperial house;

and Augustus himself, after all, when he was looking for a husband for his daughter, had considered men of equestrian rank. So, if Livia Julia was thought to be in need of a husband, would the emperor kindly think of him?

Tiberius, in answer, said he would speak plainly. Livia Julia, already in her seventies and once the wife of Gaius Caesar, would never agree to grow old with ' a mere Roman knight'. Even if he, Tiberius, agreed to it, the leading men in the state would never do so; they already thought Sejanus had been promoted well above 'the permissible levels of equestrian advancement'. Yes, Augustus might have considered equestrian suitors for his daughter. But he went no further; she had married nobles. If Sejanus continued to prove his devotion and his usefulness, 'there are no heights you may not reach'; but for the moment, nobility was out of the question.

Rebuffed, Sejanus went on plotting. Over the next months and years he persuaded Tiberius to leave the smoke and noise of Rome and go into exile in Capri, surrounded by Greek scholars; he poisoned his mind still further against Agrippina, engineering an imperial dinner party at which she refused to take apples, imagining them poisoned, from the emperor's hand; and he managed to save Tiberius' life by shielding him from a rock-fall as he dined at a villa called 'The Cave'. His sense of power was perhaps never greater than when, crouching on hands and knees, braced beneath the rocks, he found himself face to face with the terrified emperor, only inches between them; and calmly held his death away from him.

For four or five years now, Sejanus had been suggesting appointments. He had recommended men as centurions, as tribunes and as governors. At dawn the leading citizens would congregate in his house, bringing the private petitions they wished to communicate to Tiberius. It is likely that Pilate was a regular too until 26, the year that he was posted. He too must have known that hall at first light and sat on the famous couch that eventually collapsed, on New Year's Day in 31, under the weight of all the petitioners. Sejanus' recommendations to the emperor in the 20s were seldom turned down. If he had suggested Pilate for the governorship of Judea, Tiberius would have concurred.

Yet there is no firm evidence that Pilate was Sejanus' creature. He was certainly not so close to him that after his fall he had to die, as several other governors did. Sejanus would have known and presumably approved of him; Pilate for his part, whatever his private feelings, would have been careful to remain in his favour. And maybe that was all.

Tiberius was also known to make governors on a whim, on no formal recommendation. Tacitus gives some idea what his criteria were: decent behaviour, good character, but not 'outstanding merit', because that might threaten him. At times, too, 'decent behaviour' was put aside. Pomponius Flaccus was made governor of Syria on the strength of a thirty-six-hour orgy of drinking, with the immortal imperial endorsement on his commission: 'A good fellow at all hours, day or night!'

In 22, during the trial of a former governor of Asia, one senator suggested that it might be an idea if no one 'of scandalous life and reputation' were allowed to be a governor in future; it might save grief. But Tiberius disagreed. Many governors, he said, had surprised people, since 'important positions stimulate some natures and blunt others'. His candidates were often unknown quantities, clay to be moulded by fate. He preferred them that way.

Pilate's presumed Samnite origins would not have commended him. Tiberius disliked both Samnite-style gladiators and the 'old Oscan farce', a long-running series of hit shows called 'The Comedies of Atella' which featured young male actors in the grotesque roles of Bucco the Braggart, Dossenus the Hunchback, Maccus the Glutton and Pappus the Dotard; he had closed such shows down and sent the actors packing. But he seemed to trust Pilate enough (or thought him insignificant enough) to send him to his province once he had appointed him, rather than detain him in Rome on trivial excuses, which was the fate of several other governors.

So, one day, Pilate received his imperial promotion. It came on a five-leaved wax tablet, the official form; the standard response was to go to the temple to offer thanks and sacrifice. And then the knight Pilate, blooded in war, approved by the favourite, but still full of social insecurities and with his Samnite chip on his shoulder, set off for Judea.

*　　*　　*

So runs one version of Pilate's early life. But a second, proposed with equal confidence, holds that he was a Spaniard. Giovanni Rosadi, an Italian magistrate, put forward this theory fully-fledged in 1908; but several sorts of Spanishness had been claimed for Pilate centuries before.

Some said he was born in Seville, a city whose residents had the right of Roman citizenship. There is a large house off the Plaza de Arguelles, built in a mixture of gothic and Moorish styles, with marble doorways, Roman columns, Spanish balconies, iridescent blue tiles and a garden which, in nineteenth-century guide books, was running wild and scattered with sculpture like a stonemason's yard. This was known from the fifteenth century, and is still known, as Pilate's house, although it was also the palace of the dukes of Alcalá. It boasts a *praetorium*, or governor's judgement hall, and the table on which Judas is meant to have thrown down his thirty pieces of silver, as if they had been carted back as souvenirs of Pilate's time in Judea.

Alternatively he was born in Tarragona on the coast of Catalonia, the citadel city where the great Augustus wintered after his Cantabrian campaign. This was another favoured imperial town, with golden ramparts on the seaward side. Among these ramparts, in a great square tower, 'a ruin among ruins', Pilate was born. The walls were twenty feet thick in places and, as late as the 1950s, the tower was still in use as a prison. Every eastern window looked towards Rome across the crawling sea. Tarragona smelt of fish and onions; white banners of cambric fluttered from the houses, and the slow *sardana* was danced in its squares. Pilate stayed and soldiered in the region for some years, and troops from Tarragona were supposed to have formed the 'Italian legion' that later scourged Christ outside the real *praetorium*.

The little Spaniard was called Lucius: Lucius Pontius Pilate. He grew up crunching garlic, sucking on oranges and revering the black bulls of Las Marismas; but he was also taught to look on Rome as the centre of the world. His father, Marcus Pontius, fought in the Cantabrian campaign and helped to suppress the Asturians, although he should by rights have defended his fellow Iberians against the might of Rome. For this treachery he was honoured and given the title *Pilatus*. Lucius followed after him, joining the suite of Germanicus and fighting with him through the German campaigns. Then, still young, he made for Rome, intending to have fun.

Spaniards in Rome had a flashy reputation, even a dangerous one. Any brigand or robber was 'a Spaniard'. Spanish sea-captains, Ovid said, dealt only in meretricious baubles, and their wine was good only to get drunk on. Being Spanish and knowing no one, Pilate needed to ingratiate himself. He became an *adsectator cenarum*, a supper-scrounger, one of those young men found loitering in bands on street corners in the evenings, hoping to be invited to dinner; or one of those sycophantic morning greeters, all smiles and fluttering Spanish scarves. The poet Catullus described one such irritating Spaniard he knew, who would flash his bright white teeth on every occasion: in court, as the defence wound up a moving peroration, or at funerals, 'where on every side

22

heartbroken mothers weep for only sons.' Perhaps, Catullus mused, this Spaniard was merely trying to prove that he washed his teeth; but all civilised people did that. The only difference he knew was that Spaniards used their morning urine as mouthwash.

So Pilate, saturnine and ingratiating, hung around Rome, and especially round the court of the emperor. Men like him were called *umbrae*, shadows clinging to their patrons. He was at the edge of every intrigue, behind every curtain. In the interests of self-improvement, he made himself as servile as possible: there was nothing he would not do. He was prepared to cut up the courtiers' food and wait beside their litters; if the mere shadow of the emperor crossed his path, he would abase himself before it. He kept his own pride, which was considerable, locked up like a wasp in a bottle, and was prepared never to release it if that would help in his advancement.

One day, at the court of the emperor, he caught sight of a girl. Not just any girl: this was Claudia Procula, the youngest daughter of Julia, the daughter of Augustus, who had married Tiberius as her second husband. The notion that Pilate's wife came from the imperial house was popular from the earliest years of Christianity; it gave an extra edge to Christ's defiance if his judge was so close to the emperor. Julia, the story ran, had been banished by Tiberius for her passionate and adulterous behaviour; and in exile she had taken up with a Roman knight, Claudia Procula's father. At the age of thirteen, Claudia Procula was sent to Rome to acquire noble manners and to find a husband. She was spirited, pretty, curious and intelligent; at least some of her blood was royal. A marriage might have been arranged for her with any of the young men at court. But the one who asked for her, who worked his way for several years towards that tremendous request, made of the emperor himself, was the strange young Spaniard with the haunted eyes and the strained, determined servility; and Tiberius agreed.

Their courtship, socially unequal as it was, did not follow the practice of other young Romans. Ovid in his *Amores* described the usual mating games: hanging round the Palatine Hill or the Temple of Diana to lure girls from the giggling, bangle-jiggling crowd; writing words in wine on the table at parties; the endless exchange of wax tablets with scribbled notes, 'Come tonight', or 'Don't come'; the snuggles and cuddles in the close press of the race-track or the gladiator shows, fanning your partner with your programme, adjusting her stool and her cushion, letting her bury her head in your shoulder when the action became too bloody to watch. Even if Pilate enjoyed these flirtations with other girls, the daughter of the imperial house demanded a certain distance: as when a man was obliged to watch his love from a different couch at a dinner party, unable in the dim light to see the subtle sign-language used by lovers, and too far away even to touch her slippered foot with his own. He would content himself then with tiny, poignant acts. When she passed the cup, he would brush with his lips the place where she had drunk; when she passed the bread, he would touch it where she had done; at night, silently, he would leave on her doorstep the chaplet of roses he had worn at the party. And after a while she would notice him.

On the day of the wedding all was as it should have been. The auspices had been consulted. The hall of Procula's house was hung with flowers and branches, and a garland of myrtle was fixed on Pilate's door. Procula, with her hair in six braids and wreathed with flowers under a veil the colour of flame, was led into the hall. Pilate, also crowned with flowers, waited for her while the contract was signed and then took charge of her. He took her right hand in his, and they were married to each other.

Among the twelve witnesses to the wedding was Tiberius himself. The imperial signet ring was impressed into the soft wax of the marriage-seals, and the imperial litter, attended by eight slaves, waited outside the house. Procula left first, with her girlfriends, to start the procession to Pilate's house. She ran down the steps in her yellow slippers, while behind her the pitch-pine torches showered sparks into the dark. Scattered voices sang the bride-song, 'Io! Hymen Hymenaeus!', and the flutes sang out like nightingales. Pilate made to follow her, burning to possess her on the myrtle-strewn bed in his own house, but he found himself snagged by a grey, aging hand: the hand of Tiberius. The emperor said nothing. Instead, he fumbled inside the breast-fold of his toga and drew out a scroll of paper. He handed it to Pilate, climbed into his litter, and was carried unsteadily away.

The paper was Pilate's order to leave at once for Judea. A war-bireme was already in the harbour, waiting to take him to Caesarea. He was to be the governor. It seemed an important posting; but it was also an exile and a punishment for having dared to marry so far above himself.

Meanwhile, Procula and her friends were nearing the door of his house. The ill-omened torches still tossed in the darkness, far away. The happy cries were fainter; the flutes had become the whine of insects. How did Catullus describe what was meant to happen next?

Shed your concealment!
new bride,
hear our bride-speech,
see, the shower of torch-flakes!
shed your concealment!

Your husband will lie
only in the valley of your breasts,
a hero caught in your arms
as the grape pole
caught in the twisting vine.
See! the day fades:
shed your concealment!

Venus will shine for him
in the vague night,
blaze
at midday.
The day fades.
New bride, shed your concealment!

But Pilate stood in the street without her. The last onlookers watched him curiously, wondering what he would do. In one hand he held the order, in the other the bag of walnuts and confetti which the new bridegroom was meant to scatter to the crowd. His wreath of flowers was still on his head. But between conjugal love and the emperor's order there was no competition. Heartbroken, he turned and walked towards the harbour.

He did not see his wife again for six years. But out of the depths of his bitterness and sadness and sexual frustration, he tried to rule over Judea.

★   ★   ★

That is the second version. But a third, hugely popular in Europe from the Middle Ages onwards, insists that Pilate was German. He was born at Forscheim, near Mainz, on the Rhine. This was sandy country, a region of fir woods and hop gardens; the air smelled of beer and resin. A pasture near the town, with cows and horses grazing the uneven ground, is still called Pilate's Field, and his red trousers – the favourite colour for a child's first pair of trousers in this part of Germany – were still on show in 1936 in the Forscheim museum.

The story is found in the *Golden Legend*, a thirteenth-century compendium of lives of the saints, and in dozens of other chronicles and songs. Jacobus de Voraigne, the friar who compiled the *Golden Legend*, admitted even then that it was apocryphal; he had 'read it in a history'. But it was worth retelling.

Back in the days when rulers were skilled in the seven liberal arts, there was a king whose name was Tyrus. He was born in the diocese of Maginise, in a castle called Leich, in the district of Babenberg. This king loved to hunt; but in the evenings, when he could no longer see the shadowy stags among the trees, he studied philosophy, as kings do. He understood the temperance and humours of the air; he measured the span of heaven; he observed the astrological signs and the courses of the stars. He knew everything.

From his observations with his 'subtle engine', and from the vellum pages of his great books, he saw that he was going to sleep with a woman and produce a line of descendants who would rule over many lands and islands. But on the day he had this illumination he was a long way from his wife, out hunting again. Indeed, he was a long way from any woman at all. He made quickly for the nearest city of the district, sending before him the message that if anyone knew of a woman good enough to sleep with him, they should bring her at once. For Tyrus preferred to lie with anyone he could find, promptly and unfussily, rather than lose the hope of fathering a great dynasty.

His men went out, following their lord's orders, and searched the neighbourhood. At last they seized on a girl called Pila, pretty enough, the daughter of a moneyer. They led her to Tyrus, and he slept with her that night just as he slept with his wife; then, pulling on his long hunting boots, he galloped away. The deed was done. Pila conceived a child who was royal, or at least half-royal, and when she had carried the baby as long as she had to, she gave birth to him. But then a problem arose. The baby had to be given his father's name, and Pila did not know the name of the king she had slept with. So she took her own name, Pila, and the name of her own father, Atus: and called him Pilatus.

She was proud of her invention. It sounded noble and respectable, more respectable than one would suppose for the child of a moneyer's house. Indeed, in its bourgeois aspirations it smacks of nothing so much as the name Henry Boffin chose for his daughter in *Our Mutual Friend*, a name to match the garish drawing-room furniture, the too-small flowery carpet, the wax fruit under glass shades and the eight volumes of Gibbon displayed on a table: 'Henrietty Boffin, – which her father's name was Henery, and her mother's name was Hetty, and so you get it –'. The Pilate of the York mystery play required his knights to 'get it' in just the same way.

> My mother was Pila, Pila the proud,
> Pila the proud had Atus for dad,
> Pila plus Atus – how does that go?
> Yes, bold knights! That's Pilatus!

Not everyone thought the child's father was Tyrus; some thought it was 'Sir Caesar, that excellent emperor', waylaid during his German campaigns. In the York play Pilate's wife Procula purred over this 'joyful genealogy', but her dreams of connection with 'gentry' were dashed by other versions of the story. According to these, Pila was no moneyer's daughter, just a bad brothel girl, 'a lazy, stinking nurse, a piece of dung, who conceived in a night of two ribalds rolling together.' The grubby tryst was not in Babenberg but in Lyons or Mainz, near the River Zei. There the king, who was himself called Atus, stumbled out of the woods under a sky filled with stars, a long way from the city. He and his companions found an inn, where they feasted and drank prodigiously to while away the hours. After a time, the king noticed the stars that blurred and danced outside the dim window, and made his prophecy of greatness to come. There was no queen to hand; but there was Pila, a serf's daughter. His men said: 'You shouldn't miss this chance, sir.'

The king was quickly persuaded. 'Matters raced on'; in no time, Pila was pregnant, and the child was born. A messenger was sent to tell the king the news. As Atus rejoiced in the birth of his wonder-child, the bringer of victories, the messenger asked: 'Do you have a name for him, your majesty?'

'Let's have something easy,' said the king. 'I'm Atus, his mother's Pila; join them together, that makes Pilatus! Call him that.'

So the messenger returned. He went back either to the inn on the edge of the forest, or to a serf's hut, or, as some say, to the dwelling of Pila's father, a mill on a stream in the depths of the woods. There, bending over the crude wooden cradle, he bestowed the name of Pilatus on the tiny child.

As the child grew, these were his memories. In the moneyer's house, the fierce glow of the forge; hands adjusting a balance; shavings of silver that bit into the skin; the pleasurable shifting of coins in a purse. In the inn, violent nights; floors being slopped down in the morning; candles in extravagant icicles overhanging their sconces; the iron taste of wine mingling with the sweetness of milk. In the serf's hut, smoke, oatmeal, cows' breath. In the mill, water ceaselessly roaring and foaming; white meal in the folds of a dress, or on the reddish hairs of an arm; the damp green powder of moss on a fence; a boat, half-submerged, with its cargo of black leaves.

However shadowy these scenes, they had a proper geography. They belonged in Lyons, in Mainz, in Babenberg, somewhere along the wooded border of Germany fringing on Gaul. Pilate came from the edge, the appalling German forest gloomy with firs and overrun with wolves. He wore barbarians' cloth trousers, his hair was flaxen, and in his cold blue eyes was the gleam of the north. A fourteenth-century poem from Vienne, in the foothills of the Alps, left no doubt of his ancestry:

Teutonicae gentis, crucifixor omnipotentis.

This was the forest where Publius Quinctilius Varus had come with his Roman legions in AD 9 only to see them slaughtered to a man, pinned among the crowded trees; and it was where Germanicus in 15 had come to avenge him, gathering and piling up the bones of the dead for dreadful mass funerals. Tacitus described the first sight of that woodland clearing, scattered with white bones and pieces of spears, skulls grinning where the barbarians had nailed them to the mangled firs; and in the dreams of one horrified Roman commander Varus himself, coated with blood, rose up from the marshy ground.

Tiberius too had campaigned there for Augustus, eating and sleeping on the bare ground under the stars, and counting it a lucky omen if his lamp blew out in the dark. In that dark, in the depths of the forest, strange birds flashed like fire. Here the trees grew so thickly that swords and shields were caught in them, and branches snared your clothes as you tried to run away. And supposing you ran, you might blunder into one of those sacred coppices where the Germans worshipped what Tacitus called 'that mysterious something' that could not be contained within walls; or into a grove where white horses that had never been ridden raised their heads from the close-cropped grass.

Medieval listeners gave this setting an even stranger coloration. This was the land where young men, sent out on difficult journeys, became confused and enchanted. They would find their path branching in the woods, with the easier way leading to misery and the harder to treasure, honours and love. In hopes of remembering where they had come from, they would scatter crumbs behind them; but the birds would devour them. Here, behind towering thickets of thorn, princesses would prick their fingers and shed their blood in fulfilment of old prophecies; but then they were kissed awake, and every stone knight and sleeping hound would stir into life around them. Here trees talked, cloaks made men invisible, and bargains were struck that brought nothing but grief to the proposer; while, in the dark vaults of the forest, the merest touch of light was enough to send a benighted prince wandering the face of the earth for seven years.

Here Pilate grew up. Some say he was prudent and good-looking; indeed that, like the child Jesus, he increased every day in wisdom and beauty:

> *Crevit Pilatus et fit prudens adolescens,*
> *corporis et mentis gemina virtute nitescens.*

Others say that he was dragged up, never punished, and 'proud as a toad'. Cassius Parmensis' scurrilous description of the child Augustus would have suited him: 'You're a lump of your mother's meal, which a money-changer took from the nearest bake-house and kneaded into some sort of shape, with his hands all discoloured from the fingering of money.' When he was still a boy – as young as three, some say – he was sent to the king his father. The king was delighted to see him; but this was a child who dragged trouble in his wake.

The king and queen already had a son of their own, about the same age as Pilate. Pilate enjoyed playing with him, and as they grew older the two often wrestled, or boxed, or shot at birds with a sling. But the king's son was always a little better than Pilate: not only of nobler birth, but also more skilful, faster and stronger. This began to rankle. Their arguments multiplied, until they could be found in furious tangles on the grass or bleeding in the corridors. Pilate was so consumed with jealousy, and already so bilious with liver trouble, that one day he simply killed his rival with a huntsman's twist of the neck.

Prostrated with grief, the king and queen called a meeting of the royal council to determine Pilate's punishment. The councillors, however, were cautious. 'We weep for you and your wife,' they told the king.

'But if one son is dead, how will it help to kill the other? Pilate deserves punishment, for sure. Indeed, he deserves death, but it would be better to warn him never to do such a thing again. Don't kill him; send him to Rome, and make sure he never comes back.'

So the boy Pilate, the slayer of innocence, was sent to Rome. He went as blood money, replacing the annual tribute which the king his father sent to the emperor. But no sooner had he arrived there than he fell into trouble in all kinds of ways. As he himself put it later, in one of the medieval 'songs' of his life, 'My heart was boiling with all the ardour of youth, even though I was only so high. When those folk from Lyons sent me to Rome, they did what they liked and I did what I liked, for good or bad.' In fact, he fell in with a fine young nobleman, the son of the king of France, or possibly the son of the king of the Angles. He played and sparred with him, just as he had with his brother; and, more or less inevitably, jealousy overcame him again. In the course of a heated argument, he put his hands round his friend's white neck and throttled him.

Now it was the Romans who wondered what to do with him. He deserved death all over again, but they could not insult his royal father. Perhaps such a ruthless young man could be useful to the empire. They could send him somewhere safely far away to put down the enemies of Rome. There was, as it happened, a savage island called Pontus off the coast of Asia Minor, famous only for producing poisonous herbs and beaver-oil. The most poisonous weed of all, yellow aconite, grew thickly there round the mouth of the cave that was one of the back doors to the Underworld. The people were shaggy and uncivilised, roaming among trees that ran with red resin as thick as tar; in one eye they had a double pupil, in the other the image of a horse, and they could not be drowned even with their clothes on. They had never accepted a ruler; instead, they had put all their would-be lords and kings to the sword. In that same medieval song, 'Caesar' – any Caesar, any emperor with a beard and crown – sent Pilate to take charge of them, since he thought his wickedness would tame their perversity. 'And if it doesn't,' he remarked, 'then he can get what he deserves.'

Pilate, who was no fool, realised that his life hung in the balance. To everyone's surprise, once he reached Pontus he conducted himself modestly, with verbal threats and blandishments rather than killing. He even lived honestly. The people took to him, and he became popular; they obeyed his laws and behaved themselves. Pilate made such a success of the job that he was called, after the island, Sir Pilate of Pontus, or Pontius Pilate.

From afar, in Jerusalem, King Herod noticed him. He liked his methods, and invited him to be his chief justice in Judea. There Pilate amassed enormous power and huge heaps of silver. He was dangerous, clever, brittle, beautiful and cruel, 'a perilous prince' in every sense. He and Herod were friends at first, in a watchful sort of way. But when Pilate petitioned Tiberius for all the authority and privileges that Herod possessed, and tried to buy the office of justice for life – the *Golden Legend* said – 'with so much money you could hardly count it', the king fell out with him. From then on, relations were strained between them. And it was Pilate alone, with his German soul, his love of the forest, his *Wanderlust*, his huntsman's indifference to killing, who was left to rule the country where Christ had already been born.

*   *   *

This Roman or Spanish or German Pilate was pictured however men imagined him. In early Christian sarcophagi and ivories he is a stocky judge in a shoulder-clasped cloak. In a sixth-century mosaic at Ravenna he has grown a neat dark beard and has melancholy eyes; in a thirteenth-century fresco by Giotto he is clean-shaven and vigorous, with a golden chaplet on his head. In either case his face is benign, and his robes long like a lawyer's; he has thin protesting hands. The Pilate of early medieval iconography was always simply a civilian ruler, with no hint of the military about him. He was neither good nor bad but reasonable and baffled, in line with the version of his character that had sprung up in the apocryphal versions of the New Testament. There was no suggestion that he would get his way by anything other than the rule of law.

This changed around the fourteenth century, as residual neutrality about Pilate faded and he became both a dandy, and a prototype bad man. His robes began to shorten (short or girded-up robes being then, as in Roman times, the mark of a man of action) and he acquired exotic hats and weapons. Only his ghost, which haunted the shores of a little lake in the Swiss Alps, dressed plainly, in the red robes of a local magistrate. When colour was applied to Pilate, he tended to alternate between gold, the colour of nobility, and red, the colour of blood: literally becoming, as Oscar Wilde described him, 'the scarlet figure of history'.

Most medieval manuscripts show him bearded, with a decorated tunic and a nobleman's hat. Stage directions for the Lucerne passion play stipulate that he should be 'a German nobleman, finely dressed, with pointed hat, heathenish, civilian coat with sleeves down to his knees, sabre and boots, sceptre or staff.' The accounts for the Coventry Corpus Christi play show that Pilate's expenses ran to a cloak, a hat, a canvas doublet (22d), gloves (4d), gold braid (2d) and a skein of green silk for the mending of his gown. The medieval stage Pilate was an aggressive fashion-plate, treated by everyone (including himself) as the most handsome figure in the house. In the York play, he pointed out that this was only natural:

> For I'm the loveliest lapped and laid, with favour fair in my face; my forehead is brown and broad, and my eyes glitter like gleam in the glass; my hair glistens like gold wire; my cheeks are both ruddy and red, and my colour is clear as crystal.
> I'm as blithe as blossom on briar . . .

Nobody dared contradict him. 'Loveliest lord, we bow to your beauty,' was a typical greeting not only from his servants, but also from the chief priests of the Jews, who seemed to shrivel in his presence as if he sapped the life from them.

Yet apart from the mystery plays, in which the actor who played Pilate was sometimes paid more than Christ for his vigorous command of the action, his portraitists tended to make him passive and almost dreamy. Among these creations, none is stranger than the haunting Pilate of Piero della Francesca's 'The Flagellation'. At first glance, it seems that Pilate should be the man who stands in a group of disinterested observers in the foreground, a close-cropped, bull-like thug with a broken nose and a gorgeous gown of blue and gold brocade. But no; he is a lean, distant figure, in a recessed room lined with marble columns where the flagellation of Christ is taking place. He sits, as Pilate probably sat in life, on a spindly curule chair (the X-shaped chair of judgement of a principal magistrate) of blue-and-gold-painted wood. His costume is extraordinary: a short pink jacket, baggy dark blue trousers, vermilion slippers and a hard-brimmed hat with a flopping pink peak. He is lightly bearded, and wears his hair long in the style of the early Renaissance. Slightly hunched, his hands loose in his lap, he is watching the flagellation with no pleasure. Indeed, it would seem that he had nothing to do with it, were it not for the fact that the hands of the beaters break into his calm rectangle of space, drawing him into the consequences of his orders.

To make Pilate authentically Roman was not important to these artists. As a symbol of earthly authority, he made his point more dramatically if he looked like a contemporary lord. That changed in the sixteenth century, when painters began to attempt fantastical historical reconstructions. In the paintings of the high Baroque period he was put in turbans and silk robes like an Arab carpet-seller, and his beard grew long. In Tintoretto's 'Christ before Pilate' his grey beard curls almost to his waist, and he is given the high domed forehead of a philosopher. Were it not for the presence in these paintings of Pilate's universal trademark, the bowl of water, he could be mistaken for an elder of the Jews. Indeed, the mistake is made by cataloguers too. Gerrit Van Honthorst in 1617 painted a picture of Christ before a questioner who is wearing a caftan and a trimmed fez and whose finger is wagging dramatically, as if declaring the lowest price in the souk. This is a man who has been dragged out of bed, his eyes bleary, his beard tousled, and with what looks suspiciously like a night-shirt gaping under his gown. It is catalogued now as 'Christ before the High Priest', but was happily accepted by earlier generations as 'Christ before Pilate'.

Decades passed; and when the trial scene became a favourite subject again, with the rise of the startling popular religiosity of the mid-nineteenth century, Pilate had recovered proper Roman dress. His plain white toga might have made an unsatisfactory contrast with the simple white robe of Christ; but painters made sure it was elaborately draped, to suggest his vanity, and slightly over-laundered, to suggest hyper-civilisation. Against this whiteness his face could be sallow, where Christ's face against his comparatively dirty robe could glow with divine luminescence. The governor had also put on weight; and as he confronted Christ, gesturing prissily, or slumped in his chair apparently examining his fingernails, the folds of his toga could not quite disguise the middle-aged paunch and the plumpness of his thighs. His neck was thick, too, like a gourmand's, or like the neck of a man used to barking orders on the parade-ground.

This image lasted a while, until Hollywood changed it. As a figure of tragedy and perplexity, Pilate was better thin; as a representative of the gross materialism of the Roman empire, he needed dressing up. In *The Last Days of Pompeii* (1935), Basil Rathbone, better known as Sherlock Holmes, made a more-than-acceptable thin Pilate, with long tapering fingers and a long tapering nose. Subsequent Pilates, younger and better-looking, relied heavily on decoration. Gold braid was sewn round the borders of their togas; more braid and jewels were glued to their sandals. In *The Robe* (1953), Pilate's wrists were so heavy with bangles and his fingers so encrusted with rings, that he could hardly squeeze the absolving water between them.

From here it was only a small step to sexual ambivalence and foppery. Indeed, to the Roman Pilate, any man with more than one ring and a clutch of bangles would have been flagrantly effeminate. This tendency reached its apotheosis in the silly, lisping Pilate of *Monty Python's Life of Brian* of 1979 ('Whom shall I cwucify? I shall cwucify Wobert!'). In Martin Scorsese's *The Last Temptation of Christ* (1988) the governor was played by the gaunt and eerily hermaphrodite David Bowie. And the actor who played Pilate in the only film made exclusively from his point of view (the French-Italian *Ponzio Pilato* of 1962) was Jean Marais, for many years the lover of Jean Cocteau. Marais was astonishingly handsome, 'with all the characteristics,' Cocteau wrote, 'of those blue-eyed hyperboreans mentioned in Greek mythology.' It was Marais' profile that Cocteau drew again and again in the doodles that littered his notebooks: blond curling hair, the straight brow proceeding to the straight nose, the small imperious mouth. Oddly enough, that face corresponded almost exactly to Pilate's preening description of himself in the York play: the same 'noble forehead', the hair like gold wire, the hard and glittering stare.

Yet, for all this, Pilate's face remains a blank. The Christs of history bear a startling similarity: dark brown hair centrally parted, a modest beard, brooding eyes. Of Pilate only two things can be said for certain: that he was, according to the imperial fashion of the day, short-haired and clean-shaven. That in itself suggests a good deal. He would submit himself to the barber each morning, after his cursory breakfast of water and bread; and perhaps again in the course of the day, if he was dark and his beard was strong. It was always a long ritual. Julius Caesar was famous for reading reports while he was being shaved; other men wrote memoranda. The procedure included minute inspection of the skin, extraction of unwanted hairs, combing and clipping: the barber's tools of razor, scissors, strap and different sizes of tweezers covered a whole table. So, on most mornings, the barber would comb Pilate's hair, snipping it in places, and then tie a towel round his neck. A servant brought cold water, and with two or three deft movements of his hands the *tonsor* would slather it, without lubrication, on Pilate's cheeks. He then began the long slow razor work.

The blade dragged across the skin. The skin became sore, and the blade dragged across it again. In the interests of passivity, master and barber did not talk much. The only sounds were the blade dipped in water, the hiss of the strap, and the tiny scratch of metal against the beard, like a bird's claw. Quite often, the blade slipped. There was a quick, fierce pain; blood on the governor's fingers, when he instinctively raised his hand to the place; and a curling flower of blood in the water.

What would he have done? Shouted 'You criminal!'? Called for a mirror? Endured in silence? We do not know. But we know what the barber would have done: opened one of his little pots of salve made of leaves or mud or tallow or cobwebs, taken a little on the tip of a finger, dabbed the cut dry with his other hand, and smoothed the ointment over Pilate's skin. Some barbers offered patches, but these were thought as effeminate as scratching the head with one finger or wearing long-sleeved gowns; Pilate would probably have refused them. Instead he took, on the smarting cut, a strange piece of stuff like tamped grey cotton wool. And it may well have been like this – chafed, cut, sore, but mollified with a little fresh pomade – that Pilate went out on that Friday morning to have his encounter with Christ.

Even this is fancy, of course. And we have little more than that to rely on when we come to his age, or his marriage, or how bright he was. Of his age, we can only be certain that he was not younger than thirty when he went to Judea. That was the minimum age for governors. But his behaviour there – enthusiastic, sarcastic, nervous, occasionally brutal – suggests he was not much older. The two ancient Jewish sources, Philo and Josephus, whose biases we shall unravel later, recorded a remarkably similar personality. Their Pilate could behave with efficiency, but not with maturity. His trademarks were calculated affronts, crude deceptions, stubbornness to a degree. This was a character not yet made smooth by experience.

The gospels, too, suggest he had a short fuse. Roman arrogance is the implied reason for it – combined, in the case of the trial, with some early-morning grumpiness. Medieval writers recognised this as a hangover; so, in the mystery plays, Pilate is usually a prodigious drinker, urging those around him to 'sit down and wet your whistle', and sleeping the thick, drugged sleep of the sozzled man. The accounts of the Coventry play show that 'wine for Pilate' was a large expense.

Whoever played the governor seemed to go on drinking it offstage, keeping in character, while even Jesus confined himself to beer.

Pilate's wife usually drank with him. He was married, history has assumed, not just because of the legend of his callously interrupted wedding, but because Matthew introduced a message from his wife into the trial of Jesus, begging him to leave the prisoner alone. (The passage was probably invented, but it was harder to invent the wife.) Like Caesar's Calpurnia, or the trembling soothsaying wives in Babylonian fables, Pilate's wife is a harbinger of cosmic disruption: leaves wither, birds shriek, the pallid moon over-fills the tides. It was the writers of the apocryphal gospels who first suggested she was Claudia Procula, of the imperial blood of Rome. The medieval playwrights preferred to call her Procla or Percula, treating the name as if it were a diminutive in the Roman style, like *libellus* (little book) or *hortulus* (little garden). The Romans had a habit of playfully diminishing even unexpected things: Cicero's letters include 'dear little cohorts' and 'dear little mint leaves'. So Pilate's dear little woman trips through history.

Yet her character has grown alongside her husband's. The earliest Christians supposed she was fascinated by Judaism and curious about Jesus, to the point where her eagerness to see him upset her dreams. Origen thought she was the first Gentile to believe in Jesus's teaching, 'the proselyte of the Gate'. The Greeks and Copts made a saint of her because of her attempt to save Jesus, and put her among the women who went to the tomb to pray. Nineteenth-century romantics saw her as delicate and spirited, confined in the Herodian palace as if in some nunnery, but nonetheless glimpsing from the window the pale Galilean as he passed; for if she had never encountered him, how could she see him in her dreams? In the Slavonic version of Josephus she was imagined to have had a desperate illness for which both she and Pilate sought the healing of Jesus; and writers through the ages have imagined her nervous headaches, the result of hysteria and insomnia, alongside her husband's puffed and aching liver.

For centuries Procula was kept indoors, virtually confined to the bed from which she would spring after her appalling dream of the innocence of Jesus, screaming for Minerva and her maid while trying to cover her nakedness with sheets. Her only communication with the wider world was by folded notes, scribbles on tablets, whispers in a messenger's ear; she seldom, if ever, committed the indiscretion of trespassing in a man's territory. It was not until the 1930s that Procula was emancipated, attending Christian rallies in Galilee in the middle of expeditions to the carpet shops of Judea; and, on celluloid, hobnobbing in glossy lipstick with Jesus in the street.

Medieval playwrights had by far the most fun with her. Pilate and Procula were seen as classic canoodlers: lovebirds, in fact. She calls him 'my friendliest'; he calls her 'the fairest figure that ever food fed'. There is no couple they resemble so much as Chanticleer and Pertelote, the besotted cock and hen from Chaucer's 'Nun's Priest's Tale'. Beautiful Chanticleer, with his golden feathers and jet beak, his scarlet comb and azure spurs, is the king of the farmyard; pretty Pertelote is his paramour. On the top perch in the hen-house they cuddle together, sing 'My love is out faring', and mate constantly in a flurry of feathers. In their case, it is Chanticleer who has the bad dreams. But the chemistry between them, with Pertelote, the stronger-minded, building up her flashy but wavering husband in order to encourage him, is precisely mirrored in the medieval passion plays.

Procula, like Pertelote, knew she was sexually gorgeous. She was always dressed and played extravagantly. Women 'lent their gear' for the part in the Coventry play, and on one occasion 'Ryngold's man Thomas' played the part in outrageous drag. In the York cycle, just before the opening of the trial of Christ, the First Couple of Judea are found together embracing on Pilate's couch, which doubles as his bed. Procula (one imagines the extravagant sigh, the fussing with her hair) is determined to improve on Pilate's glowing description of himself:

'The Jews have never had another judge like you, darling! You doughty duke, you doomer of damnation – so nobly born, so debonair! You tell everyone where to go.'

'Certainly do.'

'I bet all the other procurators take lessons from you. If someone disobeys an order of yours, you kill them, don't you? If anyone drags their feet, you have him stoned, don't you? Just reduced to a pile of rags.'

'Try to.'

'Lucky me! Dame Precious Procula, wife of Sir Pilate, prince without peer! And wife without peer, too! Witty, wise . . .'

(Pause)

'Don't you think my skin's smooth? So comely and clear? It's just like the rest of me. And this dress . . . it's ravishing, don't you think? Though I say it myself, wouldn't you agree – no lord could have anyone sweeter than me?'

'I agree totally.'

'Love you, darling.'

'Love you, too. In fact, if I don't kiss you, I'll go crazy.'

'Kiss away then, darling. No one's stopping you.'

'Hey, fellows, see how lucky I am! These lovely lips are all mine! Luscious, lovely lips . . . all mine . . .'

(A long pause, while he kisses her)

'I just want to stay in bed all morning, loving you.'

'Me too.'

This steamy little episode was interrupted only by 'jangling Jews' at the door; but it was not only medieval playwrights who gave a high erotic temperature to Pilate's life. Edwardian commentators in their boned collars also liked to imagine him in love ('at least as a man of his nature could love') because it softened the military and legal rigours a little, and possibly also because it confirmed the governor's moral weakness. Like some character in a Galsworthy play, Pilate could struggle between cruel masculine imperatives and a clumsy desire to please his wife. The man's world would win, as it had to, but not without a moment of sentimental hesitation, when Jesus was on the brink of being handed over like a pretty necklace or a new dress.

She was vivid enough; but Procula is impossible to trace. In life she could have come from the clan of the Proculi, wealthy Roman knights of the same social background as Pilate, who lived – at least in the mid-80s – in a 'gleaming smart' house on the Palatine Hill. Martial described the journey to this house from the Quirinal, where he lived: past the Temple of Vesta, across the Via Sacra, through the Forum, until 'right before you on the left stands a building with a shining façade, the hall of a lofty house that bids you enter.' This was possibly a route Pilate took to see her, his heart pounding as he negotiated the stalls, the carts, the building sites, the muddy drains. We can imagine that Procula wished her hair blonde, wore Coan silks in pastel colours, softened her skin with bean-meal and wove Pilate's clothes with her own hands; but we are deep in the realm of conjecture here.

The presence of Procula in Judea, if she was there, has often been taken as an indicator of love. In the early years of the empire, wives did not normally accompany their husbands to the provinces. They were seen as a security risk. Augustus had enforced this law absolutely, allowing only one visit in winter, when travel was often impossible because the sea-lanes closed. In 21, not long before Pilate left, an attempt was still being made in the Senate to keep the wives at home. The proposer claimed that women were frail, extravagant, easily tired, and 'made a Roman army look like an Oriental progress'. Sternness of this sort was hard on marriages. Aelius Rufus, Cicero's friend, described the fate of one such couple in a letter. 'Paulla Valeria, the sister of Triarius, has divorced her husband without assigning any reason, on the very day that he was to arrive from his province. She is going to marry D. Brutus. She has sent back her whole wardrobe.'

Some writers suppose that Procula was there because she had asked Tiberius especially for this favour, at the end of six years of anguished correspondence from Pilate on his own in Judea. But this would not have been necessary, since by then both sentiment and the law had changed. As a spokesman for the majority put it during that same Senate debate in 21, weren't governors entitled, when they returned from their labours, to relax with their wives? Was enforced celibacy really ideal? It was true, of course, that husbands were often corrupted by bad wives, but who was the stronger party here? 'If a woman misbehaves, it's her husband's fault.'

This argument won the day, although in the minds of Roman males the women were still barely controllable: half-expected, like the medieval Procula, to scour the markets for dresses and baubles, or, like the flapper-Procula, to hitch up their skirts and run after preachers in the wild hills of Galilee. Yet Matthew's gospel suggests that Pilate took Procula not only to Judea but also on his party-and-peacekeeping trips to Jerusalem, at moments when the city was manifestly unsafe. Perhaps they loved each other with the passionate dottiness suggested by the Roman poets, whispering in the dark *mea rosa*, *mi anime*, *passerculus* (little sparrow), *melliculum* (little honey), *mea vita*, my life. Tradition has them clinging together like limpets in his uncomfortable posting; and it was in Jerusalem that Procula committed the indiscretion that invented her life and her career, as well as gaining her admittance to the canon of Greek and Coptic saints.

So Pilate, from a shadow, was given his passionate and colourful wife; and, by logical extension in the Middle Ages, he was also given children. There were usually two offspring in the Pilate household, two boys or a boy and a girl, aged somewhere between six and twelve. In the York cycle the boys are little yobs, hanging like puppies round the feet of the knights as they bring Jesus to trial. 'Here, Jesus, you caitiff,' cries one, 'why don't you fall flat on your face for fear of my father? I reckon you don't know how wise he is. But I recommend you obey him, you brawler.' In the Coventry play Pilate's son is a miniature king in gown and hat, with his own small sceptre and gilded poleaxe; but he is a child of better manners, essentially waiting on his parents, like a baffled servant in the wake of their gaudiness.

The most child-like children belong to a fifteenth-century French passion play, a boy and a girl whose role, like small chirping birds, is to be the conscience of their father as he deals with Jesus. They appear first with Procula, who wants to shoo them away as she talks to Pilate; but they tug at her skirt, demanding 'When are we going to see the prophet they want to torture?' The little boy adds: 'We know where to find him. He's where no one has pity on him, but everyone really hates him.'

The little girl then says, alarmingly, 'God, who made the world, take care of my father.'

'And God give *you* honour and grace, my lovely daughter,' Pilate happily answers her.

'Father, I'm really sad you've treated that prophet so badly. No one's complained about him except the Jews. He has such a good character, everyone says so. Let him go. Have pity on him.'

'What are you saying, sweetheart? The Jews will kill me if I do that; they'll have the eyes out of my head.'

At this point, the little boy comes in with a disturbing sing-song verse of his own:

> God who made the wind and rain
> Let my father not be ashamed.

There are echoes here of Shakespeare's fools, like Feste in *Twelfth Night* ('For the rain it raineth every day'): innocent creatures who see to the heart of the action and are somehow allowed to speak plainly, without being beaten. Pilate does not hear the warning in his son's words; he simply takes it as a sweet song, hugs the child, asks what he really wants. His son has opened a window, letting into the palace great blasts of cold air and dark water, but Pilate is always the indulgent father. In the same way, the brutish little boys of York are ignored, or flattered with the title 'Sir' and told to wait on their mother; the girls are called pretty and delightful, however disquieting their chatter. The medieval Pilate, a villain in most respects, is made pliant and disorganised by any show of goodness, in his children as well as in Jesus. He is a fearsome ranter, and yet he is domesticated: the managing director who, in the midst of some towering crisis – a takeover bid, a liability suit – comes home from work to kneel on the floor and mess around with model trains.

Lastly, there is Pilate's dog. Bulgakov's Pilate in *The Master and Margerita* has a wolfhound called Banga, a great grey dog with pointed ears and a gold-studded collar. Banga is the only creature Pilate loves, and the feeling is mutual. They sleep together on a couch out on the balcony of Herod's palace, under the stars, the governor's arms round the dog's neck; they walk together in his dreams up the long path of light towards the moon. Cruel and sharp with everyone else, with Banga Pilate is a child; and there is almost no characterisation of him that does not contain some peculiar, almost discordant, element of innocence. The man may be a schemer but, in a deep way, he has barely the faintest notion of what he is doing.

Perhaps he was not very bright. His learning, or the lack of it, is once again a subject we know nothing or everything about. He was either a rough soldier, or a philosopher of acute and sceptical intelligence, or any possible gradation in between. One phrase above all has served to pigeonhole him: the question, seemingly too strange to have been invented, which he asks Jesus in the gospel of John – 'What is truth?' And our assessments of his intelligence spring, too, from what he apparently did next; turned on his heel and, in Bacon's words, 'would not stay for an answer.'

Bacon thought he was 'jesting'. Perhaps he was. Even as a chance remark, with all deeper meanings stripped out of it, it has been taken in all kinds of ways. Most probably Pilate thought Jesus was out of his depth and was simply tossing the subject back to him, as confident men do. (This sense is wonderfully caught in the broad Yorkshire of the *Northern Passion*: 'What is sothefastness? *You* tell *me*.') Possibly he had never in his life wasted his time thinking about truth; possibly he racked his brain on the subject daily. Yet that last suggestion, that he was a thinker, seems to suit the Pilate of the ancient accounts least of all. Josephus, Philo and the gospels agree that this is a man who believes in action, even – and often – at the cost of reflection.

The author of the fourth-century *Acta Pilati* went to some lengths to make Pilate more thoughtful and intelligent. These *Acta,* which were supposedly an account of the passion events recorded by Pilate's Jewish 'friend' Nicodemus, had an interest in gilding the governor. This is a man who, largely for reasons of early Christian prejudice, is being drawn in deliberately reasonable contrast to the supposed fanaticism of the Jews. It is he who takes delivery of the priests' 'memorials', written in Hebrew and providing the conclusive evidence of the resurrection, and preserves them – with Roman efficiency – so that later Christians may make use of them. Although he knows almost nothing of Jewish culture, he is intellectually curious and sharp. He may feel occasionally at sea, but he is not about to let anything pass him by.

In the *Acta*, just before the trial of Jesus, a messenger runs in to tell Pilate and the chief priests that he has seen Jesus coming into Jerusalem and has heard the crowd cry: 'Save us, you who are in the highest! Blessed is he who comes in the name of the Lord!' The priests dispute this, and point out that the messenger must have got the message wrong; after all, the shouts were in Hebrew, and he is Greek. Stung, the messenger retorts: 'But I asked one of the Jews, and he explained it.' Pilate then butts in, throwing out a question to the Jews in the room:

'What did they cry out in Hebrew?'
'*Hosanna membrome baruchamma adonai.*'
'And what does that mean, *Hosanna* and the rest?'
'It means, save us now, you who are in the highest.'
'So, if you yourselves say your children shouted that, how has my messenger sinned?'

The chief priests cannot answer him. And this is not the last of Pilate's clever interjections. In the middle of the trial of Jesus he suddenly accuses the Jews of 'always rebelling' against their benefactors, and goes on:

According to what I've heard, your God brought you out of Egypt out of hard bondage, and led you safe through the sea as by dry land, and in the wilderness he nourished you with manna and gave you quails, and water to drink out of a rock, and gave you a law. And in all these things you provoked your God to anger, and sought out a molten calf, and angered your God and he tried to kill you; but Moses made supplication for you, and you were spared.

This breathtaking precis of Jewish history is all the more impressive because Pilate has encountered neither the Bible nor the Scriptures. His first sight of the Bible comes a day later, in the Temple itself, when the chief priests, *grammatici*, scribes and teachers of the law produce one for him. It is heavily inlaid with gold and glittering with precious stones; four ministers stagger under it. Pilate, deeply impressed, commands the chief priests to consult the book and to tell him in which year the Son of God was meant to come. The chief priests answer in arithmetic:

- from the third son of Adam to the coming of Christ, 5,500 years.
  - length of the Ark of the Covenant, $2\frac{1}{2}$ cubits.
              plus breadth, $1\frac{1}{2}$ cubits,
              plus height, $1\frac{1}{2}$ cubits
                  equals $5\frac{1}{2}$ cubits

therefore the coming of Jesus Christ in the ark of his body was to be after 5,500 years.

Alternatively –

- from the making of heaven and earth and the first man to the Flood, 2,212 years.
- from the Flood to the building of the tower, 531 years.
- from the building of the tower to Abraham, 606 years.
- from Abraham to the coming of the children of Israel out of Egypt, 470 years.
- from the leaving of Egypt to the building of the Temple, 511 years.
- from the building of the Temple to its destruction, 464 years
- from the burning of the Temple to the coming of Christ, 636 years

              equals 5,500 years [sic]

Pilate drinks all this in, and takes notes. We imagine him bent over the calculations, hanging on the numbers; he too, impatiently, can do the addition and subtraction. But that image remains less impressive than the one of Pilate, like the Inca Atahualpa, facing the Book. He is half afraid of it, half-contemptuous; he will not read it himself, open it or even touch it, because it glitters like a reptile. Yet he waits for it to enlighten him.

In the medieval plays, Pilate is seldom faced with the teachings of the Jews. When he is, it is plain that Jewish history and religion mean nothing at all to him; he has brought in something superior. The York Pilate boasts that he made his reputation among philosophers, while the Towneley Pilate still has a law teacher, a bedraggled fellow, who complains that his careful teaching about right and wrong seems to be falling on deaf ears. Yet, even when he is a buffoon, Pilate is still more intelligent and usually more cunning than anyone else on the stage. He never has much time, and does not suffer fools gladly. In the Gréban play Caiaphas, painstakingly listing the charges against Jesus, is urged, even rudely, to get to the point; as the high priest drifts again, Pilate barks, 'Keep to the matter, sir!'

But it was the nineteenth-century biographers of Jesus who drew the boldest and wildest pictures of Pilate's intellectual formation, his favourite reading and the colour of his thinking. Curiously enough, whether English or not, they often gave him an English character, as if in deference to the imperial power of the day. Thus Giovanni Papini, an Italian, stated confidently that a Pilate transplanted to Victorian London would have read John Stuart Mill and Swinburne ('Thou hast conquered, O pale Galilean; The world has grown grey from Thy breath'); that he would have enjoyed the romantic vigour of Byron and the sentimental cadences of Tennyson; and that he would have taken *The Times*. Ernest Renan, a Frenchman, was sure that Pilate would have been a Tory; Papini thought he would have voted Liberal (hence Mill); both were convinced of an overwhelming superiority complex on the British colonial model, allied to rather lush and disjointed reading. It therefore followed that Pilate was 'one of those sceptics of the Roman decadence corrupted with Pyrrhonism, a devotee of Epicurus, an encyclopaedist of Hellenism without any belief in the gods of his country'; an odd conclusion, since by their lights Pilate was almost bound to have been a card-carrying member of the Church of England.

It was provocative and fantastic, and it made Victorian writers feel closer to Christ, to dress up Pilate as a man in a top hat and astrakhan coat who worried about the Irish Question. Yet it did not shed much light in the darkness. How intelligent might this man have been? How thoughtful, and how well equipped to deal with the spiritual challenge that was set before him? In Pilate's Rome the *equites*, often new men with new money, were assumed to be magpies in the matter of knowledge too: ostentatiously organising readings of their own poems, buying pocket cribs of the philosophers, rejoicing in arcane self-improvement. A knight who was truly learned or wise was something to remark on. More typical was the man Tacitus sat next to at the races, who 'after discoursing on several learned subjects', suddenly asked, 'Are you Tacitus or Pliny?'

So to return to Pilate's own famous question, the one John says he threw out at Jesus with much the same abruptness as that racegoer threw his at Tacitus. *Ti estin aletheia?* was what he said, according to John;

and, if indeed he said it, Greek was very probably the language he used. This was the lingua franca of the eastern empire. Even a rough soldier would have a smattering of it, and a governor could not work without it, unless he dared to put himself at the mercy of interpreters. Seneca, apparently voicing the general opinion, thought Greek a bit vague and sissyish beside the forcefulness of Latin. It fitted with other soppy Greek things, such as the slippers (rather than sensible Roman shoes) that Tiberius had slopped around in during his exile in Rhodes. Cicero scattered Greek through his letters to express the sort of refined, snobbish concepts for which the English use French: *bons mots, double entendre, banal.* To him, too, it was a literary language first of all, although he noted in his treatise *On the Nature of the Gods* that 'in matters of style we've now made such progress that even in richness of vocabulary the Greeks do not surpass us.'

Perhaps Pilate thought the same. It is easy to imagine him mangling his Greek as English-speaking diplomats still mangle French, falling back into the cadence of inky blotters and tear-stained lists of verbs. The state of Pilate's Greek, possibly fluent, possibly awful, adds a peculiar poignancy to his supposed exchanges with Jesus and the Jews during the trial. Perhaps he repeated the same question over and over not out of judicial cussedness, but because his phrasebook Greek could not stretch much further; perhaps he was baffled by Jesus's answers not because he could not penetrate the philosophy, but because he could not understand the words. These 'conversations', heavily theological in any case, could well be read as the dialogue of two men adrift in a half-known language: meanings missed, questions and answers not quite connecting, like two dim-sighted explorers extending their hands to make out the shape of the other.

Even some Greek would have laid Pilate open to the influence of Homer, Plato, Aristotle and the Greek theatre; just as his Latin laid him open to Virgil, Ovid, Cicero, Propertius, Horace, Lucretius. Had he read any of them? Did he think of them at all? Did he carry in his head scraps of the *Aeneid*, as Pliny did, or Greek tags, as Augustus did? Could he debate the finer literary points of the *Odyssey*, as Tiberius could? Or was there a contemporary mish-mash of Greek and Roman adventure stories, the clashing of oars, the wine-dark sea, Scipio falling on his sword, Odysseus tied to the mast, the heartbreaking presentation of pious Aeneas as the founder and saviour of Rome? There may have been all these things, as well as the common maxims and quips that men carry round with them. The ones below came from *Cato's Collected Wisdom*, a popular little book of the time.

> What you don't need is dear, even when it's cheap.
> Know yourself.
> Be thrifty with time.
> Only a fool stubs his toe on the same rock twice.
> Forgetting trouble is the way to cure it.
> Fortune favours the brave.
> Nothing in excess.
> Expect to be treated by others as you have treated them.
> Don't ask for what you'll wish you hadn't got.

Something of this blunt practicality could have coloured Pilate's question too. For a Christian or a Jew, religion and philosophy may be one and the same; 'What is truth?' is also a religious question. For Pilate, if he meant it as anything more than a knee-jerk challenge, it would have been purely philosophical. A Roman could practise religion and pursue philosophy almost without the two colliding; for his religion, ritualistic, pragmatic and superstitious, was in a separate compartment. It was entwined not with higher thinking, but with politics; not with lofty abstractions, but with matters of practical loyalty and even of life and death.

Modern minds think of this religion – the obsessive auguries, the pompous state sacrifices, the dry decisions of the Board of Fifteen for Religious Ceremonies and the Board of Seven for Sacrificial Banquets – as essentially empty. But Augustus' reformation of Roman religion around the cult of the emperor, together with the inexorable spread of the Roman empire and the Roman peace, could make this worship in Pilate's time relevant and even affecting: the divine Augustus was the saviour of the world, and what Rome was doing was a work approved by the gods.

As a young man, Pilate may well have watched the defining scene of the cult: the moment in AD 12 when Tiberius returned from his German campaigns and, alighting from his chariot, knelt at Augustus' feet. It appears, at any rate, that the governor wore his religion on his sleeve. His god was the emperor, and he not only surrounded himself with holy imperial objects – military standards, votive shields, coins with religious insignia – but also tried to foist them, like an evangelist, on the outraged Jews. To return to the Victorian metaphor, he sometimes seems like one of those British governors of India who, partly out of nostalgia for home, partly out of desire to civilise the natives, partly out of eagerness to keep in with the establishment, built Anglican cathedrals in which to take their ostentatious Communion.

Did he really believe in Roman religion, and in the imperial cult that now coloured it from top to bottom? It is difficult to say. Public devotion was often a cover for private doubt. Several modern writers have assumed that he believed in nothing at all: 'neither gods nor men, nor Pontius Pilate', as Nikos Kazantzakis put it. It is tempting to make him indifferent, even nihilistic, if only for the satisfaction of a real intellectual clash with Christ. But the evidence of the ancient sources – both written and archaeological – suggests a different picture.

His philosophy, if he dabbled in any, is even harder to pin down. If he was a sceptic or a Pyrrhonist, he would scarcely have bothered with book-learning beyond what he had absorbed as a child; there was no point. Pyrrhon taught that certain knowledge of anything was unattainable. For any given proposition, the opposite could be proposed with equal reason; no assertion was more valid than another. The man of wisdom, rather than declaring 'This *is* so,' could only say, 'This *seems* so.' The Academicians followed this teaching later, but, said Cicero,

> We are not men whose minds wander in uncertainty and never know what principles to adopt. For what sort of mental habit, or rather what sort of life would that be which dispensed with all rules for reasoning or even for living? We don't do that; but, where other schools maintain that some things are certain and others uncertain, we . . . say that some things are probable, others improbable.
>
> What then is to stop me from accepting what seems to me probable, while rejecting what seems to be improbable, and from shunning the presumption of dogmatism, while keeping clear of that recklessness of assertion which is as far as possible removed from pure wisdom? And as to the fact that our school argues against everything, that is only because we could not get a clear view of what is 'probable' unless we could make a comparative estimate of all the arguments on both sides.

An Academician Pilate, asking 'What is truth?', would be neither mocking nor world-weary, but would simply be exposing Jesus for being so recklessly sure of himself. This philosophy was not meant to lead to sneering or superiority, only to the tranquillity of constant equilibrium and lack of dogmatism. Like Polonius, he could accept whatever seemed probable, especially if his superiors suggested it to him.

> *Hamlet.* Do you see yonder cloud, that's almost in the shape of a camel?
> *Polonius.* By the mass, and 'tis like a camel indeed.
> *Hamlet.* Methinks it is like a weasel.
> *Polonius.* It is backed like a weasel.
> *Hamlet.* Or like a whale?
> *Polonius.* Very like a whale.

Other teachings too might have flickered in Pilate's mind. Epicurus would have told him that he had no overriding obligations to the gods or the state, that no one had claims on him, that peace lay in withdrawal from outside influences and in the revealed truth of his own sensations; but that was hardly a line a Roman governor could take. The Stoics would have taught him the tranquil virtue of the wise man, so fixed on the divinity within him that he could become oblivious to pain, to money, or to promotion. Pilate did not seem to take that path either, or not successfully. Some civil servants never read philosophers.

Besides, even if we know what his references might have been, we still do not know what store he set by reading. Julius Caesar read at the games, which was thought bad form; Cicero read at picnics, lying on a blanket on the grass; Pliny (like many contemporaries) had books read during and after meals, and even took his notebooks out when he was hunting boar, 'so that I shall have something to bring home even if I catch nothing.' Among governors and proconsuls there was a presumption of literacy and cultivation. The governor Lucilius, to whom Seneca addressed his *Moral Letters*, wrote poetry and contemplated, though not without nervousness, the highest reaches of philosophical inquiry. A governor's job was not one that kept him too busy for reading or self-improvement; indeed, Cicero congratulated one friend on becoming a governor simply for the acres of leisure time he would have.

It was also a job that required much written self-expression. Letters were sent, and from the homesick they were long ones, 'filling the reader's left hand' as he unrolled them; crowds greeted the flashing white top-sails of the mail-boats as they jostled into the harbour. In Pilate's luggage too as he left home must have been the paraphernalia of his thinking life: empty scrolls, bundles of papers, waxed pocket books to be kept in the breast-fold of his toga, cuttlefish ink, iron pens.

Possibly somewhere too, among the stacks of white togas, the cloaks and shoes, the bric-à-brac and the statuettes of the household gods, were the favourite books. The best ones were usually kept in rectangular boxes impregnated with cedar oil. They may have been new, purchased for the journey, 'new books with new ivories, inscribed on Augustan Royal, the lines lead-ruled, red tabs and red wrappers, the ends shaved with pumice', as Catullus described some he had bought himself; or well-worn scrolls, cracked with constant unrolling, marked in the margins, tied with frayed string. And what was on them was whatever we want to imagine.

The journey from Rome to Caesarea, Pilate's seat of government, took at least twenty days. By tradition, a new governor set out from the temple of Mars the Avenger, the huge new temple built by Augustus from which all campaigns against 'impious foes', to the east or the west, were always started. The doors and walls were hung with weird weapons taken from defeated foreigners, all hides and feathers and spikes; while above them, serenely, Romulus and Aeneas and the rest of the heroes blessed the new hero on his journey.

From Rome to the coast the governor would pass in parade with his escort, waving to any crowds that gathered. The sea-voyage started from Brindisi. We do not know exactly what time of year Pilate left, but the elder Pliny recorded that the sea was opened to voyagers 'when the west winds soften the wintry heavens' and the sun occupied the twenty-fifth degree of Aquarius. This meant mid-February, just before the rising of the wind that brought the swallows. If a man was important or devout, he sacrificed to the waves before embarking; a man of regular piety would go on board *adoratis sideribus*, having paid his respects to the stars. The recommended route was by way of Alexandria on ships which, according to the Emperor Gaius, were sailed as swiftly as 'a charioteer handles race-horses'.

Each morning, the sun rose over the sea in the direction in which he was sailing. Above the crack of the sails and the chants of the oarsmen the night sky grew ragged, and the mottled clouds were filled with light. Did Pilate see, with Homer, the goddess of the rose-tinged dawn rising from the couch of Tithonus, harnessing her two-horse chariot and ascending the heaven to announce the coming of the sun? Did he feel, as the Stoics felt, some stirring of the divinity within himself in tune with the divinity outside? Or did he merely see, as Hamlet saw, whales and weasels in the flat and unknowable sky?

One line at least he might have remembered, common to every

school of thought, as the low coast of Judea came into view. '*Nunc animis opus, Aenea, nunc pectore firmo!*'; Ah now, Aeneas, be strong and stout of heart!'

2

Governing Judea

'But how,' you ask, 'does one attain the highest good?' You do not need to cross the Pennine or Graian hills, or traverse the Candavian waste, or face the Syrtes quicksands, or Scylla, or Charybdis, although you have travelled through all these places for the bribe of a petty governorship; the journey for which nature has equipped you is safe and pleasant. She has given you such gifts that you may, if you do not prove false to them, rise level with God. Your money, however, will not place you on a level with God; for God has no property. Your bordered robe will not do this, for God is not clad in raiment; nor your reputation, nor a display of self, nor a knowledge of your name spread throughout the world, for no one has knowledge of God. The throng of slaves which carries your litter along the city streets and in foreign places will not help you; for this God of whom I speak, though the highest and most powerful of beings, carries all things on his own shoulders. Neither can beauty or strength make you blessed, for neither of these qualities can withstand old age.

What we have to seek for, then, is that which is untouched by Time and Chance. And what is this? It is the soul – but the soul that is upright, good and great. What else could you call such a soul than a god dwelling as a guest in the human body? A soul like this may descend into a Roman knight as well as into a freedman's son or a slave. For what is a Roman knight, or a freedman's son, or a slave? They are mere titles, born of ambition or of wrong. One may leap to heaven from the very slums. Only rise,

And mould thyself to kinship with thy God.

Seneca, *Moral Letters*, XXXI

Beyond Idumea and Samaria, wrote the elder Pliny,

Judea extends far and wide. The part which joins up with Syria is called Galilee, while the part which is nearest to Arabia and Egypt is called Perea. This last is thickly covered with rugged mountains, and is separated from the rest of Judea by the River Jordan.

The River Jordan rises from the spring of Panias. It is a delightful stream and, as far as the terrain allows, it winds along its course and lingers among the dwellers on its banks. With the greatest reluctance, as it were, it moves on towards Asphaltites [the Dead Sea], a lake of a gloomy and unpropitious nature, by which it is at last swallowed up; and its celebrated waters are lost sight of as they mingle with the pestilential streams of the lake. Because it is so reluctant to get there, as soon as the valley through which it flows affords the opportunity, the Jordan discharges itself into a lake known as Genesara [Tiberias], sixteen miles long and six miles wide. This lake is skirted by the pleasant towns of Julias and Hippo on the east, Tarichea on the south ... and Tiberias on the west, where there are health-giving hot springs.

Asphaltites produces nothing whatever except bitumen, to which it owes its name. The bodies of animals will not sink in its waters, and even those of bulls and camels float there. In length it exceeds a hundred miles, being at its widest point twenty-five miles, and at its narrowest six. The country of the Arabian tent-people faces it on the east, and Macharus on the south, which was at one time the most strongly fortified place in Judea, next to Jerusalem. On the same side lies Callirrhoe, a warm spring, remarkable for its medicinal qualities.

Lying on the west of Asphaltites, and sufficiently distant to escape its noxious exhalations, are the Esseni: a people that live apart from the world, and marvellous beyond all others throughout the whole earth, for they have no women among them. To sexual desire they are complete strangers; they have no money; the palm trees are their only companions. Day after day, however, their numbers are replenished by the crowds of strangers that resort to them, driven there to adopt their customs by the tempests of fortune, and wearied with the miseries of life. So it is that through thousands of years, incredible to relate, this people eternally prolongs its existence without a single birth taking place there: so fruitful a source of population is the weariness of others.

Below the home of this people [stands] the town of Engadda, second only to Jerusalem in the fertility of its soil and its groves of palm trees . . . and next to it is Masada, a fortress on a rock, not far from Lake Asphaltites.

So much for Judea.

Strabo in his *Geography* provided a few more details. On the plain of Hiericus, near Jericho, was a wonderful grove of fruit trees and date palms one hundred stadia long, watered by streams and dotted with fine buildings, including a palace built by Herod. (Horace confirmed this: he wrote that in Herod's palm groves 'a man might idle and play and smooth himself with oil', a Roman's heaven.) Near the palace stood a 'balsam park', where workers tapped the spice-scented shrubs for their milky juice; 'and when it is put up in small quantities, it solidifies, and is remarkably good for curing headaches and incipient cataracts and dimness of sight.' But for Strabo too it was Asphaltites that summed up the strangeness of this country. He noted that the asphalt was blown to the surface, leavened with bubbles, until it looked like a hill, and that it tarnished every metal that touched it. When the local people knew it was rising they would venture out in reed boats to gather it in. This required the chanting of spells and the softening of the asphalt, with their own urine, before they could chop it in pieces and bring it home. The fire and fumes that underlay Judea also rose up in other places, so that in Gadaris the lake water corroded the hooves of sheep, and near Masada the high cliffs dripped with pitch.

Pilate arrived in this land of bitumen and balsam in about 26. We assume this date because his predecessor, according to Josephus, was appointed immediately after the death of Augustus in 14, and served for eleven years; and because when Pilate was recalled, in 36, Josephus remarks that he had been in Judea for a decade. Some think he arrived in 19, which would have made him more experienced when he encountered Christ; but Josephus' calculations seem good enough.

He was the fifth prefect – a word that is best translated, for familiarity's sake, as governor. The word in Greek was *hegemon*, the title he would officially have been addressed by, although Greek-speakers under his orders would have called him *Kratiste*, 'your Excellency'. Before him came Coponius (AD 6–9), M. Ambivius (9–12), Annius Rufus (12–15) and Valerius Gratus (15–26). Short tours were normal policy under Augustus, but Judea was not known as a place that enticed men to stay longer. Did any of his predecessors advise Pilate, give him briefings, or leave the odd warning letter in the files? Possibly. Gratus, after appointing and dismissing four high priests of Judea in as many years, had gone back to Rome. The last part of his tour was obviously bad-tempered and corrupt: the high priesthood of Judea was generally awarded for money. So Gratus may have given Pilate a lesson in graft and Sejanus, if he was his patron, may have trained him in anti-Semitism; for, according to Philo, Sejanus found it impossible to trust the Jews. He accused the Jews in Rome of plotting against the emperor, and the bad feeling was mutual: 'He knew,' wrote Philo, 'that the Jewish nation would take the principal part against his own unholy plots.'

However, no writer but Philo, an ardent Jew, suggests that Sejanus was especially anti-Jewish; and Pilate, in any case, could have picked up this everyday Roman prejudice well before his posting. A large Jewish colony lived on 'the other side' – the west side – of the Tiber, known as Ward 14, which was then as now a warren of workshops and small houses. The Jews who lived here were emancipated slaves and Roman citizens, though they were careful to preserve their Jewishness: hence the dual loyalties that Sejanus mistrusted. They ran their own synagogues, in which they received 'training in ancestral philosophy', as Philo put it, every Sabbath morning. Inside their small houses an elaborate system of enclosed rooms kept their women hidden, and hayboxes warmed their food on non-cooking days. They did not often leave their own quarter, though by the 70s (when their numbers were swollen by refugees after the Jewish War) Jewish hawkers could be seen in the city proper, trading sulphur matches for broken crockery.

Some formal respect was shown to them. According to a decree of Augustus, Jews could not be made to appear in court on the Sabbath, which was understood to start at 3 o'clock on Friday afternoons; and their sacred money from 'the first fruits' was always sent to receivers in Jerusalem and never touched by Romans. The law also dictated that 'anyone caught stealing their holy books, or their sacred money, whether out of the synagogues or from the men's apartments, shall be deemed a sacrilegious person'. Tiberius, too, was usually solicitous for these Jews, allowing them to come a day late to claim the distributions of money or corn that were made on the Sabbath.

Pilate in Rome could often have observed Jewish rhythms of life – the robes and beards, the hush of Friday evening, the hum of Saturday prayers. But he would probably not have cared to. Romans nursed some lively prejudices against Jews, based largely on misunderstanding what they believed. Sabbath observance persuaded them that the Jews were bone-idle. Petronius Arbiter, unless he was being extraordinarily offensive, thought they worshipped a 'pig-god'. Horace in his *Satires* painted Jews as proselytisers, always on the look-out for drifting Romans to draw into their prayer-groups, and deeply superstitious, believing for example that frankincense would combust spontaneously if placed on a holy stone. (Horace's friends roared with laughter at that one.) In the ninth Satire, another friend refuses to rescue Horace from a man who is annoying him because 'Today is the thirtieth Sabbath. Would you affront the circumcised Jews?'

'I don't care. Religion's nothing to me.'

'But it is to me. I'm a weaker brother, one of the many. So, if you'll excuse me, I'll talk another day.'

Despite this banter, the Jewish Sabbath was not considered inauspicious for Romans; Ovid thought it was a good day for chasing girls, though he does not say why. In the end, it was their 'proselytising', real or imagined, that rankled most. In 19 Tiberius expelled the Jews from Rome after a Roman woman of good breeding had been conned into sending her treasure to Jerusalem; but Dio Cassius, a chronicler of the early years of the empire, thought they had been banished more generally for 'flocking to Rome and converting people to their ways'. Some 4,000 Jewish men were called up for military service and sent to Sardinia, a fever-ridden place; the rest, who refused to be soldiers for religious reasons, were arrested, and their holy objects and vestments burned. At around the same time, Tiberius also banned over-priced mullets, Corinthian glass and promiscuous kissing in the street: but these eventually crept back in, and so did the Jews.

The one thing Romans knew for sure about Jews, which fascinated them in the most prurient way, was that the men were circumcised. Anyone trying to disguise himself as a Jew reckoned this was the first distinguishing mark, beyond beards or robes. But to be circumcised, for a Roman, was to lose a bit of manliness. There was therefore that suggestion too in Pilate's outraged response in John's gospel, 'Am *I* a Jew?' The very notion insulted him; the difference was physical, obvious, and there was absolutely nothing to be gained by seeking to narrow the gulf between them.

To do his job well, in his view, was not a matter of understanding the land he ruled over. He just had to use to the profit of Rome the powers he had been given. His job was not a plum appointment. It was a junior officer's billet; more experienced men got Syria or Egypt. It was also a challenge, because Judea was such a new and recalcitrant province. Although it had a mixed population of Jews, Greeks, Samarians, Syrians and Idumeans, all other ethnic conflicts paled beside the overwhelming cultural clash between the Romans and the Jews.

The Jewish nation considered itself in every way superior to Rome, especially chosen by God, and essentially untouchable. Any Roman would have been disquieted by that. All his schooling, his experience, the lines of Livy and Virgil ringing in his head, told him it was his own nation the gods had blessed and appointed: 'the Romans, the lords of creation, the togaed people'. Cicero put it with typical bluntness: 'There is no race which has not either been so utterly destroyed that it hardly exists, or so thoroughly subdued that it remains submissive, or so pacified, that it rejoices in our victory and rule.' Earlier in the same speech he dismissed the Jews explicitly as 'people born to be slaves'. It was a constant headache to Pilate that they were of the opposite opinion.

The Jewish diaspora made his job more difficult. As Philo pointed out, the Jews were spread out across almost the breadth of the habitable world. An insult to them in Judea could bring 'myriads' into open conflict with Rome, and 'the result would be something too awesome to be resisted.'

Philo, always so fierce in his defence of his people, exaggerated. The desert-sweeping Parthians on the border with Syria, darkening the sky with buzzing swarms of arrows shot backwards, were probably more of a threat in Pilate's mind than the massed crowds of the Jews. He might even have felt more nervous about Gauls and Germans, the 'godless' barbarians he had probably fought face to face. Yet Judea was fragile enough to be under the personal aegis of the emperor, rather than the Senate, and Pilate was there as his personal representative. In the interests of stability both he and his regional superiors, 'good fellow' Flaccus and Lucius Vitellius, successive governors of Syria, were bound to obey the least decree that came down from Rome. Petronius, Vitellius' successor, stated this as plainly as possible to a crowd of complaining Jews of the sort Pilate often had to face: 'The emperor has sent me, and I am under the necessity of carrying out his decrees, because disobedience to them would bring upon me inevitable destruction.'

Vitellius commanded four legions: the sixth ('Iron-Clad'), the third ('Gallica'), the twelfth ('Rolling Thunder') and the tenth, 'Fretensis', whose symbols were the bull and the boar. He was on call to intervene in Judea if things got out of hand – as, by the end of Pilate's stint, they had. For the first five years of his tour, however, the legate of Syria was detained in Rome on the emperor's orders, so Pilate had no one on hand to advise or restrain him. Not that he could get up to much mischief: the governor of Judea had, at most, 4,000 men in auxiliary units of cavalry and infantry. Only the senior officers, and perhaps not all of those, were Romans. The troops were Idumeans, Samarians and Syrians, many from Caesarea itself, where they sometimes amused themselves by insulting the local Jews and throwing stones at them.

This was a fatal flaw in Pilate's forces. They might be even more anti-Jewish than the governor himself was inclined to be, and less able to control themselves. Some years before, Varus (the same Varus who was destroyed in the German forest, who was then governor of Syria) had been only too pleased to disband similar units, 'which he had not found at all useful, for the soldiers behaved themselves in a most disorderly manner, disobeying his wishes and being intent only on the profits they could make from their misbehaviour.' The mercy was that their numbers in Judea were relatively small: so small that, in an emergency, there were simply not enough of them unless Vitellius joined in.

The point of the Roman presence in Judea was to secure tax revenues, keep the peace and establish trade with Rome; it was not to colonise or Romanise it. Most Romans knew a lost cause when they saw one. Nor was their job to act like an occupying army. Pilate's troops were more of a police force, responsible for guarding important buildings, protecting the governor, controlling sheep in the streets and, when necessary, punishing malefactors. They also carried out the duties of interrogators and secret police. In 1997 part of Pilate's palace at Caesarea was excavated, revealing a room (later than Pilate's time, but built over another of similar function) with a black and white mosaic floor. The mosaic carried the legend, 'I have come to this room in the good hope that I shall be secure'. Israeli archaeologists assumed it was an inner interrogation room, in which spies were debriefed or prisoners tortured to elicit secret information.

Pilate seemed to relish the military side of his job. Josephus showed he had a fondness for unusual strategy, even though it often went wrong. He was, after all, the prefect of Judea, the title he proudly acknowledged in the only memorial that survives of him. By the time of Claudius, around 46, the title of such officials had been changed to 'procurator', and Tacitus made the mistake, in about 115, of attaching this title to Pilate. He would have been offended. A procurator in the strict sense was a financial agent, like a purchaser of grain or a supervisor of mines. By contrast, in Caesar's armies a prefect was a cavalry commander. When Augustus redefined the office, the title was automatically attached to knightly officers who extended their military careers to become governors of provinces, as Pilate seemed to do. Strabo in his *Geography* noted that prefects of the equestrian order were usually sent to wild or mountainous regions, or to places where the people were 'entirely barbarians'. A prefect was on the front line, in harm's way: or certainly liked to assume he was.

Some of this was simply wishful thinking. As Cicero remarked, Romans were so passionate about military glory that most of their statues were in military dress. The greatest possible virtue lay in fighting and laying down your life for Rome; civilian public service could seem second-rate. Pilate would sometimes have worn his leather soldier's tunic and metal breastplate, but his public clothing was usually the *toga praetexta*, white bordered with purple, clothing so heavy and so elaborately draped that he could only move like a bureaucrat or a statesman. If he chafed at that, Cicero had comforting words for him:

> Men who in a civil capacity direct the affairs of the nation render no less important service that those who conduct its wars . . . Diplomacy in the friendly settlement of controversies is more desirable than courage in settling them on the battlefield . . . It takes a brave and resolute spirit not to be disconcerted in times of difficulty or ruffled and thrown off one's feet, as they say, but to keep one's presence of

mind and one's self-possession and not to swerve from the path of reason.

Now all this requires great personal courage; but it also calls for great intellectual ability by reflection to anticipate the future, to discover some time in advance what is going to happen, whether for good or ill, and what must be done in any possible event, and never to be reduced to having to say, 'I hadn't thought of that.'

... There are, therefore, instances of civic courage that are not inferior to the courage of the soldier. Indeed, [civic service] calls for even greater energy and even greater devotion.

In Judea he was not just the chief soldier; he was also the chief magistrate and head of the judicial system, carrying Tiberius' whole *imperium* into his tiny patch. Although most civil and criminal jurisdiction continued to be exercised by the Jews through their councils, the lesser and greater Sanhedrin, there was a tendency to refer the hardest cases to the governor, especially when they involved unrest or might require the death penalty.

Pilate routinely used his troops to carry out crucifixions, the favoured punishment for thieves, bandits and all low-class troublemakers. These were performed, in peacetime, after a cursory hearing and, at times of rebellion, immediately and *en masse*. After the uprising under Spartacus, a century before, the Appian Way in Rome was lined with crucified slaves on both sides; in Judea, after one uprising, Gratus crucified 200 Jews at once. Under Pilate there is no record of mass crucifixions, but we can assume a steady run of them. The governor would have seen this as good administration: the policy that would later enable Tacitus to sum up his tour in Judea as *sub Tiberio quies*, 'under Tiberius, peace'. Crucifixion was not done without a reason, and the reasons were advertised on the crosses themselves. The horror of this punishment, for non-Romans, was its savagery, and for Romans its disgrace; but not randomness. Rabble-rousing Jews could anticipate the cross as a matter of course. As Luke's good thief remarked, hanging beside Jesus where Pilate had put him, 'We were sentenced justly; we are paying for what we did.'

The governor's sentences were written into the record, filed in the archive and continually referred to, as were the records of his predecessors. They were annulled only if he fell into disgrace. Almost all such governors' records have vanished with the passage of time. Historians and myth-makers alike have agonised over the disappearance of Pilate's archive, and the puzzle of whether anyone saw or consulted it while it still existed. Many suspect that, if it survived for any length of time, it was suppressed for the short, sharp reference to Jesus it presumably contained.

Pilate was also the chief fiscal officer, responsible for collecting taxes, allocating revenues, and keeping the wheels of his province turning to the profit of the *princeps* in Rome. According to Philo, budget matters took up most of a governor's time. Underlings called *publicani* farmed the indirect taxes for him, and there were plenty of them: 'income' taxes, food taxes, the *tributum soli* (land taxes based on harvests), *portorium* (a transport tax on goods), purchase tax, customs duties. Among these, the most lucrative was the duty charged at Gaza on the frankincense brought by camel from Arabia. This was still raw, white and sticky, wrapped in the palm mats on which it had dropped, like foaming milk, from the wounded trees – but not so raw that it could not be diverted, in sticky samples, as an offering to the governor.

These dues came on top of the *tributum capitis*, the poll tax paid directly to Rome, for which the census was taken that led the family of Jesus to Bethlehem. In Pilate's time the tribute was set at one silver *denarius* per head, the coin that was given to Jesus to test him on the morality of Roman taxation; it raised about 400 talents a year. This heavy load was fiercely resented by the Jews, and not only for the obvious reasons. For many of them, the tribute implied an unacceptable submission to human masters rather than to God; and the census itself was the work of the Devil, since God alone had the right to know his people in that sort of statistical detail.

Venal collectors compounded the sin. In the first years of Gaius, and possibly in the last years of Tiberius and Pilate, the chief tax-collector for Judea was one Capito, who cherished according to Philo 'a spite against the population'. (Philo painted his villains black, but most tax-collectors can seem that way.) When Capito arrived in Judea he was apparently a poor man, 'but by his rapacity and peculation he amassed much wealth in various forms. Then, fearing that some charge might be brought against him, he devised a scheme to elude the charges by slandering those he had wronged.' We do not know whether Judea made a profit or a loss while Pilate was in charge, or how much ended up in his pocket as it ended up in Capito's; but peace was also construed as profit, no matter how slim the revenues were.

In other provinces governors also approved all public works, reviewed the status of slaves and freedmen, adjudicated disputed wills, saw to the welfare of abandoned babies. At least some of their time was spent picking their way through overgrown gardens and swampland to see if they could bear constructions to the greater glory of Rome. They issued, or refused, permits for clubs and societies, and gave out precious licences to use the Imperial Post. Pilate would have done all this for the Gentiles in his province, but the social government of the Jews was left exclusively to the Sanhedrin and the local councils. This greatly narrowed his scope. While the essence of his job, as he apparently saw it, was to implant the ways of Rome, in Judea he was under strict orders not only to tolerate the local culture – standard practice in the provinces – but to make his own virtually invisible, and to keep himself as much as possible out of Jewish life.

This had financial implications. Each of his actions as governor provided an excuse for a bribe, and the habit was so endemic that it is doubtful Pilate would have resisted. This was one of the paybacks of foreign service. You were stuck in the provinces, you were homesick, bored and reviled, but at least you could shake down your subjects in exchange for the blessings of straight roads and a postal service. Cicero described one governor of Syria as 'always standing with his right hand out' to get payments for favours. In official charge-sheets, the various types of extortion were all described as 'theft'; but in common parlance a governor's payments on the side were *unguentaria*, ointment money. You could also extort more straightforwardly, through taxes, as one governor of a Spanish province bragged in a letter to his mistress: 'Hooray, hooray, I'm coming back to you solvent! Because – guess what? – I've managed to screw 4 million *sesterces* out of the Baetici.'

Governors knew that their behaviour was meant to be upright, but temptation loomed on every side. Foreigners had nice things. When Verres was pro-praetor of Sicily in the 40s BC, he sent home four hundred jars of honey, fifty sofa cushions, dozens of candelabra and dozens of bales of Maltese silk, all without paying duty. Cicero was gratified and astonished that his brother Quintus, governor of Asia, should have been three years in supreme command 'and not been tempted by the offer of any statue, picture, plate, garment, or slave, or by any fascination of human beauty, or any pecuniary proposal.'

Pilate's presumed ancestor, Gavius Pontius, could have lectured him severely on the subject. Self-seeking behaviour in public office was unpardonable to him. He had complained bitterly that fate had engineered his birth too soon, in the years before the Romans started taking bribes. Had he been born later, he said, he would have had the most glorious excuse 'for suffering their supremacy no longer'. But it seems safe to say that Pilate would have taken a softer, looser line.

Besides, a certain amount of conspicuous expenditure went with the posting. Embassies had to be received, friends entertained, rituals observed with music and processions. On his birthday and at Saturnalia, in December, the governor was expected to send out presents: books or bottles for the men, alabaster perfume boxes for their wives, or figs and dates to wish them (as the Jews also wished each other) a sweet new year. He was also expected by his Gentile subjects to organise games and to decide how the prizes ought to be awarded. Under Herod, Pilate's base-city of Caesarea had been the site of a four-yearly festival in honour of Augustus, with athletic and musical competitions as well as wild-beast shows; and perhaps the new governor was expected to keep these up. Good shows, as much as brilliant campaigns, made a man's political reputation; some men imagined God himself as an *aedile*, a master of ceremonies, stringing the sky with lights and marshalling the shooting stars. Pilate would need to get wild panthers, keeping them in cages to judge their sinuous stretching and the thrilling flash of their fangs. He would need to recruit gladiators and worry about their morale, for it was not unknown for slave-fighters to throw themselves, slippery with oil, from the carts that took them to the arena, or even to kill themselves with the cleansing sticks from the latrines. Chariots would have to be built, horses trained, and elaborate naval battles staged in a few feet of frothing water. If Pilate was a true Roman, the hours spent in the circus at Caesarea – entering to the crowd's applause, throwing out coins among the spectators, hollering on his favourite racing-colour as he cheered the Blues or the Greens at home – might well have been the happiest aspect of his job.

There were certainly disappointments. Since Judea was a small and second-rate posting, he had a shoestring staff. Governors in the larger provinces commanded a staff of three secretaries (one of whom kept the accounts), three judicial officers, a military commander, ten messengers, and the usual host of guards, interpreters, clerks, military intelligence officers, torturers, spies and grooms. Flaccus, the governor of Egypt, had a 'crowd' of secretaries, and routinely took 'only' ten or fifteen household slaves with him when dining round town. Pilate's entourage was probably a shadow of this. The gospels imply that he had no lictors, the two men who usually walked before a magistrate carrying the *fasces*, bundles of elm rods bound with an axe, as symbols of his penal authority. His initial inquiries about Jesus suggest that he did not even have a *quaestor*, the man who would usually have done the background questioning for him. Pilate seems to have done things for himself, perhaps even struggling through in Greek without an interpreter, and his 'court officers' were mostly ordinary soldiers, who might also be in short supply. Pliny reported that Gavius Bassus, the prefect of the Pontic Shore, was highly annoyed to find that he could claim only ten hand-picked soldiers, or *beneficiarii*, to be exempted from their normal duties and assigned to his staff. He went moaning to Pliny for more, but Pliny could not oblige him.

Being abroad was difficult. Like most men in foreign postings, governors got homesick. They worried about the houses they had left, the estates that needed planting, unreliable tenants, and – as Cicero put it – 'being robbed in every direction by domestics in their absence'. As now, builders and architects had to be chased up at long distance. ('I urged Longilius, the contractor, to hurry up. He convinced me he was anxious to give every satisfaction . . . Diphilus is outdoing himself in dilatoriness . . . The columns he had placed were neither perpendicular nor opposite each other. Of course, he'll have to pull them down. Some day or other he'll learn the use of plumb-line and tape . . .')

Favourite foods were elusive, too. It was hard to get oysters, chipped ice or good Falernian aged in the bottle, although, like generations of expatriates before and after, it may have been smaller things that Pilate missed: nut-and-honey pastries bought on the run, hot sausage, Tuscan olives. The *Daily Gazette* was unavailable and, though friends might send it whole or in bits, the gossip was cold by the time it arrived. Foreign-service officers missed the life of Rome, 'the City', even in its tedious aspects: the endless round of dinners and recitals, the faked excitement and assiduous applause, the ritual morning greetings and emotionless embraces. 'All foreign service,' wrote Cicero to Aelius Rufus,

> (and this has been my conviction from the days of my youth), is obscurity and squalor for those whose active services at Rome can shine forth in splendour . . . All the profits of a province are not to be compared, I swear it, with one single little stroll, and one single talk, with you. . . . 'Any hope of a triumph?' you say. I should have quite a glorious triumph if only in the shortening of the period of my yearning for all that is dearest to me.
>
> Rome, my dear Rufus, Rome – stay there in that full light and *live*.

From Rome, in reply, friends tried to cheer them up. Thus Seneca to his friend Lucilius, who was feeling down about his job as procurator of Sicily:

> There's no reason why you should measure yourself according to this part of the world; concentrate on where you're living. Any point which rises above adjacent points is great at the spot where it rises . . . a ship which looms large in the river seems tiny when it's on the ocean . . .
>
> You're really important in your province, though you scorn yourself. Men are asking what you do, what you eat for dinner, how you sleep – and they find out, too.

Most governors could comfort themselves with the thought that they were gossiped about and noticed, as they could hardly fail to be: the only man in gleaming white in a crowd, the only officer to sit in judgement in the gilded curule chair, the man before whose carriage the army cleared the streets. Yet all this show meant nothing to the Jews. They were trained from the cradle, Philo wrote, 'by the far higher authority of the sacred laws and the unwritten customs, to acknowledge one God who is the Father and maker of the world.' In this frame of mind, they accepted death 'as willingly as if it were immortality, to save them from submitting to the destruction of any of their ancient traditions.' The culture that Pilate carried with him and, indeed, loved, made him despised even before he reached Judea. He could no more simulate affection for the Jews than they could for him; and as soon as he landed, mistrust enfolded him like noxious fumes from the sea.

*   *   *

It was an old story, told most vividly by Josephus, with his Jewish heart and his Roman head. Each side knew the chief events, as plainly as pictures in a child's book. The first scene was Pompey in Jerusalem in 63 BC, standing in his sweat-stained battle clothes in the very heart of the Temple, the Holy of Holies. For months the walls had been pummelled with battering rams. Faustus, Furius and Fabius, the three centurions, had finally scaled the walls and set the city on fire on the Sabbath, when the Jews were resting; 12,000 Jews had been killed, 'but of the Romans very few'. That done, Pompey and his men thrust into the Temple and made for the innermost sanctum, where they knew the treasure was.

They saw things it was not lawful for any man to see except the priests: the golden table laid with loaves of white flour topped with frankincense, the holy menorah, the pouring vessels, bowls heaped with spices. Bulls' blood was daubed on the walls. In the innermost chamber, to their surprise, they found nothing at all. But in the outer rooms, musty, dark and rancid with ancient sacrifice, they uncovered 2,000 talents of sacred money. Pompey would not touch it. He did not need to: Jerusalem was made a tribute-city, and the Romans soon extracted 10,000 talents from it. 'And so,' sighs Josephus, 'we lost our liberty, and became subject to the Romans.' The Psalms of Solomon put it even more bitterly: 'Foreign nations went up to Thy altar and trampled it proudly without removing their shoes.'

Quarrelling high priests had been the excuse for Roman intervention. Pompey confirmed one, Hyrcanus, in power, and sent his rival Aristobulus to Rome with his arms bound behind him. But Aristobulus escaped, as did his sons Antigonus and Alexander, and immediately began to whip up unrest in Galilee, Samaria and Judea. Alexander slaughtered many Romans and beseiged others who took refuge on Mount Gerizim, in Samaria – a mountain that Pilate, too, would have reason to remember. Eventually the rebels were suppressed and the land was half-quiet again.

Until the next outrage. Crassus, governor of Syria, on his way to fight the Parthians in 55 BC, broke into the Temple again and robbed it of its gold. He found between himself and the treasure nothing more than a high curtain, embroidered with gold and purple, hanging from a great rafter. The high priest Hyrcanus begged him to take the rafter. It was hollow, and held inside it a solid beam of beaten gold that weighed 700 pounds. If Crassus took this, the priest reasoned, he would not want the rest of the gold that lay inside the Temple. But Crassus took it all. His appetite for gold was so intense that when, the next year, the Parthians killed him and sent his head to their king, the king amused himself by pouring melted gold into the dead, sagging mouth.

Hyrcanus continued to preside as high priest; but at his back, increasingly, was the ambitious Antipater, the father of Herod the Great. He came from Idumea, further south towards Egypt. Under Antipater, the Jews helped Caesar against the Eyptians and provisioned his army with corn. Antipater was even wounded in the cause of Rome; he was made a Roman citizen and procurator of Judea. His headstrong son Herod, who had charge of Galilee, carried on his father's tradition of ingratiating himself with Rome. He sent money and presents to Mark

Antony, who was on campaign in the region between his trysts with Cleopatra. In return, Rome gave the Jews privileges. Governors (including Pilate when his turn came) were banned from raising auxiliaries within the borders of Judea, or from extracting money from Jews for winter quarters 'or on any other pretext'; they could not take away their property or expect tribute in sabbatical years, when the Jews did not plough their land or pick the fruit from their trees. In 47 BC, at the instigation of Hyrcanus, the whole Jewish nation was confirmed by treaty as a client-state of Rome.

In 40 BC came the apotheosis of this era of good feeling. With struggles for local control still going on in Judea, Herod decided to claim the throne in person and to seek help in Rome. Antony and Octavian (later Augustus) took him into the Senate, where he was introduced to the senators by the master of the horse. The senators heard how fond of Rome Herod's father had been and how fond he was himself, a bulwark against the Parthians; and when Antony suggested that Herod should be king of Judea, the Senate unanimously agreed. Then Antony and Octavian walked out of the Senate house with Herod between them. He was darker than they were, with his Idumaean skin, long-haired and bearded; even in the toga of an honorary Roman citizen, he looked like a merchant. But he walked between the two Romans as if this was his natural place. They went up the hill to the Capitol, followed by a crowd of consuls and magistrates, to spill the blood of lambs and goats on Jupiter's altar. It was a Roman sacrifice, but Herod was already half-Roman: made nervous by birds and auguries, in love with architects' designs for porticoes and white marble, thrilled to sit among the senators for the wild-beast shows. He was easy to deal with because he was only half a Jew.

His people resented that. They did not believe his wriggling apology that he put up fantastic buildings only to be polite to the Romans. Factions resisted him, and he fought them to the point where, in 37 BC, twenty-seven years to the day since Pompey's incursion, he had to take Jerusalem by force. The Romans under Sosius helped him. Once more they battered the walls, scaled them, set fire to the porticoes of the Temple and cut down Jews in the city's maze of alleyways; and once more, smelling gold, the Romans rushed towards the Holy of Holies. This time, the outcome was different. Herod held them back and begged them not to loot the city. 'Do you want to make me king of a desert?' he kept asking. 'Do you want to make me king of a desert?' To encourage them to leave, he pressed money into their hands and gave

Sosius a golden crown. This was an embarrassing present for a Roman, a sign of Herod's cultural obtuseness; so Sosius dedicated the crown to the gods and marched away from Jerusalem.

Herod was soon without rivals. In 31 BC he was confirmed as a client king, a dependent and ever-dependable ally, by Octavian/Augustus; and, feeling himself secure, he became more Roman than the Romans. Great palaces and public buildings in the Roman style went up at Caesarea, Sebaste and Jerusalem, featuring vast dining rooms and floors of polished stone. The king developed a Roman fixation for fittings and statues of Corinthian bronze, which was allegedly fused with gold and silver to give it a colour and patina that conoisseurs adored. His sons were sent to Rome to study. And, most offensive of all to the Jews, he instituted games at Jerusalem in honour of Augustus. At the great ampitheatre in the plain, glittering with gold and silver trophies from Herod's campaigns and inscriptions in honour of the emperor, appeared wrestlers, professional musicians, horse-races, races for two-horse and four-horse chariots and wild-beast fights. Foreigners loved these; Pilate would probably have been in heaven; but the Jews, said Josephus, lamented 'the palpable destruction of the customs they venerated'. It was no better than barefaced impiety 'to throw men to wild beasts, to afford delight to spectators', almost within sight and earshot of the holiest place in the world.

In short – at least in Josephus' view – Herod was a hedonist and a tyrant. Even his squabbling sons turned against him. When Augustus came to Syria in 20 BC a people called the Gadarenes accused Herod of violence, plunder and overthrowing of temples; but Herod was so sure of the emperor's favour that he stood in the judgement hall unconcerned. His confidence was justified, Josephus said. Augustus took him by the right hand, 'and remitted nothing of his kindness to him, despite the uproar of the crowd.' Eight years later he reconciled Herod's sons with him, when they came to Rome to accuse their father in person. Augustus beckoned to the three of them to embrace each other; and as they did so, in floods of relieved tears, a few tears glistened also on the taut imperial cheek. This did not stop Augustus remarking, on another occasion, that he would rather be Herod's pig than his son.

The reconciliation did not last long. The Herodian family soon quarrelled, and Judea broke up with them. Josephus, undoubtedly letting his hatred for Herod get the better of him, related how the man brought bad luck on himself by going one night into the musty vault of King David's tomb and taking out, from beneath the damp slabs, the golden ornaments that were buried there. Then he ventured further, towards the coffins of David and Solomon; but a great flame burst out, killing two of his bodyguards and frightening Herod out of his wits. He began to suspect that all his intimates were plotting against him, and most of them were. Eventually, worn out by his sons' misbehaviour, he fell ill. Age and bitterness ate up his body. His intestines were ulcerated, his feet gouty, his breathing laboured. Even his penis turned to stone and generated worms, and his breath stank. In desperation he tried the warm baths at Callirrhoe, where his doctors immersed him in vats of tepid oil; but it did no good.

In 4 BC he died, and his kingdom was divided among his surviving sons. Archelaus took the half containing Judea, Idumaea and Samaria; Herod Antipas became tetrarch of Galilee; Philip became tetrarch of Batanea, Trachonitis and Auranitis. Augustus confirmed the division of Herod's kingdom in the presence of fifty Jewish ambassadors in the temple of Apollo in Rome, and this was how it was still divided when Pilate arrived there, thirty years later. Archelaus had been banished after ten years of misrule, at the end of which he was haunted by a dream of ears of corn being devoured by oxen. After his banishment, in AD 6, Rome had taken over his half of the kingdom; his brothers still sat in their sections. It was not a comfortable arrangement for either side. Judea both needed Rome, and hated it. It sulked and seethed.

*   *   *

Pilate's ship docked at Caesarea, one of the most impressive cities of the eastern empire. The whole waterfront was newly built by Herod, largely of white marble. From far out at sea the buildings shone in the brilliant light: blue sky, blue sea, white stone. On the left as the ship entered harbour was a round turret, capable of withstanding the strongest sweep of the sea; on the right were two monoliths, each larger than the turret, joined together to make a sort of monumental sculpture at the entryway to Judea.

Because this coast was difficult to anchor in, buffeted by south winds and drifting sand, Herod had built a pier of huge stones 200 feet out into the sea. Each stone was at least fifty feet long, eighteen feet wide and nine feet high, and with enormous difficulty and skill they had been lowered down through twenty fathoms of water. The leeward half of the pier supported a wall and several towers, the largest named Drusus after the step-son of Augustus, who had died young. Round the harbour ran a promenade lined with arches and, behind these, with fine buildings. At the central point, facing north where the sky was clearest, a small man-made hillock was crowned with a temple of Augustus. The city was so new that even the cellars and sewers were lined with beautiful fresh-cut stone; from Pilate's latrine, the Roman filth of Caesarea's newest resident could be swiftly and neatly conveyed to the sea. The north-east side of the town held an amphitheatre and the south side a theatre, from which the audience for the nautical war-games could look out over the shining stage of waves and salt water almost as far as the Bosphorus.

The palace in Caesarea, newly built too, was Pilate's headquarters. Little dragged him away from this vision of white marble. He spent almost all his time in a city that was trying to be Rome; he could almost forget that he was in Judea. There were far fewer Jews in town than Syrians, Greeks, Romans and far-flung sailors, whose drunken night songs floated from the harbour arches into the thickening air. Pilate could walk out by the water in the evenings, along the curving promenade ('a most agreeable walk for those who like exercise', Josephus said), unless like Tiberius he preferred to be carried in his litter, round and round, for the sheer imperious fun of it. There, if he cared to, he could sniff the salt tang of the sea and feel the wind ruffle his hair. In the winter he could wrap his cloak twice round him and shroud his head from the spray; in the summer he could watch intrepid boys plunging in the blue-green water where, deep down, the great stones sent back a shimmering lattice-work of sunlight. When he offered public sacrifice it was Caesar's temple he walked to, attended by his retinue; and the statues to which he raised his eyes were of Augustus and motherly Roma, comforting and essential images of home, though touched with foreign light in a foreign place.

On the rare occasions when he left Caesarea he could still contrive to remain in this world. The way to Jerusalem, where he went to reinforce security on the Jewish festivals of Passover, Pentecost and Tabernacles, was sixty miles south-south-east along a Roman road marked reassuringly with Roman mile-posts. He did not go there willingly; few Romans did. Augustus had actually commended his grandson Gaius, when he went on tour through Judea, for not stopping in Jerusalem to pay his respects. But Pilate had to make the best of it.

His lodgings there made life easier. When he reached the city he stayed in Herod's old palace on the western hill, another wonder of white marble, where glistening terraces overlooked the city in one direction and, in the other, gardens shaded with trees. The palace afforded (as Josephus said) 'a most delightful prospect to those who wished to overlook the city', and its luxury 'baffled description'. Possibly he was exaggerating, wishing to condemn the conspicuous consumption of both Herodians and Romans; but possibly what he described was exactly what Pilate saw.

It was extraordinary. Among columns of coloured marble and glittering fountains flew sudden scattered clouds of white doves. Their feathers fell on pavements of mosaic, on floors of agate and lapis lazuli; their wings beat among improbably high ceilings where every beam was painted with gold and vermilion. The very chairs and tables were of gold or silver inlaid with jewels, uncomfortable designer objects in which no man could relax, and Herod's gifts from his emperor-friends were on display in every room. In the two great marble wings, one named after Augustus and the other after Agrippa, dining rooms with one hundred reclining couches and table settings could accommodate three hundred diners. To a visitor with a relatively small staff it was no doubt a bemusing place, easy to get lost in: the journey to bed complicated, the bedroom vast, little things like wine and snacks and writing tablets not readily to hand. And it was into this cold but fantastic hotel that Pilate brought Christ.

He did not necessarily see much of the Jews, even in Jerusalem. There they were a largely undifferentiated, potentially dangerous crowd. He stayed above them. From his terrace he could gaze down at the low grey houses, the shanties and allotments of the Holy City, studded with mangy palms and occasional cypresses like those of home. At Caesarea he felt safe, with plenty of troops around him and the blue sea offering escape. Here, although he had soldiers billeted in both the palace and the Antonia (Herod's fort, named after his friend Antony, now the headquarters of the Roman garrison), he was surrounded by enemies. Like all provincials – to a Roman nose – they had a smell about them, a sharp, foreign smell untempered by perfume sprays. When Verres was pro-praetor of Sicily he would bury his face, on unavoidable outings, in a string bag stuffed with roses; and modern writers, from Kazantzakis to Bulgakov, have imagined Pilate too seeking refuge in gardens and handkerchiefs, an aesthete suffering in an unbearable place.

Yet there was much to admire outside the palace in Jerusalem, the Temple most of all. The building was a fabulous treasure-house, replenished every year with gold and silver from every corner of the world. Herod had begun to rebuild it with the services of 10,000 workers and 1,000 priests, and the work was just finished – after 46 years – by the time Pilate first came up from Caesarea. From afar it could be seen on its hill, a giant mausoleum framed by great walls and porticoes lined with Corinthian pillars. It was impossible not to be curious.

Besides, the Romans were not without interests there. They stationed soldiers in the western porticoes during the festivals, in case of trouble; and, more strangely, they themselves sent gifts and offered sacrifice. Augustus, Livia and Tiberius sent golden vials and libation bowls to decorate the sanctuary, and the Roman administration (that is, Pilate's officers) provided the bullock and two lambs that were sacrificed there daily on Tiberius's orders for the safety of the emperor. Whether the smell of blood and incense reached the nostrils of many gods or one God was, in this case, immaterial; the emperor's subjects commended him for safety's sake to 'the Supreme God', the singular God of Israel.

So, undoubtedly, Pilate got closer. He was allowed to see the front wall of the Temple, decorated with lintels on pillars and constructed of slabs of white marble polished to such a high gloss that he might almost have seen his own gazing image reflected back. The lavish gold-plating flashed in the sun. In Mark's gospel Jesus' disciples too were amazed at that colossal outer wall: 'Master, just look! What huge stones! What huge buildings!' It was disconcerting proof of Jesus' radicalism that he seemed to take pleasure in imagining it wrecked, even if rebuilt afterwards.

If Pilate went through the entrance in that first gleaming wall, his servants clearing a path through the beggars who crouched there in hope of alms, he would arrive in the courtyard below the porticoes where pilgrims could change money, and where hawkers sold pigeons and lambs to those who wished to offer sacrifice. He could walk across this courtyard to a small flight of steps, surmounted by a wall with a door. On the wall, however, were large signs in Latin and Greek, erected by a previous Roman administration, warning him that entry beyond this point was restricted to Jews. Trespassers, it was made clear, could expect to die. Dusty couples from the countryside went through that door, dutifully carrying their pigeons in wicker cages, as Mary and Joseph had done years before to give thanks for the infant Jesus. But Pilate could do no more than watch them.

Marcus Agrippa, Tiberius' father-in-law and Augustus' second-in-command, probably saw as much of Temple business as a Roman could observe. He came in the autumn of 15 BC as a guest of Herod, and was so impressed by the Temple that he could not keep away. He had seen, wrote Philo proudly, 'something to be profoundly reverenced, something greater than words could describe.' Every day of his stay he went back to the Temple precinct, marvelling at the ritual and decorations, 'the majestic aspect of the high priest wearing the sacred vestments and conducting the holy rites.' These, presumably, were the ceremonies of the Feast of Tabernacles and the daily sacrifices made on behalf of the emperor; more than this he was not allowed to witness. Rumour had it, though, that when you proceeded through the third door, where even the ritually pure were required to take a bath and change into white clothes, the splendours were almost incredible: enormous doors hung with embroidered veils and flowers of purple, behind a great golden grille fantastically crafted to resemble a spreading vine burdened with bunches of grapes the size of a man, symbols of the fruitfulness of Israel.

Rumour had it, too, that the tiny innermost chamber called the Holy of Holies was empty, for Pompey had been disappointed. Tacitus wrote that he had found only 'a naked dome, the sanctuary unadorned and simple', though Tacitus himself was half persuaded that it really contained the head of an ass, since a herd of wild asses had led the Jews to water during the exodus. On Yom Kippur, the holiest day of the year, the high priest, in a tunic of linen and a robe of silk brocade encrusted with jewels and hemmed with gold, entered the Holy of Holies alone to burn incense and pray for the peace of the world. It was the most secret, sacred act, and so fearful that the priest would later celebrate the fact that he had emerged alive. Yet the Romans played a tiny part in that, too. For the rest of the year the high priest's gorgeous robes, including a purple *chiton* with golden bells and tassels, were kept in Roman custody, though never touched. They lay in the Antonia, kept like some magic treasure trove in a sealed stone room in a guarded tower. Every day, in one of the more peculiar courtesies of the Roman regime, the commandant lit a lamp outside the chamber. Seven days before the festivals on which they were needed, he would deliver the robes to the priests; and the priests, exhaustively, with water and incense and incantations, would rub the smell of the Romans away.

If anyone told Pilate of these secret places and rituals of the people he governed, it was probably Joseph Caiaphas, the high priest. Caiaphas was there when he arrived, the last of Gratus' string of appointments, and he was there when he left. Indeed, because he was seen as Pilate's man, he did not long outlast him. His longevity in office was unusual. Was this because he was a towering figure, impressively competent? It seems unlikely. Although he was the son-in-law of Annas, an ex-high priest and the real power behind the Sanhedrin, he seems to have been more of a trimmer and appeaser. It was Caiaphas who was said to have made the crassly pragmatic suggestion, as the priests were discussing how to handle the problem of Jesus, that it was 'expedient that one man should die for the people', to preserve them from Roman rage; and he needed to hear very little from Jesus before, like the good Sadducee he was, he stood up and carefully made a tear in his robes of the ritually required length for mourning over blasphemy.

Did he stay, then, because Pilate forswore the chance to enrich himself by selling Judea's premier appointment? Again, it seems unlikely, although Pilate is not presented as a man who was particularly interested in money. More probably the two men got on, after a fashion; the getting-on was greased by an annual bribe pitched by Caiaphas at a rate higher than his rivals; and Pilate felt it was safer not to rock the boat by replacing him. He relied on him too much. All through his rocky career in Judea, the priests and local rulers almost always stayed on Pilate's side; it was the crowd, usually without leaders, that opposed him.

For his part, Caiaphas accepted – as did all the Roman-appointed high priests, and most of the Sadducees and Pharisees – that the Romans were the best protectors of the Temple against insurgents from the more violent Jewish sects. In 5 BC a gang of young men had climbed on the Temple roof, let themselves down with ropes and vandalised a great golden eagle set by Herod above a doorway, taking it both for a sacriligious icon and for an emblem of Rome. Samaritans had attacked the Temple too a little later, getting into the forbidden courtyards 'and throwing dead men's bones around', as the horrified Josephus reported. But the Romans defended it, and Pilate played his part: in the twenty-three years of Tiberius' rule, according to Philo, no part of the Temple was disturbed.

Through Caiaphas, over the years, Pilate might have absorbed a little knowledge of Jewish faith and practice. If he had read his Strabo on the geography of Judea, he would also have picked up the notion that the Jews were originally Egyptians, led to Jerusalem by the pious Egyptian priest Moses 'because he thought the Egyptians were wrong to reproduce the image of the Divine Being by the images of beasts and cattle.' Moses believed, Strabo wrote, that God was 'this one thing alone that encompasses us all and encompasses land and sea – the thing which we call heaven, or universe, or the nature of all that exists.' Strabo evidently struggled with this concept, and he was not alone. Tacitus thought the God of the Jews was 'the great governing mind', whom they imagined in their heads; Juvenal thought the Jews worshipped 'the clouds and brightness of the heavens'.

Roman writers were less tentative, and much less kind, when it came to the religious practices of the Jews. Tacitus called their religion 'the reverse of everything known to any other age or country . . . Whatever is held sacred by the Romans, with the Jews is held profane, and what in other nations is unlawful and impure, with them is fully established.' Their festival days were 'a gloomy ceremony, full of absurd enthusiasm, rueful, mean and sordid'. They were unsociable, and seemed to hate the rest of mankind. 'Obstinate' and 'stubborn' were the words Tacitus used most often of them; and it was their 'superstitions' and 'unholy practices', he said, that had made Tiberius send them away.

Even tiny things rankled. The long finger-dates of Judea were cherished by the Romans as acceptable offerings to the gods; Pilate might have laid them among the private deities in his bedroom as he laid down quinces or apples at home. The Jews, however, called these 'common dates'; and this fact alone, the elder Pliny wrote, summed up 'their contempt for things divine'.

His attitude was common enough. At best (as in the case of Petronius, who was sent by the emperor Gaius to sort out Judea shortly after Pilate left), the Romans in Judea found the faith of the Jews impressive but baffling. At worst, they mocked it, like the detachment of soldiers described by Josephus who were sent to search a village for malefactors and, finding a copy of the Laws of Moses in one of the houses, apparently tore it up with guffaws of laughter. Between these two attitudes was insulting ignorance, of the sort displayed by Gaius in 38 when he received a delegation of Jews protesting about the proposed erection of his golden image in the Temple. This delegation included Philo, who described the scene with customary, but justified, bitterness; though he was no harder than Roman writers were on the playful, brutal man who came to meet them, waving casually from his garden gate.

'Ah, so you're the god-haters!' Gaius shouted.

When they had recovered from this he went on, between wandering upstairs and downstairs and out into the gardens of his villa, 'Why don't you eat pork?'

His hangers-on burst out laughing. The Jewish delegates, embarrassed, answered, 'Different people have different customs.'

'Yes', said someone, 'just as many don't eat lamb, though it's easy enough to get.'

'Quite right, too, because it's not nice!' cried Gaius. The company burst out laughing again; and the emperor, ignoring what the Jews were trying to say to him, wandered off into other rooms to order new windows and new paintings. 'Under such befooling and reviling we were helpless,' wrote Philo sadly.

By the end of his tour, Pilate could probably have distinguished his Pharisees from his Sadducees. Josephus in the *Antiquities* made the differences clear enough, and so did Jesus in his parables. The Pharisees were the ones with their tassels and broad phylacteries, as Jesus described them, who prayed and swayed in the streets; or who, as Josephus said, lived simply, followed the guidance of reason and directed the religious observances of the people. They were not of the highest social rank and, as far as religion went, were open to and interested in change. A Roman would suppose they were not to be trusted because, during the time of Augustus, they had refused to make a pledge of goodwill to him. Then came the Sadducees, like Caiaphas and the rest of the priests: sturdy traditionalists, keepers of the Temple ritual, rejecters of novel theories such as the immortality of the soul, and though 'a disputacious elite' to Jews like Josephus, ready and willing to accommodate with Rome. Last came the Essenes, 'addicted to virtue', Josephus said, who dressed all in white, shared everything, refused to keep slaves and lived without sex in the desert. Pilate may never have seen an Essene; yet even these may sometimes have intruded on his dreams.

When all was said, his interest in Judaism was simple. He had to know whether it was dangerous or not. Judea in his time seemed quiet, but in the vacuum left after Herod's death and before the Roman prefecture it had filled up with mavericks, prophets and impostors. A man called Judas, the son of a robber-chief, had gathered a gang together, stormed the palace at Sepphoris in Galilee, and made off with a stash of weapons in the hope that the raid would make him king. Another called Simon, one of Herod's servants ('tall, robust and handsome,' said Josephus), put a crown on his head and had himself proclaimed king; he then went on the rampage, burning down all the royal palaces he came across, until the legions stopped him. Next came a band of shepherd brothers with individual gangs of their own, who engaged in constant guerrilla warfare and, in the end, revolt against the Romans. Varus put this down by crucifying two thousand of the rebels.

Still this was not the end of it. Another hothead called Judas sprang out of Galilee when Coponius was governor, exhorting the Jews to resist Roman taxes; even if they failed they would be glorious, because

God was on their side. And in Pilate's time, just as he arrived in Judea, a man called John appeared in the desert, shouting about the Kingdom of God and the mountains tumbling. Was this dangerous? What was it supposed to mean? The 'pretext of public welfare', as Josephus called it, was intensely worrying; more so was the flammable mixture of politics and religion. All risings in Judea had this cast. The hand of God, not merely of His people, was raised against the Romans; His sword would smite them; His anointing floated about the rebel leaders, balsam and frankincense, the odour of holiness. Those prophets who seemed the maddest of all might be precisely those who could not be ignored.

Nor did these discontents ever disappear. They lay under the hide of the land. It might be true, as Josephus remarked, that Judea was a nice place in parts, with 'a light and fertile soil for agriculture, thick woods, abundant fruit, singularly sweet water and a higher milk yield than other districts'; it was true that Herod had scattered it with magnificent fortresses done up, like the palace in Jerusalem, with mosaics and swimming pools and painted marble. But to the north and east of Jerusalem the wilderness unfolded, apparently empty. The bare lime-stone hills were scattered only with stones, or with sheep that resembled stones. The dry fissures held no water, only washes of gravel. Brown thistles and thorn bushes were the only crops, and the hilltop villages were coated like the hills themselves with baked grey dust. Tacitus wrote later that the whole landscape seemed to bear the marks of 'celestial vengeance', though he himself thought it was only the exhalations from the great dead lake that withered the flowers into black dust and, near the coast, petrified the alluvial sands into rivulets of glass.

In the great Judean survey made by Quirinius in AD 6, just after Rome had assumed direct control, all these places had been inspected, their people counted and their taxes assessed. Although the governor of Judea was evidently thought too junior to carry out a census himself, it was part of Pilate's job to know these numbers: to see why this collection of mud and stones could not pay tribute, to see why that goat-infested hollow needed a road or a water supply. In practice he preferred, as any Roman would have done, to keep to the Jordan valley, the lake shores or the haven of Caesarea, where he could sit in the shade of palms with a plate of fresh dates and a flask of decent wine. But his domain was largely mountains, wilderness and trouble.

From time to time he would not have been able to avoid this part of it. Perhaps he was carried, but his litter was more suited to the streets of Caesarea; and out in the desert there was no one to impress. Few sights would have been odder, in the howling waste, than the governor's litter with its gilded wood and shimmering silk curtains, tipping this way and that among the rocks. It was safer to ride, though not alone; the imperial governor of Nearer Spain had been killed by a peasant not long before while travelling unguarded in just such country, steep, pathless, strewn with stones. Pilate therefore went surrounded by military outriders under heavy arms. Even then, the emptiness of the scene was terrifying. In the imagination of the Romans the desert was riddled with caves and the caves stuffed with *lestai* and *sicarii*, bandits with small curved swords. As you passed a hillside, armed men the colour of dust might rise up from the ground, as men had sprung from the stones thrown by Deucalion to repopulate the earth. The very goats had fire in their eyes; they bleated of Messiahs. And the far beckoning blue of the sea was no sea at all, only poisonous Asphaltites where, as over Avernus, the birds dropped dead as they flew.

It was a job; and it was a continuous bad dream.

'Every native, I verily believe, is corrupt,' wrote one governor. Another, kinder, confided to a friend: 'As you know, the vast majority of the people are ignorant and illiterate and easily swayed by sentiment and emotion. And yet, it always seems to me wonderful that in spite of trouble and disturbances, British rule in India has lasted and continues notwithstanding . . .'

To Christ's biographers of the late nineteenth and early twentieth centuries, in Europe as well as in Britain, the plume-hatted representatives of the King-Emperor seemed to be much like Pilate. Their problems were seen as comparable, different mostly in scale. A sunbaked, hard terrain in which you were forced to seek breezes, fans and shade. A surface veneer of roads, government buildings, imported legal structures and a pompous shared vernacular; but beneath that sulking clerks, untrustworthy officials, even outright bandits. Every so often – for their own good, naturally – the people's rights under law were suspended. They could be arrested without warrant and detained without trial, and officers acting in good faith against unruly elements were not obliged to justify their actions. As one writer put it in 1931, drawing an explicit comparison with Pilate and his circumstances, 'There is almost no severity of provincial repression which will not be enthusiastically supported by a cultivated upper class at home.'

Imperial power was not absolute. Local princelings ruled in their own states, controlled the local factions, were more gorgeously arrayed and had better table manners. One complained that the wife of the governor-general ate her cheese with her knife. They were schooled in England, had beautifully pointed diction, drank tea at the right time, and brimmed with courteous contempt. Yet these were the easiest Indians to get on with. In the north the Sikhs were heavily armed with knives and swords, fiercely defensive of their Golden Temple; as late as 1919, four hundred Sikh protesters, this time without arms, were killed by General Dyer's troops at Amritsar. General Dyer had been sent to restore order after rioting in the town, and was angry to find that his orders banning public meetings were ignored; after the massacre, he said he would have used the machine guns on his armoured cars if he had been able to get the vehicles into the square. Those Sikhs who continued to cause trouble were forced to crawl on hands and knees, or were publicly flogged. It was natural, our writer of 1931 continued, that contemporary scholars should seek to defend Pilate, since to condemn him 'might lead to unpleasant contemporary applications.'

Governors trained for India by cultivating social graces. A nominee for governor in the 1920s had daily riding lessons in Rotten Row; studied marksmanship, so as to be able to pick off tigers from the swaying perch of a howdah; and took up ballroom dancing. These talents were known to be appreciated. He learned no Indian language, however, and what cultural peculiarities he studied were mostly to avoid giving social offence. His day, after all, was largely diplomatic and ceremonial. A ride in the cool dawn; breakfast; council meetings, or the handling of reports; lunch with guests; more meetings, interviews, more reports; official dinners, balls and receptions. When he was travelling the state Rolls-Royces would wait in the drive with their motors running, followed by lorries for the luggage and the servants; and liveried men would stand with torches at twenty-yard intervals along the railway line.

Why were they there? To claim and hold and preserve the empire, its language and laws. To keep revenues flowing from the landowners to the coffers of the imperial government, according to Cornwallis's Permanent Settlement, which had assessed what taxes the land could sustain. To relieve famine, build aqueducts, lay roads, educate children, and set up a model of civilisation. If necessary, governors could be kingmakers; but in general they preferred to keep power out of Indian hands. Racial superiority decreed it, just as it decreed a lower level of proof in trials and harder seats in railway carriages. If you gave Indians some partnership in governing, one governor wrote, this would instil in them 'an increased feeling of existing subordination and a realisation of everything by which this subordination was expressed'.

In 1925, Lord Reading, then governor-general, concluded that 'In ultimate analysis, the strength of the British position is that we are in India for the good of India.' A year later, on his way home, he carried the thought further:

> . . . as I wend my way home, I return with a deeper realisation of the beneficent outlook of the British Empire, with a wider understanding of its duties and responsibilities, with a larger conception of the influence and power of that great commonwealth of nations. I glory in the high purpose it is our duty as citizens of the Empire to seek to achieve; in the moral standpoint of public service we try to inculcate; in the endeavour to improve the conditions of the poorer and less fortunate people, in the earnest wish that this country may be the better for our efforts, that we may have contributed to the cause of humanity, and that we may have assisted in promoting the welfare and happiness of India.

So wrote one of the better governors on one of his better days. Yet even he was not above mass arrests, racial snobbery and unbalanced trials. One of these was the trial of an inoffensive-looking, clerkish man in a dhoti, with spindly bare legs, who had come to visit him at the vice-regal palace some months before. Reading admitted that Gandhi's moral thinking was 'on a high altitude'; he was bothered by, but could not work out, his politics. What most impressed him was that when he ordered tea, Gandhi ordered hot water, and would not touch his cup until the governor-general had touched his. 'I have to admit I liked him,' he wrote afterwards. Yet he also felt he had to crush him as a fomenter of dangerous ideas, and did so as soon as he could act with impunity, immediately after an expensive and successful visit by the Prince of Wales. His standing with the King-Emperor was secure; his management of India was applauded; a nationalist uprising seemed unlikely. The chink of teacups could be replaced by the iron fist.

Gandhi was tried and convicted on a charge of sedition. It was the same charge on which Pilate tried and convicted Christ.

The fifth prefect left almost no traces behind him. No roads, no milestones, no public buildings. Some miles from Jerusalem runs an aqueduct that may be his, solidly built of brick and lined with lead. Beyond that, all that remains is a block of calcareous stone and a handful of coins.

The stone was found at Caesarea in the summer of 1961. By then, nothing remained of the fabulous city but traces of the rampart, a few scattered ruins of the temple of Augustus, and two colossal right feet from the statues of Augustus and Roma: feet that Pilate had probably grasped to give him safety, or to bring him luck. Herod's granite blocks still shone at the edge of the pier, beside the tumbled walls of his theatre.

Among those blocks was Pilate's stone. In the manner of the ancient stones built into the walls of medieval Italian buildings, this one had been hacked from its original position and put to another use. It formed a landing between flights of steps at one of the entrances to Herod's theatre when, in later years, the theatre was rebuilt to stage water sports. The endless passage of sports-fans' feet had worn away the inscription and chipped away the sides until almost nothing remained but this:

S TIBERIEVM
TIVS PILATVS
ECTVS IVDA--E

Most photographs of the stone show it against a neutral background, as in a museum. One, startlingly different, shows it as it was found at the edge of the sea. The chiselled letters on the small, smooth slab grow out of a massive rock encrusted with limpets and barnacles. Beyond it are other ruins, low spars of stone lying in shallow water. The sun, setting, bathes the scene in a light the colour of old bronze. This might be a battlefield strewn with bodies and rusted blades, except that all have been caught and half-covered by the bright evening wash of the sea.

For weeks the Italian team of archaeologists pored over the stone, cleaned it with water, brushed away the sand. They willed the letters to reveal themselves among the dancing molecules of limestone. In the end, their best guess was this:

CAESARIENSIBUS TIBERIEVM
PONTIVS PILATVS
PRAEFECTVS IVDAEAE
DEDIT

'Pontius Pilate, Prefect of Judea, has given this Tiberieum to the citizens of Caesarea.'

The second-best guess presumed that Pilate would have preferred to offer something to the gods of the imperial house rather than to the Caesareans; and perhaps that was true.

> DIS AVGVSTIS TIBERIEVM
> PONTIVS PILATVS
> PRAEFECTVS IVDAEAE
> FECIT, DEDICAVIT

'Pontius Pilate, Prefect of Judea, has made this Tiberieum and dedicated it to the Augustan gods.'

The block was of limestone quarried at Kabbara, a few miles north of the town; it was 82 cm high, 68 cm broad and 21 cm thick, with lettering 5–6cm high. This suggests it was at eye-level, where people could read it, in a building of modest size. It is strange, even revealing, that the inscription is in Latin, since Greek was the common language of all public notices at that time in the east. Even here, perhaps, Pilate's love of Rome insisted on showing itself; or his devotion to Tiberius, who, though fluent in Greek, once apologised to the Senate for using the word 'monopoly'. It is revealing, too, that at a time when abbreviation (especially of titles) was the rule and fashion in inscriptions, Pilate proudly spelt out in full the words *Praefectus Judaeae*.

That said, it was not an impressive piece of work. The lettering is deeply incised, but cramped and irregular. *Tiberieum* is elegantly done, but for the name of the governor the inscriber has let himself go: he follows the contemporary fashion of making some letters, especially the 'T' and the 'I' of *Pilatus*, taller than others, but the effect is slightly untidy. Perhaps it was hard to find good stone-cutters in Judea. But Pilate was presumably satisfied with it, and possibly even wanted his name to be inscribed that way. It would not have graced the building without his approval and a ceremony of dedication, with flowers and fat-laden smoke, on the breezy site beside the water.

The word *Tiberieum* may have been Pilate's own invention; it occurs nowhere else. Perhaps because it was new, he made sure the final 'e' carried a flamboyant accent to lengthen the vowel, and took this convention through to the fourth line (where an accent is all that remains), accenting the 'e' of *dedit* or *dedicavit* in a way that was unusual and even unnecessary. Yet the construction of the word was common enough. It meant that this was a building in honour of Tiberius, just as a Caesareum was a building in honour of Augustus. The usual centrepiece of such buildings was a shrine, but around the shrine – as in the famous Caesareum in Alexandria – might be courtyards, libraries, picture galleries, even 'sacred groves'. The budget at Caesarea would not stretch as far as that, and Pilate's Tiberieum was possibly closer to a basilica or a meeting hall. But it could well have been a temple, in which the emperor's image was worshipped every month with offerings of wine and incense, and prayers offered for his health and the prosperity of Rome.

Either way, Tiberius would have found the building embarrassing. According to Suetonius, religion meant almost nothing to him; he cared only for divination and the more obscure sides of literature. He rebuked people who called him 'Lord', was highly annoyed to be addressed as a god, and once asked a man who had called his work 'sacred' to change the word to 'laborious'. He had, of course, deified Augustus, but Pliny was of the opinion that Tiberius had given the emperor 'his place among the stars' merely to reflect upon himself the glory of the man who had adopted him, and to terrorise the people. He continued to resist suggestions of temples or cults of himself, at least in the west, maintaining that the emperor could be worshipped only after his death and that, meanwhile, 'my temples are in your hearts.'

On the other hand, people knew he did not usually mean what he said. Even in Rome his effigy was used as a sacred amulet by criminals, who knew that by clasping this image of a god they could escape prosecution; and in the eastern empire, in Asia, Tiberius had at last allowed a temple to be built to him. In Rome in 27 the Senate suggested that one of the city's hills should be given extra veneration because, when fire had ravaged it, the only object spared had been a statue of Tiberius in a house there. Far away in Caesarea, hearing these stories, Pilate might have imagined he would bolster both himself and Rome with his intemperate devotions.

His coins tell a similar story. Prefects' coins were tiny; the largest ones issued under Pilate were only 17 mm across, weighing about two grams. They were worth a demi-*quadrans*, or the eighth part of an *as*; two of them could get you into the public baths in Rome. All the coins that survive are of bronze. They were simple small change for the man in the street, but not without use as propaganda.

When Pilate arrived in Judea, the coins of Gratus were in circulation. These carried uncontroversial devices, with a wreath or a cut branch of vine on the obverse and, on the reverse, various symbols of fruitfulness: double cornucopias, lilies, branches of leaves. The emperor's name was abbreviated and given in Greek. Other, weightier coins in circulation included silver *denarii* with the head of the emperor, but these were not minted in Judea because they were offensive to the Jews.

Gratus had found a way round Jewish sensibilities with his branches and flowers, but Pilate wanted to honour Tiberius properly. Since a portrait was unacceptable to his subjects, a graven image that violated the second commandment, Pilate devised the next-best, next-most-offensive thing: images of objects used in Roman religious rites. These were not his own design. They were in circulation in other parts of the empire, but were not recommended for Judea, and were never seen there until he introduced them. Some scholars doubt whether this was his idea; they note that he issued no more coins after 31, when Sejanus fell. But Sejanus, unlike Pilate, had no motive for flaunting Roman superiority in Judea.

Some of Pilate's coins showed the *simpulum*, a small vessel used to pour out oil or wine upon the altar. Others showed the *lituus* or augur's wand, as carried in the right hand when reading the future from the slippery entrails of beasts. On the reverse of his coins he kept his symbols innocuous: three bending ears of barley, a wreath with berries. This side at least would not annoy the Jews, although it made no difference in one way: his coins would still be unacceptable in the Temple. The reason why the outer court was full of changing tables – tables soon to be upended by Jesus – was because no coin with a pagan symbol could be used, or even dropped in a box, in that holy place.

The *simpulum* was the holiest of these images: 'How pleasing to the gods are the *simpula* of the priests!' Cicero had written. These were made of clay as a mark of respect to the earth, the mother of all things. The *lituus* too was deeply sacramental: it was the wand by which Augustus had saved the world by establishing universal peace, the instrument through which the will of the gods was made manifest in him. It was also, for those who knew, a particular sop to Tiberius and his love of divination. His mother had divined his own birth by warming an egg in her hands until a cockerel hatched from it; an eagle had perched on his house in Rhodes before he was made emperor; he was warned of a popular revolt when he found his pet snake eaten by ants. As emperor, although he banned the use of astrology by others, he spent so much time in the company of his astrologer Thrasyllus, and studied the subject so avidly, Suetonius said, that he could even tell when his dreams were deceiving him. At the end of his life, he decided to depend on divination to fix the succession to the empire; it fell to Gaius because one morning he came in to Tiberius first, while his rival Drusus waited for breakfast. All the emperor's frightening fascination was caught up in that magic wand, curled like a sea-horse, that Pilate impressed upon his coins. And around the image lay his title, *Tiberius Kaisaros*, spelt out by Pilate in full, just as he had spelt out 'Prefect of Judea'.

Beyond the coins and dedicated buildings lay more routine expressions of respect. Governors made annual vows, with prayers and celebrations, on the anniversary of the emperor's accession, and at the beginning of the year they offered public prayers for his safety and that of the state. They were also bound to remember his birthday. (In his early years Tiberius would not allow any special celebration, but this changed as he got older.) As in the British Raj, imperial birthdays meant special services, ceremonies and reviews of the troops. Condemned men were usually not punished on that day, and the crucified were taken down and allowed to be buried; 'for it was thought fitting,' says Philo, 'that the dead should also have the advantage of some kind treatment on the emperor's birthday, and also that the sanctity of the festival should be maintained.' Tiberius' birthday was on the sixteenth of November, the sixteenth before the Kalends of December, and Pilate's dutiful note to Rome would doubtless have resembled Pliny's of a little later: 'It is my prayer, sir, that this birthday and many others will bring you the greatest happiness, and that in health and strength you may add to the immortal fame and glory of your reputation by ever-new achievements.' Doubtless, too, the form reply came back from the emperor's secretary: 'Thank you. I hope the gods ensure you're right.'

Between the emperor and his servant-governor there was an almost continuous stream of communication. Governors were expected to keep a minute record of everything that happened, every day. They were issued with *tabellae*, thin leaves of wood coated with wax on which to jot notes and write memoranda, and from these they drafted reports. These formed the basis of the *commentarii*, the governor's official diary. Copies of the *commentarii* were filed in the provincial archives, and edited extracts were sent to Rome. Governors – especially imperial deputies like Pilate – did not do this for their own amusement. They did it for the emperor, as his eyes and ears on the spot.

Surviving records show that the writing was done, in cursive script, on parchment or papyrus by a secretary. The governor then read them through and wrote, in his own hand, *lecta*, 'read'. These reports were sometimes posted up in public, like news-sheets, but eventually they were pasted on a long roll to be stored in the archives. Similar reports went out in letter form to the emperor or to colleagues, sometimes written by the governor himself in moments of emergency but generally, again, dictated to the secretary. These too would be scanned for errors. That done, the governor sealed the report or letter with his signet ring. This gesture was as personal as a signature and, according to Cicero, was to be used with as much circumspection: as he advised his governor-brother Quintus, 'Let your signet ring be your very self.'

Day by day, this was Pilate's routine: dictation, scanning, signing, sealing. Rummaging in his memory as he fiddled with pens at his desk, or paced the room with his hands behind his back; the squeak and scratch of a reed pen; the search for phrases that might justify, conceal, cast in a flattering light; the ring pulled from the fourth finger of his left hand and pressed into the yielding wax. The worries did not end when the letter was sent. Ships were slow, and couriers could be delayed; letters often crossed, or arrived two at a time. The most important letters were sent out in duplicate with duplicate messengers, but even this did not guarantee safe delivery. Worst of all, the governor's report was sometimes not the only version of events the emperor saw. More than once, Pilate's 'subjects' wrote their own letters to Rome complaining about him. On the last occasion, they succeeded in removing him.

Messages arrived in such quantity that the emperors were reduced to reading them as they were being shaved and while they watched the games; they seldom climbed into their litters but a sackful of letters went with them, to be read between the jolts of the journey. When Caesar was murdered, his arms were full of papers. A wise governor would have seen some virtue in not burdening the emperor with unnecessary words from the provinces. Yet alongside the temptation to leave 'the sovereign of earth and sea' alone, there was a stronger urge to get his attention and to flatter him.

None of Pilate's letters survive, as none of his reports do. Yet he presumably wrote from time to time, as Pliny wrote from his posting in Pontus and Bithynia, hoping for imperial guidance on matters large and small. An emperor, it seemed, could be bothered with most problems: the promotion of schoolfriends to the Senate, the correct form of punishment for slaves discovered in the army, permission for a wife to use the Imperial Post to visit her aunt, the site of a new bath-house. ('I've looked round Prusa and chosen one which is occupied at present by the unsightly ruins of what I am told was once a fine house. We could remove this eyesore and embellish the city without pulling down any existing structure . . .') He could be asked about suitable prizes for winning the games, and petitioned for extra troops to control traffic. Other governors sent nature notes: the governor of Gaul reported Nereids, bristling mermaids, washed up on the beaches of his province and singing sadly as they died, while the governor of Africa reported an encounter with a giant squid ('its head the size of a 90-gallon barrel, its tentacles 30 feet long and covered with suckers the size of plates') on which he had set his hunting dogs. The governor of the Alps reported a sighting of an ibis, never previously seen outside Egypt, and the governor of Lycia in Asia Minor sent an account of his night inside a giant plane tree, 'where the sound of the rain falling on the leaves was more delightful than any gleaming marble or gilded panelling.'

What could have intrigued Tiberius about Pilate's little patch? The skeleton of the sea-monster to which Andromeda had been exposed had turned up in Jaffa, forty feet long, and with ribs bigger than an elephant's; but it had been taken away long ago. A chunk of bitumen from Asphaltites, intriguing as it was, would land in the imperial palace like an insult. In any case, an emperor's interest in a small province like Judea was not expected to be great. Nonetheless, anything that touched remotely on the dignity of the emperor (such as Pilate's Tiberieum) or the enforcement of the *pax Romana* (such as all his run-ins with the Jews) demanded imperial notification and imperial instructions.

So Pilate doubtless wrote, although the only letters that 'survive' are medieval inventions. His letters probably began with the laborious official formula to someone of higher rank, S.V.B.E.V., *Si vales bene ego valeo*, 'If you are in good health, I am well, too.' They proceeded with utmost care; Augustus had once dismissed a governor for misspelling *ipsi* as *ixi* in a letter. And doubtless they ended on much the same note as Pliny's, if less elegantly expressed: 'I trust you will think that my obedience was correct, for I am anxious for every word and deed of mine to receive the sanction of your own supreme standards.' With emperors as suspicious as Tiberius and his successors, the sycophancy had to be laid on thick, not least because governors were too far away to gauge the political temperature at home. (Gauging the temperature was literally what was needed: a man who was out of favour or had lost his influence was dismissed with the single word *friget*, 'he's cold'.) When Flaccus, governor of Egypt, was trying to make things right between himself and the emperor Gaius, his written dispatches 'overflowed with flattery', according to his enemy Philo, while his public speeches were 'strings of fawning words and long screeds of insincere encomium'. And for all that, in his case as in Pilate's, it is never clear whether the emperor gave him much of a reply.

Most probably Pilate had nothing to go on, no hints of how best to communicate. By the time he was appointed, in 26, Tiberius had already been persuaded by Sejanus to retire from Rome and from much of the business of government. He was, after all, sixty-eight years old; and although his health was good he was worn out by fears, suspicions and debaucheries. The rugged cliffs of Capri and the deep blue sea entranced him, not least because access was so difficult. When a fisherman scrambled up the rocks behind him to present him with a fresh-caught mullet, Tiberius was so terrified at this breach of security that he ordered the man's face to be scrubbed raw with the fish. (When the man cried out, 'Thank goodness I didn't give him the crab,' Tiberius ordered him to be scrubbed with the crab as well.) In Capri, however, he gave plenty of receptions and entertainments, and it may have been here that Pilate was entrusted with his province. The commission was not necessarily bestowed in person, but it was a personal appointment; and it is therefore likely that, on this occasion at least, the two men met formally.

Pilate had almost certainly seen the emperor before. If he was a Praetorian he could even have walked beside him, providing part of the constant bodyguard that kept Tiberius safe from the knives he imagined under every arm. If not, he would still have seen him at a distance: perhaps at the funeral of Augustus in 14, when Tiberius had appeared, in dark robes, to offer incense before the body and to deliver the oration; or across the arena at the games Tiberius so disliked, where Pilate would have found himself, like all the others, watching every gesture, every movement, every change of colour and expression on the imperial face.

Tiberius was tall, robust and reasonably handsome, according to Suetonius, but his face was often pimply or patched with plasters. He wore his thinning hair untidily long at the nape of the neck, a style Pilate may have copied, and cut it only when the moon was in conjunction with the sun. He was shortsighted, which made him peer at people with his large unblinking eyes; though, as Dio Cassius noted, he could see well enough in the dark. When he gave receptions he liked to take leave of his guests by standing in the centre of the room with a *lictor* beside him and addressing each person by name, sometimes clasping their hands. This may have been the treatment Pilate received and the touch he remembered, as the fan remembers the touch of the star. We know, too, that Tiberius talked with deliberate slowness, a sort of affected drawl, and made slow movements with his fingers; but those fingers (which touched Pilate's?) were also strong enough, Suetonius said, to bore a hole in an apple, or to draw blood when they flicked the head of a child.

Reading this man was exceptionally difficult: indeed, it was forbidden, as some men believed it was also forbidden to explore the nature of God. Every ancient writer, no matter what their scale of objectivity about Tiberius, remarked how dour and cryptic he was. Dio spoke for all of them:

> He never let what he desired appear in his conversation, and what he said he wanted he usually did not desire at all . . . He would show anger over matters that were very far from upsetting him, and make a show of affability where he was most irritated. He would pretend to pity those whom he severely punished, and would retain a grudge against those whom he pardoned . . . in short, he thought it bad policy for a sovereign to reveal his thoughts . . . He became angry if anyone gave evidence of understanding him, and he put many to death for no other offence than that of having grasped what he meant.

His friends, confidants and helpers were very few. Suetonius estimated that he needed twenty people at close hand to help administer the empire, but that he had killed all but two or three of them. He trusted no one, and had a gloominess about him that repelled intimacy. In his early years, suspicion had made him modest and even diffident. He was shrewd and wise then, despite Augustus' reservations about his 'sourness'; he literally fell over himself to get away from flatterers. But in his killing mood, which lasted for most of the time Pilate was governor of Judea, he executed his enemies on the least word of any informer; and informers were everywhere. 'All offences were capital,' wrote Suetonius; 'even speaking a few words without any bad intention.' Tacitus said that if Tiberius' soul had been exposed it would have shown, like the scourged back of a slave, the lash-marks of his cruelty.

Those who offended him were dragged through the streets with hooks, sent sprawling down the Gemonian Steps and thrown into the Tiber, if they did not kill themselves first. Nobody could trust his favour, even if they thought they enjoyed it. There is a literal chill in the words of Seneca when he describes how Montanus, a mediocre poet known as 'the sunrise and sunset man', was famous for being touched by *amicitia Tiberii . . . et frigore*, both Tiberius' friendship and his coldness. Whatever may be true or untrue in the gospel accounts of the trial of Jesus, one moment, from John, is highly plausible: Pilate's total loss of composure when the Jews suggest that, if he spares Jesus, 'You are not Caesar's friend.'

Was he ever his friend? The Jews at the trial used the official title, *philos tou kaisaros*, which attached to members of the emperor's innermost circle, but there is no evidence that Pilate was ever so close. The Jews appear only to have meant that he was loyal to Tiberius and sensitive to his interests. The later story of an imperial connection through marriage to Procula was almost certainly invented. Yet a friendship of some sort was not socially impossible. There was always the example of the 'mere Roman knight' Sejanus: the one who had made the emperor laugh when, for others, even a tempered smile was unsafe. If Pilate had been recommended by Sejanus, he could have been Tiberius' golden boy for a time. Yet to be close to the emperor, any emperor, was no particular advantage. Juvenal said you could spot these men at a glance, by their drawn white faces. Imperial favour not only laid a man open to the emperor's jealousies, but tarred him by association with his excesses and his horrors.

These Tiberius displayed in plenty. He was nicknamed 'Biberius Caldius Mero' ('tippler of hot wine with no water added') because he drank too much, and 'The Old Goat' for his lecheries on Capri, frolics so disgusting that the Victorian translators of Suetonius could mark them only with rows of blushing asterisks. Grottoes were made in the woods where his buggery could take place unobserved, and off the rocky beaches of Capri he indulged in naked swimming-and-sex sessions with minors of both sexes. These things were the talk of Rome. Tiberius was mocked on the stage, where the goat jokes brought the house down; and in more serious vein, around 27, an anonymous poem appeared.

> *Fastidit vinum, quia iam sitit iste cruorem;*
> *Tam bibit hunc avide, quam bibit ante merum.*

All he wants now
Is undiluted gore,
Just as he guzzled
Undiluted wine before.

At some slow remove, this talk must have reached Caesarea too. By all accounts, the public so loathed Tiberius that when his death was announced they could scarcely contain themselves for joy, although they were terrified of showing it until it was confirmed. This fear and loathing also suffused the city, and the empire, when he was alive. It is not hard to imagine dinner parties in Caesarea at which Pilate's guests, visiting from Rome, would regale him with blood-soaked stories and sexual details that would make the women cover their ears; while Pilate would listen in the awful, sinking knowledge that this was the man to whom he owed his career, from whom he drew his authority, and whose safety he prayed for. Doubtless in some sense he could disconnect the man from the office, as people under any regime can close their eyes to the personal sins of their rulers. But there may have been times when he could not; when, amid the genteel litter of wine beakers, chicken bones, roses and clowns, the prefect of Judea would find himself suddenly sickened by the obscenity of his protector, as by the flopping fall of an augur's bird.

★   ★   ★

Pilate stayed in Judea ten years. This was much longer than some of his predecessors, but it did not necessarily mean that he was doing a good job. Tiberius did not believe in changing his lieutenants abroad. Suetonius supposed this was because he did not care about government in general, and because he especially wanted to avoid provoking unrest overseas. Tacitus remarked of one aged record-holder – twenty-four years in various governorships – that he was kept on 'not for any outstanding talent, but because he was competent and no more'.

Josephus had a more interesting theory. Tiberius was a man who made an art of procrastination, and could justify any form of it. He kept prisoners waiting for trials and the condemned rotting in prison, to draw out the agony of punishment. Ambassadors too were always made to hang about, in case new ones were about to be appointed who would have to be treated with all over again. The same excruciating slowness and shrewdness, Josephus supposed, coloured his attitude to the running of the empire.

Tiberius thought that all governors were grasping, out to wring as much from their provinces as they could. If they were given short tours, it meant that they would fleece their subjects unbearably in the effort to fill their pockets before they were recalled. If, on the other hand, they were left in place, they would be sated with their spoil and become less keen on pillaging. The emperor's unlovely analogy – typical of a man his schoolteacher described as 'mud mixed with blood' – was of flies swarming on a wound. If you drove the flies away, new ones would settle that were famished for food. If you left the old flies alone, they would become so gorged with blood that their bite no longer hurt.

So Pilate, trusted or ignored, remained for a decade. His job carried with it certain expectations. Clearly Tiberius assumed, and Pilate assumed, that he would enrich himself personally; his salary, of around 100,000 *sesterces* a year, was understood as a basis only. But he was not supposed to be brutal about it. This was both dangerous and counter-productive. Of one governor of Egypt, who suddenly sent the emperor more money than his province was down for, Tiberius remarked: 'I told him to shear the sheep, not flay it.' Senatorial governors, at his insistence, were regularly condemned for extortion. Contrary to his style in domestic affairs, Tiberius's advice to his men abroad was almost benevolent. Suetonius records him saying – and possibly Pilate heard him saying – words that now carry an unavoidable ring of irony and poignancy. A governor, he said, ought to be 'a good shepherd'.

Was Pilate ever that? There is no Roman assessment of his career; the chapters of Tacitus' *Annals* for 30 and 31, which might have mentioned him, have vanished. Instead the most famous summary of his career comes from Philo, that highly educated Jewish contemporary who so hated (with some reason) the treatment of his people by the Romans. He included his description of Pilate in an impassioned letter supposedly sent to the emperor Gaius by Agrippa, Prince of the Jews, in the course of his ill-fated diplomatic mission to protest against an imperial statue in the Temple. Agrippa cited Pilate as a governor who, though bad and unreasonably devoted to Roman symbols, would not have been allowed to go that far. He was, said Philo/Agrippa, 'inflexible, stubborn and cruel'. He was induced to behave decently only because he was so afraid that Tiberius would hear bad things of him, and there was plenty bad to report: 'venality, violence, robbery, assault, abusive behaviour, frequent executions without trial and endless savage ferocity.'

Philo's words have weight because he was a contemporary of Pilate's, and some of his charges are backed up elsewhere. They lose it because, in this particular case, Agrippa's letter had a purpose that depended on painting Pilate black. It was meant to show Tiberius in the best light, the mild and wise ruler contrasted with his rapacious deputy; and it was also intended to advance Agrippa's own claims to be the ruler of Judea, the soothing Jewish presence that the province needed. Philo's habit, in any case, is to present characters in fierce black and white, either good or bad. In *Flaccus*, his book-length attack on the governor who failed to prevent the pogrom of 36 in Alexandria, Roman governors are summed up as a breed in much the same words he applied to Pilate specifically. Philo may have had good reason to hate Pilate, but nor was he disposed to treat anyone impartially.

Josephus, writing forty years later and with Roman sympathies, provides a milder view. Although he does not favour Pilate, he does not object to him particularly. He relates the governor's most brutal actions in detail, but never accuses him generally of anything worse than 'tumult'. When the governor of Syria eventually sent Pilate home, Josephus reports that he rescinded the tax on grain sales; he does not say that it was burdensome, but he implies that it was part of a regime that was hated. As a Romanophile, perhaps he was even too kind to Pilate; perhaps he thought the governor's reckless and clumsy actions spoke for themselves. Yet Josephus could be sharp enough in his accusations against other governors who were violent and corrupt: witness his descriptions of the 'mad insolence' of Sabinus, or this verdict on Gessius Florus, governor of Judea under Nero:

> It was as though he had been despatched to Judea on purpose to display his crimes, ostentatiously showing his lawlessness to our nation, never omitting any rapine or unjust punishment; for he was not to be moved by pity, and was never satisfied with any amount of gain . . . but went fair shares with the robbers.

On Pilate, however, Josephus passed no judgement, and sometimes even gave him the benefit of the doubt. Over ten years, he cites three incidents in which the governor provoked his subjects, once severely enough to induce them to appeal to Rome against him. Out of this, and out of the gospel accounts, there emerges a character consistent in many ways with Philo's picture: obstinate, proud, patriotic, cunning, flippant, heavy-handed. But the obstinacy wavers, in Josephus too, even becoming repentance; the heavy-handedness is sometimes unintended, the result of incompetence and insecurity; and between the provocations, whether malicious or thoughtless, Judea is at peace. The 'endless savage ferocity' is not substantiated. What we seem to have is someone immature and hot-headed, entranced by schemes that don't work, who seems less on the edge of destroying the Jews than of destroying himself.

A temperament like this was not unknown in governors generally. Cicero rebuked his brother, a man of high intelligence, for similar 'violent outbursts of temper' and 'abusive or insulting language' in his post in Asia. These were worse in his first year because, Cicero supposed, 'the general insolence you came across took you by surprise, and struck you as intolerable'; but his second year was kinder, 'because you improved in tolerance and mildness as the result of getting used to things and reasoning things out, and also, I believe, because you read my letters . . .'

If any such progress occurred in Pilate's case, it was not recorded. He may simply have lacked the good advice Quintus had, or not listened to it when he got it. But he was not a Jew-hater as we, in our supposedly more civilised times, would understand the term. He did not like them; he felt superior to all of them. But his tour was marked by crass tactlessness, rather than a consistent policy of anti-Semitism. In some ways, he even believed he was there to make their lives better. And most of all he wanted to leave Judea in the good graces of the man-god who had sent him there. Cicero's words in *The Laws* may not have been far-fetched as a motto for Pilate's enthusiasm. 'For Rome it is our duty to die, to her to give ourselves entirely, to place on her altar and, as it were, to offer to her service all that we possess.' The most sentimental hymns of the British Empire had said exactly that.

So the devotion played itself out. It centred round the issue of the emperor's graven image. The Jews would not accept it anywhere, in any form. Pilate's predecessors, as far as we know, had respected Jewish sensibilities. The new governor, more arrogant or more desperate to please, was not inclined to.

The emperor's image belonged on all buildings, monuments, coins and insignia, and in most cities of the empire it was standard practice to put it there. Philo describes how the city of Alexandria was full of tributes to the emperor, 'shields and gilded crowns and slabs and inscriptions'. Most especially, his image belonged on the sacred standards of the army, which, along with the silver eagles, were carried with every unit and brought good luck in battle. After victories, incense was burned before them as if before gods; on holidays they were anointed with perfumed oil, despite their sharp points and cutting edges; and the very precinct of the camp where they were stored was considered holy. When Germanicus went back to Germany after the defeat of Varus to restore the honour of Rome, his piety consisted not merely in burying the dead, but in recovering the standards.

The image attached to the standards was a gold medallion about six inches across, enclosed in a border engraved like a triumphal wreath bound up with ribbons. The whole thing, about the size of a carving plate, was attached to the standard a foot from the top, where the insignia met the shaft, and could be taken off if necessary. Not only the image of Tiberius but also that of the favourite, Sejanus, glittered on the standard poles when Pilate took over in Judea; only the legions in Syria had boldly refused to display it.

Pilate's sense of security in Caesarea depended not merely on the armour and number of his men, but also on the gleaming spiritual barrier provided by the standards. He needed their protection even more on his rare visits to Jerusalem. But his predecessors had agreed that the fully decorated standards would never be taken there, into the city sacred to the Jews. Instead, they were dismantled and the images left in the guard room at Caesarea, among the extra blankets and the broken swords. Jerusalem was thus the only city in the empire where people did not bow in the public squares to the image of the emperor. Indeed, it was the only city where they had no glimpse of imperial paraphernalia at all.

The moment Pilate arrived in Judea, according to Josephus, he decided on a different policy. The next time the troops were ordered to Jerusalem for garrison duty, they would not dismantle the standards but would take them, fully accoutred, under cover of darkness. Still in the dark, they would fix them to the walls of the Antonia fortress. If Pilate was thinking tactically at this point – rather than vengefully or emotionally – he might have reasoned that the fortress was not a holy part of the city; it already had Romans in it. He was simply planting Rome's standards in a Roman-occupied place, as any conquering general would. Then, when the Jews woke up, the beauty and power of the emperor's authority would hit them in the face. The first rays of the morning sun would gild his profile all along the battlements: Tiberius, Tiberius, Tiberius, Tiberius.

Josephus in the *Antiquities* suggests that this was part of a larger, more outrageous plan: to move the army to winter quarters in Jerusalem 'to abolish the laws of the Jews'. But it would have been odd to move the troops in winter to a colder, snowier place, and Josephus in his earlier work, *The Jewish War*, does not mention any such motive. Instead, the aim of the standards policy seems to have been much simpler: to show the Jews who was in charge at the start of Pilate's term. He did not, after all, parade the standards flagrantly through the streets by day; he had enough sensitivity, just, to do it in the dark. Abolishing the laws of the Jews was nowhere in the brief of even a foolishly headstrong governor of Judea.

In any case, the new standards policy had only one airing. Some days after the garrison had gone to Jerusalem, Pilate awoke to find a huge crowd of Jews outside his palace. They were right below the walls, under the windows. Most had plainly walked the sixty miles from Jerusalem. Some had their feet bound with rags; many, since it was almost winter, were bundled in cloaks and overcoats. The crowd seethed with noise or perhaps, more unnervingly, with silence. And it stretched as far as he could see.

According to Josephus, the Jews petitioned him for days to take the standards down. For most of the time they did so with ritual swaying and incantations, praying that his soul would be softened and that he would see sense. Josephus suggests that they also negotiated directly; but perhaps they did not get too close. Pilate would have suffered them to approach and salute him with the usual deep bow of subject people; but in their eyes the Roman governor, though freshly-bathed daily and scraped with the strigil and full of the magnetism of his authority, was impurity itself, from which they wished to keep their distance.

They therefore could not really negotiate. These were, in effect, two religions colliding: two notions of the sacred that could not be reconciled. Again and again the Jews pleaded with him: 'Please, sir, remove the standards. They offend us, and they offend the laws of our ancestors. Please remove them.'

'No.'

'Your predecessors did not offend against our laws. They respected them. Please remove the standards, sir.'

'No.'

'Will you tell us why you will not remove them, sir?'

'Because it would be an insult to the emperor,' Pilate answered. 'And I will not insult him.'

The Jews stayed for five days. On each day, for hours, they petitioned him. He refused to budge, and so did they. Pilate seemed too surprised to ask his troops to clear them. He went about his duties. Then, on the sixth day, he forced a confrontation in the Great Stadium. He let himself get to the point of killing them because they would not leave; his soldiers had their swords at the Jews' throats. Then, when they showed themselves quite indifferent to death, he was so shocked that he backed down. Their invisible God was stronger than his, whose image surrounded him. The order was given for the standards to be taken out of Jerusalem, and Pilate retreated to his palace.

It was his first defeat, and perhaps the hardest to take. Not only the emperor's honour had been at stake, but his own ability to keep order and impress Roman ways on his province. His humiliation so impressed and delighted the Jews that they appointed a new feast-day, the third of Kislev, to commemorate the day 'when the standards were taken away from the pavement of the Temple'. The fact that Pilate removed them without apparent clearance from Rome suggests that the whole affair was his idea from the beginning, and that he had only himself to blame for the débâcle that resulted. The honour of Tiberius in this small, symbolic case was not worth a massacre of the Jews, and Tiberius himself would have been the first to point that out to him.

And so he returned, smarting, to his quasi-Roman chambers by the sea.

After a while he had a second idea. It was less contentious; indeed, it was benevolent and kind. It was futile to imagine that the Jews would ever like him; but perhaps a little murmur of appreciation would fall from their stubborn lips.

He would build an aqueduct. There was nothing better to mark the advent of Roman civilisation: massive masonry at the service of safe and convenient drinking water. This was a resource Judea was almost without. In the high desert, the overwhelming impression was of unwatered stone. From Beersheba to Bethel there were perhaps six tiny streams; no lake, no river, no waterfall. Shepherds led their flocks to pools that were almost illusory, trembling among improbable trees. Even in Jerusalem, where rain could fall copiously in winter, the precious water sank immediately into deep limestone, where every resource of ingenuity was needed to catch it. The city was riddled with man-made pools and cisterns, including, it was said, a fantastic complex of reservoirs sixty feet beneath the Temple: a 'fountain of perennial water', as Tacitus called it, hewn in the solid rock. Pilate may have only heard rumours of this reservoir, but there were countless others, such as the two pools beside the Antonia fortress and the two pools of Siloam, beside which lay the abandoned crutches of the men Jesus had cured.

The Jews yearned for water with a religious longing: the hart panting for waterbrooks, the torrent gushing from the rock under God's power and 'running in all the dry places'. They feared more than anything the divine anger that could turn rivers into wilderness and springs into thirsting ground. With immense labour they built conduits, tunnels and aqueducts to bring spring water to the pools of Jerusalem. Pilate evidently thought that Roman labour could help the enterprise. His enthusiasm may well have matched Pliny's, who adored the combination of beauty, utility and *Romanitas* that an aqueduct represented. Of a similar project, the linking of a lake with the sea, Pliny wrote to the emperor Trajan:

> In consideration of your noble ambition which matches your supreme position, I think I should bring to your notice any projects which are worthy of your name and glory and are likely to combine utility with magnificence . . . The king [who started it] despaired of finishing the work. This, however, only fires me with enthusiasm to see you accomplish what kings could only attempt. You will forgive my ambition for your greater glory.

The aqueduct Pilate built was, by all accounts, impressive. It ran for twenty to forty miles (Josephus ranges between two hundred and four hundred furlongs), lined with lead and lime mortar, and the water in it gleamed blue as metal. It is thought to have been the aqueduct that linked the springs in the Wadi el Arab to Solomon's pools near Bethlehem, from which two great 'high- and low-level' aqueducts, probably built by Herod, conveyed the water northwards to Jerusalem. To a Roman, the completed project would have looked wonderful. But the Jews were not grateful. According to Josephus, 'they were not pleased with what was done about the water.'

There could have been many reasons for this. Perhaps there were casualties in the building works, or perhaps the Jews were simply indulging the age-old and reasonable dislike of monstrous modern stoneworks marching across the landscape. It appears, too, that part of the aqueduct may have run through a cemetery, rendering the water ritually impure. But the main problem was that Pilate allegedly financed the project with *corban* money, the sacred treasure stored in the Temple. The account in Josephus's *Jewish War* suggests that he exhausted the treasure completely.

Corban was the adjective applied to all money that was either vowed to one holy purpose or was deliberately removed from the use of others.

It applied to other objects, too: a beast bound for sacrifice was *corban* once it had been chosen for the altar. The sacred money flowed in from Jews all over the empire, as well as from the poor widow whom Jesus saw depositing her two mites,'which make a farthing', in the box in the Temple courtyard. Every male Jew over the age of twenty paid a half-shekel tax every year towards this treasure, and people also gave their clothes, jewels and ornaments. The money could be used for public works of benefit to Jerusalem as well as for ritual observances; indeed, Jesus himself criticised the way that the notion of *corban* tended to turn spontaneous generosity and social duty into narrowly ritualistic 'gift-giving'. Cheekily, he told the collector to pluck his own Temple-tax out of the jaws of a fish. Among his followers, he suggested, the *corban* idea should be treated sceptically or even dismissed in favour of unrestricted love: but not by Romans.

The most famous misuse of the *corban* treasure was in fact not by Pilate, but by the Sanhedrin itself. It was *corban* money, thirty pieces of silver, that was said to have been given to Judas by the chief priests as payment for betraying Jesus. Whether or not such a use was legitimate in their eyes, the priests in Matthew's gospel refused to take it back from Judas when he changed his mind and tried to return it. It had become impure, and was unwanted. It would have been equally impure, of course, if Pilate had tried to give it back.

How he got hold of the treasure is unclear, but he did not seize it by force. A Roman would have known as keenly as a Jew that it was sacrilege to steal anything entrusted to a holy place; his own temples were stacked, like banks, with boxes of money. Even Philo noted that in the time of Tiberius the Temple was never disturbed. Josephus says simply that Pilate 'used' the treasure, without saying that he committed any sacrilege in getting it. Probably some secret deal was made with Caiaphas, and the money was simply transferred. But however it was done, the Jews violently objected.

When Pilate next visited Jerusalem a great crowd of them assembled, just as they had done about the standards. Yet this time there was no pretence of submission; 'God's gift', the holy money, was at stake. Enraged, they formed a ring round Pilate's tribunal and screamed abuse at him. This would have shocked Pilate; Josephus, always sensitive to etiquette, was apologetic, almost embarrassed ('crowds will do that sort of thing'). But Pilate was not proposing to apologise; he considered himself the injured party and, in his view, there was nothing to be sorry for. Instead, knowing in advance that he was going to face trouble, he had already concocted one of his plans. He had made his soldiers put on Jewish dress (long robes, head-cloths, perhaps the odd false beard; since most of them were Samaritan and Idumean auxiliaries, there was no need to touch up the skin with ink or green-walnut juice). In the *Antiquities*, Josephus says they had daggers under their costumes, but were ordered not to use them if they could help it. In the *Jewish War* he says they had swords, but that Pilate ordered them only to use their cudgels to beat 'the noisy ones'. With this sort of muddled thinking, the stage was clearly set for a calamity.

Pilate continued to face the crowd from the tribunal. He was alone, as he had been at the Great Stadium in Caesarea; yet not as alone as all that, because, as before, he had his troops hidden and ready. He loved to challenge the Jews in this way, to appear courageous, to take a risk that was, in fact, no risk at all, because he had brute force hidden up his sleeve. Yet experience would have taught him not to feel entirely secure: the Jews had quite as much cunning as he had.

He sat in his curule chair and told the Jews to go away. The reverse happened; the crowd surged forward. They came right up to him: close enough, Josephus implied, actually to hurt him. When they waved their fists, he flinched; when they spat, he felt the spittle in his face. Most of what they shouted he could not understand, but it needed no translation. He had touched the holy money; he had defiled the Temple. While the water in his aqueduct might be pure, the aqueduct itself was filthy, hateful and degraded, and so was he. The Jews came so close that they almost trampled the hem of his toga: so white, so immaculately fullered with bean-meal and potash, so uselessly clean.

He bore this for a while. He knew that when he had had enough, he could give the signal. And something broke his forbearance in the end, as it was bound to. Possibly he was frightened, or felt he was getting too close to humiliation. Possibly someone touched him, that unbearable contact of flesh against flesh that suggested equality, common humanity and the threat of capitulation. He gave the signal. At once, his legionaries-in-disguise fell upon the fringes of the crowd.

The local auxiliaries who made up his raggle-taggle army always relished such a chance. Their animosity towards the Jews was something Pilate could never control entirely; here, he could not control it at all. Instead of sticking to their cudgels, the soldiers used everything they had, and Pilate did not intervene to call them off. Of course, he should have done. As Valerius Maximus could have told him, 'The force of the empire is in the soldier; once out of the straight line, that force soon becomes oppressive unless it is swiftly controlled again.' Instead, perhaps deliberately, he froze. His men slashed and cut as if the Jews were armed, when they had no weapons at all. Many who escaped the blows were killed as they ran away, trampled by their own people as they tried to squeeze through the narrow streets to safety. The bloodshed may have extended to the courtyard of the Temple, where the pigeon-sellers and money-changers were; this may have been what Luke meant when he recorded Jesus being asked about 'the Galileans whose blood Pilate had mingled with their sacrifices.' Perhaps within the holy place, certainly outside it, Jewish blood was on the flagstones and smeared along the walls. How much water from the wonderful new aqueduct would it take to wash them clean?

Pilate had not left the scene. The brutalities took place on the edges of the crowd; it is uncertain how much he saw, except that, as Josephus noted, it was much more than he had commanded. When it was over the rest of the crowd still remained, terrified and silent, staring at him. We do not know with what feeling or with what expression Pilate looked at them.

That was his second mistake. He probably analysed the failing, if he saw it as a failing at all, as a loss of control over his men, but the Jews saw it as a violent lack of regard for the things they thought holy. This was a lesson Pilate seemed incapable of learning.

Philo records that some time later he had some shields made, coated with gold and dedicated to Tiberius, and had them put up in Herod's palace in Jerusalem. Why he did this is unclear. If it happened around 32, and Pilate was indeed a protégé of Sejanus, it may have followed on the news that the favourite's star had fallen. Sejanus had reached such heights that he seemed to share the emperor's power: receiving his own ambassadors, becoming the object of prayers and sacrifices. At the shows, he even had his own gold chair beside the emperor's. In distant Judea Pilate too would have sacrificed to him, set up his bronze statue among his household gods and entered his name in the records alongside the name of Tiberius. It was standard practice. But then Tiberius, afraid of the favourite's ambition, sent a letter to the Senate ordering his arrest. Sejanus, after a moment of stunned disbelief ('Me? You are calling me?') was accused of treason and garrotted, and his relatives and friends were rounded up and killed. If Pilate had been a friend of any sort, he desperately needed to make a show of loyalty to the emperor. What he may not have known was that Tiberius, as part of his policy of destabilising Sejanus, had actually forbidden the proposal of honours either to the favourite or to himself. To make such a gesture now was almost as dangerous as making none at all.

Yet there the shields were. The Greek word Philo used for Pilate's action was *anatithesin*, 'consecrated'; the word for shield, *aspideion*, meant one that was dedicated in thanks for services rendered. Shields like this were not normally hung up in private houses, however grand. They were hung up in public buildings or in the temple of the god who had been prayed to and had answered the prayer, as engraved tin tokens are still put up round statues of the Virgin in Catholic Europe. Horace recorded the hanging of a votive tablet, together with his dripping clothes, in the temple of the god of the sea of love in which he had just escaped drowning; Ovid promised to erect one, engraved in his own hand, in the temple of the goddess of childbirth, if only his girlfriend Corinna might be saved from dying from a self-induced abortion. They were very simply worded. 'Horace to Neptune' was all that was required to make the prayer of thanks.

What did Pilate's say? In all probability, 'Pilate thanks Tiberius'. He could have gone further: 'Dedicated by Pontius Pilate to divine Tiberius.' What he thanked him for was mysterious, and perhaps best left unspecified. His job? Hardly. Perhaps he merely thanked him for his existence, as a Roman, under Tiberius' wisdom and peace, and hoped that this would commend him.

Philo thought differently. He assumed that Pilate had put the shields up simply to annoy the Jews. This is plausible enough, but even Philo said there was nothing on the shields that was obviously offensive: 'no image work nor anything forbidden by the law, apart from the barest inscription stating two facts, the name of the person who made the dedication and of him in whose honour it was made.' They were not on public display, but seem to have been set up inside the palace in Pilate's private apartments, which he could presumably decorate as he liked. Yet some reference to divinity was likely from the mere fact of their consecration, and would have been deeply offensive. Besides, part of the penalty of being so unpopular was that anything Pilate did could be turned against him. So people began to talk about the shields and, in the end, to complain with vigour.

Such sensitivity was not new. Something similar had happened when Herod, who liked to give prizes at the games, devised some out of blocks of wood to look like miniature armed men. The Jews took enormous offence at these prizes, claiming they violated the Law. Even when Herod invited them to inspect the little 'images of men', and to tap the blocks of wood beneath the gilded decoration, several of them still accused him of profanity. A little later, the incident was cited as one of the reasons for a 'holy and pious' revolt against him. This happened all too often in Judea: out of simple decoration, martyrdom.

Philo claims that the four Herodian princes, no less, came in embassy to Pilate to ask him to take the shields down. (This must have happened at a festival; there were few other occasions when all the local rulers were in Jerusalem together.) They begged him not to violate their traditions and disturb their customs, 'which have been safeguarded through all preceding ages by kings and emperors.' But Pilate dug his heels in. Inflexibly, stubbornly, 'with his usual mixture of self-will and relentlessness', as Philo described it, he refused to do what they wanted.

The Herodian delegation is difficult to identify, but it clearly included Herod Antipas of Galilee and Philip the Tetrarch as chief spokesmen. These men were all virtual kings in their own right: bearded, gorgeously dressed, exotic, attended by trains of servants. They were not cowed by Pilate. It was their father, not his, who had once hung on the arm of Augustus and had been on gift-exchanging terms with Mark Antony. If they cared to, they could put on Roman airs and adopt Roman practice; and they knew which strings to pull at the court of Tiberius. They pulled them now.

'Don't arouse sedition,' they pleaded with him. 'Don't make war, don't destroy the peace. You don't honour the emperor by dishonouring ancient laws. Don't take Tiberius as your pretext for outraging our nation; he doesn't want any of our customs to be overthrown. If you say he does, produce an order or a letter or something of the kind, so that we can stop pestering you and can go and petition him.'

Pilate listened to all this in a cold, sulking fury. To him the shields were holy; they had been dedicated, and now he could not possibly take them down. Besides, how much fuss could the Jews make over inscriptions? How could the mere geometry of letters offend them? It was impossible to live with such exquisite sensitivity, in which the gleaming angles of an 'A' became a weapon, and the curves of an 'S' an obscenity. Besides, as the princes knew, there was no order from Tiberius. There was no letter, either. It was ridiculous to think that the emperor would send one, or the governor could produce one, ordering the customs of the Jews to be overthrown. Pilate's compulsion and enthusiasm were his only authority; it was all in his own head.

But it was the last point – the possibility of Jewish tale-telling – that most exasperated him. More than anything, he didn't want the Jews to write to Tiberius. He would have no control over what they said and there were, according to Philo, plenty of aspects of his rule that were better hidden. He was cautious in what he revealed to the emperor through his regular, cosmetic reports; he could even instruct the messenger to loiter, not to rush in, to make sure the emperor was smiling and unirritated, before handing the letter to the Praetorian guard to be delivered. He could not bear to think that anyone else should represent him. But if he did not want the Jewish princes to write, he would have to remove the shields and dishonour the emperor by removing them. He was stuck.

A silence followed, in which Pilate's conscience and his pride struggled like desperate wrestlers. 'With all his vindictiveness and furious temper,' wrote Philo, 'he was in a difficult position. He had not the courage to take down what had been dedicated; nor did he wish to do anything that would please his subjects. At the same time, he knew full well the constant policy of Tiberius in these matters . . .'

The Herodian princes watched Pilate closely: four fierce, imperious heads. He would not concede. He would not back down. The protocol for listening to requests from subject-people was to keep your head bowed and your gaze fixed on the floor, so that your expression gave nothing away. But no matter how still he sat in his curule chair, draped in the resplendent white folds of his office, his mind squirmed. Something of his torment must have shown in his face, in a twitch of the lips or a glimmer of compunction in his furious eyes. Perhaps, like many Romans, he showed his unutterable frustration by biting his nails. For somehow the princes divined, according to Philo, that for all his stony refusals he had, in fact, repented. He was sorry, but he was damned if he would ever admit it to four petty local rulers.

They left him then and wrote, as they had threatened, their letters of complaint to Tiberius. This was not an entirely hostile act. They could see that Pilate was trapped in his own pride and, to some degree, in his terror of offending the emperor, and this was a quandary from which only Tiberius could release him. Yet the moment of release, when it came, was appalling.

Tiberius would have received the letters on Capri, on his terrace dappled with the light of the sea. Philo, relishing the scene, says he read them through quickly (not in this case procrastinating, or waiting until his romp-of-the-day was done) and immediately erupted with anger.

This was not unusual. According to Suetonius, the emperor wavered between being a timid and quasi-scholarly old man, who would make a nuisance of asking abstruse questions ('What was the song the Sirens sang?' 'Who was Hecuba's mother?'), and a terrifying brute who scourged almost to death a centurion who failed to clear a road of bushes to let his litter pass. Had Pilate been there in front of him he might have dreamed up some exquisitely appropriate punishment, such as nailing him up spreadeagled to the walls like a votive shield himself. But since he was far away, Tiberius merely cursed him to the skies and tore him limb from limb with words. 'What language he used about Pilate!' crowed Philo in delight. He then dictated that language to his secretary, not caring to wait until the white heat of the moment had passed.

A letter 'full of reproaches and rebukes for his audacious violation of precedent', was sent off to Pilate. The wording can only be guessed at now, and what Philo suggests it was should probably be taken with the same grain of salt as his assessment of Pilate himself. All we know is that Pilate was told to take the shields down and transfer them to the temple of Augustus in Caesarea. But very little imperial displeasure was needed to have a petrifying effect at the other end of the line. Plainly, this was one of those communications that coats a man in a cold rush of fear from the scalp downwards: the fear of a job, or a life, in pieces.

amicitia Tiberii et frigore.

Pilate took the shields down. A man went up a ladder, prised them off the walls, packed them in boxes or wrapped them in cloth, and sent them back to Caesarea. Each time after that when Pilate stood in the temple of Caesar Augustus on the little hill above the harbour, gazing at the image of the emperor's adoptive father through the sweet rising smoke, he would see the gleaming shields along the walls. Stupid, sang the shields, stupid and rash, stupid and rash; count yourself lucky not to be fired. Or words to that effect.

Presumably he kept the letter. It was awful, but it was from Him, and so could not be part of the selective culling and cleansing of correspondence that went on from time to time. His shadow would have fallen across it as he dictated it, in his marble villa by the deep blue waters in the centre of the world. His ring had impressed his image on the heavy purple seals. Besides, the letter was not wholly critical. Tiberius had shown him mercy, which was the prerogative of great men. And if he had hurt him, that too was his prerogative. As Ovid said, when Augustus exiled him for a crime that remains obscure, *et iubet et merui*; 'he orders it and I have deserved it.'

To feel the wrath of Caesar was, the poet said, to be crushed by God. He was the *princeps,* the life of the world, the most merciful, 'he who sees all things'. It was never necessary to name him: he was *ipse,* Him, and he had the power to give or take a man's life. Although he was mortal, his soul was already divine. The stars beckoned, and he was already 'immeasurably removed' from the thin petitions of his subjects. Poets, of course, exaggerated. But if Pilate's feelings were anything like this, it could be that the idea for the Tiberieum grew out of the humiliation of the dismantled golden shields. In Jerusalem, he could not put a prayer of loyalty on an inside wall; but in Caesarea he could build in stone and put up altars.

In any case, Pilate now needed to begin the long process of working himself back into his boss's affections. It was difficult. He could try to send him something, some natural curiosity, as governors often did; the deputy-governor of Africa once sent Augustus a parcel, heavy with damp sand, of nearly 400 shoots obtained from a single grain of wheat. Tiberius had his likings, strange as they were: for Setinum wine and wild German parsnips and cucumbers grown all year under glass. Perhaps these could be grown in Judea, to save the imperial gardeners the trouble of making cucumber-beds in little carts that could be wheeled around to catch the sun. They might be grown in strange shapes that would tantalise him. Or he could be sent dates again, the famous Nicholas dates that a philosopher from Damascus had once presented to Augustus: four inches long, flesh-white when you crushed them, oozing with a juice like honey, and grander by far than those that Pilate offered to the gods beyond the clouds.

Yet he had gone wrong once, and there was always the numbing possibility of going wrong again. From distant Judea, it was impossible to tell. Tiberius, in his palace, sucked the sweet flesh from a fig and wished his name to be respected; and Pilate, far away, harried, keen for approval, put up the gleaming shields. On whose orders? the princes had asked him. But he could not answer. He could not bear to admit that there was no order, nothing in writing, only a prompting of the heart and a deep urge to ingratiate himself: as with the whispered *bon mot,* the watchful eye at the great man's back, the steer by the elbow to a place of safety, if only he were close.

3

God's secret agent

Don't bother.
It's all worked out beforehand
The match is rigged
And when he appears in the ring
surrounded by magnesium lights
they'll thunder the *Te Deum* fit to deafen you
and even before you've got out of your chair
they'll ring the bells at full tilt
they'll throw the sacred sponge in your face
and you won't have time to fly towards his feathers
they'll throw themselves on you
and you'll crumple
your arms out stupidly, like a cross
in the sawdust
and you'll never make love again

Jacques Prévert, 'The Fight with the Angel' (1949)

He may have wondered, from time to time, why he had been sent to Judea. Any number of later theologians and scholars could have told him. He was sent because the stars were in alignment and the other players in place. This was what God had planned from the beginning of the world. His son would be put to death, a symbolic death on a tree, to save sinners. But it would appear to be a routine execution by a governor who did such things all the time.

The place was set. To cite the words of Peter and John in the fourth chapter of the Acts of the Apostles, 'In [Jerusalem], in fact, both Herod and Pontius Pilate, with the Gentiles and the people of Israel, gathered together against your holy servant Jesus, whom you anointed, to do whatever your hand and your plan had predestined to take place.' Both God and, below him, the astral spirits, were involved in this design. When St Paul wrote of 'the rulers of our age' crucifying Christ, the Greek phrase he used – *archontes tou aionos toutou* – meant not only the present authorities but also the demonic powers, seated in the planets, who governed the order of the world and the lives of men. It was the *archontes* who brought about the crucifixion. The authorities, Caiaphas, Annas or Pilate, were merely their agents.

The Catholic Catechism adds: 'For the sake of accomplishing his plan of salvation, God permitted the acts that flowed from their blindness.' But this is a refinement, in which God allows free will and incorporates it into his design. The unrolling of scripture suggests a different, inexorable motion: the 'free' acts of Pilate and the others were already part of the plan. Although the Roman governor had never heard the voices of the prophets, he fulfilled them in every detail by trying Jesus and condemning him.

Even the time was prefigured. As St Thomas More confidently expressed it, 'Adam was created and fell into sin in the month of March, on Friday the sixth day of the week and at the sixth hour of the day, and Christ chose to suffer on the day in March on which his coming was announced and on which he was put to death – the sixth day, Friday, at the sixth hour.' *Christ chose to suffer.* Yet he suffered at a time apparently determined by Pilate's schedule. At a certain hour, Pilate went out on the Great Pavement outside Herod's palace to hold the tribunal that would sentence Christ to death. From the hour of that hearing, the crucifixion was set. As far as Pilate knew, the precise timing of the tribunal was determined by how quickly he came downstairs, once the Jews had summoned him; how well he had slept; whether he had paused to dip bread in wine, an elementary breakfast; whether urgent letters had arived from Rome; whether he had made love. Yet perhaps these things, too, were factored into the divine chronometer: each crumb, each kiss, each delay, each stroke of the razor, until at the appointed time Pilate took his seat, prepared to send Christ to the predetermined cross. The exact time of his sentence (which More did not 'record', but John did) was noon, the very moment that the lambs intended for Passover began to be killed in the precincts of the Temple.

Pilate would have believed in Fate, though to what degree we cannot possibly tell. As a schoolboy he would probably have repeated, as the elder Seneca said he had done, the famous epigrams of Furnus: 'The moment we are born, the day that will end our life is fixed; we are hurried off to a destiny that is not announced to us beforehand.' As a magistrate with *imperium* and the highest official in Judea, it would have been his duty from time to time to take the auspices himself: to observe the warm entrails, the flight of birds and the 'carefully designated parts of the sky', in case the gods had somehow revealed in them their plans for his province. He would know what to look for: the bad luck of a missing heart, or one spongy and distended by disease; the good luck of a liver folded at the bottom like a pocket. He was obliged on such occasions to show belief in the augur's rites and to speak the ritual words with all possible solemnity, though Cicero remarked that most men seemed to put on 'an outward show, with no belief in the reality.'

Nonetheless lists were kept, and all oddities recorded, in case their significance could be detected. Julius Obsequens kept records of portents by consulships, so that men could read how under Gaius

Valerius and Marcus Herennius a bronze statue sweated, a kite was caught in the temple of Apollo, and at Volsinii flame flashed through the sky at dawn. Some of these incidents evidently predicted the fate of Rome. During the victorious campaigns in Spain in 75 BC, blood appeared on the outside of the soldiers' shields; this meant triumph. Before the conspiracy of Catiline in 63 BC, bronze tablets containing laws were struck by lightning. Marcus Crassus in 54 BC disregarded a black fog and the sinking of a standard in the Euphrates; and so he perished, with his whole army, in the war against the Parthians. A foaling mule meant civil war, and a swarm of bees on the standards would bring ruin. Just after Pilate left for Judea the collapse of a jerry-built stadium at Fidenae, which crushed hundreds of spectators, was taken as an omen of Rome's abandonment by Tiberius.

Most Romans tended to believe there was a message of some sort in these things, something involving higher powers, even if they did not quite know how. Only an Epicurean would have no time for it, calling it old women's tales; he would claim that natural forces made the world work, while the gods basked in indifference and idleness. A Stoic would tend to believe in an unbroken chain of causation proceeding from the soul of the universe, which was Fate, or Providence, or Jupiter, or Nature, or 'every name of power'. The very beauty and organisation of the world, said Cicero, was enough to demonstrate that some intelligence was in charge of it, just as the beauty of a sun-dial or a water-clock displayed the skill of the craftsman. The very greatness of Rome was a proof that the gods had poured out their favour on her. How could this order be fortuitous? 'It would be as if by making countless copies of the twenty-one letters of the alphabet, of gold or whatever you will, and throwing them together in some receptacle and shaking them out on the ground, you could produce the *Annals* of Ennius, all ready for the reader.'

Between these views came what ordinary men believed. It was a mish-mash: the whimsical tinkerings of heavenly beings, Jupiter's nods, Mercury's tricks, Venus' breathy interruptions, and the implacable decisions of the goddess-of-what-must-be, balancing in the scales the illustrious and the lowly:

> *aequa lege Necessitas*
> *sortitur insignes et imos.*

Fortune herself was a goddess, as was Misfortune; both had temples in

Rome, and both needed propitiation. The stars themselves, scattered over the bowl of heaven, were attached to each man and displayed his fate: the brightest belonged to the rich, the dimmest to the worn-out and poor. Some flared up, flashed and vanished, like a lamp fed with too much oil. A man could be boldly rationalistic, no longer believing literally in the three old stooping Fates with their spindles and shears who paid out the thread of his life, yet certain that what happened to him was not random, and that he did not drift in time undirected. Even Trimalcho's great burlesque in the *Satyricon* of Petronius Arbiter was not without some vestige of belief:

> Under the Bull are born ox-herds and men who have to find their own food. Under the Twins tandems are born, and oxen, and debauchees . . . Under Virgo are born women, and runaway slaves, and chain gangs. Under Libra, butchers and perfumiers, and people who put things to rights; under Scorpio, poisoners and assassins; under Sagittarius cross-eyed men, who take the bacon while they look at the vegetables; under Capricorn, the poor folk whose troubles make horns sprout on them; under Aquarius innkeepers and men with water on the brain; under Pisces chefs and rhetoricians. So the world turns like a mill, and always brings some evil to pass . . .

The most stalwart believer in the power of the stars was Tiberius himself. According to Dio, he would not appoint a man to high office without first ascertaining, from the day and hour of his birth, whether he might present some danger to him in the future. He had almost certainly read Pilate's horoscope, and divined enough from it to know the limits of his ambition and potential; he could already tell, from the lines of his fate, whether he might need to kill him. And Pilate, equally, would understand what the nature of his official clearance was. It lay in the stars.

In his own mind, then, Pilate was not free from otherworldly interference. And he may not have been mistaken. We imagine we are free agents, but possibly do not realise how steadily fate moves us along the road we think we have chosen. A woman wakes in the morning, and gives her hair a hundred strokes of the brush; if she had given it seventy-five, she might not have crossed the road in front of the car that killed her. A man spills a teaspoon of sugar between the packet and the cup, and stops to sweep it off the table; if he had not bothered, he would not have been at the crossroads when the woman stepped from the pavement. A boy stoops to tie his shoelace, and avoids the bullet that passes a foot away; a businessman decides not to take the aeroplane that plunges into the sea. A young Roman makes the right contact at the right dinner party, picks an opportune moment, passes the wine bowl with acceptable obsequiousness, and finds he has ended up with a foreign posting he might as well accept: even Judea.

His life had been moving in parallel with Christ's almost from the beginning. Christ was sent to earth at just the moment when Judea was passing under Roman control. He was born as his parents submitted to the Roman tax assessors: in Luke's words, 'the decree of Caesar Augustus that all the world should be taxed, which was first made while Quirinius was governor of Syria'. His birth thus paralleled the triumph of Augustus, one divine bringer of peace beside another. When Jesus, at the age of twelve, began his precocious teaching in the Temple, Pilate in the army was impressing Roman teaching on barbarians. As Jesus hammered nails in his father's workshop, Pilate was directing men to hammer up the palisades of camps; as Jesus observed the netting of fish and their battering to death on stones beside the Sea of Galilee, Pilate saw much the same fate meted out in the circus to prisoners taken on the German campaigns. One medieval legend imagined the child Jesus at the carpenter's bench, blond curls over blond curling wood, already fashioning small models of the cross on which Pilate would hang him.

Those legends also emphasised that Pilate's father had been an astrologer. He had foreseen his child's power in the stars and had passed on to him, together with an arrogant smile and a love of hunting dogs, certain presentiments and forebodings. These trouble Bulgakov's Pilate, too. He finds himself haunted by images of death and physical dissolution, phials of poison and fearfully dissolving trees; but also strangely drawn to his philosopher-prisoner Jesus, who also has the gift of foreseeing things. 'You and I will always be together,' Jesus tells him. 'Whenever people think of me, they will think of you.' In Pilate's dreams the two walk in comforting lockstep up the long beams of light towards the moon, that twister of fate and arranger of the tides, as if they are grafted to each other.

And perhaps they were. Man's salvation was assured because at the appointed moment Pilate was ready, and in his place. As an early Russian catechism expresses it, with utmost confidence: 'God and man undertook to compass our redemption, by interceding for us with his father, by suffering for us under Pontius Pilate, and by satisfying, by his death, burial and resurrection, the demands of divine justice.' When

God had proceeded from God and the Light from the Light, when Christ had come down from heaven and was made flesh, there was Pilate, waiting: a crop-haired prefect with a grumbling liver, a pretty wife, a sarcastic streak and an obsession with clean water. Or so he was imagined. Here was a man who, like us, found his eyes bleary in the mornings, picked dirt from his fingernails, savoured a good wine, thought he made his decisions for himself; and had no notion of the part he might be playing in any higher scheme of things. Well done, thou good and faithful servant! *Ad majorem Dei gloriam.*

*   *   *

It began in a garden. In the centre of that garden, planted by God in Eden, grew the tree of knowledge of good and evil. Fruit hung from its branches. The Book of Genesis does not say what sort of fruits these were: the Arabs think they were figs, some say they were pomegranates or green plantains; but at least since the time of the apocryphal gospels men have imagined they were apples.

The apple, *malum*, also meant 'the bad thing'. It could not be evil in itself; it was the concentration of God's sweetness. But men could not cope with it. It symbolised not only dangerous knowledge, but contention and power. Men longed for it almost without knowing why. Hercules travelled the world for the golden apples of the Hesperides, which also grew in a tree guarded by a coiling serpent; he tricked Atlas into fetching them, but Atlas refused to hand them over. Eris, also called Discordia, tossed a golden apple among the gods to spoil their celebrations. Apples were irresistible, but carried risks. Men or women who longed for apples were about to get into trouble.

Adam and Eve in the garden desired the apple, ate, and fell. What is less well known is that Pilate followed them. The *Golden Legend* relates how one day he stood at the window of his palace, gazing at a nearby orchard. The trees were heavy with red apples, and Pilate was seized with such a fierce desire for the fruit that he almost fainted. He called his servant to him and said, 'I want that fruit so much that if I don't get some, I shall die.'

The scene was supposedly set in Judea, but it sounds like northern Europe. It is a version of the story of Rapunzel, where the pregnant wife longs for the wild garlic that grows in the witch's garden. Her husband, believing her when she insists that she will die without it, scales the wall. But the witch exacts a penalty for the stolen plant: she demands the child that is to be born. A bargain of the same sort was about to be made with Pilate, that loss and death would come of his desire.

He did not exactly order the apples to be stolen, but they were stolen anyway. That is the way with apples. They invite the stealing, then the excuses. ('The woman gave it to me, and I ate.' 'The serpent beguiled me, and I ate.') Typically the guardian of the apples – the owner, the higher authority, the conscience – is absent or asleep. The apples ask to be stolen, inveigle themselves into outstretched hands. Thoreau, the most moral of men, wrote in his diary of sampling apples in the woods of Massachusetts; they belonged to someone, but their very splendour made it more of a sin to leave them than to take them. 'I pluck them,' he wrote,

> fruit of old trees that have been dying ever since I was a boy and are not yet dead . . . Frequented only by the woodpecker, deserted now by the farmer, who has not faith enough to look under the boughs. Food for walkers. Sometimes apples red inside, perfused with a beautiful blush, too beautiful to eat, – apple of the evening sky, of the Hesperides . . . Let the frost come to freeze them first solid as stones, and then the sun . . . thaw them, and they will seem to have borrowed a flavour from heaven through the medium of the air in which they hang.

Stolen apples, as the proverb says, are always sweetest. They impart knowledge, love, authority, charisma, to those who are not ready to have them yet. The immature king (or the immature governor) holds the orb, the 'golden apple' of power; the teenager fondles the orbs of his girl's breasts. If apples are so bewitching, perhaps God has put them there deliberately to provoke the crime: to unleash the longing that will lead to the fall.

So Pilate, in his palace, longed for the apples beyond the wall. His servant went over to fetch them, scrambling, jumping, filling his pockets. On the way he encountered the owner of the orchard, a man he did not recognise, and killed him with a stone. Then he delivered the apples to Pilate, shining, blood-red, and watched as he cut the white flesh to the core. As Pilate ate, the servant told him what the price of the apples had been.

Adam, too, had eaten the apple boldly for a while. But it turned to ashes. He realised that he was naked; and then, *sciens bonum et malum,* knowing good and the apple, he was driven from the garden. The cost of that apple, too, was blood. According to St Augustine, 'Eve borrowed sin from the devil and wrote a bill and provided a surety, and the interest on the debt was heaped upon posterity . . . She wrote the bill when she reached out her hand to the forbidden apple.'And in the end, adds the *Golden Legend*, 'Christ took this bill and nailed it to the cross.'

That cross itself, some said, sprang from the forbidden apple tree. Centuries before, Japeth, the son of Noah, had taken into the Ark a cutting from the tree of knowledge in the garden of Eden, and planted it in the garden where Christ was arrested. By the time Pilate needed it, it was high enough to hang a man.

The Song of Songs offered a different speculation. There Christ was both the apple and the tree: the outstretched arms and the drops of blood.

> As the apple tree among the trees of the wood,
> So is my beloved among the sons.
> I sat down under his shadow with great delight,
> And his fruit was sweet to my taste.

It was sweet to Pilate also. The governor desired the apple tree and its sweet hanging burden, without knowing why, because of the job he was destined to do. Christ was the tree, Christ the apple; Christ was the temptation and the satisfaction. And if Pilate did not pluck him, peel him, pierce him, crush him till the juice flowed, he would never unleash for fallen men the possibility of salvation.

So Pilate stood at the window, longing so deeply that he thought he would faint away; and his servant stood at his shoulder. But this was no ordinary servant. He was Pilate's deputy, his soul–mate, and a man who understood at a snap of the fingers the deepest inclinations of his master's heart. His name was Judas Iscariot.

Medieval mythmakers believed the two men must have been thrown together some years before the betrayal of Christ. Their careers were bound to cross. Like evil twins, they needed to plot together and strengthen their complicity in each other's company. No one else would willingly be their associate; but in the gloomy halls and mountain passes where such lost souls met, they could comfort each other. Thus, in one modern Italian novel about Pilate, Judas tells him: 'We are the indispensable artisans of the redemption. We are the instruments of the supreme outrage required to shake the moral conscience of the world ... You will be execrated, but console yourself. He knows that he could never have redeemed mankind without my pretended betrayal and your pretended cowardice.'

Thomas de Quincey, in his opium haze, also understood this. Judas, he wrote, should never have been flung into the Potter's Field after his suicide on the elder tree. He had served Christ's purposes; he had been the force that had pushed him into action. Pilate had then pushed Christ further, towards the result that God intended.

The *Golden Legend* recounted how Judas's life, like Pilate's, had begun with portents, though they were more in the nature of bad dreams. One night, after Ruben, his father, and Cyborea, his mother, had made love, she fell into a half-sleep, only to wake up screaming. She had dreamt, she said, that she was going to have a son 'so wicked that he would bring ruin to all our people'. Ruben scoffed at this; he thought 'some divining spirit' must have infected her. But she insisted through her sobs that it was not; the son she was bound to have would be 'a revelation of the truth'.

The nine months passed, and Cyborea bore a son. His parents did not know what to do with him. His little body was perfect, but he was red-haired, a sign of criminality and bewitchment. At last, feeling that they must dispose of him, they put him in a basket woven of green rushes and set him afloat on the sea.

After a while, the basket drifted ashore on an island called Iscariot. The queen of the island, who was childless, was walking along the beach. She saw the basket bobbing on the surf, and asked her maids to bring it to her. The child's face within the basket shone with fraudulent beauty; and the queen sighed. 'If I had a child like that,' she said, 'the royal line would be secure.' So she had the child rescued and secretly put to a nurse, while she herself pretended to be pregnant. Later, amid national rejoicing, she produced Judas as her own son.

In this way, though his origins were obscure, he was brought up royally: as, at some distance, Pilate was. And in Judas' case, too, there was competition that his proud nature found unbearable. Not long after the queen's false pregnancy, she gave birth to a true son conceived with the king. So Judas, like Pilate, had a brother who was by blood and breeding superior. As they grew up and played together, Judas often mistreated the royal child and made him cry. Sometimes the Devil himself got into Judas, making him bite anyone who came near him; if there was no one near, he would bite his own arms and the backs of his freckled hands.

In despair, his mother took him at last to a child in Nazareth, Jesus, who was said to work miracles. The child touched Judas, and at once the devil slunk out of him in the shape of a black dog; but not before Judas had bitten Jesus on the hand and the right side, which made him cry. The scar of the bite in his side later provided a marker for a half-blind centurion to pierce him on Pilate's orders.

After the visit to Jesus Judas was better for a time, but it did not last. He somehow found out that he was not the queen's son but a foundling, a piece of jetsam washed up on the beach. This filled him with such shame that he secretly killed the queen's true son and fled to Jerusalem, hiding himself in a company of young men who were being sent there as tribute. Daring to emerge, he took service in the household of Pilate, who was governor. Pilate was deeply charmed by him: a strange-starred child like himself, a half-prince, a brother-killer, a tribute-boy. On every level they understood each other, 'screw to screw and false to false', as a medieval writer described it. In no time, Judas became Pilate's favourite. They walked together, drank together, laughed at each other's jokes. Pilate gave Judas the post of chief steward, and Judas did for Pilate anything he requested.

Pilate made a strange employer. He was capricious, filled with sudden longings and peculiar impulses, and each of these Judas was bound to satisfy. When he went to fetch the apples from the orchard the man he encountered was Ruben, his own father. Unwittingly, since neither man recognised the other, Judas slew him with a stone to the nape of the neck. The governor, the bright fruit at last in his hands, barely registered the cost of the errand.

When he did, after the body was discovered at dusk under the blue trees, he awarded all Ruben's goods to Judas: including Cyborea, Judas's mother. The governor, morally impervious or possibly still dreaming, seemed unaware of the enormity of what he had done. So Judas, like Oedipus, killed his father and, at Pilate's urging, married his mother, until the day when she suddenly burst into tears among the tangled sheets. Learning the truth, Judas at first had no idea what to do; but Cyborea saved him. She urged him to repent of his awful sin by joining Jesus and his band of disciples. Judas agreed, for, as it happened, that too fitted perfectly with the schemes which he and Pilate were hatching together.

For Pilate had longed for apples, the symbols of Christ; but this was nothing compared to his desire for Christ himself. He had heard reports of his disturbances but also snippets of his teachings, including the idea that this man too had a royal parentage that was distant and confused. It was impossible to make a public show of his curiosity; but repentant Iscariot could become Christ's follower, and infiltrate the group of disciples on Pilate's behalf.

He succeeded admirably. He became a favourite among the disciples, and was trusted with the group's store of cash, not that there was much of it. Meanwhile, Jesus' doings were faithfully reported back to Pilate. When those doings became too dangerous, too strange, smacking of alternative authority, it was Judas who was sent to turn Christ in: to jump over the wall, seize the fruit that so tortured Pilate, brush his lips against it and bring it before him. He would not know – as Pilate himself did not know – whether Pilate was motivated by rage, curiosity, jealousy, cruelty, or something like love. His own role was not to ask questions. It was to jump, fetch, deliver, feign and fawn, like any good little red-headed spy.

*   *   *

Perhaps the relationship was like that. The medieval playwrights, however, thought it was more distant, at least in the beginning. Their Judas did not cross Pilate's path until the passion story was already fast unfolding, with Jesus waiting outside Jerusalem and receiving the tender ministrations of Mary Magdalene. This Judas was a stranger and a pest; he had his uses, but he would not leave Pilate alone. In the York play he makes his appearance just as the Jews, mainly in the persons of Annas and Caiaphas, are trying to persuade Pilate that Jesus is dangerous. From offstage then comes that piping, whining voice: 'I hate him, Jesus, that Jew.'

Judas' fate is already clear. He wears his cloak like a shroud, and a noose is round his neck; his hair blazes red as if it is on fire. He pours out his hatred for thirty lines to the porter at the gate of the palace. While they were all at supper, a woman came and poured ointment over Jesus's feet. As treasurer, Judas objected: the ointment could have been sold for 'three hundred silver pennies to give to the poor', and he could have taken his secret cut, his ten per cent. In order to recoup it somehow, he now wants to sell his master to 'Prince Pilate and the priests'.

But the porter refuses to admit him. There is something about this 'glowering gadling', this 'beetle-browed briber' that bothers him. It is not just the beard, as Judas rather plaintively supposes, but the whole personality. So the two argue on the doorstep. Pilate meanwhile sits behind them, in his golden robes, on 'a bench with banners bright', but he can hear nothing. The man Judas has to persuade is a statue caught in amber, sitting beside the gesticulating Jews, and pouring himself the occasional drink.

'You look like an utter loser to me. If you don't clear off, I'll beat you to a pulp!'

'Look, just this time ... It's all true, I swear it is.'

'Tell me another.'

'Look, just get me a word with him. In proper council, if you like. I don't see why everybody shouldn't hear it.'

'Wait here.'

The porter goes in to Pilate, composed on his golden bench. Annas and Caiaphas are at his elbow. Two doctors in wide-brimmed Jewish hats perch on the steps, and a soldier stands guard behind them. The porter says, 'I suppose I'd better keep nothing from you, my lord.'

'Tell me,' says Pilate.

The scene is stately and sycophantic. The Jews are telling Pilate how beautiful he is, a theme as constant as sunlight in the York play; he, in turn, is being gracious. The news that there is a man at the door 'hilt-full of ire' merely intrigues him. He says, 'What has he come for?'

'I don't know him. He's wrapped in a cloak. All I know is, you wouldn't want to kiss him.'

'Go and get him, so we know what his trouble is. We'll give him an open hearing.'

The porter fetches Judas. He sidles in, cloak round his head, noose round his neck, and bows to them. 'Come on, look sharp!' the porter bellows. 'Say what you want to say, and don't make trouble! Step up lively, and take care not to upset us!'

'Flower of fortune and fame, may we all find favour with you.'

'Thank you,' says Pilate. 'Welcome. I like that.'

Caiaphas comes bustling up, in his bishop's mitre, and hooks a long finger in Judas's sleeve. 'Can't you hear, knave?' he cried. 'You should be on your knees! On your knees!'

'Don't worry about them,' says Pilate to Judas. 'Caiaphas, stop mocking him; you should be ashamed, sir. And you, fair sir – come in properly. Don't stand in the doorway and be bashful.'

They connect at once. Even in traditions like York that make the two men strangers, they understand each other. The Jews irritate Pilate, and he ignores them; Judas he wants to deal with man to man. And the deal begins when they have scarcely met. Judas makes his offer: 'If you want to bargain or buy, I'll sell you Jesus.' Some of the bystanders whoop, but Pilate simply asks: 'What's your name?'

'Judas Iscariot.'

'You're a just man. So Jesus will be justified by our judgement, Judas.'

These two conclusions are plucked from thin air. The York Pilate has seen Judas for two minutes, knows nothing about him, but is immediately prepared to do business with him. More than that, he is prepared to alter the course of history with him by 'justifying Jesus', or, in other words, letting him do his work of salvation. The partners in crime fall smoothly into each other's arms. 'Now, what shall we pay?' asks Pilate. 'Is that price all right with everyone?' 'Do you agree, Judas?' 'That's great.' He even repeats Judas' pregnant phrase, 'a knot for to knit', redolent of both the plot and the noose. Their fates are tangled together in an instant.

Only one sticky moment occurs, when it emerges that Judas is a disciple of Jesus. Pilate doesn't like that: 'Say, man, to sell your master – what has he done wrong?' Judas answers: 'Done me out of as much money as I'll get from you, if everything goes right.' Pilate wavers for a while, but as Judas describes his plan to the Jews, his motions to catch Jesus, the governor softens again. He smiles at this awful creature, this 'lurdan', this 'harlot': 'Abide in my blessing and bring what is best, Judas. It would be good to clear this little difficulty up. As soon as you can.'

'I haven't had any money yet.'

'You'll be paid soon, really soon. Then you'll have reason to love us. So, Judas, no more moaning – '

As if on sudden impulse, he takes out the bag and thrusts it at him. Judas yelps with delight; the priests rear back their mitred heads.

'Take your silver. Take it all.'

'That's fine. I feel great now. I'll bring you that traitor before you know it. I'm so happy now.'

'Keep your word, do your work well, and you'll have our love and support; that's a promise.'

The crowd presses to the door, priests, doctors, soldiers, all eager to catch Jesus. But Pilate's last words are for his agent, his new accomplice, promising precisely what he cannot give him: 'Solace to your soul.'

Let me introduce you to this Judas. He is the direct descendant of the servant-spy of the *Golden Legend* and the mystery plays, but his name is not in the newspapers. He is Judas only in his own head, in the heads of those who suspect him (but they can never be sure) and in the head of the man, the Pilate, who runs him on the Leader's behalf and in the name of internal security. It is a little drama of loyalty, cruelty and betrayal that is played out daily in the hearts of all oppressive regimes. The Cold War saw such Judases everywhere; but now you may most easily find them in a city like Havana, where there is still the same sense of people trapped like insects in historical forces larger than themselves.

You may not spot him at first. He could be the taxi-driver outside the Hotel Nacional, or the young blood who offers ham sandwiches in the street. The man lying on the sea wall, his cap over his eyes, or the one selling greenish oranges from a tilting market stall. A boy on a bicycle, chewing sugar cane like a stick of rock; or a lanky mulatto who mops, with languorous insouciance, the floor of the meeting hall of the local political committee. All these, like him, are watchers. They note who visits, who knocks, who leaves, who parks for a while in a car with foreign numberplates. But Judas is the one who reports to the man in the government office who reports to the Leader himself. He can command his attention, bother him at odd hours; and can also be sure that if trouble comes he can be disowned and brushed aside, as easily as his Pilate can be brushed aside by the Leader in the villa in Miramar.

So, carefully, Judas maps out his days. In the morning a shave with a cut-throat razor and a cup of domestic coffee, made mostly of pulverised dried peas. Down the damp peeling stairs into the street, where the heat is already rising among the tattered palm trees. A better cup of coffee at the Esplendido, where the tourists stay. A table inside, in the cavernous tiled dining room, or his customary seat on the leather sofa just inside the door. From there he can banter with the bow-tied doorman, another watcher, and with the taxi drivers, who will work only for hard currency and the promise of conversations worth recording.

He himself records other things. The room numbers of foreigners; the addresses on the cards they innocently post in the black box in the foyer, to which he has the key; descriptions of nationals consorting with tourists and the objects – a pen, a roll of Sellotape, candied peanuts in a screw of brown paper – they exchange. Since paper is scarce and thin he writes on anything he finds, including opened-out cigarette packets and the margins of his newspaper. He imagines he is safe; no one could read writing so oblique and small.

As he leaves the hotel, the sun is vertical above the streets. His lunch is a hot maize fritter from a stall in the market, washed down with weak beer. He makes it last as long as the siesta, an hour or so. After this he strolls the streets, making for the flat where he will spend his afternoons. It is this flat that holds the information his boss needs, where Pilate longs to go himself with the security of a pistol under his jacket; but instead he must sit, and smoke, and wait for the moment when Judas will report to him.

The flat is on a side street, up two flights of concrete stairs. It belongs to an eminent national philosopher, now out of favour for discoursing on free thought and democracy. He holds court there in a room bare except for his desk, two metal garden chairs, the bed where his mother sleeps, and the television set on which she watches Brazilian soap-operas. His followers cram on the bed and the floor; some stand in the kitchen, a room about the size of a small cupboard, with a sink that drains into a bucket. They talk, argue, drink glasses of sweet coffee. Everyone knows the group is infiltrated; it is their guarantee of survival, for if they were not controlled they would need to be eliminated. But no one is sure which among them is Pilate's man.

At around seven in the evening, Judas makes for Pilate's house. It is a disused embassy off Avenida Quinta; the steps to the front door are broken, the garden overgrown, the elegant balcony lined with empty drums of cooking oil. Because this man is important he merits a sentry, who sits in a glass-sided kiosk with his rifle cocked. The bushes down the avenue's central divide are rustling with girls in Lycra and lipstick; but they do not look at Judas, because he has no money.

All he has is information. And this is as good as money, as good as treasure, to the man he has come to see. Pilate wants not only the dissenters' movements but also their ideas. To him these ideas are as dangerous and as exotic as bright fruit on a tree, the tree he himself – as a good party member – has been ordered never to touch. But once he tastes them, he will not fear them; he will be able to debate them, counter them and, if necessary, crush them. Knowledge will give him the advantage over these subversive people.

So night after night they talk together; screw to screw, false to false, across a desk with only an ashtray and a packet of cigarettes. The room in which they sit was once beautiful, with the remains of cornices now crumbling in the humidity; but the black plastic sofa is party issue, and the walls are stained with nicotine. Pilate's cigarettes are Cuban, although he has the currency to buy Marlboros in the dollar shop; it is a gesture of ideological purity and solidarity. He keeps the Leader's picture on the wall behind his desk.

So, steadily, Judas stokes his curiosity. He retails the philosopher's stories and, by doing so, spreads the word himself: agent and double agent. He cannot gauge the effect he is having. Sometimes Pilate laughs, snorting smoke at the ceiling; sometimes he seems perplexed, almost afraid; more often he launches into an impassioned diatribe on some scarcely related subject. If it gets too late, a taciturn woman – perhaps his mistress, perhaps his wife – will appear and put down before him a plate with rice, fried plantain, pork, fish. Pilate scarcely notices; he is swallowing ideas. But Judas barely waits for the moment of invitation before he is eating, fast and furtively, like a small and lucky dog.

Around them the regime moves towards its inevitable dissolution. The people are resentful, the revolutionary murals fading; the soldiers are preparing to put their guns away. In the great scheme of things, Pilate and Judas are battling against ideas that will inevitably prevail. Indeed they themselves, by alternately bullying the dissenters and relaxing their grip, are agents in their state's collapse, just as a trickle of water freezing and expanding may topple the monuments of concrete and cement. They themselves are advancing the events that must come. They are part of the plan.

Were it not that the air inside is thick with tobacco and the air outside still steams, like damp laundry, you might say that you were in Judea.

In the beginning was the Word, and the Word was with God, and the word was God.

He was in the beginning with God.

All things were made by him; and nothing came into being except through him.

In him was life; and the life was the light of men.

And the light shines in darkness, and the darkness did not understand it.

There was a man sent from God, whose name was John. In 26, as Pilate's ship approached Judea, this man had just begun to preach in the Judean wilderness. He roamed in that frightening expanse east of Jerusalem, running down towards Asphaltites. People had surged out to him from the whole province, and now that delightful river, the Jordan, was full of people up to their knees in the dappling water.

The two strangers appeared together: the new governor in his rippling toga, snacking nervously on the recommended Judean dates, and the Baptist in his camel-hair loincloth, crunching locusts with wild honey. The crowds that followed both of them were not merely interested in their new, foreign faces: they wanted to hear promises, receive instructions, form some notion of what the future might be like. Auxiliary soldiers came to John, as doubtless they came to Pilate, to ask what they ought to do. He answered: 'Don't hurt anyone or accuse anyone falsely, and be content with your wages.' The *publicani*, or collectors of Roman taxes, came too, and John told them: 'Exact no more than you're supposed to.' In the wilds of Judea, they may well have obeyed him with more alacrity than they did the man who was still exploring, and mentally redecorating, the rooms of the palace in Caesarea.

Herod Antipas kept an eye on John. He was fascinated by him, and wary of his capacity to provoke disorder. If Pilate and Herod shared intelligence in those early days of cautious diplomacy, or if Pilate sent his own spies out, he would have heard that 'all Judea' was streaming out to John to hear his teaching. Much of it did not make a great deal of sense: he spoke of fire, winnowing flails, sandals. But he mentioned also 'the wrath to come', a code-word for the Roman aggressors, and spoke of someone more disturbing who was to come after him. Beyond that there was, to Roman ears, a strange perversion in his most persistent teachings. He called for straight paths and baptism by water, whose purity would make all men new. Pilate too could offer straight roads and clean water; indeed, it was almost all he could bring that would remotely interest the Jews.

Although John was on Pilate's territory, it was Antipas who took action against him, showing the new governor both how such mad creatures could get under a ruler's skin, and how hard they were to eradicate. Josephus, as well as the gospels, reported his anxiety. Herod feared, said Josephus, 'that the great influence John had over the people might lead to some rebellion'; he therefore thought it best to prevent mischief by putting him to death, 'and not bring himself into difficulties by sparing a man who might make him repent of his leniency when it would be too late.' On the other hand, according to Mark, Antipas liked John and even thought him holy, or at least possessed of spiritual powers. The fox of Galilee in his sumptuous court liked to watch and listen to this dishevelled, half-naked man; he imprisoned him as one might cage a curious animal at the zoo. He was dangerous, but he was compelling and probably in command of magic; so Antipas wavered. It was not until his new wife Herodias inveigled him, through her daughter Salome's dancing, to kill John that he found the courage to do so, and had him beheaded.

Even then, the tetrarch never got over him. He did not shed his guilt or forget his fascination with the wonder-worker. When Jesus appeared, according to Mark, there was no doubt in Herod's mind who he was. This was John risen from the dead, 'and that's why mighty works show themselves in him.'

'No, no,' said others round him. 'It's Elias.'

'It's one of the prophets.'

But Antipas insisted. 'It's John, the one I beheaded. He's risen from the dead.'

From then on his court swarmed with rumours. And perhaps it was not only the Jews who were so credulous, believing in maverick preachers who did not die but assumed different shapes. Perhaps Gratus, Coponius and Pilate were haunted also, in their elaborate beds. Not only the Jews had prophecies. Virgil in his fourth *Eclogue* had foretold the coming of a golden child 'filled with the life of the gods' who would bring in a kingdom of love, in which hounds and deer would steal to the stream to drink together. The sins of men would fade away then, and they would no longer need to struggle to make the earth fruitful: grapes would hang on brambles, the oak trees would run with honey, and soft waves of wheat would spread across the fields like sunlight. Destiny had fixed this scene: it would come, and it would come soon. Augustus had already inaugurated the Age of Gold, the *pax deorum*; Fortune had crowned him, and from his cornucopia the earth was springing already with fruit, and flowers, and peace.

Back in Rome, lines like this would be politely applauded in lecture rooms for the elegance of their metre and the niceness of their sentiment: even the golden child could be safely identified as the son of one of the consuls. There was no need to be mystical about it. Yet in Judea prophecies were shouted in the market, howled in the desert; their broken rhythms were of no importance. They were urgent and true. Ideas that would never have disquieted a governor in the mocking air of Rome gained a disturbing life from the fervour with which men believed them in Judea. At night, with the oil-lamp almost out and the bedtime reading (Livy? Propertius?) laid aside, the imposed order of the working day gave way to creeping moonlight, Hebrew songs, the cries of distant birds and, most unnerving to an urban Roman, silence. Rationalisation was no good in the dark.

Every governor ran spies and informers, but there were other means of getting information. Pilate's soldiers, on duty all through Judea and Samaria, could send reports. An odd incident in the mountains; people moving on the road like refugees but without their goods, as if called out to see something; their litter, broken bread and fish, spread over a hillside. The story would be picked up in bits and pieces from the hysterical healed woman, the surprised tax-collector, the small boy with crumbs in his pockets. These were unreliable witnesses, of course, their tales the sort of rubbish heard in drinking houses. Would you believe water turned into wine, or a herd of pigs falling arse-over-tip into the sea?

Nonetheless, the stars were in alignment, and the land of Judea swarmed with the intimation of Christ. In Isaiah, the Lord had promised that the desert would fracture into streams that were full of him, that the hills would sing with the thought of him, and that the stony beds of dragons would become soft paths of holiness on which Christ would tread. Everyone expected him, and the secret could not be kept. Reeds at the edge of Lake Tiberias took in the message and whispered it, as their cousins had once whispered the secret of the folly of Midas. The turpentine trees that grew among the rocks overheard, and impressed the message on their many-fingered leaves. The leaves shivered and, before the wind, exposed the name of Christ on their pale undersides. Some fluttered down, turning in the air like the Sybil's distracted prophecies, to carry Christ into gullies where sheep huddled, or into dry stream beds to be kicked aside by boys.

A citron tree in a garden overheard; and when its fruit was picked the name of Christ was in the pith, bitter and white. A row of bean-plants overheard and, when they blossomed, the name of Christ was inscribed on their flowers.

Shells held to the ear on the beach whispered 'Christ', and the sea itself sighed and roared him.

Lastly, the swallows heard that darted round the eaves of the houses in Caesarea. All day they swooped and dashed across the terraces and into the cool tiled halls, squeaking the name of Christ. In his palace, Pilate watched as the birds flew to and fro to their nests among the joists of the ceiling. And in his ears, on his plate, in his kitchens, in his garden, in the breast of the blue sea, past the shining piers, one name resounded: Christ, Christ, Christ.

A spy in the crowd that followed John would have seen him baptise a man whom he called 'The Lamb of God'. He dribbled the water over his head at the place where the River Jordan flowed into the dead Asphaltites. John said he had seen the spirit of God descending on him like a dove. Spirits were harder for spies to discern; but it was clear that the man began to gather disciples of his own, who also began to baptise. To a Roman governor, the names of some of these disciples were disturbing: two brothers who were called 'Sons of Thunder', and a man called 'Simon the Zealot'. Perhaps these titles had no political connotation to the disciples or to Jesus; perhaps they were even a joke. But they carried echoes of rebellion which Pilate would not have missed.

For a while, Jesus put no particular strain on him. He did not want the earthly authorities to be provoked. For most of his ministry he stayed in Galilee, out of Pilate's way. He told his disciples expressly, as he sent them out, that they were not to go 'into the way of the Gentiles', though he knew they could not help encountering them; even if they were 'prudent as serpents', as he advised them to be, they would still end up 'brought before governors and kings for my sake'.

Yet Jesus avoided Judea less for fear of the Romans than for fear of the Jews; and the gospels suggest that, but for the suspicions of the Pharisees, he would have been left alone. He is not bothered by the Romans, though he calls them 'enemies', 'wolves' and 'dogs', and they are not yet bothered by him. Their presence in the gospels is virtually invisible. They are scarcely seen, heard or even talked about, an extraordinarily muted performance for an armed occupation force. As Luke's Jesus implied in the parable of the Good Samaritan, they had not even made the main road between Jerusalem and Jericho safe for people to travel on. Only occasionally, as when Jesus invokes the carrying of crosses or, in the course of teaching, breaks the night into the four Roman watches of evening, midnight, cock-crow and morning, is there some sense that these occupiers have left a mark on Jewish life. It does not matter; they will be useful when they have to be.

Until the passion, there is no account of the Romans exercising their police powers except by implication. In Luke, the 'enemies' who must be loved slap people on the face, take their cloaks and steal their property; they are 'sinners' who, like any Roman – like Pilate – love those who love them and scratch the backs of those who scratch theirs. In the course of the Sermon on the Mount, Jesus advises his listeners that if someone asks them to go a mile, they should go two; the reference was to compulsory services demanded by Roman troops, who might, for example, get locals to carry their packs to the next village. John the Baptist told such soldiers not to intimidate or to extort money; presumably, therefore, they often did so.

In Mark, the devil driven out of a madman is asked his name; he answers, 'Legion, because we are so many.' A legion could only mean Romans, bristling, swarming, appropriately changed at last into a snorting herd of swine. On the other hand, the parables of Jesus show a Judea in which people are going about their business peacefully enough. They plant vineyards, sow seed, invest money, hire reapers for the harvest, with every expectation of profit and no suggestion of political disruption. The only sour note is provided by the local tax-collectors, the hated *publicani*, who collect Pilate's money for him. Yet even these Jesus has time for. It is a measure of his strangeness and his kindness that he talks to these people and eats with them: people he does not hesitate to call 'sick' and 'sinners' and who are usually mentioned in the gospels in the same breath as prostitutes, because they could find no better way of living than whoring for the Romans.

Jesus made a point of the gravity of their offences. The virtue of the publicans in his eyes was that, having fallen so far in collaboration with the Gentiles, they could only begin to repent and rise. Even these hardest cases could be saved. A publican who bowed in humility and dejection in the Temple, beating his breast in repentance for the money he had handled, was more surely justified before God than the Pharisee who fasted, tithed, prayed extravagantly, and was not 'an extortioner and unjust, or even like this publican.' In the grand scheme of salvation Pilate's fiscal agents had their own small role, as exemplars of the extraordinary breadth of the love of God.

The first to be saved by name was Zaccheus. He was the first indirect point of contact between Pilate and Jesus: a man who talked to, indeed took orders from, both of them. Zaccheus was a chief of the publicans, bustling, rich, and so small that he had to scramble into a sycamore tree to catch a glimpse of Jesus as he came through Jericho. Jesus spotted him in the shadow-play of the leaves, which fell on his body like coins. The hiding man was called down and persuaded (though he needed no persuasion) to host a meal for Jesus. This had an extraordinary effect on him. At once, he found himself promising that 'If I've taken anything from any man by false accusation, I'll give him back four times as much.' Then he offered to give half his goods to the poor. If he kept those promises, the effect on Pilate's receipts would not have gone unnoticed. The governor would have wanted to know what the hell Zaccheus was doing; there can be few things more unsettling than a tax-collector finding God.

On one famous occasion, Jesus was asked directly about payment of Roman taxes. The question came from 'spies', according to Luke, or from 'disciples of the Pharisees, with the Herodians', according to Matthew. Those 'spies' have usually been assumed to be Jewish, but not necessarily so; their information would have been of the deepest interest to Pilate. These men, whatever their affiliation, approached Jesus as he was teaching in the Temple. 'Master', they asked, in their wheedling way, 'we know you only teach the way of God in truth, and care nothing for men or the pretensions of men. So, tell us: Is it lawful to pay tribute to Caesar, or not?'

Jesus saw at once that this was a trick question: a ruse, as Matthew put it, 'to take hold of his words, and to deliver him into the power and authority of the governor.' But he did not want that encounter with Pilate yet; it was not yet the hour for him to court sedition and to draw his death sentence from Tiberius' devoted representative. Instead, he demanded: 'Show me a penny.'

One was brought to him. This was the coin Jews used to pay the poll-tax that went to the emperor's privy purse; it was not an acceptable currency in the Temple, but there would be a few of them on the money-changers' tables. Unlike Pilate's small change, this was solid and silver. It was probably a coin of Tiberius with, around the edge, the words TI [BERIVS] CAESAR DIVI AVG[VSTI] F[ILIVS], Tiberius, son of the divine Augustus, another son of a god; and it would have carried that same blunt-nosed profile, with the untidily cropped hair, that Pilate had paraded through Jerusalem on the standards of his army.

Here, then, was another close call. Jesus held in his palm, looked at, touched, the image of Tiberius: an image that counted as sacred to the man who was to kill him.

'Whose image and superscription is this?' he asked.

'Caesar's,' they answered.

'So give to Caesar the things that are Caesar's, and to God the things that are God's.'

This clever answer meant many things. Most obviously, it meant that Caesar could have his relatively unimportant offerings, as long as God was assured of his. But there was a strong political charge in the statement, too. The whole of Judea, after all, was God's, and the Jews his people. Jesus might have meant that the hand of the Romans on Jewish money or Jewish property was an abomination. Indeed, he may have gone further, since he acted like a man who had scarcely handled money and had no coins about him; money itself was an abomination, and a world obsessed with money was a peculiarly Roman creation. The words 'give to Caesar', may in fact have meant 'pour Caesar's money down his throat', as the Parthians had poured molten gold into the mouth of Crassus. Pay contemptuously, but keep them quiet. Play games with the money, throw it in the air, hide it in a sleeve, produce it from the sea, crack their precious *denarii* between their well-brushed Roman teeth, mock at their desperation to collect it; but in the end, kindly, let them have it.

This would have been the Essene or Zealot interpretation of the words. They fitted in precisely with the political philosophy of Judas of Galilee who, since the time of Coponius, had urged the Jews not to pay Roman taxes. Yet a Roman would have missed this bitter subtext; to him, the sentiments expressed would have been innocuous, even laudable. Rome too, Jesus seemed to be saying, had legitimate claims on these people. Pilate could demand his taxes, and the people ought to pay them. No one picked Jesus up then and there on this ambiguity; but when he came to trial, and the Jews told Pilate that he had 'forbidden them to pay tribute to Caesar,' Pilate ignored the charge, implying that he did not believe them.

That said, there was no love lost between Jesus and the Romans.

These were two different worlds coming into collision. Gentile values – Pilate's values – were the antithesis of what Jesus taught. Romans cared for worldly goods, fine clothes, power, and the hierarchies of their 'so-called rulers'. They were constantly asking 'What shall we eat?' 'What shall we drink?' 'What shall we wear?' In the parable of the wedding feast, Jesus gave the Gentiles a walk-on role as street-loafers and supper-scroungers, just as some suppose the young Pilate was; but the followers of Jesus were to be simple and self-effacing, like wild flowers. When a Roman prayed, it was a series of 'vain repetitions': Jesus's followers were to address God as 'Father', and to mention down-to-earth subjects such as debts and bread. If a brother among the disciples did something wrong, he was to be won back with love and community discipline; but if he refused to repent, he was to be treated 'like a pagan or a tax-collector', a man outside the bounds of normal contact and reasonable discourse.

Mutual antipathy was essential to God's plan. Jesus had to provoke Pilate, and Pilate had to kill him. Yet this was not (as it could have been) a police murder in an alleyway; it was a set piece, including a meeting and a conversation, and the path was prepared in advance. Before Pilate met him, there was one other close encounter: the meeting with the centurion who petitioned Jesus to heal his servant. This man was probably not a Roman, despite his title. He was more likely to have been a non-commissioned officer of Herod Antipas, since the meeting took place in Capernaum, in Galilee, under Herod's jurisdiction: a native perhaps of Syria or Sebaste, speaking Aramaic. According to Luke, his sympathies with the Jews ran deep: his Jewish friends explained that 'he loves our nation and has built us a synagogue.' Yet he was a Gentile. He was a career soldier, as Jews never were, since they had a religious exemption; he was probably tricked out by Antipas, a slavish Romanophile, in imitation Roman gear; and he knew, as a Roman would have done, that he would have to conduct his negotiations with Jews at a distance. In all these respects, he may as well have been one of Pilate's men.

In Luke, he never meets Jesus. Instead he sends the elders of the Jews, with whom he is on good terms, to petition on his behalf, and Jesus sets off for his house. When he is not far from it, the centurion sends out friends to stop him. 'Lord, please don't trouble yourself,' is the message. 'I am not worthy that you should enter under my roof.' Jesus therefore stops, and heals the servant from several hundred yards away.

Matthew tells the story differently. Here the two men meet, but elements of distance remain. The centurion makes his request; Jesus responds by remarking about the centurion's faith to his disciples. The centurion looks at Jesus; Jesus does not necessarily look at him. It is not, in any sense, a conversation.

This was how Jesus would have acted with a Roman, too. The same invisible *cordon sanitaire* would have restrained him: through which, nonetheless, he would have sensed the centurion's sincerity, and through which the servant, stiff with pain on his damp bed, could have felt that sudden inflow of life. A Roman, of course, would not have called him 'Lord'; the word *domine* was used only for evident superiors. Yet the centurion's thinking was quintessentially Roman: practical, efficient, down-to-earth. He was under orders, he told Jesus.

> I am under authority myself, and I have soldiers under me; and I say to this man, Go, and he goes, and to another Come here, and he comes, and to my slave, Do this, and he does it.

This was the authentic Gentile voice. It was obsessed with power, hierarchy, position, authority. *I am under someone, but I have people under me. This is how the world works; it depends on who is giving the orders and how strong they are. This is what counts.* Jesus did not answer these remarks directly, but he seems to have taken note of the thinking; it became the basis of the little lecture on power that he delivered later, according to John, to the Gentile who was to execute him.

Although a miracle came out of it, this was not a spiritual encounter. The centurion had heard that Jesus could do things, and he wanted him to do something for him. Although Jesus commended him for his faith, there was nothing higher in it, no glimpse of realms of light. If you can do it, do it. Just say the word. That wonderful neatness of the imperative, as soldiers knew it and as Pilate knew it: *fac, age, i, sta,* do, act, go, stay. And rise up: *surge*.

This was only the beginning of the encounter God had planned. There was not yet a proper dialogue between Christ and the Gentiles, nor even proper contact between them. Yet Jesus nevertheless heard, for the first time, the insistent Gentile mantra: Do something, say something, prove yourself, define your chain of command. He was to hear it again.

* * *

For four or possibly seven years, Pilate and Jesus shared the same territory. Although Pilate was most of the time in Caesarea and Jesus in Galilee, their paths inevitably crossed from time to time. The two antagonists were sometimes tantalisingly close. Like characters in a formulaic thriller or a farce, they seemed to miss each other by seconds: one behind a door as the other enters, one looking the wrong way as the other saunters down the street.

Jesus was noted on Pilate's turf. He was reported teaching 'on the coasts of Judea beyond Jordan' and in Jericho; he was seen 'in all the cities and villages' of the province, leaving behind him people marvelling and fainting. But in John's gospel he also visited Jerusalem, and at precisely the moments when Pilate, too, was there to keep order. Every year, his parents and his family went up to Jerusalem for Passover. They also went for Tabernacles (the feast of Sukkot, in the autumn), and with such regularity that when Jesus decided not to go for the Sukkot before his death it was thought peculiar, and he went up later secretly after the rest of his family had gone.

He took some precautions in Jerusalem, though the gospels insist that this was for fear of the Jews rather than the Romans. At dusk he would leave the city to spend the night with his friends in Bethany or on the Mount of Olives. Only in the morning would he reappear. Each time he emerged, however, he caused a commotion. He healed people, performed miracles, drew noisy and rapturous crowds. According to Matthew, 'the whole city was in turmoil, saying "Who is this?" And the crowd replied, "This is Jesus, the prophet".' As one voice.

At the pool of Bethesda, by the sheep market, he cured the sick who had gathered there in expectation that an angel would come and stir the waters. The sick shouted as they were healed. Day after day he would walk in front of the Temple and in the Temple courtyards, teaching, as he termed it, but also haranguing the Pharisees, screaming at them. On these occasions, Luke said, 'all the people hung upon him, listening.' Several times the Temple guards were scrambled to get him, but held back 'because his hour had not yet come.' Once, at the Feast of Dedication in the winter, he was walking in Solomon's Porch in the Temple when the Jews chased him, demanded to know whether he was the Christ or not, and got ready to stone him. He fled then 'beyond Jordan', but left behind a city half-crazed with him. By the time of that last fatal Passover, all the talk was of whether Jesus would come for the feast or not. The crowd knew that he had raised Lazarus from the dead, a mere two miles outside Jerusalem; they expected more wonders. Even

Greeks in Jerusalem were asking, haltingly, to see him, the most famous tourist attraction after the Temple itself. Many of the chief rulers of the Jews were said to be secret believers in this man. In short, as the Pharisees lamented, 'the world is gone after him.'

Pilate remained in Herod's palace. In that great white mausoleum, where the marble floors absorbed his footsteps and the marble walls kept out all sound, he moved as if wrapped in insulation. Yet if he was to go to the window, or venture out to inspect the troops on duty in the western porticoes of the Temple, he might have glimpsed Jesus in the motions of the crowd, which swarmed about him like ants disturbed from the ground. He could have heard (though he would not have understood) the shout of Jesus to the crowd: 'Why do you want to kill me?', and the crowd's raucous answer: 'You're mad! Who wants to kill you?' Called out to the entrance of the Temple after Jesus had argued there, he might have seen him leaving: an abrupt turn of the shoulder, a whip of the long robe, face and hands still flushed with violence. To touch him, even approach him, was impossible; it was in violation of the plan. Yet Pilate could tread in his footsteps across the Temple porch, and the same beggars who had tugged Jesus's robe might be brushed aside by Pilate too.

There were other opportunities. In the street near the Pool of Bethesda the governor's litter might have paused. Runners were meant to clear the roads, but in a seething, distracted crowd they made no headway. Pilate waited. If he parted the curtain, he might have seen by the gloomy cisterns a man whose brown hair, as some apocryphal writings described it, fell in waves about his pale face as the leaves around a filbert: a man beneath whose touch the water trembled as if the angel of the pool had indeed descended. But it was unnecessary to notice him. The only meeting that counted was the one that was scheduled: on that day in March, on the sixth day of the week, at the first hour.

The litter jolted on.

Slowly, inevitably, by rumour and report, Pilate's antagonist was introduced to him. There was a man wandering in the district before whom a Gentile soldier had more or less knelt and prayed. And back at home that soldier's servant had swung his legs out of bed, stretched his arms, and gone back to his fetching and carrying. In general, the Jews kept their magic-working and mischief-making to themselves. This man

Jesus was extending his strange ministry, in a gesture that seemed designed to catch the Romans' attention. It was as if he were embracing the cords of his own death.

Possibly the centurion delivered his own observations, to Herod Antipas or to Pilate himself: nervous, almost stammering, his helmet under his arm as he had held it, presumably, in the presence of Christ. It would not have been the usual soldier's story, but a catalogue of mystifying things. A healing at a distance, even without the touch of a hand. A magic word of some sort. And faith, that particular madness, that admission of weakness, which in the end seemed to make men strong. It could make a Jew impervious to the sword; so too it might make a centurion heedless of lying on the ground, arms out, to be whipped, as Tiberius had whipped one such jackass for stealing a peacock from his orchard. Who can feel pain when his eyes and his arms have been full of the blue of heaven?

The writers of the apocryphal gospels supposed that other men too conveyed their thoughts to Pilate. One was Nicodemus, and some sort of contact between this man and the governor may not have been so strange. The Nicodemus of the gospels and the rabbinical traditions is hard to pin down, but he was probably one of that group of ruling Jews who bothered, sometimes, to talk to Pilate, because he was their guarantor of order. The Jewish *Ta'an* contains the story of a man called Nicodemus (in Hebrew, Naqdimon ben Gurion), which illustrates his dealings with a 'Roman lord' in Jerusalem. The heathen lord, who is in authority there, is almost certainly the governor; from the presumed date of the episode, some years before the fall of Jerusalem, he may well have been Pilate.

The scene was set at one of the Jewish festivals, when thousands of pilgrims were converging on the city and there was no water for drinking. (Another clue: there was apparently no aqueduct yet, and the incident that followed may even have encouraged Pilate in his plans to build one.) Nicodemus therefore approached the governor. He asked to be lent twelve wells of water for the pilgrims, promising to repay him by sunset on a certain date either with water – presuming it would rain in time – or, if he couldn't manage that, with twelve talents of silver. The governor agreed. When the deadline came, messages kept arriving from the governor at regular intervals, morning, midday and afternoon, demanding 'Return me either the water or the money you owe me.' The last message was delivered in person by the governor, who was on his way to the baths. Nicodemus replied to each, in relaxed fashion, 'I still have time today.'

'Oh?' replied the governor. 'Seeing that no rain has fallen all year, do you suppose it will rain now?' (That sounded like Pilate, light, sarcastic, ever-happy to have trumped the Jews.) And, certain that he had won the argument, he went off blithely to the baths.

Nicodemus was depressed. He went to the Temple, wrapped his cloak round his head, and began to pray. Immediately the sky grew dark with clouds and the rain fell, until there was enough to fill the twelve wells with a good deal left over.

As Nicodemus left the Temple and the governor emerged from the baths, the two men met. Nicodemus said, 'Give me the money for the extra water you've had!' The governor replied; 'I know that the Holy One only disturbed the world for your sake, but my claim against you for the money still holds good; the sun had already set when the rain fell, so it belongs to me!'

Back to the Temple went Nicodemus, his cloak round his head, and prayed again: 'Master of the universal, make it known that you have favourites in the world.' Immediately the sun broke through. The governor was forced to admit that his claim had vanished; the rain had fallen in time. 'But I'd still have had my claim if it hadn't,' he could not resist remarking.

If there was already fraternisation of this edgy, calculated sort between rabbis and their heathen governor, rumours of an astonishing or dangerous new preacher might bring them closer. Certainly the story had spread by the fourth century, when the *Acta Pilati* were produced as the 'evidence' of Nicodemus, that Nicodemus and Pilate were associates and friends. The gospels do not substantiate this, but there is one intriguing detail. According to John, Nicodemus was a secret disciple, not wanting his allegiance known. There could hardly have been better cover than friendship with the Roman governor, who in turn could hardly have found a more useful source of information.

In John's gospel Nicodemus visited Jesus at night, and there heard the strangest things. Perhaps circumstances dictated that he visited Pilate at night too, or entertained him in his own house, to pass on what he had learned. He was enormously rich, with great estates near Jerusalem: estates so extensive, people said, that the stocks of wheat and wine from his fields could feed the whole city for a week. Out there, in the drowsy dusk on the white terraces, he and Pilate could talk without the governor sullying a Jewish living room; as a strict Pharisee, Nicodemus had to be careful to observe the proprieties. The governor's guards and attendants, among the clipped trees, could station themselves at a distance; delicacies could be ferried out on trays to fuel the secret conversations. If Pilate shared the fashionable taste for gold tableware, exquisitely transparent glass, wine cooled in snow and meat already cut from the bone, he was likely to find them here. Nicodemus's fabulous wealth was known all over Jerusalem. His sister had been given a million gold *dinars* as a dowry, and a niece had received 400 *dinars* a month to replenish her perfume basket. But he was also wise, and curious, and discreet.

John's Jesus had told him, as they sat in the whispering dark: '*Unless a man is born again, he cannot see the kingdom of God.*'

Pass that on to Pilate. What would the governor make of it? Probably nothing. A man clambering back inside his mother's womb: that was almost a ribald joke, soldiers' tent-flap stuff. Or becoming, suddenly, a baby again, the laughable bald head soft and shining and new. How could a man be born again? It was an impossibility.

Nicodemus had asked the same thing. Back came the answer: 'Unless a man is born again of water and the spirit, he cannot enter the kingdom of God.'

Pass that on. Leave aside for the moment the most troubling element, the kingdom talk. *Born of water and of the spirit.* The Jesus-followers who did what they called baptising were said to sprinkle water on people's heads as they stood up to their knees in rivers; it washed off Gentile impurity. How could such desultory, untraumatic actions add up to a birth? Venus was born of water; when Chronos had destroyed Uranus and the fragments of his body fell into the sea, the red-flecked foam gave birth to the goddess of love. She rose from the sea like a shell, like a frail skiff, her hair slicked on her white thighs. You could be born that way; or by lustration, total immersion, ritual purification, in which you rose up new, in a sense, to present yourself to the gods. That was a type of birth. The water tended to be cold, the bathing place dark and cramped, an uncomfortable womb; and when you emerged your skin was purplish and puckered like that of a new-born child.

Was that right?

Jesus went on: '*What is born of the flesh is flesh, and what is born of the spirit is spirit. Don't be surprised when I tell you that you must be born again. The wind blows where it pleases, and you hear the sound of it, but you can't tell where it comes from or where it is going. So it is with everyone who is born of the spirit.'*

Pass that on. Yes, the wind blew where it wanted, but you could tell where it came from by the feel of it. Icy, shaggy Boreas fanned the face of the earth with his tawny wings, as Ovid described it, and ruffled the wide sea. Auster was drizzling and warm, the rain-bearing wind; Zephyrus brought flowers from the soft west and the land of the evening star. Eurus blew from beyond the Euphrates towards Arabia Felix and the borders of Judea. This was the Parthian wind, the enemy wind; but it was not the worst. Boreas and Aquilo between them could sink ships, howling like war-trumpets and hurling hailstones from the north-east.

God – whichever god it was who had created them – had put these brothers on earth to stir and refresh creation, but had then restrained them, when he saw how strong they were, to their own particular quarters of the sky. Their mayhem was limited. At least, this was how the poets explained it. They also spread the story that Aeolus, king of Thessaly, was in charge of the winds, who therefore did his bidding and not their own. Aeolus could catch the winds and release them any time he chose. Most of the time he kept them locked in a mountain, but when Juno hinted he threw them at Aeneas, and when Odysseus visited he gave him the bad winds wriggling and puffing in a bag. If you didn't parcel them up like that they would certainly do as they liked: tatter your sails, whip the rain in your face, blow you off course. That was why men still sacrificed to the winds, and why from November to March the wide Mediterranean was left for Aquilo to play in, separating Pilate definitively from home.

But it was strictly a poet's fancy to put the winds in cloaks and tunics and make them men. The philosophers knew it was the damp or dry exhalations of the earth that made the wind, as they squeezed into the crowded sky and struggled to get past each other. And the wind, too, was part of the plan. The four major winds and the eight subsidiary winds had been devised by Providence so that every section of the sky would be active and scoured clean. As one fell, the next rose, moving from east to west. The north winds, being regulated by odd numbers, could not blow on odd days, and Eudoxus reckoned that the exact pattern of the winds, with their exact consequences of fruit torn from the trees or boats blown back into harbour, was repeated every four years.

So wind was the air set in motion. The air moved and blew in heaven; the air moved and blew on earth, and even under the earth. Miners reported that the rivers and lakes beneath the earth also had their exhalations; 'dead winds in the darkness', as Seneca was to call them. In the middle of the Underworld, not far from the banks of the Styx, stood a great dark elm tree in which dreams roosted like birds, hanging and trembling under every leaf. It must be the wind that touched them, just as a wind seemed to wrack the shivering army of spirits that stood pleading on the river bank, as if they were leaves stripped from the autumn trees by Boreas himself, or gulls blown inland in the winter.

Was that what the man meant, that men born of spirit were like the wind? Could you see them at all? If you couldn't, how was it that this man Jesus could be seen, who was supposed to be born of the spirit himself? Did his so-called magical powers extend to spiriting himself away?

Jesus went on, as reported: '*Do you call yourself a master of Israel, and you don't know these things? If I tell you of earthly things, and you don't believe, how will you believe me when I tell you about heavenly things?*

'*No one has gone up to heaven except the one who came down from heaven, the Son of Man. For God so loved the world that he gave his only son, that whoever believes in him shall not perish, but have everlasting life.*'

He seemed to mean immortality. That was not a foreign concept. There were plenty of immortals; they were set among the stars, engraved on the vault of the sky. Cassiopeia was there, the mother of Andromeda, whose boasting had caused her daughter to be chained to a rock to be eaten by that sea-monster that later turned up in Jaffa. Perseus, who had rescued her, was there too, with his helmet and breastplate; Castor and Pollux were there, the heavenly twins, the guardians of sailors. Hercules could be seen sprawling, littering the sky with the evidence of his labours in the shape of lions and dragons; and beyond them, in sparkling drifts, was the milk that had spilled from the breasts of Venus when Cupid had been snatched away.

According to the poets (if you believed the poets) all these characters were now immortal. They were divine in very different measures: Tiberius, in his eulogy of Augustus, had even laughed at Hercules as 'only dealing with a stag or two and, oh, yes, a lion'; but when they had met their deaths they had all been taken up to heaven to preside and shine. It was nonsense to say, as this man Jesus did, that no one had gone up to heaven; the place was overcrowded. The real gods and the comedy stunt-men jostled each other right up to the limits of the sky.

Somewhere in the dark was the Caesar-star; farmers already knew it as the herald of good weather, colouring the grapes and the corn. Augustus was there too, if you knew where to look for him. After his death his soul had been taken up to heaven by an eagle which had flown out of the funeral pyre under everyone's eyes. That soul had become a comet that had blazed for seven days, and then Tiberius had placed it among the constellations. Augustus would go on for ever; he would never die. Like the stars.

It could happen in theory to any man. The Stoics believed that each man was already a god, 'if a god is that which lives, feels, remembers, foresees, and which rules, governs and moves the body over which it is set, just as the Supreme God above us rules this universe.' But practical and public divinity was far away. It seemed essential to be of the right social class, the right *gens*, the right family, all somewhat higher than the ones to which Pilate belonged. Strength of character, achievements in the field, magisterial authority, favour in high places, could move a man steadily up the steep incline connecting mortals and immortals. Such a man could be an agent of heaven, doing the gods' work for them. As Tiberius had said of Augustus, 'his actions and his fortunes were not · such as he himself desired, but as heaven decreed.'

The gods helped, giving a man violent times or raging wars in which to prove himself. There were certain qualities too, as Cicero said, that enabled a man to ascend towards heaven: Intellect, Virtue, Piety, Fidelity. Perhaps even a governor of an obscure province could inch towards that extraordinary state. If Pilate did well in Judea, if he ruled wisely, firmly yet benevolently, if he averted some disaster to the empire, he too would begin the long ascent. People would begin to applaud him. He would be given triumphs, feel the wreaths on his forehead. The people would make him consul, then repeat the honour. He would be called *pater patriae*, father of his country. Divinity would still be far off; but his brow would gleam, his eyes would shine, and his very shadow would inspire awe as it fell on the ground before him. *Et deus factus est.*

Idle dreams. Wrong family, wrong class, no likely opportunity.

Yet his soul might be immortal. It might journey on when his body died. Most people believed that; only the Epicureans dismissed it as nonsense. Even the Stoics, who thought a man simply went out like a lamp, believed that his soul then darted back to heaven, a flying spark freed from the shackles of the body. Something in a man did not die and kept on travelling, even if he did not deserve the stars. The soul went on – if you believed all this – through the caves and corridors of the Underworld, a sad-eyed moth. It was not just children, though cynics said it was mostly children, who believed in seven-headed Cerberus barking at the gate of hell, or Charon the ferryman taking the souls across. Men's spirits had sometimes wandered there as they lay on the funeral pyre, and they had revived to report it afterwards. Aeneas too had travelled through the underworld alive, his heart broken by the sobbing spirits of the unburied dead.

There was some comfort in believing that the spirits remained. You did not quite lose the people you loved, even if you remembered them personally only at the Parentalia in February, strewing their graves with wreaths and bread and the first few violets of the spring. That was eternal life too, wasn't it? Immortality was a name and a life remembered by your children.

But that was not the trickiest part of what Jesus had said. The trickiest part was *God loved*. Could the gods love like that, sweetly and paternally? They fell in love; they lusted and rutted like beasts. Great Jupiter came down on Ganymede, on Danae, on Io and on countless women, begetting divine sons to fornicate after him. And they loved in the sense that they picked people out to be showered with honours and elevated in the state. But this was benevolence, care for a man's interests, not that clamorous pain in the heart and that aching rush to embrace someone. It was the selective, discriminating kindness of superior to inferior. A prayer to the gods was a petition to be loved in just that way. Notice *me*. Favour *me*. And, at the end, as you lowered your arms: *Propitius sit*, God be gracious to me.

How could such prayers find purchase, if God loved everyone? How could there be beggars, slaves, victims of murder, patients with rotting sores, if God loved everyone? And why should his favour be meted out to anyone who did not love him first? Love was not unconditional; it did not work like that. Tiberius would love him because he had loved him first. Favour was returned for favour. The client served the patron, the patron smiled on the client. This was the thrust of his letters home, the hardest part of his distance from Rome: *Mutuo me diligas*, love me as I love you, put in a word for me, press for this favour; if you are well, it is well, I am well. This was the whole reciprocal web of the world.

Most worryingly, this God loved him. He had not asked him to, but nevertheless he seemed to have found him. It was as unnerving as the thought that Jupiter selected you for thunderbolts, or that your fate was sealed when a snake slid out of the altar as you were sacrificing. You were trapped in someone else's arrangement, caught like a leaf in his burning, undiscriminating love.

Yet, having talked of love, Jesus went on: '*God did not send his son into the world to condemn the world, but so that through him the world might be saved.*

'*No one who believes in him is condemned; but whoever does not believe is condemned already, because he does not believe in the Name of the only Son of God.*'

So he was loved, and he was condemned too – was that right? He was condemned *already*; no chance of struggle. To Nicodemus, the rabbi, the secret believer, the words presented no difficulty. He was in the light, as the man had put it, but Pilate was in the dark: in the uncomprehending Gentiles' place. Sentence had been passed. He had failed the test.

Of course, he didn't care. He didn't believe these preposterous things. But Jesus insisted on involving him in his schemes, like a trader trying to make a bargain, or a column-lounger in the Forum trying to draw him into his pressure group. Luke's Jesus had been asked once what he thought of Pilate directly, after Pilate had cut down a crowd of Galilean pilgrims in the outer courtyard of the Temple, 'mingling their blood with their sacrifices'. This might have been the aqueduct incident, or perhaps some other rash and clumsy disciplinary action. Jesus said: 'I tell you, unless you repent, you shall all perish in the same way.'

Unless you repent. It was as if Pilate himself was doing God's work of punishment: as if he himself, despite his presence in the list under 'darkness', was the winnowing flail that John the Baptist had spoken of in the desert. He was showing Judea what the wrath of God was like; he was the implacable and violent opposite of Jesus' gentleness and healing. This made them co-conspirators. Pilate did not need to creep, like Nicodemus, to visit Jesus in the dark. He was already instructed to behave as he was meant to. He was in the plan, enlisted already, condemned already.

End of report. Will you have more wine, governor? Olives? A cloak for the cold?

⋆   ⋆   ⋆

According to the *Acta Pilati*, the leaders of the Jews came more than once to Pilate to tell him their complaints against Jesus. The list was long. A clerk could fill a whole stack of wax tablets with them: picking ears of wheat on the Sabbath, claiming to forgive sins, prophesying the destruction of the Temple. Several tablets could be filled with Jesus's remarks about the Pharisees alone, and these were much more vicious than anything he had to say about the Romans: they were whitewashed sepulchres, camel-swallowers, blind fools, filth, goats, trumpeters, dirty plates, mumblers on street corners. But, from the Jewish point of view, there was worse.

'We know this man,' said the priests in the *Acta Pilati*. 'His father's Joseph the carpenter, his mother's Mary, and he's going round this city calling himself a king and the son of God; and even though he's a Jew, he's overthrowing the scriptures and polluting the Sabbath, and says he will destroy the law of our fathers!'

'What exactly does he do that would destroy your law?' asked Pilate.

The council of the priests broke into shouts of outrage. 'We have a law that we should not heal any man on the Sabbath! This man by his evil deeds heals the lame, the crooked, the withered, the blind, the dumb, the paralytic . . . People possessed! And on the Sabbath day –'

Pilate said, 'By what evil deeds?'

'He's a sorcerer. He casts out devils by Beelzebub, the prince of devils. And they're all subject to him!'

'This is not casting out devils by an unclean spirit, but by the god Aesculapius,' countered Pilate.

The *Acta Pilati* left that observation hanging, as doubtless the Jews would have done if Pilate had ever uttered it. Their silence said, '*What?*' Roman and Jewish notions of sorcery and healing were simply incompatible. But the notion of Jesus as a miracle-worker comes not only from the gospels but also, with a slightly pagan flavour, from Josephus, in the section known as the *Testimonium Flavianum* in the *Antiquities*. 'Now about this time,' runs the passage,

there appeared a wise man called Jesus – if indeed one can speak of him as a man, for he was a doer of astonishing deeds, a healer of people who receive gladly what they want to believe. He won over many of the Jews and many of the Greeks . . .

For years, this section about Jesus (sandwiched between the reportage about Pilate) was dismissed as a Christian forgery, but modern scholars increasingly think that bits of it may be true: in particular, the parts describing Jesus as 'a wise man', a 'wonder-worker' and a healer of the simple and credulous. Josephus does not mention what effect, if any, this man had on Romans. But later writers built on the thought to suggest that Pilate was intrigued by Christ's credentials as a healer, because he himself needed help. Procula had terrible headaches and, of course, bad dreams; according to a Slavonic version of Josephus, Pilate actually summoned Jesus, like a doctor, because his wife was dying. According to the *Golden Legend*, it was his own aching liver that tortured him. In both the apocryphal gospels and in Templar lore there are suggestions that Jesus was a follower of the magi of the East, bringing with him the occult practices that captivated more susceptible minds in Rome: minds that demanded healing both physical and psychological.

Among modern writings, Bulgakov's Pilate is clearly in this tradition. He suffers from blinding migraines, hemicrania, brought on by the dry dazzling sun of Jerusalem and the smell of attar of roses. When they afflict him he can only sit perfectly still, dreaming of darkened rooms and the touch of cold water. Jesus's response to his question, 'What is truth?' is to tell him: 'The truth is chiefly that your head aches, and aches so hard that you are having cowardly thoughts about death.' Pilate immediately feels the pain subsiding. From that point on, his line of questioning wavers; the only thing he really wants to know is 'Are you a great physician?' When Jesus says he is not, he is bitterly disappointed.

St Paul himself hinted that Pilate, a man caught up in forces he did not control, may have been the prey of the demon *archontes* who ruled both his world and his body. This did not necessarily suggest that he would have dabbled in philtres or charms, but most Romans did. He may well have worn round his neck, or carried in a breast-pocket, an amulet of dried anemones to ward off tertian fever, or of black bryony against scrofula. (There were so many anemones in Judea; the Garden of Gethsemane was thick with them.) He may have drunk the local bitumen, powdered and tangy like coal-tar, in draughts of wine to treat diarrhoea. It made sense to take care abroad, since this was where strange new diseases came from, like the virulent facial pox that spread to Rome when a quaestor's secretary picked it up in Asia Minor. On this disease, which had to be treated with cauterisation, the legate of Aquitaine had spent 200,000 *sesterces*. The ill would seek a cure in anything, even other people's deaths. Some doctors would not hesitate to hang round the necks of sufferers from quartan fever little bags containing the hair of the crucified and nails from the cross.

This was getting close to the edge of accepted medical practice, but not too close. When the sensible advice of doctors had been taken to heart – rest, exercise, no wine, cold baths – most Romans fell back on folk medicine and, in effect, faith-healing. At its worst, this was a realm of hags, witches, charlatans, fake potions concocted from lizards, leaves and entrails, anointings with grease. Practitioners of the art loitered in damp caves or, more often, in basement rooms behind screens of dirty sheets. Nothing they did was miraculous, however. Everything had some rational explanation, to be attributed to some property in the ingredients of the ghastly mixtures they made. If something could not be explained it was better to suppress the worker of miracles, rather than let his power spread. A man once visited Tiberius, broke a crystal goblet and put it together again by passing his hands over it; Tiberius, horrified that he could not control this, had the man killed.

Healing by the agency of Aesculapius came as close as a Roman dared to the art of the miraculous. The god of medicine and healing had been spirited out of the fire by Mercury himself. He was the healer of all men and the raiser of the dead, reviving them with holy herbs; Jupiter killed him at last with a bolt of lightning, because as long as Aesculapius continued his work men lived for ever and would not die. In that sense (as perhaps in others), Jupiter and Tiberius responded to the threat of usurpation in exactly the same way.

The devotee of Aesculapius would hope to be healed by sleeping overnight in the temple of the god. He would approach quietly, in the dusk. It was not necessary to have the agency or presence of priests; he would stay there alone. Commonly he bathed or swam first, to present himself thoroughly cleansed at the altar. His hands would still be damp, the hair damp on the nape of his neck; if he had swum in the dusk, he might carry the memory of the glittering phosphorescence that had followed the motion of his arms. To cleave the water had given him the necessary shock of sacred purification. As he bowed before the altar, his body shivered and glowed.

'Heal me, O God of eternal life.'

In a hessian bag he had a small snake, sacred to the god. It had been doped with an infusion of poppy seeds; it flopped in his hand, opening its pale sleepy jaws. He laid it on the altar, where it coiled in on itself. Thus was Aesculapius born, hatched from the egg of a crow; then, as his powers grew, he had conjured snakes to twine round a stick. His remedy for snake-bite was inscribed on a stone at his temple in Cos: two *denarii* of wild thyme, two of all-heal, one of trefoil, aniseed, fennel and parsley, pounded with wine into pastilles to be swallowed one at a time. The yawning snake also prefigured the instruments of a human doctor: the puncturing, the pain, the mingling of blood.

Honey cakes were laid on the altar too. After that, the patient wrapped his toga round his head and sat against the wall. He hoped to sleep. Suppliants who slept in the temples of Aesculapius were visited with dreams describing the means of their cure. Some saw ghostly priests who came to them with poultices and decoctions, or surgeons sharpening their knives. Some were cured merely by dreaming. Others saw only the endless repetition of a peacock spreading its blue-green tail or milestones on the coast road, solidly marching into darkness. To calm himself, to make sure that he was lucid and not beginning to die, the patient would repeat the same words over and over: Heal me. Milestones, road, darkness, spinning circles of green and purple, the bright curve of a claw, sickness in the throat: Heal me. Heal me. Heal me.

Alone, he sweated with fear. But he did not try to leave in case the sweat itself was curative. He had brought wine, but it was dedicated and he could not drink it; besides, he wanted icy water, and the hands of a woman soothing his neck and face. His limbs were stiffening. As the night wore on he slid down the wall and rolled himself in his cloak on the unforgiving floor. Thus he would doze for a while, waiting for the touch of the god.

When dawn appeared, a slave would come to rouse him. Diffidently, as he had been trained to, he shook him by the shoulder and spoke into his ear. Then he wiped his face with a cloth that had been dipped in water, making him shiver and spit. Any cure would be more efficacious if a man first spat three times on the ground. Light was coming up over the city; there were slight tinkling morning sounds, the songs of birds. The patient would stand by the wall, aware of his unshavenness, composing himself.

The slave had brought a cockerel in a bag. He threw it down on the altar, wings and head trussed, beak tied with a leather thong. The creature continued to struggle feebly, its comb lying sideways and its eyelids flickering. The patient took the knife. He cut the thong first, to let the bird scream; but sometimes it was traumatised and made no sound. This was unnerving. By its hard yellow feet he swung it away from him, slashed down with the blade, and severed the cord on the bird's back. Instantly the cock was alive, striking out, flailing, screaming in a whirlwind of black wings. He managed to hold it, and cut off the head. For a minute the wings continued to whirl. His arms were full of pulsating feathers and rivulets of warm blood that ran down his chest and splashed on the marble floor.

He laid his sacrifice on the altar. There was a prayer to be said and he whispered it, holding out his crimsoned sleeves. Somewhere in the town, among the still trees, other cocks crowed. And the sun came up slowly over the red-rimmed bowl of the sea.

If not Aesculapius, then Jesus; if one could not heal, perhaps the other could. The Roman Pilate, like the Pilate of the *Acta*, would have understood the parallels of healing and blood sacrifice, both gateways to eternal life. In his curiosity, he might have risked a meeting with Jesus in the hope of getting well. He might have wanted to test his power, as much as to kill him in the cause of public order. In the world of relentlessly interlocking fates, one pretext was as good as another.

*   *   *

All through the gospels the net closed on Pilate. The prophets said what he would do, and he did it. Confidently, tauntingly, Jesus predicted his decisions; for he knew 'from the beginning,' according to Matthew, 'who did not believe, and who was going to betray him.' The representative of the world's most overweening power was reduced to a stage-hand who would, at a given moment – the given moment – draw back the curtain, turn the revolve, drop the scenery from the flies.

Even the smallest detail was pre-arranged. The props were laid out on the table. The blank board on which Pilate was to write 'Jesus of Nazareth' was there already, with the pen beside it, for the prophets had foretold that 'he shall be called a Nazarene'. The nails were laid out, for, according to Isaiah, 'he was pierced through for our faults'. Here were the thirty pieces of silver bulging in a bag, ready to accomplish Jeremiah: 'And they took the thirty pieces of silver, the price of him that was valued.' And there the knucklebone dice that the soldiers would roll at the foot of the cross, drunkenly fulfilling the words of the prophet: 'On my vesture they cast lots.'

It was not only the coming of Jesus that was advertised as the fulfilment of prophecy but, some thought, Pilate's too. Jesus preached that when the Jews saw 'the abomination of desolation' standing 'where it ought not', this would be the sign of afflictions to come. At the sight of it, residents of the cities of Judea would flee to the hills, not turning back even for their coats. This was not a vague general warning, but a specific prediction that Jerusalem would be trodden down by the Gentiles; and the beginning of that oppression, at least for some of the Jews, was Pilate's 'mistake' about the standards. Eusebius, citing Josephus and Philo, said that when Pilate brought the images of Caesar into Jerusalem by night, this marked 'the beginning of factions'.

The prophet Daniel had foretold all this. He said that the abomination of desolation would be set up, and that none of the wicked would understand what was happening. His particular 'abomination' was probably a statue of Zeus Olympios set up in the Temple long before Pilate, but his later verses could be taken to refer directly to Pilate's desecration of the holy city: 'Arms shall stand on his part, and they shall pollute the sanctuary of strength.'

The Romans after Pilate were to do much worse things in Jerusalem. In 70, during the Jewish war, they smashed the Temple down. But at the time of Jesus's teaching Pilate's blunders in Jerusalem, the shock of the standards glittering on the walls of the Antonia, would have been the first abomination that sprang to mind. It was the worst incident the Jews had seen since Crassus, the closest approach of armed force to the Temple. On this view, Pilate signalled precisely the beginning of those times that Jesus had come to preach about, the 'desolation' of which John the Baptist warned so repeatedly. His tactless incursion coincided almost exactly with the start of Jesus' ministry. Whatever impulse had prompted him to send those standards with their images into Jerusalem, the impulse itself was preordained, God's finger nudging his back. The infamous medallions of Tiberius were on the prop-table too.

Jesus got closer, more taunting still. He knew that he must die for these calamitous and glorious events to unfold, and he knew when it would happen. Openly, frequently, he talked about it. The timing was precise. When he refused to go up to Jerusalem for Sukkot, it was because his time had 'not yet come'. He told the Pharisees, on one of the many occasions when they came to arrest him but lost their nerve, that he would be with them 'only a little while, and then I go to him who sent me.' Before the last supper he told the people who hung on his parables that 'Yet a little while is the light with you; walk while you have the light.' Some days before his death he began to announce that the hour had come when he would be 'glorified'. In Matthew he said openly that it would come at the feast of the Passover, the day of the sacrifice of the holy and unblemished lamb.

He was often equally precise about the manner of his glorification. According to Luke, he told his disciples that 'this scripture must be fulfilled in me: "And he was reckoned with transgressors".' According to Matthew he explained what would happen to him three times, each time in a slightly different way: 'We are going up to Jerusalem, and the Son of Man shall be betrayed to the chief priests and the scribes, and they shall condemn him to death; and they shall deliver him to the Gentiles to mock, and to scourge, and to crucify him; and the third day he shall rise again.'

The manner of his trial had been foretold by the prophets down to the last detail. At the prophet Jeremiah's trial in Jerusalem, despite his warning that the priests would bring 'innocent blood' on themselves, they went ahead and accused him, saying he should die for 'prophesying against this city'. The 'princes', Pilates-to-be, demurred, saying 'This man is not worthy of death.' Nonetheless Jeremiah was bound and sent to an 'Idumaean', just as Jesus, according to Luke, was sent by Pilate to Herod Antipas. The prophet Hosea also foresaw this scene, predicting that Jesus would be sent 'bound as a present to the king'. Once he was sent back, the prophecy was carried on by Isaiah: Jesus would appear before his judge 'like a lamb that is dumb before the shearers, never opening his mouth.' For his meekness and man's sins he would then be 'punished, struck by God, brought low, pierced': exact premonitions of the orders Pilate was to give for the binding, the scourging, the laying on the cross, the nails. God struck Jesus and the governor struck him, one in the person of the other.

Jesus brooded on his Roman denouement. The cross seemed to haunt him. Although he most often told his disciples merely that he would be 'killed', he never implied that he would be stoned, which would have been his fate at the hands of the Jews, or that he would be stabbed in the street. His death was to be in the Roman fashion, administered by the Roman who happened to be in charge. Jesus told both his disciples and would-be disciples to 'take up their cross' and follow him; he was going first, another of those familiar trudgers along the roads of Judea, with Pilate's sentence round his neck. It was a horror routine enough to stand for the shouldering of any burden or disgrace, but it was also an explicit prediction. In his own case, having carried the cross and allowed himself to be nailed to it, he would be lifted up, 'as Moses lifted up the serpent in the wilderness'.

The serpent Moses lifted up was a brazen snake that looped from a pole in horizontal coils; all those who were bitten turned to the serpent and were healed. That ritual shape of upright and cross-beam had been prefigured all through the Old Testament. Sacrificial brands had been stacked in the form of a cross on the back of Isaac, the son of Abraham. Lamb's blood in the form of a cross had marked the doors of the Israelites on the eve of the first Passover, and the lamb itself, spiked with rosemary, was roasted spreadeagled on two spits set at right-angles. Moses had stretched out his arms, cross-like, before the battle with Amalek; and Elijah had met an old woman who, because she held up two pieces of wood in the form of a cross, was rewarded by God with extra meal and oil in her cupboards. St Jerome contended that the form was even older than that, elemental, suggesting birds flying in the air, a plough breaking the soil, a man swimming.

Yet the oddest prefiguring of all was that Pilate's standards, complete with their images of Tiberius, were also in the form of the cross. Justin Martyr, a converted pagan and one of the earliest apologists for Christianity, described this precisely when, in his *First Apology* of around 150, he addressed the emperor Diocletian. 'And your symbols,' he wrote, 'in what are called banners, and the trophies with which your processions are universally made, display the power of this form; and by these you show the signs of your rule and authority, even if you do it without knowing what you do. And you consecrate the images of your emperors, on their demise, by this form, and by inscriptions you term them gods.' On this reading, Pilate was the first man to carry to Jerusalem the triumphant sign of the cross that the Jews rejected.

So the form was vital: and so was the sheer spectacle, the showiness, of crucifixion. Jesus meant to be on display, so that his death could have its cosmic effect. 'When you have lifted up the Son of Man, then you will know that I am he,' he said once. Another remark was possibly even more specific: 'If I am lifted up from the earth, I will draw all men unto me.' Only one man could bring about this lifting and this irresistible attraction: the man who, as Jesus spoke, was perhaps lifting nothing heavier than the day's routine report, or a Corinthian wineglass through which, dreamily, he could see the sun.

Judas was fingered too. Jesus knew what his role was among the disciples, even before Judas was sure of it himself. He announced his betrayal as frequently as he announced his crucifixion. When the cosmic moment came at the last supper in the upper room, Jesus already knew Judas's movements to the last detail. He would take a piece of bread and dip his hand towards the dish of vinegar that stood on the table as a condiment, prefiguring the dipping of a sponge in sour wine during the crucifixion. Their fingers would brush together. In John, he would give the sop to Judas directly, already understanding his disposition: 'I know, he said, 'whom I have chosen.' Judas would ask, 'Is it I, Lord?' – the slightly tremulous question, more a statement, of the man who cannot escape. Then he would leave, skittering down the stone stairs, obeying automatically the order to 'Do what you have to do, quickly.' He went, in the apocryphal versions of the passion, to perform the various jobs allotted to him: to notify the priests, collect the tree of the cross, and warn Pilate that his turn was coming.

When Judas asked Jesus, 'Is it I, Lord?', Jesus answered: 'You said it.' Pilate was later to ask Jesus questions to which he would get the same irritating answer, as if to say: 'Of course. Those are the words I expected, the lines written in the script for you since time began. You said them. Well done.' In John, as soon as Judas had stumbled out into the dark, Jesus exclaimed: 'Now is the Son of Man glorified, and God is glorified with him.'

Each of these predictions, if he ever heard them, would have been like a dare to Pilate. He was being challenged to kill a man who was determined to die anyway; who, when his disciples cried that they would try to protect him, accused them of being the Devil in disguise. If Pilate killed him, it would be with his permission and encouragement: he was dying only to prove that he could rise. Augustine, in an extraordinary passage, had Jesus say: 'I carried you on my shoulders, gave you back to my father, laboured, sweated, pressed thorns upon my head, exposed my hands to the nails, opened my side with a spear . . .' He was totally in control of the situation. 'I lay down my life,' John's Jesus said imperiously, 'that I may take it again. No man takes it from me; I lay it down myself and I have power to take it again.'

No man takes it from me. Would Pilate stand for that? How was he meant to react to these confident predictions of how he would behave? Some were encoded, but others were blatant: Jesus was approaching, expecting, wanting crucifixion. He needed Pilate. But what if Pilate refused to play? The sulky, resentful governor of Philo would instinctively react by refusing to indulge him; the clumsy tactician of Josephus would try to get out of the trap. Perhaps Jesus would lose his authority if he didn't do it, if he refused to rise to the dare; the prophet would miss his chance of martyrdom, and his prophecies would turn out wrong. Perhaps Pilate could simply ignore him, let him get old, allow his followers to drift away. But the uncomfortable implication of Jesus was that his arrest and death were in the stars, and that Fate had already fingered Pilate as his executioner.

Someone then – perhaps his secretary, or his military aide, or Caiaphas, or his own conscience – would ask, 'So, are you going to kill him then?'

And he would burst out, furious: 'Is it up to me?'

*   *   *

Go through the props again. Reed pen, dice, money, chair of judgement; and, in the corner, the most vital prop of all: the cross. 'The tree,' wrote St Augustine, 'which had brought about the fall and the loss of Paradise, shall be the instrument of redemption.'

The type of wood did not matter. By legend and prediction, whatever timber Pilate ordered was already incorporated into God's design. The date palm, with its unwithering fronds and clustering fruit, was the model of the Tree of Life on which, according to the Archangel Michael in the Book of Enoch, the glory of the Eternal King would rest when he visited the earth. The yew was the tree of immortality. Under the oak tree, God had made his covenant with Abraham; and according to Isaiah he had promised that 'the glory of Lebanon' would come to the pine and the fir trees. The aspen tree shook with the premonition that it would carry Christ, and the apple tree was spoken for.

Five thousand two hundred and twenty years before the year of the passion – according to the *Golden Legend* and dozens of medieval variants – the tree that formed the cross was seen in a vision by Seth, the son of Adam. Seth had been asked by his father, who was then nine hundred and thirty-two years old, to find the oil of mercy that God had promised to send them. This oil would heal the sin-wounds, 'sixty and ten' of them, that still covered his body and the body of Eve as punishment for eating the apple in the garden of Eden. Adam told Seth to go to the gate of Eden and beg the oil from the angel who stood there.

Seth set out from the head of the valley of Hebron and found the soft green path that led to the gate of Paradise. The track turned eastward, and soon became bare earth; this was the route that Adam and Eve had taken out of the garden. Since then, no grass had grown on it. At the end of this track, in a light like a burning fire, stood the gate of Eden.

At the gate Seth began to pray. St Michael appeared to him. 'It's useless to pray for the oil of mercy,' he told him. 'It won't be sent for 5,220 years, until Christ dies for the sins of men. But put your head through the gate, and note what you see.'

Seth did so. Inside he saw jewel-green meadows sparkling with flowers, perfumed trees, branches hung heavily with bright fruit, and the flash and cry of extraordinary birds. He wanted to live there for ever. Only one thing spoiled the garden: a great bare tree, embraced by the withered remains of a snake like a dried and twisted creeper. This was the tree from which his parents had eaten the apple of fate.

Then he looked again, and saw that the tree had grown bark and leaves. It was immense now, filling the blue-gold sky, and at the top of the tree was a tiny baby in swaddling clothes. This, he was told, was the Son of God who would bring the oil of mercy in the fullness of time.

When Seth left, the angel gave him three pips from an apple and instructed him to put them under Adam's tongue as soon as he was dead. Seth did so, and, as Adam lay dead in the valley of Hebron, the pips began to grow into three small trees as delicate as wands, which stood in Adam's mouth in the deep earth until the time of Moses. One was a cedar, 'the tree of height', denoting the Father; one was the sweet-smelling cypress, denoting the Son; and the third, the pine or the olive, was a fruit-bearing tree, denoting the gifts of the Holy Ghost. These grew until they were an ell high, and then paused to await the passage of history.

In time the Israelites crossed the Red Sea and came to the valley of Hebron. One evening Moses, walking in the valley, came upon the tiny trees. Recognising them at once as a symbol of the Trinity, he pulled them out of the ground, and the sweetest smell came up with them. With these wands Moses healed the sick and performed miracles. When he knew he was about to die, he planted them in a stream under Mount Tabor in Arabia.

For a thousand years the wands stood in the stream, never growing. Then King David found them, on God's instructions, and took them to Jerusalem. On the way he met three blackamoors who, when touched with the rods, became white. It was evening when he carried the wands into the city, so he set them in a ditch and put a company of men to guard them. In the morning, he found that the wands had grown into one tree with three branches springing from the top. He did not try to move it, but built a strong wall around it and encircled it with a silver girdle to mark its growth each year. David wrote the whole of the

Psalter under it, sitting in its deep shade. After thirty years the tree stopped growing.

Meanwhile, the Temple was being built in Jerusalem. David began the work, and Solomon completed it. When the work was almost finished, the carpenters found that they needed one more beam; and the only wood they could find to measure was the tree that David had planted. Solomon therefore ordered it cut down and taken into the Temple. But the carpenters found that they could never cut it to the right size; it was either one cubit too long or one cubit too short. So Solomon ordered them to make a bridge with it across the Kedron ditch. The Queen of Sheba, visiting Solomon one day, saw the beam-bridge and advised him to bury it, for a man would die on it who would destroy the Mosaic law.

Solomon buried it deep. But a well sprang out of it which had miraculous powers, and the sick came to bathe in the waters. Every morning, while it was still dark, God sent his angels to stir the water so that the tree beneath would be remembered. When Jesus came to earth and began to perform miracles at the pool, the beam rose from the deep and floated. This was the tree, seasoned by water, cut down by Solomon, encircled with silver by David, uprooted by Moses, germinated under the tongue of Adam, which Pilate ordered loaded on to the back of Christ.

Others say the journey was less complicated. In the medieval *Book of the Bee*, Adam, as he was driven out of Paradise, hacked a branch from the tree, whittled off the twigs and used it as a staff for the rest of his life. The staff was passed to Abel and then to Abraham, who wielded it to smash the idols of Terah. Jacob used it, along with rods of hazel and chestnut and green poplar, to cast a fertility spell on the watering troughs where the flocks of Laban drank. For a while after that, the staff was hidden by an angel in a cave of treasures in the mountains of Moab; but it was found by Jethro as he grazed his sheep, and he passed it on to Moses. Moses used it to display the brazen serpent, and the staff then passed to Phineas, who buried it in the desert. It remained buried there until Christ was born, at which moment its whereabouts were revealed to Joseph. He dug it up, used it all his life, passed it to James the brother of Jesus, and James gave it to Judas. Judas gave it to Pilate, and it was used as one of the planks on the cross that Jesus carried to Golgotha.

Golgotha itself was also preordained. Some men, like John Donne, thought it was the site of the fateful tree itself:

> We think that Paradise and Calvarie,
> Christ's cross and Adam's tree stood in one place.

But more often it was said to be the place where Adam was buried, the bald, brownish hill that held the skull of the head of the human race. Cain and Abel had brought their offerings to this place; Noah had sacrificed there when he came out of the Ark; and it was there that Abraham was saved from sacrificing Isaac by finding, caught in the brambles, a ram that prefigured the lamb-like offering of Christ. So, although crucifixions could be carried out in any prominent site and along any public road, Pilate naturally sent Jesus to Golgotha. There was no other place.

Nor was there any other time. At a certain hour on a certain day of a certain year the sun would be eclipsed. As Amos put it, 'I will cause the sun to go down at noon, and I will darken the earth in one clear day . . . and I will make it as the mourning of an only son.' Or as Joel said, 'The earth shall quake . . . the heavens shall tremble . . . the sun and moon shall be dark, and the stars shall withdraw their shining.'

The date of this eclipse was to be the twenty-fifth of March: in the Roman calendar the sixth before the Kalends of April, in the Jewish calendar the fourteenth of Nisan, of the year 33. Or it could have been the year 30; for it was the day that mattered, rather than the year. Since the reform of the calendar by Caesar, the twenty-fifth of March was the spring equinox: the day when the sun passed the great celestial cross, the X of Plato's *Timaeus*, formed by the equator and the ecliptic. Justin Martyr actually pointed out that the X was God's son, set crosswise in the heavens. In the great scheme of things it was bound to be on Friday the twenty-fifth of March that Christ was put to death, in order that after the necessary spell of darkness he could rise on a Sunday, the day of the *sol invictus* or the unconquered sun.

The twenty-fourth of March was also known in the cult of Attis, among the Phrygians, as the 'day of blood' on which the god died. The beautiful Attis was driven so mad by the jealous Cybele, goddess of nature, that he mutilated himself beneath a pine tree. His spirit passed into the tree, a resinous flash, and at the foot of the pine sprang anemones and violets from the warm rain of his blood. On the twenty-fourth an effigy would be presented of the young man tied to a sacred pine, with wreaths of violets on its branches; for two days he would be mourned as lost; and on the third his followers would celebrate his resurrection, which was also the coming of the spring.

In the case of Christ, now, the dead wood of the cross put out flowers. The scheme of salvation was also the scheme of the seasons. It was symbolically necessary that Christ should die at the coming of the spring, not at any other time; that he should die on a tree, not in any other way; and that he should not merely hang there, as on a gibbet, but extend his arms like branches with the sap of his blood flowing from his hands.

Only Pilate could effect that. Only he could provide the *tau*-shape of the cross, the Egyptian sign of life, on which life could be proclaimed through the act of death. His role was to be the winter to Christ's spring. He could struggle, of course. He was free to do that. But the result of his struggling was already known; however he wriggled, he would end up as God's agent. To resist his role was unhelpful, as if Boreas were suddenly to sulk and abandon his job as scourer of the northern quarter. To be merciful and soft, in his case, would do nothing to advance the transformation of the world.

4

Blood on his boots

... And we are onlookers at the crime,
Callous contemporaries of the slow
Torture of God. Here is the hill
Made ghastly by His spattered blood

Whereon He hangs and suffers still:
See, the centurions wear riding-boots,
Black shirts and badges and peaked caps,
Greet one another with raised-arm salutes;
They have cold eyes, unsmiling lips;
Yet these His brothers know not what they do.

And on his either side hang dead
A labourer and a factory hand,
Or one is maybe a lynched Jew
And one a Negro or a Red,
Coolie or Ethiopian, Irishman,
Spaniard or German democrat ...

David Gascoyne,
'Ecce Homo' from 'Miserere' (1937)

We are in Victoria Street, in London, on any weekday morning. (It is any street of any capital in the northern hemisphere: glass towers above, sandwich shops below.) It is raining. On both sides of the street, workers stream on their way from the station to the desk, the computer screen, the hasty mug of coffee. Their heads and shoulders are bent forward, under jostling umbrellas, with the thought of the work that awaits them in the government department or the magistrates' court: the memos they will write, the rules they will revise, the tiny drops of lubricant they will apply to the giant wheels of the machinery of state. Try to walk against the flow of these workers, and you are buffeted as if in a current full of fish. They swim on inexorably down the long rain-slicked street.

On their right stands Westminster Cathedral, across a plaza laid with pink and grey paving. This is the Catholic Church admitted at last as part of the British establishment, a stone's throw from Parliament and right beside the Army and Navy Stores. On the corner stands a giant McDonald's with seating for 200 and a corporate presence that spans the globe from Anchorage to China. The commuters, intent, ignore both of them.

They ignore even more the young black man who stands in the cathedral porch, silently holding out a McDonald's paper cup. His belongings are stacked in a corner, under a cardboard refrigerator box which he uses to sleep on the pavement. His rancid smell mingles with others: incense, candles, cold stone. He lingers in a place where every kind of power – religious, corporate, political – is oppressively represented. And by his very presence he unsettles them all.

Sixty yards from him is another confrontation. It is in stone, a bas-relief on a pillar, the first Station of the Cross; but it is just as unsettling. Jesus, a dishevelled creature, no doubt malodorous too, stands before Pilate. Pilate sits on a high-backed marble throne engraved with the words *Senatus Populusque Romanus*; he presides in the full and solid power of the Roman empire. Before him, a boy servant with the bowl of water kneels respectfully. Behind the governor, on the wall, in Roman capitals, march the scarlet letters recording his two irreversible decisions, the release of Barabbas and the condemnation of Christ. Memo: action taken. His throne has raised him on a level with his victim, and he stares at him with a look that is arrogant, longing, confused and cold, all at once. It is the absolute bafflement of power meeting power, but not understanding how.

Eric Gill, who sculpted the relief, laboured over this expression. He worked on the piece for seventeen years in his barn at Ditchling, under the South Downs. In his working smock, with his thick-lensed glasses protecting him from chips of stone, he chiselled Pilate's features in Hoptonwood limestone. Under the soft Sussex light, the face seemed to say everything he wanted. But once it was placed in the cathedral, with 'the reflected light from the floor [and] the conflicting shadows thrown by the electric lights', it looked 'entirely different'. Gill told a friend that the expressions on both faces had been completely changed, and that the result distressed him.

He had meant to suggest galvanising, outrageous things. Pilate was supposed to be a symbol of the world Gill hated and from which he had retreated: the symbol of power, industry, capital, plutocracy, the exploitation of labour. In this first Station Christ, the lover, gazed on 'the essential dirtiness, dirtiness in its very being and nature, of the industrial capitalist world'. It was fitting that the Station was hung in the autumn of 1914, when that world had just plunged into a convulsion largely of its own making: a bloodbath made possible by pampered armaments industries and the unstoppable efficiency of the railways.

This was not the first time that Pilate had been made to symbolise power far beyond himself. The reason why he is in the Creed, a bureaucrat set down incongruously among elemental streams of light and celestial thrones, is not merely to set Christ's death in time. Pilate represented not simply his age, but the full power-structure of his age and the worst that it could do. He sat on the judgement seat of Caesar transplanted to Judea; as Tacitus put it, leaning his full weight on the Latin *imperitante*, 'Christ had, by the imperial authority of Tiberius exercised through the procurator Pontius Pilate, incurred the penalty of death.' The trial of Jesus before the imperial judge was the moment when he challenged overweening power and appeared to lose; but, as the faithful knew, he burst out of the tomb and threw that power over. It was essential not merely to express faith in Christ but in 'Christ crucified under Pontius Pilate', brutally killed but not – ha! – killed at all.

Among the early Christians the phrase *sub Pontio Pilato* was used almost as an incantation, an invocation, a magic spell. In one apocryphal gospel St Peter commanded a camel 'in the name of Jesus Christ crucified under Pontius Pilate' through the eye of the famous needle; the tiny needle, glinting in the sand, opened 'like a gate', and the camel lurched through. Demoniacs were exorcised 'by the name of Christ crucified under Pontius Pilate', and converts were plunged three times in the baptismal water while Pilate's name, as well as Christ's, washed over them. The purged demoniacs immediately began to cure the sick, where other charm-wavers had been unable to cure them. The names made devils tremble; and Justin Martyr makes it clear that they did not fall down merely at the mention of Christ, but at the name of 'Pontius Pilate the governor of Judea', who had administered his death 'by dispensation' and had then been trumped, utterly.

The victory was all the more impressive if the odds were stacked against Christ by a bigger dose of evil and portentousness in his prosecutor. Writers through the ages therefore coloured Pilate's character darker and crueller, without feeling they were exaggerating much. Tyrant Pilate is a constant. He can be traced right back to Philo's description, based after all to some extent on life, of his 'venality, violence . . . abusive behaviour . . . and endless savage ferocity.' The Dead Sea Scrolls record him with bitterness too: there, where Roman governors are generically known as 'the Wrath', Pilate appears as 'the Young Lion of Wrath', claws sharpened. Among the Jews, tyrants and lions were coterminous; both tore their subjects to pieces.

Yet this character would have grown even without Philo and even without the Scrolls. The arrogance of Pilate is there in the gospels, even starker in Greek than in English: 'Am *I* a Jew?' 'Take him and crucify him yourselves.' 'Are you refusing to speak to me? *To me?*' His pride and stubbornness were there for the inflating, and the medieval dramatists were not slow to get to work on them. To begin with, the ancient accounts of Pilate's insults and brutalities were embroidered. Eusebius in the fourth century claimed that he consecrated the standards in Jerusalem, secretly, at night; Vincent de Beauvais in the thirteenth century added that he put up images on standards in the Temple itself; and Jean Michel's *Passion* of 1486 insisted that he ordered the Jews to worship these images and killed anyone who refused. According to the *Scholastic History*, cited in the *Golden Legend,* it was Pilate who organised the Massacre of the Innocents; and the famous aqueduct was built to bring fresh water only to Pilate's own bath.

From there the governor could develop into a cartoon bad-man, culpably weak as well as culpably strong. The drama of the passion demanded a man who could be shamed and shown up by Christ, as well as a ruler whose power could be overwhelming. To the medieval mind, Pilate was dull when he doubted. It was when he was bad that he became magnificent, the first great modern villain of the European theatre. The villain-figure of Satan, with red beard and sparking black fur, had none of the contemporary edge of Pilate, who was every bad prince that everyone knew.

Pilate was Everyruler. He was a prince, a king, a duke, a knight, and the son of the emperor of Rome. What he wore on his head was not exactly a crown; it was sometimes a helmet, sometimes a chaplet, sometimes a hat. Most suggestively, in the Coventry play, he wore a headdress of glittering gold foil; for this was a man accustomed to seeing menials lower their eyes in his presence, as Suetonius wrote that men lowered them when encountering the emperor or the sun.

Not only Pilate's headgear symbolised worldly power. It was summed up, too, in the weapons he carried. He had a sword which he swung terrifyingly, threatening to cut people to ribbons. Occasionally he was kitted out with a gilded poleaxe, representing a sceptre with a sharp point, and with a set of leather 'balls' which he seems to have hurled at his audience. Most spectacularly, he wielded a huge club of green leather stuffed with wool, covered all over with floppy leather 'spikes' and ornamented with brass nails. The accounts of the Coventry play show that this was used with abandon, for almost every year it was mended at fourpence a time, or made again from scratch. In 1578 two were mended, suggesting that Pilate flourished one in each hand. Such a club, spilling out its white wool as it thwacked against pillars and heads, was a villain's trademark. The Devil was issued with one too, though at Coventry this was covered with canvas and painted. Country folk in the north of England believed that Satan usually went armed this way. When blackberries were overripe and had lost their flavour, the Devil was said to have cast his club over them.

The Devil and Pilate shared other similarities. Satan too had a set of leather balls (at Coventry, sixteen of them) to hurl around the stage. His gatekeeper at the jaws of hell was usually the same fellow, half-cut on beer, who played Pilate's porter at his palace gate. (When Raoul de Houdaing in his fifteenth-century *Dream of Hell* found himself at the brimstone entrance, there were Pilate and Beelzebub together, crying 'Raoul, welcome!') Annas and Caiaphas, gulping out their praises of Pilate in the York play, call him 'most lovely of lure', exactly the compliment paid a little later by Beelzebub to Lucifer. And Satan, like Pilate, would pace the stage roaring and swearing, promising to beat to a pulp anyone who got in his way. These two great villains never colluded; they left the stage to each other. But nobody watching them could doubt that they were spawned from the same darkness. In the Towneley plays Pilate actually described himself as *mali actoris*, the author of evil; and his terror, both at Christ's miracles and at the thought that he may be God's son, is, like Satan's, a terror that his power will be suddenly extinguished.

In the Coventry play, Pilate's temper was encouraged by the wine he was allowed to drink 'between the stages': in 1479, a whole quart of it. He was meant to be a bibber and a gourmand not just because tradition said so, but because this was how rulers lived. Then, having drunk deep, he ranted. His voice was usually pitched like a blaring trumpet, brassily loud and high. In the prologue to *The Miller's Tale* Chaucer describes how the miller, 'all pale with drink/ Began to shout in Pilate's voice/ and swore by arms and blood and bones/ "I know a noble story, now . . ."'

Pilate declaimed in several languages. One of them was sheer coarse English. Those who in any way offended him were 'losels', 'curs', 'dotards', 'vile fators' and 'harlots', whom the devil could 'hang high to dry'. On the stage even his better instincts were stained by bad language, as when he considered moderating Christ's flogging in the York play: 'Spoil not his shape, for if the sot be sinless, it behoves us to save him.'

But his ranting had another dimension. In the Chester plays he spoke French, then still the language of the English ruling classes; in the Towneley play he spoke Latin, not because he was a Roman (he was, first and foremost, a heathen, swearing by Mahound, Lucifer, Baal and 'Mohammed's blood so dear'), but because Latin was the language of oppression, bureaucracy and legalese. Tyrant-Pilate is never on better form than for his entry in the Towneley play at the stage called 'The Talents':

Leave me be! Men give place, *quia sum dominus dominorum*!
He that dares to me outface, *rapietur lux oculorum*!
Then you'd better give me space, *ne tendam vim bracchiorum*!
Or else no man will get his grace, *contestor Iura polorum*!
I rule in Jewry!
Maxime pure!
Town *quoque rure,*
Me paveatis!

Stemate regali, King Atus begat me of Pila!
Tramite legali, I'm ordained to reign in Judah!
Nomine vulgari, Pontius Pilate who holds you all in awe!
Qui bene vult fari should call me the head of all law!
Judeorum
Iura guberno!
Please me and say so,
Omnia firmo,
Sorte deorum!

It is unlikely that much, or any, of this was understood; it was swallowed up in the boos of the crowd and the manic thumpings of Pilate's club against the stage. But the very sound of legal Latin carried with it, to fourteenth-century ears, the ring of unfair property claims, exorbitant taxes and crooked lawyers: a whole world in which the ordinary man was ground up and spat out again. He couldn't win in this world. There was no mercy in it. The Spanish saying ¡*Que apela a Poncio Pilato*! still means just this; it is used, as the dictionary says, 'for decisions from which there is no appeal or for circumstances for which there's no help, because it's too late or there's nothing left or what's happened is irrevocable . . . [it means] to cry vainly and uselessly over something that cannot be avoided or cannot be corrected.'

Pilate was not imagined to do his oppressive work alone. He had accomplices and hangers-on. There were his knights, loutish and stupid, and his torturers in their black buckram jackets, who doubled (at least in the Towneley play) as the gamblers for Christ's seamless garment underneath the cross. In Towneley Pilate lists other allies too, his 'dear darlings':

> All false indicters
> Questmongers and jurors

And all these false outriders
Are welcome to my sight.

Questmongers gave information against other people for the price of a
dinner or a share in the fines. Jurors were bribed to give false evidence.
They were welcome because Pilate was crooked himself, 'full of
subtlety, falsehood, guile and treachery.' In fact, this Pilate is not really a
king any more; he is himself the type of a local officer of the shire, but
no less a tyrant for that, full of the bureaucratic and authoritarian
obsessions of a big man in a little patch. He knows the law and is
boastfully at home in it, using it both as a shield and as a tool for his
duplicity. To medieval listeners, this made him much more a tyrant than
the king was. The whole drama of the passion was that this man, whose
instruments of oppression were his law-books as much as his clubs, had
caught up Jesus too in his ghastly legalistic machinery. He was a
technician and a specialist, one of the knowledge-elite; Jesus was a
peasant, even though he was God. In earthly terms, there was no
contest.

Jesus was poor. Without money, though, Pilate had no interest in
giving him a hearing. His principles followed the warm trail of cash. As
he explained it in the Towneley play, he liked to play both sides of a
case, 'just as the hammer makes iron smooth: I'll support the right if it
will give me advantage, but the wrong if it will avail me more.' He then
makes a jaunty contemporary point:

If I say so myself, as men of court now learn,
Support a man today, tomorrow against him turn.

This is his tactic for the trial, and a clever one from the playwright's
point of view: it allows Pilate to pose as Jesus' friend, wash his hands,
even proclaim him innocent, while all the time fully intending to kill
him. He proposes to 'tack him up', but only when he has shown him a
benign contenance and flattering words. This comes easily to him
because he is, after all, 'a court man', skilled in every sort of social
unctuousness and capable of turning every vice to his advantage.

Pride, gluttony, anger, lust. Cupidity, too: in York it is Pilate, rather
than the high priests, who drives the bargain with Judas and who later
swindles the landowner out of the Potter's Field. In both Towneley and
York he purloins Christ's coat by cheating at dice, a trick everyone can

see coming: 'If Sir Pilate meddles in this,' says the third soldier in the York play, 'you can be sure you won't get much.' The fifteenth-century moralists could find not only the seven deadly sins in Pilate, but the three most corrupting appetites of crooked judges: money, self-love and fear.

All this sin was tiring. The hallmark of the medieval tyrant was a propensity to sleep: like a small child worn out with tantrums, he had to be put to bed to recoup his energy for the outbursts to come. In the Towneley play, having roared at the audience not to 'rake the ash of his anger', Pilate is sleepy and petulant within a few lines, asking to be 'wrapped up well against the cold.' In the York play he is found in his hall, where he has just said a lingering goodnight to his wife. A couch with rich draperies is at the side of the stage; Pilate is still on his throne, his leather club propped against it, with a beaker of wine in his hand. 'Now my wife's gone,' he says mournfully. Then, in a snap of the fingers, his mood changes. 'Put me to bed, beadle. It's time for you to take care of me.'

'Yes, sir.'

'Put rich robes on me, and make sure everything's as cosy as can be.'

'Of course, sir. Your servant, sir. There's nothing that can possibly annoy you, sir, once you're beautifully tucked in.'

'Come here, beadle.'

'Sir.'

'I want to go to bed. Carry me there. Just put your arms round me and carry me over. But be really careful how you handle me! Don't hurt me. Pick me up really gently.'

'You weigh a bit, sir.'

'That's because I'm wet with wine, of course! Now, put me down. Make sure the sheets are pulled over me neatly. I'm going to sleep for a while. See to it that nobody disturbs me: no servants, and nobody from outside either. I don't want the slightest noise to come near me. Understood?

'Sir, if any warlock wakes you, it would be better for him if he'd never been born.'

'If he escapes without a scratch — 'scapes without a scratch . . . I'll meet him tomorrow and kill him. I'll kill him.'

'Of course you will, sir.'

'Teach him to feel sorry for himself.'

'You just sleep, sir.'

This man was a tyrant, but he was also a buffoon. His terror was full of comic gestures, but his comedy could wound. One way and another, the audience could not take their eyes off him. He controlled the stage. Undoubtedly the crowd heckled him at every appearance, every exit and entrance, which gave him his cues to roar for silence: a cross-play with the mob that echoed accurately enough at least some of the encounters in Josephus and the gospels. He was the man they loved to hate, the cumulation of all unjust authority, and their loathing was cathartic. Thomas Nashe summed up the feeling on his visit to Rome in 1594: 'I was at Pontius Pilate's house and *piss'd* against it.'

Pilate's dominance was reflected in his wages. At Coventry he was paid 3/3d for his performance: a little less than Herod, who had to ride a horse, but almost twice as much as Jesus. This made sense, for Jesus in these plays was virtually speechless. His role was to stand there in white – sometimes in a long sheepskin, symbolising simplicity and poverty – and to be belaboured by others. Only streaks of gold paint in his hair and beard suggested his divinity. He was everything his tormentors were not: solemn where they were stupid, modest where they were vain, silent when they ranted. And so the scene was set and the metaphor displayed: pure force against pure force.

*   *   *

There was nothing physically impressive about Jesus. He was, as Isaiah had prophesied, 'without beauty, without majesty, with no looks to attract our eyes; a thing despised and rejected by men.' People 'took no account of him'. As he himself explained to Pilate, he had no servants or officers; his kingdom had none of the accoutrements of power that Pilate would have thought essential. Yet Pilate's authority, like his medieval beauty, was skin-deep. It was all violence, noise and show.

Nineteenth-century popularisers revelled in the scene of their confrontation. When they described it in words, they stressed the elements of equivocation and uncertainty; but when they painted it, as they did endlessly, filling Pilate's palace with grieving women with the faces of Rossetti angels, what was paramount was the clash of authority. In these paintings Jesus is imbued with it, a faint and almost imagined nimbus of power, though his hands are bound and his feet are bare. Pilate, on the other hand, surrounded by marble, soldiers and brass eagles, can't seem to connect; he makes the sweeping or contemptuous gestures of a man in power, but the observer knows they will not work.

The governor is in the presence of a man of child-like subversiveness who, as Oscar Wilde noted, is the first figure in history to have told his followers to live 'flower-like' lives; and he has no notion how to deal with that delicacy, that lack of substance.

Perhaps the most famous of the nineteenth-century pictures appeared in 1890 in Russia, where Tolstoy was its champion. He first saw it in the form of a sketch which Nikolay Gay senior brought to his country estate at Yasnaya Polyana in January that year. The weather was bitter, and Tolstoy was sleeping badly; he was distressed by the unfavourable reviews of *The Kreutzer Sonata*. Each morning he trudged down through the snow to the school his daughter Masha had founded in a gardener's cottage on the estate, in order to chop logs and light the stove. He then drank coffee, wrote and revised his comedy *The Fruits of Enlightenment*, and went sledging with the children on old benches. Into this white implacable landscape, marked with the straggling skeletons of orchards and birch trees, Gay carried his sketch of Jesus and Pilate in a briefcase. 'Very good,' Tolstoy noted in his diary, and returned to his struggles with the stove.

In spring the finished picture arrived. The leaves were bright green on the birch trees, and at the base of the gleaming white trunks the earth lay in ruts and pools where the carriages had passed. Overhead, the sky was the washed blue of an eggshell; beyond, the wind sighed in the forest trees. Seated in his carriage, with his painting wrapped up on the seat beside him, Gay bumped down the muddy drive towards Tolstoy's house. The great writer had written to him, telling him that he longed to know how the picture had been received. Although he had not yet seen it in a finished state, he could not stop thinking about it.

In fact, the painting had caused a scandal. It had been hung at the Wanderers' Exhibition in St Petersburg that year, but had occasioned such an uproar that it was taken down on the tsar's orders and banned from further showings in Russia. It was subversive because it showed Jesus, unkempt and fiery, flattening himself against the wall like a rat about to spring; and because it showed Pilate as a sleek, contemptible, impervious figure, every tsar facing every rebel who had only his beliefs to sustain him.

The picture was called 'What is Truth?' It represented the moment when Pilate, invited to consider 'a kingdom not of this world', had flung out his infamous retort. It was, wrote Tolstoy, 'the most simple motif: Christ and his teaching in conflict with the teaching of the world.' It was a theme that had obsessed Tolstoy ever since, in 1881, he had written to the new tsar Alexander III expressing the hope that 'out of Christian love and forgiveness' he would pardon the young revolutionaries who had murdered his father. Alexander had found it too hard. Now, in Gay's painting, Tolstoy saw another ruler who could not understand that love and truth might be applied to government. Passive resistance baffled Pilate; brute force was all he recognised. 'With a laugh and a contemptuous gesture, he throws the words carelessly at him ... and, evidently considering his remark decisive, goes out to the crowd ...'

Tolstoy then turned to the governor's body language: the plump back and the gesturing arm that took up most of the foreground of the painting. He saw there, alongside 'all the dignity of that Roman figure', 'a slavish anxiety about himself: the mean trepidation of a petty soul'. For all the toga and the height and the majesty, Pilate was the little man and Jesus the man who towered; Jesus was the brave one, while Pilate was afraid.

This delighted Tolstoy. He embraced Gay, kissed him effusively, and decided then and there to become a champion of the painting, which he believed all the cultured classes of the western powers should see. Eventually he persuaded P.M. Tretyakov, a famous collector, to buy the picture for his gallery in Moscow and, since it could no longer be publicly exhibited in Russia, to send it on tour to Europe and America. Tolstoy wrote to George Kennan, an American journalist who worked in Siberia for Western Union, to explain the picture's vital importance:

> Pilate is a Roman governor, similar to our Siberian governors of whom you know; he lives only for the interests of his mother-country and, of course, reacts with contempt and a certain disgust to those disturbances − religious disturbances to boot − among the coarse, superstitious people he governs.
>
> At this point a conversation occurs in which the good-natured governor has to lower himself *en bon prince* to the barbarous interests of his subjects and, as is natural to important people, he has formed an idea of what he is going to ask and he himself speaks first, without any interest in the answers; with a smile of condescension, I imagine, he keeps saying: 'So you are a king?'

This was not just ancient Jerusalem for Tolstoy; it was clearly also the anteroom of a palace in his Russia, where peasants in tunics and grandmothers in scarves, anxious perhaps about eviction or the price of bread, waited on hard benches. Or it was a room where a heavilymedalled army commander and his casually smoking sidekicks dealt with a conscientious objector, one who objected perhaps to firing on demonstrators.

> Jesus is exhausted and one look at this well-groomed, self-satisfied figure, dulled by his luxurious life, is sufficient to understand the gulf which divides them, and how impossible or enormously difficult it is for Pilate to understand his teaching. But Jesus remembers that even Pilate is a man and a brother, a lost one, but still a brother, and that he doesn't have the right not to reveal to him the truth which he reveals to people, and he begins to speak. But Pilate stops him at the word *truth*. What can a ragged beggar, a mere youth, tell him, the friend and companion of Roman poets and philosophers – about truth?

One look at these marble floors, these ceiling panels, the tailcoats of the flunkeys who open the doors, will convince these people that the problems which eat up their days are not worth pursuing; just as a little staged contempt, with the well-polished riding-boots kicked up on the desk and a laughing flick of the newspaper, will show the political dissenters what their arguments are worth.

> He's not interested in listening to all the rubbish which this little Jew might tell him, and it is even rather disagreeable that this vagrant can imagine that he can instruct a Roman dignitary; so he stops him immediately, and points out to him that people more intelligent, more learned, more refined than himself and his Jews have thought about the word and have decided long ago that it's impossible to know what truth is, and that truth is an empty word. Having said 'What is truth?' and turned on his heel, the good-natured and self-satisfied governor leaves the room. And Jesus feels sorry for the man and is terrified because of the gulf of lies which separates him and people like him from the truth . . .

The picture was not a success in Germany or in America. Tolstoy blamed the failure on lack of proper advertising, but there was a culture-gap at work too. Pilate, Tolstoy told Kennan, 'is what a governor should be now in . . . Massachusetts.' But he was wrong. Nowhere in America, outside the deep South where a rebellious black might have faced a white governor, was there the same yawning gulf between rulers and ruled as persisted in Russia; and perhaps nowhere else in the industrialised world was government so easily reinforced by violence. Tolstoy felt he knew many Pilates; the character was still as fresh and menacing as Gay had painted him. But to the bourgeoisie of Philadelphia, where Gay's painting was shown, he was inert and historical.

Gay went on refining his thoughts about the passion, and about Pilate, for years. He began to think that power might be better depicted without a human body at all; a figure in a toga was almost too cultured, too leisurely, as Tolstoy had said. In 1893 he produced a painting called 'Golgotha', in which the governor, pronouncing sentence, is reduced to a scrawny pointing hand that comes in from the left of the frame. The hand and the arm, though naked, represent pure power and brute force. Before it, Jesus shrivels up, and the two thieves shrink back in despair. Yet the oppression is almost disembodied.

Sixty years earlier, Turner had had the same idea. In 'Pilate Washing his Hands', painted in 1830, the governor has disappeared completely and only power is left: the square back of a golden chair, an explosion of light like ectoplasm, and the desperately pleading faces of the crowd. There is no more banter, no more condescension. Instead there is something elemental, like a storm or like the sea, which not only does not listen but, caught up in its own noise, is incapable of doing so.

*   *   *

The political analogies could be taken even further than this. Tolstoy had never quite equated Jesus with political revolutionaries, but others did. In the twentieth century Jesus was increasingly a separatist, a socialist, even a Marxist, and as he changed so too did Pilate, becoming every cynic or thug who faced him. No other age has been so convinced of the sheer brutishness of Pilate: a brutishness unmixed with majesty, physical charm or even much intelligence. If Jesus was the Spanish Republican martyred by the sniper's bullet, Pilate was the local Falangist strongman; if Jesus was the worker-priest, promoting liberation theology's 'option for the poor', Pilate was the pin-striped *caudillo* with his mistress on his arm. The Pilate of the 1959 version of *Ben Hur*, presiding languidly and sneeringly over the famous chariot race, seemed closely modelled on the Hitler footage from the 1936 Olympics. And if Jesus was the Jew gassed in Auschwitz or shot in Treblinka, Pilate was his Amon Goetz: the insomniac commandant, the reckless drinker, the man who 'went to the work of murder as calmly as a clerk goes to his office', and who thought that his exaltation after killing was because he had performed 'an act of political, racial and moral justice'. For even Goetz, in Thomas Keneally's words, had his moment of toying with restraint. The most heinous thug could be, in every sense, like Pilate.

> It seemed . . . that he was attracted by the thought of moderation – a temptation worthy of an emperor. Amon could imagine a sick slave on the trolleys, or returning prisoner from Kabelwerke, staggering – with that put-upon way one found so hard to tolerate – under a load of clothing or timber picked up at the prison gate. And the fantasy ran with a strange warmth in Amon's belly that he would forgive that laggard, that pathetic actor. As Caligula might have been tempted to see himself as Caligula the Good, so the image of Amon the Good exercised the commandant's imagination for a time. He would, in fact, always have a weakness for it. Tonight, his blood running golden with cognac and nearly all the camp asleep beyond his steps, Amon was more definitely seduced by mercy than by the fear of reprisal . . .

Restraint allows the tyrant to avoid making martyrs. Martyrs know the truth and, by dying for it, proclaim how strong it is. But if the tyrant toys with the truth, queries it, worries it, refuses to grant its importance and spares men the theatrical satisfaction of dying to uphold it, he remains the strong man and they become the fools. Most modern dramatisations of Pilate show him taking this line. He is even the originator of this approach in history, the man of apparently assured and absolute power attempting, with a bit of a joke, to jog Jesus out of his obsessive progress towards the cross. He does not always ask 'What is truth?' In Dennis Potter's play, *Son of Man*, he asks 'Aren't you afraid of the nails?' Yet the burden of the question is the same: 'Why do you want to do this ridiculous thing? Is it really worth it?'

The martyr will always answer yes. Only mercy can thwart his determination. Yet the practice of mercy can be horribly hard for the man whose first instinct is to crush the nuisance. Pilate learned that lesson right at the start of his tour in Judea, with the confrontation over the military standards. He had scarcely arrived when he found himself able to make martyrs; and at the same moment felt humiliated and disarmed, because martyrdom was precisely what the Jews demanded of him.

The protesting Jews had been camped outside his palace in Caesarea for five days. In the *Antiquities*, Josephus says they lay prostrate for all that time; but it is more likely that they camped, like sit-down strikers. They sat in the gardens and on the lower terraces, only a little tidier than the drunken sailors down by the harbour, with a constant murmur and wail of prayers that a Roman could not understand.

On the sixth day, Pilate sent a messenger to order the Jews to assemble in the Great Stadium. His patience was exhausted, and they could be dealt with more easily there. At dawn he put the soldiers in, hiding them under the stadium platform. Then he took his seat in the great chair of the tribunal. On normal occasions he would have been greeted with a standing ovation; but now the stadium was unmoved. He sat there, alone except for his attendants, facing the crowd of Jews on the vast ground where the chariots raced each other. There was a saying drawn from chariot-racing, if you felt in control of events and things were going well, that you were 'rolling with a true axle'; conversely, if you got into trouble, you 'crashed the column' that marked the turning-point at each end of the track. Roll or crash.

The Jews stood there, every eye on him. Pilate let them petition him again. 'This time,' he said, 'I will give you an answer.'

They fell for it. 'Please, *hegemon*, remove the standards,' cried their spokesman. 'They offend us, and offend the laws of our ancestors.'

Pilate said, 'Here's my answer.'

He raised his hand, as if summoning the wineboy; or perhaps, as Caesar once did when preparing for a massacre, he shook his bright white toga from his shoulder. The troops poured from beneath the platform. In an instant they had the Jews surrounded, three-deep. The Jews were terrified. They had never seen anything like this.

Now Pilate began to shout at them. 'If you continue to refuse to admit the images of Caesar,' he cried, 'I'll have you cut down! I want you to stop disturbing me, *now*! I want you to go home!'

The Jews did not move. Pilate raised his hand again.

'Soldiers, draw your swords!'

Hundred of blades flashed in the early sun. Each was pointed at the throat of a Jew.

'Are you not prepared to answer me?'

The crowd before him seemed to waver. It was like a mirage seen from a distance in the desert; or perhaps it was only his eyes, and the strain. But no, they were wavering. They were swaying, as they swayed when they prayed in the street. Then an awful thing happened. In unison, as if by agreement, the Jews fell prostrate. It looked like a wood collapsing, with an odd, crumpling, soft sound. Surely a body should make more noise when it fell. But there was almost none. They lay there, arms outstretched, faces to the ground, among the staring troops. Every man had bared the back of his neck: a white stalk, strangely vulnerable, untouched by the sun. Pilate understood, with a dreadful surprise, that they were offering themselves to the swords of his men.

'Rather than violate our law, we will die, sir,' one of them cried.

Others joined him in a confused murmur. 'Yes, we would rather die, sir.'

Some years later, when another crowd of Jews fell prostrate before another Roman governor, Philo expanded on their arguments. 'We gladly put our throats at your disposal,' they told the governor. 'Let [your cavalry and infantry] slaughter, butcher, carve our flesh without a blow struck or blood drawn by us. Let them do all the deeds that conquerors commit. But why do you need an army? We'll do the sacrifice ourselves, priests of a noble order; and then, when we've bathed ourselves in the blood of our kinsfolk, the right sort of bathing for those who want to go to Hades clean, we'll mingle our blood with theirs by the crowning slaughter of ourselves . . . We take our departure in contempt of the life that is no life.'

There was not an ounce of submission in this, not an ounce of fear. The suffering was embraced and defiantly enjoyed. Centuries before Gandhi wrote down his doctrine of non-violence, it was exactly what he recommended. 'Non-violence in its dynamic condition means conscious suffering,' he wrote in 1920, the massacre at Amritsar still in his mind. 'It does not mean meek submission to the will of the evil-doer, but it means putting of one's whole soul against the will of the tyrant. Working under this law of our being, it is possible for a single individual to defy the whole might of an unjust empire to save his honour, his religion, his soul, and lay the foundation for that empire's fall or its regeneration.'

These Jews believed, again in Gandhi's words, that 'this Government represents the activity of Satan.' That, too, was a concept they could be confident the new governor would not understand.

The commander was at Pilate's shoulder. 'All right, sir?' he was asking.

Pilate could not speak.

'Cut them now, sir?'

He was too astonished to answer. And in his astonishment all he could say was 'No'.

The commander's eyebrows would have flickered, at the least, with scepticism and surprise.

'Tell them to put their swords away.'

At once, the swords crashed back into the scabbards. Still the Jews stayed where they were. Standing Romans, prostrate subjects: the scene should have looked satisfactory to Pilate. Instead, it was almost intolerable: the Romans had lost, and the Jews had won. Pilate still wore his 'badge of the violent', as Gandhi would have called it, armed troops everywhere; but the Jews wore their shield of the non-violent, God himself.

It was possible to salvage some scrap of comfort from this. Pilate would have understood, through the raging in his head, that he had done something magnanimous: that he had spared people. 'We are a strong nation,' Propertius wrote, 'as much through humanity as through the sword': *nam quantum ferro tantum pietate potentes/stamus*. He had loosened his grip before snapping the bone; he had allowed the insect to go on its way uncrushed. This was what ancestor Gavius, *pius* Gavius, had done in the mountain pass, when the white necks before him had been Roman. They had bent down, expecting death swiftly, as Virgil in the *Aeneid* had described the death of Euryalus: the head flopping feebly on to one shoulder, as when a shining flower was cut by the ploughshare, or when fragile poppies found that the weight of a shower was too much for them.

> *purpureus veluti cum flos succisus aratro*
> *languescit moriens, lassove papavera collo*
> *demisere caput, pluvia cum forte gravantur.*

He could have mown down the protestors, just like that; he could have turned the sand of the stadium scarlet. Instead, he had stopped himself. He was, says Josephus, 'astonished at their determination to keep their laws inviolate.' The Slavonic version has him 'astonished at their God-fearing purity'. These men were not lying on the ground out of fear of him, a Roman governor; they were lying there out of fear of their God, whose anger was worse than cold steel severing the cords of the spine. He, Pilate, could do nothing to hurt them. Their zeal protected them.

The sun would have climbed higher now, perhaps clearing the rim of the stadium. The smell of sweat and unwashed clothes was all the stronger. That might bring the flies out; the soldiers would beat them away from him, if necessary, with their leather wristbands. Yes, he too would do as much as that. He would carefully keep the flies from disturbing his emperor as he sat in judgement. He would also prostrate himself before him, assuming Tiberius would ever ask him to. He would do all this, as to a god, if he wanted. But he did not think he should put these Jews to death to spare the emperor's honour or defend his holy standards. Yes, he feared Tiberius and he loved him. But this fear, and this love, were more impressive.

'Your order, sir?' asked the commander.

'Go to Jerusalem, take the standards down, remove them immediately, bring them back here.'

'Sir.'

The commander barked out the order. On hearing it, the soldiers stepped out awkwardly from behind and among the Jews. They crowded towards the tribunal, the sun now glaring from their helmets, and fell into some sort of column. They would escort Pilate away first, and then go off to Jerusalem.

He must have given some explanation, dressed up as clemency or magnanimity, but Josephus does not say what it was. Slowly, the Jews responded. After some moments, they began to register that the threat had passed. They stirred, then scrambled up, smoothing and dusting down their clothes. Pilate knew that they stared at him, but to meet their eyes would have been awful. Instead he could gaze at his soldiers regrouping, or at the neutral undemanding stones under his feet.

Perhaps the Jews thanked him. If so, it would have given him no pleasure. He would have flinched from it as from a blow. He would have left the platform with a taste in his mouth like dust, like dried blood, as if it had been he rather than they who had pushed his face into the unyielding earth.

There is no beating these people, though they seem beatable. The women have soft arms; they wear summer dresses, as if for a picnic or a day by the sea. The men wear ties and have polished their shoes. They wheel small children in pushchairs, or lead the older ones neatly decked out in Christian T-shirts. Nobody stands directly outside the abortion clinic; that would constitute illegal intimidation. Instead they stand across the road by the chain-link fence, on a piece of broken pavement that might be in Wichita, or Buffalo, or Pensacola, or Houston, in the summer of 1992.

A line of city police has taken up position down the middle of the street. They have painted a white line near the curb (not tidy, edged with little dribbles and blurs) to mark the legal limit of the demonstration. This keeps the protestors away from the clinic door, so they cannot press leaflets into the limp hands of girls escorted in for abortions, nor shout in their faces. But they have decided to drop those tactics anyway. Instead, they will simply pray and lie down in the street, daring the authorities to take violent action against them. The parallel with the Jews is not exact; these protestors face nothing worse than handcuffs and rough pushing. Yet in one respect the scenes are identical: the protestors feel themselves so empowered by God's approval that nothing can hurt or deter them.

The police are well aware of this. They know that nothing will induce these people to leave the street and go home. Even force, were they to use it – and they have been told not to – will founder against the certainty of the just and holy cause. Violence would be easy, they have been trained to counter that. But against the passive and believing, what action can they take? Facing two dozen women, a clutch of children, six preachers in suits, the Police Department knows it is of no more consequence than a wire-mesh barrier or a decorative fence.

So the officers wait. The day is hot; sweat runs down their faces from under their peaked caps, and damp patches spread on their blue shirts. Police cars have sealed off the street, and the officers carry massive padded armaments at their waists. They cannot use them. Nervously, they keep the protestors confined to a corner and a few dozen yards along the edge of a tired city park of patchy grass and magnolia trees. They treat them with as much fear, and as much distance, as if their faith were a live grenade primed to explode the moment it is thrown in their direction.

The protestors have rigged up a soap box from which, for five minutes each, the preachers speak. Each man has his own Bible, a prop as familiar as a barman's napkin, which flops open to the page confirming their enemies' damnation. They shout towards the clinic's open doors. At intervals the women sing 'Our God is an Awesome God' in voices too soft to carry far. Some, too tired to sing, lean against the fence with rosaries in their hands. They have entrusted to their children the gruesome placards of the trade: colour posters of the head of a foetus in tweezers over a petri dish.

They have spent a night and a day on this. Last night they drove their campers and church vans into the woods to the north of the city. It was raining; their wheels chewed up the lush grass under the trees. In a cheerless barn they took a communal supper of sausages, orangeade and pound cake. Then, with their children on their laps, the mothers watched a slide show of saline-solution abortions and listened to testimonies and songs. At the end of the evening they made posters, while the men tried to find beer and the children ran about outside in the dripping darkness. It was all leading up to this.

Now the six preachers move forward across the demarcation line. Just beyond it they sit down, tucking their legs beneath them. They link arms. 'We come in the Lord's name; he who comes in the Lord's name shall not be confounded,' announces one. The blow-dried heads bend together. 'Amen, brother. Let us not be moved.'

The police do not react at first. They let the preachers huddle at their feet, their heads at the level of the billy-clubs and guns. It is the contact of flesh against flesh they are waiting for: the assault that will allow them to call in reinforcements. But in fact the reinforcements are already here. They poured earlier out of cars parked just round the corner by the Rees Hardware Store, and they have spent the morning working the back rows of the protestors, the women with the pushchairs by the chain-link fence. Aimlessly, still praying, the women stray into the side-street and block the traffic. The police take their arms and lead them back to the fence, while the women go on singing in their soft thin voices.

But the preachers are determined to be arrested. They move forward a little, shuffling on their bottoms, and link arms again. A huge black policeman mutters into his crackling radio, and the blue line begins to buckle. One by one the preachers are picked up and gently hauled into station wagons. Their ties are askew, but their hair is scarcely disordered; their Bibles remain in their hands. Praying, the crowd parts to let them through.

Yet this is only the beginning. The protestors have called in their reinforcements too, and at the police station and the courthouse they are all in place. A vast assembly of bodies lies in the road, singing and praying. These are students, a tangle of jeans and trainers and bright hair; they call themselves 'Lambs of God'. All summer they have been travelling from clinic to clinic, sleeping in city parks or prevailing on the kindness of strangers. When the police pluck them from the roadway they go limp, like weeds pulled from a lake; their long hair brushes the asphalt. If they are left in an open van they escape to lie down again, languidly, wreathed in smiles, in whatever space is left among their sisters and brothers.

The police cannot cope with this. They pick the protestors up; they lie down again. To club them or beat them is uncalled for, for they offer no resistance. Dogs are available, but there is nothing to incite them. Gas would only bring water from those beatific eyes.

From an upper floor of the police station, the chief of operations watches from behind the blinds. No, you will say, he is not like Pilate: no taste for blood, no disposition to shed it, a position of studied neutrality between the right to abortion and the right to free speech. But he too is bound by the imperative to keep order, whatever the cost in terms of his own pride or his own convictions. And he too is astonished, angry, frustrated, as dozens of protestors sway and fall in the street beneath his window.

The noise from outside scarcely penetrates his sanctuary, which is lined with walnut panelling and framed certificates of service. His men have orders not to disturb him unless the situation gets out of hand. Outside is a jumble of bodies, vans and backed-up cars, confined in a criss-cross knitting of blue and white tape. Inside, all is order. At one side of his desk stands the Police Federation flag, at the other the Stars and Stripes, both hung with yellow tassels. On the desk, among the neat papers, he has placed a foil pack of dyspepsia tablets and a cooling cup of coffee. He sits in quiet dread of the press, his superiors, his chances of promotion, the damage to his city's reputation, his own aching bowels. From the bookcase his wife and children beam their encouraging smiles.

It will happen again tomorrow, and the next day. The mild and defenceless will become possessed of an idea that makes them invulnerable. The preacher is lugged by ankles and elbows towards a waiting van. The mother, bottle-feeding a wailing child, is hustled across the sun-baked street. Their posters are torn, their hymns laughed at. But outside the Rees Hardware Store they lie down in His love, and the glow of the victor is in their faces.

*   *   *

Nineteenth-century writers, and later ones too, imagined that Christ would always be judged harshly by the civil authorities. As Thoreau wrote in his essay *On the Duty of Civil Disobedience* in the revolution-year of 1848, referring to government in general, 'Why does it always crucify Christ, and excommunicate Copernicus and Luther, and pronounce Washington and Franklin rebels?'

Thoreau knew the answer perfectly well. Government could never learn to cherish its rebels, because it could not accept that the pointing out of faults or absurdities in the system might be wisdom rather than sedition. Christ's teachings made no sense in the world of power, whether Jewish or Roman. They had to be suppressed. As Pilate asks Jesus in George Bernard Shaw's preface to his play *On the Rocks* of 1933, 'Am I to spare and encourage every heretic, every rebel, every lawbreaker, every rapscallion lest he should turn out to be wiser than all the generations who made the Roman law and built up the Roman Empire on it?' When Jesus warns him against 'killing a thought that is new to you', because it may lead to the kingdom of God, Pilate's retort is immediate: 'It may also be the ruin of all kingdoms, all law, and all human society. It may be the thought of the beast of prey striving to return.'

There was a second objection, deeper and more reasonable. As a proposed framework for government, Christ's teachings did not work. Shaw, in the same preface, made the point with telling brevity. 'History has borne out the case against him; for no State has ever constituted itself on his principles or made it possible to live according to his commandments.' Supposing you could insist by government decree that evil should be countered by good and neighbours loved unconditionally, you could neither govern by that teaching nor uphold any system of punitive law. 'Politically,' as Shaw said, 'it has received no more quarter than Pilate gave it.' Christ's doctrine might be the absolute truth, but it was neither pragmatic nor practical. It couldn't give men what they wanted most urgently, security and bread.

This question was raised by Dostoevsky's Ivan Karamazov in what he called 'this absurd thing', his essay on an imaginary meeting, around 1500, between a Christ who had returned to earth and the cardinal in charge of the Spanish Inquisition. Huddled together in a prison cell in Seville, the two men talk through the night: or rather the cardinal talks, while Christ lovingly observes him. The cardinal explains why he cannot allow Christ to come back and exercise his ministry unimpeded.

He runs through Christ's refusals, during his temptation by Satan in the wilderness, to assume earthly power and, in particular, to turn stones into bread. As a result, he says, Christ has left men leaderless and hungry; he has promised them bread from heaven, when what they crave is order and solid sustenance. His work has therefore been taken over and 'corrected' by the authorities, who resent that he has now returned to bother them. They have replaced damaging freedom with predictable structures of obedience, and have thereby created a world in which, as before, Christ does not fit in.

Ivan called this a 'conversation'. It took place on a night 'heavy with laurel and lemon', and the old churchman, in his simple monk's habit, came to Christ's cell alone with a lamp in his hand. But its form and substance carried strong echoes of the confrontation with Pilate. The cardinal had arrested Jesus to get him off the streets, where his miracles were a nuisance and the adulation he inspired unnerving; and his remarks to him were couched in the form of one long, puzzled, occasionally angry accusation. Again, too, Christ would not defend himself. As it was pointed out to him that his system could not work, because it did not seem to take account of the way the world turned and what men wanted, he merely gazed at the cardinal and, at last, kissed him on the lips.

Christ's teachings threatened not just temporary disturbance, people running and shouting in the street. They also implied the overthrow of institutions and the social order. Those who followed Christ's teachings, as Tolstoy never tired of pointing out, could not logically subscribe to any state that preserved itself by force of arms. They should therefore not only refuse to do military service and protest against all armies, fortifications, monuments, trophies and celebrations, but they should also refuse to pay the taxes that kept the soldiers in readiness. Eventually, by logical extension, they should exclude themselves from any legislative or judicial body, since to vote in elections was to participate in the inherent violence of the government. Both Gandhi and Tolstoy recommended 'non-co-operation with the whole system'. For Gandhi, it was a sin even to eat the wheat that the presence of the army guaranteed for him. 'I said to myself,' he explained, in words that would have struck Pilate as forcefully as they struck the British authorities,

> there is no state either run by Nero or by Mussolini which has not good points about it, but we have to reject the whole, once we decide to non-co-operate with the system. 'There are in our country

grand public roads and palatial educational institutions,' said I to myself, 'but they are part of a system which crushes the nation. I should not have anything to do with them. They are like the fabled snake with a brilliant jewel in its head, but which has fangs full of poison.'

Ideas like this were terrifyingly subversive. They might bring the whole structure down. Jesus before Pilate, the conscientious objector before the general, Galileo before the Pope, all represented in some degree the world turned on its head. There was no way the powers-that-be could allow this, even if they suspected that these thoughts had reason in them. A man had to keep such convictions to himself. If he could not, it would be best to silence him in the name of law and order.

Jesus was therefore not so harmless or blameless, and he might well not have seemed so to Pilate. The Jews were already exceptionally resistant to the Roman state. They balked at paying their taxes, had been let off military service, showed no appreciation for public works. Then came Jesus, who threatened the established order in two ways. He proclaimed indifference to it, seeming to recognise laws of his own; and he was connected by his followers with 'kingship' of a peculiar and ungraspable sort.

The Romans had a dim view of kings, which they incongruously preserved long after the Republic had collapsed and the emperors had seized power. In principle, monarchy should have been the best form of government, one wise head governing the body as Jupiter ruled the universe; but the depraved reign of Tarquinius Superbus had reminded the Romans that where government depended on one man, the vices of that man could turn it to destruction. 'When we think of kingship, we immediately think of an unjust king,' wrote Cicero. 'All those who have power of life and death over a subject people, though they prefer to be called kings, are tyrants.' Few boys in Pilate's day would have escaped the set exercise of delivering a speech against 'The Tyrant', a figure of fantastically stylised violence who could not be confused, even for a moment, with any ruler a Roman boy might know of.

In the end, kingship was incompatible with smoothly functioning government. Caesar himself had understood that. In 44 BC, at the February Lupercalia when the priests of Pan ran naked through Rome, he was offered the crown of a king. It was Mark Antony, naked and drunk and shining with oil like a wrestler, who thrust it towards him. He turned it down. Antony offered it again, a laurel wreath threaded through with white ribbon, and again Caesar refused it. Then he rejected it a third time. Yet he did not object when a citizen placed a crown on his statue, nor to the golden throne set up for him on the rostrum; and even this flirting with crowns, this proximity to them, was suspect to any Roman who cherished the Republic.

Pilate's own relatives, in the different branches of the family, took different views. Lucius Pontius Aquila ('The Eagle'), refused to stand up for Caesar during his triumphal parade and later joined the conspirators who killed him. He spent money to provide soldiers for Brutus in the civil war and gave lodging to Brutus' mother at his house in Naples. Cicero, too, was a friend. Aquila's villa at Trebula – possibly a house Pilate knew, though by then the famous visitors were merely ghosts in the rooms – had been a haven for Republican writing and talk, from which Cicero sent letters pining for the end of tyrants and the restoration of the proper liberties of Rome.

On the other hand, that 'big-hearted centurion' Titus Pontius, a soldier of Caesar's party, had utterly refused to abandon him. When he was taken prisoner by Scipio, Caesar's enemy in the civil war, Scipio offered to spare his life if he would enter his service. Titus replied, in that gruff low-class way of his, 'Thank you, Scipio; my life's not worth that price.' Perhaps the lower down the social scale a man was, the more the thwack of dictatorship attracted him.

Caesar had got perilously close to a crown; but Augustus was more careful. He never allowed himself to be called *Domine*, lord, because it was a title of kings. Although both Caesar and Augustus had since ascended to divinity, both in their earthly lives had affected proper Republican forms. Their decrees had been debated in the Senate; they had refused applause at the games; they had sometimes walked to their business from their unpretentious houses, which, in the case of Augustus, had been decorated by the citizens themselves with garlands of laurel and oak leaves. (That was the house Pilate would have passed: ordinary enough, no Herodian palace, but already glossy and resinous with evergreens, like a sacred grove.) Tiberius too considered *Domine* an insult, monarchy 'a monstrous beast'; he described himself, at least at first, as the servant of the Senate. In contrast, contemporary kings were thought showy, tyrannical, barbarian. They could sometimes put on a gloss of civilisation, as Herod could, but it seemed superficial. They always kept something of the manners of the slaves who were allowed to be kings of every Roman household at the Saturnalia in December: sprawling at the table, coupling in the hall, throwing up at last over their bunched and gorgeous clothes.

The word *rex* was still in polite circulation in Rome: it meant a patron, a man with royal amounts of influence and money. There was also a game that children played: if you jumped or kicked a ball the right way, you were made the king. *Rex erit si recte faciet, qui non faciet non erit:* You'll be king if you do it right, if you don't you won't. But kings' crowns mostly attracted the mad and the unstable, as when in 13, at the horse races held for the Augustalia, a lunatic sat in the chair dedicated to Caesar and put on Caesar's diadem.

A year or so after Pilate's tour in Judea, Flaccus, then governor of Egypt, allowed the Alexandrians to express what civilised people thought of kings – and Jewish kings at that. Agrippa, appointed by Rome as the true King of the Jews, was breaking his voyage in Alexandria in 38, on his way back to assume power in the territories once ruled by Philip and Herod Antipas. The townsmen found a local idiot called Carabas, a gentle fellow who lived on the streets in all weathers, and set him up on a throne in the gymnasium in mockery of Agrippa. A sheet of papyrus was placed on his head as a crown, he was draped stiffly in a carpet, and a papyrus reed was put in his hand. Young men carrying rods made up a bodyguard for him; others pretended to consult him on judicial decisions and matters of state. Carabas nodded and smiled, as kings did when listening to supplicants, while the crowd yelled out '*Maranatha!*' 'Come, Lord!' to the small burbling figure in his big floppy crown.

Soldiers played 'king' games too. At Saturnalia, a man was chosen by lot from the company to be King of the Feast. He would be crowned, dressed in rich robes and allowed to indulge his every whim for thirty days. At the end of this time, puffy, liverish, pale with sexual excess, he had to crawl back to his regiment. A darker version of this rite is said to have happened at the Kronia, another celebration of Saturn: the chosen soldier, after two days' royal licence, would cut his own throat on Saturn's altar. This was known to have happened on the Danube in 303; it was a sacrifice all the more primitive and sinister for taking place in a makeshift temple in the king-haunted woods. Romans who overheard the blood-commemoration of Jesus among early Christians thought it was esentially the same thing, the mysteries of Saturn in the offering of blood.

In Judea, as elsewhere in the empire, the king-game seemed to survive as a barrack-room diversion. In the Antonia garrison, at the foot of the soldiers' stairways, rough symbols for a game called *basilinda*, 'king', have been found carved on the flagstone pavement. The pavement dates from the second century, but the symbols belonged to a game that was older, one which Pilate, too, might have watched his men play: a crown of thorns, a sabre and a 'B' for *basileus*, 'king' in Greek. *Basilinda* was apparently played with knucklebones. At the end of the game the winner would sometimes choose a victim from among the prisoners awaiting execution, crown him, robe him and call the whole company in to salute him before he was crucified.

The climax of the king-game was not complicated. It was played with whatever came to hand. The cloak was an old red army blanket, the sort Pilate would have wrapped himself in on campaigns; the crown was made of any flexible plant that could be plucked and woven quickly. Scholars have insisted on identifying the thorns of the crown that was woven for Jesus; they suppose it was made of *Zizyphus spinaChristi*, *nubk* in Arabic, a common weed round Jerusalem, with flexible twigs and a host of small sharp thorns. Medieval Europeans supposed the material was common furze, with spines like needles; and Mandeville speculated on a series of crowns for Jesus, of whitethorn, eglantine, honeysuckle and (in Pilate's *praetorium*) 'reeds of the sea, which are white, and prick as sharp as thorns.' He saw half of Christ's crown at Constantinople, where it was kept in a glass jar and brought out 'to show to great men and lords' – presumably shaming them to feel, uneasily, the crowns on their own heads.

Such crowns were also woven in mocking imitation of the crowns of leaves the emperors wore, or of the wreaths of laurel awarded to athletes at the games. For all his professed hatred of imperial titles and honours, Tiberius wore such a wreath almost all the time; he believed it kept lightning away. He was also depicted in diadems from which the rays of the sun shone out like thorns. So, by comparison, the most pathetic offenders against his power could be made even sillier and smaller. Cut the thorns, twine them, hold the coronation, and laugh.

★   ★   ★

Who could understand the exact sort of kingship that seemed to hover round Jesus? It was 'near' and 'at hand', as the Jews always said, the Messianic kingdom that was to fulfil God's purpose in Israel. The persecuted would possess it, rather than the powerful, and Pilate's tax-collectors would proceed ahead of the priests through the open gates. This was a kingdom of the poor, the afflicted and the thirsty; the lowest were set highest and the highest lowest, every rational ruler's nightmare. As Jesus pointed out, Romans were not meant to understand this sort of power:

> You know that among the Gentiles those they call their rulers lord it over them, and their great men make their authority felt. But this is not to happen with you. No; anyone who wants to become great among you must be your servant.

A king was presumably in charge of this vaporous domain, but Jesus seemed always to be seeking confirmation and encouragement rather than claiming the kingship for himself. He was the heir of the royal line of David if the people thought he was; he was the equivalent of Moses and Elias, worthy of a tabernacle to shield his divinity, if his followers insisted on it; but the mention of the word 'Messiah' made him flinch and bolt, much as Caesar had bolted from the wreath with the ribbons. After the feeding of the five thousand, according to John, Jesus escaped into the hills rather than be taken and made a king by acclamation. Only at the end, when he wanted to force the issue with Pilate, did he begin to act the king and accept the applause.

His kingdom did not seem to be in Judea, in any case. He disdained the world. The land to which he drew his followers was often the desert, almost the only part of the world still untouched by Rome, where he could shimmer like a mirage before their hunger. Among the wilder stories available to Pilate's spies was one of Jesus spurning the chance to float down through the air, borne up by angels. This single act would have won him the allegiance of the Jews; but he rejected it, just as he rejected the Devil's offer of 'all the kingdoms of the world' spread out in blue and misty ridges under his feet. Like Scipio Africanus, who in a famous dream retailed by Cicero was given an outside view of the universe, he seemed already to know how small the world was and how little space, on that drop of a globe, the Roman empire covered. Earthly realms were inconsequential. His kingdom, he told the Pharisees, was not like this. 'It doesn't come with observation,' he said. 'No one can say, "Oh, look, here it is!" or "There it is!". For the kingdom of God is within you.'

Within you. The thought was perhaps less difficult for a Roman than for a Jew. The Stoics taught that there was indeed a god within you, providing all a man could approximate of virtue and goodness. The poets felt him: 'It is when he stirs us that our breast grows warm,' Ovid wrote. But there was no political connotation in that, no sense of competing lines of authority. You might disdain death, but you did not disdain the state because you were in possession of this secret fire. It made you placid, so that you ceased to care who was promoted over you or who went to which province; but you put up no resistance to doing what the emperor required. This Jewish kingdom of God had a different ring. Interior or not, it suggested danger, as if these people carried round with them, like snakes, a tiny sac of poison in their heads.

Any more indications, any more notes on the subject? These, perhaps, now preserved on a scrap of third-century parchment as 'the Oxyrhynchus Sayings of Jesus':

Judas (not Iscariot) then said: 'Who is it that will draw us to heaven, if that kingdom is in heaven? And when shall it come?'

Jesus said: 'The birds of the air and the beasts of the earth and the fishes of the sea shall draw you to heaven, and also any creatures that are underneath the earth. And the kingdom of heaven is within you, and whoever knows God shall find it; for if you know him, you shall know yourselves. And you shall realise that you are the sons of the Father who is perfect; and you shall know yourselves to be citizens of heaven. For you are the city of God.'

He also said:

'Wherever there are two, they are not without God; and where there is one alone, I say, I am with him. Lift up the stone and there you shall find me; cleave the wood and I am there.'

This was typical of him. The man had been fed questions on what the kingdom he so continually talked of was like: what indications there were that the kingdom was close and what a seeker might look for, like signposts on a road. And he had wittered on about birds and fish! Perhaps he meant that, as before an earthquake, birds would fly in strange erratic circles and animals would dig into the hillsides with frantic claws; or perhaps he meant nothing at all, and was drunk or deliberately misleading. The kingdoms of revolutionaries were always the same. They contained no army, no police, no institutions, no bodies of law, no currency; just idlers, love, wine, curved knives. Yet they were not always easy to crush, for all that. Dreams could be slippery.

Lift up the stone and there you shall find me; cleave the wood and I am there.

Cleave the wood. In the balsam gardens of Judea the harvesters took their knives and opened the wood of the tiny crooked trees. A knife of steel would kill them; the men used only knives of bone, knives of stone, or a splinter of glass. Their hands were poised steady, not daring to tremble in case they cut too deep. Just under the bark lay perfection. It dribbled out, drop by tiny drop, bright white and viscous as olive oil, spreading on the air the perfume of heaven. Was that God? Why not? Only men and gods wept, and those white drops were called tears too, tears as precious as pearls. So you could catch God as the harvesters did, on tufts of wool, and squeeze him in a conch shell. You could adulterate him with gum, almond oil, rose oil, resin, wax, turpentine and honey that drew flies in swarms. You could sell him, inflate his price. And when he had hardened into red-white opaqueness, you broke him and ground him.

Or think about this. *Lift up the stone and there you shall find me.* God in the stone. That in itself was hard enough to picture. A creature lived and grew; a stone slept, rolled on the river bed. There was nothing motive there. It lay inert. Only with the greatest effort could man put God into a stone. But consider how a spark was struck out of it by flint, or by the metal tip of a boot. Was that divinity? By night the spark flared gold, by day ice-blue; in that tiny burst of energy, it was not impossible to believe that a god secreted himself. Epicurus said that the whole world and the gods themselves were made of atoms like these, and that somehow life flowed among them. You could not know for certain whether and when they lived or died, but in their thousands and millions, rising and subsiding, they formed the shape of everything there was. Was that God? Why not?

But wait; God *under* the stone. God in the dark damp earth, or slithering like a millipede. God like a toad, squatting immobile before moving off, hand over plump spread-fingered hand. God in the dry leaves, in the wood-ash, in the papery carapaces of woodlice that stirred and blew away. His kingdom was there even in the rubbish of creation. Every morsel of detritus smouldered with its own transferable fire.

So God was acted on, eroded, rolled on a river bed, flung out to sea, tossed in the air. You too could kick God, and flick him flatly over the waves so that he jumped like a fish. But his kingdom was coming, and at any moment you might start to feel it shift and burn under your feet.

What else did he say it was?

A sower sowing seed. Some good, some scorched, some in the thorns.
Bundles of tares burning. But the wheat is in the barn.
Birds nesting in the branches of a mustard tree.
Yeast in a loaf.
Treasure in a field.
A pearl of great price.
A net cast into the sea. Fish.
Labourers hired, different hours, same wage.
A king forgiving a debtor. (Does this happen?)
A wedding party, but nobody comes.
Oil for lamps.

You couldn't proceed against such a kingdom. It was in men's heads. To crush it with troops would make as much sense as sending the infantry in among those mustard-trees, flailing with their swords until they sent up a storm of yellow petals; or into the rush-topped houses to impale the loaves of bread. It was true that you could detect a sort of revolutionary swarming in the metaphors of yeast rising and seeds sprouting; but some of the plants were choked before they grew, and the leavening stopped at three measures of meal. This kingdom's expansive potential did not go on indefinitely. It petered out, and you were left with peculiarly placid images: an old woman baking, a merchant holding a perfect pearl. Few things were more harmless than a solitary man gloating.

Yet the stories had their violence, all the same. The tares burned, and the bad fish writhed stiff-backed on the beach. There was weeping and gnashing of teeth. Jesus said his teaching would burst old bottles like fermenting wine. He was a stone on which people would break their shins, or which would smash them to powder when it fell on them. Peace, he once said, was not his purpose. He had come to bring a sword, and his followers were sometimes urged to buy them; he had come to 'cast fire on the earth'. So much for being harmless as doves, without shoes, without even a satchel in which to carry stones; so much for turning the other cheek and disarming your enemies with love. In his sermons Jesus had preached a doctrine of passive resistance to authority. It was the meek, not the brutal, who would inherit the earth. Yet he also implied that the meek would wreak havoc before, with gentle smiles, they proclaimed themselves the winners.

What could a governor do? He could go on ignoring the trouble, let it fester. But then again, he needed to know how dangerous this man was. He needed to know how hard he should hit him. You could put a man in prison; that cooled his heels, especially if, like Tiberius, you then affected to forget him. You could cudgel the noisier elements: this was relatively restrained but, as experience had taught him, hard to control. After that you could lash with a whip or a rope, stringing up the culprits perhaps to dangle by their feet, though this was no worse than the punishment given to slaves for dropping a glass or staunching a shaving-cut with the wrong colour of wool; it was called 'reviewing the accounts'. Men survived all this easily, and women were even said to pity their scars. Like slaves who had just been emancipated, they were said still to carry the marks of their master's slaps.

When all this had failed, you could start to draw blood. Scourge with the flat blades, then with the shards of bone. Flat blades were for the better class of criminal – Alexandrians insisted on them – but bone-shards opened the skin like razors, and the flow of blood was exciting and astonishing. It was what you went to the games for, the bright sudden gash of crimson and the spattering on the sand. *Occide! Verbera!* Kill him! Flog him! You changed your seat if you couldn't see it; you cursed the organiser if the action was not right in the centre of the ring. And then you yelled, as one of the fighters began to collapse, *Adhibe!* Lay it on!

It was hard to recover from that sort of arousal except to go again, or to do it again. Yet punishment or entertainment was not the only purpose. The blood that spilled was beautiful. At certain seasons it could seem that the whole land was drenched with it to propitiate the gods. On the sea-shore it soaked into the sand, a sacrifice to Neptune, tinting with pink the floating froth of the waves. Under the pine trees it painted with dark purple the turf sacred to Diana; it ran red in the streams, bubbled thickly in the fountains. The word *sanguinis* itself was beautiful, with that aching lean on the first syllable; *sanguine donem*, wrote Horace, let me give by blood. Each pastoral had its perfect ending in sacrifice. The victim that grazed on snowy Algidus among the oaks and ilexes, or grew fat on the Alban grass, would dye with its neck's blood the axes of the priests:

> *victima pontificum securis*
> *cervice tinguet.*

There was nothing violent in this. The blood tinged the blades, barely disturbing the peace of the scene. The blood-soaked earth, like black peat, showed up the fragility of the flowers that were strewn on it. As for the victim, it was commended to the altar by its beauty and innocence: the pure white kid, the lamb with horns just budding, the boar 'just practising its first sidelong thrusts'. The sight of red against white was particularly favoured: blood against new wool, or, as Propertius wrote, scarlet petals floating on milk. The most longed-for Tyrian purple to border white robes was the colour of congealed blood, 'blackish at first glance but gleaming in the light.' It was possible, of course, bloodlessly to propitiate the gods by touching the altar with pure hands, burning incense and spreading over the stone meal mixed with rock-salt. But altars were described as yearning, like the worshippers, to see blood spilled on them at the behest of the priests.

In Judea, Pilate possessed every kind of blood-spilling power. He offered sacrifice; it was his business to sever the throat-vein and watch as the blood flowed, scarlet on white, staining his own clothes in expiation or propitiation. He held gladiatorial combats and, as magistrate or military commander, he could kill people. This was called *ius gladii*, the right of the sword, although the sword was used only for Roman citizens or, conversely, rebels *en masse*. The others got the cross. This was the ultimate punishment, the most painful, the most protracted, the most public. For the Jews in particular, it was the last curse recorded in the law of God: men crucified, by whatever authority, were supposed to have incurred God's particular emnity.

The Roman attitude was more confused. This *arbor malus* or *lignum infelix* – bad tree, unhappy wood – was not the most violent or bloody of deaths. For brutality, it could hardly compare with being torn to pieces by wild beasts, or with the punishment for parricides, which was to place the culprit in a sack with a dog, a cock, a snake and an ape and to throw the sack into the sea. (Even the morally acute Cicero could call this, without a qualm, 'bagging people'.) Against such fantastic horrors, or even in the context of the daily treatment meted out to slaves, the cross could seem almost mundane. *I ad malam crucem!* 'Go and hang yourself!' was a common insult, to which the common retort was: 'I'd *rather* be hanged' (than eat with you, or listen to your stories, or sit beside your wife). And although Cicero thought the language brutal, a hapless man was commonly said to be 'really setting up a cross for himself.' Pilate's reported retort at the trial, 'Take him and crucify him yourselves', had something of this spirit: Do what the hell you like with him.

The chief horror of the cross lay in the time it took a man to die, by asphyxiation or dehydration; and in its shame. It was a punishment for slaves, bandits, hoodlums, foreign miscreants. A man could not get lower. He was *corvorum cibia*, crow-food. As Justin Martyr put it, 'Why on earth should we believe that a crucified man is the son of God?' You might as well believe that a worm was. Once a man was on the cross his relatives would keep trying to take him down to bury him, so getting him out of the public eye; and this made crucifixion, awful as it was, also something of a black comedy. In dinner-party stories soldiers set to keep watch would fall asleep, go off to supper, get distracted by girls, and come back to find the body gone; they would then have to run around finding another, on pain of ending up on the cross themselves. In the 30s, and possibly earlier, there was a hit play called *The Crucified Bandit* in which the star was 'crucified' on stage, tried to escape, and had to vomit blood while the audience guffawed. Yet the laughter did not completely hide the terror; as Maecenas wrote, this was the worst thing a Roman could imagine happening to a man.

> Fashion me with a palsied hand,
> Weak of foot, and a cripple;
> Build upon me a crook-backed hump;
> Shake my teeth till they rattle;
> All is well, if my life remains.
> Save, oh, save it, I pray you,
> Though I sit on the piercing cross!

Seneca capped this in one sentence: 'I think he would find many excuses for dying even before mounting the cross.'

A governor could make good propaganda from this punishment. It offered maximum deterrence with minimum involvement. He could supervise a flogging, urge it on, number the strokes, but the only exercise of his power at a crucifixion was to pronounce the sentence and then dictate it for the charge-sheet. It could be done as imperiously as the emperor did it at the games: a signal, the downturned thumb, the casting down of two sticks to make the shape of the cross. '*Staurotheto*' was all that needed to be said. The accused dragged his own load to some benighted spot outside town. Florus, one of Pilate's successors, got more involved; he had some Romanised Jews crucified right in front of him, below the terrace where Pilate scourged Christ. Flaccus in Egypt, apparently not wanting to miss the details of such deaths, turned some crucifixions of Jews into a show at the circus. They were hauled to the cross through the orchestra pit; the second act featured flautists and dancers.

The governor's heavy hand was meant to be moderated by information, investigation, inquiry, even full-blown trials. Philo claimed that Pilate did not bother much with these. He may have been right. If you wanted a short cut, there were useful catch-all charges available, of which the most useful was *maiestas*. Tacitus called this the most momentous of all offences: 'the crime of damaging or threatening the majesty of the R'oman people' or doing anything that might be thought prejudicial to their interests. The majesty of the Roman people was naturally summed up in the person of the emperor, and the emperor was high magistrate, high priest and god apparent; therefore, as Ulpian wrote later, the crime of *maiestas* was next to that of sacrilege. Every Roman official in the provinces was alert to the least whiff of *maiestas*, and it is notable that wherever in the *Acta Pilati* Pilate wants to underline an order by an oath, he swears 'by the safety of Caesar', as if invoking a spell against treason.

Under Tiberius, the concept of *maiestas* had been enormously expanded: 'pushed to the bitter end', as Dio Cassius said. The death penalty was now applied for criticising anything the emperor had ever said or done, for wearing robes like his, and for allowing honours to be voted to you on the same day as they had been voted to him. In the most notorious occurrence, a man was executed for *maiestas* because, in Tiberius' own words, 'with my coin in your bosom you turned aside into a foul and loathsome latrine and emptied your bowels.' Roman officials like Pilate, who were happy in most cases to leave their subject people in charge of their own courts, were expected to intervene with the utmost brutality over a coin, a set of clothes, or a half-joking claim to a piece of the emperor's power. Any dreaming tinkerer, like Daedalus, could potter along at low altitudes, but the flier who approached the sun would plummet downwards, as Icarus had plummeted, blinded by filaments and quills.

Jesus did not make such a claim directly for many months. He refused to be the leader of any Jewish national movement. But when, in the end, he accepted the title of Messiah, he was setting himself up as an alternative centre of power. In the episode of the tribute money, Caesar's authority and God's were simply and directly opposed to each other: Jesus was offering a kingdom unstained by money, a spiritual ideal rather than an earthly place. If his title was purely spiritual, it could be tolerated by Rome; but, as Justin Martyr pointed out, when Romans heard that anyone was seeking a kingdom, they could only assume it was a human one. No other sort made sense. Besides, it was gradually becoming clear that the Jews were flocking to Jesus in the expectation, misguided or not, that he would overthrow the Romans.

Mark's gospel confirms that there was an 'insurrection' that Passover, as a result of which Barabbas was arrested for murder and other 'rebels', among them Jesus, were arrested for miscellaneous trouble-making. Offenders like this were generally called *lestai,* a word which could translate as robber, brigand or mischief-maker; the Good Samaritan soothed with his ointment a victim of *lestai,* and these were also the 'thieves' that Jesus expelled from the Temple. They were not necessarily, or even usually, political, but they were dangerous. Indeed it is hard to say how dangerous, at this point, Jesus was. Just before the disruption, outside Jerusalem, Luke's Jesus ended his parable of the king and his servants with the words: 'Bring my enemies here, the ones who do not wish me to reign over them, and kill them in front of me.' The Slavonic version of Josephus makes the trouble even more explicit: Jesus and his followers came to Jerusalem at that festival deliberately to mount a coup against Pilate and, if necessary, to kill him.

The governor was probably already in Jerusalem. The cold unused beds were being turned over, and blazing fires lit in the rooms. We know, from Peter's attempts to warm himself by a charcoal brazier in the tavern as he denied Jesus, that the weather was bitter. Some biographers have fancied that Pilate was in the city for some serious partying, but it is hard to imagine that he played any role in the Jewish holidays. He probably kept to the company of his entourage or of any Romans who happened to be in town, dining and entertaining on a small scale and nervously sniffing the air for the trouble that was predicted.

The city was filling up fast, and not only with worshippers. *Sicarii,* bandits from the wilderness, came into the city at every festival, hoping to use the crowd as a cover for the various killings they had planned. Mingling unobtrusively, they would find their man and silence him. They also had a habit of kidnapping officials' slaves on the eve of festivals, forcing them to be exchanged for *sicarii* held in prison. Governors after Pilate gave in to them simply in the hope of keeping the city quiet. That, after all, was the reason they were there and not in Caesarea.

Two days before that Passover in 33 – or perhaps in 30, for the year has never been determined exactly – thousands of Galilean pilgrims streamed towards Jerusalem. This was not unusual. What was unusual was that Jesus was in the midst of them, riding on an ass. The ass was stolen. As he rode along, the dusty peasant pilgrims threw their coats in the road. The gesture was heavy with political symbolism, as the whole scene was. Jesus had taken the ass in accordance with the words of Zachariah: 'Rejoice greatly, O daughter of Zion;/ behold/ your king comes to you . . . /He is just, and having salvation . . . /lowly, and riding upon an ass/ and his dominion shall be from sea to sea,/ and from the river even to the ends of the earth.' The strewing of coats was based on the description in the Second Book of Kings of how the king should come, 'when every man took his garment and put it under him.' The crowd then broke off palm fronds and waved them, just as they had been waved for Judas Maccabeus on his triumphal entry into Jerusalem. Judas had retaken the Temple, cleared out the filth of the Gentiles and restored the menorah with its magical oil. The cleansing Jesus proposed was of the Temple too, which for the moment the Romans were leaving alone. But there was no indication to the nervous authorities that he would stop there. He came as a king, and only Pilate in Jerusalem approximated that sort of power.

Some commentators have imagined that the procession was patently dangerous. The crowd was shouting subversive things. Over the years, 'Hosanna' has been changed into a chant of angels; but on that day, some say, it was a revolutionary slogan hurled against Rome. 'Hosanna, save us now, son of David!' The Galileans yelled it as they surged into the city, and the people coming out of the city took it up too; later, youths went rampaging through the Temple shouting 'Save us! Save us!'

Some of the noise must have carried to the western hill, where Pilate among the inlaid furniture was reading or eating or dictating reports. Whether it carried or not, the tumult would soon have been reported there. The *Acta Pilati* are probably right to suggest that Pilate had no idea what the chants meant, though once they had been translated he might have realised the significance of 'Son of David' by himself. About 'Messiah-King' there was no doubt. Caiaphas could have given him the scriptural references, and they were not encouraging. Pilate may well have imagined he faced a full-scale revolt.

It contained, from the Christian viewpoint down the centuries, disarming elements of gentleness. Jesus on the humble donkey, moving slowly. Peasants with mud-stained clothes, large hands and patient eyes, the normally unprotesting lower classes mobilised into bewildered enthusiasm. Children shouting, with their innocent piping voices. A sea of palm fronds, green and pale yellow, taken from the tree that symbolised peace. So docile was this demonstration that the authorities did nothing right away, as if transfixed by the virtue of the show. But Caesar himself had declared that palm-fronds meant victory, as well as peace. They were carried in triumphs in Rome, and many of them, in a stroke of irony, came from Herod's own great groves of trees in Judea. Real violence was likely, and as soon as the crowd was inside the city gates there came the shocking scene of Jesus in the outer court of the Temple, throwing over the money-changers' tables and freeing the beasts and birds: the creatures that would lead men to the kingdom of heaven.

Only John's gospel puts events in this order, but the sequence makes sense, especially to those who see Jesus as a revolutionary and a freedom-fighter. This was the necessary confrontation, the provocation that tyrant-Pilate would be unable to resist. Again, everything was symbolic: the trashing of the tables with their piles of dirty *denarii*, Tiberius' money and Pilate's money, and the liberation of the innocents trussed for sacrifice. Jesus laid about him as he did this with a scourge of short cords, and when the business was done he retired with his disciples. Yet neither the Jewish nor the Roman authorities intervened to arrest him; the powers-that-be were either unimpressed with this display, or they were content to wait.

Jesus, however, was already on his guard. In response to the presumed awakening of the Roman authorities, he had become slippery and secret. He led his disciples to a house with deliberately tortuous directions. ('When you enter the city, you will see a man with a pitcher of water. Follow him into the house he enters . . .') In the upper room where Jesus held the last supper and established the Eucharist, his disciples prepared the weapons. Even allowing for later suppression of the part Jesus played in the riot in Jerusalem, it is clear that there were swords about and that, few as they were, they were going to be used. Jesus may have loved his enemies and willingly arranged his death at their hands, but these dispositions were never transferred to his disciples. They hated the Romans and, if the Romans at last were provoked into lunging at Jesus, they intended to fight back.

This was a serious situation. Pilate may have been tempted to take pre-emptive steps to keep order: one of his successors, Felix, massacred 400 people after the mere appearance of an Egyptian sorcerer on the Mount of Olives. On the other hand, the priests were saying (and Pilate probably heard) that if Jesus were so much as arrested at the feast, it would cause uproar. Some scholars think Pilate must have consulted with the priests before Jesus was arrested; he needed to know what they thought of his claims, and the priests needed to be sure that the governor would get up early enough the next day to hold the trial and finish the business before the Sabbath began. It may have been Pilate, the man who had chosen the cover of night to sneak the standards into Jerusalem, who suggested that controversy might be avoided if Jesus were arrested at night too. Christ's more romantic biographers imagined that Pilate's palace was full of news of this man, deadening the dinner conversation; this was why Procula dreamed of him. And as she took the wine-cup from her husband, softly placing her lips over the mark of his own as wives and lovers did, Jesus in the garden was resisting and then accepting the cup of death that God offered him.

John's gospel put Pilate even closer, involving him in the arrest itself. When Caiaphas sent out the Temple guard by night to Gethsemane, carrying their lanterns, John suggests that 'a captain and a troop of soldiers' (the *speira*, or cohort of 600 men, responsible for festival duty in the western porticoes of the Temple) went along too as Pilate's contribution. This seems a ludicrously large number, and it is odd that they did not bring the prisoner back to him; but John was perhaps writing mystically here, of the gathering of Satan's forces in whatever guise the soldiers might have been. Certainly the gospels record Jesus' surprise that he should be subject to a full military arrest. For their part, John's soldiers, Roman-auxiliary and Jewish alike, reacted as evil forces were bound to in the presence of God. When Jesus confirmed that he was the man they were seeking ('I am he'), they staggered backwards and fell to the ground.

The disciples resisted with violence. Peter, with his sword, cut off the ear of the high priest's servant. But Jesus healed him, restoring the message of loving non-resistance. He said, 'Do you think I can't pray to my father and that he can't instantly send me twelve legions of angels? But how then shall the scripture be fulfilled?' He could have hurt them if he wanted to, as he told Pilate later, but there was nothing to be gained by hitting back. He wanted them to hit him; he was still the man in charge.

As both a man of violence and a man of love, Jesus was interrogated and mocked by Caiaphas and the priests. He stood before them saying virtually nothing. In such a situation, he had told his disciples, when they were brought before 'governors and powers', the Holy Spirit would tell them what to say. In the presence of the priests, the spirit apparently told him to say nothing. And these men, deciding that he deserved death – in fact, as Caiaphas said, that he was the 'one man' whose death might placate Pilate and forestall reprisals against the whole nation – led him bound to the governor's palace.

They could not arrange his death themselves. Blasphemy, the crime of which they accused Jesus, was a religious charge. Pilate could no more touch this than he could touch the Temple. But the penalty, stoning sometimes followed by hanging, was one the Jews had relinquished, at least in its official and judicial form. All that remained was non-judicial lynching, as when they had wanted to stone the woman taken in adultery, and when they had taken up stones to do the same to Jesus not so long before. If they had tried to kill Jesus that way, Pilate would not have tried to stop them. But Jesus had to fulfil prophecy by dying on a cross; and, even without that mystical compulsion, there were other urgent reasons why the governor should have come on the scene.

The Jews seemed to want Pilate to assuage his presumed hunger for blood with this man. So far, he had sent no armies to pursue Jesus and made no attempt to kill him in battle. Other prefects faced with would-be kings had felt no hesitation; but the claims of Jesus were perhaps too nebulous, and his followers too few. The machine that would crush Jesus would not be military. But there remained the might of the criminal law, which also fed on blood.

*　　*　　*

Meanwhile, in the York play, Judas had repented. The heavy bag of money burned him, so that he limped like a beggar. Under the tall eaves, in the dark, he skittered past. The beadle snoozed at the base of Pilate's platform, among the brocade and gilt chairs; in the chairs lounged Pilate, Annas and Caiaphas, drinking.

'Hey, Judas, what tidings?' called Pilate cheerfully.

'Painful tidings, Sir Pilate, I tell you,' he stammered.

'Oh, surely not.'

Judas, whimpering with terror, explained that he had changed his mind. He no longer wanted to sell Jesus; he wanted Pilate to let him go, take the money back. The two priests, like two fussing wimpled women, began exclaiming at once: 'No, no, no, can't have that!' But Pilate took over the conversation: he was suddenly, fiercely awake.

'Who needs what you think?' he yelled at Judas. 'You unhanged harlot, listen to me. Spare your speeches, there's no point; or get out of here and go to the devil!'

'Why, does that mean – you won't let him go? You won't take the money back?'

'No, traitor, I won't.'

Judas began to cry. 'Then I'm lost,' he whispered. 'Lost in bone, lost in blood. Why did I ever agree to get him killed?' His voice rose in pain, and in a sudden convulsion he threw down the money on the floor. It rolled everywhere. 'Please, sirs, spare him!' he screamed. 'Take back your money, all of it! Spare him, I beg you! I can't bear it!'

Pilate stood up, swaying slightly on his feet; his heavy dazzling robe seemed to hold him up, like a statue draped for a pageant. 'Now look, Judas, listen to me,' he said. 'Just take that money back again. We don't want it. What the devil's up with you? When you first came to see us, you wanted this money badly. What's changed now to make you repent?'

Judas was on his knees, scrabbling for the coins. He gathered a handful, two handfuls, jumped up, and, still sobbing, thrust the money into Pilate's hands. Those hands were limp; the coins clattered once more to the floor. 'Again, I'm giving it to you again,' wept Judas. 'It's to save him from ruin. That's what I mean.'

'You ruined him yourself,' said Pilate sharply. 'You stupid fool.'

He replenished his cup. Offstage, a drum began to beat. But Judas suddenly knelt among the coins and clung to Pilate's robe. 'I know my guilt,' he whispered. 'I wish I could save him. I would do anything. Sir, if you save him, I'll bind myself to your service. I'll be your bond man for ever. Sir Pilate, you can trust me! You'll find me utterly faithful – you know that –'

The red head buried itself in the folds of the robe; but Pilate brusquely detached himself.

'Find you faithful?' he snapped. 'By Mahound's blood, I think you'd sell us all.'

'Have mercy, lord, have mercy, have mercy!' moaned Judas. 'I'm wicked, I'm wretched, I've done wrong, but please have mercy on my master!'

'Go to hell!' cried Pilate. 'I don't want to hear any more.'

'No more, he says, no more!' twittered Annas. 'Mumbling mommet, false felon! We've expressly found you guilty!'

'You can keep the money,' gabbled Judas, stumbling backwards. 'May it bring you power. You can claim it's clean, can't you? I loathe my life, my pain torments me; I need ask no mercy, for I know I'll get none. I'll go now and kill myself, for who can I turn to? I'll go and kill myself –'

He bolted from the stage. The drums beat, and roared to a racket; the stage grew dark, and in the dark the coins gleamed on the floor.

'Come now, Sir Pilate,' chirped Caiaphas, 'what are we going to do with this money here? Can't let it lie about.'

'He's slung it, we'll save it!' trilled Annas.

'Quick, take it to the treasury!'

But Pilate said no. It was tainted money, the price of blood; he preferred to buy 'a spot of earth' with it, to give burial to pilgrims and criminals. 'What do you think of that, Sir Caiaphas and Annas?' he asked.

'Exactly as you like, my lord.'

This sounded like a virtuous idea, even one handled with diplomacy. But the York Pilate could not manage virtue. Instead, he had to make his little purchase by trickery. Just at the opportune moment, when the money was in his hands, there came a knock at the door. A squire had come to pay his respects. He bowed deeply to the governor, doffing his feathered hat, calling him 'gayest on ground' and 'loveliest of limb'; and revealed he had a piece of land to sell. Pilate's first question, having brushed the flattery aside, was typical: 'Is it freehold?'

It was. And within a few lines, Pilate had boldly and charmingly stolen it. It was a time-honoured trick; he asked to look at the deeds, on several rolls of parchment tied with ribbons and dangling with seals, and then refused to hand them back. 'I'll keep these quite safe,' he told the squire. 'Take yourself off. I own it now.'

The man stormed out, wild, sending them all to the Devil; and Pilate, with the deeds, smiled a beatific smile. He had purchased Calvary, and he had some good ideas for it. 'This is all very satisfactory,' he told Annas and Caiaphas. 'We've made a proper purchase, gentlemen. I'm going to call it the Field of Blood.' His eyes gleamed, and he snapped: 'That's an order!'

'Very nice, sir,' babbled Annas and Caiaphas. 'We'll call it whatever you like. Must go now.'

'Must go now.'

'Must do something about that lewd lad ... that gadling, that dodderer ... put him to death, you know.'

Pilate raised his cup to them. 'Walk on then, with a vengeance!'

Judas ran through the streets. He barely saw where he was going for the rain and tears that filled his eyes. The dogs barked at him, or turned tail and slunk away; slops from high windows splattered on his shoulders. In an Anglo-Saxon apocryphal gospel he reached his own house, threw himself at the flimsy door, and screamed as he entered: 'Give me a rope!'

His wife was by the fire. Over the hot coals she held a pan with a cockerel roasting in it. She said, 'What do you want a rope for, my love?'

'To kill myself for betraying my master for Pilate to put him to death; because he'll rise again on the third day, and then woe betide us!'

His wife, shaking the pan on the coals, merely laughed. 'What a thing to say. That Jesus is as likely to rise again as this cock I'm roasting on the fire is likely to crow.'

And immediately the cock spread its wings. The wings rose out of the pan among the flames, shining black and green feathers, in a great fan that filled the room; and the cock raised itself on its silver spurs, threw out its breast, and crowed.

Judas seized a halter made from a rope and ran from the house. In the Gréban play four townsmen saw him. 'There goes that Judas again, the dirty villain!' remarked one.

'Drunk again.'

'Drunk again.'

'Fetch the constable!'

'Leave him alone,' said the first. 'Let him get on with it.'

Satan came strolling along the street. 'Poor Judas,' he exclaimed, 'our long-lost brother! We'll help him put himself away. Let's find him a holly tree, where he can hang himself against a blood-red sky. Who can help him? Ah, Despair, step forward!'

Despair introduced himself to Judas; and they shook hands.

Some say he hanged himself on a tamarind tree. That tree was formerly tall and beautiful; but after the hanging it became short and worthless. Or he may have hanged himself, as Mandeville said, on an elder tree growing by the pool of Siloam: Shakespeare's 'stinking elder grief', with its burden of dark fruit. When he dropped to the ground, his blood spread over it: the true Field of Blood.

The cockerel overflew him. Its wings were the onset of night itself, its spurs and eyes the stars. The cockerel was the bridge between the night of the arrest and the morning of the resurrection: it marked the end and the beginning of the world. Its cry humiliated Peter as he sat in the tavern, reminding him that he had denied Christ and that the movement had fallen apart; but it also accompanied the women as they made for the tomb at dawn. Night fell, the cock crew, the day appeared. This bird was no spectator, but an agent in the story; this bird might indeed believe, as the children's poem has it, that his crowing made the sun rise.

Was the cockerel Christ? Yes, at one level. But at another this boastful creature, with his rasping voice, was much closer to the medieval image of Christ's executioner. It was not Christ who strutted through Jerusalem in boots, spurs, sword and glittering brocade; by contrast, Christ was the victim, unassuming as a sparrow. Only Pilate ceaselessly reminded his hearers of his power, his standing, his glow and his golden hair, the refrain of an inveterate preener.

The hour was *gallicinium*, second cock-crow, the fourth and last watch of the Roman night. Over Jerusalem, shrill as a military bugle, the Roman eagle flung his golden wings. Cocorico! *Judicetur!* Let Christ be judged!

5

The great equivocator

'The intriguing thing about Pilate is the degree to which he tried to do the good thing rather than the bad. He commands our moral attention not because he was a bad man, but because he was so nearly a good man. One can imagine him agonising, seeing that Jesus had done nothing wrong, and wishing to release him. Just as easily, however, one can envisage Pilate's advisers telling him of the risks, warning him not to cause a riot or inflame Jewish opinion. It is a timeless parable of political life.

'It is possible to view Pilate as the archetypal politician, caught on the horns of an age-old political dilemma. We know he did wrong, yet his is the struggle between what is right and what is expedient that has occurred throughout history. The Munich Agreement of 1938 was a classic example of this, as were the debates surrounding the Great Reform Act of 1832 and the Corn Laws. And it is not always clear, even in retrospect, what is, in truth, right. Should we do what appears principled or what is politically expedient? Do you apply a utilitarian test or what is morally absolute? . . .

'Christianity is optimistic about the human condition, but not naive. It can identify what is good, but knows the capacity to do evil. I believe that the endless striving to do the one and avoid the other is the purpose of human existence. Through that comes progress.'

Tony Blair, interview in the *Sunday Telegraph*, 7 April 1996

It was dark when he awoke. At the first cock-crow, at that time of year, the moon was often up and shining. At the second cock-crow, the *gallicinium*, night still hung in the silent trees. It must have been around four in the morning. A servant roused him, lighting the fire and opening the shutters to reveal the pale beginnings of the sunrise. The third legion in Syria had once adopted the local practice of saluting the rising sun; it had brought them luck in battle. The *Acta Pilati* imagined that Pilate, too, would have saluted it; later that day this account had him washing his hands 'before the sun', the god of purification. Most later writers have liked to think that he ignored it, eyes screwed up, head aching from the fun of the night before; and that it was in this state, hung-over and resentful, that he embarked on the day that was to seal his place in history.

In fact, it was not unconscionably early for him. Back in Rome it was not unusual for clients to get up and dress in the dark, in order to be the first to pay their morning respects to their patrons. Lawyers too started the court day at dawn, so that by three in the afternoon the business day would be over. Horace in one of his letters rejoiced in this arrangement: 'At Rome it was long a pleasure and a habit to be up at dawn with open door, to set forth the law for clients.' Others, to be sure, took a different view. Martial wrote that one of the chief delights of going to the country was that 'the pale defendant will not break your sleep, and you can dream all through the morning'. But Pilate's dreams had fled already, and the pale defendant was approaching.

There was not much dressing to be done. He had probably slept in his under-tunic, as was the custom in cold weather. His shoes were by the bed; a servant put them on him and laced them. This was the first essential. To walk around barefoot was slovenly, and the marble floor was cold. He splashed his face, washed his teeth, passed water in a brass pot held by a slave, made sure his nails were clean. His official tunic with its broad purple stripe (a stripe that still smelled vaguely of shellfish–dye) was put on him; a fresh toga was placed over his head and carefully arranged on his shoulders. He drank perhaps one glass of water, chewed a piece of bread. If he felt his breath was bad, he could pop in a freshening pastille; in later years, Cosmus' was the recommended brand. Then, seated in a chair by the window, he gave himself over to the attentions of his barber.

The light was still dim; too murky to see his stubble by and perhaps too bad to read, if he had wanted to try. Lamps would be lit to illuminate the scene. The razor scraped across his chin, his cheeks, the nape of his neck. Water dripped in the basin. A little aromatic oil was smoothed across his hair. All this was perfectly normal, routine. Yet it was not just another day in his life. There were perhaps 100,000 people in the city, three times the normal population, and he was in the middle of trouble. The judgements he had to make would be easy at one level but vexed at another, when he had to consider how the crowd would react. He was keeping order like a soldier, but he had to be careful like a politician; and he was not good at this.

It was – to take one of the possible dates at random – the sixth before the Kalends of April. This was not in itself inauspicious. The unlucky days were those that immediately followed the Kalends, the Ides or the Nones; these, and some others, would be marked in his calendar with the letter N as *nefastus*, unlawful. On those days, in Rome, the courts could not open. Other days were partly lawful: on NP days (*nefastus parte*) the morning was unlawful, but if the gods were propitiated with sacrifice the afternoon could be used for court business; on EN days (*endotereisi*), hearings were allowed in the middle of the day. There remained the days, like this one, that were reminders of previous troubles. It is probable that the dates around Passover were already marked in his calendar with the special dots or seals proclaiming them unlucky, *auspicio malo*.

At such times, even an unsuperstitious man might start to look for auguries and signs: the wavering flight of birds, water spilled on a table, the left shoe put on unluckily before the right in the dark. If a man of great power were about to appear, palm trees would spring from cracks in the paving stones, put out suckers and draw wild pigeons to nest in their branches. Yellowing sprays of ilex or laurel suddenly revived. Eagles perched on the roofs of houses, or were seen flying where they had never ventured before. They fought with crows and defeated them. Some even swooped down to take food, as one had snatched a piece of bread from Augustus as he dined in a wood at the fourth milestone on the Campanian Road; after soaring to a prodigious height, it dived down again and returned it to him. Before the fall of Sejanus crows had flocked round him and cawed as he took the auspices, and a weasel had darted through the crowd outside his house. Perhaps omens of this sort had already been spotted in Jerusalem and Pilate, too busy, had missed them.

Even good omens had to be received correctly. A sneeze had to be greeted with *Salve!* 'Good health!' – Tiberius insisted on this, even when out in his carriage. A sputtering lamp had to be calmed with a few careful drops of wine, an empty eggshell pierced or crushed as soon as the egg had been eaten. A bad omen – even one as slight as a misformed cloud, a dropped glass, a horse stumbling – called for certain precautions. To ensure your physical safety you could touch your hand to your heart, murmuring *salvum sit, quod tango*, 'May what I touch be safe.' You could rebuff the evil omens by saying *longe a nobis*, 'be far from us', sprinkle wine under the table, or change the rings on your right hand. If you were at dinner, you could kiss the table; at home, you could kiss the shrine of the household gods, wishing all the while for the horror to stay away.

Pilate that morning would probably have stood before the shrine anyway, with his head covered and with as many members of his household as he could gather, to pour out the wine and make the morning invocations. This was how the business day started, except in the worst emergency. His statuettes of household gods would probably have travelled with him from Caesarea, rather as Aeneas journeyed with his from Troy to Latium. And they would have included a little bronze or gold Tiberius, perhaps the one to whom Pilate directed his most earnest prayers. It did not need to take long: *Bene nos, bene te, pater patriae, optime Caesar,* was the brief and acceptable form. He would touch the altar as he prayed, or lift his arms with the palms upwards; the burning grains of incense crackled in a bowl. Servants, or children if he had any, might deck the little statues with flowers clumsily knotted together. He could give an extra touch to Apollo, the god of good luck. And perhaps all that would be enough to keep him safe.

He was probably forewarned of the delegation that brought Jesus to the palace. Since his first question to the chief priests, inquiring about the charges, was a formal one, it did not necessarily mean he was ignorant of the case. When Paul was tried before Felix and later before Festus, the Roman governor on each occasion specifically asked the accusers to bring their complaints to him beforehand. And this was how the medieval writers imagined the case of Jesus was handled.

In the York play, Annas, Caiaphas and a Jewish doctor come to Pilate complaining about Jesus before Judas has even thought of selling him. Pilate agrees that 'if that wretch in our ward has wrought any wrong', he will act. But he feels they are too angry, doesn't quite understand. 'Isn't he the one you said would come down to help you?' he asks. This prompts an exasperated remark from Caiaphas: 'Ah, please sir, shut up.'

On the evening before the trial, according to the fourth-century fantasies of the *Acta Pilati*, Pilate sat up late discussing the case of Jesus with Caiaphas, Levi, Nephlahim and the rest of the chief priests. Together, they were drawing up a charge-sheet against him; or rather, the priests were arguing the charges among themselves, while Pilate sat in bewilderment. He was still unconvinced of the danger of Jesus, and the priests were furious at his obtuseness. 'Well, then,' they cried, 'we beseech your Majesty to summon him here before your judgement seat and examine him properly. Then you can find out yourself whether what we are saying is true or not.'

'Tell me, how can I, a governor, examine a king?' asked Pilate.

'We're not calling him a king. That's what he says of himself,' said the priests.

Pilate decided to summon Jesus. He called a messenger and ordered Jesus to be brought to him, 'but with gentleness'. Then, taking off his own cloak, he handed it to the messenger. 'Go and show this to Jesus,' he told him, 'and say, "Pilate the governor asks you to come to him".'

The messenger went out and, when he found Jesus, knelt and worshipped him. He spread Pilate's cloak on the dusty ground, one more robe on the Messiah's path of triumph, and invited him to dismount and come to the *praetorium*. 'Lord,' he said, 'walk on this robe and come this way, for the governor calls you.'

Jesus began to follow him. Meanwhile, the Pilate of the *Acta* waited in the *praetorium*. In the centre stood the judgement seat; around the walls, the golden standards. Pilate had removed them from the public gaze to display them here, as if in a private sanctuary. Sometimes they were fixed to the walls; sometimes, as today, each was held by an unmoving guard. The early sun gave them the barest illumination. And among them, furious, stood the chief priests. The *Acta* and the medieval plays, heedless of the laws of ritual impurity, always put the priests right in with Pilate, even letting them give him elementary Hebrew lessons, while they waited for Jesus to appear. They had much to upbraid him about. 'Why did you send a messenger to get him?' they cried. 'That messenger spread your robe on the ground and let him walk on it like a king! Why on earth do you think him worthy of an honour like that?'

As Pilate tried to explain himself, there was a commotion at the door. The guest, or rather the prisoner, was arriving. Pilate tensed himself instinctively. But then, all of a sudden, something else happened. The standards along the wall bowed down, a long rippling wave of white and gold crested with brass; they made obeisance right to the floor, coiling like bright snakes from the arms of their astonished handlers.

The banners bowed down in the York play, too, and Pilate leapt from his seat. He was terrified. 'What the hell are you doing?' he cried. 'You're bowing to this wretch? Are you mad? Put them up again!'

'Sir, we had nothing to do with it, sir!'

'The standards bowed themselves, sir! We couldn't hold them – we tried –'

'Take the prisoner back,' ordered Pilate, in a cold fury. 'And put the standards up again. Now –' he snapped his fingers for a centurion, who came running – 'I want six men to every standard. I want you to hold them here, right in front of the judgement seat. If they bend one hair's breadth when the prisoner is brought in, I swear by the safety of Caesar that I will cut off your heads. Is that understood?'

'Sir.'

The reinforcements crowded in, six to each standard, their bodies contorted like wrestlers at a fair. The York Pilate did a tour of inspection, shaking the standards himself; they did not bend.

'I'm holding mine straight as a line, sir!'

'If mine goes the wrong way, you can hack off my hand, sir!'

'All right, you boasters. Don't pull any fast ones on me.'

Pilate returned to his chair. He stared for a while at the monoliths before him. Then he snapped his fingers for Jesus to return. The messenger of the *Acta* did exactly as he had done before: he spread Pilate's cloak on the ground and, with many entreaties, persuaded Jesus to walk on it. The two entered the *praetorium* again. At that moment, the shafts shook; the standards shivered, as though the muscled arms of the guards were no more than gossamer threads; and again they bowed to the floor, from where no man could raise them.

Something happened to Pilate, too. Involutarily, in the York play, he rose from his chair as if Tiberius had entered. He found himself standing, slightly distant and light-headed, as if in a dream of devotion. And he could not speak.

'What's up, sir?'

The centurion was holding his arm; the moment was over. Pilate murmured, sitting down again, with a nervous little laugh: 'Didn't really mean to do that. It was out of my power. I just felt I had to worship him. Something like that . . . I never saw something like that before.'

'We couldn't think what had got into you!' laughed Caiaphas. 'Reverencing that ribald.'

'I couldn't help it, I tell you. It was out of my power . . . But listen, listen. I think he should go away. I'm afraid to offend him . . . really.'

Astonished, the Jews ignored him. The hall was cleared, but the standards were left against the wall: so many long-necked birds. Pilate had promised bloodshed if they bowed again, but it seemed that everyone had been traumatised enough; and he had forgotten the logic of his order.

Besides, the prisoner stood before him.

*   *   *

Pilate presided that day, as always, 'with power', *cum potestate*. He was the emperor's agent, invested with full civil, military and criminal jurisdiction. He did not judge all cases: the Jews had been left with considerable autonomy. But he had the power of review, and in general the more serious the charge, the more likely he was to handle it. This was true even in religious cases. Later, in the early 60s when Albinus was governor, Jesus the son of Ananias went berserk and ran through Jerusalem screaming of 'voices' coming out of the west and the east; the priests took him to Albinus to get him silenced, as if this was their only hope.

This would not have made the governor comfortable. When the Jews brought Paul to Seneca's brother Gallio, proconsul of Achaia in 51–2, and accused him of 'making men worship God contrary to the law', Gallio instantly cut them off before Paul could open his mouth. 'If it were a matter of real wrong or wickedness, you Jews,' he said, 'it would be reasonable for me to involve myself; but if it is a question of words and names, and of your law, deal with it yourselves; I will be no judge of such matters.' And he drove them away from his judgement seat. Some Greeks then approached him as he sat there and, in front of his chair, beat up the chief ruler of the synagogue. 'But Gallio', said Luke, 'cared for none of those things.' They should never have brought the case to him and, if they lynched someone at the end of it, he could not be less bothered.

As he walked through the palace, Pilate probably felt much the same. Send them away, let me have a quiet life. He too would suspect that at least some of the charges that morning arose from 'words and names': from those strange Messianic slogans that had been shouted out when Jesus entered Jerusalem. And this may have been why the gospels show him initiating no proceedings on his own account, but waiting – with no great enthusiasm – for the case to be laid at his door by the Jewish priests.

Insofar as there was a Roman charge at issue here, it was *maiestas* again. In the case of non-citizens, this was automatically punishable by crucifixion. It was also an exceedingly broad charge, ('an ambiguous term', as Cicero called it), which vaguely included any act prejudicial to the interests of the Roman people and admitted no easy defence. Had Pilate been commanding troops in the field, no procedures would have been necessary: he would have disposed of the matter with his *ius gladii*, summary executions and crucifixions without trial. Both Philo and the Samaritans later accused him of partiality for acting this way, and he may well have had a soldier's instinctive liking for it. A strong body of opinion still holds that the trial of Jesus was not a trial at all, just a farce: Pope John Paul II has condemned it as 'an illegitimate tribunal'. But Jerusalem, for all its difficulties, was not a battlefield. Correct form had to be followed. And since the city was bursting with dignitaries who could report to Rome any high-handed action by the governor, Pilate had an extra motive for being careful.

By all appearances, the trial of Jesus was correctly conducted according to the rules of *cognitio extra ordinem*, the criminal-justice procedure commonly in use in provinces like Judea. *Extra ordinem* meant there was no need to follow the law books word for word; Pilate could use his own discretion. The wrongness of the verdict – if indeed it was wrong – did not make the proceedings themselves illegitimate.

A trial of this sort was abbreviated, closer to a simple hearing, as befitted non-citizens who had no rights before the law to speak of. There was no need, for example, for a written version of the accusation.

Nor was there a jury, as there would have been in Rome; Pilate was both the judge and the jury. But there still had to be a formal *accusatio*, or statement of the charge; a *cognitio*, or inquiry into that charge, either by a panel of justices or by the governor himself; statements from witnesses, and some opportunity (typically, three chances) for the accused to defend himself before sentence was passed. It was possibly routine procedure for a governor to accept charges brought by other authorities without further inquiry; but not in a case involving the death penalty. As the governor Festus proudly explained to the Jews, 'It is not the manner of the Romans to deliver any man to die, before he who is accused has faced his accusers and been able to answer for himself concerning the crimes laid against him.'

In this case, the case of Jesus the Nazarene, the Sanhedrin had already made their own preliminary enquiries of the largely silent suspect. (Luke records: 'Are you the Christ? Are you the Son of God?' And then Caiaphas's despairing exclamation, 'What need have we of further evidence?') As a result of these, they had decided that Jesus should die for blasphemy. Mark's gospel says they also tried to gather witnesses for Pilate's trial, but – in a portent of what was to come – most of those witnesses had disagreed with each other, and even those who remembered Jesus's remarks about destroying the Temple garbled them, and got them wrong.

In the grey light, groggy with lack of sleep, the small group of elders and priests now toiled up the hill to the governor's palace. Writers used to imagine the *praetorium* as part of the Antonia, the Roman military headquarters: a grimly utilitarian place. This background, with soldiers armed and waiting, added to the underlying brutality of the trial. Film-makers made good use of it, imagining an empty, echoing interrogation chamber of bare stone containing a chair and, incongruously, an executive's desk with inkstands. But the judgement hall was almost certainly in Herod's palace: a luxurious, even surreal, setting of mosaic pavements, white marble balustrades, softly sweeping servants and the intermittent fluttering of doves. To the east, over the city, the sun was rising.

The scene that followed is given differently in each gospel. It is impossible to tell how much history is preserved there. The gospel accounts, and John's in particular, are theology rather than history: the writers wished to show the clash predicted by Jesus between the powers of darkness and the powers of light, between Truth and men, like Pilate, who would never grasp it. The evangelists were not interested in characterising the governor. The four Pilates of the gospel trial differ mostly in what they do, not in what they are; and they differ in what they do because they react to the widely varying characters given to Jesus. The Pilate of Mark and Matthew is abrupt and practical because the Jesus of Mark and Matthew, the suffering servant, has nothing to say to this ruler who must brutalise him. The Pilate of John is both brimming with arrogance and touched by anxiety, because he is dealing with a Jesus who is patently king and patently God. The governor probably spoke very few of the words the evangelists, and John especially, gave him. It was what he symbolised that mattered.

Yet for generations the tortuous gospel accounts of the trial were broadly accepted as historical and true: so true that the words of the chief players remained unaltered even by the medieval playwrights, who altered everything. They revelled in the story of the Roman governor who could not decide between right and wrong, truth and falsehood: because Pilate, in this case, was all men. And other ages have followed them. The stilted 'conversations' between Pilate and Jesus have been treated as the most sacred of sacred texts, and every scholar has found a sort of thrill in retranslating them, sucking the juice out of them, uncovering every possible nuance of meaning. It was the Victorians who rejoiced to discover that when Pilate appeared to say the same thing over and over again, it was in fact never quite the same; and from those tiny differences sprang a whole psychology of doubting.

In striking contrast, Josephus in the *Testimonium Flavianum* makes it all seem practical and simple. 'Pilate condemned him to the cross upon indictment of the first-ranking men among us.' No hesitation, no deviation. This may well have been what the real trial of Jesus was like. Perhaps – as many suppose – the gospel-writers invented a vacillating Pilate only to make the Roman judge more sympathetic and the Jews worse. They had a reason for doing so, to make the vulnerable new religion more palatable to the empire. If they could not get round the fact of the Roman execution carried out by Roman troops, they could at least make Pilate waver and wonder until his hand was forced by the Jews.

There is plenty in that, as we shall see later. But the Pilate of the gospels is not just a Roman judge whose character must be softened for political reasons. That is almost the least of the roles he plays. He is also a symbol of the state, the secular power, the material world, ignorance, and darkness. He is all men facing, considering and ultimately rejecting Truth. That is why, though many modern scholars favour the kangaroo court and the instant death sentence, people continue to cling to Pilate as the great equivocator. Like an audience at a show, they love to watch him teeter, struggle, almost save himself, and fall. In some sense, they feel they are watching themselves.

Only John began the trial as it needed to begin, with Pilate emerging from the *praetorium* to meet the Jewish priests. Armed soldiers, attendants and secretaries were probably with him; a trial had to be recorded. The backless wooden curule chair, the seat of judgement, was carried outside too. There was also, perhaps, an interpreter. Although it often seems, and some scholars assume, that Pilate and Jesus spoke Greek to each other, the trial of Paul suggests that governors might stick to their safe judicial Latin, and that Latin-speakers might even be retained to make the case for the plaintiff. Theologically, it made no difference: the interpreter could be forgotten. Both Jesus and Pilate were symbols, speaking symbolic words. The actions, too, had their symbolism, including Pilate's agreement to step outside into the bracing morning air to range himself with Christ's accusers.

This was in any case required of him. The priests could not enter the *praetorium*, or indeed any Gentile building, before the Passover unless every crumb of leavened bread had been scrupulously removed from it. So Pilate had to come to them. In no other city of the empire would a governor have had to submit himself to this indignity. But Pilate, 'with his Roman smile', as one Edwardian writer put it – that imperial, tight-lipped smile of haughty condescension – came out to accommodate them. Moreover he came early, so that the bloody work of punishment, if punishment were necessary, could be finished before the festival began. Later on in John's gospel he even mentioned the name of the feast, a word one can hardly imagine falling from his lips: *to Pascha*, Passover. These concessions suggest that, over his years in Judea, he had begun to learn something. It was perhaps no humiliation after all, for him or for Rome, occasionally to be polite.

The whole Sanhedrin, if it came, would consist of seventy people, with Caiaphas to the fore and the aged Annas possibly in a litter, concealed by a curtain. It is usually assumed that Caiaphas – Pilate's man – was the spokesman. The actual delegation seems to have been just numerous enough to accompany the prisoner Jesus. As for him, he may have been led on past Pilate into the hall, or brought forward to face him; no one knows. He was, at any rate, bound and already battered, with a rope round his neck. This was the way captive kings of barbarian tribes were led through Rome in triumph; Pilate would have laughed and cheered such spectacles before. If his eyes rested on the bound king this time, they might well have registered only that he looked a mess: there was no point in gazing longer at a spectacle that was distasteful. So Pilate proceeded immediately to business, asking, 'What charges do you bring against this man?'

This was the routine but necessary beginning to any Roman trial. The response was expected to be equally formal. When Felix asked the question at the start of Paul's trial, the answer (from a Roman orator retained by the Jews for the purpose) was wrapped in honeyed obsequiousness: how much the 'most noble' governor was appreciated, what worthy deeds he had done, how deeply the Jews hoped that their 'tedious' words would not take up too much of his time. In Pilate's case, according to John, the response could hardly have been more different. The Jews were offended at the implication that they might have brought an innocent man to the *praetorium*. They flung out an insulting answer: 'If he wasn't a malefactor, we wouldn't have brought him to you.'

Pilate, stung, immediately lashed back: 'Take him yourselves, and judge him according to your law.'

This was a bad start, the old contemptuous battle-lines redrawn: the Roman hating to be used as some unthinking rubber-stamp, and showing it by acidly reminding the Jews how little ground their law actually covered. But it was also a strange beginning, because Pilate and Caiaphas relied on each other, were used to each other and had plainly worked out some mutually beneficial civility over the years; and yet here they were, instantly with their hackles up.

Both sides then seemed to take a breath and start again. The chief priests needed Pilate's help; there was no point in offending him. In Luke's gospel they delivered their verbal report, as required, wording the charges with care to make sure he understood the hefty political danger behind them.

'We found this man perverting our nation, preaching revolution, forbidding people to pay tribute to Caesar and saying that he is Christ, a king.'

Luke's chief priests obviously thought these points conclusive, and were not prepared for Pilate to hesitate. They had even made things easy by explaining to him what the word 'Christ' meant. They now expected a simple confirmation of their sentence, but he was not inclined to go so fast. He seemed to want to go through the forms, find out a bit more, handle the official questioning himself. This was the usual form with the abbreviated *cognitio* he was conducting; and, in any case, he was not about to be swept into anything. If he felt himself under pressure he was quite likely to resist, almost wilfully, doing what the Jews wanted. It was the old game again.

Besides, the claims made by the priests would not necessarily have impressed him. The first point about 'perverting the nation' was possibly true; he had probably heard of the teachings, the wild crowds, and he could also associate Jesus with the trouble-makers he had arrested. The second point, forbidding people to pay tribute, seemed to be a lie; as far as Pilate knew, Jesus had supported him in this, strange as it was. The third point, the Christ-point, was odd and intriguing; it smelled of *maiestas*. It was also highly dangerous; for if Pilate was being asked to execute a king, a popular leader of the people, it might provoke more violence. This was the point he seized on.

By some motion, from him or from the priests, Jesus was brought forward. (Felix beckoned Paul; Pilate probably beckoned Jesus.) They had not looked at each other in this way before, in the direct glance of conversation. But Jesus may not have returned the governor's stare.

Pilate asked: 'Are you the King of the Jews?'

'You said that.'

All the gospels record this exchange in almost the same words; it is virtually all they agree on. Jesus had given the same reply to the chief priests when they had asked him if he was the son of God: '*You* say that I am.' It was a cool and disturbing answer. It had driven the priests mad; they took it for insolence. Pilate did not seem to. The two men were feeling each other out. The old commentators, dissecting the Greek form of Pilate's first question – *Sy ei o Basileus ton Ioudaion?* – found in that *sy ei* tiny traces both of pity and surprise. He did not quite know what to expect from Jesus. Certainly, this king did not look the part. In the York play, Pilate actually tells Jesus not to be frightened; in the Gréban play he calls him 'the most piteous sight I ever saw'. The sense was probably more straightforward: a simple question, without coloration, to which he expected a simple yes or no. He did not get it.

Meanwhile, the high priests continued their accusations. They spoke of Jesus teaching and stirring up the people from one end of the country to the other. In the *Acta Pilati*, the priests made great play of the charge that Jesus was a bastard, that his birth had caused the Massacre of the Innocents, and that his parents had had to flee to Egypt, because they were 'ashamed of themselves before the people'. In the York play, the priests' arguments with Pilate over Jesus go on so long that Pilate is reduced to snapping at Annas, 'Sir, have you done? Then sit down and shut up.'

Amid all the hubbub, Jesus stood there silently. Matthew says 'He answered never a word to him,' implying (as his gospel bears out) that Jesus never spoke to Pilate, beyond that off-hand first answer. This silence was theologically important: the silence of the suffering servant as predicted in Isaiah, or of the God who does not want to reveal himself to men. But Pilate expected and required an answer. That initial 'You said that' was not quite the plea of guilty that he needed. Jesus did nothing to build up the tally of accusations, but nor did he offer a defence that Pilate could use. He had to confess to the whole indictment, or else contest it with facts that Pilate could verify. He did neither.

The Pilate of Mark and Matthew asked at last, 'Have you nothing to say? See how many charges they bring against you.'

He was trying to be fair, almost kind, and encourage Jesus in a defence of himself. Still Jesus said nothing. Pilate too said nothing, or nothing that is recorded; he was apparently lost in astonishment. The Greek word *thaumazein*, used by Mark, means to be surprised or astounded, as by an angel in a tree: among the usual branches, the routine leaves, creeping feathers of fire.

At last, Pilate said: 'I find no fault in this man.'

He said this in Luke and John. In Matthew and Mark he put it rather differently, challenging the chief priests to tell him what wrong Jesus had done. The later the gospel, or the more derivative, the more the writers – anxious to get this Roman on Jesus's side – pressed Pilate to declare him innocent as early and often as possible. But it was not psychologically or judicially impossible for Pilate to have said it, even if his heart felt nothing. To side with Christ peremptorily, even cynically, would have had its attractions. Besides, he may have hoped to end the business there. The morning was cold; they were standing outside; the defendant was offering no defence, the crimes alleged were trivial or didn't seem to stand up, and the crowd was growing by the minute. But the priests persisted. They probably repeated their remark that they had not brought Jesus to him for nothing; he probably repeated his initial comment that they could take care of him themselves (with the heavy implication that they could screw themselves, too). But then, at some point, the priests made their clinching argument: 'It is not lawful for us to put a man to death.'

It was the first time death had been mentioned; and not merely mentioned, but offered to Pilate explicitly as the action expected of him. Here was the real point of the exercise, laid out in the open. We can't kill him, but you can. Under Roman rule, the Sanhedrin had apparently ceded to the governor all power of life and death. They could pass sentence in a capital case, but they could not carry the sentence out. Even in blasphemy cases, all they had reserved to themselves was a type of lynch-power. A proper judicial sentence of death, properly carried out, required Pilate's permission. So, in this case, the odium of dealing with death on the high feast day could be transferred to the hated heathen governor: unless, of course, he did not want to be their executioner.

Some medieval writers were sure he did not want to be, despite his usual brutality. At the mention of the death sentence in the Chester play he bursts out, in his broad northern accent, 'What the devil of hell does that mean?' In the *Acta Pilati*, as in the York play, he tries to get to the bottom of things. He asks a group of pro-Jesus witnesses, 'Why do they want to kill him?'

'They're jealous of him, because he heals people on the Sabbath.'

'So for doing something good, they want to put him to death?'

'That's right.'

So Pilate, faced with death, hesitated. Any Roman official might have done the same. Even slaves (and Jesus, standing before him, had the status of a slave in his eyes) were owed a proper hearing in such circumstances. Juvenal pointed this out in his mock dispute between a husband and his wife, hysterical because of some slip-up in the hairdressing or wardrobe department:

> *Wife*. Crucify that slave!
> *Husband*. But what is the slave's offence
> To merit such punishment? Who has brought charges against him?
> Where are the witnesses? You must hear his defence; no
> delay can be too long when a man's life is at stake.
> *Wife*. So a slave's a *man* now, is he, you crackpot? All right, perhaps
> He didn't do anything. This is still my wish, my command . . .

Jean Michel's fifteenth-century *Mystery of the Passion* had Pilate making this point too: 'You're forgetting what danger a judge can get into when he condemns an innocent man to death. You've got to weigh up such a death properly, put it in the scales. It's no small thing, the death of a man.'

So Pilate seems to have hesitated. And something else was in play, too. John adds, at this point, that the priests' remark about legality and death was made 'so that the sayings of Jesus might be fulfilled, signifying what sort of death he would die'. He had to die, of course, on a cross. Only Pilate could put him there. The prophecies had found their mark, and forces more complex than the outrage of the Sanhedrin were clearly pushing Jesus and Pilate together. The *Acta Pilati* adds, after the Jews' statement of their own powerlessness, a rawly pertinent question from the governor: 'Has God forbidden you to kill, and allowed me?'

He received no answer. So in John's gospel Pilate, as if to clear his head – or perhaps in the hope of getting a proper confession at last – cut off the conversation with the Jewish leaders, turned his back on them, beckoned his prisoner, and shut himself up in the judgement hall with Jesus.

*   *   *

At last they were alone. It was quieter inside the *praetorium*, and the light was softer. F.W. Farrar, writing in 1850, imagined that they did not simply step inside a doorway, a few yards from the Jews. He surmised that Jesus was led 'up the noble flight of stairs, over a floor of agate and lazuli, under the gilded roofs, ceiled with cedar and painted with vermilion'. There is no reason why they should have gone so far, but part of Farrar's assumption is correct: they would have stood in a room that was sumptuous, in which the marble and gilded furniture would have convinced some men that they were now in heaven.

They would still have been on grotesquely uneven terms, Pilate in the full sweep of his authority, Jesus haltered with ropes; yet John made them equals, trading points as one power to another. Nor were they truly alone: no Roman trial, whatever its peculiarities, could be held in secret, and Pilate's guards and attendants would have stayed with him. Yet John presented them as two men in a room face to face; and, at least for a few minutes, they tried to have a conversation.

John's gospel provides three moments when Pilate, in effect, retires from the trial. On two of these occasions he leaves to question Jesus more closely, and on the third he appears to distance himself, opting out of mocking him. There is dramatic method in this. What John provides is space for relative quiet, dialogue and contemplation. In the other gospels the trial moves almost too briskly, like a public auction; Pilate interracts strenuously with the Jewish crowd, but with Jesus he has no relationship at all. John gives him the chance.

There was also more to it than that. The act of going into the *praetorium* and closing the door was highly symbolic. Jesus told his followers to pray like this, in the secrecy of their own chambers. There they too were to be face to face with God. Yet any act of retirement might have done as well. The essential was to withdraw from the world and from distraction. Romans, too, understood the importance of this act, even the possibility of divine encounters. As Seneca wrote to his governor-friend Lucilius:

> If you have ever come upon a grove full of ancient trees that have grown to an unusual height, shutting out a view of the sky with a veil of intertwining branches, then the loftiness of the forest, the seclusion of the spot, and your wonder at the thick unbroken shade in the midst of open spaces, will prove to you the presence of deity. Or if a cave, made by the deep crumbling of the rocks, holds up a mountain on its arch, a place not built with hands but hollowed out into such spaciousness by natural causes, your soul will be deeply moved by a certain intimation of the existence of God. We worship the sources of mighty rivers; we erect altars at places where great streams break suddenly from hidden sources; we adore springs of hot water as divine, and consecrate certain pools because of their dark waters or their immeasurable depth.
>
> If you see a man who is unterrified in the midst of dangers, untouched by desires, happy in adversity, peaceful amid the storm, who looks down upon men from a higher plane and views the gods on a footing of equality, will not a feeling of reverence for him steal over you? Won't you say, 'This quality is too great and too lofty to be regarded as resembling this petty body in which it dwells. A divine power has descended upon that man'?

John's staging of the scene underlines this confrontation. In the inward place, the grove, the cave or the *praetorium*, stands Jesus, who is the truth and the light; outside are the Jews in the darkness of their ignorance, refusing to enter. Between the two walks Pilate, constantly in and out, struggling to decide where he wants to be: in the howling darkness with those who do not believe, or in the holy and unsettling embrace of God. It will take the whole length of the trial for him to make his choice.

With Jesus, and for the truth, or against them. This may have been a scene that was recorded and remembered; more probably, it was a scene that John longed to have happened, in which Jesus and Pilate, light and darkness, explained themselves to each other.

It is a strangely compelling dialogue, all the same. It has the ring of real conversation between two men who find each other mystifying: polite defiance on both sides, a refusal to give ground, and a procession of *non sequiturs* in which questions and answers do not quite fit together. No man wishing to write propaganda would produce a piece of dialogue like this. It has its uses, too, for the logical structure of the trial, explaining some of the more abrupt and curious actions attributed to Pilate in the other gospels: in particular his assertion, only minutes into the trial and on no evidence at all, that he found no fault in Jesus, and his subsequent efforts to avert the fate that was bearing down on both of them.

The nineteenth-century commentators considered this scene crucial. It was, they thought, the first of several occasions in the trial when Pilate ('a man doubtless of corrupt principles and irreligious life') was touched by the divine despite himself. Caught in such proximity, looking into the eyes of Jesus and listening to his voice, the governor – they felt sure – encountered for the first time the ineffable sweetness of God. He could not, they imagined, have been indifferent to this. Jesus, after all, was a man who effortlessly drew crowds, whom even the mad and blind could recognise as a spiritual force: 'I know who you are, God's holy one!' an epileptic screamed. Lepers, noblemen, women, rulers of local synagogues, knelt down at his feet. They worshipped him. There seemed no reason, then, why a Roman should not have been affected, however proud and intransigent. In John's gospel, Pilate's soldiers in the arresting party had already fallen to the ground before Jesus. Perhaps it was not mere propaganda that the words appeared again and again in the trial, 'Pilate marvelled'.

The brevity of the conversation was misleading, therefore. It must have started something. Those who believe in Jesus have always seen small epiphanies strewn all through the trial, especially in John. However obtuse or thuggish Pilate is – however obtuse or thuggish ordinary men and their rulers are, whom he represents – there comes a moment when God, or the notion of goodness, disturbs him. He comes to a point where he can choose the higher or the lower path, the virtuous action or the sin; and he pauses. Redemption is held out to him, and the question is whether he will notice it in time before he plunges into darkness.

Even the modern playwright Dennis Potter, who rewrites the trial completely, preserves a moment of epiphany. It comes after Pilate has tauntingly reminded Jesus of the commandment to 'love your enemies'. 'What about me?' he asks. 'Do you love me?'

Pause. Jesus looks at him steadily. Pilate's chuckle dies away uncomfortably

> *Jesus.* Yes, Pontius.
> *Pilate slaps out at him in humiliation. And then suddenly covers his face in a gesture of shame*
> *Pilate:* I'm sorry, that was not necessary. That was not necessary.
> *Jesus.* Don't be afraid.
> *This really frightens Pilate*
> *Pilate.* What?
> *Jesus.* There is no need to be frightened.
> *Pilate steps back in alarm. He shouts out in bewildered anger*
> *Pilate.* Take him away! Take the idiot away!

Standing in the *praetorium*, planting the barricades of his awkward questions, Pilate becomes the prototype of every uncertain man or woman forced into a dialogue with God. He asks, only half-believing that he will ever get an answer; what comes back is elliptical, disturbing; but for a moment the heart, like a door, has been laid open.

'Are you the King of the Jews?' he asked again.

'Are you saying that yourself, or did other people tell you this about me?'

It was the same question, with almost the same answer; except that the formulation was gentler, as if Jesus were addressing a child. It was meant to be an appeal to Pilate's conscience, to make him consider for himself whether the charge should be criminal and what it might mean. It was a suggestion that the conversation could go to a different level. But John's Pilate, completely missing the point, thought he was being put down. And that was exquisitely insulting.

'Am I a Jew?' *Meti ego Judaios eimi?* He snapped it out in fury. Was he one of that tribe, bearded, atheist, fanatical, *circumcised*? All his Roman dignity burned in his face.

After an almost audible swallowing of temper, he went on: 'Your own people and the chief priests have delivered you to me. [Understood: all those people who usually despise me.] What did you do to turn them against you?'

The answer should have been straightforward. Instead, it was bizarre.

'My kingdom is not of this world. If my kingdom were of this world, then my officers would be fighting to stop me being delivered to the Jews. But my kingdom is not from here.'

What could Pilate make of this? The remark came out of the blue. But the last phrase would have snagged his attention, at least: not from here. A man might say that casually in the street, and you would not necessarily follow up. Not from here, not from Judea: a foreigner, therefore. The empire was full of foreigners and petty kings. That much distance was manageable. You might go further still, towards the end of the world the empire covered or geographers knew, petering out in wilderness and forests and ice. But Jesus had gone further even than that. He had described a kingdom not of this *kosmos*. Not of this world, not of this earth; not of this universe. Pilate was asked to consider a realm without palaces, armies, temples, roads or the Imperial Post; an utterly ethereal place in which Caesar's soldiers had no purchase, and in which invisible officers did not try to stop their master being arrested in the street.

That in itself suggested something else. (So many suggestions in a mere two sentences: how was a judge to cope with them all?) If the officers of Jesus were not fighting, this meant he expected, or possibly even wanted, to be handed over to the Jewish authorities and to Pilate. He didn't care. Perhaps he wished to be handed over for reasons Pilate could never detect, to further his purposes. Perhaps he did not want to be saved, because death was of no consequence to him; or because, on the contrary, he craved it and embraced it. Such notions were fairly otherworldly too.

The question the governor should have asked next was obvious: 'So where are you from, if you are not of this world?' But it did not occur to John's Pilate then; only later, when as it turned out he had missed his chance. For the moment, he seemed too baffled to pursue it. Out of the vast cloudiness of the answer he had been given, Pilate plucked the only solid grain: Jesus' apparent admission that he was a king after all. He seized on the question that was the least interesting to pursue but the safest to ask, the sanest to ask, out of that vertiginous trail of words.

'So,' he said, 'you *are* a king, then?'

The tone was one of doubtful surprise, bordering on scorn. You, with your bruised face and blackened eyes, your dirty robe, you're a king? The question should have made him laugh; Jesus' answer should have assured him that, in practical terms, Rome had nothing to fear from him. But the doubt was also, perhaps, a fear of the altitude from which this peculiar man might have fallen.

'You said it,' Jesus told him.

That answer again. And its subtext: There really isn't much point discussing such things with you. There's no common ground between us. There's nowhere to go here.

Then, unexpectedly, Jesus went on: 'This is what I was born for, and this is why I came into the world, to bear witness to the truth. Everyone on the side of truth listens to me.'

Pilate retorted: 'What is truth?'

The words linger. In fact they have never ceased to echo, and they have received a slightly different interpretation from almost every scholar who has considered them. Had they been uttered in the middle of the exchange and been answered, they would have had far less impact. But John's Pilate threw them out, and immediately left the *praetorium* and returned to the Jews to announce that he could find no fault in the man he had been talking to.

It is an odd moment, marked in John's original Greek by an abrupt ending to the paragraph; the words are literally left dangling. It is also a moment of acute disappointment. The conversation has been getting interesting, even extraordinary. Pilate has been fed neat Christian doctrine, baffling and astonishing: we imagine it might have the same effect on him as a shot of whisky on a child. First, he has been asked to apply his conscience ('If he had a conscience,' so many have chorused) to the meaning of the charges against Jesus; then he has been asked to consider the nature of universal truth. This was bound to be too hard for him; and so, though the world has come to hang lovingly on this exchange, he cut the conversation off.

Several writers since have thought this was a shame. The writer of the York play certainly thought he could improve on John's performance. After Jesus's remarks he has Pilate saying, with all the shortness of a Yorkshire pork-butcher, 'That sounds like the truth to me,' and rounding on the chief priests, whom he accuses of lying to him and trumping up the charges. He then falls to wondering where Jesus got such language and such imagery from: 'Perhaps his father travelled, and saw wonders, and told him about them.' Annas corrects him: 'No, no, sir, he's a workman. He's got no subtlety in him.'

The writer of the *Acta Pilati* also carried matters on a bit further. When Pilate asks, 'What is truth?', Jesus answers: 'Truth is of heaven.'

'Is there no truth on earth?'

'Well, just look at how those who speak the truth are judged by those who have worldly authority!'

In other words: Look how you are treating me. But in a slightly different version of the *Acta* Jesus adds another, devastating phrase: '*I* am the truth.'

He had said as much to his followers, of course. Would he have dared to say it to Pilate? It is not completely outside the bounds of possibility. The conversation in the *Acta Pilati* has a trace of the plausible about it. Yet Pilate's most famous remark gains that tremor of authenticity precisely because nothing follows it. Augustine supposed he left because he had suddenly remembered the custom of releasing a prisoner on the feast day, and did not want it to slip his mind before he could mention it to the Jews. John Chrysostom in the fourth century (joined by Aldous Huxley in the twentieth) thought that Pilate, though he had been in earnest for a minute, did not want to waste his time in the thousand idle disputations his question could give rise to; he had serious work to do. In other words, as John almost seems to imply, the conversation was disrupted by a technicality.

But disrupted or not, what did he mean? Was he simply, as a well-trained Sceptic, giving the proper and acceptable Sceptics' answer? It seems unlikely. A true Sceptic would have shown none of Pilate's agitation. Believing that nothing was good, nothing bad, nothing false and nothing true, he was meant to have reached a state of quietude. He was beyond choice, beyond decision; his judgement was suspended. Pilate in the trial presented completely the opposite picture. He wanted to make his own decision over true or false, right or wrong, but the choice confounded him. It would not have been the first time in his career.

Perhaps his words suggested sheer world-weariness. It is almost certain that he had read Livy's *History of Rome*, in which the preface described 'the process of our moral decline ... the sinking of the foundations of morality ... then the final collapse of the whole edifice, and the dark dawning of our modern day when we can neither endure our vices, nor face the remedies needed to cure them.' Or, by contrast,

Pilate's words could have summed up the flippancy of decadent Rome, in which good and evil, true and false, were mere dishes – as Seneca said – to be sampled by idle young men in the eating houses; where, instead of chewing the rough bread of wisdom, they dined on filleted mullet, boned chicken and rare mushrooms, sated on the riot of flavours until they could no longer distinguish them. Bacon's famous passage about 'jesting Pilate', who 'would not stay for an answer', captures this mood: 'Certainly there be, that delight in giddiness; and count it a bondage to fix a belief; affecting free-will in thinking, as well as in acting.' Yes, perhaps that was what Pilate was doing: affecting free will, when in fact he did not have any. His moments of giddiness – they seemed to be in his character, erupting even at serious junctures – only emphasised how stuck he was, unable to choose and unable to move.

Pilate's Greek, as 'relayed' by John, gives a tiny clue as to what he may have meant. The word he used for truth, *aletheia*, was not quite the construction (*i aletheia*) Jesus had used. Jesus was speaking of absolute truth; Pilate seemed to mean a truth that was narrow and particular. Jesus was referring to a truth that was overpoweringly different: as different, Polybius had once said, as when a galley-rower, trained on skeleton ships on dry land, suddenly felt in the live ocean the pull of the oar and the craft's response.

Possibly Pilate could have grasped just a thread of that: Plato's truth that was reality, not seeming. But because he was not open to metaphysical explanations, as Jesus gently inferred, the only truth he could understand was the sort a judge was confined to: facts, assertions, the evidence of eyes and ears. How could Jesus consider a truth beyond even that? How did he imagine (this was Martin Luther's interpretation) that airy speculations about truth would help him out of this particular legal mess? And, most of all, *how did he know*? Most scholars see the remark as a challenge, thrown out by a man of the world who thinks the other fellow has no idea what he is talking about. It was much like Festus' remark after Paul had proclaimed Christ's death and resurrection: 'Paul, you're beside yourself; too much learning has made you mad.'

If John's Pilate thought Jesus was mad, this would explain his precipitate exit. After all, he left the *praetorium*, according to John, not to announce Jesus's guilt and execution but to declare his innocence. A madman would not be worth bothering with any longer; they could all go home. Yet there is another possible explanation, short of a conviction of lunacy. Pilate had asked a question that departed abruptly from his one-track interest in the inquiry, which was kingship. That question threatened to engage him in Jesus's argument, on Jesus's terms. This was disturbing; it was the beginning of complicity. Therefore Pilate no sooner asked the question, than he dropped it, and left at once to cover his embarrassment. His remark was not just the symbolic statement of a man who could not see God before his face; it was the statement of a man who has had an intimation of the truth but is too afraid, or too shallow, or too self-preserving, to go on.

It is a possibility. There are a dozen possibilities. And whichever way it happened, in John's gospel, Jesus was left formulating the answer into the empty air.

★   ★   ★

By this point in the trial, Pilate seemed desperate to be released from his duties. According to the gospels, he tried to wriggle out in three different ways. In John his first device was to go outside, back to the chief priests, and say: 'I find no fault in him at all.' By this time, however, it was not just the priests who were waiting for him, but a crowd of ordinary people. From this moment on, the trial ceased to be small-scale and conversational. It became an exercise in crowd control, conducted at full volume and with increasing urgency on both sides.

When Pilate declared Jesus innocent, the crowd seemed to take it badly: so badly that he couldn't just leave it there, order the prisoner released and expect them to disperse. He had to do something else. In his long experience of getting stuck with resentful Jewish crowds, he knew there was a simple way out somewhere. There was always some trick, some deception that would work. And in his long experience, he also knew that he could never seem to find what it was.

What he appeared to be searching for was a third way: not to kill Jesus, not to release him, but to take a middle course. The other choices were too extreme, too hard. They involved a commitment he did not want to make. Pilate was, after all, a politician: he wanted to preserve his skin and please his audience and, somewhere down the line, try to do the right thing.

His Samnite forebears had agonised over a middle course on a much larger scale. Livy retailed the semi-mythical story. When Gavius Pontius trapped the Roman army at the Caudine Forks, he was so delighted that he could not think what to do next. He sent a messenger to his aged father, Herennius, the man who had talked to Plato, to seek advice.

'Dismiss them unhurt,' his father said.

Gavius rejected that.

'Kill the lot of them, then.'

Gavius rejected that too.

He asked his father to advise them in person, and Herennius was brought to the camp in a wagon. There, like the dogged old man he was, he simply repeated his advice. Spare these men, and they would make powerful friends; kill them, and the Romans would be weakened for a generation. There was, he said, 'no third plan': *tertium nullum consilium esse*.

But Gavius and the other Samnite leaders demanded one. What would happen, they asked, if they took a middle course? Let the Romans go unhurt, but imposed terms on them? Herennius was dismissive. 'That's a policy,' he said, 'that neither wins men friends nor rids them of their enemies.'

They sent the old man home. Gavius Pontius then went to the Romans with his middle way: he offered them their lives, and peace, but each of them would have to pass under the yoke, unarmed and wearing only a tunic. This was such humiliation that the Romans could scarcely bear it. They passed under the yoke while their enemies reviled them, and then lay down in the Capua road in nakedness and tears.

Yet they had their revenge. As Herennius had predicted, the middle way won the Samnites no friends, but forged so dishonourable a peace that they and the Romans were soon at war again. Before long, they too were defeated and sent under the yoke by the crowing Romans, with Gavius Pontius among them. He was later led in triumph and beheaded. His wonderful compromise had come to nothing.

'They had let slip the chance both of doing good and of doing harm,' Livy wrote. History proved that equivocation did not work. A man should either do good or bad, but not waver between them. Pilate ignored this simple lesson of history. He wanted his schemes, his escape routes; there was surely some way out.

His best idea came in Luke's gospel: he would wriggle out by passing the buck. The chief priests were still accusing Jesus of preaching 'from Galilee to this place', and Pilate's ears pricked up at that. 'Is this man a Galilean?' he asked.

When Felix heard the case of Paul, the very first question he asked was where the man was from. This was the obvious point to establish before going any further; he asked it even before requesting the accusation. It was strange, perhaps even incompetent, that Pilate left the enquiry so late. If Jesus was a Galilean, Herod Antipas could judge him;

the matter would be out of Pilate's hands. And Antipas, conveniently, was also in Jerusalem for Passover.

So Luke's Pilate, having made his inquiries and satisfied himself that this might work, sent Jesus across to the tetrarch at his lodgings in the old Asmonean palace, on the other side of the city. It looked like a diplomatic gesture, almost like a present. If he did this, it was the first such spontaneous and unpressured behaviour ever credited to Pilate. In effect, he sent Herod something he knew he was intrigued by (even, in one medieval French drama, recommending the 'great games' Jesus knew how to play), and divested himself in the process of a prisoner who was getting too difficult.

It didn't work. Jesus refused to answer Herod's eager questions about his miracles, let alone perform any; and after a brief session of abuse and mockery he was sent back to Pilate. But Herod seems to have appreciated the thought behind the gesture. He and Pilate had been enemies, Luke said. That enmity might well have sprung from the business of the votive shields and the 'sneaking' letter to Tiberius; or from Pilate's slaughter of Galileans (also mentioned only by Luke) in the Temple courtyard. There were probably many reasons. Now, however, they were 'made friends together', by a sort of grim telepathy, on opposite sides of swarming Jerusalem. By the end of the morning, according to the second-century *gospel of Peter* – the earliest uncanonical account of the passion – Herod was calling him 'Brother Pilate'.

The prophets had foretold such a day, of course, when the rulers of the world would unite against Christ. Perhaps Luke was just inventing to fulfil the prophecies; or perhaps he had a source at Herod's court, who fed him an exclusive. The scholars disagree. But the incident is not implausible. It occasionally happened in criminal trials that a prisoner was sent from the *forum apprehensionis*, the place where he was caught, to the *forum originis*, the place he was from, though this was not obligatory. And Pilate had a motive for trying to please Herod; he needed his help against Herod's nephew, the Roman-educated nationalist Agrippa. Agrippa, in Rome, was planning to assume the kingship of Judea. He had an interest in painting an unflattering picture of Pilate's administration, and he was, at that moment, much closer to Tiberius than Pilate was. The governor badly needed the tetrarch of Galilee to be his friend. That much is certain.

All the same, Jesus was returned rather quickly, and he was not returned as he had been sent. He came back dressed up in a festival robe that was 'gorgeous', or 'shining white'. Herod seems to have meant to dress him like a fool, but a white robe would have had all sorts of connotations for Pilate. A man in white, the good-luck colour, could be a candidate for election or a proper claimant to a crown; he could be one of those heroes in history or literature whose greatness of soul clothed him in radiance. Tacitus mentioned that the tribunes – so, probably, Pilate himself – wore white robes when they went before the eagles into battle. The spectacle, then, might have been unsettling. The Gréban playwright imagined that Pilate was furious to get Jesus back: 'By all the thunders of Almighty Jupiter!' he cried to his attendants. But Luke's Pilate took it more calmly. Standing beside Jesus, facing the chief priests, he made his longest and most eloquent plea for him.

'You brought this man to me as one who was stirring up the people,' he told them. 'Well, look, I've examined him in front of you and I've found him completely innocent of the things you accuse him of. Herod found no fault in him either, for I sent the case to him, and nothing worthy of death has been imputed to him. So I'm going to chastise him and let him go.'

This, in effect, was Pilate's sentence of acquittal. But there was a fatal flaw in it; he had not proved Jesus innocent at all, because Jesus had offered no defence. There was therefore no reason why the chief priests should accept it. Pilate could have taken the line that this was unimportant; Mark claims that he was already well aware that their case against Jesus was based mostly on envy. But here he apparently made a terrible mistake, an attempt at political cleverness – even, perhaps, another attempt at diplomacy – which threw the case open to the judgement of the mob. He remembered, or was reminded, according to all the gospels, that there was a custom of releasing a prisoner on the feast day.

Such a custom is not substantiated anywhere else for Judea, but it is not implausible. At Roman festivals, provision was usually made to show mercy to criminals and pity to the executed. At the Lectisternia and the Bacchanalia an amnesty was offered, and this was also done at the new emperor's accession. When Albinus was replaced as governor of Judea a little after Pilate's time, his last act of kindness was to release all those who had been arrested 'for trifling matters', in exchange for cash. ('So the prisons were emptied,' says Josephus tartly, 'and the country was filled with robbers.') The trials of Paul, too, show both the governors involved as 'keen to do the Jews a favour' by, in the first instance, keeping Paul bound, and, in the second, offering to try him on Jewish charges: in other words, treating Jewish malcontents in the way they thought the Jews wanted. There also exists the evidence of a papyrus in Greek from Egypt, in which a Roman prefect says to the accused: 'You deserve to be scourged for the crimes you have committed, but I grant you to the crowd.'

Nothing is recorded elsewhere to suggest that Pilate's gesture was a 'custom'. It is therefore possible that he had introduced it on his own initiative. If so, it showed an uncharacteristic insight into Jewish sensibilities and the meaning of Passover: releasing a prisoner from bondage, just as the Jewish people had been released by God from captivity in Egypt. In Luke and John Pilate talks of this as a Jewish practice ('You have a custom'), but in Mark and Matthew it seems to be the governor's idea: to release one prisoner, whomever the Jews wanted, at the Passover or at 'festival time', was something Pilate had 'always done for them' and which the crowd noisily demanded that he should do again. In fact, Mark suggests that the people had come to the *praetorium* expressly to ask for that, rather than merely to observe a trial; and it is possible that at least some of them, at the start, came in the hope that Jesus might be the man released. This puts a slightly different complexion on the scene, as on the dilemma that resulted. Perhaps it was not Pilate who made the suggestion of a choice to the crowd, but the crowd which made the suggestion to him.

Yet when all is said and done, the oddest part of the story is not the notion of a judicial reprieve. It is the idea that Pilate should have handed over his own authority to the whim of the crowd, thereby abandoning all forms of Roman legal procedure. It was a moment of crisis, certainly. But he had armed troops at his disposal – dozens stationed in the palace alone, more in the Antonia – and, in this case, absolute power to act. He had no need at all to ask the Jews' permission or to let them choose who would live or who would die. That was his job. Philo made the point with venom against Flaccus, the prefect of Egypt, who failed to stop the pogrom of 38 in Alexandria: 'When the governor of the country, who, if he wished, could have suppressed in a single hour the tyranny of the mob, pretended not to see what he saw and not to hear what he heard, but allowed them to wage war unrestrainedly, he wrecked the peace.'

Besides, Pilate would have been imbued with all the snobbery and distaste that Romans in high places felt for the mob. The people, the *populus*, sometimes had reason on their side; the *res publica*, after all, was meant to be the expression of the popular will in lasting laws and institutions. But even the Roman people, the best in the world, needed to be led by Caesar and represented by the senators. Left to themselves, they were just the drunken mob who took to the streets at Saturnalia; or the crowd who stayed in their seats through the intermissions at the shows, singing and skipping lunch in the hope of seeing throats cut. They were the *turba* who surrounded a man to distract him from every good purpose: the goat-reeking mass of bean- and chestnut-eaters pressing round his litter in the market, or the hee-hawing group on the bottom couch at the dinner party. Seneca wrote that even the ordinary crush of the streets disturbed him and seemed to change his character; and he felt that even Socrates and Cato might have been shaken in their moral strength by mingling with the crowd.

A Roman citizen facing the death penalty could, by the *Lex Valeria,* make an appeal to the crowd for his life. This apart, you did not ask such men for their opinions. The *Law of the Twelve Tables,* which Pilate, as a magistrate, was meant to have read, made this quite clear: *Vanae voces populi non sunt audiendae, quando aut noxium crimine absolvi, aut innocentem condemnari desiderant.* The crowd's empty voices must not be listened to. But then, as Cicero had lamented some years before Pilate was born, 'no one learns that law nowadays.'

Besides, the crowd was unteachable. With a small group of men, you could talk rationally; but the crowd had to be harangued at maximum volume, with sweeping gestures, and in the process all subtlety of thought would disappear. You threw out trinkets, just as coins and bread rolls were tossed out at the games, and watched as the audience fell on each other to seize them. Only the most primitive ideas could get through: ideas requiring 'yes' or 'no'. You roared into the answering roar. There was pleasure in it sometimes, the pleasure of rapturous applause on a grand scale. But even Caesar, when he heard it, would feel curiously weakened and afraid that the fawning throng would turn on him.

Perhaps Pilate thought he could keep control. After all, he was trying to release Jesus; and the crowd liked him, didn't they? They had made him their king, hadn't they? Despite what the priests said, perhaps governor and crowd were unexpectedly on the same side. Perhaps he saw himself in a play, one of those tragedies in which the leading actors wore *togae praetextae* just like his own, and in which the crowd was the Chorus, 'siding with the good and giving friendly advice, swaying the angry and cherishing the righteous,' as Horace said. Perhaps, after all, his choice could be offloaded on to them.

In Mark and John he tried, however clumsily, to get the crowd behind him. 'Would you like me to release the king of the Jews for you?' he enquired of them. But that leading question, apparently caught between kindness and a sneer, got him nowhere. His offer was quickly flung back in his face, contempt returned for contempt: 'No, not this man! Barabbas!'

Joshua (Jesus) Barabbas, if he was not invented, seems to have been a bandit and an outlaw. John calls him 'a robber', although Matthew says he was 'a notable prisoner', suggesting that he might have been high-born. His name translates as 'son of a distinguished father'. Whatever his lineage, he was apparently already guilty both of sedition, the crime which the priests were trying to fasten on Jesus, and of 'murder committed during the insurrection'. He had probably been flung into jail a few days before, roughed up after the disturbance in the Temple compound. A couple of other *lestai* were locked up with him, presumably to await execution when Pilate arrived from Caesarea. They became the two thieves (in medieval tradition, Gestas and Dysmas) who were crucified on either side of Jesus. The Romans sometimes preferred not to kill such people immediately, but to make a spectacle of them at a time of general holiday. Perhaps that was what was going on in this case.

The evangelists implied that Barabbas was well-known as both a patriot and a trouble-maker. This was not a man who ought to escape death. His criminality was obvious, as was his defiance of the Roman occupying power. To pardon him would therefore be an extraordinary concession by the governor. Indeed, too extraordinary: Pilate would be in the deepest trouble with Tiberius if he ordered Barabbas to be released.

Yet he ploughed on. In Matthew, to make the choice clear, Pilate spelt it out to the crowd. He also turned the decision over to them entirely. 'Which of the two do you want me to release to you?' he asked. 'Barabbas, or Jesus who is called Christ?'

These were outlandish words for a Roman to have uttered, if he ever said them. But what was he thinking by offering this choice at all? Hans Kelsen, an Austrian-American jurist and philosopher whose writing spanned most of the twentieth century, thought this was a wonderful show of democratic sensitivity: untroubled by absolutist notions of what was right or wrong, Pilate simply acquiesced in the will of the popular majority. But the German theologian Martin Niemöller disagreed. In one of his last passion sermons, preached in Berlin in 1937, Niemöller fingered Pilate as a simple coward: a man who handed the choice to the Jews because he preferred not to make it himself. They, not he, would decide whether Jesus or Barabbas died. But, as usual,

Pilate omitted something from his perfect scheme: he was still the hangman, and so could not excuse himself from making the same choice. 'No man', said Niemöller, 'has the right to put this question to other men without giving the answer himself.'

And Pilate had, in fact, given his answer. By asking the question, 'Jesus or Barabbas?', he had already rejected the claims of Jesus. By placing the two on the same level, two criminals who could be taken or left, he had already ranged himself with Christ's enemies. This choice, which he believed he had presented to the Jews in a neutral spirit, was in fact a failure of nerve: failure to commit himself to the defence of a man in whom he had found no crime. Niemöller, preaching in Nazi Germany with the storm-troopers closing in around him, saw Pilates everywhere. 'In these days and weeks,' he said, 'it seems dangerous to vote or to work openly and unequivocally for this Jesus, and human foresight and shrewdness may more than once give us the tempting counsel to imitate Pilate and to leave the decision to others. "Do choose for yourselves; you are free, you know, to decide whether you will have Barabbas or Jesus, of whom it is said he is called the Christ".'

So, in the gospels, the crowd chose Barabbas. They are presumed to have decided so quickly because the chief priests, like cheerleaders, whipped them up. There is never any hint of the crowd splitting into factions; the gospel-writers give them one loud hectoring voice. Some commentators suppose they did this to spread the supposed guilt of the Jews evenly and universally; there were no dissenters. But later embroiderers of the New Testament, writing in the same broad climate of distaste for the Jews, begged to differ. They did not forget that the crowd had recently been on Jesus's side. It did not make sense, they insisted, that no one had tried to defend him.

In the *Acta Pilati*, different factions in the crowd clamoured loudly for Pilate's ear. Nicodemus spoke first. He pushed himself forward with the request 'Might I have a few words, governor?' and recommended that Jesus should be dismissed without punishment: 'If what he does comes from God, it will stand. If it's merely human, it will come to nothing.' He reminded Pilate that Moses had performed proper miracles, but that his imitators had performed tricks and cures that had not received divine approval; and so they had perished, along with their followers. God himself would save this Jesus or damn him. Pilate could let him go.

The opponents of Jesus refused to accept this. 'You're his disciple!' they shouted. 'You're making a plea for him!'

Nicodemus countered: 'Is the governor his disciple too? He's making a plea for him, isn't he? Even though Caesar appointed him?'

Another supporter of Jesus then leapt up, describing how Jesus had made him walk after thirty-eight years of lying in his bed. 'Ah, but ask him what day he was healed on!' cried the opponents to Pilate.

'What day were you healed on?'

'The Sabbath, sir.'

'Ha!' shouted the opposition. 'Didn't we tell you that he heals and casts out demons on the Sabbath?'

'I still don't think he deserves death,' said Pilate. 'Even for that.'

'Then tell us, governor, if someone blasphemes against Caesar, should he die, or not?'

'He deserves to die, yes.'

'So how much more should he deserve to die, if he blasphemes against God?'

Pilate was silent. But the opponents of Jesus went on, insistent and insatiable: 'He said, "I can destroy this temple and raise it up again in three days!"'

'Which temple?' Pilate asked.

'The one that Solomon laboured to build for forty-six years; he says he will destroy it and build it again in three days!'

'I don't want to kill him,' Pilate insisted. 'I don't think he deserves to die.'

Supporters of Jesus were now starting up all over the crowd, waving for the governor's attention. One cried: 'I was blind, and he put his hands on my eyes, and I saw.' Another cried, 'I was bowed down, and he made me straight with a word.' The woman with the issue of blood tried to speak, but the anti-Jesus lobby cut her short: women's evidence did not count. Then came another shout, louder than the rest: 'This man is a prophet, and the demons are subject to him!'

'So why,' asked Pilate wearily, 'aren't your teachers subject to him?'

'We don't know.'

The Pilate of the *Acta* sat down in the judgement seat. He still did not know what to say. But as he sat there, he felt a whisper in his ear. An attendant murmured, 'Message from your wife, sir.'

'Not now.'

'She says, "Have nothing to do with this just man, because I've suffered many things today in a dream because of him."'

Pilate looked up at the priests and the elders. He said, 'You know that my wife is a worshipper of God, and prefers to adhere to the Jewish religion, along with you?'

'Yes,' they said. 'We know.'

'My wife says, have nothing to do with this just man. She's had a terrible dream about him.'

'Didn't we tell you he was a magician?' cried the elders, laughing. 'Now he's sent a phantom of dreams to your wife.'

It is the most fantastical element in the trial. In the gospels, only Matthew includes it. For one verse in the New Testament Pilate's wife is given, through a messenger, a voice that warns her husband to bear in mind the innocence of Jesus, revealed as she was sleeping. She then disappears, as swiftly as she has come. Everything else in the trial may be dimly plausible, but not this; not the dreams of distracted women.

Yet credulous souls supposed it happened, and that it affected Pilate; and they were right to some extent. If a dream seemed to carry a message in it, Pilate would not have discounted it. This was by all accounts a vivid morning deam, the sort that roused the sleeper, slightly nauseous, to the shock of daylight. Dreams seen after midnight were taken as true. And they were not to be ignored: even the dreams of spring, which Augustus had found 'frivolous and frightful'. Heaven still sent them as gifts and warnings. Caesar once dreamt that he was making love to his mother and that she was submissive to his embraces; it meant that he was going to be the master of the earth. On the night before the Ides when he was killed, his wife Calpurnia dreamt that the pediment of their house was crumbling and that her husband lay stabbed on her breast, his blood soaking the sheets; as she started up, the doors of their room flew open. That same night, Caesar himself dreamt that he was soaring above the clouds and joining hands with Jupiter.

The career of Augustus was also filled with presentiments and dreams. He took every one of them seriously, for his life had been shaped by them even before he was born. His mother, Alia, dreamt that she had made love to Apollo in the form of a snake; when she woke, the mark of the snake was on her body, and no amount of washing could remove it. Before she was delivered, she dreamt that her womb stretched to encompass the earth and the stars, and her husband dreamt that she gave birth to a beam of sunlight. Quintus Catulus dreamt that Jupiter chose the boy Augustus out of a group playing round his altar, blew him a kiss and wrapped him to his bosom in his cloak; Marcus Cicero dreamt that

Augustus was let down from heaven on a golden chain and was handed a whip by Jupiter as he stood at the door of the Capitol.

Spectres who appeared in dreams might have nothing to do with the gods directly, but only with private disaster. Valerius Maximus, in his *Memorable Doings and Sayings* (a highly popular work around the time Pilate left for Judea), ran through several examples. After the battle of Actium, Cassius Parmensis dreamt that a huge man came into his bedroom, black-skinned, with a dishevelled beard and straggling hair. 'Who are you?' he cried. '*Kakadaimon*,' the man howled, 'your bad demon.' Cassius yelled for his slaves, who said they had seen no one enter. He went back to sleep and saw him again. This time he called for light and kept his slaves with him; the demon did not reappear, but Cassius was sentenced to death by Caesar shortly thereafter. The Roman knight Aterius Rufus also foresaw his death in a dream, in which a gladiator pierced his breast with a sword. At the show the next day he told his friends, who were sitting in the next seats; but they laughed the dream away and made him stay. The gladiator of the dream then entered the arena, chased his rival into the knights' seats, and, lunging at him, killed Rufus instead, just as he had been killed in his dream.

Rufus could not have escaped this dream. It was his fate. But if one of his friends had dreamed of his death or his disgrace, Rufus might have been able to deflect it by propitiating the gods. A friend constantly dreamed that bad things would happen to Martial; as a result, Martial complained, he had no more wine, pigs or frankincense left to sacrifice to keep his fate at bay. 'Either stay awake, Nasidianus,' he wrote furiously, 'or dream about yourself!'

What form could Procula's dream have taken? Had Jesus appeared in her room too, bearded and loud, or dangling from a golden chain, or in easy familiarity with the gods? Had crumbling buildings suggested that his death might be important? Possibly Jesus had appeared to her with that strange intensity that characters acquire in dreams: his face sketchy, almost misty, but his body charged with physical energy and even with eroticism. He might have entered softly, in the white robe of the hero, persuading her of his holiness with a mere gesture or a glance; or in a blaze of extraordinary, embarrassing involvement, as when the gods descended to the couches of common mortals.

The nineteenth-century popularisers were convinced that Procula had dreamed of Jesus, his face appearing with all the sad-eyed solemnity of the lithographs that lined their halls. They imagined that she had gone to bed late in any case, kept up by the odd noises downstairs:

deputations, the priests' demands for help in arresting Jesus, the clanking departure of the cohort towards the garden of Gethsemane. She was interested in this man already, they surmised, already haunting the outer courtyards of the synagogues. It was no wonder he featured in her dreams. But the medieval writers dismissed all that. They believed, on the contrary, that Procula had dreamed about the Devil.

The terrifying scene was set. There she lay, centre-stage, in the half-dark. In the Gréban play Satan tiptoed up to her, softly twitching the curtain so that she moaned and moved in her sleep. 'No, don't wake, dear,' he whispered. 'I won't ravish you . . . or, at least, only through your ear . . .'

Procula moaned again.

'Your husband holds sway over the life and death of a holy and saintly man. His name's Jesus, who calls himself Christ . . . You must make sure your husband doesn't pass sentence on him, for if he does you'll both be utterly destroyed.'

Procula cried out in her sleep, covered her ears.

'Don't fret!' whispered Satan. 'I'm such a gentleman . . . I won't deflower you of anything but your peace of mind . . . Just remember what I said! Tell your husband!'

He blew her a kiss, and let the curtain fall. In the Coventry play he did the same, 'making no din', but this was out of character. In most other plays the Devil could creep up on Procula only because she, like her husband, was a drunkard, and her sleep was deep. Everyone else could hear Satan as he erupted on the stage 'in most horrible wise', hairy, obscene, red-bearded, to make his case. He was the king of hell, commanding thousands of demons, mixing up the brimstone in great brass vats; no cunning clerk could escape him. But he was worried about Jesus and his miracles. He had worked out a clever plan to get him; he had made the cross ready, 'with three nails to tack him with'; but perhaps after all it was not a good idea to entertain this wonder-worker in his kingdom. What if he defeated him? What if, as his demons fretted, Jesus 'burst the power of hell asunder'? It was better after all to save him, to make sure he didn't die, so that redemption was thwarted and hell left alone. The York Satan made the same point about this 'gentleman Jesus':

> By any sign that I see, this same is God's son.
> If he shall be slain, our solace shall cease.

> He will save man's soul from our hand,
> And ravage our realms all around.

As far as Satan was concerned, to work through a woman was not only sound psychologically, but neat theologically. As one woman, Eve, had brought death to man, so another would make sure that Satan retained his *imperium mortis*, his death-grip on the world. And so he crept up to embrace Pilate's wife.

She was terrified. The Gréban Satan, however smilingly, said she would be destroyed; the York Satan snarled that she and Pilate would lose all their power and riches; the Coventry Satan, through whose diatribe she seemed to have been snoring, screamed that they would both go to hell unless they obeyed him, and filled her dreams with 'wildfire and thunderblast'. In every case she leapt out of bed, pulling the golden drapes down and round her to cover up her nakedness. The York Procula sent her grumpy little son to tell Pilate ('Oh, *what*? I've got to go *now*?'); the Gréban Procula sent her maid, nicknamed Fluff, who had fallen in love with the dark, handsome, cloven-footed man she had just encountered on the stairs. Only in the Coventry play did Procula herself burst in on Pilate, 'her skirt and kirtle in her hand, like a mad woman'. But however the message was relayed, Pilate received it seriously. Where necessary, he calmed Procula down, but he did not discount what she told him. On the contrary, as in Matthew's gospel, his wife's dream pushed Pilate as far as he had yet dared go towards sparing Jesus.

We think of this as an attempted act of mercy: Pilate's good angel, in the form of his wife, prompting him to spare an innocent man. The medieval writers proposed a more complicated theology. It was the Devil that pushed Pilate towards mercy, to upset the plan of salvation. But the demands of divine justice were that Jesus should die; Pilate could not decide otherwise. Although it might be true, as Gerard Manley Hopkins wrote, that Jesus 'did not entrap Pilate, Caiaphas and Satan into crucifying him; . . . on the contrary he was all the time giving graces which his enemies might have used,' those graces always seemed weaker than the roar of the mob and his own silence. At various times in the trial, according to all sorts of interpretations, Pilate was tempted by the notion of being both virtuous and brave; but his good angel, brutal and effulgent, was on the other side.

There was no resolving this contradiction. The theology itself was in confusion. The judgement Pilate was to make would be wicked and damnable, but it would also be liberating and essential. In the centuries that followed, the day of his decision would be cursed: wine would turn sour, washed clothes would never be clean, baked bread would smear the oven with a trail of bloody crumbs. Yet this would also be the Friday that men called Good.

The gospels suggest dilemmas enough in any case. Pilate needed no added complications from his wife. If she was really there in Jerusalem, as Matthew says she was, her role was to keep away from the courtroom, merely giving moral support from a distance; the nearest she could get was to sit behind a curtain, hiding herself from the men's world. Pliny's wife was the ideal. 'How full of solicitude she is,' he wrote, 'when I am entering upon any cause! How kindly does she rejoice with me when it's over! When I'm pleading, she stations messengers to tell her from time to time what applause I'm getting, and how the case is going.' Procula, by contrast, had drawn Pilate's awful situation in the starkest terms, even if she obeyed Roman rules and never interrupted his business in person; even if she stayed in bed, eyes bruised, hair dishevelled, cheeks scratched with her own nails, letting the *ornatrix* dab salve on the courses of her tears. For if Jesus was just, and Pilate condemned him, he would offend the gods and the reputation of Rome. Yet if he did not give the crowd what it wanted, things might get out of hand, and he might be reported to Tiberius and lose his job; or worse.

That is the dilemma pictured in the gospels. It expressed itself in physical agitation; Pilate kept getting up, pacing round, going into the *praetorium*, coming out again. Such turbulence had no place in a trial; if the crime was serious, Pilate should have judged it sitting utterly still on his *sella curulis*, the sacred symbol of justice and of his office. And such turbulence was the very antithesis of the Roman public speaker, who was supposed to rise 'like the morning star from the eastern waters', and, before he uttered even a word, stand rapt and motionless before his audience. Instead, Pilate resembled the dreadful Verres, once pro-praetor of Sicily, who had a reputation for taking money to decide cases. In one, Verres had to decide whether to take a small bribe to acquit a just man, or a large one to condemn him. He could not decide. 'He turned himself every way,' said Cicero, prosecuting, 'not only in his mind but also in his body; so that everyone could plainly see that fear and covetousness were contending together in his heart. There was a great crowd of people present, and profound silence, and eager expectation which way his covetousness was finally going to find rest. His attendant was constantly stooping down to his ear . . .'

There must have been attendants with Pilate, too; he would not have been alone, though in the gospels it seems as though he is. There would have been people stooping down to whisper to him, too, as he sat in his chair, or walking at his shoulder as he paced about. An early apocryphal version of the trial suggests another parallel to the Verres case: that the Jews were offering Pilate money to give the decision they wanted. But the evangelists (who noticed that Festus offered to release Paul for money) would not have missed that routine Roman weakness.

Luke's Pilate asked the crowd: 'What shall I do with him?'

'Crucify him!' they shouted back. What else was a Roman governor good for? How else did he amuse himself?

'I can't find him guilty of anything. Nothing he has done is worthy of death. So I'll flog him and let him go.'

'No!' they yelled. 'Not this one! Let Barabbas go! Crucify this one! *Crucify him!*'

'*Why*?' asked Pilate. He too was shouting at top volume now; Luke says that 'he cried out in addressing them'. 'What wrong has this fellow done? I've found no cause of death in him.'

He threw out his offer again. The Greek suggests that he was as emotional and insistent as they were, but the repetition did not suggest resolve. It suggested a man who needed to convince himself that anything he did could work at all.

'I will flog him and let him go.'

*　　*　　*

Cicero, yes, had something to say on this.

Now when we meet with expediency in some specious form or other, we cannot help being influenced by it. But if on closer inspection we see that there is some immorality connected with what appears to be expediency, then we should not necessarily sacrifice expediency, but recognise that there can be no expediency where there is immorality.

For if there is nothing so repugnant to nature as immorality (for nature demands right and harmony and consistency, and abhors their opposites), and if nothing is so thoroughly in accord with nature as expediency, then surely expediency and immorality cannot co-exist in one and the same object.

Again: if we are born for moral rectitude and if that is either the only thing worth seeking, as Zeno thought, or is at least to be esteemed as infinitely outweighing everything else, as Aristotle holds, then it necessarily follows that the morally right is either the sole good or the supreme good. Now, that which is good is certainly expedient; consequently, what is morally right is also expedient.

Thus it is the error of men who are not strictly upright to seize upon something that seems to be expedient and straight away to dissociate it from the question of moral right. To this error the assassin's dagger, the poisoned cup, the forged will owe their origin; this gives rise to theft, embezzlement of public funds, exploitation and plundering of provincials and citizens; this engenders also the lust for excessive wealth, for despotic power, and finally for making oneself king even in the midst of a free people; and anything more atrocious than such a passion cannot be conceived. For with a false perspective they see the material rewards but not the punishment; I do not mean the penalty of the law, which they often escape, but the heaviest penalty of all, their own demoralisation.

Away, then, with questioners of this sort . . . who stop to consider whether to pursue the course which they see is morally right or to stain their hands with what they know is crime. For there is guilt in their very deliberation.

Did that help?

(Should Cicero have begged Antony's pardon?)

(Should the Spartans have fled when they were sent against Xerxes?)

(Should Alexander have sailed the ocean?)

*   *   *

In art and tradition, Jesus was hidden for the scourging. He was taken into an inner room of the palace, even into the basement, and whipped by soldiers in the half-dark. Yet scourging was a public punishment. In Rome it was done in the Forum itself, in front of the crowd and in front of the judgement seat, before which the victim was flung at the end. In

Judea, at least in Florus's time (a few years after Pilate), it was done precisely where Pilate was now sitting, in front of his chair.

Like crucifixion, scourging was illegal – though not unknown – for Roman citizens, because it was a punishment of slaves. The official order for scourging was *I, lictor, colliga manus*: 'Go, lictor, tie his hands.' If there were no lictors (and the gospels imply that Pilate had none), ordinary soldiers or even household servants did the job instead. The scourging was done either with the lictors' rods, switches of elm, or with leather thongs tipped with fragments of lead and bone.

This torture was not a legal requirement. It was merely a custom grown solid with repetition, and the severity of the treatment depended on what was meant to happen next. If the victim was to proceed directly to crucifixion, the scourging was relatively light to preserve his strength. If the judge intended to let him off with a flogging only, it was as brutal as he thought necessary. Matthew and Mark take the view that the scourging, as was normal, immediately preceded the crucifixion, and was therefore the preliminary to death. John supposes that Pilate, still struggling with his conviction of Christ's innocence, meant the scourging as a gesture of appeasement to his accusers, and perhaps as a last attempt to extract a confession by torture. When Paul was arrested by the Romans later, the chief captain ordered that he should be 'examined by scourging'.

Luke, too, suggests that this was the way the governor's mind was working. According to these writers, Pilate intended to reduce Jesus to a figure of pity who might be spared by the Jews. It was typical Roman thinking: in the Roman law courts an accused man would deliberately dress in black mourning clothes, grow a straggly beard, neglect to wash, in order to incite pity in the jurors. Pilate was the only jury here, but the crowd seemed to be competing with him; so, in a formula that has since become ever more useful to politicians, he scourged Jesus to save him. He had found his middle course.

To say that Pilate 'took him and scourged him', as the gospels do, is not a misstatement. Although he did not do so with his own hands, he would have attended and supervised. Having given the order to start, and knowing just how far he wanted this to go, he also had to give the order to stop. He therefore sat in his judgement seat and oversaw what was done: the stripping of Jesus to his loincloth (he would have been prudish, like most Romans, about nakedness in criminals); the tying, in a half-bent position, to a pillar; the exact loss of blood, the progress of exhaustion. Perhaps he counted aloud, as people counted at the gladiator shows, the precise number of strokes as they fell. *Unum, duo, tres, quattuor.* In the process, he may have found himself watching for stranger signs, despite his position of judicial indifference: for blood the colour of resin, for skin that did not break, for bruises of peculiar regularity, that might have confirmed the claims of this man to come from some otherworldly place. The veins of the gods were supposed to run not with blood but with ichor: Alexander had once damped down the idea that he was divine by remarking, when he was wounded, that only blood was flowing from him. In the case of Jesus, too, the blood and the weariness were human.

The medieval plays made much, even too much, of the scourging scene. They dwelt with appalled fascination on the thought that men could actually whip, and then mock, the son of God. Yet they faced a dilemma: for though Pilate was deeply involved, indeed responsible, they still needed to keep him slightly distant and sympathetic. So while the brutality of the soldiers never wavered, Pilate's did. As during the trial itself, he vacillated from confidence to sadism to sudden horror at what he was doing. In one French play, he even let Jesus in on his ruse to save him: 'Jesus, don't worry about these people. You'll be all right.'

In the York play, Pilate gives the order as tersely as one would expect: 'Right, men, get this straight. Strip him, make him bleed, and beat him black and blue. Wring him till he weeps.' The soldiers then set to work, glorying in the job, and remarking that they would go even further 'if it wasn't for Sir Pilate.' At that point, they stop and look at the governor. He gets up and comes over to inspect the work, holding his robe out of the blood.

'You, man,' he says to Jesus. 'Why do you suffer all this and never ask us for mercy? Isn't that an arrogant way to behave? You ought to be humble. We're the masters here. If men call you a king, tell us why. Tell us why the Jews want to kill you. Inform me. I want to know.'

He searches the swollen face; but Jesus will not answer.

'He's going to faint or something, sir.'

'Yes, we'd better not kill him, had we, sir?'

'Inform me!' Pilate shouts.

'Sir, I've got a great idea. He called himself a king, so let's make him one! Let's sit him here in this chair, really comfortable, as if he was in his own hall, and then we'll crown him with nice brambles, give him a lovely purple robe —'

'Do it,' says Pilate. And leaves them.

The mockery then begins: the robing, the crowning, the hailing. The silly soldiers prick their fingers on the thorns, admire the blood, make up songs.

'Hail, doughty dumb duke!'
'Hail, lord with no land!'
'Hail, fool with no force!'
'Hey, harlot. What about a bit of thanks to all of us who are working so hard to worship you?'

Just as things are getting out of hand, the door flies open. It is Pilate. He storms in, flinging the men aside. 'No more!' he cries. 'No more! No more!'

They fall back, stunned.

'Are you men of stone? Leave him alone!'

'But sir –'

'Stand aside! Leave him alone!'

In the silence that follows Pilate walks up to Jesus, his face slack with regret; and it seems for a moment as though he might touch him.

'Ah, look,' he murmurs. 'He blushes all blue.'

If the mockery happened this way, in the middle of the trial, Pilate probably watched. John gives no indication that he left the scene; he only implies that he took no active part in it. This made him no less culpable. After all, he allowed it, even if he did not order it explicitly. In Matthew and Mark, where the scourging and mocking happened at the end of the trial, he had already left; Matthew's Pilate had already washed his hands of the whole affair. That did not exculpate him, either.

In the vast hall of the palace ('the common hall', Matthew calls it), the whole cohort supposedly passed before Jesus. Hundreds of soldiers each kneeled and saluted him, some spitting and slapping his face. A man who wished to show himself superior to military rough-housing would take no part in this charade; a man who liked the ritual humiliations of the Roman shows, or who wanted to be one of the lads, might even enjoy it. We do not know which of these types Pilate was. Possibly he was either type at different times, as the mood took him. Those who endorse John's account have usually imagined that he left the soldiers to it. But perhaps, after all, the distancing was only in his head.

According to John, Pilate scourged Jesus although he thought he was innocent. Then, still thinking him innocent, he let him be mocked by his men. Assuming that this is how things were, would it have troubled Pilate's conscience? Or, to put it more brutally, did he have a conscience that could recognise when it should have been troubled? Probably. As a Roman, the concept was not foreign to him. In all the incidents of his life that are reported, violence or wilfulness or intransigence was followed by a glimmering of conscience, a shadow of repentance. Something or someone seemed to whisper to him then. Perhaps it was his *genius*, the guardian spirit who ruled his birth-star, imploring him to keep on a straight track. *Genii*, though divine, were attached as if in cages to each man's life; only death could free them. Their murmur told him not to do what he should not, and reminded him how brief life was. When a man sinned, the face of his guardian spirit changed from white to black like the demon of Cassius Parmensis; and although he could propitiate the spirit with flowers and wine, only virtuous action could restore its brightness. On every birthday he became pure again by offering, in sacrifice to the spirit, the birthday wreaths from his forehead and the honey cake from his table; and also by making resolutions to be good.

A man who revered the gods, or even one single providence, kept a natural guard over his conduct. He might be more lax if his sense of the gods was routine or distant, or if his most intense devotions were reserved for a man who could not see him. But there remained, as Seneca put it, 'his own rules'. If Pilate watched the mockery, as John suggests, it may still have been with some of that tortuous examination of the rules or of his conscience which, in other incidents, he plainly had to carry out in public.

At last, he must have stopped the horseplay. Another wave of the hand, or a snap of the fingers. And then the prisoner was brought over. The nineteenth-century writers endlessly pictured and coloured this scene. Jesus was wedged between two guards, barely standing. The cloak was askew on his shoulders, the crown of thorns lopsided on his head. Blood was drying on his face; his beard was crusted with it. Pilate, they imagined, looked at the face for a while. He searched it for whatever information it could give him, but it reflected only his own deliberate humiliations. No information, no confession. Ludicrously, some writers thought, he may have tried a small smile of encouragement, as if to say, This is your chance, I'm helping you now. But the smile wavered, his eyes pricked, and he turned away exasperated by his own weakness.

He walked out again to the balustrade. In most ages, the scene that followed – though only John described it – was the emotional peak of the trial. Pilate, having reduced Jesus to the most pitiable sight imaginable, would now present him to the crowd. He had brought him to the point where even he, Pilate, couldn't bear to hurt him any more. The judge had become the advocate, and, as Farrar wrote, 'with all the strength of a feeble pride, and all the daring of a guilty cowardice, and all the pity of which a blood-stained nature was capable, did strive to deliver him.'

Once more he faced the crowd. In one Edwardian lithograph of the scene he leans right over, throwing out his left arm, almost airborne in his attempt to persuade them. 'Look,' he shouted, 'I'm bringing him out to you, to let you know that I find no fault in him!'

Jesus was brought out, still in the cloak and the crown. He stood beside the governor now, the unbearable, piteous, ludicrous figure; Pilate could smell his unwashed skin. Medieval and Renaissance painters of this scene put the two men apart, with Jesus almost in the crowd and Pilate, flanked by aides and advisors, still discussing legal strategy in the background. But Christ's nineteenth-century biographers liked to have them close. Some writers imagined he took Jesus by the hand, the first pagan touch that was not meant to cause him pain; or that, like some thoughtless election-winner, he seized and thrust aloft the arm of his rival. But whatever he did, John's Pilate also cried out: 'Behold the man!'

What on earth did he mean? Sentimentalists thought the strangeness of the phrase was easily accounted for: Pilate, almost in tears, blurted out any brief form of words that would do as a public statement. His magisterial reserve had melted away. It was replaced by the great phrase the Victorians found so thrilling, *Ecce Homo*, words that implied man but meant God, and which even suggested adoration: although most writers accepted that Pilate himself was highly unlikely to have thought that, and may indeed have been scarcely aware of what he was doing.

John gave the words in Greek and not Latin, in any case; and *Ide, o anthropos!* could carry a variety of meanings, from 'Look at this poor fellow,' to 'What a figure of a man is this!' According to John (and again, only John) Pilate had last used the word *anthropos* at the very beginning of the trial, when he asked 'What charges do you bring against this man?' So perhaps it was more neutral, even legalistic; or perhaps John was putting the word in Pilate's mouth to make some point about glory and divinity in human shape. Only John – or Pilate, if he spoke those words – knew exactly what he meant to say.

Yet the time for introductions was short. Immediately the crowd screamed back, 'Crucify him! Crucify him!'

Pilate seems to have been stunned by their reaction. Despite his brutal scourging of a man whose case was, at best, uncertain, the crowd did not pity the victim at all. In fact, he seemed to have made things worse; for whereas before, in John, the crowd had only wanted Barabbas, they were clamouring now for the cross. His ruse had failed. He was beside himself with humiliation and anger.

'*You* take him yourselves. *You* crucify him. I find no fault in him at all.'

A ridiculous thing to say. I find him innocent, but yes, kill him. Your immorality and illegality are fine with me. I'm only a Roman judge, what do I know? Or even more ridiculous: *You* crucify him. The Jews could not crucify anyone. He meant, If you are so keen to kill him, go ahead. Don't make me do it. Like so much that day, it came out idiotic and wrong. Even his insults didn't work: his anger and his flippancy alike evaporated uselessly above the seething heads. He kept on saying, according to John, 'I find no fault in him. I find no fault in him.' In the original Greek the '*ego*' is always at the start of the phrase, suggesting that whatever the priests and the crowd might think, he proudly and passionately disagreed. But the crowd went on howling like the sea in a gale, as Virgil described that sea that wrecked Aeneas: violence brewing in great clouds, the 'mass-mind boiling over' like the spume of terrific waves. And he couldn't calm them; because the only man who could calm such a sea or such a crowd, Virgil continued, was someone 'whose goodness of heart and conduct/has won their respect.'

So he stood there, with Jesus still beside him.

The elders said: 'We have a law, and by our law he ought to die, because he made himself the Son of God.'

*　　*　　*

Pilate's answer should have been easy. The Jews' religious law had nothing to do with him or with Rome. It was their affair. They could take Jesus away and stone him for blasphemy if they wanted to; they could leave him out of it. But, according to John at least, that is not what happened. Pilate instead became 'more afraid'.

No particular fear had been registered in him before. He had been obtuse, off-hand and surprised; he had tried, in his usual way, to slide from one clever scheme to another. Now, apparently, he was afraid.

Real fear was something a Roman man tried not to show; rather than show it, he would pull his toga across to hide his face from others. Pilate's fear, in John, was not quite like that. It was an increasing anxiety that he could not postpone much longer his decision for the truth or against it. Now the stakes were mounting: he had to find out whether Jesus was the Son of God or not. It was an area in which he had no judicial competence at all, but he approached it with a sort of petrified fascination: similar, perhaps, to what Felix felt later, when Paul instructed him in the notion of faith in Christ and Felix 'trembled'.

Instead of answering the chief priests, John's Pilate went back inside the *praetorium* and beckoned Jesus to follow him. Once again, to all intents and purposes, they were alone. They could continue their earlier conversation, the one about kingdoms not of this world. But it had taken a different turn. It had gone deeper. When they had last spoken, they had got as far as 'truth' before Pilate balked. He had not wanted to go on. Now, consumed with worry, he thought he ought to try.

The question Pilate asked was *Pothen ei sy?* 'Where are you from?'

It was not meant literally. He knew as well as Jesus did that he came from Nazareth, in Galilee. It was a composite question. Bloomfield's *Recensio Synoptica* of 1826 translates it as: 'What is your origin? what are your parents? [That essential Roman question: establish the tribe and class.] terrestrial or celestial? merely human, or divine? or mixed?' All in three words, which might best be translated in English as: 'Who are you, really?'

Behind that question lay every unsettling, half-grasped phrase John's Pilate had heard that day. *Not of this world. Not from here. I came into this world to bear witness to the truth.* And now, *Son of God.* Pilate did not take chances with gods. This was why he let the Jews worship theirs, although he could neither respect nor understand a deity that was singular and could not be depicted; this was why he honoured his own with a fervour that got him into trouble again and again. That, indeed, was the Son of God he would have thought he knew: *Caesar, divi filius.*

And what of the rest? Whether or not he gave credence to the whole catalogue of characters, he had known since childhood exactly what the gods were like. Bearded Jupiter with the lightning in his pocket; sandal-winged Mercury, blue-eyed Neptune; blonde Minerva in her helmet, the goddess he had prayed to as a schoolboy to get his exercises right. Even in a Roman's dreams, as Cicero said, these details were unvarying and particular. When Pilate thought of Juno, the mother of the gods, he saw her in her goat-skin and upturned slippers, with a shield and spear in her hand; he saw Venus as a woman whose skin was soft as roses and whose hair breathed out ambrosia, even when she disguised herself as a hunting-girl, in high soft boots, among the mountains of North Africa.

For the gods did come down among men, at least in the stories he knew. At the founding of Italy they had done so constantly, as well as before it. They had lain with mortals and produced more gods, and sons of gods; but like humans, like this Jesus, they had sometimes been rebuffed, or had wept in frustration. Propertius recorded that even Jupiter had cried with disappointment once, a man rejected: *deceptus quoniam flevit et ipse deus*. As Justin Martyr pointed out, the Jewish prophecies of the suffering Christ were easily confused with these tales. The sons of Jupiter – Mercury, Aesculapius, Hercules, Dionysus – had suffered on the earth like men, fighting, torn in pieces, oppressed with labours, struck by lightning. They were taken up to heaven but then, scarcely settled among the stars, they returned again. Castor and Pollux had been sighted, two young warriors on white horses, fighting on the Roman side at the battle of Lake Regillus; Castor's horse had left a footprint in the rock. And often, Cicero added, 'the sound of the voice of the Fauns, or the apparition of a divine form, has compelled anyone who is not simple-minded to admit the real presence of the gods.'

The sons of gods could always be detected, or almost always. As soon as Aeneas, the son of Venus, approached Dido, the queen of Carthage, she knew that he was half-divine: he stood there 'in an aura of brilliant light, godlike in face and figure'. Even his small son revealed, when necessary, the touch of the gods: a halo of gently flickering fire among his curls. Although these beings might be broken, they still shone, as when the head of the murdered Orpheus sang in the crimsoned river that carried the rags of his body away. If Pilate probed a little deeper into this man Jesus, he too might find this light: a light that would seem to open a crack in the dome of the sky and let through an icy filament of air.

He could have ignored it. But it was dangerous to ignore the gods; it could bring havoc, ignominy, bad luck. They could adopt the most ludicrous disguises, from hissing snakes to toothless crones; even, perhaps, an irritating Jew in a lopsided crown. When Dionysus descended to earth, he dressed in a deerskin with a wreath of ivy on his long blond curls. It did not seem much of a disguise, but Pentheus, the king of Thebes, still failed to recognise him; he took him for another troublemaker, an imposter, leading the women into the hills to do their obscene dancing. When he had him arrested at last, and they stood face to face, he found himself marvelling at the brightness of his hair and the whiteness of his skin, the faint thrilling perfume of wine on him. He had scorned and condemned this man but now, suddenly, he wanted to know. He wanted to know who he was.

John's Pilate was now in the same position. Across the chasm of incomprehension he extended, like Pentheus, a tentative hand. He could be informed, he could keep a secret, he could be an accomplice. And he asked the same question as Pentheus, in the same words: 'Where are you from?'

But Jesus would not answer him.

The question hung between them. The non-answer seemed to say: If I told you, you would not understand. I'm weak, and it's too complicated. You had your chance earlier, and you threw it away. Remain in your ignorance; I don't want your commiseration.

Pentheus had been there too.

Pentheus. What form do they take, these mysteries of yours?
Dionysus. It is forbidden to tell the uninitiate.
Pentheus. Tell me the benefits that those who know your mysteries enjoy.
Dionysus. I am forbidden to say. But they are worth knowing.
Pentheus. Your answers are designed to make me curious.
Dionysus. No: our mysteries abhor an unbelieving man.
Pentheus. You say you saw the god. What form did he assume?
Dionysus. Whatever form he wished. The choice was his, not mine.
Pentheus. You evade the question.
Dionysus. Talk sense to a fool and he calls you foolish.

Pilate had reached the same point with Jesus, the same slap in the face. It was a rebuke, certainly. But Henry Liddon, a Victorian clergyman, interpreted the slap as kindness. This was really a child Jesus was talking to: the child to whom he had said, 'Are you saying that yourself, or did other people tell you that about me?' He had to be careful how much he told Pilate. To hand him something sacred and transcendent would be foolish; he would only drop it or misuse it. 'Do not give what is holy to dogs,' Jesus had said once, precisely meaning to Romans. Don't let them break it, even if they beg you for it. Beware those eager, slipping, dangerous fingers. 'We should all of us agree,' Liddon went on, preaching in St Paul's in 1881 as anarchist bombs exploded in Moscow, 'that there are just now people up and down Europe who are none the better for knowing something of the properties of dynamite; and a wise and kind father would not begin the education of his little boy by showing him how to fire off a loaded pistol.'

So John's Pilate, the little boy, was not handed the loaded gun. It was held silently away from him, locked up where he could not see it. He reacted accordingly. 'Won't you speak to me? *To me*? Don't you know that I have authority to release you and authority to crucify you?'

The answer to being hurt and humiliated was his usual one: to draw himself up like a wounded animal to the full height of his powers. The word he used for 'authority' was *imperium, exousia* in the Greek, the numinous power he drew from Tiberius himself; there could be nothing more impressive. He was even falling back on legal jargon, as officials tend to do at moments of crisis. Yet his question had not just been a judicial one, to which he wanted an answer as a magistrate: it was also a question in which he was interested as a man, and not to answer was, to a Roman, the height of rudeness. His hurt, however publicly expressed, was also personal.

So Jesus replied to him. His words were both tender and extraordinarily defiant: 'You have no power over me at all, except what was given to you from above; therefore he who delivered me to you has the greater sin.'

The words were fairly mystifying, and their conjunction more so. In John's Greek, each noun and verb carries several meanings. What comes through is a strange, almost thrilling, clash of egos. The word *emoi*, to me or against me, was thrown out by both men at the start of their remarks: in answer to Pilate's literal '*To me* won't you speak?' Jesus in effect replied, '*Against me*, you're powerless.' This *emoi* is so emphatic that it is, in itself, almost an admission of kingship. Pilate was unlikely to have missed it.

Yet the word 'sin', *amartia*, is the one that lingers. *Meizona amartia*, greater sin. That apparently belonged to Caiaphas, the one who had delivered Jesus to Pilate; or, as medieval writers thought, to Judas, the one who had betrayed him. But Pilate too was among 'the sinners' into whose hands Jesus had predicted he would fall. His sin was great, Jesus implied; it paled only beside the sin of Caiaphas, which was greater. Caiaphas knew with whom he was dealing; Pilate did not, so his ignorance could be used in mitigation. Caiaphas had delivered Jesus out of envy; Pilate was prepared to kill him out of fear, or even out of habit. In the exercise of his authority, he had killed men before, and this marked the beginning of his downward slide; as Gerard Manley

Hopkins noted, 'If you will murder man you may come, as Pilate did, to murder the man who is God.'

The notion of sin was not clear, however. Something was lost in translation. A Roman sin was a crime, a mistake, an aberration, from a slip of the pen to a cut throat. Sins were deeds done, and could be counted. You could fall into one sin or into many, as Cicero put it, *in peccata incidere*, as into a swarm of bees; but there was no general state of sin into which a man could sink, as in a quicksand. Pilate's day-to-day prayers would have carried no notion either of sin or of forgiveness: it was success and safety he prayed for. To the extent that he had made mistakes, his sins that day were obvious. He had vacillated; he had turned the decision about Jesus over to the crowd; in Socrates' words, he had committed sin by failing to know what was false and what was true. But he had not entered – could not imagine entering – that pervasive sense of sin that Jesus was implying.

Socrates may have haunted him in another way. At that trial, too, the accused man had become the man in charge. Socrates knew he was more virtuous than the Athenians who had gathered to condemn him for supposedly corrupting their sons. The Oracle at Delphi had pronounced him the wisest man in the world; and besides, he had a 'sign of God' in him, a divine voice of restraint that held him back from what was unwise or wrong. He could not sin, but his accusers could. It was from this height of God-touched assurance that Socrates spoke at his trial: 'not a supplicant or a witness, but the master and lord of his judges', as Cicero described him. And here, in Jerusalem, something similar was happening. The tables had been turned. It was Pilate, not Jesus, who had to acknowledge his guilt and struggle to save himself. Pilate had, as yet, found no sin in Jesus; but Jesus had found sin in him, and had stated it as a fact with no need of witnesses at all.

Jesus had also told him something else. He had said that Pilate's power came 'from above', or 'from the top'. He could have meant from the emperor – that would have been Pilate's instinctive understanding – but perhaps he meant higher still. Most scholars agree that the word meant 'from heaven, from divine power'. John's Pilate had nothing to say to this, suggesting eloquently that he couldn't fathom what Jesus was saying; but nor could he deflect it with one of his flippant remarks. The Gréban play gave him a reply of sorts:

> Well, I don't know what you're getting at.
> Who can be greater than the Emperor?

He is Apollo, Jupiter and all the gods in one.
What other Emperor could have a power like that?

Silence may have been the best reaction, for what Jesus was saying was extraordinary. He was telling Pilate that his role was not fortuitous. Divine Providence had put him there. Pilate's power over him was God-given; Pilate himself was God's vice-regent, perhaps even his instrument. (Paul, in his letter to the Romans, made that thought even more explicit: 'The powers that be are ordained of God . . . a ruler is God's servant.') And Jesus, who stood before him, was also God's instrument. Beyond the brotherhood of humanity, which Pilate may already have sensed, they were in some unfathomable way brothers in heaven. And Jesus, who knew what God's will was, was suggesting that Pilate too might come to understand and advance it. He too could be good; he could be the *candidatus* in his shining robe, ready for the wreath of divine favour to settle on his glowing hair.

But what did God, or the gods, demand of him? It was still unclear. In the *Acta Pilati* Pilate called Jesus into the *praetorium* to ask a different, almost hopeless, question: 'What shall I do with you?'

Jesus answered, 'Do as it has been given to you.'

'How has it been given?'

'Moses and the prophets said that I would die and rise again.'

This was the clearest expression of Pilate as God's agent; but it led in an impossible direction. It asked him not to save Jesus, but to kill him. In the *Acta Pilati* the chief priests, eavesdropping outside, interrupted the conversation before Jesus could explain further; and Pilate continued to believe that he could not, should not, put Jesus to death. Virtue could lie only in the act of salvation.

In John's gospel too, Pilate apparently made the same decision: to save him. Whereas before, in the literal sense of the Greek, he had merely been 'willing' to release him, he now 'sought to', earnestly and zealously. Pilate would act as the gods had moved him to. If the Jews overwhelmed him, he could call the troops out of the Antonia and suppress the unrest in the usual manner; he would think later about precisely how to explain events to Tiberius. The force of the sword was the force of right. Blood would flow in the streets again, but Rome would not be party to the execution of this innocent prisoner who was touched by God. In the name of righteousness, certainty, even happiness, he went back out to the crowd.

This was what Seneca was to call 'the adventure of being good':

He that judges right, and perseveres in it, enjoys a perpetual calm; he takes a true prospect of things; he observes order and measure in all his actions; he has a benevolence in his nature; he squares his life according to reason, and draws to himself love and admiration. Without a certain and unchangeable judgement, all the rest is pure speculation.

. . . If you could only see the mind of a good man . . . the beauty and the majesty of it . . . would not a man bless himself at the sight of such a thing, as at the encounter of some supernatural power?

. . . What I do shall be done for conscience, not ostentation . . . I will look upon the whole world as my country, and upon the gods as both the witnesses and judges of my words and deeds. I will live and die with this testimony: that I loved good studies and a good conscience; that I never invaded another man's liberty, and that I preserved my own.

It was thrilling; but it couldn't last. In an instant it fell apart. All it took was one phrase, shouted out of John's mob and then picked up in a merciless chorus: 'If you let this man go, you are not Caesar's friend. Whoever makes himself a king speaks against Caesar!'

It was the Jews' last gambit. They had tried 'evil doing', but Pilate had refused to accept their allegation. They had tried 'king of the Jews', surely seditious, but Pilate had dismissed it. Next they had tried a religious offence, but this had made Pilate even more unwilling to act. Now they had found a real nerve: the governor's private fears. And whatever else may have been imagined in John's passion story, this part rings true.

Pilate, as we have seen, was almost certainly not a friend of Caesar in the official sense. The Jews may have been remembering that Herod the Great, that half-Jewish sycophant, had styled himself 'Friend of Caesar' as well as 'Friend of Rome'; perhaps they thought the title automatic in a man who governed Judea. There was also a wider circle, a longer list from which Pilate could be struck off: *interdicta amicitia* was the phrase, debarred from the emperor's friendship, as if it was the only sort that counted. But the Jews seemed to mean no more than 'You are not loyal to him'. And that was accusation enough.

Pilate's career was characterised by an almost slavish public (and sometimes private) devotion: with Seneca, he seemed to believe that 'loyalty is the holiest good in the human heart.' But he knew that would not save him. If he slipped up, there was no doubt that people would inform against him. If the Jews did not, others would. Tiberius was known to hoard every scrap of insult, retailed from whatever source: 'whether it was a slave denouncing his master or a son his father', as Dio Cassius said. Every slighting remark was investigated, and even secret ones were published, embellished with Tiberius' own inventions. Since the death of his son Drusus by poison in 23, he had never hesitated to kill or exile people even for fictitious reasons. And by the time of the trial Pilate may also have had indelibly before him the example of the fall of Sejanus, the closest imperial friend of all: a man who had dangled in unbearable suspense between the emperor's love and his abuse.

For John's Pilate the situation was quite clear now, as indeed it had been at the outset. The chief priests had condemned Jesus, and they wanted him to die. They now had the people on their side, and the people would riot if he did not give them what they wanted. Moreover, they would tell on him. Here his past missteps and miscalculations came back to haunt him: for even if he wanted to be merciful in this case, he dared not be, if it would lead to a blistering report to Rome of everything else he had done. 'The nemesis of his past wrongdoing,' as Farrar wrote, 'was that he could no longer do right.'

Tiberius had perhaps already received unfavourable reports of him. Would he tolerate more? Did Pilate have any stock of goodwill left? If he had, was he really going to hazard it, and with it the lives of hundreds of Jews and Romans and others, on the fate of one peculiar preacher? One man's life could never be worth that. If he let his soldiers loose on people, he would be called a butcher. He might lose Judea. The crowd was already on the edge of tumult, and he was getting nowhere in his efforts to persuade them. Nor was Jesus helping: by keeping silent, offering no defence, he seemed to be asking for death.

Again, the shadow of Socrates was here. He too had wanted to die. He had gone about it in a completely different way, by arrogantly inflaming the jury, yet the aim was always in view. If a man thought nothing of death, his judge had no reason to intercede for him. There was no point in agonising over whether to release him, when the consummate release was that of the soul from the body. Besides, Pilate was not there in Judea to pursue celestial fantasies or to sift the philosophy of those he sentenced. He was there to preserve law and order in the name of Rome.

If Pilate thought Jesus guilty, the trial came down to this: a contest between defiance of the state and assertion of the state's authority. If he thought him innocent, it came down to a contest between the rights of the individual and the safety of the state. Even if Pilate was troubled by his prisoner, there was therefore no question which path he should take. The judges of Socrates had been in the same position: faced with a man whose crime was merely his teaching, in a society where different opinions were ostensibly respected, they nonetheless condemned him for turning young people against 'the gods of the city', which meant the whole apparatus of the state. The law – Pilate's law, their law, our law – stands *in extremis* always on the state's side. As Caiaphas had already pointed out in the case of Jesus, it was both right and expedient that one man should die for the people.

When Bulgakov's Pilate came before the Russian public, in 1966, it was this dilemma that intrigued the critics. Pilate was seen as a model of the spineless provincial bureaucrats of Stalinist Russia: a man who would reverence the distant tyrant, put up his tinted portrait, drink his health in bad vodka, while all the time suppressing his conscience. To save the dissident Jesus – to save Pasternak or Solzhenitsyn – was too much for him. Some Russian reviewers thought such moral cowardice could never be justified. Others disagreed. Personal morality, they wrote, could never replace civic duty as a basis for ethical behaviour in a socialist society. And a man's civic duty was to preserve the social order and promote the ideology that underpinned it. So Pilate was right: he had, in effect, nobly and firmly subjected the promptings of his conscience to the tenets of the Communist Party of the Soviet Union.

The Victorians, too, debated over many years whether Pilate was right to crucify Christ. John Stuart Mill, in his essay *On Liberty* of 1859, contended that the judges of Christ – both Jewish and Roman – could not possibly have been justified, because they had tried to stifle freedom of conscience. Like the judges of Socrates, they had simply done wrong; and, even allowing for the temper of the times, they had to be condemned as guilty. It was impossible, Mill argued, to find a principle that would justify them.

James Fitzjames Stephen, an eminent lawyer, took up the challenge. In the course of a sweeping attack on Mill in his book *Liberty, Equality, Fraternity,* published in 1873, he argued that he could certainly find 'a principle that will justify Pontius Pilate'. Pilate's paramount duty, he went on, was not to preserve anyone's freedom of conscience, or even liberty in the abstract, but to keep the peace. 'Therefore, if and insofar as he believed in good faith that what he did was necessary for the peace of Palestine, he was right.'

Stephen admitted that the word 'right' was problematic. Perhaps it could not be applied to political decisions at all; for much of what politicians did for the public good would never pass muster with 'an omnipotent, omniscient and perfectly benevolent man'. Ideas of right and duty had to be limited to allow for human weakness, for men, like Pilate, 'stuck like limpets or spinning like weathercocks'. The main problem, though, as Mill and his supporters argued back, lay in that phrase 'in good faith'. The gospels implied both that Pilate knew Jesus was innocent (understanding that the Jews had delivered him 'out of envy'), and that he said so, several times. No judge could justly condemn an innocent man, no matter how compelling the reason.

But suppose, Stephen continued, a British officer in the Punjab found himself compelled to order the execution of a native preacher who was gentle enough in himself, but whose preaching was 'dangerous to the English power'? What if he had by his side, virtually governing in association, a native ruler who was not only supporting, but actively encouraging, his decision to execute? Back came the answer from J. Taylor Innes, a practising barrister, in *The Trial of Jesus Christ*, published in 1899:

> If done judicially, it would be a judicial murder. If done administratively, what ought it to be called? . . . I believe that few British officers who considered [such an act] would, as the result, think themselves compelled or even entitled to do it.

As for the officer who examined a 'Guru or Imam' and found him innocent, but thought he would whip him anyway, and ordered his execution out of a sudden panic about his own promotion, 'suppose that the story came out fully on his arrival in London, in how many drawing rooms would he be received?'

There was still one argument left. This was that, whatever Jesus seemed to be teaching in the way of absolute moral standards, Pilate had a set of his own already, of which the highest were the preservation of the emperor and the Roman peace. Stephen imagined him unconscionably stirred by the sight of his sentries standing guard in the Temple porticoes, 'as [the Englishman's heart] beats high as he looks at the scarred and shattered walls of Delhi or at the Union Jack flying from the fort at Lahore.' What words of Virgil, 'as new and fresh as the best of Mr Tennyson's poems to us', as imperially proud and sentimental, must have come home to him then?

Tu regere imperio populos, Romane, memento
(Hae tibi erunt artes) pacique imponere morem,
Parcere subiectis et debellare superbos.

(In Dryden's translation:

> But Rome, 'tis thine alone, with awful sway,
> To rule mankind and make the world obey,
> To tame the proud, the fettered slave to free –
> These are imperial arts, and worthy thee.)

Wasn't he right to kill someone who threatened this *pax et imperium*, however indirectly? Yes, Innes answered, he would have been; but it was crystal-clear from the gospels that he had killed Jesus mostly to preserve himself.

That was how it appeared. In John the crowd reminded Pilate, who had been touched for a moment by the light, what his job was, who his boss was, what the issue was, where his reputation lay. And so he capitulated. In all the gospels, his fall was sudden. He seemed to throw up his hands; some modern writers even imagine him drowning. Bulgakov's Pilate, grieving that he has lost something even though he scarcely knows what it is, feels himself dragged down by seaweed in a purple mass of water. The Pilate of Romano Guardini, a German–Italian writing in 1956, 'is sucked into the depths of the powers of darkness, into a confusion so dark and deep that he is no longer sensible of the gruesome and ignominious folly he is committing.'

The chair of gilded wood or ivory still waited for him, set on a raised and tessellated pavement. He was out in the open air like the master of ceremonies at a show, with the same thin, wandering acoustic and the same ungrateful audience to address, whose only thought was blood. Well, he could do blood, too.

In John, he summoned Jesus out again for the last time and sat down in the chair of judgement.

'Look, your king,' he told the crowd. It was not a bitter or a mocking announcement; he was on his official platform now, obliged to be serious, and the sense was to make the Jews consider what they were asking him, a Roman, to do.

'Away with him, away with him!' they screamed. 'Crucify him!'

The endless repeated commands would have been enough to make him balk, as usual, like a child who had been lectured too much. 'Shall I crucify your *king*?' he asked, with a trace of mockery now. But the chief priests and the crowd mocked back: 'We have no king but Caesar.'

In John, this was the end. As soon as the crowd proved it was implacable, Pilate handed Jesus over to be executed. Mark and Luke said the same, and Mark suggests there were no qualms about it: 'wanting to please the people', Pilate set Barabbas free and abandoned Jesus. But in Matthew, before he did so, he called for water.

A servant brought it. This would have taken a little time; it was not a normal request in the middle of a trial. And so Pilate sat there, waiting. Traditional paintings show the servant, when he returned, kneeling to offer the bowl to the governor. It was almost noon, but he did not need water to refresh himself. Instead, he washed his hands, smoothing the water with ritual slowness over the palms and backs and between the fingers. The verb Matthew uses, *aponiptein,* means 'to wash off from'; though dirt or blood was not there, it was vividly imagined. Then Pilate took a towel from the servant and dried his hands again.

It was no part of a Roman trial for the judge to wash the blood-guilt from his hands. He should never have been in that position. If a sentence or the prospect of a sentence bothered him, Pilate could adjourn the trial to the judgement hall back in Caesarea (where Paul was tried by Felix), or refer the case to his provincial superior. If the case concerned a Roman citizen, he could even refer it to Rome. Sometimes, before they pronounced sentence, Roman judges would turn to the east or to the sun to declare their own innocence. That was as far as they could go.

The Jews, however, believed in the washing-away of blood-guilt. In Deuteronomy, when a man was found murdered within the boundaries of a city, the elders of that city were ordered to sacrifice a heifer and to wash their hands over it with the words, 'Our hands have not shed this blood.' Isaiah, too, had emphasised the redemptive power of washing. 'Wash yourself,' he wrote,

> make yourself clean,
> put away evil from your souls,
> learn to do well,
> judge for the fatherless and justify the widow,
> and come, let us reason with the Lord:
> and though your sins be scarlet, I will make them white as wool;
> and if they be red like crimson,
> I will make them white as snow.

Matthew's Pilate, with his washing, would therefore have caught the crowd's attention. Perhaps they would have grown quieter and watched him until, at last, he raised his eyes and looked at them.

'I am innocent of the blood of this just person,' he told them. 'It's your affair.'

The formulation he used seemed to echo those words from Deuteronomy, as if he meant to make a point by it; as if, despite himself, he had adopted a local custom that seemed ideal for the circumstance. If this was so, the crowd picked up the reference at once and, almost debonairly, threw back the response: 'His blood on us and on our children!'

Yet the idea of Pilate appealing to Jewish sensibilities, to the point of adopting Jewish ritual, is almost ludicrous. It would have been completely out of character, even outrageous to him. The phrase he used in Matthew, *dikaion touton*, 'this innocent person', sounded like the expression used, in Matthew again, by his wife, as she tried to divert the fate of 'this just man'. As for the action, Pilate would not have missed the fact that much of the Jewish washing that went on all round him (washing that Jesus himself had condemned as hypocritical and ineffectual) was to remove the merest trace of the Gentiles from hands, pots, tables and cups that might have been contaminated.

And so another theory holds that what Pilate did – if he did it at all – was not Jewish, but Roman. Among both the Greeks and the Romans it was customary for a man who had involuntarily committed a crime, such as homicide, to purify himself with water in order to expiate the offence. Of course, no sophisticated man believed that real guilt could be washed away by water: 'A stain on the soul cannot vanish for a long time, nor be washed away by any rivers,' Cicero wrote. Ovid agreed: it was something the forefathers and the Greeks had believed in, but modern men did not. He described how Alcmaeon, after murdering his mother, had gone to the River Achelous with a prayer to be rid of his sin; and the river god had purged him. But 'it's too easy to suppose, as you do,' he wrote, 'that those sad crimes can be carried away by water.'

Nonetheless, the notion that sin could be washed away remained. Germanicus, faced with mutiny on the German frontier in AD 14, cried out to the spirit of Augustus in heaven to 'come to these soldiers of yours and wash clean this stain.' From day to day, too, a Roman would use water to proclaim that he was pure. Holy water, ideally living, flowing water, could be used for private consecration, as Aeneas used it at the entrance to the Elysian Fields; or for ritual purification, as when priests – or magistrates, like Pilate, acting in place of priests – poured water over their right hands before the act of sacrifice. The most important prayers of the day, the morning invocations, were made fasting and with ceremonial washing of the hands. In all probability, this was how he had started his own day.

So Pilate, if he performed this action, had no need to imitate the Jews. He understood this ritual in his own heart, as part of his own practice. His offence was now apparent: he was consigning Jesus to that dim part of the underworld inhabited by those condemned on false charges, between the mewling infants and the sad suicides. And he felt he had to express to the crowd, pass on if he could, that weight of sinfulness. But perhaps he also felt moved by his own predicament to the point where some gesture of abnegation, however primitive, had to be made. It was the equivalent, compressed and in miniature, of stripping off his clothes and diving into the sea.

Indeed, the sea might have purged him. Its waters were a potent soup of every medicinal virtue of the lakes and rivers that ran into it: of salt, alum, nitre, bitumen and sulphur. Dissolved within were the waters of Campania, which cured insanity; the waters of Aenaria, which cured the stone; the freezing waters of Cutilia, stiffening the sinews and the stomach, and the warm springs of Albula, which closed up wounds. If you swam far enough you would find traces of Thessalonian springs that turned black to white and white to black; and of the twin fountains of Boetia, producing respectively remembrance and forgetfulness.

Not every water healed. The Red Fountain of Ethiopia brought delirium; the dark waters of Avernus, like those of Asphaltites which Pilate himself had looked on, perhaps touched, perhaps tasted, swallowed both leaves and birds. In Macedonia, the Lake of Insanity became salt and bitter three times a day, and crawled with white serpents twenty cubits long. The waters of the Styx brought death at once; those of Leontium killed after two days. At Tempe in Thessaly, out of a bank overhung with wild carob and purple flowers, a small stream trickled that corroded copper and ate the flesh of men.

But the water Pilate took was pure. It had flowed, perhaps, from his own aqueduct into the cisterns of the palace. This was water you could drink at once, dipping in a beaker to sip the essence of the snows on the mountains of Hebron. It was his own unwanted gift to the city of Jerusalem, civilisation and power and peace in liquid form; and its power now included the promise of renewal. The soft touch of rain, the healing wave of the sea, the cold rush of the morning drink through the drowsy pores of the body, all carried the dross of the past away. A man could start again. Desperately, half-wittingly, Matthew's Pilate plunged his hands in the cleansing mercy of God.

★ ★ ★

He goes on doing so. His gesture has never ended. It turns up in the stone-flagged passage of a castle in Scotland, where a wild-haired woman wrings her hands in imaginary water for hours at a time. It echoes in tsarist St Petersburg, where in a shattered fourth-floor apartment Raskolnikov, his murders done, scrubs away the blood with a hard piece of soap and water in a pail. It lingers in the bathroom of the grandest hotel in a grey river-port in northern Argentina, where the adulterous Dr Plarr of Graham Greene's *The Honorary Consul* washes his hands, gazes at his face in the mirror and thinks, I am like Pilate.

Political cartoonists still rejoice in it. Only the face of the hand-washer needs to change. Margaret Thatcher, nose in air, washes her hands of the Westland arms-sales affair; Ronald Reagan cleanses himself of the Iran-contra scandal; Mikhail Gorbachev, confronted with a limp victim of heavy-handed policies in the Baltics, nervously seeks a bowl of water. All these, too, are like Pilate. They are even dressed like him. They sport togas, laurel wreaths and sandals from which their toes protrude ludicrously; minions hold brimming bowls of water. Henchmen surround them, and the media crowd in with cameras to record the ritual ablutions. Sometimes the leaders look defiant, splashing the water with abandon. More often, the expression is hapless and ashamed. Try as they may to wash the guilt away, it stays there.

In nineteenth-century France, Proudhon declared that, 'like Pilate', he had washed his fingers of the germ of the Second Empire. He was possibly the only official ever to boast of the comparison. All through the Middle Ages and the Renaissance, as in the modern world, Pilate's handwashing was taken as an act of culpable buck-passing. His double was understood to sit on the bench of every weak judge surrendering to injustice, and at the desk of every official, or general, or priest of the church who saw atrocities or scandals and ignored them. The fourteenth-century *Book of the Passion* put it as well as anyone:

> He washed his hands before their eyes.
> He could have done better, but – surprise!
> He'd rather please them with a fudge

Than be a just and upright judge.
You see that everywhere today,
In every court, it's sad to say.
The godly poor get screwed again,
The wicked rich escape the pain.
And right gets shafted – what a shame!
In every country it's the same.

The washing of hands is almost the only passion scene that is found on sarcophagi or in the catacombs. These earliest reliefs and drawings of the scene show how the gesture was seen as futile, even then. On the sarcophagus of Junius Bassves, from the mid-fourth century, Pilate looks away from Jesus as the servant prepares the water. He cannot look him in the eye. Another sarcophagus in the Lateran Museum shows Pilate turning away in evident embarrassment, searching for the water, as Jesus tries to talk to him; above him hangs a laurel wreath, symbolic of Jesus' victory over his judge. Pilate knows – or almost knows – who Jesus is, but he turns away, washes his hands, and condemns him. The fact that he has doubted does not absolve him, but merely makes things worse. The ritual of cleansing is started, not completed; the blood sticks.

Is it right that it should? From the gospels onwards, the question of who had killed Jesus was made complicated. Matthew's Pilate had recused himself, and elsewhere in the gospels there were hints – for those intent on seeing them – that Jesus was delivered to the Jews to be executed. 'He handed Jesus over to them to deal with as they wished', Luke wrote.

In the centuries that followed, even up to the twentieth, Christians wishing to blame the Jews seized on this single sentence. Their names include some of the most venerated in the Church: Augustine, Aquinas, Chrysostom. And even if they accepted that Luke's grammar was ambiguous, they could nonetheless point to the pressure put on Pilate by the chief priests and the crowd. All the Jews, they argued, had killed Jesus. They had even, in Matthew, explicitly taken his blood on themselves and removed it from the Romans. And they had reaped the whirlwind. Every misfortune that subsequently befell the Jews – from the destruction of Jerusalem to the obscenity of Auschwitz – carried some echo of that blood-pact from the trial.

Yet the effect of blaming the Jews was not always – or even often – to exonerate Pilate. The evangelists knew, as their readers knew, that crucifixion was a Roman punishment, and all of them, including Luke, described it as carried out by Romans. Roman soldiers were at the foot of the cross, and Pilate wrote out the public charge-sheet. Each evangelist stressed, as was politically important, that Jesus had been found innocent of any offence under Roman law. But if that was the case, what on earth did Pilate look like? At best, spineless, and at worst a murderer.

To the unprejudiced reader of the gospels – but also to plenty of prejudiced ones, from the Middle Ages onwards – the conclusion is inescapable. As Luke said in Acts, all the rulers of the age ganged up against Christ. The Jewish priests may have been instigators, the crowd persuaders; but it was the Roman governor who killed him. In the end, Jesus did not have many executioners. He had one. That one could have refused to sentence him, but he did not refuse. This was probably not because he found Jesus guilty – though he may have done – but because he could not prove him innocent, and Jesus was no help to him. These were his choices in the end: prove Jesus innocent, strongly enough to avoid controversy or even rioting; or accept what the chief priests had already decided. The Pilate of Dorothy L. Sayers weakly summed it all up.

> I do not think there is any way out of these problems;
> One is always at the mercy of events and the world situation;
> One takes the thing as one finds it and makes the best of it;
> I do not believe there are any ultimate standards.

Not all his critics thought Pilate was so hopeless. Luther described him, not without irony, as 'a more honest and just man than any papist prince of the empire':

> I could name many of these, who are in no degree comparable with Pilate; for he kept strictly to the Roman laws. He didn't want an innocent man to be executed and slain without a hearing, and he availed himself of all just means to try and release Christ; but when they threatened him with the emperor's disfavour, he was dazzled, and forsook the imperial laws, thinking, it's only the loss of one man, who is both poor and condemned; no one is supporting him; what hurt can his death do me? Better that one man should die than that the whole nation should be against me.

The modern politician might call this pragmatism. Pilate had taken the muddled middle course, the one that looked safest, the only way out. Yet, just as Livy had concluded in the case of the Samnites and their 'third way', some nineteenth-century commentators thought this temporising was the worst thing about Pilate: much worse than simply condemning Jesus and having done with it. Pilate, in their eyes, lacked both the courage to be good and the boldness to be bad. Goodness would have saved Jesus; badness would have sent him straight to the cross; but vacillation, Pilate's middle way, led to the protracted torture of multiple interrogations, mockings and scourgings. They led to the unnecessary reed and crown of thorns.

In the fifth of his Lent lectures in 1835 at the church of Holy Trinity in Chelsea, the Rev. Henry Blunt summed up the governor.

> There was indeed, as far as we can see, nothing remarkable in Pilate; he was one of the most common characters to be met with in passing through life; a timid, time-serving man, with just conscience enough to make himself uncomfortable, and with just integrity enough to ruin the best of causes, and even to increase, as he obviously did, the sufferings of Him whom he desired to save.

And so it may have been.

At the solemn moment of sentencing, in a normal trial, the curtain behind the tribunal was drawn across. The judge would then announce, as a preliminary, that he was conceding nothing 'to bias or entreaty'. Those words might have stuck in Pilate's throat, if he had tried to say them. But no proper sentence was recorded in the gospels. The *Acta Pilati* imagined a long one: 'Your nation has accused you, and you have proclaimed yourself a king. That is why I have decided that you shall be flogged according to the laws of the pious emperors, then hanged on a cross in the garden where you were taken. Dysmas and Gestas, the two robbers, will be crucified with you.'

What must have happened would have been decidedly briefer. Pilate ordered Barabbas to be released, condemned Jesus, and saw to it that the record was changed. This was known as 'turning the pen': reversing the stylus to erase from the wax tablet the sentence of acquittal that had probably been written there before, and writing a sentence of condemnation. When the blunt end of the stylus had erased a line of words, it was sometimes possible still to read them under the new ones; and even if they were illegible, the 'fresh wounds' of the erasure still showed through. You could catch embezzlers that way, as well as judges whose timidity had got the better of them.

Nineteenth-century writers, anxious for one last confrontation between the two men, imagined that the governor's last words were addressed to Jesus directly. They wanted him to look into his eyes – those divine eyes – and say, in his best judicial Latin, *Condemno. Ibis in crucem.* He was more likely to have said, in Greek to his soldiers, *Staurotheto*, 'Let him be crucified.' Maybe, if the trial was as gruelling as it has been painted, there were no words at all.

It was only another day in his life. It was just a bad morning, like any other bad morning, in a man's long struggle to keep to some sort of moral path. As one Edwardian cleric said, 'He was tempted as we are tempted, fell as we fall, and might have overcome even as we also by the grace of God may overcome, if we will.'

And then he went to lunch.

6

Witness to Christ

You never know
Death could still dream
Dream he was alive
Dream he wasn't dead
And shaking his sheets of stone
Disengage himself
And lean out
And tumble from the tomb
Like a child out of bed
(Horror and catacombs)
Fall back into life
You would see it from here
Everything would be put in question
Affection and desolation
And what follows after . . .

Jacques Prévert,
'Nothing to Fear' from *Histoires*

I n the cellar of a house in Arnithero, near the city of Aquila in the kingdom of Naples, in the year 1580, a man was digging. We do not know why. We can imagine the cellar dark, with damp stone walls; and from the dark of the earth, under the steady blows of the spade, a stone 'of marvellous beauty' gradually emerged. Under the stone was an iron box, too heavy to shift, with rusted locks that were quickly smashed open. Inside that box was another, of finest marble; and inside this, neatly rolled up, a yellow document covered with faint and foreign writing.

Several early Spanish romances were 'found' in just this way, in costly marble tombs or under floors, unearthed completely by chance. Yet this was no romance: it was said to be Pilate's sentence from Christ's trial, which had long been rumoured to be in Aquila somewhere. A few lines of the sentence, in Hebrew, were said to have been found on a copper plaque that turned up, in excavations in the city around the year 1200, in an old vase of white marble. Other lines stated that the plaque was one of twelve copies sent to the twelve tribes of Israel. The vase was placed in an ebony box, and became so celebrated that in the eighteenth century a mere model of it was sold to Lord Howard for 2,890 francs. But the finding of Pilate's 'complete' sentence, in the late sixteenth century, caused even more excitement.

Exposed to the light of day – according to the monk who related the discovery, Fray Rodrigo de Yepes – the document turned out to be a piece of sheepskin covered with Hebrew script. At the court of Philip II in Madrid it was displayed as a curiosity. Courtiers in black, with neat pointed ruffs and beards, poked at it with their long fingers. It was agreed that the piece had its peculiarities: it was not particularly accurate on names of contemporary officials or forms of address. Some queried the signatures, in the same neat Hebrew script, of the leaders of the twelve tribes of Israel. Details that would not have gone unappreciated in Counter-Reformation Spain – the precise number of wounds to be inflicted, the options of vinegar and lance, the witnesses allowed at the foot of the cross – had been omitted by the governor. Nonetheless, among the talk of domestic plotting, of European alliances, of debasement of silver and the management of the Americas, the Sentence of Pilate circulated like a piece of treasured samizdat. Many hands translated the Hebrew original into Spanish, correcting the more manifest errors as they went. That done, the Sentence was printed and glued into other books. But the definitive version, according to Fray Yepes, was the one appended to his own *Life of Christ*, published in 1583.

In the 17th year of Tiberius Caesar, Emperor of Rome and invincible monarch of all the world, and in the two hundred and second Olympiad in the 24th Decade. From the creation of the World, according to the enumeration of the Hebrews, four times 1187, and from the establishment of the Roman Empire the year 73, and from the liberation from the Babylonish captivity 480 . . .

On the 25th of the month of March, I, Pontius Pilate, President of the Imperial Roman Empire within the Palace of the High Court, judge, condemn and sentence to death Jesus called by the people Christ the Nazarene, and of Galilean origin, a seditious man according to Mosaic law and an opponent of the great Emperor, Tiberius Caesar.

I declare and pronounce . . . that his death shall be on the cross, fixed to it with nails, as is customary with criminals; because, inviting and gathering together many men both rich and poor, he has not ceased from making a disturbance through all Judea, claiming to be the Son of God, King of Israel, threatening the destruction of Jerusalem and of the Sacred Temple, denying that one ought to pay tribute to Caesar, and in addition to this audacity, entering with palms and triumph, together with a section of the people, into the city of Jerusalem.

Wherefore I order my chief Centurion, Quintus Cornelius, to conduct Jesus publicly through the city of Jerusalem, bound and tied, and that he be crowned with sharp thorns, and carry his own cross on his shoulders, that he may be an example to all malefactors; and in his company I desire to be taken two murderous robbers, and they shall go out by the gate Golgotha, now called Antoniana: And that they shall take this Jesus to the public hill of justice, called Calvario, where being crucified and dead, his body shall remain on the cross as a spectacle to all wicked men.

We likewise order that no one of any rank, state or condition whatsoever shall have the temerity to interfere with the said judgement which is to be carried out by my order and decree according to the decrees and laws, Roman and Hebrew, under penalty of being in rebellion against Imperial Rome.

[signed]   [notarised by]

The Twelve Tribes of Israel   Notamber (for the Hebrews)
The Pharisees   Sextilius (for the Romans)
The Sadducees   Amasius Chilion

Fray Yepes – for he was most probably the forger – had had fun with this. By calling Pilate *Presidente*, he summoned up an image of the governor of some Spanish province in the old world or the new: the sort of man who, mounted on a Moorish stallion, would make a tour of his plantations or watch, from a decent distance, the slaughter of Indians. The signatures of the twelve tribes also had something of this feel: single, primitive names, like the marks of Indian chiefs appended to some charter of expropriation. And at the end, as in any Spanish legal transaction, the notaries came in with their spectacles and sealing wax.

Of course, few thought for long that the document was genuine; but Pilate was such a precious witness that his evidence, if it did not exist, had endlessly to be invented. Any prejudice against his veracity or hatred of him as a man could be set aside in the interests of historical embellishment. Besides, if he had been so close to Christ, how could he have escaped some frisson of conversion?

His first appearance in the role of witness came in the trial itself. According to all the gospels he kept saying 'Look here', *ide* or *idou* in Greek; almost all his remarks to the Jews began with it. Perhaps it was just a tic, a habit of speech, typical of an exasperated man trying to get people in order; but the gospels were not concerned with that sort of historical detail. By using the phrase in conjunction with words like 'man' and 'king' and 'king of the Jews', the evangelists were making Pilate do their pleading for them, right to the moment when, in Matthew, he washed his hands of 'this just person'. In both Luke and John he proclaimed Jesus innocent not once, but three times, a highly symbolic number. Matthew also made him the first Gentile to speak aloud the name of Jesus. Tertullian thought these scraps of recognition made Pilate a Christian in his heart, *iam pro sua consciencia christianus*; the Ethiopians thought they justified his inclusion in their calendar of saints, 'because he had confessed to the innocence of Jesus Christ.' In the *Acta Pilati*, Joseph of Arimathea proclaimed Pilate 'circumcised in heart'; and Justin Martyr elaborated on this by saying that Christ 'circumcises the hearts of all who are willing with knives of stone'.

Pilate also became, in a way, the first priest of the Eucharist of Christ. Christ offered the bread and wine as symbols of his body and blood; but Pilate offered Christ himself. He took him, showed him to the people, proclaimed him and broke him. The gospels also say he 'handed him over', to his soldiers, to the will of the crowd and, as a dead body, to Joseph of Arimathea. The first part of the trial, like the first part of the Mass, was the establishment of Christ's claims and credentials. The second part was the sacrifice itself, for which Pilate prepared by washing his hands. Every priest still repeats his action, adding the words which Pilate implied but could not say: 'Lord, wash me from my iniquity, and cleanse me from my sin.' He repeats, too, as a Roman would have had to, the centurion's mantra of uncleanness: 'Lord, I am not worthy that you should enter under my roof.' In actions small and large, routine or instinctive, the liturgy of the Church continues to shadow Pilate's performance. This is how ordinary men must deal with a God who is close enough to touch.

Medieval Christians were intrigued by the thought that Pilate had looked on Jesus, that he had talked to him and could have described him. In the eighth century, relic-hunters in Jerusalem were shown a painting on the wall of the building that was supposed to be Pilate's *praetorium*, and were told it was a portrait of Christ drawn there on the governor's orders. The guides insisted that Pilate was so fascinated by his prisoner that he had called in portrait-painters and had several likenesses done. The only written 'description' of Jesus, contained in a thirteenth- or fourteenth-century forgery called the *Letter of Lentulus*, was also supposed to be a version of a description drawn up on Pilate's orders as part of the official charge-sheet, or perhaps as part of a 'Wanted' poster before Jesus was arrested.

Some said that Publius Lentulus was a proconsular superior of Pilate's, others that he was a friend of his; but in one case the letter is just ascribed directly to Pilate, as part of a report to Rome. The purpose of this forgery seems clear. There were several unflattering portraits of Jesus around, based on questionable versions of the famous passage from Josephus, describing him as small, hunched and ugly to look at; so the early Christians turned to Pilate for a testimony to his beauty. The description ran as follows:

> There has appeared in these times a man called Christ whose name is Jesus . . . whom his disciples call Son of God, raising the dead and healing all diseases . . . fifteen palms and a half in height, with hair the colour of an unripe hazel and smooth almost to the ears; but from the ears down slightly darker-coloured corkscrew curls, more glistening, and waving downwards from the shoulders. He wears his hair parted in the centre in the manner of the Nazarenes, and has a copious but immature beard that is also forked in the middle. He has a simple and mature aspect, with blue eyes varying in colour and bright . . .

This was peculiar wording for a report but not so strange, perhaps, for a police poster. Such posters were written in black and red characters on white paper and posted up in public places, and they went into extraordinary detail. In 145 BC, for example, a slave called Hermon, aged about eighteen, went missing in Alexandria: 'of medium height, beardless, straight-legged, with a dimple in the chin, tattooed on the right wrist with foreign characters. He has with him a string purse with three *minas* of gold, ten cowrie shells, an iron ring on which hangs a flask of oil and bath-scrapers, and is wearing round his body an overcoat and a belt.' As Hermon's marks were the things he carried, filched from the baths, so the distinguishing marks of Jesus – who carried nothing – may well have been the colour and luxuriance of his hair, so strange to the eyes of a Roman.

Yet even if Pilate was implicated in that physical description of Jesus, it was not the vital part of his evidence. That was the *titulus*, or public charge-sheet, which had to be written out, paraded in front of the victim or hung round his neck, and placed over him on the cross. Before Pilate could leave the trial behind – go upstairs, sink into his reading chair, cram his mouth with olives, bread and fish – he had to sum up the offences of the man he had just sentenced.

The *titulus* board that was brought to Pilate was about two feet square, its surface whitened and smoothed with gypsum. The word for this placard was the same as that used in Roman grocer's shops, or in brothels, for the wooden display board that listed the prices of goods. When you looked at such a board you expected a little gilding, a little exaggeration: the best this, the finest that. A prosaic list was disappointing, a sign of a shopkeeper who took no joy in his job. This was a chance to embellish, as well as to have the last word.

A clerk stood by with a bottle of cuttlefish ink and a reed softened at the tip, a larger version of the sort of pen that was used for writing on papyrus. John's gospel implies that Pilate wrote the *titulus* himself in Latin, Hebrew and Greek. The mystery plays have him writing it too, in laborious mime, and in the Coventry play he goes so far as to scramble up a ladder to fix his handiwork to the top of the cross. But governors did not write out public notices, any more than they would have chalked up the price of oil or the rate for a Bithynian brunette. Even if he had lowered himself to write the Latin and Greek, Pilate could hardly have managed the odd squared-off characters of the Hebrew – a language of which it is safe to say he knew nothing. The trilingualism may just have been John's invention; and a scribe or even a soldier would have painted the words on the board while Pilate dictated.

How much thought went into it? The gospels imply that Pilate took charge to the extent of making the board say exactly what he wanted: some variant of 'Jesus of Nazareth, King of the Jews'. This was deliberately insulting to his Jewish subjects, and especially to the chief priests. He made doubly sure that the insult was not missed by crucifying Jesus between two thieves, as if to say: 'Your king, and the whole lot of you, are bandits.' There was possibly another joke-reference too to *latrunculi*, the Roman version of chess, in which the game was over when the king-piece was trapped between two robber-pieces of glass. At least one commentator imagined Pilate laughing as he thought these ideas up. 'Not lacking in witticisms,' wrote Oecolampadius in the sixteenth century, 'you made a lampoon against Christ.'

The lampoon was, in fact, inaccurate. Despite Pilate's multiple leading questions, Jesus had never acknowledged that he was the king of the Jews. Indeed, John's Pilate had been told directly that Jesus's kingdom was 'not from here'. So it is possible, after all, that Pilate had understood nothing of the few answers Jesus had given him. He had simply reverted to the third and last charge brought by the high priests as if to say, the rest is nonsense.

Medieval scholars and playwrights thought the *titulus* could bear a better gloss than that. It was Pilate's revenge, they thought; but it was also his confession. It is the moment when Pilate says, in effect, this man is indeed a king; *I* recognise him; and one day all you unbelievers will recognise him too. In the *Northern Passion* the *titulus* is written on a palm-board, the tree of victory and peace; that, says one of the bystanders, sums up what Pilate really meant to write. The governor thus becomes the first in that little procession of Romans who, in the course of the crucifixion, find their eyes suddenly opened to the innermost mysteries of the Christian God.

Most Christians still understand the *titulus* this way. No crucifix is complete without the proclamation made by John's Pilate, *Iesus Nazarenus Rex Iudaeorum*, reduced as in 'SPQR' to INRI, the four letters of dominion. (Historically, he would not have abbreviated it; it would need to be understood, and besides, he was not a man for abbreviations.) That INRI is flaunted as a banner of victory, a statement of what is obvious and permanent and true to believers: This is the Messiah. Pilate repeats, like some ghostly bureaucrat, in the three great languages of the civilised world of the time, the statement Jesus makes in sweat and blood. Even Christians will admit that he did this unwittingly. He never meant to proclaim the greatest truth of Christendom at all. But, oddly enough, there he was doing so. As Augustine put it, 'It could not . . . be torn from his heart that Jesus was the King of the Jews, but was fixed there, as in the superscription, by the truth itself.'

Augustine believed that the cross itself now proclaimed something new, and that this too was the work of 'evil men', like Pilate, suddenly made good. The traverse beam now signified the breadth of love; the upright, perseverance towards the goal of heaven; even the depth of the cross in the ground symbolised 'the depths of the grace of God, which is beyond human understanding'. Not just the *titulus*, but the whole gibbet ordered by Pilate became a means to display the glory of God. The pagan governor could not have done better if he had tried.

But of course this was not his intention. He had simply passed sentence and had settled, for the *titulus*, on a formula that was neat, obvious and mildly defiant. When it was done the business should have been over. But John's gospel says he was not left in peace; the priests came back at him in fury. In the mystery plays they leant over his shoulder, jabbing at the board, or rushed in and pointed with indignation to the *titulus* already on the cross; their beards, stiff with glue, stood out sharply from their chins. 'This isn't right!' they chorused.

'You shouldn't have put "The King of the Jews", but "*This man said* he was the King of the Jews!"'

Pilate said, 'What I have written, I have written.'

O gegrapha, gegrapha. Quod scripsi, scripsi. Whether snapped out in Greek or Latin, it carried a clear sub-text: Go away, leave me alone. Reduced to the common Roman gesture, he had put up his finger to the Jews.

Christian commentators found another subtext too. This was Pilate, the chief witness, repeating his evidence. Not only had he proclaimed Jesus as king, unequivocally, but he had meant to proclaim it; he was not to be shifted from this great shining truth. In the trial he might have wavered, but now he was stalwart. He was not going to fiddle even with the form of words. Augustine wondered whether there was not 'some hidden voice that sounded through Pilate's inner man with – if one may put it this way – a kind of loud-toned silence, the words that had been prophesied so long before in the very letter of the Psalms, "Corrupt not the inscription of the title". Here, then, you see, he did not corrupt it.' Pilate had recovered his courage; this was his own good, unalterable confession. *Quod scripsi, scripsi.*

Go away and leave me alone.

They went at last. It is tempting to imagine his relief, his heady plunge back into his ordinary life. He must have eaten something: bread, sardines, soft cheese, cold meat pepped up with fish sauce. He must have drunk something, probably the usual watered-down wine: though not to the point of stupefaction, for this was still a working day. Then he would have taken his siesta, either on the day couch with his shoes on or properly in bed, between sheets, in the merciful enveloping arms of his wife. The conversation (we imagine) might have been awkward. 'So you killed him, then? You didn't get my message?' Yes, I killed him. The crime was sedition. It was all completely straightforward. There was never any question of what I had to do, apart from not wanting the Jews to bounce me into things. 'So that was why it took six hours?' Yes, that was why it took six hours. Six hours, three more troublemakers on crosses. Another productive day in Judea.

After this, there were probably more cases to hear. By about two-thirty or three, he would have concluded the business of the day and made for the baths. This was the essential winding-down, the proper ablution. Perhaps he still felt in need of it. He could let them scrape him, pummel him, bruise him as he lay on the slab; naked too, human too, with only a towel round his shoulders. Then he could slip into the soothing water. Perhaps he ploughed ferociously up and down, still feeling his humiliation or his anger; or perhaps he merely lay in the water, watching his limbs float, letting his thoughts drift away. And when he eventually emerged, faintly fragile and glowing, his hair slicked down, it was to find that the sky was dark.

Three gospels record the 'darkness over the face of the earth'; Matthew adds that an earthquake followed. These occurrences may have been symbolic, nature in upheaval at the death of God, but they may also have happened in fact. An eclipse on the likeliest Friday in 33 was recorded in several Mediterranean countries. The *Gospel of Peter* said that people went about with lamps, thinking it was night. Lamps may have been lit too in the tall braziers round Pilate's palace, while the air outside turned thick as smoke.

Intelligent men were not afraid of eclipses. Cicero remembered soldiers in camp, always prone to superstitious fears, being instructed by their superior officers – as Pilate would have had to instruct them – that this was no miracle, but something that happened at fixed times and would continue to do so in future. All it meant, they said, was that the moon was passing between the earth and the sun. Earthquakes, too, had a rational explanation: trapped winds bursting out of the earth, like a bout of cosmic farting that made even the wells stink. Yet Romulus had died during an eclipse of the sun, as had Caesar, and similar disturbances had attended the death of Augustus in 14: a total eclipse, then the sky on fire, glowing embers that fell in showers, blood-red comets. As for earthquakes, as Pliny the elder pointed out, 'The city of Rome never experienced a shock which was not the forerunner of some great calamity.'

Jerusalem too was prone to tremors, and according to Matthew this one caused no particular damage to buildings. But the rock tombs around the city were shattered, uncovering their cargo of grey bones, and the great hanging curtain in the Temple (forty cubits high by ten cubits wide, as thick as a hand, woven of gold and purple thread) was torn from top to bottom. This was an earthquake Matthew's Pilate would have felt. Perhaps the lampstands swayed and crashed to the floor; perhaps a little gritty dust fell from the ceiling on to his hair; or perhaps he merely felt the terror of the solid marble floor not quite steady, shifting under his feet. He may have scarcely dared to look up in case he saw – as a Jewish family seated at dinner had once seen – the whole dome of the roof peel back like a soft fruit, disclosing the sky.

It passed after a while. The day began to lighten without explanation.

Fallen objects were picked up from the floor, and Pilate returned to whatever his business was. Tradition said he did not work long, however, before a stream of visitors came in to interrupt him, pestering him about the man he had caused to be nailed to the cross. The gospels 'recorded' most of them, since they wanted both the soldiers and Pilate to bear witness that Jesus had died, been taken down, buried and placed under guard. But only the Towneley playwright described the first visitors to Pilate on that particular afternoon, when the milky dust of the earthquake still hung in the trees and the air: three soldiers, one of whom carried a robe made of cobwebs and moonshine, and woven in one piece.

This was the only personal relic of Jesus that had survived intact. According to the gospels, his overcoat was cut into four by the soldiers who kept watch at the foot of the cross; but his undergarment had no seam for a knife-blade to unpick. Medieval writers took this story further. The Virgin Mary had woven the robe for Jesus when he was a child, and it had gone on growing with him. In one sense, it was his own mystical body; in another it was the magical garment woven for a loved one, as the old song said.

> I will make you a cambric shirt,
> Parsley, sage, rosemary and thyme;
> Without no seams or needlework,
> Then you'll be a true love of mine.

When the shirt was made, Mary washed it in the sea and hung it on a withered thorn bush to dry. Later, when she went to fetch it, she found the linen gently rising and falling, and the thorn bush covered with roses varying from red to white: passion and resurrection in one place.

In the Towneley play, after Christ's clothes were taken from him, they did not end up with the soldiers. Pilate had ordered the clothes to be brought back to him, together with the news that Jesus was dead. The soldiers therefore gathered up the overcoat and the seamless garment, which still carried the soft sheen of rose petals and the phosphorescence of the sea, and raced down the hill of Calvary, heading for Pilate's house. All three were wildly excited. As they pitched up, gasping, against the painted sentry box outside the *praetorium*, one complained that he had almost shat in his breeches, another that he had 'burst his bollocks' to get to Pilate and put in his claim. Each man wanted the garment badly, because whoever got it would have good luck for the rest of his life.

But Pilate wanted it too. This was intolerable. He had done nothing to deserve it; like the soft tyrant he was, he was at that moment lying in bed asleep. Together, the soldiers swore by Mohammed – the god of all villains and heathens – that they would keep it out of his clutches. That done, they knocked on the door.

Pilate's councillor answered, dressed in the robe of a scholar. The governor was slow to rouse. 'Don't call me again, you've called me twice already!' he groaned from his bed.

'My lord!' yelled the councillor again.

'Why do I seem to feel a bit bad today?' moaned Pilate.

'My lord, I entreat you, *get up!*'

'Is it traitors? Plots?'

'Not that I know of.'

'Then stop annoying me! Just pick me up, set me softly in my seat . . .'

But the councillor, grimly pulling away the sheets, had a lesson for him. 'They've come about that boy you killed, sir. You'll be in a fair amount of trouble if you killed him, and he was innocent.'

'Would you mind not mentioning that?' Pilate snapped. 'Is there any point in drawing attention to it? Why don't you look up the law about it? And show it some respect, or I'll buffet you fit to kill you!'

'I thought I should mention what I taught you, sir. I wouldn't like to see you go wrong –'

'Have you finished?' screamed Pilate into his face.

'Yes, lord.'

'Then get out, for God's sake.'

The councillor left, and the soldiers crowded in. They were welcome; they brought the news that Jesus was dead. But Pilate was strangely prickly. When the second soldier gabbled ingratiatingly that Pilate had tortured Jesus 'really well', the governor murmured 'Leave the part I played out of it, will you?' And when the third soldier held out the armful of shining clothes, asking 'Did you have any hope in your heart of having his gear, sir?', Pilate turned white.

'That belongs to me! I by no means meant you men to have this!'

The soldiers jumped back, clutching the clothes tight. 'We got there first!' they cried. But Pilate caught hold of the overcoat and pulled. Desperate, scrambling to be deferential, the soldiers agreed to tear it to shreds; and in the ensuing storm of fabric Pilate was left with the largest piece. He smiled, and thanked them.

'He can't get the other coat too,' muttered the third soldier.

'Better cut it into four parts, properly,' said the first.

But they could find no seam. The second soldier, knife ready in his hand, searched all over it. At last he went to stick the point into the middle of the garment, but Pilate caught his arm. 'I command you not to cut it!' he shouted. 'You bastards, leave it whole, or I'll kill you!'

The soldiers were shaken. 'Calm down, sir, he meant well,' they told the distraught governor. 'He'd be upset if you killed him, sir.'

'All right,' Pilate whispered. 'I forgive him.'

'Wonderful, sir! Thank you, sir!'

The first soldier was still kneeling beside the shining white robe; the folds spread round him like milk. He said, 'Shall I save it, sir?'

'I say we cast lots, and the highest wins it.'

Nobody trusted this suggestion. Dicing was touched by the Devil; in some French mystery plays, Satan actually taught the soldiers how to play. On the other hand, the third soldier had the three dice, ready in his pocket. At least Pilate had no chance to tamper with them. The first soldier imagined they all had an equal opportunity of winning. 'He can't cheat us at dicing,' he remarked.

Eager and magnanimous, Pilate sat down on the floor. 'I like this game!' he cried. 'Who's going to start?'

'You first, sir.'

'I'll win it with a single throw: just watch!'

He threw thirteen.

'I'm going to win now, for sure.'

'Maybe, sir,' said the first soldier; 'but I might just spoil your joy, if Fortune looks on me.'

He threw the dice. 'And I've seen Fortune look on great knights just the same!' crowed Pilate. 'You've only got eight there, for all your boasting!'

'Eight? What the hell's wrong with me? It must be these dice, the bitches!'

'Well, *you* don't get it,' said the second soldier. 'Let's see if luck will look on me.'

'I hope not,' said Pilate.

The second soldier threw, and fell silent. 'Mohammed's bones, you've only got seven,' the third told him.

'Oh blast, it's short!' said the thrower in despair.

The third soldier seized the dice, blew on them, and threw. 'Bitched bones, be as I tell you, or be cursed!'

He threw fifteen.

'There, fellows, just as I forecast! I win it!'

'What?' cried Pilate in scorn. 'You whistle, and the moon is waning? Where've you been? You can take your throw back again!'

The third soldier jumped to his feet. 'There are plenty of people here, law-abiding people, who can witness that I did nothing wrong. Ask them!'

His colleagues backed him: 'You didn't do any trickery that we saw.'

'Yes,' shouted Pilate, 'but I don't play this game puffing and blowing like that! I wouldn't mind if he played straight –'

The third soldier clapped him on the back, smiling. 'Calm down, sir. Don't spoil your day.'

Pilate sprang from the floor, furious; but before he seized the man he seemed to remember something, and collect himself. He took several deep breaths, straightened up, and settled his chaplet on his golden head. He was princely again; and, being princely, he turned to the winner with a perfect smile.

'Sir,' he said. The artificial humility was deeply worrying; the soldiers began to edge away. 'Since you've won this gown now, do you suppose you could be enormously generous and good, and give it to me?'

'No, sir. This you won't have.'

'Then I'll make you!' Pilate roared. 'Cursed you are and cursed you'll remain! What? You think you're free to defy me?'

The soldier grew pale. 'Your words go through me, sir,' he stammered. 'They really do. I – I'd give you three if I had them, sir.'

The robe was handed over.

'How extremely kind of you!' beamed Pilate. 'Thanks so much.'

The soldiers made their exit, grumbling and cursing. Their curses were an elegy on the folly of gambling: how Fortune threw men in the ditch, made them sell their cattle for nothing, emptied the bakers' ovens, and all for 'a sweet girl's gift'. As they reached the door, the third soldier turned back and said to Pilate: 'You should realise what comes of dicing, sir. You'd do better to leave such a vain thing and serve God instead, if you want to know the bliss of heaven. We know that the Lord is the most mighty and the gentlest of all the Jews. We believe he is holy. What do you think of that?'

Pilate stood in the hall with the garment in his arms. He smiled at them. 'I think you're wonderful,' he said, in a voice that sounded as though he were dreaming, touched by the sun. 'Of all the scholars I know, you're the most full of wisdom and subtlety. Every law you keep dutifully. I grant you all power and all the friendship I can give you. *Dieu vous garde, monseigneurs*, and may Mohammed in his castles and towers protect you. Have a good day, gentlemen.'

The soldiers disappeared. Pilate remained with his precious burden, bright as light, light as air, soft as petals, winking with the white foam of the sea, and found himself bathed in a benevolence he could not understand.

★   ★   ★

Part of the purpose of the soldiers' mission had been to tell Pilate that Jesus was dead. In their rage and excitement, the Towneley soldiers almost forgot to do so. But other messengers in other accounts, including the gospels, brought the message properly, and sometimes in disturbing ways. All had been touched by Jesus, some even converted, even in a matter of moments. In this state they approached the governor. Their very obeisance must have been troubled and unsteady; for they knew now who the man was whom Pilate had put to death.

According to Mark, the first to appear in the *praetorium* – at some time around four in the afternoon – was not a soldier at all. It was Joseph of Arimathea, who was seeking the body of Jesus for burial. Joseph's credentials were confused. Mark, most plausibly, called him a member of the Sanhedrin, 'an honourable counsellor, who also waited for the kingdom of God.' Yet it is not clear how this religious Jew could bring himself to enter the unclean Roman palace, even in emergency. *The Legend of the High Holy Grail* transformed him into a Roman soldier who had seen seven years' service with Pilate and wanted the body as his reward.

John's gospel suggested he was a friend of Nicodemus, the secret disciple, who was also to bring the unguents for the burial. In the second-century *Gospel of Peter* Joseph was called 'a friend of Pilate and of the Lord', and some modern writings on the legends of the Grail continue to surmise that he was close to the governor. The fact that he could go in 'boldly' to Pilate, as Mark says, suggests either intimacy or authority, as well as recklessness of the governor's fragile temper. But though Joseph 'begged' for the corpse of Jesus – the phrase is full of ritual subservience – Pilate could not give him the body at once. He needed to find out how things stood at Calvary, and whether Jesus was indeed dead.

Accordingly, he sent for the centurion who had kept guard at the foot of the cross. This was his second set of orders. In John he had already sent out commands, at the behest of the Jewish priests, that the legs of the victims should be broken with a heavy mallet to make sure they died before sunset. (Again, that necessary acquiescence to Jewish feelings.) The messenger sent to relay those orders could have reported back that Jesus was dead, but the centurion's report was of a different sort. He had watched Jesus all the time; he was therefore in a position to provide as much detail of this death as Pilate wanted.

The scene of the centurion's report takes only a verse in Mark, but it is heavy with implications. This man had heard Jesus call out 'My God, my God, why have you forsaken me?' He had seen him offered the sponge on a stick, noticed the confusion about whether or not he was summoning Elias, and had heard him cry out loudly as he died. In Matthew's account, he saw how at that moment the dusty twilight of the eclipse came down, and the ground shook. His reaction, in Matthew, was to say: 'Truly this man was the Son of God.' In Luke, he cried out, 'Truly this man was innocent.' Unlike his superior officer's hand-washing or his sarcastic charge-sheet, this sounded like a proper change of heart.

It was not much of a military report, however. It probably required suppressing, even though it contained the answers to Pilate's most urgent questions from the trial. So the centurion stood in the *praetorium*, not without anxiety. His conversion was fresh and sharp, his memories of the death still burning; and Mark's Pilate, for his part, also seemed to want to know exactly how events had unfolded. He had, at the least, a Roman's interest in the mechanics and the minutiae of death. There were always lessons in the way men died, sometimes more than in their lives.

He might well have asked whether Jesus had said anything before he died. Last words were important. The centurion would not have understood Jesus's Aramaic, as Pilate himself would not have done. But part of the chatter at the foot of the cross, to while away the boredom of standing there, had been to puzzle out what the crucified man was saying. At one point he cried out a word that even Pilate could have grasped: *Abba*, 'Father'. What had he meant by that? Men in pain cried out for their mothers, not their fathers. But the King of the Jews had called for his father, looking up into the dark sky. He could not have meant the Jewish God, whom nobody could see; it was more as if, improbably, he called for Jupiter, the Father and helper. *Iove* from *adiuvare*, Come here and help me. Do not forsake me. It made sense to call on such a God, with broad arms and a breast so immense that each fold of his robe was like a sweeping beach of deep, soft sand. Yet the word *Abba* suggested more intimacy than that. It was also 'Daddy', the word toddlers chirped in the market, a word you would never use to a deity who might strike you.

The faint, strange suggestion was of some sort of family feeling between the man on the cross and the company of the gods; and the next question, the counter-question, was why they had not helped him. When the servants had gone to the Tiber to drown the new-born Romulus and Remus, the future founders of Rome, they had made the same appeal as they placed the squalling babies in their little boat: 'If some god were the author of your being, he would surely come to your aid in so perilous an hour.' On that occasion, he had done so. But in the case of Jesus, Daddy seemed to have looked away.

According to Luke, Jesus had also added something to that 'Father'. He had said, 'Father, forgive them, for they know not what they do.' The prayer encompassed everyone by the cross: thieves, bystanders, Romans. The evangelist also clearly implied it went further, over the chief priests and the Jewish crowd, and that it included the governor in his palace. So Pilate had been forgiven, if he wanted to know. This Jesus had loved his enemy, even though his enemy had scarcely left him the breath or the strength to do so. And, having forgiven, he died almost instantly. Far from putting up defences against death, he seemed to invite it in.

A Roman could only admire this, even in the lowest sort of men. This was the good and acceptable death, the perfect ending. A gladiator in the ring might have lost every weapon and be staggering in circles; the crowd would be screaming *Habet!* 'He's had it!'; but with his last energies he would approach his opponent, one dragging step, two steps, and offer him his breast as if to say, Kill me. I forgive you, kill me, it's necessary. As Jesus had done.

Or Cato would tear off his bandages. This was the wonderful, heartbreaking story known to every Roman, to Pilate too, as the example of death determinedly embraced. Marcus Cato Uticensis had been a friend of Cicero's and a supporter of the Republic. In 46 BC he had found himself cornered by Caesar's troops at Utica, in Africa. The rest of Africa had already submitted to Caesar; there was no way out.

On the night before he would be forced to surrender, he laid two things beside his pillow. One was Plato's *Phaedo,* on the immortality of the soul, and the other was his sword. One gave him the will to die, as Seneca said, the other the means. He read the *Phaedo,* and then pierced his breast with the blade. A sample school exercise still exists, perhaps one Pilate too had memorised as a boy, describing Cato as 'the finest model of how to live and how to die,' and ending: 'he put into those hands, clean to the last of Roman blood, a sword to plunge into his hallowed breast.' But the thrust did not go deep enough; the doctors found him, and bandaged the wound. It was hard to imagine how a man would feel when, perfectly ready and resigned to death, the fussing doctors pulled him back from the brink. Cato could not bear it, and as soon as they had gone he ripped the bandages apart. The wound opened, and bled his life away.

Jesus had done much the same. He had rehearsed his philosophy – in Pilate's hearing – and then, quite resigned, had gone to the cross. Once there, he barely tasted the sour drugged wine and water that might have kept him alive for longer. He was impatient to die. In the end, like Cato, he almost seemed to race towards it; his final scream was an act of violent liberation, like the bandages torn away. Yet even this indifference to death – if he had truly been indifferent – was not the most beautiful or admirable thing. The most admirable was to lay down one's life, as on an altar, to save the lives of others: to be the one man, as Caiaphas said, whose death would redeem the whole nation.

This sort of death too would have been familiar to Pilate. Every Roman knew the stories. P. Decimus Mus gave up his life to save the Roman army when it was fighting the Latins, and his son Decius, a military tribune, did the same at the battle of Sentinum against the Samnites, Pilate's own tribe. To die like this was a ritual, with prescribed actions and prayers; it was not an impulse, but deliberate and controlled. A man offered himself to the gods to turn destruction aside. So, at Sentinum, Decius called for the army priest, and the priest instructed him to put on the purple-bordered toga and cover his head. A spear was laid on the ground; he stood on it, touched his finger to his lips and prayed to Jupiter, Mars, Bellona, the household gods and the shades of the dead. Then he girded up his toga with the Gabinian cincture, vaulted on to his horse and plunged into the thick of the enemy. It took his friends a day and a night to find his body; when they did, it was covered with missiles and the corpses of his attackers. But the Romans had won the day.

All these deaths had a common theme. The men who died controlled them completely, even to the way they happened and the time when they occurred. Pilate had imagined that, in the case of Jesus, these matters were in his hands. But Jesus surprised him. According to Mark, it was the quickness of Christ's death that most fascinated Pilate. He was surprised – 'astonished', Mark says – that Jesus was already dead when the officer went to break his legs. Was it really that fast? And if so, why? A death from crucifixion might easily take two or three days; Jesus had died in three hours. It was as if, in the words of Tertullian, 'he released his spirit of his own accord with a word, anticipating the duty of the executioner.' And he had died not just at the ninth hour, as the centurion could have reported, but when the sun went dark and the light too died.

Would the centurion have thought that worth adding? An eclipse was far more obvious, far more noteworthy, than hours measured on Pilate's water-clock. The centurion on Golgotha may have had no idea of the time. But he would have watched the sky. And he knew, as Pilate knew, what sort of men died when eclipses came.

There was no necessity to retail his own ideas. He was only on guard, the most boring job in the world, watching in case the relatives crept up with pliers in their pockets. But if he was asked for any further observations, would Matthew's centurion have dared to blurt out to Pilate what he had already uttered to the empty air, the weeping bystanders and his own half-listening colleages? However carefully he picked his words, however generalised the reference – heavenly heroes, Olympian stunt-men – his eyes would have met the governor's with a pained and disquieting stare: 'I thought he was the Son of God, sir.'

Behind the centurion came the lance-man, the soldier who had pierced the side of Jesus to ascertain whether he was dead. In the gospels, only John described the piercing. It may have happened, but it was also symbolically necessary: without it, not enough blood would have been spilled at a crucifixion to carry out the prophecies of sacrifice.

Once his job was done, John's anonymous lance-man vanished from the scene. But he reappeared in the *Acta Pilati* with a name, Longinus, which he kept all through the Middle Ages. Medieval playwrights joyfully made use of him, sending him into the *praetorium* to improve on the centurion's conversion. For their Longinus had been blind, or as good as blind; he had dimly glimpsed the scar of the old wound inflicted on Jesus as a child by Judas, and had used it to guide the lance home. In the York play, Pilate had instructed him: 'In Jesus' side/ Shove it this tide.' He had done so, and immediately tumbled to his knees. Out of the pierced side had flowed blood and water, though blood never flowed from a dead man; and the drops, part silver, part crimson, had fallen on the blind man's eyes. Now Longinus walked in to Pilate unaided, his chin lifted, for he could see.

But Pilate did not notice him. Longinus' witness to Christ ('Ah, mercy my succour, mercy my treasure, mercy my Saviour; thy mercy be marked in me') was heard by the audience, but not by the governor. Medieval writers put these soldiers on the stage with Pilate, but then eschewed the drama of making them report to him. He seemed preoccupied, distracted, and above all not ready to hear that he had made the worst mistake of his life. The York Pilate remarks to Caiaphas and Annas that 'I'm not very happy that he's hanging up there', but that is all. He does not elaborate. As for the Towneley Pilate, he strides in after the trial not only with no regrets, but with a roaring song of triumph:

> Mighty lord of all, *me Caesar magnificavit!*
> Down on your knees you fall, great God *me sanctificavit!*

The *Acta Pilati,* on the other hand, presumed that as the day wore on Pilate began to feel worse. When the last of the witnesses had left, Pilate and his wife were 'furious'. The servants brought food, but they ignored it. They ate nothing, drank nothing. Procula sat there like a statue, her hands in her lap or sometimes, distractedly, scratching at her pale cheeks. The only thing Pilate raised to his lips, as if they were the only sustenance he had, were his white knuckles and his fiercely bitten thumbs.

At one point he summoned the chief priests. All he asked was, 'Did you see what happened?'

'It was just an eclipse of the sun,' they answered. 'Of the usual sort.'

He knew it was not of the usual sort.

At the end of the afternoon, in the most fantastical accounts, a servant brought in a hexagonal dish of green emerald. It was empty, but the deep cross-cutting of the base suggested that it was full of green light glittering on water. This souvenir had been brought, on Pilate's orders, from the upper room in which Jesus had eaten his last meal before the trial. In this dish the roast lamb of the Passover had been passed round the table. It was now, for the moment, the property of Pilate, shining strangely on his table among the untouched food.

First the magic coat, now the magic dish. No writer imputed any special motive to Pilate for wanting these things. They seemed to come to him like war spoils, objects casually acquired because their owner had been parted from them. Yet he wanted them badly. He was prepared to lie and cheat to get them, or to rifle through the otherwise unremarkable tableware of an ordinary Jewish house. They were evidence of a kind, souvenirs of a kind, but also talismans that he did not want to fall into anyone else's hands. Though he did not understand their power, he accepted that they possessed it; just as although he had never understood the claims of Jesus, he had found himself afraid of him. He needed these objects as one might need the personal effects of a murderer or a magician, the knife, the dried herbs, the jacket with a dust of poison in the pocket, to keep the power locked up.

Yet he did not keep the dish for long. A servant brought a message, as the light faded, that Joseph of Arimathea had returned to repeat his request to take the body from the cross. All the gospels 'recorded' this scene; and according to all of them, the interview was short. Mark's Joseph asked for the body, using the word he would have used of a living man; Pilate said he could take it, using the term for a corpse. Joseph was hinting at the resurrection; Pilate was still a witness to the death. Now he was to be the chief agent of the burial, so that again the words of the Creed could be fulfilled in him: *crucified, dead and buried*. Only one Coptic text suggests that he resisted giving up the corpse, as though, like the coat and the dish, he needed to keep it under his control. That text contained a long appeal by Joseph, every clause of which began with the words 'Give me this stranger': as if Joseph meant to play Jesus down while Pilate, for some reason, suspected he might be important.

Pilate was not bound to hand the body over. Corpses were usually removed from the cross on request, but most were thrown into a common pit. The corpse of a man found guilty of sedition was often granted not even that grace, but was left to the crows and the vultures as a final humiliation. In Judea, the Jews demanded more respect for their dead criminals. This alone may have accounted for the speed of the transaction. The Jews cared, Pilate did not, and unrest had to be avoided. The decision was easy.

Yet some scholars have imagined there was more to it than that. Perhaps the handing over was so prompt because Pilate felt the beginnings of guilt, and wanted to show some respect to Jesus. John's Pilate seemed even to discern that Joseph was a secret disciple who should be 'granted' this concession. In that gospel Joseph had already discussed the burial with Nicodemus, and Nicodemus had his servants ready with ointment of myrrh and aloes in dozens of alabaster jars. It was abundantly clear that if they took this man down they were going to bury him as a king; Pilate's insulting words on the *titulus* were going to be taken literally. And he made no attempt to question it or to prevent it.

Roman piety demanded in any case that bodies – even the bodies of enemies, even sometimes the bodies of criminals – should be given some ceremony of burial or farewell. At a minimum, three handfuls of earth had to be scattered over them with the prayer *sit tibi terra levis,* may the earth lie light on you. If this was not done, the shade could not be ferried across the River Styx but had to remain among the desperate crowds on the bank, doomed to wander eternally. The worst part of the killings that were going on in Rome at that moment – the purges of the accomplices of Sejanus – was less that men died than that their bodies were left on the mud-banks of the Tiber, uncremated, untouched even by the loving hands of their relations. If you respected your enemy you handed his body over, as Aeneas handed over the body of the brave boy Lausus to the ashes and the shades:

> *teque parentum*
> *manibus et cineri, si qua est ea cura, remitto.*

It was possibly significant that no cash seemed to change hands. Mark's use of the word 'gave' or 'presented' suggests that, unusual as it was, Pilate made no charge for this service. Conspiracy theorists take this as a clue of the friendship between Joseph and Pilate, as also of Pilate's connivance in the idea that Jesus should be buried splendidly. But it could have meant anything, from *pietas* to profound indifference.

The Pilate of 'Joseph of Arimathea', a fanciful medieval poem by Robert de Borron, went a little further. He was happy to give Joseph the body, because he expected him to drag it round the streets of Jerusalem and leave it in some mean place. But when the guards at the cross proved reluctant to hand the body over, he sent Nicodemus to persuade them, and gave him an extra gift for his service. At the end of the interview he picked up the emerald dish from the table and thrust it into his hands. It was no holy relic to him, but vaguely malevolent, like a witching stone. He was almost afraid of it, with its green glittering shine. Perhaps this was something that ought to be swiftly passed on.

Nicodemus handed the dish to Joseph. He took it out to the cross, and collected in it the blood of Christ when he was taken down. The dish that had held the blood of the lamb held the blood of the Lamb again. And Pilate became the first man to seek and find – and lose again – the Holy Grail.

*　　*　　*

Once the trial was over, a record was placed in the archive. This was standard, indeed required, practice. No more than a few lines were needed to note the name, charge and sentence. And of course it has disappeared, together with everything else Pilate or his secretaries committed to wax or paper.

If the case was important, a longer version would have to be sent to the imperial archives in Rome. There is no particular reason why Pilate should have thought the case of Jesus, the sentencing of an obscure provincial, should have justified further attention. So it is probable that no report was sent; but the early Christians were predictably dissatisfied with that. Pilate, they thought, must have been moved by Jesus and troubled by the signs attending his death. He would now have to scramble both to atone, and to cover himself.

Tertullian in the second century took it as a fact that Pilate had sent a full report to the emperor, a report so persuasive that Tiberius himself had been convinced that Jesus was divine. Justin Martyr referred to the governor's written record as a matter of course, 'from which you may learn the details of the crucifixion', including especially the piercing with nails and the division of Christ's clothes. He also claimed that Pilate's own *acta* contained accounts of Jesus's miracles, his healing of the lame and blind and his raising of men from the dead, and told his Roman readers that they could easily consult them. In 311 the emperor Maximinus apparently caused certain *Memoirs of Pilate* to be forged, circulated and memorised by schoolchildren in order to rebut the claims of the Christians. It is possible, though unlikely, that the basis of this was the real, brief, judicial entry in which Pilate described the simple sedition for which Jesus had been executed.

Yet any real records had probably vanished even by the time of Maximinus; and since they were bound to be embarrassing in any case, the *Acta Pilati* were invented by early Christians to take their place. The existing versions date from the fifth century, but they are mentioned in the fourth, when Epiphanus, in a sermon of 387 on fixing the date of Easter, asserted that the correct date for the crucifixion was given in the *Acta Pilati* as the fifth before the Kalends of April.

These *Acta,* though they were supposed to be Nicodemus' official record of the passion events, were not written to resemble judicial records at all. They were a highly coloured version of the passion story, in which the role of Pilate was so far expanded that he became chief actor. They found a wide audience. Not long after their first invention they were translated into Coptic, Slav, Syriac, Armenian and Georgian, finding a wide audience all through the shaggier fringes of the disintegrating empire. As they spread, so their version of Pilate – the regretful intellectual – spread too, at least in quarters where there were no bigger and badder Pilates to compete with.

Yet there also existed, from the second century onwards, several official letters or reports the governor was supposed to have written to Tiberius. Here the forgers tried harder to make their documents look officially Roman: beginning with one 'written' right after the crucifixion, on the very day given in the *Acta* for the trial.

Pontius Pilate to Tiberius Caesar, Emperor, Greeting.

Jesus Christ, whom I mentioned in my last letter, has been executed by the will of the people. I myself was unwilling and apprehensive. By Hercules, so pious and austere a man has never been seen nor will be again. But there was an amazing unanimity in the request of the Jews and their leaders that this ambassador of truth should be crucified, even though their own prophets (who are like the Sybil with us) testified against them. When he was hanged supernatural signs appeared, and these – in the judgement of philosophers – menaced the whole world with ruin . . .

Had I not feared that the people would riot – for they were almost furious – perhaps this man would still be living with us. Although I have to say that – compelled by loyalty to your dignity, rather than my own inclination – I did not strive with all my might to prevent the sale and suffering of this innocent blood, which was guiltless of every accusation. It was an injustice, caused by the maliciousness of men, and yet, as the Scriptures say, it will destroy them.

The fifth before the Kalends of April.

As forgeries went, it was quite good. The grovelling tone, and the attempt to pass the buck, were both plausible; the Sybil was a nice touch. That 'By Hercules!' perhaps went a little far: as if a Victorian governor writing to the Foreign Office were suddenly to say, 'Damn it all, what a fine fellow he was!' And perhaps there was not enough detail for the letter to be truly persuasive. Lick the pen, roll up the sleeves, try again.

To the most potent, august, divine and awful Augustus [sic] Caesar, from Pilate, the administrator of the eastern province, greeting.

I have received information, your excellency, which fills me with fear and trembling. For in this province which I administer, my lord, according to the command of your serenity, one of whose cities is called Jerusalem, the whole multitude of Jews delivered to me a man called Jesus, and brought many accusations against him, but they would not convict him of anything. They charged him with one heresy in particular: that he said the Sabbath was not a day of rest, and was not to be observed by them. For he performed many cures on that day, and made the blind see and the lame walk, raised the dead, cleansed lepers, healed the paralytic who were wholly unable to move their bodies or brace their nerves, and gave them power to walk and run, removing their infirmity by his word alone.

There is another very mighty deed which is strange to the gods we have: he raised up a man, Lazarus, who had been dead four days, summoning him by his word alone, when the dead man had already begun to decay, and his body was corrupted by worms and stank like a dog's; but seeing him lying in the tomb he ordered him to run, and the dead man did not hesitate, but ran out of his tomb like a bridegroom out of his chamber, and the tomb was filled with sweet perfume. Moreover, he approached men who were strangers and clearly demoniacs, who lived in deserts and devoured their own flesh and wandered about among cattle and creeping things, and caused them to live in cities in their own houses, and by a word rendered them rational. He caused men who were vexed by unclean spirits to become wise and honourable, and he sent the demons that were in them into a herd of swine and pushed them into the sea and drowned them.

And again, there was another man who had a withered hand and lived in suffering, and had neither the shape of a man nor the symmetry of a body; and he healed even this man with a word and made him whole. And there was a woman too, who had had an issue of blood for a long time, and whose veins and arteries were exhausted, and the joints of her bones stuck out and shone through like glass, so that all the doctors of the district had dismissed her without hope and had not relieved her; but as Jesus passed by she mysteriously received strength by his shadow falling on her from behind, and touched the hem of his garment; and immediately, at that very moment, strength filled her exhausted limbs, and as if she had never suffered anything she began to run along towards Capernaum, her own city, and she reached it within six days.

That is how these things happened. But the Jews reported that Jesus did these things on the Sabbath; and I saw greater works of wonder done by him than by the gods whom we worship.

But Herod and Archelaus and Philip, Annas and Caiaphas, with all the people, delivered him to me to put him on trial. And because many people raised a tumult against me, I commanded that he should be crucified. I scourged him first, though I found no cause in him for evil accusations.

Now when he was crucified darkness came over all the world, and the sun was obscured for half a day, and the stars appeared, but no lustre was seen in them; and I suppose your excellency is not unaware that all over the world they lit their lamps from the sixth hour until the evening. And the moon, which was like blood, did not shine all night long, although it was full, and the stars and Orion made lamentation over the Jews, because of the crime they had committed . . .

The forgers went on trying. The more words he wrote, the less Roman and rational Pilate became; and the more medieval, credulous, open-mouthed. He walked among wonders and recognised the prophets, as if he himself were one of the shattered Jewish crowd. And although he was writing at his desk, supposedly in cultured detachment from it all, it was clear that he bent over his writing like a medieval clerk, eyes wide and head to one side, while outside the window hung stars with faces on the flat blue backcloth of the sky.

Yet the faint possibility still remains of some explanation to headquarters. Pilate had got himself into a very public difficulty, at a time when the city was full of foreigners who could carry rumours home. The Jews had already hinted at telling tales to Rome, and the release of Barabbas may also have required justification. Dealings with Tiberius were so sensitive that self-protecting cover-letters, even for small incidents, might have been essential.

Emergency letters could be scribbled on anything, even the backs of old ones, if you were in camp and paper was scarce. But a letter to the emperor, no matter how urgently self-justifying, had to be written with maximum formality. The best pen was chosen, one with decorative bronze leaf or wire chased into the iron shaft. Ink was freshly compounded from carbon, gum arabic and water. The writing paper, made of papyrus, was smoothed down with ivory and pumice until there was no risk that the pen would blot on surface imperfections. Augustan paper, the best kind, was still perilously thin, snagging the nib and showing through any writing on the other side. The task was fraught even before the explaining began.

All this done, Pilate would try to express himself directly. Secretaries wrote his letters, but a letter to the emperor might be an exception. He might try to do it himself. The cursive script of men who were usually too grand to write for themselves was often spidery and wobbly, with the letters – trailing 's's, open Greek 'e's, languid left-leaning 'd's – set nervously apart from each other. Pilate's anxiety to please, to be careful, would have been apparent in every stroke, as if he was once again the child with his slate, terrified that the wet rope would lash across his back.

When the letter was written it was rolled up, tied and sealed. A stick of wax was melted over a candle flame; the blob of hot wax was applied to the tie. Pilate would have taken the gold signet ring from the fourth finger of his left hand and pressed it into the wax. We do not know what impression it left there. Pliny's signet ring was engraved with a four-horse chariot, Tiberius' with his own profile; it was common to have animals or gods. If you did not want the engraved stone to be damaged by the wax you moistened it first with your lips, an action that became as swift and unthinking with repetition as licking a finger to turn a page. When replaced on the finger the ring was still warm, just for a moment, like the tightening flush on a man's face when he knows he has written an account that is just a little coloured, just a little false.

The sealing of this letter, in Pilate's mind, might literally have sealed up the case of Jesus. He should never have had to think about him again. But in the subsequent dramatisations of his life, that supposed letter to Tiberius merely marked the beginning of the biggest dramas of all.

*   *   *

Pilate was officially the chief witness now. He had declared Jesus king at the trial and on the cross. He had retailed his wonders to the emperor himself. Like a tourist, the first of the relic-seekers, he had gathered up souvenirs: the magic coat, the Holy Grail. With elaborate care, he had made his soldiers prove that Jesus was dead. Next he was required to lay out the most thrilling evidence of all: that he had risen, and he lived.

First, like the magician's partner, he had to lock the box to make escape impossible. Each catch had to be fastened, each bolt thrust home, the audience positioned to watch for trickery. And trickery was expected. In Matthew's gospel the chief priests came to Pilate on the Saturday morning, suddenly unafraid of being defiled by meeting him on the Sabbath. 'Your Excellency', they said, 'we remember that that deceiver said, when he was still alive, that after three days he would rise again.'

Possibly Pilate remembered. Such things could be expected of Messiahs: they never died, never lay down. Others came back in the same clothes.

'So, sir,' Matthew's priests went on, 'order the sepulchre to be made secure until the third day, or else his disciples will come by night and steal him away and tell the people he's risen from the dead, and the last error will be worse than the first.'

Pilate could see there was a grain of sense in this. If he could prevent the growth of a dangerous cult based on the rising of a man from the dead, he ought to do so. Archaeology, too, bears this out. In the nineteenth century an imperial edict was discovered in Nazareth, inscribed in Greek on marble and dating from close to Pilate's time, decreeing that tombs should be kept inviolate. Offenders would be punished especially severely for taking bodies out of tombs and putting them in other places. This suggests that, even if it did not happen in the case of Jesus, the possibility of cultic or political deception was well understood. Matthew's Pilate did not hesitate. 'Take a watch,' he told the Jews, meaning 'Take some of mine'; 'go off and make it as secure as you know how.'

Tradition says he let them have four soldiers, including a centurion. The word used by Matthew for the troop usually meant men who reported to the governor; later in Matthew's account, they dreaded that they would actually have to face Pilate afterwards. The apocryphal

Gospel of Peter says that a man called Petronius was their commander. Some scholars, translating the Greek a different way, thought Pilate told the Jews rather haughtily to use their own police force, the Temple guard. But the technical terms used by Matthew (including Pilate's *Echete koustodian*) suggest that these were his men, put for a day or so under the orders of the chief priests.

Besides, it was theologically vital that the soldiers should be Roman. It meant that Jesus, in his rising, would overthrow the power of darkness and all the obstacles it put in his way: swords, helmets, shields, the whole might of *pax et imperium*. The soldiers who would sprawl by the tomb in hundreds of later paintings, in the unguarded attitudes of sleep, had to display the weight of the old order. Not only death would be shattered, but also the earthly equipment that dealt out death. Real prisons and real stones, secured with official imperial seals, would be cracked and broken as surely as prisons of the spirit.

Matthew ignored the actual setting of the guard, but medieval writers made the most of it. At nightfall, their Pilate went to the garden to put his soldiers in place. The great storm of the day before, the cracking of the hills, the sun eclipsed, the 'mist and great weather' had cleared away. The cross still stood, empty, in the cool unelectric air. In the garden the great trees stood too, becoming their own shadows: the descendants of the trees of Eden, hung with the same golden apples and pomegranates, about to witness the new creation. Pilate walked on a path that showed dimly between them, winding upwards. In his long cloak and pillbox hat, he was the only element of agitation.

At his side trotted an attendant with wax in a bowl and a torch to melt it. In the twilight air, the torch smoked. Behind him came the soldiers, a reluctant posse. These were the same men Pilate had cheated of the seamless garment; they dragged their feet and grumbled. 'Look here,' moaned one, 'what the hell's the point of watching him, if he's dead?'

'If they're going to pay me, I don't care what he is. Just give me the money, mate.'

They marched on. Eventually, through the trees, came a glimpse of the new tomb, embedded in the hillside like a segment of the moon itself.

Pilate approached it and touched it, as if to defy any magic that lurked there. Then, stepping back, he barked: 'Set the watch, men.'

'Right, sir! They could set a whole mob on us, and we wouldn't let him out!'

'I could kill a hundred thousand with one hand, sir!'

Pilate beckoned to each in turn. The Coventry and Redentin plays, written respectively for listeners in the English Midlands and on the German Baltic coast, gave these men names that were thought to sound Jewish or heathen, together with exotic armour and big ridiculous weapons. Over these lumpen auxiliaries, Pilate fussed and fretted. Amoraunt, also known as Soloman, he placed to the west with his fine sword Mummink, which could cut through the bolts on armour and lift rings off fingers. Arfaxat, also known as Samson, he placed to the north with his sword, Strike-the-shield. Cosdram, also known as Boas von Thomar ('My good man Boas!'), the clumsiest of the soldiers, was placed to the east and ordered to be nimbler than usual. He rattled his good sword Klinger in its scabbard, promising to 'split the pants' of anyone who came past. Lastly, Affraunt, also called Sasoch, 'my faithful knight', was placed to the south. When Pilate had put them in their places, they puffed out their armour-plated chests and saluted him.

'If anyone comes here he's a dead man, sir!' cried Affraunt.

'I'll guard his feet, sir, even if both Jack and Jill come to get him!' Arfaxat shouted. 'He'd rather he had the whooping cough, I tell you!'

'I'm on the right side, and I'll kill anyone who comes!' yelled Cosdram.

'And I'll take the left,' said Affraunt; 'if anyone comes here, I'll give him some fearful blows to think about. Have a nice night, Sir Pilate, don't you worry yourself! We'll keep him safe.'

'I only hope he is really dead,' the governor muttered.

'Dead as a log, sir! He's not going anywhere.'

Pilate called for the melted wax. Along each edge of the great white tomb he smeared the wax and pushed in his ring. He did so seven times, symbolically sealing the tomb, like the scroll in the Apocalypse, so that no one in heaven or earth could break it open; save Christ. 'On every corner I've set my seal,' he said at last. 'My heart's easy now. No briber will steal away the body from under this stone. Will he, men?'

'Not likely, sir.'

Once more Pilate touched the seals. The wax had hardened; there was no chink where light could enter. The stone slab would take six men to lift it. After that the Nazarene would need to wriggle from his graveclothes, grey-faced and tousle-haired, like a snake from its skin; and then the soldiers would cut him down.

'Right, men,' said Pilate. 'Be fierce as the wind. Guard the man well. If you lose him, you and your wives and your children will regret it, believe me. If you keep him safe, I'll give you gold and silver and steel helmets; I'll be your friend without deception. Remember this especially: a good deed is never wasted. I'm going home now.'

'Sir.'

As he walked back, the knights were singing to keep themselves awake. The *Gospel of Peter* claims they arranged to keep watch two by two, and pitched a little tent among the trees. In the Redentin play they sang of gold, and the soft-skinned wife of the German emperor, and of a boat tossing in the wild sea between Hiddensee and Mone. From time to time, as they related it later, their throaty carousing seemed to be overtaken by a note of pure beauty, as if someone had tapped on the side of a glass. But perhaps it was only a bird, ruffled in its night feathers, spilling notes from a needle-like beak; or the tinkle of a rivulet of water, or the high solemn tone of the stars.

Pilate lay down in his gold bed, but he did not sleep. Beside him his wife did not sleep either. They lay in separate silences, two entombments. He too was wrapped in linen like the Nazarene, head to feet; his body was oiled too, as Christ's was, with glistening sweeps of a woman's hand. The weather had not fully settled; there were rattling thunderdrums, weird lights in the dark. Pilate's head ached with wine, and worry, and an intimation of calamity.

Before dawn had broken he heard the soldiers' voices.

'What the hell do we tell him?'

'Tell him the truth. That his disciples stole him from us −'

'There was this terrible earthquake −'

'I couldn't stand. I couldn't sit, even.'

'Why the hell did we trust the watchman to wake us? I read in a book once, never put your trust in anything.'

'So someone tell me, what do we tell him? That we've lost Jesus?'

Then, dogmatic, Affraunt's voice: 'Well, lost is lost! What are you shouting about? Things have gone wrong, but we're innocent, aren't we? Why should we get it in the neck?'

Pilate seized his cloak and went out to them. Fury began to consume him: fury, and terror. 'What!' he screamed. 'What? What? What are you saying, you bastard? What garbage are you trying to tell me? That he came back to life? When he was dead and in the tomb? What the hell happened here?'

His hands were at Arfaxat's throat. The man babbled about an earthquake, about trying not to sleep but being unable to keep his eyes open; he said he had been held to the ground as if pinioned there. Pilate let him go contemptuously, as he might have discarded a cockerel once its neck had snapped.

'What a great set of knights you are. God, what a glittering reputation you must all have. How about going to sit in the corn, to see if you can scare off a raven or two?'

'Sir,' said Arfaxat, 'please listen.'

His voice was bruised and feeble, but something made Pilate give half an ear to him.

'Sir, beautiful angels came down. They came from the highest throne, and they took the man away from us. We were terribly frightened. I don't know how, but something happened to me. I couldn't see, I couldn't hear. Look –' for he could sense Pilate's anger again, see the tick of the vein in his neck – 'believe me, sir, it wasn't our fault. There we were, all lying by the grave. We could see everything clearly, absolutely clearly. The angels came –'

'Angels,' said Pilate blankly.

'Beings came, in great force, in wonderful clearness and beauty. They shone like lightning, like the snow. They robbed us of our wits and made us fall asleep. The angels came to the grave, and they took Jesus out. He was there among them, and they led him to a bright place, singing for joy all the time. And all this –' here his voice faltered again, 'I noticed in my sleep, sir.'

'If you were asleep,' yelled Pilate, 'then how could you see it? That can't possibly make sense. When I see something, I'm not asleep! You invented that story, the lot of you, between yourselves. I've a good mind to put the thumbscrews on you! Get out of here! You're dismissed, and you're disgraced!'

Then the York Pilate thought again. Caiaphas and Annas, drawn by the noise, had hurried across to his palace and were sitting on the steps. 'Caiaphas, you're a cunning clerk,' said Pilate. 'I think we're in danger of having made a big mistake here. What do you think we should do?'

'Best if no one knows about it, for sure,' answered Caiaphas.

'I know what!' piped Annas. 'Get your men to spread the word round that he was taken by at least twenty thousand men. Get them to say they were almost killed. And we'll pay them for their lies out of our treasury.'

'Great idea!' cried Pilate. 'Now, men, listen well: here's the story. Ten thousand heavily armed men took him away by force. You tried to resist, but they would have killed you. That's the story I want told *everywhere*. And here's a reward of a thousand pounds, in cash. Oh, and – my eternal gratitude, men. You can count on it.'

'We'll tell that tale wherever we go, sir. Night and day.'

Pilate put a money bag in each hand, then paced up and down in front of them. 'Wherever you go,' he said, 'whatever country you're in, see that no man's wiser about what we've done. Remember: you didn't see anything. That sight you saw, forget it. We'll back you up. We'll tell people it's against the law to believe stupid stories of dead men rising. We'll make them think it's all lies. Remember the old motto!

> *So shall truth be bought and sold*
> *And treason shall for truth be told.*

Goodbye now!'

The idea of a plot to conceal the resurrection also originates with Matthew. It seems plausible enough: no one would have wanted the story of a Messianic miracle to spread through the Passover crowd. But Matthew's version of the plot was different. In his gospel, it was the Jewish priests, not Pilate, who gave the terrified soldiers 'a considerable sum of money' to say that the disciples had stolen Jesus in the night while they slept; 'and if this comes to the governor's ears, we will put things right with him and protect you.' Far from being the inventor of the 'stolen body' plot, Pilate was the chief victim of the exercise.

Matthew's chief priests seemed confident that they could do it. All through the trial, they had showed an acute understanding of the governor's psychology. Now they divined that they could run rings round him again. But in exactly what fashion did they hope to 'put things right' with him? The soldiers would have been bound to report to him eventually, even if they went to the priests first. Their story, shorn of the 'ten thousand armed men' of the passion plays, suggested unbelievable incompetence. It could hardly have protected them from Pilate's lashing sarcasm, or his temper. What the Jews' proposal provided, however, was an explanation for something that otherwise seemed baffling: how a nervy governor, highly sensitised at that moment to crowd hysteria and the threat of violence, could have missed the news that his difficult victim had disappeared from the tomb and was presumed to have risen from the dead.

For, according to the gospels, he did miss it. Matthew's mention of the plot that might come to the governor's ears was Pilate's last live appearance. There was no Roman reaction to the resurrection, even though the news of the body's disappearance, and the supposition that Jesus lived, burned through Jerusalem. In Luke, all Jesus's appearances were in or near the city; he materialised in rooms, but he also haunted the roads and the gardens. When two disciples met the risen Jesus a little later on the road to Emmaus, they could ask him: 'Are you the only person who doesn't know what's been happening in Jerusalem these past few days?' No, apparently he was not the only person.

Perhaps Pilate had already left, riding back in splendid and indifferent convoy to the haven of Caesarea. Or perhaps the evangelists' imaginations failed them. Again and again, through the passion naratives, they had made Pilate an unwitting witness to the divinity of Jesus. Here, with the resurrection, was their chance to make him confirm the most astonishing miracle of all. For some reason, they chose not to.

He could at least have gone to the garden. He could have sent out a search party, treated the case as a simple escape. But the gospel Pilate did not even show as much interest as that. With so many wild stories floating around, perhaps he thought there was no point. Better to withdraw from the scene, leave the Jews to it. There was, besides, the humiliation of losing face: his own *imperium* had been thrown back at him and counted for nothing.

The notion of men rising from the dead would have struck him first as Jewish fanaticism; yet it was not completely impossible. There were stories recorded. Men had been found alive in the funeral pyre; some had been claimed as corpses, though they still breathed, by relatives who wanted their money. As you placed the body in the winding sheet you would notice the soft heave of the cloth, a warm moistness when the hand was held over the face. Men had been carried to the pyre, and had then walked home and clapped their hands for the servants; or their souls had wandered from their bodies and gone to other countries, only to return and nudge their corpses back to astonishing life. But those were men who had merely been declared dead, not buried; as the elder Pliny put it, 'we are treating of the operations of nature, not of miracles.'

The Nazarene had been quite dead, of course. Pilate had had the reports. It was just conceivable that his soldiers had been deceived, and that the man had been taken down still breathing. If the claim of resurrection reached his ears at all, Pilate might have concluded that Jesus was an athlete or a trickster. He might have grudgingly admired his fortitude, like that of the gladiators whose names he yelled and whose winning bouts he argued over. But his reaction, whatever it was, was obviously beyond imagining by any of the gospel writers.

The absence of a Roman *imprimatur* does not weaken the resurrection story for those who believe it happened. Yet it will always be strange. For some early Christian writers, notably in the Coptic church, it was too strange. They insisted on having their Roman witness, *the* Roman witness, to the fact that Christ had risen. In this, according to one Edwardian scholar, they showed 'no feeling for the tragic irony of history': the irony that 'the greatest event of human history passed unnoticed by the rulers of the earth.' But this, of course, did not bother them. The story of the resurrection was undeniably stronger, they thought, if Pilate and the chief priests realised it had happened too.

The author of the *Gospel of Peter* sent the centurion, the soldiers and the chief priests racing by night to tell Pilate what had happened. 'They were in great agony,' he wrote, 'saying, "This man really was the Son of God."'

Pilate answered in a telling variant of his words as he washed his hands: 'I am clean of the blood of the Son of God, but this was what seemed good to you.'

The chief priests begged him, implored him, not to let the soldiers reveal what they had seen; if they were to do so, the people would stone them. So Pilate told the soldiers to say nothing. Apart from that he showed no curiosity, no reaction, as if his own mind too was deliberately cleansed of the affair. In most of the apocryphal gospels of the western Church, this was his attitude: proud, almost indifferent. The notable exception was the longer version of his letter to Tiberius. In this he claimed to have witnessed the resurrection; and not only that, but the harrowing of hell and the destruction of the synagogues, in one great cosmic theatre-show from the terrace of his palace.

On the first day of the week, about the third hour of the night, there came a sound from heaven, and the heavens became seven times more luminous than on all other days. And the sun blazed out more luminously than it had ever shone, lighting up the whole hemisphere. And just as lightning-flashes suddenly appear in a storm, so tall men in beautiful clothes, and of indescribable glory, appeared in the air, an uncountable crowd, crying out, 'Glory to God in the highest, and on earth peace, goodwill among men; Jesus that was crucified is risen again; come up from Hades you that were enslaved in the subterranean recesses of hell.' And at their voice the mountains and hills were moved, and the rocks were split, and great chasms were made in the earth, so that even the foundations of the earth appeared. And He that raised up all the dead and bound Hades said, 'Tell my disciples that He goes before you into Galilee, and there you shall see him.'

And amid this terror the dead appeared rising again. The Jews themselves saw it, and said it was Abraham, and Isaac, and Jacob, and the twelve patriarchs, and Moses, and Job, who had died (they say) 2,500 years ago; and we saw Noah clearly in his body, as in life. And all the crowd of men walked about and sang hymns to God in loud voices, saying 'The Lord our God, who has risen from the dead, has brought all the dead to life, and Hades has been spoiled and slain.'

All that night, my lord king, the light went on shining. And many of the Jews died in the chasm of the earth, as they were swallowed up, so that the next morning most of those who had opposed Jesus could not be found. Others saw men rising again whom none of us had ever seen. Only one Jewish synagogue was left in Jerusalem itself, for all the synagogues which had been against Jesus were destroyed.

Through that terror, therefore, amazed and seized with the most dreadful trembling, I wrote down what I saw . . . and I have sent it to your divinity, my lord.

Trembling as he was, this was still Pilate writing as a bureaucrat in detachment. His terror contained no element of remorse, because he had blamed the Jews for everything. The Coptic writers, however, knew they could do better with their witness. The Coptic hagiographies of Pilate (later read by many more people in Arabic translations) enjoyed a huge vogue in Egypt and Ethiopia from the fifth century onwards. Even in the eighteenth century, a Jesuit missionary reported that these stories were still being read in churches, and that babies were still being christened 'Pilate' after their reluctant hero. The anti-Semitism of the Copts, who lived next door to the Jews, makes these tales almost unreadable in parts; but they are not without interest for their treatment of the governor. These writers thought they could make him involved and moved; they could make him approach Jesus, even touch him. They thought they could make him sorry. The fact that the tales often came out comical, rather than affecting, does not change the fact that many Christians half-wanted matters to have happened this way.

In the *Martyrdom of Pilate*, an Egyptian fantasy of the sixth century, Pilate quickly noticed the miracles and prodigies occurring round the tomb of Jesus. He went to his house and prepared a banquet for the poor to celebrate his joy at the resurrection, and Procula, even more joyful, prepared to go to the tomb to worship. When the Jews got wind of this, they went in search of Barabbas to persuade him to ambush Procula and kill Pilate. But the author of the *Martyrdom*, one Gamaliel, passed this news to Joseph of Arimathea, who tipped off the governor; and Pilate drew up his troops in readiness.

Procula got up in the night, with her handmaids and servants, and went to the tomb. There she worshipped, spreading precious ointments and perfumes on the tomb itself and on the cross, which was propped beside it. She lit dozens of lamps and burned incense. As the women lingered by the tomb, veiled heads bending and hands upraised, Barabbas and his men attacked them. But Pilate's soldiers fell on the attackers. Barabbas himself was sentenced by the governor to be crucified upside down, his side pierced and his legs broken. The execution took place five days after the resurrection; it was, Pilate told Barabbas, revenge for 'that innocent blood which we have unjustly shed'.

Which *we* have unjustly shed. The Copts may have made a saint out of Pilate, but they did not exculpate him. He had killed Christ, certainly; but it bothered him. So in another Coptic fragment – the one that survived the wreck of HMS *Captain* – Pilate interrogated the soldiers from the tomb, dismissed their feeble excuses, threw them in prison, and went back to the garden himself.

It was still early. The bushes of the garden were soaked with dew as he brushed against them, and mist garlanded the trees like the drift that followed an explosion. It hung there, that sense of Him, moving away as he approached it. Early dawn was the time when honey fell from the air; a man out walking then would find himself sticky, under leaves that were dribbled with nectar in the colour of the scattering clouds.

He did not go down the winding paths alone. The chief priests and the centurion went with him, at least as far as the tomb, when the priests refused to go further because of the taint of pollution. They drew back, letting the two unclean Romans go ahead of them. Yet the tomb itself did not suggest uncleanness. The new stone gleamed, and under Pilate's hand the tiny grains glittered like diamond. The air was cool still; the heat of the day had not yet warmed the surface of the stone. And the neatness of its displacement, which had left the grass-blades and rose-petals unbruised beside it, caused Pilate's hand to tremble.

He needed to enter the tomb too. Perhaps it would contain evidence of a mistake: the corpse still there but somehow shifted into a corner, overlooked. He took the centurion with him to confirm whatever he found, but they were two unseeing men together. The centurion, half-blinded in battle, was now utterly blind in the enclosing darkness. As for Pilate, he was afflicted again with that temporary blindness that had overcome him at the trial; he was once more the man who had failed to see God when he had stood within a yard of him.

The tomb was filled with astonishing perfume. Before Pilate had gone even two steps inside, the air seemed to swarm with all the potions and essences of the apothecary. After he had handed the body over to Joseph, after Nicodemus had performed his own anointing, the women had crept in with their smaller jars of salve and ointment, and these were the perfumes that surrounded him. The passion plays listed them: pepper, ginger, cinnamon; new saffron powder from the purple crocus-fields of Anatolia; nutmeg, pomegranate and the wrinkled buds of cloves; raisins, garingay, violet-scented sugar, aniseed and cumin; grains of paradise; white ginger; cubes of white sugar as clear as ice; rosewater, olive oil, yellow wax, white wax, honey in the comb. And over all these was myrrh, the golden fragrance wept by Myrrha in her imprisonment under the bark of the unyielding tree.

Pilate was enraptured. 'Why is the air so sweet here?' he called to the priests. 'Where are these perfumes from?'

'It's just the wind in the garden,' they told him carelessly. 'The wind blowing through the flowers.'

He did not believe them. The three women must have compounded these scents, their long dark hair hanging down past their anguished eyes, the ground littered with little precious boxes and bags and measuring spoons. They had smeared it so thickly on the beloved body that the winding sheets appeared to be stained not with blood, but with drifts of petals and violets and dried jasmine flowers; and the sheets lay as a young man in vigour and impetuosity might have hurled them off one morning, stepping out into the glare of the light.

'If he was stolen,' Pilate murmured, 'the thieves would have taken these graveclothes, too.'

'No, no,' the priests told him. 'Those belong to someone else.'

He did not believe that, either. He knew they belonged to Jesus, who had somehow left them. Picking up the winding sheets, he pressed them to his heart and kissed them for joy as if Jesus were still wrapped in them. Then, over the holy sheets, in the intoxication of spices and flowers, he bent his head and wept.

The centurion, too, touched the winding sheet. He held it to his eye, and he saw again. At once he acknowledged Jesus, but Pilate did not do so yet. He sent for Joseph and Nicodemus, needing to consult with them. At the same time, the priests informed him that in a well elsewhere in the garden they had found the body of a crucified man. Everyone rushed to the well, where the corpse floated vertically like a white stone. The priests cried, 'Look, it's the sorcerer!'

'Is this really him?' asked Pilate.

Joseph and Nicodemus told him no. The graveclothes had belonged to Jesus; but this body in the well was that of one of the thieves who had been crucified with him.

Pilate then remembered that Jesus had said, 'The dead shall come to life in my tomb.' He ordered his men to carry the body to Jesus' tomb and to roll the stone across. The Jewish priests were outraged that a Roman governor would come meddling to a sepulchre. But as they upbraided Pilate, a voice from the tomb commanded them to take the stone away. The body of the thief had risen from the dead.

The pagan governor had, after all, witnessed a resurrection. More than that: he had helped it to occur. It had happened in the middle of a scene that seems farcical enough, with stock priests and bumbling soldiers, and with bodies, naked or in shrouds, popping up with the regularity of lovers in wardrobes in a Feydeau play. Yet it was meant to be an awakening of sorts, even the start of an apology. That was the gist of the end of the fragment, where Pilate stood in the garden and raised his hands in the praying posture of both Romans and Christians. He said nothing within earshot of the others, although they swarmed around him like characters at a carnival. Yet in his heart the phrase of recognition had already formed: *Oh, my Lord.*

*   *   *

The Pilate of the *Acta Pilati* was never quite so vulnerable. He was angry rather than sorry, and the evidence he sought was intellectual. Although it might have been an obvious step to go to the tomb, to inspect the clothes, to order his troops to check for footprints or the signs of a struggle, he did not do so. Instead he gathered the chief priests and teachers in the Temple, ordered the doors shut, and said: 'I've heard you have a great Bible here. I should like you to bring it before us.'

The chief priests brought it out. Four of them carried it, two of them struggled to open the great golden clasps. Pilate went on: 'I adjure you, by the God of your fathers who commanded you to build this Temple in the place of his sanctuary, not to hide the truth from me. You know everything that is written in this Bible. Tell me if you have found in the scriptures that this Jesus whom you crucified is the Son of God who was to come for the salvation of mankind, and in what year he was meant to come. Tell me whether you crucified him in ignorance or knowingly.'

In reply, Annas and Caiaphas immediately asked everyone in the Temple to leave. They closed the doors again. The mood was conspiratorial, the chamber dark; the great Bible lay mutely on the table. Caiaphas, leaning close to Pilate, admitted that they had found many witnesses to the resurrection among the Jews. They had even found two who had been raised from the dead and had witnessed Christ's harrowing of hell; they had taken written statements. And they had gone back to the Bible, labouring to turn the great creaking pages, to find out what God had to say on the subject. The arithmetical progression, from the creation to the flood, to the exile, to the building of the Temple, to the coming of Christ, was quite clear: it was (in a slight variant of what Michael the archangel had already told Seth, the son of Adam), exactly 5,500 years. So yes, this Jesus was the Son of God. But they had not told a soul; and they appealed to Pilate 'by your life and health' not to tell anyone either.

Pilate took this news calmly. No anger, no emotion; indeed, no reaction, except to sit down and write an account of everything the two priests had told him, 'and to lay them all up among the acts of the Lord and Saviour in the public books of his judgement hall.' Then he wrote another letter, this time to 'Claudius, king of Rome'. It was much like his other 'letters' for the first paragraph, retailing how the Jews had brought fearful judgement on themselves by ignoring the fact that 'their God would send them out of heaven his holy one who should rightly be called a king, and promised he would send him on earth by a virgin'. 'This god of the Hebrews,' he wrote, 'came when I was governor of Judea', and performed miracles for everyone to see; but the priests had told Pilate that he was a sorcerer, and Pilate had believed them.

He delivered him to death and the body was buried: 'but while my soldiers watched him he rose again on the third day.' The chief priests bribed the soldiers to say that the body had been stolen, 'but, though they took the money, they could not keep quiet about what had happened, and they testified too that they saw him when he had risen.' In his closing sentence he tried to explain himself, the only sentence that might have remotely rung true: 'I've reported these things to you, most mighty one, in case somebody else tries to tell you a pack of lies.'

There was still no conversion in this invention. Pilate had been duped into killing a god, but it was not his god, for all the signs and wonders. It was still 'the god of the Hebrews'. The execution of Jesus was an administrative lapse, not an error with any cosmic meaning; though it might be inconvenient and even dangerous to have dealt out death to a representative of divinity, Pilate's gods were still in charge here. He was going to clear up this mess, keep it under control. It was the Jews who would pay the price for snubbing their God.

Meanwhile, the Pilate of the Eastern Church had been writing letters of a different sort. In one sixth-century letter, written in Greek, he told Herod Antipas how after the resurrection he had kept track of Jesus. He followed him with spies as far as Galilee, where he learned that he was preaching. His wife Procula had gone up to Galilee to see him, together with the lance-man Longinus and the soldiers who had guarded the tomb. They found Jesus sitting in a tilled field, where the lines of rolled brown earth echoed the regular curls of his hair, with a great crowd listening to him; and though they did not dare approach, he saw them.

'What is it?' he asked them. 'Do you believe in me?'

They could not answer him.

'Procula, you should know that everyone who has died shall live by my death, which you have seen. You see that I'm alive, though you crucified me. Now, listen to me, and believe in God my father, who is with me. For I have burst the bounds of death and broken open the gates of Sheol.'

Procula returned, in tears, and told Pilate. Overwhelmed with grief, he lay on his bed and wept for a while. Then he put on black robes of mourning. Procula took off, one by one, her rings and bracelets, ripped the gold braiding from her dress, and let her hair fall in long tangled tresses. Like this, in their litter, clinging to each other, they went to Galilee. All the way there, Pilate complained: 'It's Herod's fault. It was Herod who made me judge him. It's Herod's fault.'

Fifty soldiers marched behind them. Pilate and Procula were desperate to see Jesus, but again they hardly dared to get close. They watched him from a distance, from behind the trees, until they summoned up enough courage to take the first steps in his direction. Then, at once, the heavens roared, thunder cracked, the earth moved; and in that moving of the earth came, once more, the perfume of paradise, of roses and cardamom and garingay and jasmine.

Pilate stood still in the middle of the road. He could see Jesus standing and talking to his disciples and, as he stood there, Jesus saw him. Pilate began to pray in his heart, for, as he told Herod, 'I knew that this was the lord of created things.' Then, unable to look any more, he knelt, with Procula beside him. Together, they fell on their faces on the hard ground. Pilate managed to cry out, 'I have sinned, Lord, that I judged you. I know you're God, the Son of God. I saw your humanity, but not your divinity.' And he added, again, wretchedly, 'It was Herod who made me do it.'

Jesus came across to them, bent down, and took their hands to raise them. As Pilate's fingers intertwined with his, he felt the deep wounds of the nails that he himself had ordered driven through them; and as he dared to raise his eyes to the face, a face misted with his own tears, he saw the scabbed scratches of the crown of thorns.

The hands of Jesus were now laid on his shoulders. 'All generations and families shall call you blessed,' he told him, 'because in your days the Son of Man died and rose again.' And with these astonishing words, he left them.

Unfortunately for the pathos of this scene, Herod wrote a reply to Pilate's letter. (This was also sixth-century, also in Greek, with an optional version in Syriac.) He seemed to overlook the blatant buckpassing, for he had a more urgent interest. 'Since you're seeing this man Jesus again,' he scribbled,

would you put in a word for me? I'm having a hard time at present. Lestonax, my son, is in the last stages of a decline. I've got dropsy myself, and worms are coming out of my mouth. My dear daughter Herodias was playing on the ice and fell in up to her neck; her mother caught at her head to save her, and it was cut off, and the water swept her body away. My wife is sitting with the head on her knees, weeping so much that her left eye is blinded, and the whole house is filled with sorrow.

Please intercede for me, and bury my family honourably. I'm enclosing my wife's earrings and my own signet ring.

Herod

These fantasies would be laughable if they did not carry a dark undercurrent: the determination of early Christian writers in every branch of the church, whether Greek, Coptic or western, to shift the blame for the crucifixion from Pilate to the Jews. This could reach grotesque levels, as when Origen in his commentaries on Matthew and John simply pronounces Pilate innocent, and ascribes to the Jews all the cruelties that were clearly inflicted on Christ by the Romans. Once the gospel-embroiderers had lost sight of the fact that crucifixion was a uniquely Roman punishment, uniquely in Pilate's power, they could take Jewish 'responsibility' to absurd lengths: even, in the Coptic apocrypha, causing the Jews to crucify Pilate himself as a loathesome 'Egyptian'.

The reason for these inventions, at least at first, was not simply to hurt the Jews. For at least three centuries after Christ's death, as the new religion struggled to establish itself, it was vital to have a Roman official who would say, repeatedly, that Jesus posed no threat to the empire. Pilate had to be Christ's advocate, even his friend, and this made the Jews the villains. As Christianity became accepted and official – starting with the Edict of Milan in 312, when Constantine recognised it as a *religio licita* throughout the empire – Pilate's fortunes fell into steep decline, and he became a villain in his own right. The Nicene Creed of 381 could state unequivocally that Jesus was crucified under Pontius Pilate, with no mention of the Jews.

Nonetheless, medieval anti-Semitism was still based squarely on the notion that the Jews had killed Christ. Pilate – who has always been used as men want to use him – became a witness to their supposed intractability, their emotionalism, their capacity to sow evil in the world. Although there was probably a core of truth in Pilate's reluctance to kill Jesus – for whatever reason – it was expanded and embroidered. Even the most tyrannical Pilate put the Jews in a bad light. In invented story after invented story he complained that they had misled him, made him do what he had never wanted to do. He had tried every subterfuge to save Jesus, but they had insisted on his death.

Even twentieth-century anti-Semitism, which had its roots in all kinds of prejudice both political and economic, was not free from that lingering image. A large amount of the nineteenth- and early twentieth-century literature about Pilate is in German. It could be argued that the Germans (like other imperial powers of the time) had an unhealthy fascination with him. The blond blue-eyed forest child was not forgotten. If the Germans – or, for that matter, the Russians or the Poles, or any other instigators of pogroms – wished to make a point against the Jews, their case was partly made for them by the struggles of an officer of a 'superior' and civilising power, a Gentile power, in ancient Judea. Even imperial and Nazi Germany could not beatify the governor and did not try; but he could still play the role of the besieged Aryan in the dangerous crowd, the upholder of reason against fanaticism, and a witness to the unchanging, unvarying 'problem' of the Jews.

All this reinterpretation made no hero of Pilate himself, however. Nor did it really exculpate him. In almost all the apocryphal gospels and the mystery plays, as in the New Testament, the crucifixion was a joint effort by Pilate and the Jews; but the apocryphal Pilate felt worse afterwards. Even the Coptic Pilate was only a saint because of his endless apologies and craven repentance. But this, too, inculpated the Jews: by showing how sorry one killer of Christ could be, it emphasised by contrast how strikingly unsorry the other killers were.

The idea of Repentant Pilate never caught on in western Christendom. It was too much even for fertile imaginations. But the end of the nineteenth century saw, for a few months, a sentimental revival. The Coptic fragment of his 'prayer' at the tomb was published in the *Newbery House Magazine*, a sort of clerical gazetteer, in December 1892. There, among advertisements for communion wine and warm underwear and offers of home loans for two guineas a month, the Rev. Arthur Baker RN indulged himself in some speculation.

There is surely no-one who would not wish such a tradition [of Pilate's repentance] to have at least some ground in truth. Could there be anything which would add more lustre to the triumph of the cross than the conversion of the Roman Procurator himself? ... If the story of Pilate's visit to the sepulchre ... has any foundation in fact, may we not hope that it was something more than curiosity which drew the Roman Governor to the spot, and that at least 'He was not far from the Kingdom of God'? ... Moreover, even if it be assumed that the whole thing is forgery pure and simple ... the world in the nineteenth century is the richer for a discovery which suggests ideas which, improbable as they may seem to many, must surely be sweet to every Christian mind.

The translator of the scrap for *Studia Siniatica*, Margaret Dunlop Gibson (one imagines her as a formidable woman of serge skirts and thick glasses), fervently agreed. 'We cannot but admire the author's truly Christian appreciation of the scope of Divine forgiveness, which could soften even Pilate's heart, and number him with the redeemed.'

Despite this, the more reputable sources offered the Rev. Baker and Mrs Gibson no hope whatsoever. In place of high emotion, vivid letters, silly chatter, speculation, there was only a deafening silence. In the Acts of the Apostles the disciples stayed indoors after the resurrection 'for fear of the Jews'. They might have been afraid of the authorities generally, but the Romans and their governor had disappeared from the scene. Jesus had even told his followers to stay in Jerusalem, as if he was confident that there would be no more executions and no reprisals. And there were none.

This was not the normal pattern of events. As the Pharisee Gamaliel pointed out to the council of the Jews in the fifth chapter of Acts, two previous 'prophets' and their followers had been comprehensively eliminated by the Romans. At the time of the census, under Coponius, Judas the Galilean had been executed and his followers sent to the winds. Pilate had only to consult the records to find, under his predecessor Gratus, two hundred crucifixions after one such Messianic eruption. He apparently settled for three, and then handed the matter over entirely to the Jewish authorities.

Why he did so is unclear. The accounts of the trial suggest that he did not like this case and badly wanted to offload it; but once he had judged it as political, and therefore a danger to Rome, he had to keep an eye on it. Tacitus clearly thought it was Pilate's job to nip this 'pestilent superstition' in the bud. Moreover he credited him with doing so, at least for a while. But Pilate had not even kept Jesus's supporters and sympathisers away from the scene of the crucifixion, as might have been prudent; and according to Luke the little band of apostles prospered, and grew.

In the forty days leading up to the Ascension they mostly kept quiet, but after Pentecost they were suddenly out preaching in the streets and the Temple. Astoundingly, Latin was among their languages: visitors from Rome apparently heard them and grasped what they were saying. In the normal run of events, such visitors would also have touched base in Caesarea. Romans in Judea tended to flock together, exchanging hospitality in this inhospitable land for precious news of the City. It would have been strange indeed if no one had informed Pilate that in the streets of Jerusalem people were being fed, in Latin, with extraordinary versions of recent events. According to Peter in his first public sermon, 'In accordance with his own plan God had already decided that Jesus would be handed over to you; and you killed him by letting sinful men ['outlaws' was more the sense of it] crucify him. But

God raised him from death, setting him free from its power, because it was impossible that death should keep him prisoner.'

Such teaching went beyond being merely insulting to Pilate. It raised again the disturbing idea that the God of the Jews had made use of him. It was dangerous, too. Crowds began to gather, saw miracles and became adherents of the new sect; in one day, 3,000 joined the movement. The sick on their sleeping mats were brought into the streets of Jerusalem, under the horses of Pilate's attendants and the feet of his litter-bearers, in case the shadow of Peter fell across them. Nor was this merely religious impulse. The first question the apostles asked Jesus in Acts, when they met again after the resurrection, was: 'Lord, are you now going to give the kingdom back to Israel?' Jesus replied that this was up to his father, but then added that the apostles would become his witnesses 'in Judea and Samaria and to the ends of the earth'. It cannot have been coincidence that he mentioned Pilate's patch first, as the place most in need of liberation and enlightenment; and then, in a phrase the Romans used too, sweeping from the Indies to the fog-bound Britons, suggested that his teachings would spread and surge to the very limits of the empire.

Still Pilate did nothing. He left everything to Caiaphas and the elders; and they, though desperately uncertain how best to proceed, apparently never brought a religious case before him again. When Stephen appeared, prophesying the destruction of the Temple just as Jesus had done, they simply took him outside the city and stoned him.

Again, the writers of the apocryphal gospels found the governor's absence disappointing. In the *Revelation of Stephen*, a Greek manuscript allegedly dating from 415, the author insists that Pilate played a part in the death of the first Christian martyr. In his version of the story, the crowd led Stephen to Pilate on a charge of blasphemy. Pilate stood on the steps and shouted, 'You made me crucify the Innocent One; why rage against this man? Why gnash your teeth? Are you still mad?'

Having failed to persuade the governor, the Jews took Stephen away to stone him. Meanwhile, Pilate called his wife and two children, and they baptised each other. Having done this, still damp with holy water, they joined the crowd of believers surrounding Stephen and tried to protect him from the stones. Their efforts failed. Afterwards Pilate took the body of Stephen and two others who had died with him and put them, in gold and silver coffins, in his secret sepulchre. In the morning he rose early to burn incense before them; but an angel had taken them away. As Pilate cried out to God, 'Wasn't I worthy to be your servant?' Stephen himself came in to comfort him.

In truth, though, Pilate was in Caesarea. There his days unfolded as usual: the morning shave, the afternoon bath, the letters and briefings, the dinner parties. At some point a man called Saul came through the city, under attack by Greek-speaking Jews and on his way to Tarsus. He claimed he was a Roman citizen. Pilate's successors had reason to question his credentials, but Pilate did not notice him. The future St Paul merely walked under his windows, went down to the harbour, inched across the blue sea, while the governor worried about something else: about who was living and who was dying at home, or about the phoenix that had been sighted in Egypt, its body purple, its neck gold, its tail of blue feathers picked out with rose, making its nest of frankincense and wild cinnamon before its immolation on the Altar of the Sun.

More strangely, the pernicious new superstition crept into Caesarea itself, and Pilate did not seem to notice that either. The date seems to have been between 35 and 38; Pilate was there until the end of 36, so he could well have been there to notice it, or not to notice. The Acts of the Apostles recorded that there was a deeply religious Roman in the city, a man called Cornelius, who seemed to be drawn towards Judaism. He was a captain in what Luke calls the 'Italian' regiment, the troop which, by tradition, had been with Pilate in Jerusalem during the trial of Jesus and had carried out the crucifixion. As their name implies, these were the only Roman soldiers in Judea. They made up a personal guard for the governor, a regiment of familiar faces and voices among the barely manageable auxiliaries. Cornelius and Pilate were almost certainly colleagues: mess-mates, perhaps even friends. They would have shared *castrensia verba*, camp slang, but they were already moving apart from each other.

Cornelius was constantly praying to God. He was doing so one day at about three o'clock in the afternoon (dinner time, on Roman time),when he was suddenly faced with a vision of an angel.

The angel said, 'Cornelius!'

His reaction was absolutely instinctive: 'What is it, sir?' He would have snapped to in just the same way to Pilate, another vision in white.

The angel told Cornelius to send to Joppa for Peter, and he did so. Peter came quickly to Caesarea, where he found Cornelius' house packed with relatives and close friends who had been invited to meet him. There, in a house that cannot have been far from Pilate's palace, was a crowd of men and women who must have included mutual acquaintances of the governor's, if not mutual friends; and they were waiting eagerly to hear about this Jesus, this man of God, whom Pilate had put to death.

As Peter entered, Cornelius fell at his feet before him. The emperor was greeted like that; even Pilate could be greeted like that. But Peter helped Cornelius up, saying, 'I'm only a man.' He explained that although he would not usually consider defiling himself by consorting with Gentiles, God had told him that on this occasion 'I must not consider anyone ritually unclean or defiled'. He asked Cornelius why he had sent for him. The captain told the story of the angel (he called him 'a man in bright clothes'), concluding that 'we are all here now in the presence of God, waiting to hear anything that the Lord has instructed you to say'.

Peter then preached to them, his first sermon specifically to Romans. Oddly, he assumed that they already knew everything he was going to tell them. 'You know the message of God to the people of Israel, the good news of Jesus Christ,' he told them. 'You know about Jesus of Nazareth and how God poured out on him the Holy Spirit and power . . . We are witnesses of everything that he did in the land of Israel and in Jerusalem. Then they put him to death by nailing him to a cross.'

They put him to death. Who were 'they'? The word was perhaps deliberately vague and diplomatic. Peter may not have wanted to spoil the astonishing moment of conversion, for, as he spoke, the Holy Ghost came down on everyone in the room, Jews and Romans alike. Peter ordered them immediately to be baptised. Perhaps this was done in the baths, or in the fountains in the garden. However it happened, 'believers throughout Judea', Luke said, heard of these Roman conversions. It is hard to believe that no inkling of this reached Pilate. He was Cornelius' superior officer, after all. In Cornelius' utterly Roman house in Caesarea, a house perhaps as familiar to Pilate as his own palace, Peter the apostle was breaking bread, and prayers were being offered to Jesus the Son of God.

The vivid mythology of 'secret crimes' imputed to Christians had not yet been invented. The secret meals and meetings were apparently just that, secret meals and meetings. The dangers of Christianity for the Roman power were not yet evident and, even when they became so, Roman provincial officers felt tentative in dealing with them. Perhaps this would have been Pilate's reaction. Nonetheless, it was becoming clear that a man could not worship the emperor if he believed in Christ;

and, if he did not worship the emperor, the glue of the empire would crumble. The earliest encounters of Roman officials with Christians vividly show this growing anxiety: with the difference that Pilate had met, talked to, scourged, killed, but possibly tried to save, the man his own captain now accepted as divine.

Pliny to Trajan   [sometime after 111]

It is my custom, Lord Emperor, to refer to you all questions I feel doubtful about. Who can better guide me when I am perplexed, or enlighten me when I am ignorant? . . .

This is the course I have taken with those who were accused before me as Christians. I asked them to their face whether they were Christian, and if they confessed, I asked them a second and a third time with threats of punishment. If they kept to it, I ordered them for execution; for there seemed no question to me that, whatever it was that they admitted, in any case obstinacy and unbending perversity deserve to be punished. There were others of the same insanity; but as these were Roman citizens, I noted them down to be sent to Rome.

. . . As for those who said that they neither were nor had ever been Christians, I thought it right to let them go, since they recited a prayer to the gods at my dictation, made supplication with incense and wine to your statue (which I had ordered to be brought into court for the purpose, together with images of the gods), and moreover cursed Christ – not a thing (so it is said) that those who are really Christians can be made to do.

. . . They maintained, however, that their only crime had been this: that it was their habit on a fixed day to assemble before daylight and sing by turns a hymn to Christ as a god; and that they bound themselves with an oath, not for any crime, but not to commit theft or robbery or adultery, not to break their word, and not to deny a deposit when demanded. After this was done, their custom was to leave, and meet together again to take food, but ordinary and harmless food; and even this (they said) they had given up doing after the issue of my edict, by which in accordance with your orders I had forbidden the existence of clubs. I considered it necessary to find out by torture from two maidservants (who are called deaconesses) how far this was true; but I discovered nothing else than a wicked and arrogant superstition. I have therefore adjourned the case and hastened to consult you.

The matter seemed worth deliberation to me, especially taking into account the number of those in danger; for many of all ages and every rank, and even of both sexes, are brought into present or future peril. The contagion of that superstition has penetrated not only the cities, but the villages and the countryside. Yet it seems possible to stop it and to set things right . . .

Trial of the Scillitan martyrs at Carthage, seventeenth of July 180
Consulship of Praesens (2) and Claudianus
Saturninus, proconsul, presiding

Proconsul: You can win the emperor's mercy, if you return to a sound mind.

First Christian: We have never done wrong, we have not lent ourselves to wrong, we have never spoken ill, but when ill-treated we have given thanks; because we pay heed to our emperor.

Proconsul: We too are religious, and our religion is simple, and we swear by the genius of our lord the emperor and pray for his welfare, as you should do too.

First Christian: If you will listen peaceably, I can tell you the mystery of simplicity.

Proconsul: I will not listen to you when you start to say evil things about our sacred rites; you should swear by the genius of our lord the emperor.

First Christian: I do not recognise the empire of this world; I serve that God whom no man has seen, nor can see with the eyes of the body. I have committed no theft; if I have bought anything, I pay the tax; because I know my lord, the King of Kings and Emperor of all nations.

Proconsul: Cease to be of this persuasion.

First Christian: It's a bad persuasion to do murder, and to bear false witness.

Proconsul (to the rest): Take no further part in this folly.

Second Christian: We have no one else to fear, save only our Lord God, who is in heaven.

Third Christian: Honour to Caesar as Caesar; but fear to God.

Fourth Christian: I am a Christian, and what I am I wish to be.

Proconsul: Will you have a space to consider?

First Christian: In a matter so straightforward, there is no considering.

Proconsul: Have a delay of thirty days and think about it.

First Christian: I am a Christian. *(And with this they all agreed)*

Proconsul (reading from the tablet): Having confessed that you live according to the Christian rite, and having obstinately refused to return to the custom of the Romans when you were given the chance, we sentence you to be put to the sword.

Second Christian: Today we are martyrs in heaven! Thanks be to God!

★   ★   ★

The worlds might have moved on in parallel, never meeting: the governor in his pretty palace, the Christian groups inexorably multiplying. Yet one last time, strangely, the tracks crossed. It happened not in Judea but in Samaria, the northern part of Pilate's province. This was a country most Jews looked down on as rough, volatile and infected by a rogue strain of Judaism, primitive and embarrassing. The Samaritans had a holy mountain, Mount Gerizim, on which they held gatherings and rituals; there was an ancient temple there, four hundred years old, and the site of an altar of stones where, they said, the Ark of the Covenant had rested. It was at the foot of those slopes that Jesus had sat with the Samaritan woman as she scooped water from the well, telling him with country simplicity that 'our fathers worshipped on this mountain, but you say that Jerusalem is the place where people pray'.

According to Josephus the Samaritans were a credulous lot, and they fell for the tales of a mendacious upstart who told them that, if they came to the mountain, he would show them the sacred vessels buried there by Moses. In the Acts of the Apostles one such upstart in Samaria – very probably the same man – was given a name, Simon. Some assume that this was Simon Magus, the magician. 'He claimed that he was someone great,' runs the account in Acts, 'and everyone in the city, from all classes of society, paid close attention to him. "He is that power of God known as the Great Power," they said.' The apostles kept Simon at arm's length; although they were converting many in Samaria, and even baptised Simon himself, they soon discovered that his interest in Christianity was skin-deep. He thought it was just another sort of magic in which he could be instructed, if only the apostles would accept his money. Indignantly, Peter told him that 'his heart was not right,' and that he should take his 'evil plan' away.

He apparently took it to Mount Gerizim, where the people were entranced. If the Ark had been carried there, and Moses's words had been recited there (by Joshua, as the story said), a cache of holy objects might well be there too: not only the Ark itself, but the holy oil, the jar of manna, Aaron's rod. Their discovery would have important implications. Once these objects were recovered, the proper worship of God could be re-established and he would appear as the Cloud of Glory, hovering over his new Temple on Gerizim and compelling recognition even from the pagans.

Fanatical Christian statements did not seem to get reported in Caesarea, but this, in some garbled version, did. And Josephus suggests that Pilate panicked. Mount Gerizim had its associations for him, too; it was where, eighty years before, the Romans had been besieged and cut down by rebel Jews. There was perhaps still honour to be satisfied there, as Germanicus had done in Germany: bones of the dead to be buried, rites to be performed. Perhaps, too, Pilate was uneasily aware that he should have been sharper in putting down the sect that was blossoming on all sides in the name of Jesus. Perhaps he was not inclined to get caught out again.

Josephus implies that Pilate went himself, with a unit of horse and a unit of infantry, to sort the Samaritan business out. Prefects of Judea did their own fighting. In the battle against Simon the impostor, in Gratus' time, Josephus described impostor and prefect racing on horseback through a defile, 'yet Gratus overtook him and cut off his head.' Here, in case Pilate had been missing it, was real war.

The Samaritans had gathered, feverish with expectation, in a village called Tirathana at the foot of the mountain. They carried arms. Crowds came to join them, and they prepared to go up the mountain *en masse*. But Pilate had made good speed. He got there before them, blocked the access road and seized control of the higher ground. It was a typical Pilate manoeuvre: sneak in, take by surprise, surround, cut off. His troops waited, half-hidden in the trees and the rocks. Their commander-in-chief was among them, once again chafed by a breastplate and half-deafened by helmet-flaps, while his horse shifted uneasily in the resinous shadows.

On a signal, they began to move down towards the village. At the same time, the crowd in the village began to storm the mountain. Scrambling and slipping over the rocks, the two sides met, but the contest was unequal. The crowd was repulsed. According to Josephus, some were killed, many fled, and many more were taken alive. The auxiliaries doubtless behaved with the same unmodulated brutality they had shown during the aqueduct riot, though when the battle was over Pilate himself showed some restraint: he ordered the Samaritan leaders to be killed and apparently let the rest go. There were perhaps more crucifixions, though these took time; the sword was quicker. Once the trouble was subdued, the mountain cleared and the village swept for subversives, Pilate and his troop went back to Caesarea. Simon himself – if it was he – appears to have escaped.

The province was quiet again, but that was not the end of the story. The Samaritans complained to Vitellius, who was in charge in Syria, that Pilate had committed murder. They had never had any intention of revolting against the Romans, they said. On the contrary, they had gone to Tirathana to escape Pilate, who had been violently pursuing them. Vitellius seemed to believe this story. The Samaritans had gathered out of religious enthusiasm, not revolutionary zeal, though that might have come later; and Pilate had marched on them immediately, fearing Messianic unrest.

Yet his action had not been extraordinary. When Festus, who was governor of Judea under Nero, found people 'seduced by a certain impostor, who promised them deliverance from their miseries if they followed him into the wilderness', he sent a force like Pilate's of horse and foot and 'destroyed' both the impostor and his followers. This did not draw official censure, and Josephus did not even think it worthy of a critical remark. Perhaps the difference was that Festus was new then, and Pilate's cruelty had been felt before. Or perhaps Pilate had begun to sense that his tour was nearly over, and was starting to dream of the triumphs that attended the return of officers who had performed spectacular service abroad. He, too, could go out with a bang, averting revolution; he too could enter Rome in the special chariot, in the *tunica palmata* and the purple robe, while the people cheered and clapped. Yet it was a far-fetched dream, if he had it. As one of Cicero's friends once wrote to him petulantly from Dalmatia, you could storm twenty towns and still not receive a favourable mention in the Senate.

Whatever the motivations on either side, Pilate was now in trouble. Vitellius intervened immediately, as if he had been waiting for an excuse to do so. He had been in command in the east for about a year, trying to sort out feuds among the Parthians. His reputation in Rome was scandalous, Tacitus said, and his interest in Syria seemed to revolve round exporting new strains of fig trees and pistachios for his country estates at home. But 'old-fashioned integrity', surprisingly enough, seemed to guide his actions abroad. He wanted to make a good impression on his emperor: not only by sacrificing a bull, a boar and a ram to mark Roman power on the banks of the Euphrates, but by doing a little clearing up in Judea on his way home.

Josephus records that Vitellius sent a colleague, Marcellus, to look after Judea, and ordered Pilate back to Rome 'to answer the accusations of the Jews before the emperor'. This suggests a more general set of charges from the Jews in general, not merely the Samaritans, and about other things: a list that spanned the years. 'He dared not contradict Vitellius' orders,' said Josephus; 'so, having stayed ten years in Judea, he hurried back to Rome.'

We have no other sources for the end of Pilate's tour, but Josephus' account seems convincing enough. Pilate had gone too far one last time, and now he was going home. It was only his subjects' word against his, but he put up no resistance. It seems never to have occurred to him to protest.

In the palace at Caesarea, the wall-hangings were taken down and the silverware packed in boxes. Once Marcellus was in place, Pilate had three months to get his affairs in order and get home. Although Marcellus was a stop-gap, and Pilate's case had not yet been judged, it seemed clear that he would not be returning. Governors who were recalled to Rome were seldom acquitted and usually banished; they needed to bring what they could back with them, for they would never be so rich again. After ten years of diplomatic presents, impulse-buying and ointment money, there was much to pack away, and much to regret.

His tour had not been a total disaster. Even Philo could characterise those years in Judea (though attributing them to Tiberius, not to him) as 'peace and the blessings of peace'. All the same, he was returning as a bad governor covered with disgrace. Philo summed it up: 'No lot is so hard as for . . . rulers to be accused by their former subjects; as well might masters be accused by the slaves whom they have bred in their house or purchased with their money.'

Before he left, Pilate was obliged to brief Marcellus and to go through the books with him. One set of accounts was left in the province; a duplicate had to be sent to the Treasury in Rome. A list had to be made of losses sustained by his troops or by the enemy in any battles fought, to be delivered to the Senate; street rioting may not have counted. Alongside these, within thirty days, he had to send a list of those members of his staff who qualified for *beneficia*, or special service bonuses. It was a painful duty for a man about to be reprimanded; he may not even have bothered to do it. But he would have made time, as Cicero recommended, to purge his correspondence. One of his freedmen would read through duplicate letters and destroy any that were 'inequitable, eccentric, or inconsistent . . . or insulting, or in poor taste, or bad-tempered'. Thus he would selectively rearrange the record he left behind him.

In the archive, the rolls were stacked up on the shelves with their identifying tags: accounts, *commentarii*, judicial decisions, arbitration about orphans, estates and the status of slaves: rulings from the time when he, Pilate, had been invested with power. The exercise of that power had demanded a certain discretion, a certain subtlety. Rome did not need to know exactly what deals he had made, what corners he had cut, or what cruelties he had committed in the name of order. Perhaps there had been none that he had not punctiliously reported. Perhaps there had been some that he would always suppress, even internally.

People were bound to remember him for something. They would see the Tiberieum standing above the sea, where surely it would stand for centuries. In the markets of Nablus, Nazareth and Jerusalem his coins would go on passing from hand to hand. His aqueduct would continue to snake across the dry hills, bringing clean water for which he might sometimes be thanked. And in the records of his judgements some decision would surely stand out for its usefulness, its perspicacity, its wisdom, before he disappeared forever from the consciousness of men.

7

Through brake, through briar

Survey everything that lies about you, as if it were luggage in a guest-room; you must travel on. Nature strips you as bare at your departure as at your entrance. You may take away no more than you brought in; what is more you must throw away the major part of what you brought with you into life . . .

Why love such a thing as if it were your own possession? It was merely your covering. The day will come which will tear you forth and lead you away from the company of the foul and stinking womb. Withdraw from it now too as much as you can, and withdraw from pleasure, unless it is bound up with essential and important things; estrange yourself from it even now, and ponder on something nobler and loftier. Some day the secrets of nature shall be disclosed to you, the haze will be shaken from your eyes, and from every side the bright light will break on you.

. . . You behold that light darkly now, with vision that is cramped to the last degree. And yet, far off as it is, you already look upon it in wonder; what do you think the heavenly light will be like when you see it in its proper sphere?

Seneca, *Moral Letters*, CII

He probably left Judea in December 36. The sea-lanes were closed; no quick way out. Those who were desperate sometimes dared the sea journey, as the Jewish delegation did in 41 to make their petition to Gaius. Flaccus, too, had 'tasted the terrors of the sea' – the sickening swell, the brine in the throat – on his way home from Egypt, also in disgrace, in the early months of winter. For twelve days around the winter solstice nature provided a respite, when the sea calmed down for the breeding of the halcyon birds. They floated on the water, sea-blue themselves, or took to the air at the setting of the Pleiades; their nests too floated on the surface, white and vaguely sparkling, woven of fish-bones or dried sea-foam. The ships stole past them.

Despite this chance, Pilate probably went overland. He would have travelled 2,000 Roman miles at a rate of, at most, 40 miles a day, through Anatolia and Greece, along icy military roads marked with drab military hostels. In the bitter weather, he would have needed felt overshoes, woollen socks and the sort of heavy cloak soldiers had to wear under the British rain. These would have compromised his dignity a little, but perhaps there was not much of that left: only mud, snow, slipping luggage, the frozen breath of horses, and a dull sickness in his heart.

What awaited him, for all he knew, was the sort of treatment that was dealt out in 22 to Gaius Junius Silanus, the former governor of Asia. Silanus' subjects had accused him of extortion and brutality. In fact, Tacitus wrote, he was charged with offences against the divinity of Augustus and the majesty of Tiberius. Solid accusations, which might have been countered by revenue scrolls and account books, were suddenly numinous and cloudy; defence was almost hopeless. Two members of his staff in Asia joined the case against him, and his slaves were sold to the Treasury agent for examination under torture.

Then Silanus was summoned to the Senate, before the senators and before the emperor. (Pilate would not have seen it, but the *Daily Gazette* would have been full of it.) According to Tacitus, Tiberius himself conducted the questioning. He proceeded threateningly and grimly, his thoughts as usual expressed with what seemed to be enormous effort; it was said that the grimmer he got, the more the words stuck in his throat. Whenever he was not speaking, he stared at Silanus unwaveringly with those large, dark, short-sighted eyes; that too was terrifying. Silanus found that, under the relentless imperial questioning, he did not dare as much as an evasion or a negative answer. That, in itself, was treason. Besides, the best orators in Asia were employed to argue the case against him. At last, the ex-governor – 'an inexperienced speaker, standing alone, in mortal fear' – abandoned his own defence. Before he was exiled, he sent a short letter of complaint to Tiberius. That was not something Pilate was likely to do.

In Rome it was the holiday month of Saturnalia, the month of gambling and cheap presents, when, as Martial put it, 'napkins fly about, and thin spoons, and wax tapers and paper, and pointed jars of dried damsons.' His own gifts had perhaps been sent on before him, in hopes of winning or preserving his friendships. They were probably the last smells and tastes of his province: dates from Herod's great palm grove, ointment perfumed with balsam, fine jars of aromatic leaves. Slowly, milestone by milestone, he approached the distant horror and the distant celebration.

The journey took at least two months, perhaps three; he did not reach home until March 37. When he finally arrived in Rome, Philo tells us, the city was not as he remembered it. People were laughing in the streets, dancing. They were dressed in white, with garlands on their heads, and more garlands were draped on the public buildings. All night the torches burned and the flutes played, like wild birds. It was as if Pilate had stumbled on a festival in honour of some new god; or, wrote Philo, as if the age of Saturn had really dawned at last. If he looked round for portents of this change, they were there too: the Circus and the Aventine laid waste by fire, and the houses by the Tiber still flooded with mud and refuse. Quickly enough, the explanation reached him:

Tiberius was dead, smothered in his bed-clothes at the age of 77, and the blank-eyed, monkey-haired Gaius was emperor in his place.

Rome was in a paroxysm of relief. Its citizens had poured into the streets hardly daring to believe that they could laugh again and speak openly. Pilate, who had revered the emperor with the sentimental loyalty of an expatriate, may have felt differently. He may have been devastated. Philo described vividly – too vividly, as usual – how Flaccus, still prefect in Egypt, had reacted to Tiberius' death. Flaccus had been appointed by the emperor in 31, five years after Pilate, and had looked on him as 'his closest friend'. When he heard of his death he fell into a deep depression, and wept for days. He wept all the more, Philo said, because he was terrified of suddenly finding himself on the wrong side politically. He was frightened because he had said bad things about Gaius' mother; but the worst came when Gaius put Tiberius' grandson to death, which suggested that closeness to the old emperor was no guarantee of survival. At this point, Philo claims that Flaccus flung himself down on his bed and lay sobbing and speechless, unable to begin to think straight.

Did Pilate weep too? He had missed the purges after the fall of Sejanus, purges in which he might well have died himself, and he had heard of the emperor's wanton atrocities only through dry reports. Yet he had still felt the lash of his anger at a distance, and had spent the long journey from Judea in the knowledge that he moved steadily towards that anger, as the sheep was driven to the altar of sacrifice. In the end, despite his best efforts, the last things Tiberius had heard of him had been unfavourable. As he gazed on the wax effigy of his patron on the Rostrum of the Orators, perhaps still laid in its imperial robes on the state couch of gold and ivory, jostled by images of ancestors and gods, it must have been hard to know whether to laugh or cry.

And at this point – just as Rome, wonderful and awful, filled his eyes again – Pilate disappears from the ancient accounts. Josephus follows him no further. His case disappears, too; we do not know what happened to it. Possibly the death of Tiberius made it moot and laid it aside. We only know that, a few days after the emperor's funeral, Gaius made Herod Agrippa king of the territories of Antipas and Philip, an honour Agrippa had been lobbying for for years; and that, a little later, he appointed Marullus as the new governor of Judea. Vitellius, meanwhile, had been clearing things up there. He had abolished the sales tax on grain, replaced Caiaphas as high priest, and regained for the Jews the custody of the holy vestments stored in the Antonia. Lastly, as he passed through Jerusalem on the Passover of April 20th 37, he 'sacrificed to the God of the Jews'. This seemed to mark more clearly than anything the end of Pilate's wave of Romanisation. The news would have astonished, even scandalised, the new ex-governor.

Yet despite such signs of a purge of the old ways, Pilate had not necessarily been condemned or even held to account. The death of Tiberius had legally terminated his appointment in any case, just as Rufus' had been terminated by the death of Augustus. In the first pious months of his reign, Gaius freed numbers of prisoners, put an end to charges of *maiestas* and showed no particular eagerness to prosecute outstanding cases. Shortly after that, he fell ill.When he emerged from his illness, only a year or so after his accession, he began to manifest multiple signs of madness: taking up with actors, dressing as a god, dancing at midnight before the Senate. A man without political astuteness could die easily in those days; as easily as the man who unwisely sold hot water during the mourning-days for the emperor's sister Drusilla.

Those who survived had to learn, as Pilate may have had to learn, a new craven language. Vitellius, the army commander who had ejected him from Judea, demonstrated this art in 40 – according to Suetonius – when he found himself under sentence of death for no worse offence than being more successful than Gaius. He put on low-class clothes, fell at the emperor's feet, and worshipped him. Eventually, when Gaius claimed one night to be making love to the moon, he asked Vitellius whether he could see her under his jerking body. The splendid Hammer of the Parthians, the Hammer of Pilate, began to tremble with awe. Then, with his eyes fixed on the ground, he answered in a half-whisper: 'Only you gods, master, may behold one another.'

This is where history left Pilate too, somewhere in Rome, between the moon and the fickle gods.

Again, this was not good enough for the writers of the apocryphal gospels. They wanted their witness to carry his work into Rome itself. He had, after all, written all those letters and reports to the emperor, and the emperor must have been curious to know more. Perhaps Tiberius was not quite dead yet; or, if he was, another emperor had taken up his interest in Jesus. It did not matter much who this emperor was, whether Claudius or Vespasian or merely 'Caesar', as long as he could play the antagonist to the increasingly hapless governor.

From the second century onwards, these tales seem to have multiplied. They survive now on fragments of manuscript that are impossible to date precisely or set in any context, other than popular craving for more than the gospels provided. One popular story, cited by Gregory of Tours in his sixth-century *History of the Franks*, maintained that Tiberius was so impressed by Pilate's reports that he requested the Senate to recognise Jesus as God. Not surprisingly, the Senate refused. Other accounts described the emperor as fearsomely angry. In the *Anaphora of Pilate*, a Greek text of the sixth century, Pilate was recalled because Tiberius could not believe he had been so crass as to kill a man who might have been useful. Tiberius was grievously ill with a fever, ulcers, and nine kinds of leprosy which covered his skin with purple lesions. (In the Anglo-Saxon version, the emperor was Vespasian who, true to his name, had a nest of wasps in his nose.) News had reached Rome, from sources other than Pilate, that Jesus cured people. Tiberius had already made a request for the holy veil on which a woman called Veronica had taken an impression of the face of Jesus on the way to Golgotha, for he had heard that it could work miracles. When the veil arrived, wrapped in a golden cloth in a box enclosed in a golden cage, Tiberius welcomed it with a trail of silk handkerchiefs spread along the ground. He merely looked at the relic, and at once his skin was as soft and clear as a child's. (When Vespasian looked at it, the wasps immediately dropped buzzing from his nose.) How could Pilate have executed a man whose very image, imprinted on a square of cloth, could be so powerful? What sort of idiot could he be?

Tiberius despatched a messenger with two thousand soldiers to bring Pilate home. The messenger was called Raab; he was the same man Pilate had once sent to spread his cloak at the feet of Christ. Raab also handed Pilate a letter.

Tiberius, most excellent Emperor of the Romans, to Pilate, prefect of Judea, greeting.

Since you inflicted a violent and iniquitous death on Jesus of Nazareth, showing no pity; since you received gifts to condemn him; and since you expressed sympathy with your tongue but, in your heart, delivered him up, you shall be brought home a prisoner to answer for yourself.

I have been most distressed at the reports that have reached me. A woman called Mary Magdalene has been here, a disciple of Jesus; he cast seven devils out of her, and she has told me of all his wonderful cures. How could you have allowed him to be crucified? If you did not receive him as a god, you might at least have honoured him as a doctor. Your own deceitful writing to me has condemned you.

As you unjustly sentenced him, I shall justly sentence you, and your accomplices as well. Farewell.

In the thirteenth-century *Golden Legend* and *The Healing of Tiberius*, a fantastical story from the eighth century, the scene unfolded rather differently. Tiberius assumed that Jesus was still alive and available to cure him. He sent a 'great officer' called Volusianus to Judea, not to get Pilate, but to ask Pilate to hand Jesus over. Volusianus appeared on Pilate's doorstep, asking to see 'this physician, Jesus'. This put the governor in a tailspin of fright. This man was no physician, he stammered to Volusianus; he was a troublemaker. In any case, could he have fourteen days' grace?

Volusianus agreed. Pilate used the time to send letters to Tiberius and ply him with presents, trying to persuade him to overlook the awkward fact that he had put Christ to death; but these were all caught in a shipwreck and sent to the bottom of the sea. Meanwhile, Volusianus had learned the truth from Veronica: Pilate had condemned Jesus and killed him. She assured him, however, that her veil had preserved Christ's healing powers. Immediately, Volusianus sent four quaternions of soldiers to arrest Pilate and put him in a cage. He was made to confess, publicly, that Jesus was dead and that it was his fault. Naturally, he tried to put it in the best light. 'This man you seek depised the Jews and broke Roman laws; so I found him guilty of grave crimes, and I crucified him. Tell my king that.' Or, even oilier, in another version: 'Tell Caesar that for his honour and to safeguard his prerogatives, by right judgement and by right sentence, I allowed the Jews to crucify a man called Jesus, who was a magician and made himself a king and put himself up against Caesar.' Then the three of them, with the veil laid softly in its cage of gold and Pilate bumping in his cage of iron, set off for Rome.

There was yet a third version of this 'send for Pilate' scene, and it was kinder; indeed, too kind. According to the Coptic *Martyrdom of Pilate*, the governor's days in Judea were numbered. Ever since he had begun to worship Jesus, and ever since he had put Barabbas to death, the Jews had decided that this 'foreign Egyptian' had to die too. But because they could not execute him themselves, they decided to bribe the imperial messenger either to let them do it, or to do it for them. The messenger therefore summoned Pilate. The governor advised his wife to take the children and leave town, only making sure that she recovered his body and buried it near the tomb of Jesus, 'so that his grace may overtake me.' But Procula insisted on staying with him. 'It is wrong,' she said, 'that you should love me more than you love him.'

Pilate was taken to the emperor's messenger. 'Are you Pilate?' he asked him. 'Are you the one who said, "There is no hand over my hand"? However did you kill this Jesus without consulting the emperor first?'

Pilate would not answer him. He merely said: 'I am prepared to die for his holy name. I have faith that if I die for his name I shall possess eternal life, and you will not impede me from his glory.' He was then stripped, flogged, put in chains and thrown into prison. Procula, her head bare and her clothes disordered (a deeply shaming fate for a woman) was thrown in beside him. The Jews shouted, 'Pilate, your life is like his, and your lot is his lot!' Pilate answered, 'Amen. My life is with him.'

In prison, Jesus visited them. He came down from heaven, bathed in effulgent light, and took them in his arms. Instantly, the fetters they wore flowed away like water, and the column to which they were tied bowed down to the ground. Jesus told Pilate that he would be crucified like him and crowned with thorns like him, but that his enemies would be unable to kill him at the first attempt because he would have to be taken before Tiberius. And that was how it happened. The Jews asked the imperial messenger, in exchange for a huge bribe of silver, to let them crucify Pilate. So he hung on the cross for a while, encouraged by Procula to enter heaven as a martyr and a king, before the crowds decided that it would be better if the messenger took him to Rome instead.

In a second Coptic story, Tiberius' only son was strangled by an evil spirit as he washed himself in the baths. He was buried, and his parents mourned him for three months, until the emperor's wife remembered Pilate's reports of a miracle-worker in Judea. Tiberius wrote to Jesus (whom he knew to have risen from the dead) and sent the boy's bones along in a coffin to be placed in the Holy Sepulchre. Joseph and Nicodemus placed them there, and waited for three days; on the fourth day, in a magical weaving of flesh over dry bones, the emperor's son came back to life. Pilate was fetched from prison, bowed to the ground with joy, and went to the tomb to see the boy. The emperor's vizier, who had brought the coffin from Rome, apologised to Pilate, kissed his hand and asked his forgiveness. Then the whole party went off to Rome with the newly-risen boy, his skin and hair still delicate and bright, to present the miracle to Tiberius.

When Pilate reached Rome, all these dozens of legends – Coptic, Greek, late Latin, Anglo-Saxon – agree that he was taken prisoner at once. Some say Tiberius did not even bother to see him; he simply asked why he had not been executed yet. But it was undeniably more dramatic to have the quaking governor dragged, bound with fetters of iron, into the emperor's presence. It bothered none of these writers that, historically, Tiberius had died before Pilate arrived in Rome. As the emperor most closely connected with Jesus, he was required to be there.

In the sixth-century Greek *Anaphora* the emperor received Pilate in the temple of the gods before all the Senate. He was seated on a throne with his army around him 'and all the multitude of his power'. The moment he saw Pilate, he screamed out: 'How did you dare to do such a thing? You most impious man! How could you do it, when you had seen all those signs and wonders concerning this man! Your wicked daring has destroyed the whole world!'

Pilate, standing before the judgement seat, tried his old excuses. 'Emperor, I'm blameless in this. The Jews did it.'

'What Jews?'

'Herod Archelaus, Philip, Hannan, Caiaphas, and the whole lot of them.'

'But why did you give in to them? Why did you obey them?'

'My lord, their whole nation is seditious and rebellious. They do not obey your authority.'

'Look,' thundered Tiberius, 'when they delivered him to you, it was your duty to put him in prison and keep him safe, and to send him carefully to me in the safekeeping of my soldiers! It was *not* your business to take the advice of the Jews and crucify him! This man was righteous! He did all those good works! Why, you admitted it yourself when you wrote the *titulus* for his exection, that this was Christ, the King of the Jews!'

Suddenly, all over the temple, the gods crashed down and were smashed to the floor like powder. They fell, pieces of Apollo's tunic and chunks of Jupiter's beard, at the feet of the emperor and his officers. They had tumbled at the name of Christ. The officers were terror-stricken, seized with involuntary trembling; one by one they left the building and crept to their homes. The emperor ordered Pilate thrown in prison and held for further questioning.

On the next day, Tiberius put up his judgement seat in the Capitol. Again, he convened the Senate and ordered Pilate to appear; again the governor, in chains, took up his defensive stand. 'Do you see what happened?' cried Tiberius. 'You dared to stretch out your hand over the Son of God, you villain, and now look what your wickedness has done! The gods have fallen, and been ground like dust, and have perished from the earth! Tell me, tell me truly: who was that man who was crucified? His name alone has destroyed all these gods!'

Pilate said: 'He is the Son of God. The report I sent you is true. Even I have been convinced that he is greater than the gods we worship.'

'Why then did you do those things to him, when you knew he had done nothing against us?'

'Because the Jews made me. That's why I did this to him.'

Tiberius exploded with anger. His wrath rose 'like smoke from a furnace', and he instantly issued an edict to the governor of the East that the Jews should be enslaved. Pilate was spared for the moment, and sent back to prison. Tiberius had more questions to ask him.

The *Anaphora* did not say what those supplementaries were, but the *Martyrdom of Pilate* provided a gentler line of interrogation. This Pilate, after all, had survived crucifixion; he came to Tiberius in a state of ecstatic weakness, bearing the marks of the nails and the thorns. The emperor asked: 'Are you the governor Pilate, who crucified Jesus?'

'Yes. It is I, your servant, who stands before you. As to the crucifixion of Jesus, our living God, the Jews did not listen to me, and Annas and Caiaphas decided judicially on his execution.'

Inevitably, constantly, Pilate passed the buck back to the Jews. But Tiberius let that go; he wanted to know what Jesus had looked like, 'his image, his portraiture, his picture, his majesty, his beauty.' Pilate's answer was mystifying. 'Oh Emperor, my lord, he was three days in my court, and I did not see what he looked like. Once I saw that he was the colour of fire, and once I saw him like a bird flying to the heights of heaven, where an angel spoke to him.'

He told Tiberius under questioning about his wife's dream, about the trial, about the virgin birth and the Annunciation. 'How long was he on the earth?' asked the emperor.

'Thirty years, sir.'

'And in all that length of time you saw that man, noticed the miracles and prodigies he was performing, and never told me?'

'By your life, my lord Emperor, I never saw him in all that time, and I never saw his face except on the day he was crucified.'

'Let's get this straight. They delivered him to you, and you didn't remember his miracles and prodigies. In his presence you felt no awe at all, and even the glory of his divinity did not frighten you. How high-handed can you get? *And why didn't you tell me?*'

Pilate could not answer. Tiberius therefore ordered his soldiers to take him away and kill him: 'Now I'll do to you what you did to him.' But, according to the *Golden Legend*, Pilate almost managed to escape the emperor's wrath. His buck-passing had made no impression, but he had one last trick almost literally up his sleeve. He had not cheated so hard to get this particular relic for nothing.

When he was summoned before Tiberius for the last time, he put on the seamless garment of Jesus. In some German legends, it was only a scrap of the garment that he put on, like an amulet, underneath his clothes. The effect was the same: Tiberius was disarmed completely. Raging as he was, he became unaccountably gentle; he could not savage the man who stood before him, shining and pure and quiet. Instead, he rose to greet him, without a single harsh word. He sent him away with a smile.

The moment Pilate left, Tiberius was furious again. He stormed up and down the room, swearing and calling himself a wretch for failing to show him the anger in his heart. 'Pilate is a son of death!' he screamed. 'He cannot possibly be allowed to go on living on this earth! Bring him back here! I'll sentence him to death!'

Once more Pilate came to him. He stepped in softly, like an angel, with the seamless garment a shaft of blue-white light from his shoulders to his feet. Tiberius opened his mouth, but could not speak. Again he greeted him tenderly, and his wrath subsided. Everyone stared at him; no one could understand how Tiberius could be so incensed when Pilate was absent and so gentle with him face to face. Then someone – God, or a bystander – gave Pilate's game away. Tiberius screamed for his guards; he made them tear the robe from Pilate's back, or, strip-searching him, pluck out the sacred scrap of cloth from beneath his clothes. Instantly, he saw the truth: before him stood an ordinary criminal.

Pilate's long trail of apocryphal witness was bound to end in scenes like this. The killer of Christ would put on Christ, assume his outward appearance, approximate his sufferings. Pagans too, as St Paul told the Ephesians, would share in the body of Christ; the withered thorn bush would break out in fragile blossoms of divinity. No hagiographer dared to have Pilate publicly baptised, although in the *Martyrdom of Stephen* he baptised himself privately; there was a limit even to invention. By the same token, no one dared to make Pilate's imitation of Christ completely saintly or completely faithful. In his many apocryphal trials, before the Jewish priests and before Tiberius, he sometimes tried to keep a Christ-like silence before his questioners. But his tendency was to whine and transfer the blame to others; so that when he was slapped and reviled, as Jesus had been slapped and reviled, it seemed no more than his sanctimony deserved.

The most daring approximation of Pilate to Christ was to put him on the cross, as the Copts did; to make him, in the supposed words of Herod's men, 'die on the cross like your God Jesus'. There was a pleasing, brutal symmetry in this. Pilate would be judged as he himself had judged Christ; he had already been scourged, as he had scourged Christ; his blood had been shed as he had shed Christ's. In short, as Jesus himself told him in prison, 'Everything that has happened to you is for the sole reason that you may be saved from the sin of my death.'

Yet even the Copts found this scene almost too hard to stage. Pilate's crucifixion at Herod's behest was a farce, with the governor taken twice to the brink, stripped, decked with a loincloth and flogged, before being put back in prison. When at last he got to Golgotha, and the soldiers were about to raise him on the cross, they suddenly realised that Christ's own cross would make a better gibbet; so they ran to the tomb, lugged it out, unfixed Pilate and nailed him up again. This made him more like Christ but also, by closer comparison, less like him. His prayers on Christ's cross acknowledged his deep unworthiness of this honour; if the Copts were not embarrassed to put him there, he seemed embarrassed himself. His body was 'impure', his blood 'carnal'; he had 'defiled and polluted' the sacred wood on which Christ had hung. He was a hopeless sinner who did not deserve, and should not have, the outrageous glory of dying on the very cross to which his weakness had sent Christ.

And in the end, that glory eluded him. His pending martyrdom was signalled by the sight of two crowns, one for him and one for Procula, descending from heaven, but this miracle so impressed the crowd that they cut him down before he could die. Instead of finding himself, as Procula had fervently predicted, 'lighting your lamp at the wedding of your lord Jesus Christ', Pilate found himself manhandled into a hot bath and back into his clothes, in preparation for going to Rome to explain himself to the emperor.

The seamless garment, too, made no saint of Pilate. It was simply a trick, a suit of magic clothes. Just as the mystery plays never made it quite clear why Pilate wanted the garment anyway, so the *Golden Legend* never explained his precise motivation for putting it on when Tiberius summoned him. In the legends where the garment was merely a scrap of material, it was clearly a sort of lucky charm. But to wear the whole garment was much more suggestive than this.

A gnostic document of at least the ninth century, the *Hymn of the Soul*, originally written in Syriac, described the descent of the soul to the earth in terms of leaving behind a wonderful robe 'set with gems and spangled with gold . . . which they had made for me because they loved me.' The soul, travelling through the world, constantly remembered this garment. When the earthly trials were accomplished the robe suddenly appeared again: and this time, the soul could put it on.

> I stretched forth and received it, and adorned myself with the beauty of the colours of it,
> And in my royal robe excelling in beauty I arrayed myself wholly.
> And when I had put it on, I was lifted up unto the place of peace and homage,
> and I bowed my head and worshipped the brightness of the Father who had sent it to me,
> For I had performed his commandments, and he had fulfilled his promise to me.

This, believers know, is the journey of all souls, from the brightest to the darkest. Even a man who is steeped in sin has described the same trajectory, falling to earth to ascend again; even he has come, in Wordsworth's phrase, 'trailing clouds of glory'. Wordsworth also says, a little earlier, 'not in entire forgetfulness'. The light of perfect goodness is somehow remembered. Plato, too, constantly emphasised the fall of the soul from the sphere of brightness. If Pilate, like Cato on the night he died, had read his *Phaedo*, he too – even he – would have stumbled across this idea.

The legends took it literally. So Pilate, who is still in the *Golden Legend* an unbeliever and a villain, clothes himself in the grace of Christ. He shines and is perfect; his presence touches others like a blessing. Yet he has no notion why. For just a few moments he is the model of the child at baptism or the initiate touched by heaven; he has put on, like them, the ritual white robe, the garment of light. But in his confusion and unbelief, the magic – or the grace – slips away.

The end of the governor's life is simply a mystery. He was probably only middle-aged when he returned to Rome; but his career had been interrupted, and it was not clear in what form he could pick it up again. His 'biographers', medieval and modern, provide three possibilities. Assuming he faced no penalty for the Samaritan business, he could have gone into semi-retirement, still in Rome but playing no part in public life. Assuming he was sentenced, he could have been sent into exile, in Italy or abroad. Or he could have chosen the common Roman route, and taken his own life to avoid the disgrace of punishment.

His fate was not without theological implications. If Jesus was God, the theory went, Pilate's end should have been horrible; if he had lived on in comfort, Christ's claims were not to be believed. True gods destroyed their destroyers. This was part of the great debate that took place between Origen and Celsus in 248 over the validity of Christian teaching. Celsus, the pagan, argued that if a man had killed a god, he would certainly suffer for it. What had happened to Pentheus after he had mocked Dionysus, cut off his curls, taken away his ivy wand and cast him into prison to 'dance down there in the dark'? First, he saw his palace explode in flames; but Dionysus escaped, sinuously, effortlessly, on tip-toe amid the rubble. Pentheus next did what Pilate would have done: called out the heavy infantry, the fastest cavalry, the mobile squadrons and the archers, to hunt him down. But Dionysus got the better of him even then, persuading him to dress up as a woman to observe the Bacchic rites he was so curious about. In his long dress, dazed by divine hallucinations, Pentheus was torn to pieces on the holy mountain by his mother and his sisters.

Yet Pilate had never suffered, said Celsus: 'the men who tortured and punished your God in person . . . suffered nothing afterwards as long as they lived.' It therefore stood to reason that Christ was not divine. Origen contradicted him, but not to say that Pilate had suffered. He maintained he had never been guilty. It was, he said, the Jews who had killed Christ; and their nation had suffered calamity ever since. Pilate, he implied, had ended his days in peace and in obscurity.

Only one of Pilate's biographers, and a very late one, took up that idea with enthusiasm: Anatole France in his short story of 1892, *The*

Procurator of Judea. His Pilate had been exiled, but merely to Sicily, where he lived happily enough as a farmer with his daughter looking after him. There he grew 'the fattest ears of corn in the country'. Because gout and obesity afflicted him, he would make his way slowly by litter round the cliffs of the Tyrrhenian coast towards the steaming sulphur springs at Phlegra. Yet he lived well, and his obsessive broodings about his career in Judea took place over lunches of larks in honey in the shade of terraces of roses. In his old age, he did not miss Rome. Nor, in the most famous line of the story, did he recall the trial that had fixed his place in history. He remembered the various slights of the Jews, yes, and the way they had clung to him and badgered him for favours; he remembered silk dresses, dancing girls. But 'Jesus? Jesus of Nazareth? I don't remember him.'

Philo and Josephus seemed to endorse this view. Neither mentioned any official condemnation or any violent end. Had there been one, Philo would surely have revelled in it, as he did in the lynching of the prefect Flaccus. Yet among both the early and the later Christians, a comfortable retirement for Pilate was not acceptable. Pilate would have to remember Jesus, the early Fathers fretted; he could not do otherwise. Somehow, he would have to pay the price. It was not good enough to say, with Origen, that he was innocent; everyone knew it was the Romans, not the Jews, who had actually crucified Christ. And the Romans themselves believed that guilty men never really escaped justice, even if they were not condemned by human judges. There was a sense of implacable pursuit: 'not really by the Furies with blazing torches, as in the tragedies,' Cicero said, 'but by the anguish of remorse and the torture of a bad conscience.' These guilty consciences, as Juvenal wrote, kept them in a lather of fear.

> the mind's its own best torturer,
> lays on with invisible whips, silently flays them alive.

The guilty man could not eat, Juvenal went on. His throat was dry with fear; he choked on his food, spat out his wine. At night he thrashed in his bed, dreaming of his broken vows to deities and altars, and visited by monstrous images of the men he had injured or defrauded. The slightest headache might be a visitation from the god he had offended. And there was no escaping this, no matter how far and fast he ran away.

Yet even the torment of a guilty conscience was not enough if a man was still in his own bed in his own house. Many legends of Pilate preferred to see him sent away. In *The Healing of Tiberius* the emperor exiled him at once to a place called Ameria, in Tuscany. Pilate was often associated with lakes and ponds that were disturbed or enchanted, and even little Ameria had one of these. Pliny the Younger recalled being shown by his wife's grandfather a peculiar round lake that lay at the foot of the hills outside the village. It was pale blue with a touch of green, smelled of sulphur, and was considered sacred because the water healed fractures. There were no boats on this lake because it was holy, but instead green floating islands of reeds and sedge that jostled in the wind continually. Sometimes the islands joined together to look like land, at other times they scattered; at times they were so firm, apparently, that cattle wandered out onto them as if on solid land, but at others they drifted, with the animals bucking in terror.

Ameria was disturbing, but it was neither very nasty nor very far; so a persistent tradition, found in the *Golden Legend* and in medieval manuscripts scattered all through Europe, said that Pilate was exiled to Vienne, in southern Gaul on the edge of the Alps. For once, the story was not implausible. The mountain regions of Gaul were just right, Romans thought, for trouble-makers from Palestine. Herod Antipas, who had been deprived of his tetrarchy by Gaius not long after Pilate's disgrace, was sent to Lyons with his equally troublesome wife; Archelaus, his half-brother, was exiled to Vienne itself. This town, it was said, drew its name from *via Gehennae*, the road to hell; Gehenna itself had been the name of the giant public rubbish pit in Jerusalem which Pilate, in better times, could have watched with its web of smouldering fires from the windows of his palace.

For all that, Vienne was not quite the end of the world. There were quasi-Roman buildings and bookshops there in which, according to Seneca, Caesar's works were recited. Horace dreamt that after his death he would fly over such barbarian outposts as a swan, and that even 'those who drink the waters of the Rhone' would come to read his poems. Among the Roman ruins that remain, several are said to be Pilate's, including a building that locals call his *praetorium*, and a peculiar four-sided pyramid on a base of four arches, eighty feet high, that some suppose to be his tomb. The Rhone itself has tales to tell, but that is to run ahead of the story.

One Latin verse romance of the fourteenth century, traced to Vienne, put Pilate instead in Lausanne, just over the border of modern Switzerland. There his enemies consigned him to a deep dark well that was to be his prison for at least twelve years. They delighted to think of him sweating there, loaded with chains, his hair a mess and his 'pretty feet' crippled and sunk in mud. In the dark he sobbed continually, for he could not escape. Nonetheless, in his more lucid moments he admitted that it was 'reasonable' that he should be among the rats, 'for the damnable false judgement I made, against truth and God's goodness.'

Between Lausanne and Vienne, eventually, he got out and wandered. His story was now in the realm of folklore. In villages and valleys all over Europe people made up his fate, imagined they saw him, linked his name with mountains and pools and bad weather. They still do. Very little of this was written down until, in the late nineteenth and early twentieth centuries, the folklorists made their collections. It passed instead into children's songs and shepherds' superstitions. And behind it all lay the medieval conviction that Pilate could not stay still. He was condemned to the deathless life of those who had taunted God, like the Wild Huntsman, doomed evermore to chase red deer because he had preferred this to praying; like the Man in the Moon, doomed to wander the sky eternally because he had gathered sticks on a Sunday; or like the captain of the Phantom ship, who, insisting on doubling the Cape whether God willed it or not, ploughed the great seas forever in a ship festooned with ice.

In the folklore of Europe, every living thing involved in the passion was made to suffer afterwards. The evergreen oak, because it did not resist being made into the cross, became a cursed tree that stained red the axes of anyone who cut it; the once-towering mistletoe, because it was also used for the cross, became a shrivelled bundle of parasitic twigs. As for Pilate, some thought he had been branded, literally marked on his forehead with the mark of the beast. His branding burned him; it stayed raw, like a plague sore. People fled away from it, and it forced him to wander through the world in an effort to slough off his pain.

Some men imagined he saw Christ before him all the time, or the shadow of the cross on his path; he could never sleep, never blot out these things. Perhaps he wandered where the broom grew; that too was cursed, like him, because it had revealed the whereabouts of Christ in the garden by cracking and spitting out its seeds. Or he caught his robes among brambles, condemned to bear black berries and leaves smeared with red because they had consented to be part of the crown of thorns.

After years of wandering he took to the mountains and, men assumed, lived there in solitary huts in the wilderness. In 1552 Felix Platter passed by one such house on the outskirts of Saint-Vallier in the Dauphiné, 'Pilate's house', half-way up a grim hillside, and noted that the governor had lived there 'in misery'. All over Alpine Europe, peculiar ruins and abandoned houses were given a demonic charge with the claim that Pilate had lived there. He was not imagined as old, for his age had been frozen at the date of the crucifixion; but he sat there in his toga consumed by guilt and harried by devils, in the midst of the grey woods.

Were there any facts at the base of all this fantasy? It is possible that he was exiled. If his trial took place and he was found guilty, exile was the usual punishment for erring provincial governors. It was mercifully short of death, but its pain was not to be underestimated. A man who was exiled was no longer a Roman citizen; once interdicted 'by fire and water', as the formula went, he could no longer wear the toga, and he was presumed to belong only to the provincial outpost where he lived. Unless he was merely *relegatus*, 'relegated', as the poet Ovid was in AD 8, he also lost his property. And, not least, he lost the city.

Ovid described in graphic terms the misery of leaving Rome. In his grief he forgot to shave or comb his hair, and he was too dazed to choose which clothes or which slaves (a Roman's order of priorities) to take with him. He kept forgetting things, finding hopeless excuses to go back just one more time into his house. Friends put their arms round his shoulders and wept, but he himself felt dead, 'as if I was being carried for burial without a funeral.' Flaccus, exiled to Andros, used almost the same words: 'It's as though I am carrying the corpse that is myself to the sepulchre.' Ovid realised that the numbness that held his limbs, paralysing them as if they had been severed from his body, was his love of his country.

Pilate too would have felt this pain. It went with sharp social humiliation: the word *exul* was used as a term of abuse in the Senate, and any contact with friends from home was usually forbidden. On their side, friends were forbidden even to mention the man who had been sent away. For someone who had once been important, the loss of prestige was disabling. According to Philo, Flaccus on Andros used to pace up and down, slap his thighs and clap his hands as if he were going mad; he would cry out, 'I'm Flaccus, the recent governor of Alexandria! Ruler of the blessed land of Egypt! Thousands of people respected me! I had infantry, cavalry, naval officers, men of excellence, and crowds of followers escorted me whenever I went out! Was this a phantom, then, and not the truth? Was I asleep, and just dreaming the light-heartedness of those days? Yes, I must have been . . .'

Philo always needs his grain of salt, but Ovid makes a sadder and more sober witness. Since the time of Augustus, exiles had been forbidden to go to pleasant places, such as the Greek islands; they were sent to the fringes of the empire, among barbarians with plaited hair and trousers. Ovid himself was sent to Tomis, the modern Constantza, on the western shore of the Black Sea. The place was rocky, almost treeless, and bitterly cold in winter; so cold, he wrote, that the beards of the natives tinkled with ice. Few people spoke Greek, fewer Latin; the beautiful language grew rusty with disuse. Ovid described how, rather than lose the habit of it, he would talk to himself. When he ventured out among the barbarians, past the guard at his gate, he could tell he was being talked about and laughed at; he would defend himself by nodding at them, pretending to understand their language. This fooled no one. Human contact with the natives was almost impossible, and homesickness only grew worse with time. He began to envy Ulysses for eating the lotuses that had made him forget his country: 'If only those were on offer,' he wrote, 'I would give half my life to buy them.'

Love of Rome, where his wife still was, tormented him. He imagined himself walking the streets, climbing the steps to the temples, taking down book-rolls in the libraries. Lingering like a ghost by the house of Augustus, he could touch the garlands of oak-leaves hanging over the door. In his dreams he saw the city below him, 'now the *fora*, now the temples, now the theatres sheathed in marble, now every portico with its levelled ground, now the green expanse of the Campus that looks towards the lovely gardens, the pools, the canals . . .' By day he gazed constantly on a medallion of Augustus, Livia and Tiberius that a friend had given him, trying by sheer will-power to make their expressions change from severity to mercy. In words that Pilate would have felt the force of, he explained the holy charge of these images: they were 'my eagles, my standards'.

Ovid was never to return to Rome. For any Roman, that was punishment enough; but the medieval writers had one last horror for God to inflict on Pilate. He had to die violently. In one account, after the episode of the seamless garment, Tiberius ordered Pilate to be shut up in a cave while he consulted all the princes and people of the city to decide what should be done with him. As Pilate sat there, the emperor rode out to the hunt through the greenwood, in boots and pointed hat, with his hounds baying at his heels. An old law held that if a condemned man looked on the emperor's face, he would be spared; so Pilate craned his head out from his prison, trying to see him. At the same moment,

Tiberius took aim at a hind; but the arrow missed, and tore instead through the window of Pilate's cave. It killed him instantly.

Only one other tradition, the Coptic, had Pilate dying by the violence of other people. In the *Anaphora of Pilate*, Tiberius – not content with Pilate's demi-crucifixion by Herod – decided to crucify him again, and then, for good measure, to behead him for the crime of deicide. In the midst of his torments Pilate asked the soldiers for a respite so that he could pray. He turned towards the east, knelt down and said: 'Oh my Lord Jesus Christ who took away the sins of the world, have pity on your servant Pilate and forgive all my stumblings, omissions and sins . . . I have indeed dared to judge you, just Judge, but do not rebuke me for this sin I have committed, because you are a merciful and compassionate God, and I am a created being, and I dared to say to you, "Who are you?"'

He asked mercy too for Procula, who was standing beside him: 'Pardon us and number us among thy righteous ones.' A voice from heaven then reassured him: 'All the generations and families of the Gentiles shall call thee blessed, because in thy days were fulfilled all the things which were spoken by the prophet concerning me.' Then the executioner cut off Pilate's head, and an angel received it. At the sight of the angel Procula, overwhelmed with joy, died instantly. It was the fifteenth of June by the old Syriac calendar, the twenty-fifth of June by the new, when Pilate was beheaded. He was laid in the tomb of Jesus, as he had requested, together with the bodies of Procula and their two children, who happened to have died the same day.

The western tradition had no time for such sentimental stuff; it was determined to pile up heaven's vengeance on the governor's head. In the *Golden Legend* Tiberius ordered Pilate to die by 'the basest of deaths', but Pilate forestalled him by committing suicide. ('So, he *did* die by the basest of deaths,' the emperor remarked, 'since his own hand did not spare him.') Almost all the medieval writers believed that Pilate had died this way, within a few years of his return from Judea: usually in Rome, occasionally in Vienne in a tower by the Lyons gate, where he had shut himself up to die, and sometimes in the Alpine wilderness. The German Pilate, wandering in that wilderness, came to a pool of marshy brackish water among the pine-woods south-west of Lucerne. It must have been the winter time, for in summer the little lake dried up entirely. He waded out into it, his robes growing heavier, and plunged in like a swimmer. The waters closed over him.

For the early Church Fathers, suicide seemed the only possible end to

Pilate's career. 'He fell into such misfortunes under Gaius,' wrote Eusebius, 'that he became by necessity his own murderer and his own executioner; apparently, divine justice didn't spare him long.' Eusebius confidently dated his suicide to the third year of Gaius, sometime between March 39 and March 40.

That end was not implausible. Under Tiberius' reign of terror in the early 30s, a mere charge of wrongdoing – even before the trial and sentence – was often enough to make a man retire to his house and there, with pocket knife or poison, try to put himself away. If he was guilty, the gesture was more or less expected. Pliny the elder recorded a case very close to Pilate's, of a knight recalled by Tiberius from his deputy-governorship for maladministration. 'In his extreme despair,' he wrote, *summa desperatione*, 'he swallowed a dose of leek-juice weighing three *denarii* in silver, and immediately expired without suffering any pain.'

No particular stigma was attached to suicide. On the contrary, Cicero called it the noblest of deaths, 'the course best adapted to the retention of honour and escape from unendurable sufferings.' Horace called it 'dying bravely'; Martial recalled his friend Festus, who 'closed his sacred life by a Roman's death'. The means were known and discussed: cantharides, hemlock, shoemaker's vitriol, the opening of a vein in the wrist, simple self-starvation. Almost no sentimental or patriotic story was complete without the moment when a man put his breast to the sword and, like a lover, leaned on it. The scenes would have been well known to Pilate, even favourite episodes in his reading: the moment when Scipio, in charge of the fleet off Africa and striving to avoid capture, fell on his sword but insisted on a final message to his men, 'All is well with the commander!' *Imperator se bene habet!* Or the moment when Gaius Fufius Geminus, accused of *maiestas* against Tiberius in 30, mortally wounded himself before his executioner arrived and, when the quaestor came to the door, showed him the welling blood with the words: 'Report to the Senate that this is how a man dies.'

Suicide was often a sacrifice that was performed for the sake of others. A man who was exiled could make no will, and those convicted of crimes might leave their families destitute unless they killed themselves. Those who committed suicide had their wishes honoured, and their family's reputation was unaffected. (Dio noted that, under Tiberius, most of those who killed themselves left something in their wills to the emperor who had driven them to suicide.) They could also be cremated with full rites, which was crucial. The act was not interpreted first as one of despair, but of calculated courage. Stoics invoked it to show how innocuous death was, how unimportant the dissolution of the body: 'not quite such a small matter as whether your hair should be worn evenly or unevenly', as Seneca wrote, but almost. Nor was it necessarily a sign of anomie or belief in nothing. Many suicides doubtless believed they were going into blackness; but Cato fell on his sword only when he had convinced himself of the immortality of the soul and the prospect of heaven.

So in the popular imagination Pilate, disgraced even if unsentenced, hounded by his demons, went into his room and shut the door. He lay down on the couch, not troubling this time to remove his shoes. The Pilate of Kazantzakis's novel *The Last Temptation of Christ* had always worn a sharpened razor, on a golden chain around his neck, for just this purpose: for the moment when he became weary of eating, drinking or governing, or when the emperor exiled him. He had called it, with a laugh, 'my Messiah, my liberator'. But perhaps it was with a little knife, as the medieval writers thought, that he nicked open the blue vein in his wrist. The pain was sharp, then quiet. As he let his arm sink towards the floor, he felt both faint and warm. The last salutation to the dead would have crossed his mind: *Aeternum vale*, goodbye for ever. Among the images before his eyes may have been some from Judea: but whether they were of hills, girls, crosses or temples, nobody knows. All men imagine is that he was alone, with no one to close his eyes or, in the Roman custom, brush his lips with theirs to take in his last breath. And then he went abruptly into the dark.

Raoul and Hector trudged to the lake, found a flat rock, and collapsed on it. They were not dressed for mountaineering. The summer of 1868 was hot and they were wearing the gear they had bought, more or less as a joke, as they left Paris: silk hats, wide trousers, high-fashion tunics *à la Garibaldi*, riding coats, cravats. As a precaution each also carried a woollen cape, a metal-tipped umbrella and a haversack with blister-tincture, lip-salve, a first-aid manual, several handkerchiefs and two spare pairs of slippers. Now they sweated, and waited.

On another part of the mountain a plump middle-aged woman, in black crepe and black bonnet, laboured upwards on a small English pony. Behind her came the Princess Louise, the Prince Arthur, a lady-in-waiting and several Highland attendants, one of whom carried the royal box of water-colours. The whole party was travelling incognito. A list of false names – the Countess of Kent, Lady Louise Kent, Lieutenant the Hon. Arthur Kent RE, the Marchioness of Ely – had been inscribed in the visitor's book at the Bellevue Hotel. Prince Arthur set the pace on foot, out-doing the guide and no doubt finding the view 'inexpressible grand', as did the panting hack from the *Illustrated London News*. But the royal party did not stay till the evening, when 'the sun . . . colours the whole of the snowy peaks with molten gold'; they went down again in the daylight, with Arthur dreaming of dinner.

The trek up Mount Pilatus had become a favourite day-trip from Lucerne, almost too organised and comfortable and often too crowded. Tourists started on the bridle-path at Hergiswyl and walked for three-and-a-half hours to the Klimsenhorn Hotel, through meadows and orchards and then up a zig-zagging path through pine woods. At the Klimsenhorn the path got steeper, still twisting, until it turned into fifty-two steps through a chimney of rock, at the top of which unfolded a sweeping panorama of the Bernese Alps. For any of these sections, though less successfully for the steps, mules could be hired. The paths had been widened by many boots, and difficult traverses had been fitted with iron railings. In later years the faint-hearted could take Colonel Locher's cog-wheel railway from the Pilatus Hotel right up to the Bellevue, which by then had been superseded by a better establishment with first- and second-class dining rooms. Twenty-five francs would take you in the single-coach train, at a maximum speed of eight miles an hour, from watering station to pumping station with occasional views of the gorges; and at the top it would buy you dinner, a room and breakfast, while the glowing Alps spread out below the terrace. As

Baedeker commented, the journey presented 'no danger even to novices'.

Tourists on Mount Pilatus therefore had to make excitements of their own. Wagner walked there in 1859, the third act of *Tristan* running in his head, dragging along a friend who was almost sick with vertigo. Raoul and Hector, the Paris students, made bets about blisters. The hack from the *News* hoped for a royal stumble, his own exclusive on the plump ball of black crepe rolling down the hillside. None of these had laid wagers on whether or not they would see Pilate. Yet that, for many nineteenth-century visitors, was the underlying thrill of the climb. At any bend of the path, behind any of the steeply serrated crags of the mountain, and especially near the marshy little lake known as the Pilatusee where Raoul and Hector now sat, the governor might suddenly appear. Raoul and Hector's guide told them that he materialised each Friday, when he paced round the lake with a notebook, taking down the names of visitors to pass them on to the Devil.

The lake itself was nothing much to see. According to the official history of Pilatus, published in 1913, it was just 'a gloomy puddle' surrounded by a mighty forest. But any change of weather on this temperamental mountain – a sudden squall, a descent of cloud – was attributed by the superstitious to Pilate's temper; and even the gloomy thoughts of Queen Victoria, her widow's visions of Albert in just such a gothic setting of rocks and forest light, might have been interrupted by a man in a toga washing his hands.

Some scraps of folklore suggested that Pilate had come here alive. More often, it was supposed to be the place where his spirit had reached the end of its wanderings. It was too easy to send Pilate directly to hell, though one thirteenth-century life of Judas confidently reported that he was being tortured there (together with Judas, Annas, Herod and Caiaphas) every day and night except Sundays, the Christmas season, the Easter season and the feasts of Our Lady. Like all malevolent spirits, he clearly had more walking on the earth to do.

After Pilate's suicide in Rome, according to the *Golden Legend*, the emperor ordered a millstone to be hung around the 'evil and sordid' body and the body to be thrown in the Tiber. But it was seized immediately by devils who made the air and water seethe, whipped up storms, lashed the city with hail and made the river flood. An oracle was consulted; it said the storms would continue as long as Pilate's body stayed in the river. But no one dared to fish it out. In the end a condemned man was sent in, fastened to the bank for safety with a long rope. As he went under the surface the rope jerked fantastically, as if hooked to a fighting fish; it took twenty men to hold it. At last the water quietened, the jerks could not be felt, and the men hauled in the body of the diver clamped to the dead Pilate's neck. The struggle had been terrible.

The brave diver was given a state funeral, but the body of Pilate clearly had to be burned. It was taken to Vesuvius and thrown into the crater, in the hope that it would roast slowly while waiting for the Day of Judgement. Instead, the mountain almost exploded. The earth shook, lava poured out, and the cities of Pompeii and Herculaneum were buried under ash. Again the oracle was consulted; again it answered, 'It's Pilate.' 'The bastard!' cried the Romans. 'How can we get rid of him?'

In the city's prison lay a Christian, waiting to be eaten by the lions. They ordered him to fetch Pilate out of the volcano. The man agreed, as long as all the other Christians in the prison were spared; the deal done, he set off for Vesuvius. At the edge of the crater, black and red and hissing with fire, he met the Devil.

'You want to go down there?' the Devil asked.

'Yes, I do,' the saint replied.

'You won't come up again.'

'God is with me.'

'If you go down there, you'll belong to me.'

'Get lost! You keep my body, God gets my soul.'

He climbed down. But Vesuvius was one of the gateways to hell, and the Devil reserved the right to refuse to release anyone who went in. He allowed the Christian to go down in search of Pilate and bring him to the surface, but then he decided not to let the theft go unavenged; instead, grabbing the Christian from behind, he dragged him down into the whirlpool of fire.

Pilate, or rather his body, was found the next day on the flanks of the volcano. The people decided to send him to Gaul, and either threw him into the Rhone at Vienne ('another river that has no bottom, but goes down directly to hell') or buried him near Lausanne. Once again the devils descended with a clatter of leathery wings, shrieking and spitting. They whipped up great whirlpools that sucked ships down, and racked the land with storms. Because there was no oracle at Lausanne, the locals put up with this for a hundred years until, one day, they decided they could do so no longer. One local legend says they sent a boat without oars, but filled with relics of the saints, to still the whirlpool in the river;

then, when the water was calm, they sent down a diving machine to search the bottom for Pilate. When he was found they threw him into a flaming pit somewhere in the Alps, 'where the devils were delighted to get their man back.'

Another local folk-tale says that the people of Lausanne tolerated Pilate until, after many years, the Wandering Jew came past. He knew Pilate of old. Matthew Paris, in his *Chronica Majora* of about 1260, said that the Jew had been a porter in Pilate's service in the *praetorium* during the trial. As Jesus had stumbled out of the door, he had urged him to go faster. In return for his scorn then, Jesus had condemned him to wander the world until the Second Coming. The Jew, called Cartaphilas, had long since repented; he had been baptised and spent most of his time in Armenia and the east, telling and retelling his stories of the passion. In a later German version of the fable his name was Ahasverus, and he was spotted in the fifteenth and sixteenth centuries in most of the countries of Europe. He was tall, with an unkempt beard and hair reaching past his shoulders; even in winter he went barefoot, wearing an old belted coat that trailed on the ground. This apparition now offered to rid Lausanne of its plague.

Without a tremor, he stepped into the Rhone and plunged until his long coat, beard and hair had disappeared under the water. When he resurfaced, Pilate was with him. The governor clung to him and let himself be carried, piggy-back, all over the world as the Jew wandered. Yet the odd pairing could not last. The Jew grew weary, and wanted to be carried himself. But Pilate was dead, and could not oblige him. One day, as they toiled up a mountain called Fracmont in the Alps, the Wandering Jew took a detour to a marshy little lake among the pine trees and tipped Pilate in.

Most people took this as the end of the journey. Yet all over southern Germany and Alpine Europe villages laid claim to the body of Pilate. If there was any pool, any lake, any well with a disturbing feel to it, this sense of menace was attributed to the governor. Pilate's ghost was seen in the Bavona valley, in the canton of Tessin and in Lake Joch on the Vigilijoch, four hours from Merano, where he fought with a count who lay drowned beside him. It was seen in the bottomless lake at Norcia in the Apennines, to which his body had been taken on an ox-cart, and where necromancers still resorted, even in the nineteenth century, to have their books of magic consecrated. On the island of Amrum in the North Sea the words 'Pilate is dead' became a charm to keep bad luck away; and Cornishmen thought his body had been put on a fishing boat and cast adrift for the devils to lay claim to.

Other places saw him too. Every year, around New Year's Eve, a not-unfriendly-looking man could be found travelling from Aargau to the Rhine. People said it was either the Wandering Jew or Pilate. In Lake Piller he could be heard howling for the whole of Holy Week; in Tiersee, near Kufstein, he took the shape of a roaring bull; on the mountain called Septimer he went on fighting with Herod, and in the Saarland he could be heard at night, crying 'I am innocent of the blood of this just man.' It was a muffled cry, people said, because he had been buried both deep and face-downwards; but from time to time it boomed like a foghorn, and from this the old folk of Ehsten said that Pilate had turned into a bittern, the hidden and booming bird of the empty marshlands. The bittern seemed an appropriate guise for history's Great Equivocator, 'skulking, solitary and usually crepuscular', as one observer described it; a bird that flew with reluctant, dragging wings and, when it tried to hide itself, blended with the dead reeds and sometimes swayed with them.

It was clear why Pilate could not rest. He was still stained with the blood of Christ, and could not get it off; he would have to go on journeying, struggling and shouting until the hand of mercy was extended to him. In Bulgakov's *The Master and Margarita* it was the Master, the man who had invented Pilate in his novel, who alone had the power to free the governor from the burden of guilt he had placed on his shoulders. On a high mountain ledge he found him, wringing his hands and gazing at the moon, his great dog at his feet. Pilate still had something to say to Jesus; he longed to walk along that path of light with him, as he had done long ago in his dreams. So the Master released him, shouting the words 'You are free! Free! He is waiting for you!' It was the moment of redemption. Half-laughing, half-crying, his dog bounding in front of him, Pilate stumbled into the light of the love of Christ.

Yet mercy was not always so certain. In medieval England Pilate was seen as a ghost-knight, riding with Herod and Judas through a landscape of unrelenting winter. Walter de la Mare in his poem 'The Three Traitors' described them travelling by moonlight, silvered and 'shining like hoarfrost', in search of Jesus who could wash them clean. When day broke the sun-Christ might indeed shine on them, and they might feel his mercy laid over them like fresh clothes; but their journey had not ended. They were still bound to wander on.

Babe of the Blessed Trinity
Shall smile their steeds to see:
Herod and Pilate riding by,
And Judas one of three.

Of all the sites of Pilate's wanderings, none was more haunted than the mountain of Fracmont above Lucerne. From at least the fourteenth century it was called Pilatus, apparently after him. As soon as Pilate's body arrived there, the mountain became a fearsome abode of hail and storms. People in Lucerne began to watch the peak, noting whether the clouds that drifted over it were bunched like Pilate's hat, or long like his sword. A hat meant fair weather, a bare head meant rain; but on a day of sword-clouds, no one would venture up the mountain. Some discounted the ghost, of course. They pointed out that *Pilatus* could well have come from *pileatus*, capped with clouds. But the shepherds on the higher slopes did not believe that. Their flocks were disturbed and skittish, and if men threw stones into the little lake they stirred up horrors: whirlpools, black vapours, foul smells, and devils that left the scrape-marks of their hooves on the rocks beside the water.

Every year, at noon on Good Friday, they claimed to see Pilate in his judge's robes of scarlet or purple, sitting on a throne of massive stones or in a purple armchair in the middle of the lake in which the devils had placed him. Man and throne would rise out of the water and, as they rose, Pilate would slowly and solemnly go through the motions of washing his hands. He would look only at his hands, not at any bystanders; and having stayed a little while, he would sink again below the surface of the lake. Anyone who saw him died within the year.

He had to be exorcised, but who would dare? The mountain was so cursed that the burghers of Lucerne forbade people to climb it under pain of fine. If a man had to climb it out of necessity, and needed to approach the lake, he had to be accompanied by a burgher of probity who would see that he did nothing to disturb Pilate's peace. Nothing at all – no stone, or fruit, or plant, or even gold coins – could be thrown into the lake. Some adventurers were executed for disobeying this law; and in 1307 six priests were put in prison for daring to climb the mountain by themselves, without a burgher or a licence.

The good citizens of Lucerne continued to look for a man in a state of grace who could rid the mountain of Pilate. At last, around the end of the fifteenth century, they seemed to find one. By some accounts he was a Rosicrucian recently returned from Palestine; by others he was a

Spanish scholar, who volunteered to put Pilate in a Christian frame of mind. Accordingly he set off up the mountain, completely alone. Torrents and huge chasms blocked his way; but when he made the sign of the cross, magical viaducts appeared across the gorges. He walked over them, and with each step the viaducts dissolved into the mist behind him. Confident of divine protection, he came at last to the edge of Pilate's pool.

Here a terrifying vision reared up before him. Pilate, who had gone on growing after death, was now the height of the tallest tower in Lucerne. He was in full Roman military dress of breastplate, helmet, kilt and nailed boots, and he shook a whole pine tree in his fist. But the Christian was unafraid, and engaged him in a tremendous contest that rocked the mountain like a boat on the sea. For thirty-six hours the battle raged, until a great thump ended it. There was silence, followed only by heavy breathing. Down in the valley, the terrified folk of Lucerne laid bets on the winner. It was the Christian, who had teased and harried the giant shadow until he had floored him.

Yet Pilate was dead already, of course. The new defeat merely winded him, but could not kill him, and so the ghost and the Christian came to terms. The Christian produced from his pocket a fragment of the true cross and made Pilate swear that he would stay quietly in his pool all the days of the week except Fridays. On Fridays he could roam through the mountains, and the people of Lucerne would leave him alone. Pilate agreed, and laid his ghostly fingers on the splinter of wood from the cross he had ordered for Christ.

Relieved and exhausted, the Christian went back down the mountain. In the town he found a notary to draw up the official contract between the town and Pilate, and the deed was done. But in one version of the story, the notary was suspicious of the man who came to his office; he imposed such heavy conditions for calming Pilate that the notary felt he could not record them. 'Not if you were the Devil himself,' he told him.

'Better put your gloves on to deal with people like that,' snapped his visitor.

It was Satan.

'All right,' he told the notary, 'I'll tear that agreement up. Here's another. Pilate keeps one day a week to wander in the mountains.'

'Fine. Friday.'

'Friday. But on that day, everyone is expressly forbidden to go up there.'

'Fine again.'

'Sign.'

'Sign what?'

'This paper.'

'But what about everyone who'll go up there on a Friday? Pilate will get them and give them to you.'

'Right! Then you forbid people to go up there!'

The notary scratched his ear.

'I'm sure they'll choose exactly that day to see him.'

'A thousand cauldrons!' cried the Devil. 'If I hadn't been sure of that I'd never have made this deal.'

'Bah! Too bad, I'll sign it,' said the notary. 'Those who go up on Friday will die the same year without being in a state of grace.'

'Done,' said the Devil.

After the agreement, Pilate was quiet. Matters unfolded as the notary had predicted. English tourists in particular made a point of climbing the mountain on Fridays to watch His Majesty Pontius Pilate promenading with his notebook; those who survived crawled back maimed or wounded, and they all died within the year. So the mountain was calmed, but it was not exorcised.

In 1518, a year after Holbein had used the mountain as a background to one of his paintings, four wise men decided to test the truth of the legend. Having obtained the necessary permissions from the notary and the burghers of Lucerne, they began the long climb up Pilatus – on a Friday. Their nicknames showed their seriousness; they were drawn from a study-bound world of encyclopedias, metal-rimmed spectacles and armillary spheres, in which strange phenomena, like botanical specimens, could be pinned down and explained. 'Vadianus' of St Gallen, otherwise known as Joachim von Watt, led the expedition. He had been a professor at Vienna, where he had taken a degree in medicine. Accompanying him were 'Xylotectus' of Lucerne, otherwise known as Zimmerman, ' a learned and well-bred ecclesiastic'; 'Myconius' of Lucerne, otherwise known as Genshaussler, an 'erudite and open-hearted' man; and Grebel of Zurich, 'a young man of remarkably fine character'. They went in a spirit of scientific enquiry, but they could not quite manage to be open-minded; for once on the mountain, strange fears began to assail them. Behind their bravely rational and humanist front, they were still men of the Middle Ages, and their climb became a metaphor for the struggle of Renaissance Europe to get past old ghosts.

They climbed in August. Half the route could be covered on horseback, but the riding was rough and finally impossible. Vadianus reported that they scrambled up a narrow path and over broken ground, guided by a shepherd. At last they came to Pilate's little lake, overgrown and still, with the reeds barely sighing. There seemed to be neither inflow nor outflow, and winds could not reach it; the sky was not reflected in the surface of the water. Vadianus was deeply struck by it, and even more so by the terror of his shepherd-guide, who 'practically made us bind ourselves by an oath' not to perform experiments on the lake, nor to throw anything into it. His life was in danger, he kept saying. They must all be careful, they must be reverent and quiet; they should tread as if they were on holy ground. This disturbed Vadianus: it made him 'almost pay a certain respect to the reputation of the place, though of course there is not a word of truth in the story which some have imagined concerning Pilate . . . it's utter nonsense.'

Yet barely a paragraph on he changed his mind. 'I cannot say whether or not things are as the local inhabitants say they are,' he wrote,

> because I was not allowed to carry out experiments; and even if I had been allowed, I could not have done so without great danger. Nonetheless, I am moved to accept most of their stories in view of the marvels of nature which are established by the authority of many observers . . . Not to mention that the character – and more particularly the lie – of the place seemed to me to correspond readily enough with the story that is told about it.

In this mood he went back down the mountain. In order to lay the ghost, the party took two hours over dinner at the hostelry halfway to Lucerne; they did not get back into town until after sunset. Yet in years to come Vadanius changed his mind again. 'I have ascertained from persons I can believe,' wrote a man who followed him up Pilatus, 'that he subsequently got rid of his doubts and recognised that his whole story was a superstitious legend.'

The man who followed him was Conrad Gesner, and he wrote with feeling. He considered himself not only a man of reason, but a scholar who loved mountains and refused to believe anything bad of them. 'Myconius' of Lucerne, one of the party that went up Pilatus in 1518, had been his teacher. But Gesner's approach to mountains was new.

They were no longer a necessary evil, something to be climbed if you could not avoid it; they were, on the contrary, thrilling and enchanting. He had resolved, he told a friend, 'as long as God suffers me to live . . . to climb one mountain every year, at the season when the vegetation is the best, partly for the sake of studying botany, and partly for the delight of the mind and the proper exercise of the body.' He added, 'The mind is strangely excited by the amazing altitude . . .'

But not towards imaginings of ghosts. Gesner's account of his trip up Pilatus, published in 1555, was as sunny and invigorating as all his others. In passing, he mentioned the irritating necessity of taking a guide 'because of the superstitions of the natives about people approaching the marsh of Pilate'; but he made something good even of this annoyance, getting the man to carry the party's wine. They started the trip with a night in a hayloft, the best bed of all, according to Gesner: soft and fragrant, 'compounded of the most wholesome grasses and flowers.' After breakfast of milk and cheese, they climbed beside a cold stream swarming with fat trout and crayfish. Gesner looked for chamois and mountain goats, spotted white ptarmigan; in a tiny cave he found an icy spring, in which they dipped bread. He exulted in the warmth of exercise, the shapes of the crags, the soft grass under his feet. Even in the grass he saw wonders, 'herbs that have a sweeter smell and a greater power of healing in the mountains than in the plain.' At the summit he noted that he could see 'without let or hindrance, the rising and setting of the stars'.

He refused to be alarmed by the thought of Pilate. When he approached the lake at last, he had fortified himself with a draught of 'rich but delicate milk', his favourite drink, and had tooted a few deep notes on an Alpine horn. The party passed a rock on which Pilate was sometimes supposed to sit, conjuring up storms. Gesner observed with interest 'letters carved upon it – the names of climbers who had been there, with their dates, and their family crests'. No other comment. Of the lake, he remarked that it was more like a marsh, and so small that a dozen people could barely stand in it. As for the ghost,

> This belief, having no *raison d'être* in the laws of nature, commands no credence from me. . . . I am inclined to believe that Pilate has never been here at all, and that even if he had been here he would not have been accorded the power of either helping or hurting human kind.
>
> If evil spirits accomplish evil deeds, one must not assume that they are privileged to do so, but rather that the Lord God allows it . . . If

there is any sorcery in the lake it is not the work of Nature, but of some evil spirit, whether you call that evil spirit Pilate or by some other name. The whole earth, in fact, is full of evil spirits . . . But if a man confronts them in a truly pious and believing frame of mind . . . he will assuredly remain tranquil and unharmed.

This report seemed to mark the final exorcism of Pilate, but the work was still not done. Gesner, for all his blitheness, still had his evil spirits, and even after his comforting report the mountain terrified people. In 1585 the pastor of Lucerne, John Müller, felt obliged to make the ascent to prove once again the harmlessness of the story. Before a crowd of witnesses he threw stones and rubbish into the pool, shouting, 'Pilate, come out of your den!' *Pilat, wirf aus dein Kath!* There was no answer. After that, witnesses were not needed again; the pastor climbed by himself once a year, threw in his customary pebble, and came down again. It was, as Francis Grebble wrote in *The Early Mountaineers* in 1899, 'as though men wished to mark with a solemn and appropriate ceremony the end of the dark ages of superstition and the beginning of the reign of reason and the scientific spririt.'

Yet even Pastor Müller's bold defiance of Pilate had not left the mountain calm. In 1649 the prefect of Lucerne, out watching the night sky, saw a bright dragon come out of a cave on Pilatus. It was large, with a long tail and extended neck; its head 'terminated in the serrated jaw of a serpent' and it flew about with swift flapping wings, 'throwing out sparks like a red-hot horseshoe hammered by a blacksmith.' The prefect wanted to be scientific about this. He said he thought at first it was a meteor, 'but then after careful observation I recognised it was a dragon, from the nature of its movements and the structure of its various limbs.'

I thought it was a meteor, but I recognised it was a dragon. The real Pilate too had seemed torn in just this way, between rationalism and superstition. It was deeply ironic that his ghost became a test case of the longevity of legends and the persuasive power of science. In the end, inevitably, the scientists won. The little lake became no more than a curiosity. But there were times even in the nineteenth century when shepherds and climbers out late on Pilatus were startled, like the Rosicrucian, by roaring and sighing, or like the prefect of Lucerne by red sparks showering among the crags, and realised too late that it was only the mountain train.

*   *   *

In mountain Europe Pilate survived as the wandering spirit of evil; but in Ethiopia he was enshrined in the Canon of the Saints. Once again, water was his medium. He was made a saint – or, strictly speaking, a confessor – because he had washed his hands of the blood of Christ. The Coptic liturgy reflected the fascination with water of any dry land subject to inundations. Ritual water made all things new and washed all sins away. On the Feast of the Epiphany in January, the greatest feast of the year, the whole nation of Ethiopia underwent a vast lustration. In the liturgy, towards the end, the priest washed his hands first at the south corner of the church and then towards the west, repeating almost exactly the words of Pilate: 'I wash my hands in innocence.' He did this as the people recited the last words of the Creed, so that, like Pilate, his words were barely heard above the chanting of the crowd.

The feast of Pilate and Procula was on the twenty-fifth of June: in Ethiopia the twenty-fifth *sane*, the month of the rains. It was commemorated in the Ethiopian calendar with a simple verse:

> Salutation to Pilate who washed his hands
> so that he himself was pure of the blood of Christ
> and salutation to Procula, his wife,
> who sent him the message: Do not condemn him
> because that man is pure and just.

The story of their 'conversion' was read in churches on Good Friday, the same day that children were given licence to beg for food and stage mock funerals in the street. Western visitors noticed this strange convention, as they noted too that the Ethiopians were summoned to church by kettle-drums, ate their meat cut from live cattle, got drunk on mead, and marked the highest pitch of religious excitement by firing off their rifles. Lawrence Durrell met them once in deputation in the 1940s:

> Fuzzy-wig, kink-haired, with cocoa-butter shining,
> With stoles on poles, sackbuts and silver salvers
>
> Walking the desert ways howling and shining;
> A Coptic congregation, red blue and yellow,
>
> With Saints on parchment and stove-pipe hats . . .

In the pantheon of Ethiopian saints, Pilate and Procula were almost dull. They shared the calendar with Naakueto-Laah, an emperor who was celebrated for never having died; with Aaron, who was made a saint for inducing roasted pigeons to fly into his mouth; with Batazun, who fasted so repeatedly that he made himself as light as air; and John, who extracted a serpent from the womb of a princess. Balaam and his ass each had their feast-days, as did Tecla Haimanot, a holy man who was taken up a perpendicular mountain on the back of a boa constrictor. After Pilate in the calendar came the angel Gabriel, who predicted the rising and falling of the Nile by causing the beams of his church at Dabra Naklon, in the desert, to run with drops of sweat.

Pilate was also the subject of a special kind of holy poem, known as 'effigies', in which every part of the saint's body was celebrated as a model for the devout. This poem, discovered in 1972 in the Bibliothèque Nationale in Paris, had been written down in the eighteenth century but probably went back as far as the fifteenth. It was attributed to Cyriacus, Archbishop of Oxyrhyncus, and was appended to some of his sermons. Such poems had very little to do with the physical world, although they solemnly saluted each feature of Pilate's body, including his nostrils and his teeth, 'disposed with such beauty of whiteness'. The body was only a frame for theological and metaphysical speculation, and as the poem progressed Pilate seemed to break up and dissolve into the teeming landscape of the myths that had been built around him.

'Salutation to thy brows,' wrote the poet,

> frontiers of thine eyes; like an ocean
> whose sand in its depths is a mirror of the secret mystery.
> Oh Pilate, thou showest to the Lord of Heaven and Earth
> thy behaviour, in its details . . .
> Salutation to thy breath, which was exhaling faith
> And to thy sweet throat which was open to the taste of the gospel . . .
> Salutation to thy breast, a treasure of deep understanding,
> And salutation to thy bosom, which was troubled with the vine of
> torments . . .
> Salutation to the nails of thy hands which were placed
> over thy ten fingers in equality.
> Salutation to thy heart, full of righteous love,
> and to thy kidneys, torrents of water . . .

Salutation to thy internal organs; thy interior kept the knowledge of
the gospel, the Law;
and to thy navel, a circle on the breadth of the house . . .
Salutation to the soles of thy feet in their prodigious running, faster
than a hurricane,
and to thy step which was ready for the ascetic struggle . . .
Salutation to the toes of thy feet, branches of cedar,
and to the nails of thy feet too, signs of sweet feeling and acting . . .
Oh Pilate, the thunder of thy hymn in the month of thy feast in the
season of the rains
was heard from the heavens of the tongues of men, and now let the
trumpets sound.

As in the Alps, so in Ethiopia, Pilate became the spirit of the storm. His
giant body became ghostly; his misty toga dissolved into clouds, and
rainstorms fell from his vanishing hands. In the European mountains his
form had diffused into elemental evil: the shadow behind a crag, the
darkness at the bottom of a lake. Thunder carried his voice, which rolled
round the peaks unable either to rest or to escape. Yet in Ethiopia his
body and its functions had become pure goodness, swiftness and
wisdom. The mystery he mirrored was divine, not diabolical. It was
neither opaque nor terrifying, but bright with blue-green transparency
like the depths of the sea. And the thunder was the sound of his awe and
understanding.

He was the essence of evil or the essence of goodness: God's rejecter
or God's embracer. These opposing legends had taken on lives of their
own. Yet they had both sprung, however far back, from a civil servant's
moment of uncertainty. There had been potential in Pilate at that
moment for darkness or light far beyond the routine experience of a
Roman prefect. Even he seemed to sense it. The tiny seed had lodged in
his heart or his mind, suggesting infinite possibilities. He could take
untravelled roads, open hidden doors, escape the bounds of earth and
flesh, exceed himself. Or he could stay as he was: shrug, scratch his ear,
write another memorandum.

He stayed as he was. As most of us do.

Epilogue: Pilate on the beach

How does the song go?

> *A-B-C-D-1-2-3*
> Jesus died for you and me

The scene is a beach in the north-east of England on a cardigan afternoon. The August sun should be hot, but the grey clouds will not leave it alone. Green corporation wind-breaks have been hammered up to protect the clutter of family seaside life: Sunday newspapers, plastic picnic boxes, damp drying swimsuits, flyaway footballs that strain to escape. Fathers, a little apart, perch on ruined sandcastles to smoke. Grandmothers, surrounded by a ballast of stout bags, sit on the lee side of beached fishing boats; mothers stretch out their pink veined legs. Thermos cups of tea shuttle between them. The children cry, throw sand, drip ice-cream or paddle in a pool which bears a yellow slick of scum; but out on the blue sea the spinnakers dip silently towards Whitby, images of grace.

From below the sand dunes comes the sound of an accordion. The player is a swarthy young man in a red shirt, backed by two red-shirted girls with tambourines. They jump in circles on the sand, in front of a blackboard and a crowd of small children sitting cross-legged. While their mothers and fathers caress or bicker in caravans suddenly emptied of noise, the United Beach Mission entertains their offspring on the patch of beach behind the tea-room.

A-B-C-D-1-2-3
Jesus died for you and me

Downwind the song carries to the outside tables, where a waitress in a white blouse puts down a tray with aluminium jug, pot and spoons, and a plate of cake. It carries up the bank, to where a couple in their fifties have put out two canvas chairs at an angle from each other and have settled to the lighter bits of the *Sunday Times*. They glance down in distaste at the gyrations below them. Sunday has its drawbacks, which they always forget.

Yet the wind also blows the sound away, dispersing it among the marram grass. It lies there with sweet papers, empty shells, ashes of old fires, a seagull's feathered bones: things saved from the sea, caressed by the wind, lifting and blowing.

A-B-C-D-1-2-3
Jesus died for you and me
He died to make us really free!

Is that so? Pilate might ask. (He walks in the sand–dunes; the wind and the grass snag at him.) Are you free now, jumping, shouting, saved, because I sentenced him? Did I do that for you?

Acknowledgements

This book was written on the sly, in bits and pieces of time snatched from running a family and doing my job, and there are many people to thank that it has appeared at all. First, as always, my husband Malcolm and my three sons, for not minding my odd disappearances to the shed at the bottom of the garden, or my scribbling away in bed after lights out. I tried to put the thing away whenever I was needed, but I'm sorry for the times when I wasn't as attentive as I should have been.

Second, I should thank the *Economist* for providing me with a computer on which I could type in the second draft, largely (though not entirely) by dint of coming in an hour earlier in the mornings; and I should thank all my colleagues who turned a blind eye when they caught sight of the letters 'BC', or a slug of Latin, in the story the American editor was working on. A large technical-support team, especially Ginny O'Riordan, Pauline Cuddihy and Helen Mann, helped me through the hitches with unfailing patience. Special thanks should go to Graham Bayfield, who, at a crucial stage in producing the manuscript, came in on a Saturday to fix the system which had somehow crashed around me.

The *Economist* should also be thanked for having the foresight to install itself just round the corner from the London Library, where I spent any moments I could spare. Thanks to the staff there for putting up with my queries, extending my borrowing limit, obtaining copies from other libraries of the rare articles they did not have themselves, and for getting down on their knees in the dustier parts of the stacks to find obscure volumes translated from the Syriac.

Michael Walsh, the librarian of Heythrop College in the University of London, allowed me to use the wonderfully ordered library there to unearth yet more information. And Babette Grolman translated many bizarre texts from the German, some of them in a gothic script that gave both of us a headache to read.

Once the book was done, many people encouraged me with their enthusiasm and good advice. Alexandra Pringle, my agent at Toby Eady Associates, gave her usual great moral support. Dan Franklin, my editor at Jonathan Cape, nobly extended the delivery deadline and showed unflagging faith in the enterprise; Charlotte Mendelson copy-edited with great care and good humour; and Joy de Menil, my editor at Random House in New York, happily edited many pages not once but twice when they went astray in mid-Atlantic. My thanks to them, and to Maria Wyke, senior lecturer in Classics at Reading University, who read through the manuscript with an academic's eagle eye. The mistakes that remain can only be mine.

AW

Extract from interview with Tony Blair in the *Sunday Telegraph* © Telegraph Group Ltd, London 1996.

Extract from *The Master and Margarita* by Mikhail Bulgakov, © in the English translation by Michael Glenny, The Harvill Press and Harper & Row, Publishers Inc. 1967. Reproduced by permission of The Harvill Press.

Extract from 'Ecce Homo' by David Gascoyne, from *Selected Poems* (Enitharmon Press 1994).

Extract from *Letters* by Eric Gill, ed. W. Sewring, Jonathan Cape.

Extract from *Schindler's Ark* by Thomas Keneally reproduced by permission of Hodder and Stoughton Ltd.

Extract from 'The Fight with the Angel' and 'Nothing to Fear' by Jacques Prévert by permission of Editions Gallimard.

Extract from Leo Tolstoy's 'Letter to George Kennan', Translation © R.F. Christian 1978, by permission of The Athlone Press Ltd.

Select Bibliography

The Bible quotations in this book are taken mostly from the Jerusalem Bible, sometimes from the King James. Quotations in Chapter 5 (the trial) are often Raymond L. Brown's literal translations in *The Death of the Messiah* (Doubleday, New York, 1994).

The translations or modernisations of the mystery plays are mine, with the exception of the Gréban play (cf. under 'Medieval sources').

The place of publication is London unless otherwise stated.

I: PRIMARY SOURCES (ROMAN AND GREEK)

In the bilingual Loeb editions unless otherwise stated:

Catullus	*Poems*, tr. Peter Whigham (Penguin, 1966)
Cicero	*On Duty*, tr. W. Miller
	The Nature of the Gods, tr. H. Rackham
	Against Verres, tr. L.H.G. Greenwood (2 vols.)
	On Friendship and Old Age, tr. W. A. Falconer
	Letters to Quintus, Brutus and others, tr. W. Glynn Williams
	Letters to his Friends, tr. W. Glynn Williams
	The Laws and *The Republic* (containing 'Scipio's Dream', Bks. VI, IV, IX-XXVI), tr. W. Keyes
	On Consular Provinces, tr. R. Gardner
Dio Cassius	*Roman History*, tr. E. Cary (in 9 vols.; vols. VI and VII are the relevant ones)

Euripides	*The Bacchae*, tr. W. Arrowsmith (*Complete Greek Tragedies*, ed. Grene & Lattimore: Euripides V; University of Chicago Press, 1959)
Horace	*Odes*, tr. David Ferry (Farrar, Straus & Giroux, New York, 1997)
	Epodes, tr. C.E. Bennett
	Satires and Epistles, tr. H.R. Fairclough
Julius Obsequens	*Prodigies* (appended to Vol. XIV of the Loeb edition of Livy), tr. A. Schlesinger
Juvenal	*Satires*, tr. Peter Green (Penguin, 1967)
Livy	*History of Rome* (in 14 vols.; see Books IX–XI for the wars against the Samnites), tr. B. Foster
Lucilius	*Fragments* (see E.H. Warmington, *Remains of Old Latin*, III (Heinemann, 1938)
Marcus Aurelius	*Meditations*, tr. J. Collier, rev. A. Zimmern (The Scott Library, undated)
Martial	*Epigrams*, tr. W.C.A. Ker (2 vols.)
Ovid	*The Art of Love*, tr. J.S. Mozley
	Metamorphoses, tr. H.T. Riley
	Tristia and *Letters from Pontus*, tr. A.L. Wheeler
	The Fasti, tr. Sir James Frazer
Petronius	*Satyricon* and *Poems*, tr. M. Heseltine
Plato	*The Republic*, tr. Paul Shore (2 vols.)
	Phaedo, tr. Henry Cary (Everyman edition, London 1938)
	Timaeus, tr. Desmond Lee (Penguin, 1965)
	The Trial and Death of Socrates (*Euthyphron, Apology, Crito*), tr. F.J. Church (London, 1892)
Plautus	*Plays*, tr. Paul Nixon
Pliny the Younger	*Letters*, tr. W. Melmoth, rev. W. Hutchinson (2 vols.)
Pliny the Elder	*Natural History* (in 6 vols., tr. J. Bostock & H.T. Riley, Bohn's Classical Library, 1855–98; in 10 vols., tr. H. Rackham & W.H.S. Jones, Loeb edition)
Propertius	*Elegies*, tr. G.P. Goold (1990)
Seneca	*Moral Letters to Lucilius*, tr. Richard Gummere (Heinemann, 1967)

	Natural Investigations, (tr. J. Clarke, as *Physical Science in the time of Nero*, Macmillan, 1910)
Seneca the Elder	*Suasiorae*, tr. M. Winterbottom
Strabo	*Geography* (Bk. XVI for Judea), tr. H. Jones
Suetonius	*The Twelve Caesars*, tr. Robert Graves, rev. Michael Grant (Penguin, 1979)
Tacitus	*Histories*, tr. C.H. Moore & J. Jackson
	Annals, tr. Michael Grant (Penguin, 1996)
	Germania, tr. M. Hutton
Tibullus	*Poems*, tr. J. B. Postgate
Valerius Maximus	*Memorable Doings and Sayings* (Latin/French edition, *Oeuvres Complètes de Valère Maxime*, tr. P. Charpentier (2 vols., Paris, undated, c. 1870)
Virgil	*Aeneid*, tr. C. Day Lewis (Hogarth Press, 1952); H.T. Fairclough (Loeb edition)
	Eclogues, tr. H.T. Fairclough

PRIMARY SOURCES (JEWISH)

Josephus	*The Jewish War* in *The Works of Flavius Josephus*, tr. W. Whiston, rev. A.R. Shilleto, vols. I–III (1898)
	The Antiquities (*ibid.*)
Philo of Alexandria	*Works*, tr. F. H. Colson (Loeb edition, in 10 vols.; see Vol. X for 'The Embassy to Gaius', Vol. IX for 'Flaccus')
	The Complete Dead Sea Scrolls in English ed. Geza Vermes (Penguin, 1997)

II: EARLY CHRISTIAN TEXTS

Augustine	*Sermons* in *Works*, ed. Marcus Dods (Edinburgh, 1873)
	Treatises on John's Gospel (*ibid.*)
	The Harmony of the Evangelists (tr. J. Innes, Vol. II (Edinburgh, 1874)

Bonaventura (attr.)	*Meditations on the Life of Christ* (tr. H. Frowde, 1908)
Eusebius	*The Ecclesiastical History* (tr. K. Lake, 2 vols., 1926)
	Demonstratio Evangelica (tr. K. Lake, 2 vols., 1926)
Gregory of Tours	*Histoire Ecclésiastique des Francs*, in 10 vols., Vol. I (tr. J. Guadet, Paris, 1836)
Gwatkin, H.M.	*Selections from Early Writers illustrative of Church History in the time of Constantine* (Macmillan, 1911)
Justin Martyr	*First Apology* in Ante-Nicene Christian Library: *Translations of the Writings of the Fathers down to AD 325.* Ed. A. Roberts & J. Donaldson (Edinburgh, 1868) (*ibid.*)
	Second Apology (*ibid.*)
	Dialogue with Trypho (*ibid.*)
Origen	*Against Celsus* (tr. H. Chadwick (Cambridge, 1953)
	Commentaries on Matthew (*ibid.*)
	Commentaries on John (*ibid.*)
Tertullian	*Against Marcion* in Ante-Nicene Christian Library: *Translations of the Writings of the Fathers down to AD 325.* Ed. A. Roberts & J. Donaldson (Edinburgh, 1868) Vol. VII
	Apologeticus (tr. E. Souter, Cambridge, 1917)

'The Hymn of the Robe of Glory', tr. G.R.S. Mead (in *Echoes from the Gnosis*, vol. x, 1908)

III: APOCRYPHAL GOSPELS AND HAGIOGRAPHIES

For the *Acta Pilati*, the *Gospel of Stephen*, Pilate's 'letters', fragments of the Coptic and Greek *Anaphora* and fragments of Anglo-Saxon apocrypha, see
James, M.R. *The Apocryphal New Testament* (Oxford, 1924)
For the *Anaphora of Pilate*, see *Apocrypha Siniatica*, ed. and tr. M.D. Gibson (*Studia Siniatica* 5, 1896)
For the *Gospel of Peter*, see Raymond L. Brown, *The Death of the Messiah*, Appendix 1, Vol. II, pp. 1317–1349 (Anchor Bible Reference Library, 2 vols., New York, 1994)

Bibliography

For the Martyrdom of Pilate, see E. Galtier, *Mémoires et Fragments inédits, Institut Français d'Archéologie du Caire; Mém.t. 27* (Cairo, 1912)
For Pilate's Sentence, see J.P. Lyell, *The Sentence of Pontius Pilate* (1922)
For the 'correspondence' between Pilate and Herod, see W. Wright, *Contributions to the Apocryphal Literature of the New Testament* (1865)
For Pilate's prayer at the tomb, see the *Newbery House Magazine*, vol. VII No. 6 (December 1892), pp. 641–646
For the 'Hymn of the Soul', see the Acts of Thomas in M. R. James, *op. cit.*, pp. 411–415
For Pilate's 'Effigy', see E. Cerulli, 'Tiberius and Pontius Pilate in Ethiopian Tradition and Poetry', *Proceedings of the British Academy*, LIX (1973), pp. 141–158
Budge, Sir Wallis E. *Coptic Apocrypha* (British Museum, 1913)
                     Coptic Martyrdoms (BM 1914)

IV: MEDIEVAL SOURCES, MYSTERY PLAYS AND FOLKLORE

Jabobus de Voraigne *The Golden Legend*, tr. William Granger Ryan (2 vols., Princeton, 1993)
The York Cycle of Mystery Plays: A Complete Version. ed J. S. Purvis (1957)
The Chester Plays, revised from the MSS by Dr Matthews: Part II (Early English Text Society 23, 1916)
The Corpus Christi Play of the English Middle Ages (The Coventry Play) ed. R.T. Davies (1972)
The Wakefield Mystery Plays (The Towneley Cycle), ed. Martial Rose (1961)
The Oberammergau Passion Play, official text by J. Daisenberger (1950)
The True History of the Passion, adapted from the French Medieval Mystery Cycle of Arnoul and Simon Gréban, ed. J. Kirkup (1962)
The Redentin Easter Play, tr. A.E. Zucker (Columbia University Press, New York, 1941)
Le Livre de la Passion; poème narratif du XIVe siècle ed. G. Frank (Paris, 1930)
Mystères inédits du Quinzième Siècle, ed. A. Jubinal (Paris, 1837)
A Stanzaic Life of Christ, ed. F. Foster (Early English Text Society 166, 1926)
Legends of the Holy Rood, ed. R. Morris, (EETS 46, 1871)
The High History of the Holy Grail, tr. J. Evans (1969)

Baring-Gould, S. *Curious Myths of the Middle Ages* (1868)

Du Meril, E. *Carmina Latina: Poésies Populaires Latines du Moyen Age* (Paris, 1847)

The Brothers Grimm *Household Tales*, tr. and ed. F. Hunt (2 vols., 1884)

Hasluck, F.W. *Letters on Religion and Folklore* (1926)

Manitus, M. *Geschichte der Lateinischen Literatur des Mittelalters (3)* (Munich, 1931)

Rappaport, A.S. *Medieval Legends of Christ* (1934)

Records of Early English Drama: Coventry (Manchester University Press, 1981)

V: SECONDARY SOURCES (ROMAN AND JEWISH HISTORY)

Brandon, S.G. F. *Jesus and the Zealots* (Manchester, 1967)

Brent, A. 'Luke-Acts and the Imperial Cult in Asia Minor' (*Journal of Theological Studies*, Vol. 48, 2 (Oct. 1997)

Brunt, P.A. *Roman Imperial Themes* (Oxford 1990)

Ferguson, J. *The Religions of the Roman Empire* (1970)

Foakes Jackson, F.J. *Josephus and the Jews* (1930)

Grant, M. *The Jews in the Roman World* (London 1973)
    History of Rome (1978)

Jones, A.H.M. Procurators and Prefects in the Early Principate, in *Studies in Roman Government and Law* (Oxford, 1960)

Lintoff, A. *Imperium Romanum: Politics and Administration* (1993)

Mommsen, T. *The Provinces of the Roman Empire from Caesar to Diocletian* (Vol. II, ch. XI, Judea and the Jews) (1909)

Parker, H.M.D. *The Roman Legions* (1928)

Perowne, S. *The Later Herods: The Political Background of the New Testament* (1958)

Raaflaub, K., and Toker, M. *Between Republic and Empire: Interpretations of Augustus and his Principate* (Berkeley, 1990)

Rajak, T. *Josephus* (1983)

Salmon, G.E.T. *Samnium and the Samnites* (Cambridge, 1967)

Sanders, E.P. *The Historical Figure of Jesus* (1993)

Seager, R. *Tiberius* (1972)

Sherwin-White, A.N. *Roman Society and Roman Law in the New Testament* (Oxford, 1963)

Silberman, N. A. *The Hidden Scrolls* (1995)

Scarborough, J. *Roman Medicine* (1969)

Smallwood, E. M. The Jews under Roman Rule (*Studies in Judaism in late Antiquity*, XX, 1976)

    'High Priests and Politics in Roman Palestine' (*Journal of Theological Studies*, XIII, 1962)

Smith, G.A. 'The Historical Geography of the Holy Land: IV, Judea' (*Expositor*, Series 4, Vol. v, 1892)

    'Studies in the History and Topography of Jerusalem: III, The Waters': *Ibid*, Series 4, Vol. vii, 1894)

Stevenson, G.H., 'The Administration of the Provinces', in *Cambridge Ancient History*, X, *The Augustan Empire* (Cambridge, 1934)

Suolahti, J. 'The Junior Officers of the Roman Army in the Republican Period', *Annales Academicae Scientiarum Fennicae*, Vol. 97 (Helsinki, 1955)

Thackeray, H.S.J. *Josephus, the Man and the Historian* (New York, 1929)

Webster, G. *The Roman Army* (Chester, 1956)

Wilson, A.N. *Paul: The Mind of the Apostle* (1997)

SECONDARY SOURCES: PILATE'S CAREER

Cox, E. 'A Day in Pilate's Life' (*Expositor*, Series 2, Vol. viii, 1884)

Doyle, A.D. 'Pilate's Career and the Date of the Crucifixion' (*Journal of Theological Studies*, XLII, 1941), pp. 190–193

Gonzales, Echegaray *Pilato, Poncio: Enciclopedia de la Biblia*, V (Barcelona, 1965)

Hedley, P.L. 'Pilate's Arrival in Judea' (*Journal of Theological Studies*, XXXV, 1934), pp. 56–7 (for details of Pilate's coinage)

Hoffman-Kreyer, E. & Staubli, H.-B., *Handworterbuch des Deutschen Aberglaubens* (Berlin/Leipzig, 1935–6) (for Pilate's supposed German origins)

Lemenon, P. *Pilate et le Gouvernement de la Judée: textes et monuments* (Paris, 1980)

Liberty, S. 'The Importance of Pontius Pilate in Creed and Gospel' (*Journal of Theological Studies*, XLV, 1944), pp. 38–56

Maier, P.L. 'Sejanus, Pilate and the Date of the Crucifixion' (*Church History*, XXXVII, 1968), pp. 3–13

Maier, P.L. 'The Fate of Pontius Pilate' (*Hermes*, XCIX, 1971), pp. 362–371

MacGregor, 'Christ's Three Judges: Pilate' (*Expositor*, Series 6, Vol. ii (1900)

Maskell, J. 'Pilate a Saint?' (*Notes & Queries*, 6th series, XI, 1885)

Ollivier, M.J. 'Ponce Pilate et les Pontii' (*Révue Biblique*, V, 1896)

Rosadi, G. *The Trial of Jesus*, tr. and ed. E. Reich (1905) (especially for Pilate's supposed Spanish origins)

Smallwood, E.M. 'The Date of the Dismissal of Pontius Pilate from Judea' (*Journal of Jewish Studies*, V, 1954), pp. 12–21

Spadafora, F. *Pilato* (Rovigo, 1973)

Vardaman, J. 'A new inscription which mentions Pilate as "Prefect"' (*Journal of Biblical Literature*, LXXXI, (Philadelphia 1962), pp. 70–71

Wansbrough, H. 'Suffered under Pontius Pilate' (*Scripture*, XVIII, 1966, pp. 84–93

SECONDARY SOURCES: THE TRIAL OF CHRIST

Andrews, S. *Life of Our Lord* (Edinburgh, 1892)

Bammel, E., ed., *The Trial of Jesus* (1970)

Bammel, E. & Moule, C.F.D. *Jesus and the Politics of his Day* (Cambridge, 1984)

Benoit, P. *The Passion and Resurrection of Jesus Christ* (1969)

Blinzler, J. *Der Prozess Jesu* (Stuttgart, 1951)

Bloomfield, S.T. *Recensio Synoptica Annotationis Sacrae* (Annotations on the New Testament), (1826)

Blunt, H. *Lectures upon the History of Our Lord and Saviour Jesus Christ* (1851)

Brandon, S.G.F. *The Trial of Jesus of Nazareth* (1968)

Brown, R. L. *The Death of the Messiah* (Anchor Bible Reference Library, 2 Vols., Doubleday, New York, 1994)

Catechism of the Catholic Church (Geoffrey Chapman, 1994)

Cook, F.C., ed. *The Holy Bible with Commentary, New Testament*, Vols. I and II (1878)

Craveri, M. *The Life of Jesus* (1967)

Edwards, R.A. *The Gospel According to St John: Its Criticism and Interpretation* (1954)

Edersheim, A. *Life and Times of Jesus the Messiah* (1863)

Eisler, R. *The Messiah Jesus and John the Baptist* (1931)

Ellicott, C.J. *Historical Lectures on the Life of Our Lord Jesus Christ* (1865)

Fairburn, A.M. *Studies in the Life of Christ* (1881)

Farrar, F.W. *Life of Christ* (1894)

Graves, R. and Podro, J. *The Nazarene Gospel Restored* (1953)

Hastings, J., and Clark T. & T., (eds.) *Dictionary of the Bible* (1900)

Hopkins, G.M. *The Sermons and Devotional Writings*, ed. C. Devlin (1959)

Innes, A.T. *The Trial of Jesus Christ: A Legal Monograph* (Edinburgh, 1899)

Keim, T. *The History of Jesus of Nazara*, Vol. VI (1883)

Lange, J.P. *Life of Our Lord Jesus Christ* (Eng. tr. 1864)

Morison, F. *Who Moved the Stone?* (1930)

Murray, J.O.F. *Jesus According to St John* (1936)

Papini, G. *The Life of Christ* (tr. D.C. Fisher, 1923)

Powell, Frank J. *The Trial of Jesus Christ* (1948)

Radin, M. *The Trial of Jesus of Nazareth* (Chicago, 1931)

Renan, E. *The Life of Jesus* (Eng. tr. 1863)

Ross Williamson, H. *AD 33: A Tract for the Times* (1941)

Smith, W. and Cheetham, F. *Dictionary of Christian Antiquities* (1983)

Stalker, J. *The Trial and Death of Jesus Christ* (1894)

Taylor, J. *The Whole Works, in 10 Volumes*: Vol. II, *Life of Christ* (1861)

Wilson, A.N. *Jesus* (1992)

Winter, P. *On the Trial of Jesus* (1961)

SECONDARY SOURCES (MYSTERY PLAYS)

Craig, H. *English Religious Drama* (1955)

Crosse, G. *The Arts of the Church: The Religious Drama* (Mowbray, 1913)

Clarke, S. *The Miracle Play in England: An Account of the Early Religious Drama* (1897)

Tydeman, W.M. *English Medieval Theatre* (1986)

Williams, A. *The Characterisation of Pilate in the Towneley Plays* (Michigan, 1950)

PILATUS AND THE ALPINE LEGENDS

Brockendon, W. *Journals of Excursions on the Alps* (1833)

D'Auvergne, E. *Switzerland in Sunshine and Snow* (1917)

Gribble, F. *The Early Mountaineers* (1899)

Hoffman-Krayer, E. & Staubli, H.-B., *Handworterbuch des Deutschen Aberglaubens* (Berlin/Leipzig, 1935–6)

Laporte, A. *La Suisse le sac à dos* (Paris, 1869)

Schama, S. *Landscape and Memory* (1995)

Weber, P.X. *Der Pilatus und seine Geschichte* (Lucerne, 1913)

Zurich, Comte P. de *Les Voyages en Suisse de Madame de la Briche, 1785–1788* (Neuchâtel, 1935)

PILATE FICTION

Bulgakov, M. *The Master and Margarita*, tr. M. Glenny (1967)

France, A. *Le Procurateur de la Judée* (in *L'Etui de Nacre*, 1892)

Kazantzakis, N. *The Last Temptation of Christ*, tr. P.A. Bien (1960)

Maier, P. *Pontius Pilate* (1968)

Potter, D. *Son of Man* (1970)

Sayers, D.L. *Four Sacred Plays* (1948)

VI: OTHER SOURCES, by chapter

Prologue

'Sinking of the *Captain*': *The Times*, 13/14 September 1870

Barnaby, K.C. *Some Ship Disasters and their Causes* (1968)

1: The Forum and the forest

Murray's Handbook: Spain, Part 1 (1855)

O'Shea's Guide to Spain and Portugal, ed. J. Lomas (1899)

Steegmuller, F. *Cocteau: A Biography* (1970)

Wilde, O. *De Profundis* (1905)

2: Governing Judea

Hyde, H. M. *Lord Reading* (1967)

Judd, D. *Lord Reading* (1982)

Segal, R. *The Crisis of India* (1965)

3: God's secret agent

Bauckham, R. 'Nicodemus and the Gurion Family' (*Journal of Theological Studies*, Vol. 47, Part 1, April 1996)

Frazer, J.G. *Adonis, Attis, Osiris* (1907)

Gavic, A.E. 'Studies in the "Inner life" of Jesus: XVI, The foreshadowings of the Cross' (*Expositor*, Series vii, Vol. ii, 1906)

More, T. *A Treatise upon the Passion* (ed. Haupt, Yale, 1980)

Ramsay, W.M., 'The Divine Child in Virgil' (*Expositor*, Series vii, Vol. iii, 1907)

Redpath, H. 'Christ, the Fulfilment of Prophecy' (*Expositor*, Series vii, Vol. iii, 1907)

Selwyn, E.C. 'The Trial-Narratives based on the Oracles' (*Expositor*, Series 8, Vol. ix, 1915)

Thoreau, H. *The Journal* (1850), in *Writings*, Walden Edition (New York, 1906)

4: Blood on his boots

Dostoevsky, F. *The Brothers Karamazov*, tr. D. Magarshack (1958)

Frazer, J.G. *The Golden Bough: Part 6, The Scapegoat* (1914)

Gandhi, M. *Non-Violence in Peace and War: 43, Theory and Practice of Non-Violence* (Ahmedabad, 1944)

Gill, E. *Social Justice and the Stations of the Cross* (London, 1939)
    The Stations of the Cross: Some Meditations on their Social Aspects (1944)
    Letters, ed. Walter Shewring (1947)

Keneally, T. *Schindler's Ark* (1982) (Extract reproduced by permission of Hodder and Stoughton Ltd.)

Mandeville, J. *Travels*, ed. J. Ashton (1887)

Maude, A. *The Life of Tolstoy: Later Years* (1910)

Nashe, T. *The Unfortunate Traveller* (1594)

Shaw, G. B. *On the Rocks: A Political Comedy* (1933)

Thoreau, H. *On the Duty of Civil Disobedience* (in *Writings*, Walden Edition, *op. cit.*)

Tolstoy, N. *Letters, Vol. II, 1880–1910*, selected, tr. and ed. R.F. Christian (1978)
    Writings on Civil Disobedience and Non-Violence (ed. P. Owen, 1968)

Wilson, A. N. *Tolstoy* (1988)

5: The great equivocator

Bacon, F. *Essays Civil and Moral: Of Truth* (1597), ed. W.A. Wright (1863)

Barratt, A. *Between Two Worlds: The Master and Margarita* (Oxford, 1987)

Brown, C. (ed.) *The New International Dictionary of New Testament Theology* (Vol. 3): Truth (1978)

Liddon, H. *Passiontide Sermons: X, 'The Silence of Jesus'* (1891)

Luther, M. *Table Talk*, tr. W. Hazlitt, DCCLXV (1848)

Mill, J.S. *On Liberty* (1859)

Niemöller, M. *The Gestapo Defied: The last 28 sermons* (1941)

Stephen, J. Fitzjames *Liberty, Equality, Fraternity* (1873)

Whitaker, G.H. '*Aletheia* in the New Testament and in Polybius' (*Expositor*, Series 8, Vol. xx, 1920)

6: Witness to Christ

See generally the section on apocrypha and hagiographies

Nutt, A. *Studies on the Legend of the Holy Grail* (1888)

7: Through brake, through briar

Baedeker, K. *Switzerland and the adjacent portions of Italy, Savoy and Tyrol* (1895)

Bonney, TG. *The Alpine Regions of Switzerland and Neighbouring Countries* (1868)

Baum, J.E. *Savage Abyssinia* (1928)

Bernard, F. *De Lyon à la Méditerranée* (Paris, 1855)

Dufton, H. *A Narrative of a Journey through Abyssinia in 1862–3* (1867)

Farago, L. *Abyssinia on the Eve* (1935)

LeRoy Ladurie, E. *Le siècle des Platter 1499–1628, t. 1, Le mendiant et le professeur* (Paris, 1995)

Stanley, A.P. *Lectures on the Eastern Church* (1861)

Wagner, R. *My Life* (tr. A. Gray, ed. M. Whittall (Cambridge, 1983)

Budge, Sir Wallis E. *The Book of Saints of the Ethiopian Church: A Translation of the Ethiopic Synaxarium* (Cambridge 1928)

For Queen Victoria's trip to Switzerland, see the *Illustrated London News* for 10, 29 August and 12 September, 1868

Index

Index

Index

314, 339; as healer, 120, 134–5, 146–50, 239, 335–6; as magician, 138, 142, 240; near-misses with Pilate, 133, 136–7; teachings as relayed to Nicodemus, 140–5; in the Oxyrhynchus Sayings of Jesus, 191–3; attitude to Pharisees, 146; their attitude to him, 132, 146, 201–2, 212; predictions of his death, 150–5; control of his death, 150–5, 227, 290–2; his death and the scheme of the seasons, 158–9; as overthrower of Roman power, 164–5, 198–9, 302, 318–9; as victim of a crooked lawyer, 169, 171, 206; his innocence, 169, 171, 221, 230, 231, 245, 247, 265, 269, 278, 297, 319; his physical appearance, 171, 218–9, 225, 278–9; as political revolutionary, 175–6, 184–6, 191–3, 197–200; in Dostoevsky's 'Grand Inquisitor', 184–5; refusing to be king, 190, 197; temptation in the desert, 190; entry into Jerusalem, 197–200; arrest of, 118, 200–202; Jewish trial of, 74, 202; Roman trial of, portrayals, 32–5, 164, 171; facing Pilate in, 218–9, 220; refusal to defend himself, 221, 227, 234, 269; his 'conversations' with Pilate, 223–31, 252–7; and Procula's dream, 36–7, 241–2; scourging of, 246–9; mocking of, 249–50; presentation of to the crowd, by Pilate, 250–1; his lecture to Pilate on power, 135, 256; see also Trial Proclaimed by Pilate, 278–9, 280–2; crucifixion of, see Crucifixion; burial of, 5, 288, 294–5; resurrection of, see Resurrection; meetings with Pilate after the resurrection, 314–5, 337,

346; and the Samaritan woman, 324; apocryphal reactions of emperors to, 334–42; apocryphal descriptions by Pilate of, 339–40; imitated by Pilate, 340–3; and the Wandering Jew, 355

Jethro, 157

Jews: prejudice against, and Pilate, x, 41–2, 95, 217, 221, 268–9, 297, 299, 308–9, 314–7; interacting with Pilate, in mystery plays, 42–4, 121–3, 202–4, 221, 281–2, 305–6; in Rome, 55–6; in Judea, 69–78, 92–107, Chapter 2 *passim*, Chapter 5, *passim*, 289; decree of Augustus concerning, 56; Roman attitudes to, 56–7, 74–5, 177–8; attitudes to Romans, 101, 127, 130–9, 165, 177–8, 218; exemptions from duties, 67, 134, 186; expulsion from Rome, 56, 75; as God's chosen people, 56, 65, 76–7, 133, 189; relations with local Roman troops, 58, 75; offences against their religion, 68, 75–6, 85, 102–5, 176–80; religious divisions of, 74, 76; pogrom against in Alexandria, 94, 235; reaction to Pilate's standards, 96–8, 176–80; reaction to Pilate's aqueduct, 98–102; reaction to the golden shields, 102–7; reaction to Jesus, 132, 146, 201–2, 212; readiness to die, 178–80; attitude to crucifixion, 195; and 'blood-guilt', 264–5; apocryphal reactions to the harrowing of hell, 309; witnesses to the resurrection, 313; Pilate's blaming of, 297, 299, 313–4, 338–41; apocryphal imprisonment of Pilate, 336–7; see also Law, Jewish; Messiahs

John the Baptist, 77, 127–8, 130, 145, 151

Index

My name is...

Nicole Nielsen

I got this Bible from...

My MOMMY

The date is...

4.20.03 (easter)

He has made everything beautiful in its time.

My Bible AND ME

My
name: Nicole Nielsen

My best
feature: ?

The people
I live with: mommy, sister, daddy, brother

My favorite
Bible verse: ?

Things
I'm good at: Not a lot

I like to **read the Bible**
when I'm feeling: bored in Bible class

The **Bible character**
most like me:

When I'm an adult
I'd like to: ?

Right now I try to
please God by: being myself

ten

Commandments

One
No other gods (Exodus 20:3)
I put God first in my life.

Two
No idols (Exodus 20:4–6)
No person or thing is more
important to me than God.

Three
Do not take God's name in vain (Exodus 20:7)
"God" isn't an empty word to me. I use his name only in
a loving way, and I count on him to help me every day.

Four
Keep the Sabbath holy (Exodus 20:8–11)
Each week has a special day set aside just for worshiping and praising
God, for reading his Word and for getting together with other believers.

Five
Honor my father and mother
(Exodus 20:12) I show respect
for my parents by listening to
them and trying to please them.

Six
Do not murder (Exodus 20:13)
I know life is precious. I take a
stand against anything that hurts
the life or well-being of others.

Seven
Do not commit adultery (Exodus 20:14)
I show respect for the opposite sex by keeping my thoughts and actions
pure and by remembering that sex is God's gift to married couples.

Eight
Do not steal (Exodus 20:15)
I refuse to take or keep for my own
use what doesn't belong to me:
"borrowed" clothing or money, test
or homework information, whatever.

Nine
Do not give false testimony
(Exodus 20:16) I know a
person's reputation is valuable,
and I refuse to lie or gossip
about anyone.

Ten
Do not covet (Exodus 20:17)
I like others for themselves, not because they have stylish clothes or the right
haircut. I don't think my own value depends on what I have or what I wear.

Love Is...

1 Corinthians 13:4-7

Love is willing to wait instead of demanding, "prove you care, now!"

Love keeps on being friendly to people who aren't friendly back.

Love doesn't hate the girl who goes out with the guy you like.

Love doesn't brag about your good grades or the touchdown you made in Friday night's game.

Love isn't stuck up. Love doesn't think you're better than others because your clothes are more expensive.

Love lets others have their turn talking. It never puts others down by acting like they don't count.

Love doesn't insist on getting all the credit or being one of the popular crowd.

Love doesn't lose its temper when a brother or sister hogs the phone or spends too much time in the bathroom.

Love doesn't hold grudges. It doesn't keep thinking over and over again about how someone hurt you.

Love doesn't think doing wrong is cool.

Love looks out for the interests of others.

Love keeps on trusting God even when the right choices you make don't turn out the way you want.

Love keeps on expecting the best.

Love doesn't give up just because something goes wrong or because your feelings are hurt. God is in charge, so those who love just keep right on loving.

NEW INTERNATIONAL VERSION

FEATURES WRITTEN BY:
Larry and Sue Richards

teen
study

Bible

ZONDERVAN™

GRAND RAPIDS, MICHIGAN 49530

The Holy Bible, New International Version
Copyright © 1973, 1978, 1984 by International Bible Society

ZONDERVAN™

The Teen Study Bible, New International Version
Copyright 1993, 1998 by Zondervan

All rights reserved

Published by Zondervan
Grand Rapids, Michigan 49530, U.S.A.

www.zondervan.com

Library of Congress Catalog Card Number 93-60507

---

02 03 04 / DC / 15 14 13 12 11

NEW INTERNATIONAL VERSION

teen
study

Bible

~Nicole Nielsen

WHAT is it?

YOU'RE A TEENAGER, RIGHT?

Do you ever wonder what, if anything, the Bible has to say to you? Sure, its teachings are great for your parents, and all the little kids you know love the stories.

But what about you? Does the Bible have anything to say to you?

It does.

And *The Teen Study Bible* tells you just what it has to say and where it says it. Lots of features, some very serious and some not-so serious, guide you not just *through* God's Word but *into* it.

Introduction to the book of Genesis

INTRODUCTION   At the beginning of each of the Bible's 66 books, you'll find a page of information telling you just what that book has to say to you, teenager heading toward the 21st century.

THE BIBLE SAYS   Does the Bible say anything about the problems and issues you face every day? It says plenty. "The Bible Says" shows you where and explains a passage of Scripture in the process.

The Bible Says

DIRECT LINE   You've probably already faced lots of hard situations in your life. And you've probably wondered at times, "What do I do??!" "Direct Line" covers almost every problem and situation you can think of. It does it directly and honestly, telling you what God has to say.

DEAR SAM   Are you looking for advice? Sam willingly gives it. The questions you ask most often are answered in this advice column. The answers are based on a Biblical character or situation. The characters of the Bible lived thousands of years ago. The teachings were written down thousands of years ago. But guess what! They are still relevant for today. And "Dear Sam" shows you how.

Direct Line

not for Jason

Sex

Sex (seks) n.
1: male or female; 2: the sexual urge or instinct, or sexual desire as it shows itself in behavior.

ALTERNATE DEFINITION
a three-letter word with some really l-o-n-g-range consequences

"So God created... male and female... God blessed them and said to them, 'Be fruitful.'"
GENESIS 1:27-28

God invented sex. He designed the hormones that trigger your desires. He designed every nerve ending that magnifies pleasure. Sex isn't wrong. Sex is good, a gift from a God who loves you.

Physical hunger can easily be satisfied by eating some food. However, the sex drive isn't like hunger, and intercourse isn't a ham sandwich. Sex isn't just physical—it's spiritual too.

Is all sex considered a sin? Why should you wait? Can you do everything but? What's so bad about it if you love the person and have protection? Does the Bible say anything to teens about sex?

"'This is now bone of my bones, and flesh of my flesh;'...For this reason a man will leave his father and mother and be united to his wife, and they will become one flesh."
GENESIS 2:23-24

God's design for sex is very specific: one man with one woman within the legal bonds of marriage. How special do you want sex to be with the person you marry? How much do you want to be "one" with him or her—instead of five or eighteen or thirty-three? It's easy to say, "I love you." But only "I do" says you're really one, for always.

Mon-ey (mun–ee) n.

the official currency, as coins and
paper notes issued by a government.

Money

ALTERNATE DEFINITION

what you never have enough of
when you go to the mall.

Do you always feel like you don't have
enough money? Is that because you need
more money? Or is it because the world you
live in is always pressuring you to get more,
more, more? How much are you affected by
what your friends have? How much are you
affected by what the media says you need?

*Money is important.
Sixteen of Jesus' forty
parables mention
money. Jesus told one
parable to illustrate the
truth that "a man's life
does not consist in the
abundance of his
possessions." You can
read the story in ...*

LUKE 12:13-21

How much money do
you spend each week?
How much do you
earn? How much is
your allowance? How
much money do you
think you need? How
much does your mom
or dad think you
need? Any chance of
negotiating for more?
If you got more, how
would you spend it?

Picture this situation:
You have to evacuate your
home for some reason and
you have, say, fifteen minutes
to gather up the things you want
to take with you (knowing that
everything else you own will
probably be destroyed). Beyond the
necessities what do you pack? Pictures? Books? Tapes? Money (if
you have any)? Jewelry? Now look at how much you're leaving
behind. How important is it? Really?

What does that little scene tell you about the
importance of all the things you own? You decide.

ing the forty years that I led you through the desert, your clothes did not wear out, nor did the sandals on your feet. ⁶You ate no bread and drank no wine or other fermented drink. I did this so that you might know that I am the LORD your God.

⁷When you reached this place, Sihon king of Heshbon and Og king of Bashan came out to fight against us, but we defeated them. ⁸We took their land and gave it as an inheritance to the Reubenites, the Gadites and the half-tribe of Manasseh.

⁹Carefully follow the terms of this covenant, so that you may prosper in everything you do. ¹⁰All of you are standing today in the presence of the LORD your God—your leaders and chief men, your elders and officials, and all the other men of Israel, ¹¹together with your children and your wives, and the aliens living in your camps who chop your wood and carry your water. ¹²You are standing here in order to enter into a covenant with the LORD your God, a covenant the LORD is making with you this day and sealing with an oath, ¹³to confirm you this day as his people, that he may be your God as he promised you and as he swore to your fathers, Abraham, Isaac and Jacob. ¹⁴I am making this covenant, with its oath, not only with you ¹⁵who are standing here with us today in the presence of the LORD our God but also with those who are not here today.

¹⁶You yourselves know how we lived in Egypt and how we passed through the countries on the way here. ¹⁷You saw among them their detestable images and idols of wood and stone, of silver and gold. ¹⁸Make sure there is no man or woman, clan or tribe among you today whose heart turns away from the LORD our God to go and worship the gods of those nations; make sure there is no root among you that produces such bitter poison.

¹⁹When such a person hears the words of this oath, he invokes a blessing on himself and therefore thinks, "I will be safe, even though I persist in going my own way." This will bring disaster on the watered land as well as the dry.ᵃ ²⁰The LORD will never be willing to forgive him; his wrath and zeal will burn against that man. All the curses written in this book will fall upon him, and the LORD will blot out his name from under heaven. ²¹The LORD will single him out from all the tribes of Israel for disaster, according to all the curses of the covenant written in this Book of the Law.

²²Your children who follow you in later generations and foreigners who come from distant lands will see the calamities that have fallen on the land and the diseases with which the LORD has afflicted it. ²³The whole land will be a burning waste of salt and sulfur—nothing planted, nothing sprouting, no vegetation growing on it. It will be like the destruction of Sodom and Gomorrah, Admah and Zeboiim, which the LORD overthrew in fierce anger. ²⁴All the nations will ask: "Why has the LORD done this to this land? Why this fierce, burning anger?"

²⁵And the answer will be: "It is because this people abandoned the covenant of the LORD, the God of their fathers, the covenant he made with them when he brought them out of Egypt. ²⁶They went

ᵃ19 Or way, in order to add drunkenness to thirst."

DEUTERONOMY 29:19–21

You check out one test answer in the book and get caught. Jimmy cheats regularly, and nobody catches him! Life sure isn't fair. To Jimmy. Actually, the worst thing that can happen to a person is to get away with doing wrong. Jimmy smirks when you get hauled up in front of class. He thinks he'll never get caught. The longer people get away with doing wrong, the more they think they'll never get caught. Eventually they do something serious and come face to face with disaster. If you're caught and punished when you step out of line, don't complain. God is being more than fair to you. It's Jimmy, not you, who's in trouble!

Direct Line

off and worshiped other gods and bowed down to them, gods they did not know, gods he had not given them. ²⁷Therefore the L<small>ORD</small>'s anger burned against this land, so that he brought on it all the curses written in this book. ²⁸In furious anger and in great wrath the L<small>ORD</small> uprooted them from their land and thrust them into another land, as it is now."

²⁹The secret things belong to the L<small>ORD</small> our God, but the things revealed belong to us and to our children forever, that we may follow all the words of this law.

Prosperity After Turning to the L<small>ORD</small>   When all these blessings and curses I have set before you come upon you and you take them to heart wherever the L<small>ORD</small> your God disperses you among the nations, ²and when you and your children return to the L<small>ORD</small> your God and obey him with all your heart and with all your soul according to everything I command you today, ³then the L<small>ORD</small> your God will restore your fortunes[a] and have compassion on you and gather you again from all the nations where he scattered you. ⁴Even if you have been banished to the most distant land under the heavens, from there the L<small>ORD</small> your God will gather you and bring you back. ⁵He will bring you to the land that belonged to your fathers, and you will take possession of it. He will make you more prosperous and numerous than your fathers. ⁶The L<small>ORD</small> your God will circumcise your hearts and the hearts of your descendants, so that you may love him with all your heart and with all your soul, and live. ⁷The L<small>ORD</small> your God will put all these curses on your enemies who hate and persecute you. ⁸You will again obey the L<small>ORD</small> and follow all his commands I am giving you today. ⁹Then the L<small>ORD</small> your God will make you most prosperous in all the work of your hands and in the fruit of your womb, the young of your livestock and the crops of your land. The L<small>ORD</small> will again delight in you and make you prosperous, just as he delighted in your fathers, ¹⁰if you obey the L<small>ORD</small> your God and keep his commands and decrees that are written in this Book of the Law and turn to the L<small>ORD</small> your God with all your heart and with all your soul.

The Offer of Life or Death   ¹¹Now what I am commanding you today is not too difficult for you or beyond your reach. ¹²It is not up in heaven, so that you have to ask, "Who will ascend into heaven to get it and proclaim it to us so we may obey it?" ¹³Nor is it beyond the sea, so that you have to ask, "Who will cross the sea to get it and proclaim it to us so we may obey it?" ¹⁴No, the word is very near you; it is in your mouth and in your heart so you may obey it.

¹⁵See, I set before you today life and prosperity, death and destruction. ¹⁶For I command you today to love the L<small>ORD</small> your God, to walk in his ways, and to keep his commands, decrees and laws; then you will live and increase, and the L<small>ORD</small> your God will bless you in the land you are entering to possess.

¹⁷But if your heart turns away and you are not obedient, and if you are drawn away to bow down to other gods and worship them, ¹⁸I declare to you this day that you will certainly be destroyed. You will not live long in the land you are crossing the Jordan to enter and possess.

¹⁹This day I call heaven and earth as witnesses against you that I have set before you life and death, blessings and curses. Now choose life, so that you and your children may live ²⁰and that you may love the L<small>ORD</small> your God, listen to his voice, and hold fast to him. For the L<small>ORD</small> is your life, and he will give you many years in the land he swore to give to your fathers, Abraham, Isaac and Jacob.

Joshua to Succeed Moses   Then Moses went out and spoke these words to all Israel: ²"I am now a hundred and twenty years old and I am no longer able to lead you. The L<small>ORD</small> has said to me, 'You shall not cross

---

a3 Or *will bring you back from captivity*

the Jordan.' ³The Lord your God himself will cross over ahead of you. He will destroy these nations before you, and you will take possession of their land. Joshua also will cross over ahead of you, as the Lord said. ⁴And the Lord will do to them what he did to Sihon and Og, the kings of the Amorites, whom he destroyed along with their land. ⁵The Lord will deliver them to you, and you must do to them all that I have commanded you. ⁶Be strong and courageous. Do not be afraid or terrified because of them, for the Lord your God goes with you; he will never leave you nor forsake you."

⁷Then Moses summoned Joshua and said to him in the presence of all Israel, "Be strong and courageous, for you must go with this people into the land that the Lord swore to their forefathers to give them, and you must divide it among them as their inheritance. ⁸The Lord himself goes before you and will be with you; he will never leave you nor forsake you. Do not be afraid; do not be discouraged."

The Reading of the Law ⁹So Moses wrote down this law and gave it to the priests, the sons of Levi, who carried the ark of the covenant of the Lord, and to all the elders of Israel. ¹⁰Then Moses commanded them: "At the end of every seven years, in the year for canceling debts, during the Feast of Tabernacles, ¹¹when all Israel comes to appear before the Lord your God at the place he will choose, you shall read this law before them in their hearing. ¹²Assemble the people—men, women and children, and the aliens living in your towns—so they can listen and learn to fear the Lord your God and follow carefully all the words of this law. ¹³Their children, who do not know this law, must hear it and learn to fear the Lord your God as long as you live in the land you are crossing the Jordan to possess."

Israel's Rebellion Predicted ¹⁴The Lord said to Moses, "Now the day of your death is near. Call Joshua and present yourselves at the Tent of Meeting, where I will commission him." So Moses and Joshua came and presented themselves at the Tent of Meeting.

¹⁵Then the Lord appeared at the Tent in a pillar of cloud, and the cloud stood over the entrance to the Tent. ¹⁶And the Lord said to Moses: "You are going to rest with your fathers, and these people will soon prostitute themselves to the foreign gods of the land they are entering. They will forsake me and break the covenant I made with them. ¹⁷On that day I will become angry

The Bible Says

Fear God

The Bible doesn't say, "Be scared of God." To "fear the Lord" (Deuteronomy 31:12) means something very different. And very important.

"Fear sharks" means that you don't go splashing around in the ocean when sharks are near. "Fear fire" means that you remember what fire can do and don't toss lighted matches around your bedroom. In each of these cases "fear" means "to have respect for"—to give sharks or fire serious consideration.

That's what the Bible means when it says to fear God. You give God serious consideration in your life. You have a growing respect for him. Some people don't fear God at all. They ignore him, as if he didn't exist. But you're wiser than that. You're not scared of God, because you know he loves you. But you do fear him, because you know he deserves all your respect.

with them and forsake them; I will hide my face from them, and they will be destroyed. Many disasters and difficulties will come upon them, and on that day they will ask, 'Have not these disasters come upon us because our God is not with us?' ¹⁸And I will certainly hide my face on that day because of all their wickedness in turning to other gods.

¹⁹"Now write down for yourselves this song and teach it to the Israelites and have them sing it, so that it may be a witness for me against them. ²⁰When I have brought them into the land flowing with milk and honey, the land I promised on oath to their forefathers, and when they eat their fill and thrive, they will turn to other gods and worship them, rejecting me and breaking my covenant. ²¹And when many disasters and difficulties come upon them, this song will testify against them, because it will not be forgotten by their descendants. I know what they are disposed to do, even before I bring them into the land I promised them on oath." ²²So Moses wrote down this song that day and taught it to the Israelites.

²³The LORD gave this command to Joshua son of Nun: "Be strong and courageous, for you will bring the Israelites into the land I promised them on oath, and I myself will be with you."

²⁴After Moses finished writing in a book the words of this law from beginning to end, ²⁵he gave this command to the Levites who carried the ark of the covenant of the LORD: ²⁶"Take this Book of the Law and place it beside the ark of the covenant of the LORD your God. There it will remain as a witness against you. ²⁷For I know how rebellious and stiff-necked you are. If you have been rebellious against the LORD while I am still alive and with you, how much more will you rebel after I die! ²⁸Assemble before me all the elders of your tribes and all your officials, so that I can speak these words in their hearing and call heaven and earth to testify against them. ²⁹For I know that after my death you are sure to become utterly corrupt and to turn from the way I have commanded you. In days to come, disaster will fall upon you because you will do evil in the sight of the LORD and provoke him to anger by what your hands have made."

The Song of Moses   ³⁰And Moses recited the words of this song from beginning to end in the hearing of the whole assembly of Israel:

32

Listen, O heavens, and I will speak;
　　hear, O earth, the words of my mouth.
²Let my teaching fall like rain
　　and my words descend like dew,
　like showers on new grass,
　　like abundant rain on tender plants.

³I will proclaim the name of the LORD.
　　Oh, praise the greatness of our God!
⁴He is the Rock, his works are perfect,
　　and all his ways are just.
　A faithful God who does no wrong,
　　upright and just is he.

⁵They have acted corruptly toward him;
　　to their shame they are no longer his children,
　　but a warped and crooked generation.ᵃ
⁶Is this the way you repay the LORD,
　　O foolish and unwise people?
　Is he not your Father, your Creator,ᵇ
　　who made you and formed you?

ᵃ5 Or *Corrupt are they and not his children, / a generation warped and twisted to their shame*   ᵇ6 Or *Father, who bought you*

⁷Remember the days of old;
    consider the generations long past.
Ask your father and he will tell you,
    your elders, and they will explain to you.
⁸When the Most High gave the nations their inheritance,
    when he divided all mankind,
he set up boundaries for the peoples
    according to the number of the sons of Israel.ᵃ
⁹For the Lᴏʀᴅ's portion is his people,
    Jacob his allotted inheritance.

¹⁰In a desert land he found him,
    in a barren and howling waste.
He shielded him and cared for him;
    he guarded him as the apple of his eye,
¹¹like an eagle that stirs up its nest
    and hovers over its young,
that spreads its wings to catch them
    and carries them on its pinions.
¹²The Lᴏʀᴅ alone led him;
    no foreign god was with him.

¹³He made him ride on the heights of the land
    and fed him with the fruit of the fields.
He nourished him with honey from the rock,
    and with oil from the flinty crag,
¹⁴with curds and milk from herd and flock
    and with fattened lambs and goats,
with choice rams of Bashan
    and the finest kernels of wheat.
You drank the foaming blood of the grape.

¹⁵Jeshurunᵇ grew fat and kicked;
    filled with food, he became heavy and sleek.
He abandoned the God who made him
    and rejected the Rock his Savior.
¹⁶They made him jealous with their foreign gods
    and angered him with their detestable idols.
¹⁷They sacrificed to demons, which are not God—
    gods they had not known,
    gods that recently appeared,
    gods your fathers did not fear.
¹⁸You deserted the Rock, who fathered you;
    you forgot the God who gave you birth.

¹⁹The Lᴏʀᴅ saw this and rejected them
    because he was angered by his sons and daughters.
²⁰"I will hide my face from them," he said,
    "and see what their end will be;
for they are a perverse generation,
    children who are unfaithful.
²¹They made me jealous by what is no god
    and angered me with their worthless idols.
I will make them envious by those who are not a people;
    I will make them angry by a nation that has no understanding.
²²For a fire has been kindled by my wrath,
    one that burns to the realm of deathᶜ below.

ᵃ8 Masoretic Text; Dead Sea Scrolls (see also Septuagint) *sons of God* ᵇ15 *Jeshurun* means *the upright one,*
that is, Israel. ᶜ22 Hebrew *to Sheol*

It will devour the earth and its harvests
and set afire the foundations of the mountains.

23 "I will heap calamities upon them
and spend my arrows against them.
24 I will send wasting famine against them,
consuming pestilence and deadly plague;
I will send against them the fangs of wild beasts,
the venom of vipers that glide in the dust.
25 In the street the sword will make them childless;
in their homes terror will reign.
Young men and young women will perish,
infants and gray-haired men.
26 I said I would scatter them
and blot out their memory from mankind,
27 but I dreaded the taunt of the enemy,
lest the adversary misunderstand
and say, 'Our hand has triumphed;
the LORD has not done all this.' "

28 They are a nation without sense,
there is no discernment in them.
29 If only they were wise and would understand this
and discern what their end will be!
30 How could one man chase a thousand,
or two put ten thousand to flight,
unless their Rock had sold them,
unless the LORD had given them up?
31 For their rock is not like our Rock,
as even our enemies concede.
32 Their vine comes from the vine of Sodom
and from the fields of Gomorrah.
Their grapes are filled with poison,
and their clusters with bitterness.
33 Their wine is the venom of serpents,
the deadly poison of cobras.

34 "Have I not kept this in reserve
and sealed it in my vaults?
35 It is mine to avenge; I will repay.
In due time their foot will slip;
their day of disaster is near
and their doom rushes upon them."

36 The LORD will judge his people
and have compassion on his servants
when he sees their strength is gone
and no one is left, slave or free.
37 He will say: "Now where are their gods,
the rock they took refuge in,
38 the gods who ate the fat of their sacrifices
and drank the wine of their drink offerings?
Let them rise up to help you!
Let them give you shelter!

39 "See now that I myself am He!
There is no god besides me.
I put to death and I bring to life,
I have wounded and I will heal,
and no one can deliver out of my hand.

⁴⁰I lift my hand to heaven and declare:
As surely as I live forever,
⁴¹when I sharpen my flashing sword
and my hand grasps it in judgment,
I will take vengeance on my adversaries
and repay those who hate me.
⁴²I will make my arrows drunk with blood,
while my sword devours flesh:
the blood of the slain and the captives,
the heads of the enemy leaders."

⁴³Rejoice, O nations, with his people,*ᵃ,ᵇ*
for he will avenge the blood of his servants;
he will take vengeance on his enemies
and make atonement for his land and people.

⁴⁴Moses came with Joshua*ᶜ* son of Nun and spoke all the words of this song in the hearing of the people. ⁴⁵When Moses finished reciting all these words to all Israel, ⁴⁶he said to them, "Take to heart all the words I have solemnly declared to you this day, so that you may command your children to obey carefully all the words of this law. ⁴⁷They are not just idle words for you— they are your life. By them you will live long in the land you are crossing the Jordan to possess."

Moses to Die on Mount Nebo   ⁴⁸On that same day the Lᴏʀᴅ told Moses, ⁴⁹"Go up into the Abarim Range to Mount Nebo in Moab, across from Jericho, and view Canaan, the land I am giving the Israelites as their own possession. ⁵⁰There on the mountain that you have climbed you will die and be gathered to your people, just as your brother Aaron died on Mount Hor and was gathered to his people. ⁵¹This is because both of you broke faith with me in the presence of the Israelites at the waters of Meribah Kadesh in the Desert of Zin and because you did not uphold my holiness among the Israelites. ⁵²Therefore, you will see the land only from a distance; you will not enter the land I am giving to the people of Israel."

33

Moses Blesses the Tribes   This is the blessing that Moses the man of God pronounced on the Israelites before his death. ²He said:

"The Lᴏʀᴅ came from Sinai
and dawned over them from Seir;
he shone forth from Mount Paran.
He came with*ᵈ* myriads of holy ones
from the south, from his mountain slopes.*ᵉ*
³Surely it is you who love the people;
all the holy ones are in your hand.
At your feet they all bow down,
and from you receive instruction,
⁴the law that Moses gave us,
the possession of the assembly of Jacob.
⁵He was king over Jeshurun*ᶠ*
when the leaders of the people assembled,
along with the tribes of Israel.

⁶"Let Reuben live and not die,
nor*ᵍ* his men be few."

ᵃ43 Or Make his people rejoice, O nations   ᵇ43 Masoretic Text; Dead Sea Scrolls (see also Septuagint) people, / and let all the angels worship him /   ᶜ44 Hebrew Hoshea, a variant of Joshua   ᵈ2 Or from   ᵉ2 The meaning of the Hebrew for this phrase is uncertain.   ᶠ5 Jeshurun means the upright one, that is, Israel; also in verse 26.   ᵍ6 Or but let

⁷And this he said about Judah:

> "Hear, O Lᴏʀᴅ, the cry of Judah;
>> bring him to his people.
> With his own hands he defends his cause.
>> Oh, be his help against his foes!"

⁸About Levi he said:

> "Your Thummim and Urim belong
>> to the man you favored.
> You tested him at Massah;
>> you contended with him at the waters of Meribah.
> ⁹He said of his father and mother,
>> 'I have no regard for them.'
> He did not recognize his brothers
>> or acknowledge his own children,
> but he watched over your word
>> and guarded your covenant.
> ¹⁰He teaches your precepts to Jacob
>> and your law to Israel.
> He offers incense before you
>> and whole burnt offerings on your altar.
> ¹¹Bless all his skills, O Lᴏʀᴅ,
>> and be pleased with the work of his hands.
> Smite the loins of those who rise up against him;
>> strike his foes till they rise no more."

¹²About Benjamin he said:

> "Let the beloved of the Lᴏʀᴅ rest secure in him,
>> for he shields him all day long,
>> and the one the Lᴏʀᴅ loves rests between his shoulders."

¹³About Joseph he said:

> "May the Lᴏʀᴅ bless his land
>> with the precious dew from heaven above
>> and with the deep waters that lie below;
> ¹⁴with the best the sun brings forth
>> and the finest the moon can yield;
> ¹⁵with the choicest gifts of the ancient mountains
>> and the fruitfulness of the everlasting hills;
> ¹⁶with the best gifts of the earth and its fullness
>> and the favor of him who dwelt in the burning bush.
> Let all these rest on the head of Joseph,
>> on the brow of the prince among*ᵃ* his brothers.
> ¹⁷In majesty he is like a firstborn bull;
>> his horns are the horns of a wild ox.
> With them he will gore the nations,
>> even those at the ends of the earth.
> Such are the ten thousands of Ephraim;
>> such are the thousands of Manasseh."

¹⁸About Zebulun he said:

> "Rejoice, Zebulun, in your going out,
>> and you, Issachar, in your tents.
> ¹⁹They will summon peoples to the mountain
>> and there offer sacrifices of righteousness;

ᵃ16 Or of the one separated from

> they will feast on the abundance of the seas,
>   on the treasures hidden in the sand."

²⁰About Gad he said:

> "Blessed is he who enlarges Gad's domain!
>   Gad lives there like a lion,
>   tearing at arm or head.
> ²¹He chose the best land for himself;
>   the leader's portion was kept for him.
> When the heads of the people assembled,
>   he carried out the LORD's righteous will,
>   and his judgments concerning Israel."

²²About Dan he said:

> "Dan is a lion's cub,
>   springing out of Bashan."

²³About Naphtali he said:

> "Naphtali is abounding with the favor of the LORD
>   and is full of his blessing;
>   he will inherit southward to the lake."

²⁴About Asher he said:

> "Most blessed of sons is Asher;
>   let him be favored by his brothers,
>   and let him bathe his feet in oil.
> ²⁵The bolts of your gates will be iron and bronze,
>   and your strength will equal your days.
>
> ²⁶"There is no one like the God of Jeshurun,
>   who rides on the heavens to help you
>   and on the clouds in his majesty.
> ²⁷The eternal God is your refuge,
>   and underneath are the everlasting arms.
> He will drive out your enemy before you,
>   saying, 'Destroy him!'
> ²⁸So Israel will live in safety alone;
>   Jacob's spring is secure
> in a land of grain and new wine,
>   where the heavens drop dew.
> ²⁹Blessed are you, O Israel!
>   Who is like you,
>   a people saved by the LORD?
> He is your shield and helper
>   and your glorious sword.
> Your enemies will cower before you,
>   and you will trample down their high places.ᵃ"

34

The Death of Moses Then Moses climbed Mount Nebo from the plains of Moab to the top of Pisgah, across from Jericho. There the LORD showed him the whole land—from Gilead to Dan, ²all of Naphtali, the territory of Ephraim and Manasseh, all the land of Judah as far as the western sea,ᵇ ³the Negev and the whole region from the Valley of Jericho, the City of Palms, as far as Zoar. ⁴Then the LORD said to him, "This is the land I

ᵃ29 Or *will tread upon their bodies*   ᵇ2 That is, the Mediterranean

promised on oath to Abraham, Isaac and Jacob when I said, 'I will give it to your descendants.' I have let you see it with your eyes, but you will not cross over into it."

⁵And Moses the servant of the LORD died there in Moab, as the LORD had said. ⁶He buried him*a* in Moab, in the valley opposite Beth Peor, but to this day no one knows where his grave is. ⁷Moses was a hundred and twenty years old when he died, yet his eyes were not weak nor his strength gone. ⁸The Israelites grieved for Moses in the plains of Moab thirty days, until the time of weeping and mourning was over.

⁹Now Joshua son of Nun was filled with the spirit*b* of wisdom because Moses had laid his hands on him. So the Israelites listened to him and did what the LORD had commanded Moses.

¹⁰Since then, no prophet has risen in Israel like Moses, whom the LORD knew face to face, ¹¹who did all those miraculous signs and wonders the LORD sent him to do in Egypt—to Pharaoh and to all his officials and to his whole land. ¹²For no one has ever shown the mighty power or performed the awesome deeds that Moses did in the sight of all Israel.

*a*6 Or *He was buried* *b*9 Or *Spirit*

to the

book of **Joshua**

THE WINNER!

What does it take to win? In sports it takes dedication, practice and hard work. Spiritual victories take dedication too. And something else: obedience. You can enjoy spiritual victories if you keep looking to God for guidance and then live by his Word.

Joshua is a book about victory and defeat. Moses, who led the Israelites out of slavery, has died. Now under a new leader, God's people must invade a heavily populated land. At Jericho and Ai, Israel learns the importance of obedience. It takes ten years, but finally Canaan is subdued and the promised land is divided among Israel's 12 tribes.

FAST FACTS

Joshua means "the Lord saves."

Jericho's walls tumbled down about 1390 B.C.

Only two Israelites who had been slaves in Egypt lived to see Canaan conquered: Joshua and Caleb.

Joshua 1:7 is this book's key verse.

Fundamentals

What good advice given to Joshua applies to you too (Joshua 1:9)?

Are you the only person who'll get hurt if you sin (Joshua 7)?

Should a person who kills someone else accidentally be executed (Joshua 20)?

Here's an important decision each person has to make (Joshua 24:15).

1 *The Lord Commands Joshua* After the death of Moses the servant of the Lord, the Lord said to Joshua son of Nun, Moses' aide: ²"Moses my servant is dead. Now then, you and all these people, get ready to cross the Jordan River into the land I am about to give to them—to the Israelites. ³I will give you every place where you set your foot, as I promised Moses. ⁴Your territory will extend from the desert to Lebanon, and from the great river, the Euphrates—all the Hittite country—to the Great Sea*a* on the west. ⁵No one will be able to stand up against you all the days of your life. As I was with Moses, so I will be with you; I will never leave you nor forsake you.

⁶"Be strong and courageous, because you will lead these people to inherit the land I swore to their forefathers to give them. ⁷Be strong and very courageous. Be careful to obey all the law my servant Moses gave you; do not turn from it to the right or to the left, that you may be successful wherever you go. ⁸Do not let this Book of the Law depart from your mouth; meditate on it day and night, so that you may be careful to do everything written in it. Then you will be prosperous and successful. ⁹Have I not commanded you? Be strong and courageous. Do not be terrified; do not be discouraged, for the Lord your God will be with you wherever you go."

> Be strong and very courageous . . . that you may be successful wherever you go (Joshua 1:7).

¹⁰So Joshua ordered the officers of the people: ¹¹"Go through the camp and tell the people, 'Get your supplies ready. Three days from now you will cross the Jordan here to go in and take possession of the land the Lord your God is giving you for your own.' "

¹²But to the Reubenites, the Gadites and the half-tribe of Manasseh, Joshua said, ¹³"Remember the command that Moses the servant of the Lord gave you: 'The Lord your God is giving you rest and has granted you this land.' ¹⁴Your wives, your children and your livestock may stay in the land that Moses gave you east of the Jordan, but all your fighting men, fully armed, must cross over ahead of your brothers. You are to help your brothers ¹⁵until the Lord gives them rest, as he has done for you, and until they too have taken possession of the land that the Lord your God is giving them. After that, you may go back and occupy your own land, which Moses the servant of the Lord gave you east of the Jordan toward the sunrise."

¹⁶Then they answered Joshua, "Whatever you have commanded us we will do, and wherever you send us we will go. ¹⁷Just as we fully obeyed Moses, so we will obey you. Only may the Lord your God be with you as he was with Moses. ¹⁸Whoever rebels against your word and does not obey your words, whatever you may command them, will be put to death. Only be strong and courageous!"

2 *Rahab and the Spies* Then Joshua son of Nun secretly sent two spies from Shittim. "Go, look over the land," he said, "especially Jericho." So they went and entered the house of a prostitute*b* named Rahab and stayed there.

²The king of Jericho was told, "Look! Some of the Israelites have come here tonight to spy out the land." ³So the king of Jericho sent this message to Rahab: "Bring out the men who came to you and entered your house, because they have come to spy out the whole land."

⁴But the woman had taken the two men and hidden them. She said, "Yes, the men came to me, but I did not know where they had come from. ⁵At dusk, when it was time to close the city gate, the men left. I don't know which way they went. Go after them quickly. You may catch up with them." ⁶(But she had taken them up to the roof and hidden them under the stalks of flax she had laid out on the roof.) ⁷So the men set out in pursuit of the

a4 That is, the Mediterranean   *b1* Or possibly *an innkeeper* spies on the road that leads to the fords of the Jordan, and as soon as the pursuers had gone out, the gate was shut.

⁸Before the spies lay down for the night, she went up on the roof ⁹and said to them, "I know that the Lᴏʀᴅ has given this land to you and that a great fear of you has fallen on us, so that all who live in this country are melting in fear because of you. ¹⁰We have heard how the Lᴏʀᴅ dried up the water of the Red Seaᵃ for you when you came out of Egypt, and what you did to Sihon and Og, the two kings of the Amorites east of the Jordan, whom you completely destroyed.ᵇ ¹¹When we heard of it, our hearts melted and everyone's courage failed because of you, for the Lᴏʀᴅ your God is God in heaven above and on the earth below. ¹²Now then, please swear to me by the Lᴏʀᴅ that you will show kindness to my family, because I have shown kindness to you. Give me a sure sign ¹³that you will spare the lives of my father and mother, my brothers and sisters, and all who belong to them, and that you will save us from death."

¹⁴"Our lives for your lives!" the men assured her. "If you don't tell what we are doing, we will treat you kindly and faithfully when the Lᴏʀᴅ gives us the land."

¹⁵So she let them down by a rope through the window, for the house she lived in was part of the city wall. ¹⁶Now she had said to them, "Go to the hills so the pursuers will not find you. Hide yourselves there three days until they return, and then go on your way."

¹⁷The men said to her, "This oath you made us swear will not be binding on us ¹⁸unless, when we enter the land, you have tied this scarlet cord in the window through which you let us down, and unless you have brought your father and mother, your brothers and all your family into your house. ¹⁹If anyone goes outside your house into the street, his blood will be on his own head; we will not be responsible. As for anyone who is in the house with you, his blood will be on our head if a hand is laid on him. ²⁰But if you tell what we are doing, we will be released from the oath you made us swear."

²¹"Agreed," she replied. "Let it be as you say." So she sent them away and they departed. And she tied the scarlet cord in the window.

²²When they left, they went into the hills and stayed there three days, until the pursuers had searched all along the road and returned without finding them. ²³Then the two men started back. They went down out of the hills, forded the river and came to Joshua son of Nun and told him everything that had happened to them. ²⁴They said to Joshua, "The Lᴏʀᴅ has surely given the whole land into our hands; all the people are melting in fear because of us."

JOSHUA 2

QU☺ZZER

Q: Where did Rahab hide the Israelite spies?

BONUS: Why did she hide them?

Answers on page 258

Crossing the Jordan Early in the morning Joshua and all the Israelites set out from Shittim and went to the Jordan, where they camped before crossing over. ²After three days the officers went throughout the camp, ³giving orders to the people: "When you see the ark of the covenant of the Lᴏʀᴅ your God, and the priests, who are Levites, carrying it, you are to move out from your positions and follow it. ⁴Then you will know which way to go, since you have never been this way before. But keep a distance of about a thousand yardsᶜ between you and the ark; do not go near it."

⁵Joshua told the people, "Consecrate yourselves, for tomorrow the Lᴏʀᴅ will do amazing things among you."

ᵃ10 Hebrew *Yam Suph*; that is, Sea of Reeds ᵇ10 The Hebrew term refers to the irrevocable giving over of things or persons to the Lᴏʀᴅ, often by totally destroying them. ᶜ4 Hebrew *about two thousand cubits* (about 900 meters)

⁶Joshua said to the priests, "Take up the ark of the covenant and pass on ahead of the people." So they took it up and went ahead of them.

⁷And the Lᴏʀᴅ said to Joshua, "Today I will begin to exalt you in the eyes of all Israel, so they may know that I am with you as I was with Moses. ⁸Tell the priests who carry the ark of the covenant: 'When you reach the edge of the Jordan's waters, go and stand in the river.' "

⁹Joshua said to the Israelites, "Come here and listen to the words of the Lᴏʀᴅ your God. ¹⁰This is how you will know that the living God is among you and that he will certainly drive out before you the Canaanites, Hittites, Hivites, Perizzites, Girgashites, Amorites and Jebusites. ¹¹See, the ark of the covenant of the Lord of all the earth will go into the Jordan ahead of you. ¹²Now then, choose twelve men from the tribes of Israel, one from each tribe. ¹³And as soon as the priests who carry the ark of the Lᴏʀᴅ—the Lord of all the earth—set foot in the Jordan, its waters flowing downstream will be cut off and stand up in a heap."

¹⁴So when the people broke camp to cross the Jordan, the priests carrying the ark of the covenant went ahead of them. ¹⁵Now the Jordan is at flood stage all during harvest. Yet as soon as the priests who carried the ark reached the Jordan and their feet touched the water's edge, ¹⁶the water from upstream stopped flowing. It piled up in a heap a great distance away, at a town called Adam in the vicinity of Zarethan, while the water flowing down to the Sea of the Arabah (the Salt Sea ᵃ) was completely cut off. So the people crossed over opposite Jericho. ¹⁷The priests who carried the ark of the covenant of the Lᴏʀᴅ stood firm on dry ground in the middle of the Jordan, while all Israel passed by until the whole nation had completed the crossing on dry ground.

A nswers

to Quizzer on
page 257

A: Under flax plants that were drying on her roof (Joshua 2:6).

BONUS: To protect herself. Everyone in Jericho knew God was with Israel, but only Rahab was willing to trust herself to him (Joshua 2:11-13).

When the whole nation had finished crossing the Jordan, the Lᴏʀᴅ said to Joshua, ²"Choose twelve men from among the people, one from each tribe, ³and tell them to take up twelve stones from the middle of the Jordan from right where the priests stood and to carry them over with you and put them down at the place where you stay tonight."

⁴So Joshua called together the twelve men he had appointed from the Israelites, one from each tribe, ⁵and said to them, "Go over before the ark of the Lᴏʀᴅ your God into the middle of the Jordan. Each of you is to take up a stone on his shoulder, according to the number of the tribes of the Israelites, ⁶to serve as a sign among you. In the future, when your children ask you, 'What do these stones mean?' ⁷tell them that the flow of the Jordan was cut off before the ark of the covenant of the Lᴏʀᴅ. When it crossed the Jordan, the waters of the Jordan were cut off. These stones are to be a memorial to the people of Israel forever."

⁸So the Israelites did as Joshua commanded them. They took twelve stones from the middle of the Jordan, according to the number of the tribes of the Israelites, as the Lᴏʀᴅ had told Joshua; and they carried them over with them to their camp, where they put them down. ⁹Joshua set up the twelve stones that had beenᵇ in the middle of the Jordan at the spot where the priests who carried the ark of the covenant had stood. And they are there to this day.

¹⁰Now the priests who carried the ark remained standing in the middle of the Jordan until everything the Lᴏʀᴅ had commanded Joshua was done by the people, just as Moses had directed Joshua. The people hurried over, ¹¹and as soon as all of them had crossed, the ark of the Lᴏʀᴅ and the priests came to the other side while the people watched. ¹²The men of Reuben, Gad and the half-tribe of Manasseh crossed over, armed, in front of the Israelites, as Moses had directed them. ¹³About forty thousand armed for battle crossed over before the Lᴏʀᴅ to the plains of Jericho for war.

ᵃ16 That is, the Dead Sea   ᵇ9 Or Joshua also set up twelve stones

¹⁴That day the LORD exalted Joshua in the sight of all Israel; and they revered him all the days of his life, just as they had revered Moses.

¹⁵Then the LORD said to Joshua, ¹⁶"Command the priests carrying the ark of the Testimony to come up out of the Jordan."

¹⁷So Joshua commanded the priests, "Come up out of the Jordan."

¹⁸And the priests came up out of the river carrying the ark of the covenant of the LORD. No sooner had they set their feet on the dry ground than the waters of the Jordan returned to their place and ran at flood stage as before.

¹⁹On the tenth day of the first month the people went up from the Jordan and camped at Gilgal on the eastern border of Jericho. ²⁰And Joshua set up at Gilgal the twelve stones they had taken out of the Jordan. ²¹He said to the Israelites, "In the future when your descendants ask their fathers, 'What do these stones mean?' ²²tell them, 'Israel crossed the Jordan on dry ground.' ²³For the LORD your God dried up the Jordan before you until you had crossed over. The LORD your God did to the Jordan just what he had done to the Red Sea*a* when he dried it up before us until we had crossed over. ²⁴He did this so that all the peoples of the earth might know that the hand of the LORD is powerful and so that you might always fear the LORD your God."

5 *Circumcision at Gilgal* Now when all the Amorite kings west of the Jordan and all the Canaanite kings along the coast heard how the LORD had dried up the Jordan before the Israelites until we had crossed over, their hearts melted and they no longer had the courage to face the Israelites.

²At that time the LORD said to Joshua, "Make flint knives and circumcise the Israelites again." ³So Joshua made flint knives and circumcised the Israelites at Gibeath Haaraloth.*b*

⁴Now this is why he did so: All those who came out of Egypt—all the men of military age—died in the desert on the way after leaving Egypt. ⁵All the people that came out had been circumcised, but all the people born in the desert during the journey from Egypt had not. ⁶The Israelites had moved about in the desert forty years until all the men who were of military age when they left Egypt had died, since they had not obeyed the LORD. For the LORD had sworn to them that they would not see the land that he had solemnly promised their fathers to give us, a land flowing with milk and honey. ⁷So he raised up their sons in their place, and these were the ones Joshua circumcised. They were still uncircumcised because they had not been circumcised on the way. ⁸And after the whole nation had been circumcised, they remained where they were in camp until they were healed.

⁹Then the LORD said to Joshua, "Today I have rolled away the reproach of Egypt from you." So the place has been called Gilgal*c* to this day.

¹⁰On the evening of the fourteenth day of the month, while camped at Gilgal on the plains of Jericho, the Israelites celebrated the Passover. ¹¹The day after the Passover, that very day, they ate some of the produce of the land: unleavened bread and roasted grain. ¹²The manna stopped the day after*d* they ate this food from the land; there was no longer any manna for the Israelites, but that year they ate of the produce of Canaan.

The Fall of Jericho ¹³Now when Joshua was near Jericho, he looked up and saw a man standing in front of him with a drawn sword in his hand. Joshua went up to him and asked, "Are you for us or for our enemies?"

¹⁴"Neither," he replied, "but as commander of the army of the LORD I have now come." Then Joshua fell facedown to the ground in reverence, and asked him, "What message does my Lord*e* have for his servant?"

¹⁵The commander of the LORD's army replied, "Take off your sandals, for the place where you are standing is holy." And Joshua did so.

a23 Hebrew *Yam Suph*; that is, Sea of Reeds   *b3 Gibeath Haaraloth* means *hill of foreskins.*   *c9 Gilgal* sounds like the Hebrew for *roll.*   *d12* Or *the day*   *e14* Or *lord*

6 Now Jericho was tightly shut up because of the Israelites. No one went out and no one came in.

²Then the LORD said to Joshua, "See, I have delivered Jericho into your hands, along with its king and its fighting men. ³March around the city once with all the armed men. Do this for six days. ⁴Have seven priests carry trumpets of rams' horns in front of the ark. On the seventh day, march around the city seven times, with the priests blowing the trumpets. ⁵When you hear them sound a long blast on the trumpets, have all the people give a loud shout; then the wall of the city will collapse and the people will go up, every man straight in."

⁶So Joshua son of Nun called the priests and said to them, "Take up the ark of the covenant of the LORD and have seven priests carry trumpets in front of it." ⁷And he ordered the people, "Advance! March around the city, with the armed guard going ahead of the ark of the LORD."

⁸When Joshua had spoken to the people, the seven priests carrying the seven trumpets before the LORD went forward, blowing their trumpets, and the ark of the LORD's covenant followed them. ⁹The armed guard marched ahead of the priests who blew the trumpets, and the rear guard followed the ark. All this time the trumpets were sounding. ¹⁰But Joshua had commanded the people, "Do not give a war cry, do not raise your voices, do not say a word until the day I tell you to shout. Then shout!" ¹¹So he had the ark of the LORD carried around the city, circling it once. Then the people returned to camp and spent the night there.

¹²Joshua got up early the next morning and the priests took up the ark of the LORD. ¹³The seven priests carrying the seven trumpets went forward, marching before the ark of the LORD and blowing the trumpets. The armed men went ahead of them and the rear guard followed the ark of the LORD, while the trumpets kept sounding. ¹⁴So on the second day they marched around the city once and returned to the camp. They did this for six days.

¹⁵On the seventh day, they got up at daybreak and marched around the city seven times in the same manner, except that on that day they circled the city seven times. ¹⁶The seventh time around, when the priests sounded the trumpet blast, Joshua commanded the people, "Shout! For the LORD has given you the city! ¹⁷The city and all that is in it are to be devoted*ᵃ* to the LORD. Only Rahab the prostitute*ᵇ* and all who are with her in her house shall be spared, because she hid the spies we sent. ¹⁸But keep away from the devoted things, so that you will not bring about your own destruction by taking any of them. Otherwise you will make the camp of Israel liable to destruction and bring trouble on it. ¹⁹All the silver and gold and the articles of bronze and iron are sacred to the LORD and must go into his treasury."

²⁰When the trumpets sounded, the people shouted, and at the sound of the trumpet, when the people gave a loud shout, the wall collapsed; so every man charged straight in, and they took the city. ²¹They devoted the city to the LORD and destroyed with the sword every living thing in it—men and women, young and old, cattle, sheep and donkeys.

²²Joshua said to the two men who had spied out the land, "Go into the prostitute's house and bring her out and all who belong to her, in accordance with your oath to her." ²³So the young men who had done the spying went in and brought out Rahab, her father and mother and brothers and all who belonged to her. They brought out her entire family and put them in a place outside the camp of Israel.

JOSHUA 6

QUIZZER

Q: How many times did the Israelites march around Jericho?

BONUS: What did this teach the Israelites?

Answers on page 263

ᵃ17 The Hebrew term refers to the irrevocable giving over of things or persons to the LORD, often by totally destroying them; also in verses 18 and 21.   *ᵇ17* Or possibly *innkeeper*; also in verses 22 and 25

²⁴Then they burned the whole city and everything in it, but they put the silver and gold and the articles of bronze and iron into the treasury of the LORD's house. ²⁵But Joshua spared Rahab the prostitute, with her family and all who belonged to her, because she hid the men Joshua had sent as spies to Jericho—and she lives among the Israelites to this day.

²⁶At that time Joshua pronounced this solemn oath: "Cursed before the LORD is the man who undertakes to rebuild this city, Jericho:

> "At the cost of his firstborn son
>   will he lay its foundations;
> at the cost of his youngest
>   will he set up its gates."

²⁷So the LORD was with Joshua, and his fame spread throughout the land.

Achan's Sin But the Israelites acted unfaithfully in regard to the devoted things*ᵃ*; Achan son of Carmi, the son of Zimri,*ᵇ* the son of Zerah, of the tribe of Judah, took some of them. So the LORD's anger burned against Israel.

²Now Joshua sent men from Jericho to Ai, which is near Beth Aven to the east of Bethel, and told them, "Go up and spy out the region." So the men went up and spied out Ai.

³When they returned to Joshua, they said, "Not all the people will have to go up against Ai. Send two or three thousand men to take it and do not weary all the people, for only a few men are there." ⁴So about three thousand men went up; but they were routed by the men of Ai, ⁵who killed about thirty-six of them. They chased the Israelites from the city gate as far as the stone quarries*ᶜ* and struck them down on the slopes. At this the hearts of the people melted and became like water.

⁶Then Joshua tore his clothes and fell facedown to the ground before the ark of the LORD, remaining there till evening. The elders of Israel did the same, and sprinkled dust on their heads. ⁷And Joshua said, "Ah, Sovereign LORD, why did you ever bring this people across the Jordan to deliver us into the hands of the Amorites to destroy us? If only we had been content to stay on the other side of the Jordan! ⁸O Lord, what can I say, now that Israel has been routed by its enemies? ⁹The Canaanites and the other people of the country will hear about this and they will surround us and wipe out our name from the earth. What then will you do for your own great name?"

¹⁰The LORD said to Joshua, "Stand up! What are you doing down on your face? ¹¹Israel has sinned; they have violated my covenant, which I commanded them to keep. They have taken some of the devoted things; they have stolen, they have lied, they have put them with their own possessions. ¹²That is why the Israelites

Talk about noise pollution! That band just shattered my china!

SEE JOSHUA 6:20

ᵃ1 The Hebrew term refers to the irrevocable giving over of things or persons to the LORD, often by totally destroying them; also in verses 11, 12, 13 and 15. ᵇ1 See Septuagint and 1 Chron. 2:6; Hebrew *Zabdi*; also in verses 17 and 18. ᶜ5 Or *as far as Shebarim*

cannot stand against their enemies; they turn their backs and run because they have been made liable to destruction. I will not be with you anymore unless you destroy whatever among you is devoted to destruction.

¹³"Go, consecrate the people. Tell them, 'Consecrate yourselves in preparation for tomorrow; for this is what the LORD, the God of Israel, says: That which is devoted is among you, O Israel. You cannot stand against your enemies until you remove it.

¹⁴"'In the morning, present yourselves tribe by tribe. The tribe that the LORD takes shall come forward clan by clan; the clan that the LORD takes shall come forward family by family; and the family that the LORD takes shall come forward man by man. ¹⁵He who is caught with the devoted things shall be destroyed by fire, along with all that belongs to him. He has violated the covenant of the LORD and has done a disgraceful thing in Israel!' "

¹⁶Early the next morning Joshua had Israel come forward by tribes, and Judah was taken. ¹⁷The clans of Judah came forward, and he took the Zerahites. He had the clan of the Zerahites come forward by families, and Zimri was taken. ¹⁸Joshua had his family come forward man by man, and Achan son of Carmi, the son of Zimri, the son of Zerah, of the tribe of Judah, was taken.

¹⁹Then Joshua said to Achan, "My son, give glory to the LORD,ᵃ the God of Israel, and give him the praise.ᵇ Tell me what you have done; do not hide it from me."

²⁰Achan replied, "It is true! I have sinned against the LORD, the God of Israel. This is what I have done: ²¹When I saw in the plunder a beautiful robe from Babylonia,ᶜ two hundred shekelsᵈ of silver and a wedge of gold weighing fifty shekels,ᵉ I coveted them and took them. They are hidden in the ground inside my tent, with the silver underneath."

²²So Joshua sent messengers, and they ran to the tent, and there it was, hidden in his tent, with the silver underneath. ²³They took the things from the tent, brought them to Joshua and all the Israelites and spread them out before the LORD.

²⁴Then Joshua, together with all Israel, took Achan son of Zerah, the silver, the robe, the gold wedge, his sons and daughters, his cattle, donkeys and sheep, his tent and all that he had, to the Valley of Achor. ²⁵Joshua said, "Why have you brought this trouble on us? The LORD will bring trouble on you today."

Then all Israel stoned him, and after they had stoned the rest, they burned them. ²⁶Over Achan they heaped up a large pile of rocks, which remains to this day. Then the LORD turned from his fierce anger. Therefore that place has been called the Valley of Achorᶠ ever since.

Ai Destroyed Then the LORD said to Joshua, "Do not be afraid; do not be discouraged. Take the whole army with you, and go up and attack Ai. For I have delivered into your hands the king of Ai, his people, his city and his land. ²You shall do to Ai and its king as you did to Jericho and its king, except that you

---

Direct Line

JOSHUA 7:10–12

Consider a teen who's grounded for slipping out the window at night—the third time this week. Two minutes later he goes to his dad and says, "Dad, will you take me to the mall for new basketball shoes?" He's sort of like Christians who knowingly do wrong and then can't understand why God doesn't answer their prayers. When an Israelite broke God's command, God's people suffered defeat in their next battle. God explained: "Israel has sinned . . . I will not be with you anymore" (Joshua 7:11–12). If you want God's blessing, don't make a habit of disobedience.

ᵃ19 A solemn charge to tell the truth ᵇ19 Or *and confess to him* ᶜ21 Hebrew *Shinar* ᵈ21 That is, about 5 pounds (about 2.3 kilograms) ᵉ21 That is, about 1 1/4 pounds (about 0.6 kilogram) ᶠ26 *Achor* means *trouble*.

may carry off their plunder and livestock for yourselves. Set an ambush behind the city."

³So Joshua and the whole army moved out to attack Ai. He chose thirty thousand of his best fighting men and sent them out at night ⁴with these orders: "Listen carefully. You are to set an ambush behind the city. Don't go very far from it. All of you be on the alert. ⁵I and all those with me will advance on the city, and when the men come out against us, as they did before, we will flee from them. ⁶They will pursue us until we have lured them away from the city, for they will say, 'They are running away from us as they did before.' So when we flee from them, ⁷you are to rise up from ambush and take the city. The LORD your God will give it into your hand. ⁸When you have taken the city, set it on fire. Do what the LORD has commanded. See to it; you have my orders."

⁹Then Joshua sent them off, and they went to the place of ambush and lay in wait between Bethel and Ai, to the west of Ai—but Joshua spent that night with the people.

¹⁰Early the next morning Joshua mustered his men, and he and the leaders of Israel marched before them to Ai. ¹¹The entire force that was with him marched up and approached the city and arrived in front of it. They set up camp north of Ai, with the valley between them and the city. ¹²Joshua had taken about five thousand men and set them in ambush between Bethel and Ai, to the west of the city. ¹³They had the soldiers take up their positions—all those in the camp to the north of the city and the ambush to the west of it. That night Joshua went into the valley.

¹⁴When the king of Ai saw this, he and all the men of the city hurried out early in the morning to meet Israel in battle at a certain place overlooking the Arabah. But he did not know that an ambush had been set against him behind the city. ¹⁵Joshua and all Israel let themselves be driven back before them, and they fled toward the desert. ¹⁶All the men of Ai were called to pursue them, and they pursued Joshua and were lured away from the city. ¹⁷Not a man remained in Ai or Bethel who did not go after Israel. They left the city open and went in pursuit of Israel.

¹⁸Then the LORD said to Joshua, "Hold out toward Ai the javelin that is in your hand, for into your hand I will deliver the city." So Joshua held out his javelin toward Ai. ¹⁹As soon as he did this, the men in the ambush rose quickly from their position and rushed forward. They entered the city and captured it and quickly set it on fire.

²⁰The men of Ai looked back and saw the smoke of the city rising against the sky, but they had no chance to escape in any direction, for the Israelites who had been fleeing toward the desert had turned back against their pursuers. ²¹For when Joshua and all Israel saw that the ambush had taken the city and that smoke was going up from the city, they turned around and attacked the men of Ai. ²²The men of the ambush also came out of the city against them, so that they were caught in the middle, with Israelites on both sides. Israel cut them down, leaving them neither survivors nor fugitives. ²³But they took the king of Ai alive and brought him to Joshua.

²⁴When Israel had finished killing all the men of Ai in the fields and in the desert where they had chased them, and when every one of them had been put to the sword, all the Israelites returned to Ai and killed those who were in it. ²⁵Twelve thousand men and women fell that day—all the people of Ai. ²⁶For Joshua did not draw back the hand that held out his javelin until he had destroyed*ᵃ* all who lived in Ai. ²⁷But Israel did carry off for themselves the livestock and plunder of this city, as the LORD had instructed Joshua.

²⁸So Joshua burned Ai and made it a permanent heap of ruins, a desolate

Answers
to Quizzer on
page 260

A: Thirteen times
(Joshua 6:3-4).

*BONUS: God
wanted them
to realize that
even when his
commands didn't
make sense they
were to obey and
that obedience
brought victory.*

---

*ᵃ26 The Hebrew term refers to the irrevocable giving over of things or persons to the LORD, often by totally destroying them.

place to this day. [29]He hung the king of Ai on a tree and left him there until evening. At sunset, Joshua ordered them to take his body from the tree and throw it down at the entrance of the city gate. And they raised a large pile of rocks over it, which remains to this day.

The Covenant Renewed at Mount Ebal [30]Then Joshua built on Mount Ebal an altar to the LORD, the God of Israel, [31]as Moses the servant of the LORD had commanded the Israelites. He built it according to what is written in the Book of the Law of Moses—an altar of uncut stones, on which no iron tool had been used. On it they offered to the LORD burnt offerings and sacrificed fellowship offerings.[a] [32]There, in the presence of the Israelites, Joshua copied on stones the law of Moses, which he had written. [33]All Israel, aliens and citizens alike, with their elders, officials and judges, were standing on both sides of the ark of the covenant of the LORD, facing those who carried it—the priests, who were Levites. Half of the people stood in front of Mount Gerizim and half of them in front of Mount Ebal, as Moses the servant of the LORD had formerly commanded when he gave instructions to bless the people of Israel.

[34]Afterward, Joshua read all the words of the law—the blessings and the curses—just as it is written in the Book of the Law. [35]There was not a word of all that Moses had commanded that Joshua did not read to the whole assembly of Israel, including the women and children, and the aliens who lived among them.

[9] *The Gibeonite Deception* Now when all the kings west of the Jordan heard about these things—those in the hill country, in the western foothills, and along the entire coast of the Great Sea[b] as far as Lebanon (the kings of the Hittites, Amorites, Canaanites, Perizzites, Hivites and Jebusites)— [2]they came together to make war against Joshua and Israel.

[3]However, when the people of Gibeon heard what Joshua had done to Jericho and Ai, [4]they resorted to a ruse: They went as a delegation whose donkeys were loaded[c] with worn-out sacks and old wineskins, cracked and mended. [5]The men put worn and patched sandals on their feet and wore old clothes. All the bread of their food supply was dry and moldy. [6]Then they went to Joshua in the camp at Gilgal and said to him and the men of Israel, "We have come from a distant country; make a treaty with us."

[7]The men of Israel said to the Hivites, "But perhaps you live near us. How then can we make a treaty with you?"

[8]"We are your servants," they said to Joshua.

But Joshua asked, "Who are you and where do you come from?"

[9]They answered: "Your servants have come from a very distant country because of the fame of the LORD your God. For we have heard reports of him: all that he did in Egypt, [10]and all that he did to the two kings of the Amorites east of the Jordan—Sihon king of Heshbon, and Og king

Direct Line

JOSHUA 9:16–21

Sometimes keeping your word can be hard, and sometimes it's just not fun. For instance, you promise to help Jenny with her algebra. Then another friend invites you to the mall. What do you do when keeping your word hurts? The Gibeonites fooled the leaders of Israel into making a treaty with them by pretending to live a long way away. Then the Israelites learned that the Gibeonites were neighbors. The Israelites were upset, but they kept their word. God wants you to be people of your word too. Christians represent a God who always keeps his word. You need to be trustworthy.

[a]31 Traditionally *peace offerings* [b]1 That is, the Mediterranean [c]4 Most Hebrew manuscripts; some Hebrew manuscripts, Vulgate and Syriac (see also Septuagint) *They prepared provisions and loaded their donkeys*

of Bashan, who reigned in Ashtaroth. ¹¹And our elders and all those living in our country said to us, 'Take provisions for your journey; go and meet them and say to them, "We are your servants; make a treaty with us." ' ¹²This bread of ours was warm when we packed it at home on the day we left to come to you. But now see how dry and moldy it is. ¹³And these wineskins that we filled were new, but see how cracked they are. And our clothes and sandals are worn out by the very long journey."

¹⁴The men of Israel sampled their provisions but did not inquire of the Lᴏʀᴅ. ¹⁵Then Joshua made a treaty of peace with them to let them live, and the leaders of the assembly ratified it by oath.

¹⁶Three days after they made the treaty with the Gibeonites, the Israelites heard that they were neighbors, living near them. ¹⁷So the Israelites set out and on the third day came to their cities: Gibeon, Kephirah, Beeroth and Kiriath Jearim. ¹⁸But the Israelites did not attack them, because the leaders of the assembly had sworn an oath to them by the Lᴏʀᴅ, the God of Israel.

The whole assembly grumbled against the leaders, ¹⁹but all the leaders answered, "We have given them our oath by the Lᴏʀᴅ, the God of Israel, and we cannot touch them now. ²⁰This is what we will do to them: We will let them live, so that wrath will not fall on us for breaking the oath we swore to them." ²¹They continued, "Let them live, but let them be woodcutters and water carriers for the entire community." So the leaders' promise to them was kept.

²²Then Joshua summoned the Gibeonites and said, "Why did you deceive us by saying, 'We live a long way from you,' while actually you live near us? ²³You are now under a curse: You will never cease to serve as woodcutters and water carriers for the house of my God."

²⁴They answered Joshua, "Your servants were clearly told how the Lᴏʀᴅ your God had commanded his servant Moses to give you the whole land and to wipe out all its inhabitants from before you. So we feared for our lives because of you, and that is why we did this. ²⁵We are now in your hands. Do to us whatever seems good and right to you."

²⁶So Joshua saved them from the Israelites, and they did not kill them. ²⁷That day he made the Gibeonites woodcutters and water carriers for the community and for the altar of the Lᴏʀᴅ at the place the Lᴏʀᴅ would choose. And that is what they are to this day.

10 *The Sun Stands Still* Now Adoni-Zedek king of Jerusalem heard that Joshua had taken Ai and totally destroyed[a] it, doing to Ai and its king as he had done to Jericho and its king, and that the people of Gibeon had made a treaty of peace with Israel and were living near them. ²He and his people were very much alarmed at this, because Gibeon was an important city, like one of the royal cities; it was larger than Ai, and all its men were good fighters. ³So Adoni-Zedek king of Jerusalem appealed to Hoham king of Hebron, Piram king of Jarmuth, Japhia king of Lachish and Debir king of Eglon. ⁴"Come up and help me attack Gibeon," he said, "because it has made peace with Joshua and the Israelites."

⁵Then the five kings of the Amorites—the kings of Jerusalem, Hebron, Jarmuth, Lachish and Eglon—joined forces. They moved up with all their troops and took up positions against Gibeon and attacked it.

⁶The Gibeonites then sent word to Joshua in the camp at Gilgal: "Do not abandon your servants. Come up to us quickly and save us! Help us, because all the Amorite kings from the hill country have joined forces against us."

⁷So Joshua marched up from Gilgal with his entire army, including all the best fighting men. ⁸The Lᴏʀᴅ said to Joshua, "Do not be afraid of them; I have

---

a1 The Hebrew term refers to the irrevocable giving over of things or persons to the Lᴏʀᴅ, often by totally destroying them; also in verses 28, 35, 37, 39 and 40.

given them into your hand. Not one of them will be able to withstand you."

⁹After an all-night march from Gilgal, Joshua took them by surprise. ¹⁰The LORD threw them into confusion before Israel, who defeated them in a great victory at Gibeon. Israel pursued them along the road going up to Beth Horon and cut them down all the way to Azekah and Makkedah. ¹¹As they fled before Israel on the road down from Beth Horon to Azekah, the LORD hurled large hailstones down on them from the sky, and more of them died from the hailstones than were killed by the swords of the Israelites.

¹²On the day the LORD gave the Amorites over to Israel, Joshua said to the LORD in the presence of Israel:

> "O sun, stand still over Gibeon,
> O moon, over the Valley of Aijalon."
> ¹³So the sun stood still,
> and the moon stopped,
> till the nation avenged itself on^a its enemies,

as it is written in the Book of Jashar.

The sun stopped in the middle of the sky and delayed going down about a full day. ¹⁴There has never been a day like it before or since, a day when the LORD listened to a man. Surely the LORD was fighting for Israel!

¹⁵Then Joshua returned with all Israel to the camp at Gilgal.

Five Amorite Kings Killed ¹⁶Now the five kings had fled and hidden in the cave at Makkedah. ¹⁷When Joshua was told that the five kings had been found hiding in the cave at Makkedah, ¹⁸he said, "Roll large rocks up to the mouth of the cave, and post some men there to guard it. ¹⁹But don't stop! Pursue your enemies, attack them from the rear and don't let them reach their cities, for the LORD your God has given them into your hand."

²⁰So Joshua and the Israelites destroyed them completely—almost to a man—but the few who were left reached their fortified cities. ²¹The whole army then returned safely to Joshua in the camp at Makkedah, and no one uttered a word against the Israelites.

²²Joshua said, "Open the mouth of the cave and bring those five kings out to me." ²³So they brought the five kings out of the cave—the kings of Jerusalem, Hebron, Jarmuth, Lachish and Eglon. ²⁴When they had brought these kings to Joshua, he summoned all the men of Israel and said to the army commanders who had come with him, "Come here and put your feet on the necks of these kings." So they came forward and placed their feet on their necks.

²⁵Joshua said to them, "Do not be afraid; do not be discouraged. Be strong and courageous. This is what the LORD will do to all the enemies you are going to fight." ²⁶Then Joshua struck and killed the kings and hung them on five trees, and they were left hanging on the trees until evening.

²⁷At sunset Joshua gave the order and they took them down from the trees and threw them into the cave where they had been hiding. At the mouth of the cave they placed large rocks, which are there to this day.

²⁸That day Joshua took Makkedah. He put the city and its king to the sword and totally destroyed everyone in it. He left no survivors. And he did to the king of Makkedah as he had done to the king of Jericho.

Southern Cities Conquered ²⁹Then Joshua and all Israel with him moved on from Makkedah to Libnah and attacked it. ³⁰The LORD also gave that city and its king into Israel's hand. The city and everyone in it Joshua put to the sword. He left no survivors there. And he did to its king as he had done to the king of Jericho.

³¹Then Joshua and all Israel with him moved on from Libnah to Lachish;

---

^{a}13 Or *nation triumphed over*

he took up positions against it and attacked it. ³²The Lᴏʀᴅ handed Lachish over to Israel, and Joshua took it on the second day. The city and everyone in it he put to the sword, just as he had done to Libnah. ³³Meanwhile, Horam king of Gezer had come up to help Lachish, but Joshua defeated him and his army—until no survivors were left.

³⁴Then Joshua and all Israel with him moved on from Lachish to Eglon; they took up positions against it and attacked it. ³⁵They captured it that same day and put it to the sword and totally destroyed everyone in it, just as they had done to Lachish.

³⁶Then Joshua and all Israel with him went up from Eglon to Hebron and attacked it. ³⁷They took the city and put it to the sword, together with its king, its villages and everyone in it. They left no survivors. Just as at Eglon, they totally destroyed it and everyone in it.

³⁸Then Joshua and all Israel with him turned around and attacked Debir. ³⁹They took the city, its king and its villages, and put them to the sword. Everyone in it they totally destroyed. They left no survivors. They did to Debir and its king as they had done to Libnah and its king and to Hebron.

⁴⁰So Joshua subdued the whole region, including the hill country, the Negev, the western foothills and the mountain slopes, together with all their kings. He left no survivors. He totally destroyed all who breathed, just as the Lᴏʀᴅ, the God of Israel, had commanded. ⁴¹Joshua subdued them from Kadesh Barnea to Gaza and from the whole region of Goshen to Gibeon. ⁴²All these kings and their lands Joshua conquered in one campaign, because the Lᴏʀᴅ, the God of Israel, fought for Israel.

⁴³Then Joshua returned with all Israel to the camp at Gilgal.

11 *Northern Kings Defeated* When Jabin king of Hazor heard of this, he sent word to Jobab king of Madon, to the kings of Shimron and Acshaph, ²and to the northern kings who were in the mountains, in the Arabah south of Kinnereth, in the western foothills and in Naphoth Dor*ᵃ* on the west; ³to the Canaanites in the east and west; to the Amorites, Hittites, Perizzites and Jebusites in the hill country; and to the Hivites below Hermon in the region of Mizpah. ⁴They came out with all their troops and a large number of horses and chariots—a huge army, as numerous as the sand on the seashore. ⁵All these kings joined forces and made camp together at the Waters of Merom, to fight against Israel.

⁶The Lᴏʀᴅ said to Joshua, "Do not be afraid of them, because by this time tomorrow I will hand all of them over to Israel, slain. You are to hamstring their horses and burn their chariots."

⁷So Joshua and his whole army came against them suddenly at the Waters of Merom and attacked them, ⁸and the Lᴏʀᴅ gave them into the hand of Israel. They defeated them and pursued them all the way to Greater Sidon, to Misrephoth Maim, and to the Valley of Mizpah on the east, until no survivors were left. ⁹Joshua did to them as the Lᴏʀᴅ had directed: He hamstrung their horses and burned their chariots.

¹⁰At that time Joshua turned back and captured Hazor and put its king to the sword. (Hazor had been the head of all these kingdoms.) ¹¹Everyone in it they put to the sword. They totally destroyed*ᵇ* them, not sparing anything that breathed, and he burned up Hazor itself.

¹²Joshua took all these royal cities and their kings and put them to the sword. He totally destroyed them, as Moses the servant of the Lᴏʀᴅ had commanded. ¹³Yet Israel did not burn any of the cities built on their mounds—except Hazor, which Joshua burned. ¹⁴The Israelites carried off for themselves all the plunder and livestock of these cities, but all the people

---

ᵃ2 Or *in the heights of Dor* *ᵇ11* The Hebrew term refers to the irrevocable giving over of things or persons to the Lᴏʀᴅ, often by totally destroying them; also in verses 12, 20 and 21.

they put to the sword until they completely destroyed them, not sparing anyone that breathed. [15]As the Lord commanded his servant Moses, so Moses commanded Joshua, and Joshua did it; he left nothing undone of all that the Lord commanded Moses.

[16]So Joshua took this entire land: the hill country, all the Negev, the whole region of Goshen, the western foothills, the Arabah and the mountains of Israel with their foothills, [17]from Mount Halak, which rises toward Seir, to Baal Gad in the Valley of Lebanon below Mount Hermon. He captured all their kings and struck them down, putting them to death. [18]Joshua waged war against all these kings for a long time. [19]Except for the Hivites living in Gibeon, not one city made a treaty of peace with the Israelites, who took them all in battle. [20]For it was the Lord himself who hardened their hearts to wage war against Israel, so that he might destroy them totally, exterminating them without mercy, as the Lord had commanded Moses.

[21]At that time Joshua went and destroyed the Anakites from the hill country: from Hebron, Debir and Anab, from all the hill country of Judah, and from all the hill country of Israel. Joshua totally destroyed them and their towns. [22]No Anakites were left in Israelite territory; only in Gaza, Gath and Ashdod did any survive. [23]So Joshua took the entire land, just as the Lord had directed Moses, and he gave it as an inheritance to Israel according to their tribal divisions.

Then the land had rest from war.

12

List of Defeated Kings   These are the kings of the land whom the Israelites had defeated and whose territory they took over east of the Jordan, from the Arnon Gorge to Mount Hermon, including all the eastern side of the Arabah:

[2]Sihon king of the Amorites,
who reigned in Heshbon. He ruled from Aroer on the rim of the Arnon Gorge—from the middle of the gorge—to the Jabbok River, which is the border of the Ammonites. This included half of Gilead. [3]He also ruled over the eastern Arabah from the Sea of Kinnereth[a] to the Sea of the Arabah (the Salt Sea[b]), to Beth Jeshimoth, and then southward below the slopes of Pisgah.

[4]And the territory of Og king of Bashan,
one of the last of the Rephaites, who reigned in Ashtaroth and Edrei. [5]He ruled over Mount Hermon, Salecah, all of Bashan to the border of the people of Geshur and Maacah, and half of Gilead to the border of Sihon king of Heshbon.

[6]Moses, the servant of the Lord, and the Israelites conquered them. And Moses the servant of the Lord gave their land to the Reubenites, the Gadites and the half-tribe of Manasseh to be their possession.

[7]These are the kings of the land that Joshua and the Israelites conquered on the west side of the Jordan, from Baal Gad in the Valley of Lebanon to Mount Halak, which rises toward Seir (their lands Joshua gave as an inheritance to the tribes of Israel according to their tribal divisions— [8]the hill country, the western foothills, the Arabah, the mountain slopes, the desert and the Negev—the lands of the Hittites, Amorites, Canaanites, Perizzites, Hivites and Jebusites):

[9]the king of Jericho	one
the king of Ai (near Bethel)	one
[10]the king of Jerusalem	one
the king of Hebron	one

a3 That is, Galilee   *b3* That is, the Dead Sea

¹¹ the king of Jarmuth	one
the king of Lachish	one
¹² the king of Eglon	one
the king of Gezer	one
¹³ the king of Debir	one
the king of Geder	one
¹⁴ the king of Hormah	one
the king of Arad	one
¹⁵ the king of Libnah	one
the king of Adullam	one
¹⁶ the king of Makkedah	one
the king of Bethel	one
¹⁷ the king of Tappuah	one
the king of Hepher	one
¹⁸ the king of Aphek	one
the king of Lasharon	one
¹⁹ the king of Madon	one
the king of Hazor	one
²⁰ the king of Shimron Meron	one
the king of Acshaph	one
²¹ the king of Taanach	one
the king of Megiddo	one
²² the king of Kedesh	one
the king of Jokneam in Carmel	one
²³ the king of Dor (in Naphoth Dor*ᵃ*)	one
the king of Goyim in Gilgal	one
²⁴ the king of Tirzah	one

thirty-one kings in all.

13 *Land Still to Be Taken* When Joshua was old and well advanced in years, the LORD said to him, "You are very old, and there are still very large areas of land to be taken over.

²"This is the land that remains: all the regions of the Philistines and Geshurites: ³from the Shihor River on the east of Egypt to the territory of Ekron on the north, all of it counted as Canaanite (the territory of the five Philistine rulers in Gaza, Ashdod, Ashkelon, Gath and Ekron—that of the Avvites); ⁴from the south, all the land of the Canaanites, from Arah of the Sidonians as far as Aphek, the region of the Amorites, ⁵the area of the Gebalites*ᵇ*; and all Lebanon to the east, from Baal Gad below Mount Hermon to Lebo*ᶜ* Hamath.

⁶"As for all the inhabitants of the mountain regions from Lebanon to Misrephoth Maim, that is, all the Sidonians, I myself will drive them out before the Israelites. Be sure to allocate this land to Israel for an inheritance, as I have instructed you, ⁷and divide it as an inheritance among the nine tribes and half of the tribe of Manasseh."

Division of the Land East of the Jordan ⁸The other half of Manasseh,*ᵈ* the Reubenites and the Gadites had received the inheritance that Moses had given them east of the Jordan, as he, the servant of the LORD, had assigned it to them.

⁹It extended from Aroer on the rim of the Arnon Gorge, and from the town in the middle of the gorge, and included the whole plateau of Medeba as far as Dibon, ¹⁰and all the towns of Sihon king of the Amorites,

ᵃ23 Or *in the heights of Dor*   *ᵇ5* That is, the area of Byblos   *ᶜ5* Or *to the entrance to*   *ᵈ8* Hebrew *With it* (that is, with the other half of Manasseh)

who ruled in Heshbon, out to the border of the Ammonites. ¹¹It also included Gilead, the territory of the people of Geshur and Maacah, all of Mount Hermon and all Bashan as far as Salecah— ¹²that is, the whole kingdom of Og in Bashan, who had reigned in Ashtaroth and Edrei and had survived as one of the last of the Rephaites. Moses had defeated them and taken over their land. ¹³But the Israelites did not drive out the people of Geshur and Maacah, so they continue to live among the Israelites to this day.

¹⁴But to the tribe of Levi he gave no inheritance, since the offerings made by fire to the LORD, the God of Israel, are their inheritance, as he promised them.

¹⁵This is what Moses had given to the tribe of Reuben, clan by clan:

¹⁶The territory from Aroer on the rim of the Arnon Gorge, and from the town in the middle of the gorge, and the whole plateau past Medeba ¹⁷to Heshbon and all its towns on the plateau, including Dibon, Bamoth Baal, Beth Baal Meon, ¹⁸Jahaz, Kedemoth, Mephaath, ¹⁹Kiriathaim, Sibmah, Zereth Shahar on the hill in the valley, ²⁰Beth Peor, the slopes of Pisgah, and Beth Jeshimoth ²¹—all the towns on the plateau and the entire realm of Sihon king of the Amorites, who ruled at Heshbon. Moses had defeated him and the Midianite chiefs, Evi, Rekem, Zur, Hur and Reba—princes allied with Sihon—who lived in that country. ²²In addition to those slain in battle, the Israelites had put to the sword Balaam son of Beor, who practiced divination. ²³The boundary of the Reubenites was the bank of the Jordan. These towns and their villages were the inheritance of the Reubenites, clan by clan.

²⁴This is what Moses had given to the tribe of Gad, clan by clan:

²⁵The territory of Jazer, all the towns of Gilead and half the Ammonite country as far as Aroer, near Rabbah; ²⁶and from Heshbon to Ramath Mizpah and Betonim, and from Mahanaim to the territory of Debir; ²⁷and in the valley, Beth Haram, Beth Nimrah, Succoth and Zaphon with the rest of the realm of Sihon king of Heshbon (the east side of the Jordan, the territory up to the end of the Sea of Kinnereth*ᵃ*). ²⁸These towns and their villages were the inheritance of the Gadites, clan by clan.

²⁹This is what Moses had given to the half-tribe of Manasseh, that is, to half the family of the descendants of Manasseh, clan by clan:

³⁰The territory extending from Mahanaim and including all of Bashan, the entire realm of Og king of Bashan—all the settlements of Jair in Bashan, sixty towns, ³¹half of Gilead, and Ashtaroth and Edrei (the royal cities of Og in Bashan). This was for the descendants of Makir son of Manasseh—for half of the sons of Makir, clan by clan.

³²This is the inheritance Moses had given when he was in the plains of Moab across the Jordan east of Jericho. ³³But to the tribe of Levi, Moses had given no inheritance; the LORD, the God of Israel, is their inheritance, as he promised them.

14 *Division of the Land West of the Jordan* Now these are the areas the Israelites received as an inheritance in the land of Canaan, which Eleazar the priest, Joshua son of Nun and the heads of the tribal clans of Israel allotted to them. ²Their inheritances were assigned by lot to the nine-and-a-half tribes, as the LORD had commanded through Moses. ³Moses had granted the two-and-a-half tribes their inheritance east of the Jordan but

ᵃ27 That is, Galilee

had not granted the Levites an inheritance among the rest, [4]for the sons of Joseph had become two tribes—Manasseh and Ephraim. The Levites received no share of the land but only towns to live in, with pasturelands for their flocks and herds. [5]So the Israelites divided the land, just as the LORD had commanded Moses.

Hebron Given to Caleb [6]Now the men of Judah approached Joshua at Gilgal, and Caleb son of Jephunneh the Kenizzite said to him, "You know what the LORD said to Moses the man of God at Kadesh Barnea about you and me. [7]I was forty years old when Moses the servant of the LORD sent me from Kadesh Barnea to explore the land. And I brought him back a report according to my convictions, [8]but my brothers who went up with me made the hearts of the people melt with fear. I, however, followed the LORD my God wholeheartedly. [9]So on that day Moses swore to me, 'The land on which your feet have walked will be your inheritance and that of your children forever, because you have followed the LORD my God wholeheartedly.'[a]

[10]"Now then, just as the LORD promised, he has kept me alive for forty-five years since the time he said this to Moses, while Israel moved about in the desert. So here I am today, eighty-five years old! [11]I am still as strong today as the day Moses sent me out; I'm just as vigorous to go out to battle now as I was then. [12]Now give me this hill country that the LORD promised me that day. You yourself heard then that the Anakites were there and their cities were large and fortified, but, the LORD helping me, I will drive them out just as he said."

[13]Then Joshua blessed Caleb son of Jephunneh and gave him Hebron as his inheritance. [14]So Hebron has belonged to Caleb son of Jephunneh the Kenizzite ever since, because he followed the LORD, the God of Israel, wholeheartedly. [15](Hebron used to be called Kiriath Arba after Arba, who was the greatest man among the Anakites.)

Then the land had rest from war.

Allotment for Judah **15** The allotment for the tribe of Judah, clan by clan, extended down to the territory of Edom, to the Desert of Zin in the extreme south.

[2]Their southern boundary started from the bay at the southern end of the Salt Sea,[b] [3]crossed south of Scorpion[c] Pass, continued on to Zin and went over to the south of Kadesh Barnea. Then it ran past Hezron up to Addar and curved around to Karka. [4]It then passed along to Azmon and joined the Wadi of Egypt, ending at the sea. This is their[d] southern boundary.

[5]The eastern boundary is the Salt Sea as far as the mouth of the Jordan.

The northern boundary started from the bay of the sea at the mouth of the Jordan, [6]went up to Beth Hoglah and continued north of Beth Arabah to the Stone of Bohan son of Reuben. [7]The boundary then went up to Debir from the Valley of Achor and turned north to Gilgal, which faces the Pass of Adummim south of the gorge. It continued along to the waters of En Shemesh and came out at En Rogel. [8]Then it ran up the Valley of Ben Hinnom along the southern slope of the Jebusite city (that is, Jerusalem). From there it climbed to the top of the hill west of the Hinnom Valley at the northern end of the Valley of Rephaim. [9]From the hilltop the boundary headed toward the spring of the waters of Nephtoah, came out at the towns of Mount Ephron and went down toward Baalah (that is, Kiriath Jearim). [10]Then it curved westward from Baalah to Mount Seir, ran along the northern slope of Mount Jearim (that is, Kesalon),

---

[a]9 Deut. 1:36   [b]2 That is, the Dead Sea; also in verse 5   [c]3 Hebrew *Akrabbim*   [d]4 Hebrew *your*

continued down to Beth Shemesh and crossed to Timnah. ¹¹It went to the northern slope of Ekron, turned toward Shikkeron, passed along to Mount Baalah and reached Jabneel. The boundary ended at the sea.

¹²The western boundary is the coastline of the Great Sea.ᵃ These are the boundaries around the people of Judah by their clans.

¹³In accordance with the LORD's command to him, Joshua gave to Caleb son of Jephunneh a portion in Judah—Kiriath Arba, that is, Hebron. (Arba was the forefather of Anak.) ¹⁴From Hebron Caleb drove out the three Anakites—Sheshai, Ahiman and Talmai—descendants of Anak. ¹⁵From there he marched against the people living in Debir (formerly called Kiriath Sepher). ¹⁶And Caleb said, "I will give my daughter Acsah in marriage to the man who attacks and captures Kiriath Sepher." ¹⁷Othniel son of Kenaz, Caleb's brother, took it; so Caleb gave his daughter Acsah to him in marriage.

¹⁸One day when she came to Othniel, she urged himᵇ to ask her father for a field. When she got off her donkey, Caleb asked her, "What can I do for you?"

¹⁹She replied, "Do me a special favor. Since you have given me land in the Negev, give me also springs of water." So Caleb gave her the upper and lower springs.

²⁰This is the inheritance of the tribe of Judah, clan by clan:

²¹The southernmost towns of the tribe of Judah in the Negev toward the boundary of Edom were:

Kabzeel, Eder, Jagur, ²²Kinah, Dimonah, Adadah, ²³Kedesh, Hazor, Ithnan, ²⁴Ziph, Telem, Bealoth, ²⁵Hazor Hadattah, Kerioth Hezron (that is, Hazor), ²⁶Amam, Shema, Moladah, ²⁷Hazar Gaddah, Heshmon, Beth Pelet, ²⁸Hazar Shual, Beersheba, Biziothiah, ²⁹Baalah, Iim, Ezem, ³⁰Eltolad, Kesil, Hormah, ³¹Ziklag, Madmannah, Sansannah, ³²Lebaoth, Shilhim, Ain and Rimmon—a total of twenty-nine towns and their villages.

³³In the western foothills:

Eshtaol, Zorah, Ashnah, ³⁴Zanoah, En Gannim, Tappuah, Enam, ³⁵Jarmuth, Adullam, Socoh, Azekah, ³⁶Shaaraim, Adithaim and Gederah (or Gederothaim)ᶜ—fourteen towns and their villages.

³⁷Zenan, Hadashah, Migdal Gad, ³⁸Dilean, Mizpah, Joktheel, ³⁹Lachish, Bozkath, Eglon, ⁴⁰Cabbon, Lahmas, Kitlish, ⁴¹Gederoth, Beth Dagon, Naamah and Makkedah—sixteen towns and their villages.

⁴²Libnah, Ether, Ashan, ⁴³Iphtah, Ashnah, Nezib, ⁴⁴Keilah, Aczib and Mareshah—nine towns and their villages.

⁴⁵Ekron, with its surrounding settlements and villages; ⁴⁶west of Ekron, all that were in the vicinity of Ashdod, together with their villages; ⁴⁷Ashdod, its surrounding settlements and villages; and Gaza, its settlements and villages, as far as the Wadi of Egypt and the coastline of the Great Sea.

⁴⁸In the hill country:

Shamir, Jattir, Socoh, ⁴⁹Dannah, Kiriath Sannah (that is, Debir), ⁵⁰Anab, Eshtemoh, Anim, ⁵¹Goshen, Holon and Giloh—eleven towns and their villages.

⁵²Arab, Dumah, Eshan, ⁵³Janim, Beth Tappuah, Aphekah, ⁵⁴Humtah, Kiriath Arba (that is, Hebron) and Zior—nine towns and their villages.

⁵⁵Maon, Carmel, Ziph, Juttah, ⁵⁶Jezreel, Jokdeam, Zanoah, ⁵⁷Kain, Gibeah and Timnah—ten towns and their villages.

ᵃ12 That is, the Mediterranean; also in verse 47   ᵇ18 Hebrew and some Septuagint manuscripts; other Septuagint manuscripts (see also note at Judges 1:14) *Othniel, he urged her*   ᶜ36 Or *Gederah and Gederothaim*

[58]Halhul, Beth Zur, Gedor, [59]Maarath, Beth Anoth and Eltekon—six towns and their villages.

[60]Kiriath Baal (that is, Kiriath Jearim) and Rabbah—two towns and their villages.

[61]In the desert:

Beth Arabah, Middin, Secacah, [62]Nibshan, the City of Salt and En Gedi—six towns and their villages.

[63]Judah could not dislodge the Jebusites, who were living in Jerusalem; to this day the Jebusites live there with the people of Judah.

16 *Allotment for Ephraim and Manasseh* The allotment for Joseph began at the Jordan of Jericho,[a] east of the waters of Jericho, and went up from there through the desert into the hill country of Bethel. [2]It went on from Bethel (that is, Luz),[b] crossed over to the territory of the Arkites in Ataroth, [3]descended westward to the territory of the Japhletites as far as the region of Lower Beth Horon and on to Gezer, ending at the sea.

[4]So Manasseh and Ephraim, the descendants of Joseph, received their inheritance.

[5]This was the territory of Ephraim, clan by clan:

The boundary of their inheritance went from Ataroth Addar in the east to Upper Beth Horon [6]and continued to the sea. From Micmethath on the north it curved eastward to Taanath Shiloh, passing by it to Janoah on the east. [7]Then it went down from Janoah to Ataroth and Naarah, touched Jericho and came out at the Jordan. [8]From Tappuah the border went west to the Kanah Ravine and ended at the sea. This was the inheritance of the tribe of the Ephraimites, clan by clan. [9]It also included all the towns and their villages that were set aside for the Ephraimites within the inheritance of the Manassites.

[10]They did not dislodge the Canaanites living in Gezer; to this day the Canaanites live among the people of Ephraim but are required to do forced labor.

17 This was the allotment for the tribe of Manasseh as Joseph's firstborn, that is, for Makir, Manasseh's firstborn. Makir was the ancestor of the Gileadites, who had received Gilead and Bashan because the Makirites were great soldiers. [2]So this allotment was for the rest of the people of Manasseh—the clans of Abiezer, Helek, Asriel, Shechem, Hepher and Shemida. These are the other male descendants of Manasseh son of Joseph by their clans.

[3]Now Zelophehad son of Hepher, the son of Gilead, the son of Makir, the son of Manasseh, had no sons but only daughters, whose names were Mahlah, Noah, Hoglah, Milcah and Tirzah. [4]They went to Eleazar the priest, Joshua son of Nun, and the leaders and said, "The LORD commanded Moses to give us an inheritance among our brothers." So Joshua gave them an inheritance along with the brothers of their father, according to the LORD's command. [5]Manasseh's share consisted of ten tracts of land besides Gilead and Bashan east of the Jordan, [6]because the daughters of the tribe of Manasseh received an inheritance among the sons. The land of Gilead belonged to the rest of the descendants of Manasseh.

[7]The territory of Manasseh extended from Asher to Micmethath east of Shechem. The boundary ran southward from there to include the people living at En Tappuah. [8](Manasseh had the land of Tappuah, but Tappuah itself, on the boundary of Manasseh, belonged to the Ephraim-

---

[a]*1 Jordan of Jericho* was possibly an ancient name for the Jordan River.   [b]*2 Septuagint; Hebrew Bethel to Luz*

ites.) ⁹Then the boundary continued south to the Kanah Ravine. There were towns belonging to Ephraim lying among the towns of Manasseh, but the boundary of Manasseh was the northern side of the ravine and ended at the sea. ¹⁰On the south the land belonged to Ephraim, on the north to Manasseh. The territory of Manasseh reached the sea and bordered Asher on the north and Issachar on the east.

¹¹Within Issachar and Asher, Manasseh also had Beth Shan, Ibleam and the people of Dor, Endor, Taanach and Megiddo, together with their surrounding settlements (the third in the list is Naphoth*).

¹²Yet the Manassites were not able to occupy these towns, for the Canaanites were determined to live in that region. ¹³However, when the Israelites grew stronger, they subjected the Canaanites to forced labor but did not drive them out completely.

¹⁴The people of Joseph said to Joshua, "Why have you given us only one allotment and one portion for an inheritance? We are a numerous people and the LORD has blessed us abundantly."

¹⁵"If you are so numerous," Joshua answered, "and if the hill country of Ephraim is too small for you, go up into the forest and clear land for yourselves there in the land of the Perizzites and Rephaites."

¹⁶The people of Joseph replied, "The hill country is not enough for us, and all the Canaanites who live in the plain have iron chariots, both those in Beth Shan and its settlements and those in the Valley of Jezreel."

¹⁷But Joshua said to the house of Joseph—to Ephraim and Manasseh—"You are numerous and very powerful. You will have not only one allotment ¹⁸but the forested hill country as well. Clear it, and its farthest limits will be yours; though the Canaanites have iron chariots and though they are strong, you can drive them out."

18 **Division of the Rest of the Land** The whole assembly of the Israelites gathered at Shiloh and set up the Tent of Meeting there. The country was brought under their control, ²but there were still seven Israelite tribes who had not yet received their inheritance.

³So Joshua said to the Israelites: "How long will you wait before you begin to take possession of the land that the LORD, the God of your fathers, has given you? ⁴Appoint three men from each tribe. I will send them out to make a survey of the land and to write a description of it, according to the inheritance of each. Then they will return to me. ⁵You are to divide the land into seven parts. Judah is to remain in its territory on the south and the house of Joseph in its territory on the north. ⁶After you have written descriptions of the seven parts of the land, bring them here to me and I will cast lots for you in the presence of the LORD our God. ⁷The Levites, however, do not get a portion among you, because the priestly service of the LORD is their inheritance. And Gad, Reuben and the half-tribe of Manasseh have already received their inheritance on the east side of the Jordan. Moses the servant of the LORD gave it to them."

⁸As the men started on their way to map out the land, Joshua instructed them, "Go and make a survey of the land and write a description of it. Then return to me, and I will cast lots for you here at Shiloh in the presence of the LORD." ⁹So the men left and went through the land. They wrote its description on a scroll, town by town, in seven parts, and returned to Joshua in the camp at Shiloh. ¹⁰Joshua then cast lots for them in Shiloh in the presence of

QUIZZER

JOSHUA 18

Q: What Israelite tribe was given no land of its own?

BONUS: Where did members of this tribe live?

Answers on page 275

*11 That is, Naphoth Dor

the Lord, and there he distributed the land to the Israelites according to their tribal divisions.

Allotment for Benjamin   [11]The lot came up for the tribe of Benjamin, clan by clan. Their allotted territory lay between the tribes of Judah and Joseph:

[12]On the north side their boundary began at the Jordan, passed the northern slope of Jericho and headed west into the hill country, coming out at the desert of Beth Aven. [13]From there it crossed to the south slope of Luz (that is, Bethel) and went down to Ataroth Addar on the hill south of Lower Beth Horon.

[14]From the hill facing Beth Horon on the south the boundary turned south along the western side and came out at Kiriath Baal (that is, Kiriath Jearim), a town of the people of Judah. This was the western side.

[15]The southern side began at the outskirts of Kiriath Jearim on the west, and the boundary came out at the spring of the waters of Nephtoah. [16]The boundary went down to the foot of the hill facing the Valley of Ben Hinnom, north of the Valley of Rephaim. It continued down the Hinnom Valley along the southern slope of the Jebusite city and so to En Rogel. [17]It then curved north, went to En Shemesh, continued to Geliloth, which faces the Pass of Adummim, and ran down to the Stone of Bohan son of Reuben. [18]It continued to the northern slope of Beth Arabah[a] and on down into the Arabah. [19]It then went to the northern slope of Beth Hoglah and came out at the northern bay of the Salt Sea,[b] at the mouth of the Jordan in the south. This was the southern boundary.

[20]The Jordan formed the boundary on the eastern side. These were the boundaries that marked out the inheritance of the clans of Benjamin on all sides.

[21]The tribe of Benjamin, clan by clan, had the following cities:

Jericho, Beth Hoglah, Emek Keziz, [22]Beth Arabah, Zemaraim, Bethel, [23]Avvim, Parah, Ophrah, [24]Kephar Ammoni, Ophni and Geba—twelve towns and their villages.

[25]Gibeon, Ramah, Beeroth, [26]Mizpah, Kephirah, Mozah, [27]Rekem, Irpeel, Taralah, [28]Zelah, Haeleph, the Jebusite city (that is, Jerusalem), Gibeah and Kiriath—fourteen towns and their villages.

This was the inheritance of Benjamin for its clans.

19 *Allotment for Simeon*   The second lot came out for the tribe of Simeon, clan by clan. Their inheritance lay within the territory of Judah. [2]It included:

Beersheba (or Sheba),[c] Moladah, [3]Hazar Shual, Balah, Ezem, [4]Eltolad, Bethul, Hormah, [5]Ziklag, Beth Marcaboth, Hazar Susah, [6]Beth Lebaoth and Sharuhen—thirteen towns and their villages;

[7]Ain, Rimmon, Ether and Ashan—four towns and their villages— [8]and all the villages around these towns as far as Baalath Beer (Ramah in the Negev).

This was the inheritance of the tribe of the Simeonites, clan by clan. [9]The inheritance of the Simeonites was taken from the share of Judah, because Judah's portion was more than they needed. So the Simeonites received their inheritance within the territory of Judah.

Allotment for Zebulun   [10]The third lot came up for Zebulun, clan by clan:

The boundary of their inheritance went as far as Sarid. [11]Going west it ran to Maralah, touched Dabbesheth, and extended to the ravine near

Answers
to Quizzer on
page 274

A: Every tribe but the Levites was given a plot of land (Joshua 18:7).

BONUS: The Levites had towns in the lands of the other tribes (Joshua 21:2-3), so they could teach everyone God's law (2 Chronicles 35:3).

---

[a]18 Septuagint; Hebrew *slope facing the Arabah*   [b]19 That is, the Dead Sea   [c]2 Or *Beersheba, Sheba;* 1 Chron. 4:28 does not have *Sheba*.

Jokneam. [12]It turned east from Sarid toward the sunrise to the territory of Kisloth Tabor and went on to Daberath and up to Japhia. [13]Then it continued eastward to Gath Hepher and Eth Kazin; it came out at Rimmon and turned toward Neah. [14]There the boundary went around on the north to Hannathon and ended at the Valley of Iphtah El. [15]Included were Kattath, Nahalal, Shimron, Idalah and Bethlehem. There were twelve towns and their villages.

[16]These towns and their villages were the inheritance of Zebulun, clan by clan.

Allotment for Issachar   [17]The fourth lot came out for Issachar, clan by clan. [18]Their territory included:

Jezreel, Kesulloth, Shunem, [19]Hapharaim, Shion, Anaharath, [20]Rabbith, Kishion, Ebez, [21]Remeth, En Gannim, En Haddah and Beth Pazzez. [22]The boundary touched Tabor, Shahazumah and Beth Shemesh, and ended at the Jordan. There were sixteen towns and their villages.

[23]These towns and their villages were the inheritance of the tribe of Issachar, clan by clan.

Allotment for Asher   [24]The fifth lot came out for the tribe of Asher, clan by clan. [25]Their territory included:

Helkath, Hali, Beten, Acshaph, [26]Allammelech, Amad and Mishal. On the west the boundary touched Carmel and Shihor Libnath. [27]It then turned east toward Beth Dagon, touched Zebulun and the Valley of Iphtah El, and went north to Beth Emek and Neiel, passing Cabul on the left. [28]It went to Abdon,[a] Rehob, Hammon and Kanah, as far as Greater Sidon. [29]The boundary then turned back toward Ramah and went to the fortified city of Tyre, turned toward Hosah and came out at the sea in the region of Aczib, [30]Ummah, Aphek and Rehob. There were twenty-two towns and their villages.

[31]These towns and their villages were the inheritance of the tribe of Asher, clan by clan.

Allotment for Naphtali   [32]The sixth lot came out for Naphtali, clan by clan:

[33]Their boundary went from Heleph and the large tree in Zaanannim, passing Adami Nekeb and Jabneel to Lakkum and ending at the Jordan. [34]The boundary ran west through Aznoth Tabor and came out at Hukkok. It touched Zebulun on the south, Asher on the west and the Jordan[b] on the east. [35]The fortified cities were Ziddim, Zer, Hammath, Rakkath, Kinnereth, [36]Adamah, Ramah, Hazor, [37]Kedesh, Edrei, En Hazor, [38]Iron, Migdal El, Horem, Beth Anath and Beth Shemesh. There were nineteen towns and their villages.

[39]These towns and their villages were the inheritance of the tribe of Naphtali, clan by clan.

Allotment for Dan   [40]The seventh lot came out for the tribe of Dan, clan by clan. [41]The territory of their inheritance included:

Zorah, Eshtaol, Ir Shemesh, [42]Shaalabbin, Aijalon, Ithlah, [43]Elon, Timnah, Ekron, [44]Eltekeh, Gibbethon, Baalath, [45]Jehud, Bene Berak, Gath Rimmon, [46]Me Jarkon and Rakkon, with the area facing Joppa.

[47](But the Danites had difficulty taking possession of their territory, so they went up and attacked Leshem, took it, put it to the sword and occupied it. They settled in Leshem and named it Dan after their forefather.)

[48]These towns and their villages were the inheritance of the tribe of Dan, clan by clan.

---

[a]28 Some Hebrew manuscripts (see also Joshua 21:30); most Hebrew manuscripts *Ebron*   [b]34 Septuagint; Hebrew *west, and Judah, the Jordan,*

Allotment for Joshua ⁴⁹When they had finished dividing the land into its allotted portions, the Israelites gave Joshua son of Nun an inheritance among them, ⁵⁰as the LORD had commanded. They gave him the town he asked for—Timnath Serah*ᵃ* in the hill country of Ephraim. And he built up the town and settled there.

⁵¹These are the territories that Eleazar the priest, Joshua son of Nun and the heads of the tribal clans of Israel assigned by lot at Shiloh in the presence of the LORD at the entrance to the Tent of Meeting. And so they finished dividing the land.

20 *Cities of Refuge* Then the LORD said to Joshua: ²"Tell the Israelites to designate the cities of refuge, as I instructed you through Moses, ³so that anyone who kills a person accidentally and unintentionally may flee there and find protection from the avenger of blood.

⁴"When he flees to one of these cities, he is to stand in the entrance of the city gate and state his case before the elders of that city. Then they are to admit him into their city and give him a place to live with them. ⁵If the avenger of blood pursues him, they must not surrender the one accused, because he killed his neighbor unintentionally and without malice aforethought. ⁶He is to stay in that city until he has stood trial before the assembly and until the death of the high priest who is serving at that time. Then he may go back to his own home in the town from which he fled."

⁷So they set apart Kedesh in Galilee in the hill country of Naphtali, Shechem in the hill country of Ephraim, and Kiriath Arba (that is, Hebron) in the hill country of Judah. ⁸On the east side of the Jordan of Jericho*ᵇ* they designated Bezer in the desert on the plateau in the tribe of Reuben, Ramoth in Gilead in the tribe of Gad, and Golan in Bashan in the tribe of Manasseh. ⁹Any of the Israelites or any alien living among them who killed someone accidentally could flee to these designated cities and not be killed by the avenger of blood prior to standing trial before the assembly.

21 *Towns for the Levites* Now the family heads of the Levites approached Eleazar the priest, Joshua son of Nun, and the heads of the other tribal families of Israel ²at Shiloh in Canaan and said to them, "The LORD commanded through Moses that you give us towns to live in, with pasturelands for our livestock." ³So, as the LORD had commanded, the Israelites gave the Levites the following towns and pasturelands out of their own inheritance:

⁴The first lot came out for the Kohathites, clan by clan. The Levites who were descendants of Aaron the priest were allotted thirteen towns from the tribes of Judah, Simeon and Benjamin. ⁵The rest of Kohath's descendants were allotted ten towns from the clans of the tribes of Ephraim, Dan and half of Manasseh.

⁶The descendants of Gershon were allotted thirteen towns from the clans of the tribes of Issachar, Asher, Naphtali and the half-tribe of Manasseh in Bashan.

CITIES OF REFUGE
• KEDESH
• GOLAN
• RAMOTH
SHECHEM
• BEZER
HEBRON •

SEE
JOSHUA 20:7-9

*ᵃ50 Also known as *Timnath Heres* (see Judges 2:9)
ᵇ8 Jordan of Jericho was possibly an ancient name for the Jordan River.

⁷The descendants of Merari, clan by clan, received twelve towns from the tribes of Reuben, Gad and Zebulun.

⁸So the Israelites allotted to the Levites these towns and their pasturelands, as the LORD had commanded through Moses.

⁹From the tribes of Judah and Simeon they allotted the following towns by name ¹⁰(these towns were assigned to the descendants of Aaron who were from the Kohathite clans of the Levites, because the first lot fell to them):

¹¹They gave them Kiriath Arba (that is, Hebron), with its surrounding pastureland, in the hill country of Judah. (Arba was the forefather of Anak.) ¹²But the fields and villages around the city they had given to Caleb son of Jephunneh as his possession.

¹³So to the descendants of Aaron the priest they gave Hebron (a city of refuge for one accused of murder), Libnah, ¹⁴Jattir, Eshtemoa, ¹⁵Holon, Debir, ¹⁶Ain, Juttah and Beth Shemesh, together with their pasturelands—nine towns from these two tribes.

¹⁷And from the tribe of Benjamin they gave them Gibeon, Geba, ¹⁸Anathoth and Almon, together with their pasturelands—four towns.

¹⁹All the towns for the priests, the descendants of Aaron, were thirteen, together with their pasturelands.

²⁰The rest of the Kohathite clans of the Levites were allotted towns from the tribe of Ephraim:

²¹In the hill country of Ephraim they were given Shechem (a city of refuge for one accused of murder) and Gezer, ²²Kibzaim and Beth Horon, together with their pasturelands—four towns.

²³Also from the tribe of Dan they received Eltekeh, Gibbethon, ²⁴Aijalon and Gath Rimmon, together with their pasturelands—four towns.

²⁵From half the tribe of Manasseh they received Taanach and Gath Rimmon, together with their pasturelands—two towns.

²⁶All these ten towns and their pasturelands were given to the rest of the Kohathite clans.

²⁷The Levite clans of the Gershonites were given:
from the half-tribe of Manasseh,
Golan in Bashan (a city of refuge for one accused of murder) and Be Eshtarah, together with their pasturelands—two towns;
²⁸from the tribe of Issachar,
Kishion, Daberath, ²⁹Jarmuth and En Gannim, together with their pasturelands—four towns;
³⁰from the tribe of Asher,
Mishal, Abdon, ³¹Helkath and Rehob, together with their pasturelands—four towns;
³²from the tribe of Naphtali,
Kedesh in Galilee (a city of refuge for one accused of murder), Hammoth Dor and Kartan, together with their pasturelands—three towns.

³³All the towns of the Gershonite clans were thirteen, together with their pasturelands.

³⁴The Merarite clans (the rest of the Levites) were given:
from the tribe of Zebulun,
Jokneam, Kartah, ³⁵Dimnah and Nahalal, together with their pasturelands—four towns;
³⁶from the tribe of Reuben,
Bezer, Jahaz, ³⁷Kedemoth and Mephaath, together with their pasturelands—four towns;
³⁸from the tribe of Gad,
Ramoth in Gilead (a city of refuge for one accused of murder), Mahana-

im, ³⁹Heshbon and Jazer, together with their pasturelands—four towns in all.

⁴⁰All the towns allotted to the Merarite clans, who were the rest of the Levites, were twelve.

⁴¹The towns of the Levites in the territory held by the Israelites were forty-eight in all, together with their pasturelands. ⁴²Each of these towns had pasturelands surrounding it; this was true for all these towns.

⁴³So the LORD gave Israel all the land he had sworn to give their forefathers, and they took possession of it and settled there. ⁴⁴The LORD gave them rest on every side, just as he had sworn to their forefathers. Not one of their enemies withstood them; the LORD handed all their enemies over to them. ⁴⁵Not one of all the LORD's good promises to the house of Israel failed; every one was fulfilled.

22 **Eastern Tribes Return Home** Then Joshua summoned the Reubenites, the Gadites and the half-tribe of Manasseh ²and said to them, "You have done all that Moses the servant of the LORD commanded, and you have obeyed me in everything I commanded. ³For a long time now—to this very day—you have not deserted your brothers but have carried out the mission the LORD your God gave you. ⁴Now that the LORD your God has given your brothers rest as he promised, return to your homes in the land that Moses the servant of the LORD gave you on the other side of the Jordan. ⁵But be very careful to keep the commandment and the law that Moses the servant of the LORD gave you: to love the LORD your God, to walk in all his ways, to obey his commands, to hold fast to him and to serve him with all your heart and all your soul."

⁶Then Joshua blessed them and sent them away, and they went to their homes. ⁷(To the half-tribe of Manasseh Moses had given land in Bashan, and to the other half of the tribe Joshua gave land on the west side of the Jordan with their brothers.) When Joshua sent them home, he blessed them, ⁸saying, "Return to your homes with your great wealth—with large herds of livestock, with silver, gold, bronze and iron, and a great quantity of clothing—and divide with your brothers the plunder from your enemies."

⁹So the Reubenites, the Gadites and the half-tribe of Manasseh left the Israelites at Shiloh in Canaan to return to Gilead, their own land, which they had acquired in accordance with the command of the LORD through Moses.

¹⁰When they came to Geliloth near the Jordan in the land of Canaan, the Reubenites, the Gadites and the half-tribe of Manasseh built an imposing altar there by the Jordan. ¹¹And when the Israelites heard that they had built the altar on the border of Canaan at Geliloth near the Jordan on the Israelite side, ¹²the whole assembly of Israel gathered at Shiloh to go to war against them.

¹³So the Israelites sent Phinehas son of Eleazar, the priest, to the land of Gilead—to Reuben, Gad and the half-tribe of Manasseh. ¹⁴With him they sent ten of the chief men, one for each of the tribes of Israel, each the head of a family division among the Israelite clans.

¹⁵When they went to Gilead—to Reuben, Gad and the half-tribe of Manasseh—they said to them: ¹⁶"The whole assembly of the LORD says: 'How could you break faith with the God of Israel like this? How could you turn away from the LORD and build yourselves an altar in rebellion against him now? ¹⁷Was not the sin of Peor enough for us? Up to this very day we have not cleansed ourselves from that sin, even though a plague fell on the community of the LORD! ¹⁸And are you now turning away from the LORD?

" 'If you rebel against the LORD today, tomorrow he will be angry with the

> Not one of all the LORD's good promises . . . failed; every one was fulfilled
> (Joshua 21:45).

Dear Sam,

I saw one of my girlfriends flirting with my boyfriend. I'm so mad I'm ready to blow up at her! Should I?

Faith in Fairbanks

100 Advice Lane, Anywhere, USA

Dear Faith,

You're in an unpleasant, but not very uncommon, situation. It's always best to be diplomatic and try to get accurate facts from the source, in this case your boyfriend and your girlfriend.

At least one war was prevented in this way. Two groups of Israelites settled on opposite banks of the Jordan (Joshua 22). One group saw the others building an altar and concluded that the others were deserting the Lord. They wanted to wage war on them, but first a delegation was sent to ask why they were building this altar. When their reason turned out to be a godly one, the delegation went back and told their group to cool it.

There is a tremendously important lesson to be learned here! Don't jump to conclusions. Many times things may appear to be far different from what they actually are. Before you wage a war of righteous anger, be sure you have your facts straight. Everyone then comes out a winner.

Sam

whole community of Israel. ¹⁹If the land you possess is defiled, come over to the Lord's land, where the Lord's tabernacle stands, and share the land with us. But do not rebel against the Lord or against us by building an altar for yourselves, other than the altar of the Lord our God. ²⁰When Achan son of Zerah acted unfaithfully regarding the devoted things,ᵃ did not wrath come upon the whole community of Israel? He was not the only one who died for his sin.' "

²¹Then Reuben, Gad and the half-tribe of Manasseh replied to the heads of the clans of Israel: ²²"The Mighty One, God, the Lord! The Mighty One, God, the Lord! He knows! And let Israel know! If this has been in rebellion or disobedience to the Lord, do not spare us this day. ²³If we have built our own altar to turn away from the Lord and to offer burnt offerings and grain offerings, or to sacrifice fellowship offeringsᵇ on it, may the Lord himself call us to account.

²⁴"No! We did it for fear that some day your descendants might say to ours, 'What do you have to do with the Lord, the God of Israel? ²⁵The Lord has made the Jordan a boundary between us and you—you Reubenites and Gadites! You have no share in the Lord.' So your descendants might cause ours to stop fearing the Lord.

²⁶"That is why we said, 'Let us get ready and build an altar—but not for burnt offerings or sacrifices.' ²⁷On the contrary, it is to be a witness between us and you and the generations that follow, that we will worship the Lord at his sanctuary with our burnt offerings, sacrifices and fellowship offerings. Then in the future your descendants will not be able to say to ours, 'You have no share in the Lord.'

²⁸"And we said, 'If they ever say this to us, or to our descendants, we will answer: Look at the replica of the Lord's altar, which our fathers built, not for burnt offerings and sacrifices, but as a witness between us and you.'

²⁹"Far be it from us to rebel against the Lord and turn away from him today by building an altar for burnt offerings, grain offerings and sacrifices, other than the altar of the Lord our God that stands before his tabernacle."

³⁰When Phinehas the priest and the leaders of the community—the heads of the clans of the Israelites—heard what Reuben, Gad and Manasseh had to say, they were pleased. ³¹And Phinehas son of Eleazar, the priest, said to Reuben, Gad and Manasseh, "Today we know that the Lord is with us, because you have not acted unfaithfully toward the Lord in this matter. Now you have rescued the Israelites from the Lord's hand."

³²Then Phinehas son of Eleazar, the priest, and the leaders returned to Canaan from their meeting with the Reubenites and Gadites in Gilead and reported to the Israelites. ³³They were glad to hear the report and praised God. And they talked no more about going to war against them to devastate the country where the Reubenites and the Gadites lived.

³⁴And the Reubenites and the Gadites gave the altar this name: A Witness Between Us that the Lord is God.

23 *Joshua's Farewell to the Leaders* After a long time had passed and the Lord had given Israel rest from all their enemies around them, Joshua, by then old and well advanced in years, ²summoned all Israel—their elders, leaders, judges and officials—and said to them: "I am old and well advanced in years. ³You yourselves have seen everything the Lord your God has done to all these nations for your sake; it was the Lord your God who fought for you. ⁴Remember how I have allotted as an inheritance for your tribes all the land of the nations that remain—the nations I conquered—between the Jordan and the Great Seaᶜ in the west. ⁵The Lord your

---

ᵃ20 The Hebrew term refers to the irrevocable giving over of things or persons to the Lord, often by totally destroying them.   ᵇ23 Traditionally *peace offerings*; also in verse 27   ᶜ4 That is, the Mediterranean

God himself will drive them out of your way. He will push them out before you, and you will take possession of their land, as the LORD your God promised you.

⁶"Be very strong; be careful to obey all that is written in the Book of the Law of Moses, without turning aside to the right or to the left. ⁷Do not associate with these nations that remain among you; do not invoke the names of their gods or swear by them. You must not serve them or bow down to them. ⁸But you are to hold fast to the LORD your God, as you have until now.

⁹"The LORD has driven out before you great and powerful nations; to this day no one has been able to withstand you. ¹⁰One of you routs a thousand, because the LORD your God fights for you, just as he promised. ¹¹So be very careful to love the LORD your God.

¹²"But if you turn away and ally yourselves with the survivors of these nations that remain among you and if you intermarry with them and associate with them, ¹³then you may be sure that the LORD your God will no longer drive out these nations before you. Instead, they will become snares and traps for you, whips on your backs and thorns in your eyes, until you perish from this good land, which the LORD your God has given you.

¹⁴"Now I am about to go the way of all the earth. You know with all your heart and soul that not one of all the good promises the LORD your God gave you has failed. Every promise has been fulfilled; not one has failed. ¹⁵But just as every good promise of the LORD your God has come true, so the LORD will bring on you all the evil he has threatened, until he has destroyed you from this good land he has given you. ¹⁶If you violate the covenant of the LORD your God, which he commanded you, and go and serve other gods and bow down to them, the LORD's anger will burn against you, and you will quickly perish from the good land he has given you."

24 *The Covenant Renewed at Shechem* Then Joshua assembled all the tribes of Israel at Shechem. He summoned the elders, leaders, judges and officials of Israel, and they presented themselves before God.

²Joshua said to all the people, "This is what the LORD, the God of Israel, says: 'Long ago your forefathers, including Terah the father of Abraham and Nahor, lived beyond the River[a] and worshiped other gods. ³But I took your father Abraham from the land beyond the River and led him throughout Canaan and gave him many descendants. I gave him Isaac, ⁴and to Isaac I gave Jacob and Esau. I assigned the hill country of Seir to Esau, but Jacob and his sons went down to Egypt.

⁵" 'Then I sent Moses and Aaron, and I afflicted the Egyptians by what I did there, and I brought you out. ⁶When I brought your fathers out of Egypt, you came to the sea, and the Egyptians pursued them with chariots and horsemen[b] as far as the Red Sea.[c] ⁷But they cried to the LORD for help, and he put darkness between you and the Egyptians; he brought

---

Direct Line

JOSHUA 23:6–13

Years ago a good-looking guy or gal was a "dreamboat." In the sixties he or she was "groovy." The words change year by year, but whatever you call an attractive person now, don't get carried away by mere looks. God warned his people not to intermarry with the neighboring Canaanites. They might have looked like "dreamboats," but they weren't committed to God and would draw God's people away from him. There's nothing wrong with good looks or with being attracted to good-looking guys or gals. Just make sure that the person you like loves the Lord and will help instead of hinder your Christian life.

---

[a]2 That is, the Euphrates; also in verses 3, 14 and 15
[b]6 Or *charioteers* [c]6 Hebrew *Yam Suph*; that is, Sea of Reeds

the sea over them and covered them. You saw with your own eyes what I did to the Egyptians. Then you lived in the desert for a long time.

⁸" 'I brought you to the land of the Amorites who lived east of the Jordan. They fought against you, but I gave them into your hands. I destroyed them from before you, and you took possession of their land. ⁹When Balak son of Zippor, the king of Moab, prepared to fight against Israel, he sent for Balaam son of Beor to put a curse on you. ¹⁰But I would not listen to Balaam, so he blessed you again and again, and I delivered you out of his hand.

¹¹" 'Then you crossed the Jordan and came to Jericho. The citizens of Jericho fought against you, as did also the Amorites, Perizzites, Canaanites, Hittites, Girgashites, Hivites and Jebusites, but I gave them into your hands. ¹²I sent the hornet ahead of you, which drove them out before you—also the two Amorite kings. You did not do it with your own sword and bow. ¹³So I gave you a land on which you did not toil and cities you did not build; and you live in them and eat from vineyards and olive groves that you did not plant.'

¹⁴"Now fear the LORD and serve him with all faithfulness. Throw away the gods your forefathers worshiped beyond the River and in Egypt, and serve the LORD. ¹⁵But if serving the LORD seems undesirable to you, then choose for yourselves this day whom you will serve, whether the gods your forefathers served beyond the River, or the gods of the Amorites, in whose land you are living. But as for me and my household, we will serve the LORD."

¹⁶Then the people answered, "Far be it from us to forsake the LORD to serve other gods! ¹⁷It was the LORD our God himself who brought us and our fathers up out of Egypt, from that land of slavery, and performed those great signs before our eyes. He protected us on our entire journey and among all the nations through which we traveled. ¹⁸And the LORD drove out before us all the nations, including the Amorites, who lived in the land. We too will serve the LORD, because he is our God."

¹⁹Joshua said to the people, "You are not able to serve the LORD. He is a holy God; he is a jealous God. He will not forgive your rebellion and your sins. ²⁰If you forsake the LORD and serve foreign gods, he will turn and bring disaster on you and make an end of you, after he has been good to you."

²¹But the people said to Joshua, "No! We will serve the LORD."

²²Then Joshua said, "You are witnesses against yourselves that you have chosen to serve the LORD."

"Yes, we are witnesses," they replied.

²³"Now then," said Joshua, "throw away the foreign gods that are among you and yield your hearts to the LORD, the God of Israel."

²⁴And the people said to Joshua, "We will serve the LORD our God and obey him."

²⁵On that day Joshua made a covenant for the people, and there at Shechem he drew up for them decrees and laws. ²⁶And Joshua recorded these things in the Book of the Law of God. Then he took a large stone and set it up there under the oak near the holy place of the LORD.

²⁷"See!" he said to all the people. "This stone will be a witness against us. It has

JOSHUA 24:14–21

Your parents make you go to church? Even if you don't want to? Well, that's their right as long as you live in their home. Not that they think dragging you to church makes you a Christian any more than sitting in a school classroom makes you an A student. Going to church just gives you the chance to learn about God. But you have to decide to make a personal commitment. Joshua knew this very well. When he was old and about to die, he challenged all the Israelites: "Choose for yourselves this day whom you will serve" (Joshua 24:15). That's a challenge every person faces. Including you.

Direct Line

heard all the words the LORD has said to us. It will be a witness against you if you are untrue to your God."

Buried in the Promised Land [28]Then Joshua sent the people away, each to his own inheritance.

[29]After these things, Joshua son of Nun, the servant of the LORD, died at the age of a hundred and ten. [30]And they buried him in the land of his inheritance, at Timnath Serah[a] in the hill country of Ephraim, north of Mount Gaash.

[31]Israel served the LORD throughout the lifetime of Joshua and of the elders who outlived him and who had experienced everything the LORD had done for Israel.

[32]And Joseph's bones, which the Israelites had brought up from Egypt, were buried at Shechem in the tract of land that Jacob bought for a hundred pieces of silver[b] from the sons of Hamor, the father of Shechem. This became the inheritance of Joseph's descendants.

[33]And Eleazar son of Aaron died and was buried at Gibeah, which had been allotted to his son Phinehas in the hill country of Ephraim.

---

[a]*30* Also known as *Timnath Heres* (see Judges 2:9)   [b]*32* Hebrew *hundred kesitahs*; a kesitah was a unit of money of unknown weight and value.

RULES.

What if no one at school followed the rules? What if no one obeyed traffic signs when driving? There certainly would be one big mess. And probably a lot of people would get hurt.

Judges tells about a time when the Israelites didn't follow God's rules. Again and again they forgot him and worshiped idols. Each time they got in trouble. And each time, when they turned back to the Lord, he sent a leader to save them from their enemies. Judges is a reminder that God is faithful even when you don't follow his rules. But Judges also reminds you that you're in for trouble if you don't do things God's way!

FAST FACTS

The "judges" were military and political leaders.

The time of the judges was from 1375 to 1040 B.C.

The longest stories are about Deborah, Gideon, Jephthah and Samson.

The stories have a pattern: Israel sins, suffers, turns to God, is saved by a judge, enjoys a brief peace, but soon sins again.

Fundamentals

Can women be leaders of God's people (Judges 4)?

Do you think it upsets God when people want proof that he's speaking to them (Judges 6)?

How can someone so strong be so weak (Judges 13–16)?

What would life be like in a country where most people ignored God (Judges 19)?

Israel Fights the Remaining Canaanites After the death of Joshua, the Israelites asked the LORD, "Who will be the first to go up and fight for us against the Canaanites?"

²The LORD answered, "Judah is to go; I have given the land into their hands."

³Then the men of Judah said to the Simeonites their brothers, "Come up with us into the territory allotted to us, to fight against the Canaanites. We in turn will go with you into yours." So the Simeonites went with them.

⁴When Judah attacked, the LORD gave the Canaanites and Perizzites into their hands and they struck down ten thousand men at Bezek. ⁵It was there that they found Adoni-Bezek and fought against him, putting to rout the Canaanites and Perizzites. ⁶Adoni-Bezek fled, but they chased him and caught him, and cut off his thumbs and big toes.

⁷Then Adoni-Bezek said, "Seventy kings with their thumbs and big toes cut off have picked up scraps under my table. Now God has paid me back for what I did to them." They brought him to Jerusalem, and he died there.

⁸The men of Judah attacked Jerusalem also and took it. They put the city to the sword and set it on fire.

⁹After that, the men of Judah went down to fight against the Canaanites living in the hill country, the Negev and the western foothills. ¹⁰They advanced against the Canaanites living in Hebron (formerly called Kiriath Arba) and defeated Sheshai, Ahiman and Talmai.

¹¹From there they advanced against the people living in Debir (formerly called Kiriath Sepher). ¹²And Caleb said, "I will give my daughter Acsah in marriage to the man who attacks and captures Kiriath Sepher." ¹³Othniel son of Kenaz, Caleb's younger brother, took it; so Caleb gave his daughter Acsah to him in marriage.

¹⁴One day when she came to Othniel, she urged him*ᵃ* to ask her father for a field. When she got off her donkey, Caleb asked her, "What can I do for you?"

¹⁵She replied, "Do me a special favor. Since you have given me land in the Negev, give me also springs of water." Then Caleb gave her the upper and lower springs.

¹⁶The descendants of Moses' father-in-law, the Kenite, went up from the City of Palms*ᵇ* with the men of Judah to live among the people of the Desert of Judah in the Negev near Arad.

¹⁷Then the men of Judah went with the Simeonites their brothers and attacked the Canaanites living in Zephath, and they totally destroyed*ᶜ* the city. Therefore it was called Hormah.*ᵈ* ¹⁸The men of Judah also took*ᵉ* Gaza, Ashkelon and Ekron—each city with its territory.

¹⁹The LORD was with the men of Judah. They took possession of the hill country, but they were unable to drive the people from the plains, because they had iron chariots. ²⁰As Moses had promised, Hebron was given to Caleb, who drove from it the three sons of Anak. ²¹The Benjamites, however, failed to dislodge the Jebusites, who were living in Jerusalem; to this day the Jebusites live there with the Benjamites.

²²Now the house of Joseph attacked Bethel, and the LORD was with them. ²³When they sent men to spy out Bethel (formerly called Luz), ²⁴the spies saw a man coming out of the city and they said to him, "Show us how to get into the city and we will see that you are treated well." ²⁵So he showed them, and they put the city to the sword but spared the man and his whole family. ²⁶He then went to the land of the Hittites, where he built a city and called it Luz, which is its name to this day.

ᵃ14 Hebrew; Septuagint and Vulgate *Othniel, he urged her*   *ᵇ16* That is, Jericho   *ᶜ17* The Hebrew term refers to the irrevocable giving over of things or persons to the LORD, often by totally destroying them.   *ᵈ17 Hormah* means *destruction.*   *ᵉ18* Hebrew; Septuagint *Judah did not take*

²⁷But Manasseh did not drive out the people of Beth Shan or Taanach or Dor or Ibleam or Megiddo and their surrounding settlements, for the Canaanites were determined to live in that land. ²⁸When Israel became strong, they pressed the Canaanites into forced labor but never drove them out completely. ²⁹Nor did Ephraim drive out the Canaanites living in Gezer, but the Canaanites continued to live there among them. ³⁰Neither did Zebulun drive out the Canaanites living in Kitron or Nahalol, who remained among them; but they did subject them to forced labor. ³¹Nor did Asher drive out those living in Acco or Sidon or Ahlab or Aczib or Helbah or Aphek or Rehob, ³²and because of this the people of Asher lived among the Canaanite inhabitants of the land. ³³Neither did Naphtali drive out those living in Beth Shemesh or Beth Anath; but the Naphtalites too lived among the Canaanite inhabitants of the land, and those living in Beth Shemesh and Beth Anath became forced laborers for them. ³⁴The Amorites confined the Danites to the hill country, not allowing them to come down into the plain. ³⁵And the Amorites were determined also to hold out in Mount Heres, Aijalon and Shaalbim, but when the power of the house of Joseph increased, they too were pressed into forced labor. ³⁶The boundary of the Amorites was from Scorpion*ᵃ* Pass to Sela and beyond.

The Angel of the Lord at Bokim   The angel of the Lord went up from Gilgal to Bokim and said, "I brought you up out of Egypt and led you into the land that I swore to give to your forefathers. I said, 'I will never break my covenant with you, ²and you shall not make a covenant with the people of this land, but you shall break down their altars.' Yet you have disobeyed me. Why have you done this? ³Now therefore I tell you that I will not drive them out before you; they will be ؛thorns؛ in your sides and their gods will be a snare to you."

⁴When the angel of the Lord had spoken these things to all the Israelites, the people wept aloud, ⁵and they called that place Bokim.*ᵇ* There they offered sacrifices to the Lord.

Disobedience and Defeat   ⁶After Joshua had dismissed the Israelites, they went to take possession of the land, each to his own inheritance. ⁷The people served the Lord throughout the lifetime of Joshua and of the elders who outlived him and who had seen all the great things the Lord had done for Israel.

⁸Joshua son of Nun, the servant of the Lord, died at the age of a hundred and ten. ⁹And they buried him in the land of his inheritance, at Timnath Heres*ᶜ* in the hill country of Ephraim, north of Mount Gaash.

¹⁰After that whole generation had been gathered to their fathers, another generation grew up, who knew neither the Lord nor what he had done for Israel. ¹¹Then the Israelites did evil in the eyes of the Lord and served the Baals. ¹²They forsook the Lord, the God of their fathers, who had brought them out of Egypt. They followed and worshiped various gods of the peoples around them. They provoked the Lord to anger ¹³because they forsook him and served Baal and the Ashtoreths. ¹⁴In his anger against Israel the Lord handed them over to raiders who plundered them. He sold them to their enemies all around, whom they were no longer able to resist. ¹⁵Whenever Israel went out to fight, the hand of the Lord was against them to defeat them, just as he had sworn to them. They were in great distress.

¹⁶Then the Lord raised up judges,*ᵈ* who saved them out of the hands of these raiders. ¹⁷Yet they would not listen to their judges but prostituted themselves to other gods and worshiped them. Unlike their fathers, they quickly turned from the way in which their fathers had walked, the way of

---

ᵃ36 Hebrew *Akrabbim*   *ᵇ5 Bokim* means *weepers.*   *ᶜ9* Also known as *Timnath Serah* (see Joshua 19:50 and 24:30)   *ᵈ16* Or *leaders;* similarly in verses 17-19

obedience to the Lord's commands. [18]Whenever the Lord raised up a judge for them, he was with the judge and saved them out of the hands of their enemies as long as the judge lived; for the Lord had compassion on them as they groaned under those who oppressed and afflicted them. [19]But when the judge died, the people returned to ways even more corrupt than those of their fathers, following other gods and serving and worshiping them. They refused to give up their evil practices and stubborn ways.

[20]Therefore the Lord was very angry with Israel and said, "Because this nation has violated the covenant that I laid down for their forefathers and has not listened to me, [21]I will no longer drive out before them any of the nations Joshua left when he died. [22]I will use them to test Israel and see whether they will keep the way of the Lord and walk in it as their forefathers did." [23]The Lord had allowed those nations to remain; he did not drive them out at once by giving them into the hands of Joshua.

These are the nations the Lord left to test all those Israelites who had not experienced any of the wars in Canaan [2](he did this only to teach warfare to the descendants of the Israelites who had not had previous battle experience): [3]the five rulers of the Philistines, all the Canaanites, the Sidonians, and the Hivites living in the Lebanon mountains from Mount Baal Hermon to Lebo[a] Hamath. [4]They were left to test the Israelites to see whether they would obey the Lord's commands, which he had given their forefathers through Moses.

[5]The Israelites lived among the Canaanites, Hittites, Amorites, Perizzites, Hivites and Jebusites. [6]They took their daughters in marriage and gave their own daughters to their sons, and served their gods.

Othniel   [7]The Israelites did evil in the eyes of the Lord; they forgot the Lord their God and served the Baals and the Asherahs. [8]The anger of the Lord burned against Israel so that he sold them into the hands of Cushan-Rishathaim king of Aram Naharaim,[b] to whom the Israelites were subject for eight years. [9]But when they cried out to the Lord, he raised up for them a deliverer, Othniel son of Kenaz, Caleb's younger brother, who saved them. [10]The Spirit of the Lord came upon him, so that he became Israel's judge[c] and went to war. The Lord gave Cushan-Rishathaim king of Aram into the hands of Othniel, who overpowered him. [11]So the land had peace for forty years, until Othniel son of Kenaz died.

Ehud   [12]Once again the Israelites did evil in the eyes of the Lord, and because they did this evil the Lord gave Eglon king of Moab power over Israel. [13]Getting the Ammonites and Amalekites to join him, Eglon came and attacked Israel, and they took possession of the City of Palms.[d] [14]The Israelites were subject to Eglon king of Moab for eighteen years.

[15]Again the Israelites cried out to the Lord, and he gave them a deliverer—Ehud, a left-handed man, the son of Gera the Benjamite. The Israelites sent him with tribute to Eglon king of Moab. [16]Now Ehud had made a double-edged sword about a foot and a half[e] long, which he strapped to his right thigh under his clothing. [17]He presented the tribute to Eglon king of Moab, who was a very fat man. [18]After Ehud had presented the tribute, he sent on their way the men who had carried it. [19]At the idols[f] near Gilgal he himself turned back and said, "I have a secret message for you, O king."

The king said, "Quiet!" And all his attendants left him.

[20]Ehud then approached him while he was sitting alone in the upper room of his summer palace[g] and said, "I have a message from God for you." As the

---

[a]3 Or *to the entrance to*   [b]8 That is, Northwest Mesopotamia   [c]10 Or *leader*   [d]13 That is, Jericho   [e]16 Hebrew *a cubit* (about 0.5 meter)   [f]19 Or *the stone quarries*; also in verse 26   [g]20 The meaning of the Hebrew for this phrase is uncertain.

king rose from his seat, ²¹Ehud reached with his left hand, drew the sword from his right thigh and plunged it into the king's belly. ²²Even the handle sank in after the blade, which came out his back. Ehud did not pull the sword out, and the fat closed in over it. ²³Then Ehud went out to the porch*ᵃ*; he shut the doors of the upper room behind him and locked them.

²⁴After he had gone, the servants came and found the doors of the upper room locked. They said, "He must be relieving himself in the inner room of the house." ²⁵They waited to the point of embarrassment, but when he did not open the doors of the room, they took a key and unlocked them. There they saw their lord fallen to the floor, dead.

²⁶While they waited, Ehud got away. He passed by the idols and escaped to Seirah. ²⁷When he arrived there, he blew a trumpet in the hill country of Ephraim, and the Israelites went down with him from the hills, with him leading them.

²⁸"Follow me," he ordered, "for the Lord has given Moab, your enemy, into your hands." So they followed him down and, taking possession of the fords of the Jordan that led to Moab, they allowed no one to cross over. ²⁹At that time they struck down about ten thousand Moabites, all vigorous and strong; not a man escaped. ³⁰That day Moab was made subject to Israel, and the land had peace for eighty years.

Shamgar ³¹After Ehud came Shamgar son of Anath, who struck down six hundred Philistines with an oxgoad. He too saved Israel.

4 *Deborah* After Ehud died, the Israelites once again did evil in the eyes of the Lord. ²So the Lord sold them into the hands of Jabin, a king of Canaan, who reigned in Hazor. The commander of his army was Sisera, who lived in Harosheth Haggoyim. ³Because he had nine hundred iron chariots and had cruelly oppressed the Israelites for twenty years, they cried to the Lord for help.

⁴Deborah, a prophetess, the wife of Lappidoth, was leading*ᵇ* Israel at that time. ⁵She held court under the Palm of Deborah between Ramah and Bethel in the hill country of Ephraim, and the Israelites came to her to have their disputes decided. ⁶She sent for Barak son of Abinoam from Kedesh in Naphtali and said to him, "The Lord, the God of Israel, commands you: 'Go, take with you ten thousand men of Naphtali and Zebulun and lead the way to Mount Tabor. ⁷I will lure Sisera, the commander of Jabin's army, with his chariots and his troops to the Kishon River and give him into your hands.' "

⁸Barak said to her, "If you go with me, I will go; but if you don't go with me, I won't go."

⁹"Very well," Deborah said, "I will go with you. But because of the way you are going about this,*ᶜ* the honor will not be yours, for the Lord will hand Sisera over to a woman." So Deborah went with Barak to Kedesh, ¹⁰where he summoned Zebulun and Naphtali. Ten thousand men followed him, and Deborah also went with him.

¹¹Now Heber the Kenite had left the other Kenites, the descendants of Hobab, Moses' brother-in-law,*ᵈ* and pitched his tent by the great tree in Zaanannim near Kedesh.

¹²When they told Sisera that Barak son of Abinoam had gone up to Mount Tabor, ¹³Sisera gathered together his nine hundred iron chariots and all the men with him, from Harosheth Haggoyim to the Kishon River.

JUDGES 3

Q: What strange weapon did Shamgar use to fight the Philistines?

BONUS: What other strange weapon is mentioned in Judges?

Answers on page 291

ᵃ23 The meaning of the Hebrew for this word is uncertain. *ᵇ4* Traditionally *judging*   *ᶜ9* Or *But on the expedition you are undertaking*   *ᵈ11* Or *father-in-law*

Dear Sam,

Does God get upset when women are leaders?

Monica in Montpelier

Dear Sam, Inc.

100 Advice Lane, Anywhere, USA

Dear Monica,

There has been a great deal of controversy in both society and in the church on this question. Scripture has many accounts of women in very important roles.

One excellent example is Deborah, a prophetess who led Israel at the end of 20 years of Canaanite oppression (Judges 4–5). The Lord told Deborah what had to be done to free the Israelites. But one of the men refused to follow her directions unless she went with him. Deborah agreed to go, but she predicted that a woman would be given credit for the victory. And she was right. Sisera, the enemy leader, went to a woman for help. But that woman killed him while all the military men were searching for him.

God not only permits women to be leaders, he sometimes appoints them. God gives the gift of leadership to men and women. And he calls on each to obey and to use those gifts.

Sam

¹⁴Then Deborah said to Barak, "Go! This is the day the LORD has given Sisera into your hands. Has not the LORD gone ahead of you?" So Barak went down Mount Tabor, followed by ten thousand men. ¹⁵At Barak's advance, the LORD routed Sisera and all his chariots and army by the sword, and Sisera abandoned his chariot and fled on foot. ¹⁶But Barak pursued the chariots and army as far as Harosheth Haggoyim. All the troops of Sisera fell by the sword; not a man was left.

¹⁷Sisera, however, fled on foot to the tent of Jael, the wife of Heber the Kenite, because there were friendly relations between Jabin king of Hazor and the clan of Heber the Kenite.

¹⁸Jael went out to meet Sisera and said to him, "Come, my lord, come right in. Don't be afraid." So he entered her tent, and she put a covering over him.

¹⁹"I'm thirsty," he said. "Please give me some water." She opened a skin of milk, gave him a drink, and covered him up.

²⁰"Stand in the doorway of the tent," he told her. "If someone comes by and asks you, 'Is anyone here?' say 'No.'"

²¹But Jael, Heber's wife, picked up a tent peg and a hammer and went quietly to him while he lay fast asleep, exhausted. She drove the peg through his temple into the ground, and he died.

²²Barak came by in pursuit of Sisera, and Jael went out to meet him. "Come," she said, "I will show you the man you're looking for." So he went in with her, and there lay Sisera with the tent peg through his temple—dead.

²³On that day God subdued Jabin, the Canaanite king, before the Israelites. ²⁴And the hand of the Israelites grew stronger and stronger against Jabin, the Canaanite king, until they destroyed him.

Answers
to Quizzer on
page 289

A: An oxgoad,
a long stick with
a metal point,
usually used to
guide oxen
(Judges 3:31).

BONUS: The
donkey's
jawbone Samson
used to fight
the Philistines
(Judges 15:15-17).

5 *The Song of Deborah*   On that day Deborah and Barak son of Abinoam sang this song:

> ²"When the princes in Israel take the lead,
>   when the people willingly offer themselves—
>   praise the LORD!
>
> ³"Hear this, you kings! Listen, you rulers!
>   I will sing to*ᵃ* the LORD, I will sing;
>   I will make music to*ᵇ* the LORD, the God of Israel.
>
> ⁴"O LORD, when you went out from Seir,
>   when you marched from the land of Edom,
> the earth shook, the heavens poured,
>   the clouds poured down water.
> ⁵The mountains quaked before the LORD, the One of Sinai,
>   before the LORD, the God of Israel.
>
> ⁶"In the days of Shamgar son of Anath,
>   in the days of Jael, the roads were abandoned;
>   travelers took to winding paths.
> ⁷Village life*ᶜ* in Israel ceased,
>   ceased until I,*ᵈ* Deborah, arose,
>   arose a mother in Israel.
> ⁸When they chose new gods,
>   war came to the city gates,
> and not a shield or spear was seen
>   among forty thousand in Israel.

ᵃ3 Or *of*   *ᵇ3* Or / *with song I will praise*   *ᶜ7* Or *Warriors*   *ᵈ7* Or *you*

⁹My heart is with Israel's princes,
    with the willing volunteers among the people.
Praise the LORD!

¹⁰"You who ride on white donkeys,
    sitting on your saddle blankets,
    and you who walk along the road,
consider ¹¹the voice of the singers*a* at the watering places.
    They recite the righteous acts of the LORD,
    the righteous acts of his warriors*b* in Israel.

"Then the people of the LORD
    went down to the city gates.
¹²'Wake up, wake up, Deborah!
    Wake up, wake up, break out in song!
Arise, O Barak!
    Take captive your captives, O son of Abinoam.'

¹³"Then the men who were left
    came down to the nobles;
the people of the LORD
    came to me with the mighty.
¹⁴Some came from Ephraim, whose roots were in Amalek;
    Benjamin was with the people who followed you.
From Makir captains came down,
    from Zebulun those who bear a commander's staff.
¹⁵The princes of Issachar were with Deborah;
    yes, Issachar was with Barak,
    rushing after him into the valley.
In the districts of Reuben
    there was much searching of heart.
¹⁶Why did you stay among the campfires*c*
    to hear the whistling for the flocks?
In the districts of Reuben
    there was much searching of heart.
¹⁷Gilead stayed beyond the Jordan.
    And Dan, why did he linger by the ships?
Asher remained on the coast
    and stayed in his coves.
¹⁸The people of Zebulun risked their very lives;
    so did Naphtali on the heights of the field.

¹⁹"Kings came, they fought;
    the kings of Canaan fought
at Taanach by the waters of Megiddo,
    but they carried off no silver, no plunder.
²⁰From the heavens the stars fought,
    from their courses they fought against Sisera.
²¹The river Kishon swept them away,
    the age-old river, the river Kishon.
March on, my soul; be strong!
²²Then thundered the horses' hoofs—
    galloping, galloping go his mighty steeds.
²³'Curse Meroz,' said the angel of the LORD.
    'Curse its people bitterly,
because they did not come to help the LORD,
    to help the LORD against the mighty.'

---

a11 Or archers; the meaning of the Hebrew for this word is uncertain. *b11 Or villagers* *c16 Or saddlebags*

²⁴"Most blessed of women be Jael,
    the wife of Heber the Kenite,
    most blessed of tent-dwelling women.
²⁵He asked for water, and she gave him milk;
    in a bowl fit for nobles she brought him curdled milk.
²⁶Her hand reached for the tent peg,
    her right hand for the workman's hammer.
She struck Sisera, she crushed his head,
    she shattered and pierced his temple.
²⁷At her feet he sank,
    he fell; there he lay.
At her feet he sank, he fell;
    where he sank, there he fell—dead.

²⁸"Through the window peered Sisera's mother;
    behind the lattice she cried out,
'Why is his chariot so long in coming?
    Why is the clatter of his chariots delayed?'
²⁹The wisest of her ladies answer her;
    indeed, she keeps saying to herself,
³⁰'Are they not finding and dividing the spoils:
    a girl or two for each man,
    colorful garments as plunder for Sisera,
    colorful garments embroidered,
    highly embroidered garments for my neck—
all this as plunder?'

³¹"So may all your enemies perish, O Lᴏʀᴅ!
    But may they who love you be like the sun
    when it rises in its strength."

Then the land had peace forty years.

Gideon   Again the Israelites did evil in the eyes of the Lᴏʀᴅ, and for seven years he gave them into the hands of the Midianites. ²Because the power of Midian was so oppressive, the Israelites prepared shelters for themselves in mountain clefts, caves and strongholds. ³Whenever the Israelites planted their crops, the Midianites, Amalekites and other eastern peoples invaded the country. ⁴They camped on the land and ruined the crops all the way to Gaza and did not spare a living thing for Israel, neither sheep nor cattle nor donkeys. ⁵They came up with their livestock and their tents like swarms of locusts. It was impossible to count the men and their camels; they invaded the land to ravage it. ⁶Midian so impoverished the Israelites that they cried out to the Lᴏʀᴅ for help.

⁷When the Israelites cried to the Lᴏʀᴅ because of Midian, ⁸he sent them a prophet, who said, "This is what the Lᴏʀᴅ, the God of Israel, says: I brought you up out of Egypt, out of the land of slavery. ⁹I snatched you from the power of Egypt and from the hand of all your oppressors. I drove them from before you and gave you their land. ¹⁰I said to you, 'I am the Lᴏʀᴅ your God; do not worship the gods of the Amorites, in whose land you live.' But you have not listened to me."

¹¹The angel of the Lᴏʀᴅ came and sat down under the oak in Ophrah that belonged to Joash the Abiezrite, where his son Gideon was threshing wheat in a winepress to keep it from the Midianites. ¹²When the angel of the Lᴏʀᴅ appeared to Gideon, he said, "The Lᴏʀᴅ is with you, mighty warrior."

¹³"But sir," Gideon replied, "if the Lᴏʀᴅ is with us, why has all this happened to us? Where are all his wonders that our fathers told us about when

they said, 'Did not the LORD bring us up out of Egypt?' But now the LORD has abandoned us and put us into the hand of Midian."

[14]The LORD turned to him and said, "Go in the strength you have and save Israel out of Midian's hand. Am I not sending you?"

[15]"But Lord,[a]" Gideon asked, "how can I save Israel? My clan is the weakest in Manasseh, and I am the least in my family."

[16]The LORD answered, "I will be with you, and you will strike down all the Midianites together."

[17]Gideon replied, "If now I have found favor in your eyes, give me a sign that it is really you talking to me. [18]Please do not go away until I come back and bring my offering and set it before you."

And the LORD said, "I will wait until you return."

[19]Gideon went in, prepared a young goat, and from an ephah[b] of flour he made bread without yeast. Putting the meat in a basket and its broth in a pot, he brought them out and offered them to him under the oak.

[20]The angel of God said to him, "Take the meat and the unleavened bread, place them on this rock, and pour out the broth." And Gideon did so. [21]With the tip of the staff that was in his hand, the angel of the LORD touched the meat and the unleavened bread. Fire flared from the rock, consuming the meat and the bread. And the angel of the LORD disappeared. [22]When Gideon realized that it was the angel of the LORD, he exclaimed, "Ah, Sovereign LORD! I have seen the angel of the LORD face to face!"

[23]But the LORD said to him, "Peace! Do not be afraid. You are not going to die."

[24]So Gideon built an altar to the LORD there and called it The LORD is Peace. To this day it stands in Ophrah of the Abiezrites.

[25]That same night the LORD said to him, "Take the second bull from your father's herd, the one seven years old.[c] Tear down your father's altar to Baal and cut down the Asherah pole[d] beside it. [26]Then build a proper kind of[e] altar to the LORD your God on the top of this height. Using the wood of the Asherah pole that you cut down, offer the second[f] bull as a burnt offering."

[27]So Gideon took ten of his servants and did as the LORD told him. But because he was afraid of his family and the men of the town, he did it at night rather than in the daytime.

[28]In the morning when the men of the town got up, there was Baal's altar, demolished, with the Asherah pole beside it cut down and the second bull sacrificed on the newly built altar!

[29]They asked each other, "Who did this?"

When they carefully investigated, they were told, "Gideon son of Joash did it."

[30]The men of the town demanded of Joash, "Bring out your son. He must die, because he has broken down Baal's altar and cut down the Asherah pole beside it."

[31]But Joash replied to the hostile crowd around him, "Are you going to plead Baal's cause? Are you trying to save him?

JUDEGS 6:14–16

Gideon had a problem with his self-image. When God told him to save Israel from the Midianites, Gideon responded, "My clan is the weakest in Manasseh, and I am the least in my family" (Judges 6:15). But God said, "Go in the strength you have" (Judges 6:14). Gideon had strengths he hadn't yet discovered. And so do you! God has given you abilities that make you unique and strengths that make you able to triumph over your challenges. Sure, you feel as inadequate as Gideon did sometimes. But God has given you strengths that are greater than your weaknesses. And he has said to you as he did to Gideon, "I will be with you" (Judges 6:16).

Direct Line

---

a15 Or *sir* *b19* That is, probably about 3/5 bushel (about 22 liters) *c25* Or *Take a full-grown, mature bull from your father's herd* *d25* That is, a symbol of the goddess Asherah; here and elsewhere in Judges *e26* Or *build with layers of stone an* *f26* Or *full-grown;* also in verse 28

Whoever fights for him shall be put to death by morning! If Baal really is a god, he can defend himself when someone breaks down his altar." [32]So that day they called Gideon "Jerub-Baal,[a]" saying, "Let Baal contend with him," because he broke down Baal's altar.

[33]Now all the Midianites, Amalekites and other eastern peoples joined forces and crossed over the Jordan and camped in the Valley of Jezreel. [34]Then the Spirit of the LORD came upon Gideon, and he blew a trumpet, summoning the Abiezrites to follow him. [35]He sent messengers throughout Manasseh, calling them to arms, and also into Asher, Zebulun and Naphtali, so that they too went up to meet them.

[36]Gideon said to God, "If you will save Israel by my hand as you have promised— [37]look, I will place a wool fleece on the threshing floor. If there is dew only on the fleece and all the ground is dry, then I will know that you will save Israel by my hand, as you said." [38]And that is what happened. Gideon rose early the next day; he squeezed the fleece and wrung out the dew—a bowlful of water.

[39]Then Gideon said to God, "Do not be angry with me. Let me make just one more request. Allow me one more test with the fleece. This time make the fleece dry and the ground covered with dew." [40]That night God did so. Only the fleece was dry; all the ground was covered with dew.

7 *Gideon Defeats the Midianites* Early in the morning, Jerub-Baal (that is, Gideon) and all his men camped at the spring of Harod. The camp of Midian was north of them in the valley near the hill of Moreh. [2]The LORD said to Gideon, "You have too many men for me to deliver Midian into their hands. In order that Israel may not boast against me that her own strength has saved her, [3]announce now to the people, 'Anyone who trembles with fear may turn back and leave Mount Gilead.' " So twenty-two thousand men left, while ten thousand remained.

[4]But the LORD said to Gideon, "There are still too many men. Take them down to the water, and I will sift them for you there. If I say, 'This one shall go with you,' he shall go; but if I say, 'This one shall not go with you,' he shall not go."

[5]So Gideon took the men down to the water. There the LORD told him, "Separate those who lap the water with their tongues like a dog from those who kneel down to drink." [6]Three hundred men lapped with their hands to their mouths. All the rest got down on their knees to drink.

[7]The LORD said to Gideon, "With the three hundred men that lapped I will save you and give the Midianites into your hands. Let all the other men go, each to his own place." [8]So Gideon sent the rest of the Israelites to their tents but kept the three hundred, who took over the provisions and trumpets of the others.

Now the camp of Midian lay below him in the valley. [9]During that night the LORD said to Gideon, "Get up, go down against the camp, because I am going to give it into your hands. [10]If you are afraid to attack, go down to the camp with your servant Purah [11]and listen to what they are saying. Afterward, you will be encouraged to attack the camp." So he and Purah his servant went down to the outposts of the camp. [12]The Midianites, the Amalekites and all the other eastern peoples had settled in the valley, thick as locusts. Their camels could no more be counted than the sand on the seashore.

[13]Gideon arrived just as a man was telling a friend his dream. "I had a dream," he was saying. "A round loaf of barley bread came tumbling into the Midianite camp. It struck the tent with such force that the tent overturned and collapsed."

[14]His friend responded, "This can be nothing other than the sword of Gid-

---

a32 Jerub-Baal means *let Baal contend.*

eon son of Joash, the Israelite. God has given the Midianites and the whole camp into his hands."

15When Gideon heard the dream and its interpretation, he worshiped God. He returned to the camp of Israel and called out, "Get up! The LORD has given the Midianite camp into your hands." 16Dividing the three hundred men into three companies, he placed trumpets and empty jars in the hands of all of them, with torches inside.

17"Watch me," he told them. "Follow my lead. When I get to the edge of the camp, do exactly as I do. 18When I and all who are with me blow our trumpets, then from all around the camp blow yours and shout, 'For the LORD and for Gideon.' "

19Gideon and the hundred men with him reached the edge of the camp at the beginning of the middle watch, just after they had changed the guard. They blew their trumpets and broke the jars that were in their hands. 20The three companies blew the trumpets and smashed the jars. Grasping the torches in their left hands and holding in their right hands the trumpets they were to blow, they shouted, "A sword for the LORD and for Gideon!" 21While each man held his position around the camp, all the Midianites ran, crying out as they fled.

22When the three hundred trumpets sounded, the LORD caused the men throughout the camp to turn on each other with their swords. The army fled to Beth Shittah toward Zererah as far as the border of Abel Meholah near Tabbath. 23Israelites from Naphtali, Asher and all Manasseh were called out, and they pursued the Midianites. 24Gideon sent messengers throughout the hill country of Ephraim, saying, "Come down against the Midianites and seize the waters of the Jordan ahead of them as far as Beth Barah."

So all the men of Ephraim were called out and they took the waters of the Jordan as far as Beth Barah. 25They also captured two of the Midianite leaders, Oreb and Zeeb. They killed Oreb at the rock of Oreb, and Zeeb at the winepress of Zeeb. They pursued the Midianites and brought the heads of Oreb and Zeeb to Gideon, who was by the Jordan.

Let's try one more time, key of B flat . . .

SEE
JUDGES 7:16-21

Zebah and Zalmunna Now the Ephraimites asked Gideon, "Why have you treated us like this? Why didn't you call us when you went to fight Midian?" And they criticized him sharply.

2But he answered them, "What have I accomplished compared to you? Aren't the gleanings of Ephraim's grapes better than the full grape harvest of Abiezer? 3God gave Oreb and Zeeb, the Midianite leaders, into your hands. What was I able to do compared to you?" At this, their resentment against him subsided.

4Gideon and his three hundred men, exhausted yet keeping up the pursuit, came to the Jordan and crossed it. 5He said to the men of Succoth, "Give my troops some bread; they are worn out, and I am still pursuing Zebah and Zalmunna, the kings of Midian."

6But the officials of Succoth said, "Do you already have the hands of Zebah and Zalmunna in your possession? Why should we give bread to your troops?"

⁷Then Gideon replied, "Just for that, when the LORD has given Zebah and Zalmunna into my hand, I will tear your flesh with desert thorns and briers."

⁸From there he went up to Peniel*ᵃ* and made the same request of them, but they answered as the men of Succoth had. ⁹So he said to the men of Peniel, "When I return in triumph, I will tear down this tower."

¹⁰Now Zebah and Zalmunna were in Karkor with a force of about fifteen thousand men, all that were left of the armies of the eastern peoples; a hundred and twenty thousand swordsmen had fallen. ¹¹Gideon went up by the route of the nomads east of Nobah and Jogbehah and fell upon the unsuspecting army. ¹²Zebah and Zalmunna, the two kings of Midian, fled, but he pursued them and captured them, routing their entire army.

¹³Gideon son of Joash then returned from the battle by the Pass of Heres. ¹⁴He caught a young man of Succoth and questioned him, and the young man wrote down for him the names of the seventy-seven officials of Succoth, the elders of the town. ¹⁵Then Gideon came and said to the men of Succoth, "Here are Zebah and Zalmunna, about whom you taunted me by saying, 'Do you already have the hands of Zebah and Zalmunna in your possession? Why should we give bread to your exhausted men?' " ¹⁶He took the elders of the town and taught the men of Succoth a lesson by punishing them with desert thorns and briers. ¹⁷He also pulled down the tower of Peniel and killed the men of the town.

¹⁸Then he asked Zebah and Zalmunna, "What kind of men did you kill at Tabor?"

"Men like you," they answered, "each one with the bearing of a prince."

¹⁹Gideon replied, "Those were my brothers, the sons of my own mother. As surely as the LORD lives, if you had spared their lives, I would not kill you." ²⁰Turning to Jether, his oldest son, he said, "Kill them!" But Jether did not draw his sword, because he was only a boy and was afraid.

²¹Zebah and Zalmunna said, "Come, do it yourself. 'As is the man, so is his strength.' " So Gideon stepped forward and killed them, and took the ornaments off their camels' necks.

Gideon's Ephod ²²The Israelites said to Gideon, "Rule over us—you, your son and your grandson—because you have saved us out of the hand of Midian."

²³But Gideon told them, "I will not rule over you, nor will my son rule over you. The LORD will rule over you." ²⁴And he said, "I do have one request, that each of you give me an earring from your share of the plunder." (It was the custom of the Ishmaelites to wear gold earrings.)

²⁵They answered, "We'll be glad to give them." So they spread out a garment, and each man threw a ring from his plunder onto it. ²⁶The weight of the gold rings he asked for came to seventeen hundred shekels,*ᵇ* not counting the ornaments, the pendants and the purple garments worn by the kings of Midian or the chains that were on their camels' necks. ²⁷Gideon made the gold into an ephod, which he placed in Ophrah, his town. All Israel prostituted themselves by worshiping it there, and it became a snare to Gideon and his family.

Gideon's Death ²⁸Thus Midian was subdued before the Israelites and did not raise its head again. During Gideon's lifetime, the land enjoyed peace forty years.

²⁹Jerub-Baal son of Joash went back home to live. ³⁰He had seventy sons of his own, for he had many wives. ³¹His concubine, who lived in Shechem, also bore him a son, whom he named Abimelech. ³²Gideon son of Joash died at a

---

ᵃ8 Hebrew *Penuel,* a variant of *Peniel;* also in verses 9 and 17   *ᵇ26* That is, about 43 pounds (about 19.5 kilograms)

good old age and was buried in the tomb of his father Joash in Ophrah of the Abiezrites.

³³No sooner had Gideon died than the Israelites again prostituted themselves to the Baals. They set up Baal-Berith as their god and ³⁴did not remember the LORD their God, who had rescued them from the hands of all their enemies on every side. ³⁵They also failed to show kindness to the family of Jerub-Baal (that is, Gideon) for all the good things he had done for them.

9 *Abimelech* Abimelech son of Jerub-Baal went to his mother's brothers in Shechem and said to them and to all his mother's clan, ²"Ask all the citizens of Shechem, 'Which is better for you: to have all seventy of Jerub-Baal's sons rule over you, or just one man?' Remember, I am your flesh and blood."

³When the brothers repeated all this to the citizens of Shechem, they were inclined to follow Abimelech, for they said, "He is our brother." ⁴They gave him seventy shekels*ᵃ* of silver from the temple of Baal-Berith, and Abimelech used it to hire reckless adventurers, who became his followers. ⁵He went to his father's home in Ophrah and on one stone murdered his seventy brothers, the sons of Jerub-Baal. But Jotham, the youngest son of Jerub-Baal, escaped by hiding. ⁶Then all the citizens of Shechem and Beth Millo gathered beside the great tree at the pillar in Shechem to crown Abimelech king.

⁷When Jotham was told about this, he climbed up on the top of Mount Gerizim and shouted to them, "Listen to me, citizens of Shechem, so that God may listen to you. ⁸One day the trees went out to anoint a king for themselves. They said to the olive tree, 'Be our king.'

⁹"But the olive tree answered, 'Should I give up my oil, by which both gods and men are honored, to hold sway over the trees?'

¹⁰"Next, the trees said to the fig tree, 'Come and be our king.'

¹¹"But the fig tree replied, 'Should I give up my fruit, so good and sweet, to hold sway over the trees?'

¹²"Then the trees said to the vine, 'Come and be our king.'

¹³"But the vine answered, 'Should I give up my wine, which cheers both gods and men, to hold sway over the trees?'

¹⁴"Finally all the trees said to the thornbush, 'Come and be our king.'

¹⁵"The thornbush said to the trees, 'If you really want to anoint me king over you, come and take refuge in my shade; but if not, then let fire come out of the thornbush and consume the cedars of Lebanon!'

¹⁶"Now if you have acted honorably and in good faith when you made Abimelech king, and if you have been fair to Jerub-Baal and his family, and if you have treated him as he deserves— ¹⁷and to think that my father fought for you, risked his life to rescue you from the hand of Midian ¹⁸(but today you have revolted against my father's family, murdered his seventy sons on a single stone, and made Abimelech, the son of his slave girl, king over

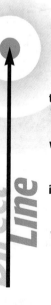

JUDGES 9

How important is it to trust people you call your friends? Judges 9 raises the question by describing the relationship between Abimelech and the citizens of Shechem, who plotted together to make Abimelech king. The story makes it very clear that people who get together to do wrong can't trust each other. True friendship is different. It's not based on doing wrong together; it's based on caring. As friendship deepens, friends share and learn that they can trust each other. What keeps you and your friends together? Can you trust them? Abimelech's "friends" weren't really friends. Are yours?

ᵃ4 That is, about 1 3/4 pounds (about 0.8 kilogram)

the citizens of Shechem because he is your brother)— [19]if then you have acted honorably and in good faith toward Jerub-Baal and his family today, may Abimelech be your joy, and may you be his, too! [20]But if you have not, let fire come out from Abimelech and consume you, citizens of Shechem and Beth Millo, and let fire come out from you, citizens of Shechem and Beth Millo, and consume Abimelech!"

[21]Then Jotham fled, escaping to Beer, and he lived there because he was afraid of his brother Abimelech.

[22]After Abimelech had governed Israel three years, [23]God sent an evil spirit between Abimelech and the citizens of Shechem, who acted treacherously against Abimelech. [24]God did this in order that the crime against Jerub-Baal's seventy sons, the shedding of their blood, might be avenged on their brother Abimelech and on the citizens of Shechem, who had helped him murder his brothers. [25]In opposition to him these citizens of Shechem set men on the hilltops to ambush and rob everyone who passed by, and this was reported to Abimelech.

[26]Now Gaal son of Ebed moved with his brothers into Shechem, and its citizens put their confidence in him. [27]After they had gone out into the fields and gathered the grapes and trodden them, they held a festival in the temple of their god. While they were eating and drinking, they cursed Abimelech. [28]Then Gaal son of Ebed said, "Who is Abimelech, and who is Shechem, that we should be subject to him? Isn't he Jerub-Baal's son, and isn't Zebul his deputy? Serve the men of Hamor, Shechem's father! Why should we serve Abimelech? [29]If only this people were under my command! Then I would get rid of him. I would say to Abimelech, 'Call out your whole army!' "[a]

[30]When Zebul the governor of the city heard what Gaal son of Ebed said, he was very angry. [31]Under cover he sent messengers to Abimelech, saying, "Gaal son of Ebed and his brothers have come to Shechem and are stirring up the city against you. [32]Now then, during the night you and your men should come and lie in wait in the fields. [33]In the morning at sunrise, advance against the city. When Gaal and his men come out against you, do whatever your hand finds to do."

[34]So Abimelech and all his troops set out by night and took up concealed positions near Shechem in four companies. [35]Now Gaal son of Ebed had gone out and was standing at the entrance to the city gate just as Abimelech and his soldiers came out from their hiding place.

[36]When Gaal saw them, he said to Zebul, "Look, people are coming down from the tops of the mountains!"

Zebul replied, "You mistake the shadows of the mountains for men."

[37]But Gaal spoke up again: "Look, people are coming down from the center of the land, and a company is coming from the direction of the soothsayers' tree."

[38]Then Zebul said to him, "Where is your big talk now, you who said, 'Who is Abimelech that we should be subject to him?' Aren't these the men you ridiculed? Go out and fight them!"

[39]So Gaal led out[b] the citizens of Shechem and fought Abimelech. [40]Abimelech chased him, and many fell wounded in the flight—all the way to the entrance to the gate. [41]Abimelech stayed in Arumah, and Zebul drove Gaal and his brothers out of Shechem.

[42]The next day the people of Shechem went out to the fields, and this was reported to Abimelech. [43]So he took his men, divided them into three companies and set an ambush in the fields. When he saw the people coming out of the city, he rose to attack them. [44]Abimelech and the companies with him rushed forward to a position at the entrance to the city gate. Then two com-

---

[a]29 Septuagint; Hebrew *him." Then he said to Abimelech, "Call out your whole army!"* [b]39 Or *Gaal went out in the sight of*

panies rushed upon those in the fields and struck them down. ⁴⁵All that day Abimelech pressed his attack against the city until he had captured it and killed its people. Then he destroyed the city and scattered salt over it.

⁴⁶On hearing this, the citizens in the tower of Shechem went into the stronghold of the temple of El-Berith. ⁴⁷When Abimelech heard that they had assembled there, ⁴⁸he and all his men went up Mount Zalmon. He took an ax and cut off some branches, which he lifted to his shoulders. He ordered the men with him, "Quick! Do what you have seen me do!" ⁴⁹So all the men cut branches and followed Abimelech. They piled them against the stronghold and set it on fire over the people inside. So all the people in the tower of Shechem, about a thousand men and women, also died.

⁵⁰Next Abimelech went to Thebez and besieged it and captured it. ⁵¹Inside the city, however, was a strong tower, to which all the men and women—all the people of the city—fled. They locked themselves in and climbed up on the tower roof. ⁵²Abimelech went to the tower and stormed it. But as he approached the entrance to the tower to set it on fire, ⁵³a woman dropped an upper millstone on his head and cracked his skull.

⁵⁴Hurriedly he called to his armor-bearer, "Draw your sword and kill me, so that they can't say, 'A woman killed him.' " So his servant ran him through, and he died. ⁵⁵When the Israelites saw that Abimelech was dead, they went home.

⁵⁶Thus God repaid the wickedness that Abimelech had done to his father by murdering his seventy brothers. ⁵⁷God also made the men of Shechem pay for all their wickedness. The curse of Jotham son of Jerub-Baal came on them.

Tola After the time of Abimelech a man of Issachar, Tola son of Puah, the son of Dodo, rose to save Israel. He lived in Shamir, in the hill country of Ephraim. ²He led[a] Israel twenty-three years; then he died, and was buried in Shamir.

Jair ³He was followed by Jair of Gilead, who led Israel twenty-two years. ⁴He had thirty sons, who rode thirty donkeys. They controlled thirty towns in Gilead, which to this day are called Havvoth Jair.[b] ⁵When Jair died, he was buried in Kamon.

QUIZZER

Q: What were Baals and Ashtoreths?

BONUS: Why was it wrong to have anything to do with them?

Answers on page 303

Jephthah ⁶Again the Israelites did evil in the eyes of the LORD. They served the Baals and the Ashtoreths, and the gods of Aram, the gods of Sidon, the gods of Moab, the gods of the Ammonites and the gods of the Philistines. And because the Israelites forsook the LORD and no longer served him, ⁷he became angry with them. He sold them into the hands of the Philistines and the Ammonites, ⁸who that year shattered and crushed them. For eighteen years they oppressed all the Israelites on the east side of the Jordan in Gilead, the land of the Amorites. ⁹The Ammonites also crossed the Jordan to fight against Judah, Benjamin and the house of Ephraim; and Israel was in great distress. ¹⁰Then the Israelites cried out to the LORD, "We have sinned against you, forsaking our God and serving the Baals."

¹¹The LORD replied, "When the Egyptians, the Amorites, the Ammonites, the Philistines, ¹²the Sidonians, the Amalekites and the Maonites[c] oppressed you and you cried to me for help, did I not save you from their hands? ¹³But you have forsaken me and served other gods, so I will no longer save you. ¹⁴Go

---

[a]2 Traditionally *judged*; also in verse 3   [b]4 Or *called the settlements of Jair*   [c]12 Hebrew; some Septuagint manuscripts *Midianites*

and cry out to the gods you have chosen. Let them save you when you are in trouble!"

¹⁵But the Israelites said to the LORD, "We have sinned. Do with us whatever you think best, but please rescue us now." ¹⁶Then they got rid of the foreign gods among them and served the LORD. And he could bear Israel's misery no longer.

¹⁷When the Ammonites were called to arms and camped in Gilead, the Israelites assembled and camped at Mizpah. ¹⁸The leaders of the people of Gilead said to each other, "Whoever will launch the attack against the Ammonites will be the head of all those living in Gilead."

11 Jephthah the Gileadite was a mighty warrior. His father was Gilead; his mother was a prostitute. ²Gilead's wife also bore him sons, and when they were grown up, they drove Jephthah away. "You are not going to get any inheritance in our family," they said, "because you are the son of another woman." ³So Jephthah fled from his brothers and settled in the land of Tob, where a group of adventurers gathered around him and followed him.

⁴Some time later, when the Ammonites made war on Israel, ⁵the elders of Gilead went to get Jephthah from the land of Tob. ⁶"Come," they said, "be our commander, so we can fight the Ammonites."

⁷Jephthah said to them, "Didn't you hate me and drive me from my father's house? Why do you come to me now, when you're in trouble?"

⁸The elders of Gilead said to him, "Nevertheless, we are turning to you now; come with us to fight the Ammonites, and you will be our head over all who live in Gilead."

⁹Jephthah answered, "Suppose you take me back to fight the Ammonites and the LORD gives them to me—will I really be your head?"

¹⁰The elders of Gilead replied, "The LORD is our witness; we will certainly do as you say." ¹¹So Jephthah went with the elders of Gilead, and the people made him head and commander over them. And he repeated all his words before the LORD in Mizpah.

¹²Then Jephthah sent messengers to the Ammonite king with the question: "What do you have against us that you have attacked our country?"

¹³The king of the Ammonites answered Jephthah's messengers, "When Israel came up out of Egypt, they took away my land from the Arnon to the Jabbok, all the way to the Jordan. Now give it back peaceably."

¹⁴Jephthah sent back messengers to the Ammonite king, ¹⁵saying:

"This is what Jephthah says: Israel did not take the land of Moab or the land of the Ammonites. ¹⁶But when they came up out of Egypt, Israel went through the desert to the Red Sea*ᵃ* and on to Kadesh. ¹⁷Then Israel sent messengers to the king of Edom, saying, 'Give us permission to go through your country,' but the king of Edom would not listen. They sent also to the king of Moab, and he refused. So Israel stayed at Kadesh.

¹⁸"Next they traveled through the desert, skirted the lands of Edom and Moab, passed along the eastern side of the country of Moab, and camped on the other side of the Arnon. They did not enter the territory of Moab, for the Arnon was its border.

¹⁹"Then Israel sent messengers to Sihon king of the Amorites, who ruled in Heshbon, and said to him, 'Let us pass through your country to our own place.' ²⁰Sihon, however, did not trust Israelᵇ to pass through his territory. He mustered all his men and encamped at Jahaz and fought with Israel.

²¹"Then the LORD, the God of Israel, gave Sihon and all his men into Is-

---

ᵃ16 Hebrew *Yam Suph*; that is, Sea of Reeds   *ᵇ20* Or *however, would not make an agreement for Israel*

DEAR SAM,

MY TWO STEPBROTHERS AND STEPSISTER GANG UP ON ME ALL THE TIME. THIS IS A REAL NO-WIN SITUATION FOR ME. WHAT CAN I DO?

DREW IN DEARBORN

100 Advice Lane, Anywhere, USA

Dear Drew,

It's always nice when problems can be solved. Unfortunately, sometimes you don't have all that much control over situations, and you just have to do the best you can.

Your letter reminds me of a young man named Jephthah (Judges 11:1-11). He too had several stepbrothers, and when his father died, they told him to leave town. They weren't going to share their inheritance with him since he had a different mother. He left town, but later his family needed him and promised him that if he would help them, he could be their leader. He finally agreed to help them; and, because he was a godly man, the Lord guided and protected him so that he succeeded in his mission.

Jephthah can be a great example for you. Through no fault of his own, he was treated unfairly. Yet he was faithful to the Lord. You may have to wait years, but, like Jephthah, the Lord will remember your faithfulness to him.

Sam

rael's hands, and they defeated them. Israel took over all the land of the Amorites who lived in that country, ²²capturing all of it from the Arnon to the Jabbok and from the desert to the Jordan.

²³"Now since the Lord, the God of Israel, has driven the Amorites out before his people Israel, what right have you to take it over? ²⁴Will you not take what your god Chemosh gives you? Likewise, whatever the Lord our God has given us, we will possess. ²⁵Are you better than Balak son of Zippor, king of Moab? Did he ever quarrel with Israel or fight with them? ²⁶For three hundred years Israel occupied Heshbon, Aroer, the surrounding settlements and all the towns along the Arnon. Why didn't you retake them during that time? ²⁷I have not wronged you, but you are doing me wrong by waging war against me. Let the Lord, the Judge,^a decide the dispute this day between the Israelites and the Ammonites."

²⁸The king of Ammon, however, paid no attention to the message Jephthah sent him.

²⁹Then the Spirit of the Lord came upon Jephthah. He crossed Gilead and Manasseh, passed through Mizpah of Gilead, and from there he advanced against the Ammonites. ³⁰And Jephthah made a vow to the Lord: "If you give the Ammonites into my hands, ³¹whatever comes out of the door of my house to meet me when I return in triumph from the Ammonites will be the Lord's, and I will sacrifice it as a burnt offering."

³²Then Jephthah went over to fight the Ammonites, and the Lord gave them into his hands. ³³He devastated twenty towns from Aroer to the vicinity of Minnith, as far as Abel Keramim. Thus Israel subdued Ammon.

³⁴When Jephthah returned to his home in Mizpah, who should come out to meet him but his daughter, dancing to the sound of tambourines! She was an only child. Except for her he had neither son nor daughter. ³⁵When he saw her, he tore his clothes and cried, "Oh! My daughter! You have made me miserable and wretched, because I have made a vow to the Lord that I cannot break."

³⁶"My father," she replied, "you have given your word to the Lord. Do to me just as you promised, now that the Lord has avenged you of your enemies, the Ammonites. ³⁷But grant me this one request," she said. "Give me two months to roam the hills and weep with my friends, because I will never marry."

³⁸"You may go," he said. And he let her go for two months. She and the girls went into the hills and wept because she would never marry. ³⁹After the two months, she returned to her father and he did to her as he had vowed. And she was a virgin.

From this comes the Israelite custom ⁴⁰that each year the young women of Israel go out for four days to commemorate the daughter of Jephthah the Gileadite.

Jephthah and Ephraim The men of Ephraim called out their 12 forces, crossed over to Zaphon and said to Jephthah, "Why did you go to fight the Ammonites without calling us to go with you? We're going to burn down your house over your head."

²Jephthah answered, "I and my people were engaged in a great struggle with the Ammonites, and although I called, you didn't save me out of their hands. ³When I saw that you wouldn't help, I took my life in my hands and crossed over to fight the Ammonites, and the Lord gave me the victory over them. Now why have you come up today to fight me?"

⁴Jephthah then called together the men of Gilead and fought against

Answers
to Quizzer on
page 300

**A: Nature gods
(Judges 10:6).
Pagans
worshiped them
and engaged in
sexual rites to try
to obtain their
blessing of fertility on the land.**

***BONUS: God
had forbidden
worship of any
false god.***

^a27 Or *Ruler*

Ephraim. The Gileadites struck them down because the Ephraimites had said, "You Gileadites are renegades from Ephraim and Manasseh." ⁵The Gileadites captured the fords of the Jordan leading to Ephraim, and whenever a survivor of Ephraim said, "Let me cross over," the men of Gilead asked him, "Are you an Ephraimite?" If he replied, "No," ⁶they said, "All right, say 'Shibboleth.'" If he said, "Sibboleth," because he could not pronounce the word correctly, they seized him and killed him at the fords of the Jordan. Forty-two thousand Ephraimites were killed at that time.

⁷Jephthah led*ᵃ* Israel six years. Then Jephthah the Gileadite died, and was buried in a town in Gilead.

Ibzan, Elon and Abdon   ⁸After him, Ibzan of Bethlehem led Israel. ⁹He had thirty sons and thirty daughters. He gave his daughters away in marriage to those outside his clan, and for his sons he brought in thirty young women as wives from outside his clan. Ibzan led Israel seven years. ¹⁰Then Ibzan died, and was buried in Bethlehem.

¹¹After him, Elon the Zebulunite led Israel ten years. ¹²Then Elon died, and was buried in Aijalon in the land of Zebulun.

¹³After him, Abdon son of Hillel, from Pirathon, led Israel. ¹⁴He had forty sons and thirty grandsons, who rode on seventy donkeys. He led Israel eight years. ¹⁵Then Abdon son of Hillel died, and was buried at Pirathon in Ephraim, in the hill country of the Amalekites.

13 *The Birth of Samson*   Again the Israelites did evil in the eyes of the LORD, so the LORD delivered them into the hands of the Philistines for forty years.

²A certain man of Zorah, named Manoah, from the clan of the Danites, had a wife who was sterile and remained childless. ³The angel of the LORD appeared to her and said, "You are sterile and childless, but you are going to conceive and have a son. ⁴Now see to it that you drink no wine or other fermented drink and that you do not eat anything unclean, ⁵because you will conceive and give birth to a son. No razor may be used on his head, because the boy is to be a Nazirite, set apart to God from birth, and he will begin the deliverance of Israel from the hands of the Philistines."

⁶Then the woman went to her husband and told him, "A man of God came to me. He looked like an angel of God, very awesome. I didn't ask him where he came from, and he didn't tell me his name. ⁷But he said to me, 'You will conceive and give birth to a son. Now then, drink no wine or other fermented drink and do not eat anything unclean, because the boy will be a Nazirite of God from birth until the day of his death.'"

⁸Then Manoah prayed to the LORD: "O Lord, I beg you, let the man of God you sent to us come again to teach us how to bring up the boy who is to be born."

⁹God heard Manoah, and the angel of God came again to the woman while she was out in the field; but her husband Manoah was not with her. ¹⁰The woman hurried to tell her husband, "He's here! The man who appeared to me the other day!"

JUDGES 13:8

How often do you thank God for your parents? Are your mom and dad like Manoah and his wife? Do they look to God "to teach [them] how to bring up" you and your brothers or sisters? If so, you've got a lot to be thankful for. That doesn't mean your parents are perfect. Maybe you feel they're a little too strict. Or that they expect too much of you. Or that they don't give you the freedom you deserve. But if you sit down and make a list, chances are the positive things about your parents will outweigh the negatives.

Direct Line

ᵃ7 Traditionally judged; *also in verses 8-14*

¹¹Manoah got up and followed his wife. When he came to the man, he said, "Are you the one who talked to my wife?"

"I am," he said.

¹²So Manoah asked him, "When your words are fulfilled, what is to be the rule for the boy's life and work?"

¹³The angel of the LORD answered, "Your wife must do all that I have told her. ¹⁴She must not eat anything that comes from the grapevine, nor drink any wine or other fermented drink nor eat anything unclean. She must do everything I have commanded her."

¹⁵Manoah said to the angel of the LORD, "We would like you to stay until we prepare a young goat for you."

¹⁶The angel of the LORD replied, "Even though you detain me, I will not eat any of your food. But if you prepare a burnt offering, offer it to the LORD." (Manoah did not realize that it was the angel of the LORD.)

¹⁷Then Manoah inquired of the angel of the LORD, "What is your name, so that we may honor you when your word comes true?"

¹⁸He replied, "Why do you ask my name? It is beyond understanding.ᵃ"

¹⁹Then Manoah took a young goat, together with the grain offering, and sacrificed it on a rock to the LORD. And the LORD did an amazing thing while Manoah and his wife watched: ²⁰As the flame blazed up from the altar toward heaven, the angel of the LORD ascended in the flame. Seeing this, Manoah and his wife fell with their faces to the ground. ²¹When the angel of the LORD did not show himself again to Manoah and his wife, Manoah realized that it was the angel of the LORD.

²²"We are doomed to die!" he said to his wife. "We have seen God!"

²³But his wife answered, "If the LORD had meant to kill us, he would not have accepted a burnt offering and grain offering from our hands, nor shown us all these things or now told us this."

²⁴The woman gave birth to a boy and named him Samson. He grew and the LORD blessed him, ²⁵and the Spirit of the LORD began to stir him while he was in Mahaneh Dan, between Zorah and Eshtaol.

14 **Samson's Marriage** Samson went down to Timnah and saw there a young Philistine woman. ²When he returned, he said to his father and mother, "I have seen a Philistine woman in Timnah; now get her for me as my wife."

³His father and mother replied, "Isn't there an acceptable woman among your relatives or among all our people? Must you go to the uncircumcised Philistines to get a wife?"

But Samson said to his father, "Get her for me. She's the right one for me." ⁴(His parents did not know that this was from the LORD, who was seeking an occasion to confront the Philistines; for at that time they were ruling over Israel.) ⁵Samson went down to Timnah together with his father and mother. As they approached the vineyards of Timnah, suddenly a young lion came roaring toward him. ⁶The Spirit of the LORD came upon him in power so that he tore the lion apart with his bare hands as he might have torn a young goat. But he told neither his father nor his mother what he had done. ⁷Then he went down and talked with the woman, and he liked her.

⁸Some time later, when he went back to marry her, he turned aside to look at the lion's carcass. In it was a swarm of bees and some honey, ⁹which he scooped out with his hands and ate as he went along. When he rejoined his parents, he gave them some, and they too ate it. But he did not tell them that he had taken the honey from the lion's carcass.

¹⁰Now his father went down to see the woman. And Samson made a feast

ᵃ18 Or *is wonderful*

there, as was customary for bridegrooms. ¹¹When he appeared, he was given thirty companions.

¹²"Let me tell you a riddle," Samson said to them. "If you can give me the answer within the seven days of the feast, I will give you thirty linen garments and thirty sets of clothes. ¹³If you can't tell me the answer, you must give me thirty linen garments and thirty sets of clothes."

"Tell us your riddle," they said. "Let's hear it."

¹⁴He replied,

> "Out of the eater, something to eat;
>   out of the strong, something sweet."

For three days they could not give the answer.

¹⁵On the fourth*ᵃ* day, they said to Samson's wife, "Coax your husband into explaining the riddle for us, or we will burn you and your father's household to death. Did you invite us here to rob us?"

¹⁶Then Samson's wife threw herself on him, sobbing, "You hate me! You don't really love me. You've given my people a riddle, but you haven't told me the answer."

"I haven't even explained it to my father or mother," he replied, "so why should I explain it to you?" ¹⁷She cried the whole seven days of the feast. So on the seventh day he finally told her, because she continued to press him. She in turn explained the riddle to her people.

¹⁸Before sunset on the seventh day the men of the town said to him,

> "What is sweeter than honey?
>   What is stronger than a lion?"

Samson said to them,

> "If you had not plowed with my heifer,
>   you would not have solved my riddle."

¹⁹Then the Spirit of the LORD came upon him in power. He went down to Ashkelon, struck down thirty of their men, stripped them of their belongings and gave their clothes to those who had explained the riddle. Burning with anger, he went up to his father's house. ²⁰And Samson's wife was given to the friend who had attended him at his wedding.

15 **Samson's Vengeance on the Philistines** Later on, at the time of wheat harvest, Samson took a young goat and went to visit his wife. He said, "I'm going to my wife's room." But her father would not let him go in.

²"I was so sure you thoroughly hated her," he said, "that I gave her to your friend. Isn't her younger sister more attractive? Take her instead."

³Samson said to them, "This time I have a right to get even with the Philistines; I will really harm them." ⁴So he went out and caught three hundred foxes and tied them tail to tail in pairs. He then fastened a torch to every pair of tails, ⁵lit the torches and let the foxes loose in the standing grain of the Philistines. He burned up the shocks and standing grain, together with the vineyards and olive groves.

⁶When the Philistines asked, "Who did this?" they were told, "Samson, the Timnite's son-in-law, because his wife was given to his friend."

So the Philistines went up and burned her and her father to death. ⁷Samson said to them, "Since you've acted like this, I won't stop until I get my revenge on you." ⁸He attacked them viciously and slaughtered many of them. Then he went down and stayed in a cave in the rock of Etam.

ᵃ15 Some Septuagint manuscripts and Syriac; Hebrew seventh

⁹The Philistines went up and camped in Judah, spreading out near Lehi. ¹⁰The men of Judah asked, "Why have you come to fight us?"

"We have come to take Samson prisoner," they answered, "to do to him as he did to us."

¹¹Then three thousand men from Judah went down to the cave in the rock of Etam and said to Samson, "Don't you realize that the Philistines are rulers over us? What have you done to us?"

He answered, "I merely did to them what they did to me."

¹²They said to him, "We've come to tie you up and hand you over to the Philistines."

Samson said, "Swear to me that you won't kill me yourselves."

¹³"Agreed," they answered. "We will only tie you up and hand you over to them. We will not kill you." So they bound him with two new ropes and led him up from the rock. ¹⁴As he approached Lehi, the Philistines came toward him shouting. The Spirit of the LORD came upon him in power. The ropes on his arms became like charred flax, and the bindings dropped from his hands. ¹⁵Finding a fresh jawbone of a donkey, he grabbed it and struck down a thousand men.

¹⁶Then Samson said,

> "With a donkey's jawbone
> I have made donkeys of them.ᵃ
> With a donkey's jawbone
> I have killed a thousand men."

¹⁷When he finished speaking, he threw away the jawbone; and the place was called Ramath Lehi.ᵇ

¹⁸Because he was very thirsty, he cried out to the LORD, "You have given your servant this great victory. Must I now die of thirst and fall into the hands of the uncircumcised?" ¹⁹Then God opened up the hollow place in Lehi, and water came out of it. When Samson drank, his strength returned and he revived. So the spring was called En Hakkore,ᶜ and it is still there in Lehi.

²⁰Samson ledᵈ Israel for twenty years in the days of the Philistines.

16 *Samson and Delilah* One day Samson went to Gaza, where he saw a prostitute. He went in to spend the night with her. ²The people of Gaza were told, "Samson is here!" So they surrounded the place and lay in wait for him all night at the city gate. They made no move during the night, saying, "At dawn we'll kill him."

³But Samson lay there only until the middle of the night. Then he got up and took hold of the doors of the city gate, together with the two posts, and tore them loose, bar and all. He lifted them to his shoulders and carried them to the top of the hill that faces Hebron.

⁴Some time later, he fell in love with a woman in the Valley of Sorek whose

JUDGES 15

Samson had great parents (see Judges 13). He had a great body. But history's super-jock was a spiritual flop. For all his exploits, Samson failed to free his people from Philistine rule. In fact, he never tried! All his battles were for personal revenge: "I merely did to them what they did to me" (Judges 15:11). You may be very talented. Athletic. Artistic. Scholastic. But how you use your talent is what counts. Use it selfishly, and in the long run your talent won't help you or anyone else. Commit your talent to God and use it to serve others, and you'll be a success.

Direct Line

ᵃ16 Or *made a heap or two*; the Hebrew for *donkey* sounds like the Hebrew for *heap*.   ᵇ17 *Ramath Lehi* means *jawbone hill*.   ᶜ19 *En Hakkore* means *caller's spring*.   ᵈ20 Traditionally *judged*

name was Delilah. ⁵The rulers of the Philistines went to her and said, "See if you can lure him into showing you the secret of his great strength and how we can overpower him so we may tie him up and subdue him. Each one of us will give you eleven hundred shekels*ᵃ* of silver."

⁶So Delilah said to Samson, "Tell me the secret of your great strength and how you can be tied up and subdued."

⁷Samson answered her, "If anyone ties me with seven fresh thongs*ᵇ* that have not been dried, I'll become as weak as any other man."

⁸Then the rulers of the Philistines brought her seven fresh thongs that had not been dried, and she tied him with them. ⁹With men hidden in the room, she called to him, "Samson, the Philistines are upon you!" But he snapped the thongs as easily as a piece of string snaps when it comes close to a flame. So the secret of his strength was not discovered.

¹⁰Then Delilah said to Samson, "You have made a fool of me; you lied to me. Come now, tell me how you can be tied."

¹¹He said, "If anyone ties me securely with new ropes that have never been used, I'll become as weak as any other man."

¹²So Delilah took new ropes and tied him with them. Then, with men hidden in the room, she called to him, "Samson, the Philistines are upon you!" But he snapped the ropes off his arms as if they were threads.

¹³Delilah then said to Samson, "Until now, you have been making a fool of me and lying to me. Tell me how you can be tied."

He replied, "If you weave the seven braids of my head into the fabric on the loom, and tighten it with the pin, I'll become as weak as any other man." So while he was sleeping, Delilah took the seven braids of his head, wove them into the fabric ¹⁴and*ᶜ* tightened it with the pin.

Again she called to him, "Samson, the Philistines are upon you!" He awoke from his sleep and pulled up the pin and the loom, with the fabric.

¹⁵Then she said to him, "How can you say, 'I love you,' when you won't confide in me? This is the third time you have made a fool of me and haven't told me the secret of your great strength." ¹⁶With such nagging she prodded him day after day until he was tired to death.

¹⁷So he told her everything. "No razor has ever been used on my head," he said, "because I have been a Nazirite set apart to God since birth. If my head were shaved, my strength would leave me, and I would become as weak as any other man."

¹⁸When Delilah saw that he had told her everything, she sent word to the rulers of the Philistines, "Come back once more; he has told me everything." So the rulers of the Philistines returned with the silver in their hands. ¹⁹Having put him to sleep on her lap, she called a man to shave off the seven braids of his hair, and so began to subdue him.*ᵈ* And his strength left him.

²⁰Then she called, "Samson, the Philistines are upon you!"

He awoke from his sleep and thought, "I'll go out as before and shake myself free." But he did not know that the LORD had left him.

²¹Then the Philistines seized him, gouged out his eyes and took him down to Gaza. Binding him with bronze shackles, they set him to grinding in the prison. ²²But the hair on his head began to grow again after it had been shaved.

QUIZZER

JUDGES 16

Q: How did Samson wear his long hair?

BONUS: Why did Samson become weak after losing his hair?

Answers on page 310

---

*ᵃ*5 That is, about 28 pounds (about 13 kilograms) *ᵇ*7 Or *bowstrings*; also in verses 8 and 9 *ᶜ*13,14 Some Septuagint manuscripts; Hebrew " ‚I can‚ if you weave the seven braids of my head into the fabric ‚on the loom‚." ¹⁴So she *ᵈ*19 Hebrew; some Septuagint manuscripts *and he began to weaken*

The Death of Samson   ²³Now the rulers of the Philistines assembled to offer a great sacrifice to Dagon their god and to celebrate, saying, "Our god has delivered Samson, our enemy, into our hands."

²⁴When the people saw him, they praised their god, saying,

> "Our god has delivered our enemy
>   into our hands,
> the one who laid waste our land
>   and multiplied our slain."

²⁵While they were in high spirits, they shouted, "Bring out Samson to entertain us." So they called Samson out of the prison, and he performed for them.

When they stood him among the pillars, ²⁶Samson said to the servant who held his hand, "Put me where I can feel the pillars that support the temple, so that I may lean against them." ²⁷Now the temple was crowded with men and women; all the rulers of the Philistines were there, and on the roof were about three thousand men and women watching Samson perform. ²⁸Then Samson prayed to the LORD, "O Sovereign LORD, remember me. O God, please strengthen me just once more, and let me with one blow get revenge on the Philistines for my two eyes." ²⁹Then Samson reached toward the two central pillars on which the temple stood. Bracing himself against them, his right hand on the one and his left hand on the other, ³⁰Samson said, "Let me die with the Philistines!" Then he pushed with all his might, and down came the temple on the rulers and all the people in it. Thus he killed many more when he died than while he lived.

³¹Then his brothers and his father's whole family went down to get him. They brought him back and buried him between Zorah and Eshtaol in the tomb of Manoah his father. He had led*ᵃ* Israel twenty years.

17 *Micah's Idols*   Now a man named Micah from the hill country of Ephraim ²said to his mother, "The eleven hundred shekels*ᵇ* of silver that were taken from you and about which I heard you utter a curse— I have that silver with me; I took it."

Then his mother said, "The LORD bless you, my son!"

³When he returned the eleven hundred shekels of silver to his mother, she said, "I solemnly consecrate my silver to the LORD for my son to make a carved image and a cast idol. I will give it back to you."

⁴So he returned the silver to his mother, and she took two hundred shekels*ᶜ* of silver and gave them to a silversmith, who made them into the image and the idol. And they were put in Micah's house.

⁵Now this man Micah had a shrine, and he made an ephod and some idols and installed one of his sons as his priest. ⁶In those days Israel had no king; everyone did as he saw fit.

⁷A young Levite from Bethlehem in Judah, who had been living within the clan of Judah, ⁸left that town in search of some other place to stay. On his way*ᵈ* he came to Micah's house in the hill country of Ephraim.

⁹Micah asked him, "Where are you from?"

"I'm a Levite from Bethlehem in Judah," he said, "and I'm looking for a place to stay."

¹⁰Then Micah said to him, "Live with me and be my father and priest, and I'll give you ten shekels*ᵉ* of silver a year, your clothes and your food." ¹¹So the Levite agreed to live with him, and the young man was to him like one of his

---

ᵃ31 Traditionally *judged*   *ᵇ2* That is, about 28 pounds (about 13 kilograms)   *ᶜ4* That is, about 5 pounds (about 2.3 kilograms)   *ᵈ8* Or *To carry on his profession*   *ᵉ10* That is, about 4 ounces (about 110 grams)

sons. ¹²Then Micah installed the Levite, and the young man became his priest and lived in his house. ¹³And Micah said, "Now I know that the LORD will be good to me, since this Levite has become my priest."

18 **Danites Settle in Laish** In those days Israel had no king. And in those days the tribe of the Danites was seeking a place of their own where they might settle, because they had not yet come into an inheritance among the tribes of Israel. ²So the Danites sent five warriors from Zorah and Eshtaol to spy out the land and explore it. These men represented all their clans. They told them, "Go, explore the land."

The men entered the hill country of Ephraim and came to the house of Micah, where they spent the night. ³When they were near Micah's house, they recognized the voice of the young Levite; so they turned in there and asked him, "Who brought you here? What are you doing in this place? Why are you here?"

⁴He told them what Micah had done for him, and said, "He has hired me and I am his priest."

⁵Then they said to him, "Please inquire of God to learn whether our journey will be successful."

⁶The priest answered them, "Go in peace. Your journey has the LORD's approval."

⁷So the five men left and came to Laish, where they saw that the people were living in safety, like the Sidonians, unsuspecting and secure. And since their land lacked nothing, they were prosperous.ᵃ Also, they lived a long way from the Sidonians and had no relationship with anyone else.ᵇ

⁸When they returned to Zorah and Eshtaol, their brothers asked them, "How did you find things?"

⁹They answered, "Come on, let's attack them! We have seen that the land is very good. Aren't you going to do something? Don't hesitate to go there and take it over. ¹⁰When you get there, you will find an unsuspecting people and a spacious land that God has put into your hands, a land that lacks nothing whatever."

¹¹Then six hundred men from the clan of the Danites, armed for battle, set out from Zorah and Eshtaol. ¹²On their way they set up camp near Kiriath Jearim in Judah. This is why the place west of Kiriath Jearim is called Mahaneh Danᶜ to this day. ¹³From there they went on to the hill country of Ephraim and came to Micah's house.

¹⁴Then the five men who had spied out the land of Laish said to their brothers, "Do you know that one of these houses has an ephod, other household gods, a carved image and a cast idol? Now you know what to do." ¹⁵So they turned in there and went to the house of the young Levite at Micah's place and greeted him. ¹⁶The six hundred Danites, armed for battle, stood at the entrance to the gate. ¹⁷The five men who had spied out the land went inside and took the carved image, the ephod, the other household gods and the cast idol while the priest and the six hundred armed men stood at the entrance to the gate.

¹⁸When these men went into Micah's house and took the carved image, the ephod, the other household gods and the cast idol, the priest said to them, "What are you doing?"

¹⁹They answered him, "Be quiet! Don't say a word. Come with us, and be our father and priest. Isn't it better that you serve a tribe and clan in Israel as priest rather than just one man's household?" ²⁰Then the priest was glad. He took the ephod, the other household gods and the carved image and

Answers

to Quizzer on page 308

A: He wore it in seven braids (Judges 16:19).

BONUS: *Long hair was a sign of special dedication to God (Numbers 6:1-5). Having lost that dedication, Samson was weak like other men.*

ᵃ7 The meaning of the Hebrew for this clause is uncertain.   ᵇ7 Hebrew; some Septuagint manuscripts *with the Arameans*   ᶜ12 Mahaneh Dan means *Dan's camp.*

went along with the people. ²¹Putting their little children, their livestock and their possessions in front of them, they turned away and left.

²²When they had gone some distance from Micah's house, the men who lived near Micah were called together and overtook the Danites. ²³As they shouted after them, the Danites turned and said to Micah, "What's the matter with you that you called out your men to fight?"

²⁴He replied, "You took the gods I made, and my priest, and went away. What else do I have? How can you ask, 'What's the matter with you?' "

²⁵The Danites answered, "Don't argue with us, or some hot-tempered men will attack you, and you and your family will lose your lives." ²⁶So the Danites went their way, and Micah, seeing that they were too strong for him, turned around and went back home.

²⁷Then they took what Micah had made, and his priest, and went on to Laish, against a peaceful and unsuspecting people. They attacked them with the sword and burned down their city. ²⁸There was no one to rescue them because they lived a long way from Sidon and had no relationship with anyone else. The city was in a valley near Beth Rehob.

The Danites rebuilt the city and settled there. ²⁹They named it Dan after their forefather Dan, who was born to Israel—though the city used to be called Laish. ³⁰There the Danites set up for themselves the idols, and Jonathan son of Gershom, the son of Moses,ᵃ and his sons were priests for the tribe of Dan until the time of the captivity of the land. ³¹They continued to use the idols Micah had made, all the time the house of God was in Shiloh.

19 A Levite and His Concubine

In those days Israel had no king.

Now a Levite who lived in a remote area in the hill country of Ephraim took a concubine from Bethlehem in Judah. ²But she was unfaithful to him. She left him and went back to her father's house in Bethlehem, Judah. After she had been there four months, ³her husband went to her to persuade her to return. He had with him his servant and two donkeys. She took him into her father's house, and when her father saw him, he gladly welcomed him. ⁴His father-in-law, the girl's father, prevailed upon him to stay; so he remained with him three days, eating and drinking, and sleeping there.

⁵On the fourth day they got up early and he prepared to leave, but the girl's father said to his son-in-law, "Refresh yourself with something to eat; then you can go." ⁶So the two of them sat down to eat and drink together. Afterward the girl's father said, "Please stay tonight and enjoy yourself." ⁷And when the man got up to go, his father-in-law persuaded him, so he stayed there that night. ⁸On the morning of the fifth day, when he rose to go, the girl's father said, "Refresh yourself. Wait till afternoon!" So the two of them ate together.

⁹Then when the man, with his concubine and his servant, got up to leave, his father-in-law, the girl's father, said, "Now look, it's almost evening. Spend the night here; the day is nearly over. Stay

---

ᵃ30 An ancient Hebrew scribal tradition, some Septuagint manuscripts and Vulgate; Masoretic Text *Manasseh*

JUDGES 19

Have you ever heard someone defend X-rated books and movies by saying the Bible has the same kinds of stories? Like this one. It's got homosexuality, gang rape, even the cutting up of a dead body. Hey, it's just like today's films! There is one difference though. X-rated books and movies cater to passion. They're intended to excite or thrill. The Bible's real-life stories, however, underline how terrible these sins are. So don't fall for the argument that sex and violence in films is the same as sex and violence in the Bible. Today's books and films try to make sin glamorous. The Bible shows sin for what it really is.

Direct Line

and enjoy yourself. Early tomorrow morning you can get up and be on your way home." ¹⁰But, unwilling to stay another night, the man left and went toward Jebus (that is, Jerusalem), with his two saddled donkeys and his concubine.

¹¹When they were near Jebus and the day was almost gone, the servant said to his master, "Come, let's stop at this city of the Jebusites and spend the night."

¹²His master replied, "No. We won't go into an alien city, whose people are not Israelites. We will go on to Gibeah." ¹³He added, "Come, let's try to reach Gibeah or Ramah and spend the night in one of those places." ¹⁴So they went on, and the sun set as they neared Gibeah in Benjamin. ¹⁵There they stopped to spend the night. They went and sat in the city square, but no one took them into his home for the night.

¹⁶That evening an old man from the hill country of Ephraim, who was living in Gibeah (the men of the place were Benjamites), came in from his work in the fields. ¹⁷When he looked and saw the traveler in the city square, the old man asked, "Where are you going? Where did you come from?"

¹⁸He answered, "We are on our way from Bethlehem in Judah to a remote area in the hill country of Ephraim where I live. I have been to Bethlehem in Judah and now I am going to the house of the LORD. No one has taken me into his house. ¹⁹We have both straw and fodder for our donkeys and bread and wine for ourselves your servants—me, your maidservant, and the young man with us. We don't need anything."

²⁰"You are welcome at my house," the old man said. "Let me supply whatever you need. Only don't spend the night in the square." ²¹So he took him into his house and fed his donkeys. After they had washed their feet, they had something to eat and drink.

²²While they were enjoying themselves, some of the wicked men of the city surrounded the house. Pounding on the door, they shouted to the old man who owned the house, "Bring out the man who came to your house so we can have sex with him."

²³The owner of the house went outside and said to them, "No, my friends, don't be so vile. Since this man is my guest, don't do this disgraceful thing. ²⁴Look, here is my virgin daughter, and his concubine. I will bring them out to you now, and you can use them and do to them whatever you wish. But to this man, don't do such a disgraceful thing."

²⁵But the men would not listen to him. So the man took his concubine and sent her outside to them, and they raped her and abused her throughout the night, and at dawn they let her go. ²⁶At daybreak the woman went back to the house where her master was staying, fell down at the door and lay there until daylight.

²⁷When her master got up in the morning and opened the door of the house and stepped out to continue on his way, there lay his concubine, fallen in the doorway of the house, with her hands on the threshold. ²⁸He said to her, "Get up; let's go." But there was no answer. Then the man put her on his donkey and set out for home.

²⁹When he reached home, he took a knife and cut up his concubine, limb by limb, into twelve parts and sent them into all the areas of Israel. ³⁰Everyone who saw it said, "Such a thing has never been seen or done, not since the day the Israelites came up out of Egypt. Think about it! Consider it! Tell us what to do!"

Israelites Fight the Benjamites   Then all the Israelites from Dan to Beersheba and from the land of Gilead came out as one man and assembled before the LORD in Mizpah. ²The leaders of all the people of the tribes of Israel took their places in the assembly of the people of God, four hundred thousand soldiers armed with swords. ³(The Benjamites heard that the Israelites had gone up to Mizpah.) Then the Israelites said, "Tell us how this awful thing happened."

⁴So the Levite, the husband of the murdered woman, said, "I and my concubine came to Gibeah in Benjamin to spend the night. ⁵During the night the men of Gibeah came after me and surrounded the house, intending to kill me. They raped my concubine, and she died. ⁶I took my concubine, cut her into pieces and sent one piece to each region of Israel's inheritance, because they committed this lewd and disgraceful act in Israel. ⁷Now, all you Israelites, speak up and give your verdict."

⁸All the people rose as one man, saying, "None of us will go home. No, not one of us will return to his house. ⁹But now this is what we'll do to Gibeah: We'll go up against it as the lot directs. ¹⁰We'll take ten men out of every hundred from all the tribes of Israel, and a hundred from a thousand, and a thousand from ten thousand, to get provisions for the army. Then, when the army arrives at Gibeah*ᵃ* in Benjamin, it can give them what they deserve for all this vileness done in Israel." ¹¹So all the men of Israel got together and united as one man against the city.

¹²The tribes of Israel sent men throughout the tribe of Benjamin, saying, "What about this awful crime that was committed among you? ¹³Now surrender those wicked men of Gibeah so that we may put them to death and purge the evil from Israel."

But the Benjamites would not listen to their fellow Israelites. ¹⁴From their towns they came together at Gibeah to fight against the Israelites. ¹⁵At once the Benjamites mobilized twenty-six thousand swordsmen from their towns, in addition to seven hundred chosen men from those living in Gibeah. ¹⁶Among all these soldiers there were seven hundred chosen men who were left-handed, each of whom could sling a stone at a hair and not miss.

¹⁷Israel, apart from Benjamin, mustered four hundred thousand swordsmen, all of them fighting men.

¹⁸The Israelites went up to Bethel*ᵇ* and inquired of God. They said, "Who of us shall go first to fight against the Benjamites?"

The LORD replied, "Judah shall go first."

¹⁹The next morning the Israelites got up and pitched camp near Gibeah. ²⁰The men of Israel went out to fight the Benjamites and took up battle positions against them at Gibeah. ²¹The Benjamites came out of Gibeah and cut down twenty-two thousand Israelites on the battlefield that day. ²²But the men of Israel encouraged one another and again took up their positions where they had stationed themselves the first day. ²³The Israelites went up and wept before the LORD until evening, and they inquired of the LORD. They said, "Shall we go up again to battle against the Benjamites, our brothers?"

The LORD answered, "Go up against them."

²⁴Then the Israelites drew near to Benjamin the second day. ²⁵This time, when the Benjamites came out from Gibeah to oppose them, they cut down another eighteen thousand Israelites, all of them armed with swords.

²⁶Then the Israelites, all the people, went up to Bethel, and there they sat weeping before the LORD. They fasted that day until evening and presented burnt offerings and fellowship offerings*ᶜ* to the LORD. ²⁷And the Israelites inquired of the LORD. (In those days the ark of the covenant of God was there, ²⁸with Phinehas son of Eleazar, the son of Aaron, ministering before it.) They asked, "Shall we go up again to battle with Benjamin our brother, or not?"

The LORD responded, "Go, for tomorrow I will give them into your hands."

²⁹Then Israel set an ambush around Gibeah. ³⁰They went up against the Benjamites on the third day and took up positions against Gibeah as they had done before. ³¹The Benjamites came out to meet them and were drawn

---

ᵃ10 One Hebrew manuscript; most Hebrew manuscripts *Geba,* a variant of *Gibeah*   *ᵇ18* Or *to the house of God*; also in verse 26   *ᶜ26* Traditionally *peace offerings*

away from the city. They began to inflict casualties on the Israelites as before, so that about thirty men fell in the open field and on the roads—the one leading to Bethel and the other to Gibeah.

³²While the Benjamites were saying, "We are defeating them as before," the Israelites were saying, "Let's retreat and draw them away from the city to the roads."

³³All the men of Israel moved from their places and took up positions at Baal Tamar, and the Israelite ambush charged out of its place on the west*a* of Gibeah.*b* ³⁴Then ten thousand of Israel's finest men made a frontal attack on Gibeah. The fighting was so heavy that the Benjamites did not realize how near disaster was. ³⁵The Lord defeated Benjamin before Israel, and on that day the Israelites struck down 25,100 Benjamites, all armed with swords. ³⁶Then the Benjamites saw that they were beaten.

Now the men of Israel had given way before Benjamin, because they relied on the ambush they had set near Gibeah. ³⁷The men who had been in ambush made a sudden dash into Gibeah, spread out and put the whole city to the sword. ³⁸The men of Israel had arranged with the ambush that they should send up a great cloud of smoke from the city, ³⁹and then the men of Israel would turn in the battle.

The Benjamites had begun to inflict casualties on the men of Israel (about thirty), and they said, "We are defeating them as in the first battle." ⁴⁰But when the column of smoke began to rise from the city, the Benjamites turned and saw the smoke of the whole city going up into the sky. ⁴¹Then the men of Israel turned on them, and the men of Benjamin were terrified, because they realized that disaster had come upon them. ⁴²So they fled before the Israelites in the direction of the desert, but they could not escape the battle. And the men of Israel who came out of the towns cut them down there. ⁴³They surrounded the Benjamites, chased them and easily*c* overran them in the vicinity of Gibeah on the east. ⁴⁴Eighteen thousand Benjamites fell, all of them valiant fighters. ⁴⁵As they turned and fled toward the desert to the rock of Rimmon, the Israelites cut down five thousand men along the roads. They kept pressing after the Benjamites as far as Gidom and struck down two thousand more.

⁴⁶On that day twenty-five thousand Benjamite swordsmen fell, all of them valiant fighters. ⁴⁷But six hundred men turned and fled into the desert to the rock of Rimmon, where they stayed four months. ⁴⁸The men of Israel went back to Benjamin and put all the towns to the sword, including the animals and everything else they found. All the towns they came across they set on fire.

21 **Wives for the Benjamites** The men of Israel had taken an oath at Mizpah: "Not one of us will give his daughter in marriage to a Benjamite."

²The people went to Bethel,*d* where they sat before God until evening, raising their voices and weeping bitterly. ³"O Lord, the God of Israel," they cried, "why has this happened to Israel? Why should one tribe be missing from Israel today?"

⁴Early the next day the people built an altar and presented burnt offerings and fellowship offerings.*e*

⁵Then the Israelites asked, "Who from all the tribes of Israel has failed to assemble before the Lord?" For they had taken a solemn oath that anyone who failed to assemble before the Lord at Mizpah should certainly be put to death.

---

a33 Some Septuagint manuscripts and Vulgate; the meaning of the Hebrew for this word is uncertain. *b33* Hebrew *Geba*, a variant of *Gibeah* *c43* The meaning of the Hebrew for this word is uncertain. *d2* Or *to the house of God* *e4* Traditionally *peace offerings*

⁶Now the Israelites grieved for their brothers, the Benjamites. "Today one tribe is cut off from Israel," they said. ⁷"How can we provide wives for those who are left, since we have taken an oath by the LORD not to give them any of our daughters in marriage?" ⁸Then they asked, "Which one of the tribes of Israel failed to assemble before the LORD at Mizpah?" They discovered that no one from Jabesh Gilead had come to the camp for the assembly. ⁹For when they counted the people, they found that none of the people of Jabesh Gilead were there.

¹⁰So the assembly sent twelve thousand fighting men with instructions to go to Jabesh Gilead and put to the sword those living there, including the women and children. ¹¹"This is what you are to do," they said. "Kill every male and every woman who is not a virgin." ¹²They found among the people living in Jabesh Gilead four hundred young women who had never slept with a man, and they took them to the camp at Shiloh in Canaan.

¹³Then the whole assembly sent an offer of peace to the Benjamites at the rock of Rimmon. ¹⁴So the Benjamites returned at that time and were given the women of Jabesh Gilead who had been spared. But there were not enough for all of them.

¹⁵The people grieved for Benjamin, because the LORD had made a gap in the tribes of Israel. ¹⁶And the elders of the assembly said, "With the women of Benjamin destroyed, how shall we provide wives for the men who are left? ¹⁷The Benjamite survivors must have heirs," they said, "so that a tribe of Israel will not be wiped out. ¹⁸We can't give them our daughters as wives, since we Israelites have taken this oath: 'Cursed be anyone who gives a wife to a Benjamite.' ¹⁹But look, there is the annual festival of the LORD in Shiloh, to the north of Bethel, and east of the road that goes from Bethel to Shechem, and to the south of Lebonah."

²⁰So they instructed the Benjamites, saying, "Go and hide in the vineyards ²¹and watch. When the girls of Shiloh come out to join in the dancing, then rush from the vineyards and each of you seize a wife from the girls of Shiloh and go to the land of Benjamin. ²²When their fathers or brothers complain to us, we will say to them, 'Do us a kindness by helping them, because we did not get wives for them during the war, and you are innocent, since you did not give your daughters to them.' "

²³So that is what the Benjamites did. While the girls were dancing, each man caught one and carried her off to be his wife. Then they returned to their inheritance and rebuilt the towns and settled in them.

²⁴At that time the Israelites left that place and went home to their tribes and clans, each to his own inheritance.

²⁵In those days Israel had no king; everyone did as he saw fit.

Introduction

to the

book of Ruth

FRIENDS.

What makes someone a good friend?

A friend is someone you like being with and can talk to. Someone you can count on when you're feeling down, need help or just want to have fun. Ruth was a Moabite widow who was a true friend to her Israelite mother-in-law, Naomi. That friendship led Ruth to accept Naomi's God and to go and live with Naomi in Israel. People admired Ruth for her devotion to Naomi, and Ruth soon remarried. But Ruth is remembered for more than friendship: she was an ancestor of King David and of Jesus Christ.

Fundamentals

How can you tell a real friend from a false one (Ruth 1)?

Is a good reputation worth keeping (Ruth 2)?

Who in this story is better than seven sons (Ruth 4:15)?

FAST FACTS

Ruth means "friendship."

Ruth lived during the time of the judges.

In Old Testament times a close relative would help a widow. He was called the "kinsman-redeemer."

God's Son became a man so he could be our kinsman-redeemer.

Naomi and Ruth In the days when the judges ruled,[a] there was a famine in the land, and a man from Bethlehem in Judah, together with his wife and two sons, went to live for a while in the country of Moab. [2]The man's name was Elimelech, his wife's name Naomi, and the names of his two sons were Mahlon and Kilion. They were Ephrathites from Bethlehem, Judah. And they went to Moab and lived there.

[3]Now Elimelech, Naomi's husband, died, and she was left with her two sons. [4]They married Moabite women, one named Orpah and the other Ruth. After they had lived there about ten years, [5]both Mahlon and Kilion also died, and Naomi was left without her two sons and her husband.

[6]When she heard in Moab that the LORD had come to the aid of his people by providing food for them, Naomi and her daughters-in-law prepared to return home from there. [7]With her two daughters-in-law she left the place where she had been living and set out on the road that would take them back to the land of Judah.

[8]Then Naomi said to her two daughters-in-law, "Go back, each of you, to your mother's home. May the LORD show kindness to you, as you have shown to your dead and to me. [9]May the LORD grant that each of you will find rest in the home of another husband."

Then she kissed them and they wept aloud [10]and said to her, "We will go back with you to your people."

[11]But Naomi said, "Return home, my daughters. Why would you come with me? Am I going to have any more sons, who could become your husbands? [12]Return home, my daughters; I am too old to have another husband. Even if I thought there was still hope for me—even if I had a husband tonight and then gave birth to sons— [13]would you wait until they grew up? Would you remain unmarried for them? No, my daughters. It is more bitter for me than for you, because the LORD's hand has gone out against me!"

[14]At this they wept again. Then Orpah kissed her mother-in-law good-by, but Ruth clung to her.

[15]"Look," said Naomi, "your sister-in-law is going back to her people and her gods. Go back with her."

[16]But Ruth replied, "Don't urge me to leave you or to turn back from you. Where you go I will go, and where you stay I will stay. Your people will be my people and your God my God. [17]Where you die I will die, and there I will be buried. May the LORD deal with me, be it ever so severely, if anything but death separates you and me." [18]When Naomi realized that Ruth was determined to go with her, she stopped urging her.

[19]So the two women went on until they came to Bethlehem. When they arrived in Bethlehem, the whole town was stirred because of them, and the women exclaimed, "Can this be Naomi?"

[20]"Don't call me Naomi,[b]" she told them. "Call me Mara,[c] because the Almighty[d] has made my life very bitter. [21]I went away full, but the LORD has brought me back empty. Why call me Naomi? The LORD has afflicted[e] me; the Almighty has brought misfortune upon me."

[22]So Naomi returned from Moab accompanied by Ruth the Moabitess, her daughter-in-law, arriving in Bethlehem as the barley harvest was beginning.

Ruth Meets Boaz Now Naomi had a relative on her husband's side, from the clan of Elimelech, a man of standing, whose name was Boaz. [2]And Ruth the Moabitess said to Naomi, "Let me go to the fields and pick up the leftover grain behind anyone in whose eyes I find favor."

Naomi said to her, "Go ahead, my daughter." [3]So she went out and began to glean in the fields behind the harvesters. As it turned out, she found her-

---

[a]1 Traditionally *judged* [b]20 *Naomi* means *pleasant;* also in verse 21. [c]20 *Mara* means *bitter.*
[d]20 Hebrew *Shaddai;* also in verse 21 [e]21 Or *has testified against*

self working in a field belonging to Boaz, who was from the clan of Elimelech.

⁴Just then Boaz arrived from Bethlehem and greeted the harvesters, "The LORD be with you!"

"The LORD bless you!" they called back.

⁵Boaz asked the foreman of his harvesters, "Whose young woman is that?"

⁶The foreman replied, "She is the Moabitess who came back from Moab with Naomi. ⁷She said, 'Please let me glean and gather among the sheaves behind the harvesters.' She went into the field and has worked steadily from morning till now, except for a short rest in the shelter."

⁸So Boaz said to Ruth, "My daughter, listen to me. Don't go and glean in another field and don't go away from here. Stay here with my servant girls. ⁹Watch the field where the men are harvesting, and follow along after the girls. I have told the men not to touch you. And whenever you are thirsty, go and get a drink from the water jars the men have filled."

¹⁰At this, she bowed down with her face to the ground. She exclaimed, "Why have I found such favor in your eyes that you notice me—a foreigner?"

¹¹Boaz replied, "I've been told all about what you have done for your mother-in-law since the death of your husband—how you left your father and mother and your homeland and came to live with a people you did not know before. ¹²May the LORD repay you for what you have done. May you be richly rewarded by the LORD, the God of Israel, under whose wings you have come to take refuge."

¹³"May I continue to find favor in your eyes, my lord," she said. "You have given me comfort and have spoken kindly to your servant—though I do not have the standing of one of your servant girls."

¹⁴At mealtime Boaz said to her, "Come over here. Have some bread and dip it in the wine vinegar."

When she sat down with the harvesters, he offered her some roasted grain. She ate all she wanted and had some left over. ¹⁵As she got up to glean, Boaz gave orders to his men, "Even if she gathers among the sheaves, don't embarrass her. ¹⁶Rather, pull out some stalks for her from the bundles and leave them for her to pick up, and don't rebuke her."

¹⁷So Ruth gleaned in the field until evening. Then she threshed the barley she had gathered, and it amounted to about an ephah.ᵃ ¹⁸She carried it back to town, and her mother-in-law saw how much she had gathered. Ruth also brought out and gave her what she had left over after she had eaten enough.

¹⁹Her mother-in-law asked her, "Where did you glean today? Where did you work? Blessed be the man who took notice of you!"

Then Ruth told her mother-in-law about the one at whose place she had been working. "The name of the man I worked with today is Boaz," she said.

²⁰"The LORD bless him!" Naomi said to her daughter-in-law. "He has not stopped showing his kindness to the living and the dead." She added, "That man is our close relative; he is one of our kinsman-redeemers."

²¹Then Ruth the Moabitess said, "He even said to me, 'Stay with my workers until they finish harvesting all my grain.' "

²²Naomi said to Ruth her daughter-in-law, "It will be good for you, my daughter, to go with his girls, because in someone else's field you might be harmed."

²³So Ruth stayed close to the servant girls of Boaz to glean until the barley and wheat harvests were finished. And she lived with her mother-in-law.

Ruth and Boaz at the Threshing Floor One day Naomi her mother-in-law said to her, "My daughter, should I not try to find a homeᵇ for you, where you will be well provided for? ²Is not Boaz, with whose servant girls

---

ᵃ17 That is, probably about 3/5 bushel (about 22 liters) ᵇ1 Hebrew *find rest* (see Ruth 1:9)

you have been, a kinsman of ours? Tonight he will be winnowing barley on the threshing floor. ³Wash and perfume yourself, and put on your best clothes. Then go down to the threshing floor, but don't let him know you are there until he has finished eating and drinking. ⁴When he lies down, note the place where he is lying. Then go and uncover his feet and lie down. He will tell you what to do."

⁵"I will do whatever you say," Ruth answered. ⁶So she went down to the threshing floor and did everything her mother-in-law told her to do.

⁷When Boaz had finished eating and drinking and was in good spirits, he went over to lie down at the far end of the grain pile. Ruth approached quietly, uncovered his feet and lay down. ⁸In the middle of the night something startled the man, and he turned and discovered a woman lying at his feet.

⁹"Who are you?" he asked.

"I am your servant Ruth," she said. "Spread the corner of your garment over me, since you are a kinsman-redeemer."

¹⁰"The LORD bless you, my daughter," he replied. "This kindness is greater than that which you showed earlier: You have not run after the younger men, whether rich or poor. ¹¹And now, my daughter, don't be afraid. I will do for you all you ask. All my fellow townsmen know that you are a woman of noble character. ¹²Although it is true that I am near of kin, there is a kinsman-redeemer nearer than I. ¹³Stay here for the night, and in the morning if he wants to redeem, good; let him redeem. But if he is not willing, as surely as the LORD lives I will do it. Lie here until morning."

¹⁴So she lay at his feet until morning, but got up before anyone could be recognized; and he said, "Don't let it be known that a woman came to the threshing floor."

¹⁵He also said, "Bring me the shawl you are wearing and hold it out." When she did so, he poured into it six measures of barley and put it on her. Then he*ᵃ* went back to town.

¹⁶When Ruth came to her mother-in-law, Naomi asked, "How did it go, my daughter?"

Then she told her everything Boaz had done for her ¹⁷and added, "He gave me these six measures of barley, saying, 'Don't go back to your mother-in-law empty-handed.' "

¹⁸Then Naomi said, "Wait, my daughter, until you find out what happens. For the man will not rest until the matter is settled today."

Boaz Marries Ruth Meanwhile Boaz went up to the town gate and sat there. When the kinsman-redeemer he had mentioned came along, Boaz said, "Come over here, my friend, and sit down." So he went over and sat down.

²Boaz took ten of the elders of the town and said, "Sit here," and they did so. ³Then he said to the kinsman-redeemer, "Naomi, who has come back from Moab, is selling the piece of land that belonged to our brother Elimelech. ⁴I thought I should bring the matter to your attention and suggest that you buy it in the presence of these seated here and in the pres-

---

*ᵃ15 Most Hebrew manuscripts; many Hebrew manuscripts, Vulgate and Syriac *she**

RUTH 3:11

Do you get upset if you hear someone is gossiping about you? Maybe saying things that aren't true? No one could blame you for being upset. A good reputation is precious. But there's an important fact to remember: Your reputation doesn't depend on what a gossip says about you. It depends on how you live. Ruth earned her reputation, and Boaz could say, "All my fellow townsmen know that you are a woman of noble character" (Ruth 3:11). Live a noble life and the only reputation that will be ruined is the reputation of the person who gossips and lies!

Direct Line

Dear Sam,

    Is it all right for a girl to let a guy know she likes him? My mom says, "Girls shouldn't chase boys." I think she's old-fashioned. Who's right?

Melanie in Madison

100 Advice Lane, Anywhere, USA

Dear Melanie,

    I can give you an opinion, but in the end you need to remember that God gave you your parents for guidance—and he expects you to be obedient to them. However, reading the book of Ruth may give you and your mother some insight.

    A young woman named Ruth was a widow. She lived with her mother-in-law Naomi. Ruth was an honorable woman who loved Naomi as a mother and even came to know the Lord through her. She worked hard to try to provide food for herself and Naomi. As you read Ruth 3, be sure to notice that while Ruth dressed and perfumed herself to get the attention of Boaz, she always acted with obedience and respect toward both Naomi and God.

    Maybe you and your mother need to have a talk about what she means by chasing guys. If you make yourself look nice, if you're kind and friendly to the guys around you, they'll know you like them. And your mother probably won't object either.

Sam

ence of the elders of my people. If you will redeem it, do so. But if you[a] will not, tell me, so I will know. For no one has the right to do it except you, and I am next in line."

"I will redeem it," he said.

[5]Then Boaz said, "On the day you buy the land from Naomi and from Ruth the Moabitess, you acquire[b] the dead man's widow, in order to maintain the name of the dead with his property."

[6]At this, the kinsman-redeemer said, "Then I cannot redeem it because I might endanger my own estate. You redeem it yourself. I cannot do it."

[7](Now in earlier times in Israel, for the redemption and transfer of property to become final, one party took off his sandal and gave it to the other. This was the method of legalizing transactions in Israel.)

[8]So the kinsman-redeemer said to Boaz, "Buy it yourself." And he removed his sandal.

[9]Then Boaz announced to the elders and all the people, "Today you are witnesses that I have bought from Naomi all the property of Elimelech, Kilion and Mahlon. [10]I have also acquired Ruth the Moabitess, Mahlon's widow, as my wife, in order to maintain the name of the dead with his property, so that his name will not disappear from among his family or from the town records. Today you are witnesses!"

[11]Then the elders and all those at the gate said, "We are witnesses. May the Lord make the woman who is coming into your home like Rachel and Leah, who together built up the house of Israel. May you have standing in Ephrathah and be famous in Bethlehem. [12]Through the offspring the Lord gives you by this young woman, may your family be like that of Perez, whom Tamar bore to Judah."

The Genealogy of David

[13]So Boaz took Ruth and she became his wife. Then he went to her, and the Lord enabled her to conceive, and she gave birth to a son. [14]The women said to Naomi: "Praise be to the Lord, who this day has not left you without a kinsman-redeemer. May he become famous throughout Israel! [15]He will renew your life and sustain you in your old age. For your daughter-in-law, who loves you and who is better to you than seven sons, has given him birth."

[16]Then Naomi took the child, laid him in her lap and cared for him. [17]The women living there said, "Naomi has a son." And they named him Obed. He was the father of Jesse, the father of David.

[18]This, then, is the family line of Perez:

Perez was the father of Hezron,
[19]Hezron the father of Ram,
   Ram the father of Amminadab,
[20]Amminadab the father of Nahshon,
   Nahshon the father of Salmon,[c]
[21]Salmon the father of Boaz,
   Boaz the father of Obed,
[22]Obed the father of Jesse,
   and Jesse the father of David.

---

[a]4 Many Hebrew manuscripts, Septuagint, Vulgate and Syriac; most Hebrew manuscripts *he* [b]5 Hebrew; Vulgate and Syriac *Naomi, you acquire Ruth the Moabitess,* [c]20 A few Hebrew manuscripts, some Septuagint manuscripts and Vulgate (see also verse 21 and Septuagint of 1 Chron. 2:11); most Hebrew manuscripts *Salma*

Introduction

to the

book of 1 Samuel

CHANGE.

Change can be hard. Especially big changes such as moving or changing schools, living through your parents' divorce or trying to adjust to a stepmother or stepfather.

Israel and David were experiencing some big changes. When Samuel, Israel's last judge, grew old, the people demanded a king. Saul, the first king, was disobedient. So God chose a young man named David to replace him. But many difficult years passed before David became king, because Saul was jealous of David and became hostile. The book of 1 Samuel tells the story of those difficult years.

Fundamentals

Did your parents dedicate you to God (1 Samuel 1:24-28)?

Do young people sometimes have more faith in God than grown-ups do (1 Samuel 17)?

What is the best way to deal with someone who is angry (1 Samuel 25)?

FAST FACTS

The main characters of 1 Samuel are Samuel, Saul and David.

The events took place between 1060 and 1010 B.C.

The Israelites were weak because they had no iron weapons. Their enemy the Philistines did!

David was the youngest in his family.

Saul was the tallest man in Israel.

The Birth of Samuel There was a certain man from Ramathaim, a Zuphite[a] from the hill country of Ephraim, whose name was Elkanah son of Jeroham, the son of Elihu, the son of Tohu, the son of Zuph, an Ephraimite. [2]He had two wives; one was called Hannah and the other Peninnah. Peninnah had children, but Hannah had none.

[3]Year after year this man went up from his town to worship and sacrifice to the LORD Almighty at Shiloh, where Hophni and Phinehas, the two sons of Eli, were priests of the LORD. [4]Whenever the day came for Elkanah to sacrifice, he would give portions of the meat to his wife Peninnah and to all her sons and daughters. [5]But to Hannah he gave a double portion because he loved her, and the LORD had closed her womb. [6]And because the LORD had closed her womb, her rival kept provoking her in order to irritate her. [7]This went on year after year. Whenever Hannah went up to the house of the LORD, her rival provoked her till she wept and would not eat. [8]Elkanah her husband would say to her, "Hannah, why are you weeping? Why don't you eat? Why are you downhearted? Don't I mean more to you than ten sons?"

[9]Once when they had finished eating and drinking in Shiloh, Hannah stood up. Now Eli the priest was sitting on a chair by the doorpost of the LORD's temple.[b] [10]In bitterness of soul Hannah wept much and prayed to the LORD. [11]And she made a vow, saying, "O LORD Almighty, if you will only look upon your servant's misery and remember me, and not forget your servant but give her a son, then I will give him to the LORD for all the days of his life, and no razor will ever be used on his head."

[12]As she kept on praying to the LORD, Eli observed her mouth. [13]Hannah was praying in her heart, and her lips were moving but her voice was not heard. Eli thought she was drunk [14]and said to her, "How long will you keep on getting drunk? Get rid of your wine."

[15]"Not so, my lord," Hannah replied, "I am a woman who is deeply troubled. I have not been drinking wine or beer; I was pouring out my soul to the LORD. [16]Do not take your servant for a wicked woman; I have been praying here out of my great anguish and grief."

[17]Eli answered, "Go in peace, and may the God of Israel grant you what you have asked of him."

[18]She said, "May your servant find favor in your eyes." Then she went her way and ate something, and her face was no longer downcast.

[19]Early the next morning they arose and worshiped before the LORD and then went back to their home at Ramah. Elkanah lay with Hannah his wife, and the LORD remembered her. [20]So in the course of time Hannah conceived and gave birth to a son. She named him Samuel,[c] saying, "Because I asked the LORD for him."

Hannah Dedicates Samuel [21]When the man Elkanah went up with all his family to offer the annual sacrifice to the LORD and to fulfill his vow, [22]Hannah did not go. She said to her husband, "After the boy is weaned, I will take him and present him before the LORD, and he will live there always."

[23]"Do what seems best to you," Elkanah her husband told her. "Stay here until you have weaned him; only may the LORD make good his[d] word." So the woman stayed at home and nursed her son until she had weaned him. [24]After he was weaned, she took the boy with her, young as he was, along with a three-year-old bull,[e] an ephah[f] of flour and a skin of wine, and brought him to the house of the LORD at Shiloh. [25]When they had slaughtered the bull, they brought the boy to Eli, [26]and she said to him, "As surely as you live, my lord, I am the woman who stood here beside you praying to the LORD. [27]I

*a1 Or from Ramathaim Zuphim *b9 That is, tabernacle *c20 Samuel sounds like the Hebrew for heard of God. *d23 Masoretic Text; Dead Sea Scrolls, Septuagint and Syriac your *e24 Dead Sea Scrolls, Septuagint and Syriac; Masoretic Text with three bulls *f24 That is, probably about 3/5 bushel (about 22 liters)

Dear Sam,

I think I'll die if my parents get a divorce.
If I promise God I'll be a missionary, do you
think he'd make them stay together?

Derek in Decatur

100 Advice Lane, Anywhere, USA

Dear Derek,

You are in a stressful situation right now, and I can sense your panic and pain. But God allows people to make choices, and sometimes those choices are not the best. Remember Eve's disobedience? God doesn't force his people. He will give them guidance, but he will not make puppets of them with no choice but to obey.

In 1 Samuel 1 a woman named Hannah bargained with God. God answered her prayer, but then she had to fulfill her part of the bargain and give up the very thing (a son) for which she was praying.

Instead of bargaining with God, why not surrender your parents to him? Ask him to fill their hearts with tenderness for one another. A tender heart can love and forgive. But remember, God won't force your parents to stay together.

Only God knows what's ahead for you. But you can be sure he will always be there. He will not abandon you. If your parents do divorce, God will help you through it.

Sam

prayed for this child, and the LORD has granted me what I asked of him. ²⁸So now I give him to the LORD. For his whole life he will be given over to the LORD." And he worshiped the LORD there.

Hannah's Prayer   Then Hannah prayed and said:

"My heart rejoices in the LORD;
  in the LORD my horn*ᵃ* is lifted high.
My mouth boasts over my enemies,
  for I delight in your deliverance.

²"There is no one holy*ᵇ* like the LORD;
  there is no one besides you;
  there is no Rock like our God.

³"Do not keep talking so proudly
  or let your mouth speak such arrogance,
for the LORD is a God who knows,
  and by him deeds are weighed.

⁴"The bows of the warriors are broken,
  but those who stumbled are armed with strength.
⁵Those who were full hire themselves out for food,
  but those who were hungry hunger no more.
She who was barren has borne seven children,
  but she who has had many sons pines away.

⁶"The LORD brings death and makes alive;
  he brings down to the grave*ᶜ* and raises up.
⁷The LORD sends poverty and wealth;
  he humbles and he exalts.
⁸He raises the poor from the dust
  and lifts the needy from the ash heap;
he seats them with princes
  and has them inherit a throne of honor.

"For the foundations of the earth are the LORD's;
  upon them he has set the world.
⁹He will guard the feet of his saints,
  but the wicked will be silenced in darkness.

"It is not by strength that one prevails;
¹⁰ those who oppose the LORD will be shattered.
He will thunder against them from heaven;
  the LORD will judge the ends of the earth.

"He will give strength to his king
  and exalt the horn of his anointed."

> He will guard the feet of his saints, but the wicked will be silenced in darkness (1 Samuel 2:9).

¹¹Then Elkanah went home to Ramah, but the boy ministered before the LORD under Eli the priest.

Eli's Wicked Sons   ¹²Eli's sons were wicked men; they had no regard for the LORD. ¹³Now it was the practice of the priests with the people that whenever anyone offered a sacrifice and while the meat was being boiled, the servant of the priest would come with a three-pronged fork in his hand. ¹⁴He would plunge it into the pan or kettle or caldron or pot, and the priest would take for himself whatever the fork brought up. This is how they treated all the Israelites who came to Shiloh. ¹⁵But even before the fat was burned, the ser-

---

ᵃ1 Horn here symbolizes strength; also in verse 10.   *ᵇ2 Or no Holy One   ᶜ6 Hebrew Sheol*

vant of the priest would come and say to the man who was sacrificing, "Give the priest some meat to roast; he won't accept boiled meat from you, but only raw."

[16]If the man said to him, "Let the fat be burned up first, and then take whatever you want," the servant would then answer, "No, hand it over now; if you don't, I'll take it by force."

[17]This sin of the young men was very great in the LORD's sight, for they[a] were treating the LORD's offering with contempt.

[18]But Samuel was ministering before the LORD—a boy wearing a linen ephod. [19]Each year his mother made him a little robe and took it to him when she went up with her husband to offer the annual sacrifice. [20]Eli would bless Elkanah and his wife, saying, "May the LORD give you children by this woman to take the place of the one she prayed for and gave to the LORD." Then they would go home. [21]And the LORD was gracious to Hannah; she conceived and gave birth to three sons and two daughters. Meanwhile, the boy Samuel grew up in the presence of the LORD.

[22]Now Eli, who was very old, heard about everything his sons were doing to all Israel and how they slept with the women who served at the entrance to the Tent of Meeting. [23]So he said to them, "Why do you do such things? I hear from all the people about these wicked deeds of yours. [24]No, my sons; it is not a good report that I hear spreading among the LORD's people. [25]If a man sins against another man, God[b] may mediate for him; but if a man sins against the LORD, who will intercede for him?" His sons, however, did not listen to their father's rebuke, for it was the LORD's will to put them to death.

[26]And the boy Samuel continued to grow in stature and in favor with the LORD and with men.

Prophecy Against the House of Eli   [27]Now a man of God came to Eli and said to him, "This is what the LORD says: 'Did I not clearly reveal myself to your father's house when they were in Egypt under Pharaoh? [28]I chose your father out of all the tribes of Israel to be my priest, to go up to my altar, to burn incense, and to wear an ephod in my presence. I also gave your father's house all the offerings made with fire by the Israelites. [29]Why do you[c] scorn my sacrifice and offering that I prescribed for my dwelling? Why do you honor your sons more than me by fattening yourselves on the choice parts of every offering made by my people Israel?'

[30]"Therefore the LORD, the God of Israel, declares: 'I promised that your house and your father's house would minister before me forever.' But now the LORD declares: 'Far be it from me! Those who honor me I will honor, but those who despise me will be disdained. [31]The time is coming when I will cut short your strength and the strength of your father's house, so that there will not be an old man in your family line [32]and you will see distress in my dwelling. Although good will be done to Israel, in your family line there will never be an old man. [33]Every one of you that I do not cut off from my altar will be spared only to blind your eyes with tears and to grieve your heart, and all your descendants will die in the prime of life.

[34]" 'And what happens to your two sons, Hophni and Phinehas, will be a sign to you—they will both die on the same day. [35]I will raise up for myself a faithful priest, who will do according to what is in my heart and mind. I will firmly establish his house, and he will minister before my anointed one always. [36]Then everyone left in your family line will come and bow down before him for a piece of silver and a crust of bread and plead, "Appoint me to some priestly office so I can have food to eat." ' "

---

a17 Or *men*   *b25* Or *the judges*   *c29* The Hebrew is plural.

The LORD Calls Samuel The boy Samuel ministered before the LORD under Eli. In those days the word of the LORD was rare; there were not many visions.

²One night Eli, whose eyes were becoming so weak that he could barely see, was lying down in his usual place. ³The lamp of God had not yet gone out, and Samuel was lying down in the temple*a* of the LORD, where the ark of God was. ⁴Then the LORD called Samuel.

Samuel answered, "Here I am." ⁵And he ran to Eli and said, "Here I am; you called me."

But Eli said, "I did not call; go back and lie down." So he went and lay down.

⁶Again the LORD called, "Samuel!" And Samuel got up and went to Eli and said, "Here I am; you called me."

"My son," Eli said, "I did not call; go back and lie down."

⁷Now Samuel did not yet know the LORD: The word of the LORD had not yet been revealed to him.

⁸The LORD called Samuel a third time, and Samuel got up and went to Eli and said, "Here I am; you called me."

Then Eli realized that the LORD was calling the boy. ⁹So Eli told Samuel, "Go and lie down, and if he calls you, say, 'Speak, LORD, for your servant is listening.' " So Samuel went and lay down in his place.

¹⁰The LORD came and stood there, calling as at the other times, "Samuel! Samuel!"

Then Samuel said, "Speak, for your servant is listening."

¹¹And the LORD said to Samuel: "See, I am about to do something in Israel that will make the ears of everyone who hears of it tingle. ¹²At that time I will carry out against Eli everything I spoke against his family—from beginning to end. ¹³For I told him that I would judge his family forever because of the sin he knew about; his sons made themselves contemptible,*b* and he failed to restrain them. ¹⁴Therefore, I swore to the house of Eli, 'The guilt of Eli's house will never be atoned for by sacrifice or offering.' "

¹⁵Samuel lay down until morning and then opened the doors of the house of the LORD. He was afraid to tell Eli the vision, ¹⁶but Eli called him and said, "Samuel, my son."

Samuel answered, "Here I am."

¹⁷"What was it he said to you?" Eli asked. "Do not hide it from me. May God deal with you, be it ever so severely, if you hide from me anything he told you." ¹⁸So Samuel told him everything, hiding nothing from him. Then Eli said, "He is the LORD; let him do what is good in his eyes."

¹⁹The LORD was with Samuel as he grew up, and he let none of his words fall to the ground. ²⁰And all Israel from Dan to Beersheba recognized that Samuel was attested as a prophet of the LORD. ²¹The LORD continued to appear at Shiloh, and there he revealed himself to Samuel through his word.

---

a3 That is, tabernacle *b13* Masoretic Text; an ancient Hebrew scribal tradition and Septuagint *sons blasphemed God*

---

1 SAMUEL 2:35

If you were to build a house and knew you had to live in it for the next 50 years, wouldn't you be very careful when laying the foundation? Of course. Why risk cracks and tumbledown walls? It's the same with your life. The choices you make each day are the foundation you lay for your future. The choices made by a priest named Eli and by his two sons are described in 1 Samuel 2. Their choices ruined their lives. But 1 Samuel 2:35 tells how you can guarantee a very different future. If you "do according to what is in [God's] heart and mind," then God will "firmly establish" you and make your life worthwhile.

Direct Line

4 And Samuel's word came to all Israel.

The Philistines Capture the Ark   Now the Israelites went out to fight against the Philistines. The Israelites camped at Ebenezer, and the Philistines at Aphek. ²The Philistines deployed their forces to meet Israel, and as the battle spread, Israel was defeated by the Philistines, who killed about four thousand of them on the battlefield. ³When the soldiers returned to camp, the elders of Israel asked, "Why did the Lord bring defeat upon us today before the Philistines? Let us bring the ark of the Lord's covenant from Shiloh, so that it*ᵃ* may go with us and save us from the hand of our enemies."

⁴So the people sent men to Shiloh, and they brought back the ark of the covenant of the Lord Almighty, who is enthroned between the cherubim. And Eli's two sons, Hophni and Phinehas, were there with the ark of the covenant of God.

⁵When the ark of the Lord's covenant came into the camp, all Israel raised such a great shout that the ground shook. ⁶Hearing the uproar, the Philistines asked, "What's all this shouting in the Hebrew camp?"

When they learned that the ark of the Lord had come into the camp, ⁷the Philistines were afraid. "A god has come into the camp," they said. "We're in trouble! Nothing like this has happened before. ⁸Woe to us! Who will deliver us from the hand of these mighty gods? They are the gods who struck the Egyptians with all kinds of plagues in the desert. ⁹Be strong, Philistines! Be men, or you will be subject to the Hebrews, as they have been to you. Be men, and fight!"

¹⁰So the Philistines fought, and the Israelites were defeated and every man fled to his tent. The slaughter was very great; Israel lost thirty thousand foot soldiers. ¹¹The ark of God was captured, and Eli's two sons, Hophni and Phinehas, died.

Death of Eli   ¹²That same day a Benjamite ran from the battle line and went to Shiloh, his clothes torn and dust on his head. ¹³When he arrived, there was Eli sitting on his chair by the side of the road, watching, because his heart feared for the ark of God. When the man entered the town and told what had happened, the whole town sent up a cry.

¹⁴Eli heard the outcry and asked, "What is the meaning of this uproar?"

The man hurried over to Eli, ¹⁵who was ninety-eight years old and whose eyes were set so that he could not see. ¹⁶He told Eli, "I have just come from the battle line; I fled from it this very day."

Eli asked, "What happened, my son?"

¹⁷The man who brought the news replied, "Israel fled before the Philistines, and the army has suffered heavy losses. Also your two sons, Hophni and Phinehas, are dead, and the ark of God has been captured."

¹⁸When he mentioned the ark of God, Eli fell backward off his chair by the side of the gate. His neck was broken and he died, for he was an old man and heavy. He had led*ᵇ* Israel forty years.

¹⁹His daughter-in-law, the wife of Phine-

Direct Line

1 SAMUEL 3:13

Do you think your dad is too strict? In 1 Samuel 3:13 God told Eli that he would judge Eli's family forever because his sons were sinful and because Eli had failed to restrain them. Maybe that strict dad of yours is just taking his responsibility seriously! Most parents don't enjoy "restraining" their children. Saying no isn't parents' idea of a good time. It's a lot easier to be laid back and let kids do whatever they want. It may be easier, but it's not right. Failing to "restrain" fails God, and as Eli realized when both his sons died, failing to restrain means failing one's children as well.

ᵃ3 Or he   ᵇ18 Traditionally judged

has, was pregnant and near the time of delivery. When she heard the news that the ark of God had been captured and that her father-in-law and her husband were dead, she went into labor and gave birth, but was overcome by her labor pains. ²⁰As she was dying, the women attending her said, "Don't despair; you have given birth to a son." But she did not respond or pay any attention.

²¹She named the boy Ichabod,ᵃ saying, "The glory has departed from Israel"—because of the capture of the ark of God and the deaths of her father-in-law and her husband. ²²She said, "The glory has departed from Israel, for the ark of God has been captured."

The Ark in Ashdod and Ekron   After the Philistines had captured the ark of God, they took it from Ebenezer to Ashdod. ²Then they carried the ark into Dagon's temple and set it beside Dagon. ³When the people of Ashdod rose early the next day, there was Dagon, fallen on his face on the ground before the ark of the LORD! They took Dagon and put him back in his place. ⁴But the following morning when they rose, there was Dagon, fallen on his face on the ground before the ark of the LORD! His head and hands had been broken off and were lying on the threshold; only his body remained. ⁵That is why to this day neither the priests of Dagon nor any others who enter Dagon's temple at Ashdod step on the threshold.

⁶The LORD's hand was heavy upon the people of Ashdod and its vicinity; he brought devastation upon them and afflicted them with tumors.ᵇ ⁷When the men of Ashdod saw what was happening, they said, "The ark of the god of Israel must not stay here with us, because his hand is heavy upon us and upon Dagon our god." ⁸So they called together all the rulers of the Philistines and asked them, "What shall we do with the ark of the god of Israel?"

They answered, "Have the ark of the god of Israel moved to Gath." So they moved the ark of the God of Israel.

⁹But after they had moved it, the LORD's hand was against that city, throwing it into a great panic. He afflicted the people of the city, both young and old, with an outbreak of tumors.ᶜ ¹⁰So they sent the ark of God to Ekron.

As the ark of God was entering Ekron, the people of Ekron cried out, "They have brought the ark of the god of Israel around to us to kill us and our people." ¹¹So they called together all the rulers of the Philistines and said, "Send the ark of the god of Israel away; let it go back to its own place, or itᵈ will kill us and our people." For death had filled the city with panic; God's hand was very heavy upon it. ¹²Those who did not die were afflicted with tumors, and the outcry of the city went up to heaven.

The Ark Returned to Israel   When the ark of the LORD had been in Philistine territory seven months, ²the Philistines called for the priests and the diviners and said, "What shall we do with the ark of the LORD? Tell us how we should send it back to its place."

³They answered, "If you return the ark of the god of Israel, do not send it away empty, but by all means send a guilt offering to him. Then you will be healed, and you will know why his hand has not been lifted from you."

⁴The Philistines asked, "What guilt offering should we send to him?"

They replied, "Five gold tumors and five gold rats, according to the

ᵃ21 Ichabod means no glory.   ᵇ6 Hebrew; Septuagint and Vulgate tumors. And rats appeared in their land, and death and destruction were throughout the city   ᶜ9 Or with tumors in the groin (see Septuagint)   ᵈ11 Or he

number of the Philistine rulers, because the same plague has struck both you and your rulers. [5]Make models of the tumors and of the rats that are destroying the country, and pay honor to Israel's god. Perhaps he will lift his hand from you and your gods and your land. [6]Why do you harden your hearts as the Egyptians and Pharaoh did? When he[a] treated them harshly, did they not send the Israelites out so they could go on their way?

[7]"Now then, get a new cart ready, with two cows that have calved and have never been yoked. Hitch the cows to the cart, but take their calves away and pen them up. [8]Take the ark of the LORD and put it on the cart, and in a chest beside it put the gold objects you are sending back to him as a guilt offering. Send it on its way, [9]but keep watching it. If it goes up to its own territory, toward Beth Shemesh, then the LORD has brought this great disaster on us. But if it does not, then we will know that it was not his hand that struck us and that it happened to us by chance."

[10]So they did this. They took two such cows and hitched them to the cart and penned up their calves. [11]They placed the ark of the LORD on the cart and along with it the chest containing the gold rats and the models of the tumors. [12]Then the cows went straight up toward Beth Shemesh, keeping on the road and lowing all the way; they did not turn to the right or to the left. The rulers of the Philistines followed them as far as the border of Beth Shemesh.

[13]Now the people of Beth Shemesh were harvesting their wheat in the valley, and when they looked up and saw the ark, they rejoiced at the sight. [14]The cart came to the field of Joshua of Beth Shemesh, and there it stopped beside a large rock. The people chopped up the wood of the cart and sacrificed the cows as a burnt offering to the LORD. [15]The Levites took down the ark of the LORD, together with the chest containing the gold objects, and placed them on the large rock. On that day the people of Beth Shemesh offered burnt offerings and made sacrifices to the LORD. [16]The five rulers of the Philistines saw all this and then returned that same day to Ekron.

[17]These are the gold tumors the Philistines sent as a guilt offering to the LORD—one each for Ashdod, Gaza, Ashkelon, Gath and Ekron. [18]And the number of the gold rats was according to the number of Philistine towns belonging to the five rulers—the fortified towns with their country villages. The large rock, on which[b] they set the ark of the LORD, is a witness to this day in the field of Joshua of Beth Shemesh.

[19]But God struck down some of the men of Beth Shemesh, putting seventy[c] of them to death because they had looked into the ark of the LORD. The people mourned because of the heavy blow the LORD had dealt them, [20]and the men of Beth Shemesh asked, "Who can stand in the presence of the LORD, this holy God? To whom will the ark go up from here?"

[21]Then they sent messengers to the people of Kiriath Jearim, saying, "The Philistines have returned the ark of the LORD. Come down and take it up to your place." [1]So the men of Kiriath Jearim came and took up the ark of the LORD. They took it to Abinadab's house on the hill and consecrated Eleazar his son to guard the ark of the LORD.

Samuel Subdues the Philistines at Mizpah [2]It was a long time, twenty years in all, that the ark remained at Kiriath Jearim, and all the people of Israel mourned and sought after the LORD. [3]And Samuel said to the whole house of Israel, "If you are returning to the LORD with all your hearts, then rid yourselves of the foreign gods and the Ashtoreths and commit yourselves to the LORD and serve him only, and he will deliver you out of the hand of the Phi-

---

Answers
to Quizzer on page 329

A: The idol Dagon fell down when the ark was placed in his temple (1 Samuel 5:4).

BONUS: They sent it back to the Israelites. They were afraid because many people in that area were suffering from tumors (1 Samuel 5:6-8).

---

[a]6 That is, God [b]18 A few Hebrew manuscripts (see also Septuagint); most Hebrew manuscripts *villages as far as Greater Abel, where* [c]19 A few Hebrew manuscripts; most Hebrew manuscripts and Septuagint 50,070

listines." ⁴So the Israelites put away their Baals and Ashtoreths, and served the LORD only.

⁵Then Samuel said, "Assemble all Israel at Mizpah and I will intercede with the LORD for you." ⁶When they had assembled at Mizpah, they drew water and poured it out before the LORD. On that day they fasted and there they confessed, "We have sinned against the LORD." And Samuel was leader*a* of Israel at Mizpah.

⁷When the Philistines heard that Israel had assembled at Mizpah, the rulers of the Philistines came up to attack them. And when the Israelites heard of it, they were afraid because of the Philistines. ⁸They said to Samuel, "Do not stop crying out to the LORD our God for us, that he may rescue us from the hand of the Philistines." ⁹Then Samuel took a suckling lamb and offered it up as a whole burnt offering to the LORD. He cried out to the LORD on Israel's behalf, and the LORD answered him.

¹⁰While Samuel was sacrificing the burnt offering, the Philistines drew near to engage Israel in battle. But that day the LORD thundered with loud thunder against the Philistines and threw them into such a panic that they were routed before the Israelites. ¹¹The men of Israel rushed out of Mizpah and pursued the Philistines, slaughtering them along the way to a point below Beth Car.

¹²Then Samuel took a stone and set it up between Mizpah and Shen. He named it Ebenezer,*b* saying, "Thus far has the LORD helped us." ¹³So the Philistines were subdued and did not invade Israelite territory again.

Throughout Samuel's lifetime, the hand of the LORD was against the Philistines. ¹⁴The towns from Ekron to Gath that the Philistines had captured from Israel were restored to her, and Israel delivered the neighboring territory from the power of the Philistines. And there was peace between Israel and the Amorites.

¹⁵Samuel continued as judge over Israel all the days of his life. ¹⁶From year to year he went on a circuit from Bethel to Gilgal to Mizpah, judging Israel in all those places. ¹⁷But he always went back to Ramah, where his home was, and there he also judged Israel. And he built an altar there to the LORD.

Israel Asks for a King When Samuel grew old, he appointed his sons as judges for Israel. ²The name of his firstborn was Joel and the name of his second was Abijah, and they served at Beersheba. ³But his sons did not walk in his ways. They turned aside after dishonest gain and accepted bribes and perverted justice.

⁴So all the elders of Israel gathered together and came to Samuel at Ramah. ⁵They said to him, "You are old, and your sons do not walk in your ways; now appoint a king to lead*c* us, such as all the other nations have."

⁶But when they said, "Give us a king to lead us," this displeased Samuel; so he prayed to the LORD. ⁷And the LORD told

---

1 SAMUEL 8

Want to be a cheerleader? Eager to be accepted by the popular kids in your class? Want to be elected class president? Great! There's nothing wrong with those ambitions—in themselves. Of course, you have to watch your motives. The people of Israel wanted a king. That wasn't wrong in itself, but they wanted a king to "be like all the other nations" (1 Samuel 8:20). They weren't satisfied to be different, even though God's people are supposed to be different in very special ways. Motives do count. It's OK to have ambitions. Just be sure your ambition isn't to "be like all the others," rather than to be different in a positive, godly way.

Direct Line

---

a6 Traditionally judge   *b12 Ebenezer means stone of help.*
c5 Traditionally judge; also in verses 6 and 20

him: "Listen to all that the people are saying to you; it is not you they have rejected, but they have rejected me as their king. [8]As they have done from the day I brought them up out of Egypt until this day, forsaking me and serving other gods, so they are doing to you. [9]Now listen to them; but warn them solemnly and let them know what the king who will reign over them will do."

[10]Samuel told all the words of the LORD to the people who were asking him for a king. [11]He said, "This is what the king who will reign over you will do: He will take your sons and make them serve with his chariots and horses, and they will run in front of his chariots. [12]Some he will assign to be commanders of thousands and commanders of fifties, and others to plow his ground and reap his harvest, and still others to make weapons of war and equipment for his chariots. [13]He will take your daughters to be perfumers and cooks and bakers. [14]He will take the best of your fields and vineyards and olive groves and give them to his attendants. [15]He will take a tenth of your grain and of your vintage and give it to his officials and attendants. [16]Your menservants and maidservants and the best of your cattle[a] and donkeys he will take for his own use. [17]He will take a tenth of your flocks, and you yourselves will become his slaves. [18]When that day comes, you will cry out for relief from the king you have chosen, and the LORD will not answer you in that day."

[19]But the people refused to listen to Samuel. "No!" they said. "We want a king over us. [20]Then we will be like all the other nations, with a king to lead us and to go out before us and fight our battles."

[21]When Samuel heard all that the people said, he repeated it before the LORD. [22]The LORD answered, "Listen to them and give them a king."

Then Samuel said to the men of Israel, "Everyone go back to his town."

Samuel Anoints Saul There was a Benjamite, a man of standing, whose name was Kish son of Abiel, the son of Zeror, the son of Becorath, the son of Aphiah of Benjamin. [2]He had a son named Saul, an impressive young man without equal among the Israelites—a head taller than any of the others.

[3]Now the donkeys belonging to Saul's father Kish were lost, and Kish said to his son Saul, "Take one of the servants with you and go and look for the donkeys." [4]So he passed through the hill country of Ephraim and through the area around Shalisha, but they did not find them. They went on into the district of Shaalim, but the donkeys were not there. Then he passed through the territory of Benjamin, but they did not find them.

[5]When they reached the district of Zuph, Saul said to the servant who was with him, "Come, let's go back, or my father will stop thinking about the donkeys and start worrying about us."

[6]But the servant replied, "Look, in this town there is a man of God; he is highly respected, and everything he says comes true. Let's go there now. Perhaps he will tell us what way to take."

[7]Saul said to his servant, "If we go, what can we give the man? The food in our sacks is gone. We have no gift to take to the man of God. What do we have?"

[8]The servant answered him again. "Look," he said, "I have a quarter of a shekel[b] of silver. I will give it to the man of God so that he will tell us what way to take." [9](Formerly in Israel, if a man went to inquire of God, he would say, "Come, let us go to the seer," because the prophet of today used to be called a seer.)

[10]"Good," Saul said to his servant. "Come, let's go." So they set out for the town where the man of God was.

---

[a]16 Septuagint; Hebrew *young men* [b]8 That is, about 1/10 ounce (about 3 grams)

¹¹As they were going up the hill to the town, they met some girls coming out to draw water, and they asked them, "Is the seer here?"

¹²"He is," they answered. "He's ahead of you. Hurry now; he has just come to our town today, for the people have a sacrifice at the high place. ¹³As soon as you enter the town, you will find him before he goes up to the high place to eat. The people will not begin eating until he comes, because he must bless the sacrifice; afterward, those who are invited will eat. Go up now; you should find him about this time."

¹⁴They went up to the town, and as they were entering it, there was Samuel, coming toward them on his way up to the high place.

¹⁵Now the day before Saul came, the Lord had revealed this to Samuel: ¹⁶"About this time tomorrow I will send you a man from the land of Benjamin. Anoint him leader over my people Israel; he will deliver my people from the hand of the Philistines. I have looked upon my people, for their cry has reached me."

¹⁷When Samuel caught sight of Saul, the Lord said to him, "This is the man I spoke to you about; he will govern my people."

¹⁸Saul approached Samuel in the gateway and asked, "Would you please tell me where the seer's house is?"

¹⁹"I am the seer," Samuel replied. "Go up ahead of me to the high place, for today you are to eat with me, and in the morning I will let you go and will tell you all that is in your heart. ²⁰As for the donkeys you lost three days ago, do not worry about them; they have been found. And to whom is all the desire of Israel turned, if not to you and all your father's family?"

²¹Saul answered, "But am I not a Benjamite, from the smallest tribe of Israel, and is not my clan the least of all the clans of the tribe of Benjamin? Why do you say such a thing to me?"

²²Then Samuel brought Saul and his servant into the hall and seated them at the head of those who were invited—about thirty in number. ²³Samuel said to the cook, "Bring the piece of meat I gave you, the one I told you to lay aside."

²⁴So the cook took up the leg with what was on it and set it in front of Saul. Samuel said, "Here is what has been kept for you. Eat, because it was set aside for you for this occasion, from the time I said, 'I have invited guests.' " And Saul dined with Samuel that day.

²⁵After they came down from the high place to the town, Samuel talked with Saul on the roof of his house. ²⁶They rose about daybreak and Samuel called to Saul on the roof, "Get ready, and I will send you on your way." When Saul got ready, he and Samuel went outside together. ²⁷As they were going down to the edge of the town, Samuel said to Saul, "Tell the servant to go on ahead of us"—and the servant did so—"but you stay here awhile, so that I may give you a message from God."

10 Then Samuel took a flask of oil and poured it on Saul's head and kissed him, saying, "Has not the Lord anointed you leader over his inheritance?ᵃ ²When you leave me today, you will meet two men near Rachel's tomb, at Zelzah on the border of Benjamin. They will say to you, 'The donkeys you set out to look for have been found. And now your father has stopped thinking about them and is worried about you. He is asking, "What shall I do about my son?" '

³"Then you will go on from there until you reach the great tree of Tabor. Three men going up to God at Bethel will meet you there. One will be carrying three young goats, another three loaves of bread, and another a skin of

---

ᵃ1 Hebrew; Septuagint and Vulgate *over his people Israel? You will reign over the* Lord's *people and save them from the power of their enemies round about. And this will be a sign to you that the* Lord *has anointed you leader over his inheritance:*

wine. ⁴They will greet you and offer you two loaves of bread, which you will accept from them.

⁵"After that you will go to Gibeah of God, where there is a Philistine outpost. As you approach the town, you will meet a procession of prophets coming down from the high place with lyres, tambourines, flutes and harps being played before them, and they will be prophesying. ⁶The Spirit of the LORD will come upon you in power, and you will prophesy with them; and you will be changed into a different person. ⁷Once these signs are fulfilled, do whatever your hand finds to do, for God is with you.

⁸"Go down ahead of me to Gilgal. I will surely come down to you to sacrifice burnt offerings and fellowship offerings,ᵃ but you must wait seven days until I come to you and tell you what you are to do."

> The Spirit of the LORD will come upon you in power . . . and you will be changed into a different person (1 Samuel 10:6).

Saul Made King ⁹As Saul turned to leave Samuel, God changed Saul's heart, and all these signs were fulfilled that day. ¹⁰When they arrived at Gibeah, a procession of prophets met him; the Spirit of God came upon him in power, and he joined in their prophesying. ¹¹When all those who had formerly known him saw him prophesying with the prophets, they asked each other, "What is this that has happened to the son of Kish? Is Saul also among the prophets?"

¹²A man who lived there answered, "And who is their father?" So it became a saying: "Is Saul also among the prophets?" ¹³After Saul stopped prophesying, he went to the high place.

¹⁴Now Saul's uncle asked him and his servant, "Where have you been?"

"Looking for the donkeys," he said. "But when we saw they were not to be found, we went to Samuel."

¹⁵Saul's uncle said, "Tell me what Samuel said to you."

¹⁶Saul replied, "He assured us that the donkeys had been found." But he did not tell his uncle what Samuel had said about the kingship.

¹⁷Samuel summoned the people of Israel to the LORD at Mizpah ¹⁸and said to them, "This is what the LORD, the God of Israel, says: 'I brought Israel up out of Egypt, and I delivered you from the power of Egypt and all the kingdoms that oppressed you.' ¹⁹But you have now rejected your God, who saves you out of all your calamities and distresses. And you have said, 'No, set a king over us.' So now present yourselves before the LORD by your tribes and clans."

²⁰When Samuel brought all the tribes of Israel near, the tribe of Benjamin was chosen. ²¹Then he brought forward the tribe of Benjamin, clan by clan, and Matri's clan was chosen. Finally Saul son of Kish was chosen. But when they looked for him, he was not to be found. ²²So they inquired further of the LORD, "Has the man come here yet?"

And the LORD said, "Yes, he has hidden himself among the baggage."

²³They ran and brought him out, and as he stood among the people he was a head taller than any of the others. ²⁴Samuel said to all the people, "Do you see the man the LORD has chosen? There is no one like him among all the people."

Then the people shouted, "Long live the king!"

²⁵Samuel explained to the people the regulations of the kingship. He wrote them down on a scroll and deposited it before the LORD. Then Samuel dismissed the people, each to his own home.

²⁶Saul also went to his home in Gibeah, accompanied by valiant men whose hearts God had touched. ²⁷But some troublemakers said, "How can this fellow save us?" They despised him and brought him no gifts. But Saul kept silent.

ᵃ8 Traditionally *peace offerings*

11 Saul Rescues the City of Jabesh

Nahash the Ammonite went up and besieged Jabesh Gilead. And all the men of Jabesh said to him, "Make a treaty with us, and we will be subject to you."

²But Nahash the Ammonite replied, "I will make a treaty with you only on the condition that I gouge out the right eye of every one of you and so bring disgrace on all Israel."

³The elders of Jabesh said to him, "Give us seven days so we can send messengers throughout Israel; if no one comes to rescue us, we will surrender to you."

⁴When the messengers came to Gibeah of Saul and reported these terms to the people, they all wept aloud. ⁵Just then Saul was returning from the fields, behind his oxen, and he asked, "What is wrong with the people? Why are they weeping?" Then they repeated to him what the men of Jabesh had said.

⁶When Saul heard their words, the Spirit of God came upon him in power, and he burned with anger. ⁷He took a pair of oxen, cut them into pieces, and sent the pieces by messengers throughout Israel, proclaiming, "This is what will be done to the oxen of anyone who does not follow Saul and Samuel." Then the terror of the Lord fell on the people, and they turned out as one man. ⁸When Saul mustered them at Bezek, the men of Israel numbered three hundred thousand and the men of Judah thirty thousand.

⁹They told the messengers who had come, "Say to the men of Jabesh Gilead, 'By the time the sun is hot tomorrow, you will be delivered.' " When the messengers went and reported this to the men of Jabesh, they were elated. ¹⁰They said to the Ammonites, "Tomorrow we will surrender to you, and you can do to us whatever seems good to you."

¹¹The next day Saul separated his men into three divisions; during the last watch of the night they broke into the camp of the Ammonites and slaughtered them until the heat of the day. Those who survived were scattered, so that no two of them were left together.

Saul Confirmed as King

¹²The people then said to Samuel, "Who was it that asked, 'Shall Saul reign over us?' Bring these men to us and we will put them to death."

¹³But Saul said, "No one shall be put to death today, for this day the Lord has rescued Israel."

¹⁴Then Samuel said to the people, "Come, let us go to Gilgal and there reaffirm the kingship." ¹⁵So all the people went to Gilgal and confirmed Saul as king in the presence of the Lord. There they sacrificed fellowship offerings*a* before the Lord, and Saul and all the Israelites held a great celebration.

12 Samuel's Farewell Speech

Samuel said to all Israel, "I have listened to everything you said to me and have set a king over you. ²Now you have a king as your leader. As for me, I am old and gray, and my sons are here with you. I have been your leader from my youth until this day. ³Here I stand. Testify against me in the presence of the Lord and his anointed. Whose ox have I taken? Whose donkey have I taken? Whom have I cheated? Whom have I op-

a15 Traditionally peace offerings

1 SAMUEL 12:1–4

Surveys show that lots of teens are concerned about improving their self-image, but they wonder how to go about it. Probably the best way to begin to feel good about yourself is to keep making good choices. Take a look at what Samuel says in this farewell speech to Israel, and how the people responded. Then, like Samuel, live a caring, honest and godly life. You'll not only develop a good self-image, other people will respect you too.

Direct Line

pressed? From whose hand have I accepted a bribe to make me shut my eyes? If I have done any of these, I will make it right."

⁴"You have not cheated or oppressed us," they replied. "You have not taken anything from anyone's hand."

⁵Samuel said to them, "The Lᴏʀᴅ is witness against you, and also his anointed is witness this day, that you have not found anything in my hand."

"He is witness," they said.

⁶Then Samuel said to the people, "It is the Lᴏʀᴅ who appointed Moses and Aaron and brought your forefathers up out of Egypt. ⁷Now then, stand here, because I am going to confront you with evidence before the Lᴏʀᴅ as to all the righteous acts performed by the Lᴏʀᴅ for you and your fathers.

⁸"After Jacob entered Egypt, they cried to the Lᴏʀᴅ for help, and the Lᴏʀᴅ sent Moses and Aaron, who brought your forefathers out of Egypt and settled them in this place.

⁹"But they forgot the Lᴏʀᴅ their God; so he sold them into the hand of Sisera, the commander of the army of Hazor, and into the hands of the Philistines and the king of Moab, who fought against them. ¹⁰They cried out to the Lᴏʀᴅ and said, 'We have sinned; we have forsaken the Lᴏʀᴅ and served the Baals and the Ashtoreths. But now deliver us from the hands of our enemies, and we will serve you.' ¹¹Then the Lᴏʀᴅ sent Jerub-Baal,ᵃ Barak,ᵇ Jephthah and Samuel,ᶜ and he delivered you from the hands of your enemies on every side, so that you lived securely.

¹²"But when you saw that Nahash king of the Ammonites was moving against you, you said to me, 'No, we want a king to rule over us'—even though the Lᴏʀᴅ your God was your king. ¹³Now here is the king you have chosen, the one you asked for; see, the Lᴏʀᴅ has set a king over you. ¹⁴If you fear the Lᴏʀᴅ and serve and obey him and do not rebel against his commands, and if both you and the king who reigns over you follow the Lᴏʀᴅ your God—good! ¹⁵But if you do not obey the Lᴏʀᴅ, and if you rebel against his commands, his hand will be against you, as it was against your fathers.

¹⁶"Now then, stand still and see this great thing the Lᴏʀᴅ is about to do before your eyes! ¹⁷Is it not wheat harvest now? I will call upon the Lᴏʀᴅ to send thunder and rain. And you will realize what an evil thing you did in the eyes of the Lᴏʀᴅ when you asked for a king."

¹⁸Then Samuel called upon the Lᴏʀᴅ, and that same day the Lᴏʀᴅ sent thunder and rain. So all the people stood in awe of the Lᴏʀᴅ and of Samuel.

¹⁹The people all said to Samuel, "Pray to the Lᴏʀᴅ your God for your servants so that we will not die, for we have added to all our other sins the evil of asking for a king."

²⁰"Do not be afraid," Samuel replied. "You have done all this evil; yet do not turn away from the Lᴏʀᴅ, but serve the Lᴏʀᴅ with all your heart. ²¹Do not turn away after useless idols. They can do you no good, nor can they rescue you, because they are useless. ²²For the sake of his great name the Lᴏʀᴅ will not reject his people, because the Lᴏʀᴅ was pleased to make you his own. ²³As for me, far be it from me that I should sin against the Lᴏʀᴅ by failing to pray for you. And I will teach you the way that is good and right. ²⁴But be sure to fear the Lᴏʀᴅ and serve him faithfully with all your heart; consider what great things he has done for you. ²⁵Yet if you persist in doing evil, both you and your king will be swept away."

13 **Samuel Rebukes Saul** Saul was ⸆thirty⸅ᵈ years old when he became king, and he reigned over Israel ⸆forty-⸅ᵉ two years.

²Saulᶠ chose three thousand men from Israel; two thousand were with him

---

ᵃ11 Also called *Gideon*   ᵇ11 Some Septuagint manuscripts and Syriac; Hebrew *Bedan*   ᶜ11 Hebrew; some Septuagint manuscripts and Syriac *Samson*   ᵈ1 A few late manuscripts of the Septuagint; Hebrew does not have *thirty*.   ᵉ1 See the round number in Acts 13:21; Hebrew does not have *forty-*.   ᶠ1,2 Or *and when he had reigned over Israel two years,* ²*he*

at Micmash and in the hill country of Bethel, and a thousand were with Jonathan at Gibeah in Benjamin. The rest of the men he sent back to their homes.

³Jonathan attacked the Philistine outpost at Geba, and the Philistines heard about it. Then Saul had the trumpet blown throughout the land and said, "Let the Hebrews hear!" ⁴So all Israel heard the news: "Saul has attacked the Philistine outpost, and now Israel has become a stench to the Philistines." And the people were summoned to join Saul at Gilgal.

⁵The Philistines assembled to fight Israel, with three thousand*ᵃ* chariots, six thousand charioteers, and soldiers as numerous as the sand on the seashore. They went up and camped at Micmash, east of Beth Aven. ⁶When the men of Israel saw that their situation was critical and that their army was hard pressed, they hid in caves and thickets, among the rocks, and in pits and cisterns. ⁷Some Hebrews even crossed the Jordan to the land of Gad and Gilead.

Saul remained at Gilgal, and all the troops with him were quaking with fear. ⁸He waited seven days, the time set by Samuel; but Samuel did not come to Gilgal, and Saul's men began to scatter. ⁹So he said, "Bring me the burnt offering and the fellowship offerings.*ᵇ*" And Saul offered up the burnt offering. ¹⁰Just as he finished making the offering, Samuel arrived, and Saul went out to greet him.

¹¹"What have you done?" asked Samuel.

Saul replied, "When I saw that the men were scattering, and that you did not come at the set time, and that the Philistines were assembling at Micmash, ¹²I thought, 'Now the Philistines will come down against me at Gilgal, and I have not sought the LORD's favor.' So I felt compelled to offer the burnt offering."

¹³"You acted foolishly," Samuel said. "You have not kept the command the LORD your God gave you; if you had, he would have established your kingdom over Israel for all time. ¹⁴But now your kingdom will not endure; the LORD has sought out a man after his own heart and appointed him leader of his people, because you have not kept the LORD's command."

¹⁵Then Samuel left Gilgal*ᶜ* and went up to Gibeah in Benjamin, and Saul counted the men who were with him. They numbered about six hundred.

Israel Without Weapons ¹⁶Saul and his son Jonathan and the men with them were staying in Gibeah*ᵈ* in Benjamin, while the Philistines camped at Micmash. ¹⁷Raiding parties went out from the Philistine camp in three detachments. One turned toward Ophrah in the vicinity of Shual, ¹⁸another toward Beth Horon, and the third toward the borderland overlooking the Valley of Zeboim facing the desert.

¹⁹Not a blacksmith could be found in the whole land of Israel, because the Philistines had said, "Otherwise the Hebrews will make swords or spears!" ²⁰So all Israel went down to the Philistines to have their plowshares, mattocks, axes and sickles*ᵉ* sharpened. ²¹The price was two thirds of a shekel*ᶠ* for sharpening plowshares and mattocks, and a third of a shekel*ᵍ* for sharpening forks and axes and for repointing goads.

²²So on the day of the battle not a soldier with Saul and Jonathan had a sword or spear in his hand; only Saul and his son Jonathan had them.

1 SAMUEL 13

QUIZZER

Q: Why didn't Saul's army carry swords or spears?

BONUS: What two men did have a sword or spear?

Answers on page 338

---

*ᵃ*5 Some Septuagint manuscripts and Syriac; Hebrew *thirty thousand*   *ᵇ*9 Traditionally *peace offerings*
*ᶜ*15 Hebrew; Septuagint *Gilgal and went his way; the rest of the people went after Saul to meet the army, and they went out of Gilgal*   *ᵈ*16 Two Hebrew manuscripts; most Hebrew manuscripts *Geba*, a variant of *Gibeah*   *ᵉ*20 Septuagint; Hebrew *plowshares*   *ᶠ*21 Hebrew *pim*; that is, about 1/4 ounce (about 8 grams)
*ᵍ*21 That is, about 1/8 ounce (about 4 grams)

Jonathan Attacks the Philistines 23Now a detachment of Philistines had gone out to the pass at Micmash. 1One day Jonathan son of Saul said to the young man bearing his armor, "Come, let's go over to the Philistine outpost on the other side." But he did not tell his father.

2Saul was staying on the outskirts of Gibeah under a pomegranate tree in Migron. With him were about six hundred men, 3among whom was Ahijah, who was wearing an ephod. He was a son of Ichabod's brother Ahitub son of Phinehas, the son of Eli, the LORD's priest in Shiloh. No one was aware that Jonathan had left.

4On each side of the pass that Jonathan intended to cross to reach the Philistine outpost was a cliff; one was called Bozez, and the other Seneh. 5One cliff stood to the north toward Micmash, the other to the south toward Geba.

6Jonathan said to his young armor-bearer, "Come, let's go over to the outpost of those uncircumcised fellows. Perhaps the LORD will act in our behalf. Nothing can hinder the LORD from saving, whether by many or by few."

7"Do all that you have in mind," his armor-bearer said. "Go ahead; I am with you heart and soul."

8Jonathan said, "Come, then; we will cross over toward the men and let them see us. 9If they say to us, 'Wait there until we come to you,' we will stay where we are and not go up to them. 10But if they say, 'Come up to us,' we will climb up, because that will be our sign that the LORD has given them into our hands."

11So both of them showed themselves to the Philistine outpost. "Look!" said the Philistines. "The Hebrews are crawling out of the holes they were hiding in." 12The men of the outpost shouted to Jonathan and his armor-bearer, "Come up to us and we'll teach you a lesson."

So Jonathan said to his armor-bearer, "Climb up after me; the LORD has given them into the hand of Israel."

13Jonathan climbed up, using his hands and feet, with his armor-bearer right behind him. The Philistines fell before Jonathan, and his armor-bearer followed and killed behind him. 14In that first attack Jonathan and his armor-bearer killed some twenty men in an area of about half an acre.[a]

Israel Routs the Philistines 15Then panic struck the whole army—those in the camp and field, and those in the outposts and raiding parties—and the ground shook. It was a panic sent by God.[b]

16Saul's lookouts at Gibeah in Benjamin saw the army melting away in all directions. 17Then Saul said to the men who were with him, "Muster the forces and see who has left us." When they did, it was Jonathan and his armor-bearer who were not there.

18Saul said to Ahijah, "Bring the ark of God." (At that time it was with the Israelites.)[c] 19While Saul was talking to the priest, the tumult in the Philistine camp increased more and more. So Saul said to the priest, "Withdraw your hand."

20Then Saul and all his men assembled and went to the battle. They found the Philistines in total confusion, striking each other with their swords. 21Those Hebrews who had previously been with the Philistines and had gone up with them to their camp went over to the Israelites who were with Saul and Jonathan. 22When all the Israelites who had hidden in the hill country of Ephraim heard that the Philistines were on the run, they joined the battle in hot pursuit. 23So the LORD rescued Israel that day, and the battle moved on beyond Beth Aven.

nswers
to Quizzer on page 337

A: The Israelites didn't have metalworking skills (1 Samuel 13:19).

BONUS: King Saul and his son Jonathan were the only two soldiers who carried a sword or spear (1 Samuel 13:22).

---

[a]14 Hebrew *half a yoke*; a "yoke" was the land plowed by a yoke of oxen in one day. [b]15 Or *a terrible panic* [c]18 Hebrew; Septuagint *"Bring the ephod."* (At that time he wore the ephod before the Israelites.)

Jonathan Eats Honey ²⁴Now the men of Israel were in distress that day, because Saul had bound the people under an oath, saying, "Cursed be any man who eats food before evening comes, before I have avenged myself on my enemies!" So none of the troops tasted food.

²⁵The entire army*ᵃ* entered the woods, and there was honey on the ground. ²⁶When they went into the woods, they saw the honey oozing out, yet no one put his hand to his mouth, because they feared the oath. ²⁷But Jonathan had not heard that his father had bound the people with the oath, so he reached out the end of the staff that was in his hand and dipped it into the honeycomb. He raised his hand to his mouth, and his eyes brightened.*ᵇ* ²⁸Then one of the soldiers told him, "Your father bound the army under a strict oath, saying, 'Cursed be any man who eats food today!' That is why the men are faint."

²⁹Jonathan said, "My father has made trouble for the country. See how my eyes brightened*ᶜ* when I tasted a little of this honey. ³⁰How much better it would have been if the men had eaten today some of the plunder they took from their enemies. Would not the slaughter of the Philistines have been even greater?"

³¹That day, after the Israelites had struck down the Philistines from Micmash to Aijalon, they were exhausted. ³²They pounced on the plunder and, taking sheep, cattle and calves, they butchered them on the ground and ate them, together with the blood. ³³Then someone said to Saul, "Look, the men are sinning against the LORD by eating meat that has blood in it."

"You have broken faith," he said. "Roll a large stone over here at once." ³⁴Then he said, "Go out among the men and tell them, 'Each of you bring me your cattle and sheep, and slaughter them here and eat them. Do not sin against the LORD by eating meat with blood still in it.' "

So everyone brought his ox that night and slaughtered it there. ³⁵Then Saul built an altar to the LORD; it was the first time he had done this.

³⁶Saul said, "Let us go down after the Philistines by night and plunder them till dawn, and let us not leave one of them alive."

"Do whatever seems best to you," they replied.

But the priest said, "Let us inquire of God here."

³⁷So Saul asked God, "Shall I go down after the Philistines? Will you give them into Israel's hand?" But God did not answer him that day.

³⁸Saul therefore said, "Come here, all you who are leaders of the army, and let us find out what sin has been committed today. ³⁹As surely as the LORD who rescues Israel lives, even if it lies with my son Jonathan, he must die." But not one of the men said a word.

⁴⁰Saul then said to all the Israelites, "You stand over there; I and Jonathan my son will stand over here."

"Do what seems best to you," the men replied.

⁴¹Then Saul prayed to the LORD, the God of Israel, "Give me the right answer."*ᵈ* And Jonathan and Saul were taken by lot, and the men were cleared. ⁴²Saul said, "Cast the lot between me and Jonathan my son." And Jonathan was taken.

⁴³Then Saul said to Jonathan, "Tell me what you have done."

So Jonathan told him, "I merely tasted a little honey with the end of my staff. And now must I die?"

⁴⁴Saul said, "May God deal with me, be it ever so severely, if you do not die, Jonathan."

⁴⁵But the men said to Saul, "Should Jonathan die—he who has brought about this great deliverance in Israel? Never! As surely as the LORD lives, not

---

ᵃ25 Or Now all the people of the land *ᵇ27 Or his strength was renewed* *ᶜ29 Or my strength was renewed* *ᵈ41 Hebrew; Septuagint "Why have you not answered your servant today? If the fault is in me or my son Jonathan, respond with Urim, but if the men of Israel are at fault, respond with Thummim."*

a hair of his head will fall to the ground, for he did this today with God's help." So the men rescued Jonathan, and he was not put to death.

⁴⁶Then Saul stopped pursuing the Philistines, and they withdrew to their own land.

⁴⁷After Saul had assumed rule over Israel, he fought against their enemies on every side: Moab, the Ammonites, Edom, the kings*a* of Zobah, and the Philistines. Wherever he turned, he inflicted punishment on them.*b* ⁴⁸He fought valiantly and defeated the Amalekites, delivering Israel from the hands of those who had plundered them.

Saul's Family ⁴⁹Saul's sons were Jonathan, Ishvi and Malki-Shua. The name of his older daughter was Merab, and that of the younger was Michal. ⁵⁰His wife's name was Ahinoam daughter of Ahimaaz. The name of the commander of Saul's army was Abner son of Ner, and Ner was Saul's uncle. ⁵¹Saul's father Kish and Abner's father Ner were sons of Abiel.

⁵²All the days of Saul there was bitter war with the Philistines, and whenever Saul saw a mighty or brave man, he took him into his service.

15 *The LORD Rejects Saul as King* Samuel said to Saul, "I am the one the LORD sent to anoint you king over his people Israel; so listen now to the message from the LORD. ²This is what the LORD Almighty says: 'I will punish the Amalekites for what they did to Israel when they waylaid them as they came up from Egypt. ³Now go, attack the Amalekites and totally destroy*c* everything that belongs to them. Do not spare them; put to death men and women, children and infants, cattle and sheep, camels and donkeys.' "

⁴So Saul summoned the men and mustered them at Telaim—two hundred thousand foot soldiers and ten thousand men from Judah. ⁵Saul went to the city of Amalek and set an ambush in the ravine. ⁶Then he said to the Kenites, "Go away, leave the Amalekites so that I do not destroy you along with them; for you showed kindness to all the Israelites when they came up out of Egypt." So the Kenites moved away from the Amalekites.

⁷Then Saul attacked the Amalekites all the way from Havilah to Shur, to the east of Egypt. ⁸He took Agag king of the Amalekites alive, and all his people he totally destroyed with the sword. ⁹But Saul and the army spared Agag and the best of the sheep and cattle, the fat calves*d* and lambs—everything that was good. These they were unwilling to destroy completely, but everything that was despised and weak they totally destroyed.

¹⁰Then the word of the LORD came to Samuel: ¹¹"I am grieved that I have made Saul king, because he has turned away from me and has not carried out my instructions." Samuel was troubled, and he cried out to the LORD all that night.

¹²Early in the morning Samuel got up and went to meet Saul, but he was told,

---

Direct Line

1 SAMUEL 14:44

Your mom tells you to put your dirty dishes in the dishwasher, then goes off to watch TV and leaves her dishes on the table. That can be upsetting. It doesn't seem fair to hold others to a higher standard than you hold yourself. That's what Saul did. Saul knowingly disobeyed God (1 Samuel 13). But when Jonathan unknowingly violated Saul's command, Saul was ready to execute him! Before you get too upset with Saul, or with your mom, stop and think. Do you get upset with friends for gossiping about you—when you gossip just as much about them? Don't use the Bible as a hammer to beat up on others. Use it as a mirror to better see yourself!

---

a47 Masoretic Text; Dead Sea Scrolls and Septuagint *king*   *b47* Hebrew; Septuagint *he was victorious*   *c3* The Hebrew term refers to the irrevocable giving over of things or persons to the LORD, often by totally destroying them; also in verses 8, 9, 15, 18, 20 and 21.   *d9* Or *the grown bulls*; the meaning of the Hebrew for this phrase is uncertain.

"Saul has gone to Carmel. There he has set up a monument in his own honor and has turned and gone on down to Gilgal."

¹³When Samuel reached him, Saul said, "The Lᴏʀᴅ bless you! I have carried out the Lᴏʀᴅ's instructions."

¹⁴But Samuel said, "What then is this bleating of sheep in my ears? What is this lowing of cattle that I hear?"

¹⁵Saul answered, "The soldiers brought them from the Amalekites; they spared the best of the sheep and cattle to sacrifice to the Lᴏʀᴅ your God, but we totally destroyed the rest."

¹⁶"Stop!" Samuel said to Saul. "Let me tell you what the Lᴏʀᴅ said to me last night."

"Tell me," Saul replied.

¹⁷Samuel said, "Although you were once small in your own eyes, did you not become the head of the tribes of Israel? The Lᴏʀᴅ anointed you king over Israel. ¹⁸And he sent you on a mission, saying, 'Go and completely destroy those wicked people, the Amalekites; make war on them until you have wiped them out.' ¹⁹Why did you not obey the Lᴏʀᴅ? Why did you pounce on the plunder and do evil in the eyes of the Lᴏʀᴅ?"

²⁰"But I did obey the Lᴏʀᴅ," Saul said. "I went on the mission the Lᴏʀᴅ assigned me. I completely destroyed the Amalekites and brought back Agag their king. ²¹The soldiers took sheep and cattle from the plunder, the best of what was devoted to God, in order to sacrifice them to the Lᴏʀᴅ your God at Gilgal."

²²But Samuel replied:

> "Does the Lᴏʀᴅ delight in burnt offerings and sacrifices
>   as much as in obeying the voice of the Lᴏʀᴅ?
> To obey is better than sacrifice,
>   and to heed is better than the fat of rams.
> ²³ For rebellion is like the sin of divination,
>   and arrogance like the evil of idolatry.
> Because you have rejected the word of the Lᴏʀᴅ,
>   he has rejected you as king."

²⁴Then Saul said to Samuel, "I have sinned. I violated the Lᴏʀᴅ's command and your instructions. I was afraid of the people and so I gave in to them. ²⁵Now I beg you, forgive my sin and come back with me, so that I may worship the Lᴏʀᴅ."

²⁶But Samuel said to him, "I will not go back with you. You have rejected the word of the Lᴏʀᴅ, and the Lᴏʀᴅ has rejected you as king over Israel!"

²⁷As Samuel turned to leave, Saul caught hold of the hem of his robe, and it tore. ²⁸Samuel said to him, "The Lᴏʀᴅ has torn the kingdom of Israel from you today and has given it to one of your neighbors—to one better than you. ²⁹He who is the Glory of Israel does not lie or change his mind; for he is not a man, that he should change his mind."

³⁰Saul replied, "I have sinned. But please honor me before the elders of my people and before Israel; come back with me, so that I may worship the Lᴏʀᴅ your God." ³¹So Samuel went back with Saul, and Saul worshiped the Lᴏʀᴅ.

³²Then Samuel said, "Bring me Agag king of the Amalekites."

Agag came to him confidently,ᵃ thinking, "Surely the bitterness of death is past."

³³But Samuel said,

> "As your sword has made women childless,
>   so will your mother be childless among women."

And Samuel put Agag to death before the Lᴏʀᴅ at Gilgal.

ᵃ*32 Or* him trembling, yet

³⁴Then Samuel left for Ramah, but Saul went up to his home in Gibeah of Saul. ³⁵Until the day Samuel died, he did not go to see Saul again, though Samuel mourned for him. And the LORD was grieved that he had made Saul king over Israel.

16 **Samuel Anoints David** The LORD said to Samuel, "How long will you mourn for Saul, since I have rejected him as king over Israel? Fill your horn with oil and be on your way; I am sending you to Jesse of Bethlehem. I have chosen one of his sons to be king."

²But Samuel said, "How can I go? Saul will hear about it and kill me."

The LORD said, "Take a heifer with you and say, 'I have come to sacrifice to the LORD.' ³Invite Jesse to the sacrifice, and I will show you what to do. You are to anoint for me the one I indicate."

⁴Samuel did what the LORD said. When he arrived at Bethlehem, the elders of the town trembled when they met him. They asked, "Do you come in peace?"

⁵Samuel replied, "Yes, in peace; I have come to sacrifice to the LORD. Consecrate yourselves and come to the sacrifice with me." Then he consecrated Jesse and his sons and invited them to the sacrifice.

⁶When they arrived, Samuel saw Eliab and thought, "Surely the LORD's anointed stands here before the LORD."

⁷But the LORD said to Samuel, "Do not consider his appearance or his height, for I have rejected him. The LORD does not look at the things man looks at. Man looks at the outward appearance, but the LORD looks at the heart."

⁸Then Jesse called Abinadab and had him pass in front of Samuel. But Samuel said, "The LORD has not chosen this one either." ⁹Jesse then had Shammah pass by, but Samuel said, "Nor has the LORD chosen this one." ¹⁰Jesse had seven of his sons pass before Samuel, but Samuel said to him, "The LORD has not chosen these." ¹¹So he asked Jesse, "Are these all the sons you have?"

"There is still the youngest," Jesse answered, "but he is tending the sheep."

Samuel said, "Send for him; we will not sit down*ᵃ* until he arrives."

¹²So he sent and had him brought in. He was ruddy, with a fine appearance and handsome features.

Then the LORD said, "Rise and anoint him; he is the one."

¹³So Samuel took the horn of oil and anointed him in the presence of his brothers, and from that day on the Spirit of the LORD came upon David in power. Samuel then went to Ramah.

David in Saul's Service ¹⁴Now the Spirit of the LORD had departed from Saul, and an evil*ᵇ* spirit from the LORD tormented him.

¹⁵Saul's attendants said to him, "See, an evil spirit from God is tormenting you. ¹⁶Let our lord command his servants here to search for someone who can play the harp. He will play when the evil spirit from God comes upon you, and you will feel better."

¹⁷So Saul said to his attendants, "Find someone who plays well and bring him to me."

¹⁸One of the servants answered, "I have seen a son of Jesse of Bethlehem who knows how to play the harp. He is a brave man and a warrior. He speaks well and is a fine-looking man. And the LORD is with him."

¹⁹Then Saul sent messengers to Jesse and said, "Send me your son David, who is with the sheep." ²⁰So Jesse took a donkey loaded with bread, a skin of wine and a young goat and sent them with his son David to Saul.

ᵃ11 Some Septuagint manuscripts; Hebrew *not gather around*   *ᵇ14* Or *injurious*; also in verses 15, 16 and 23

who kills this Philistine and removes this disgrace from Israel? Who is this uncircumcised Philistine that he should defy the armies of the living God?"

²⁷They repeated to him what they had been saying and told him, "This is what will be done for the man who kills him."

²⁸When Eliab, David's oldest brother, heard him speaking with the men, he burned with anger at him and asked, "Why have you come down here? And with whom did you leave those few sheep in the desert? I know how conceited you are and how wicked your heart is; you came down only to watch the battle."

²⁹"Now what have I done?" said David. "Can't I even speak?" ³⁰He then turned away to someone else and brought up the same matter, and the men answered him as before. ³¹What David said was overheard and reported to Saul, and Saul sent for him.

³²David said to Saul, "Let no one lose heart on account of this Philistine; your servant will go and fight him."

³³Saul replied, "You are not able to go out against this Philistine and fight him; you are only a boy, and he has been a fighting man from his youth."

³⁴But David said to Saul, "Your servant has been keeping his father's sheep. When a lion or a bear came and carried off a sheep from the flock, ³⁵I went after it, struck it and rescued the sheep from its mouth. When it turned on me, I seized it by its hair, struck it and killed it. ³⁶Your servant has killed both the lion and the bear; this uncircumcised Philistine will be like one of them, because he has defied the armies of the living God. ³⁷The LORD who delivered me from the paw of the lion and the paw of the bear will deliver me from the hand of this Philistine."

Saul said to David, "Go, and the LORD be with you."

³⁸Then Saul dressed David in his own tunic. He put a coat of armor on him and a bronze helmet on his head. ³⁹David fastened on his sword over the tunic and tried walking around, because he was not used to them.

"I cannot go in these," he said to Saul, "because I am not used to them." So he took them off. ⁴⁰Then he took his staff in his hand, chose five smooth stones from the stream, put them in the pouch of his shepherd's bag and, with his sling in his hand, approached the Philistine.

⁴¹Meanwhile, the Philistine, with his shield bearer in front of him, kept coming closer to David. ⁴²He looked David over and saw that he was only a boy, ruddy and handsome, and he despised him. ⁴³He said to David, "Am I a dog, that you come at me with sticks?" And the Philistine cursed David by his gods. ⁴⁴"Come here," he said, "and I'll give your flesh to the birds of the air and the beasts of the field!"

⁴⁵David said to the Philistine, "You come against me with sword and spear and javelin, but I come against you in the name of the LORD Almighty, the God of the armies of Israel, whom you have defied. ⁴⁶This day the LORD will hand you over to me, and I'll strike you down and cut off your head. Today I will give the carcasses of the Philistine army to the birds of the air and the beasts of the earth, and the whole world will know that there is a God in Israel. ⁴⁷All those gathered here will know that it is not by sword or spear that the LORD saves; for the battle is the LORD's, and he will give all of you into our hands."

⁴⁸As the Philistine moved closer to attack him, David ran quickly toward the battle line to meet him. ⁴⁹Reaching into his bag and taking out a stone, he slung it and struck the Philistine on the forehead. The stone sank into his forehead, and he fell facedown on the ground.

⁵⁰So David triumphed over the Philistine with a sling and a stone; without a sword in his hand he struck down the Philistine and killed him.

1 SAMUEL 17

QUIZZER

Q: Was Goliath tall enough to play NBA basketball?

BONUS: Was the stone David used to kill Goliath closer to the size of a Ping-Pong ball or a tennis ball?

Answers on page 346

⁵¹David ran and stood over him. He took hold of the Philistine's sword and drew it from the scabbard. After he killed him, he cut off his head with the sword.

When the Philistines saw that their hero was dead, they turned and ran. ⁵²Then the men of Israel and Judah surged forward with a shout and pursued the Philistines to the entrance of Gath*a* and to the gates of Ekron. Their dead were strewn along the Shaaraim road to Gath and Ekron. ⁵³When the Israelites returned from chasing the Philistines, they plundered their camp. ⁵⁴David took the Philistine's head and brought it to Jerusalem, and he put the Philistine's weapons in his own tent.

⁵⁵As Saul watched David going out to meet the Philistine, he said to Abner, commander of the army, "Abner, whose son is that young man?"

Abner replied, "As surely as you live, O king, I don't know."

⁵⁶The king said, "Find out whose son this young man is."

⁵⁷As soon as David returned from killing the Philistine, Abner took him and brought him before Saul, with David still holding the Philistine's head. ⁵⁸"Whose son are you, young man?" Saul asked him.

David said, "I am the son of your servant Jesse of Bethlehem."

Answers

to Quizzer on
page 345

A: You bet!
He was over
nine feet tall
(1 Samuel 17:4)!

BONUS: Many
sling stones have
been found on
battlegrounds in
Israel. These
heavy stones
were just a little
smaller than a
tennis ball.

18 *Saul's Jealousy of David* After David had finished talking with Saul, Jonathan became one in spirit with David, and he loved him as himself. ²From that day Saul kept David with him and did not let him return to his father's house. ³And Jonathan made a covenant with David because he loved him as himself. ⁴Jonathan took off the robe he was wearing and gave it to David, along with his tunic, and even his sword, his bow and his belt.

⁵Whatever Saul sent him to do, David did it so successfully*b* that Saul gave him a high rank in the army. This pleased all the people, and Saul's officers as well.

⁶When the men were returning home after David had killed the Philistine, the women came out from all the towns of Israel to meet King Saul with singing and dancing, with joyful songs and with tambourines and lutes. ⁷As they danced, they sang:

"Saul has slain his thousands,
and David his tens of thousands."

⁸Saul was very angry; this refrain galled him. "They have credited David with tens of thousands," he thought, "but me with only thousands. What more can he get but the kingdom?" ⁹And from that time on Saul kept a jealous eye on David.

¹⁰The next day an evil*c* spirit from God came forcefully upon Saul. He was prophesying in his house, while David was playing the harp, as he usually did. Saul had a spear in his hand ¹¹and he hurled it, saying to himself, "I'll pin David to the wall." But David eluded him twice.

¹²Saul was afraid of David, because the LORD was with David but had left Saul. ¹³So he sent David away from him and gave him command over a thousand men, and David led the troops in their campaigns. ¹⁴In everything he did he had great success,*d* because the LORD was with him. ¹⁵When Saul saw how successful*e* he was, he was afraid of him. ¹⁶But all Israel and Judah loved David, because he led them in their campaigns.

¹⁷Saul said to David, "Here is my older daughter Merab. I will give her to you in marriage; only serve me bravely and fight the battles of the LORD." For

---

*a*52 Some Septuagint manuscripts; Hebrew *a valley*   *b*5 Or *wisely*   *c*10 Or *injurious*   *d*14 Or *he was very
wise*   *e*15 Or *wise*

Saul said to himself, "I will not raise a hand against him. Let the Philistines do that!"

¹⁸But David said to Saul, "Who am I, and what is my family or my father's clan in Israel, that I should become the king's son-in-law?" ¹⁹So*ᵃ* when the time came for Merab, Saul's daughter, to be given to David, she was given in marriage to Adriel of Meholah.

²⁰Now Saul's daughter Michal was in love with David, and when they told Saul about it, he was pleased. ²¹"I will give her to him," he thought, "so that she may be a snare to him and so that the hand of the Philistines may be against him." So Saul said to David, "Now you have a second opportunity to become my son-in-law."

²²Then Saul ordered his attendants: "Speak to David privately and say, 'Look, the king is pleased with you, and his attendants all like you; now become his son-in-law.' "

²³They repeated these words to David. But David said, "Do you think it is a small matter to become the king's son-in-law? I'm only a poor man and little known."

²⁴When Saul's servants told him what David had said, ²⁵Saul replied, "Say to David, 'The king wants no other price for the bride than a hundred Philistine foreskins, to take revenge on his enemies.' " Saul's plan was to have David fall by the hands of the Philistines.

²⁶When the attendants told David these things, he was pleased to become the king's son-in-law. So before the allotted time elapsed, ²⁷David and his men went out and killed two hundred Philistines. He brought their foreskins and presented the full number to the king so that he might become the king's son-in-law. Then Saul gave him his daughter Michal in marriage.

²⁸When Saul realized that the LORD was with David and that his daughter Michal loved David, ²⁹Saul became still more afraid of him, and he remained his enemy the rest of his days.

³⁰The Philistine commanders continued to go out to battle, and as often as they did, David met with more success*ᵇ* than the rest of Saul's officers, and his name became well known.

19 **Saul Tries to Kill David** Saul told his son Jonathan and all the attendants to kill David. But Jonathan was very fond of David ²and warned him, "My father Saul is looking for a chance to kill you. Be on your guard tomorrow morning; go into hiding and stay there. ³I will go out and stand with my father in the field where you are. I'll speak to him about you and will tell you what I find out."

⁴Jonathan spoke well of David to Saul his father and said to him, "Let not the king do wrong to his servant David; he has not wronged you, and what he has done has benefited you greatly. ⁵He took his life in his hands when he killed the Philistine. The LORD won a great victory for all Israel, and you saw it and were

ᵃ19 Or However,   ᵇ30 Or David acted more wisely

---

1 SAMUEL 18:1–15

She's going out with the guy you like. He's the quarterback and you're on the bench. These are just two reasons why teens get jealous of each other. You could probably name more. King Saul was jealous of David because David was successful. But what's important here is to see what jealousy leads to. Instead of being David's friend, he became David's enemy (1 Samuel 18:15). Jealousy drives people apart. It creates suspicion and fear. What can you do about jealousy? First, remember that God loves you and gives you what's best for you. Second, pray for the person you're jealous of. It's really hard to hate or fear someone you're praying for!

Direct Line

glad. Why then would you do wrong to an innocent man like David by killing him for no reason?"

⁶Saul listened to Jonathan and took this oath: "As surely as the LORD lives, David will not be put to death."

⁷So Jonathan called David and told him the whole conversation. He brought him to Saul, and David was with Saul as before.

⁸Once more war broke out, and David went out and fought the Philistines. He struck them with such force that they fled before him.

⁹But an evilᵃ spirit from the LORD came upon Saul as he was sitting in his house with his spear in his hand. While David was playing the harp, ¹⁰Saul tried to pin him to the wall with his spear, but David eluded him as Saul drove the spear into the wall. That night David made good his escape.

¹¹Saul sent men to David's house to watch it and to kill him in the morning. But Michal, David's wife, warned him, "If you don't run for your life tonight, tomorrow you'll be killed." ¹²So Michal let David down through a window, and he fled and escaped. ¹³Then Michal took an idolᵇ and laid it on the bed, covering it with a garment and putting some goats' hair at the head.

¹⁴When Saul sent the men to capture David, Michal said, "He is ill."

¹⁵Then Saul sent the men back to see David and told them, "Bring him up to me in his bed so that I may kill him." ¹⁶But when the men entered, there was the idol in the bed, and at the head was some goats' hair.

¹⁷Saul said to Michal, "Why did you deceive me like this and send my enemy away so that he escaped?"

Michal told him, "He said to me, 'Let me get away. Why should I kill you?'"

¹⁸When David had fled and made his escape, he went to Samuel at Ramah and told him all that Saul had done to him. Then he and Samuel went to Naioth and stayed there. ¹⁹Word came to Saul: "David is in Naioth at Ramah"; ²⁰so he sent men to capture him. But when they saw a group of prophets prophesying, with Samuel standing there as their leader, the Spirit of God came upon Saul's men and they also prophesied. ²¹Saul was told about it, and he sent more men, and they prophesied too. Saul sent men a third time, and they also prophesied. ²²Finally, he himself left for Ramah and went to the great cistern at Secu. And he asked, "Where are Samuel and David?"

"Over in Naioth at Ramah," they said.

²³So Saul went to Naioth at Ramah. But the Spirit of God came even upon him, and he walked along prophesying until he came to Naioth. ²⁴He stripped off his robes and also prophesied in Samuel's presence. He lay that way all that day and night. This is why people say, "Is Saul also among the prophets?"

20 ***David and Jonathan*** Then David fled from Naioth at Ramah and went to Jonathan and asked, "What have I done? What is my crime? How have I wronged your father, that he is trying to take my life?"

²"Never!" Jonathan replied. "You are not going to die! Look, my father doesn't do anything, great or small, without confiding in me. Why would he hide this from me? It's not so!"

³But David took an oath and said, "Your father knows very well that I have found favor in your eyes, and he has said to himself, 'Jonathan must not know this or he will be grieved.' Yet as surely as the LORD lives and as you live, there is only a step between me and death."

⁴Jonathan said to David, "Whatever you want me to do, I'll do for you."

⁵So David said, "Look, tomorrow is the New Moon festival, and I am supposed to dine with the king; but let me go and hide in the field until the eve-

---

ᵃ9 Or *injurious* ᵇ13 Hebrew *teraphim*; also in verse 16

ning of the day after tomorrow. ⁶If your father misses me at all, tell him, 'David earnestly asked my permission to hurry to Bethlehem, his hometown, because an annual sacrifice is being made there for his whole clan.' ⁷If he says, 'Very well,' then your servant is safe. But if he loses his temper, you can be sure that he is determined to harm me. ⁸As for you, show kindness to your servant, for you have brought him into a covenant with you before the LORD. If I am guilty, then kill me yourself! Why hand me over to your father?"

⁹"Never!" Jonathan said. "If I had the least inkling that my father was determined to harm you, wouldn't I tell you?"

¹⁰David asked, "Who will tell me if your father answers you harshly?"

¹¹"Come," Jonathan said, "let's go out into the field." So they went there together.

¹²Then Jonathan said to David: "By the LORD, the God of Israel, I will surely sound out my father by this time the day after tomorrow! If he is favorably disposed toward you, will I not send you word and let you know? ¹³But if my father is inclined to harm you, may the LORD deal with me, be it ever so severely, if I do not let you know and send you away safely. May the LORD be with you as he has been with my father. ¹⁴But show me unfailing kindness like that of the LORD as long as I live, so that I may not be killed, ¹⁵and do not ever cut off your kindness from my family—not even when the LORD has cut off every one of David's enemies from the face of the earth."

¹⁶So Jonathan made a covenant with the house of David, saying, "May the LORD call David's enemies to account." ¹⁷And Jonathan had David reaffirm his oath out of love for him, because he loved him as he loved himself.

¹⁸Then Jonathan said to David: "Tomorrow is the New Moon festival. You will be missed, because your seat will be empty. ¹⁹The day after tomorrow, toward evening, go to the place where you hid when this trouble began, and wait by the stone Ezel. ²⁰I will shoot three arrows to the side of it, as though I were shooting at a target. ²¹Then I will send a boy and say, 'Go, find the arrows.' If I say to him, 'Look, the arrows are on this side of you; bring them here,' then come, because, as surely as the LORD lives, you are safe; there is no danger. ²²But if I say to the boy, 'Look, the arrows are beyond you,' then you must go, because the LORD has sent you away. ²³And about the matter you and I discussed—remember, the LORD is witness between you and me forever."

²⁴So David hid in the field, and when the New Moon festival came, the king sat down to eat. ²⁵He sat in his customary place by the wall, opposite Jonathan,ᵃ and Abner sat next to Saul, but David's place was empty. ²⁶Saul said nothing that day, for he thought, "Something must have happened to David to make him ceremonially unclean—surely he is unclean." ²⁷But the next day, the second day of the month, David's place was empty again. Then Saul said to his son Jonathan, "Why hasn't the son of Jesse come to the meal, either yesterday or today?"

²⁸Jonathan answered, "David earnestly asked me for permission to go to Bethlehem. ²⁹He said, 'Let me go, because our family is observing a sacrifice in the town and my

ᵃ25 Septuagint; Hebrew *wall. Jonathan arose*

SEE 1 SAMUEL 20:18-23

brother has ordered me to be there. If I have found favor in your eyes, let me get away to see my brothers.' That is why he has not come to the king's table."

³⁰Saul's anger flared up at Jonathan and he said to him, "You son of a perverse and rebellious woman! Don't I know that you have sided with the son of Jesse to your own shame and to the shame of the mother who bore you? ³¹As long as the son of Jesse lives on this earth, neither you nor your kingdom will be established. Now send and bring him to me, for he must die!"

³²"Why should he be put to death? What has he done?" Jonathan asked his father. ³³But Saul hurled his spear at him to kill him. Then Jonathan knew that his father intended to kill David.

³⁴Jonathan got up from the table in fierce anger; on that second day of the month he did not eat, because he was grieved at his father's shameful treatment of David.

³⁵In the morning Jonathan went out to the field for his meeting with David. He had a small boy with him, ³⁶and he said to the boy, "Run and find the arrows I shoot." As the boy ran, he shot an arrow beyond him. ³⁷When the boy came to the place where Jonathan's arrow had fallen, Jonathan called out after him, "Isn't the arrow beyond you?" ³⁸Then he shouted, "Hurry! Go quickly! Don't stop!" The boy picked up the arrow and returned to his master. ³⁹(The boy knew nothing of all this; only Jonathan and David knew.) ⁴⁰Then Jonathan gave his weapons to the boy and said, "Go, carry them back to town."

⁴¹After the boy had gone, David got up from the south side of the stone, and bowed down before Jonathan three times, with his face to the ground. Then they kissed each other and wept together—but David wept the most.

⁴²Jonathan said to David, "Go in peace, for we have sworn friendship with each other in the name of the LORD, saying, 'The LORD is witness between you and me, and between your descendants and my descendants forever.'" Then David left, and Jonathan went back to the town.

21 **David at Nob** David went to Nob, to Ahimelech the priest. Ahimelech trembled when he met him, and asked, "Why are you alone? Why is no one with you?"

²David answered Ahimelech the priest, "The king charged me with a certain matter and said to me, 'No one is to know anything about your mission and your instructions.' As for my men, I have told them to meet me at a certain place. ³Now then, what do you have on hand? Give me five loaves of bread, or whatever you can find."

⁴But the priest answered David, "I don't have any ordinary bread on hand; however, there is some consecrated bread here—provided the men have kept themselves from women."

⁵David replied, "Indeed women have been kept from us, as usual whenever*a* I set out. The men's things*b* are holy even on missions that are not holy. How much more so today!" ⁶So the priest gave him the consecrated bread, since there was no bread there except the bread of the Presence that had been removed from before the LORD and replaced by hot bread on the day it was taken away.

⁷Now one of Saul's servants was there that day, detained before the LORD; he was Doeg the Edomite, Saul's head shepherd.

⁸David asked Ahimelech, "Don't you have a spear or a sword here? I haven't brought my sword or any other weapon, because the king's business was urgent."

⁹The priest replied, "The sword of Goliath the Philistine, whom you killed

---

*a*5 Or *from us in the past few days since*   *b*5 Or *bodies* in the Valley of Elah, is here; it is wrapped in a cloth behind the ephod. If you want it, take it; there is no sword here but that one."

David said, "There is none like it; give it to me."

David at Gath   ¹⁰That day David fled from Saul and went to Achish king of Gath. ¹¹But the servants of Achish said to him, "Isn't this David, the king of the land? Isn't he the one they sing about in their dances:

> " 'Saul has slain his thousands,
>   and David his tens of thousands'?"

¹²David took these words to heart and was very much afraid of Achish king of Gath. ¹³So he pretended to be insane in their presence; and while he was in their hands he acted like a madman, making marks on the doors of the gate and letting saliva run down his beard.

¹⁴Achish said to his servants, "Look at the man! He is insane! Why bring him to me? ¹⁵Am I so short of madmen that you have to bring this fellow here to carry on like this in front of me? Must this man come into my house?"

22 *David at Adullam and Mizpah*   David left Gath and escaped to the cave of Adullam. When his brothers and his father's household heard about it, they went down to him there. ²All those who were in distress or in debt or discontented gathered around him, and he became their leader. About four hundred men were with him.

³From there David went to Mizpah in Moab and said to the king of Moab, "Would you let my father and mother come and stay with you until I learn what God will do for me?" ⁴So he left them with the king of Moab, and they stayed with him as long as David was in the stronghold.

⁵But the prophet Gad said to David, "Do not stay in the stronghold. Go into the land of Judah." So David left and went to the forest of Hereth.

Saul Kills the Priests of Nob   ⁶Now Saul heard that David and his men had been discovered. And Saul, spear in hand, was seated under the tamarisk tree on the hill at Gibeah, with all his officials standing around him. ⁷Saul said to them, "Listen, men of Benjamin! Will the son of Jesse give all of you fields and vineyards? Will he make all of you commanders of thousands and commanders of hundreds? ⁸Is that why you have all conspired against me? No one tells me when my son makes a covenant with the son of Jesse. None of you is concerned about me or tells me that my son has incited my servant to lie in wait for me, as he does today."

Have you ever been tempted to get out of trouble by telling a lie? Most everyone has. Even Bible heroes were tempted to lie.

* Abram lied and said Sarai was his sister—and got into trouble in Egypt (Genesis 12:10–20).
* Jacob lied to his father—and made his brother so angry that Jacob had to run to safety (Genesis 27:34–45).
* David lied in order to get help from Ahimelech the priest—and later King Saul killed the innocent priest and his family for helping David escape (1 Samuel 21—22).

When tempted to lie, remember: "The LORD detests lying lips, but he delights in men who are truthful" (Proverbs 12:22).

The Bible Says

Lies Don't Help

⁹But Doeg the Edomite, who was standing with Saul's officials, said, "I saw the son of Jesse come to Ahimelech son of Ahitub at Nob. ¹⁰Ahimelech inquired of the LORD for him; he also gave him provisions and the sword of Goliath the Philistine."

¹¹Then the king sent for the priest Ahimelech son of Ahitub and his father's whole family, who were the priests at Nob, and they all came to the king. ¹²Saul said, "Listen now, son of Ahitub."

"Yes, my lord," he answered.

¹³Saul said to him, "Why have you conspired against me, you and the son of Jesse, giving him bread and a sword and inquiring of God for him, so that he has rebelled against me and lies in wait for me, as he does today?"

¹⁴Ahimelech answered the king, "Who of all your servants is as loyal as David, the king's son-in-law, captain of your bodyguard and highly respected in your household? ¹⁵Was that day the first time I inquired of God for him? Of course not! Let not the king accuse your servant or any of his father's family, for your servant knows nothing at all about this whole affair."

¹⁶But the king said, "You will surely die, Ahimelech, you and your father's whole family."

¹⁷Then the king ordered the guards at his side: "Turn and kill the priests of the LORD, because they too have sided with David. They knew he was fleeing, yet they did not tell me."

But the king's officials were not willing to raise a hand to strike the priests of the LORD.

¹⁸The king then ordered Doeg, "You turn and strike down the priests." So Doeg the Edomite turned and struck them down. That day he killed eighty-five men who wore the linen ephod. ¹⁹He also put to the sword Nob, the town of the priests, with its men and women, its children and infants, and its cattle, donkeys and sheep.

²⁰But Abiathar, a son of Ahimelech son of Ahitub, escaped and fled to join David. ²¹He told David that Saul had killed the priests of the LORD. ²²Then David said to Abiathar: "That day, when Doeg the Edomite was there, I knew he would be sure to tell Saul. I am responsible for the death of your father's whole family. ²³Stay with me; don't be afraid; the man who is seeking your life is seeking mine also. You will be safe with me."

Direct Line

1 SAMUEL 23:1–13

You helped the neighbor wash her car, and she didn't pay you? You rescued a cat stuck up in a tree, and it bit you? You worked all day cleaning up at church, and they left your name out of the bulletin? Then look what happened to David: David and his men rescued the people of a little town, yet the people of that town were ready to turn him over to Saul. But so what? Did the ingratitude of those people make David's rescue foolish? Or even more noble? Sure, you want to be recognized for the good things you do. But even when you don't get credit or appreciation, you have the inner satisfaction of knowing you did right.

23 *David Saves Keilah* When David was told, "Look, the Philistines are fighting against Keilah and are looting the threshing floors," ²he inquired of the LORD, saying, "Shall I go and attack these Philistines?"

The LORD answered him, "Go, attack the Philistines and save Keilah."

³But David's men said to him, "Here in Judah we are afraid. How much more, then, if we go to Keilah against the Philistine forces!"

⁴Once again David inquired of the LORD, and the LORD answered him, "Go down to Keilah, for I am going to give the Philistines into your hand." ⁵So David and his men went to Keilah, fought the Philistines and carried off their livestock. He inflicted heavy losses on the Philistines and saved the people of Keilah. ⁶(Now Abia-

thar son of Ahimelech had brought the ephod down with him when he fled to David at Keilah.)

Saul Pursues David   ⁷Saul was told that David had gone to Keilah, and he said, "God has handed him over to me, for David has imprisoned himself by entering a town with gates and bars." ⁸And Saul called up all his forces for battle, to go down to Keilah to besiege David and his men.

⁹When David learned that Saul was plotting against him, he said to Abiathar the priest, "Bring the ephod." ¹⁰David said, "O LORD, God of Israel, your servant has heard definitely that Saul plans to come to Keilah and destroy the town on account of me. ¹¹Will the citizens of Keilah surrender me to him? Will Saul come down, as your servant has heard? O LORD, God of Israel, tell your servant."

And the LORD said, "He will."

¹²Again David asked, "Will the citizens of Keilah surrender me and my men to Saul?"

And the LORD said, "They will."

¹³So David and his men, about six hundred in number, left Keilah and kept moving from place to place. When Saul was told that David had escaped from Keilah, he did not go there.

¹⁴David stayed in the desert strongholds and in the hills of the Desert of Ziph. Day after day Saul searched for him, but God did not give David into his hands.

¹⁵While David was at Horesh in the Desert of Ziph, he learned that Saul had come out to take his life. ¹⁶And Saul's son Jonathan went to David at Horesh and helped him find strength in God. ¹⁷"Don't be afraid," he said. "My father Saul will not lay a hand on you. You will be king over Israel, and I will be second to you. Even my father Saul knows this." ¹⁸The two of them made a covenant before the LORD. Then Jonathan went home, but David remained at Horesh.

¹⁹The Ziphites went up to Saul at Gibeah and said, "Is not David hiding among us in the strongholds at Horesh, on the hill of Hakilah, south of Jeshimon? ²⁰Now, O king, come down whenever it pleases you to do so, and we will be responsible for handing him over to the king."

²¹Saul replied, "The LORD bless you for your concern for me. ²²Go and make further preparation. Find out where David usually goes and who has seen him there. They tell me he is very crafty. ²³Find out about all the hiding places he uses and come back to me with definite information.*ᵃ* Then I will go with you; if he is in the area, I will track him down among all the clans of Judah."

²⁴So they set out and went to Ziph ahead of Saul. Now David and his men were in the Desert of Maon, in the Arabah south of Jeshimon. ²⁵Saul and his men began the search, and when David was told about it, he went down to the rock and stayed in the Desert of Maon. When Saul heard this, he went into the Desert of Maon in pursuit of David.

²⁶Saul was going along one side of the mountain, and David and his men were on the other side, hurrying to get away from Saul. As Saul and his forces were closing in on David and his men to capture them, ²⁷a messenger came to Saul, saying, "Come quickly! The Philistines are raiding the land." ²⁸Then Saul broke off his pursuit of David and went to meet the Philistines. That is why they call this place Sela Hammahlekoth.*ᵇ* ²⁹And David went up from there and lived in the strongholds of En Gedi.

24 *David Spares Saul's Life*   After Saul returned from pursuing the Philistines, he was told, "David is in the Desert of En Gedi." ²So Saul took three thousand chosen men from all Israel and set out to look for David and his men near the Crags of the Wild Goats.

ᵃ23 Or me at Nacon   ᵇ28 Sela Hammahlekoth means rock of parting.

³He came to the sheep pens along the way; a cave was there, and Saul went in to relieve himself. David and his men were far back in the cave. ⁴The men said, "This is the day the LORD spoke of when he said*ᵃ* to you, 'I will give your enemy into your hands for you to deal with as you wish.' " Then David crept up unnoticed and cut off a corner of Saul's robe.

⁵Afterward, David was conscience-stricken for having cut off a corner of his robe. ⁶He said to his men, "The LORD forbid that I should do such a thing to my master, the LORD's anointed, or lift my hand against him; for he is the anointed of the LORD." ⁷With these words David rebuked his men and did not allow them to attack Saul. And Saul left the cave and went his way.

⁸Then David went out of the cave and called out to Saul, "My lord the king!" When Saul looked behind him, David bowed down and prostrated himself with his face to the ground. ⁹He said to Saul, "Why do you listen when men say, 'David is bent on harming you'? ¹⁰This day you have seen with your own eyes how the LORD delivered you into my hands in the cave. Some urged me to kill you, but I spared you; I said, 'I will not lift my hand against my master, because he is the LORD's anointed.' ¹¹See, my father, look at this piece of your robe in my hand! I cut off the corner of your robe but did not kill you. Now understand and recognize that I am not guilty of wrongdoing or rebellion. I have not wronged you, but you are hunting me down to take my life. ¹²May the LORD judge between you and me. And may the LORD avenge the wrongs you have done to me, but my hand will not touch you. ¹³As the old saying goes, 'From evildoers come evil deeds,' so my hand will not touch you.

¹⁴"Against whom has the king of Israel come out? Whom are you pursuing? A dead dog? A flea? ¹⁵May the LORD be our judge and decide between us. May he consider my cause and uphold it; may he vindicate me by delivering me from your hand."

¹⁶When David finished saying this, Saul asked, "Is that your voice, David my son?" And he wept aloud. ¹⁷"You are more righteous than I," he said. "You have treated me well, but I have treated you badly. ¹⁸You have just now told me of the good you did to me; the LORD delivered me into your hands, but you did not kill me. ¹⁹When a man finds his enemy, does he let him get away unharmed? May the LORD reward you well for the way you treated me today. ²⁰I know that you will surely be king and that the kingdom of Israel will be established in your hands. ²¹Now swear to me by the LORD that you will not cut off my descendants or wipe out my name from my father's family."

²²So David gave his oath to Saul. Then Saul returned home, but David and his men went up to the stronghold.

David, Nabal and Abigail Now Samuel died, and all Israel assembled and mourned for him; and they buried him at his home in Ramah.

Then David moved down into the Desert of Maon.*ᵇ* ²A certain man in Maon, who had property there at Carmel, was

1 SAMUEL 24

What's the first thing you want to do when someone tells a lie about you? You want to talk to the people who heard the lie and tell them it isn't true. And you may want to beat up the person who told the lie. David gives you another option. Saul labeled David a traitor and set out to kill him. But when David had the chance to kill Saul, he let him live. David's action did more to disprove the lies told about him than anything he could have said. Sure, it's upsetting to hear someone is saying bad things about you. But keep on living a good life and prove by your actions how wrong those accusations are.

Direct Line

ᵃ4 Or "Today the LORD is saying *ᵇ1 Some Septuagint manuscripts; Hebrew Paran*

very wealthy. He had a thousand goats and three thousand sheep, which he was shearing in Carmel. ³His name was Nabal and his wife's name was Abigail. She was an intelligent and beautiful woman, but her husband, a Calebite, was surly and mean in his dealings.

⁴While David was in the desert, he heard that Nabal was shearing sheep. ⁵So he sent ten young men and said to them, "Go up to Nabal at Carmel and greet him in my name. ⁶Say to him: 'Long life to you! Good health to you and your household! And good health to all that is yours!

⁷" 'Now I hear that it is sheep-shearing time. When your shepherds were with us, we did not mistreat them, and the whole time they were at Carmel nothing of theirs was missing. ⁸Ask your own servants and they will tell you. Therefore be favorable toward my young men, since we come at a festive time. Please give your servants and your son David whatever you can find for them.' "

⁹When David's men arrived, they gave Nabal this message in David's name. Then they waited.

¹⁰Nabal answered David's servants, "Who is this David? Who is this son of Jesse? Many servants are breaking away from their masters these days. ¹¹Why should I take my bread and water, and the meat I have slaughtered for my shearers, and give it to men coming from who knows where?"

¹²David's men turned around and went back. When they arrived, they reported every word. ¹³David said to his men, "Put on your swords!" So they put on their swords, and David put on his. About four hundred men went up with David, while two hundred stayed with the supplies.

¹⁴One of the servants told Nabal's wife Abigail: "David sent messengers from the desert to give our master his greetings, but he hurled insults at them. ¹⁵Yet these men were very good to us. They did not mistreat us, and the whole time we were out in the fields near them nothing was missing. ¹⁶Night and day they were a wall around us all the time we were herding our sheep near them. ¹⁷Now think it over and see what you can do, because disaster is hanging over our master and his whole household. He is such a wicked man that no one can talk to him."

¹⁸Abigail lost no time. She took two hundred loaves of bread, two skins of wine, five dressed sheep, five seahs*ᵃ* of roasted grain, a hundred cakes of raisins and two hundred cakes of pressed figs, and loaded them on donkeys. ¹⁹Then she told her servants, "Go on ahead; I'll follow you." But she did not tell her husband Nabal.

²⁰As she came riding her donkey into a mountain ravine, there were David and his men descending toward her, and she met them. ²¹David had just said, "It's been useless—all my watching over this fellow's property in the desert so that nothing of his was missing. He has paid me back evil for good. ²²May God deal with David,ᵇ be it ever so severely, if by morning I leave alive one male of all who belong to him!"

²³When Abigail saw David, she quickly got off her donkey and bowed down before David with her face to the ground. ²⁴She fell at his feet and said: "My lord, let the blame be on me alone. Please let your servant speak to you; hear what your servant has to say. ²⁵May my lord pay no attention to that wicked man Nabal. He is just like his name—his name is Fool, and folly goes with him. But as for me, your servant, I did not see the men my master sent.

²⁶"Now since the LORD has kept you, my master, from bloodshed and from avenging yourself with your own hands, as surely as the LORD lives and as you live, may your enemies and all who intend to harm my master be like Nabal. ²⁷And let this gift, which your servant has brought to my master, be given to the men who follow you. ²⁸Please forgive your servant's offense, for

---

ᵃ18 That is, probably about a bushel (about 37 liters) *ᵇ22* Some Septuagint manuscripts; Hebrew *with David's enemies*

Dear Sam,

I have a problem controlling my anger. Afterward I'm sorry, but what's been said can't be changed. How can I learn to be in control?

Max in Macon

100 Advice Lane, Anywhere, USA

Dear Max,

Your problem is not uncommon, and your letter shows you've done some thinking about it. You probably realize anger is a choice. Everyone gets into upsetting situations from time to time. How you choose to react makes the difference.

When David was angry about the way he had been treated by a wealthy fool, he decided to go and kill him (1 Samuel 25). Abigail, that man's wife, immediately went to David, taking him many gifts and begging his forgiveness for her foolish husband. Wisely, she told David that just because her husband was a fool didn't mean that David should become a murderer. David agreed and said, "May you be blessed . . . for keeping me from bloodshed this day" (1 Samuel 25:33).

Instead of lashing out at people when you're angry, try doing something physical like running, riding your bike or playing tennis. Some people find it helpful to count mentally until their angry feelings subside. Plan ahead, and next time you get angry you'll have some options to try besides losing your cool.

Sam

the LORD will certainly make a lasting dynasty for my master, because he fights the LORD's battles. Let no wrongdoing be found in you as long as you live. ²⁹Even though someone is pursuing you to take your life, the life of my master will be bound securely in the bundle of the living by the LORD your God. But the lives of your enemies he will hurl away as from the pocket of a sling. ³⁰When the LORD has done for my master every good thing he promised concerning him and has appointed him leader over Israel, ³¹my master will not have on his conscience the staggering burden of needless bloodshed or of having avenged himself. And when the LORD has brought my master success, remember your servant."

³²David said to Abigail, "Praise be to the LORD, the God of Israel, who has sent you today to meet me. ³³May you be blessed for your good judgment and for keeping me from bloodshed this day and from avenging myself with my own hands. ³⁴Otherwise, as surely as the LORD, the God of Israel, lives, who has kept me from harming you, if you had not come quickly to meet me, not one male belonging to Nabal would have been left alive by daybreak."

³⁵Then David accepted from her hand what she had brought him and said, "Go home in peace. I have heard your words and granted your request."

³⁶When Abigail went to Nabal, he was in the house holding a banquet like that of a king. He was in high spirits and very drunk. So she told him nothing until daybreak. ³⁷Then in the morning, when Nabal was sober, his wife told him all these things, and his heart failed him and he became like a stone. ³⁸About ten days later, the LORD struck Nabal and he died.

³⁹When David heard that Nabal was dead, he said, "Praise be to the LORD, who has upheld my cause against Nabal for treating me with contempt. He has kept his servant from doing wrong and has brought Nabal's wrongdoing down on his own head."

Then David sent word to Abigail, asking her to become his wife. ⁴⁰His servants went to Carmel and said to Abigail, "David has sent us to you to take you to become his wife."

⁴¹She bowed down with her face to the ground and said, "Here is your maidservant, ready to serve you and wash the feet of my master's servants." ⁴²Abigail quickly got on a donkey and, attended by her five maids, went with David's messengers and became his wife. ⁴³David had also married Ahinoam of Jezreel, and they both were his wives. ⁴⁴But Saul had given his daughter Michal, David's wife, to Paltiel*ᵃ* son of Laish, who was from Gallim.

David Again Spares Saul's Life The Ziphites went to Saul at Gibeah and said, "Is not David hiding on the hill of Hakilah, which faces Jeshimon?"

²So Saul went down to the Desert of Ziph, with his three thousand chosen men of Israel, to search there for David. ³Saul made his camp beside the road on the hill of Hakilah facing Jeshimon, but David stayed in the desert. When he saw that Saul had followed him there, ⁴he sent out scouts and learned that Saul had definitely arrived.*ᵇ*

⁵Then David set out and went to the place where Saul had camped. He saw where Saul and Abner son of Ner, the commander of the army, had lain down. Saul was lying inside the camp, with the army encamped around him.

⁶David then asked Ahimelech the Hittite and Abishai son of Zeruiah, Joab's brother, "Who will go down into the camp with me to Saul?"

"I'll go with you," said Abishai.

⁷So David and Abishai went to the army by night, and there was Saul, lying asleep inside the camp with his spear stuck in the ground near his head. Abner and the soldiers were lying around him.

---

*ᵃ*44 Hebrew *Palti*, a variant of *Paltiel*   *ᵇ*4 Or *had come to Nacon*

[8]Abishai said to David, "Today God has delivered your enemy into your hands. Now let me pin him to the ground with one thrust of my spear; I won't strike him twice."

[9]But David said to Abishai, "Don't destroy him! Who can lay a hand on the LORD's anointed and be guiltless? [10]As surely as the LORD lives," he said, "the LORD himself will strike him; either his time will come and he will die, or he will go into battle and perish. [11]But the LORD forbid that I should lay a hand on the LORD's anointed. Now get the spear and water jug that are near his head, and let's go."

[12]So David took the spear and water jug near Saul's head, and they left. No one saw or knew about it, nor did anyone wake up. They were all sleeping, because the LORD had put them into a deep sleep.

[13]Then David crossed over to the other side and stood on top of the hill some distance away; there was a wide space between them. [14]He called out to the army and to Abner son of Ner, "Aren't you going to answer me, Abner?"

Abner replied, "Who are you who calls to the king?"

[15]David said, "You're a man, aren't you? And who is like you in Israel? Why didn't you guard your lord the king? Someone came to destroy your lord the king. [16]What you have done is not good. As surely as the LORD lives, you and your men deserve to die, because you did not guard your master, the LORD's anointed. Look around you. Where are the king's spear and water jug that were near his head?"

[17]Saul recognized David's voice and said, "Is that your voice, David my son?"

David replied, "Yes it is, my lord the king." [18]And he added, "Why is my lord pursuing his servant? What have I done, and what wrong am I guilty of? [19]Now let my lord the king listen to his servant's words. If the LORD has incited you against me, then may he accept an offering. If, however, men have done it, may they be cursed before the LORD! They have now driven me from my share in the LORD's inheritance and have said, 'Go, serve other gods.'

[20]Now do not let my blood fall to the ground far from the presence of the LORD. The king of Israel has come out to look for a flea—as one hunts a partridge in the mountains."

[21]Then Saul said, "I have sinned. Come back, David my son. Because you considered my life precious today, I will not try to harm you again. Surely I have acted like a fool and have erred greatly."

[22]"Here is the king's spear," David answered. "Let one of your young men come over and get it. [23]The LORD rewards every man for his righteousness and faithfulness. The LORD delivered you into my hands today, but I would not lay a hand on the LORD's anointed. [24]As surely as I valued your life today, so may the LORD value my life and deliver me from all trouble."

[25]Then Saul said to David, "May you be blessed, my son David; you will do great things and surely triumph."

So David went on his way, and Saul returned home.

Direct Line

1 SAMUEL 26:9–12

Sometimes being nice doesn't work. Just look at David. Twice David had the chance to kill Saul. Twice David let Saul live. But Saul kept on trying to kill David anyway. Being nice to Saul didn't change Saul one bit. So what do you do when nice doesn't work? David states a basic principle: "I would not lay a hand on the LORD's anointed" (1 Samuel 26:11,23). Nice didn't work. But revenge or getting even doesn't work either! Instead what David says is "may the LORD avenge the wrongs you have done to me" (1 Samuel 24:12). Any payback for being wronged is to come from God. Not from David. And not from you or me.

27 *David Among the Philistines* But David thought to himself, "One of these days I will be destroyed by the hand of Saul. The best thing I can do is to escape to the land of the Philistines. Then Saul will give up searching for me anywhere in Israel, and I will slip out of his hand."

²So David and the six hundred men with him left and went over to Achish son of Maoch king of Gath. ³David and his men settled in Gath with Achish. Each man had his family with him, and David had his two wives: Ahinoam of Jezreel and Abigail of Carmel, the widow of Nabal. ⁴When Saul was told that David had fled to Gath, he no longer searched for him.

⁵Then David said to Achish, "If I have found favor in your eyes, let a place be assigned to me in one of the country towns, that I may live there. Why should your servant live in the royal city with you?"

⁶So on that day Achish gave him Ziklag, and it has belonged to the kings of Judah ever since. ⁷David lived in Philistine territory a year and four months.

⁸Now David and his men went up and raided the Geshurites, the Girzites and the Amalekites. (From ancient times these peoples had lived in the land extending to Shur and Egypt.) ⁹Whenever David attacked an area, he did not leave a man or woman alive, but took sheep and cattle, donkeys and camels, and clothes. Then he returned to Achish.

¹⁰When Achish asked, "Where did you go raiding today?" David would say, "Against the Negev of Judah" or "Against the Negev of Jerahmeel" or "Against the Negev of the Kenites." ¹¹He did not leave a man or woman alive to be brought to Gath, for he thought, "They might inform on us and say, 'This is what David did.'" And such was his practice as long as he lived in Philistine territory. ¹²Achish trusted David and said to himself, "He has become so odious to his people, the Israelites, that he will be my servant forever."

28 *Saul and the Witch of Endor* In those days the Philistines gathered their forces to fight against Israel. Achish said to David, "You must understand that you and your men will accompany me in the army."

²David said, "Then you will see for yourself what your servant can do."

Achish replied, "Very well, I will make you my bodyguard for life."

³Now Samuel was dead, and all Israel had mourned for him and buried him in his own town of Ramah. Saul had expelled the mediums and spiritists from the land.

⁴The Philistines assembled and came and set up camp at Shunem, while Saul gathered all the Israelites and set up camp at Gilboa. ⁵When Saul saw the Philistine army, he was afraid; terror filled his heart. ⁶He inquired of the Lord, but the Lord did not answer him by dreams or Urim or prophets. ⁷Saul then said to his attendants, "Find me a woman who is a medium, so I may go and inquire of her."

"There is one in Endor," they said.

⁸So Saul disguised himself, putting on other clothes, and at night he and two men went to the woman. "Consult a spirit for me," he said, "and bring up for me the one I name."

⁹But the woman said to him, "Surely you know what Saul has done. He has cut off the mediums and spiritists from the land. Why have you set a trap for my life to bring about my death?"

¹⁰Saul swore to her by the Lord, "As surely as the Lord lives, you will not be punished for this."

¹¹Then the woman asked, "Whom shall I bring up for you?"

"Bring up Samuel," he said.

¹²When the woman saw Samuel, she cried out at the top of her voice and said to Saul, "Why have you deceived me? You are Saul!"

¹³The king said to her, "Don't be afraid. What do you see?"

The woman said, "I see a spirit*ᵃ* coming up out of the ground."

¹⁴"What does he look like?" he asked.

"An old man wearing a robe is coming up," she said.

Then Saul knew it was Samuel, and he bowed down and prostrated himself with his face to the ground.

¹⁵Samuel said to Saul, "Why have you disturbed me by bringing me up?"

"I am in great distress," Saul said. "The Philistines are fighting against me, and God has turned away from me. He no longer answers me, either by prophets or by dreams. So I have called on you to tell me what to do."

¹⁶Samuel said, "Why do you consult me, now that the LORD has turned away from you and become your enemy? ¹⁷The LORD has done what he predicted through me. The LORD has torn the kingdom out of your hands and given it to one of your neighbors—to David. ¹⁸Because you did not obey the LORD or carry out his fierce wrath against the Amalekites, the LORD has done this to you today. ¹⁹The LORD will hand over both Israel and you to the Philistines, and tomorrow you and your sons will be with me. The LORD will also hand over the army of Israel to the Philistines."

²⁰Immediately Saul fell full length on the ground, filled with fear because of Samuel's words. His strength was gone, for he had eaten nothing all that day and night.

²¹When the woman came to Saul and saw that he was greatly shaken, she said, "Look, your maidservant has obeyed you. I took my life in my hands and did what you told me to do. ²²Now please listen to your servant and let me give you some food so you may eat and have the strength to go on your way."

²³He refused and said, "I will not eat."

But his men joined the woman in urging him, and he listened to them. He got up from the ground and sat on the couch.

²⁴The woman had a fattened calf at the house, which she butchered at once. She took some flour, kneaded it and baked bread without yeast. ²⁵Then she set it before Saul and his men, and they ate. That same night they got up and left.

Direct Line

1 SAMUEL 28

How much power do witches have? Didn't the witch of Endor call Samuel back from the dead? Doesn't that prove spiritists and mediums really can reach the dead, as they claim? Read the story closely, and you discover the most surprised person in the witch's house was the witch herself (1 Samuel 28:12–14)! She may have expected some evil spirit to manifest itself, but she surely didn't expect Samuel himself to appear. Don't be fooled. People who dabble in the occult may touch supernatural powers, but they're dabbling with danger.

29

Achish Sends David Back to Ziklag The Philistines gathered all their forces at Aphek, and Israel camped by the spring in Jezreel. ²As the Philistine rulers marched with their units of hundreds and thousands, David and his men were marching at the rear with Achish. ³The commanders of the Philistines asked, "What about these Hebrews?"

Achish replied, "Is this not David, who was an officer of Saul king of Israel? He has already been with me for over a year, and from the day he left Saul until now, I have found no fault in him."

⁴But the Philistine commanders were angry with him and said, "Send the man back, that he may return to the place you assigned him. He must not go with us into battle, or he will turn against us during the fighting. How better could he re-

ᵃ13 Or see spirits; or see gods

gain his master's favor than by taking the heads of our own men? 5Isn't this the David they sang about in their dances:

> " 'Saul has slain his thousands,
> and David his tens of thousands'?"

6So Achish called David and said to him, "As surely as the LORD lives, you have been reliable, and I would be pleased to have you serve with me in the army. From the day you came to me until now, I have found no fault in you, but the rulers don't approve of you. 7Turn back and go in peace; do nothing to displease the Philistine rulers."

8"But what have I done?" asked David. "What have you found against your servant from the day I came to you until now? Why can't I go and fight against the enemies of my lord the king?"

9Achish answered, "I know that you have been as pleasing in my eyes as an angel of God; nevertheless, the Philistine commanders have said, 'He must not go up with us into battle.' 10Now get up early, along with your master's servants who have come with you, and leave in the morning as soon as it is light."

11So David and his men got up early in the morning to go back to the land of the Philistines, and the Philistines went up to Jezreel.

30 David Destroys the Amalekites

David and his men reached Ziklag on the third day. Now the Amalekites had raided the Negev and Ziklag. They had attacked Ziklag and burned it, 2and had taken captive the women and all who were in it, both young and old. They killed none of them, but carried them off as they went on their way.

3When David and his men came to Ziklag, they found it destroyed by fire and their wives and sons and daughters taken captive. 4So David and his men wept aloud until they had no strength left to weep. 5David's two wives had been captured—Ahinoam of Jezreel and Abigail, the widow of Nabal of Carmel. 6David was greatly distressed because the men were talking of stoning him; each one was bitter in spirit because of his sons and daughters. But David found strength in the LORD his God.

7Then David said to Abiathar the priest, the son of Ahimelech, "Bring me the ephod." Abiathar brought it to him, 8and David inquired of the LORD, "Shall I pursue this raiding party? Will I overtake them?"

"Pursue them," he answered. "You will certainly overtake them and succeed in the rescue."

The story in 1 Samuel 29 illustrates God's providence, how he works to make sure things turn out according to his plan.

David had fled his homeland and settled with the Philistines. When the Philistines went to war against Israel, David was expected to fight against his own people. But God had chosen David to be the king of Israel (1 Samuel 16). He would never become king if he fought on the side of the Philistines. Then, because some Philistine rulers questioned David's loyalties, they refused to let him go to war with them. God was at work, making sure that David became king.

It's comforting to know that God is at work for you too, isn't it? You may not see miracles. You may not hear God speak. But in all that happens, God is at work for your good (Romans 8:28).

The
Bible
Says

God Is at Work

⁹David and the six hundred men with him came to the Besor Ravine, where some stayed behind, ¹⁰for two hundred men were too exhausted to cross the ravine. But David and four hundred men continued the pursuit.

¹¹They found an Egyptian in a field and brought him to David. They gave him water to drink and food to eat— ¹²part of a cake of pressed figs and two cakes of raisins. He ate and was revived, for he had not eaten any food or drunk any water for three days and three nights.

¹³David asked him, "To whom do you belong, and where do you come from?"

He said, "I am an Egyptian, the slave of an Amalekite. My master abandoned me when I became ill three days ago. ¹⁴We raided the Negev of the Kerethites and the territory belonging to Judah and the Negev of Caleb. And we burned Ziklag."

¹⁵David asked him, "Can you lead me down to this raiding party?"

He answered, "Swear to me before God that you will not kill me or hand me over to my master, and I will take you down to them."

¹⁶He led David down, and there they were, scattered over the countryside, eating, drinking and reveling because of the great amount of plunder they had taken from the land of the Philistines and from Judah. ¹⁷David fought them from dusk until the evening of the next day, and none of them got away, except four hundred young men who rode off on camels and fled. ¹⁸David recovered everything the Amalekites had taken, including his two wives. ¹⁹Nothing was missing: young or old, boy or girl, plunder or anything else they had taken. David brought everything back. ²⁰He took all the flocks and herds, and his men drove them ahead of the other livestock, saying, "This is David's plunder."

²¹Then David came to the two hundred men who had been too exhausted to follow him and who were left behind at the Besor Ravine. They came out to meet David and the people with him. As David and his men approached, he greeted them. ²²But all the evil men and troublemakers among David's followers said, "Because they did not go out with us, we will not share with them the plunder we recovered. However, each man may take his wife and children and go."

²³David replied, "No, my brothers, you must not do that with what the Lord has given us. He has protected us and handed over to us the forces that came against us. ²⁴Who will listen to what you say? The share of the man who stayed with the supplies is to be the same as that of him who went down to the battle. All will share alike." ²⁵David made this a statute and ordinance for Israel from that day to this.

²⁶When David arrived in Ziklag, he sent some of the plunder to the elders of Judah, who were his friends, saying, "Here is a present for you from the plunder of the Lord's enemies."

²⁷He sent it to those who were in Bethel, Ramoth Negev and Jattir; ²⁸to those in Aroer, Siphmoth, Eshtemoa ²⁹and Racal; to those in the towns of the Jerahmeelites and the Kenites; ³⁰to those in Hormah, Bor Ashan, Athach ³¹and Hebron; and to those in all the other places where David and his men had roamed.

31 *Saul Takes His Life* Now the Philistines fought against Israel; the Israelites fled before them, and many fell slain on Mount Gilboa. ²The Philistines pressed hard after Saul and his sons, and they killed his sons Jonathan, Abinadab and Malki-Shua. ³The fighting grew fierce around Saul, and when the archers overtook him, they wounded him critically.

⁴Saul said to his armor-bearer, "Draw your sword and run me through, or these uncircumcised fellows will come and run me through and abuse me."

But his armor-bearer was terrified and would not do it; so Saul took his own sword and fell on it. ⁵When the armor-bearer saw that Saul was dead, he too fell on his sword and died with him. ⁶So Saul and his three sons and his armor-bearer and all his men died together that same day.

⁷When the Israelites along the valley and those across the Jordan saw that the Israelite army had fled and that Saul and his sons had died, they abandoned their towns and fled. And the Philistines came and occupied them.

⁸The next day, when the Philistines came to strip the dead, they found Saul and his three sons fallen on Mount Gilboa. ⁹They cut off his head and stripped off his armor, and they sent messengers throughout the land of the Philistines to proclaim the news in the temple of their idols and among their people. ¹⁰They put his armor in the temple of the Ashtoreths and fastened his body to the wall of Beth Shan.

¹¹When the people of Jabesh Gilead heard of what the Philistines had done to Saul, ¹²all their valiant men journeyed through the night to Beth Shan. They took down the bodies of Saul and his sons from the wall of Beth Shan and went to Jabesh, where they burned them. ¹³Then they took their bones and buried them under a tamarisk tree at Jabesh, and they fasted seven days.

DREAM ON.

What if all your dreams were to come true? You make it in the movies or become president. You become the next Mother Teresa, or your process for turning sunlight into energy makes you a billionaire. Will your life be easier then?

David's dreams did come true. Saul died; David was crowned king over all Israel. His armies pushed back Israel's enemies until Israel had ten times as much land as before. And David led his people to worship God in Jerusalem. But despite his successes, David's life wasn't easy. He made some choices that hurt him and his people.

Fundamentals

What if someone was willing to do wrong to help you (2 Samuel 4)?

What is the best thing to do if you're caught doing wrong (2 Samuel 12:13)?

Can someone who loves God still sin (2 Samuel 24)?

FAST FACTS

In the Hebrew Bible, 1 and 2 Samuel are one book.

Samuel didn't write the books bearing his name. It is unknown who did.

David expresses sorrow for his sins in Psalms 32 and 51.

God promised David one of his descendants would rule forever.

David Hears of Saul's Death After the death of Saul, David returned from defeating the Amalekites and stayed in Ziklag two days. ²On the third day a man arrived from Saul's camp, with his clothes torn and with dust on his head. When he came to David, he fell to the ground to pay him honor.

³"Where have you come from?" David asked him.

He answered, "I have escaped from the Israelite camp."

⁴"What happened?" David asked. "Tell me."

He said, "The men fled from the battle. Many of them fell and died. And Saul and his son Jonathan are dead."

⁵Then David said to the young man who brought him the report, "How do you know that Saul and his son Jonathan are dead?"

⁶"I happened to be on Mount Gilboa," the young man said, "and there was Saul, leaning on his spear, with the chariots and riders almost upon him. ⁷When he turned around and saw me, he called out to me, and I said, 'What can I do?'

⁸"He asked me, 'Who are you?'

" 'An Amalekite,' I answered.

⁹"Then he said to me, 'Stand over me and kill me! I am in the throes of death, but I'm still alive.'

¹⁰"So I stood over him and killed him, because I knew that after he had fallen he could not survive. And I took the crown that was on his head and the band on his arm and have brought them here to my lord."

¹¹Then David and all the men with him took hold of their clothes and tore them. ¹²They mourned and wept and fasted till evening for Saul and his son Jonathan, and for the army of the Lord and the house of Israel, because they had fallen by the sword.

¹³David said to the young man who brought him the report, "Where are you from?"

"I am the son of an alien, an Amalekite," he answered.

¹⁴David asked him, "Why were you not afraid to lift your hand to destroy the Lord's anointed?"

¹⁵Then David called one of his men and said, "Go, strike him down!" So he struck him down, and he died. ¹⁶For David had said to him, "Your blood be on your own head. Your own mouth testified against you when you said, 'I killed the Lord's anointed.' "

David's Lament for Saul and Jonathan ¹⁷David took up this lament concerning Saul and his son Jonathan, ¹⁸and ordered that the men of Judah be taught this lament of the bow (it is written in the Book of Jashar):

> ¹⁹"Your glory, O Israel, lies slain on your heights.
> How the mighty have fallen!

> ²⁰"Tell it not in Gath,
> proclaim it not in the streets of Ashkelon,
> lest the daughters of the Philistines be glad,
> lest the daughters of the uncircumcised rejoice.

> ²¹"O mountains of Gilboa,
> may you have neither dew nor rain,
> nor fields that yield offerings of grain.
> For there the shield of the mighty was defiled,
> the shield of Saul—no longer rubbed with oil.
> ²²From the blood of the slain,
> from the flesh of the mighty,
> the bow of Jonathan did not turn back,
> the sword of Saul did not return unsatisfied.

> [23] "Saul and Jonathan—
>> in life they were loved and gracious,
>> and in death they were not parted.
> They were swifter than eagles,
>> they were stronger than lions.
>
> [24] "O daughters of Israel,
>> weep for Saul,
> who clothed you in scarlet and finery,
>> who adorned your garments with ornaments of gold.
>
> [25] "How the mighty have fallen in battle!
>> Jonathan lies slain on your heights.
> [26] I grieve for you, Jonathan my brother;
>> you were very dear to me.
> Your love for me was wonderful,
>> more wonderful than that of women.
>
> [27] "How the mighty have fallen!
>> The weapons of war have perished!"

David Anointed King Over Judah   In the course of time, David inquired of the Lord. "Shall I go up to one of the towns of Judah?" he asked.
The Lord said, "Go up."

David asked, "Where shall I go?"

"To Hebron," the Lord answered.

[2] So David went up there with his two wives, Ahinoam of Jezreel and Abigail, the widow of Nabal of Carmel. [3] David also took the men who were with him, each with his family, and they settled in Hebron and its towns. [4] Then the men of Judah came to Hebron and there they anointed David king over the house of Judah.

When David was told that it was the men of Jabesh Gilead who had buried Saul, [5] he sent messengers to the men of Jabesh Gilead to say to them, "The Lord bless you for showing this kindness to Saul your master by burying him. [6] May the Lord now show you kindness and faithfulness, and I too will show you the same favor because you have done this. [7] Now then, be strong and brave, for Saul your master is dead, and the house of Judah has anointed me king over them."

War Between the Houses of David and Saul   [8] Meanwhile, Abner son of Ner, the commander of Saul's army, had taken Ish-Bosheth son of Saul and brought him over to Mahanaim. [9] He made him king over Gilead, Ashuri[a] and Jezreel, and also over Ephraim, Benjamin and all Israel.

[10] Ish-Bosheth son of Saul was forty years old when he became king over Israel, and he reigned two years. The house of Judah, however, followed David. [11] The length of time David was king in Hebron over the house of Judah was seven years and six months.

[12] Abner son of Ner, together with the men of Ish-Bosheth son of Saul, left Mahanaim and went to Gibeon. [13] Joab son of Zeruiah and David's men went out and met them at the pool of Gibeon. One group sat down on one side of the pool and one group on the other side.

[14] Then Abner said to Joab, "Let's have some of the young men get up and fight hand to hand in front of us."

"All right, let them do it," Joab said.

[15] So they stood up and were counted off—twelve men for Benjamin and Ish-Bosheth son of Saul, and twelve for David. [16] Then each man grabbed

a9 Or Asher

his opponent by the head and thrust his dagger into his opponent's side, and they fell down together. So that place in Gibeon was called Helkath Hazzurim.*

¹⁷The battle that day was very fierce, and Abner and the men of Israel were defeated by David's men.

¹⁸The three sons of Zeruiah were there: Joab, Abishai and Asahel. Now Asahel was as fleet-footed as a wild gazelle. ¹⁹He chased Abner, turning neither to the right nor to the left as he pursued him. ²⁰Abner looked behind him and asked, "Is that you, Asahel?"

"It is," he answered.

²¹Then Abner said to him, "Turn aside to the right or to the left; take on one of the young men and strip him of his weapons." But Asahel would not stop chasing him.

²²Again Abner warned Asahel, "Stop chasing me! Why should I strike you down? How could I look your brother Joab in the face?"

²³But Asahel refused to give up the pursuit; so Abner thrust the butt of his spear into Asahel's stomach, and the spear came out through his back. He fell there and died on the spot. And every man stopped when he came to the place where Asahel had fallen and died.

²⁴But Joab and Abishai pursued Abner, and as the sun was setting, they came to the hill of Ammah, near Giah on the way to the wasteland of Gibeon. ²⁵Then the men of Benjamin rallied behind Abner. They formed themselves into a group and took their stand on top of a hill.

²⁶Abner called out to Joab, "Must the sword devour forever? Don't you realize that this will end in bitterness? How long before you order your men to stop pursuing their brothers?"

²⁷Joab answered, "As surely as God lives, if you had not spoken, the men would have continued the pursuit of their brothers until morning.*"

²⁸So Joab blew the trumpet, and all the men came to a halt; they no longer pursued Israel, nor did they fight anymore.

²⁹All that night Abner and his men marched through the Arabah. They crossed the Jordan, continued through the whole Bithron* and came to Mahanaim.

³⁰Then Joab returned from pursuing Abner and assembled all his men. Besides Asahel, nineteen of David's men were found missing. ³¹But David's men had killed three hundred and sixty Benjamites who were with Abner. ³²They took Asahel and buried him in his father's tomb at Bethlehem. Then Joab and his men marched all night and arrived at Hebron by daybreak.

The war between the house of Saul and the house of David lasted a long time. David grew stronger and stronger, while the house of Saul grew weaker and weaker.

²Sons were born to David in Hebron:

His firstborn was Amnon the son of Ahinoam of Jezreel;

³his second, Kileab the son of Abigail the widow of Nabal of Carmel;

the third, Absalom the son of Maacah daughter of Talmai king of Geshur;

⁴the fourth, Adonijah the son of Haggith;

the fifth, Shephatiah the son of Abital;

⁵and the sixth, Ithream the son of David's wife Eglah.

These were born to David in Hebron.

---

*16 Helkath Hazzurim means field of daggers or field of hostilities.   *27 Or spoken this morning, the men would not have taken up the pursuit of their brothers; or spoken, the men would have given up the pursuit of their brothers by morning   *29 Or morning; or ravine; the meaning of the Hebrew for this word is uncertain.

Abner Goes Over to David ⁶During the war between the house of Saul and the house of David, Abner had been strengthening his own position in the house of Saul. ⁷Now Saul had had a concubine named Rizpah daughter of Aiah. And Ish-Bosheth said to Abner, "Why did you sleep with my father's concubine?"

⁸Abner was very angry because of what Ish-Bosheth said and he answered, "Am I a dog's head—on Judah's side? This very day I am loyal to the house of your father Saul and to his family and friends. I haven't handed you over to David. Yet now you accuse me of an offense involving this woman! ⁹May God deal with Abner, be it ever so severely, if I do not do for David what the LORD promised him on oath ¹⁰and transfer the kingdom from the house of Saul and establish David's throne over Israel and Judah from Dan to Beersheba." ¹¹Ish-Bosheth did not dare to say another word to Abner, because he was afraid of him.

¹²Then Abner sent messengers on his behalf to say to David, "Whose land is it? Make an agreement with me, and I will help you bring all Israel over to you."

¹³"Good," said David. "I will make an agreement with you. But I demand one thing of you: Do not come into my presence unless you bring Michal daughter of Saul when you come to see me." ¹⁴Then David sent messengers to Ish-Bosheth son of Saul, demanding, "Give me my wife Michal, whom I betrothed to myself for the price of a hundred Philistine foreskins."

¹⁵So Ish-Bosheth gave orders and had her taken away from her husband Paltiel son of Laish. ¹⁶Her husband, however, went with her, weeping behind her all the way to Bahurim. Then Abner said to him, "Go back home!" So he went back.

¹⁷Abner conferred with the elders of Israel and said, "For some time you have wanted to make David your king. ¹⁸Now do it! For the LORD promised David, 'By my servant David I will rescue my people Israel from the hand of the Philistines and from the hand of all their enemies.' "

¹⁹Abner also spoke to the Benjamites in person. Then he went to Hebron to tell David everything that Israel and the whole house of Benjamin wanted to do. ²⁰When Abner, who had twenty men with him, came to David at Hebron, David prepared a feast for him and his men. ²¹Then Abner said to David, "Let me go at once and assemble all Israel for my lord the king, so that they may make a compact with you, and that you may rule over all that your heart desires." So David sent Abner away, and he went in peace.

Joab Murders Abner ²²Just then David's men and Joab returned from a raid and brought with them a great deal of plunder. But Abner was no longer with David in Hebron, because David had sent him away, and he had gone in peace. ²³When Joab and all the soldiers with him arrived, he was told that Abner son of Ner had come to the king and that the king had sent him away and that he had gone in peace.

²⁴So Joab went to the king and said, "What have you done? Look, Abner came to you. Why did you let him go? Now he is gone! ²⁵You know Abner son of Ner; he came to deceive you and observe your movements and find out everything you are doing."

²⁶Joab then left David and sent messengers after Abner, and they brought him back from the well of Sirah. But David did not know it. ²⁷Now when Abner returned to Hebron, Joab took him aside into the gateway, as though to speak with him privately. And there, to avenge the blood of his brother Asahel, Joab stabbed him in the stomach, and he died.

²⁸Later, when David heard about this, he said, "I and my kingdom are forever innocent before the LORD concerning the blood of Abner son of Ner. ²⁹May his blood fall upon the head of Joab and upon all his father's house!

May Joab's house never be without someone who has a running sore or lep-rosy*^a* or who leans on a crutch or who falls by the sword or who lacks food."

³⁰(Joab and his brother Abishai murdered Abner because he had killed their brother Asahel in the battle at Gibeon.)

³¹Then David said to Joab and all the people with him, "Tear your clothes and put on sackcloth and walk in mourning in front of Abner." King David himself walked behind the bier. ³²They buried Abner in Hebron, and the king wept aloud at Abner's tomb. All the people wept also.

³³The king sang this lament for Abner:

> "Should Abner have died as the lawless die?
> ³⁴   Your hands were not bound,
>   your feet were not fettered.
>   You fell as one falls before wicked men."

And all the people wept over him again.

³⁵Then they all came and urged David to eat something while it was still day; but David took an oath, saying, "May God deal with me, be it ever so se-verely, if I taste bread or anything else before the sun sets!"

³⁶All the people took note and were pleased; indeed, everything the king did pleased them. ³⁷So on that day all the people and all Israel knew that the king had no part in the murder of Abner son of Ner.

³⁸Then the king said to his men, "Do you not realize that a prince and a great man has fallen in Israel this day? ³⁹And today, though I am the anoint-ed king, I am weak, and these sons of Zeruiah are too strong for me. May the LORD repay the evildoer according to his evil deeds!"

Ish-Bosheth Murdered   When Ish-Bosheth son of Saul heard that Ab-ner had died in Hebron, he lost courage, and all Israel became alarmed. ²Now Saul's son had two men who were leaders of raiding bands. One was named Baanah and the other Recab; they were sons of Rimmon the Beeroth-ite from the tribe of Benjamin—Beeroth is considered part of Benjamin, ³be-cause the people of Beeroth fled to Gittaim and have lived there as aliens to this day.

⁴(Jonathan son of Saul had a son who was lame in both feet. He was five years old when the news about Saul and Jonathan came from Jezreel. His nurse picked him up and fled, but as she hurried to leave, he fell and became crippled. His name was Mephibosheth.)

⁵Now Recab and Baanah, the sons of Rimmon the Beerothite, set out for the house of Ish-Bosheth, and they arrived there in the heat of the day while he was taking his noonday rest. ⁶They went into the inner part of the house as if to get some wheat, and they stabbed him in the stomach. Then Recab and his brother Baanah slipped away.

⁷They had gone into the house while he was lying on the bed in his bed-room. After they stabbed and killed him, they cut off his head. Taking it with them, they traveled all night by way of the Arabah. ⁸They brought the head of Ish-Bosheth to David at Hebron and said to the king, "Here is the head of Ish-Bosheth son of Saul, your enemy, who tried to take your life. This day the LORD has avenged my lord the king against Saul and his offspring."

⁹David answered Recab and his brother Baanah, the sons of Rimmon the Beerothite, "As surely as the LORD lives, who has delivered me out of all trou-ble, ¹⁰when a man told me, 'Saul is dead,' and thought he was bringing good news, I seized him and put him to death in Ziklag. That was the reward I gave him for his news! ¹¹How much more—when wicked men have killed an inno-cent man in his own house and on his own bed—should I not now demand his blood from your hand and rid the earth of you!"

---

^a29 The Hebrew word was used for various diseases affecting the skin—not necessarily leprosy.

¹²So David gave an order to his men, and they killed them. They cut off their hands and feet and hung the bodies by the pool in Hebron. But they took the head of Ish-Bosheth and buried it in Abner's tomb at Hebron.

David Becomes King Over Israel

All the tribes of Israel came to David at Hebron and said, "We are your own flesh and blood. ²In the past, while Saul was king over us, you were the one who led Israel on their military campaigns. And the Lord said to you, 'You will shepherd my people Israel, and you will become their ruler.' "

³When all the elders of Israel had come to King David at Hebron, the king made a compact with them at Hebron before the Lord, and they anointed David king over Israel.

⁴David was thirty years old when he became king, and he reigned forty years. ⁵In Hebron he reigned over Judah seven years and six months, and in Jerusalem he reigned over all Israel and Judah thirty-three years.

David Conquers Jerusalem

⁶The king and his men marched to Jerusalem to attack the Jebusites, who lived there. The Jebusites said to David, "You will not get in here; even the blind and the lame can ward you off." They thought, "David cannot get in here." ⁷Nevertheless, David captured the fortress of Zion, the City of David.

⁸On that day, David said, "Anyone who conquers the Jebusites will have to use the water shaft*a* to reach those 'lame and blind' who are David's enemies.*b*" That is why they say, "The 'blind and lame' will not enter the palace."

⁹David then took up residence in the fortress and called it the City of David. He built up the area around it, from the supporting terraces*c* inward. ¹⁰And he became more and more powerful, because the Lord God Almighty was with him.

¹¹Now Hiram king of Tyre sent messengers to David, along with cedar logs and carpenters and stonemasons, and they built a palace for David. ¹²And David knew that the Lord had established him as king over Israel and had exalted his kingdom for the sake of his people Israel.

¹³After he left Hebron, David took more concubines and wives in Jerusalem, and more sons and daughters were born to him. ¹⁴These are the names of the children born to him there: Shammua, Shobab, Nathan, Solomon, ¹⁵Ibhar, Elishua, Nepheg, Japhia, ¹⁶Elishama, Eliada and Eliphelet.

David Defeats the Philistines

¹⁷When the Philistines heard that David had been anointed king over Israel, they went up in full force to search for him, but David heard about it and went down to the stronghold. ¹⁸Now the Philistines had come and spread out in the Valley of Rephaim; ¹⁹so David inquired of the Lord, "Shall I go and attack the Philistines? Will you hand them over to me?"

The Lord answered him, "Go, for I will surely hand the Philistines over to you."

²⁰So David went to Baal Perazim, and there he defeated them. He said, "As waters break out, the Lord has broken out against my enemies before me." So that place was called Baal Perazim.*d* ²¹The Philistines abandoned their idols there, and David and his men carried them off.

²²Once more the Philistines came up and spread out in the Valley of Rephaim; ²³so David inquired of the Lord, and he answered, "Do not go straight

---

2 SAMUEL 5

QUIZZER

Q: How many years did David reign over the tribe of Judah?

BONUS: How many years did he reign over the rest of the tribes of Israel?

Answers on page 371

---

*a*8 Or *use scaling hooks*   *b*8 Or *are hated by David*   *c*9 Or *the Millo*   *d*20 Baal Perazim means *the lord who breaks out.*

up, but circle around behind them and attack them in front of the balsam trees. ²⁴As soon as you hear the sound of marching in the tops of the balsam trees, move quickly, because that will mean the LORD has gone out in front of you to strike the Philistine army." ²⁵So David did as the LORD commanded him, and he struck down the Philistines all the way from Gibeon[a] to Gezer.

6 *The Ark Brought to Jerusalem*   David again brought together out of Israel chosen men, thirty thousand in all. ²He and all his men set out from Baalah of Judah[b] to bring up from there the ark of God, which is called by the Name,[c] the name of the LORD Almighty, who is enthroned between the cherubim that are on the ark. ³They set the ark of God on a new cart and brought it from the house of Abinadab, which was on the hill. Uzzah and Ahio, sons of Abinadab, were guiding the new cart ⁴with the ark of God on it,[d] and Ahio was walking in front of it. ⁵David and the whole house of Israel were celebrating with all their might before the LORD, with songs[e] and with harps, lyres, tambourines, sistrums and cymbals.

⁶When they came to the threshing floor of Nacon, Uzzah reached out and took hold of the ark of God, because the oxen stumbled. ⁷The LORD's anger burned against Uzzah because of his irreverent act; therefore God struck him down and he died there beside the ark of God.

⁸Then David was angry because the LORD's wrath had broken out against Uzzah, and to this day that place is called Perez Uzzah.[f]

⁹David was afraid of the LORD that day and said, "How can the ark of the LORD ever come to me?" ¹⁰He was not willing to take the ark of the LORD to be with him in the City of David. Instead, he took it aside to the house of Obed-Edom the Gittite. ¹¹The ark of the LORD remained in the house of Obed-Edom the Gittite for three months, and the LORD blessed him and his entire household.

¹²Now King David was told, "The LORD has blessed the household of Obed-Edom and everything he has, because of the ark of God." So David went down and brought up the ark of God from the house of Obed-Edom to the City of David with rejoicing. ¹³When those who were carrying the ark of the LORD had taken six steps, he sacrificed a bull and a fattened calf. ¹⁴David, wearing a linen ephod, danced before the LORD with all his might, ¹⁵while he and the entire house of Israel brought up the ark of the LORD with shouts and the sound of trumpets.

¹⁶As the ark of the LORD was entering the City of David, Michal daughter of Saul watched from a window. And when she saw King David leaping and dancing before the LORD, she despised him in her heart.

¹⁷They brought the ark of the LORD and set it in its place inside the tent that David had pitched for it, and David sacrificed burnt offerings and fellowship offerings[g] before the LORD. ¹⁸After he had finished sacrificing the burnt offerings and fellowship offerings, he blessed the people in the name of the LORD Almighty. ¹⁹Then he gave a loaf of bread, a cake of dates and a cake of raisins to each person in the whole crowd of Israelites, both men and women. And all the people went to their homes.

²⁰When David returned home to bless his household, Michal daughter of Saul came out to meet him and said, "How the king of Israel has distinguished himself today, disrobing in the sight of the slave girls of his servants as any vulgar fellow would!"

Answers
to Quizzer on page 370

A: Forty years (2 Samuel 5:4).

BONUS: Thirty-three years (2 Samuel 5:5). It took seven years before the other eleven tribes accepted him as king.

---

a25 Septuagint (see also 1 Chron. 14:16); Hebrew *Geba*   *b2* That is, Kiriath Jearim; Hebrew *Baale Judah*, a variant of *Baalah of Judah*   *c2* Hebrew; Septuagint and Vulgate do not have *the Name*.   *d3,4* Dead Sea Scrolls and some Septuagint manuscripts; Masoretic Text *cart* *and they brought it with the ark of God from the house of Abinadab, which was on the hill*   *e5* See Dead Sea Scrolls, Septuagint and 1 Chronicles 13:8; Masoretic Text *celebrating before the LORD with all kinds of instruments made of pine.*   *f8 Perez Uzzah* means *outbreak against Uzzah.*   *g17* Traditionally *peace offerings*; also in verse 18

²¹David said to Michal, "It was before the Lord, who chose me rather than your father or anyone from his house when he appointed me ruler over the Lord's people Israel—I will celebrate before the Lord. ²²I will become even more undignified than this, and I will be humiliated in my own eyes. But by these slave girls you spoke of, I will be held in honor."

²³And Michal daughter of Saul had no children to the day of her death.

God's Promise to David   After the king was settled in his palace and the Lord had given him rest from all his enemies around him, ²he said to Nathan the prophet, "Here I am, living in a palace of cedar, while the ark of God remains in a tent."

³Nathan replied to the king, "Whatever you have in mind, go ahead and do it, for the Lord is with you."

⁴That night the word of the Lord came to Nathan, saying:

⁵"Go and tell my servant David, 'This is what the Lord says: Are you the one to build me a house to dwell in? ⁶I have not dwelt in a house from the day I brought the Israelites up out of Egypt to this day. I have been moving from place to place with a tent as my dwelling. ⁷Wherever I have moved with all the Israelites, did I ever say to any of their rulers whom I commanded to shepherd my people Israel, "Why have you not built me a house of cedar?" '

⁸"Now then, tell my servant David, 'This is what the Lord Almighty says: I took you from the pasture and from following the flock to be ruler over my people Israel. ⁹I have been with you wherever you have gone, and I have cut off all your enemies from before you. Now I will make your name great, like the names of the greatest men of the earth. ¹⁰And I will provide a place for my people Israel and will plant them so that they can have a home of their own and no longer be disturbed. Wicked people will not oppress them anymore, as they did at the beginning ¹¹and have done ever since the time I appointed leaders*ª* over my people Israel. I will also give you rest from all your enemies.

" 'The Lord declares to you that the Lord himself will establish a house for you: ¹²When your days are over and you rest with your fathers, I will raise up your offspring to succeed you, who will come from your own body, and I will establish his kingdom. ¹³He is the one who will build a

---

ª11 Traditionally *judges*

The Bible Says

David's Son Will Rule!

Sometimes words in the Bible are hard to understand. Take God's promise to David, "Your *house* and your kingdom will endure forever before me; your *throne* will be established *forever*" (2 Samuel 7:16, italics added). David knew what God was saying, but do you?

❋ In the Bible, *house* can mean "family" as well as a building.
❋ In the Bible, *throne* often stands for a king's rule.
❋ In the Bible, *forever* means forever.

This verse promises that someone born into David's family will be a king who will rule forever. Does anyone qualify? Yes! Jesus was a descendant of David (Matthew 1:1). Raised from the dead, he is "KING OF KINGS AND LORD OF LORDS"(Revelation 19:16). "And he will reign for ever and ever" (Revelation 11:15).

house for my Name, and I will establish the throne of his kingdom forever. [14]I will be his father, and he will be my son. When he does wrong, I will punish him with the rod of men, with floggings inflicted by men. [15]But my love will never be taken away from him, as I took it away from Saul, whom I removed from before you. [16]Your house and your kingdom will endure forever before me[a]; your throne will be established forever.' "

[17]Nathan reported to David all the words of this entire revelation.

David's Prayer [18]Then King David went in and sat before the LORD, and he said:

"Who am I, O Sovereign LORD, and what is my family, that you have brought me this far? [19]And as if this were not enough in your sight, O Sovereign LORD, you have also spoken about the future of the house of your servant. Is this your usual way of dealing with man, O Sovereign LORD?

[20]"What more can David say to you? For you know your servant, O Sovereign LORD. [21]For the sake of your word and according to your will, you have done this great thing and made it known to your servant.

[22]"How great you are, O Sovereign LORD! There is no one like you, and there is no God but you, as we have heard with our own ears. [23]And who is like your people Israel—the one nation on earth that God went out to redeem as a people for himself, and to make a name for himself, and to perform great and awesome wonders by driving out nations and their gods from before your people, whom you redeemed from Egypt?[b] [24]You have established your people Israel as your very own forever, and you, O LORD, have become their God.

[25]"And now, LORD God, keep forever the promise you have made concerning your servant and his house. Do as you promised, [26]so that your name will be great forever. Then men will say, 'The LORD Almighty is God over Israel!' And the house of your servant David will be established before you.

[27]"O LORD Almighty, God of Israel, you have revealed this to your servant, saying, 'I will build a house for you.' So your servant has found courage to offer you this prayer. [28]O Sovereign LORD, you are God! Your words are trustworthy, and you have promised these good things to your servant. [29]Now be pleased to bless the house of your servant, that it may continue forever in your sight; for you, O Sovereign LORD, have spoken, and with your blessing the house of your servant will be blessed forever."

David's Victories In the course of time, David defeated the Philistines and subdued them, and he took Metheg Ammah from the control of the Philistines.

[2]David also defeated the Moabites. He

---

[a]16 Some Hebrew manuscripts and Septuagint; most Hebrew manuscripts *you* [b]23 See Septuagint and 1 Chron. 17:21; Hebrew *wonders for your land and before your people, whom you redeemed from Egypt, from the nations and their gods*

2 SAMUEL 7:25-26

Do you ever wonder if what you're asking for in prayer is OK with God? You can gain confidence in prayer by "claiming God's promises." This is what David did in 2 Samuel 7:25-26. God through the prophet Nathan gave David a wonderful promise. So David thanked God and then claimed the promise: he asked God to "keep forever the promise you have made." In keeping his promises God shows the universe that he is faithful to his word, that he can be trusted. As you read your Bible, underline the promises you find. Then when you pray, claim God's promises and become more and more confident about prayer.

Direct Line

made them lie down on the ground and measured them off with a length of cord. Every two lengths of them were put to death, and the third length was allowed to live. So the Moabites became subject to David and brought tribute.

³Moreover, David fought Hadadezer son of Rehob, king of Zobah, when he went to restore his control along the Euphrates River. ⁴David captured a thousand of his chariots, seven thousand charioteers*ᵃ* and twenty thousand foot soldiers. He hamstrung all but a hundred of the chariot horses.

⁵When the Arameans of Damascus came to help Hadadezer king of Zobah, David struck down twenty-two thousand of them. ⁶He put garrisons in the Aramean kingdom of Damascus, and the Arameans became subject to him and brought tribute. The LORD gave David victory wherever he went.

⁷David took the gold shields that belonged to the officers of Hadadezer and brought them to Jerusalem. ⁸From Tebah*ᵇ* and Berothai, towns that belonged to Hadadezer, King David took a great quantity of bronze.

⁹When Tou*ᶜ* king of Hamath heard that David had defeated the entire army of Hadadezer, ¹⁰he sent his son Joram*ᵈ* to King David to greet him and congratulate him on his victory in battle over Hadadezer, who had been at war with Tou. Joram brought with him articles of silver and gold and bronze.

¹¹King David dedicated these articles to the LORD, as he had done with the silver and gold from all the nations he had subdued: ¹²Edom*ᵉ* and Moab, the Ammonites and the Philistines, and Amalek. He also dedicated the plunder taken from Hadadezer son of Rehob, king of Zobah.

¹³And David became famous after he returned from striking down eighteen thousand Edomites*ᶠ* in the Valley of Salt.

¹⁴He put garrisons throughout Edom, and all the Edomites became subject to David. The LORD gave David victory wherever he went.

David's Officials   ¹⁵David reigned over all Israel, doing what was just and right for all his people. ¹⁶Joab son of Zeruiah was over the army; Jehoshaphat son of Ahilud was recorder; ¹⁷Zadok son of Ahitub and Ahimelech son of Abiathar were priests; Seraiah was secretary; ¹⁸Benaiah son of Jehoiada was over the Kerethites and Pelethites; and David's sons were royal advisers.*ᵍ*

9 *David and Mephibosheth*   David asked, "Is there anyone still left of the house of Saul to whom I can show kindness for Jonathan's sake?"

²Now there was a servant of Saul's household named Ziba. They called him to appear before David, and the king said to him, "Are you Ziba?"

"Your servant," he replied.

³The king asked, "Is there no one still left of the house of Saul to whom I can show God's kindness?"

Ziba answered the king, "There is still a son of Jonathan; he is crippled in both feet."

⁴"Where is he?" the king asked.

Ziba answered, "He is at the house of Makir son of Ammiel in Lo Debar."

⁵So King David had him brought from Lo Debar, from the house of Makir son of Ammiel.

⁶When Mephibosheth son of Jonathan, the son of Saul, came to David, he bowed down to pay him honor.

David said, "Mephibosheth!"

"Your servant," he replied.

ᵃ4 Septuagint (see also Dead Sea Scrolls and 1 Chron. 18:4); Masoretic Text *captured seventeen hundred of his charioteers*   *ᵇ8* See some Septuagint manuscripts (see also 1 Chron. 18:8); Hebrew *Betah.*   *ᶜ9* Hebrew *Toi,* a variant of *Tou;* also in verse 10   *ᵈ10* A variant of *Hadoram*   *ᵉ12* Some Hebrew manuscripts, Septuagint and Syriac (see also 1 Chron. 18:11); most Hebrew manuscripts *Aram*   *ᶠ13* A few Hebrew manuscripts, Septuagint and Syriac (see also 1 Chron. 18:12); most Hebrew manuscripts *Aram* (that is, Arameans)   *ᵍ18* Or *were priests*

[7]"Don't be afraid," David said to him, "for I will surely show you kindness for the sake of your father Jonathan. I will restore to you all the land that belonged to your grandfather Saul, and you will always eat at my table."

[8]Mephibosheth bowed down and said, "What is your servant, that you should notice a dead dog like me?"

[9]Then the king summoned Ziba, Saul's servant, and said to him, "I have given your master's grandson everything that belonged to Saul and his family. [10]You and your sons and your servants are to farm the land for him and bring in the crops, so that your master's grandson may be provided for. And Mephibosheth, grandson of your master, will always eat at my table." (Now Ziba had fifteen sons and twenty servants.)

[11]Then Ziba said to the king, "Your servant will do whatever my lord the king commands his servant to do." So Mephibosheth ate at David's[a] table like one of the king's sons.

[12]Mephibosheth had a young son named Mica, and all the members of Ziba's household were servants of Mephibosheth. [13]And Mephibosheth lived in Jerusalem, because he always ate at the king's table, and he was crippled in both feet.

10 *David Defeats the Ammonites* In the course of time, the king of the Ammonites died, and his son Hanun succeeded him as king. [2]David thought, "I will show kindness to Hanun son of Nahash, just as his father showed kindness to me." So David sent a delegation to express his sympathy to Hanun concerning his father.

When David's men came to the land of the Ammonites, [3]the Ammonite nobles said to Hanun their lord, "Do you think David is honoring your father by sending men to you to express sympathy? Hasn't David sent them to you to explore the city and spy it out and overthrow it?" [4]So Hanun seized David's men, shaved off half of each man's beard, cut off their garments in the middle at the buttocks, and sent them away.

[5]When David was told about this, he sent messengers to meet the men, for they were greatly humiliated. The king said, "Stay at Jericho till your beards have grown, and then come back."

[6]When the Ammonites realized that they had become a stench in David's nostrils, they hired twenty thousand Aramean foot soldiers from Beth Rehob and Zobah, as well as the king of Maacah with a thousand men, and also twelve thousand men from Tob.

[7]On hearing this, David sent Joab out with the entire army of fighting men. [8]The Ammonites came out and drew up in battle formation at the entrance to their city gate, while the Arameans of Zobah and Rehob and the men of Tob and Maacah were by themselves in the open country.

[9]Joab saw that there were battle lines in front of him and behind him; so he selected some of the best troops in Israel

2 SAMUEL 9:1–11

Sure, Christians should be "different." But how? By carrying a Bible with your books? By listening to Christian rock CDs? By writing Bible verses on your homework? When David became king over Israel, he searched for descendants of Saul in order to show kindness to them (2 Samuel 9:1). Rulers in that day usually searched for members of the previous king's family, not to show kindness but to kill them! David was different, in a godly way. How can you be different? You can be pleasant to classmates who don't like you. You can be polite to unpopular teachers. Keep on being "different," and you'll be surprised how many of your friends will be attracted to you and to Christ.

Direct Line

[a]11 Septuagint; Hebrew *my*

and deployed them against the Arameans. ¹⁰He put the rest of the men under the command of Abishai his brother and deployed them against the Ammonites. ¹¹Joab said, "If the Arameans are too strong for me, then you are to come to my rescue; but if the Ammonites are too strong for you, then I will come to rescue you. ¹²Be strong and let us fight bravely for our people and the cities of our God. The Lord will do what is good in his sight."

¹³Then Joab and the troops with him advanced to fight the Arameans, and they fled before him. ¹⁴When the Ammonites saw that the Arameans were fleeing, they fled before Abishai and went inside the city. So Joab returned from fighting the Ammonites and came to Jerusalem.

¹⁵After the Arameans saw that they had been routed by Israel, they regrouped. ¹⁶Hadadezer had Arameans brought from beyond the River[a]; they went to Helam, with Shobach the commander of Hadadezer's army leading them.

¹⁷When David was told of this, he gathered all Israel, crossed the Jordan and went to Helam. The Arameans formed their battle lines to meet David and fought against him. ¹⁸But they fled before Israel, and David killed seven hundred of their charioteers and forty thousand of their foot soldiers.[b] He also struck down Shobach the commander of their army, and he died there. ¹⁹When all the kings who were vassals of Hadadezer saw that they had been defeated by Israel, they made peace with the Israelites and became subject to them.

So the Arameans were afraid to help the Ammonites anymore.

11 *David and Bathsheba*   In the spring, at the time when kings go off to war, David sent Joab out with the king's men and the whole Israelite army. They destroyed the Ammonites and besieged Rabbah. But David remained in Jerusalem.

²One evening David got up from his bed and walked around on the roof of the palace. From the roof he saw a woman bathing. The woman was very beautiful, ³and David sent someone to find out about her. The man said, "Isn't this Bathsheba, the daughter of Eliam and the wife of Uriah the Hittite?" ⁴Then David sent messengers to get her. She came to him, and he slept with her. (She had purified herself from her uncleanness.) Then[c] she went back home. ⁵The woman conceived and sent word to David, saying, "I am pregnant."

⁶So David sent this word to Joab: "Send me Uriah the Hittite." And Joab sent him to David. ⁷When Uriah came to him, David asked him how Joab was, how the soldiers were and how the war was going. ⁸Then David said to Uriah, "Go down to your house and wash your feet." So Uriah left the palace, and a gift from the king was sent after him. ⁹But Uriah slept at the entrance to the palace with all his master's servants and did not go down to his house.

¹⁰When David was told, "Uriah did not go home," he asked him, "Haven't you just come from a distance? Why didn't you go home?"

¹¹Uriah said to David, "The ark and Israel and Judah are staying in tents, and my master Joab and my lord's men are camped in the open fields. How could I go to my house to eat and drink and lie with my wife? As surely as you live, I will not do such a thing!"

¹²Then David said to him, "Stay here one more day, and tomorrow I will send you back." So Uriah remained in Jerusalem that day and the next. ¹³At David's invitation, he ate and drank with him, and David made him drunk. But in the evening Uriah went out to sleep on his mat among his master's servants; he did not go home.

¹⁴In the morning David wrote a letter to Joab and sent it with Uriah. ¹⁵In it

---

[a]16 That is, the Euphrates   [b]18 Some Septuagint manuscripts (see also 1 Chron. 19:18); Hebrew *horsemen*   [c]4 Or *with her. When she purified herself from her uncleanness,*

he wrote, "Put Uriah in the front line where the fighting is fiercest. Then withdraw from him so he will be struck down and die."

¹⁶So while Joab had the city under siege, he put Uriah at a place where he knew the strongest defenders were. ¹⁷When the men of the city came out and fought against Joab, some of the men in David's army fell; moreover, Uriah the Hittite died.

¹⁸Joab sent David a full account of the battle. ¹⁹He instructed the messenger: "When you have finished giving the king this account of the battle, ²⁰the king's anger may flare up, and he may ask you, 'Why did you get so close to the city to fight? Didn't you know they would shoot arrows from the wall? ²¹Who killed Abimelech son of Jerub-Besheth*? Didn't a woman throw an upper millstone on him from the wall, so that he died in Thebez? Why did you get so close to the wall?' If he asks you this, then say to him, 'Also, your servant Uriah the Hittite is dead.' "

²²The messenger set out, and when he arrived he told David everything Joab had sent him to say. ²³The messenger said to David, "The men overpowered us and came out against us in the open, but we drove them back to the entrance to the city gate. ²⁴Then the archers shot arrows at your servants from the wall, and some of the king's men died. Moreover, your servant Uriah the Hittite is dead."

²⁵David told the messenger, "Say this to Joab: 'Don't let this upset you; the sword devours one as well as another. Press the attack against the city and destroy it.' Say this to encourage Joab."

²⁶When Uriah's wife heard that her husband was dead, she mourned for him. ²⁷After the time of mourning was over, David had her brought to his house, and she became his wife and bore him a son. But the thing David had done displeased the LORD.

Nathan Rebukes David The LORD sent Nathan to David. When he came to him, he said, "There were two men in a certain town, one rich and the other poor. ²The rich man had a very large number of sheep and cattle, ³but the poor man had nothing except one little ewe lamb he had bought. He raised it, and it grew up with him and his children. It shared his food, drank from his cup and even slept in his arms. It was like a daughter to him.

⁴"Now a traveler came to the rich man, but the rich man refrained from taking one of his own sheep or cattle to prepare a meal for the traveler who had come to him. Instead, he took the ewe lamb that belonged to the poor man and prepared it for the one who had come to him."

⁵David burned with anger against the man and said to Nathan, "As surely as the LORD lives, the man who did this deserves to die! ⁶He must pay for that lamb four times over, because he did such a thing and had no pity."

⁷Then Nathan said to David, "You are the man! This is what the LORD, the God of Israel, says: 'I anointed you king over Israel, and I delivered you from the hand of Saul. ⁸I gave your master's house to you, and your master's wives into your arms. I gave you the house of Israel and Judah. And if all this had been too little, I would have given you even more. ⁹Why did you despise the word of the LORD by doing what is evil in his eyes? You struck down Uriah the Hittite with the sword and took his wife to be your own. You killed him with the sword of the Ammonites. ¹⁰Now, therefore, the sword will never depart from your house, because you despised me and took the wife of Uriah the Hittite to be your own.'

¹¹"This is what the LORD says: 'Out of your own household I am going to bring calamity upon you. Before your very eyes I will take your wives and

---

*21 Also known as *Jerub-Baal* (that is, Gideon)

give them to one who is close to you, and he will lie with your wives in broad daylight. ¹²You did it in secret, but I will do this thing in broad daylight before all Israel.' "

¹³Then David said to Nathan, "I have sinned against the LORD."

Nathan replied, "The LORD has taken away your sin. You are not going to die. ¹⁴But because by doing this you have made the enemies of the LORD show utter contempt,ᵃ the son born to you will die."

¹⁵After Nathan had gone home, the LORD struck the child that Uriah's wife had borne to David, and he became ill. ¹⁶David pleaded with God for the child. He fasted and went into his house and spent the nights lying on the ground. ¹⁷The elders of his household stood beside him to get him up from the ground, but he refused, and he would not eat any food with them.

¹⁸On the seventh day the child died. David's servants were afraid to tell him that the child was dead, for they thought, "While the child was still living, we spoke to David but he would not listen to us. How can we tell him the child is dead? He may do something desperate."

¹⁹David noticed that his servants were whispering among themselves and he realized the child was dead. "Is the child dead?" he asked.

"Yes," they replied, "he is dead."

²⁰Then David got up from the ground. After he had washed, put on lotions and changed his clothes, he went into the house of the LORD and worshiped. Then he went to his own house, and at his request they served him food, and he ate.

²¹His servants asked him, "Why are you acting this way? While the child was alive, you fasted and wept, but now that the child is dead, you get up and eat!"

²²He answered, "While the child was still alive, I fasted and wept. I thought, 'Who knows? The LORD may be gracious to me and let the child live.' ²³But now that he is dead, why should I fast? Can I bring him back again? I will go to him, but he will not return to me."

²⁴Then David comforted his wife Bathsheba, and he went to her and lay with her. She gave birth to a son, and they named him Solomon. The LORD loved him; ²⁵and because the LORD loved him, he sent word through Nathan the prophet to name him Jedidiah.ᵇ

²⁶Meanwhile Joab fought against Rabbah of the Ammonites and captured the royal citadel. ²⁷Joab then sent messengers to David, saying, "I have fought against Rabbah and taken its water supply. ²⁸Now muster the rest of the troops and besiege the city and capture it. Otherwise I will take the city, and it will be named after me."

²⁹So David mustered the entire army and went to Rabbah, and attacked and captured it. ³⁰He took the crown from the head of their kingᶜ—its weight was a talentᵈ of gold, and it was set with precious stones—and it was placed on David's

Direct Line

2 SAMUEL 12:13

The brownies your sister baked are half gone. You're the only one home, yet you look her in the eye and say, "But I didn't eat them." Even without that brown smear on your upper lip, she knows you did it. What's worse, God knows. And you know. When David tried to hide his sin with Bathsheba, God didn't let him rest. Finally, when confronted by the prophet Nathan, David confessed his sin. Then he wrote Psalm 51 to describe the sense of release that came when he admitted his sin and let God cleanse him. Check out this psalm, and you may find a better way to react than to claim, "But I didn't do it," when you really did.

ᵃ14 Masoretic Text; an ancient Hebrew scribal tradition *this you have shown utter contempt for the LORD*   ᵇ25 *Jedidiah* means *loved by the LORD.*   ᶜ30 Or *of Milcom* (that is, Molech)   ᵈ30 That is, about 75 pounds (about 34 kilograms)

head. He took a great quantity of plunder from the city ³¹and brought out the people who were there, consigning them to labor with saws and with iron picks and axes, and he made them work at brickmaking.*a* He did this to all the Ammonite towns. Then David and his entire army returned to Jerusalem.

13 *Amnon and Tamar* In the course of time, Amnon son of David fell in love with Tamar, the beautiful sister of Absalom son of David. ²Amnon became frustrated to the point of illness on account of his sister Tamar, for she was a virgin, and it seemed impossible for him to do anything to her.

³Now Amnon had a friend named Jonadab son of Shimeah, David's brother. Jonadab was a very shrewd man. ⁴He asked Amnon, "Why do you, the king's son, look so haggard morning after morning? Won't you tell me?"

Amnon said to him, "I'm in love with Tamar, my brother Absalom's sister."

⁵"Go to bed and pretend to be ill," Jonadab said. "When your father comes to see you, say to him, 'I would like my sister Tamar to come and give me something to eat. Let her prepare the food in my sight so I may watch her and then eat it from her hand.' "

⁶So Amnon lay down and pretended to be ill. When the king came to see him, Amnon said to him, "I would like my sister Tamar to come and make some special bread in my sight, so I may eat from her hand."

⁷David sent word to Tamar at the palace: "Go to the house of your brother Amnon and prepare some food for him." ⁸So Tamar went to the house of her brother Amnon, who was lying down. She took some dough, kneaded it, made the bread in his sight and baked it. ⁹Then she took the pan and served him the bread, but he refused to eat.

"Send everyone out of here," Amnon said. So everyone left him. ¹⁰Then Amnon said to Tamar, "Bring the food here into my bedroom so I may eat from your hand." And Tamar took the bread she had prepared and brought it to her brother Amnon in his bedroom. ¹¹But when she took it to him to eat, he grabbed her and said, "Come to bed with me, my sister."

¹²"Don't, my brother!" she said to him. "Don't force me. Such a thing should not be done in Israel! Don't do this wicked thing. ¹³What about me? Where could I get rid of my disgrace? And what about you? You would be like one of the wicked fools in Israel. Please speak to the king; he will not keep me from being married to you." ¹⁴But he refused to listen to her, and since he was stronger than she, he raped her.

¹⁵Then Amnon hated her with intense hatred. In fact, he hated her more than he had loved her. Amnon said to her, "Get up and get out!"

¹⁶"No!" she said to him. "Sending me away would be a greater wrong than what you have already done to me."

But he refused to listen to her. ¹⁷He called his personal servant and said, "Get this woman out of here and bolt the door after her." ¹⁸So his servant put her out and bolted the door after her. She was wearing a richly ornamented*b* robe, for this was the kind of garment the virgin daughters of the king wore. ¹⁹Tamar put ashes on her head and tore the ornamented*c* robe she was wearing. She put her hand on her head and went away, weeping aloud as she went.

²⁰Her brother Absalom said to her, "Has that Amnon, your brother, been with you? Be quiet now, my sister; he is your brother. Don't take this thing to heart." And Tamar lived in her brother Absalom's house, a desolate woman.

²¹When King David heard all this, he was furious. ²²Absalom never said a word to Amnon, either good or bad; he hated Amnon because he had disgraced his sister Tamar.

---

a31 The meaning of the Hebrew for this clause is uncertain. *b18* The meaning of the Hebrew for this phrase is uncertain. *c19* The meaning of the Hebrew for this word is uncertain.

Dear Sam,

My boyfriend keeps telling me if I loved him, I would let him go all the way. I don't want to lose him. What do you think?

Lori in Lexington

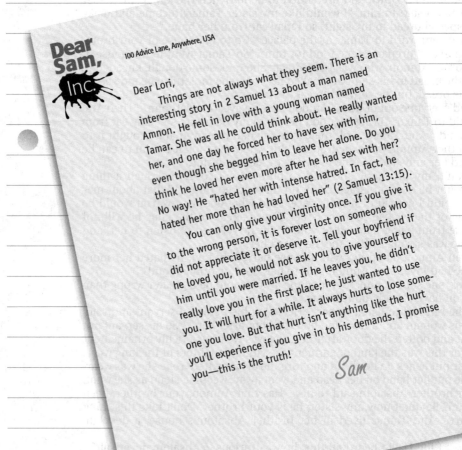

Dear Sam, Inc.

100 Advice Lane, Anywhere, USA

Dear Lori,

Things are not always what they seem. There is an interesting story in 2 Samuel 13 about a man named Amnon. He fell in love with a young woman named Tamar. She was all he could think about. He really wanted her, and one day he forced her to have sex with him, even though she begged him to leave her alone. Do you think he loved her even more after he had sex with her? No way! He "hated her with intense hatred. In fact, he hated her more than he had loved her" (2 Samuel 13:15).

You can only give your virginity once. If you give it to the wrong person, it is forever lost on someone who did not appreciate it or deserve it. Tell your boyfriend if he loved you, he would not ask you to give yourself to him until you were married. If he leaves you, he didn't really love you in the first place; he just wanted to use you. It will hurt for a while. It always hurts to lose some-one you love. But that hurt isn't anything like the hurt you'll experience if you give in to his demands. I promise you—this is the truth!

Sam

Absalom Kills Amnon ²³Two years later, when Absalom's sheepshearers were at Baal Hazor near the border of Ephraim, he invited all the king's sons to come there. ²⁴Absalom went to the king and said, "Your servant has had shearers come. Will the king and his officials please join me?"

²⁵"No, my son," the king replied. "All of us should not go; we would only be a burden to you." Although Absalom urged him, he still refused to go, but gave him his blessing.

²⁶Then Absalom said, "If not, please let my brother Amnon come with us."

The king asked him, "Why should he go with you?" ²⁷But Absalom urged him, so he sent with him Amnon and the rest of the king's sons.

²⁸Absalom ordered his men, "Listen! When Amnon is in high spirits from drinking wine and I say to you, 'Strike Amnon down,' then kill him. Don't be afraid. Have not I given you this order? Be strong and brave." ²⁹So Absalom's men did to Amnon what Absalom had ordered. Then all the king's sons got up, mounted their mules and fled.

³⁰While they were on their way, the report came to David: "Absalom has struck down all the king's sons; not one of them is left." ³¹The king stood up, tore his clothes and lay down on the ground; and all his servants stood by with their clothes torn.

³²But Jonadab son of Shimeah, David's brother, said, "My lord should not think that they killed all the princes; only Amnon is dead. This has been Absalom's expressed intention ever since the day Amnon raped his sister Tamar. ³³My lord the king should not be concerned about the report that all the king's sons are dead. Only Amnon is dead."

³⁴Meanwhile, Absalom had fled.

Now the man standing watch looked up and saw many people on the road west of him, coming down the side of the hill. The watchman went and told the king, "I see men in the direction of Horonaim, on the side of the hill."ᵃ

³⁵Jonadab said to the king, "See, the king's sons are here; it has happened just as your servant said."

³⁶As he finished speaking, the king's sons came in, wailing loudly. The king, too, and all his servants wept very bitterly.

³⁷Absalom fled and went to Talmai son of Ammihud, the king of Geshur. But King David mourned for his son every day.

³⁸After Absalom fled and went to Geshur, he stayed there three years. ³⁹And the spirit of the kingᵇ longed to go to Absalom, for he was consoled concerning Amnon's death.

14 *Absalom Returns to Jerusalem* Joab son of Zeruiah knew that the king's heart longed for Absalom. ²So Joab sent someone to Tekoa and had a wise woman brought from there. He said to her, "Pretend you are in mourning. Dress in mourning clothes, and don't use any cosmetic lotions. Act like a woman who has spent many days grieving for the dead. ³Then go to the king and speak these words to him." And Joab put the words in her mouth.

⁴When the woman from Tekoa wentᶜ to the king, she fell with her face to the ground to pay him honor, and she said, "Help me, O king!"

⁵The king asked her, "What is troubling you?"

She said, "I am indeed a widow; my husband is dead. ⁶I your servant had two sons. They got into a fight with each other in the field, and no one was there to separate them. One struck the other and killed him. ⁷Now the whole clan has risen up against your servant; they say, 'Hand over the one who struck his brother down, so that we may put him to death for the life of his

---

ᵃ*34* Septuagint; Hebrew does not have this sentence.   ᵇ*39* Dead Sea Scrolls and some Septuagint manuscripts; Masoretic Text *But the spirit of David the king*   ᶜ*4* Many Hebrew manuscripts, Septuagint, Vulgate and Syriac; most Hebrew manuscripts *spoke*

brother whom he killed; then we will get rid of the heir as well.' They would put out the only burning coal I have left, leaving my husband neither name nor descendant on the face of the earth."

⁸The king said to the woman, "Go home, and I will issue an order in your behalf."

⁹But the woman from Tekoa said to him, "My lord the king, let the blame rest on me and on my father's family, and let the king and his throne be without guilt."

¹⁰The king replied, "If anyone says anything to you, bring him to me, and he will not bother you again."

¹¹She said, "Then let the king invoke the LORD his God to prevent the avenger of blood from adding to the destruction, so that my son will not be destroyed."

"As surely as the LORD lives," he said, "not one hair of your son's head will fall to the ground."

¹²Then the woman said, "Let your servant speak a word to my lord the king."

"Speak," he replied.

¹³The woman said, "Why then have you devised a thing like this against the people of God? When the king says this, does he not convict himself, for the king has not brought back his banished son? ¹⁴Like water spilled on the ground, which cannot be recovered, so we must die. But God does not take away life; instead, he devises ways so that a banished person may not remain estranged from him.

¹⁵"And now I have come to say this to my lord the king because the people have made me afraid. Your servant thought, 'I will speak to the king; perhaps he will do what his servant asks. ¹⁶Perhaps the king will agree to deliver his servant from the hand of the man who is trying to cut off both me and my son from the inheritance God gave us.'

¹⁷"And now your servant says, 'May the word of my lord the king bring me rest, for my lord the king is like an angel of God in discerning good and evil. May the LORD your God be with you.' "

¹⁸Then the king said to the woman, "Do not keep from me the answer to what I am going to ask you."

"Let my lord the king speak," the woman said.

¹⁹The king asked, "Isn't the hand of Joab with you in all this?"

The woman answered, "As surely as you live, my lord the king, no one can turn to the right or to the left from anything my lord the king says. Yes, it was your servant Joab who instructed me to do this and who put all these words into the mouth of your servant. ²⁰Your servant Joab did this to change the present situation. My lord has wisdom like that of an angel of God—he knows everything that happens in the land."

²¹The king said to Joab, "Very well, I will do it. Go, bring back the young man Absalom."

²²Joab fell with his face to the ground to pay him honor, and he blessed the king. Joab said, "Today your servant knows

2 SAMUEL 14:23–24

Parents do make mistakes. David made a big one with his son Absalom. When Absalom killed his brother Amnon, David neither punished Absalom nor forgave him. By failing to act, David left Absalom without moral direction and was at least partly responsible when his son later rebelled. Are your parents quick to ground you when you get out of line? Or are they more likely to talk it over and give you a hug? Believe it or not, both kinds of discipline work. What counts is that Mom and Dad have well-defined moral standards and let you know by their actions that they care whether the choices you make are right or wrong.

Direct Line

that he has found favor in your eyes, my lord the king, because the king has granted his servant's request."

²³Then Joab went to Geshur and brought Absalom back to Jerusalem. ²⁴But the king said, "He must go to his own house; he must not see my face." So Absalom went to his own house and did not see the face of the king.

²⁵In all Israel there was not a man so highly praised for his handsome appearance as Absalom. From the top of his head to the sole of his foot there was no blemish in him. ²⁶Whenever he cut the hair of his head—he used to cut his hair from time to time when it became too heavy for him—he would weigh it, and its weight was two hundred shekels*a* by the royal standard.

²⁷Three sons and a daughter were born to Absalom. The daughter's name was Tamar, and she became a beautiful woman.

²⁸Absalom lived two years in Jerusalem without seeing the king's face. ²⁹Then Absalom sent for Joab in order to send him to the king, but Joab refused to come to him. So he sent a second time, but he refused to come. ³⁰Then he said to his servants, "Look, Joab's field is next to mine, and he has barley there. Go and set it on fire." So Absalom's servants set the field on fire.

³¹Then Joab did go to Absalom's house and he said to him, "Why have your servants set my field on fire?"

³²Absalom said to Joab, "Look, I sent word to you and said, 'Come here so I can send you to the king to ask, "Why have I come from Geshur? It would be better for me if I were still there!"' Now then, I want to see the king's face, and if I am guilty of anything, let him put me to death."

³³So Joab went to the king and told him this. Then the king summoned Absalom, and he came in and bowed down with his face to the ground before the king. And the king kissed Absalom.

Absalom's Conspiracy In the course of time, Absalom provided himself with a chariot and horses and with fifty men to run ahead of him. ²He would get up early and stand by the side of the road leading to the city gate. Whenever anyone came with a complaint to be placed before the king for a decision, Absalom would call out to him, "What town are you from?" He would answer, "Your servant is from one of the tribes of Israel." ³Then Absalom would say to him, "Look, your claims are valid and proper, but there is no representative of the king to hear you." ⁴And Absalom would add, "If only I were appointed judge in the land! Then everyone who has a complaint or case could come to me and I would see that he gets justice."

⁵Also, whenever anyone approached him to bow down before him, Absalom would reach out his hand, take hold of him and kiss him. ⁶Absalom behaved in this way toward all the Israelites who came to the king asking for justice, and so he stole the hearts of the men of Israel.

⁷At the end of four*b* years, Absalom said to the king, "Let me go to Hebron and fulfill a vow I made to the LORD. ⁸While your servant was living at Geshur in Aram, I made this vow: 'If the LORD takes me back to Jerusalem, I will worship the LORD in Hebron.*c* '"

⁹The king said to him, "Go in peace." So he went to Hebron.

¹⁰Then Absalom sent secret messengers throughout the tribes of Israel to say, "As soon as you hear the sound of the trumpets, then say, 'Absalom is king in Hebron.'" ¹¹Two hundred men from Jerusalem had accompanied Absalom. They had been invited as guests and went quite innocently, knowing nothing about the matter. ¹²While Absalom was offering sacrifices, he also sent for Ahithophel the Gilonite, David's counselor, to come from Giloh, his hometown. And so the conspiracy gained strength, and Absalom's following kept on increasing.

---

a26 That is, about 5 pounds (about 2.3 kilograms) *b7* Some Septuagint manuscripts, Syriac and Josephus; Hebrew *forty* *c8* Some Septuagint manuscripts; Hebrew does not have *in Hebron.*

David Flees ¹³A messenger came and told David, "The hearts of the men of Israel are with Absalom."

¹⁴Then David said to all his officials who were with him in Jerusalem, "Come! We must flee, or none of us will escape from Absalom. We must leave immediately, or he will move quickly to overtake us and bring ruin upon us and put the city to the sword."

¹⁵The king's officials answered him, "Your servants are ready to do whatever our lord the king chooses."

2 SAMUEL 15

QUIZZER

Q: What foreigner remained faithful when David's son Absalom led a rebellion against his father?

BONUS: How did David feel as he fled Jerusalem?

Answers on page 385

¹⁶The king set out, with his entire household following him; but he left ten concubines to take care of the palace. ¹⁷So the king set out, with all the people following him, and they halted at a place some distance away. ¹⁸All his men marched past him, along with all the Kerethites and Pelethites; and all the six hundred Gittites who had accompanied him from Gath marched before the king.

¹⁹The king said to Ittai the Gittite, "Why should you come along with us? Go back and stay with King Absalom. You are a foreigner, an exile from your homeland. ²⁰You came only yesterday. And today shall I make you wander about with us, when I do not know where I am going? Go back, and take your countrymen. May kindness and faithfulness be with you."

²¹But Ittai replied to the king, "As surely as the LORD lives, and as my lord the king lives, wherever my lord the king may be, whether it means life or death, there will your servant be."

²²David said to Ittai, "Go ahead, march on." So Ittai the Gittite marched on with all his men and the families that were with him.

²³The whole countryside wept aloud as all the people passed by. The king also crossed the Kidron Valley, and all the people moved on toward the desert.

²⁴Zadok was there, too, and all the Levites who were with him were carrying the ark of the covenant of God. They set down the ark of God, and Abiathar offered sacrifices*a* until all the people had finished leaving the city.

²⁵Then the king said to Zadok, "Take the ark of God back into the city. If I find favor in the LORD's eyes, he will bring me back and let me see it and his dwelling place again. ²⁶But if he says, 'I am not pleased with you,' then I am ready; let him do to me whatever seems good to him."

²⁷The king also said to Zadok the priest, "Aren't you a seer? Go back to the city in peace, with your son Ahimaaz and Jonathan son of Abiathar. You and Abiathar take your two sons with you. ²⁸I will wait at the fords in the desert until word comes from you to inform me." ²⁹So Zadok and Abiathar took the ark of God back to Jerusalem and stayed there.

³⁰But David continued up the Mount of Olives, weeping as he went; his head was covered and he was barefoot. All the people with him covered their heads too and were weeping as they went up. ³¹Now David had been told, "Ahithophel is among the conspirators with Absalom." So David prayed, "O LORD, turn Ahithophel's counsel into foolishness."

³²When David arrived at the summit, where people used to worship God, Hushai the Arkite was there to meet him, his robe torn and dust on his head. ³³David said to him, "If you go with me, you will be a burden to me. ³⁴But if you return to the city and say to Absalom, 'I will be your servant, O king; I was your father's servant in the past, but now I will be your servant,' then you can help me by frustrating Ahithophel's advice. ³⁵Won't the priests Zadok and Abiathar be there with you? Tell them anything you hear

a24 Or Abiathar went up

in the king's palace. [36]Their two sons, Ahimaaz son of Zadok and Jonathan son of Abiathar, are there with them. Send them to me with anything you hear."

[37]So David's friend Hushai arrived at Jerusalem as Absalom was entering the city.

16 *David and Ziba*   When David had gone a short distance beyond the summit, there was Ziba, the steward of Mephibosheth, waiting to meet him. He had a string of donkeys saddled and loaded with two hundred loaves of bread, a hundred cakes of raisins, a hundred cakes of figs and a skin of wine.

[2]The king asked Ziba, "Why have you brought these?"

Ziba answered, "The donkeys are for the king's household to ride on, the bread and fruit are for the men to eat, and the wine is to refresh those who become exhausted in the desert."

[3]The king then asked, "Where is your master's grandson?"

Ziba said to him, "He is staying in Jerusalem, because he thinks, 'Today the house of Israel will give me back my grandfather's kingdom.'"

[4]Then the king said to Ziba, "All that belonged to Mephibosheth is now yours."

"I humbly bow," Ziba said. "May I find favor in your eyes, my lord the king."

Shimei Curses David   [5]As King David approached Bahurim, a man from the same clan as Saul's family came out from there. His name was Shimei son of Gera, and he cursed as he came out. [6]He pelted David and all the king's officials with stones, though all the troops and the special guard were on David's right and left. [7]As he cursed, Shimei said, "Get out, get out, you man of blood, you scoundrel! [8]The LORD has repaid you for all the blood you shed in the household of Saul, in whose place you have reigned. The LORD has handed the kingdom over to your son Absalom. You have come to ruin because you are a man of blood!"

[9]Then Abishai son of Zeruiah said to the king, "Why should this dead dog curse my lord the king? Let me go over and cut off his head."

[10]But the king said, "What do you and I have in common, you sons of Zeruiah? If he is cursing because the LORD said to him, 'Curse David,' who can ask, 'Why do you do this?'"

[11]David then said to Abishai and all his officials, "My son, who is of my own flesh, is trying to take my life. How much more, then, this Benjamite! Leave him alone; let him curse, for the LORD has told him to. [12]It may be that the LORD will see my distress and repay me with good for the cursing I am receiving today."

[13]So David and his men continued along the road while Shimei was going along the hillside opposite him, cursing as he went and throwing stones at him and showering him with dirt. [14]The king and all the people with him arrived at their destination exhausted. And there he refreshed himself.

The Advice of Hushai and Ahithophel   [15]Meanwhile, Absalom and all the men of Israel came to Jerusalem, and Ahithophel was with him. [16]Then Hushai the Arkite, David's friend, went to Absalom and said to him, "Long live the king! Long live the king!"

[17]Absalom asked Hushai, "Is this the love you show your friend? Why didn't you go with your friend?"

[18]Hushai said to Absalom, "No, the one chosen by the LORD, by these people, and by all the men of Israel—his I will be, and I will remain with him. [19]Furthermore, whom should I serve? Should I not serve the son? Just as I served your father, so I will serve you."

Answers
to Quizzer on page 384

A: Ittai the Gittite. This foreign soldier was more loyal to King David than David's own people (2 Samuel 15:19-21).

BONUS: Although David felt abandoned, he trusted God to deliver him (Psalm 3).

²⁰Absalom said to Ahithophel, "Give us your advice. What should we do?" ²¹Ahithophel answered, "Lie with your father's concubines whom he left to take care of the palace. Then all Israel will hear that you have made yourself a stench in your father's nostrils, and the hands of everyone with you will be strengthened." ²²So they pitched a tent for Absalom on the roof, and he lay with his father's concubines in the sight of all Israel.

²³Now in those days the advice Ahithophel gave was like that of one who inquires of God. That was how both David and Absalom regarded all of Ahithophel's advice.

17 Ahithophel said to Absalom, "I would[a] choose twelve thousand men and set out tonight in pursuit of David. ²I would[b] attack him while he is weary and weak. I would[b] strike him with terror, and then all the people with him will flee. I would[b] strike down only the king ³and bring all the people back to you. The death of the man you seek will mean the return of all; all the people will be unharmed." ⁴This plan seemed good to Absalom and to all the elders of Israel.

⁵But Absalom said, "Summon also Hushai the Arkite, so we can hear what he has to say." ⁶When Hushai came to him, Absalom said, "Ahithophel has given this advice. Should we do what he says? If not, give us your opinion."

⁷Hushai replied to Absalom, "The advice Ahithophel has given is not good this time. ⁸You know your father and his men; they are fighters, and as fierce as a wild bear robbed of her cubs. Besides, your father is an experienced fighter; he will not spend the night with the troops. ⁹Even now, he is hidden in a cave or some other place. If he should attack your troops first,[c] whoever hears about it will say, 'There has been a slaughter among the troops who follow Absalom.' ¹⁰Then even the bravest soldier, whose heart is like the heart of a lion, will melt with fear, for all Israel knows that your father is a fighter and that those with him are brave.

¹¹"So I advise you: Let all Israel, from Dan to Beersheba—as numerous as the sand on the seashore—be gathered to you, with you yourself leading them into battle. ¹²Then we will attack him wherever he may be found, and we will fall on him as dew settles on the ground. Neither he nor any of his men will be left alive. ¹³If he withdraws into a city, then all Israel will bring ropes to that city, and we will drag it down to the valley until not even a piece of it can be found."

¹⁴Absalom and all the men of Israel said, "The advice of Hushai the Arkite is better than that of Ahithophel." For the LORD had determined to frustrate the good advice of Ahithophel in order to bring disaster on Absalom.

¹⁵Hushai told Zadok and Abiathar, the priests, "Ahithophel has advised Absalom and the elders of Israel to do such and such, but I have advised them to do so and so. ¹⁶Now send a message immediately and tell David, 'Do not spend the night at the fords in the desert; cross

---

Direct Line

2 SAMUEL 17:1–14

You ask Jenny what she thinks, and she says you should tell. Kendra says don't tell. You ask Karen, and she says you should tell only if you're asked. Sarah says you should pick up the phone and tell right away. So you ask Chrissy, and she . . . Somehow, when you want advice, everyone seems to have a different opinion. It may be good to get different views, but in the end you're the one who has to make the decision. Even if all agree that one choice is better (2 Samuel 17:14), they may be wrong. In the end you have to decide. Ask God for help with your decisions. And do what you think is right.

---

[a]1 Or *Let me*   [b]2 Or *will*   [c]9 Or *When some of the men fall at the first attack*

over without fail, or the king and all the people with him will be swallowed up.' "

[17]Jonathan and Ahimaaz were staying at En Rogel. A servant girl was to go and inform them, and they were to go and tell King David, for they could not risk being seen entering the city. [18]But a young man saw them and told Absalom. So the two of them left quickly and went to the house of a man in Bahurim. He had a well in his courtyard, and they climbed down into it. [19]His wife took a covering and spread it out over the opening of the well and scattered grain over it. No one knew anything about it.

[20]When Absalom's men came to the woman at the house, they asked, "Where are Ahimaaz and Jonathan?"

The woman answered them, "They crossed over the brook."[a] The men searched but found no one, so they returned to Jerusalem.

[21]After the men had gone, the two climbed out of the well and went to inform King David. They said to him, "Set out and cross the river at once; Ahithophel has advised such and such against you." [22]So David and all the people with him set out and crossed the Jordan. By daybreak, no one was left who had not crossed the Jordan.

[23]When Ahithophel saw that his advice had not been followed, he saddled his donkey and set out for his house in his hometown. He put his house in order and then hanged himself. So he died and was buried in his father's tomb.

[24]David went to Mahanaim, and Absalom crossed the Jordan with all the men of Israel. [25]Absalom had appointed Amasa over the army in place of Joab. Amasa was the son of a man named Jether,[b] an Israelite[c] who had married Abigail,[d] the daughter of Nahash and sister of Zeruiah the mother of Joab. [26]The Israelites and Absalom camped in the land of Gilead.

[27]When David came to Mahanaim, Shobi son of Nahash from Rabbah of the Ammonites, and Makir son of Ammiel from Lo Debar, and Barzillai the Gileadite from Rogelim [28]brought bedding and bowls and articles of pottery. They also brought wheat and barley, flour and roasted grain, beans and lentils,[e] [29]honey and curds, sheep, and cheese from cows' milk for David and his people to eat. For they said, "The people have become hungry and tired and thirsty in the desert."

18 **Absalom's Death** David mustered the men who were with him and appointed over them commanders of thousands and commanders of hundreds. [2]David sent the troops out—a third under the command of Joab, a third under Joab's brother Abishai son of Zeruiah, and a third under Ittai the Gittite. The king told the troops, "I myself will surely march out with you."

[3]But the men said, "You must not go out; if we are forced to flee, they won't care about us. Even if half of us die, they won't care; but you are worth ten thousand of us.[f] It would be better now for you to give us support from the city."

[4]The king answered, "I will do whatever seems best to you."

So the king stood beside the gate while all the men marched out in units of hundreds and of thousands. [5]The king commanded Joab, Abishai and Ittai, "Be gentle with the young man Absalom for my sake." And all the troops heard the king giving orders concerning Absalom to each of the commanders.

---

[a]20 Or *"They passed by the sheep pen toward the water."*   [b]25 Hebrew *Ithra*, a variant of *Jether*
[c]25 Hebrew and some Septuagint manuscripts; other Septuagint manuscripts (see also 1 Chron. 2:17)
Ishmaelite or *Jezreelite*   [d]25 Hebrew *Abigal*, a variant of *Abigail*   [e]28 Most Septuagint manuscripts and
Syriac; Hebrew *lentils, and roasted grain*   [f]3 Two Hebrew manuscripts, some Septuagint manuscripts and
Vulgate; most Hebrew manuscripts *care; for now there are ten thousand like us*

⁶The army marched into the field to fight Israel, and the battle took place in the forest of Ephraim. ⁷There the army of Israel was defeated by David's men, and the casualties that day were great—twenty thousand men. ⁸The battle spread out over the whole countryside, and the forest claimed more lives that day than the sword.

⁹Now Absalom happened to meet David's men. He was riding his mule, and as the mule went under the thick branches of a large oak, Absalom's head got caught in the tree. He was left hanging in midair, while the mule he was riding kept on going.

¹⁰When one of the men saw this, he told Joab, "I just saw Absalom hanging in an oak tree."

¹¹Joab said to the man who had told him this, "What! You saw him? Why didn't you strike him to the ground right there? Then I would have had to give you ten shekels*ᵃ* of silver and a warrior's belt."

¹²But the man replied, "Even if a thousand shekels*ᵇ* were weighed out into my hands, I would not lift my hand against the king's son. In our hearing the king commanded you and Abishai and Ittai, 'Protect the young man Absalom for my sake.'*ᶜ* ¹³And if I had put my life in jeopardy*ᵈ*—and nothing is hidden from the king—you would have kept your distance from me."

¹⁴Joab said, "I'm not going to wait like this for you." So he took three javelins in his hand and plunged them into Absalom's heart while Absalom was still alive in the oak tree. ¹⁵And ten of Joab's armor-bearers surrounded Absalom, struck him and killed him.

¹⁶Then Joab sounded the trumpet, and the troops stopped pursuing Israel, for Joab halted them. ¹⁷They took Absalom, threw him into a big pit in the forest and piled up a large heap of rocks over him. Meanwhile, all the Israelites fled to their homes.

¹⁸During his lifetime Absalom had taken a pillar and erected it in the King's Valley as a monument to himself, for he thought, "I have no son to carry on the memory of my name." He named the pillar after himself, and it is called Absalom's Monument to this day.

David Mourns ¹⁹Now Ahimaaz son of Zadok said, "Let me run and take the news to the king that the LORD has delivered him from the hand of his enemies."

²⁰"You are not the one to take the news today," Joab told him. "You may take the news another time, but you must not do so today, because the king's son is dead."

²¹Then Joab said to a Cushite, "Go, tell the king what you have seen." The Cushite bowed down before Joab and ran off.

²²Ahimaaz son of Zadok again said to Joab, "Come what may, please let me run behind the Cushite."

But Joab replied, "My son, why do you want to go? You don't have any news that will bring you a reward."

²³He said, "Come what may, I want to run."

So Joab said, "Run!" Then Ahimaaz ran by way of the plain*ᵉ* and outran the Cushite.

²⁴While David was sitting between the inner and outer gates, the watchman went up to the roof of the gateway by the wall. As he looked out, he saw a man running alone. ²⁵The watchman called out to the king and reported it.

ᵃ11 That is, about 4 ounces (about 115 grams)   *ᵇ12* That is, about 25 pounds (about 11 kilograms)
ᶜ12 A few Hebrew manuscripts, Septuagint, Vulgate and Syriac; most Hebrew manuscripts may be translated *Absalom, whoever you may be.*   *ᵈ13* Or *Otherwise, if I had acted treacherously toward him*
ᵉ23 That is, the plain of the Jordan

The king said, "If he is alone, he must have good news." And the man came closer and closer.

²⁶Then the watchman saw another man running, and he called down to the gatekeeper, "Look, another man running alone!"

The king said, "He must be bringing good news, too."

²⁷The watchman said, "It seems to me that the first one runs like Ahimaaz son of Zadok."

"He's a good man," the king said. "He comes with good news."

²⁸Then Ahimaaz called out to the king, "All is well!" He bowed down before the king with his face to the ground and said, "Praise be to the Lord your God! He has delivered up the men who lifted their hands against my lord the king."

²⁹The king asked, "Is the young man Absalom safe?"

Ahimaaz answered, "I saw great confusion just as Joab was about to send the king's servant and me, your servant, but I don't know what it was."

³⁰The king said, "Stand aside and wait here." So he stepped aside and stood there.

³¹Then the Cushite arrived and said, "My lord the king, hear the good news! The Lord has delivered you today from all who rose up against you."

³²The king asked the Cushite, "Is the young man Absalom safe?"

The Cushite replied, "May the enemies of my lord the king and all who rise up to harm you be like that young man."

³³The king was shaken. He went up to the room over the gateway and wept. As he went, he said: "O my son Absalom! My son, my son Absalom! If only I had died instead of you—O Absalom, my son, my son!"

19 Joab was told, "The king is weeping and mourning for Absalom." ²And for the whole army the victory that day was turned into mourning, because on that day the troops heard it said, "The king is grieving for his son." ³The men stole into the city that day as men steal in who are ashamed when they flee from battle. ⁴The king covered his face and cried aloud, "O my son Absalom! O Absalom, my son, my son!"

⁵Then Joab went into the house to the king and said, "Today you have humiliated all your men, who have just saved your life and the lives of your sons and daughters and the lives of your wives and concubines. ⁶You love those who hate you and hate those who love you. You have made it clear today that the commanders and their men mean nothing to you. I see that you would be pleased if Absalom were alive today and all of us were dead. ⁷Now go out and encourage your men. I swear by the Lord that if you don't go out, not a man will be left with you by nightfall. This will be worse for you than all the calamities that have come upon you from your youth till now."

⁸So the king got up and took his seat in the gateway. When the men were told, "The king is sitting in the gateway," they all came before him.

David Returns to Jerusalem Meanwhile, the Israelites had fled to their homes. ⁹Throughout the tribes of Israel, the people were all arguing with each other, saying, "The king delivered us from the hand of our enemies; he is the one who rescued us from the hand of the Philistines. But now he has fled the country because of Absalom; ¹⁰and Absalom, whom we anointed to rule over us, has died in battle. So why do you say nothing about bringing the king back?"

¹¹King David sent this message to Zadok and Abiathar, the priests: "Ask the elders of Judah, 'Why should you be the last to bring the king back to his palace, since what is being said throughout Israel has reached the king at his quarters? ¹²You are my brothers, my own flesh and blood. So why should you be the last to bring back the king?' ¹³And say to Amasa, 'Are you not my own flesh and blood? May God deal with me, be it ever so severely, if from now on you are not the commander of my army in place of Joab.'"

¹⁴He won over the hearts of all the men of Judah as though they were one man. They sent word to the king, "Return, you and all your men." ¹⁵Then the king returned and went as far as the Jordan.

Now the men of Judah had come to Gilgal to go out and meet the king and bring him across the Jordan. ¹⁶Shimei son of Gera, the Benjamite from Bahurim, hurried down with the men of Judah to meet King David. ¹⁷With him were a thousand Benjamites, along with Ziba, the steward of Saul's household, and his fifteen sons and twenty servants. They rushed to the Jordan, where the king was. ¹⁸They crossed at the ford to take the king's household over and to do whatever he wished.

When Shimei son of Gera crossed the Jordan, he fell prostrate before the king ¹⁹and said to him, "May my lord not hold me guilty. Do not remember how your servant did wrong on the day my lord the king left Jerusalem. May the king put it out of his mind. ²⁰For I your servant know that I have sinned, but today I have come here as the first of the whole house of Joseph to come down and meet my lord the king."

²¹Then Abishai son of Zeruiah said, "Shouldn't Shimei be put to death for this? He cursed the LORD's anointed."

²²David replied, "What do you and I have in common, you sons of Zeruiah? This day you have become my adversaries! Should anyone be put to death in Israel today? Do I not know that today I am king over Israel?" ²³So the king said to Shimei, "You shall not die." And the king promised him on oath.

²⁴Mephibosheth, Saul's grandson, also went down to meet the king. He had not taken care of his feet or trimmed his mustache or washed his clothes from the day the king left until the day he returned safely. ²⁵When he came from Jerusalem to meet the king, the king asked him, "Why didn't you go with me, Mephibosheth?"

²⁶He said, "My lord the king, since I your servant am lame, I said, 'I will have my donkey saddled and will ride on it, so I can go with the king.' But Ziba my servant betrayed me. ²⁷And he has slandered your servant to my lord the king. My lord the king is like an angel of God; so do whatever pleases you. ²⁸All my grandfather's descendants deserved nothing but death from my lord the king, but you gave your servant a place among those who eat at your table. So what right do I have to make any more appeals to the king?"

²⁹The king said to him, "Why say more? I order you and Ziba to divide the fields."

³⁰Mephibosheth said to the king, "Let him take everything, now that my lord the king has arrived home safely."

³¹Barzillai the Gileadite also came down from Rogelim to cross the Jordan with the king and to send him on his way from there. ³²Now Barzillai was a very old man, eighty years of age. He had provided for the king during his stay in Mahanaim, for he was a very wealthy man. ³³The king said to Barzillai, "Cross over with me and stay with me in Jerusalem, and I will provide for you."

³⁴But Barzillai answered the king, "How many more years will I live, that I should go up to Jerusalem with the king? ³⁵I am now eighty years old. Can I tell the difference between what is good and what is not? Can your servant taste what he eats and drinks? Can I still hear the voices of men and women singers? Why should your servant be an added burden to my lord the king? ³⁶Your servant will cross over the Jordan with the king for a short distance, but why should the king reward me in this way? ³⁷Let your servant return, that I may die in my own town near the tomb of my father and mother. But here is your servant Kimham. Let him cross over with my lord the king. Do for him whatever pleases you."

³⁸The king said, "Kimham shall cross over with me, and I will do for him whatever pleases you. And anything you desire from me I will do for you."

³⁹So all the people crossed the Jordan, and then the king crossed over. The

Answers
to Quizzer on
page 388

A: Joab, David's army general, plunged three javelins into his heart (2 Samuel 18:14).

BONUS: Absalom had his head caught in the branches of a tree when he was attacked and killed by Joab.

king kissed Barzillai and gave him his blessing, and Barzillai returned to his home.

⁴⁰When the king crossed over to Gilgal, Kimham crossed with him. All the troops of Judah and half the troops of Israel had taken the king over.

⁴¹Soon all the men of Israel were coming to the king and saying to him, "Why did our brothers, the men of Judah, steal the king away and bring him and his household across the Jordan, together with all his men?"

⁴²All the men of Judah answered the men of Israel, "We did this because the king is closely related to us. Why are you angry about it? Have we eaten any of the king's provisions? Have we taken anything for ourselves?"

⁴³Then the men of Israel answered the men of Judah, "We have ten shares in the king; and besides, we have a greater claim on David than you have. So why do you treat us with contempt? Were we not the first to speak of bringing back our king?"

But the men of Judah responded even more harshly than the men of Israel.

20 *Sheba Rebels Against David* Now a troublemaker named Sheba son of Bicri, a Benjamite, happened to be there. He sounded the trumpet and shouted,

> "We have no share in David,
> no part in Jesse's son!
> Every man to his tent, O Israel!"

²So all the men of Israel deserted David to follow Sheba son of Bicri. But the men of Judah stayed by their king all the way from the Jordan to Jerusalem.

³When David returned to his palace in Jerusalem, he took the ten concubines he had left to take care of the palace and put them in a house under guard. He provided for them, but did not lie with them. They were kept in confinement till the day of their death, living as widows.

⁴Then the king said to Amasa, "Summon the men of Judah to come to me within three days, and be here yourself." ⁵But when Amasa went to summon Judah, he took longer than the time the king had set for him.

⁶David said to Abishai, "Now Sheba son of Bicri will do us more harm than Absalom did. Take your master's men and pursue him, or he will find fortified cities and escape from us." ⁷So Joab's men and the Kerethites and Pelethites and all the mighty warriors went out under the command of Abishai. They marched out from Jerusalem to pursue Sheba son of Bicri.

⁸While they were at the great rock in Gibeon, Amasa came to meet them. Joab was wearing his military tunic, and strapped over it at his waist was a belt with a dagger in its sheath. As he stepped forward, it dropped out of its sheath.

⁹Joab said to Amasa, "How are you, my brother?" Then Joab took Amasa by the beard with his right hand to kiss him. ¹⁰Amasa was not on his guard against the dagger in Joab's hand, and Joab plunged it into his belly, and his intestines spilled out on the ground. Without being stabbed again, Amasa died. Then Joab and his brother Abishai pursued Sheba son of Bicri.

¹¹One of Joab's men stood beside Amasa and said, "Whoever favors Joab, and whoever is for David, let him follow Joab!" ¹²Amasa lay wallowing in his blood in the middle of the road, and the man saw that all the troops came to a halt there. When he realized that everyone who came up to Amasa stopped, he dragged him from the road into a field and threw a garment over him. ¹³After Amasa had been removed from the road, all the men went on with Joab to pursue Sheba son of Bicri.

¹⁴Sheba passed through all the tribes of Israel to Abel Beth Maacah*ᵃ* and

ᵃ14 Or *Abel, even Beth Maacah*; also in verse 15

through the entire region of the Berites, who gathered together and followed him. ¹⁵All the troops with Joab came and besieged Sheba in Abel Beth Maacah. They built a siege ramp up to the city, and it stood against the outer fortifications. While they were battering the wall to bring it down, ¹⁶a wise woman called from the city, "Listen! Listen! Tell Joab to come here so I can speak to him." ¹⁷He went toward her, and she asked, "Are you Joab?"

"I am," he answered.

She said, "Listen to what your servant has to say."

"I'm listening," he said.

¹⁸She continued, "Long ago they used to say, 'Get your answer at Abel,' and that settled it. ¹⁹We are the peaceful and faithful in Israel. You are trying to destroy a city that is a mother in Israel. Why do you want to swallow up the Lord's inheritance?"

²⁰"Far be it from me!" Joab replied, "Far be it from me to swallow up or destroy! ²¹That is not the case. A man named Sheba son of Bicri, from the hill country of Ephraim, has lifted up his hand against the king, against David. Hand over this one man, and I'll withdraw from the city."

The woman said to Joab, "His head will be thrown to you from the wall."

²²Then the woman went to all the people with her wise advice, and they cut off the head of Sheba son of Bicri and threw it to Joab. So he sounded the trumpet, and his men dispersed from the city, each returning to his home. And Joab went back to the king in Jerusalem.

²³Joab was over Israel's entire army; Benaiah son of Jehoiada was over the Kerethites and Pelethites; ²⁴Adoniram*ᵃ* was in charge of forced labor; Jehoshaphat son of Ahilud was recorder; ²⁵Sheva was secretary; Zadok and Abiathar were priests; ²⁶and Ira the Jairite was David's priest.

The Gibeonites Avenged

21 During the reign of David, there was a famine for three successive years; so David sought the face of the Lord. The Lord said, "It is on account of Saul and his blood-stained house; it is because he put the Gibeonites to death."

²The king summoned the Gibeonites and spoke to them. (Now the Gibeonites were not a part of Israel but were survivors of the Amorites; the Israelites had sworn to spare them, but Saul in his zeal for Israel and Judah had tried to annihilate them.) ³David asked the Gibeonites, "What shall I do for you? How shall I make amends so that you will bless the Lord's inheritance?"

⁴The Gibeonites answered him, "We have no right to demand silver or gold from Saul or his family, nor do we have the right to put anyone in Israel to death."

"What do you want me to do for you?" David asked.

⁵They answered the king, "As for the man who destroyed us and plotted against us so that we have been decimated and have no place anywhere in Israel, ⁶let seven of his male descendants be given to us to be killed and exposed before the Lord at Gibeah of Saul—the Lord's chosen one."

So the king said, "I will give them to you."

⁷The king spared Mephibosheth son of Jonathan, the son of Saul, because of the oath before the Lord between David and Jonathan son of Saul. ⁸But the king took Armoni and Mephibosheth, the two sons of Aiah's daughter Rizpah, whom she had borne to Saul, together with the five sons of Saul's daughter Merab,ᵇ whom she had borne to Adriel son of Barzillai the Meholathite. ⁹He handed them over to the Gibeonites, who killed and exposed them on a hill before the Lord. All seven of them fell together; they were put to death during the first days of the harvest, just as the barley harvest was beginning.

ᵃ*24* Some Septuagint manuscripts (see also 1 Kings 4:6 and 5:14); Hebrew *Adoram*   ᵇ*8* Two Hebrew manuscripts, some Septuagint manuscripts and Syriac (see also 1 Samuel 18:19); most Hebrew and Septuagint manuscripts *Michal*

¹⁰Rizpah daughter of Aiah took sackcloth and spread it out for herself on a rock. From the beginning of the harvest till the rain poured down from the heavens on the bodies, she did not let the birds of the air touch them by day or the wild animals by night. ¹¹When David was told what Aiah's daughter Rizpah, Saul's concubine, had done, ¹²he went and took the bones of Saul and his son Jonathan from the citizens of Jabesh Gilead. (They had taken them secretly from the public square at Beth Shan, where the Philistines had hung them after they struck Saul down on Gilboa.) ¹³David brought the bones of Saul and his son Jonathan from there, and the bones of those who had been killed and exposed were gathered up.

¹⁴They buried the bones of Saul and his son Jonathan in the tomb of Saul's father Kish, at Zela in Benjamin, and did everything the king commanded. After that, God answered prayer in behalf of the land.

Wars Against the Philistines ¹⁵Once again there was a battle between the Philistines and Israel. David went down with his men to fight against the Philistines, and he became exhausted. ¹⁶And Ishbi-Benob, one of the descendants of Rapha, whose bronze spearhead weighed three hundred shekels*a* and who was armed with a new sword, said he would kill David. ¹⁷But Abishai son of Zeruiah came to David's rescue; he struck the Philistine down and killed him. Then David's men swore to him, saying, "Never again will you go out with us to battle, so that the lamp of Israel will not be extinguished."

¹⁸In the course of time, there was another battle with the Philistines, at Gob. At that time Sibbecai the Hushathite killed Saph, one of the descendants of Rapha.

¹⁹In another battle with the Philistines at Gob, Elhanan son of Jaare-Oregim*b* the Bethlehemite killed Goliath*c* the Gittite, who had a spear with a shaft like a weaver's rod.

²⁰In still another battle, which took place at Gath, there was a huge man with six fingers on each hand and six toes on each foot—twenty-four in all. He also was descended from Rapha. ²¹When he taunted Israel, Jonathan son of Shimeah, David's brother, killed him.

²²These four were descendants of Rapha in Gath, and they fell at the hands of David and his men.

22 *David's Song of Praise* David sang to the LORD the words of this song when the LORD delivered him from the hand of all his enemies and from the hand of Saul. ²He said:

> "The LORD is my rock, my fortress and my deliverer;
> ³   my God is my rock, in whom I take refuge,
>   my shield and the horn*d* of my salvation.
> He is my stronghold, my refuge and my savior—
>   from violent men you save me.
> ⁴I call to the LORD, who is worthy of praise,
>   and I am saved from my enemies.
>
> ⁵ "The waves of death swirled about me;
>   the torrents of destruction overwhelmed me.
> ⁶The cords of the grave*e* coiled around me;
>   the snares of death confronted me.
> ⁷In my distress I called to the LORD;
>   I called out to my God.
> From his temple he heard my voice;
>   my cry came to his ears.

My God is my rock, in whom I take refuge (2 Samuel 22:3).

a16 That is, about 7 1/2 pounds (about 3.5 kilograms) *b19* Or *son of Jair the weaver* *c19* Hebrew and Septuagint; 1 Chron. 20:5 *son of Jair killed Lahmi the brother of Goliath* *d3 Horn* here symbolizes strength. *e6* Hebrew *Sheol*

⁸"The earth trembled and quaked,
  the foundations of the heavens*ᵃ* shook;
  they trembled because he was angry.
⁹Smoke rose from his nostrils;
  consuming fire came from his mouth,
  burning coals blazed out of it.
¹⁰He parted the heavens and came down;
  dark clouds were under his feet.
¹¹He mounted the cherubim and flew;
  he soared*ᵇ* on the wings of the wind.
¹²He made darkness his canopy around him—
  the dark*ᶜ* rain clouds of the sky.
¹³Out of the brightness of his presence
  bolts of lightning blazed forth.
¹⁴The LORD thundered from heaven;
  the voice of the Most High resounded.
¹⁵He shot arrows and scattered the enemies,
  bolts of lightning and routed them.
¹⁶The valleys of the sea were exposed
  and the foundations of the earth laid bare
  at the rebuke of the LORD,
  at the blast of breath from his nostrils.

¹⁷"He reached down from on high and took hold of me;
  he drew me out of deep waters.
¹⁸He rescued me from my powerful enemy,
  from my foes, who were too strong for me.
¹⁹They confronted me in the day of my disaster,
  but the LORD was my support.
²⁰He brought me out into a spacious place;
  he rescued me because he delighted in me.

²¹"The LORD has dealt with me according to my righteousness;
  according to the cleanness of my hands he has rewarded me.
²²For I have kept the ways of the LORD;
  I have not done evil by turning from my God.
²³All his laws are before me;
  I have not turned away from his decrees.
²⁴I have been blameless before him
  and have kept myself from sin.
²⁵The LORD has rewarded me according to my righteousness,
  according to my cleanness*ᵈ* in his sight.

²⁶"To the faithful you show yourself faithful,
  to the blameless you show yourself blameless,
²⁷to the pure you show yourself pure,
  but to the crooked you show yourself shrewd.
²⁸You save the humble,
  but your eyes are on the haughty to bring them low.
²⁹You are my lamp, O LORD;
  the LORD turns my darkness into light.
³⁰With your help I can advance against a troop*ᵉ*;
  with my God I can scale a wall.

ᵃ8 Hebrew; Vulgate and Syriac (see also Psalm 18:7) *mountains* *ᵇ11* Many Hebrew manuscripts (see also Psalm 18:10); most Hebrew manuscripts *appeared* *ᶜ12* Septuagint and Vulgate (see also Psalm 18:11); Hebrew *massed* *ᵈ25* Hebrew; Septuagint and Vulgate (see also Psalm 18:24) *to the cleanness of my hands* *ᵉ30* Or *can run through a barricade*

31 "As for God, his way is perfect;
  the word of the LORD is flawless.
He is a shield
  for all who take refuge in him.
32 For who is God besides the LORD?
  And who is the Rock except our God?
33 It is God who arms me with strength^a
  and makes my way perfect.
34 He makes my feet like the feet of a deer;
  he enables me to stand on the heights.
35 He trains my hands for battle;
  my arms can bend a bow of bronze.
36 You give me your shield of victory;
  you stoop down to make me great.
37 You broaden the path beneath me,
  so that my ankles do not turn.

38 "I pursued my enemies and crushed them;
  I did not turn back till they were destroyed.
39 I crushed them completely, and they could not rise;
  they fell beneath my feet.
40 You armed me with strength for battle;
  you made my adversaries bow at my feet.
41 You made my enemies turn their backs in flight,
  and I destroyed my foes.
42 They cried for help, but there was no one to save
    them—
  to the LORD, but he did not answer.
43 I beat them as fine as the dust of the earth;
  I pounded and trampled them like mud in the
    streets.

44 "You have delivered me from the attacks of my
    people;
  you have preserved me as the head of nations.
People I did not know are subject to me,
45   and foreigners come cringing to me;
  as soon as they hear me, they obey me.
46 They all lose heart;
  they come trembling^b from their strongholds.

47 "The LORD lives! Praise be to my Rock!
  Exalted be God, the Rock, my Savior!
48 He is the God who avenges me,
  who puts the nations under me,
49   who sets me free from my enemies.
You exalted me above my foes;
  from violent men you rescued me.
50 Therefore I will praise you, O LORD, among the
    nations;
  I will sing praises to your name.
51 He gives his king great victories;
  he shows unfailing kindness to his anointed,
    to David and his descendants forever."

> As for God, his way is perfect . . . He is a shield for all who take refuge in him (2 Samuel 22:31).

^a33 Dead Sea Scrolls, some Septuagint manuscripts, Vulgate and Syriac (see also Psalm 18:32); Masoretic Text *who is my strong refuge*   ^b46 Some Septuagint manuscripts and Vulgate (see also Psalm 18:45); Masoretic Text *they arm themselves.*

23 *The Last Words of David* These are the last words of David:

"The oracle of David son of Jesse,
  the oracle of the man exalted by the Most High,
the man anointed by the God of Jacob,
  Israel's singer of songs[a]:

[2] "The Spirit of the LORD spoke through me;
  his word was on my tongue.
[3] The God of Israel spoke,
  the Rock of Israel said to me:
'When one rules over men in righteousness,
  when he rules in the fear of God,
[4] he is like the light of morning at sunrise
  on a cloudless morning,
like the brightness after rain
  that brings the grass from the earth.'

[5] "Is not my house right with God?
  Has he not made with me an everlasting covenant,
  arranged and secured in every part?
Will he not bring to fruition my salvation
  and grant me my every desire?
[6] But evil men are all to be cast aside like thorns,
  which are not gathered with the hand.
[7] Whoever touches thorns
  uses a tool of iron or the shaft of a spear;
  they are burned up where they lie."

David's Mighty Men [8] These are the names of David's mighty men:

Josheb-Basshebeth,[b] a Tahkemonite,[c] was chief of the Three; he raised his spear against eight hundred men, whom he killed[d] in one encounter.

[9] Next to him was Eleazar son of Dodai the Ahohite. As one of the three mighty men, he was with David when they taunted the Philistines gathered at Pas Dammim[e] for battle. Then the men of Israel retreated, [10] but he stood his ground and struck down the Philistines till his hand grew tired and froze to the sword. The LORD brought about a great victory that day. The troops returned to Eleazar, but only to strip the dead.

[11] Next to him was Shammah son of Agee the Hararite. When the Philistines banded together at a place where there was a field full of lentils, Israel's troops fled from them. [12] But Shammah took his stand in the middle of the field. He defended it and struck the Philistines down, and the LORD brought about a great victory.

[13] During harvest time, three of the thirty chief men came down to David at the cave of Adullam, while a band of Philistines was encamped in the Valley of Rephaim. [14] At that time David was in the stronghold, and the Philistine garrison was at Bethlehem. [15] David longed for water and said, "Oh, that someone would get me a drink of water from the well near the gate of Bethlehem!" [16] So the three mighty men broke through the Philistine lines, drew water from the well near the gate of Bethlehem and carried it back to David. But he refused to drink it; instead, he poured it out before the LORD. [17] "Far

---

[a]1 Or *Israel's beloved singer* [b]8 Hebrew; some Septuagint manuscripts suggest *Ish-Bosheth,* that is, *Esh-Baal* (see also 1 Chron. 11:11 *Jashobeam*). [c]8 Probably a variant of *Hacmonite* (see 1 Chron. 11:11) [d]8 Some Septuagint manuscripts (see also 1 Chron. 11:11); Hebrew and other Septuagint manuscripts *Three; it was Adino the Eznite who killed eight hundred men* [e]9 See 1 Chron. 11:13; Hebrew *gathered there.*

be it from me, O LORD, to do this!" he said. "Is it not the blood of men who went at the risk of their lives?" And David would not drink it.

Such were the exploits of the three mighty men.

[18]Abishai the brother of Joab son of Zeruiah was chief of the Three.[a] He raised his spear against three hundred men, whom he killed, and so he became as famous as the Three. [19]Was he not held in greater honor than the Three? He became their commander, even though he was not included among them.

[20]Benaiah son of Jehoiada was a valiant fighter from Kabzeel, who performed great exploits. He struck down two of Moab's best men. He also went down into a pit on a snowy day and killed a lion. [21]And he struck down a huge Egyptian. Although the Egyptian had a spear in his hand, Benaiah went against him with a club. He snatched the spear from the Egyptian's hand and killed him with his own spear. [22]Such were the exploits of Benaiah son of Jehoiada; he too was as famous as the three mighty men. [23]He was held in greater honor than any of the Thirty, but he was not included among the Three. And David put him in charge of his bodyguard.

[24]Among the Thirty were:

    Asahel the brother of Joab,
    Elhanan son of Dodo from Bethlehem,
[25]Shammah the Harodite,
    Elika the Harodite,
[26]Helez the Paltite,
    Ira son of Ikkesh from Tekoa,
[27]Abiezer from Anathoth,
    Mebunnai[b] the Hushathite,
[28]Zalmon the Ahohite,
    Maharai the Netophathite,
[29]Heled[c] son of Baanah the Netophathite,
    Ithai son of Ribai from Gibeah in Benjamin,
[30]Benaiah the Pirathonite,
    Hiddai[d] from the ravines of Gaash,
[31]Abi-Albon the Arbathite,
    Azmaveth the Barhumite,
[32]Eliahba the Shaalbonite,
    the sons of Jashen,
    Jonathan [33]son of[e] Shammah the Hararite,
    Ahiam son of Sharar[f] the Hararite,
[34]Eliphelet son of Ahasbai the Maacathite,
    Eliam son of Ahithophel the Gilonite,
[35]Hezro the Carmelite,
    Paarai the Arbite,
[36]Igal son of Nathan from Zobah,
    the son of Hagri,[g]
[37]Zelek the Ammonite,
    Naharai the Beerothite, the armor-bearer of Joab son of Zeruiah,
[38]Ira the Ithrite,
    Gareb the Ithrite
[39]and Uriah the Hittite.

  There were thirty-seven in all.

---

[a]18 Most Hebrew manuscripts (see also 1 Chron. 11:20); two Hebrew manuscripts and Syriac *Thirty* [b]27 Hebrew; some Septuagint manuscripts (see also 1 Chron. 11:29) *Sibbecai* [c]29 Some Hebrew manuscripts and Vulgate (see also 1 Chron. 11:30); most Hebrew manuscripts *Heleb* [d]30 Hebrew; some Septuagint manuscripts (see also 1 Chron. 11:32) *Hurai* [e]33 Some Septuagint manuscripts (see also 1 Chron. 11:34); Hebrew does not have *son of*. [f]33 Hebrew; some Septuagint manuscripts (see also 1 Chron. 11:35) *Sacar* [g]36 Some Septuagint manuscripts (see also 1 Chron. 11:38); Hebrew *Haggadi*

24 *David Counts the Fighting Men* Again the anger of the Lord burned against Israel, and he incited David against them, saying, "Go and take a census of Israel and Judah."

²So the king said to Joab and the army commanders*ᵃ* with him, "Go throughout the tribes of Israel from Dan to Beersheba and enroll the fighting men, so that I may know how many there are."

³But Joab replied to the king, "May the Lord your God multiply the troops a hundred times over, and may the eyes of my lord the king see it. But why does my lord the king want to do such a thing?"

⁴The king's word, however, overruled Joab and the army commanders; so they left the presence of the king to enroll the fighting men of Israel.

⁵After crossing the Jordan, they camped near Aroer, south of the town in the gorge, and then went through Gad and on to Jazer. ⁶They went to Gilead and the region of Tahtim Hodshi, and on to Dan Jaan and around toward Sidon. ⁷Then they went toward the fortress of Tyre and all the towns of the Hivites and Canaanites. Finally, they went on to Beersheba in the Negev of Judah.

⁸After they had gone through the entire land, they came back to Jerusalem at the end of nine months and twenty days.

⁹Joab reported the number of the fighting men to the king: In Israel there were eight hundred thousand able-bodied men who could handle a sword, and in Judah five hundred thousand.

¹⁰David was conscience-stricken after he had counted the fighting men, and he said to the Lord, "I have sinned greatly in what I have done. Now, O Lord, I beg you, take away the guilt of your servant. I have done a very foolish thing."

¹¹Before David got up the next morning, the word of the Lord had come to Gad the prophet, David's seer: ¹²"Go and tell David, 'This is what the Lord says: I am giving you three options. Choose one of them for me to carry out against you.' "

¹³So Gad went to David and said to him, "Shall there come upon you three*ᵇ* years of famine in your land? Or three months of fleeing from your enemies while they pursue you? Or three days of plague in your land? Now then, think it over and decide how I should answer the one who sent me."

¹⁴David said to Gad, "I am in deep distress. Let us fall into the hands of the Lord, for his mercy is great; but do not let me fall into the hands of men."

¹⁵So the Lord sent a plague on Israel from that morning until the end of the time designated, and seventy thousand of the people from Dan to Beersheba died. ¹⁶When the angel stretched out his hand to destroy Jerusalem, the Lord was grieved because of the calamity and said to the angel who was afflicting the people, "Enough! Withdraw your hand." The angel of the Lord was then at the threshing floor of Araunah the Jebusite.

Direct Line

2 SAMUEL 24:1–10

Have you ever wondered if something you wanted to do was right or wrong? How can you tell if there's no commandment about it in the Bible? There's no commandment in the Old Testament against taking a military census. But after David counted the fighting men in Israel, the Bible says he "was conscience-stricken" (2 Samuel 24:10). Somehow David knew he'd done wrong. Even though there was no command against a census, David's motive was wrong. He had begun to rely on numbers instead of on God. When you have a decision to make and there's no clear command in the Bible, check your motive. Even right things done for the wrong reasons are wrong.

ᵃ2 Septuagint (see also verse 4 and 1 Chron. 21:2); Hebrew *Joab the army commander*   ᵇ13 Septuagint (see also 1 Chron. 21:12); Hebrew *seven*

¹⁷When David saw the angel who was striking down the people, he said to the LORD, "I am the one who has sinned and done wrong. These are but sheep. What have they done? Let your hand fall upon me and my family."

David Builds an Altar ¹⁸On that day Gad went to David and said to him, "Go up and build an altar to the LORD on the threshing floor of Araunah the Jebusite." ¹⁹So David went up, as the LORD had commanded through Gad. ²⁰When Araunah looked and saw the king and his men coming toward him, he went out and bowed down before the king with his face to the ground.

²¹Araunah said, "Why has my lord the king come to his servant?"

"To buy your threshing floor," David answered, "so I can build an altar to the LORD, that the plague on the people may be stopped."

²²Araunah said to David, "Let my lord the king take whatever pleases him and offer it up. Here are oxen for the burnt offering, and here are threshing sledges and ox yokes for the wood. ²³O king, Araunah gives all this to the king." Araunah also said to him, "May the LORD your God accept you."

²⁴But the king replied to Araunah, "No, I insist on paying you for it. I will not sacrifice to the LORD my God burnt offerings that cost me nothing."

So David bought the threshing floor and the oxen and paid fifty shekels*ᵃ* of silver for them. ²⁵David built an altar to the LORD there and sacrificed burnt offerings and fellowship offerings.*ᵇ* Then the LORD answered prayer in behalf of the land, and the plague on Israel was stopped.

ᵃ24 That is, about 1 1/4 pounds (about 0.6 kilogram) *ᵇ25* Traditionally *peace offerings*

JUSTICE.

Sometimes you see other kids do wrong and get away with it, and you wonder, why doesn't the school do something? Why don't their parents? Why doesn't God? But just because someone doesn't get punished doesn't mean justice won't be done.

Solomon held on to the great kingdom of his father David. But after Solomon died the kingdom split in two, Israel and Judah. God sent prophets to warn both kingdoms to return to him. But they didn't listen. Would both kingdoms get away with abandoning God? The stories in this book are a reminder: no one gets away with anything! Justice will be done.

Fundamentals

Can children learn from their fathers' mistakes (1 Kings 11)?

What do you say when people argue that they have a right to worship God their own way (1 Kings 12:25-33)?

Can a strong Christian ever get depressed (1 Kings 19:1-9)?

FAST FACTS

The author used royal records, called "annals," to write this history.

Solomon's personal income was 50,000 pounds of gold a year.

Baal means "lord" or "master" or "god."

Child sacrifice was part of some Baal worship.

1 *Adonijah Sets Himself Up as King* When King David was old and well advanced in years, he could not keep warm even when they put covers over him. ²So his servants said to him, "Let us look for a young virgin to attend the king and take care of him. She can lie beside him so that our lord the king may keep warm."

³Then they searched throughout Israel for a beautiful girl and found Abishag, a Shunammite, and brought her to the king. ⁴The girl was very beautiful; she took care of the king and waited on him, but the king had no intimate relations with her.

⁵Now Adonijah, whose mother was Haggith, put himself forward and said, "I will be king." So he got chariots and horses*a* ready, with fifty men to run ahead of him. ⁶(His father had never interfered with him by asking, "Why do you behave as you do?" He was also very handsome and was born next after Absalom.)

⁷Adonijah conferred with Joab son of Zeruiah and with Abiathar the priest, and they gave him their support. ⁸But Zadok the priest, Benaiah son of Jehoiada, Nathan the prophet, Shimei and Rei*b* and David's special guard did not join Adonijah.

⁹Adonijah then sacrificed sheep, cattle and fattened calves at the Stone of Zoheleth near En Rogel. He invited all his brothers, the king's sons, and all the men of Judah who were royal officials, ¹⁰but he did not invite Nathan the prophet or Benaiah or the special guard or his brother Solomon.

¹¹Then Nathan asked Bathsheba, Solomon's mother, "Have you not heard that Adonijah, the son of Haggith, has become king without our lord David's knowing it? ¹²Now then, let me advise you how you can save your own life and the life of your son Solomon. ¹³Go in to King David and say to him, 'My lord the king, did you not swear to me your servant: "Surely Solomon your son shall be king after me, and he will sit on my throne"? Why then has Adonijah become king?' ¹⁴While you are still there talking to the king, I will come in and confirm what you have said."

¹⁵So Bathsheba went to see the aged king in his room, where Abishag the Shunammite was attending him. ¹⁶Bathsheba bowed low and knelt before the king.

"What is it you want?" the king asked.

¹⁷She said to him, "My lord, you yourself swore to me your servant by the Lord your God: 'Solomon your son shall be king after me, and he will sit on my throne.' ¹⁸But now Adonijah has become king, and you, my lord the king, do not know about it. ¹⁹He has sacrificed great numbers of cattle, fattened calves, and sheep, and has invited all the king's sons, Abiathar the priest and Joab the commander of the army, but he has not invited Solomon your servant. ²⁰My lord the king, the eyes of all Israel are on you, to learn from you who will sit on the throne of my lord the

1 KINGS 1:1–27

You know you have to get your homework done. But maybe later, after your favorite TV show. And you have to write a report for English. But right now the guys want you to play B-ball. Guess you can write it later. David took the "maybe later" approach, and it almost cost the life of Bathsheba and Solomon. Because David put off announcing a successor, another son tried to steal the throne. Fortunately, Bathsheba and the prophet Nathan stepped in. (Sort of like Mom or Dad making you study!) Putting off homework or even missing a report probably won't ruin your life. But if putting things off becomes a habit, it might!

Direct Line

*a*5 Or *charioteers* *b*8 Or *and his friends*

king after him. ²¹Otherwise, as soon as my lord the king is laid to rest with his fathers, I and my son Solomon will be treated as criminals."

²²While she was still speaking with the king, Nathan the prophet arrived. ²³And they told the king, "Nathan the prophet is here." So he went before the king and bowed with his face to the ground.

²⁴Nathan said, "Have you, my lord the king, declared that Adonijah shall be king after you, and that he will sit on your throne? ²⁵Today he has gone down and sacrificed great numbers of cattle, fattened calves, and sheep. He has invited all the king's sons, the commanders of the army and Abiathar the priest. Right now they are eating and drinking with him and saying, 'Long live King Adonijah!' ²⁶But me your servant, and Zadok the priest, and Benaiah son of Jehoiada, and your servant Solomon he did not invite. ²⁷Is this something my lord the king has done without letting his servants know who should sit on the throne of my lord the king after him?"

David Makes Solomon King ²⁸Then King David said, "Call in Bathsheba." So she came into the king's presence and stood before him.

²⁹The king then took an oath: "As surely as the LORD lives, who has delivered me out of every trouble, ³⁰I will surely carry out today what I swore to you by the LORD, the God of Israel: Solomon your son shall be king after me, and he will sit on my throne in my place."

³¹Then Bathsheba bowed low with her face to the ground and, kneeling before the king, said, "May my lord King David live forever!"

³²King David said, "Call in Zadok the priest, Nathan the prophet and Benaiah son of Jehoiada." When they came before the king, ³³he said to them: "Take your lord's servants with you and set Solomon my son on my own mule and take him down to Gihon. ³⁴There have Zadok the priest and Nathan the prophet anoint him king over Israel. Blow the trumpet and shout, 'Long live King Solomon!' ³⁵Then you are to go up with him, and he is to come and sit on my throne and reign in my place. I have appointed him ruler over Israel and Judah."

³⁶Benaiah son of Jehoiada answered the king, "Amen! May the LORD, the God of my lord the king, so declare it. ³⁷As the LORD was with my lord the king, so may he be with Solomon to make his throne even greater than the throne of my lord King David!"

³⁸So Zadok the priest, Nathan the prophet, Benaiah son of Jehoiada, the Kerethites and the Pelethites went down and put Solomon on King David's mule and escorted him to Gihon. ³⁹Zadok the priest took the horn of oil from the sacred tent and anointed Solomon. Then they sounded the trumpet and all the people shouted, "Long live King Solomon!" ⁴⁰And all the people went up after him, playing flutes and rejoicing greatly, so that the ground shook with the sound.

⁴¹Adonijah and all the guests who were with him heard it as they were finishing their feast. On hearing the sound of the trumpet, Joab asked, "What's the meaning of all the noise in the city?"

⁴²Even as he was speaking, Jonathan son of Abiathar the priest arrived. Adonijah said, "Come in. A worthy man like you must be bringing good news."

⁴³"Not at all!" Jonathan answered. "Our lord King David has made Solomon king. ⁴⁴The king has sent with him Zadok the priest, Nathan the prophet, Benaiah son of Jehoiada, the Kerethites and the Pelethites, and they have put him on the king's mule, ⁴⁵and Zadok the priest and Nathan the prophet have anointed him king at Gihon. From there they have gone up cheering, and the city resounds with it. That's the noise you hear. ⁴⁶Moreover, Solomon has taken his seat on the royal throne. ⁴⁷Also, the royal officials have come to congratulate our lord King David, saying, 'May your God make Solomon's name more famous than yours and his throne greater than yours!' And the king

bowed in worship on his bed [48]and said, 'Praise be to the LORD, the God of Israel, who has allowed my eyes to see a successor on my throne today.' "

[49]At this, all Adonijah's guests rose in alarm and dispersed. [50]But Adonijah, in fear of Solomon, went and took hold of the horns of the altar. [51]Then Solomon was told, "Adonijah is afraid of King Solomon and is clinging to the horns of the altar. He says, 'Let King Solomon swear to me today that he will not put his servant to death with the sword.' "

[52]Solomon replied, "If he shows himself to be a worthy man, not a hair of his head will fall to the ground; but if evil is found in him, he will die." [53]Then King Solomon sent men, and they brought him down from the altar. And Adonijah came and bowed down to King Solomon, and Solomon said, "Go to your home."

David's Charge to Solomon When the time drew near for David to die, he gave a charge to Solomon his son.

[2]"I am about to go the way of all the earth," he said. "So be strong, show yourself a man, [3]and observe what the LORD your God requires: Walk in his ways, and keep his decrees and commands, his laws and requirements, as written in the Law of Moses, so that you may prosper in all you do and wherever you go, [4]and that the LORD may keep his promise to me: 'If your descendants watch how they live, and if they walk faithfully before me with all their heart and soul, you will never fail to have a man on the throne of Israel.'

> Walk in his ways . . . so that you may prosper in all you do
> (1 Kings 2:3).

[5]"Now you yourself know what Joab son of Zeruiah did to me—what he did to the two commanders of Israel's armies, Abner son of Ner and Amasa son of Jether. He killed them, shedding their blood in peacetime as if in battle, and with that blood stained the belt around his waist and the sandals on his feet. [6]Deal with him according to your wisdom, but do not let his gray head go down to the grave*a* in peace.

[7]"But show kindness to the sons of Barzillai of Gilead and let them be among those who eat at your table. They stood by me when I fled from your brother Absalom.

[8]"And remember, you have with you Shimei son of Gera, the Benjamite from Bahurim, who called down bitter curses on me the day I went to Mahanaim. When he came down to meet me at the Jordan, I swore to him by the LORD: 'I will not put you to death by the sword.' [9]But now, do not consider him innocent. You are a man of wisdom; you will know what to do to him. Bring his gray head down to the grave in blood."

[10]Then David rested with his fathers and was buried in the City of David. [11]He had reigned forty years over Israel—seven years in Hebron and thirty-three in Jerusalem. [12]So Solomon sat on the throne of his father David, and his rule was firmly established.

Solomon's Throne Established [13]Now Adonijah, the son of Haggith, went to Bathsheba, Solomon's mother. Bathsheba asked him, "Do you come peacefully?"

He answered, "Yes, peacefully." [14]Then he added, "I have something to say to you."

"You may say it," she replied.

[15]"As you know," he said, "the kingdom was mine. All Israel looked to me as their king. But things changed, and the kingdom has gone to my brother; for it has come to him from the LORD. [16]Now I have one request to make of you. Do not refuse me."

"You may make it," she said.

---

*a*6 Hebrew *Sheol*; also in verse 9

¹⁷So he continued, "Please ask King Solomon—he will not refuse you—to give me Abishag the Shunammite as my wife."

¹⁸"Very well," Bathsheba replied, "I will speak to the king for you."

¹⁹When Bathsheba went to King Solomon to speak to him for Adonijah, the king stood up to meet her, bowed down to her and sat down on his throne. He had a throne brought for the king's mother, and she sat down at his right hand.

²⁰"I have one small request to make of you," she said. "Do not refuse me."

The king replied, "Make it, my mother; I will not refuse you."

²¹So she said, "Let Abishag the Shunammite be given in marriage to your brother Adonijah."

²²King Solomon answered his mother, "Why do you request Abishag the Shunammite for Adonijah? You might as well request the kingdom for him—after all, he is my older brother—yes, for him and for Abiathar the priest and Joab son of Zeruiah!"

²³Then King Solomon swore by the LORD: "May God deal with me, be it ever so severely, if Adonijah does not pay with his life for this request! ²⁴And now, as surely as the LORD lives—he who has established me securely on the throne of my father David and has founded a dynasty for me as he promised—Adonijah shall be put to death today!" ²⁵So King Solomon gave orders to Benaiah son of Jehoiada, and he struck down Adonijah and he died.

²⁶To Abiathar the priest the king said, "Go back to your fields in Anathoth. You deserve to die, but I will not put you to death now, because you carried the ark of the Sovereign LORD before my father David and shared all my father's hardships." ²⁷So Solomon removed Abiathar from the priesthood of the LORD, fulfilling the word the LORD had spoken at Shiloh about the house of Eli.

²⁸When the news reached Joab, who had conspired with Adonijah though not with Absalom, he fled to the tent of the LORD and took hold of the horns of the altar. ²⁹King Solomon was told that Joab had fled to the tent of the LORD and was beside the altar. Then Solomon ordered Benaiah son of Jehoiada, "Go, strike him down!"

³⁰So Benaiah entered the tent of the LORD and said to Joab, "The king says, 'Come out!' "

But he answered, "No, I will die here."

Benaiah reported to the king, "This is how Joab answered me."

³¹Then the king commanded Benaiah, "Do as he says. Strike him down and bury him, and so clear me and my father's house of the guilt of the innocent blood that Joab shed. ³²The LORD will repay him for the blood he shed, because without the knowledge of my father David he attacked two men and killed them with the sword. Both of them—Abner son of Ner, commander of Israel's army, and Amasa son of Jether, commander of Judah's army—were better men and more upright than he. ³³May the guilt of their blood rest on the head of Joab and his descendants forever. But on David and his descendants, his house and his throne, may there be the LORD's peace forever."

³⁴So Benaiah son of Jehoiada went up and struck down Joab and killed him, and he was buried on his own land*ᵃ* in the desert. ³⁵The king put Benaiah son of Jehoiada over the army in Joab's position and replaced Abiathar with Zadok the priest.

³⁶Then the king sent for Shimei and said to him, "Build yourself a house in Jerusalem and live there, but do not go anywhere else. ³⁷The day you leave and cross the Kidron Valley, you can be sure you will die; your blood will be on your own head."

ᵃ34 Or *buried in his tomb*

³⁸Shimei answered the king, "What you say is good. Your servant will do as my lord the king has said." And Shimei stayed in Jerusalem for a long time.

³⁹But three years later, two of Shimei's slaves ran off to Achish son of Maacah, king of Gath, and Shimei was told, "Your slaves are in Gath." ⁴⁰At this, he saddled his donkey and went to Achish at Gath in search of his slaves. So Shimei went away and brought the slaves back from Gath.

⁴¹When Solomon was told that Shimei had gone from Jerusalem to Gath and had returned, ⁴²the king summoned Shimei and said to him, "Did I not make you swear by the LORD and warn you, 'On the day you leave to go anywhere else, you can be sure you will die'? At that time you said to me, 'What you say is good. I will obey.' ⁴³Why then did you not keep your oath to the LORD and obey the command I gave you?"

⁴⁴The king also said to Shimei, "You know in your heart all the wrong you did to my father David. Now the LORD will repay you for your wrongdoing. ⁴⁵But King Solomon will be blessed, and David's throne will remain secure before the LORD forever."

⁴⁶Then the king gave the order to Benaiah son of Jehoiada, and he went out and struck Shimei down and killed him.

The kingdom was now firmly established in Solomon's hands.

Solomon Asks for Wisdom Solomon made an alliance with Pharaoh king of Egypt and married his daughter. He brought her to the City of David until he finished building his palace and the temple of the LORD, and the wall around Jerusalem. ²The people, however, were still sacrificing at the high places, because a temple had not yet been built for the Name of the LORD. ³Solomon showed his love for the LORD by walking according to the statutes of his father David, except that he offered sacrifices and burned incense on the high places.

⁴The king went to Gibeon to offer sacrifices, for that was the most important high place, and Solomon offered a thousand burnt offerings on that altar. ⁵At Gibeon the LORD appeared to Solomon during the night in a dream, and God said, "Ask for whatever you want me to give you."

⁶Solomon answered, "You have shown great kindness to your servant, my father David, because he was faithful to you and righteous and upright in heart. You have continued this great kindness to him and have given him a son to sit on his throne this very day.

⁷"Now, O LORD my God, you have made your servant king in place of my father David. But I am only a little child and do not know how to carry out my duties. ⁸Your servant is here among the people you have chosen, a great people, too numerous to count or number. ⁹So give your servant a discerning heart to govern your people and to distinguish between right and wrong. For who is able to govern this great people of yours?"

¹⁰The Lord was pleased that Solomon had asked for this. ¹¹So God said to him, "Since you have asked for this and not for long life or wealth for yourself, nor have asked for the death of your enemies but for discernment in administering justice, ¹²I will do what you have asked. I will give you a wise and discerning heart, so that there will never have been anyone like you, nor will there ever be. ¹³Moreover, I will give you what you have not asked for—both riches and honor—so that in your lifetime you will have no equal among kings. ¹⁴And if you walk in my ways and obey my statutes and commands as David your father did, I will give you a long life." ¹⁵Then Solomon awoke—and he realized it had been a dream.

He returned to Jerusalem, stood before the ark of the Lord's covenant and sacrificed burnt offerings and fellowship offerings.^a Then he gave a feast for all his court.

---

^a15 Traditionally *peace offerings*

A Wise Ruling ¹⁶Now two prostitutes came to the king and stood before him. ¹⁷One of them said, "My lord, this woman and I live in the same house. I had a baby while she was there with me. ¹⁸The third day after my child was born, this woman also had a baby. We were alone; there was no one in the house but the two of us.

¹⁹"During the night this woman's son died because she lay on him. ²⁰So she got up in the middle of the night and took my son from my side while I your servant was asleep. She put him by her breast and put her dead son by my breast. ²¹The next morning, I got up to nurse my son—and he was dead! But when I looked at him closely in the morning light, I saw that it wasn't the son I had borne."

²²The other woman said, "No! The living one is my son; the dead one is yours."

But the first one insisted, "No! The dead one is yours; the living one is mine." And so they argued before the king.

²³The king said, "This one says, 'My son is alive and your son is dead,' while that one says, 'No! Your son is dead and mine is alive.' "

²⁴Then the king said, "Bring me a sword." So they brought a sword for the king. ²⁵He then gave an order: "Cut the living child in two and give half to one and half to the other."

²⁶The woman whose son was alive was filled with compassion for her son and said to the king, "Please, my lord, give her the living baby! Don't kill him!"

But the other said, "Neither I nor you shall have him. Cut him in two!"

²⁷Then the king gave his ruling: "Give the living baby to the first woman. Do not kill him; she is his mother."

²⁸When all Israel heard the verdict the king had given, they held the king in awe, because they saw that he had wisdom from God to administer justice.

QUIZZER

1 KINGS 3

Q:What did Solomon get that he hadn't asked for?

BONUS:
What was Solomon's yearly income?

Answers on page 408

Solomon's Officials and Governors So King Solomon ruled over all Israel. ²And these were his chief officials:

Azariah son of Zadok—the priest;
³Elihoreph and Ahijah, sons of Shisha—secretaries;
Jehoshaphat son of Ahilud—recorder;
⁴Benaiah son of Jehoiada—commander in chief;
Zadok and Abiathar—priests;
⁵Azariah son of Nathan—in charge of the district officers;
Zabud son of Nathan—a priest and personal adviser to the king;
⁶Ahishar—in charge of the palace;
Adoniram son of Abda—in charge of forced labor.

⁷Solomon also had twelve district governors over all Israel, who supplied provisions for the king and the royal household. Each one had to provide supplies for one month in the year. ⁸These are their names:

Ben-Hur—in the hill country of Ephraim;
⁹Ben-Deker—in Makaz, Shaalbim, Beth Shemesh and Elon Bethhanan;
¹⁰Ben-Hesed—in Arubboth (Socoh and all the land of Hepher were his);
¹¹Ben-Abinadab—in Naphoth Dorᵃ (he was married to Taphath daughter of Solomon);

ᵃ11 Or *in the heights of Dor*

¹²Baana son of Ahilud—in Taanach and Megiddo, and in all of Beth Shan next to Zarethan below Jezreel, from Beth Shan to Abel Meholah across to Jokmeam;

¹³Ben-Geber—in Ramoth Gilead (the settlements of Jair son of Manasseh in Gilead were his, as well as the district of Argob in Bashan and its sixty large walled cities with bronze gate bars);

¹⁴Ahinadab son of Iddo—in Mahanaim;

¹⁵Ahimaaz—in Naphtali (he had married Basemath daughter of Solomon);

¹⁶Baana son of Hushai—in Asher and in Aloth;

¹⁷Jehoshaphat son of Paruah—in Issachar;

¹⁸Shimei son of Ela—in Benjamin;

¹⁹Geber son of Uri—in Gilead (the country of Sihon king of the Amorites and the country of Og king of Bashan). He was the only governor over the district.

Solomon's Daily Provisions ²⁰The people of Judah and Israel were as numerous as the sand on the seashore; they ate, they drank and they were happy. ²¹And Solomon ruled over all the kingdoms from the River*ᵃ* to the land of the Philistines, as far as the border of Egypt. These countries brought tribute and were Solomon's subjects all his life.

²²Solomon's daily provisions were thirty cors*ᵇ* of fine flour and sixty cors*ᶜ* of meal, ²³ten head of stall-fed cattle, twenty of pasture-fed cattle and a hundred sheep and goats, as well as deer, gazelles, roebucks and choice fowl. ²⁴For he ruled over all the kingdoms west of the River, from Tiphsah to Gaza, and had peace on all sides. ²⁵During Solomon's lifetime Judah and Israel, from Dan to Beersheba, lived in safety, each man under his own vine and fig tree.

²⁶Solomon had four*ᵈ* thousand stalls for chariot horses, and twelve thousand horses.*ᵉ*

²⁷The district officers, each in his month, supplied provisions for King Solomon and all who came to the king's table. They saw to it that nothing was lacking. ²⁸They also brought to the proper place their quotas of barley and straw for the chariot horses and the other horses.

Solomon's Wisdom ²⁹God gave Solomon wisdom and very great insight, and a breadth of understanding as measureless as the sand on the seashore. ³⁰Solomon's wisdom was greater than the wisdom of all the men of the East, and greater than all the wisdom of Egypt. ³¹He was wiser than any other man, including Ethan the Ezrahite—wiser than Heman, Calcol and Darda, the sons of Mahol. And his fame spread to all the surrounding nations. ³²He spoke three thousand proverbs and his songs numbered a thousand and five. ³³He described plant life, from the cedar of Lebanon to the hyssop that grows out of walls. He also taught about animals and birds, reptiles and fish. ³⁴Men of all nations came to listen to Solomon's wisdom, sent by all the kings of the world, who had heard of his wisdom.

Preparations for Building the Temple When Hiram king of Tyre heard that Solomon had been anointed king to succeed his father David, he sent his envoys to Solomon, because he had always been on friendly terms with David. ²Solomon sent back this message to Hiram:

³"You know that because of the wars waged against my father David from all sides, he could not build a temple for the Name of the LORD his God until the LORD put his enemies under his feet. ⁴But now the LORD my God has given me rest on every side, and there is no adversary or disas-

---

ᵃ21 That is, the Euphrates; also in verse 24   *ᵇ22* That is, probably about 185 bushels (about 6.6 kiloliters)
ᶜ22 That is, probably about 375 bushels (about 13.2 kiloliters)   *ᵈ26* Some Septuagint manuscripts (see also 2 Chron. 9:25); Hebrew *forty*   *ᵉ26* Or *charioteers*

ter. ⁵I intend, therefore, to build a temple for the Name of the Lord my God, as the Lord told my father David, when he said, 'Your son whom I will put on the throne in your place will build the temple for my Name.'

⁶"So give orders that cedars of Lebanon be cut for me. My men will work with yours, and I will pay you for your men whatever wages you set. You know that we have no one so skilled in felling timber as the Sidonians."

⁷When Hiram heard Solomon's message, he was greatly pleased and said, "Praise be to the Lord today, for he has given David a wise son to rule over this great nation."

⁸So Hiram sent word to Solomon:

"I have received the message you sent me and will do all you want in providing the cedar and pine logs. ⁹My men will haul them down from Lebanon to the sea, and I will float them in rafts by sea to the place you specify. There I will separate them and you can take them away. And you are to grant my wish by providing food for my royal household."

¹⁰In this way Hiram kept Solomon supplied with all the cedar and pine logs he wanted, ¹¹and Solomon gave Hiram twenty thousand cors*a* of wheat as food for his household, in addition to twenty thousand baths*b,c* of pressed olive oil. Solomon continued to do this for Hiram year after year. ¹²The Lord gave Solomon wisdom, just as he had promised him. There were peaceful relations between Hiram and Solomon, and the two of them made a treaty.

¹³King Solomon conscripted laborers from all Israel—thirty thousand men. ¹⁴He sent them off to Lebanon in shifts of ten thousand a month, so that they spent one month in Lebanon and two months at home. Adoniram was in charge of the forced labor. ¹⁵Solomon had seventy thousand carriers and eighty thousand stonecutters in the hills, ¹⁶as well as thirty-three hundred*d* foremen who supervised the project and directed the workmen. ¹⁷At the king's command they removed from the quarry large blocks of quality stone to provide a foundation of dressed stone for the temple. ¹⁸The craftsmen of Solomon and Hiram and the men of Gebal*e* cut and prepared the timber and stone for the building of the temple.

6 **Solomon Builds the Temple** In the four hundred and eightieth*f* year after the Israelites had come out of Egypt, in the fourth year of Solomon's reign over Israel, in the month of Ziv, the second month, he began to build the temple of the Lord.

²The temple that King Solomon built for the Lord was sixty cubits long, twenty wide and thirty high.*g* ³The portico at the front of the main hall of the temple extended the width of the temple, that is twenty cubits,*h* and projected ten cubits*i* from the front of the temple. ⁴He made narrow clerestory windows in the temple. ⁵Against the walls of the main hall and inner sanctuary he built a structure around the building, in which there were side rooms. ⁶The lowest floor was five cubits*j* wide, the middle floor six cubits*k* and the third floor seven.*l* He made offset ledges around the outside of the temple so that nothing would be inserted into the temple walls.

⁷In building the temple, only blocks dressed at the quarry were used, and no hammer, chisel or any other iron tool was heard at the temple site while it was being built.

Answers
to Quizzer on page 406

A: Solomon asked for wisdom but God also gave him "riches and honor" (1 Kings 3:13).

BONUS: Solomon earned about 25 tons of gold per year (1 Kings 10:14)! At $350 an ounce, that's about $2.8 million a year!

---

a11 That is, probably about 125,000 bushels (about 4,400 kiloliters) *b11* Septuagint (see also 2 Chron. 2:10); Hebrew *twenty cors* *c11* That is, about 115,000 gallons (about 440 kiloliters) *d16* Hebrew; some Septuagint manuscripts (see also 2 Chron. 2:2, 18) *thirty-six hundred* *e18* That is, Byblos *f1* Hebrew; Septuagint *four hundred and fortieth* *g2* That is, about 90 feet (about 27 meters) long and 30 feet (about 9 meters) wide and 45 feet (about 13.5 meters) high *h3* That is, about 30 feet (about 9 meters) *i3* That is, about 15 feet (about 4.5 meters) *j6* That is, about 7 1/2 feet (about 2.3 meters); also in verses 10 and 24 *k6* That is, about 9 feet (about 2.7 meters) *l6* That is, about 10 1/2 feet (about 3.1 meters)

Dear Sam,

I've just become a Christian, but none of my friends have accepted Christ. Should I still be friends with them?

Jason in Jacksonville

Dear Sam, Inc.

100 Advice Lane, Anywhere, USA

Dear Jason,

Many Christians have this same question. I like to look at the example that wise King Solomon gives. He had a friend, Hiram king of Tyre, who did not worship God. Solomon explained in a message to Hiram that he was building a temple for the Lord and needed raw materials that Israel did not have (1 Kings 5:3-6). Hiram gladly supplied his friend with what was needed.

These men had a cordial relationship for many years (1 Kings 5:10-11) even though they did not worship the same God. Their relationship was obviously based on mutual respect. Each man dealt honestly with the other. Solomon was open about the purpose for the materials he needed, and the king of Tyre did nothing that would entice or encourage Solomon to disobey his God.

If you have friends who are not Christians, God doesn't expect you to abandon them unless they are tempting you to sin. In fact, perhaps they will notice a change in you and you will be able to lead them to the Lord. You must decide about each friendship individually. If it is like the one between Hiram and Solomon, keep it.

Sam

⁸The entrance to the lowest*ᵃ* floor was on the south side of the temple; a stairway led up to the middle level and from there to the third. ⁹So he built the temple and completed it, roofing it with beams and cedar planks. ¹⁰And he built the side rooms all along the temple. The height of each was five cubits, and they were attached to the temple by beams of cedar.

¹¹The word of the Lᴏʀᴅ came to Solomon: ¹²"As for this temple you are building, if you follow my decrees, carry out my regulations and keep all my commands and obey them, I will fulfill through you the promise I gave to David your father. ¹³And I will live among the Israelites and will not abandon my people Israel."

¹⁴So Solomon built the temple and completed it. ¹⁵He lined its interior walls with cedar boards, paneling them from the floor of the temple to the ceiling, and covered the floor of the temple with planks of pine. ¹⁶He partitioned off twenty cubits*ᵇ* at the rear of the temple with cedar boards from floor to ceiling to form within the temple an inner sanctuary, the Most Holy Place. ¹⁷The main hall in front of this room was forty cubits*ᶜ* long. ¹⁸The inside of the temple was cedar, carved with gourds and open flowers. Everything was cedar; no stone was to be seen.

¹⁹He prepared the inner sanctuary within the temple to set the ark of the covenant of the Lᴏʀᴅ there. ²⁰The inner sanctuary was twenty cubits long, twenty wide and twenty high.*ᵈ* He overlaid the inside with pure gold, and he also overlaid the altar of cedar. ²¹Solomon covered the inside of the temple with pure gold, and he extended gold chains across the front of the inner sanctuary, which was overlaid with gold. ²²So he overlaid the whole interior with gold. He also overlaid with gold the altar that belonged to the inner sanctuary.

²³In the inner sanctuary he made a pair of cherubim of olive wood, each ten cubits*ᵉ* high. ²⁴One wing of the first cherub was five cubits long, and the other wing five cubits—ten cubits from wing tip to wing tip. ²⁵The second cherub also measured ten cubits, for the two cherubim were identical in size and shape. ²⁶The height of each cherub was ten cubits. ²⁷He placed the cherubim inside the innermost room of the temple, with their wings spread out. The wing of one cherub touched one wall, while the wing of the other touched the other wall, and their wings touched each other in the middle of the room. ²⁸He overlaid the cherubim with gold.

²⁹On the walls all around the temple, in both the inner and outer rooms, he carved cherubim, palm trees and open flowers. ³⁰He also covered the floors of both the inner and outer rooms of the temple with gold.

³¹For the entrance of the inner sanctuary he made doors of olive wood with five-sided jambs. ³²And on the two olive wood doors he carved cherubim, palm trees and open flowers, and overlaid the cherubim and palm trees with beaten gold. ³³In the same way he made four-sided jambs of olive wood for the entrance to the main hall. ³⁴He also made two pine doors, each having two leaves that turned in sockets. ³⁵He carved cherubim, palm trees and open flowers on them and overlaid them with gold hammered evenly over the carvings.

³⁶And he built the inner courtyard of three courses of dressed stone and one course of trimmed cedar beams.

³⁷The foundation of the temple of the Lᴏʀᴅ was laid in the fourth year, in the month of Ziv. ³⁸In the eleventh year in the month of Bul, the eighth month, the temple was finished in all its details according to its specifications. He had spent seven years building it.

ᵃ8 Septuagint; Hebrew *middle*   *ᵇ16* That is, about 30 feet (about 9 meters)   *ᶜ17* That is, about 60 feet (about 18 meters)   *ᵈ20* That is, about 30 feet (about 9 meters) long, wide and high   *ᵉ23* That is, about 15 feet (about 4.5 meters)

7 *Solomon Builds His Palace*   It took Solomon thirteen years, however, to complete the construction of his palace. ²He built the Palace of the Forest of Lebanon a hundred cubits long, fifty wide and thirty high,*ᵃ* with four rows of cedar columns supporting trimmed cedar beams. ³It was roofed with cedar above the beams that rested on the columns—forty-five beams, fifteen to a row. ⁴Its windows were placed high in sets of three, facing each other. ⁵All the doorways had rectangular frames; they were in the front part in sets of three, facing each other.*ᵇ*

⁶He made a colonnade fifty cubits long and thirty wide.*ᶜ* In front of it was a portico, and in front of that were pillars and an overhanging roof.

⁷He built the throne hall, the Hall of Justice, where he was to judge, and he covered it with cedar from floor to ceiling.*ᵈ* ⁸And the palace in which he was to live, set farther back, was similar in design. Solomon also made a palace like this hall for Pharaoh's daughter, whom he had married.

⁹All these structures, from the outside to the great courtyard and from foundation to eaves, were made of blocks of high-grade stone cut to size and trimmed with a saw on their inner and outer faces. ¹⁰The foundations were laid with large stones of good quality, some measuring ten cubits*ᵉ* and some eight.*ᶠ* ¹¹Above were high-grade stones, cut to size, and cedar beams. ¹²The great courtyard was surrounded by a wall of three courses of dressed stone and one course of trimmed cedar beams, as was the inner courtyard of the temple of the Lᴏʀᴅ with its portico.

The Temple's Furnishings   ¹³King Solomon sent to Tyre and brought Huram,*ᵍ* ¹⁴whose mother was a widow from the tribe of Naphtali and whose father was a man of Tyre and a craftsman in bronze. Huram was highly skilled and experienced in all kinds of bronze work. He came to King Solomon and did all the work assigned to him.

¹⁵He cast two bronze pillars, each eighteen cubits high and twelve cubits around,*ʰ* by line. ¹⁶He also made two capitals of cast bronze to set on the tops of the pillars; each capital was five cubits*ⁱ* high. ¹⁷A network of interwoven chains festooned the capitals on top of the pillars, seven for each capital. ¹⁸He made pomegranates in two rows*ʲ* encircling each network to decorate the capitals on top of the pillars.*ᵏ* He did the same for each capital. ¹⁹The capitals on top of the pillars in the portico were in the shape of lilies, four cubits*ˡ* high. ²⁰On the capitals of both pillars, above the bowl-shaped part next to the network, were the two hundred pomegranates in rows all around. ²¹He erected the pillars at the portico of the temple. The pillar to the south he named Jakin*ᵐ* and the one to the north Boaz.*ⁿ* ²²The capitals on top were in the shape of lilies. And so the work on the pillars was completed.

²³He made the Sea of cast metal, circular in shape, measuring ten cubits*ᵉ* from rim to rim and five cubits high. It took a line of thirty cubits*ᵒ* to measure around it. ²⁴Below the rim, gourds encircled it—ten to a cubit. The gourds were cast in two rows in one piece with the Sea.

²⁵The Sea stood on twelve bulls, three facing north, three facing west, three facing south and three facing east. The Sea rested on top of them, and their hindquarters were toward the center. ²⁶It was a handbreadth*ᵖ* in thickness,

ᵃ2 That is, about 150 feet (about 46 meters) long, 75 feet (about 23 meters) wide and 45 feet (about 13.5 meters) high   *ᵇ5* The meaning of the Hebrew for this verse is uncertain.   *ᶜ6* That is, about 75 feet (about 23 meters) long and 45 feet (about 13.5 meters) wide   *ᵈ7* Vulgate and Syriac; Hebrew *floor*   *ᵉ10,23* That is, about 15 feet (about 4.5 meters)   *ᶠ10* That is, about 12 feet (about 3.6 meters)   *ᵍ13* Hebrew *Hiram*, a variant of *Huram*; also in verses 40 and 45   *ʰ15* That is, about 27 feet (about 8.1 meters) high and 18 feet (about 5.4 meters) around   *ⁱ16* That is, about 7 1/2 feet (about 2.3 meters); also in verse 23   *ʲ18* Two Hebrew manuscripts and Septuagint; most Hebrew manuscripts *made the pillars, and there were two rows*   *ᵏ18* Many Hebrew manuscripts and Syriac; most Hebrew manuscripts *pomegranates*   *ˡ19* That is, about 6 feet (about 1.8 meters); also in verse 38   *ᵐ21 Jakin* probably means *he establishes.*   *ⁿ21 Boaz* probably means *in him is strength.*   *ᵒ23* That is, about 45 feet (about 13.5 meters)   *ᵖ26* That is, about 3 inches (about 8 centimeters)

and its rim was like the rim of a cup, like a lily blossom. It held two thousand baths.*

²⁷He also made ten movable stands of bronze; each was four cubits long, four wide and three high.* ²⁸This is how the stands were made: They had side panels attached to uprights. ²⁹On the panels between the uprights were lions, bulls and cherubim—and on the uprights as well. Above and below the lions and bulls were wreaths of hammered work. ³⁰Each stand had four bronze wheels with bronze axles, and each had a basin resting on four supports, cast with wreaths on each side. ³¹On the inside of the stand there was an opening that had a circular frame one cubit deep. This opening was round, and with its basework it measured a cubit and a half.* Around its opening there was engraving. The panels of the stands were square, not round. ³²The four wheels were under the panels, and the axles of the wheels were attached to the stand. The diameter of each wheel was a cubit and a half. ³³The wheels were made like chariot wheels; the axles, rims, spokes and hubs were all of cast metal.

³⁴Each stand had four handles, one on each corner, projecting from the stand. ³⁵At the top of the stand there was a circular band half a cubit deep. The supports and panels were attached to the top of the stand. ³⁶He engraved cherubim, lions and palm trees on the surfaces of the supports and on the panels, in every available space, with wreaths all around. ³⁷This is the way he made the ten stands. They were all cast in the same molds and were identical in size and shape.

³⁸He then made ten bronze basins, each holding forty baths* and measuring four cubits across, one basin to go on each of the ten stands. ³⁹He placed five of the stands on the south side of the temple and five on the north. He placed the Sea on the south side, at the southeast corner of the temple. ⁴⁰He also made the basins and shovels and sprinkling bowls.

So Huram finished all the work he had undertaken for King Solomon in the temple of the Lord:

⁴¹the two pillars;
  the two bowl-shaped capitals on top of the pillars;
  the two sets of network decorating the two bowl-shaped capitals on top of the pillars;
⁴²the four hundred pomegranates for the two sets of network (two rows of pomegranates for each network, decorating the bowl-shaped capitals on top of the pillars);
⁴³the ten stands with their ten basins;
⁴⁴the Sea and the twelve bulls under it;
⁴⁵the pots, shovels and sprinkling bowls.

All these objects that Huram made for King Solomon for the temple of the Lord were of burnished bronze. ⁴⁶The king had them cast in clay molds in the plain of the Jordan between Succoth and Zarethan. ⁴⁷Solomon left all these things unweighed, because there were so many; the weight of the bronze was not determined.

⁴⁸Solomon also made all the furnishings that were in the Lord's temple:

the golden altar;
the golden table on which was the bread of the Presence;
⁴⁹the lampstands of pure gold (five on the right and five on the left, in front of the inner sanctuary);
the gold floral work and lamps and tongs;

---

*26 That is, probably about 11,500 gallons (about 44 kiloliters); the Septuagint does not have this sentence. *27 That is, about 6 feet (about 1.8 meters) long and wide and about 4 1/2 feet (about 1.3 meters) high *31 That is, about 1 1/2 feet (about 0.5 meter) *31 That is, about 2 1/4 feet (about 0.7 meter); also in verse 32 *35 That is, about 3/4 foot (about 0.2 meter) *38 That is, about 230 gallons (about 880 liters)

⁵⁰the pure gold basins, wick trimmers, sprinkling bowls, dishes and
censers;
and the gold sockets for the doors of the innermost room, the Most
Holy Place, and also for the doors of the main hall of the temple.

⁵¹When all the work King Solomon had done for the temple of the Lord was
finished, he brought in the things his father David had dedicated—the silver
and gold and the furnishings—and he placed them in the treasuries of the
Lord's temple.

The Ark Brought to the Temple Then King Solomon summoned into
his presence at Jerusalem the elders of Israel, all the heads of the
tribes and the chiefs of the Israelite families, to bring up the ark of the
Lord's covenant from Zion, the City of David. ²All the men of Israel came together to King Solomon at the time of the festival in the month of Ethanim,
the seventh month.

³When all the elders of Israel had arrived, the priests took up the ark, ⁴and
they brought up the ark of the Lord and the Tent of Meeting and all the sa-
cred furnishings in it. The priests and Levites carried them up, ⁵and King Solomon and the entire assembly of Israel that had gathered about him were
before the ark, sacrificing so many sheep and cattle that they could not be
recorded or counted.

⁶The priests then brought the ark of the Lord's covenant to its place in the
inner sanctuary of the temple, the Most Holy Place, and put it beneath the
wings of the cherubim. ⁷The cherubim spread their wings over the place of
the ark and overshadowed the ark and its carrying poles. ⁸These poles were
so long that their ends could be seen from the Holy Place in front of the inner sanctuary, but not from outside the Holy Place; and they are still there
today. ⁹There was nothing in the ark except the two stone tablets that Moses had placed in it at Horeb, where the Lord made a covenant with the Israelites after they came out of Egypt.

¹⁰When the priests withdrew from the Holy Place, the cloud filled the tem-
ple of the Lord. ¹¹And the priests could not perform their service because of
the cloud, for the glory of the Lord filled his temple.

¹²Then Solomon said, "The Lord has said that he would dwell in a dark
cloud; ¹³I have indeed built a magnificent temple for you, a place for you to
dwell forever."

¹⁴While the whole assembly of Israel was standing there, the king turned
around and blessed them. ¹⁵Then he said:

"Praise be to the Lord, the God of Israel, who with his own hand has
fulfilled what he promised with his own mouth to my father David. For
he said, ¹⁶'Since the day I brought my people Israel out of Egypt, I have
not chosen a city in any tribe of Israel to have a temple built for my
Name to be there, but I have chosen David to rule my people Israel.'

¹⁷"My father David had it in his heart to build a temple for the Name
of the Lord, the God of Israel. ¹⁸But the Lord said to my father David, 'Because it was in your heart to build a temple for my Name, you did well
to have this in your heart. ¹⁹Nevertheless, you are not the one to build
the temple, but your son, who is your own flesh and blood—he is the
one who will build the temple for my Name.'

²⁰"The Lord has kept the promise he made: I have succeeded David my
father and now I sit on the throne of Israel, just as the Lord promised,
and I have built the temple for the Name of the Lord, the God of Israel.
²¹I have provided a place there for the ark, in which is the covenant of
the Lord that he made with our fathers when he brought them out of
Egypt."

Solomon's Prayer of Dedication   ²²Then Solomon stood before the altar of the LORD in front of the whole assembly of Israel, spread out his hands toward heaven ²³and said:

"O LORD, God of Israel, there is no God like you in heaven above or on earth below—you who keep your covenant of love with your servants who continue wholeheartedly in your way. ²⁴You have kept your promise to your servant David my father; with your mouth you have promised and with your hand you have fulfilled it—as it is today.

²⁵"Now LORD, God of Israel, keep for your servant David my father the promises you made to him when you said, 'You shall never fail to have a man to sit before me on the throne of Israel, if only your sons are careful in all they do to walk before me as you have done.' ²⁶And now, O God of Israel, let your word that you promised your servant David my father come true.

> There is no God like you in heaven above or on earth below—you who keep your covenant of love
> (1 Kings 8:23).

²⁷"But will God really dwell on earth? The heavens, even the highest heaven, cannot contain you. How much less this temple I have built! ²⁸Yet give attention to your servant's prayer and his plea for mercy, O LORD my God. Hear the cry and the prayer that your servant is praying in your presence this day. ²⁹May your eyes be open toward this temple night and day, this place of which you said, 'My Name shall be there,' so that you will hear the prayer your servant prays toward this place. ³⁰Hear the supplication of your servant and of your people Israel when they pray toward this place. Hear from heaven, your dwelling place, and when you hear, forgive.

³¹"When a man wrongs his neighbor and is required to take an oath and he comes and swears the oath before your altar in this temple, ³²then hear from heaven and act. Judge between your servants, condemning the guilty and bringing down on his own head what he has done. Declare the innocent not guilty, and so establish his innocence.

³³"When your people Israel have been defeated by an enemy because they have sinned against you, and when they turn back to you and confess your name, praying and making supplication to you in this temple, ³⁴then hear from heaven and forgive the sin of your people Israel and bring them back to the land you gave to their fathers.

³⁵"When the heavens are shut up and there is no rain because your people have sinned against you, and when they pray toward this place and confess your name and turn from their sin because you have afflicted them, ³⁶then hear from heaven and forgive the sin of your servants, your people Israel. Teach them the right way to live, and send rain on the land you gave your people for an inheritance.

³⁷"When famine or plague comes to the land, or blight or mildew, locusts or grasshoppers, or when an enemy besieges them in any of their cities, whatever disaster or disease may come, ³⁸and when a prayer or plea is made by any of your people Israel—each one aware of the afflictions of his own heart, and spreading out his hands toward this temple— ³⁹then hear from heaven, your dwelling place. Forgive and act; deal with each man according to all he does, since you know his heart (for you alone know the hearts of all men), ⁴⁰so that they will fear you all the time they live in the land you gave our fathers.

⁴¹"As for the foreigner who does not belong to your people Israel but has come from a distant land because of your name— ⁴²for men will hear of your great name and your mighty hand and your outstretched arm— when he comes and prays toward this temple, ⁴³then hear from heaven, your dwelling place, and do whatever the foreigner asks of you, so that

all the peoples of the earth may know your name and fear you, as do your own people Israel, and may know that this house I have built bears your Name.

⁴⁴"When your people go to war against their enemies, wherever you send them, and when they pray to the Lord toward the city you have chosen and the temple I have built for your Name, ⁴⁵then hear from heaven their prayer and their plea, and uphold their cause.

⁴⁶"When they sin against you—for there is no one who does not sin— and you become angry with them and give them over to the enemy, who takes them captive to his own land, far away or near; ⁴⁷and if they have a change of heart in the land where they are held captive, and repent and plead with you in the land of their conquerors and say, 'We have sinned, we have done wrong, we have acted wickedly'; ⁴⁸and if they turn back to you with all their heart and soul in the land of their enemies who took them captive, and pray to you toward the land you gave their fathers, to- ward the city you have chosen and the temple I have built for your Name; ⁴⁹then from heaven, your dwelling place, hear their prayer and their plea, and uphold their cause. ⁵⁰And forgive your people, who have sinned against you; forgive all the offenses they have committed against you, and cause their conquerors to show them mercy; ⁵¹for they are your people and your inheritance, whom you brought out of Egypt, out of that iron-smelting furnace.

⁵²"May your eyes be open to your servant's plea and to the plea of your people Israel, and may you listen to them whenever they cry out to you. ⁵³For you singled them out from all the nations of the world to be your own inheritance, just as you declared through your servant Moses when you, O Sovereign Lord, brought our fathers out of Egypt."

⁵⁴When Solomon had finished all these prayers and supplications to the Lord, he rose from before the altar of the Lord, where he had been kneeling with his hands spread out toward heaven. ⁵⁵He stood and blessed the whole assembly of Israel in a loud voice, saying:

⁵⁶"Praise be to the Lord, who has given rest to his people Israel just as he promised. Not one word has failed of all the good promises he gave through his servant Moses. ⁵⁷May the Lord our God be with us as he was with our fathers; may he never leave us nor forsake us. ⁵⁸May he turn our hearts to him, to walk in all his ways and to keep the commands, decrees and regulations he gave our fathers. ⁵⁹And may these words of mine, which I have prayed before the Lord, be near to the Lord our God day and night, that he may uphold the cause of his servant and the cause of his peo- ple Israel according to each day's need, ⁶⁰so that all the peoples of the earth may know that the Lord is God and that there is no other. ⁶¹But your hearts must be fully com- mitted to the Lord our God, to live by his decrees and obey his com- mands, as at this time."

> May the Lord our God . . . never leave us nor forsake us
> (1 Kings 8:57).

The Dedication of the Temple ⁶²Then the king and all Israel with him offered sacrifices before the Lord. ⁶³Solomon offered a sacrifice of fellowship offer- ingsᵃ to the Lord: twenty-two thousand cattle and a hundred and twenty thousand sheep and goats. So the king and all the Israelites dedicated the temple of the Lord.

⁶⁴On that same day the king consecrated the middle part of the courtyard in front of the temple of the Lord, and there he offered burnt offerings,

---

ᵃ*63* Traditionally *peace offerings*; also in verse 64

grain offerings and the fat of the fellowship offerings, because the bronze altar before the LORD was too small to hold the burnt offerings, the grain offerings and the fat of the fellowship offerings.

⁶⁵So Solomon observed the festival at that time, and all Israel with him— a vast assembly, people from Lebo*ᵃ* Hamath to the Wadi of Egypt. They celebrated it before the LORD our God for seven days and seven days more, fourteen days in all. ⁶⁶On the following day he sent the people away. They blessed the king and then went home, joyful and glad in heart for all the good things the LORD had done for his servant David and his people Israel.

The LORD Appears to Solomon When Solomon had finished building the temple of the LORD and the royal palace, and had achieved all he had desired to do, ²the LORD appeared to him a second time, as he had appeared to him at Gibeon. ³The LORD said to him:

"I have heard the prayer and plea you have made before me; I have consecrated this temple, which you have built, by putting my Name there forever. My eyes and my heart will always be there.

⁴"As for you, if you walk before me in integrity of heart and uprightness, as David your father did, and do all I command and observe my decrees and laws, ⁵I will establish your royal throne over Israel forever, as I promised David your father when I said, 'You shall never fail to have a man on the throne of Israel.'

⁶"But if you*ᵇ* or your sons turn away from me and do not observe the commands and decrees I have given you*ᵇ* and go off to serve other gods and worship them, ⁷then I will cut off Israel from the land I have given them and will reject this temple I have consecrated for my Name. Israel will then become a byword and an object of ridicule among all peoples. ⁸And though this temple is now imposing, all who pass by will be appalled and will scoff and say, 'Why has the LORD done such a thing to this land and to this temple?' ⁹People will answer, 'Because they have forsaken the LORD their God, who brought their fathers out of Egypt, and have embraced other gods, worshiping and serving them—that is why the LORD brought all this disaster on them.' "

Solomon's Other Activities ¹⁰At the end of twenty years, during which Solomon built these two buildings—the temple of the LORD and the royal palace— ¹¹King Solomon gave twenty towns in Galilee to Hiram king of Tyre, because Hiram had supplied him with all the cedar and pine and gold he wanted. ¹²But when Hiram went from Tyre to see the towns that Solomon had given him, he was not pleased with them. ¹³"What kind of towns are these you have given me, my brother?" he asked. And he called them the Land of Cabul,*ᶜ* a name they have to this day. ¹⁴Now Hiram had sent to the king 120 talents*ᵈ* of gold.

¹⁵Here is the account of the forced labor King Solomon conscripted to build the LORD's temple, his own palace, the supporting terraces,*ᵉ* the wall of Jerusalem, and Hazor, Megiddo and Gezer. ¹⁶(Pharaoh king of Egypt had attacked and captured Gezer. He had set it on fire. He killed its Canaanite inhabitants and then gave it as a wedding gift to his daughter, Solomon's wife. ¹⁷And Solomon rebuilt Gezer.) He built up Lower Beth Horon, ¹⁸Baalath, and Tadmor*ᶠ* in the desert, within his land, ¹⁹as well as all his store cities and the towns for his chariots and for his horses*ᵍ*—whatever he desired to build in Jerusalem, in Lebanon and throughout all the territory he ruled.

²⁰All the people left from the Amorites, Hittites, Perizzites, Hivites and Jeb-

---

ᵃ65 Or from the entrance to ᵇ6 The Hebrew is plural. ᶜ13 Cabul sounds like the Hebrew for good-for-nothing. ᵈ14 That is, about 4 1/2 tons (about 4 metric tons) ᵉ15 Or the Millo; also in verse 24 ᶠ18 The Hebrew may also be read Tamar. ᵍ19 Or charioteers

usites (these peoples were not Israelites), ²¹that is, their descendants remaining in the land, whom the Israelites could not exterminate*ᵃ*—these Solomon conscripted for his slave labor force, as it is to this day. ²²But Solomon did not make slaves of any of the Israelites; they were his fighting men, his government officials, his officers, his captains, and the commanders of his chariots and charioteers. ²³They were also the chief officials in charge of Solomon's projects—550 officials supervising the men who did the work.

²⁴After Pharaoh's daughter had come up from the City of David to the palace Solomon had built for her, he constructed the supporting terraces.

²⁵Three times a year Solomon sacrificed burnt offerings and fellowship offerings*ᵇ* on the altar he had built for the LORD, burning incense before the LORD along with them, and so fulfilled the temple obligations.

²⁶King Solomon also built ships at Ezion Geber, which is near Elath in Edom, on the shore of the Red Sea.*ᶜ* ²⁷And Hiram sent his men—sailors who knew the sea—to serve in the fleet with Solomon's men. ²⁸They sailed to Ophir and brought back 420 talents*ᵈ* of gold, which they delivered to King Solomon.

10 *The Queen of Sheba Visits Solomon* When the queen of Sheba heard about the fame of Solomon and his relation to the name of the LORD, she came to test him with hard questions. ²Arriving at Jerusalem with a very great caravan—with camels carrying spices, large quantities of gold, and precious stones—she came to Solomon and talked with him about all that she had on her mind. ³Solomon answered all her questions; nothing was too hard for the king to explain to her. ⁴When the queen of Sheba saw all the wisdom of Solomon and the palace he had built, ⁵the food on his table, the seating of his officials, the attending servants in their robes, his cupbearers, and the burnt offerings he made at*ᵉ* the temple of the LORD, she was overwhelmed.

⁶She said to the king, "The report I heard in my own country about your achievements and your wisdom is true. ⁷But I did not believe these things until I came and saw with my own eyes. Indeed, not even half was told me; in wisdom and wealth you have far exceeded the report I heard. ⁸How happy your men must be! How happy your officials, who continually stand before you and hear your wisdom! ⁹Praise be to the LORD your God, who has delighted in you and placed you on the throne of Israel. Because of the LORD's eternal love for Israel, he has made you king, to maintain justice and righteousness."

¹⁰And she gave the king 120 talents*ᶠ* of gold, large quantities of spices, and precious stones. Never again were so many spices brought in as those the queen of Sheba gave to King Solomon.

¹¹(Hiram's ships brought gold from Ophir; and from there they brought great cargoes of almugwood*ᵍ* and precious

---

*ᵃ*21 The Hebrew term refers to the irrevocable giving over of things or persons to the LORD, often by totally destroying them.   *ᵇ*25 Traditionally *peace offerings*   *ᶜ*26 Hebrew *Yam Suph*; that is, Sea of Reeds   *ᵈ*28 That is, about 16 tons (about 14.5 metric tons)   *ᵉ*5 Or *the ascent by which he went up to*   *ᶠ*10 That is, about 4 1/2 tons (about 4 metric tons)   *ᵍ*11 Probably a variant of *algumwood*; also in verse 12

stones. ¹²The king used the almugwood to make supports for the temple of the LORD and for the royal palace, and to make harps and lyres for the musicians. So much almugwood has never been imported or seen since that day.)

¹³King Solomon gave the queen of Sheba all she desired and asked for, besides what he had given her out of his royal bounty. Then she left and returned with her retinue to her own country.

Solomon's Splendor   ¹⁴The weight of the gold that Solomon received yearly was 666 talents,ᵃ ¹⁵not including the revenues from merchants and traders and from all the Arabian kings and the governors of the land.

¹⁶King Solomon made two hundred large shields of hammered gold; six hundred bekasᵇ of gold went into each shield. ¹⁷He also made three hundred small shields of hammered gold, with three minasᶜ of gold in each shield. The king put them in the Palace of the Forest of Lebanon.

¹⁸Then the king made a great throne inlaid with ivory and overlaid with fine gold. ¹⁹The throne had six steps, and its back had a rounded top. On both sides of the seat were armrests, with a lion standing beside each of them. ²⁰Twelve lions stood on the six steps, one at either end of each step. Nothing like it had ever been made for any other kingdom. ²¹All King Solomon's goblets were gold, and all the household articles in the Palace of the Forest of Lebanon were pure gold. Nothing was made of silver, because silver was considered of little value in Solomon's days. ²²The king had a fleet of trading shipsᵈ at sea along with the ships of Hiram. Once every three years it returned, carrying gold, silver and ivory, and apes and baboons.

²³King Solomon was greater in riches and wisdom than all the other kings of the earth. ²⁴The whole world sought audience with Solomon to hear the wisdom God had put in his heart. ²⁵Year after year, everyone who came brought a gift—articles of silver and gold, robes, weapons and spices, and horses and mules.

²⁶Solomon accumulated chariots and horses; he had fourteen hundred chariots and twelve thousand horses,ᵉ which he kept in the chariot cities and also with him in Jerusalem. ²⁷The king made silver as common in Jerusalem as stones, and cedar as plentiful as sycamore-fig trees in the foothills. ²⁸Solomon's horses were imported from Egyptᶠ and from Kueᵍ—the royal merchants purchased them from Kue. ²⁹They imported a chariot from Egypt for six hundred shekelsʰ of silver, and a horse for a hundred and fifty.ⁱ They also exported them to all the kings of the Hittites and of the Arameans.

11 *Solomon's Wives*   King Solomon, however, loved many foreign women besides Pharaoh's daughter—Moabites, Ammonites, Edomites, Sidonians and Hittites. ²They were from nations about which the LORD had told the Israelites, "You must not intermarry with them, because they will surely turn your hearts after their gods." Nevertheless, Solomon held fast to them in love. ³He had seven hundred wives of royal birth and three hundred concubines, and his wives led him astray. ⁴As Solomon grew old, his wives turned his heart after other gods, and his heart was not fully devoted to the LORD his God, as the heart of David his father had been. ⁵He followed Ashtoreth the goddess of the Sidonians, and Molechʲ the detestable god of the Ammonites. ⁶So Solomon did evil in the eyes of the LORD; he did not follow the LORD completely, as David his father had done.

⁷On a hill east of Jerusalem, Solomon built a high place for Chemosh the

---

ᵃ14 That is, about 25 tons (about 23 metric tons)   ᵇ16 That is, about 7 1/2 pounds (about 3.5 kilograms)   ᶜ17 That is, about 3 3/4 pounds (about 1.7 kilograms)   ᵈ22 Hebrew *of ships of Tarshish*   ᵉ26 Or *charioteers*   ᶠ28 Or possibly *Muzur*, a region in Cilicia; also in verse 29   ᵍ28 Probably *Cilicia*   ʰ29 That is, about 15 pounds (about 7 kilograms)   ⁱ29 That is, about 3 3/4 pounds (about 1.7 kilograms)   ʲ5 Hebrew *Milcom*; also in verse 33

detestable god of Moab, and for Molech the detestable god of the Ammonites. [8]He did the same for all his foreign wives, who burned incense and offered sacrifices to their gods.

[9]The LORD became angry with Solomon because his heart had turned away from the LORD, the God of Israel, who had appeared to him twice. [10]Although he had forbidden Solomon to follow other gods, Solomon did not keep the LORD's command. [11]So the LORD said to Solomon, "Since this is your attitude and you have not kept my covenant and my decrees, which I commanded you, I will most certainly tear the kingdom away from you and give it to one of your subordinates. [12]Nevertheless, for the sake of David your father, I will not do it during your lifetime. I will tear it out of the hand of your son. [13]Yet I will not tear the whole kingdom from him, but will give him one tribe for the sake of David my servant and for the sake of Jerusalem, which I have chosen."

Solomon's Adversaries [14]Then the LORD raised up against Solomon an adversary, Hadad the Edomite, from the royal line of Edom. [15]Earlier when David was fighting with Edom, Joab the commander of the army, who had gone up to bury the dead, had struck down all the men in Edom. [16]Joab and all the Israelites stayed there for six months, until they had destroyed all the men in Edom. [17]But Hadad, still only a boy, fled to Egypt with some Edomite officials who had served his father. [18]They set out from Midian and went to Paran. Then taking men from Paran with them, they went to Egypt, to Pharaoh king of Egypt, who gave Hadad a house and land and provided him with food.

[19]Pharaoh was so pleased with Hadad that he gave him a sister of his own wife, Queen Tahpenes, in marriage. [20]The sister of Tahpenes bore him a son named Genubath, whom Tahpenes brought up in the royal palace. There Genubath lived with Pharaoh's own children.

[21]While he was in Egypt, Hadad heard that David rested with his fathers and that Joab the commander of the army was also dead. Then Hadad said to Pharaoh, "Let me go, that I may return to my own country."

[22]"What have you lacked here that you want to go back to your own country?" Pharaoh asked.

"Nothing," Hadad replied, "but do let me go!"

[23]And God raised up against Solomon another adversary, Rezon son of Eliada, who had fled from his master, Hadadezer king of Zobah. [24]He gathered men around him and became the leader of a band of rebels when David destroyed the forces[a] of Zobah; the rebels went to Damascus, where they settled and took control. [25]Rezon was Israel's adversary as long as Solomon lived, adding to the trouble caused by Hadad. So Rezon ruled in Aram and was hostile toward Israel.

Jeroboam Rebels Against Solomon
[26]Also, Jeroboam son of Nebat rebelled against the king. He was one of Solo-

[a]24 Hebrew *destroyed them*

---

1 KINGS 11:1–10

Holding hands. Kissing. A hug or kiss is exciting, even if you don't really like the guy or girl that much. Your hormones are pumping. Add the stimulation from TV, music and movies, and it's no surprise they pump overtime. Solomon's hormones pumped too, and he didn't control them. The king may have been wise, but he sure wasn't smart when it came to women. "His wives turned his heart after other gods" (1 Kings 11:4). You don't need to be ashamed of your hormones. It was God who designed you this way. But you do need to be careful that hormones don't turn your heart away from obedience to the Lord.

Direct Line

mon's officials, an Ephraimite from Zeredah, and his mother was a widow named Zeruah.

²⁷Here is the account of how he rebelled against the king: Solomon had built the supporting terraces*a* and had filled in the gap in the wall of the city of David his father. ²⁸Now Jeroboam was a man of standing, and when Solomon saw how well the young man did his work, he put him in charge of the whole labor force of the house of Joseph.

²⁹About that time Jeroboam was going out of Jerusalem, and Ahijah the prophet of Shiloh met him on the way, wearing a new cloak. The two of them were alone out in the country, ³⁰and Ahijah took hold of the new cloak he was wearing and tore it into twelve pieces. ³¹Then he said to Jeroboam, "Take ten pieces for yourself, for this is what the LORD, the God of Israel, says: 'See, I am going to tear the kingdom out of Solomon's hand and give you ten tribes. ³²But for the sake of my servant David and the city of Jerusalem, which I have chosen out of all the tribes of Israel, he will have one tribe. ³³I will do this because they have*b* forsaken me and worshiped Ashtoreth the goddess of the Sidonians, Chemosh the god of the Moabites, and Molech the god of the Ammonites, and have not walked in my ways, nor done what is right in my eyes, nor kept my statutes and laws as David, Solomon's father, did.

³⁴" 'But I will not take the whole kingdom out of Solomon's hand; I have made him ruler all the days of his life for the sake of David my servant, whom I chose and who observed my commands and statutes. ³⁵I will take the kingdom from his son's hands and give you ten tribes. ³⁶I will give one tribe to his son so that David my servant may always have a lamp before me in Jerusalem, the city where I chose to put my Name. ³⁷However, as for you, I will take you, and you will rule over all that your heart desires; you will be king over Israel. ³⁸If you do whatever I command you and walk in my ways and do what is right in my eyes by keeping my statutes and commands, as David my servant did, I will be with you. I will build you a dynasty as enduring as the one I built for David and will give Israel to you. ³⁹I will humble David's descendants because of this, but not forever.' "

⁴⁰Solomon tried to kill Jeroboam, but Jeroboam fled to Egypt, to Shishak the king, and stayed there until Solomon's death.

Solomon's Death ⁴¹As for the other events of Solomon's reign—all he did and the wisdom he displayed—are they not written in the book of the annals of Solomon? ⁴²Solomon reigned in Jerusalem over all Israel forty years. ⁴³Then he rested with his fathers and was buried in the city of David his father. And Rehoboam his son succeeded him as king.

Israel Rebels Against Rehoboam
12 Rehoboam went to Shechem, for all the Israelites had gone there to make him king. ²When Jeroboam son of Nebat heard this (he was still in Egypt,

---

Direct Line

1 KINGS 11:29–33

Have you ever noticed how some of your friends look like their parents? Or have their mannerisms? Like Melissa, who has her mom's way of sputtering when she's upset. If you were to make a list of ways you want to be like your dad or your mom, what would the top three traits be? How might you go about developing those traits? Solomon's problems can be traced to the fact that he failed to imitate his father David in one thing. David was faithful to God all his life and "walked in [God's] ways" (1Kings 11:33). David wasn't perfect. But he honestly tried to put God first. That's a family tradition you'll want to follow. Or begin!

---

*a*27 Or *the Millo* *b*33 Hebrew; Septuagint, Vulgate and Syriac *because he has*

where he had fled from King Solomon), he returned from*a* Egypt. ³So they sent for Jeroboam, and he and the whole assembly of Israel went to Rehoboam and said to him: ⁴"Your father put a heavy yoke on us, but now lighten the harsh labor and the heavy yoke he put on us, and we will serve you."

⁵Rehoboam answered, "Go away for three days and then come back to me." So the people went away.

⁶Then King Rehoboam consulted the elders who had served his father Solomon during his lifetime. "How would you advise me to answer these people?" he asked.

⁷They replied, "If today you will be a servant to these people and serve them and give them a favorable answer, they will always be your servants."

⁸But Rehoboam rejected the advice the elders gave him and consulted the young men who had grown up with him and were serving him. ⁹He asked them, "What is your advice? How should we answer these people who say to me, 'Lighten the yoke your father put on us'?"

¹⁰The young men who had grown up with him replied, "Tell these people who have said to you, 'Your father put a heavy yoke on us, but make our yoke lighter'—tell them, 'My little finger is thicker than my father's waist. ¹¹My father laid on you a heavy yoke; I will make it even heavier. My father scourged you with whips; I will scourge you with scorpions.' "

¹²Three days later Jeroboam and all the people returned to Rehoboam, as the king had said, "Come back to me in three days." ¹³The king answered the people harshly. Rejecting the advice given him by the elders, ¹⁴he followed the advice of the young men and said, "My father made your yoke heavy; I will make it even heavier. My father scourged you with whips; I will scourge you with scorpions." ¹⁵So the king did not listen to the people, for this turn of events was from the LORD, to fulfill the word the LORD had spoken to Jeroboam son of Nebat through Ahijah the Shilonite.

¹⁶When all Israel saw that the king refused to listen to them, they answered the king:

> "What share do we have in David,
>   what part in Jesse's son?
> To your tents, O Israel!
>   Look after your own house, O David!"

So the Israelites went home. ¹⁷But as for the Israelites who were living in the towns of Judah, Rehoboam still ruled over them.

¹⁸King Rehoboam sent out Adoniram,*b* who was in charge of forced labor, but all Israel stoned him to death. King Rehoboam, however, managed to get into his chariot and escape to Jerusalem. ¹⁹So Israel has been in rebellion against the house of David to this day.

²⁰When all the Israelites heard that Jeroboam had returned, they sent and called him to the assembly and made him king over all Israel. Only the tribe of Judah remained loyal to the house of David.

²¹When Rehoboam arrived in Jerusalem, he mustered the whole house of Judah and the tribe of Benjamin—a hundred and eighty thousand fighting men—to make war against the house of Israel and to regain the kingdom for Rehoboam son of Solomon.

²²But this word of God came to Shemaiah the man of God: ²³"Say to Rehoboam son of Solomon king of Judah, to the whole house of Judah and Benjamin, and to the rest of the people, ²⁴'This is what the LORD says: Do not go up to fight against your brothers, the Israelites. Go home, every one of you, for this is my doing.' " So they obeyed the word of the LORD and went home again, as the LORD had ordered.

---

*a2 Or he remained in   *b18 Some Septuagint manuscripts and Syriac (see also 1 Kings 4:6 and 5:14); Hebrew *Adoram*

Golden Calves at Bethel and Dan ²⁵Then Jeroboam fortified Shechem in the hill country of Ephraim and lived there. From there he went out and built up Peniel.ᵃ

²⁶Jeroboam thought to himself, "The kingdom will now likely revert to the house of David. ²⁷If these people go up to offer sacrifices at the temple of the LORD in Jerusalem, they will again give their allegiance to their lord, Rehoboam king of Judah. They will kill me and return to King Rehoboam."

²⁸After seeking advice, the king made two golden calves. He said to the people, "It is too much for you to go up to Jerusalem. Here are your gods, O Israel, who brought you up out of Egypt." ²⁹One he set up in Bethel, and the other in Dan. ³⁰And this thing became a sin; the people went even as far as Dan to worship the one there.

³¹Jeroboam built shrines on high places and appointed priests from all sorts of people, even though they were not Levites. ³²He instituted a festival on the fifteenth day of the eighth month, like the festival held in Judah, and offered sacrifices on the altar. This he did in Bethel, sacrificing to the calves he had made. And at Bethel he also installed priests at the high places he had made. ³³On the fifteenth day of the eighth month, a month of his own choosing, he offered sacrifices on the altar he had built at Bethel. So he instituted the festival for the Israelites and went up to the altar to make offerings.

13 **The Man of God From Judah** By the word of the LORD a man of God came from Judah to Bethel, as Jeroboam was standing by the altar to make an offering. ²He cried out against the altar by the word of the LORD: "O altar, altar! This is what the LORD says: 'A son named Josiah will be born to the house of David. On you he will sacrifice the priests of the high places who now make offerings here, and human bones will be burned on you.' " ³That same day the man of God gave a sign: "This is the sign the LORD has declared: The altar will be split apart and the ashes on it will be poured out."

⁴When King Jeroboam heard what the man of God cried out against the altar at Bethel, he stretched out his hand from the altar and said, "Seize him!" But the hand he stretched out toward the man shriveled up, so that he could not pull it back. ⁵Also, the altar was split apart and its ashes poured out according to the sign given by the man of God by the word of the LORD.

⁶Then the king said to the man of God, "Intercede with the LORD your God and pray for me that my hand may be restored." So the man of God interceded with the LORD, and the king's hand was restored and became as it was before.

⁷The king said to the man of God, "Come home with me and have something to eat, and I will give you a gift."

⁸But the man of God answered the king, "Even if you were to give me half your possessions, I would not go with you, nor would I eat bread or drink water here. ⁹For I was commanded by the word of the LORD: 'You must not eat bread or drink water or return by the way you came.' " ¹⁰So he took another road and did not return by the way he had come to Bethel.

THE DIVIDED KINGDOM

GREAT SEA

ISRAEL

SAMARIA

JERUSALEM

JUDAH

SEE 1 KINGS 12:16-24

ᵃ25 Hebrew *Penuel*, a variant of *Peniel*

¹¹Now there was a certain old prophet living in Bethel, whose sons came and told him all that the man of God had done there that day. They also told their father what he had said to the king. ¹²Their father asked them, "Which way did he go?" And his sons showed him which road the man of God from Judah had taken. ¹³So he said to his sons, "Saddle the donkey for me." And when they had saddled the donkey for him, he mounted it ¹⁴and rode after the man of God. He found him sitting under an oak tree and asked, "Are you the man of God who came from Judah?"

"I am," he replied.

¹⁵So the prophet said to him, "Come home with me and eat."

¹⁶The man of God said, "I cannot turn back and go with you, nor can I eat bread or drink water with you in this place. ¹⁷I have been told by the word of the LORD: 'You must not eat bread or drink water there or return by the way you came.' "

¹⁸The old prophet answered, "I too am a prophet, as you are. And an angel said to me by the word of the LORD: 'Bring him back with you to your house so that he may eat bread and drink water.' " (But he was lying to him.) ¹⁹So the man of God returned with him and ate and drank in his house.

²⁰While they were sitting at the table, the word of the LORD came to the old prophet who had brought him back. ²¹He cried out to the man of God who had come from Judah, "This is what the LORD says: 'You have defied the word of the LORD and have not kept the command the LORD your God gave you. ²²You came back and ate bread and drank water in the place where he told you not to eat or drink. Therefore your body will not be buried in the tomb of your fathers.' "

²³When the man of God had finished eating and drinking, the prophet who had brought him back saddled his donkey for him. ²⁴As he went on his way, a lion met him on the road and killed him, and his body was thrown down on the road, with both the donkey and the lion standing beside it. ²⁵Some people who passed by saw the body thrown down there, with the lion standing beside the body, and they went and reported it in the city where the old prophet lived.

²⁶When the prophet who had brought him back from his journey heard of it, he said, "It is the man of God who defied the word of the LORD. The LORD has given him over to the lion, which has mauled him and killed him, as the word of the LORD had warned him."

²⁷The prophet said to his sons, "Saddle the donkey for me," and they did so. ²⁸Then he went out and found the body thrown down on the road, with the donkey and the lion standing beside it. The lion had neither eaten the body nor mauled the donkey. ²⁹So the prophet picked up the body of the man of God, laid it on the donkey, and brought it back to his own city to mourn for him and bury him. ³⁰Then he laid the body in his own tomb, and they mourned over him and said, "Oh, my brother!"

³¹After burying him, he said to his sons, "When I die, bury me in the grave where the man of God is buried; lay my bones beside his bones. ³²For the message he declared by the word of the LORD against the altar in Bethel and against all the shrines on the high places in the towns of Samaria will certainly come true."

³³Even after this, Jeroboam did not change his evil ways, but once more appointed priests for the high places from all sorts of people. Anyone who wanted to become a priest he consecrated for the high places. ³⁴This was the sin of the house of Jeroboam that led to its downfall and to its destruction from the face of the earth.

14

Ahijah's Prophecy Against Jeroboam At that time Abijah Jeroboam became ill, ²and Jeroboam said to his wife, "Go yourself, so you won't be recognized as the wife of Jeroboam. Then

loh. Ahijah the prophet is there—the one who told me I would be king over this people. ³Take ten loaves of bread with you, some cakes and a jar of honey, and go to him. He will tell you what will happen to the boy." ⁴So Jeroboam's wife did what he said and went to Ahijah's house in Shiloh.

Now Ahijah could not see; his sight was gone because of his age. ⁵But the LORD had told Ahijah, "Jeroboam's wife is coming to ask you about her son, for he is ill, and you are to give her such and such an answer. When she arrives, she will pretend to be someone else."

⁶So when Ahijah heard the sound of her footsteps at the door, he said, "Come in, wife of Jeroboam. Why this pretense? I have been sent to you with bad news. ⁷Go, tell Jeroboam that this is what the LORD, the God of Israel, says: 'I raised you up from among the people and made you a leader over my people Israel. ⁸I tore the kingdom away from the house of David and gave it to you, but you have not been like my servant David, who kept my commands and followed me with all his heart, doing only what was right in my eyes. ⁹You have done more evil than all who lived before you. You have made for yourself other gods, idols made of metal; you have provoked me to anger and thrust me behind your back.

¹⁰'Because of this, I am going to bring disaster on the house of Jeroboam. I will cut off from Jeroboam every last male in Israel—slave or free. I will burn up the house of Jeroboam as one burns dung, until it is all gone. ¹¹Dogs will eat those belonging to Jeroboam who die in the city, and the birds of the air will feed on those who die in the country. The LORD has spoken!'

¹²"As for you, go back home. When you set foot in your city, the boy will die. ¹³All Israel will mourn for him and bury him. He is the only one belonging to Jeroboam who will be buried, because he is the only one in the house of Jeroboam in whom the LORD, the God of Israel, has found anything good.

¹⁴"The LORD will raise up for himself a king over Israel who will cut off the family of Jeroboam. This is the day! What? Yes, even now.ᵃ ¹⁵And the LORD will strike Israel, so that it will be like a reed swaying in the water. He will uproot Israel from this good land that he gave to their forefathers and scatter them beyond the River,ᵇ because they provoked the LORD to anger by making Asherah poles.ᶜ ¹⁶And he will give Israel up because of the sins Jeroboam has committed and has caused Israel to commit."

¹⁷Then Jeroboam's wife got up and left and went to Tirzah. As soon as she stepped over the threshold of the house, the boy died. ¹⁸They buried him, and all Israel mourned for him, as the LORD had said through his servant the prophet Ahijah.

¹⁹The other events of Jeroboam's reign, his wars and how he ruled, are written in the book of the annals of the kings of Israel. ²⁰He reigned for twenty-two years and then rested with his fathers. And Nadab his son succeeded him as king.

Rehoboam King of Judah ²¹Rehoboam son of Solomon was king in Judah. He was forty-one years old when he became king, and he reigned seventeen years in Jerusalem, the city the LORD had chosen out of all the tribes of Israel in which to put his Name. His mother's name was Naamah; she was an Ammonite.

²²Judah did evil in the eyes of the LORD. By the sins they committed they stirred up his jealous anger more than their fathers had done. ²³They also set up for themselves high places, sacred stones and Asherah poles on every

QUIZZER

1 KINGS 14

Q: What happened to all of Solomon's gold?

BONUS: What was all that gold used for?

Answers on page 426

ᵃ14 The meaning of the Hebrew for this sentence is uncertain.   ᵇ15 That is, the Euphrates   ᶜ15 That is, symbols of the goddess Asherah; here and elsewhere in 1 Kings

high hill and under every spreading tree. ²⁴There were even male shrine prostitutes in the land; the people engaged in all the detestable practices of the nations the Lᴏʀᴅ had driven out before the Israelites.

²⁵In the fifth year of King Rehoboam, Shishak king of Egypt attacked Jerusalem. ²⁶He carried off the treasures of the temple of the Lᴏʀᴅ and the treasures of the royal palace. He took everything, including all the gold shields Solomon had made. ²⁷So King Rehoboam made bronze shields to replace them and assigned these to the commanders of the guard on duty at the entrance to the royal palace. ²⁸Whenever the king went to the Lᴏʀᴅ's temple, the guards bore the shields, and afterward they returned them to the guardroom.

²⁹As for the other events of Rehoboam's reign, and all he did, are they not written in the book of the annals of the kings of Judah? ³⁰There was continual warfare between Rehoboam and Jeroboam. ³¹And Rehoboam rested with his fathers and was buried with them in the City of David. His mother's name was Naamah; she was an Ammonite. And Abijah*ᵃ* his son succeeded him as king.

15 *Abijah King of Judah*   In the eighteenth year of the reign of Jeroboam son of Nebat, Abijah*ᵇ* became king of Judah, ²and he reigned in Jerusalem three years. His mother's name was Maacah daughter of Abishalom.*ᶜ*

³He committed all the sins his father had done before him; his heart was not fully devoted to the Lᴏʀᴅ his God, as the heart of David his forefather had been. ⁴Nevertheless, for David's sake the Lᴏʀᴅ his God gave him a lamp in Jerusalem by raising up a son to succeed him and by making Jerusalem strong. ⁵For David had done what was right in the eyes of the Lᴏʀᴅ and had not failed to keep any of the Lᴏʀᴅ's commands all the days of his life—except in the case of Uriah the Hittite.

⁶There was war between Rehoboam*ᵈ* and Jeroboam throughout ͺAbijah's͵ lifetime. ⁷As for the other events of Abijah's reign, and all he did, are they not written in the book of the annals of the kings of Judah? There was war between Abijah and Jeroboam. ⁸And Abijah rested with his fathers and was buried in the City of David. And Asa his son succeeded him as king.

Asa King of Judah   ⁹In the twentieth year of Jeroboam king of Israel, Asa became king of Judah, ¹⁰and he reigned in Jerusalem forty-one years. His grandmother's name was Maacah daughter of Abishalom.

¹¹Asa did what was right in the eyes of the Lᴏʀᴅ, as his father David had done. ¹²He expelled the male shrine prostitutes from the land and got rid of all the idols his fathers had made. ¹³He even deposed his grandmother Maacah from her position as queen mother, because she had made a repulsive Asherah pole. Asa cut the pole down and burned it in the Kidron Valley. ¹⁴Although he did not remove the high places, Asa's heart was fully committed to the Lᴏʀᴅ all his life. ¹⁵He brought into the temple of the Lᴏʀᴅ the silver and gold and the articles that he and his father had dedicated.

¹⁶There was war between Asa and Baasha king of Israel throughout their reigns. ¹⁷Baasha king of Israel went up against Judah and fortified Ramah to prevent anyone from leaving or entering the territory of Asa king of Judah. ¹⁸Asa then took all the silver and gold that was left in the treasuries of the Lᴏʀᴅ's temple and of his own palace. He entrusted it to his officials and sent them to Ben-Hadad son of Tabrimmon, the son of Hezion, the king of Aram, who was ruling in Damascus. ¹⁹"Let there be a treaty between me and you," he said, "as there was between my father and your father. See, I am sendinͼ

ᵃ31 Some Hebrew manuscripts and Septuagint (see also 2 Chron. 12:16); most Hebrew manuscriptˢ *Abijam* *ᵇ1* Some Hebrew manuscripts and Septuagint (see also 2 Chron. 12:16); most Hebrew manuscripts *Abijam*; also in verses 7 and 8 *ᶜ2* A variant of *Absalom*; also in verse 10 *ᵈ6* Moˢ manuscripts; some Hebrew manuscripts and Syriac *Abijam* (that is, Abijah)

you a gift of silver and gold. Now break your treaty with Baasha king of Israel so he will withdraw from me."

²⁰Ben-Hadad agreed with King Asa and sent the commanders of his forces against the towns of Israel. He conquered Ijon, Dan, Abel Beth Maacah and all Kinnereth in addition to Naphtali. ²¹When Baasha heard this, he stopped building Ramah and withdrew to Tirzah. ²²Then King Asa issued an order to all Judah—no one was exempt—and they carried away from Ramah the stones and timber Baasha had been using there. With them King Asa built up Geba in Benjamin, and also Mizpah.

²³As for all the other events of Asa's reign, all his achievements, all he did and the cities he built, are they not written in the book of the annals of the kings of Judah? In his old age, however, his feet became diseased. ²⁴Then Asa rested with his fathers and was buried with them in the city of his father David. And Jehoshaphat his son succeeded him as king.

Answers

to Quizzer on
page 424

**A: After Judah
abandoned the
Lord, Pharaoh
Shishak captured
Jerusalem and
took Solomon's
gold to Egypt
(1 Kings
14:25-26).**

**BONUS: It was
used to beautify
the temples of
Egypt's gods.**

Nadab King of Israel ²⁵Nadab son of Jeroboam became king of Israel in the second year of Asa king of Judah, and he reigned over Israel two years. ²⁶He did evil in the eyes of the LORD, walking in the ways of his father and in his sin, which he had caused Israel to commit.

²⁷Baasha son of Ahijah of the house of Issachar plotted against him, and he struck him down at Gibbethon, a Philistine town, while Nadab and all Israel were besieging it. ²⁸Baasha killed Nadab in the third year of Asa king of Judah and succeeded him as king.

²⁹As soon as he began to reign, he killed Jeroboam's whole family. He did not leave Jeroboam anyone that breathed, but destroyed them all, according to the word of the LORD given through his servant Ahijah the Shilonite— ³⁰because of the sins Jeroboam had committed and had caused Israel to commit, and because he provoked the LORD, the God of Israel, to anger.

³¹As for the other events of Nadab's reign, and all he did, are they not written in the book of the annals of the kings of Israel? ³²There was war between Asa and Baasha king of Israel throughout their reigns.

Baasha King of Israel ³³In the third year of Asa king of Judah, Baasha son of Ahijah became king of all Israel in Tirzah, and he reigned twenty-four years. ³⁴He did evil in the eyes of the LORD, walking in the ways of Jeroboam and in his sin, which he had caused Israel to commit.

16 Then the word of the LORD came to Jehu son of Hanani against Baasha: ²"I lifted you up from the dust and made you leader of my people Israel, but you walked in the ways of Jeroboam and caused my people Israel to sin and to provoke me to anger by their sins. ³So I am about to consume Baasha and his house, and I will make your house like that of Jeroboam son of Nebat. ⁴Dogs will eat those belonging to Baasha who die in the city, and the birds of the air will feed on those who die in the country."

⁵As for the other events of Baasha's reign, what he did and his achievements, are they not written in the book of the annals of the kings of Israel? ⁶Baasha rested with his fathers and was buried in Tirzah. And Elah his son succeeded him as king.

⁷Moreover, the word of the LORD came through the prophet Jehu son of Hanani to Baasha and his house, because of all the evil he had done in the eyes of the LORD, provoking him to anger by the things he did, and becoming like the house of Jeroboam—and also because he destroyed it.

Elah King of Israel ⁸In the twenty-sixth year of Asa king of Judah, Elah son of Baasha became king of Israel, and he reigned in Tirzah two years.

⁹Zimri, one of his officials, who had command of half his chariots, plotted against him. Elah was in Tirzah at the time, getting drunk in the home of Arza, the man in charge of the palace at Tirzah. ¹⁰Zimri came in, struck him

down and killed him in the twenty-seventh year of Asa king of Judah. Then he succeeded him as king.

[11]As soon as he began to reign and was seated on the throne, he killed off Baasha's whole family. He did not spare a single male, whether relative or friend. [12]So Zimri destroyed the whole family of Baasha, in accordance with the word of the LORD spoken against Baasha through the prophet Jehu— [13]because of all the sins Baasha and his son Elah had committed and had caused Israel to commit, so that they provoked the LORD, the God of Israel, to anger by their worthless idols.

[14]As for the other events of Elah's reign, and all he did, are they not written in the book of the annals of the kings of Israel?

Zimri King of Israel   [15]In the twenty-seventh year of Asa king of Judah, Zimri reigned in Tirzah seven days. The army was encamped near Gibbethon, a Philistine town. [16]When the Israelites in the camp heard that Zimri had plotted against the king and murdered him, they proclaimed Omri, the commander of the army, king over Israel that very day there in the camp. [17]Then Omri and all the Israelites with him withdrew from Gibbethon and laid siege to Tirzah. [18]When Zimri saw that the city was taken, he went into the citadel of the royal palace and set the palace on fire around him. So he died, [19]because of the sins he had committed, doing evil in the eyes of the LORD and walking in the ways of Jeroboam and in the sin he had committed and had caused Israel to commit.

[20]As for the other events of Zimri's reign, and the rebellion he carried out, are they not written in the book of the annals of the kings of Israel?

Omri King of Israel   [21]Then the people of Israel were split into two factions; half supported Tibni son of Ginath for king, and the other half supported Omri. [22]But Omri's followers proved stronger than those of Tibni son of Ginath. So Tibni died and Omri became king.

[23]In the thirty-first year of Asa king of Judah, Omri became king of Israel, and he reigned twelve years, six of them in Tirzah. [24]He bought the hill of Samaria from Shemer for two talents*a* of silver and built a city on the hill, calling it Samaria, after Shemer, the name of the former owner of the hill.

[25]But Omri did evil in the eyes of the LORD and sinned more than all those before him. [26]He walked in all the ways of Jeroboam son of Nebat and in his sin, which he had caused Israel to commit, so that they provoked the LORD, the God of Israel, to anger by their worthless idols.

[27]As for the other events of Omri's reign, what he did and the things he achieved, are they not written in the book of the annals of the kings of Israel? [28]Omri rested with his fathers and was buried in Samaria. And Ahab his son succeeded him as king.

Ahab Becomes King of Israel   [29]In the thirty-eighth year of Asa king of Judah, Ahab son of Omri became king of Israel, and he reigned in Samaria over Israel twenty-two years. [30]Ahab son of Omri did more evil in the eyes of the LORD than any of those before him. [31]He not only considered it trivial to commit the sins of Jeroboam son of Nebat, but he also married Jezebel daughter of Ethbaal king of the Sidonians, and began to serve Baal and worship him. [32]He set up an altar for Baal in the temple of Baal that he built in Samaria. [33]Ahab also made an Asherah pole and did more to provoke the LORD, the God of Israel, to anger than did all the kings of Israel before him.

[34]In Ahab's time, Hiel of Bethel rebuilt Jericho. He laid its foundations at the cost of his firstborn son Abiram, and he set up its gates at the cost of his youngest son Segub, in accordance with the word of the LORD spoken by Joshua son of Nun.

---

a24 That is, about 150 pounds (about 70 kilograms)

17

Elijah Fed by Ravens Now Elijah the Tishbite, from Tishbe*a* in Gilead, said to Ahab, "As the Lord, the God of Israel, lives, whom I serve, there will be neither dew nor rain in the next few years except at my word."

²Then the word of the Lord came to Elijah: ³"Leave here, turn eastward and hide in the Kerith Ravine, east of the Jordan. ⁴You will drink from the brook, and I have ordered the ravens to feed you there."

⁵So he did what the Lord had told him. He went to the Kerith Ravine, east of the Jordan, and stayed there. ⁶The ravens brought him bread and meat in the morning and bread and meat in the evening, and he drank from the brook.

The Widow at Zarephath ⁷Some time later the brook dried up because there had been no rain in the land. ⁸Then the word of the Lord came to him: ⁹"Go at once to Zarephath of Sidon and stay there. I have commanded a widow in that place to supply you with food." ¹⁰So he went to Zarephath. When he came to the town gate, a widow was there gathering sticks. He called to her and asked, "Would you bring me a little water in a jar so I may have a drink?" ¹¹As she was going to get it, he called, "And bring me, please, a piece of bread."

¹²"As surely as the Lord your God lives," she replied, "I don't have any bread—only a handful of flour in a jar and a little oil in a jug. I am gathering a few sticks to take home and make a meal for myself and my son, that we may eat it—and die."

¹³Elijah said to her, "Don't be afraid. Go home and do as you have said. But first make a small cake of bread for me from what you have and bring it to me, and then make something for yourself and your son. ¹⁴For this is what the Lord, the God of Israel, says: 'The jar of flour will not be used up and the jug of oil will not run dry until the day the Lord gives rain on the land.' "

¹⁵She went away and did as Elijah had told her. So there was food every day for Elijah and for the woman and her family. ¹⁶For the jar of flour was not used up and the jug of oil did not run dry, in keeping with the word of the Lord spoken by Elijah.

¹⁷Some time later the son of the woman who owned the house became ill. He grew worse and worse, and finally stopped breathing. ¹⁸She said to Elijah, "What do you have against me, man of God? Did you come to remind me of my sin and kill my son?"

¹⁹"Give me your son," Elijah replied. He took him from her arms, carried him to the upper room where he was staying, and laid him on his bed. ²⁰Then he cried out to the Lord, "O Lord my God, have you brought tragedy also upon this widow I am staying with, by causing her son to die?" ²¹Then he stretched himself out on the boy three times and cried to the Lord, "O Lord my God, let this boy's life return to him!"

²²The Lord heard Elijah's cry, and the boy's life returned to him, and he lived. ²³Elijah picked up the child and carried

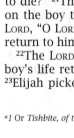

Direct Line

1 KINGS 17:13-14

A widow in a town called Zarephath had just enough food for one meal for herself and her son. The prophet Elijah told her not to be afraid, but to "first make a small cake of bread for me" (1 Kings 17:13). Put God's prophet first? When there wasn't enough for the woman and her son? If you remember the story, you know that God made the woman's pot of oil and jar of flour last for years. She put God first, and God provided for her needs. Can you apply this story to your life? You bet! Don't act because you feel you have to have something "right now." Put God first in all you do, and he'll meet your needs too.

a1 Or *Tishbite, of the settlers*

him down from the room into the house. He gave him to his mother and said, "Look, your son is alive!"

²⁴Then the woman said to Elijah, "Now I know that you are a man of God and that the word of the LORD from your mouth is the truth."

18 *Elijah and Obadiah* After a long time, in the third year, the word of the LORD came to Elijah: "Go and present yourself to Ahab, and I will send rain on the land." ²So Elijah went to present himself to Ahab.

Now the famine was severe in Samaria, ³and Ahab had summoned Obadiah, who was in charge of his palace. (Obadiah was a devout believer in the LORD. ⁴While Jezebel was killing off the LORD's prophets, Obadiah had taken a hundred prophets and hidden them in two caves, fifty in each, and had supplied them with food and water.) ⁵Ahab had said to Obadiah, "Go through the land to all the springs and valleys. Maybe we can find some grass to keep the horses and mules alive so we will not have to kill any of our animals." ⁶So they divided the land they were to cover, Ahab going in one direction and Obadiah in another.

⁷As Obadiah was walking along, Elijah met him. Obadiah recognized him, bowed down to the ground, and said, "Is it really you, my lord Elijah?"

⁸"Yes," he replied. "Go tell your master, 'Elijah is here.'"

⁹"What have I done wrong," asked Obadiah, "that you are handing your servant over to Ahab to be put to death? ¹⁰As surely as the LORD your God lives, there is not a nation or kingdom where my master has not sent someone to look for you. And whenever a nation or kingdom claimed you were not there, he made them swear they could not find you. ¹¹But now you tell me to go to my master and say, 'Elijah is here.' ¹²I don't know where the Spirit of the LORD may carry you when I leave you. If I go and tell Ahab and he doesn't find you, he will kill me. Yet I your servant have worshiped the LORD since my youth. ¹³Haven't you heard, my lord, what I did while Jezebel was killing the prophets of the LORD? I hid a hundred of the LORD's prophets in two caves, fifty in each, and supplied them with food and water. ¹⁴And now you tell me to go to my master and say, 'Elijah is here.' He will kill me!"

¹⁵Elijah said, "As the LORD Almighty lives, whom I serve, I will surely present myself to Ahab today."

Elijah on Mount Carmel ¹⁶So Obadiah went to meet Ahab and told him, and Ahab went to meet Elijah. ¹⁷When he saw Elijah, he said to him, "Is that you, you troubler of Israel?"

¹⁸"I have not made trouble for Israel," Elijah replied. "But you and your father's family have. You have abandoned the LORD's commands and have followed the Baals. ¹⁹Now summon the people from all over Israel to meet me on Mount Carmel. And bring the four hundred and fifty prophets of Baal and the four hundred prophets of Asherah, who eat at Jezebel's table."

²⁰So Ahab sent word throughout all Israel and assembled the prophets on Mount Carmel. ²¹Elijah went before the people and said, "How long will you waver between two opinions? If the LORD is God, follow him; but if Baal is God, follow him."

But the people said nothing.

²²Then Elijah said to them, "I am the only one of the LORD's prophets left, but Baal has four hundred and fifty prophets. ²³Get two bulls for us. Let them choose one for themselves, and let them cut it into pieces and put it on the wood but not set fire to it. I will prepare the other bull and put it on the wood but not set fire to it. ²⁴Then you call on the name of your god, and I will call on the name of the LORD. The god who answers by fire—he is God."

Then all the people said, "What you say is good."

²⁵Elijah said to the prophets of Baal, "Choose one of the bulls and prepare it first, since there are so many of you. Call on the name of your god, but do not light the fire." ²⁶So they took the bull given them and prepared it.

Then they called on the name of Baal from morning till noon. "O Baal, answer us!" they shouted. But there was no response; no one answered. And they danced around the altar they had made.

²⁷At noon Elijah began to taunt them. "Shout louder!" he said. "Surely he is a god! Perhaps he is deep in thought, or busy, or traveling. Maybe he is sleeping and must be awakened." ²⁸So they shouted louder and slashed themselves with swords and spears, as was their custom, until their blood flowed. ²⁹Midday passed, and they continued their frantic prophesying until the time for the evening sacrifice. But there was no response, no one answered, no one paid attention.

³⁰Then Elijah said to all the people, "Come here to me." They came to him, and he repaired the altar of the LORD, which was in ruins. ³¹Elijah took twelve stones, one for each of the tribes descended from Jacob, to whom the word of the LORD had come, saying, "Your name shall be Israel." ³²With the stones he built an altar in the name of the LORD, and he dug a trench around it large enough to hold two seahs*ᵃ* of seed. ³³He arranged the wood, cut the bull into pieces and laid it on the wood. Then he said to them, "Fill four large jars with water and pour it on the offering and on the wood."

³⁴"Do it again," he said, and they did it again.

"Do it a third time," he ordered, and they did it the third time. ³⁵The water ran down around the altar and even filled the trench.

³⁶At the time of sacrifice, the prophet Elijah stepped forward and prayed: "O LORD, God of Abraham, Isaac and Israel, let it be known today that you are God in Israel and that I am your servant and have done all these things at your command. ³⁷Answer me, O LORD, answer me, so these people will know that you, O LORD, are God, and that you are turning their hearts back again."

³⁸Then the fire of the LORD fell and burned up the sacrifice, the wood, the stones and the soil, and also licked up the water in the trench.

³⁹When all the people saw this, they fell prostrate and cried, "The LORD— he is God! The LORD—he is God!"

⁴⁰Then Elijah commanded them, "Seize the prophets of Baal. Don't let anyone get away!" They seized them, and Elijah had them brought down to the Kishon Valley and slaughtered there.

⁴¹And Elijah said to Ahab, "Go, eat and drink, for there is the sound of a heavy rain." ⁴²So Ahab went off to eat and drink, but Elijah climbed to the top of Carmel, bent down to the ground and put his face between his knees.

⁴³"Go and look toward the sea," he told his servant. And he went up and looked.

"There is nothing there," he said.

Seven times Elijah said, "Go back."

⁴⁴The seventh time the servant reported, "A cloud as small as a man's hand is rising from the sea."

So Elijah said, "Go and tell Ahab, 'Hitch up your chariot and go down before the rain stops you.'"

⁴⁵Meanwhile, the sky grew black with clouds, the wind rose, a heavy rain came on and Ahab rode off to Jezreel. ⁴⁶The power of the LORD came upon Elijah and, tucking his cloak into his belt, he ran ahead of Ahab all the way to Jezreel.

19 **Elijah Flees to Horeb** Now Ahab told Jezebel everything Elijah had done and how he had killed all the prophets with the sword. ²So Jezebel sent a messenger to Elijah to say, "May the gods deal with me, be it ever so severely, if by this time tomorrow I do not make your life like that of one of them."

ᵃ32 That is, probably about 13 quarts (about 15 liters)

³Elijah was afraid*a* and ran for his life. When he came to Beersheba in Judah, he left his servant there, ⁴while he himself went a day's journey into the desert. He came to a broom tree, sat down under it and prayed that he might die. "I have had enough, LORD," he said. "Take my life; I am no better than my ancestors." ⁵Then he lay down under the tree and fell asleep.

All at once an angel touched him and said, "Get up and eat." ⁶He looked around, and there by his head was a cake of bread baked over hot coals, and a jar of water. He ate and drank and then lay down again.

⁷The angel of the LORD came back a second time and touched him and said, "Get up and eat, for the journey is too much for you." ⁸So he got up and ate and drank. Strengthened by that food, he traveled forty days and forty nights until he reached Horeb, the mountain of God. ⁹There he went into a cave and spent the night.

The LORD Appears to Elijah   And the word of the LORD came to him: "What are you doing here, Elijah?"

¹⁰He replied, "I have been very zealous for the LORD God Almighty. The Israelites have rejected your covenant, broken down your altars, and put your prophets to death with the sword. I am the only one left, and now they are trying to kill me too."

¹¹The LORD said, "Go out and stand on the mountain in the presence of the LORD, for the LORD is about to pass by."

Then a great and powerful wind tore the mountains apart and shattered the rocks before the LORD, but the LORD was not in the wind. After the wind there was an earthquake, but the LORD was not in the earthquake. ¹²After the earthquake came a fire, but the LORD was not in the fire. And after the fire came a gentle whisper. ¹³When Elijah heard it, he pulled his cloak over his face and went out and stood at the mouth of the cave.

Then a voice said to him, "What are you doing here, Elijah?"

¹⁴He replied, "I have been very zealous for the LORD God Almighty. The Israelites have rejected your covenant, broken down your altars, and put your prophets to death with the sword. I am the only one left, and now they are trying to kill me too."

¹⁵The LORD said to him, "Go back the way you came, and go to the Desert of Damascus. When you get there, anoint Hazael king over Aram. ¹⁶Also, anoint Jehu son of Nimshi king over Israel, and anoint Elisha son of Shaphat from Abel Meholah to succeed you as prophet. ¹⁷Jehu will put to death any who escape the sword of Hazael, and Elisha will put to death any who escape the sword of Jehu. ¹⁸Yet I reserve seven thousand in Israel—all whose knees have not bowed down to Baal and all whose mouths have not kissed him."

The Call of Elisha   ¹⁹So Elijah went from there and found Elisha son of Shaphat. He was plowing with twelve yoke of oxen, and he himself was driving the twelfth pair. Elijah went up to him and threw his cloak around him. ²⁰Elisha then left his oxen and ran after Elijah. "Let me kiss my father and mother good-by," he said, "and then I will come with you."

"Go back," Elijah replied. "What have I done to you?"

²¹So Elisha left him and went back. He took his yoke of oxen and slaughtered them. He burned the plowing equipment to cook the meat and gave it to the people, and they ate. Then he set out to follow Elijah and became his attendant.

20 *Ben-Hadad Attacks Samaria*   Now Ben-Hadad king of Aram mustered his entire army. Accompanied by thirty-two kings with their horses and chariots, he went up and besieged Samaria and attacked it. ²He

---

*a*3 Or *Elijah saw*

Dear Sam,

I get so depressed sometimes. One of my friends says that Christians don't get depressed. Does that mean I'm not really a Christian?

Brett in Boise

Dear Sam, Inc.

100 Advice Lane, Anywhere, USA

Dear Brett,

I think that people who have never felt depressed can't understand what it's like. Many great believers have had periods of depression. Elijah, one of Israel's greatest prophets, was so depressed that he prayed that he would die (1 Kings 19:4). But God did not get angry with Elijah. He loved him. He fed him a nourishing meal so that he wouldn't be weak. He whispered to him gently and led him to a friend, Elisha. A good friend, good nutrition, communing with God—all can help depression.

You don't say why you're depressed. Has someone in your family died recently? Have your parents divorced? Have you moved? If so, you may be experiencing grief, which should not be confused with depression.

Much depression is caused by a chemical imbalance in the brain and can be helped by medications. Are you wrestling with a problem you can't handle on your own? Talking to a parent, pastor or counselor may help you find some answers. Look for the Elisha God may be sending your way.

Sam

sent messengers into the city to Ahab king of Israel, saying, "This is what Ben-Hadad says: ³'Your silver and gold are mine, and the best of your wives and children are mine.' "

⁴The king of Israel answered, "Just as you say, my lord the king. I and all I have are yours."

⁵The messengers came again and said, "This is what Ben-Hadad says: 'I sent to demand your silver and gold, your wives and your children. ⁶But about this time tomorrow I am going to send my officials to search your palace and the houses of your officials. They will seize everything you value and carry it away.' "

⁷The king of Israel summoned all the elders of the land and said to them, "See how this man is looking for trouble! When he sent for my wives and my children, my silver and my gold, I did not refuse him."

⁸The elders and the people all answered, "Don't listen to him or agree to his demands."

⁹So he replied to Ben-Hadad's messengers, "Tell my lord the king, 'Your servant will do all you demanded the first time, but this demand I cannot meet.' " They left and took the answer back to Ben-Hadad.

¹⁰Then Ben-Hadad sent another message to Ahab: "May the gods deal with me, be it ever so severely, if enough dust remains in Samaria to give each of my men a handful."

¹¹The king of Israel answered, "Tell him: 'One who puts on his armor should not boast like one who takes it off.' "

¹²Ben-Hadad heard this message while he and the kings were drinking in their tents,ᵃ and he ordered his men: "Prepare to attack." So they prepared to attack the city.

Ahab Defeats Ben-Hadad ¹³Meanwhile a prophet came to Ahab king of Israel and announced, "This is what the Lᴏʀᴅ says: 'Do you see this vast army? I will give it into your hand today, and then you will know that I am the Lᴏʀᴅ.' "

¹⁴"But who will do this?" asked Ahab.

The prophet replied, "This is what the Lᴏʀᴅ says: 'The young officers of the provincial commanders will do it.' "

"And who will start the battle?" he asked.

The prophet answered, "You will."

¹⁵So Ahab summoned the young officers of the provincial commanders, 232 men. Then he assembled the rest of the Israelites, 7,000 in all. ¹⁶They set out at noon while Ben-Hadad and the 32 kings allied with him were in their tents getting drunk. ¹⁷The young officers of the provincial commanders went out first.

Now Ben-Hadad had dispatched scouts, who reported, "Men are advancing from Samaria."

¹⁸He said, "If they have come out for peace, take them alive; if they have come out for war, take them alive."

¹⁹The young officers of the provincial commanders marched out of the city with the army behind them ²⁰and each one struck down his opponent. At that, the Arameans fled, with the Israelites in pursuit. But Ben-Hadad king of Aram escaped on horseback with some of his horsemen.

Shhhhh. One susurration from God is worth a thousand siroccos. (Look 'em up!)

SEE
1 KINGS 19:11-13

ᵃ12 Or *in Succoth*; also in verse 16

²¹The king of Israel advanced and overpowered the horses and chariots and inflicted heavy losses on the Arameans.

²²Afterward, the prophet came to the king of Israel and said, "Strengthen your position and see what must be done, because next spring the king of Aram will attack you again."

²³Meanwhile, the officials of the king of Aram advised him, "Their gods are gods of the hills. That is why they were too strong for us. But if we fight them on the plains, surely we will be stronger than they. ²⁴Do this: Remove all the kings from their commands and replace them with other officers. ²⁵You must also raise an army like the one you lost—horse for horse and chariot for chariot—so we can fight Israel on the plains. Then surely we will be stronger than they." He agreed with them and acted accordingly.

²⁶The next spring Ben-Hadad mustered the Arameans and went up to Aphek to fight against Israel. ²⁷When the Israelites were also mustered and given provisions, they marched out to meet them. The Israelites camped opposite them like two small flocks of goats, while the Arameans covered the countryside.

²⁸The man of God came up and told the king of Israel, "This is what the Lord says: 'Because the Arameans think the Lord is a god of the hills and not a god of the valleys, I will deliver this vast army into your hands, and you will know that I am the Lord.' "

²⁹For seven days they camped opposite each other, and on the seventh day the battle was joined. The Israelites inflicted a hundred thousand casualties on the Aramean foot soldiers in one day. ³⁰The rest of them escaped to the city of Aphek, where the wall collapsed on twenty-seven thousand of them. And Ben-Hadad fled to the city and hid in an inner room.

³¹His officials said to him, "Look, we have heard that the kings of the house of Israel are merciful. Let us go to the king of Israel with sackcloth around our waists and ropes around our heads. Perhaps he will spare your life."

³²Wearing sackcloth around their waists and ropes around their heads, they went to the king of Israel and said, "Your servant Ben-Hadad says: 'Please let me live.' "

The king answered, "Is he still alive? He is my brother."

³³The men took this as a good sign and were quick to pick up his word. "Yes, your brother Ben-Hadad!" they said.

"Go and get him," the king said. When Ben-Hadad came out, Ahab had him come up into his chariot.

³⁴"I will return the cities my father took from your father," Ben-Hadad offered. "You may set up your own market areas in Damascus, as my father did in Samaria."

Ahab said, "On the basis of a treaty I will set you free." So he made a treaty with him, and let him go.

A Prophet Condemns Ahab   ³⁵By the word of the Lord one of the sons of the prophets said to his companion, "Strike me with your weapon," but the man refused.

³⁶So the prophet said, "Because you have not obeyed the Lord, as soon as you leave me a lion will kill you." And after the man went away, a lion found him and killed him.

³⁷The prophet found another man and said, "Strike me, please." So the man struck him and wounded him. ³⁸Then the prophet went and stood by the road waiting for the king. He disguised himself with his headband down over his eyes. ³⁹As the king passed by, the prophet called out to him, "Your servant went into the thick of the battle, and someone came to me with a captive and said, 'Guard this man. If he is missing, it will be your life for his

life, or you must pay a talent*ª* of silver.' ⁴⁰While your servant was busy here and there, the man disappeared."

"That is your sentence," the king of Israel said. "You have pronounced it yourself."

⁴¹Then the prophet quickly removed the headband from his eyes, and the king of Israel recognized him as one of the prophets. ⁴²He said to the king, "This is what the Lᴏʀᴅ says: 'You have set free a man I had determined should die.*ᵇ* Therefore it is your life for his life, your people for his people.' " ⁴³Sullen and angry, the king of Israel went to his palace in Samaria.

21 *Naboth's Vineyard* Some time later there was an incident involving a vineyard belonging to Naboth the Jezreelite. The vineyard was in Jezreel, close to the palace of Ahab king of Samaria. ²Ahab said to Naboth, "Let me have your vineyard to use for a vegetable garden, since it is close to my palace. In exchange I will give you a better vineyard or, if you prefer, I will pay you whatever it is worth."

³But Naboth replied, "The Lᴏʀᴅ forbid that I should give you the inheritance of my fathers."

⁴So Ahab went home, sullen and angry because Naboth the Jezreelite had said, "I will not give you the inheritance of my fathers." He lay on his bed sulking and refused to eat.

⁵His wife Jezebel came in and asked him, "Why are you so sullen? Why won't you eat?"

⁶He answered her, "Because I said to Naboth the Jezreelite, 'Sell me your vineyard; or if you prefer, I will give you another vineyard in its place.' But he said, 'I will not give you my vineyard.' "

⁷Jezebel his wife said, "Is this how you act as king over Israel? Get up and eat! Cheer up. I'll get you the vineyard of Naboth the Jezreelite."

⁸So she wrote letters in Ahab's name, placed his seal on them, and sent them to the elders and nobles who lived in Naboth's city with him. ⁹In those letters she wrote:

"Proclaim a day of fasting and seat Naboth in a prominent place among the people. ¹⁰But seat two scoundrels opposite him and have them testify that he has cursed both God and the king. Then take him out and stone him to death."

¹¹So the elders and nobles who lived in Naboth's city did as Jezebel directed in the letters she had written to them. ¹²They proclaimed a fast and seated Naboth in a prominent place among the people. ¹³Then two scoundrels came and sat opposite him and brought charges against Naboth before the people, saying, "Naboth has cursed both God and the king." So they took him outside the city and stoned him to death. ¹⁴Then they sent word to Jezebel: "Naboth has been stoned and is dead."

¹⁵As soon as Jezebel heard that Naboth had been stoned to death, she said to Ahab, "Get up and take possession of the vineyard of Naboth the Jezreelite that he refused to sell you. He is no longer alive, but dead." ¹⁶When Ahab heard that Naboth was dead, he got up and went down to take possession of Naboth's vineyard.

¹⁷Then the word of the Lᴏʀᴅ came to Elijah the Tishbite: ¹⁸"Go down to meet Ahab king of Israel, who rules in Samaria. He is now in Naboth's vineyard, where he has gone to take possession of it. ¹⁹Say to him, 'This is what the Lᴏʀᴅ says: Have you not murdered a man and seized his property?' Then say to him, 'This is what the Lᴏʀᴅ says: In the place where dogs licked up Naboth's blood, dogs will lick up your blood—yes, yours!' "

ª39 That is, about 75 pounds (about 34 kilograms)   *ᵇ42* The Hebrew term refers to the irrevocable giving over of things or persons to the Lᴏʀᴅ, often by totally destroying them.

²⁰Ahab said to Elijah, "So you have found me, my enemy!"

"I have found you," he answered, "because you have sold yourself to do evil in the eyes of the Lord. ²¹'I am going to bring disaster on you. I will consume your descendants and cut off from Ahab every last male in Israel—slave or free. ²²I will make your house like that of Jeroboam son of Nebat and that of Baasha son of Ahijah, because you have provoked me to anger and have caused Israel to sin.'

²³"And also concerning Jezebel the Lord says: 'Dogs will devour Jezebel by the wall ofᵃ Jezreel.'

²⁴"Dogs will eat those belonging to Ahab who die in the city, and the birds of the air will feed on those who die in the country."

²⁵(There was never a man like Ahab, who sold himself to do evil in the eyes of the Lord, urged on by Jezebel his wife. ²⁶He behaved in the vilest manner by going after idols, like the Amorites the Lord drove out before Israel.)

²⁷When Ahab heard these words, he tore his clothes, put on sackcloth and fasted. He lay in sackcloth and went around meekly.

²⁸Then the word of the Lord came to Elijah the Tishbite: ²⁹"Have you noticed how Ahab has humbled himself before me? Because he has humbled himself, I will not bring this disaster in his day, but I will bring it on his house in the days of his son."

22 *Micaiah Prophesies Against Ahab* For three years there was no war between Aram and Israel. ²But in the third year Jehoshaphat king of Judah went down to see the king of Israel. ³The king of Israel had said to his officials, "Don't you know that Ramoth Gilead belongs to us and yet we are doing nothing to retake it from the king of Aram?"

⁴So he asked Jehoshaphat, "Will you go with me to fight against Ramoth Gilead?"

Jehoshaphat replied to the king of Israel, "I am as you are, my people as your people, my horses as your horses." ⁵But Jehoshaphat also said to the king of Israel, "First seek the counsel of the Lord."

⁶So the king of Israel brought together the prophets—about four hundred men—and asked them, "Shall I go to war against Ramoth Gilead, or shall I refrain?"

"Go," they answered, "for the Lord will give it into the king's hand."

⁷But Jehoshaphat asked, "Is there not a prophet of the Lord here whom we can inquire of?"

⁸The king of Israel answered Jehoshaphat, "There is still one man through whom we can inquire of the Lord, but I hate him because he never prophesies anything good about me, but always bad. He is Micaiah son of Imlah."

"The king should not say that," Jehoshaphat replied.

⁹So the king of Israel called one of his officials and said, "Bring Micaiah son of Imlah at once."

¹⁰Dressed in their royal robes, the king

Direct Line

1 KINGS 22

Who is a real friend? Someone who tells you what you want to hear? Or someone who tells you the truth? King Ahab didn't want to hear the truth, so he locked out a prophet of God and invited some prophets of Baal to speak. When he did finally hear what God's prophet had to say, Ahab learned he was going to die. If only Ahab had listened to God's prophet earlier, he might have had a very different end. God made sure that Ahab heard the truth. But even when Ahab heard, he refused to believe. Value friends who tell you the truth even when it isn't pleasant. Act on what they say, and you may avoid tragedy in your life.

ᵃ23 Most Hebrew manuscripts; a few Hebrew manuscripts, Vulgate and Syriac (see also 2 Kings 9:26) *the plot of ground at*

of Israel and Jehoshaphat king of Judah were sitting on their thrones at the threshing floor by the entrance of the gate of Samaria, with all the prophets prophesying before them. ¹¹Now Zedekiah son of Kenaanah had made iron horns and he declared, "This is what the LORD says: 'With these you will gore the Arameans until they are destroyed.' "

¹²All the other prophets were prophesying the same thing. "Attack Ramoth Gilead and be victorious," they said, "for the LORD will give it into the king's hand."

¹³The messenger who had gone to summon Micaiah said to him, "Look, as one man the other prophets are predicting success for the king. Let your word agree with theirs, and speak favorably."

¹⁴But Micaiah said, "As surely as the LORD lives, I can tell him only what the LORD tells me."

¹⁵When he arrived, the king asked him, "Micaiah, shall we go to war against Ramoth Gilead, or shall I refrain?"

"Attack and be victorious," he answered, "for the LORD will give it into the king's hand."

¹⁶The king said to him, "How many times must I make you swear to tell me nothing but the truth in the name of the LORD?"

¹⁷Then Micaiah answered, "I saw all Israel scattered on the hills like sheep without a shepherd, and the LORD said, 'These people have no master. Let each one go home in peace.' "

¹⁸The king of Israel said to Jehoshaphat, "Didn't I tell you that he never prophesies anything good about me, but only bad?"

¹⁹Micaiah continued, "Therefore hear the word of the LORD: I saw the LORD sitting on his throne with all the host of heaven standing around him on his right and on his left. ²⁰And the LORD said, 'Who will entice Ahab into attacking Ramoth Gilead and going to his death there?'

"One suggested this, and another that. ²¹Finally, a spirit came forward, stood before the LORD and said, 'I will entice him.'

²²" 'By what means?' the LORD asked.

" 'I will go out and be a lying spirit in the mouths of all his prophets,' he said.

" 'You will succeed in enticing him,' said the LORD. 'Go and do it.'

²³"So now the LORD has put a lying spirit in the mouths of all these prophets of yours. The LORD has decreed disaster for you."

²⁴Then Zedekiah son of Kenaanah went up and slapped Micaiah in the face. "Which way did the spirit from*a* the LORD go when he went from me to speak to you?" he asked.

²⁵Micaiah replied, "You will find out on the day you go to hide in an inner room."

²⁶The king of Israel then ordered, "Take Micaiah and send him back to Amon the ruler of the city and to Joash the king's son ²⁷and say, 'This is what the king says: Put this fellow in prison and give him nothing but bread and water until I return safely.' "

²⁸Micaiah declared, "If you ever return safely, the LORD has not spoken through me." Then he added, "Mark my words, all you people!"

Ahab Killed at Ramoth Gilead ²⁹So the king of Israel and Jehoshaphat king of Judah went up to Ramoth Gilead. ³⁰The king of Israel said to Jehoshaphat, "I will enter the battle in disguise, but you wear your royal robes." So the king of Israel disguised himself and went into battle.

³¹Now the king of Aram had ordered his thirty-two chariot commanders, "Do not fight with anyone, small or great, except the king of Israel." ³²When the chariot commanders saw Jehoshaphat, they thought, "Surely this is the

a24 Or Spirit of

king of Israel." So they turned to attack him, but when Jehoshaphat cried out, ³³the chariot commanders saw that he was not the king of Israel and stopped pursuing him.

³⁴But someone drew his bow at random and hit the king of Israel between the sections of his armor. The king told his chariot driver, "Wheel around and get me out of the fighting. I've been wounded." ³⁵All day long the battle raged, and the king was propped up in his chariot facing the Arameans. The blood from his wound ran onto the floor of the chariot, and that evening he died. ³⁶As the sun was setting, a cry spread through the army: "Every man to his town; everyone to his land!"

³⁷So the king died and was brought to Samaria, and they buried him there. ³⁸They washed the chariot at a pool in Samaria (where the prostitutes bathed),ᵃ and the dogs licked up his blood, as the word of the LORD had declared.

³⁹As for the other events of Ahab's reign, including all he did, the palace he built and inlaid with ivory, and the cities he fortified, are they not written in the book of the annals of the kings of Israel? ⁴⁰Ahab rested with his fathers. And Ahaziah his son succeeded him as king.

Jehoshaphat King of Judah ⁴¹Jehoshaphat son of Asa became king of Judah in the fourth year of Ahab king of Israel. ⁴²Jehoshaphat was thirty-five years old when he became king, and he reigned in Jerusalem twenty-five years. His mother's name was Azubah daughter of Shilhi. ⁴³In everything he walked in the ways of his father Asa and did not stray from them; he did what was right in the eyes of the LORD. The high places, however, were not removed, and the people continued to offer sacrifices and burn incense there. ⁴⁴Jehoshaphat was also at peace with the king of Israel.

⁴⁵As for the other events of Jehoshaphat's reign, the things he achieved and his military exploits, are they not written in the book of the annals of the kings of Judah? ⁴⁶He rid the land of the rest of the male shrine prostitutes who remained there even after the reign of his father Asa. ⁴⁷There was then no king in Edom; a deputy ruled.

⁴⁸Now Jehoshaphat built a fleet of trading shipsᵇ to go to Ophir for gold, but they never set sail—they were wrecked at Ezion Geber. ⁴⁹At that time Ahaziah son of Ahab said to Jehoshaphat, "Let my men sail with your men," but Jehoshaphat refused.

⁵⁰Then Jehoshaphat rested with his fathers and was buried with them in the city of David his father. And Jehoram his son succeeded him.

Ahaziah King of Israel ⁵¹Ahaziah son of Ahab became king of Israel in Samaria in the seventeenth year of Jehoshaphat king of Judah, and he reigned over Israel two years. ⁵²He did evil in the eyes of the LORD, because he walked in the ways of his father and mother and in the ways of Jeroboam son of Nebat, who caused Israel to sin. ⁵³He served and worshiped Baal and provoked the LORD, the God of Israel, to anger, just as his father had done.

ᵃ38 Or *Samaria and cleaned the weapons* ᵇ48 Hebrew *of ships of Tarshish*

WARNINGS?

You don't want to hear them? Nothing will happen to you? Actually, most people think this way when they're determined to do something they know is dangerous or wrong.

The book of 2 Kings is full of stories telling how God warned his people and how they refused to listen. Even when the northern Israelite kingdom was taken into captivity by the Assyrians in 722 B.C., the southern kingdom wouldn't change its ways. Some people think the stories about these kings are boring. But what you can learn from them might save your life.

Fundamentals

Do you think God really takes care of his people in hard times (2 Kings 4:1-7)?

Can you think of anything that God isn't able to do (2 Kings 7:5-9)?

What is the first thing you do when you're in trouble (2 Kings 19:14-19)?

How would you describe a person who wants to please God (2 Kings 23:24-25)?

FAST FACTS

For 108 years the northern kingdom didn't have one good king!

The southern kingdom was led by godly kings for 234 of its 344 years.

Judah was conquered by Nebuchadnezzar in 586 B.C.

Nebuchadnezzar deported the people to Babylon where they stayed for 70 years.

The LORD's Judgment on Ahaziah After Ahab's death, Moab rebelled against Israel. ²Now Ahaziah had fallen through the lattice of his upper room in Samaria and injured himself. So he sent messengers, saying to them, "Go and consult Baal-Zebub, the god of Ekron, to see if I will recover from this injury."

³But the angel of the LORD said to Elijah the Tishbite, "Go up and meet the messengers of the king of Samaria and ask them, 'Is it because there is no God in Israel that you are going off to consult Baal-Zebub, the god of Ekron?' ⁴Therefore this is what the LORD says: 'You will not leave the bed you are lying on. You will certainly die!' " So Elijah went.

⁵When the messengers returned to the king, he asked them, "Why have you come back?"

⁶"A man came to meet us," they replied. "And he said to us, 'Go back to the king who sent you and tell him, "This is what the LORD says: Is it because there is no God in Israel that you are sending men to consult Baal-Zebub, the god of Ekron? Therefore you will not leave the bed you are lying on. You will certainly die!" ' "

⁷The king asked them, "What kind of man was it who came to meet you and told you this?"

⁸They replied, "He was a man with a garment of hair and with a leather belt around his waist."

The king said, "That was Elijah the Tishbite."

⁹Then he sent to Elijah a captain with his company of fifty men. The captain went up to Elijah, who was sitting on the top of a hill, and said to him, "Man of God, the king says, 'Come down!' "

¹⁰Elijah answered the captain, "If I am a man of God, may fire come down from heaven and consume you and your fifty men!" Then fire fell from heaven and consumed the captain and his men.

¹¹At this the king sent to Elijah another captain with his fifty men. The captain said to him, "Man of God, this is what the king says, 'Come down at once!' "

¹²"If I am a man of God," Elijah replied, "may fire come down from heaven and consume you and your fifty men!" Then the fire of God fell from heaven and consumed him and his fifty men.

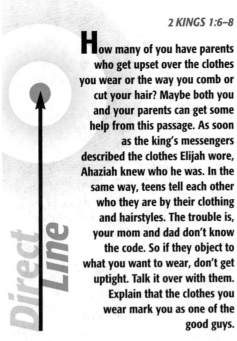

2 KINGS 1:6–8

How many of you have parents who get upset over the clothes you wear or the way you comb or cut your hair? Maybe both you and your parents can get some help from this passage. As soon as the king's messengers described the clothes Elijah wore, Ahaziah knew who he was. In the same way, teens tell each other who they are by their clothing and hairstyles. The trouble is, your mom and dad don't know the code. So if they object to what you want to wear, don't get uptight. Talk it over with them. Explain that the clothes you wear mark you as one of the good guys.

Direct Line

¹³So the king sent a third captain with his fifty men. This third captain went up and fell on his knees before Elijah. "Man of God," he begged, "please have respect for my life and the lives of these fifty men, your servants! ¹⁴See, fire has fallen from heaven and consumed the first two captains and all their men. But now have respect for my life!"

¹⁵The angel of the LORD said to Elijah, "Go down with him; do not be afraid of him." So Elijah got up and went down with him to the king.

¹⁶He told the king, "This is what the LORD says: Is it because there is no God in Israel for you to consult that you have sent messengers to consult Baal-Zebub, the god of Ek-

ron? Because you have done this, you will never leave the bed you are lying on. You will certainly die!" ¹⁷So he died, according to the word of the Lᴏʀᴅ that Elijah had spoken.

Because Ahaziah had no son, Joramᵃ succeeded him as king in the second year of Jehoram son of Jehoshaphat king of Judah. ¹⁸As for all the other events of Ahaziah's reign, and what he did, are they not written in the book of the annals of the kings of Israel?

Elijah Taken Up to Heaven When the Lᴏʀᴅ was about to take Elijah up to heaven in a whirlwind, Elijah and Elisha were on their way from Gilgal. ²Elijah said to Elisha, "Stay here; the Lᴏʀᴅ has sent me to Bethel."

But Elisha said, "As surely as the Lᴏʀᴅ lives and as you live, I will not leave you." So they went down to Bethel.

³The company of the prophets at Bethel came out to Elisha and asked, "Do you know that the Lᴏʀᴅ is going to take your master from you today?"

"Yes, I know," Elisha replied, "but do not speak of it."

⁴Then Elijah said to him, "Stay here, Elisha; the Lᴏʀᴅ has sent me to Jericho."

And he replied, "As surely as the Lᴏʀᴅ lives and as you live, I will not leave you." So they went to Jericho.

⁵The company of the prophets at Jericho went up to Elisha and asked him, "Do you know that the Lᴏʀᴅ is going to take your master from you today?"

"Yes, I know," he replied, "but do not speak of it."

⁶Then Elijah said to him, "Stay here; the Lᴏʀᴅ has sent me to the Jordan."

And he replied, "As surely as the Lᴏʀᴅ lives and as you live, I will not leave you." So the two of them walked on.

⁷Fifty men of the company of the prophets went and stood at a distance, facing the place where Elijah and Elisha had stopped at the Jordan. ⁸Elijah took his cloak, rolled it up and struck the water with it. The water divided to the right and to the left, and the two of them crossed over on dry ground.

⁹When they had crossed, Elijah said to Elisha, "Tell me, what can I do for you before I am taken from you?"

"Let me inherit a double portion of your spirit," Elisha replied.

¹⁰"You have asked a difficult thing," Elijah said, "yet if you see me when I am taken from you, it will be yours—otherwise not."

¹¹As they were walking along and talking together, suddenly a chariot of fire and horses of fire appeared and separated the two of them, and Elijah went up to heaven in a whirlwind. ¹²Elisha saw this and cried out, "My father! My father! The chariots and horsemen of Israel!" And Elisha saw him no more. Then he took hold of his own clothes and tore them apart.

¹³He picked up the cloak that had fallen from Elijah and went back and stood on the bank of the Jordan. ¹⁴Then he took the cloak that had fallen from him and struck the water with it. "Where now is the Lᴏʀᴅ, the God of Elijah?" he asked. When he struck the water, it divided to the right and to the left, and he crossed over.

¹⁵The company of the prophets from Jericho, who were watching, said, "The spirit of Elijah is resting on Elisha." And they went to meet him and bowed to the ground before him. ¹⁶"Look," they said, "we your servants have fifty able men. Let them go and look for your master. Perhaps the Spirit of the Lᴏʀᴅ has picked him up and set him down on some mountain or in some valley."

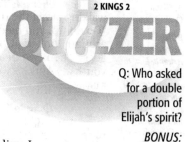

2 KINGS 2

Q: Who asked for a double portion of Elijah's spirit?

BONUS: What did that request mean?

Answers on page 442

ᵃ17 Hebrew *Jehoram*, a variant of *Joram*

"No," Elisha replied, "do not send them."

[17]But they persisted until he was too ashamed to refuse. So he said, "Send them." And they sent fifty men, who searched for three days but did not find him. [18]When they returned to Elisha, who was staying in Jericho, he said to them, "Didn't I tell you not to go?"

Healing of the Water [19]The men of the city said to Elisha, "Look, our lord, this town is well situated, as you can see, but the water is bad and the land is unproductive."

[20]"Bring me a new bowl," he said, "and put salt in it." So they brought it to him.

[21]Then he went out to the spring and threw the salt into it, saying, "This is what the LORD says: 'I have healed this water. Never again will it cause death or make the land unproductive.' " [22]And the water has remained wholesome to this day, according to the word Elisha had spoken.

Answers
to Quizzer on page 441

Elisha Is Jeered [23]From there Elisha went up to Bethel. As he was walking along the road, some youths came out of the town and jeered at him. "Go on up, you baldhead!" they said. "Go on up, you baldhead!" [24]He turned around, looked at them and called down a curse on them in the name of the LORD. Then two bears came out of the woods and mauled forty-two of the youths. [25]And he went on to Mount Carmel and from there returned to Samaria.

Moab Revolts Joram[a] son of Ahab became king of Israel in Samaria in the eighteenth year of Jehoshaphat king of Judah, and he reigned twelve years. [2]He did evil in the eyes of the LORD, but not as his father and mother had done. He got rid of the sacred stone of Baal that his father had made. [3]Nevertheless he clung to the sins of Jeroboam son of Nebat, which he had caused Israel to commit; he did not turn away from them.

[4]Now Mesha king of Moab raised sheep, and he had to supply the king of Israel with a hundred thousand lambs and with the wool of a hundred thousand rams. [5]But after Ahab died, the king of Moab rebelled against the king of Israel. [6]So at that time King Joram set out from Samaria and mobilized all Israel. [7]He also sent this message to Jehoshaphat king of Judah: "The king of Moab has rebelled against me. Will you go with me to fight against Moab?"

"I will go with you," he replied. "I am as you are, my people as your people, my horses as your horses."

[8]"By what route shall we attack?" he asked.

"Through the Desert of Edom," he answered.

[9]So the king of Israel set out with the king of Judah and the king of Edom. After a roundabout march of seven days, the army had no more water for themselves or for the animals with them.

[10]"What!" exclaimed the king of Israel. "Has the LORD called us three kings together only to hand us over to Moab?"

[11]But Jehoshaphat asked, "Is there no prophet of the LORD here, that we may inquire of the LORD through him?"

An officer of the king of Israel answered, "Elisha son of Shaphat is here. He used to pour water on the hands of Elijah.[b]"

[12]Jehoshaphat said, "The word of the LORD is with him." So the king of Israel and Jehoshaphat and the king of Edom went down to him.

[13]Elisha said to the king of Israel, "What do we have to do with each other? Go to the prophets of your father and the prophets of your mother."

---

[a]1 Hebrew Jehoram, a variant of Joram; also in verse 6 [b]11 That is, he was Elijah's personal servant.

"No," the king of Israel answered, "because it was the LORD who called us three kings together to hand us over to Moab."

¹⁴Elisha said, "As surely as the LORD Almighty lives, whom I serve, if I did not have respect for the presence of Jehoshaphat king of Judah, I would not look at you or even notice you. ¹⁵But now bring me a harpist."

While the harpist was playing, the hand of the LORD came upon Elisha ¹⁶and he said, "This is what the LORD says: Make this valley full of ditches. ¹⁷For this is what the LORD says: You will see neither wind nor rain, yet this valley will be filled with water, and you, your cattle and your other animals will drink. ¹⁸This is an easy thing in the eyes of the LORD; he will also hand Moab over to you. ¹⁹You will overthrow every fortified city and every major town. You will cut down every good tree, stop up all the springs, and ruin every good field with stones."

²⁰The next morning, about the time for offering the sacrifice, there it was—water flowing from the direction of Edom! And the land was filled with water.

²¹Now all the Moabites had heard that the kings had come to fight against them; so every man, young and old, who could bear arms was called up and stationed on the border. ²²When they got up early in the morning, the sun was shining on the water. To the Moabites across the way, the water looked red—like blood. ²³"That's blood!" they said. "Those kings must have fought and slaughtered each other. Now to the plunder, Moab!"

²⁴But when the Moabites came to the camp of Israel, the Israelites rose up and fought them until they fled. And the Israelites invaded the land and slaughtered the Moabites. ²⁵They destroyed the towns, and each man threw a stone on every good field until it was covered. They stopped up all the springs and cut down every good tree. Only Kir Hareseth was left with its stones in place, but men armed with slings surrounded it and attacked it as well.

²⁶When the king of Moab saw that the battle had gone against him, he took with him seven hundred swordsmen to break through to the king of Edom, but they failed. ²⁷Then he took his firstborn son, who was to succeed him as king, and offered him as a sacrifice on the city wall. The fury against Israel was great; they withdrew and returned to their own land.

The Widow's Oil The wife of a man from the company of the prophets cried out to Elisha, "Your servant my husband is dead, and you know that he revered the LORD. But now his creditor is coming to take my two boys as his slaves."

²Elisha replied to her, "How can I help you? Tell me, what do you have in your house?"

"Your servant has nothing there at all," she said, "except a little oil."

³Elisha said, "Go around and ask all your neighbors for empty jars. Don't ask for just a few. ⁴Then go inside and shut the door behind you and your sons. Pour oil into all the jars, and as each is filled, put it to one side."

⁵She left him and afterward shut the door behind her and her sons. They brought the jars to her and she kept pouring. ⁶When all the jars were full, she said to her son, "Bring me another one."

But he replied, "There is not a jar left." Then the oil stopped flowing.

⁷She went and told the man of God, and he said, "Go, sell the oil and pay your debts. You and your sons can live on what is left."

The Shunammite's Son Restored to Life ⁸One day Elisha went to Shunem. And a well-to-do woman was there, who urged him to stay for a meal. So whenever he came by, he stopped there to eat. ⁹She said to her husband, "I know that this man who often comes our way is a holy man of God. ¹⁰Let's make a small room on the roof and put in it a bed and a table, a chair and a lamp for him. Then he can stay there whenever he comes to us."

¹¹One day when Elisha came, he went up to his room and lay down there. ¹²He said to his servant Gehazi, "Call the Shunammite." So he called her,

and she stood before him. ¹³Elisha said to him, "Tell her, 'You have gone to all this trouble for us. Now what can be done for you? Can we speak on your behalf to the king or the commander of the army?' "

She replied, "I have a home among my own people."

¹⁴"What can be done for her?" Elisha asked.

Gehazi said, "Well, she has no son and her husband is old."

¹⁵Then Elisha said, "Call her." So he called her, and she stood in the door-way. ¹⁶"About this time next year," Elisha said, "you will hold a son in your arms."

"No, my lord," she objected. "Don't mislead your servant, O man of God!"

¹⁷But the woman became pregnant, and the next year about that same time she gave birth to a son, just as Elisha had told her.

¹⁸The child grew, and one day he went out to his father, who was with the reapers. ¹⁹"My head! My head!" he said to his father.

His father told a servant, "Carry him to his mother." ²⁰After the servant had lifted him up and carried him to his mother, the boy sat on her lap un-til noon, and then he died. ²¹She went up and laid him on the bed of the man of God, then shut the door and went out.

²²She called her husband and said, "Please send me one of the servants and a donkey so I can go to the man of God quickly and return."

²³"Why go to him today?" he asked. "It's not the New Moon or the Sabbath."

"It's all right," she said.

²⁴She saddled the donkey and said to her servant, "Lead on; don't slow down for me unless I tell you." ²⁵So she set out and came to the man of God at Mount Carmel.

When he saw her in the distance, the man of God said to his servant Ge-hazi, "Look! There's the Shunammite! ²⁶Run to meet her and ask her, 'Are you all right? Is your husband all right? Is your child all right?' "

"Everything is all right," she said.

²⁷When she reached the man of God at the mountain, she took hold of his feet. Gehazi came over to push her away, but the man of God said, "Leave her alone! She is in bitter distress, but the LORD has hidden it from me and has not told me why."

²⁸"Did I ask you for a son, my lord?" she said. "Didn't I tell you, 'Don't raise my hopes'?"

²⁹Elisha said to Gehazi, "Tuck your cloak into your belt, take my staff in your hand and run. If you meet anyone, do not greet him, and if anyone greets you, do not answer. Lay my staff on the boy's face."

³⁰But the child's mother said, "As surely as the LORD lives and as you live, I will not leave you." So he got up and followed her.

³¹Gehazi went on ahead and laid the staff on the boy's face, but there was no sound or response. So Gehazi went back to meet Elisha and told him, "The boy has not awakened."

³²When Elisha reached the house, there was the boy lying dead on his couch. ³³He went in, shut the door on the two of them and prayed to the LORD. ³⁴Then he got on the bed and lay upon the boy, mouth to mouth, eyes to eyes, hands to hands. As he stretched himself out upon him, the boy's body grew warm. ³⁵Elisha turned away and walked back and forth in the room and then got on the bed and stretched out upon him once more. The boy sneezed seven times and opened his eyes.

³⁶Elisha summoned Gehazi and said, "Call the Shunammite." And he did. When she came, he said, "Take your son." ³⁷She came in, fell at his feet and bowed to the ground. Then she took her son and went out.

Death in the Pot ³⁸Elisha returned to Gilgal and there was a famine in that region. While the company of the prophets was meeting with him, he said to his servant, "Put on the large pot and cook some stew for these men."

Dear Sam,

Sometimes when I'm stressed out my friend will ask me what's wrong. Should I blurt out my problem or smile and say everything's just fine?

Holly in Houston

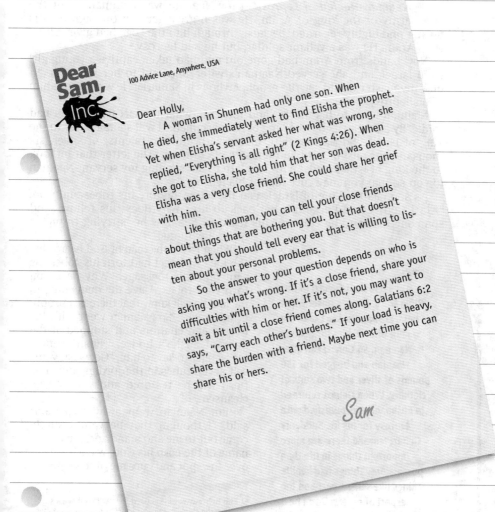

100 Advice Lane, Anywhere, USA

Dear Holly,

A woman in Shunem had only one son. When he died, she immediately went to find Elisha the prophet. Yet when Elisha's servant asked her what was wrong, she replied, "Everything is all right" (2 Kings 4:26). When she got to Elisha, she told him that her son was dead. Elisha was a very close friend. She could share her grief with him.

Like this woman, you can tell your close friends about things that are bothering you. But that doesn't mean that you should tell every ear that is willing to listen about your personal problems.

So the answer to your question depends on who is asking you what's wrong. If it's a close friend, share your difficulties with him or her. If it's not, you may want to wait a bit until a close friend comes along. Galatians 6:2 says, "Carry each other's burdens." If your load is heavy, share the burden with a friend. Maybe next time you can share his or hers.

Sam

³⁹One of them went out into the fields to gather herbs and found a wild vine. He gathered some of its gourds and filled the fold of his cloak. When he returned, he cut them up into the pot of stew, though no one knew what they were. ⁴⁰The stew was poured out for the men, but as they began to eat it, they cried out, "O man of God, there is death in the pot!" And they could not eat it.

⁴¹Elisha said, "Get some flour." He put it into the pot and said, "Serve it to the people to eat." And there was nothing harmful in the pot.

Feeding of a Hundred ⁴²A man came from Baal Shalishah, bringing the man of God twenty loaves of barley bread baked from the first ripe grain, along with some heads of new grain. "Give it to the people to eat," Elisha said.

⁴³"How can I set this before a hundred men?" his servant asked.

But Elisha answered, "Give it to the people to eat. For this is what the LORD says: 'They will eat and have some left over.' " ⁴⁴Then he set it before them, and they ate and had some left over, according to the word of the LORD.

Naaman Healed of Leprosy Now Naaman was commander of the army of the king of Aram. He was a great man in the sight of his master and highly regarded, because through him the LORD had given victory to Aram. He was a valiant soldier, but he had leprosy.ᵃ

²Now bands from Aram had gone out and had taken captive a young girl from Israel, and she served Naaman's wife. ³She said to her mistress, "If only my master would see the prophet who is in Samaria! He would cure him of his leprosy."

⁴Naaman went to his master and told him what the girl from Israel had said. ⁵"By all means, go," the king of Aram replied. "I will send a letter to the king of Israel." So Naaman left, taking with him ten talentsᵇ of silver, six thousand shekelsᶜ of gold and ten sets of clothing. ⁶The letter that he took to the king of Israel read: "With this letter I am sending my servant Naaman to you so that you may cure him of his leprosy."

⁷As soon as the king of Israel read the letter, he tore his robes and said, "Am I God? Can I kill and bring back to life? Why does this fellow send someone to me to be cured of his leprosy? See how he is trying to pick a quarrel with me!"

⁸When Elisha the man of God heard that the king of Israel had torn his robes, he sent him this message: "Why have you torn your robes? Have the man come to me and he will know that there is a prophet in Israel." ⁹So Naaman went with his horses and chariots and stopped at the door of Elisha's house. ¹⁰Elisha sent a messenger to say to him, "Go, wash yourself seven times in the Jordan, and your flesh will be restored and you will be cleansed."

¹¹But Naaman went away angry and said, "I thought that he would surely come out to me and stand and call on the name of the LORD his God, wave his hand over the spot and cure me of my leprosy.

2 KINGS 5

Take a look at Gehazi in this Bible story. He was upset when his boss, Elisha, wouldn't take the wealth offered him for healing Naaman. So Gehazi ran after Naaman and begged for 150 pounds of silver and two suits of clothing. When Gehazi returned to Elisha, he was punished with leprosy for his lie. Suddenly Gehazi learned there are more important things in life than possessions. Things like health. Things like self-respect and the respect of others. Don't be a Gehazi. Don't buy into the notion that possessions are the most important things in life.

Direct Line

ᵃ1 The Hebrew word was used for various diseases affecting the skin—not necessarily leprosy; also in verses 3, 6, 7, 11 and 27. ᵇ5 That is, about 750 pounds (about 340 kilograms) ᶜ5 That is, about 150 pounds (about 70 kilograms)

¹²Are not Abana and Pharpar, the rivers of Damascus, better than any of the waters of Israel? Couldn't I wash in them and be cleansed?" So he turned and went off in a rage.

¹³Naaman's servants went to him and said, "My father, if the prophet had told you to do some great thing, would you not have done it? How much more, then, when he tells you, 'Wash and be cleansed'!" ¹⁴So he went down and dipped himself in the Jordan seven times, as the man of God had told him, and his flesh was restored and became clean like that of a young boy.

¹⁵Then Naaman and all his attendants went back to the man of God. He stood before him and said, "Now I know that there is no God in all the world except in Israel. Please accept now a gift from your servant."

¹⁶The prophet answered, "As surely as the LORD lives, whom I serve, I will not accept a thing." And even though Naaman urged him, he refused.

¹⁷"If you will not," said Naaman, "please let me, your servant, be given as much earth as a pair of mules can carry, for your servant will never again make burnt offerings and sacrifices to any other god but the LORD. ¹⁸But may the LORD forgive your servant for this one thing: When my master enters the temple of Rimmon to bow down and he is leaning on my arm and I bow there also—when I bow down in the temple of Rimmon, may the LORD forgive your servant for this."

¹⁹"Go in peace," Elisha said.

After Naaman had traveled some distance, ²⁰Gehazi, the servant of Elisha the man of God, said to himself, "My master was too easy on Naaman, this Aramean, by not accepting from him what he brought. As surely as the LORD lives, I will run after him and get something from him."

²¹So Gehazi hurried after Naaman. When Naaman saw him running toward him, he got down from the chariot to meet him. "Is everything all right?" he asked.

²²"Everything is all right," Gehazi answered. "My master sent me to say, 'Two young men from the company of the prophets have just come to me from the hill country of Ephraim. Please give them a talent*ᵃ* of silver and two sets of clothing.' "

²³"By all means, take two talents," said Naaman. He urged Gehazi to accept them, and then tied up the two talents of silver in two bags, with two sets of clothing. He gave them to two of his servants, and they carried them ahead of Gehazi. ²⁴When Gehazi came to the hill, he took the things from the servants and put them away in the house. He sent the men away and they left. ²⁵Then he went in and stood before his master Elisha.

"Where have you been, Gehazi?" Elisha asked.

"Your servant didn't go anywhere," Gehazi answered.

²⁶But Elisha said to him, "Was not my spirit with you when the man got down from his chariot to meet you? Is this the time to take money, or to accept clothes, olive groves, vineyards, flocks, herds, or menservants and maidservants? ²⁷Naaman's leprosy will cling to you and to your descendants forever." Then Gehazi went from Elisha's presence and he was leprous, as white as snow.

6 *An Axhead Floats* The company of the prophets said to Elisha, "Look, the place where we meet with you is too small for us. ²Let us go to the Jordan, where each of us can get a pole; and let us build a place there for us to live."

And he said, "Go."

³Then one of them said, "Won't you please come with your servants?"

"I will," Elisha replied. ⁴And he went with them.

ᵃ22 That is, about 75 pounds (about 34 kilograms)

They went to the Jordan and began to cut down trees. ⁵As one of them was cutting down a tree, the iron axhead fell into the water. "Oh, my lord," he cried out, "it was borrowed!"

⁶The man of God asked, "Where did it fall?" When he showed him the place, Elisha cut a stick and threw it there, and made the iron float. ⁷"Lift it out," he said. Then the man reached out his hand and took it.

Elisha Traps Blinded Arameans   ⁸Now the king of Aram was at war with Israel. After conferring with his officers, he said, "I will set up my camp in such and such a place."

⁹The man of God sent word to the king of Israel: "Beware of passing that place, because the Arameans are going down there." ¹⁰So the king of Israel checked on the place indicated by the man of God. Time and again Elisha warned the king, so that he was on his guard in such places.

¹¹This enraged the king of Aram. He summoned his officers and demanded of them, "Will you not tell me which of us is on the side of the king of Israel?"

¹²"None of us, my lord the king," said one of his officers, "but Elisha, the prophet who is in Israel, tells the king of Israel the very words you speak in your bedroom."

¹³"Go, find out where he is," the king ordered, "so I can send men and capture him." The report came back: "He is in Dothan." ¹⁴Then he sent horses and chariots and a strong force there. They went by night and surrounded the city.

¹⁵When the servant of the man of God got up and went out early the next morning, an army with horses and chariots had surrounded the city. "Oh, my lord, what shall we do?" the servant asked.

¹⁶"Don't be afraid," the prophet answered. "Those who are with us are more than those who are with them."

¹⁷And Elisha prayed, "O LORD, open his eyes so he may see." Then the LORD opened the servant's eyes, and he looked and saw the hills full of horses and chariots of fire all around Elisha.

¹⁸As the enemy came down toward him, Elisha prayed to the LORD, "Strike these people with blindness." So he struck them with blindness, as Elisha had asked.

¹⁹Elisha told them, "This is not the road and this is not the city. Follow me, and I will lead you to the man you are looking for." And he led them to Samaria.

The Bible Says

Angels Are Around

Elisha's servant couldn't see God's protecting army until God opened his eyes. Then he saw "horses and chariots of fire all around" (2 Kings 6:15–17), protecting Elisha from the enemy army. Do God's angels protect ordinary people like you and me, or just prophets? Here are some things the Bible says about angels:

✳ Angels minister to Christians (Hebrews 1:14).
✳ Angels protect people from their enemies (Psalm 91:11–14).
✳ Angels guard children (Matthew 18:10) and churches (Revelation 2–3).

Pretty exciting, isn't it? Look around you. You may not see them with your eyes, but you can be sure they are there.

²⁰After they entered the city, Elisha said, "Lᴏʀᴅ, open the eyes of these men so they can see." Then the Lᴏʀᴅ opened their eyes and they looked, and there they were, inside Samaria.

²¹When the king of Israel saw them, he asked Elisha, "Shall I kill them, my father? Shall I kill them?"

²²"Do not kill them," he answered. "Would you kill men you have captured with your own sword or bow? Set food and water before them so that they may eat and drink and then go back to their master." ²³So he prepared a great feast for them, and after they had finished eating and drinking, he sent them away, and they returned to their master. So the bands from Aram stopped raiding Israel's territory.

Famine in Besieged Samaria ²⁴Some time later, Ben-Hadad king of Aram mobilized his entire army and marched up and laid siege to Samaria. ²⁵There was a great famine in the city; the siege lasted so long that a donkey's head sold for eighty shekelsᵃ of silver, and a quarter of a cabᵇ of seed podsᶜ for five shekels.ᵈ

²⁶As the king of Israel was passing by on the wall, a woman cried to him, "Help me, my lord the king!"

²⁷The king replied, "If the Lᴏʀᴅ does not help you, where can I get help for you? From the threshing floor? From the winepress?" ²⁸Then he asked her, "What's the matter?"

She answered, "This woman said to me, 'Give up your son so we may eat him today, and tomorrow we'll eat my son.' ²⁹So we cooked my son and ate him. The next day I said to her, 'Give up your son so we may eat him,' but she had hidden him."

³⁰When the king heard the woman's words, he tore his robes. As he went along the wall, the people looked, and there, underneath, he had sackcloth on his body. ³¹He said, "May God deal with me, be it ever so severely, if the head of Elisha son of Shaphat remains on his shoulders today!"

³²Now Elisha was sitting in his house, and the elders were sitting with him. The king sent a messenger ahead, but before he arrived, Elisha said to the elders, "Don't you see how this murderer is sending someone to cut off my head? Look, when the messenger comes, shut the door and hold it shut against him. Is not the sound of his master's footsteps behind him?"

³³While he was still talking to them, the messenger came down to him. And ₜthe king₎ said, "This disaster is from the Lᴏʀᴅ. Why should I wait for the Lᴏʀᴅ any longer?"

Elisha said, "Hear the word of the Lᴏʀᴅ. This is what the Lᴏʀᴅ says: About this time tomorrow, a seahᵉ of flour will sell for a shekelᶠ and two seahsᵍ of barley for a shekel at the gate of Samaria."

²The officer on whose arm the king was leaning said to the man of God, "Look, even if the Lᴏʀᴅ should open the floodgates of the heavens, could this happen?"

"You will see it with your own eyes," answered Elisha, "but you will not eat any of it!"

The Siege Lifted ³Now there were four men with leprosyʰ at the entrance of the city gate. They said to each other, "Why stay here until we die? ⁴If we say, 'We'll go into the city'—the famine is there, and we will die. And if we stay here, we will die. So let's go over to the camp of the Arameans and surrender. If they spare us, we live; if they kill us, then we die."

ᵃ25 That is, about 2 pounds (about 1 kilogram)   ᵇ25 That is, probably about 1/2 pint (about 0.3 liter)
ᶜ25 Or *of doves' dung*   ᵈ25 That is, about 2 ounces (about 55 grams)   ᵉ1 That is, probably about 7 quarts (about 7.3 liters); also in verses 16 and 18   ᶠ1 That is, about 2/5 ounce (about 11 grams); also in verses 16 and 18   ᵍ1 That is, probably about 13 quarts (about 15 liters); also in verses 16 and 18   ʰ3 The Hebrew word is used for various diseases affecting the skin—not necessarily leprosy; also in verse 8.

⁵At dusk they got up and went to the camp of the Arameans. When they reached the edge of the camp, not a man was there, ⁶for the Lord had caused the Arameans to hear the sound of chariots and horses and a great army, so that they said to one another, "Look, the king of Israel has hired the Hittite and Egyptian kings to attack us!" ⁷So they got up and fled in the dusk and abandoned their tents and their horses and donkeys. They left the camp as it was and ran for their lives.

⁸The men who had leprosy reached the edge of the camp and entered one of the tents. They ate and drank, and carried away silver, gold and clothes, and went off and hid them. They returned and entered another tent and took some things from it and hid them also.

⁹Then they said to each other, "We're not doing right. This is a day of good news and we are keeping it to ourselves. If we wait until daylight, punishment will overtake us. Let's go at once and report this to the royal palace."

¹⁰So they went and called out to the city gatekeepers and told them, "We went into the Aramean camp and not a man was there—not a sound of anyone—only tethered horses and donkeys, and the tents left just as they were." ¹¹The gatekeepers shouted the news, and it was reported within the palace.

¹²The king got up in the night and said to his officers, "I will tell you what the Arameans have done to us. They know we are starving; so they have left the camp to hide in the countryside, thinking, 'They will surely come out, and then we will take them alive and get into the city.' "

¹³One of his officers answered, "Have some men take five of the horses that are left in the city. Their plight will be like that of all the Israelites left here—yes, they will only be like all these Israelites who are doomed. So let us send them to find out what happened."

¹⁴So they selected two chariots with their horses, and the king sent them after the Aramean army. He commanded the drivers, "Go and find out what has happened." ¹⁵They followed them as far as the Jordan, and they found the whole road strewn with the clothing and equipment the Arameans had thrown away in their headlong flight. So the messengers returned and reported to the king. ¹⁶Then the people went out and plundered the camp of the Arameans. So a seah of flour sold for a shekel, and two seahs of barley sold for a shekel, as the Lord had said.

¹⁷Now the king had put the officer on whose arm he leaned in charge of the gate, and the people trampled him in the gateway, and he died, just as the man of God had foretold when the king came down to his house. ¹⁸It happened as the man of God had said to the king: "About this time tomorrow, a seah of flour will sell for a shekel and two seahs of barley for a shekel at the gate of Samaria."

¹⁹The officer had said to the man of God, "Look, even if the Lord should open the floodgates of the heavens, could this happen?" The man of God had replied, "You will see it with your own eyes, but you will not eat any of it!" ²⁰And that is exactly what happened to him, for the people trampled him in the gateway, and he died.

2 KINGS 7:9

Probably the most common idea people have about salvation is that as long as you believe in God, you'll be OK; as long as you live a reasonably good life, God will just have to accept you. Of course that's not what the Bible teaches. Jesus made it very clear that there's only one way to approach God, and that is through faith in him (John 14:6). After all, why would Christ have had to die if there were other ways to heaven? Like people who have food while others are starving, it's not right for Christians to "keep to ourselves" the good news that Jesus, and only Jesus, saves.

Direct Line

8 *The Shunammite's Land Restored* Now Elisha had said to the woman whose son he had restored to life, "Go away with your family and stay for a while wherever you can, because the LORD has decreed a famine in the land that will last seven years." ²The woman proceeded to do as the man of God said. She and her family went away and stayed in the land of the Philistines seven years.

³At the end of the seven years she came back from the land of the Philistines and went to the king to beg for her house and land. ⁴The king was talking to Gehazi, the servant of the man of God, and had said, "Tell me about all the great things Elisha has done." ⁵Just as Gehazi was telling the king how Elisha had restored the dead to life, the woman whose son Elisha had brought back to life came to beg the king for her house and land.

Gehazi said, "This is the woman, my lord the king, and this is her son whom Elisha restored to life." ⁶The king asked the woman about it, and she told him.

Then he assigned an official to her case and said to him, "Give back everything that belonged to her, including all the income from her land from the day she left the country until now."

Hazael Murders Ben-Hadad ⁷Elisha went to Damascus, and Ben-Hadad king of Aram was ill. When the king was told, "The man of God has come all the way up here," ⁸he said to Hazael, "Take a gift with you and go to meet the man of God. Consult the LORD through him; ask him, 'Will I recover from this illness?' "

⁹Hazael went to meet Elisha, taking with him as a gift forty camel-loads of all the finest wares of Damascus. He went in and stood before him, and said, "Your son Ben-Hadad king of Aram has sent me to ask, 'Will I recover from this illness?' "

¹⁰Elisha answered, "Go and say to him, 'You will certainly recover'; but*ᵃ* the LORD has revealed to me that he will in fact die." ¹¹He stared at him with a fixed gaze until Hazael felt ashamed. Then the man of God began to weep.

¹²"Why is my lord weeping?" asked Hazael.

"Because I know the harm you will do to the Israelites," he answered. "You will set fire to their fortified places, kill their young men with the sword, dash their little children to the ground, and rip open their pregnant women." ¹³Hazael said, "How could your servant, a mere dog, accomplish such a feat?"

"The LORD has shown me that you will become king of Aram," answered Elisha.

¹⁴Then Hazael left Elisha and returned to his master. When Ben-Hadad asked, "What did Elisha say to you?" Hazael replied, "He told me that you would certainly recover." ¹⁵But the next day he took a thick cloth, soaked it in water and spread it over the king's face, so that he died. Then Hazael succeeded him as king.

Jehoram King of Judah ¹⁶In the fifth year of Joram son of Ahab king of Israel, when Jehoshaphat was king of Judah, Jehoram son of Jehoshaphat began his reign as king of Judah. ¹⁷He was thirty-two years old when he became king, and he reigned in Jerusalem eight years. ¹⁸He walked in the ways of the kings of Israel, as the house of Ahab had done, for he married a daughter of Ahab. He did evil in the eyes of the LORD. ¹⁹Nevertheless, for the sake of his servant David, the LORD was not willing to destroy Judah. He had promised to maintain a lamp for David and his descendants forever.

²⁰In the time of Jehoram, Edom rebelled against Judah and set up its own king. ²¹So Jehoram*ᵇ* went to Zair with all his chariots. The Edomites sur-

---

ᵃ10 The Hebrew may also be read *Go and say, 'You will certainly not recover,' for.* *ᵇ21* Hebrew *Joram,* a variant of *Jehoram;* also in verses 23 and 24

rounded him and his chariot commanders, but he rose up and broke through by night; his army, however, fled back home. ²²To this day Edom has been in rebellion against Judah. Libnah revolted at the same time.

²³As for the other events of Jehoram's reign, and all he did, are they not written in the book of the annals of the kings of Judah? ²⁴Jehoram rested with his fathers and was buried with them in the City of David. And Ahaziah his son succeeded him as king.

Ahaziah King of Judah ²⁵In the twelfth year of Joram son of Ahab king of Israel, Ahaziah son of Jehoram king of Judah began to reign. ²⁶Ahaziah was twenty-two years old when he became king, and he reigned in Jerusalem one year. His mother's name was Athaliah, a granddaughter of Omri king of Israel. ²⁷He walked in the ways of the house of Ahab and did evil in the eyes of the LORD, as the house of Ahab had done, for he was related by marriage to Ahab's family.

²⁸Ahaziah went with Joram son of Ahab to war against Hazael king of Aram at Ramoth Gilead. The Arameans wounded Joram; ²⁹so King Joram returned to Jezreel to recover from the wounds the Arameans had inflicted on him at Ramoth*ᵃ* in his battle with Hazael king of Aram.

Then Ahaziah son of Jehoram king of Judah went down to Jezreel to see Joram son of Ahab, because he had been wounded.

9 *Jehu Anointed King of Israel* The prophet Elisha summoned a man from the company of the prophets and said to him, "Tuck your cloak into your belt, take this flask of oil with you and go to Ramoth Gilead. ²When you get there, look for Jehu son of Jehoshaphat, the son of Nimshi. Go to him, get him away from his companions and take him into an inner room. ³Then take the flask and pour the oil on his head and declare, 'This is what the LORD says: I anoint you king over Israel.' Then open the door and run; don't delay!"

⁴So the young man, the prophet, went to Ramoth Gilead. ⁵When he arrived, he found the army officers sitting together. "I have a message for you, commander," he said.

"For which of us?" asked Jehu.

"For you, commander," he replied.

⁶Jehu got up and went into the house. Then the prophet poured the oil on Jehu's head and declared, "This is what the LORD, the God of Israel, says: 'I anoint you king over the LORD's people Israel. ⁷You are to destroy the house of Ahab your master, and I will avenge the blood of my servants the prophets and the blood of all the LORD's servants shed by Jezebel. ⁸The whole house of Ahab will perish. I will cut off from Ahab every last male in Israel—slave or free. ⁹I will make the house of Ahab like the house of Jeroboam son of Nebat and like the house of Baasha son of Ahijah. ¹⁰As for Jezebel, dogs will devour her on the plot of ground at Jezreel, and no one will bury her.' " Then he opened the door and ran.

¹¹When Jehu went out to his fellow officers, one of them asked him, "Is everything all right? Why did this madman come to you?"

"You know the man and the sort of things he says," Jehu replied.

¹²"That's not true!" they said. "Tell us."

Jehu said, "Here is what he told me: 'This is what the LORD says: I anoint you king over Israel.' "

¹³They hurried and took their cloaks and spread them under him on the bare steps. Then they blew the trumpet and shouted, "Jehu is king!"

Jehu Kills Joram and Ahaziah ¹⁴So Jehu son of Jehoshaphat, the son of Nimshi, conspired against Joram. (Now Joram and all Israel had been defending

---

ᵃ29 Hebrew *Ramah,* a variant of *Ramoth*

Ramoth Gilead against Hazael king of Aram, ¹⁵but King Joram^a had returned to Jezreel to recover from the wounds the Arameans had inflicted on him in the battle with Hazael king of Aram.) Jehu said, "If this is the way you feel, don't let anyone slip out of the city to go and tell the news in Jezreel." ¹⁶Then he got into his chariot and rode to Jezreel, because Joram was resting there and Ahaziah king of Judah had gone down to see him.

¹⁷When the lookout standing on the tower in Jezreel saw Jehu's troops approaching, he called out, "I see some troops coming."

"Get a horseman," Joram ordered. "Send him to meet them and ask, 'Do you come in peace?' "

¹⁸The horseman rode off to meet Jehu and said, "This is what the king says: 'Do you come in peace?' "

"What do you have to do with peace?" Jehu replied. "Fall in behind me."

The lookout reported, "The messenger has reached them, but he isn't coming back."

¹⁹So the king sent out a second horseman. When he came to them he said, "This is what the king says: 'Do you come in peace?' "

Jehu replied, "What do you have to do with peace? Fall in behind me."

²⁰The lookout reported, "He has reached them, but he isn't coming back either. The driving is like that of Jehu son of Nimshi—he drives like a madman."

²¹"Hitch up my chariot," Joram ordered. And when it was hitched up, Joram king of Israel and Ahaziah king of Judah rode out, each in his own chariot, to meet Jehu. They met him at the plot of ground that had belonged to Naboth the Jezreelite. ²²When Joram saw Jehu he asked, "Have you come in peace, Jehu?"

"How can there be peace," Jehu replied, "as long as all the idolatry and witchcraft of your mother Jezebel abound?"

²³Joram turned about and fled, calling out to Ahaziah, "Treachery, Ahaziah!"

²⁴Then Jehu drew his bow and shot Joram between the shoulders. The arrow pierced his heart and he slumped down in his chariot. ²⁵Jehu said to Bidkar, his chariot officer, "Pick him up and throw him on the field that belonged to Naboth the Jezreelite. Remember how you and I were riding together in chariots behind Ahab his father when the LORD made this prophecy about him: ²⁶'Yesterday I saw the blood of Naboth and the blood of his sons, declares the LORD, and I will surely make you pay for it on this plot of ground, declares the LORD.'^b Now then, pick him up and throw him on that plot, in accordance with the word of the LORD."

²⁷When Ahaziah king of Judah saw what had happened, he fled up the road to Beth Haggan.^c Jehu chased him, shouting, "Kill him too!" They wounded him in his chariot on the way up to Gur near Ibleam, but he escaped to Megiddo and died there. ²⁸His servants took him by chariot to Jerusalem and buried him with his fathers in his tomb in the City of David. ²⁹(In the eleventh year of Joram son of Ahab, Ahaziah had become king of Judah.)

Jezebel Killed ³⁰Then Jehu went to Jezreel. When Jezebel heard about it, she painted her eyes, arranged her hair and looked out of a window. ³¹As Jehu entered the gate, she asked, "Have you come in peace, Zimri, you murderer of your master?"^d

2 KINGS 9

QU**i**ZZER

Q: Who was the first woman in the Bible reported to use cosmetics?

BONUS: What cosmetics did women use in Old Testament times?

Answers on page 454

---

^a15 Hebrew *Jehoram*, a variant of *Joram*; also in verses 17 and 21-24   ^b26 See 1 Kings 21:19.   ^c27 Or *fled by way of the garden house*   ^d31 Or *"Did Zimri have peace, who murdered his master?"*

³²He looked up at the window and called out, "Who is on my side? Who?" Two or three eunuchs looked down at him. ³³"Throw her down!" Jehu said. So they threw her down, and some of her blood spattered the wall and the horses as they trampled her underfoot.

³⁴Jehu went in and ate and drank. "Take care of that cursed woman," he said, "and bury her, for she was a king's daughter." ³⁵But when they went out to bury her, they found nothing except her skull, her feet and her hands. ³⁶They went back and told Jehu, who said, "This is the word of the LORD that he spoke through his servant Elijah the Tishbite: On the plot of ground at Jezreel dogs will devour Jezebel's flesh.ᵃ ³⁷Jezebel's body will be like refuse on the ground in the plot at Jezreel, so that no one will be able to say, 'This is Jezebel.' "

10 **Ahab's Family Killed** Now there were in Samaria seventy sons of the house of Ahab. So Jehu wrote letters and sent them to Samaria: to the officials of Jezreel,ᵇ to the elders and to the guardians of Ahab's children. He said, ²"As soon as this letter reaches you, since your master's sons are with you and you have chariots and horses, a fortified city and weapons, ³choose the best and most worthy of your master's sons and set him on his father's throne. Then fight for your master's house."

⁴But they were terrified and said, "If two kings could not resist him, how can we?"

⁵So the palace administrator, the city governor, the elders and the guardians sent this message to Jehu: "We are your servants and we will do anything you say. We will not appoint anyone as king; you do whatever you think best."

⁶Then Jehu wrote them a second letter, saying, "If you are on my side and will obey me, take the heads of your master's sons and come to me in Jezreel by this time tomorrow."

Now the royal princes, seventy of them, were with the leading men of the city, who were rearing them. ⁷When the letter arrived, these men took the princes and slaughtered all seventy of them. They put their heads in baskets and sent them to Jehu in Jezreel. ⁸When the messenger arrived, he told Jehu, "They have brought the heads of the princes."

Then Jehu ordered, "Put them in two piles at the entrance of the city gate until morning."

⁹The next morning Jehu went out. He stood before all the people and said, "You are innocent. It was I who conspired against my master and killed him, but who killed all these? ¹⁰Know then, that not a word the LORD has spoken against the house of Ahab will fail. The LORD has done what he promised through his servant Elijah." ¹¹So Jehu killed everyone in Jezreel who remained of the house of Ahab, as well as all his chief men, his close friends and his priests, leaving him no survivor.

¹²Jehu then set out and went toward Samaria. At Beth Eked of the Shepherds, ¹³he met some relatives of Ahaziah king of Judah and asked, "Who are you?"

They said, "We are relatives of Ahaziah, and we have come down to greet the families of the king and of the queen mother."

¹⁴"Take them alive!" he ordered. So they took them alive and slaughtered them by the well of Beth Eked—forty-two men. He left no survivor.

¹⁵After he left there, he came upon Jehonadab son of Recab, who was on his way to meet him. Jehu greeted him and said, "Are you in accord with me, as I am with you?"

"I am," Jehonadab answered.

Answers
to Quizzer on
page 453

A: Queen Jezebel (2 Kings 9:30).

BONUS:
Archaeologists have found cosmetic kits containing kohl to darken the eyes, crushed colored stones to powder the face, and henna to color the palms of the hands bright orange.

ᵃ36 See 1 Kings 21:23.   ᵇ1 Hebrew; some Septuagint manuscripts and Vulgate *of the city*

"If so," said Jehu, "give me your hand." So he did, and Jehu helped him up into the chariot. ¹⁶Jehu said, "Come with me and see my zeal for the LORD." Then he had him ride along in his chariot.

¹⁷When Jehu came to Samaria, he killed all who were left there of Ahab's family; he destroyed them, according to the word of the LORD spoken to Elijah.

Ministers of Baal Killed   ¹⁸Then Jehu brought all the people together and said to them, "Ahab served Baal a little; Jehu will serve him much. ¹⁹Now summon all the prophets of Baal, all his ministers and all his priests. See that no one is missing, because I am going to hold a great sacrifice for Baal. Anyone who fails to come will no longer live." But Jehu was acting deceptively in order to destroy the ministers of Baal.

²⁰Jehu said, "Call an assembly in honor of Baal." So they proclaimed it. ²¹Then he sent word throughout Israel, and all the ministers of Baal came; not one stayed away. They crowded into the temple of Baal until it was full from one end to the other. ²²And Jehu said to the keeper of the wardrobe, "Bring robes for all the ministers of Baal." So he brought out robes for them.

²³Then Jehu and Jehonadab son of Recab went into the temple of Baal. Jehu said to the ministers of Baal, "Look around and see that no servants of the LORD are here with you—only ministers of Baal." ²⁴So they went in to make sacrifices and burnt offerings. Now Jehu had posted eighty men outside with this warning: "If one of you lets any of the men I am placing in your hands escape, it will be your life for his life."

²⁵As soon as Jehu had finished making the burnt offering, he ordered the guards and officers: "Go in and kill them; let no one escape." So they cut them down with the sword. The guards and officers threw the bodies out and then entered the inner shrine of the temple of Baal. ²⁶They brought the sacred stone out of the temple of Baal and burned it. ²⁷They demolished the sacred stone of Baal and tore down the temple of Baal, and people have used it for a latrine to this day.

²⁸So Jehu destroyed Baal worship in Israel. ²⁹However, he did not turn away from the sins of Jeroboam son of Nebat, which he had caused Israel to commit—the worship of the golden calves at Bethel and Dan.

³⁰The LORD said to Jehu, "Because you have done well in accomplishing what is right in my eyes and have done to the house of Ahab all I had in mind to do, your descendants will sit on the throne of Israel to the fourth generation." ³¹Yet Jehu was not careful to keep the law of the LORD, the God of Israel, with all his heart. He did not turn away from the sins of Jeroboam, which he had caused Israel to commit.

³²In those days the LORD began to reduce the size of Israel. Hazael overpowered the Israelites throughout their territory ³³east of the Jordan in all the land of Gilead (the region of Gad, Reuben and Manasseh), from Aroer by the Arnon Gorge through Gilead to Bashan.

³⁴As for the other events of Jehu's reign, all he did, and all his achievements, are they not written in the book of the annals of the kings of Israel?

³⁵Jehu rested with his fathers and was buried in Samaria. And Jehoahaz his son succeeded him as king. ³⁶The time that Jehu reigned over Israel in Samaria was twenty-eight years.

Athaliah and Joash   When Athaliah the mother of Ahaziah saw that her son was dead, she proceeded to destroy the whole royal family. ²But Jehosheba, the daughter of King Jehoram*ᵃ* and sister of Ahaziah, took Joash son of Ahaziah and stole him away from among the royal princes, who were about to be murdered. She put him and his nurse in a bedroom to

*ᵃ2 Hebrew *Joram,* a variant of *Jehoram

hide him from Athaliah; so he was not killed. ³He remained hidden with his nurse at the temple of the Lord for six years while Athaliah ruled the land.

⁴In the seventh year Jehoiada sent for the commanders of units of a hundred, the Carites and the guards and had them brought to him at the temple of the Lord. He made a covenant with them and put them under oath at the temple of the Lord. Then he showed them the king's son. ⁵He commanded them, saying, "This is what you are to do: You who are in the three companies that are going on duty on the Sabbath—a third of you guarding the royal palace, ⁶a third at the Sur Gate, and a third at the gate behind the guard, who take turns guarding the temple— ⁷and you who are in the other two companies that normally go off Sabbath duty are all to guard the temple for the king. ⁸Station yourselves around the king, each man with his weapon in his hand. Anyone who approaches your ranks*ᵃ* must be put to death. Stay close to the king wherever he goes."

⁹The commanders of units of a hundred did just as Jehoiada the priest ordered. Each one took his men—those who were going on duty on the Sabbath and those who were going off duty—and came to Jehoiada the priest. ¹⁰Then he gave the commanders the spears and shields that had belonged to King David and that were in the temple of the Lord. ¹¹The guards, each with his weapon in his hand, stationed themselves around the king—near the altar and the temple, from the south side to the north side of the temple.

¹²Jehoiada brought out the king's son and put the crown on him; he presented him with a copy of the covenant and proclaimed him king. They anointed him, and the people clapped their hands and shouted, "Long live the king!"

¹³When Athaliah heard the noise made by the guards and the people, she went to the people at the temple of the Lord. ¹⁴She looked and there was the king, standing by the pillar, as the custom was. The officers and the trumpeters were beside the king, and all the people of the land were rejoicing and blowing trumpets. Then Athaliah tore her robes and called out, "Treason! Treason!"

¹⁵Jehoiada the priest ordered the commanders of units of a hundred, who were in charge of the troops: "Bring her out between the ranks*ᵇ* and put to the sword anyone who follows her." For the priest had said, "She must not be put to death in the temple of the Lord." ¹⁶So they seized her as she reached the place where the horses enter the palace grounds, and there she was put to death.

¹⁷Jehoiada then made a covenant between the Lord and the king and people that they would be the Lord's people. He also made a covenant between the king and the people. ¹⁸All the people of the land went to the temple of Baal and tore it down. They smashed the altars and idols to pieces and killed Mattan the priest of Baal in front of the altars.

Then Jehoiada the priest posted guards at the temple of the Lord. ¹⁹He took with him the commanders of hundreds, the Carites, the guards and all the people of the land, and together they brought the

---

Direct Line

2 KINGS 11:1-12

There are some things you just have to wait for. Like a license to drive. Like graduating from school and getting a good job. Marriage is another "wait" kind of thing. After all, it would be hard to have a home or raise kids on wages you'd earn flipping burgers at the local fast-food joint. It was hard for the priest Jehoiada to wait for six long years during the rule of evil Queen Athaliah until he was able to reveal the hidden boy king, Joash. But Jehoiada had to wait. Waiting is always hard. But the outcome of this Bible story reminds you that waiting on God's timing in life really is best.

ᵃ8 Or approaches the precincts ᵇ15 Or out from the precincts

king down from the temple of the LORD and went into the palace, entering by way of the gate of the guards. The king then took his place on the royal throne, ²⁰and all the people of the land rejoiced. And the city was quiet, because Athaliah had been slain with the sword at the palace.

²¹Joash*ᵃ* was seven years old when he began to reign.

Joash Repairs the Temple In the seventh year of Jehu, Joash*ᵇ* became king, and he reigned in Jerusalem forty years. His mother's name was Zibiah; she was from Beersheba. ²Joash did what was right in the eyes of the LORD all the years Jehoiada the priest instructed him. ³The high places, however, were not removed; the people continued to offer sacrifices and burn incense there.

⁴Joash said to the priests, "Collect all the money that is brought as sacred offerings to the temple of the LORD—the money collected in the census, the money received from personal vows and the money brought voluntarily to the temple. ⁵Let every priest receive the money from one of the treasurers, and let it be used to repair whatever damage is found in the temple."

⁶But by the twenty-third year of King Joash the priests still had not repaired the temple. ⁷Therefore King Joash summoned Jehoiada the priest and the other priests and asked them, "Why aren't you repairing the damage done to the temple? Take no more money from your treasurers, but hand it over for repairing the temple." ⁸The priests agreed that they would not collect any more money from the people and that they would not repair the temple themselves.

⁹Jehoiada the priest took a chest and bored a hole in its lid. He placed it beside the altar, on the right side as one enters the temple of the LORD. The priests who guarded the entrance put into the chest all the money that was brought to the temple of the LORD. ¹⁰Whenever they saw that there was a large amount of money in the chest, the royal secretary and the high priest came, counted the money that had been brought into the temple of the LORD and put it into bags. ¹¹When the amount had been determined, they gave the money to the men appointed to supervise the work on the temple. With it they paid those who worked on the temple of the LORD—the carpenters and builders, ¹²the masons and stonecutters. They purchased timber and dressed stone for the repair of the temple of the LORD, and met all the other expenses of restoring the temple.

¹³The money brought into the temple was not spent for making silver basins, wick trimmers, sprinkling bowls, trumpets or any other articles of gold or silver for the temple of the LORD; ¹⁴it was paid to the workmen, who used it to repair the temple. ¹⁵They did not require an accounting from those to whom they gave the money to pay the workers, because they acted with complete honesty. ¹⁶The money from the guilt offerings and sin offerings was not brought into the temple of the LORD; it belonged to the priests.

¹⁷About this time Hazael king of Aram went up and attacked Gath and captured it. Then he turned to attack Jerusalem. ¹⁸But Joash king of Judah took all the sacred objects dedicated by his fathers—Jehoshaphat, Jehoram and Ahaziah, the kings of Judah—and the gifts he himself had dedicated and all the gold found in the treasuries of the temple of the LORD and of the royal palace, and he sent them to Hazael king of Aram, who then withdrew from Jerusalem.

¹⁹As for the other events of the reign of Joash, and all he did, are they not written in the book of the annals of the kings of Judah? ²⁰His officials con-

---

ᵃ21 Hebrew *Jehoash,* a variant of *Joash*   *ᵇ1* Hebrew *Jehoash,* a variant of *Joash*; also in verses 2, 4, 6, 7 and 18

spired against him and assassinated him at Beth Millo, on the road down to Silla. ²¹The officials who murdered him were Jozabad son of Shimeath and Jehozabad son of Shomer. He died and was buried with his fathers in the City of David. And Amaziah his son succeeded him as king.

Jehoahaz King of Israel In the twenty-third year of Joash son of Ahaziah king of Judah, Jehoahaz son of Jehu became king of Israel in Samaria, and he reigned seventeen years. ²He did evil in the eyes of the LORD by following the sins of Jeroboam son of Nebat, which he had caused Israel to commit, and he did not turn away from them. ³So the LORD's anger burned against Israel, and for a long time he kept them under the power of Hazael king of Aram and Ben-Hadad his son.

⁴Then Jehoahaz sought the LORD's favor, and the LORD listened to him, for he saw how severely the king of Aram was oppressing Israel. ⁵The LORD provided a deliverer for Israel, and they escaped from the power of Aram. So the Israelites lived in their own homes as they had before. ⁶But they did not turn away from the sins of the house of Jeroboam, which he had caused Israel to commit; they continued in them. Also, the Asherah pole*a* remained standing in Samaria.

⁷Nothing had been left of the army of Jehoahaz except fifty horsemen, ten chariots and ten thousand foot soldiers, for the king of Aram had destroyed the rest and made them like the dust at threshing time.

⁸As for the other events of the reign of Jehoahaz, all he did and his achievements, are they not written in the book of the annals of the kings of Israel? ⁹Jehoahaz rested with his fathers and was buried in Samaria. And Jehoash*b* his son succeeded him as king.

Jehoash King of Israel ¹⁰In the thirty-seventh year of Joash king of Judah, Jehoash son of Jehoahaz became king of Israel in Samaria, and he reigned sixteen years. ¹¹He did evil in the eyes of the LORD and did not turn away from any of the sins of Jeroboam son of Nebat, which he had caused Israel to commit; he continued in them.

¹²As for the other events of the reign of Jehoash, all he did and his achievements, including his war against Amaziah king of Judah, are they not written in the book of the annals of the kings of Israel? ¹³Jehoash rested with his fathers, and Jeroboam succeeded him on the throne. Jehoash was buried in Samaria with the kings of Israel.

¹⁴Now Elisha was suffering from the illness from which he died. Jehoash king of Israel went down to see him and wept over him. "My father! My father!" he cried. "The chariots and horsemen of Israel!"

¹⁵Elisha said, "Get a bow and some arrows," and he did so. ¹⁶"Take the bow in your hands," he said to the king of Israel. When he had taken it, Elisha put his hands on the king's hands.

¹⁷"Open the east window," he said, and he opened it. "Shoot!" Elisha said, and he shot. "The LORD's arrow of victory, the arrow of victory over Aram!" Elisha declared. "You will completely destroy the Arameans at Aphek."

¹⁸Then he said, "Take the arrows," and the king took them. Elisha told him, "Strike the ground." He struck it three times and stopped. ¹⁹The man of God was angry with him and said, "You should have struck the ground five or six times; then you would have defeated Aram and completely destroyed it. But now you will defeat it only three times."

²⁰Elisha died and was buried.

Now Moabite raiders used to enter the country every spring. ²¹Once while some Israelites were burying a man, suddenly they saw a band of raiders; so

---

a6 That is, a symbol of the goddess Asherah; here and elsewhere in 2 Kings   *b9* Hebrew *Joash*, a variant of *Jehoash*; also in verses 12-14 and 25

they threw the man's body into Elisha's tomb. When the body touched Elisha's bones, the man came to life and stood up on his feet.

²²Hazael king of Aram oppressed Israel throughout the reign of Jehoahaz. ²³But the LORD was gracious to them and had compassion and showed concern for them because of his covenant with Abraham, Isaac and Jacob. To this day he has been unwilling to destroy them or banish them from his presence.

²⁴Hazael king of Aram died, and Ben-Hadad his son succeeded him as king. ²⁵Then Jehoash son of Jehoahaz recaptured from Ben-Hadad son of Hazael the towns he had taken in battle from his father Jehoahaz. Three times Jehoash defeated him, and so he recovered the Israelite towns.

14 *Amaziah King of Judah* In the second year of Jehoash[a] son of Jehoahaz king of Israel, Amaziah son of Joash king of Judah began to reign. ²He was twenty-five years old when he became king, and he reigned in Jerusalem twenty-nine years. His mother's name was Jehoaddin; she was from Jerusalem. ³He did what was right in the eyes of the LORD, but not as his father David had done. In everything he followed the example of his father Joash. ⁴The high places, however, were not removed; the people continued to offer sacrifices and burn incense there.

⁵After the kingdom was firmly in his grasp, he executed the officials who had murdered his father the king. ⁶Yet he did not put the sons of the assassins to death, in accordance with what is written in the Book of the Law of Moses where the LORD commanded: "Fathers shall not be put to death for their children, nor children put to death for their fathers; each is to die for his own sins."[b]

⁷He was the one who defeated ten thousand Edomites in the Valley of Salt and captured Sela in battle, calling it Joktheel, the name it has to this day.

⁸Then Amaziah sent messengers to Jehoash son of Jehoahaz, the son of Jehu, king of Israel, with the challenge: "Come, meet me face to face."

⁹But Jehoash king of Israel replied to Amaziah king of Judah: "A thistle in Lebanon sent a message to a cedar in Lebanon, 'Give your daughter to my son in marriage.' Then a wild beast in Lebanon came along and trampled the thistle underfoot. ¹⁰You have indeed defeated Edom and now you are arrogant. Glory in your victory, but stay at home! Why ask for trouble and cause your own downfall and that of Judah also?"

¹¹Amaziah, however, would not listen, so Jehoash king of Israel attacked. He and Amaziah king of Judah faced each other at Beth Shemesh in Judah. ¹²Judah was routed by Israel, and every man fled to his home. ¹³Jehoash king of Israel captured Amaziah king of Judah, the son of Joash, the son of Ahaziah, at Beth Shemesh. Then Jehoash went to Jerusalem and broke down the wall of Jerusalem from the Ephraim Gate to the Corner Gate—a section about six hundred feet long.[c] ¹⁴He took all the gold and silver and all the articles found in the temple of the LORD and in the treasuries of the royal palace. He also took hostages and returned to Samaria.

¹⁵As for the other events of the reign of Jehoash, what he did and his achievements, including his war against Amaziah king of Judah, are they not written in the book of the annals of the kings of Israel? ¹⁶Jehoash rested with his fathers and was buried in Samaria with the kings of Israel. And Jeroboam his son succeeded him as king.

¹⁷Amaziah son of Joash king of Judah lived for fifteen years after the death of Jehoash son of Jehoahaz king of Israel. ¹⁸As for the other events of Amaziah's reign, are they not written in the book of the annals of the kings of Judah?

---

a1 Hebrew *Joash,* a variant of *Jehoash;* also in verses 13, 23 and 27   *b6* Deut. 24:16   *c13* Hebrew *four hundred cubits* (about 180 meters)

¹⁹They conspired against him in Jerusalem, and he fled to Lachish, but they sent men after him to Lachish and killed him there. ²⁰He was brought back by horse and was buried in Jerusalem with his fathers, in the City of David.

²¹Then all the people of Judah took Azariah,ᵃ who was sixteen years old, and made him king in place of his father Amaziah. ²²He was the one who rebuilt Elath and restored it to Judah after Amaziah rested with his fathers.

Jeroboam II King of Israel ²³In the fifteenth year of Amaziah son of Joash king of Judah, Jeroboam son of Jehoash king of Israel became king in Samaria, and he reigned forty-one years. ²⁴He did evil in the eyes of the LORD and did not turn away from any of the sins of Jeroboam son of Nebat, which he had caused Israel to commit. ²⁵He was the one who restored the boundaries of Israel from Leboᵇ Hamath to the Sea of the Arabah,ᶜ in accordance with the word of the LORD, the God of Israel, spoken through his servant Jonah son of Amittai, the prophet from Gath Hepher.

²⁶The LORD had seen how bitterly everyone in Israel, whether slave or free, was suffering; there was no one to help them. ²⁷And since the LORD had not said he would blot out the name of Israel from under heaven, he saved them by the hand of Jeroboam son of Jehoash.

²⁸As for the other events of Jeroboam's reign, all he did, and his military achievements, including how he recovered for Israel both Damascus and Hamath, which had belonged to Yaudi,ᵈ are they not written in the book of the annals of the kings of Israel? ²⁹Jeroboam rested with his fathers, the kings of Israel. And Zechariah his son succeeded him as king.

15 ***Azariah King of Judah*** In the twenty-seventh year of Jeroboam king of Israel, Azariah son of Amaziah king of Judah began to reign. ²He was sixteen years old when he became king, and he reigned in Jerusalem fifty-two years. His mother's name was Jecoliah; she was from Jerusalem. ³He did what was right in the eyes of the LORD, just as his father Amaziah had done. ⁴The high places, however, were not removed; the people continued to offer sacrifices and burn incense there.

⁵The LORD afflicted the king with leprosyᵉ until the day he died, and he lived in a separate house.ᶠ Jotham the king's son had charge of the palace and governed the people of the land.

⁶As for the other events of Azariah's reign, and all he did, are they not written in the book of the annals of the kings of Judah? ⁷Azariah rested with his fathers and was buried near them in the City of David. And Jotham his son succeeded him as king.

Zechariah King of Israel ⁸In the thirty-eighth year of Azariah king of Judah, Zechariah son of Jeroboam became king of Israel in Samaria, and he reigned six months. ⁹He did evil in the eyes of the LORD, as his fathers had done. He did not turn away from the sins of Jeroboam son of Nebat, which he had caused Israel to commit.

JUDAH
ISRAEL
ANNALS OF THE KIN
ANNALS OF THE

SEE
2 KINGS 15

ᵃ21 Also called *Uzziah* ᵇ25 Or *from the entrance to* ᶜ25 That is, the Dead Sea ᵈ28 Or *Judah* ᵉ5 The Hebrew word was used for various diseases affecting the skin—not necessarily leprosy. ᶠ5 Or *in a house where he was relieved of responsibility*

[10]Shallum son of Jabesh conspired against Zechariah. He attacked him in front of the people,[a] assassinated him and succeeded him as king. [11]The other events of Zechariah's reign are written in the book of the annals of the kings of Israel. [12]So the word of the LORD spoken to Jehu was fulfilled: "Your descendants will sit on the throne of Israel to the fourth generation."[b]

Shallum King of Israel   [13]Shallum son of Jabesh became king in the thirty-ninth year of Uzziah king of Judah, and he reigned in Samaria one month. [14]Then Menahem son of Gadi went from Tirzah up to Samaria. He attacked Shallum son of Jabesh in Samaria, assassinated him and succeeded him as king.

[15]The other events of Shallum's reign, and the conspiracy he led, are written in the book of the annals of the kings of Israel.

[16]At that time Menahem, starting out from Tirzah, attacked Tiphsah and everyone in the city and its vicinity, because they refused to open their gates. He sacked Tiphsah and ripped open all the pregnant women.

Menahem King of Israel   [17]In the thirty-ninth year of Azariah king of Judah, Menahem son of Gadi became king of Israel, and he reigned in Samaria ten years. [18]He did evil in the eyes of the LORD. During his entire reign he did not turn away from the sins of Jeroboam son of Nebat, which he had caused Israel to commit.

[19]Then Pul[c] king of Assyria invaded the land, and Menahem gave him a thousand talents[d] of silver to gain his support and strengthen his own hold on the kingdom. [20]Menahem exacted this money from Israel. Every wealthy man had to contribute fifty shekels[e] of silver to be given to the king of Assyria. So the king of Assyria withdrew and stayed in the land no longer.

[21]As for the other events of Menahem's reign, and all he did, are they not written in the book of the annals of the kings of Israel? [22]Menahem rested with his fathers. And Pekahiah his son succeeded him as king.

Pekahiah King of Israel   [23]In the fiftieth year of Azariah king of Judah, Pekahiah son of Menahem became king of Israel in Samaria, and he reigned two years. [24]Pekahiah did evil in the eyes of the LORD. He did not turn away from the sins of Jeroboam son of Nebat, which he had caused Israel to commit. [25]One of his chief officers, Pekah son of Remaliah, conspired against him. Taking fifty men of Gilead with him, he assassinated Pekahiah, along with Argob and Arieh, in the citadel of the royal palace at Samaria. So Pekah killed Pekahiah and succeeded him as king.

[26]The other events of Pekahiah's reign, and all he did, are written in the book of the annals of the kings of Israel.

Pekah King of Israel   [27]In the fifty-second year of Azariah king of Judah, Pekah son of Remaliah became king of Israel in Samaria, and he reigned twenty years. [28]He did evil in the eyes of the LORD. He did not turn away from the sins of Jeroboam son of Nebat, which he had caused Israel to commit.

[29]In the time of Pekah king of Israel, Tiglath-Pileser king of Assyria came and took Ijon, Abel Beth Maacah, Janoah, Kedesh and Hazor. He took Gilead and Galilee, including all the land of Naphtali, and deported the people to Assyria. [30]Then Hoshea son of Elah conspired against Pekah son of Remaliah. He attacked and assassinated him, and then succeeded him as king in the twentieth year of Jotham son of Uzziah.

[31]As for the other events of Pekah's reign, and all he did, are they not written in the book of the annals of the kings of Israel?

---

[a]*10* Hebrew; some Septuagint manuscripts *in Ibleam*   [b]*12* 2 Kings 10:30   [c]*19* Also called *Tiglath-Pileser*   [d]*19* That is, about 37 tons (about 34 metric tons)   [e]*20* That is, about 1 1/4 pounds (about 0.6 kilogram)

Jotham King of Judah ³²In the second year of Pekah son of Remaliah king of Israel, Jotham son of Uzziah king of Judah began to reign. ³³He was twenty-five years old when he became king, and he reigned in Jerusalem sixteen years. His mother's name was Jerusha daughter of Zadok. ³⁴He did what was right in the eyes of the LORD, just as his father Uzziah had done. ³⁵The high places, however, were not removed; the people continued to offer sacrifices and burn incense there. Jotham rebuilt the Upper Gate of the temple of the LORD.

³⁶As for the other events of Jotham's reign, and what he did, are they not written in the book of the annals of the kings of Judah? ³⁷(In those days the LORD began to send Rezin king of Aram and Pekah son of Remaliah against Judah.) ³⁸Jotham rested with his fathers and was buried with them in the City of David, the city of his father. And Ahaz his son succeeded him as king.

16 *Ahaz King of Judah* In the seventeenth year of Pekah son of Remaliah, Ahaz son of Jotham king of Judah began to reign. ²Ahaz was twenty years old when he became king, and he reigned in Jerusalem sixteen years. Unlike David his father, he did not do what was right in the eyes of the LORD his God. ³He walked in the ways of the kings of Israel and even sacrificed his son in*ᵃ* the fire, following the detestable ways of the nations the LORD had driven out before the Israelites. ⁴He offered sacrifices and burned incense at the high places, on the hilltops and under every spreading tree.

⁵Then Rezin king of Aram and Pekah son of Remaliah king of Israel marched up to fight against Jerusalem and besieged Ahaz, but they could not overpower him. ⁶At that time, Rezin king of Aram recovered Elath for Aram by driving out the men of Judah. Edomites then moved into Elath and have lived there to this day.

⁷Ahaz sent messengers to say to Tiglath-Pileser king of Assyria, "I am your servant and vassal. Come up and save me out of the hand of the king of Aram and of the king of Israel, who are attacking me." ⁸And Ahaz took the silver and gold found in the temple of the LORD and in the treasuries of the royal palace and sent it as a gift to the king of Assyria. ⁹The king of Assyria complied by attacking Damascus and capturing it. He deported its inhabitants to Kir and put Rezin to death.

¹⁰Then King Ahaz went to Damascus to meet Tiglath-Pileser king of Assyria. He saw an altar in Damascus and sent to Uriah the priest a sketch of the altar, with detailed plans for its construction. ¹¹So Uriah the priest built an altar in accordance with all the plans that King Ahaz had sent from Damascus and finished it before King Ahaz returned. ¹²When the king came back from Damascus and saw the altar, he approached it and presented offerings*ᵇ* on it. ¹³He offered up his burnt offering and grain offering, poured out his drink offering, and sprinkled the blood of his fellowship offerings*ᶜ* on the altar. ¹⁴The bronze altar that stood before the LORD he brought from the front of the temple—from between the new altar and the temple of the LORD—and put it on the north side of the new altar.

¹⁵King Ahaz then gave these orders to Uriah the priest: "On the large new altar, offer the morning burnt offering and the evening grain offering, the king's burnt offering and his grain offering, and the burnt offering of all the people of the land, and their grain offering and their drink offering. Sprinkle on the altar all the blood of the burnt offerings and sacrifices. But I will use the bronze altar for seeking guidance." ¹⁶And Uriah the priest did just as King Ahaz had ordered.

¹⁷King Ahaz took away the side panels and removed the basins from the

---

ᵃ3 Or even made his son pass through ᵇ12 Or and went up ᶜ13 Traditionally peace offerings

movable stands. He removed the Sea from the bronze bulls that supported it and set it on a stone base. ¹⁸He took away the Sabbath canopy*a* that had been built at the temple and removed the royal entryway outside the temple of the LORD, in deference to the king of Assyria.

¹⁹As for the other events of the reign of Ahaz, and what he did, are they not written in the book of the annals of the kings of Judah? ²⁰Ahaz rested with his fathers and was buried with them in the City of David. And Hezekiah his son succeeded him as king.

17

Hoshea Last King of Israel In the twelfth year of Ahaz king of Judah, Hoshea son of Elah became king of Israel in Samaria, and he reigned nine years. ²He did evil in the eyes of the LORD, but not like the kings of Israel who preceded him.

³Shalmaneser king of Assyria came up to attack Hoshea, who had been Shalmaneser's vassal and had paid him tribute. ⁴But the king of Assyria discovered that Hoshea was a traitor, for he had sent envoys to So*b* king of Egypt, and he no longer paid tribute to the king of Assyria, as he had done year by year. Therefore Shalmaneser seized him and put him in prison. ⁵The king of Assyria invaded the entire land, marched against Samaria and laid siege to it for three years. ⁶In the ninth year of Hoshea, the king of Assyria captured Samaria and deported the Israelites to Assyria. He settled them in Halah, in Gozan on the Habor River and in the towns of the Medes.

Israel Exiled Because of Sin ⁷All this took place because the Israelites had sinned against the LORD their God, who had brought them up out of Egypt from under the power of Pharaoh king of Egypt. They worshiped other gods ⁸and followed the practices of the nations the LORD had driven out before them, as well as the practices that the kings of Israel had introduced. ⁹The Israelites secretly did things against the LORD their God that were not right. From watchtower to fortified city they built themselves high places in all their towns. ¹⁰They set up sacred stones and Asherah poles on every high hill and under every spreading tree. ¹¹At every high place they burned incense, as the nations whom the LORD had driven out before them had done. They did wicked things that provoked the LORD to anger. ¹²They worshiped idols, though the LORD had said, "You shall not do this."*c* ¹³The LORD warned Israel and Judah through all his prophets and seers: "Turn from your evil ways. Observe my commands and decrees, in accordance with the entire Law that I commanded your fathers to obey and that I delivered to you through my servants the prophets."

¹⁴But they would not listen and were as stiff-necked as their fathers, who did not trust in the LORD their God. ¹⁵They rejected his decrees and the covenant he had made with their fathers and the warnings he had given them. They followed worthless idols and themselves became worthless. They imitated the nations around them although the LORD had ordered them, "Do not do as they do," and they did the things the LORD had forbidden them to do.

¹⁶They forsook all the commands of the LORD their God and made for themselves two idols cast in the shape of calves, and an Asherah pole. They bowed down to all the starry hosts, and they worshiped Baal. ¹⁷They sacrificed their sons and daughters in*d* the fire. They practiced divination and sorcery and sold themselves to do evil in the eyes of the LORD, provoking him to anger.

¹⁸So the LORD was very angry with Israel and removed them from his presence. Only the tribe of Judah was left, ¹⁹and even Judah did not keep the commands of the LORD their God. They followed the practices Israel had in-

---

a18 Or the dais of his throne (see Septuagint) *b4 Or to Sais, to the; So* is possibly an abbreviation for *Osorkon.* *c12 Exodus 20:4, 5 d17 Or They made their sons and daughters pass through*

troduced. [20]Therefore the LORD rejected all the people of Israel; he afflicted them and gave them into the hands of plunderers, until he thrust them from his presence.

[21]When he tore Israel away from the house of David, they made Jeroboam son of Nebat their king. Jeroboam enticed Israel away from following the LORD and caused them to commit a great sin. [22]The Israelites persisted in all the sins of Jeroboam and did not turn away from them [23]until the LORD removed them from his presence, as he had warned through all his servants the prophets. So the people of Israel were taken from their homeland into exile in Assyria, and they are still there.

Samaria Resettled   [24]The king of Assyria brought people from Babylon, Cuthah, Avva, Hamath and Sepharvaim and settled them in the towns of Samaria to replace the Israelites. They took over Samaria and lived in its towns. [25]When they first lived there, they did not worship the LORD; so he sent lions among them and they killed some of the people. [26]It was reported to the king of Assyria: "The people you deported and resettled in the towns of Samaria do not know what the god of that country requires. He has sent lions among them, which are killing them off, because the people do not know what he requires."

[27]Then the king of Assyria gave this order: "Have one of the priests you took captive from Samaria go back to live there and teach the people what the god of the land requires." [28]So one of the priests who had been exiled from Samaria came to live in Bethel and taught them how to worship the LORD.

[29]Nevertheless, each national group made its own gods in the several towns where they settled, and set them up in the shrines the people of Samaria had made at the high places. [30]The men from Babylon made Succoth Benoth, the men from Cuthah made Nergal, and the men from Hamath made Ashima; [31]the Avvites made Nibhaz and Tartak, and the Sepharvites burned their children in the fire as sacrifices to Adrammelech and Anammelech, the gods of Sepharvaim. [32]They worshiped the LORD, but they also appointed all sorts of their own people to officiate for them as priests in the shrines at the high places. [33]They worshiped the LORD, but they also served their own gods in accordance with the customs of the nations from which they had been brought.

The Bible Says

Not Like Dad

Are you destined to become just like your parents? Abusive? Alcoholic? Generous? Loving? Bitter? For some teens, turning out like their parents would be terrible; for others, terrific. You can have terrific parents and go wrong, or you can have terrible parents and become a good person. Follow this family's story (2 Kings 8–21):

* Ahaz was a wicked king; his son Joash was godly.
* Joash's son Amaziah was godly, and so was Amaziah's son Uzziah.
* Uzziah's son Jotham was godly, but Jotham's son Ahaz was wicked.
* Ahaz's son Hezekiah was godly, but Hezekiah's son Manasseh was the most wicked of all Judah's kings.

What does this pattern tell you? Having good parents won't make you good. And bad parents won't make you bad. The kind of person you become is up to you.

³⁴To this day they persist in their former practices. They neither worship the Lord nor adhere to the decrees and ordinances, the laws and commands that the Lord gave the descendants of Jacob, whom he named Israel. ³⁵When the Lord made a covenant with the Israelites, he commanded them: "Do not worship any other gods or bow down to them, serve them or sacrifice to them. ³⁶But the Lord, who brought you up out of Egypt with mighty power and outstretched arm, is the one you must worship. To him you shall bow down and to him offer sacrifices. ³⁷You must always be careful to keep the decrees and ordinances, the laws and commands he wrote for you. Do not worship other gods. ³⁸Do not forget the covenant I have made with you, and do not worship other gods. ³⁹Rather, worship the Lord your God; it is he who will deliver you from the hand of all your enemies."

⁴⁰They would not listen, however, but persisted in their former practices. ⁴¹Even while these people were worshiping the Lord, they were serving their idols. To this day their children and grandchildren continue to do as their fathers did.

18 *Hezekiah King of Judah* In the third year of Hoshea son of Elah king of Israel, Hezekiah son of Ahaz king of Judah began to reign. ²He was twenty-five years old when he became king, and he reigned in Jerusalem twenty-nine years. His mother's name was Abijah*a* daughter of Zechariah. ³He did what was right in the eyes of the Lord, just as his father David had done. ⁴He removed the high places, smashed the sacred stones and cut down the Asherah poles. He broke into pieces the bronze snake Moses had made, for up to that time the Israelites had been burning incense to it. (It was called*b* Nehushtan.*c*)

⁵Hezekiah trusted in the Lord, the God of Israel. There was no one like him among all the kings of Judah, either before him or after him. ⁶He held fast to the Lord and did not cease to follow him; he kept the commands the Lord had given Moses. ⁷And the Lord was with him; he was successful in whatever he undertook. He rebelled against the king of Assyria and did not serve him. ⁸From watchtower to fortified city, he defeated the Philistines, as far as Gaza and its territory.

⁹In King Hezekiah's fourth year, which was the seventh year of Hoshea son of Elah king of Israel, Shalmaneser king of Assyria marched against Samaria and laid siege to it. ¹⁰At the end of three years the Assyrians took it. So Samaria was captured in Hezekiah's sixth year, which was the ninth year of Hoshea king of Israel. ¹¹The king of Assyria deported Israel to Assyria and settled them in Halah, in Gozan on the Habor River and in towns of the Medes. ¹²This happened because they had not obeyed the Lord their God, but had violated his covenant—all that Moses the servant of the Lord commanded. They neither listened to the commands nor carried them out.

¹³In the fourteenth year of King Hezekiah's reign, Sennacherib king of Assyria attacked all the fortified cities of Judah and captured them. ¹⁴So Hezekiah king of Judah sent this message to the king of Assyria at Lachish: "I have done wrong. Withdraw from me, and I will pay whatever you demand of me." The king of Assyria exacted from Hezekiah king of Judah three hundred talents*d* of silver and thirty talents*e* of gold. ¹⁵So Hezekiah gave him all the silver that was found in the temple of the Lord and in the treasuries of the royal palace.

¹⁶At this time Hezekiah king of Judah stripped off the gold with which he had covered the doors and doorposts of the temple of the Lord, and gave it to the king of Assyria.

---

a2 Hebrew *Abi*, a variant of *Abijah* *b4* Or *He called it* *c4 Nehushtan* sounds like the Hebrew for *bronze* and *snake* and *unclean thing*. *d14* That is, about 11 tons (about 10 metric tons) *e14* That is, about 1 ton (about 1 metric ton)

Sennacherib Threatens Jerusalem ¹⁷The king of Assyria sent his supreme commander, his chief officer and his field commander with a large army, from Lachish to King Hezekiah at Jerusalem. They came up to Jerusalem and stopped at the aqueduct of the Upper Pool, on the road to the Washerman's Field. ¹⁸They called for the king; and Eliakim son of Hilkiah the palace administrator, Shebna the secretary, and Joah son of Asaph the recorder went out to them.

¹⁹The field commander said to them, "Tell Hezekiah:

" 'This is what the great king, the king of Assyria, says: On what are you basing this confidence of yours? ²⁰You say you have strategy and military strength—but you speak only empty words. On whom are you depending, that you rebel against me? ²¹Look now, you are depending on Egypt, that splintered reed of a staff, which pierces a man's hand and wounds him if he leans on it! Such is Pharaoh king of Egypt to all who depend on him. ²²And if you say to me, "We are depending on the Lord our God"—isn't he the one whose high places and altars Hezekiah removed, saying to Judah and Jerusalem, "You must worship before this altar in Jerusalem"?

²³" 'Come now, make a bargain with my master, the king of Assyria: I will give you two thousand horses—if you can put riders on them! ²⁴How can you repulse one officer of the least of my master's officials, even though you are depending on Egypt for chariots and horsemen*? ²⁵Furthermore, have I come to attack and destroy this place without word from the Lord? The Lord himself told me to march against this country and destroy it.' "

²⁶Then Eliakim son of Hilkiah, and Shebna and Joah said to the field commander, "Please speak to your servants in Aramaic, since we understand it. Don't speak to us in Hebrew in the hearing of the people on the wall."

²⁷But the commander replied, "Was it only to your master and you that my master sent me to say these things, and not to the men sitting on the wall—who, like you, will have to eat their own filth and drink their own urine?"

²⁸Then the commander stood and called out in Hebrew: "Hear the word of the great king, the king of Assyria! ²⁹This is what the king says: Do not let Hezekiah deceive you. He cannot deliver you from my hand. ³⁰Do not let Hezekiah persuade you to trust in the Lord when he says, 'The Lord will surely deliver us; this city will not be given into the hand of the king of Assyria.'

³¹"Do not listen to Hezekiah. This is what the king of Assyria says: Make peace with me and come out to me. Then every one of you will eat from his own vine and fig tree and drink water from his own cistern, ³²until I come and take you to a land like your own, a land of grain and new wine, a land of bread and vineyards, a land of olive trees and honey. Choose life and not death!

"Do not listen to Hezekiah, for he is misleading you when he says, 'The Lord will deliver us.' ³³Has the god of any nation ever delivered his land from the hand of the king of Assyria? ³⁴Where are the gods of Hamath and Arpad? Where are the gods of Sepharvaim, Hena and Ivvah? Have they rescued Samaria from my hand? ³⁵Who of all the gods of these countries has been able to save his land from me? How then can the Lord deliver Jerusalem from my hand?"

³⁶But the people remained silent and said nothing in reply, because the king had commanded, "Do not answer him."

³⁷Then Eliakim son of Hilkiah the palace administrator, Shebna the secretary and Joah son of Asaph the recorder went to Hezekiah, with their clothes torn, and told him what the field commander had said.

*24 Or *charioteers*

19 *Jerusalem's Deliverance Foretold* When King Hezekiah heard this, he tore his clothes and put on sackcloth and went into the temple of the LORD. ²He sent Eliakim the palace administrator, Shebna the secretary and the leading priests, all wearing sackcloth, to the prophet Isaiah son of Amoz. ³They told him, "This is what Hezekiah says: This day is a day of distress and rebuke and disgrace, as when children come to the point of birth and there is no strength to deliver them. ⁴It may be that the LORD your God will hear all the words of the field commander, whom his master, the king of Assyria, has sent to ridicule the living God, and that he will rebuke him for the words the LORD your God has heard. Therefore pray for the remnant that still survives."

⁵When King Hezekiah's officials came to Isaiah, ⁶Isaiah said to them, "Tell your master, 'This is what the LORD says: Do not be afraid of what you have heard—those words with which the underlings of the king of Assyria have blasphemed me. ⁷Listen! I am going to put such a spirit in him that when he hears a certain report, he will return to his own country, and there I will have him cut down with the sword.' "

⁸When the field commander heard that the king of Assyria had left Lachish, he withdrew and found the king fighting against Libnah.

⁹Now Sennacherib received a report that Tirhakah, the Cushite*ᵃ* king of Egypt,, was marching out to fight against him. So he again sent messengers to Hezekiah with this word: ¹⁰"Say to Hezekiah king of Judah: Do not let the god you depend on deceive you when he says, 'Jerusalem will not be handed over to the king of Assyria.' ¹¹Surely you have heard what the kings of Assyria have done to all the countries, destroying them completely. And will you be delivered? ¹²Did the gods of the nations that were destroyed by my forefathers deliver them: the gods of Gozan, Haran, Rezeph and the people of Eden who were in Tel Assar? ¹³Where is the king of Hamath, the king of Arpad, the king of the city of Sepharvaim, or of Hena or Ivvah?"

Hezekiah's Prayer ¹⁴Hezekiah received the letter from the messengers and read it. Then he went up to the temple of the LORD and spread it out before the LORD. ¹⁵And Hezekiah prayed to the LORD: "O LORD, God of Israel, enthroned between the cherubim, you alone are God over all the kingdoms of the earth. You have made heaven and earth. ¹⁶Give ear, O LORD, and hear; open your eyes, O LORD, and see; listen to the words Sennacherib has sent to insult the living God.

¹⁷"It is true, O LORD, that the Assyrian kings have laid waste these nations and their lands. ¹⁸They have thrown their gods into the fire and destroyed them, for they were not gods but only wood and stone, fashioned by men's hands. ¹⁹Now, O LORD our God, deliver us from his hand, so that all kingdoms on earth may know that you alone, O LORD, are God."

Isaiah Prophesies Sennacherib's Fall

²⁰Then Isaiah son of Amoz sent a message to Hezekiah: "This is what the LORD,

ᵃ9 That is, from the upper Nile region

2 KINGS 19:14–19

Have you ever wondered why God answers prayers? Because he loves you? Because you've been good and deserve a reward? Because you keep on asking? Because you ask in faith? It's not really possible to say why God chooses to answer a particular prayer. But King Hezekiah's experience is educational. An Assyrian army threatened Jerusalem, yet Hezekiah didn't plead for the lives of his people. He asked God to deliver the city "so that all kingdoms on earth may know that you alone, O LORD, are God" (2 Kings 19:19). When you can honestly ask God to answer your prayers for his glory, there's a good chance he will say yes.

Direct Line

the God of Israel, says: I have heard your prayer concerning Sennacherib king of Assyria. ²¹This is the word that the LORD has spoken against him:

> " 'The Virgin Daughter of Zion
> despises you and mocks you.
> The Daughter of Jerusalem
> tosses her head as you flee.
> ²²Who is it you have insulted and blasphemed?
> Against whom have you raised your voice
> and lifted your eyes in pride?
> Against the Holy One of Israel!
> ²³By your messengers
> you have heaped insults on the Lord.
> And you have said,
> "With my many chariots
> I have ascended the heights of the mountains,
> the utmost heights of Lebanon.
> I have cut down its tallest cedars,
> the choicest of its pines.
> I have reached its remotest parts,
> the finest of its forests.
> ²⁴I have dug wells in foreign lands
> and drunk the water there.
> With the soles of my feet
> I have dried up all the streams of Egypt."

> ²⁵ " 'Have you not heard?
> Long ago I ordained it.
> In days of old I planned it;
> now I have brought it to pass,
> that you have turned fortified cities
> into piles of stone.
> ²⁶Their people, drained of power,
> are dismayed and put to shame.
> They are like plants in the field,
> like tender green shoots,
> like grass sprouting on the roof,
> scorched before it grows up.

> ²⁷ " 'But I know where you stay
> and when you come and go
> and how you rage against me.
> ²⁸Because you rage against me
> and your insolence has reached my ears,
> I will put my hook in your nose
> and my bit in your mouth,
> and I will make you return
> by the way you came.'

²⁹"This will be the sign for you, O Hezekiah:

> "This year you will eat what grows by itself,
> and the second year what springs from that.
> But in the third year sow and reap,
> plant vineyards and eat their fruit.
> ³⁰Once more a remnant of the house of Judah
> will take root below and bear fruit above.
> ³¹For out of Jerusalem will come a remnant,
> and out of Mount Zion a band of survivors.

The zeal of the LORD Almighty will accomplish this.

³²"Therefore this is what the LORD says concerning the king of Assyria:

"He will not enter this city
　　or shoot an arrow here.
He will not come before it with shield
　　or build a siege ramp against it.
³³By the way that he came he will return;
　　he will not enter this city,

declares the LORD.

³⁴I will defend this city and save it,
　　for my sake and for the sake of David my servant."

³⁵That night the angel of the LORD went out and put to death a hundred and eighty-five thousand men in the Assyrian camp. When the people got up the next morning—there were all the dead bodies! ³⁶So Sennacherib king of Assyria broke camp and withdrew. He returned to Nineveh and stayed there.

³⁷One day, while he was worshiping in the temple of his god Nisroch, his sons Adrammelech and Sharezer cut him down with the sword, and they escaped to the land of Ararat. And Esarhaddon his son succeeded him as king.

Hezekiah's Illness In those days Hezekiah became ill and was at the point of death. The prophet Isaiah son of Amoz went to him and said, "This is what the LORD says: Put your house in order, because you are going to die; you will not recover."

²Hezekiah turned his face to the wall and prayed to the LORD, ³"Remember, O LORD, how I have walked before you faithfully and with wholehearted devotion and have done what is good in your eyes." And Hezekiah wept bitterly.

⁴Before Isaiah had left the middle court, the word of the LORD came to him: ⁵"Go back and tell Hezekiah, the leader of my people, 'This is what the LORD, the God of your father David, says: I have heard your prayer and seen your tears; I will heal you. On the third day from now you will go up to the temple of the LORD. ⁶I will add fifteen years to your life. And I will deliver you and this city from the hand of the king of Assyria. I will defend this city for my sake and for the sake of my servant David.' "

⁷Then Isaiah said, "Prepare a poultice of figs." They did so and applied it to the boil, and he recovered.

⁸Hezekiah had asked Isaiah, "What will be the sign that the LORD will heal me and that I will go up to the temple of the LORD on the third day from now?"

⁹Isaiah answered, "This is the LORD's sign to you that the LORD will do what he has promised: Shall the shadow go forward ten steps, or shall it go back ten steps?"

¹⁰"It is a simple matter for the shadow to go forward ten steps," said Hezekiah. "Rather, have it go back ten steps."

¹¹Then the prophet Isaiah called upon the LORD, and the LORD made the shadow go back the ten steps it had gone down on the stairway of Ahaz.

Envoys From Babylon ¹²At that time Merodach-Baladan son of Baladan king of Babylon sent Hezekiah letters and a gift, because he had heard of Hezekiah's illness. ¹³Hezekiah received the messengers and showed them all that was in his storehouses—the silver, the gold, the spices and the fine oil—his armory and everything found among his treasures. There was nothing in his palace or in all his kingdom that Hezekiah did not show them.

¹⁴Then Isaiah the prophet went to King Hezekiah and asked, "What did those men say, and where did they come from?"

"From a distant land," Hezekiah replied. "They came from Babylon."

¹⁵The prophet asked, "What did they see in your palace?"

"They saw everything in my palace," Hezekiah said. "There is nothing among my treasures that I did not show them."

¹⁶Then Isaiah said to Hezekiah, "Hear the word of the Lord: ¹⁷The time will surely come when everything in your palace, and all that your fathers have stored up until this day, will be carried off to Babylon. Nothing will be left, says the Lord. ¹⁸And some of your descendants, your own flesh and blood, that will be born to you, will be taken away, and they will become eunuchs in the palace of the king of Babylon."

¹⁹"The word of the Lord you have spoken is good," Hezekiah replied. For he thought, "Will there not be peace and security in my lifetime?"

²⁰As for the other events of Hezekiah's reign, all his achievements and how he made the pool and the tunnel by which he brought water into the city, are they not written in the book of the annals of the kings of Judah? ²¹Hezekiah rested with his fathers. And Manasseh his son succeeded him as king.

21 *Manasseh King of Judah* Manasseh was twelve years old when he became king, and he reigned in Jerusalem fifty-five years. His mother's name was Hephzibah. ²He did evil in the eyes of the Lord, following the detestable practices of the nations the Lord had driven out before the Israelites. ³He rebuilt the high places his father Hezekiah had destroyed; he also erected altars to Baal and made an Asherah pole, as Ahab king of Israel had done. He bowed down to all the starry hosts and worshiped them. ⁴He built altars in the temple of the Lord, of which the Lord had said, "In Jerusalem I will put my Name." ⁵In both courts of the temple of the Lord, he built altars to all the starry hosts. ⁶He sacrificed his own son in*ᵃ* the fire, practiced sorcery and divination, and consulted mediums and spiritists. He did much evil in the eyes of the Lord, provoking him to anger.

⁷He took the carved Asherah pole he had made and put it in the temple, of which the Lord had said to David and to his son Solomon, "In this temple and in Jerusalem, which I have chosen out of all the tribes of Israel, I will put my Name forever. ⁸I will not again make the feet of the Israelites wander from the land I gave their forefathers, if only they will be careful to do everything I commanded them and will keep the whole Law that my servant Moses gave them." ⁹But the people did not listen. Manasseh led them astray, so that they did more evil than the nations the Lord had destroyed before the Israelites.

¹⁰The Lord said through his servants the prophets: ¹¹"Manasseh king of Judah has committed these detestable sins. He has done more evil than the Amorites who preceded him and has led Judah into sin with his idols. ¹²Therefore this is what the Lord, the God of Israel, says: I am going to bring such disaster on Jerusalem and Judah that the ears of everyone who hears of it will tingle. ¹³I will stretch out over Jerusalem the measuring line used against Samaria and the plumb line used against the house of Ahab. I will wipe out Jerusalem as one wipes a dish, wiping it and turning it upside down. ¹⁴I will forsake the remnant of my inheritance and hand them over to their enemies. They will be looted and plundered by all their foes, ¹⁵because they have done evil in my eyes and have provoked me to anger from the day their forefathers came out of Egypt until this day."

¹⁶Moreover, Manasseh also shed so much innocent blood that he filled Jerusalem from end to end—besides the sin that he had caused Judah to commit, so that they did evil in the eyes of the Lord.

¹⁷As for the other events of Manasseh's reign, and all he did, including the

---

ᵃ6 Or He made his own son pass through

sin he committed, are they not written in the book of the annals of the kings of Judah? [18]Manasseh rested with his fathers and was buried in his palace garden, the garden of Uzza. And Amon his son succeeded him as king.

Amon King of Judah [19]Amon was twenty-two years old when he became king, and he reigned in Jerusalem two years. His mother's name was Meshullemeth daughter of Haruz; she was from Jotbah. [20]He did evil in the eyes of the LORD, as his father Manasseh had done. [21]He walked in all the ways of his father; he worshiped the idols his father had worshiped, and bowed down to them. [22]He forsook the LORD, the God of his fathers, and did not walk in the way of the LORD.

[23]Amon's officials conspired against him and assassinated the king in his palace. [24]Then the people of the land killed all who had plotted against King Amon, and they made Josiah his son king in his place.

[25]As for the other events of Amon's reign, and what he did, are they not written in the book of the annals of the kings of Judah? [26]He was buried in his grave in the garden of Uzza. And Josiah his son succeeded him as king.

22 *The Book of the Law Found* Josiah was eight years old when he became king, and he reigned in Jerusalem thirty-one years. His mother's name was Jedidah daughter of Adaiah; she was from Bozkath. [2]He did what was right in the eyes of the LORD and walked in all the ways of his father David, not turning aside to the right or to the left.

[3]In the eighteenth year of his reign, King Josiah sent the secretary, Shaphan son of Azaliah, the son of Meshullam, to the temple of the LORD. He said: [4]"Go up to Hilkiah the high priest and have him get ready the money that has been brought into the temple of the LORD, which the doorkeepers have collected from the people. [5]Have them entrust it to the men appointed to supervise the work on the temple. And have these men pay the workers who repair the temple of the LORD— [6]the carpenters, the builders and the masons. Also have them purchase timber and dressed stone to repair the temple. [7]But they need not account for the money entrusted to them, because they are acting faithfully."

[8]Hilkiah the high priest said to Shaphan the secretary, "I have found the Book of the Law in the temple of the LORD." He gave it to Shaphan, who read it. [9]Then Shaphan the secretary went to the king and reported to him: "Your officials have paid out the money that was in the temple of the LORD and have entrusted it to the workers and supervisors at the temple." [10]Then Shaphan the secretary informed the king, "Hilkiah the priest has given me a book." And Shaphan read from it in the presence of the king.

[11]When the king heard the words of the Book of the Law, he tore his robes. [12]He gave these orders to Hilkiah the priest, Ahikam son of Shaphan, Acbor son of Micaiah, Shaphan the secretary and Asaiah the king's attendant: [13]"Go and inquire of the LORD for me and for the people and for all Judah about what is written in this book that has been found. Great is the LORD's anger that burns against us because our fathers have not obeyed the words of this book; they have not acted in accordance with all that is written there concerning us."

[14]Hilkiah the priest, Ahikam, Acbor, Shaphan and Asaiah went to speak to the prophetess Huldah, who was the wife of Shallum son of Tikvah, the son of Harhas, keeper of the wardrobe. She lived in Jerusalem, in the Second District.

[15]She said to them, "This is what the LORD, the God of Israel, says: Tell the man who sent you to me, [16]'This is what the LORD says: I am going to bring disaster on this place and its people, according to everything written in the book the king of Judah has read. [17]Because they have forsaken me and burned incense to other gods and provoked me to anger by all the idols

Dear Sam,

Whenever I do something wrong or if one of my parents gets really upset, my parents beat me. They never hit my brother or my sister. Why?

Leslie in Laramie

Dear Sam, Inc.

100 Advice Lane, Anywhere, USA

Dear Leslie,

Child abuse has been going on for thousands of years. In the time of King Josiah of Israel (640-609 B.C.) parents were taking their children to be burned alive to pagan gods (2 Kings 23:10). Those children did nothing to deserve being burned alive. And you do not deserve to be beaten.

Child abuse is a big problem today. Unfortunately, the situation you describe is common: one child is some-how chosen to be abused while the others are not. While it is good your siblings aren't being physically abused, that doesn't make it any easier for you.

Chances are that one or both of your parents were abused as children. I hope you will be able to get some counseling or join a support group at your school so that you can put an end to the cycle of abuse in your family. Tell your teacher or your pastor how you feel. Remember that God loves you and will never forsake you despite how your parents act (Psalm 27:10).

Sam

their hands have made,*ᵃ* my anger will burn against this place and will not be quenched.' ¹⁸Tell the king of Judah, who sent you to inquire of the LORD, 'This is what the LORD, the God of Israel, says concerning the words you heard: ¹⁹Because your heart was responsive and you humbled yourself before the LORD when you heard what I have spoken against this place and its people, that they would become accursed and laid waste, and because you tore your robes and wept in my presence, I have heard you, declares the LORD. ²⁰Therefore I will gather you to your fathers, and you will be buried in peace. Your eyes will not see all the disaster I am going to bring on this place.' "

So they took her answer back to the king.

23

Josiah Renews the Covenant Then the king called together all the elders of Judah and Jerusalem. ²He went up to the temple of the LORD with the men of Judah, the people of Jerusalem, the priests and the prophets—all the people from the least to the greatest. He read in their hearing all the words of the Book of the Covenant, which had been found in the temple of the LORD. ³The king stood by the pillar and renewed the covenant in the presence of the LORD—to follow the LORD and keep his commands, regulations and decrees with all his heart and all his soul, thus confirming the words of the covenant written in this book. Then all the people pledged themselves to the covenant.

⁴The king ordered Hilkiah the high priest, the priests next in rank and the doorkeepers to remove from the temple of the LORD all the articles made for Baal and Asherah and all the starry hosts. He burned them outside Jerusalem in the fields of the Kidron Valley and took the ashes to Bethel. ⁵He did away with the pagan priests appointed by the kings of Judah to burn incense on the high places of the towns of Judah and on those around Jerusalem— those who burned incense to Baal, to the sun and moon, to the constellations and to all the starry hosts. ⁶He took the Asherah pole from the temple of the LORD to the Kidron Valley outside Jerusalem and burned it there. He ground it to powder and scattered the dust over the graves of the common people. ⁷He also tore down the quarters of the male shrine prostitutes, which were in the temple of the LORD and where women did weaving for Asherah.

⁸Josiah brought all the priests from the towns of Judah and desecrated the high places, from Geba to Beersheba, where the priests had burned incense. He broke down the shrines*ᵇ* at the gates—at the entrance to the Gate of Joshua, the city governor, which is on the left of the city gate. ⁹Although the priests of the high places did not serve at the altar of the LORD in Jerusalem, they ate unleavened bread with their fellow priests.

¹⁰He desecrated Topheth, which was in the Valley of Ben Hinnom, so no one could use it to sacrifice his son or daughter in*ᶜ* the fire to Molech. ¹¹He removed from the entrance to the temple of the LORD the horses that the kings of Judah had dedicated to the sun. They were in the court near the room of an official named Nathan-Melech. Josiah then burned the chariots dedicated to the sun.

¹²He pulled down the altars the kings of Judah had erected on the roof near the upper room of Ahaz, and the altars Manasseh had built in the two courts of the temple of the LORD. He removed them from there, smashed them to pieces and threw the rubble into the Kidron Valley. ¹³The king also desecrated the high places that were east of Jerusalem on the south of the Hill of Corruption—the ones Solomon king of Israel had built for Ashtoreth the vile goddess of the Sidonians, for Chemosh the vile god of Moab, and for Molech*ᵈ* the detestable god of the people of Ammon. ¹⁴Josiah smashed the sacred stones and cut down the Asherah poles and covered the sites with human bones.

ᵃ17 Or *by everything they have done*   *ᵇ8* Or *high places*   *ᶜ10* Or *to make his son or daughter pass through*
ᵈ13 Hebrew *Milcom*

¹⁵Even the altar at Bethel, the high place made by Jeroboam son of Nebat, who had caused Israel to sin—even that altar and high place he demolished. He burned the high place and ground it to powder, and burned the Asherah pole also. ¹⁶Then Josiah looked around, and when he saw the tombs that were there on the hillside, he had the bones removed from them and burned on the altar to defile it, in accordance with the word of the LORD proclaimed by the man of God who foretold these things.

¹⁷The king asked, "What is that tombstone I see?"

The men of the city said, "It marks the tomb of the man of God who came from Judah and pronounced against the altar of Bethel the very things you have done to it."

¹⁸"Leave it alone," he said. "Don't let anyone disturb his bones." So they spared his bones and those of the prophet who had come from Samaria.

¹⁹Just as he had done at Bethel, Josiah removed and defiled all the shrines at the high places that the kings of Israel had built in the towns of Samaria that had provoked the LORD to anger. ²⁰Josiah slaughtered all the priests of those high places on the altars and burned human bones on them. Then he went back to Jerusalem.

²¹The king gave this order to all the people: "Celebrate the Passover to the LORD your God, as it is written in this Book of the Covenant." ²²Not since the days of the judges who led Israel, nor throughout the days of the kings of Israel and the kings of Judah, had any such Passover been observed. ²³But in the eighteenth year of King Josiah, this Passover was celebrated to the LORD in Jerusalem.

²⁴Furthermore, Josiah got rid of the mediums and spiritists, the household gods, the idols and all the other detestable things seen in Judah and Jerusalem. This he did to fulfill the requirements of the law written in the book that Hilkiah the priest had discovered in the temple of the LORD. ²⁵Neither before nor after Josiah was there a king like him who turned to the LORD as he did—with all his heart and with all his soul and with all his strength, in accordance with all the Law of Moses.

²⁶Nevertheless, the LORD did not turn away from the heat of his fierce anger, which burned against Judah because of all that Manasseh had done to provoke him to anger. ²⁷So the LORD said, "I will remove Judah also from my presence as I removed Israel, and I will reject Jerusalem, the city I chose, and this temple, about which I said, 'There shall my Name be.'ᵃ"

²⁸As for the other events of Josiah's reign, and all he did, are they not written in the book of the annals of the kings of Judah?

²⁹While Josiah was king, Pharaoh Neco king of Egypt went up to the Euphrates River to help the king of Assyria. King Josiah marched out to meet him in battle, but Neco faced him and killed him at Megiddo. ³⁰Josiah's servants brought his body in a chariot from Megiddo to Jerusalem and buried him in his own tomb. And

Direct Line

2 Kings 23:25

Chris was a popular guy in high school. He was on the varsity football and baseball teams. He was elected to the student council and was president of a few school clubs. Oh, yes, Chris is now studying for the ministry. Maybe Chris doesn't fit the stereotype some people have of a "godly" teenager, but he fits this description of young King Josiah. Josiah was committed to getting rid of everything in Judah that was corrupting and sinful. Chris is just as committed to being personally pure. Josiah was committed to worship. Chris is committed to worship too. Commitment to the Lord does bring challenges. But it also brings a satisfying lifestyle.

ᵃ*27* 1 Kings 8:29

the people of the land took Jehoahaz son of Josiah and anointed him and made him king in place of his father.

Jehoahaz King of Judah   ³¹Jehoahaz was twenty-three years old when he became king, and he reigned in Jerusalem three months. His mother's name was Hamutal daughter of Jeremiah; she was from Libnah. ³²He did evil in the eyes of the LORD, just as his fathers had done. ³³Pharaoh Neco put him in chains at Riblah in the land of Hamath*ᵃ* so that he might not reign in Jerusalem, and he imposed on Judah a levy of a hundred talents*ᵇ* of silver and a talent*ᶜ* of gold. ³⁴Pharaoh Neco made Eliakim son of Josiah king in place of his father Josiah and changed Eliakim's name to Jehoiakim. But he took Jehoahaz and carried him off to Egypt, and there he died. ³⁵Jehoiakim paid Pharaoh Neco the silver and gold he demanded. In order to do so, he taxed the land and exacted the silver and gold from the people of the land according to their assessments.

Jehoiakim King of Judah   ³⁶Jehoiakim was twenty-five years old when he became king, and he reigned in Jerusalem eleven years. His mother's name was Zebidah daughter of Pedaiah; she was from Rumah. ³⁷And he did evil in the eyes of the LORD, just as his fathers had done.

24 During Jehoiakim's reign, Nebuchadnezzar king of Babylon invaded the land, and Jehoiakim became his vassal for three years. But then he changed his mind and rebelled against Nebuchadnezzar. ²The LORD sent Babylonian,*ᵈ* Aramean, Moabite and Ammonite raiders against him. He sent them to destroy Judah, in accordance with the word of the LORD proclaimed by his servants the prophets. ³Surely these things happened to Judah according to the LORD's command, in order to remove them from his presence because of the sins of Manasseh and all he had done, ⁴including the shedding of innocent blood. For he had filled Jerusalem with innocent blood, and the LORD was not willing to forgive.

⁵As for the other events of Jehoiakim's reign, and all he did, are they not written in the book of the annals of the kings of Judah? ⁶Jehoiakim rested with his fathers. And Jehoiachin his son succeeded him as king.

⁷The king of Egypt did not march out from his own country again, because the king of Babylon had taken all his territory, from the Wadi of Egypt to the Euphrates River.

Jehoiachin King of Judah   ⁸Jehoiachin was eighteen years old when he became king, and he reigned in Jerusalem three months. His mother's name was Nehushta daughter of Elnathan; she was from Jerusalem. ⁹He did evil in the eyes of the LORD, just as his father had done.

¹⁰At that time the officers of Nebuchadnezzar king of Babylon advanced on Jerusalem and laid siege to it, ¹¹and Nebuchadnezzar himself came up to the city while his officers were besieging it. ¹²Jehoiachin king of Judah, his mother, his attendants, his nobles and his officials all surrendered to him.

In the eighth year of the reign of the king of Babylon, he took Jehoiachin prisoner. ¹³As the LORD had declared, Nebuchadnezzar removed all the treasures from the temple of the LORD and from the royal palace, and took away all the gold articles that Solomon king of Israel had made for the temple of the LORD. ¹⁴He carried into exile all Jerusalem: all the officers and fighting men, and all the craftsmen and artisans—a total of ten thousand. Only the poorest people of the land were left.

¹⁵Nebuchadnezzar took Jehoiachin captive to Babylon. He also took from

---

ᵃ33 Hebrew; Septuagint (see also 2 Chron. 36:3) *Neco at Riblah in Hamath removed him*   *ᵇ33* That is, about 3 3/4 tons (about 3.4 metric tons)   *ᶜ33* That is, about 75 pounds (about 34 kilograms)   *ᵈ2* Or *Chaldean*

Jerusalem to Babylon the king's mother, his wives, his officials and the leading men of the land. [16]The king of Babylon also deported to Babylon the entire force of seven thousand fighting men, strong and fit for war, and a thousand craftsmen and artisans. [17]He made Mattaniah, Jehoiachin's uncle, king in his place and changed his name to Zedekiah.

Zedekiah King of Judah   [18]Zedekiah was twenty-one years old when he became king, and he reigned in Jerusalem eleven years. His mother's name was Hamutal daughter of Jeremiah; she was from Libnah. [19]He did evil in the eyes of the LORD, just as Jehoiakim had done. [20]It was because of the LORD's anger that all this happened to Jerusalem and Judah, and in the end he thrust them from his presence.

The Fall of Jerusalem   Now Zedekiah rebelled against the king of Babylon.

25 So in the ninth year of Zedekiah's reign, on the tenth day of the tenth month, Nebuchadnezzar king of Babylon marched against Jerusalem with his whole army. He encamped outside the city and built siege works all around it. [2]The city was kept under siege until the eleventh year of King Zedekiah. [3]By the ninth day of the ⌊fourth⌋[a] month the famine in the city had become so severe that there was no food for the people to eat. [4]Then the city wall was broken through, and the whole army fled at night through the gate between the two walls near the king's garden, though the Babylonians[b] were surrounding the city. They fled toward the Arabah,[c] [5]but the Babylonian[d] army pursued the king and overtook him in the plains of Jericho. All his soldiers were separated from him and scattered, [6]and he was captured. He was taken to the king of Babylon at Riblah, where sentence was pronounced on him. [7]They killed the sons of Zedekiah before his eyes. Then they put out his eyes, bound him with bronze shackles and took him to Babylon.

[8]On the seventh day of the fifth month, in the nineteenth year of Nebuchadnezzar king of Babylon, Nebuzaradan commander of the imperial guard, an official of the king of Babylon, came to Jerusalem. [9]He set fire to the temple of the LORD, the royal palace and all the houses of Jerusalem. Every important building he burned down. [10]The whole Babylonian army, under the commander of the imperial guard, broke down the walls around Jerusalem. [11]Nebuzaradan the commander of the guard carried into exile the people who remained in the city, along with the rest of the populace and those who had gone over to the king of Babylon. [12]But the commander left behind some of the poorest people of the land to work the vineyards and fields.

[13]The Babylonians broke up the bronze pillars, the movable stands and the bronze Sea that were at the temple of the LORD and they carried the bronze to Babylon. [14]They also took away the pots, shovels, wick trimmers, dishes and all the bronze articles used in the temple service. [15]The commander of the imperial guard took away the censers and sprinkling bowls— all that were made of pure gold or silver.

[16]The bronze from the two pillars, the Sea

Do you think he had to mow the lawn and clean his room like I do?

SEE
2 KINGS 25:30

[a]3 See Jer. 52:6.   [b]4 Or *Chaldeans*; also in verses 13, 25 and 26
[c]4 Or *the Jordan Valley*   [d]5 Or *Chaldean*; also in verses 10 and 24

and the movable stands, which Solomon had made for the temple of the LORD, was more than could be weighed. ¹⁷Each pillar was twenty-seven feet*ᵃ* high. The bronze capital on top of one pillar was four and a half feet*ᵇ* high and was decorated with a network and pomegranates of bronze all around. The other pillar, with its network, was similar.

¹⁸The commander of the guard took as prisoners Seraiah the chief priest, Zephaniah the priest next in rank and the three doorkeepers. ¹⁹Of those still in the city, he took the officer in charge of the fighting men and five royal advisers. He also took the secretary who was chief officer in charge of conscripting the people of the land and sixty of his men who were found in the city. ²⁰Nebuzaradan the commander took them all and brought them to the king of Babylon at Riblah. ²¹There at Riblah, in the land of Hamath, the king had them executed.

So Judah went into captivity, away from her land.

²²Nebuchadnezzar king of Babylon appointed Gedaliah son of Ahikam, the son of Shaphan, to be over the people he had left behind in Judah. ²³When all the army officers and their men heard that the king of Babylon had appointed Gedaliah as governor, they came to Gedaliah at Mizpah—Ishmael son of Nethaniah, Johanan son of Kareah, Seraiah son of Tanhumeth the Netophathite, Jaazaniah the son of the Maacathite, and their men. ²⁴Gedaliah took an oath to reassure them and their men. "Do not be afraid of the Babylonian officials," he said. "Settle down in the land and serve the king of Babylon, and it will go well with you."

²⁵In the seventh month, however, Ishmael son of Nethaniah, the son of Elishama, who was of royal blood, came with ten men and assassinated Gedaliah and also the men of Judah and the Babylonians who were with him at Mizpah. ²⁶At this, all the people from the least to the greatest, together with the army officers, fled to Egypt for fear of the Babylonians.

Jehoiachin Released   ²⁷In the thirty-seventh year of the exile of Jehoiachin king of Judah, in the year Evil-Merodach*ᶜ* became king of Babylon, he released Jehoiachin from prison on the twenty-seventh day of the twelfth month. ²⁸He spoke kindly to him and gave him a seat of honor higher than those of the other kings who were with him in Babylon. ²⁹So Jehoiachin put aside his prison clothes and for the rest of his life ate regularly at the king's table. ³⁰Day by day the king gave Jehoiachin a regular allowance as long as he lived.

ᵃ17 Hebrew *eighteen cubits* (about 8.1 meters)   *ᵇ17* Hebrew *three cubits* (about 1.3 meters)   *ᶜ27* Also called *Amel-Marduk*

Introduction

to the

book of 1 Chronicles

DIARIES.

Some teens like to keep a diary. They write down not only what happens to them but also what they think about it and how they feel. Wouldn't it be interesting if God kept a diary about you? What do you suppose he'd think was important enough to write down?

The book of 1 Chronicles contains, in genealogies, a religious history of the Israelite nation from creation to the return of the captives in 538 B.C. In a way it's God's diary, his record of what was important in his people's lives. This book emphasizes good kings and good things rather than sins. Isn't it good to know that God is more interested in your successes than your failures?

Fundamentals

Do you ever feel that God is being unfair (1 Chronicles 13:9-11; 15:13)?

How do you react when someone makes you a promise (1 Chronicles 17)?

What is more important to God than any offering (1 Chronicles 22)?

How do you think people will remember you (1 Chronicles 29:28)?

FAST FACTS

This book was written after the Babylonian captivity, about 440 B.C.

Forty passages repeat material from Samuel and Kings.

Genealogies trace a family tree.

The long genealogy here (1 Chronicles 1–9) traces Israel's roots.

1 *Historical Records From Adam to Abraham*
To Noah's Sons Adam, Seth, Enosh, [2]Kenan, Mahalalel, Jared, [3]Enoch, Methuselah, Lamech, Noah.

[4]The sons of Noah:[a]
Shem, Ham and Japheth.

The Japhethites

[5]The sons[b] of Japheth:
Gomer, Magog, Madai, Javan, Tubal, Meshech and Tiras.
[6]The sons of Gomer:
Ashkenaz, Riphath[c] and Togarmah.
[7]The sons of Javan:
Elishah, Tarshish, the Kittim and the Rodanim.

The Hamites

[8]The sons of Ham:
Cush, Mizraim,[d] Put and Canaan.
[9]The sons of Cush:
Seba, Havilah, Sabta, Raamah and Sabteca.
The sons of Raamah:
Sheba and Dedan.
[10]Cush was the father[e] of
Nimrod, who grew to be a mighty warrior on earth.
[11]Mizraim was the father of
the Ludites, Anamites, Lehabites, Naphtuhites, [12]Pathrusites, Casluhites (from whom the Philistines came) and Caphtorites.
[13]Canaan was the father of
Sidon his firstborn,[f] and of the Hittites, [14]Jebusites, Amorites, Girgashites, [15]Hivites, Arkites, Sinites, [16]Arvadites, Zemarites and Hamathites.

The Semites

[17]The sons of Shem:
Elam, Asshur, Arphaxad, Lud and Aram.
The sons of Aram[g]:
Uz, Hul, Gether and Meshech.
[18]Arphaxad was the father of Shelah,
and Shelah the father of Eber.
[19]Two sons were born to Eber:
One was named Peleg,[h] because in his time the earth was divided; his brother was named Joktan.

This is one massive family tree!

SEE
1 CHRONICLES 1–9

[a]4 Septuagint; Hebrew does not have *The sons of Noah:* [b]5 *Sons* may mean *descendants* or *successors* or *nations*; also in verses 6-10, 17 and 20. [c]6 Many Hebrew manuscripts and Vulgate (see also Septuagint and Gen. 10:3); most Hebrew manuscripts *Diphath* [d]8 That is, Egypt; also in verse 11 [e]10 *Father* may mean *ancestor* or *predecessor* or *founder*; also in verses 11, 13, 18 and 20. [f]13 Or *of the Sidonians, the foremost* [g]17 One Hebrew manuscript and some Septuagint manuscripts (see also Gen. 10:23); most Hebrew manuscripts do not have this line. [h]19 *Peleg* means *division*.

²⁰ Joktan was the father of
Almodad, Sheleph, Hazarmaveth, Jerah, ²¹Hadoram, Uzal, Diklah, ²²Obal,ᵃ Abimael, Sheba, ²³Ophir, Havilah and Jobab. All these were sons of Joktan.

²⁴ Shem, Arphaxad,ᵇ Shelah,
²⁵ Eber, Peleg, Reu,
²⁶ Serug, Nahor, Terah
²⁷ and Abram (that is, Abraham).

The Family of Abraham

²⁸ The sons of Abraham:
Isaac and Ishmael.

Descendants of Hagar

²⁹ These were their descendants:
Nebaioth the firstborn of Ishmael, Kedar, Adbeel, Mibsam, ³⁰Mishma, Dumah, Massa, Hadad, Tema, ³¹Jetur, Naphish and Kedemah. These were the sons of Ishmael.

Descendants of Keturah

³² The sons born to Keturah, Abraham's concubine:
Zimran, Jokshan, Medan, Midian, Ishbak and Shuah.
The sons of Jokshan:
Sheba and Dedan.
³³ The sons of Midian:
Ephah, Epher, Hanoch, Abida and Eldaah.
All these were descendants of Keturah.

Descendants of Sarah

³⁴ Abraham was the father of Isaac.
The sons of Isaac:
Esau and Israel.

Esau's Sons

³⁵ The sons of Esau:
Eliphaz, Reuel, Jeush, Jalam and Korah.
³⁶ The sons of Eliphaz:
Teman, Omar, Zepho,ᶜ Gatam and Kenaz;
by Timna: Amalek.ᵈ
³⁷ The sons of Reuel:
Nahath, Zerah, Shammah and Mizzah.

The People of Seir in Edom

³⁸ The sons of Seir:
Lotan, Shobal, Zibeon, Anah, Dishon, Ezer and Dishan.
³⁹ The sons of Lotan:
Hori and Homam. Timna was Lotan's sister.
⁴⁰ The sons of Shobal:
Alvan,ᵉ Manahath, Ebal, Shepho and Onam.
The sons of Zibeon:
Aiah and Anah.

ᵃ22 Some Hebrew manuscripts and Syriac (see also Gen. 10:28); most Hebrew manuscripts *Ebal*
ᵇ24 Hebrew; some Septuagint manuscripts *Arphaxad, Cainan* (see also note at Gen. 11:10)   ᶜ36 Many Hebrew manuscripts, some Septuagint manuscripts and Syriac (see also Gen. 36:11); most Hebrew manuscripts *Zephi*   ᵈ36 Some Septuagint manuscripts (see also Gen. 36:12); Hebrew *Gatam, Kenaz, Timna and Amalek*   ᵉ40 Many Hebrew manuscripts and some Septuagint manuscripts (see also Gen. 36:23); most Hebrew manuscripts *Alian*

⁴¹The son of Anah:
   Dishon.
   The sons of Dishon:
   Hemdan,ª Eshban, Ithran and Keran.
⁴²The sons of Ezer:
   Bilhan, Zaavan and Akan.ᵇ
   The sons of Dishanᶜ:
   Uz and Aran.

The Rulers of Edom

⁴³These were the kings who reigned in Edom before any Israelite king
reignedᵈ:
   Bela son of Beor, whose city was named Dinhabah.
⁴⁴When Bela died, Jobab son of Zerah from Bozrah succeeded him as
   king.
⁴⁵When Jobab died, Husham from the land of the Temanites succeeded
   him as king.
⁴⁶When Husham died, Hadad son of Bedad, who defeated Midian in the
   country of Moab, succeeded him as king. His city was named Avith.
⁴⁷When Hadad died, Samlah from Masrekah succeeded him as king.
⁴⁸When Samlah died, Shaul from Rehoboth on the riverᵉ succeeded him
   as king.
⁴⁹When Shaul died, Baal-Hanan son of Acbor succeeded him as king.
⁵⁰When Baal-Hanan died, Hadad succeeded him as king. His city was
   named Pau,ᶠ and his wife's name was Mehetabel daughter of Matred,
   the daughter of Me-Zahab. ⁵¹Hadad also died.

   The chiefs of Edom were:
   Timna, Alvah, Jetheth, ⁵²Oholibamah, Elah, Pinon, ⁵³Kenaz, Teman,
   Mibzar, ⁵⁴Magdiel and Iram. These were the chiefs of Edom.

2 *Israel's Sons*   These were the sons of Israel:
   Reuben, Simeon, Levi, Judah, Issachar, Zebulun, ²Dan, Joseph, Benjamin, Naphtali, Gad and Asher.

Judah
To Hezron's Sons

³The sons of Judah:
   Er, Onan and Shelah. These three were born to him by a Canaanite
   woman, the daughter of Shua. Er, Judah's firstborn, was wicked in the
   Lᴏʀᴅ's sight; so the Lᴏʀᴅ put him to death. ⁴Tamar, Judah's daughter-
   in-law, bore him Perez and Zerah. Judah had five sons in all.

⁵The sons of Perez:
   Hezron and Hamul.
⁶The sons of Zerah:
   Zimri, Ethan, Heman, Calcol and Dardaᵍ—five in all.
⁷The son of Carmi:
   Achar,ʰ who brought trouble on Israel by violating the ban on taking
   devoted things.ⁱ

ª*41* Many Hebrew manuscripts and some Septuagint manuscripts (see also Gen. 36:26); most Hebrew
manuscripts *Hamran*   ᵇ*42* Many Hebrew and Septuagint manuscripts (see also Gen. 36:27); most Hebrew
manuscripts *Zaavan, Jaakan*   ᶜ*42* Hebrew *Dishon,* a variant of *Dishan*   ᵈ*43* Or *before an Israelite king
reigned over them*   ᵉ*48* Possibly the Euphrates   ᶠ*50* Many Hebrew manuscripts, some Septuagint
manuscripts, Vulgate and Syriac (see also Gen. 36:39); most Hebrew manuscripts *Pai*   ᵍ*6* Many Hebrew
manuscripts, some Septuagint manuscripts and Syriac (see also 1 Kings 4:31); most Hebrew manuscripts
Dara   ʰ*7 Achar* means *trouble*; *Achar* is called *Achan* in Joshua.   ⁱ*7* The Hebrew term refers to the
irrevocable giving over of things or persons to the Lᴏʀᴅ, often by totally destroying them.

⁸The son of Ethan:
    Azariah.
⁹The sons born to Hezron were:
    Jerahmeel, Ram and Caleb.ᵃ

From Ram Son of Hezron
¹⁰Ram was the father of
    Amminadab, and Amminadab the father of Nahshon, the leader of
    the people of Judah. ¹¹Nahshon was the father of Salmon,ᵇ Salmon
    the father of Boaz, ¹²Boaz the father of Obed and Obed the father of
    Jesse.
¹³Jesse was the father of
    Eliab his firstborn; the second son was Abinadab, the third Shimea,
    ¹⁴the fourth Nethanel, the fifth Raddai, ¹⁵the sixth Ozem and the
    seventh David. ¹⁶Their sisters were Zeruiah and Abigail. Zeruiah's
    three sons were Abishai, Joab and Asahel. ¹⁷Abigail was the mother
    of Amasa, whose father was Jether the Ishmaelite.

Caleb Son of Hezron
¹⁸Caleb son of Hezron had children by his wife Azubah (and by Jerioth).
    These were her sons: Jesher, Shobab and Ardon. ¹⁹When Azubah
    died, Caleb married Ephrath, who bore him Hur. ²⁰Hur was the father
    of Uri, and Uri the father of Bezalel.
²¹Later, Hezron lay with the daughter of Makir the father of Gilead (he
    had married her when he was sixty years old), and she bore him Se-
    gub. ²²Segub was the father of Jair, who controlled twenty-three
    towns in Gilead. ²³(But Geshur and Aram captured Havvoth Jair,ᶜ as
    well as Kenath with its surrounding settlements—sixty towns.) All
    these were descendants of Makir the father of Gilead.

²⁴After Hezron died in Caleb Ephrathah, Abijah the wife of Hezron bore
    him Ashhur the fatherᵈ of Tekoa.

Jerahmeel Son of Hezron
²⁵The sons of Jerahmeel the firstborn of Hezron:
    Ram his firstborn, Bunah, Oren, Ozem andᵉ Ahijah. ²⁶Jerahmeel had
    another wife, whose name was Atarah; she was the mother of Onam.
²⁷The sons of Ram the firstborn of Jerahmeel:
    Maaz, Jamin and Eker.
²⁸The sons of Onam:
    Shammai and Jada.
   The sons of Shammai:
    Nadab and Abishur.
²⁹Abishur's wife was named Abihail, who bore him Ahban and Molid.
³⁰The sons of Nadab:
    Seled and Appaim. Seled died without children.
³¹The son of Appaim:
    Ishi, who was the father of Sheshan.
    Sheshan was the father of Ahlai.
³²The sons of Jada, Shammai's brother:
    Jether and Jonathan. Jether died without children.
³³The sons of Jonathan:
    Peleth and Zaza.
   These were the descendants of Jerahmeel.

ᵃ9 Hebrew *Kelubai*, a variant of *Caleb* ᵇ11 Septuagint (see also Ruth 4:21); Hebrew *Salma* ᶜ23 Or
captured the settlements of Jair ᵈ24 *Father* may mean *civic leader* or *military leader*; also in verses 42, 45,
49-52 and possibly elsewhere. ᵉ25 Or *Oren and Ozem, by*

³⁴Sheshan had no sons—only daughters.
He had an Egyptian servant named Jarha. ³⁵Sheshan gave his daughter in marriage to his servant Jarha, and she bore him Attai.
³⁶Attai was the father of Nathan,
Nathan the father of Zabad,
³⁷Zabad the father of Ephlal,
Ephlal the father of Obed,
³⁸Obed the father of Jehu,
Jehu the father of Azariah,
³⁹Azariah the father of Helez,
Helez the father of Eleasah,
⁴⁰Eleasah the father of Sismai,
Sismai the father of Shallum,
⁴¹Shallum the father of Jekamiah,
and Jekamiah the father of Elishama.

The Clans of Caleb

⁴²The sons of Caleb the brother of Jerahmeel:
Mesha his firstborn, who was the father of Ziph, and his son Mareshah,^a who was the father of Hebron.
⁴³The sons of Hebron:
Korah, Tappuah, Rekem and Shema. ⁴⁴Shema was the father of Raham, and Raham the father of Jorkeam. Rekem was the father of Shammai. ⁴⁵The son of Shammai was Maon, and Maon was the father of Beth Zur.
⁴⁶Caleb's concubine Ephah was the mother of Haran, Moza and Gazez. Haran was the father of Gazez.
⁴⁷The sons of Jahdai:
Regem, Jotham, Geshan, Pelet, Ephah and Shaaph.
⁴⁸Caleb's concubine Maacah was the mother of Sheber and Tirhanah. ⁴⁹She also gave birth to Shaaph the father of Madmannah and to Sheva the father of Macbenah and Gibea. Caleb's daughter was Acsah. ⁵⁰These were the descendants of Caleb.

The sons of Hur the firstborn of Ephrathah:
Shobal the father of Kiriath Jearim, ⁵¹Salma the father of Bethlehem, and Hareph the father of Beth Gader.
⁵²The descendants of Shobal the father of Kiriath Jearim were:
Haroeh, half the Manahathites, ⁵³and the clans of Kiriath Jearim: the Ithrites, Puthites, Shumathites and Mishraites. From these descended the Zorathites and Eshtaolites.
⁵⁴The descendants of Salma:
Bethlehem, the Netophathites, Atroth Beth Joab, half the Manahathites, the Zorites, ⁵⁵and the clans of scribes^b who lived at Jabez: the Tirathites, Shimeathites and Sucathites. These are the Kenites who came from Hammath, the father of the house of Recab.^c

3 ### The Sons of David These were the sons of David born to him in Hebron:
The firstborn was Amnon the son of Ahinoam of Jezreel;
the second, Daniel the son of Abigail of Carmel;
²the third, Absalom the son of Maacah daughter of Talmai king of Geshur;
the fourth, Adonijah the son of Haggith;
³the fifth, Shephatiah the son of Abital;
and the sixth, Ithream, by his wife Eglah.

^a42 The meaning of the Hebrew for this phrase is uncertain. ^b55 Or *of the Sopherites* ^c55 Or *father of Beth Recab*

⁴These six were born to David in Hebron, where he reigned seven years and six months.

David reigned in Jerusalem thirty-three years, ⁵and these were the children born to him there:

Shammua,ᵃ Shobab, Nathan and Solomon. These four were by Bath-shebaᵇ daughter of Ammiel. ⁶There were also Ibhar, Elishua,ᶜ Eliphelet, ⁷Nogah, Nepheg, Japhia, ⁸Elishama, Eliada and Eliphelet—nine in all. ⁹All these were the sons of David, besides his sons by his concubines. And Tamar was their sister.

The Kings of Judah

¹⁰Solomon's son was Rehoboam,
Abijah his son,
Asa his son,
Jehoshaphat his son,
¹¹Jehoramᵈ his son,
Ahaziah his son,
Joash his son,
¹²Amaziah his son,
Azariah his son,
Jotham his son,
¹³Ahaz his son,
Hezekiah his son,
Manasseh his son,
¹⁴Amon his son,
Josiah his son.
¹⁵The sons of Josiah:
Johanan the firstborn,
Jehoiakim the second son,
Zedekiah the third,
Shallum the fourth.
¹⁶The successors of Jehoiakim:
Jehoiachinᵉ his son,
and Zedekiah.

The Royal Line After the Exile

¹⁷The descendants of Jehoiachin the captive:
Shealtiel his son, ¹⁸Malkiram, Pedaiah, Shenazzar, Jekamiah, Hoshama and Nedabiah.
¹⁹The sons of Pedaiah:
Zerubbabel and Shimei.
The sons of Zerubbabel:
Meshullam and Hananiah.
Shelomith was their sister.
²⁰There were also five others:
Hashubah, Ohel, Berekiah, Hasadiah and Jushab-Hesed.
²¹The descendants of Hananiah:
Pelatiah and Jeshaiah, and the sons of Rephaiah, of Arnan, of Obadiah and of Shecaniah.
²²The descendants of Shecaniah:
Shemaiah and his sons:
Hattush, Igal, Bariah, Neariah and Shaphat—six in all.

ᵃ5 Hebrew *Shimea,* a variant of *Shammua*   ᵇ5 One Hebrew manuscript and Vulgate (see also Septuagint and 2 Samuel 11:3); most Hebrew manuscripts *Bathshua*   ᶜ6 Two Hebrew manuscripts (see also 2 Samuel 5:15 and 1 Chron. 14:5); most Hebrew manuscripts *Elishama*   ᵈ11 Hebrew *Joram,* a variant of *Jehoram*
ᵉ16 Hebrew *Jeconiah,* a variant of *Jehoiachin;* also in verse 17

²³The sons of Neariah:
Elioenai, Hizkiah and Azrikam—three in all.
²⁴The sons of Elioenai:
Hodaviah, Eliashib, Pelaiah, Akkub, Johanan, Delaiah and Anani—
seven in all.

Other Clans of Judah   The descendants of Judah:
Perez, Hezron, Carmi, Hur and Shobal.
²Reaiah son of Shobal was the father of Jahath, and Jahath the father
of Ahumai and Lahad. These were the clans of the Zorathites.
³These were the sons[a] of Etam:
Jezreel, Ishma and Idbash. Their sister was named Hazzelelponi.
⁴Penuel was the father of Gedor, and Ezer the father of Hushah.
These were the descendants of Hur, the firstborn of Ephrathah and father[b] of Bethlehem.
⁵Ashhur the father of Tekoa had two wives, Helah and Naarah.
⁶Naarah bore him Ahuzzam, Hepher, Temeni and Haahashtari. These
were the descendants of Naarah.
⁷The sons of Helah:
Zereth, Zohar, Ethnan, ⁸and Koz, who was the father of Anub and
Hazzobebah and of the clans of Aharhel son of Harum.

⁹Jabez was more honorable than his brothers. His mother had named him
Jabez,[c] saying, "I gave birth to him in pain." ¹⁰Jabez cried out to the God of
Israel, "Oh, that you would bless me and enlarge my territory! Let your hand
be with me, and keep me from harm so that I will be free from pain." And
God granted his request.

¹¹Kelub, Shuhah's brother, was the father of Mehir, who was the father
of Eshton. ¹²Eshton was the father of Beth Rapha, Paseah and Tehin-
nah the father of Ir Nahash.[d] These were the men of Recah.

¹³The sons of Kenaz:
Othniel and Seraiah.
The sons of Othniel:
Hathath and Meonothai.[e] ¹⁴Meonothai was the father of Ophrah.
Seraiah was the father of Joab,
the father of Ge Harashim.[f] It was called this because its people were
craftsmen.
¹⁵The sons of Caleb son of Jephunneh:
Iru, Elah and Naam.
The son of Elah:
Kenaz.
¹⁶The sons of Jehallelel:
Ziph, Ziphah, Tiria and Asarel.
¹⁷The sons of Ezrah:
Jether, Mered, Epher and Jalon. One of Mered's wives gave birth to
Miriam, Shammai and Ishbah the father of Eshtemoa. ¹⁸(His Judean
wife gave birth to Jered the father of Gedor, Heber the father of
Soco, and Jekuthiel the father of Zanoah.) These were the children of
Pharaoh's daughter Bithiah, whom Mered had married.
¹⁹The sons of Hodiah's wife, the sister of Naham:
the father of Keilah the Garmite, and Eshtemoa the Maacathite.

---

[a]3 Some Septuagint manuscripts (see also Vulgate); Hebrew *father*   [b]4 *Father* may mean *civic leader* or
military leader, also in verses 12, 14, 17, 18 and possibly elsewhere.   [c]9 *Jabez* sounds like the Hebrew for
pain.   [d]12 Or *of the city of Nahash*   [e]13 Some Septuagint manuscripts and Vulgate; Hebrew does not have
and Meonothai.   [f]14 *Ge Harashim* means *valley of craftsmen.*

²⁰ The sons of Shimon:

Amnon, Rinnah, Ben-Hanan and Tilon.

The descendants of Ishi:

Zoheth and Ben-Zoheth.

²¹ The sons of Shelah son of Judah:

Er the father of Lecah, Laadah the father of Mareshah and the clans of the linen workers at Beth Ashbea, ²²Jokim, the men of Cozeba, and Joash and Saraph, who ruled in Moab and Jashubi Lehem. (These records are from ancient times.) ²³They were the potters who lived at Netaim and Gederah; they stayed there and worked for the king.

Simeon

²⁴ The descendants of Simeon:

Nemuel, Jamin, Jarib, Zerah and Shaul;

²⁵ Shallum was Shaul's son, Mibsam his son and Mishma his son.

²⁶ The descendants of Mishma:

Hammuel his son, Zaccur his son and Shimei his son.

²⁷Shimei had sixteen sons and six daughters, but his brothers did not have many children; so their entire clan did not become as numerous as the people of Judah. ²⁸They lived in Beersheba, Moladah, Hazar Shual, ²⁹Bilhah, Ezem, Tolad, ³⁰Bethuel, Hormah, Ziklag, ³¹Beth Marcaboth, Hazar Susim, Beth Biri and Shaaraim. These were their towns until the reign of David. ³²Their surrounding villages were Etam, Ain, Rimmon, Token and Ashan—five towns— ³³and all the villages around these towns as far as Baalath.ᵃ These were their settlements. And they kept a genealogical record.

³⁴Meshobab, Jamlech, Joshah son of Amaziah, ³⁵Joel, Jehu son of Joshibiah, the son of Seraiah, the son of Asiel, ³⁶also Elioenai, Jaakobah, Jeshohaiah, Asaiah, Adiel, Jesimiel, Benaiah, ³⁷and Ziza son of Shiphi, the son of Allon, the son of Jedaiah, the son of Shimri, the son of Shemaiah.

³⁸The men listed above by name were leaders of their clans. Their families increased greatly, ³⁹and they went to the outskirts of Gedor to the east of the valley in search of pasture for their flocks. ⁴⁰They found rich, good pasture, and the land was spacious, peaceful and quiet. Some Hamites had lived there formerly.

⁴¹The men whose names were listed came in the days of Hezekiah king of Judah. They attacked the Hamites in their dwellings and also the Meunites who were there and completely destroyedᵇ them, as is evident to this day. Then they settled in their place, because there was pasture for their flocks. ⁴²And five hundred of these Simeonites, led by Pelatiah, Neariah, Rephaiah and Uzziel, the sons of Ishi, invaded the hill country of Seir. ⁴³They killed the remaining Amalekites who had escaped, and they have lived there to this day.

Reuben

The sons of Reuben the firstborn of Israel (he was the firstborn, but when he defiled his father's marriage bed, his rights as firstborn were given to the sons of Joseph son of Israel; so he could not be listed in the genealogical record in accordance with his birthright, ²and though Judah was the strongest of his brothers and a ruler came from him, the rights of the firstborn belonged to Joseph)— ³the sons of Reuben the firstborn of Israel:

Hanoch, Pallu, Hezron and Carmi.

⁴ The descendants of Joel:

Shemaiah his son, Gog his son,

Shimei his son, ⁵Micah his son,

Reaiah his son, Baal his son,

ᵃ33 Some Septuagint manuscripts (see also Joshua 19:8); Hebrew Baal   ᵇ41 The Hebrew term refers to the irrevocable giving over of things or persons to the Lord, often by totally destroying them.

⁶and Beerah his son, whom Tiglath-Pileser*ᵃ* king of Assyria took into exile. Beerah was a leader of the Reubenites.

⁷Their relatives by clans, listed according to their genealogical records:

Jeiel the chief, Zechariah, ⁸and Bela son of Azaz, the son of Shema, the son of Joel. They settled in the area from Aroer to Nebo and Baal Meon. ⁹To the east they occupied the land up to the edge of the desert that extends to the Euphrates River, because their livestock had increased in Gilead.

¹⁰During Saul's reign they waged war against the Hagrites, who were defeated at their hands; they occupied the dwellings of the Hagrites throughout the entire region east of Gilead.

Gad

¹¹The Gadites lived next to them in Bashan, as far as Salecah:

¹²Joel was the chief, Shapham the second, then Janai and Shaphat, in Bashan.

¹³Their relatives, by families, were:

Michael, Meshullam, Sheba, Jorai, Jacan, Zia and Eber—seven in all. ¹⁴These were the sons of Abihail son of Huri, the son of Jaroah, the son of Gilead, the son of Michael, the son of Jeshishai, the son of Jahdo, the son of Buz.

¹⁵Ahi son of Abdiel, the son of Guni, was head of their family.

¹⁶The Gadites lived in Gilead, in Bashan and its outlying villages, and on all the pasturelands of Sharon as far as they extended.

¹⁷All these were entered in the genealogical records during the reigns of Jotham king of Judah and Jeroboam king of Israel.

¹⁸The Reubenites, the Gadites and the half-tribe of Manasseh had 44,760 men ready for military service—able-bodied men who could handle shield and sword, who could use a bow, and who were trained for battle. ¹⁹They waged war against the Hagrites, Jetur, Naphish and Nodab. ²⁰They were helped in fighting them, and God handed the Hagrites and all their allies over to them, because they cried out to him during the battle. He answered their prayers, because they trusted in him. ²¹They seized the livestock of the Hagrites—fifty thousand camels, two hundred fifty thousand sheep and two thousand donkeys. They also took one hundred thousand people captive, ²²and many others fell slain, because the battle was God's. And they occupied the land until the exile.

The Half-Tribe of Manasseh

²³The people of the half-tribe of Manasseh were numerous; they settled in the land from Bashan to Baal Hermon, that is, to Senir (Mount Hermon).

²⁴These were the heads of their families: Epher, Ishi, Eliel, Azriel, Jeremiah, Hodaviah and Jahdiel. They were brave warriors, famous men, and heads of their families. ²⁵But they were unfaithful to the God of their fathers and prostituted themselves to the gods of the peoples of the land, whom God had destroyed before them. ²⁶So the God of Israel stirred up the spirit of Pul king of Assyria (that is, Tiglath-Pileser king of Assyria), who took the Reubenites, the Gadites and the half-tribe of Manasseh into exile. He took them to Halah, Habor, Hara and the river of Gozan, where they are to this day.

6 **Levi** The sons of Levi:

Gershon, Kohath and Merari.

²The sons of Kohath:

Amram, Izhar, Hebron and Uzziel.

ᵃ6 Hebrew Tilgath-Pilneser, a variant of Tiglath-Pileser; also in verse 26

³The children of Amram:
    Aaron, Moses and Miriam.
The sons of Aaron:
    Nadab, Abihu, Eleazar and Ithamar.
⁴Eleazar was the father of Phinehas,
    Phinehas the father of Abishua,
⁵Abishua the father of Bukki,
    Bukki the father of Uzzi,
⁶Uzzi the father of Zerahiah,
    Zerahiah the father of Meraioth,
⁷Meraioth the father of Amariah,
    Amariah the father of Ahitub,
⁸Ahitub the father of Zadok,
    Zadok the father of Ahimaaz,
⁹Ahimaaz the father of Azariah,
    Azariah the father of Johanan,
¹⁰Johanan the father of Azariah (it was he who served as priest in the
    temple Solomon built in Jerusalem),
¹¹Azariah the father of Amariah,
    Amariah the father of Ahitub,
¹²Ahitub the father of Zadok,
    Zadok the father of Shallum,
¹³Shallum the father of Hilkiah,
    Hilkiah the father of Azariah,
¹⁴Azariah the father of Seraiah,
    and Seraiah the father of Jehozadak.
¹⁵Jehozadak was deported when the LORD sent Judah and Jerusalem into
    exile by the hand of Nebuchadnezzar.

¹⁶The sons of Levi:
    Gershon,ᵃ Kohath and Merari.
¹⁷These are the names of the sons of Gershon:
    Libni and Shimei.
¹⁸The sons of Kohath:
    Amram, Izhar, Hebron and Uzziel.
¹⁹The sons of Merari:
    Mahli and Mushi.
These are the clans of the Levites listed according to their fathers:
²⁰Of Gershon:
    Libni his son, Jehath his son,
    Zimmah his son, ²¹Joah his son,
    Iddo his son, Zerah his son
    and Jeatherai his son.
²²The descendants of Kohath:
    Amminadab his son, Korah his son,
    Assir his son, ²³Elkanah his son,
    Ebiasaph his son, Assir his son,
    ²⁴Tahath his son, Uriel his son,
    Uzziah his son and Shaul his son.
²⁵The descendants of Elkanah:
    Amasai, Ahimoth,
    ²⁶Elkanah his son,ᵇ Zophai his son,
    Nahath his son, ²⁷Eliab his son,

ᵃ16 Hebrew *Gershom*, a variant of *Gershon*; also in verses 17, 20, 43, 62 and 71   ᵇ26 Some Hebrew
manuscripts, Septuagint and Syriac; most Hebrew manuscripts *Ahimoth ²⁶and Elkanah. The sons of
Elkanah:*

Jeroham his son, Elkanah his son
and Samuel his son.*ᵃ*
²⁸The sons of Samuel:
Joel*ᵇ* the firstborn
and Abijah the second son.
²⁹The descendants of Merari:
Mahli, Libni his son,
Shimei his son, Uzzah his son,
³⁰Shimea his son, Haggiah his son
and Asaiah his son.

The Temple Musicians ³¹These are the men David put in charge of the music in the house of the Lᴏʀᴅ after the ark came to rest there. ³²They ministered with music before the tabernacle, the Tent of Meeting, until Solomon built the temple of the Lᴏʀᴅ in Jerusalem. They performed their duties according to the regulations laid down for them.

³³Here are the men who served, together with their sons:
From the Kohathites:
Heman, the musician,
the son of Joel, the son of Samuel,
³⁴the son of Elkanah, the son of Jeroham,
the son of Eliel, the son of Toah,
³⁵the son of Zuph, the son of Elkanah,
the son of Mahath, the son of Amasai,
³⁶the son of Elkanah, the son of Joel,
the son of Azariah, the son of Zephaniah,
³⁷the son of Tahath, the son of Assir,
the son of Ebiasaph, the son of Korah,
³⁸the son of Izhar, the son of Kohath,
the son of Levi, the son of Israel;
³⁹and Heman's associate Asaph, who served at his right hand:
Asaph son of Berekiah, the son of Shimea,
⁴⁰the son of Michael, the son of Baaseiah,*ᶜ*
the son of Malkijah, ⁴¹the son of Ethni,
the son of Zerah, the son of Adaiah,
⁴²the son of Ethan, the son of Zimmah,
the son of Shimei, ⁴³the son of Jahath,
the son of Gershon, the son of Levi;
⁴⁴and from their associates, the Merarites, at his left hand:
Ethan son of Kishi, the son of Abdi,
the son of Malluch, ⁴⁵the son of Hashabiah,
the son of Amaziah, the son of Hilkiah,
⁴⁶the son of Amzi, the son of Bani,
the son of Shemer, ⁴⁷the son of Mahli,
the son of Mushi, the son of Merari,
the son of Levi.

⁴⁸Their fellow Levites were assigned to all the other duties of the tabernacle, the house of God. ⁴⁹But Aaron and his descendants were the ones who presented offerings on the altar of burnt offering and on the altar of incense in connection with all that was done in the Most Holy Place, making atonement for Israel, in accordance with all that Moses the servant of God had commanded.

ᵃ27 Some Septuagint manuscripts (see also 1 Samuel 1:19,20 and 1 Chron. 6:33,34); Hebrew does not have *and Samuel his son.* *ᵇ28* Some Septuagint manuscripts and Syriac (see also 1 Samuel 8:2 and 1 Chron. 6:33); Hebrew does not have *Joel.* *ᶜ40* Most Hebrew manuscripts; some Hebrew manuscripts, one Septuagint manuscript and Syriac *Maaseiah*

⁵⁰These were the descendants of Aaron:

Eleazar his son, Phinehas his son,
Abishua his son, ⁵¹Bukki his son,
Uzzi his son, Zerahiah his son,
⁵²Meraioth his son, Amariah his son,
Ahitub his son, ⁵³Zadok his son
and Ahimaaz his son.

⁵⁴These were the locations of their settlements allotted as their territory (they were assigned to the descendants of Aaron who were from the Kohathite clan, because the first lot was for them):

⁵⁵They were given Hebron in Judah with its surrounding pasturelands. ⁵⁶But the fields and villages around the city were given to Caleb son of Jephunneh.

⁵⁷So the descendants of Aaron were given Hebron (a city of refuge), and Libnah,ᵃ Jattir, Eshtemoa, ⁵⁸Hilen, Debir, ⁵⁹Ashan, Juttahᵇ and Beth Shemesh, together with their pasturelands. ⁶⁰And from the tribe of Benjamin they were given Gibeon,ᶜ Geba, Alemeth and Anathoth, together with their pasturelands.

These towns, which were distributed among the Kohathite clans, were thirteen in all.

⁶¹The rest of Kohath's descendants were allotted ten towns from the clans of half the tribe of Manasseh.

⁶²The descendants of Gershon, clan by clan, were allotted thirteen towns from the tribes of Issachar, Asher and Naphtali, and from the part of the tribe of Manasseh that is in Bashan.

⁶³The descendants of Merari, clan by clan, were allotted twelve towns from the tribes of Reuben, Gad and Zebulun.

⁶⁴So the Israelites gave the Levites these towns and their pasturelands. ⁶⁵From the tribes of Judah, Simeon and Benjamin they allotted the previously named towns.

⁶⁶Some of the Kohathite clans were given as their territory towns from the tribe of Ephraim.

⁶⁷In the hill country of Ephraim they were given Shechem (a city of refuge), and Gezer,ᵈ ⁶⁸Jokmeam, Beth Horon, ⁶⁹Aijalon and Gath Rimmon, together with their pasturelands.

⁷⁰And from half the tribe of Manasseh the Israelites gave Aner and Bileam, together with their pasturelands, to the rest of the Kohathite clans.

⁷¹The Gershonites received the following:

From the clan of the half-tribe of Manasseh
   they received Golan in Bashan and also Ashtaroth, together with their pasturelands;
⁷²from the tribe of Issachar
   they received Kedesh, Daberath, ⁷³Ramoth and Anem, together with their pasturelands;
⁷⁴from the tribe of Asher
   they received Mashal, Abdon, ⁷⁵Hukok and Rehob, together with their pasturelands;
⁷⁶and from the tribe of Naphtali
   they received Kedesh in Galilee, Hammon and Kiriathaim, together with their pasturelands.

⁷⁷The Merarites (the rest of the Levites) received the following:

From the tribe of Zebulun

ᵃ57 See Joshua 21:13; Hebrew *given the cities of refuge: Hebron, Libnah.* ᵇ59 Syriac (see also Septuagint and Joshua 21:16); Hebrew does not have *Juttah.* ᶜ60 See Joshua 21:17; Hebrew does not have *Gibeon.* ᵈ67 See Joshua 21:21; Hebrew *given the cities of refuge: Shechem, Gezer.*

they received Jokneam, Kartah,*a* Rimmono and Tabor, together with their pasturelands;
78 from the tribe of Reuben across the Jordan east of Jericho
they received Bezer in the desert, Jahzah, 79Kedemoth and Mephaath, together with their pasturelands;
80 and from the tribe of Gad
they received Ramoth in Gilead, Mahanaim, 81Heshbon and Jazer, together with their pasturelands.

Issachar   The sons of Issachar:
Tola, Puah, Jashub and Shimron—four in all.
2The sons of Tola:
Uzzi, Rephaiah, Jeriel, Jahmai, Ibsam and Samuel—heads of their families. During the reign of David, the descendants of Tola listed as fighting men in their genealogy numbered 22,600.
3The son of Uzzi:
Izrahiah.
The sons of Izrahiah:
Michael, Obadiah, Joel and Isshiah. All five of them were chiefs. 4According to their family genealogy, they had 36,000 men ready for battle, for they had many wives and children.
5The relatives who were fighting men belonging to all the clans of Issachar, as listed in their genealogy, were 87,000 in all.

Benjamin
6Three sons of Benjamin:
Bela, Beker and Jediael.
7The sons of Bela:
Ezbon, Uzzi, Uzziel, Jerimoth and Iri, heads of families—five in all. Their genealogical record listed 22,034 fighting men.
8The sons of Beker:
Zemirah, Joash, Eliezer, Elioenai, Omri, Jeremoth, Abijah, Anathoth and Alemeth. All these were the sons of Beker. 9Their genealogical record listed the heads of families and 20,200 fighting men.
10The son of Jediael:
Bilhan.
The sons of Bilhan:
Jeush, Benjamin, Ehud, Kenaanah, Zethan, Tarshish and Ahishahar. 11All these sons of Jediael were heads of families. There were 17,200 fighting men ready to go out to war.
12The Shuppites and Huppites were the descendants of Ir, and the Hushites the descendants of Aher.

Naphtali
13The sons of Naphtali:
Jahziel, Guni, Jezer and Shillem*b*—the descendants of Bilhah.

Manasseh
14The descendants of Manasseh:
Asriel was his descendant through his Aramean concubine. She gave birth to Makir the father of Gilead. 15Makir took a wife from among the Huppites and Shuppites. His sister's name was Maacah.
Another descendant was named Zelophehad, who had only daughters.
16Makir's wife Maacah gave birth to a son and named him Peresh. His brother was named Sheresh, and his sons were Ulam and Rakem.

---

a77 See Septuagint and Joshua 21:34; Hebrew does not have *Jokneam, Kartah.*   *b13* Some Hebrew and Septuagint manuscripts (see also Gen. 46:24 and Num. 26:49); most Hebrew manuscripts *Shallum*

¹⁷The son of Ulam:

Bedan.

These were the sons of Gilead son of Makir, the son of Manasseh. ¹⁸His sister Hammoleketh gave birth to Ishhod, Abiezer and Mahlah.

¹⁹The sons of Shemida were:

Ahian, Shechem, Likhi and Aniam.

Ephraim

²⁰The descendants of Ephraim:

Shuthelah, Bered his son,

Tahath his son, Eleadah his son,

Tahath his son, ²¹Zabad his son

and Shuthelah his son.

Ezer and Elead were killed by the native-born men of Gath, when they went down to seize their livestock. ²²Their father Ephraim mourned for them many days, and his relatives came to comfort him. ²³Then he lay with his wife again, and she became pregnant and gave birth to a son. He named him Beriah,[a] because there had been misfortune in his family. ²⁴His daughter was Sheerah, who built Lower and Upper Beth Horon as well as Uzzen Sheerah.

²⁵Rephah was his son, Resheph his son,[b]

Telah his son, Tahan his son,

²⁶Ladan his son, Ammihud his son,

Elishama his son, ²⁷Nun his son

and Joshua his son.

²⁸Their lands and settlements included Bethel and its surrounding villages, Naaran to the east, Gezer and its villages to the west, and Shechem and its villages all the way to Ayyah and its villages. ²⁹Along the borders of Manasseh were Beth Shan, Taanach, Megiddo and Dor, together with their villages. The descendants of Joseph son of Israel lived in these towns.

Asher

³⁰The sons of Asher:

Imnah, Ishvah, Ishvi and Beriah. Their sister was Serah.

³¹The sons of Beriah:

Heber and Malkiel, who was the father of Birzaith.

³²Heber was the father of Japhlet, Shomer and Hotham and of their sister Shua.

³³The sons of Japhlet:

Pasach, Bimhal and Ashvath.

These were Japhlet's sons.

³⁴The sons of Shomer:

Ahi, Rohgah,[c] Hubbah and Aram.

³⁵The sons of his brother Helem:

Zophah, Imna, Shelesh and Amal.

³⁶The sons of Zophah:

Suah, Harnepher, Shual, Beri, Imrah, ³⁷Bezer, Hod, Shamma, Shilshah, Ithran[d] and Beera.

³⁸The sons of Jether:

Jephunneh, Pispah and Ara.

³⁹The sons of Ulla:

Arah, Hanniel and Rizia.

⁴⁰All these were descendants of Asher—heads of families, choice men, brave warriors and outstanding leaders. The number of men ready for battle, as listed in their genealogy, was 26,000.

---

[a]23 Beriah sounds like the Hebrew for *misfortune*. [b]25 Some Septuagint manuscripts; Hebrew does not have *his son*. [c]34 Or *of his brother Shomer: Rohgah* [d]37 Possibly a variant of *Jether*

8

The Genealogy of Saul the Benjamite   Benjamin was the father of Bela his firstborn,

Ashbel the second son, Aharah the third, ²Nohah the fourth and Rapha the fifth.

³The sons of Bela were:

Addar, Gera, Abihud,ᵃ ⁴Abishua, Naaman, Ahoah, ⁵Gera, Shephuphan and Huram.

⁶These were the descendants of Ehud, who were heads of families of those living in Geba and were deported to Manahath:

⁷Naaman, Ahijah, and Gera, who deported them and who was the father of Uzza and Ahihud.

⁸Sons were born to Shaharaim in Moab after he had divorced his wives Hushim and Baara. ⁹By his wife Hodesh he had Jobab, Zibia, Mesha, Malcam, ¹⁰Jeuz, Sakia and Mirmah. These were his sons, heads of families. ¹¹By Hushim he had Abitub and Elpaal.

¹²The sons of Elpaal:

Eber, Misham, Shemed (who built Ono and Lod with its surrounding villages), ¹³and Beriah and Shema, who were heads of families of those living in Aijalon and who drove out the inhabitants of Gath.

¹⁴Ahio, Shashak, Jeremoth, ¹⁵Zebadiah, Arad, Eder, ¹⁶Michael, Ishpah and Joha were the sons of Beriah.

¹⁷Zebadiah, Meshullam, Hizki, Heber, ¹⁸Ishmerai, Izliah and Jobab were the sons of Elpaal.

¹⁹Jakim, Zicri, Zabdi, ²⁰Elienai, Zillethai, Eliel, ²¹Adaiah, Beraiah and Shimrath were the sons of Shimei.

²²Ishpan, Eber, Eliel, ²³Abdon, Zicri, Hanan, ²⁴Hananiah, Elam, Anthothijah, ²⁵Iphdeiah and Penuel were the sons of Shashak.

²⁶Shamsherai, Shehariah, Athaliah, ²⁷Jaareshiah, Elijah and Zicri were the sons of Jeroham.

²⁸All these were heads of families, chiefs as listed in their genealogy, and they lived in Jerusalem.

²⁹Jeielᵇ the fatherᶜ of Gibeon lived in Gibeon.

His wife's name was Maacah, ³⁰and his firstborn son was Abdon, followed by Zur, Kish, Baal, Ner,ᵈ Nadab, ³¹Gedor, Ahio, Zeker ³²and Mikloth, who was the father of Shimeah. They too lived near their relatives in Jerusalem.

³³Ner was the father of Kish, Kish the father of Saul, and Saul the father of Jonathan, Malki-Shua, Abinadab and Esh-Baal.ᵉ

³⁴The son of Jonathan:

Merib-Baal,ᶠ who was the father of Micah.

³⁵The sons of Micah:

Pithon, Melech, Tarea and Ahaz.

³⁶Ahaz was the father of Jehoaddah, Jehoaddah was the father of Alemeth, Azmaveth and Zimri, and Zimri was the father of Moza. ³⁷Moza was the father of Binea; Raphah was his son, Eleasah his son and Azel his son.

³⁸Azel had six sons, and these were their names:

Azrikam, Bokeru, Ishmael, Sheariah, Obadiah and Hanan. All these were the sons of Azel.

³⁹The sons of his brother Eshek:

Ulam his firstborn, Jeush the second son and Eliphelet the third.

ᵃ3 Or *Gera the father of Ehud*   ᵇ29 Some Septuagint manuscripts (see also 1 Chron. 9:35); Hebrew does not have *Jeiel*.   ᶜ29 *Father* may mean *civic leader* or *military leader*.   ᵈ30 Some Septuagint manuscripts (see also 1 Chron. 9:36); Hebrew does not have *Ner*.   ᵉ33 Also known as *Ish-Bosheth*   ᶠ34 Also known as *Mephibosheth*

⁴⁰The sons of Ulam were brave warriors who could handle the bow. They had many sons and grandsons—150 in all.

All these were the descendants of Benjamin.

9 All Israel was listed in the genealogies recorded in the book of the kings of Israel.

The People in Jerusalem The people of Judah were taken captive to Babylon because of their unfaithfulness. ²Now the first to resettle on their own property in their own towns were some Israelites, priests, Levites and temple servants.

³Those from Judah, from Benjamin, and from Ephraim and Manasseh who lived in Jerusalem were:

⁴Uthai son of Ammihud, the son of Omri, the son of Imri, the son of Bani, a descendant of Perez son of Judah.

⁵Of the Shilonites:

Asaiah the firstborn and his sons.

⁶Of the Zerahites:

Jeuel.

The people from Judah numbered 690.

⁷Of the Benjamites:

Sallu son of Meshullam, the son of Hodaviah, the son of Hassenuah; ⁸Ibneiah son of Jeroham; Elah son of Uzzi, the son of Micri; and Meshullam son of Shephatiah, the son of Reuel, the son of Ibnijah.

⁹The people from Benjamin, as listed in their genealogy, numbered 956. All these men were heads of their families.

¹⁰Of the priests:

Jedaiah; Jehoiarib; Jakin;

¹¹Azariah son of Hilkiah, the son of Meshullam, the son of Zadok, the son of Meraioth, the son of Ahitub, the official in charge of the house of God;

¹²Adaiah son of Jeroham, the son of Pashhur, the son of Malkijah; and Maasai son of Adiel, the son of Jahzerah, the son of Meshullam, the son of Meshillemith, the son of Immer.

¹³The priests, who were heads of families, numbered 1,760. They were able men, responsible for ministering in the house of God.

¹⁴Of the Levites:

Shemaiah son of Hasshub, the son of Azrikam, the son of Hashabiah, a Merarite; ¹⁵Bakbakkar, Heresh, Galal and Mattaniah son of Mica, the son of Zicri, the son of Asaph; ¹⁶Obadiah son of Shemaiah, the son of Galal, the son of Jeduthun; and Berekiah son of Asa, the son of Elkanah, who lived in the villages of the Netophathites.

¹⁷The gatekeepers:

Shallum, Akkub, Talmon, Ahiman and their brothers, Shallum their chief ¹⁸being stationed at the King's Gate on the east, up to the present time. These were the gatekeepers belonging to the camp of the Levites. ¹⁹Shallum son of Kore, the son of Ebiasaph, the son of Korah, and his fellow gatekeepers from his family (the Korahites) were responsible for guarding the thresholds of the Tent*ᵃ* just as their fathers had been responsible for guarding the entrance to the dwelling of the Lᴏʀᴅ. ²⁰In earlier times Phinehas son of Eleazar was in charge of the gatekeepers, and the Lᴏʀᴅ was with him. ²¹Zechariah son of Meshelemiah was the gatekeeper at the entrance to the Tent of Meeting.

ᵃ19 That is, the temple; also in verses 21 and 23

[22]Altogether, those chosen to be gatekeepers at the thresholds numbered 212. They were registered by genealogy in their villages. The gatekeepers had been assigned to their positions of trust by David and Samuel the seer. [23]They and their descendants were in charge of guarding the gates of the house of the LORD—the house called the Tent. [24]The gatekeepers were on the four sides: east, west, north and south. [25]Their brothers in their villages had to come from time to time and share their duties for seven-day periods. [26]But the four principal gatekeepers, who were Levites, were entrusted with the responsibility for the rooms and treasuries in the house of God. [27]They would spend the night stationed around the house of God, because they had to guard it; and they had charge of the key for opening it each morning.

[28]Some of them were in charge of the articles used in the temple service; they counted them when they were brought in and when they were taken out. [29]Others were assigned to take care of the furnishings and all the other articles of the sanctuary, as well as the flour and wine, and the oil, incense and spices. [30]But some of the priests took care of mixing the spices. [31]A Levite named Mattithiah, the firstborn son of Shallum the Korahite, was entrusted with the responsibility for baking the offering bread. [32]Some of their Kohathite brothers were in charge of preparing for every Sabbath the bread set out on the table.

[33]Those who were musicians, heads of Levite families, stayed in the rooms of the temple and were exempt from other duties because they were responsible for the work day and night.

[34]All these were heads of Levite families, chiefs as listed in their genealogy, and they lived in Jerusalem.

The Genealogy of Saul

[35]Jeiel the father[a] of Gibeon lived in Gibeon.

His wife's name was Maacah, [36]and his firstborn son was Abdon, followed by Zur, Kish, Baal, Ner, Nadab, [37]Gedor, Ahio, Zechariah and Mikloth. [38]Mikloth was the father of Shimeam. They too lived near their relatives in Jerusalem.

[39]Ner was the father of Kish, Kish the father of Saul, and Saul the father of Jonathan, Malki-Shua, Abinadab and Esh-Baal.[b]

[40]The son of Jonathan:

Merib-Baal,[c] who was the father of Micah.

[41]The sons of Micah:

Pithon, Melech, Tahrea and Ahaz.[d]

[42]Ahaz was the father of Jadah, Jadah[e] was the father of Alemeth, Azmaveth and Zimri, and Zimri was the father of Moza. [43]Moza was the father of Binea; Rephaiah was his son, Eleasah his son and Azel his son.

[44]Azel had six sons, and these were their names:

Azrikam, Bokeru, Ishmael, Sheariah, Obadiah and Hanan. These were the sons of Azel.

10 **Saul Takes His Life** Now the Philistines fought against Israel; the Israelites fled before them, and many fell slain on Mount Gilboa. [2]The Philistines pressed hard after Saul and his sons, and they killed his sons Jonathan, Abinadab and Malki-Shua. [3]The fighting grew fierce around Saul, and when the archers overtook him, they wounded him.

[4]Saul said to his armor-bearer, "Draw your sword and run me through, or these uncircumcised fellows will come and abuse me."

---

[a]35 *Father* may mean *civic leader* or *military leader.*   [b]39 Also known as *Ish-Bosheth*   [c]40 Also known as *Mephibosheth*   [d]41 Vulgate and Syriac (see also Septuagint and 1 Chron. 8:35); Hebrew does not have *and Ahaz.*   [e]42 Some Hebrew manuscripts and Septuagint (see also 1 Chron. 8:36); most Hebrew manuscripts *Jarah, Jarah*

But his armor-bearer was terrified and would not do it; so Saul took his own sword and fell on it. ⁵When the armor-bearer saw that Saul was dead, he too fell on his sword and died. ⁶So Saul and his three sons died, and all his house died together.

⁷When all the Israelites in the valley saw that the army had fled and that Saul and his sons had died, they abandoned their towns and fled. And the Philistines came and occupied them.

⁸The next day, when the Philistines came to strip the dead, they found Saul and his sons fallen on Mount Gilboa. ⁹They stripped him and took his head and his armor, and sent messengers throughout the land of the Philistines to proclaim the news among their idols and their people. ¹⁰They put his armor in the temple of their gods and hung up his head in the temple of Dagon.

¹¹When all the inhabitants of Jabesh Gilead heard of everything the Philistines had done to Saul, ¹²all their valiant men went and took the bodies of Saul and his sons and brought them to Jabesh. Then they buried their bones under the great tree in Jabesh, and they fasted seven days.

¹³Saul died because he was unfaithful to the LORD; he did not keep the word of the LORD and even consulted a medium for guidance, ¹⁴and did not inquire of the LORD. So the LORD put him to death and turned the kingdom over to David son of Jesse.

11 *David Becomes King Over Israel* All Israel came together to David at Hebron and said, "We are your own flesh and blood. ²In the past, even while Saul was king, you were the one who led Israel on their military campaigns. And the LORD your God said to you, 'You will shepherd my people Israel, and you will become their ruler.' "

³When all the elders of Israel had come to King David at Hebron, he made a compact with them at Hebron before the LORD, and they anointed David king over Israel, as the LORD had promised through Samuel.

David Conquers Jerusalem ⁴David and all the Israelites marched to Jerusalem (that is, Jebus). The Jebusites who lived there ⁵said to David, "You will not get in here." Nevertheless, David captured the fortress of Zion, the City of David.

⁶David had said, "Whoever leads the attack on the Jebusites will become commander-in-chief." Joab son of Zeruiah went up first, and so he received the command.

⁷David then took up residence in the fortress, and so it was called the City of David. ⁸He built up the city around it, from the supporting terraces*a* to the surrounding wall, while Joab restored the rest of the city. ⁹And David became more and more powerful, because the LORD Almighty was with him.

David's Mighty Men ¹⁰These were the chiefs of David's mighty men—they, together with all Israel, gave his kingship strong support to extend it over the whole land, as the LORD had promised— ¹¹this is the list of David's mighty men:

Jashobeam,*b* a Hacmonite, was chief of the officers*c*; he raised his spear against three hundred men, whom he killed in one encounter.

¹²Next to him was Eleazar son of Dodai the Ahohite, one of the three mighty men. ¹³He was with David at Pas Dammim when the Philistines gathered there for battle. At a place where there was a field full of barley, the troops fled from the Philistines. ¹⁴But they took their stand in the middle of the field. They defended it and struck the Philistines down, and the LORD brought about a great victory.

---

a8 Or the Millo *b11 Possibly a variant of Jashob-Baal* *c11 Or Thirty;* some Septuagint manuscripts *Three* (see also 2 Samuel 23:8)

¹⁵Three of the thirty chiefs came down to David to the rock at the cave of Adullam, while a band of Philistines was encamped in the Valley of Rephaim. ¹⁶At that time David was in the stronghold, and the Philistine garrison was at Bethlehem. ¹⁷David longed for water and said, "Oh, that someone would get me a drink of water from the well near the gate of Bethlehem!" ¹⁸So the Three broke through the Philistine lines, drew water from the well near the gate of Bethlehem and carried it back to David. But he refused to drink it; instead, he poured it out before the LORD. ¹⁹"God forbid that I should do this!" he said. "Should I drink the blood of these men who went at the risk of their lives?" Because they risked their lives to bring it back, David would not drink it.

Such were the exploits of the three mighty men.

²⁰Abishai the brother of Joab was chief of the Three. He raised his spear against three hundred men, whom he killed, and so he became as famous as the Three. ²¹He was doubly honored above the Three and became their commander, even though he was not included among them.

²²Benaiah son of Jehoiada was a valiant fighter from Kabzeel, who performed great exploits. He struck down two of Moab's best men. He also went down into a pit on a snowy day and killed a lion. ²³And he struck down an Egyptian who was seven and a half feet*ᵃ* tall. Although the Egyptian had a spear like a weaver's rod in his hand, Benaiah went against him with a club. He snatched the spear from the Egyptian's hand and killed him with his own spear. ²⁴Such were the exploits of Benaiah son of Jehoiada; he too was as famous as the three mighty men. ²⁵He was held in greater honor than any of the Thirty, but he was not included among the Three. And David put him in charge of his bodyguard.

²⁶The mighty men were:

Asahel the brother of Joab,
Elhanan son of Dodo from Bethlehem,
²⁷Shammoth the Harorite,
Helez the Pelonite,
²⁸Ira son of Ikkesh from Tekoa,
Abiezer from Anathoth,
²⁹Sibbecai the Hushathite,
Ilai the Ahohite,
³⁰Maharai the Netophathite,
Heled son of Baanah the Netophathite,
³¹Ithai son of Ribai from Gibeah in Benjamin,
Benaiah the Pirathonite,
³²Hurai from the ravines of Gaash,
Abiel the Arbathite,
³³Azmaveth the Baharumite,
Eliahba the Shaalbonite,
³⁴the sons of Hashem the Gizonite,
Jonathan son of Shagee the Hararite,
³⁵Ahiam son of Sacar the Hararite,
Eliphal son of Ur,
³⁶Hepher the Mekerathite,
Ahijah the Pelonite,
³⁷Hezro the Carmelite,
Naarai son of Ezbai,
³⁸Joel the brother of Nathan,
Mibhar son of Hagri,
³⁹Zelek the Ammonite,
Naharai the Berothite, the armor-bearer of Joab son of Zeruiah,

---

ᵃ23 Hebrew *five cubits* (about 2.3 meters)

⁴⁰Ira the Ithrite,
Gareb the Ithrite,
⁴¹Uriah the Hittite,
Zabad son of Ahlai,
⁴²Adina son of Shiza the Reubenite, who was chief of the Reubenites,
and the thirty with him,
⁴³Hanan son of Maacah,
Joshaphat the Mithnite,
⁴⁴Uzzia the Ashterathite,
Shama and Jeiel the sons of Hotham the Aroerite,
⁴⁵Jediael son of Shimri,
his brother Joha the Tizite,
⁴⁶Eliel the Mahavite,
Jeribai and Joshaviah the sons of Elnaam,
Ithmah the Moabite,
⁴⁷Eliel, Obed and Jaasiel the Mezobaite.

12

Warriors Join David   These were the men who came to David at Ziklag, while he was banished from the presence of Saul son of Kish (they were among the warriors who helped him in battle; ²they were armed with bows and were able to shoot arrows or to sling stones right-handed or left-handed; they were kinsmen of Saul from the tribe of Benjamin):

³Ahiezer their chief and Joash the sons of Shemaah the Gibeathite; Jeziel and Pelet the sons of Azmaveth; Beracah, Jehu the Anathothite, ⁴and Ishmaiah the Gibeonite, a mighty man among the Thirty, who was a leader of the Thirty; Jeremiah, Jahaziel, Johanan, Jozabad the Gederathite, ⁵Eluzai, Jerimoth, Bealiah, Shemariah and Shephatiah the Haruphite; ⁶Elkanah, Isshiah, Azarel, Joezer and Jashobeam the Korahites; ⁷and Joelah and Zebadiah the sons of Jeroham from Gedor.

⁸Some Gadites defected to David at his stronghold in the desert. They were brave warriors, ready for battle and able to handle the shield and spear. Their faces were the faces of lions, and they were as swift as gazelles in the mountains.
⁹Ezer was the chief,
Obadiah the second in command, Eliab the third,
¹⁰Mishmannah the fourth, Jeremiah the fifth,
¹¹Attai the sixth, Eliel the seventh,
¹²Johanan the eighth, Elzabad the ninth,
¹³Jeremiah the tenth and Macbannai the eleventh.

¹⁴These Gadites were army commanders; the least was a match for a hundred, and the greatest for a thousand. ¹⁵It was they who crossed the Jordan in the first month when it was overflowing all its banks, and they put to flight everyone living in the valleys, to the east and to the west.

¹⁶Other Benjamites and some men from Judah also came to David in his stronghold. ¹⁷David went out to meet them and said to them, "If you have come to me in peace, to help me, I am ready to have you unite with me. But if you have come to betray me to my enemies when my hands are free from violence, may the God of our fathers see it and judge you."

¹⁸Then the Spirit came upon Amasai, chief of the Thirty, and he said:

> Success, success to you, and success to those who help you, for your God will help you
>
> (1 Chronicles 12:18).

"We are yours, O David!
We are with you, O son of Jesse!
Success, success to you,

and success to those who help you,
for your God will help you."

So David received them and made them leaders of his raiding bands.

[19] Some of the men of Manasseh defected to David when he went with the Philistines to fight against Saul. (He and his men did not help the Philistines because, after consultation, their rulers sent him away. They said, "It will cost us our heads if he deserts to his master Saul.") [20] When David went to Ziklag, these were the men of Manasseh who defected to him: Adnah, Jozabad, Jediael, Michael, Jozabad, Elihu and Zillethai, leaders of units of a thousand in Manasseh. [21] They helped David against raiding bands, for all of them were brave warriors, and they were commanders in his army. [22] Day after day men came to help David, until he had a great army, like the army of God.[a]

Others Join David at Hebron [23] These are the numbers of the men armed for battle who came to David at Hebron to turn Saul's kingdom over to him, as the LORD had said:

[24] men of Judah, carrying shield and spear—6,800 armed for battle;

[25] men of Simeon, warriors ready for battle—7,100;

[26] men of Levi—4,600, [27] including Jehoiada, leader of the family of Aaron, with 3,700 men, [28] and Zadok, a brave young warrior, with 22 officers from his family;

[29] men of Benjamin, Saul's kinsmen—3,000, most of whom had remained loyal to Saul's house until then;

[30] men of Ephraim, brave warriors, famous in their own clans—20,800;

[31] men of half the tribe of Manasseh, designated by name to come and make David king—18,000;

[32] men of Issachar, who understood the times and knew what Israel should do—200 chiefs, with all their relatives under their command;

[33] men of Zebulun, experienced soldiers prepared for battle with every type of weapon, to help David with undivided loyalty—50,000;

[34] men of Naphtali—1,000 officers, together with 37,000 men carrying shields and spears;

[35] men of Dan, ready for battle—28,600;

[36] men of Asher, experienced soldiers prepared for battle—40,000;

[37] and from east of the Jordan, men of Reuben, Gad and the half-tribe of Manasseh, armed with every type of weapon—120,000.

[38] All these were fighting men who volunteered to serve in the ranks. They came to Hebron fully determined to make David king over all Israel. All the rest of the Israelites were also of one mind to make David king. [39] The men spent three days there with David, eating and drinking, for their families had supplied provisions for them. [40] Also, their neighbors from as far away as Issachar, Zebulun and Naphtali came bringing food on donkeys, camels, mules and oxen. There were plentiful supplies of flour, fig cakes, raisin cakes, wine, oil, cattle and sheep, for there was joy in Israel.

[a] 22 Or *a great and mighty army*

1 CHRONICLES 12:22

If you've been a leader in your youth group, you've probably found out how frustrating leadership can be. You've pushed and prodded and poked, and you've probably found out that it just doesn't work. David's way of leading is better. David set out to accomplish a task. When others saw what he was doing, they joined him. His volunteer team grew "until he had a great army." That's how spiritual leadership works. Set out to accomplish something important, and rely on those who are willing to volunteer. Leading by example is always more effective than getting behind others and trying to push.

Direct Line

Bringing Back the Ark David conferred with each of his officers, the commanders of thousands and commanders of hundreds. ²He then said to the whole assembly of Israel, "If it seems good to you and if it is the will of the LORD our God, let us send word far and wide to the rest of our brothers throughout the territories of Israel, and also to the priests and Levites who are with them in their towns and pasturelands, to come and join us. ³Let us bring the ark of our God back to us, for we did not inquire of*a* it*b* during the reign of Saul." ⁴The whole assembly agreed to do this, because it seemed right to all the people.

⁵So David assembled all the Israelites, from the Shihor River in Egypt to Le-bo*c* Hamath, to bring the ark of God from Kiriath Jearim. ⁶David and all the Israelites with him went to Baalah of Judah (Kiriath Jearim) to bring up from there the ark of God the LORD, who is enthroned between the cherubim—the ark that is called by the Name.

⁷They moved the ark of God from Abinadab's house on a new cart, with Uzzah and Ahio guiding it. ⁸David and all the Israelites were celebrating with all their might before God, with songs and with harps, lyres, tambourines, cymbals and trumpets.

⁹When they came to the threshing floor of Kidon, Uzzah reached out his hand to steady the ark, because the oxen stumbled. ¹⁰The LORD's anger burned against Uzzah, and he struck him down because he had put his hand on the ark. So he died there before God.

¹¹Then David was angry because the LORD's wrath had broken out against Uzzah, and to this day that place is called Perez Uzzah.*d*

¹²David was afraid of God that day and asked, "How can I ever bring the ark of God to me?" ¹³He did not take the ark to be with him in the City of David. Instead, he took it aside to the house of Obed-Edom the Gittite. ¹⁴The ark of God remained with the family of Obed-Edom in his house for three months, and the LORD blessed his household and everything he had.

David's House and Family Now Hiram king of Tyre sent messengers to David, along with cedar logs, stonemasons and carpenters to build a palace for him. ²And David knew that the LORD had established him as king over Israel and that his kingdom had been highly exalted for the sake of his people Israel.

³In Jerusalem David took more wives and became the father of more sons and daughters. ⁴These are the names of the children born to him there: Shammua, Shobab, Nathan, Solomon, ⁵Ibhar, Elishua, Elpelet, ⁶Nogah, Nepheg, Japhia, ⁷Elishama, Beeliada*e* and Eliphelet.

David Defeats the Philistines ⁸When the Philistines heard that David had been anointed king over all Israel, they went up in full force to search for him, but David heard about it and went out to meet them. ⁹Now the Philistines had come and raided the Valley of Rephaim; ¹⁰so David inquired of God: "Shall I go and attack the Philistines? Will you hand them over to me?"

The LORD answered him, "Go, I will hand them over to you."

¹¹So David and his men went up to Baal Perazim, and there he defeated them. He said, "As waters break out, God has broken out against my enemies by my hand." So that place was called Baal Perazim.*f* ¹²The Philistines had abandoned their gods there, and David gave orders to burn them in the fire.

QUIZZER

1 CHRONICLES 13

Q: Why did God kill Uzzah?

BONUS: How are we to understand that punishment?

Answers on page 502

---

a3 Or we neglected *b3 Or him* *c5 Or to the entrance to* *d11 Perez Uzzah means outbreak against Uzzah.* *e7 A variant of Eliada* *f11 Baal Perazim means the lord who breaks out.*

Answers
to Quizzer

QUIZZER   If you like trivia, this feature is for you. "Quizzer" asks and then answers interesting Bible trivia questions.

BIBLE PROMISES   There are loads of great verses in the Bible. This feature highlights some of them for you.

> I am with you and will watch over you wherever you go (Genesis 28:15).

JERICHO JOE   Jericho Joe is just a little bit off-the-wall. (Get it?? Wall/Jericho?) Look to him for a unique and often funny perspective on certain passages.

COLOR PAGES   Some at the front, some at the back, some in the middle. These pages make you stop and think about contemporary issues. Whether covering money or school or sex or death??, these pages will help you look for answers to some of life's most difficult problems, and help you find those answers in God's Word.

WHAT DO I READ TODAY?   If you've been wondering what to read in the Bible or where to start, there's a reading plan on page 1638 to get you going.

WHERE DO I LOOK FOR THAT?   Better known as a subject index, you'll find this feature way in the back of *The Teen Study Bible* on page 1642. Think of a topic—look it up—locate the information within the text.

Best of all, *The Teen Study Bible* contains the full text of the New International Version of the Bible. It's contemporary, it's accurate, and it's written in language you can understand.

The Teen Study Bible, New International Version. It really is all you need to add excitement to your study of God's Word.

PREFACE

*T*HE NEW INTERNATIONAL VERSION is a completely new translation of the Holy Bible made by over a hundred scholars working directly from the best available Hebrew, Aramaic and Greek texts. It had its beginning in 1965 when, after several years of exploratory study by committees from the Christian Reformed Church and the National Association of Evangelicals, a group of scholars met at Palos Heights, Illinois, and concurred in the need for a new translation of the Bible in contemporary English. This group, though not made up of official church representatives, was transdenominational. Its conclusion was endorsed by a large number of leaders from many denominations who met in Chicago in 1966.

Responsibility for the new version was delegated by the Palos Heights group to a self-governing body of fifteen, the Committee on Bible Translation, composed for the most part of biblical scholars from colleges, universities and seminaries. In 1967 the New York Bible Society (now the International Bible Society) generously undertook the financial sponsorship of the project—a sponsorship that made it possible to enlist the help of many distinguished scholars. The fact that participants from the United States, Great Britain, Canada, Australia and New Zealand worked together gave the project its international scope. That they were from many denominations—including Anglican, Assemblies of God, Baptist, Brethren, Christian Reformed, Church of Christ, Evangelical Free, Lutheran, Mennonite, Methodist, Nazarene, Presbyterian, Wesleyan and other churches—helped to safeguard the translation from sectarian bias.

How it was made helps to give the New International Version its distinctiveness. The translation of each book was assigned to a team of scholars. Next, one of the Intermediate Editorial Committees revised the initial translation, with constant reference to the Hebrew, Aramaic or Greek. Their work then went to one of the General Editorial Committees, which checked it in detail and made another thorough revision. This revision in turn was carefully reviewed by the Committee on Bible Translation, which made further changes and then released the final version for publication. In this way the entire Bible underwent three revisions, during each of which the translation was examined for its faithfulness to the original languages and for its English style.

All this involved many thousands of hours of research and discussion regarding the meaning of the texts and the precise way of putting them into English. It may well be that no other translation has been made by a more thorough process of review and revision from committee to committee than this one.

From the beginning of the project, the Committee on Bible Translation held to certain goals for the New International Version: that it would be an accurate translation and one that would have clarity and literary quality and so prove suitable for public and private reading, teaching, preaching, memorizing and liturgical use. The Committee also sought to preserve some measure of continuity with the long tradition of translating the Scriptures into English.

In working toward these goals, the translators were united in their commitment to the authority and infallibility of the Bible as God's Word in written form. They believe that it contains the divine answer to the deepest needs of humanity, that it sheds unique light on our path in a dark world, and that it sets forth the way to our eternal well-being.

The first concern of the translators has been the accuracy of the translation and its fidelity to the thought of the biblical writers. They have weighed the significance of the lexical and grammatical details of the Hebrew, Aramaic and Greek texts. At the same time, they have striven for more than a word-for-word translation. Because thought patterns and syntax differ from language to language, faithful communication of the meaning of the writers of the Bible demands frequent modifications in sentence structure and constant regard for the contextual meanings of words.

A sensitive feeling for style does not always accompany scholarship. Accordingly the Committee on Bible Translation submitted the developing version to a number of stylistic consultants. Two of them read every book of both Old and New Testaments twice—once before and once after the last major revision—and made invaluable suggestions. Samples of the translation were tested for clarity and ease of reading by various kinds of people—young and old, highly educated and less well educated, ministers and laymen.

Concern for clear and natural English—that the New International Version should be idiomatic but not idiosyncratic, contemporary but not dated—motivated the translators and consultants. At the same time, they tried to reflect the differing styles of the biblical writers. In view of the international use of English, the translators sought to avoid obvious

Americanisms on the one hand and obvious Anglicisms on the other. A British edition reflects the comparatively few differences of significant idiom and of spelling.

As for the traditional pronouns "thou," "thee" and "thine" in reference to the Deity, the translators judged that to use these archaisms (along with the old verb forms such as "doest," "wouldest" and "hadst") would violate accuracy in translation. Neither Hebrew, Aramaic nor Greek uses special pronouns for the persons of the Godhead. A present-day translation is not enhanced by forms that in the time of the King James Version were used in everyday speech, whether referring to God or man.

For the Old Testament the standard Hebrew text, the Masoretic Text as published in the latest editions of Biblia Hebraica, was used throughout. The Dead Sea Scrolls contain material bearing on an earlier stage of the Hebrew text. They were consulted, as were the Samaritan Pentateuch and the ancient scribal traditions relating to textual changes. Sometimes a variant Hebrew reading in the margin of the Masoretic Text was followed instead of the text itself. Such instances, being variants within the Masoretic tradition, are not specified by footnotes. In rare cases, words in the consonantal text were divided differently from the way they appear in the Masoretic Text. Footnotes indicate this. The translators also consulted the more important early versions—the Septuagint; Aquila, Symmachus and Theodotion; the Vulgate; the Syriac Peshitta; the Targums; and for the Psalms the Juxta Hebraica of Jerome. Readings from these versions were occasionally followed where the Masoretic Text seemed doubtful and where accepted principles of textual criticism showed that one or more of these textual witnesses appeared to provide the correct reading. Such instances are footnoted. Sometimes vowel letters and vowel signs did not, in the judgment of the translators, represent the correct vowels for the original consonantal text. Accordingly some words were read with a different set of vowels. These instances are usually not indicated by footnotes.

The Greek text used in translating the New Testament was an eclectic one. No other piece of ancient literature has such an abundance of manuscript witnesses as does the New Testament. Where existing manuscripts differ, the translators made their choice of readings according to accepted principles of New Testament textual criticism. Footnotes call attention to places where there was uncertainty about what the original text was. The best current printed texts of the Greek New Testament were used.

There is a sense in which the work of translation is never wholly finished. This applies to all great literature and uniquely so to the Bible. In 1973 the New Testament in the New International Version was published. Since then, suggestions for corrections and revisions have been received from various sources. The Committee on Bible Translation carefully considered the suggestions and adopted a number of them. These were incorporated in the first printing of the entire Bible in 1978. Additional revisions were made by the Committee on Bible Translation in 1983 and appear in printings after that date.

As in other ancient documents, the precise meaning of the biblical texts is sometimes uncertain. This is more often the case with the Hebrew and Aramaic texts than with the Greek text. Although archaeological and linguistic discoveries in this century aid in understanding difficult passages, some uncertainties remain. The more significant of these have been called to the reader's attention in the footnotes.

In regard to the divine name YHWH, commonly referred to as the Tetragrammaton, the translators adopted the device used in most English versions of rendering that name as "Lord" in capital letters to distinguish it from Adonai, another Hebrew word rendered "Lord," for which small letters are used. Wherever the two names stand together in the Old Testament as a compound name of God, they are rendered "Sovereign Lord."

Because for most readers today the phrases "the Lord of hosts" and "God of hosts" have little meaning, this version renders them "the Lord Almighty" and "God Almighty." These renderings convey the sense of the Hebrew, namely, "he who is sovereign over all the 'hosts' (powers) in heaven and on earth, especially over the 'hosts' (armies) of Israel." For readers unacquainted with Hebrew this does not make clear the distinction between Sabaoth ("hosts" or "Almighty") and Shaddai (which can also be translated "Almighty"), but the latter occurs infrequently and is always footnoted. When Adonai and YHWH Sabaoth occur together, they are rendered "the Lord, the Lord Almighty."

As for other proper nouns, the familiar spellings of the King James Version are generally retained. Names traditionally spelled with "ch," except where it is final, are usually spelled in this translation with "k" or "c," since the biblical languages do not have the sound that "ch" frequently indicates in English—for example, in chant. For well-known names such as Zechariah, however, the traditional spelling has been retained. Variation in the spelling of names in the original languages has usually not been indicated. Where a person or place has two or more different names in the Hebrew, Aramaic or Greek texts, the more familiar one has generally been used, with footnotes where needed.

To achieve clarity the translators sometimes supplied words not in the original texts but required by the context. If there was uncertainty about such material, it is enclosed in brackets. Also for the sake of clarity or style, nouns, including some proper nouns, are sometimes substituted for pronouns, and vice versa. And though the Hebrew writers often shifted back and forth between first, second and third personal pronouns without change of antecedent, this translation often makes them uniform, in accordance with English style and without the use of footnotes.

Poetical passages are printed as poetry, that is, with indentation of lines and with separate stanzas. These are generally designed to reflect the structure of Hebrew poetry. This poetry is normally characterized by parallelism in balanced lines. Most of the poetry in the Bible is in the Old Testament, and scholars differ regarding the scansion of Hebrew lines. The translators determined the stanza divisions for the most part by analysis of the subject matter. The stanzas therefore serve as poetic paragraphs.

As an aid to the reader, italicized sectional headings are inserted in most of the books. They are not to be regarded as part of the NIV text, are not for oral reading, and are not intended to dictate the interpretation of the sections they head.

The footnotes in this version are of several kinds, most of which need no explanation. Those giving alternative translations begin with "Or" and generally introduce the alternative with the last word preceding it in the text, except when it is a single-word alternative; in poetry quoted in a footnote a slant mark indicates a line division. Footnotes introduced by "Or" do not have uniform significance. In some cases two possible translations were considered to have about equal validity. In other cases, though the translators were convinced that the translation in the text was correct, they judged that another interpretation was possible and of sufficient importance to be represented in a footnote.

In the New Testament, footnotes that refer to uncertainty regarding the original text are introduced by "Some manuscripts" or similar expressions. In the Old Testament, evidence for the reading chosen is given first and evidence for the alternative is added after a semicolon (for example: Septuagint; Hebrew father). In such notes the term "Hebrew" refers to the Masoretic Text.

It should be noted that minerals, flora and fauna, architectural details, articles of clothing and jewelry, musical instruments and other articles cannot always be identified with precision. Also measures of capacity in the biblical period are particularly uncertain (see the table of weights and measures following the text).

Like all translations of the Bible, made as they are by imperfect man, this one undoubtedly falls short of its goals. Yet we are grateful to God for the extent to which he has enabled us to realize these goals and for the strength he has given us and our colleagues to complete our task. We offer this version of the Bible to him in whose name and for whose glory it has been made. We pray that it will lead many into a better understanding of the Holy Scriptures and a fuller knowledge of Jesus Christ the incarnate Word, of whom the Scriptures so faithfully testify.

The Committee on Bible Translation
June 1978
(Revised August 1983)

Names of the translators and editors may be secured
from the International Bible Society,
translation sponsors of the New International Version,
1820 Jet Stream Drive, Colorado Springs, Colorado
80921-3696 U.S.A.

The OLD Testament

THE NAME MEANS "BEGINNINGS."

And the book answers some of life's biggest questions. Where did the universe come from? How can there be evil in a world a good God created? One of the biggest questions Genesis answers is whether or not God truly cares about the people he created. That question is answered when God promises to bless Abraham and all his descendants.

Genesis is also the story of how God's promises to Abraham were passed on to the generations after him. The people you will meet in Genesis don't always do what's right, but God keeps his promises to them. Just as he keeps his promises to you today.

FAST FACTS

Genesis doesn't give a date for creation.

Famous people in Genesis? Adam and Eve, Noah, Abraham, Isaac, Jacob and Joseph.

Today's Jews are descended from Abraham's son Isaac.

Today's Arabs are descended from Abraham's son Ishmael.

Moses wrote this book about 1400 B.C.

Fundamentals

What makes you and other people so special (Genesis 2:7)?

How do God's promises to Abraham affect you (Genesis 12:3)?

What sometimes makes brothers and sisters jealous (Genesis 37:3)?

What is the best way to treat people who hurt you (Genesis 50:20)?

The Beginning In the beginning God created the heavens and the earth. ²Now the earth was*ᵃ* formless and empty, darkness was over the surface of the deep, and the Spirit of God was hovering over the waters.

³And God said, "Let there be light," and there was light. ⁴God saw that the light was good, and he separated the light from the darkness. ⁵God called the light "day," and the darkness he called "night." And there was evening, and there was morning—the first day.

⁶And God said, "Let there be an expanse between the waters to separate water from water." ⁷So God made the expanse and separated the water under the expanse from the water above it. And it was so. ⁸God called the expanse "sky." And there was evening, and there was morning—the second day.

⁹And God said, "Let the water under the sky be gathered to one place, and let dry ground appear." And it was so. ¹⁰God called the dry ground "land," and the gathered waters he called "seas." And God saw that it was good.

¹¹Then God said, "Let the land produce vegetation: seed-bearing plants and trees on the land that bear fruit with seed in it, according to their various kinds." And it was so. ¹²The land produced vegetation: plants bearing seed according to their kinds and trees bearing fruit with seed in it according to their kinds. And God saw that it was good. ¹³And there was evening, and there was morning—the third day.

¹⁴And God said, "Let there be lights in the expanse of the sky to separate the day from the night, and let them serve as signs to mark seasons and days and years, ¹⁵and let them be lights in the expanse of the sky to give light on the earth." And it was so. ¹⁶God made two great lights—the greater light to govern the day and the lesser light to govern the night. He also made the stars. ¹⁷God set them in the expanse of the sky to give light on the earth, ¹⁸to govern the day and the night, and to separate light from darkness. And God saw that it was good. ¹⁹And there was evening, and there was morning—the fourth day.

²⁰And God said, "Let the water teem with living creatures, and let birds fly

---

ᵃ2 Or possibly became

The Bible Says

It Didn't Just Happen!

Genesis 1 teaches that God created the universe. Life didn't "just happen" as molecules bumped into each other. How do you know? Psalm 19:1 and Romans 1:18–20 suggest that you look around. If you saw a shiny new Cadillac in a junkyard, would you think it "evolved" from the junkyard parts? The universe is thousands of times more complex than a Cadillac. It didn't "just happen." God designed this world—all of it:

* God created the universe from nothing (Psalm 33:6,8–9).
* Creation reminds you of the greatness of your God (Isaiah 40:26,28).
* You accept the evidence that God created the universe by faith (Hebrews 11:3).

Isn't it great to know that the heavenly Father who loves you is the all-powerful Creator of the universe?

above the earth across the expanse of the sky." ²¹So God created the great creatures of the sea and every living and moving thing with which the water teems, according to their kinds, and every winged bird according to its kind. And God saw that it was good. ²²God blessed them and said, "Be fruitful and increase in number and fill the water in the seas, and let the birds increase on the earth." ²³And there was evening, and there was morning—the fifth day.

²⁴And God said, "Let the land produce living creatures according to their kinds: livestock, creatures that move along the ground, and wild animals, each according to its kind." And it was so. ²⁵God made the wild animals according to their kinds, the livestock according to their kinds, and all the creatures that move along the ground according to their kinds. And God saw that it was good.

²⁶Then God said, "Let us make man in our image, in our likeness, and let them rule over the fish of the sea and the birds of the air, over the livestock, over all the earth,*ᵃ* and over all the creatures that move along the ground."

²⁷So God created man in his own image,
in the image of God he created him;
male and female he created them.

²⁸God blessed them and said to them, "Be fruitful and increase in number; fill the earth and subdue it. Rule over the fish of the sea and the birds of the air and over every living creature that moves on the ground."

²⁹Then God said, "I give you every seed-bearing plant on the face of the whole earth and every tree that has fruit with seed in it. They will be yours for food. ³⁰And to all the beasts of the earth and all the birds of the air and all the creatures that move on the ground—everything that has the breath of life in it—I give every green plant for food." And it was so.

³¹God saw all that he had made, and it was very good. And there was evening, and there was morning—the sixth day.

Thus the heavens and the earth were completed in all their vast array.

2 ²By the seventh day God had finished the work he had been doing; so on the seventh day he rested*ᵇ* from all his work. ³And God blessed the seventh day and made it holy, because on it he rested from all the work of creating that he had done.

Adam and Eve ⁴This is the account of the heavens and the earth when they were created.

When the LORD God made the earth and the heavens— ⁵and no shrub of the field had yet appeared on the earth*ᶜ* and no plant of the field had yet sprung up, for the LORD God had not sent rain on the earth*ᶜ* and there was no man to work the ground, ⁶but streams*ᵈ* came up from the earth and watered the whole surface of the ground— ⁷the LORD God formed the man*ᵉ* from the dust of the ground and breathed into his nostrils the breath of life, and the man became a living being.

⁸Now the LORD God had planted a garden in the east, in Eden; and there he put the man he had formed. ⁹And the LORD God made all kinds of trees grow out of the ground—trees that were pleasing to the eye and good for food. In

---

ᵃ26 Hebrew; Syriac *all the wild animals* *ᵇ2* Or *ceased*; also in verse 3 *ᶜ5* Or *land*; also in verse 6 *ᵈ6* Or *mist* *ᵉ7* The Hebrew for *man (adam)* sounds like and may be related to the Hebrew for *ground (adamah)*; it is also the name *Adam* (see Gen. 2:20).

the middle of the garden were the tree of life and the tree of the knowledge of good and evil.

¹⁰A river watering the garden flowed from Eden; from there it was separated into four headwaters. ¹¹The name of the first is the Pishon; it winds through the entire land of Havilah, where there is gold. ¹²(The gold of that land is good; aromatic resin⁰ and onyx are also there.) ¹³The name of the second river is the Gihon; it winds through the entire land of Cush.ᵇ ¹⁴The name of the third river is the Tigris; it runs along the east side of Asshur. And the fourth river is the Euphrates.

¹⁵The LORD God took the man and put him in the Garden of Eden to work it and take care of it. ¹⁶And the LORD God commanded the man, "You are free to eat from any tree in the garden; ¹⁷but you must not eat from the tree of the knowledge of good and evil, for when you eat of it you will surely die."

¹⁸The LORD God said, "It is not good for the man to be alone. I will make a helper suitable for him."

¹⁹Now the LORD God had formed out of the ground all the beasts of the field and all the birds of the air. He brought them to the man to see what he would name them; and whatever the man called each living creature, that was its name. ²⁰So the man gave names to all the livestock, the birds of the air and all the beasts of the field.

But for Adamᶜ no suitable helper was found. ²¹So the LORD God caused the man to fall into a deep sleep; and while he was sleeping, he took one of the man's ribsᵈ and closed up the place with flesh. ²²Then the LORD God made a woman from the ribᵉ he had taken out of the man, and he brought her to the man.

²³The man said,

> "This is now bone of my bones
>   and flesh of my flesh;
> she shall be called 'woman,ᶠ'
>   for she was taken out of man."

²⁴For this reason a man will leave his father and mother and be united to his wife, and they will become one flesh.

²⁵The man and his wife were both naked, and they felt no shame.

The Fall of Man Now the serpent was more crafty than any of the wild animals the LORD God had made. He said to the woman, "Did God really say, 'You must not eat from any tree in the garden'?"

²The woman said to the serpent, "We may eat fruit from the trees in the garden, ³but God did say, 'You must not eat fruit from the tree that is in the middle of the garden, and you must not touch it, or you will die.' "

⁴"You will not surely die," the serpent said to the woman. ⁵"For God knows that

Direct Line

GENESIS 2:7

Sometimes you don't feel very special. You say something stupid in class. You look in the mirror and see a giant zit on the end of your nose. You? Special? You bet! You're a human being, totally special to God. When God made animals he simply spoke them into existence. But when he made Adam, God personally fashioned Adam's body from clay and then breathed the gift of life into him, a human being made in the image and likeness of God (Genesis 1:27). Oh, you'll get zits. And maybe you'll say a stupid thing or two. But don't let things like that rob you of feeling special, because you are!

ᵃ12 Or good; pearls ᵇ13 Possibly southeast Mesopotamia ᶜ20 Or the man ᵈ21 Or took part of the man's side ᵉ22 Or part ᶠ23 The Hebrew for woman sounds like the Hebrew for man.

when you eat of it your eyes will be opened, and you will be like God, knowing good and evil."

⁶When the woman saw that the fruit of the tree was good for food and pleasing to the eye, and also desirable for gaining wisdom, she took some and ate it. She also gave some to her husband, who was with her, and he ate it. ⁷Then the eyes of both of them were opened, and they realized they were naked; so they sewed fig leaves together and made coverings for themselves.

⁸Then the man and his wife heard the sound of the LORD God as he was walking in the garden in the cool of the day, and they hid from the LORD God among the trees of the garden. ⁹But the LORD God called to the man, "Where are you?"

¹⁰He answered, "I heard you in the garden, and I was afraid because I was naked; so I hid."

¹¹And he said, "Who told you that you were naked? Have you eaten from the tree that I commanded you not to eat from?"

¹²The man said, "The woman you put here with me—she gave me some fruit from the tree, and I ate it."

¹³Then the LORD God said to the woman, "What is this you have done?"

The woman said, "The serpent deceived me, and I ate."

¹⁴So the LORD God said to the serpent, "Because you have done this,

> "Cursed are you above all the livestock
>   and all the wild animals!
> You will crawl on your belly
>   and you will eat dust
>   all the days of your life.
> ¹⁵ And I will put enmity
>   between you and the woman,
>   and between your offspring*a* and hers;
> he will crush*b* your head,
>   and you will strike his heel."

¹⁶To the woman he said,

> "I will greatly increase your pains in
>   childbearing;
>   with pain you will give birth to children.
> Your desire will be for your husband,
>   and he will rule over you."

¹⁷To Adam he said, "Because you listened to your wife and ate from the tree about which I commanded you, 'You must not eat of it,'

> "Cursed is the ground because of you;
>   through painful toil you will eat of it
>   all the days of your life.
> ¹⁸It will produce thorns and thistles for you,
>   and you will eat the plants of the field.
> ¹⁹By the sweat of your brow
>   you will eat your food
> until you return to the ground,
>   since from it you were taken;
> for dust you are
>   and to dust you will return."

²⁰Adam*c* named his wife Eve,*d* because she would become the mother of all the living.

"So they ate the fruit anyway . . . that's the pits!"

SEE GENESIS 3:6

---

*a*15 Or *seed* *b*15 Or *strike* *c*20 Or *The man* *d*20 *Eve* probably means *living.*

[21]The Lord God made garments of skin for Adam and his wife and clothed them. [22]And the Lord God said, "The man has now become like one of us, knowing good and evil. He must not be allowed to reach out his hand and take also from the tree of life and eat, and live forever." [23]So the Lord God banished him from the Garden of Eden to work the ground from which he had been taken. [24]After he drove the man out, he placed on the east side[a] of the Garden of Eden cherubim and a flaming sword flashing back and forth to guard the way to the tree of life.

4 *Cain and Abel* Adam[b] lay with his wife Eve, and she became pregnant and gave birth to Cain.[c] She said, "With the help of the Lord I have brought forth[d] a man." [2]Later she gave birth to his brother Abel.

Now Abel kept flocks, and Cain worked the soil. [3]In the course of time Cain brought some of the fruits of the soil as an offering to the Lord. [4]But Abel brought fat portions from some of the firstborn of his flock. The Lord looked with favor on Abel and his offering, [5]but on Cain and his offering he did not look with favor. So Cain was very angry, and his face was downcast.

[6]Then the Lord said to Cain, "Why are you angry? Why is your face downcast? [7]If you do what is right, will you not be accepted? But if you do not do what is right, sin is crouching at your door; it desires to have you, but you must master it."

[8]Now Cain said to his brother Abel, "Let's go out to the field."[e] And while they were in the field, Cain attacked his brother Abel and killed him.

[9]Then the Lord said to Cain, "Where is your brother Abel?"

"I don't know," he replied. "Am I my brother's keeper?"

[10]The Lord said, "What have you done? Listen! Your brother's blood cries out to me from the ground. [11]Now you are under a curse and driven from the ground, which opened its mouth to receive your brother's blood from your hand. [12]When you work the ground, it will no longer yield its crops for you. You will be a restless wanderer on the earth."

[13]Cain said to the Lord, "My punishment is more than I can bear. [14]Today you are driving me from the land, and I will be hidden from your presence; I will be a restless wanderer on the earth, and whoever finds me will kill me."

[15]But the Lord said to him, "Not so[f]; if anyone kills Cain, he will suffer vengeance seven times over." Then the Lord put a mark on Cain so that no one who found him would kill him. [16]So Cain went out from the Lord's presence and lived in the land of Nod,[g] east of Eden.

[17]Cain lay with his wife, and she became pregnant and gave birth to Enoch. Cain was then building a city, and he named it after his son Enoch. [18]To Enoch was born Irad, and Irad was the father of Mehujael, and Mehujael was the father of Methushael, and Methushael was the father of Lamech.

GENESIS 3:12–13

Adam and Eve felt scared and guilty when God confronted them after they ate the forbidden fruit (Genesis 3:1–13). They probably felt a little like you do when your mom or dad says, "Hey, why are you kids fighting?" Or when one of your friends says, "Why did you tell Sarah?" Adam and Eve acted like people do today. When confronted with his sin, Adam blamed Eve. And Eve in turn blamed the serpent. Sound familiar? Sort of like, "Mom, he started it." Or, "Dad, it's not my fault." But try to remember, you're responsible for your own choices. And, as Adam and Eve found out, the consequences of bad choices can hurt!

Direct Line

---

[a]24 Or *placed in front* [b]1 Or *The man* [c]1 *Cain* sounds like the Hebrew for *brought forth* or *acquired*. [d]1 Or *have acquired* [e]8 Samaritan Pentateuch, Septuagint, Vulgate and Syriac; Masoretic Text does not have *"Let's go out to the field."* [f]15 Septuagint, Vulgate and Syriac; Hebrew *Very well* [g]16 *Nod* means *wandering* (see verses 12 and 14).

¹⁹Lamech married two women, one named Adah and the other Zillah. ²⁰Adah gave birth to Jabal; he was the father of those who live in tents and raise livestock. ²¹His brother's name was Jubal; he was the father of all who play the harp and flute. ²²Zillah also had a son, Tubal-Cain, who forged all kinds of tools out of*ᵃ* bronze and iron. Tubal-Cain's sister was Naamah.

²³Lamech said to his wives,

> "Adah and Zillah, listen to me;
>   wives of Lamech, hear my words.
> I have killed*ᵇ* a man for wounding me,
>   a young man for injuring me.
> ²⁴If Cain is avenged seven times,
>   then Lamech seventy-seven times."

²⁵Adam lay with his wife again, and she gave birth to a son and named him Seth,*ᶜ* saying, "God has granted me another child in place of Abel, since Cain killed him." ²⁶Seth also had a son, and he named him Enosh.

At that time men began to call on*ᵈ* the name of the LORD.

From Adam to Noah   This is the written account of Adam's line.

When God created man, he made him in the likeness of God. ²He created them male and female and blessed them. And when they were created, he called them "man.*ᵉ*"

³When Adam had lived 130 years, he had a son in his own likeness, in his own image; and he named him Seth. ⁴After Seth was born, Adam lived 800 years and had other sons and daughters. ⁵Altogether, Adam lived 930 years, and then he died.

⁶When Seth had lived 105 years, he became the father*ᶠ* of Enosh. ⁷And after he became the father of Enosh, Seth lived 807 years and had other sons and daughters. ⁸Altogether, Seth lived 912 years, and then he died.

⁹When Enosh had lived 90 years, he became the father of Kenan. ¹⁰And after he became the father of Kenan, Enosh lived 815 years and had other sons and daughters. ¹¹Altogether, Enosh lived 905 years, and then he died.

¹²When Kenan had lived 70 years, he became the father of Mahalalel. ¹³And after he became the father of Mahalalel, Kenan lived 840 years and had other sons and daughters. ¹⁴Altogether, Kenan lived 910 years, and then he died.

¹⁵When Mahalalel had lived 65 years, he became the father of Jared. ¹⁶And after he became the father of Jared, Mahalalel lived 830 years and had other sons and daughters. ¹⁷Altogether, Mahalalel lived 895 years, and then he died.

¹⁸When Jared had lived 162 years, he became the father of Enoch. ¹⁹And after he became the father of Enoch, Jared lived 800 years and had other sons and daughters. ²⁰Altogether, Jared lived 962 years, and then he died.

²¹When Enoch had lived 65 years, he became the father of Methuselah. ²²And after he became the father of Methuselah, Enoch walked with God 300 years and had other sons and daughters. ²³Altogether, Enoch lived 365 years. ²⁴Enoch walked with God; then he was no more, because God took him away.

²⁵When Methuselah had lived 187 years, he became the father of Lamech. ²⁶And after he became the father of Lamech, Methuselah lived 782 years and had other sons and daughters. ²⁷Altogether, Methuselah lived 969 years, and then he died.

²⁸When Lamech had lived 182 years, he had a son. ²⁹He named him Noah*ᵍ*

ᵃ22 Or *who instructed all who work in*   *ᵇ23* Or *I will kill*   *ᶜ25 Seth* probably means *granted.*   *ᵈ26* Or *to proclaim*   *ᵉ2* Hebrew *adam*   *ᶠ6 Father* may mean *ancestor;* also in verses 7-26.   *ᵍ29 Noah* sounds like the Hebrew for *comfort.*

and said, "He will comfort us in the labor and painful toil of our hands caused by the ground the LORD has cursed." ³⁰After Noah was born, Lamech lived 595 years and had other sons and daughters. ³¹Altogether, Lamech lived 777 years, and then he died.

³²After Noah was 500 years old, he became the father of Shem, Ham and Japheth.

The Flood When men began to increase in number on the earth and daughters were born to them, ²the sons of God saw that the daughters of men were beautiful, and they married any of them they chose. ³Then the LORD said, "My Spirit will not contend with*ᵃ* man forever, for he is mortal*ᵇ*; his days will be a hundred and twenty years."

⁴The Nephilim were on the earth in those days—and also afterward—when the sons of God went to the daughters of men and had children by them. They were the heroes of old, men of renown.

⁵The LORD saw how great man's wickedness on the earth had become, and that every inclination of the thoughts of his heart was only evil all the time. ⁶The LORD was grieved that he had made man on the earth, and his heart was filled with pain. ⁷So the LORD said, "I will wipe mankind, whom I have created, from the face of the earth—men and animals, and creatures that move along the ground, and birds of the air—for I am grieved that I have made them." ⁸But Noah found favor in the eyes of the LORD.

⁹This is the account of Noah.

Noah was a righteous man, blameless among the people of his time, and he walked with God. ¹⁰Noah had three sons: Shem, Ham and Japheth.

¹¹Now the earth was corrupt in God's sight and was full of violence. ¹²God saw how corrupt the earth had become, for all the people on earth had corrupted their ways. ¹³So God said to Noah, "I am going to put an end to all people, for the earth is filled with violence because of them. I am surely going to destroy both them and the earth. ¹⁴So make yourself an ark of cypress*ᶜ* wood; make rooms in it and coat it with pitch inside and out. ¹⁵This is how you are to build it: The ark is to be 450 feet long, 75 feet wide and 45 feet high.*ᵈ* ¹⁶Make a roof for it and finish*ᵉ* the ark to within 18 inches*ᶠ* of the top. Put a door in the side of the ark and make lower, middle and upper decks. ¹⁷I am going to bring floodwaters on the earth to destroy all life under the heavens, every creature that has the breath of life in it. Everything on earth will perish. ¹⁸But I will establish my covenant with you, and you will enter the ark—you and your sons and your wife and your sons' wives with you. ¹⁹You are to bring into the ark two of all living creatures, male and female, to keep them alive with you. ²⁰Two of every kind of bird, of every kind of animal and of every kind of creature that moves along the ground will come to you to be kept alive. ²¹You are to take every kind of food that is to be eaten and store it away as food for you and for them."

²²Noah did everything just as God commanded him.

The LORD then said to Noah, "Go into the ark, you and your whole family, because I have found you righteous in this generation. ²Take with you seven*ᵍ* of every kind of clean animal, a male and its mate, and two of every kind of unclean animal, a male and its mate, ³and also seven of every kind of bird, male and female, to keep their various kinds alive throughout

---

ᵃ3 Or My spirit will not remain in *ᵇ3 Or corrupt* *ᶜ14 The meaning of the Hebrew for this word is uncertain.* *ᵈ15 Hebrew 300 cubits long, 50 cubits wide and 30 cubits high (about 140 meters long, 23 meters wide and 13.5 meters high)* *ᵉ16 Or Make an opening for light by finishing* *ᶠ16 Hebrew a cubit (about 0.5 meter)* *ᵍ2 Or seven pairs; also in verse 3*

the earth. ⁴Seven days from now I will send rain on the earth for forty days and forty nights, and I will wipe from the face of the earth every living creature I have made."

⁵And Noah did all that the LORD commanded him.

⁶Noah was six hundred years old when the floodwaters came on the earth. ⁷And Noah and his sons and his wife and his sons' wives entered the ark to escape the waters of the flood. ⁸Pairs of clean and unclean animals, of birds and of all creatures that move along the ground, ⁹male and female, came to Noah and entered the ark, as God had commanded Noah. ¹⁰And after the seven days the floodwaters came on the earth.

¹¹In the six hundredth year of Noah's life, on the seventeenth day of the second month—on that day all the springs of the great deep burst forth, and the floodgates of the heavens were opened. ¹²And rain fell on the earth forty days and forty nights.

¹³On that very day Noah and his sons, Shem, Ham and Japheth, together with his wife and the wives of his three sons, entered the ark. ¹⁴They had with them every wild animal according to its kind, all livestock according to their kinds, every creature that moves along the ground according to its kind and every bird according to its kind, everything with wings. ¹⁵Pairs of all creatures that have the breath of life in them came to Noah and entered the ark. ¹⁶The animals going in were male and female of every living thing, as God had commanded Noah. Then the LORD shut him in.

¹⁷For forty days the flood kept coming on the earth, and as the waters increased they lifted the ark high above the earth. ¹⁸The waters rose and increased greatly on the earth, and the ark floated on the surface of the water. ¹⁹They rose greatly on the earth, and all the high mountains under the entire heavens were covered. ²⁰The waters rose and covered the mountains to a depth of more than twenty feet.[a,b] ²¹Every living thing that moved on the earth perished—birds, livestock, wild animals, all the creatures that swarm over the earth, and all mankind. ²²Everything on dry land that had the breath of life in its nostrils died. ²³Every living thing on the face of the earth was wiped out; men and animals and the creatures that move along the ground and the birds of the air were wiped from the earth. Only Noah was left, and those with him in the ark.

²⁴The waters flooded the earth for a hundred and fifty days.

8 But God remembered Noah and all the wild animals and the livestock that were with him in the ark, and he sent a wind over the earth, and the waters receded. ²Now the springs of the deep and the floodgates of the heavens had been closed, and the rain had stopped falling from the sky. ³The water receded steadily from the earth. At the end of the hundred and fifty days the water had gone down, ⁴and on the seventeenth day of the seventh month the ark came to rest on the mountains of Ararat. ⁵The waters continued to recede until the tenth month, and on the first day of the tenth month the tops of the mountains became visible.

⁶After forty days Noah opened the window he had made in the ark ⁷and sent out a raven, and it kept flying back and forth until the water had dried up from the earth. ⁸Then he sent out a dove to see if the water had receded from the surface of the ground. ⁹But the dove could find no place to set its feet because there was water over all the surface of the earth; so it returned to Noah in the ark. He reached out his hand and took the dove and brought

GENESIS 7

QUIZZER

Q: How many days would a person have to tread water to survive the flood?

BONUS: What happened to all that water?

Answers on page 10

---

[a]20 Hebrew *fifteen cubits* (about 6.9 meters)   [b]20 Or *rose more than twenty feet, and the mountains were covered*

it back to himself in the ark. [10]He waited seven more days and again sent out the dove from the ark. [11]When the dove returned to him in the evening, there in its beak was a freshly plucked olive leaf! Then Noah knew that the water had receded from the earth. [12]He waited seven more days and sent the dove out again, but this time it did not return to him.

Answers
*to Quizzer on
page 9*

A: About five
months (compare
Genesis 7:11
and 8:4).

BONUS: Many
think it fills our
oceans. The
weight of the
waters pressed
down the
seabeds and
thrust up the
mountains.

[13]By the first day of the first month of Noah's six hundred and first year, the water had dried up from the earth. Noah then removed the covering from the ark and saw that the surface of the ground was dry. [14]By the twenty-seventh day of the second month the earth was completely dry.

[15]Then God said to Noah, [16]"Come out of the ark, you and your wife and your sons and their wives. [17]Bring out every kind of living creature that is with you—the birds, the animals, and all the creatures that move along the ground—so they can multiply on the earth and be fruitful and increase in number upon it."

[18]So Noah came out, together with his sons and his wife and his sons' wives. [19]All the animals and all the creatures that move along the ground and all the birds—everything that moves on the earth—came out of the ark, one kind after another.

[20]Then Noah built an altar to the LORD and, taking some of all the clean animals and clean birds, he sacrificed burnt offerings on it. [21]The LORD smelled the pleasing aroma and said in his heart: "Never again will I curse the ground because of man, even though[a] every inclination of his heart is evil from childhood. And never again will I destroy all living creatures, as I have done.

[22]"As long as the earth endures,
seedtime and harvest,
cold and heat,
summer and winter,
day and night
will never cease."

God's Covenant With Noah   Then God blessed Noah and his sons, saying to them, "Be fruitful and increase in number and fill the earth. [2]The fear and dread of you will fall upon all the beasts of the earth and all the birds of the air, upon every creature that moves along the ground, and upon all the fish of the sea; they are given into your hands. [3]Everything that lives and moves will be food for you. Just as I gave you the green plants, I now give you everything.

[4]"But you must not eat meat that has its lifeblood still in it. [5]And for your lifeblood I will surely demand an accounting. I will demand an accounting from every animal. And from each man, too, I will demand an accounting for the life of his fellow man.

[6]"Whoever sheds the blood of man,
by man shall his blood be shed;
for in the image of God
has God made man.

[7]As for you, be fruitful and increase in number; multiply on the earth and increase upon it."

[8]Then God said to Noah and to his sons with him: [9]"I now establish my covenant with you and with your descendants after you [10]and with every living creature that was with you—the birds, the livestock and all the wild animals, all those that came out of the ark with you—every living creature on earth.

[a]21 Or *man, for*

¹¹I establish my covenant with you: Never again will all life be cut off by the waters of a flood; never again will there be a flood to destroy the earth."

¹²And God said, "This is the sign of the covenant I am making between me and you and every living creature with you, a covenant for all generations to come: ¹³I have set my rainbow in the clouds, and it will be the sign of the covenant between me and the earth. ¹⁴Whenever I bring clouds over the earth and the rainbow appears in the clouds, ¹⁵I will remember my covenant between me and you and all living creatures of every kind. Never again will the waters become a flood to destroy all life. ¹⁶Whenever the rainbow appears in the clouds, I will see it and remember the everlasting covenant between God and all living creatures of every kind on the earth."

¹⁷So God said to Noah, "This is the sign of the covenant I have established between me and all life on the earth."

> Never again will
> there be a
> flood to destroy
> the earth
> (Genesis 9:11).

The Sons of Noah   ¹⁸The sons of Noah who came out of the ark were Shem, Ham and Japheth. (Ham was the father of Canaan.) ¹⁹These were the three sons of Noah, and from them came the people who were scattered over the earth.

²⁰Noah, a man of the soil, proceeded[a] to plant a vineyard. ²¹When he drank some of its wine, he became drunk and lay uncovered inside his tent. ²²Ham, the father of Canaan, saw his father's nakedness and told his two brothers outside. ²³But Shem and Japheth took a garment and laid it across their shoulders; then they walked in backward and covered their father's nakedness. Their faces were turned the other way so that they would not see their father's nakedness.

²⁴When Noah awoke from his wine and found out what his youngest son had done to him, ²⁵he said,

> "Cursed be Canaan!
>   The lowest of slaves
>   will he be to his brothers."

²⁶He also said,

> "Blessed be the LORD, the God of Shem!
>   May Canaan be the slave of Shem.[b]
> ²⁷May God extend the territory of Japheth[c];
>   may Japheth live in the tents of Shem,
>   and may Canaan be his[d] slave."

²⁸After the flood Noah lived 350 years. ²⁹Altogether, Noah lived 950 years, and then he died.

10 **The Table of Nations**   This is the account of Shem, Ham and Japheth, Noah's sons, who themselves had sons after the flood.

The Japhethites

²The sons[e] of Japheth:

Gomer, Magog, Madai, Javan, Tubal, Meshech and Tiras.

³The sons of Gomer:

Ashkenaz, Riphath and Togarmah.

ᵃ20 Or *soil, was the first*   ᵇ26 Or *be his slave*   ᶜ27 *Japheth* sounds like the Hebrew for *extend.*
ᵈ27 Or *their*   ᵉ2 *Sons* may mean *descendants* or *successors* or *nations*; also in verses 3, 4, 6, 7, 20-23, 29 and 31.

⁴The sons of Javan:

Elishah, Tarshish, the Kittim and the Rodanim.^a ⁵(From these the maritime peoples spread out into their territories by their clans within their nations, each with its own language.)

The Hamites

⁶The sons of Ham:

Cush, Mizraim,^b Put and Canaan.

⁷The sons of Cush:

Seba, Havilah, Sabtah, Raamah and Sabteca.

The sons of Raamah:

Sheba and Dedan.

⁸Cush was the father^c of Nimrod, who grew to be a mighty warrior on the earth. ⁹He was a mighty hunter before the Lᴏʀᴅ; that is why it is said, "Like Nimrod, a mighty hunter before the Lᴏʀᴅ." ¹⁰The first centers of his kingdom were Babylon, Erech, Akkad and Calneh, in^d Shinar.^e ¹¹From that land he went to Assyria, where he built Nineveh, Rehoboth Ir,^f Calah ¹²and Resen, which is between Nineveh and Calah; that is the great city.

¹³Mizraim was the father of

the Ludites, Anamites, Lehabites, Naphtuhites, ¹⁴Pathrusites, Casluhites (from whom the Philistines came) and Caphtorites.

¹⁵Canaan was the father of

Sidon his firstborn,^g and of the Hittites, ¹⁶Jebusites, Amorites, Girgashites, ¹⁷Hivites, Arkites, Sinites, ¹⁸Arvadites, Zemarites and Hamathites.

Later the Canaanite clans scattered ¹⁹and the borders of Canaan reached from Sidon toward Gerar as far as Gaza, and then toward Sodom, Gomorrah, Admah and Zeboiim, as far as Lasha.

²⁰These are the sons of Ham by their clans and languages, in their territories and nations.

The Semites
²¹Sons were also born to Shem, whose older brother was^h Japheth; Shem was the ancestor of all the sons of Eber.

²²The sons of Shem:

Elam, Asshur, Arphaxad, Lud and Aram.

²³The sons of Aram:

Uz, Hul, Gether and Meshech.ⁱ

²⁴Arphaxad was the father of^j Shelah,

and Shelah the father of Eber.

²⁵Two sons were born to Eber:

One was named Peleg,^k because in his time the earth was divided; his brother was named Joktan.

²⁶Joktan was the father of

Almodad, Sheleph, Hazarmaveth, Jerah, ²⁷Hadoram, Uzal, Diklah, ²⁸Obal, Abimael, Sheba, ²⁹Ophir, Havilah and Jobab. All these were sons of Joktan.

³⁰The region where they lived stretched from Mesha toward Sephar, in the eastern hill country.

---

^a4 Some manuscripts of the Masoretic Text and Samaritan Pentateuch (see also Septuagint and 1 Chron. 1:7); most manuscripts of the Masoretic Text *Dodanim*   ^b6 That is, Egypt; also in verse 13   ^c8 *Father* may mean *ancestor* or *predecessor* or *founder*; also in verses 13, 15, 24 and 26.   ^d10 Or *Erech and Akkad—all of them in*   ^e10 That is, Babylonia   ^f11 Or *Nineveh with its city squares*   ^g15 Or *of the Sidonians, the foremost*   ^h21 Or *Shem, the older brother of*   ⁱ23 See Septuagint and 1 Chron. 1:17; Hebrew *Mash*   ^j24 Hebrew; Septuagint *father of Cainan, and Cainan was the father of*   ^k25 *Peleg* means *division.*

³¹These are the sons of Shem by their clans and languages, in their territories and nations.

³²These are the clans of Noah's sons, according to their lines of descent, within their nations. From these the nations spread out over the earth after the flood.

11 *The Tower of Babel*   Now the whole world had one language and a common speech. ²As men moved eastward,*ᵃ* they found a plain in Shinar*ᵇ* and settled there.

³They said to each other, "Come, let's make bricks and bake them thoroughly." They used brick instead of stone, and tar for mortar. ⁴Then they said, "Come, let us build ourselves a city, with a tower that reaches to the heavens, so that we may make a name for ourselves and not be scattered over the face of the whole earth."

⁵But the LORD came down to see the city and the tower that the men were building. ⁶The LORD said, "If as one people speaking the same language they have begun to do this, then nothing they plan to do will be impossible for them. ⁷Come, let us go down and confuse their language so they will not understand each other."

⁸So the LORD scattered them from there over all the earth, and they stopped building the city. ⁹That is why it was called Babel*ᶜ*—because there the LORD confused the language of the whole world. From there the LORD scattered them over the face of the whole earth.

From Shem to Abram   ¹⁰This is the account of Shem.

Two years after the flood, when Shem was 100 years old, he became the father*ᵈ* of Arphaxad. ¹¹And after he became the father of Arphaxad, Shem lived 500 years and had other sons and daughters.

¹²When Arphaxad had lived 35 years, he became the father of Shelah. ¹³And after he became the father of Shelah, Arphaxad lived 403 years and had other sons and daughters.*ᵉ*

¹⁴When Shelah had lived 30 years, he became the father of Eber. ¹⁵And after he became the father of Eber, Shelah lived 403 years and had other sons and daughters.

¹⁶When Eber had lived 34 years, he became the father of Peleg. ¹⁷And after he became the father of Peleg, Eber lived 430 years and had other sons and daughters.

¹⁸When Peleg had lived 30 years, he became the father of Reu. ¹⁹And after he became the father of Reu, Peleg lived 209 years and had other sons and daughters.

²⁰When Reu had lived 32 years, he became the father of Serug. ²¹And after he became the father of Serug, Reu lived 207 years and had other sons and daughters.

²²When Serug had lived 30 years, he became the father of Nahor. ²³And after he became the father of Nahor, Serug lived 200 years and had other sons and daughters.

²⁴When Nahor had lived 29 years, he became the father of Terah. ²⁵And after he became the father of Terah, Nahor lived 119 years and had other sons and daughters.

ᵃ2 Or from the east; or in the east   ᵇ2 That is, Babylonia   ᶜ9 That is, Babylon; Babel sounds like the Hebrew for confused.   ᵈ10 Father may mean ancestor; also in verses 11-25.   ᵉ12,13 Hebrew; Septuagint (see also Luke 3:35, 36 and note at Gen. 10:24) 35 years, he became the father of Cainan. ¹³And after he became the father of Cainan, Arphaxad lived 430 years and had other sons and daughters, and then he died. When Cainan had lived 130 years, he became the father of Shelah. And after he became the father of Shelah, Cainan lived 330 years and had other sons and daughters

²⁶After Terah had lived 70 years, he became the father of Abram, Nahor and Haran.

²⁷This is the account of Terah.

Terah became the father of Abram, Nahor and Haran. And Haran became the father of Lot. ²⁸While his father Terah was still alive, Haran died in Ur of the Chaldeans, in the land of his birth. ²⁹Abram and Nahor both married. The name of Abram's wife was Sarai, and the name of Nahor's wife was Milcah; she was the daughter of Haran, the father of both Milcah and Iscah. ³⁰Now Sarai was barren; she had no children.

³¹Terah took his son Abram, his grandson Lot son of Haran, and his daughter-in-law Sarai, the wife of his son Abram, and together they set out from Ur of the Chaldeans to go to Canaan. But when they came to Haran, they settled there.

³²Terah lived 205 years, and he died in Haran.

12 *The Call of Abram*   The LORD had said to Abram, "Leave your country, your people and your father's household and go to the land I will show you.

² "I will make you into a great nation
   and I will bless you;
 I will make your name great,
   and you will be a blessing.
³ I will bless those who bless you,
   and whoever curses you I will curse;
 and all peoples on earth
   will be blessed through you."

⁴So Abram left, as the LORD had told him; and Lot went with him. Abram was seventy-five years old when he set out from Haran. ⁵He took his wife Sarai, his nephew Lot, all the possessions they had accumulated and the people they had acquired in Haran, and they set out for the land of Canaan, and they arrived there.

⁶Abram traveled through the land as far as the site of the great tree of Moreh at Shechem. At that time the Canaanites were in the land. ⁷The LORD appeared to Abram and said, "To your offspring*ᵃ* I will give this land." So he built an altar there to the LORD, who had appeared to him.

⁸From there he went on toward the hills east of Bethel and pitched his tent, with Bethel on the west and Ai on the east. There he built an altar to the LORD and called on the name of the LORD. ⁹Then Abram set out and continued toward the Negev.

Abram in Egypt   ¹⁰Now there was a famine in the land, and Abram went down to Egypt to live there for a while because the famine

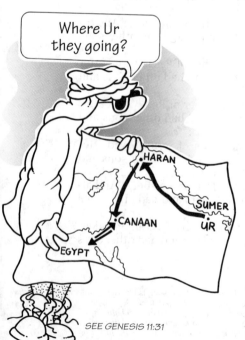

Where Ur they going?

HARAN

SUMER

CANAAN

UR

EGYPT

SEE GENESIS 11:31

ᵃ7 Or seed

was severe. ¹¹As he was about to enter Egypt, he said to his wife Sarai, "I know what a beautiful woman you are. ¹²When the Egyptians see you, they will say, 'This is his wife.' Then they will kill me but will let you live. ¹³Say you are my sister, so that I will be treated well for your sake and my life will be spared because of you."

¹⁴When Abram came to Egypt, the Egyptians saw that she was a very beautiful woman. ¹⁵And when Pharaoh's officials saw her, they praised her to Pharaoh, and she was taken into his palace. ¹⁶He treated Abram well for her sake, and Abram acquired sheep and cattle, male and female donkeys, menservants and maidservants, and camels.

¹⁷But the LORD inflicted serious diseases on Pharaoh and his household because of Abram's wife Sarai. ¹⁸So Pharaoh summoned Abram. "What have you done to me?" he said. "Why didn't you tell me she was your wife? ¹⁹Why did you say, 'She is my sister,' so that I took her to be my wife? Now then, here is your wife. Take her and go!" ²⁰Then Pharaoh gave orders about Abram to his men, and they sent him on his way, with his wife and everything he had.

13 **Abram and Lot Separate** So Abram went up from Egypt to the Negev, with his wife and everything he had, and Lot went with him. ²Abram had become very wealthy in livestock and in silver and gold.

³From the Negev he went from place to place until he came to Bethel, to the place between Bethel and Ai where his tent had been earlier ⁴and where he had first built an altar. There Abram called on the name of the LORD.

⁵Now Lot, who was moving about with Abram, also had flocks and herds and tents. ⁶But the land could not support them while they stayed together, for their possessions were so great that they were not able to stay together. ⁷And quarreling arose between Abram's herdsmen and the herdsmen of Lot. The Canaanites and Perizzites were also living in the land at that time.

⁸So Abram said to Lot, "Let's not have any quarreling between you and me, or between your herdsmen and mine, for we are brothers. ⁹Is not the whole land before you? Let's part company. If you go to the left, I'll go to the right; if you go to the right, I'll go to the left."

God made Abraham several promises in Genesis 12:2–3, and he has kept every one!

* Abraham's descendants, the Jews, are still a distinct and numerous people today.
* Abraham was wealthy and protected by the Lord throughout his long life.
* Even after 4,000 years, three world religions—Christianity, Judaism and Islam—honor Abraham.
* The Hitlers of history who have tried to destroy the Jews have been destroyed themselves.
* Jesus, a descendant of Abraham, brings salvation to all who will believe.

The Bible Says

God Keeps His Promises

God's Word is full of his promises to you—and you can count on him to keep every one.

¹⁰Lot looked up and saw that the whole plain of the Jordan was well watered, like the garden of the LORD, like the land of Egypt, toward Zoar. (This was before the LORD destroyed Sodom and Gomorrah.) ¹¹So Lot chose for himself the whole plain of the Jordan and set out toward the east. The two men parted company: ¹²Abram lived in the land of Canaan, while Lot lived among the cities of the plain and pitched his tents near Sodom. ¹³Now the men of Sodom were wicked and were sinning greatly against the LORD.

¹⁴The LORD said to Abram after Lot had parted from him, "Lift up your eyes from where you are and look north and south, east and west. ¹⁵All the land that you see I will give to you and your offspring*ᵃ* forever. ¹⁶I will make your offspring like the dust of the earth, so that if anyone could count the dust, then your offspring could be counted. ¹⁷Go, walk through the length and breadth of the land, for I am giving it to you."

¹⁸So Abram moved his tents and went to live near the great trees of Mamre at Hebron, where he built an altar to the LORD.

Abram Rescues Lot At this time Amraphel king of Shinar,*ᵇ* Arioch king of Ellasar, Kedorlaomer king of Elam and Tidal king of Goiim ²went to war against Bera king of Sodom, Birsha king of Gomorrah, Shinab king of Admah, Shemeber king of Zeboiim, and the king of Bela (that is, Zoar). ³All these latter kings joined forces in the Valley of Siddim (the Salt Sea*ᶜ*). ⁴For twelve years they had been subject to Kedorlaomer, but in the thirteenth year they rebelled.

⁵In the fourteenth year, Kedorlaomer and the kings allied with him went out and defeated the Rephaites in Ashteroth Karnaim, the Zuzites in Ham, the Emites in Shaveh Kiriathaim ⁶and the Horites in the hill country of Seir, as far as El Paran near the desert. ⁷Then they turned back and went to En Mishpat (that is, Kadesh), and they conquered the whole territory of the Amalekites, as well as the Amorites who were living in Hazazon Tamar.

⁸Then the king of Sodom, the king of Gomorrah, the king of Admah, the king of Zeboiim and the king of Bela (that is, Zoar) marched out and drew up their battle lines in the Valley of Siddim ⁹against Kedorlaomer king of Elam, Tidal king of Goiim, Amraphel king of Shinar and Arioch king of Ellasar— four kings against five. ¹⁰Now the Valley of Siddim was full of tar pits, and when the kings of Sodom and Gomorrah fled, some of the men fell into them and the rest fled to the hills. ¹¹The four kings seized all the goods of Sodom and Gomorrah and all their food; then they went away. ¹²They also carried off Abram's nephew Lot and his possessions, since he was living in Sodom.

¹³One who had escaped came and reported this to Abram the Hebrew. Now Abram was living near the great trees of Mamre the Amorite, a brother*ᵈ* of Eshcol and Aner, all of whom were allied with Abram. ¹⁴When Abram heard that his relative had been taken captive, he called out the 318 trained men born in his household and went in pursuit as far as Dan. ¹⁵During the night Abram divided his men to attack them and he routed them, pursuing them as far as Hobah, north of Damascus. ¹⁶He recovered all the goods and brought back his relative Lot and his possessions, together with the women and the other people.

¹⁷After Abram returned from defeating Kedorlaomer and the kings allied with him, the king of Sodom came out to meet him in the Valley of Shaveh (that is, the King's Valley).

¹⁸Then Melchizedek king of Salem*ᵉ* brought out bread and wine. He was priest of God Most High, ¹⁹and he blessed Abram, saying,

---

ᵃ15 Or *seed*; also in verse 16 *ᵇ1* That is, Babylonia; also in verse 9 *ᶜ3* That is, the Dead Sea *ᵈ13* Or *a relative*; or *an ally* *ᵉ18* That is, Jerusalem

Dear Sam,

This sounds terrible, but I hate my older sisters.
I never get to do the things they get to do, and
they're always picking on me. I can't stand it.

Paula in Pittsburgh

Dear Sam, Inc

100 Advice Lane, Anywhere, USA

Dear Paula,

You have one of the oldest problems in history—getting along with your siblings. Adam and Eve's two sons Cain and Abel didn't get along at all. Cain finally killed his brother Abel—obviously not a good model to follow.

In Genesis 13–14 you'll find a story about Abram and Lot. Lot was Abram's nephew, not his brother, but they lived together, and they were having problems. These men had herds so huge that the land could not support all the animals, so Abram and Lot had to split up. Abram, as the older man, should have had first choice. But instead he told Lot to choose. Lot chose the best grazing land in the area, and Abram went another way. But the Lord still took care of Abram and his herds.

Abram's example is a good one to follow. Try to be loving to your sisters, even when it means you get the short end of the stick. Another option is to call a family meeting. Let everyone speak, and try to meet everyone's needs. You just might all be surprised at how much you like each other when you're not fighting!

Sam

"Blessed be Abram by God Most High,
　Creator[a] of heaven and earth.
²⁰And blessed be[b] God Most High,
　who delivered your enemies into your hand."

Then Abram gave him a tenth of everything.

²¹The king of Sodom said to Abram, "Give me the people and keep the goods for yourself."

²²But Abram said to the king of Sodom, "I have raised my hand to the LORD, God Most High, Creator of heaven and earth, and have taken an oath ²³that I will accept nothing belonging to you, not even a thread or the thong of a sandal, so that you will never be able to say, 'I made Abram rich.' ²⁴I will accept nothing but what my men have eaten and the share that belongs to the men who went with me—to Aner, Eshcol and Mamre. Let them have their share."

15 *God's Covenant With Abram*　After this, the word of the LORD came to Abram in a vision:

"Do not be afraid, Abram.
　I am your shield,[c]
　your very great reward.[d]"

²But Abram said, "O Sovereign LORD, what can you give me since I remain childless and the one who will inherit[e] my estate is Eliezer of Damascus?" ³And Abram said, "You have given me no children; so a servant in my household will be my heir."

⁴Then the word of the LORD came to him: "This man will not be your heir, but a son coming from your own body will be your heir." ⁵He took him outside and said, "Look up at the heavens and count the stars—if indeed you can count them." Then he said to him, "So shall your offspring be."

⁶Abram believed the LORD, and he credited it to him as righteousness.

⁷He also said to him, "I am the LORD, who brought you out of Ur of the Chaldeans to give you this land to take possession of it."

⁸But Abram said, "O Sovereign LORD, how can I know that I will gain possession of it?"

⁹So the LORD said to him, "Bring me a heifer, a goat and a ram, each three years old, along with a dove and a young pigeon."

¹⁰Abram brought all these to him, cut them in two and arranged the halves opposite each other; the birds, however, he did not cut in half. ¹¹Then birds of prey came down on the carcasses, but Abram drove them away.

> Abram believed the LORD, and he credited it to him as righteousness (Genesis 15:6).

¹²As the sun was setting, Abram fell into a deep sleep, and a thick and dreadful darkness came over him. ¹³Then the LORD said to him, "Know for certain that your descendants will be strangers in a country not their own, and they will be enslaved and mistreated four hundred years. ¹⁴But I will punish the nation they serve as slaves, and afterward they will come out with great possessions. ¹⁵You, however, will go to your fathers in peace and be buried at a good old age. ¹⁶In the fourth generation your descendants will come back here, for the sin of the Amorites has not yet reached its full measure."

¹⁷When the sun had set and darkness had fallen, a smoking firepot with a blazing torch appeared and passed between the pieces. ¹⁸On that day the

---

a19 Or *Possessor*; also in verse 22　*b20* Or *And praise be to*　*c1* Or *sovereign*　*d1* Or *shield; / your reward will be very great*　*e2* The meaning of the Hebrew for this phrase is uncertain.

Lord made a covenant with Abram and said, "To your descendants I give this land, from the river*a* of Egypt to the great river, the Euphrates— ¹⁹the land of the Kenites, Kenizzites, Kadmonites, ²⁰Hittites, Perizzites, Rephaites, ²¹Amorites, Canaanites, Girgashites and Jebusites."

16 *Hagar and Ishmael* Now Sarai, Abram's wife, had borne him no children. But she had an Egyptian maidservant named Hagar; ²so she said to Abram, "The Lord has kept me from having children. Go, sleep with my maidservant; perhaps I can build a family through her."

Abram agreed to what Sarai said. ³So after Abram had been living in Canaan ten years, Sarai his wife took her Egyptian maidservant Hagar and gave her to her husband to be his wife. ⁴He slept with Hagar, and she conceived.

When she knew she was pregnant, she began to despise her mistress. ⁵Then Sarai said to Abram, "You are responsible for the wrong I am suffering. I put my servant in your arms, and now that she knows she is pregnant, she despises me. May the Lord judge between you and me."

⁶"Your servant is in your hands," Abram said. "Do with her whatever you think best." Then Sarai mistreated Hagar; so she fled from her.

⁷The angel of the Lord found Hagar near a spring in the desert; it was the spring that is beside the road to Shur. ⁸And he said, "Hagar, servant of Sarai, where have you come from, and where are you going?"

"I'm running away from my mistress Sarai," she answered.

⁹Then the angel of the Lord told her, "Go back to your mistress and submit to her." ¹⁰The angel added, "I will so increase your descendants that they will be too numerous to count."

¹¹The angel of the Lord also said to her:

> "You are now with child
>   and you will have a son.
> You shall name him Ishmael,*b*
>   for the Lord has heard of
>   your misery.
> ¹²He will be a wild donkey of a
>   man;
>   his hand will be against
>   everyone
>   and everyone's hand against
>   him,
> and he will live in hostility
>   toward*c* all his brothers."

¹³She gave this name to the Lord who spoke to her: "You are the God who sees me," for she said, "I have now seen*d* the One who sees me." ¹⁴That is why the well was called Beer Lahai Roi*e*; it is still there, between Kadesh and Bered.

¹⁵So Hagar bore Abram a son, and Abram gave the name Ishmael to the son she had borne. ¹⁶Abram was eighty-six years old when Hagar bore him Ishmael.

a18 Or Wadi b11 Ishmael means God hears. c12 Or live to the east / of d13 Or seen the back of e14 Beer Lahai Roi means well of the Living One who sees me.

GENESIS 16:6-10

Do you ever feel like running away? Probably. Your brothers and sisters bug you. Mom doesn't understand. Dad yells at you. Things are so bad at home you can't get your schoolwork done, and your grades have dropped so low you have to look up to see the bottom. But is taking off the only option? In this Bible story, Hagar was so hurt by Abram's jealous wife Sarah that she ran away. But God's angel told Hagar to go back and submit. The angel added, "I will increase your descendants" (Genesis 16:10). Running away when things are tough may seem like the only way out. But usually it's staying in there that leads to God's blessing.

Direct Line

17 **The Covenant of Circumcision**   When Abram was ninety-nine years old, the LORD appeared to him and said, "I am God Almighty*ᵃ*; walk before me and be blameless. ²I will confirm my covenant between me and you and will greatly increase your numbers."

³Abram fell facedown, and God said to him, ⁴"As for me, this is my covenant with you: You will be the father of many nations. ⁵No longer will you be called Abram*ᵇ*; your name will be Abraham,*ᶜ* for I have made you a father of many nations. ⁶I will make you very fruitful; I will make nations of you, and kings will come from you. ⁷I will establish my covenant as an everlasting covenant between me and you and your descendants after you for the generations to come, to be your God and the God of your descendants after you. ⁸The whole land of Canaan, where you are now an alien, I will give as an everlasting possession to you and your descendants after you; and I will be their God."

⁹Then God said to Abraham, "As for you, you must keep my covenant, you and your descendants after you for the generations to come. ¹⁰This is my covenant with you and your descendants after you, the covenant you are to keep: Every male among you shall be circumcised. ¹¹You are to undergo circumcision, and it will be the sign of the covenant between me and you. ¹²For the generations to come every male among you who is eight days old must be circumcised, including those born in your household or bought with money from a foreigner—those who are not your offspring. ¹³Whether born in your household or bought with your money, they must be circumcised. My covenant in your flesh is to be an everlasting covenant. ¹⁴Any uncircumcised male, who has not been circumcised in the flesh, will be cut off from his people; he has broken my covenant."

¹⁵God also said to Abraham, "As for Sarai your wife, you are no longer to call her Sarai; her name will be Sarah. ¹⁶I will bless her and will surely give you a son by her. I will bless her so that she will be the mother of nations; kings of peoples will come from her."

¹⁷Abraham fell facedown; he laughed and said to himself, "Will a son be born to a man a hundred years old? Will Sarah bear a child at the age of ninety?" ¹⁸And Abraham said to God, "If only Ishmael might live under your blessing!"

¹⁹Then God said, "Yes, but your wife Sarah will bear you a son, and you will call him Isaac.*ᵈ* I will establish my covenant with him as an everlasting covenant for his descendants after him. ²⁰And as for Ishmael, I have heard you: I will surely bless him; I will make him fruitful and will greatly increase his numbers. He will be the father of twelve rulers, and I will make him into a great nation. ²¹But my covenant I will establish with Isaac, whom Sarah will bear to you by this time next year." ²²When he had finished speaking with Abraham, God went up from him.

²³On that very day Abraham took his son Ishmael and all those born in his household or bought with his money, every male in his household, and circumcised them, as God told him. ²⁴Abraham was ninety-nine years old when he was circumcised, ²⁵and his son Ishmael was thirteen; ²⁶Abraham and his son Ishmael were both circumcised on that same day. ²⁷And every male in Abraham's household, including those born in his household or bought from a foreigner, was circumcised with him.

18 **The Three Visitors**   The LORD appeared to Abraham near the great trees of Mamre while he was sitting at the entrance to his tent in the heat of the day. ²Abraham looked up and saw three men standing nearby. When he saw them, he hurried from the entrance of his tent to meet them and bowed low to the ground.

ᵃ1 Hebrew *El-Shaddai*   *ᵇ5 Abram* means *exalted father.*   *ᶜ5 Abraham* means *father of many.*   *ᵈ19 Isaac* means *he laughs.*

³He said, "If I have found favor in your eyes, my lord,ᵃ do not pass your servant by. ⁴Let a little water be brought, and then you may all wash your feet and rest under this tree. ⁵Let me get you something to eat, so you can be refreshed and then go on your way—now that you have come to your servant."

"Very well," they answered, "do as you say."

⁶So Abraham hurried into the tent to Sarah. "Quick," he said, "get three seahsᵇ of fine flour and knead it and bake some bread."

⁷Then he ran to the herd and selected a choice, tender calf and gave it to a servant, who hurried to prepare it. ⁸He then brought some curds and milk and the calf that had been prepared, and set these before them. While they ate, he stood near them under a tree.

⁹"Where is your wife Sarah?" they asked him.

"There, in the tent," he said.

¹⁰Then the Lordᶜ said, "I will surely return to you about this time next year, and Sarah your wife will have a son."

Now Sarah was listening at the entrance to the tent, which was behind him. ¹¹Abraham and Sarah were already old and well advanced in years, and Sarah was past the age of childbearing. ¹²So Sarah laughed to herself as she thought, "After I am worn out and my masterᵈ is old, will I now have this pleasure?"

¹³Then the Lord said to Abraham, "Why did Sarah laugh and say, 'Will I really have a child, now that I am old?' ¹⁴Is anything too hard for the Lord? I will return to you at the appointed time next year and Sarah will have a son."

¹⁵Sarah was afraid, so she lied and said, "I did not laugh."

But he said, "Yes, you did laugh."

Abraham Pleads for Sodom   ¹⁶When the men got up to leave, they looked down toward Sodom, and Abraham walked along with them to see them on their way. ¹⁷Then the Lord said, "Shall I hide from Abraham what I am about to do? ¹⁸Abraham will surely become a great and powerful nation, and all nations on earth will be blessed through him. ¹⁹For I have chosen him, so that he will direct his children and his household after him to keep the way of the Lord by doing what is right and just, so that the Lord will bring about for Abraham what he has promised him."

²⁰Then the Lord said, "The outcry against Sodom and Gomorrah is so great and their sin so grievous ²¹that I will go down and see if what they have done is as bad as the outcry that has reached me. If not, I will know."

²²The men turned away and went toward Sodom, but Abraham remained standing before the Lord.ᵉ ²³Then Abraham approached him and said: "Will you sweep away the righteous with the wicked? ²⁴What if there are fifty righteous people in the city? Will you really sweep it away and not spareᶠ the place for the sake of the fifty righteous people in it? ²⁵Far be it from you to do such a thing—to kill the righteous with the wicked, treating the righteous and the wicked alike. Far be it from you! Will not the Judgeᵍ of all the earth do right?"

²⁶The Lord said, "If I find fifty righteous people in the city of Sodom, I will spare the whole place for their sake."

²⁷Then Abraham spoke up again: "Now that I have been so bold as to speak to the Lord, though I am nothing but dust and ashes, ²⁸what if the number of the righteous is five less than fifty? Will you destroy the whole city because of five people?"

"If I find forty-five there," he said, "I will not destroy it."

ᵃ3 Or *O Lord*   ᵇ6 That is, probably about 20 quarts (about 22 liters)   ᶜ10 Hebrew *Then he*   ᵈ12 Or *husband*   ᵉ22 Masoretic Text; an ancient Hebrew scribal tradition *but the Lord remained standing before Abraham*   ᶠ24 Or *forgive*; also in verse 26   ᵍ25 Or *Ruler*

²⁹Once again he spoke to him, "What if only forty are found there?"

He said, "For the sake of forty, I will not do it."

³⁰Then he said, "May the Lord not be angry, but let me speak. What if only thirty can be found there?"

He answered, "I will not do it if I find thirty there."

³¹Abraham said, "Now that I have been so bold as to speak to the Lord, what if only twenty can be found there?"

He said, "For the sake of twenty, I will not destroy it."

³²Then he said, "May the Lord not be angry, but let me speak just once more. What if only ten can be found there?"

He answered, "For the sake of ten, I will not destroy it."

³³When the LORD had finished speaking with Abraham, he left, and Abraham returned home.

19 *Sodom and Gomorrah Destroyed*

The two angels arrived at Sodom in the evening, and Lot was sitting in the gateway of the city. When he saw them, he got up to meet them and bowed down with his face to the ground. ²"My lords," he said, "please turn aside to your servant's house. You can wash your feet and spend the night and then go on your way early in the morning."

"No," they answered, "we will spend the night in the square."

³But he insisted so strongly that they did go with him and entered his house. He prepared a meal for them, baking bread without yeast, and they ate. ⁴Before they had gone to bed, all the men from every part of the city of Sodom—both young and old—surrounded the house. ⁵They called to Lot, "Where are the men who came to you tonight? Bring them out to us so that we can have sex with them."

⁶Lot went outside to meet them and shut the door behind him ⁷and said, "No, my friends. Don't do this wicked thing. ⁸Look, I have two daughters who have never slept with a man. Let me bring them out to you, and you can do what you like with them. But don't do anything to these men, for they have come under the protection of my roof."

⁹"Get out of our way," they replied. And they said, "This fellow came here as an alien, and now he wants to play the judge! We'll treat you worse than them." They kept bringing pressure on Lot and moved forward to break down the door.

¹⁰But the men inside reached out and pulled Lot back into the house and shut the door. ¹¹Then they struck the men who were at the door of the house, young and old, with blindness so that they could not find the door.

¹²The two men said to Lot, "Do you have anyone else here—sons-in-law, sons or daughters, or anyone else in the city who belongs to you? Get them out of here, ¹³because we are going to destroy this place. The outcry to the LORD against its people is so great that he has sent us to destroy it."

¹⁴So Lot went out and spoke to his sons-in-law, who were pledged to marry[a]

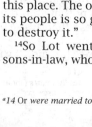

GENESIS 18:32

Do you ever worry that God might be upset when you keep on asking for something? Abraham felt the same way. He said, "May the Lord not be angry, but let me speak just once more" (Genesis 18:32). God wasn't angry at all. For one thing, Abraham was asking God to be merciful. Abraham asked God to spare Sodom for the sake of ten righteous people. God could find only one: Lot. So he made sure Lot and his family escaped before fire destroyed the wicked city. If you know that what you're praying for honors God and is the kind of thing he wants to do, you don't need to be anxious. Your prayers are pleasing to the Lord.

ᵃ14 Or *were married to*

his daughters. He said, "Hurry and get out of this place, because the Lord is about to destroy the city!" But his sons-in-law thought he was joking.

¹⁵With the coming of dawn, the angels urged Lot, saying, "Hurry! Take your wife and your two daughters who are here, or you will be swept away when the city is punished."

¹⁶When he hesitated, the men grasped his hand and the hands of his wife and of his two daughters and led them safely out of the city, for the Lord was merciful to them. ¹⁷As soon as they had brought them out, one of them said, "Flee for your lives! Don't look back, and don't stop anywhere in the plain! Flee to the mountains or you will be swept away!"

¹⁸But Lot said to them, "No, my lords,ᵃ please! ¹⁹Yourᵇ servant has found favor in yourᵇ eyes, and youᵇ have shown great kindness to me in sparing my life. But I can't flee to the mountains; this disaster will overtake me, and I'll die. ²⁰Look, here is a town near enough to run to, and it is small. Let me flee to it—it is very small, isn't it? Then my life will be spared."

²¹He said to him, "Very well, I will grant this request too; I will not overthrow the town you speak of. ²²But flee there quickly, because I cannot do anything until you reach it." (That is why the town was called Zoar.ᶜ)

²³By the time Lot reached Zoar, the sun had risen over the land. ²⁴Then the Lord rained down burning sulfur on Sodom and Gomorrah—from the Lord out of the heavens. ²⁵Thus he overthrew those cities and the entire plain, including all those living in the cities—and also the vegetation in the land. ²⁶But Lot's wife looked back, and she became a pillar of salt.

²⁷Early the next morning Abraham got up and returned to the place where he had stood before the Lord. ²⁸He looked down toward Sodom and Gomorrah, toward all the land of the plain, and he saw dense smoke rising from the land, like smoke from a furnace.

²⁹So when God destroyed the cities of the plain, he remembered Abraham, and he brought Lot out of the catastrophe that overthrew the cities where Lot had lived.

Lot and His Daughters ³⁰Lot and his two daughters left Zoar and settled in the mountains, for he was afraid to stay in Zoar. He and his two daughters lived in a cave. ³¹One day the older daughter said to the younger, "Our father is old, and there is no man around here to lie with us, as is the custom all over the earth. ³²Let's get our father to drink wine and then lie with him and preserve our family line through our father."

³³That night they got their father to drink wine, and the older daughter went in and lay with him. He was not aware of it when she lay down or when she got up.

³⁴The next day the older daughter said to the younger, "Last night I lay with my father. Let's get him to drink wine again tonight, and you go in and lie with him so we can preserve our family line through our father." ³⁵So they got their father to drink wine that night also, and the younger daughter went and lay with him. Again he was not aware of it when she lay down or when she got up.

³⁶So both of Lot's daughters became pregnant by their father. ³⁷The older daughter had a son, and she named him Moabᵈ; he is the father of the Moabites of today. ³⁸The younger daughter also had a son, and she named him Ben-Ammiᵉ; he is the father of the Ammonites of today.

ᵃ18 Or *No, Lord*; or *No, my lord* ᵇ19 The Hebrew is singular. ᶜ22 *Zoar* means *small*. ᵈ37 *Moab* sounds like the Hebrew for *from father*. ᵉ38 *Ben-Ammi* means *son of my people*.

20

Abraham and Abimelech Now Abraham moved on from there into the region of the Negev and lived between Kadesh and Shur. For a while he stayed in Gerar, ²and there Abraham said of his wife Sarah, "She is my sister." Then Abimelech king of Gerar sent for Sarah and took her.

³But God came to Abimelech in a dream one night and said to him, "You are as good as dead because of the woman you have taken; she is a married woman."

⁴Now Abimelech had not gone near her, so he said, "Lord, will you destroy an innocent nation? ⁵Did he not say to me, 'She is my sister,' and didn't she also say, 'He is my brother'? I have done this with a clear conscience and clean hands."

⁶Then God said to him in the dream, "Yes, I know you did this with a clear conscience, and so I have kept you from sinning against me. That is why I did not let you touch her. ⁷Now return the man's wife, for he is a prophet, and he will pray for you and you will live. But if you do not return her, you may be sure that you and all yours will die."

⁸Early the next morning Abimelech summoned all his officials, and when he told them all that had happened, they were very much afraid. ⁹Then Abimelech called Abraham in and said, "What have you done to us? How have I wronged you that you have brought such great guilt upon me and my kingdom? You have done things to me that should not be done." ¹⁰And Abimelech asked Abraham, "What was your reason for doing this?"

¹¹Abraham replied, "I said to myself, 'There is surely no fear of God in this place, and they will kill me because of my wife.' ¹²Besides, she really is my sister, the daughter of my father though not of my mother; and she became my wife. ¹³And when God had me wander from my father's household, I said to her, 'This is how you can show your love to me: Everywhere we go, say of me, "He is my brother." ' "

¹⁴Then Abimelech brought sheep and cattle and male and female slaves and gave them to Abraham, and he returned Sarah his wife to him. ¹⁵And Abimelech said, "My land is before you; live wherever you like."

¹⁶To Sarah he said, "I am giving your brother a thousand shekels*a* of silver. This is to cover the offense against you before all who are with you; you are completely vindicated."

¹⁷Then Abraham prayed to God, and God healed Abimelech, his wife and his slave girls so they could have children again, ¹⁸for the LORD had closed up every womb in Abimelech's household because of Abraham's wife Sarah.

21

The Birth of Isaac Now the LORD was gracious to Sarah as he had said, and the LORD did for Sarah what he had promised. ²Sarah became pregnant and bore a son to Abraham in his old age, at the very time God had promised him. ³Abraham gave the name Isaac*b* to the son Sarah bore him. ⁴When his son Isaac was eight days old, Abraham circumcised him, as God commanded him. ⁵Abraham was a hundred years old when his son Isaac was born to him.

Direct Line

GENESIS 20:11

Moving to a new school can be pretty scary. Abraham was afraid when he moved to a new area of Palestine. He was so afraid that he asked his wife Sarah to lie for him. And that lie got him into all sorts of trouble. Abraham was afraid of the strangers because they didn't know God. But he forgot that God knew them! If you find yourself in places where people don't know God or live godly lives, don't forget that God is there already. Read this story, and remember that, like Abraham, wherever you go, God goes too.

a16 That is, about 25 pounds (about 11.5 kilograms)
b3 Isaac means *he laughs.*

⁶Sarah said, "God has brought me laughter, and everyone who hears about this will laugh with me." ⁷And she added, "Who would have said to Abraham that Sarah would nurse children? Yet I have borne him a son in his old age."

Hagar and Ishmael Sent Away

⁸The child grew and was weaned, and on the day Isaac was weaned Abraham held a great feast. ⁹But Sarah saw that the son whom Hagar the Egyptian had borne to Abraham was mocking, ¹⁰and she said to Abraham, "Get rid of that slave woman and her son, for that slave woman's son will never share in the inheritance with my son Isaac."

¹¹The matter distressed Abraham greatly because it concerned his son. ¹²But God said to him, "Do not be so distressed about the boy and your maidservant. Listen to whatever Sarah tells you, because it is through Isaac that your offspring^a will be reckoned. ¹³I will make the son of the maidservant into a nation also, because he is your offspring."

¹⁴Early the next morning Abraham took some food and a skin of water and gave them to Hagar. He set them on her shoulders and then sent her off with the boy. She went on her way and wandered in the desert of Beersheba.

¹⁵When the water in the skin was gone, she put the boy under one of the bushes. ¹⁶Then she went off and sat down nearby, about a bowshot away, for she thought, "I cannot watch the boy die." And as she sat there nearby, she^b began to sob.

¹⁷God heard the boy crying, and the angel of God called to Hagar from heaven and said to her, "What is the matter, Hagar? Do not be afraid; God has heard the boy crying as he lies there. ¹⁸Lift the boy up and take him by the hand, for I will make him into a great nation."

¹⁹Then God opened her eyes and she saw a well of water. So she went and filled the skin with water and gave the boy a drink.

²⁰God was with the boy as he grew up. He lived in the desert and became an archer. ²¹While he was living in the Desert of Paran, his mother got a wife for him from Egypt.

The Treaty at Beersheba

²²At that time Abimelech and Phicol the commander of his forces said to Abraham, "God is with you in everything you do. ²³Now swear to me here before God that you will not deal falsely with me or my children or my descendants. Show to me and the country where you are living as an alien the same kindness I have shown to you."

²⁴Abraham said, "I swear it."

²⁵Then Abraham complained to Abimelech about a well of water that Abimelech's servants had seized. ²⁶But Abimelech said, "I don't know who has done this. You did not tell me, and I heard about it only today."

²⁷So Abraham brought sheep and cattle and gave them to Abimelech, and the two men made a treaty. ²⁸Abraham set apart

---

GENESIS 21:8–18

Probably nothing hurts so much as rejection. Lots of kids whose parents divorce feel like their parents divorced them instead of each other. And sometimes a child actually *is* rejected or abandoned. Abraham didn't want to send Hagar or Ishmael away, but God told him to do what Sarah insisted. It hurt Abraham to be separated from his son. It also hurt Ishmael, who was a teenager. But God spoke to each of them to make the hurt easier to bear. You will at times feel rejected by someone you love. When that happens, try to remember this story. Whatever happens, God will remain at your side.

Direct Line

---

^a12 Or *seed*   ^b16 Hebrew; Septuagint *the child*

seven ewe lambs from the flock, ²⁹and Abimelech asked Abraham, "What is the meaning of these seven ewe lambs you have set apart by themselves?"

³⁰He replied, "Accept these seven lambs from my hand as a witness that I dug this well."

³¹So that place was called Beersheba,ᵃ because the two men swore an oath there.

³²After the treaty had been made at Beersheba, Abimelech and Phicol the commander of his forces returned to the land of the Philistines. ³³Abraham planted a tamarisk tree in Beersheba, and there he called upon the name of the Lᴏʀᴅ, the Eternal God. ³⁴And Abraham stayed in the land of the Philistines for a long time.

22 *Abraham Tested* Some time later God tested Abraham. He said to him, "Abraham!"

"Here I am," he replied.

²Then God said, "Take your son, your only son, Isaac, whom you love, and go to the region of Moriah. Sacrifice him there as a burnt offering on one of the mountains I will tell you about."

³Early the next morning Abraham got up and saddled his donkey. He took with him two of his servants and his son Isaac. When he had cut enough wood for the burnt offering, he set out for the place God had told him about. ⁴On the third day Abraham looked up and saw the place in the distance. ⁵He said to his servants, "Stay here with the donkey while I and the boy go over there. We will worship and then we will come back to you."

⁶Abraham took the wood for the burnt offering and placed it on his son Isaac, and he himself carried the fire and the knife. As the two of them went on together, ⁷Isaac spoke up and said to his father Abraham, "Father?"

"Yes, my son?" Abraham replied.

"The fire and wood are here," Isaac said, "but where is the lamb for the burnt offering?"

⁸Abraham answered, "God himself will provide the lamb for the burnt offering, my son." And the two of them went on together.

⁹When they reached the place God had told him about, Abraham built an altar there and arranged the wood on it. He bound his son Isaac and laid him on the altar, on top of the wood. ¹⁰Then he reached out his hand and took the knife to slay his son. ¹¹But the angel of the Lᴏʀᴅ called out to him from heaven, "Abraham! Abraham!"

"Here I am," he replied.

¹²"Do not lay a hand on the boy," he said. "Do not do anything to him. Now I know that you fear God, because you have not withheld from me your son, your only son."

¹³Abraham looked up and there in a thicket he saw a ramᵇ caught by its horns. He went over and took the ram and sacrificed it as a burnt offering instead of his son. ¹⁴So Abraham called that place The

---

GENESIS 22:5

Faith is doing right even when you don't know how God is going to work things out. Abraham had that kind of faith. God promised Abraham that his descendants would come through Isaac. But when God told Abraham to offer his son Isaac as a sacrifice, Abraham didn't hesitate. Abraham was sure that God would keep his promises even though he didn't know how God could if Isaac were dead. That's the kind of faith that will give you the courage to always do what's right. You don't have to know how God will work things out. You only need to know that, if you obey, *God will.*

Direct Line

ᵃ*31 Beersheba* can mean *well of seven* or *well of the oath.*
ᵇ*13* Many manuscripts of the Masoretic Text, Samaritan Pentateuch, Septuagint and Syriac; most manuscripts of the Masoretic Text *a ram behind him,*

L ord Will Provide. And to this day it is said, "On the mountain of the L ord it will be provided."

¹⁵The angel of the L ord called to Abraham from heaven a second time ¹⁶and said, "I swear by myself, declares the L ord, that because you have done this and have not withheld your son, your only son, ¹⁷I will surely bless you and make your descendants as numerous as the stars in the sky and as the sand on the seashore. Your descendants will take possession of the cities of their enemies, ¹⁸and through your offspring*a* all nations on earth will be blessed, because you have obeyed me."

¹⁹Then Abraham returned to his servants, and they set off together for Beersheba. And Abraham stayed in Beersheba.

Nahor's Sons ²⁰Some time later Abraham was told, "Milcah is also a mother; she has borne sons to your brother Nahor: ²¹Uz the firstborn, Buz his brother, Kemuel (the father of Aram), ²²Kesed, Hazo, Pildash, Jidlaph and Bethuel." ²³Bethuel became the father of Rebekah. Milcah bore these eight sons to Abraham's brother Nahor. ²⁴His concubine, whose name was Reumah, also had sons: Tebah, Gaham, Tahash and Maacah.

The Death of Sarah Sarah lived to be a hundred and twenty-seven years old. ²She died at Kiriath Arba (that is, Hebron) in the land of Canaan, and Abraham went to mourn for Sarah and to weep over her.

³Then Abraham rose from beside his dead wife and spoke to the Hittites.*b* He said, ⁴"I am an alien and a stranger among you. Sell me some property for a burial site here so I can bury my dead."

⁵The Hittites replied to Abraham, ⁶"Sir, listen to us. You are a mighty prince among us. Bury your dead in the choicest of our tombs. None of us will refuse you his tomb for burying your dead."

⁷Then Abraham rose and bowed down before the people of the land, the Hittites. ⁸He said to them, "If you are willing to let me bury my dead, then listen to me and intercede with Ephron son of Zohar on my behalf ⁹so he will sell me the cave of Machpelah, which belongs to him and is at the end of his field. Ask him to sell it to me for the full price as a burial site among you."

¹⁰Ephron the Hittite was sitting among his people and he replied to Abraham in the hearing of all the Hittites who had come to the gate of his city. ¹¹"No, my lord," he said. "Listen to me; I give*c* you the field, and I give*c* you the cave that is in it. I give*c* it to you in the presence of my people. Bury your dead."

¹²Again Abraham bowed down before the people of the land ¹³and he said to Ephron in their hearing, "Listen to me, if you will. I will pay the price of the field. Accept it from me so I can bury my dead there."

¹⁴Ephron answered Abraham, ¹⁵"Listen to me, my lord; the land is worth four hundred shekels*d* of silver, but what is that between me and you? Bury your dead."

¹⁶Abraham agreed to Ephron's terms and weighed out for him the price he had named in the hearing of the Hittites: four hundred shekels of silver, according to the weight current among the merchants.

¹⁷So Ephron's field in Machpelah near Mamre—both the field and the cave in it, and all the trees within the borders of the field—was deeded ¹⁸to Abraham as his property in the presence of all the Hittites who had come to the gate of the city. ¹⁹Afterward Abraham buried his wife Sarah in the cave in the

---

a18 Or *seed* *b3* Or *the sons of Heth*; also in verses 5, 7, 10, 16, 18 and 20 *c11* Or *sell* *d15* That is, about 10 pounds (about 4.5 kilograms)

field of Machpelah near Mamre (which is at Hebron) in the land of Canaan. [20]So the field and the cave in it were deeded to Abraham by the Hittites as a burial site.

24 *Isaac and Rebekah*   Abraham was now old and well advanced in years, and the LORD had blessed him in every way. [2]He said to the chief[a] servant in his household, the one in charge of all that he had, "Put your hand under my thigh. [3]I want you to swear by the LORD, the God of heaven and the God of earth, that you will not get a wife for my son from the daughters of the Canaanites, among whom I am living, [4]but will go to my country and my own relatives and get a wife for my son Isaac."

[5]The servant asked him, "What if the woman is unwilling to come back with me to this land? Shall I then take your son back to the country you came from?"

[6]"Make sure that you do not take my son back there," Abraham said. [7]"The LORD, the God of heaven, who brought me out of my father's household and my native land and who spoke to me and promised me on oath, saying, 'To your offspring[b] I will give this land'—he will send his angel before you so that you can get a wife for my son from there. [8]If the woman is unwilling to come back with you, then you will be released from this oath of mine. Only do not take my son back there." [9]So the servant put his hand under the thigh of his master Abraham and swore an oath to him concerning this matter.

[10]Then the servant took ten of his master's camels and left, taking with him all kinds of good things from his master. He set out for Aram Naharaim[c] and made his way to the town of Nahor. [11]He had the camels kneel down near the well outside the town; it was toward evening, the time the women go out to draw water.

[12]Then he prayed, "O LORD, God of my master Abraham, give me success today, and show kindness to my master Abraham. [13]See, I am standing beside this spring, and the daughters of the townspeople are coming out to draw water. [14]May it be that when I say to a girl, 'Please let down your jar that I may have a drink,' and she says, 'Drink, and I'll water your camels too'—let her be the one you have chosen for your servant Isaac. By this I will know that you have shown kindness to my master."

[15]Before he had finished praying, Rebekah came out with her jar on her shoulder. She was the daughter of Bethuel son of Milcah, who was the wife of Abraham's brother Nahor. [16]The girl was very beautiful, a virgin; no man had ever lain with her. She went down to the spring, filled her jar and came up again.

[17]The servant hurried to meet her and said, "Please give me a little water from your jar."

[18]"Drink, my lord," she said, and quickly lowered the jar to her hands and gave him a drink.

[19]After she had given him a drink, she said, "I'll draw water for your camels too, until they have finished drinking." [20]So she quickly emptied her jar into the trough, ran back to the well to draw more

GENESIS 24:14

Choosing the person you will marry is serious business. A good choice will bring you a happy, rewarding life. A poor choice can make you miserable. That's why it's important to involve God in your dating life even when you're young. I know. You're not planning to get married yet. Dating is a time for fun and for getting to know lots of kids of the opposite sex. But it's also a time when you develop attitudes that will shape your choice of a mate. Genesis 24 teaches that God will lead you if you ask his help in choosing a mate.

Direct Line

[a]2 Or *oldest*   [b]7 Or *seed*   [c]10 That is, Northwest Mesopotamia

water, and drew enough for all his camels. ²¹Without saying a word, the man watched her closely to learn whether or not the LORD had made his journey successful.

²²When the camels had finished drinking, the man took out a gold nose ring weighing a beka*a* and two gold bracelets weighing ten shekels.*b* ²³Then he asked, "Whose daughter are you? Please tell me, is there room in your father's house for us to spend the night?"

²⁴She answered him, "I am the daughter of Bethuel, the son that Milcah bore to Nahor." ²⁵And she added, "We have plenty of straw and fodder, as well as room for you to spend the night."

²⁶Then the man bowed down and worshiped the LORD, ²⁷saying, "Praise be to the LORD, the God of my master Abraham, who has not abandoned his kindness and faithfulness to my master. As for me, the LORD has led me on the journey to the house of my master's relatives."

²⁸The girl ran and told her mother's household about these things. ²⁹Now Rebekah had a brother named Laban, and he hurried out to the man at the spring. ³⁰As soon as he had seen the nose ring, and the bracelets on his sister's arms, and had heard Rebekah tell what the man said to her, he went out to the man and found him standing by the camels near the spring. ³¹"Come, you who are blessed by the LORD," he said. "Why are you standing out here? I have prepared the house and a place for the camels."

³²So the man went to the house, and the camels were unloaded. Straw and fodder were brought for the camels, and water for him and his men to wash their feet. ³³Then food was set before him, but he said, "I will not eat until I have told you what I have to say."

"Then tell us," Laban said.

³⁴So he said, "I am Abraham's servant. ³⁵The LORD has blessed my master abundantly, and he has become wealthy. He has given him sheep and cattle, silver and gold, menservants and maidservants, and camels and donkeys. ³⁶My master's wife Sarah has borne him a son in her*c* old age, and he has given him everything he owns. ³⁷And my master made me swear an oath, and said, 'You must not get a wife for my son from the daughters of the Canaanites, in whose land I live, ³⁸but go to my father's family and to my own clan, and get a wife for my son.'

³⁹"Then I asked my master, 'What if the woman will not come back with me?'

⁴⁰"He replied, 'The LORD, before whom I have walked, will send his angel with you and make your journey a success, so that you can get a wife for my son from my own clan and from my father's family. ⁴¹Then, when you go to my clan, you will be released from my oath even if they refuse to give her to you—you will be released from my oath.'

⁴²"When I came to the spring today, I said, 'O LORD, God of my master Abraham, if you will, please grant success to the journey on which I have come. ⁴³See, I am standing beside this spring; if a maiden comes out to draw water and I say to her, "Please let me drink a little water from your jar," ⁴⁴and if she says to me, "Drink, and I'll draw water for your camels too," let her be the one the LORD has chosen for my master's son.'

⁴⁵"Before I finished praying in my heart, Rebekah came out, with her jar on her shoulder. She went down to the spring and drew water, and I said to her, 'Please give me a drink.'

⁴⁶"She quickly lowered her jar from her shoulder and said, 'Drink, and I'll water your camels too.' So I drank, and she watered the camels also.

⁴⁷"I asked her, 'Whose daughter are you?'

"She said, 'The daughter of Bethuel son of Nahor, whom Milcah bore to him.'

---

a22 That is, about 1/5 ounce (about 5.5 grams)   *b22* That is, about 4 ounces (about 110 grams)   *c36* Or *his*

"Then I put the ring in her nose and the bracelets on her arms, ⁴⁸and I bowed down and worshiped the LORD. I praised the LORD, the God of my master Abraham, who had led me on the right road to get the granddaughter of my master's brother for his son. ⁴⁹Now if you will show kindness and faithfulness to my master, tell me; and if not, tell me, so I may know which way to turn."

⁵⁰Laban and Bethuel answered, "This is from the LORD; we can say nothing to you one way or the other. ⁵¹Here is Rebekah; take her and go, and let her become the wife of your master's son, as the LORD has directed."

⁵²When Abraham's servant heard what they said, he bowed down to the ground before the LORD. ⁵³Then the servant brought out gold and silver jewelry and articles of clothing and gave them to Rebekah; he also gave costly gifts to her brother and to her mother. ⁵⁴Then he and the men who were with him ate and drank and spent the night there.

When they got up the next morning, he said, "Send me on my way to my master."

⁵⁵But her brother and her mother replied, "Let the girl remain with us ten days or so; then you*ᵃ* may go."

⁵⁶But he said to them, "Do not detain me, now that the LORD has granted success to my journey. Send me on my way so I may go to my master."

⁵⁷Then they said, "Let's call the girl and ask her about it." ⁵⁸So they called Rebekah and asked her, "Will you go with this man?"

"I will go," she said.

⁵⁹So they sent their sister Rebekah on her way, along with her nurse and Abraham's servant and his men. ⁶⁰And they blessed Rebekah and said to her,

> "Our sister, may you increase
>   to thousands upon thousands;
> may your offspring possess
>   the gates of their enemies."

⁶¹Then Rebekah and her maids got ready and mounted their camels and went back with the man. So the servant took Rebekah and left.

⁶²Now Isaac had come from Beer Lahai Roi, for he was living in the Negev. ⁶³He went out to the field one evening to meditate,*ᵇ* and as he looked up, he saw camels approaching. ⁶⁴Rebekah also looked up and saw Isaac. She got down from her camel ⁶⁵and asked the servant, "Who is that man in the field coming to meet us?"

"He is my master," the servant answered. So she took her veil and covered herself.

⁶⁶Then the servant told Isaac all he had done. ⁶⁷Isaac brought her into the tent of his mother Sarah, and he married Rebekah. So she became his wife, and he loved her; and Isaac was comforted after his mother's death.

The Death of Abraham Abraham took*ᶜ* another wife, whose name was Keturah. ²She bore him Zimran, Jokshan, Medan, Midian, Ishbak and Shuah. ³Jokshan was the father of Sheba and Dedan; the descendants of Dedan were the Asshurites, the Letushites and the Leummites. ⁴The sons of Midian were Ephah, Epher, Hanoch, Abida and Eldaah. All these were descendants of Keturah.

⁵Abraham left everything he owned to Isaac. ⁶But while he was still living, he gave gifts to the sons of his concubines and sent them away from his son Isaac to the land of the east.

⁷Altogether, Abraham lived a hundred and seventy-five years. ⁸Then Abraham breathed his last and died at a good old age, an old man and full of

---

ᵃ55 Or *she* ᵇ63 The meaning of the Hebrew for this word is uncertain. ᶜ1 Or *had taken* years; and he was gathered to his people. ⁹His sons Isaac and Ishmael buried him in the cave of Machpelah near Mamre, in the field of Ephron son of Zohar the Hittite, ¹⁰the field Abraham had bought from the Hittites.ᵃ There Abraham was buried with his wife Sarah. ¹¹After Abraham's death, God blessed his son Isaac, who then lived near Beer Lahai Roi.

Ishmael's Sons ¹²This is the account of Abraham's son Ishmael, whom Sarah's maidservant, Hagar the Egyptian, bore to Abraham.

¹³These are the names of the sons of Ishmael, listed in the order of their birth: Nebaioth the firstborn of Ishmael, Kedar, Adbeel, Mibsam, ¹⁴Mishma, Dumah, Massa, ¹⁵Hadad, Tema, Jetur, Naphish and Kedemah. ¹⁶These were the sons of Ishmael, and these are the names of the twelve tribal rulers according to their settlements and camps. ¹⁷Altogether, Ishmael lived a hundred and thirty-seven years. He breathed his last and died, and he was gathered to his people. ¹⁸His descendants settled in the area from Havilah to Shur, near the border of Egypt, as you go toward Asshur. And they lived in hostility towardᵇ all their brothers.

Jacob and Esau ¹⁹This is the account of Abraham's son Isaac.

Abraham became the father of Isaac, ²⁰and Isaac was forty years old when he married Rebekah daughter of Bethuel the Aramean from Paddan Aramᶜ and sister of Laban the Aramean.

²¹Isaac prayed to the Lᴏʀᴅ on behalf of his wife, because she was barren. The Lᴏʀᴅ answered his prayer, and his wife Rebekah became pregnant. ²²The babies jostled each other within her, and she said, "Why is this happening to me?" So she went to inquire of the Lᴏʀᴅ.

²³The Lᴏʀᴅ said to her,

> "Two nations are in your womb,
>   and two peoples from within you will be separated;
> one people will be stronger than the other,
>   and the older will serve the
>   younger."

²⁴When the time came for her to give birth, there were twin boys in her womb. ²⁵The first to come out was red, and his whole body was like a hairy garment; so they named him Esau.ᵈ ²⁶After this, his brother came out, with his hand grasping Esau's heel; so he was named Jacob.ᵉ Isaac was sixty years old when Rebekah gave birth to them.

²⁷The boys grew up, and Esau became a skillful hunter, a man of the open country, while Jacob was a quiet man, staying among the tents. ²⁸Isaac, who had a taste for wild game, loved Esau, but Rebekah loved Jacob.

²⁹Once when Jacob was cooking some

ᵃ10 Or *the sons of Heth*   ᵇ18 Or *lived to the east of*
ᶜ20 That is, Northwest Mesopotamia   ᵈ25 *Esau* may mean *hairy*; he was also called Edom, which means *red*.
ᵉ26 *Jacob* means *he grasps the heel* (figuratively, *he deceives*).

GENESIS 25:24–34

Picture Esau, hungry after being out hunting, and his brother Jacob, holding a pot of stew and offering a trade: a bowlful for a birthright. As the oldest son Esau had the right to inherit his father Isaac's possessions as well as God's promises to his grandfather Abraham. Esau looked at that stew and, without giving a second thought to God, told Jacob, "Take the birthright. I'm famished!" Dumb? You bet. Just as dumb as the choices some teens make today, trading away what's important for an immediate thrill. They trade away their tomorrow for cheap thrills today.

Direct Line

stew, Esau came in from the open country, famished. ³⁰He said to Jacob, "Quick, let me have some of that red stew! I'm famished!" (That is why he was also called Edom.ᵃ)

³¹Jacob replied, "First sell me your birthright."

³²"Look, I am about to die," Esau said. "What good is the birthright to me?"

³³But Jacob said, "Swear to me first." So he swore an oath to him, selling his birthright to Jacob.

³⁴Then Jacob gave Esau some bread and some lentil stew. He ate and drank, and then got up and left.

So Esau despised his birthright.

26 *Isaac and Abimelech*   Now there was a famine in the land—besides the earlier famine of Abraham's time—and Isaac went to Abimelech king of the Philistines in Gerar. ²The LORD appeared to Isaac and said, "Do not go down to Egypt; live in the land where I tell you to live. ³Stay in this land for a while, and I will be with you and will bless you. For to you and your descendants I will give all these lands and will confirm the oath I swore to your father Abraham. ⁴I will make your descendants as numerous as the stars in the sky and will give them all these lands, and through your offspringᵇ all nations on earth will be blessed, ⁵because Abraham obeyed me and kept my requirements, my commands, my decrees and my laws." ⁶So Isaac stayed in Gerar.

⁷When the men of that place asked him about his wife, he said, "She is my sister," because he was afraid to say, "She is my wife." He thought, "The men of this place might kill me on account of Rebekah, because she is beautiful."

⁸When Isaac had been there a long time, Abimelech king of the Philistines looked down from a window and saw Isaac caressing his wife Rebekah. ⁹So Abimelech summoned Isaac and said, "She is really your wife! Why did you say, 'She is my sister'?"

Isaac answered him, "Because I thought I might lose my life on account of her."

¹⁰Then Abimelech said, "What is this you have done to us? One of the men might well have slept with your wife, and you would have brought guilt upon us."

¹¹So Abimelech gave orders to all the people: "Anyone who molests this man or his wife shall surely be put to death."

¹²Isaac planted crops in that land and the same year reaped a hundredfold, because the LORD blessed him. ¹³The man became rich, and his wealth continued to grow until he became very wealthy. ¹⁴He had so many flocks and herds and servants that the Philistines envied him. ¹⁵So all the wells that his father's servants had dug in the time of his father Abraham, the Philistines stopped up, filling them with earth.

¹⁶Then Abimelech said to Isaac, "Move away from us; you have become too powerful for us."

¹⁷So Isaac moved away from there and encamped in the Valley of Gerar and settled there. ¹⁸Isaac reopened the wells that had been dug in the time of his father Abraham, which the Philistines had stopped up after Abraham died, and he gave them the same names his father had given them.

¹⁹Isaac's servants dug in the valley and discovered a well of fresh water there. ²⁰But the herdsmen of Gerar quarreled with Isaac's herdsmen and said, "The water is ours!" So he named the well Esek,ᶜ because they disputed with him. ²¹Then they dug another well, but they quarreled over that one also; so he named it Sitnah.ᵈ ²²He moved on from there and dug another well,

---

ᵃ30 Edom means *red.*   *ᵇ4* Or *seed*   *ᶜ20 Esek* means *dispute.*   *ᵈ21 Sitnah* means *opposition.*

Dear Sam,

My mom and dad favor my sister. She gets to do everything. Also, I get punished for things, but when she does the same thing, it's always overlooked. It's not fair.

Tracey in Trenton

100 Advice Lane, Anywhere, USA

Dear Tracey,

Sometimes parents really do favor one child over another. And you're right: it's not fair! Most parents try to be as fair as possible, but at times they fail. It's an ancient problem. In Genesis 25:28 the Bible says very plainly that Isaac and Rebekah each favored one of their twin sons. All this favoritism led to lies and trickery and trouble between these brothers. (You can read Genesis 27 to get the sordid details.)

If both parents favor your sister, after praying for the right words, write your parents a letter explaining how you feel. Tell them that you want to feel equally loved and appreciated. Let them know what needs of yours aren't being met, then ask if you can meet to discuss the problem.

Now comes the hard part. Be sure to let your parents and your sister know that you love them. And do your best not to become bitter or angry over the whole situation.

Sam

and no one quarreled over it. He named it Rehoboth,ᵃ saying, "Now the LORD has given us room and we will flourish in the land."

²³From there he went up to Beersheba. ²⁴That night the LORD appeared to him and said, "I am the God of your father Abraham. Do not be afraid, for I am with you; I will bless you and will increase the number of your descendants for the sake of my servant Abraham."

²⁵Isaac built an altar there and called on the name of the LORD. There he pitched his tent, and there his servants dug a well.

²⁶Meanwhile, Abimelech had come to him from Gerar, with Ahuzzath his personal adviser and Phicol the commander of his forces. ²⁷Isaac asked them, "Why have you come to me, since you were hostile to me and sent me away?"

²⁸They answered, "We saw clearly that the LORD was with you; so we said, 'There ought to be a sworn agreement between us'—between us and you. Let us make a treaty with you ²⁹that you will do us no harm, just as we did not molest you but always treated you well and sent you away in peace. And now you are blessed by the LORD."

³⁰Isaac then made a feast for them, and they ate and drank. ³¹Early the next morning the men swore an oath to each other. Then Isaac sent them on their way, and they left him in peace.

³²That day Isaac's servants came and told him about the well they had dug. They said, "We've found water!" ³³He called it Shibah,ᵇ and to this day the name of the town has been Beersheba.ᶜ

³⁴When Esau was forty years old, he married Judith daughter of Beeri the Hittite, and also Basemath daughter of Elon the Hittite. ³⁵They were a source of grief to Isaac and Rebekah.

Jacob Gets Isaac's Blessing When Isaac was old and his eyes were so weak that he could no longer see, he called for Esau his older son and said to him, "My son."

"Here I am," he answered.

²Isaac said, "I am now an old man and don't know the day of my death. ³Now then, get your weapons—your quiver and bow—and go out to the open country to hunt some wild game for me. ⁴Prepare me the kind of tasty food I like and bring it to me to eat, so that I may give you my blessing before I die."

⁵Now Rebekah was listening as Isaac spoke to his son Esau. When Esau left for the open country to hunt game and bring it back, ⁶Rebekah said to her son Jacob, "Look, I overheard your father say to your brother Esau, ⁷'Bring me some game and prepare me some tasty food to eat, so that I may give you my blessing in the presence of the LORD before I die.' ⁸Now, my son, listen carefully and do what I tell you: ⁹Go out to the flock and bring me two choice young goats, so I can prepare some tasty food for your father, just the way he likes it. ¹⁰Then take it to your father to eat, so that he may give you his blessing before he dies."

¹¹Jacob said to Rebekah his mother, "But my brother Esau is a hairy man, and I'm a man with smooth skin. ¹²What if my father touches me? I would appear to be tricking him and would bring down a curse on myself rather than a blessing."

¹³His mother said to him, "My son, let the curse fall on me. Just do what I say; go and get them for me."

¹⁴So he went and got them and brought them to his mother, and she prepared some tasty food, just the way his father liked it. ¹⁵Then Rebekah took the best clothes of Esau her older son, which she had in the house, and put them on her younger son Jacob. ¹⁶She also covered his hands and the smooth

ᵃ22 Rehoboth means room. ᵇ33 Shibah can mean oath or seven. ᶜ33 Beersheba can mean well of the oath or well of seven.

part of his neck with the goatskins. ¹⁷Then she handed to her son Jacob the tasty food and the bread she had made.

¹⁸He went to his father and said, "My father."

"Yes, my son," he answered. "Who is it?"

¹⁹Jacob said to his father, "I am Esau your firstborn. I have done as you told me. Please sit up and eat some of my game so that you may give me your blessing."

²⁰Isaac asked his son, "How did you find it so quickly, my son?"

"The LORD your God gave me success," he replied.

²¹Then Isaac said to Jacob, "Come near so I can touch you, my son, to know whether you really are my son Esau or not."

²²Jacob went close to his father Isaac, who touched him and said, "The voice is the voice of Jacob, but the hands are the hands of Esau." ²³He did not recognize him, for his hands were hairy like those of his brother Esau; so he blessed him. ²⁴"Are you really my son Esau?" he asked.

"I am," he replied.

²⁵Then he said, "My son, bring me some of your game to eat, so that I may give you my blessing."

Jacob brought it to him and he ate; and he brought some wine and he drank. ²⁶Then his father Isaac said to him, "Come here, my son, and kiss me."

²⁷So he went to him and kissed him. When Isaac caught the smell of his clothes, he blessed him and said,

> "Ah, the smell of my son
>   is like the smell of a field
>   that the LORD has blessed.
> ²⁸May God give you of heaven's dew
>   and of earth's richness—
>   an abundance of grain and new wine.
> ²⁹May nations serve you
>   and peoples bow down to
>   you.
> Be lord over your brothers,
>   and may the sons of your
>   mother bow down to
>   you.
> May those who curse you be
>   cursed
>   and those who bless you be
>   blessed."

³⁰After Isaac finished blessing him and Jacob had scarcely left his father's presence, his brother Esau came in from hunting. ³¹He too prepared some tasty food and brought it to his father. Then he said to him, "My father, sit up and eat some of my game, so that you may give me your blessing."

³²His father Isaac asked him, "Who are you?"

"I am your son," he answered, "your firstborn, Esau."

³³Isaac trembled violently and said, "Who was it, then, that hunted game and brought it to me? I ate it just before you came and I blessed him—and indeed he will be blessed!"

GENESIS 27:1–41

Are you admiring that guy in the next row? You know, the one with the cheat sheet? All the answers written on his hand? He got an A on the last test! But before you decide cheating pays off, check what happened when Jacob cheated his brother Esau out of their father's blessing. In Old Testament times a father's "blessing" was both a will and a prophecy. It guaranteed the success of the son who received it. And Jacob got that blessing—by cheating. But read verse 41 and you'll see that Jacob got more than he bargained for. Sure, some people cheat and get away with it, but usually cheating brings more negative results than you expect.

Direct Line

³⁴When Esau heard his father's words, he burst out with a loud and bitter cry and said to his father, "Bless me—me too, my father!"

³⁵But he said, "Your brother came deceitfully and took your blessing."

³⁶Esau said, "Isn't he rightly named Jacob*ᵃ*? He has deceived me these two times: He took my birthright, and now he's taken my blessing!" Then he asked, "Haven't you reserved any blessing for me?"

³⁷Isaac answered Esau, "I have made him lord over you and have made all his relatives his servants, and I have sustained him with grain and new wine. So what can I possibly do for you, my son?"

³⁸Esau said to his father, "Do you have only one blessing, my father? Bless me too, my father!" Then Esau wept aloud.

³⁹His father Isaac answered him,

> "Your dwelling will be
>   away from the earth's richness,
>   away from the dew of heaven above.
> ⁴⁰You will live by the sword
>   and you will serve your brother.
> But when you grow restless,
>   you will throw his yoke
>   from off your neck."

Jacob Flees to Laban ⁴¹Esau held a grudge against Jacob because of the blessing his father had given him. He said to himself, "The days of mourning for my father are near; then I will kill my brother Jacob."

⁴²When Rebekah was told what her older son Esau had said, she sent for her younger son Jacob and said to him, "Your brother Esau is consoling himself with the thought of killing you. ⁴³Now then, my son, do what I say: Flee at once to my brother Laban in Haran. ⁴⁴Stay with him for a while until your brother's fury subsides. ⁴⁵When your brother is no longer angry with you and forgets what you did to him, I'll send word for you to come back from there. Why should I lose both of you in one day?"

⁴⁶Then Rebekah said to Isaac, "I'm disgusted with living because of these Hittite women. If Jacob takes a wife from among the women of this land, from Hittite women like these, my life will not be worth living."

28 So Isaac called for Jacob and blessed*ᵇ* him and commanded him: "Do not marry a Canaanite woman. ²Go at once to Paddan Aram,*ᶜ* to the house of your mother's father Bethuel. Take a wife for yourself there, from among the daughters of Laban, your mother's brother. ³May God Almighty*ᵈ* bless you and make you fruitful and increase your numbers until you become a community of peoples. ⁴May he give you and your descendants the blessing given to Abraham, so that you may take possession of the land where you now live as an alien, the land God gave to Abraham." ⁵Then Isaac sent Jacob on his way, and he went to Paddan Aram, to Laban son of Bethuel the Aramean, the brother of Rebekah, who was the mother of Jacob and Esau.

⁶Now Esau learned that Isaac had blessed Jacob and had sent him to Paddan Aram to take a wife from there, and that when he blessed him he commanded him, "Do not marry a Canaanite woman," ⁷and that Jacob had obeyed his father and mother and had gone to Paddan Aram. ⁸Esau then realized how displeasing the Canaanite women were to his father Isaac; ⁹so he went to Ishmael and married Mahalath, the sister of Nebaioth and daughter of Ishmael son of Abraham, in addition to the wives he already had.

ᵃ36 Jacob means *he grasps the heel* (figuratively, *he deceives*). *ᵇ1* Or *greeted* *ᶜ2* That is, Northwest Mesopotamia; also in verses 5, 6 and 7 *ᵈ3* Hebrew *El-Shaddai*

Jacob's Dream at Bethel ¹⁰Jacob left Beersheba and set out for Haran. ¹¹When he reached a certain place, he stopped for the night because the sun had set. Taking one of the stones there, he put it under his head and lay down to sleep. ¹²He had a dream in which he saw a stairway*ᵃ* resting on the earth, with its top reaching to heaven, and the angels of God were ascending and descending on it. ¹³There above it*ᵇ* stood the LORD, and he said: "I am the LORD, the God of your father Abraham and the God of Isaac. I will give you and your descendants the land on which you are lying. ¹⁴Your descendants will be like the dust of the earth, and you will spread out to the west and to the east, to the north and to the south. All peoples on earth will be blessed through you and your offspring. ¹⁵I am with you and will watch over you wherever you go, and I will bring you back to this land. I will not leave you until I have done what I have promised you."

I am with you and will watch over you wherever you go (Genesis 28:15).

¹⁶When Jacob awoke from his sleep, he thought, "Surely the LORD is in this place, and I was not aware of it." ¹⁷He was afraid and said, "How awesome is this place! This is none other than the house of God; this is the gate of heaven."

¹⁸Early the next morning Jacob took the stone he had placed under his head and set it up as a pillar and poured oil on top of it. ¹⁹He called that place Bethel,*ᶜ* though the city used to be called Luz.

²⁰Then Jacob made a vow, saying, "If God will be with me and will watch over me on this journey I am taking and will give me food to eat and clothes to wear ²¹so that I return safely to my father's house, then the LORD*ᵈ* will be my God ²²and*ᵉ* this stone that I have set up as a pillar will be God's house, and of all that you give me I will give you a tenth."

29 *Jacob Arrives in Paddan Aram* Then Jacob continued on his journey and came to the land of the eastern peoples. ²There he saw a well in the field, with three flocks of sheep lying near it because the flocks were watered from that well. The stone over the mouth of the well was large. ³When all the flocks were gathered there, the shepherds would roll the stone away from the well's mouth and water the sheep. Then they would return the stone to its place over the mouth of the well.

⁴Jacob asked the shepherds, "My brothers, where are you from?"

"We're from Haran," they replied.

⁵He said to them, "Do you know Laban, Nahor's grandson?"

"Yes, we know him," they answered.

⁶Then Jacob asked them, "Is he well?"

"Yes, he is," they said, "and here comes his daughter Rachel with the sheep."

⁷"Look," he said, "the sun is still high; it is not time for the flocks to be gathered. Water the sheep and take them back to pasture."

⁸"We can't," they replied, "until all the flocks are gathered and the stone has been rolled away from the mouth of the well. Then we will water the sheep."

⁹While he was still talking with them, Rachel came with her father's sheep, for she was a shepherdess. ¹⁰When Jacob saw Rachel daughter of Laban, his mother's brother, and Laban's sheep, he went over and rolled the stone away from the mouth of the well and watered his uncle's sheep. ¹¹Then Jacob kissed Rachel and began to weep aloud. ¹²He had told Rachel that he was a relative of her father and a son of Rebekah. So she ran and told her father.

ᵃ12 Or ladder ᵇ13 Or There beside him ᶜ19 Bethel means house of God. ᵈ20,21 Or Since God . . . father's house, the LORD ᵉ21,22 Or house, and the LORD will be my God, ²²then

¹³As soon as Laban heard the news about Jacob, his sister's son, he hurried to meet him. He embraced him and kissed him and brought him to his home, and there Jacob told him all these things. ¹⁴Then Laban said to him, "You are my own flesh and blood."

Jacob Marries Leah and Rachel   After Jacob had stayed with him for a whole month, ¹⁵Laban said to him, "Just because you are a relative of mine, should you work for me for nothing? Tell me what your wages should be."

¹⁶Now Laban had two daughters; the name of the older was Leah, and the name of the younger was Rachel. ¹⁷Leah had weak*ᵃ* eyes, but Rachel was lovely in form, and beautiful. ¹⁸Jacob was in love with Rachel and said, "I'll work for you seven years in return for your younger daughter Rachel."

¹⁹Laban said, "It's better that I give her to you than to some other man. Stay here with me." ²⁰So Jacob served seven years to get Rachel, but they seemed like only a few days to him because of his love for her.

²¹Then Jacob said to Laban, "Give me my wife. My time is completed, and I want to lie with her."

²²So Laban brought together all the people of the place and gave a feast. ²³But when evening came, he took his daughter Leah and gave her to Jacob, and Jacob lay with her. ²⁴And Laban gave his servant girl Zilpah to his daughter as her maidservant.

²⁵When morning came, there was Leah! So Jacob said to Laban, "What is this you have done to me? I served you for Rachel, didn't I? Why have you deceived me?"

²⁶Laban replied, "It is not our custom here to give the younger daughter in marriage before the older one. ²⁷Finish this daughter's bridal week; then we will give you the younger one also, in return for another seven years of work."

²⁸And Jacob did so. He finished the week with Leah, and then Laban gave him his daughter Rachel to be his wife. ²⁹Laban gave his servant girl Bilhah to his daughter Rachel as her maidservant. ³⁰Jacob lay with Rachel also, and he loved Rachel more than Leah. And he worked for Laban another seven years.

ᵃ17 Or delicate

The Bible Says

One Man, One Woman

Jacob had four wives (Rachel, Leah, Bilhah and Zilpah). Why shouldn't people today have more than one spouse?

Bear in mind that the historical books of the Bible report that what happened in history didn't always go according to what God had in mind for his creation.

Jesus taught that God's best is for "the two" to "become one flesh" (Matthew 19:5). God wants one man and one woman to love each other completely and to grow closer through the years.

If you think it would be fun to have more than one husband or wife, read Jacob's story closely (Genesis 29:30—30:24). You'll find that there was more competition than love going on.

God's ideal of a lifetime marriage between one man and one woman is best. Choose your future husband or wife wisely. If you do, you'll find more happiness with one person than with any number of marriage partners.

Jacob's Children ³¹When the Lord saw that Leah was not loved, he opened her womb, but Rachel was barren. ³²Leah became pregnant and gave birth to a son. She named him Reuben,^a for she said, "It is because the Lord has seen my misery. Surely my husband will love me now."

³³She conceived again, and when she gave birth to a son she said, "Because the Lord heard that I am not loved, he gave me this one too." So she named him Simeon.^b

³⁴Again she conceived, and when she gave birth to a son she said, "Now at last my husband will become attached to me, because I have borne him three sons." So he was named Levi.^c

³⁵She conceived again, and when she gave birth to a son she said, "This time I will praise the Lord." So she named him Judah.^d Then she stopped having children.

30 When Rachel saw that she was not bearing Jacob any children, she became jealous of her sister. So she said to Jacob, "Give me children, or I'll die!"

²Jacob became angry with her and said, "Am I in the place of God, who has kept you from having children?"

³Then she said, "Here is Bilhah, my maidservant. Sleep with her so that she can bear children for me and that through her I too can build a family."

⁴So she gave him her servant Bilhah as a wife. Jacob slept with her, ⁵and she became pregnant and bore him a son. ⁶Then Rachel said, "God has vindicated me; he has listened to my plea and given me a son." Because of this she named him Dan.^e

⁷Rachel's servant Bilhah conceived again and bore Jacob a second son. ⁸Then Rachel said, "I have had a great struggle with my sister, and I have won." So she named him Naphtali.^f

⁹When Leah saw that she had stopped having children, she took her maidservant Zilpah and gave her to Jacob as a wife. ¹⁰Leah's servant Zilpah bore Jacob a son. ¹¹Then Leah said, "What good fortune!"^g So she named him Gad.^h

¹²Leah's servant Zilpah bore Jacob a second son. ¹³Then Leah said, "How happy I am! The women will call me happy." So she named him Asher.ⁱ

¹⁴During wheat harvest, Reuben went out into the fields and found some mandrake plants, which he brought to his mother Leah. Rachel said to Leah, "Please give me some of your son's mandrakes."

¹⁵But she said to her, "Wasn't it enough that you took away my husband? Will you take my son's mandrakes too?"

"Very well," Rachel said, "he can sleep with you tonight in return for your son's mandrakes."

¹⁶So when Jacob came in from the fields that evening, Leah went out to meet him. "You must sleep with me," she said. "I have hired you with my son's mandrakes." So he slept with her that night.

¹⁷God listened to Leah, and she became pregnant and bore Jacob a fifth son. ¹⁸Then Leah said, "God has rewarded me for giving my maidservant to my husband." So she named him Issachar.^j

¹⁹Leah conceived again and bore Jacob a sixth son. ²⁰Then Leah said, "God has presented me with a precious gift. This time my husband will treat me with honor, because I have borne him six sons." So she named him Zebulun.^k

²¹Some time later she gave birth to a daughter and named her Dinah.

²²Then God remembered Rachel; he listened to her and opened her womb.

^a*32 Reuben* sounds like the Hebrew for *he has seen my misery*; the name means *see, a son.* ^b*33 Simeon* probably means *one who hears.* ^c*34 Levi* sounds like and may be derived from the Hebrew for *attached.* ^d*35 Judah* sounds like and may be derived from the Hebrew for *praise.* ^e*6 Dan* here means *he has vindicated.* ^f*8 Naphtali* means *my struggle.* ^g*11* Or *"A troop is coming!"* ^h*11 Gad* can mean *good fortune* or *a troop.* ⁱ*13 Asher* means *happy.* ^j*18 Issachar* sounds like the Hebrew for *reward.* ^k*20 Zebulun* probably means *honor.*

²³She became pregnant and gave birth to a son and said, "God has taken away my disgrace." ²⁴She named him Joseph,[a] and said, "May the LORD add to me another son."

Jacob's Flocks Increase   ²⁵After Rachel gave birth to Joseph, Jacob said to Laban, "Send me on my way so I can go back to my own homeland. ²⁶Give me my wives and children, for whom I have served you, and I will be on my way. You know how much work I've done for you."

²⁷But Laban said to him, "If I have found favor in your eyes, please stay. I have learned by divination that[b] the LORD has blessed me because of you." ²⁸He added, "Name your wages, and I will pay them."

²⁹Jacob said to him, "You know how I have worked for you and how your livestock has fared under my care. ³⁰The little you had before I came has increased greatly, and the LORD has blessed you wherever I have been. But now, when may I do something for my own household?"

³¹"What shall I give you?" he asked.

"Don't give me anything," Jacob replied. "But if you will do this one thing for me, I will go on tending your flocks and watching over them: ³²Let me go through all your flocks today and remove from them every speckled or spotted sheep, every dark-colored lamb and every spotted or speckled goat. They will be my wages. ³³And my honesty will testify for me in the future, whenever you check on the wages you have paid me. Any goat in my possession that is not speckled or spotted, or any lamb that is not dark-colored, will be considered stolen."

³⁴"Agreed," said Laban. "Let it be as you have said." ³⁵That same day he removed all the male goats that were streaked or spotted, and all the speckled or spotted female goats (all that had white on them) and all the dark-colored lambs, and he placed them in the care of his sons. ³⁶Then he put a three-day journey between himself and Jacob, while Jacob continued to tend the rest of Laban's flocks.

³⁷Jacob, however, took fresh-cut branches from poplar, almond and plane trees and made white stripes on them by peeling the bark and exposing the white inner wood of the branches. ³⁸Then he placed the peeled branches in all the watering troughs, so that they would be directly in front of the flocks when they came to drink. When the flocks were in heat and came to drink, ³⁹they mated in front of the branches. And they bore young that were streaked or speckled or spotted. ⁴⁰Jacob set apart the young of the flock by themselves, but made the rest face the streaked and dark-colored animals that belonged to Laban. Thus he made separate flocks for himself and did not put them with Laban's animals. ⁴¹Whenever the stronger females were in heat, Jacob would place the branches in the troughs in front of the animals so they would mate near the branches, ⁴²but if the animals were weak, he would not place them there. So the weak animals went to Laban and the strong ones to Jacob. ⁴³In this way the man grew exceedingly prosperous and came to own large flocks, and maidservants and menservants, and camels and donkeys.

31   *Jacob Flees From Laban*   Jacob heard that Laban's sons were saying, "Jacob has taken everything our father owned and has gained all this wealth from what belonged to our father." ²And Jacob noticed that Laban's attitude toward him was not what it had been.

³Then the LORD said to Jacob, "Go back to the land of your fathers and to your relatives, and I will be with you."

---

a24 Joseph means *may he add.*   *b27* Or possibly *have become rich and*

4So Jacob sent word to Rachel and Leah to come out to the fields where his flocks were. 5He said to them, "I see that your father's attitude toward me is not what it was before, but the God of my father has been with me. 6You know that I've worked for your father with all my strength, 7yet your father has cheated me by changing my wages ten times. However, God has not allowed him to harm me. 8If he said, 'The speckled ones will be your wages,' then all the flocks gave birth to speckled young; and if he said, 'The streaked ones will be your wages,' then all the flocks bore streaked young. 9So God has taken away your father's livestock and has given them to me.

10"In breeding season I once had a dream in which I looked up and saw that the male goats mating with the flock were streaked, speckled or spotted. 11The angel of God said to me in the dream, 'Jacob.' I answered, 'Here I am.' 12And he said, 'Look up and see that all the male goats mating with the flock are streaked, speckled or spotted, for I have seen all that Laban has been doing to you. 13I am the God of Bethel, where you anointed a pillar and where you made a vow to me. Now leave this land at once and go back to your native land.' "

14Then Rachel and Leah replied, "Do we still have any share in the inheritance of our father's estate? 15Does he not regard us as foreigners? Not only has he sold us, but he has used up what was paid for us. 16Surely all the wealth that God took away from our father belongs to us and our children. So do whatever God has told you."

17Then Jacob put his children and his wives on camels, 18and he drove all his livestock ahead of him, along with all the goods he had accumulated in Paddan Aram,a to go to his father Isaac in the land of Canaan.

19When Laban had gone to shear his sheep, Rachel stole her father's household gods. 20Moreover, Jacob deceived Laban the Aramean by not telling him he was running away. 21So he fled with all he had, and crossing the River,b he headed for the hill country of Gilead.

Laban Pursues Jacob 22On the third day Laban was told that Jacob had fled. 23Taking his relatives with him, he pursued Jacob for seven days and caught up with him in the hill country of Gilead. 24Then God came to Laban the Aramean in a dream at night and said to him, "Be careful not to say anything to Jacob, either good or bad."

25Jacob had pitched his tent in the hill country of Gilead when Laban overtook him, and Laban and his relatives camped there too. 26Then Laban said to Jacob, "What have you done? You've deceived me, and you've carried off my daughters like captives in war. 27Why did you run off secretly and deceive me? Why didn't you tell me, so I could send you away with joy and singing to the music of tambourines and harps? 28You didn't even let me kiss my grandchildren and my daughters good-by. You have done a foolish thing. 29I have the power to harm you; but last night the God of your father said to me, 'Be careful not to say anything to Jacob, either good or bad.' 30Now you have gone off because you longed to return to your father's house. But why did you steal my gods?"

31Jacob answered Laban, "I was afraid, because I thought you would take your daughters away from me by force. 32But if you find anyone who has your gods, he shall not live. In the presence of our relatives, see for yourself whether there is anything of yours here with me; and if so, take it." Now Jacob did not know that Rachel had stolen the gods.

GENESIS 31:14-35

QUIZZER

Q: What did Rachel take from her father when the family left town?

BONUS: Why did she take these particular things?

Answers on page 42

a18 That is, Northwest Mesopotamia   b21 That is, the Euphrates

³³So Laban went into Jacob's tent and into Leah's tent and into the tent of the two maidservants, but he found nothing. After he came out of Leah's tent, he entered Rachel's tent. ³⁴Now Rachel had taken the household gods and put them inside her camel's saddle and was sitting on them. Laban searched through everything in the tent but found nothing.

³⁵Rachel said to her father, "Don't be angry, my lord, that I cannot stand up in your presence; I'm having my period." So he searched but could not find the household gods.

³⁶Jacob was angry and took Laban to task. "What is my crime?" he asked Laban. "What sin have I committed that you hunt me down? ³⁷Now that you have searched through all my goods, what have you found that belongs to your household? Put it here in front of your relatives and mine, and let them judge between the two of us.

³⁸"I have been with you for twenty years now. Your sheep and goats have not miscarried, nor have I eaten rams from your flocks. ³⁹I did not bring you animals torn by wild beasts; I bore the loss myself. And you demanded payment from me for whatever was stolen by day or night. ⁴⁰This was my situation: The heat consumed me in the daytime and the cold at night, and sleep fled from my eyes. ⁴¹It was like this for the twenty years I was in your household. I worked for you fourteen years for your two daughters and six years for your flocks, and you changed my wages ten times. ⁴²If the God of my father, the God of Abraham and the Fear of Isaac, had not been with me, you would surely have sent me away empty-handed. But God has seen my hardship and the toil of my hands, and last night he rebuked you."

⁴³Laban answered Jacob, "The women are my daughters, the children are my children, and the flocks are my flocks. All you see is mine. Yet what can I do today about these daughters of mine, or about the children they have borne? ⁴⁴Come now, let's make a covenant, you and I, and let it serve as a witness between us."

⁴⁵So Jacob took a stone and set it up as a pillar. ⁴⁶He said to his relatives, "Gather some stones." So they took stones and piled them in a heap, and they ate there by the heap. ⁴⁷Laban called it Jegar Sahadutha,^a and Jacob called it Galeed.^b

⁴⁸Laban said, "This heap is a witness between you and me today." That is why it was called Galeed. ⁴⁹It was also called Mizpah,^c because he said, "May the LORD keep watch between you and me when we are away from each other. ⁵⁰If you mistreat my daughters or if you take any wives besides my daughters, even though no one is with us, remember that God is a witness between you and me."

⁵¹Laban also said to Jacob, "Here is this heap, and here is this pillar I have set up between you and me. ⁵²This heap is a witness, and this pillar is a witness, that I will not go past this heap to your side to harm you and that you will not go past this heap and pillar to my side to harm me. ⁵³May the God of Abraham and the God of Nahor, the God of their father, judge between us."

So Jacob took an oath in the name of the Fear of his father Isaac. ⁵⁴He offered a sacrifice there in the hill country and invited his relatives to a meal. After they had eaten, they spent the night there.

⁵⁵Early the next morning Laban kissed his grandchildren and his daughters and blessed them. Then he left and returned home.

Jacob Prepares to Meet Esau   Jacob also went on his way, and the angels of God met him. ²When Jacob saw them, he said, "This is the camp of God!" So he named that place Mahanaim.^d

³Jacob sent messengers ahead of him to his brother Esau in the land of

---

Answers

to Quizzer on page 41

A: Her father's household gods (Genesis 31:19).

BONUS: She wanted them for her children. The person who owned the family gods was the heir of the family fortune.

---

^a47 The Aramaic *Jegar Sahadutha* means *witness heap.*   ^b47 The Hebrew *Galeed* means *witness heap.*
^c49 *Mizpah* means *watchtower.*   ^d2 *Mahanaim* means *two camps.*

Seir, the country of Edom. ⁴He instructed them: "This is what you are to say to my master Esau: 'Your servant Jacob says, I have been staying with Laban and have remained there till now. ⁵I have cattle and donkeys, sheep and goats, menservants and maidservants. Now I am sending this message to my lord, that I may find favor in your eyes.'"

⁶When the messengers returned to Jacob, they said, "We went to your brother Esau, and now he is coming to meet you, and four hundred men are with him."

⁷In great fear and distress Jacob divided the people who were with him into two groups,ᵃ and the flocks and herds and camels as well. ⁸He thought, "If Esau comes and attacks one group,ᵇ the groupᵇ that is left may escape."

⁹Then Jacob prayed, "O God of my father Abraham, God of my father Isaac, O Lᴏʀᴅ, who said to me, 'Go back to your country and your relatives, and I will make you prosper,' ¹⁰I am unworthy of all the kindness and faithfulness you have shown your servant. I had only my staff when I crossed this Jordan, but now I have become two groups. ¹¹Save me, I pray, from the hand of my brother Esau, for I am afraid he will come and attack me, and also the mothers with their children. ¹²But you have said, 'I will surely make you prosper and will make your descendants like the sand of the sea, which cannot be counted.'"

¹³He spent the night there, and from what he had with him he selected a gift for his brother Esau: ¹⁴two hundred female goats and twenty male goats, two hundred ewes and twenty rams, ¹⁵thirty female camels with their young, forty cows and ten bulls, and twenty female donkeys and ten male donkeys. ¹⁶He put them in the care of his servants, each herd by itself, and said to his servants, "Go ahead of me, and keep some space between the herds."

¹⁷He instructed the one in the lead: "When my brother Esau meets you and asks, 'To whom do you belong, and where are you going, and who owns all these animals in front of you?' ¹⁸then you are to say, 'They belong to your servant Jacob. They are a gift sent to my lord Esau, and he is coming behind us.'"

¹⁹He also instructed the second, the third and all the others who followed the herds: "You are to say the same thing to Esau when you meet him. ²⁰And be sure to say, 'Your servant Jacob is coming behind us.'" For he thought, "I will pacify him with these gifts I am sending on ahead; later, when I see him, perhaps he will receive me." ²¹So Jacob's gifts went on ahead of him, but he himself spent the night in the camp.

Jacob Wrestles With God ²²That night Jacob got up and took his two wives, his two maidservants and his eleven sons and crossed the ford of the Jabbok. ²³After he had sent them across the stream, he sent over all his possessions. ²⁴So Jacob was left alone, and a man wrestled with him till daybreak. ²⁵When the man saw that he could not overpower him, he touched the socket of Jacob's hip so that his hip was wrenched as he wrestled with the man. ²⁶Then the man said, "Let me go, for it is daybreak."

ᵃ7 Or camps; also in verse 10 ᵇ8 Or camp

GENESIS 32:1–12

When is the last time you were terrified enough to pray hard? How did you pray? Jacob was terrified when returning to his home in Canaan. He had cheated his brother Esau 20 years before, and Esau had sworn to kill him. Would Esau still be angry? Here's how Jacob prayed when he was afraid: Jacob reminded God that he was being obedient (Genesis 32:9). Jacob remembered all the good things God had done for him (Genesis 32:10). Jacob begged God to save him (Genesis 32:11). Jacob quoted God's promises (Genesis 32:12). What a model for your prayers when you're anxious or afraid!

Direct Line

But Jacob replied, "I will not let you go unless you bless me."

²⁷The man asked him, "What is your name?"

"Jacob," he answered.

²⁸Then the man said, "Your name will no longer be Jacob, but Israel,ᵃ because you have struggled with God and with men and have overcome."

²⁹Jacob said, "Please tell me your name."

But he replied, "Why do you ask my name?" Then he blessed him there.

³⁰So Jacob called the place Peniel,ᵇ saying, "It is because I saw God face to face, and yet my life was spared."

³¹The sun rose above him as he passed Peniel,ᶜ and he was limping because of his hip. ³²Therefore to this day the Israelites do not eat the tendon attached to the socket of the hip, because the socket of Jacob's hip was touched near the tendon.

33 *Jacob Meets Esau* Jacob looked up and there was Esau, coming with his four hundred men; so he divided the children among Leah, Rachel and the two maidservants. ²He put the maidservants and their children in front, Leah and her children next, and Rachel and Joseph in the rear. ³He himself went on ahead and bowed down to the ground seven times as he approached his brother.

⁴But Esau ran to meet Jacob and embraced him; he threw his arms around his neck and kissed him. And they wept. ⁵Then Esau looked up and saw the women and children. "Who are these with you?" he asked.

Jacob answered, "They are the children God has graciously given your servant."

⁶Then the maidservants and their children approached and bowed down. ⁷Next, Leah and her children came and bowed down. Last of all came Joseph and Rachel, and they too bowed down.

⁸Esau asked, "What do you mean by all these droves I met?"

"To find favor in your eyes, my lord," he said.

⁹But Esau said, "I already have plenty, my brother. Keep what you have for yourself."

¹⁰"No, please!" said Jacob. "If I have found favor in your eyes, accept this gift from me. For to see your face is like seeing the face of God, now that you have received me favorably. ¹¹Please accept the present that was brought to you, for God has been gracious to me and I have all I need." And because Jacob insisted, Esau accepted it.

¹²Then Esau said, "Let us be on our way; I'll accompany you."

¹³But Jacob said to him, "My lord knows that the children are tender and that I must care for the ewes and cows that are nursing their young. If they are driven hard just one day, all the animals will die. ¹⁴So let my lord go on ahead of his servant, while I move along slowly at the pace of the droves before me and that of the children, until I come to my lord in Seir."

¹⁵Esau said, "Then let me leave some of my men with you."

"But why do that?" Jacob asked. "Just let me find favor in the eyes of my lord."

¹⁶So that day Esau started on his way back to Seir. ¹⁷Jacob, however, went to Succoth, where he built a place for himself and made shelters for his livestock. That is why the place is called Succoth.ᵈ

¹⁸After Jacob came from Paddan Aram,ᵉ he arrived safely at theᶠ city of Shechem in Canaan and camped within sight of the city. ¹⁹For a hundred pieces of silver,ᵍ he bought from the sons of Hamor, the father of Shechem, the plot

---

ᵃ28 *Israel* means *he struggles with God.* ᵇ30 *Peniel* means *face of God.* ᶜ31 Hebrew *Penuel,* a variant of *Peniel* ᵈ17 *Succoth* means *shelters.* ᵉ18 That is, Northwest Mesopotamia ᶠ18 Or *arrived at Shalem, a* ᵍ19 Hebrew *hundred kesitahs;* a kesitah was a unit of money of unknown weight and value.

of ground where he pitched his tent. ²⁰There he set up an altar and called it El Elohe Israel.ᵃ

34 *Dinah and the Shechemites* Now Dinah, the daughter Leah had borne to Jacob, went out to visit the women of the land. ²When Shechem son of Hamor the Hivite, the ruler of that area, saw her, he took her and violated her. ³His heart was drawn to Dinah daughter of Jacob, and he loved the girl and spoke tenderly to her. ⁴And Shechem said to his father Hamor, "Get me this girl as my wife."

⁵When Jacob heard that his daughter Dinah had been defiled, his sons were in the fields with his livestock; so he kept quiet about it until they came home.

⁶Then Shechem's father Hamor went out to talk with Jacob. ⁷Now Jacob's sons had come in from the fields as soon as they heard what had happened. They were filled with grief and fury, because Shechem had done a disgraceful thing inᵇ Israel by lying with Jacob's daughter—a thing that should not be done.

⁸But Hamor said to them, "My son Shechem has his heart set on your daughter. Please give her to him as his wife. ⁹Intermarry with us; give us your daughters and take our daughters for yourselves. ¹⁰You can settle among us; the land is open to you. Live in it, tradeᶜ in it, and acquire property in it."

¹¹Then Shechem said to Dinah's father and brothers, "Let me find favor in your eyes, and I will give you whatever you ask. ¹²Make the price for the bride and the gift I am to bring as great as you like, and I'll pay whatever you ask me. Only give me the girl as my wife."

¹³Because their sister Dinah had been defiled, Jacob's sons replied deceitfully as they spoke to Shechem and his father Hamor. ¹⁴They said to them, "We can't do such a thing; we can't give our sister to a man who is not circumcised. That would be a disgrace to us. ¹⁵We will give our consent to you on one condition only: that you become like us by circumcising all your males. ¹⁶Then we will give you our daughters and take your daughters for ourselves. We'll settle among you and become one people with you. ¹⁷But if you will not agree to be circumcised, we'll take our sisterᵈ and go."

¹⁸Their proposal seemed good to Hamor and his son Shechem. ¹⁹The young man, who was the most honored of all his father's household, lost no time in doing what they said, because he was delighted with Jacob's daughter. ²⁰So Hamor and his son Shechem went to the gate of their city to speak to their fellow townsmen. ²¹"These men are friendly toward us," they said. "Let them live in our land and trade in it; the land has plenty of room for them. We can marry their daughters and they can marry ours. ²²But the men will consent to live with us as one people only on the condition that our males be circumcised, as they themselves are. ²³Won't their livestock, their property and all their other animals become ours? So let us give our consent to them, and they will settle among us."

²⁴All the men who went out of the city gate agreed with Hamor and his son Shechem, and every male in the city was circumcised.

²⁵Three days later, while all of them were still in pain, two of Jacob's sons, Simeon and Levi, Dinah's brothers, took their swords and attacked the unsuspecting city, killing every male. ²⁶They put Hamor and his son Shechem to the sword and took Dinah from Shechem's house and left. ²⁷The sons of Jacob came upon the dead bodies and looted the city whereᵉ their sister had been defiled. ²⁸They seized their flocks and herds and donkeys and everything else of theirs in the city and out in the fields. ²⁹They carried off all their

---

ᵃ20 *El Elohe Israel* can mean *God, the God of Israel* or *mighty is the God of Israel.* ᵇ7 Or *against* ᶜ10 Or *move about freely,* also in verse 21 ᵈ17 Hebrew *daughter* ᵉ27 Or *because*

wealth and all their women and children, taking as plunder everything in the houses.

³⁰Then Jacob said to Simeon and Levi, "You have brought trouble on me by making me a stench to the Canaanites and Perizzites, the people living in this land. We are few in number, and if they join forces against me and attack me, I and my household will be destroyed."

³¹But they replied, "Should he have treated our sister like a prostitute?"

Jacob Returns to Bethel   Then God said to Jacob, "Go up to Bethel and settle there, and build an altar there to God, who appeared to you when you were fleeing from your brother Esau."

²So Jacob said to his household and to all who were with him, "Get rid of the foreign gods you have with you, and purify yourselves and change your clothes. ³Then come, let us go up to Bethel, where I will build an altar to God, who answered me in the day of my distress and who has been with me wherever I have gone." ⁴So they gave Jacob all the foreign gods they had and the rings in their ears, and Jacob buried them under the oak at Shechem. ⁵Then they set out, and the terror of God fell upon the towns all around them so that no one pursued them.

⁶Jacob and all the people with him came to Luz (that is, Bethel) in the land of Canaan. ⁷There he built an altar, and he called the place El Bethel,ᵃ because it was there that God revealed himself to him when he was fleeing from his brother.

⁸Now Deborah, Rebekah's nurse, died and was buried under the oak below Bethel. So it was named Allon Bacuth.ᵇ

⁹After Jacob returned from Paddan Aram,ᶜ God appeared to him again and blessed him. ¹⁰God said to him, "Your name is Jacob,ᵈ but you will no longer be called Jacob; your name will be Israel.ᵉ" So he named him Israel.

¹¹And God said to him, "I am God Almightyᶠ; be fruitful and increase in number. A nation and a community of nations will come from you, and kings will come from your body. ¹²The land I gave to Abraham and Isaac I also give to you, and I will give this land to your descendants after you." ¹³Then God went up from him at the place where he had talked with him.

¹⁴Jacob set up a stone pillar at the place where God had talked with him, and he poured out a drink offering on it; he also poured oil on it. ¹⁵Jacob called the place where God had talked with him Bethel.ᵍ

The Deaths of Rachel and Isaac   ¹⁶Then they moved on from Bethel. While they were still some distance from Ephrath, Rachel began to give birth and had great difficulty. ¹⁷And as she was having great difficulty in childbirth, the midwife said to her, "Don't be afraid, for you have another son." ¹⁸As she breathed her last—for she was dying—she named her son Ben-Oni.ʰ But his father named him Benjamin.ⁱ

¹⁹So Rachel died and was buried on the way to Ephrath (that is, Bethlehem). ²⁰Over her tomb Jacob set up a pillar, and to this day that pillar marks Rachel's tomb.

²¹Israel moved on again and pitched his tent beyond Migdal Eder. ²²While Israel was living in that region, Reuben went in and slept with his father's concubine Bilhah, and Israel heard of it.

Jacob had twelve sons:

²³ The sons of Leah:

Reuben the firstborn of Jacob,
Simeon, Levi, Judah, Issachar and Zebulun.

ᵃ7 *El Bethel* means *God of Bethel.*   ᵇ8 *Allon Bacuth* means *oak of weeping.*   ᶜ9 That is, Northwest Mesopotamia; also in verse 26   ᵈ10 *Jacob* means *he grasps the heel* (figuratively, *he deceives*).   ᵉ10 *Israel* means *he struggles with God.*   ᶠ11 Hebrew *El-Shaddai*   ᵍ15 *Bethel* means *house of God.*   ʰ18 *Ben-Oni* means *son of my trouble.*   ⁱ18 *Benjamin* means *son of my right hand.*

²⁴The sons of Rachel:
  Joseph and Benjamin.
²⁵The sons of Rachel's maidservant Bilhah:
  Dan and Naphtali.
²⁶The sons of Leah's maidservant Zilpah:
  Gad and Asher.
These were the sons of Jacob, who were born to him in Paddan Aram.

²⁷Jacob came home to his father Isaac in Mamre, near Kiriath Arba (that is, Hebron), where Abraham and Isaac had stayed. ²⁸Isaac lived a hundred and eighty years. ²⁹Then he breathed his last and died and was gathered to his people, old and full of years. And his sons Esau and Jacob buried him.

36 *Esau's Descendants* This is the account of Esau (that is, Edom).

²Esau took his wives from the women of Canaan: Adah daughter of Elon the Hittite, and Oholibamah daughter of Anah and granddaughter of Zibeon the Hivite— ³also Basemath daughter of Ishmael and sister of Nebaioth.

⁴Adah bore Eliphaz to Esau, Basemath bore Reuel, ⁵and Oholibamah bore Jeush, Jalam and Korah. These were the sons of Esau, who were born to him in Canaan.

⁶Esau took his wives and sons and daughters and all the members of his household, as well as his livestock and all his other animals and all the goods he had acquired in Canaan, and moved to a land some distance from his brother Jacob. ⁷Their possessions were too great for them to remain together; the land where they were staying could not support them both because of their livestock. ⁸So Esau (that is, Edom) settled in the hill country of Seir.

⁹This is the account of Esau the father of the Edomites in the hill country of Seir.

¹⁰These are the names of Esau's sons:
  Eliphaz, the son of Esau's wife Adah, and Reuel, the son of Esau's wife Basemath.
¹¹The sons of Eliphaz:
  Teman, Omar, Zepho, Gatam and Kenaz.
  ¹²Esau's son Eliphaz also had a concubine named Timna, who bore him Amalek. These were grandsons of Esau's wife Adah.
¹³The sons of Reuel:
  Nahath, Zerah, Shammah and Mizzah. These were grandsons of Esau's wife Basemath.
¹⁴The sons of Esau's wife Oholibamah daughter of Anah and granddaughter of Zibeon, whom she bore to Esau:
  Jeush, Jalam and Korah.

¹⁵These were the chiefs among Esau's descendants:
The sons of Eliphaz the firstborn of Esau:
  Chiefs Teman, Omar, Zepho, Kenaz, ¹⁶Korah,ᵃ Gatam and Amalek. These were the chiefs descended from Eliphaz in Edom; they were grandsons of Adah.
¹⁷The sons of Esau's son Reuel:
  Chiefs Nahath, Zerah, Shammah and Mizzah. These were the chiefs descended from Reuel in Edom; they were grandsons of Esau's wife Basemath.

ᵃ16 Masoretic Text; Samaritan Pentateuch (see also Gen. 36:11 and 1 Chron. 1:36) does not have *Korah*.

¹⁸The sons of Esau's wife Oholibamah:

Chiefs Jeush, Jalam and Korah. These were the chiefs descended from Esau's wife Oholibamah daughter of Anah.

¹⁹These were the sons of Esau (that is, Edom), and these were their chiefs.

²⁰These were the sons of Seir the Horite, who were living in the region:

Lotan, Shobal, Zibeon, Anah, ²¹Dishon, Ezer and Dishan. These sons of Seir in Edom were Horite chiefs.

²²The sons of Lotan:

Hori and Homam.*a* Timna was Lotan's sister.

²³The sons of Shobal:

Alvan, Manahath, Ebal, Shepho and Onam.

²⁴The sons of Zibeon:

Aiah and Anah. This is the Anah who discovered the hot springs*b* in the desert while he was grazing the donkeys of his father Zibeon.

²⁵The children of Anah:

Dishon and Oholibamah daughter of Anah.

²⁶The sons of Dishon*c*:

Hemdan, Eshban, Ithran and Keran.

²⁷The sons of Ezer:

Bilhan, Zaavan and Akan.

²⁸The sons of Dishan:

Uz and Aran.

²⁹These were the Horite chiefs:

Lotan, Shobal, Zibeon, Anah, ³⁰Dishon, Ezer and Dishan. These were the Horite chiefs, according to their divisions, in the land of Seir.

The Rulers of Edom ³¹These were the kings who reigned in Edom before any Israelite king reigned*d*:

³²Bela son of Beor became king of Edom. His city was named Dinhabah.

³³When Bela died, Jobab son of Zerah from Bozrah succeeded him as king.

³⁴When Jobab died, Husham from the land of the Temanites succeeded him as king.

³⁵When Husham died, Hadad son of Bedad, who defeated Midian in the country of Moab, succeeded him as king. His city was named Avith.

³⁶When Hadad died, Samlah from Masrekah succeeded him as king.

³⁷When Samlah died, Shaul from Rehoboth on the river*e* succeeded him as king.

³⁸When Shaul died, Baal-Hanan son of Acbor succeeded him as king.

³⁹When Baal-Hanan son of Acbor died, Hadad*f* succeeded him as king. His city was named Pau, and his wife's name was Mehetabel daughter of Matred, the daughter of Me-Zahab.

⁴⁰These were the chiefs descended from Esau, by name, according to their clans and regions:

Timna, Alvah, Jetheth, ⁴¹Oholibamah, Elah, Pinon, ⁴²Kenaz, Teman, Mibzar, ⁴³Magdiel and Iram. These were the chiefs of Edom, according to their settlements in the land they occupied.

This was Esau the father of the Edomites.

---

a22 Hebrew *Hemam,* a variant of *Homam* (see 1 Chron. 1:39)   *b24* Vulgate; Syriac *discovered water;* the meaning of the Hebrew for this word is uncertain.   *c26* Hebrew *Dishan,* a variant of *Dishon*   *d31* Or *before an Israelite king reigned over them*   *e37* Possibly the Euphrates   *f39* Many manuscripts of the Masoretic Text, Samaritan Pentateuch and Syriac (see also 1 Chron. 1:50); most manuscripts of the Masoretic Text *Hadar*

37 *Joseph's Dreams* Jacob lived in the land where his father had stayed, the land of Canaan.

²This is the account of Jacob.

Joseph, a young man of seventeen, was tending the flocks with his brothers, the sons of Bilhah and the sons of Zilpah, his father's wives, and he brought their father a bad report about them. ³Now Israel loved Joseph more than any of his other sons, because he had been born to him in his old age; and he made a richly ornamented*ᵃ* robe for him. ⁴When his brothers saw that their father loved him more than any of them, they hated him and could not speak a kind word to him.

⁵Joseph had a dream, and when he told it to his brothers, they hated him all the more. ⁶He said to them, "Listen to this dream I had: ⁷We were binding sheaves of grain out in the field when suddenly my sheaf rose and stood upright, while your sheaves gathered around mine and bowed down to it."

⁸His brothers said to him, "Do you intend to reign over us? Will you actually rule us?" And they hated him all the more because of his dream and what he had said.

⁹Then he had another dream, and he told it to his brothers. "Listen," he said, "I had another dream, and this time the sun and moon and eleven stars were bowing down to me."

¹⁰When he told his father as well as his brothers, his father rebuked him and said, "What is this dream you had? Will your mother and I and your brothers actually come and bow down to the ground before you?" ¹¹His brothers were jealous of him, but his father kept the matter in mind.

Joseph Sold by His Brothers ¹²Now his brothers had gone to graze their father's flocks near Shechem, ¹³and Israel said to Joseph, "As you know, your brothers are grazing the flocks near Shechem. Come, I am going to send you to them."

"Very well," he replied.

¹⁴So he said to him, "Go and see if all is well with your brothers and with the flocks, and bring word back to me." Then he sent him off from the Valley of Hebron.

When Joseph arrived at Shechem, ¹⁵a man found him wandering around in the fields and asked him, "What are you looking for?"

¹⁶He replied, "I'm looking for my brothers. Can you tell me where they are grazing their flocks?"

¹⁷"They have moved on from here," the man answered. "I heard them say, 'Let's go to Dothan.' "

So Joseph went after his brothers and found them near Dothan. ¹⁸But they saw him in the distance, and before he reached them, they plotted to kill him.

¹⁹"Here comes that dreamer!" they said to each other. ²⁰"Come now, let's kill him and throw him into one of these cisterns and say that a ferocious animal devoured him. Then we'll see what comes of his dreams."

²¹When Reuben heard this, he tried to rescue him from their hands. "Let's not take his life," he said. ²²"Don't shed any blood. Throw him into this cistern here in the desert, but don't lay a hand on him." Reuben said this to rescue him from them and take him back to his father.

²³So when Joseph came to his brothers, they stripped him of his robe—the richly ornamented robe he was wearing— ²⁴and they took him and threw him into the cistern. Now the cistern was empty; there was no water in it.

²⁵As they sat down to eat their meal, they looked up and saw a caravan of

---

ᵃ3 The meaning of the Hebrew for *richly ornamented* is uncertain; also in verses 23 and 32.

Dear Sam,

This will sound conceited, but it's true. I am much better looking and a better student than my sister and my brother. They both hate me. Am I supposed to fail to make them feel better?

Felicia in Fremont

100 Advice Lane, Anywhere, USA

Dear Felicia,

Genesis 37 tells the story of Joseph. He was in a situation similar to yours. He was his father's favorite, and his older brothers hated him so much that they sold him into slavery.

Joseph would probably have been better off if he had toned down his arrogant attitude and kept quiet about his dreams. Do you ever remind your siblings of your beauty and brilliance? Your relationship with them will probably improve if you stop. Take a close look at your attitude. Maybe you never do any outright bragging, but your attitude in ordinary situations can do a lot of harm.

Also, be willing to use your beauty and brilliance to help, not alienate, your brother and sister. Could you teach them a few good study skills? Or show them a new hairdo? Or give some pointers on how to coordinate clothing? Just be sure that when you offer help you do it with love, not with a superior attitude.

You may not be able to completely control what your brother and sister feel toward you. But with these loving attitudes and actions, you'll feel a lot better about them.

Sam

Ishmaelites coming from Gilead. Their camels were loaded with spices, balm and myrrh, and they were on their way to take them down to Egypt.

²⁶Judah said to his brothers, "What will we gain if we kill our brother and cover up his blood? ²⁷Come, let's sell him to the Ishmaelites and not lay our hands on him; after all, he is our brother, our own flesh and blood." His brothers agreed.

²⁸So when the Midianite merchants came by, his brothers pulled Joseph up out of the cistern and sold him for twenty shekels*a* of silver to the Ishmaelites, who took him to Egypt.

²⁹When Reuben returned to the cistern and saw that Joseph was not there, he tore his clothes. ³⁰He went back to his brothers and said, "The boy isn't there! Where can I turn now?"

³¹Then they got Joseph's robe, slaughtered a goat and dipped the robe in the blood. ³²They took the ornamented robe back to their father and said, "We found this. Examine it to see whether it is your son's robe."

³³He recognized it and said, "It is my son's robe! Some ferocious animal has devoured him. Joseph has surely been torn to pieces."

³⁴Then Jacob tore his clothes, put on sackcloth and mourned for his son many days. ³⁵All his sons and daughters came to comfort him, but he refused to be comforted. "No," he said, "in mourning will I go down to the grave*b* to my son." So his father wept for him.

³⁶Meanwhile, the Midianites*c* sold Joseph in Egypt to Potiphar, one of Pharaoh's officials, the captain of the guard.

38 *Judah and Tamar* At that time, Judah left his brothers and went down to stay with a man of Adullam named Hirah. ²There Judah met the daughter of a Canaanite man named Shua. He married her and lay with her; ³she became pregnant and gave birth to a son, who was named Er. ⁴She conceived again and gave birth to a son and named him Onan. ⁵She gave birth to still another son and named him Shelah. It was at Kezib that she gave birth to him.

⁶Judah got a wife for Er, his firstborn, and her name was Tamar. ⁷But Er, Judah's firstborn, was wicked in the Lord's sight; so the Lord put him to death.

⁸Then Judah said to Onan, "Lie with your brother's wife and fulfill your duty to her as a brother-in-law to produce offspring for your brother." ⁹But Onan knew that the offspring would not be his; so whenever he lay with his brother's wife, he spilled his semen on the ground to keep from producing offspring for his brother. ¹⁰What he did was wicked in the Lord's sight; so he put him to death also.

¹¹Judah then said to his daughter-in-law Tamar, "Live as a widow in your father's house until my son Shelah grows up." For he thought, "He may die too, just like his brothers." So Tamar went to live in her father's house.

¹²After a long time Judah's wife, the daughter of Shua, died. When Judah had recovered from his grief, he went up to Timnah, to the men who were shearing his sheep, and his friend Hirah the Adullamite went with him.

¹³When Tamar was told, "Your father-in-law is on his way to Timnah to shear his sheep," ¹⁴she took off her widow's clothes, covered herself with a veil to disguise herself, and then sat down at the entrance to Enaim, which is on the road to Timnah. For she saw that, though Shelah had now grown up, she had not been given to him as his wife.

¹⁵When Judah saw her, he thought she was a prostitute, for she had covered her face. ¹⁶Not realizing that she was his daughter-in-law, he went over to her by the roadside and said, "Come now, let me sleep with you."

a28 That is, about 8 ounces (about 0.2 kilogram) *b35* Hebrew *Sheol* *c36* Samaritan Pentateuch, Septuagint, Vulgate and Syriac (see also verse 28); Masoretic Text *Medanites*

"And what will you give me to sleep with you?" she asked.

[17]"I'll send you a young goat from my flock," he said.

"Will you give me something as a pledge until you send it?" she asked.

[18]He said, "What pledge should I give you?"

"Your seal and its cord, and the staff in your hand," she answered. So he gave them to her and slept with her, and she became pregnant by him. [19]After she left, she took off her veil and put on her widow's clothes again.

[20]Meanwhile Judah sent the young goat by his friend the Adullamite in order to get his pledge back from the woman, but he did not find her. [21]He asked the men who lived there, "Where is the shrine prostitute who was beside the road at Enaim?"

"There hasn't been any shrine prostitute here," they said.

[22]So he went back to Judah and said, "I didn't find her. Besides, the men who lived there said, 'There hasn't been any shrine prostitute here.' "

[23]Then Judah said, "Let her keep what she has, or we will become a laughingstock. After all, I did send her this young goat, but you didn't find her."

[24]About three months later Judah was told, "Your daughter-in-law Tamar is guilty of prostitution, and as a result she is now pregnant."

Judah said, "Bring her out and have her burned to death!"

[25]As she was being brought out, she sent a message to her father-in-law. "I am pregnant by the man who owns these," she said. And she added, "See if you recognize whose seal and cord and staff these are."

[26]Judah recognized them and said, "She is more righteous than I, since I wouldn't give her to my son Shelah." And he did not sleep with her again.

[27]When the time came for her to give birth, there were twin boys in her womb. [28]As she was giving birth, one of them put out his hand; so the midwife took a scarlet thread and tied it on his wrist and said, "This one came out first." [29]But when he drew back his hand, his brother came out, and she said, "So this is how you have broken out!" And he was named Perez.[a] [30]Then his brother, who had the scarlet thread on his wrist, came out and he was given the name Zerah.[b]

39

Joseph and Potiphar's Wife
Now Joseph had been taken down to Egypt. Potiphar, an Egyptian who was one of Pharaoh's officials, the captain of the guard, bought him from the Ishmaelites who had taken him there.

[2]The LORD was with Joseph and he prospered, and he lived in the house of his Egyptian master. [3]When his master saw that the LORD was with him and that the LORD gave him success in everything he did, [4]Joseph found favor in his eyes and became his attendant. Potiphar put him in charge of his household, and he entrusted to his care everything he owned. [5]From the time he put him in charge of his household and of all that he owned, the LORD blessed the household of the Egyptian because of Joseph. The blessing of the LORD was on everything Potiphar had, both in the house and in the field.

GENESIS 39:6–23

Have you ever noticed that our society seems to run on sex? Advertisers sell everything from toothpaste to tires by appealing to society's obsession with things sexual. The story of Joseph can teach you two things about sex. First, the pressure to have sex outside of marriage isn't new. And second, you don't have to give in to the pressure. Joseph didn't. He refused to "do such a wicked thing and sin against God" (Genesis 39:9). That decision cost him a lot: his job and his freedom. But he was brave enough to handle it. Are you?

Direct Line

---

[a]29 *Perez* means *breaking out.*   [b]30 *Zerah* can mean *scarlet* or *brightness.*

⁶So he left in Joseph's care everything he had; with Joseph in charge, he did not concern himself with anything except the food he ate.

Now Joseph was well-built and handsome, ⁷and after a while his master's wife took notice of Joseph and said, "Come to bed with me!"

⁸But he refused. "With me in charge," he told her, "my master does not concern himself with anything in the house; everything he owns he has entrusted to my care. ⁹No one is greater in this house than I am. My master has withheld nothing from me except you, because you are his wife. How then could I do such a wicked thing and sin against God?" ¹⁰And though she spoke to Joseph day after day, he refused to go to bed with her or even be with her.

¹¹One day he went into the house to attend to his duties, and none of the household servants was inside. ¹²She caught him by his cloak and said, "Come to bed with me!" But he left his cloak in her hand and ran out of the house.

¹³When she saw that he had left his cloak in her hand and had run out of the house, ¹⁴she called her household servants. "Look," she said to them, "this Hebrew has been brought to us to make sport of us! He came in here to sleep with me, but I screamed. ¹⁵When he heard me scream for help, he left his cloak beside me and ran out of the house."

¹⁶She kept his cloak beside her until his master came home. ¹⁷Then she told him this story: "That Hebrew slave you brought us came to me to make sport of me. ¹⁸But as soon as I screamed for help, he left his cloak beside me and ran out of the house."

¹⁹When his master heard the story his wife told him, saying, "This is how your slave treated me," he burned with anger. ²⁰Joseph's master took him and put him in prison, the place where the king's prisoners were confined.

But while Joseph was there in the prison, ²¹the LORD was with him; he showed him kindness and granted him favor in the eyes of the prison warden. ²²So the warden put Joseph in charge of all those held in the prison, and he was made responsible for all that was done there. ²³The warden paid no attention to anything under Joseph's care, because the LORD was with Joseph and gave him success in whatever he did.

40 *The Cupbearer and the Baker* Some time later, the cupbearer and the baker of the king of Egypt offended their master, the king of Egypt. ²Pharaoh was angry with his two officials, the chief cupbearer and the chief baker, ³and put them in custody in the house of the captain of the guard, in the same prison where Joseph was confined. ⁴The captain of the guard assigned them to Joseph, and he attended them.

After they had been in custody for some time, ⁵each of the two men—the cupbearer and the baker of the king of Egypt, who were being held in prison—had a dream the same night, and each dream had a meaning of its own.

⁶When Joseph came to them the next morning, he saw that they were dejected. ⁷So he asked Pharaoh's officials who were in custody with him in his master's house, "Why are your faces so sad today?"

⁸"We both had dreams," they answered, "but there is no one to interpret them."

Then Joseph said to them, "Do not interpretations belong to God? Tell me your dreams."

⁹So the chief cupbearer told Joseph his dream. He said to him, "In my dream I saw a vine in front of me, ¹⁰and on the vine were three branches. As soon as it budded, it blossomed, and its clusters ripened into grapes. ¹¹Pharaoh's cup was in my hand, and I took the grapes, squeezed them into Pharaoh's cup and put the cup in his hand."

¹²"This is what it means," Joseph said to him. "The three branches are three days. ¹³Within three days Pharaoh will lift up your head and restore you to your position, and you will put Pharaoh's cup in his hand, just as you used to do when you were his cupbearer. ¹⁴But when all goes well with you, re-

member me and show me kindness; mention me to Pharaoh and get me out of this prison. ¹⁵For I was forcibly carried off from the land of the Hebrews, and even here I have done nothing to deserve being put in a dungeon."

¹⁶When the chief baker saw that Joseph had given a favorable interpretation, he said to Joseph, "I too had a dream: On my head were three baskets of bread.*ᵃ* ¹⁷In the top basket were all kinds of baked goods for Pharaoh, but the birds were eating them out of the basket on my head."

¹⁸"This is what it means," Joseph said. "The three baskets are three days. ¹⁹Within three days Pharaoh will lift off your head and hang you on a tree.*ᵇ* And the birds will eat away your flesh."

²⁰Now the third day was Pharaoh's birthday, and he gave a feast for all his officials. He lifted up the heads of the chief cupbearer and the chief baker in the presence of his officials: ²¹He restored the chief cupbearer to his position, so that he once again put the cup into Pharaoh's hand, ²²but he hanged*ᶜ* the chief baker, just as Joseph had said to them in his interpretation.

²³The chief cupbearer, however, did not remember Joseph; he forgot him.

41 **_Pharaoh's Dreams_** When two full years had passed, Pharaoh had a dream: He was standing by the Nile, ²when out of the river there came up seven cows, sleek and fat, and they grazed among the reeds. ³After them, seven other cows, ugly and gaunt, came up out of the Nile and stood beside those on the riverbank. ⁴And the cows that were ugly and gaunt ate up the seven sleek, fat cows. Then Pharaoh woke up.

⁵He fell asleep again and had a second dream: Seven heads of grain, healthy and good, were growing on a single stalk. ⁶After them, seven other heads of grain sprouted—thin and scorched by the east wind. ⁷The thin heads of grain swallowed up the seven healthy, full heads. Then Pharaoh woke up; it had been a dream.

⁸In the morning his mind was troubled, so he sent for all the magicians and wise men of Egypt. Pharaoh told them his dreams, but no one could interpret them for him.

⁹Then the chief cupbearer said to Pharaoh, "Today I am reminded of my shortcomings. ¹⁰Pharaoh was once angry with his servants, and he imprisoned me and the chief baker in the house of the captain of the guard. ¹¹Each of us had a dream the same night, and each dream had a meaning of its own. ¹²Now a young Hebrew was there with us, a servant of the captain of the guard. We told him our dreams, and he interpreted them for us, giving each man the interpretation of his dream. ¹³And things turned out exactly as he interpreted them to us: I was restored to my position, and the other man was hanged.*ᶜ*"

¹⁴So Pharaoh sent for Joseph, and he was quickly brought from the dungeon. When he had shaved and changed his clothes, he came before Pharaoh.

¹⁵Pharaoh said to Joseph, "I had a dream, and no one can interpret it. But I have heard it said of you that when you hear a dream you can interpret it."

¹⁶"I cannot do it," Joseph replied to Pharaoh, "but God will give Pharaoh the answer he desires."

¹⁷Then Pharaoh said to Joseph, "In my dream I was standing on the bank of the Nile, ¹⁸when out of the river there came up seven cows, fat and sleek, and they grazed among the reeds. ¹⁹After them, seven other cows came up—scrawny and very ugly and lean. I had never seen such ugly cows in all the land of Egypt. ²⁰The lean, ugly cows ate up the seven fat cows that came up first. ²¹But even after they ate them, no one could tell that they had done so; they looked just as ugly as before. Then I woke up.

²²"In my dreams I also saw seven heads of grain, full and good, growing on a single stalk. ²³After them, seven other heads sprouted—withered and thin

---

ᵃ16 Or three wicker baskets ᵇ19 Or and impale you on a pole ᶜ22 Or impaled and scorched by the east wind. ²⁴The thin heads of grain swallowed up the seven good heads. I told this to the magicians, but none could explain it to me."

²⁵Then Joseph said to Pharaoh, "The dreams of Pharaoh are one and the same. God has revealed to Pharaoh what he is about to do. ²⁶The seven good cows are seven years, and the seven good heads of grain are seven years; it is one and the same dream. ²⁷The seven lean, ugly cows that came up afterward are seven years, and so are the seven worthless heads of grain scorched by the east wind: They are seven years of famine.

²⁸"It is just as I said to Pharaoh: God has shown Pharaoh what he is about to do. ²⁹Seven years of great abundance are coming throughout the land of Egypt, ³⁰but seven years of famine will follow them. Then all the abundance in Egypt will be forgotten, and the famine will ravage the land. ³¹The abundance in the land will not be remembered, because the famine that follows it will be so severe. ³²The reason the dream was given to Pharaoh in two forms is that the matter has been firmly decided by God, and God will do it soon.

³³"And now let Pharaoh look for a discerning and wise man and put him in charge of the land of Egypt. ³⁴Let Pharaoh appoint commissioners over the land to take a fifth of the harvest of Egypt during the seven years of abundance. ³⁵They should collect all the food of these good years that are coming and store up the grain under the authority of Pharaoh, to be kept in the cities for food. ³⁶This food should be held in reserve for the country, to be used during the seven years of famine that will come upon Egypt, so that the country may not be ruined by the famine."

³⁷The plan seemed good to Pharaoh and to all his officials. ³⁸So Pharaoh asked them, "Can we find anyone like this man, one in whom is the spirit of God*ᵃ*?"

³⁹Then Pharaoh said to Joseph, "Since God has made all this known to you, there is no one so discerning and wise as you. ⁴⁰You shall be in charge of my palace, and all my people are to submit to your orders. Only with respect to the throne will I be greater than you."

Joseph in Charge of Egypt ⁴¹So Pharaoh said to Joseph, "I hereby put you in charge of the whole land of Egypt." ⁴²Then Pharaoh took his signet ring from his finger and put it on Joseph's finger. He dressed him in robes of fine linen and put a gold chain around his neck. ⁴³He had him ride in a chariot as his second-in-command,*ᵇ* and men shouted before him, "Make way*ᶜ*!" Thus he put him in charge of the whole land of Egypt.

⁴⁴Then Pharaoh said to Joseph, "I am Pharaoh, but without your word no one will lift hand or foot in all Egypt." ⁴⁵Pharaoh gave Joseph the name Zaphenath-Paneah and gave him Asenath daughter of Potiphera, priest of On,*ᵈ* to be his wife. And Joseph went throughout the land of Egypt.

⁴⁶Joseph was thirty years old when he entered the service of Pharaoh king of Egypt. And Joseph went out from Pharaoh's presence and traveled through-

GENESIS 41:46

School bores you to death? Mom and Dad treat you like a child? Your friends are driving cars, and you're stuck with a bike? Life is passing you by, and you're stuck forever in the slow lane? Joseph probably felt the same way. He was sold into slavery as a young teen and jailed unfairly in his early twenties. Life was passing him by too, but he stuck it out and did his best. Genesis 41:46 says that at age 30 "he entered the service of Pharaoh king of Egypt" to become that country's second most powerful man. Age 30 may seem like forever, but doing your best in little things is the way God prepares you for great things.

Direct Line

ᵃ38 Or of the gods ᵇ43 Or in the chariot of his second-in-command; or in his second chariot ᶜ43 Or Bow down
ᵈ45 That is, Heliopolis; also in verse 50

out Egypt. ⁴⁷During the seven years of abundance the land produced plentifully. ⁴⁸Joseph collected all the food produced in those seven years of abundance in Egypt and stored it in the cities. In each city he put the food grown in the fields surrounding it. ⁴⁹Joseph stored up huge quantities of grain, like the sand of the sea; it was so much that he stopped keeping records because it was beyond measure.

⁵⁰Before the years of famine came, two sons were born to Joseph by Asenath daughter of Potiphera, priest of On. ⁵¹Joseph named his firstborn Manasseh*a* and said, "It is because God has made me forget all my trouble and all my father's household." ⁵²The second son he named Ephraim*b* and said, "It is because God has made me fruitful in the land of my suffering."

⁵³The seven years of abundance in Egypt came to an end, ⁵⁴and the seven years of famine began, just as Joseph had said. There was famine in all the other lands, but in the whole land of Egypt there was food. ⁵⁵When all Egypt began to feel the famine, the people cried to Pharaoh for food. Then Pharaoh told all the Egyptians, "Go to Joseph and do what he tells you."

⁵⁶When the famine had spread over the whole country, Joseph opened the storehouses and sold grain to the Egyptians, for the famine was severe throughout Egypt. ⁵⁷And all the countries came to Egypt to buy grain from Joseph, because the famine was severe in all the world.

Joseph's Brothers Go to Egypt   When Jacob learned that there was grain in Egypt, he said to his sons, "Why do you just keep looking at each other?" ²He continued, "I have heard that there is grain in Egypt. Go down there and buy some for us, so that we may live and not die."

³Then ten of Joseph's brothers went down to buy grain from Egypt. ⁴But Jacob did not send Benjamin, Joseph's brother, with the others, because he was afraid that harm might come to him. ⁵So Israel's sons were among those who went to buy grain, for the famine was in the land of Canaan also.

⁶Now Joseph was the governor of the land, the one who sold grain to all its people. So when Joseph's brothers arrived, they bowed down to him with their faces to the ground. ⁷As soon as Joseph saw his brothers, he recognized them, but he pretended to be a stranger and spoke harshly to them. "Where do you come from?" he asked.

"From the land of Canaan," they replied, "to buy food."

⁸Although Joseph recognized his brothers, they did not recognize him. ⁹Then he remembered his dreams about them and said to them, "You are spies! You have come to see where our land is unprotected."

¹⁰"No, my lord," they answered. "Your servants have come to buy food. ¹¹We are all the sons of one man. Your servants are honest men, not spies."

¹²"No!" he said to them. "You have come to see where our land is unprotected."

¹³But they replied, "Your servants were twelve brothers, the sons of one man, who lives in the land of Canaan. The youngest is now with our father, and one is no more."

¹⁴Joseph said to them, "It is just as I told you: You are spies! ¹⁵And this is how you will be tested: As surely as Pharaoh lives, you will not leave this place unless your youngest brother comes here. ¹⁶Send one of your number to get your brother; the rest of you will be kept in prison, so that your words may be tested to see if you are telling the truth. If you are not, then as surely as Pharaoh lives, you are spies!" ¹⁷And he put them all in custody for three days.

¹⁸On the third day, Joseph said to them, "Do this and you will live, for I fear God: ¹⁹If you are honest men, let one of your brothers stay here in prison,

---

a51 Manasseh sounds like and may be derived from the Hebrew for *forget.*   *b52 Ephraim* sounds like the Hebrew for *twice fruitful.*

while the rest of you go and take grain back for your starving households. ²⁰But you must bring your youngest brother to me, so that your words may be verified and that you may not die." This they proceeded to do.

²¹They said to one another, "Surely we are being punished because of our brother. We saw how distressed he was when he pleaded with us for his life, but we would not listen; that's why this distress has come upon us."

²²Reuben replied, "Didn't I tell you not to sin against the boy? But you wouldn't listen! Now we must give an accounting for his blood." ²³They did not realize that Joseph could understand them, since he was using an interpreter.

²⁴He turned away from them and began to weep, but then turned back and spoke to them again. He had Simeon taken from them and bound before their eyes.

²⁵Joseph gave orders to fill their bags with grain, to put each man's silver back in his sack, and to give them provisions for their journey. After this was done for them, ²⁶they loaded their grain on their donkeys and left.

²⁷At the place where they stopped for the night one of them opened his sack to get feed for his donkey, and he saw his silver in the mouth of his sack. ²⁸"My silver has been returned," he said to his brothers. "Here it is in my sack."

Their hearts sank and they turned to each other trembling and said, "What is this that God has done to us?"

²⁹When they came to their father Jacob in the land of Canaan, they told him all that had happened to them. They said, ³⁰"The man who is lord over the land spoke harshly to us and treated us as though we were spying on the land. ³¹But we said to him, 'We are honest men; we are not spies. ³²We were twelve brothers, sons of one father. One is no more, and the youngest is now with our father in Canaan.'

³³"Then the man who is lord over the land said to us, 'This is how I will know whether you are honest men: Leave one of your brothers here with me, and take food for your starving households and go. ³⁴But bring your youngest brother to me so I will know that you are not spies but honest men. Then I will give your brother back to you, and you can trade*a* in the land.' "

³⁵As they were emptying their sacks, there in each man's sack was his pouch of silver! When they and their father saw the money pouches, they were frightened. ³⁶Their father Jacob said to them, "You have deprived me of my children. Joseph is no more and Simeon is no more, and now you want to take Benjamin. Everything is against me!"

³⁷Then Reuben said to his father, "You may put both of my sons to death if I do not bring him back to you. Entrust him to my care, and I will bring him back."

³⁸But Jacob said, "My son will not go down there with you; his brother is dead and he is the only one left. If harm comes to him on the journey you are taking, you will bring my gray head down to the grave*b* in sorrow."

43 *The Second Journey to Egypt* Now the famine was still severe in the land. ²So when they had eaten all the grain they had brought from Egypt, their father said to them, "Go back and buy us a little more food."

³But Judah said to him, "The man warned us solemnly, 'You will not see my face again unless your brother is with you.' ⁴If you will send our brother along with us, we will go down and buy food for you. ⁵But if you will not send him, we will not go down, because the man said to us, 'You will not see my face again unless your brother is with you.' "

---

a34 Or move about freely   *b38 Hebrew Sheol*

⁶Israel asked, "Why did you bring this trouble on me by telling the man you had another brother?"

⁷They replied, "The man questioned us closely about ourselves and our family. 'Is your father still living?' he asked us. 'Do you have another brother?' We simply answered his questions. How were we to know he would say, 'Bring your brother down here'?"

⁸Then Judah said to Israel his father, "Send the boy along with me and we will go at once, so that we and you and our children may live and not die. ⁹I myself will guarantee his safety; you can hold me personally responsible for him. If I do not bring him back to you and set him here before you, I will bear the blame before you all my life. ¹⁰As it is, if we had not delayed, we could have gone and returned twice."

¹¹Then their father Israel said to them, "If it must be, then do this: Put some of the best products of the land in your bags and take them down to the man as a gift—a little balm and a little honey, some spices and myrrh, some pistachio nuts and almonds. ¹²Take double the amount of silver with you, for you must return the silver that was put back into the mouths of your sacks. Perhaps it was a mistake. ¹³Take your brother also and go back to the man at once. ¹⁴And may God Almighty*a* grant you mercy before the man so that he will let your other brother and Benjamin come back with you. As for me, if I am bereaved, I am bereaved."

¹⁵So the men took the gifts and double the amount of silver, and Benjamin also. They hurried down to Egypt and presented themselves to Joseph. ¹⁶When Joseph saw Benjamin with them, he said to the steward of his house, "Take these men to my house, slaughter an animal and prepare dinner; they are to eat with me at noon."

¹⁷The man did as Joseph told him and took the men to Joseph's house. ¹⁸Now the men were frightened when they were taken to his house. They thought, "We were brought here because of the silver that was put back into our sacks the first time. He wants to attack us and overpower us and seize us as slaves and take our donkeys."

¹⁹So they went up to Joseph's steward and spoke to him at the entrance to the house. ²⁰"Please, sir," they said, "we came down here the first time to buy food. ²¹But at the place where we stopped for the night we opened our sacks and each of us found his silver—the exact weight—in the mouth of his sack. So we have brought it back with us. ²²We have also brought additional silver with us to buy food. We don't know who put our silver in our sacks."

²³"It's all right," he said. "Don't be afraid. Your God, the God of your father, has given you treasure in your sacks; I received your silver." Then he brought Simeon out to them.

²⁴The steward took the men into Joseph's house, gave them water to wash their feet and provided fodder for their donkeys. ²⁵They prepared their gifts for Joseph's arrival at noon, because they had heard that they were to eat there.

²⁶When Joseph came home, they presented to him the gifts they had brought into the house, and they bowed down before him to the ground. ²⁷He asked them how they were, and then he said, "How is your aged father you told me about? Is he still living?"

²⁸They replied, "Your servant our father is still alive and well." And they bowed low to pay him honor.

²⁹As he looked about and saw his brother Benjamin, his own mother's son, he asked, "Is this your youngest brother, the one you told me about?" And he said, "God be gracious to you, my son." ³⁰Deeply moved at the sight of his

---

a14 Hebrew *El-Shaddai*

brother, Joseph hurried out and looked for a place to weep. He went into his private room and wept there.

³¹After he had washed his face, he came out and, controlling himself, said, "Serve the food."

³²They served him by himself, the brothers by themselves, and the Egyptians who ate with him by themselves, because Egyptians could not eat with Hebrews, for that is detestable to Egyptians. ³³The men had been seated before him in the order of their ages, from the firstborn to the youngest; and they looked at each other in astonishment. ³⁴When portions were served to them from Joseph's table, Benjamin's portion was five times as much as anyone else's. So they feasted and drank freely with him.

44 *A Silver Cup in a Sack* Now Joseph gave these instructions to the steward of his house: "Fill the men's sacks with as much food as they can carry, and put each man's silver in the mouth of his sack. ²Then put my cup, the silver one, in the mouth of the youngest one's sack, along with the silver for his grain." And he did as Joseph said.

³As morning dawned, the men were sent on their way with their donkeys. ⁴They had not gone far from the city when Joseph said to his steward, "Go after those men at once, and when you catch up with them, say to them, 'Why have you repaid good with evil? ⁵Isn't this the cup my master drinks from and also uses for divination? This is a wicked thing you have done.' "

⁶When he caught up with them, he repeated these words to them. ⁷But they said to him, "Why does my lord say such things? Far be it from your servants to do anything like that! ⁸We even brought back to you from the land of Canaan the silver we found inside the mouths of our sacks. So why would we steal silver or gold from your master's house? ⁹If any of your servants is found to have it, he will die; and the rest of us will become my lord's slaves."

¹⁰"Very well, then," he said, "let it be as you say. Whoever is found to have it will become my slave; the rest of you will be free from blame."

¹¹Each of them quickly lowered his sack to the ground and opened it. ¹²Then the steward proceeded to search, beginning with the oldest and ending with the youngest. And the cup was found in Benjamin's sack. ¹³At this, they tore their clothes. Then they all loaded their donkeys and returned to the city.

¹⁴Joseph was still in the house when Judah and his brothers came in, and they threw themselves to the ground before him. ¹⁵Joseph said to them, "What is this you have done? Don't you know that a man like me can find things out by divination?"

¹⁶"What can we say to my lord?" Judah replied. "What can we say? How can we prove our innocence? God has uncovered your servants' guilt. We are now my lord's slaves—we ourselves and the one who was found to have the cup."

¹⁷But Joseph said, "Far be it from me to do such a thing! Only the man who was found to have the cup will become my slave. The rest of you, go back to your father in peace."

¹⁸Then Judah went up to him and said: "Please, my lord, let your servant speak a word to my lord. Do not be angry with your servant, though you are equal to Pharaoh himself. ¹⁹My lord asked his servants, 'Do you have a father or a brother?' ²⁰And we answered, 'We have an aged father, and there is a young son born to him in his old age. His brother is dead, and he is the only one of his mother's sons left, and his father loves him.'

²¹"Then you said to your servants, 'Bring him down to me so I can see him for myself.' ²²And we said to my lord, 'The boy cannot leave his father; if he leaves him, his father will die.' ²³But you told your servants, 'Unless your youngest brother comes down with you, you will not see my face again.' ²⁴When we went back to your servant my father, we told him what my lord had said.

²⁵"Then our father said, 'Go back and buy a little more food.' ²⁶But we said, 'We cannot go down. Only if our youngest brother is with us will we go. We cannot see the man's face unless our youngest brother is with us.'

²⁷"Your servant my father said to us, 'You know that my wife bore me two sons. ²⁸One of them went away from me, and I said, "He has surely been torn to pieces." And I have not seen him since. ²⁹If you take this one from me too and harm comes to him, you will bring my gray head down to the grave*ᵃ* in misery.'

³⁰"So now, if the boy is not with us when I go back to your servant my father and if my father, whose life is closely bound up with the boy's life, ³¹sees that the boy isn't there, he will die. Your servants will bring the gray head of our father down to the grave in sorrow. ³²Your servant guaranteed the boy's safety to my father. I said, 'If I do not bring him back to you, I will bear the blame before you, my father, all my life!'

³³"Now then, please let your servant remain here as my lord's slave in place of the boy, and let the boy return with his brothers. ³⁴How can I go back to my father if the boy is not with me? No! Do not let me see the misery that would come upon my father."

45 *Joseph Makes Himself Known* Then Joseph could no longer control himself before all his attendants, and he cried out, "Have everyone leave my presence!" So there was no one with Joseph when he made himself known to his brothers. ²And he wept so loudly that the Egyptians heard him, and Pharaoh's household heard about it.

³Joseph said to his brothers, "I am Joseph! Is my father still living?" But his brothers were not able to answer him, because they were terrified at his presence.

⁴Then Joseph said to his brothers, "Come close to me." When they had done so, he said, "I am your brother Joseph, the one you sold into Egypt! ⁵And now, do not be distressed and do not be angry with yourselves for selling me here, because it was to save lives that God sent me ahead of you. ⁶For two years now there has been famine in the land, and for the next five years there will not be plowing and reaping. ⁷But God sent me ahead of you to preserve for you a remnant on earth and to save your lives by a great deliverance.*ᵇ*

⁸"So then, it was not you who sent me here, but God. He made me father to Pharaoh, lord of his entire household and ruler of all Egypt. ⁹Now hurry back to my father and say to him, 'This is what your son Joseph says: God has made me lord of all Egypt. Come down to me; don't delay. ¹⁰You shall live in the region of Goshen and be near me—you, your children and grandchildren, your flocks and herds, and all you have. ¹¹I will provide for you there, because five years of famine are still to come. Otherwise you and your household and all who belong to you will become destitute.'

¹²"You can see for yourselves, and so can my brother Benjamin, that it is really

GENESIS 44:27–34

Participants at one church camp asked these questions about their brothers and sisters: "Why are they so mean?" "How can we keep from fighting?" Joseph knew all about that. His brothers sold him into slavery, and in all the years that followed, the brothers never tried to find Joseph or help him. But this chapter reminds you of something important: people can change. Years later in Egypt the very brother who suggested Joseph be sold as a slave was willing to give up his own freedom to protect his youngest brother. So don't give up. There really is hope for your siblings. And for you!

Direct Line

---

*ᵃ*29 Hebrew *Sheol*; also in verse 31 *ᵇ*7 Or *save you as a great band of survivors*

I who am speaking to you. ¹³Tell my father about all the honor accorded me in Egypt and about everything you have seen. And bring my father down here quickly."

¹⁴Then he threw his arms around his brother Benjamin and wept, and Benjamin embraced him, weeping. ¹⁵And he kissed all his brothers and wept over them. Afterward his brothers talked with him.

¹⁶When the news reached Pharaoh's palace that Joseph's brothers had come, Pharaoh and all his officials were pleased. ¹⁷Pharaoh said to Joseph, "Tell your brothers, 'Do this: Load your animals and return to the land of Canaan, ¹⁸and bring your father and your families back to me. I will give you the best of the land of Egypt and you can enjoy the fat of the land.'

¹⁹"You are also directed to tell them, 'Do this: Take some carts from Egypt for your children and your wives, and get your father and come. ²⁰Never mind about your belongings, because the best of all Egypt will be yours.' "

²¹So the sons of Israel did this. Joseph gave them carts, as Pharaoh had commanded, and he also gave them provisions for their journey. ²²To each of them he gave new clothing, but to Benjamin he gave three hundred shekels*ᵃ* of silver and five sets of clothes. ²³And this is what he sent to his father: ten donkeys loaded with the best things of Egypt, and ten female donkeys loaded with grain and bread and other provisions for his journey. ²⁴Then he sent his brothers away, and as they were leaving he said to them, "Don't quarrel on the way!"

²⁵So they went up out of Egypt and came to their father Jacob in the land of Canaan. ²⁶They told him, "Joseph is still alive! In fact, he is ruler of all Egypt." Jacob was stunned; he did not believe them. ²⁷But when they told him everything Joseph had said to them, and when he saw the carts Joseph had sent to carry him back, the spirit of their father Jacob revived. ²⁸And Israel said, "I'm convinced! My son Joseph is still alive. I will go and see him before I die."

46 **Jacob Goes to Egypt** So Israel set out with all that was his, and when he reached Beersheba, he offered sacrifices to the God of his father Isaac.

²And God spoke to Israel in a vision at night and said, "Jacob! Jacob!"

"Here I am," he replied.

³"I am God, the God of your father," he said. "Do not be afraid to go down to Egypt, for I will make you into a great nation there. ⁴I will go down to Egypt with you, and I will surely bring you back again. And Joseph's own hand will close your eyes."

⁵Then Jacob left Beersheba, and Israel's sons took their father Jacob and their children and their wives in the carts that Pharaoh had sent to transport him. ⁶They also took with them their livestock and the possessions they had acquired in Canaan, and Jacob and all his offspring went to Egypt. ⁷He took with him to Egypt

ᵃ22 That is, about 7 1/2 pounds (about 3.5 kilograms)

GENESIS 45:1–20

"**S**he ate my whole box of candy. So I'm taking her CD!" It's not that you want the CD. It's just that you're angry and you want revenge. After all, she did you wrong. You have a right to be upset. If anyone had a right to hold a grudge, it was Joseph. His own brothers sold him into slavery. Years later, when his brothers were starving, Joseph ruled Egypt, the only country that had food. What a chance to get revenge! But Joseph chose a better way. He threw his arms around his brothers and promised them the best of Egypt. When someone hurts you, try reacting like Joseph. Don't get even. Do good to them instead.

Direct Line

his sons and grandsons and his daughters and granddaughters—all his offspring.

[8]These are the names of the sons of Israel (Jacob and his descendants) who went to Egypt:

Reuben the firstborn of Jacob.
[9]The sons of Reuben:
Hanoch, Pallu, Hezron and Carmi.
[10]The sons of Simeon:
Jemuel, Jamin, Ohad, Jakin, Zohar and Shaul the son of a Canaanite woman.
[11]The sons of Levi:
Gershon, Kohath and Merari.
[12]The sons of Judah:
Er, Onan, Shelah, Perez and Zerah (but Er and Onan had died in the land of Canaan).
The sons of Perez:
Hezron and Hamul.
[13]The sons of Issachar:
Tola, Puah,[a] Jashub[b] and Shimron.
[14]The sons of Zebulun:
Sered, Elon and Jahleel.

[15]These were the sons Leah bore to Jacob in Paddan Aram,[c] besides his daughter Dinah. These sons and daughters of his were thirty-three in all.

[16]The sons of Gad:
Zephon,[d] Haggi, Shuni, Ezbon, Eri, Arodi and Areli.
[17]The sons of Asher:
Imnah, Ishvah, Ishvi and Beriah.
Their sister was Serah.
The sons of Beriah:
Heber and Malkiel.

[18]These were the children born to Jacob by Zilpah, whom Laban had given to his daughter Leah—sixteen in all.

[19]The sons of Jacob's wife Rachel:
Joseph and Benjamin. [20]In Egypt, Manasseh and Ephraim were born to Joseph by Asenath daughter of Potiphera, priest of On.[e]
[21]The sons of Benjamin:
Bela, Beker, Ashbel, Gera, Naaman, Ehi, Rosh, Muppim, Huppim and Ard.

[22]These were the sons of Rachel who were born to Jacob—fourteen in all.

[23]The son of Dan:
Hushim.
[24]The sons of Naphtali:
Jahziel, Guni, Jezer and Shillem.

[25]These were the sons born to Jacob by Bilhah, whom Laban had given to his daughter Rachel—seven in all.

[26]All those who went to Egypt with Jacob—those who were his direct descendants, not counting his sons' wives—numbered sixty-six persons. [27]With the two sons[f] who had been born to Joseph in Egypt, the members of Jacob's family, which went to Egypt, were seventy[g] in all.

---

[a]13 Samaritan Pentateuch and Syriac (see also 1 Chron. 7:1); Masoretic Text *Puvah*   [b]13 Samaritan Pentateuch and some Septuagint manuscripts (see also Num. 26:24 and 1 Chron. 7:1); Masoretic Text *Iob*   [c]15 That is, Northwest Mesopotamia   [d]16 Samaritan Pentateuch and Septuagint (see also Num. 26:15); Masoretic Text *Ziphion*   [e]20 That is, Heliopolis   [f]27 Hebrew; Septuagint *the nine children*   [g]27 Hebrew (see also Exodus 1:5 and footnote); Septuagint (see also Acts 7:14) *seventy-five*

²⁸Now Jacob sent Judah ahead of him to Joseph to get directions to Goshen. When they arrived in the region of Goshen, ²⁹Joseph had his chariot made ready and went to Goshen to meet his father Israel. As soon as Joseph appeared before him, he threw his arms around his father[a] and wept for a long time.

³⁰Israel said to Joseph, "Now I am ready to die, since I have seen for myself that you are still alive."

³¹Then Joseph said to his brothers and to his father's household, "I will go up and speak to Pharaoh and will say to him, 'My brothers and my father's household, who were living in the land of Canaan, have come to me. ³²The men are shepherds; they tend livestock, and they have brought along their flocks and herds and everything they own.' ³³When Pharaoh calls you in and asks, 'What is your occupation?' ³⁴you should answer, 'Your servants have tended livestock from our boyhood on, just as our fathers did.' Then you will be allowed to settle in the region of Goshen, for all shepherds are detestable to the Egyptians."

47 Joseph went and told Pharaoh, "My father and brothers, with their flocks and herds and everything they own, have come from the land of Canaan and are now in Goshen." ²He chose five of his brothers and presented them before Pharaoh.

³Pharaoh asked the brothers, "What is your occupation?"

"Your servants are shepherds," they replied to Pharaoh, "just as our fathers were." ⁴They also said to him, "We have come to live here awhile, because the famine is severe in Canaan and your servants' flocks have no pasture. So now, please let your servants settle in Goshen."

⁵Pharaoh said to Joseph, "Your father and your brothers have come to you, ⁶and the land of Egypt is before you; settle your father and your brothers in the best part of the land. Let them live in Goshen. And if you know of any among them with special ability, put them in charge of my own livestock."

⁷Then Joseph brought his father Jacob in and presented him before Pharaoh. After Jacob blessed[b] Pharaoh, ⁸Pharaoh asked him, "How old are you?"

⁹And Jacob said to Pharaoh, "The years of my pilgrimage are a hundred and thirty. My years have been few and difficult, and they do not equal the years of the pilgrimage of my fathers." ¹⁰Then Jacob blessed[c] Pharaoh and went out from his presence.

¹¹So Joseph settled his father and his brothers in Egypt and gave them property in the best part of the land, the district of Rameses, as Pharaoh directed. ¹²Joseph also provided his father and his brothers and all his father's household with food, according to the number of their children.

Joseph and the Famine ¹³There was no food, however, in the whole region because the famine was severe; both Egypt and Canaan wasted away because of the famine. ¹⁴Joseph collected all the money that was to be found in Egypt and Canaan in payment for the grain they were buying, and he brought it to Pharaoh's palace. ¹⁵When the money of the people of Egypt and Canaan was gone, all Egypt came to Joseph and said, "Give us food. Why should we die before your eyes? Our money is used up."

¹⁶"Then bring your livestock," said Joseph. "I will sell you food in exchange for your livestock, since your money is gone." ¹⁷So they brought their livestock to Joseph, and he gave them food in exchange for their horses, their sheep and goats, their cattle and donkeys. And he brought them through that year with food in exchange for all their livestock.

¹⁸When that year was over, they came to him the following year and said,

[a]29 Hebrew around him [b]7 Or greeted [c]10 Or said farewell to

"We cannot hide from our lord the fact that since our money is gone and our livestock belongs to you, there is nothing left for our lord except our bodies and our land. ¹⁹Why should we perish before your eyes—we and our land as well? Buy us and our land in exchange for food, and we with our land will be in bondage to Pharaoh. Give us seed so that we may live and not die, and that the land may not become desolate."

²⁰So Joseph bought all the land in Egypt for Pharaoh. The Egyptians, one and all, sold their fields, because the famine was too severe for them. The land became Pharaoh's, ²¹and Joseph reduced the people to servitude,ᵃ from one end of Egypt to the other. ²²However, he did not buy the land of the priests, because they received a regular allotment from Pharaoh and had food enough from the allotment Pharaoh gave them. That is why they did not sell their land.

²³Joseph said to the people, "Now that I have bought you and your land today for Pharaoh, here is seed for you so you can plant the ground. ²⁴But when the crop comes in, give a fifth of it to Pharaoh. The other four-fifths you may keep as seed for the fields and as food for yourselves and your households and your children."

²⁵"You have saved our lives," they said. "May we find favor in the eyes of our lord; we will be in bondage to Pharaoh."

²⁶So Joseph established it as a law concerning land in Egypt—still in force today—that a fifth of the produce belongs to Pharaoh. It was only the land of the priests that did not become Pharaoh's.

²⁷Now the Israelites settled in Egypt in the region of Goshen. They acquired property there and were fruitful and increased greatly in number.

²⁸Jacob lived in Egypt seventeen years, and the years of his life were a hundred and forty-seven. ²⁹When the time drew near for Israel to die, he called for his son Joseph and said to him, "If I have found favor in your eyes, put your hand under my thigh and promise that you will show me kindness and faithfulness. Do not bury me in Egypt, ³⁰but when I rest with my fathers, carry me out of Egypt and bury me where they are buried."

"I will do as you say," he said.

³¹"Swear to me," he said. Then Joseph swore to him, and Israel worshiped as he leaned on the top of his staff.ᵇ

48 *Manasseh and Ephraim* Some time later Joseph was told, "Your father is ill." So he took his two sons Manasseh and Ephraim along with him. ²When Jacob was told, "Your son Joseph has come to you," Israel rallied his strength and sat up on the bed.

³Jacob said to Joseph, "God Almightyᶜ appeared to me at Luz in the land of Canaan, and there he blessed me ⁴and said to me, 'I am going to make you fruitful and will increase your numbers. I will make you a community of peoples, and I will give this land as an everlasting possession to your descendants after you.'

⁵"Now then, your two sons born to you in Egypt before I came to you here will be reckoned as mine; Ephraim and Manasseh will be mine, just as Reuben and Simeon are mine. ⁶Any children born to you after them will be yours; in the territory they inherit they will be reckoned under the names of their brothers. ⁷As I was returning from Paddan,ᵈ to my sorrow Rachel died in the land of Canaan while we were still on the way, a little distance from Ephrath. So I buried her there beside the road to Ephrath" (that is, Bethlehem).

⁸When Israel saw the sons of Joseph, he asked, "Who are these?"

⁹"They are the sons God has given me here," Joseph said to his father.

ᵃ*21* Samaritan Pentateuch and Septuagint (see also Vulgate); Masoretic Text *and he moved the people into the cities* ᵇ*31* Or *Israel bowed down at the head of his bed* ᶜ*3* Hebrew *El-Shaddai* ᵈ*7* That is, Northwest Mesopotamia

Then Israel said, "Bring them to me so I may bless them."

¹⁰Now Israel's eyes were failing because of old age, and he could hardly see. So Joseph brought his sons close to him, and his father kissed them and embraced them.

¹¹Israel said to Joseph, "I never expected to see your face again, and now God has allowed me to see your children too."

¹²Then Joseph removed them from Israel's knees and bowed down with his face to the ground. ¹³And Joseph took both of them, Ephraim on his right toward Israel's left hand and Manasseh on his left toward Israel's right hand, and brought them close to him. ¹⁴But Israel reached out his right hand and put it on Ephraim's head, though he was the younger, and crossing his arms, he put his left hand on Manasseh's head, even though Manasseh was the firstborn.

¹⁵Then he blessed Joseph and said,

"May the God before whom my fathers
    Abraham and Isaac walked,
the God who has been my shepherd
    all my life to this day,
¹⁶the Angel who has delivered me from all harm
    —may he bless these boys.
May they be called by my name
    and the names of my fathers Abraham and Isaac,
and may they increase greatly
    upon the earth."

¹⁷When Joseph saw his father placing his right hand on Ephraim's head he was displeased; so he took hold of his father's hand to move it from Ephraim's head to Manasseh's head. ¹⁸Joseph said to him, "No, my father, this one is the firstborn; put your right hand on his head."

¹⁹But his father refused and said, "I know, my son, I know. He too will become a people, and he too will become great. Nevertheless, his younger brother will be greater than he, and his descendants will become a group of nations." ²⁰He blessed them that day and said,

"In your*a* name will Israel
        pronounce this blessing:
    'May God make you like
            Ephraim and Manasseh.' "

So he put Ephraim ahead of Manasseh.

²¹Then Israel said to Joseph, "I am about to die, but God will be with you*b* and take you*b* back to the land of your*b* fathers. ²²And to you, as one who is over your brothers, I give the ridge of land*c* I took from the Amorites with my sword and my bow."

49 *Jacob Blesses His Sons* Then Jacob called for his sons and said: "Gather around so I can tell you what will happen to you in days to come.

---

*a20 The Hebrew is singular. b21 The Hebrew is plural.
c22 Or And to you I give one portion more than to your brothers—the portion*

GENESIS 48:21

Losing a parent hurts. You just didn't expect your mom or dad to die. And it's not just the feeling of emptiness and loss. You suddenly discover that your mom or dad did more around the house than you imagined. Now you have to take on some of those jobs. And you wonder: *Who's going to take care of me? Who's going to help me get through college?* Death brings much uncertainty along with all of the pain. If that kind of tragedy strikes your household, what Israel told his son when he was about to die is something to hang on to: "God will be with you." God will not only comfort you, he will see you through.

Direct Line

²"Assemble and listen, sons of Jacob;
    listen to your father Israel.

³"Reuben, you are my firstborn,
    my might, the first sign of my strength,
    excelling in honor, excelling in power.
⁴Turbulent as the waters, you will no longer excel,
    for you went up onto your father's bed,
    onto my couch and defiled it.

⁵"Simeon and Levi are brothers—
    their swords^a are weapons of violence.
⁶Let me not enter their council,
    let me not join their assembly,
for they have killed men in their anger
    and hamstrung oxen as they pleased.
⁷Cursed be their anger, so fierce,
    and their fury, so cruel!
I will scatter them in Jacob
    and disperse them in Israel.

⁸"Judah,^b your brothers will praise you;
    your hand will be on the neck of your enemies;
    your father's sons will bow down to you.
⁹You are a lion's cub, O Judah;
    you return from the prey, my son.
Like a lion he crouches and lies down,
    like a lioness—who dares to rouse him?
¹⁰The scepter will not depart from Judah,
    nor the ruler's staff from between his feet,
until he comes to whom it belongs^c
    and the obedience of the nations is his.
¹¹He will tether his donkey to a vine,
    his colt to the choicest branch;
he will wash his garments in wine,
    his robes in the blood of grapes.
¹²His eyes will be darker than wine,
    his teeth whiter than milk.^d

¹³"Zebulun will live by the seashore
    and become a haven for ships;
    his border will extend toward Sidon.

¹⁴"Issachar is a rawboned^e donkey
    lying down between two saddlebags.^f
¹⁵When he sees how good is his resting place
    and how pleasant is his land,
he will bend his shoulder to the burden
    and submit to forced labor.

¹⁶"Dan^g will provide justice for his people
    as one of the tribes of Israel.
¹⁷Dan will be a serpent by the roadside,
    a viper along the path,
that bites the horse's heels
    so that its rider tumbles backward.

---

^a5 The meaning of the Hebrew for this word is uncertain. ^b8 *Judah* sounds like and may be derived from the Hebrew for *praise*. ^c10 Or *until Shiloh comes*; or *until he comes to whom tribute belongs* ^d12 Or *will be dull from wine, / his teeth white from milk* ^e14 Or *strong* ^f14 Or *campfires* ^g16 *Dan* here means *he provides justice*.

¹⁸"I look for your deliverance, O L<small>ORD</small>.

¹⁹"Gad^a will be attacked by a band of raiders,
    but he will attack them at their heels.

²⁰"Asher's food will be rich;
    he will provide delicacies fit for a king.

²¹"Naphtali is a doe set free
    that bears beautiful fawns.^b

²²"Joseph is a fruitful vine,
    a fruitful vine near a spring,
    whose branches climb over a wall.^c
²³With bitterness archers attacked him;
    they shot at him with hostility.
²⁴But his bow remained steady,
    his strong arms stayed^d limber,
  because of the hand of the Mighty One of Jacob,
    because of the Shepherd, the Rock of Israel,
²⁵because of your father's God, who helps you,
    because of the Almighty,^e who blesses you
  with blessings of the heavens above,
    blessings of the deep that lies below,
    blessings of the breast and womb.
²⁶Your father's blessings are greater
    than the blessings of the ancient mountains,
    than^f the bounty of the age-old hills.
  Let all these rest on the head of Joseph,
    on the brow of the prince among^g his brothers.

²⁷"Benjamin is a ravenous wolf;
    in the morning he devours the prey,
    in the evening he divides the plunder."

²⁸All these are the twelve tribes of Israel, and this is what their father said to them when he blessed them, giving each the blessing appropriate to him.

The Death of Jacob ²⁹Then he gave them these instructions: "I am about to be gathered to my people. Bury me with my fathers in the cave in the field of Ephron the Hittite, ³⁰the cave in the field of Machpelah, near Mamre in Canaan, which Abraham bought as a burial place from Ephron the Hittite, along with the field. ³¹There Abraham and his wife Sarah were buried, there Isaac and his wife Rebekah were buried, and there I buried Leah. ³²The field and the cave in it were bought from the Hittites.^h"

³³When Jacob had finished giving instructions to his sons, he drew his feet up into the bed, breathed his last and was gathered to his people.

GENESIS 50

Q: How was Jacob prepared for burial?

BONUS: Why did the Egyptians use this method?

Answers on page 68

50 Joseph threw himself upon his father and wept over him and kissed him. ²Then Joseph directed the physicians in his service to embalm his father Israel. So the physicians embalmed him, ³taking a full

---

^a19 Gad *can mean* attack *and* band of raiders. ^b21 Or free; / he utters beautiful words ^c22 Or Joseph is a wild colt, / a wild colt near a spring, / a wild donkey on a terraced hill ^d23,24 Or archers will attack . . . will shoot . . . will remain . . . will stay ^e25 Hebrew Shaddai ^f26 Or of my progenitors, / as great as ^g26 Or the one separated from ^h32 Or the sons of Heth

forty days, for that was the time required for embalming. And the Egyptians mourned for him seventy days.

[4]When the days of mourning had passed, Joseph said to Pharaoh's court, "If I have found favor in your eyes, speak to Pharaoh for me. Tell him, [5]'My father made me swear an oath and said, "I am about to die; bury me in the tomb I dug for myself in the land of Canaan." Now let me go up and bury my father; then I will return.' "

[6]Pharaoh said, "Go up and bury your father, as he made you swear to do."

[7]So Joseph went up to bury his father. All Pharaoh's officials accompanied him—the dignitaries of his court and all the dignitaries of Egypt— [8]besides all the members of Joseph's household and his brothers and those belonging to his father's household. Only their children and their flocks and herds were left in Goshen. [9]Chariots and horsemen[a] also went up with him. It was a very large company.

[10]When they reached the threshing floor of Atad, near the Jordan, they lamented loudly and bitterly; and there Joseph observed a seven-day period of mourning for his father. [11]When the Canaanites who lived there saw the mourning at the threshing floor of Atad, they said, "The Egyptians are holding a solemn ceremony of mourning." That is why that place near the Jordan is called Abel Mizraim.[b]

[12]So Jacob's sons did as he had commanded them: [13]They carried him to the land of Canaan and buried him in the cave in the field of Machpelah, near Mamre, which Abraham had bought as a burial place from Ephron the Hittite, along with the field. [14]After burying his father, Joseph returned to Egypt, together with his brothers and all the others who had gone with him to bury his father.

Joseph Reassures His Brothers   [15]When Joseph's brothers saw that their father was dead, they said, "What if Joseph holds a grudge against us and pays us back for all the wrongs we did to him?" [16]So they sent word to Joseph, saying, "Your father left these instructions before he died: [17]'This is what you are to say to Joseph: I ask you to forgive your brothers the sins and the wrongs they committed in treating you so badly.' Now please forgive the sins of the servants of the God of your father." When their message came to him, Joseph wept.

[18]His brothers then came and threw themselves down before him. "We are your slaves," they said.

[19]But Joseph said to them, "Don't be afraid. Am I in the place of God? [20]You intended to harm me, but God intended it for good to accomplish what is now being done, the saving of many lives. [21]So then, don't be afraid. I will provide for you and your children." And he reassured them and spoke kindly to them.

The Death of Joseph   [22]Joseph stayed in Egypt, along with all his father's family. He lived a hundred and ten years [23]and saw the third generation of Ephraim's children. Also the children of Makir son of Manasseh were placed at birth on Joseph's knees.[c]

[24]Then Joseph said to his brothers, "I am about to die. But God will surely come to your aid and take you up out of this land to the land he promised on oath to Abraham, Isaac and Jacob." [25]And Joseph made the sons of Israel swear an oath and said, "God will surely come to your aid, and then you must carry my bones up from this place."

[26]So Joseph died at the age of a hundred and ten. And after they embalmed him, he was placed in a coffin in Egypt.

Answers
to Quizzer on
page 67

A: He was embalmed (Genesis 50:2-3).

BONUS: To preserve the body. The Egyptians believed that the soul existed only as long as the body survived.

---

[a]9 Or *charioteers*   [b]11 Abel Mizraim means *mourning of the Egyptians.*   [c]23 That is, were counted as his

FREEDOM!

God sets you free—not free to do anything you feel like doing—free to live a happy and meaningful life. The Israelites' road map of Exodus 20 can be your road map as well. You don't have to keep trying things in order to discover what's good and what's bad. Your map tells you.

The book of Exodus tells how God stepped in with stunning miracles to free the Israelites. Exodus contains the Ten Commandments, God's road map to the good life. Then Exodus moves on to record, in striking detail, the Israelites' decision at times to follow that road map and at other times to ignore it.

Fundamentals

What is slavery like (Exodus 1:14)?

Are you the only one who sometimes finds it hard to obey God (Exodus 4:10,13)?

Road map? What road map (Exodus 20:1-17)?

What happens when you know something is right but choose to do wrong (Exodus 32)?

FAST FACTS

Moses, the son of a Hebrew slave, was raised as an Egyptian prince.

Moses was 80 years old when he led Israel out of Egypt.

God sent ten plagues to punish Egypt for persecuting his people and to show that Egypt's gods were powerless.

Mount Sinai is 7,500 feet high.

Moses wrote this book about 1440 B.C.

The Israelites Oppressed These are the names of the sons of Israel who went to Egypt with Jacob, each with his family: ²Reuben, Simeon, Levi and Judah; ³Issachar, Zebulun and Benjamin; ⁴Dan and Naphtali; Gad and Asher. ⁵The descendants of Jacob numbered seventy[a] in all; Joseph was already in Egypt.

⁶Now Joseph and all his brothers and all that generation died, ⁷but the Israelites were fruitful and multiplied greatly and became exceedingly numerous, so that the land was filled with them.

⁸Then a new king, who did not know about Joseph, came to power in Egypt. ⁹"Look," he said to his people, "the Israelites have become much too numerous for us. ¹⁰Come, we must deal shrewdly with them or they will become even more numerous and, if war breaks out, will join our enemies, fight against us and leave the country."

¹¹So they put slave masters over them to oppress them with forced labor, and they built Pithom and Rameses as store cities for Pharaoh. ¹²But the more they were oppressed, the more they multiplied and spread; so the Egyptians came to dread the Israelites ¹³and worked them ruthlessly. ¹⁴They made their lives bitter with hard labor in brick and mortar and with all kinds of work in the fields; in all their hard labor the Egyptians used them ruthlessly.

¹⁵The king of Egypt said to the Hebrew midwives, whose names were Shiphrah and Puah, ¹⁶"When you help the Hebrew women in childbirth and observe them on the delivery stool, if it is a boy, kill him; but if it is a girl, let her live." ¹⁷The midwives, however, feared God and did not do what the king of Egypt had told them to do; they let the boys live. ¹⁸Then the king of Egypt summoned the midwives and asked them, "Why have you done this? Why have you let the boys live?"

¹⁹The midwives answered Pharaoh, "Hebrew women are not like Egyptian women; they are vigorous and give birth before the midwives arrive."

²⁰So God was kind to the midwives and the people increased and became even more numerous. ²¹And because the midwives feared God, he gave them families of their own.

²²Then Pharaoh gave this order to all his people: "Every boy that is born[b] you must throw into the Nile, but let every girl live."

The Birth of Moses Now a man of the house of Levi married a Levite woman, ²and she became pregnant and gave birth to a son. When she saw that he was a fine child, she hid him for three months. ³But when she could hide him no longer, she got a papyrus basket for him and coated it with tar and pitch. Then she placed the child in it and put it among the reeds along the bank of the Nile. ⁴His sister stood at a distance to see what would happen to him.

⁵Then Pharaoh's daughter went down to the Nile to bathe, and her attendants were walking along the river bank. She saw the basket among the reeds and sent

---

Direct Line

EXODUS 1:15–17

Do you ever feel like it's hard to be friends with other teens, especially when they ask you to do something you know is wrong? The midwives in Egypt had a similar problem. The king had ordered them to kill any boy baby born to an Israelite. No question about that being wrong, and no question that it would be dangerous to disobey. What happened? "The midwives feared God and did not do what the king of Egypt had told them to do" (Exodus 1:17). The next time someone tries to get you to do something wrong, think about the midwives of Egypt and do what's right.

---

[a]5 Masoretic Text (see also Gen. 46:27); Dead Sea Scrolls and Septuagint (see also Acts 7:14 and note at Gen. 46:27) *seventy-five* [b]22 Masoretic Text; Samaritan Pentateuch, Septuagint and Targums *born to the Hebrews*

her slave girl to get it. ⁶She opened it and saw the baby. He was crying, and she felt sorry for him. "This is one of the Hebrew babies," she said.

⁷Then his sister asked Pharaoh's daughter, "Shall I go and get one of the Hebrew women to nurse the baby for you?"

⁸"Yes, go," she answered. And the girl went and got the baby's mother. ⁹Pharaoh's daughter said to her, "Take this baby and nurse him for me, and I will pay you." So the woman took the baby and nursed him. ¹⁰When the child grew older, she took him to Pharaoh's daughter and he became her son. She named him Moses,ᵃ saying, "I drew him out of the water."

Moses Flees to Midian ¹¹One day, after Moses had grown up, he went out to where his own people were and watched them at their hard labor. He saw an Egyptian beating a Hebrew, one of his own people. ¹²Glancing this way and that and seeing no one, he killed the Egyptian and hid him in the sand. ¹³The next day he went out and saw two Hebrews fighting. He asked the one in the wrong, "Why are you hitting your fellow Hebrew?"

¹⁴The man said, "Who made you ruler and judge over us? Are you thinking of killing me as you killed the Egyptian?" Then Moses was afraid and thought, "What I did must have become known."

¹⁵When Pharaoh heard of this, he tried to kill Moses, but Moses fled from Pharaoh and went to live in Midian, where he sat down by a well. ¹⁶Now a priest of Midian had seven daughters, and they came to draw water and fill the troughs to water their father's flock. ¹⁷Some shepherds came along and drove them away, but Moses got up and came to their rescue and watered their flock.

¹⁸When the girls returned to Reuel their father, he asked them, "Why have you returned so early today?"

¹⁹They answered, "An Egyptian rescued us from the shepherds. He even drew water for us and watered the flock."

²⁰"And where is he?" he asked his daughters. "Why did you leave him? Invite him to have something to eat."

²¹Moses agreed to stay with the man, who gave his daughter Zipporah to Moses in marriage. ²²Zipporah gave birth to a son, and Moses named him Gershom,ᵇ saying, "I have become an alien in a foreign land."

²³During that long period, the king of Egypt died. The Israelites groaned in their slavery and cried out, and their cry for help because of their slavery went up to God. ²⁴God heard their groaning and he remembered his covenant with Abraham, with Isaac and with Jacob. ²⁵So God looked on the Israelites and was concerned about them.

Moses and the Burning Bush Now Moses was tending the flock of Jethro his father-in-law, the priest of Midian, and he led the flock to the far side of the desert and came to Horeb, the mountain of God. ²There the angel of the LORD appeared to him in flames of fire from within a bush. Moses saw that though the bush was on fire it did not burn up. ³So Moses thought, "I will go over and see this strange sight—why the bush does not burn up."

⁴When the LORD saw that he had gone over to look, God called to him from within the bush, "Moses! Moses!"

And Moses said, "Here I am."

⁵"Do not come any closer," God said. "Take off your sandals, for the place where you are standing is holy ground." ⁶Then he said, "I am the God of your father, the God of Abraham, the God of Isaac and the God of Jacob." At this, Moses hid his face, because he was afraid to look at God.

⁷The LORD said, "I have indeed seen the misery of my people in Egypt. I

ᵃ10 *Moses* sounds like the Hebrew for *draw out.*   ᵇ22 *Gershom* sounds like the Hebrew for *an alien there.*

have heard them crying out because of their slave drivers, and I am concerned about their suffering. [8]So I have come down to rescue them from the hand of the Egyptians and to bring them up out of that land into a good and spacious land, a land flowing with milk and honey—the home of the Canaanites, Hittites, Amorites, Perizzites, Hivites and Jebusites. [9]And now the cry of the Israelites has reached me, and I have seen the way the Egyptians are oppressing them. [10]So now, go. I am sending you to Pharaoh to bring my people the Israelites out of Egypt."

[11]But Moses said to God, "Who am I, that I should go to Pharaoh and bring the Israelites out of Egypt?"

[12]And God said, "I will be with you. And this will be the sign to you that it is I who have sent you: When you have brought the people out of Egypt, you[a] will worship God on this mountain."

[13]Moses said to God, "Suppose I go to the Israelites and say to them, 'The God of your fathers has sent me to you,' and they ask me, 'What is his name?' Then what shall I tell them?"

[14]God said to Moses, "I AM WHO I AM.[b] This is what you are to say to the Israelites: 'I AM has sent me to you.' "

[15]God also said to Moses, "Say to the Israelites, 'The LORD,[c] the God of your fathers—the God of Abraham, the God of Isaac and the God of Jacob—has sent me to you.' This is my name forever, the name by which I am to be remembered from generation to generation.

[16]"Go, assemble the elders of Israel and say to them, 'The LORD, the God of your fathers—the God of Abraham, Isaac and Jacob—appeared to me and said: I have watched over you and have seen what has been done to you in Egypt. [17]And I have promised to bring you up out of your misery in Egypt into the land of the Canaanites, Hittites, Amorites, Perizzites, Hivites and Jebusites—a land flowing with milk and honey.'

[18]"The elders of Israel will listen to you. Then you and the elders are to go to the king of Egypt and say to him, 'The LORD, the God of the Hebrews, has met with us. Let us take a three-day journey into the desert to offer sacrifices to the LORD our God.' [19]But I know that the king of Egypt will not let you go unless a mighty hand compels him. [20]So I will stretch out my hand and strike the Egyptians with all the wonders that I will perform among them. After that, he will let you go.

[21]"And I will make the Egyptians favorably disposed toward this people, so

---

[a]12 The Hebrew is plural.   [b]14 Or *I WILL BE WHAT I WILL BE*   [c]15 The Hebrew for LORD sounds like and may be derived from the Hebrew for *I AM* in verse 14.

The Bible Says

God's Name Is "I AM"

In Exodus 3:14–15 God declares the name by which he is to be remembered forever: "I AM." What does "I AM" mean? Why is this name special?

I AM (the Hebrew "Yahweh") means that God is always present with you. When you were a baby, God was I AM, right there with you. Wherever you are today, God is I AM, right there with you. And when you grow old, God will still be I AM, right there with you.

This special name is found many times in the Old Testament. Every time you see the word LORD in small capital letters, the Hebrew text used this special name.

How wonderful to have a God who is I AM, always there for you!

that when you leave you will not go empty-handed. ²²Every woman is to ask her neighbor and any woman living in her house for articles of silver and gold and for clothing, which you will put on your sons and daughters. And so you will plunder the Egyptians."

Signs for Moses   Moses answered, "What if they do not believe me or listen to me and say, 'The Lord did not appear to you'?"

²Then the Lord said to him, "What is that in your hand?"

"A staff," he replied.

³The Lord said, "Throw it on the ground."

Moses threw it on the ground and it became a snake, and he ran from it. ⁴Then the Lord said to him, "Reach out your hand and take it by the tail." So Moses reached out and took hold of the snake and it turned back into a staff in his hand. ⁵"This," said the Lord, "is so that they may believe that the Lord, the God of their fathers—the God of Abraham, the God of Isaac and the God of Jacob—has appeared to you."

⁶Then the Lord said, "Put your hand inside your cloak." So Moses put his hand into his cloak, and when he took it out, it was leprous,ᵃ like snow.

⁷"Now put it back into your cloak," he said. So Moses put his hand back into his cloak, and when he took it out, it was restored, like the rest of his flesh.

⁸Then the Lord said, "If they do not believe you or pay attention to the first miraculous sign, they may believe the second. ⁹But if they do not believe these two signs or listen to you, take some water from the Nile and pour it on the dry ground. The water you take from the river will become blood on the ground."

¹⁰Moses said to the Lord, "O Lord, I have never been eloquent, neither in the past nor since you have spoken to your servant. I am slow of speech and tongue."

¹¹The Lord said to him, "Who gave man his mouth? Who makes him deaf or mute? Who gives him sight or makes him blind? Is it not I, the Lord? ¹²Now go; I will help you speak and will teach you what to say."

¹³But Moses said, "O Lord, please send someone else to do it."

¹⁴Then the Lord's anger burned against Moses and he said, "What about your brother, Aaron the Levite? I know he can speak well. He is already on his way to meet you, and his heart will be glad when he sees you. ¹⁵You shall speak to him and put words in his mouth; I will help both of you speak and will teach you what to do. ¹⁶He will speak to the people for you, and it will be as if he were your mouth and as if you were God to him. ¹⁷But take this staff in your hand so you can perform miraculous signs with it."

> I will . . . teach you what to do (Exodus 4:15).

Moses Returns to Egypt   ¹⁸Then Moses went back to Jethro his father-in-law and said to him, "Let me go back to my own people in Egypt to see if any of them are still alive."

Jethro said, "Go, and I wish you well."

¹⁹Now the Lord had said to Moses in Midian, "Go back to Egypt, for all the men who wanted to kill you are dead." ²⁰So Moses took his wife and sons, put them on a donkey and started back to Egypt. And he took the staff of God in his hand.

²¹The Lord said to Moses, "When you return to Egypt, see that you perform before Pharaoh all the wonders I have given you the power to do. But I will harden his heart so that he will not let the people go. ²²Then say to Pharaoh, 'This is what the Lord says: Israel is my firstborn son, ²³and I told you, "Let my son go, so he may worship me." But you refused to let him go; so I will kill your firstborn son.' "

ᵃ6 The Hebrew word was used for various diseases affecting the skin—not necessarily leprosy.

²⁴At a lodging place on the way, the LORD met Moses, ᵃ and was about to kill him. ²⁵But Zipporah took a flint knife, cut off her son's foreskin and touched Moses' feet with it.ᵇ "Surely you are a bridegroom of blood to me," she said. ²⁶So the LORD let him alone. (At that time she said "bridegroom of blood," referring to circumcision.)

²⁷The LORD said to Aaron, "Go into the desert to meet Moses." So he met Moses at the mountain of God and kissed him. ²⁸Then Moses told Aaron everything the LORD had sent him to say, and also about all the miraculous signs he had commanded him to perform.

²⁹Moses and Aaron brought together all the elders of the Israelites, ³⁰and Aaron told them everything the LORD had said to Moses. He also performed the signs before the people, ³¹and they believed. And when they heard that the LORD was concerned about them and had seen their misery, they bowed down and worshiped.

Bricks Without Straw Afterward Moses and Aaron went to Pharaoh and said, "This is what the LORD, the God of Israel, says: 'Let my people go, so that they may hold a festival to me in the desert.' "

²Pharaoh said, "Who is the LORD, that I should obey him and let Israel go? I do not know the LORD and I will not let Israel go."

³Then they said, "The God of the Hebrews has met with us. Now let us take a three-day journey into the desert to offer sacrifices to the LORD our God, or he may strike us with plagues or with the sword."

⁴But the king of Egypt said, "Moses and Aaron, why are you taking the people away from their labor? Get back to your work!" ⁵Then Pharaoh said, "Look, the people of the land are now numerous, and you are stopping them from working."

⁶That same day Pharaoh gave this order to the slave drivers and foremen in charge of the people: ⁷"You are no longer to supply the people with straw for making bricks; let them go and gather their own straw. ⁸But require them to make the same number of bricks as before; don't reduce the quota. They are lazy; that is why they are crying out, 'Let us go and sacrifice to our God.' ⁹Make the work harder for the men so that they keep working and pay no attention to lies."

¹⁰Then the slave drivers and the foremen went out and said to the people, "This is what Pharaoh says: 'I will not give you any more straw. ¹¹Go and get your own straw wherever you can find it, but your work will not be reduced at all.' " ¹²So the people scattered all over Egypt to gather stubble to use for straw. ¹³The slave drivers kept pressing them, saying, "Complete the work required of you for each day, just as when you had straw." ¹⁴The Israelite foremen appointed by Pharaoh's slave drivers were beaten and were asked, "Why didn't you meet your quota of bricks yesterday or today, as before?"

¹⁵Then the Israelite foremen went and appealed to Pharaoh: "Why have you treated your servants this way? ¹⁶Your servants are given no straw, yet we are told, 'Make bricks!' Your servants are being beaten, but the fault is with your own people."

¹⁷Pharaoh said, "Lazy, that's what you are—lazy! That is why you keep saying, 'Let us go and sacrifice to the LORD.' ¹⁸Now get to work. You will not be given any straw, yet you must produce your full quota of bricks."

¹⁹The Israelite foremen realized they were in trouble when they were told, "You are not to reduce the number of bricks required of you for each day." ²⁰When they left Pharaoh, they found Moses and Aaron waiting to meet them, ²¹and they said, "May the LORD look upon you and judge you! You have made us a stench to Pharaoh and his officials and have put a sword in their hand to kill us."

ᵃ24 Or Moses' son; Hebrew him   ᵇ25 Or and drew near Moses' feet

God Promises Deliverance ²²Moses returned to the LORD and said, "O Lord, why have you brought trouble upon this people? Is this why you sent me? ²³Ever since I went to Pharaoh to speak in your name, he has brought trouble upon this people, and you have not rescued your people at all."

Then the LORD said to Moses, "Now you will see what I will do to Pharaoh: Because of my mighty hand he will let them go; because of my mighty hand he will drive them out of his country."

²God also said to Moses, "I am the LORD. ³I appeared to Abraham, to Isaac and to Jacob as God Almighty,ᵃ but by my name the LORDᵇ I did not make myself known to them.ᶜ ⁴I also established my covenant with them to give them the land of Canaan, where they lived as aliens. ⁵Moreover, I have heard the groaning of the Israelites, whom the Egyptians are enslaving, and I have remembered my covenant.

⁶"Therefore, say to the Israelites: 'I am the LORD, and I will bring you out from under the yoke of the Egyptians. I will free you from being slaves to them, and I will redeem you with an outstretched arm and with mighty acts of judgment. ⁷I will take you as my own people, and I will be your God. Then you will know that I am the LORD your God, who brought you out from under the yoke of the Egyptians. ⁸And I will bring you to the land I swore with uplifted hand to give to Abraham, to Isaac and to Jacob. I will give it to you as a possession. I am the LORD.' "

⁹Moses reported this to the Israelites, but they did not listen to him because of their discouragement and cruel bondage.

¹⁰Then the LORD said to Moses, ¹¹"Go, tell Pharaoh king of Egypt to let the Israelites go out of his country."

¹²But Moses said to the LORD, "If the Israelites will not listen to me, why would Pharaoh listen to me, since I speak with faltering lipsᵈ?"

Family Record of Moses and Aaron ¹³Now the LORD spoke to Moses and Aaron about the Israelites and Pharaoh king of Egypt, and he commanded them to bring the Israelites out of Egypt.

¹⁴These were the heads of their familiesᵉ:

The sons of Reuben the firstborn son of Israel were Hanoch and Pallu, Hezron and Carmi. These were the clans of Reuben.

¹⁵The sons of Simeon were Jemuel, Jamin, Ohad, Jakin, Zohar and Shaul the son of a Canaanite woman. These were the clans of Simeon.

¹⁶These were the names of the sons of Levi according to their records: Gershon, Kohath and Merari. Levi lived 137 years.

¹⁷The sons of Gershon, by clans, were Libni and Shimei.

¹⁸The sons of Kohath were Amram, Izhar, Hebron and Uzziel. Kohath lived 133 years.

Exodus 5:22—6:8

Do you ever get discouraged? You study hard for a science test and still get a D? You clean your room, and your mom still finds 103 things you need to do before it passes inspection? Is it worth it to even try? Does anyone care? Moses felt that way. He told Egypt's king to let God's people go, but the king just made them work harder. And that made the Israelites angry with Moses. Nothing was working out like it was supposed to. God had a word for Moses: "I will free you . . . I will take you as my own" (Exodus 6:6–7). If you belong to God, he's on your side. He'll bring you through discouraging times to a better tomorrow.

Direct Line

ᵃ3 Hebrew *El-Shaddai* ᵇ3 See note at Exodus 3:15. ᶜ3 Or *Almighty, and by my name the LORD did I not let myself be known to them?* ᵈ12 Hebrew *I am uncircumcised of lips;* also in verse 30 ᵉ14 The Hebrew for *families* here and in verse 25 refers to units larger than clans.

¹⁹The sons of Merari were Mahli and Mushi.

These were the clans of Levi according to their records.

²⁰Amram married his father's sister Jochebed, who bore him Aaron and Moses. Amram lived 137 years.

²¹The sons of Izhar were Korah, Nepheg and Zicri.

²²The sons of Uzziel were Mishael, Elzaphan and Sithri.

²³Aaron married Elisheba, daughter of Amminadab and sister of Nahshon, and she bore him Nadab and Abihu, Eleazar and Ithamar.

²⁴The sons of Korah were Assir, Elkanah and Abiasaph. These were the Korahite clans.

²⁵Eleazar son of Aaron married one of the daughters of Putiel, and she bore him Phinehas.

These were the heads of the Levite families, clan by clan.

²⁶It was this same Aaron and Moses to whom the Lᴏʀᴅ said, "Bring the Israelites out of Egypt by their divisions." ²⁷They were the ones who spoke to Pharaoh king of Egypt about bringing the Israelites out of Egypt. It was the same Moses and Aaron.

Aaron to Speak for Moses   ²⁸Now when the Lᴏʀᴅ spoke to Moses in Egypt, ²⁹he said to him, "I am the Lᴏʀᴅ. Tell Pharaoh king of Egypt everything I tell you."

³⁰But Moses said to the Lᴏʀᴅ, "Since I speak with faltering lips, why would Pharaoh listen to me?"

7 Then the Lᴏʀᴅ said to Moses, "See, I have made you like God to Pharaoh, and your brother Aaron will be your prophet. ²You are to say everything I command you, and your brother Aaron is to tell Pharaoh to let the Israelites go out of his country. ³But I will harden Pharaoh's heart, and though I multiply my miraculous signs and wonders in Egypt, ⁴he will not listen to you. Then I will lay my hand on Egypt and with mighty acts of judgment I will bring out my divisions, my people the Israelites. ⁵And the Egyptians will know that I am the Lᴏʀᴅ when I stretch out my hand against Egypt and bring the Israelites out of it."

⁶Moses and Aaron did just as the Lᴏʀᴅ commanded them. ⁷Moses was eighty years old and Aaron eighty-three when they spoke to Pharaoh.

Aaron's Staff Becomes a Snake   ⁸The Lᴏʀᴅ said to Moses and Aaron, ⁹"When Pharaoh says to you, 'Perform a miracle,' then say to Aaron, 'Take your staff and throw it down before Pharaoh,' and it will become a snake."

¹⁰So Moses and Aaron went to Pharaoh and did just as the Lᴏʀᴅ commanded. Aaron threw his staff down in front of Pharaoh and his officials, and it became a snake. ¹¹Pharaoh then summoned wise men and sorcerers, and the Egyptian magicians also did the same things by their secret arts: ¹²Each one threw down his staff and it became a snake. But Aaron's staff swallowed up their staffs. ¹³Yet Pharaoh's heart became hard and he would not listen to them, just as the Lᴏʀᴅ had said.

The Plague of Blood   ¹⁴Then the Lᴏʀᴅ said to Moses, "Pharaoh's heart is unyielding; he refuses to let the people go. ¹⁵Go to Pharaoh in the morning as he goes out to the water. Wait on the bank of the Nile to meet him, and take in your hand the staff that was changed into a snake. ¹⁶Then say to him, 'The Lᴏʀᴅ, the God of the Hebrews, has sent me to say to you: Let my people go, so that they may worship me in the desert. But until now you have not listened. ¹⁷This is what the Lᴏʀᴅ says: By this you will know that I am the Lᴏʀᴅ: With the staff that is in my hand I will strike the water of the Nile, and it will be changed into blood. ¹⁸The fish in the Nile will die, and the river will stink; the Egyptians will not be able to drink its water.' "

¹⁹The Lord said to Moses, "Tell Aaron, 'Take your staff and stretch out your hand over the waters of Egypt—over the streams and canals, over the ponds and all the reservoirs'—and they will turn to blood. Blood will be everywhere in Egypt, even in the wooden buckets and stone jars."

²⁰Moses and Aaron did just as the Lord had commanded. He raised his staff in the presence of Pharaoh and his officials and struck the water of the Nile, and all the water was changed into blood. ²¹The fish in the Nile died, and the river smelled so bad that the Egyptians could not drink its water. Blood was everywhere in Egypt.

²²But the Egyptian magicians did the same things by their secret arts, and Pharaoh's heart became hard; he would not listen to Moses and Aaron, just as the Lord had said. ²³Instead, he turned and went into his palace, and did not take even this to heart. ²⁴And all the Egyptians dug along the Nile to get drinking water, because they could not drink the water of the river.

The Plague of Frogs ²⁵Seven days passed after the Lord struck the Nile. ¹Then the Lord said to Moses, "Go to Pharaoh and say to him, 'This is what the Lord says: Let my people go, so that they may worship me. ²If you refuse to let them go, I will plague your whole country with frogs. ³The Nile will teem with frogs. They will come up into your palace and your bedroom and onto your bed, into the houses of your officials and on your people, and into your ovens and kneading troughs. ⁴The frogs will go up on you and your people and all your officials.' "

⁵Then the Lord said to Moses, "Tell Aaron, 'Stretch out your hand with your staff over the streams and canals and ponds, and make frogs come up on the land of Egypt.' "

⁶So Aaron stretched out his hand over the waters of Egypt, and the frogs came up and covered the land. ⁷But the magicians did the same things by their secret arts; they also made frogs come up on the land of Egypt.

⁸Pharaoh summoned Moses and Aaron and said, "Pray to the Lord to take the frogs away from me and my people, and I will let your people go to offer sacrifices to the Lord."

⁹Moses said to Pharaoh, "I leave to you the honor of setting the time for me to pray for you and your officials and your people that you and your houses may be rid of the frogs, except for those that remain in the Nile."

¹⁰"Tomorrow," Pharaoh said.

Moses replied, "It will be as you say, so that you may know there is no one like the Lord our God. ¹¹The frogs will leave you and your houses, your officials and your people; they will remain only in the Nile."

¹²After Moses and Aaron left Pharaoh, Moses cried out to the Lord about the frogs he had brought on Pharaoh. ¹³And the Lord did what Moses asked. The frogs died in the houses, in the courtyards and in the fields. ¹⁴They were piled into heaps, and the land reeked of them. ¹⁵But when Pharaoh saw that there was relief, he hardened his heart and would not listen to Moses and Aaron, just as the Lord had said.

EXODUS 8:15

When you say, "I'll do my homework at six," do you keep your word? Or when you promise to be home at ten, are you there? True, these are little things. But they're important because they're issues of character. And character is shaped day by day, choice by choice. Egypt's king was a young man at the time of the exodus. The land of Egypt suffered plague after plague because its king kept refusing to do what he said he would. Oh, God probably won't send plagues your way if you don't keep every promise you make. But you can be sure he doesn't want you to be like Egypt's untrustworthy king.

Direct Line

The Plague of Gnats ¹⁶Then the LORD said to Moses, "Tell Aaron, 'Stretch out your staff and strike the dust of the ground,' and throughout the land of Egypt the dust will become gnats." ¹⁷They did this, and when Aaron stretched out his hand with the staff and struck the dust of the ground, gnats came upon men and animals. All the dust throughout the land of Egypt became gnats. ¹⁸But when the magicians tried to produce gnats by their secret arts, they could not. And the gnats were on men and animals.

¹⁹The magicians said to Pharaoh, "This is the finger of God." But Pharaoh's heart was hard and he would not listen, just as the LORD had said.

The Plague of Flies ²⁰Then the LORD said to Moses, "Get up early in the morning and confront Pharaoh as he goes to the water and say to him, 'This is what the LORD says: Let my people go, so that they may worship me. ²¹If you do not let my people go, I will send swarms of flies on you and your officials, on your people and into your houses. The houses of the Egyptians will be full of flies, and even the ground where they are.

²²" 'But on that day I will deal differently with the land of Goshen, where my people live; no swarms of flies will be there, so that you will know that I, the LORD, am in this land. ²³I will make a distinction*a* between my people and your people. This miraculous sign will occur tomorrow.' "

²⁴And the LORD did this. Dense swarms of flies poured into Pharaoh's palace and into the houses of his officials, and throughout Egypt the land was ruined by the flies.

²⁵Then Pharaoh summoned Moses and Aaron and said, "Go, sacrifice to your God here in the land."

²⁶But Moses said, "That would not be right. The sacrifices we offer the LORD our God would be detestable to the Egyptians. And if we offer sacrifices that are detestable in their eyes, will they not stone us? ²⁷We must take a three-day journey into the desert to offer sacrifices to the LORD our God, as he commands us."

²⁸Pharaoh said, "I will let you go to offer sacrifices to the LORD your God in the desert, but you must not go very far. Now pray for me."

²⁹Moses answered, "As soon as I leave you, I will pray to the LORD, and tomorrow the flies will leave Pharaoh and his officials and his people. Only be sure that Pharaoh does not act deceitfully again by not letting the people go to offer sacrifices to the LORD."

³⁰Then Moses left Pharaoh and prayed to the LORD, ³¹and the LORD did what Moses asked: The flies left Pharaoh and his officials and his people; not a fly remained. ³²But this time also Pharaoh hardened his heart and would not let the people go.

The Plague on Livestock Then the LORD said to Moses, "Go to Pharaoh and say to him, 'This is what the LORD, the God of the Hebrews, says: "Let my people go, so that they may worship me." ²If you refuse to let them go and continue to hold them back, ³the hand of the LORD will bring a terrible plague on your livestock in the field—on your horses and donkeys and camels and on your cattle and sheep and goats. ⁴But the LORD will make a distinction between the livestock of Israel and that of Egypt, so that no animal belonging to the Israelites will die.' "

⁵The LORD set a time and said, "Tomorrow the LORD will do this in the land." ⁶And the next day the LORD did it: All the livestock of the Egyptians died, but not one animal belonging to the Israelites died. ⁷Pharaoh sent men to investigate and found that not even one of the animals of the Israelites had died. Yet his heart was unyielding and he would not let the people go.

a23 Septuagint and Vulgate; Hebrew will put a deliverance

The Plague of Boils   ⁸Then the LORD said to Moses and Aaron, "Take handfuls of soot from a furnace and have Moses toss it into the air in the presence of Pharaoh. ⁹It will become fine dust over the whole land of Egypt, and festering boils will break out on men and animals throughout the land."

¹⁰So they took soot from a furnace and stood before Pharaoh. Moses tossed it into the air, and festering boils broke out on men and animals. ¹¹The magicians could not stand before Moses because of the boils that were on them and on all the Egyptians. ¹²But the LORD hardened Pharaoh's heart and he would not listen to Moses and Aaron, just as the LORD had said to Moses.

The Plague of Hail   ¹³Then the LORD said to Moses, "Get up early in the morning, confront Pharaoh and say to him, 'This is what the LORD, the God of the Hebrews, says: Let my people go, so that they may worship me, ¹⁴or this time I will send the full force of my plagues against you and against your officials and your people, so you may know that there is no one like me in all the earth. ¹⁵For by now I could have stretched out my hand and struck you and your people with a plague that would have wiped you off the earth. ¹⁶But I have raised you up*a* for this very purpose, that I might show you my power and that my name might be proclaimed in all the earth. ¹⁷You still set yourself against my people and will not let them go. ¹⁸Therefore, at this time tomorrow I will send the worst hailstorm that has ever fallen on Egypt, from the day it was founded till now. ¹⁹Give an order now to bring your livestock and everything you have in the field to a place of shelter, because the hail will fall on every man and animal that has not been brought in and is still out in the field, and they will die.' "

²⁰Those officials of Pharaoh who feared the word of the LORD hurried to bring their slaves and their livestock inside. ²¹But those who ignored the word of the LORD left their slaves and livestock in the field.

²²Then the LORD said to Moses, "Stretch out your hand toward the sky so that hail will fall all over Egypt—on men and animals and on everything growing in the fields of Egypt." ²³When Moses stretched out his staff toward the sky, the LORD sent thunder and hail, and lightning flashed down to the ground. So the LORD rained hail on the land of Egypt; ²⁴hail fell and lightning flashed back and forth. It was the worst storm in all the land of Egypt since it had become a nation. ²⁵Throughout Egypt hail struck everything in the fields—both men and animals; it beat down everything growing in the fields and stripped every tree. ²⁶The only place it did not hail was the land of Goshen, where the Israelites were.

²⁷Then Pharaoh summoned Moses and Aaron. "This time I have sinned," he said to them. "The LORD is in the right, and I and my people are in the wrong. ²⁸Pray to the LORD, for we have had enough thunder and hail. I will let you go; you don't have to stay any longer."

²⁹Moses replied, "When I have gone out of the city, I will spread out my hands in prayer to the LORD. The thunder will stop and there will be no more hail, so you

EXODUS 9:13-21

How do you know if someone really believes in God? *Not by what they say, but by what they do.* When Moses announced a hailstorm, the Egyptians who believed in God rushed to get their flocks and herds inside (Exodus 9:20-21). This is a pretty good test to apply to yourself as well as to others. Are you eager to obey God's commands? Do you make choices by asking yourself what's right, what will please the Lord? There's no wiser way to live your life, as the people of Egypt found out. The animals of the believing Egyptians survived. The Egyptians who didn't believe God lost all they owned.

Direct Line

---

a16 Or have spared you

may know that the earth is the LORD's. ³⁰But I know that you and your officials still do not fear the LORD God."

³¹(The flax and barley were destroyed, since the barley had headed and the flax was in bloom. ³²The wheat and spelt, however, were not destroyed, because they ripen later.)

³³Then Moses left Pharaoh and went out of the city. He spread out his hands toward the LORD; the thunder and hail stopped, and the rain no longer poured down on the land. ³⁴When Pharaoh saw that the rain and hail and thunder had stopped, he sinned again: He and his officials hardened their hearts. ³⁵So Pharaoh's heart was hard and he would not let the Israelites go, just as the LORD had said through Moses.

The Plague of Locusts Then the LORD said to Moses, "Go to Pharaoh, for I have hardened his heart and the hearts of his officials so that I may perform these miraculous signs of mine among them ²that you may tell your children and grandchildren how I dealt harshly with the Egyptians and how I performed my signs among them, and that you may know that I am the LORD."

³So Moses and Aaron went to Pharaoh and said to him, "This is what the LORD, the God of the Hebrews, says: 'How long will you refuse to humble yourself before me? Let my people go, so that they may worship me. ⁴If you refuse to let them go, I will bring locusts into your country tomorrow. ⁵They will cover the face of the ground so that it cannot be seen. They will devour what little you have left after the hail, including every tree that is growing in your fields. ⁶They will fill your houses and those of all your officials and all the Egyptians—something neither your fathers nor your forefathers have ever seen from the day they settled in this land till now.'" Then Moses turned and left Pharaoh.

⁷Pharaoh's officials said to him, "How long will this man be a snare to us? Let the people go, so that they may worship the LORD their God. Do you not yet realize that Egypt is ruined?"

⁸Then Moses and Aaron were brought back to Pharaoh. "Go, worship the LORD your God," he said. "But just who will be going?"

⁹Moses answered, "We will go with our young and old, with our sons and daughters, and with our flocks and herds, because we are to celebrate a festival to the LORD."

¹⁰Pharaoh said, "The LORD be with you—if I let you go, along with your women and children! Clearly you are bent on evil.*a* ¹¹No! Have only the men go; and worship the LORD, since that's what you have been asking for." Then Moses and Aaron were driven out of Pharaoh's presence.

¹²And the LORD said to Moses, "Stretch out your hand over Egypt so that locusts will swarm over the land and devour everything growing in the fields, everything left by the hail."

¹³So Moses stretched out his staff over Egypt, and the LORD made an east wind blow across the land all that day and all that night. By morning the wind had brought the locusts; ¹⁴they invaded all Egypt and settled down in every area of the country in great numbers. Never before had there been such a plague of locusts, nor will there ever be again. ¹⁵They covered all the ground until it was black. They devoured all that was left after the hail—everything growing in the fields and the fruit on the trees. Nothing green remained on tree or plant in all the land of Egypt.

¹⁶Pharaoh quickly summoned Moses and Aaron and said, "I have sinned against the LORD your God and against you. ¹⁷Now forgive my sin once more and pray to the LORD your God to take this deadly plague away from me."

---

a10 Or Be careful, trouble is in store for you!

¹⁸Moses then left Pharaoh and prayed to the LORD. ¹⁹And the LORD changed the wind to a very strong west wind, which caught up the locusts and carried them into the Red Sea.ᵃ Not a locust was left anywhere in Egypt. ²⁰But the LORD hardened Pharaoh's heart, and he would not let the Israelites go.

The Plague of Darkness ²¹Then the LORD said to Moses, "Stretch out your hand toward the sky so that darkness will spread over Egypt—darkness that can be felt." ²²So Moses stretched out his hand toward the sky, and total darkness covered all Egypt for three days. ²³No one could see anyone else or leave his place for three days. Yet all the Israelites had light in the places where they lived.

²⁴Then Pharaoh summoned Moses and said, "Go, worship the LORD. Even your women and children may go with you; only leave your flocks and herds behind."

²⁵But Moses said, "You must allow us to have sacrifices and burnt offerings to present to the LORD our God. ²⁶Our livestock too must go with us; not a hoof is to be left behind. We have to use some of them in worshiping the LORD our God, and until we get there we will not know what we are to use to worship the LORD."

²⁷But the LORD hardened Pharaoh's heart, and he was not willing to let them go. ²⁸Pharaoh said to Moses, "Get out of my sight! Make sure you do not appear before me again! The day you see my face you will die."

²⁹"Just as you say," Moses replied, "I will never appear before you again."

11 *The Plague on the Firstborn* Now the LORD had said to Moses, "I will bring one more plague on Pharaoh and on Egypt. After that, he will let you go from here, and when he does, he will drive you out completely. ²Tell the people that men and women alike are to ask their neighbors for articles of silver and gold." ³(The LORD made the Egyptians favorably disposed toward the people, and Moses himself was highly regarded in Egypt by Pharaoh's officials and by the people.)

⁴So Moses said, "This is what the LORD says: 'About midnight I will go throughout Egypt. ⁵Every firstborn son in Egypt will die, from the firstborn son of Pharaoh, who sits on the throne, to the firstborn son of the slave girl,

---

ᵃ*19* Hebrew *Yam Suph*; that is, Sea of Reeds

These chapters in Exodus tell of several miracles God performed. Certainly there had been locusts and hailstorms in Egypt before. Why then did people think these were miracles? Because Moses predicted the events and because he commanded them to end.

Exodus gives three reasons for these miracles:

✳ To show that God is Lord of all (Exodus 7:5).
✳ To show that God cares for his people (Exodus 6:7).
✳ To show that the gods of Egypt were powerless (Exodus 12:12).

Do you ever wonder why God doesn't do miracles every day? Does it seem like more people would believe in him if he did? Read John 9:28–34 and 11:1–53 to see if more people believed in Jesus because of his miracles. Miracles don't create faith. Faith comes when you hear what God says to you in the Bible and believe it.

The
Bible
Says

**God Does
Miracles**

who is at her hand mill, and all the firstborn of the cattle as well. ⁶There will be loud wailing throughout Egypt—worse than there has ever been or ever will be again. ⁷But among the Israelites not a dog will bark at any man or animal.' Then you will know that the LORD makes a distinction between Egypt and Israel. ⁸All these officials of yours will come to me, bowing down before me and saying, 'Go, you and all the people who follow you!' After that I will leave." Then Moses, hot with anger, left Pharaoh.

⁹The LORD had said to Moses, "Pharaoh will refuse to listen to you—so that my wonders may be multiplied in Egypt." ¹⁰Moses and Aaron performed all these wonders before Pharaoh, but the LORD hardened Pharaoh's heart, and he would not let the Israelites go out of his country.

The Passover The LORD said to Moses and Aaron in Egypt, ²"This month is to be for you the first month, the first month of your year. ³Tell the whole community of Israel that on the tenth day of this month each man is to take a lamb*ᵃ* for his family, one for each household. ⁴If any household is too small for a whole lamb, they must share one with their nearest neighbor, having taken into account the number of people there are. You are to determine the amount of lamb needed in accordance with what each person will eat. ⁵The animals you choose must be year-old males without defect, and you may take them from the sheep or the goats. ⁶Take care of them until the fourteenth day of the month, when all the people of the community of Israel must slaughter them at twilight. ⁷Then they are to take some of the blood and put it on the sides and tops of the doorframes of the houses where they eat the lambs. ⁸That same night they are to eat the meat roasted over the fire, along with bitter herbs, and bread made without yeast. ⁹Do not eat the meat raw or cooked in water, but roast it over the fire—head, legs and inner parts. ¹⁰Do not leave any of it till morning; if some is left till morning, you must burn it. ¹¹This is how you are to eat it: with your cloak tucked into your belt, your sandals on your feet and your staff in your hand. Eat it in haste; it is the LORD's Passover.

¹²"On that same night I will pass through Egypt and strike down every firstborn—both men and animals—and I will bring judgment on all the gods of Egypt. I am the LORD. ¹³The blood will be a sign for you on the houses where you are; and when I see the blood, I will pass over you. No destructive plague will touch you when I strike Egypt.

¹⁴"This is a day you are to commemorate; for the generations to come you shall celebrate it as a festival to the LORD—a lasting ordinance. ¹⁵For seven days you are to eat bread made without yeast. On the first day remove the yeast from your houses, for whoever eats anything with yeast in it from the first day through the seventh must be cut off from Israel. ¹⁶On the first day hold a sacred assembly, and another one on the seventh day. Do no work at all on these days, except to prepare food for everyone to eat—that is all you may do.

¹⁷"Celebrate the Feast of Unleavened Bread, because it was on this very day

---

Direct Line

EXODUS 12:14–16

Some occasions are so important you celebrate them every year. Birthdays. Marriages. Christmas. Did you know that God ordered the Israelites to celebrate a special holiday? He told them to celebrate every year their release from slavery. What has God done for you that's worth remembering and celebrating? Some people celebrate the day they accepted Christ as Savior, a "spiritual birthday." Some record answers to prayer and look back over that record at least once a year. God is good, and it's good to celebrate the things he does for you.

ᵃ3 The Hebrew word can mean lamb or kid; also in verse 4.

that I brought your divisions out of Egypt. Celebrate this day as a lasting ordinance for the generations to come. [18]In the first month you are to eat bread made without yeast, from the evening of the fourteenth day until the evening of the twenty-first day. [19]For seven days no yeast is to be found in your houses. And whoever eats anything with yeast in it must be cut off from the community of Israel, whether he is an alien or native-born. [20]Eat nothing made with yeast. Wherever you live, you must eat unleavened bread."

[21]Then Moses summoned all the elders of Israel and said to them, "Go at once and select the animals for your families and slaughter the Passover lamb. [22]Take a bunch of hyssop, dip it into the blood in the basin and put some of the blood on the top and on both sides of the doorframe. Not one of you shall go out the door of his house until morning. [23]When the LORD goes through the land to strike down the Egyptians, he will see the blood on the top and sides of the doorframe and will pass over that doorway, and he will not permit the destroyer to enter your houses and strike you down.

[24]"Obey these instructions as a lasting ordinance for you and your descendants. [25]When you enter the land that the LORD will give you as he promised, observe this ceremony. [26]And when your children ask you, 'What does this ceremony mean to you?' [27]then tell them, 'It is the Passover sacrifice to the LORD, who passed over the houses of the Israelites in Egypt and spared our homes when he struck down the Egyptians.' " Then the people bowed down and worshiped. [28]The Israelites did just what the LORD commanded Moses and Aaron.

[29]At midnight the LORD struck down all the firstborn in Egypt, from the firstborn of Pharaoh, who sat on the throne, to the firstborn of the prisoner, who was in the dungeon, and the firstborn of all the livestock as well. [30]Pharaoh and all his officials and all the Egyptians got up during the night, and there was loud wailing in Egypt, for there was not a house without someone dead.

The Exodus [31]During the night Pharaoh summoned Moses and Aaron and said, "Up! Leave my people, you and the Israelites! Go, worship the LORD as you have requested. [32]Take your flocks and herds, as you have said, and go. And also bless me."

[33]The Egyptians urged the people to hurry and leave the country. "For otherwise," they said, "we will all die!" [34]So the people took their dough before the yeast was added, and carried it on their shoulders in kneading troughs wrapped in clothing. [35]The Israelites did as Moses instructed and asked the Egyptians for articles of silver and gold and for clothing. [36]The LORD had made the Egyptians favorably disposed toward the people, and they gave them what they asked for; so they plundered the Egyptians.

[37]The Israelites journeyed from Rameses to Succoth. There were about six hundred thousand men on foot, besides women and children. [38]Many other people went up with them, as well as large droves of livestock, both flocks and herds. [39]With the dough they had brought from Egypt, they baked cakes of unleavened bread. The dough was without yeast because they had been driven out of Egypt and did not have time to prepare food for themselves.

[40]Now the length of time the Israelite people lived in Egypt[a] was 430 years. [41]At the end of the 430 years, to the very day, all the LORD's divisions left Egypt. [42]Because the LORD kept vigil that night to bring them out of Egypt, on this night all the Israelites are to keep vigil to honor the LORD for the generations to come.

EXODUS 12

QUIZZER

Q: How long were the Israelites in Egypt?

BONUS: Why didn't God rescue his people sooner?

Answers on page 84

a40 Masoretic Text; Samaritan Pentateuch and Septuagint *Egypt and Canaan*

Passover Restrictions ⁴³The Lᴏʀᴅ said to Moses and Aaron, "These are the regulations for the Passover:

"No foreigner is to eat of it. ⁴⁴Any slave you have bought may eat of it after you have circumcised him, ⁴⁵but a temporary resident and a hired worker may not eat of it.

⁴⁶"It must be eaten inside one house; take none of the meat outside the house. Do not break any of the bones. ⁴⁷The whole community of Israel must celebrate it.

⁴⁸"An alien living among you who wants to celebrate the Lᴏʀᴅ's Passover must have all the males in his household circumcised; then he may take part like one born in the land. No uncircumcised male may eat of it. ⁴⁹The same law applies to the native-born and to the alien living among you."

⁵⁰All the Israelites did just what the Lᴏʀᴅ had commanded Moses and Aaron. ⁵¹And on that very day the Lᴏʀᴅ brought the Israelites out of Egypt by their divisions.

Answers
to Quizzer on page 83

A: They were there for 430 years (Exodus 12:40).

BONUS: Only 70 descendants of Abraham entered Egypt. It took 430 years before their numbers had grown enough to attack and capture the promised land (Exodus 1:1-7).

Consecration of the Firstborn The Lᴏʀᴅ said to Moses, ²"Consecrate to me every firstborn male. The first offspring of every womb among the Israelites belongs to me, whether man or animal."

³Then Moses said to the people, "Commemorate this day, the day you came out of Egypt, out of the land of slavery, because the Lᴏʀᴅ brought you out of it with a mighty hand. Eat nothing containing yeast. ⁴Today, in the month of Abib, you are leaving. ⁵When the Lᴏʀᴅ brings you into the land of the Canaanites, Hittites, Amorites, Hivites and Jebusites—the land he swore to your forefathers to give you, a land flowing with milk and honey—you are to observe this ceremony in this month: ⁶For seven days eat bread made without yeast and on the seventh day hold a festival to the Lᴏʀᴅ. ⁷Eat unleavened bread during those seven days; nothing with yeast in it is to be seen among you, nor shall any yeast be seen anywhere within your borders. ⁸On that day tell your son, 'I do this because of what the Lᴏʀᴅ did for me when I came out of Egypt.' ⁹This observance will be for you like a sign on your hand and a reminder on your forehead that the law of the Lᴏʀᴅ is to be on your lips. For the Lᴏʀᴅ brought you out of Egypt with his mighty hand. ¹⁰You must keep this ordinance at the appointed time year after year.

¹¹"After the Lᴏʀᴅ brings you into the land of the Canaanites and gives it to you, as he promised on oath to you and your forefathers, ¹²you are to give over to the Lᴏʀᴅ the first offspring of every womb. All the firstborn males of your livestock belong to the Lᴏʀᴅ. ¹³Redeem with a lamb every firstborn donkey, but if you do not redeem it, break its neck. Redeem every firstborn among your sons.

¹⁴"In days to come, when your son asks you, 'What does this mean?' say to him, 'With a mighty hand the Lᴏʀᴅ brought us out of Egypt, out of the land of slavery. ¹⁵When Pharaoh stubbornly refused to let us go, the Lᴏʀᴅ killed every firstborn in Egypt, both man and animal. This is why I sacrifice to the Lᴏʀᴅ the first male offspring of every womb and redeem each of my firstborn sons.' ¹⁶And it will be like a sign on your hand and a symbol on your forehead that the Lᴏʀᴅ brought us out of Egypt with his mighty hand."

Crossing the Sea ¹⁷When Pharaoh let the people go, God did not lead them on the road through the Philistine country, though that was shorter. For God said, "If they face war, they might change their minds and return to Egypt." ¹⁸So God led the people around by the desert road toward the Red Sea.ᵃ The Israelites went up out of Egypt armed for battle.

ᵃ18 Hebrew *Yam Suph*; that is, Sea of Reeds

[19]Moses took the bones of Joseph with him because Joseph had made the sons of Israel swear an oath. He had said, "God will surely come to your aid, and then you must carry my bones up with you from this place."[a]

[20]After leaving Succoth they camped at Etham on the edge of the desert. [21]By day the LORD went ahead of them in a pillar of cloud to guide them on their way and by night in a pillar of fire to give them light, so that they could travel by day or night. [22]Neither the pillar of cloud by day nor the pillar of fire by night left its place in front of the people.

14 Then the LORD said to Moses, [2]"Tell the Israelites to turn back and encamp near Pi Hahiroth, between Migdol and the sea. They are to encamp by the sea, directly opposite Baal Zephon. [3]Pharaoh will think, 'The Israelites are wandering around the land in confusion, hemmed in by the desert.' [4]And I will harden Pharaoh's heart, and he will pursue them. But I will gain glory for myself through Pharaoh and all his army, and the Egyptians will know that I am the LORD." So the Israelites did this.

[5]When the king of Egypt was told that the people had fled, Pharaoh and his officials changed their minds about them and said, "What have we done? We have let the Israelites go and have lost their services!" [6]So he had his chariot made ready and took his army with him. [7]He took six hundred of the best chariots, along with all the other chariots of Egypt, with officers over all of them. [8]The LORD hardened the heart of Pharaoh king of Egypt, so that he pursued the Israelites, who were marching out boldly. [9]The Egyptians—all Pharaoh's horses and chariots, horsemen[b] and troops—pursued the Israelites and overtook them as they camped by the sea near Pi Hahiroth, opposite Baal Zephon.

[10]As Pharaoh approached, the Israelites looked up, and there were the Egyptians, marching after them. They were terrified and cried out to the LORD. [11]They said to Moses, "Was it because there were no graves in Egypt that you brought us to the desert to die? What have you done to us by bringing us out of Egypt? [12]Didn't we say to you in Egypt, 'Leave us alone; let us serve the Egyptians'? It would have been better for us to serve the Egyptians than to die in the desert!"

[13]Moses answered the people, "Do not be afraid. Stand firm and you will see the deliverance the LORD will bring you today. The Egyptians you see today you will never see again. [14]The LORD will fight for you; you need only to be still."

[15]Then the LORD said to Moses, "Why are you crying out to me? Tell the Israelites to move on. [16]Raise your staff and stretch out your hand over the sea to divide the water so that the Israelites can go through the sea on dry ground. [17]I will harden the hearts of the Egyptians so that they will go in after them. And I will gain glory through Pharaoh and all his army, through his chariots and his horsemen. [18]The Egyptians will know that I am the LORD when I gain glory through Pharaoh, his chariots and his horsemen."

[19]Then the angel of God, who had been traveling in front of Israel's army, withdrew

Has that wall of water sprung a leak?!

SEE EXODUS 14:21-22

[a]19 See Gen. 50:25. [b]9 Or charioteers; also in verses 17, 18, 23, 26 and 28

and went behind them. The pillar of cloud also moved from in front and stood behind them, ²⁰coming between the armies of Egypt and Israel. Throughout the night the cloud brought darkness to the one side and light to the other side; so neither went near the other all night long.

²¹Then Moses stretched out his hand over the sea, and all that night the Lᴏʀᴅ drove the sea back with a strong east wind and turned it into dry land. The waters were divided, ²²and the Israelites went through the sea on dry ground, with a wall of water on their right and on their left.

²³The Egyptians pursued them, and all Pharaoh's horses and chariots and horsemen followed them into the sea. ²⁴During the last watch of the night the Lᴏʀᴅ looked down from the pillar of fire and cloud at the Egyptian army and threw it into confusion. ²⁵He made the wheels of their chariots come off ᵃ so that they had difficulty driving. And the Egyptians said, "Let's get away from the Israelites! The Lᴏʀᴅ is fighting for them against Egypt."

²⁶Then the Lᴏʀᴅ said to Moses, "Stretch out your hand over the sea so that the waters may flow back over the Egyptians and their chariots and horsemen." ²⁷Moses stretched out his hand over the sea, and at daybreak the sea went back to its place. The Egyptians were fleeing toward ᵇ it, and the Lᴏʀᴅ swept them into the sea. ²⁸The water flowed back and covered the chariots and horsemen—the entire army of Pharaoh that had followed the Israelites into the sea. Not one of them survived.

²⁹But the Israelites went through the sea on dry ground, with a wall of water on their right and on their left. ³⁰That day the Lᴏʀᴅ saved Israel from the hands of the Egyptians, and Israel saw the Egyptians lying dead on the shore. ³¹And when the Israelites saw the great power the Lᴏʀᴅ displayed against the Egyptians, the people feared the Lᴏʀᴅ and put their trust in him and in Moses his servant.

The Song of Moses and Miriam Then Moses and the Israelites sang this song to the Lᴏʀᴅ:

"I will sing to the Lᴏʀᴅ,
    for he is highly exalted.
The horse and its rider
    he has hurled into the sea.
²The Lᴏʀᴅ is my strength and my song;
    he has become my salvation.
He is my God, and I will praise him,
    my father's God, and I will exalt him.
³The Lᴏʀᴅ is a warrior;
    the Lᴏʀᴅ is his name.
⁴Pharaoh's chariots and his army
    he has hurled into the sea.
The best of Pharaoh's officers
    are drowned in the Red Sea.ᶜ
⁵The deep waters have covered them;
    they sank to the depths like a stone.

⁶"Your right hand, O Lᴏʀᴅ,
    was majestic in power.
Your right hand, O Lᴏʀᴅ,
    shattered the enemy.
⁷In the greatness of your majesty
    you threw down those who opposed you.

ᵃ25 Or *He jammed the wheels of their chariots* (see Samaritan Pentateuch, Septuagint and Syriac) ᵇ27 Or *from* ᶜ4 Hebrew *Yam Suph*; that is, Sea of Reeds; also in verse 22

You unleashed your burning anger;
    it consumed them like stubble.
⁸By the blast of your nostrils
    the waters piled up.
The surging waters stood firm like a wall;
    the deep waters congealed in the heart of the sea.

⁹"The enemy boasted,
    'I will pursue, I will overtake them.
I will divide the spoils;
    I will gorge myself on them.
I will draw my sword
    and my hand will destroy them.'
¹⁰But you blew with your breath,
    and the sea covered them.
They sank like lead
    in the mighty waters.

¹¹"Who among the gods is like you, O LORD?
    Who is like you—
        majestic in holiness,
        awesome in glory,
        working wonders?
¹²You stretched out your right hand
    and the earth swallowed them.

¹³"In your unfailing love you will lead
    the people you have redeemed.
In your strength you will guide them
    to your holy dwelling.
¹⁴The nations will hear and tremble;
    anguish will grip the people of Philistia.
¹⁵The chiefs of Edom will be terrified,
    the leaders of Moab will be seized with trembling,
the people*a* of Canaan will melt away;
¹⁶   terror and dread will fall upon them.
By the power of your arm
    they will be as still as a stone—
until your people pass by, O LORD,
    until the people you bought*b* pass by.
¹⁷You will bring them in and plant them
    on the mountain of your inheritance—
the place, O LORD, you made for your dwelling,
    the sanctuary, O Lord, your hands established.
¹⁸The LORD will reign
    for ever and ever."

¹⁹When Pharaoh's horses, chariots and horsemen*c* went into the sea, the LORD brought the waters of the sea back over them, but the Israelites walked through the sea on dry ground. ²⁰Then Miriam the prophetess, Aaron's sister, took a tambourine in her hand, and all the women followed her, with tambourines and dancing. ²¹Miriam sang to them:

    "Sing to the LORD,
        for he is highly exalted.
    The horse and its rider
        he has hurled into the sea."

a15 Or rulers b16 Or created c19 Or charioteers

The Waters of Marah and Elim 22Then Moses led Israel from the Red Sea and they went into the Desert of Shur. For three days they traveled in the desert without finding water. 23When they came to Marah, they could not drink its water because it was bitter. (That is why the place is called Marah.*a*) 24So the people grumbled against Moses, saying, "What are we to drink?"

25Then Moses cried out to the LORD, and the LORD showed him a piece of wood. He threw it into the water, and the water became sweet.

There the LORD made a decree and a law for them, and there he tested them. 26He said, "If you listen carefully to the voice of the LORD your God and do what is right in his eyes, if you pay attention to his commands and keep all his decrees, I will not bring on you any of the diseases I brought on the Egyptians, for I am the LORD, who heals you."

27Then they came to Elim, where there were twelve springs and seventy palm trees, and they camped there near the water.

Manna and Quail The whole Israelite community set out from Elim and came to the Desert of Sin, which is between Elim and Sinai, on the fifteenth day of the second month after they had come out of Egypt. 2In the desert the whole community grumbled against Moses and Aaron. 3The Israelites said to them, "If only we had died by the LORD's hand in Egypt! There we sat around pots of meat and ate all the food we wanted, but you have brought us out into this desert to starve this entire assembly to death."

4Then the LORD said to Moses, "I will rain down bread from heaven for you. The people are to go out each day and gather enough for that day. In this way I will test them and see whether they will follow my instructions. 5On the sixth day they are to prepare what they bring in, and that is to be twice as much as they gather on the other days."

6So Moses and Aaron said to all the Israelites, "In the evening you will know that it was the LORD who brought you out of Egypt, 7and in the morning you will see the glory of the LORD, because he has heard your grumbling against him. Who are we, that you should grumble against us?" 8Moses also said, "You will know that it was the LORD when he gives you meat to eat in the evening and all the bread you want in the morning, because he has heard your grumbling against him. Who are we? You are not grumbling against us, but against the LORD."

9Then Moses told Aaron, "Say to the entire Israelite community, 'Come before the LORD, for he has heard your grumbling.' "

10While Aaron was speaking to the whole Israelite community, they looked toward the desert, and there was the glory of the LORD appearing in the cloud.

11The LORD said to Moses, 12"I have heard the grumbling of the Israelites. Tell them, 'At twilight you will eat meat, and in the morning you will be filled with bread. Then you will know that I am the LORD your God.' "

13That evening quail came and covered the camp, and in the morning there was a layer of dew around the camp. 14When the dew was gone, thin flakes like frost on the ground appeared on the

This stuff looks like frosted flakes! Wonder where I can get some cold goat's milk?

SEE
EXODUS 16:14-15

*a*23 *Marah* means *bitter.*

desert floor. ¹⁵When the Israelites saw it, they said to each other, "What is it?" For they did not know what it was.

Moses said to them, "It is the bread the LORD has given you to eat. ¹⁶This is what the LORD has commanded: 'Each one is to gather as much as he needs. Take an omer*a* for each person you have in your tent.' "

¹⁷The Israelites did as they were told; some gathered much, some little. ¹⁸And when they measured it by the omer, he who gathered much did not have too much, and he who gathered little did not have too little. Each one gathered as much as he needed.

¹⁹Then Moses said to them, "No one is to keep any of it until morning."

²⁰However, some of them paid no attention to Moses; they kept part of it until morning, but it was full of maggots and began to smell. So Moses was angry with them.

²¹Each morning everyone gathered as much as he needed, and when the sun grew hot, it melted away. ²²On the sixth day, they gathered twice as much—two omers*b* for each person—and the leaders of the community came and reported this to Moses. ²³He said to them, "This is what the LORD commanded: 'Tomorrow is to be a day of rest, a holy Sabbath to the LORD. So bake what you want to bake and boil what you want to boil. Save whatever is left and keep it until morning.' "

²⁴So they saved it until morning, as Moses commanded, and it did not stink or get maggots in it. ²⁵"Eat it today," Moses said, "because today is a Sabbath to the LORD. You will not find any of it on the ground today. ²⁶Six days you are to gather it, but on the seventh day, the Sabbath, there will not be any."

²⁷Nevertheless, some of the people went out on the seventh day to gather it, but they found none. ²⁸Then the LORD said to Moses, "How long will you*c* refuse to keep my commands and my instructions? ²⁹Bear in mind that the LORD has given you the Sabbath; that is why on the sixth day he gives you bread for two days. Everyone is to stay where he is on the seventh day; no one is to go out." ³⁰So the people rested on the seventh day.

³¹The people of Israel called the bread manna.*d* It was white like coriander seed and tasted like wafers made with honey. ³²Moses said, "This is what the LORD has commanded: 'Take an omer of manna and keep it for the generations to come, so they can see the bread I gave you to eat in the desert when I brought you out of Egypt.' "

³³So Moses said to Aaron, "Take a jar and put an omer of manna in it. Then place it before the LORD to be kept for the generations to come."

³⁴As the LORD commanded Moses, Aaron put the manna in front of the Testimony, that it might be kept. ³⁵The Israelites ate manna forty years, until they came to a land that was settled; they ate manna until they reached the border of Canaan.

³⁶(An omer is one tenth of an ephah.)

Water From the Rock The whole Israelite community set out from the Desert of Sin, traveling from place to place as the LORD commanded. They camped at Rephidim, but there was no water for the people to drink. ²So they quarreled with Moses and said, "Give us water to drink."

Moses replied, "Why do you quarrel with me? Why do you put the LORD to the test?"

³But the people were thirsty for water there, and they grumbled against Moses. They said, "Why did you bring us up out of Egypt to make us and our children and livestock die of thirst?"

---

a16 That is, probably about 2 quarts (about 2 liters); also in verses 18, 32, 33 and 36   *b22* That is, probably about 4 quarts (about 4.5 liters)   *c28* The Hebrew is plural.   *d31* *Manna* means *What is it?* (see verse 15).

⁴Then Moses cried out to the Lord, "What am I to do with these people? They are almost ready to stone me."

⁵The Lord answered Moses, "Walk on ahead of the people. Take with you some of the elders of Israel and take in your hand the staff with which you struck the Nile, and go. ⁶I will stand there before you by the rock at Horeb. Strike the rock, and water will come out of it for the people to drink." So Moses did this in the sight of the elders of Israel. ⁷And he called the place Massah*ᵃ* and Meribah*ᵇ* because the Israelites quarreled and because they tested the Lord saying, "Is the Lord among us or not?"

The Amalekites Defeated ⁸The Amalekites came and attacked the Israelites at Rephidim. ⁹Moses said to Joshua, "Choose some of our men and go out to fight the Amalekites. Tomorrow I will stand on top of the hill with the staff of God in my hands."

¹⁰So Joshua fought the Amalekites as Moses had ordered, and Moses, Aaron and Hur went to the top of the hill. ¹¹As long as Moses held up his hands, the Israelites were winning, but whenever he lowered his hands, the Amalekites were winning. ¹²When Moses' hands grew tired, they took a stone and put it under him and he sat on it. Aaron and Hur held his hands up—one on one side, one on the other—so that his hands remained steady till sunset. ¹³So Joshua overcame the Amalekite army with the sword.

¹⁴Then the Lord said to Moses, "Write this on a scroll as something to be remembered and make sure that Joshua hears it, because I will completely blot out the memory of Amalek from under heaven."

¹⁵Moses built an altar and called it The Lord is my Banner. ¹⁶He said, "For hands were lifted up to the throne of the Lord. The*ᶜ* Lord will be at war against the Amalekites from generation to generation."

Jethro Visits Moses Now Jethro, the priest of Midian and father-in-law of Moses, heard of everything God had done for Moses and for his people Israel, and how the Lord had brought Israel out of Egypt.

²After Moses had sent away his wife Zipporah, his father-in-law Jethro received her ³and her two sons. One son was named Gershom,*ᵈ* for Moses said, "I have become an alien in a foreign land"; ⁴and the other was named Eliezer,*ᵉ* for he said, "My father's God was my helper; he saved me from the sword of Pharaoh."

⁵Jethro, Moses' father-in-law, together with Moses' sons and wife, came to him in the desert, where he was camped near the mountain of God. ⁶Jethro had sent word to him, "I, your father-in-law Jethro, am coming to you with your wife and her two sons."

⁷So Moses went out to meet his father-in-law and bowed down and kissed him. They greeted each other and then went into the tent. ⁸Moses told his father-in-law about everything the Lord had done to Pharaoh and the Egyptians for Israel's sake and about all the hardships they had met along the way and how the Lord had saved them.

⁹Jethro was delighted to hear about all the good things the Lord had done for Israel in rescuing them from the hand of the Egyptians. ¹⁰He said, "Praise be to the Lord, who rescued you from the hand of the Egyptians and of Pharaoh, and who rescued the people from the hand of the Egyptians. ¹¹Now I know that the Lord is greater than all other gods, for he did this to those who had treated Israel arrogantly." ¹²Then Jethro, Moses' father-in-law, brought a burnt offering and other sacrifices to God, and Aaron came with all the elders of Israel to eat bread with Moses' father-in-law in the presence of God.

ᵃ7 Massah means *testing.* *ᵇ7 Meribah* means *quarreling.* *ᶜ16* Or *"Because a hand was against the throne of the* Lord, *the* *ᵈ3 Gershom* sounds like the Hebrew for *an alien there.* *ᵉ4 Eliezer* means *my God is helper.*

¹³The next day Moses took his seat to serve as judge for the people, and they stood around him from morning till evening. ¹⁴When his father-in-law saw all that Moses was doing for the people, he said, "What is this you are doing for the people? Why do you alone sit as judge, while all these people stand around you from morning till evening?"

¹⁵Moses answered him, "Because the people come to me to seek God's will. ¹⁶Whenever they have a dispute, it is brought to me, and I decide between the parties and inform them of God's decrees and laws."

¹⁷Moses' father-in-law replied, "What you are doing is not good. ¹⁸You and these people who come to you will only wear yourselves out. The work is too heavy for you; you cannot handle it alone. ¹⁹Listen now to me and I will give you some advice, and may God be with you. You must be the people's representative before God and bring their disputes to him. ²⁰Teach them the decrees and laws, and show them the way to live and the duties they are to perform. ²¹But select capable men from all the people—men who fear God, trustworthy men who hate dishonest gain—and appoint them as officials over thousands, hundreds, fifties and tens. ²²Have them serve as judges for the people at all times, but have them bring every difficult case to you; the simple cases they can decide themselves. That will make your load lighter, because they will share it with you. ²³If you do this and God so commands, you will be able to stand the strain, and all these people will go home satisfied."

²⁴Moses listened to his father-in-law and did everything he said. ²⁵He chose capable men from all Israel and made them leaders of the people, officials over thousands, hundreds, fifties and tens. ²⁶They served as judges for the people at all times. The difficult cases they brought to Moses, but the simple ones they decided themselves.

²⁷Then Moses sent his father-in-law on his way, and Jethro returned to his own country.

19 *At Mount Sinai* In the third month after the Israelites left Egypt—on the very day—they came to the Desert of Sinai. ²After they set out from Rephidim, they entered the Desert of Sinai, and Israel camped there in the desert in front of the mountain.

³Then Moses went up to God, and the LORD called to him from the mountain and said, "This is what you are to say to the house of Jacob and what you are to tell the people of Israel: ⁴'You yourselves have seen what I did to Egypt, and how I carried you on eagles' wings and brought you to myself. ⁵Now if you obey me fully and keep my covenant, then out of all nations you will be my treasured possession. Although the whole earth is mine, ⁶you*ᵃ* will be for me a kingdom of priests and a holy nation.' These are the words you are to speak to the Israelites."

⁷So Moses went back and summoned the elders of the people and set before them all the words the LORD had com-

ᵃ5,6 Or *possession, for the whole earth is mine.* ⁶*You*

EXODUS 18:17-19

Advice is often hard to take. Dad wants to show you how to bowl. Mom says she knows a better way to study. Your older brother says your sweater is out of style. Hey, whose life is it, anyway? Check out how Moses reacted when his father-in-law Jethro offered advice. Jethro started out in the worst way possible: he said, "What you are doing is not good" (Exodus 18:17). Talk about criticism! But Moses listened. He didn't get hostile. Instead he realized that Jethro was right, and he followed his advice. If one of the Bible's truly great men, Moses, can take advice without feeling attacked or getting hostile, maybe you can too.

Direct Line

manded him to speak. ⁸The people all responded together, "We will do everything the LORD has said." So Moses brought their answer back to the LORD.

⁹The LORD said to Moses, "I am going to come to you in a dense cloud, so that the people will hear me speaking with you and will always put their trust in you." Then Moses told the LORD what the people had said.

¹⁰And the LORD said to Moses, "Go to the people and consecrate them today and tomorrow. Have them wash their clothes ¹¹and be ready by the third day, because on that day the LORD will come down on Mount Sinai in the sight of all the people. ¹²Put limits for the people around the mountain and tell them, 'Be careful that you do not go up the mountain or touch the foot of it. Whoever touches the mountain shall surely be put to death. ¹³He shall surely be stoned or shot with arrows; not a hand is to be laid on him. Whether man or animal, he shall not be permitted to live.' Only when the ram's horn sounds a long blast may they go up to the mountain."

¹⁴After Moses had gone down the mountain to the people, he consecrated them, and they washed their clothes. ¹⁵Then he said to the people, "Prepare yourselves for the third day. Abstain from sexual relations."

> You will be my treasured possession (Exodus 19:5).

¹⁶On the morning of the third day there was thunder and lightning, with a thick cloud over the mountain, and a very loud trumpet blast. Everyone in the camp trembled. ¹⁷Then Moses led the people out of the camp to meet with God, and they stood at the foot of the mountain. ¹⁸Mount Sinai was covered with smoke, because the LORD descended on it in fire. The smoke billowed up from it like smoke from a furnace, the whole mountain*a* trembled violently, ¹⁹and the sound of the trumpet grew louder and louder. Then Moses spoke and the voice of God answered him.*b*

²⁰The LORD descended to the top of Mount Sinai and called Moses to the top of the mountain. So Moses went up ²¹and the LORD said to him, "Go down and warn the people so they do not force their way through to see the LORD and many of them perish. ²²Even the priests, who approach the LORD, must consecrate themselves, or the LORD will break out against them."

²³Moses said to the LORD, "The people cannot come up Mount Sinai, because you yourself warned us, 'Put limits around the mountain and set it apart as holy.'"

²⁴The LORD replied, "Go down and bring Aaron up with you. But the priests and the people must not force their way through to come up to the LORD, or he will break out against them."

²⁵So Moses went down to the people and told them.

20 *The Ten Commandments* And God spoke all these words:

²"I am the LORD your God, who brought you out of Egypt, out of the land of slavery.

³"You shall have no other gods before*c* me.

⁴"You shall not make for yourself an idol in the form of anything in heaven above or on the earth beneath or in the waters below. ⁵You shall not bow down to them or worship them; for I, the LORD your God, am a jealous God, punishing the children for the sin of the fathers to the third and fourth generation of those who hate me, ⁶but showing love to a thousand ˌgenerationsˌ of those who love me and keep my commandments.

---

a18 Most Hebrew manuscripts; a few Hebrew manuscripts and Septuagint *all the people*   *b19* Or *and God answered him with thunder*   *c3* Or *besides*

⁷"You shall not misuse the name of the LORD your God, for the LORD will not hold anyone guiltless who misuses his name.

⁸"Remember the Sabbath day by keeping it holy. ⁹Six days you shall labor and do all your work, ¹⁰but the seventh day is a Sabbath to the LORD your God. On it you shall not do any work, neither you, nor your son or daughter, nor your manservant or maidservant, nor your animals, nor the alien within your gates. ¹¹For in six days the LORD made the heavens and the earth, the sea, and all that is in them, but he rested on the seventh day. Therefore the LORD blessed the Sabbath day and made it holy.

¹²"Honor your father and your mother, so that you may live long in the land the LORD your God is giving you.

¹³"You shall not murder.

¹⁴"You shall not commit adultery.

¹⁵"You shall not steal.

¹⁶"You shall not give false testimony against your neighbor.

¹⁷"You shall not covet your neighbor's house. You shall not covet your neighbor's wife, or his manservant or maidservant, his ox or donkey, or anything that belongs to your neighbor."

¹⁸When the people saw the thunder and lightning and heard the trumpet and saw the mountain in smoke, they trembled with fear. They stayed at a distance ¹⁹and said to Moses, "Speak to us yourself and we will listen. But do not have God speak to us or we will die."

²⁰Moses said to the people, "Do not be afraid. God has come to test you, so that the fear of God will be with you to keep you from sinning."

²¹The people remained at a distance, while Moses approached the thick darkness where God was.

Idols and Altars ²²Then the LORD said to Moses, "Tell the Israelites this: 'You have seen for yourselves that I have spoken to you from heaven: ²³Do not make any gods to be alongside me; do not make for yourselves gods of silver or gods of gold.

²⁴" 'Make an altar of earth for me and sacrifice on it your burnt offerings and fellowship offerings,ᵃ your sheep and goats and your cattle. Wherever I cause my name to be honored, I will come to you and bless you. ²⁵If you make an altar of stones for me, do not build it with dressed stones, for you will defile it if you use a tool on it. ²⁶And do not go up to my altar on steps, lest your nakedness be exposed on it.'

21 "These are the laws you are to set before them:

Hebrew Servants ²"If you buy a Hebrew servant, he is to serve you for six years. But in the seventh year, he shall go free, without paying anything. ³If he comes alone, he is to go free alone; but if he has a wife when he comes, she is to go with him. ⁴If his master gives him a wife and she bears him sons or daughters, the woman and her children shall belong to her master, and only the man shall go free.

⁵"But if the servant declares, 'I love my master and my wife and children and do not want to go free,' ⁶then his master must take him before the judges.ᵇ He shall take him to the door or the doorpost and pierce his ear with an awl. Then he will be his servant for life.

⁷"If a man sells his daughter as a servant, she is not to go free as menservants do. ⁸If she does not please the master who has selected her for himself,ᶜ he must let her be redeemed. He has no right to sell her to foreigners,

ᵃ24 Traditionally *peace offerings* ᵇ6 Or *before God* ᶜ8 Or *master so that he does not choose her* because he has broken faith with her. ⁹If he selects her for his son, he must grant her the rights of a daughter. ¹⁰If he marries another woman, he must not deprive the first one of her food, clothing and marital rights. ¹¹If he does not provide her with these three things, she is to go free, without any payment of money.

Personal Injuries ¹²"Anyone who strikes a man and kills him shall surely be put to death. ¹³However, if he does not do it intentionally, but God lets it happen, he is to flee to a place I will designate. ¹⁴But if a man schemes and kills another man deliberately, take him away from my altar and put him to death.

¹⁵"Anyone who attacks*a* his father or his mother must be put to death.

¹⁶"Anyone who kidnaps another and either sells him or still has him when he is caught must be put to death.

¹⁷"Anyone who curses his father or mother must be put to death.

¹⁸"If men quarrel and one hits the other with a stone or with his fist*b* and he does not die but is confined to bed, ¹⁹the one who struck the blow will not be held responsible if the other gets up and walks around outside with his staff; however, he must pay the injured man for the loss of his time and see that he is completely healed.

²⁰"If a man beats his male or female slave with a rod and the slave dies as a direct result, he must be punished, ²¹but he is not to be punished if the slave gets up after a day or two, since the slave is his property.

²²"If men who are fighting hit a pregnant woman and she gives birth prematurely*c* but there is no serious injury, the offender must be fined whatever the woman's husband demands and the court allows. ²³But if there is serious injury, you are to take life for life, ²⁴eye for eye, tooth for tooth, hand for hand, foot for foot, ²⁵burn for burn, wound for wound, bruise for bruise.

²⁶"If a man hits a manservant or maidservant in the eye and destroys it, he must let the servant go free to compensate for the eye. ²⁷And if he knocks out the tooth of a manservant or maidservant, he must let the servant go free to compensate for the tooth.

²⁸"If a bull gores a man or a woman to death, the bull must be stoned to death, and its meat must not be eaten. But the owner of the bull will not be held responsible. ²⁹If, however, the bull has had the habit of goring and the owner has been warned but has not kept it penned up and it kills a man or woman, the bull must be stoned and the owner also must be put to death. ³⁰However, if payment is demanded of him, he may redeem his life by paying whatever is demanded. ³¹This law also applies if the bull gores a son or daughter. ³²If the bull gores a male or female slave, the owner must pay thirty shekels*d* of silver to the master of the slave, and the bull must be stoned.

³³"If a man uncovers a pit or digs one and fails to cover it and an ox or a donkey falls into it, ³⁴the owner of the pit must pay for the loss; he must pay its owner, and the dead animal will be his.

³⁵"If a man's bull injures the bull of another and it dies, they are to sell the live one and divide both the money and the dead animal equally. ³⁶However, if it was known that the bull had the habit of goring, yet the owner did not keep it penned up, the owner must pay, animal for animal, and the dead animal will be his.

22 ***Protection of Property*** "If a man steals an ox or a sheep and slaughters it or sells it, he must pay back five head of cattle for the ox and four sheep for the sheep.

²"If a thief is caught breaking in and is struck so that he dies, the defender

---

a15 Or kills *b18 Or with a tool* *c22 Or she has a miscarriage* *d32 That is, about 12 ounces (about 0.3 kilogram)*

Dear Sam,

Some of my friends say bad things about others just because of their skin color or nationality. Does the Bible mention prejudice?

Cara in Carson City

100 Advice Lane, Anywhere, USA

Dear Sam, Inc.

Dear Cara,

God made many different races, giving each distinctive characteristics. Even within the same race there are differences—short or tall, thin or heavy. God made some people extroverts and others introverts. No two people are alike. But all are made in the image of God.

You asked what the Bible teaches. Check out Exodus 22:21 to see how the Israelites were instructed to interact with people of other races. John 4 tells how Jesus treated a Samaritan woman (the Samaritans were a despised race, and women were held in very low esteem). And Paul makes it very clear that everyone who believes in Jesus is equally accepted by God (Galatians 3:26-29; Ephesians 2:11-20; Colossians 3:11).

So when you are tempted to put people down because of their skin color, remember—you would be mocking God's creation! Instead praise him for the variety he's given.

Sam

is not guilty of bloodshed; ³but if it happens*ᵃ* after sunrise, he is guilty of bloodshed.

"A thief must certainly make restitution, but if he has nothing, he must be sold to pay for his theft.

⁴"If the stolen animal is found alive in his possession—whether ox or donkey or sheep—he must pay back double.

⁵"If a man grazes his livestock in a field or vineyard and lets them stray and they graze in another man's field, he must make restitution from the best of his own field or vineyard.

⁶"If a fire breaks out and spreads into thornbushes so that it burns shocks of grain or standing grain or the whole field, the one who started the fire must make restitution.

⁷"If a man gives his neighbor silver or goods for safekeeping and they are stolen from the neighbor's house, the thief, if he is caught, must pay back double. ⁸But if the thief is not found, the owner of the house must appear before the judges*ᵇ* to determine whether he has laid his hands on the other man's property. ⁹In all cases of illegal possession of an ox, a donkey, a sheep, a garment, or any other lost property about which somebody says, 'This is mine,' both parties are to bring their cases before the judges. The one whom the judges declare*ᶜ* guilty must pay back double to his neighbor.

¹⁰"If a man gives a donkey, an ox, a sheep or any other animal to his neighbor for safekeeping and it dies or is injured or is taken away while no one is looking, ¹¹the issue between them will be settled by the taking of an oath before the Lᴏʀᴅ that the neighbor did not lay hands on the other person's property. The owner is to accept this, and no restitution is required. ¹²But if the animal was stolen from the neighbor, he must make restitution to the owner. ¹³If it was torn to pieces by a wild animal, he shall bring in the remains as evidence and he will not be required to pay for the torn animal.

¹⁴"If a man borrows an animal from his neighbor and it is injured or dies while the owner is not present, he must make restitution. ¹⁵But if the owner is with the animal, the borrower will not have to pay. If the animal was hired, the money paid for the hire covers the loss.

Social Responsibility   ¹⁶"If a man seduces a virgin who is not pledged to be married and sleeps with her, he must pay the bride-price, and she shall be his wife. ¹⁷If her father absolutely refuses to give her to him, he must still pay the bride-price for virgins.

¹⁸"Do not allow a sorceress to live.

¹⁹"Anyone who has sexual relations with an animal must be put to death.

²⁰"Whoever sacrifices to any god other than the Lᴏʀᴅ must be destroyed.*ᵈ*

²¹"Do not mistreat an alien or oppress him, for you were aliens in Egypt.

²²"Do not take advantage of a widow or an orphan. ²³If you do and they cry out to me, I will certainly hear their cry. ²⁴My anger will be aroused, and I will kill you with the sword; your wives will become widows and your children fatherless.

²⁵"If you lend money to one of my people among you who is needy, do not be like a moneylender; charge him no interest.*ᵉ* ²⁶If you take your neighbor's cloak as a pledge, return it to him by sunset, ²⁷because his cloak is the only covering he has for his body. What else will he sleep in? When he cries out to me, I will hear, for I am compassionate.

²⁸"Do not blaspheme God*ᶠ* or curse the ruler of your people.

²⁹"Do not hold back offerings from your granaries or your vats.*ᵍ*

"You must give me the firstborn of your sons. ³⁰Do the same with your cat-

---

ᵃ3 Or if he strikes him   ᵇ8 Or before God; also in verse 9   ᶜ9 Or whom God declares   ᵈ20 The Hebrew term refers to the irrevocable giving over of things or persons to the Lᴏʀᴅ, often by totally destroying them.   ᵉ25 Or excessive interest   ᶠ28 Or Do not revile the judges   ᵍ29 The meaning of the Hebrew for this phrase is uncertain.

tle and your sheep. Let them stay with their mothers for seven days, but give them to me on the eighth day.

³¹"You are to be my holy people. So do not eat the meat of an animal torn by wild beasts; throw it to the dogs.

23 *Laws of Justice and Mercy* "Do not spread false reports. Do not help a wicked man by being a malicious witness.

²"Do not follow the crowd in doing wrong. When you give testimony in a lawsuit, do not pervert justice by siding with the crowd, ³and do not show favoritism to a poor man in his lawsuit.

⁴"If you come across your enemy's ox or donkey wandering off, be sure to take it back to him. ⁵If you see the donkey of someone who hates you fallen down under its load, do not leave it there; be sure you help him with it.

⁶"Do not deny justice to your poor people in their lawsuits. ⁷Have nothing to do with a false charge and do not put an innocent or honest person to death, for I will not acquit the guilty.

⁸"Do not accept a bribe, for a bribe blinds those who see and twists the words of the righteous.

⁹"Do not oppress an alien; you yourselves know how it feels to be aliens, because you were aliens in Egypt.

Sabbath Laws ¹⁰"For six years you are to sow your fields and harvest the crops, ¹¹but during the seventh year let the land lie unplowed and unused. Then the poor among your people may get food from it, and the wild animals may eat what they leave. Do the same with your vineyard and your olive grove.

¹²"Six days do your work, but on the seventh day do not work, so that your ox and your donkey may rest and the slave born in your household, and the alien as well, may be refreshed.

¹³"Be careful to do everything I have said to you. Do not invoke the names of other gods; do not let them be heard on your lips.

The Three Annual Festivals ¹⁴"Three times a year you are to celebrate a festival to me.

¹⁵"Celebrate the Feast of Unleavened Bread; for seven days eat bread made without yeast, as I commanded you. Do this at the appointed time in the month of Abib, for in that month you came out of Egypt.

"No one is to appear before me empty-handed.

¹⁶"Celebrate the Feast of Harvest with the firstfruits of the crops you sow in your field.

"Celebrate the Feast of Ingathering at the end of the year, when you gather in your crops from the field.

¹⁷"Three times a year all the men are to appear before the Sovereign Lord.

¹⁸"Do not offer the blood of a sacrifice to me along with anything containing yeast.

"The fat of my festival offerings must not be kept until morning.

¹⁹"Bring the best of the firstfruits of your soil to the house of the Lord your God.

"Do not cook a young goat in its mother's milk.

EXODUS 23:4–5

You find the lost term paper of a classmate who hates you—and give it back to him. You say nice things about the girl who's spreading terrible rumors about you. To most people that's crazy. They say you ought to tear up the term paper and get even with that nasty girl. But you don't, because you're following a pattern established in Exodus 23:4–5. Why does God tell you to do good to people who don't like you? Maybe because God wants you to be like *him*, not like those around you who like to hurt you. And maybe because the best way to get rid of an enemy is to make him or her your friend.

Direct Line

God's Angel to Prepare the Way [20]"See, I am sending an angel ahead of you to guard you along the way and to bring you to the place I have prepared. [21]Pay attention to him and listen to what he says. Do not rebel against him; he will not forgive your rebellion, since my Name is in him. [22]If you listen carefully to what he says and do all that I say, I will be an enemy to your enemies and will oppose those who oppose you. [23]My angel will go ahead of you and bring you into the land of the Amorites, Hittites, Perizzites, Canaanites, Hivites and Jebusites, and I will wipe them out. [24]Do not bow down before their gods or worship them or follow their practices. You must demolish them and break their sacred stones to pieces. [25]Worship the LORD your God, and his blessing will be on your food and water. I will take away sickness from among you, [26]and none will miscarry or be barren in your land. I will give you a full life span.

[27]"I will send my terror ahead of you and throw into confusion every nation you encounter. I will make all your enemies turn their backs and run. [28]I will send the hornet ahead of you to drive the Hivites, Canaanites and Hittites out of your way. [29]But I will not drive them out in a single year, because the land would become desolate and the wild animals too numerous for you. [30]Little by little I will drive them out before you, until you have increased enough to take possession of the land.

[31]"I will establish your borders from the Red Sea[a] to the Sea of the Philistines,[b] and from the desert to the River.[c] I will hand over to you the people who live in the land and you will drive them out before you. [32]Do not make a covenant with them or with their gods. [33]Do not let them live in your land, or they will cause you to sin against me, because the worship of their gods will certainly be a snare to you."

The Covenant Confirmed Then he said to Moses, "Come up to the LORD, you and Aaron, Nadab and Abihu, and seventy of the elders of Israel. You are to worship at a distance, [2]but Moses alone is to approach the LORD; the others must not come near. And the people may not come up with him."

[3]When Moses went and told the people all the LORD's words and laws, they responded with one voice, "Everything the LORD has said we will do." [4]Moses then wrote down everything the LORD had said.

He got up early the next morning and built an altar at the foot of the mountain and set up twelve stone pillars representing the twelve tribes of Israel. [5]Then he sent young Israelite men, and they offered burnt offerings and sacrificed young bulls as fellowship offerings[d] to the LORD. [6]Moses took half of the blood and put it in bowls, and the other half he sprinkled on the altar. [7]Then he took the Book of the Covenant and read it to the people. They responded, "We will do everything the LORD has said; we will obey."

[8]Moses then took the blood, sprinkled it on the people and said, "This is the blood of the covenant that the LORD has made with you in accordance with all these words."

[9]Moses and Aaron, Nadab and Abihu, and the seventy elders of Israel went up [10]and saw the God of Israel. Under his feet was something like a pavement made of sapphire,[e] clear as the sky itself. [11]But God did not raise his hand against these leaders of the Israelites; they saw God, and they ate and drank.

[12]The LORD said to Moses, "Come up to me on the mountain and stay here, and I will give you the tablets of stone, with the law and commands I have written for their instruction."

[13]Then Moses set out with Joshua his aide, and Moses went up on the mountain of God. [14]He said to the elders, "Wait here for us until we come

---

[a]31 Hebrew *Yam Suph*; that is, Sea of Reeds [b]31 That is, the Mediterranean [c]31 That is, the Euphrates [d]5 Traditionally *peace offerings* [e]10 Or *lapis lazuli*

back to you. Aaron and Hur are with you, and anyone involved in a dispute can go to them."

¹⁵When Moses went up on the mountain, the cloud covered it, ¹⁶and the glory of the LORD settled on Mount Sinai. For six days the cloud covered the mountain, and on the seventh day the LORD called to Moses from within the cloud. ¹⁷To the Israelites the glory of the LORD looked like a consuming fire on top of the mountain. ¹⁸Then Moses entered the cloud as he went on up the mountain. And he stayed on the mountain forty days and forty nights.

25 *Offerings for the Tabernacle* The LORD said to Moses, ²"Tell the Israelites to bring me an offering. You are to receive the offering for me from each man whose heart prompts him to give. ³These are the offerings you are to receive from them: gold, silver and bronze; ⁴blue, purple and scarlet yarn and fine linen; goat hair; ⁵ram skins dyed red and hides of sea cows*ᵃ* ; acacia wood; ⁶olive oil for the light; spices for the anointing oil and for the fragrant incense; ⁷and onyx stones and other gems to be mounted on the ephod and breastpiece.

⁸"Then have them make a sanctuary for me, and I will dwell among them. ⁹Make this tabernacle and all its furnishings exactly like the pattern I will show you.

The Ark ¹⁰"Have them make a chest of acacia wood—two and a half cubits long, a cubit and a half wide, and a cubit and a half high.*ᵇ* ¹¹Overlay it with pure gold, both inside and out, and make a gold molding around it. ¹²Cast four gold rings for it and fasten them to its four feet, with two rings on one side and two rings on the other. ¹³Then make poles of acacia wood and overlay them with gold. ¹⁴Insert the poles into the rings on the sides of the chest to carry it. ¹⁵The poles are to remain in the rings of this ark; they are not to be removed. ¹⁶Then put in the ark the Testimony, which I will give you.

¹⁷"Make an atonement cover*ᶜ* of pure gold—two and a half cubits long and a cubit and a half wide.*ᵈ* ¹⁸And make two cherubim out of hammered gold at the ends of the cover. ¹⁹Make one cherub on one end and the second cherub on the other; make the cherubim of one piece with the cover, at the two ends. ²⁰The cherubim are to have their wings spread upward, overshadowing the cover with them. The cherubim are to face each other, looking toward the cover. ²¹Place the cover on top of the ark and put in the ark the Testimony, which I will give you. ²²There, above the cover between the two cherubim that are over the ark of the Testimony, I will meet with you and give you all my commands for the Israelites.

The Table ²³"Make a table of acacia wood—two cubits long, a cubit wide and a cubit and a half high.*ᵉ* ²⁴Overlay it with pure gold and make a gold molding around it. ²⁵Also make around it a rim a handbreadth*ᶠ* wide and put a gold molding on the rim. ²⁶Make four gold rings for the table and fasten them to the four corners, where the four legs are. ²⁷The rings are to be close to the rim to hold the poles used in carrying the table. ²⁸Make the poles of acacia wood, overlay them with gold and carry the table with them. ²⁹And make its plates and dishes of pure gold, as well as its pitchers and bowls for the pouring out of offerings. ³⁰Put the bread of the Presence on this table to be before me at all times.

EXODUS 25

QUIZZER

Q: What did the ark of God look like?

BONUS: Why isn't the ark in Jerusalem today?

Answers on page 100

---

*ᵃ5 That is, dugongs *ᵇ10 That is, about 3 3/4 feet (about 1.1 meters) long and 2 1/4 feet (about 0.7 meter) wide and high *ᶜ17 Traditionally *a mercy seat* *ᵈ17 That is, about 3 3/4 feet (about 1.1 meters) long and 2 1/4 feet (about 0.7 meter) wide *ᵉ23 That is, about 3 feet (about 0.9 meter) long and 1 1/2 feet (about 0.5 meter) wide and 2 1/4 feet (about 0.7 meter) high *ᶠ25 That is, about 3 inches (about 8 centimeters)

The Lampstand ³¹"Make a lampstand of pure gold and hammer it out, base and shaft; its flowerlike cups, buds and blossoms shall be of one piece with it. ³²Six branches are to extend from the sides of the lampstand—three on one side and three on the other. ³³Three cups shaped like almond flowers with buds and blossoms are to be on one branch, three on the next branch, and the same for all six branches extending from the lampstand. ³⁴And on the lampstand there are to be four cups shaped like almond flowers with buds and blossoms. ³⁵One bud shall be under the first pair of branches extending from the lampstand, a second bud under the second pair, and a third bud under the third pair—six branches in all. ³⁶The buds and branches shall all be of one piece with the lampstand, hammered out of pure gold.

³⁷"Then make its seven lamps and set them up on it so that they light the space in front of it. ³⁸Its wick trimmers and trays are to be of pure gold. ³⁹A talent^a of pure gold is to be used for the lampstand and all these accessories. ⁴⁰See that you make them according to the pattern shown you on the mountain.

The Tabernacle "Make the tabernacle with ten curtains of finely twisted linen and blue, purple and scarlet yarn, with cherubim worked into them by a skilled craftsman. ²All the curtains are to be the same size—twenty-eight cubits long and four cubits wide.^b ³Join five of the curtains together, and do the same with the other five. ⁴Make loops of blue material along the edge of the end curtain in one set, and do the same with the end curtain in the other set. ⁵Make fifty loops on one curtain and fifty loops on the end curtain of the other set, with the loops opposite each other. ⁶Then make fifty gold clasps and use them to fasten the curtains together so that the tabernacle is a unit.

⁷"Make curtains of goat hair for the tent over the tabernacle— eleven altogether. ⁸All eleven curtains are to be the same size—thirty cubits long and four cubits wide.^c ⁹Join five of the curtains together into one set and the other six into another set. Fold the sixth curtain double at the front of the tent. ¹⁰Make fifty loops along the edge of the end curtain in one set and also along the edge of the end curtain in the other set. ¹¹Then make fifty bronze clasps and put them in the loops to fasten the tent together as a unit. ¹²As for the additional length of the tent curtains, the half curtain that is left over is to hang down at the rear of the tabernacle. ¹³The tent curtains will be a cubit^d longer on both sides; what is left will hang over the sides of the tabernacle so as to cover it. ¹⁴Make for the tent a covering of ram skins dyed red, and over that a covering of hides of sea cows.^e

¹⁵"Make upright frames of acacia wood for the tabernacle. ¹⁶Each frame is to be ten cubits long and a cubit and a half wide,^f ¹⁷with two projections set parallel to each other. Make all the frames of the tabernacle in this way. ¹⁸Make twenty frames for the south side of the tabernacle ¹⁹and make forty silver bases to go under them—two bases for each frame, one under each projection. ²⁰For the other side, the north side of the tabernacle, make twenty frames ²¹and forty silver bases—two under each frame. ²²Make six frames for the far end, that is, the west end of the tabernacle, ²³and make two frames for the corners at the far end. ²⁴At these two corners they must be double from the bottom all the way to the top, and fitted into a single ring; both shall be like that. ²⁵So there will be eight frames and sixteen silver bases—two under each frame.

²⁶"Also make crossbars of acacia wood: five for the frames on one side of

Answers
to Quizzer on
page 99

A: It was a small, gold-covered box topped with two gold angels (Exodus 25:10-22).

BONUS: It was taken to Babylon when the two tribes of Judah went into captivity (2 Chronicles 36:18) and has never been found since.

---

^a39 That is, about 75 pounds (about 34 kilograms) ^b2 That is, about 42 feet (about 12.5 meters) long and 6 feet (about 1.8 meters) wide ^c8 That is, about 45 feet (about 13.5 meters) long and 6 feet (about 1.8 meters) wide ^d13 That is, about 1 1/2 feet (about 0.5 meter) ^e14 That is, dugongs ^f16 That is, about 15 feet (about 4.5 meters) long and 2 1/4 feet (about 0.7 meter) wide

the tabernacle, ²⁷five for those on the other side, and five for the frames on the west, at the far end of the tabernacle. ²⁸The center crossbar is to extend from end to end at the middle of the frames. ²⁹Overlay the frames with gold and make gold rings to hold the crossbars. Also overlay the crossbars with gold.

³⁰"Set up the tabernacle according to the plan shown you on the mountain.

³¹"Make a curtain of blue, purple and scarlet yarn and finely twisted linen, with cherubim worked into it by a skilled craftsman. ³²Hang it with gold hooks on four posts of acacia wood overlaid with gold and standing on four silver bases. ³³Hang the curtain from the clasps and place the ark of the Testimony behind the curtain. The curtain will separate the Holy Place from the Most Holy Place. ³⁴Put the atonement cover on the ark of the Testimony in the Most Holy Place. ³⁵Place the table outside the curtain on the north side of the tabernacle and put the lampstand opposite it on the south side.

³⁶"For the entrance to the tent make a curtain of blue, purple and scarlet yarn and finely twisted linen—the work of an embroiderer. ³⁷Make gold hooks for this curtain and five posts of acacia wood overlaid with gold. And cast five bronze bases for them.

The Altar of Burnt Offering "Build an altar of acacia wood, three cubits*ᵃ* high; it is to be square, five cubits long and five cubits wide.*ᵇ* ²Make a horn at each of the four corners, so that the horns and the altar are of one piece, and overlay the altar with bronze. ³Make all its utensils of bronze—its pots to remove the ashes, and its shovels, sprinkling bowls, meat forks and firepans. ⁴Make a grating for it, a bronze network, and make a bronze ring at each of the four corners of the network. ⁵Put it under the ledge of the altar so that it is halfway up the altar. ⁶Make poles of acacia wood for the altar and overlay them with bronze. ⁷The poles are to be inserted into the rings so they will be on two sides of the altar when it is carried. ⁸Make the altar hollow, out of boards. It is to be made just as you were shown on the mountain.

The Courtyard ⁹"Make a courtyard for the tabernacle. The south side shall be a hundred cubits*ᶜ* long and is to have curtains of finely twisted linen, ¹⁰with twenty posts and twenty bronze bases and with silver hooks and bands on the posts. ¹¹The north side shall also be a hundred cubits long and is to have curtains, with twenty posts and twenty bronze bases and with silver hooks and bands on the posts.

¹²"The west end of the courtyard shall be fifty cubits*ᵈ* wide and have curtains, with ten posts and ten bases. ¹³On the east end, toward the sunrise, the courtyard shall also be fifty cubits wide. ¹⁴Curtains fifteen cubits*ᵉ* long are to be on one side of the entrance, with three posts and three bases, ¹⁵and curtains fifteen cubits long are to be on the other side, with three posts and three bases.

¹⁶"For the entrance to the courtyard, provide a curtain twenty cubits*ᶠ* long, of blue, purple and scarlet yarn and finely twisted linen—the work of an embroiderer—with four posts and four bases. ¹⁷All the posts around the courtyard are to have silver bands and hooks, and bronze bases. ¹⁸The courtyard shall be a hundred cubits long and fifty cubits wide,*ᵍ* with curtains of finely twisted linen five cubits*ʰ* high, and with bronze bases. ¹⁹All the other articles used in the service of the tabernacle, whatever their function, including all the tent pegs for it and those for the courtyard, are to be of bronze.

Oil for the Lampstand   ²⁰"Command the Israelites to bring you clear oil of pressed olives for the light so that the lamps may be kept burning. ²¹In the Tent of Meeting, outside the curtain that is in front of the Testimony, Aaron and his sons are to keep the lamps burning before the LORD from evening till morning. This is to be a lasting ordinance among the Israelites for the generations to come.

28 *The Priestly Garments*   "Have Aaron your brother brought to you from among the Israelites, along with his sons Nadab and Abihu, Eleazar and Ithamar, so they may serve me as priests. ²Make sacred garments for your brother Aaron, to give him dignity and honor. ³Tell all the skilled men to whom I have given wisdom in such matters that they are to make garments for Aaron, for his consecration, so he may serve me as priest. ⁴These are the garments they are to make: a breastpiece, an ephod, a robe, a woven tunic, a turban and a sash. They are to make these sacred garments for your brother Aaron and his sons, so they may serve me as priests. ⁵Have them use gold, and blue, purple and scarlet yarn, and fine linen.

The Ephod   ⁶"Make the ephod of gold, and of blue, purple and scarlet yarn, and of finely twisted linen—the work of a skilled craftsman. ⁷It is to have two shoulder pieces attached to two of its corners, so it can be fastened. ⁸Its skillfully woven waistband is to be like it—of one piece with the ephod and made with gold, and with blue, purple and scarlet yarn, and with finely twisted linen.

⁹"Take two onyx stones and engrave on them the names of the sons of Israel ¹⁰in the order of their birth—six names on one stone and the remaining six on the other. ¹¹Engrave the names of the sons of Israel on the two stones the way a gem cutter engraves a seal. Then mount the stones in gold filigree settings ¹²and fasten them on the shoulder pieces of the ephod as memorial stones for the sons of Israel. Aaron is to bear the names on his shoulders as a memorial before the LORD. ¹³Make gold filigree settings ¹⁴and two braided chains of pure gold, like a rope, and attach the chains to the settings.

The Breastpiece   ¹⁵"Fashion a breastpiece for making decisions—the work of a skilled craftsman. Make it like the ephod: of gold, and of blue, purple and scarlet yarn, and of finely twisted linen. ¹⁶It is to be square—a span*a* long and a span wide—and folded double. ¹⁷Then mount four rows of precious stones on it. In the first row there shall be a ruby, a topaz and a beryl; ¹⁸in the second row a turquoise, a sapphire*b* and an emerald; ¹⁹in the third row a jacinth, an agate and an amethyst; ²⁰in the fourth row a chrysolite, an onyx and a jasper.*c* Mount them in gold filigree settings. ²¹There are to be twelve stones, one for each of the names of the sons of Israel, each engraved like a seal with the name of one of the twelve tribes.

²²"For the breastpiece make braided chains of pure gold, like a rope. ²³Make two gold rings for it and fasten them to two corners of the breastpiece. ²⁴Fasten the two gold chains to the rings at the corners of the breastpiece, ²⁵and the other ends of the chains to the two settings, attaching them to the shoulder pieces of the ephod at the front. ²⁶Make two gold rings and attach them to the other two corners of the breastpiece on the inside edge next to the ephod. ²⁷Make two more gold rings and attach them to the bottom of the shoulder pieces on the front of the ephod, close to the seam just above the waistband of the ephod. ²⁸The rings of the breastpiece are to be tied to the rings of the ephod with blue cord, connecting it to the waistband, so that the breastpiece will not swing out from the ephod.

²⁹"Whenever Aaron enters the Holy Place, he will bear the names of the

---

a16 That is, about 9 inches (about 22 centimeters)   *b18* Or *lapis lazuli*   *c20* The precise identification of some of these precious stones is uncertain.

sons of Israel over his heart on the breastpiece of decision as a continuing memorial before the LORD. ³⁰Also put the Urim and the Thummim in the breastpiece, so they may be over Aaron's heart whenever he enters the presence of the LORD. Thus Aaron will always bear the means of making decisions for the Israelites over his heart before the LORD.

Other Priestly Garments ³¹"Make the robe of the ephod entirely of blue cloth, ³²with an opening for the head in its center. There shall be a woven edge like a collar*ᵃ* around this opening, so that it will not tear. ³³Make pomegranates of blue, purple and scarlet yarn around the hem of the robe, with gold bells between them. ³⁴The gold bells and the pomegranates are to alternate around the hem of the robe. ³⁵Aaron must wear it when he ministers. The sound of the bells will be heard when he enters the Holy Place before the LORD and when he comes out, so that he will not die.

³⁶"Make a plate of pure gold and engrave on it as on a seal: HOLY TO THE LORD. ³⁷Fasten a blue cord to it to attach it to the turban; it is to be on the front of the turban. ³⁸It will be on Aaron's forehead, and he will bear the guilt involved in the sacred gifts the Israelites consecrate, whatever their gifts may be. It will be on Aaron's forehead continually so that they will be acceptable to the LORD.

³⁹"Weave the tunic of fine linen and make the turban of fine linen. The sash is to be the work of an embroiderer. ⁴⁰Make tunics, sashes and headbands for Aaron's sons, to give them dignity and honor. ⁴¹After you put these clothes on your brother Aaron and his sons, anoint and ordain them. Consecrate them so they may serve me as priests.

⁴²"Make linen undergarments as a covering for the body, reaching from the waist to the thigh. ⁴³Aaron and his sons must wear them whenever they enter the Tent of Meeting or approach the altar to minister in the Holy Place, so that they will not incur guilt and die.

"This is to be a lasting ordinance for Aaron and his descendants.

29 *Consecration of the Priests* "This is what you are to do to consecrate them, so they may serve me as priests: Take a young bull and two rams without defect. ²And from fine wheat flour, without yeast, make bread, and cakes mixed with oil, and wafers spread with oil. ³Put them in a basket and present them in it—along with the bull and the two rams. ⁴Then bring Aaron and his sons to the entrance to the Tent of Meeting and wash them with water. ⁵Take the garments and dress Aaron with the tunic, the robe of the ephod, the ephod itself and the breastpiece. Fasten the ephod on him by its skillfully woven waistband. ⁶Put the turban on his head and attach the sacred diadem to the turban. ⁷Take the anointing oil and anoint him by pouring it on his head. ⁸Bring his sons and dress them in tunics ⁹and put headbands on them. Then tie sashes on Aaron and his sons.*ᵇ* The priesthood is theirs by a lasting ordinance. In this way you shall ordain Aaron and his sons.

¹⁰"Bring the bull to the front of the Tent of Meeting, and Aaron and his sons shall lay their hands on its head. ¹¹Slaughter it in the LORD's presence at the entrance to the Tent of Meeting. ¹²Take some of the bull's blood and put it on the horns of the altar with your finger, and pour out the rest of it at the base of the altar. ¹³Then take all the fat around the inner parts, the covering of the liver, and both kidneys with the fat on them, and burn them on the altar. ¹⁴But burn the bull's flesh and its hide and its offal outside the camp. It is a sin offering.

¹⁵"Take one of the rams, and Aaron and his sons shall lay their hands on its head. ¹⁶Slaughter it and take the blood and sprinkle it against the altar on

ᵃ32 The meaning of the Hebrew for this word is uncertain. ᵇ9 Hebrew; Septuagint on them all sides. ¹⁷Cut the ram into pieces and wash the inner parts and the legs, putting them with the head and the other pieces. ¹⁸Then burn the entire ram on the altar. It is a burnt offering to the Lord, a pleasing aroma, an offering made to the Lord by fire.

¹⁹"Take the other ram, and Aaron and his sons shall lay their hands on its head. ²⁰Slaughter it, take some of its blood and put it on the lobes of the right ears of Aaron and his sons, on the thumbs of their right hands, and on the big toes of their right feet. Then sprinkle blood against the altar on all sides. ²¹And take some of the blood on the altar and some of the anointing oil and sprinkle it on Aaron and his garments and on his sons and their garments. Then he and his sons and their garments will be consecrated.

²²"Take from this ram the fat, the fat tail, the fat around the inner parts, the covering of the liver, both kidneys with the fat on them, and the right thigh. (This is the ram for the ordination.) ²³From the basket of bread made without yeast, which is before the Lord, take a loaf, and a cake made with oil, and a wafer. ²⁴Put all these in the hands of Aaron and his sons and wave them before the Lord as a wave offering. ²⁵Then take them from their hands and burn them on the altar along with the burnt offering for a pleasing aroma to the Lord, an offering made to the Lord by fire. ²⁶After you take the breast of the ram for Aaron's ordination, wave it before the Lord as a wave offering, and it will be your share.

²⁷"Consecrate those parts of the ordination ram that belong to Aaron and his sons: the breast that was waved and the thigh that was presented. ²⁸This is always to be the regular share from the Israelites for Aaron and his sons. It is the contribution the Israelites are to make to the Lord from their fellowship offerings.^a

²⁹"Aaron's sacred garments will belong to his descendants so that they can be anointed and ordained in them. ³⁰The son who succeeds him as priest and comes to the Tent of Meeting to minister in the Holy Place is to wear them seven days.

³¹"Take the ram for the ordination and cook the meat in a sacred place. ³²At the entrance to the Tent of Meeting, Aaron and his sons are to eat the meat of the ram and the bread that is in the basket. ³³They are to eat these offerings by which atonement was made for their ordination and consecration. But no one else may eat them, because they are sacred. ³⁴And if any of the meat of the ordination ram or any bread is left over till morning, burn it up. It must not be eaten, because it is sacred.

³⁵"Do for Aaron and his sons everything I have commanded you, taking seven days to ordain them. ³⁶Sacrifice a bull each day as a sin offering to make atonement. Purify the altar by making atonement for it, and anoint it to consecrate it. ³⁷For seven days make atonement for the altar and consecrate it. Then the altar will be most holy, and whatever touches it will be holy.

³⁸"This is what you are to offer on the altar regularly each day: two lambs a year old. ³⁹Offer one in the morning and the other at twilight. ⁴⁰With the first lamb offer a tenth of an ephah^b of fine flour mixed with a quarter of a hin^c of oil from pressed olives, and a quarter of a hin of wine as a drink offering. ⁴¹Sacrifice the other lamb at twilight with the same grain offering and its drink offering as in the morning—a pleasing aroma, an offering made to the Lord by fire.

⁴²"For the generations to come this burnt offering is to be made regularly at the entrance to the Tent of Meeting before the Lord. There I will meet you and speak to you; ⁴³there also I will meet with the Israelites, and the place will be consecrated by my glory.

---

^a28 Traditionally *peace offerings*   ^b40 That is, probably about 2 quarts (about 2 liters)   ^c40 That is, probably about 1 quart (about 1 liter)

⁴⁴"So I will consecrate the Tent of Meeting and the altar and will consecrate Aaron and his sons to serve me as priests. ⁴⁵Then I will dwell among the Israelites and be their God. ⁴⁶They will know that I am the LORD their God, who brought them out of Egypt so that I might dwell among them. I am the LORD their God.

The Altar of Incense "Make an altar of acacia wood for burning incense. ²It is to be square, a cubit long and a cubit wide, and two cubits high*ᵃ*—its horns of one piece with it. ³Overlay the top and all the sides and the horns with pure gold, and make a gold molding around it. ⁴Make two gold rings for the altar below the molding—two on opposite sides—to hold the poles used to carry it. ⁵Make the poles of acacia wood and overlay them with gold. ⁶Put the altar in front of the curtain that is before the ark of the Testimony—before the atonement cover that is over the Testimony—where I will meet with you.

⁷"Aaron must burn fragrant incense on the altar every morning when he tends the lamps. ⁸He must burn incense again when he lights the lamps at twilight so incense will burn regularly before the LORD for the generations to come. ⁹Do not offer on this altar any other incense or any burnt offering or grain offering, and do not pour a drink offering on it. ¹⁰Once a year Aaron shall make atonement on its horns. This annual atonement must be made with the blood of the atoning sin offering for the generations to come. It is most holy to the LORD."

Atonement Money ¹¹Then the LORD said to Moses, ¹²"When you take a census of the Israelites to count them, each one must pay the LORD a ransom for his life at the time he is counted. Then no plague will come on them when you number them. ¹³Each one who crosses over to those already counted is to give a half shekel,*ᵇ* according to the sanctuary shekel, which weighs twenty gerahs. This half shekel is an offering to the LORD. ¹⁴All who cross over, those twenty years old or more, are to give an offering to the LORD. ¹⁵The rich are not to give more than a half shekel and the poor are not to give less when you make the offering to the LORD to atone for your lives. ¹⁶Receive the atonement money from the Israelites and use it for the service of the Tent of Meeting. It will be a memorial for the Israelites before the LORD, making atonement for your lives."

Basin for Washing ¹⁷Then the LORD said to Moses, ¹⁸"Make a bronze basin, with its bronze stand, for washing. Place it between the Tent of Meeting and the altar, and put water in it. ¹⁹Aaron and his sons are to wash their hands and feet with water from it. ²⁰Whenever they enter the Tent of Meeting, they shall wash with water so that they will not die. Also, when they approach the altar to minister by presenting an offering made to the LORD by fire, ²¹they shall wash their hands and feet so that they will not die. This is to be a lasting ordinance for Aaron and his descendants for the generations to come."

Anointing Oil ²²Then the LORD said to Moses, ²³"Take the following fine spices: 500 shekels*ᶜ* of liquid myrrh, half as much (that is, 250 shekels) of fragrant cinnamon, 250 shekels of fragrant cane, ²⁴500 shekels of cassia—all according to the sanctuary shekel—and a hin*ᵈ* of olive oil. ²⁵Make these into a sacred anointing oil, a fragrant blend, the work of a perfumer. It will be the sacred anointing oil. ²⁶Then use it to anoint the Tent of Meeting, the ark of the Testimony, ²⁷the table and all its articles, the lampstand and its accessories, the altar of incense, ²⁸the altar of burnt offering and all its uten-

---

ᵃ2 That is, about 1 1/2 feet (about 0.5 meter) long and wide and about 3 feet (about 0.9 meter) high
ᵇ13 That is, about 1/5 ounce (about 6 grams); also in verse 15   *ᶜ23* That is, about 12 1/2 pounds (about 6 kilograms)   *ᵈ24* That is, probably about 4 quarts (about 4 liters)

sils, and the basin with its stand. ²⁹You shall consecrate them so they will be most holy, and whatever touches them will be holy.

³⁰"Anoint Aaron and his sons and consecrate them so they may serve me as priests. ³¹Say to the Israelites, 'This is to be my sacred anointing oil for the generations to come. ³²Do not pour it on men's bodies and do not make any oil with the same formula. It is sacred, and you are to consider it sacred. ³³Whoever makes perfume like it and whoever puts it on anyone other than a priest must be cut off from his people.' "

Incense ³⁴Then the LORD said to Moses, "Take fragrant spices—gum resin, onycha and galbanum—and pure frankincense, all in equal amounts, ³⁵and make a fragrant blend of incense, the work of a perfumer. It is to be salted and pure and sacred. ³⁶Grind some of it to powder and place it in front of the Testimony in the Tent of Meeting, where I will meet with you. It shall be most holy to you. ³⁷Do not make any incense with this formula for yourselves; consider it holy to the LORD. ³⁸Whoever makes any like it to enjoy its fragrance must be cut off from his people."

31 *Bezalel and Oholiab* Then the LORD said to Moses, ²"See, I have chosen Bezalel son of Uri, the son of Hur, of the tribe of Judah, ³and I have filled him with the Spirit of God, with skill, ability and knowledge in all kinds of crafts— ⁴to make artistic designs for work in gold, silver and bronze, ⁵to cut and set stones, to work in wood, and to engage in all kinds of craftsmanship. ⁶Moreover, I have appointed Oholiab son of Ahisamach, of the tribe of Dan, to help him. Also I have given skill to all the craftsmen to make everything I have commanded you: ⁷the Tent of Meeting, the ark of the Testimony with the atonement cover on it, and all the other furnishings of the tent— ⁸the table and its articles, the pure gold lampstand and all its accessories, the altar of incense, ⁹the altar of burnt offering and all its utensils, the basin with its stand— ¹⁰and also the woven garments, both the sacred garments for Aaron the priest and the garments for his sons when they serve as priests, ¹¹and the anointing oil and fragrant incense for the Holy Place. They are to make them just as I commanded you."

The Sabbath ¹²Then the LORD said to Moses, ¹³"Say to the Israelites, 'You must observe my Sabbaths. This will be a sign between me and you for the generations to come, so you may know that I am the LORD, who makes you holy.ᵃ

¹⁴" 'Observe the Sabbath, because it is holy to you. Anyone who desecrates it must be put to death; whoever does any work on that day must be cut off from his people. ¹⁵For six days, work is to be done, but the seventh day is a Sabbath of rest, holy to the LORD. Whoever does any work on the Sabbath day must be put to death. ¹⁶The Israelites are to observe the Sabbath, celebrating it for the generations to come as a lasting covenant. ¹⁷It will be a sign between me and the Israelites forever, for in six days the LORD made the heavens and the earth, and on the seventh day he abstained from work and rested.' "

¹⁸When the LORD finished speaking to Moses on Mount Sinai, he gave him the

---

Direct Line

EXODUS 31:1–11

Ken gets all A's. You don't. Shelly is a good speaker. You're not. Karen has a good voice. You can't sing a note. Kind of makes you think you'll never amount to much, doesn't it? Of course, you work harder at school than Ken. You may not be a good speaker, but you can fix just about anything on a car. This passage speaks about Bezalel. God gave him talent in all kinds of crafts— from metal work to jewelry design. Bezalel used his talent for God. Any talent you have is a gift from God. He can use your talent. He can use you.

ᵃ13 Or *who sanctifies you;* or *who sets you apart as holy*

two tablets of the Testimony, the tablets of stone inscribed by the finger of God.

32 **The Golden Calf** When the people saw that Moses was so long in coming down from the mountain, they gathered around Aaron and said, "Come, make us gods*a* who will go before us. As for this fellow Moses who brought us up out of Egypt, we don't know what has happened to him."

²Aaron answered them, "Take off the gold earrings that your wives, your sons and your daughters are wearing, and bring them to me." ³So all the people took off their earrings and brought them to Aaron. ⁴He took what they handed him and made it into an idol cast in the shape of a calf, fashioning it with a tool. Then they said, "These are your gods,*b* O Israel, who brought you up out of Egypt."

⁵When Aaron saw this, he built an altar in front of the calf and announced, "Tomorrow there will be a festival to the LORD." ⁶So the next day the people rose early and sacrificed burnt offerings and presented fellowship offerings.*c* Afterward they sat down to eat and drink and got up to indulge in revelry.

⁷Then the LORD said to Moses, "Go down, because your people, whom you brought up out of Egypt, have become corrupt. ⁸They have been quick to turn away from what I commanded them and have made themselves an idol cast in the shape of a calf. They have bowed down to it and sacrificed to it and have said, 'These are your gods, O Israel, who brought you up out of Egypt.'

⁹"I have seen these people," the LORD said to Moses, "and they are a stiff-necked people. ¹⁰Now leave me alone so that my anger may burn against them and that I may destroy them. Then I will make you into a great nation."

¹¹But Moses sought the favor of the LORD his God. "O LORD," he said, "why should your anger burn against your people, whom you brought out of Egypt with great power and a mighty hand? ¹²Why should the Egyptians say, 'It was with evil intent that he brought them out, to kill them in the mountains and to wipe them off the face of the earth'? Turn from your fierce anger; relent and do not bring disaster on your people. ¹³Remember your servants Abraham, Isaac and Israel, to whom you swore by your own self: 'I will make your descendants as numerous as the stars in the sky and I will give your descendants all this land I promised them, and it will be their inheritance forever.'"
¹⁴Then the LORD relented and did not bring on his people the disaster he had threatened.

¹⁵Moses turned and went down the mountain with the two tablets of the Testimony in his hands. They were inscribed on both sides, front and back. ¹⁶The tablets were the work of God; the writing was the writing of God, engraved on the tablets.

¹⁷When Joshua heard the noise of the people shouting, he said to Moses, "There is the sound of war in the camp."

¹⁸Moses replied:

> "It is not the sound of victory,
> it is not the sound of defeat;
> it is the sound of singing that I hear."

¹⁹When Moses approached the camp and saw the calf and the dancing, his anger burned and he threw the tablets out of his hands, breaking them to

EXODUS 32

QUIZZER

Q: Where did slaves get enough gold to make a golden calf?

BONUS: How much gold did the Israelites have?

Answers on page 108

---

a1 Or a god; also in verses 23 and 31 *b4 Or This is your god; also in verse 8* *c6 Traditionally peace offerings*

pieces at the foot of the mountain. ²⁰And he took the calf they had made and burned it in the fire; then he ground it to powder, scattered it on the water and made the Israelites drink it.

²¹He said to Aaron, "What did these people do to you, that you led them into such great sin?"

²²"Do not be angry, my lord," Aaron answered. "You know how prone these people are to evil. ²³They said to me, 'Make us gods who will go before us. As for this fellow Moses who brought us up out of Egypt, we don't know what has happened to him.' ²⁴So I told them, 'Whoever has any gold jewelry, take it off.' Then they gave me the gold, and I threw it into the fire, and out came this calf!"

²⁵Moses saw that the people were running wild and that Aaron had let them get out of control and so become a laughingstock to their enemies. ²⁶So he stood at the entrance to the camp and said, "Whoever is for the LORD, come to me." And all the Levites rallied to him.

²⁷Then he said to them, "This is what the LORD, the God of Israel, says: 'Each man strap a sword to his side. Go back and forth through the camp from one end to the other, each killing his brother and friend and neighbor.' " ²⁸The Levites did as Moses commanded, and that day about three thousand of the people died. ²⁹Then Moses said, "You have been set apart to the LORD today, for you were against your own sons and brothers, and he has blessed you this day."

³⁰The next day Moses said to the people, "You have committed a great sin. But now I will go up to the LORD; perhaps I can make atonement for your sin."

³¹So Moses went back to the LORD and said, "Oh, what a great sin these people have committed! They have made themselves gods of gold. ³²But now, please forgive their sin—but if not, then blot me out of the book you have written."

³³The LORD replied to Moses, "Whoever has sinned against me I will blot out of my book. ³⁴Now go, lead the people to the place I spoke of, and my angel will go before you. However, when the time comes for me to punish, I will punish them for their sin."

³⁵And the LORD struck the people with a plague because of what they did with the calf Aaron had made.

33 Then the LORD said to Moses, "Leave this place, you and the people you brought up out of Egypt, and go up to the land I promised on oath to Abraham, Isaac and Jacob, saying, 'I will give it to your descendants.' ²I will send an angel before you and drive out the Canaanites, Amorites, Hittites, Perizzites, Hivites and Jebusites. ³Go up to the land flowing with milk and honey. But I will not go with you, because you are a stiff-necked people and I might destroy you on the way."

⁴When the people heard these distressing words, they began to mourn and no one put on any ornaments. ⁵For the LORD had said to Moses, "Tell the Israelites, 'You are a stiff-necked people. If I were to go with you even for a moment, I might destroy you. Now take off your ornaments and I will decide what to do with you.' " ⁶So the Israelites stripped off their ornaments at Mount Horeb.

The Tent of Meeting ⁷Now Moses used to take a tent and pitch it outside the camp some distance away, calling it the "tent of meeting." Anyone inquiring of the LORD would go to the tent of meeting outside the camp. ⁸And whenever Moses went out to the tent, all the people rose and stood at the entrances to their tents, watching Moses until he entered the tent. ⁹As Moses went into the tent, the pillar of cloud would come down and stay at the entrance, while the LORD spoke with Moses. ¹⁰Whenever the people saw the pillar of cloud standing at the entrance to the tent, they all stood and worshiped, each at the entrance to his tent. ¹¹The LORD would speak to Mo-

---

Answers

to Quizzer on page 107

A: They got it from Egyptians who were terrified by the plagues (Exodus 12:35-36).

BONUS: Besides the gold used for the calf, they had about a ton for constructing the tabernacle (Exodus 38:21-31).

ses face to face, as a man speaks with his friend. Then Moses would return to the camp, but his young aide Joshua son of Nun did not leave the tent.

Moses and the Glory of the LORD ¹²Moses said to the LORD, "You have been telling me, 'Lead these people,' but you have not let me know whom you will send with me. You have said, 'I know you by name and you have found favor with me.' ¹³If you are pleased with me, teach me your ways so I may know you and continue to find favor with you. Remember that this nation is your people."

¹⁴The LORD replied, "My Presence will go with you, and I will give you rest."

¹⁵Then Moses said to him, "If your Presence does not go with us, do not send us up from here. ¹⁶How will anyone know that you are pleased with me and with your people unless you go with us? What else will distinguish me and your people from all the other people on the face of the earth?"

¹⁷And the LORD said to Moses, "I will do the very thing you have asked, because I am pleased with you and I know you by name."

¹⁸Then Moses said, "Now show me your glory."

¹⁹And the LORD said, "I will cause all my goodness to pass in front of you, and I will proclaim my name, the LORD, in your presence. I will have mercy on whom I will have mercy, and I will have compassion on whom I will have compassion. ²⁰But," he said, "you cannot see my face, for no one may see me and live."

²¹Then the LORD said, "There is a place near me where you may stand on a rock. ²²When my glory passes by, I will put you in a cleft in the rock and cover you with my hand until I have passed by. ²³Then I will remove my hand and you will see my back; but my face must not be seen."

34 *The New Stone Tablets* The LORD said to Moses, "Chisel out two stone tablets like the first ones, and I will write on them the words that were on the first tablets, which you broke. ²Be ready in the morning, and then come up on Mount Sinai. Present yourself to me there on top of the mountain. ³No one is to come with you or be seen anywhere on the mountain; not even the flocks and herds may graze in front of the mountain."

⁴So Moses chiseled out two stone tablets like the first ones and went up Mount Sinai early in the morning, as the LORD had commanded him; and he carried the two stone tablets in his hands. ⁵Then the LORD came down in the cloud and stood there with him and proclaimed his name, the LORD. ⁶And he passed in front of Moses, proclaiming, "The LORD, the LORD, the compassionate and gracious God, slow to anger, abounding in love and faithfulness, ⁷maintaining love to thousands, and forgiving wickedness, rebellion and sin. Yet he does not leave the guilty unpunished; he punishes the children and their children for the sin of the fathers to the third and fourth generation."

⁸Moses bowed to the ground at once and worshiped. ⁹"O Lord, if I have found favor in your eyes," he said, "then let the Lord go with us. Although this is a stiff-necked people, forgive our wickedness and our sin, and take us as your inheritance."

¹⁰Then the LORD said: "I am making a covenant with you. Before all your people I will do wonders never before done in any nation in all the world. The people you live among will see how awesome is the work that I, the LORD, will do for you. ¹¹Obey what I command you today. I will drive out before you the Amorites, Canaanites, Hittites, Perizzites, Hivites and Jebusites. ¹²Be careful not to make a treaty with those who live in the land where you are going, or they will be a snare among you. ¹³Break down their altars, smash their sacred stones and cut down their Asherah poles.ᵃ ¹⁴Do not worship any other god, for the LORD, whose name is Jealous, is a jealous God.

ᵃ13 That is, symbols of the goddess Asherah

¹⁵"Be careful not to make a treaty with those who live in the land; for when they prostitute themselves to their gods and sacrifice to them, they will invite you and you will eat their sacrifices. ¹⁶And when you choose some of their daughters as wives for your sons and those daughters prostitute themselves to their gods, they will lead your sons to do the same.

¹⁷"Do not make cast idols.

¹⁸"Celebrate the Feast of Unleavened Bread. For seven days eat bread made without yeast, as I commanded you. Do this at the appointed time in the month of Abib, for in that month you came out of Egypt.

¹⁹"The first offspring of every womb belongs to me, including all the first-born males of your livestock, whether from herd or flock. ²⁰Redeem the first-born donkey with a lamb, but if you do not redeem it, break its neck. Redeem all your firstborn sons.

"No one is to appear before me empty-handed.

²¹"Six days you shall labor, but on the seventh day you shall rest; even during the plowing season and harvest you must rest.

²²"Celebrate the Feast of Weeks with the firstfruits of the wheat harvest, and the Feast of Ingathering at the turn of the year.ᵃ ²³Three times a year all your men are to appear before the Sovereign LORD, the God of Israel. ²⁴I will drive out nations before you and enlarge your territory, and no one will covet your land when you go up three times each year to appear before the LORD your God.

²⁵"Do not offer the blood of a sacrifice to me along with anything containing yeast, and do not let any of the sacrifice from the Passover Feast remain until morning.

²⁶"Bring the best of the firstfruits of your soil to the house of the LORD your God.

"Do not cook a young goat in its mother's milk."

²⁷Then the LORD said to Moses, "Write down these words, for in accordance with these words I have made a covenant with you and with Israel." ²⁸Moses was there with the LORD forty days and forty nights without eating bread or drinking water. And he wrote on the tablets the words of the covenant—the Ten Commandments.

The Radiant Face of Moses ²⁹When Moses came down from Mount Sinai with the two tablets of the Testimony in his hands, he was not aware that his face was radiant because he had spoken with the LORD. ³⁰When Aaron and all the Israelites saw Moses, his face was radiant, and they were afraid to come near him. ³¹But Moses called to them; so Aaron and all the leaders of the community came back to him, and he spoke to them. ³²Afterward all the Israelites came near him, and he gave them all the commands the LORD had given him on Mount Sinai.

³³When Moses finished speaking to them, he put a veil over his face. ³⁴But whenever he entered the LORD's presence to speak with him, he removed the veil until he came out. And when he came out and told the Israelites what he had been

---

EXODUS 34:14

Jealousy is one of those "bad" emotions, isn't it? Why then does the Bible say, "the LORD, whose name is Jealous, is a jealous God"? The Hebrew word here describes an intense love. In human beings jealousy usually is selfish. God's jealousy is different. God's jealousy is intense love, a love so strong that he wants only what is best for you. That's why God gets so upset when you sin. He loves you too much to just stand by and see you mess up your life. His intense love makes him jealous of anything in your life that pulls you away from him and the wonderful things he has planned for you.

Direct Line

ᵃ22 That is, in the fall

commanded, ³⁵they saw that his face was radiant. Then Moses would put the veil back over his face until he went in to speak with the LORD.

Sabbath Regulations   Moses assembled the whole Israelite community and said to them, "These are the things the LORD has commanded you to do: ²For six days, work is to be done, but the seventh day shall be your holy day, a Sabbath of rest to the LORD. Whoever does any work on it must be put to death. ³Do not light a fire in any of your dwellings on the Sabbath day."

Materials for the Tabernacle   ⁴Moses said to the whole Israelite community, "This is what the LORD has commanded: ⁵From what you have, take an offering for the LORD. Everyone who is willing is to bring to the LORD an offering of gold, silver and bronze; ⁶blue, purple and scarlet yarn and fine linen; goat hair; ⁷ram skins dyed red and hides of sea cows*ª*; acacia wood; ⁸olive oil for the light; spices for the anointing oil and for the fragrant incense; ⁹and onyx stones and other gems to be mounted on the ephod and breastpiece.

¹⁰"All who are skilled among you are to come and make everything the LORD has commanded: ¹¹the tabernacle with its tent and its covering, clasps, frames, crossbars, posts and bases; ¹²the ark with its poles and the atonement cover and the curtain that shields it; ¹³the table with its poles and all its articles and the bread of the Presence; ¹⁴the lampstand that is for light with its accessories, lamps and oil for the light; ¹⁵the altar of incense with its poles, the anointing oil and the fragrant incense; the curtain for the doorway at the entrance to the tabernacle; ¹⁶the altar of burnt offering with its bronze grating, its poles and all its utensils; the bronze basin with its stand; ¹⁷the curtains of the courtyard with its posts and bases, and the curtain for the entrance to the courtyard; ¹⁸the tent pegs for the tabernacle and for the courtyard, and their ropes; ¹⁹the woven garments worn for ministering in the sanctuary—both the sacred garments for Aaron the priest and the garments for his sons when they serve as priests."

²⁰Then the whole Israelite community withdrew from Moses' presence, ²¹and everyone who was willing and whose heart moved him came and brought an offering to the LORD for the work on the Tent of Meeting, for all its service, and for the sacred garments. ²²All who were willing, men and women alike, came and brought gold jewelry of all kinds: brooches, earrings, rings and ornaments. They all presented their gold as a wave offering to the LORD. ²³Everyone who had blue, purple or scarlet yarn or fine linen, or goat hair, ram skins dyed red or hides of sea cows brought them. ²⁴Those presenting an offering of silver or bronze brought it as an offering to the LORD, and everyone who had acacia wood for any part of the work brought it. ²⁵Every skilled woman spun with her hands and brought what she had spun—blue, purple or scarlet yarn or fine linen. ²⁶And all the women who were willing and had the skill spun the goat hair. ²⁷The leaders brought onyx stones and other gems to be mounted on the ephod and breastpiece. ²⁸They also brought spices and olive oil for the light and for the anointing oil and for the fragrant incense. ²⁹All the Israelite men and women who were willing brought to the LORD freewill offerings for all the work the LORD through Moses had commanded them to do.

Bezalel and Oholiab   ³⁰Then Moses said to the Israelites, "See, the LORD has chosen Bezalel son of Uri, the son of Hur, of the tribe of Judah, ³¹and he has filled him with the Spirit of God, with skill, ability and knowledge in all kinds of crafts— ³²to make artistic designs for work in gold, silver and bronze, ³³to cut and set stones, to work in wood and to engage in all kinds of artistic

---

ª7 That is, dugongs; also in verse 23

craftsmanship. ³⁴And he has given both him and Oholiab son of Ahisamach, of the tribe of Dan, the ability to teach others. ³⁵He has filled them with skill to do all kinds of work as craftsmen, designers, embroiderers in blue, purple and scarlet yarn and fine linen, and weavers—all of them master craftsmen and designers. ¹So Bezalel, Oholiab and every skilled person to whom the LORD has given skill and ability to know how to carry out all the work of constructing the sanctuary are to do the work just as the Lord has commanded."

²Then Moses summoned Bezalel and Oholiab and every skilled person to whom the LORD had given ability and who was willing to come and do the work. ³They received from Moses all the offerings the Israelites had brought to carry out the work of constructing the sanctuary. And the people continued to bring freewill offerings morning after morning. ⁴So all the skilled craftsmen who were doing all the work on the sanctuary left their work ⁵and said to Moses, "The people are bringing more than enough for doing the work the LORD commanded to be done."

⁶Then Moses gave an order and they sent this word throughout the camp: "No man or woman is to make anything else as an offering for the sanctuary." And so the people were restrained from bringing more, ⁷because what they already had was more than enough to do all the work.

The Tabernacle ⁸All the skilled men among the workmen made the tabernacle with ten curtains of finely twisted linen and blue, purple and scarlet yarn, with cherubim worked into them by a skilled craftsman. ⁹All the curtains were the same size—twenty-eight cubits long and four cubits wide.ᵃ ¹⁰They joined five of the curtains together and did the same with the other five. ¹¹Then they made loops of blue material along the edge of the end curtain in one set, and the same was done with the end curtain in the other set. ¹²They also made fifty loops on one curtain and fifty loops on the end curtain of the other set, with the loops opposite each other. ¹³Then they made fifty gold clasps and used them to fasten the two sets of curtains together so that the tabernacle was a unit.

¹⁴They made curtains of goat hair for the tent over the tabernacle—eleven altogether. ¹⁵All eleven curtains were the same size—thirty cubits long and four cubits wide.ᵇ ¹⁶They joined five of the curtains into one set and the other six into another set. ¹⁷Then they made fifty loops along the edge of the end curtain in one set and also along the edge of the end curtain in the other set. ¹⁸They made fifty bronze clasps to fasten the tent together as a unit. ¹⁹Then they made for the tent a covering of ram skins dyed red, and over that a covering of hides of sea cows.ᶜ

²⁰They made upright frames of acacia wood for the tabernacle. ²¹Each frame was ten cubits long and a cubit and a half wide,ᵈ ²²with two projections set parallel to each other. They made all the frames of the tabernacle in this way. ²³They made twenty frames for the south side of the tabernacle ²⁴and made forty silver bases to go under them—two bases for each frame, one under each projection. ²⁵For the other side, the north side of the tabernacle, they made twenty frames ²⁶and forty silver bases—two under each frame. ²⁷They made six frames for the far end, that is, the west end of the tabernacle, ²⁸and two frames were made for the corners of the tabernacle at the far end. ²⁹At these two corners the frames were double from the bottom all the way to the top and fitted into a single ring; both were made alike. ³⁰So there were eight frames and sixteen silver bases—two under each frame.

³¹They also made crossbars of acacia wood: five for the frames on one side of the tabernacle, ³²five for those on the other side, and five for the frames

---

ᵃ9 That is, about 42 feet (about 12.5 meters) long and 6 feet (about 1.8 meters) wide   ᵇ15 That is, about 45 feet (about 13.5 meters) long and 6 feet (about 1.8 meters) wide   ᶜ19 That is, dugongs   ᵈ21 That is, about 15 feet (about 4.5 meters) long and 2 1/4 feet (about 0.7 meter) wide

on the west, at the far end of the tabernacle. ³³They made the center cross-bar so that it extended from end to end at the middle of the frames. ³⁴They overlaid the frames with gold and made gold rings to hold the crossbars. They also overlaid the crossbars with gold.

³⁵They made the curtain of blue, purple and scarlet yarn and finely twisted linen, with cherubim worked into it by a skilled craftsman. ³⁶They made four posts of acacia wood for it and overlaid them with gold. They made gold hooks for them and cast their four silver bases. ³⁷For the entrance to the tent they made a curtain of blue, purple and scarlet yarn and finely twisted linen—the work of an embroiderer; ³⁸and they made five posts with hooks for them. They overlaid the tops of the posts and their bands with gold and made their five bases of bronze.

The Ark   Bezalel made the ark of acacia wood—two and a half cubits long, a cubit and a half wide, and a cubit and a half high.ᵃ ²He overlaid it with pure gold, both inside and out, and made a gold molding around it. ³He cast four gold rings for it and fastened them to its four feet, with two rings on one side and two rings on the other. ⁴Then he made poles of acacia wood and overlaid them with gold. ⁵And he inserted the poles into the rings on the sides of the ark to carry it.

⁶He made the atonement cover of pure gold—two and a half cubits long and a cubit and a half wide.ᵇ ⁷Then he made two cherubim out of hammered gold at the ends of the cover. ⁸He made one cherub on one end and the second cherub on the other; at the two ends he made them of one piece with the cover. ⁹The cherubim had their wings spread upward, overshadowing the cover with them. The cherubim faced each other, looking toward the cover.

The Table   ¹⁰Theyᶜ made the table of acacia wood—two cubits long, a cubit wide, and a cubit and a half high.ᵈ ¹¹Then they overlaid it with pure gold and made a gold molding around it. ¹²They also made around it a rim a handbreadthᵉ wide and put a gold molding on the rim. ¹³They cast four gold rings for the table and fastened them to the four corners, where the four legs were. ¹⁴The rings were put close to the rim to hold the poles used in carrying the table. ¹⁵The poles for carrying the table were made of acacia wood and were overlaid with gold. ¹⁶And they made from pure gold the articles for the table—its plates and dishes and bowls and its pitchers for the pouring out of drink offerings.

The Lampstand   ¹⁷They made the lampstand of pure gold and hammered it out, base and shaft; its flowerlike cups, buds and blossoms were of one piece with it. ¹⁸Six branches extended from the sides of the lampstand—three on one side and three on the other. ¹⁹Three cups shaped like almond flowers with buds and blossoms were on one branch, three on the next branch and the same for all six branches extending from the lampstand. ²⁰And on the lampstand were four cups shaped like almond flowers with buds and blossoms. ²¹One bud was under the first pair of branches extending from the lampstand, a second bud under the second pair, and a third bud under the third pair—six branches in all. ²²The buds and the branches were all of one piece with the lampstand, hammered out of pure gold.

²³They made its seven lamps, as well as its wick trimmers and trays, of pure gold. ²⁴They made the lampstand and all its accessories from one talentᶠ of pure gold.

ᵃ1 That is, about 3 3/4 feet (about 1.1 meters) long and 2 1/4 feet (about 0.7 meter) wide and high   ᵇ6 That is, about 3 3/4 feet (about 1.1 meters) long and 2 1/4 feet (about 0.7 meter) wide   ᶜ10 Or He; also in verses 11-29   ᵈ10 That is, about 3 feet (about 0.9 meter) long, 1 1/2 feet (about 0.5 meter) wide, and 2 1/4 feet (about 0.7 meter) high   ᵉ12 That is, about 3 inches (about 8 centimeters)   ᶠ24 That is, about 75 pounds (about 34 kilograms)

The Altar of Incense   ²⁵They made the altar of incense out of acacia wood. It was square, a cubit long and a cubit wide, and two cubits high*ᵃ*—its horns of one piece with it. ²⁶They overlaid the top and all the sides and the horns with pure gold, and made a gold molding around it. ²⁷They made two gold rings below the molding—two on opposite sides—to hold the poles used to carry it. ²⁸They made the poles of acacia wood and overlaid them with gold.

²⁹They also made the sacred anointing oil and the pure, fragrant incense—the work of a perfumer.

The Altar of Burnt Offering   They*ᵇ* built the altar of burnt offering of acacia wood, three cubits*ᶜ* high; it was square, five cubits long and five cubits wide.*ᵈ* ²They made a horn at each of the four corners, so that the horns and the altar were of one piece, and they overlaid the altar with bronze. ³They made all its utensils of bronze—its pots, shovels, sprinkling bowls, meat forks and firepans. ⁴They made a grating for the altar, a bronze network, to be under its ledge, halfway up the altar. ⁵They cast bronze rings to hold the poles for the four corners of the bronze grating. ⁶They made the poles of acacia wood and overlaid them with bronze. ⁷They inserted the poles into the rings so they would be on the sides of the altar for carrying it. They made it hollow, out of boards.

Basin for Washing   ⁸They made the bronze basin and its bronze stand from the mirrors of the women who served at the entrance to the Tent of Meeting.

The Courtyard   ⁹Next they made the courtyard. The south side was a hundred cubits*ᵉ* long and had curtains of finely twisted linen, ¹⁰with twenty posts and twenty bronze bases, and with silver hooks and bands on the posts. ¹¹The north side was also a hundred cubits long and had twenty posts and twenty bronze bases, with silver hooks and bands on the posts.

¹²The west end was fifty cubits*ᶠ* wide and had curtains, with ten posts and ten bases, with silver hooks and bands on the posts. ¹³The east end, toward the sunrise, was also fifty cubits wide. ¹⁴Curtains fifteen cubits*ᵍ* long were on one side of the entrance, with three posts and three bases, ¹⁵and curtains fifteen cubits long were on the other side of the entrance to the courtyard, with three posts and three bases. ¹⁶All the curtains around the courtyard were of finely twisted linen. ¹⁷The bases for the posts were bronze. The hooks and bands on the posts were silver, and their tops were overlaid with silver; so all the posts of the courtyard had silver bands.

¹⁸The curtain for the entrance to the courtyard was of blue, purple and scarlet yarn and finely twisted linen—the work of an embroiderer. It was twenty cubits*ʰ* long and, like the curtains of the courtyard, five cubits*ⁱ* high, ¹⁹with four posts and four bronze bases. Their hooks and bands were silver, and their tops were overlaid with silver. ²⁰All the tent pegs of the tabernacle and of the surrounding courtyard were bronze.

The Materials Used   ²¹These are the amounts of the materials used for the tabernacle, the tabernacle of the Testimony, which were recorded at Moses' command by the Levites under the direction of Ithamar son of Aaron, the priest. ²²(Bezalel son of Uri, the son of Hur, of the tribe of Judah, made everything the LORD commanded Moses; ²³with him was Oholiab son of Ahisamach, of the tribe of Dan—a craftsman and designer, and an embroiderer in blue, purple and scarlet yarn and fine linen.) ²⁴The total amount of the gold

---

ᵃ25 That is, about 1 1/2 feet (about 0.5 meter) long and wide, and about 3 feet (about 0.9 meter) high   *ᵇ1* Or *He*; also in verses 2-9   *ᶜ1* That is, about 4 1/2 feet (about 1.3 meters)   *ᵈ1* That is, about 7 1/2 feet (about 2.3 meters) long and wide   *ᵉ9* That is, about 150 feet (about 46 meters)   *ᶠ12* That is, about 75 feet (about 23 meters)   *ᵍ14* That is, about 22 1/2 feet (about 6.9 meters)   *ʰ18* That is, about 30 feet (about 9 meters)   *ⁱ18* That is, about 7 1/2 feet (about 2.3 meters)

from the wave offering used for all the work on the sanctuary was 29 talents and 730 shekels,*a* according to the sanctuary shekel.

²⁵The silver obtained from those of the community who were counted in the census was 100 talents and 1,775 shekels,*b* according to the sanctuary shekel— ²⁶one beka per person, that is, half a shekel,*c* according to the sanctuary shekel, from everyone who had crossed over to those counted, twenty years old or more, a total of 603,550 men. ²⁷The 100 talents*d* of silver were used to cast the bases for the sanctuary and for the curtain—100 bases from the 100 talents, one talent for each base. ²⁸They used the 1,775 shekels*e* to make the hooks for the posts, to overlay the tops of the posts, and to make their bands.

²⁹The bronze from the wave offering was 70 talents and 2,400 shekels.*f* ³⁰They used it to make the bases for the entrance to the Tent of Meeting, the bronze altar with its bronze grating and all its utensils, ³¹the bases for the surrounding courtyard and those for its entrance and all the tent pegs for the tabernacle and those for the surrounding courtyard.

The Priestly Garments From the blue, purple and scarlet yarn they made woven garments for ministering in the sanctuary. They also made sacred garments for Aaron, as the LORD commanded Moses.

The Ephod ²They*g* made the ephod of gold, and of blue, purple and scarlet yarn, and of finely twisted linen. ³They hammered out thin sheets of gold and cut strands to be worked into the blue, purple and scarlet yarn and fine linen—the work of a skilled craftsman. ⁴They made shoulder pieces for the ephod, which were attached to two of its corners, so it could be fastened. ⁵Its skillfully woven waistband was like it—of one piece with the ephod and made with gold, and with blue, purple and scarlet yarn, and with finely twisted linen, as the LORD commanded Moses.

⁶They mounted the onyx stones in gold filigree settings and engraved them like a seal with the names of the sons of Israel. ⁷Then they fastened them on the shoulder pieces of the ephod as memorial stones for the sons of Israel, as the LORD commanded Moses.

The Breastpiece ⁸They fashioned the breastpiece—the work of a skilled craftsman. They made it like the ephod: of gold, and of blue, purple and scarlet yarn, and of finely twisted linen. ⁹It was square—a span*h* long and a span wide—and folded double. ¹⁰Then they mounted four rows of precious stones on it. In the first row there was a ruby, a topaz and a beryl; ¹¹in the second row a turquoise, a sapphire*i* and an emerald; ¹²in the third row a jacinth, an agate and an amethyst; ¹³in the fourth row a chrysolite, an onyx and a jasper.*j* They were mounted in gold filigree settings. ¹⁴There were twelve stones, one for each of the names of the sons of Israel, each engraved like a seal with the name of one of the twelve tribes.

¹⁵For the breastpiece they made braided chains of pure gold, like a rope. ¹⁶They made two gold filigree settings and two gold rings, and fastened the rings to two of the corners of the breastpiece. ¹⁷They fastened the two gold chains to the rings at the corners of the breastpiece, ¹⁸and the other ends of the chains to the two settings, attaching them to the shoulder pieces of the ephod at the front. ¹⁹They made two gold rings and attached them to the other two corners of the breastpiece on the inside edge next to the ephod. ²⁰Then they made two more gold rings and attached them to the bottom of

---

a24 The weight of the gold was a little over one ton (about 1 metric ton). b25 The weight of the silver was a little over 3 3/4 tons (about 3.4 metric tons). c26 That is, about 1/5 ounce (about 5.5 grams) d27 That is, about 3 3/4 tons (about 3.4 metric tons) e28 That is, about 45 pounds (about 20 kilograms) f29 The weight of the bronze was about 2 1/2 tons (about 2.4 metric tons). g2 Or He; also in verses 7, 8 and 22 h9 That is, about 9 inches (about 22 centimeters) i11 Or lapis lazuli j13 The precise identification of some of these precious stones is uncertain.

the shoulder pieces on the front of the ephod, close to the seam just above the waistband of the ephod. ²¹They tied the rings of the breastpiece to the rings of the ephod with blue cord, connecting it to the waistband so that the breastpiece would not swing out from the ephod—as the LORD commanded Moses.

Other Priestly Garments ²²They made the robe of the ephod entirely of blue cloth—the work of a weaver— ²³with an opening in the center of the robe like the opening of a collar,ᵃ and a band around this opening, so that it would not tear. ²⁴They made pomegranates of blue, purple and scarlet yarn and finely twisted linen around the hem of the robe. ²⁵And they made bells of pure gold and attached them around the hem between the pomegranates. ²⁶The bells and pomegranates alternated around the hem of the robe to be worn for ministering, as the LORD commanded Moses.

²⁷For Aaron and his sons, they made tunics of fine linen—the work of a weaver— ²⁸and the turban of fine linen, the linen headbands and the undergarments of finely twisted linen. ²⁹The sash was of finely twisted linen and blue, purple and scarlet yarn—the work of an embroiderer—as the LORD commanded Moses.

³⁰They made the plate, the sacred diadem, out of pure gold and engraved on it, like an inscription on a seal: HOLY TO THE LORD. ³¹Then they fastened a blue cord to it to attach it to the turban, as the LORD commanded Moses.

Moses Inspects the Tabernacle ³²So all the work on the tabernacle, the Tent of Meeting, was completed. The Israelites did everything just as the LORD commanded Moses. ³³Then they brought the tabernacle to Moses: the tent and all its furnishings, its clasps, frames, crossbars, posts and bases; ³⁴the covering of ram skins dyed red, the covering of hides of sea cowsᵇ and the shielding curtain; ³⁵the ark of the Testimony with its poles and the atonement cover; ³⁶the table with all its articles and the bread of the Presence; ³⁷the pure gold lampstand with its row of lamps and all its accessories, and the oil for the light; ³⁸the gold altar, the anointing oil, the fragrant incense, and the curtain for the entrance to the tent; ³⁹the bronze altar with its bronze grating, its poles and all its utensils; the basin with its stand; ⁴⁰the curtains of the courtyard with its posts and bases, and the curtain for the entrance to the courtyard; the ropes and tent pegs for the courtyard; all the furnishings for the tabernacle, the Tent of Meeting; ⁴¹and the woven garments worn for ministering in the sanctuary, both the sacred garments for Aaron the priest and the garments for his sons when serving as priests.

⁴²The Israelites had done all the work just as the LORD had commanded Moses. ⁴³Moses inspected the work and saw that they had done it just as the LORD had commanded. So Moses blessed them.

Setting Up the Tabernacle

40 Then the LORD said to Moses: ²"Set up the tabernacle, the Tent of Meeting, on the first day of the first month. ³Place the ark of the Testimony in it and

---

Direct Line

EXODUS 39:42-43

Have you ever finished a job and then stood back and looked at it with pride and satisfaction? When the Israelites finished building the tabernacle, Exodus says they did all the work "just as the LORD had commanded" and "Moses inspected the work." Can you imagine the people standing there as Moses looked over their work, proud and happy that they'd done such a good job? Life is pretty similar. You want to be able to look back at the choices you've made and feel great satisfaction. You want to watch with pride as God inspects your life and says you've lived it "just as the LORD commanded."

ᵃ*23* The meaning of the Hebrew for this word is uncertain. ᵇ*34* That is, dugongs

shield the ark with the curtain. ⁴Bring in the table and set out what belongs on it. Then bring in the lampstand and set up its lamps. ⁵Place the gold altar of incense in front of the ark of the Testimony and put the curtain at the entrance to the tabernacle.

⁶"Place the altar of burnt offering in front of the entrance to the tabernacle, the Tent of Meeting; ⁷place the basin between the Tent of Meeting and the altar and put water in it. ⁸Set up the courtyard around it and put the curtain at the entrance to the courtyard.

⁹"Take the anointing oil and anoint the tabernacle and everything in it; consecrate it and all its furnishings, and it will be holy. ¹⁰Then anoint the altar of burnt offering and all its utensils; consecrate the altar, and it will be most holy. ¹¹Anoint the basin and its stand and consecrate them.

¹²"Bring Aaron and his sons to the entrance to the Tent of Meeting and wash them with water. ¹³Then dress Aaron in the sacred garments, anoint him and consecrate him so he may serve me as priest. ¹⁴Bring his sons and dress them in tunics. ¹⁵Anoint them just as you anointed their father, so they may serve me as priests. Their anointing will be to a priesthood that will continue for all generations to come." ¹⁶Moses did everything just as the Lord commanded him.

¹⁷So the tabernacle was set up on the first day of the first month in the second year. ¹⁸When Moses set up the tabernacle, he put the bases in place, erected the frames, inserted the crossbars and set up the posts. ¹⁹Then he spread the tent over the tabernacle and put the covering over the tent, as the Lord commanded him.

²⁰He took the Testimony and placed it in the ark, attached the poles to the ark and put the atonement cover over it. ²¹Then he brought the ark into the tabernacle and hung the shielding curtain and shielded the ark of the Testimony, as the Lord commanded him.

²²Moses placed the table in the Tent of Meeting on the north side of the tabernacle outside the curtain ²³and set out the bread on it before the Lord, as the Lord commanded him.

²⁴He placed the lampstand in the Tent of Meeting opposite the table on the south side of the tabernacle ²⁵and set up the lamps before the Lord, as the Lord commanded him.

²⁶Moses placed the gold altar in the Tent of Meeting in front of the curtain ²⁷and burned fragrant incense on it, as the Lord commanded him. ²⁸Then he put up the curtain at the entrance to the tabernacle.

²⁹He set the altar of burnt offering near the entrance to the tabernacle, the Tent of Meeting, and offered on it burnt offerings and grain offerings, as the Lord commanded him.

³⁰He placed the basin between the Tent of Meeting and the altar and put water in it for washing, ³¹and Moses and Aaron and his sons used it to wash their hands and feet. ³²They washed whenever they entered the Tent of Meeting or approached the altar, as the Lord commanded Moses.

³³Then Moses set up the courtyard around the tabernacle and altar and put up the curtain at the entrance to the courtyard. And so Moses finished the work.

The Glory of the Lord   ³⁴Then the cloud covered the Tent of Meeting, and the glory of the Lord filled the tabernacle. ³⁵Moses could not enter the Tent of Meeting because the cloud had settled upon it, and the glory of the Lord filled the tabernacle.

³⁶In all the travels of the Israelites, whenever the cloud lifted from above the tabernacle, they would set out; ³⁷but if the cloud did not lift, they did not set out—until the day it lifted. ³⁸So the cloud of the Lord was over the tabernacle by day, and fire was in the cloud by night, in the sight of all the house of Israel during all their travels.

Introduction

to the

book of Leviticus

WORSHIP.

That's what the book of Leviticus is all about. God wants you to worship him. But how do you go about it? Well, you get together with other believers and sing God's praises. You talk about what God is like and about the things he's done for you. You pray and tell God how wonderful he is. It's really quite simple.

But Leviticus will take you back to a time when worship wasn't so simple. This book is filled with rules that Israel's priests and people had to follow. It describes the required yearly religious holidays, and it lists practices that set the Hebrews apart from all the other people of the world.

Fundamentals

What wouldn't you find on the menu at an Old Testament banquet (Leviticus 11)?

Can you ever be forgiven if you sin on purpose (Leviticus 16:30)?

What would be more likely to make you do right: God's rewards for obedience or his punishments for doing wrong (Leviticus 26)?

FAST FACTS

Leviticus quotes God's words to Moses 38 times.

About half the book is addressed to priests and half to all the people.

The word holy occurs 87 times. It means to be set apart to God, showing loyalty by keeping his commands.

The command to "love your neighbor as yourself" is found in Leviticus 19:18.

The Burnt Offering   The LORD called to Moses and spoke to him from the Tent of Meeting. He said, ²"Speak to the Israelites and say to them: 'When any of you brings an offering to the LORD, bring as your offering an animal from either the herd or the flock.

³" 'If the offering is a burnt offering from the herd, he is to offer a male without defect. He must present it at the entrance to the Tent of Meeting so that it*ᵃ* will be acceptable to the LORD. ⁴He is to lay his hand on the head of the burnt offering, and it will be accepted on his behalf to make atonement for him. ⁵He is to slaughter the young bull before the LORD, and then Aaron's sons the priests shall bring the blood and sprinkle it against the altar on all sides at the entrance to the Tent of Meeting. ⁶He is to skin the burnt offering and cut it into pieces. ⁷The sons of Aaron the priest are to put fire on the altar and arrange wood on the fire. ⁸Then Aaron's sons the priests shall arrange the pieces, including the head and the fat, on the burning wood that is on the altar. ⁹He is to wash the inner parts and the legs with water, and the priest is to burn all of it on the altar. It is a burnt offering, an offering made by fire, an aroma pleasing to the LORD.

¹⁰" 'If the offering is a burnt offering from the flock, from either the sheep or the goats, he is to offer a male without defect. ¹¹He is to slaughter it at the north side of the altar before the LORD, and Aaron's sons the priests shall sprinkle its blood against the altar on all sides. ¹²He is to cut it into pieces, and the priest shall arrange them, including the head and the fat, on the burning wood that is on the altar. ¹³He is to wash the inner parts and the legs with water, and the priest is to bring all of it and burn it on the altar. It is a burnt offering, an offering made by fire, an aroma pleasing to the LORD.

¹⁴" 'If the offering to the LORD is a burnt offering of birds, he is to offer a dove or a young pigeon. ¹⁵The priest shall bring it to the altar, wring off the head and burn it on the altar; its blood shall be drained out on the side of the altar. ¹⁶He is to remove the crop with its contents*ᵇ* and throw it to the east side of the altar, where the ashes are. ¹⁷He shall tear it open by the wings, not severing it completely, and then the priest shall burn it on the wood that is on the fire on the altar. It is a burnt offering, an offering made by fire, an aroma pleasing to the LORD.

The Grain Offering   " 'When someone brings a grain offering to the LORD, his offering is to be of fine flour. He is to pour oil on it, put incense on it ²and take it to Aaron's sons the priests. The priest shall take a handful of the fine flour and oil, together with all the incense, and burn this as a memorial portion on the altar, an offering made by fire, an aroma pleasing to the LORD. ³The rest of the grain offering belongs to Aaron and his sons; it is a most holy part of the offerings made to the LORD by fire.

⁴" 'If you bring a grain offering baked in an oven, it is to consist of fine flour: cakes made without yeast and mixed with oil, or*ᶜ* wafers made without yeast and spread with oil. ⁵If your grain offering is prepared on a griddle, it is to be made of fine flour mixed with oil, and without yeast. ⁶Crumble it and pour oil on it; it is a grain offering. ⁷If your grain offering is cooked in a pan, it is to be made of fine flour and oil. ⁸Bring the grain offering made of these things to the LORD; present it to the priest, who shall take it to the altar. ⁹He shall take out the memorial portion from the grain offering and burn it on the altar as an offering made by fire, an aroma pleasing to the LORD. ¹⁰The rest of the grain offering belongs to Aaron and his sons; it is a most holy part of the offerings made to the LORD by fire.

¹¹" 'Every grain offering you bring to the LORD must be made without yeast, for you are not to burn any yeast or honey in an offering made to the LORD

ᵃ3 Or *he*   *ᵇ16* Or *crop and the feathers*; the meaning of the Hebrew for this word is uncertain.   *ᶜ4* Or *and* by fire. ¹²You may bring them to the LORD as an offering of the firstfruits, but they are not to be offered on the altar as a pleasing aroma. ¹³Season all your grain offerings with salt. Do not leave the salt of the covenant of your God out of your grain offerings; add salt to all your offerings.

¹⁴" 'If you bring a grain offering of firstfruits to the LORD, offer crushed heads of new grain roasted in the fire. ¹⁵Put oil and incense on it; it is a grain offering. ¹⁶The priest shall burn the memorial portion of the crushed grain and the oil, together with all the incense, as an offering made to the LORD by fire.

The Fellowship Offering " 'If someone's offering is a fellowship offering,ᵃ and he offers an animal from the herd, whether male or female, he is to present before the LORD an animal without defect. ²He is to lay his hand on the head of his offering and slaughter it at the entrance to the Tent of Meeting. Then Aaron's sons the priests shall sprinkle the blood against the altar on all sides. ³From the fellowship offering he is to bring a sacrifice made to the LORD by fire: all the fat that covers the inner parts or is connected to them, ⁴both kidneys with the fat on them near the loins, and the covering of the liver, which he will remove with the kidneys. ⁵Then Aaron's sons are to burn it on the altar on top of the burnt offering that is on the burning wood, as an offering made by fire, an aroma pleasing to the LORD.

⁶" 'If he offers an animal from the flock as a fellowship offering to the LORD, he is to offer a male or female without defect. ⁷If he offers a lamb, he is to present it before the LORD. ⁸He is to lay his hand on the head of his offering and slaughter it in front of the Tent of Meeting. Then Aaron's sons shall sprinkle its blood against the altar on all sides. ⁹From the fellowship offering he is to bring a sacrifice made to the LORD by fire: its fat, the entire fat tail cut off close to the backbone, all the fat that covers the inner parts or is connected to them, ¹⁰both kidneys with the fat on them near the loins, and the covering of the liver, which he will remove with the kidneys. ¹¹The priest shall burn them on the altar as food, an offering made to the LORD by fire.

¹²" 'If his offering is a goat, he is to present it before the LORD. ¹³He is to lay his hand on its head and slaughter it in front of the Tent of Meeting. Then Aaron's sons shall sprinkle its blood against the altar on all sides. ¹⁴From what he offers he is to make this offering to the LORD by fire: all the fat that covers the inner parts or is connected to them, ¹⁵both kidneys with the fat on them near the loins, and the covering of the liver, which he will remove with the kidneys. ¹⁶The priest shall burn them on the altar as food, an offering made by fire, a pleasing aroma. All the fat is the LORD's.

¹⁷" 'This is a lasting ordinance for the generations to come, wherever you live: You must not eat any fat or any blood.' "

The Sin Offering The LORD said to Moses, ²"Say to the Israelites: 'When anyone sins unintentionally and does what is forbidden in any of the LORD's commands—

³" 'If the anointed priest sins, bringing guilt on the people, he must bring to the LORD a young bull without defect as a sin offering for the sin he has committed. ⁴He is to present the bull at the entrance to the Tent of Meeting before the LORD. He is to lay his hand on its head and slaughter it before the LORD. ⁵Then the anointed priest shall take some of the bull's blood and carry it into the Tent of Meeting. ⁶He is to dip his finger into the blood and sprinkle some of it seven times before the LORD, in front of the curtain of the sanctuary. ⁷The priest shall then put some of the blood on the horns of the altar of fragrant incense that is before the LORD in the Tent of Meeting. The

---

ᵃ1 Traditionally *peace offering*; also in verses 3, 6 and 9

rest of the bull's blood he shall pour out at the base of the altar of burnt of-fering at the entrance to the Tent of Meeting. [8]He shall remove all the fat from the bull of the sin offering—the fat that covers the inner parts or is con-nected to them, [9]both kidneys with the fat on them near the loins, and the covering of the liver, which he will remove with the kidneys— [10]just as the fat is removed from the ox[a] sacrificed as a fellowship offering.[b] Then the priest shall burn them on the altar of burnt offering. [11]But the hide of the bull and all its flesh, as well as the head and legs, the inner parts and offal— [12]that is, all the rest of the bull—he must take outside the camp to a place ceremonially clean, where the ashes are thrown, and burn it in a wood fire on the ash heap.

[13]'If the whole Israelite community sins unintentionally and does what is forbidden in any of the LORD's commands, even though the community is un-aware of the matter, they are guilty. [14]When they become aware of the sin they committed, the assembly must bring a young bull as a sin offering and present it before the Tent of Meeting. [15]The elders of the community are to lay their hands on the bull's head before the LORD, and the bull shall be slaughtered before the LORD. [16]Then the anointed priest is to take some of the bull's blood into the Tent of Meeting. [17]He shall dip his finger into the blood and sprinkle it before the LORD seven times in front of the curtain. [18]He is to put some of the blood on the horns of the altar that is before the LORD in the Tent of Meeting. The rest of the blood he shall pour out at the base of the altar of burnt offering at the entrance to the Tent of Meeting. [19]He shall re-move all the fat from it and burn it on the altar, [20]and do with this bull just as he did with the bull for the sin offering. In this way the priest will make atonement for them, and they will be forgiven. [21]Then he shall take the bull outside the camp and burn it as he burned the first bull. This is the sin of-fering for the community.

[22]'When a leader sins unintentionally and does what is forbidden in any of the commands of the LORD his God, he is guilty. [23]When he is made aware of the sin he committed, he must bring as his offering a male goat without defect. [24]He is to lay his hand on the goat's head and slaughter it at the place where the burnt offering is slaughtered before the LORD. It is a sin of-fering. [25]Then the priest shall take some of the blood of the sin offering with his finger and put it on the horns of the altar of burnt offering and pour out the rest of the blood at the base of the altar. [26]He shall burn all the fat on the altar as he burned the fat of the fellowship offering. In this way the priest will make atonement for the man's sin, and he will be forgiven.

[27]'If a member of the community sins unintentionally and does what is forbidden in any of the LORD's commands, he is guilty. [28]When he is made aware of the sin he committed, he must bring as his offering for the sin he committed a female goat without defect. [29]He is to lay his hand on the head of the sin offering and slaughter it at the place of the burnt offering. [30]Then the priest is to take some of the blood with his finger and put it on the horns of the altar of burnt offering and pour out the rest of the blood at the base of the altar. [31]He shall remove all the fat, just as the fat is removed from the fellowship offering, and the priest shall burn it on the altar as an aroma pleasing to the LORD. In this way the priest will make atonement for him, and he will be forgiven.

[32]'If he brings a lamb as his sin offering, he is to bring a female without defect. [33]He is to lay his hand on its head and slaughter it for a sin offering at the place where the burnt offering is slaughtered. [34]Then the priest shall

---

[a]10 The Hebrew word can include both male and female.   [b]10 Traditionally *peace offering*; also in verses 26, 31 and 35

take some of the blood of the sin offering with his finger and put it on the horns of the altar of burnt offering and pour out the rest of the blood at the base of the altar. ³⁵He shall remove all the fat, just as the fat is removed from the lamb of the fellowship offering, and the priest shall burn it on the altar on top of the offerings made to the LORD by fire. In this way the priest will make atonement for him for the sin he has committed, and he will be forgiven.

5 " 'If a person sins because he does not speak up when he hears a public charge to testify regarding something he has seen or learned about, he will be held responsible.

²" 'Or if a person touches anything ceremonially unclean—whether the carcasses of unclean wild animals or of unclean livestock or of unclean creatures that move along the ground—even though he is unaware of it, he has become unclean and is guilty.

³" 'Or if he touches human uncleanness—anything that would make him unclean—even though he is unaware of it, when he learns of it he will be guilty.

⁴" 'Or if a person thoughtlessly takes an oath to do anything, whether good or evil—in any matter one might carelessly swear about—even though he is unaware of it, in any case when he learns of it he will be guilty.

⁵" 'When anyone is guilty in any of these ways, he must confess in what way he has sinned ⁶and, as a penalty for the sin he has committed, he must bring to the LORD a female lamb or goat from the flock as a sin offering; and the priest shall make atonement for him for his sin.

⁷" 'If he cannot afford a lamb, he is to bring two doves or two young pigeons to the LORD as a penalty for his sin—one for a sin offering and the other for a burnt offering. ⁸He is to bring them to the priest, who shall first offer the one for the sin offering. He is to wring its head from its neck, not severing it completely, ⁹and is to sprinkle some of the blood of the sin offering against the side of the altar; the rest of the blood must be drained out at the base of the altar. It is a sin offering. ¹⁰The priest shall then offer the other as a burnt offering in the prescribed way and make atonement for him for the sin he has committed, and he will be forgiven.

¹¹" 'If, however, he cannot afford two doves or two young pigeons, he is to bring as an offering for his sin a tenth of an ephah*a* of fine flour for a sin offering. He must not put oil or incense on it, because it is a sin offering. ¹²He is to bring it to the priest, who shall take a handful of it as a memorial portion and burn it on the altar on top of the offerings made to the LORD by fire. It is a sin offering. ¹³In this way the priest will make atonement for him for any of these sins he has committed, and he will be forgiven. The rest of the offering will belong to the priest, as in the case of the grain offering.' "

The Guilt Offering   ¹⁴The LORD said to Moses: ¹⁵"When a person commits a violation and sins unintentionally in regard to any of the LORD's holy things, he is to bring to the LORD as a penalty a ram from the flock, one without defect and of the proper value in silver, according to the sanctuary shekel.*b* It is a guilt offering. ¹⁶He must make restitution for what he has failed to do in regard to the holy things, add a fifth of the value to that and give it all to the priest, who will make atonement for him with the ram as a guilt offering, and he will be forgiven.

¹⁷"If a person sins and does what is forbidden in any of the LORD's commands, even though he does not know it, he is guilty and will be held responsible. ¹⁸He is to bring to the priest as a guilt offering a ram from the flock, one without defect and of the proper value. In this way the priest will make

---

*a11 That is, probably about 2 quarts (about 2 liters)   *b15 That is, about 2/5 ounce (about 11.5 grams)

Dear Sam,

I saw someone at school do something he shouldn't have. I kept my mouth shut, but now I feel guilty. What should I have done?

Stan in Sacramento

Dear Sam, Inc.

100 Advice Lane, Anywhere, USA

Dear Stan,

This is a tough situation because if you do tell, you may take a lot of abuse from your classmates. Was anyone hurt? Were anyone's belongings damaged or stolen? If so, you really must find a way to go forward and tell what you know.

God puts responsibility on you in these situations. Old Testament law required all residents in a community to live up to and help others live up to the law (Leviticus 5:1).

If you refuse your responsibility, you allow evil a foothold in your school. Perhaps you can find a discreet way to tell an administrator or other responsible adult without taking abuse for doing what is truly right.

Sam

atonement for him for the wrong he has committed unintentionally, and he will be forgiven. [19]It is a guilt offering; he has been guilty of[a] wrongdoing against the LORD."

6 The LORD said to Moses: [2]"If anyone sins and is unfaithful to the LORD by deceiving his neighbor about something entrusted to him or left in his care or stolen, or if he cheats him, [3]or if he finds lost property and lies about it, or if he swears falsely, or if he commits any such sin that people may do— [4]when he thus sins and becomes guilty, he must return what he has stolen or taken by extortion, or what was entrusted to him, or the lost property he found, [5]or whatever it was he swore falsely about. He must make restitution in full, add a fifth of the value to it and give it all to the owner on the day he presents his guilt offering. [6]And as a penalty he must bring to the priest, that is, to the LORD, his guilt offering, a ram from the flock, one without defect and of the proper value. [7]In this way the priest will make atonement for him before the LORD, and he will be forgiven for any of these things he did that made him guilty."

The Burnt Offering [8]The LORD said to Moses: [9]"Give Aaron and his sons this command: 'These are the regulations for the burnt offering: The burnt offering is to remain on the altar hearth throughout the night, till morning, and the fire must be kept burning on the altar. [10]The priest shall then put on his linen clothes, with linen undergarments next to his body, and shall remove the ashes of the burnt offering that the fire has consumed on the altar and place them beside the altar. [11]Then he is to take off these clothes and put on others, and carry the ashes outside the camp to a place that is ceremonially clean. [12]The fire on the altar must be kept burning; it must not go out. Every morning the priest is to add firewood and arrange the burnt offering on the fire and burn the fat of the fellowship offerings[b] on it. [13]The fire must be kept burning on the altar continuously; it must not go out.

The Grain Offering [14]" 'These are the regulations for the grain offering: Aaron's sons are to bring it before the LORD, in front of the altar. [15]The priest is to take a handful of fine flour and oil, together with all the incense on the grain offering, and burn the memorial portion on the altar as an aroma pleasing to the LORD. [16]Aaron and his sons shall eat the rest of it, but it is to be eaten without yeast in a holy place; they are to eat it in the courtyard of the Tent of Meeting. [17]It must not be baked with yeast; I have given it as their share of the offerings made to me by fire. Like the sin offering and the guilt offering, it is most holy. [18]Any male descendant of Aaron may eat it. It is his regular share of the offerings made to the LORD by fire for the generations to come. Whatever touches them will become holy.[c]' "

[19]The LORD also said to Moses, [20]"This is the offering Aaron and his sons are to bring to the LORD on the day he[d] is anointed: a tenth of an ephah[e] of fine flour as a regular grain offering, half of it in the morning and half in the evening. [21]Prepare it with oil on a griddle; bring it well-mixed and present the grain offering broken[f] in pieces as an aroma pleasing to the LORD. [22]The son who is to succeed him as anointed priest shall prepare it. It is the LORD's regular share and is to be burned completely. [23]Every grain offering of a priest shall be burned completely; it must not be eaten."

The Sin Offering [24]The LORD said to Moses, [25]"Say to Aaron and his sons: 'These are the regulations for the sin offering: The sin offering is to be slaughtered before the LORD in the place the burnt offering is slaughtered; it

---

[a]*19 Or has made full expiation for his* [b]*12 Traditionally peace offerings* [c]*18 Or Whoever touches them must be holy; similarly in verse 27* [d]*20 Or each* [e]*20 That is, probably about 2 quarts (about 2 liters)* [f]*21 The meaning of the Hebrew for this word is uncertain.*

is most holy. ²⁶The priest who offers it shall eat it; it is to be eaten in a holy place, in the courtyard of the Tent of Meeting. ²⁷Whatever touches any of the flesh will become holy, and if any of the blood is spattered on a garment, you must wash it in a holy place. ²⁸The clay pot the meat is cooked in must be broken; but if it is cooked in a bronze pot, the pot is to be scoured and rinsed with water. ²⁹Any male in a priest's family may eat it; it is most holy. ³⁰But any sin offering whose blood is brought into the Tent of Meeting to make atonement in the Holy Place must not be eaten; it must be burned.

The Guilt Offering   " 'These are the regulations for the guilt offering, which is most holy: ²The guilt offering is to be slaughtered in the place where the burnt offering is slaughtered, and its blood is to be sprinkled against the altar on all sides. ³All its fat shall be offered: the fat tail and the fat that covers the inner parts, ⁴both kidneys with the fat on them near the loins, and the covering of the liver, which is to be removed with the kidneys. ⁵The priest shall burn them on the altar as an offering made to the Lord by fire. It is a guilt offering. ⁶Any male in a priest's family may eat it, but it must be eaten in a holy place; it is most holy.

⁷" 'The same law applies to both the sin offering and the guilt offering: They belong to the priest who makes atonement with them. ⁸The priest who offers a burnt offering for anyone may keep its hide for himself. ⁹Every grain offering baked in an oven or cooked in a pan or on a griddle belongs to the priest who offers it, ¹⁰and every grain offering, whether mixed with oil or dry, belongs equally to all the sons of Aaron.

The Fellowship Offering   ¹¹" 'These are the regulations for the fellowship offering^a a person may present to the Lord:

¹²" 'If he offers it as an expression of thankfulness, then along with this thank offering he is to offer cakes of bread made without yeast and mixed with oil, wafers made without yeast and spread with oil, and cakes of fine flour well-kneaded and mixed with oil. ¹³Along with his fellowship offering of thanksgiving he is to present an offering with cakes of bread made with yeast. ¹⁴He is to bring one of each kind as an offering, a contribution to the Lord; it belongs to the priest who sprinkles the blood of the fellowship offerings. ¹⁵The meat of his fellowship offering of thanksgiving must be eaten on the day it is offered; he must leave none of it till morning.

¹⁶" 'If, however, his offering is the result of a vow or is a freewill offering, the sacrifice shall be eaten on the day he offers it, but anything left over may be eaten on the next day. ¹⁷Any meat of the sacrifice left over till the third day must be burned up. ¹⁸If any meat of the fellowship offering is eaten on the third day, it will not be accepted. It will not be credited to the one who offered it, for it is impure; the person who eats any of it will be held responsible.

¹⁹" 'Meat that touches anything ceremonially unclean must not be eaten; it must be burned up. As for other meat, anyone ceremonially clean may eat it. ²⁰But if anyone who is unclean eats any meat of the fellowship offering belonging to the Lord, that person must be cut off from his people. ²¹If anyone touches something unclean—whether human uncleanness or an unclean animal or any unclean, detestable thing—and then eats any of the meat of the fellowship offering belonging to the Lord, that person must be cut off from his people.' "

Eating Fat and Blood Forbidden   ²²The Lord said to Moses, ²³"Say to the Israelites: 'Do not eat any of the fat of cattle, sheep or goats. ²⁴The fat of an animal found dead or torn by wild animals may be used for any other purpose,

---

^a11 Traditionally *peace offering*; also in verses 13-37

but you must not eat it. ²⁵Anyone who eats the fat of an animal from which an offering by fire may be* made to the LORD must be cut off from his people. ²⁶And wherever you live, you must not eat the blood of any bird or animal. ²⁷If anyone eats blood, that person must be cut off from his people.' "

The Priests' Share ²⁸The LORD said to Moses, ²⁹"Say to the Israelites: 'Anyone who brings a fellowship offering to the LORD is to bring part of it as his sacrifice to the LORD. ³⁰With his own hands he is to bring the offering made to the LORD by fire; he is to bring the fat, together with the breast, and wave the breast before the LORD as a wave offering. ³¹The priest shall burn the fat on the altar, but the breast belongs to Aaron and his sons. ³²You are to give the right thigh of your fellowship offerings to the priest as a contribution. ³³The son of Aaron who offers the blood and the fat of the fellowship offering shall have the right thigh as his share. ³⁴From the fellowship offerings of the Israelites, I have taken the breast that is waved and the thigh that is presented and have given them to Aaron the priest and his sons as their regular share from the Israelites.' "

³⁵This is the portion of the offerings made to the LORD by fire that were allotted to Aaron and his sons on the day they were presented to serve the LORD as priests. ³⁶On the day they were anointed, the LORD commanded that the Israelites give this to them as their regular share for the generations to come.

³⁷These, then, are the regulations for the burnt offering, the grain offering, the sin offering, the guilt offering, the ordination offering and the fellowship offering, ³⁸which the LORD gave Moses on Mount Sinai on the day he commanded the Israelites to bring their offerings to the LORD, in the Desert of Sinai.

The Ordination of Aaron and His Sons The LORD said to Moses, ²"Bring Aaron and his sons, their garments, the anointing oil, the bull for the sin offering, the two rams and the basket containing bread made without yeast, ³and gather the entire assembly at the entrance to the Tent of Meeting." ⁴Moses did as the LORD commanded him, and the assembly gathered at the entrance to the Tent of Meeting.

⁵Moses said to the assembly, "This is what the LORD has commanded to be done." ⁶Then Moses brought Aaron and his sons forward and washed them with water. ⁷He put the tunic on Aaron, tied the sash around him, clothed him with the robe and put the ephod on him. He also tied the ephod to him by its skillfully woven waistband; so it was fastened on him. ⁸He placed the breastpiece on him and put the Urim and Thummim in the breastpiece. ⁹Then he placed the turban on Aaron's head and set the gold plate, the sacred diadem, on the front of it, as the LORD commanded Moses.

¹⁰Then Moses took the anointing oil and anointed the tabernacle and everything in it, and so consecrated them. ¹¹He sprinkled some of the oil on the altar seven times, anointing the altar and all its utensils and the basin with its stand, to consecrate them. ¹²He poured some of the anointing oil on Aaron's head and anointed him to consecrate him. ¹³Then he brought Aaron's sons forward, put tunics on them, tied sashes around them and put headbands on them, as the LORD commanded Moses.

¹⁴He then presented the bull for the sin offering, and Aaron and his sons laid their hands on its head. ¹⁵Moses slaughtered the bull and took some of the blood, and with his finger he put it on all the horns of the altar to purify the altar. He poured out the rest of the blood at the base of the altar. So he consecrated it to make atonement for it. ¹⁶Moses also took all the fat around the inner parts, the covering of the liver, and both kidneys and their

ª25 Or fire is

fat, and burned it on the altar. [17]But the bull with its hide and its flesh and its offal he burned up outside the camp, as the LORD commanded Moses.

[18]He then presented the ram for the burnt offering, and Aaron and his sons laid their hands on its head. [19]Then Moses slaughtered the ram and sprinkled the blood against the altar on all sides. [20]He cut the ram into pieces and burned the head, the pieces and the fat. [21]He washed the inner parts and the legs with water and burned the whole ram on the altar as a burnt offering, a pleasing aroma, an offering made to the LORD by fire, as the LORD commanded Moses.

[22]He then presented the other ram, the ram for the ordination, and Aaron and his sons laid their hands on its head. [23]Moses slaughtered the ram and took some of its blood and put it on the lobe of Aaron's right ear, on the thumb of his right hand and on the big toe of his right foot. [24]Moses also brought Aaron's sons forward and put some of the blood on the lobes of their right ears, on the thumbs of their right hands and on the big toes of their right feet. Then he sprinkled blood against the altar on all sides. [25]He took the fat, the fat tail, all the fat around the inner parts, the covering of the liver, both kidneys and their fat and the right thigh. [26]Then from the basket of bread made without yeast, which was before the LORD, he took a cake of bread, and one made with oil, and a wafer; he put these on the fat portions and on the right thigh. [27]He put all these in the hands of Aaron and his sons and waved them before the LORD as a wave offering. [28]Then Moses took them from their hands and burned them on the altar on top of the burnt offering as an ordination offering, a pleasing aroma, an offering made to the LORD by fire. [29]He also took the breast—Moses' share of the ordination ram—and waved it before the LORD as a wave offering, as the LORD commanded Moses.

[30]Then Moses took some of the anointing oil and some of the blood from the altar and sprinkled them on Aaron and his garments and on his sons and their garments. So he consecrated Aaron and his garments and his sons and their garments.

[31]Moses then said to Aaron and his sons, "Cook the meat at the entrance to the Tent of Meeting and eat it there with the bread from the basket of ordination offerings, as I commanded, saying,[a] 'Aaron and his sons are to eat it.' [32]Then burn up the rest of the meat and the bread. [33]Do not leave the entrance to the Tent of Meeting for seven days, until the days of your ordination are completed, for your ordination will last seven days. [34]What has been done today was commanded by the LORD to make atonement for you. [35]You must stay at the entrance to the Tent of Meeting day and night for seven days and do what the LORD requires, so you will not die; for that is what I have been commanded." [36]So Aaron and his sons did everything the LORD commanded through Moses.

9 *The Priests Begin Their Ministry* On the eighth day Moses summoned Aaron and his sons and the elders of Israel. [2]He said to Aaron, "Take a bull calf for your sin offering and a ram for your burnt offering, both without defect, and present them before the LORD. [3]Then say to the Israelites: 'Take a male goat for a sin offering, a calf and a lamb—both a year old and without defect—for a burnt offering, [4]and an ox[b] and a ram for a fellowship offering[c] to sacrifice before the LORD, together with a grain offering mixed with oil. For today the LORD will appear to you.' "

[5]They took the things Moses commanded to the front of the Tent of Meeting, and the entire assembly came near and stood before the LORD. [6]Then Moses said, "This is what the LORD has commanded you to do, so that the glory of the LORD may appear to you."

---

a31 Or I was commanded: *b4 The Hebrew word can include both male and female; also in verses 18 and 19. c4 Traditionally* peace offering; *also in verses 18 and 22*

⁷Moses said to Aaron, "Come to the altar and sacrifice your sin offering and your burnt offering and make atonement for yourself and the people; sacrifice the offering that is for the people and make atonement for them, as the LORD has commanded."

⁸So Aaron came to the altar and slaughtered the calf as a sin offering for himself. ⁹His sons brought the blood to him, and he dipped his finger into the blood and put it on the horns of the altar; the rest of the blood he poured out at the base of the altar. ¹⁰On the altar he burned the fat, the kidneys and the covering of the liver from the sin offering, as the LORD commanded Moses; ¹¹the flesh and the hide he burned up outside the camp.

¹²Then he slaughtered the burnt offering. His sons handed him the blood, and he sprinkled it against the altar on all sides. ¹³They handed him the burnt offering piece by piece, including the head, and he burned them on the altar. ¹⁴He washed the inner parts and the legs and burned them on top of the burnt offering on the altar.

¹⁵Aaron then brought the offering that was for the people. He took the goat for the people's sin offering and slaughtered it and offered it for a sin offering as he did with the first one.

¹⁶He brought the burnt offering and offered it in the prescribed way. ¹⁷He also brought the grain offering, took a handful of it and burned it on the altar in addition to the morning's burnt offering.

¹⁸He slaughtered the ox and the ram as the fellowship offering for the people. His sons handed him the blood, and he sprinkled it against the altar on all sides. ¹⁹But the fat portions of the ox and the ram—the fat tail, the layer of fat, the kidneys and the covering of the liver— ²⁰these they laid on the breasts, and then Aaron burned the fat on the altar. ²¹Aaron waved the breasts and the right thigh before the LORD as a wave offering, as Moses commanded.

²²Then Aaron lifted his hands toward the people and blessed them. And having sacrificed the sin offering, the burnt offering and the fellowship offering, he stepped down.

²³Moses and Aaron then went into the Tent of Meeting. When they came out, they blessed the people; and the glory of the LORD appeared to all the people. ²⁴Fire came out from the presence of the LORD and consumed the burnt offering and the fat portions on the altar. And when all the people saw it, they shouted for joy and fell facedown.

10 *The Death of Nadab and Abihu* Aaron's sons Nadab and Abihu took their censers, put fire in them and added incense; and they offered unauthorized fire before the LORD, contrary to his command. ²So fire came out from the presence of the LORD and consumed them, and they died before the LORD. ³Moses then said to Aaron, "This is what the LORD spoke of when he said:

> " 'Among those who approach me
> I will show myself holy;
> in the sight of all the people
> I will be honored.' "

Aaron remained silent.

⁴Moses summoned Mishael and Elzaphan, sons of Aaron's uncle Uzziel, and said to them, "Come here; carry your cousins outside the camp, away from the front of the sanctuary." ⁵So they came and carried them, still in their tunics, outside the camp, as Moses ordered.

⁶Then Moses said to Aaron and his sons Eleazar and Ithamar, "Do not let your hair become unkempt,ᵃ and do not tear your clothes, or you will die and

---

ᵃ6 Or *Do not uncover your heads*

the LORD will be angry with the whole community. But your relatives, all the house of Israel, may mourn for those the LORD has destroyed by fire. [7]Do not leave the entrance to the Tent of Meeting or you will die, because the LORD's anointing oil is on you." So they did as Moses said.

[8]Then the LORD said to Aaron, [9]"You and your sons are not to drink wine or other fermented drink whenever you go into the Tent of Meeting, or you will die. This is a lasting ordinance for the generations to come. [10]You must distinguish between the holy and the common, between the unclean and the clean, [11]and you must teach the Israelites all the decrees the LORD has given them through Moses."

[12]Moses said to Aaron and his remaining sons, Eleazar and Ithamar, "Take the grain offering left over from the offerings made to the LORD by fire and eat it prepared without yeast beside the altar, for it is most holy. [13]Eat it in a holy place, because it is your share and your sons' share of the offerings made to the LORD by fire; for so I have been commanded. [14]But you and your sons and your daughters may eat the breast that was waved and the thigh that was presented. Eat them in a ceremonially clean place; they have been given to you and your children as your share of the Israelites' fellowship offerings.[a] [15]The thigh that was presented and the breast that was waved must be brought with the fat portions of the offerings made by fire, to be waved before the LORD as a wave offering. This will be the regular share for you and your children, as the LORD has commanded."

[16]When Moses inquired about the goat of the sin offering and found that it had been burned up, he was angry with Eleazar and Ithamar, Aaron's remaining sons, and asked, [17]"Why didn't you eat the sin offering in the sanctuary area? It is most holy; it was given to you to take away the guilt of the community by making atonement for them before the LORD. [18]Since its blood was not taken into the Holy Place, you should have eaten the goat in the sanctuary area, as I commanded."

[19]Aaron replied to Moses, "Today they sacrificed their sin offering and their burnt offering before the LORD, but such things as this have happened to me. Would the LORD have been pleased if I had eaten the sin offering today?" [20]When Moses heard this, he was satisfied.

11 *Clean and Unclean Food* The LORD said to Moses and Aaron, [2]"Say to the Israelites: 'Of all the animals that live on land, these are the ones you may eat: [3]You may eat any animal that has a split hoof completely divided and that chews the cud.

[4]" 'There are some that only chew the cud or only have a split hoof, but you must not eat them. The camel, though it chews the cud, does not have a split hoof; it is ceremonially unclean for you. [5]The coney,[b] though it chews the cud, does not have a split hoof; it is unclean for you. [6]The rabbit, though it chews the cud, does not have a split hoof; it is unclean for you. [7]And the pig, though it has a

[a]14 Traditionally *peace offerings*   [b]5 That is, the hyrax or rock badger

LEVITICUS 10:1-11

Do you ever wonder about some of the grisly stories in the Bible? This is one. Aaron's sons violated God's command about offerings and were destroyed by fire. Why such a terrible penalty? Because these men were priests, responsible to teach God's decrees to others. How unthinkable that these men should show contempt for God by ignoring his commands. The greater the privileges given to you, the more responsibility you have. Christians have the wonderful privilege of knowing God personally, of drawing on God for strength, of coming to God in prayer. Let Nadab and Abihu remind you of your responsibilities because of those great privileges.

Direct Line

split hoof completely divided, does not chew the cud; it is unclean for you. [8]You must not eat their meat or touch their carcasses; they are unclean for you.

[9]" 'Of all the creatures living in the water of the seas and the streams, you may eat any that have fins and scales. [10]But all creatures in the seas or streams that do not have fins and scales—whether among all the swarming things or among all the other living creatures in the water—you are to detest. [11]And since you are to detest them, you must not eat their meat and you must detest their carcasses. [12]Anything living in the water that does not have fins and scales is to be detestable to you.

[13]" 'These are the birds you are to detest and not eat because they are detestable: the eagle, the vulture, the black vulture, [14]the red kite, any kind of black kite, [15]any kind of raven, [16]the horned owl, the screech owl, the gull, any kind of hawk, [17]the little owl, the cormorant, the great owl, [18]the white owl, the desert owl, the osprey, [19]the stork, any kind of heron, the hoopoe and the bat.[a]

[20]" 'All flying insects that walk on all fours are to be detestable to you. [21]There are, however, some winged creatures that walk on all fours that you may eat: those that have jointed legs for hopping on the ground. [22]Of these you may eat any kind of locust, katydid, cricket or grasshopper. [23]But all other winged creatures that have four legs you are to detest.

[24]" 'You will make yourselves unclean by these; whoever touches their carcasses will be unclean till evening. [25]Whoever picks up one of their carcasses must wash his clothes, and he will be unclean till evening.

[26]" 'Every animal that has a split hoof not completely divided or that does not chew the cud is unclean for you; whoever touches the carcass of any of them will be unclean. [27]Of all the animals that walk on all fours, those that walk on their paws are unclean for you; whoever touches their carcasses will be unclean till evening. [28]Anyone who picks up their carcasses must wash his clothes, and he will be unclean till evening. They are unclean for you.

[29]" 'Of the animals that move about on the ground, these are unclean for you: the weasel, the rat, any kind of great lizard, [30]the gecko, the monitor lizard, the wall lizard, the skink and the chameleon. [31]Of all those that move along the ground, these are unclean for you. Whoever touches them when they are dead will be unclean till evening. [32]When one of them dies and falls on something, that article, whatever its use, will be unclean, whether it is made of wood, cloth, hide or sackcloth. Put it in water; it will be unclean till evening, and then it will be clean. [33]If one of them falls into a clay pot, everything in it will be unclean, and you must break the pot. [34]Any food that could be eaten but has water on it from such a pot is unclean, and any liquid that could be drunk from it is unclean. [35]Anything that one of their carcasses falls on becomes unclean; an oven or cooking pot must be broken up. They are unclean, and you are to regard them as unclean. [36]A spring, however, or a cistern for collecting water remains clean, but anyone who touches one of these carcasses is unclean. [37]If a carcass falls on any seeds that are to be planted, they remain clean. [38]But if water has been put on the seed and a carcass falls on it, it is unclean for you.

[39]" 'If an animal that you are allowed to eat dies, anyone who touches the carcass will be unclean till evening. [40]Anyone who eats some of the carcass must wash his clothes, and he will be unclean till evening. Anyone who picks up the carcass must wash his clothes, and he will be unclean till evening.

LEVITICUS 11

QUIZZER

Q: What do rabbits and camels have in common?

BONUS: Why did God give the Jews dietary laws?

Answers on page 131

---

[a]19 The precise identification of some of the birds, insects and animals in this chapter is uncertain.

⁴¹" 'Every creature that moves about on the ground is detestable; it is not to be eaten. ⁴²You are not to eat any creature that moves about on the ground, whether it moves on its belly or walks on all fours or on many feet; it is detestable. ⁴³Do not defile yourselves by any of these creatures. Do not make yourselves unclean by means of them or be made unclean by them. ⁴⁴I am the LORD your God; consecrate yourselves and be holy, because I am holy. Do not make yourselves unclean by any creature that moves about on the ground. ⁴⁵I am the LORD who brought you up out of Egypt to be your God; therefore be holy, because I am holy.

⁴⁶" 'These are the regulations concerning animals, birds, every living thing that moves in the water and every creature that moves about on the ground. ⁴⁷You must distinguish between the unclean and the clean, between living creatures that may be eaten and those that may not be eaten.' "

Purification After Childbirth The LORD said to Moses, ²"Say to the Israelites: 'A woman who becomes pregnant and gives birth to a son will be ceremonially unclean for seven days, just as she is unclean during her monthly period. ³On the eighth day the boy is to be circumcised. ⁴Then the woman must wait thirty-three days to be purified from her bleeding. She must not touch anything sacred or go to the sanctuary until the days of her purification are over. ⁵If she gives birth to a daughter, for two weeks the woman will be unclean, as during her period. Then she must wait sixty-six days to be purified from her bleeding.

⁶" 'When the days of her purification for a son or daughter are over, she is to bring to the priest at the entrance to the Tent of Meeting a year-old lamb for a burnt offering and a young pigeon or a dove for a sin offering. ⁷He shall offer them before the LORD to make atonement for her, and then she will be ceremonially clean from her flow of blood.

" 'These are the regulations for the woman who gives birth to a boy or a girl. ⁸If she cannot afford a lamb, she is to bring two doves or two young pigeons, one for a burnt offering and the other for a sin offering. In this way the priest will make atonement for her, and she will be clean.' "

Regulations About Infectious Skin Diseases The LORD said to Moses and Aaron, ²"When anyone has a swelling or a rash or a bright spot on his skin that may become an infectious skin disease,ᵃ he must be brought to Aaron the priest or to one of his sonsᵇ who is a priest. ³The priest is to examine the sore on his skin, and if the hair in the sore has turned white and the sore appears to be more than skin deep,ᶜ it is an infectious skin disease. When the priest examines him, he shall pronounce him ceremonially unclean. ⁴If the spot on his skin is white but does not appear to be more than skin deep and the hair in it has not turned white, the priest is to put the infected person in isolation for seven days. ⁵On the seventh day the priest is to examine him, and if he sees that the sore is unchanged and has not spread in the skin, he is to keep him in isolation another seven days. ⁶On the seventh day the priest is to examine him again, and if the sore has faded and has not spread in the skin, the priest shall pronounce him clean; it is only a rash. The man must wash his clothes, and he will be clean. ⁷But if the rash does spread in his skin after he has shown himself to the priest to be pronounced clean, he must appear before the priest again. ⁸The priest is to examine him, and if the rash has spread in the skin, he shall pronounce him unclean; it is an infectious disease.

Answers
to Quizzer on page 130

A: Both chew the cud but have no split hoof, and so could not be eaten by the Jews (Leviticus 11:4,6).

BONUS: To remind them that belonging to God made them different from other people (Leviticus 11:44-45).

ᵃ2 Traditionally *leprosy*; the Hebrew word was used for various diseases affecting the skin—not necessarily leprosy; also elsewhere in this chapter. ᵇ2 Or *descendants* ᶜ3 Or *be lower than the rest of the skin*; also elsewhere in this chapter

⁹"When anyone has an infectious skin disease, he must be brought to the priest. ¹⁰The priest is to examine him, and if there is a white swelling in the skin that has turned the hair white and if there is raw flesh in the swelling, ¹¹it is a chronic skin disease and the priest shall pronounce him unclean. He is not to put him in isolation, because he is already unclean.

¹²"If the disease breaks out all over his skin and, so far as the priest can see, it covers all the skin of the infected person from head to foot, ¹³the priest is to examine him, and if the disease has covered his whole body, he shall pronounce that person clean. Since it has all turned white, he is clean. ¹⁴But whenever raw flesh appears on him, he will be unclean. ¹⁵When the priest sees the raw flesh, he shall pronounce him unclean. The raw flesh is unclean; he has an infectious disease. ¹⁶Should the raw flesh change and turn white, he must go to the priest. ¹⁷The priest is to examine him, and if the sores have turned white, the priest shall pronounce the infected person clean; then he will be clean.

¹⁸"When someone has a boil on his skin and it heals, ¹⁹and in the place where the boil was, a white swelling or reddish-white spot appears, he must present himself to the priest. ²⁰The priest is to examine it, and if it appears to be more than skin deep and the hair in it has turned white, the priest shall pronounce him unclean. It is an infectious skin disease that has broken out where the boil was. ²¹But if, when the priest examines it, there is no white hair in it and it is not more than skin deep and has faded, then the priest is to put him in isolation for seven days. ²²If it is spreading in the skin, the priest shall pronounce him unclean; it is infectious. ²³But if the spot is unchanged and has not spread, it is only a scar from the boil, and the priest shall pronounce him clean.

²⁴"When someone has a burn on his skin and a reddish-white or white spot appears in the raw flesh of the burn, ²⁵the priest is to examine the spot, and if the hair in it has turned white, and it appears to be more than skin deep, it is an infectious disease that has broken out in the burn. The priest shall pronounce him unclean; it is an infectious skin disease. ²⁶But if the priest examines it and there is no white hair in the spot and if it is not more than skin deep and has faded, then the priest is to put him in isolation for seven days. ²⁷On the seventh day the priest is to examine him, and if it is spreading in the skin, the priest shall pronounce him unclean; it is an infectious skin disease. ²⁸If, however, the spot is unchanged and has not spread in the skin but has faded, it is a swelling from the burn, and the priest shall pronounce him clean; it is only a scar from the burn.

²⁹"If a man or woman has a sore on the head or on the chin, ³⁰the priest is to examine the sore, and if it appears to be more than skin deep and the hair in it is yellow and thin, the priest shall pronounce that person unclean; it is an itch, an infectious disease of the head or chin. ³¹But if, when the priest examines this kind of sore, it does not seem to be more than skin deep and there is no black hair in it, then the priest is to put the infected person in isolation for seven days.

LEVITICUS 12:8

Do you ever feel kind of funny about putting a quarter in the church offering? Do you think maybe you should wait to give until you have a job and can give more? If you've thought that way, Leviticus 12:8 shares a good insight. In Old Testament times a mother brought a special offering to God right after the birth of a child. The best offering was a lamb, but if the family was poor, she could bring "two doves or two young pigeons," a very inexpensive offering. What counted was not how much the mother gave but the fact that she did give. How much you give is not most important. Giving even a little is a way of saying thank you to God.

Direct Line

[32]On the seventh day the priest is to examine the sore, and if the itch has not spread and there is no yellow hair in it and it does not appear to be more than skin deep, [33]he must be shaved except for the diseased area, and the priest is to keep him in isolation another seven days. [34]On the seventh day the priest is to examine the itch, and if it has not spread in the skin and appears to be no more than skin deep, the priest shall pronounce him clean. He must wash his clothes, and he will be clean. [35]But if the itch does spread in the skin after he is pronounced clean, [36]the priest is to examine him, and if the itch has spread in the skin, the priest does not need to look for yellow hair; the person is unclean. [37]If, however, in his judgment it is unchanged and black hair has grown in it, the itch is healed. He is clean, and the priest shall pronounce him clean.

[38]"When a man or woman has white spots on the skin, [39]the priest is to examine them, and if the spots are dull white, it is a harmless rash that has broken out on the skin; that person is clean.

[40]"When a man has lost his hair and is bald, he is clean. [41]If he has lost his hair from the front of his scalp and has a bald forehead, he is clean. [42]But if he has a reddish-white sore on his bald head or forehead, it is an infectious disease breaking out on his head or forehead. [43]The priest is to examine him, and if the swollen sore on his head or forehead is reddish-white like an infectious skin disease, [44]the man is diseased and is unclean. The priest shall pronounce him unclean because of the sore on his head.

[45]"The person with such an infectious disease must wear torn clothes, let his hair be unkempt,[a] cover the lower part of his face and cry out, 'Unclean! Unclean!' [46]As long as he has the infection he remains unclean. He must live alone; he must live outside the camp.

Regulations About Mildew [47]"If any clothing is contaminated with mildew— any woolen or linen clothing, [48]any woven or knitted material of linen or wool, any leather or anything made of leather— [49]and if the contamination in the clothing, or leather, or woven or knitted material, or any leather article, is greenish or reddish, it is a spreading mildew and must be shown to the priest. [50]The priest is to examine the mildew and isolate the affected article for seven days. [51]On the seventh day he is to examine it, and if the mildew

[a]45 Or *clothes, uncover his head*

The Bible Says "Unclean!"

In Old Testament times, people with a disease that might harm others were expected to be responsible. To avoid giving the disease to someone else, they lived alone and warned others of their condition, calling out, "Unclean!" to anyone who came near.

The word *unclean* in the Bible is used to describe several conditions that affected a person's relationship with others:

* physical (Leviticus 13:45–46)
* religious (Leviticus 16; Numbers 19)
* moral (Psalm 106:34–39).

Old Testament laws of uncleanness aren't in effect today, but by reading about them you can learn responsibility and respect for others.

has spread in the clothing, or the woven or knitted material, or the leather, whatever its use, it is a destructive mildew; the article is unclean. ⁵²He must burn up the clothing, or the woven or knitted material of wool or linen, or any leather article that has the contamination in it, because the mildew is destructive; the article must be burned up.

⁵³"But if, when the priest examines it, the mildew has not spread in the clothing, or the woven or knitted material, or the leather article, ⁵⁴he shall order that the contaminated article be washed. Then he is to isolate it for another seven days. ⁵⁵After the affected article has been washed, the priest is to examine it, and if the mildew has not changed its appearance, even though it has not spread, it is unclean. Burn it with fire, whether the mildew has affected one side or the other. ⁵⁶If, when the priest examines it, the mildew has faded after the article has been washed, he is to tear the contaminated part out of the clothing, or the leather, or the woven or knitted material. ⁵⁷But if it reappears in the clothing, or in the woven or knitted material, or in the leather article, it is spreading, and whatever has the mildew must be burned with fire. ⁵⁸The clothing, or the woven or knitted material, or any leather article that has been washed and is rid of the mildew, must be washed again, and it will be clean."

⁵⁹These are the regulations concerning contamination by mildew in woolen or linen clothing, woven or knitted material, or any leather article, for pronouncing them clean or unclean.

14 ***Cleansing From Infectious Skin Diseases*** The LORD said to Moses, ²"These are the regulations for the diseased person at the time of his ceremonial cleansing, when he is brought to the priest: ³The priest is to go outside the camp and examine him. If the person has been healed of his infectious skin disease,ᵃ ⁴the priest shall order that two live clean birds and some cedar wood, scarlet yarn and hyssop be brought for the one to be cleansed. ⁵Then the priest shall order that one of the birds be killed over fresh water in a clay pot. ⁶He is then to take the live bird and dip it, together with the cedar wood, the scarlet yarn and the hyssop, into the blood of the bird that was killed over the fresh water. ⁷Seven times he shall sprinkle the one to be cleansed of the infectious disease and pronounce him clean. Then he is to release the live bird in the open fields.

Oooh! You mean that green stuff that grows on my socks?

SEE LEVITICUS 13:47-59

⁸"The person to be cleansed must wash his clothes, shave off all his hair and bathe with water; then he will be ceremonially clean. After this he may come into the camp, but he must stay outside his tent for seven days. ⁹On the seventh day he must shave off all his hair; he must shave his head, his beard, his eyebrows and the rest of his hair. He must wash his clothes and bathe himself with water, and he will be clean.

¹⁰"On the eighth day he must bring two male lambs and one ewe lamb a year old, each without defect, along with three-tenths of an ephahᵇ of

ᵃ3 Traditionally *leprosy*; the Hebrew word was used for various diseases affecting the skin—not necessarily leprosy; also elsewhere in this chapter. ᵇ10 That is, probably about 6 quarts (about 6.5 liters)

fine flour mixed with oil for a grain offering, and one log*a* of oil. ¹¹The priest who pronounces him clean shall present both the one to be cleansed and his offerings before the LORD at the entrance to the Tent of Meeting.

¹²"Then the priest is to take one of the male lambs and offer it as a guilt offering, along with the log of oil; he shall wave them before the LORD as a wave offering. ¹³He is to slaughter the lamb in the holy place where the sin offering and the burnt offering are slaughtered. Like the sin offering, the guilt offering belongs to the priest; it is most holy. ¹⁴The priest is to take some of the blood of the guilt offering and put it on the lobe of the right ear of the one to be cleansed, on the thumb of his right hand and on the big toe of his right foot. ¹⁵The priest shall then take some of the log of oil, pour it in the palm of his own left hand, ¹⁶dip his right forefinger into the oil in his palm, and with his finger sprinkle some of it before the LORD seven times. ¹⁷The priest is to put some of the oil remaining in his palm on the lobe of the right ear of the one to be cleansed, on the thumb of his right hand and on the big toe of his right foot, on top of the blood of the guilt offering. ¹⁸The rest of the oil in his palm the priest shall put on the head of the one to be cleansed and make atonement for him before the LORD.

¹⁹"Then the priest is to sacrifice the sin offering and make atonement for the one to be cleansed from his uncleanness. After that, the priest shall slaughter the burnt offering ²⁰and offer it on the altar, together with the grain offering, and make atonement for him, and he will be clean.

²¹"If, however, he is poor and cannot afford these, he must take one male lamb as a guilt offering to be waved to make atonement for him, together with a tenth of an ephah*b* of fine flour mixed with oil for a grain offering, a log of oil, ²²and two doves or two young pigeons, which he can afford, one for a sin offering and the other for a burnt offering.

²³"On the eighth day he must bring them for his cleansing to the priest at the entrance to the Tent of Meeting, before the LORD. ²⁴The priest is to take the lamb for the guilt offering, together with the log of oil, and wave them before the LORD as a wave offering. ²⁵He shall slaughter the lamb for the guilt offering and take some of its blood and put it on the lobe of the right ear of the one to be cleansed, on the thumb of his right hand and on the big toe of his right foot. ²⁶The priest is to pour some of the oil into the palm of his own left hand, ²⁷and with his right forefinger sprinkle some of the oil from his palm seven times before the LORD. ²⁸Some of the oil in his palm he is to put on the same places he put the blood of the guilt offering—on the lobe of the right ear of the one to be cleansed, on the thumb of his right hand and on the big toe of his right foot. ²⁹The rest of the oil in his palm the priest shall put on the head of the one to be cleansed, to make atonement for him before the LORD. ³⁰Then he shall sacrifice the doves or the young pigeons, which the person can afford, ³¹one*c* as a sin offering and the other as a burnt offering, together with the grain offering. In this way the priest will make atonement before the LORD on behalf of the one to be cleansed."

³²These are the regulations for anyone who has an infectious skin disease and who cannot afford the regular offerings for his cleansing.

Cleansing From Mildew ³³The LORD said to Moses and Aaron, ³⁴"When you enter the land of Canaan, which I am giving you as your possession, and I put a spreading mildew in a house in that land, ³⁵the owner of the house must go and tell the priest, 'I have seen something that looks like mildew in my house.' ³⁶The priest is to order the house to be emptied before he goes in to

a10 That is, probably about 2/3 pint (about 0.3 liter); also in verses 12, 15, 21 and 24   *b21* That is, probably about 2 quarts (about 2 liters)   *c31* Septuagint and Syriac; Hebrew *31such as the person can afford, one* examine the mildew, so that nothing in the house will be pronounced unclean. After this the priest is to go in and inspect the house. [37]He is to examine the mildew on the walls, and if it has greenish or reddish depressions that appear to be deeper than the surface of the wall, [38]the priest shall go out the doorway of the house and close it up for seven days. [39]On the seventh day the priest shall return to inspect the house. If the mildew has spread on the walls, [40]he is to order that the contaminated stones be torn out and thrown into an unclean place outside the town. [41]He must have all the inside walls of the house scraped and the material that is scraped off dumped into an unclean place outside the town. [42]Then they are to take other stones to replace these and take new clay and plaster the house.

[43]"If the mildew reappears in the house after the stones have been torn out and the house scraped and plastered, [44]the priest is to go and examine it and, if the mildew has spread in the house, it is a destructive mildew; the house is unclean. [45]It must be torn down—its stones, timbers and all the plaster—and taken out of the town to an unclean place.

[46]"Anyone who goes into the house while it is closed up will be unclean till evening. [47]Anyone who sleeps or eats in the house must wash his clothes.

[48]"But if the priest comes to examine it and the mildew has not spread after the house has been plastered, he shall pronounce the house clean, because the mildew is gone. [49]To purify the house he is to take two birds and some cedar wood, scarlet yarn and hyssop. [50]He shall kill one of the birds over fresh water in a clay pot. [51]Then he is to take the cedar wood, the hyssop, the scarlet yarn and the live bird, dip them into the blood of the dead bird and the fresh water, and sprinkle the house seven times. [52]He shall purify the house with the bird's blood, the fresh water, the live bird, the cedar wood, the hyssop and the scarlet yarn. [53]Then he is to release the live bird in the open fields outside the town. In this way he will make atonement for the house, and it will be clean."

[54]These are the regulations for any infectious skin disease, for an itch, [55]for mildew in clothing or in a house, [56]and for a swelling, a rash or a bright spot, [57]to determine when something is clean or unclean.

These are the regulations for infectious skin diseases and mildew.

Discharges Causing Uncleanness The LORD said to Moses and Aaron, [2]"Speak to the Israelites and say to them: 'When any man has a bodily discharge, the discharge is unclean. [3]Whether it continues flowing from his body or is blocked, it will make him unclean. This is how his discharge will bring about uncleanness:

[4]"'Any bed the man with a discharge lies on will be unclean, and anything he sits on will be unclean. [5]Anyone who touches his bed must wash his clothes and bathe with water, and he will be unclean till evening. [6]Whoever sits on anything that the man with a discharge sat on must wash his clothes and bathe with water, and he will be unclean till evening.

[7]"'Whoever touches the man who has a discharge must wash his clothes and bathe with water, and he will be unclean till evening.

[8]"'If the man with the discharge spits on someone who is clean, that person must wash his clothes and bathe with water, and he will be unclean till evening.

[9]"'Everything the man sits on when riding will be unclean, [10]and whoever touches any of the things that were under him will be unclean till evening; whoever picks up those things must wash his clothes and bathe with water, and he will be unclean till evening.

[11]"'Anyone the man with a discharge touches without rinsing his hands with water must wash his clothes and bathe with water, and he will be unclean till evening.

¹²" 'A clay pot that the man touches must be broken, and any wooden article is to be rinsed with water.

¹³" 'When a man is cleansed from his discharge, he is to count off seven days for his ceremonial cleansing; he must wash his clothes and bathe himself with fresh water, and he will be clean. ¹⁴On the eighth day he must take two doves or two young pigeons and come before the LORD to the entrance to the Tent of Meeting and give them to the priest. ¹⁵The priest is to sacrifice them, the one for a sin offering and the other for a burnt offering. In this way he will make atonement before the LORD for the man because of his discharge.

¹⁶" 'When a man has an emission of semen, he must bathe his whole body with water, and he will be unclean till evening. ¹⁷Any clothing or leather that has semen on it must be washed with water, and it will be unclean till evening. ¹⁸When a man lies with a woman and there is an emission of semen, both must bathe with water, and they will be unclean till evening.

¹⁹" 'When a woman has her regular flow of blood, the impurity of her monthly period will last seven days, and anyone who touches her will be unclean till evening.

²⁰" 'Anything she lies on during her period will be unclean, and anything she sits on will be unclean. ²¹Whoever touches her bed must wash his clothes and bathe with water, and he will be unclean till evening. ²²Whoever touches anything she sits on must wash his clothes and bathe with water, and he will be unclean till evening. ²³Whether it is the bed or anything she was sitting on, when anyone touches it, he will be unclean till evening.

²⁴" 'If a man lies with her and her monthly flow touches him, he will be unclean for seven days; any bed he lies on will be unclean.

²⁵" 'When a woman has a discharge of blood for many days at a time other than her monthly period or has a discharge that continues beyond her period, she will be unclean as long as she has the discharge, just as in the days of her period. ²⁶Any bed she lies on while her discharge continues will be unclean, as is her bed during her monthly period, and anything she sits on will be unclean, as during her period. ²⁷Whoever touches them will be unclean; he must wash his clothes and bathe with water, and he will be unclean till evening.

²⁸" 'When she is cleansed from her discharge, she must count off seven days, and after that she will be ceremonially clean. ²⁹On the eighth day she must take two doves or two young pigeons and bring them to the priest at the entrance to the Tent of Meeting. ³⁰The priest is to sacrifice one for a sin offering and the other for a burnt offering. In this way he will make atonement for her before the LORD for the uncleanness of her discharge.

³¹" 'You must keep the Israelites separate from things that make them unclean, so they will not die in their uncleanness for defiling my dwelling place,^a which is among them.' "

³²These are the regulations for a man with a discharge, for anyone made unclean by an emission of semen, ³³for a woman in her monthly period, for a man or a woman with a discharge, and for a man who lies with a woman who is ceremonially unclean.

16 *The Day of Atonement* The LORD spoke to Moses after the death of the two sons of Aaron who died when they approached the LORD. ²The LORD said to Moses: "Tell your brother Aaron not to come whenever he chooses into the Most Holy Place behind the curtain in front of the atonement cover on the ark, or else he will die, because I appear in the cloud over the atonement cover.

a31 Or my tabernacle

³"This is how Aaron is to enter the sanctuary area: with a young bull for a sin offering and a ram for a burnt offering. ⁴He is to put on the sacred linen tunic, with linen undergarments next to his body; he is to tie the linen sash around him and put on the linen turban. These are sacred garments; so he must bathe himself with water before he puts them on. ⁵From the Israelite community he is to take two male goats for a sin offering and a ram for a burnt offering.

⁶"Aaron is to offer the bull for his own sin offering to make atonement for himself and his household. ⁷Then he is to take the two goats and present them before the Lord at the entrance to the Tent of Meeting. ⁸He is to cast lots for the two goats—one lot for the Lord and the other for the scapegoat.ᵃ ⁹Aaron shall bring the goat whose lot falls to the Lord and sacrifice it for a sin offering. ¹⁰But the goat chosen by lot as the scapegoat shall be presented alive before the Lord to be used for making atonement by sending it into the desert as a scapegoat.

¹¹"Aaron shall bring the bull for his own sin offering to make atonement for himself and his household, and he is to slaughter the bull for his own sin offering. ¹²He is to take a censer full of burning coals from the altar before the Lord and two handfuls of finely ground fragrant incense and take them behind the curtain. ¹³He is to put the incense on the fire before the Lord, and the smoke of the incense will conceal the atonement cover above the Testimony, so that he will not die. ¹⁴He is to take some of the bull's blood and with his finger sprinkle it on the front of the atonement cover; then he shall sprinkle some of it with his finger seven times before the atonement cover.

¹⁵"He shall then slaughter the goat for the sin offering for the people and take its blood behind the curtain and do with it as he did with the bull's blood: He shall sprinkle it on the atonement cover and in front of it. ¹⁶In this way he will make atonement for the Most Holy Place because of the uncleanness and rebellion of the Israelites, whatever their sins have been. He is to do the same for the Tent of Meeting, which is among them in the midst of their uncleanness. ¹⁷No one is to be in the Tent of Meeting from the time Aaron goes in to make atonement in the Most Holy Place until he comes out, having made atonement for himself, his household and the whole community of Israel.

¹⁸"Then he shall come out to the altar that is before the Lord and make atonement for it. He shall take some of the bull's blood and some of the goat's blood and put it on all the horns of the altar. ¹⁹He shall sprinkle some of the blood on it with his finger seven times to cleanse it and to consecrate it from the uncleanness of the Israelites.

²⁰"When Aaron has finished making atonement for the Most Holy Place, the Tent of Meeting and the altar, he shall bring forward the live goat. ²¹He is to lay both hands on the head of the live goat and confess over it all the wickedness and rebellion of the Israelites—all their sins—and put them on the goat's head. He shall send the goat away into the desert in the care of a man appointed for the task. ²²The goat will carry on itself all their sins to a solitary place; and the man shall release it in the desert.

²³"Then Aaron is to go into the Tent of Meeting and take off the linen garments he put on before he entered the Most Holy Place, and he is to leave them there. ²⁴He shall bathe himself with water in a holy place and put on his regular garments. Then he shall come out and sacrifice the burnt offering for himself and the burnt offering for the people, to make atonement for himself and for the people. ²⁵He shall also burn the fat of the sin offering on the altar.

²⁶"The man who releases the goat as a scapegoat must wash his clothes

---

ᵃ8 That is, the goat of removal; Hebrew *azazel*; also in verses 10 and 26

and bathe himself with water; afterward he may come into the camp. ²⁷The bull and the goat for the sin offerings, whose blood was brought into the Most Holy Place to make atonement, must be taken outside the camp; their hides, flesh and offal are to be burned up. ²⁸The man who burns them must wash his clothes and bathe himself with water; afterward he may come into the camp.

²⁹"This is to be a lasting ordinance for you: On the tenth day of the seventh month you must deny yourselves^a and not do any work—whether native-born or an alien living among you— ³⁰because on this day atonement will be made for you, to cleanse you. Then, before the LORD, you will be clean from all your sins. ³¹It is a sabbath of rest, and you must deny yourselves; it is a lasting ordinance. ³²The priest who is anointed and ordained to succeed his father as high priest is to make atonement. He is to put on the sacred linen garments ³³and make atonement for the Most Holy Place, for the Tent of Meeting and the altar, and for the priests and all the people of the community.

³⁴"This is to be a lasting ordinance for you: Atonement is to be made once a year for all the sins of the Israelites."

And it was done, as the LORD commanded Moses.

Eating Blood Forbidden The LORD said to Moses, ²"Speak to Aaron and his sons and to all the Israelites and say to them: 'This is what the LORD has commanded: ³Any Israelite who sacrifices an ox,^b a lamb or a goat in the camp or outside of it ⁴instead of bringing it to the entrance to the Tent of Meeting to present it as an offering to the LORD in front of the tabernacle of the LORD—that man shall be considered guilty of bloodshed; he has shed blood and must be cut off from his people. ⁵This is so the Israelites will bring to the LORD the sacrifices they are now making in the open fields. They must bring them to the priest, that is, to the LORD, at the entrance to the Tent of Meeting and sacrifice them as fellowship offerings.^c ⁶The priest is to sprinkle the blood against the altar of the LORD at the entrance to the Tent of Meeting and burn the fat as an aroma pleasing to the LORD. ⁷They must no longer offer any of their sacrifices to the goat idols^d to whom they prostitute themselves. This is to be a lasting ordinance for them and for the generations to come.'

⁸"Say to them: 'Any Israelite or any alien living among them who offers a burnt offering or sacrifice ⁹and does not bring it to the entrance to the Tent of Meeting to sacrifice it to the LORD—that man must be cut off from his people.

¹⁰"'Any Israelite or any alien living among them who eats any blood—I will set my face against that person who eats blood and will cut him off from his people. ¹¹For the life of a creature is in the blood, and I have given it to you to make atonement for yourselves on the altar; it is the blood that makes atonement for one's life. ¹²Therefore I say to the Israelites, "None of you may eat blood, nor may an alien living among you eat blood."

¹³"'Any Israelite or any alien living among you who hunts any animal or bird that may be eaten must drain out the blood and cover it with earth, ¹⁴because the life of every creature is its blood. That is why I have said to the Israelites, "You must not eat the blood of any creature, because the life of every creature is its blood; anyone who eats it must be cut off."

¹⁵"'Anyone, whether native-born or alien, who eats anything found dead or torn by wild animals must wash his clothes and bathe with water, and he will be ceremonially unclean till evening; then he will be clean. ¹⁶But if he does not wash his clothes and bathe himself, he will be held responsible.'"

---

^a29 Or *must fast*; also in verse 31   ^b3 The Hebrew word can include both male and female.
^c5 Traditionally *peace offerings*   ^d7 Or *demons*

18 *Unlawful Sexual Relations* The L ORD said to Moses, ²"Speak to the Israelites and say to them: 'I am the L ORD your God. ³You must not do as they do in Egypt, where you used to live, and you must not do as they do in the land of Canaan, where I am bringing you. Do not follow their practices. ⁴You must obey my laws and be careful to follow my decrees. I am the L ORD your God. ⁵Keep my decrees and laws, for the man who obeys them will live by them. I am the L ORD.

⁶"'No one is to approach any close relative to have sexual relations. I am the L ORD.

⁷"'Do not dishonor your father by having sexual relations with your mother. She is your mother; do not have relations with her.

⁸"'Do not have sexual relations with your father's wife; that would dishonor your father.

⁹"'Do not have sexual relations with your sister, either your father's daughter or your mother's daughter, whether she was born in the same home or elsewhere.

¹⁰"'Do not have sexual relations with your son's daughter or your daughter's daughter; that would dishonor you.

¹¹"'Do not have sexual relations with the daughter of your father's wife, born to your father; she is your sister.

¹²"'Do not have sexual relations with your father's sister; she is your father's close relative.

¹³"'Do not have sexual relations with your mother's sister, because she is your mother's close relative.

¹⁴"'Do not dishonor your father's brother by approaching his wife to have sexual relations; she is your aunt.

¹⁵"'Do not have sexual relations with your daughter-in-law. She is your son's wife; do not have relations with her.

¹⁶"'Do not have sexual relations with your brother's wife; that would dishonor your brother.

¹⁷"'Do not have sexual relations with both a woman and her daughter. Do not have sexual relations with either her son's daughter or her daughter's daughter; they are her close relatives. That is wickedness.

¹⁸"'Do not take your wife's sister as a rival wife and have sexual relations with her while your wife is living.

¹⁹"'Do not approach a woman to have sexual relations during the uncleanness of her monthly period.

The Bible Says

Only One Right Choice

"Alternative lifestyle" usually refers to making a sexual choice. The impression is that any choice is all right. It's just a matter of preference. When it comes to sex, don't kid yourself about some of those choices being morally all right:

* It's wrong to have sex with any close relative (Leviticus 18:6–18).
* It's wrong to have sex with animals (Leviticus 18:23).
* It's wrong to have homosexual sex (Leviticus 18:22).

This isn't the only Bible passage that says homosexual sex is a sin. Read also Romans 1:26–27. If someone tells you homosexuality is an alternative lifestyle—meaning that it's OK—don't let those words fool you. It's an alternative all right. A sinful one.

²⁰" 'Do not have sexual relations with your neighbor's wife and defile your-self with her.

²¹" 'Do not give any of your children to be sacrificed^ᵃ to Molech, for you must not profane the name of your God. I am the LORD.

²²" 'Do not lie with a man as one lies with a woman; that is detestable.

²³" 'Do not have sexual relations with an animal and defile yourself with it. A woman must not present herself to an animal to have sexual relations with it; that is a perversion.

²⁴" 'Do not defile yourselves in any of these ways, because this is how the nations that I am going to drive out before you became defiled. ²⁵Even the land was defiled; so I punished it for its sin, and the land vomited out its in-habitants. ²⁶But you must keep my decrees and my laws. The native-born and the aliens living among you must not do any of these detestable things, ²⁷for all these things were done by the people who lived in the land before you, and the land became defiled. ²⁸And if you defile the land, it will vomit you out as it vomited out the nations that were before you.

²⁹" 'Everyone who does any of these detestable things—such persons must be cut off from their people. ³⁰Keep my requirements and do not follow any of the detestable customs that were practiced before you came and do not defile yourselves with them. I am the LORD your God.' "

Various Laws The LORD said to Moses, ²"Speak to the entire as-sembly of Israel and say to them: 'Be holy because I, the LORD your God, am holy.

³" 'Each of you must respect his mother and father, and you must observe my Sabbaths. I am the LORD your God.

⁴" 'Do not turn to idols or make gods of cast metal for yourselves. I am the LORD your God.

⁵" 'When you sacrifice a fellowship offering^ᵇ to the LORD, sacrifice it in such a way that it will be accepted on your behalf. ⁶It shall be eaten on the day you sacrifice it or on the next day; anything left over until the third day must be burned up. ⁷If any of it is eaten on the third day, it is impure and will not be accepted. ⁸Whoever eats it will be held responsible because he has desecrated what is holy to the LORD; that person must be cut off from his people.

⁹" 'When you reap the harvest of your land, do not reap to the very edges of your field or gather the gleanings of your harvest. ¹⁰Do not go over your vineyard a second time or pick up the grapes that have fallen. Leave them for the poor and the alien. I am the LORD your God.

¹¹" 'Do not steal.

" 'Do not lie.

" 'Do not deceive one another.

¹²" 'Do not swear falsely by my name and so profane the name of your God. I am the LORD.

¹³" 'Do not defraud your neighbor or rob him.

" 'Do not hold back the wages of a hired man overnight.

¹⁴" 'Do not curse the deaf or put a stumbling block in front of the blind, but fear your God. I am the LORD.

¹⁵" 'Do not pervert justice; do not show partiality to the poor or favoritism to the great, but judge your neighbor fairly.

¹⁶" 'Do not go about spreading slander among your people.

" 'Do not do anything that endangers your neighbor's life. I am the LORD.

¹⁷" 'Do not hate your brother in your heart. Rebuke your neighbor frankly so you will not share in his guilt.

---

^ᵃ21 Or to be passed through the fire, ^ᵇ5 Traditionally peace offering

¹⁸" 'Do not seek revenge or bear a grudge against one of your people, but love your neighbor as yourself. I am the LORD.

¹⁹" 'Keep my decrees.

" 'Do not mate different kinds of animals.

" 'Do not plant your field with two kinds of seed.

" 'Do not wear clothing woven of two kinds of material.

²⁰" 'If a man sleeps with a woman who is a slave girl promised to another man but who has not been ransomed or given her freedom, there must be due punishment. Yet they are not to be put to death, because she had not been freed. ²¹The man, however, must bring a ram to the entrance to the Tent of Meeting for a guilt offering to the LORD. ²²With the ram of the guilt offering the priest is to make atonement for him before the LORD for the sin he has committed, and his sin will be forgiven.

²³" 'When you enter the land and plant any kind of fruit tree, regard its fruit as forbidden.^a For three years you are to consider it forbidden^a; it must not be eaten. ²⁴In the fourth year all its fruit will be holy, an offering of praise to the LORD. ²⁵But in the fifth year you may eat its fruit. In this way your harvest will be increased. I am the LORD your God.

²⁶" 'Do not eat any meat with the blood still in it.

" 'Do not practice divination or sorcery.

²⁷" 'Do not cut the hair at the sides of your head or clip off the edges of your beard.

²⁸" 'Do not cut your bodies for the dead or put tattoo marks on yourselves. I am the LORD.

²⁹" 'Do not degrade your daughter by making her a prostitute, or the land will turn to prostitution and be filled with wickedness.

³⁰" 'Observe my Sabbaths and have reverence for my sanctuary. I am the LORD.

³¹" 'Do not turn to mediums or seek out spiritists, for you will be defiled by them. I am the LORD your God.

³²" 'Rise in the presence of the aged, show respect for the elderly and revere your God. I am the LORD.

³³" 'When an alien lives with you in your land, do not mistreat him. ³⁴The alien living with you must be treated as one of your native-born. Love him as yourself, for you were aliens in Egypt. I am the LORD your God.

³⁵" 'Do not use dishonest standards when measuring length, weight or quantity. ³⁶Use honest scales and honest weights, an honest ephah^b and an honest hin.^c I am the LORD your God, who brought you out of Egypt.

³⁷" 'Keep all my decrees and all my laws and follow them. I am the LORD.' "

20 *Punishments for Sin* The LORD said to Moses, ²"Say to the Israelites: 'Any Israelite or any alien living in Israel who gives^d any of his children to Molech must be put to death. The people of the community are to stone him. ³I will set my face against that man and I will cut him off from his people; for by giving his children to Molech, he has defiled my sanctuary and profaned my holy name. ⁴If the people of the community close their eyes when that man gives one of his children to Molech and they fail to put him to death, ⁵I will set my face against that man and his family and will cut off from their people both him and all who follow him in prostituting themselves to Molech.

⁶" 'I will set my face against the person who turns to mediums and spiritists to prostitute himself by following them, and I will cut him off from his people.

⁷" 'Consecrate yourselves and be holy, because I am the LORD your God.

---

^a23 Hebrew *uncircumcised*   ^b36 An ephah was a dry measure.   ^c36 A hin was a liquid measure.   ^d2 Or *sacrifices*; also in verses 3 and 4

⁸Keep my decrees and follow them. I am the Lord, who makes you holy.ᵃ

⁹" 'If anyone curses his father or mother, he must be put to death. He has cursed his father or his mother, and his blood will be on his own head.

¹⁰" 'If a man commits adultery with another man's wife—with the wife of his neighbor—both the adulterer and the adulteress must be put to death.

¹¹" 'If a man sleeps with his father's wife, he has dishonored his father. Both the man and the woman must be put to death; their blood will be on their own heads.

¹²" 'If a man sleeps with his daughter-in-law, both of them must be put to death. What they have done is a perversion; their blood will be on their own heads.

¹³" 'If a man lies with a man as one lies with a woman, both of them have done what is detestable. They must be put to death; their blood will be on their own heads.

¹⁴" 'If a man marries both a woman and her mother, it is wicked. Both he and they must be burned in the fire, so that no wickedness will be among you.

¹⁵" 'If a man has sexual relations with an animal, he must be put to death, and you must kill the animal.

¹⁶" 'If a woman approaches an animal to have sexual relations with it, kill both the woman and the animal. They must be put to death; their blood will be on their own heads.

¹⁷" 'If a man marries his sister, the daughter of either his father or his mother, and they have sexual relations, it is a disgrace. They must be cut off before the eyes of their people. He has dishonored his sister and will be held responsible.

¹⁸" 'If a man lies with a woman during her monthly period and has sexual relations with her, he has exposed the source of her flow, and she has also uncovered it. Both of them must be cut off from their people.

¹⁹" 'Do not have sexual relations with the sister of either your mother or your father, for that would dishonor a close relative; both of you would be held responsible.

²⁰" 'If a man sleeps with his aunt, he has dishonored his uncle. They will be held responsible; they will die childless.

²¹" 'If a man marries his brother's wife, it is an act of impurity; he has dishonored his brother. They will be childless.

²²" 'Keep all my decrees and laws and follow them, so that the land where I am bringing you to live may not vomit you out. ²³You must not live according to the customs of the nations I am going to drive out before you. Because they did all these things, I abhorred them. ²⁴But I said to you, "You will possess their land; I will give it to you as an inheritance, a land flowing with milk and honey." I am the Lord your God, who has set you apart from the nations.

²⁵" 'You must therefore make a distinction between clean and unclean animals and between unclean and clean birds. Do not defile yourselves by any animal or bird or anything that moves along the ground—those which I have set apart as unclean for you. ²⁶You are to be holy to meᵇ because I, the Lord, am holy, and I have set you apart from the nations to be my own.

²⁷" 'A man or woman who is a medium or spiritist among you must be put to death. You are to stone them; their blood will be on their own heads.' "

21 *Rules for Priests* The Lord said to Moses, "Speak to the priests, the sons of Aaron, and say to them: 'A priest must not make himself ceremonially unclean for any of his people who die, ²except for a close relative, such as his mother or father, his son or daughter, his brother, ³or an unmarried sister who is dependent on him since she has no husband—

ᵃ8 Or *who sanctifies you;* or *who sets you apart as holy* ᵇ26 Or *be my holy ones*

Dear Sam,
I'm confused. If I'm supposed to love everyone, should I love homosexuals? Is that an acceptable alternative lifestyle?

Chris in Crystal Springs

Dear Sam, Inc.

100 Advice Lane, Anywhere, USA

Dear Chris,

I see why you're confused, but really you're dealing with two separate issues here. God wants you to love others as you love yourself. That means caring about them as people God created. But it does not mean that you approve of or get involved with their lifestyle.

While there are many things not forbidden in Scripture, things about which you can make up your own mind, homosexuality is not one of them. There are many passages discussing this "alternative," and every passage makes it clear that this is a sinful and unacceptable lifestyle (Leviticus 18:22; 20:13; Romans 1:26-27).

You can't approve of something evil that God has forbidden. But you can love people, pray for them and witness to those who will listen.

Sam

for her he may make himself unclean. ⁴He must not make himself unclean for people related to him by marriage,ᵃ and so defile himself.

⁵“ 'Priests must not shave their heads or shave off the edges of their beards or cut their bodies. ⁶They must be holy to their God and must not profane the name of their God. Because they present the offerings made to the Lᴏʀᴅ by fire, the food of their God, they are to be holy.

⁷“ 'They must not marry women defiled by prostitution or divorced from their husbands, because priests are holy to their God. ⁸Regard them as holy, because they offer up the food of your God. Consider them holy, because I the Lᴏʀᴅ am holy—I who make you holy.ᵇ

⁹“ 'If a priest's daughter defiles herself by becoming a prostitute, she disgraces her father; she must be burned in the fire.

¹⁰“ 'The high priest, the one among his brothers who has had the anointing oil poured on his head and who has been ordained to wear the priestly garments, must not let his hair become unkemptᶜ or tear his clothes. ¹¹He must not enter a place where there is a dead body. He must not make himself unclean, even for his father or mother, ¹²nor leave the sanctuary of his God or desecrate it, because he has been dedicated by the anointing oil of his God. I am the Lᴏʀᴅ.

¹³“ 'The woman he marries must be a virgin. ¹⁴He must not marry a widow, a divorced woman, or a woman defiled by prostitution, but only a virgin from his own people, ¹⁵so he will not defile his offspring among his people. I am the Lᴏʀᴅ, who makes him holy.ᵈ' ”

¹⁶The Lᴏʀᴅ said to Moses, ¹⁷“Say to Aaron: 'For the generations to come none of your descendants who has a defect may come near to offer the food of his God. ¹⁸No man who has any defect may come near: no man who is blind or lame, disfigured or deformed; ¹⁹no man with a crippled foot or hand, ²⁰or who is hunchbacked or dwarfed, or who has any eye defect, or who has festering or running sores or damaged testicles. ²¹No descendant of Aaron the priest who has any defect is to come near to present the offerings made to the Lᴏʀᴅ by fire. He has a defect; he must not come near to offer the food of his God. ²²He may eat the most holy food of his God, as well as the holy food; ²³yet because of his defect, he must not go near the curtain or approach the altar, and so desecrate my sanctuary. I am the Lᴏʀᴅ, who makes them holy.ᵉ' ”

²⁴So Moses told this to Aaron and his sons and to all the Israelites.

22 The Lᴏʀᴅ said to Moses, ²“Tell Aaron and his sons to treat with respect the sacred offerings the Israelites consecrate to me, so they will not profane my holy name. I am the Lᴏʀᴅ.

³“Say to them: 'For the generations to come, if any of your descendants is ceremonially unclean and yet comes near the sacred offerings that the Israelites consecrate to the Lᴏʀᴅ, that person must be cut off from my presence. I am the Lᴏʀᴅ.

⁴“ 'If a descendant of Aaron has an infectious skin diseaseᶠ or a bodily discharge, he may not eat the sacred offerings until he is cleansed. He will also be unclean if he touches something defiled by a corpse or by anyone who has an emission of semen, ⁵or if he touches any crawling thing that makes him unclean, or any person who makes him unclean, whatever the uncleanness may be. ⁶The one who touches any such thing will be unclean till evening. He must not eat any of the sacred offerings unless he has bathed himself with water. ⁷When the sun goes down, he will be clean, and after that he may eat

---

ᵃ4 Or *unclean as a leader among his people* ᵇ8 Or *who sanctify you;* or *who set you apart as holy* ᶜ10 Or *not uncover his head* ᵈ15 Or *who sanctifies him;* or *who sets him apart as holy* ᵉ23 Or *who sanctifies them;* or *who sets them apart as holy* ᶠ4 Traditionally *leprosy;* the Hebrew word was used for various diseases affecting the skin—not necessarily leprosy.

the sacred offerings, for they are his food. [8]He must not eat anything found dead or torn by wild animals, and so become unclean through it. I am the Lord.

[9]" 'The priests are to keep my requirements so that they do not become guilty and die for treating them with contempt. I am the Lord, who makes them holy.[a]

[10]" 'No one outside a priest's family may eat the sacred offering, nor may the guest of a priest or his hired worker eat it. [11]But if a priest buys a slave with money, or if a slave is born in his household, that slave may eat his food. [12]If a priest's daughter marries anyone other than a priest, she may not eat any of the sacred contributions. [13]But if a priest's daughter becomes a widow or is divorced, yet has no children, and she returns to live in her father's house as in her youth, she may eat of her father's food. No unauthorized person, however, may eat any of it.

[14]" 'If anyone eats a sacred offering by mistake, he must make restitution to the priest for the offering and add a fifth of the value to it. [15]The priests must not desecrate the sacred offerings the Israelites present to the Lord [16]by allowing them to eat the sacred offerings and so bring upon them guilt requiring payment. I am the Lord, who makes them holy.' "

Unacceptable Sacrifices   [17]The Lord said to Moses, [18]"Speak to Aaron and his sons and to all the Israelites and say to them: 'If any of you—either an Israelite or an alien living in Israel—presents a gift for a burnt offering to the Lord, either to fulfill a vow or as a freewill offering, [19]you must present a male without defect from the cattle, sheep or goats in order that it may be accepted on your behalf. [20]Do not bring anything with a defect, because it will not be accepted on your behalf. [21]When anyone brings from the herd or flock a fellowship offering[b] to the Lord to fulfill a special vow or as a freewill offering, it must be without defect or blemish to be acceptable. [22]Do not offer to the Lord the blind, the injured or the maimed, or anything with warts or festering or running sores. Do not place any of these on the altar as an offering made to the Lord by fire. [23]You may, however, present as a freewill offering an ox[c] or a sheep that is deformed or stunted, but it will not be accepted in fulfillment of a vow. [24]You must not offer to the Lord an animal whose testicles are bruised, crushed, torn or cut. You must not do this in your own land, [25]and you must not accept such animals from the hand of a foreigner and offer them as the food of your God. They will not be accepted on your behalf, because they are deformed and have defects.' "

[26]The Lord said to Moses, [27]"When a calf, a lamb or a goat is born, it is to remain with its mother for seven days. From the eighth day on, it will be acceptable as an offering made to the Lord by fire. [28]Do not slaughter a cow or a sheep and its young on the same day.

[29]"When you sacrifice a thank offering to the Lord, sacrifice it in such a way that it will be accepted on your behalf. [30]It must be eaten that same day; leave none of it till morning. I am the Lord.

[31]"Keep my commands and follow them. I am the Lord. [32]Do not profane my holy name. I must be acknowledged as holy by the Israelites. I am the Lord, who makes[d] you holy[e] [33]and who brought you out of Egypt to be your God. I am the Lord."

23   The Lord said to Moses, [2]"Speak to the Israelites and say to them: 'These are my appointed feasts, the appointed feasts of the Lord, which you are to proclaim as sacred assemblies.

---

[a]9 Or *who sanctifies them;* or *who sets them apart as holy;* also in verse 16   [b]21 Traditionally *peace offering*   [c]23 The Hebrew word can include both male and female.   [d]32 Or *made*   [e]32 Or *who sanctifies you;* or *who sets you apart as holy*

The Sabbath   ³" 'There are six days when you may work, but the seventh day is a Sabbath of rest, a day of sacred assembly. You are not to do any work; wherever you live, it is a Sabbath to the LORD.

The Passover and Unleavened Bread   ⁴" 'These are the LORD's appointed feasts, the sacred assemblies you are to proclaim at their appointed times: ⁵The LORD's Passover begins at twilight on the fourteenth day of the first month. ⁶On the fifteenth day of that month the LORD's Feast of Unleavened Bread begins; for seven days you must eat bread made without yeast. ⁷On the first day hold a sacred assembly and do no regular work. ⁸For seven days present an offering made to the LORD by fire. And on the seventh day hold a sacred assembly and do no regular work.' "

Firstfruits   ⁹The LORD said to Moses, ¹⁰"Speak to the Israelites and say to them: 'When you enter the land I am going to give you and you reap its harvest, bring to the priest a sheaf of the first grain you harvest. ¹¹He is to wave the sheaf before the LORD so it will be accepted on your behalf; the priest is to wave it on the day after the Sabbath. ¹²On the day you wave the sheaf, you must sacrifice as a burnt offering to the LORD a lamb a year old without defect, ¹³together with its grain offering of two-tenths of an ephah*ᵃ* of fine flour mixed with oil—an offering made to the LORD by fire, a pleasing aroma—and its drink offering of a quarter of a hin*ᵇ* of wine. ¹⁴You must not eat any bread, or roasted or new grain, until the very day you bring this offering to your God. This is to be a lasting ordinance for the generations to come, wherever you live.

Feast of Weeks   ¹⁵" 'From the day after the Sabbath, the day you brought the sheaf of the wave offering, count off seven full weeks. ¹⁶Count off fifty days up to the day after the seventh Sabbath, and then present an offering of new grain to the LORD. ¹⁷From wherever you live, bring two loaves made of two-tenths of an ephah of fine flour, baked with yeast, as a wave offering of firstfruits to the LORD. ¹⁸Present with this bread seven male lambs, each a year old and without defect, one young bull and two rams. They will be a burnt offering to the LORD, together with their grain offerings and drink offerings—an offering made by fire, an aroma pleasing to the LORD. ¹⁹Then sacrifice one male goat for a sin offering and two lambs, each a year old, for a fellowship offering.*ᶜ* ²⁰The priest is to wave the two lambs before the LORD as a wave offering, together with the bread of the firstfruits. They are a sacred offering to the LORD for the priest. ²¹On that same day you are to proclaim a sacred assembly and do no regular work. This is to be a lasting ordinance for the generations to come, wherever you live.

²²" 'When you reap the harvest of your land, do not reap to the very edges of your field or gather the gleanings of your harvest. Leave them for the poor and the alien. I am the LORD your God.' "

Feast of Trumpets   ²³The LORD said to Moses, ²⁴"Say to the Israelites: 'On the first day of the seventh month you are to have a day of rest, a sacred assembly commemorated with trumpet blasts. ²⁵Do no regular work, but present an offering made to the LORD by fire.' "

Day of Atonement   ²⁶The LORD said to Moses, ²⁷"The tenth day of this seventh month is the Day of Atonement. Hold a sacred assembly and deny yourselves,*ᵈ* and present an offering made to the LORD by fire. ²⁸Do no work on that day, because it is the Day of Atonement, when atonement is made for you before the LORD your God. ²⁹Anyone who does not deny himself on that day must be cut off from his people. ³⁰I will destroy from among his people

---

ᵃ13 That is, probably about 4 quarts (about 4.5 liters); also in verse 17   *ᵇ13* That is, probably about 1 quart (about 1 liter)   *ᶜ19* Traditionally *peace offering*   *ᵈ27* Or *and fast;* also in verses 29 and 32

anyone who does any work on that day. ³¹You shall do no work at all. This is to be a lasting ordinance for the generations to come, wherever you live. ³²It is a sabbath of rest for you, and you must deny yourselves. From the evening of the ninth day of the month until the following evening you are to observe your sabbath."

Feast of Tabernacles ³³The LORD said to Moses, ³⁴"Say to the Israelites: 'On the fifteenth day of the seventh month the LORD's Feast of Tabernacles begins, and it lasts for seven days. ³⁵The first day is a sacred assembly; do no regular work. ³⁶For seven days present offerings made to the LORD by fire, and on the eighth day hold a sacred assembly and present an offering made to the LORD by fire. It is the closing assembly; do no regular work.

³⁷(" 'These are the LORD's appointed feasts, which you are to proclaim as sacred assemblies for bringing offerings made to the LORD by fire—the burnt offerings and grain offerings, sacrifices and drink offerings required for each day. ³⁸These offerings are in addition to those for the LORD's Sabbaths andᵃ in addition to your gifts and whatever you have vowed and all the freewill offerings you give to the LORD.)

³⁹" 'So beginning with the fifteenth day of the seventh month, after you have gathered the crops of the land, celebrate the festival to the LORD for seven days; the first day is a day of rest, and the eighth day also is a day of rest. ⁴⁰On the first day you are to take choice fruit from the trees, and palm fronds, leafy branches and poplars, and rejoice before the LORD your God for seven days. ⁴¹Celebrate this as a festival to the LORD for seven days each year. This is to be a lasting ordinance for the generations to come; celebrate it in the seventh month. ⁴²Live in booths for seven days: All native-born Israelites are to live in booths ⁴³so your descendants will know that I had the Israelites live in booths when I brought them out of Egypt. I am the LORD your God.' "

⁴⁴So Moses announced to the Israelites the appointed feasts of the LORD.

Oil and Bread Set Before the LORD The LORD said to Moses, ²"Command the Israelites to bring you clear oil of pressed olives for the light so that the lamps may be kept burning continually. ³Outside the curtain of the Testimony in the Tent of Meeting, Aaron is to tend the lamps before the LORD from evening till morning, continually. This is to be a lasting ordinance for the generations to come. ⁴The lamps on the pure gold lampstand before the LORD must be tended continually.

⁵"Take fine flour and bake twelve loaves of bread, using two-tenths of an ephahᵇ for each loaf. ⁶Set them in two rows, six in each row, on the table of pure gold before the LORD. ⁷Along each row put some pure incense as a memorial portion to represent the bread and to be an offering made to the LORD by fire. ⁸This bread is to be set out before the LORD regularly, Sabbath after Sabbath, on behalf of the Israelites, as a lasting covenant. ⁹It belongs to Aaron and his sons, who are to eat it in a holy place, because it is a most holy part of their regular share of the offerings made to the LORD by fire."

A Blasphemer Stoned ¹⁰Now the son of an Israelite mother and an Egyptian fa-

Direct Line

LEVITICUS 24:10–16

Some people are upset by this story of a young man who was stoned because he "blasphemed the Name with a curse" (Leviticus 24:11). What they don't realize is that the word *curse* doesn't mean "swear." This man used God's name as a magic word in a curse aimed to harm the man he had fought with. Swearing certainly isn't acceptable behavior for a Christian, but cursing goes much further. That's why God required the death penalty for it.

ᵃ38 Or *These feasts are in addition to the LORD's Sabbaths, and these offerings are* ᵇ5 That is, probably about 4 quarts (about 4.5 liters)

ther went out among the Israelites, and a fight broke out in the camp between him and an Israelite. ¹¹The son of the Israelite woman blasphemed the Name with a curse; so they brought him to Moses. (His mother's name was Shelomith, the daughter of Dibri the Danite.) ¹²They put him in custody until the will of the LORD should be made clear to them.

¹³Then the LORD said to Moses: ¹⁴"Take the blasphemer outside the camp. All those who heard him are to lay their hands on his head, and the entire assembly is to stone him. ¹⁵Say to the Israelites: 'If anyone curses his God, he will be held responsible; ¹⁶anyone who blasphemes the name of the LORD must be put to death. The entire assembly must stone him. Whether an alien or native-born, when he blasphemes the Name, he must be put to death.

¹⁷" 'If anyone takes the life of a human being, he must be put to death. ¹⁸Anyone who takes the life of someone's animal must make restitution—life for life. ¹⁹If anyone injures his neighbor, whatever he has done must be done to him: ²⁰fracture for fracture, eye for eye, tooth for tooth. As he has injured the other, so he is to be injured. ²¹Whoever kills an animal must make restitution, but whoever kills a man must be put to death. ²²You are to have the same law for the alien and the native-born. I am the LORD your God.' "

²³Then Moses spoke to the Israelites, and they took the blasphemer outside the camp and stoned him. The Israelites did as the LORD commanded Moses.

25 *The Sabbath Year* The LORD said to Moses on Mount Sinai, ²"Speak to the Israelites and say to them: 'When you enter the land I am going to give you, the land itself must observe a sabbath to the LORD. ³For six years sow your fields, and for six years prune your vineyards and gather their crops. ⁴But in the seventh year the land is to have a sabbath of rest, a sabbath to the LORD. Do not sow your fields or prune your vineyards. ⁵Do not reap what grows of itself or harvest the grapes of your untended vines. The land is to have a year of rest. ⁶Whatever the land yields during the sabbath year will be food for you—for yourself, your manservant and maidservant, and the hired worker and temporary resident who live among you, ⁷as well as for your livestock and the wild animals in your land. Whatever the land produces may be eaten.

The Year of Jubilee ⁸" 'Count off seven sabbaths of years—seven times seven years—so that the seven sabbaths of years amount to a period of forty-nine years. ⁹Then have the trumpet sounded everywhere on the tenth day of the seventh month; on the Day of Atonement sound the trumpet throughout your land. ¹⁰Consecrate the fiftieth year and proclaim liberty throughout the land to all its inhabitants. It shall be a jubilee for you; each one of you is to return to his family property and each to his own clan. ¹¹The fiftieth year shall be a jubilee for you; do not sow and do not reap what grows of itself or harvest the untended vines. ¹²For it is a jubilee and is to be holy for you; eat only what is taken directly from the fields.

¹³" 'In this Year of Jubilee everyone is to return to his own property.

¹⁴" 'If you sell land to one of your countrymen or buy any from him, do not take advantage of each other. ¹⁵You are to buy from your countryman on the basis of the number of years since the Jubilee. And he is to sell to you on the basis of the number of years left for harvesting crops. ¹⁶When the years are many, you are to increase the price, and when the years are few, you are to decrease the price, because what he is really selling you is the number of crops. ¹⁷Do not take advantage of each other, but fear your God. I am the LORD your God.

¹⁸" 'Follow my decrees and be careful to obey my laws, and you will live safely in the land. ¹⁹Then the land will yield its fruit, and you will eat your fill and live there in safety. ²⁰You may ask, "What will we eat in the seventh year if we do not plant or harvest our crops?" ²¹I will send you such a bless-

ing in the sixth year that the land will yield enough for three years. ²²While you plant during the eighth year, you will eat from the old crop and will continue to eat from it until the harvest of the ninth year comes in.

²³" 'The land must not be sold permanently, because the land is mine and you are but aliens and my tenants. ²⁴Throughout the country that you hold as a possession, you must provide for the redemption of the land.

²⁵" 'If one of your countrymen becomes poor and sells some of his property, his nearest relative is to come and redeem what his countryman has sold. ²⁶If, however, a man has no one to redeem it for him but he himself prospers and acquires sufficient means to redeem it, ²⁷he is to determine the value for the years since he sold it and refund the balance to the man to whom he sold it; he can then go back to his own property. ²⁸But if he does not acquire the means to repay him, what he sold will remain in the possession of the buyer until the Year of Jubilee. It will be returned in the Jubilee, and he can then go back to his property.

²⁹" 'If a man sells a house in a walled city, he retains the right of redemption a full year after its sale. During that time he may redeem it. ³⁰If it is not redeemed before a full year has passed, the house in the walled city shall belong permanently to the buyer and his descendants. It is not to be returned in the Jubilee. ³¹But houses in villages without walls around them are to be considered as open country. They can be redeemed, and they are to be returned in the Jubilee.

³²" 'The Levites always have the right to redeem their houses in the Levitical towns, which they possess. ³³So the property of the Levites is redeemable—that is, a house sold in any town they hold—and is to be returned in the Jubilee, because the houses in the towns of the Levites are their property among the Israelites. ³⁴But the pastureland belonging to their towns must not be sold; it is their permanent possession.

³⁵" 'If one of your countrymen becomes poor and is unable to support himself among you, help him as you would an alien or a temporary resident, so he can continue to live among you. ³⁶Do not take interest of any kind[a] from him, but fear your God, so that your countryman may continue to live among you. ³⁷You must not lend him money at interest or sell him food at a profit. ³⁸I am the LORD your God, who brought you out of Egypt to give you the land of Canaan and to be your God.

³⁹" 'If one of your countrymen becomes poor among you and sells himself to you, do not make him work as a slave. ⁴⁰He is to be treated as a hired worker or a temporary resident among you; he is to work for you until the Year of Jubilee. ⁴¹Then he and his children are to be released, and he will go back to his own clan and to the property of his forefathers. ⁴²Because the Israelites are my servants, whom I brought out of Egypt, they must not be sold as slaves. ⁴³Do not rule over them ruthlessly, but fear your God.

⁴⁴" 'Your male and female slaves are to come from the nations around you; from them you may buy slaves. ⁴⁵You may also buy some of the temporary residents living among you and members of their clans born in your country, and they will become your property. ⁴⁶You can will them to your children as inherited property and can make them slaves for life, but you must not rule over your fellow Israelites ruthlessly.

⁴⁷" 'If an alien or a temporary resident among you becomes rich and one of your countrymen becomes poor and sells himself to the alien living among you or to a member of the alien's clan, ⁴⁸he retains the right of redemption after he has sold himself. One of his relatives may redeem him: ⁴⁹An uncle or a cousin or any blood relative in his clan may redeem him. Or if he prospers, he may redeem himself. ⁵⁰He and his buyer are to count the time from the year he sold himself up to the Year of Jubilee. The price for

---

a36 Or take excessive interest; similarly in verse 37

his release is to be based on the rate paid to a hired man for that number of years. ⁵¹If many years remain, he must pay for his redemption a larger share of the price paid for him. ⁵²If only a few years remain until the Year of Jubilee, he is to compute that and pay for his redemption accordingly. ⁵³He is to be treated as a man hired from year to year; you must see to it that his owner does not rule over him ruthlessly.

⁵⁴ 'Even if he is not redeemed in any of these ways, he and his children are to be released in the Year of Jubilee, ⁵⁵for the Israelites belong to me as servants. They are my servants, whom I brought out of Egypt. I am the LORD your God.

Reward for Obedience

26 " 'Do not make idols or set up an image or a sacred stone for yourselves, and do not place a carved stone in your land to bow down before it. I am the LORD your God.

²" 'Observe my Sabbaths and have reverence for my sanctuary. I am the LORD.

³" 'If you follow my decrees and are careful to obey my commands, ⁴I will send you rain in its season, and the ground will yield its crops and the trees of the field their fruit. ⁵Your threshing will continue until grape harvest and the grape harvest will continue until planting, and you will eat all the food you want and live in safety in your land.

⁶" 'I will grant peace in the land, and you will lie down and no one will make you afraid. I will remove savage beasts from the land, and the sword will not pass through your country. ⁷You will pursue your enemies, and they will fall by the sword before you. ⁸Five of you will chase a hundred, and a hundred of you will chase ten thousand, and your enemies will fall by the sword before you.

⁹" 'I will look on you with favor and make you fruitful and increase your numbers, and I will keep my covenant with you. ¹⁰You will still be eating last year's harvest when you will have to move it out to make room for the new. ¹¹I will put my dwelling place[a] among you, and I will not abhor you. ¹²I will walk among you and be your God, and you will be my people. ¹³I am the LORD your God, who brought you out of Egypt so that you would no longer be slaves to the Egyptians; I broke the bars of your yoke and enabled you to walk with heads held high.

Punishment for Disobedience

¹⁴" 'But if you will not listen to me and carry out all these commands, ¹⁵and if you reject my decrees and abhor my laws and fail to carry out all my commands and so violate my covenant, ¹⁶then I will do this to you: I will bring upon you sudden terror, wasting diseases and fever that will destroy your sight and drain away your life. You will plant seed in vain, because your enemies will eat it. ¹⁷I will set my face against you so that you will be defeated by your enemies; those who hate you will rule over you, and you will flee even when no one is pursuing you.

¹⁸" 'If after all this you will not listen to me, I will punish you for your sins seven times over. ¹⁹I will break down your stubborn pride and make the sky above you like iron and the ground beneath you like bronze. ²⁰Your strength will be spent in vain, because your soil will not yield its crops, nor will the trees of the land yield their fruit.

²¹" 'If you remain hostile toward me and refuse to listen to me, I will multiply your afflictions seven times over, as your sins deserve. ²²I will send wild animals against you, and they will rob you of your children, destroy your cattle and make you so few in number that your roads will be deserted.

²³" 'If in spite of these things you do not accept my correction but continue to be hostile toward me, ²⁴I myself will be hostile toward you and will afflict

---

a 11 Or my tabernacle

you for your sins seven times over. ²⁵And I will bring the sword upon you to avenge the breaking of the covenant. When you withdraw into your cities, I will send a plague among you, and you will be given into enemy hands. ²⁶When I cut off your supply of bread, ten women will be able to bake your bread in one oven, and they will dole out the bread by weight. You will eat, but you will not be satisfied.

²⁷" 'If in spite of this you still do not listen to me but continue to be hostile toward me, ²⁸then in my anger I will be hostile toward you, and I myself will punish you for your sins seven times over. ²⁹You will eat the flesh of your sons and the flesh of your daughters. ³⁰I will destroy your high places, cut down your incense altars and pile your dead bodies on the lifeless forms of your idols, and I will abhor you. ³¹I will turn your cities into ruins and lay waste your sanctuaries, and I will take no delight in the pleasing aroma of your offerings. ³²I will lay waste the land, so that your enemies who live there will be appalled. ³³I will scatter you among the nations and will draw out my sword and pursue you. Your land will be laid waste, and your cities will lie in ruins. ³⁴Then the land will enjoy its sabbath years all the time that it lies desolate and you are in the country of your enemies; then the land will rest and enjoy its sabbaths. ³⁵All the time that it lies desolate, the land will have the rest it did not have during the sabbaths you lived in it.

³⁶" 'As for those of you who are left, I will make their hearts so fearful in the lands of their enemies that the sound of a windblown leaf will put them to flight. They will run as though fleeing from the sword, and they will fall, even though no one is pursuing them. ³⁷They will stumble over one another as though fleeing from the sword, even though no one is pursuing them. So you will not be able to stand before your enemies. ³⁸You will perish among the nations; the land of your enemies will devour you. ³⁹Those of you who are left will waste away in the lands of their enemies because of their sins; also because of their fathers' sins they will waste away.

⁴⁰" 'But if they will confess their sins and the sins of their fathers—their treachery against me and their hostility toward me, ⁴¹which made me hostile toward them so that I sent them into the land of their enemies—then when their uncircumcised hearts are humbled and they pay for their sin, ⁴²I will remember my covenant with Jacob and my covenant with Isaac and my covenant with Abraham, and I will remember the land. ⁴³For the land will be deserted by them and will enjoy its sabbaths while it lies desolate without them. They will pay for their sins because they rejected my laws and abhorred my decrees. ⁴⁴Yet in spite of this, when they are in the land of their enemies, I will not reject them or abhor them so as to destroy them completely, breaking my covenant with them. I am the Lord their God. ⁴⁵But for their sake I will remember the covenant with their ancestors whom I brought out of Egypt in the sight of the nations to be their God. I am the Lord.' "

⁴⁶These are the decrees, the laws and the regulations that the Lord established on Mount Sinai between himself and the Israelites through Moses.

Direct Line

LEVITICUS 26:42-44

Usually when you do the right thing, good things happen. But what if you make some bad choices? I mean, really bad choices. Like stealing and getting in trouble with the police. Or drinking and driving and wrecking the family car. Or going too far sexually and discovering that you're pregnant. Are you ruined for life? This Bible chapter warns that there are tragic consequences for disobeying God. But it also promises that God will not totally reject you, even for serious sins. You don't want to commit any of those serious sins. But if you do something wrong, remember God's promise. God will welcome you home and bless you again.

27 *Redeeming What Is the Lord's* The Lord said to Moses, ²"Speak to the Israelites and say to them: 'If anyone makes a special vow to dedicate persons to the Lord by giving equivalent values, ³set the value of a male between the ages of twenty and sixty at fifty shekels*ᵃ* of silver, according to the sanctuary shekel*ᵇ*; ⁴and if it is a female, set her value at thirty shekels.*ᶜ* ⁵If it is a person between the ages of five and twenty, set the value of a male at twenty shekels*ᵈ* and of a female at ten shekels.*ᵉ* ⁶If it is a person between one month and five years, set the value of a male at five shekels*ᶠ* of silver and that of a female at three shekels*ᵍ* of silver. ⁷If it is a person sixty years old or more, set the value of a male at fifteen shekels*ʰ* and of a female at ten shekels. ⁸If anyone making the vow is too poor to pay the specified amount, he is to present the person to the priest, who will set the value for him according to what the man making the vow can afford.

⁹"'If what he vowed is an animal that is acceptable as an offering to the Lord, such an animal given to the Lord becomes holy. ¹⁰He must not exchange it or substitute a good one for a bad one, or a bad one for a good one; if he should substitute one animal for another, both it and the substitute become holy. ¹¹If what he vowed is a ceremonially unclean animal—one that is not acceptable as an offering to the Lord—the animal must be presented to the priest, ¹²who will judge its quality as good or bad. Whatever value the priest then sets, that is what it will be. ¹³If the owner wishes to redeem the animal, he must add a fifth to its value.

¹⁴"'If a man dedicates his house as something holy to the Lord, the priest will judge its quality as good or bad. Whatever value the priest then sets, so it will remain. ¹⁵If the man who dedicates his house redeems it, he must add a fifth to its value, and the house will again become his.

¹⁶"'If a man dedicates to the Lord part of his family land, its value is to be set according to the amount of seed required for it—fifty shekels of silver to a homer*ⁱ* of barley seed. ¹⁷If he dedicates his field during the Year of Jubilee, the value that has been set remains. ¹⁸But if he dedicates his field after the Jubilee, the priest will determine the value according to the number of years that remain until the next Year of Jubilee, and its set value will be reduced. ¹⁹If the man who dedicates the field wishes to redeem it, he must add a fifth to its value, and the field will again become his. ²⁰If, however, he does not redeem the field, or if he has sold it to someone else, it can never be redeemed. ²¹When the field is released in the Jubilee, it will become holy, like a field devoted to the Lord; it will become the property of the priests.*ʲ*

²²"'If a man dedicates to the Lord a field he has bought, which is not part of his family land, ²³the priest will determine its value up to the Year of Jubilee, and the man must pay its value on that day as something holy to the Lord. ²⁴In the Year of Jubilee the field will revert to the person from whom he bought it, the one whose land it was. ²⁵Every value is to be set according to the sanctuary shekel, twenty gerahs to the shekel.

²⁶"'No one, however, may dedicate the firstborn of an animal, since the firstborn already belongs to the Lord; whether an ox*ᵏ* or a sheep, it is the Lord's. ²⁷If it is one of the unclean animals, he may buy it back at its set value, adding a fifth of the value to it. If he does not redeem it, it is to be sold at its set value.

²⁸"'But nothing that a man owns and devotes*ˡ* to the Lord—whether man

---

ᵃ3 That is, about 1 1/4 pounds (about 0.6 kilogram); also in verse 16   *ᵇ3* That is, about 2/5 ounce (about 11.5 grams); also in verse 25   *ᶜ4* That is, about 12 ounces (about 0.3 kilogram)   *ᵈ5* That is, about 8 ounces (about 0.2 kilogram)   *ᵉ5* That is, about 4 ounces (about 110 grams); also in verse 7   *ᶠ6* That is, about 2 ounces (about 55 grams)   *ᵍ6* That is, about 1 1/4 ounces (about 35 grams)   *ʰ7* That is, about 6 ounces (about 170 grams)   *ⁱ16* That is, probably about 6 bushels (about 220 liters)   *ʲ21* Or *priest*   *ᵏ26* The Hebrew word can include both male and female.   *ˡ28* The Hebrew term refers to the irrevocable giving over of things or persons to the Lord.

or animal or family land—may be sold or redeemed; everything so devoted is most holy to the Lord.

[29]" 'No person devoted to destruction[a] may be ransomed; he must be put to death.

[30]" 'A tithe of everything from the land, whether grain from the soil or fruit from the trees, belongs to the Lord; it is holy to the Lord. [31]If a man redeems any of his tithe, he must add a fifth of the value to it. [32]The entire tithe of the herd and flock—every tenth animal that passes under the shepherd's rod—will be holy to the Lord. [33]He must not pick out the good from the bad or make any substitution. If he does make a substitution, both the animal and its substitute become holy and cannot be redeemed.' "

[34]These are the commands the Lord gave Moses on Mount Sinai for the Israelites.

---

[a]29 The Hebrew term refers to the irrevocable giving over of things or persons to the Lord, often by totally destroying them.

BON VOYAGE!

Think of life as a long trip. You have a good start, but you still have a long way to go. Along the way you have some big choices to make. A detour may take you years out of the way or even keep you from reaching your goal.

That's something the Israelites discovered. Numbers tells about their journey toward the promised land. It tells about choices they made, especially one particular choice that led to 38 years of wandering before God finally got them back on track. God didn't desert his people in their wilderness, and he won't desert you either. But life will be a lot better if you stay on the right road.

FAST FACTS

The name Numbers comes from a census of the people taken at Mount Sinai.

Moses led about two million people out of slavery.

Numbers has three parts: preparing to go (Numbers 1–9), wandering in the wilderness (Numbers 10–20), and getting back on track (Numbers 21–36).

The journey described here took place about 1440 to 1400 B.C.

Fundamentals

Can you be as sure as the Israelites that God is with you (Numbers 9:15-23)?

What's wrong with that familiar excuse, "I just can't do it" (Numbers 14:9)?

How was a snake on a pole like Jesus on the cross (Numbers 21:4-9)?

Can evil spirits harm God's own (Numbers 22–24)?

The Census The LORD spoke to Moses in the Tent of Meeting in the Desert of Sinai on the first day of the second month of the second year after the Israelites came out of Egypt. He said: ²"Take a census of the whole Israelite community by their clans and families, listing every man by name, one by one. ³You and Aaron are to number by their divisions all the men in Israel twenty years old or more who are able to serve in the army. ⁴One man from each tribe, each the head of his family, is to help you. ⁵These are the names of the men who are to assist you:

  from Reuben, Elizur son of Shedeur;
  ⁶from Simeon, Shelumiel son of Zurishaddai;
  ⁷from Judah, Nahshon son of Amminadab;
  ⁸from Issachar, Nethanel son of Zuar;
  ⁹from Zebulun, Eliab son of Helon;
  ¹⁰from the sons of Joseph:
    from Ephraim, Elishama son of Ammihud;
    from Manasseh, Gamaliel son of Pedahzur;
  ¹¹from Benjamin, Abidan son of Gideoni;
  ¹²from Dan, Ahiezer son of Ammishaddai;
  ¹³from Asher, Pagiel son of Ocran;
  ¹⁴from Gad, Eliasaph son of Deuel;
  ¹⁵from Naphtali, Ahira son of Enan."

¹⁶These were the men appointed from the community, the leaders of their ancestral tribes. They were the heads of the clans of Israel.

¹⁷Moses and Aaron took these men whose names had been given, ¹⁸and they called the whole community together on the first day of the second month. The people indicated their ancestry by their clans and families, and the men twenty years old or more were listed by name, one by one, ¹⁹as the LORD commanded Moses. And so he counted them in the Desert of Sinai:

²⁰From the descendants of Reuben the firstborn son of Israel:
  All the men twenty years old or more who were able to serve in the army were listed by name, one by one, according to the records of their clans and families. ²¹The number from the tribe of Reuben was 46,500.

²²From the descendants of Simeon:
  All the men twenty years old or more who were able to serve in the army were counted and listed by name, one by one, according to the records of their clans and families. ²³The number from the tribe of Simeon was 59,300.

²⁴From the descendants of Gad:
  All the men twenty years old or more who were able to serve in the army were listed by name, according to the records of their clans and families. ²⁵The number from the tribe of Gad was 45,650.

²⁶From the descendants of Judah:
  All the men twenty years old or more who were able to serve in the army were listed by name, according to the records of their clans and families. ²⁷The number from the tribe of Judah was 74,600.

²⁸From the descendants of Issachar:
  All the men twenty years old or more who were able to serve in the army were listed by name, according to the records of their clans and families. ²⁹The number from the tribe of Issachar was 54,400.

³⁰From the descendants of Zebulun:
  All the men twenty years old or more who were able to serve in the

army were listed by name, according to the records of their clans and families. ³¹The number from the tribe of Zebulun was 57,400.

³²From the sons of Joseph:

From the descendants of Ephraim:

All the men twenty years old or more who were able to serve in the army were listed by name, according to the records of their clans and families. ³³The number from the tribe of Ephraim was 40,500.

³⁴From the descendants of Manasseh:

All the men twenty years old or more who were able to serve in the army were listed by name, according to the records of their clans and families. ³⁵The number from the tribe of Manasseh was 32,200.

³⁶From the descendants of Benjamin:

All the men twenty years old or more who were able to serve in the army were listed by name, according to the records of their clans and families. ³⁷The number from the tribe of Benjamin was 35,400.

³⁸From the descendants of Dan:

All the men twenty years old or more who were able to serve in the army were listed by name, according to the records of their clans and families. ³⁹The number from the tribe of Dan was 62,700.

⁴⁰From the descendants of Asher:

All the men twenty years old or more who were able to serve in the army were listed by name, according to the records of their clans and families. ⁴¹The number from the tribe of Asher was 41,500.

⁴²From the descendants of Naphtali:

All the men twenty years old or more who were able to serve in the army were listed by name, according to the records of their clans and families. ⁴³The number from the tribe of Naphtali was 53,400.

NUMBERS

QUIZZER

Q: How many Israelite men of military age escaped from Egypt?

BONUS: How many people did Moses lead out to freedom?

Answers on page 159

⁴⁴These were the men counted by Moses and Aaron and the twelve leaders of Israel, each one representing his family. ⁴⁵All the Israelites twenty years old or more who were able to serve in Israel's army were counted according to their families. ⁴⁶The total number was 603,550.

⁴⁷The families of the tribe of Levi, however, were not counted along with the others. ⁴⁸The Lord had said to Moses: ⁴⁹"You must not count the tribe of Levi or include them in the census of the other Israelites. ⁵⁰Instead, appoint the Levites to be in charge of the tabernacle of the Testimony—over all its furnishings and everything belonging to it. They are to carry the tabernacle and all its furnishings; they are to take care of it and encamp around it. ⁵¹Whenever the tabernacle is to move, the Levites are to take it down, and whenever the tabernacle is to be set up, the Levites shall do it. Anyone else who goes near it shall be put to death. ⁵²The Israelites are to set up their tents by divisions, each man in his own camp under his own standard. ⁵³The Levites, however, are to set up their tents around the tabernacle of the Testimony so that wrath will not fall on the Israelite community. The Levites are to be responsible for the care of the tabernacle of the Testimony."

⁵⁴The Israelites did all this just as the Lord commanded Moses.

The Arrangement of the Tribal Camps The Lord said to Moses and Aaron: ²"The Israelites are to camp around the Tent of Meeting some distance from it, each man under his standard with the banners of his family."

³On the east, toward the sunrise, the divisions of the camp of Judah are to encamp under their standard. The leader of the people of Judah is Nahshon son of Amminadab. ⁴His division numbers 74,600.

⁵The tribe of Issachar will camp next to them. The leader of the people of Issachar is Nethanel son of Zuar. ⁶His division numbers 54,400.

⁷The tribe of Zebulun will be next. The leader of the people of Zebulun is Eliab son of Helon. ⁸His division numbers 57,400.

⁹All the men assigned to the camp of Judah, according to their divisions, number 186,400. They will set out first.

¹⁰On the south will be the divisions of the camp of Reuben under their standard. The leader of the people of Reuben is Elizur son of Shedeur. ¹¹His division numbers 46,500.

¹²The tribe of Simeon will camp next to them. The leader of the people of Simeon is Shelumiel son of Zurishaddai. ¹³His division numbers 59,300.

¹⁴The tribe of Gad will be next. The leader of the people of Gad is Eliasaph son of Deuel.ᵃ ¹⁵His division numbers 45,650.

¹⁶All the men assigned to the camp of Reuben, according to their divisions, number 151,450. They will set out second.

¹⁷Then the Tent of Meeting and the camp of the Levites will set out in the middle of the camps. They will set out in the same order as they encamp, each in his own place under his standard.

¹⁸On the west will be the divisions of the camp of Ephraim under their standard. The leader of the people of Ephraim is Elishama son of Ammihud. ¹⁹His division numbers 40,500.

²⁰The tribe of Manasseh will be next to them. The leader of the people of Manasseh is Gamaliel son of Pedahzur. ²¹His division numbers 32,200.

²²The tribe of Benjamin will be next. The leader of the people of Benjamin is Abidan son of Gideoni. ²³His division numbers 35,400.

²⁴All the men assigned to the camp of Ephraim, according to their divisions, number 108,100. They will set out third.

²⁵On the north will be the divisions of the camp of Dan, under their standard. The leader of the people of Dan is Ahiezer son of Ammishaddai. ²⁶His division numbers 62,700.

²⁷The tribe of Asher will camp next to them. The leader of the people of Asher is Pagiel son of Ocran. ²⁸His division numbers 41,500.

²⁹The tribe of Naphtali will be next. The leader of the people of Naphtali is Ahira son of Enan. ³⁰His division numbers 53,400.

³¹All the men assigned to the camp of Dan number 157,600. They will set out last, under their standards.

³²These are the Israelites, counted according to their families. All those in the camps, by their divisions, number 603,550. ³³The Levites, however, were not counted along with the other Israelites, as the LORD commanded Moses.

³⁴So the Israelites did everything the LORD commanded Moses; that is the way they encamped under their standards, and that is the way they set out, each with his clan and family.

3 **The Levites** This is the account of the family of Aaron and Moses at the time the LORD talked with Moses on Mount Sinai.

²The names of the sons of Aaron were Nadab the firstborn and Abihu, Eleazar and Ithamar. ³Those were the names of Aaron's sons, the anointed

---

ᵃ14 Many manuscripts of the Masoretic Text, Samaritan Pentateuch and Vulgate (see also Num. 1:14); most manuscripts of the Masoretic Text *Reuel*

priests, who were ordained to serve as priests. ⁴Nadab and Abihu, however, fell dead before the LORD when they made an offering with unauthorized fire before him in the Desert of Sinai. They had no sons; so only Eleazar and Ithamar served as priests during the lifetime of their father Aaron.

⁵The LORD said to Moses, ⁶"Bring the tribe of Levi and present them to Aaron the priest to assist him. ⁷They are to perform duties for him and for the whole community at the Tent of Meeting by doing the work of the tabernacle. ⁸They are to take care of all the furnishings of the Tent of Meeting, fulfilling the obligations of the Israelites by doing the work of the tabernacle. ⁹Give the Levites to Aaron and his sons; they are the Israelites who are to be given wholly to him.ᵃ ¹⁰Appoint Aaron and his sons to serve as priests; anyone else who approaches the sanctuary must be put to death."

¹¹The LORD also said to Moses, ¹²"I have taken the Levites from among the Israelites in place of the first male offspring of every Israelite woman. The Levites are mine, ¹³for all the firstborn are mine. When I struck down all the firstborn in Egypt, I set apart for myself every firstborn in Israel, whether man or animal. They are to be mine. I am the LORD."

¹⁴The LORD said to Moses in the Desert of Sinai, ¹⁵"Count the Levites by their families and clans. Count every male a month old or more." ¹⁶So Moses counted them, as he was commanded by the word of the LORD.

¹⁷These were the names of the sons of Levi:

Gershon, Kohath and Merari.

¹⁸These were the names of the Gershonite clans:

Libni and Shimei.

¹⁹The Kohathite clans:

Amram, Izhar, Hebron and Uzziel.

²⁰The Merarite clans:

Mahli and Mushi.

These were the Levite clans, according to their families.

²¹To Gershon belonged the clans of the Libnites and Shimeites; these were the Gershonite clans. ²²The number of all the males a month old or more who were counted was 7,500. ²³The Gershonite clans were to camp on the west, behind the tabernacle. ²⁴The leader of the families of the Gershonites was Eliasaph son of Lael. ²⁵At the Tent of Meeting the Gershonites were responsible for the care of the tabernacle and tent, its coverings, the curtain at the entrance to the Tent of Meeting, ²⁶the curtains of the courtyard, the curtain at the entrance to the courtyard surrounding the tabernacle and altar, and the ropes—and everything related to their use.

²⁷To Kohath belonged the clans of the Amramites, Izharites, Hebronites and Uzzielites; these were the Kohathite clans. ²⁸The number of all the males a month old or more was 8,600.ᵇ The Kohathites were responsible for the care of the sanctuary. ²⁹The Kohathite clans were to camp on the south side of the tabernacle. ³⁰The leader of the families of the Kohathite clans was Elizaphan son of Uzziel. ³¹They were responsible for the care of the ark, the table, the lampstand, the altars, the articles of the sanctuary used in ministering, the curtain, and everything related to their use. ³²The chief leader of the Levites was Eleazar son of Aaron, the priest. He was appointed over those who were responsible for the care of the sanctuary.

³³To Merari belonged the clans of the Mahlites and the Mushites; these were the Merarite clans. ³⁴The number of all the males a month old or more

Answers
to Quizzer on
page 157

A: Over half a million— 603,550 to be exact (Numbers 1:44-46).

BONUS: If each man had a wife and only two children, there were about 2.5 million Israelites.

ᵃ9 Most manuscripts of the Masoretic Text; some manuscripts of the Masoretic Text, Samaritan Pentateuch and Septuagint (see also Num. 8:16) *to me*   ᵇ28 Hebrew; some Septuagint manuscripts *8,300*

who were counted was 6,200. ³⁵The leader of the families of the Merarite clans was Zuriel son of Abihail; they were to camp on the north side of the tabernacle. ³⁶The Merarites were appointed to take care of the frames of the tabernacle, its crossbars, posts, bases, all its equipment, and everything related to their use, ³⁷as well as the posts of the surrounding courtyard with their bases, tent pegs and ropes.

³⁸Moses and Aaron and his sons were to camp to the east of the tabernacle, toward the sunrise, in front of the Tent of Meeting. They were responsible for the care of the sanctuary on behalf of the Israelites. Anyone else who approached the sanctuary was to be put to death.

³⁹The total number of Levites counted at the LORD's command by Moses and Aaron according to their clans, including every male a month old or more, was 22,000.

⁴⁰The LORD said to Moses, "Count all the firstborn Israelite males who are a month old or more and make a list of their names. ⁴¹Take the Levites for me in place of all the firstborn of the Israelites, and the livestock of the Levites in place of all the firstborn of the livestock of the Israelites. I am the LORD."

⁴²So Moses counted all the firstborn of the Israelites, as the LORD commanded him. ⁴³The total number of firstborn males a month old or more, listed by name, was 22,273.

⁴⁴The LORD also said to Moses, ⁴⁵"Take the Levites in place of all the firstborn of Israel, and the livestock of the Levites in place of their livestock. The Levites are to be mine. I am the LORD. ⁴⁶To redeem the 273 firstborn Israelites who exceed the number of the Levites, ⁴⁷collect five shekels[a] for each one, according to the sanctuary shekel, which weighs twenty gerahs. ⁴⁸Give the money for the redemption of the additional Israelites to Aaron and his sons."

⁴⁹So Moses collected the redemption money from those who exceeded the number redeemed by the Levites. ⁵⁰From the firstborn of the Israelites he collected silver weighing 1,365 shekels,[b] according to the sanctuary shekel. ⁵¹Moses gave the redemption money to Aaron and his sons, as he was commanded by the word of the LORD.

The Kohathites The LORD said to Moses and Aaron: ²"Take a census of the Kohathite branch of the Levites by their clans and families. ³Count all the men from thirty to fifty years of age who come to serve in the work in the Tent of Meeting.

⁴"This is the work of the Kohathites in the Tent of Meeting: the care of the most holy things. ⁵When the camp is to move, Aaron and his sons are to go in and take down the shielding curtain and cover the ark of the Testimony with it. ⁶Then they are to cover this with hides of sea cows,[c] spread a cloth of solid blue over that and put the poles in place.

⁷"Over the table of the Presence they are to spread a blue cloth and put on it the plates, dishes and bowls, and the jars for drink offerings; the bread that is continually there is to remain on it. ⁸Over these they are to spread a scarlet cloth, cover that with hides of sea cows and put its poles in place.

⁹"They are to take a blue cloth and cover the lampstand that is for light, together with its lamps, its wick trimmers and trays, and all its jars for the

---

[a]47 That is, about 2 ounces (about 55 grams)   [b]50 That is, about 35 pounds (about 15.5 kilograms)   [c]6 That is, dugongs; also in verses 8, 10, 11, 12, 14 and 25

oil used to supply it. ¹⁰Then they are to wrap it and all its accessories in a covering of hides of sea cows and put it on a carrying frame.

¹¹"Over the gold altar they are to spread a blue cloth and cover that with hides of sea cows and put its poles in place.

¹²"They are to take all the articles used for ministering in the sanctuary, wrap them in a blue cloth, cover that with hides of sea cows and put them on a carrying frame.

¹³"They are to remove the ashes from the bronze altar and spread a purple cloth over it. ¹⁴Then they are to place on it all the utensils used for ministering at the altar, including the firepans, meat forks, shovels and sprinkling bowls. Over it they are to spread a covering of hides of sea cows and put its poles in place.

¹⁵"After Aaron and his sons have finished covering the holy furnishings and all the holy articles, and when the camp is ready to move, the Kohathites are to come to do the carrying. But they must not touch the holy things or they will die. The Kohathites are to carry those things that are in the Tent of Meeting.

¹⁶"Eleazar son of Aaron, the priest, is to have charge of the oil for the light, the fragrant incense, the regular grain offering and the anointing oil. He is to be in charge of the entire tabernacle and everything in it, including its holy furnishings and articles."

¹⁷The LORD said to Moses and Aaron, ¹⁸"See that the Kohathite tribal clans are not cut off from the Levites. ¹⁹So that they may live and not die when they come near the most holy things, do this for them: Aaron and his sons are to go into the sanctuary and assign to each man his work and what he is to carry. ²⁰But the Kohathites must not go in to look at the holy things, even for a moment, or they will die."

The Gershonites   ²¹The LORD said to Moses, ²²"Take a census also of the Gershonites by their families and clans. ²³Count all the men from thirty to fifty years of age who come to serve in the work at the Tent of Meeting.

²⁴"This is the service of the Gershonite clans as they work and carry burdens: ²⁵They are to carry the curtains of the tabernacle, the Tent of Meeting, its covering and the outer covering of hides of sea cows, the curtains for the entrance to the Tent of Meeting, ²⁶the curtains of the courtyard surrounding the tabernacle and altar, the curtain for the entrance, the ropes and all the equipment used in its service. The Gershonites are to do all that needs to be done with these things. ²⁷All their service, whether carrying or doing other work, is to be done under the direction of Aaron and his sons. You shall assign to them as their responsibility all they are to carry. ²⁸This is the service of the Gershonite clans at the Tent of Meeting. Their duties are to be under the direction of Ithamar son of Aaron, the priest.

The Merarites   ²⁹"Count the Merarites by their clans and families. ³⁰Count all the men from thirty to fifty years of age who come to serve in the work at the Tent of Meeting. ³¹This is their duty as they perform service at the Tent of Meeting: to carry the frames of the tabernacle, its crossbars, posts and bases, ³²as well as the posts of the surrounding courtyard with their bases, tent pegs, ropes, all their equipment and everything related to their use. Assign to each man the specific things he is to carry. ³³This is the service of the Merarite clans as they work at the Tent of Meeting under the direction of Ithamar son of Aaron, the priest."

The Numbering of the Levite Clans   ³⁴Moses, Aaron and the leaders of the community counted the Kohathites by their clans and families. ³⁵All the men from thirty to fifty years of age who came to serve in the work in the Tent of Meeting, ³⁶counted by clans, were 2,750. ³⁷This was the total of all those in the Kohathite clans who served in the Tent of Meeting. Moses and Aaron counted them according to the Lord's command through Moses.

³⁸The Gershonites were counted by their clans and families. ³⁹All the men from thirty to fifty years of age who came to serve in the work at the Tent of Meeting, ⁴⁰counted by their clans and families, were 2,630. ⁴¹This was the total of those in the Gershonite clans who served at the Tent of Meeting. Moses and Aaron counted them according to the Lord's command.

⁴²The Merarites were counted by their clans and families. ⁴³All the men from thirty to fifty years of age who came to serve in the work at the Tent of Meeting, ⁴⁴counted by their clans, were 3,200. ⁴⁵This was the total of those in the Merarite clans. Moses and Aaron counted them according to the Lord's command through Moses.

⁴⁶So Moses, Aaron and the leaders of Israel counted all the Levites by their clans and families. ⁴⁷All the men from thirty to fifty years of age who came to do the work of serving and carrying the Tent of Meeting ⁴⁸numbered 8,580. ⁴⁹At the Lord's command through Moses, each was assigned his work and told what to carry.

Thus they were counted, as the Lord commanded Moses.

The Purity of the Camp   The Lord said to Moses, ²"Command the Israelites to send away from the camp anyone who has an infectious skin disease*ᵃ* or a discharge of any kind, or who is ceremonially unclean because of a dead body. ³Send away male and female alike; send them outside the camp so they will not defile their camp, where I dwell among them." ⁴The Israelites did this; they sent them outside the camp. They did just as the Lord had instructed Moses.

Restitution for Wrongs   ⁵The Lord said to Moses, ⁶"Say to the Israelites: 'When a man or woman wrongs another in any way*ᵇ* and so is unfaithful to the Lord, that person is guilty ⁷and must confess the sin he has committed. He must make full restitution for his wrong, add one fifth to it and give it all to the person he has wronged. ⁸But if that person has no close relative to whom restitution can be made for the wrong, the restitution belongs to the Lord and must be given to the priest, along with the ram with which atonement is made for him. ⁹All the sacred contributions the Israelites bring to a priest will belong to him. ¹⁰Each man's sacred gifts are his own, but what he gives to the priest will belong to the priest.' "

The Test for an Unfaithful Wife   ¹¹Then the Lord said to Moses, ¹²"Speak to the Israelites and say to them: 'If a man's wife goes astray and is unfaithful to him ¹³by sleeping with another man, and this is hidden from her husband and her impurity is undetected (since there is no witness against her and she has not been caught in the act), ¹⁴and if feelings of jealousy come over her husband and he suspects his wife and she is impure—or if he

Direct Line

NUMBERS 5:5–8

You didn't mean for Keri to see the note you wrote about her. You didn't even mean what you wrote. But Keri saw the note, and she's hurt. This passage says that when you "wrong another in any way" (Numbers 5:6), you have to make up for it. First, admit you're guilty of doing wrong. Then make "full restitution" for the wrong, with a bonus. How? You start by telling Keri you know you did wrong. Then you tell everyone who saw the note you were wrong. You apologize to Keri in front of them and ask her to forgive you. It may be hard. It may be tough. But it's the right thing to do.

ᵃ2 Traditionally *leprosy*; the Hebrew word was used for various diseases affecting the skin—not necessarily leprosy.   ᵇ6 Or *woman commits any wrong common to mankind*

is jealous and suspects her even though she is not impure— ¹⁵then he is to take his wife to the priest. He must also take an offering of a tenth of an ephah*ᵃ* of barley flour on her behalf. He must not pour oil on it or put incense on it, because it is a grain offering for jealousy, a reminder offering to draw attention to guilt.

¹⁶ 'The priest shall bring her and have her stand before the LORD. ¹⁷Then he shall take some holy water in a clay jar and put some dust from the tabernacle floor into the water. ¹⁸After the priest has had the woman stand before the LORD, he shall loosen her hair and place in her hands the reminder offering, the grain offering for jealousy, while he himself holds the bitter water that brings a curse. ¹⁹Then the priest shall put the woman under oath and say to her, "If no other man has slept with you and you have not gone astray and become impure while married to your husband, may this bitter water that brings a curse not harm you. ²⁰But if you have gone astray while married to your husband and you have defiled yourself by sleeping with a man other than your husband"— ²¹here the priest is to put the woman under this curse of the oath—"may the LORD cause your people to curse and denounce you when he causes your thigh to waste away and your abdomen to swell.*ᵇ* ²²May this water that brings a curse enter your body so that your abdomen swells and your thigh wastes away.*ᶜ*"

" 'Then the woman is to say, "Amen. So be it."

²³ 'The priest is to write these curses on a scroll and then wash them off into the bitter water. ²⁴He shall have the woman drink the bitter water that brings a curse, and this water will enter her and cause bitter suffering. ²⁵The priest is to take from her hands the grain offering for jealousy, wave it before the LORD and bring it to the altar. ²⁶The priest is then to take a handful of the grain offering as a memorial offering and burn it on the altar; after that, he is to have the woman drink the water. ²⁷If she has defiled herself and been unfaithful to her husband, then when she is made to drink the water that brings a curse, it will go into her and cause bitter suffering; her abdomen will swell and her thigh waste away,*ᵈ* and she will become accursed among her people. ²⁸If, however, the woman has not defiled herself and is free from impurity, she will be cleared of guilt and will be able to have children.

²⁹ 'This, then, is the law of jealousy when a woman goes astray and defiles herself while married to her husband, ³⁰or when feelings of jealousy come over a man because he suspects his wife. The priest is to have her stand before the LORD and is to apply this entire law to her. ³¹The husband will be innocent of any wrongdoing, but the woman will bear the consequences of her sin.' "

The Nazirite   The LORD said to Moses, ²"Speak to the Israelites and say to them: 'If a man or woman wants to make a special vow, a vow of separation to the LORD as a Nazirite, ³he must abstain from wine and other fermented drink and must not drink vinegar made from wine or from other fermented drink. He must not drink grape juice or eat grapes or raisins. ⁴As long as he is a Nazirite, he must not eat anything that comes from the grapevine, not even the seeds or skins.

⁵ 'During the entire period of his vow of separation no razor may be used on his head. He must be holy until the period of his separation to the LORD is over; he must let the hair of his head grow long. ⁶Throughout the period of his separation to the LORD he must not go near a dead body. ⁷Even if his own father or mother or brother or sister dies, he must not make himself

---

ᵃ15 That is, probably about 2 quarts (about 2 liters)   *ᵇ21* Or *causes you to have a miscarrying womb and barrenness*   *ᶜ22* Or *body and cause you to be barren and have a miscarrying womb*   *ᵈ27* Or *suffering; she will have barrenness and a miscarrying womb*

ceremonially unclean on account of them, because the symbol of his separation to God is on his head. [8]Throughout the period of his separation he is consecrated to the LORD.

[9]" 'If someone dies suddenly in his presence, thus defiling the hair he has dedicated, he must shave his head on the day of his cleansing—the seventh day. [10]Then on the eighth day he must bring two doves or two young pigeons to the priest at the entrance to the Tent of Meeting. [11]The priest is to offer one as a sin offering and the other as a burnt offering to make atonement for him because he sinned by being in the presence of the dead body. That same day he is to consecrate his head. [12]He must dedicate himself to the LORD for the period of his separation and must bring a year-old male lamb as a guilt offering. The previous days do not count, because he became defiled during his separation.

[13]" 'Now this is the law for the Nazirite when the period of his separation is over. He is to be brought to the entrance to the Tent of Meeting. [14]There he is to present his offerings to the LORD: a year-old male lamb without defect for a burnt offering, a year-old ewe lamb without defect for a sin offering, a ram without defect for a fellowship offering,[a] [15]together with their grain offerings and drink offerings, and a basket of bread made without yeast—cakes made of fine flour mixed with oil, and wafers spread with oil.

[16]" 'The priest is to present them before the LORD and make the sin offering and the burnt offering. [17]He is to present the basket of unleavened bread and is to sacrifice the ram as a fellowship offering to the LORD, together with its grain offering and drink offering.

[18]" 'Then at the entrance to the Tent of Meeting, the Nazirite must shave off the hair that he dedicated. He is to take the hair and put it in the fire that is under the sacrifice of the fellowship offering.

[19]" 'After the Nazirite has shaved off the hair of his dedication, the priest is to place in his hands a boiled shoulder of the ram, and a cake and a wafer from the basket, both made without yeast. [20]The priest shall then wave them before the LORD as a wave offering; they are holy and belong to the priest, together with the breast that was waved and the thigh that was presented. After that, the Nazirite may drink wine.

[21]" 'This is the law of the Nazirite who vows his offering to the LORD in accordance with his separation, in addition to whatever else he can afford. He must fulfill the vow he has made, according to the law of the Nazirite.' "

The Priestly Blessing   [22]The LORD said to Moses, [23]"Tell Aaron and his sons, 'This is how you are to bless the Israelites. Say to them:

> [24]" ' "The LORD bless you
>   and keep you;
> [25]the LORD make his face shine upon you
>   and be gracious to you;
> [26]the LORD turn his face toward you
>   and give you peace." '

[27]"So they will put my name on the Israelites, and I will bless them."

7 *Offerings at the Dedication of the Tabernacle*   When Moses finished setting up the tabernacle, he anointed it and consecrated it and all its furnishings. He also anointed and consecrated the altar and all its utensils. [2]Then the leaders of Israel, the heads of families who were the tribal leaders in charge of those who were counted, made offerings. [3]They brought as their gifts before the LORD six covered carts and twelve oxen—an ox from each leader and a cart from every two. These they presented before the tabernacle.

---

[a]14 Traditionally *peace offering*; also in verses 17 and 18

[4]The LORD said to Moses, [5]"Accept these from them, that they may be used in the work at the Tent of Meeting. Give them to the Levites as each man's work requires."

[6]So Moses took the carts and oxen and gave them to the Levites. [7]He gave two carts and four oxen to the Gershonites, as their work required, [8]and he gave four carts and eight oxen to the Merarites, as their work required. They were all under the direction of Ithamar son of Aaron, the priest. [9]But Moses did not give any to the Kohathites, because they were to carry on their shoulders the holy things, for which they were responsible.

[10]When the altar was anointed, the leaders brought their offerings for its dedication and presented them before the altar. [11]For the LORD had said to Moses, "Each day one leader is to bring his offering for the dedication of the altar."

The LORD bless you and keep you (Numbers 6:24).

[12]The one who brought his offering on the first day was Nahshon son of Amminadab of the tribe of Judah.

[13]His offering was one silver plate weighing a hundred and thirty shekels,[a] and one silver sprinkling bowl weighing seventy shekels,[b] both according to the sanctuary shekel, each filled with fine flour mixed with oil as a grain offering; [14]one gold dish weighing ten shekels,[c] filled with incense; [15]one young bull, one ram and one male lamb a year old, for a burnt offering; [16]one male goat for a sin offering; [17]and two oxen, five rams, five male goats and five male lambs a year old, to be sacrificed as a fellowship offering.[d] This was the offering of Nahshon son of Amminadab.

[18]On the second day Nethanel son of Zuar, the leader of Issachar, brought his offering.

[19]The offering he brought was one silver plate weighing a hundred and thirty shekels, and one silver sprinkling bowl weighing seventy shekels, both according to the sanctuary shekel, each filled with fine flour mixed with oil as a grain offering; [20]one gold dish weighing ten shekels, filled with incense; [21]one young bull, one ram and one male lamb a year old, for a burnt offering; [22]one male goat for a sin offering; [23]and two oxen, five rams, five male goats and five male lambs a year old, to be sacrificed as a fellowship offering. This was the offering of Nethanel son of Zuar.

[24]On the third day, Eliab son of Helon, the leader of the people of Zebulun, brought his offering.

[25]His offering was one silver plate weighing a hundred and thirty shekels, and one silver sprinkling bowl weighing seventy shekels, both according to the sanctuary shekel, each filled with fine flour mixed with oil as a grain offering; [26]one gold dish weighing ten shekels, filled with incense; [27]one young bull, one ram and one male lamb a year old, for a burnt offering; [28]one male goat for a sin offering; [29]and two oxen, five rams, five male goats and five male lambs a year old, to be sacrificed as a fellowship offering. This was the offering of Eliab son of Helon.

[30]On the fourth day Elizur son of Shedeur, the leader of the people of Reuben, brought his offering.

[31]His offering was one silver plate weighing a hundred and thirty shekels, and one silver sprinkling bowl weighing seventy shekels, both according to the sanctuary shekel, each filled with fine flour mixed with oil as a grain offering; [32]one gold dish weighing ten shekels, filled with incense; [33]one young bull, one ram and one male lamb a year old, for a burnt offering; [34]one male goat for a sin offering; [35]and two oxen, five

[a]13 That is, about 3 1/4 pounds (about 1.5 kilograms); also elsewhere in this chapter [b]13 That is, about 1 3/4 pounds (about 0.8 kilogram); also elsewhere in this chapter [c]14 That is, about 4 ounces (about 110 grams); also elsewhere in this chapter [d]17 Traditionally *peace offering*; also elsewhere in this chapter

rams, five male goats and five male lambs a year old, to be sacrificed as a fellowship offering. This was the offering of Elizur son of Shedeur.

³⁶On the fifth day Shelumiel son of Zurishaddai, the leader of the people of Simeon, brought his offering.

³⁷His offering was one silver plate weighing a hundred and thirty shekels, and one silver sprinkling bowl weighing seventy shekels, both according to the sanctuary shekel, each filled with fine flour mixed with oil as a grain offering; ³⁸one gold dish weighing ten shekels, filled with incense; ³⁹one young bull, one ram and one male lamb a year old, for a burnt offering; ⁴⁰one male goat for a sin offering; ⁴¹and two oxen, five rams, five male goats and five male lambs a year old, to be sacrificed as a fellowship offering. This was the offering of Shelumiel son of Zurishaddai.

⁴²On the sixth day Eliasaph son of Deuel, the leader of the people of Gad, brought his offering.

⁴³His offering was one silver plate weighing a hundred and thirty shekels, and one silver sprinkling bowl weighing seventy shekels, both according to the sanctuary shekel, each filled with fine flour mixed with oil as a grain offering; ⁴⁴one gold dish weighing ten shekels, filled with incense; ⁴⁵one young bull, one ram and one male lamb a year old, for a burnt offering; ⁴⁶one male goat for a sin offering; ⁴⁷and two oxen, five rams, five male goats and five male lambs a year old, to be sacrificed as a fellowship offering. This was the offering of Eliasaph son of Deuel.

⁴⁸On the seventh day Elishama son of Ammihud, the leader of the people of Ephraim, brought his offering.

⁴⁹His offering was one silver plate weighing a hundred and thirty shekels, and one silver sprinkling bowl weighing seventy shekels, both according to the sanctuary shekel, each filled with fine flour mixed with oil as a grain offering; ⁵⁰one gold dish weighing ten shekels, filled with incense; ⁵¹one young bull, one ram and one male lamb a year old, for a burnt offering; ⁵²one male goat for a sin offering; ⁵³and two oxen, five rams, five male goats and five male lambs a year old, to be sacrificed as a fellowship offering. This was the offering of Elishama son of Ammihud.

⁵⁴On the eighth day Gamaliel son of Pedahzur, the leader of the people of Manasseh, brought his offering.

⁵⁵His offering was one silver plate weighing a hundred and thirty shekels, and one silver sprinkling bowl weighing seventy shekels, both according to the sanctuary shekel, each filled with fine flour mixed with oil as a grain offering; ⁵⁶one gold dish weighing ten shekels, filled with incense; ⁵⁷one young bull, one ram and one male lamb a year old, for a burnt offering; ⁵⁸one male goat for a sin offering; ⁵⁹and two oxen, five rams, five male goats and five male lambs a year old, to be sacrificed as a fellowship offering. This was the offering of Gamaliel son of Pedahzur.

⁶⁰On the ninth day Abidan son of Gideoni, the leader of the people of Benjamin, brought his offering.

⁶¹His offering was one silver plate weighing a hundred and thirty shekels, and one silver sprinkling bowl weighing seventy shekels, both according to the sanctuary shekel, each filled with fine flour mixed with oil as a grain offering; ⁶²one gold dish weighing ten shekels, filled with incense; ⁶³one young bull, one ram and one male lamb a year old, for a burnt offering; ⁶⁴one male goat for a sin offering; ⁶⁵and two oxen, five rams, five male goats and five male lambs a year old, to be sacrificed as a fellowship offering. This was the offering of Abidan son of Gideoni.

⁶⁶On the tenth day Ahiezer son of Ammishaddai, the leader of the people of Dan, brought his offering.

⁶⁷His offering was one silver plate weighing a hundred and thirty shekels, and one silver sprinkling bowl weighing seventy shekels, both according to the sanctuary shekel, each filled with fine flour mixed with oil as a grain offering; ⁶⁸one gold dish weighing ten shekels, filled with incense; ⁶⁹one young bull, one ram and one male lamb a year old, for a burnt offering; ⁷⁰one male goat for a sin offering; ⁷¹and two oxen, five rams, five male goats and five male lambs a year old, to be sacrificed as a fellowship offering. This was the offering of Ahiezer son of Ammishaddai.

⁷²On the eleventh day Pagiel son of Ocran, the leader of the people of Asher, brought his offering.

⁷³His offering was one silver plate weighing a hundred and thirty shekels, and one silver sprinkling bowl weighing seventy shekels, both according to the sanctuary shekel, each filled with fine flour mixed with oil as a grain offering; ⁷⁴one gold dish weighing ten shekels, filled with incense; ⁷⁵one young bull, one ram and one male lamb a year old, for a burnt offering; ⁷⁶one male goat for a sin offering; ⁷⁷and two oxen, five rams, five male goats and five male lambs a year old, to be sacrificed as a fellowship offering. This was the offering of Pagiel son of Ocran.

⁷⁸On the twelfth day Ahira son of Enan, the leader of the people of Naphtali, brought his offering.

⁷⁹His offering was one silver plate weighing a hundred and thirty shekels, and one silver sprinkling bowl weighing seventy shekels, both according to the sanctuary shekel, each filled with fine flour mixed with oil as a grain offering; ⁸⁰one gold dish weighing ten shekels, filled with incense; ⁸¹one young bull, one ram and one male lamb a year old, for a burnt offering; ⁸²one male goat for a sin offering; ⁸³and two oxen, five rams, five male goats and five male lambs a year old, to be sacrificed as a fellowship offering. This was the offering of Ahira son of Enan.

⁸⁴These were the offerings of the Israelite leaders for the dedication of the altar when it was anointed: twelve silver plates, twelve silver sprinkling bowls and twelve gold dishes. ⁸⁵Each silver plate weighed a hundred and thirty shekels, and each sprinkling bowl seventy shekels. Altogether, the silver dishes weighed two thousand four hundred shekels,ᵃ according to the sanctuary shekel. ⁸⁶The twelve gold dishes filled with incense weighed ten shekels each, according to the sanctuary shekel. Altogether, the gold dishes weighed a hundred and twenty shekels.ᵇ ⁸⁷The total number of animals for the burnt offering came to twelve young bulls, twelve rams and twelve male lambs a year old, together with their grain offering. Twelve male goats were used for the sin offering. ⁸⁸The total number of animals for the sacrifice of the fellowship offering came to twenty-four oxen, sixty rams, sixty male goats and sixty male lambs a year old. These were the offerings for the dedication of the altar after it was anointed.

⁸⁹When Moses entered the Tent of Meeting to speak with the LORD, he heard the voice speaking to him from between the two cherubim above the atonement cover on the ark of the Testimony. And he spoke with him.

Setting Up the Lamps   The LORD said to Moses, ²"Speak to Aaron and say to him, 'When you set up the seven lamps, they are to light the area in front of the lampstand.' "

³Aaron did so; he set up the lamps so that they faced forward on the lampstand, just as the LORD commanded Moses. ⁴This is how the lampstand was made: It was made of hammered gold—from its base to its blossoms. The lampstand was made exactly like the pattern the LORD had shown Moses.

ᵃ85 That is, about 60 pounds (about 28 kilograms)   ᵇ86 That is, about 3 pounds (about 1.4 kilograms)

The Setting Apart of the Levites ⁵The Lᴏʀᴅ said to Moses: ⁶"Take the Levites from among the other Israelites and make them ceremonially clean. ⁷To purify them, do this: Sprinkle the water of cleansing on them; then have them shave their whole bodies and wash their clothes, and so purify themselves. ⁸Have them take a young bull with its grain offering of fine flour mixed with oil; then you are to take a second young bull for a sin offering. ⁹Bring the Levites to the front of the Tent of Meeting and assemble the whole Israelite community. ¹⁰You are to bring the Levites before the Lᴏʀᴅ, and the Israelites are to lay their hands on them. ¹¹Aaron is to present the Levites before the Lᴏʀᴅ as a wave offering from the Israelites, so that they may be ready to do the work of the Lᴏʀᴅ.

¹²"After the Levites lay their hands on the heads of the bulls, use the one for a sin offering to the Lᴏʀᴅ and the other for a burnt offering, to make atonement for the Levites. ¹³Have the Levites stand in front of Aaron and his sons and then present them as a wave offering to the Lᴏʀᴅ. ¹⁴In this way you are to set the Levites apart from the other Israelites, and the Levites will be mine.

¹⁵"After you have purified the Levites and presented them as a wave offering, they are to come to do their work at the Tent of Meeting. ¹⁶They are the Israelites who are to be given wholly to me. I have taken them as my own in place of the firstborn, the first male offspring from every Israelite woman. ¹⁷Every firstborn male in Israel, whether man or animal, is mine. When I struck down all the firstborn in Egypt, I set them apart for myself. ¹⁸And I have taken the Levites in place of all the firstborn sons in Israel. ¹⁹Of all the Israelites, I have given the Levites as gifts to Aaron and his sons to do the work at the Tent of Meeting on behalf of the Israelites and to make atonement for them so that no plague will strike the Israelites when they go near the sanctuary."

²⁰Moses, Aaron and the whole Israelite community did with the Levites just as the Lᴏʀᴅ commanded Moses. ²¹The Levites purified themselves and washed their clothes. Then Aaron presented them as a wave offering before the Lᴏʀᴅ and made atonement for them to purify them. ²²After that, the Levites came to do their work at the Tent of Meeting under the supervision of Aaron and his sons. They did with the Levites just as the Lᴏʀᴅ commanded Moses.

²³The Lᴏʀᴅ said to Moses, ²⁴"This applies to the Levites: Men twenty-five years old or more shall come to take part in the work at the Tent of Meeting, ²⁵but at the age of fifty, they must retire from their regular service and work no longer. ²⁶They may assist their brothers in performing their duties at the Tent of Meeting, but they themselves must not do the work. This, then, is how you are to assign the responsibilities of the Levites."

That totals 12 bulls, 12 rams, 12 lambs, 24 oxen, 60 more rams . . . that's one monster barbecue!

SEE NUMBERS 7:87-88

The Passover The Lᴏʀᴅ spoke to Moses in the Desert of Sinai in the first month of the second year after they came out of Egypt. He said, ²"Have the Israelites celebrate the Passover at the appointed time. ³Celebrate it at the appointed time, at twilight on the fourteenth day of this month, in accordance with all its rules and regulations."

⁴So Moses told the Israelites to celebrate the Passover, ⁵and they did so in the Desert of Sinai at twilight on the fourteenth day of the first month. The Israelites did everything just as the LORD commanded Moses.

⁶But some of them could not celebrate the Passover on that day because they were ceremonially unclean on account of a dead body. So they came to Moses and Aaron that same day ⁷and said to Moses, "We have become unclean because of a dead body, but why should we be kept from presenting the LORD's offering with the other Israelites at the appointed time?"

⁸Moses answered them, "Wait until I find out what the LORD commands concerning you."

⁹Then the LORD said to Moses, ¹⁰"Tell the Israelites: 'When any of you or your descendants are unclean because of a dead body or are away on a journey, they may still celebrate the LORD's Passover. ¹¹They are to celebrate it on the fourteenth day of the second month at twilight. They are to eat the lamb, together with unleavened bread and bitter herbs. ¹²They must not leave any of it till morning or break any of its bones. When they celebrate the Passover, they must follow all the regulations. ¹³But if a man who is ceremonially clean and not on a journey fails to celebrate the Passover, that person must be cut off from his people because he did not present the LORD's offering at the appointed time. That man will bear the consequences of his sin.

¹⁴" 'An alien living among you who wants to celebrate the LORD's Passover must do so in accordance with its rules and regulations. You must have the same regulations for the alien and the native-born.' "

The Cloud Above the Tabernacle ¹⁵On the day the tabernacle, the Tent of the Testimony, was set up, the cloud covered it. From evening till morning the cloud above the tabernacle looked like fire. ¹⁶That is how it continued to be; the cloud covered it, and at night it looked like fire. ¹⁷Whenever the cloud lifted from above the Tent, the Israelites set out; wherever the cloud settled, the Israelites encamped. ¹⁸At the LORD's command the Israelites set out, and at his command they encamped. As long as the cloud stayed over the tabernacle, they remained in camp. ¹⁹When the cloud remained over the tabernacle a long time, the Israelites obeyed the LORD's order and did not set out. ²⁰Sometimes the cloud was over the tabernacle only a few days; at the LORD's command they would encamp, and then at his command they would set out. ²¹Sometimes the cloud stayed only from evening till morning, and when it lifted in the morning, they set out. Whether by day or by night, whenever the cloud lifted, they set out. ²²Whether the cloud stayed over the tabernacle for two days or a month or a year, the Israelites would remain in camp and not set out; but when it lifted, they would set out. ²³At the LORD's command they encamped, and at the LORD's command they set out. They obeyed the LORD's order, in accordance with his command through Moses.

NUMBERS 9:15–23

Do you ever feel like you're out there all alone? That even God isn't around? Hey, wouldn't it be great at times to have a fiery cloud floating nearby as proof that God is right there with you? And have it move to show you just where God wants you to go? Well, it won't happen. God isn't in the fiery cloud business these days. But you can still know that God is with you, for sure. Just memorize his promise: "Never will I leave you; never will I forsake you" (Deuteronomy 31:6; Hebrews 13:5). With a promise like that, you don't need a fiery cloud.

10 *The Silver Trumpets* The Lord said to Moses: ²"Make two trumpets of hammered silver, and use them for calling the community together and for having the camps set out. ³When both are sounded, the whole community is to assemble before you at the entrance to the Tent of Meeting. ⁴If only one is sounded, the leaders—the heads of the clans of Israel—are to assemble before you. ⁵When a trumpet blast is sounded, the tribes camping on the east are to set out. ⁶At the sounding of a second blast, the camps on the south are to set out. The blast will be the signal for setting out. ⁷To gather the assembly, blow the trumpets, but not with the same signal.

⁸"The sons of Aaron, the priests, are to blow the trumpets. This is to be a lasting ordinance for you and the generations to come. ⁹When you go into battle in your own land against an enemy who is oppressing you, sound a blast on the trumpets. Then you will be remembered by the Lord your God and rescued from your enemies. ¹⁰Also at your times of rejoicing—your appointed feasts and New Moon festivals—you are to sound the trumpets over your burnt offerings and fellowship offerings,ª and they will be a memorial for you before your God. I am the Lord your God."

The Israelites Leave Sinai ¹¹On the twentieth day of the second month of the second year, the cloud lifted from above the tabernacle of the Testimony. ¹²Then the Israelites set out from the Desert of Sinai and traveled from place to place until the cloud came to rest in the Desert of Paran. ¹³They set out, this first time, at the Lord's command through Moses.

¹⁴The divisions of the camp of Judah went first, under their standard. Nahshon son of Amminadab was in command. ¹⁵Nethanel son of Zuar was over the division of the tribe of Issachar, ¹⁶and Eliab son of Helon was over the division of the tribe of Zebulun. ¹⁷Then the tabernacle was taken down, and the Gershonites and Merarites, who carried it, set out.

¹⁸The divisions of the camp of Reuben went next, under their standard. Elizur son of Shedeur was in command. ¹⁹Shelumiel son of Zurishaddai was over the division of the tribe of Simeon, ²⁰and Eliasaph son of Deuel was over the division of the tribe of Gad. ²¹Then the Kohathites set out, carrying the holy things. The tabernacle was to be set up before they arrived.

²²The divisions of the camp of Ephraim went next, under their standard. Elishama son of Ammihud was in command. ²³Gamaliel son of Pedahzur was over the division of the tribe of Manasseh, ²⁴and Abidan son of Gideoni was over the division of the tribe of Benjamin.

²⁵Finally, as the rear guard for all the units, the divisions of the camp of Dan set out, under their standard. Ahiezer son of Ammishaddai was in command. ²⁶Pagiel son of Ocran was over the division of the tribe of Asher, ²⁷and Ahira son of Enan was over the division of the tribe of Naphtali. ²⁸This was the order of march for the Israelite divisions as they set out.

²⁹Now Moses said to Hobab son of Reuel the Midianite, Moses' father-in-law, "We are setting out for the place about which the Lord said, 'I will give it to you.' Come with us and we will treat you well, for the Lord has promised good things to Israel."

³⁰He answered, "No, I will not go; I am going back to my own land and my own people."

³¹But Moses said, "Please do not leave us. You know where we should camp in the desert, and you can be our eyes. ³²If you come with us, we will share with you whatever good things the Lord gives us."

³³So they set out from the mountain of the Lord and traveled for three days. The ark of the covenant of the Lord went before them during those three days to find them a place to rest. ³⁴The cloud of the Lord was over them by day when they set out from the camp.

ª10 Traditionally *peace offerings*

³⁵Whenever the ark set out, Moses said,

"Rise up, O Lᴏʀᴅ!
May your enemies be scattered;
may your foes flee before you."

³⁶Whenever it came to rest, he said,

"Return, O Lᴏʀᴅ,
to the countless thousands of Israel."

Fire From the Lᴏʀᴅ Now the people complained about their hardships in the hearing of the Lᴏʀᴅ, and when he heard them his anger was aroused. Then fire from the Lᴏʀᴅ burned among them and consumed some of the outskirts of the camp. ²When the people cried out to Moses, he prayed to the Lᴏʀᴅ and the fire died down. ³So that place was called Taberah,ᵃ because fire from the Lᴏʀᴅ had burned among them.

Quail From the Lᴏʀᴅ ⁴The rabble with them began to crave other food, and again the Israelites started wailing and said, "If only we had meat to eat! ⁵We remember the fish we ate in Egypt at no cost—also the cucumbers, melons, leeks, onions and garlic. ⁶But now we have lost our appetite; we never see anything but this manna!"

⁷The manna was like coriander seed and looked like resin. ⁸The people went around gathering it, and then ground it in a handmill or crushed it in a mortar. They cooked it in a pot or made it into cakes. And it tasted like something made with olive oil. ⁹When the dew settled on the camp at night, the manna also came down.

¹⁰Moses heard the people of every family wailing, each at the entrance to his tent. The Lᴏʀᴅ became exceedingly angry, and Moses was troubled. ¹¹He asked the Lᴏʀᴅ, "Why have you brought this trouble on your servant? What have I done to displease you that you put the burden of all these people on me? ¹²Did I conceive all these people? Did I give them birth? Why do you tell me to carry them in my arms, as a nurse carries an infant, to the land you promised on oath to their forefathers? ¹³Where can I get meat for all these people? They keep wailing to me, 'Give us meat to eat!' ¹⁴I cannot carry all these people by myself; the burden is too heavy for me. ¹⁵If this is how you are going to treat me, put me to death right now—if I have found favor in your eyes—and do not let me face my own ruin."

¹⁶The Lᴏʀᴅ said to Moses: "Bring me seventy of Israel's elders who are known to you as leaders and officials among the people. Have them come to the Tent of Meeting, that they may stand there with you. ¹⁷I will come down and speak with you there, and I will take of the Spirit that is on you and put the Spirit on them. They will help you carry the burden of the people so that you will not have to carry it alone.

¹⁸"Tell the people: 'Consecrate yourselves in preparation for tomorrow, when you will eat meat. The Lᴏʀᴅ heard you when you wailed, "If only we had meat to eat! We were better off in Egypt!" Now the Lᴏʀᴅ will give you meat, and you will eat it. ¹⁹You will not eat it for just one day, or two days, or five, ten or twenty days, ²⁰but for a whole month—until it comes out of your nostrils and you loathe it—because you have rejected the Lᴏʀᴅ, who is among you, and have wailed before him, saying, "Why did we ever leave Egypt?" ' "

²¹But Moses said, "Here I am among six hundred thousand men on foot, and you say, 'I will give them meat to eat for a whole month!' ²²Would they have enough if flocks and herds were slaughtered for them? Would they have enough if all the fish in the sea were caught for them?"

ᵃ*3 Taberah* means *burning*.

Dear Sam,

My parents say I complain too much. Is it always wrong to complain? Is there a good way to complain?

Emily in Edmonton

100 Advice Lane, Anywhere, USA

Dear Emily,

Sometimes people have a right to complain, but sometimes they complain no matter what. Try to hear yourself as others do. Do you complain about things that really don't matter much? Or about things over which no one has control? If you don't complain about every little thing, people are more likely to pay attention.

Remember when God put Moses in charge of Israel as they left captivity in Egypt and wandered in the wilderness for 40 years? God provided the Israelites with special food called manna. But when they got sick of eating it every day, they complained constantly about it and about Moses' leadership. Finally poor Moses was so sick of their complaints that he asked God to put him to death so he wouldn't have to hear them any more (Numbers 11:15)!

Some parents feel the same way when their kids complain over and over again. So listen to yourself. Do a complaint check every day. When you have a legitimate complaint, make it. But if you don't, try being positive and supportive instead. You'll feel better and so will all those around you.

Sam

²³The Lord answered Moses, "Is the Lord's arm too short? You will now see whether or not what I say will come true for you."

²⁴So Moses went out and told the people what the Lord had said. He brought together seventy of their elders and had them stand around the Tent. ²⁵Then the Lord came down in the cloud and spoke with him, and he took of the Spirit that was on him and put the Spirit on the seventy elders. When the Spirit rested on them, they prophesied, but they did not do so again.ᵃ

²⁶However, two men, whose names were Eldad and Medad, had remained in the camp. They were listed among the elders, but did not go out to the Tent. Yet the Spirit also rested on them, and they prophesied in the camp. ²⁷A young man ran and told Moses, "Eldad and Medad are prophesying in the camp."

²⁸Joshua son of Nun, who had been Moses' aide since youth, spoke up and said, "Moses, my lord, stop them!"

²⁹But Moses replied, "Are you jealous for my sake? I wish that all the Lord's people were prophets and that the Lord would put his Spirit on them!" ³⁰Then Moses and the elders of Israel returned to the camp.

³¹Now a wind went out from the Lord and drove quail in from the sea. It brought themᵇ down all around the camp to about three feetᶜ above the ground, as far as a day's walk in any direction. ³²All that day and night and all the next day the people went out and gathered quail. No one gathered less than ten homers.ᵈ Then they spread them out all around the camp. ³³But while the meat was still between their teeth and before it could be consumed, the anger of the Lord burned against the people, and he struck them with a severe plague. ³⁴Therefore the place was named Kibroth Hattaavah,ᵉ because there they buried the people who had craved other food.

³⁵From Kibroth Hattaavah the people traveled to Hazeroth and stayed there.

Miriam and Aaron Oppose Moses Miriam and Aaron began to talk against Moses because of his Cushite wife, for he had married a Cushite. ²"Has the Lord spoken only through Moses?" they asked. "Hasn't he also spoken through us?" And the Lord heard this.

³(Now Moses was a very humble man, more humble than anyone else on the face of the earth.)

⁴At once the Lord said to Moses, Aaron and Miriam, "Come out to the Tent of Meeting, all three of you." So the three of them came out. ⁵Then the Lord came down in a pillar of cloud; he stood at the entrance to the Tent and summoned Aaron and Miriam. When both of them stepped forward, ⁶he said, "Listen to my words:

> "When a prophet of the Lord
>   is among you,
> I reveal myself to him in
>   visions,
> I speak to him in dreams.

ᵃ25 Or prophesied and continued to do so   ᵇ31 Or They flew   ᶜ31 Hebrew two cubits (about 1 meter)   ᵈ32 That is, probably about 60 bushels (about 2.2 kiloliters)   ᵉ34 Kibroth Hattaavah means graves of craving.

NUMBERS 12

It's a good thing to be an officer in your youth group or school club. Being an officer is an opportunity to help your group reach its goals. It's a way to serve God and others. Miriam and Aaron didn't see leadership that way. They were already important leaders in Israel. But they were jealous of Moses, who had the top job. They were like teens who want to be elected youth group officers so they can feel important instead of so they can contribute. It's OK to run for office, but watch your motives. And if someone else wins, try not to be jealous. Instead, get behind that person 100 percent.

Direct Line

⁷But this is not true of my servant Moses;
    he is faithful in all my house.
⁸With him I speak face to face,
    clearly and not in riddles;
    he sees the form of the Lord.
Why then were you not afraid
    to speak against my servant Moses?"

⁹The anger of the Lord burned against them, and he left them.

¹⁰When the cloud lifted from above the Tent, there stood Miriam—leprous,ᵃ like snow. Aaron turned toward her and saw that she had leprosy; ¹¹and he said to Moses, "Please, my lord, do not hold against us the sin we have so foolishly committed. ¹²Do not let her be like a stillborn infant coming from its mother's womb with its flesh half eaten away."

¹³So Moses cried out to the Lord, "O God, please heal her!"

¹⁴The Lord replied to Moses, "If her father had spit in her face, would she not have been in disgrace for seven days? Confine her outside the camp for seven days; after that she can be brought back." ¹⁵So Miriam was confined outside the camp for seven days, and the people did not move on till she was brought back.

¹⁶After that, the people left Hazeroth and encamped in the Desert of Paran.

13   *Exploring Canaan* The Lord said to Moses, ²"Send some men to explore the land of Canaan, which I am giving to the Israelites. From each ancestral tribe send one of its leaders."

³So at the Lord's command Moses sent them out from the Desert of Paran. All of them were leaders of the Israelites. ⁴These are their names:

    from the tribe of Reuben, Shammua son of Zaccur;
⁵from the tribe of Simeon, Shaphat son of Hori;
⁶from the tribe of Judah, Caleb son of Jephunneh;
⁷from the tribe of Issachar, Igal son of Joseph;
⁸from the tribe of Ephraim, Hoshea son of Nun;
⁹from the tribe of Benjamin, Palti son of Raphu;
¹⁰from the tribe of Zebulun, Gaddiel son of Sodi;
¹¹from the tribe of Manasseh (a tribe of Joseph), Gaddi son of Susi;
¹²from the tribe of Dan, Ammiel son of Gemalli;
¹³from the tribe of Asher, Sethur son of Michael;
¹⁴from the tribe of Naphtali, Nahbi son of Vophsi;
¹⁵from the tribe of Gad, Geuel son of Maki.

¹⁶These are the names of the men Moses sent to explore the land. (Moses gave Hoshea son of Nun the name Joshua.)

¹⁷When Moses sent them to explore Canaan, he said, "Go up through the Negev and on into the hill country. ¹⁸See what the land is like and whether the people who live there are strong or weak, few or many. ¹⁹What kind of land do they live in? Is it good or bad? What kind of towns do they live in? Are they unwalled or fortified? ²⁰How is the soil? Is it fertile or poor? Are there trees on it or not? Do your best to bring back some of the fruit of the land." (It was the season for the first ripe grapes.)

²¹So they went up and explored the land from the Desert of Zin as far as Rehob, toward Leboᵇ Hamath. ²²They went up through the Negev and came to Hebron, where Ahiman, Sheshai and Talmai, the descendants of Anak, lived. (Hebron had been built seven years before Zoan in Egypt.) ²³When they reached the Valley of Eshcol,ᶜ they cut off a branch bearing a single cluster

---

ᵃ10 The Hebrew word was used for various diseases affecting the skin—not necessarily leprosy. ᵇ21 Or *toward the entrance to* ᶜ23 Eshcol means *cluster*; also in verse 24.

of grapes. Two of them carried it on a pole between them, along with some pomegranates and figs. ²⁴That place was called the Valley of Eshcol because of the cluster of grapes the Israelites cut off there. ²⁵At the end of forty days they returned from exploring the land.

Report on the Exploration ²⁶They came back to Moses and Aaron and the whole Israelite community at Kadesh in the Desert of Paran. There they reported to them and to the whole assembly and showed them the fruit of the land. ²⁷They gave Moses this account: "We went into the land to which you sent us, and it does flow with milk and honey! Here is its fruit. ²⁸But the people who live there are powerful, and the cities are fortified and very large. We even saw descendants of Anak there. ²⁹The Amalekites live in the Negev; the Hittites, Jebusites and Amorites live in the hill country; and the Canaanites live near the sea and along the Jordan."

³⁰Then Caleb silenced the people before Moses and said, "We should go up and take possession of the land, for we can certainly do it."

³¹But the men who had gone up with him said, "We can't attack those people; they are stronger than we are." ³²And they spread among the Israelites a bad report about the land they had explored. They said, "The land we explored devours those living in it. All the people we saw there are of great size. ³³We saw the Nephilim there (the descendants of Anak come from the Nephilim). We seemed like grasshoppers in our own eyes, and we looked the same to them."

14 *The People Rebel* That night all the people of the community raised their voices and wept aloud. ²All the Israelites grumbled against Moses and Aaron, and the whole assembly said to them, "If only we had died in Egypt! Or in this desert! ³Why is the LORD bringing us to this land only to let us fall by the sword? Our wives and children will be taken as plunder. Wouldn't it be better for us to go back to Egypt?" ⁴And they said to each other, "We should choose a leader and go back to Egypt."

⁵Then Moses and Aaron fell facedown in front of the whole Israelite assembly gathered there. ⁶Joshua son of Nun and Caleb son of Jephunneh, who were among those who had explored the land, tore their clothes ⁷and said to the entire Israelite assembly, "The land we passed through and explored is exceedingly good. ⁸If the LORD is pleased with us, he will lead us into that land, a land flowing with milk and honey, and will give it to us. ⁹Only do not rebel against the LORD. And do not be afraid of the people of the land, because we will swallow them up. Their protection is gone, but the LORD is with us. Do not be afraid of them."

¹⁰But the whole assembly talked about stoning them. Then the glory of the LORD appeared at the Tent of Meeting to all the Israelites. ¹¹The LORD said to Moses, "How long will these people treat me with contempt? How long will they refuse to believe in me, in spite of all the miraculous signs I have performed among them? ¹²I will strike them down with a plague and

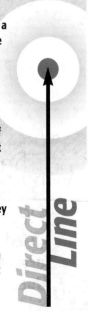

NUMBERS 13:31–14:9

Are you afraid when you have to do something you've never done before? What if you make a mistake? What if you don't have all the answers or don't know what to do next? It's a real temptation to focus on the obstacles. That's what the Israelite spies did when they traveled through Canaan. Ten of the spies could only think about how strong the cities were and how big the people looked. But two of the spies, Caleb and Joshua, didn't see obstacles—they saw God. They said, "The LORD will lead us" (Numbers 14:8). That's the best way to approach something new. Remember that God will lead you. And then jump in.

Direct Line

destroy them, but I will make you into a nation greater and stronger than they."

¹³Moses said to the Lord, "Then the Egyptians will hear about it! By your power you brought these people up from among them. ¹⁴And they will tell the inhabitants of this land about it. They have already heard that you, O Lord, are with these people and that you, O Lord, have been seen face to face, that your cloud stays over them, and that you go before them in a pillar of cloud by day and a pillar of fire by night. ¹⁵If you put these people to death all at one time, the nations who have heard this report about you will say, ¹⁶'The Lord was not able to bring these people into the land he promised them on oath; so he slaughtered them in the desert.'

¹⁷"Now may the Lord's strength be displayed, just as you have declared: ¹⁸'The Lord is slow to anger, abounding in love and forgiving sin and rebellion. Yet he does not leave the guilty unpunished; he punishes the children for the sin of the fathers to the third and fourth generation.' ¹⁹In accordance with your great love, forgive the sin of these people, just as you have pardoned them from the time they left Egypt until now."

²⁰The Lord replied, "I have forgiven them, as you asked. ²¹Nevertheless, as surely as I live and as surely as the glory of the Lord fills the whole earth, ²²not one of the men who saw my glory and the miraculous signs I performed in Egypt and in the desert but who disobeyed me and tested me ten times— ²³not one of them will ever see the land I promised on oath to their forefathers. No one who has treated me with contempt will ever see it. ²⁴But because my servant Caleb has a different spirit and follows me wholeheartedly, I will bring him into the land he went to, and his descendants will inherit it. ²⁵Since the Amalekites and Canaanites are living in the valleys, turn back tomorrow and set out toward the desert along the route to the Red Sea.ᵃ"

²⁶The Lord said to Moses and Aaron: ²⁷"How long will this wicked community grumble against me? I have heard the complaints of these grumbling Israelites. ²⁸So tell them, 'As surely as I live, declares the Lord, I will do to you the very things I heard you say: ²⁹In this desert your bodies will fall— every one of you twenty years old or more who was counted in the census and who has grumbled against me. ³⁰Not one of you will enter the land I swore with uplifted hand to make your home, except Caleb son of Jephunneh and Joshua son of Nun. ³¹As for your children that you said would be taken as plunder, I will bring them in to enjoy the land you have rejected.

ᵃ25 Hebrew *Yam Suph*; that is, Sea of Reeds

The Bible Says

God Forgives, But . . .

One of life's greatest wonders is this: because God loves you he forgives, again and again. But there's something very important to remember about forgiveness: You can be forgiven for making a bad choice, but that choice still has its consequences.

That's something the Israelites learned when they rebelled against God and refused to attack Canaan (Numbers 14:1–4). God forgave them (Numbers 14:18), but he turned them back to wander in the desert. Their sin even had consequences for their children, who wandered with their parents.

You can sin and know that God will forgive you. But remember, every choice has its consequences.

³²But you—your bodies will fall in this desert. ³³Your children will be shepherds here for forty years, suffering for your unfaithfulness, until the last of your bodies lies in the desert. ³⁴For forty years—one year for each of the forty days you explored the land—you will suffer for your sins and know what it is like to have me against you.' ³⁵I, the LORD, have spoken, and I will surely do these things to this whole wicked community, which has banded together against me. They will meet their end in this desert; here they will die."

³⁶So the men Moses had sent to explore the land, who returned and made the whole community grumble against him by spreading a bad report about it— ³⁷these men responsible for spreading the bad report about the land were struck down and died of a plague before the LORD. ³⁸Of the men who went to explore the land, only Joshua son of Nun and Caleb son of Jephunneh survived.

³⁹When Moses reported this to all the Israelites, they mourned bitterly. ⁴⁰Early the next morning they went up toward the high hill country. "We have sinned," they said. "We will go up to the place the LORD promised."

⁴¹But Moses said, "Why are you disobeying the LORD's command? This will not succeed! ⁴²Do not go up, because the LORD is not with you. You will be defeated by your enemies, ⁴³for the Amalekites and Canaanites will face you there. Because you have turned away from the LORD, he will not be with you and you will fall by the sword."

⁴⁴Nevertheless, in their presumption they went up toward the high hill country, though neither Moses nor the ark of the LORD's covenant moved from the camp. ⁴⁵Then the Amalekites and Canaanites who lived in that hill country came down and attacked them and beat them down all the way to Hormah.

15 **Supplementary Offerings** The LORD said to Moses, ²"Speak to the Israelites and say to them: 'After you enter the land I am giving you as a home ³and you present to the LORD offerings made by fire, from the herd or the flock, as an aroma pleasing to the LORD—whether burnt offerings or sacrifices, for special vows or freewill offerings or festival offerings— ⁴then the one who brings his offering shall present to the LORD a grain offering of a tenth of an ephah*ᵃ* of fine flour mixed with a quarter of a hin*ᵇ* of oil. ⁵With each lamb for the burnt offering or the sacrifice, prepare a quarter of a hin of wine as a drink offering.

⁶" 'With a ram prepare a grain offering of two-tenths of an ephah*ᶜ* of fine flour mixed with a third of a hin*ᵈ* of oil, ⁷and a third of a hin of wine as a drink offering. Offer it as an aroma pleasing to the LORD.

⁸" 'When you prepare a young bull as a burnt offering or sacrifice, for a special vow or a fellowship offering*ᵉ* to the LORD, ⁹bring with the bull a grain offering of three-tenths of an ephah*ᶠ* of fine flour mixed with half a hin*ᵍ* of oil. ¹⁰Also bring half a hin of wine as a drink offering. It will be an offering made by fire, an aroma pleasing to the LORD. ¹¹Each bull or ram, each lamb or young goat, is to be prepared in this manner. ¹²Do this for each one, for as many as you prepare.

¹³" 'Everyone who is native-born must do these things in this way when he brings an offering made by fire as an aroma pleasing to the LORD. ¹⁴For the generations to come, whenever an alien or anyone else living among you presents an offering made by fire as an aroma pleasing to the LORD, he must do exactly as you do. ¹⁵The community is to have the same rules for you and

---

ᵃ4 That is, probably about 2 quarts (about 2 liters)   *ᵇ4* That is, probably about 1 quart (about 1 liter); also in verse 5   *ᶜ6* That is, probably about 4 quarts (about 4.5 liters)   *ᵈ6* That is, probably about 1 1/4 quarts (about 1.2 liters); also in verse 7   *ᵉ8* Traditionally *peace offering*   *ᶠ9* That is, probably about 6 quarts (about 6.5 liters)   *ᵍ9* That is, probably about 2 quarts (about 2 liters); also in verse 10

for the alien living among you; this is a lasting ordinance for the generations to come. You and the alien shall be the same before the LORD: ¹⁶The same laws and regulations will apply both to you and to the alien living among you.' "

¹⁷The LORD said to Moses, ¹⁸"Speak to the Israelites and say to them: 'When you enter the land to which I am taking you ¹⁹and you eat the food of the land, present a portion as an offering to the LORD. ²⁰Present a cake from the first of your ground meal and present it as an offering from the threshing floor. ²¹Throughout the generations to come you are to give this offering to the LORD from the first of your ground meal.

Offerings for Unintentional Sins ²²" 'Now if you unintentionally fail to keep any of these commands the LORD gave Moses— ²³any of the LORD's commands to you through him, from the day the LORD gave them and continuing through the generations to come— ²⁴and if this is done unintentionally without the community being aware of it, then the whole community is to offer a young bull for a burnt offering as an aroma pleasing to the LORD, along with its prescribed grain offering and drink offering, and a male goat for a sin offering. ²⁵The priest is to make atonement for the whole Israelite community, and they will be forgiven, for it was not intentional and they have brought to the LORD for their wrong an offering made by fire and a sin offering. ²⁶The whole Israelite community and the aliens living among them will be forgiven, because all the people were involved in the unintentional wrong.

²⁷" 'But if just one person sins unintentionally, he must bring a year-old female goat for a sin offering. ²⁸The priest is to make atonement before the LORD for the one who erred by sinning unintentionally, and when atonement has been made for him, he will be forgiven. ²⁹One and the same law applies to everyone who sins unintentionally, whether he is a native-born Israelite or an alien.

³⁰" 'But anyone who sins defiantly, whether native-born or alien, blasphemes the LORD, and that person must be cut off from his people. ³¹Because he has despised the LORD's word and broken his commands, that person must surely be cut off; his guilt remains on him.' "

The Sabbath-Breaker Put to Death

³²While the Israelites were in the desert, a man was found gathering wood on the Sabbath day. ³³Those who found him gathering wood brought him to Moses and Aaron and the whole assembly, ³⁴and they kept him in custody, because it was not clear what should be done to him. ³⁵Then the LORD said to Moses, "The man must die. The whole assembly must stone him outside the camp." ³⁶So the assembly took him outside the camp and stoned him to death, as the LORD commanded Moses.

Tassels on Garments ³⁷The LORD said to Moses, ³⁸"Speak to the Israelites and say to them: 'Throughout the generations to come you are to make tassels on the corners of your garments, with a blue cord on each tassel. ³⁹You will have these tas-

Direct Line

NUMBERS 15:37-41

Are your parents totally out of style when it comes to the clothes you wear? Or are they pretty stylish? It's true that teens know better what's in at school than their parents do. But there's a little more to choosing clothing than copying what your friends wear. The Israelites were told to wear tassels with a blue cord on the corners of their garments. The tassels were to remind the Israelites they were God's people. The clothing was a sign of their identity. Your clothes identify you too. Your clothes say, "This is who I am." The important thing is to be sure that your clothes say, "I'm a Christian who tries always to please God."

sels to look at and so you will remember all the commands of the Lᴏʀᴅ, that you may obey them and not prostitute yourselves by going after the lusts of your own hearts and eyes. ⁴⁰Then you will remember to obey all my commands and will be consecrated to your God. ⁴¹I am the Lᴏʀᴅ your God, who brought you out of Egypt to be your God. I am the Lᴏʀᴅ your God.' "

Korah, Dathan and Abiram Korah son of Izhar, the son of Kohath, the son of Levi, and certain Reubenites—Dathan and Abiram, sons of Eliab, and On son of Peleth—became insolent*ᵃ* ²and rose up against Moses. With them were 250 Israelite men, well-known community leaders who had been appointed members of the council. ³They came as a group to oppose Moses and Aaron and said to them, "You have gone too far! The whole community is holy, every one of them, and the Lᴏʀᴅ is with them. Why then do you set yourselves above the Lᴏʀᴅ's assembly?"

⁴When Moses heard this, he fell facedown. ⁵Then he said to Korah and all his followers: "In the morning the Lᴏʀᴅ will show who belongs to him and who is holy, and he will have that person come near him. The man he chooses he will cause to come near him. ⁶You, Korah, and all your followers are to do this: Take censers ⁷and tomorrow put fire and incense in them before the Lᴏʀᴅ. The man the Lᴏʀᴅ chooses will be the one who is holy. You Levites have gone too far!"

⁸Moses also said to Korah, "Now listen, you Levites! ⁹Isn't it enough for you that the God of Israel has separated you from the rest of the Israelite community and brought you near himself to do the work at the Lᴏʀᴅ's tabernacle and to stand before the community and minister to them? ¹⁰He has brought you and all your fellow Levites near himself, but now you are trying to get the priesthood too. ¹¹It is against the Lᴏʀᴅ that you and all your followers have banded together. Who is Aaron that you should grumble against him?"

¹²Then Moses summoned Dathan and Abiram, the sons of Eliab. But they said, "We will not come! ¹³Isn't it enough that you have brought us up out of a land flowing with milk and honey to kill us in the desert? And now you also want to lord it over us? ¹⁴Moreover, you haven't brought us into a land flowing with milk and honey or given us an inheritance of fields and vineyards. Will you gouge out the eyes of*ᵇ* these men? No, we will not come!"

¹⁵Then Moses became very angry and said to the Lᴏʀᴅ, "Do not accept their offering. I have not taken so much as a donkey from them, nor have I wronged any of them."

¹⁶Moses said to Korah, "You and all your followers are to appear before the Lᴏʀᴅ tomorrow—you and they and Aaron. ¹⁷Each man is to take his censer and put incense in it—250 censers in all—and present it before the Lᴏʀᴅ. You and Aaron are to present your censers also." ¹⁸So each man took his censer, put fire and incense in it, and stood with Moses and Aaron at the entrance to the Tent of Meeting. ¹⁹When Korah had gathered all his followers in opposition to them at the entrance to the Tent of Meeting, the glory of the Lᴏʀᴅ appeared to the entire assembly. ²⁰The Lᴏʀᴅ said to Moses and Aaron, ²¹"Separate yourselves from this assembly so I can put an end to them at once."

²²But Moses and Aaron fell facedown and cried out, "O God, God of the spirits of all mankind, will you be angry with the entire assembly when only one man sins?"

²³Then the Lᴏʀᴅ said to Moses, ²⁴"Say to the assembly, 'Move away from the tents of Korah, Dathan and Abiram.' "

²⁵Moses got up and went to Dathan and Abiram, and the elders of Israel followed him. ²⁶He warned the assembly, "Move back from the tents of these

---

ᵃ1 Or Peleth—took men   *ᵇ14 Or you make slaves of; or you deceive*

wicked men! Do not touch anything belonging to them, or you will be swept away because of all their sins." ²⁷So they moved away from the tents of Korah, Dathan and Abiram. Dathan and Abiram had come out and were standing with their wives, children and little ones at the entrances to their tents.

²⁸Then Moses said, "This is how you will know that the LORD has sent me to do all these things and that it was not my idea: ²⁹If these men die a natural death and experience only what usually happens to men, then the LORD has not sent me. ³⁰But if the LORD brings about something totally new, and the earth opens its mouth and swallows them, with everything that belongs to them, and they go down alive into the grave,ᵃ then you will know that these men have treated the LORD with contempt."

³¹As soon as he finished saying all this, the ground under them split apart ³²and the earth opened its mouth and swallowed them, with their households and all Korah's men and all their possessions. ³³They went down alive into the grave, with everything they owned; the earth closed over them, and they perished and were gone from the community. ³⁴At their cries, all the Israelites around them fled, shouting, "The earth is going to swallow us too!"

³⁵And fire came out from the LORD and consumed the 250 men who were offering the incense.

³⁶The LORD said to Moses, ³⁷"Tell Eleazar son of Aaron, the priest, to take the censers out of the smoldering remains and scatter the coals some distance away, for the censers are holy— ³⁸the censers of the men who sinned at the cost of their lives. Hammer the censers into sheets to overlay the altar, for they were presented before the LORD and have become holy. Let them be a sign to the Israelites."

³⁹So Eleazar the priest collected the bronze censers brought by those who had been burned up, and he had them hammered out to overlay the altar, ⁴⁰as the LORD directed him through Moses. This was to remind the Israelites that no one except a descendant of Aaron should come to burn incense before the LORD, or he would become like Korah and his followers.

⁴¹The next day the whole Israelite community grumbled against Moses and Aaron. "You have killed the LORD's people," they said.

⁴²But when the assembly gathered in opposition to Moses and Aaron and turned toward the Tent of Meeting, suddenly the cloud covered it and the glory of the LORD appeared. ⁴³Then Moses and Aaron went to the front of the Tent of Meeting, ⁴⁴and the LORD said to Moses, ⁴⁵"Get away from this assembly so I can put an end to them at once." And they fell facedown.

⁴⁶Then Moses said to Aaron, "Take your censer and put incense in it, along with fire from the altar, and hurry to the assembly to make atonement for them. Wrath has come out from the LORD; the plague has started." ⁴⁷So Aaron did as Moses said, and ran into the midst of the assembly. The plague had already started among the people, but Aaron offered the incense and made atonement for them.

NUMBERS 16:23-24

Have you ever wondered why your mom or dad wants to meet the guy or girl you're dating? Or the kids you hang around with after school? Do you think they're just hassling you? Being mean? Or is there more to it? God told the Israelites to "move away from the tents of Korah, Dathan and Abiram" when these men organized a rebellion. Then the ground opened up beneath them, and they were killed. Your parents want to know your friends in case you ever need the same warning. They don't want you in the middle of big problems or messy situations. When they say, "Stay away from there," stop a minute to listen— and obey.

Direct Line

ᵃ30 Hebrew *Sheol*; also in verse 33

⁴⁸He stood between the living and the dead, and the plague stopped. ⁴⁹But 14,700 people died from the plague, in addition to those who had died because of Korah. ⁵⁰Then Aaron returned to Moses at the entrance to the Tent of Meeting, for the plague had stopped.

The Budding of Aaron's Staff The LORD said to Moses, ²"Speak to the Israelites and get twelve staffs from them, one from the leader of each of their ancestral tribes. Write the name of each man on his staff. ³On the staff of Levi write Aaron's name, for there must be one staff for the head of each ancestral tribe. ⁴Place them in the Tent of Meeting in front of the Testimony, where I meet with you. ⁵The staff belonging to the man I choose will sprout, and I will rid myself of this constant grumbling against you by the Israelites."

⁶So Moses spoke to the Israelites, and their leaders gave him twelve staffs, one for the leader of each of their ancestral tribes, and Aaron's staff was among them. ⁷Moses placed the staffs before the LORD in the Tent of the Testimony.

⁸The next day Moses entered the Tent of the Testimony and saw that Aaron's staff, which represented the house of Levi, had not only sprouted but had budded, blossomed and produced almonds. ⁹Then Moses brought out all the staffs from the LORD's presence to all the Israelites. They looked at them, and each man took his own staff.

¹⁰The LORD said to Moses, "Put back Aaron's staff in front of the Testimony, to be kept as a sign to the rebellious. This will put an end to their grumbling against me, so that they will not die." ¹¹Moses did just as the LORD commanded him.

¹²The Israelites said to Moses, "We will die! We are lost, we are all lost! ¹³Anyone who even comes near the tabernacle of the LORD will die. Are we all going to die?"

Duties of Priests and Levites The LORD said to Aaron, "You, your sons and your father's family are to bear the responsibility for offenses against the sanctuary, and you and your sons alone are to bear the responsibility for offenses against the priesthood. ²Bring your fellow Levites from your ancestral tribe to join you and assist you when you and your sons minister before the Tent of the Testimony. ³They are to be responsible to you and are to perform all the duties of the Tent, but they must not go near the furnishings of the sanctuary or the altar, or both they and you will die. ⁴They are to join you and be responsible for the care of the Tent of Meeting—all the work at the Tent—and no one else may come near where you are.

⁵"You are to be responsible for the care of the sanctuary and the altar, so that wrath will not fall on the Israelites again. ⁶I myself have selected your fellow Levites from among the Israelites as a gift to you, dedicated to the LORD to do the work at the Tent of Meeting. ⁷But only you and your sons may serve as priests in connection with everything at the altar and inside the curtain. I am giving you the service of the priesthood as a gift. Anyone else who comes near the sanctuary must be put to death."

Offerings for Priests and Levites ⁸Then the LORD said to Aaron, "I myself have put you in charge of the offerings presented to me; all the holy offerings the Israelites give me I give to you and your sons as your portion and regular share. ⁹You are to have the part of the most holy offerings that is kept from the fire. From all the gifts they bring me as most holy offerings, whether grain or sin or guilt offerings, that part belongs to you and your sons. ¹⁰Eat it as something most holy; every male shall eat it. You must regard it as holy.

¹¹"This also is yours: whatever is set aside from the gifts of all the wave offerings of the Israelites. I give this to you and your sons and daughters as

your regular share. Everyone in your household who is ceremonially clean may eat it.

¹²"I give you all the finest olive oil and all the finest new wine and grain they give the LORD as the firstfruits of their harvest. ¹³All the land's firstfruits that they bring to the LORD will be yours. Everyone in your household who is ceremonially clean may eat it.

¹⁴"Everything in Israel that is devoted*a* to the LORD is yours. ¹⁵The first offspring of every womb, both man and animal, that is offered to the LORD is yours. But you must redeem every firstborn son and every firstborn male of unclean animals. ¹⁶When they are a month old, you must redeem them at the redemption price set at five shekels*b* of silver, according to the sanctuary shekel, which weighs twenty gerahs.

¹⁷"But you must not redeem the firstborn of an ox, a sheep or a goat; they are holy. Sprinkle their blood on the altar and burn their fat as an offering made by fire, an aroma pleasing to the LORD. ¹⁸Their meat is to be yours, just as the breast of the wave offering and the right thigh are yours. ¹⁹Whatever is set aside from the holy offerings the Israelites present to the LORD I give to you and your sons and daughters as your regular share. It is an everlasting covenant of salt before the LORD for both you and your offspring."

²⁰The LORD said to Aaron, "You will have no inheritance in their land, nor will you have any share among them; I am your share and your inheritance among the Israelites.

²¹"I give to the Levites all the tithes in Israel as their inheritance in return for the work they do while serving at the Tent of Meeting. ²²From now on the Israelites must not go near the Tent of Meeting, or they will bear the consequences of their sin and will die. ²³It is the Levites who are to do the work at the Tent of Meeting and bear the responsibility for offenses against it. This is a lasting ordinance for the generations to come. They will receive no inheritance among the Israelites. ²⁴Instead, I give to the Levites as their inheritance the tithes that the Israelites present as an offering to the LORD. That is why I said concerning them: 'They will have no inheritance among the Israelites.' "

²⁵The LORD said to Moses, ²⁶"Speak to the Levites and say to them: 'When you receive from the Israelites the tithe I give you as your inheritance, you must present a tenth of that tithe as the LORD's offering. ²⁷Your offering will be reckoned to you as grain from the threshing floor or juice from the winepress. ²⁸In this way you also will present an offering to the LORD from all the tithes you receive from the Israelites. From these tithes you must give the LORD's portion to Aaron the priest. ²⁹You must present as the LORD's portion the best and holiest part of everything given to you.'

³⁰"Say to the Levites: 'When you present the best part, it will be reckoned to you as the product of the threshing floor or the winepress. ³¹You and your households may eat the rest of it anywhere, for it is your wages for your work at the Tent of Meeting. ³²By presenting the best part of it you will not be guilty in this matter; then you will not defile the holy offerings of the Israelites, and you will not die.' "

19 **The Water of Cleansing** The LORD said to Moses and Aaron: ²"This is a requirement of the law that the LORD has commanded: Tell the Israelites to bring you a red heifer without defect or blemish and that has never been under a yoke. ³Give it to Eleazar the priest; it is to be taken outside the camp and slaughtered in his presence. ⁴Then Eleazar the priest is to take some of its blood on his finger and sprinkle it seven times toward the front of the Tent of Meeting. ⁵While he watches, the heifer is to be burned—its hide, flesh, blood and offal. ⁶The priest is to take some cedar wood, hys-

---

a14 The Hebrew term refers to the irrevocable giving over of things or persons to the LORD.   *b16* That is, about 2 ounces (about 55 grams) sop and scarlet wool and throw them onto the burning heifer. [7]After that, the priest must wash his clothes and bathe himself with water. He may then come into the camp, but he will be ceremonially unclean till evening. [8]The man who burns it must also wash his clothes and bathe with water, and he too will be unclean till evening.

[9]"A man who is clean shall gather up the ashes of the heifer and put them in a ceremonially clean place outside the camp. They shall be kept by the Israelite community for use in the water of cleansing; it is for purification from sin. [10]The man who gathers up the ashes of the heifer must also wash his clothes, and he too will be unclean till evening. This will be a lasting ordinance both for the Israelites and for the aliens living among them.

[11]"Whoever touches the dead body of anyone will be unclean for seven days. [12]He must purify himself with the water on the third day and on the seventh day; then he will be clean. But if he does not purify himself on the third and seventh days, he will not be clean. [13]Whoever touches the dead body of anyone and fails to purify himself defiles the LORD's tabernacle. That person must be cut off from Israel. Because the water of cleansing has not been sprinkled on him, he is unclean; his uncleanness remains on him.

[14]"This is the law that applies when a person dies in a tent: Anyone who enters the tent and anyone who is in it will be unclean for seven days, [15]and every open container without a lid fastened on it will be unclean.

[16]"Anyone out in the open who touches someone who has been killed with a sword or someone who has died a natural death, or anyone who touches a human bone or a grave, will be unclean for seven days.

[17]"For the unclean person, put some ashes from the burned purification offering into a jar and pour fresh water over them. [18]Then a man who is ceremonially clean is to take some hyssop, dip it in the water and sprinkle the tent and all the furnishings and the people who were there. He must also sprinkle anyone who has touched a human bone or a grave or someone who has been killed or someone who has died a natural death. [19]The man who is clean is to sprinkle the unclean person on the third and seventh days, and on the seventh day he is to purify him. The person being cleansed must wash his clothes and bathe with water, and that evening he will be clean. [20]But if a person who is unclean does not purify himself, he must be cut off from the community, because he has defiled the sanctuary of the LORD. The water of cleansing has not been sprinkled on him, and he is unclean. [21]This is a lasting ordinance for them.

"The man who sprinkles the water of cleansing must also wash his clothes, and anyone who touches the water of cleansing will be unclean till evening. [22]Anything that an unclean person touches becomes unclean, and anyone who touches it becomes unclean till evening."

20 *Water From the Rock* In the first month the whole Israelite community arrived at the Desert of Zin, and they stayed at Kadesh. There Miriam died and was buried.

[2]Now there was no water for the community, and the people gathered in opposition to Moses and Aaron. [3]They quarreled with Moses and said, "If only we had died when our brothers fell dead before the LORD! [4]Why did you bring the LORD's community into this desert, that we and our livestock should die here? [5]Why did you bring us up out of Egypt to this terrible place? It has no grain or figs, grapevines or pomegranates. And there is no water to drink!"

[6]Moses and Aaron went from the assembly to the entrance to the Tent of Meeting and fell facedown, and the glory of the LORD appeared to them. [7]The LORD said to Moses, [8]"Take the staff, and you and your brother Aaron gather the assembly together. Speak to that rock before their eyes and it will pour

out its water. You will bring water out of the rock for the community so they and their livestock can drink."

⁹So Moses took the staff from the LORD's presence, just as he commanded him. ¹⁰He and Aaron gathered the assembly together in front of the rock and Moses said to them, "Listen, you rebels, must we bring you water out of this rock?" ¹¹Then Moses raised his arm and struck the rock twice with his staff. Water gushed out, and the community and their livestock drank.

¹²But the LORD said to Moses and Aaron, "Because you did not trust in me enough to honor me as holy in the sight of the Israelites, you will not bring this community into the land I give them."

¹³These were the waters of Meribah,ᵃ where the Israelites quarreled with the LORD and where he showed himself holy among them.

Edom Denies Israel Passage ¹⁴Moses sent messengers from Kadesh to the king of Edom, saying:

"This is what your brother Israel says: You know about all the hardships that have come upon us. ¹⁵Our forefathers went down into Egypt, and we lived there many years. The Egyptians mistreated us and our fathers, ¹⁶but when we cried out to the LORD, he heard our cry and sent an angel and brought us out of Egypt.

"Now we are here at Kadesh, a town on the edge of your territory. ¹⁷Please let us pass through your country. We will not go through any field or vineyard, or drink water from any well. We will travel along the king's highway and not turn to the right or to the left until we have passed through your territory."

¹⁸But Edom answered:

"You may not pass through here; if you try, we will march out and attack you with the sword."

¹⁹The Israelites replied:

"We will go along the main road, and if we or our livestock drink any of your water, we will pay for it. We only want to pass through on foot— nothing else."

²⁰Again they answered:

"You may not pass through."

Then Edom came out against them with a large and powerful army. ²¹Since Edom refused to let them go through their territory, Israel turned away from them.

The Death of Aaron ²²The whole Israelite community set out from Kadesh and came to Mount Hor. ²³At Mount Hor, near the border of Edom, the LORD said to Moses and Aaron, ²⁴"Aaron will be gathered to his people. He will not enter the land I give the Israelites, because both of you rebelled against my command at the waters of Meribah. ²⁵Get Aaron and his son Eleazar and take them up Mount Hor. ²⁶Remove Aaron's garments and put them on his son Eleazar, for Aaron will be gathered to his people; he will die there."

²⁷Moses did as the LORD commanded: They went up Mount Hor in the sight of the whole community. ²⁸Moses removed Aaron's garments and put them on his son Eleazar. And Aaron died there on top of the mountain. Then Moses and Eleazar came down from the mountain, ²⁹and when the whole community learned that Aaron had died, the entire house of Israel mourned for him thirty days.

ᵃ*13 Meribah* means *quarreling.*

21 *Arad Destroyed* When the Canaanite king of Arad, who lived in the Negev, heard that Israel was coming along the road to Atharim, he attacked the Israelites and captured some of them. ²Then Israel made this vow to the LORD: "If you will deliver these people into our hands, we will totally destroy*ᵃ* their cities." ³The LORD listened to Israel's plea and gave the Canaanites over to them. They completely destroyed them and their towns; so the place was named Hormah.*ᵇ*

The Bronze Snake ⁴They traveled from Mount Hor along the route to the Red Sea,*ᶜ* to go around Edom. But the people grew impatient on the way; ⁵they spoke against God and against Moses, and said, "Why have you brought us up out of Egypt to die in the desert? There is no bread! There is no water! And we detest this miserable food!"

⁶Then the LORD sent venomous snakes among them; they bit the people and many Israelites died. ⁷The people came to Moses and said, "We sinned when we spoke against the LORD and against you. Pray that the LORD will take the snakes away from us." So Moses prayed for the people.

⁸The LORD said to Moses, "Make a snake and put it up on a pole; anyone who is bitten can look at it and live." ⁹So Moses made a bronze snake and put it up on a pole. Then when anyone was bitten by a snake and looked at the bronze snake, he lived.

The Journey to Moab ¹⁰The Israelites moved on and camped at Oboth. ¹¹Then they set out from Oboth and camped in Iye Abarim, in the desert that faces Moab toward the sunrise. ¹²From there they moved on and camped in the Zered Valley. ¹³They set out from there and camped alongside the Arnon, which is in the desert extending into Amorite territory. The Arnon is the border of Moab, between Moab and the Amorites. ¹⁴That is why the Book of the Wars of the LORD says:

> ". . . Waheb in Suphah*ᵈ* and the ravines,
> the Arnon ¹⁵and*ᵉ* the slopes of the ravines
> that lead to the site of Ar
> and lie along the border of Moab."

¹⁶From there they continued on to Beer, the well where the LORD said to Moses, "Gather the people together and I will give them water."

¹⁷Then Israel sang this song:

> "Spring up, O well!
> Sing about it,
> ¹⁸about the well that the princes dug,
> that the nobles of the people sank—
> the nobles with scepters and staffs."

Then they went from the desert to Mattanah, ¹⁹from Mattanah to Nahaliel, from Nahaliel to Bamoth, ²⁰and from Bamoth to the valley in Moab where the top of Pisgah overlooks the wasteland.

Defeat of Sihon and Og ²¹Israel sent messengers to say to Sihon king of the Amorites:

²²"Let us pass through your country. We will not turn aside into any

NUMBERS 21

QUIZZER

Q: Why did Moses make a bronze snake?

BONUS: Who destroyed that snake, and why?

Answers on page 186

ᵃ2 The Hebrew term refers to the irrevocable giving over of things or persons to the LORD, often by totally destroying them; also in verse 3. ᵇ3 Hormah means destruction. ᶜ4 Hebrew Yam Suph; that is, Sea of Reeds ᵈ14 The meaning of the Hebrew for this phrase is uncertain. ᵉ14,15 Or "I have been given from Suphah and the ravines / of the Arnon ¹⁵to

field or vineyard, or drink water from any well. We will travel along the king's highway until we have passed through your territory."

²³But Sihon would not let Israel pass through his territory. He mustered his entire army and marched out into the desert against Israel. When he reached Jahaz, he fought with Israel. ²⁴Israel, however, put him to the sword and took over his land from the Arnon to the Jabbok, but only as far as the Ammonites, because their border was fortified. ²⁵Israel captured all the cities of the Amorites and occupied them, including Heshbon and all its surrounding settlements. ²⁶Heshbon was the city of Sihon king of the Amorites, who had fought against the former king of Moab and had taken from him all his land as far as the Arnon.

²⁷That is why the poets say:

> "Come to Heshbon and let it be rebuilt;
>   let Sihon's city be restored.
>
> ²⁸ "Fire went out from Heshbon,
>   a blaze from the city of Sihon.
> It consumed Ar of Moab,
>   the citizens of Arnon's heights.
> ²⁹Woe to you, O Moab!
>   You are destroyed, O people of Chemosh!
> He has given up his sons as fugitives
>   and his daughters as captives
>   to Sihon king of the Amorites.
>
> ³⁰ "But we have overthrown them;
>   Heshbon is destroyed all the way to Dibon.
> We have demolished them as far as Nophah,
>   which extends to Medeba."

³¹So Israel settled in the land of the Amorites.

³²After Moses had sent spies to Jazer, the Israelites captured its surrounding settlements and drove out the Amorites who were there. ³³Then they turned and went up along the road toward Bashan, and Og king of Bashan and his whole army marched out to meet them in battle at Edrei.

³⁴The LORD said to Moses, "Do not be afraid of him, for I have handed him over to you, with his whole army and his land. Do to him what you did to Sihon king of the Amorites, who reigned in Heshbon."

³⁵So they struck him down, together with his sons and his whole army, leaving them no survivors. And they took possession of his land.

A nswers
to Quizzer on page 185

A: God promised to heal those who had been bitten by snakes if they looked at the bronze snake (Numbers 21:8).

BONUS: Hezekiah destroyed it about 680 years later. The Israelites were worshiping it as an idol (2 Kings 18:4).

22 *Balak Summons Balaam* Then the Israelites traveled to the plains of Moab and camped along the Jordan across from Jericho.ᵃ ²Now Balak son of Zippor saw all that Israel had done to the Amorites, ³and Moab was terrified because there were so many people. Indeed, Moab was filled with dread because of the Israelites.

⁴The Moabites said to the elders of Midian, "This horde is going to lick up everything around us, as an ox licks up the grass of the field."

So Balak son of Zippor, who was king of Moab at that time, ⁵sent messengers to summon Balaam son of Beor, who was at Pethor, near the River,ᵇ in his native land. Balak said:

> "A people has come out of Egypt; they cover the face of the land and have settled next to me. ⁶Now come and put a curse on these people, be-

---

ᵃ1 Hebrew *Jordan of Jericho*; possibly an ancient name for the Jordan River   ᵇ5 That is, the Euphrates

cause they are too powerful for me. Perhaps then I will be able to defeat them and drive them out of the country. For I know that those you bless are blessed, and those you curse are cursed."

⁷The elders of Moab and Midian left, taking with them the fee for divination. When they came to Balaam, they told him what Balak had said.

⁸"Spend the night here," Balaam said to them, "and I will bring you back the answer the Lᴏʀᴅ gives me." So the Moabite princes stayed with him.

⁹God came to Balaam and asked, "Who are these men with you?"

¹⁰Balaam said to God, "Balak son of Zippor, king of Moab, sent me this message: ¹¹'A people that has come out of Egypt covers the face of the land. Now come and put a curse on them for me. Perhaps then I will be able to fight them and drive them away.' "

¹²But God said to Balaam, "Do not go with them. You must not put a curse on those people, because they are blessed."

¹³The next morning Balaam got up and said to Balak's princes, "Go back to your own country, for the Lᴏʀᴅ has refused to let me go with you."

¹⁴So the Moabite princes returned to Balak and said, "Balaam refused to come with us."

¹⁵Then Balak sent other princes, more numerous and more distinguished than the first. ¹⁶They came to Balaam and said:

"This is what Balak son of Zippor says: Do not let anything keep you from coming to me, ¹⁷because I will reward you handsomely and do whatever you say. Come and put a curse on these people for me."

¹⁸But Balaam answered them, "Even if Balak gave me his palace filled with silver and gold, I could not do anything great or small to go beyond the command of the Lᴏʀᴅ my God. ¹⁹Now stay here tonight as the others did, and I will find out what else the Lᴏʀᴅ will tell me."

²⁰That night God came to Balaam and said, "Since these men have come to summon you, go with them, but do only what I tell you."

Balaam's Donkey   ²¹Balaam got up in the morning, saddled his donkey and went with the princes of Moab. ²²But God was very angry when he went, and the angel of the Lᴏʀᴅ stood in the road to oppose him. Balaam was riding on his donkey, and his two servants were with him. ²³When the donkey saw the angel of the Lᴏʀᴅ standing in the road with a drawn sword in his hand, she turned off the road into a field. Balaam beat her to get her back on the road.

²⁴Then the angel of the Lᴏʀᴅ stood in a narrow path between two vineyards, with walls on both sides. ²⁵When the donkey saw the angel of the Lᴏʀᴅ, she pressed close to the wall, crushing Balaam's foot against it. So he beat her again.

²⁶Then the angel of the Lᴏʀᴅ moved on ahead and stood in a narrow place where there was no room to turn, either to the right or to the left. ²⁷When the donkey saw the angel of the Lᴏʀᴅ, she lay down under Balaam, and he was angry and beat her with his staff. ²⁸Then the Lᴏʀᴅ opened the donkey's mouth, and she said to Balaam, "What have I done to you to make you beat me these three times?"

²⁹Balaam answered the donkey, "You have made a fool of me! If I had a sword in my hand, I would kill you right now."

³⁰The donkey said to Balaam, "Am I not your own donkey, which you have always ridden, to this day? Have I been in the habit of doing this to you?"

"No," he said.

³¹Then the Lᴏʀᴅ opened Balaam's eyes, and he saw the angel of the Lᴏʀᴅ

NUMBERS 22

QUIZZER

Q: Who rode on an animal that talked to him?

BONUS: What did that animal do to his foot?

Answers on page 188

standing in the road with his sword drawn. So he bowed low and fell face-down.

³²The angel of the Lord asked him, "Why have you beaten your donkey these three times? I have come here to oppose you because your path is a reckless one before me.ᵃ ³³The donkey saw me and turned away from me these three times. If she had not turned away, I would certainly have killed you by now, but I would have spared her."

³⁴Balaam said to the angel of the Lord, "I have sinned. I did not realize you were standing in the road to oppose me. Now if you are displeased, I will go back."

³⁵The angel of the Lord said to Balaam, "Go with the men, but speak only what I tell you." So Balaam went with the princes of Balak.

³⁶When Balak heard that Balaam was coming, he went out to meet him at the Moabite town on the Arnon border, at the edge of his territory. ³⁷Balak said to Balaam, "Did I not send you an urgent summons? Why didn't you come to me? Am I really not able to reward you?"

³⁸"Well, I have come to you now," Balaam replied. "But can I say just anything? I must speak only what God puts in my mouth."

³⁹Then Balaam went with Balak to Kiriath Huzoth. ⁴⁰Balak sacrificed cattle and sheep, and gave some to Balaam and the princes who were with him. ⁴¹The next morning Balak took Balaam up to Bamoth Baal, and from there he saw part of the people.

23 *Balaam's First Oracle* Balaam said, "Build me seven altars here, and prepare seven bulls and seven rams for me." ²Balak did as Balaam said, and the two of them offered a bull and a ram on each altar.

³Then Balaam said to Balak, "Stay here beside your offering while I go aside. Perhaps the Lord will come to meet with me. Whatever he reveals to me I will tell you." Then he went off to a barren height.

⁴God met with him, and Balaam said, "I have prepared seven altars, and on each altar I have offered a bull and a ram."

⁵The Lord put a message in Balaam's mouth and said, "Go back to Balak and give him this message."

⁶So he went back to him and found him standing beside his offering, with all the princes of Moab. ⁷Then Balaam uttered his oracle:

> "Balak brought me from Aram,
>   the king of Moab from the eastern mountains.
> 'Come,' he said, 'curse Jacob for me;
>   come, denounce Israel.'
> ⁸How can I curse
>   those whom God has not cursed?
> How can I denounce
>   those whom the Lord has not denounced?
> ⁹From the rocky peaks I see them,
>   from the heights I view them.
> I see a people who live apart
>   and do not consider themselves one of the nations.
> ¹⁰Who can count the dust of Jacob
>   or number the fourth part of Israel?
> Let me die the death of the righteous,
>   and may my end be like theirs!"

¹¹Balak said to Balaam, "What have you done to me? I brought you to curse my enemies, but you have done nothing but bless them!"

¹²He answered, "Must I not speak what the Lord puts in my mouth?"

Answers
to Quizzer on page 187

A: The pagan prophet Balaam (Numbers 22:21-35).

BONUS: The donkey crushed his foot against a wall (Numbers 22:25).

ᵃ32 The meaning of the Hebrew for this clause is uncertain.

Balaam's Second Oracle ¹³Then Balak said to him, "Come with me to another place where you can see them; you will see only a part but not all of them. And from there, curse them for me." ¹⁴So he took him to the field of Zophim on the top of Pisgah, and there he built seven altars and offered a bull and a ram on each altar.

¹⁵Balaam said to Balak, "Stay here beside your offering while I meet with him over there."

¹⁶The LORD met with Balaam and put a message in his mouth and said, "Go back to Balak and give him this message."

¹⁷So he went to him and found him standing beside his offering, with the princes of Moab. Balak asked him, "What did the LORD say?"

¹⁸Then he uttered his oracle:

> "Arise, Balak, and listen;
>   hear me, son of Zippor.
> ¹⁹God is not a man, that he should lie,
>   nor a son of man, that he should change his mind.
> Does he speak and then not act?
>   Does he promise and not fulfill?
> ²⁰I have received a command to bless;
>   he has blessed, and I cannot change it.
>
> ²¹ "No misfortune is seen in Jacob,
>   no misery observed in Israel.ᵃ
> The LORD their God is with them;
>   the shout of the King is among them.
> ²²God brought them out of Egypt;
>   they have the strength of a wild ox.
> ²³There is no sorcery against Jacob,
>   no divination against Israel.
> It will now be said of Jacob
>   and of Israel, 'See what God has done!'
> ²⁴The people rise like a lioness;
>   they rouse themselves like a lion
> that does not rest till he devours his prey
>   and drinks the blood of his victims."

²⁵Then Balak said to Balaam, "Neither curse them at all nor bless them at all!"

²⁶Balaam answered, "Did I not tell you I must do whatever the LORD says?"

Balaam's Third Oracle ²⁷Then Balak said to Balaam, "Come, let me take you to another place. Perhaps it will please God to let you curse them for me from there." ²⁸And Balak took Balaam to the top of Peor, overlooking the wasteland.

²⁹Balaam said, "Build me seven altars here, and prepare seven bulls and seven rams for me." ³⁰Balak did as Balaam had said, and offered a bull and a ram on each altar.

24 Now when Balaam saw that it pleased the LORD to bless Israel, he did not resort to sorcery as at other times, but turned his face toward the desert. ²When Balaam looked out and saw Israel encamped tribe by tribe, the Spirit of God came upon him ³and he uttered his oracle:

> "The oracle of Balaam son of Beor,
>   the oracle of one whose eye sees clearly,

ᵃ21 Or *He has not looked on Jacob's offenses / or on the wrongs found in Israel.*

⁴the oracle of one who hears the words of God,
who sees a vision from the Almighty,ᵃ
who falls prostrate, and whose eyes are opened:

⁵"How beautiful are your tents, O Jacob,
your dwelling places, O Israel!

⁶"Like valleys they spread out,
like gardens beside a river,
like aloes planted by the LORD,
like cedars beside the waters.
⁷Water will flow from their buckets;
their seed will have abundant water.

"Their king will be greater than Agag;
their kingdom will be exalted.

⁸"God brought them out of Egypt;
they have the strength of a wild ox.
They devour hostile nations
and break their bones in pieces;
with their arrows they pierce them.
⁹Like a lion they crouch and lie down,
like a lioness—who dares to rouse them?

"May those who bless you be blessed
and those who curse you be cursed!"

¹⁰Then Balak's anger burned against Balaam. He struck his hands together and said to him, "I summoned you to curse my enemies, but you have blessed them these three times. ¹¹Now leave at once and go home! I said I would reward you handsomely, but the LORD has kept you from being rewarded."

¹²Balaam answered Balak, "Did I not tell the messengers you sent me, ¹³'Even if Balak gave me his palace filled with silver and gold, I could not do anything of my own accord, good or bad, to go beyond the command of the LORD—and I must say only what the LORD says'? ¹⁴Now I am going back to my people, but come, let me warn you of what this people will do to your people in days to come."

> May those who bless you be blessed and those who curse you be cursed (Numbers 24:9)!

Balaam's Fourth Oracle ¹⁵Then he uttered his oracle:

"The oracle of Balaam son of Beor,
the oracle of one whose eye sees clearly,
¹⁶the oracle of one who hears the words of God,
who has knowledge from the Most High,
who sees a vision from the Almighty,
who falls prostrate, and whose eyes are opened:

¹⁷"I see him, but not now;
I behold him, but not near.
A star will come out of Jacob;
a scepter will rise out of Israel.
He will crush the foreheads of Moab,
the skullsᵇ ofᶜ all the sons of Sheth.ᵈ
¹⁸Edom will be conquered;
Seir, his enemy, will be conquered,
but Israel will grow strong.

ᵃ4 Hebrew *Shaddai*; also in verse 16   ᵇ17 Samaritan Pentateuch (see also Jer. 48:45); the meaning of the word in the Masoretic Text is uncertain.   ᶜ17 Or possibly *Moab, / batter*   ᵈ17 Or *all the noisy boasters*

¹⁹A ruler will come out of Jacob
and destroy the survivors of the city."

Balaam's Final Oracles ²⁰Then Balaam saw Amalek and uttered his oracle:

"Amalek was first among the nations,
but he will come to ruin at last."

²¹Then he saw the Kenites and uttered his oracle:

"Your dwelling place is secure,
your nest is set in a rock;
²²yet you Kenites will be destroyed
when Asshur takes you captive."

²³Then he uttered his oracle:

"Ah, who can live when God does this?*a*
24   Ships will come from the shores of Kittim;
they will subdue Asshur and Eber,
but they too will come to ruin."

²⁵Then Balaam got up and returned home and Balak went his own way.

Moab Seduces Israel While Israel was staying in Shittim, the men began to indulge in sexual immorality with Moabite women, ²who invited them to the sacrifices to their gods. The people ate and bowed down before these gods. ³So Israel joined in worshiping the Baal of Peor. And the LORD's anger burned against them.

⁴The LORD said to Moses, "Take all the leaders of these people, kill them and expose them in broad daylight before the LORD, so that the LORD's fierce anger may turn away from Israel."

⁵So Moses said to Israel's judges, "Each of you must put to death those of your men who have joined in worshiping the Baal of Peor."

⁶Then an Israelite man brought to his family a Midianite woman right before the eyes of Moses and the whole assembly of Israel while they were weeping at the entrance to the Tent of Meeting. ⁷When Phinehas son of Eleazar, the son of Aaron, the priest, saw this, he left the assembly, took a spear in his hand ⁸and followed the Israelite into the tent. He drove the spear through both of them—through the Israelite and into the woman's body. Then the plague against the Israelites was stopped; ⁹but those who died in the plague numbered 24,000.

¹⁰The LORD said to Moses, ¹¹"Phinehas son of Eleazar, the son of Aaron, the priest, has turned my anger away from the Israelites; for he was as zealous as I am for my honor among them, so that in my zeal I did not put an end to them. ¹²Therefore tell him I am making my covenant of peace with him. ¹³He and his descendants will have a covenant of a lasting priesthood, because he was zealous for the honor of his God and made atonement for the Israelites."

¹⁴The name of the Israelite who was killed with the Midianite woman was Zimri son of Salu, the leader of a Simeonite family. ¹⁵And the name of the Midianite woman who was put to death was Cozbi daughter of Zur, a tribal chief of a Midianite family.

¹⁶The LORD said to Moses, ¹⁷"Treat the Midianites as enemies and kill them, ¹⁸because they treated you as enemies when they deceived you in the affair of Peor and their sister Cozbi, the daughter of a Midianite leader, the woman who was killed when the plague came as a result of Peor."

---

a23 Masoretic Text; with a different word division of the Hebrew A people will gather from the north.

The Second Census   After the plague the LORD said to Moses and Eleazar son of Aaron, the priest, ²"Take a census of the whole Israelite community by families—all those twenty years old or more who are able to serve in the army of Israel." ³So on the plains of Moab by the Jordan across from Jericho,ᵃ Moses and Eleazar the priest spoke with them and said, ⁴"Take a census of the men twenty years old or more, as the LORD commanded Moses."

These were the Israelites who came out of Egypt:

⁵The descendants of Reuben, the firstborn son of Israel, were:
    through Hanoch, the Hanochite clan;
    through Pallu, the Palluite clan;
    ⁶through Hezron, the Hezronite clan;
    through Carmi, the Carmite clan.
⁷These were the clans of Reuben; those numbered were 43,730.

⁸The son of Pallu was Eliab, ⁹and the sons of Eliab were Nemuel, Dathan and Abiram. The same Dathan and Abiram were the community officials who rebelled against Moses and Aaron and were among Korah's followers when they rebelled against the LORD. ¹⁰The earth opened its mouth and swallowed them along with Korah, whose followers died when the fire devoured the 250 men. And they served as a warning sign. ¹¹The line of Korah, however, did not die out.

¹²The descendants of Simeon by their clans were:
    through Nemuel, the Nemuelite clan;
    through Jamin, the Jaminite clan;
    through Jakin, the Jakinite clan;
    ¹³through Zerah, the Zerahite clan;
    through Shaul, the Shaulite clan.
¹⁴These were the clans of Simeon; there were 22,200 men.

¹⁵The descendants of Gad by their clans were:
    through Zephon, the Zephonite clan;
    through Haggi, the Haggite clan;
    through Shuni, the Shunite clan;
    ¹⁶through Ozni, the Oznite clan;
    through Eri, the Erite clan;
    ¹⁷through Arodi,ᵇ the Arodite clan;
    through Areli, the Arelite clan.
¹⁸These were the clans of Gad; those numbered were 40,500.

¹⁹Er and Onan were sons of Judah, but they died in Canaan. ²⁰The descendants of Judah by their clans were:
    through Shelah, the Shelanite clan;
    through Perez, the Perezite clan;
    through Zerah, the Zerahite clan.
    ²¹The descendants of Perez were:
      through Hezron, the Hezronite clan;
      through Hamul, the Hamulite clan.
²²These were the clans of Judah; those numbered were 76,500.

²³The descendants of Issachar by their clans were:
    through Tola, the Tolaite clan;
    through Puah, the Puiteᶜ clan;

ᵃ3 Hebrew *Jordan of Jericho;* possibly an ancient name for the Jordan River; also in verse 63   ᵇ17 Samaritan Pentateuch and Syriac (see also Gen. 46:16); Masoretic Text *Arod*   ᶜ23 Samaritan Pentateuch, Septuagint, Vulgate and Syriac (see also 1 Chron. 7:1); Masoretic Text *through Puvah, the Punite*

²⁴through Jashub, the Jashubite clan;
    through Shimron, the Shimronite clan.
²⁵These were the clans of Issachar; those numbered were 64,300.

²⁶The descendants of Zebulun by their clans were:
    through Sered, the Seredite clan;
    through Elon, the Elonite clan;
    through Jahleel, the Jahleelite clan.
²⁷These were the clans of Zebulun; those numbered were 60,500.

²⁸The descendants of Joseph by their clans through Manasseh and Ephraim were:

²⁹The descendants of Manasseh:
    through Makir, the Makirite clan (Makir was the father of Gilead);
    through Gilead, the Gileadite clan.
    ³⁰These were the descendants of Gilead:
      through Iezer, the Iezerite clan;
      through Helek, the Helekite clan;
      ³¹through Asriel, the Asrielite clan;
      through Shechem, the Shechemite clan;
      ³²through Shemida, the Shemidaite clan;
      through Hepher, the Hepherite clan.
    ³³(Zelophehad son of Hepher had no sons; he had only daughters, whose names were Mahlah, Noah, Hoglah, Milcah and Tirzah.)
³⁴These were the clans of Manasseh; those numbered were 52,700.

³⁵These were the descendants of Ephraim by their clans:
    through Shuthelah, the Shuthelahite clan;
    through Beker, the Bekerite clan;
    through Tahan, the Tahanite clan.
    ³⁶These were the descendants of Shuthelah:
      through Eran, the Eranite clan.
³⁷These were the clans of Ephraim; those numbered were 32,500.

These were the descendants of Joseph by their clans.

³⁸The descendants of Benjamin by their clans were:
    through Bela, the Belaite clan;
    through Ashbel, the Ashbelite clan;
    through Ahiram, the Ahiramite clan;
    ³⁹through Shupham,[a] the Shuphamite clan;
    through Hupham, the Huphamite clan.
    ⁴⁰The descendants of Bela through Ard and Naaman were:
      through Ard,[b] the Ardite clan;
      through Naaman, the Naamite clan.
⁴¹These were the clans of Benjamin; those numbered were 45,600.

⁴²These were the descendants of Dan by their clans:
    through Shuham, the Shuhamite clan.
These were the clans of Dan: ⁴³All of them were Shuhamite clans; and those numbered were 64,400.

⁴⁴The descendants of Asher by their clans were:
    through Imnah, the Imnite clan;
    through Ishvi, the Ishvite clan;
    through Beriah, the Beriite clan;

---

a 39 A few manuscripts of the Masoretic Text, Samaritan Pentateuch, Vulgate and Syriac (see also Septuagint); most manuscripts of the Masoretic Text *Shephupham*   *b 40* Samaritan Pentateuch and Vulgate (see also Septuagint); Masoretic Text does not have *through Ard.*

⁴⁵and through the descendants of Beriah:

through Heber, the Heberite clan;

through Malkiel, the Malkielite clan.

⁴⁶(Asher had a daughter named Serah.)

⁴⁷These were the clans of Asher; those numbered were 53,400.

⁴⁸The descendants of Naphtali by their clans were:

through Jahzeel, the Jahzeelite clan;

through Guni, the Gunite clan;

⁴⁹through Jezer, the Jezerite clan;

through Shillem, the Shillemite clan.

⁵⁰These were the clans of Naphtali; those numbered were 45,400.

⁵¹The total number of the men of Israel was 601,730.

⁵²The Lᴏʀᴅ said to Moses, ⁵³"The land is to be allotted to them as an inheritance based on the number of names. ⁵⁴To a larger group give a larger inheritance, and to a smaller group a smaller one; each is to receive its inheritance according to the number of those listed. ⁵⁵Be sure that the land is distributed by lot. What each group inherits will be according to the names for its ancestral tribe. ⁵⁶Each inheritance is to be distributed by lot among the larger and smaller groups."

⁵⁷These were the Levites who were counted by their clans:

through Gershon, the Gershonite clan;

through Kohath, the Kohathite clan;

through Merari, the Merarite clan.

⁵⁸These also were Levite clans:

the Libnite clan,

the Hebronite clan,

the Mahlite clan,

the Mushite clan,

the Korahite clan.

(Kohath was the forefather of Amram; ⁵⁹the name of Amram's wife was Jochebed, a descendant of Levi, who was born to the Levites*ᵃ* in Egypt. To Amram she bore Aaron, Moses and their sister Miriam. ⁶⁰Aaron was the father of Nadab and Abihu, Eleazar and Ithamar. ⁶¹But Nadab and Abihu died when they made an offering before the Lᴏʀᴅ with unauthorized fire.)

⁶²All the male Levites a month old or more numbered 23,000. They were not counted along with the other Israelites because they received no inheritance among them.

⁶³These are the ones counted by Moses and Eleazar the priest when they counted the Israelites on the plains of Moab by the Jordan across from Jericho. ⁶⁴Not one of them was among those counted by Moses and Aaron the priest when they counted the Israelites in the Desert of Sinai. ⁶⁵For the Lᴏʀᴅ had told those Israelites they would surely die in the desert, and not one of them was left except Caleb son of Jephunneh and Joshua son of Nun.

27 *Zelophehad's Daughters* The daughters of Zelophehad son of Hepher, the son of Gilead, the son of Makir, the son of Manasseh, belonged to the clans of Manasseh son of Joseph. The names of the daughters were Mahlah, Noah, Hoglah, Milcah and Tirzah. They approached ²the entrance to the Tent of Meeting and stood before Moses, Eleazar the priest,

---

ᵃ59 Or *Jochebed, a daughter of Levi, who was born to Levi*

the leaders and the whole assembly, and said, ³"Our father died in the desert. He was not among Korah's followers, who banded together against the LORD, but he died for his own sin and left no sons. ⁴Why should our father's name disappear from his clan because he had no son? Give us property among our father's relatives."

⁵So Moses brought their case before the LORD ⁶and the LORD said to him, ⁷"What Zelophehad's daughters are saying is right. You must certainly give them property as an inheritance among their father's relatives and turn their father's inheritance over to them.

⁸"Say to the Israelites, 'If a man dies and leaves no son, turn his inheritance over to his daughter. ⁹If he has no daughter, give his inheritance to his brothers. ¹⁰If he has no brothers, give his inheritance to his father's brothers. ¹¹If his father had no brothers, give his inheritance to the nearest relative in his clan, that he may possess it. This is to be a legal requirement for the Israelites, as the LORD commanded Moses.' "

Joshua to Succeed Moses ¹²Then the LORD said to Moses, "Go up this mountain in the Abarim range and see the land I have given the Israelites. ¹³After you have seen it, you too will be gathered to your people, as your brother Aaron was, ¹⁴for when the community rebelled at the waters in the Desert of Zin, both of you disobeyed my command to honor me as holy before their eyes." (These were the waters of Meribah Kadesh, in the Desert of Zin.)

¹⁵Moses said to the LORD, ¹⁶"May the LORD, the God of the spirits of all mankind, appoint a man over this community ¹⁷to go out and come in before them, one who will lead them out and bring them in, so the LORD's people will not be like sheep without a shepherd."

¹⁸So the LORD said to Moses, "Take Joshua son of Nun, a man in whom is the spirit,*ᵃ* and lay your hand on him. ¹⁹Have him stand before Eleazar the priest and the entire assembly and commission him in their presence. ²⁰Give him some of your authority so the whole Israelite community will obey him. ²¹He is to stand before Eleazar the priest, who will obtain decisions for him by inquiring of the Urim before the LORD. At his command he and the entire community of the Israelites will go out, and at his command they will come in."

²²Moses did as the LORD commanded him. He took Joshua and had him stand before Eleazar the priest and the whole assembly. ²³Then he laid his hands on him and commissioned him, as the LORD instructed through Moses.

28 *Daily Offerings* The LORD said to Moses, ²"Give this command to the Israelites and say to them: 'See that you present to me at the appointed time the food for my offerings made by fire, as an aroma pleasing to me.' ³Say to them: 'This is the offering made by fire that you are to present to the LORD: two lambs a year old without defect, as a regular burnt offering each day. ⁴Prepare one lamb in the morning and the other at twilight, ⁵together with a grain offering of a tenth of an ephah*ᵇ* of fine flour mixed with a quarter of a hin*ᶜ* of oil from pressed olives. ⁶This is the regular burnt offering instituted at Mount Sinai as a pleasing aroma, an offering made to the LORD by fire. ⁷The accompanying drink offering is to be a quarter of a hin of fermented drink with each lamb. Pour out the drink offering to the LORD at the sanctuary. ⁸Prepare the second lamb at twilight, along with the same kind of grain offering and drink offering that you prepare in the morning. This is an offering made by fire, an aroma pleasing to the LORD.

Sabbath Offerings ⁹" 'On the Sabbath day, make an offering of two lambs a year old without defect, together with its drink offering and a grain offering

ᵃ18 Or Spirit   ᵇ5 That is, probably about 2 quarts (about 2 liters); also in verses 13, 21 and 29   ᶜ5 That is, probably about 1 quart (about 1 liter); also in verses 7 and 14

Dear Sam,

I raise my hand at school, but my teachers always call on the boys in class first. It's not fair to the girls. What can I do?

Mary in Montreal

100 Advice Lane, Anywhere, USA

Dear Mary,

You are the victim of sexual prejudice. Of course you feel angry. But don't give up. God cares about girls too!

When Zelophehad died, he had no sons to inherit his property as was the custom. So his daughters went to Moses and said they should be able to inherit the land of their father. Moses asked God what to do, and God said the women should get the property (Numbers 27:7).

Recent research shows that boys are given preferential treatment by both male and female teachers. Most teachers are totally unaware of what they are doing. Do you think you could talk to your teacher about this? Could you send him or her a note explaining how you feel? Making a teacher aware of the problem is the first step toward solving it. Be courteous. Be respectful. But don't be afraid to stand up for what you know is right.

Sam

of two-tenths of an ephah*a* of fine flour mixed with oil. ¹⁰This is the burnt offering for every Sabbath, in addition to the regular burnt offering and its drink offering.

Monthly Offerings　¹¹" 'On the first of every month, present to the LORD a burnt offering of two young bulls, one ram and seven male lambs a year old, all without defect. ¹²With each bull there is to be a grain offering of three-tenths of an ephah*b* of fine flour mixed with oil; with the ram, a grain offering of two-tenths of an ephah of fine flour mixed with oil; ¹³and with each lamb, a grain offering of a tenth of an ephah of fine flour mixed with oil. This is for a burnt offering, a pleasing aroma, an offering made to the LORD by fire. ¹⁴With each bull there is to be a drink offering of half a hin*c* of wine; with the ram, a third of a hin*d*; and with each lamb, a quarter of a hin. This is the monthly burnt offering to be made at each new moon during the year. ¹⁵Besides the regular burnt offering with its drink offering, one male goat is to be presented to the LORD as a sin offering.

The Passover　¹⁶" 'On the fourteenth day of the first month the LORD's Passover is to be held. ¹⁷On the fifteenth day of this month there is to be a festival; for seven days eat bread made without yeast. ¹⁸On the first day hold a sacred assembly and do no regular work. ¹⁹Present to the LORD an offering made by fire, a burnt offering of two young bulls, one ram and seven male lambs a year old, all without defect. ²⁰With each bull prepare a grain offering of three-tenths of an ephah of fine flour mixed with oil; with the ram, two-tenths; ²¹and with each of the seven lambs, one-tenth. ²²Include one male goat as a sin offering to make atonement for you. ²³Prepare these in addition to the regular morning burnt offering. ²⁴In this way prepare the food for the offering made by fire every day for seven days as an aroma pleasing to the LORD; it is to be prepared in addition to the regular burnt offering and its drink offering. ²⁵On the seventh day hold a sacred assembly and do no regular work.

Feast of Weeks　²⁶" 'On the day of firstfruits, when you present to the LORD an offering of new grain during the Feast of Weeks, hold a sacred assembly and do no regular work. ²⁷Present a burnt offering of two young bulls, one ram and seven male lambs a year old as an aroma pleasing to the LORD. ²⁸With each bull there is to be a grain offering of three-tenths of an ephah of fine flour mixed with oil; with the ram, two-tenths; ²⁹and with each of the seven lambs, one-tenth. ³⁰Include one male goat to make atonement for you. ³¹Prepare these together with their drink offerings, in addition to the regular burnt offering and its grain offering. Be sure the animals are without defect.

29 *Feast of Trumpets*　" 'On the first day of the seventh month hold a sacred assembly and do no regular work. It is a day for you to sound the trumpets. ²As an aroma pleasing to the LORD, prepare a burnt offering of one young bull, one ram and seven male lambs a year old, all without defect. ³With the bull prepare a grain offering of three-tenths of an ephah*e* of fine flour mixed with oil; with the ram, two-tenths*f*; ⁴and with each of the seven lambs, one-tenth.*g* ⁵Include one male goat as a sin offering to make atonement for you. ⁶These are in addition to the monthly and daily burnt offerings with their grain offerings and drink offerings as specified. They are offerings made to the LORD by fire—a pleasing aroma.

a9 That is, probably about 4 quarts (about 4.5 liters); also in verses 12, 20 and 28　b12 That is, probably about 6 quarts (about 6.5 liters); also in verses 20 and 28　c14 That is, probably about 2 quarts (about 2 liters)　d14 That is, probably about 1 1/4 quarts (about 1.2 liters)　e3 That is, probably about 6 quarts (about 6.5 liters); also in verses 9 and 14　f3 That is, probably about 4 quarts (about 4.5 liters); also in verses 9 and 14　g4 That is, probably about 2 quarts (about 2 liters); also in verses 10 and 15

Day of Atonement ⁷" 'On the tenth day of this seventh month hold a sacred assembly. You must deny yourselves*ᵃ* and do no work. ⁸Present as an aroma pleasing to the LORD a burnt offering of one young bull, one ram and seven male lambs a year old, all without defect. ⁹With the bull prepare a grain offering of three-tenths of an ephah of fine flour mixed with oil; with the ram, two-tenths; ¹⁰and with each of the seven lambs, one-tenth. ¹¹Include one male goat as a sin offering, in addition to the sin offering for atonement and the regular burnt offering with its grain offering, and their drink offerings.

Feast of Tabernacles ¹²" 'On the fifteenth day of the seventh month, hold a sacred assembly and do no regular work. Celebrate a festival to the LORD for seven days. ¹³Present an offering made by fire as an aroma pleasing to the LORD, a burnt offering of thirteen young bulls, two rams and fourteen male lambs a year old, all without defect. ¹⁴With each of the thirteen bulls prepare a grain offering of three-tenths of an ephah of fine flour mixed with oil; with each of the two rams, two-tenths; ¹⁵and with each of the fourteen lambs, one-tenth. ¹⁶Include one male goat as a sin offering, in addition to the regular burnt offering with its grain offering and drink offering.

¹⁷" 'On the second day prepare twelve young bulls, two rams and fourteen male lambs a year old, all without defect. ¹⁸With the bulls, rams and lambs, prepare their grain offerings and drink offerings according to the number specified. ¹⁹Include one male goat as a sin offering, in addition to the regular burnt offering with its grain offering, and their drink offerings.

²⁰" 'On the third day prepare eleven bulls, two rams and fourteen male lambs a year old, all without defect. ²¹With the bulls, rams and lambs, prepare their grain offerings and drink offerings according to the number specified. ²²Include one male goat as a sin offering, in addition to the regular burnt offering with its grain offering and drink offering.

²³" 'On the fourth day prepare ten bulls, two rams and fourteen male lambs a year old, all without defect. ²⁴With the bulls, rams and lambs, prepare their grain offerings and drink offerings according to the number specified. ²⁵Include one male goat as a sin offering, in addition to the regular burnt offering with its grain offering and drink offering.

²⁶" 'On the fifth day prepare nine bulls, two rams and fourteen male lambs a year old, all without defect. ²⁷With the bulls, rams and lambs, prepare their grain offerings and drink offerings according to the number specified. ²⁸Include one male goat as a sin offering, in addition to the regular burnt offering with its grain offering and drink offering.

²⁹" 'On the sixth day prepare eight bulls, two rams and fourteen male lambs a year old, all without defect. ³⁰With the bulls, rams and lambs, prepare their grain offerings and drink offerings according to the number specified. ³¹Include one male goat as a sin offering, in addition to the regular burnt offering with its grain offering and drink offering.

³²" 'On the seventh day prepare seven bulls, two rams and fourteen male lambs a year old, all without defect. ³³With the bulls, rams and lambs, prepare their grain offerings and drink offerings according to the number specified. ³⁴Include one male goat as a sin offering, in addition to the regular burnt offering with its grain offering and drink offering.

³⁵" 'On the eighth day hold an assembly and do no regular work. ³⁶Present an offering made by fire as an aroma pleasing to the LORD, a burnt offering of one bull, one ram and seven male lambs a year old, all without defect. ³⁷With the bull, the ram and the lambs, prepare their grain offerings and drink offerings according to the number specified. ³⁸Include one male goat as a sin offering, in addition to the regular burnt offering with its grain offering and drink offering.

ᵃ7 Or must fast

³⁹" 'In addition to what you vow and your freewill offerings, prepare these for the L<small>ORD</small> at your appointed feasts: your burnt offerings, grain offerings, drink offerings and fellowship offerings.*a*' "

⁴⁰Moses told the Israelites all that the L<small>ORD</small> commanded him.

Vows Moses said to the heads of the tribes of Israel: "This is what the L<small>ORD</small> commands: ²When a man makes a vow to the L<small>ORD</small> or takes an oath to obligate himself by a pledge, he must not break his word but must do everything he said.

³"When a young woman still living in her father's house makes a vow to the L<small>ORD</small> or obligates herself by a pledge ⁴and her father hears about her vow or pledge but says nothing to her, then all her vows and every pledge by which she obligated herself will stand. ⁵But if her father forbids her when he hears about it, none of her vows or the pledges by which she obligated herself will stand; the L<small>ORD</small> will release her because her father has forbidden her.

⁶"If she marries after she makes a vow or after her lips utter a rash promise by which she obligates herself ⁷and her husband hears about it but says nothing to her, then her vows or the pledges by which she obligated herself will stand. ⁸But if her husband forbids her when he hears about it, he nullifies the vow that obligates her or the rash promise by which she obligates herself, and the L<small>ORD</small> will release her.

⁹"Any vow or obligation taken by a widow or divorced woman will be binding on her.

¹⁰"If a woman living with her husband makes a vow or obligates herself by a pledge under oath ¹¹and her husband hears about it but says nothing to her and does not forbid her, then all her vows or the pledges by which she obligated herself will stand. ¹²But if her husband nullifies them when he hears about them, then none of the vows or pledges that came from her lips will stand. Her husband has nullified them, and the L<small>ORD</small> will release her. ¹³Her husband may confirm or nullify any vow she makes or any sworn pledge to deny herself. ¹⁴But if her husband says nothing to her about it from day to day, then he confirms all her vows or the pledges binding on her. He confirms them by saying nothing to her when he hears about them. ¹⁵If, however, he nullifies them some time after he hears about them, then he is responsible for her guilt."

¹⁶These are the regulations the L<small>ORD</small> gave Moses concerning relationships between a man and his wife, and between a father and his young daughter still living in his house.

Vengeance on the Midianites The L<small>ORD</small> said to Moses, ²"Take vengeance on the Midianites for the Israelites. After that, you will be gathered to your people."

³So Moses said to the people, "Arm some of your men to go to war against the Midianites and to carry out the L<small>ORD</small>'s vengeance on them. ⁴Send into battle a thousand men from each of the tribes of Israel." ⁵So twelve thousand men armed for battle, a thousand from each tribe, were supplied from the clans of Israel.

NUMBERS 30

Some promises are hard to keep. You say, "I'll be there. I promise." And then your mom makes you stay home. Or you say, "I'll do that tomorrow. I promise." And then you completely forget about it. Sometimes your broken promises are serious. Sometimes they're no big deal. But making a promise to God is a serious thing. When you make God a promise, whether to give regularly, to read the Bible, to witness to a particular person, whatever—be sure to do what you say.

a39 Traditionally *peace offerings*

⁶Moses sent them into battle, a thousand from each tribe, along with Phinehas son of Eleazar, the priest, who took with him articles from the sanctuary and the trumpets for signaling.

⁷They fought against Midian, as the LORD commanded Moses, and killed every man. ⁸Among their victims were Evi, Rekem, Zur, Hur and Reba—the five kings of Midian. They also killed Balaam son of Beor with the sword. ⁹The Israelites captured the Midianite women and children and took all the Midianite herds, flocks and goods as plunder. ¹⁰They burned all the towns where the Midianites had settled, as well as all their camps. ¹¹They took all the plunder and spoils, including the people and animals, ¹²and brought the captives, spoils and plunder to Moses and Eleazar the priest and the Israelite assembly at their camp on the plains of Moab, by the Jordan across from Jericho.ᵃ

¹³Moses, Eleazar the priest and all the leaders of the community went to meet them outside the camp. ¹⁴Moses was angry with the officers of the army—the commanders of thousands and commanders of hundreds—who returned from the battle.

¹⁵"Have you allowed all the women to live?" he asked them. ¹⁶"They were the ones who followed Balaam's advice and were the means of turning the Israelites away from the LORD in what happened at Peor, so that a plague struck the LORD's people. ¹⁷Now kill all the boys. And kill every woman who has slept with a man, ¹⁸but save for yourselves every girl who has never slept with a man.

¹⁹"All of you who have killed anyone or touched anyone who was killed must stay outside the camp seven days. On the third and seventh days you must purify yourselves and your captives. ²⁰Purify every garment as well as everything made of leather, goat hair or wood."

²¹Then Eleazar the priest said to the soldiers who had gone into battle, "This is the requirement of the law that the LORD gave Moses: ²²Gold, silver, bronze, iron, tin, lead ²³and anything else that can withstand fire must be put through the fire, and then it will be clean. But it must also be purified with the water of cleansing. And whatever cannot withstand fire must be put through that water. ²⁴On the seventh day wash your clothes and you will be clean. Then you may come into the camp."

Dividing the Spoils   ²⁵The LORD said to Moses, ²⁶"You and Eleazar the priest and the family heads of the community are to count all the people and animals that were captured. ²⁷Divide the spoils between the soldiers who took part in the battle and the rest of the community. ²⁸From the soldiers who fought in the battle, set apart as tribute for the LORD one out of every five hundred, whether persons, cattle, donkeys, sheep or goats. ²⁹Take this tribute from their half share and give it to Eleazar the priest as the LORD's part. ³⁰From the Israelites' half, select one out of every fifty, whether persons, cattle, donkeys, sheep, goats or other animals. Give them to the Levites, who are responsible for the care of the LORD's tabernacle." ³¹So Moses and Eleazar the priest did as the LORD commanded Moses.

³²The plunder remaining from the spoils that the soldiers took was 675,000 sheep, ³³72,000 cattle, ³⁴61,000 donkeys ³⁵and 32,000 women who had never slept with a man. ³⁶The half share of those who fought in the battle was:

337,500 sheep, ³⁷of which the tribute for the LORD was 675;
³⁸36,000 cattle, of which the tribute for the LORD was 72;
³⁹30,500 donkeys, of which the tribute for the LORD was 61;
⁴⁰16,000 people, of which the tribute for the LORD was 32.

ᵃ12 Hebrew *Jordan of Jericho*; possibly an ancient name for the Jordan River

⁴¹Moses gave the tribute to Eleazar the priest as the LORD's part, as the LORD commanded Moses.

⁴²The half belonging to the Israelites, which Moses set apart from that of the fighting men— ⁴³the community's half—was 337,500 sheep, ⁴⁴36,000 cattle, ⁴⁵30,500 donkeys ⁴⁶and 16,000 people. ⁴⁷From the Israelites' half, Moses selected one out of every fifty persons and animals, as the LORD commanded him, and gave them to the Levites, who were responsible for the care of the LORD's tabernacle.

⁴⁸Then the officers who were over the units of the army—the commanders of thousands and commanders of hundreds—went to Moses ⁴⁹and said to him, "Your servants have counted the soldiers under our command, and not one is missing. ⁵⁰So we have brought as an offering to the LORD the gold articles each of us acquired—armlets, bracelets, signet rings, earrings and necklaces—to make atonement for ourselves before the LORD."

⁵¹Moses and Eleazar the priest accepted from them the gold—all the crafted articles. ⁵²All the gold from the commanders of thousands and commanders of hundreds that Moses and Eleazar presented as a gift to the LORD weighed 16,750 shekels.ª ⁵³Each soldier had taken plunder for himself. ⁵⁴Moses and Eleazar the priest accepted the gold from the commanders of thousands and commanders of hundreds and brought it into the Tent of Meeting as a memorial for the Israelites before the LORD.

32 *The Transjordan Tribes* The Reubenites and Gadites, who had very large herds and flocks, saw that the lands of Jazer and Gilead were suitable for livestock. ²So they came to Moses and Eleazar the priest and to the leaders of the community, and said, ³"Ataroth, Dibon, Jazer, Nimrah, Heshbon, Elealeh, Sebam, Nebo and Beon— ⁴the land the LORD subdued before the people of Israel—are suitable for livestock, and your servants have livestock. ⁵If we have found favor in your eyes," they said, "let this land be given to your servants as our possession. Do not make us cross the Jordan."

⁶Moses said to the Gadites and Reubenites, "Shall your countrymen go to war while you sit here? ⁷Why do you discourage the Israelites from going over into the land the LORD has given them? ⁸This is what your fathers did when I sent them from Kadesh Barnea to look over the land. ⁹After they went up to the Valley of Eshcol and viewed the land, they discouraged the Israelites from entering the land the LORD had given them. ¹⁰The LORD's anger was aroused that day and he swore this oath: ¹¹'Because they have not followed me wholeheartedly, not one of the men twenty years old or more who came up out of Egypt will see the land I promised on oath to Abraham, Isaac and Jacob— ¹²not one except Caleb son of Jephunneh the Kenizzite and Joshua son of Nun, for they followed the LORD wholeheartedly.' ¹³The LORD's anger burned against Israel and he made them wander in the desert forty years, until the whole generation of those who had done evil in his sight was gone.

NUMBERS 32:1-24

When your youth group has a service project, do you show up? How about when your youth group goes out visiting? Or delivers Christmas baskets? Can others count on you to do your share? The Israelite tribes who settled east of the Jordan River didn't just settle there and stay. First they crossed to the west side of the river and helped their fellow Israelites conquer that land. Whenever something important is accomplished, it's because everyone contributes and does his or her fair share. Your youth group needs your support.

Direct Line

ª52 That is, about 420 pounds (about 190 kilograms)

[14]"And here you are, a brood of sinners, standing in the place of your fathers and making the LORD even more angry with Israel. [15]If you turn away from following him, he will again leave all this people in the desert, and you will be the cause of their destruction."

[16]Then they came up to him and said, "We would like to build pens here for our livestock and cities for our women and children. [17]But we are ready to arm ourselves and go ahead of the Israelites until we have brought them to their place. Meanwhile our women and children will live in fortified cities, for protection from the inhabitants of the land. [18]We will not return to our homes until every Israelite has received his inheritance. [19]We will not receive any inheritance with them on the other side of the Jordan, because our inheritance has come to us on the east side of the Jordan."

[20]Then Moses said to them, "If you will do this—if you will arm yourselves before the LORD for battle, [21]and if all of you will go armed over the Jordan before the LORD until he has driven his enemies out before him— [22]then when the land is subdued before the LORD, you may return and be free from your obligation to the LORD and to Israel. And this land will be your possession before the LORD.

[23]"But if you fail to do this, you will be sinning against the LORD; and you may be sure that your sin will find you out. [24]Build cities for your women and children, and pens for your flocks, but do what you have promised."

[25]The Gadites and Reubenites said to Moses, "We your servants will do as our lord commands. [26]Our children and wives, our flocks and herds will remain here in the cities of Gilead. [27]But your servants, every man armed for battle, will cross over to fight before the LORD, just as our lord says."

[28]Then Moses gave orders about them to Eleazar the priest and Joshua son of Nun and to the family heads of the Israelite tribes. [29]He said to them, "If the Gadites and Reubenites, every man armed for battle, cross over the Jordan with you before the LORD, then when the land is subdued before you, give them the land of Gilead as their possession. [30]But if they do not cross over with you armed, they must accept their possession with you in Canaan."

[31]The Gadites and Reubenites answered, "Your servants will do what the LORD has said. [32]We will cross over before the LORD into Canaan armed, but the property we inherit will be on this side of the Jordan."

[33]Then Moses gave to the Gadites, the Reubenites and the half-tribe of Manasseh son of Joseph the kingdom of Sihon king of the Amorites and the kingdom of Og king of Bashan—the whole land with its cities and the territory around them.

[34]The Gadites built up Dibon, Ataroth, Aroer, [35]Atroth Shophan, Jazer, Jogbehah, [36]Beth Nimrah and Beth Haran as fortified cities, and built pens for their flocks. [37]And the Reubenites rebuilt Heshbon, Elealeh and Kiriathaim, [38]as well as Nebo and Baal Meon (these names were changed) and Sibmah. They gave names to the cities they rebuilt.

[39]The descendants of Makir son of Manasseh went to Gilead, captured it and drove out the Amorites who were there. [40]So Moses gave Gilead to the Makirites, the descendants of Manasseh, and they settled there. [41]Jair, a descendant of Manasseh, captured their settlements and called them Havvoth Jair.[a] [42]And Nobah captured Kenath and its surrounding settlements and called it Nobah after himself.

Stages in Israel's Journey Here are the stages in the journey of the Israelites when they came out of Egypt by divisions under the leadership of Moses and Aaron. [2]At the LORD's command Moses recorded the stages in their journey. This is their journey by stages:

---

[a]41 Or them the settlements of Jair

³The Israelites set out from Rameses on the fifteenth day of the first month, the day after the Passover. They marched out boldly in full view of all the Egyptians, ⁴who were burying all their firstborn, whom the Lord had struck down among them; for the Lord had brought judgment on their gods.

⁵The Israelites left Rameses and camped at Succoth.

⁶They left Succoth and camped at Etham, on the edge of the desert.

⁷They left Etham, turned back to Pi Hahiroth, to the east of Baal Zephon, and camped near Migdol.

⁸They left Pi Hahiroth*ᵃ* and passed through the sea into the desert, and when they had traveled for three days in the Desert of Etham, they camped at Marah.

⁹They left Marah and went to Elim, where there were twelve springs and seventy palm trees, and they camped there.

¹⁰They left Elim and camped by the Red Sea.*ᵇ*

¹¹They left the Red Sea and camped in the Desert of Sin.

¹²They left the Desert of Sin and camped at Dophkah.

¹³They left Dophkah and camped at Alush.

¹⁴They left Alush and camped at Rephidim, where there was no water for the people to drink.

¹⁵They left Rephidim and camped in the Desert of Sinai.

¹⁶They left the Desert of Sinai and camped at Kibroth Hattaavah.

¹⁷They left Kibroth Hattaavah and camped at Hazeroth.

¹⁸They left Hazeroth and camped at Rithmah.

¹⁹They left Rithmah and camped at Rimmon Perez.

²⁰They left Rimmon Perez and camped at Libnah.

²¹They left Libnah and camped at Rissah.

²²They left Rissah and camped at Kehelathah.

²³They left Kehelathah and camped at Mount Shepher.

²⁴They left Mount Shepher and camped at Haradah.

²⁵They left Haradah and camped at Makheloth.

²⁶They left Makheloth and camped at Tahath.

²⁷They left Tahath and camped at Terah.

²⁸They left Terah and camped at Mithcah.

²⁹They left Mithcah and camped at Hashmonah.

³⁰They left Hashmonah and camped at Moseroth.

³¹They left Moseroth and camped at Bene Jaakan.

³²They left Bene Jaakan and camped at Hor Haggidgad.

³³They left Hor Haggidgad and camped at Jotbathah.

³⁴They left Jotbathah and camped at Abronah.

³⁵They left Abronah and camped at Ezion Geber.

³⁶They left Ezion Geber and camped at Kadesh, in the Desert of Zin.

³⁷They left Kadesh and camped at Mount Hor, on the border of Edom. ³⁸At the Lord's command Aaron the priest went up Mount Hor, where he died on the first day of the fifth month of the fortieth year after the Israelites came out of Egypt. ³⁹Aaron was a hundred and twenty-three years old when he died on Mount Hor.

⁴⁰The Canaanite king of Arad, who lived in the Negev of Canaan, heard that the Israelites were coming.

⁴¹They left Mount Hor and camped at Zalmonah.

⁴²They left Zalmonah and camped at Punon.

⁴³They left Punon and camped at Oboth.

I have given you the land to possess (Numbers 33:53).

ᵃ8 Many manuscripts of the Masoretic Text, Samaritan Pentateuch and Vulgate; most manuscripts of the Masoretic Text *left from before Hahiroth*   *ᵇ10* Hebrew *Yam Suph;* that is, Sea of Reeds; also in verse 11

⁴⁴They left Oboth and camped at Iye Abarim, on the border of Moab.
⁴⁵They left Iyim*a* and camped at Dibon Gad.
⁴⁶They left Dibon Gad and camped at Almon Diblathaim.
⁴⁷They left Almon Diblathaim and camped in the mountains of Abarim, near Nebo.
⁴⁸They left the mountains of Abarim and camped on the plains of Moab by the Jordan across from Jericho.*b* ⁴⁹There on the plains of Moab they camped along the Jordan from Beth Jeshimoth to Abel Shittim.

⁵⁰On the plains of Moab by the Jordan across from Jericho the Lord said to Moses, ⁵¹"Speak to the Israelites and say to them: 'When you cross the Jordan into Canaan, ⁵²drive out all the inhabitants of the land before you. Destroy all their carved images and their cast idols, and demolish all their high places. ⁵³Take possession of the land and settle in it, for I have given you the land to possess. ⁵⁴Distribute the land by lot, according to your clans. To a larger group give a larger inheritance, and to a smaller group a smaller one. Whatever falls to them by lot will be theirs. Distribute it according to your ancestral tribes.

⁵⁵" 'But if you do not drive out the inhabitants of the land, those you allow to remain will become barbs in your eyes and thorns in your sides. They will give you trouble in the land where you will live. ⁵⁶And then I will do to you what I plan to do to them.' "

34 **Boundaries of Canaan** The Lord said to Moses, ²"Command the Israelites and say to them: 'When you enter Canaan, the land that will be allotted to you as an inheritance will have these boundaries:

³" 'Your southern side will include some of the Desert of Zin along the border of Edom. On the east, your southern boundary will start from the end of the Salt Sea,*c* ⁴cross south of Scorpion*d* Pass, continue on to Zin and go south of Kadesh Barnea. Then it will go to Hazar Addar and over to Azmon, ⁵where it will turn, join the Wadi of Egypt and end at the Sea.*e*

⁶" 'Your western boundary will be the coast of the Great Sea. This will be your boundary on the west.

⁷" 'For your northern boundary, run a line from the Great Sea to Mount Hor ⁸and from Mount Hor to Lebo*f* Hamath. Then the boundary will go to Zedad, ⁹continue to Ziphron and end at Hazar Enan. This will be your boundary on the north.

¹⁰" 'For your eastern boundary, run a line from Hazar Enan to Shepham. ¹¹The boundary will go down from Shepham to Riblah on the east side of Ain and continue along the slopes east of the Sea of Kinnereth.*g* ¹²Then the boundary will go down along the Jordan and end at the Salt Sea.

" 'This will be your land, with its boundaries on every side.' "

¹³Moses commanded the Israelites: "Assign this land by lot as an inheritance. The Lord has ordered that it be given to the nine and a half tribes, ¹⁴because the families of the tribe of Reuben, the tribe of Gad and the half-tribe of Manasseh have received their inheritance. ¹⁵These two and a half tribes have received their inheritance on the east side of the Jordan of Jericho,*h* toward the sunrise."

¹⁶The Lord said to Moses, ¹⁷"These are the names of the men who are to assign the land for you as an inheritance: Eleazar the priest and Joshua son of Nun. ¹⁸And appoint one leader from each tribe to help assign the land. ¹⁹These are their names:

---

a45 That is, Iye Abarim *b48* Hebrew *Jordan of Jericho,* possibly an ancient name for the Jordan River; also in verse 50 *c3* That is, the Dead Sea; also in verse 12 *d4* Hebrew *Akrabbim* *e5* That is, the Mediterranean; also in verses 6 and 7 *f8* Or *to the entrance to* *g11* That is, Galilee *h15* Jordan of Jericho was possibly an ancient name for the Jordan River.

Caleb son of Jephunneh,
   from the tribe of Judah;
20 Shemuel son of Ammihud,
   from the tribe of Simeon;
21 Elidad son of Kislon,
   from the tribe of Benjamin;
22 Bukki son of Jogli,
   the leader from the tribe of Dan;
23 Hanniel son of Ephod,
   the leader from the tribe of Manasseh son of Joseph;
24 Kemuel son of Shiphtan,
   the leader from the tribe of Ephraim son of Joseph;
25 Elizaphan son of Parnach,
   the leader from the tribe of Zebulun;
26 Paltiel son of Azzan,
   the leader from the tribe of Issachar;
27 Ahihud son of Shelomi,
   the leader from the tribe of Asher;
28 Pedahel son of Ammihud,
   the leader from the tribe of Naphtali."

29 These are the men the Lord commanded to assign the inheritance to the Israelites in the land of Canaan.

Towns for the Levites   On the plains of Moab by the Jordan across from Jericho,ᵃ the Lord said to Moses, 2"Command the Israelites to give the Levites towns to live in from the inheritance the Israelites will possess. And give them pasturelands around the towns. 3Then they will have towns to live in and pasturelands for their cattle, flocks and all their other livestock.

4"The pasturelands around the towns that you give the Levites will extend out fifteen hundred feetᵇ from the town wall. 5Outside the town, measure three thousand feetᶜ on the east side, three thousand on the south side, three thousand on the west and three thousand on the north, with the town in the center. They will have this area as pastureland for the towns.

Cities of Refuge   6"Six of the towns you give the Levites will be cities of refuge, to which a person who has killed someone may flee. In addition, give them forty-two other towns. 7In all you must give the Levites forty-eight towns, together with their pasturelands. 8The towns you give the Levites from the land the Israelites possess are to be given in proportion to the inheritance of each tribe: Take many towns from a tribe that has many, but few from one that has few."

9Then the Lord said to Moses: 10"Speak to the Israelites and say to them: 'When you cross the Jordan into Canaan, 11select some towns to be your cities of refuge, to which a person who has killed someone accidentally may flee. 12They will be places of refuge from the avenger, so that a person accused of murder may not die before he stands trial before the assembly. 13These six towns you give will be your cities of refuge. 14Give three on this side of the Jordan and three in Canaan as cities of refuge. 15These six towns will be a place of refuge for Israelites, aliens and any other people living among them, so that anyone who has killed another accidentally can flee there.

NUMBERS 35

QU ZZER

Q: What was a "city of refuge"?

BONUS: Who wasn't safe there?

Answers on page 206

ᵃ1 Hebrew *Jordan of Jericho;* possibly an ancient name for the Jordan River   ᵇ4 Hebrew *a thousand cubits* (about 450 meters)   ᶜ5 Hebrew *two thousand cubits* (about 900 meters)

¹⁶ 'If a man strikes someone with an iron object so that he dies, he is a murderer; the murderer shall be put to death. ¹⁷Or if anyone has a stone in his hand that could kill, and he strikes someone so that he dies, he is a murderer; the murderer shall be put to death. ¹⁸Or if anyone has a wooden object in his hand that could kill, and he hits someone so that he dies, he is a murderer; the murderer shall be put to death. ¹⁹The avenger of blood shall put the murderer to death; when he meets him, he shall put him to death. ²⁰If anyone with malice aforethought shoves another or throws something at him intentionally so that he dies ²¹or if in hostility he hits him with his fist so that he dies, that person shall be put to death; he is a murderer. The avenger of blood shall put the murderer to death when he meets him.

²² 'But if without hostility someone suddenly shoves another or throws something at him unintentionally ²³or, without seeing him, drops a stone on him that could kill him, and he dies, then since he was not his enemy and he did not intend to harm him, ²⁴the assembly must judge between him and the avenger of blood according to these regulations. ²⁵The assembly must protect the one accused of murder from the avenger of blood and send him back to the city of refuge to which he fled. He must stay there until the death of the high priest, who was anointed with the holy oil.

²⁶ 'But if the accused ever goes outside the limits of the city of refuge to which he has fled ²⁷and the avenger of blood finds him outside the city, the avenger of blood may kill the accused without being guilty of murder. ²⁸The accused must stay in his city of refuge until the death of the high priest; only after the death of the high priest may he return to his own property.

²⁹ 'These are to be legal requirements for you throughout the generations to come, wherever you live.

³⁰ 'Anyone who kills a person is to be put to death as a murderer only on the testimony of witnesses. But no one is to be put to death on the testimony of only one witness.

³¹ 'Do not accept a ransom for the life of a murderer, who deserves to die. He must surely be put to death.

³² 'Do not accept a ransom for anyone who has fled to a city of refuge and so allow him to go back and live on his own land before the death of the high priest.

³³ 'Do not pollute the land where you are. Bloodshed pollutes the land, and atonement cannot be made for the land on which blood has been shed, except by the blood of the one who shed it. ³⁴Do not defile the land where you live and where I dwell, for I, the LORD, dwell among the Israelites.' "

36 *Inheritance of Zelophehad's Daughters* The family heads of the clan of Gilead son of Makir, the son of Manasseh, who were from the clans of the descendants of Joseph, came and spoke before Moses and the leaders, the heads of the Israelite families. ²They said, "When the LORD commanded my lord to give the land as an inheritance to the Israelites by lot, he ordered you to give the inheritance of our brother Zelophehad to his daughters. ³Now suppose they marry men from other Israelite tribes; then their inheritance will be taken from our ancestral inheritance and added to that of the tribe they marry into. And so part of the inheritance allotted to us will be taken away. ⁴When the Year of Jubilee for the Israelites comes, their inheritance will be added to that of the tribe into which they marry, and their property will be taken from the tribal inheritance of our forefathers."

⁵Then at the LORD's command Moses gave this order to the Israelites: "What the tribe of the descendants of Joseph is saying is right. ⁶This is what the LORD commands for Zelophehad's daughters: They may marry anyone they please as long as they marry within the tribal clan of their father. ⁷No inheritance in Israel is to pass from tribe to tribe, for every Israelite shall keep the

tribal land inherited from his forefathers. [8]Every daughter who inherits land in any Israelite tribe must marry someone in her father's tribal clan, so that every Israelite will possess the inheritance of his fathers. [9]No inheritance may pass from tribe to tribe, for each Israelite tribe is to keep the land it inherits."

[10]So Zelophehad's daughters did as the LORD commanded Moses. [11]Zelophehad's daughters—Mahlah, Tirzah, Hoglah, Milcah and Noah—married their cousins on their father's side. [12]They married within the clans of the descendants of Manasseh son of Joseph, and their inheritance remained in their father's clan and tribe.

[13]These are the commands and regulations the LORD gave through Moses to the Israelites on the plains of Moab by the Jordan across from Jericho.[a]

---

[a]13 Hebrew *Jordan of Jericho;* possibly an ancient name for the Jordan River

Introduction

to the

book of Deuteronomy

SAY IT!

Some things are important enough to say two or three times. Like reminding your parents you have plans for Friday night. Or reminding them that they promised to take you to the mall.

Deuteronomy means "second law." This book contains teachings Moses felt were important enough to repeat. Sort of like a TV rerun. Deuteronomy repeats the Ten Commandments. And it reminds you that love prompted God to choose his people. And love prompted God to give them his law. Why is that important? Because rules made by someone who loves you will have your best interest at heart.

Fundamentals

You can prove that you are loved (Deuteronomy 2:7).

Loving God pays big dividends (Deuteronomy 11).

Ever think about playing with a Ouija board (Deuteronomy 18:10-12)?

What is the best reason to bring offerings to God (Deuteronomy 26:8-11)?

FAST FACTS

At this time Israel was camped just outside Canaan (the promised land).

Moses was 120 years old when he wrote Deuteronomy. Jesus quoted this book three times when tempted by Satan (Matthew 4).

Deuteronomy is quoted about 80 times in the New Testament.

Jewish rabbis honored Deuteronomy as "five-fifths of the law."

1

The Command to Leave Horeb These are the words Moses spoke to all Israel in the desert east of the Jordan—that is, in the Arabah—opposite Suph, between Paran and Tophel, Laban, Hazeroth and Dizahab. ²(It takes eleven days to go from Horeb to Kadesh Barnea by the Mount Seir road.)

³In the fortieth year, on the first day of the eleventh month, Moses proclaimed to the Israelites all that the Lord had commanded him concerning them. ⁴This was after he had defeated Sihon king of the Amorites, who reigned in Heshbon, and at Edrei had defeated Og king of Bashan, who reigned in Ashtaroth.

⁵East of the Jordan in the territory of Moab, Moses began to expound this law, saying:

⁶The Lord our God said to us at Horeb, "You have stayed long enough at this mountain. ⁷Break camp and advance into the hill country of the Amorites; go to all the neighboring peoples in the Arabah, in the mountains, in the western foothills, in the Negev and along the coast, to the land of the Canaanites and to Lebanon, as far as the great river, the Euphrates. ⁸See, I have given you this land. Go in and take possession of the land that the Lord swore he would give to your fathers—to Abraham, Isaac and Jacob—and to their descendants after them."

The Appointment of Leaders ⁹At that time I said to you, "You are too heavy a burden for me to carry alone. ¹⁰The Lord your God has increased your numbers so that today you are as many as the stars in the sky. ¹¹May the Lord, the God of your fathers, increase you a thousand times and bless you as he has promised! ¹²But how can I bear your problems and your burdens and your disputes all by myself? ¹³Choose some wise, understanding and respected men from each of your tribes, and I will set them over you."

¹⁴You answered me, "What you propose to do is good."

¹⁵So I took the leading men of your tribes, wise and respected men, and appointed them to have authority over you—as commanders of thousands, of hundreds, of fifties and of tens and as tribal officials. ¹⁶And I charged your judges at that time: Hear the disputes between your brothers and judge fairly, whether the case is between brother Israelites or between one of them and an alien. ¹⁷Do not show partiality in judging; hear both small and great alike. Do not be afraid of any man, for judgment belongs to God. Bring me any case too hard for you, and I will hear it. ¹⁸And at that time I told you everything you were to do.

Spies Sent Out ¹⁹Then, as the Lord our God commanded us, we set out from Horeb and went toward the hill country of the Amorites through all that vast and dreadful desert that you have seen, and so we reached Kadesh Barnea. ²⁰Then I said to you, "You have reached the hill country of the Amorites, which the Lord our God is giving us. ²¹See, the Lord your God has given you the land. Go up and take possession of it as the Lord, the God of your fathers, told you. Do not be afraid; do not be discouraged."

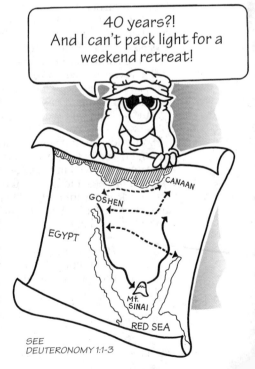

SEE
DEUTERONOMY 1:1-3

²²Then all of you came to me and said, "Let us send men ahead to spy out the land for us and bring back a report about the route we are to take and the towns we will come to."

²³The idea seemed good to me; so I selected twelve of you, one man from each tribe. ²⁴They left and went up into the hill country, and came to the Valley of Eshcol and explored it. ²⁵Taking with them some of the fruit of the land, they brought it down to us and reported, "It is a good land that the LORD our God is giving us."

Rebellion Against the LORD   ²⁶But you were unwilling to go up; you rebelled against the command of the LORD your God. ²⁷You grumbled in your tents and said, "The LORD hates us; so he brought us out of Egypt to deliver us into the hands of the Amorites to destroy us. ²⁸Where can we go? Our brothers have made us lose heart. They say, 'The people are stronger and taller than we are; the cities are large, with walls up to the sky. We even saw the Anakites there.' "

²⁹Then I said to you, "Do not be terrified; do not be afraid of them. ³⁰The LORD your God, who is going before you, will fight for you, as he did for you in Egypt, before your very eyes, ³¹and in the desert. There you saw how the LORD your God carried you, as a father carries his son, all the way you went until you reached this place."

³²In spite of this, you did not trust in the LORD your God, ³³who went ahead of you on your journey, in fire by night and in a cloud by day, to search out places for you to camp and to show you the way you should go.

³⁴When the LORD heard what you said, he was angry and solemnly swore: ³⁵"Not a man of this evil generation shall see the good land I swore to give your forefathers, ³⁶except Caleb son of Jephunneh. He will see it, and I will give him and his descendants the land he set his feet on, because he followed the LORD wholeheartedly."

³⁷Because of you the LORD became angry with me also and said, "You shall not enter it, either. ³⁸But your assistant, Joshua son of Nun, will enter it. Encourage him, because he will lead Israel to inherit it. ³⁹And the little ones that you said would be taken captive, your children who do not yet know good from bad—they will enter the land. I will give it to them and they will take possession of it. ⁴⁰But as for you, turn around and set out toward the desert along the route to the Red Sea.ᵃ"

⁴¹Then you replied, "We have sinned against the LORD. We will go up and fight, as the LORD our God commanded us." So every one of you put on his weapons, thinking it easy to go up into the hill country.

⁴²But the LORD said to me, "Tell them, 'Do not go up and fight, because I will not be with you. You will be defeated by your enemies.' "

⁴³So I told you, but you would not listen. You rebelled against the LORD's command and in your arrogance you marched up into the hill country. ⁴⁴The Amorites who lived in those hills came out against you; they chased you like a swarm of bees and beat you down from Seir all the way to Hormah. ⁴⁵You came back and wept before the LORD, but he paid no attention to your weeping and turned a deaf ear to you. ⁴⁶And so you stayed in Kadesh many days— all the time you spent there.

Wanderings in the Desert   Then we turned back and set out toward the desert along the route to the Red Sea,ᵃ as the LORD had directed me. For a long time we made our way around the hill country of Seir.

²Then the LORD said to me, ³"You have made your way around this hill country long enough; now turn north. ⁴Give the people these orders: 'You are about to pass through the territory of your brothers the descendants of

---

ᵃ40,1 Hebrew *Yam Suph*; that is, Sea of Reeds

Esau, who live in Seir. They will be afraid of you, but be very careful. ⁵Do not provoke them to war, for I will not give you any of their land, not even enough to put your foot on. I have given Esau the hill country of Seir as his own. ⁶You are to pay them in silver for the food you eat and the water you drink.' "

⁷The LORD your God has blessed you in all the work of your hands. He has watched over your journey through this vast desert. These forty years the LORD your God has been with you, and you have not lacked anything.

⁸So we went on past our brothers the descendants of Esau, who live in Seir. We turned from the Arabah road, which comes up from Elath and Ezion Geber, and traveled along the desert road of Moab.

⁹Then the LORD said to me, "Do not harass the Moabites or provoke them to war, for I will not give you any part of their land. I have given Ar to the descendants of Lot as a possession."

¹⁰(The Emites used to live there—a people strong and numerous, and as tall as the Anakites. ¹¹Like the Anakites, they too were considered Rephaites, but the Moabites called them Emites. ¹²Horites used to live in Seir, but the descendants of Esau drove them out. They destroyed the Horites from before them and settled in their place, just as Israel did in the land the LORD gave them as their possession.)

¹³And the LORD said, "Now get up and cross the Zered Valley." So we crossed the valley.

¹⁴Thirty-eight years passed from the time we left Kadesh Barnea until we crossed the Zered Valley. By then, that entire generation of fighting men had perished from the camp, as the LORD had sworn to them. ¹⁵The LORD's hand was against them until he had completely eliminated them from the camp.

¹⁶Now when the last of these fighting men among the people had died, ¹⁷the LORD said to me, ¹⁸"Today you are to pass by the region of Moab at Ar. ¹⁹When you come to the Ammonites, do not harass them or provoke them to war, for I will not give you possession of any land belonging to the Ammonites. I have given it as a possession to the descendants of Lot."

²⁰(That too was considered a land of the Rephaites, who used to live there; but the Ammonites called them Zamzummites. ²¹They were a people strong and numerous, and as tall as the Anakites. The LORD destroyed them from before the Ammonites, who drove them out and settled in their place. ²²The LORD had done the same for the descendants of Esau, who lived in Seir, when he destroyed the Horites from before them. They drove them out and have lived in their place to this day. ²³And as for the Avvites who lived in villages as far as Gaza, the Caphtorites coming out from Caphtor*ᵃ* destroyed them and settled in their place.)

Defeat of Sihon King of Heshbon   ²⁴"Set out now and cross the Arnon Gorge. See, I have given into your hand Sihon the Amorite, king of Heshbon, and his country. Begin to take possession of it and engage him in battle. ²⁵This very day I will begin to put the terror and fear of you on all the nations under heaven. They will hear reports of you and will tremble and be in anguish because of you."

²⁶From the desert of Kedemoth I sent messengers to Sihon king of Heshbon offering peace and saying, ²⁷"Let us pass through your country. We will stay on the main road; we will not turn aside to the right or to the left. ²⁸Sell us food to eat and water to drink for their price in silver. Only let us pass through on foot— ²⁹as the descendants of Esau, who live in Seir, and the Moabites, who live in Ar, did for us—until we cross the Jordan into the land the

> The LORD your God has blessed you in all the work of your hands (Deuteronomy 2:7).

LORD our God is giving us." ³⁰But Sihon king of Heshbon refused to let us pass through. For the LORD your God had made his spirit stubborn and his heart obstinate in order to give him into your hands, as he has now done.

³¹The LORD said to me, "See, I have begun to deliver Sihon and his country over to you. Now begin to conquer and possess his land."

³²When Sihon and all his army came out to meet us in battle at Jahaz, ³³the LORD our God delivered him over to us and we struck him down, together with his sons and his whole army. ³⁴At that time we took all his towns and completely destroyed*a* them—men, women and children. We left no survivors. ³⁵But the livestock and the plunder from the towns we had captured we carried off for ourselves. ³⁶From Aroer on the rim of the Arnon Gorge, and from the town in the gorge, even as far as Gilead, not one town was too strong for us. The LORD our God gave us all of them. ³⁷But in accordance with the command of the LORD our God, you did not encroach on any of the land of the Ammonites, neither the land along the course of the Jabbok nor that around the towns in the hills.

Defeat of Og King of Bashan Next we turned and went up along the road toward Bashan, and Og king of Bashan with his whole army marched out to meet us in battle at Edrei. ²The LORD said to me, "Do not be afraid of him, for I have handed him over to you with his whole army and his land. Do to him what you did to Sihon king of the Amorites, who reigned in Heshbon."

³So the LORD our God also gave into our hands Og king of Bashan and all his army. We struck them down, leaving no survivors. ⁴At that time we took all his cities. There was not one of the sixty cities that we did not take from them—the whole region of Argob, Og's kingdom in Bashan. ⁵All these cities were fortified with high walls and with gates and bars, and there were also a great many unwalled villages. ⁶We completely destroyed*a* them, as we had done with Sihon king of Heshbon, destroying*a* every city—men, women and children. ⁷But all the livestock and the plunder from their cities we carried off for ourselves.

⁸So at that time we took from these two kings of the Amorites the territory east of the Jordan, from the Arnon Gorge as far as Mount Hermon. ⁹(Hermon is called Sirion by the Sidonians; the Amorites call it Senir.) ¹⁰We took all the towns on the plateau, and all Gilead, and all Bashan as far as Salecah and Edrei, towns of Og's kingdom in Bashan. ¹¹(Only Og king of Bashan was left of the remnant of the Rephaites. His bed*b* was made of iron and was more than thirteen feet long and six feet wide.*c* It is still in Rabbah of the Ammonites.)

Division of the Land ¹²Of the land that we took over at that time, I gave the Reubenites and the Gadites the territory north of Aroer by the Arnon Gorge, including half the hill country of Gilead, together with its towns. ¹³The rest of Gilead and also all of Bashan, the kingdom of Og, I gave to the half tribe of Manasseh. (The whole region of Argob in Bashan used to be known as a land of the Rephaites. ¹⁴Jair, a descendant of Manasseh, took the whole region of Argob as far as the border of the Geshurites and the Maacathites; it was named after him, so that to this day Bashan is called Havvoth Jair.*d*) ¹⁵And I gave Gilead to Makir. ¹⁶But to the Reubenites and the Gadites I gave the territory extending from Gilead down to the Arnon Gorge (the middle of the gorge being the border) and out to the Jabbok River, which is the bor-

---

a34,6 The Hebrew term refers to the irrevocable giving over of things or persons to the LORD, often by totally destroying them. *b11* Or *sarcophagus* *c11* Hebrew *nine cubits long and four cubits wide* (about 4 meters long and 1.8 meters wide) *d14* Or *called the settlements of Jair*

der of the Ammonites. ¹⁷Its western border was the Jordan in the Arabah, from Kinnereth to the Sea of the Arabah (the Salt Sea*), below the slopes of Pisgah.

¹⁸I commanded you at that time: "The Lord your God has given you this land to take possession of it. But all your able-bodied men, armed for battle, must cross over ahead of your brother Israelites. ¹⁹However, your wives, your children and your livestock (I know you have much livestock) may stay in the towns I have given you, ²⁰until the Lord gives rest to your brothers as he has to you, and they too have taken over the land that the Lord your God is giving them, across the Jordan. After that, each of you may go back to the possession I have given you."

Moses Forbidden to Cross the Jordan ²¹At that time I commanded Joshua: "You have seen with your own eyes all that the Lord your God has done to these two kings. The Lord will do the same to all the kingdoms over there where you are going. ²²Do not be afraid of them; the Lord your God himself will fight for you."

²³At that time I pleaded with the Lord: ²⁴"O Sovereign Lord, you have begun to show to your servant your greatness and your strong hand. For what god is there in heaven or on earth who can do the deeds and mighty works you do? ²⁵Let me go over and see the good land beyond the Jordan—that fine hill country and Lebanon."

²⁶But because of you the Lord was angry with me and would not listen to me. "That is enough," the Lord said. "Do not speak to me anymore about this matter. ²⁷Go up to the top of Pisgah and look west and north and south and east. Look at the land with your own eyes, since you are not going to cross this Jordan. ²⁸But commission Joshua, and encourage and strengthen him, for he will lead this people across and will cause them to inherit the land that you will see." ²⁹So we stayed in the valley near Beth Peor.

Obedience Commanded Hear now, O Israel, the decrees and laws I am about to teach you. Follow them so that you may live and may go in and take possession of the land that the Lord, the God of your fathers, is giving you. ²Do not add to what I command you and do not subtract from it, but keep the commands of the Lord your God that I give you.

³You saw with your own eyes what the Lord did at Baal Peor. The Lord your God destroyed from among you everyone who followed the Baal of Peor, ⁴but all of you who held fast to the Lord your God are still alive today.

⁵See, I have taught you decrees and laws as the Lord my God commanded me, so that you may follow them in the land you are entering to take possession of it. ⁶Observe them carefully, for this will show your wisdom and understanding to the nations, who will hear about all these decrees and say, "Surely this great nation is a wise and understanding people." ⁷What other nation is so great as to have their gods near them the way the Lord our God is near us whenever we pray to him? ⁸And what other nation is so great as to have such righteous decrees and laws as this body of laws I am setting before you today?

⁹Only be careful, and watch yourselves closely so that you do not forget the things your eyes have seen or let them slip from your heart as long as you live. Teach them to your children and to their children after them. ¹⁰Remember the day you stood before the Lord your God at Horeb, when he said to me, "Assemble the people before me to hear my words so that they may learn to revere me as long as they live in the land and may teach them to their children." ¹¹You came near and stood at the foot of the mountain while it blazed with fire to the very heavens, with black clouds and deep darkness.

*17 That is, the Dead Sea

¹²Then the LORD spoke to you out of the fire. You heard the sound of words but saw no form; there was only a voice. ¹³He declared to you his covenant, the Ten Commandments, which he commanded you to follow and then wrote them on two stone tablets. ¹⁴And the LORD directed me at that time to teach you the decrees and laws you are to follow in the land that you are crossing the Jordan to possess.

Idolatry Forbidden ¹⁵You saw no form of any kind the day the LORD spoke to you at Horeb out of the fire. Therefore watch yourselves very carefully, ¹⁶so that you do not become corrupt and make for yourselves an idol, an image of any shape, whether formed like a man or a woman, ¹⁷or like any animal on earth or any bird that flies in the air, ¹⁸or like any creature that moves along the ground or any fish in the waters below. ¹⁹And when you look up to the sky and see the sun, the moon and the stars—all the heavenly array—do not be enticed into bowing down to them and worshiping things the LORD your God has apportioned to all the nations under heaven. ²⁰But as for you, the LORD took you and brought you out of the iron-smelting furnace, out of Egypt, to be the people of his inheritance, as you now are.

²¹The LORD was angry with me because of you, and he solemnly swore that I would not cross the Jordan and enter the good land the LORD your God is giving you as your inheritance. ²²I will die in this land; I will not cross the Jordan; but you are about to cross over and take possession of that good land. ²³Be careful not to forget the covenant of the LORD your God that he made with you; do not make for yourselves an idol in the form of anything the LORD your God has forbidden. ²⁴For the LORD your God is a consuming fire, a jealous God.

²⁵After you have had children and grandchildren and have lived in the land a long time—if you then become corrupt and make any kind of idol, doing evil in the eyes of the LORD your God and provoking him to anger, ²⁶I call heaven and earth as witnesses against you this day that you will quickly perish from the land that you are crossing the Jordan to possess. You will not live there long but will certainly be destroyed. ²⁷The LORD will scatter you among the peoples, and only a few of you will survive among the nations to which the LORD will drive you. ²⁸There you will worship man-made gods of wood and stone, which cannot see or hear or eat or smell. ²⁹But if from there you seek the LORD your God, you will find him if you look for him with all your heart and with all your soul. ³⁰When you are in distress and all these things have happened to you, then in later days you will return to the LORD

The Bible Says

God Is Merciful

Deuteronomy 4:31 says that "the LORD your God is a merciful God." Hebrew words translated "mercy" picture a love that reaches down to help people in need—even those who have done nothing to deserve help. The Greek word translated "mercy" emphasizes compassion—caring enough about another's suffering to help.

When the Bible says the Lord is merciful, it's saying that he cares when you're feeling hurt or helpless. He cares enough to help.

* He gives you eternal life through Jesus (Ephesians 2:4–5).
* You can pray with confidence, knowing the Lord will listen to you (Hebrews 4:16).
* He expects you to be merciful toward others (Luke 6:36).

your God and obey him. ³¹For the LORD your God is a merciful God; he will not abandon or destroy you or forget the covenant with your forefathers, which he confirmed to them by oath.

The LORD Is God   ³²Ask now about the former days, long before your time, from the day God created man on the earth; ask from one end of the heavens to the other. Has anything so great as this ever happened, or has anything like it ever been heard of? ³³Has any other people heard the voice of God*ᵃ* speaking out of fire, as you have, and lived? ³⁴Has any god ever tried to take for himself one nation out of another nation, by testings, by miraculous signs and wonders, by war, by a mighty hand and an outstretched arm, or by great and awesome deeds, like all the things the LORD your God did for you in Egypt before your very eyes?

³⁵You were shown these things so that you might know that the LORD is God; besides him there is no other. ³⁶From heaven he made you hear his voice to discipline you. On earth he showed you his great fire, and you heard his words from out of the fire. ³⁷Because he loved your forefathers and chose their descendants after them, he brought you out of Egypt by his Presence and his great strength, ³⁸to drive out before you nations greater and stronger than you and to bring you into their land to give it to you for your inheritance, as it is today.

³⁹Acknowledge and take to heart this day that the LORD is God in heaven above and on the earth below. There is no other. ⁴⁰Keep his decrees and commands, which I am giving you today, so that it may go well with you and your children after you and that you may live long in the land the LORD your God gives you for all time.

Cities of Refuge   ⁴¹Then Moses set aside three cities east of the Jordan, ⁴²to which anyone who had killed a person could flee if he had unintentionally killed his neighbor without malice aforethought. He could flee into one of these cities and save his life. ⁴³The cities were these: Bezer in the desert plateau, for the Reubenites; Ramoth in Gilead, for the Gadites; and Golan in Bashan, for the Manassites.

Introduction to the Law   ⁴⁴This is the law Moses set before the Israelites. ⁴⁵These are the stipulations, decrees and laws Moses gave them when they came out of Egypt ⁴⁶and were in the valley near Beth Peor east of the Jordan, in the land of Sihon king of the Amorites, who reigned in Heshbon and was defeated by Moses and the Israelites as they came out of Egypt. ⁴⁷They took possession of his land and the land of Og king of Bashan, the two Amorite kings east of the Jordan. ⁴⁸This land extended from Aroer on the rim of the Arnon Gorge to Mount Siyon*ᵇ* (that is, Hermon), ⁴⁹and included all the Arabah east of the Jordan, as far as the Sea of the Arabah,*ᶜ* below the slopes of Pisgah.

5 *The Ten Commandments*   Moses summoned all Israel and said:

Hear, O Israel, the decrees and laws I declare in your hearing today. Learn them and be sure to follow them. ²The LORD our God made a covenant with us at Horeb. ³It was not with our fathers that the LORD made this covenant, but with us, with all of us who are alive here today. ⁴The LORD spoke to you face to face out of the fire on the mountain. ⁵(At that time I stood between the LORD and you to declare to you the word of the LORD, because you were afraid of the fire and did not go up the mountain.) And he said:

⁶"I am the LORD your God, who brought you out of Egypt, out of the land of slavery.

⁷"You shall have no other gods before*ᵈ* me.

ᵃ33 Or of a god   ᵇ48 Hebrew; Syriac (see also Deut. 3:9) Sirion   ᶜ49 That is, the Dead Sea   ᵈ7 Or besides

⁸"You shall not make for yourself an idol in the form of anything in heaven above or on the earth beneath or in the waters below. ⁹You shall not bow down to them or worship them; for I, the LORD your God, am a jealous God, punishing the children for the sin of the fathers to the third and fourth generation of those who hate me, ¹⁰but showing love to a thousand ˌgenerationsˌ of those who love me and keep my commandments.

¹¹"You shall not misuse the name of the LORD your God, for the LORD will not hold anyone guiltless who misuses his name.

¹²"Observe the Sabbath day by keeping it holy, as the LORD your God has commanded you. ¹³Six days you shall labor and do all your work, ¹⁴but the seventh day is a Sabbath to the LORD your God. On it you shall not do any work, neither you, nor your son or daughter, nor your manservant or maidservant, nor your ox, your donkey or any of your animals, nor the alien within your gates, so that your manservant and maidservant may rest, as you do. ¹⁵Remember that you were slaves in Egypt and that the LORD your God brought you out of there with a mighty hand and an outstretched arm. Therefore the LORD your God has commanded you to observe the Sabbath day.

¹⁶"Honor your father and your mother, as the LORD your God has commanded you, so that you may live long and that it may go well with you in the land the LORD your God is giving you.

¹⁷"You shall not murder.

¹⁸"You shall not commit adultery.

¹⁹"You shall not steal.

²⁰"You shall not give false testimony against your neighbor.

²¹"You shall not covet your neighbor's wife. You shall not set your desire on your neighbor's house or land, his manservant or maidservant, his ox or donkey, or anything that belongs to your neighbor."

²²These are the commandments the LORD proclaimed in a loud voice to your whole assembly there on the mountain from out of the fire, the cloud and the deep darkness; and he added nothing more. Then he wrote them on two stone tablets and gave them to me.

²³When you heard the voice out of the darkness, while the mountain was ablaze with fire, all the leading men of your tribes and your elders came to me. ²⁴And you said, "The LORD our God has shown us his glory and his majesty, and we have heard his voice from the fire. Today we have seen that a man can live even if God speaks with him. ²⁵But now, why should we die? This great fire will consume us, and we will die if we hear the voice of the LORD our God any longer. ²⁶For what mortal man has ever heard the voice of the living God speaking out of fire, as we have, and survived? ²⁷Go near and listen to all that the LORD our God says. Then tell us whatever the LORD our God tells you. We will listen and obey."

²⁸The LORD heard you when you spoke to me and the LORD said to me, "I have heard what this people said to you. Everything they said was good. ²⁹Oh, that their hearts would be inclined to fear me and keep all my commands always, so that it might go well with them and their children forever!

³⁰"Go, tell them to return to their tents. ³¹But you stay here with me so that I may give you all the commands, decrees and laws you are to teach them to follow in the land I am giving them to possess."

³²So be careful to do what the LORD your God has commanded you; do not turn aside to the right or to the left. ³³Walk in all the way that the LORD your God has commanded you, so that you may live and prosper and prolong your days in the land that you will possess.

6 *Love the Lord Your God* These are the commands, decrees and laws the Lord your God directed me to teach you to observe in the land that you are crossing the Jordan to possess, ²so that you, your children and their children after them may fear the Lord your God as long as you live by keeping all his decrees and commands that I give you, and so that you may enjoy long life. ³Hear, O Israel, and be careful to obey so that it may go well with you and that you may increase greatly in a land flowing with milk and honey, just as the Lord, the God of your fathers, promised you.

⁴Hear, O Israel: The Lord our God, the Lord is one.*ᵃ* ⁵Love the Lord your God with all your heart and with all your soul and with all your strength. ⁶These commandments that I give you today are to be upon your hearts. ⁷Impress them on your children. Talk about them when you sit at home and when you walk along the road, when you lie down and when you get up. ⁸Tie them as symbols on your hands and bind them on your foreheads. ⁹Write them on the doorframes of your houses and on your gates.

¹⁰When the Lord your God brings you into the land he swore to your fathers, to Abraham, Isaac and Jacob, to give you—a land with large, flourishing cities you did not build, ¹¹houses filled with all kinds of good things you did not provide, wells you did not dig, and vineyards and olive groves you did not plant—then when you eat and are satisfied, ¹²be careful that you do not forget the Lord, who brought you out of Egypt, out of the land of slavery.

¹³Fear the Lord your God, serve him only and take your oaths in his name. ¹⁴Do not follow other gods, the gods of the peoples around you; ¹⁵for the Lord your God, who is among you, is a jealous God and his anger will burn against you, and he will destroy you from the face of the land. ¹⁶Do not test the Lord your God as you did at Massah. ¹⁷Be sure to keep the commands of the Lord your God and the stipulations and decrees he has given you. ¹⁸Do what is right and good in the Lord's sight, so that it may go well with you and you may go in and take over the good land that the Lord promised on oath to your forefathers, ¹⁹thrusting out all your enemies before you, as the Lord said.

²⁰In the future, when your son asks you, "What is the meaning of the stipulations, decrees and laws the Lord our God has commanded you?" ²¹tell him: "We were slaves of Pharaoh in Egypt, but the Lord brought us out of Egypt with a mighty hand. ²²Before our eyes the Lord sent miraculous signs and wonders—great and terrible—upon Egypt and Pharaoh and his whole household. ²³But he brought us out from there to bring us in and give us the land that he promised on oath to our forefathers. ²⁴The Lord commanded us to obey all these decrees and to fear the Lord our God, so that we might always prosper and be kept alive, as is the case today. ²⁵And if we are careful to obey all this law before the Lord our God, as he has commanded us, that will be our righteousness."

ᵃ4 Or The Lord our God is one Lord; or The Lord is our God, the Lord is one; or The Lord is our God, the Lord alone

---

DEUTERONOMY 6:4–9

Moses told God's Old Testament people to love the Lord and live by his words. Then as they sat at home or walked along the road or stretched out to relax, they talked about those words of God that shaped their lives. This is still the best way to share your faith with others. Have an answer to prayer? Mention it to your friend when you're riding the bus to school. Do you have a different outlook on sex? Tell your friends the choice you've made, and why. You don't have to argue. All you have to do is talk naturally about the place God has in your own life.

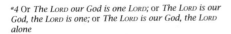

Direct Line

7 *Driving Out the Nations* When the LORD your God brings you into the land you are entering to possess and drives out before you many nations—the Hittites, Girgashites, Amorites, Canaanites, Perizzites, Hivites and Jebusites, seven nations larger and stronger than you— ²and when the LORD your God has delivered them over to you and you have defeated them, then you must destroy them totally.*ᵃ* Make no treaty with them, and show them no mercy. ³Do not intermarry with them. Do not give your daughters to their sons or take their daughters for your sons, ⁴for they will turn your sons away from following me to serve other gods, and the LORD's anger will burn against you and will quickly destroy you. ⁵This is what you are to do to them: Break down their altars, smash their sacred stones, cut down their Asherah poles*ᵇ* and burn their idols in the fire. ⁶For you are a people holy to the LORD your God. The LORD your God has chosen you out of all the peoples on the face of the earth to be his people, his treasured possession.

⁷The LORD did not set his affection on you and choose you because you were more numerous than other peoples, for you were the fewest of all peoples. ⁸But it was because the LORD loved you and kept the oath he swore to your forefathers that he brought you out with a mighty hand and redeemed you from the land of slavery, from the power of Pharaoh king of Egypt. ⁹Know therefore that the LORD your God is God; he is the faithful God, keeping his covenant of love to a thousand generations of those who love him and keep his commands. ¹⁰But

> those who hate him he will repay to their face by destruction;
> he will not be slow to repay to their face those who hate him.

¹¹Therefore, take care to follow the commands, decrees and laws I give you today.

¹²If you pay attention to these laws and are careful to follow them, then the LORD your God will keep his covenant of love with you, as he swore to your forefathers. ¹³He will love you and bless you and increase your numbers. He will bless the fruit of your womb, the crops of your land—your grain, new wine and oil—the calves of your herds and the lambs of your flocks in the land that he swore to your forefathers to give you. ¹⁴You will be blessed more than any other people; none of your men or women will be childless, nor any of your livestock without young. ¹⁵The LORD will keep you free from every disease. He will not inflict on you the horrible diseases you knew in Egypt, but he will inflict them on all who hate you. ¹⁶You must destroy all the peoples the LORD your God gives over to you. Do not look on them with pity and do not serve their gods, for that will be a snare to you.

¹⁷You may say to yourselves, "These nations are stronger than we are. How can we drive them out?" ¹⁸But do not be afraid of them; remember well what the LORD your God did to Pharaoh and to all Egypt. ¹⁹You saw with your own eyes the great trials, the miraculous signs and wonders, the mighty hand and outstretched arm, with which the LORD your God brought you out. The LORD your God will do the same to all the peoples you now fear. ²⁰Moreover, the LORD your God will send the hornet among them until even the survivors who hide from you have perished. ²¹Do not be terrified by them, for the LORD your God, who is among you, is a great and awesome God. ²²The

> He is the faithful God, keeping his covenant of love to a thousand generations (Deuteronomy 7:9).

ᵃ2 The Hebrew term refers to the irrevocable giving over of things or persons to the LORD, often by totally destroying them; also in verse 26.   *ᵇ5* That is, symbols of the goddess Asherah; here and elsewhere in Deuteronomy

LORD your God will drive out those nations before you, little by little. You will not be allowed to eliminate them all at once, or the wild animals will multiply around you. ²³But the LORD your God will deliver them over to you, throwing them into great confusion until they are destroyed. ²⁴He will give their kings into your hand, and you will wipe out their names from under heaven. No one will be able to stand up against you; you will destroy them. ²⁵The images of their gods you are to burn in the fire. Do not covet the silver and gold on them, and do not take it for yourselves, or you will be ensnared by it, for it is detestable to the LORD your God. ²⁶Do not bring a detestable thing into your house or you, like it, will be set apart for destruction. Utterly abhor and detest it, for it is set apart for destruction.

8 *Do Not Forget the LORD* Be careful to follow every command I am giving you today, so that you may live and increase and may enter and possess the land that the LORD promised on oath to your forefathers. ²Remember how the LORD your God led you all the way in the desert these forty years, to humble you and to test you in order to know what was in your heart, whether or not you would keep his commands. ³He humbled you, causing you to hunger and then feeding you with manna, which neither you nor your fathers had known, to teach you that man does not live on bread alone but on every word that comes from the mouth of the LORD. ⁴Your clothes did not wear out and your feet did not swell during these forty years. ⁵Know then in your heart that as a man disciplines his son, so the LORD your God disciplines you.

⁶Observe the commands of the LORD your God, walking in his ways and revering him. ⁷For the LORD your God is bringing you into a good land—a land with streams and pools of water, with springs flowing in the valleys and hills; ⁸a land with wheat and barley, vines and fig trees, pomegranates, olive oil and honey; ⁹a land where bread will not be scarce and you will lack nothing; a land where the rocks are iron and you can dig copper out of the hills.

¹⁰When you have eaten and are satisfied, praise the LORD your God for the good land he has given you. ¹¹Be careful that you do not forget the LORD your God, failing to observe his commands, his laws and his decrees that I am giving you this day. ¹²Otherwise, when you eat and are satisfied, when you build fine houses and settle down, ¹³and when your herds and flocks grow large and your silver and gold increase and all you have is multiplied, ¹⁴then your heart will become proud and you will forget the LORD your God, who brought you out of Egypt, out of the land of slavery. ¹⁵He led you through the vast and dreadful desert, that thirsty and waterless land, with its venomous snakes and scorpions. He brought you water out of hard rock. ¹⁶He gave you manna to eat in the desert, something your fathers had never known, to humble and to test you so that in the end it might go well with you. ¹⁷You may say to yourself, "My power and the strength of my hands have produced this wealth for me." ¹⁸But remember the LORD your God, for it is he

DEUTERONOMY 8:10–18

You just got all A's on your report card, the guy you like finally asked you out, and your dad just said you can get your license as soon as you turn 16! God? Who needs him now? But maybe this is the time you need God most. The Bible warns that when things go well there's a danger that "then your heart will become proud and you will forget the LORD your God" (Deuteronomy 8:14). And if you forget God, you'll probably soon be in trouble. Why not write yourself a note? Remind yourself that when something really great happens, enjoy. Then stop a moment to thank God and give him credit for the good things in your life.

Direct Line

who gives you the ability to produce wealth, and so confirms his covenant, which he swore to your forefathers, as it is today.

[19]If you ever forget the LORD your God and follow other gods and worship and bow down to them, I testify against you today that you will surely be destroyed. [20]Like the nations the LORD destroyed before you, so you will be destroyed for not obeying the LORD your God.

Not Because of Israel's Righteousness Hear, O Israel. You are now about to cross the Jordan to go in and dispossess nations greater and stronger than you, with large cities that have walls up to the sky. [2]The people are strong and tall—Anakites! You know about them and have heard it said: "Who can stand up against the Anakites?" [3]But be assured today that the LORD your God is the one who goes across ahead of you like a devouring fire. He will destroy them; he will subdue them before you. And you will drive them out and annihilate them quickly, as the LORD has promised you.

[4]After the LORD your God has driven them out before you, do not say to yourself, "The LORD has brought me here to take possession of this land because of my righteousness." No, it is on account of the wickedness of these nations that the LORD is going to drive them out before you. [5]It is not because of your righteousness or your integrity that you are going in to take possession of their land; but on account of the wickedness of these nations, the LORD your God will drive them out before you, to accomplish what he swore to your fathers, to Abraham, Isaac and Jacob. [6]Understand, then, that it is not because of your righteousness that the LORD your God is giving you this good land to possess, for you are a stiff-necked people.

The Golden Calf [7]Remember this and never forget how you provoked the LORD your God to anger in the desert. From the day you left Egypt until you arrived here, you have been rebellious against the LORD. [8]At Horeb you aroused the LORD's wrath so that he was angry enough to destroy you. [9]When I went up on the mountain to receive the tablets of stone, the tablets of the covenant that the LORD had made with you, I stayed on the mountain forty days and forty nights; I ate no bread and drank no water. [10]The LORD gave me two stone tablets inscribed by the finger of God. On them were all the commandments the LORD proclaimed to you on the mountain out of the fire, on the day of the assembly.

[11]At the end of the forty days and forty nights, the LORD gave me the two stone tablets, the tablets of the covenant. [12]Then the LORD told me, "Go down from here at once, because your people whom you brought out of Egypt have become corrupt. They have turned away quickly from what I commanded them and have made a cast idol for themselves."

[13]And the LORD said to me, "I have seen this people, and they are a stiff-necked people indeed! [14]Let me alone, so that I may destroy them and blot out their name from under heaven. And I will make you into a nation stronger and more numerous than they."

[15]So I turned and went down from the mountain while it was ablaze with fire. And the two tablets of the covenant were in my hands.[a] [16]When I looked, I saw that you had sinned against the LORD your God; you had made for yourselves an idol cast in the shape of a calf. You had turned aside quickly from the way that the LORD had commanded you. [17]So I took the two tablets and threw them out of my hands, breaking them to pieces before your eyes.

[18]Then once again I fell prostrate before the LORD for forty days and forty nights; I ate no bread and drank no water, because of all the sin you had committed, doing what was evil in the LORD's sight and so provoking him to

---

*a*15 Or *And I had the two tablets of the covenant with me, one in each hand*

anger. ¹⁹I feared the anger and wrath of the Lord, for he was angry enough with you to destroy you. But again the Lord listened to me. ²⁰And the Lord was angry enough with Aaron to destroy him, but at that time I prayed for Aaron too. ²¹Also I took that sinful thing of yours, the calf you had made, and burned it in the fire. Then I crushed it and ground it to powder as fine as dust and threw the dust into a stream that flowed down the mountain.

²²You also made the Lord angry at Taberah, at Massah and at Kibroth Hattaavah.

²³And when the Lord sent you out from Kadesh Barnea, he said, "Go up and take possession of the land I have given you." But you rebelled against the command of the Lord your God. You did not trust him or obey him. ²⁴You have been rebellious against the Lord ever since I have known you.

²⁵I lay prostrate before the Lord those forty days and forty nights because the Lord had said he would destroy you. ²⁶I prayed to the Lord and said, "O Sovereign Lord, do not destroy your people, your own inheritance that you redeemed by your great power and brought out of Egypt with a mighty hand. ²⁷Remember your servants Abraham, Isaac and Jacob. Overlook the stubbornness of this people, their wickedness and their sin. ²⁸Otherwise, the country from which you brought us will say, 'Because the Lord was not able to take them into the land he had promised them, and because he hated them, he brought them out to put them to death in the desert.' ²⁹But they are your people, your inheritance that you brought out by your great power and your outstretched arm."

10 *Tablets Like the First Ones*   At that time the Lord said to me, "Chisel out two stone tablets like the first ones and come up to me on the mountain. Also make a wooden chest.ᵃ ²I will write on the tablets the words that were on the first tablets, which you broke. Then you are to put them in the chest."

³So I made the ark out of acacia wood and chiseled out two stone tablets like the first ones, and I went up on the mountain with the two tablets in my hands. ⁴The Lord wrote on these tablets what he had written before, the Ten Commandments he had proclaimed to you on the mountain, out of the fire, on the day of the assembly. And the Lord gave them to me. ⁵Then I came back down the mountain and put the tablets in the ark I had made, as the Lord commanded me, and they are there now.

⁶(The Israelites traveled from the wells of the Jaakanites to Moserah. There Aaron died and was buried, and Eleazar his son succeeded him as priest. ⁷From there they traveled to Gudgodah and on to Jotbathah, a land with streams of water. ⁸At that time the Lord set apart the tribe of Levi to carry the ark of the covenant of the Lord, to stand before the Lord to minister and to pronounce blessings in his name, as they still do today. ⁹That is why the Levites have no share or inheritance among their brothers; the Lord is their inheritance, as the Lord your God told them.)

¹⁰Now I had stayed on the mountain forty days and nights, as I did the first time, and the Lord listened to me at this time also. It was not his will to destroy you. ¹¹"Go," the Lord said to me, "and lead the people on their way, so that they may enter and possess the land that I swore to their fathers to give them."

Fear the Lord   ¹²And now, O Israel, what does the Lord your God ask of you but to fear the Lord your God, to walk in all his ways, to love him, to serve the Lord your God with all your heart and with all your soul, ¹³and to observe the Lord's commands and decrees that I am giving you today for your own good?

¹⁴To the Lord your God belong the heavens, even the highest heavens, the earth and everything in it. ¹⁵Yet the Lord set his affection on your forefathers

ᵃ*1* That is, an ark

and loved them, and he chose you, their descendants, above all the nations, as it is today. [16]Circumcise your hearts, therefore, and do not be stiff-necked any longer. [17]For the LORD your God is God of gods and Lord of lords, the great God, mighty and awesome, who shows no partiality and accepts no bribes. [18]He defends the cause of the fatherless and the widow, and loves the alien, giving him food and clothing. [19]And you are to love those who are aliens, for you yourselves were aliens in Egypt. [20]Fear the LORD your God and serve him. Hold fast to him and take your oaths in his name. [21]He is your praise; he is your God, who performed for you those great and awesome wonders you saw with your own eyes. [22]Your forefathers who went down into Egypt were seventy in all, and now the LORD your God has made you as numerous as the stars in the sky.

11 *Love and Obey the LORD* Love the LORD your God and keep his requirements, his decrees, his laws and his commands always. [2]Remember today that your children were not the ones who saw and experienced the discipline of the LORD your God: his majesty, his mighty hand, his outstretched arm; [3]the signs he performed and the things he did in the heart of Egypt, both to Pharaoh king of Egypt and to his whole country; [4]what he did to the Egyptian army, to its horses and chariots, how he overwhelmed them with the waters of the Red Sea[a] as they were pursuing you, and how the LORD brought lasting ruin on them. [5]It was not your children who saw what he did for you in the desert until you arrived at this place, [6]and what he did to Dathan and Abiram, sons of Eliab the Reubenite, when the earth opened its mouth right in the middle of all Israel and swallowed them up with their households, their tents and every living thing that belonged to them. [7]But it was your own eyes that saw all these great things the LORD has done.

[8]Observe therefore all the commands I am giving you today, so that you may have the strength to go in and take over the land that you are crossing the Jordan to possess, [9]and so that you may live long in the land that the LORD swore to your forefathers to give to them and their descendants, a land flowing with milk and honey. [10]The land you are entering to take over is not like the land of Egypt, from which you have come, where you planted your seed and irrigated it by foot as in a vegetable garden. [11]But the land you are

---

[a]4 Hebrew *Yam Suph*; that is, Sea of Reeds

The Bible Says

Love Comes First

Don't let all the Old Testament laws confuse you. God isn't sitting in heaven keeping score of your wins and losses. And believers aren't moral athletes who make points by jumping over his hurdles. The relationship between God and the believer is one of love.

Deuteronomy 11 tells you that God's commands were given to show you what is right and good so he can bless you. That's one way God shows his love for you. Obedience is one way you show your love for God. That's why Deuteronomy 11:13 tells you that the call to obedience is a call to "love the LORD your God and to serve him with all your heart and with all your soul."

Love led God to give the law. He wants your love in return—love that expresses itself by doing what he says.

crossing the Jordan to take possession of is a land of mountains and valleys that drinks rain from heaven. [12]It is a land the LORD your God cares for; the eyes of the LORD your God are continually on it from the beginning of the year to its end.

[13]So if you faithfully obey the commands I am giving you today—to love the LORD your God and to serve him with all your heart and with all your soul— [14]then I will send rain on your land in its season, both autumn and spring rains, so that you may gather in your grain, new wine and oil. [15]I will provide grass in the fields for your cattle, and you will eat and be satisfied.

[16]Be careful, or you will be enticed to turn away and worship other gods and bow down to them. [17]Then the LORD's anger will burn against you, and he will shut the heavens so that it will not rain and the ground will yield no produce, and you will soon perish from the good land the LORD is giving you. [18]Fix these words of mine in your hearts and minds; tie them as symbols on your hands and bind them on your foreheads. [19]Teach them to your children, talking about them when you sit at home and when you walk along the road, when you lie down and when you get up. [20]Write them on the doorframes of your houses and on your gates, [21]so that your days and the days of your children may be many in the land that the LORD swore to give your forefathers, as many as the days that the heavens are above the earth.

[22]If you carefully observe all these commands I am giving you to follow— to love the LORD your God, to walk in all his ways and to hold fast to him— [23]then the LORD will drive out all these nations before you, and you will dispossess nations larger and stronger than you. [24]Every place where you set your foot will be yours: Your territory will extend from the desert to Lebanon, and from the Euphrates River to the western sea.[a] [25]No man will be able to stand against you. The LORD your God, as he promised you, will put the terror and fear of you on the whole land, wherever you go.

[26]See, I am setting before you today a blessing and a curse— [27]the blessing if you obey the commands of the LORD your God that I am giving you today; [28]the curse if you disobey the commands of the LORD your God and turn from the way that I command you today by following other gods, which you have not known. [29]When the LORD your God has brought you into the land you are entering to possess, you are to proclaim on Mount Gerizim the blessings, and on Mount Ebal the curses. [30]As you know, these mountains are across the Jordan, west of the road,[b] toward the setting sun, near the great trees of Moreh, in the territory of those Canaanites living in the Arabah in the vicinity of Gilgal. [31]You are about to cross the Jordan to enter and take possession of the land the LORD your God is giving you. When you have taken it over and are living there, [32]be sure that you obey all the decrees and laws I am setting before you today.

12 **The One Place of Worship** These are the decrees and laws you must be careful to follow in the land that the LORD, the God of your fathers, has given you to possess—as long as you live in the land. [2]Destroy completely all the places on the high mountains and on the hills and under every spreading tree where the nations you are dispossessing worship their gods. [3]Break down their altars, smash their sacred stones and burn their Asherah poles in the fire; cut down the idols of their gods and wipe out their names from those places.

[4]You must not worship the LORD your God in their way. [5]But you are to seek the place the LORD your God will choose from among all your tribes to put his Name there for his dwelling. To that place you must go; [6]there bring your burnt offerings and sacrifices, your tithes and special gifts, what you

---

[a]24 That is, the Mediterranean   *[b]30* Or *Jordan, westward*

have vowed to give and your freewill offerings, and the firstborn of your herds and flocks. ⁷There, in the presence of the LORD your God, you and your families shall eat and shall rejoice in everything you have put your hand to, because the LORD your God has blessed you.

⁸You are not to do as we do here today, everyone as he sees fit, ⁹since you have not yet reached the resting place and the inheritance the LORD your God is giving you. ¹⁰But you will cross the Jordan and settle in the land the LORD your God is giving you as an inheritance, and he will give you rest from all your enemies around you so that you will live in safety. ¹¹Then to the place the LORD your God will choose as a dwelling for his Name—there you are to bring everything I command you: your burnt offerings and sacrifices, your tithes and special gifts, and all the choice possessions you have vowed to the LORD. ¹²And there rejoice before the LORD your God, you, your sons and daughters, your menservants and maidservants, and the Levites from your towns, who have no allotment or inheritance of their own. ¹³Be careful not to sacrifice your burnt offerings anywhere you please. ¹⁴Offer them only at the place the LORD will choose in one of your tribes, and there observe everything I command you.

¹⁵Nevertheless, you may slaughter your animals in any of your towns and eat as much of the meat as you want, as if it were gazelle or deer, according to the blessing the LORD your God gives you. Both the ceremonially unclean and the clean may eat it. ¹⁶But you must not eat the blood; pour it out on the ground like water. ¹⁷You must not eat in your own towns the tithe of your grain and new wine and oil, or the firstborn of your herds and flocks, or whatever you have vowed to give, or your freewill offerings or special gifts. ¹⁸Instead, you are to eat them in the presence of the LORD your God at the place the LORD your God will choose—you, your sons and daughters, your menservants and maidservants, and the Levites from your towns—and you are to rejoice before the LORD your God in everything you put your hand to. ¹⁹Be careful not to neglect the Levites as long as you live in your land.

²⁰When the LORD your God has enlarged your territory as he promised you, and you crave meat and say, "I would like some meat," then you may eat as much of it as you want. ²¹If the place where the LORD your God chooses to put his Name is too far away from you, you may slaughter animals from the herds and flocks the LORD has given you, as I have commanded you, and in your own towns you may eat as much of them as you want. ²²Eat them as you would gazelle or deer. Both the ceremonially unclean and the clean may eat. ²³But be sure you do not eat the blood, because the blood is the life, and you must not eat the life with the meat. ²⁴You must not eat the blood; pour it out on the ground like water. ²⁵Do not eat it, so that it may go well with you and your children after you, because you will be doing what is right in the eyes of the LORD.

²⁶But take your consecrated things and whatever you have vowed to give, and go to the place the LORD will choose. ²⁷Present your burnt offerings on the altar of the LORD your God, both the meat and the blood. The blood of your sacrifices must be poured beside the altar of the LORD your God, but you may eat the meat. ²⁸Be careful to obey all these regulations I am giving you, so that it may always go well with you and your children after you, because you will be doing what is good and right in the eyes of the LORD your God.

²⁹The LORD your God will cut off before you the nations you are about to invade and dispossess. But when you have driven them out and settled in their land, ³⁰and after they have been destroyed before you, be careful not to be ensnared by inquiring about their gods, saying, "How do these nations serve their gods? We will do the same." ³¹You must not worship the LORD your God in their way, because in worshiping their gods, they do all kinds of detestable things the LORD hates. They even burn their sons and daughters in the fire as sacrifices to their gods.

³²See that you do all I command you; do not add to it or take away from it.

13 *Worshiping Other Gods* If a prophet, or one who foretells by dreams, appears among you and announces to you a miraculous sign or wonder, ²and if the sign or wonder of which he has spoken takes place, and he says, "Let us follow other gods" (gods you have not known) "and let us worship them," ³you must not listen to the words of that prophet or dreamer. The LORD your God is testing you to find out whether you love him with all your heart and with all your soul. ⁴It is the LORD your God you must follow, and him you must revere. Keep his commands and obey him; serve him and hold fast to him. ⁵That prophet or dreamer must be put to death, because he preached rebellion against the LORD your God, who brought you out of Egypt and redeemed you from the land of slavery; he has tried to turn you from the way the LORD your God commanded you to follow. You must purge the evil from among you.

⁶If your very own brother, or your son or daughter, or the wife you love, or your closest friend secretly entices you, saying, "Let us go and worship other gods" (gods that neither you nor your fathers have known, ⁷gods of the peoples around you, whether near or far, from one end of the land to the other), ⁸do not yield to him or listen to him. Show him no pity. Do not spare him or shield him. ⁹You must certainly put him to death. Your hand must be the first in putting him to death, and then the hands of all the people. ¹⁰Stone him to death, because he tried to turn you away from the LORD your God, who brought you out of Egypt, out of the land of slavery. ¹¹Then all Israel will hear and be afraid, and no one among you will do such an evil thing again.

¹²If you hear it said about one of the towns the LORD your God is giving you to live in ¹³that wicked men have arisen among you and have led the people of their town astray, saying, "Let us go and worship other gods" (gods you have not known), ¹⁴then you must inquire, probe and investigate it thoroughly. And if it is true and it has been proved that this detestable thing has been done among you, ¹⁵you must certainly put to the sword all who live in that town. Destroy it completely,ᵃ both its people and its livestock. ¹⁶Gather all the plunder of the town into the middle of the public square and completely burn the town and all its plunder as a whole burnt offering to the LORD your God. It is to remain a ruin forever, never to be rebuilt. ¹⁷None of those condemned thingsᵃ shall be found in your hands, so that the LORD will turn from his fierce anger; he will show you mercy, have compassion on you, and increase your numbers, as he promised on oath to your forefathers, ¹⁸because you obey the LORD your God, keeping all his commands that I am giving you today and doing what is right in his eyes.

14 *Clean and Unclean Food* You are the children of the LORD your God. Do not cut yourselves or shave the front of your heads for the dead, ²for you are a people holy to the LORD your

---

ᵃ15,17 The Hebrew term refers to the irrevocable giving over of things or persons to the LORD, often by totally destroying them.

DEUTERONOMY 13:6–11

What if an acquaintance asks for the answer to a test question? You shake your head no. But he whispers, "I was sick last night and couldn't study. Help me just this once." Would you still say no? What if he was a close friend? When it comes to doing wrong, the person who asks may be "your son or daughter, or the wife you love, or your closest friend" (Deuteronomy 13:6). It makes no difference. This Bible passage says, "Do not yield to him or listen to him" (Deuteronomy 13:8). Acting on your convictions rather than giving in to peer pressure is tough. But it's an important part of becoming a mature adult and a mature Christian.

Direct Line

God. Out of all the peoples on the face of the earth, the Lᴏʀᴅ has chosen you to be his treasured possession.

³Do not eat any detestable thing. ⁴These are the animals you may eat: the ox, the sheep, the goat, ⁵the deer, the gazelle, the roe deer, the wild goat, the ibex, the antelope and the mountain sheep.ᵃ ⁶You may eat any animal that has a split hoof divided in two and that chews the cud. ⁷However, of those that chew the cud or that have a split hoof completely divided you may not eat the camel, the rabbit or the coney.ᵇ Although they chew the cud, they do not have a split hoof; they are ceremonially unclean for you. ⁸The pig is also unclean; although it has a split hoof, it does not chew the cud. You are not to eat their meat or touch their carcasses.

⁹Of all the creatures living in the water, you may eat any that has fins and scales. ¹⁰But anything that does not have fins and scales you may not eat; for you it is unclean.

¹¹You may eat any clean bird. ¹²But these you may not eat: the eagle, the vulture, the black vulture, ¹³the red kite, the black kite, any kind of falcon, ¹⁴any kind of raven, ¹⁵the horned owl, the screech owl, the gull, any kind of hawk, ¹⁶the little owl, the great owl, the white owl, ¹⁷the desert owl, the osprey, the cormorant, ¹⁸the stork, any kind of heron, the hoopoe and the bat.

¹⁹All flying insects that swarm are unclean to you; do not eat them. ²⁰But any winged creature that is clean you may eat.

²¹Do not eat anything you find already dead. You may give it to an alien living in any of your towns, and he may eat it, or you may sell it to a foreigner. But you are a people holy to the Lᴏʀᴅ your God.

Do not cook a young goat in its mother's milk.

Tithes ²²Be sure to set aside a tenth of all that your fields produce each year. ²³Eat the tithe of your grain, new wine and oil, and the firstborn of your herds and flocks in the presence of the Lᴏʀᴅ your God at the place he will choose as a dwelling for his Name, so that you may learn to revere the Lᴏʀᴅ your God always. ²⁴But if that place is too distant and you have been blessed by the Lᴏʀᴅ your God and cannot carry your tithe (because the place where the Lᴏʀᴅ will choose to put his Name is so far away), ²⁵then exchange your tithe for silver, and take the silver with you and go to the place the Lᴏʀᴅ your God will choose. ²⁶Use the silver to buy whatever you like: cattle, sheep, wine or other fermented drink, or anything you wish. Then you and your household shall eat there in the presence of the Lᴏʀᴅ your God and rejoice. ²⁷And do not neglect the Levites living in your towns, for they have no allotment or inheritance of their own.

²⁸At the end of every three years, bring all the tithes of that year's produce and store it in your towns, ²⁹so that the Levites (who have no allotment or inheritance of their own) and the aliens, the fatherless and the widows who live in your towns may come and eat and be satisfied, and so that the Lᴏʀᴅ your God may bless you in all the work of your hands.

DEUTERONOMY 14:28–29

Do you ever wonder what happens to the money people give at church? Probably some goes to pay for the building and the pastor's salary and educational materials. But what else? In Old Testament times 10 percent of the harvest was set aside to support the temple and the priests. But every third year the tithe was kept in the village to feed "the aliens, the fatherless and the widows who live in your towns" (Deuteronomy 14:29). Many churches show the same concern for the needy people in their communities. Helping others is a priority with God. Why not check out what your church does?

Direct Line

ᵃ5 The precise identification of some of the birds and animals in this chapter is uncertain. ᵇ7 That is, the hyrax or rock badger

15 *The Year for Canceling Debts* At the end of every seven years you must cancel debts. [2]This is how it is to be done: Every creditor shall cancel the loan he has made to his fellow Israelite. He shall not require payment from his fellow Israelite or brother, because the LORD's time for canceling debts has been proclaimed. [3]You may require payment from a foreigner, but you must cancel any debt your brother owes you. [4]However, there should be no poor among you, for in the land the LORD your God is giving you to possess as your inheritance, he will richly bless you, [5]if only you fully obey the LORD your God and are careful to follow all these commands I am giving you today. [6]For the LORD your God will bless you as he has promised, and you will lend to many nations but will borrow from none. You will rule over many nations but none will rule over you.

[7]If there is a poor man among your brothers in any of the towns of the land that the LORD your God is giving you, do not be hardhearted or tightfisted toward your poor brother. [8]Rather be openhanded and freely lend him whatever he needs. [9]Be careful not to harbor this wicked thought: "The seventh year, the year for canceling debts, is near," so that you do not show ill will toward your needy brother and give him nothing. He may then appeal to the LORD against you, and you will be found guilty of sin. [10]Give generously to him and do so without a grudging heart; then because of this the LORD your God will bless you in all your work and in everything you put your hand to. [11]There will always be poor people in the land. Therefore I command you to be openhanded toward your brothers and toward the poor and needy in your land.

Freeing Servants [12]If a fellow Hebrew, a man or a woman, sells himself to you and serves you six years, in the seventh year you must let him go free. [13]And when you release him, do not send him away empty-handed. [14]Supply him liberally from your flock, your threshing floor and your winepress. Give to him as the LORD your God has blessed you. [15]Remember that you were slaves in Egypt and the LORD your God redeemed you. That is why I give you this command today.

[16]But if your servant says to you, "I do not want to leave you," because he loves you and your family and is well off with you, [17]then take an awl and push it through his ear lobe into the door, and he will become your servant for life. Do the same for your maidservant.

[18]Do not consider it a hardship to set your servant free, because his service to you these six years has been worth twice as much as that of a hired hand. And the LORD your God will bless you in everything you do.

The Firstborn Animals [19]Set apart for the LORD your God every firstborn male of your herds and flocks. Do not put the firstborn of your oxen to work, and do not shear the firstborn of your sheep. [20]Each year you and your family are to eat them in the presence of the LORD your God at the place he will choose. [21]If an animal has a defect, is lame or blind, or has any serious flaw, you must not sacrifice it to the LORD your God. [22]You are to eat it in your own towns. Both the ceremonially unclean and the clean may eat it, as if it were gazelle or deer. [23]But you must not eat the blood; pour it out on the ground like water.

16 *Passover* Observe the month of Abib and celebrate the Passover of the LORD your God, because in the month of Abib he brought you out of Egypt by night. [2]Sacrifice as the Passover to the LORD your God an animal from your flock or herd at the place the LORD will choose as a dwelling for his Name. [3]Do not eat it with bread made with yeast, but for seven days eat unleavened bread, the bread of affliction, because you left Egypt in haste—so that all the days of your life you may remember the time of your departure from Egypt. [4]Let no yeast be found in your possession in all your land for seven days. Do not let any of the meat you sacrifice on the evening of the first day remain until morning.

⁵You must not sacrifice the Passover in any town the LORD your God gives you ⁶except in the place he will choose as a dwelling for his Name. There you must sacrifice the Passover in the evening, when the sun goes down, on the anniversary*ᵃ* of your departure from Egypt. ⁷Roast it and eat it at the place the LORD your God will choose. Then in the morning return to your tents. ⁸For six days eat unleavened bread and on the seventh day hold an assembly to the LORD your God and do no work.

Feast of Weeks   ⁹Count off seven weeks from the time you begin to put the sickle to the standing grain. ¹⁰Then celebrate the Feast of Weeks to the LORD your God by giving a freewill offering in proportion to the blessings the LORD your God has given you. ¹¹And rejoice before the LORD your God at the place he will choose as a dwelling for his Name—you, your sons and daughters, your menservants and maidservants, the Levites in your towns, and the aliens, the fatherless and the widows living among you. ¹²Remember that you were slaves in Egypt, and follow carefully these decrees.

Feast of Tabernacles   ¹³Celebrate the Feast of Tabernacles for seven days after you have gathered the produce of your threshing floor and your winepress. ¹⁴Be joyful at your Feast—you, your sons and daughters, your menservants and maidservants, and the Levites, the aliens, the fatherless and the widows who live in your towns. ¹⁵For seven days celebrate the Feast to the LORD your God at the place the LORD will choose. For the LORD your God will bless you in all your harvest and in all the work of your hands, and your joy will be complete.

¹⁶Three times a year all your men must appear before the LORD your God at the place he will choose: at the Feast of Unleavened Bread, the Feast of Weeks and the Feast of Tabernacles. No man should appear before the LORD empty-handed: ¹⁷Each of you must bring a gift in proportion to the way the LORD your God has blessed you.

Judges   ¹⁸Appoint judges and officials for each of your tribes in every town the LORD your God is giving you, and they shall judge the people fairly. ¹⁹Do not pervert justice or show partiality. Do not accept a bribe, for a bribe blinds the eyes of the wise and twists the words of the righteous. ²⁰Follow justice and justice alone, so that you may live and possess the land the LORD your God is giving you.

Worshiping Other Gods   ²¹Do not set up any wooden Asherah pole*ᵇ* beside the altar you build to the LORD your God, ²²and do not erect a sacred stone, for these the LORD your God hates.

17 Do not sacrifice to the LORD your God an ox or a sheep that has any defect or flaw in it, for that would be detestable to him.

²If a man or woman living among you in one of the towns the LORD gives you is

---

DEUTERONOMY 16:16–17

Many families plan a Christmas gift for Jesus. Some have jars for loose change, and at Christmas they count it up and give it to missions. There are many ways to make your "holidays" true "holy-days," but one of the best is to show gratitude by making a special, extra gift to the Lord. Three times a year God's people were invited to great national holidays where "no man should appear before the LORD empty-handed. Each of you must bring a gift in proportion to the way the LORD your God has blessed you." What a good reminder that God is the source of all your blessings. And what a good way to say, "Thanks!"

Direct Line

ᵃ6 Or *down, at the time of day*   ᵇ21 Or *Do not plant any tree dedicated to Asherah*

found doing evil in the eyes of the LORD your God in violation of his covenant, ³and contrary to my command has worshiped other gods, bowing down to them or to the sun or the moon or the stars of the sky, ⁴and this has been brought to your attention, then you must investigate it thoroughly. If it is true and it has been proved that this detestable thing has been done in Israel, ⁵take the man or woman who has done this evil deed to your city gate and stone that person to death. ⁶On the testimony of two or three witnesses a man shall be put to death, but no one shall be put to death on the testimony of only one witness. ⁷The hands of the witnesses must be the first in putting him to death, and then the hands of all the people. You must purge the evil from among you.

Law Courts ⁸If cases come before your courts that are too difficult for you to judge—whether bloodshed, lawsuits or assaults—take them to the place the LORD your God will choose. ⁹Go to the priests, who are Levites, and to the judge who is in office at that time. Inquire of them and they will give you the verdict. ¹⁰You must act according to the decisions they give you at the place the LORD will choose. Be careful to do everything they direct you to do. ¹¹Act according to the law they teach you and the decisions they give you. Do not turn aside from what they tell you, to the right or to the left. ¹²The man who shows contempt for the judge or for the priest who stands ministering there to the LORD your God must be put to death. You must purge the evil from Israel. ¹³All the people will hear and be afraid, and will not be contemptuous again.

The King ¹⁴When you enter the land the LORD your God is giving you and have taken possession of it and settled in it, and you say, "Let us set a king over us like all the nations around us," ¹⁵be sure to appoint over you the king the LORD your God chooses. He must be from among your own brothers. Do not place a foreigner over you, one who is not a brother Israelite. ¹⁶The king, moreover, must not acquire great numbers of horses for himself or make the people return to Egypt to get more of them, for the LORD has told you, "You are not to go back that way again." ¹⁷He must not take many wives, or his heart will be led astray. He must not accumulate large amounts of silver and gold.

¹⁸When he takes the throne of his kingdom, he is to write for himself on a scroll a copy of this law, taken from that of the priests, who are Levites. ¹⁹It is to be with him, and he is to read it all the days of his life so that he may learn to revere the LORD his God and follow carefully all the words of this law and these decrees ²⁰and not consider himself better than his brothers and turn from the law to the right or to the left. Then he and his descendants will reign a long time over his kingdom in Israel.

18 *Offerings for Priests and Levites* The priests, who are Levites—indeed the whole tribe of Levi—are to have no allotment or inheritance with Israel. They shall live on the offerings made to the LORD by fire, for that is their inheritance. ²They shall have no inheritance among their brothers; the LORD is their inheritance, as he promised them.

³This is the share due the priests from the people who sacrifice a bull or a sheep: the shoulder, the jowls and the inner parts. ⁴You are to give them the firstfruits of your grain, new wine and oil, and the first wool from the shearing of your sheep, ⁵for the LORD your God has chosen them and their descendants out of all your tribes to stand and minister in the LORD's name always.

⁶If a Levite moves from one of your towns anywhere in Israel where he is living, and comes in all earnestness to the place the LORD will choose, ⁷he may minister in the name of the LORD his God like all his fellow Levites who serve there in the presence of the LORD. ⁸He is to share equally in their benefits, even though he has received money from the sale of family possessions.

Dear Sam,

My friends use a Ouija board at parties. When my mom heard, she said I couldn't go to any more parties. How can I persuade my mom not to be so old-fashioned?

Brad in Bradenton

Dear Sam, Inc.

100 Advice Lane, Anywhere, USA

Dear Brad,

Everyone wants to fit in. It's hard to be different. It doesn't seem fair when your friends seem to be having fun and you can't join them.

But did you know that Ouija boards are part of the occult? The spirit world is very real and is divided into two groups—the spirits who belong to God's kingdom and those who don't. God has given a strong message about trying to communicate with those spirits who are not part of his kingdom (Deuteronomy 18:10-12).

God is a spirit, and you don't need a Ouija board to talk to him. You can talk to him in prayer anytime and anyplace. God wants you to come to him for advice. When you turn to a Ouija board, a fortune teller, a horoscope or a palm reader, you are turning from God to seek advice from a kingdom God hates.

The Ouija board seems like an innocent toy. But it isn't. It is really an instrument used to contact spirits who are not of God. Your mother isn't being mean or old-fashioned. She is trying to keep you safe from something that is dangerous and evil.

Sam

Detestable Practices   ⁹When you enter the land the LORD your God is giving you, do not learn to imitate the detestable ways of the nations there. ¹⁰Let no one be found among you who sacrifices his son or daughter in*ᵃ* the fire, who practices divination or sorcery, interprets omens, engages in witchcraft, ¹¹or casts spells, or who is a medium or spiritist or who consults the dead. ¹²Anyone who does these things is detestable to the LORD, and because of these detestable practices the LORD your God will drive out those nations before you. ¹³You must be blameless before the LORD your God.

The Prophet   ¹⁴The nations you will dispossess listen to those who practice sorcery or divination. But as for you, the LORD your God has not permitted you to do so. ¹⁵The LORD your God will raise up for you a prophet like me from among your own brothers. You must listen to him. ¹⁶For this is what you asked of the LORD your God at Horeb on the day of the assembly when you said, "Let us not hear the voice of the LORD our God nor see this great fire anymore, or we will die."

¹⁷The LORD said to me: "What they say is good. ¹⁸I will raise up for them a prophet like you from among their brothers; I will put my words in his mouth, and he will tell them everything I command him. ¹⁹If anyone does not listen to my words that the prophet speaks in my name, I myself will call him to account. ²⁰But a prophet who presumes to speak in my name anything I have not commanded him to say, or a prophet who speaks in the name of other gods, must be put to death."

²¹You may say to yourselves, "How can we know when a message has not been spoken by the LORD?" ²²If what a prophet proclaims in the name of the LORD does not take place or come true, that is a message the LORD has not spoken. That prophet has spoken presumptuously. Do not be afraid of him.

Cities of Refuge   When the LORD your God has destroyed the nations whose land he is giving you, and when you have driven them out and settled in their towns and houses, ²then set aside for yourselves three cities centrally located in the land the LORD your God is giving you to possess. ³Build roads to them and divide into three parts the land the LORD your God is giving you as an inheritance, so that anyone who kills a man may flee there.

⁴This is the rule concerning the man who kills another and flees there to save his life—one who kills his neighbor unintentionally, without malice aforethought. ⁵For instance, a man may go into the forest with his neighbor to cut wood, and as he swings his ax to fell a tree, the head may fly off and hit his neighbor and kill him. That man may flee to one of these cities and save his life. ⁶Otherwise, the avenger of blood might pursue him in a rage, overtake him if the distance is too great, and kill him even though he is not deserving of death, since he did it to his neighbor without malice aforethought. ⁷This is why I command you to set aside for yourselves three cities.

⁸If the LORD your God enlarges your territory, as he promised on oath to your forefathers, and gives you the whole land he promised them, ⁹because you carefully follow all these laws I command you today—to love the LORD your God and to walk always in his ways—then you are to set aside three more cities. ¹⁰Do this so that innocent blood will not be shed in your land, which the LORD your God is giving you as your inheritance, and so that you will not be guilty of bloodshed.

¹¹But if a man hates his neighbor and lies in wait for him, assaults and kills him, and then flees to one of these cities, ¹²the elders of his town shall send for him, bring him back from the city, and hand him over to the avenger of

---

ᵃ10 Or who makes his son or daughter pass through

blood to die. [13]Show him no pity. You must purge from Israel the guilt of shedding innocent blood, so that it may go well with you.

[14]Do not move your neighbor's boundary stone set up by your predecessors in the inheritance you receive in the land the LORD your God is giving you to possess.

Witnesses [15]One witness is not enough to convict a man accused of any crime or offense he may have committed. A matter must be established by the testimony of two or three witnesses.

[16]If a malicious witness takes the stand to accuse a man of a crime, [17]the two men involved in the dispute must stand in the presence of the LORD before the priests and the judges who are in office at the time. [18]The judges must make a thorough investigation, and if the witness proves to be a liar, giving false testimony against his brother, [19]then do to him as he intended to do to his brother. You must purge the evil from among you. [20]The rest of the people will hear of this and be afraid, and never again will such an evil thing be done among you. [21]Show no pity: life for life, eye for eye, tooth for tooth, hand for hand, foot for foot.

20 *Going to War* When you go to war against your enemies and see horses and chariots and an army greater than yours, do not be afraid of them, because the LORD your God, who brought you up out of Egypt, will be with you. [2]When you are about to go into battle, the priest shall come forward and address the army. [3]He shall say: "Hear, O Israel, today you are going into battle against your enemies. Do not be fainthearted or afraid; do not be terrified or give way to panic before them. [4]For the LORD your God is the one who goes with you to fight for you against your enemies to give you victory."

[5]The officers shall say to the army: "Has anyone built a new house and not dedicated it? Let him go home, or he may die in battle and someone else may dedicate it. [6]Has anyone planted a vineyard and not begun to enjoy it? Let him go home, or he may die in battle and someone else enjoy it. [7]Has anyone become pledged to a woman and not married her? Let him go home, or he may die in battle and someone else marry her." [8]Then the officers shall add, "Is any man afraid or fainthearted? Let him go home so that his brothers will

---

The Bible Says

Destroy Them?

How could a loving God tell his people to "completely destroy" the Canaanites (Deuteronomy 20:16–17)? God gave this command to protect his people. Deuteronomy 20:18 explains clearly that if any Canaanites were left alive they would teach the Israelites to worship idols.

Archaeology has revealed much about Canaanite religion, which featured prostitution, immorality, even burning children alive to please their gods. And because the Israelites did not exterminate these people, exactly what God warned about did happen. The Canaanites turned the Israelites to idolatry.

So was God being brutal and bloodthirsty when he gave this command? Not at all. It was the Canaanites who were bloodthirsty, brutal and immoral. God was protecting his people and punishing the Canaanites, as they deserved.

not become disheartened too." ⁹When the officers have finished speaking to the army, they shall appoint commanders over it.

¹⁰When you march up to attack a city, make its people an offer of peace. ¹¹If they accept and open their gates, all the people in it shall be subject to forced labor and shall work for you. ¹²If they refuse to make peace and they engage you in battle, lay siege to that city. ¹³When the LORD your God delivers it into your hand, put to the sword all the men in it. ¹⁴As for the women, the children, the livestock and everything else in the city, you may take these as plunder for yourselves. And you may use the plunder the LORD your God gives you from your enemies. ¹⁵This is how you are to treat all the cities that are at a distance from you and do not belong to the nations nearby.

¹⁶However, in the cities of the nations the LORD your God is giving you as an inheritance, do not leave alive anything that breathes. ¹⁷Completely destroy*a* them—the Hittites, Amorites, Canaanites, Perizzites, Hivites and Jebusites—as the LORD your God has commanded you. ¹⁸Otherwise, they will teach you to follow all the detestable things they do in worshiping their gods, and you will sin against the LORD your God.

¹⁹When you lay siege to a city for a long time, fighting against it to capture it, do not destroy its trees by putting an ax to them, because you can eat their fruit. Do not cut them down. Are the trees of the field people, that you should besiege them?*b* ²⁰However, you may cut down trees that you know are not fruit trees and use them to build siege works until the city at war with you falls.

21 *Atonement for an Unsolved Murder* If a man is found slain, lying in a field in the land the LORD your God is giving you to possess, and it is not known who killed him, ²your elders and judges shall go out and measure the distance from the body to the neighboring towns. ³Then the elders of the town nearest the body shall take a heifer that has never been worked and has never worn a yoke ⁴and lead her down to a valley that has not been plowed or planted and where there is a flowing stream. There in the valley they are to break the heifer's neck. ⁵The priests, the sons of Levi, shall step forward, for the LORD your God has chosen them to minister and to pronounce blessings in the name of the LORD and to decide all cases of dispute and assault. ⁶Then all the elders of the town nearest the body shall wash their hands over the heifer whose neck was broken in the valley, ⁷and they shall declare: "Our hands did not shed this blood, nor did our eyes see it done. ⁸Accept this atonement for your people Israel, whom you have redeemed, O LORD, and do not hold your people guilty of the blood of an innocent man." And the bloodshed will be atoned for. ⁹So you will purge from yourselves the guilt of shedding innocent blood, since you have done what is right in the eyes of the LORD.

Marrying a Captive Woman ¹⁰When you go to war against your enemies and the LORD your God delivers them into your hands and you take captives, ¹¹if you notice among the captives a beautiful woman and are attracted to her, you may take her as your wife. ¹²Bring her into your home and have her shave her head, trim her nails ¹³and put aside the clothes she was wearing when captured. After she has lived in your house and mourned her father and mother for a full month, then you may go to her and be her husband and she shall be your wife. ¹⁴If you are not pleased with her, let her go wherever she wishes. You must not sell her or treat her as a slave, since you have dishonored her.

---

a 17 The Hebrew term refers to the irrevocable giving over of things or persons to the LORD, often by totally destroying them. *b 19* Or *down to use in the siege, for the fruit trees are for the benefit of man.*

The Right of the Firstborn ¹⁵If a man has two wives, and he loves one but not the other, and both bear him sons but the firstborn is the son of the wife he does not love, ¹⁶when he wills his property to his sons, he must not give the rights of the firstborn to the son of the wife he loves in preference to his actual firstborn, the son of the wife he does not love. ¹⁷He must acknowledge the son of his unloved wife as the firstborn by giving him a double share of all he has. That son is the first sign of his father's strength. The right of the firstborn belongs to him.

A Rebellious Son ¹⁸If a man has a stubborn and rebellious son who does not obey his father and mother and will not listen to them when they discipline him, ¹⁹his father and mother shall take hold of him and bring him to the elders at the gate of his town. ²⁰They shall say to the elders, "This son of ours is stubborn and rebellious. He will not obey us. He is a profligate and a drunkard." ²¹Then all the men of his town shall stone him to death. You must purge the evil from among you. All Israel will hear of it and be afraid.

Various Laws ²²If a man guilty of a capital offense is put to death and his body is hung on a tree, ²³you must not leave his body on the tree overnight. Be sure to bury him that same day, because anyone who is hung on a tree is under God's curse. You must not desecrate the land the LORD your God is giving you as an inheritance.

22 If you see your brother's ox or sheep straying, do not ignore it but be sure to take it back to him. ²If the brother does not live near you or if you do not know who he is, take it home with you and keep it until he comes looking for it. Then give it back to him. ³Do the same if you find your brother's donkey or his cloak or anything he loses. Do not ignore it.

⁴If you see your brother's donkey or his ox fallen on the road, do not ignore it. Help him get it to its feet.

⁵A woman must not wear men's clothing, nor a man wear women's clothing, for the LORD your God detests anyone who does this.

⁶If you come across a bird's nest beside the road, either in a tree or on the ground, and the mother is sitting on the young or on the eggs, do not take the mother with the young. ⁷You may take the young, but be sure to let the mother go, so that it may go well with you and you may have a long life.

⁸When you build a new house, make a parapet around your roof so that you may not bring the guilt of bloodshed on your house if someone falls from the roof.

⁹Do not plant two kinds of seed in your vineyard; if you do, not only the crops you plant but also the fruit of the vineyard will be defiled.[a]

¹⁰Do not plow with an ox and a donkey yoked together.

¹¹Do not wear clothes of wool and linen woven together.

¹²Make tassels on the four corners of the cloak you wear.

Marriage Violations ¹³If a man takes a wife and, after lying with her, dislikes her ¹⁴and slanders her and gives her a bad

Direct Line

DEUTERONOMY 21:18–21

Dad says, "Be home at 10:00." And you get home at 10:45. Mom says, "No MTV." And you sneak in a music video while she's in the kitchen. Even though your parents might not be too happy with you, chances are you won't get grounded—much less stoned to death. But what about open rebellion? Dad says be in by 10:45, and son is gone all night. Every day Mom says, "Get up and go to school," and every day daughter rolls over and ignores her. Now that's disobedience. Is it serious? Check out this passage, and never think rebellion at home is minor sin.

[a]9 Or be forfeited to the sanctuary

name, saying, "I married this woman, but when I approached her, I did not find proof of her virginity," ¹⁵then the girl's father and mother shall bring proof that she was a virgin to the town elders at the gate. ¹⁶The girl's father will say to the elders, "I gave my daughter in marriage to this man, but he dislikes her. ¹⁷Now he has slandered her and said, 'I did not find your daughter to be a virgin.' But here is the proof of my daughter's virginity." Then her parents shall display the cloth before the elders of the town, ¹⁸and the elders shall take the man and punish him. ¹⁹They shall fine him a hundred shekels of silver[a] and give them to the girl's father, because this man has given an Israelite virgin a bad name. She shall continue to be his wife; he must not divorce her as long as he lives.

²⁰If, however, the charge is true and no proof of the girl's virginity can be found, ²¹she shall be brought to the door of her father's house and there the men of her town shall stone her to death. She has done a disgraceful thing in Israel by being promiscuous while still in her father's house. You must purge the evil from among you.

²²If a man is found sleeping with another man's wife, both the man who slept with her and the woman must die. You must purge the evil from Israel.

²³If a man happens to meet in a town a virgin pledged to be married and he sleeps with her, ²⁴you shall take both of them to the gate of that town and stone them to death—the girl because she was in a town and did not scream for help, and the man because he violated another man's wife. You must purge the evil from among you.

²⁵But if out in the country a man happens to meet a girl pledged to be married and rapes her, only the man who has done this shall die. ²⁶Do nothing to the girl; she has committed no sin deserving death. This case is like that of someone who attacks and murders his neighbor, ²⁷for the man found the girl out in the country, and though the betrothed girl screamed, there was no one to rescue her.

²⁸If a man happens to meet a virgin who is not pledged to be married and rapes her and they are discovered, ²⁹he shall pay the girl's father fifty shekels of silver.[b] He must marry the girl, for he has violated her. He can never divorce her as long as he lives.

³⁰A man is not to marry his father's wife; he must not dishonor his father's bed.

Exclusion From the Assembly

23 No one who has been emasculated by crushing or cutting may enter the assembly of the LORD.

²No one born of a forbidden marriage[c] nor any of his descendants may enter the assembly of the LORD, even down to the tenth generation.

³No Ammonite or Moabite or any of his descendants may enter the assembly of the LORD, even down to the tenth generation. ⁴For they did not come to meet you with bread and water on your way when you came out of Egypt, and they hired Balaam son of Beor from Pethor in Aram Naharaim[d] to pronounce a curse on you.

This command is really for the birds!

SEE DEUTERONOMY 22:6-7

[a]19 That is, about 2 1/2 pounds (about 1 kilogram)
[b]29 That is, about 1 1/4 pounds (about 0.6 kilogram)
[c]2 Or *one of illegitimate birth*   [d]4 That is, Northwest Mesopotamia

Dear Sam,

A guy I really liked forced me to have sex with him on a date. I yelled and said no, but he did it any way. Now I feel so dirty and used and guilty. Help!

Anne in Annapolis

100 Advice Lane, Anywhere, USA

Dear Anne,

You are a victim of date rape. You were personally violated, and the feelings you describe are a normal reaction. Rape is emotionally very damaging. I encourage you to talk to your mom or another responsible adult, someone you can trust. This person can give you guidance or direct you to seek professional help. You have a long life ahead of you, and it's important for healing to take place so that you can have healthy relationships in the future.

One thing you must understand is that you are not at fault. Your date made the choice to yield to physical desires; the fault is his. Deuteronomy 22:25-27 discusses rape and God's reaction to it. He places the blame for rape firmly on the male involved, while the female is the innocent victim.

I encourage you to seek the help I mentioned earlier. And don't forget to also seek God in prayer. He is the great healer of physical, emotional and spiritual wounds.

Sam

⁵However, the Lᴏʀᴅ your God would not listen to Balaam but turned the curse into a blessing for you, because the Lᴏʀᴅ your God loves you. ⁶Do not seek a treaty of friendship with them as long as you live.

⁷Do not abhor an Edomite, for he is your brother. Do not abhor an Egyptian, because you lived as an alien in his country. ⁸The third generation of children born to them may enter the assembly of the Lᴏʀᴅ.

Uncleanness in the Camp ⁹When you are encamped against your enemies, keep away from everything impure. ¹⁰If one of your men is unclean because of a nocturnal emission, he is to go outside the camp and stay there. ¹¹But as evening approaches he is to wash himself, and at sunset he may return to the camp.

¹²Designate a place outside the camp where you can go to relieve yourself. ¹³As part of your equipment have something to dig with, and when you relieve yourself, dig a hole and cover up your excrement. ¹⁴For the Lᴏʀᴅ your God moves about in your camp to protect you and to deliver your enemies to you. Your camp must be holy, so that he will not see among you anything indecent and turn away from you.

Miscellaneous Laws ¹⁵If a slave has taken refuge with you, do not hand him over to his master. ¹⁶Let him live among you wherever he likes and in whatever town he chooses. Do not oppress him.

¹⁷No Israelite man or woman is to become a shrine prostitute. ¹⁸You must not bring the earnings of a female prostitute or of a male prostitute[a] into the house of the Lᴏʀᴅ your God to pay any vow, because the Lᴏʀᴅ your God detests them both.

¹⁹Do not charge your brother interest, whether on money or food or anything else that may earn interest. ²⁰You may charge a foreigner interest, but not a brother Israelite, so that the Lᴏʀᴅ your God may bless you in everything you put your hand to in the land you are entering to possess.

²¹If you make a vow to the Lᴏʀᴅ your God, do not be slow to pay it, for the Lᴏʀᴅ your God will certainly demand it of you and you will be guilty of sin. ²²But if you refrain from making a vow, you will not be guilty. ²³Whatever your lips utter you must be sure to do, because you made your vow freely to the Lᴏʀᴅ your God with your own mouth.

²⁴If you enter your neighbor's vineyard, you may eat all the grapes you want, but do not put any in your basket. ²⁵If you enter your neighbor's grainfield, you may pick kernels with your hands, but you must not put a sickle to his standing grain.

24 If a man marries a woman who becomes displeasing to him because he finds something indecent about her, and he writes her a certificate of divorce, gives it to her and sends her from his house, ²and if after she leaves his house she becomes the wife of another man, ³and her second husband dislikes her and writes her a certificate of divorce, gives it to her and sends her from his house, or if he dies, ⁴then her first husband, who divorced her, is not allowed to marry her again after she has been defiled. That would be detestable in the eyes of the Lᴏʀᴅ. Do not bring sin upon the land the Lᴏʀᴅ your God is giving you as an inheritance.

⁵If a man has recently married, he must not be sent to war or have any other duty laid on him. For one year he is to be free to stay at home and bring happiness to the wife he has married.

DEUTERONOMY 24

QUIZZER

Q: How long a honeymoon did the Old Testament law permit?

BONUS: What was the purpose of the honeymoon?

Answers on page 238

ᵃ18 Hebrew *of a dog*

⁶Do not take a pair of millstones—not even the upper one—as security for a debt, because that would be taking a man's livelihood as security.

⁷If a man is caught kidnapping one of his brother Israelites and treats him as a slave or sells him, the kidnapper must die. You must purge the evil from among you.

⁸In cases of leprous[a] diseases be very careful to do exactly as the priests, who are Levites, instruct you. You must follow carefully what I have commanded them. ⁹Remember what the LORD your God did to Miriam along the way after you came out of Egypt.

¹⁰When you make a loan of any kind to your neighbor, do not go into his house to get what he is offering as a pledge. ¹¹Stay outside and let the man to whom you are making the loan bring the pledge out to you. ¹²If the man is poor, do not go to sleep with his pledge in your possession. ¹³Return his cloak to him by sunset so that he may sleep in it. Then he will thank you, and it will be regarded as a righteous act in the sight of the LORD your God.

¹⁴Do not take advantage of a hired man who is poor and needy, whether he is a brother Israelite or an alien living in one of your towns. ¹⁵Pay him his wages each day before sunset, because he is poor and is counting on it. Otherwise he may cry to the LORD against you, and you will be guilty of sin.

¹⁶Fathers shall not be put to death for their children, nor children put to death for their fathers; each is to die for his own sin.

¹⁷Do not deprive the alien or the fatherless of justice, or take the cloak of the widow as a pledge. ¹⁸Remember that you were slaves in Egypt and the LORD your God redeemed you from there. That is why I command you to do this.

¹⁹When you are harvesting in your field and you overlook a sheaf, do not go back to get it. Leave it for the alien, the fatherless and the widow, so that the LORD your God may bless you in all the work of your hands. ²⁰When you beat the olives from your trees, do not go over the branches a second time. Leave what remains for the alien, the fatherless and the widow. ²¹When you harvest the grapes in your vineyard, do not go over the vines again. Leave what remains for the alien, the fatherless and the widow. ²²Remember that you were slaves in Egypt. That is why I command you to do this.

When men have a dispute, they are to take it to court and the judges will decide the case, acquitting the innocent and condemning the guilty. ²If the guilty man deserves to be beaten, the judge shall make him lie down and have him flogged in his presence with the number of lashes his crime deserves, ³but he must not give him more than forty lashes. If he is flogged more than that, your brother will be degraded in your eyes.

⁴Do not muzzle an ox while it is treading out the grain.

⁵If brothers are living together and one of them dies without a son, his widow must not marry outside the family. Her husband's brother shall take her and marry her and fulfill the duty of a brother-in-law to her. ⁶The first son she bears shall carry on the name of the dead brother so that his name will not be blotted out from Israel.

⁷However, if a man does not want to marry his brother's wife, she shall go to the elders at the town gate and say, "My husband's brother refuses to carry on his brother's name in Israel. He will not fulfill the duty of a brother-in-law to me." ⁸Then the elders of his town shall summon him and talk to him. If he persists in saying, "I do not want to marry her," ⁹his brother's widow shall go up to him in the presence of the elders, take off one of his sandals, spit in his face and say, "This is what is done to the man who will not build

Answers

to Quizzer on
page 237

**A: One year
(Deuteronomy
24:5)!**

**BONUS: To let
the man "bring
happiness" to
his wife before
going to war
or having any
other civic duty.**

---

[a]8 The Hebrew word was used for various diseases affecting the skin—not necessarily leprosy.

up his brother's family line." ¹⁰That man's line shall be known in Israel as The Family of the Unsandaled.

¹¹If two men are fighting and the wife of one of them comes to rescue her husband from his assailant, and she reaches out and seizes him by his private parts, ¹²you shall cut off her hand. Show her no pity.

¹³Do not have two differing weights in your bag—one heavy, one light. ¹⁴Do not have two differing measures in your house—one large, one small. ¹⁵You must have accurate and honest weights and measures, so that you may live long in the land the LORD your God is giving you. ¹⁶For the LORD your God detests anyone who does these things, anyone who deals dishonestly.

¹⁷Remember what the Amalekites did to you along the way when you came out of Egypt. ¹⁸When you were weary and worn out, they met you on your journey and cut off all who were lagging behind; they had no fear of God. ¹⁹When the LORD your God gives you rest from all the enemies around you in the land he is giving you to possess as an inheritance, you shall blot out the memory of Amalek from under heaven. Do not forget!

26 *Firstfruits and Tithes*

When you have entered the land the LORD your God is giving you as an inheritance and have taken possession of it and settled in it, ²take some of the firstfruits of all that you produce from the soil of the land the LORD your God is giving you and put them in a basket. Then go to the place the LORD your God will choose as a dwelling for his Name ³and say to the priest in office at the time, "I declare today to the LORD your God that I have come to the land the LORD swore to our forefathers to give us." ⁴The priest shall take the basket from your hands and set it down in front of the altar of the LORD your God. ⁵Then you shall declare before the LORD your God: "My father was a wandering Aramean, and he went down into Egypt with a few people and lived there and became a great nation, powerful and numerous. ⁶But the Egyptians mistreated us and made us suffer, putting us to hard labor. ⁷Then we cried out to the LORD, the God of our fathers, and the LORD heard our voice and saw our misery, toil and oppression. ⁸So the LORD brought us out of Egypt with a mighty hand and an outstretched arm, with great terror and with miraculous signs and wonders. ⁹He brought us to this place and gave us this land, a land flowing with milk and honey; ¹⁰and now I bring the firstfruits of the soil that you, O LORD, have given me." Place the basket before the LORD your God and bow down before him. ¹¹And you and the Levites and the aliens among you shall rejoice in all the good things the LORD your God has given to you and your household.

¹²When you have finished setting aside a tenth of all your produce in the third year, the year of the tithe, you shall give it to the Levite, the alien, the fatherless and the widow, so that they may eat in your towns and be satisfied. ¹³Then say to the LORD your God: "I have removed from my house the sacred portion and have given it to the Levite, the alien, the fatherless and the widow, according to all you commanded. I have not turned aside from your commands nor have I forgotten any of them. ¹⁴I

DEUTERONOMY 26:16–19

Does it bother you when kids who go to church regularly swear or tell dirty stories at school? When an officer in your youth group cheats on tests? Or when a teen who is oh-so-pious at church mocks Christian kids at school? Maybe you wonder if they're real Christians at all. That question is one you and I can't answer. But in real Christians, walk and talk are supposed to be the same. Maybe you can't judge whether another person is a real Christian or not. But you *can* make sure that no one has any doubts about you! If you say you're a Christian, live a Christian life at school, at home, everywhere!

Direct Line

have not eaten any of the sacred portion while I was in mourning, nor have I removed any of it while I was unclean, nor have I offered any of it to the dead. I have obeyed the LORD my God; I have done everything you commanded me. ¹⁵Look down from heaven, your holy dwelling place, and bless your people Israel and the land you have given us as you promised on oath to our forefathers, a land flowing with milk and honey."

Follow the LORD's Commands ¹⁶The LORD your God commands you this day to follow these decrees and laws; carefully observe them with all your heart and with all your soul. ¹⁷You have declared this day that the LORD is your God and that you will walk in his ways, that you will keep his decrees, commands and laws, and that you will obey him. ¹⁸And the LORD has declared this day that you are his people, his treasured possession as he promised, and that you are to keep all his commands. ¹⁹He has declared that he will set you in praise, fame and honor high above all the nations he has made and that you will be a people holy to the LORD your God, as he promised.

The Altar on Mount Ebal Moses and the elders of Israel commanded the people: "Keep all these commands that I give you today. ²When you have crossed the Jordan into the land the LORD your God is giving you, set up some large stones and coat them with plaster. ³Write on them all the words of this law when you have crossed over to enter the land the LORD your God is giving you, a land flowing with milk and honey, just as the LORD, the God of your fathers, promised you. ⁴And when you have crossed the Jordan, set up these stones on Mount Ebal, as I command you today, and coat them with plaster. ⁵Build there an altar to the LORD your God, an altar of stones. Do not use any iron tool upon them. ⁶Build the altar of the LORD your God with fieldstones and offer burnt offerings on it to the LORD your God. ⁷Sacrifice fellowship offerings*ᵃ* there, eating them and rejoicing in the presence of the LORD your God. ⁸And you shall write very clearly all the words of this law on these stones you have set up."

Curses From Mount Ebal ⁹Then Moses and the priests, who are Levites, said to all Israel, "Be silent, O Israel, and listen! You have now become the people of the LORD your God. ¹⁰Obey the LORD your God and follow his commands and decrees that I give you today."

¹¹On the same day Moses commanded the people:

¹²When you have crossed the Jordan, these tribes shall stand on Mount Gerizim to bless the people: Simeon, Levi, Judah, Issachar, Joseph and Benjamin. ¹³And these tribes shall stand on Mount Ebal to pronounce curses: Reuben, Gad, Asher, Zebulun, Dan and Naphtali.

¹⁴The Levites shall recite to all the people of Israel in a loud voice:

¹⁵"Cursed is the man who carves an image or casts an idol—a thing detestable to the LORD, the work of the craftsman's hands—and sets it up in secret."

Then all the people shall say, "Amen!"
¹⁶"Cursed is the man who dishonors his father or his mother."

Then all the people shall say, "Amen!"
¹⁷"Cursed is the man who moves his neighbor's boundary stone."

Then all the people shall say, "Amen!"
¹⁸"Cursed is the man who leads the blind astray on the road."

Then all the people shall say, "Amen!"
¹⁹"Cursed is the man who withholds justice from the alien, the fatherless or the widow."

Then all the people shall say, "Amen!"

ᵃ7 Traditionally *peace offerings*

²⁰"Cursed is the man who sleeps with his father's wife, for he dishonors his father's bed."

Then all the people shall say, "Amen!"

²¹"Cursed is the man who has sexual relations with any animal."

Then all the people shall say, "Amen!"

²²"Cursed is the man who sleeps with his sister, the daughter of his father or the daughter of his mother."

Then all the people shall say, "Amen!"

²³"Cursed is the man who sleeps with his mother-in-law."

Then all the people shall say, "Amen!"

²⁴"Cursed is the man who kills his neighbor secretly."

Then all the people shall say, "Amen!"

²⁵"Cursed is the man who accepts a bribe to kill an innocent person."

Then all the people shall say, "Amen!"

²⁶"Cursed is the man who does not uphold the words of this law by carrying them out."

Then all the people shall say, "Amen!"

28 *Blessings for Obedience* If you fully obey the Lord your God and carefully follow all his commands I give you today, the Lord your God will set you high above all the nations on earth. ²All these blessings will come upon you and accompany you if you obey the Lord your God:

³You will be blessed in the city and blessed in the country.

⁴The fruit of your womb will be blessed, and the crops of your land and the young of your livestock—the calves of your herds and the lambs of your flocks.

⁵Your basket and your kneading trough will be blessed.

⁶You will be blessed when you come in and blessed when you go out.

⁷The Lord will grant that the enemies who rise up against you will be defeated before you. They will come at you from one direction but flee from you in seven.

⁸The Lord will send a blessing on your barns and on everything you put your hand to. The Lord your God will bless you in the land he is giving you.

⁹The Lord will establish you as his holy people, as he promised you on oath, if you keep the commands of the Lord your God and walk in his ways. ¹⁰Then all the peoples on earth will see that you are called by the name of the Lord, and they will fear you. ¹¹The Lord will grant you abundant prosperity—in the fruit of your womb, the young of your livestock and the crops of your ground—in the land he swore to your forefathers to give you.

¹²The Lord will open the heavens, the storehouse of his bounty, to send rain on your land in season and to bless all the work of your hands. You will lend to many nations but will borrow from none. ¹³The Lord will make you the head, not the tail. If you pay attention to the commands of the Lord your God that I give you this day and carefully follow them, you will always be at the top, never at the bottom. ¹⁴Do not turn aside from any of the commands I give you today, to the right or to the left, following other gods and serving them.

> The Lord will establish you as his holy people (Deuteronomy 28:9).

Curses for Disobedience ¹⁵However, if you do not obey the Lord your God and do not carefully follow all his commands and decrees I am giving you today, all these curses will come upon you and overtake you:

¹⁶You will be cursed in the city and cursed in the country.

¹⁷Your basket and your kneading trough will be cursed.

Dear Sam,

What's the big deal about obedience?
Isn't it just another way to make
kids feel guilty?

Marc in Muncie

100 Advice Lane, Anywhere, USA

Dear Marc,

What would this world be like without rules? Imagine if there were no speed limits, if stealing and murder were legal, if kidnapping were OK. You would live in a world of total chaos. If you really think about it, most laws aren't there to make you feel guilty but to protect you. If you look at rules from that viewpoint, perhaps you'll see them as a protection rather than as a roadblock. Their purpose is to protect, not control.

Is it possible that some of your parents' rules are to protect you?

Everyone in society must obey rules and laws. Some laws are given by God; some, by government; others, by parents. Many rules and laws are made to protect you. Regardless of the reason for the law, God promises to bless obedience and discipline disobedience (Deuteronomy 28:1,15).

Sam

¹⁸The fruit of your womb will be cursed, and the crops of your land, and the calves of your herds and the lambs of your flocks.

¹⁹You will be cursed when you come in and cursed when you go out.

²⁰The LORD will send on you curses, confusion and rebuke in everything you put your hand to, until you are destroyed and come to sudden ruin because of the evil you have done in forsaking him.ᵃ ²¹The LORD will plague you with diseases until he has destroyed you from the land you are entering to possess. ²²The LORD will strike you with wasting disease, with fever and inflammation, with scorching heat and drought, with blight and mildew, which will plague you until you perish. ²³The sky over your head will be bronze, the ground beneath you iron. ²⁴The LORD will turn the rain of your country into dust and powder; it will come down from the skies until you are destroyed.

²⁵The LORD will cause you to be defeated before your enemies. You will come at them from one direction but flee from them in seven, and you will become a thing of horror to all the kingdoms on earth. ²⁶Your carcasses will be food for all the birds of the air and the beasts of the earth, and there will be no one to frighten them away. ²⁷The LORD will afflict you with the boils of Egypt and with tumors, festering sores and the itch, from which you cannot be cured. ²⁸The LORD will afflict you with madness, blindness and confusion of mind. ²⁹At midday you will grope about like a blind man in the dark. You will be unsuccessful in everything you do; day after day you will be oppressed and robbed, with no one to rescue you.

³⁰You will be pledged to be married to a woman, but another will take her and ravish her. You will build a house, but you will not live in it. You will plant a vineyard, but you will not even begin to enjoy its fruit. ³¹Your ox will be slaughtered before your eyes, but you will eat none of it. Your donkey will be forcibly taken from you and will not be returned. Your sheep will be given to your enemies, and no one will rescue them. ³²Your sons and daughters will be given to another nation, and you will wear out your eyes watching for them day after day, powerless to lift a hand. ³³A people that you do not know will eat what your land and labor produce, and you will have nothing but cruel oppression all your days. ³⁴The sights you see will drive you mad. ³⁵The LORD will afflict your knees and legs with painful boils that cannot be cured, spreading from the soles of your feet to the top of your head.

³⁶The LORD will drive you and the king you set over you to a nation unknown to you or your fathers. There you will worship other gods, gods of wood and stone. ³⁷You will become a thing of horror and an object of scorn and ridicule to all the nations where the LORD will drive you.

³⁸You will sow much seed in the field but you will harvest little, because locusts will devour it. ³⁹You will plant vineyards and cultivate them but you will not drink the wine or gather the grapes, because worms will eat them. ⁴⁰You will have olive trees throughout your country but you will not use the oil, because the olives will drop off. ⁴¹You will have sons and daughters but you will not keep them, because they will go into captivity. ⁴²Swarms of locusts will take over all your trees and the crops of your land.

⁴³The alien who lives among you will rise above you higher and higher, but you will sink lower and lower. ⁴⁴He will lend to you, but you will not lend to him. He will be the head, but you will be the tail.

⁴⁵All these curses will come upon you. They will pursue you and overtake you until you are destroyed, because you did not obey the LORD your God and observe the commands and decrees he gave you. ⁴⁶They will be a sign and a wonder to you and your descendants forever. ⁴⁷Because you did not serve the LORD your God joyfully and gladly in the time of prosperity, ⁴⁸therefore in hunger and thirst, in nakedness and dire poverty, you will serve the enemies

ᵃ20 Hebrew *me*

the LORD sends against you. He will put an iron yoke on your neck until he has destroyed you.

⁴⁹The LORD will bring a nation against you from far away, from the ends of the earth, like an eagle swooping down, a nation whose language you will not understand, ⁵⁰a fierce-looking nation without respect for the old or pity for the young. ⁵¹They will devour the young of your livestock and the crops of your land until you are destroyed. They will leave you no grain, new wine or oil, nor any calves of your herds or lambs of your flocks until you are ruined. ⁵²They will lay siege to all the cities throughout your land until the high fortified walls in which you trust fall down. They will besiege all the cities throughout the land the LORD your God is giving you.

⁵³Because of the suffering that your enemy will inflict on you during the siege, you will eat the fruit of the womb, the flesh of the sons and daughters the LORD your God has given you. ⁵⁴Even the most gentle and sensitive man among you will have no compassion on his own brother or the wife he loves or his surviving children, ⁵⁵and he will not give to one of them any of the flesh of his children that he is eating. It will be all he has left because of the suffering your enemy will inflict on you during the siege of all your cities. ⁵⁶The most gentle and sensitive woman among you—so sensitive and gentle that she would not venture to touch the ground with the sole of her foot— will begrudge the husband she loves and her own son or daughter ⁵⁷the afterbirth from her womb and the children she bears. For she intends to eat them secretly during the siege and in the distress that your enemy will inflict on you in your cities.

⁵⁸If you do not carefully follow all the words of this law, which are written in this book, and do not revere this glorious and awesome name—the LORD your God— ⁵⁹the LORD will send fearful plagues on you and your descendants, harsh and prolonged disasters, and severe and lingering illnesses. ⁶⁰He will bring upon you all the diseases of Egypt that you dreaded, and they will cling to you. ⁶¹The LORD will also bring on you every kind of sickness and disaster not recorded in this Book of the Law, until you are destroyed. ⁶²You who were as numerous as the stars in the sky will be left but few in number, because you did not obey the LORD your God. ⁶³Just as it pleased the LORD to make you prosper and increase in number, so it will please him to ruin and destroy you. You will be uprooted from the land you are entering to possess.

⁶⁴Then the LORD will scatter you among all nations, from one end of the earth to the other. There you will worship other gods—gods of wood and stone, which neither you nor your fathers have known. ⁶⁵Among those nations you will find no repose, no resting place for the sole of your foot. There the LORD will give you an anxious mind, eyes weary with longing, and a despairing heart. ⁶⁶You will live in constant suspense, filled with dread both night and day, never sure of your life. ⁶⁷In the morning you will say, "If only it were evening!" and in the evening, "If only it were morning!"—because of the terror that will fill your hearts and the sights that your eyes will see. ⁶⁸The LORD will send you back in ships to Egypt on a journey I said you should never make again. There you will offer yourselves for sale to your enemies as male and female slaves, but no one will buy you.

29 *Renewal of the Covenant* These are the terms of the covenant the LORD commanded Moses to make with the Israelites in Moab, in addition to the covenant he had made with them at Horeb.

²Moses summoned all the Israelites and said to them:

Your eyes have seen all that the LORD did in Egypt to Pharaoh, to all his officials and to all his land. ³With your own eyes you saw those great trials, those miraculous signs and great wonders. ⁴But to this day the LORD has not given you a mind that understands or eyes that see or ears that hear. ⁵Dur-

Death

You see death all the time. On TV, on a video, at the movies. But that's not real death. It's just "pretend." Real death is far from "pretend." Real death is painful and can be frightening.

Death (deth) n.
the act of dying; the termination of life; the state of being dead.

ALTERNATE DEFINITION
they're gone, and it seems like the end

Death always brings sorrow. But a Christian's sorrow is eased by hope: "We do not want you to...grieve like the rest of men, who have no hope. We believe that Jesus died and rose again and so we believe that God will bring with Jesus those who have fallen asleep in him."
1 THESSALONIANS 4:13-14

In this world nothing is certain but death...
—Benjamin Franklin

Most teenagers first experience death when a grandparent dies. Some lose one or both parents. Others lose a close friend. The death of someone you love leaves an aching, empty hole in your life.

If you're honest with yourself, would you be willing to admit that death frightens you? At least a little? Well, you're not alone. Death, your own or that of someone you love, gives most everyone a shiver at one time or another.

Death is an enemy. But when Jesus returns, God has promised to "wipe every tear from their eyes. There will be no more death or mourning or crying or pain, for the old order of things has passed away."
REVELATIONS 21:4

Stress

(stres) n.
a mentally or emotionally disruptive
or disquieting influence.

ALTERNATE DEFINITION
that tightness in your stomach when
it's test time—and you didn't study!

Mom and Dad fighting. Trying to squeeze in both school and a job. Having to stay home with your little brother when you want to be out with your friends. Getting up on time for school. Make a list of what stresses you out.

You can't get away from stress completely. Some stress is good for you. But don't punish yourself. Do what you can to relieve some of the pressures. And about those things you can't change...

"I have learned to be content whatever the circumstances. I know what it is to be in need, and I know what it is to have plenty...I can do everything through him who gives me strength."
PHILIPPIANS 4:11-13

Check each source of stress. How can you avoid it? By planning ahead? By making a change in your priorities? Your lifestyle? Your relationship with a family member?

Or is the stress in your life caused by something out of control?

What would life be like if you had no stress? Sounds pretty good sometimes, doesn't it? No challenges to meet. No tough choices. No hassles. No need for God?

¹³Once more the Philistines raided the valley; ¹⁴so David inquired of God again, and God answered him, "Do not go straight up, but circle around them and attack them in front of the balsam trees. ¹⁵As soon as you hear the sound of marching in the tops of the balsam trees, move out to battle, because that will mean God has gone out in front of you to strike the Philistine army." ¹⁶So David did as God commanded him, and they struck down the Philistine army, all the way from Gibeon to Gezer.

¹⁷So David's fame spread throughout every land, and the LORD made all the nations fear him.

15 *The Ark Brought to Jerusalem* After David had constructed buildings for himself in the City of David, he prepared a place for the ark of God and pitched a tent for it. ²Then David said, "No one but the Levites may carry the ark of God, because the LORD chose them to carry the ark of the LORD and to minister before him forever."

³David assembled all Israel in Jerusalem to bring up the ark of the LORD to the place he had prepared for it. ⁴He called together the descendants of Aaron and the Levites:

⁵From the descendants of Kohath,
    Uriel the leader and 120 relatives;
⁶from the descendants of Merari,
    Asaiah the leader and 220 relatives;
⁷from the descendants of Gershon,*
    Joel the leader and 130 relatives;
⁸from the descendants of Elizaphan,
    Shemaiah the leader and 200 relatives;
⁹from the descendants of Hebron,
    Eliel the leader and 80 relatives;
¹⁰from the descendants of Uzziel,
    Amminadab the leader and 112 relatives.

¹¹Then David summoned Zadok and Abiathar the priests, and Uriel, Asaiah, Joel, Shemaiah, Eliel and Amminadab the Levites. ¹²He said to them, "You are the heads of the Levitical families; you and your fellow Levites are to consecrate yourselves and bring up the ark of the LORD, the God of Israel, to the place I have prepared for it. ¹³It was because you, the Levites, did not bring it up the first time that the LORD our God broke out in anger against us. We did not inquire of him about how to do it in the prescribed way." ¹⁴So the priests and Levites consecrated themselves in order to bring up the ark of the LORD, the God of Israel. ¹⁵And the Levites carried the ark of God with the poles on their shoulders, as Moses had commanded in accordance with the word of the LORD.

¹⁶David told the leaders of the Levites to appoint their brothers as singers to sing joyful songs, accompanied by musical instruments: lyres, harps and cymbals.

¹⁷So the Levites appointed Heman son of Joel; from his brothers, Asaph son of Berekiah; and from their brothers the Merarites, Ethan son of Kushaiah; ¹⁸and with them their brothers next in rank: Zechariah,ᵇ Jaaziel, Shemiramoth, Jehiel, Unni, Eliab, Benaiah, Maaseiah, Mattithiah, Eliphelehu, Mikneiah, Obed-Edom and Jeiel,ᶜ the gatekeepers.

¹⁹The musicians Heman, Asaph and Ethan were to sound the bronze cymbals; ²⁰Zechariah, Aziel, Shemiramoth, Jehiel, Unni, Eliab, Maaseiah and Benaiah were to play the lyres according to *alamoth,*ᵈ ²¹and Mattithiah,

---

*7 Hebrew *Gershom,* a variant of *Gershon*   ᵇ18 Three Hebrew manuscripts and most Septuagint manuscripts (see also verse 20 and 1 Chron. 16:5); most Hebrew manuscripts *Zechariah son and* or *Zechariah, Ben and*   ᶜ18 Hebrew; Septuagint (see also verse 21) *Jeiel and Azaziah*   ᵈ20 Probably a musical term

Eliphelehu, Mikneiah, Obed-Edom, Jeiel and Azaziah were to play the harps, directing according to *sheminith.ª* ²²Kenaniah the head Levite was in charge of the singing; that was his responsibility because he was skillful at it.

²³Berekiah and Elkanah were to be doorkeepers for the ark. ²⁴Shebaniah, Joshaphat, Nethanel, Amasai, Zechariah, Benaiah and Eliezer the priests were to blow trumpets before the ark of God. Obed-Edom and Jehiah were also to be doorkeepers for the ark.

²⁵So David and the elders of Israel and the commanders of units of a thousand went to bring up the ark of the covenant of the LORD from the house of Obed-Edom, with rejoicing. ²⁶Because God had helped the Levites who were carrying the ark of the covenant of the LORD, seven bulls and seven rams were sacrificed. ²⁷Now David was clothed in a robe of fine linen, as were all the Levites who were carrying the ark, and as were the singers, and Kenaniah, who was in charge of the singing of the choirs. David also wore a linen ephod. ²⁸So all Israel brought up the ark of the covenant of the LORD with shouts, with the sounding of rams' horns and trumpets, and of cymbals, and the playing of lyres and harps.

²⁹As the ark of the covenant of the LORD was entering the City of David, Michal daughter of Saul watched from a window. And when she saw King David dancing and celebrating, she despised him in her heart.

nswers

to Quizzer on page 500

A: Uzzah put his hand on the ark of the covenant, which no one was allowed to touch (1 Chronicles 13:9-10).

BONUS: God is holy and his commands must be obeyed (1 Chronicles 15:11-15).

16 They brought the ark of God and set it inside the tent that David had pitched for it, and they presented burnt offerings and fellowship offerings*ᵇ* before God. ²After David had finished sacrificing the burnt offerings and fellowship offerings, he blessed the people in the name of the LORD. ³Then he gave a loaf of bread, a cake of dates and a cake of raisins to each Israelite man and woman.

⁴He appointed some of the Levites to minister before the ark of the LORD, to make petition, to give thanks, and to praise the LORD, the God of Israel: ⁵Asaph was the chief, Zechariah second, then Jeiel, Shemiramoth, Jehiel, Mattithiah, Eliab, Benaiah, Obed-Edom and Jeiel. They were to play the lyres and harps, Asaph was to sound the cymbals, ⁶and Benaiah and Jahaziel the priests were to blow the trumpets regularly before the ark of the covenant of God.

David's Psalm of Thanks ⁷That day David first committed to Asaph and his associates this psalm of thanks to the LORD:

⁸Give thanks to the LORD, call on his name;
    make known among the nations what he has done.
⁹Sing to him, sing praise to him;
    tell of all his wonderful acts.
¹⁰Glory in his holy name;
    let the hearts of those who seek the LORD rejoice.
¹¹Look to the LORD and his strength;
    seek his face always.
¹²Remember the wonders he has done,
    his miracles, and the judgments he pronounced,
¹³O descendants of Israel his servant,
    O sons of Jacob, his chosen ones.

¹⁴He is the LORD our God;
    his judgments are in all the earth.
¹⁵He remembers*ᶜ* his covenant forever,
    the word he commanded, for a thousand generations,

ª21 Probably a musical term   *ᵇ1* Traditionally *peace offerings*; also in verse 2   *ᶜ15* Some Septuagint manuscripts (see also Psalm 105:8); Hebrew *Remember*

DEAR SAM,

I HAVE THE ABSOLUTE WORST CHORES IN
THE HOUSE. IS THERE ANYTHING I CAN
DO BESIDES COMPLAIN OR REFUSE?

GREG IN GREAT FALLS

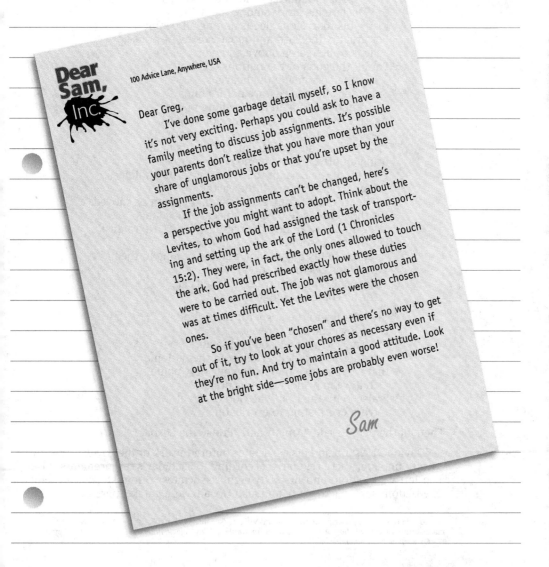

Dear Sam, Inc.

100 Advice Lane, Anywhere, USA

Dear Greg,

I've done some garbage detail myself, so I know it's not very exciting. Perhaps you could ask to have a family meeting to discuss job assignments. It's possible your parents don't realize that you have more than your share of unglamorous jobs or that you're upset by the assignments.

If the job assignments can't be changed, here's a perspective you might want to adopt. Think about the Levites, to whom God had assigned the task of transporting and setting up the ark of the Lord (1 Chronicles 15:2). They were, in fact, the only ones allowed to touch the ark. God had prescribed exactly how these duties were to be carried out. The job was not glamorous and was at times difficult. Yet the Levites were the chosen ones.

So if you've been "chosen" and there's no way to get out of it, try to look at your chores as necessary even if they're no fun. And try to maintain a good attitude. Look at the bright side—some jobs are probably even worse!

Sam

¹⁶the covenant he made with Abraham,
the oath he swore to Isaac.
¹⁷He confirmed it to Jacob as a decree,
to Israel as an everlasting covenant:
¹⁸"To you I will give the land of Canaan
as the portion you will inherit."

¹⁹When they were but few in number,
few indeed, and strangers in it,
²⁰they^a wandered from nation to nation,
from one kingdom to another.
²¹He allowed no man to oppress them;
for their sake he rebuked kings:
²²"Do not touch my anointed ones;
do my prophets no harm."

²³Sing to the LORD, all the earth;
proclaim his salvation day after day.
²⁴Declare his glory among the nations,
his marvelous deeds among all peoples.
²⁵For great is the Lord and most worthy of praise;
he is to be feared above all gods.
²⁶For all the gods of the nations are idols,
but the LORD made the heavens.
²⁷Splendor and majesty are before him;
strength and joy in his dwelling place.
²⁸Ascribe to the LORD, O families of nations,
ascribe to the LORD glory and strength,
²⁹   ascribe to the LORD the glory due his name.
Bring an offering and come before him;
worship the LORD in the splendor of his^b holiness.
³⁰Tremble before him, all the earth!
The world is firmly established; it cannot be moved.
³¹Let the heavens rejoice, let the earth be glad;
let them say among the nations, "The LORD reigns!"
³²Let the sea resound, and all that is in it;
let the fields be jubilant, and everything in them!
³³Then the trees of the forest will sing,
they will sing for joy before the LORD,
for he comes to judge the earth.

³⁴Give thanks to the LORD, for he is good;
his love endures forever.
³⁵Cry out, "Save us, O God our Savior;
gather us and deliver us from the nations,
that we may give thanks to your holy name,
that we may glory in your praise."
³⁶Praise be to the LORD, the God of Israel,
from everlasting to everlasting.

Then all the people said "Amen" and "Praise the LORD."

³⁷David left Asaph and his associates before the ark of the covenant of the LORD to minister there regularly, according to each day's requirements. ³⁸He also left Obed-Edom and his sixty-eight associates to minister with them. Obed-Edom son of Jeduthun, and also Hosah, were gatekeepers.

> Let the hearts of those who seek the LORD rejoice (1 Chronicles 16:10).

---

^a18-20 One Hebrew manuscript, Septuagint and Vulgate (see also Psalm 105:12); most Hebrew manuscripts *inherit,* / ¹⁹*though you are but few in number,* / *few indeed, and strangers in it."* / ²⁰*They*
^b29 Or *LORD with the splendor of*

[39]David left Zadok the priest and his fellow priests before the tabernacle of the LORD at the high place in Gibeon [40]to present burnt offerings to the LORD on the altar of burnt offering regularly, morning and evening, in accordance with everything written in the Law of the LORD, which he had given Israel. [41]With them were Heman and Jeduthun and the rest of those chosen and designated by name to give thanks to the LORD, "for his love endures forever." [42]Heman and Jeduthun were responsible for the sounding of the trumpets and cymbals and for the playing of the other instruments for sacred song. The sons of Jeduthun were stationed at the gate.

[43]Then all the people left, each for his own home, and David returned home to bless his family.

God's Promise to David After David was settled in his palace, he said to Nathan the prophet, "Here I am, living in a palace of cedar, while the ark of the covenant of the LORD is under a tent."

[2]Nathan replied to David, "Whatever you have in mind, do it, for God is with you."

[3]That night the word of God came to Nathan, saying:

> Give thanks to the LORD, for he is good; his love endures forever
> (1 Chronicles 16:34).

[4]"Go and tell my servant David, 'This is what the LORD says: You are not the one to build me a house to dwell in. [5]I have not dwelt in a house from the day I brought Israel up out of Egypt to this day. I have moved from one tent site to another, from one dwelling place to another. [6]Wherever I have moved with all the Israelites, did I ever say to any of their leaders*a* whom I commanded to shepherd my people, "Why have you not built me a house of cedar?" '

[7]"Now then, tell my servant David, 'This is what the LORD Almighty says: I took you from the pasture and from following the flock, to be ruler over my people Israel. [8]I have been with you wherever you have gone, and I have cut off all your enemies from before you. Now I will make your name like the names of the greatest men of the earth. [9]And I will provide a place for my people Israel and will plant them so that they can have a home of their own and no longer be disturbed. Wicked people will not oppress them anymore, as they did at the beginning [10]and have done ever since the time I appointed leaders over my people Israel. I will also subdue all your enemies.

" 'I declare to you that the LORD will build a house for you: [11]When your days are over and you go to be with your fathers, I will raise up your offspring to succeed you, one of your own sons, and I will establish his kingdom. [12]He is the one who will build a house for me, and I will establish his throne forever. [13]I will be his father, and he will be my son. I will never take my love away from him, as I took it away from your predecessor. [14]I will set him over my house and my kingdom forever; his throne will be established forever.' "

[15]Nathan reported to David all the words of this entire revelation.

David's Prayer [16]Then King David went in and sat before the LORD, and he said:

"Who am I, O LORD God, and what is my family, that you have brought me this far? [17]And as if this were not enough in your sight, O God, you have spoken about the future of the house of your servant. You have looked on me as though I were the most exalted of men, O LORD God.

---

*a*6 Traditionally *judges*; also in verse 10

¹⁸"What more can David say to you for honoring your servant? For you know your servant, ¹⁹O Lᴏʀᴅ. For the sake of your servant and according to your will, you have done this great thing and made known all these great promises.

²⁰"There is no one like you, O Lᴏʀᴅ, and there is no God but you, as we have heard with our own ears. ²¹And who is like your people Israel—the one nation on earth whose God went out to redeem a people for himself, and to make a name for yourself, and to perform great and awesome wonders by driving out nations from before your people, whom you redeemed from Egypt? ²²You made your people Israel your very own forever, and you, O Lᴏʀᴅ, have become their God.

²³"And now, Lᴏʀᴅ, let the promise you have made concerning your servant and his house be established forever. Do as you promised, ²⁴so that it will be established and that your name will be great forever. Then men will say, 'The Lᴏʀᴅ Almighty, the God over Israel, is Israel's God!' And the house of your servant David will be established before you.

²⁵"You, my God, have revealed to your servant that you will build a house for him. So your servant has found courage to pray to you. ²⁶O Lᴏʀᴅ, you are God! You have promised these good things to your servant. ²⁷Now you have been pleased to bless the house of your servant, that it may continue forever in your sight; for you, O Lᴏʀᴅ, have blessed it, and it will be blessed forever."

18 *David's Victories*   In the course of time, David defeated the Philistines and subdued them, and he took Gath and its surrounding villages from the control of the Philistines.

²David also defeated the Moabites, and they became subject to him and brought tribute.

³Moreover, David fought Hadadezer king of Zobah, as far as Hamath, when he went to establish his control along the Euphrates River. ⁴David captured a thousand of his chariots, seven thousand charioteers and twenty thousand foot soldiers. He hamstrung all but a hundred of the chariot horses.

⁵When the Arameans of Damascus came to help Hadadezer king of Zobah, David struck down twenty-two thousand of them. ⁶He put garrisons in the Aramean kingdom of Damascus, and the Arameans became subject to him and brought tribute. The Lᴏʀᴅ gave David victory everywhere he went.

⁷David took the gold shields carried by the officers of Hadadezer and brought them to Jerusalem. ⁸From Tebah*ᵃ* and Cun, towns that belonged to Hadadezer, David took a great quantity of bronze, which Solomon used to make the bronze Sea, the pillars and various bronze articles.

⁹When Tou king of Hamath heard that David had defeated the entire army of Hadadezer king of Zobah, ¹⁰he sent his son Hadoram to King David to greet him and congratulate him on his victory in battle over Hadadezer, who had been at war with Tou. Hadoram brought all kinds of articles of gold and silver and bronze.

¹¹King David dedicated these articles to the Lᴏʀᴅ, as he had done with the silver and gold he had taken from all these nations: Edom and Moab, the Ammonites and the Philistines, and Amalek.

¹²Abishai son of Zeruiah struck down eighteen thousand Edomites in the Valley of Salt. ¹³He put garrisons in Edom, and all the Edomites became subject to David. The Lᴏʀᴅ gave David victory everywhere he went.

David's Officials   ¹⁴David reigned over all Israel, doing what was just and right for all his people. ¹⁵Joab son of Zeruiah was over the army; Jehoshaphat son of Ahilud was recorder; ¹⁶Zadok son of Ahitub and Ahimelech*ᵇ* son of

---

ᵃ8 Hebrew *Tibhath,* a variant of *Tebah*   *ᵇ16* Some Hebrew manuscripts, Vulgate and Syriac (see also 2 Samuel 8:17); most Hebrew manuscripts *Abimelech*

Abiathar were priests; Shavsha was secretary; ¹⁷Benaiah son of Jehoiada was over the Kerethites and Pelethites; and David's sons were chief officials at the king's side.

19 **The Battle Against the Ammonites** In the course of time, Nahash king of the Ammonites died, and his son succeeded him as king. ²David thought, "I will show kindness to Hanun son of Nahash, because his father showed kindness to me." So David sent a delegation to express his sympathy to Hanun concerning his father.

When David's men came to Hanun in the land of the Ammonites to express sympathy to him, ³the Ammonite nobles said to Hanun, "Do you think David is honoring your father by sending men to you to express sympathy? Haven't his men come to you to explore and spy out the country and overthrow it?" ⁴So Hanun seized David's men, shaved them, cut off their garments in the middle at the buttocks, and sent them away.

⁵When someone came and told David about the men, he sent messengers to meet them, for they were greatly humiliated. The king said, "Stay at Jericho till your beards have grown, and then come back."

⁶When the Ammonites realized that they had become a stench in David's nostrils, Hanun and the Ammonites sent a thousand talents*a* of silver to hire chariots and charioteers from Aram Naharaim,*b* Aram Maacah and Zobah. ⁷They hired thirty-two thousand chariots and charioteers, as well as the king of Maacah with his troops, who came and camped near Medeba, while the Ammonites were mustered from their towns and moved out for battle.

⁸On hearing this, David sent Joab out with the entire army of fighting men. ⁹The Ammonites came out and drew up in battle formation at the entrance to their city, while the kings who had come were by themselves in the open country.

¹⁰Joab saw that there were battle lines in front of him and behind him; so he selected some of the best troops in Israel and deployed them against the Arameans. ¹¹He put the rest of the men under the command of Abishai his brother, and they were deployed against the Ammonites. ¹²Joab said, "If the Arameans are too strong for me, then you are to rescue me; but if the Ammonites are too strong for you, then I will rescue you. ¹³Be strong and let us fight bravely for our people and the cities of our God. The LORD will do what is good in his sight."

¹⁴Then Joab and the troops with him advanced to fight the Arameans, and they fled before him. ¹⁵When the Ammonites saw that the Arameans were fleeing, they too fled before his brother Abishai and went inside the city. So Joab went back to Jerusalem.

¹⁶After the Arameans saw that they had been routed by Israel, they sent messengers and had Arameans brought from beyond the River,*c* with Shophach the commander of Hadadezer's army leading them.

¹⁷When David was told of this, he gathered all Israel and crossed the Jordan; he

a6 That is, about 37 tons (about 34 metric tons) b6 That is, Northwest Mesopotamia c16 That is, the Euphrates

---

1 CHRONICLES 19:4–5

Do your parents have trouble understanding why you just can't wear the clothes they think you should wear? Try this Bible story. A foreign king humiliated David's messengers by shaving off their beards and cutting up their clothes. David let his messengers stay in Jericho until their beards had grown back and they could return to Jerusalem without embarrassment. Ask your mom and dad to be as sensitive as David. It can be humiliating if your clothing is too different from that of other teens. If your parents understand just how you feel, they just might give you more freedom to dress the way you want.

Direct Line

advanced against them and formed his battle lines opposite them. David formed his lines to meet the Arameans in battle, and they fought against him. [18]But they fled before Israel, and David killed seven thousand of their charioteers and forty thousand of their foot soldiers. He also killed Shophach the commander of their army.

[19]When the vassals of Hadadezer saw that they had been defeated by Israel, they made peace with David and became subject to him.

So the Arameans were not willing to help the Ammonites anymore.

20 *The Capture of Rabbah* In the spring, at the time when kings go off to war, Joab led out the armed forces. He laid waste the land of the Ammonites and went to Rabbah and besieged it, but David remained in Jerusalem. Joab attacked Rabbah and left it in ruins. [2]David took the crown from the head of their king[a] —its weight was found to be a talent[b] of gold, and it was set with precious stones—and it was placed on David's head. He took a great quantity of plunder from the city [3]and brought out the people who were there, consigning them to labor with saws and with iron picks and axes. David did this to all the Ammonite towns. Then David and his entire army returned to Jerusalem.

War With the Philistines [4]In the course of time, war broke out with the Philistines, at Gezer. At that time Sibbecai the Hushathite killed Sippai, one of the descendants of the Rephaites, and the Philistines were subjugated.

[5]In another battle with the Philistines, Elhanan son of Jair killed Lahmi the brother of Goliath the Gittite, who had a spear with a shaft like a weaver's rod.

[6]In still another battle, which took place at Gath, there was a huge man with six fingers on each hand and six toes on each foot—twenty-four in all. He also was descended from Rapha. [7]When he taunted Israel, Jonathan son of Shimea, David's brother, killed him.

[8]These were descendants of Rapha in Gath, and they fell at the hands of David and his men.

---

[a]2 Or *of Milcom,* that is, Molech   [b]2 That is, about 75 pounds (about 34 kilograms)

The Bible Says

The Devil Didn't Make You

"The devil made me do it!" Some people actually believe that Satan is responsible when they do something that's wrong. But is he?

First Chronicles 21:1 tells you that Satan "incited" David to do something wrong. When David was later confronted by God, he didn't say, "The devil made me do it." He said, "I am the one who has sinned and done wrong" (1 Chronicles 21:17). Satan may tempt you, but he can't make you sin. It's your choice, and you don't have to choose to do wrong. You're free to choose what is right.

So what should you do when Satan tempts you?

* Remember what the Bible teaches and act on it (Matthew 4:1–11).
* "Resist the devil, and he will flee" (James 4:7).
* Remember: Christ is far more powerful than Satan (1 John 4:4).

21 *David Numbers the Fighting Men* Satan rose up against Israel and incited David to take a census of Israel. ²So David said to Joab and the commanders of the troops, "Go and count the Israelites from Beersheba to Dan. Then report back to me so that I may know how many there are."

³But Joab replied, "May the LORD multiply his troops a hundred times over. My lord the king, are they not all my lord's subjects? Why does my lord want to do this? Why should he bring guilt on Israel?"

⁴The king's word, however, overruled Joab; so Joab left and went throughout Israel and then came back to Jerusalem. ⁵Joab reported the number of the fighting men to David: In all Israel there were one million one hundred thousand men who could handle a sword, including four hundred and seventy thousand in Judah.

⁶But Joab did not include Levi and Benjamin in the numbering, because the king's command was repulsive to him. ⁷This command was also evil in the sight of God; so he punished Israel.

⁸Then David said to God, "I have sinned greatly by doing this. Now, I beg you, take away the guilt of your servant. I have done a very foolish thing."

⁹The LORD said to Gad, David's seer, ¹⁰"Go and tell David, 'This is what the LORD says: I am giving you three options. Choose one of them for me to carry out against you.' "

¹¹So Gad went to David and said to him, "This is what the LORD says: 'Take your choice: ¹²three years of famine, three months of being swept away*a* before your enemies, with their swords overtaking you, or three days of the sword of the LORD—days of plague in the land, with the angel of the LORD ravaging every part of Israel.' Now then, decide how I should answer the one who sent me."

¹³David said to Gad, "I am in deep distress. Let me fall into the hands of the LORD, for his mercy is very great; but do not let me fall into the hands of men."

¹⁴So the LORD sent a plague on Israel, and seventy thousand men of Israel fell dead. ¹⁵And God sent an angel to destroy Jerusalem. But as the angel was doing so, the LORD saw it and was grieved because of the calamity and said to the angel who was destroying the people, "Enough! Withdraw your hand." The angel of the LORD was then standing at the threshing floor of Araunah*b* the Jebusite.

¹⁶David looked up and saw the angel of the LORD standing between heaven and earth, with a drawn sword in his hand extended over Jerusalem. Then David and the elders, clothed in sackcloth, fell facedown.

¹⁷David said to God, "Was it not I who ordered the fighting men to be counted? I am the one who has sinned and done wrong. These are but sheep. What have they done? O LORD my God, let your hand fall upon me and my family, but do not let this plague remain on your people."

¹⁸Then the angel of the LORD ordered Gad to tell David to go up and build an altar to the LORD on the threshing floor of Araunah the Jebusite. ¹⁹So David went up in obedience to the word that Gad had spoken in the name of the LORD.

²⁰While Araunah was threshing wheat, he turned and saw the angel; his four sons who were with him hid themselves. ²¹Then David approached, and when Araunah looked and saw him, he left the threshing floor and bowed down before David with his face to the ground.

²²David said to him, "Let me have the site of your threshing floor so I can build an altar to the LORD, that the plague on the people may be stopped. Sell it to me at the full price."

---

a12 Hebrew; Septuagint and Vulgate (see also 2 Samuel 24:13) *of fleeing*   *b15* Hebrew *Ornan,* a variant of *Araunah;* also in verses 18-28

²³Araunah said to David, "Take it! Let my lord the king do whatever pleases him. Look, I will give the oxen for the burnt offerings, the threshing sledges for the wood, and the wheat for the grain offering. I will give all this."

²⁴But King David replied to Araunah, "No, I insist on paying the full price. I will not take for the LORD what is yours, or sacrifice a burnt offering that costs me nothing."

²⁵So David paid Araunah six hundred shekels[a] of gold for the site. ²⁶David built an altar to the LORD there and sacrificed burnt offerings and fellowship offerings.[b] He called on the LORD, and the LORD answered him with fire from heaven on the altar of burnt offering.

²⁷Then the LORD spoke to the angel, and he put his sword back into its sheath. ²⁸At that time, when David saw that the LORD had answered him on the threshing floor of Araunah the Jebusite, he offered sacrifices there. ²⁹The tabernacle of the LORD, which Moses had made in the desert, and the altar of burnt offering were at that time on the high place at Gibeon. ³⁰But David could not go before it to inquire of God, because he was afraid of the sword of the angel of the LORD.

22 Then David said, "The house of the LORD God is to be here, and also the altar of burnt offering for Israel."

Preparations for the Temple ²So David gave orders to assemble the aliens living in Israel, and from among them he appointed stonecutters to prepare dressed stone for building the house of God. ³He provided a large amount of iron to make nails for the doors of the gateways and for the fittings, and more bronze than could be weighed. ⁴He also provided more cedar logs than could be counted, for the Sidonians and Tyrians had brought large numbers of them to David.

⁵David said, "My son Solomon is young and inexperienced, and the house to be built for the LORD should be of great magnificence and fame and splendor in the sight of all the nations. Therefore I will make preparations for it." So David made extensive preparations before his death.

⁶Then he called for his son Solomon and charged him to build a house for the LORD, the God of Israel. ⁷David said to Solomon: "My son, I had it in my heart to build a house for the Name of the LORD my God. ⁸But this word of the LORD came to me: 'You have shed much blood and have fought many wars. You are not to build a house for my Name, because you have shed much blood on the earth in my sight. ⁹But you will have a son who will be a man of peace and rest, and I will give him rest from all his enemies on every side. His name will be Solomon,[c] and I will grant Israel peace and quiet during his reign. ¹⁰He is the one who will build a house for my Name. He will be my son, and I will be his father. And I will establish the throne of his kingdom over Israel forever.'

Direct Line

1 CHRONICLES 22:5

Can you sense David's concern in this verse: "My son Solomon is young and inexperienced"? We know Solomon as history's wisest man, but to David, Solomon was still his little boy. Most parents worry about their children. "He's gone for the evening with all his friends. Will he be OK?" "This is her first real date. I won't sleep until she gets home safely." It's not that they don't trust you. It's just love. Yes, it can be irritating at times, but part of loving is being concerned about the person you love. Maybe if you sense the love, the feeling that Mom or Dad is hanging over your shoulder watching will be a little easier to bear.

---

[a]25 That is, about 15 pounds (about 7 kilograms)
[b]26 Traditionally *peace offerings* [c]9 *Solomon* sounds like and may be derived from the Hebrew for *peace.*

¹¹"Now, my son, the LORD be with you, and may you have success and build the house of the LORD your God, as he said you would. ¹²May the LORD give you discretion and understanding when he puts you in command over Israel, so that you may keep the law of the LORD your God. ¹³Then you will have success if you are careful to observe the decrees and laws that the LORD gave Moses for Israel. Be strong and courageous. Do not be afraid or discouraged.

¹⁴"I have taken great pains to provide for the temple of the LORD a hundred thousand talents*a* of gold, a million talents*b* of silver, quantities of bronze and iron too great to be weighed, and wood and stone. And you may add to them. ¹⁵You have many workmen: stonecutters, masons and carpenters, as well as men skilled in every kind of work ¹⁶in gold and silver, bronze and iron—craftsmen beyond number. Now begin the work, and the LORD be with you."

¹⁷Then David ordered all the leaders of Israel to help his son Solomon. ¹⁸He said to them, "Is not the LORD your God with you? And has he not granted you rest on every side? For he has handed the inhabitants of the land over to me, and the land is subject to the LORD and to his people. ¹⁹Now devote your heart and soul to seeking the LORD your God. Begin to build the sanctuary of the LORD God, so that you may bring the ark of the covenant of the LORD and the sacred articles belonging to God into the temple that will be built for the Name of the LORD."

23 **The Levites** When David was old and full of years, he made his son Solomon king over Israel.

²He also gathered together all the leaders of Israel, as well as the priests and Levites. ³The Levites thirty years old or more were counted, and the total number of men was thirty-eight thousand. ⁴David said, "Of these, twenty-four thousand are to supervise the work of the temple of the LORD and six thousand are to be officials and judges. ⁵Four thousand are to be gatekeepers and four thousand are to praise the LORD with the musical instruments I have provided for that purpose."

⁶David divided the Levites into groups corresponding to the sons of Levi: Gershon, Kohath and Merari.

Gershonites

⁷Belonging to the Gershonites:
Ladan and Shimei.
⁸The sons of Ladan:
Jehiel the first, Zetham and Joel—three in all.
⁹The sons of Shimei:
Shelomoth, Haziel and Haran—three in all.
These were the heads of the families of Ladan.
¹⁰And the sons of Shimei:
Jahath, Ziza,*c* Jeush and Beriah.
These were the sons of Shimei—four in all.
¹¹Jahath was the first and Ziza the second, but Jeush and Beriah did not have many sons; so they were counted as one family with one assignment.

Kohathites

¹²The sons of Kohath:
Amram, Izhar, Hebron and Uzziel—four in all.
¹³The sons of Amram:
Aaron and Moses.
Aaron was set apart, he and his descendants forever, to consecrate

---

a14 That is, about 3,750 tons (about 3,450 metric tons) *b14* That is, about 37,500 tons (about 34,500 metric tons) *c10* One Hebrew manuscript, Septuagint and Vulgate (see also verse 11); most Hebrew manuscripts *Zina*

the most holy things, to offer sacrifices before the LORD, to minister before him and to pronounce blessings in his name forever. ¹⁴The sons of Moses the man of God were counted as part of the tribe of Levi.

¹⁵ The sons of Moses:

Gershom and Eliezer.

¹⁶ The descendants of Gershom:

Shubael was the first.

¹⁷ The descendants of Eliezer:

Rehabiah was the first.

Eliezer had no other sons, but the sons of Rehabiah were very numerous.

¹⁸ The sons of Izhar:

Shelomith was the first.

¹⁹ The sons of Hebron:

Jeriah the first, Amariah the second, Jahaziel the third and Jekameam the fourth.

²⁰ The sons of Uzziel:

Micah the first and Isshiah the second.

Merarites

²¹The sons of Merari:

Mahli and Mushi.

The sons of Mahli:

Eleazar and Kish.

²²Eleazar died without having sons: he had only daughters. Their cousins, the sons of Kish, married them.

²³ The sons of Mushi:

Mahli, Eder and Jerimoth—three in all.

²⁴These were the descendants of Levi by their families—the heads of families as they were registered under their names and counted individually, that is, the workers twenty years old or more who served in the temple of the LORD. ²⁵For David had said, "Since the LORD, the God of Israel, has granted rest to his people and has come to dwell in Jerusalem forever, ²⁶the Levites no longer need to carry the tabernacle or any of the articles used in its service." ²⁷According to the last instructions of David, the Levites were counted from those twenty years old or more.

²⁸The duty of the Levites was to help Aaron's descendants in the service of the temple of the LORD: to be in charge of the courtyards, the side rooms, the purification of all sacred things and the performance of other duties at the house of God. ²⁹They were in charge of the bread set out on the table, the flour for the grain offerings, the unleavened wafers, the baking and the mixing, and all measurements of quantity and size. ³⁰They were also to stand every morning to thank and praise the LORD. They were to do the same in the evening ³¹and whenever burnt offerings were presented to the LORD on Sabbaths and at New Moon festivals and at appointed feasts. They were to serve before the LORD regularly in the proper number and in the way prescribed for them.

³²And so the Levites carried out their responsibilities for the Tent of Meeting, for the Holy Place and, under their brothers the descendants of Aaron, for the service of the temple of the LORD.

24

The Divisions of Priests These were the divisions of the sons of Aaron:

The sons of Aaron were Nadab, Abihu, Eleazar and Ithamar. ²But Nadab and Abihu died before their father did, and they had no sons; so Eleazar and Ithamar served as the priests. ³With the help of Zadok a descendant of Eleazar and Ahimelech a descendant of Ithamar, David separated them into divisions for their appointed order of ministering. [4]A larger number of leaders were found among Eleazar's descendants than among Ithamar's, and they were divided accordingly: sixteen heads of families from Eleazar's descendants and eight heads of families from Ithamar's descendants. [5]They divided them impartially by drawing lots, for there were officials of the sanctuary and officials of God among the descendants of both Eleazar and Ithamar.

[6]The scribe Shemaiah son of Nethanel, a Levite, recorded their names in the presence of the king and of the officials: Zadok the priest, Ahimelech son of Abiathar and the heads of families of the priests and of the Levites—one family being taken from Eleazar and then one from Ithamar.

[7]The first lot fell to Jehoiarib,
the second to Jedaiah,
[8]the third to Harim,
the fourth to Seorim,
[9]the fifth to Malkijah,
the sixth to Mijamin,
[10]the seventh to Hakkoz,
the eighth to Abijah,
[11]the ninth to Jeshua,
the tenth to Shecaniah,
[12]the eleventh to Eliashib,
the twelfth to Jakim,
[13]the thirteenth to Huppah,
the fourteenth to Jeshebeab,
[14]the fifteenth to Bilgah,
the sixteenth to Immer,
[15]the seventeenth to Hezir,
the eighteenth to Happizzez,
[16]the nineteenth to Pethahiah,
the twentieth to Jehezkel,
[17]the twenty-first to Jakin,
the twenty-second to Gamul,
[18]the twenty-third to Delaiah
and the twenty-fourth to Maaziah.

[19]This was their appointed order of ministering when they entered the temple of the LORD, according to the regulations prescribed for them by their forefather Aaron, as the LORD, the God of Israel, had commanded him.

The Rest of the Levites

[20]As for the rest of the descendants of Levi:
from the sons of Amram: Shubael;
from the sons of Shubael: Jehdeiah.
[21]As for Rehabiah, from his sons:
Isshiah was the first.
[22]From the Izharites: Shelomoth;
from the sons of Shelomoth: Jahath.
[23]The sons of Hebron: Jeriah the first,[a] Amariah the second, Jahaziel the third and Jekameam the fourth.
[24]The son of Uzziel: Micah;
from the sons of Micah: Shamir.
[25]The brother of Micah: Isshiah;
from the sons of Isshiah: Zechariah.

---

[a]23 Two Hebrew manuscripts and some Septuagint manuscripts (see also 1 Chron. 23:19); most Hebrew manuscripts *The sons of Jeriah:*

26 The sons of Merari: Mahli and Mushi.
   The son of Jaaziah: Beno.
27 The sons of Merari:
   from Jaaziah: Beno, Shoham, Zaccur and Ibri.
28 From Mahli: Eleazar, who had no sons.
29 From Kish: the son of Kish:
   Jerahmeel.
30 And the sons of Mushi: Mahli, Eder and Jerimoth.

These were the Levites, according to their families. 31 They also cast lots, just as their brothers the descendants of Aaron did, in the presence of King David and of Zadok, Ahimelech, and the heads of families of the priests and of the Levites. The families of the oldest brother were treated the same as those of the youngest.

25 *The Singers* David, together with the commanders of the army, set apart some of the sons of Asaph, Heman and Jeduthun for the ministry of prophesying, accompanied by harps, lyres and cymbals. Here is the list of the men who performed this service:

2 From the sons of Asaph:
   Zaccur, Joseph, Nethaniah and Asarelah. The sons of Asaph were under the supervision of Asaph, who prophesied under the king's supervision.
3 As for Jeduthun, from his sons:
   Gedaliah, Zeri, Jeshaiah, Shimei,*a* Hashabiah and Mattithiah, six in all, under the supervision of their father Jeduthun, who prophesied, using the harp in thanking and praising the LORD.
4 As for Heman, from his sons:
   Bukkiah, Mattaniah, Uzziel, Shubael and Jerimoth; Hananiah, Hanani, Eliathah, Giddalti and Romamti-Ezer; Joshbekashah, Mallothi, Hothir and Mahazioth. 5 All these were sons of Heman the king's seer. They were given him through the promises of God to exalt him.*b* God gave Heman fourteen sons and three daughters.

6 All these men were under the supervision of their fathers for the music of the temple of the LORD, with cymbals, lyres and harps, for the ministry at the house of God. Asaph, Jeduthun and Heman were under the supervision of the king. 7 Along with their relatives—all of them trained and skilled in music for the LORD—they numbered 288. 8 Young and old alike, teacher as well as student, cast lots for their duties.

9 The first lot, which was for
   Asaph, fell to Joseph,
      his sons and relatives,*c*   12*d*
   the second to Gedaliah,
      he and his relatives and sons, 12

1 CHRONICLES 25:1–7

It's easy to feel lost in church. You sit there in the pew. You stand up to sing or read the responsive reading. And nobody cares if you're there or not. Or so it may seem. Read some of the weird names in this passage: Zeri, Shimei, Hashabiah, Uzziel, Jerimoth, Mallothi, Hothir, and so on. Who in the world are these people, and why are they in the Bible? They're people who served God by leading in worship. And, although no one today knows who they are, God knows them and gave them a place in his Word. Don't ever feel lost in church. God knows you're there. And he lists you among his worshipers.

a3 One Hebrew manuscript and some Septuagint manuscripts (see also verse 17); most Hebrew manuscripts do not have *Shimei.* *b5* Hebrew *exalt the horn* *c9* See Septuagint; Hebrew does not have *his sons and relatives.* *d9* See the total in verse 7; Hebrew does not have *twelve.*

¹⁰the third to Zaccur,
    his sons and relatives,   12
¹¹the fourth to Izri,^{*a*}
    his sons and relatives,   12
¹²the fifth to Nethaniah,
    his sons and relatives,   12
¹³the sixth to Bukkiah,
    his sons and relatives,   12
¹⁴the seventh to Jesarelah,^{*b*}
    his sons and relatives,   12
¹⁵the eighth to Jeshaiah,
    his sons and relatives,   12
¹⁶the ninth to Mattaniah,
    his sons and relatives,   12
¹⁷the tenth to Shimei,
    his sons and relatives,   12
¹⁸the eleventh to Azarel,^{*c*}
    his sons and relatives,   12
¹⁹the twelfth to Hashabiah,
    his sons and relatives,   12
²⁰the thirteenth to Shubael,
    his sons and relatives,   12
²¹the fourteenth to Mattithiah,
    his sons and relatives,   12
²²the fifteenth to Jerimoth,
    his sons and relatives,   12
²³the sixteenth to Hananiah,
    his sons and relatives,   12
²⁴the seventeenth to Joshbekashah,
    his sons and relatives,   12
²⁵the eighteenth to Hanani,
    his sons and relatives,   12
²⁶the nineteenth to Mallothi,
    his sons and relatives,   12
²⁷the twentieth to Eliathah,
    his sons and relatives,   12
²⁸the twenty-first to Hothir,
    his sons and relatives,   12
²⁹the twenty-second to Giddalti,
    his sons and relatives,   12
³⁰the twenty-third to Mahazioth,
    his sons and relatives,   12
³¹the twenty-fourth to Romamti-Ezer,
    his sons and relatives,   12

26

The Gatekeepers The divisions of the gatekeepers:

From the Korahites: Meshelemiah son of Kore, one of the sons of Asaph. ²Meshelemiah had sons:
    Zechariah the firstborn,
    Jediael the second,
    Zebadiah the third,
    Jathniel the fourth,
    ³Elam the fifth,

---

^a11 A variant of Zeri ^b14 A variant of Asarelah ^c18 A variant of Uzziel

Jehohanan the sixth
and Eliehoenai the seventh.
⁴Obed-Edom also had sons:
Shemaiah the firstborn,
Jehozabad the second,
Joah the third,
Sacar the fourth,
Nethanel the fifth,
⁵Ammiel the sixth,
Issachar the seventh
and Peullethai the eighth.
(For God had blessed Obed-Edom.)

⁶His son Shemaiah also had sons, who were leaders in their father's family because they were very capable men. ⁷The sons of Shemaiah: Othni, Rephael, Obed and Elzabad; his relatives Elihu and Semakiah were also able men. ⁸All these were descendants of Obed-Edom; they and their sons and their relatives were capable men with the strength to do the work—descendants of Obed-Edom, 62 in all.
⁹Meshelemiah had sons and relatives, who were able men—18 in all.

¹⁰Hosah the Merarite had sons: Shimri the first (although he was not the firstborn, his father had appointed him the first), ¹¹Hilkiah the second, Tabaliah the third and Zechariah the fourth. The sons and relatives of Hosah were 13 in all.
¹²These divisions of the gatekeepers, through their chief men, had duties for ministering in the temple of the Lord, just as their relatives had. ¹³Lots were cast for each gate, according to their families, young and old alike.
¹⁴The lot for the East Gate fell to Shelemiah.ᵃ Then lots were cast for his son Zechariah, a wise counselor, and the lot for the North Gate fell to him. ¹⁵The lot for the South Gate fell to Obed-Edom, and the lot for the storehouse fell to his sons. ¹⁶The lots for the West Gate and the Shalleketh Gate on the upper road fell to Shuppim and Hosah.
Guard was alongside of guard: ¹⁷There were six Levites a day on the east, four a day on the north, four a day on the south and two at a time at the storehouse. ¹⁸As for the court to the west, there were four at the road and two at the court itself.
¹⁹These were the divisions of the gatekeepers who were descendants of Korah and Merari.

The Treasurers and Other Officials ²⁰Their fellow Levites wereᵇ in charge of the treasuries of the house of God and the treasuries for the dedicated things.
²¹The descendants of Ladan, who were Gershonites through Ladan and who were heads of families belonging to Ladan the Gershonite, were Jehieli, ²²the sons of Jehieli, Zetham and his brother Joel. They were in charge of the treasuries of the temple of the Lord.
²³From the Amramites, the Izharites, the Hebronites and the Uzzielites:

²⁴Shubael, a descendant of Gershom son of Moses, was the officer in charge of the treasuries. ²⁵His relatives through Eliezer: Rehabiah his son, Jeshaiah his son, Joram his son, Zicri his son and Shelomith his son. ²⁶Shelomith and his relatives were in charge of all the treasuries for the things dedicated by King David, by the heads of families who were the commanders of thousands and commanders of hundreds, and by the other army commanders. ²⁷Some of the plunder taken in battle they dedicated for the repair of the temple of the

---

ᵃ14 A variant of *Meshelemiah* ᵇ20 Septuagint; Hebrew *As for the Levites, Ahijah was*

Lord. ²⁸And everything dedicated by Samuel the seer and by Saul son of Kish, Abner son of Ner and Joab son of Zeruiah, and all the other dedicated things were in the care of Shelomith and his relatives.

²⁹From the Izharites: Kenaniah and his sons were assigned duties away from the temple, as officials and judges over Israel.

³⁰From the Hebronites: Hashabiah and his relatives—seventeen hundred able men—were responsible in Israel west of the Jordan for all the work of the Lord and for the king's service. ³¹As for the Hebronites, Jeriah was their chief according to the genealogical records of their families. In the fortieth year of David's reign a search was made in the records, and capable men among the Hebronites were found at Jazer in Gilead. ³²Jeriah had twenty-seven hundred relatives, who were able men and heads of families, and King David put them in charge of the Reubenites, the Gadites and the half-tribe of Manasseh for every matter pertaining to God and for the affairs of the king.

27 *Army Divisions* This is the list of the Israelites—heads of families, commanders of thousands and commanders of hundreds, and their officers, who served the king in all that concerned the army divisions that were on duty month by month throughout the year. Each division consisted of 24,000 men.

²In charge of the first division, for the first month, was Jashobeam son of Zabdiel. There were 24,000 men in his division. ³He was a descendant of Perez and chief of all the army officers for the first month.

⁴In charge of the division for the second month was Dodai the Ahohite; Mikloth was the leader of his division. There were 24,000 men in his division.

⁵The third army commander, for the third month, was Benaiah son of Jehoiada the priest. He was chief and there were 24,000 men in his division. ⁶This was the Benaiah who was a mighty man among the Thirty and was over the Thirty. His son Ammizabad was in charge of his division.

⁷The fourth, for the fourth month, was Asahel the brother of Joab; his son Zebadiah was his successor. There were 24,000 men in his division.

⁸The fifth, for the fifth month, was the commander Shamhuth the Izrahite. There were 24,000 men in his division.

⁹The sixth, for the sixth month, was Ira the son of Ikkesh the Tekoite. There were 24,000 men in his division.

¹⁰The seventh, for the seventh month, was Helez the Pelonite, an Ephraimite. There were 24,000 men in his division.

¹¹The eighth, for the eighth month, was Sibbecai the Hushathite, a Zerahite. There were 24,000 men in his division.

¹²The ninth, for the ninth month, was Abiezer the Anathothite, a Benjamite. There were 24,000 men in his division.

¹³The tenth, for the tenth month, was Maharai the Netophathite, a Zerahite. There were 24,000 men in his division.

¹⁴The eleventh, for the eleventh month, was Benaiah the Pirathonite, an Ephraimite. There were 24,000 men in his division.

¹⁵The twelfth, for the twelfth month, was Heldai the Netophathite, from the family of Othniel. There were 24,000 men in his division.

Officers of the Tribes

¹⁶The officers over the tribes of Israel:

over the Reubenites: Eliezer son of Zicri;
over the Simeonites: Shephatiah son of Maacah;
¹⁷over Levi: Hashabiah son of Kemuel;
over Aaron: Zadok;

¹⁸over Judah: Elihu, a brother of David;
  over Issachar: Omri son of Michael;
¹⁹over Zebulun: Ishmaiah son of Obadiah;
  over Naphtali: Jerimoth son of Azriel;
²⁰over the Ephraimites: Hoshea son of Azaziah;
  over half the tribe of Manasseh: Joel son of Pedaiah;
²¹over the half-tribe of Manasseh in Gilead: Iddo son of Zechariah;
  over Benjamin: Jaasiel son of Abner;
²²over Dan: Azarel son of Jeroham.
These were the officers over the tribes of Israel.

²³David did not take the number of the men twenty years old or less, because the Lᴏʀᴅ had promised to make Israel as numerous as the stars in the sky. ²⁴Joab son of Zeruiah began to count the men but did not finish. Wrath came on Israel on account of this numbering, and the number was not entered in the book*a* of the annals of King David.

The King's Overseers ²⁵Azmaveth son of Adiel was in charge of the royal storehouses.

Jonathan son of Uzziah was in charge of the storehouses in the outlying districts, in the towns, the villages and the watchtowers.

²⁶Ezri son of Kelub was in charge of the field workers who farmed the land.

²⁷Shimei the Ramathite was in charge of the vineyards.

Zabdi the Shiphmite was in charge of the produce of the vineyards for the wine vats.

²⁸Baal-Hanan the Gederite was in charge of the olive and sycamore-fig trees in the western foothills.

Joash was in charge of the supplies of olive oil.

²⁹Shitrai the Sharonite was in charge of the herds grazing in Sharon.

Shaphat son of Adlai was in charge of the herds in the valleys.

³⁰Obil the Ishmaelite was in charge of the camels.

Jehdeiah the Meronothite was in charge of the donkeys.

³¹Jaziz the Hagrite was in charge of the flocks.

All these were the officials in charge of King David's property.

³²Jonathan, David's uncle, was a counselor, a man of insight and a scribe. Jehiel son of Hacmoni took care of the king's sons.

³³Ahithophel was the king's counselor.

Hushai the Arkite was the king's friend. ³⁴Ahithophel was succeeded by Jehoiada son of Benaiah and by Abiathar.

Joab was the commander of the royal army.

28 *David's Plans for the Temple* David summoned all the officials of Israel to assemble at Jerusalem: the officers over the tribes, the commanders of the divisions in the service of the king, the commanders of thousands and commanders of hundreds, and the officials in charge of all the property and livestock belonging to the king and his sons, together with the palace officials, the mighty men and all the brave warriors.

²King David rose to his feet and said: "Listen to me, my brothers and my people. I had it in my heart to build a house as a place of rest for the ark of the covenant of the Lᴏʀᴅ, for the footstool of our God, and I made plans to build it. ³But God said to me, 'You are not to build a house for my Name, because you are a warrior and have shed blood.'

⁴"Yet the Lᴏʀᴅ, the God of Israel, chose me from my whole family to be king over Israel forever. He chose Judah as leader, and from the house of Judah he chose my family, and from my father's sons he was pleased to make

---

a24 Septuagint; Hebrew *number*

me king over all Israel. [5]Of all my sons—and the LORD has given me many—he has chosen my son Solomon to sit on the throne of the kingdom of the LORD over Israel. [6]He said to me: 'Solomon your son is the one who will build my house and my courts, for I have chosen him to be my son, and I will be his father. [7]I will establish his kingdom forever if he is unswerving in carrying out my commands and laws, as is being done at this time.'

[8]"So now I charge you in the sight of all Israel and of the assembly of the LORD, and in the hearing of our God: Be careful to follow all the commands of the LORD your God, that you may possess this good land and pass it on as an inheritance to your descendants forever.

[9]"And you, my son Solomon, acknowledge the God of your father, and serve him with wholehearted devotion and with a willing mind, for the LORD searches every heart and understands every motive behind the thoughts. If you seek him, he will be found by you; but if you forsake him, he will reject you forever. [10]Consider now, for the LORD has chosen you to build a temple as a sanctuary. Be strong and do the work."

[11]Then David gave his son Solomon the plans for the portico of the temple, its buildings, its storerooms, its upper parts, its inner rooms and the place of atonement. [12]He gave him the plans of all that the Spirit had put in his mind for the courts of the temple of the LORD and all the surrounding rooms, for the treasuries of the temple of God and for the treasuries for the dedicated things. [13]He gave him instructions for the divisions of the priests and Levites, and for all the work of serving in the temple of the LORD, as well as for all the articles to be used in its service. [14]He designated the weight of gold for all the gold articles to be used in various kinds of service, and the weight of silver for all the silver articles to be used in various kinds of service: [15]the weight of gold for the gold lampstands and their lamps, with the weight for each lampstand and its lamps; and the weight of silver for each silver lampstand and its lamps, according to the use of each lampstand; [16]the weight of gold for each table for consecrated bread; the weight of silver for the silver tables; [17]the weight of pure gold for the forks, sprinkling bowls and pitchers; the weight of gold for each gold dish; the weight of silver for each silver dish; [18]and the weight of the refined gold for the altar of incense. He also gave him the plan for the chariot, that is, the cherubim of gold that spread their wings and shelter the ark of the covenant of the LORD.

[19]"All this," David said, "I have in writing from the hand of the LORD upon me, and he gave me understanding in all the details of the plan."

[20]David also said to Solomon his son, "Be strong and courageous, and do the work. Do not be afraid or discouraged, for the LORD God, my God, is with you. He will not fail you or forsake you until all the work for the service of the temple of the LORD is finished. [21]The divisions of the priests and Levites are ready for all the work on the temple of God, and every willing man skilled in any craft will help you in all the work. The officials and all the people will obey your every command."

1 CHRONICLES 28:9

Can God truly be real to you? Lots of kids believe in God but aren't sure how to experience him. Listen a minute to David's advice to Solomon: "Acknowledge God" and "serve him with wholehearted devotion and with a willing mind." Then David promises: "If you seek him, he will be found by you." And he gives this assurance: that God "searches every heart and understands every motive." You won't always obey the Lord. You'll fall short at times. But God won't evaluate you only by what you do. He'll look deeper. And if you are committed to serving God with wholehearted devotion, he'll know you. And you'll know him.

Direct Line

29 **Gifts for Building the Temple** Then King David said to the whole assembly: "My son Solomon, the one whom God has chosen, is young and inexperienced. The task is great, because this palatial structure is not for man but for the LORD God. ²With all my resources I have provided for the temple of my God—gold for the gold work, silver for the silver, bronze for the bronze, iron for the iron and wood for the wood, as well as onyx for the settings, turquoise,*ª* stones of various colors, and all kinds of fine stone and marble—all of these in large quantities. ³Besides, in my devotion to the temple of my God I now give my personal treasures of gold and silver for the temple of my God, over and above everything I have provided for this holy temple: ⁴three thousand talents*ᵇ* of gold (gold of Ophir) and seven thousand talents*ᶜ* of refined silver, for the overlaying of the walls of the buildings, ⁵for the gold work and the silver work, and for all the work to be done by the craftsmen. Now, who is willing to consecrate himself today to the LORD?"

⁶Then the leaders of families, the officers of the tribes of Israel, the commanders of thousands and commanders of hundreds, and the officials in charge of the king's work gave willingly. ⁷They gave toward the work on the temple of God five thousand talents*ᵈ* and ten thousand darics*ᵉ* of gold, ten thousand talents*ᶠ* of silver, eighteen thousand talents*ᵍ* of bronze and a hundred thousand talents*ʰ* of iron. ⁸Any who had precious stones gave them to the treasury of the temple of the LORD in the custody of Jehiel the Gershonite. ⁹The people rejoiced at the willing response of their leaders, for they had given freely and wholeheartedly to the LORD. David the king also rejoiced greatly.

David's Prayer ¹⁰David praised the LORD in the presence of the whole assembly, saying,

> "Praise be to you, O LORD,
>   God of our father Israel,
>   from everlasting to everlasting.
> ¹¹Yours, O LORD, is the greatness and the power
>   and the glory and the majesty and the splendor,
>   for everything in heaven and earth is yours.
> Yours, O LORD, is the kingdom;
>   you are exalted as head over all.
> ¹²Wealth and honor come from you;
>   you are the ruler of all things.
> In your hands are strength and power
>   to exalt and give strength to all.
> ¹³Now, our God, we give you thanks,
>   and praise your glorious name.

¹⁴"But who am I, and who are my people, that we should be able to give as generously as this? Everything comes from you, and we have given you only what comes from your hand. ¹⁵We are aliens and strangers in your sight, as were all our forefathers. Our days on earth are like a shadow, without hope. ¹⁶O LORD our God, as for all this abundance that we have provided for building you a temple for your Holy Name, it comes from your hand, and all of it belongs to you. ¹⁷I know, my God, that you test the heart and are pleased with integrity. All these things have I given willingly and with hon-

> Now, our God, we give you thanks, and praise your glorious name
> (1 Chronicles 29:13).

ª2 The meaning of the Hebrew for this word is uncertain. *ᵇ4* That is, about 110 tons (about 100 metric tons) *ᶜ4* That is, about 260 tons (about 240 metric tons) *ᵈ7* That is, about 190 tons (about 170 metric tons) *ᵉ7* That is, about 185 pounds (about 84 kilograms) *ᶠ7* That is, about 375 tons (about 345 metric tons) *ᵍ7* That is, about 675 tons (about 610 metric tons) *ʰ7* That is, about 3,750 tons (about 3,450 metric tons)

est intent. And now I have seen with joy how willingly your people who are here have given to you. ¹⁸O Lord, God of our fathers Abraham, Isaac and Israel, keep this desire in the hearts of your people forever, and keep their hearts loyal to you. ¹⁹And give my son Solomon the wholehearted devotion to keep your commands, requirements and decrees and to do everything to build the palatial structure for which I have provided."

²⁰Then David said to the whole assembly, "Praise the Lord your God." So they all praised the Lord, the God of their fathers; they bowed low and fell prostrate before the Lord and the king.

Solomon Acknowledged as King   ²¹The next day they made sacrifices to the Lord and presented burnt offerings to him: a thousand bulls, a thousand rams and a thousand male lambs, together with their drink offerings, and other sacrifices in abundance for all Israel. ²²They ate and drank with great joy in the presence of the Lord that day.

Then they acknowledged Solomon son of David as king a second time, anointing him before the Lord to be ruler and Zadok to be priest. ²³So Solomon sat on the throne of the Lord as king in place of his father David. He prospered and all Israel obeyed him. ²⁴All the officers and mighty men, as well as all of King David's sons, pledged their submission to King Solomon.

²⁵The Lord highly exalted Solomon in the sight of all Israel and bestowed on him royal splendor such as no king over Israel ever had before.

The Death of David   ²⁶David son of Jesse was king over all Israel. ²⁷He ruled over Israel forty years—seven in Hebron and thirty-three in Jerusalem. ²⁸He died at a good old age, having enjoyed long life, wealth and honor. His son Solomon succeeded him as king.

²⁹As for the events of King David's reign, from beginning to end, they are written in the records of Samuel the seer, the records of Nathan the prophet and the records of Gad the seer, ³⁰together with the details of his reign and power, and the circumstances that surrounded him and Israel and the kingdoms of all the other lands.

2 Chronicles

FRIENDS.

Probably you have some friends who are good examples and others who are not so good. Even bad. If you could study one of these groups of kids to see what made them like they are, which would you study: the kids who are good examples or the kids who are bad?

The book of 2 Chronicles tells the story of the southern kingdom of Judah from Solomon to the Babylonian captivity. The writer quickly passes over Judah's bad kings. But he looks in depth at the godly rulers, all to make an important point. When the nation's rulers and people were faithful to God, he blessed them. Get the picture?

Fundamentals

What prayers are you most eager to have God answer (2 Chronicles 6)?

What prayers can you be sure God will answer (2 Chronicles 7:11-22)?

Bad friends can't mess up good people, can they (2 Chronicles 24:17-19)?

FAST FACTS

The two books of Chronicles are one book in the Hebrew Bible.

Restoring worship was a key to every good king's success.

The most godly kings were Asa, Jehoshaphat, Joash, Hezekiah and Josiah.

Five kings began their reigns when in their teens or younger: Joash (7), Uzziah (16), Manasseh (12), Josiah (8) and Jehoiachin (18).

1 *Solomon Asks for Wisdom* Solomon son of David established himself firmly over his kingdom, for the Lord his God was with him and made him exceedingly great.

²Then Solomon spoke to all Israel—to the commanders of thousands and commanders of hundreds, to the judges and to all the leaders in Israel, the heads of families— ³and Solomon and the whole assembly went to the high place at Gibeon, for God's Tent of Meeting was there, which Moses the Lord's servant had made in the desert. ⁴Now David had brought up the ark of God from Kiriath Jearim to the place he had prepared for it, because he had pitched a tent for it in Jerusalem. ⁵But the bronze altar that Bezalel son of Uri, the son of Hur, had made was in Gibeon in front of the tabernacle of the Lord; so Solomon and the assembly inquired of him there. ⁶Solomon went up to the bronze altar before the Lord in the Tent of Meeting and offered a thousand burnt offerings on it.

⁷That night God appeared to Solomon and said to him, "Ask for whatever you want me to give you."

⁸Solomon answered God, "You have shown great kindness to David my father and have made me king in his place. ⁹Now, Lord God, let your promise to my father David be confirmed, for you have made me king over a people who are as numerous as the dust of the earth. ¹⁰Give me wisdom and knowledge, that I may lead this people, for who is able to govern this great people of yours?"

¹¹God said to Solomon, "Since this is your heart's desire and you have not asked for wealth, riches or honor, nor for the death of your enemies, and since you have not asked for a long life but for wisdom and knowledge to govern my people over whom I have made you king, ¹²therefore wisdom and knowledge will be given you. And I will also give you wealth, riches and honor, such as no king who was before you ever had and none after you will have."

¹³Then Solomon went to Jerusalem from the high place at Gibeon, from before the Tent of Meeting. And he reigned over Israel.

¹⁴Solomon accumulated chariots and horses; he had fourteen hundred chariots and twelve thousand horses,ᵃ which he kept in the chariot cities and also with him in Jerusalem. ¹⁵The king made silver and gold as common in Jerusalem as stones, and cedar as plentiful as sycamore-fig trees in the foothills. ¹⁶Solomon's horses were imported from Egyptᵇ and from Kueᶜ—the royal merchants purchased them from Kue. ¹⁷They imported a chariot from Egypt for six hundred shekelsᵈ of silver, and a horse for a hundred and fifty.ᵉ They also exported them to all the kings of the Hittites and of the Arameans.

2 *Preparations for Building the Temple* Solomon gave orders to build a temple for the Name of the Lord and a royal palace for himself. ²He conscripted

ᵃ*14* Or *charioteers* ᵇ*16* Or possibly *Muzur,* a region in Cilicia; also in verse 17 ᶜ*16* Probably Cilicia ᵈ*17* That is, about 15 pounds (about 7 kilograms) ᵉ*17* That is, about 3 3/4 pounds (about 1.7 kilograms)

"Silver and gold as common as stones"? Where can I find a place like that?

SEE 2 CHRONICLES 1:15

seventy thousand men as carriers and eighty thousand as stonecutters in the hills and thirty-six hundred as foremen over them.

[3]Solomon sent this message to Hiram[a] king of Tyre:

"Send me cedar logs as you did for my father David when you sent him cedar to build a palace to live in. [4]Now I am about to build a temple for the Name of the LORD my God and to dedicate it to him for burning fragrant incense before him, for setting out the consecrated bread regularly, and for making burnt offerings every morning and evening and on Sabbaths and New Moons and at the appointed feasts of the LORD our God. This is a lasting ordinance for Israel.

[5]"The temple I am going to build will be great, because our God is greater than all other gods. [6]But who is able to build a temple for him, since the heavens, even the highest heavens, cannot contain him? Who then am I to build a temple for him, except as a place to burn sacrifices before him?

[7]"Send me, therefore, a man skilled to work in gold and silver, bronze and iron, and in purple, crimson and blue yarn, and experienced in the art of engraving, to work in Judah and Jerusalem with my skilled craftsmen, whom my father David provided.

[8]"Send me also cedar, pine and algum[b] logs from Lebanon, for I know that your men are skilled in cutting timber there. My men will work with yours [9]to provide me with plenty of lumber, because the temple I build must be large and magnificent. [10]I will give your servants, the woodsmen who cut the timber, twenty thousand cors[c] of ground wheat, twenty thousand cors of barley, twenty thousand baths[d] of wine and twenty thousand baths of olive oil."

> Our God is greater than all other gods
> (2 Chronicles 2:5).

[11]Hiram king of Tyre replied by letter to Solomon:

"Because the LORD loves his people, he has made you their king."

[12]And Hiram added:

"Praise be to the LORD, the God of Israel, who made heaven and earth! He has given King David a wise son, endowed with intelligence and discernment, who will build a temple for the LORD and a palace for himself.

[13]"I am sending you Huram-Abi, a man of great skill, [14]whose mother was from Dan and whose father was from Tyre. He is trained to work in gold and silver, bronze and iron, stone and wood, and with purple and blue and crimson yarn and fine linen. He is experienced in all kinds of engraving and can execute any design given to him. He will work with your craftsmen and with those of my lord, David your father.

[15]"Now let my lord send his servants the wheat and barley and the olive oil and wine he promised, [16]and we will cut all the logs from Lebanon that you need and will float them in rafts by sea down to Joppa. You can then take them up to Jerusalem."

[17]Solomon took a census of all the aliens who were in Israel, after the census his father David had taken; and they were found to be 153,600. [18]He assigned 70,000 of them to be carriers and 80,000 to be stonecutters in the hills, with 3,600 foremen over them to keep the people working.

---

[a]3 Hebrew *Huram*, a variant of *Hiram*; also in verses 11 and 12   [b]8 Probably a variant of *almug*; possibly juniper   [c]10 That is, probably about 125,000 bushels (about 4,400 kiloliters)   [d]10 That is, probably about 115,000 gallons (about 440 kiloliters)

3 ***Solomon Builds the Temple*** Then Solomon began to build the temple
of the LORD in Jerusalem on Mount Moriah, where the LORD had appeared to his father David. It was on the threshing floor of Araunah[a] the Jebusite, the place provided by David. [2]He began building on the second day of
the second month in the fourth year of his reign.
[3]The foundation Solomon laid for building the temple of God was sixty cubits long and twenty cubits wide[b] (using the cubit of the old standard). [4]The
portico at the front of the temple was twenty cubits[c] long across the width
of the building and twenty cubits[d] high.
He overlaid the inside with pure gold. [5]He paneled the main hall with pine
and covered it with fine gold and decorated it with palm tree and chain designs. [6]He adorned the temple with precious stones. And the gold he used
was gold of Parvaim. [7]He overlaid the ceiling beams, doorframes, walls and
doors of the temple with gold, and he carved cherubim on the walls.
[8]He built the Most Holy Place, its length corresponding to the width of the
temple—twenty cubits long and twenty cubits wide. He overlaid the inside
with six hundred talents[e] of fine gold. [9]The gold nails weighed fifty shekels.[f]
He also overlaid the upper parts with gold.
[10]In the Most Holy Place he made a pair of sculptured cherubim and overlaid them with gold. [11]The total wingspan of the cherubim was twenty cubits.
One wing of the first cherub was five cubits[g] long and touched the temple
wall, while its other wing, also five cubits long, touched the wing of the other cherub. [12]Similarly one wing of the second cherub was five cubits long and
touched the other temple wall, and its other wing, also five cubits long,
touched the wing of the first cherub. [13]The wings of these cherubim extended twenty cubits. They stood on their feet, facing the main hall.[h]
[14]He made the curtain of blue, purple and crimson yarn and fine linen, with
cherubim worked into it.
[15]In the front of the temple he made two pillars, which ⌊together⌋ were
thirty-five cubits[i] long, each with a capital on top measuring five cubits. [16]He
made interwoven chains[j] and put them on top of the pillars. He also made a
hundred pomegranates and attached them to the chains. [17]He erected the pillars in the front of the temple, one to the south and one to the north. The
one to the south he named Jakin[k] and the one to the north Boaz.[l]

4 ***The Temple's Furnishings*** He made a bronze altar twenty cubits long,
twenty cubits wide and ten cubits high.[m] [2]He made the Sea of cast
metal, circular in shape, measuring ten cubits from rim to rim and five cubits[n] high. It took a line of thirty cubits[o] to measure around it. [3]Below the rim,
figures of bulls encircled it—ten to a cubit.[p] The bulls were cast in two rows
in one piece with the Sea.
[4]The Sea stood on twelve bulls, three facing north, three facing west, three
facing south and three facing east. The Sea rested on top of them, and their
hindquarters were toward the center. [5]It was a handbreadth[q] in thickness,
and its rim was like the rim of a cup, like a lily blossom. It held three thousand baths.[r]
[6]He then made ten basins for washing and placed five on the south side

[a] *1* Hebrew *Ornan,* a variant of *Araunah* [b] *3* That is, about 90 feet (about 27 meters) long and 30 feet (about 9 meters) wide [c] *4* That is, about 30 feet (about 9 meters); also in verses 8, 11 and 13 [d] *4* Some Septuagint and Syriac manuscripts; Hebrew *and a hundred and twenty* [e] *8* That is, about 23 tons (about 21 metric tons) [f] *9* That is, about 1 1/4 pounds (about 0.6 kilogram) [g] *11* That is, about 7 1/2 feet (about 2.3 meters); also in verse 15 [h] *13* Or *facing inward* [i] *15* That is, about 52 feet (about 16 meters) [j] *16* Or possibly *made chains in the inner sanctuary;* the meaning of the Hebrew for this phrase is uncertain. [k] *17 Jakin* probably means *he establishes.* [l] *17 Boaz* probably means *in him is strength.* [m] *1* That is, about 30 feet (about 9 meters) long and wide, and about 15 feet (about 4.5 meters) high [n] *2* That is, about 7 1/2 feet (about 2.3 meters) [o] *2* That is, about 45 feet (about 13.5 meters) [p] *3* That is, about 1 1/2 feet (about 0.5 meter) [q] *5* That is, about 3 inches (about 8 centimeters) [r] *5* That is, about 17,500 gallons (about 66 kiloliters)

and five on the north. In them the things to be used for the burnt offerings were rinsed, but the Sea was to be used by the priests for washing.

⁷He made ten gold lampstands according to the specifications for them and placed them in the temple, five on the south side and five on the north.

⁸He made ten tables and placed them in the temple, five on the south side and five on the north. He also made a hundred gold sprinkling bowls.

⁹He made the courtyard of the priests, and the large court and the doors for the court, and overlaid the doors with bronze. ¹⁰He placed the Sea on the south side, at the southeast corner.

¹¹He also made the pots and shovels and sprinkling bowls.

So Huram finished the work he had undertaken for King Solomon in the temple of God:

¹²the two pillars;
  the two bowl-shaped capitals on top of the pillars;
  the two sets of network decorating the two bowl-shaped capitals on top of the pillars;
¹³the four hundred pomegranates for the two sets of network (two rows of pomegranates for each network, decorating the bowl-shaped capitals on top of the pillars);
¹⁴the stands with their basins;
¹⁵the Sea and the twelve bulls under it;
¹⁶the pots, shovels, meat forks and all related articles.

All the objects that Huram-Abi made for King Solomon for the temple of the Lord were of polished bronze. ¹⁷The king had them cast in clay molds in the plain of the Jordan between Succoth and Zarethan.ᵃ ¹⁸All these things that Solomon made amounted to so much that the weight of the bronze was not determined.

¹⁹Solomon also made all the furnishings that were in God's temple:

the golden altar;
the tables on which was the bread of the Presence;
²⁰ the lampstands of pure gold with their lamps, to burn in front of the inner sanctuary as prescribed;
²¹ the gold floral work and lamps and tongs (they were solid gold);
²² the pure gold wick trimmers, sprinkling bowls, dishes and censers; and the gold doors of the temple: the inner doors to the Most Holy Place and the doors of the main hall.

When all the work Solomon had done for the temple of the Lord was finished, he brought in the things his father David had dedicated—the silver and gold and all the furnishings—and he placed them in the treasuries of God's temple.

The Ark Brought to the Temple ²Then Solomon summoned to Jerusalem the

SEE
2 CHRONICLES 3-4

ᵃ17 Hebrew *Zeredatha*, a variant of *Zarethan*

elders of Israel, all the heads of the tribes and the chiefs of the Israelite families, to bring up the ark of the Lord's covenant from Zion, the City of David. ³And all the men of Israel came together to the king at the time of the festival in the seventh month.

⁴When all the elders of Israel had arrived, the Levites took up the ark, ⁵and they brought up the ark and the Tent of Meeting and all the sacred furnishings in it. The priests, who were Levites, carried them up; ⁶and King Solomon and the entire assembly of Israel that had gathered about him were before the ark, sacrificing so many sheep and cattle that they could not be recorded or counted.

⁷The priests then brought the ark of the Lord's covenant to its place in the inner sanctuary of the temple, the Most Holy Place, and put it beneath the wings of the cherubim. ⁸The cherubim spread their wings over the place of the ark and covered the ark and its carrying poles. ⁹These poles were so long that their ends, extending from the ark, could be seen from in front of the inner sanctuary, but not from outside the Holy Place; and they are still there today. ¹⁰There was nothing in the ark except the two tablets that Moses had placed in it at Horeb, where the Lord made a covenant with the Israelites after they came out of Egypt.

¹¹The priests then withdrew from the Holy Place. All the priests who were there had consecrated themselves, regardless of their divisions. ¹²All the Levites who were musicians—Asaph, Heman, Jeduthun and their sons and relatives—stood on the east side of the altar, dressed in fine linen and playing cymbals, harps and lyres. They were accompanied by 120 priests sounding trumpets. ¹³The trumpeters and singers joined in unison, as with one voice, to give praise and thanks to the Lord. Accompanied by trumpets, cymbals and other instruments, they raised their voices in praise to the Lord and sang:

> "He is good;
>   his love endures forever."

Then the temple of the Lord was filled with a cloud, ¹⁴and the priests could not perform their service because of the cloud, for the glory of the Lord filled the temple of God.

Then Solomon said, "The Lord has said that he would dwell in a dark cloud; ²I have built a magnificent temple for you, a place for you to dwell forever."

³While the whole assembly of Israel was standing there, the king turned around and blessed them. ⁴Then he said:

"Praise be to the Lord, the God of Israel, who with his hands has fulfilled what he promised with his mouth to my father David. For he said, ⁵'Since the day I brought my people out of Egypt, I have not chosen a city in any tribe of Israel to have a temple built for my Name to be there, nor have I chosen anyone to be the leader over my people Israel. ⁶But now I have chosen Jerusalem for my Name to be there, and I have chosen David to rule my people Israel.'

⁷"My father David had it in his heart to build a temple for the Name of the Lord, the God of Israel. ⁸But the Lord said to my father David, 'Because it was in your heart to build a temple for my Name, you did well to have this in your heart. ⁹Nevertheless, you are not the one to build the temple, but your son, who is your own flesh and blood—he is the one who will build the temple for my Name.'

¹⁰"The Lord has kept the promise he made. I have succeeded David my father and now I sit on the throne of Israel, just as the Lord promised, and I have built the temple for the Name of the Lord, the God of Israel. ¹¹There I have placed the ark, in which is the covenant of the Lord that he made with the people of Israel."

Solomon's Prayer of Dedication ¹²Then Solomon stood before the altar of the Lᴏʀᴅ in front of the whole assembly of Israel and spread out his hands. ¹³Now he had made a bronze platform, five cubits*ᵃ* long, five cubits wide and three cubits*ᵇ* high, and had placed it in the center of the outer court. He stood on the platform and then knelt down before the whole assembly of Israel and spread out his hands toward heaven. ¹⁴He said:

"O Lᴏʀᴅ, God of Israel, there is no God like you in heaven or on earth— you who keep your covenant of love with your servants who continue wholeheartedly in your way. ¹⁵You have kept your promise to your servant David my father; with your mouth you have promised and with your hand you have fulfilled it—as it is today.

¹⁶"Now Lᴏʀᴅ, God of Israel, keep for your servant David my father the promises you made to him when you said, 'You shall never fail to have a man to sit before me on the throne of Israel, if only your sons are careful in all they do to walk before me according to my law, as you have done.' ¹⁷And now, O Lᴏʀᴅ, God of Israel, let your word that you promised your servant David come true.

¹⁸"But will God really dwell on earth with men? The heavens, even the highest heavens, cannot contain you. How much less this temple I have built! ¹⁹Yet give attention to your servant's prayer and his plea for mercy, O Lᴏʀᴅ my God. Hear the cry and the prayer that your servant is praying in your presence. ²⁰May your eyes be open toward this temple day and night, this place of which you said you would put your Name there. May you hear the prayer your servant prays toward this place. ²¹Hear the supplications of your servant and of your people Israel when they pray toward this place. Hear from heaven, your dwelling place; and when you hear, forgive.

²²"When a man wrongs his neighbor and is required to take an oath and he comes and swears the oath before your altar in this temple, ²³then hear from heaven and act. Judge between your servants, repaying the guilty by bringing down on his own head what he has done. Declare the innocent not guilty and so establish his innocence.

²⁴"When your people Israel have been defeated by an enemy because they have sinned against you and when they turn back and confess your name, praying and making supplication before you in this temple, ²⁵then hear from heaven and forgive the sin of your people Israel and bring them back to the land you gave to them and their fathers.

²⁶"When the heavens are shut up and there is no rain because your people have sinned against you, and when they pray toward this place and confess your name and turn from their sin because you have afflicted them, ²⁷then hear from heaven and forgive the sin of your servants, your people Israel. Teach them the right way to live, and send rain on the land you gave your people for an inheritance.

²⁸"When famine or plague comes to the land, or blight or mildew, locusts or grasshoppers, or when enemies besiege them in any of their cities, whatever disaster or disease may come, ²⁹and when a prayer or plea is made by any of your people Israel—each one aware of his afflictions and pains, and spreading out his hands toward this temple— ³⁰then hear from heaven, your dwelling place. Forgive, and deal with each man according to all he does, since you know his heart (for you alone know the hearts of men), ³¹so that they will fear you and walk in your ways all the time they live in the land you gave our fathers.

³²"As for the foreigner who does not belong to your people Israel but has come from a distant land because of your great name and your

---

ᵃ13 That is, about 7 1/2 feet (about 2.3 meters)   *ᵇ13* That is, about 4 1/2 feet (about 1.3 meters)

Dear Sam,

My parents told me I can't hang around with certain kids. I think I should be able to choose my own friends, so I've been lying and sneaking out. Now I don't feel comfortable talking to God. Help!

Shawn in Sheldon

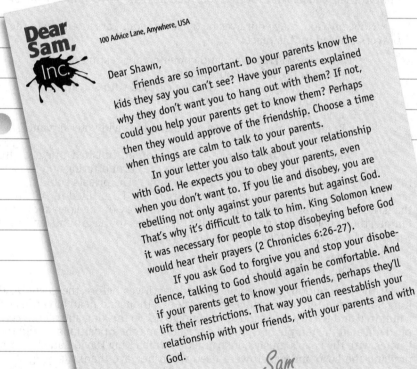

Dear Sam, Inc.

100 Advice Lane, Anywhere, USA

Dear Shawn,

Friends are so important. Do your parents know the kids they say you can't see? Have your parents explained why they don't want you to hang out with them? If not, could you help your parents get to know them? Perhaps then they would approve of the friendship. Choose a time when things are calm to talk to your parents.

In your letter you also talk about your relationship with God. He expects you to obey your parents, even when you don't want to. If you lie and disobey, you are rebelling not only against your parents but against God. That's why it's difficult to talk to him. King Solomon knew it was necessary for people to stop disobeying before God would hear their prayers (2 Chronicles 6:26-27).

If you ask God to forgive you and stop your disobedience, talking to God should again be comfortable. And if your parents get to know your friends, perhaps they'll lift their restrictions. That way you can reestablish your relationship with your friends, with your parents and with God.

Sam

mighty hand and your outstretched arm—when he comes and prays toward this temple, [33]then hear from heaven, your dwelling place, and do whatever the foreigner asks of you, so that all the peoples of the earth may know your name and fear you, as do your own people Israel, and may know that this house I have built bears your Name.

[34]"When your people go to war against their enemies, wherever you send them, and when they pray to you toward this city you have chosen and the temple I have built for your Name, [35]then hear from heaven their prayer and their plea, and uphold their cause.

[36]"When they sin against you—for there is no one who does not sin—and you become angry with them and give them over to the enemy, who takes them captive to a land far away or near; [37]and if they have a change of heart in the land where they are held captive, and repent and plead with you in the land of their captivity and say, 'We have sinned, we have done wrong and acted wickedly'; [38]and if they turn back to you with all their heart and soul in the land of their captivity where they were taken, and pray toward the land you gave their fathers, toward the city you have chosen and toward the temple I have built for your Name; [39]then from heaven, your dwelling place, hear their prayer and their pleas, and uphold their cause. And forgive your people, who have sinned against you.

[40]"Now, my God, may your eyes be open and your ears attentive to the prayers offered in this place.

> [41]"Now arise, O Lord God, and come to your resting place,
>   you and the ark of your might.
> May your priests, O Lord God, be clothed with salvation,
>   may your saints rejoice in your goodness.
> [42]O Lord God, do not reject your anointed one.
>   Remember the great love promised to David your servant."

7 **The Dedication of the Temple** When Solomon finished praying, fire came down from heaven and consumed the burnt offering and the sacrifices, and the glory of the Lord filled the temple. [2]The priests could not enter the temple of the Lord because the glory of the Lord filled it. [3]When all the Israelites saw the fire coming down and the glory of the Lord above the temple, they knelt on the pavement with their faces to the ground, and they worshiped and gave thanks to the Lord, saying,

> "He is good;
>   his love endures forever."

[4]Then the king and all the people offered sacrifices before the Lord. [5]And King Solomon offered a sacrifice of twenty-two thousand head of cattle and a hundred and twenty thousand sheep and goats. So the king and all the people dedicated the temple of God. [6]The priests took their positions, as did the Levites with the Lord's musical instruments, which King David had made for praising the Lord and which were used when he gave thanks, saying, "His love endures forever." Opposite the Levites, the priests blew their trumpets, and all the Israelites were standing.

[7]Solomon consecrated the middle part of the courtyard in front of the temple of the Lord, and there he offered burnt offerings and the fat of the fellowship offerings,[a] because the bronze altar he had made could not hold the burnt offerings, the grain offerings and the fat portions.

[8]So Solomon observed the festival at that time for seven days, and all Israel with him—a vast assembly, people from Lebo[b] Hamath to the Wadi of

---

[a]7 Traditionally *peace offerings*   [b]8 Or *from the entrance to*

Egypt. ⁹On the eighth day they held an assembly, for they had celebrated the dedication of the altar for seven days and the festival for seven days more. ¹⁰On the twenty-third day of the seventh month he sent the people to their homes, joyful and glad in heart for the good things the Lᴏʀᴅ had done for David and Solomon and for his people Israel.

The Lᴏʀᴅ Appears to Solomon ¹¹When Solomon had finished the temple of the Lᴏʀᴅ and the royal palace, and had succeeded in carrying out all he had in mind to do in the temple of the Lᴏʀᴅ and in his own palace, ¹²the Lᴏʀᴅ appeared to him at night and said:

"I have heard your prayer and have chosen this place for myself as a temple for sacrifices.

¹³"When I shut up the heavens so that there is no rain, or command locusts to devour the land or send a plague among my people, ¹⁴if my people, who are called by my name, will humble themselves and pray and seek my face and turn from their wicked ways, then will I hear from heaven and will forgive their sin and will heal their land. ¹⁵Now my eyes will be open and my ears attentive to the prayers offered in this place. ¹⁶I have chosen and consecrated this temple so that my Name may be there forever. My eyes and my heart will always be there.

¹⁷"As for you, if you walk before me as David your father did, and do all I command, and observe my decrees and laws, ¹⁸I will establish your royal throne, as I covenanted with David your father when I said, 'You shall never fail to have a man to rule over Israel.'

¹⁹"But if youᵃ turn away and forsake the decrees and commands I have given youᵃ and go off to serve other gods and worship them, ²⁰then I will uproot Israel from my land, which I have given them, and will reject this temple I have consecrated for my Name. I will make it a byword and an object of ridicule among all peoples. ²¹And though this temple is now so imposing, all who pass by will be appalled and say, 'Why has the Lᴏʀᴅ done such a thing to this land and to this temple?' ²²People will answer, 'Because they have forsaken the Lᴏʀᴅ, the God of their fathers, who brought them out of Egypt, and have embraced other gods, worshiping and serving them— that is why he brought all this disaster on them.' "

2 CHRONICLES 7

QUIZZER

Q: How many animals did Solomon sacrifice to God at the dedication of the temple?

BONUS: How did God reveal his presence in the temple?

Answers on page 533

Solomon's Other Activities At the end of twenty years, during which Solomon built the temple of the Lᴏʀᴅ and his own palace, ²Solomon rebuilt the villages that Hiramᵇ had given him, and settled Israelites in them. ³Solomon then went to Hamath Zobah and captured it. ⁴He also built up Tadmor in the desert and all the store cities he had built in Hamath. ⁵He rebuilt Upper Beth Horon and Lower Beth Horon as fortified cities, with walls and with gates and bars, ⁶as well as Baalath and all his store cities, and all the cities for his chariots and for his horsesᶜ—whatever he desired to build in Jerusalem, in Lebanon and throughout all the territory he ruled.

⁷All the people left from the Hittites, Amorites, Perizzites, Hivites and Jebusites (these peoples were not Israelites), ⁸that is, their descendants remaining in the land, whom the Israelites had not destroyed—these Solomon conscripted for his slave labor force, as it is to this day. ⁹But Solomon did not make slaves of the Israelites for his work; they were his fighting men, commanders of his captains, and commanders of his chariots and charioteers.

ᵃ19 The Hebrew is plural. ᵇ2 Hebrew *Huram*, a variant of *Hiram*; also in verse 18 ᶜ6 Or *charioteers*

[10]They were also King Solomon's chief officials—two hundred and fifty officials supervising the men.

[11]Solomon brought Pharaoh's daughter up from the City of David to the palace he had built for her, for he said, "My wife must not live in the palace of David king of Israel, because the places the ark of the LORD has entered are holy."

[12]On the altar of the LORD that he had built in front of the portico, Solomon sacrificed burnt offerings to the LORD, [13]according to the daily requirement for offerings commanded by Moses for Sabbaths, New Moons and the three annual feasts—the Feast of Unleavened Bread, the Feast of Weeks and the Feast of Tabernacles. [14]In keeping with the ordinance of his father David, he appointed the divisions of the priests for their duties, and the Levites to lead the praise and to assist the priests according to each day's requirement. He also appointed the gatekeepers by divisions for the various gates, because this was what David the man of God had ordered. [15]They did not deviate from the king's commands to the priests or to the Levites in any matter, including that of the treasuries.

[16]All Solomon's work was carried out, from the day the foundation of the temple of the LORD was laid until its completion. So the temple of the LORD was finished.

[17]Then Solomon went to Ezion Geber and Elath on the coast of Edom. [18]And Hiram sent him ships commanded by his own officers, men who knew the sea. These, with Solomon's men, sailed to Ophir and brought back four hundred and fifty talents[a] of gold, which they delivered to King Solomon.

The Queen of Sheba Visits Solomon   When the queen of Sheba heard of Solomon's fame, she came to Jerusalem to test him with hard questions. Arriving with a very great caravan—with camels carrying spices, large quantities of gold, and precious stones—she came to Solomon and talked with him about all she had on her mind. [2]Solomon answered all her questions; nothing was too hard for him to explain to her. [3]When the queen of Sheba saw the wisdom of Solomon, as well as the palace he had built, [4]the food on his table, the seating of his officials, the attending servants in their robes, the cupbearers in their robes and the burnt offerings he made at[b] the temple of the LORD, she was overwhelmed.

[5]She said to the king, "The report I heard in my own country about your achievements and your wisdom is true. [6]But I did not believe what they said until I came and saw with my own eyes. Indeed, not even half the greatness of your wisdom was told me; you have far exceeded the report I heard. [7]How happy your men must be! How happy your officials, who continually stand before you and hear your wisdom! [8]Praise be to the LORD your God, who has delighted in you and placed you on his throne as king to rule for the LORD your God. Because of the love of your God for Israel and his desire

---

2 CHRONICLES 7:14

Some prayers are always answered with an enthusiastic "Yes!" God promises: "If my people, who are called by my name, will humble themselves and pray and seek my face and turn from their wicked ways, then will I hear from heaven and will forgive their sin." What a great promise for those times when guilt gets you down. You feel ashamed. Even dirty. You wonder how you'll ever be able to face yourself or God. And then you hear the promise: "Pray. Seek my face. Turn from your wicked ways." And you remember God always answers "Yes!" to prayers for forgiveness. He has promised, "I will hear and will forgive."

Direct Line

---

[a]18 That is, about 17 tons (about 16 metric tons)   [b]4 Or *the ascent by which he went up to*

to uphold them forever, he has made you king over them, to maintain justice and righteousness."

⁹Then she gave the king 120 talents*ᵃ* of gold, large quantities of spices, and precious stones. There had never been such spices as those the queen of Sheba gave to King Solomon.

¹⁰(The men of Hiram and the men of Solomon brought gold from Ophir; they also brought algumwood*ᵇ* and precious stones. ¹¹The king used the algumwood to make steps for the temple of the LORD and for the royal palace, and to make harps and lyres for the musicians. Nothing like them had ever been seen in Judah.)

¹²King Solomon gave the queen of Sheba all she desired and asked for; he gave her more than she had brought to him. Then she left and returned with her retinue to her own country.

Solomon's Splendor ¹³The weight of the gold that Solomon received yearly was 666 talents,*ᶜ* ¹⁴not including the revenues brought in by merchants and traders. Also all the kings of Arabia and the governors of the land brought gold and silver to Solomon.

¹⁵King Solomon made two hundred large shields of hammered gold; six hundred bekas*ᵈ* of hammered gold went into each shield. ¹⁶He also made three hundred small shields of hammered gold, with three hundred bekas*ᵉ* of gold in each shield. The king put them in the Palace of the Forest of Lebanon.

¹⁷Then the king made a great throne inlaid with ivory and overlaid with pure gold. ¹⁸The throne had six steps, and a footstool of gold was attached to it. On both sides of the seat were armrests, with a lion standing beside each of them. ¹⁹Twelve lions stood on the six steps, one at either end of each step. Nothing like it had ever been made for any other kingdom. ²⁰All King Solomon's goblets were gold, and all the household articles in the Palace of the Forest of Lebanon were pure gold. Nothing was made of silver, because silver was considered of little value in Solomon's day. ²¹The king had a fleet of trading ships*ᶠ* manned by Hiram's*ᵍ* men. Once every three years it returned, carrying gold, silver and ivory, and apes and baboons.

²²King Solomon was greater in riches and wisdom than all the other kings of the earth. ²³All the kings of the earth sought audience with Solomon to hear the wisdom God had put in his heart. ²⁴Year after year, everyone who came brought a gift—articles of silver and gold, and robes, weapons and spices, and horses and mules.

²⁵Solomon had four thousand stalls for horses and chariots, and twelve thousand horses,*ʰ* which he kept in the chariot cities and also with him in Jerusalem. ²⁶He ruled over all the kings from the River*ⁱ* to the land of the Philistines, as far as the border of Egypt. ²⁷The king made silver as common in Jerusalem as stones, and cedar as plentiful as sycamore-fig trees in the foothills. ²⁸Solomon's horses were imported from Egypt*ʲ* and from all other countries.

Solomon's Death ²⁹As for the other events of Solomon's reign, from beginning to end, are they not written in the records of Nathan the prophet, in the prophecy of Ahijah the Shilonite and in the visions of Iddo the seer concerning Jeroboam son of Nebat? ³⁰Solomon reigned in Jerusalem over all Israel forty years. ³¹Then he rested with his fathers and was buried in the city of David his father. And Rehoboam his son succeeded him as king.

Answers

to Quizzer on page 531

A: He sacrificed 22,000 head of cattle and 120,000 sheep and goats (2 Chronicles 7:5).

BONUS: The "glory of the LORD," a bright, glowing cloud, filled the temple (2 Chronicles 7:1-3).

ᵃ9 That is, about 4 1/2 tons (about 4 metric tons) *ᵇ10* Probably a variant of *almugwood* *ᶜ13* That is, about 25 tons (about 23 metric tons) *ᵈ15* That is, about 7 1/2 pounds (about 3.5 kilograms) *ᵉ16* That is, about 3 3/4 pounds (about 1.7 kilograms) *ᶠ21* Hebrew *of ships that could go to Tarshish* *ᵍ21* Hebrew *Huram*, a variant of *Hiram* *ʰ25* Or *charioteers* *ⁱ26* That is, the Euphrates *ʲ28* Or possibly *Muzur*, a region in Cilicia

10 *Israel Rebels Against Rehoboam* Rehoboam went to Shechem, for all the Israelites had gone there to make him king. ²When Jeroboam son of Nebat heard this (he was in Egypt, where he had fled from King Solomon), he returned from Egypt. ³So they sent for Jeroboam, and he and all Israel went to Rehoboam and said to him: ⁴"Your father put a heavy yoke on us, but now lighten the harsh labor and the heavy yoke he put on us, and we will serve you."

⁵Rehoboam answered, "Come back to me in three days." So the people went away.

⁶Then King Rehoboam consulted the elders who had served his father Solomon during his lifetime. "How would you advise me to answer these people?" he asked.

⁷They replied, "If you will be kind to these people and please them and give them a favorable answer, they will always be your servants."

⁸But Rehoboam rejected the advice the elders gave him and consulted the young men who had grown up with him and were serving him. ⁹He asked them, "What is your advice? How should we answer these people who say to me, 'Lighten the yoke your father put on us'?"

¹⁰The young men who had grown up with him replied, "Tell the people who have said to you, 'Your father put a heavy yoke on us, but make our yoke lighter'—tell them, 'My little finger is thicker than my father's waist. ¹¹My father laid on you a heavy yoke; I will make it even heavier. My father scourged you with whips; I will scourge you with scorpions.' "

¹²Three days later Jeroboam and all the people returned to Rehoboam, as the king had said, "Come back to me in three days." ¹³The king answered them harshly. Rejecting the advice of the elders, ¹⁴he followed the advice of the young men and said, "My father made your yoke heavy; I will make it even heavier. My father scourged you with whips; I will scourge you with scorpions." ¹⁵So the king did not listen to the people, for this turn of events was from God, to fulfill the word the Lᴏʀᴅ had spoken to Jeroboam son of Nebat through Ahijah the Shilonite.

¹⁶When all Israel saw that the king refused to listen to them, they answered the king:

> "What share do we have in David,
>   what part in Jesse's son?
> To your tents, O Israel!
> Look after your own house, O David!"

So all the Israelites went home. ¹⁷But as for the Israelites who were living in the towns of Judah, Rehoboam still ruled over them.

¹⁸King Rehoboam sent out Adoniram,ᵃ who was in charge of forced labor, but the Israelites stoned him to death. King Rehoboam, however, managed to get into his chariot and escape to Jerusalem. ¹⁹So Israel has been in rebellion against the house of David to this day.

11 When Rehoboam arrived in Jerusalem, he mustered the house of Judah and Benjamin—a hundred and eighty thousand fighting men—to make war against Israel and to regain the kingdom for Rehoboam.

²But this word of the Lᴏʀᴅ came to Shemaiah the man of God: ³"Say to Rehoboam son of Solomon king of Judah and to all the Israelites in Judah and

2 CHRONICLES 9

QUIZZER

Q: What animals did Solomon's trading ships bring back to Jerusalem?

BONUS: How many horses did Solomon own?

Answers on page 535

ᵃ18 Hebrew *Hadoram,* a variant of *Adoniram*

Benjamin, ⁴"This is what the LORD says: Do not go up to fight against your brothers. Go home, every one of you, for this is my doing.' " So they obeyed the words of the LORD and turned back from marching against Jeroboam.

Rehoboam Fortifies Judah   ⁵Rehoboam lived in Jerusalem and built up towns for defense in Judah: ⁶Bethlehem, Etam, Tekoa, ⁷Beth Zur, Soco, Adullam, ⁸Gath, Mareshah, Ziph, ⁹Adoraim, Lachish, Azekah, ¹⁰Zorah, Aijalon and Hebron. These were fortified cities in Judah and Benjamin. ¹¹He strengthened their defenses and put commanders in them, with supplies of food, olive oil and wine. ¹²He put shields and spears in all the cities, and made them very strong. So Judah and Benjamin were his.

¹³The priests and Levites from all their districts throughout Israel sided with him. ¹⁴The Levites even abandoned their pasturelands and property, and came to Judah and Jerusalem because Jeroboam and his sons had rejected them as priests of the LORD. ¹⁵And he appointed his own priests for the high places and for the goat and calf idols he had made. ¹⁶Those from every tribe of Israel who set their hearts on seeking the LORD, the God of Israel, followed the Levites to Jerusalem to offer sacrifices to the LORD, the God of their fathers. ¹⁷They strengthened the kingdom of Judah and supported Rehoboam son of Solomon three years, walking in the ways of David and Solomon during this time.

Rehoboam's Family   ¹⁸Rehoboam married Mahalath, who was the daughter of David's son Jerimoth and of Abihail, the daughter of Jesse's son Eliab. ¹⁹She bore him sons: Jeush, Shemariah and Zaham. ²⁰Then he married Maacah daughter of Absalom, who bore him Abijah, Attai, Ziza and Shelomith. ²¹Rehoboam loved Maacah daughter of Absalom more than any of his other wives and concubines. In all, he had eighteen wives and sixty concubines, twenty-eight sons and sixty daughters.

²²Rehoboam appointed Abijah son of Maacah to be the chief prince among his brothers, in order to make him king. ²³He acted wisely, dispersing some of his sons throughout the districts of Judah and Benjamin, and to all the fortified cities. He gave them abundant provisions and took many wives for them.

Answers

to Quizzer on page 534

A: Apes and baboons (2 Chronicles 9:21).

BONUS: He owned 12,000 horses (2 Chronicles 9:25).

12 *Shishak Attacks Jerusalem*   After Rehoboam's position as king was established and he had become strong, he and all Israel[a] with him abandoned the law of the LORD. ²Because they had been unfaithful to the LORD, Shishak king of Egypt attacked Jerusalem in the fifth year of King Rehoboam. ³With twelve hundred chariots and sixty thousand horsemen and the innumerable troops of Libyans, Sukkites and Cushites[b] that came with him from Egypt, ⁴he captured the fortified cities of Judah and came as far as Jerusalem.

⁵Then the prophet Shemaiah came to Rehoboam and to the leaders of Judah who had assembled in Jerusalem for fear of Shishak, and he said to them, "This is what the LORD says, 'You have abandoned me; therefore, I now abandon you to Shishak.' "

⁶The leaders of Israel and the king humbled themselves and said, "The LORD is just."

⁷When the LORD saw that they humbled themselves, this word of the LORD came to Shemaiah: "Since they have humbled themselves, I will not destroy them but will soon give them deliverance. My wrath will not be poured out on Jerusalem through Shishak. ⁸They will, however, become subject to him, so that they may learn the difference between serving me and serving the kings of other lands."

---

[a]1 That is, Judah, as frequently in 2 Chronicles   [b]3 That is, people from the upper Nile region

Dear Sam,

Why are my parents always saying, "Don't do this. Don't do that"? Why can't I live and find out things for myself?

Trisha in Troy

Dear Sam, Inc.

100 Advice Lane, Anywhere, USA

Dear Trisha,

Of course you can choose to learn every lesson the hard way. But your life will probably be full of pain and suffering. Suppose you want to jump off a roof to see if you'll bounce. Is it easier and smarter to find out the results for yourself or to take the advice of someone who loves you? If your parents said, "Don't try it. Trust us, you won't bounce," would you try it anyway?

A young king in Israel, Rehoboam, felt much the same as you. When some people came to him with a request, he sought the advice of those who had served his father and had much experience and wisdom. But then he talked to his friends and decided to take their advice instead. Disaster followed (2 Chronicles 10:16-19).

God gives you parents and other adults to teach you how to make wise choices. Try to keep in mind that they aren't trying to cramp your style, they're trying to help.

Sam

⁹When Shishak king of Egypt attacked Jerusalem, he carried off the treasures of the temple of the LORD and the treasures of the royal palace. He took everything, including the gold shields Solomon had made. ¹⁰So King Rehoboam made bronze shields to replace them and assigned these to the commanders of the guard on duty at the entrance to the royal palace. ¹¹Whenever the king went to the LORD's temple, the guards went with him, bearing the shields, and afterward they returned them to the guardroom.

¹²Because Rehoboam humbled himself, the LORD's anger turned from him, and he was not totally destroyed. Indeed, there was some good in Judah.

¹³King Rehoboam established himself firmly in Jerusalem and continued as king. He was forty-one years old when he became king, and he reigned seventeen years in Jerusalem, the city the LORD had chosen out of all the tribes of Israel in which to put his Name. His mother's name was Naamah; she was an Ammonite. ¹⁴He did evil because he had not set his heart on seeking the LORD.

¹⁵As for the events of Rehoboam's reign, from beginning to end, are they not written in the records of Shemaiah the prophet and of Iddo the seer that deal with genealogies? There was continual warfare between Rehoboam and Jeroboam. ¹⁶Rehoboam rested with his fathers and was buried in the City of David. And Abijah his son succeeded him as king.

13 *Abijah King of Judah*   In the eighteenth year of the reign of Jeroboam, Abijah became king of Judah, ²and he reigned in Jerusalem three years. His mother's name was Maacah,ª a daughterᵇ of Uriel of Gibeah.

There was war between Abijah and Jeroboam. ³Abijah went into battle with a force of four hundred thousand able fighting men, and Jeroboam drew up a battle line against him with eight hundred thousand able troops.

⁴Abijah stood on Mount Zemaraim, in the hill country of Ephraim, and said, "Jeroboam and all Israel, listen to me! ⁵Don't you know that the LORD, the God of Israel, has given the kingship of Israel to David and his descendants forever by a covenant of salt? ⁶Yet Jeroboam son of Nebat, an official of Solomon son of David, rebelled against his master. ⁷Some worthless scoundrels gathered around him and opposed Rehoboam son of Solomon when he was young and indecisive and not strong enough to resist them.

⁸"And now you plan to resist the kingdom of the LORD, which is in the hands of David's descendants. You are indeed a vast army and have with you the golden calves that Jeroboam made to be your gods. ⁹But didn't you drive out the priests of the LORD, the sons of Aaron, and the Levites, and make priests of your own as the peoples of other lands do? Whoever comes to consecrate himself with a young bull and seven rams may become a priest of what are not gods.

¹⁰"As for us, the LORD is our God, and we have not forsaken him. The priests who serve the LORD are sons of Aaron, and the Levites assist them. ¹¹Every

ª2 Most Septuagint manuscripts and Syriac (see also 2 Chron. 11:20 and 1 Kings 15:2); Hebrew *Micaiah*
ᵇ2 Or *granddaughter*

2 CHRONICLES 13:10–18

Do you ever feel the odds are stacked against you? The guys in the locker room mock you because you don't join in the sex talk? Everyone in your science class laughs at you when you say you believe in creation? You face hostile kids when you get on the bus? How do you keep your courage up? When one king of Judah was forced to face an army twice as big as his (2 Chronicles 13:3), he was absolutely confident. He cried out, "The LORD is our God . . . God is with us" (1 Chronicles 13:10–12). Keep on being faithful to the Lord and have courage. The odds may seem to be against you, but one person plus God is a majority!

Direct Line

morning and evening they present burnt offerings and fragrant incense to the Lord. They set out the bread on the ceremonially clean table and light the lamps on the gold lampstand every evening. We are observing the requirements of the Lord our God. But you have forsaken him. ¹²God is with us; he is our leader. His priests with their trumpets will sound the battle cry against you. Men of Israel, do not fight against the Lord, the God of your fathers, for you will not succeed."

¹³Now Jeroboam had sent troops around to the rear, so that while he was in front of Judah the ambush was behind them. ¹⁴Judah turned and saw that they were being attacked at both front and rear. Then they cried out to the Lord. The priests blew their trumpets ¹⁵and the men of Judah raised the battle cry. At the sound of their battle cry, God routed Jeroboam and all Israel before Abijah and Judah. ¹⁶The Israelites fled before Judah, and God delivered them into their hands. ¹⁷Abijah and his men inflicted heavy losses on them, so that there were five hundred thousand casualties among Israel's able men. ¹⁸The men of Israel were subdued on that occasion, and the men of Judah were victorious because they relied on the Lord, the God of their fathers.

¹⁹Abijah pursued Jeroboam and took from him the towns of Bethel, Jeshanah and Ephron, with their surrounding villages. ²⁰Jeroboam did not regain power during the time of Abijah. And the Lord struck him down and he died.

²¹But Abijah grew in strength. He married fourteen wives and had twenty-two sons and sixteen daughters.

²²The other events of Abijah's reign, what he did and what he said, are written in the annotations of the prophet Iddo.

14 And Abijah rested with his fathers and was buried in the City of David. Asa his son succeeded him as king, and in his days the country was at peace for ten years.

Asa King of Judah ²Asa did what was good and right in the eyes of the Lord his God. ³He removed the foreign altars and the high places, smashed the sacred stones and cut down the Asherah poles.ª ⁴He commanded Judah to seek the Lord, the God of their fathers, and to obey his laws and commands. ⁵He removed the high places and incense altars in every town in Judah, and the kingdom was at peace under him. ⁶He built up the fortified cities of Judah, since the land was at peace. No one was at war with him during those years, for the Lord gave him rest.

⁷"Let us build up these towns," he said to Judah, "and put walls around them, with towers, gates and bars. The land is still ours, because we have sought the Lord our God; we sought him and he has given us rest on every side." So they built and prospered.

⁸Asa had an army of three hundred thousand men from Judah, equipped with large shields and with spears, and two hundred and eighty thousand from Benjamin, armed with small shields and with bows. All these were brave fighting men.

⁹Zerah the Cushite marched out against them with a vast army*b* and three hundred chariots, and came as far as Mareshah. ¹⁰Asa went out to meet him, and they took up battle positions in the Valley of Zephathah near Mareshah.

¹¹Then Asa called to the Lord his God and said, "Lord, there is no one like you to help the powerless against the mighty. Help us, O Lord our God, for we rely on you, and in your name we have come against this vast army. O Lord, you are our God; do not let man prevail against you."

ª3 That is, symbols of the goddess Asherah; here and elsewhere in 2 Chronicles ᵇ9 Hebrew *with an army of a thousand thousands* or *with an army of thousands upon thousands*

¹²The Lord struck down the Cushites before Asa and Judah. The Cushites fled, ¹³and Asa and his army pursued them as far as Gerar. Such a great number of Cushites fell that they could not recover; they were crushed before the Lord and his forces. The men of Judah carried off a large amount of plunder. ¹⁴They destroyed all the villages around Gerar, for the terror of the Lord had fallen upon them. They plundered all these villages, since there was much booty there. ¹⁵They also attacked the camps of the herdsmen and carried off droves of sheep and goats and camels. Then they returned to Jerusalem.

15 ***Asa's Reform*** The Spirit of God came upon Azariah son of Oded. ²He went out to meet Asa and said to him, "Listen to me, Asa and all Judah and Benjamin. The Lord is with you when you are with him. If you seek him, he will be found by you, but if you forsake him, he will forsake you. ³For a long time Israel was without the true God, without a priest to teach and without the law. ⁴But in their distress they turned to the Lord, the God of Israel, and sought him, and he was found by them. ⁵In those days it was not safe to travel about, for all the inhabitants of the lands were in great turmoil. ⁶One nation was being crushed by another and one city by another, because God was troubling them with every kind of distress. ⁷But as for you, be strong and do not give up, for your work will be rewarded."

> The Lord is with you when you are with him. If you seek him, he will be found by you
> (2 Chronicles 15:2).

⁸When Asa heard these words and the prophecy of Azariah son of[a] Oded the prophet, he took courage. He removed the detestable idols from the whole land of Judah and Benjamin and from the towns he had captured in the hills of Ephraim. He repaired the altar of the Lord that was in front of the portico of the Lord's temple.

⁹Then he assembled all Judah and Benjamin and the people from Ephraim, Manasseh and Simeon who had settled among them, for large numbers had come over to him from Israel when they saw that the Lord his God was with him.

¹⁰They assembled at Jerusalem in the third month of the fifteenth year of Asa's reign. ¹¹At that time they sacrificed to the Lord seven hundred head of cattle and seven thousand sheep and goats from the plunder they had brought back. ¹²They entered into a covenant to seek the Lord, the God of their fathers, with all their heart and soul. ¹³All who would not seek the Lord, the God of Israel, were to be put to death, whether small or great, man or woman. ¹⁴They took an oath to the Lord with loud acclamation, with shouting and with trumpets and horns. ¹⁵All Judah rejoiced about the oath because they had sworn it wholeheartedly. They sought God eagerly, and he was found by them. So the Lord gave them rest on every side.

¹⁶King Asa also deposed his grandmother Maacah from her position as queen mother, because she had made a repulsive Asherah pole. Asa cut the pole down, broke it up and burned it in the Kidron Valley. ¹⁷Although he did not remove the high places from Israel, Asa's heart was fully committed to the Lord all his life. ¹⁸He brought into the temple of God the silver and gold and the articles that he and his father had dedicated.

¹⁹There was no more war until the thirty-fifth year of Asa's reign.

16 ***Asa's Last Years*** In the thirty-sixth year of Asa's reign Baasha king of Israel went up against Judah and fortified Ramah to prevent anyone from leaving or entering the territory of Asa king of Judah. ²Asa then took the silver and gold out of the treasuries of the Lord's tem-

---

a 8 Vulgate and Syriac (see also Septuagint and verse 1); Hebrew does not have *Azariah son of*.

Dear Sam,

I'm one of Two Trombonists in our school band. The oTher player Thinks I'm hopeless. Should I quiT?

Brenda in Brooklyn

Dear Sam, Inc.

100 Advice Lane, Anywhere, USA

Dear Brenda,

Don't give up! First, don't you think your band director is a better judge of your ability? Ask his or her opinion. Second, here's a good Biblical principle you can apply: Do your best, don't give up, and your hard work will be rewarded (2 Chronicles 15:7).

This passage is a great promise. You can depend on it every day as life's discouragements come your way. The world's values are so different from yours. Do you ever feel like you're swimming against the current? Like you're going the wrong way on a one-way street? (Or perhaps you're the one going the right way!) It's good to remember that your work will be rewarded by God if you stay strong and don't give up.

Isn't it great of God to put such encouraging words in the Bible?

Sam

ple and of his own palace and sent it to Ben-Hadad king of Aram, who was ruling in Damascus. ³"Let there be a treaty between me and you," he said, "as there was between my father and your father. See, I am sending you silver and gold. Now break your treaty with Baasha king of Israel so he will withdraw from me."

⁴Ben-Hadad agreed with King Asa and sent the commanders of his forces against the towns of Israel. They conquered Ijon, Dan, Abel Maim*ᵃ* and all the store cities of Naphtali. ⁵When Baasha heard this, he stopped building Ramah and abandoned his work. ⁶Then King Asa brought all the men of Judah, and they carried away from Ramah the stones and timber Baasha had been using. With them he built up Geba and Mizpah.

⁷At that time Hanani the seer came to Asa king of Judah and said to him: "Because you relied on the king of Aram and not on the LORD your God, the army of the king of Aram has escaped from your hand. ⁸Were not the Cushites*ᵇ* and Libyans a mighty army with great numbers of chariots and horsemen*ᶜ*? Yet when you relied on the LORD, he delivered them into your hand. ⁹For the eyes of the LORD range throughout the earth to strengthen those whose hearts are fully committed to him. You have done a foolish thing, and from now on you will be at war."

¹⁰Asa was angry with the seer because of this; he was so enraged that he put him in prison. At the same time Asa brutally oppressed some of the people.

¹¹The events of Asa's reign, from beginning to end, are written in the book of the kings of Judah and Israel. ¹²In the thirty-ninth year of his reign Asa was afflicted with a disease in his feet. Though his disease was severe, even in his illness he did not seek help from the LORD, but only from the physicians. ¹³Then in the forty-first year of his reign Asa died and rested with his fathers. ¹⁴They buried him in the tomb that he had cut out for himself in the City of David. They laid him on a bier covered with spices and various blended perfumes, and they made a huge fire in his honor.

17 *Jehoshaphat King of Judah* Jehoshaphat his son succeeded him as king and strengthened himself against Israel. ²He stationed troops in all the fortified cities of Judah and put garrisons in Judah and in the towns of Ephraim that his father Asa had captured.

ᵃ4 Also known as Abel Beth Maacah *ᵇ8 That is, people from the upper Nile region* *ᶜ8 Or charioteers*

Some people think going to a doctor shows a lack of faith. They think someone who's sick should just pray. They point to 2 Chronicles 16:12 and say that if Asa had relied only on God he would have been healed for sure. Of course, the Bible actually says that Asa was wrong to rely *only* on doctors and not to ask for God's help.

Jesus' miracles show that God can heal even the most terrible sicknesses. Many Christians will tell you that God answered their prayers for healing. But most of them will also tell you that they followed the doctors' orders and expected God to use the knowledge of the doctors to make them well. (Who do you suppose gave them that knowledge in the first place?)

It's always important to rely on the Lord. But that doesn't mean you can't seek and find help from doctors.

The Bible Says

Doctors and God

³The LORD was with Jehoshaphat because in his early years he walked in the ways his father David had followed. He did not consult the Baals ⁴but sought the God of his father and followed his commands rather than the practices of Israel. ⁵The LORD established the kingdom under his control; and all Judah brought gifts to Jehoshaphat, so that he had great wealth and honor. ⁶His heart was devoted to the ways of the LORD; furthermore, he removed the high places and the Asherah poles from Judah.

⁷In the third year of his reign he sent his officials Ben-Hail, Obadiah, Zechariah, Nethanel and Micaiah to teach in the towns of Judah. ⁸With them were certain Levites—Shemaiah, Nethaniah, Zebadiah, Asahel, Shemiramoth, Jehonathan, Adonijah, Tobijah and Tob-Adonijah—and the priests Elishama and Jehoram. ⁹They taught throughout Judah, taking with them the Book of the Law of the LORD; they went around to all the towns of Judah and taught the people.

¹⁰The fear of the LORD fell on all the kingdoms of the lands surrounding Judah, so that they did not make war with Jehoshaphat. ¹¹Some Philistines brought Jehoshaphat gifts and silver as tribute, and the Arabs brought him flocks: seven thousand seven hundred rams and seven thousand seven hundred goats.

¹²Jehoshaphat became more and more powerful; he built forts and store cities in Judah ¹³and had large supplies in the towns of Judah. He also kept experienced fighting men in Jerusalem. ¹⁴Their enrollment by families was as follows:

> From Judah, commanders of units of 1,000:
>> Adnah the commander, with 300,000 fighting men;
> ¹⁵next, Jehohanan the commander, with 280,000;
> ¹⁶next, Amasiah son of Zicri, who volunteered himself for the service of the LORD, with 200,000.
> ¹⁷From Benjamin:
>> Eliada, a valiant soldier, with 200,000 men armed with bows and shields;
> ¹⁸next, Jehozabad, with 180,000 men armed for battle.

¹⁹These were the men who served the king, besides those he stationed in the fortified cities throughout Judah.

18 *Micaiah Prophesies Against Ahab* Now Jehoshaphat had great wealth and honor, and he allied himself with Ahab by marriage. ²Some years later he went down to visit Ahab in Samaria. Ahab slaughtered many sheep and cattle for him and the people with him and urged him to attack Ramoth Gilead. ³Ahab king of Israel asked Jehoshaphat king of Judah, "Will you go with me against Ramoth Gilead?"

Jehoshaphat replied, "I am as you are, and my people as your people; we will join you in the war." ⁴But Jehoshaphat also said to the king of Israel, "First seek the counsel of the LORD."

⁵So the king of Israel brought together the prophets—four hundred men—and asked them, "Shall we go to war against Ramoth Gilead, or shall I refrain?"

"Go," they answered, "for God will give it into the king's hand."

⁶But Jehoshaphat asked, "Is there not a prophet of the LORD here whom we can inquire of?"

⁷The king of Israel answered Jehoshaphat, "There is still one man through whom we can inquire of the LORD, but I hate him because he never prophesies anything good about me, but always bad. He is Micaiah son of Imlah."

"The king should not say that," Jehoshaphat replied.

⁸So the king of Israel called one of his officials and said, "Bring Micaiah son of Imlah at once."

⁹Dressed in their royal robes, the king of Israel and Jehoshaphat king of Judah were sitting on their thrones at the threshing floor by the entrance to the gate of Samaria, with all the prophets prophesying before them. ¹⁰Now Zedekiah son of Kenaanah had made iron horns, and he declared, "This is what the LORD says: 'With these you will gore the Arameans until they are destroyed.' "

¹¹All the other prophets were prophesying the same thing. "Attack Ramoth Gilead and be victorious," they said, "for the LORD will give it into the king's hand."

¹²The messenger who had gone to summon Micaiah said to him, "Look, as one man the other prophets are predicting success for the king. Let your word agree with theirs, and speak favorably."

¹³But Micaiah said, "As surely as the LORD lives, I can tell him only what my God says."

¹⁴When he arrived, the king asked him, "Micaiah, shall we go to war against Ramoth Gilead, or shall I refrain?"

"Attack and be victorious," he answered, "for they will be given into your hand."

¹⁵The king said to him, "How many times must I make you swear to tell me nothing but the truth in the name of the LORD?"

¹⁶Then Micaiah answered, "I saw all Israel scattered on the hills like sheep without a shepherd, and the LORD said, 'These people have no master. Let each one go home in peace.' "

¹⁷The king of Israel said to Jehoshaphat, "Didn't I tell you that he never prophesies anything good about me, but only bad?"

¹⁸Micaiah continued, "Therefore hear the word of the LORD: I saw the LORD sitting on his throne with all the host of heaven standing on his right and on his left. ¹⁹And the LORD said, 'Who will entice Ahab king of Israel into attacking Ramoth Gilead and going to his death there?'

"One suggested this, and another that. ²⁰Finally, a spirit came forward, stood before the LORD and said, 'I will entice him.'

" 'By what means?' the LORD asked.

²¹" 'I will go and be a lying spirit in the mouths of all his prophets,' he said.

" 'You will succeed in enticing him,' said the LORD. 'Go and do it.'

²²"So now the LORD has put a lying spirit in the mouths of these prophets of yours. The LORD has decreed disaster for you."

²³Then Zedekiah son of Kenaanah went up and slapped Micaiah in the face. "Which way did the spirit from[a] the LORD go when he went from me to speak to you?" he asked.

²⁴Micaiah replied, "You will find out on the day you go to hide in an inner room."

²⁵The king of Israel then ordered, "Take Micaiah and send him back to Amon the ruler of the city and to Joash the king's son, ²⁶and say, 'This is what the king says: Put this fellow in prison and give him nothing but bread and water until I return safely.' "

²⁷Micaiah declared, "If you ever return safely, the LORD has not spoken through me." Then he added, "Mark my words, all you people!"

Ahab Killed at Ramoth Gilead   ²⁸So the king of Israel and Jehoshaphat king of Judah went up to Ramoth Gilead. ²⁹The king of Israel said to Jehoshaphat, "I will enter the battle in disguise, but you wear your royal robes." So the king of Israel disguised himself and went into battle.

³⁰Now the king of Aram had ordered his chariot commanders, "Do not fight with anyone, small or great, except the king of Israel." ³¹When the chariot commanders saw Jehoshaphat, they thought, "This is the king of Israel."

---

a 23 Or Spirit of

So they turned to attack him, but Jehoshaphat cried out, and the Lord helped him. God drew them away from him, ³²for when the chariot commanders saw that he was not the king of Israel, they stopped pursuing him.

³³But someone drew his bow at random and hit the king of Israel between the sections of his armor. The king told the chariot driver, "Wheel around and get me out of the fighting. I've been wounded." ³⁴All day long the battle raged, and the king of Israel propped himself up in his chariot facing the Arameans until evening. Then at sunset he died.

19 When Jehoshaphat king of Judah returned safely to his palace in Jerusalem, ²Jehu the seer, the son of Hanani, went out to meet him and said to the king, "Should you help the wicked and love*ᵃ* those who hate the Lord? Because of this, the wrath of the Lord is upon you. ³There is, however, some good in you, for you have rid the land of the Asherah poles and have set your heart on seeking God."

Jehoshaphat Appoints Judges ⁴Jehoshaphat lived in Jerusalem, and he went out again among the people from Beersheba to the hill country of Ephraim and turned them back to the Lord, the God of their fathers. ⁵He appointed judges in the land, in each of the fortified cities of Judah. ⁶He told them, "Consider carefully what you do, because you are not judging for man but for the Lord, who is with you whenever you give a verdict. ⁷Now let the fear of the Lord be upon you. Judge carefully, for with the Lord our God there is no injustice or partiality or bribery."

⁸In Jerusalem also, Jehoshaphat appointed some of the Levites, priests and heads of Israelite families to administer the law of the Lord and to settle disputes. And they lived in Jerusalem. ⁹He gave them these orders: "You must serve faithfully and wholeheartedly in the fear of the Lord. ¹⁰In every case that comes before you from your fellow countrymen who live in the cities—whether bloodshed or other concerns of the law, commands, decrees or ordinances—you are to warn them not to sin against the Lord; otherwise his wrath will come on you and your brothers. Do this, and you will not sin.

¹¹"Amariah the chief priest will be over you in any matter concerning the Lord, and Zebadiah son of Ishmael, the leader of the tribe of Judah, will be over you in any matter concerning the king, and the Levites will serve as officials before you. Act with courage, and may the Lord be with those who do well."

20 *Jehoshaphat Defeats Moab and Ammon* After this, the Moabites and Ammonites with some of the Meunites*ᵇ* came to make war on Jehoshaphat.

²Some men came and told Jehoshaphat, "A vast army is coming against you from Edom,*ᶜ* from the other side of the Sea.*ᵈ* It is already in Hazazon Tamar" (that is, En Gedi). ³Alarmed, Jehoshaphat resolved to inquire of the Lord, and he proclaimed a fast for all Judah. ⁴The people of Judah came together to seek help from the Lord; indeed, they came from every town in Judah to seek him.

⁵Then Jehoshaphat stood up in the assembly of Judah and Jerusalem at the temple of the Lord in the front of the new courtyard ⁶and said:

"O Lord, God of our fathers, are you not the God who is in heaven? You rule over all the kingdoms of the nations. Power and might are in your hand, and no one can withstand you. ⁷O our God, did you not drive out the inhabitants of this land before your people Israel and give it forever to the descendants of Abraham your friend? ⁸They have lived in

---

ᵃ2 Or *and make alliances with* *ᵇ1* Some Septuagint manuscripts; Hebrew *Ammonites* *ᶜ2* One Hebrew manuscript; most Hebrew manuscripts, Septuagint and Vulgate *Aram* *ᵈ2* That is, the Dead Sea

it and have built in it a sanctuary for your Name, saying, ⁹'If calamity comes upon us, whether the sword of judgment, or plague or famine, we will stand in your presence before this temple that bears your Name and will cry out to you in our distress, and you will hear us and save us.'

¹⁰"But now here are men from Ammon, Moab and Mount Seir, whose territory you would not allow Israel to invade when they came from Egypt; so they turned away from them and did not destroy them. ¹¹See how they are repaying us by coming to drive us out of the possession you gave us as an inheritance. ¹²O our God, will you not judge them? For we have no power to face this vast army that is attacking us. We do not know what to do, but our eyes are upon you."

¹³All the men of Judah, with their wives and children and little ones, stood there before the Lord.

¹⁴Then the Spirit of the Lord came upon Jahaziel son of Zechariah, the son of Benaiah, the son of Jeiel, the son of Mattaniah, a Levite and descendant of Asaph, as he stood in the assembly.

¹⁵He said: "Listen, King Jehoshaphat and all who live in Judah and Jerusalem! This is what the Lord says to you: 'Do not be afraid or discouraged because of this vast army. For the battle is not yours, but God's. ¹⁶Tomorrow march down against them. They will be climbing up by the Pass of Ziz, and you will find them at the end of the gorge in the Desert of Jeruel. ¹⁷You will not have to fight this battle. Take up your positions; stand firm and see the deliverance the Lord will give you, O Judah and Jerusalem. Do not be afraid; do not be discouraged. Go out to face them tomorrow, and the Lord will be with you.' "

¹⁸Jehoshaphat bowed with his face to the ground, and all the people of Judah and Jerusalem fell down in worship before the Lord. ¹⁹Then some Levites from the Kohathites and Korahites stood up and praised the Lord, the God of Israel, with very loud voice.

²⁰Early in the morning they left for the Desert of Tekoa. As they set out, Jehoshaphat stood and said, "Listen to me, Judah and people of Jerusalem! Have faith in the Lord your God and you will be upheld; have faith in his prophets and you will be successful." ²¹After consulting the people, Jehoshaphat appointed men to sing to the Lord and to praise him for the splendor of his*ᵃ* holiness as they went out at the head of the army, saying:

> "Give thanks to the Lord,
>   for his love endures forever."

²²As they began to sing and praise, the Lord set ambushes against the men of Ammon and Moab and Mount Seir who were invading Judah, and they were defeated. ²³The men of Ammon and Moab rose up against the men from Mount Seir to destroy and annihilate them. After they finished slaughtering the men from Seir, they helped to destroy one another.

²⁴When the men of Judah came to the place that overlooks the desert and looked toward the vast army, they saw only dead bodies lying on the ground; no one had escaped. ²⁵So Jehoshaphat and his men went to carry off their plunder, and they found among them a great amount of equipment and clothing*ᵇ* and also articles of value—more than they could take away. There was so much plunder that it took three days to collect it. ²⁶On the fourth day they assembled in the Valley of Beracah, where they praised the Lord. This is why it is called the Valley of Beracah*ᶜ* to this day.

> Have faith in
> the Lord your God
> and you will
> be upheld
> (2 Chronicles 20:20).

ᵃ21 Or him with the splendor of ᵇ25 Some Hebrew manuscripts and Vulgate; most Hebrew manuscripts corpses ᶜ26 Beracah means praise.

²⁷Then, led by Jehoshaphat, all the men of Judah and Jerusalem returned joyfully to Jerusalem, for the LORD had given them cause to rejoice over their enemies. ²⁸They entered Jerusalem and went to the temple of the LORD with harps and lutes and trumpets.

²⁹The fear of God came upon all the kingdoms of the countries when they heard how the LORD had fought against the enemies of Israel. ³⁰And the kingdom of Jehoshaphat was at peace, for his God had given him rest on every side.

The End of Jehoshaphat's Reign   ³¹So Jehoshaphat reigned over Judah. He was thirty-five years old when he became king of Judah, and he reigned in Jerusalem twenty-five years. His mother's name was Azubah daughter of Shilhi. ³²He walked in the ways of his father Asa and did not stray from them; he did what was right in the eyes of the LORD. ³³The high places, however, were not removed, and the people still had not set their hearts on the God of their fathers.

³⁴The other events of Jehoshaphat's reign, from beginning to end, are written in the annals of Jehu son of Hanani, which are recorded in the book of the kings of Israel.

³⁵Later, Jehoshaphat king of Judah made an alliance with Ahaziah king of Israel, who was guilty of wickedness. ³⁶He agreed with him to construct a fleet of trading ships.ᵃ After these were built at Ezion Geber, ³⁷Eliezer son of Dodavahu of Mareshah prophesied against Jehoshaphat, saying, "Because you have made an alliance with Ahaziah, the LORD will destroy what you have made." The ships were wrecked and were not able to set sail to trade.ᵇ

21 Then Jehoshaphat rested with his fathers and was buried with them in the City of David. And Jehoram his son succeeded him as king. ²Jehoram's brothers, the sons of Jehoshaphat, were Azariah, Jehiel, Zechariah, Azariahu, Michael and Shephatiah. All these were sons of Jehoshaphat king of Israel.ᶜ ³Their father had given them many gifts of silver and gold and articles of value, as well as fortified cities in Judah, but he had given the kingdom to Jehoram because he was his firstborn son.

Jehoram King of Judah   ⁴When Jehoram established himself firmly over his father's kingdom, he put all his brothers to the sword along with some of the princes of Israel. ⁵Jehoram was thirty-two years old when he became king, and he reigned in Jerusalem eight years. ⁶He walked in the ways of the kings of Israel, as the house of Ahab had done, for he married a daughter of Ahab. He did evil in the eyes of the LORD. ⁷Nevertheless, because of the covenant the LORD had made with David, the LORD was not willing to destroy the house of David. He had promised to maintain a lamp for him and his descendants forever.

⁸In the time of Jehoram, Edom rebelled against Judah and set up its own king. ⁹So Jehoram went there with his officers and all his chariots. The Edomites surrounded him and his chariot commanders, but he rose up and broke through by night. ¹⁰To this day Edom has been in rebellion against Judah.

Libnah revolted at the same time, because Jehoram had forsaken the LORD, the God of his fathers. ¹¹He had also built high places on the hills of Judah and had caused the people of Jerusalem to prostitute themselves and had led Judah astray.

¹²Jehoram received a letter from Elijah the prophet, which said:

"This is what the LORD, the God of your father David, says: 'You have not walked in the ways of your father Jehoshaphat or of Asa king of Judah.

ᵃ36 Hebrew *of ships that could go to Tarshish*   ᵇ37 Hebrew *sail for Tarshish*   ᶜ2 That is, Judah, as frequently in 2 Chronicles

¹³But you have walked in the ways of the kings of Israel, and you have led Judah and the people of Jerusalem to prostitute themselves, just as the house of Ahab did. You have also murdered your own brothers, members of your father's house, men who were better than you. ¹⁴So now the LORD is about to strike your people, your sons, your wives and everything that is yours, with a heavy blow. ¹⁵You yourself will be very ill with a lingering disease of the bowels, until the disease causes your bowels to come out.' "

¹⁶The LORD aroused against Jehoram the hostility of the Philistines and of the Arabs who lived near the Cushites. ¹⁷They attacked Judah, invaded it and carried off all the goods found in the king's palace, together with his sons and wives. Not a son was left to him except Ahaziah,ᵃ the youngest.

¹⁸After all this, the LORD afflicted Jehoram with an incurable disease of the bowels. ¹⁹In the course of time, at the end of the second year, his bowels came out because of the disease, and he died in great pain. His people made no fire in his honor, as they had for his fathers.

²⁰Jehoram was thirty-two years old when he became king, and he reigned in Jerusalem eight years. He passed away, to no one's regret, and was buried in the City of David, but not in the tombs of the kings.

22 *Ahaziah King of Judah* The people of Jerusalem made Ahaziah, Jehoram's youngest son, king in his place, since the raiders, who came with the Arabs into the camp, had killed all the older sons. So Ahaziah son of Jehoram king of Judah began to reign.

²Ahaziah was twenty-twoᵇ years old when he became king, and he reigned in Jerusalem one year. His mother's name was Athaliah, a granddaughter of Omri.

³He too walked in the ways of the house of Ahab, for his mother encouraged him in doing wrong. ⁴He did evil in the eyes of the LORD, as the house of Ahab had done, for after his father's death they became his advisers, to his undoing. ⁵He also followed their counsel when he went with Joramᶜ son of Ahab king of Israel to war against Hazael king of Aram at Ramoth Gilead. The Arameans wounded Joram; ⁶so he returned to Jezreel to recover from the wounds they had inflicted on him at Ramothᵈ in his battle with Hazael king of Aram.

Then Ahaziahᵉ son of Jehoram king of Judah went down to Jezreel to see Joram son of Ahab because he had been wounded.

⁷Through Ahaziah's visit to Joram, God brought about Ahaziah's downfall. When Ahaziah arrived, he went out with Joram to meet Jehu son of Nimshi, whom the LORD had anointed to destroy the house of Ahab. ⁸While Jehu was executing judgment on the house of Ahab, he found the princes of Judah and the sons of Ahaziah's relatives, who had been attending Ahaziah, and he killed them. ⁹He then went in search of Ahaziah, and his men captured him while he was hiding in Samaria. He was brought to Jehu and put to death. They buried him, for they said, "He was a son of Jehoshaphat, who sought the LORD with all his heart." So there was no one in the house of Ahaziah powerful enough to retain the kingdom.

Athaliah and Joash ¹⁰When Athaliah the mother of Ahaziah saw that her son was dead, she proceeded to destroy the whole royal family of the house of Judah. ¹¹But Jehosheba,ᶠ the daughter of King Jehoram, took Joash son of Ahaziah and stole him away from among the royal princes who were about

---

ᵃ17 Hebrew *Jehoahaz*, a variant of *Ahaziah* ᵇ2 Some Septuagint manuscripts and Syriac (see also 2 Kings 8:26); Hebrew *forty-two* ᶜ5 Hebrew *Jehoram*, a variant of *Joram*; also in verses 6 and 7 ᵈ6 Hebrew *Ramah*, a variant of *Ramoth* ᵉ6 Some Hebrew manuscripts, Septuagint, Vulgate and Syriac (see also 2 Kings 8:29); most Hebrew manuscripts *Azariah* ᶠ11 Hebrew *Jehoshabeath*, a variant of *Jehosheba*

to be murdered and put him and his nurse in a bedroom. Because Jehosheba,[a] the daughter of King Jehoram and wife of the priest Jehoiada, was Ahaziah's sister, she hid the child from Athaliah so she could not kill him. [12]He remained hidden with them at the temple of God for six years while Athaliah ruled the land.

23 In the seventh year Jehoiada showed his strength. He made a covenant with the commanders of units of a hundred: Azariah son of Jeroham, Ishmael son of Jehohanan, Azariah son of Obed, Maaseiah son of Adaiah, and Elishaphat son of Zicri. [2]They went throughout Judah and gathered the Levites and the heads of Israelite families from all the towns. When they came to Jerusalem, [3]the whole assembly made a covenant with the king at the temple of God.

Jehoiada said to them, "The king's son shall reign, as the LORD promised concerning the descendants of David. [4]Now this is what you are to do: A third of you priests and Levites who are going on duty on the Sabbath are to keep watch at the doors, [5]a third of you at the royal palace and a third at the Foundation Gate, and all the other men are to be in the courtyards of the temple of the LORD. [6]No one is to enter the temple of the LORD except the priests and Levites on duty; they may enter because they are consecrated, but all the other men are to guard what the LORD has assigned to them.[b] [7]The Levites are to station themselves around the king, each man with his weapons in his hand. Anyone who enters the temple must be put to death. Stay close to the king wherever he goes."

[8]The Levites and all the men of Judah did just as Jehoiada the priest ordered. Each one took his men—those who were going on duty on the Sabbath and those who were going off duty—for Jehoiada the priest had not released any of the divisions. [9]Then he gave the commanders of units of a hundred the spears and the large and small shields that had belonged to King David and that were in the temple of God. [10]He stationed all the men, each with his weapon in his hand, around the king—near the altar and the temple, from the south side to the north side of the temple.

[11]Jehoiada and his sons brought out the king's son and put the crown on him; they presented him with a copy of the covenant and proclaimed him king. They anointed him and shouted, "Long live the king!"

[12]When Athaliah heard the noise of the people running and cheering the king, she went to them at the temple of the LORD. [13]She looked, and there was the king, standing by his pillar at the entrance. The officers and the trumpeters were beside the king, and all the people of the land were rejoicing and blowing trumpets, and singers with musical instruments were leading the praises. Then Athaliah tore her robes and shouted, "Treason! Treason!"

[14]Jehoiada the priest sent out the commanders of units of a hundred, who were in charge of the troops, and said to them: "Bring her out between the ranks[c] and put to the sword anyone who follows her." For the priest had said, "Do not put her to death at the temple of the LORD." [15]So they seized her as she reached the entrance of the Horse Gate on the palace grounds, and there they put her to death.

[16]Jehoiada then made a covenant that he and the people and the king[d] would be the LORD's people. [17]All the people went to the temple of Baal and tore it down. They smashed the altars and idols and killed Mattan the priest of Baal in front of the altars.

[18]Then Jehoiada placed the oversight of the temple of the LORD in the hands of the priests, who were Levites, to whom David had made assign-

---

[a]11 Hebrew *Jehoshabeath,* a variant of *Jehosheba*   [b]6 Or *to observe the LORD's command ,not to enter,*   [c]14 Or *out from the precincts*   [d]16 Or *covenant between ,the LORD, and the people and the king that they* (see 2 Kings 11:17)

Dear Sam,

When my parents are drunk, they verbally and physically abuse me. I've tried to tell a few people, but they don't believe me. I need help!

Missy in Miami

Dear Sam, Inc

100 Advice Lane, Anywhere, USA

Dear Missy,

Your letter breaks my heart. Perhaps knowing what happened to Joash may help. There was a wicked woman named Athaliah whose son, the king, had just been killed. She decided that if she killed all his children (her own grandchildren), she could rule the kingdom. Fortunately, Jehosheba, the dead king's sister, took Joash (son of the dead king) and hid him from Athaliah. Joash remained hidden in the temple for six years while Athaliah ruled (2 Chronicles 22:12).

Just as Joash was protected, there must be a place of safety for you. If those you told didn't believe you, you must find another trustworthy and responsible adult who will. Do you have an aunt or grandmother who might be able to help? Perhaps your pastor or a teacher? Or do you have a good friend whose parents would be willing to offer you a safe place?

Please, don't give up. No one deserves verbal or physical abuse.

Sam

ments in the temple, to present the burnt offerings of the LORD as written in the Law of Moses, with rejoicing and singing, as David had ordered. ¹⁹He also stationed doorkeepers at the gates of the LORD's temple so that no one who was in any way unclean might enter.

²⁰He took with him the commanders of hundreds, the nobles, the rulers of the people and all the people of the land and brought the king down from the temple of the LORD. They went into the palace through the Upper Gate and seated the king on the royal throne, ²¹and all the people of the land rejoiced. And the city was quiet, because Athaliah had been slain with the sword.

24 *Joash Repairs the Temple* Joash was seven years old when he became king, and he reigned in Jerusalem forty years. His mother's name was Zibiah; she was from Beersheba. ²Joash did what was right in the eyes of the LORD all the years of Jehoiada the priest. ³Jehoiada chose two wives for him, and he had sons and daughters.

⁴Some time later Joash decided to restore the temple of the LORD. ⁵He called together the priests and Levites and said to them, "Go to the towns of Judah and collect the money due annually from all Israel, to repair the temple of your God. Do it now." But the Levites did not act at once.

⁶Therefore the king summoned Jehoiada the chief priest and said to him, "Why haven't you required the Levites to bring in from Judah and Jerusalem the tax imposed by Moses the servant of the LORD and by the assembly of Israel for the Tent of the Testimony?"

⁷Now the sons of that wicked woman Athaliah had broken into the temple of God and had used even its sacred objects for the Baals.

⁸At the king's command, a chest was made and placed outside, at the gate of the temple of the LORD. ⁹A proclamation was then issued in Judah and Jerusalem that they should bring to the LORD the tax that Moses the servant of God had required of Israel in the desert. ¹⁰All the officials and all the people brought their contributions gladly, dropping them into the chest until it was full. ¹¹Whenever the chest was brought in by the Levites to the king's officials and they saw that there was a large amount of money, the royal secretary and the officer of the chief priest would come and empty the chest and carry it back to its place. They did this regularly and collected a great amount of money. ¹²The king and Jehoiada gave it to the men who carried out the work required for the temple of the LORD. They hired masons and carpenters to restore the LORD's temple, and also workers in iron and bronze to repair the temple.

¹³The men in charge of the work were diligent, and the repairs progressed under them. They rebuilt the temple of God according to its original design and reinforced it. ¹⁴When they had finished, they brought the rest of the money to the king and Jehoiada, and with it were made articles for the LORD's temple: articles for the service and for the burnt offerings, and also dishes and other objects of gold and silver. As long as Jehoiada lived, burnt offerings were presented continually in the temple of the LORD.

¹⁵Now Jehoiada was old and full of years, and he died at the age of a hundred and thirty. ¹⁶He was buried with the kings in the City of David, because of the good he had done in Israel for God and his temple.

The Wickedness of Joash ¹⁷After the death of Jehoiada, the officials of Judah came and paid homage to the king, and he listened to them. ¹⁸They abandoned the temple of the LORD, the God of their fathers, and worshiped Asherah poles and idols. Because of their guilt, God's anger came upon Judah and Jerusalem. ¹⁹Although the LORD sent prophets to the people to bring them back to him, and though they testified against them, they would not listen.

²⁰Then the Spirit of God came upon Zechariah son of Jehoiada the priest. He stood before the people and said, "This is what God says: 'Why do you disobey the LORD's commands? You will not prosper. Because you have forsaken the LORD, he has forsaken you.' "

²¹But they plotted against him, and by order of the king they stoned him to death in the courtyard of the LORD's temple. ²²King Joash did not remember the kindness Zechariah's father Jehoiada had shown him but killed his son, who said as he lay dying, "May the LORD see this and call you to account."

²³At the turn of the year,ᵃ the army of Aram marched against Joash; it invaded Judah and Jerusalem and killed all the leaders of the people. They sent all the plunder to their king in Damascus. ²⁴Although the Aramean army had come with only a few men, the LORD delivered into their hands a much larger army. Because Judah had forsaken the LORD, the God of their fathers, judgment was executed on Joash. ²⁵When the Arameans withdrew, they left Joash severely wounded. His officials conspired against him for murdering the son of Jehoiada the priest, and they killed him in his bed. So he died and was buried in the City of David, but not in the tombs of the kings.

²⁶Those who conspired against him were Zabad,ᵇ son of Shimeath an Ammonite woman, and Jehozabad, son of Shimrithᶜ a Moabite woman. ²⁷The account of his sons, the many prophecies about him, and the record of the restoration of the temple of God are written in the annotations on the book of the kings. And Amaziah his son succeeded him as king.

25 *Amaziah King of Judah*

Amaziah was twenty-five years old when he became king, and he reigned in Jerusalem twenty-nine years. His mother's name was Jehoaddinᵈ; she was from Jerusalem. ²He did what was right in the eyes of the LORD, but not wholeheartedly. ³After the kingdom was firmly in his control, he executed the officials who had murdered his father the king. ⁴Yet he did not put their sons to death, but acted in accordance with what is written in the Law, in the Book of Moses, where the LORD commanded: "Fathers shall not be put to death for their children, nor children put to death for their fathers; each is to die for his own sins."ᵉ

⁵Amaziah called the people of Judah together and assigned them according to their families to commanders of thousands and commanders of hundreds for all Judah and Benjamin. He then mustered those twenty years old or more and found that there were three hundred thousand men ready for military service, able to handle the spear and shield. ⁶He also hired a hundred thousand fighting men from Israel for a hundred talentsᶠ of silver.

⁷But a man of God came to him and said, "O king, these troops from Israel must not march with you, for the LORD is not with Israel—not with any of the people of Ephraim. ⁸Even if you go and fight

2 CHRONICLES 24:17

You look so beautiful today!" Words like that can make you feel good–that is, until the person who said them adds, "Can you loan me your Top-10 CD for Friday night?" Then you realize the compliment was only flattery. Your friend was buttering you up. Some people are susceptible to flattery. King Joash was. After the death of his adviser, Judah's officials came and "paid homage to" (meaning "flattered") the king. And Joash let his people manipulate him into serving pagan gods. Watch out when insincere people rush up to compliment you. That's flattery. You don't have to pay flatterers back by doing what they want.

Direct Line

ᵃ23 Probably in the spring   ᵇ26 A variant of *Jozabad*
ᶜ26 A variant of *Shomer*   ᵈ1 Hebrew *Jehoaddan*, a variant of *Jehoaddin*   ᵉ4 Deut. 24:16   ᶠ6 That is, about 3 3/4 tons (about 3.4 metric tons); also in verse 9

courageously in battle, God will overthrow you before the enemy, for God has the power to help or to overthrow."

⁹Amaziah asked the man of God, "But what about the hundred talents I paid for these Israelite troops?"

The man of God replied, "The LORD can give you much more than that."

¹⁰So Amaziah dismissed the troops who had come to him from Ephraim and sent them home. They were furious with Judah and left for home in a great rage.

¹¹Amaziah then marshaled his strength and led his army to the Valley of Salt, where he killed ten thousand men of Seir. ¹²The army of Judah also captured ten thousand men alive, took them to the top of a cliff and threw them down so that all were dashed to pieces.

¹³Meanwhile the troops that Amaziah had sent back and had not allowed to take part in the war raided Judean towns from Samaria to Beth Horon. They killed three thousand people and carried off great quantities of plunder.

¹⁴When Amaziah returned from slaughtering the Edomites, he brought back the gods of the people of Seir. He set them up as his own gods, bowed down to them and burned sacrifices to them. ¹⁵The anger of the LORD burned against Amaziah, and he sent a prophet to him, who said, "Why do you consult this people's gods, which could not save their own people from your hand?"

¹⁶While he was still speaking, the king said to him, "Have we appointed you an adviser to the king? Stop! Why be struck down?"

So the prophet stopped but said, "I know that God has determined to destroy you, because you have done this and have not listened to my counsel."

¹⁷After Amaziah king of Judah consulted his advisers, he sent this challenge to Jehoash*ᵃ* son of Jehoahaz, the son of Jehu, king of Israel: "Come, meet me face to face."

¹⁸But Jehoash king of Israel replied to Amaziah king of Judah: "A thistle in Lebanon sent a message to a cedar in Lebanon, 'Give your daughter to my son in marriage.' Then a wild beast in Lebanon came along and trampled the thistle underfoot. ¹⁹You say to yourself that you have defeated Edom, and now you are arrogant and proud. But stay at home! Why ask for trouble and cause your own downfall and that of Judah also?"

²⁰Amaziah, however, would not listen, for God so worked that he might hand them over to Jehoash, because they sought the gods of Edom. ²¹So Jehoash king of Israel attacked. He and Amaziah king of Judah faced each other at Beth Shemesh in Judah. ²²Judah was routed by Israel, and every man fled to his home. ²³Jehoash king of Israel captured Amaziah king of Judah, the son of Joash, the son of Ahaziah,*ᵇ* at Beth Shemesh. Then Jehoash brought him to Jerusalem and broke down the wall of Jerusalem from the Ephraim Gate to the Corner Gate—a section about six hundred feet*ᶜ* long. ²⁴He took all the gold and silver and all the articles found in the temple of God that had been in the care of Obed-Edom, together with the palace treasures and the hostages, and returned to Samaria.

²⁵Amaziah son of Joash king of Judah lived for fifteen years after the death of Jehoash son of Jehoahaz king of Israel. ²⁶As for the other events of Amaziah's reign, from beginning to end, are they not written in the book of the kings of Judah and Israel? ²⁷From the time that Amaziah turned away from following the LORD, they conspired against him in Jerusalem and he fled to Lachish, but they sent men after him to Lachish and killed him there. ²⁸He was brought back by horse and was buried with his fathers in the City of Judah.

ᵃ17 Hebrew *Joash,* a variant of *Jehoash;* also in verses 18, 21, 23 and 25   *ᵇ23* Hebrew *Jehoahaz,* a variant of *Ahaziah*   *ᶜ23* Hebrew *four hundred cubits* (about 180 meters)

26

Uzziah King of Judah   Then all the people of Judah took Uzziah,[a] who was sixteen years old, and made him king in place of his father Amaziah. [2]He was the one who rebuilt Elath and restored it to Judah after Amaziah rested with his fathers.

[3]Uzziah was sixteen years old when he became king, and he reigned in Jerusalem fifty-two years. His mother's name was Jecoliah; she was from Jerusalem. [4]He did what was right in the eyes of the LORD, just as his father Amaziah had done. [5]He sought God during the days of Zechariah, who instructed him in the fear[b] of God. As long as he sought the LORD, God gave him success.

[6]He went to war against the Philistines and broke down the walls of Gath, Jabneh and Ashdod. He then rebuilt towns near Ashdod and elsewhere among the Philistines. [7]God helped him against the Philistines and against the Arabs who lived in Gur Baal and against the Meunites. [8]The Ammonites brought tribute to Uzziah, and his fame spread as far as the border of Egypt, because he had become very powerful.

> As long as he sought the LORD, God gave him success
> (2 Chronicles 26:5).

[9]Uzziah built towers in Jerusalem at the Corner Gate, at the Valley Gate and at the angle of the wall, and he fortified them. [10]He also built towers in the desert and dug many cisterns, because he had much livestock in the foothills and in the plain. He had people working his fields and vineyards in the hills and in the fertile lands, for he loved the soil.

[11]Uzziah had a well-trained army, ready to go out by divisions according to their numbers as mustered by Jeiel the secretary and Maaseiah the officer under the direction of Hananiah, one of the royal officials. [12]The total number of family leaders over the fighting men was 2,600. [13]Under their command was an army of 307,500 men trained for war, a powerful force to support the king against his enemies. [14]Uzziah provided shields, spears, helmets, coats of armor, bows and slingstones for the entire army. [15]In Jerusalem he made machines designed by skillful men for use on the towers and on the corner defenses to shoot arrows and hurl large stones. His fame spread far and wide, for he was greatly helped until he became powerful.

[16]But after Uzziah became powerful, his pride led to his downfall. He was unfaithful to the LORD his God, and entered the temple of the LORD to burn incense on the altar of incense. [17]Azariah the priest with eighty other courageous priests of the LORD followed him in. [18]They confronted him and said, "It is not right for you, Uzziah, to burn incense to the LORD. That is for the priests, the descendants of Aaron, who have been consecrated to burn incense. Leave the sanctuary, for you have been unfaithful; and you will not be honored by the LORD God."

[19]Uzziah, who had a censer in his hand ready to burn incense, became angry. While he was raging at the priests in their presence before the incense altar in the LORD's temple, leprosy[c] broke out on his forehead. [20]When Azariah the chief priest and all the other priests looked at him, they saw that he had leprosy on his forehead, so they hurried him out. Indeed, he himself was eager to leave, because the LORD had afflicted him.

[21]King Uzziah had leprosy until the day he died. He lived in a separate house[d]—leprous, and excluded from the temple of the LORD. Jotham his son had charge of the palace and governed the people of the land.

[22]The other events of Uzziah's reign, from beginning to end, are recorded by the prophet Isaiah son of Amoz. [23]Uzziah rested with his fathers and was buried near them in a field for burial that belonged to the kings, for people said, "He had leprosy." And Jotham his son succeeded him as king.

---

[a]1 Also called *Azariah*   [b]5 Many Hebrew manuscripts, Septuagint and Syriac; other Hebrew manuscripts *vision*   [c]19 The Hebrew word was used for various diseases affecting the skin—not necessarily leprosy; also in verses 20, 21 and 23.   [d]21 Or *in a house where he was relieved of responsibilities*

27 Jotham King of Judah

Jotham was twenty-five years old when he became king, and he reigned in Jerusalem sixteen years. His mother's name was Jerusha daughter of Zadok. ²He did what was right in the eyes of the LORD, just as his father Uzziah had done, but unlike him he did not enter the temple of the LORD. The people, however, continued their corrupt practices. ³Jotham rebuilt the Upper Gate of the temple of the LORD and did extensive work on the wall at the hill of Ophel. ⁴He built towns in the Judean hills and forts and towers in the wooded areas.

⁵Jotham made war on the king of the Ammonites and conquered them. That year the Ammonites paid him a hundred talents*a* of silver, ten thousand cors*b* of wheat and ten thousand cors of barley. The Ammonites brought him the same amount also in the second and third years.

⁶Jotham grew powerful because he walked steadfastly before the LORD his God.

⁷The other events in Jotham's reign, including all his wars and the other things he did, are written in the book of the kings of Israel and Judah. ⁸He was twenty-five years old when he became king, and he reigned in Jerusalem sixteen years. ⁹Jotham rested with his fathers and was buried in the City of David. And Ahaz his son succeeded him as king.

28 Ahaz King of Judah

Ahaz was twenty years old when he became king, and he reigned in Jerusalem sixteen years. Unlike David his father, he did not do what was right in the eyes of the LORD. ²He walked in the ways of the kings of Israel and also made cast idols for worshiping the Baals. ³He burned sacrifices in the Valley of Ben Hinnom and sacrificed his sons in the fire, following the detestable ways of the nations the LORD had driven out before the Israelites. ⁴He offered sacrifices and burned incense at the high places, on the hilltops and under every spreading tree.

⁵Therefore the LORD his God handed him over to the king of Aram. The Arameans defeated him and took many of his people as prisoners and brought them to Damascus.

He was also given into the hands of the king of Israel, who inflicted heavy casualties on him. ⁶In one day Pekah son of Remaliah killed a hundred and twenty thousand soldiers in Judah—because Judah had forsaken the LORD, the God of their fathers. ⁷Zicri, an Ephraimite warrior, killed Maaseiah the king's son, Azrikam the officer in charge of the palace, and Elkanah, second to the king. ⁸The Israelites took captive from their kinsmen two hundred thousand wives, sons and daughters. They also took a great deal of plunder, which they carried back to Samaria.

⁹But a prophet of the LORD named Oded was there, and he went out to meet the army when it returned to Samaria. He said to them, "Because the LORD, the God of your fathers, was angry with Judah, he gave them into your hand. But you have slaughtered them in a rage that reaches to heaven. ¹⁰And now you intend to make

Direct Line

2 CHRONICLES 26:16–21

Sometimes even Christians can become proud. Of good grades. Of popularity. Of athletic ability. Want to know if you are proud? You can recognize pride by the feeling that you don't have to live by normal rules. You're so beautiful you don't have to be nice to "ugly" people. You're so popular you don't talk to kids who are "out" socially. King Uzziah became so rich and powerful that he didn't think he had to live by the rules either. He found out the hard way that pride does go before a painful fall (Proverbs 16:18). Watch out for pride. It hurts others first. Then it really hurts–you.

*a*5 That is, about 3 3/4 tons (about 3.4 metric tons)
*b*5 That is, probably about 62,000 bushels (about 2,200 kiloliters)

the men and women of Judah and Jerusalem your slaves. But aren't you also guilty of sins against the LORD your God? ¹¹Now listen to me! Send back your fellow countrymen you have taken as prisoners, for the LORD's fierce anger rests on you."

¹²Then some of the leaders in Ephraim—Azariah son of Jehohanan, Berekiah son of Meshillemoth, Jehizkiah son of Shallum, and Amasa son of Hadlai—confronted those who were arriving from the war. ¹³"You must not bring those prisoners here," they said, "or we will be guilty before the LORD. Do you intend to add to our sin and guilt? For our guilt is already great, and his fierce anger rests on Israel."

¹⁴So the soldiers gave up the prisoners and plunder in the presence of the officials and all the assembly. ¹⁵The men designated by name took the prisoners, and from the plunder they clothed all who were naked. They provided them with clothes and sandals, food and drink, and healing balm. All those who were weak they put on donkeys. So they took them back to their fellow countrymen at Jericho, the City of Palms, and returned to Samaria.

¹⁶At that time King Ahaz sent to the king^a of Assyria for help. ¹⁷The Edomites had again come and attacked Judah and carried away prisoners, ¹⁸while the Philistines had raided towns in the foothills and in the Negev of Judah. They captured and occupied Beth Shemesh, Aijalon and Gederoth, as well as Soco, Timnah and Gimzo, with their surrounding villages. ¹⁹The LORD had humbled Judah because of Ahaz king of Israel,^b for he had promoted wickedness in Judah and had been most unfaithful to the LORD. ²⁰Tiglath-Pileser^c king of Assyria came to him, but he gave him trouble instead of help. ²¹Ahaz took some of the things from the temple of the LORD and from the royal palace and from the princes and presented them to the king of Assyria, but that did not help him.

²²In his time of trouble King Ahaz became even more unfaithful to the LORD. ²³He offered sacrifices to the gods of Damascus, who had defeated him; for he thought, "Since the gods of the kings of Aram have helped them, I will sacrifice to them so they will help me." But they were his downfall and the downfall of all Israel.

²⁴Ahaz gathered together the furnishings from the temple of God and took them away.^d He shut the doors of the LORD's temple and set up altars at every street corner in Jerusalem. ²⁵In every town in Judah he built high places to burn sacrifices to other gods and provoked the LORD, the God of his fathers, to anger.

²⁶The other events of his reign and all his ways, from beginning to end, are written in the book of the kings of Judah and Israel. ²⁷Ahaz rested with his fathers and was buried in the city of Jerusalem, but he was not placed in the tombs of the kings of Israel. And Hezekiah his son succeeded him as king.

29 *Hezekiah Purifies the Temple* Hezekiah was twenty-five years old when he became king, and he reigned in Jerusalem twenty-nine years. His mother's name was Abijah daughter of Zechariah. ²He did what was right in the eyes of the LORD, just as his father David had done.

³In the first month of the first year of his reign, he opened the doors of the temple of the LORD and repaired them. ⁴He brought in the priests and the Levites, assembled them in the square on the east side ⁵and said: "Listen to me, Levites! Consecrate yourselves now and consecrate the temple of the LORD, the God of your fathers. Remove all defilement from the sanctuary. ⁶Our fathers were unfaithful; they did evil in the eyes of the LORD our God and forsook him. They turned their faces away from the LORD's dwelling place and

^a16 One Hebrew manuscript, Septuagint and Vulgate (see also 2 Kings 16:7); most Hebrew manuscripts *kings* ^b19 That is, Judah, as frequently in 2 Chronicles ^c20 Hebrew *Tilgath-Pilneser*, a variant of *Tiglath-Pileser* ^d24 Or *and cut them up*

turned their backs on him. ⁷They also shut the doors of the portico and put out the lamps. They did not burn incense or present any burnt offerings at the sanctuary to the God of Israel. ⁸Therefore, the anger of the LORD has fallen on Judah and Jerusalem; he has made them an object of dread and horror and scorn, as you can see with your own eyes. ⁹This is why our fathers have fallen by the sword and why our sons and daughters and our wives are in captivity. ¹⁰Now I intend to make a covenant with the LORD, the God of Israel, so that his fierce anger will turn away from us. ¹¹My sons, do not be negligent now, for the LORD has chosen you to stand before him and serve him, to minister before him and to burn incense."

¹²Then these Levites set to work:

from the Kohathites,
    Mahath son of Amasai and Joel son of Azariah;
from the Merarites,
    Kish son of Abdi and Azariah son of Jehallelel;
from the Gershonites,
    Joah son of Zimmah and Eden son of Joah;
¹³from the descendants of Elizaphan,
    Shimri and Jeiel;
from the descendants of Asaph,
    Zechariah and Mattaniah;
¹⁴from the descendants of Heman,
    Jehiel and Shimei;
from the descendants of Jeduthun,
    Shemaiah and Uzziel.

¹⁵When they had assembled their brothers and consecrated themselves, they went in to purify the temple of the LORD, as the king had ordered, following the word of the LORD. ¹⁶The priests went into the sanctuary of the LORD to purify it. They brought out to the courtyard of the LORD's temple everything unclean that they found in the temple of the LORD. The Levites took it and carried it out to the Kidron Valley. ¹⁷They began the consecration on the first day of the first month, and by the eighth day of the month they reached the portico of the LORD. For eight more days they consecrated the temple of the LORD itself, finishing on the sixteenth day of the first month.

¹⁸Then they went in to King Hezekiah and reported: "We have purified the entire temple of the LORD, the altar of burnt offering with all its utensils, and the table for setting out the consecrated bread, with all its articles. ¹⁹We have prepared and consecrated all the articles that King Ahaz removed in his unfaithfulness while he was king. They are now in front of the LORD's altar."

²⁰Early the next morning King Hezekiah gathered the city officials together and went up to the temple of the LORD. ²¹They brought seven bulls, seven rams, seven male lambs and seven male goats as a sin offering for the kingdom, for the sanctuary and for Judah. The king commanded the priests, the descendants of Aaron, to offer these on the altar of the LORD. ²²So they slaughtered the bulls, and the priests took the blood and sprinkled it on the altar; next they slaughtered the rams and sprinkled their blood on the altar; then they slaughtered the lambs and sprinkled their blood on the altar. ²³The goats for the sin offering were brought before the king and the assembly, and they laid their hands on them. ²⁴The priests then slaughtered the goats and presented their blood on the altar for a sin offering to atone for all Israel, because the king had ordered the burnt offering and the sin offering for all Israel.

²⁵He stationed the Levites in the temple of the LORD with cymbals, harps and lyres in the way prescribed by David and Gad the king's seer and Nathan the prophet; this was commanded by the LORD through his prophets. ²⁶So the Levites stood ready with David's instruments, and the priests with their trumpets.

²⁷Hezekiah gave the order to sacrifice the burnt offering on the altar. As

the offering began, singing to the Lord began also, accompanied by trumpets and the instruments of David king of Israel. ²⁸The whole assembly bowed in worship, while the singers sang and the trumpeters played. All this continued until the sacrifice of the burnt offering was completed.

²⁹When the offerings were finished, the king and everyone present with him knelt down and worshiped. ³⁰King Hezekiah and his officials ordered the Levites to praise the Lord with the words of David and of Asaph the seer. So they sang praises with gladness and bowed their heads and worshiped.

³¹Then Hezekiah said, "You have now dedicated yourselves to the Lord. Come and bring sacrifices and thank offerings to the temple of the Lord." So the assembly brought sacrifices and thank offerings, and all whose hearts were willing brought burnt offerings.

³²The number of burnt offerings the assembly brought was seventy bulls, a hundred rams and two hundred male lambs—all of them for burnt offerings to the Lord. ³³The animals consecrated as sacrifices amounted to six hundred bulls and three thousand sheep and goats. ³⁴The priests, however, were too few to skin all the burnt offerings; so their kinsmen the Levites helped them until the task was finished and until other priests had been consecrated, for the Levites had been more conscientious in consecrating themselves than the priests had been. ³⁵There were burnt offerings in abundance, together with the fat of the fellowship offerings*ᵃ* and the drink offerings that accompanied the burnt offerings.

So the service of the temple of the Lord was reestablished. ³⁶Hezekiah and all the people rejoiced at what God had brought about for his people, because it was done so quickly.

30 *Hezekiah Celebrates the Passover* Hezekiah sent word to all Israel and Judah and also wrote letters to Ephraim and Manasseh, inviting them to come to the temple of the Lord in Jerusalem and celebrate the Passover to the Lord, the God of Israel. ²The king and his officials and the whole assembly in Jerusalem decided to celebrate the Passover in the second month. ³They had not been able to celebrate it at the regular time because not enough priests had consecrated themselves and the people had not assembled in Jerusalem. ⁴The plan seemed right both to the king and to the whole assembly. ⁵They decided to send a proclamation throughout Israel, from Beersheba to Dan, calling the people to come to Jerusalem and celebrate the Passover to the Lord, the God of Israel. It had not been celebrated in large numbers according to what was written.

⁶At the king's command, couriers went throughout Israel and Judah with letters from the king and from his officials, which read:

"People of Israel, return to the Lord, the God of Abraham, Isaac and Israel, that he may return to you who are left, who have escaped from the hand of the kings of Assyria. ⁷Do not be like your fathers and brothers, who were unfaithful to the Lord, the God of their fathers, so that he made them an object of horror, as you see. ⁸Do not be stiff-necked, as your fathers were; submit to the Lord. Come to the sanctuary, which he has consecrated forever. Serve the Lord your God, so that his fierce anger will turn away from you. ⁹If you return to the Lord, then your brothers and your children will be shown compassion by their captors and will come back to this land, for the Lord your God is gracious and compassionate. He will not turn his face from you if you return to him."

¹⁰The couriers went from town to town in Ephraim and Manasseh, as far as Zebulun, but the people scorned and ridiculed them. ¹¹Nevertheless, some men of Asher, Manasseh and Zebulun humbled themselves and went to Je-

---

*ᵃ35 Traditionally *peace offerings*

rusalem. [12]Also in Judah the hand of God was on the people to give them unity of mind to carry out what the king and his officials had ordered, following the word of the LORD.

[13]A very large crowd of people assembled in Jerusalem to celebrate the Feast of Unleavened Bread in the second month. [14]They removed the altars in Jerusalem and cleared away the incense altars and threw them into the Kidron Valley.

[15]They slaughtered the Passover lamb on the fourteenth day of the second month. The priests and the Levites were ashamed and consecrated themselves and brought burnt offerings to the temple of the LORD. [16]Then they took up their regular positions as prescribed in the Law of Moses the man of God. The priests sprinkled the blood handed to them by the Levites. [17]Since many in the crowd had not consecrated themselves, the Levites had to kill the Passover lambs for all those who were not ceremonially clean and could not consecrate their lambs to the LORD. [18]Although most of the many people who came from Ephraim, Manasseh, Issachar and Zebulun had not purified themselves, yet they ate the Passover, contrary to what was written. But Hezekiah prayed for them, saying, "May the LORD, who is good, pardon everyone [19]who sets his heart on seeking God—the LORD, the God of his fathers—even if he is not clean according to the rules of the sanctuary." [20]And the LORD heard Hezekiah and healed the people.

[21]The Israelites who were present in Jerusalem celebrated the Feast of Unleavened Bread for seven days with great rejoicing, while the Levites and priests sang to the LORD every day, accompanied by the LORD's instruments of praise.[a]

[22]Hezekiah spoke encouragingly to all the Levites, who showed good understanding of the service of the LORD. For the seven days they ate their assigned portion and offered fellowship offerings[b] and praised the LORD, the God of their fathers.

[23]The whole assembly then agreed to celebrate the festival seven more days; so for another seven days they celebrated joyfully. [24]Hezekiah king of Judah provided a thousand bulls and seven thousand sheep and goats for the assembly, and the officials provided them with a thousand bulls and ten thousand sheep and goats. A great number of priests consecrated themselves. [25]The entire assembly of Judah rejoiced, along with the priests and Levites and all who had assembled from Israel, including the aliens who had come from Israel and those who lived in Judah. [26]There was great joy in Jerusalem, for since the days of Solomon son of David king of Israel there had been nothing like this in Jerusalem. [27]The priests and the Levites stood to bless the people, and God heard them, for their prayer reached heaven, his holy dwelling place.

31 When all this had ended, the Israelites who were there went out to the towns of Judah, smashed the sacred stones and cut down the Asherah poles. They destroyed the high places and the altars throughout Judah and Benjamin and in Ephraim and Manasseh. After they had destroyed all of them, the Israelites returned to their own towns and to their own property.

Contributions for Worship [2]Hezekiah assigned the priests and Levites to divisions—each of them according to their duties as priests or Levites—to offer burnt offerings and fellowship offerings,[b] to minister, to give thanks and to sing praises at the gates of the LORD's dwelling. [3]The king contributed from his own possessions for the morning and evening burnt offerings and

[a]21 Or *priests praised the LORD every day with resounding instruments belonging to the LORD*
[b]22,2 Traditionally *peace offerings*

for the burnt offerings on the Sabbaths, New Moons and appointed feasts as written in the Law of the Lord. ⁴He ordered the people living in Jerusalem to give the portion due the priests and Levites so they could devote themselves to the Law of the Lord. ⁵As soon as the order went out, the Israelites generously gave the firstfruits of their grain, new wine, oil and honey and all that the fields produced. They brought a great amount, a tithe of everything. ⁶The men of Israel and Judah who lived in the towns of Judah also brought a tithe of their herds and flocks and a tithe of the holy things dedicated to the Lord their God, and they piled them in heaps. ⁷They began doing this in the third month and finished in the seventh month. ⁸When Hezekiah and his officials came and saw the heaps, they praised the Lord and blessed his people Israel.

⁹Hezekiah asked the priests and Levites about the heaps; ¹⁰and Azariah the chief priest, from the family of Zadok, answered, "Since the people began to bring their contributions to the temple of the Lord, we have had enough to eat and plenty to spare, because the Lord has blessed his people, and this great amount is left over."

¹¹Hezekiah gave orders to prepare storerooms in the temple of the Lord, and this was done. ¹²Then they faithfully brought in the contributions, tithes and dedicated gifts. Conaniah, a Levite, was in charge of these things, and his brother Shimei was next in rank. ¹³Jehiel, Azaziah, Nahath, Asahel, Jerimoth, Jozabad, Eliel, Ismakiah, Mahath and Benaiah were supervisors under Conaniah and Shimei his brother, by appointment of King Hezekiah and Azariah the official in charge of the temple of God.

¹⁴Kore son of Imnah the Levite, keeper of the East Gate, was in charge of the freewill offerings given to God, distributing the contributions made to the Lord and also the consecrated gifts. ¹⁵Eden, Miniamin, Jeshua, Shemaiah, Amariah and Shecaniah assisted him faithfully in the towns of the priests, distributing to their fellow priests according to their divisions, old and young alike.

¹⁶In addition, they distributed to the males three years old or more whose names were in the genealogical records—all who would enter the temple of the Lord to perform the daily duties of their various tasks, according to their responsibilities and their divisions. ¹⁷And they distributed to the priests enrolled by their families in the genealogical records and likewise to the Levites twenty years old or more, according to their responsibilities and their divisions. ¹⁸They included all the little ones, the wives, and the sons and daughters of the whole community listed in these genealogical records. For they were faithful in consecrating themselves.

¹⁹As for the priests, the descendants of Aaron, who lived on the farm lands around their towns or in any other towns, men were designated by name to distribute portions to every male among them and to all who were recorded in the genealogies of the Levites.

²⁰This is what Hezekiah did throughout Judah, doing what was good and right and faithful before the Lord his God. ²¹In everything that he undertook in the service of God's temple and in obedience to the law and the commands, he sought his God and worked wholeheartedly. And so he prospered.

32 *Sennacherib Threatens Jerusalem* After all that Hezekiah had so faithfully done, Sennacherib king of Assyria came and invaded Judah. He laid siege to the fortified cities, thinking to conquer them for himself. ²When Hezekiah saw that Sennacherib had come and that he intended to make war on Jerusalem, ³he consulted with his officials and military staff about blocking off the water from the springs outside the city, and they helped him. ⁴A large force of men assembled, and they blocked all the springs and the stream that flowed through the land. "Why should the kings*ᵃ* of Assyria come and find plenty of water?" they said. ⁵Then he worked hard repairing all the broken sections of the wall and building towers on it. He built another wall outside that one and reinforced the supporting terraces*ᵇ* of the City of David. He also made large numbers of weapons and shields.

⁶He appointed military officers over the people and assembled them before him in the square at the city gate and encouraged them with these words: ⁷"Be strong and courageous. Do not be afraid or discouraged because of the king of Assyria and the vast army with him, for there is a greater power with us than with him. ⁸With him is only the arm of flesh, but with us is the Lᴏʀᴅ our God to help us and to fight our battles." And the people gained confidence from what Hezekiah the king of Judah said.

⁹Later, when Sennacherib king of Assyria and all his forces were laying siege to Lachish, he sent his officers to Jerusalem with this message for Hezekiah king of Judah and for all the people of Judah who were there:

¹⁰"This is what Sennacherib king of Assyria says: On what are you basing your confidence, that you remain in Jerusalem under siege? ¹¹When Hezekiah says, 'The Lᴏʀᴅ our God will save us from the hand of the king of Assyria,' he is misleading you, to let you die of hunger and thirst. ¹²Did not Hezekiah himself remove this god's high places and altars, saying to Judah and Jerusalem, 'You must worship before one altar and burn sacrifices on it'?

¹³"Do you not know what I and my fathers have done to all the peoples of the other lands? Were the gods of those nations ever able to deliver their land from my hand? ¹⁴Who of all the gods of these nations that my fathers destroyed has been able to save his people from me? How then can your god deliver you from my hand? ¹⁵Now do not let Hezekiah deceive you and mislead you like this. Do not believe him, for no god of any nation or kingdom has been able to deliver his people from my hand or the hand of my fathers. How much less will your god deliver you from my hand!"

¹⁶Sennacherib's officers spoke further against the Lᴏʀᴅ God and against his servant Hezekiah. ¹⁷The king also wrote letters insulting the Lᴏʀᴅ, the God of Israel, and saying this against him: "Just as the gods of the peoples of the other lands did not rescue their people from my hand, so the god of Hezekiah will not rescue his people from my hand." ¹⁸Then they called out in Hebrew to the people of Jerusalem who were on the wall, to terrify them and make them afraid in order to capture the city. ¹⁹They spoke about the God of Jerusalem as they did about the gods of the other peoples of the world—the work of men's hands.

²⁰King Hezekiah and the prophet Isaiah son of Amoz cried out in prayer to heaven about this. ²¹And the Lᴏʀᴅ sent an angel, who annihilated all the fighting men and the leaders and officers in the camp of the Assyrian king. So he withdrew to his own land in disgrace. And when he went into the temple of his god, some of his sons cut him down with the sword.

²²So the Lᴏʀᴅ saved Hezekiah and the people of Jerusalem from the hand of Sennacherib king of Assyria and from the hand of all others. He took care of them*ᶜ* on every side. ²³Many brought offerings to Jerusalem for the Lᴏʀᴅ and valuable gifts for Hezekiah king of Judah. From then on he was highly regarded by all the nations.

Hezekiah's Pride, Success and Death ²⁴In those days Hezekiah became ill and was at the point of death. He prayed to the Lᴏʀᴅ, who answered him and gave him a miraculous sign. ²⁵But Hezekiah's heart was proud and he did not

ᵃ4 Hebrew; Septuagint and Syriac king ᵇ5 Or the Millo ᶜ22 Hebrew; Septuagint and Vulgate He gave them rest

respond to the kindness shown him; therefore the LORD's wrath was on him and on Judah and Jerusalem. ²⁶Then Hezekiah repented of the pride of his heart, as did the people of Jerusalem; therefore the LORD's wrath did not come upon them during the days of Hezekiah.

²⁷Hezekiah had very great riches and honor, and he made treasuries for his silver and gold and for his precious stones, spices, shields and all kinds of valuables. ²⁸He also made buildings to store the harvest of grain, new wine and oil; and he made stalls for various kinds of cattle, and pens for the flocks. ²⁹He built villages and acquired great numbers of flocks and herds, for God had given him very great riches.

³⁰It was Hezekiah who blocked the upper outlet of the Gihon spring and channeled the water down to the west side of the City of David. He succeeded in everything he undertook. ³¹But when envoys were sent by the rulers of Babylon to ask him about the miraculous sign that had occurred in the land, God left him to test him and to know everything that was in his heart.

³²The other events of Hezekiah's reign and his acts of devotion are written in the vision of the prophet Isaiah son of Amoz in the book of the kings of Judah and Israel. ³³Hezekiah rested with his fathers and was buried on the hill where the tombs of David's descendants are. All Judah and the people of Jerusalem honored him when he died. And Manasseh his son succeeded him as king.

33 *Manasseh King of Judah* Manasseh was twelve years old when he became king, and he reigned in Jerusalem fifty-five years. ²He did evil in the eyes of the LORD, following the detestable practices of the nations the LORD had driven out before the Israelites. ³He rebuilt the high places his father Hezekiah had demolished; he also erected altars to the Baals and made Asherah poles. He bowed down to all the starry hosts and worshiped them. ⁴He built altars in the temple of the LORD, of which the LORD had said, "My Name will remain in Jerusalem forever." ⁵In both courts of the temple of the LORD, he built altars to all the starry hosts. ⁶He sacrificed his sons in*ᵃ* the fire in the Valley of Ben Hinnom, practiced sorcery, divination and witchcraft, and consulted mediums and spiritists. He did much evil in the eyes of the LORD, provoking him to anger.

⁷He took the carved image he had made and put it in God's temple, of which God had said to David and to his son Solomon, "In this temple and in Jerusalem, which I have chosen out of all the tribes of Israel, I will put my Name forever. ⁸I will not again make the feet of the Israelites leave the land I assigned to your forefathers, if only they will be careful to do everything I commanded them concerning all the laws, decrees and ordinances given through Moses." ⁹But Manasseh led Judah and the people of Jerusalem astray, so that they did more evil than the nations the LORD had destroyed before the Israelites.

¹⁰The LORD spoke to Manasseh and his people, but they paid no attention. ¹¹So the LORD brought against them the army commanders of the king of Assyria, who took Manasseh prisoner, put a hook in his nose, bound him with bronze shackles and took him to Babylon. ¹²In his distress he sought the favor of the LORD his God and humbled himself greatly before the God of his fathers. ¹³And when he prayed to him, the LORD was moved by his entreaty and listened to his plea; so he brought him back to Jerusalem and to his kingdom. Then Manasseh knew that the LORD is God.

¹⁴Afterward he rebuilt the outer wall of the City of David, west of the Gihon spring in the valley, as far as the entrance of the Fish Gate and encircling the hill of Ophel; he also made it much higher. He stationed military commanders in all the fortified cities in Judah.

ᵃ6 Or He made his sons pass through

[15]He got rid of the foreign gods and removed the image from the temple of the Lord, as well as all the altars he had built on the temple hill and in Jerusalem; and he threw them out of the city. [16]Then he restored the altar of the Lord and sacrificed fellowship offerings[a] and thank offerings on it, and told Judah to serve the Lord, the God of Israel. [17]The people, however, continued to sacrifice at the high places, but only to the Lord their God.

[18]The other events of Manasseh's reign, including his prayer to his God and the words the seers spoke to him in the name of the Lord, the God of Israel, are written in the annals of the kings of Israel.[b] [19]His prayer and how God was moved by his entreaty, as well as all his sins and unfaithfulness, and the sites where he built high places and set up Asherah poles and idols before he humbled himself—all are written in the records of the seers.[c] [20]Manasseh rested with his fathers and was buried in his palace. And Amon his son succeeded him as king.

Amon King of Judah [21]Amon was twenty-two years old when he became king, and he reigned in Jerusalem two years. [22]He did evil in the eyes of the Lord, as his father Manasseh had done. Amon worshiped and offered sacrifices to all the idols Manasseh had made. [23]But unlike his father Manasseh, he did not humble himself before the Lord; Amon increased his guilt.

[24]Amon's officials conspired against him and assassinated him in his palace. [25]Then the people of the land killed all who had plotted against King Amon, and they made Josiah his son king in his place.

34 **Josiah's Reforms** Josiah was eight years old when he became king, and he reigned in Jerusalem thirty-one years. [2]He did what was right in the eyes of the Lord and walked in the ways of his father David, not turning aside to the right or to the left.

[3]In the eighth year of his reign, while he was still young, he began to seek the God of his father David. In his twelfth year he began to purge Judah and Jerusalem of high places, Asherah poles, carved idols and cast images. [4]Under his direction the altars of the Baals were torn down; he cut to pieces the incense altars that were above them, and smashed the Asherah poles, the idols and the images. These he broke to pieces and scattered over the graves of those who had sacrificed to them. [5]He burned the bones of the priests on their altars, and so he purged Judah and Jerusalem. [6]In the towns of Manasseh, Ephraim and Simeon, as far as Naphtali, and in the ruins around them, [7]he tore down the altars and the Asherah poles and crushed the idols to powder and cut to pieces all the incense altars throughout Israel. Then he went back to Jerusalem.

[8]In the eighteenth year of Josiah's reign, to purify the land and the temple, he sent Shaphan son of Azaliah and Maaseiah the ruler of the city, with Joah son of Joahaz, the recorder, to repair the temple of the Lord his God.

[9]They went to Hilkiah the high priest and gave him the money that had been brought into the temple of God, which the Levites who were the doorkeepers had collected from the people of Manas-

Direct Line

2 CHRONICLES 34:1–3

You don't have to be an adult for God to use you. Six-year-old Sarah explained to her cousin that "Jesus loves you." And it was a 12-year-old who was so moved by the plight of the homeless that he launched a winter crusade to supply street people with blankets. At age 16 young King Josiah "began to seek the God of his father," and before he was 21 he led his nation in a great religious revival. Seek God now, and look for ways to serve him. God uses faithful followers of any age.

[a]16 Traditionally *peace offerings* [b]18 That is, Judah, as frequently in 2 Chronicles [c]19 One Hebrew manuscript and Septuagint; most Hebrew manuscripts *of Hozai*

seh, Ephraim and the entire remnant of Israel and from all the people of Judah and Benjamin and the inhabitants of Jerusalem. [10]Then they entrusted it to the men appointed to supervise the work on the LORD's temple. These men paid the workers who repaired and restored the temple. [11]They also gave money to the carpenters and builders to purchase dressed stone, and timber for joists and beams for the buildings that the kings of Judah had allowed to fall into ruin.

[12]The men did the work faithfully. Over them to direct them were Jahath and Obadiah, Levites descended from Merari, and Zechariah and Meshullam, descended from Kohath. The Levites—all who were skilled in playing musical instruments— [13]had charge of the laborers and supervised all the workers from job to job. Some of the Levites were secretaries, scribes and doorkeepers.

The Book of the Law Found   [14]While they were bringing out the money that had been taken into the temple of the LORD, Hilkiah the priest found the Book of the Law of the LORD that had been given through Moses. [15]Hilkiah said to Shaphan the secretary, "I have found the Book of the Law in the temple of the LORD." He gave it to Shaphan.

[16]Then Shaphan took the book to the king and reported to him: "Your officials are doing everything that has been committed to them. [17]They have paid out the money that was in the temple of the LORD and have entrusted it to the supervisors and workers." [18]Then Shaphan the secretary informed the king, "Hilkiah the priest has given me a book." And Shaphan read from it in the presence of the king.

[19]When the king heard the words of the Law, he tore his robes. [20]He gave these orders to Hilkiah, Ahikam son of Shaphan, Abdon son of Micah,[a] Shaphan the secretary and Asaiah the king's attendant: [21]"Go and inquire of the LORD for me and for the remnant in Israel and Judah about what is written in this book that has been found. Great is the LORD's anger that is poured out on us because our fathers have not kept the word of the LORD; they have not acted in accordance with all that is written in this book."

[22]Hilkiah and those the king had sent with him[b] went to speak to the prophetess Huldah, who was the wife of Shallum son of Tokhath,[c] the son of Hasrah,[d] keeper of the wardrobe. She lived in Jerusalem, in the Second District.

[23]She said to them, "This is what the LORD, the God of Israel, says: Tell the man who sent you to me, [24]'This is what the LORD says: I am going to bring disaster on this place and its people—all the curses written in the book that has been read in the presence of the king of Judah. [25]Because they have forsaken me and burned incense to other gods and provoked me to anger by all that their hands have made,[e] my anger will be poured out on this place and will not be quenched.' [26]Tell the king of Judah, who sent you to inquire of the LORD, 'This is what the LORD, the God of Israel, says concerning the words you heard: [27]Because your heart was responsive and you humbled yourself before God when you heard what he spoke against this place and its people, and because you humbled yourself before me and tore your robes and wept in my presence, I have heard you, declares the LORD. [28]Now I will gather you to your fathers, and you will be buried in peace. Your eyes will not see all the disaster I am going to bring on this place and on those who live here.' "

So they took her answer back to the king.

[29]Then the king called together all the elders of Judah and Jerusalem. [30]He went up to the temple of the LORD with the men of Judah, the people of Jerusalem, the priests and the Levites—all the people from the least to the

---

[a]20 Also called *Acbor son of Micaiah* [b]22 One Hebrew manuscript, Vulgate and Syriac; most Hebrew manuscripts do not have *had sent with him.* [c]22 Also called *Tikvah* [d]22 Also called *Harhas* [e]25 Or *by everything they have done*

greatest. He read in their hearing all the words of the Book of the Covenant, which had been found in the temple of the LORD. ³¹The king stood by his pillar and renewed the covenant in the presence of the LORD—to follow the LORD and keep his commands, regulations and decrees with all his heart and all his soul, and to obey the words of the covenant written in this book.

³²Then he had everyone in Jerusalem and Benjamin pledge themselves to it; the people of Jerusalem did this in accordance with the covenant of God, the God of their fathers.

³³Josiah removed all the detestable idols from all the territory belonging to the Israelites, and he had all who were present in Israel serve the LORD their God. As long as he lived, they did not fail to follow the LORD, the God of their fathers.

35 *Josiah Celebrates the Passover* Josiah celebrated the Passover to the LORD in Jerusalem, and the Passover lamb was slaughtered on the fourteenth day of the first month. ²He appointed the priests to their duties and encouraged them in the service of the LORD's temple. ³He said to the Levites, who instructed all Israel and who had been consecrated to the LORD: "Put the sacred ark in the temple that Solomon son of David king of Israel built. It is not to be carried about on your shoulders. Now serve the LORD your God and his people Israel. ⁴Prepare yourselves by families in your divisions, according to the directions written by David king of Israel and by his son Solomon.

⁵"Stand in the holy place with a group of Levites for each subdivision of the families of your fellow countrymen, the lay people. ⁶Slaughter the Passover lambs, consecrate yourselves and prepare the lambs for your fellow countrymen, doing what the LORD commanded through Moses."

⁷Josiah provided for all the lay people who were there a total of thirty thousand sheep and goats for the Passover offerings, and also three thousand cattle—all from the king's own possessions.

⁸His officials also contributed voluntarily to the people and the priests and Levites. Hilkiah, Zechariah and Jehiel, the administrators of God's temple, gave the priests twenty-six hundred Passover offerings and three hundred cattle. ⁹Also Conaniah along with Shemaiah and Nethanel, his brothers, and Hashabiah, Jeiel and Jozabad, the leaders of the Levites, provided five thousand Passover offerings and five hundred head of cattle for the Levites.

¹⁰The service was arranged and the priests stood in their places with the

The Bible Says

Keep Passover

Second Chronicles 35 tells a story of a very special Passover in Israel. What was Passover anyway, and why was it important? When God's angel killed the firstborn sons of the Egyptians, the angel "passed over" the homes of God's people (Exodus 12:13). Passover was a celebration of that event.

On the first Passover the blood of a lamb was used to tell the angel that the people who lived there were God's own. The New Testament calls Jesus your "Passover lamb" (1 Corinthians 5:7). Because Jesus shed his blood, you are now God's own.

Did you know that it was the very week of Passover that Jesus was crucified? So every Easter Christians have their own special Passover. Easter can remind you of Jesus, your Passover lamb, and of God's promise that through Jesus you have everlasting life.

Levites in their divisions as the king had ordered. [11]The Passover lambs were slaughtered, and the priests sprinkled the blood handed to them, while the Levites skinned the animals. [12]They set aside the burnt offerings to give them to the subdivisions of the families of the people to offer to the LORD, as is written in the Book of Moses. They did the same with the cattle. [13]They roasted the Passover animals over the fire as prescribed, and boiled the holy offerings in pots, caldrons and pans and served them quickly to all the people. [14]After this, they made preparations for themselves and for the priests, because the priests, the descendants of Aaron, were sacrificing the burnt offerings and the fat portions until nightfall. So the Levites made preparations for themselves and for the Aaronic priests.

[15]The musicians, the descendants of Asaph, were in the places prescribed by David, Asaph, Heman and Jeduthun the king's seer. The gatekeepers at each gate did not need to leave their posts, because their fellow Levites made the preparations for them.

[16]So at that time the entire service of the LORD was carried out for the celebration of the Passover and the offering of burnt offerings on the altar of the LORD, as King Josiah had ordered. [17]The Israelites who were present celebrated the Passover at that time and observed the Feast of Unleavened Bread for seven days. [18]The Passover had not been observed like this in Israel since the days of the prophet Samuel; and none of the kings of Israel had ever celebrated such a Passover as did Josiah, with the priests, the Levites and all Judah and Israel who were there with the people of Jerusalem. [19]This Passover was celebrated in the eighteenth year of Josiah's reign.

The Death of Josiah   [20]After all this, when Josiah had set the temple in order, Neco king of Egypt went up to fight at Carchemish on the Euphrates, and Josiah marched out to meet him in battle. [21]But Neco sent messengers to him, saying, "What quarrel is there between you and me, O king of Judah? It is not you I am attacking at this time, but the house with which I am at war. God has told me to hurry; so stop opposing God, who is with me, or he will destroy you."

[22]Josiah, however, would not turn away from him, but disguised himself to engage him in battle. He would not listen to what Neco had said at God's command but went to fight him on the plain of Megiddo.

[23]Archers shot King Josiah, and he told his officers, "Take me away; I am badly wounded." [24]So they took him out of his chariot, put him in the other chariot he had and brought him to Jerusalem, where he died. He was buried in the tombs of his fathers, and all Judah and Jerusalem mourned for him.

[25]Jeremiah composed laments for Josiah, and to this day all the men and women singers commemorate Josiah in the laments. These became a tradition in Israel and are written in the Laments.

[26]The other events of Josiah's reign and his acts of devotion, according to what is written in the Law of the LORD— [27]all the events, from beginning to end, are written in the book of the kings of Israel and Judah. [1]And the people of the land took Jehoahaz son of Josiah and made him king in Jerusalem in place of his father.

Jehoahaz King of Judah   [2]Jehoahaz[a] was twenty-three years old when he became king, and he reigned in Jerusalem three months. [3]The king of Egypt dethroned him in Jerusalem and imposed on Judah a levy of a hundred talents[b] of silver and a talent[c] of gold. [4]The king of Egypt made Eliakim, a brother of Jehoahaz, king over Judah and Jerusalem and changed Eliakim's name to Jehoiakim. But Neco took Eliakim's brother Jehoahaz and carried him off to Egypt.

---

[a]2 Hebrew *Joahaz*, a variant of *Jehoahaz*; also in verse 4   [b]3 That is, about 3 3/4 tons (about 3.4 metric tons)   [c]3 That is, about 75 pounds (about 34 kilograms)

Jehoiakim King of Judah ⁵Jehoiakim was twenty-five years old when he became king, and he reigned in Jerusalem eleven years. He did evil in the eyes of the LORD his God. ⁶Nebuchadnezzar king of Babylon attacked him and bound him with bronze shackles to take him to Babylon. ⁷Nebuchadnezzar also took to Babylon articles from the temple of the LORD and put them in his temple*ᵃ* there.

⁸The other events of Jehoiakim's reign, the detestable things he did and all that was found against him, are written in the book of the kings of Israel and Judah. And Jehoiachin his son succeeded him as king.

Jehoiachin King of Judah ⁹Jehoiachin was eighteen*ᵇ* years old when he became king, and he reigned in Jerusalem three months and ten days. He did evil in the eyes of the LORD. ¹⁰In the spring, King Nebuchadnezzar sent for him and brought him to Babylon, together with articles of value from the temple of the LORD, and he made Jehoiachin's uncle,*ᶜ* Zedekiah, king over Judah and Jerusalem.

Zedekiah King of Judah ¹¹Zedekiah was twenty-one years old when he became king, and he reigned in Jerusalem eleven years. ¹²He did evil in the eyes of the LORD his God and did not humble himself before Jeremiah the prophet, who spoke the word of the LORD. ¹³He also rebelled against King Nebuchadnezzar, who had made him take an oath in God's name. He became stiff-necked and hardened his heart and would not turn to the LORD, the God of Israel. ¹⁴Furthermore, all the leaders of the priests and the people became more and more unfaithful, following all the detestable practices of the nations and defiling the temple of the LORD, which he had consecrated in Jerusalem.

The Fall of Jerusalem ¹⁵The LORD, the God of their fathers, sent word to them through his messengers again and again, because he had pity on his people and on his dwelling place. ¹⁶But they mocked God's messengers, despised his words and scoffed at his prophets until the wrath of the LORD was aroused against his people and there was no remedy. ¹⁷He brought up against them the king of the Babylonians,*ᵈ* who killed their young men with the sword in the sanctuary, and spared neither young man nor young woman, old man or aged. God handed all of them over to Nebuchadnezzar. ¹⁸He carried to Babylon all the articles from the temple of God, both large and small, and the treasures of the LORD's temple and the treasures of the king and his officials. ¹⁹They set fire to God's temple and broke down the wall of Jerusalem; they burned all the palaces and destroyed everything of value there.

²⁰He carried into exile to Babylon the remnant, who escaped from the sword, and they became servants to him and his sons until the kingdom of Persia came to power. ²¹The land enjoyed its sabbath rests; all the time of its desolation it rested, until the seventy years were completed in fulfillment of the word of the LORD spoken by Jeremiah.

²²In the first year of Cyrus king of Persia, in order to fulfill the word of the LORD spoken by Jeremiah, the LORD moved the heart of Cyrus king of Persia to make a proclamation throughout his realm and to put it in writing:

²³"This is what Cyrus king of Persia says:

" 'The LORD, the God of heaven, has given me all the kingdoms of the earth and he has appointed me to build a temple for him at Jerusalem in Judah. Anyone of his people among you—may the LORD his God be with him, and let him go up.' "

ᵃ7 Or *palace* *ᵇ9* One Hebrew manuscript, some Septuagint manuscripts and Syriac (see also 2 Kings 24:8); most Hebrew manuscripts *eight* *ᶜ10* Hebrew *brother,* that is, relative (see 2 Kings 24:17) *ᵈ17* Or *Chaldeans*

COMING HOME.

After a rough day at school or a long trip, it feels pretty good to come home, doesn't it? But what if you were gone for years, and when you got back your house had burned down and your hometown was deserted? You might be glad to get back, but you'd be disappointed too.

Ezra tells the story of the Israelites' return to their empty and ruined homeland after 70 years of captivity in Babylon. It was especially tough because the Jews' neighbors were hostile. If their attempt to rebuild their homeland was going to succeed in the face of harsh opposition, they had to remain faithful to God!

Fun damentals

Have you set any goals for your life (Ezra 7:10)?

Is there any reason why you should hesitate to date non-Christians (Ezra 9)?

How can you help someone who is involved in some sin (Ezra 10:1-5)?

FAST FACTS

Isaiah predicted Cyrus's victory over Babylon 100 years before it happened.

Cyrus permitted the Israelites to go home in 538 B.C.

The Israelites wanted to go home in order to rebuild God's temple.

Only 50,000 Israelites returned. Hundreds of thousands stayed because they had become wealthy in Babylon.

Cyrus Helps the Exiles to Return In the first year of Cyrus king of Persia, in order to fulfill the word of the Lord spoken by Jeremiah, the Lord moved the heart of Cyrus king of Persia to make a proclamation throughout his realm and to put it in writing:

²"This is what Cyrus king of Persia says:

" 'The Lord, the God of heaven, has given me all the kingdoms of the earth and he has appointed me to build a temple for him at Jerusalem in Judah. ³Anyone of his people among you—may his God be with him, and let him go up to Jerusalem in Judah and build the temple of the Lord, the God of Israel, the God who is in Jerusalem. ⁴And the people of any place where survivors may now be living are to provide him with silver and gold, with goods and livestock, and with freewill offerings for the temple of God in Jerusalem.' "

⁵Then the family heads of Judah and Benjamin, and the priests and Levites—everyone whose heart God had moved—prepared to go up and build the house of the Lord in Jerusalem. ⁶All their neighbors assisted them with articles of silver and gold, with goods and livestock, and with valuable gifts, in addition to all the freewill offerings. ⁷Moreover, King Cyrus brought out the articles belonging to the temple of the Lord, which Nebuchadnezzar had carried away from Jerusalem and had placed in the temple of his god.*a* ⁸Cyrus king of Persia had them brought by Mithredath the treasurer, who counted them out to Sheshbazzar the prince of Judah.

⁹This was the inventory:

gold dishes	30
silver dishes	1,000
silver pans*b*	29
¹⁰gold bowls	30
matching silver bowls	410
other articles	1,000

¹¹In all, there were 5,400 articles of gold and of silver. Sheshbazzar brought all these along when the exiles came up from Babylon to Jerusalem.

The List of the Exiles Who Returned Now these are the people of the province who came up from the captivity of the exiles, whom Nebuchadnezzar king of Babylon had taken captive to Babylon (they returned to Jerusalem and Judah, each to his own town, ²in company with Zerubbabel, Jeshua, Nehemiah, Seraiah, Reelaiah, Mordecai, Bilshan, Mispar, Bigvai, Rehum and Baanah):

The list of the men of the people of Israel:

³the descendants of Parosh	2,172
⁴of Shephatiah	372
⁵of Arah	775
⁶of Pahath-Moab (through the line of Jeshua and Joab)	2,812
⁷of Elam	1,254
⁸of Zattu	945
⁹of Zaccai	760

4,361,
4,362,
Sigh...,
4,363...

SEE
EZRA 1:9-11

*a*7 Or *gods* *b*9 The meaning of the Hebrew for this word is uncertain.

¹⁰of Bani	642
¹¹of Bebai	623
¹²of Azgad	1,222
¹³of Adonikam	666
¹⁴of Bigvai	2,056
¹⁵of Adin	454
¹⁶of Ater (through Hezekiah)	98
¹⁷of Bezai	323
¹⁸of Jorah	112
¹⁹of Hashum	223
²⁰of Gibbar	95
²¹the men of Bethlehem	123
²²of Netophah	56
²³of Anathoth	128
²⁴of Azmaveth	42
²⁵of Kiriath Jearim,ᵃ Kephirah and Beeroth	743
²⁶of Ramah and Geba	621
²⁷of Micmash	122
²⁸of Bethel and Ai	223
²⁹of Nebo	52
³⁰of Magbish	156
³¹of the other Elam	1,254
³²of Harim	320
³³of Lod, Hadid and Ono	725
³⁴of Jericho	345
³⁵of Senaah	3,630

³⁶The priests:

the descendants of Jedaiah (through the family of Jeshua)	973
³⁷of Immer	1,052
³⁸of Pashhur	1,247
³⁹of Harim	1,017

⁴⁰The Levites:

the descendants of Jeshua and Kadmiel (through the line of Hodaviah)	74

⁴¹The singers:

the descendants of Asaph	128

⁴²The gatekeepers of the temple:

the descendants of Shallum, Ater, Talmon, Akkub, Hatita and Shobai	139

⁴³The temple servants:

the descendants of
Ziha, Hasupha, Tabbaoth,
⁴⁴Keros, Siaha, Padon,
⁴⁵Lebanah, Hagabah, Akkub,
⁴⁶Hagab, Shalmai, Hanan,
⁴⁷Giddel, Gahar, Reaiah,
⁴⁸Rezin, Nekoda, Gazzam,
⁴⁹Uzza, Paseah, Besai,

ᵃ25 See Septuagint (see also Neh. 7:29); Hebrew *Kiriath Arim.*

⁵⁰Asnah, Meunim, Nephussim,
⁵¹Bakbuk, Hakupha, Harhur,
⁵²Bazluth, Mehida, Harsha,
⁵³Barkos, Sisera, Temah,
⁵⁴Neziah and Hatipha

⁵⁵The descendants of the servants of Solomon:

the descendants of
Sotai, Hassophereth, Peruda,
⁵⁶Jaala, Darkon, Giddel,
⁵⁷Shephatiah, Hattil,
Pokereth-Hazzebaim and Ami

⁵⁸The temple servants and the descendants
of the servants of Solomon   392

⁵⁹The following came up from the towns of Tel Melah, Tel Harsha, Kerub, Addon and Immer, but they could not show that their families were descended from Israel:

⁶⁰The descendants of
Delaiah, Tobiah and Nekoda   652

⁶¹And from among the priests:

The descendants of
Hobaiah, Hakkoz and Barzillai (a man who had married
a daughter of Barzillai the Gileadite and was called by
that name).

⁶²These searched for their family records, but they could not find them and so were excluded from the priesthood as unclean. ⁶³The governor ordered them not to eat any of the most sacred food until there was a priest ministering with the Urim and Thummim.

⁶⁴The whole company numbered 42,360, ⁶⁵besides their 7,337 menservants and maidservants; and they also had 200 men and women singers. ⁶⁶They had 736 horses, 245 mules, ⁶⁷435 camels and 6,720 donkeys.

⁶⁸When they arrived at the house of the LORD in Jerusalem, some of the heads of the families gave freewill offerings toward the rebuilding of the house of God on its site. ⁶⁹According to their ability they gave to the treasury for this work 61,000 drachmas*ᵃ* of gold, 5,000 minas*ᵇ* of silver and 100 priestly garments.

⁷⁰The priests, the Levites, the singers, the gatekeepers and the temple servants settled in their own towns, along with some of the other people, and the rest of the Israelites settled in their towns.

3 *Rebuilding the Altar* When the seventh month came and the Israelites had settled in their towns, the people as-

---

Direct Line

EZRA 3:1-6

You woke up grumpy. Called your sister a name. Talked back to your mother. Got in a fight at the bus stop. Tripped a kid in gym. You feel awful. If only you could start the day over! No one can go back and live a day over again. But you can make a fresh start, even in the middle of a bad day. The people of Judah had a bad century. They sinned willfully. Their homeland was destroyed, and they were carried as captives to Babylon. Now they were back. And the first thing they did was worship the Lord. Fresh starts begin by turning to the Lord. Admit your failures. Thank God for his forgiveness. And the rest of the day really will be new.

ᵃ69 That is, about 1,100 pounds (about 500 kilograms)
ᵇ69 That is, about 3 tons (about 2.9 metric tons)

sembled as one man in Jerusalem. ²Then Jeshua son of Jozadak and his fellow priests and Zerubbabel son of Shealtiel and his associates began to build the altar of the God of Israel to sacrifice burnt offerings on it, in accordance with what is written in the Law of Moses the man of God. ³Despite their fear of the peoples around them, they built the altar on its foundation and sacrificed burnt offerings on it to the LORD, both the morning and evening sacrifices. ⁴Then in accordance with what is written, they celebrated the Feast of Tabernacles with the required number of burnt offerings prescribed for each day. ⁵After that, they presented the regular burnt offerings, the New Moon sacrifices and the sacrifices for all the appointed sacred feasts of the LORD, as well as those brought as freewill offerings to the LORD. ⁶On the first day of the seventh month they began to offer burnt offerings to the LORD, though the foundation of the LORD's temple had not yet been laid.

Rebuilding the Temple ⁷Then they gave money to the masons and carpenters, and gave food and drink and oil to the people of Sidon and Tyre, so that they would bring cedar logs by sea from Lebanon to Joppa, as authorized by Cyrus king of Persia.

⁸In the second month of the second year after their arrival at the house of God in Jerusalem, Zerubbabel son of Shealtiel, Jeshua son of Jozadak and the rest of their brothers (the priests and the Levites and all who had returned from the captivity to Jerusalem) began the work, appointing Levites twenty years of age and older to supervise the building of the house of the LORD. ⁹Jeshua and his sons and brothers and Kadmiel and his sons (descendants of Hodaviah*ᵃ*) and the sons of Henadad and their sons and brothers—all Levites—joined together in supervising those working on the house of God.

¹⁰When the builders laid the foundation of the temple of the LORD, the priests in their vestments and with trumpets, and the Levites (the sons of Asaph) with cymbals, took their places to praise the LORD, as prescribed by David king of Israel. ¹¹With praise and thanksgiving they sang to the LORD:

> "He is good;
> his love to Israel endures forever."

And all the people gave a great shout of praise to the LORD, because the foundation of the house of the LORD was laid. ¹²But many of the older priests and Levites and family heads, who had seen the former temple, wept aloud when they saw the foundation of this temple being laid, while many others shouted for joy. ¹³No one could distinguish the sound of the shouts of joy from the sound of weeping, because the people made so much noise. And the sound was heard far away.

Opposition to the Rebuilding When the enemies of Judah and Benjamin heard that the exiles were building a temple for the LORD, the God of Israel, ²they came to Zerubbabel and to the heads of the families and said, "Let us help you build because, like you, we seek your God and have been sacrificing to him since the time of Esarhaddon king of Assyria, who brought us here."

³But Zerubbabel, Jeshua and the rest of the heads of the families of Israel answered, "You have no part with us in building a temple to our God. We alone will build it for the LORD, the God of Israel, as King Cyrus, the king of Persia, commanded us."

⁴Then the peoples around them set out to discourage the people of Judah and make them afraid to go on building.*ᵇ* ⁵They hired counselors to work against them and frustrate their plans during the entire reign of Cyrus king of Persia and down to the reign of Darius king of Persia.

ᵃ9 Hebrew Yehudah, probably a variant of Hodaviah   ᵇ4 Or and troubled them as they built

Later Opposition Under Xerxes and Artaxerxes ⁶At the beginning of the reign of Xerxes,ᵃ they lodged an accusation against the people of Judah and Jerusalem.

⁷And in the days of Artaxerxes king of Persia, Bishlam, Mithredath, Tabeel and the rest of his associates wrote a letter to Artaxerxes. The letter was written in Aramaic script and in the Aramaic language.ᵇ,ᶜ

⁸Rehum the commanding officer and Shimshai the secretary wrote a letter against Jerusalem to Artaxerxes the king as follows:

⁹Rehum the commanding officer and Shimshai the secretary, together with the rest of their associates—the judges and officials over the men from Tripolis, Persia,ᵈ Erech and Babylon, the Elamites of Susa, ¹⁰and the other people whom the great and honorable Ashurbanipalᵉ deported and settled in the city of Samaria and elsewhere in Trans-Euphrates.

¹¹(This is a copy of the letter they sent him.)

To King Artaxerxes,

From your servants, the men of Trans-Euphrates:

¹²The king should know that the Jews who came up to us from you have gone to Jerusalem and are rebuilding that rebellious and wicked city. They are restoring the walls and repairing the foundations.

¹³Furthermore, the king should know that if this city is built and its walls are restored, no more taxes, tribute or duty will be paid, and the royal revenues will suffer. ¹⁴Now since we are under obligation to the palace and it is not proper for us to see the king dishonored, we are sending this message to inform the king, ¹⁵so that a search may be made in the archives of your predecessors. In these records you will find that this city is a rebellious city, troublesome to kings and provinces, a place of rebellion from ancient times. That is why this city was destroyed. ¹⁶We inform the king that if this city is built and its walls are restored, you will be left with nothing in Trans-Euphrates.

¹⁷The king sent this reply:

To Rehum the commanding officer, Shimshai the secretary and the rest of their associates living in Samaria and elsewhere in Trans-Euphrates:

Greetings.

¹⁸The letter you sent us has been read and translated in my presence. ¹⁹I issued an order and a search was made, and it was found that this city has a long history of revolt against kings and has been a place of rebellion and sedition. ²⁰Jerusalem has had powerful kings ruling over the whole of Trans-Euphrates, and taxes, tribute and duty were paid to them. ²¹Now issue an order to these men to stop work, so that this city will not be rebuilt until I so order. ²²Be careful not to neglect this matter. Why let this threat grow, to the detriment of the royal interests?

²³As soon as the copy of the letter of King Artaxerxes was read to Rehum and Shimshai the secretary and their associates, they went immediately to the Jews in Jerusalem and compelled them by force to stop.

²⁴Thus the work on the house of God in Jerusalem came to a standstill until the second year of the reign of Darius king of Persia.

ᵃ6 Hebrew *Ahasuerus,* a variant of Xerxes' Persian name   ᵇ7 Or *written in Aramaic and translated*   ᶜ7 The text of Ezra 4:8—6:18 is in Aramaic.   ᵈ9 Or *officials, magistrates and governors over the men from*   ᵉ10 Aramaic *Osnappar,* a variant of *Ashurbanipal*

5 *Tattenai's Letter to Darius* Now Haggai the prophet and Zechariah the prophet, a descendant of Iddo, prophesied to the Jews in Judah and Jerusalem in the name of the God of Israel, who was over them. ²Then Zerubbabel son of Shealtiel and Jeshua son of Jozadak set to work to rebuild the house of God in Jerusalem. And the prophets of God were with them, helping them.

³At that time Tattenai, governor of Trans-Euphrates, and Shethar-Bozenai and their associates went to them and asked, "Who authorized you to rebuild this temple and restore this structure?" ⁴They also asked, "What are the names of the men constructing this building?"ᵃ ⁵But the eye of their God was watching over the elders of the Jews, and they were not stopped until a report could go to Darius and his written reply be received.

⁶This is a copy of the letter that Tattenai, governor of Trans-Euphrates, and Shethar-Bozenai and their associates, the officials of Trans-Euphrates, sent to King Darius. ⁷The report they sent him read as follows:

To King Darius:

Cordial greetings.

⁸The king should know that we went to the district of Judah, to the temple of the great God. The people are building it with large stones and placing the timbers in the walls. The work is being carried on with diligence and is making rapid progress under their direction.

⁹We questioned the elders and asked them, "Who authorized you to rebuild this temple and restore this structure?" ¹⁰We also asked them their names, so that we could write down the names of their leaders for your information.

¹¹This is the answer they gave us:

"We are the servants of the God of heaven and earth, and we are rebuilding the temple that was built many years ago, one that a great king of Israel built and finished. ¹²But because our fathers angered the God of heaven, he handed them over to Nebuchadnezzar the Chaldean, king of Babylon, who destroyed this temple and deported the people to Babylon.

¹³"However, in the first year of Cyrus king of Babylon, King Cyrus issued a decree to rebuild this house of God. ¹⁴He even removed from the templeᵇ of Babylon the gold and silver articles of the house of God, which Nebuchadnezzar had taken from the temple in Jerusalem and brought to the templeᵇ in Babylon.

"Then King Cyrus gave them to a man named Sheshbazzar, whom he had appointed governor, ¹⁵and he told him, 'Take these articles and go and deposit them in the temple in Jerusalem. And rebuild the house of God on its site.' ¹⁶So this Sheshbazzar came and laid the foundations of the house of God in Jerusalem. From that day to the present it has been under construction but is not yet finished."

¹⁷Now if it pleases the king, let a search be made in the royal archives of Babylon to see if King Cyrus did in fact issue a decree to rebuild this house of God in Jerusalem. Then let the king send us his decision in this matter.

6 *The Decree of Darius* King Darius then issued an order, and they searched in the archives stored in the treasury at Babylon. ²A scroll was found in the citadel of Ecbatana in the province of Media, and this was written on it:

ᵃ4 See Septuagint; Aramaic *We told them the names of the men constructing this building.* ᵇ14 Or *palace*

Dear Sam,

My brother's been telling everyone I was at a mental hospital when I was really on vacation. My reputation is ruined! What can I do?

Dirk in Des Moines

100 Advice Lane, Anywhere, USA

Dear Dirk,

Rumors can be vicious. That's one reason God warns people not to gossip. This is obviously an embarrassing situation, but I don't think your reputation is really ruined.

Do you know how the people of Israel stopped a bad rumor? The Israelites were rebuilding the temple. Their enemies wrote letters to the ruler Artaxerxes and started a rumor that the Israelites were rebellious and wicked (Ezra 4:11-16). Artaxerxes ordered the rebuilding to stop until the rumor was checked out. Eventually another king verified that the Israelites had permission to rebuild. In fact, the enemies were ordered to help them (Ezra 6:3-10)! Of course this took a great deal of time and caused much stress for the Israelites, but after a while, the truth came out and they were vindicated.

When the truth is known about where you were, your reputation will be restored. That's not to say you won't experience some stress or be teased, but things will get back to normal. Remember how hurtful rumors can be, and be sure you never start one.

Sam

Memorandum:

³In the first year of King Cyrus, the king issued a decree concerning the temple of God in Jerusalem:

Let the temple be rebuilt as a place to present sacrifices, and let its foundations be laid. It is to be ninety feet*a* high and ninety feet wide, ⁴with three courses of large stones and one of timbers. The costs are to be paid by the royal treasury. ⁵Also, the gold and silver articles of the house of God, which Nebuchadnezzar took from the temple in Jerusalem and brought to Babylon, are to be returned to their places in the temple in Jerusalem; they are to be deposited in the house of God.

⁶Now then, Tattenai, governor of Trans-Euphrates, and Shethar-Bozenai and you, their fellow officials of that province, stay away from there. ⁷Do not interfere with the work on this temple of God. Let the governor of the Jews and the Jewish elders rebuild this house of God on its site.

⁸Moreover, I hereby decree what you are to do for these elders of the Jews in the construction of this house of God:

The expenses of these men are to be fully paid out of the royal treasury, from the revenues of Trans-Euphrates, so that the work will not stop. ⁹Whatever is needed—young bulls, rams, male lambs for burnt offerings to the God of heaven, and wheat, salt, wine and oil, as requested by the priests in Jerusalem—must be given them daily without fail, ¹⁰so that they may offer sacrifices pleasing to the God of heaven and pray for the well-being of the king and his sons.

¹¹Furthermore, I decree that if anyone changes this edict, a beam is to be pulled from his house and he is to be lifted up and impaled on it. And for this crime his house is to be made a pile of rubble. ¹²May God, who has caused his Name to dwell there, overthrow any king or people who lifts a hand to change this decree or to destroy this temple in Jerusalem.

I Darius have decreed it. Let it be carried out with diligence.

Completion and Dedication of the Temple ¹³Then, because of the decree King Darius had sent, Tattenai, governor of Trans-Euphrates, and Shethar-Bozenai and their associates carried it out with diligence. ¹⁴So the elders of the Jews continued to build and prosper under the preaching of Haggai the prophet and Zechariah, a descendant of Iddo. They finished building the temple according to the command of the God of Israel and the decrees of Cyrus, Darius and Artaxerxes, kings of Persia. ¹⁵The temple was completed on the third day of the month Adar, in the sixth year of the reign of King Darius.

¹⁶Then the people of Israel—the priests, the Levites and the rest of the exiles—celebrated the dedication of the house of God with joy. ¹⁷For the dedication of this house of God they offered a hundred bulls, two hundred rams, four hundred male lambs and, as a sin offering for all Israel, twelve male goats, one for each of the tribes of Israel. ¹⁸And they installed the priests in their divisions and the Levites in their groups for the service of God at Jerusalem, according to what is written in the Book of Moses.

The Passover ¹⁹On the fourteenth day of the first month, the exiles celebrated the Passover. ²⁰The priests and Levites had purified themselves and were all ceremonially clean. The Levites slaughtered the Passover lamb for all the exiles, for their brothers the priests and for themselves. ²¹So the Israelites who had returned from the exile ate it, together with all who had separated themselves from the unclean practices of their Gentile neighbors in

---

a3 Aramaic *sixty cubits* (about 27 meters)

order to seek the Lord, the God of Israel. ²²For seven days they celebrated with joy the Feast of Unleavened Bread, because the Lord had filled them with joy by changing the attitude of the king of Assyria, so that he assisted them in the work on the house of God, the God of Israel.

Ezra Comes to Jerusalem After these things, during the reign of Artaxerxes king of Persia, Ezra son of Seraiah, the son of Azariah, the son of Hilkiah, ²the son of Shallum, the son of Zadok, the son of Ahitub, ³the son of Amariah, the son of Azariah, the son of Meraioth, ⁴the son of Zerahiah, the son of Uzzi, the son of Bukki, ⁵the son of Abishua, the son of Phinehas, the son of Eleazar, the son of Aaron the chief priest— ⁶this Ezra came up from Babylon. He was a teacher well versed in the Law of Moses, which the Lord, the God of Israel, had given. The king had granted him everything he asked, for the hand of the Lord his God was on him. ⁷Some of the Israelites, including priests, Levites, singers, gatekeepers and temple servants, also came up to Jerusalem in the seventh year of King Artaxerxes.

⁸Ezra arrived in Jerusalem in the fifth month of the seventh year of the king. ⁹He had begun his journey from Babylon on the first day of the first month, and he arrived in Jerusalem on the first day of the fifth month, for the gracious hand of his God was on him. ¹⁰For Ezra had devoted himself to the study and observance of the Law of the Lord, and to teaching its decrees and laws in Israel.

King Artaxerxes' Letter to Ezra ¹¹This is a copy of the letter King Artaxerxes had given to Ezra the priest and teacher, a man learned in matters concerning the commands and decrees of the Lord for Israel:

¹²ᵃArtaxerxes, king of kings,

To Ezra the priest, a teacher of the Law of the God of heaven:

Greetings.

¹³Now I decree that any of the Israelites in my kingdom, including priests and Levites, who wish to go to Jerusalem with you, may go. ¹⁴You are sent by the king and his seven advisers to inquire about Judah and Jerusalem with regard to the Law of your God, which is in your hand. ¹⁵Moreover, you are to take with you the silver and gold that the king and his advisers have freely given to the God of Israel, whose dwelling is in Jerusalem, ¹⁶together with all the silver and gold you may obtain from the province of Babylon, as well as the freewill offerings of the people and priests for the temple of their God in Jerusalem. ¹⁷With this money be sure to buy bulls, rams and male lambs, together with their grain offerings and drink offerings, and sacrifice them on the altar of the temple of your God in Jerusalem.

¹⁸You and your brother Jews may then do whatever seems best with the rest of the silver and gold, in accordance with the will of your God. ¹⁹Deliver to the God of Jerusalem all the

Direct Line

EZRA 7:10

You want to be a leader? It doesn't just happen. You have to prepare yourself to be a leader. To be a leading scientist, you'd better start now to master math. To be a top athlete, you'd better practice daily. It's the same way with the spiritual. If you want to be a leader in God's kingdom, you need to follow Ezra's path. He devoted himself to studying and practicing God's Word and to teaching it to others. Leaders aren't born. People become leaders because they're dedicated to excellence in their field. Wouldn't it be great to follow Ezra's path to leadership?

ᵃ12 The text of Ezra 7:12-26 is in Aramaic.

articles entrusted to you for worship in the temple of your God. ²⁰And anything else needed for the temple of your God that you may have occasion to supply, you may provide from the royal treasury.

²¹Now I, King Artaxerxes, order all the treasurers of Trans-Euphrates to provide with diligence whatever Ezra the priest, a teacher of the Law of the God of heaven, may ask of you— ²²up to a hundred talents*ᵃ* of silver, a hundred cors*ᵇ* of wheat, a hundred baths*ᶜ* of wine, a hundred baths*ᶜ* of olive oil, and salt without limit. ²³Whatever the God of heaven has prescribed, let it be done with diligence for the temple of the God of heaven. Why should there be wrath against the realm of the king and of his sons? ²⁴You are also to know that you have no authority to impose taxes, tribute or duty on any of the priests, Levites, singers, gatekeepers, temple servants or other workers at this house of God.

²⁵And you, Ezra, in accordance with the wisdom of your God, which you possess, appoint magistrates and judges to administer justice to all the people of Trans-Euphrates—all who know the laws of your God. And you are to teach any who do not know them. ²⁶Whoever does not obey the law of your God and the law of the king must surely be punished by death, banishment, confiscation of property, or imprisonment.

²⁷Praise be to the Lᴏʀᴅ, the God of our fathers, who has put it into the king's heart to bring honor to the house of the Lᴏʀᴅ in Jerusalem in this way ²⁸and who has extended his good favor to me before the king and his advisers and all the king's powerful officials. Because the hand of the Lᴏʀᴅ my God was on me, I took courage and gathered leading men from Israel to go up with me.

8 *List of the Family Heads Returning With Ezra* These are the family heads and those registered with them who came up with me from Babylon during the reign of King Artaxerxes:

² of the descendants of Phinehas, Gershom;
of the descendants of Ithamar, Daniel;
of the descendants of David, Hattush ³of the descendants of Shecaniah;

of the descendants of Parosh, Zechariah, and with him were registered 150 men;
⁴ of the descendants of Pahath-Moab, Eliehoenai son of Zerahiah, and with him 200 men;
⁵ of the descendants of Zattu,*ᵈ* Shecaniah son of Jahaziel, and with him 300 men;
⁶ of the descendants of Adin, Ebed son of Jonathan, and with him 50 men;
⁷ of the descendants of Elam, Jeshaiah son of Athaliah, and with him 70 men;
⁸ of the descendants of Shephatiah, Zebadiah son of Michael, and with him 80 men;
⁹ of the descendants of Joab, Obadiah son of Jehiel, and with him 218 men;
¹⁰ of the descendants of Bani,*ᵉ* Shelomith son of Josiphiah, and with him 160 men;
¹¹ of the descendants of Bebai, Zechariah son of Bebai, and with him 28 men;

ᵃ22 That is, about 3 3/4 tons (about 3.4 metric tons) *ᵇ22* That is, probably about 600 bushels (about 22 kiloliters) *ᶜ22* That is, probably about 600 gallons (about 2.2 kiloliters) *ᵈ5* Some Septuagint manuscripts (also 1 Esdras 8:32); Hebrew does not have *Zattu*. *ᵉ10* Some Septuagint manuscripts (also 1 Esdras 8:36); Hebrew does not have *Bani*.

¹²of the descendants of Azgad, Johanan son of Hakkatan, and with him 110 men;

¹³of the descendants of Adonikam, the last ones, whose names were Eliphelet, Jeuel and Shemaiah, and with them 60 men;

¹⁴of the descendants of Bigvai, Uthai and Zaccur, and with them 70 men.

The Return to Jerusalem ¹⁵I assembled them at the canal that flows toward Ahava, and we camped there three days. When I checked among the people and the priests, I found no Levites there. ¹⁶So I summoned Eliezer, Ariel, Shemaiah, Elnathan, Jarib, Elnathan, Nathan, Zechariah and Meshullam, who were leaders, and Joiarib and Elnathan, who were men of learning, ¹⁷and I sent them to Iddo, the leader in Casiphia. I told them what to say to Iddo and his kinsmen, the temple servants in Casiphia, so that they might bring attendants to us for the house of our God. ¹⁸Because the gracious hand of our God was on us, they brought us Sherebiah, a capable man, from the descendants of Mahli son of Levi, the son of Israel, and Sherebiah's sons and brothers, 18 men; ¹⁹and Hashabiah, together with Jeshaiah from the descendants of Merari, and his brothers and nephews, 20 men. ²⁰They also brought 220 of the temple servants—a body that David and the officials had established to assist the Levites. All were registered by name.

²¹There, by the Ahava Canal, I proclaimed a fast, so that we might humble ourselves before our God and ask him for a safe journey for us and our children, with all our possessions. ²²I was ashamed to ask the king for soldiers and horsemen to protect us from enemies on the road, because we had told the king, "The gracious hand of our God is on everyone who looks to him, but his great anger is against all who forsake him." ²³So we fasted and petitioned our God about this, and he answered our prayer.

²⁴Then I set apart twelve of the leading priests, together with Sherebiah, Hashabiah and ten of their brothers, ²⁵and I weighed out to them the offering of silver and gold and the articles that the king, his advisers, his officials and all Israel present there had donated for the house of our God. ²⁶I weighed out to them 650 talents*ᵃ* of silver, silver articles weighing 100 talents,*ᵇ* 100 talents*ᵇ* of gold, ²⁷20 bowls of gold valued at 1,000 darics,*ᶜ* and two fine articles of polished bronze, as precious as gold.

²⁸I said to them, "You as well as these articles are consecrated to the LORD. The silver and gold are a freewill offering to the LORD, the God of your fathers. ²⁹Guard them carefully until you weigh them out in the chambers of the house of the LORD in Jerusalem before the leading priests and the Levites and the family heads of Israel." ³⁰Then the priests and Levites received the silver and gold and sacred articles that had been weighed out to be taken to the house of our God in Jerusalem.

³¹On the twelfth day of the first month we set out from the Ahava Canal to go to Jerusalem. The hand of our God was on us, and he protected us from enemies and bandits along the way. ³²So we arrived in Jerusalem, where we rested three days.

³³On the fourth day, in the house of our God, we weighed out the silver and gold and the sacred articles into the hands of Meremoth son of Uriah, the priest. Eleazar son of Phinehas was with him, and so were the Levites Jozabad son of Jeshua and Noadiah son of Binnui. ³⁴Everything was accounted for by number and weight, and the entire weight was recorded at that time.

³⁵Then the exiles who had returned from captivity sacrificed burnt offerings to the God of Israel: twelve bulls for all Israel, ninety-six rams, seventy-

---

ᵃ26 That is, about 25 tons (about 22 metric tons)   *ᵇ26* That is, about 3 3/4 tons (about 3.4 metric tons)   *ᶜ27* That is, about 19 pounds (about 8.5 kilograms)

seven male lambs and, as a sin offering, twelve male goats. All this was a burnt offering to the LORD. ³⁶They also delivered the king's orders to the royal satraps and to the governors of Trans-Euphrates, who then gave assistance to the people and to the house of God.

Ezra's Prayer About Intermarriage After these things had been done, the leaders came to me and said, "The people of Israel, including the priests and the Levites, have not kept themselves separate from the neighboring peoples with their detestable practices, like those of the Canaanites, Hittites, Perizzites, Jebusites, Ammonites, Moabites, Egyptians and Amorites. ²They have taken some of their daughters as wives for themselves and their sons, and have mingled the holy race with the peoples around them. And the leaders and officials have led the way in this unfaithfulness."

³When I heard this, I tore my tunic and cloak, pulled hair from my head and beard and sat down appalled. ⁴Then everyone who trembled at the words of the God of Israel gathered around me because of this unfaithfulness of the exiles. And I sat there appalled until the evening sacrifice.

⁵Then, at the evening sacrifice, I rose from my self-abasement, with my tunic and cloak torn, and fell on my knees with my hands spread out to the LORD my God ⁶and prayed:

"O my God, I am too ashamed and disgraced to lift up my face to you, my God, because our sins are higher than our heads and our guilt has reached to the heavens. ⁷From the days of our forefathers until now, our guilt has been great. Because of our sins, we and our kings and our priests have been subjected to the sword and captivity, to pillage and humiliation at the hand of foreign kings, as it is today.

⁸"But now, for a brief moment, the LORD our God has been gracious in leaving us a remnant and giving us a firm place in his sanctuary, and so our God gives light to our eyes and a little relief in our bondage. ⁹Though we are slaves, our God has not deserted us in our bondage. He has shown us kindness in the sight of the kings of Persia: He has granted us new life to rebuild the house of our God and repair its ruins, and he has given us a wall of protection in Judah and Jerusalem.

¹⁰"But now, O our God, what can we say after this? For we have disregarded the commands ¹¹you gave through your servants the prophets when you said: 'The land you are entering to possess is a land polluted by the corruption of its peoples. By their detestable practices they have filled it with their impurity from one end to the other. ¹²Therefore, do not give your daughters in marriage to their sons or take their daughters for your sons. Do not seek a treaty of friendship with them at any time, that you may be strong and eat the good things of the land and leave it to your children as an everlasting inheritance.'

¹³"What has happened to us is a result of our evil deeds and our great guilt, and yet, our God, you have punished us less than our sins have deserved and have given us a remnant like this. ¹⁴Shall we again break your commands and intermarry with the peoples who commit such detestable practices? Would you not be angry enough with us to destroy us, leaving us no remnant or survivor? ¹⁵O LORD, God of Israel, you are righteous! We are left this day as a remnant. Here we are before you in our guilt, though because of it not one of us can stand in your presence."

The People's Confession of Sin While Ezra was praying and confessing, weeping and throwing himself down before the house of God, a large crowd of Israelites—men, women and children—gathered around him. They too wept bitterly. ²Then Shecaniah son of Jehiel, one of the descendants of Elam, said to Ezra, "We have been unfaithful to our God by marrying foreign women from the peoples around us. But in spite of this,

Dear Sam,

My parents get really bent out
of shape when I date non-Christians.
What does the Bible say about this?

Jennifer in Jersey City

100 Advice Lane, Anywhere, USA

Dear Jennifer,

Dating was one problem young people in Biblical times didn't worry about. Marriages were prearranged by parents. While dating isn't discussed, intermarriage is. God told the Israelites not to marry outside of their faith. Unfortunately, they didn't pay much attention. Over and over again they adopted pagan religions and were punished for their sins (Ezra 9).

Dating isn't marriage, you're probably thinking. And probably those you date aren't worshiping idols. Then again, maybe they are. Materialism, for instance, is a type of modern idolatry. The values of this world are not the values of God. Scripture is clear about forbidding marriage between Christians and non-Christians (Ezra 9; 2 Corinthians 6:14).

If you are dating an unbeliever, be very careful. Perhaps he has good morals. Perhaps he doesn't tempt you to go against God's teaching. Perhaps you will even be able to lead him to Christ. But you're in dangerous territory. Be very careful.

Sam

there is still hope for Israel. ³Now let us make a covenant before our God to send away all these women and their children, in accordance with the counsel of my lord and of those who fear the commands of our God. Let it be done according to the Law. ⁴Rise up; this matter is in your hands. We will support you, so take courage and do it."

⁵So Ezra rose up and put the leading priests and Levites and all Israel under oath to do what had been suggested. And they took the oath. ⁶Then Ezra withdrew from before the house of God and went to the room of Jehohanan son of Eliashib. While he was there, he ate no food and drank no water, because he continued to mourn over the unfaithfulness of the exiles.

⁷A proclamation was then issued throughout Judah and Jerusalem for all the exiles to assemble in Jerusalem. ⁸Anyone who failed to appear within three days would forfeit all his property, in accordance with the decision of the officials and elders, and would himself be expelled from the assembly of the exiles.

⁹Within the three days, all the men of Judah and Benjamin had gathered in Jerusalem. And on the twentieth day of the ninth month, all the people were sitting in the square before the house of God, greatly distressed by the occasion and because of the rain. ¹⁰Then Ezra the priest stood up and said to them, "You have been unfaithful; you have married foreign women, adding to Israel's guilt. ¹¹Now make confession to the LORD, the God of your fathers, and do his will. Separate yourselves from the peoples around you and from your foreign wives."

¹²The whole assembly responded with a loud voice: "You are right! We must do as you say. ¹³But there are many people here and it is the rainy season; so we cannot stand outside. Besides, this matter cannot be taken care of in a day or two, because we have sinned greatly in this thing. ¹⁴Let our officials act for the whole assembly. Then let everyone in our towns who has married a foreign woman come at a set time, along with the elders and judges of each town, until the fierce anger of our God in this matter is turned away from us." ¹⁵Only Jonathan son of Asahel and Jahzeiah son of Tikvah, supported by Meshullam and Shabbethai the Levite, opposed this.

¹⁶So the exiles did as was proposed. Ezra the priest selected men who were family heads, one from each family division, and all of them designated by name. On the first day of the tenth month they sat down to investigate the cases, ¹⁷and by the first day of the first month they finished dealing with all the men who had married foreign women.

Those Guilty of Intermarriage

¹⁸Among the descendants of the priests, the following had married foreign women:

From the descendants of Jeshua son of Jozadak, and his brothers: Maaseiah, Eliezer, Jarib and Gedaliah. ¹⁹(They all gave their hands in pledge to put away their wives, and for their guilt they each presented a ram from the flock as a guilt offering.)

²⁰From the descendants of Immer: Hanani and Zebadiah.

EZRA 10:12

Jim comes home, and his dad says, "Looks like you've got a lot of homework." "You're right," Jim says (and heads out to play B-ball). "Jenny, it's your turn to empty the dishwasher." "OK," Jenny says (and picks up the phone to call Keri). Knowing you should do something, and doing it, are two different things. The people of Ezra's time set a good example. Ezra pointed out an area in which many had disobeyed God. The people not only said, "You are right," but added, "We must do as you say." Be a Christian who not only says, "You're right," but also says, "We should do that." Then do it!

Direct Line

²¹ From the descendants of Harim:
   Maaseiah, Elijah, Shemaiah, Jehiel and Uzziah.
²² From the descendants of Pashhur:
   Elioenai, Maaseiah, Ishmael, Nethanel, Jozabad and Elasah.

²³ Among the Levites:

   Jozabad, Shimei, Kelaiah (that is, Kelita), Pethahiah, Judah and
   Eliezer.
²⁴ From the singers:
   Eliashib.
   From the gatekeepers:
   Shallum, Telem and Uri.

²⁵ And among the other Israelites:

   From the descendants of Parosh:
   Ramiah, Izziah, Malkijah, Mijamin, Eleazar, Malkijah and Benaiah.
²⁶ From the descendants of Elam:
   Mattaniah, Zechariah, Jehiel, Abdi, Jeremoth and Elijah.
²⁷ From the descendants of Zattu:
   Elioenai, Eliashib, Mattaniah, Jeremoth, Zabad and Aziza.
²⁸ From the descendants of Bebai:
   Jehohanan, Hananiah, Zabbai and Athlai.
²⁹ From the descendants of Bani:
   Meshullam, Malluch, Adaiah, Jashub, Sheal and Jeremoth.
³⁰ From the descendants of Pahath-Moab:
   Adna, Kelal, Benaiah, Maaseiah, Mattaniah, Bezalel, Binnui and Manasseh.
³¹ From the descendants of Harim:
   Eliezer, Ishijah, Malkijah, Shemaiah, Shimeon, ³²Benjamin, Malluch
   and Shemariah.
³³ From the descendants of Hashum:
   Mattenai, Mattattah, Zabad, Eliphelet, Jeremai, Manasseh and
   Shimei.
³⁴ From the descendants of Bani:
   Maadai, Amram, Uel, ³⁵Benaiah, Bedeiah, Keluhi, ³⁶Vaniah, Meremoth,
   Eliashib, ³⁷Mattaniah, Mattenai and Jaasu.
³⁸ From the descendants of Binnui:[a]
   Shimei, ³⁹Shelemiah, Nathan, Adaiah, ⁴⁰Macnadebai, Shashai, Sharai,
   ⁴¹Azarel, Shelemiah, Shemariah, ⁴²Shallum, Amariah and Joseph.
⁴³ From the descendants of Nebo:
   Jeiel, Mattithiah, Zabad, Zebina, Jaddai, Joel and Benaiah.

⁴⁴ All these had married foreign women, and some of them had children by
these wives.[b]

---

[a]37,38 See Septuagint (also 1 Esdras 9:34); Hebrew *Jaasu* ³⁸*and Bani and Binnui,*   [b]44 Or *and they sent them away with their children*

COURAGE.

So many things call for courage. Speaking up in class. Saying no when friends pressure you to do something wrong. Making a decision and sticking with it when things don't turn out as you expect.

This book is about one man's courage. Nehemiah was a high official in the Persian empire. He was so upset when he heard of poverty and weakness in his homeland that he asked to be made governor of that tiny province. There Nehemiah battled hostile neighbors, threats and the indifference of his own people. Nehemiah's success reminds you that faith plus courage wins.

Fun damentals

What is most important: praying or doing or both (Nehemiah 1)?

Is courage catching? How can you infect others (Nehemiah 4:12-15)?

What can you learn by an honest look at your past choices (Nehemiah 9:1-6)?

What kind of reward would you want if you did something great (Nehemiah 13)?

FAST FACTS

Nehemiah was governor of Judah from 444 to 433 B.C.

City walls symbolized strength in Bible times. No walls, no respect!

This is the only Old Testament book written in the first person, "I."

Nehemiah's Prayer The words of Nehemiah son of Hacaliah:

In the month of Kislev in the twentieth year, while I was in the citadel of Susa, ²Hanani, one of my brothers, came from Judah with some other men, and I questioned them about the Jewish remnant that survived the exile, and also about Jerusalem.

³They said to me, "Those who survived the exile and are back in the province are in great trouble and disgrace. The wall of Jerusalem is broken down, and its gates have been burned with fire."

⁴When I heard these things, I sat down and wept. For some days I mourned and fasted and prayed before the God of heaven. ⁵Then I said:

"O LORD, God of heaven, the great and awesome God, who keeps his covenant of love with those who love him and obey his commands, ⁶let your ear be attentive and your eyes open to hear the prayer your servant is praying before you day and night for your servants, the people of Israel. I confess the sins we Israelites, including myself and my father's house, have committed against you. ⁷We have acted very wickedly toward you. We have not obeyed the commands, decrees and laws you gave your servant Moses.

⁸"Remember the instruction you gave your servant Moses, saying, 'If you are unfaithful, I will scatter you among the nations, ⁹but if you return to me and obey my commands, then even if your exiled people are at the farthest horizon, I will gather them from there and bring them to the place I have chosen as a dwelling for my Name.'

¹⁰"They are your servants and your people, whom you redeemed by your great strength and your mighty hand. ¹¹O Lord, let your ear be attentive to the prayer of this your servant and to the prayer of your servants who delight in revering your name. Give your servant success today by granting him favor in the presence of this man."

I was cupbearer to the king.

Direct Line

NEHEMIAH 1:1-11

Martin Luther once said, "I've got so much work to do today, I'd better spend two hours in prayer instead of one." Got tons of homework? Feel overwhelmed and rushed? Maybe the best way to get everything done is to stop and pray. Nehemiah was a man of action. He became governor of Judah and quickly got everyone to work building the walls of Jerusalem. But the first thing Nehemiah did "for some days" was to mourn and fast and pray (Nehemiah 1:4). If you're going to get any job done well, you need God's help. The time you take to pray before you act isn't wasted. It's the most important time of all.

Artaxerxes Sends Nehemiah to Jerusalem In the month of Nisan in the twentieth year of King Artaxerxes, when wine was brought for him, I took the wine and gave it to the king. I had not been sad in his presence before; ²so the king asked me, "Why does your face look so sad when you are not ill? This can be nothing but sadness of heart."

I was very much afraid, ³but I said to the king, "May the king live forever! Why should my face not look sad when the city where my fathers are buried lies in ruins, and its gates have been destroyed by fire?"

⁴The king said to me, "What is it you want?"

Then I prayed to the God of heaven, ⁵and I answered the king, "If it pleases the king and if your servant has found favor in his sight, let him send me to the city in Judah where my fathers are buried so that I can rebuild it."

⁶Then the king, with the queen sitting beside him, asked me, "How long will your

journey take, and when will you get back?" It pleased the king to send me; so I set a time.

⁷I also said to him, "If it pleases the king, may I have letters to the governors of Trans-Euphrates, so that they will provide me safe-conduct until I arrive in Judah? ⁸And may I have a letter to Asaph, keeper of the king's forest, so he will give me timber to make beams for the gates of the citadel by the temple and for the city wall and for the residence I will occupy?" And because the gracious hand of my God was upon me, the king granted my requests. ⁹So I went to the governors of Trans-Euphrates and gave them the king's letters. The king had also sent army officers and cavalry with me.

¹⁰When Sanballat the Horonite and Tobiah the Ammonite official heard about this, they were very much disturbed that someone had come to promote the welfare of the Israelites.

Nehemiah Inspects Jerusalem's Walls ¹¹I went to Jerusalem, and after staying there three days ¹²I set out during the night with a few men. I had not told anyone what my God had put in my heart to do for Jerusalem. There were no mounts with me except the one I was riding on.

¹³By night I went out through the Valley Gate toward the Jackal*ᵃ* Well and the Dung Gate, examining the walls of Jerusalem, which had been broken down, and its gates, which had been destroyed by fire. ¹⁴Then I moved on toward the Fountain Gate and the King's Pool, but there was not enough room for my mount to get through; ¹⁵so I went up the valley by night, examining the wall. Finally, I turned back and reentered through the Valley Gate. ¹⁶The officials did not know where I had gone or what I was doing, because as yet I had said nothing to the Jews or the priests or nobles or officials or any others who would be doing the work.

¹⁷Then I said to them, "You see the trouble we are in: Jerusalem lies in ruins, and its gates have been burned with fire. Come, let us rebuild the wall of Jerusalem, and we will no longer be in disgrace." ¹⁸I also told them about the gracious hand of my God upon me and what the king had said to me.

They replied, "Let us start rebuilding." So they began this good work.

¹⁹But when Sanballat the Horonite, Tobiah the Ammonite official and Geshem the Arab heard about it, they mocked and ridiculed us. "What is this you are doing?" they asked. "Are you rebelling against the king?"

²⁰I answered them by saying, "The God of heaven will give us success. We his servants will start rebuilding, but as for you, you have no share in Jerusalem or any claim or historic right to it."

> The God of heaven will give us success (Nehemiah 2:20).

Builders of the Wall Eliashib the high priest and his fellow priests went to work and rebuilt the Sheep Gate. They dedicated it and set its doors in place, building as far as the Tower of the Hundred, which they dedicated, and as far as the Tower of Hananel. ²The men of Jericho built the adjoining section, and Zaccur son of Imri built next to them.

³The Fish Gate was rebuilt by the sons of Hassenaah. They laid its beams and put its doors and bolts and bars in place. ⁴Meremoth son of Uriah, the son of Hakkoz, repaired the next section. Next to him Meshullam son of Berekiah, the son of Meshezabel, made repairs, and next to him Zadok son of Baana also made repairs. ⁵The next section was repaired by the men of Tekoa, but their nobles would not put their shoulders to the work under their supervisors.*ᵇ*

⁶The Jeshanah*ᶜ* Gate was repaired by Joiada son of Paseah and Meshullam son of Besodeiah. They laid its beams and put its doors and bolts and bars

*ᵃ13 Or *Serpent* or *Fig*   ᵇ5 Or *their Lord* or *the governor*   ᶜ6 Or *Old**

in place. [7]Next to them, repairs were made by men from Gibeon and Mizpah—Melatiah of Gibeon and Jadon of Meronoth—places under the authority of the governor of Trans-Euphrates. [8]Uzziel son of Harhaiah, one of the goldsmiths, repaired the next section; and Hananiah, one of the perfumemakers, made repairs next to that. They restored[a] Jerusalem as far as the Broad Wall. [9]Rephaiah son of Hur, ruler of a half-district of Jerusalem, repaired the next section. [10]Adjoining this, Jedaiah son of Harumaph made repairs opposite his house, and Hattush son of Hashabneiah made repairs next to him. [11]Malkijah son of Harim and Hasshub son of Pahath-Moab repaired another section and the Tower of the Ovens. [12]Shallum son of Hallohesh, ruler of a half-district of Jerusalem, repaired the next section with the help of his daughters.

[13]The Valley Gate was repaired by Hanun and the residents of Zanoah. They rebuilt it and put its doors and bolts and bars in place. They also repaired five hundred yards[b] of the wall as far as the Dung Gate.

[14]The Dung Gate was repaired by Malkijah son of Recab, ruler of the district of Beth Hakkerem. He rebuilt it and put its doors and bolts and bars in place.

[15]The Fountain Gate was repaired by Shallun son of Col-Hozeh, ruler of the district of Mizpah. He rebuilt it, roofing it over and putting its doors and bolts and bars in place. He also repaired the wall of the Pool of Siloam,[c] by the King's Garden, as far as the steps going down from the City of David. [16]Beyond him, Nehemiah son of Azbuk, ruler of a half-district of Beth Zur, made repairs up to a point opposite the tombs[d] of David, as far as the artificial pool and the House of the Heroes.

[17]Next to him, the repairs were made by the Levites under Rehum son of Bani. Beside him, Hashabiah, ruler of half the district of Keilah, carried out repairs for his district. [18]Next to him, the repairs were made by their countrymen under Binnui[e] son of Henadad, ruler of the other half-district of Keilah. [19]Next to him, Ezer son of Jeshua, ruler of Mizpah, repaired another section, from a point facing the ascent to the armory as far as the angle. [20]Next to him, Baruch son of Zabbai zealously repaired another section, from the angle to the entrance of the house of Eliashib the high priest. [21]Next to him, Meremoth son of Uriah, the son of Hakkoz, repaired another section, from the entrance of Eliashib's house to the end of it.

[22]The repairs next to him were made by the priests from the surrounding region. [23]Beyond them, Benjamin and Hasshub made repairs in front of their house; and next to them, Azariah son of Maaseiah, the son of Ananiah, made repairs beside his house. [24]Next to him, Binnui son of Henadad repaired another section, from Azariah's house to the angle and the corner, [25]and Palal son of Uzai worked opposite the angle and the tower projecting from the upper palace near the court of the guard. Next to him, Pedaiah son of Parosh [26]and the temple servants living on the hill of Ophel made repairs up to a point opposite the Water Gate toward the east and the projecting tower. [27]Next to them, the men of Tekoa repaired another section, from the great projecting tower to the wall of Ophel.

[28]Above the Horse Gate, the priests made repairs, each in front of his own house. [29]Next to them, Zadok son of Immer made repairs opposite his house. Next to him, Shemaiah son of Shecaniah, the guard at the East Gate, made

---

[a]8 Or *They left out part of* [b]13 Hebrew *a thousand cubits* (about 450 meters) [c]15 Hebrew *Shelah*, a variant of *Shiloah*, that is, Siloam [d]16 Hebrew; Septuagint, some Vulgate manuscripts and Syriac *tomb* [e]18 Two Hebrew manuscripts and Syriac (see also Septuagint and verse 24); most Hebrew manuscripts *Bavvai*

repairs. ³⁰Next to him, Hananiah son of Shelemiah, and Hanun, the sixth son of Zalaph, repaired another section. Next to them, Meshullam son of Berekiah made repairs opposite his living quarters. ³¹Next to him, Malkijah, one of the goldsmiths, made repairs as far as the house of the temple servants and the merchants, opposite the Inspection Gate, and as far as the room above the corner; ³²and between the room above the corner and the Sheep Gate the goldsmiths and merchants made repairs.

Opposition to the Rebuilding When Sanballat heard that we were rebuilding the wall, he became angry and was greatly incensed. He ridiculed the Jews, ²and in the presence of his associates and the army of Samaria, he said, "What are those feeble Jews doing? Will they restore their wall? Will they offer sacrifices? Will they finish in a day? Can they bring the stones back to life from those heaps of rubble—burned as they are?"

³Tobiah the Ammonite, who was at his side, said, "What they are building—if even a fox climbed up on it, he would break down their wall of stones!"

⁴Hear us, O our God, for we are despised. Turn their insults back on their own heads. Give them over as plunder in a land of captivity. ⁵Do not cover up their guilt or blot out their sins from your sight, for they have thrown insults in the face of*ᵃ* the builders.

⁶So we rebuilt the wall till all of it reached half its height, for the people worked with all their heart.

⁷But when Sanballat, Tobiah, the Arabs, the Ammonites and the men of Ashdod heard that the repairs to Jerusalem's walls had gone ahead and that the gaps were being closed, they were very angry. ⁸They all plotted together to come and fight against Jerusalem and stir up trouble against it. ⁹But we prayed to our God and posted a guard day and night to meet this threat.

¹⁰Meanwhile, the people in Judah said, "The strength of the laborers is giving out, and there is so much rubble that we cannot rebuild the wall."

¹¹Also our enemies said, "Before they know it or see us, we will be right there among them and will kill them and put an end to the work."

¹²Then the Jews who lived near them came and told us ten times over, "Wherever you turn, they will attack us."

¹³Therefore I stationed some of the people behind the lowest points of the wall at the exposed places, posting them by families, with their swords, spears and bows. ¹⁴After I looked things over, I stood up and said to the nobles, the officials and the rest of the people, "Don't be afraid of them. Remember the Lord, who is great and awesome, and fight for your brothers, your sons and your daughters, your wives and your homes."

¹⁵When our enemies heard that we were aware of their plot and that God had frustrated it, we all returned to the wall, each to his own work.

¹⁶From that day on, half of my men did the work, while the other half were equipped with spears, shields, bows and armor. The officers posted themselves behind all the people of Judah ¹⁷who were building the wall. Those who carried materials did their work with one hand and held a weapon in the other, ¹⁸and each of the builders wore his sword at his side as he worked. But the man who sounded the trumpet stayed with me.

¹⁹Then I said to the nobles, the officials and the rest of the people, "The work is extensive and spread out, and we are widely separated from each other along the wall. ²⁰Wherever you hear the sound of the trumpet, join us there. Our God will fight for us!"

ᵃ5 Or have provoked you to anger before

²¹So we continued the work with half the men holding spears, from the first light of dawn till the stars came out. ²²At that time I also said to the people, "Have every man and his helper stay inside Jerusalem at night, so they can serve us as guards by night and workmen by day." ²³Neither I nor my brothers nor my men nor the guards with me took off our clothes; each had his weapon, even when he went for water.*

Nehemiah Helps the Poor Now the men and their wives raised a great outcry against their Jewish brothers. ²Some were saying, "We and our sons and daughters are numerous; in order for us to eat and stay alive, we must get grain."

³Others were saying, "We are mortgaging our fields, our vineyards and our homes to get grain during the famine."

⁴Still others were saying, "We have had to borrow money to pay the king's tax on our fields and vineyards. ⁵Although we are of the same flesh and blood as our countrymen and though our sons are as good as theirs, yet we have to subject our sons and daughters to slavery. Some of our daughters have already been enslaved, but we are powerless, because our fields and our vineyards belong to others."

⁶When I heard their outcry and these charges, I was very angry. ⁷I pondered them in my mind and then accused the nobles and officials. I told them, "You are exacting usury from your own countrymen!" So I called together a large meeting to deal with them ⁸and said: "As far as possible, we have bought back our Jewish brothers who were sold to the Gentiles. Now you are selling your brothers, only for them to be sold back to us!" They kept quiet, because they could find nothing to say.

⁹So I continued, "What you are doing is not right. Shouldn't you walk in the fear of our God to avoid the reproach of our Gentile enemies? ¹⁰I and my brothers and my men are also lending the people money and grain. But let the exacting of usury stop! ¹¹Give back to them immediately their fields, vineyards, olive groves and houses, and also the usury you are charging them— the hundredth part of the money, grain, new wine and oil."

¹²"We will give it back," they said. "And we will not demand anything more from them. We will do as you say."

Then I summoned the priests and made the nobles and officials take an oath to do what they had promised. ¹³I also shook out the folds of my robe and said, "In this way may God shake out of his house and possessions every man who does not keep this promise. So may such a man be shaken out and emptied!"

At this the whole assembly said, "Amen," and praised the LORD. And the people did as they had promised.

¹⁴Moreover, from the twentieth year of King Artaxerxes, when I was appointed to be their governor in the land of Judah, until his thirty-second year—twelve years—neither I nor my brothers ate the food allotted to the governor. ¹⁵But the

SEE NEHEMIAH 4:16-18

*23 The meaning of the Hebrew for this clause is uncertain.

earlier governors—those preceding me—placed a heavy burden on the people and took forty shekels[a] of silver from them in addition to food and wine. Their assistants also lorded it over the people. But out of reverence for God I did not act like that. [16]Instead, I devoted myself to the work on this wall. All my men were assembled there for the work; we[b] did not acquire any land.

[17]Furthermore, a hundred and fifty Jews and officials ate at my table, as well as those who came to us from the surrounding nations. [18]Each day one ox, six choice sheep and some poultry were prepared for me, and every ten days an abundant supply of wine of all kinds. In spite of all this, I never demanded the food allotted to the governor, because the demands were heavy on these people.

[19]Remember me with favor, O my God, for all I have done for these people.

6 *Further Opposition to the Rebuilding* When word came to Sanballat, Tobiah, Geshem the Arab and the rest of our enemies that I had rebuilt the wall and not a gap was left in it—though up to that time I had not set the doors in the gates— [2]Sanballat and Geshem sent me this message: "Come, let us meet together in one of the villages[c] on the plain of Ono."

But they were scheming to harm me; [3]so I sent messengers to them with this reply: "I am carrying on a great project and cannot go down. Why should the work stop while I leave it and go down to you?" [4]Four times they sent me the same message, and each time I gave them the same answer.

[5]Then, the fifth time, Sanballat sent his aide to me with the same message, and in his hand was an unsealed letter [6]in which was written:

"It is reported among the nations—and Geshem[d] says it is true—that you and the Jews are plotting to revolt, and therefore you are building the wall. Moreover, according to these reports you are about to become their king [7]and have even appointed prophets to make this proclamation about you in Jerusalem: 'There is a king in Judah!' Now this report will get back to the king; so come, let us confer together."

[8]I sent him this reply: "Nothing like what you are saying is happening; you are just making it up out of your head."

[9]They were all trying to frighten us, thinking, "Their hands will get too weak for the work, and it will not be completed."

But I prayed, "Now strengthen my hands."

[10]One day I went to the house of Shemaiah son of Delaiah, the son of Mehetabel, who was shut in at his home. He said, "Let us meet in the house of God, inside the temple, and let us close the temple doors, because men are coming to kill you—by night they are coming to kill you."

[11]But I said, "Should a man like me run away? Or should one like me go into the temple to save his life? I will not go!" [12]I realized that God had not sent him, but that he had

---

NEHEMIAH 6:11

Have you ever looked in the mirror and thought to yourself, "I am so ugly"? Or have you done something at school and later in the day thought, "I am such a jerk"? Most people, both adults and teens, at times have trouble dealing with their self-image. Nehemiah had a strong, positive self-image. He wasn't about to be frightened into doing something he knew was wrong. Wouldn't it be great to have such a strong self-image that you would do what's right no matter what? Nehemiah wasn't born with a strong self-image. He developed it by making right choices. If you want a strong, positive self-image, you can build one the same way.

Direct Line

---

[a]15 That is, about 1 pound (about 0.5 kilogram)   [b]16 Most Hebrew manuscripts; some Hebrew manuscripts, Septuagint, Vulgate and Syriac I   [c]2 Or *in Kephirim*   [d]6 Hebrew *Gashmu,* a variant of *Geshem*

prophesied against me because Tobiah and Sanballat had hired him. ¹³He had been hired to intimidate me so that I would commit a sin by doing this, and then they would give me a bad name to discredit me.

¹⁴Remember Tobiah and Sanballat, O my God, because of what they have done; remember also the prophetess Noadiah and the rest of the prophets who have been trying to intimidate me.

The Completion of the Wall ¹⁵So the wall was completed on the twenty-fifth of Elul, in fifty-two days. ¹⁶When all our enemies heard about this, all the surrounding nations were afraid and lost their self-confidence, because they realized that this work had been done with the help of our God.

¹⁷Also, in those days the nobles of Judah were sending many letters to Tobiah, and replies from Tobiah kept coming to them. ¹⁸For many in Judah were under oath to him, since he was son-in-law to Shecaniah son of Arah, and his son Jehohanan had married the daughter of Meshullam son of Berekiah. ¹⁹Moreover, they kept reporting to me his good deeds and then telling him what I said. And Tobiah sent letters to intimidate me.

After the wall had been rebuilt and I had set the doors in place, the gatekeepers and the singers and the Levites were appointed. ²I put in charge of Jerusalem my brother Hanani, along with*ᵃ* Hananiah the commander of the citadel, because he was a man of integrity and feared God more than most men do. ³I said to them, "The gates of Jerusalem are not to be opened until the sun is hot. While the gatekeepers are still on duty, have them shut the doors and bar them. Also appoint residents of Jerusalem as guards, some at their posts and some near their own houses."

The List of the Exiles Who Returned ⁴Now the city was large and spacious, but there were few people in it, and the houses had not yet been rebuilt. ⁵So my God put it into my heart to assemble the nobles, the officials and the common people for registration by families. I found the genealogical record of those who had been the first to return. This is what I found written there:

⁶These are the people of the province who came up from the captivity of the exiles whom Nebuchadnezzar king of Babylon had taken captive (they returned to Jerusalem and Judah, each to his own town, ⁷in company with Zerubbabel, Jeshua, Nehemiah, Azariah, Raamiah, Nahamani, Mordecai, Bilshan, Mispereth, Bigvai, Nehum and Baanah):

The list of the men of Israel:

⁸the descendants of Parosh	2,172
⁹of Shephatiah	372
¹⁰of Arah	652
¹¹of Pahath-Moab (through the line of Jeshua and Joab)	2,818
¹²of Elam	1,254
¹³of Zattu	845
¹⁴of Zaccai	760
¹⁵of Binnui	648
¹⁶of Bebai	628
¹⁷of Azgad	2,322
¹⁸of Adonikam	667
¹⁹of Bigvai	2,067
²⁰of Adin	655
²¹of Ater (through Hezekiah)	98

ᵃ2 Or *Hanani, that is,*

22 of Hashum	328
23 of Bezai	324
24 of Hariph	112
25 of Gibeon	95
26 the men of Bethlehem and Netophah	188
27 of Anathoth	128
28 of Beth Azmaveth	42
29 of Kiriath Jearim, Kephirah and Beeroth	743
30 of Ramah and Geba	621
31 of Micmash	122
32 of Bethel and Ai	123
33 of the other Nebo	52
34 of the other Elam	1,254
35 of Harim	320
36 of Jericho	345
37 of Lod, Hadid and Ono	721
38 of Senaah	3,930

39 The priests:

the descendants of Jedaiah (through the family of Jeshua)	973
40 of Immer	1,052
41 of Pashhur	1,247
42 of Harim	1,017

43 The Levites:

the descendants of Jeshua (through Kadmiel through the line of Hodaviah)	74

44 The singers:

the descendants of Asaph	148

45 The gatekeepers:

the descendants of Shallum, Ater, Talmon, Akkub, Hatita and Shobai	138

46 The temple servants:

the descendants of
Ziha, Hasupha, Tabbaoth,
47 Keros, Sia, Padon,
48 Lebana, Hagaba, Shalmai,
49 Hanan, Giddel, Gahar,
50 Reaiah, Rezin, Nekoda,
51 Gazzam, Uzza, Paseah,
52 Besai, Meunim, Nephussim,
53 Bakbuk, Hakupha, Harhur,
54 Bazluth, Mehida, Harsha,
55 Barkos, Sisera, Temah,
56 Neziah and Hatipha

57 The descendants of the servants of Solomon:

the descendants of
Sotai, Sophereth, Perida,
58 Jaala, Darkon, Giddel,
59 Shephatiah, Hattil,
Pokereth-Hazzebaim and Amon

⁶⁰ The temple servants and the descendants of the
servants of Solomon   392

⁶¹The following came up from the towns of Tel Melah, Tel Harsha, Kerub, Addon and Immer, but they could not show that their families were descended from Israel:

⁶² the descendants of
Delaiah, Tobiah and Nekoda   642

⁶³And from among the priests:

the descendants of
Hobaiah, Hakkoz and Barzillai (a man who had married
a daughter of Barzillai the Gileadite and was called by
that name).

⁶⁴These searched for their family records, but they could not find them and so were excluded from the priesthood as unclean. ⁶⁵The governor, therefore, ordered them not to eat any of the most sacred food until there should be a priest ministering with the Urim and Thummim.

⁶⁶The whole company numbered 42,360, ⁶⁷besides their 7,337 menservants and maidservants; and they also had 245 men and women singers. ⁶⁸There were 736 horses, 245 mules,^a ⁶⁹435 camels and 6,720 donkeys.

⁷⁰Some of the heads of the families contributed to the work. The governor gave to the treasury 1,000 drachmas^b of gold, 50 bowls and 530 garments for priests. ⁷¹Some of the heads of the families gave to the treasury for the work 20,000 drachmas^c of gold and 2,200 minas^d of silver. ⁷²The total given by the rest of the people was 20,000 drachmas of gold, 2,000 minas^e of silver and 67 garments for priests.

⁷³The priests, the Levites, the gatekeepers, the singers and the temple servants, along with certain of the people and the rest of the Israelites, settled in their own towns.

Ezra Reads the Law When the seventh month came and the Israelites had settled in their towns, ¹all the people assembled as one man in the square before the Water Gate. They told Ezra the scribe to bring out the Book of the Law of Moses, which the LORD had commanded for Israel.

²So on the first day of the seventh month Ezra the priest brought the Law before the assembly, which was made up of men and women and all who were able to understand. ³He read it aloud from daybreak till noon as he faced the square before the Water Gate in the presence of the men, women and others who could understand. And all the people listened attentively to the Book of the Law.

⁴Ezra the scribe stood on a high wooden platform built for the occasion. Beside him on his right stood Mattithiah, Shema, Anaiah, Uriah, Hilkiah and Maaseiah; and on his left were Pedaiah, Mishael, Malkijah, Hashum, Hashbaddanah, Zechariah and Meshullam.

⁵Ezra opened the book. All the people could see him because he was standing above them; and as he opened it, the people all stood up. ⁶Ezra praised the LORD, the great God; and all the people lifted their hands and responded, "Amen! Amen!" Then they bowed down and worshiped the LORD with their faces to the ground.

⁷The Levites—Jeshua, Bani, Sherebiah, Jamin, Akkub, Shabbethai, Hodiah,

---

^a68 Some Hebrew manuscripts (see also Ezra 2:66); most Hebrew manuscripts do not have this verse. ^b70 That is, about 19 pounds (about 8.5 kilograms) ^c71 That is, about 375 pounds (about 170 kilograms); also in verse 72 ^d71 That is, about 1 1/3 tons (about 1.2 metric tons) ^e72 That is, about 1 1/4 tons (about 1.1 metric tons)

Maaseiah, Kelita, Azariah, Jozabad, Hanan and Pelaiah—instructed the people in the Law while the people were standing there. [8]They read from the Book of the Law of God, making it clear[a] and giving the meaning so that the people could understand what was being read.

[9]Then Nehemiah the governor, Ezra the priest and scribe, and the Levites who were instructing the people said to them all, "This day is sacred to the LORD your God. Do not mourn or weep." For all the people had been weeping as they listened to the words of the Law.

[10]Nehemiah said, "Go and enjoy choice food and sweet drinks, and send some to those who have nothing prepared. This day is sacred to our Lord. Do not grieve, for the joy of the LORD is your strength."

[11]The Levites calmed all the people, saying, "Be still, for this is a sacred day. Do not grieve."

[12]Then all the people went away to eat and drink, to send portions of food and to celebrate with great joy, because they now understood the words that had been made known to them.

[13]On the second day of the month, the heads of all the families, along with the priests and the Levites, gathered around Ezra the scribe to give attention to the words of the Law. [14]They found written in the Law, which the LORD had commanded through Moses, that the Israelites were to live in booths during the feast of the seventh month [15]and that they should proclaim this word and spread it throughout their towns and in Jerusalem: "Go out into the hill country and bring back branches from olive and wild olive trees, and from myrtles, palms and shade trees, to make booths"—as it is written.[b]

[16]So the people went out and brought back branches and built themselves booths on their own roofs, in their courtyards, in the courts of the house of God and in the square by the Water Gate and the one by the Gate of Ephraim. [17]The whole company that had returned from exile built booths and lived in them. From the days of Joshua son of Nun until that day, the Israelites had not celebrated it like this. And their joy was very great.

[18]Day after day, from the first day to the last, Ezra read from the Book of the Law of God. They celebrated the feast for seven days, and on the eighth day, in accordance with the regulation, there was an assembly.

The Israelites Confess Their Sins

9 On the twenty-fourth day of the same month, the Israelites gathered together, fasting and wearing sackcloth and having dust on their heads. [2]Those of Israelite descent had separated themselves from all foreigners. They stood in their places and confessed their sins and the wickedness of their fathers. [3]They stood where they were and read from the Book of the Law of the LORD their God for a quarter of the day, and spent another quarter in confession and in worshiping the LORD their God. [4]Standing on the stairs were the Levites—Jeshua, Bani, Kadmiel, Shebaniah, Bunni, Sherebiah, Bani and Kenani—who called with loud voices to the LORD their God. [5]And the Levites—Jeshua, Kadmiel, Bani, Hashab-

[a]8 Or *God, translating it*   [b]15 See Lev. 23:37-40.

NEHEMIAH 8:10

How would you describe a good time? What would you do? Who would you do it with? Think about it for a minute—what's the most fun thing you can think of to do? Fun! Just because you're a Christian doesn't mean you aren't supposed to have fun. Sure there are some activities you shouldn't participate in, but there are plenty of things you *can* do. Nehemiah told his people, "Go and enjoy choice food and sweet drinks." Par-tay! Have a good time and enjoy yourselves, for "this day is sacred to our Lord." Don't ever apologize for having a good time. God has given you life. Celebrate it, and enjoy God's good gifts.

Direct Line

neiah, Sherebiah, Hodiah, Shebaniah and Pethahiah—said: "Stand up and praise the LORD your God, who is from everlasting to everlasting.*"

"Blessed be your glorious name, and may it be exalted above all blessing and praise. [6]You alone are the LORD. You made the heavens, even the highest heavens, and all their starry host, the earth and all that is on it, the seas and all that is in them. You give life to everything, and the multitudes of heaven worship you.

[7]"You are the LORD God, who chose Abram and brought him out of Ur of the Chaldeans and named him Abraham. [8]You found his heart faithful to you, and you made a covenant with him to give to his descendants the land of the Canaanites, Hittites, Amorites, Perizzites, Jebusites and Girgashites. You have kept your promise because you are righteous.

[9]"You saw the suffering of our forefathers in Egypt; you heard their cry at the Red Sea.[b] [10]You sent miraculous signs and wonders against Pharaoh, against all his officials and all the people of his land, for you knew how arrogantly the Egyptians treated them. You made a name for yourself, which remains to this day. [11]You divided the sea before them, so that they passed through it on dry ground, but you hurled their pursuers into the depths, like a stone into mighty waters. [12]By day you led them with a pillar of cloud, and by night with a pillar of fire to give them light on the way they were to take.

[13]"You came down on Mount Sinai; you spoke to them from heaven. You gave them regulations and laws that are just and right, and decrees and commands that are good. [14]You made known to them your holy Sabbath and gave them commands, decrees and laws through your servant Moses. [15]In their hunger you gave them bread from heaven and in their thirst you brought them water from the rock; you told them to go in and take possession of the land you had sworn with uplifted hand to give them.

[16]"But they, our forefathers, became arrogant and stiff-necked, and did not obey your commands. [17]They refused to listen and failed to remember the miracles you performed among them. They became stiff-necked and in their rebellion appointed a leader in order to return to their slavery. But you are a forgiving God, gracious and compassionate, slow to anger and abounding in love. Therefore you did not desert them, [18]even when they cast for themselves an image of a calf and said, 'This is your god, who brought you up out of Egypt,' or when they committed awful blasphemies.

[19]"Because of your great compassion you did not abandon them in the desert. By day the pillar of cloud did not cease to guide them on their path, nor the pillar of fire by night to shine on the way they were to take. [20]You gave your good Spirit to instruct them. You did not withhold your manna from their mouths, and you gave them water for their thirst. [21]For forty years you sustained them in the desert; they lacked nothing, their clothes did not wear out nor did their feet become swollen.

[22]"You gave them kingdoms and nations, allotting to them even the remotest frontiers. They took over the country of Sihon[c] king of Heshbon and the country of Og king of Bashan. [23]You made their sons as numerous as the stars in the sky, and you brought them into the land that you told their fathers to enter and possess. [24]Their sons went in and took possession of the land. You subdued before them the Canaanites, who lived in the land; you handed the Canaanites over to them, along with their kings and the peoples of the land, to deal with them as they

---

[a]5 Or *God for ever and ever*   [b]9 Hebrew *Yam Suph*; that is, Sea of Reeds   [c]22 One Hebrew manuscript and Septuagint; most Hebrew manuscripts *Sihon, that is, the country of the*

pleased. 25They captured fortified cities and fertile land; they took possession of houses filled with all kinds of good things, wells already dug, vineyards, olive groves and fruit trees in abundance. They ate to the full and were well-nourished; they reveled in your great goodness.

26"But they were disobedient and rebelled against you; they put your law behind their backs. They killed your prophets, who had admonished them in order to turn them back to you; they committed awful blasphemies. 27So you handed them over to their enemies, who oppressed them. But when they were oppressed they cried out to you. From heaven you heard them, and in your great compassion you gave them deliverers, who rescued them from the hand of their enemies.

28"But as soon as they were at rest, they again did what was evil in your sight. Then you abandoned them to the hand of their enemies so that they ruled over them. And when they cried out to you again, you heard from heaven, and in your compassion you delivered them time after time.

29"You warned them to return to your law, but they became arrogant and disobeyed your commands. They sinned against your ordinances, by which a man will live if he obeys them. Stubbornly they turned their backs on you, became stiff-necked and refused to listen. 30For many years you were patient with them. By your Spirit you admonished them through your prophets. Yet they paid no attention, so you handed them over to the neighboring peoples. 31But in your great mercy you did not put an end to them or abandon them, for you are a gracious and merciful God.

32"Now therefore, O our God, the great, mighty and awesome God, who keeps his covenant of love, do not let all this hardship seem trifling in your eyes—the hardship that has come upon us, upon our kings and leaders, upon our priests and prophets, upon our fathers and all your people, from the days of the kings of Assyria until today. 33In all that has happened to us, you have been just; you have acted faithfully, while we did wrong. 34Our kings, our leaders, our priests and our fathers did not follow your law; they did not pay attention to your commands or the warnings you gave them. 35Even while they were in their kingdom, enjoying your great goodness to them in the spacious and fertile land you gave them, they did not serve you or turn from their evil ways.

36"But see, we are slaves today, slaves in the land you gave our forefathers so they could eat its fruit and the other good things it produces. 37Because of our sins, its abundant harvest goes to the kings you have placed over us. They rule over our bodies and our cattle as they please. We are in great distress.

The Agreement of the People 38"In view of all this, we are making a binding agreement, putting it in writing, and our leaders, our Levites and our priests are affixing their seals to it."

10 Those who sealed it were:

Nehemiah the governor, the son of Hacaliah.

Zedekiah, 2Seraiah, Azariah, Jeremiah,
3Pashhur, Amariah, Malkijah,
4Hattush, Shebaniah, Malluch,
5Harim, Meremoth, Obadiah,
6Daniel, Ginnethon, Baruch,
7Meshullam, Abijah, Mijamin,
8Maaziah, Bilgai and Shemaiah.
These were the priests.

⁹The Levites:

Jeshua son of Azaniah, Binnui of the sons of Henadad, Kadmiel,
¹⁰and their associates: Shebaniah,
Hodiah, Kelita, Pelaiah, Hanan,
¹¹Mica, Rehob, Hashabiah,
¹²Zaccur, Sherebiah, Shebaniah,
¹³Hodiah, Bani and Beninu.

¹⁴The leaders of the people:

Parosh, Pahath-Moab, Elam, Zattu, Bani,
¹⁵Bunni, Azgad, Bebai,
¹⁶Adonijah, Bigvai, Adin,
¹⁷Ater, Hezekiah, Azzur,
¹⁸Hodiah, Hashum, Bezai,
¹⁹Hariph, Anathoth, Nebai,
²⁰Magpiash, Meshullam, Hezir,
²¹Meshezabel, Zadok, Jaddua,
²²Pelatiah, Hanan, Anaiah,
²³Hoshea, Hananiah, Hasshub,
²⁴Hallohesh, Pilha, Shobek,
²⁵Rehum, Hashabnah, Maaseiah,
²⁶Ahiah, Hanan, Anan,
²⁷Malluch, Harim and Baanah.

²⁸"The rest of the people—priests, Levites, gatekeepers, singers, temple servants and all who separated themselves from the neighboring peoples for the sake of the Law of God, together with their wives and all their sons and daughters who are able to understand— ²⁹all these now join their brothers the nobles, and bind themselves with a curse and an oath to follow the Law of God given through Moses the servant of God and to obey carefully all the commands, regulations and decrees of the LORD our Lord.

³⁰"We promise not to give our daughters in marriage to the peoples around us or take their daughters for our sons.

³¹"When the neighboring peoples bring merchandise or grain to sell on the Sabbath, we will not buy from them on the Sabbath or on any holy day. Every seventh year we will forgo working the land and will cancel all debts.

³²"We assume the responsibility for carrying out the commands to give a third of a shekel*a* each year for the service of the house of our God: ³³for the bread set out on the table; for the regular grain offerings and burnt offerings; for the offerings on the Sabbaths, New Moon festivals and appointed feasts; for the holy offerings; for sin offerings to make atonement for Israel; and for all the duties of the house of our God.

Direct Line

NEHEMIAH 10:28-39

New Year's resolutions are kind of a joke. Give up candy? Sure. Do your homework right away—all of it? You bet. Of course, you know those resolutions will be broken by January 2! There's another kind of resolution you're more likely to keep. You make a bad mistake, and you say, "Boy, I won't do that again." You hurt a friend, and you say, "I'm sorry, I'll never do it again." The mistakes made you feel bad, and you resolved not to make them again. Nehemiah 10:28-39 lists seven resolutions the people of Judah made because of past mistakes. Now think of mistakes you've made. What personal resolutions will you make to avoid them in the future?

a32 That is, about 1/8 ounce (about 4 grams)

34"We—the priests, the Levites and the people—have cast lots to determine when each of our families is to bring to the house of our God at set times each year a contribution of wood to burn on the altar of the LORD our God, as it is written in the Law.

35"We also assume responsibility for bringing to the house of the LORD each year the firstfruits of our crops and of every fruit tree.

36"As it is also written in the Law, we will bring the firstborn of our sons and of our cattle, of our herds and of our flocks to the house of our God, to the priests ministering there.

37"Moreover, we will bring to the storerooms of the house of our God, to the priests, the first of our ground meal, of our ˌgrainˌ offerings, of the fruit of all our trees and of our new wine and oil. And we will bring a tithe of our crops to the Levites, for it is the Levites who collect the tithes in all the towns where we work. 38A priest descended from Aaron is to accompany the Levites when they receive the tithes, and the Levites are to bring a tenth of the tithes up to the house of our God, to the storerooms of the treasury. 39The people of Israel, including the Levites, are to bring their contributions of grain, new wine and oil to the storerooms where the articles for the sanctuary are kept and where the ministering priests, the gatekeepers and the singers stay.

"We will not neglect the house of our God."

11 *The New Residents of Jerusalem* Now the leaders of the people settled in Jerusalem, and the rest of the people cast lots to bring one out of every ten to live in Jerusalem, the holy city, while the remaining nine were to stay in their own towns. 2The people commended all the men who volunteered to live in Jerusalem.

3These are the provincial leaders who settled in Jerusalem (now some Israelites, priests, Levites, temple servants and descendants of Solomon's servants lived in the towns of Judah, each on his own property in the various towns, 4while other people from both Judah and Benjamin lived in Jerusalem):

From the descendants of Judah:

Athaiah son of Uzziah, the son of Zechariah, the son of Amariah, the son of Shephatiah, the son of Mahalalel, a descendant of Perez; 5and Maaseiah son of Baruch, the son of Col-Hozeh, the son of Hazaiah, the son of Adaiah, the son of Joiarib, the son of Zechariah, a descendant of Shelah. 6The descendants of Perez who lived in Jerusalem totaled 468 able men.

7From the descendants of Benjamin:

Sallu son of Meshullam, the son of Joed, the son of Pedaiah, the son of Kolaiah, the son of Maaseiah, the son of Ithiel, the son of Jeshaiah, 8and his followers, Gabbai and Sallai—928 men. 9Joel son of Zicri was their chief officer, and Judah son of Hassenuah was over the Second District of the city.

10From the priests:

Jedaiah; the son of Joiarib; Jakin; 11Seraiah son of Hilkiah, the son of Meshullam, the son of Zadok, the son of Meraioth, the son of Ahitub, supervisor in the house of God, 12and their associates, who carried on work for the temple—822 men; Adaiah son of Jeroham, the son of Pelaliah, the son of Amzi, the son of Zechariah, the son of Pashhur, the son of Malkijah, 13and his associates, who were heads of families—242 men; Amashsai son of Azarel, the son of Ahzai, the son of Meshillemoth, the

NEHEMIAH 11

QUIZZER

Q: How did the returning exiles decide who would live in Jerusalem?

BONUS: Why did they have to do this?

Answers on page 598

son of Immer, [14]and his[a] associates, who were able men—128. Their chief officer was Zabdiel son of Haggedolim.

[15]From the Levites:

Shemaiah son of Hasshub, the son of Azrikam, the son of Hashabiah, the son of Bunni; [16]Shabbethai and Jozabad, two of the heads of the Levites, who had charge of the outside work of the house of God; [17]Mattaniah son of Mica, the son of Zabdi, the son of Asaph, the director who led in thanksgiving and prayer; Bakbukiah, second among his associates; and Abda son of Shammua, the son of Galal, the son of Jeduthun. [18]The Levites in the holy city totaled 284.

[19]The gatekeepers:

Akkub, Talmon and their associates, who kept watch at the gates—172 men.

[20]The rest of the Israelites, with the priests and Levites, were in all the towns of Judah, each on his ancestral property.

Answers

to Quizzer on
page 597

A: They cast lots to bring one out of every ten men to live in Jerusalem (Nehemiah 11:1).

BONUS: Apparently Jerusalem was sparsely populated because many men wanted to settle in their own native towns rather than Jerusalem.

[21]The temple servants lived on the hill of Ophel, and Ziha and Gishpa were in charge of them.

[22]The chief officer of the Levites in Jerusalem was Uzzi son of Bani, the son of Hashabiah, the son of Mattaniah, the son of Mica. Uzzi was one of Asaph's descendants, who were the singers responsible for the service of the house of God. [23]The singers were under the king's orders, which regulated their daily activity.

[24]Pethahiah son of Meshezabel, one of the descendants of Zerah son of Judah, was the king's agent in all affairs relating to the people.

[25]As for the villages with their fields, some of the people of Judah lived in Kiriath Arba and its surrounding settlements, in Dibon and its settlements, in Jekabzeel and its villages, [26]in Jeshua, in Moladah, in Beth Pelet, [27]in Hazar Shual, in Beersheba and its settlements, [28]in Ziklag, in Meconah and its settlements, [29]in En Rimmon, in Zorah, in Jarmuth, [30]Zanoah, Adullam and their villages, in Lachish and its fields, and in Azekah and its settlements. So they were living all the way from Beersheba to the Valley of Hinnom.

[31]The descendants of the Benjamites from Geba lived in Micmash, Aija, Bethel and its settlements, [32]in Anathoth, Nob and Ananiah, [33]in Hazor, Ramah and Gittaim, [34]in Hadid, Zeboim and Neballat, [35]in Lod and Ono, and in the Valley of the Craftsmen.

[36]Some of the divisions of the Levites of Judah settled in Benjamin.

12 ***Priests and Levites*** These were the priests and Levites who returned with Zerubbabel son of Shealtiel and with Jeshua: Seraiah, Jeremiah, Ezra,
[2]Amariah, Malluch, Hattush,
[3]Shecaniah, Rehum, Meremoth,
[4]Iddo, Ginnethon,[b] Abijah,
[5]Mijamin,[c] Moadiah, Bilgah,
[6]Shemaiah, Joiarib, Jedaiah,
[7]Sallu, Amok, Hilkiah and Jedaiah.
These were the leaders of the priests and their associates in the days of Jeshua.

[8]The Levites were Jeshua, Binnui, Kadmiel, Sherebiah, Judah, and also Mattaniah, who, together with his associates, was in charge of the songs of thanksgiving. [9]Bakbukiah and Unni, their associates, stood opposite them in the services.

---

[a]14 Most Septuagint manuscripts; Hebrew *their* [b]4 Many Hebrew manuscripts and Vulgate (see also Neh. 12:16); most Hebrew manuscripts *Ginnethoi* [c]5 A variant of *Miniamin*

¹⁰Jeshua was the father of Joiakim, Joiakim the father of Eliashib, Eliashib the father of Joiada, ¹¹Joiada the father of Jonathan, and Jonathan the father of Jaddua.

¹²In the days of Joiakim, these were the heads of the priestly families:

of Seraiah's family, Meraiah;

of Jeremiah's, Hananiah;

¹³of Ezra's, Meshullam;

of Amariah's, Jehohanan;

¹⁴of Malluch's, Jonathan;

of Shecaniah's,ᵃ Joseph;

¹⁵of Harim's, Adna;

of Meremoth's,ᵇ Helkai;

¹⁶of Iddo's, Zechariah;

of Ginnethon's, Meshullam;

¹⁷of Abijah's, Zicri;

of Miniamin's and of Moadiah's, Piltai;

¹⁸of Bilgah's, Shammua;

of Shemaiah's, Jehonathan;

¹⁹of Joiarib's, Mattenai;

of Jedaiah's, Uzzi;

²⁰of Sallu's, Kallai;

of Amok's, Eber;

²¹of Hilkiah's, Hashabiah;

of Jedaiah's, Nethanel.

²²The family heads of the Levites in the days of Eliashib, Joiada, Johanan and Jaddua, as well as those of the priests, were recorded in the reign of Darius the Persian. ²³The family heads among the descendants of Levi up to the time of Johanan son of Eliashib were recorded in the book of the annals. ²⁴And the leaders of the Levites were Hashabiah, Sherebiah, Jeshua son of Kadmiel, and their associates, who stood opposite them to give praise and thanksgiving, one section responding to the other, as prescribed by David the man of God.

²⁵Mattaniah, Bakbukiah, Obadiah, Meshullam, Talmon and Akkub were gatekeepers who guarded the storerooms at the gates. ²⁶They served in the days of Joiakim son of Jeshua, the son of Jozadak, and in the days of Nehemiah the governor and of Ezra the priest and scribe.

Dedication of the Wall of Jerusalem
²⁷At the dedication of the wall of Jerusalem, the Levites were sought out from where they lived and were brought to Jerusalem to celebrate joyfully the dedication with songs of thanksgiving and with the music of cymbals, harps and lyres. ²⁸The singers also were brought together from the region around Jerusalem—from the villages of the Netophathites, ²⁹from Beth Gilgal, and from the area of Geba and Azmaveth, for the singers had built villages for themselves around Jerusalem. ³⁰When the priests and Levites had purified themselves ceremonially, they purified the people, the gates and the wall.

³¹I had the leaders of Judah go up on topᶜ of the wall. I also assigned two large choirs to give thanks. One was to proceed on topᵈ of the wall to the right, toward the Dung Gate. ³²Hoshaiah and half the leaders of Judah followed them, ³³along with Azariah, Ezra, Meshullam, ³⁴Judah, Benjamin, Shemaiah, Jeremiah, ³⁵as well as some priests with trumpets, and also Zechariah son of Jonathan, the son of Shemaiah, the son of Mattaniah, the son of Micaiah, the son of Zaccur, the son of Asaph, ³⁶and his associates—Shemaiah,

---

ᵃ14 Very many Hebrew manuscripts, some Septuagint manuscripts and Syriac (see also Neh. 12:3); most Hebrew manuscripts *Shebaniah's* ᵇ15 Some Septuagint manuscripts (see also Neh. 12:3); Hebrew *Meraioth's* ᶜ31 Or *go alongside* ᵈ31 Or *proceed alongside*

Azarel, Milalai, Gilalai, Maai, Nethanel, Judah and Hanani—with musical instruments prescribed by David the man of God. Ezra the scribe led the procession. ³⁷At the Fountain Gate they continued directly up the steps of the City of David on the ascent to the wall and passed above the house of David to the Water Gate on the east.

³⁸The second choir proceeded in the opposite direction. I followed them on top*ᵃ* of the wall, together with half the people—past the Tower of the Ovens to the Broad Wall, ³⁹over the Gate of Ephraim, the Jeshanah*ᵇ* Gate, the Fish Gate, the Tower of Hananel and the Tower of the Hundred, as far as the Sheep Gate. At the Gate of the Guard they stopped.

⁴⁰The two choirs that gave thanks then took their places in the house of God; so did I, together with half the officials, ⁴¹as well as the priests—Eliakim, Maaseiah, Miniamin, Micaiah, Elioenai, Zechariah and Hananiah with their trumpets— ⁴²and also Maaseiah, Shemaiah, Eleazar, Uzzi, Jehohanan, Malkijah, Elam and Ezer. The choirs sang under the direction of Jezrahiah. ⁴³And on that day they offered great sacrifices, rejoicing because God had given them great joy. The women and children also rejoiced. The sound of rejoicing in Jerusalem could be heard far away.

⁴⁴At that time men were appointed to be in charge of the storerooms for the contributions, firstfruits and tithes. From the fields around the towns they were to bring into the storerooms the portions required by the Law for the priests and the Levites, for Judah was pleased with the ministering priests and Levites. ⁴⁵They performed the service of their God and the service of purification, as did also the singers and gatekeepers, according to the commands of David and his son Solomon. ⁴⁶For long ago, in the days of David and Asaph, there had been directors for the singers and for the songs of praise and thanksgiving to God. ⁴⁷So in the days of Zerubbabel and of Nehemiah, all Israel contributed the daily portions for the singers and gatekeepers. They also set aside the portion for the other Levites, and the Levites set aside the portion for the descendants of Aaron.

13 *Nehemiah's Final Reforms* On that day the Book of Moses was read aloud in the hearing of the people and there it was found written that no Ammonite or Moabite should ever be admitted into the assembly of God, ²because they had not met the Israelites with food and water but had hired Balaam to call a curse down on them. (Our God, however, turned the curse into a blessing.) ³When the people heard this law, they excluded from Israel all who were of foreign descent.

⁴Before this, Eliashib the priest had been put in charge of the storerooms of the house of our God. He was closely associated with Tobiah, ⁵and he had provided him with a large room formerly used to store the grain offerings and incense and temple articles, and also the tithes of grain, new wine and oil prescribed for the Levites, singers and gatekeepers, as well as the contributions for the priests.

⁶But while all this was going on, I was not in Jerusalem, for in the thirty-second year of Artaxerxes king of Babylon I had returned to the king. Some time later I asked his permission ⁷and came back to Jerusalem. Here I learned about the evil thing Eliashib had done in providing Tobiah a room in the courts of the house of God. ⁸I was greatly displeased and threw all Tobiah's household goods out of the room. ⁹I gave orders to purify the rooms, and then I put back into them the equipment of the house of God, with the grain offerings and the incense.

¹⁰I also learned that the portions assigned to the Levites had not been given to them, and that all the Levites and singers responsible for the ser-

---

ᵃ38 Or them alongside ᵇ39 Or Old

vice had gone back to their own fields. ¹¹So I rebuked the officials and asked them, "Why is the house of God neglected?" Then I called them together and stationed them at their posts.

¹²All Judah brought the tithes of grain, new wine and oil into the storerooms. ¹³I put Shelemiah the priest, Zadok the scribe, and a Levite named Pedaiah in charge of the storerooms and made Hanan son of Zaccur, the son of Mattaniah, their assistant, because these men were considered trustworthy. They were made responsible for distributing the supplies to their brothers.

¹⁴Remember me for this, O my God, and do not blot out what I have so faithfully done for the house of my God and its services.

¹⁵In those days I saw men in Judah treading winepresses on the Sabbath and bringing in grain and loading it on donkeys, together with wine, grapes, figs and all other kinds of loads. And they were bringing all this into Jerusalem on the Sabbath. Therefore I warned them against selling food on that day. ¹⁶Men from Tyre who lived in Jerusalem were bringing in fish and all kinds of merchandise and selling them in Jerusalem on the Sabbath to the people of Judah. ¹⁷I rebuked the nobles of Judah and said to them, "What is this wicked thing you are doing—desecrating the Sabbath day? ¹⁸Didn't your forefathers do the same things, so that our God brought all this calamity upon us and upon this city? Now you are stirring up more wrath against Israel by desecrating the Sabbath."

¹⁹When evening shadows fell on the gates of Jerusalem before the Sabbath, I ordered the doors to be shut and not opened until the Sabbath was over. I stationed some of my own men at the gates so that no load could be brought in on the Sabbath day. ²⁰Once or twice the merchants and sellers of all kinds of goods spent the night outside Jerusalem. ²¹But I warned them and said, "Why do you spend the night by the wall? If you do this again, I will lay hands on you." From that time on they no longer came on the Sabbath. ²²Then I commanded the Levites to purify themselves and go and guard the gates in order to keep the Sabbath day holy.

Remember me for this also, O my God, and show mercy to me according to your great love.

²³Moreover, in those days I saw men of Judah who had married women from Ashdod, Ammon and Moab. ²⁴Half of their children spoke the language of Ashdod or the language of one of the other peoples, and did not know how to speak the language of Judah. ²⁵I rebuked them and called curses down on them. I beat some of the men and pulled out their hair. I made them take an oath in God's name and said: "You are not to give your daughters in marriage to their sons, nor are you to take their daughters in marriage for your sons or for yourselves. ²⁶Was it not because of marriages like these that Solomon king of Israel sinned? Among the many nations there was no king like him. He was loved by his God, and God made him king over all Israel, but even he was led into sin by foreign women. ²⁷Must we hear now that you too are doing all this terrible wickedness and are being unfaithful to our God by marrying foreign women?"

²⁸One of the sons of Joiada son of Eliashib the high priest was son-in-law to Sanballat the Horonite. And I drove him away from me.

²⁹Remember them, O my God, because they defiled the priestly office and the covenant of the priesthood and of the Levites.

³⁰So I purified the priests and the Levites of everything foreign, and assigned them duties, each to his own task. ³¹I also made provision for contributions of wood at designated times, and for the firstfruits.

Remember me with favor, O my God.

MAKING PLANS.

Is God putting your life together according to some plan? Or do you "just happen" to have your looks, your brain, your talents and abilities? You can't look ahead and know what God is preparing you for. But God definitely has something special in mind.

Esther was an orphan, raised by her uncle. Yet she became Queen of Persia and saved an entire nation. God isn't mentioned once in this book named for the orphan queen. But it's clear that God was at work, arranging things behind the scenes, just as he's at work behind the scenes in your life.

FAST FACTS

Esther means "star."

Esther's husband, Xerxes, ruled Persia 486-465 B.C.

Xerxes was known for his bad temper. Esther really was in danger!

Xerxes invaded Europe and was defeated by the Greeks.

Providence is the belief that God guides all that happens.

Fundamentals

Do you suppose it is better to be a woman now than in ancient times (Esther 1)?

Can remaining loyal to God get a person in trouble (Esther 3)?

When others are in trouble, it can be scary to think maybe you ought to help (Esther 4:1-5).

Some people set a trap for others and catch themselves (Esther 7).

Queen Vashti Deposed This is what happened during the time of Xerxes,[a] the Xerxes who ruled over 127 provinces stretching from India to Cush[b]: [2]At that time King Xerxes reigned from his royal throne in the citadel of Susa, [3]and in the third year of his reign he gave a banquet for all his nobles and officials. The military leaders of Persia and Media, the princes, and the nobles of the provinces were present.

[4]For a full 180 days he displayed the vast wealth of his kingdom and the splendor and glory of his majesty. [5]When these days were over, the king gave a banquet, lasting seven days, in the enclosed garden of the king's palace, for all the people from the least to the greatest, who were in the citadel of Susa. [6]The garden had hangings of white and blue linen, fastened with cords of white linen and purple material to silver rings on marble pillars. There were couches of gold and silver on a mosaic pavement of porphyry, marble, mother-of-pearl and other costly stones. [7]Wine was served in goblets of gold, each one different from the other, and the royal wine was abundant, in keeping with the king's liberality. [8]By the king's command each guest was allowed to drink in his own way, for the king instructed all the wine stewards to serve each man what he wished.

[9]Queen Vashti also gave a banquet for the women in the royal palace of King Xerxes.

[10]On the seventh day, when King Xerxes was in high spirits from wine, he commanded the seven eunuchs who served him—Mehuman, Biztha, Harbona, Bigtha, Abagtha, Zethar and Carcas— [11]to bring before him Queen Vashti, wearing her royal crown, in order to display her beauty to the people and nobles, for she was lovely to look at. [12]But when the attendants delivered the king's command, Queen Vashti refused to come. Then the king became furious and burned with anger.

[13]Since it was customary for the king to consult experts in matters of law and justice, he spoke with the wise men who understood the times [14]and were closest to the king—Carshena, Shethar, Admatha, Tarshish, Meres, Marsena and Memucan, the seven nobles of Persia and Media who had special access to the king and were highest in the kingdom.

[15]"According to law, what must be done to Queen Vashti?" he asked. "She has not obeyed the command of King Xerxes that the eunuchs have taken to her."

[16]Then Memucan replied in the presence of the king and the nobles, "Queen Vashti has done wrong, not only against the king but also against all the nobles and the peoples of all the provinces of King Xerxes. [17]For the queen's conduct will become known to all the women, and so they will despise their husbands and say, 'King Xerxes commanded Queen Vashti to be brought before him, but she would not come.' [18]This very day the Persian and Median women of the nobility who have heard about the queen's conduct will respond to all the king's nobles in the same way. There will be no end of disrespect and discord.

[19]"Therefore, if it pleases the king, let him issue a royal decree and let it be written in the laws of Persia and Media, which cannot be repealed, that Vashti is never again to enter the presence of King Xerxes. Also let the king give her royal position to someone else who is better than she. [20]Then when the king's edict is proclaimed throughout all his vast realm, all the women will respect their husbands, from the least to the greatest."

[21]The king and his nobles were pleased with this advice, so the king did as

ESTHER 1

QU?ZER

Q: Who was one of the first women's rights advocates?

BONUS: What happened to her?

Answers on page 604

[a]1 Hebrew *Ahasuerus*, a variant of Xerxes' Persian name; here and throughout Esther   [b]1 That is, the upper Nile region

Memucan proposed. [22]He sent dispatches to all parts of the kingdom, to each province in its own script and to each people in its own language, proclaiming in each people's tongue that every man should be ruler over his own household.

Esther Made Queen Later when the anger of King Xerxes had subsided, he remembered Vashti and what she had done and what he had decreed about her. [2]Then the king's personal attendants proposed, "Let a search be made for beautiful young virgins for the king. [3]Let the king appoint commissioners in every province of his realm to bring all these beautiful girls into the harem at the citadel of Susa. Let them be placed under the care of Hegai, the king's eunuch, who is in charge of the women; and let beauty treatments be given to them. [4]Then let the girl who pleases the king be queen instead of Vashti." This advice appealed to the king, and he followed it.

[5]Now there was in the citadel of Susa a Jew of the tribe of Benjamin, named Mordecai son of Jair, the son of Shimei, the son of Kish, [6]who had been carried into exile from Jerusalem by Nebuchadnezzar king of Babylon, among those taken captive with Jehoiachin[a] king of Judah. [7]Mordecai had a cousin named Hadassah, whom he had brought up because she had neither father nor mother. This girl, who was also known as Esther, was lovely in form and features, and Mordecai had taken her as his own daughter when her father and mother died.

Answers
*to Quizzer on
page 603*

A: Vashti, the
Queen of Persia,
who refused her
husband Xerxes'
command to
show off her
beauty (Esther
1:10-12).

*BONUS: Xerxes
divorced her.*

[8]When the king's order and edict had been proclaimed, many girls were brought to the citadel of Susa and put under the care of Hegai. Esther also was taken to the king's palace and entrusted to Hegai, who had charge of the harem. [9]The girl pleased him and won his favor. Immediately he provided her with her beauty treatments and special food. He assigned to her seven maids selected from the king's palace and moved her and her maids into the best place in the harem.

[10]Esther had not revealed her nationality and family background, because Mordecai had forbidden her to do so. [11]Every day he walked back and forth near the courtyard of the harem to find out how Esther was and what was happening to her.

[12]Before a girl's turn came to go in to King Xerxes, she had to complete twelve months of beauty treatments prescribed for the women, six months with oil of myrrh and six with perfumes and cosmetics. [13]And this is how she would go to the king: Anything she wanted was given her to take with her from the harem to the king's palace. [14]In the evening she would go there and in the morning return to another part of the harem to the care of Shaashgaz, the king's eunuch who was in charge of the concubines. She would not return to the king unless he was pleased with her and summoned her by name.

[15]When the turn came for Esther (the girl Mordecai had adopted, the daughter of his uncle Abihail) to go to the king, she asked for nothing other than what Hegai, the king's eunuch who was in charge of the harem, suggested. And Esther won the favor of everyone who saw her. [16]She was taken to King Xerxes in the royal residence in the tenth month, the month of Tebeth, in the seventh year of his reign.

[17]Now the king was attracted to Esther more than to any of the other women, and she won his favor and approval more than any of the other virgins. So he set a royal crown on her head and made her queen instead of Vashti. [18]And the king gave a great banquet, Esther's banquet, for all his nobles and officials. He proclaimed a holiday throughout the provinces and distributed gifts with royal liberality.

---

[a]6 Hebrew *Jeconiah*, a variant of *Jehoiachin*

Mordecai Uncovers a Conspiracy ¹⁹When the virgins were assembled a second time, Mordecai was sitting at the king's gate. ²⁰But Esther had kept secret her family background and nationality just as Mordecai had told her to do, for she continued to follow Mordecai's instructions as she had done when he was bringing her up.

²¹During the time Mordecai was sitting at the king's gate, Bigthana*a* and Teresh, two of the king's officers who guarded the doorway, became angry and conspired to assassinate King Xerxes. ²²But Mordecai found out about the plot and told Queen Esther, who in turn reported it to the king, giving credit to Mordecai. ²³And when the report was investigated and found to be true, the two officials were hanged on a gallows.*b* All this was recorded in the book of the annals in the presence of the king.

Haman's Plot to Destroy the Jews After these events, King Xerxes honored Haman son of Hammedatha, the Agagite, elevating him and giving him a seat of honor higher than that of all the other nobles. ²All the royal officials at the king's gate knelt down and paid honor to Haman, for the king had commanded this concerning him. But Mordecai would not kneel down or pay him honor.

³Then the royal officials at the king's gate asked Mordecai, "Why do you disobey the king's command?" ⁴Day after day they spoke to him but he refused to comply. Therefore they told Haman about it to see whether Mordecai's behavior would be tolerated, for he had told them he was a Jew.

⁵When Haman saw that Mordecai would not kneel down or pay him honor, he was enraged. ⁶Yet having learned who Mordecai's people were, he scorned the idea of killing only Mordecai. Instead Haman looked for a way to destroy all Mordecai's people, the Jews, throughout the whole kingdom of Xerxes.

⁷In the twelfth year of King Xerxes, in the first month, the month of Nisan, they cast the *pur* (that is, the lot) in the presence of Haman to select a day and month. And the lot fell on*c* the twelfth month, the month of Adar.

⁸Then Haman said to King Xerxes, "There is a certain people dispersed and scattered among the peoples in all the provinces of your kingdom whose customs are different from those of all other people and who do not obey the king's laws; it is not in the king's best interest to tolerate them. ⁹If it pleases the king, let a decree be issued to destroy them, and I will put ten thousand talents*d* of silver into the royal treasury for the men who carry out this business."

¹⁰So the king took his signet ring from his finger and gave it to Haman son of Hammedatha, the Agagite, the enemy of the Jews. ¹¹"Keep the money," the king said to Haman, "and do with the people as you please."

¹²Then on the thirteenth day of the first month the royal secretaries were sum-

---

ESTHER 3:1–6

Have you ever noticed that some friends get over being mad at you quickly? Then there are others who get mad and hold a grudge for days or weeks. Their pride is hurt, and they're not about to forgive you. The pagan official Haman was like that. He thought the Jew Mordecai had insulted him, and he held such a grudge that he plotted to wipe out the whole Jewish race. He didn't succeed, but holding that grudge was the sign of a hateful and wicked man. Aren't you glad God doesn't hold grudges when you do something wrong? God is eager to forgive. And God is eager for his people to follow his example of forgiveness and to not hold grudges.

Direct Line

---

*a*21 Hebrew *Bigthan,* a variant of *Bigthana*   *b*23 Or *were hung* (or *impaled*) *on poles;* similarly elsewhere in Esther
*c*7 Septuagint; Hebrew does not have *And the lot fell on.*
*d*9 That is, about 375 tons (about 345 metric tons)

moned. They wrote out in the script of each province and in the language of each people all Haman's orders to the king's satraps, the governors of the various provinces and the nobles of the various peoples. These were written in the name of King Xerxes himself and sealed with his own ring. ¹³Dispatches were sent by couriers to all the king's provinces with the order to destroy, kill and annihilate all the Jews—young and old, women and little children—on a single day, the thirteenth day of the twelfth month, the month of Adar, and to plunder their goods. ¹⁴A copy of the text of the edict was to be issued as law in every province and made known to the people of every nationality so they would be ready for that day.

¹⁵Spurred on by the king's command, the couriers went out, and the edict was issued in the citadel of Susa. The king and Haman sat down to drink, but the city of Susa was bewildered.

Mordecai Persuades Esther to Help When Mordecai learned of all that had been done, he tore his clothes, put on sackcloth and ashes, and went out into the city, wailing loudly and bitterly. ²But he went only as far as the king's gate, because no one clothed in sackcloth was allowed to enter it. ³In every province to which the edict and order of the king came, there was great mourning among the Jews, with fasting, weeping and wailing. Many lay in sackcloth and ashes.

⁴When Esther's maids and eunuchs came and told her about Mordecai, she was in great distress. She sent clothes for him to put on instead of his sackcloth, but he would not accept them. ⁵Then Esther summoned Hathach, one of the king's eunuchs assigned to attend her, and ordered him to find out what was troubling Mordecai and why.

⁶So Hathach went out to Mordecai in the open square of the city in front of the king's gate. ⁷Mordecai told him everything that had happened to him, including the exact amount of money Haman had promised to pay into the royal treasury for the destruction of the Jews. ⁸He also gave him a copy of the text of the edict for their annihilation, which had been published in Susa, to show to Esther and explain it to her, and he told him to urge her to go into the king's presence to beg for mercy and plead with him for her people.

⁹Hathach went back and reported to Esther what Mordecai had said. ¹⁰Then she instructed him to say to Mordecai, ¹¹"All the king's officials and the people of the royal provinces know that for any man or woman who approaches the king in the inner court without being summoned the king has but one law: that he be put to death. The only exception to this is for the king to extend the gold scepter to him and spare his life. But thirty days have passed since I was called to go to the king."

¹²When Esther's words were reported to Mordecai, ¹³he sent back this answer: "Do not think that because you are in the king's house you alone of all the Jews will escape. ¹⁴For if you remain silent at this time, relief and deliverance for the Jews will arise from another place, but you and your father's family will perish. And who

ESTHER 4

Three big bullies are pushing around a little kid. You feel like you ought to step in. But it's scary. So you . . . Queen Esther was frightened when her Uncle Mordecai asked her to see the king about Haman's plot. King Xerxes was unpredictable. If Esther went to see him uninvited, she might very well be killed! Mordecai had an answer for her: "Who knows but that you have come to royal position for such a time as this?" (Esther 4:14). Did God make Esther queen so she could step in and help? Ask yourself the same thing the next time you feel you ought to speak up but are afraid. Maybe God put you in that situation just so you could help.

Direct Line

knows but that you have come to royal position for such a time as this?" ¹⁵Then Esther sent this reply to Mordecai: ¹⁶"Go, gather together all the Jews who are in Susa, and fast for me. Do not eat or drink for three days, night or day. I and my maids will fast as you do. When this is done, I will go to the king, even though it is against the law. And if I perish, I perish." ¹⁷So Mordecai went away and carried out all of Esther's instructions.

Esther's Request to the King   On the third day Esther put on her royal robes and stood in the inner court of the palace, in front of the king's hall. The king was sitting on his royal throne in the hall, facing the entrance. ²When he saw Queen Esther standing in the court, he was pleased with her and held out to her the gold scepter that was in his hand. So Esther approached and touched the tip of the scepter.

³Then the king asked, "What is it, Queen Esther? What is your request? Even up to half the kingdom, it will be given you."

⁴"If it pleases the king," replied Esther, "let the king, together with Haman, come today to a banquet I have prepared for him."

⁵"Bring Haman at once," the king said, "so that we may do what Esther asks."

So the king and Haman went to the banquet Esther had prepared. ⁶As they were drinking wine, the king again asked Esther, "Now what is your petition? It will be given you. And what is your request? Even up to half the kingdom, it will be granted."

⁷Esther replied, "My petition and my request is this: ⁸If the king regards me with favor and if it pleases the king to grant my petition and fulfill my request, let the king and Haman come tomorrow to the banquet I will prepare for them. Then I will answer the king's question."

Haman's Rage Against Mordecai   ⁹Haman went out that day happy and in high spirits. But when he saw Mordecai at the king's gate and observed that he neither rose nor showed fear in his presence, he was filled with rage against Mordecai. ¹⁰Nevertheless, Haman restrained himself and went home.

Calling together his friends and Zeresh, his wife, ¹¹Haman boasted to them about his vast wealth, his many sons, and all the ways the king had honored him and how he had elevated him above the other nobles and officials. ¹²"And that's not all," Haman added. "I'm the only person Queen Esther invited to accompany the king to the banquet she gave. And she has invited me along with the king tomorrow. ¹³But all this gives me no satisfaction as long as I see that Jew Mordecai sitting at the king's gate."

¹⁴His wife Zeresh and all his friends said to him, "Have a gallows built, seventy-five feet*ᵃ* high, and ask the king in the morning to have Mordecai hanged on it. Then go with the king to the dinner and be happy." This suggestion delighted Haman, and he had the gallows built.

Mordecai Honored   That night the king could not sleep; so he ordered the book of the chronicles, the record of his reign, to be brought in and read to him. ²It was found recorded there that Mordecai had exposed Bigthana and Teresh, two of the king's officers who guarded the doorway, who had conspired to assassinate King Xerxes.

³"What honor and recognition has Mordecai received for this?" the king asked.

"Nothing has been done for him," his attendants answered.

⁴The king said, "Who is in the court?" Now Haman had just entered the outer court of the palace to speak to the king about hanging Mordecai on the gallows he had erected for him.

---

*ᵃ*14 Hebrew *fifty cubits* (about 23 meters)

Dear Sam,

My family moved this summer and school is about to start. I'm so lonely. I don't know anyone, and I feel so out of place. What can I do?

Kim in Kenosha

100 Advice Lane, Anywhere, USA

Dear Kim,

Moving is a very stressful experience. Your feelings are certainly valid. Has your family found a church yet? If the church youth group meets in the summer, perhaps you could make some friends there. Get their phone numbers and call them to talk or to get together. Take a bike ride through the neighborhood to locate other kids your age. Be brave. Stop and talk to teens you see.

As soon as school begins find out what clubs are available. Join a club or two with others who have similar interests. Smiles are the best way to look friendly. Try to smile even if you're feeling lonely.

There's always the chance that you're at this new school because God needs you there. Esther found that God had prepared her for a very special job (Esther 4:14). It wasn't easy, and she wasn't sure that she wanted it, but she followed God and served him and saved a whole nation of people.

Now perhaps you won't be used to save a whole nation, but you could be in this school to have a particular impact on the life of a particular person. Be ready for God to use you.

Sam

⁵His attendants answered, "Haman is standing in the court."

"Bring him in," the king ordered.

⁶When Haman entered, the king asked him, "What should be done for the man the king delights to honor?"

Now Haman thought to himself, "Who is there that the king would rather honor than me?" ⁷So he answered the king, "For the man the king delights to honor, ⁸have them bring a royal robe the king has worn and a horse the king has ridden, one with a royal crest placed on its head. ⁹Then let the robe and horse be entrusted to one of the king's most noble princes. Let them robe the man the king delights to honor, and lead him on the horse through the city streets, proclaiming before him, 'This is what is done for the man the king delights to honor!' "

¹⁰"Go at once," the king commanded Haman. "Get the robe and the horse and do just as you have suggested for Mordecai the Jew, who sits at the king's gate. Do not neglect anything you have recommended."

¹¹So Haman got the robe and the horse. He robed Mordecai, and led him on horseback through the city streets, proclaiming before him, "This is what is done for the man the king delights to honor!"

¹²Afterward Mordecai returned to the king's gate. But Haman rushed home, with his head covered in grief, ¹³and told Zeresh his wife and all his friends everything that had happened to him.

His advisers and his wife Zeresh said to him, "Since Mordecai, before whom your downfall has started, is of Jewish origin, you cannot stand against him—you will surely come to ruin!" ¹⁴While they were still talking with him, the king's eunuchs arrived and hurried Haman away to the banquet Esther had prepared.

7 **Haman Hanged** So the king and Haman went to dine with Queen Esther, ²and as they were drinking wine on that second day, the king again asked, "Queen Esther, what is your petition? It will be given you. What is your request? Even up to half the kingdom, it will be granted."

³Then Queen Esther answered, "If I have found favor with you, O king, and if it pleases your majesty, grant me my life—this is my petition. And spare my people—this is my request. ⁴For I and my people have been sold for destruction and slaughter and annihilation. If we had merely been sold as male and female slaves, I would have kept quiet, because no such distress would justify disturbing the king.ᵃ"

⁵King Xerxes asked Queen Esther, "Who is he? Where is the man who has dared to do such a thing?"

⁶Esther said, "The adversary and enemy is this vile Haman."

Then Haman was terrified before the king and queen. ⁷The king got up in a rage, left his wine and went out into the palace garden. But Haman, realizing that the king had already decided his fate, stayed behind to beg Queen Esther for his life.

⁸Just as the king returned from the palace garden to the banquet hall, Haman was falling on the couch where Esther was reclining.

The king exclaimed, "Will he even molest the queen while she is with me in the house?"

As soon as the word left the king's mouth, they covered Haman's face. ⁹Then Harbona, one of the eunuchs attending the king, said, "A gallows seventy-five feetᵇ high stands by Haman's house. He had it made for Mordecai, who spoke up to help the king."

The king said, "Hang him on it!" ¹⁰So they hanged Haman on the gallows he had prepared for Mordecai. Then the king's fury subsided.

ᵃ4 Or *quiet, but the compensation our adversary offers cannot be compared with the loss the king would suffer* ᵇ9 Hebrew *fifty cubits* (about 23 meters)

8 *The King's Edict in Behalf of the Jews* That same day King Xerxes gave Queen Esther the estate of Haman, the enemy of the Jews. And Mordecai came into the presence of the king, for Esther had told how he was related to her. [2]The king took off his signet ring, which he had reclaimed from Haman, and presented it to Mordecai. And Esther appointed him over Haman's estate.

[3]Esther again pleaded with the king, falling at his feet and weeping. She begged him to put an end to the evil plan of Haman the Agagite, which he had devised against the Jews. [4]Then the king extended the gold scepter to Esther and she arose and stood before him.

[5]"If it pleases the king," she said, "and if he regards me with favor and thinks it the right thing to do, and if he is pleased with me, let an order be written overruling the dispatches that Haman son of Hammedatha, the Agagite, devised and wrote to destroy the Jews in all the king's provinces. [6]For how can I bear to see disaster fall on my people? How can I bear to see the destruction of my family?"

[7]King Xerxes replied to Queen Esther and to Mordecai the Jew, "Because Haman attacked the Jews, I have given his estate to Esther, and they have hanged him on the gallows. [8]Now write another decree in the king's name in behalf of the Jews as seems best to you, and seal it with the king's signet ring—for no document written in the king's name and sealed with his ring can be revoked."

[9]At once the royal secretaries were summoned—on the twenty-third day of the third month, the month of Sivan. They wrote out all Mordecai's orders to the Jews, and to the satraps, governors and nobles of the 127 provinces stretching from India to Cush.[a] These orders were written in the script of each province and the language of each people and also to the Jews in their own script and language. [10]Mordecai wrote in the name of King Xerxes, sealed the dispatches with the king's signet ring, and sent them by mounted couriers, who rode fast horses especially bred for the king.

[11]The king's edict granted the Jews in every city the right to assemble and protect themselves; to destroy, kill and annihilate any armed force of any nationality or province that might attack them and their women and children; and to plunder the property of their enemies. [12]The day appointed for the Jews to do this in all the provinces of King Xerxes was the thirteenth day of the twelfth month, the month of Adar. [13]A copy of the text of the edict was to be issued as law in every province and made known to the people of every nationality so that the Jews would be ready on that day to avenge themselves on their enemies.

[14]The couriers, riding the royal horses, raced out, spurred on by the king's command. And the edict was also issued in the citadel of Susa.

[15]Mordecai left the king's presence wearing royal garments of

---

Direct Line

ESTHER 7

A voice swears in the back of the bus and someone says, "Carl did it!" Everybody snickers. Carl didn't do it, but the bus driver still writes him up. Someone may even try to get you in trouble because they don't like you. They don't want a laugh. They want to hurt you. And sometimes they succeed. If you've ever been the victim of a prank or a plot, you know how unfair it is. But take comfort in this Bible story. The more someone tries to harm you, the more likely it is the plot will backfire. Like Haman, hung on the gallows he built for Mordecai, your tormentor is more likely to hurt him or herself!

---

[a]9 That is, the upper Nile region

blue and white, a large crown of gold and a purple robe of fine linen. And the city of Susa held a joyous celebration. ¹⁶For the Jews it was a time of happiness and joy, gladness and honor. ¹⁷In every province and in every city, wherever the edict of the king went, there was joy and gladness among the Jews, with feasting and celebrating. And many people of other nationalities became Jews because fear of the Jews had seized them.

9 *Triumph of the Jews* On the thirteenth day of the twelfth month, the month of Adar, the edict commanded by the king was to be carried out. On this day the enemies of the Jews had hoped to overpower them, but now the tables were turned and the Jews got the upper hand over those who hated them. ²The Jews assembled in their cities in all the provinces of King Xerxes to attack those seeking their destruction. No one could stand against them, because the people of all the other nationalities were afraid of them. ³And all the nobles of the provinces, the satraps, the governors and the king's administrators helped the Jews, because fear of Mordecai had seized them. ⁴Mordecai was prominent in the palace; his reputation spread throughout the provinces, and he became more and more powerful.

⁵The Jews struck down all their enemies with the sword, killing and destroying them, and they did what they pleased to those who hated them. ⁶In the citadel of Susa, the Jews killed and destroyed five hundred men. ⁷They also killed Parshandatha, Dalphon, Aspatha, ⁸Poratha, Adalia, Aridatha, ⁹Parmashta, Arisai, Aridai and Vaizatha, ¹⁰the ten sons of Haman son of Hammedatha, the enemy of the Jews. But they did not lay their hands on the plunder.

¹¹The number of those slain in the citadel of Susa was reported to the king that same day. ¹²The king said to Queen Esther, "The Jews have killed and destroyed five hundred men and the ten sons of Haman in the citadel of Susa. What have they done in the rest of the king's provinces? Now what is your petition? It will be given you. What is your request? It will also be granted."

¹³"If it pleases the king," Esther answered, "give the Jews in Susa permission to carry out this day's edict tomorrow also, and let Haman's ten sons be hanged on gallows."

¹⁴So the king commanded that this be done. An edict was issued in Susa, and they hanged the ten sons of Haman. ¹⁵The Jews in Susa came together on the fourteenth day of the month of Adar, and they put to death in Susa three hundred men, but they did not lay their hands on the plunder.

¹⁶Meanwhile, the remainder of the Jews who were in the king's provinces also assembled to protect themselves and get relief from their enemies. They killed seventy-five thousand of them but did not lay their hands on the plunder. ¹⁷This happened on the thirteenth day of the month of Adar, and on the fourteenth they rested and made it a day of feasting and joy.

ESTHER 9 QUIZZER

Q: What Jewish holiday is mentioned in this book?

BONUS: What did it celebrate?

Answers on page 612

Purim Celebrated ¹⁸The Jews in Susa, however, had assembled on the thirteenth and fourteenth, and then on the fifteenth they rested and made it a day of feasting and joy.

¹⁹That is why rural Jews—those living in villages—observe the fourteenth of the month of Adar as a day of joy and feasting, a day for giving presents to each other.

²⁰Mordecai recorded these events, and he sent letters to all the Jews throughout the provinces of King Xerxes, near and far, ²¹to have them celebrate annually the fourteenth and fifteenth days of the month of Adar ²²as

the time when the Jews got relief from their enemies, and as the month when their sorrow was turned into joy and their mourning into a day of celebration. He wrote them to observe the days as days of feasting and joy and giving presents of food to one another and gifts to the poor.

²³So the Jews agreed to continue the celebration they had begun, doing what Mordecai had written to them. ²⁴For Haman son of Hammedatha, the Agagite, the enemy of all the Jews, had plotted against the Jews to destroy them and had cast the *pur* (that is, the lot) for their ruin and destruction. ²⁵But when the plot came to the king's attention,[a] he issued written orders that the evil scheme Haman had devised against the Jews should come back onto his own head, and that he and his sons should be hanged on the gallows. ²⁶(Therefore these days were called Purim, from the word *pur*.) Because of everything written in this letter and because of what they had seen and what had happened to them, ²⁷the Jews took it upon themselves to establish the custom that they and their descendants and all who join them should without fail observe these two days every year, in the way prescribed and at the time appointed. ²⁸These days should be remembered and observed in every generation by every family, and in every province and in every city. And these days of Purim should never cease to be celebrated by the Jews, nor should the memory of them die out among their descendants.

²⁹So Queen Esther, daughter of Abihail, along with Mordecai the Jew, wrote with full authority to confirm this second letter concerning Purim. ³⁰And Mordecai sent letters to all the Jews in the 127 provinces of the kingdom of Xerxes—words of goodwill and assurance— ³¹to establish these days of Purim at their designated times, as Mordecai the Jew and Queen Esther had decreed for them, and as they had established for themselves and their descendants in regard to their times of fasting and lamentation. ³²Esther's decree confirmed these regulations about Purim, and it was written down in the records.

The Greatness of Mordecai King Xerxes imposed tribute throughout the empire, to its distant shores. ²And all his acts of power and might, together with a full account of the greatness of Mordecai to which the king had raised him, are they not written in the book of the annals of the kings of Media and Persia? ³Mordecai the Jew was second in rank to King Xerxes, preeminent among the Jews, and held in high esteem by his many fellow Jews, because he worked for the good of his people and spoke up for the welfare of all the Jews.

Answers
to Quizzer on
page 611

A: Purim
(Esther 9:28).

BONUS: It
celebrated the
deliverance of
the Jews from
mass execution,
won for them by
the bravery of
Queen Esther.

---

[a]25 Or *when Esther came before the king*

TOUGH TIMES.

You plan a vacation and get sick the day before you're supposed to leave. Your grandma gets cancer, and even though you pray hard, she dies. Your dad, a good person, loses his job and can't find work. Do you ever wonder why God lets bad things happen to good people?

Job wondered too. He was a good person, but one day he lost all his wealth, all his children and his health. Job's friends said God must be punishing him for secret sins. Job knew he'd been faithful to God, but he couldn't explain why God was letting him suffer.

Fundamentals

Does being a good person protect you from troubles (Job 1)?

When something bad does happen, do you ever think God must be punishing you (Job 4:8-9)?

Do you feel that God hasn't been fair to you (Job 19)?

How could things turn out in the end for the person committed to pleasing God (Job 42:7-17)?

FAST FACTS

Most of Job is a long poem.

God himself called Job "blameless and upright." Satan is mentioned only in Job 1 and 2.

Troubles need not be punishment for sins. God can use suffering to teach you and help you grow.

1 *Prologue* In the land of Uz there lived a man whose name was Job. This man was blameless and upright; he feared God and shunned evil. ²He had seven sons and three daughters, ³and he owned seven thousand sheep, three thousand camels, five hundred yoke of oxen and five hundred donkeys, and had a large number of servants. He was the greatest man among all the people of the East.

⁴His sons used to take turns holding feasts in their homes, and they would invite their three sisters to eat and drink with them. ⁵When a period of feasting had run its course, Job would send and have them purified. Early in the morning he would sacrifice a burnt offering for each of them, thinking, "Perhaps my children have sinned and cursed God in their hearts." This was Job's regular custom.

Job's First Test ⁶One day the angels*ᵃ* came to present themselves before the LORD, and Satan*ᵇ* also came with them. ⁷The LORD said to Satan, "Where have you come from?"

Satan answered the LORD, "From roaming through the earth and going back and forth in it."

⁸Then the LORD said to Satan, "Have you considered my servant Job? There is no one on earth like him; he is blameless and upright, a man who fears God and shuns evil."

⁹"Does Job fear God for nothing?" Satan replied. ¹⁰"Have you not put a hedge around him and his household and everything he has? You have blessed the work of his hands, so that his flocks and herds are spread throughout the land. ¹¹But stretch out your hand and strike everything he has, and he will surely curse you to your face."

¹²The LORD said to Satan, "Very well, then, everything he has is in your hands, but on the man himself do not lay a finger."

Then Satan went out from the presence of the LORD.

¹³One day when Job's sons and daughters were feasting and drinking wine at the oldest brother's house, ¹⁴a messenger came to Job and said, "The oxen were plowing and the donkeys were grazing nearby, ¹⁵and the Sabeans attacked and carried them off. They put the servants to the sword, and I am the only one who has escaped to tell you!"

¹⁶While he was still speaking, another messenger came and said, "The fire of God fell from the sky and burned up the sheep and the servants, and I am the only one who has escaped to tell you!"

¹⁷While he was still speaking, another messenger came and said, "The Chaldeans formed three raiding parties and swept down on your camels and carried them off. They put the servants to the sword, and I am the only one who has escaped to tell you!"

¹⁸While he was still speaking, yet another messenger came and said, "Your sons and daughters were feasting and drinking wine at the oldest brother's house, ¹⁹when suddenly a mighty wind swept in from the desert and struck the four corners of the house. It collapsed on them and they are dead, and I am the only one who has escaped to tell you!"

²⁰At this, Job got up and tore his robe and shaved his head. Then he fell to the ground in worship ²¹and said:

> "Naked I came from my mother's womb,
> and naked I will depart.*ᶜ*
> The LORD gave and the LORD has taken away;
> may the name of the LORD be praised."

²²In all this, Job did not sin by charging God with wrongdoing.

ᵃ6 Hebrew *the sons of God* *ᵇ6 Satan* means *accuser.* *ᶜ21* Or *will return there*

2 *Job's Second Test* On another day the angels*ᵃ* came to present themselves before the LORD, and Satan also came with them to present himself before him. ²And the LORD said to Satan, "Where have you come from?"

Satan answered the LORD, "From roaming through the earth and going back and forth in it."

³Then the LORD said to Satan, "Have you considered my servant Job? There is no one on earth like him; he is blameless and upright, a man who fears God and shuns evil. And he still maintains his integrity, though you incited me against him to ruin him without any reason."

⁴"Skin for skin!" Satan replied. "A man will give all he has for his own life. ⁵But stretch out your hand and strike his flesh and bones, and he will surely curse you to your face."

⁶The LORD said to Satan, "Very well, then, he is in your hands; but you must spare his life."

⁷So Satan went out from the presence of the LORD and afflicted Job with painful sores from the soles of his feet to the top of his head. ⁸Then Job took a piece of broken pottery and scraped himself with it as he sat among the ashes.

⁹His wife said to him, "Are you still holding on to your integrity? Curse God and die!"

¹⁰He replied, "You are talking like a foolish*ᵇ* woman. Shall we accept good from God, and not trouble?"

In all this, Job did not sin in what he said.

Job's Three Friends ¹¹When Job's three friends, Eliphaz the Temanite, Bildad the Shuhite and Zophar the Naamathite, heard about all the troubles that had come upon him, they set out from their homes and met together by agreement to go and sympathize with him and comfort him. ¹²When they saw him from a distance, they could hardly recognize him; they began to weep aloud, and they tore their robes and sprinkled dust on their heads. ¹³Then they sat on the ground with him for seven days and seven nights. No one said a word to him, because they saw how great his suffering was.

3 *Job Speaks* After this, Job opened his mouth and cursed the day of his birth. ²He said:

³"May the day of my birth perish,
    and the night it was said, 'A boy is born!'
⁴That day—may it turn to darkness;
    may God above not care about it;
    may no light shine upon it.
⁵May darkness and deep shadow*ᶜ* claim it once more;
    may a cloud settle over it;
    may blackness overwhelm its light.
⁶That night—may thick darkness seize it;
    may it not be included among the days of the year
    nor be entered in any of the months.
⁷May that night be barren;
    may no shout of joy be heard in it.
⁸May those who curse days*ᵈ* curse that day,
    those who are ready to rouse Leviathan.
⁹May its morning stars become dark;
    may it wait for daylight in vain
    and not see the first rays of dawn,

---

*ᵃ1 Hebrew *the sons of God* *ᵇ10 The Hebrew word rendered *foolish* denotes moral deficiency. *ᶜ5 Or *and the shadow of death* *ᵈ8 Or *the sea*

Dear Sam,

I'm a Christian. I'm not perfect, but there are lots of people worse than I am. How come I had to get cancer? It's totally unfair!

Chad in Chattanooga

100 Advice Lane, Anywhere, USA

Dear Sam, Inc.

Dear Chad,

I can't imagine what being in your position must feel like. Job would know though. Job was a good man who loved the Lord. Satan was sure that if God would let him ruin Job's life and health, Job would curse God. God was sure Job would remain faithful. He allowed Satan to test Job by taking the lives of his children and then destroying his wealth and health (Job 1–2). Job had times when he wished he'd never been born (Job 3:2-3). But even though he felt God was being totally unfair, he still refused to curse him (Job 27:1-4). Job had done nothing to deserve his suffering, and so he waited patiently for God to help him.

Job is a fascinating book to read, and I do love the epilogue (Job 42:7-17). Job's health was restored, his wealth was doubled, and he had ten more children.

When you look at your situation, it's easy to see only the here and now. God sees way beyond that. God loves you, and in the end those who love him get not only justice, but grace and mercy and heaven.

Sam

¹⁰for it did not shut the doors of the womb on me
to hide trouble from my eyes.

¹¹"Why did I not perish at birth,
and die as I came from the womb?
¹²Why were there knees to receive me
and breasts that I might be nursed?
¹³For now I would be lying down in peace;
I would be asleep and at rest
¹⁴with kings and counselors of the earth,
who built for themselves places now lying in ruins,
¹⁵with rulers who had gold,
who filled their houses with silver.
¹⁶Or why was I not hidden in the ground like a stillborn child,
like an infant who never saw the light of day?
¹⁷There the wicked cease from turmoil,
and there the weary are at rest.
¹⁸Captives also enjoy their ease;
they no longer hear the slave driver's shout.
¹⁹The small and the great are there,
and the slave is freed from his master.

²⁰"Why is light given to those in misery,
and life to the bitter of soul,
²¹to those who long for death that does not come,
who search for it more than for hidden treasure,
²²who are filled with gladness
and rejoice when they reach the grave?
²³Why is life given to a man
whose way is hidden,
whom God has hedged in?
²⁴For sighing comes to me
instead of food;
my groans pour out like
water.
²⁵What I feared has come upon
me;
what I dreaded has
happened to me.
²⁶I have no peace, no quietness;
I have no rest, but only
turmoil."

4 *Eliphaz* Then Eliphaz the Temanite replied:

²"If someone ventures a word
with you, will you be
impatient?
But who can keep from
speaking?
³Think how you have
instructed many,
how you have strengthened
feeble hands.
⁴Your words have supported
those who stumbled;
you have strengthened
faltering knees.

JOB 2:11–13

Your friend's mother died yesterday. You know you should go over and talk to her, comfort her. But you just can't. You don't have any idea what to say. Well, this passage suggests that maybe you don't need to say anything! Job was so sad that when his friends came to comfort him, "they could hardly recognize him" (Job 2:12). What did they do? They sat "with him for seven days and seven nights. No one said a word to him" (Job 2:13)! Many times, when someone is sad or upset, words aren't necessary. Just your presence speaks of your love and caring. Don't be afraid. Go visit your friend. You don't have to say a word.

Direct Line

⁵But now trouble comes to you, and you are discouraged;
 it strikes you, and you are dismayed.
⁶Should not your piety be your confidence
 and your blameless ways your hope?

⁷"Consider now: Who, being innocent, has ever perished?
 Where were the upright ever destroyed?
⁸As I have observed, those who plow evil
 and those who sow trouble reap it.
⁹At the breath of God they are destroyed;
 at the blast of his anger they perish.
¹⁰The lions may roar and growl,
 yet the teeth of the great lions are broken.
¹¹The lion perishes for lack of prey,
 and the cubs of the lioness are scattered.

¹²"A word was secretly brought to me,
 my ears caught a whisper of it.
¹³Amid disquieting dreams in the night,
 when deep sleep falls on men,
¹⁴fear and trembling seized me
 and made all my bones shake.
¹⁵A spirit glided past my face,
 and the hair on my body stood on end.
¹⁶It stopped,
 but I could not tell what it was.
A form stood before my eyes,
 and I heard a hushed voice:
¹⁷'Can a mortal be more righteous than God?
 Can a man be more pure than his Maker?
¹⁸If God places no trust in his servants,
 if he charges his angels with error,
¹⁹how much more those who live in houses of clay,
 whose foundations are in the dust,
 who are crushed more readily than a moth!
²⁰Between dawn and dusk they are broken to pieces;
 unnoticed, they perish forever.
²¹Are not the cords of their tent pulled up,
 so that they die without wisdom?'ᵃ

5 "Call if you will, but who will answer you?
 To which of the holy ones will you turn?
²Resentment kills a fool,
 and envy slays the simple.
³I myself have seen a fool taking root,
 but suddenly his house was cursed.
⁴His children are far from safety,
 crushed in court without a defender.
⁵The hungry consume his harvest,
 taking it even from among thorns,
 and the thirsty pant after his wealth.
⁶For hardship does not spring from the soil,
 nor does trouble sprout from the ground.
⁷Yet man is born to trouble
 as surely as sparks fly upward.

ᵃ21 Some interpreters end the quotation after verse 17.

8 "But if it were I, I would appeal to God;
  I would lay my cause before him.
9 He performs wonders that cannot be fathomed,
  miracles that cannot be counted.
10 He bestows rain on the earth;
  he sends water upon the countryside.
11 The lowly he sets on high,
  and those who mourn are lifted to safety.
12 He thwarts the plans of the crafty,
  so that their hands achieve no success.
13 He catches the wise in their craftiness,
  and the schemes of the wily are swept away.
14 Darkness comes upon them in the daytime;
  at noon they grope as in the night.
15 He saves the needy from the sword in their mouth;
  he saves them from the clutches of the powerful.
16 So the poor have hope,
  and injustice shuts its mouth.

17 "Blessed is the man whom God corrects;
  so do not despise the discipline of the Almighty.*
18 For he wounds, but he also binds up;
  he injures, but his hands also heal.
19 From six calamities he will rescue you;
  in seven no harm will befall you.
20 In famine he will ransom you from death,
  and in battle from the stroke of the sword.
21 You will be protected from the lash of the tongue,
  and need not fear when destruction comes.
22 You will laugh at destruction and famine,
  and need not fear the beasts of the earth.
23 For you will have a covenant with the stones of the field,
  and the wild animals will be at peace with you.
24 You will know that your tent is secure;
  you will take stock of your property and find nothing
    missing.
25 You will know that your children will be many,
  and your descendants like the grass of the earth.
26 You will come to the grave in full vigor,
  like sheaves gathered in season.

27 "We have examined this, and it is true.
  So hear it and apply it to yourself."

6 *Job* Then Job replied:

2 "If only my anguish could be weighed
  and all my misery be placed on the scales!
3 It would surely outweigh the sand of the seas—
  no wonder my words have been impetuous.
4 The arrows of the Almighty are in me,
  my spirit drinks in their poison;
  God's terrors are marshaled against me.
5 Does a wild donkey bray when it has grass,
  or an ox bellow when it has fodder?

---

*17 Hebrew *Shaddai*, here and throughout Job

⁶ Is tasteless food eaten without salt,
  or is there flavor in the white of an egg*?
⁷ I refuse to touch it;
  such food makes me ill.

⁸ "Oh, that I might have my request,
  that God would grant what I hope for,
⁹ that God would be willing to crush me,
  to let loose his hand and cut me off!
¹⁰ Then I would still have this consolation—
  my joy in unrelenting pain—
  that I had not denied the words of the Holy One.

¹¹ "What strength do I have, that I should still hope?
  What prospects, that I should be patient?
¹² Do I have the strength of stone?
  Is my flesh bronze?
¹³ Do I have any power to help myself,
  now that success has been driven from me?

¹⁴ "A despairing man should have the devotion of his friends,
  even though he forsakes the fear of the Almighty.
¹⁵ But my brothers are as undependable as intermittent streams,
  as the streams that overflow
¹⁶ when darkened by thawing ice
  and swollen with melting snow,
¹⁷ but that cease to flow in the dry season,
  and in the heat vanish from their channels.
¹⁸ Caravans turn aside from their routes;
  they go up into the wasteland and perish.
¹⁹ The caravans of Tema look for water,
  the traveling merchants of Sheba look in hope.
²⁰ They are distressed, because they had been confident;
  they arrive there, only to be disappointed.
²¹ Now you too have proved to be of no help;
  you see something dreadful and are afraid.
²² Have I ever said, 'Give something on my behalf,
  pay a ransom for me from your wealth,
²³ deliver me from the hand of the enemy,
  ransom me from the clutches of the ruthless'?

²⁴ "Teach me, and I will be quiet;
  show me where I have been wrong.
²⁵ How painful are honest words!
  But what do your arguments prove?
²⁶ Do you mean to correct what I say,
  and treat the words of a despairing man as wind?
²⁷ You would even cast lots for the fatherless
  and barter away your friend.

²⁸ "But now be so kind as to look at me.
  Would I lie to your face?
²⁹ Relent, do not be unjust;
  reconsider, for my integrity is at stake.ᵇ
³⁰ Is there any wickedness on my lips?
  Can my mouth not discern malice?

---

*6 The meaning of the Hebrew for this phrase is uncertain. ᵇ29 Or *my righteousness still stands*

7

"Does not man have hard service on earth?
    Are not his days like those of a hired man?
²Like a slave longing for the evening shadows,
    or a hired man waiting eagerly for his wages,
³so I have been allotted months of futility,
    and nights of misery have been assigned to me.
⁴When I lie down I think, 'How long before I get up?'
    The night drags on, and I toss till dawn.
⁵My body is clothed with worms and scabs,
    my skin is broken and festering.

⁶"My days are swifter than a weaver's shuttle,
    and they come to an end without hope.
⁷Remember, O God, that my life is but a breath;
    my eyes will never see happiness again.
⁸The eye that now sees me will see me no longer;
    you will look for me, but I will be no more.
⁹As a cloud vanishes and is gone,
    so he who goes down to the graveᵃ does not return.
¹⁰He will never come to his house again;
    his place will know him no more.

¹¹"Therefore I will not keep silent;
    I will speak out in the anguish of my spirit,
    I will complain in the bitterness of my soul.
¹²Am I the sea, or the monster of the deep,
    that you put me under guard?
¹³When I think my bed will comfort me
    and my couch will ease my complaint,
¹⁴even then you frighten me with dreams
    and terrify me with visions,
¹⁵so that I prefer strangling and death,
    rather than this body of mine.
¹⁶I despise my life; I would not live forever.
    Let me alone; my days have no meaning.

¹⁷"What is man that you make so much of him,
    that you give him so much attention,
¹⁸that you examine him every morning
    and test him every moment?
¹⁹Will you never look away from me,
    or let me alone even for an instant?
²⁰If I have sinned, what have I done to you,
    O watcher of men?
Why have you made me your target?
    Have I become a burden to you?ᵇ
²¹Why do you not pardon my offenses
    and forgive my sins?
For I will soon lie down in the dust;
    you will search for me, but I will be no more."

8 *Bildad*   Then Bildad the Shuhite replied:

²"How long will you say such things?
    Your words are a blustering wind.

ᵃ9 Hebrew *Sheol* ᵇ20 A few manuscripts of the Masoretic Text, an ancient Hebrew scribal tradition and Septuagint; most manuscripts of the Masoretic Text *I have become a burden to myself.*

³Does God pervert justice?
  Does the Almighty pervert what is right?
⁴When your children sinned against him,
  he gave them over to the penalty of their sin.
⁵But if you will look to God
  and plead with the Almighty,
⁶if you are pure and upright,
  even now he will rouse himself on your behalf
  and restore you to your rightful place.
⁷Your beginnings will seem humble,
  so prosperous will your future be.

⁸"Ask the former generations
  and find out what their fathers learned,
⁹for we were born only yesterday and know nothing,
  and our days on earth are but a shadow.
¹⁰Will they not instruct you and tell you?
  Will they not bring forth words from their understanding?
¹¹Can papyrus grow tall where there is no marsh?
  Can reeds thrive without water?
¹²While still growing and uncut,
  they wither more quickly than grass.
¹³Such is the destiny of all who forget God;
  so perishes the hope of the godless.
¹⁴What he trusts in is fragile*;
  what he relies on is a spider's web.
¹⁵He leans on his web, but it gives way;
  he clings to it, but it does not hold.
¹⁶He is like a well-watered plant in the sunshine,
  spreading its shoots over the garden;
¹⁷it entwines its roots around a pile of rocks
  and looks for a place among the stones.
¹⁸But when it is torn from its spot,
  that place disowns it and says, 'I never saw you.'
¹⁹Surely its life withers away,
  and*ᵇ* from the soil other plants grow.

²⁰"Surely God does not reject a blameless man
  or strengthen the hands of evildoers.
²¹He will yet fill your mouth with laughter
  and your lips with shouts of joy.
²²Your enemies will be clothed in shame,
  and the tents of the wicked will be no more."

9

Job Then Job replied:

²"Indeed, I know that this is true.
  But how can a mortal be righteous before God?
³Though one wished to dispute with him,
  he could not answer him one time out of a thousand.
⁴His wisdom is profound, his power is vast.
  Who has resisted him and come out unscathed?
⁵He moves mountains without their knowing it
  and overturns them in his anger.
⁶He shakes the earth from its place
  and makes its pillars tremble.

ᵃ14 The meaning of the Hebrew for this word is uncertain. ᵇ19 Or Surely all the joy it has / is that

⁷He speaks to the sun and it does not shine;
    he seals off the light of the stars.
⁸He alone stretches out the heavens
    and treads on the waves of the sea.
⁹He is the Maker of the Bear and Orion,
    the Pleiades and the constellations of the south.
¹⁰He performs wonders that cannot be fathomed,
    miracles that cannot be counted.
¹¹When he passes me, I cannot see him;
    when he goes by, I cannot perceive him.
¹²If he snatches away, who can stop him?
    Who can say to him, 'What are you doing?'
¹³God does not restrain his anger;
    even the cohorts of Rahab cowered at his feet.

¹⁴"How then can I dispute with him?
    How can I find words to argue with him?
¹⁵Though I were innocent, I could not answer him;
    I could only plead with my Judge for mercy.
¹⁶Even if I summoned him and he responded,
    I do not believe he would give me a hearing.
¹⁷He would crush me with a storm
    and multiply my wounds for no reason.
¹⁸He would not let me regain my breath
    but would overwhelm me with misery.
¹⁹If it is a matter of strength, he is mighty!
    And if it is a matter of justice, who will summon him[a]?
²⁰Even if I were innocent, my mouth would condemn me;
    if I were blameless, it would pronounce me guilty.

²¹"Although I am blameless,
    I have no concern for myself;
    I despise my own life.
²²It is all the same; that is why I say,
    'He destroys both the blameless and the wicked.'
²³When a scourge brings sudden death,
    he mocks the despair of the innocent.
²⁴When a land falls into the hands of the wicked,
    he blindfolds its judges.
    If it is not he, then who is it?

²⁵"My days are swifter than a runner;
    they fly away without a glimpse of joy.
²⁶They skim past like boats of papyrus,
    like eagles swooping down on their prey.
²⁷If I say, 'I will forget my complaint,
    I will change my expression, and smile,'
²⁸I still dread all my sufferings,
    for I know you will not hold me innocent.
²⁹Since I am already found guilty,
    why should I struggle in vain?
³⁰Even if I washed myself with soap[b]
    and my hands with washing soda,
³¹you would plunge me into a slime pit
    so that even my clothes would detest me.

[a]*19* See Septuagint; Hebrew *me*. [b]*30* Or *snow*

³²"He is not a man like me that I might answer him,
  that we might confront each other in court.
³³If only there were someone to arbitrate between us,
  to lay his hand upon us both,
³⁴someone to remove God's rod from me,
  so that his terror would frighten me no more.
³⁵Then I would speak up without fear of him,
  but as it now stands with me, I cannot.

10 "I loathe my very life;
  therefore I will give free rein to my complaint
  and speak out in the bitterness of my soul.
²I will say to God: Do not condemn me,
  but tell me what charges you have against me.
³Does it please you to oppress me,
  to spurn the work of your hands,
  while you smile on the schemes of the wicked?
⁴Do you have eyes of flesh?
  Do you see as a mortal sees?
⁵Are your days like those of a mortal
  or your years like those of a man,
⁶that you must search out my faults
  and probe after my sin—
⁷though you know that I am not guilty
  and that no one can rescue me from your hand?

⁸"Your hands shaped me and made me.
  Will you now turn and destroy me?
⁹Remember that you molded me like clay.
  Will you now turn me to dust again?
¹⁰Did you not pour me out like milk
  and curdle me like cheese,
¹¹clothe me with skin and flesh
  and knit me together with bones and sinews?
¹²You gave me life and showed me kindness,
  and in your providence watched over my spirit.

¹³"But this is what you concealed in your heart,
  and I know that this was in your mind:
¹⁴If I sinned, you would be watching me
  and would not let my offense go unpunished.
¹⁵If I am guilty—woe to me!
  Even if I am innocent, I cannot lift my head,
  for I am full of shame
  and drowned inª my affliction.
¹⁶If I hold my head high, you stalk me like a lion
  and again display your awesome power against me.
¹⁷You bring new witnesses against me
  and increase your anger toward me;
  your forces come against me wave upon wave.

¹⁸"Why then did you bring me out of the womb?
  I wish I had died before any eye saw me.
¹⁹If only I had never come into being,
  or had been carried straight from the womb to the grave!
²⁰Are not my few days almost over?

> You gave me
> life and showed
> me kindness, and
> in your providence
> watched over
> my spirit
> (Job 10:12).

ª15 Or *and aware of*

Turn away from me so I can have a moment's
         joy
²¹before I go to the place of no return,
      to the land of gloom and deep shadow,ᵃ
²²to the land of deepest night,
      of deep shadow and disorder,
      where even the light is like darkness."

11 *Zophar* Then Zophar the Naamathite replied:

²"Are all these words to go unanswered?
      Is this talker to be vindicated?
³Will your idle talk reduce men to silence?
      Will no one rebuke you when you mock?
⁴You say to God, 'My beliefs are flawless
      and I am pure in your sight.'
⁵Oh, how I wish that God would speak,
      that he would open his lips against you
⁶and disclose to you the secrets of wisdom,
      for true wisdom has two sides.
      Know this: God has even forgotten some of your sin.

⁷"Can you fathom the mysteries of God?
      Can you probe the limits of the Almighty?
⁸They are higher than the heavens—what can you do?
      They are deeper than the depths of the graveᵇ—what can
         you know?
⁹Their measure is longer than the earth
      and wider than the sea.

¹⁰"If he comes along and confines you in prison
      and convenes a court, who can oppose him?
¹¹Surely he recognizes deceitful men;
      and when he sees evil, does he not take note?
¹²But a witless man can no more become wise
      than a wild donkey's colt can be born a man.ᶜ

¹³"Yet if you devote your heart to him
      and stretch out your hands to him,
¹⁴if you put away the sin that is in your hand
      and allow no evil to dwell in your tent,
¹⁵then you will lift up your face without shame;
      you will stand firm and without fear.
¹⁶You will surely forget your trouble,
      recalling it only as waters gone by.
¹⁷Life will be brighter than noonday,
      and darkness will become like morning.
¹⁸You will be secure, because there is hope;
      you will look about you and take your rest in safety.
¹⁹You will lie down, with no one to make you afraid,
      and many will court your favor.
²⁰But the eyes of the wicked will fail,
      and escape will elude them;
      their hope will become a dying gasp."

ᵃ21 Or *and the shadow of death*; also in verse 22   ᵇ8 Hebrew *than Sheol*   ᶜ12 Or *wild donkey can be born tame*

12 **Job** Then Job replied:

²"Doubtless you are the people,
and wisdom will die with you!
³But I have a mind as well as you;
I am not inferior to you.
Who does not know all these things?

⁴"I have become a laughingstock to my friends,
though I called upon God and he answered—
a mere laughingstock, though righteous and blameless!
⁵Men at ease have contempt for misfortune
as the fate of those whose feet are slipping.
⁶The tents of marauders are undisturbed,
and those who provoke God are secure—
those who carry their god in their hands.ᵃ

⁷"But ask the animals, and they will teach you,
or the birds of the air, and they will tell you;
⁸or speak to the earth, and it will teach you,
or let the fish of the sea inform you.
⁹Which of all these does not know
that the hand of the LORD has done this?
¹⁰In his hand is the life of every creature
and the breath of all mankind.
¹¹Does not the ear test words
as the tongue tastes food?
¹²Is not wisdom found among the aged?
Does not long life bring understanding?

¹³"To God belong wisdom and power;
counsel and understanding are his.
¹⁴What he tears down cannot be rebuilt;
the man he imprisons cannot be released.
¹⁵If he holds back the waters, there is drought;
if he lets them loose, they devastate the land.
¹⁶To him belong strength and victory;
both deceived and deceiver are his.
¹⁷He leads counselors away stripped
and makes fools of judges.
¹⁸He takes off the shackles put on by kings
and ties a loinclothᵇ around their waist.
¹⁹He leads priests away stripped
and overthrows men long established.
²⁰He silences the lips of trusted advisers
and takes away the discernment of elders.
²¹He pours contempt on nobles
and disarms the mighty.
²²He reveals the deep things of darkness
and brings deep shadows into the light.
²³He makes nations great, and destroys them;
he enlarges nations, and disperses them.
²⁴He deprives the leaders of the earth of their reason;
he sends them wandering through a trackless waste.
²⁵They grope in darkness with no light;
he makes them stagger like drunkards.

ᵃ6 Or *secure / in what God's hand brings them*   ᵇ18 Or *shackles of kings / and ties a belt*

13 "My eyes have seen all this,
my ears have heard and understood it.
²What you know, I also know;
I am not inferior to you.
³But I desire to speak to the Almighty
and to argue my case with God.
⁴You, however, smear me with lies;
you are worthless physicians, all of you!
⁵If only you would be altogether silent!
For you, that would be wisdom.
⁶Hear now my argument;
listen to the plea of my lips.
⁷Will you speak wickedly on God's behalf?
Will you speak deceitfully for him?
⁸Will you show him partiality?
Will you argue the case for God?
⁹Would it turn out well if he examined you?
Could you deceive him as you might deceive men?
¹⁰He would surely rebuke you
if you secretly showed partiality.
¹¹Would not his splendor terrify you?
Would not the dread of him fall on you?
¹²Your maxims are proverbs of ashes;
your defenses are defenses of clay.

¹³"Keep silent and let me speak;
then let come to me what may.
¹⁴Why do I put myself in jeopardy
and take my life in my hands?
¹⁵Though he slay me, yet will I hope in him;
I will surely*ᵃ* defend my ways to his face.
¹⁶Indeed, this will turn out for my deliverance,
for no godless man would dare come before him!
¹⁷Listen carefully to my words;
let your ears take in what I say.
¹⁸Now that I have prepared my case,
I know I will be vindicated.
¹⁹Can anyone bring charges against me?
If so, I will be silent and die.

²⁰"Only grant me these two things, O God,
and then I will not hide from you:
²¹Withdraw your hand far from me,
and stop frightening me with your terrors.
²²Then summon me and I will answer,
or let me speak, and you reply.
²³How many wrongs and sins have I committed?
Show me my offense and my sin.
²⁴Why do you hide your face
and consider me your enemy?
²⁵Will you torment a windblown leaf?
Will you chase after dry chaff?
²⁶For you write down bitter things against me
and make me inherit the sins of my youth.
²⁷You fasten my feet in shackles;

ᵃ15 Or He will surely slay me; I have no hope — / yet I will

you keep close watch on all my paths
by putting marks on the soles of my feet.

28 "So man wastes away like something rotten,
like a garment eaten by moths.

14 "Man born of woman
is of few days and full of trouble.
2 He springs up like a flower and withers away;
like a fleeting shadow, he does not endure.
3 Do you fix your eye on such a one?
Will you bring him*a* before you for judgment?
4 Who can bring what is pure from the impure?
No one!
5 Man's days are determined;
you have decreed the number of his months
and have set limits he cannot exceed.
6 So look away from him and let him alone,
till he has put in his time like a hired man.

7 "At least there is hope for a tree:
If it is cut down, it will sprout again,
and its new shoots will not fail.
8 Its roots may grow old in the ground
and its stump die in the soil,
9 yet at the scent of water it will bud
and put forth shoots like a plant.
10 But man dies and is laid low;
he breathes his last and is no more.
11 As water disappears from the sea
or a riverbed becomes parched and dry,
12 so man lies down and does not rise;
till the heavens are no more, men will not awake
or be roused from their sleep.

13 "If only you would hide me in the grave*b*
and conceal me till your anger has passed!
If only you would set me a time
and then remember me!
14 If a man dies, will he live again?
All the days of my hard service
I will wait for my renewal*c* to come.
15 You will call and I will answer you;
you will long for the creature your hands have made.
16 Surely then you will count my steps
but not keep track of my sin.
17 My offenses will be sealed up in a bag;
you will cover over my sin.

18 "But as a mountain erodes and crumbles
and as a rock is moved from its place,
19 as water wears away stones
and torrents wash away the soil,
so you destroy man's hope.
20 You overpower him once for all, and he is gone;
you change his countenance and send him away.

*a*3 Septuagint, Vulgate and Syriac; Hebrew *me*   *b*13 Hebrew *Sheol*   *c*14 Or *release*

²¹If his sons are honored, he does not know it;
    if they are brought low, he does not see it.
²²He feels but the pain of his own body
    and mourns only for himself."

15 *Eliphaz*   Then Eliphaz the Temanite replied:

²"Would a wise man answer with empty notions
    or fill his belly with the hot east wind?
³Would he argue with useless words,
    with speeches that have no value?
⁴But you even undermine piety
    and hinder devotion to God.
⁵Your sin prompts your mouth;
    you adopt the tongue of the crafty.
⁶Your own mouth condemns you, not mine;
    your own lips testify against you.

⁷"Are you the first man ever born?
    Were you brought forth before the hills?
⁸Do you listen in on God's council?
    Do you limit wisdom to yourself?
⁹What do you know that we do not know?
    What insights do you have that we do not have?
¹⁰The gray-haired and the aged are on our side,
    men even older than your father.
¹¹Are God's consolations not enough for you,
    words spoken gently to you?
¹²Why has your heart carried you away,
    and why do your eyes flash,
¹³so that you vent your rage against God
    and pour out such words from your mouth?

¹⁴"What is man, that he could be pure,
    or one born of woman, that he could be righteous?
¹⁵If God places no trust in his holy ones,
    if even the heavens are not pure in his eyes,
¹⁶how much less man, who is vile and corrupt,
    who drinks up evil like water!

¹⁷"Listen to me and I will explain to you;
    let me tell you what I have seen,
¹⁸what wise men have declared,
    hiding nothing received from their fathers
¹⁹(to whom alone the land was given
    when no alien passed among them):
²⁰All his days the wicked man suffers torment,
    the ruthless through all the years stored up for him.
²¹Terrifying sounds fill his ears;
    when all seems well, marauders attack him.
²²He despairs of escaping the darkness;
    he is marked for the sword.
²³He wanders about—food for vultures*ᵃ*;
    he knows the day of darkness is at hand.
²⁴Distress and anguish fill him with terror;
    they overwhelm him, like a king poised to attack,

ᵃ23 Or about, looking for food

²⁵ because he shakes his fist at God
and vaunts himself against the Almighty,
²⁶ defiantly charging against him
with a thick, strong shield.

²⁷ "Though his face is covered with fat
and his waist bulges with flesh,
²⁸ he will inhabit ruined towns
and houses where no one lives,
houses crumbling to rubble.
²⁹ He will no longer be rich and his wealth will not endure,
nor will his possessions spread over the land.
³⁰ He will not escape the darkness;
a flame will wither his shoots,
and the breath of God's mouth will carry him away.
³¹ Let him not deceive himself by trusting what is worthless,
for he will get nothing in return.
³² Before his time he will be paid in full,
and his branches will not flourish.
³³ He will be like a vine stripped of its unripe grapes,
like an olive tree shedding its blossoms.
³⁴ For the company of the godless will be barren,
and fire will consume the tents of those who love bribes.
³⁵ They conceive trouble and give birth to evil;
their womb fashions deceit."

16

Job Then Job replied:

² "I have heard many things like these;
miserable comforters are you all!
³ Will your long-winded speeches never end?
What ails you that you keep on arguing?
⁴ I also could speak like you,
if you were in my place;
I could make fine speeches against you
and shake my head at you.
⁵ But my mouth would encourage you;
comfort from my lips would bring you relief.

⁶ "Yet if I speak, my pain is not relieved;
and if I refrain, it does not go away.
⁷ Surely, O God, you have worn me out;
you have devastated my entire household.
⁸ You have bound me—and it has become a witness;
my gauntness rises up and testifies against me.
⁹ God assails me and tears me in his anger
and gnashes his teeth at me;
my opponent fastens on me his piercing eyes.
¹⁰ Men open their mouths to jeer at me;
they strike my cheek in scorn
and unite together against me.
¹¹ God has turned me over to evil men
and thrown me into the clutches of the wicked.
¹² All was well with me, but he shattered me;
he seized me by the neck and crushed me.
He has made me his target;

¹³ his archers surround me.
    Without pity, he pierces my kidneys
       and spills my gall on the ground.
¹⁴ Again and again he bursts upon me;
       he rushes at me like a warrior.

¹⁵ "I have sewed sackcloth over my skin
       and buried my brow in the dust.
¹⁶ My face is red with weeping,
       deep shadows ring my eyes;
¹⁷ yet my hands have been free of violence
       and my prayer is pure.

¹⁸ "O earth, do not cover my blood;
       may my cry never be laid to rest!
¹⁹ Even now my witness is in heaven;
       my advocate is on high.
²⁰ My intercessor is my friend[a]
       as my eyes pour out tears to God;
²¹ on behalf of a man he pleads with God
       as a man pleads for his friend.

²² "Only a few years will pass
       before I go on the journey of no return.

17 ¹ My spirit is broken,
       my days are cut short,
       the grave awaits me.
² Surely mockers surround me;
       my eyes must dwell on their hostility.

³ "Give me, O God, the pledge you demand.
       Who else will put up security for me?
⁴ You have closed their minds to understanding;
       therefore you will not let them triumph.
⁵ If a man denounces his friends for reward,
       the eyes of his children will fail.

⁶ "God has made me a byword to everyone,
       a man in whose face people spit.
⁷ My eyes have grown dim with grief;
       my whole frame is but a shadow.
⁸ Upright men are appalled at this;
       the innocent are aroused against the ungodly.
⁹ Nevertheless, the righteous will hold to their
          ways,
       and those with clean hands will grow stronger.

¹⁰ "But come on, all of you, try again!
       I will not find a wise man among you.
¹¹ My days have passed, my plans are shattered,
       and so are the desires of my heart.
¹² These men turn night into day;
       in the face of darkness they say, 'Light is near.'
¹³ If the only home I hope for is the grave,[b]
       if I spread out my bed in darkness,
¹⁴ if I say to corruption, 'You are my father,'
       and to the worm, 'My mother' or 'My sister,'

---

a20 Or My friends treat me with scorn   *b13 Hebrew Sheol*

¹⁵where then is my hope?
      Who can see any hope for me?
¹⁶Will it go down to the gates of death[a]?
      Will we descend together into the dust?"

18

Bildad Then Bildad the Shuhite replied:

²"When will you end these speeches?
      Be sensible, and then we can talk.
³Why are we regarded as cattle
      and considered stupid in your sight?
⁴You who tear yourself to pieces in your anger,
      is the earth to be abandoned for your sake?
      Or must the rocks be moved from their place?

⁵"The lamp of the wicked is snuffed out;
      the flame of his fire stops burning.
⁶The light in his tent becomes dark;
      the lamp beside him goes out.
⁷The vigor of his step is weakened;
      his own schemes throw him down.
⁸His feet thrust him into a net
      and he wanders into its mesh.
⁹A trap seizes him by the heel;
      a snare holds him fast.
¹⁰A noose is hidden for him on the ground;
      a trap lies in his path.
¹¹Terrors startle him on every side
      and dog his every step.
¹²Calamity is hungry for him;
      disaster is ready for him when he falls.
¹³It eats away parts of his skin;
      death's firstborn devours his limbs.
¹⁴He is torn from the security of his tent
      and marched off to the king of terrors.
¹⁵Fire resides[b] in his tent;
      burning sulfur is scattered over his dwelling.
¹⁶His roots dry up below
      and his branches wither above.
¹⁷The memory of him perishes from the earth;
      he has no name in the land.
¹⁸He is driven from light into darkness
      and is banished from the world.
¹⁹He has no offspring or descendants among his people,
      no survivor where once he lived.
²⁰Men of the west are appalled at his fate;
      men of the east are seized with horror.
²¹Surely such is the dwelling of an evil man;
      such is the place of one who knows not God."

19

Job Then Job replied:

²"How long will you torment me
      and crush me with words?
³Ten times now you have reproached me;
      shamelessly you attack me.

---

[a]16 Hebrew *Sheol*   [b]15 Or *Nothing he had remains*

⁴If it is true that I have gone astray,
  my error remains my concern alone.
⁵If indeed you would exalt yourselves above me
  and use my humiliation against me,
⁶then know that God has wronged me
  and drawn his net around me.

⁷"Though I cry, 'I've been wronged!' I get no response;
  though I call for help, there is no justice.
⁸He has blocked my way so I cannot pass;
  he has shrouded my paths in darkness.
⁹He has stripped me of my honor
  and removed the crown from my head.
¹⁰He tears me down on every side till I am gone;
  he uproots my hope like a tree.
¹¹His anger burns against me;
  he counts me among his enemies.
¹²His troops advance in force;
  they build a siege ramp against me
  and encamp around my tent.

¹³"He has alienated my brothers from me;
  my acquaintances are completely estranged from me.
¹⁴My kinsmen have gone away;
  my friends have forgotten me.
¹⁵My guests and my maidservants count me a stranger;
  they look upon me as an alien.
¹⁶I summon my servant, but he does not answer,
  though I beg him with my own mouth.
¹⁷My breath is offensive to my wife;
  I am loathsome to my own brothers.
¹⁸Even the little boys scorn me;
  when I appear, they ridicule me.
¹⁹All my intimate friends detest me;
  those I love have turned against me.
²⁰I am nothing but skin and bones;
  I have escaped with only the skin of my teeth.ᵃ

²¹"Have pity on me, my friends, have pity,
  for the hand of God has struck me.
²²Why do you pursue me as God does?
  Will you never get enough of my flesh?

²³"Oh, that my words were recorded,
  that they were written on a scroll,
²⁴that they were inscribed with an iron tool onᵇ lead,
  or engraved in rock forever!
²⁵I know that my Redeemerᶜ lives,
  and that in the end he will stand upon the earth.ᵈ
²⁶And after my skin has been destroyed,
  yetᵉ inᶠ my flesh I will see God;
²⁷I myself will see him
  with my own eyes—I, and not another.
  How my heart yearns within me!

²⁸"If you say, 'How we will hound him,
  since the root of the trouble lies in him,ᵍ'

> I myself will see
> him with my
> own eyes—I, and
> not another. How
> my heart yearns
> within me
> (Job 19:27)!

ᵃ20 Or *only my gums* ᵇ24 Or *and* ᶜ25 Or *defender* ᵈ25 Or *upon my grave* ᵉ26 Or *And after I awake, / though this body has been destroyed, / then* ᶠ26 Or */ apart from* ᵍ28 Many Hebrew manuscripts, Septuagint and Vulgate; most Hebrew manuscripts *me*

²⁹you should fear the sword yourselves;
  for wrath will bring punishment by the sword,
  and then you will know that there is judgment.ᵃ"

20 *Zophar* Then Zophar the Naamathite replied:

²"My troubled thoughts prompt me to answer
  because I am greatly disturbed.
³I hear a rebuke that dishonors me,
  and my understanding inspires me to reply.

⁴"Surely you know how it has been from of old,
  ever since manᵇ was placed on the earth,
⁵that the mirth of the wicked is brief,
  the joy of the godless lasts but a moment.
⁶Though his pride reaches to the heavens
  and his head touches the clouds,
⁷he will perish forever, like his own dung;
  those who have seen him will say, 'Where is he?'
⁸Like a dream he flies away, no more to be found,
  banished like a vision of the night.
⁹The eye that saw him will not see him again;
  his place will look on him no more.
¹⁰His children must make amends to the poor;
  his own hands must give back his wealth.
¹¹The youthful vigor that fills his bones
  will lie with him in the dust.

¹²"Though evil is sweet in his mouth
  and he hides it under his tongue,
¹³though he cannot bear to let it go
  and keeps it in his mouth,
¹⁴yet his food will turn sour in his stomach;
  it will become the venom of serpents within him.
¹⁵He will spit out the riches he swallowed;
  God will make his stomach vomit them up.
¹⁶He will suck the poison of serpents;
  the fangs of an adder will kill him.
¹⁷He will not enjoy the streams,
  the rivers flowing with honey and cream.
¹⁸What he toiled for he must give back uneaten;
  he will not enjoy the profit from his trading.
¹⁹For he has oppressed the poor and left them destitute;
  he has seized houses he did not build.

²⁰"Surely he will have no respite from his craving;
  he cannot save himself by his treasure.
²¹Nothing is left for him to devour;
  his prosperity will not endure.
²²In the midst of his plenty, distress will overtake him;
  the full force of misery will come upon him.
²³When he has filled his belly,
  God will vent his burning anger against him
  and rain down his blows upon him.
²⁴Though he flees from an iron weapon,
  a bronze-tipped arrow pierces him.

ᵃ29 Or / that you may come to know the Almighty   ᵇ4 Or Adam

²⁵ He pulls it out of his back,
    the gleaming point out of his liver.
  Terrors will come over him;
²⁶   total darkness lies in wait for his treasures.
  A fire unfanned will consume him
    and devour what is left in his tent.
²⁷ The heavens will expose his guilt;
    the earth will rise up against him.
²⁸ A flood will carry off his house,
    rushing waters^a on the day of God's wrath.
²⁹ Such is the fate God allots the wicked,
    the heritage appointed for them by God."

21

Job   Then Job replied:

² "Listen carefully to my words;
    let this be the consolation you give me.
³ Bear with me while I speak,
    and after I have spoken, mock on.

⁴ "Is my complaint directed to man?
    Why should I not be impatient?
⁵ Look at me and be astonished;
    clap your hand over your mouth.
⁶ When I think about this, I am terrified;
    trembling seizes my body.
⁷ Why do the wicked live on,
    growing old and increasing in power?
⁸ They see their children established around them,
    their offspring before their eyes.
⁹ Their homes are safe and free from fear;
    the rod of God is not upon them.
¹⁰ Their bulls never fail to breed;
    their cows calve and do not miscarry.
¹¹ They send forth their children as a flock;
    their little ones dance about.
¹² They sing to the music of tambourine and harp;
    they make merry to the sound of the flute.
¹³ They spend their years in prosperity
    and go down to the grave^b in peace.^c
¹⁴ Yet they say to God, 'Leave us alone!
    We have no desire to know your ways.
¹⁵ Who is the Almighty, that we should serve him?
    What would we gain by praying to him?'
¹⁶ But their prosperity is not in their own hands,
    so I stand aloof from the counsel of the wicked.

¹⁷ "Yet how often is the lamp of the wicked snuffed out?
    How often does calamity come upon them,
    the fate God allots in his anger?
¹⁸ How often are they like straw before the wind,
    like chaff swept away by a gale?
¹⁹ It is said, 'God stores up a man's punishment for his sons.'
    Let him repay the man himself, so that he will know it!

---

^a28 Or *The possessions in his house will be carried off, / washed away* ^b13 Hebrew *Sheol* ^c13 Or *in an instant*

²⁰Let his own eyes see his destruction;
  let him drink of the wrath of the Almighty.ᵃ
²¹For what does he care about the family he leaves behind
  when his allotted months come to an end?

²²"Can anyone teach knowledge to God,
  since he judges even the highest?
²³One man dies in full vigor,
  completely secure and at ease,
²⁴his bodyᵇ well nourished,
  his bones rich with marrow.
²⁵Another man dies in bitterness of soul,
  never having enjoyed anything good.
²⁶Side by side they lie in the dust,
  and worms cover them both.

²⁷"I know full well what you are thinking,
  the schemes by which you would wrong me.
²⁸You say, 'Where now is the great man's house,
  the tents where wicked men lived?'
²⁹Have you never questioned those who travel?
  Have you paid no regard to their accounts—
³⁰that the evil man is spared from the day of calamity,
  that he is delivered fromᶜ the day of wrath?
³¹Who denounces his conduct to his face?
  Who repays him for what he has done?
³²He is carried to the grave,
  and watch is kept over his tomb.
³³The soil in the valley is sweet to him;
  all men follow after him,
  and a countless throng goesᵈ before him.

³⁴"So how can you console me with your nonsense?
  Nothing is left of your answers but falsehood!"

22 *Eliphaz* Then Eliphaz the Temanite replied:

²"Can a man be of benefit to God?
  Can even a wise man benefit him?
³What pleasure would it give the Almighty if you were righteous?
  What would he gain if your ways were blameless?

⁴"Is it for your piety that he rebukes you
  and brings charges against you?
⁵Is not your wickedness great?
  Are not your sins endless?
⁶You demanded security from your brothers for no reason;
  you stripped men of their clothing, leaving them naked.
⁷You gave no water to the weary
  and you withheld food from the hungry,
⁸though you were a powerful man, owning land—
  an honored man, living on it.
⁹And you sent widows away empty-handed
  and broke the strength of the fatherless.

ᵃ17-20 Verses 17 and 18 may be taken as exclamations and 19 and 20 as declarations.   ᵇ24 The meaning of the Hebrew for this word is uncertain.   ᶜ30 Or *man is reserved for the day of calamity, / that he is brought forth to*   ᵈ33 Or / *as a countless throng went*

¹⁰ That is why snares are all around you,
    why sudden peril terrifies you,
¹¹ why it is so dark you cannot see,
    and why a flood of water covers you.

¹² "Is not God in the heights of heaven?
    And see how lofty are the highest stars!
¹³ Yet you say, 'What does God know?
    Does he judge through such darkness?
¹⁴ Thick clouds veil him, so he does not see us
    as he goes about in the vaulted heavens.'
¹⁵ Will you keep to the old path
    that evil men have trod?
¹⁶ They were carried off before their time,
    their foundations washed away by a flood.
¹⁷ They said to God, 'Leave us alone!
    What can the Almighty do to us?'
¹⁸ Yet it was he who filled their houses with good things,
    so I stand aloof from the counsel of the wicked.

¹⁹ "The righteous see their ruin and rejoice;
    the innocent mock them, saying,
²⁰ 'Surely our foes are destroyed,
    and fire devours their wealth.'

²¹ "Submit to God and be at peace with him;
    in this way prosperity will come to you.
²² Accept instruction from his mouth
    and lay up his words in your heart.
²³ If you return to the Almighty, you will be restored:
    If you remove wickedness far from your tent
²⁴ and assign your nuggets to the dust,
    your gold of Ophir to the rocks in the ravines,
²⁵ then the Almighty will be your gold,
    the choicest silver for you.
²⁶ Surely then you will find delight in the Almighty
    and will lift up your face to God.
²⁷ You will pray to him, and he will hear you,
    and you will fulfill your vows.
²⁸ What you decide on will be done,
    and light will shine on your ways.
²⁹ When men are brought low and you say, 'Lift them up!'
    then he will save the downcast.
³⁰ He will deliver even one who is not innocent,
    who will be delivered through the cleanness of your hands."

23 *Job* Then Job replied:

² "Even today my complaint is bitter;
    his hand[a] is heavy in spite of[b] my groaning.
³ If only I knew where to find him;
    if only I could go to his dwelling!
⁴ I would state my case before him
    and fill my mouth with arguments.
⁵ I would find out what he would answer me,
    and consider what he would say.

---

a2 Septuagint and Syriac; Hebrew / *the hand on me*   *b2* Or *heavy on me in*

⁶Would he oppose me with great power?
No, he would not press charges against me.
⁷There an upright man could present his case before him,
and I would be delivered forever from my judge.

⁸"But if I go to the east, he is not there;
if I go to the west, I do not find him.
⁹When he is at work in the north, I do not see him;
when he turns to the south, I catch no glimpse of him.
¹⁰But he knows the way that I take;
when he has tested me, I will come forth as gold.
¹¹My feet have closely followed his steps;
I have kept to his way without turning aside.
¹²I have not departed from the commands of his lips;
I have treasured the words of his mouth more than my daily
bread.

¹³"But he stands alone, and who can oppose him?
He does whatever he pleases.
¹⁴He carries out his decree against me,
and many such plans he still has in store.
¹⁵That is why I am terrified before him;
when I think of all this, I fear him.
¹⁶God has made my heart faint;
the Almighty has terrified me.
¹⁷Yet I am not silenced by the darkness,
by the thick darkness that covers my face.

24 "Why does the Almighty not set times for judgment?
Why must those who know him look in vain for such days?
²Men move boundary stones;
they pasture flocks they have stolen.
³They drive away the orphan's donkey
and take the widow's ox in pledge.
⁴They thrust the needy from the path
and force all the poor of the land into hiding.
⁵Like wild donkeys in the desert,
the poor go about their labor of foraging food;
the wasteland provides food for their children.
⁶They gather fodder in the fields
and glean in the vineyards of the wicked.
⁷Lacking clothes, they spend the night naked;
they have nothing to cover themselves in the cold.
⁸They are drenched by mountain rains
and hug the rocks for lack of shelter.
⁹The fatherless child is snatched from the breast;
the infant of the poor is seized for a debt.
¹⁰Lacking clothes, they go about naked;
they carry the sheaves, but still go hungry.
¹¹They crush olives among the terraces*ᵃ*;
they tread the winepresses, yet suffer thirst.
¹²The groans of the dying rise from the city,
and the souls of the wounded cry out for help.
But God charges no one with wrongdoing.

ᵃ11 Or olives between the millstones; the meaning of the Hebrew for this word is uncertain.

13 "There are those who rebel against the light,
   who do not know its ways
   or stay in its paths.
14 When daylight is gone, the murderer rises up
   and kills the poor and needy;
   in the night he steals forth like a thief.
15 The eye of the adulterer watches for dusk;
   he thinks, 'No eye will see me,'
   and he keeps his face concealed.
16 In the dark, men break into houses,
   but by day they shut themselves in;
   they want nothing to do with the light.
17 For all of them, deep darkness is their morning*ᵃ*;
   they make friends with the terrors of darkness.*ᵇ*

18 "Yet they are foam on the surface of the water;
   their portion of the land is cursed,
   so that no one goes to the vineyards.
19 As heat and drought snatch away the melted snow,
   so the grave*ᶜ* snatches away those who have sinned.
20 The womb forgets them,
   the worm feasts on them;
 evil men are no longer remembered
   but are broken like a tree.
21 They prey on the barren and childless woman,
   and to the widow show no kindness.
22 But God drags away the mighty by his power;
   though they become established, they have no assurance of
      life.
23 He may let them rest in a feeling of security,
   but his eyes are on their ways.
24 For a little while they are exalted, and then they are gone;
   they are brought low and gathered up like all others;
   they are cut off like heads of grain.

25 "If this is not so, who can prove me false
   and reduce my words to nothing?"

25   *Bildad*   Then Bildad the Shuhite replied:

2 "Dominion and awe belong to God;
   he establishes order in the heights of heaven.
3 Can his forces be numbered?
   Upon whom does his light not rise?
4 How then can a man be righteous before God?
   How can one born of woman be pure?
5 If even the moon is not bright
   and the stars are not pure in his eyes,
6 how much less man, who is but a maggot—
   a son of man, who is only a worm!"

26   *Job*   Then Job replied:

2 "How you have helped the powerless!
   How you have saved the arm that is feeble!

---

*ᵃ17 Or them, their morning is like the shadow of death   *ᵇ17 Or of the shadow of death   *ᶜ19 Hebrew Sheol

³What advice you have offered to one without wisdom!
  And what great insight you have displayed!
⁴Who has helped you utter these words?
  And whose spirit spoke from your mouth?

⁵"The dead are in deep anguish,
  those beneath the waters and all that live in them.
⁶Death*ᵃ* is naked before God;
  Destruction*ᵇ* lies uncovered.
⁷He spreads out the northern skies over empty space;
  he suspends the earth over nothing.
⁸He wraps up the waters in his clouds,
  yet the clouds do not burst under their weight.
⁹He covers the face of the full moon,
  spreading his clouds over it.
¹⁰He marks out the horizon on the face of the waters
  for a boundary between light and darkness.
¹¹The pillars of the heavens quake,
  aghast at his rebuke.
¹²By his power he churned up the sea;
  by his wisdom he cut Rahab to pieces.
¹³By his breath the skies became fair;
  his hand pierced the gliding serpent.
¹⁴And these are but the outer fringe of his works;
  how faint the whisper we hear of him!
  Who then can understand the thunder of his power?"

27 And Job continued his discourse:

²"As surely as God lives, who has denied me justice,
  the Almighty, who has made me taste bitterness of soul,
³as long as I have life within me,
  the breath of God in my nostrils,
⁴my lips will not speak wickedness,
  and my tongue will utter no deceit.
⁵I will never admit you are in the right;
  till I die, I will not deny my integrity.
⁶I will maintain my righteousness and never let go of it;
  my conscience will not reproach me as long as I live.

⁷"May my enemies be like the wicked,
  my adversaries like the unjust!
⁸For what hope has the godless when he is cut off,
  when God takes away his life?
⁹Does God listen to his cry
  when distress comes upon him?
¹⁰Will he find delight in the Almighty?
  Will he call upon God at all times?

¹¹"I will teach you about the power of God;
  the ways of the Almighty I will not conceal.
¹²You have all seen this yourselves.
  Why then this meaningless talk?

¹³"Here is the fate God allots to the wicked,
  the heritage a ruthless man receives from the Almighty:

ᵃ6 Hebrew *Sheol* *ᵇ6* Hebrew *Abaddon*

¹⁴However many his children, their fate is the sword;
  his offspring will never have enough to eat.
¹⁵The plague will bury those who survive him,
  and their widows will not weep for them.
¹⁶Though he heaps up silver like dust
  and clothes like piles of clay,
¹⁷what he lays up the righteous will wear,
  and the innocent will divide his silver.
¹⁸The house he builds is like a moth's cocoon,
  like a hut made by a watchman.
¹⁹He lies down wealthy, but will do so no more;
  when he opens his eyes, all is gone.
²⁰Terrors overtake him like a flood;
  a tempest snatches him away in the night.
²¹The east wind carries him off, and he is gone;
  it sweeps him out of his place.
²²It hurls itself against him without mercy
  as he flees headlong from its power.
²³It claps its hands in derision
  and hisses him out of his place.

28 "There is a mine for silver
  and a place where gold is refined.
²Iron is taken from the earth,
  and copper is smelted from ore.
³Man puts an end to the darkness;
  he searches the farthest recesses
  for ore in the blackest darkness.
⁴Far from where people dwell he cuts a shaft,
  in places forgotten by the foot of man;
  far from men he dangles and sways.
⁵The earth, from which food comes,
  is transformed below as by fire;
⁶sapphires^a come from its rocks,
  and its dust contains nuggets of gold.
⁷No bird of prey knows that hidden path,
  no falcon's eye has seen it.
⁸Proud beasts do not set foot on it,
  and no lion prowls there.
⁹Man's hand assaults the flinty rock
  and lays bare the roots of the mountains.
¹⁰He tunnels through the rock;
  his eyes see all its treasures.
¹¹He searches^b the sources of the rivers
  and brings hidden things to light.

¹²"But where can wisdom be found?
  Where does understanding dwell?
¹³Man does not comprehend its worth;
  it cannot be found in the land of the living.
¹⁴The deep says, 'It is not in me';
  the sea says, 'It is not with me.'
¹⁵It cannot be bought with the finest gold,
  nor can its price be weighed in silver.

---

^a6 Or *lapis lazuli*; also in verse 16   ^b11 Septuagint, Aquila and Vulgate; Hebrew *He dams up*

¹⁶It cannot be bought with the gold of Ophir,
  with precious onyx or sapphires.
¹⁷Neither gold nor crystal can compare with it,
  nor can it be had for jewels of gold.
¹⁸Coral and jasper are not worthy of mention;
  the price of wisdom is beyond rubies.
¹⁹The topaz of Cush cannot compare with it;
  it cannot be bought with pure gold.

²⁰"Where then does wisdom come from?
  Where does understanding dwell?
²¹It is hidden from the eyes of every living thing,
  concealed even from the birds of the air.
²²Destruction^a and Death say,
  'Only a rumor of it has reached our ears.'
²³God understands the way to it
  and he alone knows where it dwells,
²⁴for he views the ends of the earth
  and sees everything under the heavens.
²⁵When he established the force of the wind
  and measured out the waters,
²⁶when he made a decree for the rain
  and a path for the thunderstorm,
²⁷then he looked at wisdom and appraised it;
  he confirmed it and tested it.
²⁸And he said to man,
  'The fear of the Lord—that is wisdom,
  and to shun evil is understanding.' "

29 Job continued his discourse:

²"How I long for the months gone by,
  for the days when God watched over me,
³when his lamp shone upon my head
  and by his light I walked through darkness!
⁴Oh, for the days when I was in my prime,
  when God's intimate friendship blessed my house,
⁵when the Almighty was still with me
  and my children were around me,
⁶when my path was drenched with cream
  and the rock poured out for me streams of olive oil.

⁷"When I went to the gate of the city
  and took my seat in the public square,
⁸the young men saw me and stepped aside
  and the old men rose to their feet;
⁹the chief men refrained from speaking
  and covered their mouths with their hands;
¹⁰the voices of the nobles were hushed,
  and their tongues stuck to the roof of their mouths.
¹¹Whoever heard me spoke well of me,
  and those who saw me commended me,
¹²because I rescued the poor who cried for help,
  and the fatherless who had none to assist him.
¹³The man who was dying blessed me;
  I made the widow's heart sing.

Are you guys still arguing?

SEE
JOB 29

^a22 Hebrew *Abaddon*

¹⁴I put on righteousness as my clothing;
　justice was my robe and my turban.
¹⁵I was eyes to the blind
　and feet to the lame.
¹⁶I was a father to the needy;
　I took up the case of the stranger.
¹⁷I broke the fangs of the wicked
　and snatched the victims from their teeth.

¹⁸"I thought, 'I will die in my own house,
　my days as numerous as the grains of sand.
¹⁹My roots will reach to the water,
　and the dew will lie all night on my branches.
²⁰My glory will remain fresh in me,
　the bow ever new in my hand.'

²¹"Men listened to me expectantly,
　waiting in silence for my counsel.
²²After I had spoken, they spoke no more;
　my words fell gently on their ears.
²³They waited for me as for showers
　and drank in my words as the spring rain.
²⁴When I smiled at them, they scarcely believed it;
　the light of my face was precious to them.ᵃ
²⁵I chose the way for them and sat as their chief;
　I dwelt as a king among his troops;
　I was like one who comforts mourners.

30 "But now they mock me,
　men younger than I,
whose fathers I would have disdained
　to put with my sheep dogs.
²Of what use was the strength of their hands to me,
　since their vigor had gone from them?
³Haggard from want and hunger,
　they roamedᵇ the parched land
　in desolate wastelands at night.
⁴In the brush they gathered salt herbs,
　and their foodᶜ was the root of the broom tree.
⁵They were banished from their fellow men,
　shouted at as if they were thieves.
⁶They were forced to live in the dry stream beds,
　among the rocks and in holes in the ground.
⁷They brayed among the bushes
　and huddled in the undergrowth.
⁸A base and nameless brood,
　they were driven out of the land.

⁹"And now their sons mock me in song;
　I have become a byword among them.
¹⁰They detest me and keep their distance;
　they do not hesitate to spit in my face.
¹¹Now that God has unstrung my bow and afflicted me,
　they throw off restraint in my presence.

ᵃ24 The meaning of the Hebrew for this clause is uncertain.　ᵇ3 Or *gnawed*　ᶜ4 Or *fuel*

¹²On my right the tribe^{*a*} attacks;
    they lay snares for my feet,
    they build their siege ramps against me.
¹³They break up my road;
    they succeed in destroying me—
    without anyone's helping them.^{*b*}
¹⁴They advance as through a gaping breach;
    amid the ruins they come rolling in.
¹⁵Terrors overwhelm me;
    my dignity is driven away as by the wind,
    my safety vanishes like a cloud.

¹⁶"And now my life ebbs away;
    days of suffering grip me.
¹⁷Night pierces my bones;
    my gnawing pains never rest.
¹⁸In his great power God becomes like clothing to me^{*c*};
    he binds me like the neck of my garment.
¹⁹He throws me into the mud,
    and I am reduced to dust and ashes.

²⁰"I cry out to you, O God, but you do not answer;
    I stand up, but you merely look at me.
²¹You turn on me ruthlessly;
    with the might of your hand you attack me.
²²You snatch me up and drive me before the wind;
    you toss me about in the storm.
²³I know you will bring me down to death,
    to the place appointed for all the living.

²⁴"Surely no one lays a hand on a broken man
    when he cries for help in his distress.
²⁵Have I not wept for those in trouble?
    Has not my soul grieved for the poor?
²⁶Yet when I hoped for good, evil came;
    when I looked for light, then came darkness.
²⁷The churning inside me never stops;
    days of suffering confront me.
²⁸I go about blackened, but not by the sun;
    I stand up in the assembly and cry for help.
²⁹I have become a brother of jackals,
    a companion of owls.
³⁰My skin grows black and peels;
    my body burns with fever.
³¹My harp is tuned to mourning,
    and my flute to the sound of wailing.

31 "I made a covenant with my eyes
    not to look lustfully at a girl.
²For what is man's lot from God above,
    his heritage from the Almighty on high?
³Is it not ruin for the wicked,
    disaster for those who do wrong?
⁴Does he not see my ways
    and count my every step?

---

a12 The meaning of the Hebrew for this word is uncertain. *b13* Or *me. / 'No one can help him,' they say* .
c18 Hebrew; Septuagint *God grasps my clothing*

⁵"If I have walked in falsehood
  or my foot has hurried after deceit—
⁶let God weigh me in honest scales
  and he will know that I am blameless—
⁷if my steps have turned from the path,
  if my heart has been led by my eyes,
  or if my hands have been defiled,
⁸then may others eat what I have sown,
  and may my crops be uprooted.

⁹"If my heart has been enticed by a woman,
  or if I have lurked at my neighbor's door,
¹⁰then may my wife grind another man's grain,
  and may other men sleep with her.
¹¹For that would have been shameful,
  a sin to be judged.
¹²It is a fire that burns to Destruction*;
  it would have uprooted my harvest.

¹³"If I have denied justice to my menservants and maidservants
  when they had a grievance against me,
¹⁴what will I do when God confronts me?
  What will I answer when called to account?
¹⁵Did not he who made me in the womb make them?
  Did not the same one form us both within our mothers?

¹⁶"If I have denied the desires of the poor
  or let the eyes of the widow grow weary,
¹⁷if I have kept my bread to myself,
  not sharing it with the fatherless—
¹⁸but from my youth I reared him as would a father,
  and from my birth I guided the widow—
¹⁹if I have seen anyone perishing for lack of clothing,
  or a needy man without a garment,
²⁰and his heart did not bless me
  for warming him with the fleece from my sheep,
²¹if I have raised my hand against the fatherless,
  knowing that I had influence in court,
²²then let my arm fall from the shoulder,
  let it be broken off at the joint.
²³For I dreaded destruction from God,
  and for fear of his splendor I could not do such
    things.

²⁴"If I have put my trust in gold
  or said to pure gold, 'You are my security,'
²⁵if I have rejoiced over my great wealth,
  the fortune my hands had gained,
²⁶if I have regarded the sun in its radiance
  or the moon moving in splendor,
²⁷so that my heart was secretly enticed
  and my hand offered them a kiss of homage,
²⁸then these also would be sins to be judged,
  for I would have been unfaithful to God on high.

²⁹"If I have rejoiced at my enemy's misfortune
  or gloated over the trouble that came to him—

*12 Hebrew *Abaddon*

³⁰I have not allowed my mouth to sin
 by invoking a curse against his life—
³¹if the men of my household have never said,
 'Who has not had his fill of Job's meat?'—
³²but no stranger had to spend the night in the street,
 for my door was always open to the traveler—
³³if I have concealed my sin as men do,^a
 by hiding my guilt in my heart
³⁴because I so feared the crowd
 and so dreaded the contempt of the clans
 that I kept silent and would not go outside

³⁵("Oh, that I had someone to hear me!
 I sign now my defense—let the Almighty answer me;
 let my accuser put his indictment in writing.
³⁶Surely I would wear it on my shoulder,
 I would put it on like a crown.
³⁷I would give him an account of my every step;
 like a prince I would approach him.)—

³⁸"if my land cries out against me
 and all its furrows are wet with tears,
³⁹if I have devoured its yield without payment
 or broken the spirit of its tenants,
⁴⁰then let briers come up instead of wheat
 and weeds instead of barley."

The words of Job are ended.

32 *Elihu* So these three men stopped answering Job, because he was righteous in his own eyes. ²But Elihu son of Barakel the Buzite, of the family of Ram, became very angry with Job for justifying himself rather than God. ³He was also angry with the three friends, because they had found no way to refute Job, and yet had condemned him.^b ⁴Now Elihu had waited before speaking to Job because they were older than he. ⁵But when he saw that the three men had nothing more to say, his anger was aroused.

⁶So Elihu son of Barakel the Buzite said:

 "I am young in years,
 and you are old;
 that is why I was fearful,
 not daring to tell you what I know.
⁷I thought, 'Age should speak;
 advanced years should teach wisdom.'
⁸But it is the spirit^c in a man,
 the breath of the Almighty, that gives him understanding.
⁹It is not only the old^d who are wise,
 not only the aged who understand what is right.

¹⁰"Therefore I say: Listen to me;
 I too will tell you what I know.
¹¹I waited while you spoke,
 I listened to your reasoning;
 while you were searching for words,
¹² I gave you my full attention.

---

^a33 Or *as Adam did* ^b3 Masoretic Text; an ancient Hebrew scribal tradition *Job, and so had condemned God* ^c8 Or *Spirit*; also in verse 18 ^d9 Or *many*, or *great*

But not one of you has proved Job wrong;
    none of you has answered his arguments.
13 Do not say, 'We have found wisdom;
    let God refute him, not man.'
14 But Job has not marshaled his words against me,
    and I will not answer him with your arguments.

15 "They are dismayed and have no more to say;
    words have failed them.
16 Must I wait, now that they are silent,
    now that they stand there with no reply?
17 I too will have my say;
    I too will tell what I know.
18 For I am full of words,
    and the spirit within me compels me;
19 inside I am like bottled-up wine,
    like new wineskins ready to burst.
20 I must speak and find relief;
    I must open my lips and reply.
21 I will show partiality to no one,
    nor will I flatter any man;
22 for if I were skilled in flattery,
    my Maker would soon take me away.

33

"But now, Job, listen to my words;
    pay attention to everything I say.
2 I am about to open my mouth;
    my words are on the tip of my tongue.
3 My words come from an upright heart;
    my lips sincerely speak what I know.
4 The Spirit of God has made me;
    the breath of the Almighty gives me life.
5 Answer me then, if you can;
    prepare yourself and confront me.
6 I am just like you before God;
    I too have been taken from clay.
7 No fear of me should alarm you,
    nor should my hand be heavy upon you.

8 "But you have said in my hearing—
    I heard the very words—
9 'I am pure and without sin;
    I am clean and free from guilt.
10 Yet God has found fault with me;
    he considers me his enemy.
11 He fastens my feet in shackles;
    he keeps close watch on all my paths.'

12 "But I tell you, in this you are not right,
    for God is greater than man.
13 Why do you complain to him
    that he answers none of man's words[a]?
14 For God does speak—now one way, now another—
    though man may not perceive it.
15 In a dream, in a vision of the night,
    when deep sleep falls on men
    as they slumber in their beds,

---

[a]13 Or *that he does not answer for any of his actions*

¹⁶he may speak in their ears
and terrify them with warnings,
¹⁷to turn man from wrongdoing
and keep him from pride,
¹⁸to preserve his soul from the pit,^a
his life from perishing by the sword.^b
¹⁹Or a man may be chastened on a bed of pain
with constant distress in his bones,
²⁰so that his very being finds food repulsive
and his soul loathes the choicest meal.
²¹His flesh wastes away to nothing,
and his bones, once hidden, now stick out.
²²His soul draws near to the pit,^c
and his life to the messengers of death.^d

²³"Yet if there is an angel on his side
as a mediator, one out of a thousand,
to tell a man what is right for him,
²⁴to be gracious to him and say,
'Spare him from going down to the pit^e;
I have found a ransom for him'—
²⁵then his flesh is renewed like a child's;
it is restored as in the days of his youth.
²⁶He prays to God and finds favor with him,
he sees God's face and shouts for joy;
he is restored by God to his righteous state.
²⁷Then he comes to men and says,
'I sinned, and perverted what was right,
but I did not get what I deserved.
²⁸He redeemed my soul from going down to the pit,^f
and I will live to enjoy the light.'

²⁹"God does all these things to a man—
twice, even three times—
³⁰to turn back his soul from the pit,^g
that the light of life may shine on him.

³¹"Pay attention, Job, and listen to me;
be silent, and I will speak.
³²If you have anything to say, answer me;
speak up, for I want you to be cleared.
³³But if not, then listen to me;
be silent, and I will teach you wisdom."

34 Then Elihu said:

²"Hear my words, you wise men;
listen to me, you men of learning.
³For the ear tests words
as the tongue tastes food.
⁴Let us discern for ourselves what is right;
let us learn together what is good.

⁵"Job says, 'I am innocent,
but God denies me justice.

---

^a18 Or *preserve him from the grave*   ^b18 Or *from crossing the River*   ^c22 Or *He draws near to the grave*
^d22 Or *to the dead*   ^e24 Or *grave*   ^f28 Or *redeemed me from going down to the grave*   ^g30 Or *turn him back from the grave*

⁶Although I am right,
    I am considered a liar;
  although I am guiltless,
    his arrow inflicts an incurable wound.'
⁷What man is like Job,
    who drinks scorn like water?
⁸He keeps company with evildoers;
    he associates with wicked men.
⁹For he says, 'It profits a man nothing
    when he tries to please God.'

¹⁰"So listen to me, you men of understanding.
    Far be it from God to do evil,
    from the Almighty to do wrong.
¹¹He repays a man for what he has done;
    he brings upon him what his conduct deserves.
¹²It is unthinkable that God would do wrong,
    that the Almighty would pervert justice.
¹³Who appointed him over the earth?
    Who put him in charge of the whole world?
¹⁴If it were his intention
    and he withdrew his spirit*a* and breath,
¹⁵all mankind would perish together
    and man would return to the dust.

¹⁶"If you have understanding, hear this;
    listen to what I say.
¹⁷Can he who hates justice govern?
    Will you condemn the just and mighty One?
¹⁸Is he not the One who says to kings, 'You are worthless,'
    and to nobles, 'You are wicked,'
¹⁹who shows no partiality to princes
    and does not favor the rich over the poor,
    for they are all the work of his hands?
²⁰They die in an instant, in the middle of the night;
    the people are shaken and they pass away;
    the mighty are removed without human hand.

²¹"His eyes are on the ways of men;
    he sees their every step.
²²There is no dark place, no deep shadow,
    where evildoers can hide.
²³God has no need to examine men further,
    that they should come before him for judgment.
²⁴Without inquiry he shatters the mighty
    and sets up others in their place.
²⁵Because he takes note of their deeds,
    he overthrows them in the night and they are crushed.
²⁶He punishes them for their wickedness
    where everyone can see them,
²⁷because they turned from following him
    and had no regard for any of his ways.
²⁸They caused the cry of the poor to come before him,
    so that he heard the cry of the needy.
²⁹But if he remains silent, who can condemn him?
    If he hides his face, who can see him?
  Yet he is over man and nation alike,

a14 Or Spirit

³⁰ to keep a godless man from ruling,
from laying snares for the people.

³¹ "Suppose a man says to God,
'I am guilty but will offend no more.
³² Teach me what I cannot see;
if I have done wrong, I will not do so again.'
³³ Should God then reward you on your terms,
when you refuse to repent?
You must decide, not I;
so tell me what you know.

³⁴ "Men of understanding declare,
wise men who hear me say to me,
³⁵ 'Job speaks without knowledge;
his words lack insight.'
³⁶ Oh, that Job might be tested to the utmost
for answering like a wicked man!
³⁷ To his sin he adds rebellion;
scornfully he claps his hands among us
and multiplies his words against God."

35 Then Elihu said:

² "Do you think this is just?
You say, 'I will be cleared by God.'^a
³ Yet you ask him, 'What profit is it to me,^b
and what do I gain by not sinning?'

⁴ "I would like to reply to you
and to your friends with you.
⁵ Look up at the heavens and see;
gaze at the clouds so high above you.
⁶ If you sin, how does that affect him?
If your sins are many, what does that do to him?
⁷ If you are righteous, what do you give to him,
or what does he receive from your hand?
⁸ Your wickedness affects only a man like yourself,
and your righteousness only the sons of men.

⁹ "Men cry out under a load of oppression;
they plead for relief from the arm of the powerful.
¹⁰ But no one says, 'Where is God my Maker,
who gives songs in the night,
¹¹ who teaches more to us than to^c the beasts of the earth
and makes us wiser than^d the birds of the air?'
¹² He does not answer when men cry out
because of the arrogance of the wicked.
¹³ Indeed, God does not listen to their empty plea;
the Almighty pays no attention to it.
¹⁴ How much less, then, will he listen
when you say that you do not see him,
that your case is before him
and you must wait for him,
¹⁵ and further, that his anger never punishes

---

^a2 Or *My righteousness is more than God's* ^b3 Or *you* ^c11 Or *teaches us by* ^d11 Or *us wise by*

and he does not take the least notice of
 wickedness.*
16 So Job opens his mouth with empty talk;
 without knowledge he multiplies words."

36 Elihu continued:

2 "Bear with me a little longer and I will show you
 that there is more to be said in God's behalf.
3 I get my knowledge from afar;
 I will ascribe justice to my Maker.
4 Be assured that my words are not false;
 one perfect in knowledge is with you.

5 "God is mighty, but does not despise men;
 he is mighty, and firm in his purpose.
6 He does not keep the wicked alive
 but gives the afflicted their rights.
7 He does not take his eyes off the righteous;
 he enthrones them with kings
 and exalts them forever.
8 But if men are bound in chains,
 held fast by cords of affliction,
9 he tells them what they have done—
 that they have sinned arrogantly.
10 He makes them listen to correction
 and commands them to repent of their evil.
11 If they obey and serve him,
 they will spend the rest of their days in prosperity
 and their years in contentment.
12 But if they do not listen,
 they will perish by the sword[b]
 and die without knowledge.

13 "The godless in heart harbor resentment;
 even when he fetters them, they do not cry for help.
14 They die in their youth,
 among male prostitutes of the shrines.
15 But those who suffer he delivers in their suffering;
 he speaks to them in their affliction.

16 "He is wooing you from the jaws of distress
 to a spacious place free from restriction,
 to the comfort of your table laden with choice food.
17 But now you are laden with the judgment due the wicked;
 judgment and justice have taken hold of you.
18 Be careful that no one entices you by riches;
 do not let a large bribe turn you aside.
19 Would your wealth
 or even all your mighty efforts
 sustain you so you would not be in distress?
20 Do not long for the night,
 to drag people away from their homes.[c]
21 Beware of turning to evil,
 which you seem to prefer to affliction.

---

[a]15 Symmachus, Theodotion and Vulgate; the meaning of the Hebrew for this word is uncertain. [b]12 Or
will cross the River [c]20 The meaning of the Hebrew for verses 18-20 is uncertain.

²²"God is exalted in his power.
　　Who is a teacher like him?
²³Who has prescribed his ways for him,
　　or said to him, 'You have done wrong'?
²⁴Remember to extol his work,
　　which men have praised in song.
²⁵All mankind has seen it;
　　men gaze on it from afar.
²⁶How great is God—beyond our understanding!
　　The number of his years is past finding out.

²⁷"He draws up the drops of water,
　　which distill as rain to the streams*a*;
²⁸the clouds pour down their moisture
　　and abundant showers fall on mankind.
²⁹Who can understand how he spreads out the clouds,
　　how he thunders from his pavilion?
³⁰See how he scatters his lightning about him,
　　bathing the depths of the sea.
³¹This is the way he governs*b* the nations
　　and provides food in abundance.
³²He fills his hands with lightning
　　and commands it to strike its mark.
³³His thunder announces the coming storm;
　　even the cattle make known its approach.*c*

37 "At this my heart pounds
　　and leaps from its place.
²Listen! Listen to the roar of his voice,
　　to the rumbling that comes from his mouth.
³He unleashes his lightning beneath the whole heaven
　　and sends it to the ends of the earth.
⁴After that comes the sound of his roar;
　　he thunders with his majestic voice.
　When his voice resounds,
　　he holds nothing back.
⁵God's voice thunders in marvelous ways;
　　he does great things beyond our understanding.
⁶He says to the snow, 'Fall on the earth,'
　　and to the rain shower, 'Be a mighty downpour.'
⁷So that all men he has made may know his work,
　　he stops every man from his labor.*d*
⁸The animals take cover;
　　they remain in their dens.
⁹The tempest comes out from its chamber,
　　the cold from the driving winds.
¹⁰The breath of God produces ice,
　　and the broad waters become frozen.
¹¹He loads the clouds with moisture;
　　he scatters his lightning through them.
¹²At his direction they swirl around
　　over the face of the whole earth
　　to do whatever he commands them.

---

a27 Or distill from the mist as rain *b31 Or nourishes* *c33 Or announces his coming— / the One zealous against evil* *d7 Or / he fills all men with fear by his power*

¹³He brings the clouds to punish men,
   or to water his earthᵃ and show his love.

¹⁴"Listen to this, Job;
   stop and consider God's wonders.
¹⁵Do you know how God controls the clouds
   and makes his lightning flash?
¹⁶Do you know how the clouds hang poised,
   those wonders of him who is perfect in knowledge?
¹⁷You who swelter in your clothes
   when the land lies hushed under the south wind,
¹⁸can you join him in spreading out the skies,
   hard as a mirror of cast bronze?

¹⁹"Tell us what we should say to him;
   we cannot draw up our case because of our darkness.
²⁰Should he be told that I want to speak?
   Would any man ask to be swallowed up?
²¹Now no one can look at the sun,
   bright as it is in the skies
   after the wind has swept them clean.
²²Out of the north he comes in golden splendor;
   God comes in awesome majesty.
²³The Almighty is beyond our reach and exalted in power;
   in his justice and great righteousness, he does not oppress.
²⁴Therefore, men revere him,
   for does he not have regard for all the wise in heart?ᵇ"

38   *The Lord Speaks*   Then the Lord answered Job out of the storm. He said:

²"Who is this that darkens my counsel
   with words without knowledge?
³Brace yourself like a man;
   I will question you,
   and you shall answer me.

⁴"Where were you when I laid the earth's foundation?
   Tell me, if you understand.

ᵃ13 Or *to favor them*   ᵇ24 Or *for he does not have regard for any who think they are wise.*

Many of today's science books discuss evolution as if scientists know what happened at creation years ago. But God once asked Job, "Where were you when I laid the earth's foundation?" (Job 38:4).

Scientists have only one way of learning things. They observe things and develop hypotheses. Then they run and rerun experiments to test the hypotheses. Does water boil at 212°F? Test it and see. Of course, there's no way to experiment with creation or evolution. So this "best way" can't be used by scientists to find out what happened long ago.

"Where were you?" is still a good question to ask when scientists talk as if they know for sure how the earth came to be. It's good for everyone to remember that while scientists weren't there, *God* was.

The Bible Says

Where Were You?

⁵Who marked off its dimensions? Surely you know!
  Who stretched a measuring line across it?
⁶On what were its footings set,
  or who laid its cornerstone—
⁷while the morning stars sang together
  and all the angelsᵃ shouted for joy?

⁸"Who shut up the sea behind doors
  when it burst forth from the womb,
⁹when I made the clouds its garment
  and wrapped it in thick darkness,
¹⁰when I fixed limits for it
  and set its doors and bars in place,
¹¹when I said, 'This far you may come and no farther;
  here is where your proud waves halt'?

¹²"Have you ever given orders to the morning,
  or shown the dawn its place,
¹³that it might take the earth by the edges
  and shake the wicked out of it?
¹⁴The earth takes shape like clay under a seal;
  its features stand out like those of a garment.
¹⁵The wicked are denied their light,
  and their upraised arm is broken.

¹⁶"Have you journeyed to the springs of the sea
  or walked in the recesses of the deep?
¹⁷Have the gates of death been shown to you?
  Have you seen the gates of the shadow of deathᵇ?
¹⁸Have you comprehended the vast expanses of the
      earth?
  Tell me, if you know all this.

¹⁹"What is the way to the abode of light?
  And where does darkness reside?
²⁰Can you take them to their places?
  Do you know the paths to their dwellings?
²¹Surely you know, for you were already born!
  You have lived so many years!

²²"Have you entered the storehouses of the snow
  or seen the storehouses of the hail,
²³which I reserve for times of trouble,
  for days of war and battle?
²⁴What is the way to the place where the lightning is dispersed,
  or the place where the east winds are scattered over the
      earth?
²⁵Who cuts a channel for the torrents of rain,
  and a path for the thunderstorm,
²⁶to water a land where no man lives,
  a desert with no one in it,
²⁷to satisfy a desolate wasteland
  and make it sprout with grass?
²⁸Does the rain have a father?
  Who fathers the drops of dew?
²⁹From whose womb comes the ice?
  Who gives birth to the frost from the heavens

ᵃ7 Hebrew *the sons of God* ᵇ17 Or *gates of deep shadows*

³⁰when the waters become hard as stone,
  when the surface of the deep is frozen?

³¹"Can you bind the beautiful^a Pleiades?
  Can you loose the cords of Orion?
³²Can you bring forth the constellations in their seasons^b
  or lead out the Bear^c with its cubs?
³³Do you know the laws of the heavens?
  Can you set up ⌊God's^d⌋ dominion over the earth?

³⁴"Can you raise your voice to the clouds
  and cover yourself with a flood of water?
³⁵Do you send the lightning bolts on their way?
  Do they report to you, 'Here we are'?
³⁶Who endowed the heart^e with wisdom
  or gave understanding to the mind^e?
³⁷Who has the wisdom to count the clouds?
  Who can tip over the water jars of the heavens
³⁸when the dust becomes hard
  and the clods of earth stick together?

³⁹"Do you hunt the prey for the lioness
  and satisfy the hunger of the lions
⁴⁰when they crouch in their dens
  or lie in wait in a thicket?
⁴¹Who provides food for the raven
  when its young cry out to God
  and wander about for lack of food?

39 "Do you know when the mountain goats give birth?
  Do you watch when the doe bears her fawn?
²Do you count the months till they bear?
  Do you know the time they give birth?
³They crouch down and bring forth their young;
  their labor pains are ended.
⁴Their young thrive and grow strong in the wilds;
  they leave and do not return.

⁵"Who let the wild donkey go free?
  Who untied his ropes?
⁶I gave him the wasteland as his home,
  the salt flats as his habitat.
⁷He laughs at the commotion in the town;
  he does not hear a driver's shout.
⁸He ranges the hills for his pasture
  and searches for any green thing.

⁹"Will the wild ox consent to serve you?
  Will he stay by your manger at night?
¹⁰Can you hold him to the furrow with a harness?
  Will he till the valleys behind you?
¹¹Will you rely on him for his great strength?
  Will you leave your heavy work to him?
¹²Can you trust him to bring in your grain
  and gather it to your threshing floor?

¹³"The wings of the ostrich flap joyfully,
    but they cannot compare with the pinions and feathers of
       the stork.
¹⁴She lays her eggs on the ground
    and lets them warm in the sand,
¹⁵unmindful that a foot may crush them,
    that some wild animal may trample them.
¹⁶She treats her young harshly, as if they were not hers;
    she cares not that her labor was in vain,
¹⁷for God did not endow her with wisdom
    or give her a share of good sense.
¹⁸Yet when she spreads her feathers to run,
    she laughs at horse and rider.

¹⁹"Do you give the horse his strength
    or clothe his neck with a flowing mane?
²⁰Do you make him leap like a locust,
    striking terror with his proud snorting?
²¹He paws fiercely, rejoicing in his strength,
    and charges into the fray.
²²He laughs at fear, afraid of nothing;
    he does not shy away from the sword.
²³The quiver rattles against his side,
    along with the flashing spear and lance.
²⁴In frenzied excitement he eats up the ground;
    he cannot stand still when the trumpet sounds.
²⁵At the blast of the trumpet he snorts, 'Aha!'
    He catches the scent of battle from afar,
    the shout of commanders and the battle cry.

²⁶"Does the hawk take flight by your wisdom
    and spread his wings toward the south?
²⁷Does the eagle soar at your command
    and build his nest on high?
²⁸He dwells on a cliff and stays there at night;
    a rocky crag is his stronghold.
²⁹From there he seeks out his food;
    his eyes detect it from afar.
³⁰His young ones feast on blood,
    and where the slain are, there is he."

40 The LORD said to Job:

²"Will the one who contends with the Almighty correct him?
    Let him who accuses God answer him!"

³Then Job answered the LORD:

⁴"I am unworthy—how can I reply to you?
    I put my hand over my mouth.
⁵I spoke once, but I have no answer—
    twice, but I will say no more."

⁶Then the LORD spoke to Job out of the storm:

⁷"Brace yourself like a man;
    I will question you,
    and you shall answer me.

⁸"Would you discredit my justice?
    Would you condemn me to justify yourself?

⁹Do you have an arm like God's,
  and can your voice thunder like his?
¹⁰Then adorn yourself with glory and splendor,
  and clothe yourself in honor and majesty.
¹¹Unleash the fury of your wrath,
  look at every proud man and bring him low,
¹²look at every proud man and humble him,
  crush the wicked where they stand.
¹³Bury them all in the dust together;
  shroud their faces in the grave.
¹⁴Then I myself will admit to you
  that your own right hand can save you.

¹⁵"Look at the behemoth,^a
  which I made along with you
  and which feeds on grass like an ox.
¹⁶What strength he has in his loins,
  what power in the muscles of his belly!
¹⁷His tail^b sways like a cedar;
  the sinews of his thighs are close-knit.
¹⁸His bones are tubes of bronze,
  his limbs like rods of iron.
¹⁹He ranks first among the works of God,
  yet his Maker can approach him with his sword.
²⁰The hills bring him their produce,
  and all the wild animals play nearby.
²¹Under the lotus plants he lies,
  hidden among the reeds in the marsh.
²²The lotuses conceal him in their shadow;
  the poplars by the stream surround him.
²³When the river rages, he is not alarmed;
  he is secure, though the Jordan should surge against his
    mouth.
²⁴Can anyone capture him by the eyes,^c
  or trap him and pierce his nose?

41 "Can you pull in the leviathan^d with a fishhook
  or tie down his tongue with a rope?
²Can you put a cord through his nose
  or pierce his jaw with a hook?
³Will he keep begging you for mercy?
  Will he speak to you with gentle words?
⁴Will he make an agreement with you
  for you to take him as your slave for life?
⁵Can you make a pet of him like a bird
  or put him on a leash for your girls?
⁶Will traders barter for him?
  Will they divide him up among the merchants?
⁷Can you fill his hide with harpoons
  or his head with fishing spears?
⁸If you lay a hand on him,
  you will remember the struggle and never do it again!
⁹Any hope of subduing him is false;
  the mere sight of him is overpowering.

---

^a15 Possibly the hippopotamus or the elephant ^b17 Possibly trunk ^c24 Or *by a water hole* ^d1 Possibly
the crocodile

¹⁰No one is fierce enough to rouse him.
  Who then is able to stand against me?
¹¹Who has a claim against me that I must pay?
  Everything under heaven belongs to me.

¹²"I will not fail to speak of his limbs,
  his strength and his graceful form.
¹³Who can strip off his outer coat?
  Who would approach him with a bridle?
¹⁴Who dares open the doors of his mouth,
  ringed about with his fearsome teeth?
¹⁵His back has* rows of shields
  tightly sealed together;
¹⁶each is so close to the next
  that no air can pass between.
¹⁷They are joined fast to one another;
  they cling together and cannot be parted.
¹⁸His snorting throws out flashes of light;
  his eyes are like the rays of dawn.
¹⁹Firebrands stream from his mouth;
  sparks of fire shoot out.
²⁰Smoke pours from his nostrils
  as from a boiling pot over a fire of reeds.
²¹His breath sets coals ablaze,
  and flames dart from his mouth.
²²Strength resides in his neck;
  dismay goes before him.
²³The folds of his flesh are tightly joined;
  they are firm and immovable.
²⁴His chest is hard as rock,
  hard as a lower millstone.
²⁵When he rises up, the mighty are terrified;
  they retreat before his thrashing.
²⁶The sword that reaches him has no effect,
  nor does the spear or the dart or the javelin.
²⁷Iron he treats like straw
  and bronze like rotten wood.
²⁸Arrows do not make him flee;
  slingstones are like chaff to him.
²⁹A club seems to him but a piece of straw;
  he laughs at the rattling of the lance.
³⁰His undersides are jagged potsherds,
  leaving a trail in the mud like a threshing sledge.
³¹He makes the depths churn like a boiling caldron
  and stirs up the sea like a pot of ointment.
³²Behind him he leaves a glistening wake;
  one would think the deep had white hair.
³³Nothing on earth is his equal—
  a creature without fear.
³⁴He looks down on all that are haughty;
  he is king over all that are proud."

42 *Job* Then Job replied to the LORD:

²"I know that you can do all things;
  no plan of yours can be thwarted.

15 Or His pride is his

³ ⌊You asked,⌋ 'Who is this that obscures my counsel without
     knowledge?'
  Surely I spoke of things I did not understand,
  things too wonderful for me to know.

⁴ ⌊"You said,⌋ 'Listen now, and I will speak;
  I will question you,
  and you shall answer me.'
⁵ My ears had heard of you
  but now my eyes have seen you.
⁶ Therefore I despise myself
  and repent in dust and ashes."

Epilogue ⁷After the Lᴏʀᴅ had said these things to Job, he said to Eliphaz the Temanite, "I am angry with you and your two friends, because you have not spoken of me what is right, as my servant Job has. ⁸So now take seven bulls and seven rams and go to my servant Job and sacrifice a burnt offering for yourselves. My servant Job will pray for you, and I will accept his prayer and not deal with you according to your folly. You have not spoken of me what is right, as my servant Job has." ⁹So Eliphaz the Temanite, Bildad the Shuhite and Zophar the Naamathite did what the Lᴏʀᴅ told them; and the Lᴏʀᴅ accepted Job's prayer.

¹⁰After Job had prayed for his friends, the Lᴏʀᴅ made him prosperous again and gave him twice as much as he had before. ¹¹All his brothers and sisters and everyone who had known him before came and ate with him in his house. They comforted and consoled him over all the trouble the Lᴏʀᴅ had brought upon him, and each one gave him a piece of silver*ᵃ* and a gold ring.

¹²The Lᴏʀᴅ blessed the latter part of Job's life more than the first. He had fourteen thousand sheep, six thousand camels, a thousand yoke of oxen and a thousand donkeys. ¹³And he also had seven sons and three daughters. ¹⁴The first daughter he named Jemimah, the second Keziah and the third Keren-Happuch. ¹⁵Nowhere in all the land were there found women as beautiful as Job's daughters, and their father granted them an inheritance along with their brothers.

¹⁶After this, Job lived a hundred and forty years; he saw his children and their children to the fourth generation. ¹⁷And so he died, old and full of years.

A piece of silver and a gold ring. How original!

SILVER

SILVER   SILVER

SEE
JOB 42:11

ᵃ11 Hebrew *him a kesitah*; a kesitah was a unit of money of unknown weight and value.

Psalms

FRIENDS.

Friends are people to whom you can really talk. You can tell a friend when you feel upset or afraid. You know a friend won't criticize you for being angry and will be patient when you mess up. A friend is someone with whom you can laugh—or cry.

Maybe that's why believers have loved the book of Psalms for thousands of years. The psalmists talk to God as a friend. They tell him just how they feel. And they praise God, not only for listening but also for his help. One of the best ways to grow close to God is to read a psalm every day and then use that psalm as a model for your own prayers.

Fun
damentals

Is it all right to tell God when you get angry at someone (Psalms 35, 69, 137)?

How does a person praise God (Psalms 33, 103, 139)?

How can you learn to think about God as a friend (Psalms 16, 20, 23)?

Will God hear your prayer when you know you've done something wrong (Psalms 32, 51)?

FAST FACTS

David wrote 73 psalms.

Hebrew poetry does not rhyme.

Many psalms were set to music for temple worship.

Psalm 119 is the longest Bible chapter.

The Hebrew name for Psalms is "Book of Praises."

BOOK I

Psalms 1–41

PSALM 1

¹ Blessed is the man
    who does not walk in the counsel of the wicked
  or stand in the way of sinners
    or sit in the seat of mockers.
² But his delight is in the law of the LORD,
    and on his law he meditates day and night.
³ He is like a tree planted by streams of water,
    which yields its fruit in season
  and whose leaf does not wither.
    Whatever he does prospers.

⁴ Not so the wicked!
    They are like chaff
    that the wind blows away.
⁵ Therefore the wicked will not stand in the judgment,
    nor sinners in the assembly of the righteous.

⁶ For the LORD watches over the way of the righteous,
    but the way of the wicked will perish.

PSALM 2

¹ Why do the nations conspire*ᵃ*
    and the peoples plot in vain?
² The kings of the earth take their stand
    and the rulers gather together
  against the LORD
    and against his Anointed One.*ᵇ*
³ "Let us break their chains," they say,
    "and throw off their fetters."

⁴ The One enthroned in heaven laughs;
    the Lord scoffs at them.
⁵ Then he rebukes them in his anger
    and terrifies them in his wrath, saying,
⁶ "I have installed my King*ᶜ*
    on Zion, my holy hill."

⁷ I will proclaim the decree of the LORD:

  He said to me, "You are my Son*ᵈ*;
    today I have become your Father.*ᵉ*
⁸ Ask of me,
    and I will make the nations your inheritance,
    the ends of the earth your possession.
⁹ You will rule them with an iron scepter*ᶠ*;
    you will dash them to pieces like pottery."

ᵃ1 Hebrew; Septuagint *rage*   *ᵇ2* Or *anointed one*   *ᶜ6* Or *king*   *ᵈ7* Or *son;* also in verse 12   *ᵉ7* Or *have begotten you*   *ᶠ9* Or *will break them with a rod of iron*

¹⁰Therefore, you kings, be wise;
  be warned, you rulers of the earth.
¹¹Serve the Lord with fear
  and rejoice with trembling.
¹²Kiss the Son, lest he be angry
  and you be destroyed in your way,
 for his wrath can flare up in a moment.
  Blessed are all who take refuge in him.

PSALM 3

A psalm of David. When he fled from his son Absalom.

¹O Lord, how many are my foes!
  How many rise up against me!
²Many are saying of me,
  "God will not deliver him."   *Selah*ᵃ

³But you are a shield around me, O Lord;
  you bestow glory on me and lift*ᵇ up my head.
⁴To the Lord I cry aloud,
  and he answers me from his holy hill.   *Selah*

⁵I lie down and sleep;
  I wake again, because the Lord sustains me.
⁶I will not fear the tens of thousands
  drawn up against me on every side.

⁷Arise, O Lord!
  Deliver me, O my God!

Strike all my enemies on the jaw;
  break the teeth of the wicked.

⁸From the Lord comes deliverance.
  May your blessing be on your
    people.   *Selah*

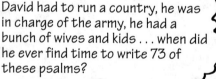

David had to run a country, he was in charge of the army, he had a bunch of wives and kids . . . when did he ever find time to write 73 of these psalms?

*SEE VARIOUS PSALM TITLES
FOR THOSE WRITTEN BY DAVID*

PSALM 4

For the director of music.
With stringed instruments.
A psalm of David.

¹Answer me when I call to you,
  O my righteous God.
 Give me relief from my distress;
  be merciful to me and hear my
    prayer.
²How long, O men, will you turn my
    glory into shameᶜ?
 How long will you love delusions
    and seek false godsᵈ?   *Selah*

ᵃ2 A word of uncertain meaning, occurring frequently in
the Psalms; possibly a musical term   ᵇ3 Or Lord, / my
Glorious One, who lifts   ᶜ2 Or you dishonor my Glorious
One   ᵈ2 Or seek lies

³Know that the Lord has set apart the godly for himself;
    the LORD will hear when I call to him.

⁴In your anger do not sin;
    when you are on your beds,
    search your hearts and be silent.   *Selah*
⁵Offer right sacrifices
    and trust in the LORD.

⁶Many are asking, "Who can show us any good?"
    Let the light of your face shine upon us, O LORD.
⁷You have filled my heart with greater joy
    than when their grain and new wine abound.
⁸I will lie down and sleep in peace,
    for you alone, O LORD,
    make me dwell in safety.

> The LORD has set apart the godly for himself; the LORD will hear when I call to him (Psalm 4:3).

PSALM 5

For the director of music. For flutes. A psalm of David.

¹Give ear to my words, O LORD,
    consider my sighing.
²Listen to my cry for help,
    my King and my God,
    for to you I pray.
³In the morning, O LORD, you hear my voice;
    in the morning I lay my requests before you
    and wait in expectation.

⁴You are not a God who takes pleasure in evil;
    with you the wicked cannot dwell.
⁵The arrogant cannot stand in your presence;
    you hate all who do wrong.
⁶You destroy those who tell lies;
    bloodthirsty and deceitful men
    the LORD abhors.

⁷But I, by your great mercy,
    will come into your house;
 in reverence will I bow down
    toward your holy temple.
⁸Lead me, O LORD, in your righteousness
    because of my enemies—
    make straight your way before me.

⁹Not a word from their mouth can be trusted;
    their heart is filled with destruction.
 Their throat is an open grave;
    with their tongue they speak deceit.
¹⁰Declare them guilty, O God!
    Let their intrigues be their downfall.
 Banish them for their many sins,
    for they have rebelled against you.
¹¹But let all who take refuge in you be glad;
    let them ever sing for joy.

Spread your protection over them,
that those who love your name may rejoice in you.
¹² For surely, O Lord, you bless the righteous;
you surround them with your favor as with a shield.

PSALM 6

For the director of music. With stringed instruments. According
to *sheminith.*^a A psalm of David.

¹ O Lord, do not rebuke me in your anger
or discipline me in your wrath.
² Be merciful to me, Lord, for I am faint;
O Lord, heal me, for my bones are in agony.
³ My soul is in anguish.
How long, O Lord, how long?

⁴ Turn, O Lord, and deliver me;
save me because of your unfailing love.
⁵ No one remembers you when he is dead.
Who praises you from the grave^b?

⁶ I am worn out from groaning;
all night long I flood my bed with weeping
and drench my couch with tears.
⁷ My eyes grow weak with sorrow;
they fail because of all my foes.

⁸ Away from me, all you who do evil,
for the Lord has heard my weeping.
⁹ The Lord has heard my cry for mercy;
the Lord accepts my prayer.
¹⁰ All my enemies will be ashamed and dismayed;
they will turn back in sudden disgrace.

PSALM 7

A *shiggaion*^c of David, which he sang to the Lord concerning Cush,
a Benjamite.

¹ O Lord my God, I take refuge in you;
save and deliver me from all who pursue me,
² or they will tear me like a lion
and rip me to pieces with no one to rescue me.

³ O Lord my God, if I have done this
and there is guilt on my hands—
⁴ if I have done evil to him who is at peace with me
or without cause have robbed my foe—
⁵ then let my enemy pursue and overtake me;
let him trample my life to the ground
and make me sleep in the dust.   *Selah*

---

^aTitle: Probably a musical term   ^b5 Hebrew *Sheol*   ^cTitle: Probably a literary or musical term

⁶Arise, O L<small>ORD</small>, in your anger;
    rise up against the rage of my enemies.
    Awake, my God; decree justice.
⁷Let the assembled peoples gather around you.
    Rule over them from on high;
⁸ let the L<small>ORD</small> judge the peoples.
  Judge me, O L<small>ORD</small>, according to my righteousness,
    according to my integrity, O Most High.
⁹O righteous God,
    who searches minds and hearts,
  bring to an end the violence of the wicked
    and make the righteous secure.

¹⁰My shield^{*a*} is God Most High,
    who saves the upright in heart.
¹¹God is a righteous judge,
    a God who expresses his wrath every day.
¹²If he does not relent,
    he^{*b*} will sharpen his sword;
    he will bend and string his bow.
¹³He has prepared his deadly weapons;
    he makes ready his flaming arrows.

¹⁴He who is pregnant with evil
    and conceives trouble gives birth to disillusionment.
¹⁵He who digs a hole and scoops it out
    falls into the pit he has made.
¹⁶The trouble he causes recoils on himself;
    his violence comes down on his own head.

¹⁷I will give thanks to the L<small>ORD</small> because of his righteousness
    and will sing praise to the name of the L<small>ORD</small> Most High.

PSALM 8

For the director of music. According to *gittith.*^{*c*} A psalm of David.

¹O L<small>ORD</small>, our Lord,
    how majestic is your name in all the earth!

---

^{*a*}10 Or *sovereign* ^{*b*}12 Or *If a man does not repent, / God* ^{*c*}Title: Probably a musical term

---

"Ecology" is a familiar word these days. More and more people have begun to realize that we are seriously polluting and damaging the earth on which we live.

When God first created human beings in his image, he said, "Rule over the fish of the sea and the birds of the air and over every living creature" (Genesis 1:28). That word *rule* doesn't mean "use." It means "take care of." That's what Psalm 8 is saying. God gave you a special honor (Psalm 8:5). God made you the ruler over all he made, to take care of it for him for the benefit of future generations and for the benefit of the other living creatures he created (Psalm 8:6–9).

The Bible Says

Guard the Earth

You have set your glory
   above the heavens.
²From the lips of children and infants
   you have ordained praise*ᵃ*
because of your enemies,
   to silence the foe and the avenger.

³When I consider your heavens,
   the work of your fingers,
the moon and the stars,
   which you have set in place,
⁴what is man that you are mindful of him,
   the son of man that you care for him?
⁵You made him a little lower than the heavenly beings*ᵇ*
   and crowned him with glory and honor.

⁶You made him ruler over the works of your hands;
   you put everything under his feet:
⁷all flocks and herds,
   and the beasts of the field,
⁸the birds of the air,
   and the fish of the sea,
   all that swim the paths of the seas.

⁹O LORD, our Lord,
   how majestic is your name in all the earth!

PSALM 9*ᶜ*

For the director of music. To the tune of, "The Death of the Son."
A psalm of David.

¹I will praise you, O LORD, with all my heart;
   I will tell of all your wonders.
²I will be glad and rejoice in you;
   I will sing praise to your name, O Most High.

³My enemies turn back;
   they stumble and perish before you.
⁴For you have upheld my right and my cause;
   you have sat on your throne, judging righteously.
⁵You have rebuked the nations and destroyed the wicked;
   you have blotted out their name for ever and ever.
⁶Endless ruin has overtaken the enemy,
   you have uprooted their cities;
   even the memory of them has perished.

⁷The LORD reigns forever;
   he has established his throne for judgment.
⁸He will judge the world in righteousness;
   he will govern the peoples with justice.
⁹The LORD is a refuge for the oppressed,
   a stronghold in times of trouble.
¹⁰Those who know your name will trust in you,
   for you, LORD, have never forsaken those who seek you.

ᵃ2 Or *strength* *ᵇ5* Or *than God* *ᶜ*Psalms 9 and 10 may have been originally a single acrostic poem, the stanzas of which begin with the successive letters of the Hebrew alphabet. In the Septuagint they constitute one psalm.

¹¹Sing praises to the LORD, enthroned in Zion;
> proclaim among the nations what he has done.
¹²For he who avenges blood remembers;
> he does not ignore the cry of the afflicted.

¹³O LORD, see how my enemies persecute me!
> Have mercy and lift me up from the gates of death,
¹⁴that I may declare your praises
> in the gates of the Daughter of Zion
> and there rejoice in your salvation.
¹⁵The nations have fallen into the pit they have dug;
> their feet are caught in the net they have hidden.
¹⁶The LORD is known by his justice;
> the wicked are ensnared by the work of their hands.

Higgaion.^a Selah

¹⁷The wicked return to the grave,^b
> all the nations that forget God.
¹⁸But the needy will not always be forgotten,
> nor the hope of the afflicted ever perish.

¹⁹Arise, O LORD, let not man triumph;
> let the nations be judged in your presence.
²⁰Strike them with terror, O LORD;
> let the nations know they are but men.

Selah

PSALM 10^c

¹Why, O LORD, do you stand far off?
> Why do you hide yourself in times of trouble?

²In his arrogance the wicked man hunts down the weak,
> who are caught in the schemes he devises.
³He boasts of the cravings of his heart;
> he blesses the greedy and reviles the LORD.
⁴In his pride the wicked does not seek him;
> in all his thoughts there is no room for God.
⁵His ways are always prosperous;
> he is haughty and your laws are far from him;
> he sneers at all his enemies.
⁶He says to himself, "Nothing will shake me;
> I'll always be happy and never have trouble."
⁷His mouth is full of curses and lies and threats;
> trouble and evil are under his tongue.
⁸He lies in wait near the villages;
> from ambush he murders the innocent,
> watching in secret for his victims.
⁹He lies in wait like a lion in cover;
> he lies in wait to catch the helpless;
> he catches the helpless and drags them off in his net.
¹⁰His victims are crushed, they collapse;
> they fall under his strength.
¹¹He says to himself, "God has forgotten;
> he covers his face and never sees."

You hear, O LORD, the desire of the afflicted; you encourage them, and you listen to their cry (Psalm 10:17).

---

^a*16* Or *Meditation*; possibly a musical notation ^b*17* Hebrew *Sheol* ^c*Psalms 9 and 10 may have been originally a single acrostic poem, the stanzas of which begin with the successive letters of the Hebrew alphabet. In the Septuagint they constitute one psalm.

¹²Arise, LORD! Lift up your hand, O God.
  Do not forget the helpless.
¹³Why does the wicked man revile God?
  Why does he say to himself,
  "He won't call me to account"?
¹⁴But you, O God, do see trouble and grief;
  you consider it to take it in hand.
The victim commits himself to you;
  you are the helper of the fatherless.
¹⁵Break the arm of the wicked and evil man;
  call him to account for his wickedness
  that would not be found out.

¹⁶The LORD is King for ever and ever;
  the nations will perish from his land.
¹⁷You hear, O LORD, the desire of the afflicted;
  you encourage them, and you listen to their cry,
¹⁸defending the fatherless and the oppressed,
  in order that man, who is of the earth, may terrify no more.

PSALM 11

For the director of music. Of David.

¹In the LORD I take refuge.
  How then can you say to me:
  "Flee like a bird to your mountain.
²For look, the wicked bend their bows;
  they set their arrows against the strings
to shoot from the shadows
  at the upright in heart.
³When the foundations are being destroyed,
  what can the righteous do*ᵃ?"

⁴The LORD is in his holy temple;
  the LORD is on his heavenly throne.
He observes the sons of men;
  his eyes examine them.
⁵The LORD examines the righteous,
  but the wicked*ᵇ and those who love violence
  his soul hates.
⁶On the wicked he will rain
  fiery coals and burning sulfur;
  a scorching wind will be their lot.

⁷For the LORD is righteous,
  he loves justice;
  upright men will see his face.

PSALM 12

For the director of music. According to *sheminith.*ᶜ A psalm
of David.

¹Help, LORD, for the godly are no more;
  the faithful have vanished from among men.

---

*ᵃ3 Or *what is the Righteous One doing* *ᵇ5 Or *The LORD, the Righteous One, examines the wicked,* /
ᶜTitle: Probably a musical term

²Everyone lies to his neighbor;
   their flattering lips speak with deception.

³May the LORD cut off all flattering lips
   and every boastful tongue
⁴that says, "We will triumph with our tongues;
   we own our lips*—who is our master?"

⁵"Because of the oppression of the weak
   and the groaning of the needy,
 I will now arise," says the LORD.
   "I will protect them from those who malign them."
⁶And the words of the LORD are flawless,
   like silver refined in a furnace of clay,
   purified seven times.

⁷O LORD, you will keep us safe
   and protect us from such people forever.
⁸The wicked freely strut about
   when what is vile is honored among men.

PSALM 13

For the director of music. A psalm of David.

¹How long, O LORD? Will you forget me forever?
   How long will you hide your face from me?
²How long must I wrestle with my thoughts
   and every day have sorrow in my heart?
   How long will my enemy triumph over me?

³Look on me and answer, O LORD my God.
   Give light to my eyes, or I will sleep in death;
⁴my enemy will say, "I have overcome him,"
   and my foes will rejoice when I fall.

⁵But I trust in your unfailing love;
   my heart rejoices in your salvation.
⁶I will sing to the LORD,
   for he has been good to me.

PSALM 14

For the director of music. Of David.

¹The fool*ᵇ says in his heart,
   "There is no God."
 They are corrupt, their deeds are vile;
   there is no one who does good.

²The LORD looks down from heaven
   on the sons of men
 to see if there are any who understand,
   any who seek God.

*ᵃ4 Or */ our lips are our plowshares* *ᵇ1 The Hebrew words rendered *fool* in Psalms denote one who is
morally deficient.

³All have turned aside,
    they have together become corrupt;
  there is no one who does good,
    not even one.

⁴Will evildoers never learn—
    those who devour my people as men eat bread
    and who do not call on the LORD?
⁵There they are, overwhelmed with dread,
    for God is present in the company of the righteous.
⁶You evildoers frustrate the plans of the poor,
    but the LORD is their refuge.

⁷Oh, that salvation for Israel would come out of Zion!
    When the LORD restores the fortunes of his people,
    let Jacob rejoice and Israel be glad!

PSALM 15

A psalm of David.

¹LORD, who may dwell in your sanctuary?
    Who may live on your holy hill?

²He whose walk is blameless
    and who does what is righteous,
  who speaks the truth from his heart
³   and has no slander on his tongue,
  who does his neighbor no wrong
    and casts no slur on his fellowman,
⁴who despises a vile man
    but honors those who fear the LORD,
  who keeps his oath
    even when it hurts,
⁵who lends his money without usury
    and does not accept a bribe against the innocent.

He who does these things
    will never be shaken.

The Bible Says

Don't Be Foolish

Very intelligent people can also be very foolish. In fact, the Old Testament uses several different words for *fool*, and none of them has anything to do with intelligence.

The word *fool* used in Psalm 14:1 describes the person who commits gross sins. The actions of such persons show that they don't believe God exists. If they believed in God and knew that one day God would declare judgment, they would change.

Believing in God makes a moral difference. It won't make you more intelligent, but it will make a difference in the way you live your life. And that's what's really important.

PSALM 16

A *miktam*[a] of David.

1 Keep me safe, O God,
    for in you I take refuge.

2 I said to the LORD, "You are my Lord;
    apart from you I have no good thing."
3 As for the saints who are in the land,
    they are the glorious ones in whom is all my delight.[b]
4 The sorrows of those will increase
    who run after other gods.
  I will not pour out their libations of blood
    or take up their names on my lips.

5 LORD, you have assigned me my portion and my cup;
    you have made my lot secure.
6 The boundary lines have fallen for me in pleasant places;
    surely I have a delightful inheritance.

7 I will praise the LORD, who counsels me;
    even at night my heart instructs me.
8 I have set the LORD always before me.
    Because he is at my right hand,
    I will not be shaken.

9 Therefore my heart is glad and my tongue rejoices;
    my body also will rest secure,
10 because you will not abandon me to the grave,[c]
    nor will you let your Holy One[d] see decay.
11 You have made[e] known to me the path of life;
    you will fill me with joy in your presence,
    with eternal pleasures at your right hand.

PSALM 17

A prayer of David.

1 Hear, O LORD, my righteous plea;
    listen to my cry.
  Give ear to my prayer—
    it does not rise from deceitful lips.
2 May my vindication come from you;
    may your eyes see what is right.

3 Though you probe my heart and examine me at night,
    though you test me, you will find nothing;
    I have resolved that my mouth will not sin.
4 As for the deeds of men—
    by the word of your lips
  I have kept myself
    from the ways of the violent.

> I call on you,
> O God, for you
> will answer me;
> give ear to me and
> hear my prayer
> (Psalm 17:6).

---

*a*Title: Probably a literary or musical term   *b*3 Or *As for the pagan priests who are in the land / and the nobles in whom all delight, I said:*   *c*10 Hebrew *Sheol*   *d*10 Or *your faithful one*   *e*11 Or *You will make*

⁵My steps have held to your paths;
   my feet have not slipped.

⁶I call on you, O God, for you will answer me;
   give ear to me and hear my prayer.
⁷Show the wonder of your great love,
   you who save by your right hand
   those who take refuge in you from their foes.
⁸Keep me as the apple of your eye;
   hide me in the shadow of your wings
⁹from the wicked who assail me,
   from my mortal enemies who surround me.

¹⁰They close up their callous hearts,
   and their mouths speak with arrogance.
¹¹They have tracked me down, they now surround me,
   with eyes alert, to throw me to the ground.
¹²They are like a lion hungry for prey,
   like a great lion crouching in cover.

¹³Rise up, O Lord, confront them, bring them down;
   rescue me from the wicked by your sword.
¹⁴O Lord, by your hand save me from such men,
   from men of this world whose reward is in this life.

You still the hunger of those you cherish;
   their sons have plenty,
   and they store up wealth for their children.
¹⁵And I—in righteousness I will see your face;
   when I awake, I will be satisfied with seeing your likeness.

PSALM 18

For the director of music. Of David the servant of the Lord. He sang to the Lord the words of this song when the Lord delivered him from the hand of all his enemies and from the hand of Saul. He said:

¹I love you, O Lord, my strength.

²The Lord is my rock, my fortress and my deliverer;
   my God is my rock, in whom I take refuge.
   He is my shield and the horn*ᵃ* of my salvation, my
      stronghold.
³I call to the Lord, who is worthy of praise,
   and I am saved from my enemies.

⁴The cords of death entangled me;
   the torrents of destruction overwhelmed me.
⁵The cords of the grave*ᵇ* coiled around me;
   the snares of death confronted me.
⁶In my distress I called to the Lord;
   I cried to my God for help.
From his temple he heard my voice;
   my cry came before him, into his ears.

⁷The earth trembled and quaked,
   and the foundations of the mountains shook;
   they trembled because he was angry.

ᵃ2 Horn here symbolizes strength.   *ᵇ5 Hebrew Sheol*

⁸Smoke rose from his nostrils;
    consuming fire came from his mouth,
    burning coals blazed out of it.
⁹He parted the heavens and came down;
    dark clouds were under his feet.
¹⁰He mounted the cherubim and flew;
    he soared on the wings of the wind.
¹¹He made darkness his covering, his canopy around him—
    the dark rain clouds of the sky.
¹²Out of the brightness of his presence clouds advanced,
    with hailstones and bolts of lightning.
¹³The Lord thundered from heaven;
    the voice of the Most High resounded.ᵃ
¹⁴He shot his arrows and scattered the enemies,
    great bolts of lightning and routed them.
¹⁵The valleys of the sea were exposed
    and the foundations of the earth laid bare
at your rebuke, O Lord,
    at the blast of breath from your nostrils.

¹⁶He reached down from on high and took hold of me;
    he drew me out of deep waters.
¹⁷He rescued me from my powerful enemy,
    from my foes, who were too strong for me.
¹⁸They confronted me in the day of my disaster,
    but the Lord was my support.
¹⁹He brought me out into a spacious place;
    he rescued me because he delighted in me.

²⁰The Lord has dealt with me according to my righteousness;
    according to the cleanness of my hands he has rewarded
      me.
²¹For I have kept the ways of the Lord;
    I have not done evil by turning from my God.
²²All his laws are before me;
    I have not turned away from his decrees.
²³I have been blameless before him
    and have kept myself from sin.
²⁴The Lord has rewarded me according to my righteousness,
    according to the cleanness of my hands in his sight.

²⁵To the faithful you show yourself faithful,
    to the blameless you show yourself blameless,
²⁶to the pure you show yourself pure,
    but to the crooked you show yourself shrewd.
²⁷You save the humble
    but bring low those whose eyes are haughty.
²⁸You, O Lord, keep my lamp burning;
    my God turns my darkness into light.
²⁹With your help I can advance against a troopᵇ;
    with my God I can scale a wall.

³⁰As for God, his way is perfect;
    the word of the Lord is flawless.
He is a shield
    for all who take refuge in him.

As for God, his
way is perfect . . .
He is a shield for
all who take
refuge in him
(Psalm 18:30).

ᵃ13 Some Hebrew manuscripts and Septuagint (see also 2 Samuel 22:14); most Hebrew manuscripts
resounded, / amid hailstones and bolts of lightning ᵇ29 Or *can run through a barricade*

³¹For who is God besides the LORD?
  And who is the Rock except our God?
³²It is God who arms me with strength
  and makes my way perfect.
³³He makes my feet like the feet of a deer;
  he enables me to stand on the heights.
³⁴He trains my hands for battle;
  my arms can bend a bow of bronze.
³⁵You give me your shield of victory,
  and your right hand sustains me;
  you stoop down to make me great.
³⁶You broaden the path beneath me,
  so that my ankles do not turn.

³⁷I pursued my enemies and overtook them;
  I did not turn back till they were destroyed.
³⁸I crushed them so that they could not rise;
  they fell beneath my feet.
³⁹You armed me with strength for battle;
  you made my adversaries bow at my feet.
⁴⁰You made my enemies turn their backs in flight,
  and I destroyed my foes.
⁴¹They cried for help, but there was no one to save them—
  to the LORD, but he did not answer.
⁴²I beat them as fine as dust borne on the wind;
  I poured them out like mud in the streets.

⁴³You have delivered me from the attacks of the people;
  you have made me the head of nations;
  people I did not know are subject to me.
⁴⁴As soon as they hear me, they obey me;
  foreigners cringe before me.
⁴⁵They all lose heart;
  they come trembling from their strongholds.

⁴⁶The LORD lives! Praise be to my Rock!
  Exalted be God my Savior!
⁴⁷He is the God who avenges me,
  who subdues nations under me,
⁴⁸ who saves me from my enemies.
  You exalted me above my foes;
  from violent men you rescued me.
⁴⁹Therefore I will praise you among the nations, O LORD;
  I will sing praises to your name.
⁵⁰He gives his king great victories;
  he shows unfailing kindness to his anointed,
  to David and his descendants forever.

PSALM 19

For the director of music. A psalm of David.

¹The heavens declare the glory of God;
  the skies proclaim the work of his hands.
²Day after day they pour forth speech;
  night after night they display knowledge.

³There is no speech or language
    where their voice is not heard.ᵃ
⁴Their voiceᵇ goes out into all the earth,
    their words to the ends of the world.

 In the heavens he has pitched a tent for the sun,
⁵ which is like a bridegroom coming forth from his pavilion,
    like a champion rejoicing to run his course.
⁶It rises at one end of the heavens
    and makes its circuit to the other;
    nothing is hidden from its heat.

⁷The law of the Lord is perfect,
    reviving the soul.
 The statutes of the Lord are trustworthy,
    making wise the simple.
⁸The precepts of the Lord are right,
    giving joy to the heart.
 The commands of the Lord are radiant,
    giving light to the eyes.
⁹The fear of the Lord is pure,
    enduring forever.
 The ordinances of the Lord are sure
    and altogether righteous.
¹⁰They are more precious than gold,
    than much pure gold;
 they are sweeter than honey,
    than honey from the comb.
¹¹By them is your servant warned;
    in keeping them there is great reward.

¹²Who can discern his errors?
    Forgive my hidden faults.
¹³Keep your servant also from willful sins;
    may they not rule over me.
 Then will I be blameless,
    innocent of great transgression.

¹⁴May the words of my mouth and the meditation of my heart
    be pleasing in your sight,
    O Lord, my Rock and my Redeemer.

PSALM 20

For the director of music. A psalm of David.

¹May the Lord answer you when you are in distress;
    may the name of the God of Jacob protect you.
²May he send you help from the sanctuary
    and grant you support from Zion.
³May he remember all your sacrifices
    and accept your burnt offerings.   *Selah*

ᵃ3 Or *They have no speech, there are no words; / no sound is heard from them* ᵇ4 Septuagint, Jerome and
Syriac; Hebrew *line*

⁴May he give you the desire of your heart
    and make all your plans succeed.
⁵We will shout for joy when you are victorious
    and will lift up our banners in the name of our God.
  May the LORD grant all your requests.

⁶Now I know that the LORD saves his anointed;
    he answers him from his holy heaven
    with the saving power of his right hand.
⁷Some trust in chariots and some in horses,
    but we trust in the name of the LORD our God.
⁸They are brought to their knees and fall,
    but we rise up and stand firm.

⁹O LORD, save the king!
    Answer*a* us when we call!

PSALM 21

For the director of music. A psalm of David.

¹O LORD, the king rejoices in your strength.
    How great is his joy in the victories you give!
²You have granted him the desire of his heart
    and have not withheld the request of his lips.   *Selah*
³You welcomed him with rich blessings
    and placed a crown of pure gold on his head.
⁴He asked you for life, and you gave it to him—
    length of days, for ever and ever.
⁵Through the victories you gave, his glory is great;
    you have bestowed on him splendor and majesty.
⁶Surely you have granted him eternal blessings
    and made him glad with the joy of your presence.
⁷For the king trusts in the LORD;
    through the unfailing love of the Most High
    he will not be shaken.

⁸Your hand will lay hold on all your enemies;
    your right hand will seize your foes.
⁹At the time of your appearing
    you will make them like a fiery furnace.
  In his wrath the LORD will swallow them up,
    and his fire will consume them.
¹⁰You will destroy their descendants from the earth,
    their posterity from mankind.
¹¹Though they plot evil against you
    and devise wicked schemes, they cannot succeed;
¹²for you will make them turn their backs
    when you aim at them with drawn bow.

¹³Be exalted, O LORD, in your strength;
    we will sing and praise your might.

---

a9 Or save! / O King, answer

PSALM 22

For the director of music. To the tune of, "The Doe of the Morning."
A psalm of David.

¹ My God, my God, why have you forsaken me?
Why are you so far from saving me,
so far from the words of my groaning?
² O my God, I cry out by day, but you do not answer,
by night, and am not silent.

³ Yet you are enthroned as the Holy One;
you are the praise of Israel.*a*
⁴ In you our fathers put their trust;
they trusted and you delivered them.
⁵ They cried to you and were saved;
in you they trusted and were not disappointed.

⁶ But I am a worm and not a man,
scorned by men and despised by the people.
⁷ All who see me mock me;
they hurl insults, shaking their heads:
⁸ "He trusts in the LORD;
let the LORD rescue him.
Let him deliver him,
since he delights in him."

⁹ Yet you brought me out of the womb;
you made me trust in you
even at my mother's breast.
¹⁰ From birth I was cast upon you;
from my mother's womb you have been my God.
¹¹ Do not be far from me,
for trouble is near
and there is no one to help.

¹² Many bulls surround me;
strong bulls of Bashan encircle me.
¹³ Roaring lions tearing their prey
open their mouths wide against me.
¹⁴ I am poured out like water,
and all my bones are out of joint.
My heart has turned to wax;
it has melted away within me.
¹⁵ My strength is dried up like a potsherd,
and my tongue sticks to the roof of my mouth;
you lay me*b* in the dust of death.
¹⁶ Dogs have surrounded me;
a band of evil men has encircled me,
they have pierced*c* my hands and my feet.
¹⁷ I can count all my bones;
people stare and gloat over me.
¹⁸ They divide my garments among them
and cast lots for my clothing.

---

*a3 Or Yet you are holy, / enthroned on the praises of Israel *b15 Or / I am laid *c16 Some Hebrew
manuscripts, Septuagint and Syriac; most Hebrew manuscripts / like the lion,

¹⁹But you, O Lord, be not far off;
O my Strength, come quickly to help me.
²⁰Deliver my life from the sword,
my precious life from the power of the dogs.
²¹Rescue me from the mouth of the lions;
save*ª* me from the horns of the wild oxen.

²²I will declare your name to my brothers;
in the congregation I will praise you.
²³You who fear the Lord, praise him!
All you descendants of Jacob, honor him!
Revere him, all you descendants of Israel!
²⁴For he has not despised or disdained
the suffering of the afflicted one;
he has not hidden his face from him
but has listened to his cry for help.

²⁵From you comes the theme of my praise in the great
assembly;
before those who fear you*ᵇ* will I fulfill my vows.
²⁶The poor will eat and be satisfied;
they who seek the Lord will praise him—
may your hearts live forever!
²⁷All the ends of the earth
will remember and turn to the Lord,
and all the families of the nations
will bow down before him,
²⁸for dominion belongs to the Lord
and he rules over the nations.

²⁹All the rich of the earth will feast and worship;
all who go down to the dust will kneel before him—
those who cannot keep themselves alive.
³⁰Posterity will serve him;
future generations will be told about the Lord.
³¹They will proclaim his righteousness
to a people yet unborn—
for he has done it.

PSALM 23

A psalm of David.

¹The Lord is my shepherd, I shall not be in want.
²   He makes me lie down in green pastures,
he leads me beside quiet waters,
³   he restores my soul.
He guides me in paths of righteousness
for his name's sake.
⁴Even though I walk
through the valley of the shadow of death,*ᶜ*
I will fear no evil,
for you are with me;
your rod and your staff,
they comfort me.

ª21 Or / you have heard ᵇ25 Hebrew him ᶜ4 Or through the darkest valley

⁵You prepare a table before me
  in the presence of my enemies.
 You anoint my head with oil;
  my cup overflows.
⁶Surely goodness and love will follow me
  all the days of my life,
 and I will dwell in the house of the LORD
  forever.

PSALM 24

Of David. A psalm.

¹The earth is the LORD's, and everything in it,
  the world, and all who live in it;
²for he founded it upon the seas
  and established it upon the waters.

³Who may ascend the hill of the LORD?
  Who may stand in his holy place?
⁴He who has clean hands and a pure heart,
  who does not lift up his soul to an idol
  or swear by what is false.ᵃ
⁵He will receive blessing from the LORD
  and vindication from God his Savior.
⁶Such is the generation of those who seek him,
  who seek your face, O God of Jacob.ᵇ   Selah

⁷Lift up your heads, O you gates;
  be lifted up, you ancient doors,
  that the King of glory may come in.
⁸Who is this King of glory?
  The LORD strong and mighty,
  the LORD mighty in battle.
⁹Lift up your heads, O you gates;
  lift them up, you ancient doors,
  that the King of glory may come in.
¹⁰Who is he, this King of glory?
  The LORD Almighty—
  he is the King of glory.   Selah

PSALM 25ᶜ

Of David.

¹To you, O LORD, I lift up my soul;
² in you I trust, O my God.
 Do not let me be put to shame,
  nor let my enemies triumph over me.
³No one whose hope is in you
  will ever be put to shame,

ᵃ4 Or *swear falsely* ᵇ6 Two Hebrew manuscripts and Syriac (see also Septuagint); most Hebrew manuscripts *face, Jacob* ᶜThis psalm is an acrostic poem, the verses of which begin with the successive letters of the Hebrew alphabet.

but they will be put to shame
who are treacherous without excuse.

⁴Show me your ways, O Lord,
teach me your paths;
⁵guide me in your truth and teach me,
for you are God my Savior,
and my hope is in you all day long.
⁶Remember, O Lord, your great mercy and love,
for they are from of old.
⁷Remember not the sins of my youth
and my rebellious ways;
according to your love remember me,
for you are good, O Lord.

⁸Good and upright is the Lord;
therefore he instructs sinners in his ways.
⁹He guides the humble in what is right
and teaches them his way.
¹⁰All the ways of the Lord are loving and faithful
for those who keep the demands of his covenant.
¹¹For the sake of your name, O Lord,
forgive my iniquity, though it is great.
¹²Who, then, is the man that fears the Lord?
He will instruct him in the way chosen for him.
¹³He will spend his days in prosperity,
and his descendants will inherit the land.
¹⁴The Lord confides in those who fear him;
he makes his covenant known to them.
¹⁵My eyes are ever on the Lord,
for only he will release my feet from the snare.

¹⁶Turn to me and be gracious to me,
for I am lonely and afflicted.
¹⁷The troubles of my heart have multiplied;
free me from my anguish.
¹⁸Look upon my affliction and my distress
and take away all my sins.
¹⁹See how my enemies have increased
and how fiercely they hate me!
²⁰Guard my life and rescue me;
let me not be put to shame,
for I take refuge in you.
²¹May integrity and uprightness protect me,
because my hope is in you.

²²Redeem Israel, O God,
from all their troubles!

PSALM 26

Of David.

¹Vindicate me, O Lord,
for I have led a blameless life;
I have trusted in the Lord
without wavering.

²Test me, O Lᴏʀᴅ, and try me,
 examine my heart and my mind;
³for your love is ever before me,
 and I walk continually in your truth.
⁴I do not sit with deceitful men,
 nor do I consort with hypocrites;
⁵I abhor the assembly of evildoers
 and refuse to sit with the wicked.
⁶I wash my hands in innocence,
 and go about your altar, O Lᴏʀᴅ,
⁷proclaiming aloud your praise
 and telling of all your wonderful deeds.
⁸I love the house where you live, O Lᴏʀᴅ,
 the place where your glory dwells.

⁹Do not take away my soul along with sinners,
 my life with bloodthirsty men,
¹⁰in whose hands are wicked schemes,
 whose right hands are full of bribes.
¹¹But I lead a blameless life;
 redeem me and be merciful to me.

¹²My feet stand on level ground;
 in the great assembly I will praise the Lᴏʀᴅ.

PSALM 27

Of David.

¹The Lᴏʀᴅ is my light and my salvation—
 whom shall I fear?
The Lᴏʀᴅ is the stronghold of my life—
 of whom shall I be afraid?
²When evil men advance against me
 to devour my flesh,ᵃ
when my enemies and my foes attack me,
 they will stumble and fall.
³Though an army besiege me,
 my heart will not fear;
though war break out against me,
 even then will I be confident.

⁴One thing I ask of the Lᴏʀᴅ,
 this is what I seek:
that I may dwell in the house of the Lᴏʀᴅ
 all the days of my life,
to gaze upon the beauty of the Lᴏʀᴅ
 and to seek him in his temple.
⁵For in the day of trouble
 he will keep me safe in his dwelling;
he will hide me in the shelter of his tabernacle
 and set me high upon a rock.
⁶Then my head will be exalted
 above the enemies who surround me;

ᵃ2 Or *to slander me*

at his tabernacle will I sacrifice with shouts of joy;
    I will sing and make music to the LORD.

[7] Hear my voice when I call, O LORD;
    be merciful to me and answer me.
[8] My heart says of you, "Seek his[a] face!"
    Your face, LORD, I will seek.
[9] Do not hide your face from me,
    do not turn your servant away in anger;
    you have been my helper.
Do not reject me or forsake me,
    O God my Savior.
[10] Though my father and mother forsake me,
    the LORD will receive me.
[11] Teach me your way, O LORD;
    lead me in a straight path
    because of my oppressors.
[12] Do not turn me over to the desire of my foes,
    for false witnesses rise up against me,
    breathing out violence.

[13] I am still confident of this:
    I will see the goodness of the LORD
    in the land of the living.
[14] Wait for the LORD;
    be strong and take heart
    and wait for the LORD.

PSALM

Of David.

[1] To you I call, O LORD my Rock;
    do not turn a deaf ear to me.
For if you remain silent,
    I will be like those who have gone down to the pit.
[2] Hear my cry for mercy
    as I call to you for help,
as I lift up my hands
    toward your Most Holy Place.

[3] Do not drag me away with the wicked,
    with those who do evil,
who speak cordially with their neighbors
    but harbor malice in their hearts.
[4] Repay them for their deeds
    and for their evil work;
repay them for what their hands have done
    and bring back upon them what they deserve.
[5] Since they show no regard for the works of the LORD
    and what his hands have done,
he will tear them down
    and never build them up again.

a 8 Or To you, O my heart, he has said, "Seek my

⁶Praise be to the Lord,
    for he has heard my cry for mercy.
⁷The Lord is my strength and my shield;
    my heart trusts in him, and I am helped.
My heart leaps for joy
    and I will give thanks to him in song.

⁸The Lord is the strength of his people,
    a fortress of salvation for his anointed one.
⁹Save your people and bless your inheritance;
    be their shepherd and carry them forever.

PSALM 29

A psalm of David.

¹Ascribe to the Lord, O mighty ones,
    ascribe to the Lord glory and strength.
²Ascribe to the Lord the glory due his name;
    worship the Lord in the splendor of his*a* holiness.

³The voice of the Lord is over the waters;
    the God of glory thunders,
    the Lord thunders over the mighty waters.
⁴The voice of the Lord is powerful;
    the voice of the Lord is majestic.
⁵The voice of the Lord breaks the cedars;
    the Lord breaks in pieces the cedars of Lebanon.
⁶He makes Lebanon skip like a calf,
    Sirion*b* like a young wild ox.
⁷The voice of the Lord strikes
    with flashes of lightning.
⁸The voice of the Lord shakes the desert;
    the Lord shakes the Desert of Kadesh.
⁹The voice of the Lord twists the oaks*c*
    and strips the forests bare.
And in his temple all cry, "Glory!"

¹⁰The Lord sits*d* enthroned over the flood;
    the Lord is enthroned as King forever.
¹¹The Lord gives strength to his people;
    the Lord blesses his people with peace.

PSALM 30

A psalm. A song. For the dedication of the temple.*e* Of David.

¹I will exalt you, O Lord,
    for you lifted me out of the depths
    and did not let my enemies gloat over me.
²O Lord my God, I called to you for help
    and you healed me.

a2 Or Lord with the splendor of b6 That is, Mount Hermon c9 Or Lord makes the deer give birth
d10 Or sat eTitle: Or palace

³O Lᴏʀᴅ, you brought me up from the grave*ᵃ*;
　　you spared me from going down into the pit.

⁴Sing to the Lᴏʀᴅ, you saints of his;
　　praise his holy name.
⁵For his anger lasts only a moment,
　　but his favor lasts a lifetime;
　weeping may remain for a night,
　　but rejoicing comes in the morning.

⁶When I felt secure, I said,
　　"I will never be shaken."
⁷O Lᴏʀᴅ, when you favored me,
　　you made my mountain*ᵇ* stand firm;
　but when you hid your face,
　　I was dismayed.

⁸To you, O Lᴏʀᴅ, I called;
　　to the Lord I cried for mercy:
⁹"What gain is there in my destruction,*ᶜ*
　　in my going down into the pit?
　Will the dust praise you?
　　Will it proclaim your faithfulness?
¹⁰Hear, O Lᴏʀᴅ, and be merciful to me;
　　O Lᴏʀᴅ, be my help."

¹¹You turned my wailing into dancing;
　　you removed my sackcloth and clothed me with joy,
¹²that my heart may sing to you and not be silent.
　　O Lᴏʀᴅ my God, I will give you thanks forever.

PSALM 31

For the director of music. A psalm of David.

¹In you, O Lᴏʀᴅ, I have taken refuge;
　　let me never be put to shame;
　　deliver me in your righteousness.
²Turn your ear to me,
　　come quickly to my rescue;
　be my rock of refuge,
　　a strong fortress to save me.
³Since you are my rock and my fortress,
　　for the sake of your name lead and guide me.
⁴Free me from the trap that is set for me,
　　for you are my refuge.
⁵Into your hands I commit my spirit;
　　redeem me, O Lᴏʀᴅ, the God of truth.

⁶I hate those who cling to worthless idols;
　　I trust in the Lᴏʀᴅ.
⁷I will be glad and rejoice in your love,
　　for you saw my affliction
　　and knew the anguish of my soul.
⁸You have not handed me over to the enemy
　　but have set my feet in a spacious place.

ᵃ3 Hebrew *Sheol*　*ᵇ7* Or *hill country*　*ᶜ9* Or *there if I am silenced*

⁹Be merciful to me, O Lᴏʀᴅ, for I am in distress;
    my eyes grow weak with sorrow,
    my soul and my body with grief.
¹⁰My life is consumed by anguish
    and my years by groaning;
  my strength fails because of my affliction,ᵃ
    and my bones grow weak.
¹¹Because of all my enemies,
    I am the utter contempt of my neighbors;
  I am a dread to my friends—
    those who see me on the street flee from me.
¹²I am forgotten by them as though I were dead;
    I have become like broken pottery.
¹³For I hear the slander of many;
    there is terror on every side;
  they conspire against me
    and plot to take my life.

¹⁴But I trust in you, O Lᴏʀᴅ;
    I say, "You are my God."
¹⁵My times are in your hands;
    deliver me from my enemies
    and from those who pursue me.
¹⁶Let your face shine on your servant;
    save me in your unfailing love.
¹⁷Let me not be put to shame, O Lᴏʀᴅ,
    for I have cried out to you;
  but let the wicked be put to shame
    and lie silent in the grave.ᵇ
¹⁸Let their lying lips be silenced,
    for with pride and contempt
    they speak arrogantly against the righteous.

¹⁹How great is your goodness,
    which you have stored up for those who fear you,
  which you bestow in the sight of men
    on those who take refuge in you.
²⁰In the shelter of your presence you hide them
    from the intrigues of men;
  in your dwelling you keep them safe
    from accusing tongues.

²¹Praise be to the Lᴏʀᴅ,
    for he showed his wonderful love to me
    when I was in a besieged city.
²²In my alarm I said,
    "I am cut off from your sight!"
  Yet you heard my cry for mercy
    when I called to you for help.

²³Love the Lᴏʀᴅ, all his saints!
    The Lᴏʀᴅ preserves the faithful,
    but the proud he pays back in full.
²⁴Be strong and take heart,
    all you who hope in the Lᴏʀᴅ.

ᵃ10 Or *guilt* ᵇ17 Hebrew *Sheol*

PSALM 32

Of David. A *maskil*.[a]

¹Blessed is he
   whose transgressions are forgiven,
   whose sins are covered.
²Blessed is the man
   whose sin the LORD does not count against him
   and in whose spirit is no deceit.

³When I kept silent,
   my bones wasted away
   through my groaning all day long.
⁴For day and night
   your hand was heavy upon me;
 my strength was sapped
   as in the heat of summer.   *Selah*
⁵Then I acknowledged my sin to you
   and did not cover up my iniquity.
 I said, "I will confess
   my transgressions to the LORD"—
 and you forgave
   the guilt of my sin.   *Selah*

⁶Therefore let everyone who is godly pray to you
   while you may be found;
 surely when the mighty waters rise,
   they will not reach him.
⁷You are my hiding place;
   you will protect me from trouble
   and surround me with songs of deliverance.   *Selah*

⁸I will instruct you and teach you in the way you should go;
   I will counsel you and watch over you.
⁹Do not be like the horse or the mule,
   which have no understanding
 but must be controlled by bit and bridle
   or they will not come to you.
¹⁰Many are the woes of the wicked,
   but the LORD's unfailing love
   surrounds the man who trusts in him.

¹¹Rejoice in the LORD and be glad, you righteous;
   sing, all you who are upright in heart!

PSALM 33

¹Sing joyfully to the LORD, you righteous;
   it is fitting for the upright to praise him.
²Praise the LORD with the harp;
   make music to him on the ten-stringed lyre.

[a]Title: Probably a literary or musical term

Dear Sam,

It seems like I spend most of my time feeling guilty about one thing or another. How can I stop? It's driving me crazy.

Sarah in Sarasota

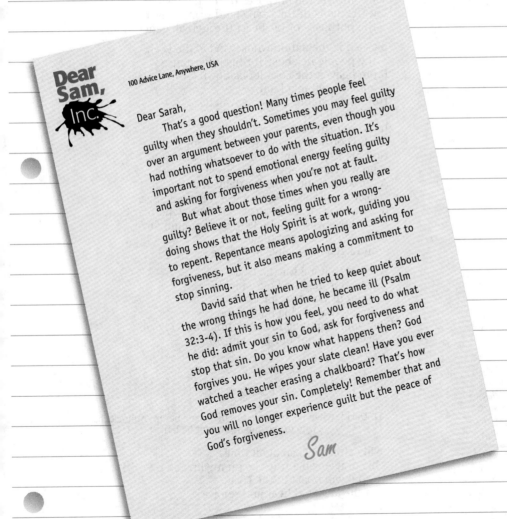

Dear Sam, Inc.

100 Advice Lane, Anywhere, USA

Dear Sarah,

That's a good question! Many times people feel guilty when they shouldn't. Sometimes you may feel guilty over an argument between your parents, even though you had nothing whatsoever to do with the situation. It's important not to spend emotional energy feeling guilty and asking for forgiveness when you're not at fault.

But what about those times when you really are guilty? Believe it or not, feeling guilt for a wrong-doing shows that the Holy Spirit is at work, guiding you to repent. Repentance means apologizing and asking for forgiveness, but it also means making a commitment to stop sinning.

David said that when he tried to keep quiet about the wrong things he had done, he became ill (Psalm 32:3-4). If this is how you feel, you need to do what he did: admit your sin to God, ask for forgiveness and stop that sin. Do you know what happens then? God forgives you. He wipes your slate clean! Have you ever watched a teacher erasing a chalkboard? That's how God removes your sin. Completely! Remember that and you will no longer experience guilt but the peace of God's forgiveness.

Sam

³Sing to him a new song;
    play skillfully, and shout for joy.

⁴For the word of the Lord is right and true;
    he is faithful in all he does.
⁵The Lord loves righteousness and justice;
    the earth is full of his unfailing love.

⁶By the word of the Lord were the heavens made,
    their starry host by the breath of his mouth.
⁷He gathers the waters of the sea into jars^a;
    he puts the deep into storehouses.
⁸Let all the earth fear the Lord;
    let all the people of the world revere him.
⁹For he spoke, and it came to be;
    he commanded, and it stood firm.
¹⁰The Lord foils the plans of the nations;
    he thwarts the purposes of the peoples.
¹¹But the plans of the Lord stand firm forever,
    the purposes of his heart through all generations.

¹²Blessed is the nation whose God is the Lord,
    the people he chose for his inheritance.
¹³From heaven the Lord looks down
    and sees all mankind;
¹⁴from his dwelling place he watches
    all who live on earth—
¹⁵he who forms the hearts of all,
    who considers everything they do.
¹⁶No king is saved by the size of his army;
    no warrior escapes by his great strength.
¹⁷A horse is a vain hope for deliverance;
    despite all its great strength it cannot save.
¹⁸But the eyes of the Lord are on those who fear him,
    on those whose hope is in his unfailing love,
¹⁹to deliver them from death
    and keep them alive in famine.

²⁰We wait in hope for the Lord;
    he is our help and our shield.
²¹In him our hearts rejoice,
    for we trust in his holy name.
²²May your unfailing love rest upon us, O Lord,
    even as we put our hope in you.

PSALM ^b

Of David. When he pretended to be insane before Abimelech,
who drove him away, and he left.

¹I will extol the Lord at all times;
    his praise will always be on my lips.
²My soul will boast in the Lord;
    let the afflicted hear and rejoice.

---

^a7 Or *sea as into a heap* ^bThis psalm is an acrostic poem, the verses of which begin with the successive letters of the Hebrew alphabet.

³Glorify the LORD with me;
    let us exalt his name together.

⁴I sought the LORD, and he answered me;
    he delivered me from all my fears.
⁵Those who look to him are radiant;
    their faces are never covered with shame.
⁶This poor man called, and the LORD heard him;
    he saved him out of all his troubles.
⁷The angel of the LORD encamps around those who fear
        him,
    and he delivers them.

⁸Taste and see that the LORD is good;
    blessed is the man who takes refuge in him.
⁹Fear the LORD, you his saints,
    for those who fear him lack nothing.
¹⁰The lions may grow weak and hungry,
    but those who seek the LORD lack no good thing.

¹¹Come, my children, listen to me;
    I will teach you the fear of the LORD.
¹²Whoever of you loves life
    and desires to see many good days,
¹³keep your tongue from evil
    and your lips from speaking lies.
¹⁴Turn from evil and do good;
    seek peace and pursue it.

¹⁵The eyes of the LORD are on the righteous
    and his ears are attentive to their cry;
¹⁶the face of the LORD is against those who do evil,
    to cut off the memory of them from the earth.

¹⁷The righteous cry out, and the LORD hears them;
    he delivers them from all their troubles.
¹⁸The LORD is close to the brokenhearted
    and saves those who are crushed in spirit.

¹⁹A righteous man may have many troubles,
    but the LORD delivers him from them all;
²⁰he protects all his bones,
    not one of them will be broken.

²¹Evil will slay the wicked;
    the foes of the righteous will be condemned.
²²The LORD redeems his servants;
    no one will be condemned who takes refuge in
        him.

PSALM

Of David.

¹Contend, O LORD, with those who contend with me;
    fight against those who fight against me.
²Take up shield and buckler;
    arise and come to my aid.

³Brandish spear and javelin*
    against those who pursue me.
  Say to my soul,
    "I am your salvation."

⁴May those who seek my life
    be disgraced and put to shame;
  may those who plot my ruin
    be turned back in dismay.
⁵May they be like chaff before the wind,
    with the angel of the LORD driving them away;
⁶may their path be dark and slippery,
    with the angel of the LORD pursuing them.
⁷Since they hid their net for me without cause
    and without cause dug a pit for me,
⁸may ruin overtake them by surprise—
    may the net they hid entangle them,
    may they fall into the pit, to their ruin.
⁹Then my soul will rejoice in the LORD
    and delight in his salvation.
¹⁰My whole being will exclaim,
    "Who is like you, O LORD?
  You rescue the poor from those too strong for them,
    the poor and needy from those who rob them."

¹¹Ruthless witnesses come forward;
    they question me on things I know nothing about.
¹²They repay me evil for good
    and leave my soul forlorn.
¹³Yet when they were ill, I put on sackcloth
    and humbled myself with fasting.
  When my prayers returned to me unanswered,
¹⁴   I went about mourning
    as though for my friend or brother.
  I bowed my head in grief
    as though weeping for my mother.
¹⁵But when I stumbled, they gathered in glee;
    attackers gathered against me when I was unaware.
    They slandered me without ceasing.
¹⁶Like the ungodly they maliciously mocked*;
    they gnashed their teeth at me.
¹⁷O Lord, how long will you look on?
    Rescue my life from their ravages,
    my precious life from these lions.
¹⁸I will give you thanks in the great assembly;
    among throngs of people I will praise you.

¹⁹Let not those gloat over me
    who are my enemies without cause;
  let not those who hate me without reason
    maliciously wink the eye.
²⁰They do not speak peaceably,
    but devise false accusations
    against those who live quietly in the land.
²¹They gape at me and say, "Aha! Aha!
    With our own eyes we have seen it."

---

*3 Or *and block the way* *16 Septuagint; Hebrew may mean *ungodly circle of mockers.*

²²O Lord, you have seen this; be not silent.
  Do not be far from me, O Lord.
²³Awake, and rise to my defense!
  Contend for me, my God and Lord.
²⁴Vindicate me in your righteousness, O Lord my God;
  do not let them gloat over me.
²⁵Do not let them think, "Aha, just what we wanted!"
  or say, "We have swallowed him up."

²⁶May all who gloat over my distress
  be put to shame and confusion;
 may all who exalt themselves over me
  be clothed with shame and disgrace.
²⁷May those who delight in my vindication
  shout for joy and gladness;
 may they always say, "The Lord be exalted,
  who delights in the well-being of his servant."
²⁸My tongue will speak of your righteousness
  and of your praises all day long.

PSALM 36

For the director of music. Of David the servant of the Lord.

¹An oracle is within my heart
  concerning the sinfulness of the wicked:ᵃ
 There is no fear of God
  before his eyes.
²For in his own eyes he flatters himself
  too much to detect or hate his sin.
³The words of his mouth are wicked and deceitful;
  he has ceased to be wise and to do good.
⁴Even on his bed he plots evil;
  he commits himself to a sinful course
  and does not reject what is wrong.

⁵Your love, O Lord, reaches to the heavens,
  your faithfulness to the skies.
⁶Your righteousness is like the mighty mountains,
  your justice like the great deep.
 O Lord, you preserve both man and beast.
⁷ How priceless is your unfailing love!
 Both high and low among men
  findᵇ refuge in the shadow of your wings.
⁸They feast on the abundance of your house;
  you give them drink from your river of delights.
⁹For with you is the fountain of life;
  in your light we see light.

¹⁰Continue your love to those who know you,
  your righteousness to the upright in heart.
¹¹May the foot of the proud not come against me,
  nor the hand of the wicked drive me away.
¹²See how the evildoers lie fallen—
  thrown down, not able to rise!

ᵃ1 Or heart: / Sin proceeds from the wicked.   ᵇ7 Or love, O God! / Men find; or love! / Both heavenly beings and men / find

PSALM 37 [a]

Of David.

¹Do not fret because of evil men
  or be envious of those who do wrong;
²for like the grass they will soon wither,
  like green plants they will soon die away.

³Trust in the Lord and do good;
  dwell in the land and enjoy safe pasture.
⁴Delight yourself in the Lord
  and he will give you the desires of your heart.

⁵Commit your way to the Lord;
  trust in him and he will do this:
⁶He will make your righteousness shine like the
    dawn,
  the justice of your cause like the noonday sun.

⁷Be still before the Lord and wait patiently for him;
  do not fret when men succeed in their ways,
  when they carry out their wicked schemes.

⁸Refrain from anger and turn from wrath;
  do not fret—it leads only to evil.
⁹For evil men will be cut off,
  but those who hope in the Lord will inherit the land.

¹⁰A little while, and the wicked will be no more;
  though you look for them, they will not be found.
¹¹But the meek will inherit the land
  and enjoy great peace.

¹²The wicked plot against the righteous
  and gnash their teeth at them;
¹³but the Lord laughs at the wicked,
  for he knows their day is coming.

¹⁴The wicked draw the sword
  and bend the bow
 to bring down the poor and needy,
  to slay those whose ways are upright.
¹⁵But their swords will pierce their own hearts,
  and their bows will be broken.

¹⁶Better the little that the righteous have
  than the wealth of many wicked;
¹⁷for the power of the wicked will be broken,
  but the Lord upholds the righteous.

¹⁸The days of the blameless are known to the Lord,
  and their inheritance will endure forever.
¹⁹In times of disaster they will not wither;
  in days of famine they will enjoy plenty.

---

[a]This psalm is an acrostic poem, the stanzas of which begin with the successive letters of the Hebrew alphabet.

²⁰But the wicked will perish:
The LORD's enemies will be like the beauty of the fields,
they will vanish—vanish like smoke.

²¹The wicked borrow and do not repay,
but the righteous give generously;
²²those the LORD blesses will inherit the land,
but those he curses will be cut off.

²³If the LORD delights in a man's way,
he makes his steps firm;
²⁴though he stumble, he will not fall,
for the LORD upholds him with his hand.

²⁵I was young and now I am old,
yet I have never seen the righteous forsaken
or their children begging bread.
²⁶They are always generous and lend freely;
their children will be blessed.

²⁷Turn from evil and do good;
then you will dwell in the land forever.
²⁸For the LORD loves the just
and will not forsake his faithful ones.

They will be protected forever,
but the offspring of the wicked will be cut off;
²⁹the righteous will inherit the land
and dwell in it forever.

³⁰The mouth of the righteous man utters wisdom,
and his tongue speaks what is just.
³¹The law of his God is in his heart;
his feet do not slip.

³²The wicked lie in wait for the righteous,
seeking their very lives;
³³but the LORD will not leave them in their power
or let them be condemned when brought to trial.

³⁴Wait for the LORD
and keep his way.
He will exalt you to inherit the land;
when the wicked are cut off, you will see it.

³⁵I have seen a wicked and ruthless man
flourishing like a green tree in its native soil,
³⁶but he soon passed away and was no more;
though I looked for him, he could not be found.

³⁷Consider the blameless, observe the upright;
there is a future^a for the man of peace.
³⁸But all sinners will be destroyed;
the future^b of the wicked will be cut off.

³⁹The salvation of the righteous comes from the LORD;
he is their stronghold in time of trouble.
⁴⁰The LORD helps them and delivers them;
he delivers them from the wicked and saves them,
because they take refuge in him.

^a37 Or there will be posterity ^b38 Or posterity

PSALM 38

A psalm of David. A petition.

¹O LORD, do not rebuke me in your anger
  or discipline me in your wrath.
²For your arrows have pierced me,
  and your hand has come down upon me.
³Because of your wrath there is no health in my
      body;
  my bones have no soundness because of my sin.
⁴My guilt has overwhelmed me
  like a burden too heavy to bear.

⁵My wounds fester and are loathsome
  because of my sinful folly.
⁶I am bowed down and brought very low;
  all day long I go about mourning.
⁷My back is filled with searing pain;
  there is no health in my body.
⁸I am feeble and utterly crushed;
  I groan in anguish of heart.

⁹All my longings lie open before you, O Lord;
  my sighing is not hidden from you.
¹⁰My heart pounds, my strength fails me;
  even the light has gone from my eyes.
¹¹My friends and companions avoid me because of my wounds;
  my neighbors stay far away.
¹²Those who seek my life set their traps,
  those who would harm me talk of my ruin;
  all day long they plot deception.

¹³I am like a deaf man, who cannot hear,
  like a mute, who cannot open his mouth;
¹⁴I have become like a man who does not hear,
  whose mouth can offer no reply.
¹⁵I wait for you, O LORD;
  you will answer, O Lord my God.
¹⁶For I said, "Do not let them gloat
  or exalt themselves over me when my foot slips."

¹⁷For I am about to fall,
  and my pain is ever with me.
¹⁸I confess my iniquity;
  I am troubled by my sin.
¹⁹Many are those who are my vigorous enemies;
  those who hate me without reason are numerous.
²⁰Those who repay my good with evil
  slander me when I pursue what is good.

²¹O LORD, do not forsake me;
  be not far from me, O my God.
²²Come quickly to help me,
  O Lord my Savior.

PSALM 39

For the director of music. For Jeduthun. A psalm of David.

1 I said, "I will watch my ways
   and keep my tongue from sin;
 I will put a muzzle on my mouth
   as long as the wicked are in my presence."
2 But when I was silent and still,
   not even saying anything good,
   my anguish increased.
3 My heart grew hot within me,
   and as I meditated, the fire burned;
   then I spoke with my tongue:

4 "Show me, O LORD, my life's end
   and the number of my days;
   let me know how fleeting is my life.
5 You have made my days a mere handbreadth;
   the span of my years is as nothing before you.
   Each man's life is but a breath.   *Selah*
6 Man is a mere phantom as he goes to and fro:
   He bustles about, but only in vain;
   he heaps up wealth, not knowing who will get it.

7 "But now, Lord, what do I look for?
   My hope is in you.
8 Save me from all my
        transgressions;
   do not make me the scorn of
        fools.
9 I was silent; I would not open my
        mouth,
   for you are the one who has
        done this.
10 Remove your scourge from me;
   I am overcome by the blow of
        your hand.
11 You rebuke and discipline men
        for their sin;
   you consume their wealth like
        a moth—
   each man is but a breath.
                    Selah

12 "Hear my prayer, O LORD,
   listen to my cry for help;
   be not deaf to my weeping.
 For I dwell with you as an alien,
   a stranger, as all my fathers
        were.
13 Look away from me, that I may
        rejoice again
   before I depart and am no
        more."

Can I borrow your muzzle?

SEE
PSALM 39:1

PSALM 40

For the director of music. Of David. A psalm.

¹I waited patiently for the Lord;
    he turned to me and heard my cry.
²He lifted me out of the slimy pit,
    out of the mud and mire;
  he set my feet on a rock
    and gave me a firm place to stand.
³He put a new song in my mouth,
    a hymn of praise to our God.
  Many will see and fear
    and put their trust in the Lord.

⁴Blessed is the man
    who makes the Lord his trust,
  who does not look to the proud,
    to those who turn aside to false gods.ᵃ
⁵Many, O Lord my God,
    are the wonders you have done.
  The things you planned for us
    no one can recount to you;
  were I to speak and tell of them,
    they would be too many to declare.

⁶Sacrifice and offering you did not desire,
    but my ears you have piercedᵇʾᶜ;
  burnt offerings and sin offerings
    you did not require.
⁷Then I said, "Here I am, I have come—
    it is written about me in the scroll.ᵈ
⁸I desire to do your will, O my God;
    your law is within my heart."

⁹I proclaim righteousness in the great assembly;
    I do not seal my lips,
    as you know, O Lord.
¹⁰I do not hide your righteousness in my heart;
    I speak of your faithfulness and salvation.
  I do not conceal your love and your truth
    from the great assembly.

¹¹Do not withhold your mercy from me, O Lord;
    may your love and your truth always protect me.
¹²For troubles without number surround me;
    my sins have overtaken me, and I cannot see.
  They are more than the hairs of my head,
    and my heart fails within me.

¹³Be pleased, O Lord, to save me;
    O Lord, come quickly to help me.

ᵃ4 Or *to falsehood*   ᵇ6 Hebrew; Septuagint *but a body you have prepared for me* (see also Symmachus and Theodotion)   ᶜ6 Or *opened*   ᵈ7 Or *come / with the scroll written for me*

¹⁴May all who seek to take my life
   be put to shame and confusion;
  may all who desire my ruin
   be turned back in disgrace.
¹⁵May those who say to me, "Aha! Aha!"
   be appalled at their own shame.
¹⁶But may all who seek you
   rejoice and be glad in you;
  may those who love your salvation always say,
   "The LORD be exalted!"

¹⁷Yet I am poor and needy;
   may the Lord think of me.
  You are my help and my deliverer;
   O my God, do not delay.

PSALM 41

For the director of music. A psalm of David.

¹Blessed is he who has regard for the weak;
   the LORD delivers him in times of trouble.
²The LORD will protect him and preserve his life;
   he will bless him in the land
   and not surrender him to the desire of his foes.
³The LORD will sustain him on his sickbed
   and restore him from his bed of illness.

⁴I said, "O LORD, have mercy on me;
   heal me, for I have sinned against you."
⁵My enemies say of me in malice,
   "When will he die and his name perish?"
⁶Whenever one comes to see me,
   he speaks falsely, while his heart gathers slander;
   then he goes out and spreads it abroad.

⁷All my enemies whisper together against me;
   they imagine the worst for me, saying,
⁸"A vile disease has beset him;
   he will never get up from the place where he
      lies."
⁹Even my close friend, whom I trusted,
   he who shared my bread,
   has lifted up his heel against me.

¹⁰But you, O LORD, have mercy on me;
   raise me up, that I may repay them.
¹¹I know that you are pleased with me,
   for my enemy does not triumph over me.
¹²In my integrity you uphold me
   and set me in your presence forever.

¹³Praise be to the LORD, the God of Israel,
   from everlasting to everlasting.
        Amen and Amen.

BOOK II
Psalm 42–72

PSALM 42[a]

For the director of music. A *maskil*[b] of the Sons of Korah.

[1]As the deer pants for streams of water,
   so my soul pants for you, O God.
[2]My soul thirsts for God, for the living God.
   When can I go and meet with God?
[3]My tears have been my food
      day and night,
   while men say to me all day long,
      "Where is your God?"
[4]These things I remember
      as I pour out my soul:
   how I used to go with the multitude,
      leading the procession to the house of God,
   with shouts of joy and thanksgiving
      among the festive throng.

[5]Why are you downcast, O my soul?
   Why so disturbed within me?
Put your hope in God,
   for I will yet praise him,
   my Savior and [6]my God.

My[c] soul is downcast within me;
   therefore I will remember you
from the land of the Jordan,
   the heights of Hermon—from Mount
      Mizar.
[7]Deep calls to deep
   in the roar of your waterfalls;
all your waves and breakers
   have swept over me.

[8]By day the LORD directs his love,
   at night his song is with me—
   a prayer to the God of my life.

[9]I say to God my Rock,
   "Why have you forgotten me?
Why must I go about mourning,
   oppressed by the enemy?"
[10]My bones suffer mortal agony
   as my foes taunt me,
saying to me all day long,
   "Where is your God?"

[11]Why are you downcast, O my soul?
   Why so disturbed within me?

Had a tough day? Feeling more than a bit "downcast"? Here's a sure-fire remedy.

SEE PSALM 42:11

[a]In many Hebrew manuscripts Psalms 42 and 43 constitute one psalm. [b]Title: Probably a literary or musical term [c]5,6 A few Hebrew manuscripts, Septuagint and Syriac; most Hebrew manuscripts *praise him for his saving help. /* [6]*O my God, my*

Put your hope in God,
    for I will yet praise him,
    my Savior and my God.

PSALM 43 [a]

¹Vindicate me, O God,
    and plead my cause against an ungodly
        nation;
  rescue me from deceitful and wicked men.
²You are God my stronghold.
    Why have you rejected me?
  Why must I go about mourning,
    oppressed by the enemy?
³Send forth your light and your truth,
    let them guide me;
  let them bring me to your holy mountain,
    to the place where you dwell.
⁴Then will I go to the altar of God,
    to God, my joy and my delight.
  I will praise you with the harp,
    O God, my God.

⁵Why are you downcast, O my soul?
    Why so disturbed within me?
  Put your hope in God,
    for I will yet praise him,
    my Savior and my God.

PSALM 44

For the director of music. Of the Sons of Korah. A *maskil*. [b]

¹We have heard with our ears, O God;
    our fathers have told us
  what you did in their days,
    in days long ago.
²With your hand you drove out the nations
    and planted our fathers;
  you crushed the peoples
    and made our fathers flourish.
³It was not by their sword that they won the land,
    nor did their arm bring them victory;
  it was your right hand, your arm,
    and the light of your face, for you loved them.

⁴You are my King and my God,
    who decrees [c] victories for Jacob.
⁵Through you we push back our enemies;
    through your name we trample our foes.

---

[a]In many Hebrew manuscripts Psalms 42 and 43 constitute one psalm.   [b]Title: Probably a literary or musical term   [c]4 Septuagint, Aquila and Syriac; Hebrew *King, O God; / command*

⁶I do not trust in my bow,
    my sword does not bring me victory;
⁷but you give us victory over our enemies,
    you put our adversaries to shame.
⁸In God we make our boast all day long,
    and we will praise your name forever.   *Selah*

⁹But now you have rejected and humbled us;
    you no longer go out with our armies.
¹⁰You made us retreat before the enemy,
    and our adversaries have plundered us.
¹¹You gave us up to be devoured like sheep
    and have scattered us among the nations.
¹²You sold your people for a pittance,
    gaining nothing from their sale.

¹³You have made us a reproach to our neighbors,
    the scorn and derision of those around us.
¹⁴You have made us a byword among the nations;
    the peoples shake their heads at us.
¹⁵My disgrace is before me all day long,
    and my face is covered with shame
¹⁶at the taunts of those who reproach and
        revile me,
    because of the enemy, who is bent on
        revenge.

¹⁷All this happened to us,
    though we had not forgotten you
    or been false to your covenant.
¹⁸Our hearts had not turned back;
    our feet had not strayed from your path.
¹⁹But you crushed us and made us a haunt for
        jackals
    and covered us over with deep darkness.

²⁰If we had forgotten the name of our God
    or spread out our hands to a foreign god,
²¹would not God have discovered it,
    since he knows the secrets of the heart?
²²Yet for your sake we face death all day
        long;
    we are considered as sheep to be slaughtered.

²³Awake, O Lord! Why do you sleep?
    Rouse yourself! Do not reject us forever.
²⁴Why do you hide your face
    and forget our misery and oppression?

²⁵We are brought down to the dust;
    our bodies cling to the ground.
²⁶Rise up and help us;
    redeem us because of your unfailing
        love.

PSALM 45

For the director of music. To the tune of, "Lilies." Of the Sons
of Korah. A *maskil.*[a] A wedding song.

¹My heart is stirred by a noble theme
   as I recite my verses for the king;
   my tongue is the pen of a skillful writer.

²You are the most excellent of men
   and your lips have been anointed with grace,
   since God has blessed you forever.
³Gird your sword upon your side, O mighty one;
   clothe yourself with splendor and majesty.
⁴In your majesty ride forth victoriously
   in behalf of truth, humility and righteousness;
   let your right hand display awesome deeds.
⁵Let your sharp arrows pierce the hearts of the king's enemies;
   let the nations fall beneath your feet.
⁶Your throne, O God, will last for ever and ever;
   a scepter of justice will be the scepter of your kingdom.
⁷You love righteousness and hate wickedness;
   therefore God, your God, has set you above your
      companions
   by anointing you with the oil of joy.
⁸All your robes are fragrant with myrrh and aloes and
      cassia;
   from palaces adorned with ivory
   the music of the strings makes you glad.
⁹Daughters of kings are among your honored women;
   at your right hand is the royal bride in gold of Ophir.

¹⁰Listen, O daughter, consider and give ear:
   Forget your people and your father's house.
¹¹The king is enthralled by your beauty;
   honor him, for he is your lord.
¹²The Daughter of Tyre will come with a gift,[b]
   men of wealth will seek your favor.

¹³All glorious is the princess within her chamber;
   her gown is interwoven with gold.
¹⁴In embroidered garments she is led to the king;
   her virgin companions follow her
   and are brought to you.
¹⁵They are led in with joy and gladness;
   they enter the palace of the king.

¹⁶Your sons will take the place of your fathers;
   you will make them princes throughout the land.
¹⁷I will perpetuate your memory through all generations;
   therefore the nations will praise you for ever and
      ever.

---

[a]Title: Probably a literary or musical term [b]12 Or *A Tyrian robe is among the gifts*

PSALM 46

For the director of music. Of the Sons of Korah.
According to *alamoth.*ᵃ A song.

¹God is our refuge and strength,
an ever-present help in trouble.
²Therefore we will not fear, though the earth give way
and the mountains fall into the heart of the sea,
³though its waters roar and foam
and the mountains quake with their surging.   *Selah*

⁴There is a river whose streams make glad the city of God,
the holy place where the Most High dwells.
⁵God is within her, she will not fall;
God will help her at break of day.
⁶Nations are in uproar, kingdoms fall;
he lifts his voice, the earth melts.

⁷The Lᴏʀᴅ Almighty is with us;
the God of Jacob is our fortress.   *Selah*

⁸Come and see the works of the Lᴏʀᴅ,
the desolations he has brought on the
earth.
⁹He makes wars cease to the ends of the earth;
he breaks the bow and shatters the spear,
he burns the shields*ᵇ* with fire.
¹⁰"Be still, and know that I am God;
I will be exalted among the nations,
I will be exalted in the earth."

¹¹The Lᴏʀᴅ Almighty is with us;
the God of Jacob is our fortress.   *Selah*

God is our refuge
and strength,
an ever-present
help in trouble
(Psalm 46:1).

PSALM 47

For the director of music. Of the Sons of Korah. A psalm.

¹Clap your hands, all you nations;
shout to God with cries of joy.
²How awesome is the Lᴏʀᴅ Most High,
the great King over all the earth!
³He subdued nations under us,
peoples under our feet.
⁴He chose our inheritance for us,
the pride of Jacob, whom he loved.   *Selah*

⁵God has ascended amid shouts of joy,
the Lᴏʀᴅ amid the sounding of trumpets.
⁶Sing praises to God, sing praises;
sing praises to our King, sing praises.

⁷For God is the King of all the earth;
sing to him a psalmᶜ of praise.

ᵃTitle: Probably a musical term   *ᵇ*9 Or *chariots*   ᶜ7 Or *a maskil* (probably a literary or musical term)

[8] God reigns over the nations;
    God is seated on his holy throne.
[9] The nobles of the nations assemble
    as the people of the God of Abraham,
  for the kings[a] of the earth belong to God;
    he is greatly exalted.

PSALM 48

A song. A psalm of the Sons of Korah.

[1] Great is the LORD, and most worthy of praise,
    in the city of our God, his holy mountain.
[2] It is beautiful in its loftiness,
    the joy of the whole earth.
  Like the utmost heights of Zaphon[b] is Mount Zion,
    the[c] city of the Great King.
[3] God is in her citadels;
    he has shown himself to be her fortress.

[4] When the kings joined forces,
    when they advanced together,
[5] they saw her, and were astounded;
    they fled in terror.
[6] Trembling seized them there,
    pain like that of a woman in labor.
[7] You destroyed them like ships of Tarshish
    shattered by an east wind.

[8] As we have heard,
    so have we seen
  in the city of the LORD Almighty,
    in the city of our God:
    God makes her secure forever.   *Selah*

[9] Within your temple, O God,
    we meditate on your unfailing love.
[10] Like your name, O God,
    your praise reaches to the ends of the earth;
    your right hand is filled with righteousness.
[11] Mount Zion rejoices,
    the villages of Judah are glad
    because of your judgments.

[12] Walk about Zion, go around her,
    count her towers,
[13] consider well her ramparts,
    view her citadels,
    that you may tell of them to the next generation.
[14] For this God is our God for ever and ever;
    he will be our guide even to the end.

---

[a] 9 Or *shields*   [b] 2 *Zaphon* can refer to a sacred mountain or the direction north.   [c] 2 Or *earth, / Mount Zion, on the northern side / of the*

PSALM 49

For the director of music. Of the Sons of Korah. A psalm.

¹Hear this, all you peoples;
  listen, all who live in this world,
²both low and high,
  rich and poor alike:
³My mouth will speak words of wisdom;
  the utterance from my heart will give understanding.
⁴I will turn my ear to a proverb;
  with the harp I will expound my riddle:

⁵Why should I fear when evil days come,
  when wicked deceivers surround me—
⁶those who trust in their wealth
  and boast of their great riches?
⁷No man can redeem the life of another
  or give to God a ransom for him—
⁸the ransom for a life is costly,
  no payment is ever enough—
⁹that he should live on forever
  and not see decay.

¹⁰For all can see that wise men die;
  the foolish and the senseless alike perish
  and leave their wealth to others.
¹¹Their tombs will remain their houses[a] forever,
  their dwellings for endless generations,
  though they had[b] named lands after themselves.

¹²But man, despite his riches, does not endure;
  he is[c] like the beasts that perish.

¹³This is the fate of those who trust in themselves,
  and of their followers, who approve their sayings.   *Selah*
¹⁴Like sheep they are destined for the grave,[d]
  and death will feed on them.
 The upright will rule over them in the morning;
  their forms will decay in the grave,[d]
  far from their princely mansions.
¹⁵But God will redeem my life[e] from the grave;
  he will surely take me to himself.   *Selah*

¹⁶Do not be overawed when a man grows rich,
  when the splendor of his house increases;
¹⁷for he will take nothing with him when he dies,
  his splendor will not descend with him.
¹⁸Though while he lived he counted himself blessed—
  and men praise you when you prosper—
¹⁹he will join the generation of his fathers,
  who will never see the light of life.

²⁰A man who has riches without understanding
  is like the beasts that perish.

---

[a]11 Septuagint and Syriac; Hebrew *In their thoughts their houses will remain*   [b]11 Or / *for they have*
[c]12 Hebrew; Septuagint and Syriac read verse 12 the same as verse 20.   [d]14 Hebrew *Sheol*; also in verse 15
[e]15 Or *soul*

PSALM 50

A psalm of Asaph.

¹ The Mighty One, God, the LORD,
  speaks and summons the earth
  from the rising of the sun to the place where it sets.
² From Zion, perfect in beauty,
  God shines forth.
³ Our God comes and will not be silent;
  a fire devours before him,
  and around him a tempest rages.
⁴ He summons the heavens above,
  and the earth, that he may judge his people:
⁵ "Gather to me my consecrated ones,
  who made a covenant with me by sacrifice."
⁶ And the heavens proclaim his righteousness,
  for God himself is judge.   *Selah*

⁷ "Hear, O my people, and I will speak,
  O Israel, and I will testify against you:
  I am God, your God.
⁸ I do not rebuke you for your sacrifices
  or your burnt offerings, which are ever before me.
⁹ I have no need of a bull from your stall
  or of goats from your pens,
¹⁰ for every animal of the forest is mine,
  and the cattle on a thousand hills.
¹¹ I know every bird in the mountains,
  and the creatures of the field are mine.
¹² If I were hungry I would not tell you,
  for the world is mine, and all that is in it.
¹³ Do I eat the flesh of bulls
  or drink the blood of goats?
¹⁴ Sacrifice thank offerings to God,
  fulfill your vows to the Most High,
¹⁵ and call upon me in the day of trouble;
  I will deliver you, and you will honor me."

¹⁶ But to the wicked, God says:

  "What right have you to recite my laws
  or take my covenant on your lips?
¹⁷ You hate my instruction
  and cast my words behind you.
¹⁸ When you see a thief, you join with him;
  you throw in your lot with adulterers.
¹⁹ You use your mouth for evil
  and harness your tongue to deceit.
²⁰ You speak continually against your brother
  and slander your own mother's son.
²¹ These things you have done and I kept silent;
  you thought I was altogether*ᵃ* like you.
  But I will rebuke you
  and accuse you to your face.

ᵃ21 Or thought the 'I AM' was

²²"Consider this, you who forget God,
  or I will tear you to pieces, with none to rescue:
²³He who sacrifices thank offerings honors me,
  and he prepares the way
  so that I may show him^a the salvation of God."

PSALM 51

For the director of music. A psalm of David. When the
prophet Nathan came to him after David had committed
adultery with Bathsheba.

¹Have mercy on me, O God,
  according to your unfailing love;
 according to your great compassion
  blot out my transgressions.
²Wash away all my iniquity
  and cleanse me from my sin.

³For I know my transgressions,
  and my sin is always before me.
⁴Against you, you only, have I sinned
  and done what is evil in your sight,
 so that you are proved right when you speak
  and justified when you judge.
⁵Surely I was sinful at birth,
  sinful from the time my mother conceived me.
⁶Surely you desire truth in the inner parts^b;
  you teach^c me wisdom in the inmost place.

⁷Cleanse me with hyssop, and I will be clean;
  wash me, and I will be whiter than snow.
⁸Let me hear joy and gladness;
  let the bones you have crushed rejoice.

---

^a23 Or *and to him who considers his way / I will show* ^b6 The meaning of the Hebrew for this phrase is uncertain. ^c6 Or *you desired . . . ; / you taught*

The Bible Says

Confess Sins

When David confessed his sin with Bathsheba to the Lord, he asked God to cleanse him, to purify his heart and to restore the joy of salvation (Psalm 51:7–12). And God did forgive him.

But King David didn't only confess to God. Other people knew what he had done, and his sin set a terrible example for his people. That's why the introduction to this psalm is important. David sent it to "the director of music." David's confession wasn't made just to God. It was made publicly as well.

If you sin in a way that doesn't involve others, confess it to God and accept his forgiveness. But if others know what you've done, you need to make sure they also know you've confessed to God and received forgiveness—and you need to ask them to forgive you too.

⁹Hide your face from my sins
  and blot out all my iniquity.

¹⁰Create in me a pure heart, O God,
  and renew a steadfast spirit within me.
¹¹Do not cast me from your presence
  or take your Holy Spirit from me.
¹²Restore to me the joy of your salvation
  and grant me a willing spirit, to sustain me.

¹³Then I will teach transgressors your ways,
  and sinners will turn back to you.
¹⁴Save me from bloodguilt, O God,
  the God who saves me,
  and my tongue will sing of your righteousness.
¹⁵O Lord, open my lips,
  and my mouth will declare your praise.
¹⁶You do not delight in sacrifice, or I would bring it;
  you do not take pleasure in burnt offerings.
¹⁷The sacrifices of God are*ᵃ* a broken spirit;
  a broken and contrite heart,
  O God, you will not despise.

¹⁸In your good pleasure make Zion prosper;
  build up the walls of Jerusalem.
¹⁹Then there will be righteous sacrifices,
  whole burnt offerings to delight you;
  then bulls will be offered on your altar.

PSALM 52

For the director of music. A *maskil*ᵇ of David. When Doeg
the Edomite had gone to Saul and told him: "David has
gone to the house of Ahimelech."

¹Why do you boast of evil, you mighty man?
  Why do you boast all day long,
  you who are a disgrace in the eyes of God?
²Your tongue plots destruction;
  it is like a sharpened razor,
  you who practice deceit.
³You love evil rather than good,
  falsehood rather than speaking the truth.   *Selah*
⁴You love every harmful word,
  O you deceitful tongue!

⁵Surely God will bring you down to everlasting ruin:
  He will snatch you up and tear you from your tent;
  he will uproot you from the land of the living.   *Selah*
⁶The righteous will see and fear;
  they will laugh at him, saying,
⁷"Here now is the man
  who did not make God his stronghold
  but trusted in his great wealth
  and grew strong by destroying others!"

ᵃ*17* Or *My sacrifice, O God, is*   ᵇTitle: Probably a literary or musical term

⁸But I am like an olive tree
    flourishing in the house of God;
  I trust in God's unfailing love
    for ever and ever.
⁹I will praise you forever for what you have done;
    in your name I will hope, for your name is good.
  I will praise you in the presence of your saints.

PSALM 53

For the director of music. According to *mahalath*.ᵃ A *maskil*ᵇ
of David.

¹The fool says in his heart,
  "There is no God."
They are corrupt, and their ways are vile;
  there is no one who does good.

²God looks down from heaven
    on the sons of men
  to see if there are any who understand,
    any who seek God.
³Everyone has turned away,
    they have together become corrupt;
  there is no one who does good,
    not even one.

⁴Will the evildoers never learn—
    those who devour my people as men eat bread
    and who do not call on God?
⁵There they were, overwhelmed with dread,
    where there was nothing to dread.
  God scattered the bones of those who attacked you;
    you put them to shame, for God despised them.

⁶Oh, that salvation for Israel would come out of Zion!
    When God restores the fortunes of his people,
    let Jacob rejoice and Israel be glad!

PSALM 54

For the director of music. With stringed instruments. A *maskil*ᵇ
of David. When the Ziphites had gone to Saul and said, "Is not
David hiding among us?"

¹Save me, O God, by your name;
    vindicate me by your might.
²Hear my prayer, O God;
    listen to the words of my mouth.

³Strangers are attacking me;
    ruthless men seek my life—
    men without regard for God.   *Selah*

ᵃTitle: Probably a musical term ᵇTitle: Probably a literary or musical term

⁴Surely God is my help;
　　the Lord is the one who sustains me.

⁵Let evil recoil on those who slander me;
　　in your faithfulness destroy them.

⁶I will sacrifice a freewill offering to you;
　　I will praise your name, O LORD,
　　for it is good.
⁷For he has delivered me from all my troubles,
　　and my eyes have looked in triumph on my
　　　　foes.

PSALM 55

For the director of music. With stringed instruments.
A *maskil*ᵃ of David.

¹Listen to my prayer, O God,
　　do not ignore my plea;
²　　hear me and answer me.
My thoughts trouble me and I am distraught
³　　at the voice of the enemy,
　　at the stares of the wicked;
for they bring down suffering upon me
　　and revile me in their anger.

⁴My heart is in anguish within me;
　　the terrors of death assail me.
⁵Fear and trembling have beset me;
　　horror has overwhelmed me.
⁶I said, "Oh, that I had the
　　　　wings of a dove!
　　I would fly away and be at
　　　　rest—
⁷I would flee far away
　　and stay in the desert;
　　　　　　　　　　　Selah
⁸I would hurry to my place of
　　　　shelter,
　　far from the tempest and
　　　　storm."

⁹Confuse the wicked, O Lord,
　　　　confound their speech,
　　for I see violence and strife
　　　　in the city.
¹⁰Day and night they prowl
　　　　about on its walls;
　　malice and abuse are within
　　　　it.
¹¹Destructive forces are at work
　　　　in the city;
　　threats and lies never leave
　　　　its streets.

ᵃTitle: Probably a literary or musical term

PSALM 55:1–8

How do you handle feelings? Strong feelings, like anger. Or fear. Or loneliness. Or shame. Feelings that are hard to share with parents or even close friends. The book of Psalms can show you what to do with strong feelings. David knew that however he felt, he could express his emotions to God. God wouldn't be angry with him or say, "You shouldn't feel that way!" God cares how you feel, and just expressing your emotions to him can often make you feel better. You could look for feeling words in different psalms and make a list. Then when you have one of those feelings, read that psalm as your prayer.

Direct
Line

¹²If an enemy were insulting me,
    I could endure it;
  if a foe were raising himself against me,
    I could hide from him.
¹³But it is you, a man like myself,
    my companion, my close friend,
¹⁴with whom I once enjoyed sweet fellowship
    as we walked with the throng at the house of God.

¹⁵Let death take my enemies by surprise;
    let them go down alive to the grave,^a
    for evil finds lodging among them.

¹⁶But I call to God,
    and the Lord saves me.
¹⁷Evening, morning and noon
    I cry out in distress,
    and he hears my voice.
¹⁸He ransoms me unharmed
    from the battle waged against me,
    even though many oppose me.
¹⁹God, who is enthroned forever,
    will hear them and afflict them—   *Selah*
  men who never change their ways
    and have no fear of God.

²⁰My companion attacks his friends;
    he violates his covenant.
²¹His speech is smooth as butter,
    yet war is in his heart;
  his words are more soothing than oil,
    yet they are drawn swords.

²²Cast your cares on the Lord
    and he will sustain you;
    he will never let the righteous fall.
²³But you, O God, will bring down the wicked
    into the pit of corruption;
  bloodthirsty and deceitful men
    will not live out half their days.

  But as for me, I trust in you.

PSALM 56

For the director of music. To the tune of, "A Dove on Distant Oaks."
Of David. A *miktam.*^b When the Philistines had seized him in Gath.

¹Be merciful to me, O God, for men hotly pursue me;
    all day long they press their attack.
²My slanderers pursue me all day long;
    many are attacking me in their pride.

³When I am afraid,
    I will trust in you.
⁴In God, whose word I praise,

^a*15* Hebrew *Sheol*   ^bTitle: Probably a literary or musical term

in God I trust; I will not be afraid.
What can mortal man do to me?

⁵All day long they twist my words;
they are always plotting to harm me.
⁶They conspire, they lurk,
they watch my steps,
eager to take my life.

⁷On no account let them escape;
in your anger, O God, bring down the nations.
⁸Record my lament;
list my tears on your scroll*—
are they not in your record?

⁹Then my enemies will turn back
when I call for help.
By this I will know that God is for me.
¹⁰In God, whose word I praise,
in the LORD, whose word I praise—
¹¹in God I trust; I will not be afraid.
What can man do to me?

¹²I am under vows to you, O God;
I will present my thank offerings to you.
¹³For you have delivered me*b* from death
and my feet from stumbling,
that I may walk before God
in the light of life.*c*

PSALM 57

For the director of music. To the tune of, "Do Not Destroy."
Of David. A *miktam.*d When he had fled from Saul into the cave.

¹Have mercy on me, O God, have mercy on me,
for in you my soul takes refuge.
I will take refuge in the shadow of your wings
until the disaster has passed.

²I cry out to God Most High,
to God, who fulfills his purpose for me.
³He sends from heaven and saves me,
rebuking those who hotly pursue me;   *Selah*
God sends his love and his faithfulness.

⁴I am in the midst of lions;
I lie among ravenous beasts—
men whose teeth are spears and arrows,
whose tongues are sharp swords.

⁵Be exalted, O God, above the heavens;
let your glory be over all the earth.

⁶They spread a net for my feet—
I was bowed down in distress.

*a8 Or / put my tears in your wineskin   b13 Or my soul   c13 Or the land of the living   dTitle: Probably a
literary or musical term*

They dug a pit in my path—
    but they have fallen into it themselves.   *Selah*

⁷My heart is steadfast, O God,
    my heart is steadfast;
    I will sing and make music.
⁸Awake, my soul!
    Awake, harp and lyre!
    I will awaken the dawn.

⁹I will praise you, O Lord, among the nations;
    I will sing of you among the peoples.
¹⁰For great is your love, reaching to the heavens;
    your faithfulness reaches to the skies.

¹¹Be exalted, O God, above the heavens;
    let your glory be over all the earth.

PSALM

For the director of music. To the tune of, "Do Not Destroy."
Of David. A *miktam.*ᵃ

¹Do you rulers indeed speak justly?
    Do you judge uprightly among men?
²No, in your heart you devise injustice,
    and your hands mete out violence on the earth.
³Even from birth the wicked go astray;
    from the womb they are wayward and speak lies.
⁴Their venom is like the venom of a snake,
    like that of a cobra that has stopped its ears,
⁵that will not heed the tune of the charmer,
    however skillful the enchanter may be.

⁶Break the teeth in their mouths, O God;
    tear out, O Lᴏʀᴅ, the fangs of the lions!
⁷Let them vanish like water that flows away;
    when they draw the bow, let their arrows be blunted.
⁸Like a slug melting away as it moves along,
    like a stillborn child, may they not see the sun.

⁹Before your pots can feel the heat of the thorns—
    whether they be green or dry—the wicked will be swept
        away.ᵇ
¹⁰The righteous will be glad when they are avenged,
    when they bathe their feet in the blood of the wicked.
¹¹Then men will say,
    "Surely the righteous still are rewarded;
    surely there is a God who judges the earth."

PSALM

For the director of music. To the tune of, "Do Not Destroy."
Of David. A *miktam.*ᵃ When Saul had sent men to watch
David's house in order to kill him.

¹Deliver me from my enemies, O God;
    protect me from those who rise up against me.

ᵃTitle: Probably a literary or musical term   ᵇ9 The meaning of the Hebrew for this verse is uncertain.

²Deliver me from evildoers
and save me from bloodthirsty men.

³See how they lie in wait for me!
Fierce men conspire against me
for no offense or sin of mine, O Lord.
⁴I have done no wrong, yet they are ready to
attack me.
Arise to help me; look on my plight!
⁵O Lord God Almighty, the God of Israel,
rouse yourself to punish all the nations;
show no mercy to wicked traitors.   *Selah*

⁶They return at evening,
snarling like dogs,
and prowl about the city.
⁷See what they spew from their mouths—
they spew out swords from their lips,
and they say, "Who can hear us?"
⁸But you, O Lord, laugh at them;
you scoff at all those nations.

⁹O my Strength, I watch for you;
you, O God, are my fortress, ¹⁰my loving
God.

God will go before me
and will let me gloat over those who slander me.
¹¹But do not kill them, O Lord our shield,ᵃ
or my people will forget.
In your might make them wander about,
and bring them down.
¹²For the sins of their mouths,
for the words of their lips,
let them be caught in their pride.
For the curses and lies they utter,
¹³   consume them in wrath,
consume them till they are no more.
Then it will be known to the ends of the
earth
that God rules over Jacob.   *Selah*

¹⁴They return at evening,
snarling like dogs,
and prowl about the city.
¹⁵They wander about for food
and howl if not satisfied.
¹⁶But I will sing of your strength,
in the morning I will sing of your love;
for you are my fortress,
my refuge in times of trouble.

¹⁷O my Strength, I sing praise to you;
you, O God, are my fortress, my loving
God.

ᵃ*11 Or* sovereign

PSALM 60

For the director of music. To the tune of, "The Lily of the Covenant."
A *miktam*[a] of David. For teaching. When he fought Aram
Naharaim[b] and Aram Zobah,[c] and when Joab returned and struck
down twelve thousand Edomites in the Valley of Salt.

¹You have rejected us, O God, and burst forth upon us;
   you have been angry—now restore us!
²You have shaken the land and torn it open;
   mend its fractures, for it is quaking.
³You have shown your people desperate times;
   you have given us wine that makes us stagger.

⁴But for those who fear you, you have raised a banner
   to be unfurled against the bow.   *Selah*

⁵Save us and help us with your right hand,
   that those you love may be delivered.
⁶God has spoken from his sanctuary:
   "In triumph I will parcel out Shechem
   and measure off the Valley of Succoth.
⁷Gilead is mine, and Manasseh is mine;
   Ephraim is my helmet,
   Judah my scepter.
⁸Moab is my washbasin,
   upon Edom I toss my sandal;
   over Philistia I shout in triumph."

⁹Who will bring me to the fortified city?
   Who will lead me to Edom?
¹⁰Is it not you, O God, you who have rejected us
   and no longer go out with our armies?
¹¹Give us aid against the enemy,
   for the help of man is worthless.
¹²With God we will gain the victory,
   and he will trample down our enemies.

PSALM 61

For the director of music. With stringed instruments. Of David.

¹Hear my cry, O God;
   listen to my prayer.

²From the ends of the earth I call to you,
   I call as my heart grows faint;
   lead me to the rock that is higher than I.
³For you have been my refuge,
   a strong tower against the foe.

⁴I long to dwell in your tent forever
   and take refuge in the shelter of your wings.   *Selah*

---

[a]Title: Probably a literary or musical term   [b]Title: That is, Arameans of Northwest Mesopotamia
[c]Title: That is, Arameans of central Syria

⁵For you have heard my vows, O God;
>you have given me the heritage of those who fear your
>>name.

⁶Increase the days of the king's life,
>his years for many generations.
⁷May he be enthroned in God's presence forever;
>appoint your love and faithfulness to protect him.

⁸Then will I ever sing praise to your name
>and fulfill my vows day after day.

PSALM 62

For the director of music. For Jeduthun. A psalm of David.

¹My soul finds rest in God alone;
>my salvation comes from him.
²He alone is my rock and my salvation;
>he is my fortress, I will never be shaken.

³How long will you assault a man?
>Would all of you throw him down—
>this leaning wall, this tottering fence?
⁴They fully intend to topple him
>from his lofty place;
>they take delight in lies.
With their mouths they bless,
>but in their hearts they curse.   *Selah*

⁵Find rest, O my soul, in God alone;
>my hope comes from him.
⁶He alone is my rock and my salvation;
>he is my fortress, I will not be shaken.
⁷My salvation and my honor depend on God*a*;
>he is my mighty rock, my refuge.
⁸Trust in him at all times, O people;
>pour out your hearts to him,
>for God is our refuge.   *Selah*

⁹Lowborn men are but a breath,
>the highborn are but a lie;
if weighed on a balance, they are nothing;
>together they are only a breath.
¹⁰Do not trust in extortion
>or take pride in stolen goods;
though your riches increase,
>do not set your heart on them.

¹¹One thing God has spoken,
>two things have I heard:
that you, O God, are strong,
¹²   and that you, O Lord, are loving.
Surely you will reward each person
>according to what he has done.

> Trust in him at all
> times, O people;
> pour out your
> hearts to him, for
> God is our refuge
> (Psalm 62:8).

---

a7 Or / God Most High is my salvation and my honor

PSALM 63

A psalm of David. When he was in the Desert of Judah.

¹O God, you are my God,
    earnestly I seek you;
my soul thirsts for you,
    my body longs for you,
in a dry and weary land
    where there is no water.

²I have seen you in the sanctuary
    and beheld your power and your glory.
³Because your love is better than life,
    my lips will glorify you.
⁴I will praise you as long as I live,
    and in your name I will lift up my hands.
⁵My soul will be satisfied as with the richest of foods;
    with singing lips my mouth will praise you.

⁶On my bed I remember you;
    I think of you through the watches of the night.
⁷Because you are my help,
    I sing in the shadow of your wings.
⁸My soul clings to you;
    your right hand upholds me.

⁹They who seek my life will be destroyed;
    they will go down to the depths of the earth.
¹⁰They will be given over to the sword
    and become food for jackals.

¹¹But the king will rejoice in God;
    all who swear by God's name will praise him,
    while the mouths of liars will be silenced.

PSALM 64

For the director of music. A psalm of David.

¹Hear me, O God, as I voice my complaint;
    protect my life from the threat of the enemy.
²Hide me from the conspiracy of the wicked,
    from that noisy crowd of evildoers.

³They sharpen their tongues like swords
    and aim their words like deadly arrows.
⁴They shoot from ambush at the innocent man;
    they shoot at him suddenly, without fear.

⁵They encourage each other in evil plans,
    they talk about hiding their snares;
    they say, "Who will see them[a]?"
⁶They plot injustice and say,

a5 Or us

"We have devised a perfect plan!"
    Surely the mind and heart of man are cunning.

⁷But God will shoot them with arrows;
    suddenly they will be struck down.
⁸He will turn their own tongues against them
    and bring them to ruin;
    all who see them will shake their heads in scorn.

⁹All mankind will fear;
    they will proclaim the works of God
    and ponder what he has done.
¹⁰Let the righteous rejoice in the LORD
    and take refuge in him;
    let all the upright in heart praise him!

PSALM 65

For the director of music. A psalm of David. A song.

¹Praise awaits*ᵃ* you, O God, in Zion;
    to you our vows will be fulfilled.
²O you who hear prayer,
    to you all men will come.
³When we were overwhelmed by sins,
    you forgave*ᵇ* our transgressions.
⁴Blessed are those you choose
    and bring near to live in your courts!
We are filled with the good things of your house,
    of your holy temple.

⁵You answer us with awesome deeds of righteousness,
    O God our Savior,
the hope of all the ends of the earth
    and of the farthest seas,
⁶who formed the mountains by your power,
    having armed yourself with strength,
⁷who stilled the roaring of the seas,
    the roaring of their waves,
    and the turmoil of the nations.
⁸Those living far away fear your wonders;
    where morning dawns and evening fades
    you call forth songs of joy.

⁹You care for the land and water it;
    you enrich it abundantly.
The streams of God are filled with water
    to provide the people with grain,
    for so you have ordained it.*ᶜ*
¹⁰You drench its furrows
    and level its ridges;
you soften it with showers
    and bless its crops.

ᵃ1 Or befits; the meaning of the Hebrew for this word is uncertain. ᵇ3 Or made atonement for ᶜ9 Or for that is how you prepare the land

¹¹You crown the year with your bounty,
  and your carts overflow with abundance.
¹²The grasslands of the desert overflow;
  the hills are clothed with gladness.
¹³The meadows are covered with flocks
  and the valleys are mantled with grain;
  they shout for joy and sing.

PSALM 66

For the director of music. A song. A psalm.

¹Shout with joy to God, all the earth!
² Sing the glory of his name;
  make his praise glorious!
³Say to God, "How awesome are your deeds!
  So great is your power
  that your enemies cringe before you.
⁴All the earth bows down to you;
  they sing praise to you,
  they sing praise to your name."   *Selah*

⁵Come and see what God has done,
  how awesome his works in man's behalf!
⁶He turned the sea into dry land,
  they passed through the waters on foot—
  come, let us rejoice in him.
⁷He rules forever by his power,
  his eyes watch the nations—
  let not the rebellious rise up against him.   *Selah*

⁸Praise our God, O peoples,
  let the sound of his praise be heard;
⁹he has preserved our lives
  and kept our feet from slipping.
¹⁰For you, O God, tested us;
  you refined us like silver.
¹¹You brought us into prison
  and laid burdens on our backs.
¹²You let men ride over our heads;
  we went through fire and water,
  but you brought us to a place of abundance.

¹³I will come to your temple with burnt offerings
  and fulfill my vows to you—
¹⁴vows my lips promised and my mouth spoke
  when I was in trouble.
¹⁵I will sacrifice fat animals to you
  and an offering of rams;
  I will offer bulls and goats.   *Selah*

¹⁶Come and listen, all you who fear God;
  let me tell you what he has done for me.
¹⁷I cried out to him with my mouth;
  his praise was on my tongue.
¹⁸If I had cherished sin in my heart,
  the Lord would not have listened;

¹⁹but God has surely listened
    and heard my voice in prayer.
²⁰Praise be to God,
    who has not rejected my prayer
    or withheld his love from me!

PSALM 67

For the director of music. With stringed instruments. A psalm.
A song.

¹May God be gracious to us and bless us
    and make his face shine upon us,   *Selah*
²that your ways may be known on earth,
    your salvation among all nations.

³May the peoples praise you, O God;
    may all the peoples praise you.
⁴May the nations be glad and sing for joy,
    for you rule the peoples justly
    and guide the nations of the earth.   *Selah*
⁵May the peoples praise you, O God;
    may all the peoples praise you.

⁶Then the land will yield its harvest,
    and God, our God, will bless us.
⁷God will bless us,
    and all the ends of the earth will fear him.

PSALM 68

For the director of music. Of David. A psalm. A song.

¹May God arise, may his enemies be scattered;
    may his foes flee before him.
²As smoke is blown away by the wind,
    may you blow them away;
  as wax melts before the fire,
    may the wicked perish before God.
³But may the righteous be glad
    and rejoice before God;
    may they be happy and joyful.

⁴Sing to God, sing praise to his name,
    extol him who rides on the clouds*ᵃ*—
  his name is the LORD—
    and rejoice before him.
⁵A father to the fatherless, a defender of widows,
    is God in his holy dwelling.
⁶God sets the lonely in families,*ᵇ*
    he leads forth the prisoners with singing;
    but the rebellious live in a sun-scorched land.

⁷When you went out before your people, O God,
    when you marched through the wasteland,   *Selah*

ᵃ4 Or / prepare the way for him who rides through the deserts   ᵇ6 Or the desolate in a homeland

⁸the earth shook,
    the heavens poured down rain,
  before God, the One of Sinai,
    before God, the God of Israel.
⁹You gave abundant showers, O God;
    you refreshed your weary inheritance.
¹⁰Your people settled in it,
    and from your bounty, O God, you provided for the poor.

¹¹The Lord announced the word,
    and great was the company of those who proclaimed it:
¹²"Kings and armies flee in haste;
    in the camps men divide the plunder.
¹³Even while you sleep among the campfires,*a*
    the wings of ˌmyˌ dove are sheathed with silver,
    its feathers with shining gold."
¹⁴When the Almighty*b* scattered the kings in the land,
    it was like snow fallen on Zalmon.

¹⁵The mountains of Bashan are majestic mountains;
    rugged are the mountains of Bashan.
¹⁶Why gaze in envy, O rugged mountains,
    at the mountain where God chooses to reign,
    where the Lᴏʀᴅ himself will dwell forever?
¹⁷The chariots of God are tens of thousands
    and thousands of thousands;
    the Lord ˌhas comeˌ from Sinai into his sanctuary.
¹⁸When you ascended on high,
    you led captives in your train;
    you received gifts from men,
  even from*c* the rebellious—
    that you,*d* O Lᴏʀᴅ God, might dwell there.

¹⁹Praise be to the Lord, to God our Savior,
    who daily bears our burdens.   *Selah*
²⁰Our God is a God who saves;
    from the Sovereign Lᴏʀᴅ comes escape from death.

²¹Surely God will crush the heads of his enemies,
    the hairy crowns of those who go on in their sins.
²²The Lord says, "I will bring them from Bashan;
    I will bring them from the depths of the sea,
²³that you may plunge your feet in the blood of your foes,
    while the tongues of your dogs have their share."

²⁴Your procession has come into view, O God,
    the procession of my God and King into the sanctuary.
²⁵In front are the singers, after them the musicians;
    with them are the maidens playing tambourines.
²⁶Praise God in the great congregation;
    praise the Lᴏʀᴅ in the assembly of Israel.
²⁷There is the little tribe of Benjamin, leading them,
    there the great throng of Judah's princes,
    and there the princes of Zebulun and of Naphtali.

²⁸Summon your power, O God*e*;
    show us your strength, O God, as you have done before.

---

a13 Or *saddlebags*   *b14* Hebrew *Shaddai*   *c18* Or *gifts for men, / even*   *d18* Or *they*   *e28* Many Hebrew
manuscripts, Septuagint and Syriac; most Hebrew manuscripts *Your God has summoned power for you*

²⁹Because of your temple at Jerusalem
    kings will bring you gifts.
³⁰Rebuke the beast among the reeds,
    the herd of bulls among the calves of the nations.
Humbled, may it bring bars of silver.
    Scatter the nations who delight in war.
³¹Envoys will come from Egypt;
    Cushᵃ will submit herself to God.

³²Sing to God, O kingdoms of the earth,
    sing praise to the Lord,   *Selah*
³³to him who rides the ancient skies above,
    who thunders with mighty voice.
³⁴Proclaim the power of God,
    whose majesty is over Israel,
    whose power is in the skies.
³⁵You are awesome, O God, in your sanctuary;
    the God of Israel gives power and strength to his people.

Praise be to God!

PSALM **69**

For the director of music. To the tune of, "Lilies." Of David.

¹Save me, O God,
    for the waters have come up to my neck.
²I sink in the miry depths,
    where there is no foothold.
I have come into the deep waters;
    the floods engulf me.
³I am worn out calling for help;
    my throat is parched.
My eyes fail,
    looking for my God.
⁴Those who hate me without reason
    outnumber the hairs of my head;
many are my enemies without cause,
    those who seek to destroy me.
I am forced to restore
    what I did not steal.

⁵You know my folly, O God;
    my guilt is not hidden from you.

⁶May those who hope in you
    not be disgraced because of me,
    O Lord, the LORD Almighty;
may those who seek you
    not be put to shame because of me,
    O God of Israel.
⁷For I endure scorn for your sake,
    and shame covers my face.
⁸I am a stranger to my brothers,
    an alien to my own mother's sons;

ᵃ*31* That is, the upper Nile region

⁹for zeal for your house consumes me,
and the insults of those who insult you fall on me.
¹⁰When I weep and fast,
I must endure scorn;
¹¹when I put on sackcloth,
people make sport of me.
¹²Those who sit at the gate mock me,
and I am the song of the drunkards.

¹³But I pray to you, O LORD,
in the time of your favor;
in your great love, O God,
answer me with your sure salvation.
¹⁴Rescue me from the mire,
do not let me sink;
deliver me from those who hate me,
from the deep waters.
¹⁵Do not let the floodwaters engulf me
or the depths swallow me up
or the pit close its mouth over me.
¹⁶Answer me, O LORD, out of the goodness of your love;
in your great mercy turn to me.
¹⁷Do not hide your face from your servant;
answer me quickly, for I am in trouble.
¹⁸Come near and rescue me;
redeem me because of my foes.

¹⁹You know how I am scorned, disgraced and shamed;
all my enemies are before you.
²⁰Scorn has broken my heart
and has left me helpless;
I looked for sympathy, but there was none,
for comforters, but I found none.
²¹They put gall in my food
and gave me vinegar for my thirst.

²²May the table set before them become a snare;
may it become retribution and*a* a trap.
²³May their eyes be darkened so they cannot see,
and their backs be bent forever.
²⁴Pour out your wrath on them;
let your fierce anger overtake them.
²⁵May their place be deserted;
let there be no one to dwell in their tents.
²⁶For they persecute those you wound
and talk about the pain of those you hurt.
²⁷Charge them with crime upon crime;
do not let them share in your salvation.
²⁸May they be blotted out of the book of life
and not be listed with the righteous.

²⁹I am in pain and distress;
may your salvation, O God, protect me.

³⁰I will praise God's name in song
and glorify him with thanksgiving.

---

a22 Or snare / and their fellowship become

³¹This will please the Lord more than an ox,
    more than a bull with its horns and hoofs.
³²The poor will see and be glad—
    you who seek God, may your hearts live!
³³The Lord hears the needy
    and does not despise his captive people.

³⁴Let heaven and earth praise him,
    the seas and all that move in them,
³⁵for God will save Zion
    and rebuild the cities of Judah.
Then people will settle there and possess it;
³⁶   the children of his servants will inherit it,
    and those who love his name will dwell there.

PSALM 70

For the director of music. Of David. A petition.

¹Hasten, O God, to save me;
    O Lord, come quickly to help me.
²May those who seek my life
    be put to shame and confusion;
may all who desire my ruin
    be turned back in disgrace.
³May those who say to me, "Aha! Aha!"
    turn back because of their shame.
⁴But may all who seek you
    rejoice and be glad in you;
may those who love your salvation always say,
    "Let God be exalted!"

⁵Yet I am poor and needy;
    come quickly to me, O God.
You are my help and my deliverer;
    O Lord, do not delay.

PSALM 71

¹In you, O Lord, I have taken refuge;
    let me never be put to shame.
²Rescue me and deliver me in your righteousness;
    turn your ear to me and save me.
³Be my rock of refuge,
    to which I can always go;
give the command to save me,
    for you are my rock and my fortress.
⁴Deliver me, O my God, from the hand of the wicked,
    from the grasp of evil and cruel men.

⁵For you have been my hope, O Sovereign Lord,
    my confidence since my youth.
⁶From birth I have relied on you;

you brought me forth from my mother's womb.
I will ever praise you.
⁷I have become like a portent to many,
but you are my strong refuge.
⁸My mouth is filled with your praise,
declaring your splendor all day long.

⁹Do not cast me away when I am old;
do not forsake me when my strength is gone.
¹⁰For my enemies speak against me;
those who wait to kill me conspire together.
¹¹They say, "God has forsaken him;
pursue him and seize him,
for no one will rescue him."
¹²Be not far from me, O God;
come quickly, O my God, to help me.
¹³May my accusers perish in shame;
may those who want to harm me
be covered with scorn and disgrace.

¹⁴But as for me, I will always have hope;
I will praise you more and more.
¹⁵My mouth will tell of your righteousness,
of your salvation all day long,
though I know not its measure.
¹⁶I will come and proclaim your mighty acts, O Sovereign
Lord;
I will proclaim your righteousness, yours alone.
¹⁷Since my youth, O God, you have taught me,
and to this day I declare your marvelous deeds.
¹⁸Even when I am old and gray,
do not forsake me, O God,
till I declare your power to the next generation,
your might to all who are to come.

¹⁹Your righteousness reaches to the skies, O God,
you who have done great things.
Who, O God, is like you?
²⁰Though you have made me see troubles, many and
bitter,
you will restore my life again;
from the depths of the earth
you will again bring me up.
²¹You will increase my honor
and comfort me once again.

²²I will praise you with the harp
for your faithfulness, O my God;
I will sing praise to you with the lyre,
O Holy One of Israel.
²³My lips will shout for joy
when I sing praise to you—
I, whom you have redeemed.
²⁴My tongue will tell of your righteous acts
all day long,
for those who wanted to harm me
have been put to shame and confusion.

PSALM 72

Of Solomon.

¹Endow the king with your justice, O God,
the royal son with your righteousness.
²He will^a judge your people in righteousness,
your afflicted ones with justice.
³The mountains will bring prosperity to the people,
the hills the fruit of righteousness.
⁴He will defend the afflicted among the people
and save the children of the needy;
he will crush the oppressor.

⁵He will endure^b as long as the sun,
as long as the moon, through all generations.
⁶He will be like rain falling on a mown field,
like showers watering the earth.
⁷In his days the righteous will flourish;
prosperity will abound till the moon is no more.

⁸He will rule from sea to sea
and from the River^c to the ends of the earth.^d
⁹The desert tribes will bow before him
and his enemies will lick the dust.
¹⁰The kings of Tarshish and of distant shores
will bring tribute to him;
the kings of Sheba and Seba
will present him gifts.
¹¹All kings will bow down to him
and all nations will serve him.

¹²For he will deliver the needy who cry out,
the afflicted who have no one to help.
¹³He will take pity on the weak and the needy
and save the needy from death.
¹⁴He will rescue them from oppression and violence,
for precious is their blood in his sight.

¹⁵Long may he live!
May gold from Sheba be given him.
May people ever pray for him
and bless him all day long.
¹⁶Let grain abound throughout the land;
on the tops of the hills may it sway.
Let its fruit flourish like Lebanon;
let it thrive like the grass of the field.
¹⁷May his name endure forever;
may it continue as long as the sun.

All nations will be blessed through him,
and they will call him blessed.

¹⁸Praise be to the Lord God, the God of Israel,
who alone does marvelous deeds.

^a2 Or *May he*; similarly in verses 3-11 and 17   ^b5 Septuagint; Hebrew *You will be feared*   ^c8 That is, the
Euphrates   ^d8 Or *the end of the land*

¹⁹Praise be to his glorious name forever;
    may the whole earth be filled with his glory.
        Amen and Amen.

²⁰This concludes the prayers of David son of Jesse.

BOOK III

Psalms 73–89

PSALM 73

A psalm of Asaph.

¹Surely God is good to Israel,
    to those who are pure in heart.

²But as for me, my feet had almost slipped;
    I had nearly lost my foothold.
³For I envied the arrogant
    when I saw the prosperity of the wicked.

⁴They have no struggles;
    their bodies are healthy and strong.[a]
⁵They are free from the burdens common to man;
    they are not plagued by human ills.
⁶Therefore pride is their necklace;
    they clothe themselves with violence.
⁷From their callous hearts comes iniquity[b];
    the evil conceits of their minds know no limits.
⁸They scoff, and speak with malice;
    in their arrogance they threaten oppression.
⁹Their mouths lay claim to heaven,
    and their tongues take possession of the earth.
¹⁰Therefore their people turn to them
    and drink up waters in abundance.[c]
¹¹They say, "How can God know?
    Does the Most High have knowledge?"

¹²This is what the wicked are like—
    always carefree, they increase in wealth.

¹³Surely in vain have I kept my heart pure;
    in vain have I washed my hands in innocence.
¹⁴All day long I have been plagued;
    I have been punished every morning.

¹⁵If I had said, "I will speak thus,"
    I would have betrayed your children.
¹⁶When I tried to understand all this,
    it was oppressive to me
¹⁷till I entered the sanctuary of God;
    then I understood their final destiny.

¹⁸Surely you place them on slippery ground;
    you cast them down to ruin.

---

a4 With a different word division of the Hebrew; Masoretic Text *struggles at their death; / their bodies are healthy* *b7* Syriac (see also Septuagint); Hebrew *Their eyes bulge with fat* *c10* The meaning of the Hebrew for this verse is uncertain.

Dear Sam,

It's a lot harder to grow up with Christian values today than when my parents were growing up. It's so much easier to be popular if you go along with the crowd. My parents just don't understand!

Rick in Richmond

100 Advice Lane, Anywhere, USA

Dear Rick,

I definitely agree; it's tougher to grow up with Christian values today. Teens today are bombarded with immoral messages so constantly that the messages no longer seem immoral, but acceptable. Music, movies, music videos, drugs, alcohol, promiscuous sex, abortion—they all mock Christian values. And those who are most immoral are often most popular.

This is nothing new, however. Many years ago the psalmist said he was jealous of wicked people because they seemed to have everything (Psalm 73:3-12). And he also felt he had gained nothing by trying to do right (Psalm 73:13).

It wasn't until he entered "the sanctuary of God" that God gave him understanding. Eventually the wicked get into trouble so deep they are destroyed (Psalm 73:16-19). God does not help them. But those who seek to obey God are always helped by him and will be rewarded some-day. It is better to be loved by God than to be liked by any number of kids.

Sam

¹⁹How suddenly are they destroyed,
  completely swept away by terrors!
²⁰As a dream when one awakes,
  so when you arise, O Lord,
  you will despise them as fantasies.

²¹When my heart was grieved
  and my spirit embittered,
²²I was senseless and ignorant;
  I was a brute beast before you.

²³Yet I am always with you;
  you hold me by my right hand.
²⁴You guide me with your counsel,
  and afterward you will take me into glory.
²⁵Whom have I in heaven but you?
  And earth has nothing I desire besides you.
²⁶My flesh and my heart may fail,
  but God is the strength of my heart
  and my portion forever.

²⁷Those who are far from you will perish;
  you destroy all who are unfaithful to you.
²⁸But as for me, it is good to be near God.
  I have made the Sovereign Lord my refuge;
  I will tell of all your deeds.

PSALM 74

A *maskil*[a] of Asaph.

¹Why have you rejected us forever, O God?
  Why does your anger smolder against the sheep of your
    pasture?
²Remember the people you purchased of old,
  the tribe of your inheritance, whom you redeemed—
  Mount Zion, where you dwelt.
³Turn your steps toward these everlasting ruins,
  all this destruction the enemy has brought on the
    sanctuary.

⁴Your foes roared in the place where you met with us;
  they set up their standards as signs.
⁵They behaved like men wielding axes
  to cut through a thicket of trees.
⁶They smashed all the carved paneling
  with their axes and hatchets.
⁷They burned your sanctuary to the ground;
  they defiled the dwelling place of your Name.
⁸They said in their hearts, "We will crush them completely!"
  They burned every place where God was worshiped in the
    land.
⁹We are given no miraculous signs;
  no prophets are left,
  and none of us knows how long this will be.

─────────────────

ªTitle: Probably a literary or musical term

¹⁰How long will the enemy mock you, O God?
  Will the foe revile your name forever?
¹¹Why do you hold back your hand, your right hand?
  Take it from the folds of your garment and destroy them!

¹²But you, O God, are my king from of old;
  you bring salvation upon the earth.
¹³It was you who split open the sea by your power;
  you broke the heads of the monster in the waters.
¹⁴It was you who crushed the heads of Leviathan
  and gave him as food to the creatures of the desert.
¹⁵It was you who opened up springs and streams;
  you dried up the ever flowing rivers.
¹⁶The day is yours, and yours also the night;
  you established the sun and moon.
¹⁷It was you who set all the boundaries of the earth;
  you made both summer and winter.

¹⁸Remember how the enemy has mocked you, O Lᴏʀᴅ,
  how foolish people have reviled your name.
¹⁹Do not hand over the life of your dove to wild beasts;
  do not forget the lives of your afflicted people forever.
²⁰Have regard for your covenant,
  because haunts of violence fill the dark places of the land.
²¹Do not let the oppressed retreat in disgrace;
  may the poor and needy praise your name.

²²Rise up, O God, and defend your cause;
  remember how fools mock you all day long.
²³Do not ignore the clamor of your adversaries,
  the uproar of your enemies, which rises continually.

PSALM 75

For the director of music. To the tune of, "Do Not Destroy."
A psalm of Asaph. A song.

¹We give thanks to you, O God,
  we give thanks, for your Name is near;
  men tell of your wonderful deeds.

²You say, "I choose the appointed time;
  it is I who judge uprightly.
³When the earth and all its people quake,
  it is I who hold its pillars firm.   *Selah*
⁴To the arrogant I say, 'Boast no more,'
  and to the wicked, 'Do not lift up your horns.
⁵Do not lift your horns against heaven;
  do not speak with outstretched neck.' "

⁶No one from the east or the west
  or from the desert can exalt a man.
⁷But it is God who judges:
  He brings one down, he exalts another.
⁸In the hand of the Lᴏʀᴅ is a cup
  full of foaming wine mixed with spices;
he pours it out, and all the wicked of the earth
  drink it down to its very dregs.

⁹As for me, I will declare this forever;
　　I will sing praise to the God of Jacob.
¹⁰I will cut off the horns of all the wicked,
　　but the horns of the righteous will be lifted up.

PSALM 76

For the director of music. With stringed instruments.
A psalm of Asaph. A song.

¹In Judah God is known;
　　his name is great in Israel.
²His tent is in Salem,
　　his dwelling place in Zion.
³There he broke the flashing arrows,
　　the shields and the swords, the weapons of war.　　　　*Selah*

⁴You are resplendent with light,
　　more majestic than mountains rich with game.
⁵Valiant men lie plundered,
　　they sleep their last sleep;
　not one of the warriors
　　can lift his hands.
⁶At your rebuke, O God of Jacob,
　　both horse and chariot lie still.
⁷You alone are to be feared.
　　Who can stand before you when you are angry?
⁸From heaven you pronounced judgment,
　　and the land feared and was quiet—
⁹when you, O God, rose up to judge,
　　to save all the afflicted of the land.　　　　*Selah*
¹⁰Surely your wrath against men brings you praise,
　　and the survivors of your wrath are restrained.*ᵃ*

¹¹Make vows to the LORD your God and fulfill them;
　　let all the neighboring lands
　　bring gifts to the One to be feared.
¹²He breaks the spirit of rulers;
　　he is feared by the kings of the earth.

PSALM 77

For the director of music. For Jeduthun. Of Asaph. A psalm.

¹I cried out to God for help;
　　I cried out to God to hear me.
²When I was in distress, I sought the Lord;
　　at night I stretched out untiring hands
　　and my soul refused to be comforted.

³I remembered you, O God, and I groaned;
　　I mused, and my spirit grew faint.　　　　*Selah*

ᵃ10 Or Surely the wrath of men brings you praise, / and with the remainder of wrath you arm yourself

⁴You kept my eyes from closing;
  I was too troubled to speak.
⁵I thought about the former days,
  the years of long ago;
⁶I remembered my songs in the night.
  My heart mused and my spirit inquired:

⁷"Will the Lord reject forever?
  Will he never show his favor again?
⁸Has his unfailing love vanished forever?
  Has his promise failed for all time?
⁹Has God forgotten to be merciful?
  Has he in anger withheld his compassion?"   *Selah*

¹⁰Then I thought, "To this I will appeal:
  the years of the right hand of the Most High."
¹¹I will remember the deeds of the LORD;
  yes, I will remember your miracles of long ago.
¹²I will meditate on all your works
  and consider all your mighty deeds.

¹³Your ways, O God, are holy.
  What god is so great as our God?
¹⁴You are the God who performs miracles;
  you display your power among the peoples.
¹⁵With your mighty arm you redeemed your people,
  the descendants of Jacob and Joseph.   *Selah*

¹⁶The waters saw you, O God,
  the waters saw you and writhed;
  the very depths were convulsed.
¹⁷The clouds poured down water,
  the skies resounded with thunder;
  your arrows flashed back and forth.
¹⁸Your thunder was heard in the whirlwind,
  your lightning lit up the world;
  the earth trembled and quaked.
¹⁹Your path led through the sea,
  your way through the mighty waters,
  though your footprints were not seen.

²⁰You led your people like a flock
  by the hand of Moses and Aaron.

PSALM 78

A *maskil*ᵃ of Asaph.

¹O my people, hear my teaching;
  listen to the words of my mouth.
²I will open my mouth in parables,
  I will utter hidden things, things from of old—
³what we have heard and known,
  what our fathers have told us.
⁴We will not hide them from their children;
  we will tell the next generation

ᵃTitle: Probably a literary or musical term

the praiseworthy deeds of the Lord,
his power, and the wonders he has done.
⁵He decreed statutes for Jacob
and established the law in Israel,
which he commanded our forefathers
to teach their children,
⁶so the next generation would know them,
even the children yet to be born,
and they in turn would tell their children.
⁷Then they would put their trust in God
and would not forget his deeds
but would keep his commands.
⁸They would not be like their forefathers—
a stubborn and rebellious generation,
whose hearts were not loyal to God,
whose spirits were not faithful to him.

⁹The men of Ephraim, though armed with bows,
turned back on the day of battle;
¹⁰they did not keep God's covenant
and refused to live by his law.
¹¹They forgot what he had done,
the wonders he had shown them.
¹²He did miracles in the sight of their fathers
in the land of Egypt, in the region of Zoan.
¹³He divided the sea and led them through;
he made the water stand firm like a wall.
¹⁴He guided them with the cloud by day
and with light from the fire all night.
¹⁵He split the rocks in the desert
and gave them water as abundant as the
seas;
¹⁶he brought streams out of a rocky crag
and made water flow down like rivers.

¹⁷But they continued to sin against him,
rebelling in the desert against the Most High.
¹⁸They willfully put God to the test
by demanding the food they craved.
¹⁹They spoke against God, saying,
"Can God spread a table in the desert?
²⁰When he struck the rock, water gushed out,
and streams flowed abundantly.
But can he also give us food?
Can he supply meat for his people?"
²¹When the Lord heard them, he was very angry;
his fire broke out against Jacob,
and his wrath rose against Israel,
²²for they did not believe in God
or trust in his deliverance.
²³Yet he gave a command to the skies above
and opened the doors of the heavens;
²⁴he rained down manna for the people to eat,
he gave them the grain of heaven.
²⁵Men ate the bread of angels;
he sent them all the food they could eat.
²⁶He let loose the east wind from the heavens
and led forth the south wind by his power.

²⁷He rained meat down on them like dust,
  flying birds like sand on the seashore.
²⁸He made them come down inside their camp,
  all around their tents.
²⁹They ate till they had more than enough,
  for he had given them what they craved.
³⁰But before they turned from the food they craved,
  even while it was still in their mouths,
³¹God's anger rose against them;
  he put to death the sturdiest among them,
  cutting down the young men of Israel.

³²In spite of all this, they kept on sinning;
  in spite of his wonders, they did not believe.
³³So he ended their days in futility
  and their years in terror.
³⁴Whenever God slew them, they would seek him;
  they eagerly turned to him again.
³⁵They remembered that God was their Rock,
  that God Most High was their Redeemer.
³⁶But then they would flatter him with their mouths,
  lying to him with their tongues;
³⁷their hearts were not loyal to him,
  they were not faithful to his covenant.
³⁸Yet he was merciful;
  he forgave their iniquities
  and did not destroy them.
  Time after time he restrained his anger
  and did not stir up his full wrath.
³⁹He remembered that they were but flesh,
  a passing breeze that does not return.

⁴⁰How often they rebelled against him in the desert
  and grieved him in the wasteland!
⁴¹Again and again they put God to the test;
  they vexed the Holy One of Israel.
⁴²They did not remember his power—
  the day he redeemed them from the oppressor,
⁴³the day he displayed his miraculous signs in Egypt,
  his wonders in the region of Zoan.
⁴⁴He turned their rivers to blood;
  they could not drink from their streams.
⁴⁵He sent swarms of flies that devoured them,
  and frogs that devastated them.
⁴⁶He gave their crops to the grasshopper,
  their produce to the locust.
⁴⁷He destroyed their vines with hail
  and their sycamore-figs with sleet.
⁴⁸He gave over their cattle to the hail,
  their livestock to bolts of lightning.
⁴⁹He unleashed against them his hot anger,
  his wrath, indignation and hostility—
  a band of destroying angels.
⁵⁰He prepared a path for his anger;
  he did not spare them from death
  but gave them over to the plague.
⁵¹He struck down all the firstborn of Egypt,
  the firstfruits of manhood in the tents of Ham.

⁵²But he brought his people out like a flock;
  he led them like sheep through the desert.
⁵³He guided them safely, so they were unafraid;
  but the sea engulfed their enemies.
⁵⁴Thus he brought them to the border of his holy land,
  to the hill country his right hand had taken.
⁵⁵He drove out nations before them
  and allotted their lands to them as an inheritance;
  he settled the tribes of Israel in their homes.

⁵⁶But they put God to the test
  and rebelled against the Most High;
  they did not keep his statutes.
⁵⁷Like their fathers they were disloyal and faithless,
  as unreliable as a faulty bow.
⁵⁸They angered him with their high places;
  they aroused his jealousy with their idols.
⁵⁹When God heard them, he was very angry;
  he rejected Israel completely.
⁶⁰He abandoned the tabernacle of Shiloh,
  the tent he had set up among men.
⁶¹He sent ͵the ark of͵ his might into captivity,
  his splendor into the hands of the enemy.
⁶²He gave his people over to the sword;
  he was very angry with his inheritance.
⁶³Fire consumed their young men,
  and their maidens had no wedding songs;
⁶⁴their priests were put to the sword,
  and their widows could not weep.

⁶⁵Then the Lord awoke as from sleep,
  as a man wakes from the stupor of wine.
⁶⁶He beat back his enemies;
  he put them to everlasting shame.
⁶⁷Then he rejected the tents of Joseph,
  he did not choose the tribe of Ephraim;
⁶⁸but he chose the tribe of Judah,
  Mount Zion, which he loved.
⁶⁹He built his sanctuary like the heights,
  like the earth that he established forever.
⁷⁰He chose David his servant
  and took him from the sheep pens;
⁷¹from tending the sheep he brought him
  to be the shepherd of his people Jacob,
  of Israel his inheritance.
⁷²And David shepherded them with integrity of heart;
  with skillful hands he led them.

PSALM 79

A psalm of Asaph.

¹O God, the nations have invaded your inheritance;
  they have defiled your holy temple,
  they have reduced Jerusalem to rubble.
²They have given the dead bodies of your servants

as food to the birds of the air,
the flesh of your saints to the beasts of the earth.
³They have poured out blood like water
all around Jerusalem,
and there is no one to bury the dead.
⁴We are objects of reproach to our neighbors,
of scorn and derision to those around us.

⁵How long, O LORD? Will you be angry forever?
How long will your jealousy burn like fire?
⁶Pour out your wrath on the nations
that do not acknowledge you,
on the kingdoms
that do not call on your name;
⁷for they have devoured Jacob
and destroyed his homeland.
⁸Do not hold against us the sins of the fathers;
may your mercy come quickly to meet us,
for we are in desperate need.

⁹Help us, O God our Savior,
for the glory of your name;
deliver us and forgive our sins
for your name's sake.
¹⁰Why should the nations say,
"Where is their God?"
Before our eyes, make known among the nations
that you avenge the outpoured blood of your servants.
¹¹May the groans of the prisoners come before you;
by the strength of your arm
preserve those condemned to die.

¹²Pay back into the laps of our neighbors seven times
the reproach they have hurled at you, O Lord.
¹³Then we your people, the sheep of your pasture,
will praise you forever;
from generation to generation
we will recount your praise.

PSALM 80

For the director of music. To the tune of, "The Lilies
of the Covenant." Of Asaph. A psalm.

¹Hear us, O Shepherd of Israel,
you who lead Joseph like a flock;
you who sit enthroned between the cherubim, shine forth
²   before Ephraim, Benjamin and Manasseh.
Awaken your might;
come and save us.

³Restore us, O God;
make your face shine upon us,
that we may be saved.

⁴O LORD God Almighty,
how long will your anger smolder
against the prayers of your people?

⁵You have fed them with the bread of tears;
 you have made them drink tears by the bowlful.
⁶You have made us a source of contention to our neighbors,
 and our enemies mock us.

⁷Restore us, O God Almighty;
 make your face shine upon us,
 that we may be saved.

⁸You brought a vine out of Egypt;
 you drove out the nations and planted it.
⁹You cleared the ground for it,
 and it took root and filled the land.
¹⁰The mountains were covered with its shade,
 the mighty cedars with its branches.
¹¹It sent out its boughs to the Sea,ᵃ
 its shoots as far as the River.ᵇ

¹²Why have you broken down its walls
 so that all who pass by pick its grapes?
¹³Boars from the forest ravage it
 and the creatures of the field feed on it.
¹⁴Return to us, O God Almighty!
 Look down from heaven and see!
 Watch over this vine,
¹⁵   the root your right hand has planted,
 the sonᶜ you have raised up for yourself.

¹⁶Your vine is cut down, it is burned with fire;
 at your rebuke your people perish.
¹⁷Let your hand rest on the man at your right hand,
 the son of man you have raised up for yourself.
¹⁸Then we will not turn away from you;
 revive us, and we will call on your name.

¹⁹Restore us, O Lᴏʀᴅ God Almighty;
 make your face shine upon us,
 that we may be saved.

PSALM

For the director of music. According to *gittith*.ᵈ Of Asaph.

¹Sing for joy to God our strength;
 shout aloud to the God of Jacob!
²Begin the music, strike the tambourine,
 play the melodious harp and lyre.

³Sound the ram's horn at the New Moon,
 and when the moon is full, on the day of our Feast;
⁴this is a decree for Israel,
 an ordinance of the God of Jacob.
⁵He established it as a statute for Joseph
 when he went out against Egypt,
 where we heard a language we did not understand.ᵉ

ᵃ11 Probably the Mediterranean ᵇ11 That is, the Euphrates ᶜ15 Or *branch* ᵈTitle: Probably a musical
term ᵉ5 Or / *and we heard a voice we had not known*

⁶He says, "I removed the burden from their shoulders;
    their hands were set free from the basket.
⁷In your distress you called and I rescued you,
    I answered you out of a thundercloud;
    I tested you at the waters of Meribah.   *Selah*

⁸"Hear, O my people, and I will warn you—
    if you would but listen to me, O Israel!
⁹You shall have no foreign god among you;
    you shall not bow down to an alien god.
¹⁰I am the LORD your God,
    who brought you up out of Egypt.
    Open wide your mouth and I will fill it.

¹¹"But my people would not listen to me;
    Israel would not submit to me.
¹²So I gave them over to their stubborn hearts
    to follow their own devices.

¹³"If my people would but listen to me,
    if Israel would follow my ways,
¹⁴how quickly would I subdue their enemies
    and turn my hand against their foes!
¹⁵Those who hate the LORD would cringe before him,
    and their punishment would last forever.
¹⁶But you would be fed with the finest of wheat;
    with honey from the rock I would satisfy you."

PSALM 82

A psalm of Asaph.

¹God presides in the great assembly;
    he gives judgment among the "gods":

²"How long will you*ᵃ* defend the unjust
    and show partiality to the wicked?   *Selah*

*ᵃ2 The Hebrew is plural.

Sometimes Christians are criticized for being "pro-life." Abortion advocates talk about how terrible it is to be an "unwanted" child. They think if a child is unwanted, he or she is sure to be abused. They suggest that it's better to kill an unborn child than to let him or her live without love.

We need to remember that adoption is an option. Believers are called to "defend the cause of the weak and fatherless" and to "rescue the weak and needy" (Psalm 82:3–4). If you should ever face the choice, don't choose an abortion. Many Christian couples want a baby to love—couples who would be glad to do God's will by caring for a fatherless child and rescuing you, the weak and needy.

The Bible Says

Adoption's an Option

³Defend the cause of the weak and fatherless;
    maintain the rights of the poor and oppressed.
⁴Rescue the weak and needy;
    deliver them from the hand of the wicked.

⁵"They know nothing, they understand nothing.
    They walk about in darkness;
    all the foundations of the earth are shaken.

⁶"I said, 'You are "gods";
    you are all sons of the Most High.'
⁷But you will die like mere men;
    you will fall like every other ruler."

⁸Rise up, O God, judge the earth,
    for all the nations are your inheritance.

PSALM 83

A song. A psalm of Asaph.

¹O God, do not keep silent;
    be not quiet, O God, be not still.
²See how your enemies are astir,
    how your foes rear their heads.
³With cunning they conspire against your people;
    they plot against those you cherish.
⁴"Come," they say, "let us destroy them as a nation,
    that the name of Israel be remembered no more."

⁵With one mind they plot together;
    they form an alliance against you—
⁶the tents of Edom and the Ishmaelites,
    of Moab and the Hagrites,
⁷Gebal,ᵃ Ammon and Amalek,
    Philistia, with the people of Tyre.
⁸Even Assyria has joined them
    to lend strength to the descendants of Lot.   *Selah*

⁹Do to them as you did to Midian,
    as you did to Sisera and Jabin at the river Kishon,
¹⁰who perished at Endor
    and became like refuse on the ground.
¹¹Make their nobles like Oreb and Zeeb,
    all their princes like Zebah and Zalmunna,
¹²who said, "Let us take possession
    of the pasturelands of God."

¹³Make them like tumbleweed, O my God,
    like chaff before the wind.
¹⁴As fire consumes the forest
    or a flame sets the mountains ablaze,
¹⁵so pursue them with your tempest
    and terrify them with your storm.
¹⁶Cover their faces with shame
    so that men will seek your name, O LORD.

ᵃ7 That is, Byblos

¹⁷May they ever be ashamed and dismayed;
　　may they perish in disgrace.
¹⁸Let them know that you, whose name is the Lᴏʀᴅ—
　　that you alone are the Most High over all the earth.

PSALM 84

For the director of music. According to *gittith.*ᵃ
Of the Sons of Korah. A psalm.

¹How lovely is your dwelling place,
　　O Lᴏʀᴅ Almighty!
²My soul yearns, even faints,
　　for the courts of the Lᴏʀᴅ;
my heart and my flesh cry out
　　for the living God.

³Even the sparrow has found a home,
　　and the swallow a nest for herself,
　　where she may have her young—
a place near your altar,
　　O Lᴏʀᴅ Almighty, my King and my God.
⁴Blessed are those who dwell in your house;
　　they are ever praising you.　　　　　　　　　　　　　　*Selah*

⁵Blessed are those whose strength is in you,
　　who have set their hearts on pilgrimage.
⁶As they pass through the Valley of Baca,
　　they make it a place of springs;
　　the autumn rains also cover it with pools.ᵇ
⁷They go from strength to strength,
　　till each appears before God in Zion.

⁸Hear my prayer, O Lᴏʀᴅ God Almighty;
　　listen to me, O God of Jacob.　　　　　　　　　　　　*Selah*
⁹Look upon our shield,ᶜ O God;
　　look with favor on your anointed one.

¹⁰Better is one day in your courts
　　than a thousand elsewhere;
I would rather be a doorkeeper in the house of my God
　　than dwell in the tents of the wicked.
¹¹For the Lᴏʀᴅ God is a sun and shield;
　　the Lᴏʀᴅ bestows favor and honor;
no good thing does he withhold
　　from those whose walk is blameless.

¹²O Lᴏʀᴅ Almighty,
　　blessed is the man who trusts in you.

> The Lᴏʀᴅ bestows favor and honor; no good thing does he withhold (Psalm 84:11).

PSALM 85

For the director of music. Of the Sons of Korah. A psalm.

¹You showed favor to your land, O Lᴏʀᴅ;
　　you restored the fortunes of Jacob.

ᵃTitle: Probably a musical term　ᵇ6 Or *blessings*　ᶜ9 Or *sovereign*

²You forgave the iniquity of your people
and covered all their sins.   *Selah*
³You set aside all your wrath
and turned from your fierce anger.

⁴Restore us again, O God our Savior,
and put away your displeasure toward us.
⁵Will you be angry with us forever?
Will you prolong your anger through all generations?
⁶Will you not revive us again,
that your people may rejoice in you?
⁷Show us your unfailing love, O Lord,
and grant us your salvation.

⁸I will listen to what God the Lord will say;
he promises peace to his people, his saints—
but let them not return to folly.
⁹Surely his salvation is near those who fear him,
that his glory may dwell in our land.

¹⁰Love and faithfulness meet together;
righteousness and peace kiss each other.
¹¹Faithfulness springs forth from the earth,
and righteousness looks down from heaven.
¹²The Lord will indeed give what is good,
and our land will yield its harvest.
¹³Righteousness goes before him
and prepares the way for his steps.

PSALM 86

A prayer of David.

¹Hear, O Lord, and answer me,
for I am poor and needy.
²Guard my life, for I am devoted to you.
You are my God; save your servant
who trusts in you.
³Have mercy on me, O Lord,
for I call to you all day long.
⁴Bring joy to your servant,
for to you, O Lord,
I lift up my soul.

⁵You are forgiving and good, O Lord,
abounding in love to all who call to you.
⁶Hear my prayer, O Lord;
listen to my cry for mercy.
⁷In the day of my trouble I will call to you,
for you will answer me.

⁸Among the gods there is none like you, O Lord;
no deeds can compare with yours.
⁹All the nations you have made
will come and worship before you, O Lord;
they will bring glory to your name.
¹⁰For you are great and do marvelous deeds;
you alone are God.

¹¹Teach me your way, O Lord,
and I will walk in your truth;

give me an undivided heart,
    that I may fear your name.
¹²I will praise you, O Lord my God, with all my heart;
    I will glorify your name forever.
¹³For great is your love toward me;
    you have delivered me from the depths of the grave.ᵃ

¹⁴The arrogant are attacking me, O God;
    a band of ruthless men seeks my life—
    men without regard for you.
¹⁵But you, O Lord, are a compassionate and gracious God,
    slow to anger, abounding in love and
        faithfulness.
¹⁶Turn to me and have mercy on me;
    grant your strength to your servant
    and save the son of your maidservant.ᵇ
¹⁷Give me a sign of your goodness,
    that my enemies may see it and be put to shame,
    for you, O Lord, have helped me and
        comforted me.

> I will glorify your
> name forever.
> For great is your
> love toward me
> (Psalm 86:12-13).

PSALM 87

Of the Sons of Korah. A psalm. A song.

¹He has set his foundation on the holy mountain;
²   the Lord loves the gates of Zion
        more than all the dwellings of Jacob.
³Glorious things are said of you,
    O city of God: *Selah*
⁴"I will record Rahabᶜ and Babylon
    among those who acknowledge me—
Philistia too, and Tyre, along with Cushᵈ—
    and will say, 'Thisᵉ one was born in Zion.' "

⁵Indeed, of Zion it will be said,
    "This one and that one were born in her,
    and the Most High himself will establish her."
⁶The Lord will write in the register of the peoples:
    "This one was born in Zion."   *Selah*
⁷As they make music they will sing,
    "All my fountains are in you."

PSALM 88

A song. A psalm of the Sons of Korah. For the director of music.
According to *mahalath leannoth.*ᶠ A *maskil*ᵍ of
Heman the Ezrahite.

¹O Lord, the God who saves me,
    day and night I cry out before you.

ᵃ*13* Hebrew *Sheol*   ᵇ*16* Or *save your faithful son*   ᶜ*4* A poetic name for Egypt   ᵈ*4* That is, the upper Nile region   ᵉ*4* Or *"O Rahab and Babylon, / Philistia, Tyre and Cush, / I will record concerning those who acknowledge me: / 'This*   ᶠTitle: Possibly a tune, "The Suffering of Affliction"   ᵍTitle: Probably a literary or musical term

²May my prayer come before you;
    turn your ear to my cry.

³For my soul is full of trouble
    and my life draws near the grave.ᵃ
⁴I am counted among those who go down to the pit;
    I am like a man without strength.
⁵I am set apart with the dead,
    like the slain who lie in the grave,
  whom you remember no more,
    who are cut off from your care.

⁶You have put me in the lowest pit,
    in the darkest depths.
⁷Your wrath lies heavily upon me;
    you have overwhelmed me with all your waves.   *Selah*
⁸You have taken from me my closest friends
    and have made me repulsive to them.
  I am confined and cannot escape;
⁹   my eyes are dim with grief.

  I call to you, O Lᴏʀᴅ, every day;
    I spread out my hands to you.
¹⁰Do you show your wonders to the dead?
    Do those who are dead rise up and praise you?   *Selah*
¹¹Is your love declared in the grave,
    your faithfulness in Destructionᵇ?
¹²Are your wonders known in the place of darkness,
    or your righteous deeds in the land of oblivion?

¹³But I cry to you for help, O Lᴏʀᴅ;
    in the morning my prayer comes before you.
¹⁴Why, O Lᴏʀᴅ, do you reject me
    and hide your face from me?

¹⁵From my youth I have been afflicted and close to death;
    I have suffered your terrors and am in despair.
¹⁶Your wrath has swept over me;
    your terrors have destroyed me.
¹⁷All day long they surround me like a flood;
    they have completely engulfed me.
¹⁸You have taken my companions and loved ones from me;
    the darkness is my closest friend.

PSALM 89

A *maskil*ᶜ of Ethan the Ezrahite.

¹I will sing of the Lᴏʀᴅ's great love forever;
    with my mouth I will make your faithfulness known through
        all generations.
²I will declare that your love stands firm forever,
    that you established your faithfulness in heaven itself.

³You said, "I have made a covenant with my chosen one,
    I have sworn to David my servant,

ᵃ3 Hebrew *Sheol* ᵇ11 Hebrew *Abaddon* ᶜTitle: Probably a literary or musical term

⁴'I will establish your line forever
and make your throne firm through all generations.'" *Selah*

⁵The heavens praise your wonders, O LORD,
your faithfulness too, in the assembly of the holy ones.
⁶For who in the skies above can compare with the LORD?
Who is like the LORD among the heavenly beings?
⁷In the council of the holy ones God is greatly feared;
he is more awesome than all who surround him.
⁸O LORD God Almighty, who is like you?
You are mighty, O LORD, and your faithfulness surrounds
you.

⁹You rule over the surging sea;
when its waves mount up, you still them.
¹⁰You crushed Rahab like one of the slain;
with your strong arm you scattered your enemies.
¹¹The heavens are yours, and yours also the earth;
you founded the world and all that is in it.
¹²You created the north and the south;
Tabor and Hermon sing for joy at your name.
¹³Your arm is endued with power;
your hand is strong, your right hand exalted.

¹⁴Righteousness and justice are the foundation of your throne;
love and faithfulness go before you.
¹⁵Blessed are those who have learned to acclaim you,
who walk in the light of your presence, O LORD.
¹⁶They rejoice in your name all day long;
they exult in your righteousness.
¹⁷For you are their glory and strength,
and by your favor you exalt our horn.ᵃ
¹⁸Indeed, our shieldᵇ belongs to the LORD,
our king to the Holy One of Israel.

¹⁹Once you spoke in a vision,
to your faithful people you said:
"I have bestowed strength on a warrior;
I have exalted a young man from among the people.
²⁰I have found David my servant;
with my sacred oil I have anointed him.
²¹My hand will sustain him;
surely my arm will strengthen him.
²²No enemy will subject him to tribute;
no wicked man will oppress him.
²³I will crush his foes before him
and strike down his adversaries.
²⁴My faithful love will be with him,
and through my name his hornᶜ will be exalted.
²⁵I will set his hand over the sea,
his right hand over the rivers.
²⁶He will call out to me, 'You are my Father,
my God, the Rock my Savior.'
²⁷I will also appoint him my firstborn,
the most exalted of the kings of the earth.
²⁸I will maintain my love to him forever,
and my covenant with him will never fail.

ᵃ17 *Horn* here symbolizes strong one.   ᵇ18 Or *sovereign*   ᶜ24 *Horn* here symbolizes strength.

²⁹I will establish his line forever,
  his throne as long as the heavens endure.

³⁰"If his sons forsake my law
  and do not follow my statutes,
³¹if they violate my decrees
  and fail to keep my commands,
³²I will punish their sin with the rod,
  their iniquity with flogging;
³³but I will not take my love from him,
  nor will I ever betray my faithfulness.
³⁴I will not violate my covenant
  or alter what my lips have uttered.
³⁵Once for all, I have sworn by my holiness—
  and I will not lie to David—
³⁶that his line will continue forever
  and his throne endure before me like the sun;
³⁷it will be established forever like the moon,
  the faithful witness in the sky."   *Selah*

³⁸But you have rejected, you have spurned,
  you have been very angry with your anointed one.
³⁹You have renounced the covenant with your servant
  and have defiled his crown in the dust.
⁴⁰You have broken through all his walls
  and reduced his strongholds to ruins.
⁴¹All who pass by have plundered him;
  he has become the scorn of his neighbors.
⁴²You have exalted the right hand of his foes;
  you have made all his enemies rejoice.
⁴³You have turned back the edge of his sword
  and have not supported him in battle.
⁴⁴You have put an end to his splendor
  and cast his throne to the ground.
⁴⁵You have cut short the days of his youth;
  you have covered him with a mantle of shame.   *Selah*

⁴⁶How long, O Lᴏʀᴅ? Will you hide yourself forever?
  How long will your wrath burn like fire?
⁴⁷Remember how fleeting is my life.
  For what futility you have created all men!
⁴⁸What man can live and not see death,
  or save himself from the power of the grave*ᵃ*?   *Selah*
⁴⁹O Lord, where is your former great love,
  which in your faithfulness you swore to David?
⁵⁰Remember, Lord, how your servant has*ᵇ* been mocked,
  how I bear in my heart the taunts of all the nations,
⁵¹the taunts with which your enemies have mocked,
  O Lᴏʀᴅ,
  with which they have mocked every step of your
    anointed one.

⁵²Praise be to the Lᴏʀᴅ forever!
    Amen and Amen.

ᵃ48 Hebrew Sheol ᵇ50 Or your servants have

BOOK IV

Psalms 90–106

PSALM 90

A prayer of Moses the man of God.

¹Lord, you have been our dwelling place
  throughout all generations.
²Before the mountains were born
  or you brought forth the earth and the world,
  from everlasting to everlasting you are God.

³You turn men back to dust,
  saying, "Return to dust, O sons of men."
⁴For a thousand years in your sight
  are like a day that has just gone by,
  or like a watch in the night.
⁵You sweep men away in the sleep of death;
  they are like the new grass of the morning—
⁶though in the morning it springs up new,
  by evening it is dry and withered.

⁷We are consumed by your anger
  and terrified by your indignation.
⁸You have set our iniquities before you,
  our secret sins in the light of your presence.
⁹All our days pass away under your wrath;
  we finish our years with a moan.
¹⁰The length of our days is seventy years—
  or eighty, if we have the strength;
  yet their span*a* is but trouble and sorrow,
  for they quickly pass, and we fly away.

¹¹Who knows the power of your anger?
  For your wrath is as great as the fear that is due
    you.
¹²Teach us to number our days aright,
  that we may gain a heart of wisdom.

¹³Relent, O Lᴏʀᴅ! How long will it be?
  Have compassion on your servants.
¹⁴Satisfy us in the morning with your unfailing love,
  that we may sing for joy and be glad all our days.
¹⁵Make us glad for as many days as you have afflicted us,
  for as many years as we have seen trouble.
¹⁶May your deeds be shown to your servants,
  your splendor to their children.

¹⁷May the favor*b* of the Lord our God rest upon us;
  establish the work of our hands for us—
  yes, establish the work of our hands.

a10 Or yet the best of them b17 Or beauty

PSALM 91

¹He who dwells in the shelter of the Most High
    will rest in the shadow of the Almighty.ᵃ
²I will sayᵇ of the LORD, "He is my refuge and my fortress,
    my God, in whom I trust."

³Surely he will save you from the fowler's snare
    and from the deadly pestilence.
⁴He will cover you with his feathers,
    and under his wings you will find refuge;
    his faithfulness will be your shield and rampart.
⁵You will not fear the terror of night,
    nor the arrow that flies by day,
⁶nor the pestilence that stalks in the darkness,
    nor the plague that destroys at midday.
⁷A thousand may fall at your side,
    ten thousand at your right hand,
    but it will not come near you.
⁸You will only observe with your eyes
    and see the punishment of the wicked.

⁹If you make the Most High your dwelling—
    even the LORD, who is my refuge—
¹⁰then no harm will befall you,
    no disaster will come near your tent.
¹¹For he will command his angels concerning you
    to guard you in all your ways;
¹²they will lift you up in their hands,
    so that you will not strike your foot against a stone.
¹³You will tread upon the lion and the cobra;
    you will trample the great lion and the
        serpent.

¹⁴"Because he loves me," says the LORD, "I will
        rescue him;
    I will protect him, for he acknowledges my
        name.
¹⁵He will call upon me, and I will answer him;
    I will be with him in trouble,
    I will deliver him and honor him.
¹⁶With long life will I satisfy him
    and show him my salvation."

He will command
his angels
concerning you
to guard you in
all your ways
(Psalm 91:11).

PSALM 92

A psalm. A song. For the Sabbath day.

¹It is good to praise the LORD
    and make music to your name, O Most High,
²to proclaim your love in the morning
    and your faithfulness at night,
³to the music of the ten-stringed lyre
    and the melody of the harp.

ᵃ1 Hebrew Shaddai   ᵇ2 Or He says

⁴For you make me glad by your deeds, O Lᴏʀᴅ;
  I sing for joy at the works of your hands.
⁵How great are your works, O Lᴏʀᴅ,
  how profound your thoughts!
⁶The senseless man does not know,
  fools do not understand,
⁷that though the wicked spring up like grass
  and all evildoers flourish,
 they will be forever destroyed.

⁸But you, O Lᴏʀᴅ, are exalted forever.

⁹For surely your enemies, O Lᴏʀᴅ,
  surely your enemies will perish;
  all evildoers will be scattered.
¹⁰You have exalted my horn*ᵃ like that of a wild ox;
  fine oils have been poured upon me.
¹¹My eyes have seen the defeat of my adversaries;
  my ears have heard the rout of my wicked foes.

¹²The righteous will flourish like a palm tree,
  they will grow like a cedar of Lebanon;
¹³planted in the house of the Lᴏʀᴅ,
  they will flourish in the courts of our God.
¹⁴They will still bear fruit in old age,
  they will stay fresh and green,
¹⁵proclaiming, "The Lᴏʀᴅ is upright;
  he is my Rock, and there is no wickedness
    in him."

PSALM 93

¹The Lᴏʀᴅ reigns, he is robed in majesty;
  the Lᴏʀᴅ is robed in majesty
  and is armed with strength.
 The world is firmly established;
  it cannot be moved.
²Your throne was established
    long ago;
  you are from all eternity.

³The seas have lifted up, O Lᴏʀᴅ,
  the seas have lifted up their
    voice;
  the seas have lifted up their
    pounding waves.
⁴Mightier than the thunder of
    the great waters,
  mightier than the breakers of
    the sea—
  the Lᴏʀᴅ on high is mighty.

⁵Your statutes stand firm;
  holiness adorns your house
  for endless days, O Lᴏʀᴅ.

ᵃ10 Horn here symbolizes strength.

PSALM 92

Have you ever gotten up in the morning and felt just great? Like everything was A-OK with your world and you wanted to shout about it? All right then, maybe not first thing in the morning but a bit later in the day? Why not be like the psalmist and express it? You don't have to write a poem, but you could give your mom a big smile and a hug. You could thump a friend on the back. You could punch your brother in the arm. Or sing. Or dance. However you feel comfortable expressing your joy. The psalmist praised God for his happiness. Maybe you could do that too!

Direct Line

¹O Lord, the God who avenges,
  O God who avenges, shine forth.
²Rise up, O Judge of the earth;
  pay back to the proud what they deserve.
³How long will the wicked, O Lord,
  how long will the wicked be jubilant?

⁴They pour out arrogant words;
  all the evildoers are full of boasting.
⁵They crush your people, O Lord;
  they oppress your inheritance.
⁶They slay the widow and the alien;
  they murder the fatherless.
⁷They say, "The Lord does not see;
  the God of Jacob pays no heed."

⁸Take heed, you senseless ones among the people;
  you fools, when will you become wise?
⁹Does he who implanted the ear not hear?
  Does he who formed the eye not see?
¹⁰Does he who disciplines nations not punish?
  Does he who teaches man lack knowledge?
¹¹The Lord knows the thoughts of man;
  he knows that they are futile.

¹²Blessed is the man you discipline, O Lord,
  the man you teach from your law;
¹³you grant him relief from days of trouble,
  till a pit is dug for the wicked.
¹⁴For the Lord will not reject his people;
  he will never forsake his inheritance.
¹⁵Judgment will again be founded on righteousness,
  and all the upright in heart will follow it.

¹⁶Who will rise up for me against the wicked?
  Who will take a stand for me against evildoers?
¹⁷Unless the Lord had given me help,
  I would soon have dwelt in the silence of
    death.
¹⁸When I said, "My foot is slipping,"
  your love, O Lord, supported me.
¹⁹When anxiety was great within me,
  your consolation brought joy to my soul.

²⁰Can a corrupt throne be allied with you—
  one that brings on misery by its decrees?
²¹They band together against the righteous
  and condemn the innocent to death.
²²But the Lord has become my fortress,
  and my God the rock in whom I take refuge.
²³He will repay them for their sins
  and destroy them for their wickedness;
  the Lord our God will destroy them.

PSALM 95

¹Come, let us sing for joy to the LORD;
    let us shout aloud to the Rock of our salvation.
²Let us come before him with thanksgiving
    and extol him with music and song.

³For the LORD is the great God,
    the great King above all gods.
⁴In his hand are the depths of the earth,
    and the mountain peaks belong to him.
⁵The sea is his, for he made it,
    and his hands formed the dry land.

⁶Come, let us bow down in worship,
    let us kneel before the LORD our Maker;
⁷for he is our God
    and we are the people of his pasture,
    the flock under his care.

    Today, if you hear his voice,
⁸   do not harden your hearts as you did at Meribah,*a*
    as you did that day at Massah*b* in the desert,
⁹where your fathers tested and tried me,
    though they had seen what I did.
¹⁰For forty years I was angry with that generation;
    I said, "They are a people whose hearts go astray,
    and they have not known my ways."
¹¹So I declared on oath in my anger,
    "They shall never enter my rest."

PSALM 96

¹Sing to the LORD a new song;
    sing to the LORD, all the earth.
²Sing to the LORD, praise his name;
    proclaim his salvation day after day.
³Declare his glory among the nations,
    his marvelous deeds among all peoples.

⁴For great is the LORD and most worthy of praise;
    he is to be feared above all gods.
⁵For all the gods of the nations are idols,
    but the LORD made the heavens.
⁶Splendor and majesty are before him;
    strength and glory are in his sanctuary.

⁷Ascribe to the LORD, O families of nations,
    ascribe to the LORD glory and strength.
⁸Ascribe to the LORD the glory due his name;
    bring an offering and come into his courts.
⁹Worship the LORD in the splendor of his*c* holiness;
    tremble before him, all the earth.

---

a8 Meribah means *quarreling.* *b8 Massah* means *testing.* *c9* Or LORD *with the splendor of*

¹⁰Say among the nations, "The LORD reigns."
 The world is firmly established, it cannot be moved;
 he will judge the peoples with equity.
¹¹Let the heavens rejoice, let the earth be glad;
 let the sea resound, and all that is in it;
¹² let the fields be jubilant, and everything in them.
 Then all the trees of the forest will sing for joy;
¹³ they will sing before the LORD, for he comes,
 he comes to judge the earth.
 He will judge the world in righteousness
 and the peoples in his truth.

PSALM 97

¹The LORD reigns, let the earth be glad;
 let the distant shores rejoice.

²Clouds and thick darkness surround him;
 righteousness and justice are the foundation of his throne.
³Fire goes before him
 and consumes his foes on every side.
⁴His lightning lights up the world;
 the earth sees and trembles.
 ⁵The mountains melt like wax before the LORD,
 before the Lord of all the earth.
 ⁶The heavens proclaim his righteousness,
 and all the peoples see his glory.

⁷All who worship images are put to shame,
 those who boast in idols—
 worship him, all you gods!

⁸Zion hears and rejoices
 and the villages of Judah are glad
 because of your judgments, O LORD.
⁹For you, O LORD, are the Most High over all the earth;
 you are exalted far above all gods.

¹⁰Let those who love the LORD hate evil,
 for he guards the lives of his faithful ones
 and delivers them from the hand of the wicked.
¹¹Light is shed upon the righteous
 and joy on the upright in heart.
¹²Rejoice in the LORD, you who are righteous,
 and praise his holy name.

> Let those who love the LORD hate evil, for he guards the lives of his faithful ones (Psalm 97:10).

PSALM 98

A psalm.

¹Sing to the LORD a new song,
 for he has done marvelous things;
 his right hand and his holy arm
 have worked salvation for him.
²The LORD has made his salvation known
 and revealed his righteousness to the nations.

³He has remembered his love
  and his faithfulness to the house of Israel;
all the ends of the earth have seen
  the salvation of our God.

⁴Shout for joy to the LORD, all the earth,
  burst into jubilant song with music;
⁵make music to the LORD with the harp,
  with the harp and the sound of singing,
⁶with trumpets and the blast of the ram's horn—
  shout for joy before the LORD, the King.

⁷Let the sea resound, and everything in it,
  the world, and all who live in it.
⁸Let the rivers clap their hands,
  let the mountains sing together for joy;
⁹let them sing before the LORD,
  for he comes to judge the earth.
He will judge the world in righteousness
  and the peoples with equity.

PSALM 99

¹The LORD reigns,
  let the nations tremble;
he sits enthroned between the cherubim,
  let the earth shake.
²Great is the LORD in Zion;
  he is exalted over all the nations.
³Let them praise your great and awesome name—
  he is holy.

⁴The King is mighty, he loves justice—
  you have established equity;
in Jacob you have done
  what is just and right.
⁵Exalt the LORD our God
  and worship at his footstool;
  he is holy.

⁶Moses and Aaron were among his priests,
  Samuel was among those who called on his name;
they called on the LORD
  and he answered them.
⁷He spoke to them from the pillar of cloud;
  they kept his statutes and the decrees he gave them.

⁸O LORD our God,
  you answered them;
you were to Israel*ᵃ* a forgiving God,
  though you punished their misdeeds.*ᵇ*
⁹Exalt the LORD our God
  and worship at his holy mountain,
  for the LORD our God is holy.

---

*ᵃ8 Hebrew *them*   *ᵇ8 Or / *an avenger of the wrongs done to them*

PSALM 100

A psalm. For giving thanks.

¹ Shout for joy to the Lord, all the earth.
²   Worship the Lord with gladness;
    come before him with joyful songs.
³ Know that the Lord is God.
    It is he who made us, and we are his*a*;
    we are his people, the sheep of his pasture.

⁴ Enter his gates with thanksgiving
    and his courts with praise;
    give thanks to him and praise his name.
⁵ For the Lord is good and his love endures forever;
    his faithfulness continues through all generations.

PSALM 101

Of David. A psalm.

¹ I will sing of your love and justice;
    to you, O Lord, I will sing praise.
² I will be careful to lead a blameless life—
    when will you come to me?

  I will walk in my house
    with blameless heart.
³ I will set before my eyes
    no vile thing.

  The deeds of faithless men I hate;
    they will not cling to me.
⁴ Men of perverse heart shall be far from me;
    I will have nothing to do with evil.

⁵ Whoever slanders his neighbor in secret,
    him will I put to silence;
  whoever has haughty eyes and a proud heart,
    him will I not endure.

⁶ My eyes will be on the faithful in the land,
    that they may dwell with me;
  he whose walk is blameless
    will minister to me.

⁷ No one who practices deceit
    will dwell in my house;
  no one who speaks falsely
    will stand in my presence.

⁸ Every morning I will put to silence
    all the wicked in the land;
  I will cut off every evildoer
    from the city of the Lord.

a3 Or and not we ourselves

PSALM 102

A prayer of an afflicted man. When he is faint and pours
out his lament before the LORD.

¹Hear my prayer, O LORD;
  let my cry for help come to you.
²Do not hide your face from me
  when I am in distress.
 Turn your ear to me;
  when I call, answer me quickly.

³For my days vanish like smoke;
  my bones burn like glowing embers.
⁴My heart is blighted and withered like grass;
  I forget to eat my food.
⁵Because of my loud groaning
  I am reduced to skin and bones.
⁶I am like a desert owl,
  like an owl among the ruins.
⁷I lie awake; I have become
  like a bird alone on a roof.
⁸All day long my enemies taunt me;
  those who rail against me use my name as a curse.
⁹For I eat ashes as my food
  and mingle my drink with tears
¹⁰because of your great wrath,
  for you have taken me up and thrown me aside.
¹¹My days are like the evening shadow;
  I wither away like grass.

¹²But you, O LORD, sit enthroned forever;
  your renown endures through all generations.
¹³You will arise and have compassion on Zion,
   for it is time to show favor to her;
   the appointed time has come.
¹⁴For her stones are dear to your servants;
   her very dust moves them to pity.
¹⁵The nations will fear the name of the LORD,
   all the kings of the earth will revere your glory.
¹⁶For the LORD will rebuild Zion
   and appear in his glory.
¹⁷He will respond to the prayer of the destitute;
   he will not despise their plea.

¹⁸Let this be written for a future generation,
   that a people not yet created may praise the LORD:
¹⁹"The LORD looked down from his sanctuary on high,
   from heaven he viewed the earth,
²⁰to hear the groans of the prisoners
   and release those condemned to death."
²¹So the name of the LORD will be declared in Zion
   and his praise in Jerusalem
²²when the peoples and the kingdoms
   assemble to worship the LORD.

²³In the course of my life^a he broke my strength;
he cut short my days.
²⁴So I said:
"Do not take me away, O my God, in the midst of my days;
your years go on through all generations.
²⁵In the beginning you laid the foundations of the earth,
and the heavens are the work of your hands.
²⁶They will perish, but you remain;
they will all wear out like a garment.
Like clothing you will change them
and they will be discarded.
²⁷But you remain the same,
and your years will never end.
²⁸The children of your servants will live in your presence;
their descendants will be established before you."

PSALM 103

Of David.

¹Praise the L ORD, O my soul;
all my inmost being, praise his holy name.
²Praise the L ORD, O my soul,
and forget not all his benefits—
³who forgives all your sins
and heals all your diseases,

How far?!

⁴who redeems your life from the pit
and crowns you with love and
compassion,
⁵who satisfies your desires with good things
so that your youth is renewed like the
eagle's.

⁶The L ORD works righteousness
and justice for all the oppressed.

⁷He made known his ways to Moses,
his deeds to the people of Israel:
⁸The L ORD is compassionate and gracious,
slow to anger, abounding in love.
⁹He will not always accuse,
nor will he harbor his anger forever;
¹⁰he does not treat us as our sins deserve
or repay us according to our iniquities.
¹¹For as high as the heavens are above the
earth,
so great is his love for those who fear
him;
¹²as far as the east is from the west,
so far has he removed our transgressions
from us.
¹³As a father has compassion on his children,
so the L ORD has compassion on those
who fear him;

*SEE
PSALM 103:12*

^a23 Or *By his power*

¹⁴for he knows how we are formed,
he remembers that we are dust.
¹⁵As for man, his days are like grass,
he flourishes like a flower of the field;
¹⁶the wind blows over it and it is gone,
and its place remembers it no more.
¹⁷But from everlasting to everlasting
the Lord's love is with those who fear him,
and his righteousness with their children's children—
¹⁸with those who keep his covenant
and remember to obey his precepts.

¹⁹The Lord has established his throne in heaven,
and his kingdom rules over all.

²⁰Praise the Lord, you his angels,
you mighty ones who do his bidding,
who obey his word.
²¹Praise the Lord, all his heavenly hosts,
you his servants who do his will.
²²Praise the Lord, all his works
everywhere in his dominion.

Praise the Lord, O my soul.

PSALM 104

¹Praise the Lord, O my soul.

O Lord my God, you are very great;
you are clothed with splendor and majesty.
²He wraps himself in light as with a garment;
he stretches out the heavens like a tent
³ and lays the beams of his upper chambers on their waters.
He makes the clouds his chariot
and rides on the wings of the wind.
⁴He makes winds his messengers,ᵃ
flames of fire his servants.

⁵He set the earth on its foundations;
it can never be moved.
⁶You covered it with the deep as with a garment;
the waters stood above the mountains.
⁷But at your rebuke the waters fled,
at the sound of your thunder they took to flight;
⁸they flowed over the mountains,
they went down into the valleys,
to the place you assigned for them.
⁹You set a boundary they cannot cross;
never again will they cover the earth.

¹⁰He makes springs pour water into the ravines;
it flows between the mountains.
¹¹They give water to all the beasts of the field;
the wild donkeys quench their thirst.
¹²The birds of the air nest by the waters;
they sing among the branches.

ᵃ4 Or angels

¹³ He waters the mountains from his upper
        chambers;
    the earth is satisfied by the fruit of his work.
¹⁴ He makes grass grow for the cattle,
    and plants for man to cultivate—
    bringing forth food from the earth:
¹⁵ wine that gladdens the heart of man,
    oil to make his face shine,
    and bread that sustains his heart.
¹⁶ The trees of the LORD are well watered,
    the cedars of Lebanon that he planted.
¹⁷ There the birds make their nests;
    the stork has its home in the pine trees.
¹⁸ The high mountains belong to the wild
        goats;
    the crags are a refuge for the coneys.ᵃ

¹⁹ The moon marks off the seasons,
    and the sun knows when to go down.
²⁰ You bring darkness, it becomes night,
    and all the beasts of the forest prowl.
²¹ The lions roar for their prey
    and seek their food from God.
²² The sun rises, and they steal away;
    they return and lie down in their dens.
²³ Then man goes out to his work,
    to his labor until evening.

²⁴ How many are your works, O LORD!
    In wisdom you made them all;
    the earth is full of your creatures.
²⁵ There is the sea, vast and spacious,
    teeming with creatures beyond number—
    living things both large and small.
²⁶ There the ships go to and fro,
    and the leviathan, which you formed to frolic
        there.

²⁷ These all look to you
    to give them their food at the proper time.
²⁸ When you give it to them,
    they gather it up;
  when you open your hand,
    they are satisfied with good things.
²⁹ When you hide your face,
    they are terrified;
  when you take away their breath,
    they die and return to the dust.
³⁰ When you send your Spirit,
    they are created,
    and you renew the face of the earth.

³¹ May the glory of the LORD endure forever;
    may the LORD rejoice in his works—
³² he who looks at the earth, and it trembles,
    who touches the mountains, and they
        smoke.

ᵃ18 That is, the hyrax or rock badger

Guilt

Guilt (gilt) n.
the fact of being responsible
for an offense or wrongdoing.

What's real guilt? It's doing something
you know is wrong. That makes you
responsible. Deep inside you know you
should be punished for what you did.
How can you stop feeling guilty?

Lots of psychiatrists
blame society or parents.
They say if others didn't
blame you for your
failures, you wouldn't
blame yourself. So, since
how you feel is their fault,
let them feel guilty!

Wouldn't it be great
if your failures and the wrong
things you've done were gone forever?
Taken away and forgotten? That's
what God does when
he forgives.

**"Their sins and lawless
acts I will remember no
more."**
HEBREWS 10:17

Some guilt is false
guilt. False guilt is
feeling anxious or to
blame even when you
didn't do anything
wrong. Like, your mom
and dad get a divorce.
Hey, that's their
choice. It isn't your
fault they didn't make
a go of their marriage.

**God's way is better.
"'I will confess my
transgressions to the
Lord'— and you
forgave the guilt of
my sin."**
PSALM 32:5

It takes time to learn to live with
forgiveness instead of guilt. Just
remember when you do wrong to
face up to it. Confess it to God, and
let him forgive you. Jesus died to
take your sins away. He'll take your
guilty feelings too.

School (skool) n.
an institution for the instruction or education of children or young people.

School

For some teens school is a place to meet friends. For some it's a chance to be on a sports team. For some it's a path to college and a great job. For some it's a place to nap before going to work to earn money to support their car. What's school to you?

What's your favorite subject? Do you like it because it's easy? Because you get good grades? Because of the teacher? Because it's interesting? Can you use what you learn in your favorite subject now, or will you be able to use it later?

"Whatever you do, whether in word or deed, do it all in the name of the Lord Jesus, giving thanks to God the Father through him."
COLOSSIANS 3:17

Public prayer is against the law in public schools in the United States. But private prayer cannot be legislated against or banned and is your right. You can pray privately, and you can live your Christian life openly in your public school.

Try to think of school as an opportunity to practice your faith. Like in the way you study. Or with that teacher you just can't stand. You can figure out the "how" by yourself. But one thing's for sure, "Whatever you do" includes school!

³³I will sing to the L<small>ORD</small> all my life;
I will sing praise to my God as long as I live.
³⁴May my meditation be pleasing to him,
as I rejoice in the L<small>ORD</small>.
³⁵But may sinners vanish from the earth
and the wicked be no more.

Praise the L<small>ORD</small>, O my soul.

Praise the L<small>ORD</small>.^a

PSALM 105

¹Give thanks to the L<small>ORD</small>, call on his name;
make known among the nations what he has
done.
²Sing to him, sing praise to him;
tell of all his wonderful acts.
³Glory in his holy name;
let the hearts of those who seek the L<small>ORD</small> rejoice.
⁴Look to the L<small>ORD</small> and his strength;
seek his face always.

⁵Remember the wonders he has done,
his miracles, and the judgments he pronounced,
⁶O descendants of Abraham his servant,
O sons of Jacob, his chosen ones.
⁷He is the L<small>ORD</small> our God;
his judgments are in all the earth.

⁸He remembers his covenant forever,
the word he commanded, for a thousand
generations,
⁹the covenant he made with Abraham,
the oath he swore to Isaac.
¹⁰He confirmed it to Jacob as a decree,
to Israel as an everlasting covenant:
¹¹"To you I will give the land of Canaan
as the portion you will inherit."

¹²When they were but few in number,
few indeed, and strangers in it,
¹³they wandered from nation to nation,
from one kingdom to another.
¹⁴He allowed no one to oppress them;
for their sake he rebuked kings:
¹⁵"Do not touch my anointed ones;
do my prophets no harm."

¹⁶He called down famine on the land
and destroyed all their supplies of food;
¹⁷and he sent a man before them—
Joseph, sold as a slave.
¹⁸They bruised his feet with shackles,
his neck was put in irons,
¹⁹till what he foretold came to pass,
till the word of the L<small>ORD</small> proved him true.

^a35 Hebrew *Hallelu Yah*; in the Septuagint this line stands at the beginning of Psalm 105.

²⁰ The king sent and released him,
  the ruler of peoples set him free.
²¹ He made him master of his household,
  ruler over all he possessed,
²² to instruct his princes as he pleased
  and teach his elders wisdom.

²³ Then Israel entered Egypt;
  Jacob lived as an alien in the land of Ham.
²⁴ The Lord made his people very fruitful;
  he made them too numerous for their foes,
²⁵ whose hearts he turned to hate his people,
  to conspire against his servants.
²⁶ He sent Moses his servant,
  and Aaron, whom he had chosen.
²⁷ They performed his miraculous signs among them,
  his wonders in the land of Ham.
²⁸ He sent darkness and made the land dark—
  for had they not rebelled against his words?
²⁹ He turned their waters into blood,
  causing their fish to die.
³⁰ Their land teemed with frogs,
  which went up into the bedrooms of their rulers.
³¹ He spoke, and there came swarms of flies,
  and gnats throughout their country.
³² He turned their rain into hail,
  with lightning throughout their land;
³³ he struck down their vines and fig trees
  and shattered the trees of their country.
³⁴ He spoke, and the locusts came,
  grasshoppers without number;
³⁵ they ate up every green thing in their land,
  ate up the produce of their soil.
³⁶ Then he struck down all the firstborn in their land,
  the firstfruits of all their manhood.

³⁷ He brought out Israel, laden with silver and gold,
  and from among their tribes no one faltered.
³⁸ Egypt was glad when they left,
  because dread of Israel had fallen on them.
³⁹ He spread out a cloud as a covering,
  and a fire to give light at night.
⁴⁰ They asked, and he brought them quail
  and satisfied them with the bread of heaven.
⁴¹ He opened the rock, and water gushed out;
  like a river it flowed in the desert.

⁴² For he remembered his holy promise
  given to his servant Abraham.
⁴³ He brought out his people with rejoicing,
  his chosen ones with shouts of joy;
⁴⁴ he gave them the lands of the nations,
  and they fell heir to what others had toiled for—
⁴⁵ that they might keep his precepts
  and observe his laws.

  Praise the Lord.ᵃ

ᵃ45 Hebrew *Hallelu Yah*

PSALM *106*

¹Praise the LORD.*ᵃ*

Give thanks to the LORD, for he is good;
   his love endures forever.
²Who can proclaim the mighty acts of the LORD
   or fully declare his praise?
³Blessed are they who maintain justice,
   who constantly do what is right.
⁴Remember me, O LORD, when you show favor to your people,
   come to my aid when you save them,
⁵that I may enjoy the prosperity of your chosen ones,
   that I may share in the joy of your nation
   and join your inheritance in giving praise.

⁶We have sinned, even as our fathers did;
   we have done wrong and acted wickedly.
⁷When our fathers were in Egypt,
   they gave no thought to your miracles;
   they did not remember your many kindnesses,
   and they rebelled by the sea, the Red Sea.*ᵇ*
⁸Yet he saved them for his name's sake,
   to make his mighty power known.
⁹He rebuked the Red Sea, and it dried up;
   he led them through the depths as through a desert.
¹⁰He saved them from the hand of the foe;
   from the hand of the enemy he redeemed them.
¹¹The waters covered their adversaries;
   not one of them survived.
¹²Then they believed his promises
   and sang his praise.

¹³But they soon forgot what he had done
   and did not wait for his counsel.
¹⁴In the desert they gave in to their craving;
   in the wasteland they put God to the test.
¹⁵So he gave them what they asked for,
   but sent a wasting disease upon them.

¹⁶In the camp they grew envious of Moses
   and of Aaron, who was consecrated to the LORD.
¹⁷The earth opened up and swallowed Dathan;
   it buried the company of Abiram.
¹⁸Fire blazed among their followers;
   a flame consumed the wicked.

¹⁹At Horeb they made a calf
   and worshiped an idol cast from metal.
²⁰They exchanged their Glory
   for an image of a bull, which eats grass.
²¹They forgot the God who saved them,
   who had done great things in Egypt,
²²miracles in the land of Ham
   and awesome deeds by the Red Sea.

ᵃ1 Hebrew *Hallelu Yah*; also in verse 48 *ᵇ7* Hebrew *Yam Suph*; that is, Sea of Reeds; also in verses 9 and 22

²³ So he said he would destroy them—
　　had not Moses, his chosen one,
　　stood in the breach before him
　　to keep his wrath from destroying them.

²⁴ Then they despised the pleasant land;
　　they did not believe his promise.
²⁵ They grumbled in their tents
　　and did not obey the LORD.
²⁶ So he swore to them with uplifted hand
　　that he would make them fall in the desert,
²⁷ make their descendants fall among the nations
　　and scatter them throughout the lands.

²⁸ They yoked themselves to the Baal of Peor
　　and ate sacrifices offered to lifeless gods;
²⁹ they provoked the LORD to anger by their wicked deeds,
　　and a plague broke out among them.
³⁰ But Phinehas stood up and intervened,
　　and the plague was checked.
³¹ This was credited to him as righteousness
　　for endless generations to come.

³² By the waters of Meribah they angered the LORD,
　　and trouble came to Moses because of them;
³³ for they rebelled against the Spirit of God,
　　and rash words came from Moses' lips.ª

³⁴ They did not destroy the peoples
　　as the LORD had commanded them,
³⁵ but they mingled with the nations
　　and adopted their customs.
³⁶ They worshiped their idols,
　　which became a snare to them.
³⁷ They sacrificed their sons
　　and their daughters to demons.
³⁸ They shed innocent blood,
　　the blood of their sons and daughters,
　whom they sacrificed to the idols of Canaan,
　　and the land was desecrated by their blood.
³⁹ They defiled themselves by what they did;
　　by their deeds they prostituted themselves.

⁴⁰ Therefore the LORD was angry with his people
　　and abhorred his inheritance.
⁴¹ He handed them over to the nations,
　　and their foes ruled over them.
⁴² Their enemies oppressed them
　　and subjected them to their power.
⁴³ Many times he delivered them,
　　but they were bent on rebellion
　　and they wasted away in their sin.

⁴⁴ But he took note of their distress
　　when he heard their cry;
⁴⁵ for their sake he remembered his covenant
　　and out of his great love he relented.

ª 33 Or *against his spirit, / and rash words came from his lips*

⁴⁶He caused them to be pitied
    by all who held them captive.

⁴⁷Save us, O Lord our God,
    and gather us from the nations,
  that we may give thanks to your holy name
    and glory in your praise.

⁴⁸Praise be to the Lord, the God of Israel,
    from everlasting to everlasting.
  Let all the people say, "Amen!"

  Praise the Lord.

BOOK V

Psalms 107–150

PSALM 107

¹Give thanks to the Lord, for he is good;
    his love endures forever.
²Let the redeemed of the Lord say this—
    those he redeemed from the hand of the foe,
³those he gathered from the lands,
    from east and west, from north and south.^a

⁴Some wandered in desert wastelands,
    finding no way to a city where they could settle.
⁵They were hungry and thirsty,
    and their lives ebbed away.
⁶Then they cried out to the Lord in their trouble,
    and he delivered them from their distress.
⁷He led them by a straight way
    to a city where they could settle.
⁸Let them give thanks to the Lord for his unfailing love
    and his wonderful deeds for men,
⁹for he satisfies the thirsty
    and fills the hungry with good things.

¹⁰Some sat in darkness and the deepest gloom,
    prisoners suffering in iron chains,
¹¹for they had rebelled against the words of God
    and despised the counsel of the Most High.
¹²So he subjected them to bitter labor;
    they stumbled, and there was no one to help.
¹³Then they cried to the Lord in their trouble,
    and he saved them from their distress.
¹⁴He brought them out of darkness and the deepest
      gloom
    and broke away their chains.
¹⁵Let them give thanks to the Lord for his unfailing love
    and his wonderful deeds for men,
¹⁶for he breaks down gates of bronze
    and cuts through bars of iron.

> Let them give
> thanks to the
> Lord . . . for he
> satisfies the
> thirsty and fills
> the hungry with
> good things
> (Psalm 107:8-9).

---

^a3 Hebrew *north and the sea*

¹⁷Some became fools through their rebellious ways
    and suffered affliction because of their iniquities.
¹⁸They loathed all food
    and drew near the gates of death.
¹⁹Then they cried to the LORD in their trouble,
    and he saved them from their distress.
²⁰He sent forth his word and healed them;
    he rescued them from the grave.
²¹Let them give thanks to the LORD for his unfailing love
    and his wonderful deeds for men.
²²Let them sacrifice thank offerings
    and tell of his works with songs of joy.

²³Others went out on the sea in ships;
    they were merchants on the mighty waters.
²⁴They saw the works of the LORD,
    his wonderful deeds in the deep.
²⁵For he spoke and stirred up a tempest
    that lifted high the waves.
²⁶They mounted up to the heavens and went down to the depths;
    in their peril their courage melted away.
²⁷They reeled and staggered like drunken men;
    they were at their wits' end.
²⁸Then they cried out to the LORD in their trouble,
    and he brought them out of their distress.
²⁹He stilled the storm to a whisper;
    the waves of the sea were hushed.
³⁰They were glad when it grew calm,
    and he guided them to their desired haven.
³¹Let them give thanks to the LORD for his unfailing love
    and his wonderful deeds for men.
³²Let them exalt him in the assembly of the people
    and praise him in the council of the elders.

³³He turned rivers into a desert,
    flowing springs into thirsty ground,
³⁴and fruitful land into a salt waste,
    because of the wickedness of those who lived there.
³⁵He turned the desert into pools of water
    and the parched ground into flowing springs;
³⁶there he brought the hungry to live,
    and they founded a city where they could settle.
³⁷They sowed fields and planted vineyards
    that yielded a fruitful harvest;
³⁸he blessed them, and their numbers greatly increased,
    and he did not let their herds diminish.

³⁹Then their numbers decreased, and they were humbled
    by oppression, calamity and sorrow;
⁴⁰he who pours contempt on nobles
    made them wander in a trackless waste.
⁴¹But he lifted the needy out of their affliction
    and increased their families like flocks.
⁴²The upright see and rejoice,
    but all the wicked shut their mouths.

⁴³Whoever is wise, let him heed these things
    and consider the great love of the LORD.

PSALM *108*

A song. A psalm of David.

¹My heart is steadfast, O God;
    I will sing and make music with all my soul.
²Awake, harp and lyre!
    I will awaken the dawn.
³I will praise you, O LORD, among the nations;
    I will sing of you among the peoples.
⁴For great is your love, higher than the heavens;
    your faithfulness reaches to the skies.
⁵Be exalted, O God, above the heavens,
    and let your glory be over all the earth.

⁶Save us and help us with your right hand,
    that those you love may be delivered.
⁷God has spoken from his sanctuary:
    "In triumph I will parcel out Shechem
    and measure off the Valley of Succoth.
⁸Gilead is mine, Manasseh is mine;
    Ephraim is my helmet,
    Judah my scepter.
⁹Moab is my washbasin,
    upon Edom I toss my sandal;
    over Philistia I shout in triumph."

¹⁰Who will bring me to the fortified city?
    Who will lead me to Edom?
¹¹Is it not you, O God, you who have rejected us
    and no longer go out with our armies?
¹²Give us aid against the enemy,
    for the help of man is worthless.
¹³With God we will gain the victory,
    and he will trample down our enemies.

PSALM *109*

For the director of music. Of David. A psalm.

¹O God, whom I praise,
    do not remain silent,
²for wicked and deceitful men
    have opened their mouths against me;
    they have spoken against me with lying tongues.
³With words of hatred they surround me;
    they attack me without cause.
⁴In return for my friendship they accuse me,
    but I am a man of prayer.
⁵They repay me evil for good,
    and hatred for my friendship.

⁶Appoint*ᵃ* an evil man*ᵇ* to oppose him;
    let an accuser*ᶜ* stand at his right hand.

ᵃ6 Or *ˌThey say:ˌ "Appoint* (with quotation marks at the end of verse 19) *ᵇ6* Or *the Evil One* *ᶜ6* Or *let
Satan*

⁷When he is tried, let him be found guilty,
    and may his prayers condemn him.
⁸May his days be few;
    may another take his place of leadership.
⁹May his children be fatherless
    and his wife a widow.
¹⁰May his children be wandering beggars;
    may they be driven*ᵃ* from their ruined homes.
¹¹May a creditor seize all he has;
    may strangers plunder the fruits of his labor.
¹²May no one extend kindness to him
    or take pity on his fatherless children.
¹³May his descendants be cut off,
    their names blotted out from the next generation.
¹⁴May the iniquity of his fathers be remembered before the
        LORD;
    may the sin of his mother never be blotted out.
¹⁵May their sins always remain before the LORD,
    that he may cut off the memory of them from the earth.

¹⁶For he never thought of doing a kindness,
    but hounded to death the poor
    and the needy and the brokenhearted.
¹⁷He loved to pronounce a curse—
    may it*ᵇ* come on him;
  he found no pleasure in blessing—
    may it be*ᶜ* far from him.
¹⁸He wore cursing as his garment;
    it entered into his body like water,
    into his bones like oil.
¹⁹May it be like a cloak wrapped about him,
    like a belt tied forever around him.
²⁰May this be the LORD's payment to my accusers,
    to those who speak evil of me.

²¹But you, O Sovereign LORD,
    deal well with me for your name's sake;
    out of the goodness of your love, deliver me.
²²For I am poor and needy,
    and my heart is wounded within me.
²³I fade away like an evening shadow;
    I am shaken off like a locust.
²⁴My knees give way from fasting;
    my body is thin and gaunt.
²⁵I am an object of scorn to my accusers;
    when they see me, they shake their heads.

²⁶Help me, O LORD my God;
    save me in accordance with your love.
²⁷Let them know that it is your hand,
    that you, O LORD, have done it.
²⁸They may curse, but you will bless;
    when they attack they will be put to shame,
    but your servant will rejoice.
²⁹My accusers will be clothed with disgrace
    and wrapped in shame as in a cloak.

ᵃ10 Septuagint; Hebrew *sought*   *ᵇ17* Or *curse, / and it has*   *ᶜ17* Or *blessing, / and it is*

³⁰With my mouth I will greatly extol the Lord;
in the great throng I will praise him.
³¹For he stands at the right hand of the needy one,
to save his life from those who condemn him.

PSALM 110

Of David. A psalm.

¹The Lord says to my Lord:
"Sit at my right hand
until I make your enemies
a footstool for your feet."

²The Lord will extend your mighty scepter from
Zion;
you will rule in the midst of your enemies.
³Your troops will be willing
on your day of battle.
Arrayed in holy majesty,
from the womb of the dawn
you will receive the dew of your youth.^a

⁴The Lord has sworn
and will not change his mind:
"You are a priest forever,
in the order of Melchizedek."

⁵The Lord is at your right hand;
he will crush kings on the day of his wrath.
⁶He will judge the nations, heaping up the dead
and crushing the rulers of the whole earth.
⁷He will drink from a brook beside the way^b;
therefore he will lift up his head.

PSALM 111 ^c

¹Praise the Lord.^d

I will extol the Lord with all my heart
in the council of the upright and in the assembly.

²Great are the works of the Lord;
they are pondered by all who delight in them.
³Glorious and majestic are his deeds,
and his righteousness endures forever.
⁴He has caused his wonders to be remembered;
the Lord is gracious and compassionate.
⁵He provides food for those who fear him;
he remembers his covenant forever.
⁶He has shown his people the power of his works,
giving them the lands of other nations.

> With my mouth
> I will greatly extol
> the Lord . . . For
> he stands at the
> right hand of the
> needy one
> (Psalm 109:30-31).

^a3 Or / your young men will come to you like the dew   ^b7 Or / The One who grants succession will set him
in authority   ^cThis psalm is an acrostic poem, the lines of which begin with the successive letters of the
Hebrew alphabet.   ^d1 Hebrew Hallelu Yah

⁷The works of his hands are faithful and just;
    all his precepts are trustworthy.
⁸They are steadfast for ever and ever,
    done in faithfulness and uprightness.
⁹He provided redemption for his people;
    he ordained his covenant forever—
    holy and awesome is his name.

¹⁰The fear of the Lord is the beginning of wisdom;
    all who follow his precepts have good understanding.
    To him belongs eternal praise.

PSALM 112 [a]

¹Praise the Lord.[b]

Blessed is the man who fears the Lord,
    who finds great delight in his commands.

²His children will be mighty in the land;
    the generation of the upright will be blessed.
³Wealth and riches are in his house,
    and his righteousness endures forever.
⁴Even in darkness light dawns for the upright,
    for the gracious and compassionate and righteous man.[c]
⁵Good will come to him who is generous and lends freely,
    who conducts his affairs with justice.
⁶Surely he will never be shaken;
    a righteous man will be remembered forever.
⁷He will have no fear of bad news;
    his heart is steadfast, trusting in the Lord.
⁸His heart is secure, he will have no fear;
    in the end he will look in triumph on his foes.
⁹He has scattered abroad his gifts to the poor,
    his righteousness endures forever;
    his horn[d] will be lifted high in honor.

¹⁰The wicked man will see and be vexed,
    he will gnash his teeth and waste away;
    the longings of the wicked will come to nothing.

PSALM 113

¹Praise the Lord.[e]

Praise, O servants of the Lord,
    praise the name of the Lord.
²Let the name of the Lord be praised,
    both now and forevermore.
³From the rising of the sun to the place where it sets,
    the name of the Lord is to be praised.

⁴The Lord is exalted over all the nations,
    his glory above the heavens.

---

[a] This psalm is an acrostic poem, the lines of which begin with the successive letters of the Hebrew alphabet. [b] 1 Hebrew *Hallelu Yah* [c] 4 Or / *for the* Lord, *is gracious and compassionate and righteous* [d] 9 *Horn* here symbolizes dignity. [e] 1 Hebrew *Hallelu Yah*; also in verse 9

⁵Who is like the Lᴏʀᴅ our God,
  the One who sits enthroned on high,
⁶who stoops down to look
  on the heavens and the earth?

⁷He raises the poor from the dust
  and lifts the needy from the ash heap;
⁸he seats them with princes,
  with the princes of their people.
⁹He settles the barren woman in her home
  as a happy mother of children.

  Praise the Lᴏʀᴅ.

PSALM 114

¹When Israel came out of Egypt,
  the house of Jacob from a people of foreign tongue,
²Judah became God's sanctuary,
  Israel his dominion.

³The sea looked and fled,
  the Jordan turned back;
⁴the mountains skipped like rams,
  the hills like lambs.

⁵Why was it, O sea, that you fled,
  O Jordan, that you turned back,
⁶you mountains, that you skipped like rams,
  you hills, like lambs?

⁷Tremble, O earth, at the presence of the Lord,
  at the presence of the God of Jacob,
⁸who turned the rock into a pool,
  the hard rock into springs of water.

PSALM 115

¹Not to us, O Lᴏʀᴅ, not to us
  but to your name be the glory,
  because of your love and faithfulness.

²Why do the nations say,
  "Where is their God?"
³Our God is in heaven;
  he does whatever pleases him.
⁴But their idols are silver and gold,
  made by the hands of men.
⁵They have mouths, but cannot speak,
  eyes, but they cannot see;
⁶they have ears, but cannot hear,
  noses, but they cannot smell;
⁷they have hands, but cannot feel,
  feet, but they cannot walk;
  nor can they utter a sound with their throats.
⁸Those who make them will be like them,
  and so will all who trust in them.

⁹O house of Israel, trust in the Lord—
    he is their help and shield.
¹⁰O house of Aaron, trust in the Lord—
    he is their help and shield.
¹¹You who fear him, trust in the Lord—
    he is their help and shield.

¹²The Lord remembers us and will bless us:
    He will bless the house of Israel,
    he will bless the house of Aaron,
¹³he will bless those who fear the Lord—
    small and great alike.

¹⁴May the Lord make you increase,
    both you and your children.
¹⁵May you be blessed by the Lord,
    the Maker of heaven and earth.

¹⁶The highest heavens belong to the Lord,
    but the earth he has given to man.
¹⁷It is not the dead who praise the Lord,
    those who go down to silence;
¹⁸it is we who extol the Lord,
    both now and forevermore.

    Praise the Lord.ᵃ

PSALM 116

¹I love the Lord, for he heard my voice;
    he heard my cry for mercy.
²Because he turned his ear to me,
    I will call on him as long as I live.

³The cords of death entangled me,
    the anguish of the graveᵇ came upon me;
    I was overcome by trouble and sorrow.
⁴Then I called on the name of the Lord:
    "O Lord, save me!"

⁵The Lord is gracious and righteous;
    our God is full of compassion.
⁶The Lord protects the simplehearted;
    when I was in great need, he saved me.

⁷Be at rest once more, O my soul,
    for the Lord has been good to you.

⁸For you, O Lord, have delivered my soul from death,
    my eyes from tears,
    my feet from stumbling,
⁹that I may walk before the Lord
    in the land of the living.
¹⁰I believed; thereforeᶜ I said,
    "I am greatly afflicted."

ᵃ18 Hebrew *Hallelu Yah* ᵇ3 Hebrew *Sheol* ᶜ10 Or *believed even when*

¹¹And in my dismay I said,
  "All men are liars."

¹²How can I repay the LORD
  for all his goodness to me?
¹³I will lift up the cup of salvation
  and call on the name of the LORD.
¹⁴I will fulfill my vows to the LORD
  in the presence of all his people.

¹⁵Precious in the sight of the LORD
  is the death of his saints.
¹⁶O LORD, truly I am your servant;
  I am your servant, the son of your maidservant[a];
  you have freed me from my chains.

¹⁷I will sacrifice a thank offering to you
  and call on the name of the LORD.
¹⁸I will fulfill my vows to the LORD
  in the presence of all his people,
¹⁹in the courts of the house of the LORD—
  in your midst, O Jerusalem.

  Praise the LORD.[b]

PSALM 117

¹Praise the LORD, all you nations;
  extol him, all you peoples.
²For great is his love toward us,
  and the faithfulness of the LORD endures forever.

  Praise the LORD.[b]

PSALM 118

¹Give thanks to the LORD, for he is good;
  his love endures forever.

²Let Israel say:
  "His love endures forever."
³Let the house of Aaron say:
  "His love endures forever."
⁴Let those who fear the LORD say:
  "His love endures forever."

⁵In my anguish I cried to the LORD,
  and he answered by setting me free.
⁶The LORD is with me; I will not be afraid.
  What can man do to me?
⁷The LORD is with me; he is my helper.
  I will look in triumph on my enemies.

[a]16 Or *servant, your faithful son* [b]19 Hebrew *Hallelu Yah*

⁸It is better to take refuge in the LORD
    than to trust in man.
⁹It is better to take refuge in the LORD
    than to trust in princes.

¹⁰All the nations surrounded me,
    but in the name of the LORD I cut them off.
¹¹They surrounded me on every side,
    but in the name of the LORD I cut them off.
¹²They swarmed around me like bees,
    but they died out as quickly as burning thorns;
    in the name of the LORD I cut them off.

¹³I was pushed back and about to fall,
    but the LORD helped me.
¹⁴The LORD is my strength and my song;
    he has become my salvation.

¹⁵Shouts of joy and victory
    resound in the tents of the righteous:
  "The LORD's right hand has done mighty things!
¹⁶   The LORD's right hand is lifted high;
    the LORD's right hand has done mighty things!"

¹⁷I will not die but live,
    and will proclaim what the LORD has done.
¹⁸The LORD has chastened me severely,
    but he has not given me over to death.

¹⁹Open for me the gates of righteousness;
    I will enter and give thanks to the LORD.
²⁰This is the gate of the LORD
    through which the righteous may enter.
²¹I will give you thanks, for you answered me;
    you have become my salvation.

²²The stone the builders rejected
    has become the capstone;
²³the LORD has done this,
    and it is marvelous in our eyes.
²⁴This is the day the LORD has made;
    let us rejoice and be glad in it.

²⁵O LORD, save us;
    O LORD, grant us success.
²⁶Blessed is he who comes in the name of the LORD.
    From the house of the LORD we bless you.ᵃ
²⁷The LORD is God,
    and he has made his light shine upon us.
  With boughs in hand, join in the festal procession
    upᵇ to the horns of the altar.

²⁸You are my God, and I will give you thanks;
    you are my God, and I will exalt you.

²⁹Give thanks to the LORD, for he is good;
    his love endures forever.

ᵃ26 The Hebrew is plural. ᵇ27 Or *Bind the festal sacrifice with ropes / and take it*

PSALM 119 [a]

א Aleph

¹Blessed are they whose ways are blameless,
    who walk according to the law of the LORD.
²Blessed are they who keep his statutes
    and seek him with all their heart.
³They do nothing wrong;
    they walk in his ways.
⁴You have laid down precepts
    that are to be fully obeyed.
⁵Oh, that my ways were steadfast
    in obeying your decrees!
⁶Then I would not be put to shame
    when I consider all your commands.
⁷I will praise you with an upright heart
    as I learn your righteous laws.
⁸I will obey your decrees;
    do not utterly forsake me.

ב Beth

⁹How can a young man keep his way pure?
    By living according to your word.
¹⁰I seek you with all my heart;
    do not let me stray from your commands.
¹¹I have hidden your word in my heart
    that I might not sin against you.
¹²Praise be to you, O LORD;
    teach me your decrees.
¹³With my lips I recount
    all the laws that come from your mouth.
¹⁴I rejoice in following your statutes
    as one rejoices in great riches.
¹⁵I meditate on your precepts
    and consider your ways.
¹⁶I delight in your decrees;
    I will not neglect your word.

ג Gimel

¹⁷Do good to your servant, and I will live;
    I will obey your word.
¹⁸Open my eyes that I may see
    wonderful things in your law.
¹⁹I am a stranger on earth;
    do not hide your commands from me.
²⁰My soul is consumed with longing
    for your laws at all times.
²¹You rebuke the arrogant, who are cursed
    and who stray from your commands.
²²Remove from me scorn and contempt,
    for I keep your statutes.

[a] This psalm is an acrostic poem; the verses of each stanza begin with the same letter of the Hebrew alphabet.

²³Though rulers sit together and slander me,
  your servant will meditate on your decrees.
²⁴Your statutes are my delight;
  they are my counselors.

ד Daleth

²⁵I am laid low in the dust;
  preserve my life according to your word.
²⁶I recounted my ways and you answered me;
  teach me your decrees.
²⁷Let me understand the teaching of your precepts;
  then I will meditate on your wonders.
²⁸My soul is weary with sorrow;
  strengthen me according to your word.
²⁹Keep me from deceitful ways;
  be gracious to me through your law.
³⁰I have chosen the way of truth;
  I have set my heart on your laws.
³¹I hold fast to your statutes, O LORD;
  do not let me be put to shame.
³²I run in the path of your commands,
  for you have set my heart free.

ה He

³³Teach me, O LORD, to follow your decrees;
  then I will keep them to the end.
³⁴Give me understanding, and I will keep your law
  and obey it with all my heart.
³⁵Direct me in the path of your commands,
  for there I find delight.
³⁶Turn my heart toward your statutes
  and not toward selfish gain.
³⁷Turn my eyes away from worthless things;
  preserve my life according to your word.[a]

---

[a]37 Two manuscripts of the Masoretic Text and Dead Sea Scrolls; most manuscripts of the Masoretic Text *life in your way*

The Bible Says

Use God's Word

It's great to know that God's Word is trustworthy, but how do you use it? Psalm 119:105 says, "Your word is a lamp to my feet and a light for my path." For a lamp to do you any good, you have to light it and hold it so its light can show you the way. For God's Word to do you any good, you have to read it and let it show you the way to live. Here is what the longest chapter in the Bible tells you about how to use God's Word:

* Live according to its laws (Psalm 119:1).
* Hide its words in your heart (Psalm 119:11).
* Obey its words (Psalm 119:57).
* Meditate on its teachings (Psalm 119:78).
* Rejoice in its promises (Psalm 119:162).

³⁸ Fulfill your promise to your servant,
  so that you may be feared.
³⁹ Take away the disgrace I dread,
  for your laws are good.
⁴⁰ How I long for your precepts!
  Preserve my life in your righteousness.

ו Waw

⁴¹ May your unfailing love come to me, O Lord,
  your salvation according to your promise;
⁴² then I will answer the one who taunts me,
  for I trust in your word.
⁴³ Do not snatch the word of truth from my mouth,
  for I have put my hope in your laws.
⁴⁴ I will always obey your law,
  for ever and ever.
⁴⁵ I will walk about in freedom,
  for I have sought out your precepts.
⁴⁶ I will speak of your statutes before kings
  and will not be put to shame,
⁴⁷ for I delight in your commands
  because I love them.
⁴⁸ I lift up my hands to^a your commands, which I love,
  and I meditate on your decrees.

ז Zayin

⁴⁹ Remember your word to your servant,
  for you have given me hope.
⁵⁰ My comfort in my suffering is this:
  Your promise preserves my life.
⁵¹ The arrogant mock me without restraint,
  but I do not turn from your law.
⁵² I remember your ancient laws, O Lord,
  and I find comfort in them.
⁵³ Indignation grips me because of the wicked,
  who have forsaken your law.
⁵⁴ Your decrees are the theme of my song
  wherever I lodge.
⁵⁵ In the night I remember your name, O Lord,
  and I will keep your law.
⁵⁶ This has been my practice:
  I obey your precepts.

ח Heth

⁵⁷ You are my portion, O Lord;
  I have promised to obey your words.
⁵⁸ I have sought your face with all my heart;
  be gracious to me according to your promise.
⁵⁹ I have considered my ways
  and have turned my steps to your statutes.
⁶⁰ I will hasten and not delay
  to obey your commands.
⁶¹ Though the wicked bind me with ropes,
  I will not forget your law.

---

a48 Or *for*

⁶²At midnight I rise to give you thanks
for your righteous laws.
⁶³I am a friend to all who fear you,
to all who follow your precepts.
⁶⁴The earth is filled with your love, O Lord;
teach me your decrees.

ט Teth

⁶⁵Do good to your servant
according to your word, O Lord.
⁶⁶Teach me knowledge and good judgment,
for I believe in your commands.
⁶⁷Before I was afflicted I went astray,
but now I obey your word.
⁶⁸You are good, and what you do is good;
teach me your decrees.
⁶⁹Though the arrogant have smeared me with lies,
I keep your precepts with all my heart.
⁷⁰Their hearts are callous and unfeeling,
but I delight in your law.
⁷¹It was good for me to be afflicted
so that I might learn your decrees.
⁷²The law from your mouth is more precious to me
than thousands of pieces of silver and gold.

י Yodh

⁷³Your hands made me and formed me;
give me understanding to learn your commands.
⁷⁴May those who fear you rejoice when they see me,
for I have put my hope in your word.
⁷⁵I know, O Lord, that your laws are righteous,
and in faithfulness you have afflicted me.
⁷⁶May your unfailing love be my comfort,
according to your promise to your servant.
⁷⁷Let your compassion come to me that I may live,
for your law is my delight.
⁷⁸May the arrogant be put to shame for wronging me without
cause;
but I will meditate on your precepts.
⁷⁹May those who fear you turn to me,
those who understand your statutes.
⁸⁰May my heart be blameless toward your decrees,
that I may not be put to shame.

כ Kaph

⁸¹My soul faints with longing for your salvation,
but I have put my hope in your word.
⁸²My eyes fail, looking for your promise;
I say, "When will you comfort me?"
⁸³Though I am like a wineskin in the smoke,
I do not forget your decrees.
⁸⁴How long must your servant wait?
When will you punish my persecutors?
⁸⁵The arrogant dig pitfalls for me,
contrary to your law.
⁸⁶All your commands are trustworthy;
help me, for men persecute me without cause.

⁸⁷They almost wiped me from the earth,
    but I have not forsaken your precepts.
⁸⁸Preserve my life according to your love,
    and I will obey the statutes of your mouth.

ל Lamedh

⁸⁹Your word, O Lord, is eternal;
    it stands firm in the heavens.
⁹⁰Your faithfulness continues through all generations;
    you established the earth, and it endures.
⁹¹Your laws endure to this day,
    for all things serve you.
⁹²If your law had not been my delight,
    I would have perished in my affliction.
⁹³I will never forget your precepts,
    for by them you have preserved my life.
⁹⁴Save me, for I am yours;
    I have sought out your precepts.
⁹⁵The wicked are waiting to destroy me,
    but I will ponder your statutes.
⁹⁶To all perfection I see a limit;
    but your commands are boundless.

מ Mem

⁹⁷Oh, how I love your law!
    I meditate on it all day long.
⁹⁸Your commands make me wiser than my enemies,
    for they are ever with me.
⁹⁹I have more insight than all my teachers,
    for I meditate on your statutes.
¹⁰⁰I have more understanding than the elders,
    for I obey your precepts.
¹⁰¹I have kept my feet from every evil path
    so that I might obey your word.
¹⁰²I have not departed from your laws,
    for you yourself have taught me.
¹⁰³How sweet are your words to my taste,
    sweeter than honey to my mouth!
¹⁰⁴I gain understanding from your precepts;
    therefore I hate every wrong path.

נ Nun

¹⁰⁵Your word is a lamp to my feet
    and a light for my path.
¹⁰⁶I have taken an oath and confirmed it,
    that I will follow your righteous laws.
¹⁰⁷I have suffered much;
    preserve my life, O Lord, according to your word.
¹⁰⁸Accept, O Lord, the willing praise of my mouth,
    and teach me your laws.
¹⁰⁹Though I constantly take my life in my hands,
    I will not forget your law.
¹¹⁰The wicked have set a snare for me,
    but I have not strayed from your precepts.
¹¹¹Your statutes are my heritage forever;
    they are the joy of my heart.
¹¹²My heart is set on keeping your decrees
    to the very end.

ס Samekh

¹¹³I hate double-minded men,
    but I love your law.
¹¹⁴You are my refuge and my shield;
    I have put my hope in your word.
¹¹⁵Away from me, you evildoers,
    that I may keep the commands of my God!
¹¹⁶Sustain me according to your promise, and I will live;
    do not let my hopes be dashed.
¹¹⁷Uphold me, and I will be delivered;
    I will always have regard for your decrees.
¹¹⁸You reject all who stray from your decrees,
    for their deceitfulness is in vain.
¹¹⁹All the wicked of the earth you discard like dross;
    therefore I love your statutes.
¹²⁰My flesh trembles in fear of you;
    I stand in awe of your laws.

ע Ayin

¹²¹I have done what is righteous and just;
    do not leave me to my oppressors.
¹²²Ensure your servant's well-being;
    let not the arrogant oppress me.
¹²³My eyes fail, looking for your salvation,
    looking for your righteous promise.
¹²⁴Deal with your servant according to your love
    and teach me your decrees.
¹²⁵I am your servant; give me discernment
    that I may understand your statutes.
¹²⁶It is time for you to act, O Lord;
    your law is being broken.
¹²⁷Because I love your commands
    more than gold, more than pure gold,
¹²⁸and because I consider all your precepts right,
    I hate every wrong path.

פ Pe

¹²⁹Your statutes are wonderful;
    therefore I obey them.
¹³⁰The unfolding of your words gives light;
    it gives understanding to the simple.
¹³¹I open my mouth and pant,
    longing for your commands.
¹³²Turn to me and have mercy on me,
    as you always do to those who love your name.
¹³³Direct my footsteps according to your word;
    let no sin rule over me.
¹³⁴Redeem me from the oppression of men,
    that I may obey your precepts.
¹³⁵Make your face shine upon your servant
    and teach me your decrees.
¹³⁶Streams of tears flow from my eyes,
    for your law is not obeyed.

צ Tsadhe

¹³⁷Righteous are you, O Lord,
    and your laws are right.

¹³⁸The statutes you have laid down are righteous;
they are fully trustworthy.
¹³⁹My zeal wears me out,
for my enemies ignore your words.
¹⁴⁰Your promises have been thoroughly tested,
and your servant loves them.
¹⁴¹Though I am lowly and despised,
I do not forget your precepts.
¹⁴²Your righteousness is everlasting
and your law is true.
¹⁴³Trouble and distress have come upon me,
but your commands are my delight.
¹⁴⁴Your statutes are forever right;
give me understanding that I may live.

ק Qoph

¹⁴⁵I call with all my heart; answer me, O Lord,
and I will obey your decrees.
¹⁴⁶I call out to you; save me
and I will keep your statutes.
¹⁴⁷I rise before dawn and cry for help;
I have put my hope in your word.
¹⁴⁸My eyes stay open through the watches of the night,
that I may meditate on your promises.
¹⁴⁹Hear my voice in accordance with your love;
preserve my life, O Lord, according to your laws.
¹⁵⁰Those who devise wicked schemes are near,
but they are far from your law.
¹⁵¹Yet you are near, O Lord,
and all your commands are true.
¹⁵²Long ago I learned from your statutes
that you established them to last forever.

ר Resh

¹⁵³Look upon my suffering and deliver me,
for I have not forgotten your law.
¹⁵⁴Defend my cause and redeem me;
preserve my life according to your promise.
¹⁵⁵Salvation is far from the wicked,
for they do not seek out your decrees.
¹⁵⁶Your compassion is great, O Lord;
preserve my life according to your laws.
¹⁵⁷Many are the foes who persecute me,
but I have not turned from your statutes.
¹⁵⁸I look on the faithless with loathing,
for they do not obey your word.
¹⁵⁹See how I love your precepts;
preserve my life, O Lord, according to your love.
¹⁶⁰All your words are true;
all your righteous laws are eternal.

ש Sin and Shin

¹⁶¹Rulers persecute me without cause,
but my heart trembles at your word.
¹⁶²I rejoice in your promise
like one who finds great spoil.

¹⁶³I hate and abhor falsehood
    but I love your law.
¹⁶⁴Seven times a day I praise you
    for your righteous laws.
¹⁶⁵Great peace have they who love your law,
    and nothing can make them stumble.
¹⁶⁶I wait for your salvation, O LORD,
    and I follow your commands.
      ¹⁶⁷I obey your statutes,
        for I love them greatly.
      ¹⁶⁸I obey your precepts and your statutes,
        for all my ways are known to you.

> Great peace have they who love your law, and nothing can make them stumble (Psalm 119:165).

ת Taw

¹⁶⁹May my cry come before you, O LORD;
    give me understanding according to your
      word.
¹⁷⁰May my supplication come before you;
    deliver me according to your promise.
¹⁷¹May my lips overflow with praise,
    for you teach me your decrees.
¹⁷²May my tongue sing of your word,
    for all your commands are righteous.
¹⁷³May your hand be ready to help me,
    for I have chosen your precepts.
¹⁷⁴I long for your salvation, O LORD,
    and your law is my delight.
¹⁷⁵Let me live that I may praise you,
    and may your laws sustain me.
¹⁷⁶I have strayed like a lost sheep.
    Seek your servant,
    for I have not forgotten your commands.

PSALM 120

A song of ascents.

¹I call on the LORD in my distress,
    and he answers me.
²Save me, O LORD, from lying lips
    and from deceitful tongues.

³What will he do to you,
    and what more besides, O deceitful tongue?
⁴He will punish you with a warrior's sharp
      arrows,
    with burning coals of the broom tree.

⁵Woe to me that I dwell in Meshech,
    that I live among the tents of Kedar!
⁶Too long have I lived
    among those who hate peace.
⁷I am a man of peace;
    but when I speak, they are for war.

PSALM *121*

A song of ascents.

¹I lift up my eyes to the hills—
    where does my help come from?
²My help comes from the Lord,
    the Maker of heaven and earth.

³He will not let your foot slip—
    he who watches over you will not slumber;
⁴indeed, he who watches over Israel
    will neither slumber nor sleep.

⁵The Lord watches over you—
    the Lord is your shade at your right hand;
⁶the sun will not harm you by day,
    nor the moon by night.

⁷The Lord will keep you from all harm—
    he will watch over your life;
⁸the Lord will watch over your coming and going
    both now and forevermore.

PSALM *122*

A song of ascents. Of David.

¹I rejoiced with those who said to me,
    "Let us go to the house of the Lord."
²Our feet are standing
    in your gates, O Jerusalem.

³Jerusalem is built like a city
    that is closely compacted together.
⁴That is where the tribes go up,
    the tribes of the Lord,
  to praise the name of the Lord
    according to the statute given to Israel.
⁵There the thrones for judgment stand,
    the thrones of the house of David.

⁶Pray for the peace of Jerusalem:
    "May those who love you be secure.
⁷May there be peace within your walls
    and security within your citadels."
⁸For the sake of my brothers and friends,
    I will say, "Peace be within you."
⁹For the sake of the house of the Lord our God,
    I will seek your prosperity.

PSALM 123

A song of ascents.

¹I lift up my eyes to you,
　to you whose throne is in heaven.
²As the eyes of slaves look to the hand of their master,
　as the eyes of a maid look to the hand of her mistress,
so our eyes look to the LORD our God,
　till he shows us his mercy.

³Have mercy on us, O LORD, have mercy on us,
　for we have endured much contempt.
⁴We have endured much ridicule from the proud,
　much contempt from the arrogant.

PSALM 124

A song of ascents. Of David.

¹If the LORD had not been on our side—
　let Israel say—
²if the LORD had not been on our side
　when men attacked us,
³when their anger flared against us,
　they would have swallowed us alive;
⁴the flood would have engulfed us,
　the torrent would have swept over us,
⁵the raging waters
　would have swept us away.

⁶Praise be to the LORD,
　who has not let us be torn by their teeth.
⁷We have escaped like a bird
　out of the fowler's snare;
the snare has been broken,
　and we have escaped.
⁸Our help is in the name of the LORD,
　the Maker of heaven and earth.

PSALM 125

A song of ascents.

¹Those who trust in the LORD are like Mount Zion,
　which cannot be shaken but endures forever.
²As the mountains surround Jerusalem,
　so the LORD surrounds his people
　both now and forevermore.

³The scepter of the wicked will not remain
　over the land allotted to the righteous,
for then the righteous might use
　their hands to do evil.

⁴Do good, O Lᴏʀᴅ, to those who are good,
  to those who are upright in heart.
⁵But those who turn to crooked ways
  the Lᴏʀᴅ will banish with the evildoers.

Peace be upon Israel.

PSALM 126

A song of ascents.

¹When the Lᴏʀᴅ brought back the captives to*ᵃ* Zion,
  we were like men who dreamed.*ᵇ*
²Our mouths were filled with laughter,
  our tongues with songs of joy.
Then it was said among the nations,
  "The Lᴏʀᴅ has done great things for them."
³The Lᴏʀᴅ has done great things for us,
  and we are filled with joy.

⁴Restore our fortunes,*ᶜ* O Lᴏʀᴅ,
  like streams in the Negev.
⁵Those who sow in tears
  will reap with songs of joy.
⁶He who goes out weeping,
  carrying seed to sow,
will return with songs of joy,
  carrying sheaves with him.

PSALM 127

A song of ascents. Of Solomon.

¹Unless the Lᴏʀᴅ builds the house,
  its builders labor in vain.
Unless the Lᴏʀᴅ watches over the city,
  the watchmen stand guard in vain.
²In vain you rise early
  and stay up late,
toiling for food to eat—
  for he grants sleep to*ᵈ* those he loves.

³Sons are a heritage from the Lᴏʀᴅ,
  children a reward from him.
⁴Like arrows in the hands of a warrior
  are sons born in one's youth.
⁵Blessed is the man
  whose quiver is full of them.
They will not be put to shame
  when they contend with their enemies in the
    gate.

ᵃ1 Or Lᴏʀᴅ restored the fortunes of   ᵇ1 Or men restored to health   ᶜ4 Or Bring back our captives   ᵈ2 Or
eat— / for while they sleep he provides for

PSALM 128

A song of ascents.

[1] Blessed are all who fear the LORD,
  who walk in his ways.
[2] You will eat the fruit of your labor;
  blessings and prosperity will be yours.
[3] Your wife will be like a fruitful vine
  within your house;
 your sons will be like olive shoots
  around your table.
[4] Thus is the man blessed
  who fears the LORD.

[5] May the LORD bless you from Zion
  all the days of your life;
 may you see the prosperity of Jerusalem,
 [6]   and may you live to see your children's children.

 Peace be upon Israel.

PSALM 129

A song of ascents.

[1] They have greatly oppressed me from my youth—
  let Israel say—
[2] they have greatly oppressed me from my youth,
  but they have not gained the victory over me.
[3] Plowmen have plowed my back
  and made their furrows long.
[4] But the LORD is righteous;
  he has cut me free from the cords of the wicked.

[5] May all who hate Zion
  be turned back in shame.
[6] May they be like grass on the roof,
  which withers before it can grow;
[7] with it the reaper cannot fill his hands,
  nor the one who gathers fill his arms.
[8] May those who pass by not say,
  "The blessing of the LORD be upon you;
  we bless you in the name of the LORD."

PSALM 130

A song of ascents.

[1] Out of the depths I cry to you, O LORD;
[2]   O Lord, hear my voice.
 Let your ears be attentive
  to my cry for mercy.

³If you, O Lᴏʀᴅ, kept a record of sins,
    O Lord, who could stand?
⁴But with you there is forgiveness;
    therefore you are feared.

⁵I wait for the Lᴏʀᴅ, my soul waits,
    and in his word I put my hope.
⁶My soul waits for the Lord
    more than watchmen wait for the morning,
    more than watchmen wait for the morning.

⁷O Israel, put your hope in the Lᴏʀᴅ,
    for with the Lᴏʀᴅ is unfailing love
    and with him is full redemption.
⁸He himself will redeem Israel
    from all their sins.

PSALM 131

A song of ascents. Of David.

¹My heart is not proud, O Lᴏʀᴅ,
    my eyes are not haughty;
 I do not concern myself with great matters
    or things too wonderful for me.
²But I have stilled and quieted my soul;
    like a weaned child with its mother,
    like a weaned child is my soul within me.

³O Israel, put your hope in the Lᴏʀᴅ
    both now and forevermore.

PSALM 132

A song of ascents.

¹O Lᴏʀᴅ, remember David
    and all the hardships he endured.

²He swore an oath to the Lᴏʀᴅ
    and made a vow to the Mighty One of Jacob:
³"I will not enter my house
    or go to my bed—
⁴I will allow no sleep to my eyes,
    no slumber to my eyelids,
⁵till I find a place for the Lᴏʀᴅ,
    a dwelling for the Mighty One of Jacob."

⁶We heard it in Ephrathah,
    we came upon it in the fields of Jaar*ᵃ:ᵇ*
⁷"Let us go to his dwelling place;
    let us worship at his footstool—
⁸arise, O Lᴏʀᴅ, and come to your resting place,
    you and the ark of your might.

ᵃ6 That is, Kiriath Jearim   ᵇ6 Or heard of it in Ephrathah, / we found it in the fields of Jaar. (And no quotes around verses 7-9)

⁹May your priests be clothed with righteousness;
    may your saints sing for joy."

¹⁰For the sake of David your servant,
    do not reject your anointed one.

¹¹The LORD swore an oath to David,
    a sure oath that he will not revoke:
"One of your own descendants
    I will place on your throne—
¹²if your sons keep my covenant
    and the statutes I teach them,
then their sons will sit
    on your throne for ever and ever."

¹³For the LORD has chosen Zion,
    he has desired it for his dwelling:
¹⁴"This is my resting place for ever and ever;
    here I will sit enthroned, for I have desired it—
¹⁵I will bless her with abundant provisions;
    her poor will I satisfy with food.
¹⁶I will clothe her priests with salvation,
    and her saints will ever sing for joy.

¹⁷"Here I will make a horn*ᵃ* grow for David
    and set up a lamp for my anointed one.
¹⁸I will clothe his enemies with shame,
    but the crown on his head will be resplendent."

PSALM 133

A song of ascents. Of David.

¹How good and pleasant it is
    when brothers live together in unity!
²It is like precious oil poured on the head,
    running down on the beard,
running down on Aaron's beard,
    down upon the collar of his robes.
³It is as if the dew of Hermon
    were falling on Mount Zion.
For there the LORD bestows his blessing,
    even life forevermore.

PSALM 134

A song of ascents.

¹Praise the LORD, all you servants of the LORD
    who minister by night in the house of the LORD.
²Lift up your hands in the sanctuary
    and praise the LORD.

³May the LORD, the Maker of heaven and earth,
    bless you from Zion.

ᵃ17 Horn here symbolizes strong one, that is, king.

PSALM 135

¹ Praise the LORD.ᵃ

Praise the name of the LORD;
  praise him, you servants of the LORD,
² you who minister in the house of the LORD,
  in the courts of the house of our God.

³ Praise the LORD, for the LORD is good;
  sing praise to his name, for that is pleasant.
⁴ For the LORD has chosen Jacob to be his own,
  Israel to be his treasured possession.

⁵ I know that the LORD is great,
  that our Lord is greater than all gods.
⁶ The LORD does whatever pleases him,
  in the heavens and on the earth,
  in the seas and all their depths.
⁷ He makes clouds rise from the ends of the earth;
  he sends lightning with the rain
  and brings out the wind from his storehouses.

⁸ He struck down the firstborn of Egypt,
  the firstborn of men and animals.
⁹ He sent his signs and wonders into your midst, O Egypt,
  against Pharaoh and all his servants.
¹⁰ He struck down many nations
  and killed mighty kings—
¹¹ Sihon king of the Amorites,
  Og king of Bashan
  and all the kings of Canaan—
¹² and he gave their land as an inheritance,
  an inheritance to his people Israel.

¹³ Your name, O LORD, endures forever,
  your renown, O LORD, through all generations.
¹⁴ For the LORD will vindicate his people
  and have compassion on his servants.

¹⁵ The idols of the nations are silver and gold,
  made by the hands of men.
¹⁶ They have mouths, but cannot speak,
  eyes, but they cannot see;
¹⁷ they have ears, but cannot hear,
  nor is there breath in their mouths.
¹⁸ Those who make them will be like them,
  and so will all who trust in them.

¹⁹ O house of Israel, praise the LORD;
  O house of Aaron, praise the LORD;
²⁰ O house of Levi, praise the LORD;
  you who fear him, praise the LORD.
²¹ Praise be to the LORD from Zion,
  to him who dwells in Jerusalem.

Praise the LORD.

ᵃ1 Hebrew *Hallelu Yah*; also in verses 3 and 21

PSALM *136*

¹ Give thanks to the LORD, for he is good.
> *His love endures forever.*

² Give thanks to the God of gods.
> *His love endures forever.*

³ Give thanks to the Lord of lords:
> *His love endures forever.*

⁴ to him who alone does great wonders,
> *His love endures forever.*

⁵ who by his understanding made the heavens,
> *His love endures forever.*

⁶ who spread out the earth upon the waters,
> *His love endures forever.*

⁷ who made the great lights—
> *His love endures forever.*

⁸ the sun to govern the day,
> *His love endures forever.*

⁹ the moon and stars to govern the night;
> *His love endures forever.*

¹⁰ to him who struck down the firstborn of Egypt
> *His love endures forever.*

¹¹ and brought Israel out from among them
> *His love endures forever.*

¹² with a mighty hand and outstretched arm;
> *His love endures forever.*

¹³ to him who divided the Red Sea*ᵃ* asunder
> *His love endures forever.*

¹⁴ and brought Israel through the midst of it,
> *His love endures forever.*

¹⁵ but swept Pharaoh and his army into the Red Sea;
> *His love endures forever.*

¹⁶ to him who led his people through the desert,
> *His love endures forever.*

¹⁷ who struck down great kings,
> *His love endures forever.*

¹⁸ and killed mighty kings—
> *His love endures forever.*

¹⁹ Sihon king of the Amorites
> *His love endures forever.*

²⁰ and Og king of Bashan—
> *His love endures forever.*

²¹ and gave their land as an inheritance,
> *His love endures forever.*

²² an inheritance to his servant Israel;
> *His love endures forever.*

²³ to the One who remembered us in our low estate
> *His love endures forever.*

²⁴ and freed us from our enemies,
> *His love endures forever.*

Give thanks to the LORD, for he is good. His love endures forever (Psalm 136:1).

ᵃ13 Hebrew *Yam Suph*; that is, Sea of Reeds; also in verse 15

²⁵and who gives food to every creature.

His love endures forever.

²⁶Give thanks to the God of heaven.

His love endures forever.

PSALM 137

¹By the rivers of Babylon we sat and wept
    when we remembered Zion.
²There on the poplars
    we hung our harps,
³for there our captors asked us for songs,
    our tormentors demanded songs of joy;
    they said, "Sing us one of the songs of Zion!"

⁴How can we sing the songs of the Lord
    while in a foreign land?
⁵If I forget you, O Jerusalem,
    may my right hand forget its skill.
⁶May my tongue cling to the roof of my mouth
    if I do not remember you,
  if I do not consider Jerusalem
    my highest joy.

⁷Remember, O Lord, what the Edomites did
    on the day Jerusalem fell.
  "Tear it down," they cried,
    "tear it down to its foundations!"

⁸O Daughter of Babylon, doomed to destruction,
    happy is he who repays you
    for what you have done to us—
⁹he who seizes your infants
    and dashes them against the rocks.

PSALM 138

Of David.

¹I will praise you, O Lord, with all my heart;
    before the "gods" I will sing your praise.
²I will bow down toward your holy temple
    and will praise your name
    for your love and your faithfulness,
  for you have exalted above all things
    your name and your word.
³When I called, you answered me;
    you made me bold and stouthearted.

⁴May all the kings of the earth praise you, O Lord,
    when they hear the words of your mouth.
⁵May they sing of the ways of the Lord,
    for the glory of the Lord is great.

⁶Though the Lord is on high, he looks upon the lowly,
    but the proud he knows from afar.

⁷Though I walk in the midst of trouble,
  you preserve my life;
you stretch out your hand against the anger of my foes,
  with your right hand you save me.
⁸The LORD will fulfill his purpose for me;
  your love, O LORD, endures forever—
  do not abandon the works of your hands.

PSALM 139

For the director of music. Of David. A psalm.

¹O LORD, you have searched me
  and you know me.
²You know when I sit and when I rise;
  you perceive my thoughts from afar.
³You discern my going out and my lying down;
  you are familiar with all my ways.
⁴Before a word is on my tongue
  you know it completely, O LORD.

⁵You hem me in—behind and before;
  you have laid your hand upon me.
⁶Such knowledge is too wonderful for me,
  too lofty for me to attain.

⁷Where can I go from your Spirit?
  Where can I flee from your presence?
⁸If I go up to the heavens, you are there;
  if I make my bed in the depths,ᵃ you are there.
⁹If I rise on the wings of the dawn,
  if I settle on the far side of the sea,
¹⁰even there your hand will guide me,
  your right hand will hold me fast.

ᵃ8 Hebrew *Sheol*

The Bible Says

God Is Pro-life

The whole abortion debate hinges on one issue. Is a fetus really part of the woman's body, so she can do what she chooses with it? Or is the fetus a separate, distinct human being?

Every human being throughout history has had a unique, individual genetic code stamped on every cell in his or her body. Both the mother and the fetus she carries have a genetic code stamped on their genes and chromosomes. Are they the same? No! The fetus's genetic code is different from the mother's. To say a woman can do whatever she wants with her own body may be true. But it is not true that a fetus is merely part of the mother's body.

As Psalm 139 teaches, even in his mother's womb, David was David, a unique person being shaped by God for a special role in God's plan. There's no doubt: God is pro-life!

¹¹If I say, "Surely the darkness will hide me
  and the light become night around me,"
¹²even the darkness will not be dark to you;
  the night will shine like the day,
  for darkness is as light to you.

¹³For you created my inmost being;
  you knit me together in my mother's womb.
¹⁴I praise you because I am fearfully and wonderfully made;
  your works are wonderful,
  I know that full well.
¹⁵My frame was not hidden from you
  when I was made in the secret place.
  When I was woven together in the depths of the earth,
¹⁶   your eyes saw my unformed body.
  All the days ordained for me
    were written in your book
    before one of them came to be.

¹⁷How precious to*a* me are your thoughts, O God!
  How vast is the sum of them!
¹⁸Were I to count them,
  they would outnumber the grains of sand.
  When I awake,
    I am still with you.

¹⁹If only you would slay the wicked, O God!
  Away from me, you bloodthirsty men!
²⁰They speak of you with evil intent;
  your adversaries misuse your name.
²¹Do I not hate those who hate you, O LORD,
  and abhor those who rise up against you?
²²I have nothing but hatred for them;
  I count them my enemies.

²³Search me, O God, and know my heart;
  test me and know my anxious thoughts.
²⁴See if there is any offensive way in me,
  and lead me in the way everlasting.

PSALM 140

For the director of music. A psalm of David.

¹Rescue me, O LORD, from evil men;
  protect me from men of violence,
²who devise evil plans in their hearts
  and stir up war every day.
³They make their tongues as sharp as a serpent's;
  the poison of vipers is on their lips.   *Selah*

⁴Keep me, O LORD, from the hands of the wicked;
  protect me from men of violence
  who plan to trip my feet.
⁵Proud men have hidden a snare for me;

---

a17 Or *concerning*

they have spread out the cords of their net
>and have set traps for me along my path. *Selah*

⁶O LORD, I say to you, "You are my God."
>Hear, O LORD, my cry for mercy.
⁷O Sovereign LORD, my strong deliverer,
>who shields my head in the day of battle—
⁸do not grant the wicked their desires, O LORD;
>do not let their plans succeed,
>or they will become proud. *Selah*

⁹Let the heads of those who surround me
>be covered with the trouble their lips have caused.
¹⁰Let burning coals fall upon them;
>may they be thrown into the fire,
>into miry pits, never to rise.
¹¹Let slanderers not be established in the land;
>may disaster hunt down men of violence.

¹²I know that the LORD secures justice for the poor
>and upholds the cause of the needy.
¹³Surely the righteous will praise your name
>and the upright will live before you.

PSALM 141

A psalm of David.

¹O LORD, I call to you; come quickly to me.
>Hear my voice when I call to you.
²May my prayer be set before you like incense;
>may the lifting up of my hands be like the evening sacrifice.

³Set a guard over my mouth, O LORD;
>keep watch over the door of my lips.
⁴Let not my heart be drawn to what is evil,
>to take part in wicked deeds
with men who are evildoers;
>let me not eat of their delicacies.

⁵Let a righteous man[a] strike me—it is a kindness;
>let him rebuke me—it is oil on my head.
>My head will not refuse it.

Yet my prayer is ever against the deeds of evildoers;
⁶ their rulers will be thrown down from the cliffs,
>and the wicked will learn that my words were well spoken.
⁷ They will say, "As one plows and breaks up the earth,
>so our bones have been scattered at the mouth of the
> grave.[b]"

⁸But my eyes are fixed on you, O Sovereign LORD;
>in you I take refuge—do not give me over to death.
⁹Keep me from the snares they have laid for me,
>from the traps set by evildoers.
¹⁰Let the wicked fall into their own nets,
>while I pass by in safety.

[a]5 Or *Let the Righteous One* [b]7 Hebrew *Sheol*

PSALM 142

A *maskil*ᵃ of David. When he was in the cave. A prayer.

¹I cry aloud to the LORD;
    I lift up my voice to the LORD for mercy.
²I pour out my complaint before him;
    before him I tell my trouble.

³When my spirit grows faint within me,
    it is you who know my way.
 In the path where I walk
    men have hidden a snare for me.
⁴Look to my right and see;
    no one is concerned for me.
 I have no refuge;
    no one cares for my life.

⁵I cry to you, O LORD;
    I say, "You are my refuge,
    my portion in the land of the living."
⁶Listen to my cry,
    for I am in desperate need;
 rescue me from those who pursue me,
    for they are too strong for me.
⁷Set me free from my prison,
    that I may praise your name.

 Then the righteous will gather about me
    because of your goodness to me.

PSALM 143

A psalm of David.

¹O LORD, hear my prayer,
    listen to my cry for mercy;
 in your faithfulness and righteousness
    come to my relief.
²Do not bring your servant into judgment,
    for no one living is righteous before you.

³The enemy pursues me,
    he crushes me to the ground;
 he makes me dwell in darkness
    like those long dead.
⁴So my spirit grows faint within me;
    my heart within me is dismayed.

⁵I remember the days of long ago;
    I meditate on all your works
    and consider what your hands have done.
⁶I spread out my hands to you;
    my soul thirsts for you like a parched land.   *Selah*

ᵃTitle: Probably a literary or musical term

⁷Answer me quickly, O Lᴏʀᴅ;
　　my spirit fails.
　Do not hide your face from me
　　or I will be like those who go down to the pit.
⁸Let the morning bring me word of your unfailing love,
　　for I have put my trust in you.
　Show me the way I should go,
　　for to you I lift up my soul.
⁹Rescue me from my enemies, O Lᴏʀᴅ,
　　for I hide myself in you.
¹⁰Teach me to do your will,
　　for you are my God;
　may your good Spirit
　　lead me on level ground.

¹¹For your name's sake, O Lᴏʀᴅ, preserve my life;
　　in your righteousness, bring me out of trouble.
¹²In your unfailing love, silence my enemies;
　　destroy all my foes,
　　for I am your servant.

PSALM 144

Of David.

¹Praise be to the Lᴏʀᴅ my Rock,
　　who trains my hands for war,
　　my fingers for battle.
²He is my loving God and my fortress,
　　my stronghold and my deliverer,
　my shield, in whom I take refuge,
　　who subdues peoplesᵃ under me.

³O Lᴏʀᴅ, what is man that you care for him,
　　the son of man that you think of him?
⁴Man is like a breath;
　　his days are like a fleeting shadow.

⁵Part your heavens, O Lᴏʀᴅ, and come down;
　　touch the mountains, so that they smoke.
⁶Send forth lightning and scatter ⌞the enemies⌟;
　　shoot your arrows and rout them.
⁷Reach down your hand from on high;
　　deliver me and rescue me
　from the mighty waters,
　　from the hands of foreigners
⁸whose mouths are full of lies,
　　whose right hands are deceitful.

⁹I will sing a new song to you, O God;
　　on the ten-stringed lyre I will make music to you,
¹⁰to the One who gives victory to kings,
　　who delivers his servant David from the deadly sword.

¹¹Deliver me and rescue me
　　from the hands of foreigners

ᵃ2 Many manuscripts of the Masoretic Text, Dead Sea Scrolls, Aquila, Jerome and Syriac; most manuscripts
of the Masoretic Text subdues my people

whose mouths are full of lies,
whose right hands are deceitful.

¹²Then our sons in their youth
will be like well-nurtured plants,
and our daughters will be like pillars
carved to adorn a palace.
¹³Our barns will be filled
with every kind of provision.
Our sheep will increase by thousands,
by tens of thousands in our fields;
¹⁴   our oxen will draw heavy loads.ᵃ
There will be no breaching of walls,
no going into captivity,
no cry of distress in our streets.

¹⁵Blessed are the people of whom this is true;
blessed are the people whose God is the LORD.

PSALM 145ᵇ

A psalm of praise. Of David.

¹I will exalt you, my God the King;
I will praise your name for ever and ever.
²Every day I will praise you
and extol your name for ever and ever.

³Great is the LORD and most worthy of praise;
his greatness no one can fathom.
⁴One generation will commend your works to another;
they will tell of your mighty acts.
⁵They will speak of the glorious splendor of your majesty,
and I will meditate on your wonderful works.ᶜ
⁶They will tell of the power of your awesome works,
and I will proclaim your great deeds.
⁷They will celebrate your abundant goodness
and joyfully sing of your righteousness.

⁸The LORD is gracious and compassionate,
slow to anger and rich in love.
⁹The LORD is good to all;
he has compassion on all he has made.
¹⁰All you have made will praise you, O LORD;
your saints will extol you.
¹¹They will tell of the glory of your kingdom
and speak of your might,
¹²so that all men may know of your mighty acts
and the glorious splendor of your kingdom.
¹³Your kingdom is an everlasting kingdom,
and your dominion endures through all generations.

> The LORD is faithful to all his promises and loving toward all he has made (Psalm 145:13).

ᵃ14 Or *our chieftains will be firmly established*   ᵇThis psalm is an acrostic poem, the verses of which (including verse 13b) begin with the successive letters of the Hebrew alphabet.   ᶜ5 Dead Sea Scrolls and Syriac (see also Septuagint); Masoretic Text *On the glorious splendor of your majesty / and on your wonderful works I will meditate*

The Lord is faithful to all his promises
and loving toward all he has made.*

¹⁴The Lord upholds all those who fall
and lifts up all who are bowed down.
¹⁵The eyes of all look to you,
and you give them their food at the proper time.
¹⁶You open your hand
and satisfy the desires of every living thing.

¹⁷The Lord is righteous in all his ways
and loving toward all he has made.
¹⁸The Lord is near to all who call on him,
to all who call on him in truth.
¹⁹He fulfills the desires of those who fear him;
he hears their cry and saves them.
²⁰The Lord watches over all who love him,
but all the wicked he will destroy.

²¹My mouth will speak in praise of the Lord.
Let every creature praise his holy name
for ever and ever.

PSALM 146

¹Praise the Lord.ᵇ

Praise the Lord, O my soul.
²   I will praise the Lord all my life;
I will sing praise to my God as long as I live.

³Do not put your trust in princes,
in mortal men, who cannot save.
⁴When their spirit departs, they return to the ground;
on that very day their plans come to nothing.

⁵Blessed is he whose help is the God of Jacob,
whose hope is in the Lord his God,
⁶the Maker of heaven and earth,
the sea, and everything in them—
the Lord, who remains faithful forever.
⁷He upholds the cause of the oppressed
and gives food to the hungry.
The Lord sets prisoners free,
⁸   the Lord gives sight to the blind,
the Lord lifts up those who are bowed down,
the Lord loves the righteous.
⁹The Lord watches over the alien
and sustains the fatherless and the widow,
but he frustrates the ways of the wicked.

¹⁰The Lord reigns forever,
your God, O Zion, for all generations.

Praise the Lord.

*13 One manuscript of the Masoretic Text, Dead Sea Scrolls and Syriac (see also Septuagint); most manuscripts of the Masoretic Text do not have the last two lines of verse 13.   ᵇ1 Hebrew *Hallelu Yah*; also in verse 10

PSALM *147*

¹Praise the LORD.ᵃ

How good it is to sing praises to our God,
how pleasant and fitting to praise him!

²The LORD builds up Jerusalem;
he gathers the exiles of Israel.
³He heals the brokenhearted
and binds up their wounds.

⁴He determines the number of the stars
and calls them each by name.
⁵Great is our Lord and mighty in power;
his understanding has no limit.
⁶The LORD sustains the humble
but casts the wicked to the ground.

⁷Sing to the LORD with thanksgiving;
make music to our God on the harp.
⁸He covers the sky with clouds;
he supplies the earth with rain
and makes grass grow on the hills.
⁹He provides food for the cattle
and for the young ravens when they call.

¹⁰His pleasure is not in the strength of the horse,
nor his delight in the legs of a man;
¹¹the LORD delights in those who fear him,
who put their hope in his unfailing love.

¹²Extol the LORD, O Jerusalem;
praise your God, O Zion,
¹³for he strengthens the bars of your gates
and blesses your people within you.
¹⁴He grants peace to your borders
and satisfies you with the finest of wheat.

¹⁵He sends his command to the earth;
his word runs swiftly.
¹⁶He spreads the snow like wool
and scatters the frost like ashes.
¹⁷He hurls down his hail like pebbles.
Who can withstand his icy blast?
¹⁸He sends his word and melts them;
he stirs up his breezes, and the waters flow.

¹⁹He has revealed his word to Jacob,
his laws and decrees to Israel.
²⁰He has done this for no other nation;
they do not know his laws.

Praise the LORD.

ᵃ1 Hebrew *Hallelu Yah*; also in verse 20

Dear Sam,

I have been sexually abused. Sometimes I feel so angry I could scream, and other times I just feel used and worthless. What can I do?

Terry in Terre Haute

100 Advice Lane, Anywhere, USA

Dear Terry,

There are a few things you must do. First, you need to try to make sure it doesn't happen again. Tell a responsible adult, someone you trust. If that person doesn't believe you, find someone else. No one deserves to be sexually abused. Most victims are abused by someone they know. The person who abused you might threaten you or tell you it was your fault (that's a lie!) in order to try to keep you quiet. But you must tell someone.

Second, pray often. Pour out your heart to God. He made you, and he will heal you. Psalm 147:3 has a wonderful promise for you: "He heals the brokenhearted and binds up their wounds."

Third, it is also helpful for abuse victims to seek counseling from a professional experienced in dealing with sexual abuse. You need help working through your anger. Give your anger to God. You don't need to take revenge; God will take care of that (Romans 12:19). God is angrier at what happened than you are, and he has the power to handle it.

Sam

PSALM 148

¹Praise the LORD.ᵃ

Praise the LORD from the heavens,
  praise him in the heights above.
²Praise him, all his angels,
  praise him, all his heavenly hosts.
³Praise him, sun and moon,
  praise him, all you shining stars.
⁴Praise him, you highest heavens
  and you waters above the skies.
⁵Let them praise the name of the LORD,
  for he commanded and they were created.
⁶He set them in place for ever and ever;
  he gave a decree that will never pass away.

⁷Praise the LORD from the earth,
  you great sea creatures and all ocean depths,
⁸lightning and hail, snow and clouds,
  stormy winds that do his bidding,
⁹you mountains and all hills,
  fruit trees and all cedars,
¹⁰wild animals and all cattle,
  small creatures and flying birds,
¹¹kings of the earth and all nations,
  you princes and all rulers on earth,
¹²young men and maidens,
  old men and children.

¹³Let them praise the name of the LORD,
  for his name alone is exalted;
  his splendor is above the earth and the heavens.
¹⁴He has raised up for his people a horn,ᵇ
  the praise of all his saints,
  of Israel, the people close to his heart.

  Praise the LORD.

PSALM 149

¹Praise the LORD.ᶜ

Sing to the LORD a new song,
  his praise in the assembly of the saints.

²Let Israel rejoice in their Maker;
  let the people of Zion be glad in their King.
³Let them praise his name with dancing
  and make music to him with tambourine and harp.
⁴For the LORD takes delight in his people;
  he crowns the humble with salvation.
⁵Let the saints rejoice in this honor
  and sing for joy on their beds.

ᵃ1 Hebrew *Hallelu Yah;* also in verse 14   ᵇ14 *Horn* here symbolizes strong one, that is, king.   ᶜ1 Hebrew
Hallelu Yah; also in verse 9

⁶May the praise of God be in their mouths
    and a double-edged sword in their hands,
⁷to inflict vengeance on the nations
    and punishment on the peoples,
⁸to bind their kings with fetters,
    their nobles with shackles of iron,
⁹to carry out the sentence written against them.
    This is the glory of all his saints.

Praise the LORD.

PSALM 150

¹Praise the LORD.ᵃ

Praise God in his sanctuary;
    praise him in his mighty heavens.
²Praise him for his acts of power;
    praise him for his surpassing greatness.
³Praise him with the sounding of the trumpet,
    praise him with the harp and lyre,
⁴praise him with tambourine and dancing,
    praise him with the strings and flute,
⁵praise him with the clash of cymbals,
    praise him with resounding cymbals.

⁶Let everything that has breath praise the LORD.

Praise the LORD.

ᵃ1 Hebrew *Hallelu Yah*; also in verse 6

Introduction

to the

book of Proverbs

GOOD ADVICE.

How can you get along with someone who doesn't like you? What is the best way to make friends? Lots of good advice is what you'll find in the book of Proverbs.

Proverbs are short sayings that help people make wise choices. The advice found in Proverbs makes good sense for both Christians and non-Christians. Take, for example, "a gentle answer turns away wrath" (Proverbs 15:1). It's better to be polite than to yell back insults when someone is angry at you. Usually this will stop a fight. But not always. Proverbs describe what usually happens, not necessarily what God promises to do.

What is the good of "wisdom"? Why not just do anything that feels good (Proverbs 2)?

You can't tell the truth all the time, can you (Proverbs 6:16-17; 12:17-19; 17:4,20)?

If you want to be rich, here's some-thing to think about (Proverbs 10:4; 11:4,28; 15:16).

FAST FACTS

Solomon contributed many of the proverbs.

The collection was finished 250 years after Solomon's death.

To "fear the Lord" means to respect him by living a moral life.

Proverbs identifies four kinds of fools: the ignorant, the stubborn, the proud and the immoral.

Prologue: Purpose and Theme

1 The proverbs of Solomon son of David, king of Israel:

² for attaining wisdom and discipline;
    for understanding words of insight;
³ for acquiring a disciplined and prudent life,
    doing what is right and just and fair;
⁴ for giving prudence to the simple,
    knowledge and discretion to the young—
⁵ let the wise listen and add to their learning,
    and let the discerning get guidance—
⁶ for understanding proverbs and parables,
    the sayings and riddles of the wise.

⁷ The fear of the Lᴏʀᴅ is the beginning of knowledge,
    but fools*ᵃ* despise wisdom and discipline.

Exhortations to Embrace Wisdom

Warning Against Enticement

⁸ Listen, my son, to your father's instruction
    and do not forsake your mother's teaching.
⁹ They will be a garland to grace your head
    and a chain to adorn your neck.

¹⁰ My son, if sinners entice you,
    do not give in to them.
¹¹ If they say, "Come along with us;
    let's lie in wait for someone's blood,
    let's waylay some harmless soul;
¹² let's swallow them alive, like the grave,*ᵇ*
    and whole, like those who go down to the pit;
¹³ we will get all sorts of valuable things
    and fill our houses with plunder;
¹⁴ throw in your lot with us,
    and we will share a common purse"—
¹⁵ my son, do not go along with them,
    do not set foot on their paths;
¹⁶ for their feet rush into sin,
    they are swift to shed blood.
¹⁷ How useless to spread a net
    in full view of all the birds!
¹⁸ These men lie in wait for their own blood;
    they waylay only themselves!
¹⁹ Such is the end of all who go after ill-gotten gain;
    it takes away the lives of those who get it.

Warning Against Rejecting Wisdom

²⁰ Wisdom calls aloud in the street,
    she raises her voice in the public squares;
²¹ at the head of the noisy streets*ᶜ* she cries out,
    in the gateways of the city she makes her speech:

²² "How long will you simple ones*ᵈ* love your simple ways?
    How long will mockers delight in mockery
    and fools hate knowledge?

ᵃ7 The Hebrew words rendered *fool* in Proverbs, and often elsewhere in the Old Testament, denote one who is morally deficient. *ᵇ12* Hebrew *Sheol* *ᶜ21* Hebrew; Septuagint */ on the tops of the walls* *ᵈ22* The Hebrew word rendered *simple* in Proverbs generally denotes one without moral direction and inclined to evil.

²³ If you had responded to my rebuke,
    I would have poured out my heart to you
    and made my thoughts known to you.
²⁴ But since you rejected me when I called
    and no one gave heed when I stretched out my hand,
²⁵ since you ignored all my advice
    and would not accept my rebuke,
²⁶ I in turn will laugh at your disaster;
    I will mock when calamity overtakes you—
²⁷ when calamity overtakes you like a storm,
    when disaster sweeps over you like a whirlwind,
    when distress and trouble overwhelm you.

²⁸ "Then they will call to me but I will not answer;
    they will look for me but will not find me.
²⁹ Since they hated knowledge
    and did not choose to fear the LORD,
³⁰ since they would not accept my advice
    and spurned my rebuke,
³¹ they will eat the fruit of their ways
    and be filled with the fruit of their schemes.
³² For the waywardness of the simple will kill them,
    and the complacency of fools will destroy them;
³³ but whoever listens to me will live in safety
    and be at ease, without fear of harm."

2

Moral Benefits of Wisdom

My son, if you accept my words
    and store up my commands within you,
² turning your ear to wisdom
    and applying your heart to understanding,
³ and if you call out for insight
    and cry aloud for understanding,
⁴ and if you look for it as for silver
    and search for it as for hidden treasure,
⁵ then you will understand the fear of the LORD
    and find the knowledge of God.

Most of you aren't wild about getting advice. Especially from your parents. Sure they've lived longer, you say, but do they really understand the world I live in?

Of course, you can't say that about God. When you read God's Word, you listen to God and learn how to live right every day. What will you gain if you read the Bible for advice?

✳ You will understand what is right and just (Proverbs 2:9).
✳ You will gain wisdom and be protected by it (Proverbs 2:10–11).
✳ You will be saved from the ways of the wicked (Proverbs 2:12).

The Bible is filled with treasures that can be yours if only you look (Proverbs 2:4).

The Bible Says

God Gives Advice

⁶For the Lᴏʀᴅ gives wisdom,
  and from his mouth come knowledge and understanding.
⁷He holds victory in store for the upright,
  he is a shield to those whose walk is blameless,
⁸for he guards the course of the just
  and protects the way of his faithful ones.

⁹Then you will understand what is right and just
  and fair—every good path.
¹⁰For wisdom will enter your heart,
  and knowledge will be pleasant to your soul.
¹¹Discretion will protect you,
  and understanding will guard you.

¹²Wisdom will save you from the ways of wicked men,
  from men whose words are perverse,
¹³who leave the straight paths
  to walk in dark ways,
¹⁴who delight in doing wrong
  and rejoice in the perverseness of evil,
¹⁵whose paths are crooked
  and who are devious in their ways.

¹⁶It will save you also from the adulteress,
  from the wayward wife with her seductive words,
¹⁷who has left the partner of her youth
  and ignored the covenant she made before God.ᵃ
¹⁸For her house leads down to death
  and her paths to the spirits of the dead.
¹⁹None who go to her return
  or attain the paths of life.

²⁰Thus you will walk in the ways of good men
  and keep to the paths of the righteous.
²¹For the upright will live in the land,
  and the blameless will remain in it;
²²but the wicked will be cut off from the land,
  and the unfaithful will be torn from it.

3 *Further Benefits of Wisdom*
  My son, do not forget my teaching,
    but keep my commands in your heart,
  ²for they will prolong your life many years
    and bring you prosperity.

³Let love and faithfulness never leave you;
  bind them around your neck,
  write them on the tablet of your heart.
⁴Then you will win favor and a good name
  in the sight of God and man.

⁵Trust in the Lᴏʀᴅ with all your heart
  and lean not on your own understanding;
⁶in all your ways acknowledge him,
  and he will make your paths straight.ᵇ

⁷Do not be wise in your own eyes;
  fear the Lᴏʀᴅ and shun evil.

ᵃ17 Or *covenant of her God* ᵇ6 Or *will direct your paths*

⁸This will bring health to your body
    and nourishment to your bones.

⁹Honor the LORD with your wealth,
    with the firstfruits of all your crops;
¹⁰then your barns will be filled to overflowing,
    and your vats will brim over with new wine.

¹¹My son, do not despise the LORD's discipline
    and do not resent his rebuke,
¹²because the LORD disciplines those he loves,
    as a father*ᵃ* the son he delights in.

¹³Blessed is the man who finds wisdom,
    the man who gains understanding,
¹⁴for she is more profitable than silver
    and yields better returns than gold.
¹⁵She is more precious than rubies;
    nothing you desire can compare with her.
¹⁶Long life is in her right hand;
    in her left hand are riches and honor.
¹⁷Her ways are pleasant ways,
    and all her paths are peace.
¹⁸She is a tree of life to those who embrace her;
    those who lay hold of her will be blessed.

¹⁹By wisdom the LORD laid the earth's foundations,
    by understanding he set the heavens in place;
²⁰by his knowledge the deeps were divided,
    and the clouds let drop the dew.

²¹My son, preserve sound judgment and discernment,
    do not let them out of your sight;
²²they will be life for you,
    an ornament to grace your neck.
²³Then you will go on your way in safety,
    and your foot will not stumble;
²⁴when you lie down, you will not be afraid;
    when you lie down, your sleep will be sweet.
²⁵Have no fear of sudden disaster
    or of the ruin that overtakes the wicked,
²⁶for the LORD will be your confidence
    and will keep your foot from being snared.

²⁷Do not withhold good from those who deserve it,
    when it is in your power to act.
²⁸Do not say to your neighbor,
    "Come back later; I'll give it tomorrow"—
    when you now have it with you.

²⁹Do not plot harm against your neighbor,
    who lives trustfully near you.
³⁰Do not accuse a man for no reason—
    when he has done you no harm.

³¹Do not envy a violent man
    or choose any of his ways,
³²for the LORD detests a perverse man
    but takes the upright into his confidence.

ᵃ12 Hebrew; Septuagint / *and he punishes*

³³The Lord's curse is on the house of the wicked,
　　but he blesses the home of the righteous.
³⁴He mocks proud mockers
　　but gives grace to the humble.
³⁵The wise inherit honor,
　　but fools he holds up to shame.

Wisdom Is Supreme

Listen, my sons, to a father's instruction;
　　pay attention and gain understanding.
²I give you sound learning,
　　so do not forsake my teaching.
³When I was a boy in my father's house,
　　still tender, and an only child of my mother,
⁴he taught me and said,
　　"Lay hold of my words with all your heart;
　　keep my commands and you will live.
⁵Get wisdom, get understanding;
　　do not forget my words or swerve from them.
⁶Do not forsake wisdom, and she will protect you;
　　love her, and she will watch over you.
⁷Wisdom is supreme; therefore get wisdom.
　　Though it cost all you have,^a get understanding.
⁸Esteem her, and she will exalt you;
　　embrace her, and she will honor you.
⁹She will set a garland of grace on your head
　　and present you with a crown of splendor."

¹⁰Listen, my son, accept what I say,
　　and the years of your life will be many.
¹¹I guide you in the way of wisdom
　　and lead you along straight paths.
¹²When you walk, your steps will not be hampered;
　　when you run, you will not stumble.
¹³Hold on to instruction, do not let it go;
　　guard it well, for it is your life.
¹⁴Do not set foot on the path of the wicked
　　or walk in the way of evil men.
¹⁵Avoid it, do not travel on it;
　　turn from it and go on your way.
¹⁶For they cannot sleep till they do evil;
　　they are robbed of slumber till they make someone fall.
¹⁷They eat the bread of wickedness
　　and drink the wine of violence.

¹⁸The path of the righteous is like the first gleam of dawn,
　　shining ever brighter till the full light of day.
¹⁹But the way of the wicked is like deep darkness;
　　they do not know what makes them stumble.

²⁰My son, pay attention to what I say;
　　listen closely to my words.
²¹Do not let them out of your sight,
　　keep them within your heart;
²²for they are life to those who find them
　　and health to a man's whole body.

^a7 Or *Whatever else you get*

²³ Above all else, guard your heart,
     for it is the wellspring of life.
²⁴ Put away perversity from your mouth;
     keep corrupt talk far from your lips.
²⁵ Let your eyes look straight ahead,
     fix your gaze directly before you.
²⁶ Make level*ᵃ* paths for your feet
     and take only ways that are firm.
²⁷ Do not swerve to the right or the left;
     keep your foot from evil.

Warning Against Adultery

5   My son, pay attention to my wisdom,
     listen well to my words of insight,
² that you may maintain discretion
     and your lips may preserve knowledge.
³ For the lips of an adulteress drip honey,
     and her speech is smoother than oil;
⁴ but in the end she is bitter as gall,
     sharp as a double-edged sword.
⁵ Her feet go down to death;
     her steps lead straight to the grave.*ᵇ*
⁶ She gives no thought to the way of life;
     her paths are crooked, but she knows it not.

⁷ Now then, my sons, listen to me;
     do not turn aside from what I say.
⁸ Keep to a path far from her,
     do not go near the door of her house,
⁹ lest you give your best strength to others
     and your years to one who is cruel,
¹⁰ lest strangers feast on your wealth
     and your toil enrich another man's house.
¹¹ At the end of your life you will groan,
     when your flesh and body are spent.
¹² You will say, "How I hated discipline!
     How my heart spurned correction!
¹³ I would not obey my teachers
     or listen to my instructors.
¹⁴ I have come to the brink of utter ruin
     in the midst of the whole assembly."

¹⁵ Drink water from your own cistern,
     running water from your own well.
¹⁶ Should your springs overflow in the streets,
     your streams of water in the public squares?
¹⁷ Let them be yours alone,
     never to be shared with strangers.
¹⁸ May your fountain be blessed,
     and may you rejoice in the wife of your youth.
¹⁹ A loving doe, a graceful deer—
     may her breasts satisfy you always,
     may you ever be captivated by her love.
²⁰ Why be captivated, my son, by an adulteress?
     Why embrace the bosom of another man's wife?

ᵃ26 Or *Consider the*   *ᵇ5* Hebrew *Sheol*

²¹For a man's ways are in full view of the LORD,
and he examines all his paths.
²²The evil deeds of a wicked man ensnare him;
the cords of his sin hold him fast.
²³He will die for lack of discipline,
led astray by his own great folly.

Warnings Against Folly

My son, if you have put up security for your neighbor,
if you have struck hands in pledge for another,
²if you have been trapped by what you said,
ensnared by the words of your mouth,
³then do this, my son, to free yourself,
since you have fallen into your neighbor's hands:
Go and humble yourself;
press your plea with your neighbor!
⁴Allow no sleep to your eyes,
no slumber to your eyelids.
⁵Free yourself, like a gazelle from the hand of the
hunter,
like a bird from the snare of the fowler.

⁶Go to the ant, you sluggard;
consider its ways and be wise!
⁷It has no commander,
no overseer or ruler,
⁸yet it stores its provisions in summer
and gathers its food at harvest.

⁹How long will you lie there, you sluggard?
When will you get up from your sleep?
¹⁰A little sleep, a little slumber,
a little folding of the hands to rest—
¹¹and poverty will come on you like a bandit
and scarcity like an armed man.ᵃ

¹²A scoundrel and villain,
who goes about with a corrupt mouth,
¹³   who winks with his eye,
signals with his feet
and motions with his fingers,
¹⁴   who plots evil with deceit in his heart—
he always stirs up dissension.
¹⁵Therefore disaster will overtake him in an instant;
he will suddenly be destroyed—without remedy.

¹⁶There are six things the LORD hates,
seven that are detestable to him:
¹⁷   haughty eyes,
a lying tongue,
hands that shed innocent blood,
¹⁸   a heart that devises wicked schemes,
feet that are quick to rush into evil,
¹⁹   a false witness who pours out lies
and a man who stirs up dissension among brothers.

ᵃ11 Or like a vagrant / and scarcity like a beggar

²⁰My son, keep your father's commands
and do not forsake your mother's teaching.
²¹Bind them upon your heart forever;
fasten them around your neck.
²²When you walk, they will guide you;
when you sleep, they will watch over you;
when you awake, they will speak to you.
²³For these commands are a lamp,
this teaching is a light,
and the corrections of discipline
are the way to life,
²⁴keeping you from the immoral woman,
from the smooth tongue of the wayward wife.
²⁵Do not lust in your heart after her beauty
or let her captivate you with her eyes,
²⁶for the prostitute reduces you to a loaf of bread,
and the adulteress preys upon your very life.
²⁷Can a man scoop fire into his lap
without his clothes being burned?
²⁸Can a man walk on hot coals
without his feet being scorched?
²⁹So is he who sleeps with another man's wife;
no one who touches her will go unpunished.

³⁰Men do not despise a thief if he steals
to satisfy his hunger when he is starving.
³¹Yet if he is caught, he must pay sevenfold,
though it costs him all the wealth of his house.
³²But a man who commits adultery lacks judgment;
whoever does so destroys himself.
³³Blows and disgrace are his lot,
and his shame will never be wiped away;
³⁴for jealousy arouses a husband's fury,
and he will show no mercy when he takes revenge.
³⁵He will not accept any compensation;
he will refuse the bribe, however great it is.

Warning Against the Adulteress

My son, keep my words
and store up my commands within you.
²Keep my commands and you will live;
guard my teachings as the apple of your eye.
³Bind them on your fingers;
write them on the tablet of your heart.
⁴Say to wisdom, "You are my sister,"
and call understanding your kinsman;
⁵they will keep you from the adulteress,
from the wayward wife with her seductive words.

⁶At the window of my house
I looked out through the lattice.
⁷I saw among the simple,
I noticed among the young men,
a youth who lacked judgment.
⁸He was going down the street near her corner,
walking along in the direction of her house

Dear Sam,

> If God made sex for people to enjoy,
> why do people get AIDS and other
> STDs (sexually transmitted diseases)?

> Rory in Riverside

100 Advice Lane, Anywhere, USA

Dear Rory,

Good question! God gave men and women a strong desire to have sex with one another. He also gave them instructions on how to use this gift.

When microwaves were first available, a woman used one to warm her cat. It thawed the pet out, but she had to bury it. The oven was wonderful, but she didn't read the instructions on how to use it. Does that mean microwaves are dangerous or that you shouldn't use them? No, but you need to follow the instructions in order to enjoy them without getting hurt.

The drive to have sex is like that. You need to know and follow God's instructions for using this wonderful gift. Marriage is a difficult, lifelong commitment. God knew that. So he gave men and women a special gift, a way to bond together, to renew their feelings and remain mates, not only of the flesh but also of the soul.

When people who aren't married to each other have sex, it's sort of like putting a pet into the microwave. Someone is going to get burned (Proverbs 6:26-28), perhaps by an unwanted pregnancy or by STDs or even by death. Why take the chance? How much better is it to follow God's instructions and enjoy the gift he's given.

Sam

⁹at twilight, as the day was fading,
    as the dark of night set in.

¹⁰Then out came a woman to meet him,
    dressed like a prostitute and with crafty intent.
¹¹(She is loud and defiant,
    her feet never stay at home;
¹²now in the street, now in the squares,
    at every corner she lurks.)
¹³She took hold of him and kissed him
    and with a brazen face she said:

¹⁴"I have fellowship offerings*a* at home;
    today I fulfilled my vows.
¹⁵So I came out to meet you;
    I looked for you and have found you!
¹⁶I have covered my bed
    with colored linens from Egypt.
¹⁷I have perfumed my bed
    with myrrh, aloes and cinnamon.
¹⁸Come, let's drink deep of love till
      morning;
    let's enjoy ourselves with love!
¹⁹My husband is not at home;
    he has gone on a long journey.
²⁰He took his purse filled with money
    and will not be home till full moon."

²¹With persuasive words she led him astray;
    she seduced him with her smooth talk.
²²All at once he followed her
    like an ox going to the slaughter,
  like a deer*b* stepping into a noose*c*
²³   till an arrow pierces his liver,
  like a bird darting into a snare,
    little knowing it will cost him his life.

²⁴Now then, my sons, listen to me;
    pay attention to what I say.
²⁵Do not let your heart turn to her ways
    or stray into her paths.
²⁶Many are the victims she has brought down;
    her slain are a mighty throng.
²⁷Her house is a highway to the grave,*d*
    leading down to the chambers of death.

8 Wisdom's Call

    Does not wisdom call out?
    Does not understanding raise her voice?
²On the heights along the way,
    where the paths meet, she takes her stand;
³beside the gates leading into the city,
    at the entrances, she cries aloud:
⁴"To you, O men, I call out;
    I raise my voice to all mankind.

PROVERBS 8

QUIZZER

Q: What is more valuable than gold, silver or rubies?

BONUS: What's the difference between being smart and being wise?

Answers on page 811

---

a14 Traditionally *peace offerings* *b22* Syriac (see also Septuagint); Hebrew *fool* *c22* The meaning of the Hebrew for this line is uncertain. *d27* Hebrew *Sheol*

⁵You who are simple, gain prudence;
    you who are foolish, gain understanding.
⁶Listen, for I have worthy things to say;
    I open my lips to speak what is right.
⁷My mouth speaks what is true,
    for my lips detest wickedness.
⁸All the words of my mouth are just;
    none of them is crooked or perverse.
⁹To the discerning all of them are right;
    they are faultless to those who have knowledge.
¹⁰Choose my instruction instead of silver,
    knowledge rather than choice gold,
¹¹for wisdom is more precious than rubies,
    and nothing you desire can compare with her.

¹²"I, wisdom, dwell together with prudence;
    I possess knowledge and discretion.
¹³To fear the LORD is to hate evil;
    I hate pride and arrogance,
    evil behavior and perverse speech.
¹⁴Counsel and sound judgment are mine;
    I have understanding and power.
¹⁵By me kings reign
    and rulers make laws that are just;
¹⁶by me princes govern,
    and all nobles who rule on earth.ᵃ
¹⁷I love those who love me,
    and those who seek me find me.
¹⁸With me are riches and honor,
    enduring wealth and prosperity.
¹⁹My fruit is better than fine gold;
    what I yield surpasses choice silver.
²⁰I walk in the way of righteousness,
    along the paths of justice,
²¹bestowing wealth on those who love me
    and making their treasuries full.

²²"The LORD brought me forth as the first of his works,ᵇ,ᶜ
    before his deeds of old;
²³I was appointedᵈ from eternity,
    from the beginning, before the world began.
²⁴When there were no oceans, I was given birth,
    when there were no springs abounding with water;
²⁵before the mountains were settled in place,
    before the hills, I was given birth,
²⁶before he made the earth or its fields
    or any of the dust of the world.
²⁷I was there when he set the heavens in place,
    when he marked out the horizon on the face of the deep,
²⁸when he established the clouds above
    and fixed securely the fountains of the deep,
²⁹when he gave the sea its boundary
    so the waters would not overstep his command,
    and when he marked out the foundations of the earth.
³⁰   Then I was the craftsman at his side.

ᵃ16 Many Hebrew manuscripts and Septuagint; most Hebrew manuscripts *and nobles—all righteous rulers*
ᵇ22 Or *way*; or *dominion*   ᶜ22 Or *The LORD possessed me at the beginning of his work*; or *The LORD brought me forth at the beginning of his work*   ᵈ23 Or *fashioned*

I was filled with delight day after day,
  rejoicing always in his presence,
31 rejoicing in his whole world
  and delighting in mankind.

32 "Now then, my sons, listen to me;
  blessed are those who keep my ways.
33 Listen to my instruction and be wise;
  do not ignore it.
34 Blessed is the man who listens to me,
  watching daily at my doors,
  waiting at my doorway.
35 For whoever finds me finds life
  and receives favor from the LORD.
36 But whoever fails to find me harms himself;
  all who hate me love death."

9 Invitations of Wisdom and of Folly

Wisdom has built her house;
  she has hewn out its seven pillars.
2 She has prepared her meat and mixed her wine;
  she has also set her table.
3 She has sent out her maids, and she calls
  from the highest point of the city.
4 "Let all who are simple come in here!"
  she says to those who lack judgment.
5 "Come, eat my food
  and drink the wine I have mixed.
6 Leave your simple ways and you will live;
  walk in the way of understanding.

7 "Whoever corrects a mocker invites insult;
  whoever rebukes a wicked man incurs abuse.
8 Do not rebuke a mocker or he will hate you;
  rebuke a wise man and he will love you.
9 Instruct a wise man and he will be wiser still;
  teach a righteous man and he will add to his learning.

10 "The fear of the LORD is the beginning of wisdom,
  and knowledge of the Holy One is understanding.
11 For through me your days will be many,
  and years will be added to your life.
12 If you are wise, your wisdom will reward you;
  if you are a mocker, you alone will suffer."

13 The woman Folly is loud;
  she is undisciplined and without knowledge.
14 She sits at the door of her house,
  on a seat at the highest point of the city,
15 calling out to those who pass by,
  who go straight on their way.
16 "Let all who are simple come in here!"
  she says to those who lack judgment.
17 "Stolen water is sweet;
  food eaten in secret is delicious!"
18 But little do they know that the dead are there,
  that her guests are in the depths of the grave.ᵃ

nswers

to Quizzer on
page 809

A: Knowledge
and wisdom
(Proverbs
8:10-11).

BONUS:
Smarts might
earn you good
grades in school,
but wisdom will
guide you to
good choices all
your life.

ᵃ18 Hebrew *Sheol*

10 The proverbs of Solomon:

A wise son brings joy to his father,
but a foolish son grief to his mother.

²Ill-gotten treasures are of no value,
but righteousness delivers from death.

³The LORD does not let the righteous go hungry
but he thwarts the craving of the wicked.

⁴Lazy hands make a man poor,
but diligent hands bring wealth.

⁵He who gathers crops in summer is a wise son,
but he who sleeps during harvest is a disgraceful
son.

⁶Blessings crown the head of the righteous,
but violence overwhelms the mouth of the wicked.ᵃ

⁷The memory of the righteous will be a blessing,
but the name of the wicked will rot.

⁸The wise in heart accept commands,
but a chattering fool comes to ruin.

⁹The man of integrity walks securely,
but he who takes crooked paths will be found out.

¹⁰He who winks maliciously causes grief,
and a chattering fool comes to ruin.

¹¹The mouth of the righteous is a fountain of life,
but violence overwhelms the mouth of the wicked.

¹²Hatred stirs up dissension,
but love covers over all wrongs.

¹³Wisdom is found on the lips of the discerning,
but a rod is for the back of him who lacks judgment.

¹⁴Wise men store up knowledge,
but the mouth of a fool invites ruin.

¹⁵The wealth of the rich is their fortified city,
but poverty is the ruin of the poor.

¹⁶The wages of the righteous bring them life,
but the income of the wicked brings them punishment.

¹⁷He who heeds discipline shows the way to life,
but whoever ignores correction leads others astray.

¹⁸He who conceals his hatred has lying lips,
and whoever spreads slander is a fool.

¹⁹When words are many, sin is not absent,
but he who holds his tongue is wise.

²⁰The tongue of the righteous is choice silver,
but the heart of the wicked is of little value.

ᵃ6 Or *but the mouth of the wicked conceals violence*; also in verse 11

²¹ The lips of the righteous nourish many,
  but fools die for lack of judgment.

²² The blessing of the LORD brings wealth,
  and he adds no trouble to it.

²³ A fool finds pleasure in evil conduct,
  but a man of understanding delights in wisdom.

²⁴ What the wicked dreads will overtake him;
  what the righteous desire will be granted.

²⁵ When the storm has swept by, the wicked are gone,
  but the righteous stand firm forever.

²⁶ As vinegar to the teeth and smoke to the eyes,
  so is a sluggard to those who send him.

²⁷ The fear of the LORD adds length to life,
  but the years of the wicked are cut short.

²⁸ The prospect of the righteous is joy,
  but the hopes of the wicked come to nothing.

²⁹ The way of the LORD is a refuge for the righteous,
  but it is the ruin of those who do evil.

³⁰ The righteous will never be uprooted,
  but the wicked will not remain in the land.

³¹ The mouth of the righteous brings forth wisdom,
  but a perverse tongue will be cut out.

³² The lips of the righteous know what is fitting,
  but the mouth of the wicked only what is perverse.

11 The LORD abhors dishonest scales,
  but accurate weights are his delight.

² When pride comes, then comes disgrace,
  but with humility comes wisdom.

³ The integrity of the upright guides them,
  but the unfaithful are destroyed by their duplicity.

⁴ Wealth is worthless in the day of wrath,
  but righteousness delivers from death.

⁵ The righteousness of the blameless makes a straight way for
    them,
  but the wicked are brought down by their own wickedness.

⁶ The righteousness of the upright delivers them,
  but the unfaithful are trapped by evil desires.

⁷ When a wicked man dies, his hope perishes;
  all he expected from his power comes to nothing.

⁸ The righteous man is rescued from trouble,
  and it comes on the wicked instead.

⁹ With his mouth the godless destroys his neighbor,
  but through knowledge the righteous escape.

¹⁰ When the righteous prosper, the city rejoices;
  when the wicked perish, there are shouts of joy.

¹¹ Through the blessing of the upright a city is exalted,
but by the mouth of the wicked it is destroyed.

¹² A man who lacks judgment derides his neighbor,
but a man of understanding holds his tongue.

¹³ A gossip betrays a confidence,
but a trustworthy man keeps a secret.

¹⁴ For lack of guidance a nation falls,
but many advisers make victory sure.

¹⁵ He who puts up security for another will surely suffer,
but whoever refuses to strike hands in pledge is safe.

¹⁶ A kindhearted woman gains respect,
but ruthless men gain only wealth.

¹⁷ A kind man benefits himself,
but a cruel man brings trouble on himself.

¹⁸ The wicked man earns deceptive wages,
but he who sows righteousness reaps a sure reward.

¹⁹ The truly righteous man attains life,
but he who pursues evil goes to his death.

²⁰ The LORD detests men of perverse heart
but he delights in those whose ways are blameless.

²¹ Be sure of this: The wicked will not go unpunished,
but those who are righteous will go free.

²² Like a gold ring in a pig's snout
is a beautiful woman who shows no discretion.

²³ The desire of the righteous ends only in good,
but the hope of the wicked only in wrath.

²⁴ One man gives freely, yet gains even more;
another withholds unduly, but comes to poverty.

²⁵ A generous man will prosper;
he who refreshes others will himself be refreshed.

²⁶ People curse the man who hoards grain,
but blessing crowns him who is willing to sell.

²⁷ He who seeks good finds goodwill,
but evil comes to him who searches for it.

²⁸ Whoever trusts in his riches will fall,
but the righteous will thrive like a green leaf.

²⁹ He who brings trouble on his family will inherit only wind,
and the fool will be servant to the wise.

³⁰ The fruit of the righteous is a tree of life,
and he who wins souls is wise.

³¹ If the righteous receive their due on earth,
how much more the ungodly and the sinner!

12 Whoever loves discipline loves knowledge,
but he who hates correction is stupid.

² A good man obtains favor from the LORD,
but the LORD condemns a crafty man.

³A man cannot be established through wickedness,
但 but the righteous cannot be uprooted.

⁴A wife of noble character is her husband's crown,
but a disgraceful wife is like decay in his bones.

⁵The plans of the righteous are just,
but the advice of the wicked is deceitful.

⁶The words of the wicked lie in wait for blood,
but the speech of the upright rescues them.

⁷Wicked men are overthrown and are no more,
but the house of the righteous stands firm.

⁸A man is praised according to his wisdom,
but men with warped minds are despised.

⁹Better to be a nobody and yet have a servant
than pretend to be somebody and have no food.

¹⁰A righteous man cares for the needs of his animal,
but the kindest acts of the wicked are cruel.

¹¹He who works his land will have abundant food,
but he who chases fantasies lacks judgment.

¹²The wicked desire the plunder of evil men,
but the root of the righteous flourishes.

¹³An evil man is trapped by his sinful talk,
but a righteous man escapes trouble.

¹⁴From the fruit of his lips a man is filled with good things
as surely as the work of his hands rewards him.

¹⁵The way of a fool seems right to him,
but a wise man listens to advice.

¹⁶A fool shows his annoyance at once,
but a prudent man overlooks an
insult.

¹⁷A truthful witness gives honest
testimony,
but a false witness tells lies.

¹⁸Reckless words pierce like a sword,
but the tongue of the wise brings healing.

¹⁹Truthful lips endure forever,
but a lying tongue lasts only a moment.

²⁰There is deceit in the hearts of those who plot evil,
but joy for those who promote peace.

²¹No harm befalls the righteous,
but the wicked have their fill of trouble.

²²The Lord detests lying lips,
but he delights in men who are truthful.

²³A prudent man keeps his knowledge to himself,
but the heart of fools blurts out folly.

²⁴Diligent hands will rule,
but laziness ends in slave labor.

PROVERBS 12

QUIZZER

Q: What
affect does
a noble wife
have on her
husband?

*BONUS:
What affect
does a
disgraceful
wife have on
her husband?*

**Answers on
page 817**

²⁵ An anxious heart weighs a man down,
but a kind word cheers him up.

²⁶ A righteous man is cautious in friendship,^a
but the way of the wicked leads them astray.

²⁷ The lazy man does not roast^b his game,
but the diligent man prizes his possessions.

²⁸ In the way of righteousness there is life;
along that path is immortality.

13 A wise son heeds his father's instruction,
but a mocker does not listen to rebuke.

² From the fruit of his lips a man enjoys good things,
but the unfaithful have a craving for violence.

³ He who guards his lips guards his life,
but he who speaks rashly will come to ruin.

⁴ The sluggard craves and gets nothing,
but the desires of the diligent are fully satisfied.

⁵ The righteous hate what is false,
but the wicked bring shame and disgrace.

⁶ Righteousness guards the man of integrity,
but wickedness overthrows the sinner.

⁷ One man pretends to be rich, yet has nothing;
another pretends to be poor, yet has great wealth.

⁸ A man's riches may ransom his life,
but a poor man hears no threat.

⁹ The light of the righteous shines brightly,
but the lamp of the wicked is snuffed out.

¹⁰ Pride only breeds quarrels,
but wisdom is found in those who take advice.

¹¹ Dishonest money dwindles away,
but he who gathers money little by little makes it grow.

¹² Hope deferred makes the heart sick,
but a longing fulfilled is a tree of life.

¹³ He who scorns instruction will pay for it,
but he who respects a command is rewarded.

¹⁴ The teaching of the wise is a fountain of life,
turning a man from the snares of death.

¹⁵ Good understanding wins favor,
but the way of the unfaithful is hard.^c

¹⁶ Every prudent man acts out of knowledge,
but a fool exposes his folly.

¹⁷ A wicked messenger falls into trouble,
but a trustworthy envoy brings healing.

¹⁸ He who ignores discipline comes to poverty and shame,
but whoever heeds correction is honored.

---

a26 Or man is a guide to his neighbor   b27 The meaning of the Hebrew for this word is uncertain.   c15 Or unfaithful does not endure

¹⁹ A longing fulfilled is sweet to the soul,
but fools detest turning from evil.

²⁰ He who walks with the wise grows wise,
but a companion of fools suffers harm.

²¹ Misfortune pursues the sinner,
but prosperity is the reward of the righteous.

²² A good man leaves an inheritance for his children's children,
but a sinner's wealth is stored up for the righteous.

²³ A poor man's field may produce abundant food,
but injustice sweeps it away.

²⁴ He who spares the rod hates his son,
but he who loves him is careful to discipline him.

²⁵ The righteous eat to their hearts' content,
but the stomach of the wicked goes hungry.

14 The wise woman builds her house,
but with her own hands the foolish one tears hers down.

² He whose walk is upright fears the LORD,
but he whose ways are devious despises him.

³ A fool's talk brings a rod to his back,
but the lips of the wise protect them.

⁴ Where there are no oxen, the manger is empty,
but from the strength of an ox comes an abundant
harvest.

⁵ A truthful witness does not deceive,
but a false witness pours out lies.

⁶ The mocker seeks wisdom and finds none,
but knowledge comes easily to the discerning.

⁷ Stay away from a foolish man,
for you will not find knowledge on his lips.

⁸ The wisdom of the prudent is to give thought to their ways,
but the folly of fools is deception.

⁹ Fools mock at making amends for sin,
but goodwill is found among the upright.

¹⁰ Each heart knows its own bitterness,
and no one else can share its joy.

¹¹ The house of the wicked will be destroyed,
but the tent of the upright will flourish.

¹² There is a way that seems right to a man,
but in the end it leads to death.

¹³ Even in laughter the heart may ache,
and joy may end in grief.

¹⁴ The faithless will be fully repaid for their ways,
and the good man rewarded for his.

¹⁵ A simple man believes anything,
but a prudent man gives thought to his steps.

Answers

to Quizzer on
page 815

**A: She is her
husband's crown;
she makes him
look good**
(Proverbs 12:4).

***BONUS: She
makes him sick.***

¹⁶ A wise man fears the LORD and shuns evil,
    but a fool is hotheaded and reckless.

¹⁷ A quick-tempered man does foolish things,
    and a crafty man is hated.

¹⁸ The simple inherit folly,
    but the prudent are crowned with knowledge.

¹⁹ Evil men will bow down in the presence of the good,
    and the wicked at the gates of the righteous.

²⁰ The poor are shunned even by their neighbors,
    but the rich have many friends.

²¹ He who despises his neighbor sins,
    but blessed is he who is kind to the needy.

²² Do not those who plot evil go astray?
    But those who plan what is good find^a love and faithfulness.

²³ All hard work brings a profit,
    but mere talk leads only to poverty.

²⁴ The wealth of the wise is their crown,
    but the folly of fools yields folly.

²⁵ A truthful witness saves lives,
    but a false witness is deceitful.

²⁶ He who fears the LORD has a secure fortress,
    and for his children it will be a refuge.

²⁷ The fear of the LORD is a fountain of life,
    turning a man from the snares of death.

²⁸ A large population is a king's glory,
    but without subjects a prince is ruined.

²⁹ A patient man has great understanding,
    but a quick-tempered man displays folly.

³⁰ A heart at peace gives life to the body,
    but envy rots the bones.

³¹ He who oppresses the poor shows contempt for their Maker,
    but whoever is kind to the needy honors God.

³² When calamity comes, the wicked are brought down,
    but even in death the righteous have a refuge.

³³ Wisdom reposes in the heart of the discerning
    and even among fools she lets herself be known.^b

³⁴ Righteousness exalts a nation,
    but sin is a disgrace to any people.

³⁵ A king delights in a wise servant,
    but a shameful servant incurs his wrath.

15 A gentle answer turns away wrath,
    but a harsh word stirs up anger.

² The tongue of the wise commends knowledge,
    but the mouth of the fool gushes folly.

^a22 Or *show* ^b33 Hebrew; Septuagint and Syriac / *but in the heart of fools she is not known*

³The eyes of the LORD are everywhere,
  keeping watch on the wicked and the good.

⁴The tongue that brings healing is a tree of life,
  but a deceitful tongue crushes the spirit.

⁵A fool spurns his father's discipline,
  but whoever heeds correction shows prudence.

⁶The house of the righteous contains great treasure,
  but the income of the wicked brings them trouble.

⁷The lips of the wise spread knowledge;
  not so the hearts of fools.

⁸The LORD detests the sacrifice of the wicked,
  but the prayer of the upright pleases him.

⁹The LORD detests the way of the wicked
  but he loves those who pursue righteousness.

¹⁰Stern discipline awaits him who leaves the path;
  he who hates correction will die.

¹¹Death and Destruction*a* lie open before the LORD—
  how much more the hearts of men!

¹²A mocker resents correction;
  he will not consult the wise.

¹³A happy heart makes the face cheerful,
  but heartache crushes the spirit.

¹⁴The discerning heart seeks knowledge,
  but the mouth of a fool feeds on folly.

¹⁵All the days of the oppressed are wretched,
  but the cheerful heart has a continual feast.

¹⁶Better a little with the fear of the LORD
  than great wealth with turmoil.

¹⁷Better a meal of vegetables where there is love
  than a fattened calf with hatred.

¹⁸A hot-tempered man stirs up dissension,
  but a patient man calms a quarrel.

¹⁹The way of the sluggard is blocked with thorns,
  but the path of the upright is a highway.

²⁰A wise son brings joy to his father,
  but a foolish man despises his mother.

²¹Folly delights a man who lacks judgment,
  but a man of understanding keeps a straight course.

²²Plans fail for lack of counsel,
  but with many advisers they succeed.

²³A man finds joy in giving an apt reply—
  and how good is a timely word!

²⁴The path of life leads upward for the wise
  to keep him from going down to the grave.*b*

a11 Hebrew Sheol and Abaddon   *b24 Hebrew* Sheol

²⁵ The LORD tears down the proud man's house
but he keeps the widow's boundaries intact.

²⁶ The LORD detests the thoughts of the wicked,
but those of the pure are pleasing to him.

²⁷ A greedy man brings trouble to his family,
but he who hates bribes will live.

²⁸ The heart of the righteous weighs its answers,
but the mouth of the wicked gushes evil.

²⁹ The LORD is far from the wicked
but he hears the prayer of the righteous.

³⁰ A cheerful look brings joy to the heart,
and good news gives health to the bones.

³¹ He who listens to a life-giving rebuke
will be at home among the wise.

³² He who ignores discipline despises himself,
but whoever heeds correction gains understanding.

³³ The fear of the LORD teaches a man wisdom,ᵃ
and humility comes before honor.

16 To man belong the plans of the heart,
but from the LORD comes the reply of the tongue.

² All a man's ways seem innocent to him,
but motives are weighed by the LORD.

³ Commit to the LORD whatever you do,
and your plans will succeed.

> Commit to the LORD whatever you do, and your plans will succeed (Proverbs 16:3).

⁴ The LORD works out everything for his own ends—
even the wicked for a day of disaster.

⁵ The LORD detests all the proud of heart.
Be sure of this: They will not go unpunished.

⁶ Through love and faithfulness sin is atoned for;
through the fear of the LORD a man avoids evil.

⁷ When a man's ways are pleasing to the LORD,
he makes even his enemies live at peace with him.

⁸ Better a little with righteousness
than much gain with injustice.

⁹ In his heart a man plans his course,
but the LORD determines his steps.

¹⁰ The lips of a king speak as an oracle,
and his mouth should not betray justice.

¹¹ Honest scales and balances are from the LORD;
all the weights in the bag are of his making.

¹² Kings detest wrongdoing,
for a throne is established through righteousness.

¹³ Kings take pleasure in honest lips;
they value a man who speaks the truth.

ᵃ33 Or *Wisdom teaches the fear of the* LORD

¹⁴A king's wrath is a messenger of death,
   but a wise man will appease it.

¹⁵When a king's face brightens, it means life;
   his favor is like a rain cloud in spring.

¹⁶How much better to get wisdom than gold,
   to choose understanding rather than silver!

¹⁷The highway of the upright avoids evil;
   he who guards his way guards his life.

¹⁸Pride goes before destruction,
   a haughty spirit before a fall.

¹⁹Better to be lowly in spirit and among the oppressed
   than to share plunder with the proud.

²⁰Whoever gives heed to instruction prospers,
   and blessed is he who trusts in the LORD.

²¹The wise in heart are called discerning,
   and pleasant words promote instruction.ᵃ

²²Understanding is a fountain of life to those who have it,
   but folly brings punishment to fools.

²³A wise man's heart guides his mouth,
   and his lips promote instruction.ᵇ

²⁴Pleasant words are a honeycomb,
   sweet to the soul and healing to the bones.

²⁵There is a way that seems right to a man,
   but in the end it leads to death.

²⁶The laborer's appetite works for him;
   his hunger drives him on.

²⁷A scoundrel plots evil,
   and his speech is like a scorching fire.

²⁸A perverse man stirs up dissension,
   and a gossip separates close friends.

²⁹A violent man entices his neighbor
   and leads him down a path that is not good.

³⁰He who winks with his eye is plotting perversity;
   he who purses his lips is bent on evil.

³¹Gray hair is a crown of splendor;
   it is attained by a righteous life.

³²Better a patient man than a warrior,
   a man who controls his temper than one who takes a city.

³³The lot is cast into the lap,
   but its every decision is from the LORD.

17 Better a dry crust with peace and quiet
   than a house full of feasting,ᶜ with strife.

²A wise servant will rule over a disgraceful son,
   and will share the inheritance as one of the brothers.

ᵃ21 Or *words make a man persuasive*   ᵇ23 Or *mouth / and makes his lips persuasive*   ᶜ1 Hebrew *sacrifices*

³The crucible for silver and the furnace for gold,
   but the Lord tests the heart.

⁴A wicked man listens to evil lips;
   a liar pays attention to a malicious tongue.

⁵He who mocks the poor shows contempt for their Maker;
   whoever gloats over disaster will not go unpunished.

⁶Children's children are a crown to the aged,
   and parents are the pride of their children.

⁷Arrogant*a* lips are unsuited to a fool—
   how much worse lying lips to a ruler!

⁸A bribe is a charm to the one who gives it;
   wherever he turns, he succeeds.

⁹He who covers over an offense promotes love,
   but whoever repeats the matter separates close friends.

¹⁰A rebuke impresses a man of discernment
   more than a hundred lashes a fool.

¹¹An evil man is bent only on rebellion;
   a merciless official will be sent against him.

¹²Better to meet a bear robbed of her cubs
   than a fool in his folly.

¹³If a man pays back evil for good,
   evil will never leave his house.

¹⁴Starting a quarrel is like breaching a dam;
   so drop the matter before a dispute breaks out.

¹⁵Acquitting the guilty and condemning the innocent—
   the Lord detests them both.

¹⁶Of what use is money in the hand of a fool,
   since he has no desire to get wisdom?

¹⁷A friend loves at all times,
   and a brother is born for adversity.

¹⁸A man lacking in judgment strikes hands in pledge
   and puts up security for his neighbor.

¹⁹He who loves a quarrel loves sin;
   he who builds a high gate invites destruction.

²⁰A man of perverse heart does not prosper;
   he whose tongue is deceitful falls into trouble.

²¹To have a fool for a son brings grief;
   there is no joy for the father of a fool.

²²A cheerful heart is good medicine,
   but a crushed spirit dries up the bones.

²³A wicked man accepts a bribe in secret
   to pervert the course of justice.

²⁴A discerning man keeps wisdom in view,
   but a fool's eyes wander to the ends of the earth.

A cheerful heart
is good medicine
(Proverbs 17:22).

a7 Or Eloquent

²⁵ A foolish son brings grief to his father
  and bitterness to the one who bore him.

²⁶ It is not good to punish an innocent man,
  or to flog officials for their integrity.

²⁷ A man of knowledge uses words with restraint,
  and a man of understanding is even-tempered.

²⁸ Even a fool is thought wise if he keeps silent,
  and discerning if he holds his tongue.

18 An unfriendly man pursues selfish ends;
  he defies all sound judgment.

² A fool finds no pleasure in understanding
  but delights in airing his own opinions.

³ When wickedness comes, so does contempt,
  and with shame comes disgrace.

⁴ The words of a man's mouth are deep waters,
  but the fountain of wisdom is a bubbling brook.

⁵ It is not good to be partial to the wicked
  or to deprive the innocent of justice.

⁶ A fool's lips bring him strife,
  and his mouth invites a beating.

⁷ A fool's mouth is his undoing,
  and his lips are a snare to his soul.

⁸ The words of a gossip are like choice morsels;
  they go down to a man's inmost parts.

⁹ One who is slack in his work
  is brother to one who destroys.

¹⁰ The name of the Lord is a strong tower;
  the righteous run to it and are safe.

¹¹ The wealth of the rich is their fortified city;
  they imagine it an unscalable wall.

¹² Before his downfall a man's heart is proud,
  but humility comes before honor.

¹³ He who answers before listening—
  that is his folly and his shame.

¹⁴ A man's spirit sustains him in sickness,
  but a crushed spirit who can bear?

¹⁵ The heart of the discerning acquires knowledge;
  the ears of the wise seek it out.

¹⁶ A gift opens the way for the giver
  and ushers him into the presence of the great.

¹⁷ The first to present his case seems right,
  till another comes forward and questions him.

¹⁸ Casting the lot settles disputes
  and keeps strong opponents apart.

¹⁹ An offended brother is more unyielding than a fortified city,
  and disputes are like the barred gates of a citadel.

²⁰From the fruit of his mouth a man's stomach is filled;
   with the harvest from his lips he is satisfied.

²¹The tongue has the power of life and death,
   and those who love it will eat its fruit.

²²He who finds a wife finds what is good
   and receives favor from the Lord.

²³A poor man pleads for mercy,
   but a rich man answers harshly.

²⁴A man of many companions may come to ruin,
   but there is a friend who sticks closer than a brother.

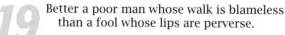

Better a poor man whose walk is blameless
   than a fool whose lips are perverse.

²It is not good to have zeal without knowledge,
   nor to be hasty and miss the way.

³A man's own folly ruins his life,
   yet his heart rages against the Lord.

⁴Wealth brings many friends,
   but a poor man's friend deserts him.

⁵A false witness will not go unpunished,
   and he who pours out lies will not go free.

⁶Many curry favor with a ruler,
   and everyone is the friend of a man who gives gifts.

⁷A poor man is shunned by all his relatives—
   how much more do his friends avoid him!
Though he pursues them with pleading,
   they are nowhere to be found.^a

⁸He who gets wisdom loves his own soul;
   he who cherishes understanding prospers.

⁹A false witness will not go unpunished,
   and he who pours out lies will perish.

¹⁰It is not fitting for a fool to live in luxury—
   how much worse for a slave to rule over princes!

¹¹A man's wisdom gives him patience;
   it is to his glory to overlook an offense.

¹²A king's rage is like the roar of a lion,
   but his favor is like dew on the grass.

¹³A foolish son is his father's ruin,
   and a quarrelsome wife is like a constant dripping.

¹⁴Houses and wealth are inherited from parents,
   but a prudent wife is from the Lord.

¹⁵Laziness brings on deep sleep,
   and the shiftless man goes hungry.

¹⁶He who obeys instructions guards his life,
   but he who is contemptuous of his ways will die.

^a7 The meaning of the Hebrew for this sentence is uncertain.

¹⁷He who is kind to the poor lends to the LORD,
  and he will reward him for what he has done.

¹⁸Discipline your son, for in that there is hope;
  do not be a willing party to his death.

¹⁹A hot-tempered man must pay the penalty;
  if you rescue him, you will have to do it again.

²⁰Listen to advice and accept instruction,
  and in the end you will be wise.

²¹Many are the plans in a man's heart,
  but it is the LORD's purpose that prevails.

²²What a man desires is unfailing love*;
  better to be poor than a liar.

²³The fear of the LORD leads to life:
  Then one rests content, untouched by trouble.

²⁴The sluggard buries his hand in the dish;
  he will not even bring it back to his mouth!

²⁵Flog a mocker, and the simple will learn prudence;
  rebuke a discerning man, and he will gain knowledge.

²⁶He who robs his father and drives out his mother
  is a son who brings shame and disgrace.

²⁷Stop listening to instruction, my son,
  and you will stray from the words of knowledge.

²⁸A corrupt witness mocks at justice,
  and the mouth of the wicked gulps down evil.

²⁹Penalties are prepared for mockers,
  and beatings for the backs of fools.

20 Wine is a mocker and beer a brawler;
  whoever is led astray by them is not wise.

²A king's wrath is like the roar of a lion;
  he who angers him forfeits his life.

³It is to a man's honor to avoid strife,
  but every fool is quick to quarrel.

⁴A sluggard does not plow in season;
  so at harvest time he
    looks but finds
    nothing.

⁵The purposes of a man's
    heart are deep
    waters,
  but a man of
    understanding
    draws them out.

⁶Many a man claims to
    have unfailing love,
  but a faithful man who
    can find?

SEE
PROVERBS 19:15

*22 Or *A man's greed is his shame*

Dear Sam,

My boyfriend usually offers me a glass of wine when we go out. He says drinking is okay as long as we don't get drunk. What do you think?

Wendy in Winnipeg

100 Advice Lane, Anywhere, USA

Dear Wendy,

The Bible certainly says drunkenness is wrong (Galatians 5:19-21). But it also has other warnings about alcohol. Proverbs 20:1 says, "Wine is a mocker and beer a brawler; whoever is led astray by them is not wise."

To understand that verse you have to understand how alcohol works. Alcohol affects the part of your brain that inhibits or stops you from getting involved in behaviors that you know are wrong and that you wouldn't be involved in otherwise. And that's where the danger lies. You don't have to be drunk to lose your inhibitions. In fact, sometimes just a little alcohol is all it takes. When inhibitions are numbed away, many people become sexually active, only to regret it the next day. Your virginity can only be given once; it cannot be restored.

Of course, let's not forget that drinking if you're a teen is against the law as well. Just as you have to wait to drive a car or vote, you must be a certain age to drink legally. And even then, you may choose not to drink.

My advice is to tell your boyfriend you don't want to drink alcohol. If he really cares about you, he won't try to get you to do something you don't want to do.

Sam

⁷The righteous man leads a blameless life;
  blessed are his children after him.

⁸When a king sits on his throne to judge,
  he winnows out all evil with his eyes.

⁹Who can say, "I have kept my heart pure;
  I am clean and without sin"?

¹⁰Differing weights and differing measures—
  the LORD detests them both.

¹¹Even a child is known by his actions,
  by whether his conduct is pure and right.

¹²Ears that hear and eyes that see—
  the LORD has made them both.

¹³Do not love sleep or you will grow poor;
  stay awake and you will have food to spare.

¹⁴"It's no good, it's no good!" says the buyer;
  then off he goes and boasts about his
    purchase.

¹⁵Gold there is, and rubies in abundance,
  but lips that speak knowledge are a
    rare jewel.

¹⁶Take the garment of one who puts up
    security for a stranger;
  hold it in pledge if he does it for a wayward
    woman.

¹⁷Food gained by fraud tastes sweet to a man,
  but he ends up with a mouth full of gravel.

¹⁸Make plans by seeking advice;
  if you wage war, obtain guidance.

¹⁹A gossip betrays a confidence;
  so avoid a man who talks too much.

²⁰If a man curses his father or mother,
  his lamp will be snuffed out in pitch darkness.

²¹An inheritance quickly gained at the beginning
  will not be blessed at the end.

²²Do not say, "I'll pay you back for this wrong!"
  Wait for the LORD, and he will deliver you.

²³The LORD detests differing weights,
  and dishonest scales do not please him.

²⁴A man's steps are directed by the LORD.
  How then can anyone understand his own
    way?

²⁵It is a trap for a man to dedicate something rashly
  and only later to consider his vows.

²⁶A wise king winnows out the wicked;
  he drives the threshing wheel over them.

PROVERBS 20

QUIZZER

Q: What kind
of person
is it good to
avoid?

BONUS:
What does
a gossip do
with the
secret you
told him
or her?

Answers on
page 829

²⁷The lamp of the L<small>ORD</small> searches the spirit of a man^a;
    it searches out his inmost being.

²⁸Love and faithfulness keep a king safe;
    through love his throne is made secure.

²⁹The glory of young men is their strength,
    gray hair the splendor of the old.

³⁰Blows and wounds cleanse away evil,
    and beatings purge the inmost being.

21 The king's heart is in the hand of the L<small>ORD</small>;
    he directs it like a watercourse wherever he pleases.

²All a man's ways seem right to him,
    but the L<small>ORD</small> weighs the heart.

³To do what is right and just
    is more acceptable to the L<small>ORD</small> than sacrifice.

⁴Haughty eyes and a proud heart,
    the lamp of the wicked, are sin!

⁵The plans of the diligent lead to profit
    as surely as haste leads to poverty.

⁶A fortune made by a lying tongue
    is a fleeting vapor and a deadly snare.^b

⁷The violence of the wicked will drag them away,
    for they refuse to do what is right.

⁸The way of the guilty is devious,
    but the conduct of the innocent is upright.

⁹Better to live on a corner of the roof
    than share a house with a quarrelsome wife.

¹⁰The wicked man craves evil;
    his neighbor gets no mercy from him.

¹¹When a mocker is punished, the simple gain wisdom;
    when a wise man is instructed, he gets knowledge.

¹²The Righteous One^c takes note of the house of the wicked
    and brings the wicked to ruin.

¹³If a man shuts his ears to the cry of the poor,
    he too will cry out and not be answered.

¹⁴A gift given in secret soothes anger,
    and a bribe concealed in the cloak pacifies great wrath.

¹⁵When justice is done, it brings joy to the righteous
    but terror to evildoers.

¹⁶A man who strays from the path of understanding
    comes to rest in the company of the dead.

¹⁷He who loves pleasure will become poor;
    whoever loves wine and oil will never be rich.

¹⁸The wicked become a ransom for the righteous,
    and the unfaithful for the upright.

---

^a27 Or *The spirit of man is the L*<small>ORD</small>*'s lamp* ^b6 Some Hebrew manuscripts, Septuagint and Vulgate; most Hebrew manuscripts *vapor for those who seek death* ^c12 Or *The righteous man*

¹⁹ Better to live in a desert
    than with a quarrelsome and ill-tempered wife.

²⁰ In the house of the wise are stores of choice food and oil,
    but a foolish man devours all he has.

²¹ He who pursues righteousness and love
    finds life, prosperity*ᵃ* and honor.

²² A wise man attacks the city of the mighty
    and pulls down the stronghold in which they trust.

²³ He who guards his mouth and his tongue
    keeps himself from calamity.

²⁴ The proud and arrogant man—"Mocker" is his name;
    he behaves with overweening pride.

²⁵ The sluggard's craving will be the death of him,
    because his hands refuse to work.
²⁶ All day long he craves for more,
    but the righteous give without sparing.

²⁷ The sacrifice of the wicked is detestable—
    how much more so when brought with evil intent!

²⁸ A false witness will perish,
    and whoever listens to him will be destroyed forever.*ᵇ*

²⁹ A wicked man puts up a bold front,
    but an upright man gives thought to his ways.

³⁰ There is no wisdom, no insight, no plan
    that can succeed against the LORD.

³¹ The horse is made ready for the day of battle,
    but victory rests with the LORD.

22 A good name is more desirable than great riches;
    to be esteemed is better than silver or gold.

² Rich and poor have this in common:
    The LORD is the Maker of them all.

³ A prudent man sees danger and takes refuge,
    but the simple keep going and suffer for it.

⁴ Humility and the fear of the LORD
    bring wealth and honor and life.

⁵ In the paths of the wicked lie thorns and snares,
    but he who guards his soul stays far from them.

⁶ Train*ᶜ* a child in the way he should go,
    and when he is old he will not turn from it.

⁷ The rich rule over the poor,
    and the borrower is servant to the lender.

⁸ He who sows wickedness reaps trouble,
    and the rod of his fury will be destroyed.

⁹ A generous man will himself be blessed,
    for he shares his food with the poor.

Answers
to Quizzer on
page 827

**A: A person who
talks too much
(Proverbs 20:19).**

**BONUS: He or
she "betrays a
confidence" and
shares your
secret with
someone else.**

---

*ᵃ21 Or righteousness   *ᵇ28 Or / but the words of an obedient man will live on   *ᶜ6 Or Start

¹⁰Drive out the mocker, and out goes strife;
  quarrels and insults are ended.

¹¹He who loves a pure heart and whose speech is gracious
  will have the king for his friend.

¹²The eyes of the LORD keep watch over knowledge,
  but he frustrates the words of the unfaithful.

¹³The sluggard says, "There is a lion outside!"
  or, "I will be murdered in the streets!"

¹⁴The mouth of an adulteress is a deep pit;
  he who is under the LORD's wrath will fall into it.

¹⁵Folly is bound up in the heart of a child,
  but the rod of discipline will drive it far from him.

¹⁶He who oppresses the poor to increase his wealth
  and he who gives gifts to the rich—both come to poverty.

Sayings of the Wise

¹⁷Pay attention and listen to the sayings of the wise;
  apply your heart to what I teach,
¹⁸for it is pleasing when you keep them in your heart
  and have all of them ready on your lips.
¹⁹So that your trust may be in the LORD,
  I teach you today, even you.
²⁰Have I not written thirty[a] sayings for you,
  sayings of counsel and knowledge,
²¹teaching you true and reliable words,
  so that you can give sound answers
  to him who sent you?

²²Do not exploit the poor because they are poor
  and do not crush the needy in court,
²³for the LORD will take up their case
  and will plunder those who plunder them.

²⁴Do not make friends with a hot-tempered man,
  do not associate with one easily angered,
²⁵or you may learn his ways
  and get yourself ensnared.

²⁶Do not be a man who strikes hands in pledge
  or puts up security for debts;
²⁷if you lack the means to pay,
  your very bed will be snatched from under you.

²⁸Do not move an ancient boundary stone
  set up by your forefathers.

²⁹Do you see a man skilled in his work?
  He will serve before kings;
  he will not serve before obscure men.

23 When you sit to dine with a ruler,
  note well what[b] is before you,
  ²and put a knife to your throat
  if you are given to gluttony.

---

[a]20 Or *not formerly written;* or *not written excellent* [b]1 Or *who*

³Do not crave his delicacies,
 for that food is deceptive.

⁴Do not wear yourself out to get rich;
 have the wisdom to show restraint.
⁵Cast but a glance at riches, and they are gone,
 for they will surely sprout wings
 and fly off to the sky like an eagle.

⁶Do not eat the food of a stingy man,
 do not crave his delicacies;
⁷for he is the kind of man
 who is always thinking about the cost.^a
"Eat and drink," he says to you,
 but his heart is not with you.
⁸You will vomit up the little you have eaten
 and will have wasted your compliments.

⁹Do not speak to a fool,
 for he will scorn the wisdom of your words.

¹⁰Do not move an ancient boundary stone
 or encroach on the fields of the fatherless,
¹¹for their Defender is strong;
 he will take up their case against you.

¹²Apply your heart to instruction
 and your ears to words of knowledge.

¹³Do not withhold discipline from a child;
 if you punish him with the rod, he will not die.
¹⁴Punish him with the rod
 and save his soul from death.^b

¹⁵My son, if your heart is wise,
 then my heart will be glad;
¹⁶my inmost being will rejoice
 when your lips speak what is right.

¹⁷Do not let your heart envy sinners,
 but always be zealous for the fear of the LORD.
¹⁸There is surely a future hope for you,
 and your hope will not be cut off.

¹⁹Listen, my son, and be wise,
 and keep your heart on the right path.
²⁰Do not join those who drink too much wine
 or gorge themselves on meat,
²¹for drunkards and gluttons become poor,
 and drowsiness clothes them in rags.

²²Listen to your father, who gave you life,
 and do not despise your mother when she is old.
²³Buy the truth and do not sell it;
 get wisdom, discipline and understanding.
²⁴The father of a righteous man has great joy;
 he who has a wise son delights in him.
²⁵May your father and mother be glad;
 may she who gave you birth rejoice!

---

^a7 Or for as he thinks within himself, / so he is; or for as he puts on a feast, / so he is *^b14 Hebrew Sheol*

²⁶My son, give me your heart
  and let your eyes keep to my ways,
²⁷for a prostitute is a deep pit
  and a wayward wife is a narrow well.
²⁸Like a bandit she lies in wait,
  and multiplies the unfaithful among men.

²⁹Who has woe? Who has sorrow?
  Who has strife? Who has complaints?
  Who has needless bruises? Who has bloodshot eyes?
³⁰Those who linger over wine,
  who go to sample bowls of mixed wine.
³¹Do not gaze at wine when it is red,
  when it sparkles in the cup,
  when it goes down smoothly!
³²In the end it bites like a snake
  and poisons like a viper.
³³Your eyes will see strange sights
  and your mind imagine confusing things.
³⁴You will be like one sleeping on the high seas,
  lying on top of the rigging.
³⁵"They hit me," you will say, "but I'm not hurt!
  They beat me, but I don't feel it!
  When will I wake up
  so I can find another drink?"

24 Do not envy wicked men,
  do not desire their company;
²for their hearts plot violence,
  and their lips talk about making trouble.

³By wisdom a house is built,
  and through understanding it is established;
⁴through knowledge its rooms are filled
  with rare and beautiful treasures.

⁵A wise man has great power,
  and a man of knowledge increases strength;
⁶for waging war you need guidance,
  and for victory many advisers.

⁷Wisdom is too high for a fool;
  in the assembly at the gate he has nothing to say.

⁸He who plots evil
  will be known as a schemer.
⁹The schemes of folly are sin,
  and men detest a mocker.

¹⁰If you falter in times of trouble,
  how small is your strength!

¹¹Rescue those being led away to death;
  hold back those staggering toward slaughter.
¹²If you say, "But we knew nothing about this,"
  does not he who weighs the heart perceive it?
  Does not he who guards your life know it?
  Will he not repay each person according to what he has
    done?

¹³Eat honey, my son, for it is good;
    honey from the comb is sweet to your taste.
¹⁴Know also that wisdom is sweet to your soul;
    if you find it, there is a future hope for you,
    and your hope will not be cut off.

¹⁵Do not lie in wait like an outlaw against a righteous man's
        house,
    do not raid his dwelling place;
¹⁶for though a righteous man falls seven times, he rises again,
    but the wicked are brought down by calamity.

¹⁷Do not gloat when your enemy falls;
    when he stumbles, do not let your heart rejoice,
¹⁸or the Lord will see and disapprove
    and turn his wrath away from him.

¹⁹Do not fret because of evil men
    or be envious of the wicked,
²⁰for the evil man has no future hope,
    and the lamp of the wicked will be snuffed out.

²¹Fear the Lord and the king, my son,
    and do not join with the rebellious,
²²for those two will send sudden destruction upon them,
    and who knows what calamities they can bring?

Further Sayings of the Wise

²³These also are sayings of the wise:

    To show partiality in judging is not good:
²⁴Whoever says to the guilty, "You are innocent"—
    peoples will curse him and nations denounce him.
²⁵But it will go well with those who convict the guilty,
    and rich blessing will come upon them.

²⁶An honest answer
    is like a kiss on the lips.

²⁷Finish your outdoor work
    and get your fields ready;
    after that, build your house.

²⁸Do not testify against your neighbor without cause,
    or use your lips to deceive.
²⁹Do not say, "I'll do to him as he has done to me;
    I'll pay that man back for what he did."

³⁰I went past the field of the sluggard,
    past the vineyard of the man who lacks judgment;
³¹thorns had come up everywhere,
    the ground was covered with weeds,
    and the stone wall was in ruins.
³²I applied my heart to what I observed
    and learned a lesson from what I saw:
³³A little sleep, a little slumber,
    a little folding of the hands to rest—
³⁴and poverty will come on you like a bandit
    and scarcity like an armed man.^a

An honest
answer is like a
kiss on the lips
(Proverbs 24:26).

^a34 Or like a vagrant / and scarcity like a beggar

25 These are more proverbs of Solomon, copied by the men of Hezekiah king of Judah:

²It is the glory of God to conceal a matter;
   to search out a matter is the glory of kings.

³As the heavens are high and the earth is deep,
   so the hearts of kings are unsearchable.

⁴Remove the dross from the silver,
   and out comes material for*a* the silversmith;
⁵remove the wicked from the king's presence,
   and his throne will be established through righteousness.

⁶Do not exalt yourself in the king's presence,
   and do not claim a place among great men;
⁷it is better for him to say to you, "Come up here,"
   than for him to humiliate you before a nobleman.

 What you have seen with your eyes
⁸ do not bring*b* hastily to court,
 for what will you do in the end
   if your neighbor puts you to shame?

⁹If you argue your case with a neighbor,
   do not betray another man's confidence,
¹⁰or he who hears it may shame you
   and you will never lose your bad reputation.

¹¹A word aptly spoken
   is like apples of gold in settings of silver.

¹²Like an earring of gold or an ornament of fine gold
   is a wise man's rebuke to a listening ear.

¹³Like the coolness of snow at harvest time
   is a trustworthy messenger to those who send him;
   he refreshes the spirit of his masters.

¹⁴Like clouds and wind without rain
   is a man who boasts of gifts he does not give.

¹⁵Through patience a ruler can be persuaded,
   and a gentle tongue can break a bone.

¹⁶If you find honey, eat just enough—
   too much of it, and you will vomit.
¹⁷Seldom set foot in your neighbor's house—
   too much of you, and he will hate you.

¹⁸Like a club or a sword or a sharp arrow
   is the man who gives false testimony against his
      neighbor.

¹⁹Like a bad tooth or a lame foot
   is reliance on the unfaithful in times of trouble.

²⁰Like one who takes away a garment on a cold day,
   or like vinegar poured on soda,
   is one who sings songs to a heavy heart.

---

*a*4 Or *comes a vessel from*   *b*7,8 Or *nobleman / on whom you had set your eyes. / ⁸Do not go*

²¹If your enemy is hungry, give him food to eat;
    if he is thirsty, give him water to drink.
²²In doing this, you will heap burning coals on his head,
    and the LORD will reward you.

²³As a north wind brings rain,
    so a sly tongue brings angry looks.

²⁴Better to live on a corner of the roof
    than share a house with a quarrelsome wife.

²⁵Like cold water to a weary soul
    is good news from a distant land.

²⁶Like a muddied spring or a polluted well
    is a righteous man who gives way to the wicked.

²⁷It is not good to eat too much honey,
    nor is it honorable to seek one's own honor.

²⁸Like a city whose walls are broken down
    is a man who lacks self-control.

26 Like snow in summer or rain in harvest,
    honor is not fitting for a fool.
²Like a fluttering sparrow or a darting swallow,
    an undeserved curse does not come to rest.

³A whip for the horse, a halter for the donkey,
    and a rod for the backs of fools!

⁴Do not answer a fool according to his folly,
    or you will be like him yourself.

⁵Answer a fool according to his folly,
    or he will be wise in his own eyes.

⁶Like cutting off one's feet or drinking violence
    is the sending of a message by the hand of a fool.

⁷Like a lame man's legs that hang limp
    is a proverb in the mouth of a fool.

⁸Like tying a stone in a sling
    is the giving of honor to a fool.

⁹Like a thornbush in a drunkard's hand
    is a proverb in the mouth of a fool.

¹⁰Like an archer who wounds at random
    is he who hires a fool or any passer-by.

¹¹As a dog returns to its vomit,
    so a fool repeats his folly.

¹²Do you see a man wise in his own eyes?
    There is more hope for a fool than for him.

¹³The sluggard says, "There is a lion in the road,
    a fierce lion roaming the streets!"

¹⁴As a door turns on its hinges,
    so a sluggard turns on his bed.

¹⁵The sluggard buries his hand in the dish;
    he is too lazy to bring it back to his mouth.

¹⁶The sluggard is wiser in his own eyes
    than seven men who answer discreetly.

¹⁷Like one who seizes a dog by the ears
    is a passer-by who meddles in a quarrel not his own.

¹⁸Like a madman shooting
    firebrands or deadly arrows
¹⁹is a man who deceives his neighbor
    and says, "I was only joking!"

²⁰Without wood a fire goes out;
    without gossip a quarrel dies down.

²¹As charcoal to embers and as wood to fire,
    so is a quarrelsome man for kindling strife.

²²The words of a gossip are like choice morsels;
    they go down to a man's inmost parts.

²³Like a coating of glaze^a over earthenware
    are fervent lips with an evil heart.

²⁴A malicious man disguises himself with his lips,
    but in his heart he harbors deceit.
²⁵Though his speech is charming, do not believe him,
    for seven abominations fill his heart.
²⁶His malice may be concealed by deception,
    but his wickedness will be exposed in the assembly.

²⁷If a man digs a pit, he will fall into it;
    if a man rolls a stone, it will roll back on him.

²⁸A lying tongue hates those it hurts,
    and a flattering mouth works ruin.

27

Do not boast about tomorrow,
    for you do not know what a day may bring forth.

²Let another praise you, and not your own mouth;
    someone else, and not your own lips.

³Stone is heavy and sand a burden,
    but provocation by a fool is heavier than both.

⁴Anger is cruel and fury overwhelming,
    but who can stand before jealousy?

⁵Better is open rebuke
    than hidden love.

⁶Wounds from a friend can be trusted,
    but an enemy multiplies kisses.

⁷He who is full loathes honey,
    but to the hungry even what is bitter tastes sweet.

⁸Like a bird that strays from its nest
    is a man who strays from his home.

⁹Perfume and incense bring joy to the heart,
    and the pleasantness of one's friend springs from his
        earnest counsel.

---

^a23 With a different word division of the Hebrew; Masoretic Text *of silver dross*

¹⁰Do not forsake your friend and the friend of your father,
  and do not go to your brother's house when disaster strikes
    you—
  better a neighbor nearby than a brother far away.

¹¹Be wise, my son, and bring joy to my heart;
  then I can answer anyone who treats me with contempt.

¹²The prudent see danger and take refuge,
  but the simple keep going and suffer for it.

¹³Take the garment of one who puts up security for a stranger;
  hold it in pledge if he does it for a wayward woman.

¹⁴If a man loudly blesses his neighbor early in the morning,
  it will be taken as a curse.

¹⁵A quarrelsome wife is like
  a constant dripping on a rainy day;
¹⁶restraining her is like restraining the wind
  or grasping oil with the hand.

¹⁷As iron sharpens iron,
  so one man sharpens another.

¹⁸He who tends a fig tree will eat its fruit,
  and he who looks after his master will be honored.

¹⁹As water reflects a face,
  so a man's heart reflects the man.

²⁰Death and Destruction[a] are never satisfied,
  and neither are the eyes of man.

²¹The crucible for silver and the furnace for gold,
  but man is tested by the praise he receives.

²²Though you grind a fool in a mortar,
  grinding him like grain with a pestle,
  you will not remove his
    folly from him.

²³Be sure you know the
    condition of your
    flocks,
  give careful attention to
    your herds;
²⁴for riches do not endure
    forever,
  and a crown is not
    secure for all
    generations.
²⁵When the hay is removed
    and new growth
    appears
  and the grass from the
    hills is gathered in,
²⁶the lambs will provide you
    with clothing,
  and the goats with the
    price of a field.

Hey, handsome!

SEE
PROVERBS 27:19

[a]20 Hebrew *Sheol and Abaddon*

²⁷You will have plenty of goats' milk
   to feed you and your family
   and to nourish your servant girls.

28 The wicked man flees though no one pursues,
   but the righteous are as bold as a lion.

²When a country is rebellious, it has many rulers,
   but a man of understanding and knowledge maintains
     order.

³A ruler^a who oppresses the poor
   is like a driving rain that leaves no crops.

⁴Those who forsake the law praise the wicked,
   but those who keep the law resist them.

⁵Evil men do not understand justice,
   but those who seek the LORD understand it fully.

⁶Better a poor man whose walk is blameless
   than a rich man whose ways are perverse.

⁷He who keeps the law is a discerning son,
   but a companion of gluttons disgraces his father.

⁸He who increases his wealth by exorbitant interest
   amasses it for another, who will be kind to the poor.

⁹If anyone turns a deaf ear to the law,
   even his prayers are detestable.

¹⁰He who leads the upright along an evil path
   will fall into his own trap,
   but the blameless will receive a good inheritance.

¹¹A rich man may be wise in his own eyes,
   but a poor man who has discernment sees through him.

¹²When the righteous triumph, there is great elation;
   but when the wicked rise to power, men go into hiding.

¹³He who conceals his sins does not prosper,
   but whoever confesses and renounces them finds mercy.

¹⁴Blessed is the man who always fears the LORD,
   but he who hardens his heart falls into trouble.

¹⁵Like a roaring lion or a charging bear
   is a wicked man ruling over a helpless people.

¹⁶A tyrannical ruler lacks judgment,
   but he who hates ill-gotten gain will enjoy a long life.

¹⁷A man tormented by the guilt of murder
   will be a fugitive till death;
   let no one support him.

¹⁸He whose walk is blameless is kept safe,
   but he whose ways are perverse will suddenly fall.

¹⁹He who works his land will have abundant food,
   but the one who chases fantasies will have his fill of
     poverty.

^a3 Or *A poor man*

²⁰ A faithful man will be richly blessed,
   but one eager to get rich will not go unpunished.

²¹ To show partiality is not good—
   yet a man will do wrong for a piece of bread.

²² A stingy man is eager to get rich
   and is unaware that poverty awaits him.

²³ He who rebukes a man will in the end gain more favor
   than he who has a flattering tongue.

²⁴ He who robs his father or mother
   and says, "It's not wrong"—
   he is partner to him who destroys.

²⁵ A greedy man stirs up dissension,
   but he who trusts in the Lord will prosper.

²⁶ He who trusts in himself is a fool,
   but he who walks in wisdom is kept safe.

²⁷ He who gives to the poor will lack nothing,
   but he who closes his eyes to them receives many curses.

²⁸ When the wicked rise to power, people go into hiding;
   but when the wicked perish, the righteous thrive.

> A faithful man will be richly blessed (Proverbs 28:20).

29 A man who remains stiff-necked after many rebukes
   will suddenly be destroyed—without remedy.

² When the righteous thrive, the people rejoice;
   when the wicked rule, the people groan.

³ A man who loves wisdom brings joy to his father,
   but a companion of prostitutes squanders his wealth.

⁴ By justice a king gives a country stability,
   but one who is greedy for bribes tears it down.

⁵ Whoever flatters his neighbor
   is spreading a net for his feet.

⁶ An evil man is snared by his own sin,
   but a righteous one can sing and be glad.

⁷ The righteous care about justice for the poor,
   but the wicked have no such concern.

⁸ Mockers stir up a city,
   but wise men turn away anger.

⁹ If a wise man goes to court with a fool,
   the fool rages and scoffs, and there is no peace.

¹⁰ Bloodthirsty men hate a man of integrity
   and seek to kill the upright.

¹¹ A fool gives full vent to his anger,
   but a wise man keeps himself under control.

¹² If a ruler listens to lies,
   all his officials become wicked.

¹³ The poor man and the oppressor have this in common:
   The Lord gives sight to the eyes of both.

¹⁴If a king judges the poor with fairness,
  his throne will always be secure.

¹⁵The rod of correction imparts wisdom,
  but a child left to himself disgraces his mother.

¹⁶When the wicked thrive, so does sin,
  but the righteous will see their downfall.

¹⁷Discipline your son, and he will give you peace;
  he will bring delight to your soul.

¹⁸Where there is no revelation, the people cast off restraint;
  but blessed is he who keeps the law.

¹⁹A servant cannot be corrected by mere words;
  though he understands, he will not respond.

²⁰Do you see a man who speaks in haste?
  There is more hope for a fool than for him.

²¹If a man pampers his servant from youth,
  he will bring grief*ᵃ* in the end.

²²An angry man stirs up dissension,
  and a hot-tempered one commits many sins.

²³A man's pride brings him low,
  but a man of lowly spirit gains honor.

²⁴The accomplice of a thief is his own enemy;
  he is put under oath and dare not testify.

²⁵Fear of man will prove to be a snare,
  but whoever trusts in the Lᴏʀᴅ is kept safe.

²⁶Many seek an audience with a ruler,
  but it is from the Lᴏʀᴅ that man gets justice.

²⁷The righteous detest the dishonest;
  the wicked detest the upright.

Sayings of Agur

30 The sayings of Agur son of Jakeh—an oracle*ᵇ*:

This man declared to Ithiel,
  to Ithiel and to Ucal:*ᶜ*

²"I am the most ignorant of men;
  I do not have a man's understanding.
³I have not learned wisdom,
  nor have I knowledge of the Holy One.
⁴Who has gone up to heaven and come down?
  Who has gathered up the wind in the hollow of his
    hands?
Who has wrapped up the waters in his cloak?
  Who has established all the ends of the earth?
What is his name, and the name of his son?
  Tell me if you know!

ᵃ21 The meaning of the Hebrew for this word is uncertain.   *ᵇ1* Or *Jakeh of Massa*   *ᶜ1* Masoretic Text; with
a different word division of the Hebrew *declared, "I am weary, O God; / I am weary, O God, and faint.*

⁵ "Every word of God is flawless;
   he is a shield to those who take refuge in him.
⁶ Do not add to his words,
   or he will rebuke you and prove you a liar.

⁷ "Two things I ask of you, O Lord;
   do not refuse me before I die:
⁸ Keep falsehood and lies far from me;
   give me neither poverty nor riches,
   but give me only my daily bread.
⁹ Otherwise, I may have too much and disown you
   and say, 'Who is the Lord?'
 Or I may become poor and steal,
   and so dishonor the name of my God.

¹⁰ "Do not slander a servant to his master,
   or he will curse you, and you will pay for it.

¹¹ "There are those who curse their fathers
   and do not bless their mothers;
¹² those who are pure in their own eyes
   and yet are not cleansed of their filth;
¹³ those whose eyes are ever so haughty,
   whose glances are so disdainful;
¹⁴ those whose teeth are swords
   and whose jaws are set with knives
 to devour the poor from the earth,
   the needy from among mankind.

¹⁵ "The leech has two daughters.
   'Give! Give!' they cry.

 "There are three things that are never satisfied,
   four that never say, 'Enough!':
¹⁶ the grave,ᵃ the barren womb,
   land, which is never satisfied with water,
   and fire, which never says, 'Enough!'

¹⁷ "The eye that mocks a father,
   that scorns obedience to a mother,
 will be pecked out by the ravens of the valley,
   will be eaten by the vultures.

¹⁸ "There are three things that are too amazing for me,
   four that I do not understand:
¹⁹ the way of an eagle in the sky,
   the way of a snake on a rock,
 the way of a ship on the high seas,
   and the way of a man with a maiden.

²⁰ "This is the way of an adulteress:
   She eats and wipes her mouth
   and says, 'I've done nothing wrong.'

²¹ "Under three things the earth trembles,
   under four it cannot bear up:
²² a servant who becomes king,
   a fool who is full of food,
²³ an unloved woman who is married,
   and a maidservant who displaces her mistress.

ᵃ16 Hebrew *Sheol*

²⁴"Four things on earth are small,
  yet they are extremely wise:
²⁵Ants are creatures of little strength,
  yet they store up their food in the summer;
²⁶coneys*ᵃ* are creatures of little power,
  yet they make their home in the crags;
²⁷locusts have no king,
  yet they advance together in ranks;
²⁸a lizard can be caught with the hand,
  yet it is found in kings' palaces.

²⁹"There are three things that are stately in their stride,
  four that move with stately bearing:
³⁰a lion, mighty among beasts,
  who retreats before nothing;
³¹a strutting rooster, a he-goat,
  and a king with his army around him.*ᵇ*

³²"If you have played the fool and exalted yourself,
  or if you have planned evil,
  clap your hand over your mouth!
³³For as churning the milk produces butter,
  and as twisting the nose produces blood,
  so stirring up anger produces strife."

Sayings of King Lemuel

31 The sayings of King Lemuel—an oracle*ᶜ* his mother taught him:

²"O my son, O son of my womb,
  O son of my vows,*ᵈ*

ᵃ26 That is, the hyrax or rock badger   *ᵇ31* Or *king secure against revolt*   *ᶜ1* Or *of Lemuel king of Massa, which*   *ᵈ2* Or / *the answer to my prayers*

The Bible Says

No "Men's Work"

Have you ever heard that women aren't supposed to do "men's work"? That they are supposed to stay home, clean house and cook?

In Old Testament times most men worked the land. They hired workers, they bought and sold produce, they gave to the poor, they took care of their families. That's what is fascinating about Proverbs 31. The noble wife does much the same work as her husband:

* She supervises employees (Proverbs 31:15).
* She buys and sells land (Proverbs 31:16).
* She invests her earnings (Proverbs 31:16).
* She makes a profit trading her produce (Proverbs 31:18).
* She gives to the poor (Proverbs 31:20).
* And she cares for the needs of her family (Proverbs 31:21).

God has given abilities to both men and women. There is nothing wrong with being a stay-at-home mom, or with having a career.

³do not spend your strength on women,
    your vigor on those who ruin kings.

⁴"It is not for kings, O Lemuel—
    not for kings to drink wine,
    not for rulers to crave beer,
⁵lest they drink and forget what the law decrees,
    and deprive all the oppressed of their rights.
⁶Give beer to those who are perishing,
    wine to those who are in anguish;
⁷let them drink and forget their poverty
    and remember their misery no more.

⁸"Speak up for those who cannot speak for themselves,
    for the rights of all who are destitute.
⁹Speak up and judge fairly;
    defend the rights of the poor and needy."

Epilogue: The Wife of Noble Character

¹⁰^aA wife of noble character who can find?
    She is worth far more than rubies.
¹¹Her husband has full confidence in her
    and lacks nothing of value.
¹²She brings him good, not harm,
    all the days of her life.
¹³She selects wool and flax
    and works with eager hands.
¹⁴She is like the merchant ships,
    bringing her food from afar.
¹⁵She gets up while it is still dark;
    she provides food for her family
    and portions for her servant girls.
¹⁶She considers a field
      and buys it;
    out of her earnings
      she plants a
      vineyard.
¹⁷She sets about her work
      vigorously;
    her arms are strong
      for her tasks.
¹⁸She sees that her
      trading is
      profitable,
    and her lamp does
      not go out at
      night.
¹⁹In her hand she holds
      the distaff
    and grasps the
      spindle with her
      fingers.

*SEE
PROVERBS 31:10-31*

^a*10* Verses 10-31 are an acrostic, each verse
beginning with a successive letter of the Hebrew
alphabet.

[20] She opens her arms to the poor
    and extends her hands to the needy.
[21] When it snows, she has no fear for her household;
    for all of them are clothed in scarlet.
[22] She makes coverings for her bed;
    she is clothed in fine linen and purple.
[23] Her husband is respected at the city gate,
    where he takes his seat among the elders of the land.
[24] She makes linen garments and sells them,
    and supplies the merchants with sashes.
[25] She is clothed with strength and dignity;
    she can laugh at the days to come.
[26] She speaks with wisdom,
    and faithful instruction is on her tongue.
[27] She watches over the affairs of her household
    and does not eat the bread of idleness.
[28] Her children arise and call her blessed;
    her husband also, and he praises her:
[29] "Many women do noble things,
    but you surpass them all."
[30] Charm is deceptive, and beauty is fleeting;
    but a woman who fears the Lord is to be praised.
[31] Give her the reward she has earned,
    and let her works bring her praise at the city gate.

Introduction

to the

book of **Ecclesiastes**

WHAT'S THE USE?

Have you ever asked yourself that question? What's the use of studying? What's the use of trying to get along with others? What's the use of trying to do the right thing when all your friends just laugh at you? Do you ever feel that life is meaningless?

One book in the Bible agrees: life is empty. Everything is meaningless. At least that's what King Solomon thought after he'd turned away from God. But Solomon was wrong! If you listen to what God's Word tells about the Lord and his plan for you, you'll find life isn't meaningless at all.

Fundamentals

If you could have every pleasure your heart desired, would you be happy (Ecclesiastes 2:1-11)?

If you had all the money in the world, what would you do with it (Ecclesiastes 5:8-20)?

Why is it important to think about God when you're young (Ecclesiastes 12:1-8)?

FAST FACTS

The "Teacher" in this book is Solomon.

Solomon wrote this book when he was far from God.

How Solomon turned from God is recorded in 1 Kings 11.

Reason can prove that God exists, but it takes God's Word to prove that he loves you.

Everything Is Meaningless The words of the Teacher,[a] son of David, king in Jerusalem:

2 "Meaningless! Meaningless!"
    says the Teacher.
  "Utterly meaningless!
    Everything is meaningless."

3 What does man gain from all his labor
    at which he toils under the sun?
4 Generations come and generations go,
    but the earth remains forever.
5 The sun rises and the sun sets,
    and hurries back to where it rises.
6 The wind blows to the south
    and turns to the north;
  round and round it goes,
    ever returning on its course.
7 All streams flow into the sea,
    yet the sea is never full.
  To the place the streams come from,
    there they return again.
8 All things are wearisome,
    more than one can say.
  The eye never has enough of seeing,
    nor the ear its fill of hearing.
9 What has been will be again,
    what has been done will be done again;
    there is nothing new under the sun.
10 Is there anything of which one can say,
    "Look! This is something new"?
  It was here already, long ago;
    it was here before our time.
11 There is no remembrance of men of old,
    and even those who are yet to come
  will not be remembered
    by those who follow.

Wisdom Is Meaningless 12 I, the Teacher, was king over Israel in Jerusalem. 13 I devoted myself to study and to explore by wisdom all that is done under heaven. What a heavy burden God has laid on men! 14 I have seen all the things that are done under the sun; all of them are meaningless, a chasing after the wind.

15 What is twisted cannot be straightened;
    what is lacking cannot be counted.

16 I thought to myself, "Look, I have grown and increased in wisdom more than anyone who has ruled over Jerusalem before me; I have experienced much of wisdom and knowledge." 17 Then I applied myself to the understanding of wisdom, and also of madness and folly, but I learned that this, too, is a chasing after the wind.

18 For with much wisdom comes much sorrow;
    the more knowledge, the more grief.

a 1 Or leader of the assembly; also in verses 2 and 12

Pleasures Are Meaningless   I thought in my heart, "Come now, I will test you with pleasure to find out what is good." But that also proved to be meaningless. ²"Laughter," I said, "is foolish. And what does pleasure accomplish?" ³I tried cheering myself with wine, and embracing folly—my mind still guiding me with wisdom. I wanted to see what was worthwhile for men to do under heaven during the few days of their lives.

⁴I undertook great projects: I built houses for myself and planted vineyards. ⁵I made gardens and parks and planted all kinds of fruit trees in them. ⁶I made reservoirs to water groves of flourishing trees. ⁷I bought male and female slaves and had other slaves who were born in my house. I also owned more herds and flocks than anyone in Jerusalem before me. ⁸I amassed silver and gold for myself, and the treasure of kings and provinces. I acquired men and women singers, and a harem*ᵃ* as well—the delights of the heart of man. ⁹I became greater by far than anyone in Jerusalem before me. In all this my wisdom stayed with me.

¹⁰I denied myself nothing my eyes desired;
   I refused my heart no pleasure.
My heart took delight in all my work,
   and this was the reward for all my labor.
¹¹Yet when I surveyed all that my hands had done
   and what I had toiled to achieve,
everything was meaningless, a chasing after the wind;
   nothing was gained under the sun.

Wisdom and Folly Are Meaningless
¹²Then I turned my thoughts to consider wisdom,
   and also madness and folly.
What more can the king's successor do
   than what has already been done?
¹³I saw that wisdom is better than folly,
   just as light is better than
      darkness.
¹⁴The wise man has eyes in his
      head,
   while the fool walks in the
      darkness;
but I came to realize
   that the same fate overtakes
      them both.

¹⁵Then I thought in my heart,

"The fate of the fool will
      overtake me also.
   What then do I gain by being
      wise?"
I said in my heart,
   "This too is meaningless."
¹⁶For the wise man, like the fool,
      will not be long
      remembered;
   in days to come both will be
      forgotten.
Like the fool, the wise man too
      must die!

ᵃ8 The meaning of the Hebrew for this phrase is uncertain.

ECCLESIASTES 2:1–11

Toys. That tractor you loved when you were three. That game you played all the time when you were five. Your baby doll with all the clothes. A popular bumper sticker says, "The one who has the most toys when he dies, wins." Some adults never grow up. Their toys just change. Solomon had so much money and power that he got anything he wanted. Later in life he looked back and decided everything he had was meaningless. Possessions hadn't made him happy at all. Those who feel like they just have to have "things" haven't grown up spiritually. It's not the things you have, but the kind of person you are that makes life worthwhile.

Direct Line

Toil Is Meaningless   ¹⁷So I hated life, because the work that is done under the sun was grievous to me. All of it is meaningless, a chasing after the wind. ¹⁸I hated all the things I had toiled for under the sun, because I must leave them to the one who comes after me. ¹⁹And who knows whether he will be a wise man or a fool? Yet he will have control over all the work into which I have poured my effort and skill under the sun. This too is meaningless. ²⁰So my heart began to despair over all my toilsome labor under the sun. ²¹For a man may do his work with wisdom, knowledge and skill, and then he must leave all he owns to someone who has not worked for it. This too is meaningless and a great misfortune. ²²What does a man get for all the toil and anxious striving with which he labors under the sun? ²³All his days his work is pain and grief; even at night his mind does not rest. This too is meaningless.

²⁴A man can do nothing better than to eat and drink and find satisfaction in his work. This too, I see, is from the hand of God, ²⁵for without him, who can eat or find enjoyment? ²⁶To the man who pleases him, God gives wisdom, knowledge and happiness, but to the sinner he gives the task of gathering and storing up wealth to hand it over to the one who pleases God. This too is meaningless, a chasing after the wind.

A Time for Everything

There is a time for everything,
  and a season for every activity under heaven:

² a time to be born and a time to die,
  a time to plant and a time to uproot,
³ a time to kill and a time to heal,
  a time to tear down and a time to build,
⁴ a time to weep and a time to laugh,
  a time to mourn and a time to dance,
⁵ a time to scatter stones and a time to gather
    them,
  a time to embrace and a time to refrain,
⁶ a time to search and a time to give up,
  a time to keep and a time to throw away,
⁷ a time to tear and a time to mend,
  a time to be silent and a time to speak,
⁸ a time to love and a time to hate,
  a time for war and a time for peace.

⁹What does the worker gain from his toil? ¹⁰I have seen the burden God has laid on men. ¹¹He has made everything beautiful in its time. He has also set eternity in the hearts of men; yet they cannot fathom what God has done from beginning to end. ¹²I know that there is nothing better for men than to be happy and do good while they live. ¹³That everyone may eat and drink, and find satisfaction in all his toil—this is the gift of God. ¹⁴I know that everything God does will endure forever; nothing can be added to it and nothing taken from it. God does it so that men will revere him.

¹⁵Whatever is has already been,
  and what will be has been before;
  and God will call the past to account.ª

ª15 Or *God calls back the past*

DEAR SAM,

I'M ALWAYS WAITING TO BE OLD ENOUGH TO DO THINGS:
DATE, GET A JOB, DRIVE, GET MY BRACES OFF. WILL
I EVER BE THE RIGHT AGE?

TIM IN TORONTO

Dear Sam, Inc.

100 Advice Lane, Anywhere, USA

Dear Tim,

Don't wish your youth away! Did you notice that sixth grade went by faster than kindergarten? And eighth grade went by faster than sixth? Of course they didn't really go any faster, it just seems that way. When you were five years old, a year was 1/5 of your life. When you were ten, it was only 1/10 of your life. So the more years you live, the shorter a year seems. The older you get, the faster time seems to pass.

Be happy for each day. Do the things this year that you can do, and when next year comes, enjoy new opportunities. But don't be so impatient for things that one day you regret you didn't take the time to enjoy each step. Remember: "There is a time for everything, and a season for every activity under heaven" (Ecclesiastes 3:1).

Sam

¹⁶And I saw something else under the sun:

> In the place of judgment—wickedness was there,
> in the place of justice—wickedness was there.

¹⁷I thought in my heart,

> "God will bring to judgment
> both the righteous and the wicked,
> for there will be a time for every activity,
> a time for every deed."

¹⁸I also thought, "As for men, God tests them so that they may see that they are like the animals. ¹⁹Man's fate is like that of the animals; the same fate awaits them both: As one dies, so dies the other. All have the same breathᵃ; man has no advantage over the animal. Everything is meaningless. ²⁰All go to the same place; all come from dust, and to dust all return. ²¹Who knows if the spirit of man rises upward and if the spirit of the animalᵇ goes down into the earth?"

²²So I saw that there is nothing better for a man than to enjoy his work, because that is his lot. For who can bring him to see what will happen after him?

 Oppression, Toil, Friendlessness Again I looked and saw all the oppression that was taking place under the sun:

> I saw the tears of the oppressed—
> and they have no comforter;
> power was on the side of their oppressors—
> and they have no comforter.
> ²And I declared that the dead,
> who had already died,
> are happier than the living,
> who are still alive.
> ³But better than both
> is he who has not yet been,
> who has not seen the evil
> that is done under the sun.

⁴And I saw that all labor and all achievement spring from man's envy of his neighbor. This too is meaningless, a chasing after the wind.

> ⁵The fool folds his hands
> and ruins himself.
> ⁶Better one handful with tranquillity
> than two handfuls with toil
> and chasing after the wind.

⁷Again I saw something meaningless under the sun:

> ⁸There was a man all alone;
> he had neither son nor brother.
> There was no end to his toil,
> yet his eyes were not content with his wealth.
> "For whom am I toiling," he asked,
> "and why am I depriving myself of enjoyment?"
> This too is meaningless—
> a miserable business!

> ⁹Two are better than one,
> because they have a good return for their work:

ᵃ19 Or *spirit* ᵇ21 Or *Who knows the spirit of man, which rises upward, or the spirit of the animal, which*

¹⁰If one falls down,
> his friend can help him up.
> But pity the man who falls
> and has no one to help him up!
¹¹Also, if two lie down together, they will keep warm.
> But how can one keep warm alone?
¹²Though one may be overpowered,
> two can defend themselves.
> A cord of three strands is not quickly broken.

Advancement Is Meaningless   ¹³Better a poor but wise youth than an old but foolish king who no longer knows how to take warning. ¹⁴The youth may have come from prison to the kingship, or he may have been born in poverty within his kingdom. ¹⁵I saw that all who lived and walked under the sun followed the youth, the king's successor. ¹⁶There was no end to all the people who were before them. But those who came later were not pleased with the successor. This too is meaningless, a chasing after the wind.

Stand in Awe of God   Guard your steps when you go to the house of God. Go near to listen rather than to offer the sacrifice of fools, who do not know that they do wrong.

²Do not be quick with your mouth,
> do not be hasty in your heart
> to utter anything before God.
> God is in heaven
> and you are on earth,
> so let your words be few.
³As a dream comes when there are many cares,
> so the speech of a fool when there are many words.

⁴When you make a vow to God, do not delay in fulfilling it. He has no pleasure in fools; fulfill your vow. ⁵It is better not to vow than to make a vow and not fulfill it. ⁶Do not let your mouth lead you into sin. And do not protest to the temple messenger, "My vow was a mistake." Why should God be angry at what you say and destroy the work of your hands? ⁷Much dreaming and many words are meaningless. Therefore stand in awe of God.

Solomon's income was probably over $200 million a year. He says, "I denied myself nothing my eyes desired; I refused my heart no pleasure" (Ecclesiastes 2:10). But in despair he also wrote, "Meaningless! Everything is meaningless." What good is money anyway? A lot, if you follow a few simple rules:

The Bible Says

Can't Buy Happiness

* Work so you won't be dependent on anyone (1 Thessalonians 4:11–12).
* Rely on God, not on your money (1 Timothy 6:17).
* Be generous and willing to share (1 Timothy 6:18).
* Store up treasures in heaven, not on earth (Matthew 6:19–21).

If money is the most important thing in your life, you'll be miserable. But if God's values are most important, and if his values shape the way you use your money, you'll be happy indeed.

Riches Are Meaningless ⁸If you see the poor oppressed in a district, and justice and rights denied, do not be surprised at such things; for one official is eyed by a higher one, and over them both are others higher still. ⁹The increase from the land is taken by all; the king himself profits from the fields.

> ¹⁰Whoever loves money never has money enough;
>> whoever loves wealth is never satisfied with his income.
>> This too is meaningless.

> ¹¹As goods increase,
>> so do those who consume them.
> And what benefit are they to the owner
>> except to feast his eyes on them?

> ¹²The sleep of a laborer is sweet,
>> whether he eats little or much,
> but the abundance of a rich man
>> permits him no sleep.

¹³I have seen a grievous evil under the sun:

> wealth hoarded to the harm of its owner,
> ¹⁴ or wealth lost through some misfortune,
> so that when he has a son
>> there is nothing left for him.
> ¹⁵Naked a man comes from his mother's womb,
>> and as he comes, so he departs.
> He takes nothing from his labor
>> that he can carry in his hand.

¹⁶This too is a grievous evil:

> As a man comes, so he departs,
>> and what does he gain,
>> since he toils for the wind?
> ¹⁷All his days he eats in darkness,
>> with great frustration, affliction and anger.

¹⁸Then I realized that it is good and proper for a man to eat and drink, and to find satisfaction in his toilsome labor under the sun during the few days of life God has given him—for this is his lot. ¹⁹Moreover, when God gives any man wealth and possessions, and enables him to enjoy them, to accept his lot and be happy in his work—this is a gift of God. ²⁰He seldom reflects on the days of his life, because God keeps him occupied with gladness of heart.

I have seen another evil under the sun, and it weighs heavily on men: ²God gives a man wealth, possessions and honor, so that he lacks nothing his heart desires, but God does not enable him to enjoy them, and a stranger enjoys them instead. This is meaningless, a grievous evil.

³A man may have a hundred children and live many years; yet no matter how long he lives, if he cannot enjoy his prosperity and does not receive proper burial, I say that a stillborn child is better off than he. ⁴It comes without meaning, it departs in darkness, and in darkness its name is shrouded. ⁵Though it never saw the sun or knew anything, it has more rest than does that man— ⁶even if he lives a thousand years twice over but fails to enjoy his prosperity. Do not all go to the same place?

> ⁷All man's efforts are for his mouth,
>> yet his appetite is never satisfied.
> ⁸What advantage has a wise man
>> over a fool?

What does a poor man gain
   by knowing how to conduct himself before others?
⁹Better what the eye sees
   than the roving of the appetite.
This too is meaningless,
   a chasing after the wind.

¹⁰Whatever exists has already been named,
   and what man is has been known;
no man can contend
   with one who is stronger than he.
¹¹The more the words,
   the less the meaning,
   and how does that profit anyone?

¹²For who knows what is good for a man in life, during the few and mean-ingless days he passes through like a shadow? Who can tell him what will happen under the sun after he is gone?

7 Wisdom

A good name is better than fine perfume,
   and the day of death better than the day of birth.
²It is better to go to a house of mourning
   than to go to a house of feasting,
for death is the destiny of every man;
   the living should take this to heart.
³Sorrow is better than laughter,
   because a sad face is good for the heart.
⁴The heart of the wise is in the house of mourning,
   but the heart of fools is in the
      house of pleasure.
⁵It is better to heed a wise man's
      rebuke
   than to listen to the song of
      fools.
⁶Like the crackling of thorns
      under the pot,
   so is the laughter of fools.
   This too is meaningless.

⁷Extortion turns a wise man into
      a fool,
   and a bribe corrupts the heart.

⁸The end of a matter is better
      than its beginning,
   and patience is better than
      pride.
⁹Do not be quickly provoked in
      your spirit,
   for anger resides in the lap of
      fools.

¹⁰Do not say, "Why were the old
      days better than these?"
   For it is not wise to ask such
      questions.

ECCLESIASTES 7:21–22

Have you ever heard someone say something bad about you? Or have you ever overheard someone you like say something about you and then laugh? It's hard not to be sensitive to what others say about you. Maybe sometimes you're too sensitive. Solomon says, "Do not pay attention to every word people say." He's wise, because lots of times people say things they don't really mean. If you think about it, you can probably remember times when you have said things about others that you didn't mean. If you remember that human beings are weak and often say things they don't really mean, it will help you follow Solomon's good advice.

Direct Line

¹¹Wisdom, like an inheritance, is a good thing
    and benefits those who see the sun.
¹²Wisdom is a shelter
    as money is a shelter,
  but the advantage of knowledge is this:
    that wisdom preserves the life of its possessor.

¹³Consider what God has done:

  Who can straighten
    what he has made crooked?
¹⁴When times are good, be happy;
    but when times are bad, consider:
  God has made the one
    as well as the other.
  Therefore, a man cannot discover
    anything about his future.

¹⁵In this meaningless life of mine I have seen both of these:

  a righteous man perishing in his righteousness,
    and a wicked man living long in his wickedness.
¹⁶Do not be overrighteous,
    neither be overwise—
    why destroy yourself?
¹⁷Do not be overwicked,
    and do not be a fool—
    why die before your time?
¹⁸It is good to grasp the one
    and not let go of the other.
  The man who fears God will avoid all extremes.^a

¹⁹Wisdom makes one wise man more powerful
    than ten rulers in a city.

²⁰There is not a righteous man on earth
    who does what is right and never sins.

²¹Do not pay attention to every word people say,
    or you may hear your servant cursing you—
²²for you know in your heart
    that many times you yourself have cursed others.

²³All this I tested by wisdom and I said,

  "I am determined to be wise"—
    but this was beyond me.
²⁴Whatever wisdom may be,
    it is far off and most profound—
    who can discover it?
²⁵So I turned my mind to understand,
    to investigate and to search out wisdom and the scheme of
        things
  and to understand the stupidity of wickedness
    and the madness of folly.

²⁶I find more bitter than death
    the woman who is a snare,
  whose heart is a trap
    and whose hands are chains.

---

^a18 Or *will follow them both*

> The man who pleases God will escape her,
> but the sinner she will ensnare.

[27]"Look," says the Teacher,[a] "this is what I have discovered:

> "Adding one thing to another to discover the scheme of things—
> [28]   while I was still searching
> but not finding—
> I found one ˌuprightˌ man among a thousand,
> but not one ˌuprightˌ woman among them all.
> [29]This only have I found:
> God made mankind upright,
> but men have gone in search of many schemes."

8

> Who is like the wise man?
> Who knows the explanation of things?
> Wisdom brightens a man's face
> and changes its hard appearance.

Obey the King   [2]Obey the king's command, I say, because you took an oath before God. [3]Do not be in a hurry to leave the king's presence. Do not stand up for a bad cause, for he will do whatever he pleases. [4]Since a king's word is supreme, who can say to him, "What are you doing?"

> [5]Whoever obeys his command will come to no harm,
> and the wise heart will know the proper time and procedure.
> [6]For there is a proper time and procedure for every matter,
> though a man's misery weighs heavily upon him.

> [7]Since no man knows the future,
> who can tell him what is to come?
> [8]No man has power over the wind to contain it[b];
> so no one has power over the day of his death.
> As no one is discharged in time of war,
> so wickedness will not release those who practice it.

[9]All this I saw, as I applied my mind to everything done under the sun. There is a time when a man lords it over others to his own[c] hurt. [10]Then too, I saw the wicked buried—those who used to come and go from the holy place and receive praise[d] in the city where they did this. This too is meaningless.

[11]When the sentence for a crime is not quickly carried out, the hearts of the people are filled with schemes to do wrong. [12]Although a wicked man commits a hundred crimes and still lives a long time, I know that it will go better with God-fearing men, who are reverent before God. [13]Yet because the wicked do not fear God, it will not go well with them, and their days will not lengthen like a shadow.

[14]There is something else meaningless that occurs on earth: righteous men who get what the wicked deserve, and wicked men who get what the righteous deserve. This too, I say, is meaningless. [15]So I commend the enjoyment of life, because nothing is better for a man under the sun than to eat and drink and be glad. Then joy will accompany him in his work all the days of the life God has given him under the sun.

[16]When I applied my mind to know wisdom and to observe man's labor on earth—his eyes not seeing sleep day or night— [17]then I saw all that God has done. No one can comprehend what goes on under the sun. Despite all his efforts to search it out, man cannot discover its meaning. Even if a wise man claims he knows, he cannot really comprehend it.

---

[a]27 Or *leader of the assembly*   [b]8 Or *over his spirit to retain it*   [c]9 Or *to their*   [d]10 Some Hebrew manuscripts and Septuagint (Aquila); most Hebrew manuscripts *and are forgotten*

9 *A Common Destiny for All* So I reflected on all this and concluded that the righteous and the wise and what they do are in God's hands, but no man knows whether love or hate awaits him. ²All share a common destiny—the righteous and the wicked, the good and the bad,ᵃ the clean and the unclean, those who offer sacrifices and those who do not.

> As it is with the good man,
> so with the sinner;
> as it is with those who take oaths,
> so with those who are afraid to take them.

³This is the evil in everything that happens under the sun: The same destiny overtakes all. The hearts of men, moreover, are full of evil and there is madness in their hearts while they live, and afterward they join the dead. ⁴Anyone who is among the living has hopeᵇ—even a live dog is better off than a dead lion!

> ⁵For the living know that they will die,
> but the dead know nothing;
> they have no further reward,
> and even the memory of them is forgotten.
> ⁶Their love, their hate
> and their jealousy have long since vanished;
> never again will they have a part
> in anything that happens under the sun.

⁷Go, eat your food with gladness, and drink your wine with a joyful heart, for it is now that God favors what you do. ⁸Always be clothed in white, and always anoint your head with oil. ⁹Enjoy life with your wife, whom you love, all the days of this meaningless life that God has given you under the sun— all your meaningless days. For this is your lot in life and in your toilsome labor under the sun. ¹⁰Whatever your hand finds to do, do it with all your might, for in the grave,ᶜ where you are going, there is neither working nor planning nor knowledge nor wisdom.

ᵃ2 Septuagint (Aquila), Vulgate and Syriac; Hebrew does not have *and the bad.* ᵇ4 Or *What then is to be chosen? With all who live, there is hope* ᶜ10 Hebrew *Sheol*

The Bible Says

Look Again

When Solomon wrote this book, he chose to depend only on what he could observe, and he came to an upsetting conclusion. It didn't seem to matter how a person lived. Both the good and the wicked die. Before long even the memory of them fades (Ecclesiastes 9:1–6).

That's what's special about the Bible. In it God pulls back the curtain and lets you look beyond the physical. You learn that there is a very real invisible world. You learn that every person who has died still exists. The body dies. But the person—the real person, who thinks and feels and remembers—continues to exist.

You don't have to be a Solomon to know that things aren't always fair here on earth. But don't be discouraged. This life isn't the end, and God promises you "an inheritance" (1 Peter 1:4).

¹¹I have seen something else under the sun:

> The race is not to the swift
>> or the battle to the strong,
> nor does food come to the wise
>> or wealth to the brilliant
>> or favor to the learned;
> but time and chance happen to them all.

¹²Moreover, no man knows when his hour will come:

> As fish are caught in a cruel net,
>> or birds are taken in a snare,
> so men are trapped by evil times
>> that fall unexpectedly upon them.

Wisdom Better Than Folly ¹³I also saw under the sun this example of wisdom that greatly impressed me: ¹⁴There was once a small city with only a few people in it. And a powerful king came against it, surrounded it and built huge siegeworks against it. ¹⁵Now there lived in that city a man poor but wise, and he saved the city by his wisdom. But nobody remembered that poor man. ¹⁶So I said, "Wisdom is better than strength." But the poor man's wisdom is despised, and his words are no longer heeded.

> ¹⁷The quiet words of the wise are more to be heeded
>> than the shouts of a ruler of fools.
> ¹⁸Wisdom is better than weapons of war,
>> but one sinner destroys much good.

10 As dead flies give perfume a bad smell,
>> so a little folly outweighs wisdom and honor.
> ²The heart of the wise inclines to the right,
>> but the heart of the fool to the left.
> ³Even as he walks along the road,
>> the fool lacks sense
>> and shows everyone how stupid he is.
> ⁴If a ruler's anger rises against you,
>> do not leave your post;
>> calmness can lay great errors to rest.

> ⁵There is an evil I have seen under the sun,
>> the sort of error that arises from a ruler:
> ⁶Fools are put in many high positions,
>> while the rich occupy the low ones.
> ⁷I have seen slaves on horseback,
>> while princes go on foot like slaves.

> ⁸Whoever digs a pit may fall into it;
>> whoever breaks through a wall may be bitten by a snake.
> ⁹Whoever quarries stones may be injured by them;
>> whoever splits logs may be endangered by them.

> ¹⁰If the ax is dull
>> and its edge unsharpened,
> more strength is needed
>> but skill will bring success.

> ¹¹If a snake bites before it is charmed,
>> there is no profit for the charmer.

> ¹²Words from a wise man's mouth are gracious,
>> but a fool is consumed by his own lips.

¹³At the beginning his words are folly;
   at the end they are wicked madness—
¹⁴   and the fool multiplies words.

No one knows what is coming—
   who can tell him what will happen after him?

¹⁵A fool's work wearies him;
   he does not know the way to town.

¹⁶Woe to you, O land whose king was a servant[a]
   and whose princes feast in the morning.
¹⁷Blessed are you, O land whose king is of noble birth
   and whose princes eat at a proper time—
   for strength and not for drunkenness.

¹⁸If a man is lazy, the rafters sag;
   if his hands are idle, the house leaks.

¹⁹A feast is made for laughter,
   and wine makes life merry,
   but money is the answer for everything.

²⁰Do not revile the king even in your thoughts,
   or curse the rich in your bedroom,
   because a bird of the air may carry your words,
   and a bird on the wing may report what you say.

11

Bread Upon the Waters

Cast your bread upon the waters,
   for after many days you will find it again.
²Give portions to seven, yes to eight,
         for you do not know what disaster
            may come upon the land.

³If clouds are full of water,
   they pour rain upon the earth.
Whether a tree falls to the south or to
      the north,
   in the place where it falls, there will
      it lie.
⁴Whoever watches the wind will not
      plant;
   whoever looks at the clouds will not
      reap.

⁵As you do not know the path of the
      wind,
   or how the body is formed[b] in a
      mother's womb,
   so you cannot understand the work of
      God,
   the Maker of all things.

⁶Sow your seed in the morning,
   and at evening let not your hands
      be idle,
   for you do not know which will succeed,

Direct Line

ECCLESIASTES 11:5

If God is "the Maker of all things," why did he make you like you are? Oh, there are some things about yourself you don't like? That nose just a bit off center? You have to study hard while your older sister breezes through school without cracking a book? OK, you're not perfect. But that's not the point. The point is that God, "the Maker of all things," shaped you from the beginning. Instead of worrying about flaws, why not make a list of good things about yourself? You may not get a lot of things down the first time you try. But keep the list around and add things when you think of them. Then enjoy—and celebrate—yourself!

[a]16 Or *king is a child* [b]5 Or *know how life* (or *the spirit*) /
enters the body being formed

whether this or that,
or whether both will do equally well.

Remember Your Creator While Young

⁷Light is sweet,
and it pleases the eyes to see the sun.
⁸However many years a man may live,
let him enjoy them all.
But let him remember the days of darkness,
for they will be many.
Everything to come is meaningless.

⁹Be happy, young man, while you are young,
and let your heart give you joy in the days of your youth.
Follow the ways of your heart
and whatever your eyes see,
but know that for all these things
God will bring you to judgment.
¹⁰So then, banish anxiety from your heart
and cast off the troubles of your body,
for youth and vigor are meaningless.

12 Remember your Creator
in the days of your youth,
before the days of trouble come
and the years approach when you will say,
"I find no pleasure in them"—
²before the sun and the light
and the moon and the
stars grow dark,
and the clouds return after
the rain;
³when the keepers of the
house tremble,
and the strong men stoop,
when the grinders cease
because they are few,
and those looking through
the windows grow dim;
⁴when the doors to the street
are closed
and the sound of grinding
fades;
when men rise up at the
sound of birds,
but all their songs grow
faint;
⁵when men are afraid of
heights
and of dangers in the
streets;
when the almond tree
blossoms
and the grasshopper drags
himself along
and desire no longer is
stirred.

"Be happy, young man."
No problem!

SEE
ECCLESIASTES 11:9

Then man goes to his eternal home
 and mourners go about the streets.

⁶Remember him—before the silver cord is severed,
 or the golden bowl is broken;
before the pitcher is shattered at the spring,
 or the wheel broken at the well,
⁷and the dust returns to the ground it came from,
 and the spirit returns to God who gave it.

⁸"Meaningless! Meaningless!" says the Teacher.ᵃ
 "Everything is meaningless!"

The Conclusion of the Matter ⁹Not only was the Teacher wise, but also he imparted knowledge to the people. He pondered and searched out and set in order many proverbs. ¹⁰The Teacher searched to find just the right words, and what he wrote was upright and true.

¹¹The words of the wise are like goads, their collected sayings like firmly embedded nails—given by one Shepherd. ¹²Be warned, my son, of anything in addition to them.

Of making many books there is no end, and much study wearies the body.

¹³Now all has been heard;
 here is the conclusion of the matter:
Fear God and keep his commandments,
 for this is the whole ˌdutyˌ of man.
¹⁴For God will bring every deed into judgment,
 including every hidden thing,
 whether it is good or evil.

ᵃ8 Or *the leader of the assembly*; also in verses 9 and 10

LOVE LETTERS.

Have you ever written one? Have you ever received one? Love is great! No wonder there are so many popular songs about love between a man and woman.

You don't need to be surprised to find love poems in the Bible. God made human beings male and female. He intended love between men and women to be a wonderful, beautiful thing. Song of Songs is a collection of love poems, telling how a man (the Lover) and his bride (the Beloved) feel about each other.

FAST FACTS

Solomon wrote Song of Songs.

Jewish rabbis said a person should be 30 before reading this book about love.

Gardens were prized in Bible times. These love poems feature garden trees, plants and flowers.

Some Christians see Song of Songs as a picture of Christ's love for the church.

Fundamentals

What beautiful things can a man say to his wife (see "Lover" portions)?

What wonderful things can a woman say to her husband (see "Beloved" portions)?

Do you like someone for who he or she is or just because it's fun to be "in love"?

Solomon's Song of Songs.

Beloved[a]

²Let him kiss me with the kisses of his mouth—
  for your love is more delightful than wine.
³Pleasing is the fragrance of your perfumes;
  your name is like perfume poured out.
  No wonder the maidens love you!
⁴Take me away with you—let us hurry!
  Let the king bring me into his chambers.

Friends

We rejoice and delight in you[b];
  we will praise your love more than wine.

Beloved

How right they are to adore you!

⁵Dark am I, yet lovely,
  O daughters of Jerusalem,
  dark like the tents of Kedar,
  like the tent curtains of Solomon.[c]
⁶Do not stare at me because I am dark,
  because I am darkened by the sun.
My mother's sons were angry with me
  and made me take care of the vineyards;
  my own vineyard I have neglected.
⁷Tell me, you whom I love, where you graze your flock
  and where you rest your sheep at midday.
Why should I be like a veiled woman
  beside the flocks of your friends?

Friends

⁸If you do not know, most beautiful of women,
  follow the tracks of the sheep
and graze your young goats
  by the tents of the shepherds.

Lover

⁹I liken you, my darling, to a mare
  harnessed to one of the chariots of Pharaoh.
¹⁰Your cheeks are beautiful with earrings,
  your neck with strings of jewels.
¹¹We will make you earrings of gold,
  studded with silver.

Beloved

¹²While the king was at his table,
  my perfume spread its fragrance.
¹³My lover is to me a sachet of myrrh
  resting between my breasts.
¹⁴My lover is to me a cluster of henna blossoms
  from the vineyards of En Gedi.

---

[a]Primarily on the basis of the gender of the Hebrew pronouns used, male and female speakers are indicated in the margins by the captions *Lover* and *Beloved* respectively. The words of others are marked *Friends*. In some instances the divisions and their captions are debatable.   [b]4 The Hebrew is masculine singular.   [c]5 Or *Salma*

Lover

¹⁵How beautiful you are, my darling!
    Oh, how beautiful!
    Your eyes are doves.

Beloved

¹⁶How handsome you are, my lover!
    Oh, how charming!
    And our bed is verdant.

Lover

¹⁷The beams of our house are cedars;
    our rafters are firs.

2 *Beloved*^a
    I am a rose^b of Sharon,
      a lily of the valleys.

Lover

²Like a lily among thorns
    is my darling among the maidens.

Beloved

³Like an apple tree among the trees of the forest
    is my lover among the young men.
I delight to sit in his shade,
    and his fruit is sweet to my taste.
⁴He has taken me to the banquet hall,
    and his banner over me is love.
⁵Strengthen me with raisins,
    refresh me with apples,
    for I am faint with love.
⁶His left arm is under my head,
    and his right arm embraces me.
⁷Daughters of Jerusalem, I charge you
    by the gazelles and by the does of the field:
Do not arouse or awaken love
    until it so desires.

⁸Listen! My lover!
    Look! Here he comes,
leaping across the mountains,
    bounding over the hills.
⁹My lover is like a gazelle or a
    young stag.
    Look! There he stands
      behind our wall,
gazing through the windows,
    peering through the lattice.
¹⁰My lover spoke and said to
    me,
    "Arise, my darling,
    my beautiful one, and come
      with me.
¹¹See! The winter is past;
    the rains are over and gone.

^a*1 Or Lover* ^b*1 Possibly a member of the crocus family*

SONG OF SONGS 2:8–13

How can each time you fall in love seem like the first time? That's part of the magic. Each time it's exciting, fresh and new. The song that Solomon wrote to celebrate love can help you realize that God isn't a prude, frowning at you when your heart beats faster. It can also help you realize that when Hollywood tries to tell you it's all just sex, Hollywood is dead wrong. Solomon is right: that "Look, here he [or she] comes" that sets your heart beating is something special you can enjoy no matter what your age.

Direct Line

¹²Flowers appear on the earth;
    the season of singing has come,
  the cooing of doves
    is heard in our land.
¹³The fig tree forms its early fruit;
    the blossoming vines spread their fragrance.
  Arise, come, my darling;
    my beautiful one, come with me."

Lover

¹⁴My dove in the clefts of the rock,
    in the hiding places on the mountainside,
  show me your face,
    let me hear your voice;
  for your voice is sweet,
    and your face is lovely.
¹⁵Catch for us the foxes,
    the little foxes
  that ruin the vineyards,
    our vineyards that are in bloom.

Beloved

¹⁶My lover is mine and I am his;
    he browses among the lilies.
¹⁷Until the day breaks
    and the shadows flee,
  turn, my lover,
    and be like a gazelle
  or like a young stag
    on the rugged hills.^a

3 All night long on my bed
    I looked for the one my heart loves;
    I looked for him but did not find him.
²I will get up now and go about the city,
    through its streets and squares;
  I will search for the one my heart loves.
    So I looked for him but did not find him.
³The watchmen found me
    as they made their rounds in the city.
  "Have you seen the one my heart loves?"
⁴Scarcely had I passed them
    when I found the one my heart loves.
  I held him and would not let him go
    till I had brought him to my mother's house,
    to the room of the one who conceived me.
⁵Daughters of Jerusalem, I charge you
    by the gazelles and by the does of the field:
  Do not arouse or awaken love
    until it so desires.

⁶Who is this coming up from the desert
    like a column of smoke,
  perfumed with myrrh and incense
    made from all the spices of the merchant?
⁷Look! It is Solomon's carriage,

---

^a*17 Or the hills of Bether*

escorted by sixty warriors,
    the noblest of Israel,
⁸all of them wearing the sword,
    all experienced in battle,
  each with his sword at his side,
    prepared for the terrors of the night.
⁹King Solomon made for himself the carriage;
    he made it of wood from Lebanon.
¹⁰Its posts he made of silver,
    its base of gold.
  Its seat was upholstered with purple,
    its interior lovingly inlaid
    by*a* the daughters of Jerusalem.
¹¹Come out, you daughters of Zion,
    and look at King Solomon wearing the crown,
    the crown with which his mother crowned him
  on the day of his wedding,
    the day his heart rejoiced.

Lover

4 How beautiful you are, my darling!
    Oh, how beautiful!
    Your eyes behind your veil are doves.
  Your hair is like a flock of goats
    descending from Mount Gilead.
²Your teeth are like a flock of sheep just shorn,
    coming up from the washing.
  Each has its twin;
    not one of them is alone.
³Your lips are like a scarlet ribbon;
    your mouth is lovely.
  Your temples behind your veil
    are like the halves of a pomegranate.
⁴Your neck is like the tower of David,
    built with elegance*b*;
  on it hang a thousand shields,
    all of them shields of warriors.
⁵Your two breasts are like two fawns,
    like twin fawns of a gazelle
    that browse among the lilies.
⁶Until the day breaks
    and the shadows flee,
  I will go to the mountain of myrrh
    and to the hill of incense.
⁷All beautiful you are, my darling;
    there is no flaw in you.

⁸Come with me from Lebanon, my bride,
    come with me from Lebanon.
  Descend from the crest of Amana,
    from the top of Senir, the summit of Hermon,
  from the lions' dens
    and the mountain haunts of the leopards.
⁹You have stolen my heart, my sister, my bride;
    you have stolen my heart

---

a10 Or its inlaid interior a gift of love / from   b4 The meaning of the Hebrew for this word is uncertain.

with one glance of your eyes,
with one jewel of your necklace.
¹⁰How delightful is your love, my sister, my bride!
How much more pleasing is your love than wine,
and the fragrance of your perfume than any spice!
¹¹Your lips drop sweetness as the honeycomb, my bride;
milk and honey are under your tongue.
The fragrance of your garments is like that of Lebanon.
¹²You are a garden locked up, my sister, my bride;
you are a spring enclosed, a sealed fountain.
¹³Your plants are an orchard of pomegranates
with choice fruits,
with henna and nard,
¹⁴   nard and saffron,
calamus and cinnamon,
with every kind of incense tree,
with myrrh and aloes
and all the finest spices.
¹⁵You are*a garden fountain,
a well of flowing water
streaming down from Lebanon.

Beloved

¹⁶Awake, north wind,
and come, south wind!
Blow on my garden,
that its fragrance may spread abroad.
Let my lover come into his garden
and taste its choice fruits.

Lover

5 I have come into my garden, my sister, my bride;
I have gathered my myrrh with my spice.
I have eaten my honeycomb and my honey;
I have drunk my wine and my milk.

Friends

Eat, O friends, and drink;
drink your fill, O lovers.

Beloved

²I slept but my heart was awake.
Listen! My lover is knocking:
"Open to me, my sister, my darling,
my dove, my flawless one.
My head is drenched with dew,
my hair with the dampness of the night."
³I have taken off my robe—
must I put it on again?
I have washed my feet—
must I soil them again?
⁴My lover thrust his hand through the latch-opening;
my heart began to pound for him.
⁵I arose to open for my lover,
and my hands dripped with myrrh,

ᵃ15 Or *I am* (spoken by the *Beloved*)

my fingers with flowing myrrh,
    on the handles of the lock.
⁶I opened for my lover,
    but my lover had left; he was gone.
    My heart sank at his departure.ᵃ
I looked for him but did not find him.
    I called him but he did not answer.
⁷The watchmen found me
    as they made their rounds in the city.
They beat me, they bruised me;
    they took away my cloak,
    those watchmen of the walls!
⁸O daughters of Jerusalem, I charge you—
    if you find my lover,
what will you tell him?
    Tell him I am faint with love.

Friends

⁹How is your beloved better than others,
    most beautiful of women?
How is your beloved better than others,
    that you charge us so?

Beloved

¹⁰My lover is radiant and ruddy,
    outstanding among ten thousand.
¹¹His head is purest gold;
    his hair is wavy
    and black as a raven.
¹²His eyes are like doves
    by the water streams,
washed in milk,
    mounted like jewels.
¹³His cheeks are like beds of spice
    yielding perfume.
His lips are like lilies
    dripping with myrrh.

ᵃ6 Or *heart had gone out to him when he spoke*

The Bible Says

Romance Ahead

Romance is a pretty special thing. You know, those feelings that grow as you get to know a special person.

Song of Songs gives you a preview of what romance is all about. In this book the "beloved" is the woman, and the "lover" is the man. She talks about being "faint with love," and he talks about how beautiful and wonderful she is (Song of Songs 5:8; 6:4).

Some teens miss out on romantic love altogether. They confuse romantic love with sex and think that having sex is love. They never realize that sex can spoil their chances to find lasting romantic love.

Don't make that mistake. Read Song of Songs to discover how special romantic love can be. If you want that kind of love, you'll be wise enough to wait for it.

¹⁴His arms are rods of gold
    set with chrysolite.
His body is like polished ivory
    decorated with sapphires.ᵃ
¹⁵His legs are pillars of marble
    set on bases of pure gold.
His appearance is like Lebanon,
    choice as its cedars.
¹⁶His mouth is sweetness itself;
    he is altogether lovely.
This is my lover, this my friend,
    O daughters of Jerusalem.

6

Friends

Where has your lover gone,
    most beautiful of women?
Which way did your lover turn,
    that we may look for him with you?

Beloved

²My lover has gone down to his garden,
    to the beds of spices,
to browse in the gardens
    and to gather lilies.
³I am my lover's and my lover is mine;
    he browses among the lilies.

Lover

⁴You are beautiful, my darling, as Tirzah,
    lovely as Jerusalem,
    majestic as troops with banners.
⁵Turn your eyes from me;
    they overwhelm me.
Your hair is like a flock of goats
    descending from Gilead.
⁶Your teeth are like a flock of sheep
    coming up from the washing.
Each has its twin,
    not one of them is alone.
⁷Your temples behind your veil
    are like the halves of a pomegranate.
⁸Sixty queens there may be,
    and eighty concubines,
    and virgins beyond number;
⁹but my dove, my perfect one, is unique,
    the only daughter of her mother,
    the favorite of the one who bore her.
The maidens saw her and called her blessed;
    the queens and concubines praised her.

Friends

¹⁰Who is this that appears like the dawn,
    fair as the moon, bright as the sun,
    majestic as the stars in procession?

ᵃ14 Or *lapis lazuli*

Lover

¹¹I went down to the grove of nut trees
    to look at the new growth in the valley,
  to see if the vines had budded
    or the pomegranates were in bloom.
¹²Before I realized it,
    my desire set me among the royal chariots of my people.[a]

Friends

¹³Come back, come back, O Shulammite;
    come back, come back, that we may gaze on you!

Lover

Why would you gaze on the Shulammite
  as on the dance of Mahanaim?

7 How beautiful your sandaled feet,
  O prince's daughter!
Your graceful legs are like jewels,
  the work of a craftsman's hands.
²Your navel is a rounded goblet
  that never lacks blended wine.
Your waist is a mound of wheat
  encircled by lilies.
³Your breasts are like two fawns,
  twins of a gazelle.
⁴Your neck is like an ivory tower.
Your eyes are the pools of Heshbon
  by the gate of Bath Rabbim.
Your nose is like the tower of
    Lebanon
  looking toward Damascus.
⁵Your head crowns you like
    Mount Carmel.
  Your hair is like royal
    tapestry;
  the king is held captive by its
    tresses.
⁶How beautiful you are and how
    pleasing,
  O love, with your delights!
⁷Your stature is like that of the
    palm,
  and your breasts like clusters
    of fruit.
⁸I said, "I will climb the palm
    tree;
  I will take hold of its fruit."
May your breasts be like the
    clusters of the vine,
  the fragrance of your breath
    like apples,
⁹ and your mouth like the best
    wine.

[a]12 Or *among the chariots of Amminadab;* or *among the chariots of the people of the prince*

SEE
SONG OF SONGS 7:4

Beloved

May the wine go straight to my lover,
   flowing gently over lips and teeth.*ᵃ*
¹⁰I belong to my lover,
   and his desire is for me.
¹¹Come, my lover, let us go to the countryside,
   let us spend the night in the villages.*ᵇ*
¹²Let us go early to the vineyards
   to see if the vines have budded,
if their blossoms have opened,
   and if the pomegranates are in bloom—
there I will give you my love.
¹³The mandrakes send out their fragrance,
   and at our door is every delicacy,
both new and old,
   that I have stored up for you, my lover.

8

If only you were to me like a brother,
   who was nursed at my mother's breasts!
Then, if I found you outside,
   I would kiss you,
   and no one would despise me.
²I would lead you
   and bring you to my mother's house—
   she who has taught me.
I would give you spiced wine to drink,
   the nectar of my pomegranates.
³His left arm is under my head
   and his right arm embraces me.
⁴Daughters of Jerusalem, I charge you:
   Do not arouse or awaken love
   until it so desires.

Friends

⁵Who is this coming up from the
     desert
   leaning on her lover?

Beloved

Under the apple tree I roused you;
   there your mother conceived you,
   there she who was in labor gave
     you birth.
⁶Place me like a seal over your heart,
   like a seal on your arm;
for love is as strong as death,
   its jealousy*ᶜ* unyielding as the
     grave.*ᵈ*
It burns like blazing fire,
   like a mighty flame.*ᵉ*
⁷Many waters cannot quench love;
   rivers cannot wash it away.
If one were to give
   all the wealth of his house for love,
   it*ᶠ* would be utterly scorned.

Direct Line

SONG OF SONGS 8:6–7

Someday you'll stop falling in love with someone new every month. Someday love will last for weeks and months and stretch on into years. When that lasting love comes—a love "as strong as death," a love "many waters cannot quench"—then you'll know you've found the right one. Then love will lead you to the commitment of marriage. You'll want to be with that one person for the rest of your life. Don't get "being in love" mixed up with "lasting love." It's so tempting to think the guy you met last week is "the one." But you can't tell until being "in love" has stood the test of time and become "lasting love."

ᵃ9 Septuagint, Aquila, Vulgate and Syriac; Hebrew lips of sleepers ᵇ11 Or henna bushes ᶜ6 Or ardor ᵈ6 Hebrew Sheol ᵉ6 Or / like the very flame of the Lᴏʀᴅ ᶠ7 Or he

⁸We have a young sister,
and her breasts are not yet grown.
What shall we do for our sister
for the day she is spoken for?
⁹If she is a wall,
we will build towers of silver on her.
If she is a door,
we will enclose her with panels of cedar.

Beloved

¹⁰I am a wall,
and my breasts are like towers.
Thus I have become in his eyes
like one bringing contentment.
¹¹Solomon had a vineyard in Baal Hamon;
he let out his vineyard to tenants.
Each was to bring for its fruit
a thousand shekels*a* of silver.
¹²But my own vineyard is mine to give;
the thousand shekels are for you, O Solomon,
and two hundred*b* are for those who tend its fruit.

Lover

¹³You who dwell in the gardens
with friends in attendance,
let me hear your voice!

Beloved

¹⁴Come away, my lover,
and be like a gazelle
or like a young stag
on the spice-laden mountains.

a11 That is, about 25 pounds (about 11.5 kilograms); also in verse 12   *b12* That is, about 5 pounds (about 2.3 kilograms)

Introduction

to the

book of Isaiah

BULLIES.

Sooner or later you'll probably meet one—someone who's mean and just doesn't like you. Wouldn't it be great to know ahead of time that everything will turn out OK next time you're confronted by a bully?

In Isaiah's time, Assyria was a bully, a powerful nation determined to invade Israel. In 722 B.C. Assyria crushed the northern kingdom of Israel. Isaiah made it clear that the southern kingdom of Judah would be invaded too. But the nation would survive. Isaiah also promised that one day God would send a Savior to deliver his people from sin and to set up God's kingdom on earth.

FAST FACTS

Isaiah means "the Lord saves."

Isaiah prophesied from about 740-681 B.C. Jesus was born years later in 4 B.C., but Isaiah predicted his birth and death.

Assyria destroyed Israel in 722 B.C. and attacked Judah in 701 B.C.

Fundamentals

It's just plain smart to be afraid of a bully, isn't it (Isaiah 8:12-13)?

How will the animals act when Christ comes to reign on earth (Isaiah 11:6-9)?

Does the Bible tell the future (Isaiah 53)?

What will the end of the world be like (Isaiah 65:17-25)?

1 The vision concerning Judah and Jerusalem that Isaiah son of Amoz saw during the reigns of Uzziah, Jotham, Ahaz and Hezekiah, kings of Judah.

A Rebellious Nation

² Hear, O heavens! Listen, O earth!
  For the LORD has spoken:
"I reared children and brought them up,
  but they have rebelled against me.
³ The ox knows his master,
  the donkey his owner's manger,
but Israel does not know,
  my people do not understand."

⁴ Ah, sinful nation,
  a people loaded with guilt,
a brood of evildoers,
  children given to corruption!
They have forsaken the LORD;
  they have spurned the Holy One of Israel
  and turned their backs on him.

⁵ Why should you be beaten anymore?
  Why do you persist in rebellion?
Your whole head is injured,
  your whole heart afflicted.
⁶ From the sole of your foot to the top of your head
  there is no soundness—
only wounds and welts
  and open sores,
not cleansed or bandaged
  or soothed with oil.

⁷ Your country is desolate,
  your cities burned with fire;
your fields are being stripped by foreigners
  right before you,
  laid waste as when overthrown by strangers.
⁸ The Daughter of Zion is left
  like a shelter in a vineyard,
like a hut in a field of melons,
  like a city under siege.
⁹ Unless the LORD Almighty
  had left us some survivors,
we would have become like Sodom,
  we would have been like Gomorrah.

¹⁰ Hear the word of the LORD,
  you rulers of Sodom;
listen to the law of our God,
  you people of Gomorrah!
¹¹ "The multitude of your sacrifices—
  what are they to me?" says the LORD.
"I have more than enough of burnt offerings,
  of rams and the fat of fattened animals;
I have no pleasure
  in the blood of bulls and lambs and goats.
¹² When you come to appear before me,
  who has asked this of you,
  this trampling of my courts?

¹³Stop bringing meaningless offerings!
　Your incense is detestable to me.
New Moons, Sabbaths and convocations—
　I cannot bear your evil assemblies.
¹⁴Your New Moon festivals and your appointed feasts
　my soul hates.
They have become a burden to me;
　I am weary of bearing them.
¹⁵When you spread out your hands in prayer,
　I will hide my eyes from you;
even if you offer many prayers,
　I will not listen.
Your hands are full of blood;
¹⁶　wash and make yourselves clean.
Take your evil deeds
　out of my sight!
Stop doing wrong,
¹⁷　learn to do right!
Seek justice,
　encourage the oppressed.ᵃ
Defend the cause of the fatherless,
　plead the case of the widow.

¹⁸"Come now, let us reason together,"
　says the Lᴏʀᴅ.
"Though your sins are like scarlet,
　they shall be as white as snow;
though they are red as crimson,
　they shall be like wool.
¹⁹If you are willing and obedient,
　you will eat the best from the land;
²⁰but if you resist and rebel,
　you will be devoured by the sword."
　　　　　　For the mouth of the Lᴏʀᴅ has spoken.

²¹See how the faithful city
　has become a harlot!
She once was full of justice;
　righteousness used to dwell in
　　her—
　but now murderers!
²²Your silver has become dross,
　your choice wine is diluted with
　　water.
²³Your rulers are rebels,
　companions of thieves;
they all love bribes
　and chase after gifts.
They do not defend the cause of the
　　fatherless;
　the widow's case does not come
　　before them.
²⁴Therefore the Lord, the Lᴏʀᴅ Almighty,
　the Mighty One of Israel, declares:
"Ah, I will get relief from my foes
　and avenge myself on my enemies.

ISAIAH 1:15–20

How bad is too bad? When do you step over the line, so there's no chance of turning back? When you take the family car and wreck it? When you try that new drug and find you're hooked? When you flunk out of school? Hey, it's best not to take any of those steps. But even if you have, it's never too late. God cried out to a sinful Judah, whose hands were "full of blood" (Isaiah 1:15), and urged them to change. "Though your sins are like scarlet," God promised, "they shall be as white as snow" (Isaiah 1:18). Don't give up. It's not too late to experience God's forgiveness, and to change.

Direct Line

ᵃ17 Or / rebuke the oppressor

²⁵I will turn my hand against you;
        I will thoroughly purge away your dross
        and remove all your impurities.
²⁶I will restore your judges as in days of old,
        your counselors as at the beginning.
    Afterward you will be called
        the City of Righteousness,
        the Faithful City."

²⁷Zion will be redeemed with justice,
        her penitent ones with righteousness.
²⁸But rebels and sinners will both be broken,
        and those who forsake the Lord will perish.

²⁹"You will be ashamed because of the sacred oaks
        in which you have delighted;
    you will be disgraced because of the gardens
        that you have chosen.
³⁰You will be like an oak with fading leaves,
        like a garden without water.
³¹The mighty man will become tinder
        and his work a spark;
    both will burn together,
        with no one to quench the fire."

The Mountain of the Lord This is what Isaiah son of Amoz saw concerning Judah and Jerusalem:

²In the last days

        the mountain of the Lord's temple will be established
            as chief among the mountains;
        it will be raised above the hills,
            and all nations will stream to it.

³Many peoples will come and say,

        "Come, let us go up to the mountain of the Lord,
            to the house of the God of Jacob.
        He will teach us his ways,
            so that we may walk in his paths."
        The law will go out from Zion,
            the word of the Lord from Jerusalem.
    ⁴He will judge between the nations
            and will settle disputes for many peoples.
        They will beat their swords into plowshares
            and their spears into pruning hooks.
        Nation will not take up sword against nation,
            nor will they train for war anymore.

    ⁵Come, O house of Jacob,
            let us walk in the light of the Lord.

The Day of the Lord
        ⁶You have abandoned your people,
            the house of Jacob.
        They are full of superstitions from the East;
            they practice divination like the Philistines
            and clasp hands with pagans.
        ⁷Their land is full of silver and gold;
            there is no end to their treasures.

Their land is full of horses;
  there is no end to their chariots.
⁸Their land is full of idols;
  they bow down to the work of their hands,
  to what their fingers have made.
⁹So man will be brought low
  and mankind humbled—
  do not forgive them.*ᵃ*

¹⁰Go into the rocks,
  hide in the ground
from dread of the Lᴏʀᴅ
  and the splendor of his majesty!
¹¹The eyes of the arrogant man will be humbled
  and the pride of men brought low;
the Lᴏʀᴅ alone will be exalted in that day.

¹²The Lᴏʀᴅ Almighty has a day in store
  for all the proud and lofty,
  for all that is exalted
  (and they will be humbled),
¹³for all the cedars of Lebanon, tall and lofty,
  and all the oaks of Bashan,
¹⁴for all the towering mountains
  and all the high hills,
¹⁵for every lofty tower
  and every fortified wall,
¹⁶for every trading ship*ᵇ*
  and every stately vessel.
¹⁷The arrogance of man will be brought low
  and the pride of men humbled;
the Lᴏʀᴅ alone will be exalted in that day,
¹⁸   and the idols will totally disappear.

¹⁹Men will flee to caves in the rocks
  and to holes in the ground
from dread of the Lᴏʀᴅ
  and the splendor of his majesty,
  when he rises to shake the earth.
²⁰In that day men will throw away
  to the rodents and bats
their idols of silver and idols of gold,
  which they made to worship.
²¹They will flee to caverns in the rocks
  and to the overhanging crags
from dread of the Lᴏʀᴅ
  and the splendor of his majesty,
  when he rises to shake the earth.
²²Stop trusting in man,
  who has but a breath in his nostrils.
  Of what account is he?

Judgment on Jerusalem and Judah

3 See now, the Lord,
  the Lᴏʀᴅ Almighty,
is about to take from Jerusalem and Judah
  both supply and support:
all supplies of food and all supplies of water,

ᵃ9 Or not raise them up   ᵇ16 Hebrew every ship of Tarshish

² the hero and warrior,
   the judge and prophet,
     the soothsayer and elder,
³ the captain of fifty and man of rank,
     the counselor, skilled craftsman and clever enchanter.

⁴ I will make boys their officials;
     mere children will govern them.
⁵ People will oppress each other—
     man against man, neighbor against neighbor.
The young will rise up against the old,
     the base against the honorable.

⁶ A man will seize one of his brothers
     at his father's home, and say,
"You have a cloak, you be our leader;
     take charge of this heap of ruins!"
⁷ But in that day he will cry out,
     "I have no remedy.
I have no food or clothing in my house;
     do not make me the leader of the people."

⁸ Jerusalem staggers,
     Judah is falling;
their words and deeds are against the Lᴏʀᴅ,
     defying his glorious presence.
⁹ The look on their faces testifies against them;
     they parade their sin like Sodom;
     they do not hide it.
Woe to them!
     They have brought disaster upon themselves.

¹⁰ Tell the righteous it will be well with them,
     for they will enjoy the fruit of their deeds.
¹¹ Woe to the wicked! Disaster is upon them!
They will be paid back for what their hands have done.

¹² Youths oppress my people,
     women rule over them.
O my people, your guides lead
     you astray;
     they turn you from the path.

¹³ The Lᴏʀᴅ takes his place in
     court;
     he rises to judge the people.
¹⁴ The Lᴏʀᴅ enters into judgment
     against the elders and
     leaders of his people:
"It is you who have ruined my
     vineyard;
     the plunder from the poor is
     in your houses.
¹⁵ What do you mean by
     crushing my people
     and grinding the faces of
     the poor?"
          declares the Lord,
          the Lᴏʀᴅ Almighty.

ISAIAH 3:8–10

Your school is rough. Drugs. Fights. Even guns and knives. Your neighborhood is rough too. There is pressure to join a gang just for safety. It's not easy to live like a Christian in a hostile world. Isaiah knew what it meant to live in a society where the "words and deeds" of the people are against everything God stands for. But the Lord had a word of encouragement for the Jews of Isaiah's day and for you: "Tell the righteous it will be well with them, for they will enjoy the fruit of their deeds" (Isaiah 3:10).

Direct Line

¹⁶The LORD says,
"The women of Zion are haughty,
   walking along with outstretched necks,
      flirting with their eyes,
   tripping along with mincing steps,
      with ornaments jingling on their ankles.
¹⁷Therefore the Lord will bring sores on the heads of the women
         of Zion;
      the LORD will make their scalps bald."

¹⁸In that day the Lord will snatch away their finery: the bangles and head-bands and crescent necklaces, ¹⁹the earrings and bracelets and veils, ²⁰the headdresses and ankle chains and sashes, the perfume bottles and charms, ²¹the signet rings and nose rings, ²²the fine robes and the capes and cloaks, the purses ²³and mirrors, and the linen garments and tiaras and shawls.

²⁴Instead of fragrance there will be a stench;
      instead of a sash, a rope;
   instead of well-dressed hair, baldness;
      instead of fine clothing, sackcloth;
      instead of beauty, branding.
²⁵Your men will fall by the sword,
      your warriors in battle.
²⁶The gates of Zion will lament and mourn;
      destitute, she will sit on the ground.

In that day seven women
      will take hold of one man
   and say, "We will eat our own food
      and provide our own clothes;
   only let us be called by your name.
      Take away our disgrace!"

The Branch of the LORD   ²In that day the Branch of the LORD will be beautiful and glorious, and the fruit of the land will be the pride and glory of the survivors in Israel. ³Those who are left in Zion, who remain in Jerusalem, will be called holy, all who are recorded among the living in Jerusalem. ⁴The Lord will wash away the filth of the women of Zion; he will cleanse the bloodstains from Jerusalem by a spirit*ᵃ* of judgment and a spirit*ᵃ* of fire. ⁵Then the LORD will create over all of Mount Zion and over those who assemble there a cloud of smoke by day and a glow of flaming fire by night; over all the glory will be a canopy. ⁶It will be a shelter and shade from the heat of the day, and a refuge and hiding place from the storm and rain.

The Song of the Vineyard
   I will sing for the one I love
      a song about his vineyard:
   My loved one had a vineyard
      on a fertile hillside.
²He dug it up and cleared it of stones
      and planted it with the choicest vines.
   He built a watchtower in it
      and cut out a winepress as well.
   Then he looked for a crop of good grapes,
      but it yielded only bad fruit.

³"Now you dwellers in Jerusalem and men of Judah,
      judge between me and my vineyard.

ᵃ4 Or the Spirit

⁴What more could have been done for my vineyard
   than I have done for it?
 When I looked for good grapes,
   why did it yield only bad?
⁵Now I will tell you
   what I am going to do to my vineyard:
 I will take away its hedge,
   and it will be destroyed;
 I will break down its wall,
   and it will be trampled.
⁶I will make it a wasteland,
   neither pruned nor cultivated,
   and briers and thorns will grow there.
 I will command the clouds
   not to rain on it."

⁷The vineyard of the LORD Almighty
   is the house of Israel,
 and the men of Judah
   are the garden of his delight.
 And he looked for justice, but saw bloodshed;
   for righteousness, but heard cries of distress.

Woes and Judgments

⁸Woe to you who add house to house
   and join field to field
 till no space is left
   and you live alone in the land.

⁹The LORD Almighty has declared in my hearing:

 "Surely the great houses will become desolate,
   the fine mansions left without occupants.
¹⁰A ten-acre*ᵃ* vineyard will produce only a bath*ᵇ* of wine,
   a homer*ᶜ* of seed only an ephah*ᵈ* of grain."

ᵃ10 Hebrew *ten-yoke,* that is, the land plowed by 10 yoke of oxen in one day   *ᵇ10* That is, probably about 6 gallons (about 22 liters)   *ᶜ10* That is, probably about 6 bushels (about 220 liters)   *ᵈ10* That is, probably about 3/5 bushel (about 22 liters)

Lots of people think being holy means never having any fun. They think God is disgusted whenever they enjoy themselves.

Actually, God enjoys a good time. The Bible says that God "provides us with everything for our enjoyment" (1 Timothy 6:17). When Jesus was on earth, he was criticized for going to dinner parties (Matthew 9:9–11). No, holiness doesn't mean being miserable.

To say that God is holy means that he is committed to doing what is right and loving—and that he wants his people to do what is right and loving too. Isaiah describes rich people who care nothing for the poor, then goes on to warn that "the holy God will show himself holy by his righteousness" (Isaiah 5:16). Because God is holy, he will punish the wicked and will see justice done.

The Bible Says
God Is Holy

¹¹Woe to those who rise early in the morning
   to run after their drinks,
who stay up late at night
   till they are inflamed with wine.
¹²They have harps and lyres at their banquets,
   tambourines and flutes and wine,
but they have no regard for the deeds of the Lord,
   no respect for the work of his hands.
¹³Therefore my people will go into exile
   for lack of understanding;
their men of rank will die of hunger
   and their masses will be parched with thirst.
¹⁴Therefore the grave*ᵃ* enlarges its appetite
   and opens its mouth without limit;
into it will descend their nobles and masses
   with all their brawlers and revelers.
¹⁵So man will be brought low
   and mankind humbled,
   the eyes of the arrogant humbled.
¹⁶But the Lord Almighty will be exalted by his justice,
   and the holy God will show himself holy by his
      righteousness.
¹⁷Then sheep will graze as in their own pasture;
   lambs will feed*ᵇ* among the ruins of the rich.

¹⁸Woe to those who draw sin along with cords of deceit,
   and wickedness as with cart ropes,
¹⁹to those who say, "Let God hurry,
   let him hasten his work
   so we may see it.
Let it approach,
   let the plan of the Holy One of Israel come,
   so we may know it."

²⁰Woe to those who call evil good
   and good evil,
who put darkness for light
   and light for darkness,
who put bitter for sweet
   and sweet for bitter.

²¹Woe to those who are wise in their own eyes
   and clever in their own sight.

²²Woe to those who are heroes at drinking wine
   and champions at mixing drinks,
²³who acquit the guilty for a bribe,
   but deny justice to the innocent.
²⁴Therefore, as tongues of fire lick up straw
   and as dry grass sinks down in the flames,
so their roots will decay
   and their flowers blow away like dust;
for they have rejected the law of the Lord Almighty
   and spurned the word of the Holy One of Israel.
²⁵Therefore the Lord's anger burns against his people;
   his hand is raised and he strikes them down.

ᵃ14 Hebrew *Sheol*   *ᵇ17* Septuagint; Hebrew / *strangers will eat*

The mountains shake,
    and the dead bodies are like refuse in the streets.

Yet for all this, his anger is not turned away,
    his hand is still upraised.

²⁶He lifts up a banner for the distant nations,
    he whistles for those at the ends of the earth.
Here they come,
    swiftly and speedily!
²⁷Not one of them grows tired or stumbles,
    not one slumbers or sleeps;
not a belt is loosened at the waist,
    not a sandal thong is broken.
²⁸Their arrows are sharp,
    all their bows are strung;
their horses' hoofs seem like flint,
    their chariot wheels like a whirlwind.
²⁹Their roar is like that of the lion,
    they roar like young lions;
they growl as they seize their prey
    and carry it off with no one to rescue.
³⁰In that day they will roar over it
    like the roaring of the sea.
And if one looks at the land,
    he will see darkness and distress;
    even the light will be darkened by the clouds.

Isaiah's Commission In the year that King Uzziah died, I saw the Lord seated on a throne, high and exalted, and the train of his robe filled the temple. ²Above him were seraphs, each with six wings: With two wings they covered their faces, with two they covered their feet, and with two they were flying. ³And they were calling to one another:

"Holy, holy, holy is the LORD
    Almighty;
the whole earth is full of his
    glory."

⁴At the sound of their voices the doorposts and thresholds shook and the temple was filled with smoke.

⁵"Woe to me!" I cried. "I am ruined! For I am a man of unclean lips, and I live among a people of unclean lips, and my eyes have seen the King, the LORD Almighty."

⁶Then one of the seraphs flew to me with a live coal in his hand, which he had taken with tongs from the altar. ⁷With it he touched my mouth and said, "See, this has touched your lips; your guilt is taken away and your sin atoned for."

⁸Then I heard the voice of the Lord saying, "Whom shall I send? And who will go for us?"

And I said, "Here am I. Send me!"
⁹He said, "Go and tell this people:

SEE
ISAIAH 6:8

" 'Be ever hearing, but never understanding;
　　be ever seeing, but never perceiving.'
¹⁰Make the heart of this people calloused;
　　make their ears dull
　　and close their eyes.ᵃ
Otherwise they might see with their eyes,
　　hear with their ears,
　　understand with their hearts,
and turn and be healed."

¹¹Then I said, "For how long, O Lord?"
And he answered:

"Until the cities lie ruined
　　and without inhabitant,
until the houses are left deserted
　　and the fields ruined and ravaged,
¹²until the LORD has sent everyone far away
　　and the land is utterly forsaken.
¹³And though a tenth remains in the land,
　　it will again be laid waste.
But as the terebinth and oak
　　leave stumps when they are cut down,
　　so the holy seed will be the stump in the land."

The Sign of Immanuel　When Ahaz son of Jotham, the son of Uzziah, was king of Judah, King Rezin of Aram and Pekah son of Remaliah king of Israel marched up to fight against Jerusalem, but they could not overpower it.

²Now the house of David was told, "Aram has allied itself withᵇ Ephraim"; so the hearts of Ahaz and his people were shaken, as the trees of the forest are shaken by the wind.

³Then the LORD said to Isaiah, "Go out, you and your son Shear-Jashub,ᶜ to meet Ahaz at the end of the aqueduct of the Upper Pool, on the road to the Washerman's Field. ⁴Say to him, 'Be careful, keep calm and don't be afraid. Do not lose heart because of these two smoldering stubs of firewood—because of the fierce anger of Rezin and Aram and of the son of Remaliah. ⁵Aram, Ephraim and Remaliah's son have plotted your ruin, saying, ⁶"Let us invade Judah; let us tear it apart and divide it among ourselves, and make the son of Tabeel king over it." ⁷Yet this is what the Sovereign LORD says:

" 'It will not take place,
　　it will not happen,
⁸for the head of Aram is Damascus,
　　and the head of Damascus is only Rezin.
Within sixty-five years
　　Ephraim will be too shattered to be a people.
⁹The head of Ephraim is Samaria,
　　and the head of Samaria is only Remaliah's son.
If you do not stand firm in your faith,
　　you will not stand at all.' "

¹⁰Again the LORD spoke to Ahaz, ¹¹"Ask the LORD your God for a sign, whether in the deepest depths or in the highest heights."

¹²But Ahaz said, "I will not ask; I will not put the LORD to the test."

ᵃ9,10 Hebrew; Septuagint 'You will be ever hearing, but never understanding; / you will be ever seeing, but never perceiving.' / ¹⁰This people's heart has become calloused; / they hardly hear with their ears, / and they have closed their eyes   ᵇ2 Or has set up camp in   ᶜ3 Shear-Jashub means a remnant will return.

¹³Then Isaiah said, "Hear now, you house of David! Is it not enough to try the patience of men? Will you try the patience of my God also? ¹⁴Therefore the Lord himself will give you*a* a sign: The virgin will be with child and will give birth to a son, and*b* will call him Immanuel.*c* ¹⁵He will eat curds and honey when he knows enough to reject the wrong and choose the right. ¹⁶But before the boy knows enough to reject the wrong and choose the right, the land of the two kings you dread will be laid waste. ¹⁷The Lord will bring on you and on your people and on the house of your father a time unlike any since Ephraim broke away from Judah—he will bring the king of Assyria."

¹⁸In that day the Lord will whistle for flies from the distant streams of Egypt and for bees from the land of Assyria. ¹⁹They will all come and settle in the steep ravines and in the crevices in the rocks, on all the thornbushes and at all the water holes. ²⁰In that day the Lord will use a razor hired from beyond the River*d*—the king of Assyria—to shave your head and the hair of your legs, and to take off your beards also. ²¹In that day, a man will keep alive a young cow and two goats. ²²And because of the abundance of the milk they give, he will have curds to eat. All who remain in the land will eat curds and honey. ²³In that day, in every place where there were a thousand vines worth a thousand silver shekels,*e* there will be only briers and thorns. ²⁴Men will go there with bow and arrow, for the land will be covered with briers and thorns. ²⁵As for all the hills once cultivated by the hoe, you will no longer go there for fear of the briers and thorns; they will become places where cattle are turned loose and where sheep run.

Assyria, the Lord's Instrument The Lord said to me, "Take a large scroll and write on it with an ordinary pen: Maher-Shalal-Hash-Baz.*f* ²And I will call in Uriah the priest and Zechariah son of Jeberekiah as reliable witnesses for me."

³Then I went to the prophetess, and she conceived and gave birth to a son. And the Lord said to me, "Name him Maher-Shalal-Hash-Baz. ⁴Before the boy knows how to say 'My father' or 'My mother,' the wealth of Damascus and the plunder of Samaria will be carried off by the king of Assyria."

⁵The Lord spoke to me again:

⁶"Because this people has rejected
   the gently flowing waters of Shiloah
and rejoices over Rezin
   and the son of Remaliah,
⁷therefore the Lord is about to bring against them
   the mighty floodwaters of the River*d*—
   the king of Assyria with all his pomp.
It will overflow all its channels,
   run over all its banks
⁸and sweep on into Judah, swirling over it,
   passing through it and reaching up to the neck.
Its outspread wings will cover the breadth of your land,
   O Immanuel*c*!"

⁹Raise the war cry,*g* you nations, and be shattered!
   Listen, all you distant lands.

ISAIAH 7

QUIZZER

Q: What does the name Immanuel mean?

BONUS: When was the prophecy of Isaiah 7:14 fulfilled?

Answers on page 885

---

*a*14 The Hebrew is plural. *b*14 Masoretic Text; Dead Sea Scrolls *and he* or *and they* *c*14,8 *Immanuel* means *God with us.* *d*20,7 That is, the Euphrates *e*23 That is, about 25 pounds (about 11.5 kilograms) *f*1 *Maher-Shalal-Hash-Baz* means *quick to the plunder, swift to the spoil*; also in verse 3. *g*9 Or *Do your worst*

Prepare for battle, and be shattered!
Prepare for battle, and be shattered!
[10]Devise your strategy, but it will be thwarted;
propose your plan, but it will not stand,
for God is with us.[a]

Fear God [11]The LORD spoke to me with his strong hand upon me, warning me not to follow the way of this people. He said:

[12]"Do not call conspiracy
everything that these people call conspiracy[b];
do not fear what they fear,
and do not dread it.
[13]The LORD Almighty is the one you are to regard as holy,
he is the one you are to fear,
he is the one you are to dread,
[14]and he will be a sanctuary;
but for both houses of Israel he will be
a stone that causes men to stumble
and a rock that makes them fall.
And for the people of Jerusalem he will be
a trap and a snare.
[15]Many of them will stumble;
they will fall and be broken,
they will be snared and captured."

[16]Bind up the testimony
and seal up the law among my disciples.
[17]I will wait for the LORD,
who is hiding his face from the house of Jacob.
I will put my trust in him.

[18]Here am I, and the children the LORD has given me. We are signs and symbols in Israel from the LORD Almighty, who dwells on Mount Zion.
[19]When men tell you to consult mediums and spiritists, who whisper and mutter, should not a people inquire of their God? Why consult the dead on behalf of the living? [20]To the law and to the testimony! If they do not speak according to this word, they have no light of dawn. [21]Distressed and hungry, they will roam through the land; when they are famished, they will become enraged and, looking upward, will curse their king and their God. [22]Then they will look toward the earth and see only distress and darkness and fearful gloom, and they will be thrust into utter darkness.

To Us a Child Is Born Nevertheless, there will be no more gloom for those who were in distress. In the past he humbled the land of Zebulun and the land of Naphtali, but in the future he will honor Galilee of the Gentiles, by the way of the sea, along the Jordan—

[2]The people walking in darkness
have seen a great light;
on those living in the land of the shadow of death[c]
a light has dawned.
[3]You have enlarged the nation
and increased their joy;
they rejoice before you
as people rejoice at the harvest,

---

[a]10 Hebrew *Immanuel*   [b]12 Or *Do not call for a treaty / every time these people call for a treaty*   [c]2 Or *land of darkness*

as men rejoice
　　when dividing the plunder.
⁴For as in the day of Midian's defeat,
　　you have shattered
the yoke that burdens them,
　　the bar across their shoulders,
　　the rod of their oppressor.
⁵Every warrior's boot used in battle
　　and every garment rolled in blood
will be destined for burning,
　　will be fuel for the fire.
⁶For to us a child is born,
　　to us a son is given,
　　and the government will be on his shoulders.
And he will be called
　　Wonderful Counselor,ᵃ Mighty God,
　　Everlasting Father, Prince of Peace.
⁷Of the increase of his government and peace
　　there will be no end.
He will reign on David's throne
　　and over his kingdom,
establishing and upholding it
　　with justice and righteousness
　　from that time on and forever.
The zeal of the Lᴏʀᴅ Almighty
　　will accomplish this.

The Lᴏʀᴅ's Anger Against Israel

⁸The Lord has sent a message against Jacob;
　　it will fall on Israel.
⁹All the people will know it—
　　Ephraim and the inhabitants of Samaria—
who say with pride
　　and arrogance of heart,
¹⁰"The bricks have fallen down,
　　but we will rebuild with dressed stone;
the fig trees have been felled,
　　but we will replace them with cedars."
¹¹But the Lᴏʀᴅ has strengthened Rezin's foes against them
　　and has spurred their enemies on.
¹²Arameans from the east and Philistines from the west
　　have devoured Israel with open mouth.

Yet for all this, his anger is not turned away,
　　his hand is still upraised.

¹³But the people have not returned to him who struck them,
　　nor have they sought the Lᴏʀᴅ Almighty.
¹⁴So the Lᴏʀᴅ will cut off from Israel both head and tail,
　　both palm branch and reed in a single day;
¹⁵the elders and prominent men are the head,
　　the prophets who teach lies are the tail.
¹⁶Those who guide this people mislead them,
　　and those who are guided are led astray.
¹⁷Therefore the Lord will take no pleasure in the young men,
　　nor will he pity the fatherless and widows,

Answers

*to Quizzer on
page 883*

**A: God is with us
(Isaiah 7:14).**

**BONUS: In 4 ʙ.ᴄ.
when Jesus was
born. (Our
calendar miscal-
culates the
date of
Jesus' birth.)**

ᵃ6 Or *Wonderful, Counselor*

for everyone is ungodly and wicked,
 every mouth speaks vileness.

Yet for all this, his anger is not turned away,
 his hand is still upraised.

¹⁸Surely wickedness burns like a fire;
 it consumes briers and thorns,
it sets the forest thickets ablaze,
 so that it rolls upward in a column of smoke.
¹⁹By the wrath of the LORD Almighty
 the land will be scorched
and the people will be fuel for the fire;
 no one will spare his brother.
²⁰On the right they will devour,
 but still be hungry;
on the left they will eat,
 but not be satisfied.
Each will feed on the flesh of his own offspring*:
²¹ Manasseh will feed on Ephraim, and Ephraim on Manasseh;
 together they will turn against Judah.

Yet for all this, his anger is not turned away,
 his hand is still upraised.

10 Woe to those who make unjust laws,
 to those who issue oppressive decrees,
²to deprive the poor of their rights
 and withhold justice from the oppressed of my people,
making widows their prey
 and robbing the fatherless.
³What will you do on the day of reckoning,
 when disaster comes from afar?
To whom will you run for help?
 Where will you leave your riches?
⁴Nothing will remain but to cringe among the captives
 or fall among the slain.

Yet for all this, his anger is not turned away,
 his hand is still upraised.

God's Judgment on Assyria
⁵"Woe to the Assyrian, the rod of my anger,
 in whose hand is the club of my wrath!
⁶I send him against a godless nation,
 I dispatch him against a people who anger me,
to seize loot and snatch plunder,
 and to trample them down like mud in the streets.
⁷But this is not what he intends,
 this is not what he has in mind;
his purpose is to destroy,
 to put an end to many nations.
⁸'Are not my commanders all kings?' he says.
⁹ 'Has not Calno fared like Carchemish?
Is not Hamath like Arpad,
 and Samaria like Damascus?
¹⁰As my hand seized the kingdoms of the idols,

---

*20 Or *arm*

kingdoms whose images excelled those of Jerusalem and
    Samaria—
¹¹shall I not deal with Jerusalem and her images
    as I dealt with Samaria and her idols?' "

¹²When the Lord has finished all his work against Mount Zion and Jerusalem, he will say, "I will punish the king of Assyria for the willful pride of his heart and the haughty look in his eyes. ¹³For he says:

    " 'By the strength of my hand I have done this,
        and by my wisdom, because I have understanding.
    I removed the boundaries of nations,
        I plundered their treasures;
        like a mighty one I subdued*^a* their kings.
¹⁴As one reaches into a nest,
        so my hand reached for the wealth of the nations;
    as men gather abandoned eggs,
        so I gathered all the countries;
    not one flapped a wing,
        or opened its mouth to chirp.' "

¹⁵Does the ax raise itself above him who swings it,
        or the saw boast against him who uses it?
    As if a rod were to wield him who lifts it up,
        or a club brandish him who is not wood!
¹⁶Therefore, the Lord, the LORD Almighty,
        will send a wasting disease upon his sturdy warriors;
    under his pomp a fire will be kindled
        like a blazing flame.
¹⁷The Light of Israel will become a fire,
        their Holy One a flame;
    in a single day it will burn and consume
        his thorns and his briers.
¹⁸The splendor of his forests and fertile fields
        it will completely destroy,
    as when a sick man wastes away.
¹⁹And the remaining trees of his forests will be so few
        that a child could write them down.

The Remnant of Israel
²⁰In that day the remnant of Israel,
        the survivors of the house of Jacob,
    will no longer rely on him
        who struck them down
    but will truly rely on the LORD,
        the Holy One of Israel.
²¹A remnant will return,^b a remnant of Jacob
        will return to the Mighty God.
²²Though your people, O Israel, be like the sand by the sea,
        only a remnant will return.
    Destruction has been decreed,
        overwhelming and righteous.
²³The Lord, the LORD Almighty, will carry out
        the destruction decreed upon the whole land.

²⁴Therefore, this is what the Lord, the LORD Almighty, says:

---

^a13 Or / *I subdued the mighty,*   *^b21* Hebrew *shear-jashub,* also in verse 22

"O my people who live in Zion,
    do not be afraid of the Assyrians,
who beat you with a rod
    and lift up a club against you, as Egypt did.
²⁵Very soon my anger against you will end
    and my wrath will be directed to their destruction."

²⁶The LORD Almighty will lash them with a whip,
    as when he struck down Midian at the rock of Oreb;
and he will raise his staff over the waters,
    as he did in Egypt.
²⁷In that day their burden will be lifted from your shoulders,
    their yoke from your neck;
the yoke will be broken
    because you have grown so fat.ª

²⁸They enter Aiath;
    they pass through Migron;
    they store supplies at Micmash.
²⁹They go over the pass, and say,
    "We will camp overnight at Geba."
Ramah trembles;
    Gibeah of Saul flees.
³⁰Cry out, O Daughter of Gallim!
    Listen, O Laishah!
    Poor Anathoth!
³¹Madmenah is in flight;
    the people of Gebim take cover.
³²This day they will halt at Nob;
    they will shake their fist
at the mount of the Daughter of Zion,
    at the hill of Jerusalem.

³³See, the Lord, the LORD Almighty,
    will lop off the boughs with great power.
The lofty trees will be felled,
    the tall ones will be brought low.
³⁴He will cut down the forest thickets with an ax;
    Lebanon will fall before the Mighty One.

ª27 Hebrew; Septuagint *broken / from your shoulders*

The Bible Says

Animals Fell Too

Why is nature so cruel? Predators kill weaker animals. Why did God create animals that hurt and kill other animals? The Bible tells you that the sin of Adam and Eve spoiled nature as well as the human race. The ground itself was cursed, and even vegetation changed (Genesis 3:17). When Adam and Eve fell, plants and animals fell too.

Take a look at Isaiah 11:6–9. In the future God will actually change the nature of wild animals. "The wolf will live with the lamb," and "the cow will feed with the bear."

This world is beautiful now. Imagine how beautiful it was before Adam and Eve sinned. One day this world will be perfect again. No wonder Romans 8:19–21 says that creation itself can hardly wait.

11

The Branch From Jesse

A shoot will come up from the stump of Jesse;
  from his roots a Branch will bear fruit.
[2] The Spirit of the Lord will rest on him—
  the Spirit of wisdom and of understanding,
  the Spirit of counsel and of power,
  the Spirit of knowledge and of the fear of the Lord—
[3] and he will delight in the fear of the Lord.

He will not judge by what he sees with his eyes,
  or decide by what he hears with his ears;
[4] but with righteousness he will judge the needy,
  with justice he will give decisions for the poor of the earth.
He will strike the earth with the rod of his mouth;
  with the breath of his lips he will slay the wicked.
[5] Righteousness will be his belt
  and faithfulness the sash around his waist.

[6] The wolf will live with the lamb,
  the leopard will lie down with the goat,
the calf and the lion and the yearling[a] together;
  and a little child will lead them.
[7] The cow will feed with the bear,
  their young will lie down together,
  and the lion will eat straw like the ox.
[8] The infant will play near the hole of the cobra,
  and the young child put his hand into the viper's nest.
[9] They will neither harm nor destroy
  on all my holy mountain,
for the earth will be full of the knowledge of the Lord
  as the waters cover the sea.

[10] In that day the Root of Jesse will stand as a banner for the peoples; the nations will rally to him, and his place of rest will be glorious. [11] In that day the Lord will reach out his hand a second time to reclaim the remnant that is left of his people from Assyria, from Lower Egypt, from Upper Egypt,[b] from Cush,[c] from Elam, from Babylonia,[d] from Hamath and from the islands of the sea.

[12] He will raise a banner for the nations
  and gather the exiles of Israel;
he will assemble the scattered people of Judah
  from the four quarters of the earth.
[13] Ephraim's jealousy will vanish,
  and Judah's enemies[e] will be cut off;
Ephraim will not be jealous of Judah,
  nor Judah hostile toward Ephraim.
[14] They will swoop down on the slopes of Philistia to the west;
  together they will plunder the people to the east.
They will lay hands on Edom and Moab,
  and the Ammonites will be subject to them.
[15] The Lord will dry up
  the gulf of the Egyptian sea;
with a scorching wind he will sweep his hand
  over the Euphrates River.[f]

---

[a]6 Hebrew; Septuagint *lion will feed*   [b]11 Hebrew *from Pathros*   [c]11 That is, the upper Nile region   [d]11 Hebrew *Shinar*   [e]13 Or *hostility*   [f]15 Hebrew *the River*

He will break it up into seven streams
    so that men can cross over in sandals.
[16] There will be a highway for the remnant of his people
    that is left from Assyria,
as there was for Israel
    when they came up from Egypt.

Songs of Praise   In that day you will say:

"I will praise you, O LORD.
    Although you were angry with me,
your anger has turned away
    and you have comforted me.
[2] Surely God is my salvation;
    I will trust and not be afraid.
The LORD, the LORD, is my strength and my song;
    he has become my salvation."
[3] With joy you will draw water
    from the wells of salvation.

[4] In that day you will say:

"Give thanks to the LORD, call on his name;
    make known among the nations what he has done,
    and proclaim that his name is exalted.
[5] Sing to the LORD, for he has done glorious things;
    let this be known to all the world.
[6] Shout aloud and sing for joy, people of Zion,
    for great is the Holy One of Israel among you."

A Prophecy Against Babylon   An oracle concerning Babylon that Isaiah son of Amoz saw:

[2] Raise a banner on a bare hilltop,
    shout to them;
beckon to them
    to enter the gates of the nobles.
[3] I have commanded my holy ones;
    I have summoned my warriors to carry out my wrath—
    those who rejoice in my triumph.

[4] Listen, a noise on the mountains,
    like that of a great multitude!
Listen, an uproar among the kingdoms,
    like nations massing together!
The LORD Almighty is mustering
    an army for war.
[5] They come from faraway lands,
    from the ends of the heavens—
the LORD and the weapons of his wrath—
    to destroy the whole country.

[6] Wail, for the day of the LORD is near;
    it will come like destruction from the Almighty.[a]
[7] Because of this, all hands will go limp,
    every man's heart will melt.
[8] Terror will seize them,

[a]6 Hebrew *Shaddai*

pain and anguish will grip them;
  they will writhe like a woman in labor.
They will look aghast at each other,
  their faces aflame.

⁹See, the day of the LORD is coming
  —a cruel day, with wrath and fierce anger—
to make the land desolate
  and destroy the sinners within it.
¹⁰The stars of heaven and their constellations
  will not show their light.
The rising sun will be darkened
  and the moon will not give its light.
¹¹I will punish the world for its evil,
  the wicked for their sins.
I will put an end to the arrogance of the haughty
  and will humble the pride of the ruthless.
¹²I will make man scarcer than pure gold,
  more rare than the gold of Ophir.
¹³Therefore I will make the heavens tremble;
  and the earth will shake from its place
at the wrath of the LORD Almighty,
  in the day of his burning anger.

¹⁴Like a hunted gazelle,
  like sheep without a shepherd,
each will return to his own people,
  each will flee to his native land.
¹⁵Whoever is captured will be thrust through;
  all who are caught will fall by the sword.
¹⁶Their infants will be dashed to pieces before their eyes;
  their houses will be looted and their wives ravished.

¹⁷See, I will stir up against them the Medes,
  who do not care for silver
  and have no delight in gold.
¹⁸Their bows will strike down the young men;
  they will have no mercy on infants
  nor will they look with compassion on children.
¹⁹Babylon, the jewel of kingdoms,
  the glory of the Babylonians'ᵃ pride,
will be overthrown by God
  like Sodom and Gomorrah.
²⁰She will never be inhabited
  or lived in through all generations;
no Arab will pitch his tent there,
  no shepherd will rest his flocks there.
²¹But desert creatures will lie there,
  jackals will fill her houses;
there the owls will dwell,
  and there the wild goats will leap about.
²²Hyenas will howl in her strongholds,
  jackals in her luxurious palaces.
Her time is at hand,
  and her days will not be prolonged.

ᵃ19 Or Chaldeans'

14 The Lord will have compassion on Jacob;
    once again he will choose Israel
    and will settle them in their own land.
Aliens will join them
    and unite with the house of Jacob.
² Nations will take them
    and bring them to their own place.
And the house of Israel will possess the nations
    as menservants and maidservants in the Lord's land.
They will make captives of their captors
    and rule over their oppressors.

³On the day the Lord gives you relief from suffering and turmoil and cruel bondage, ⁴you will take up this taunt against the king of Babylon:

How the oppressor has come to an end!
    How his fury*ᵃ* has ended!
⁵ The Lord has broken the rod of the wicked,
    the scepter of the rulers,
⁶ which in anger struck down peoples
    with unceasing blows,
and in fury subdued nations
    with relentless aggression.
⁷ All the lands are at rest and at peace;
    they break into singing.
⁸ Even the pine trees and the cedars of Lebanon
    exult over you and say,
"Now that you have been laid low,
    no woodsman comes to cut us down."

⁹ The grave*ᵇ* below is all astir
    to meet you at your coming;
it rouses the spirits of the departed to greet you—
    all those who were leaders in the world;
it makes them rise from their thrones—
    all those who were kings over the nations.
¹⁰ They will all respond,
    they will say to you,
"You also have become weak, as we are;
    you have become like us."
¹¹ All your pomp has been brought down to the grave,
    along with the noise of your harps;
maggots are spread out beneath you
    and worms cover you.

¹² How you have fallen from heaven,
    O morning star, son of the dawn!
You have been cast down to the earth,
    you who once laid low the nations!
¹³ You said in your heart,
    "I will ascend to heaven;
I will raise my throne
    above the stars of God;
I will sit enthroned on the mount of assembly,
    on the utmost heights of the sacred mountain.*ᶜ*

ᵃ4 Dead Sea Scrolls, Septuagint and Syriac; the meaning of the word in the Masoretic Text is uncertain.
ᵇ9 Hebrew *Sheol*; also in verses 11 and 15   *ᶜ13* Or *the north*; Hebrew *Zaphon*

¹⁴I will ascend above the tops of the clouds;
    I will make myself like the Most High."
¹⁵But you are brought down to the grave,
    to the depths of the pit.

¹⁶Those who see you stare at you,
    they ponder your fate:
  "Is this the man who shook the earth
    and made kingdoms tremble,
¹⁷the man who made the world a desert,
    who overthrew its cities
    and would not let his captives go home?"

¹⁸All the kings of the nations lie in state,
    each in his own tomb.
¹⁹But you are cast out of your tomb
    like a rejected branch;
  you are covered with the slain,
    with those pierced by the sword,
    those who descend to the stones of the pit.
  Like a corpse trampled underfoot,
²⁰   you will not join them in burial,
  for you have destroyed your land
    and killed your people.

  The offspring of the wicked
    will never be mentioned again.
²¹Prepare a place to slaughter his sons
    for the sins of their forefathers;
  they are not to rise to inherit the land
    and cover the earth with their cities.

²²"I will rise up against them,"
    declares the LORD Almighty.
  "I will cut off from Babylon her name and survivors,
    her offspring and descendants,"
                    declares the LORD.
²³"I will turn her into a place for owls
    and into swampland;
  I will sweep her with the broom of destruction,"
    declares the LORD Almighty.

A Prophecy Against Assyria   ²⁴The LORD Almighty has sworn,

  "Surely, as I have planned, so it will be,
    and as I have purposed, so it will stand.
²⁵I will crush the Assyrian in my land;
    on my mountains I will trample him down.
  His yoke will be taken from my people,
    and his burden removed from their shoulders."

²⁶This is the plan determined for the whole world;
    this is the hand stretched out over all nations.
²⁷For the LORD Almighty has purposed, and who can thwart him?
    His hand is stretched out, and who can turn it back?

A Prophecy Against the Philistines   ²⁸This oracle came in the year King Ahaz
died:

²⁹Do not rejoice, all you Philistines,
    that the rod that struck you is broken;

from the root of that snake will spring up a viper,
    its fruit will be a darting, venomous serpent.
[30]The poorest of the poor will find pasture,
    and the needy will lie down in safety.
But your root I will destroy by famine;
    it will slay your survivors.

[31]Wail, O gate! Howl, O city!
    Melt away, all you Philistines!
A cloud of smoke comes from the north,
    and there is not a straggler in its ranks.
[32]What answer shall be given
    to the envoys of that nation?
"The LORD has established Zion,
    and in her his afflicted people will find refuge."

15 *A Prophecy Against Moab* An oracle concerning Moab:

Ar in Moab is ruined,
    destroyed in a night!
Kir in Moab is ruined,
    destroyed in a night!
[2]Dibon goes up to its temple,
    to its high places to weep;
Moab wails over Nebo and Medeba.
Every head is shaved
    and every beard cut off.
[3]In the streets they wear sackcloth;
    on the roofs and in the public squares
they all wail,
    prostrate with weeping.
[4]Heshbon and Elealeh cry out,
    their voices are heard all the way to Jahaz.
Therefore the armed men of Moab cry out,
    and their hearts are faint.

[5]My heart cries out over Moab;
    her fugitives flee as far as Zoar,
    as far as Eglath Shelishiyah.
They go up the way to Luhith,
    weeping as they go;
on the road to Horonaim
    they lament their destruction.
[6]The waters of Nimrim are dried up
    and the grass is withered;
the vegetation is gone
    and nothing green is left.
[7]So the wealth they have acquired and stored up
    they carry away over the Ravine of the Poplars.
[8]Their outcry echoes along the border of Moab;
    their wailing reaches as far as Eglaim,
    their lamentation as far as Beer Elim.
[9]Dimon's[a] waters are full of blood,
    but I will bring still more upon Dimon[a]—
a lion upon the fugitives of Moab
    and upon those who remain in the land.

---

[a]9 Masoretic Text; Dead Sea Scrolls, some Septuagint manuscripts and Vulgate *Dibon*

16 Send lambs as tribute
to the ruler of the land,
from Sela, across the desert,
to the mount of the Daughter of Zion.
² Like fluttering birds
pushed from the nest,
so are the women of Moab
at the fords of the Arnon.

³ "Give us counsel,
render a decision.
Make your shadow like night—
at high noon.
Hide the fugitives,
do not betray the refugees.
⁴ Let the Moabite fugitives stay with you;
be their shelter from the destroyer."

The oppressor will come to an end,
and destruction will cease;
the aggressor will vanish from the land.
⁵ In love a throne will be established;
in faithfulness a man will sit on it—
one from the house^a of David—
one who in judging seeks justice
and speeds the cause of righteousness.

⁶ We have heard of Moab's pride—
her overweening pride and conceit,
her pride and her insolence—
but her boasts are empty.
⁷ Therefore the Moabites wail,
they wail together for Moab.
Lament and grieve
for the men^b of Kir Hareseth.
⁸ The fields of Heshbon wither,
the vines of Sibmah also.
The rulers of the nations
have trampled down the choicest vines,
which once reached Jazer
and spread toward the desert.
Their shoots spread out
and went as far as the sea.
⁹ So I weep, as Jazer weeps,
for the vines of Sibmah.
O Heshbon, O Elealeh,
I drench you with tears!
The shouts of joy over your ripened fruit
and over your harvests have been stilled.
¹⁰ Joy and gladness are taken away from the orchards;
no one sings or shouts in the vineyards;
no one treads out wine at the presses,
for I have put an end to the shouting.
¹¹ My heart laments for Moab like a harp,
my inmost being for Kir Hareseth.

^a5 Hebrew *tent*   ^b7 Or *"raisin cakes,"* a wordplay

¹²When Moab appears at her high place,
  she only wears herself out;
when she goes to her shrine to pray,
  it is to no avail.

¹³This is the word the LORD has already spoken concerning Moab. ¹⁴But now the LORD says: "Within three years, as a servant bound by contract would count them, Moab's splendor and all her many people will be despised, and her survivors will be very few and feeble."

17 An Oracle Against Damascus An oracle concerning Damascus:

"See, Damascus will no longer be a city
  but will become a heap of ruins.
²The cities of Aroer will be deserted
  and left to flocks, which will lie down,
  with no one to make them afraid.
³The fortified city will disappear from Ephraim,
  and royal power from Damascus;
the remnant of Aram will be
  like the glory of the Israelites,"
                    declares the LORD Almighty.

⁴"In that day the glory of Jacob will fade;
  the fat of his body will waste away.
⁵It will be as when a reaper gathers the standing grain
  and harvests the grain with his arm—
as when a man gleans heads of grain
  in the Valley of Rephaim.
⁶Yet some gleanings will remain,
  as when an olive tree is beaten,
leaving two or three olives on the topmost branches,
  four or five on the fruitful boughs,"
                    declares the LORD, the God of Israel.

⁷In that day men will look to their Maker
  and turn their eyes to the Holy One of Israel.
⁸They will not look to the altars,
  the work of their hands,
and they will have no regard for the Asherah poles*
  and the incense altars their fingers have made.

⁹In that day their strong cities, which they left because of the Israelites, will be like places abandoned to thickets and undergrowth. And all will be desolation.

¹⁰You have forgotten God your Savior;
  you have not remembered the Rock, your fortress.
Therefore, though you set out the finest plants
  and plant imported vines,
¹¹though on the day you set them out, you make them grow,
  and on the morning when you plant them, you bring them
    to bud,
yet the harvest will be as nothing
  in the day of disease and incurable pain.

¹²Oh, the raging of many nations—
  they rage like the raging sea!

*8 That is, symbols of the goddess Asherah

Oh, the uproar of the peoples—
    they roar like the roaring of great waters!
¹³Although the peoples roar like the roar of surging waters,
    when he rebukes them they flee far away,
driven before the wind like chaff on the hills,
    like tumbleweed before a gale.
¹⁴In the evening, sudden terror!
    Before the morning, they are gone!
This is the portion of those who loot us,
    the lot of those who plunder us.

A Prophecy Against Cush

18 Woe to the land of whirring wings*ᵃ*
    along the rivers of Cush,*ᵇ*
²which sends envoys by sea
    in papyrus boats over the water.

Go, swift messengers,
to a people tall and smooth-skinned,
    to a people feared far and wide,
an aggressive nation of strange speech,
    whose land is divided by rivers.

³All you people of the world,
    you who live on the earth,
when a banner is raised on the mountains,
    you will see it,
and when a trumpet sounds,
    you will hear it.
⁴This is what the Lord says to me:
    "I will remain quiet and will look on from my dwelling place,
like shimmering heat in the sunshine,
    like a cloud of dew in the heat of harvest."
⁵For, before the harvest, when the blossom is gone
    and the flower becomes a ripening grape,
he will cut off the shoots with pruning knives,
    and cut down and take away the spreading branches.
⁶They will all be left to the mountain birds of prey
    and to the wild animals;
the birds will feed on them all summer,
    the wild animals all winter.

⁷At that time gifts will be brought to the Lord Almighty

from a people tall and smooth-skinned,
    from a people feared far and wide,
an aggressive nation of strange speech,
    whose land is divided by rivers—

the gifts will be brought to Mount Zion, the place of the Name of the Lord Almighty.

A Prophecy About Egypt

19 An oracle concerning Egypt:

See, the Lord rides on a swift cloud
    and is coming to Egypt.
The idols of Egypt tremble before him,
    and the hearts of the Egyptians melt within them.

ᵃ1 Or of locusts ᵇ1 That is, the upper Nile region

² "I will stir up Egyptian against Egyptian—
    brother will fight against brother,
    neighbor against neighbor,
    city against city,
    kingdom against kingdom.
³ The Egyptians will lose heart,
    and I will bring their plans to nothing;
  they will consult the idols and the spirits of the dead,
    the mediums and the spiritists.
⁴ I will hand the Egyptians over
    to the power of a cruel master,
  and a fierce king will rule over them,"
    declares the Lord, the Lᴏʀᴅ Almighty.

⁵ The waters of the river will dry up,
    and the riverbed will be parched and dry.
⁶ The canals will stink;
    the streams of Egypt will dwindle and dry up.
  The reeds and rushes will wither,
⁷   also the plants along the Nile,
    at the mouth of the river.
  Every sown field along the Nile
    will become parched, will blow away and be no more.
⁸ The fishermen will groan and lament,
    all who cast hooks into the Nile;
  those who throw nets on the water
    will pine away.
⁹ Those who work with combed flax will despair,
    the weavers of fine linen will lose hope.
¹⁰ The workers in cloth will be dejected,
    and all the wage earners will be sick at heart.

¹¹ The officials of Zoan are nothing but fools;
    the wise counselors of Pharaoh give senseless advice.
  How can you say to Pharaoh,
    "I am one of the wise men,
    a disciple of the ancient kings"?

¹² Where are your wise men now?
    Let them show you and make known
  what the Lᴏʀᴅ Almighty
    has planned against Egypt.
¹³ The officials of Zoan have become fools,
    the leaders of Memphis^a are deceived;
  the cornerstones of her peoples
    have led Egypt astray.
¹⁴ The Lᴏʀᴅ has poured into them
    a spirit of dizziness;
  they make Egypt stagger in all that she does,
    as a drunkard staggers around in his vomit.
¹⁵ There is nothing Egypt can do—
    head or tail, palm branch or reed.

¹⁶In that day the Egyptians will be like women. They will shudder with fear at the uplifted hand that the Lᴏʀᴅ Almighty raises against them. ¹⁷And the land of Judah will bring terror to the Egyptians; everyone to whom Ju-

^a*13* Hebrew *Noph*

dah is mentioned will be terrified, because of what the LORD Almighty is planning against them.

¹⁸In that day five cities in Egypt will speak the language of Canaan and swear allegiance to the LORD Almighty. One of them will be called the City of Destruction.ᵃ

¹⁹In that day there will be an altar to the LORD in the heart of Egypt, and a monument to the LORD at its border. ²⁰It will be a sign and witness to the LORD Almighty in the land of Egypt. When they cry out to the LORD because of their oppressors, he will send them a savior and defender, and he will rescue them. ²¹So the LORD will make himself known to the Egyptians, and in that day they will acknowledge the LORD. They will worship with sacrifices and grain offerings; they will make vows to the LORD and keep them. ²²The LORD will strike Egypt with a plague; he will strike them and heal them. They will turn to the LORD, and he will respond to their pleas and heal them.

²³In that day there will be a highway from Egypt to Assyria. The Assyrians will go to Egypt and the Egyptians to Assyria. The Egyptians and Assyrians will worship together. ²⁴In that day Israel will be the third, along with Egypt and Assyria, a blessing on the earth. ²⁵The LORD Almighty will bless them, saying, "Blessed be Egypt my people, Assyria my handiwork, and Israel my inheritance."

20 *A Prophecy Against Egypt and Cush* In the year that the supreme commander, sent by Sargon king of Assyria, came to Ashdod and attacked and captured it— ²at that time the LORD spoke through Isaiah son of Amoz. He said to him, "Take off the sackcloth from your body and the sandals from your feet." And he did so, going around stripped and barefoot.

³Then the LORD said, "Just as my servant Isaiah has gone stripped and barefoot for three years, as a sign and portent against Egypt and Cush,ᵇ ⁴so the king of Assyria will lead away stripped and barefoot the Egyptian captives and Cushite exiles, young and old, with buttocks bared—to Egypt's shame. ⁵Those who trusted in Cush and boasted in Egypt will be afraid and put to shame. ⁶In that day the people who live on this coast will say, 'See what has happened to those we relied on, those we fled to for help and deliverance from the king of Assyria! How then can we escape?' "

21 *A Prophecy Against Babylon* An oracle concerning the Desert by the Sea:

Like whirlwinds sweeping through the southland,
    an invader comes from the desert,
    from a land of terror.

²A dire vision has been shown to me:
    The traitor betrays, the looter takes loot.
Elam, attack! Media, lay siege!
    I will bring to an end all the groaning she caused.

³At this my body is racked with pain,
    pangs seize me, like those of a woman in labor;
I am staggered by what I hear,
    I am bewildered by what I see.
⁴My heart falters,
    fear makes me tremble;
the twilight I longed for
    has become a horror to me.

ᵃ*18* Most manuscripts of the Masoretic Text; some manuscripts of the Masoretic Text, Dead Sea Scrolls and Vulgate *City of the Sun* (that is, Heliopolis)   ᵇ*3* That is, the upper Nile region; also in verse 5

⁵ They set the tables,
    they spread the rugs,
    they eat, they drink!
Get up, you officers,
    oil the shields!

⁶This is what the Lord says to me:

"Go, post a lookout
    and have him report what he sees.
⁷When he sees chariots
    with teams of horses,
riders on donkeys
    or riders on camels,
let him be alert,
    fully alert."

⁸And the lookout*a* shouted,

"Day after day, my lord, I stand on the watchtower;
    every night I stay at my post.
⁹Look, here comes a man in a chariot
    with a team of horses.
And he gives back the answer:
    'Babylon has fallen, has fallen!
All the images of its gods
    lie shattered on the ground!' "

¹⁰O my people, crushed on the threshing floor,
    I tell you what I have heard
from the Lord Almighty,
    from the God of Israel.

A Prophecy Against Edom   ¹¹An oracle concerning Dumah*b*:

Someone calls to me from Seir,
    "Watchman, what is left of the night?
    Watchman, what is left of the night?"
¹²The watchman replies,
    "Morning is coming, but also the night.
If you would ask, then ask;
    and come back yet again."

A Prophecy Against Arabia   ¹³An oracle concerning Arabia:

You caravans of Dedanites,
    who camp in the thickets of Arabia,
¹⁴   bring water for the thirsty;
you who live in Tema,
    bring food for the fugitives.
¹⁵They flee from the sword,
    from the drawn sword,
from the bent bow
    and from the heat of battle.

¹⁶This is what the Lord says to me: "Within one year, as a servant bound by contract would count it, all the pomp of Kedar will come to an end. ¹⁷The survivors of the bowmen, the warriors of Kedar, will be few." The Lord, the God of Israel, has spoken.

---

a8 Dead Sea Scrolls and Syriac; Masoretic Text *A lion*   *b11 Dumah* means *silence* or *stillness,* a wordplay on *Edom.*

22

A Prophecy About Jerusalem An oracle concerning the Valley of Vision:

What troubles you now,
    that you have all gone up on the roofs,
²O town full of commotion,
    O city of tumult and revelry?
Your slain were not killed by the sword,
    nor did they die in battle.
³All your leaders have fled together;
    they have been captured without using the bow.
All you who were caught were taken prisoner together,
    having fled while the enemy was still far away.
⁴Therefore I said, "Turn away from me;
    let me weep bitterly.
Do not try to console me
    over the destruction of my people."

⁵The Lord, the Lord Almighty, has a day
    of tumult and trampling and terror
    in the Valley of Vision,
a day of battering down walls
    and of crying out to the mountains.
⁶Elam takes up the quiver,
    with her charioteers and horses;
    Kir uncovers the shield.
⁷Your choicest valleys are full of chariots,
    and horsemen are posted at the city gates;
⁸   the defenses of Judah are stripped away.

And you looked in that day
    to the weapons in the Palace of the Forest;
⁹you saw that the City of David
    had many breaches in its defenses;
you stored up water
    in the Lower Pool.
¹⁰You counted the buildings in Jerusalem
    and tore down houses to strengthen the wall.
¹¹You built a reservoir between the two walls
    for the water of the Old Pool,
but you did not look to the One who made it,
    or have regard for the One who planned it long ago.

¹²The Lord, the Lord Almighty,
    called you on that day
to weep and to wail,
    to tear out your hair and put on sackcloth.
¹³But see, there is joy and revelry,
    slaughtering of cattle and killing of sheep,
    eating of meat and drinking of wine!
"Let us eat and drink," you say,
    "for tomorrow we die!"

¹⁴The Lord Almighty has revealed this in my hearing: "Till your dying day this sin will not be atoned for," says the Lord, the Lord Almighty.

¹⁵This is what the Lord, the Lord Almighty, says:

"Go, say to this steward,
    to Shebna, who is in charge of the palace:

¹⁶What are you doing here and who gave you permission
to cut out a grave for yourself here,
hewing your grave on the height
and chiseling your resting place in the rock?

¹⁷"Beware, the Lord is about to take firm hold of you
and hurl you away, O you mighty man.
¹⁸He will roll you up tightly like a ball
and throw you into a large country.
There you will die
and there your splendid chariots will remain—
you disgrace to your master's house!
¹⁹I will depose you from your office,
and you will be ousted from your position.

²⁰"In that day I will summon my servant, Eliakim son of Hilkiah. ²¹I will clothe him with your robe and fasten your sash around him and hand your authority over to him. He will be a father to those who live in Jerusalem and to the house of Judah. ²²I will place on his shoulder the key to the house of David; what he opens no one can shut, and what he shuts no one can open. ²³I will drive him like a peg into a firm place; he will be a seat[a] of honor for the house of his father. ²⁴All the glory of his family will hang on him: its offspring and offshoots—all its lesser vessels, from the bowls to all the jars.

²⁵"In that day," declares the Lord Almighty, "the peg driven into the firm place will give way; it will be sheared off and will fall, and the load hanging on it will be cut down." The Lord has spoken.

23 A Prophecy About Tyre   An oracle concerning Tyre:

Wail, O ships of Tarshish!
For Tyre is destroyed
and left without house or harbor.
From the land of Cyprus[b]
word has come to them.

²Be silent, you people of the island
and you merchants of Sidon,
whom the seafarers have enriched.
³On the great waters
came the grain of the Shihor;
the harvest of the Nile[c] was the revenue of Tyre,
and she became the marketplace of the nations.

⁴Be ashamed, O Sidon, and you, O fortress of the sea,
for the sea has spoken:
"I have neither been in labor nor given birth;
I have neither reared sons nor brought up daughters."
⁵When word comes to Egypt,
they will be in anguish at the report from Tyre.

⁶Cross over to Tarshish;
wail, you people of the island.
⁷Is this your city of revelry,
the old, old city,
whose feet have taken her
to settle in far-off lands?

---

*a*23 Or *throne*   *b*1 Hebrew *Kittim*   *c*2,3 Masoretic Text; one Dead Sea Scroll *Sidon, / who cross over the sea;
/ your envoys* ³*are on the great waters. / The grain of the Shihor, / the harvest of the Nile,*

⁸Who planned this against Tyre,
　　the bestower of crowns,
　whose merchants are princes,
　　whose traders are renowned in the earth?
⁹The Lord Almighty planned it,
　　to bring low the pride of all glory
　　and to humble all who are renowned on the earth.

¹⁰Till*a* your land as along the Nile,
　　O Daughter of Tarshish,
　　for you no longer have a harbor.
¹¹The Lord has stretched out his hand over the sea
　　and made its kingdoms tremble.
　He has given an order concerning Phoenicia*b*
　　that her fortresses be destroyed.
¹²He said, "No more of your reveling,
　　O Virgin Daughter of Sidon, now crushed!

　"Up, cross over to Cyprus*c*;
　　even there you will find no rest."
¹³Look at the land of the Babylonians,*d*
　　this people that is now of no account!
　The Assyrians have made it
　　a place for desert creatures;
　they raised up their siege towers,
　　they stripped its fortresses bare
　　and turned it into a ruin.

¹⁴Wail, you ships of Tarshish;
　　your fortress is destroyed!

¹⁵At that time Tyre will be forgotten for seventy years, the span of a king's life. But at the end of these seventy years, it will happen to Tyre as in the song of the prostitute:

　　¹⁶"Take up a harp, walk through the city,
　　　O prostitute forgotten;
　　play the harp well, sing many a song,
　　　so that you will be remembered."

¹⁷At the end of seventy years, the Lord will deal with Tyre. She will return to her hire as a prostitute and will ply her trade with all the kingdoms on the face of the earth. ¹⁸Yet her profit and her earnings will be set apart for the Lord; they will not be stored up or hoarded. Her profits will go to those who live before the Lord, for abundant food and fine clothes.

24 **The Lord's Devastation of the Earth**
See, the Lord is going to lay waste the earth
　　and devastate it;
　he will ruin its face
　　and scatter its inhabitants—
²it will be the same
　　for priest as for people,
　　for master as for servant,
　　for mistress as for maid,
　　for seller as for buyer,

---

a10 Dead Sea Scrolls and some Septuagint manuscripts; Masoretic Text *Go through*
b11 Hebrew *Canaan* *c12* Hebrew *Kittim* *d13* Or *Chaldeans*

for borrower as for lender,
for debtor as for creditor.
³ The earth will be completely laid waste
and totally plundered.

The LORD has spoken this word.

⁴ The earth dries up and withers,
the world languishes and withers,
the exalted of the earth languish.
⁵ The earth is defiled by its people;
they have disobeyed the laws,
violated the statutes
and broken the everlasting covenant.
⁶ Therefore a curse consumes the earth;
its people must bear their guilt.
Therefore earth's inhabitants are burned up,
and very few are left.
⁷ The new wine dries up and the vine withers;
all the merrymakers groan.
⁸ The gaiety of the tambourines is stilled,
the noise of the revelers has stopped,
the joyful harp is silent.
⁹ No longer do they drink wine with a song;
the beer is bitter to its drinkers.
¹⁰ The ruined city lies desolate;
the entrance to every house is barred.
¹¹ In the streets they cry out for wine;
all joy turns to gloom,
all gaiety is banished from the earth.
¹² The city is left in ruins,
its gate is battered to pieces.
¹³ So will it be on the earth
and among the nations,
as when an olive tree is beaten,
or as when gleanings are left
after the grape harvest.

¹⁴ They raise their voices, they shout
for joy;
from the west they acclaim the
LORD's majesty.
¹⁵ Therefore in the east give glory to
the LORD;
exalt the name of the LORD, the
God of Israel,
in the islands of the sea.
¹⁶ From the ends of the earth we hear
singing:
"Glory to the Righteous One."

But I said, "I waste away, I waste
away!
Woe to me!
The treacherous betray!
With treachery the treacherous
betray!"
¹⁷ Terror and pit and snare await you,
O people of the earth.

This makes it sound like I'm not going to have to worry about retirement!

SEE ISAIAH 24-27

¹⁸Whoever flees at the sound of terror
    will fall into a pit;
whoever climbs out of the pit
    will be caught in a snare.

The floodgates of the heavens are opened,
    the foundations of the earth shake.
¹⁹The earth is broken up,
    the earth is split asunder,
    the earth is thoroughly shaken.
²⁰The earth reels like a drunkard,
    it sways like a hut in the wind;
so heavy upon it is the guilt of its rebellion
    that it falls—never to rise again.

²¹In that day the LORD will punish
    the powers in the heavens above
    and the kings on the earth below.
²²They will be herded together
    like prisoners bound in a dungeon;
they will be shut up in prison
    and be punished*ᵃ* after many days.
²³The moon will be abashed, the sun ashamed;
    for the LORD Almighty will reign
on Mount Zion and in Jerusalem,
    and before its elders, gloriously.

25 *Praise to the LORD*

O LORD, you are my God;
    I will exalt you and praise your name,
for in perfect faithfulness
    you have done marvelous things,
    things planned long ago.
²You have made the city a heap of rubble,
    the fortified town a ruin,
the foreigners' stronghold a city no more;
    it will never be rebuilt.
³Therefore strong peoples will honor you;
    cities of ruthless nations will revere you.
⁴You have been a refuge for the poor,
    a refuge for the needy in his distress,
a shelter from the storm
    and a shade from the heat.
For the breath of the ruthless
    is like a storm driving against a wall
⁵   and like the heat of the desert.
You silence the uproar of foreigners;
    as heat is reduced by the shadow of a cloud,
    so the song of the ruthless is stilled.

⁶On this mountain the LORD Almighty will prepare
    a feast of rich food for all peoples,
a banquet of aged wine—
    the best of meats and the finest of wines.
⁷On this mountain he will destroy

> O LORD, you are
> my God . . .
> in perfect
> faithfulness you
> have done
> marvelous things
> (Isaiah 25:1).

ᵃ*22 Or* released

  the shroud that enfolds all peoples,
  the sheet that covers all nations;
8 he will swallow up death forever.
  The Sovereign LORD will wipe away the tears
   from all faces;
  he will remove the disgrace of his people
   from all the earth.

            The LORD has spoken.

9In that day they will say,

  "Surely this is our God;
   we trusted in him, and he saved us.
  This is the LORD, we trusted in him;
   let us rejoice and be glad in his salvation."

10The hand of the LORD will rest on this mountain;
  but Moab will be trampled under him
  as straw is trampled down in the manure.
11They will spread out their hands in it,
  as a swimmer spreads out his hands to swim.
  God will bring down their pride
   despite the cleverness*a* of their hands.
12He will bring down your high fortified walls
  and lay them low;
  he will bring them down to the ground,
   to the very dust.

26

A Song of Praise In that day this song will be sung in the land of
Judah:

  We have a strong city;
   God makes salvation
   its walls and ramparts.
2Open the gates
  that the righteous nation may enter,
  the nation that keeps faith.
3You will keep in perfect peace
  him whose mind is steadfast,
  because he trusts in you.
4Trust in the LORD forever,
  for the LORD, the LORD, is the Rock eternal.
5He humbles those who dwell on high,
  he lays the lofty city low;
  he levels it to the ground
  and casts it down to the dust.
6Feet trample it down—
  the feet of the oppressed,
  the footsteps of the poor.

7The path of the righteous is level;
  O upright One, you make the way of the righteous smooth.
8Yes, LORD, walking in the way of your laws,*b*
  we wait for you;
  your name and renown
   are the desire of our hearts.

a11 The meaning of the Hebrew for this word is uncertain. *b8* Or *judgments*

⁹My soul yearns for you in the night;
 in the morning my spirit longs for you.
When your judgments come upon the earth,
 the people of the world learn righteousness.
¹⁰Though grace is shown to the wicked,
 they do not learn righteousness;
even in a land of uprightness they go on doing evil
 and regard not the majesty of the LORD.
¹¹O LORD, your hand is lifted high,
 but they do not see it.
Let them see your zeal for your people and be put to
  shame;
 let the fire reserved for your enemies consume them.

¹²LORD, you establish peace for us;
 all that we have accomplished you have done for us.
¹³O LORD, our God, other lords besides you have ruled
  over us,
 but your name alone do we honor.
¹⁴They are now dead, they live no more;
 those departed spirits do not rise.
You punished them and brought them to ruin;
 you wiped out all memory of them.
¹⁵You have enlarged the nation, O LORD;
 you have enlarged the nation.
You have gained glory for yourself;
 you have extended all the borders of the land.

¹⁶LORD, they came to you in their distress;
 when you disciplined them,
 they could barely whisper a prayer.*
¹⁷As a woman with child and about to give birth
 writhes and cries out in her pain,
 so were we in your presence, O LORD.
¹⁸We were with child, we writhed in pain,
 but we gave birth to wind.
We have not brought salvation to the earth;
 we have not given birth to people of the world.

¹⁹But your dead will live;
 their bodies will rise.
You who dwell in the dust,
 wake up and shout for joy.
Your dew is like the dew of the morning;
 the earth will give birth to her dead.

²⁰Go, my people, enter your rooms
 and shut the doors behind you;
hide yourselves for a little while
 until his wrath has passed by.
²¹See, the LORD is coming out of his dwelling
 to punish the people of the earth for their sins.
The earth will disclose the blood shed upon her;
 she will conceal her slain no longer.

*16 The meaning of the Hebrew for this clause is uncertain.

27 *Deliverance of Israel* In that day,

the LORD will punish with his sword,
  his fierce, great and powerful sword,
Leviathan the gliding serpent,
  Leviathan the coiling serpent;
he will slay the monster of the sea.

²In that day—

"Sing about a fruitful vineyard:
³ I, the LORD, watch over it;
  I water it continually.
I guard it day and night
  so that no one may harm it.
⁴ I am not angry.
If only there were briers and thorns confronting me!
  I would march against them in battle;
  I would set them all on fire.
⁵Or else let them come to me for refuge;
  let them make peace with me,
  yes, let them make peace with me."

⁶In days to come Jacob will take root,
  Israel will bud and blossom
  and fill all the world with fruit.

⁷Has ⸢the LORD⸣ struck her
  as he struck down those who struck her?
Has she been killed
  as those were killed who killed her?
⁸By warfare*a* and exile you contend with her—
  with his fierce blast he drives her out,
  as on a day the east wind blows.
⁹By this, then, will Jacob's guilt be atoned for,
  and this will be the full fruitage of the removal of his sin:
When he makes all the altar stones
  to be like chalk stones crushed to pieces,
no Asherah poles*b* or incense altars
  will be left standing.
¹⁰The fortified city stands desolate,
  an abandoned settlement, forsaken like the desert;
there the calves graze,
  there they lie down;
  they strip its branches bare.
¹¹When its twigs are dry, they are broken off
  and women come and make fires with them.
For this is a people without understanding;
  so their Maker has no compassion on them,
  and their Creator shows them no favor.

¹²In that day the LORD will thresh from the flowing Euphrates*c* to the Wadi of Egypt, and you, O Israelites, will be gathered up one by one. ¹³And in that day a great trumpet will sound. Those who were perishing in Assyria and those who were exiled in Egypt will come and worship the LORD on the holy mountain in Jerusalem.

---

a8 See Septuagint; the meaning of the Hebrew for this word is uncertain. *b9* That is, symbols of the goddess Asherah *c12* Hebrew *River*

28 Woe to Ephraim

Woe to that wreath, the pride of Ephraim's drunkards,
   to the fading flower, his glorious beauty,
set on the head of a fertile valley—
   to that city, the pride of those laid low by wine!
²See, the Lord has one who is powerful and strong.
   Like a hailstorm and a destructive wind,
like a driving rain and a flooding downpour,
   he will throw it forcefully to the ground.
³That wreath, the pride of Ephraim's drunkards,
   will be trampled underfoot.
⁴That fading flower, his glorious beauty,
   set on the head of a fertile valley,
will be like a fig ripe before harvest—
   as soon as someone sees it and takes it in his hand,
   he swallows it.

⁵In that day the LORD Almighty
   will be a glorious crown,
a beautiful wreath
   for the remnant of his people.
⁶He will be a spirit of justice
   to him who sits in judgment,
a source of strength
   to those who turn back the battle at the gate.

⁷And these also stagger from wine
   and reel from beer:
Priests and prophets stagger from beer
   and are befuddled with wine;
they reel from beer,
   they stagger when seeing visions,
   they stumble when rendering decisions.
⁸All the tables are covered with vomit
   and there is not a spot without filth.

⁹"Who is it he is trying to teach?
   To whom is he explaining his message?
To children weaned from their milk,
   to those just taken from the breast?
¹⁰For it is:
   Do and do, do and do,
   rule on rule, rule on rule*ᵃ*;
   a little here, a little there."

¹¹Very well then, with foreign lips and strange tongues
   God will speak to this people,
¹²to whom he said,
   "This is the resting place, let the weary rest";
and, "This is the place of repose"—
   but they would not listen.
¹³So then, the word of the LORD to them will become:
   Do and do, do and do,
   rule on rule, rule on rule;
   a little here, a little there—
so that they will go and fall backward,
   be injured and snared and captured.

*ᵃ10 Hebrew / sav lasav sav lasav / kav lakav kav lakav (possibly meaningless sounds; perhaps a
mimicking of the prophet's words); also in verse 13*

¹⁴Therefore hear the word of the LORD, you scoffers
who rule this people in Jerusalem.
¹⁵You boast, "We have entered into a covenant with death,
with the grave*ᵃ* we have made an agreement.
When an overwhelming scourge sweeps by,
it cannot touch us,
for we have made a lie our refuge
and falsehood*ᵇ* our hiding place."

¹⁶So this is what the Sovereign LORD says:

"See, I lay a stone in Zion,
a tested stone,
a precious cornerstone for a sure foundation;
the one who trusts will never be dismayed.
¹⁷I will make justice the measuring line
and righteousness the plumb line;
hail will sweep away your refuge, the lie,
and water will overflow your hiding place.
¹⁸Your covenant with death will be annulled;
your agreement with the grave will not stand.
When the overwhelming scourge sweeps by,
you will be beaten down by it.
¹⁹As often as it comes it will carry you away;
morning after morning, by day and by night,
it will sweep through."

The understanding of this message
will bring sheer terror.
²⁰The bed is too short to stretch out on,
the blanket too narrow to wrap around you.
²¹The LORD will rise up as he did at Mount Perazim,
he will rouse himself as in the Valley of Gibeon—
to do his work, his strange work,
and perform his task, his alien task.
²²Now stop your mocking,
or your chains will become heavier;
the Lord, the LORD Almighty, has told me
of the destruction decreed against the whole land.

²³Listen and hear my voice;
pay attention and hear what I say.
²⁴When a farmer plows for planting, does he plow
continually?
Does he keep on breaking up and harrowing the soil?
²⁵When he has leveled the surface,
does he not sow caraway and scatter cummin?
Does he not plant wheat in its place,*ᶜ*
barley in its plot,*ᶜ*
and spelt in its field?
²⁶His God instructs him
and teaches him the right way.

²⁷Caraway is not threshed with a sledge,
nor is a cartwheel rolled over cummin;

ᵃ15 Hebrew *Sheol*; also in verse 18   *ᵇ15* Or *false gods*   *ᶜ25* The meaning of the Hebrew for this word is
uncertain.

caraway is beaten out with a rod,
and cummin with a stick.
²⁸ Grain must be ground to make bread;
so one does not go on threshing it forever.
Though he drives the wheels of his threshing cart over it,
his horses do not grind it.
²⁹ All this also comes from the LORD Almighty,
wonderful in counsel and magnificent in wisdom.

29 Woe to David's City

Woe to you, Ariel, Ariel,
the city where David settled!
Add year to year
and let your cycle of festivals go on.
² Yet I will besiege Ariel;
she will mourn and lament,
she will be to me like an altar hearth.ᵃ
³ I will encamp against you all around;
I will encircle you with towers
and set up my siege works against you.
⁴ Brought low, you will speak from the ground;
your speech will mumble out of the dust.
Your voice will come ghostlike from the earth;
out of the dust your speech will whisper.

⁵ But your many enemies will become like fine dust,
the ruthless hordes like blown chaff.
Suddenly, in an instant,
⁶   the LORD Almighty will come
with thunder and earthquake and great noise,
with windstorm and tempest and flames of a devouring
fire.
⁷ Then the hordes of all the nations that fight against Ariel,
that attack her and her fortress and besiege her,
will be as it is with a dream,
with a vision in the night—
⁸ as when a hungry man dreams that he is eating,
but he awakens, and his hunger remains;
as when a thirsty man dreams that he is drinking,
but he awakens faint, with his thirst unquenched.
So will it be with the hordes of all the nations
that fight against Mount Zion.

⁹ Be stunned and amazed,
blind yourselves and be sightless;
be drunk, but not from wine,
stagger, but not from beer.
¹⁰ The LORD has brought over you a deep sleep:
He has sealed your eyes (the prophets);
he has covered your heads (the seers).

¹¹ For you this whole vision is nothing but words sealed in a scroll. And if you give the scroll to someone who can read, and say to him, "Read this, please," he will answer, "I can't; it is sealed." ¹² Or if you give the scroll to someone who cannot read, and say, "Read this, please," he will answer, "I don't know how to read."

ᵃ2 The Hebrew for *altar hearth* sounds like the Hebrew for *Ariel.*

¹³The Lord says:

"These people come near to me with their mouth
and honor me with their lips,
but their hearts are far from me.
Their worship of me
is made up only of rules taught by men.*

¹⁴Therefore once more I will astound these people
with wonder upon wonder;
the wisdom of the wise will perish,
the intelligence of the intelligent will vanish."

¹⁵Woe to those who go to great depths
to hide their plans from the LORD,
who do their work in darkness and think,
"Who sees us? Who will know?"

¹⁶You turn things upside down,
as if the potter were thought to be like the clay!
Shall what is formed say to him who formed it,
"He did not make me"?
Can the pot say of the potter,
"He knows nothing"?

¹⁷In a very short time, will not Lebanon be turned into a fertile
field
and the fertile field seem like a forest?

¹⁸In that day the deaf will hear the words of the scroll,
and out of gloom and darkness
the eyes of the blind will see.

¹⁹Once more the humble will rejoice in the LORD;
the needy will rejoice in the Holy One of Israel.

²⁰The ruthless will vanish,
the mockers will disappear,
and all who have an eye for evil will be cut down—

²¹those who with a word make a man out to be guilty,
who ensnare the defender in court
and with false testimony deprive the innocent of justice.

²²Therefore this is what the LORD, who redeemed Abraham, says to the
house of Jacob:

"No longer will Jacob be ashamed;
no longer will their faces grow pale.

²³When they see among them their children,
the work of my hands,
they will keep my name holy;
they will acknowledge the holiness of the Holy One of Jacob,
and will stand in awe of the God of Israel.

²⁴Those who are wayward in spirit will gain understanding;
those who complain will accept instruction."

30

Woe to the Obstinate Nation

"Woe to the obstinate children,"
declares the LORD,
"to those who carry out plans that are not mine,
forming an alliance, but not by my Spirit,
heaping sin upon sin;

---

*a13 Hebrew; Septuagint *They worship me in vain; / their teachings are but rules taught by men*

²who go down to Egypt
without consulting me;
who look for help to Pharaoh's protection,
to Egypt's shade for refuge.
³But Pharaoh's protection will be to your shame,
Egypt's shade will bring you disgrace.
⁴Though they have officials in Zoan
and their envoys have arrived in Hanes,
⁵everyone will be put to shame
because of a people useless to them,
who bring neither help nor advantage,
but only shame and disgrace."

⁶An oracle concerning the animals of the Negev:

Through a land of hardship and distress,
of lions and lionesses,
of adders and darting snakes,
the envoys carry their riches on donkeys' backs,
their treasures on the humps of camels,
to that unprofitable nation,
⁷   to Egypt, whose help is utterly useless.
Therefore I call her
Rahab the Do-Nothing.

⁸Go now, write it on a tablet for them,
inscribe it on a scroll,
that for the days to come
it may be an everlasting witness.
⁹These are rebellious people, deceitful children,
children unwilling to listen to the LORD's instruction.
¹⁰They say to the seers,
"See no more visions!"
and to the prophets,
"Give us no more visions of what is right!
Tell us pleasant things,
prophesy illusions.
¹¹Leave this way,
get off this path,
and stop confronting us
with the Holy One of Israel!"

¹²Therefore, this is what the Holy One of Israel says:

"Because you have rejected this message,
relied on oppression
and depended on deceit,
¹³this sin will become for you
like a high wall, cracked and bulging,
that collapses suddenly, in an instant.
¹⁴It will break in pieces like pottery,
shattered so mercilessly
that among its pieces not a fragment will be found
for taking coals from a hearth
or scooping water out of a cistern."

¹⁵This is what the Sovereign LORD, the Holy One of Israel, says:

"In repentance and rest is your salvation,
in quietness and trust is your strength,
but you would have none of it.

¹⁶You said, 'No, we will flee on horses.'
   Therefore you will flee!
You said, 'We will ride off on swift horses.'
   Therefore your pursuers will be swift!
¹⁷A thousand will flee
   at the threat of one;
at the threat of five
   you will all flee away,
till you are left
   like a flagstaff on a mountaintop,
   like a banner on a hill."

¹⁸Yet the Lord longs to be gracious to you;
   he rises to show you compassion.
For the Lord is a God of justice.
   Blessed are all who wait for him!

¹⁹O people of Zion, who live in Jerusalem, you will weep no more. How gracious he will be when you cry for help! As soon as he hears, he will answer you. ²⁰Although the Lord gives you the bread of adversity and the water of affliction, your teachers will be hidden no more; with your own eyes you will see them. ²¹Whether you turn to the right or to the left, your ears will hear a voice behind you, saying, "This is the way; walk in it." ²²Then you will defile your idols overlaid with silver and your images covered with gold; you will throw them away like a menstrual cloth and say to them, "Away with you!"

²³He will also send you rain for the seed you sow in the ground, and the food that comes from the land will be rich and plentiful. In that day your cattle will graze in broad meadows. ²⁴The oxen and donkeys that work the soil will eat fodder and mash, spread out with fork and shovel. ²⁵In the day of great slaughter, when the towers fall, streams of water will flow on every high mountain and every lofty hill. ²⁶The moon will shine like the sun, and the sunlight will be seven times brighter, like the light of seven full days, when the Lord binds up the bruises of his people and heals the wounds he inflicted.

²⁷See, the Name of the Lord comes from afar,
   with burning anger and dense clouds of smoke;
his lips are full of wrath,
   and his tongue is a consuming fire.
²⁸His breath is like a rushing torrent,
   rising up to the neck.
He shakes the nations in the sieve of destruction;
   he places in the jaws of the peoples
   a bit that leads them astray.
²⁹And you will sing
   as on the night you celebrate a holy festival;
your hearts will rejoice
   as when people go up with flutes
to the mountain of the Lord,
   to the Rock of Israel.
³⁰The Lord will cause men to hear his majestic voice
   and will make them see his arm coming down
with raging anger and consuming fire,
   with cloudburst, thunderstorm and hail.
³¹The voice of the Lord will shatter Assyria;
   with his scepter he will strike them down.
³²Every stroke the Lord lays on them
   with his punishing rod

will be to the music of tambourines and harps,
    as he fights them in battle with the blows of his arm.
³³Topheth has long been prepared;
    it has been made ready for the king.
Its fire pit has been made deep and wide,
    with an abundance of fire and wood;
the breath of the LORD,
    like a stream of burning sulfur,
    sets it ablaze.

31

Woe to Those Who Rely on Egypt

Woe to those who go down to Egypt for help,
    who rely on horses,
who trust in the multitude of their chariots
    and in the great strength of their horsemen,
but do not look to the Holy One of Israel,
    or seek help from the LORD.
²Yet he too is wise and can bring disaster;
    he does not take back his words.
He will rise up against the house of the wicked,
    against those who help evildoers.
³But the Egyptians are men and not God;
    their horses are flesh and not spirit.
When the LORD stretches out his hand,
    he who helps will stumble,
    he who is helped will fall;
    both will perish together.

⁴This is what the LORD says to me:

    "As a lion growls,
      a great lion over his prey—
    and though a whole band of shepherds
      is called together against him,
    he is not frightened by their shouts
      or disturbed by their clamor—
    so the LORD Almighty will come down
      to do battle on Mount Zion and on its heights.
⁵Like birds hovering overhead,
    the LORD Almighty will shield Jerusalem;
he will shield it and deliver it,
    he will 'pass over' it and will rescue it."

⁶Return to him you have so greatly revolted against, O Israelites. ⁷For in that day every one of you will reject the idols of silver and gold your sinful hands have made.

    ⁸"Assyria will fall by a sword that is not of man;
      a sword, not of mortals, will devour them.
They will flee before the sword
      and their young men will be put to forced labor.
⁹Their stronghold will fall because of terror;
      at sight of the battle standard their commanders will
        panic,"
declares the LORD,
    whose fire is in Zion,
    whose furnace is in Jerusalem.

32 *The Kingdom of Righteousness*
See, a king will reign in righteousness
    and rulers will rule with justice.
²Each man will be like a shelter from the wind
    and a refuge from the storm,
like streams of water in the desert
    and the shadow of a great rock in a thirsty land.

³Then the eyes of those who see will no longer be
        closed,
    and the ears of those who hear will listen.
⁴The mind of the rash will know and understand,
    and the stammering tongue will be fluent and clear.
⁵No longer will the fool be called noble
    nor the scoundrel be highly respected.
⁶For the fool speaks folly,
    his mind is busy with evil:
He practices ungodliness
    and spreads error concerning the LORD;
the hungry he leaves empty
    and from the thirsty he withholds water.
⁷The scoundrel's methods are wicked,
    he makes up evil schemes
to destroy the poor with lies,
    even when the plea of the needy is just.
⁸But the noble man makes noble plans,
    and by noble deeds he stands.

The Women of Jerusalem
⁹You women who are so complacent,
    rise up and listen to me;
you daughters who feel secure,
    hear what I have to say!
¹⁰In little more than a year
    you who feel secure will tremble;
the grape harvest will fail,
    and the harvest of fruit will not come.
¹¹Tremble, you complacent women;
    shudder, you daughters who feel secure!
Strip off your clothes,
    put sackcloth around your waists.
¹²Beat your breasts for the pleasant fields,
    for the fruitful vines
¹³and for the land of my people,
    a land overgrown with thorns and briers—
yes, mourn for all houses of merriment
    and for this city of revelry.
¹⁴The fortress will be abandoned,
    the noisy city deserted;
citadel and watchtower will become a wasteland forever,
    the delight of donkeys, a pasture for flocks,
¹⁵till the Spirit is poured upon us from on high,
    and the desert becomes a fertile field,
    and the fertile field seems like a forest.
¹⁶Justice will dwell in the desert
    and righteousness live in the fertile field.
¹⁷The fruit of righteousness will be peace;

the effect of righteousness will be quietness and confidence
    forever.
¹⁸ My people will live in peaceful dwelling places,
    in secure homes,
    in undisturbed places of rest.
¹⁹ Though hail flattens the forest
    and the city is leveled completely,
²⁰ how blessed you will be,
    sowing your seed by every stream,
    and letting your cattle and donkeys range free.

33 Distress and Help

Woe to you, O destroyer,
    you who have not been destroyed!
Woe to you, O traitor,
    you who have not been betrayed!
When you stop destroying,
    you will be destroyed;
when you stop betraying,
    you will be betrayed.

² O LORD, be gracious to us;
    we long for you.
Be our strength every morning,
    our salvation in time of distress.
³ At the thunder of your voice, the peoples flee;
    when you rise up, the nations scatter.
⁴ Your plunder, O nations, is harvested as by young locusts;
    like a swarm of locusts men pounce on it.

⁵ The LORD is exalted, for he dwells on high;
    he will fill Zion with justice and righteousness.
⁶ He will be the sure foundation for your times,
    a rich store of salvation and wisdom and knowledge;
    the fear of the LORD is the key to this treasure.ᵃ

ᵃ6 Or *is a treasure from him*

The Bible Says

Yes to World Peace

Today world peace seems closer than it did when the United States and the Soviet Union had missiles aimed at each other. However, every day thousands of people live in terror. You might feel safer, but someone on the other side of the world might not. *World* peace is peace everywhere, for all people.

When the United Nations tries to stop a battle or sends help to the victims of war, you can be glad. But however hard they try, they'll never be able to bring world peace. As long as people are moved by anger and hatred and a lust for power, peace is impossible.

When Jesus returns to rule, he'll bring world peace by changing the hearts of those who live in this world. "The fruit of righteousness will be peace; the effect of righteousness will be quietness and confidence forever" (Isaiah 32:17).

⁷Look, their brave men cry aloud in the streets;
    the envoys of peace weep bitterly.
⁸The highways are deserted,
    no travelers are on the roads.
The treaty is broken,
    its witnesses*ᵃ* are despised,
    no one is respected.
⁹The land mourns*ᵇ* and wastes away,
    Lebanon is ashamed and withers;
Sharon is like the Arabah,
    and Bashan and Carmel drop their leaves.

¹⁰"Now will I arise," says the LORD.
    "Now will I be exalted;
    now will I be lifted up.
¹¹You conceive chaff,
    you give birth to straw;
    your breath is a fire that consumes you.
¹²The peoples will be burned as if to lime;
    like cut thornbushes they will be set ablaze."

¹³You who are far away, hear what I have done;
    you who are near, acknowledge my power!
¹⁴The sinners in Zion are terrified;
    trembling grips the godless:
"Who of us can dwell with the consuming fire?
    Who of us can dwell with everlasting burning?"
¹⁵He who walks righteously
    and speaks what is right,
who rejects gain from extortion
    and keeps his hand from accepting bribes,
who stops his ears against plots of murder
    and shuts his eyes against contemplating evil—
¹⁶this is the man who will dwell on the heights,
    whose refuge will be the mountain fortress.
His bread will be supplied,
    and water will not fail him.

¹⁷Your eyes will see the king in his beauty
    and view a land that stretches afar.
¹⁸In your thoughts you will ponder the former terror:
    "Where is that chief officer?
    Where is the one who took the revenue?
    Where is the officer in charge of the towers?"
¹⁹You will see those arrogant people no more,
    those people of an obscure speech,
    with their strange, incomprehensible tongue.

²⁰Look upon Zion, the city of our festivals;
    your eyes will see Jerusalem,
    a peaceful abode, a tent that will not be moved;
its stakes will never be pulled up,
    nor any of its ropes broken.
²¹There the LORD will be our Mighty One.
    It will be like a place of broad rivers and streams.
No galley with oars will ride them,
    no mighty ship will sail them.

ᵃ8 Dead Sea Scrolls; Masoretic Text / the cities   ᵇ9 Or dries up

²²For the L ORD is our judge,
the L ORD is our lawgiver,
the L ORD is our king;
it is he who will save us.

²³Your rigging hangs loose:
The mast is not held secure,
the sail is not spread.
Then an abundance of spoils will be divided
and even the lame will carry off plunder.
²⁴No one living in Zion will say, "I am ill";
and the sins of those who dwell there will be
forgiven.

34 Judgment Against the Nations

Come near, you nations, and listen;
pay attention, you peoples!
Let the earth hear, and all that is in it,
the world, and all that comes out of it!
²The L ORD is angry with all nations;
his wrath is upon all their armies.
He will totally destroy[a] them,
he will give them over to slaughter.
³Their slain will be thrown out,
their dead bodies will send up a stench;
the mountains will be soaked with their blood.
⁴All the stars of the heavens will be dissolved
and the sky rolled up like a scroll;
all the starry host will fall
like withered leaves from the vine,
like shriveled figs from the fig tree.

⁵My sword has drunk its fill in the heavens;
see, it descends in judgment on Edom,
the people I have totally destroyed.
⁶The sword of the L ORD is bathed in blood,
it is covered with fat—
the blood of lambs and goats,
fat from the kidneys of rams.
For the L ORD has a sacrifice in Bozrah
and a great slaughter in Edom.
⁷And the wild oxen will fall with them,
the bull calves and the great bulls.
Their land will be drenched with blood,
and the dust will be soaked with fat.

⁸For the L ORD has a day of vengeance,
a year of retribution, to uphold Zion's cause.
⁹Edom's streams will be turned into pitch,
her dust into burning sulfur;
her land will become blazing pitch!
¹⁰It will not be quenched night and day;
its smoke will rise forever.
From generation to generation it will lie desolate;
no one will ever pass through it again.

ᵃ2 The Hebrew term refers to the irrevocable giving over of things or persons to the L ORD, often by totally
destroying them; also in verse 5.

¹¹The desert owl*ᵃ* and screech owl*ᵃ* will possess it;
  the great owl*ᵃ* and the raven will nest there.
God will stretch out over Edom
  the measuring line of chaos
  and the plumb line of desolation.
¹²Her nobles will have nothing there to be called a kingdom,
  all her princes will vanish away.
¹³Thorns will overrun her citadels,
  nettles and brambles her strongholds.
She will become a haunt for jackals,
  a home for owls.
¹⁴Desert creatures will meet with hyenas,
  and wild goats will bleat to each other;
there the night creatures will also repose
  and find for themselves places of rest.
¹⁵The owl will nest there and lay eggs,
  she will hatch them, and care for her young under the
      shadow of her wings;
there also the falcons will gather,
  each with its mate.

¹⁶Look in the scroll of the Lᴏʀᴅ and read:

None of these will be missing,
  not one will lack her mate.
For it is his mouth that has given the order,
  and his Spirit will gather them together.
¹⁷He allots their portions;
  his hand distributes them by measure.
They will possess it forever
  and dwell there from generation to generation.

35 *Joy of the Redeemed*

The desert and the parched land will be glad;
  the wilderness will rejoice and blossom.
Like the crocus, ²it will burst into bloom;
  it will rejoice greatly and shout for joy.
The glory of Lebanon will be given to it,
  the splendor of Carmel and Sharon;
        they will see the glory of the Lᴏʀᴅ,
          the splendor of our God.

³Strengthen the feeble hands,
  steady the knees that give way;
⁴say to those with fearful hearts,
  "Be strong, do not fear;
your God will come,
  he will come with vengeance;
with divine retribution
  he will come to save you."

⁵Then will the eyes of the blind be opened
  and the ears of the deaf unstopped.
⁶Then will the lame leap like a deer,
  and the mute tongue shout for joy.

SEE ISAIAH 35

ᵃ11 The precise identification of these birds is uncertain.

Water will gush forth in the wilderness
  and streams in the desert.
⁷The burning sand will become a pool,
  the thirsty ground bubbling springs.
In the haunts where jackals once lay,
  grass and reeds and papyrus will grow.

⁸And a highway will be there;
  it will be called the Way of Holiness.
The unclean will not journey on it;
  it will be for those who walk in that Way;
  wicked fools will not go about on it.*
⁹No lion will be there,
  nor will any ferocious beast get up on it;
  they will not be found there.
But only the redeemed will walk there,
¹⁰ and the ransomed of the LORD will return.
They will enter Zion with singing;
  everlasting joy will crown their heads.
Gladness and joy will overtake them,
  and sorrow and sighing will flee away.

> The ransomed
> of the LORD will
> return . . . sorrow
> and sighing
> will flee away
> (Isaiah 35:10).

36 **Sennacherib Threatens Jerusalem** In the fourteenth year of King Hezekiah's reign, Sennacherib king of Assyria attacked all the fortified cities of Judah and captured them. ²Then the king of Assyria sent his field commander with a large army from Lachish to King Hezekiah at Jerusalem. When the commander stopped at the aqueduct of the Upper Pool, on the road to the Washerman's Field, ³Eliakim son of Hilkiah the palace administrator, Shebna the secretary, and Joah son of Asaph the recorder went out to him.

⁴The field commander said to them, "Tell Hezekiah,

" 'This is what the great king, the king of Assyria, says: On what are you basing this confidence of yours? ⁵You say you have strategy and military strength—but you speak only empty words. On whom are you depending, that you rebel against me? ⁶Look now, you are depending on Egypt, that splintered reed of a staff, which pierces a man's hand and wounds him if he leans on it! Such is Pharaoh king of Egypt to all who depend on him. ⁷And if you say to me, "We are depending on the LORD our God"—isn't he the one whose high places and altars Hezekiah removed, saying to Judah and Jerusalem, "You must worship before this altar"?

⁸" 'Come now, make a bargain with my master, the king of Assyria: I will give you two thousand horses—if you can put riders on them! ⁹How then can you repulse one officer of the least of my master's officials, even though you are depending on Egypt for chariots and horsemen? ¹⁰Furthermore, have I come to attack and destroy this land without the LORD? The LORD himself told me to march against this country and destroy it.' "

¹¹Then Eliakim, Shebna and Joah said to the field commander, "Please speak to your servants in Aramaic, since we understand it. Don't speak to us in Hebrew in the hearing of the people on the wall."

¹²But the commander replied, "Was it only to your master and you that my master sent me to say these things, and not to the men sitting on the wall— who, like you, will have to eat their own filth and drink their own urine?"

---

8 Or / the simple will not stray from it

¹³Then the commander stood and called out in Hebrew, "Hear the words of the great king, the king of Assyria! ¹⁴This is what the king says: Do not let Hezekiah deceive you. He cannot deliver you! ¹⁵Do not let Hezekiah persuade you to trust in the LORD when he says, 'The LORD will surely deliver us; this city will not be given into the hand of the king of Assyria.'

¹⁶"Do not listen to Hezekiah. This is what the king of Assyria says: Make peace with me and come out to me. Then every one of you will eat from his own vine and fig tree and drink water from his own cistern, ¹⁷until I come and take you to a land like your own—a land of grain and new wine, a land of bread and vineyards.

¹⁸"Do not let Hezekiah mislead you when he says, 'The LORD will deliver us.' Has the god of any nation ever delivered his land from the hand of the king of Assyria? ¹⁹Where are the gods of Hamath and Arpad? Where are the gods of Sepharvaim? Have they rescued Samaria from my hand? ²⁰Who of all the gods of these countries has been able to save his land from me? How then can the LORD deliver Jerusalem from my hand?"

²¹But the people remained silent and said nothing in reply, because the king had commanded, "Do not answer him."

²²Then Eliakim son of Hilkiah the palace administrator, Shebna the secretary, and Joah son of Asaph the recorder went to Hezekiah, with their clothes torn, and told him what the field commander had said.

37 *Jerusalem's Deliverance Foretold* When King Hezekiah heard this, he tore his clothes and put on sackcloth and went into the temple of the LORD. ²He sent Eliakim the palace administrator, Shebna the secretary, and the leading priests, all wearing sackcloth, to the prophet Isaiah son of Amoz. ³They told him, "This is what Hezekiah says: This day is a day of distress and rebuke and disgrace, as when children come to the point of birth and there is no strength to deliver them. ⁴It may be that the LORD your God will hear the words of the field commander, whom his master, the king of Assyria, has sent to ridicule the living God, and that he will rebuke him for the words the LORD your God has heard. Therefore pray for the remnant that still survives."

⁵When King Hezekiah's officials came to Isaiah, ⁶Isaiah said to them, "Tell your master, 'This is what the LORD says: Do not be afraid of what you have heard—those words with which the underlings of the king of Assyria have blasphemed me. ⁷Listen! I am going to put a spirit in him so that when he hears a certain report, he will return to his own country, and there I will have him cut down with the sword.' "

⁸When the field commander heard that the king of Assyria had left Lachish, he withdrew and found the king fighting against Libnah.

⁹Now Sennacherib received a report that Tirhakah, the Cushite*a* king of Egypt, was marching out to fight against him. When he heard it, he sent messengers to Hezekiah with this word: ¹⁰"Say to Hezekiah king of Judah: Do not let the god you depend on deceive you when he says, 'Jerusalem will not be handed over to the king of Assyria.' ¹¹Surely you have heard what the kings of Assyria have done to all the countries, destroying them completely. And will you be delivered? ¹²Did the gods of the nations that were destroyed by my forefathers deliver them—the gods of Gozan, Haran, Rezeph and the people of Eden who were in Tel Assar? ¹³Where is the king of Hamath, the king of Arpad, the king of the city of Sepharvaim, or of Hena or Ivvah?"

Hezekiah's Prayer ¹⁴Hezekiah received the letter from the messengers and read it. Then he went up to the temple of the LORD and spread it out before the LORD. ¹⁵And Hezekiah prayed to the LORD: ¹⁶"O LORD Almighty, God of Is-

a9 That is, from the upper Nile region

rael, enthroned between the cherubim, you alone are God over all the kingdoms of the earth. You have made heaven and earth. [17]Give ear, O LORD, and hear; open your eyes, O LORD, and see; listen to all the words Sennacherib has sent to insult the living God.

[18]"It is true, O LORD, that the Assyrian kings have laid waste all these peoples and their lands. [19]They have thrown their gods into the fire and destroyed them, for they were not gods but only wood and stone, fashioned by human hands. [20]Now, O LORD our God, deliver us from his hand, so that all kingdoms on earth may know that you alone, O LORD, are God.[a]"

Sennacherib's Fall [21]Then Isaiah son of Amoz sent a message to Hezekiah: "This is what the LORD, the God of Israel, says: Because you have prayed to me concerning Sennacherib king of Assyria, [22]this is the word the LORD has spoken against him:

> "The Virgin Daughter of Zion
> despises and mocks you.
> The Daughter of Jerusalem
> tosses her head as you flee.
> [23]Who is it you have insulted and blasphemed?
> Against whom have you raised your voice
> and lifted your eyes in pride?
> Against the Holy One of Israel!
> [24]By your messengers
> you have heaped insults on the Lord.
> And you have said,
> 'With my many chariots
> I have ascended the heights of the mountains,
> the utmost heights of Lebanon.
> I have cut down its tallest cedars,
> the choicest of its pines.
> I have reached its remotest heights,
> the finest of its forests.
> [25]I have dug wells in foreign lands[b]
> and drunk the water there.
> With the soles of my feet
> I have dried up all the streams of Egypt.'
>
> [26]"Have you not heard?
> Long ago I ordained it.
> In days of old I planned it;
> now I have brought it to pass,
> that you have turned fortified cities
> into piles of stone.
> [27]Their people, drained of power,
> are dismayed and put to shame.
> They are like plants in the field,
> like tender green shoots,
> like grass sprouting on the roof,
> scorched[c] before it grows up.
>
> [28]"But I know where you stay
> and when you come and go
> and how you rage against me.

ISAIAH 37

QUIZZER

Q: How many Assyrian soldiers did the angel of the Lord kill?

BONUS: Do any other historical sources report this incident?

Answers on page 927

---

[a]20 Dead Sea Scrolls (see also 2 Kings 19:19); Masoretic Text *alone are the* LORD [b]25 Dead Sea Scrolls (see also 2 Kings 19:24); Masoretic Text does not have *in foreign lands.* [c]27 Some manuscripts of the Masoretic Text, Dead Sea Scrolls and some Septuagint manuscripts (see also 2 Kings 19:26); most manuscripts of the Masoretic Text *roof / and terraced fields*

²⁹Because you rage against me
    and because your insolence has reached my ears,
I will put my hook in your nose
    and my bit in your mouth,
and I will make you return
    by the way you came.

³⁰"This will be the sign for you, O Hezekiah:

"This year you will eat what grows by itself,
    and the second year what springs from that.
But in the third year sow and reap,
    plant vineyards and eat their fruit.
³¹Once more a remnant of the house of Judah
    will take root below and bear fruit above.
³²For out of Jerusalem will come a remnant,
    and out of Mount Zion a band of survivors.
The zeal of the Lord Almighty
    will accomplish this.

³³"Therefore this is what the Lord says concerning the king of Assyria:

"He will not enter this city
    or shoot an arrow here.
He will not come before it with shield
    or build a siege ramp against it.
³⁴By the way that he came he will return;
    he will not enter this city,"

                      declares the Lord.
³⁵"I will defend this city and save it,
    for my sake and for the sake of David my servant!"

³⁶Then the angel of the Lord went out and put to death a hundred and eighty-five thousand men in the Assyrian camp. When the people got up the next morning—there were all the dead bodies! ³⁷So Sennacherib king of Assyria broke camp and withdrew. He returned to Nineveh and stayed there.

³⁸One day, while he was worshiping in the temple of his god Nisroch, his sons Adrammelech and Sharezer cut him down with the sword, and they escaped to the land of Ararat. And Esarhaddon his son succeeded him as king.

38 *Hezekiah's Illness* In those days Hezekiah became ill and was at the point of death. The prophet Isaiah son of Amoz went to him and said, "This is what the Lord says: Put your house in order, because you are going to die; you will not recover."

²Hezekiah turned his face to the wall and prayed to the Lord, ³"Remember, O Lord, how I have walked before you faithfully and with wholehearted devotion and have done what is good in your eyes." And Hezekiah wept bitterly.

⁴Then the word of the Lord came to Isaiah: ⁵"Go and tell Hezekiah, 'This is what the Lord, the God of your father David, says: I have heard your prayer and seen your tears; I will add fifteen years to your life. ⁶And I will deliver you and this city from the hand of the king of Assyria. I will defend this city.

⁷"'This is the Lord's sign to you that the Lord will do what he has promised: ⁸I will make the shadow cast by the sun go back the ten steps it has gone down on the stairway of Ahaz.'" So the sunlight went back the ten steps it had gone down.

⁹A writing of Hezekiah king of Judah after his illness and recovery:

¹⁰I said, "In the prime of my life
must I go through the gates of death*ᵃ*
and be robbed of the rest of my years?"
¹¹I said, "I will not again see the LORD,
the LORD, in the land of the living;
no longer will I look on mankind,
or be with those who now dwell in this world.*ᵇ*
¹²Like a shepherd's tent my house
has been pulled down and taken from me.
Like a weaver I have rolled up my life,
and he has cut me off from the loom;
day and night you made an end of me.
¹³I waited patiently till dawn,
but like a lion he broke all my bones;
day and night you made an end of me.
¹⁴I cried like a swift or thrush,
I moaned like a mourning dove.
My eyes grew weak as I looked to the heavens.
I am troubled; O Lord, come to my aid!"

¹⁵But what can I say?
He has spoken to me, and he himself has done this.
I will walk humbly all my years
because of this anguish of my soul.
¹⁶Lord, by such things men live;
and my spirit finds life in them too.
You restored me to health
and let me live.
¹⁷Surely it was for my benefit
that I suffered such anguish.
In your love you kept me
from the pit of destruction;
you have put all my sins
behind your back.
¹⁸For the grave*ᵃ* cannot praise you,
death cannot sing your praise;
those who go down to the pit
cannot hope for your faithfulness.
¹⁹The living, the living—they praise you,
as I am doing today;
fathers tell their children
about your faithfulness.

²⁰The LORD will save me,
and we will sing with stringed instruments
all the days of our lives
in the temple of the LORD.

²¹Isaiah had said, "Prepare a poultice of figs and apply it to the boil, and he will recover."
²²Hezekiah had asked, "What will be the sign that I will go up to the temple of the LORD?"

39 *Envoys From Babylon* At that time Merodach-Baladan son of Baladan king of Babylon sent Hezekiah letters and a gift, because he had heard of his illness and recovery. ²Hezekiah received the envoys gladly

ᵃ10,18 Hebrew *Sheol* *ᵇ11* A few Hebrew manuscripts; most Hebrew manuscripts *in the place of cessation*

and showed them what was in his storehouses—the silver, the gold, the spices, the fine oil, his entire armory and everything found among his treasures. There was nothing in his palace or in all his kingdom that Hezekiah did not show them.

³Then Isaiah the prophet went to King Hezekiah and asked, "What did those men say, and where did they come from?"

"From a distant land," Hezekiah replied. "They came to me from Babylon."

⁴The prophet asked, "What did they see in your palace?"

"They saw everything in my palace," Hezekiah said. "There is nothing among my treasures that I did not show them."

⁵Then Isaiah said to Hezekiah, "Hear the word of the LORD Almighty: ⁶The time will surely come when everything in your palace, and all that your fathers have stored up until this day, will be carried off to Babylon. Nothing will be left, says the LORD. ⁷And some of your descendants, your own flesh and blood who will be born to you, will be taken away, and they will become eunuchs in the palace of the king of Babylon."

⁸"The word of the LORD you have spoken is good," Hezekiah replied. For he thought, "There will be peace and security in my lifetime."

40 Comfort for God's People

Comfort, comfort my people,
    says your God.
²Speak tenderly to Jerusalem,
    and proclaim to her
that her hard service has been completed,
    that her sin has been paid for,
that she has received from the LORD's hand
    double for all her sins.

³A voice of one calling:
"In the desert prepare
    the way for the LORDᵃ;
make straight in the wilderness
    a highway for our God.ᵇ
⁴Every valley shall be raised up,
    every mountain and hill made low;
the rough ground shall become level,
    the rugged places a plain.
⁵And the glory of the LORD will be revealed,
    and all mankind together will see it.
                 For the mouth of the LORD has spoken."

⁶A voice says, "Cry out."
    And I said, "What shall I cry?"

"All men are like grass,
    and all their glory is like the flowers of the field.
⁷The grass withers and the flowers fall,
    because the breath of the LORD blows on them.
    Surely the people are grass.
⁸The grass withers and the flowers fall,
    but the word of our God stands forever."

⁹You who bring good tidings to Zion,
    go up on a high mountain.

ᵃ3 Or *A voice of one calling in the desert: / "Prepare the way for the* LORD ᵇ3 Hebrew; Septuagint *make straight the paths of our God*

You who bring good tidings to Jerusalem,^a
    lift up your voice with a shout,
lift it up, do not be afraid;
    say to the towns of Judah,
    "Here is your God!"
¹⁰See, the Sovereign Lord comes with power,
    and his arm rules for him.
See, his reward is with him,
    and his recompense accompanies him.
¹¹He tends his flock like a shepherd:
    He gathers the lambs in his arms
and carries them close to his heart;
    he gently leads those that have young.

¹²Who has measured the waters in the hollow of his hand,
    or with the breadth of his hand marked off the heavens?
Who has held the dust of the earth in a basket,
    or weighed the mountains on the scales
    and the hills in a balance?
¹³Who has understood the mind^b of the Lord,
    or instructed him as his counselor?
¹⁴Whom did the Lord consult to enlighten him,
    and who taught him the right way?
Who was it that taught him knowledge
    or showed him the path of understanding?

¹⁵Surely the nations are like a drop in a bucket;
    they are regarded as dust on the scales;
    he weighs the islands as though they were fine dust.
¹⁶Lebanon is not sufficient for altar fires,
    nor its animals enough for burnt offerings.
¹⁷Before him all the nations are as nothing;
    they are regarded by him as worthless
    and less than nothing.

¹⁸To whom, then, will you compare God?
    What image will you compare him to?
¹⁹As for an idol, a craftsman casts it,
    and a goldsmith overlays it with gold
    and fashions silver chains for it.
²⁰A man too poor to present such an offering
    selects wood that will not rot.
He looks for a skilled craftsman
    to set up an idol that will not topple.

²¹Do you not know?
    Have you not heard?
Has it not been told you from the beginning?
    Have you not understood since the earth was founded?
²²He sits enthroned above the circle of the earth,
    and its people are like grasshoppers.
He stretches out the heavens like a canopy,
    and spreads them out like a tent to live in.
²³He brings princes to naught
    and reduces the rulers of this world to nothing.

Answers
*to Quizzer on
page 923*

**A: He killed
185,000
(Isaiah 37:36)!**

***BONUS:
According to the
Greek historian
Herodotus, field
mice attacked
Sennacherib's
army and ate
their weapons.
Perhaps God
used plague-
infested mice to
deliver his
people.***

---

^a9 Or *O Zion, bringer of good tidings, / go up on a high mountain. / O Jerusalem, bringer of good tidings*
^b13 Or *Spirit*; or *spirit*

²⁴No sooner are they planted,
    no sooner are they sown,
    no sooner do they take root in the ground,
than he blows on them and they wither,
    and a whirlwind sweeps them away like chaff.

²⁵"To whom will you compare me?
    Or who is my equal?" says the Holy One.
²⁶Lift your eyes and look to the heavens:
    Who created all these?
He who brings out the starry host one by one,
    and calls them each by name.
Because of his great power and mighty strength,
    not one of them is missing.

²⁷Why do you say, O Jacob,
    and complain, O Israel,
"My way is hidden from the LORD;
    my cause is disregarded by my God"?
²⁸Do you not know?
    Have you not heard?
The LORD is the everlasting God,
    the Creator of the ends of the earth.
        He will not grow tired or weary,
            and his understanding no one can fathom.
²⁹He gives strength to the weary
    and increases the power of the weak.
³⁰Even youths grow tired and weary,
    and young men stumble and fall;
³¹but those who hope in the LORD
    will renew their strength.
They will soar on wings like eagles;
    they will run and not grow weary,
    they will walk and not be faint.

> Those who hope in the LORD will renew their strength. They will soar on wings like eagles (Isaiah 40:31).

41 *The Helper of Israel*
"Be silent before me, you islands!
    Let the nations renew their strength!
Let them come forward and speak;
    let us meet together at the place of judgment.

²"Who has stirred up one from the east,
    calling him in righteousness to his service*ᵃ*?
He hands nations over to him
    and subdues kings before him.
He turns them to dust with his sword,
    to windblown chaff with his bow.
³He pursues them and moves on unscathed,
    by a path his feet have not traveled before.
⁴Who has done this and carried it through,
    calling forth the generations from the beginning?
I, the LORD—with the first of them
    and with the last—I am he."

ᵃ2 Or / whom victory meets at every step

Dear Sam,

Because I don't have sex with the girls I date, the guys in the locker room ask me if I'm gay. And they're always after me to go out drinking with them. I am so worn down from saying no.

Larry in Lawrence

Dear Sam, Inc.

100 Advice Lane, Anywhere, USA

Dear Larry,

You have really been doing a great job of living up to your beliefs! But I'm concerned that you're feeling so worn down. Here are some suggestions that might help. Next time the guys get on your case, try saying something like this: "Guys, I don't bug you because of the choices you make. Can't you do the same for me? I'm not into drinking and premarital sex. Please respect my right to live according to my values." You may not say it exactly that way, but I suspect after a while they'll leave you alone.

You need to get together with friends who share your values. Then you can support each other. Does your church have a youth group? If so, work on friendships with some of those teens, both girls and guys.

God will give you the strength to live by his standards, so when you're tired of being hassled, turn to him. Isaiah 40:28-31 is a great passage of encouragement. Try reading it whenever you think you can't say no one more time.

Sam

⁵The islands have seen it and fear;
  the ends of the earth tremble.
They approach and come forward;
⁶ each helps the other
  and says to his brother, "Be strong!"
⁷The craftsman encourages the goldsmith,
  and he who smooths with the hammer
  spurs on him who strikes the anvil.
He says of the welding, "It is good."
  He nails down the idol so it will not topple.

⁸"But you, O Israel, my servant,
  Jacob, whom I have chosen,
  you descendants of Abraham my friend,
⁹I took you from the ends of the earth,
  from its farthest corners I called you.
I said, 'You are my servant';
  I have chosen you and have not rejected you.
¹⁰So do not fear, for I am with you;
  do not be dismayed, for I am your God.
I will strengthen you and help you;
  I will uphold you with my righteous right hand.

¹¹"All who rage against you
  will surely be ashamed and disgraced;
those who oppose you
  will be as nothing and perish.
¹²Though you search for your enemies,
  you will not find them.
Those who wage war against you
  will be as nothing at all.
¹³For I am the LORD, your God,
  who takes hold of your right hand
and says to you, Do not fear;
  I will help you.
¹⁴Do not be afraid, O worm Jacob,
  O little Israel,
for I myself will help you," declares the LORD,
  your Redeemer, the Holy One of Israel.
¹⁵"See, I will make you into a threshing sledge,
  new and sharp, with many teeth.
You will thresh the mountains and crush them,
  and reduce the hills to chaff.
¹⁶You will winnow them, the wind will pick them up,
  and a gale will blow them away.
But you will rejoice in the LORD
  and glory in the Holy One of Israel.

¹⁷"The poor and needy search for water,
  but there is none;
  their tongues are parched with thirst.
But I the LORD will answer them;
  I, the God of Israel, will not forsake them.
¹⁸I will make rivers flow on barren heights,
  and springs within the valleys.
I will turn the desert into pools of water,
  and the parched ground into springs.
¹⁹I will put in the desert
  the cedar and the acacia, the myrtle and the olive.

I will set pines in the wasteland,
the fir and the cypress together,
²⁰ so that people may see and know,
may consider and understand,
that the hand of the LORD has done this,
that the Holy One of Israel has created it.

²¹ "Present your case," says the LORD.
"Set forth your arguments," says Jacob's King.
²² "Bring in ˌyour idolsˌ to tell us
what is going to happen.
Tell us what the former things were,
so that we may consider them
and know their final outcome.
Or declare to us the things to come,
²³   tell us what the future holds,
so we may know that you are gods.
Do something, whether good or bad,
so that we will be dismayed and filled with fear.
²⁴ But you are less than nothing
and your works are utterly worthless;
he who chooses you is detestable.

²⁵ "I have stirred up one from the north, and he comes—
one from the rising sun who calls on my name.
He treads on rulers as if they were mortar,
as if he were a potter treading the clay.
²⁶ Who told of this from the beginning, so we could know,
or beforehand, so we could say, 'He was right'?
No one told of this,
no one foretold it,
no one heard any words from you.
²⁷ I was the first to tell Zion, 'Look,
here they are!'
I gave to Jerusalem a messenger
of good tidings.
²⁸ I look but there is no one—
no one among them to give
counsel,
no one to give answer when I ask
them.
²⁹ See, they are all false!
Their deeds amount to nothing;
their images are but wind and
confusion.

42 The Servant of the LORD

"Here is my servant, whom I
uphold,
my chosen one in whom I
delight;
I will put my Spirit on him
and he will bring justice to the
nations.
² He will not shout or cry out,
or raise his voice in the streets.
³ A bruised reed he will not break,

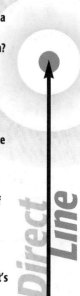

ISAIAH 42:3

When you go to school
tomorrow or the next day, take a
look around you. What about
that girl with the bad reputation?
Or the guy with the bad
complexion? Or the little group
that dresses radically and walks
around looking ornery? They're
outsiders who make you feel
uncomfortable. Do you just write
them off? This passage in Isaiah
describes the outsider as a
"bruised reed" and as a
"smoldering wick." Neither is of
much use. Isaiah is saying that
people whom society sees as
worthless are important to the
Lord. Try to look at the
"outsiders" at school with Christ's
eyes, and reach out to them.

Direct Line

and a smoldering wick he will not snuff out.
In faithfulness he will bring forth justice;
⁴   he will not falter or be discouraged
till he establishes justice on earth.
In his law the islands will put their hope."

⁵ This is what God the LORD says—
he who created the heavens and stretched them out,
    who spread out the earth and all that comes out of it,
who gives breath to its people,
    and life to those who walk on it:
⁶ "I, the LORD, have called you in righteousness;
    I will take hold of your hand.
I will keep you and will make you
    to be a covenant for the people
    and a light for the Gentiles,
⁷ to open eyes that are blind,
    to free captives from prison
    and to release from the dungeon those who sit in darkness.

⁸ "I am the LORD; that is my name!
    I will not give my glory to another
    or my praise to idols.
⁹ See, the former things have taken place,
    and new things I declare;
before they spring into being
    I announce them to you."

Song of Praise to the LORD

¹⁰ Sing to the LORD a new song,
    his praise from the ends of the earth,
you who go down to the sea, and all that is in it,
    you islands, and all who live in them.
¹¹ Let the desert and its towns raise their voices;
    let the settlements where Kedar lives rejoice.
Let the people of Sela sing for joy;
    let them shout from the mountaintops.
¹² Let them give glory to the LORD
    and proclaim his praise in the islands.
¹³ The LORD will march out like a mighty man,
    like a warrior he will stir up his zeal;
with a shout he will raise the battle cry
    and will triumph over his enemies.

¹⁴ "For a long time I have kept silent,
    I have been quiet and held myself back.
But now, like a woman in childbirth,
    I cry out, I gasp and pant.
¹⁵ I will lay waste the mountains and hills
    and dry up all their vegetation;
I will turn rivers into islands
    and dry up the pools.
¹⁶ I will lead the blind by ways they have not known,
    along unfamiliar paths I will guide them;
I will turn the darkness into light before them
    and make the rough places smooth.
These are the things I will do;
    I will not forsake them.

¹⁷But those who trust in idols,
who say to images, 'You are our gods,'
will be turned back in utter shame.

Israel Blind and Deaf

¹⁸"Hear, you deaf;
look, you blind, and see!
¹⁹Who is blind but my servant,
and deaf like the messenger I send?
Who is blind like the one committed to me,
blind like the servant of the LORD?
²⁰You have seen many things, but have paid no attention;
your ears are open, but you hear nothing."
²¹It pleased the LORD
for the sake of his righteousness
to make his law great and glorious.
²²But this is a people plundered and looted,
all of them trapped in pits
or hidden away in prisons.
They have become plunder,
with no one to rescue them;
they have been made loot,
with no one to say, "Send them back."

²³Which of you will listen to this
or pay close attention in time to come?
²⁴Who handed Jacob over to become loot,
and Israel to the plunderers?
Was it not the LORD,
against whom we have sinned?
For they would not follow his ways;
they did not obey his law.
²⁵So he poured out on them his burning anger,
the violence of war.
It enveloped them in flames, yet they did not
understand;
it consumed them, but they did not take it to heart.

43 Israel's Only Savior

But now, this is what the LORD says—
he who created you, O Jacob,
he who formed you, O Israel:
"Fear not, for I have redeemed you;
I have summoned you by name; you are mine.
²When you pass through the waters,
I will be with you;
and when you pass through the rivers,
they will not sweep over you.
When you walk through the fire,
you will not be burned;
the flames will not set you ablaze.
³For I am the LORD, your God,
the Holy One of Israel, your Savior;
I give Egypt for your ransom,
Cush^a and Seba in your stead.

^a3 That is, the upper Nile region

⁴Since you are precious and honored in my sight,
and because I love you,
I will give men in exchange for you,
and people in exchange for your life.
⁵Do not be afraid, for I am with you;
I will bring your children from the east
and gather you from the west.
⁶I will say to the north, 'Give them up!'
and to the south, 'Do not hold them back.'
Bring my sons from afar
and my daughters from the ends of the earth—
⁷everyone who is called by my name,
whom I created for my glory,
whom I formed and made."

⁸Lead out those who have eyes but are blind,
who have ears but are deaf.
⁹All the nations gather together
and the peoples assemble.
Which of them foretold this
and proclaimed to us the former things?
Let them bring in their witnesses to prove they were right,
so that others may hear and say, "It is true."
¹⁰"You are my witnesses," declares the LORD,
"and my servant whom I have chosen,
so that you may know and believe me
and understand that I am he.
Before me no god was formed,
nor will there be one after me.
¹¹I, even I, am the LORD,
and apart from me there is no savior.
¹²I have revealed and saved and proclaimed—
I, and not some foreign god among you.
You are my witnesses," declares the LORD, "that I am God.
¹³   Yes, and from ancient days I am he.
No one can deliver out of my hand.
When I act, who can reverse it?"

God's Mercy and Israel's Unfaithfulness

¹⁴This is what the LORD says—
your Redeemer, the Holy One of Israel:
"For your sake I will send to Babylon
and bring down as fugitives all the Babylonians,ᵃ
in the ships in which they took pride.
¹⁵I am the LORD, your Holy One,
Israel's Creator, your King."

¹⁶This is what the LORD says—
he who made a way through the sea,
a path through the mighty waters,
¹⁷who drew out the chariots and horses,
the army and reinforcements together,
and they lay there, never to rise again,
extinguished, snuffed out like a wick:
¹⁸"Forget the former things;
do not dwell on the past.

ᵃ14 Or *Chaldeans*

¹⁹ See, I am doing a new thing!
    Now it springs up; do you not perceive it?
I am making a way in the desert
    and streams in the wasteland.
²⁰ The wild animals honor me,
    the jackals and the owls,
because I provide water in the desert
    and streams in the wasteland,
to give drink to my people, my chosen,
²¹   the people I formed for myself
    that they may proclaim my praise.

²² "Yet you have not called upon me, O Jacob,
    you have not wearied yourselves for me, O Israel.
²³ You have not brought me sheep for burnt offerings,
    nor honored me with your sacrifices.
I have not burdened you with grain offerings
    nor wearied you with demands for incense.
²⁴ You have not bought any fragrant calamus for me,
    or lavished on me the fat of your sacrifices.
But you have burdened me with your sins
    and wearied me with your offenses.

²⁵ "I, even I, am he who blots out
    your transgressions, for my own sake,
    and remembers your sins no more.
²⁶ Review the past for me,
    let us argue the matter together;
    state the case for your innocence.
²⁷ Your first father sinned;
    your spokesmen rebelled against me.
²⁸ So I will disgrace the dignitaries of your temple,
    and I will consign Jacob to destruction^a
    and Israel to scorn.

Israel the Chosen

44 "But now listen, O Jacob, my servant,
    Israel, whom I have chosen.
² This is what the Lord says—
    he who made you, who formed you in the womb,
    and who will help you:
Do not be afraid, O Jacob, my servant,
    Jeshurun, whom I have chosen.
³ For I will pour water on the thirsty land,
    and streams on the dry ground;
I will pour out my Spirit on your offspring,
    and my blessing on your descendants.
⁴ They will spring up like grass in a meadow,
    like poplar trees by flowing streams.
⁵ One will say, 'I belong to the Lord';
    another will call himself by the name of Jacob;
still another will write on his hand, 'The Lord's,'
    and will take the name Israel.

The Lord, Not Idols

⁶ "This is what the Lord says—
    Israel's King and Redeemer, the Lord Almighty:

---

^a28 The Hebrew term refers to the irrevocable giving over of things or persons to the Lord, often by totally destroying them.

I am the first and I am the last;
    apart from me there is no God.
[7]Who then is like me? Let him proclaim it.
    Let him declare and lay out before me
what has happened since I established my ancient people,
    and what is yet to come—
    yes, let him foretell what will come.
[8]Do not tremble, do not be afraid.
    Did I not proclaim this and foretell it long ago?
You are my witnesses. Is there any God besides me?
    No, there is no other Rock; I know not one."

[9]All who make idols are nothing,
    and the things they treasure are worthless.
Those who would speak up for them are blind;
    they are ignorant, to their own shame.
[10]Who shapes a god and casts an idol,
    which can profit him nothing?
[11]He and his kind will be put to shame;
    craftsmen are nothing but men.
Let them all come together and take their stand;
    they will be brought down to terror and infamy.

[12]The blacksmith takes a tool
    and works with it in the coals;
he shapes an idol with hammers,
    he forges it with the might of his arm.
He gets hungry and loses his strength;
    he drinks no water and grows faint.
[13]The carpenter measures with a line
    and makes an outline with a marker;
he roughs it out with chisels
    and marks it with compasses.
He shapes it in the form of man,
    of man in all his glory,
    that it may dwell in a shrine.
[14]He cut down cedars,
    or perhaps took a cypress or oak.

The Bible Says

Idols Can't Help

In Isaiah 44:6–20, Isaiah pokes fun at people who cut down a tree, use part of it for firewood, and then carve an idol from the rest. Then they bow down and pray to that hunk of wood!

People today are often just as foolish, counting on the wrong things to help them. Some count on wealth, others on popularity. Some count on stylish clothes, others on athletic ability. But in the end, you can't count on any of these things.

What you can count on is God. Don't misunderstand. It's not wrong to have money or nice clothes. What's wrong is to count on these things as if they are what life is all about. That's idolatry. And that's foolish. Living God's way and making what's important to him important to you will lead you to a happy tomorrow and a happy forever.

He let it grow among the trees of the forest,
    or planted a pine, and the rain made it grow.
¹⁵ It is man's fuel for burning;
    some of it he takes and warms himself,
    he kindles a fire and bakes bread.
But he also fashions a god and worships it;
    he makes an idol and bows down to it.
¹⁶ Half of the wood he burns in the fire;
    over it he prepares his meal,
    he roasts his meat and eats his fill.
He also warms himself and says,
    "Ah! I am warm; I see the fire."
¹⁷ From the rest he makes a god, his idol;
    he bows down to it and worships.
He prays to it and says,
    "Save me; you are my god."
¹⁸ They know nothing, they understand nothing;
    their eyes are plastered over so they cannot see,
    and their minds closed so they cannot understand.
¹⁹ No one stops to think,
    no one has the knowledge or understanding to say,
"Half of it I used for fuel;
    I even baked bread over its coals,
    I roasted meat and I ate.
Shall I make a detestable thing from what is left?
    Shall I bow down to a block of wood?"
²⁰ He feeds on ashes, a deluded heart misleads him;
    he cannot save himself, or say,
    "Is not this thing in my right hand a lie?"

²¹ "Remember these things, O Jacob,
    for you are my servant, O Israel.
I have made you, you are my servant;
    O Israel, I will not forget you.
²² I have swept away your offenses like a cloud,
    your sins like the morning mist.
Return to me,
    for I have redeemed you."

²³ Sing for joy, O heavens, for the LORD has done this;
    shout aloud, O earth beneath.
Burst into song, you mountains,
    you forests and all your trees,
for the LORD has redeemed Jacob,
    he displays his glory in Israel.

Jerusalem to Be Inhabited

²⁴ "This is what the LORD says—
    your Redeemer, who formed you in the womb:

I am the LORD,
who has made all things,
who alone stretched out the heavens,
who spread out the earth by myself,

²⁵ who foils the signs of false prophets
    and makes fools of diviners,
who overthrows the learning of the wise
    and turns it into nonsense,

²⁶who carries out the words of his servants
  and fulfills the predictions of his messengers,

who says of Jerusalem, 'It shall be inhabited,'
  of the towns of Judah, 'They shall be built,'
  and of their ruins, 'I will restore them,'
²⁷who says to the watery deep, 'Be dry,
  and I will dry up your streams,'
²⁸who says of Cyrus, 'He is my shepherd
  and will accomplish all that I please;
  he will say of Jerusalem, "Let it be rebuilt,"
  and of the temple, "Let its foundations be laid." '

45 "This is what the LORD says to his anointed,
  to Cyrus, whose right hand I take hold of
to subdue nations before him
  and to strip kings of their armor,
to open doors before him
  so that gates will not be shut:
²I will go before you
  and will level the mountains^a;
I will break down gates of bronze
  and cut through bars of iron.
³I will give you the treasures of darkness,
  riches stored in secret places,
so that you may know that I am the LORD,
  the God of Israel, who summons you by name.
⁴For the sake of Jacob my servant,
  of Israel my chosen,
I summon you by name
  and bestow on you a title of honor,
  though you do not acknowledge me.
⁵I am the LORD, and there is no other;
  apart from me there is no God.
I will strengthen you,
  though you have not acknowledged me,
⁶so that from the rising of the sun
  to the place of its setting
men may know there is none besides me.
  I am the LORD, and there is no other.
⁷I form the light and create darkness,
  I bring prosperity and create disaster;
  I, the LORD, do all these things.

⁸"You heavens above, rain down righteousness;
  let the clouds shower it down.
Let the earth open wide,
  let salvation spring up,
let righteousness grow with it;
  I, the LORD, have created it.

⁹"Woe to him who quarrels with his Maker,
  to him who is but a potsherd among the potsherds on the
    ground.
Does the clay say to the potter,
  'What are you making?'

---

^a2 Dead Sea Scrolls and Septuagint; the meaning of the word in the Masoretic Text is uncertain.

Does your work say,
  'He has no hands'?
¹⁰Woe to him who says to his father,
  'What have you begotten?'
or to his mother,
  'What have you brought to birth?'

¹¹"This is what the Lord says—
  the Holy One of Israel, and its Maker:
Concerning things to come,
  do you question me about my children,
  or give me orders about the work of my hands?
¹²It is I who made the earth
  and created mankind upon it.
My own hands stretched out the heavens;
  I marshaled their starry hosts.
¹³I will raise up Cyrus*ᵃ* in my righteousness:
  I will make all his ways straight.
He will rebuild my city
  and set my exiles free,
but not for a price or reward,
  says the Lord Almighty."

¹⁴This is what the Lord says:

  "The products of Egypt and the merchandise of Cush,*ᵇ*
    and those tall Sabeans—
  they will come over to you
    and will be yours;
  they will trudge behind you,
    coming over to you in chains.
  They will bow down before you
    and plead with you, saying,
  'Surely God is with you, and there is no other;
    there is no other god.' "

¹⁵Truly you are a God who hides himself,
  O God and Savior of Israel.
¹⁶All the makers of idols will be put to shame and disgraced;
  they will go off into disgrace together.
¹⁷But Israel will be saved by the Lord
  with an everlasting salvation;
you will never be put to shame or disgraced,
  to ages everlasting.

¹⁸For this is what the Lord says—
  he who created the heavens,
    he is God;
he who fashioned and made the earth,
    he founded it;
he did not create it to be empty,
    but formed it to be inhabited—
  he says:
  "I am the Lord,
    and there is no other.
¹⁹I have not spoken in secret,
  from somewhere in a land of darkness;

ᵃ13 Hebrew *him* *ᵇ14* That is, the upper Nile region

I have not said to Jacob's descendants,
    'Seek me in vain.'
I, the LORD, speak the truth;
    I declare what is right.

20 "Gather together and come;
    assemble, you fugitives from the nations.
Ignorant are those who carry about idols of wood,
    who pray to gods that cannot save.
21 Declare what is to be, present it—
    let them take counsel together.
Who foretold this long ago,
    who declared it from the distant past?
Was it not I, the LORD?
    And there is no God apart from me,
a righteous God and a Savior;
    there is none but me.

22 "Turn to me and be saved,
    all you ends of the earth;
    for I am God, and there is no other.
23 By myself I have sworn,
    my mouth has uttered in all integrity
    a word that will not be revoked:
Before me every knee will bow;
    by me every tongue will swear.
24 They will say of me, 'In the LORD alone
    are righteousness and strength.' "
All who have raged against him
    will come to him and be put to shame.
25 But in the LORD all the descendants of Israel
    will be found righteous and will exult.

Gods of Babylon

46 Bel bows down, Nebo stoops low;
    their idols are borne by beasts of burden.[a]
The images that are carried about are burdensome,
    a burden for the weary.
2 They stoop and bow down together;
    unable to rescue the burden,
    they themselves go off into captivity.

3 "Listen to me, O house of Jacob,
    all you who remain of the house of Israel,
you whom I have upheld since you were conceived,
    and have carried since your birth.
4 Even to your old age and gray hairs
    I am he, I am he who will sustain you.
I have made you and I will carry you;
    I will sustain you and I will rescue you.

5 "To whom will you compare me or count me equal?
    To whom will you liken me that we may be compared?
6 Some pour out gold from their bags
    and weigh out silver on the scales;

---

a 1 Or are but beasts and cattle

they hire a goldsmith to make it into a god,
    and they bow down and worship it.
⁷They lift it to their shoulders and carry it;
    they set it up in its place, and there it stands.
    From that spot it cannot move.
Though one cries out to it, it does not answer;
    it cannot save him from his troubles.

⁸"Remember this, fix it in mind,
    take it to heart, you rebels.
⁹Remember the former things, those of long ago;
    I am God, and there is no other;
    I am God, and there is none like me.
¹⁰I make known the end from the beginning,
    from ancient times, what is still to come.
I say: My purpose will stand,
    and I will do all that I please.
¹¹From the east I summon a bird of prey;
    from a far-off land, a man to fulfill my purpose.
What I have said, that will I bring about;
    what I have planned, that will I do.
¹²Listen to me, you stubborn-hearted,
    you who are far from righteousness.
¹³I am bringing my righteousness near,
    it is not far away;
    and my salvation will not be delayed.
I will grant salvation to Zion,
    my splendor to Israel.

> I am he who will sustain you. I have made you and I will carry you (Isaiah 46:4).

47 The Fall of Babylon

"Go down, sit in the dust,
    Virgin Daughter of Babylon;
sit on the ground without a throne,
    Daughter of the Babylonians.ᵃ
No more will you be called
    tender or delicate.
²Take millstones and grind flour;
    take off your veil.
Lift up your skirts, bare your legs,
    and wade through the streams.
³Your nakedness will be exposed
    and your shame uncovered.
I will take vengeance;
    I will spare no one."

⁴Our Redeemer—the LORD Almighty is his name—
    is the Holy One of Israel.

⁵"Sit in silence, go into darkness,
    Daughter of the Babylonians;
no more will you be called
    queen of kingdoms.
⁶I was angry with my people
    and desecrated my inheritance;
I gave them into your hand,
    and you showed them no mercy.

ᵃ1 Or Chaldeans; also in verse 5

Even on the aged
    you laid a very heavy yoke.
⁷You said, 'I will continue forever—
    the eternal queen!'
But you did not consider these things
    or reflect on what might happen.

⁸"Now then, listen, you wanton creature,
    lounging in your security
and saying to yourself,
    'I am, and there is none besides me.
I will never be a widow
    or suffer the loss of children.'
⁹Both of these will overtake you
    in a moment, on a single day:
    loss of children and widowhood.
They will come upon you in full measure,
    in spite of your many sorceries
    and all your potent spells.
¹⁰You have trusted in your wickedness
    and have said, 'No one sees me.'
Your wisdom and knowledge mislead you
    when you say to yourself,
    'I am, and there is none besides me.'
¹¹Disaster will come upon you,
    and you will not know how to conjure it away.
A calamity will fall upon you
    that you cannot ward off with a ransom;
a catastrophe you cannot foresee
    will suddenly come upon you.

¹²"Keep on, then, with your magic spells
    and with your many sorceries,
    which you have labored at since childhood.
Perhaps you will succeed,
    perhaps you will cause terror.
¹³All the counsel you have received has only worn
        you out!
    Let your astrologers come forward,
    those stargazers who make predictions month by month,
    let them save you from what is coming upon you.
¹⁴Surely they are like stubble;
    the fire will burn them up.
They cannot even save themselves
    from the power of the flame.
Here are no coals to warm anyone;
    here is no fire to sit by.
¹⁵That is all they can do for you—
    these you have labored with
    and trafficked with since childhood.
Each of them goes on in his error;
    there is not one that can save you.

48

Stubborn Israel
"Listen to this, O house of Jacob,
    you who are called by the name of Israel
    and come from the line of Judah,
you who take oaths in the name of the LORD

and invoke the God of Israel—
but not in truth or righteousness—
² you who call yourselves citizens of the holy city
and rely on the God of Israel—
the Lord Almighty is his name:
³ I foretold the former things long ago,
my mouth announced them and I made them
known;
then suddenly I acted, and they came to pass.
⁴ For I knew how stubborn you were;
the sinews of your neck were iron,
your forehead was bronze.
⁵ Therefore I told you these things long ago;
before they happened I announced them to you
so that you could not say,
'My idols did them;
my wooden image and metal god ordained them.'
⁶ You have heard these things; look at them all.
Will you not admit them?

"From now on I will tell you of new things,
of hidden things unknown to you.
⁷ They are created now, and not long ago;
you have not heard of them before today.
So you cannot say,
'Yes, I knew of them.'
⁸ You have neither heard nor understood;
from of old your ear has not been open.
Well do I know how treacherous you are;
you were called a rebel from birth.
⁹ For my own name's sake I delay my wrath;
for the sake of my praise I hold it back from
you,
so as not to cut you off.
¹⁰ See, I have refined you, though
not as silver;
I have tested you in the
furnace of affliction.
¹¹ For my own sake, for my own
sake, I do this.
How can I let myself be
defamed?
I will not yield my glory to
another.

Israel Freed

¹² "Listen to me, O Jacob,
Israel, whom I have called:
I am he;
I am the first and I am the
last.
¹³ My own hand laid the
foundations of the earth,
and my right hand spread
out the heavens;
when I summon them,
they all stand up together.

ISAIAH 48:17

Do you wish you had more independence? That's good. You're not a child anymore. You make many decisions on your own. But probably not all of them. So it's easy to see why some kids resent authority. It's your life, and you want to make your own decisions. But remember one thing: even adults need guidance. Not someone to say, "You have to do this!" But someone to suggest, "This way is best." Don't resent God's authority. He isn't standing over you with a whip. He's standing beside you saying, "Let me help you. I just want what's best for you."

Direct Line

¹⁴"Come together, all of you, and listen:
    Which of ͵the idols͵ has foretold these things?
The Lord's chosen ally
    will carry out his purpose against Babylon;
    his arm will be against the Babylonians.^a
¹⁵I, even I, have spoken;
    yes, I have called him.
I will bring him,
    and he will succeed in his mission.

¹⁶"Come near me and listen to this:

"From the first announcement I have not spoken in secret;
    at the time it happens, I am there."

And now the Sovereign Lord has sent me,
    with his Spirit.

¹⁷This is what the Lord says—
    your Redeemer, the Holy One of Israel:
"I am the Lord your God,
    who teaches you what is best for you,
    who directs you in the way you should go.
¹⁸If only you had paid attention to my commands,
    your peace would have been like a river,
    your righteousness like the waves of the sea.
¹⁹Your descendants would have been like the sand,
    your children like its numberless grains;
their name would never be cut off
    nor destroyed from before me."

²⁰Leave Babylon,
    flee from the Babylonians!
Announce this with shouts of joy
    and proclaim it.
Send it out to the ends of the earth;
    say, "The Lord has redeemed his servant Jacob."
²¹They did not thirst when he led them through the deserts;
    he made water flow for them from the rock;
he split the rock
    and water gushed out.

²²"There is no peace," says the Lord, "for the wicked."

49 The Servant of the Lord

Listen to me, you islands;
    hear this, you distant nations:
Before I was born the Lord called me;
    from my birth he has made mention of my name.
²He made my mouth like a sharpened sword,
    in the shadow of his hand he hid me;
he made me into a polished arrow
    and concealed me in his quiver.
³He said to me, "You are my servant,
    Israel, in whom I will display my splendor."
⁴But I said, "I have labored to no purpose;
    I have spent my strength in vain and for nothing.
Yet what is due me is in the Lord's hand,
    and my reward is with my God."

---

^a14 Or *Chaldeans*; also in verse 20

⁵And now the LORD says—
    he who formed me in the womb to be his servant
to bring Jacob back to him
    and gather Israel to himself,
for I am honored in the eyes of the LORD
    and my God has been my strength—
⁶he says:

"It is too small a thing for you to be my servant
    to restore the tribes of Jacob
    and bring back those of Israel I have kept.
I will also make you a light for the Gentiles,
    that you may bring my salvation to the ends of the earth."

⁷This is what the LORD says—
    the Redeemer and Holy One of Israel—
to him who was despised and abhorred by the nation,
    to the servant of rulers:
"Kings will see you and rise up,
    princes will see and bow down,
because of the LORD, who is faithful,
    the Holy One of Israel, who has chosen you."

Restoration of Israel   ⁸This is what the LORD says:

"In the time of my favor I will answer you,
    and in the day of salvation I will help you;
I will keep you and will make you
    to be a covenant for the people,
to restore the land
    and to reassign its desolate inheritances,
⁹to say to the captives, 'Come out,'
    and to those in darkness, 'Be free!'

"They will feed beside the roads
    and find pasture on every barren hill.
¹⁰They will neither hunger nor thirst,
    nor will the desert heat or the sun beat upon them.
He who has compassion on them will guide them
    and lead them beside springs of water.
¹¹I will turn all my mountains into roads,
    and my highways will be raised up.
¹²See, they will come from afar—
    some from the north, some from the west,
    some from the region of Aswan.ᵃ"

¹³Shout for joy, O heavens;
    rejoice, O earth;
    burst into song, O mountains!
For the LORD comforts his people
    and will have compassion on his afflicted ones.

¹⁴But Zion said, "The LORD has forsaken me,
    the Lord has forgotten me."

¹⁵"Can a mother forget the baby at her breast
    and have no compassion on the child she has borne?
Though she may forget,
    I will not forget you!

ᵃ12 Dead Sea Scrolls; Masoretic Text *Sinim*

¹⁶See, I have engraved you on the palms of my hands;
your walls are ever before me.
¹⁷Your sons hasten back,
and those who laid you waste depart from you.
¹⁸Lift up your eyes and look around;
all your sons gather and come to you.
As surely as I live," declares the Lord,
"you will wear them all as ornaments;
you will put them on, like a bride.

¹⁹"Though you were ruined and made desolate
and your land laid waste,
now you will be too small for your people,
and those who devoured you will be far away.
²⁰The children born during your bereavement
will yet say in your hearing,
'This place is too small for us;
give us more space to live in.'
²¹Then you will say in your heart,
'Who bore me these?
I was bereaved and barren;
I was exiled and rejected.
Who brought these up?
I was left all alone,
but these—where have they come from?' "

²²This is what the Sovereign Lord says:

"See, I will beckon to the Gentiles,
I will lift up my banner to the peoples;
they will bring your sons in their arms
and carry your daughters on their shoulders.
²³Kings will be your foster fathers,
and their queens your nursing mothers.
They will bow down before you with their faces to the ground;
they will lick the dust at your feet.
Then you will know that I am the Lord;
those who hope in me will not be disappointed."

²⁴Can plunder be taken from warriors,
or captives rescued from the fierce[a]?

²⁵But this is what the Lord says:

"Yes, captives will be taken from warriors,
and plunder retrieved from the fierce;
I will contend with those who contend with you,
and your children I will save.
²⁶I will make your oppressors eat their own flesh;
they will be drunk on their own blood, as with wine.
Then all mankind will know
that I, the Lord, am your Savior,
your Redeemer, the Mighty One of Jacob."

50

Israel's Sin and the Servant's Obedience This is what the Lord
says:

"Where is your mother's certificate of divorce
with which I sent her away?

---

[a]24 Dead Sea Scrolls, Vulgate and Syriac (see also Septuagint and verse 25); Masoretic Text *righteous*

Or to which of my creditors
  did I sell you?
Because of your sins you were sold;
  because of your transgressions your mother was sent
    away.
² When I came, why was there no one?
  When I called, why was there no one to answer?
Was my arm too short to ransom you?
  Do I lack the strength to rescue you?
By a mere rebuke I dry up the sea,
  I turn rivers into a desert;
their fish rot for lack of water
  and die of thirst.
³ I clothe the sky with darkness
  and make sackcloth its covering."

⁴ The Sovereign Lord has given me an instructed tongue,
  to know the word that sustains the weary.
He wakens me morning by morning,
  wakens my ear to listen like one being taught.
⁵ The Sovereign Lord has opened my ears,
  and I have not been rebellious;
  I have not drawn back.
⁶ I offered my back to those who beat me,
  my cheeks to those who pulled out my beard;
I did not hide my face
  from mocking and spitting.
⁷ Because the Sovereign Lord helps me,
  I will not be disgraced.
Therefore have I set my face like flint,
  and I know I will not be put to shame.
⁸ He who vindicates me is near.
  Who then will bring charges against me?
  Let us face each other!
Who is my accuser?
  Let him confront me!
⁹ It is the Sovereign Lord who helps me.
  Who is he that will condemn me?
They will all wear out like a garment;
  the moths will eat them up.

¹⁰ Who among you fears the Lord
  and obeys the word of his servant?
Let him who walks in the dark,
  who has no light,
trust in the name of the Lord
  and rely on his God.
¹¹ But now, all you who light fires
  and provide yourselves with flaming torches,
go, walk in the light of your fires
  and of the torches you have set ablaze.
This is what you shall receive from my hand:
  You will lie down in torment.

51

Everlasting Salvation for Zion

"Listen to me, you who pursue righteousness
  and who seek the Lord:
Look to the rock from which you were cut

and to the quarry from which you were
hewn;
²look to Abraham, your father,
and to Sarah, who gave you birth.
When I called him he was but one,
and I blessed him and made him many.
³The Lord will surely comfort Zion
and will look with compassion on all her ruins;
he will make her deserts like Eden,
her wastelands like the garden of the Lord.
Joy and gladness will be found in her,
thanksgiving and the sound of singing.

⁴"Listen to me, my people;
hear me, my nation:
The law will go out from me;
my justice will become a light to the nations.
⁵My righteousness draws near speedily,
my salvation is on the way,
and my arm will bring justice to the nations.
The islands will look to me
and wait in hope for my arm.
⁶Lift up your eyes to the heavens,
look at the earth beneath;
the heavens will vanish like smoke,
the earth will wear out like a garment
and its inhabitants die like flies.
But my salvation will last forever,
my righteousness will never fail.

⁷"Hear me, you who know what is right,
you people who have my law in your hearts:
Do not fear the reproach of men
or be terrified by their insults.
⁸For the moth will eat them up like a garment;
the worm will devour them like wool.
But my righteousness will last forever,
my salvation through all generations."

⁹Awake, awake! Clothe yourself with strength,
O arm of the Lord;
awake, as in days gone by,
as in generations of old.
Was it not you who cut Rahab to pieces,
who pierced that monster through?
¹⁰Was it not you who dried up the sea,
the waters of the great deep,
who made a road in the depths of the sea
so that the redeemed might cross over?
¹¹The ransomed of the Lord will return.
They will enter Zion with singing;
everlasting joy will crown their heads.
Gladness and joy will overtake them,
and sorrow and sighing will flee away.

¹²"I, even I, am he who comforts you.
Who are you that you fear mortal men,
the sons of men, who are but grass,
¹³that you forget the Lord your Maker,

> My righteousness
> draws near
> speedily, my
> salvation is on
> the way
> (Isaiah 51:5).

who stretched out the heavens
and laid the foundations of the earth,
that you live in constant terror every day
because of the wrath of the oppressor,
who is bent on destruction?
For where is the wrath of the oppressor?
¹⁴ The cowering prisoners will soon be set free;
they will not die in their dungeon,
nor will they lack bread.
¹⁵ For I am the Lord your God,
who churns up the sea so that its waves roar—
the Lord Almighty is his name.
¹⁶ I have put my words in your mouth
and covered you with the shadow of my hand—
I who set the heavens in place,
who laid the foundations of the earth,
and who say to Zion, 'You are my people.' "

The Cup of the Lord's Wrath

¹⁷ Awake, awake!
Rise up, O Jerusalem,
you who have drunk from the hand of the Lord
the cup of his wrath,
you who have drained to its dregs
the goblet that makes men stagger.
¹⁸ Of all the sons she bore
there was none to guide her;
of all the sons she reared
there was none to take her by the hand.
¹⁹ These double calamities have come upon you—
who can comfort you?—
ruin and destruction, famine and sword—
who can*ᵃ* console you?
²⁰ Your sons have fainted;
they lie at the head of every street,
like antelope caught in a net.
They are filled with the wrath of the Lord
and the rebuke of your God.

²¹ Therefore hear this, you afflicted one,
made drunk, but not with wine.
²² This is what your Sovereign Lord says,
your God, who defends his people:
"See, I have taken out of your hand
the cup that made you stagger;
from that cup, the goblet of my wrath,
you will never drink again.
²³ I will put it into the hands of your tormentors,
who said to you,
'Fall prostrate that we may walk over you.'
And you made your back like the ground,
like a street to be walked over."

52 Awake, awake, O Zion,
clothe yourself with strength.
Put on your garments of splendor,

ᵃ19 Dead Sea Scrolls, Septuagint, Vulgate and Syriac; Masoretic Text / *how can I*

O Jerusalem, the holy city.
The uncircumcised and defiled
　will not enter you again.
² Shake off your dust;
　rise up, sit enthroned, O Jerusalem.
Free yourself from the chains on your neck,
　O captive Daughter of Zion.

³ For this is what the LORD says:

"You were sold for nothing,
　and without money you will be redeemed."

⁴ For this is what the Sovereign LORD says:

"At first my people went down to Egypt to live;
　lately, Assyria has oppressed them.

⁵ "And now what do I have here?" declares the LORD.

"For my people have been taken away for nothing,
　and those who rule them mock,ᵃ"
　　　　　　　　　　　　　　　　　declares the LORD.

"And all day long
　my name is constantly blasphemed.
⁶ Therefore my people will know my name;
　therefore in that day they will know
that it is I who foretold it.
　Yes, it is I."

⁷ How beautiful on the mountains
　are the feet of those who bring good news,
who proclaim peace,
　who bring good tidings,
　who proclaim salvation,
who say to Zion,
　"Your God reigns!"
⁸ Listen! Your watchmen lift up their voices;
　together they shout for joy.
When the LORD returns to Zion,
　they will see it with their own eyes.
⁹ Burst into songs of joy together,
　you ruins of Jerusalem,
for the LORD has comforted his people,
　he has redeemed Jerusalem.
¹⁰ The LORD will lay bare his holy arm
　in the sight of all the nations,
and all the ends of the earth will see
　the salvation of our God.

¹¹ Depart, depart, go out from there!
　Touch no unclean thing!
Come out from it and be pure,
　you who carry the vessels of the LORD.
¹² But you will not leave in haste
　or go in flight;
for the LORD will go before you,
　the God of Israel will be your rear guard.

ᵃ5 Dead Sea Scrolls and Vulgate; Masoretic Text *wail*

The Suffering and Glory of the Servant

¹³See, my servant will act wisely*^a*;
　　he will be raised and lifted up and highly exalted.
¹⁴Just as there were many who were appalled at him*^b*—
　　his appearance was so disfigured beyond that of any man
　　and his form marred beyond human likeness—
¹⁵so will he sprinkle many nations,*^c*
　　and kings will shut their mouths because of him.
For what they were not told, they will see,
　　and what they have not heard, they will understand.

53 Who has believed our message
　　and to whom has the arm of the LORD been revealed?
²He grew up before him like a tender shoot,
　　and like a root out of dry ground.
He had no beauty or majesty to attract us to him,
　　nothing in his appearance that we should desire him.
³He was despised and rejected by men,
　　a man of sorrows, and familiar with suffering.
Like one from whom men hide their faces
　　he was despised, and we esteemed him not.

⁴Surely he took up our infirmities
　　and carried our sorrows,
yet we considered him stricken by God,
　　smitten by him, and afflicted.
⁵But he was pierced for our transgressions,
　　he was crushed for our iniquities;
the punishment that brought us peace was upon him,
　　and by his wounds we are healed.
⁶We all, like sheep, have gone astray,
　　each of us has turned to his own way;
and the LORD has laid on him
　　the iniquity of us all.

⁷He was oppressed and afflicted,
　　yet he did not open his mouth;

a13 Or will prosper b14 Hebrew you c15 Hebrew; Septuagint so will many nations marvel at him

Seven hundred years before it happened the prophet Isaiah described how Jesus would die:

✸ Standing silent before his accusers (Isaiah 53:7)
✸ Hands and feet pierced (Isaiah 53:5)
✸ Hanging between two criminals (Isaiah 53:9)
✸ Buried in a rich man's tomb (Isaiah 53:9)

　Isaiah also described why Jesus had to die. He took the punishment you deserved, so you could have peace with God (Isaiah 53:4–6). Also, Isaiah saw beyond the cross. After all Jesus' pain, he rose from the grave, knew that your salvation had been won and said, "It was worth it" (Isaiah 53:11).

The Bible Says

He Was Pierced for You

he was led like a lamb to the slaughter,
    and as a sheep before her shearers is silent,
    so he did not open his mouth.
⁸By oppression*ᵃ* and judgment he was taken away.
    And who can speak of his descendants?
For he was cut off from the land of the living;
    for the transgression of my people he was stricken.*ᵇ*
⁹He was assigned a grave with the wicked,
    and with the rich in his death,
though he had done no violence,
    nor was any deceit in his mouth.

¹⁰Yet it was the Lᴏʀᴅ's will to crush him and cause him to
        suffer,
    and though the Lᴏʀᴅ makes*ᶜ* his life a guilt offering,
he will see his offspring and prolong his days,
    and the will of the Lᴏʀᴅ will prosper in his hand.
¹¹After the suffering of his soul,
    he will see the light of life*ᵈ* and be satisfied*ᵉ*;
by his knowledge*ᶠ* my righteous servant will justify many,
    and he will bear their iniquities.
¹²Therefore I will give him a portion among the great,*ᵍ*
    and he will divide the spoils with the strong,*ʰ*
because he poured out his life unto death,
    and was numbered with the transgressors.
For he bore the sin of many,
    and made intercession for the transgressors.

The Future Glory of Zion

54 "Sing, O barren woman,
    you who never bore a child;
burst into song, shout for joy,
    you who were never in labor;
because more are the children of the desolate woman
    than of her who has a husband,"

                                says the Lᴏʀᴅ.

² "Enlarge the place of your tent,
    stretch your tent curtains wide,
    do not hold back;
lengthen your cords,
    strengthen your stakes.
³For you will spread out to the right and to the left;
    your descendants will dispossess nations
    and settle in their desolate cities.

⁴"Do not be afraid; you will not suffer shame.
    Do not fear disgrace; you will not be humiliated.
You will forget the shame of your youth
    and remember no more the reproach of your widowhood.
⁵For your Maker is your husband—
    the Lᴏʀᴅ Almighty is his name—
the Holy One of Israel is your Redeemer;
    he is called the God of all the earth.

ᵃ8 Or From arrest ᵇ8 Or away. / Yet who of his generation considered / that he was cut off from the land of the living / for the transgression of my people, / to whom the blow was due? ᶜ10 Hebrew though you make ᵈ11 Dead Sea Scrolls (see also Septuagint); Masoretic Text does not have the light of life, ᵉ11 Or (with Masoretic Text) ¹¹He will see the result of the suffering of his soul / and be satisfied ᶠ11 Or by knowledge of him ᵍ12 Or many ʰ12 Or numerous

⁶The LORD will call you back
   as if you were a wife deserted and distressed in spirit—
a wife who married young,
   only to be rejected," says your God.
⁷"For a brief moment I abandoned you,
   but with deep compassion I will bring you back.
⁸In a surge of anger
   I hid my face from you for a moment,
but with everlasting kindness
   I will have compassion on you,"
   says the LORD your Redeemer.

⁹"To me this is like the days of Noah,
   when I swore that the waters of Noah would never again
      cover the earth.
So now I have sworn not to be angry with you,
   never to rebuke you again.
¹⁰Though the mountains be shaken
   and the hills be removed,
yet my unfailing love for you will not be shaken
   nor my covenant of peace be removed,"
   says the LORD, who has compassion on you.

¹¹"O afflicted city, lashed by storms and not comforted,
   I will build you with stones of turquoise,ᵃ
   your foundations with sapphires.ᵇ
¹²I will make your battlements of rubies,
   your gates of sparkling jewels,
   and all your walls of precious stones.
¹³All your sons will be taught by the LORD,
   and great will be your children's peace.
¹⁴In righteousness you will be established:
Tyranny will be far from you;
   you will have nothing to fear.
Terror will be far removed;
   it will not come near you.
¹⁵If anyone does attack you, it will not be my doing;
   whoever attacks you will surrender to you.

¹⁶"See, it is I who created the blacksmith
   who fans the coals into flame
   and forges a weapon fit for its work.
And it is I who have created the destroyer to work havoc;
¹⁷   no weapon forged against you will prevail,
   and you will refute every tongue that accuses you.
This is the heritage of the servants of the LORD,
   and this is their vindication from me,"
                                    declares the LORD.

55 *Invitation to the Thirsty*
"Come, all you who are thirsty,
   come to the waters;
and you who have no money,
   come, buy and eat!
Come, buy wine and milk
   without money and without cost.

ᵃ11 The meaning of the Hebrew for this word is uncertain.   ᵇ11 Or *lapis lazuli*

²Why spend money on what is not bread,
and your labor on what does not satisfy?
Listen, listen to me, and eat what is good,
and your soul will delight in the richest of fare.
³Give ear and come to me;
hear me, that your soul may live.
I will make an everlasting covenant with you,
my faithful love promised to David.
⁴See, I have made him a witness to the peoples,
a leader and commander of the peoples.
⁵Surely you will summon nations you know not,
and nations that do not know you will hasten to you,
because of the LORD your God,
the Holy One of Israel,
for he has endowed you with splendor."

⁶Seek the LORD while he may be found;
call on him while he is near.
⁷Let the wicked forsake his way
and the evil man his thoughts.
Let him turn to the LORD, and he will have mercy on him,
and to our God, for he will freely pardon.

> Let the wicked forsake his way . . . Let him turn to the LORD, and he will . . . freely pardon (Isaiah 55:7).

⁸"For my thoughts are not your thoughts,
neither are your ways my ways,"

declares the LORD.

⁹"As the heavens are higher than the earth,
so are my ways higher than your ways
and my thoughts than your thoughts.
¹⁰As the rain and the snow
come down from heaven,
and do not return to it
without watering the earth
and making it bud and flourish,
so that it yields seed for the sower and bread for the eater,
¹¹so is my word that goes out from my mouth:
It will not return to me empty,
but will accomplish what I desire
and achieve the purpose for which I sent it.
¹²You will go out in joy
and be led forth in peace;
the mountains and hills
will burst into song before you,
and all the trees of the field
will clap their hands.
¹³Instead of the thornbush will grow the pine tree,
and instead of briers the myrtle will grow.
This will be for the LORD's renown,
for an everlasting sign,
which will not be destroyed."

56 *Salvation for Others*   This is what the LORD says:

"Maintain justice
and do what is right,
for my salvation is close at hand
and my righteousness will soon be revealed.

²Blessed is the man who does this,
  the man who holds it fast,
who keeps the Sabbath without desecrating it,
  and keeps his hand from doing any evil."

³Let no foreigner who has bound himself to the LORD say,
  "The LORD will surely exclude me from his people."
And let not any eunuch complain,
  "I am only a dry tree."

⁴For this is what the LORD says:

"To the eunuchs who keep my Sabbaths,
  who choose what pleases me
  and hold fast to my covenant—
⁵to them I will give within my temple and its walls
  a memorial and a name
  better than sons and daughters;
I will give them an everlasting name
  that will not be cut off.
⁶And foreigners who bind themselves to the LORD
  to serve him,
to love the name of the LORD,
  and to worship him,
all who keep the Sabbath without desecrating it
  and who hold fast to my covenant—
⁷these I will bring to my holy mountain
  and give them joy in my house of prayer.
Their burnt offerings and sacrifices
  will be accepted on my altar;
for my house will be called
  a house of prayer for all nations."
⁸The Sovereign LORD declares—
  he who gathers the exiles of Israel:
"I will gather still others to them
  besides those already gathered."

God's Accusation Against the Wicked

⁹Come, all you beasts of the field,
  come and devour, all you beasts of the forest!
¹⁰Israel's watchmen are blind,
  they all lack knowledge;
they are all mute dogs,
  they cannot bark;
they lie around and dream,
  they love to sleep.
¹¹They are dogs with mighty appetites;
  they never have enough.
They are shepherds who lack understanding;
  they all turn to their own way,
  each seeks his own gain.
¹²"Come," each one cries, "let me get wine!
  Let us drink our fill of beer!
And tomorrow will be like today,
  or even far better."

57 The righteous perish,
  and no one ponders it in his heart;
devout men are taken away,
  and no one understands

that the righteous are taken away
to be spared from evil.
²Those who walk uprightly
enter into peace;
they find rest as they lie in death.

³"But you—come here, you sons of a sorceress,
you offspring of adulterers and prostitutes!
⁴Whom are you mocking?
At whom do you sneer
and stick out your tongue?
Are you not a brood of rebels,
the offspring of liars?
⁵You burn with lust among the oaks
and under every spreading tree;
you sacrifice your children in the ravines
and under the overhanging crags.
⁶ The idols, among the smooth stones of the ravines are your
portion;
they, they are your lot.
Yes, to them you have poured out drink offerings
and offered grain offerings.
In the light of these things, should I relent?
⁷You have made your bed on a high and lofty hill;
there you went up to offer your sacrifices.
⁸Behind your doors and your doorposts
you have put your pagan symbols.
Forsaking me, you uncovered your bed,
you climbed into it and opened it wide;
you made a pact with those whose beds you love,
and you looked on their nakedness.
⁹You went to Molech*ᵃ* with olive oil
and increased your perfumes.
You sent your ambassadors*ᵇ* far away;
you descended to the grave*ᶜ* itself!
¹⁰You were wearied by all your ways,
but you would not say, 'It is hopeless.'
You found renewal of your strength,
and so you did not faint.

¹¹"Whom have you so dreaded and feared
that you have been false to me,
and have neither remembered me
nor pondered this in your hearts?
Is it not because I have long been silent
that you do not fear me?
¹²I will expose your righteousness and your works,
and they will not benefit you.
¹³When you cry out for help,
let your collection of idols, save you!
The wind will carry all of them off,
a mere breath will blow them away.
But the man who makes me his refuge
will inherit the land
and possess my holy mountain."

ᵃ9 Or to the king ᵇ9 Or idols ᶜ9 Hebrew Sheol

¹⁴And it will be said:

"Build up, build up, prepare the road!
    Remove the obstacles out of the way of my people."
¹⁵For this is what the high and lofty One says—
    he who lives forever, whose name is holy:
"I live in a high and holy place,
    but also with him who is contrite and lowly in spirit,
to revive the spirit of the lowly
    and to revive the heart of the contrite.
¹⁶I will not accuse forever,
    nor will I always be angry,
for then the spirit of man would grow faint before me—
    the breath of man that I have created.
¹⁷I was enraged by his sinful greed;
    I punished him, and hid my face in anger,
    yet he kept on in his willful ways.
¹⁸I have seen his ways, but I will heal him;
    I will guide him and restore comfort to him,
¹⁹   creating praise on the lips of the mourners in
        Israel.
    Peace, peace, to those far and near,"
        says the Lᴏʀᴅ. "And I will heal them."
²⁰But the wicked are like the tossing sea,
    which cannot rest,
    whose waves cast up mire and mud.
²¹"There is no peace," says my God, "for the wicked."

58

True Fasting

"Shout it aloud, do not hold back.
    Raise your voice like a trumpet.
Declare to my people their rebellion
    and to the house of Jacob their sins.
²For day after day they seek me out;
    they seem eager to know my ways,
as if they were a nation that does what is right
    and has not forsaken the commands of its God.
They ask me for just decisions
    and seem eager for God to come near them.
³'Why have we fasted,' they say,
    'and you have not seen it?
Why have we humbled ourselves,
    and you have not noticed?'

"Yet on the day of your fasting, you do as you please
    and exploit all your workers.
⁴Your fasting ends in quarreling and strife,
    and in striking each other with wicked fists.
You cannot fast as you do today
    and expect your voice to be heard on high.
⁵Is this the kind of fast I have chosen,
    only a day for a man to humble himself?
Is it only for bowing one's head like a reed
    and for lying on sackcloth and ashes?
Is that what you call a fast,
    a day acceptable to the Lᴏʀᴅ?

⁶"Is not this the kind of fasting I have chosen:
to loose the chains of injustice

and untie the cords of the yoke,
to set the oppressed free
and break every yoke?
⁷Is it not to share your food with the hungry
and to provide the poor wanderer with shelter—
when you see the naked, to clothe him,
and not to turn away from your own flesh and
blood?
⁸Then your light will break forth like the dawn,
and your healing will quickly appear;
then your righteousness*a* will go before you,
and the glory of the LORD will be your rear
guard.
⁹Then you will call, and the LORD will answer;
you will cry for help, and he will say: Here
am I.

> You will call,
> and the LORD
> will answer; you
> will cry for help,
> and he will say:
> Here am I
> (Isaiah 58:9).

"If you do away with the yoke of oppression,
with the pointing finger and malicious talk,
¹⁰and if you spend yourselves in behalf of the hungry
and satisfy the needs of the oppressed,
then your light will rise in the darkness,
and your night will become like the noonday.
¹¹The LORD will guide you always;
he will satisfy your needs in a sun-scorched land
and will strengthen your frame.
You will be like a well-watered garden,
like a spring whose waters never fail.
¹²Your people will rebuild the ancient ruins
and will raise up the age-old foundations;
you will be called Repairer of Broken Walls,
Restorer of Streets with Dwellings.

¹³"If you keep your feet from breaking the Sabbath
and from doing as you please on my holy day,
if you call the Sabbath a delight
and the LORD's holy day honorable,
and if you honor it by not going your own way
and not doing as you please or speaking idle words,
¹⁴then you will find your joy in the LORD,
and I will cause you to ride on the heights of the land
and to feast on the inheritance of your father Jacob."
The mouth of the LORD has spoken.

59

Sin, Confession and Redemption

Surely the arm of the LORD is not too short to save,
nor his ear too dull to hear.
²But your iniquities have separated
you from your God;
your sins have hidden his face from you,
so that he will not hear.
³For your hands are stained with blood,
your fingers with guilt.
Your lips have spoken lies,
and your tongue mutters wicked things.

---

a8 Or your righteous One

⁴No one calls for justice;
  no one pleads his case with integrity.
They rely on empty arguments and speak lies;
  they conceive trouble and give birth to evil.
⁵They hatch the eggs of vipers
  and spin a spider's web.
Whoever eats their eggs will die,
  and when one is broken, an adder is hatched.
⁶Their cobwebs are useless for clothing;
  they cannot cover themselves with what they make.
Their deeds are evil deeds,
  and acts of violence are in their hands.
⁷Their feet rush into sin;
  they are swift to shed innocent blood.
Their thoughts are evil thoughts;
  ruin and destruction mark their ways.
⁸The way of peace they do not know;
  there is no justice in their paths.
They have turned them into crooked roads;
  no one who walks in them will know peace.

⁹So justice is far from us,
  and righteousness does not reach us.
We look for light, but all is darkness;
  for brightness, but we walk in deep shadows.
¹⁰Like the blind we grope along the wall,
  feeling our way like men without eyes.
At midday we stumble as if it were twilight;
  among the strong, we are like the dead.
¹¹We all growl like bears;
  we moan mournfully like doves.
We look for justice, but find none;
  for deliverance, but it is far away.

¹²For our offenses are many in your sight,
  and our sins testify against us.
Our offenses are ever with us,
  and we acknowledge our iniquities:
¹³rebellion and treachery against the LORD,
  turning our backs on our God,
fomenting oppression and revolt,
  uttering lies our hearts have conceived.
¹⁴So justice is driven back,
  and righteousness stands at a distance;
truth has stumbled in the streets,
  honesty cannot enter.
¹⁵Truth is nowhere to be found,
  and whoever shuns evil becomes a prey.

The LORD looked and was displeased
  that there was no justice.
¹⁶He saw that there was no one,
  he was appalled that there was no one to intervene;
so his own arm worked salvation for him,
  and his own righteousness sustained him.
¹⁷He put on righteousness as his breastplate,
  and the helmet of salvation on his head;
he put on the garments of vengeance
  and wrapped himself in zeal as in a cloak.

[18] According to what they have done,
  so will he repay
wrath to his enemies
  and retribution to his foes;
  he will repay the islands their due.
[19] From the west, men will fear the name of the LORD,
  and from the rising of the sun, they will revere his glory.
For he will come like a pent-up flood
  that the breath of the LORD drives along.[a]

[20] "The Redeemer will come to Zion,
  to those in Jacob who repent of their sins,"

declares the LORD.

[21] "As for me, this is my covenant with them," says the LORD. "My Spirit, who is on you, and my words that I have put in your mouth will not depart from your mouth, or from the mouths of your children, or from the mouths of their descendants from this time on and forever," says the LORD.

60

The Glory of Zion

"Arise, shine, for your light has come,
  and the glory of the LORD rises upon you.
[2] See, darkness covers the earth
  and thick darkness is over the peoples,
but the LORD rises upon you
  and his glory appears over you.
[3] Nations will come to your light,
  and kings to the brightness of your dawn.

[4] "Lift up your eyes and look about you:
  All assemble and come to you;
your sons come from afar,
  and your daughters are carried on the arm.
[5] Then you will look and be radiant,
  your heart will throb and swell with joy;
the wealth on the seas will be brought to you,
  to you the riches of the nations will come.
[6] Herds of camels will cover your land,
  young camels of Midian and Ephah.
And all from Sheba will come,
  bearing gold and incense
  and proclaiming the praise of the LORD.
[7] All Kedar's flocks will be gathered to you,
  the rams of Nebaioth will serve you;
they will be accepted as offerings on my altar,
  and I will adorn my glorious temple.

[8] "Who are these that fly along like clouds,
  like doves to their nests?
[9] Surely the islands look to me;
  in the lead are the ships of Tarshish,[b]
bringing your sons from afar,
  with their silver and gold,
to the honor of the LORD your God,

---

[a] 19 Or *When the enemy comes in like a flood, / the Spirit of the* LORD *will put him to flight*   [b] 9 Or *the trading ships*

the Holy One of Israel,
for he has endowed you with splendor.

10 "Foreigners will rebuild your walls,
and their kings will serve you.
Though in anger I struck you,
in favor I will show you compassion.
11 Your gates will always stand open,
they will never be shut, day or night,
so that men may bring you the wealth of the nations—
their kings led in triumphal procession.
12 For the nation or kingdom that will not serve you will perish;
it will be utterly ruined.

13 "The glory of Lebanon will come to you,
the pine, the fir and the cypress together,
to adorn the place of my sanctuary;
and I will glorify the place of my feet.
14 The sons of your oppressors will come bowing before you;
all who despise you will bow down at your feet
and will call you the City of the LORD,
Zion of the Holy One of Israel.

15 "Although you have been forsaken and hated,
with no one traveling through,
I will make you the everlasting pride
and the joy of all generations.
16 You will drink the milk of nations
and be nursed at royal breasts.
Then you will know that I, the LORD, am your Savior,
your Redeemer, the Mighty One of Jacob.
17 Instead of bronze I will bring you gold,
and silver in place of iron.
Instead of wood I will bring you
bronze,
and iron in place of stones.
I will make peace your governor
and righteousness your ruler.
18 No longer will violence be heard in
your land,
nor ruin or destruction within
your borders,
but you will call your walls
Salvation
and your gates Praise.
19 The sun will no more be your light
by day,
nor will the brightness of the
moon shine on you,
for the LORD will be your everlasting
light,
and your God will be your glory.
20 Your sun will never set again,
and your moon will wane no
more;
the LORD will be your everlasting
light,
and your days of sorrow will end.

I'll be hanging on to these shades—I think I'm gonna be needing them.

SEE ISAIAH 60:20

²¹ Then will all your people be righteous
    and they will possess the land forever.
They are the shoot I have planted,
    the work of my hands,
    for the display of my splendor.
²² The least of you will become a thousand,
    the smallest a mighty nation.
I am the LORD;
    in its time I will do this swiftly."

The Year of the LORD's Favor

61 The Spirit of the Sovereign LORD is on me,
    because the LORD has anointed me
    to preach good news to the poor.
He has sent me to bind up the brokenhearted,
    to proclaim freedom for the captives
    and release from darkness for the prisoners,ᵃ
² to proclaim the year of the LORD's favor
    and the day of vengeance of our God,
to comfort all who mourn,
³   and provide for those who grieve in Zion—
to bestow on them a crown of beauty
    instead of ashes,
the oil of gladness
    instead of mourning,
and a garment of praise
    instead of a spirit of despair.
They will be called oaks of righteousness,
    a planting of the LORD
    for the display of his splendor.

⁴ They will rebuild the ancient ruins
    and restore the places long devastated;
they will renew the ruined cities
    that have been devastated for generations.
⁵ Aliens will shepherd your flocks;
    foreigners will work your fields and vineyards.
⁶ And you will be called priests of the LORD,
    you will be named ministers of our God.
You will feed on the wealth of nations,
    and in their riches you will boast.

⁷ Instead of their shame
    my people will receive a double portion,
and instead of disgrace
    they will rejoice in their inheritance;
and so they will inherit a double portion in their land,
    and everlasting joy will be theirs.

⁸ "For I, the LORD, love justice;
    I hate robbery and iniquity.
In my faithfulness I will reward them
    and make an everlasting covenant with them.
⁹ Their descendants will be known among the nations
    and their offspring among the peoples.

ᵃ1 Hebrew; Septuagint *the blind*

All who see them will acknowledge
    that they are a people the Lord has blessed."

¹⁰I delight greatly in the Lord;
    my soul rejoices in my God.
For he has clothed me with garments of salvation
    and arrayed me in a robe of righteousness,
as a bridegroom adorns his head like a priest,
    and as a bride adorns herself with her jewels.
¹¹For as the soil makes the sprout come up
    and a garden causes seeds to grow,
so the Sovereign Lord will make righteousness and praise
    spring up before all nations.

62

Zion's New Name

For Zion's sake I will not keep silent,
    for Jerusalem's sake I will not remain quiet,
till her righteousness shines out like the dawn,
    her salvation like a blazing torch.
²The nations will see your righteousness,
    and all kings your glory;
you will be called by a new name
    that the mouth of the Lord will bestow.
³You will be a crown of splendor in the Lord's hand,
    a royal diadem in the hand of your God.
⁴No longer will they call you Deserted,
    or name your land Desolate.
But you will be called Hephzibah,ᵃ
    and your land Beulahᵇ;
for the Lord will take delight in you,
    and your land will be married.
⁵As a young man marries a maiden,
    so will your sonsᶜ marry you;
as a bridegroom rejoices over his bride,
    so will your God rejoice over you.

⁶I have posted watchmen on your walls, O Jerusalem;
    they will never be silent day or night.
You who call on the Lord,
    give yourselves no rest,
⁷and give him no rest till he establishes Jerusalem
    and makes her the praise of the earth.

⁸The Lord has sworn by his right hand
    and by his mighty arm:
"Never again will I give your grain
    as food for your enemies,
and never again will foreigners drink the new wine
    for which you have toiled;
⁹but those who harvest it will eat it
    and praise the Lord,
and those who gather the grapes will drink it
    in the courts of my sanctuary."

¹⁰Pass through, pass through the gates!
    Prepare the way for the people.

ᵃ4 Hephzibah means *my delight is in her.* ᵇ4 Beulah means *married.* ᶜ5 Or Builder

Build up, build up the highway!
  Remove the stones.
Raise a banner for the nations.

[11] The LORD has made proclamation
    to the ends of the earth:
"Say to the Daughter of Zion,
    'See, your Savior comes!
See, his reward is with him,
    and his recompense accompanies him.' "
[12] They will be called the Holy People,
    the Redeemed of the LORD;
and you will be called Sought After,
    the City No Longer Deserted.

63 God's Day of Vengeance and Redemption

Who is this coming from Edom,
    from Bozrah, with his garments stained crimson?
Who is this, robed in splendor,
    striding forward in the greatness of his strength?

"It is I, speaking in righteousness,
    mighty to save."

[2] Why are your garments red,
    like those of one treading the winepress?

[3] "I have trodden the winepress alone;
    from the nations no one was with me.
I trampled them in my anger
    and trod them down in my wrath;
their blood spattered my garments,
    and I stained all my clothing.
[4] For the day of vengeance was in my heart,
    and the year of my redemption has come.
[5] I looked, but there was no one to help,
    I was appalled that no one gave support;
so my own arm worked salvation for me,
    and my own wrath sustained me.
[6] I trampled the nations in my anger;
    in my wrath I made them drunk
    and poured their blood on the ground."

Praise and Prayer

[7] I will tell of the kindnesses of the LORD,
    the deeds for which he is to be praised,
    according to all the LORD has done for us—
yes, the many good things he has done
    for the house of Israel,
    according to his compassion and many kindnesses.
[8] He said, "Surely they are my people,
    sons who will not be false to me";
    and so he became their Savior.
[9] In all their distress he too was distressed,
    and the angel of his presence saved them.
In his love and mercy he redeemed them;
    he lifted them up and carried them
    all the days of old.

¹⁰ Yet they rebelled
    and grieved his Holy Spirit.
So he turned and became their enemy
    and he himself fought against them.

¹¹ Then his people recalled^{*a*} the days of old,
    the days of Moses and his people—
where is he who brought them through the sea,
    with the shepherd of his flock?
Where is he who set
    his Holy Spirit among them,
¹² who sent his glorious arm of power
    to be at Moses' right hand,
who divided the waters before them,
    to gain for himself everlasting renown,
¹³ who led them through the depths?
Like a horse in open country,
    they did not stumble;
¹⁴ like cattle that go down to the plain,
    they were given rest by the Spirit of the LORD.
This is how you guided your people
    to make for yourself a glorious name.

¹⁵ Look down from heaven and see
    from your lofty throne, holy and glorious.
Where are your zeal and your might?
    Your tenderness and compassion are withheld from us.
¹⁶ But you are our Father,
    though Abraham does not know us
    or Israel acknowledge us;
you, O LORD, are our Father,
    our Redeemer from of old is your name.
¹⁷ Why, O LORD, do you make us wander from your ways
    and harden our hearts so we do not revere you?
Return for the sake of your servants,
    the tribes that are your inheritance.
¹⁸ For a little while your people possessed your holy place,
    but now our enemies have trampled down your sanctuary.
¹⁹ We are yours from of old;
    but you have not ruled over them,
    they have not been called by your name.^{*b*}

64 Oh, that you would rend the heavens and come down,
    that the mountains would tremble before you!
² As when fire sets twigs ablaze
    and causes water to boil,
come down to make your name known to your enemies
    and cause the nations to quake before you!
³ For when you did awesome things that we did not expect,
    you came down, and the mountains trembled before you.
⁴ Since ancient times no one has heard,
    no ear has perceived,
no eye has seen any God besides you,
    who acts on behalf of those who wait for him.

---

a 11 Or But may he recall   *b 19 Or We are like those you have never ruled, / like those never called by your name*

⁵You come to the help of those who gladly do right,
who remember your ways.
But when we continued to sin against them,
you were angry.
How then can we be saved?
⁶All of us have become like one who is unclean,
and all our righteous acts are like filthy rags;
we all shrivel up like a leaf,
and like the wind our sins sweep us away.
⁷No one calls on your name
or strives to lay hold of you;
for you have hidden your face from us
and made us waste away because of our sins.

⁸Yet, O LORD, you are our Father.
We are the clay, you are the potter;
we are all the work of your hand.
⁹Do not be angry beyond measure, O LORD;
do not remember our sins forever.
Oh, look upon us, we pray,
for we are all your people.
¹⁰Your sacred cities have become a desert;
even Zion is a desert, Jerusalem a desolation.
¹¹Our holy and glorious temple, where our fathers
praised you,
has been burned with fire,
and all that we treasured lies in ruins.
¹²After all this, O LORD, will you hold yourself back?
Will you keep silent and punish us beyond measure?

65 *Judgment and Salvation*
"I revealed myself to those who did not ask for me;
I was found by those who did not seek me.
To a nation that did not call on my name,
I said, 'Here am I, here am I.'
²All day long I have held out my hands
to an obstinate people,
who walk in ways not good,
pursuing their own imaginations—
³a people who continually provoke me
to my very face,
offering sacrifices in gardens
and burning incense on altars of brick;
⁴who sit among the graves
and spend their nights keeping secret vigil;
who eat the flesh of pigs,
and whose pots hold broth of unclean meat;
⁵who say, 'Keep away; don't come near me,
for I am too sacred for you!'
Such people are smoke in my nostrils,
a fire that keeps burning all day.

⁶"See, it stands written before me:
I will not keep silent but will pay back in full;
I will pay it back into their laps—
⁷both your sins and the sins of your fathers,"
says the LORD.

"Because they burned sacrifices on the mountains
and defied me on the hills,
I will measure into their laps
the full payment for their former deeds."

⁸This is what the LORD says:

"As when juice is still found in a cluster of grapes
and men say, 'Don't destroy it,
there is yet some good in it,'
so will I do in behalf of my servants;
I will not destroy them all.
⁹I will bring forth descendants from Jacob,
and from Judah those who will possess my mountains;
my chosen people will inherit them,
and there will my servants live.
¹⁰Sharon will become a pasture for flocks,
and the Valley of Achor a resting place for herds,
for my people who seek me.

¹¹"But as for you who forsake the LORD
and forget my holy mountain,
who spread a table for Fortune
and fill bowls of mixed wine for Destiny,
¹²I will destine you for the sword,
and you will all bend down for the slaughter;
for I called but you did not answer,
I spoke but you did not listen.
You did evil in my sight
and chose what displeases me."

¹³Therefore this is what the Sovereign LORD says:

"My servants will eat,
but you will go hungry;
my servants will drink,
but you will go thirsty;
my servants will rejoice,
but you will be put to shame.
¹⁴My servants will sing
out of the joy of their hearts,
but you will cry out
from anguish of heart
and wail in brokenness of spirit.
¹⁵You will leave your name
to my chosen ones as a curse;
the Sovereign LORD will put you to death,
but to his servants he will give another name.
¹⁶Whoever invokes a blessing in the land
will do so by the God of truth;
he who takes an oath in the land
will swear by the God of truth.
For the past troubles will be forgotten
and hidden from my eyes.

ISAIAH 65

QU ZZER

Q: Where
will some
Jewish people
be living at
history's end?

*BONUS:
Between 1840
and 1980
the world's
population
doubled.
During this
time how
much did
the Jewish
population of
Israel grow?*

**Answers on
page 969**

New Heavens and a New Earth

¹⁷"Behold, I will create
new heavens and a new earth.
The former things will not be remembered,
nor will they come to mind.

¹⁸ But be glad and rejoice forever
    in what I will create,
  for I will create Jerusalem to be a delight
    and its people a joy.
¹⁹ I will rejoice over Jerusalem
    and take delight in my people;
  the sound of weeping and of crying
    will be heard in it no more.

²⁰ "Never again will there be in it
    an infant who lives but a few days,
    or an old man who does not live out his years;
  he who dies at a hundred
    will be thought a mere youth;
  he who fails to reach*a* a hundred
    will be considered accursed.
²¹ They will build houses and dwell in them;
    they will plant vineyards and eat their fruit.
²² No longer will they build houses and others live in them,
    or plant and others eat.
  For as the days of a tree,
    so will be the days of my people;
  my chosen ones will long enjoy
    the works of their hands.
²³ They will not toil in vain
    or bear children doomed to misfortune;
  for they will be a people blessed by the Lord,
    they and their descendants with them.
²⁴ Before they call I will answer;
    while they are still speaking I will hear.
²⁵ The wolf and the lamb will feed together,
    and the lion will eat straw like the ox,
    but dust will be the serpent's food.
  They will neither harm nor destroy
    on all my holy mountain,"
                             says the Lord.

66

Judgment and Hope   This is what the Lord says:

"Heaven is my throne,
    and the earth is my footstool.
  Where is the house you will build for me?
    Where will my resting place be?
² Has not my hand made all these things,
    and so they came into being?"
                             declares the Lord.

"This is the one I esteem:
    he who is humble and contrite in spirit,
    and trembles at my word.
³ But whoever sacrifices a bull
    is like one who kills a man,
  and whoever offers a lamb,
    like one who breaks a dog's neck;

a20 Or / the sinner who reaches

whoever makes a grain offering
 is like one who presents pig's blood,
and whoever burns memorial incense,
 like one who worships an idol.
They have chosen their own ways,
 and their souls delight in their abominations;
⁴so I also will choose harsh treatment for them
 and will bring upon them what they dread.
For when I called, no one answered,
 when I spoke, no one listened.
They did evil in my sight
 and chose what displeases me."

⁵Hear the word of the LORD,
 you who tremble at his word:
"Your brothers who hate you,
 and exclude you because of my name, have said,
'Let the LORD be glorified,
 that we may see your joy!'
 Yet they will be put to shame.
⁶Hear that uproar from the city,
 hear that noise from the temple!
It is the sound of the LORD
 repaying his enemies all they deserve.

⁷"Before she goes into labor,
 she gives birth;
before the pains come upon her,
 she delivers a son.
⁸Who has ever heard of such a thing?
 Who has ever seen such things?
Can a country be born in a day
 or a nation be brought forth in a moment?
Yet no sooner is Zion in labor
 than she gives birth to her children.
⁹Do I bring to the moment of birth
 and not give delivery?" says the LORD.
"Do I close up the womb
 when I bring to delivery?" says your God.
¹⁰"Rejoice with Jerusalem and be glad for her,
 all you who love her;
rejoice greatly with her,
 all you who mourn over her.
¹¹For you will nurse and be satisfied
 at her comforting breasts;
you will drink deeply
 and delight in her overflowing abundance."

¹²For this is what the LORD says:

"I will extend peace to her like a river,
 and the wealth of nations like a flooding stream;
you will nurse and be carried on her arm
 and dandled on her knees.
¹³As a mother comforts her child,
 so will I comfort you;
 and you will be comforted over Jerusalem."

¹⁴When you see this, your heart will rejoice
 and you will flourish like grass;

Answers
*to Quizzer on
page 967*

**A: In Israel,
according to
Isaiah and other
prophets
(Isaiah 65:9).**

**BONUS: It grew
1500 percent!**

the hand of the Lord will be made known to his servants,
> but his fury will be shown to his foes.
[15] See, the Lord is coming with fire,
> and his chariots are like a whirlwind;
he will bring down his anger with fury,
> and his rebuke with flames of fire.
[16] For with fire and with his sword
> the Lord will execute judgment upon all men,
> and many will be those slain by the Lord.

[17] "Those who consecrate and purify themselves to go into the gardens, following the one in the midst of[a] those who eat the flesh of pigs and rats and other abominable things—they will meet their end together," declares the Lord.

[18] "And I, because of their actions and their imaginations, am about to come[b] and gather all nations and tongues, and they will come and see my glory.

[19] "I will set a sign among them, and I will send some of those who survive to the nations—to Tarshish, to the Libyans[c] and Lydians (famous as archers), to Tubal and Greece, and to the distant islands that have not heard of my fame or seen my glory. They will proclaim my glory among the nations. [20] And they will bring all your brothers, from all the nations, to my holy mountain in Jerusalem as an offering to the Lord—on horses, in chariots and wagons, and on mules and camels," says the Lord. "They will bring them, as the Israelites bring their grain offerings, to the temple of the Lord in ceremonially clean vessels. [21] And I will select some of them also to be priests and Levites," says the Lord.

[22] "As the new heavens and the new earth that I make will endure before me," declares the Lord, "so will your name and descendants endure. [23] From one New Moon to another and from one Sabbath to another, all mankind will come and bow down before me," says the Lord. [24] "And they will go out and look upon the dead bodies of those who rebelled against me; their worm will not die, nor will their fire be quenched, and they will be loathsome to all mankind."

Direct Line

ISAIAH 66:22

Have you heard the latest on the "end of the world"? Global warming? A new ice age? Giant asteroids that knock the earth out of its orbit? All these theories make the future sound pretty grim. And then you turn to the Bible and get a different view. Yes, this earth will be destroyed (Isaiah 51:6; 2 Peter 3:10–13). But by God, who will then create a new heaven and earth to be the home of a purified humanity. What will life on earth be like after God acts? Check it out in Isaiah 65:17–25. Sure, scientists throw out scary pictures of the end of the world. But what God has in store for you is nothing but good!

---

[a]17 Or *gardens behind one of your temples, and* [b]18 The meaning of the Hebrew for this clause is uncertain. [c]19 Some Septuagint manuscripts *Put* (Libyans); Hebrew *Pul*

CHANGE.

Is it ever too late to change? No, but sometimes it's too late to avoid punishment. You can say you're sorry and you'll never do it again, but you'll probably still be punished. And if you refuse to change, well, then you can be sure there's more trouble ahead!

Jeremiah's contemporaries refused to change. For 40 years God's prophet urged the people of Judah to turn back to God. If they didn't change, God was going to destroy the nation. Instead of changing, the people of Judah got mad at Jeremiah. Finally what Jeremiah predicted happened. Judah and Jerusalem were destroyed by Babylon, and the people were taken captive.

FAST FACTS

Jeremiah is called the weeping prophet because he was so sad over what was happening to his country.

God told Jeremiah not to marry so he wouldn't have to see his children suffer.

Near the end of Jeremiah's life the Babylonians destroyed Jerusalem and took the people captive.

Fundamentals

What does the Bible have to say about hypocrites (Jeremiah 7:1-19)?

Read this verse when you think things are so bad you can't take it anymore (Jeremiah 29:11).

What will happen if you put someone or something other than God first in your life (Jeremiah 43)?

1 The words of Jeremiah son of Hilkiah, one of the priests at Anathoth in the territory of Benjamin. ²The word of the LORD came to him in the thirteenth year of the reign of Josiah son of Amon king of Judah, ³and through the reign of Jehoiakim son of Josiah king of Judah, down to the fifth month of the eleventh year of Zedekiah son of Josiah king of Judah, when the people of Jerusalem went into exile.

The Call of Jeremiah   ⁴The word of the LORD came to me, saying,

> ⁵ "Before I formed you in the womb I knew*ᵃ* you,
>   before you were born I set you apart;
>   I appointed you as a prophet to the nations."

⁶"Ah, Sovereign LORD," I said, "I do not know how to speak; I am only a child."

⁷But the LORD said to me, "Do not say, 'I am only a child.' You must go to everyone I send you to and say whatever I command you. ⁸Do not be afraid of them, for I am with you and will rescue you," declares the LORD.

⁹Then the LORD reached out his hand and touched my mouth and said to me, "Now, I have put my words in your mouth. ¹⁰See, today I appoint you over nations and kingdoms to uproot and tear down, to destroy and overthrow, to build and to plant."

¹¹The word of the LORD came to me: "What do you see, Jeremiah?"

"I see the branch of an almond tree," I replied.

¹²The LORD said to me, "You have seen correctly, for I am watching*ᵇ* to see that my word is fulfilled."

¹³The word of the LORD came to me again: "What do you see?"

"I see a boiling pot, tilting away from the north," I answered.

¹⁴The LORD said to me, "From the north disaster will be poured out on all who live in the land. ¹⁵I am about to summon all the peoples of the northern kingdoms," declares the LORD.

> "Their kings will come and set up their thrones
>   in the entrance of the gates of Jerusalem;
> they will come against all her surrounding walls
>   and against all the towns of Judah.
> ¹⁶I will pronounce my judgments on my people
>   because of their wickedness in forsaking me,
> in burning incense to other gods
>   and in worshiping what their hands have made.

¹⁷"Get yourself ready! Stand up and say to them whatever I command you. Do not be terrified by them, or I will terrify you before them. ¹⁸Today I have made you a fortified city, an iron pillar and a bronze wall to stand against the whole land—against the kings of Judah, its officials, its priests and the people of the land. ¹⁹They will fight against you but will not overcome you, for I am with you and will rescue you," declares the LORD.

2 *Israel Forsakes God*   The word of the LORD came to me: ²"Go and proclaim in the hearing of Jerusalem:

> " 'I remember the devotion of your youth,
>   how as a bride you loved me
> and followed me through the desert,
>   through a land not sown.
> ³Israel was holy to the LORD,
>   the firstfruits of his harvest;

ᵃ5 Or *chose*   *ᵇ12* The Hebrew for *watching* sounds like the Hebrew for *almond tree.*

Dear Sam,

If the U.S. Supreme Court says abortions are legal, why shouldn't Christians have them? Does the Bible really speak about this important issue?

Nancy in Naperville

Dear Sam, Inc.

100 Advice Lane, Anywhere, USA

Dear Nancy,

You're right. Abortion is an important issue! Even people who don't believe in the Bible should reconsider the facts of abortion. Pro-choicers who defend abortion by saying that a woman has the right to control her own body are not being honest about medical facts. Each cell in your body has your unique genetic stamp. Whether a living cell is taken from your tongue or toe, it contains the stamp of your identity. A baby, from the second the sperm meets the egg, carries its own genetic code, different from its mother's. A fetus is not a part of the woman's "own body."

Old Testament laws said if someone caused a woman's unborn child to die, compensation should be paid. The fetus was seen as more than just an extension of the woman's body (Exodus 21:22-23).

For Christians, the issue is even clearer. The Bible says God formed you in the womb and prepared you for your life before you were born (Jeremiah 1:5). You were carefully made by God from the moment of conception (Psalm 139:13-16). The unborn are spiritual individuals known by God. No one has the right to destroy them.

Sam

all who devoured her were held guilty,
and disaster overtook them,' "

declares the LORD.

⁴Hear the word of the LORD, O house of Jacob,
all you clans of the house of Israel.

⁵This is what the LORD says:

"What fault did your fathers find in me,
that they strayed so far from me?
They followed worthless idols
and became worthless themselves.
⁶They did not ask, 'Where is the LORD,
who brought us up out of Egypt
and led us through the barren wilderness,
through a land of deserts and rifts,
a land of drought and darkness,ᵃ
a land where no one travels and no one lives?'
⁷I brought you into a fertile land
to eat its fruit and rich produce.
But you came and defiled my land
and made my inheritance detestable.
⁸The priests did not ask,
'Where is the LORD?'
Those who deal with the law did not know me;
the leaders rebelled against me.
The prophets prophesied by Baal,
following worthless idols.

⁹"Therefore I bring charges against you again,"

declares the LORD.

"And I will bring charges against your children's children.
¹⁰Cross over to the coasts of Kittimᵇ and look,
send to Kedarᶜ and observe closely;
see if there has ever been anything like this:
¹¹Has a nation ever changed its gods?
(Yet they are not gods at all.)
But my people have exchanged theirᵈ Glory
for worthless idols.
¹²Be appalled at this, O heavens,
and shudder with great horror,"

declares the LORD.

¹³"My people have committed two sins:
They have forsaken me,
the spring of living water,
and have dug their own cisterns,
broken cisterns that cannot hold water.
¹⁴Is Israel a servant, a slave by birth?
Why then has he become plunder?
¹⁵Lions have roared;
they have growled at him.
They have laid waste his land;
his towns are burned and deserted.
¹⁶Also, the men of Memphisᵉ and Tahpanhes

ᵃ6 Or *and the shadow of death*   ᵇ10 That is, Cyprus and western coastlands   ᶜ10 The home of Bedouin tribes in the Syro-Arabian desert   ᵈ11 Masoretic Text; an ancient Hebrew scribal tradition *my*
ᵉ16 Hebrew *Noph*

have shaved the crown of your head.*

17 Have you not brought this on yourselves
by forsaking the Lord your God
when he led you in the way?
18 Now why go to Egypt
to drink water from the Shihor*?
And why go to Assyria
to drink water from the River*?
19 Your wickedness will punish you;
your backsliding will rebuke you.
Consider then and realize
how evil and bitter it is for you
when you forsake the Lord your God
and have no awe of me,"
declares the Lord, the Lord Almighty.

20 "Long ago you broke off your yoke
and tore off your bonds;
you said, 'I will not serve you!'
Indeed, on every high hill
and under every spreading tree
you lay down as a prostitute.
21 I had planted you like a choice vine
of sound and reliable stock.
How then did you turn against me
into a corrupt, wild vine?
22 Although you wash yourself with soda
and use an abundance of soap,
the stain of your guilt is still before me,"
declares the Sovereign Lord.

23 "How can you say, 'I am not defiled;
I have not run after the Baals'?
See how you behaved in the valley;
consider what you have done.
You are a swift she-camel
running here and there,
24 a wild donkey accustomed to the desert,
sniffing the wind in her craving—
in her heat who can restrain her?
Any males that pursue her need not tire themselves;
at mating time they will find her.
25 Do not run until your feet are bare
and your throat is dry.
But you said, 'It's no use!
I love foreign gods,
and I must go after them.'

26 "As a thief is disgraced when he is caught,
so the house of Israel is disgraced—
they, their kings and their officials,
their priests and their prophets.
27 They say to wood, 'You are my father,'
and to stone, 'You gave me birth.'
They have turned their backs to me
and not their faces;

---

*16 Or *have cracked your skull*   *18 That is, a branch of the Nile   *18 That is, the Euphrates

yet when they are in trouble, they say,
'Come and save us!'
²⁸ Where then are the gods you made for yourselves?
Let them come if they can save you
when you are in trouble!
For you have as many gods
as you have towns, O Judah.

²⁹ "Why do you bring charges against me?
You have all rebelled against me,"

declares the Lord.

³⁰ "In vain I punished your people;
they did not respond to correction.
Your sword has devoured your prophets
like a ravening lion.

³¹ "You of this generation, consider the word of the Lord:

"Have I been a desert to Israel
or a land of great darkness?
Why do my people say, 'We are free to roam;
we will come to you no more'?
³² Does a maiden forget her jewelry,
a bride her wedding ornaments?
Yet my people have forgotten me,
days without number.
³³ How skilled you are at pursuing love!
Even the worst of women can learn from your ways.
³⁴ On your clothes men find
the lifeblood of the innocent poor,
though you did not catch them breaking in.
Yet in spite of all this
³⁵ you say, 'I am innocent;
he is not angry with me.'
But I will pass judgment on you
because you say, 'I have not sinned.'
³⁶ Why do you go about so much,
changing your ways?
You will be disappointed by Egypt
as you were by Assyria.
³⁷ You will also leave that place
with your hands on your head,
for the Lord has rejected those you trust;
you will not be helped by them.

3 "If a man divorces his wife
and she leaves him and marries another man,
should he return to her again?
Would not the land be completely defiled?
But you have lived as a prostitute with many lovers—
would you now return to me?"

declares the Lord.

² "Look up to the barren heights and see.
Is there any place where you have not been ravished?
By the roadside you sat waiting for lovers,
sat like a nomadᵃ in the desert.
You have defiled the land

ᵃ2 Or an Arab

with your prostitution and wickedness.
³Therefore the showers have been withheld,
and no spring rains have fallen.
Yet you have the brazen look of a prostitute;
you refuse to blush with shame.
⁴Have you not just called to me:
'My Father, my friend from my youth,
⁵will you always be angry?
Will your wrath continue forever?'
This is how you talk,
but you do all the evil you can."

Unfaithful Israel ⁶During the reign of King Josiah, the Lᴏʀᴅ said to me, "Have you seen what faithless Israel has done? She has gone up on every high hill and under every spreading tree and has committed adultery there. ⁷I thought that after she had done all this she would return to me but she did not, and her unfaithful sister Judah saw it. ⁸I gave faithless Israel her certificate of divorce and sent her away because of all her adulteries. Yet I saw that her unfaithful sister Judah had no fear; she also went out and committed adultery. ⁹Because Israel's immorality mattered so little to her, she defiled the land and committed adultery with stone and wood. ¹⁰In spite of all this, her unfaithful sister Judah did not return to me with all her heart, but only in pretense," declares the Lᴏʀᴅ.

¹¹The Lᴏʀᴅ said to me, "Faithless Israel is more righteous than unfaithful Judah. ¹²Go, proclaim this message toward the north:

" 'Return, faithless Israel,' declares the Lᴏʀᴅ,
'I will frown on you no longer,
for I am merciful,' declares the Lᴏʀᴅ,
'I will not be angry forever.
¹³Only acknowledge your guilt—
you have rebelled against the Lᴏʀᴅ your God,
you have scattered your favors to foreign gods
under every spreading tree,
and have not obeyed me,' "
declares the Lᴏʀᴅ.

¹⁴"Return, faithless people," declares the Lᴏʀᴅ, "for I am your husband. I will choose you—one from a town and two from a clan—and bring you to Zion. ¹⁵Then I will give you shepherds after my own heart, who will lead you with knowledge and understanding. ¹⁶In those days, when your numbers have increased greatly in the land," declares the Lᴏʀᴅ, "men will no longer say, 'The ark of the covenant of the Lᴏʀᴅ.' It will never enter their minds or be remembered; it will not be missed, nor will another one be made. ¹⁷At that time they will call Jerusalem The Throne of the Lᴏʀᴅ, and all nations will gather in Jerusalem to honor the name of the Lᴏʀᴅ. No longer will they follow the stubbornness of their evil hearts. ¹⁸In those days the house of Judah will join the house of Israel, and together they will come from a northern land to the land I gave your forefathers as an inheritance.

JEREMIAH 3:6–13

Show pictures of a car wrecked by a drunk driver and lots of people who drink will think, "Sure, but that won't happen to me!" Many who are sexually promiscuous think to themselves, "Hey, AIDS won't happen to me!" Assyria had destroyed the Israelites. It was God's judgment on them for their idolatry. But the idolaters in Judah thought, "Hey, that can't happen to us," and went right on sinning. It's wise to learn from your own mistakes. But it's better to learn from others' mistakes. The next time you catch yourself thinking, "That can't happen to me," think again!

Direct Line

¹⁹"I myself said,

" 'How gladly would I treat you like sons
and give you a desirable land,
the most beautiful inheritance of any nation.'
I thought you would call me 'Father'
and not turn away from following me.
²⁰But like a woman unfaithful to her husband,
so you have been unfaithful to me, O house of Israel,"

declares the LORD.

²¹A cry is heard on the barren heights,
the weeping and pleading of the people of Israel,
because they have perverted their ways
and have forgotten the LORD their God.

²²"Return, faithless people;
I will cure you of backsliding."

"Yes, we will come to you,
for you are the LORD our God.
²³Surely the idolatrous commotion on the hills
and mountains is a deception;
surely in the LORD our God
is the salvation of Israel.
²⁴From our youth shameful gods have consumed
the fruits of our fathers' labor—
their flocks and herds,
their sons and daughters.
²⁵Let us lie down in our shame,
and let our disgrace cover us.
We have sinned against the LORD our God,
both we and our fathers;
from our youth till this day
we have not obeyed the LORD our God."

4 "If you will return, O Israel,
return to me,"

declares the LORD.

"If you put your detestable idols out of my sight
and no longer go astray,
²and if in a truthful, just and righteous way
you swear, 'As surely as the LORD lives,'
then the nations will be blessed by him
and in him they will glory."

³This is what the LORD says to the men of Judah and to Jerusalem:

"Break up your unplowed ground
and do not sow among thorns.
⁴Circumcise yourselves to the LORD,
circumcise your hearts,
you men of Judah and people of Jerusalem,
or my wrath will break out and burn like fire
because of the evil you have done—
burn with no one to quench it.

Disaster From the North

⁵"Announce in Judah and proclaim in Jerusalem and say:
'Sound the trumpet throughout the land!'
Cry aloud and say:

'Gather together!
    Let us flee to the fortified cities!'
⁶Raise the signal to go to Zion!
    Flee for safety without delay!
For I am bringing disaster from the north,
    even terrible destruction."

⁷A lion has come out of his lair;
    a destroyer of nations has set out.
He has left his place
    to lay waste your land.
Your towns will lie in ruins
    without inhabitant.
⁸So put on sackcloth,
    lament and wail,
for the fierce anger of the LORD
    has not turned away from us.

⁹"In that day," declares the LORD,
    "the king and the officials will lose heart,
the priests will be horrified,
    and the prophets will be appalled."

¹⁰Then I said, "Ah, Sovereign LORD, how completely you have deceived this people and Jerusalem by saying, 'You will have peace,' when the sword is at our throats."

¹¹At that time this people and Jerusalem will be told, "A scorching wind from the barren heights in the desert blows toward my people, but not to winnow or cleanse; ¹²a wind too strong for that comes from me.ᵃ Now I pronounce my judgments against them."

¹³Look! He advances like the clouds,
    his chariots come like a whirlwind,
his horses are swifter than eagles.
    Woe to us! We are ruined!
¹⁴O Jerusalem, wash the evil from your heart and be saved.
    How long will you harbor wicked thoughts?
¹⁵A voice is announcing from Dan,
    proclaiming disaster from the hills of Ephraim.
¹⁶"Tell this to the nations,
    proclaim it to Jerusalem:
'A besieging army is coming from a distant land,
    raising a war cry against the cities of Judah.
¹⁷They surround her like men guarding a field,
    because she has rebelled against me,' "

                declares the LORD.

¹⁸"Your own conduct and actions
    have brought this upon you.
This is your punishment.
    How bitter it is!
    How it pierces to the heart!"

¹⁹Oh, my anguish, my anguish!
    I writhe in pain.
Oh, the agony of my heart!
    My heart pounds within me,
    I cannot keep silent.

ᵃ12 Or *comes at my command*

For I have heard the sound of the trumpet;
  I have heard the battle cry.
²⁰ Disaster follows disaster;
  the whole land lies in ruins.
In an instant my tents are destroyed,
  my shelter in a moment.
²¹ How long must I see the battle standard
  and hear the sound of the trumpet?

²² "My people are fools;
  they do not know me.
They are senseless children;
  they have no understanding.
They are skilled in doing evil;
  they know not how to do good."

²³ I looked at the earth,
  and it was formless and empty;
and at the heavens,
  and their light was gone.
²⁴ I looked at the mountains,
  and they were quaking;
  all the hills were swaying.
²⁵ I looked, and there were no people;
  every bird in the sky had flown away.
²⁶ I looked, and the fruitful land was a desert;
  all its towns lay in ruins
  before the Lord, before his fierce anger.

²⁷ This is what the Lord says:

"The whole land will be ruined,
  though I will not destroy it completely.
²⁸ Therefore the earth will mourn
  and the heavens above grow dark,
because I have spoken and will not relent,
  I have decided and will not turn back."

²⁹ At the sound of horsemen and archers
  every town takes to flight.
Some go into the thickets;
  some climb up among the rocks.
All the towns are deserted;
  no one lives in them.

³⁰ What are you doing, O devastated one?
  Why dress yourself in scarlet
  and put on jewels of gold?
Why shade your eyes with paint?
  You adorn yourself in vain.
Your lovers despise you;
  they seek your life.

³¹ I hear a cry as of a woman in labor,
  a groan as of one bearing her first child—
the cry of the Daughter of Zion gasping for breath,
  stretching out her hands and saying,
"Alas! I am fainting;
  my life is given over to murderers."

5 Not One Is Upright

"Go up and down the streets of Jerusalem,
    look around and consider,
    search through her squares.
If you can find but one person
    who deals honestly and seeks the truth,
    I will forgive this city.
² Although they say, 'As surely as the LORD lives,'
    still they are swearing falsely."

³ O LORD, do not your eyes look for truth?
    You struck them, but they felt no pain;
    you crushed them, but they refused correction.
They made their faces harder than stone
    and refused to repent.
⁴ I thought, "These are only the poor;
    they are foolish,
for they do not know the way of the LORD,
    the requirements of their God.
⁵ So I will go to the leaders
    and speak to them;
surely they know the way of the LORD,
    the requirements of their God."
But with one accord they too had broken off the yoke
    and torn off the bonds.
⁶ Therefore a lion from the forest will attack them,
    a wolf from the desert will ravage them,
a leopard will lie in wait near their towns
    to tear to pieces any who venture out,
for their rebellion is great
    and their backslidings many.

⁷ "Why should I forgive you?
    Your children have forsaken
        me
    and sworn by gods that are not
        gods.
I supplied all their needs,
    yet they committed adultery
    and thronged to the houses of
        prostitutes.
⁸ They are well-fed, lusty stallions,
    each neighing for another
        man's wife.
⁹ Should I not punish them for
        this?"
    declares the LORD.
"Should I not avenge myself
    on such a nation as this?

¹⁰ "Go through her vineyards and
        ravage them,
    but do not destroy them
        completely.
Strip off her branches,
    for these people do not belong
        to the LORD.

JEREMIAH 5:11–17

What does God do all day? Sit back and watch you? Make lists of the good and bad things you do? Or does he ignore you and think his own thoughts? Whatever God does, many people pretty much ignore him. They may not consciously think it, but their actions show that they assume, "He will do nothing. No harm will come to us." It's not safe to think of the Lord as a do-nothing God. God may be patient and delay punishment while he gives people a chance to repent. But people who persist in doing wrong aren't safe at all. God really is the judge of his universe, and there are painful consequences for people who keep on doing wrong.

Direct Line

¹¹ The house of Israel and the house of Judah
　　have been utterly unfaithful to me,"

　　　　　　　　　　　　　　　　　declares the Lord.

¹² They have lied about the Lord;
　　they said, "He will do nothing!
　No harm will come to us;
　　we will never see sword or famine.
¹³ The prophets are but wind
　　and the word is not in them;
　　so let what they say be done to them."

¹⁴Therefore this is what the Lord God Almighty says:

"Because the people have spoken these words,
　I will make my words in your mouth a fire
　and these people the wood it consumes.
¹⁵ O house of Israel," declares the Lord,
　"I am bringing a distant nation against you—
an ancient and enduring nation,
　a people whose language you do not know,
　whose speech you do not understand.
¹⁶ Their quivers are like an open grave;
　all of them are mighty warriors.
¹⁷ They will devour your harvests and food,
　devour your sons and daughters;
they will devour your flocks and herds,
　devour your vines and fig trees.
With the sword they will destroy
　the fortified cities in which you trust.

¹⁸"Yet even in those days," declares the Lord, "I will not destroy you completely. ¹⁹And when the people ask, 'Why has the Lord our God done all this to us?' you will tell them, 'As you have forsaken me and served foreign gods in your own land, so now you will serve foreigners in a land not your own.'

²⁰"Announce this to the house of Jacob
　and proclaim it in Judah:
²¹ Hear this, you foolish and senseless people,
　who have eyes but do not see,
　who have ears but do not hear:
²² Should you not fear me?" declares the Lord.
　"Should you not tremble in my presence?
I made the sand a boundary for the sea,
　an everlasting barrier it cannot cross.
The waves may roll, but they cannot prevail;
　they may roar, but they cannot cross it.
²³ But these people have stubborn and rebellious hearts;
　they have turned aside and gone away.
²⁴ They do not say to themselves,
　'Let us fear the Lord our God,
who gives autumn and spring rains in season,
　who assures us of the regular weeks of harvest.'
²⁵ Your wrongdoings have kept these away;
　your sins have deprived you of good.

²⁶"Among my people are wicked men
　who lie in wait like men who snare birds
　and like those who set traps to catch men.

²⁷Like cages full of birds,
    their houses are full of deceit;
  they have become rich and powerful
²⁸   and have grown fat and sleek.
  Their evil deeds have no limit;
    they do not plead the case of the fatherless to win it,
    they do not defend the rights of the poor.
²⁹Should I not punish them for this?"
    declares the LORD.
  "Should I not avenge myself
    on such a nation as this?

³⁰"A horrible and shocking thing
    has happened in the land:
³¹The prophets prophesy lies,
    the priests rule by their own authority,
  and my people love it this way.
    But what will you do in the end?

Jerusalem Under Siege

6   "Flee for safety, people of Benjamin!
    Flee from Jerusalem!
  Sound the trumpet in Tekoa!
    Raise the signal over Beth Hakkerem!
  For disaster looms out of the north,
    even terrible destruction.
²I will destroy the Daughter of Zion,
    so beautiful and delicate.
³Shepherds with their flocks will come against her;
    they will pitch their tents around her,
    each tending his own portion."

⁴"Prepare for battle against her!
    Arise, let us attack at noon!
  But, alas, the daylight is fading,
    and the shadows of evening grow long.
⁵So arise, let us attack at night
    and destroy her fortresses!"

⁶This is what the LORD Almighty says:

  "Cut down the trees
    and build siege ramps against Jerusalem.
  This city must be punished;
    it is filled with oppression.
⁷As a well pours out its water,
    so she pours out her wickedness.
  Violence and destruction resound in her;
    her sickness and wounds are ever before me.
⁸Take warning, O Jerusalem,
    or I will turn away from you
  and make your land desolate
    so no one can live in it."

⁹This is what the LORD Almighty says:

  "Let them glean the remnant of Israel
    as thoroughly as a vine;

pass your hand over the branches again,
like one gathering grapes.”

¹⁰To whom can I speak and give warning?
Who will listen to me?
Their ears are closed*ᵃ*
so they cannot hear.
The word of the LORD is offensive to them;
they find no pleasure in it.
¹¹But I am full of the wrath of the LORD,
and I cannot hold it in.

“Pour it out on the children in the street
and on the young men gathered together;
both husband and wife will be caught in it,
and the old, those weighed down with years.
¹²Their houses will be turned over to others,
together with their fields and their wives,
when I stretch out my hand
against those who live in the land,”

declares the LORD.

¹³“From the least to the greatest,
all are greedy for gain;
prophets and priests alike,
all practice deceit.
¹⁴They dress the wound of my people
as though it were not serious.
‘Peace, peace,’ they say,
when there is no peace.
¹⁵Are they ashamed of their loathsome conduct?
No, they have no shame at all;
they do not even know how to blush.
So they will fall among the fallen;
they will be brought down when I punish them,”

says the LORD.

¹⁶This is what the LORD says:

“Stand at the crossroads and look;
ask for the ancient paths,
ask where the good way is, and walk in it,
and you will find rest for your souls.
But you said, ‘We will not walk in it.’
¹⁷I appointed watchmen over you and said,
‘Listen to the sound of the trumpet!’
But you said, ‘We will not listen.’
¹⁸Therefore hear, O nations;
observe, O witnesses,
what will happen to them.
¹⁹Hear, O earth:
I am bringing disaster on this people,
the fruit of their schemes,
because they have not listened to my words
and have rejected my law.
²⁰What do I care about incense from Sheba
or sweet calamus from a distant land?

ᵃ10 Hebrew *uncircumcised*

Your burnt offerings are not acceptable;
your sacrifices do not please me."

²¹Therefore this is what the Lᴏʀᴅ says:

"I will put obstacles before this people.
Fathers and sons alike will stumble over them;
neighbors and friends will perish."

²²This is what the Lᴏʀᴅ says:

"Look, an army is coming
from the land of the north;
a great nation is being stirred up
from the ends of the earth.
²³They are armed with bow and spear;
they are cruel and show no mercy.
They sound like the roaring sea
as they ride on their horses;
they come like men in battle formation
to attack you, O Daughter of Zion."

²⁴We have heard reports about them,
and our hands hang limp.
Anguish has gripped us,
pain like that of a woman in labor.
²⁵Do not go out to the fields
or walk on the roads,
for the enemy has a sword,
and there is terror on every side.
²⁶O my people, put on sackcloth
and roll in ashes;
mourn with bitter wailing
as for an only son,
for suddenly the destroyer
will come upon us.

²⁷"I have made you a tester of metals
and my people the ore,
that you may observe
and test their ways.
²⁸They are all hardened rebels,
going about to slander.
They are bronze and iron;
they all act corruptly.
²⁹The bellows blow fiercely
to burn away the lead with fire,
but the refining goes on in vain;
the wicked are not purged out.
³⁰They are called rejected silver,
because the Lᴏʀᴅ has rejected them."

7 *False Religion Worthless* This is the word that came to Jeremiah from the Lᴏʀᴅ: ²"Stand at the gate of the Lᴏʀᴅ's house and there proclaim this message:

" 'Hear the word of the Lᴏʀᴅ, all you people of Judah who come through these gates to worship the Lᴏʀᴅ. ³This is what the Lᴏʀᴅ Almighty, the God of Israel, says: Reform your ways and your actions, and I will let you live in this place. ⁴Do not trust in deceptive words and say, "This is the temple of the Lᴏʀᴅ, the temple of the Lᴏʀᴅ, the temple of the Lᴏʀᴅ!" ⁵If you really change your ways and your actions and deal with each other justly, ⁶if you do not oppress the alien, the fatherless or the widow and do not shed innocent blood in this place, and if you do not follow other gods to your own harm, ⁷then I will let you live in this place, in the land I gave your forefathers for ever and ever. ⁸But look, you are trusting in deceptive words that are worthless.

⁹ 'Will you steal and murder, commit adultery and perjury,ᵃ burn incense to Baal and follow other gods you have not known, ¹⁰and then come and stand before me in this house, which bears my Name, and say, "We are safe"—safe to do all these detestable things? ¹¹Has this house, which bears my Name, become a den of robbers to you? But I have been watching! declares the LORD.

¹² 'Go now to the place in Shiloh where I first made a dwelling for my Name, and see what I did to it because of the wickedness of my people Israel. ¹³While you were doing all these things, declares the LORD, I spoke to you again and again, but you did not listen; I called you, but you did not answer. ¹⁴Therefore, what I did to Shiloh I will now do to the house that bears my Name, the temple you trust in, the place I gave to you and your fathers. ¹⁵I will thrust you from my presence, just as I did all your brothers, the people of Ephraim.'

¹⁶ "So do not pray for this people nor offer any plea or petition for them; do not plead with me, for I will not listen to you. ¹⁷Do you not see what they are doing in the towns of Judah and in the streets of Jerusalem? ¹⁸The children gather wood, the fathers light the fire, and the women knead the dough and make cakes of bread for the Queen of Heaven. They pour out drink offerings to other gods to provoke me to anger. ¹⁹But am I the one they are provoking? declares the LORD. Are they not rather harming themselves, to their own shame?

²⁰ 'Therefore this is what the Sovereign LORD says: My anger and my wrath will be poured out on this place, on man and beast, on the trees of the field and on the fruit of the ground, and it will burn and not be quenched.

²¹ 'This is what the LORD Almighty, the God of Israel, says: Go ahead, add your burnt offerings to your other sacrifices and eat the meat yourselves! ²²For when I brought your forefathers out of Egypt and spoke to them, I did not just give them commands about burnt offerings and sacrifices, ²³but I gave them this command: Obey me, and I will be your God and you will be my people. Walk in all the ways I command you, that it may go well with you. ²⁴But they did not listen or pay attention; instead, they followed the stubborn inclinations of their evil hearts. They went backward and not forward. ²⁵From the time your forefathers left Egypt until now, day after day, again and again I sent you my servants the prophets. ²⁶But they did not listen to me or pay attention. They were stiff-necked and did more evil than their forefathers.'

²⁷ "When you tell them all this, they will not listen to you; when you call to them, they will not answer. ²⁸Therefore say to them, 'This is the nation that has not obeyed the LORD its God or responded to correction. Truth has perished; it has vanished from their lips. ²⁹Cut off your hair and throw it away; take up a lament on the barren heights, for the LORD has rejected and abandoned this generation that is under his wrath.

The Valley of Slaughter   ³⁰ 'The people of Judah have done evil in my eyes, declares the LORD. They have set up their detestable idols in the house that bears my Name and have defiled it. ³¹They have built the high places of Topheth in the Valley of Ben Hinnom to burn their sons and daughters in the fire—something I did not command, nor did it enter my mind. ³²So beware, the days are coming, declares the LORD, when people will no longer call it To-

ᵃ9 Or *and swear by false gods*

pheth or the Valley of Ben Hinnom, but the Valley of Slaughter, for they will bury the dead in Topheth until there is no more room. ³³Then the carcasses of this people will become food for the birds of the air and the beasts of the earth, and there will be no one to frighten them away. ³⁴I will bring an end to the sounds of joy and gladness and to the voices of bride and bridegroom in the towns of Judah and the streets of Jerusalem, for the land will become desolate.

8 " 'At that time, declares the Lord, the bones of the kings and officials of Judah, the bones of the priests and prophets, and the bones of the people of Jerusalem will be removed from their graves. ²They will be exposed to the sun and the moon and all the stars of the heavens, which they have loved and served and which they have followed and consulted and worshiped. They will not be gathered up or buried, but will be like refuse lying on the ground. ³Wherever I banish them, all the survivors of this evil nation will prefer death to life, declares the Lord Almighty.'

Sin and Punishment ⁴"Say to them, 'This is what the Lord says:

" 'When men fall down, do they not get up?
  When a man turns away, does he not return?
⁵Why then have these people turned away?
  Why does Jerusalem always turn away?
They cling to deceit;
  they refuse to return.
⁶I have listened attentively,
  but they do not say what is right.
No one repents of his wickedness,
  saying, "What have I done?"
Each pursues his own course
  like a horse charging into battle.
⁷Even the stork in the sky
  knows her appointed seasons,
and the dove, the swift and the thrush
  observe the time of their migration.
But my people do not know
  the requirements of the Lord.

⁸" 'How can you say, "We are wise,
  for we have the law of the Lord,"
when actually the lying pen of the scribes
  has handled it falsely?
⁹The wise will be put to shame;
  they will be dismayed and trapped.
Since they have rejected the word of the Lord,
  what kind of wisdom do they have?
¹⁰Therefore I will give their wives to other men
  and their fields to new owners.
From the least to the greatest,
  all are greedy for gain;
prophets and priests alike,
  all practice deceit.
¹¹They dress the wound of my people
  as though it were not serious.
"Peace, peace," they say,
  when there is no peace.
¹²Are they ashamed of their loathsome conduct?
  No, they have no shame at all;
  they do not even know how to blush.

So they will fall among the fallen;
    they will be brought down when they are punished,

                  says the LORD.

13 " 'I will take away their harvest,

              declares the LORD.

    There will be no grapes on the vine.
There will be no figs on the tree,
    and their leaves will wither.
What I have given them
    will be taken from them.*' "

14 "Why are we sitting here?
    Gather together!
Let us flee to the fortified cities
    and perish there!
For the LORD our God has doomed us to perish
    and given us poisoned water to drink,
    because we have sinned against him.
15 We hoped for peace
    but no good has come,
for a time of healing
    but there was only terror.
16 The snorting of the enemy's horses
    is heard from Dan;
at the neighing of their stallions
    the whole land trembles.
They have come to devour
    the land and everything in it,
    the city and all who live there."

17 "See, I will send venomous snakes among you,
    vipers that cannot be charmed,
    and they will bite you,"

              declares the LORD.

18 O my Comforter*b* in sorrow,
    my heart is faint within me.
19 Listen to the cry of my people
    from a land far away:
"Is the LORD not in Zion?
    Is her King no longer there?"

    "Why have they provoked me to anger with their images,
    with their worthless foreign idols?"

20 "The harvest is past,
    the summer has ended,
    and we are not saved."

21 Since my people are crushed, I am crushed;
    I mourn, and horror grips me.
22 Is there no balm in Gilead?
    Is there no physician there?
Why then is there no healing
    for the wound of my people?

---

*13 The meaning of the Hebrew for this sentence is uncertain.   *b18 The meaning of the Hebrew for this word is uncertain.

9 ¹Oh, that my head were a spring of water
and my eyes a fountain of tears!
I would weep day and night
for the slain of my people.
²Oh, that I had in the desert
a lodging place for travelers,
so that I might leave my people
and go away from them;
for they are all adulterers,
a crowd of unfaithful people.

³"They make ready their tongue
like a bow, to shoot lies;
it is not by truth
that they triumph*ᵃ* in the land.
They go from one sin to another;
they do not acknowledge me,"

declares the LORD.

⁴"Beware of your friends;
do not trust your brothers.
For every brother is a deceiver,*ᵇ*
and every friend a slanderer.
⁵Friend deceives friend,
and no one speaks the truth.
They have taught their tongues to lie;
they weary themselves with sinning.
⁶You*ᶜ* live in the midst of deception;
in their deceit they refuse to acknowledge me,"

declares the LORD.

⁷Therefore this is what the LORD Almighty says:

"See, I will refine and test them,
for what else can I do
because of the sin of my people?
⁸Their tongue is a deadly arrow;
it speaks with deceit.
With his mouth each speaks cordially to his neighbor,
but in his heart he sets a trap for him.
⁹Should I not punish them for this?"
declares the LORD.
"Should I not avenge myself
on such a nation as this?"

¹⁰I will weep and wail for the mountains
and take up a lament concerning the desert pastures.
They are desolate and untraveled,
and the lowing of cattle is not heard.
The birds of the air have fled
and the animals are gone.

¹¹"I will make Jerusalem a heap of ruins,
a haunt of jackals;
and I will lay waste the towns of Judah
so no one can live there."

ᵃ3 Or lies; / they are not valiant for truth *ᵇ4 Or a deceiving Jacob* *ᶜ6 That is, Jeremiah (the Hebrew is singular)*

¹²What man is wise enough to understand this? Who has been instructed by the LORD and can explain it? Why has the land been ruined and laid waste like a desert that no one can cross?

¹³The LORD said, "It is because they have forsaken my law, which I set before them; they have not obeyed me or followed my law. ¹⁴Instead, they have followed the stubbornness of their hearts; they have followed the Baals, as their fathers taught them." ¹⁵Therefore, this is what the LORD Almighty, the God of Israel, says: "See, I will make this people eat bitter food and drink poisoned water. ¹⁶I will scatter them among nations that neither they nor their fathers have known, and I will pursue them with the sword until I have destroyed them."

¹⁷This is what the LORD Almighty says:

> "Consider now! Call for the wailing women to come;
>   send for the most skillful of them.
> ¹⁸Let them come quickly
>   and wail over us
> till our eyes overflow with tears
>   and water streams from our eyelids.
> ¹⁹The sound of wailing is heard from Zion:
>   'How ruined we are!
>   How great is our shame!
> We must leave our land
>   because our houses are in ruins.' "

> ²⁰Now, O women, hear the word of the LORD;
>   open your ears to the words of his mouth.
> Teach your daughters how to wail;
>   teach one another a lament.
> ²¹Death has climbed in through our windows
>   and has entered our fortresses;
> it has cut off the children from the streets
>   and the young men from the public squares.

²²Say, "This is what the LORD declares:

> " 'The dead bodies of men will lie
>   like refuse on the open field,
> like cut grain behind the reaper,
>   with no one to gather them.' "

²³This is what the LORD says:

> "Let not the wise man boast of his wisdom
>   or the strong man boast of his strength
>   or the rich man boast of his riches,
> ²⁴but let him who boasts boast about this:
>   that he understands and knows me,
> that I am the LORD, who exercises kindness,
>   justice and righteousness on earth,
>   for in these I delight,"

declares the LORD.

²⁵"The days are coming," declares the LORD, "when I will punish all who are circumcised only in the flesh— ²⁶Egypt, Judah, Edom, Ammon, Moab and all who live in the desert in distant places.ᵃ For all these nations are really uncircumcised, and even the whole house of Israel is uncircumcised in heart."

ᵃ26 Or *desert and who clip the hair by their foreheads*

10 *God and Idols* Hear what the LORD says to you, O house of Israel. [2]This is what the LORD says:

"Do not learn the ways of the nations
or be terrified by signs in the sky,
though the nations are terrified by them.
[3]For the customs of the peoples are worthless;
they cut a tree out of the forest,
and a craftsman shapes it with his chisel.
[4]They adorn it with silver and gold;
they fasten it with hammer and nails
so it will not totter.
[5]Like a scarecrow in a melon patch,
their idols cannot speak;
they must be carried
because they cannot walk.
Do not fear them;
they can do no harm
nor can they do any good."

[6]No one is like you, O LORD;
you are great,
and your name is mighty in power.
[7]Who should not revere you,
O King of the nations?
This is your due.
Among all the wise men of the nations
and in all their kingdoms,
there is no one like you.
[8]They are all senseless and foolish;
they are taught by worthless wooden idols.
[9]Hammered silver is brought from Tarshish
and gold from Uphaz.
What the craftsman and
goldsmith have made
is then dressed in blue and
purple—
all made by skilled workers.
[10]But the LORD is the true God;
he is the living God, the
eternal King.
When he is angry, the earth
trembles;
the nations cannot endure his
wrath.

[11]"Tell them this: 'These gods, who did not make the heavens and the earth, will perish from the earth and from under the heavens.' "[a]

[12]But God made the earth by his
power;
he founded the world by his
wisdom
and stretched out the heavens
by his understanding.

[a]*11 The text of this verse is in Aramaic.*

JEREMIAH 9:23–24

Only about 1 person out of 100 comes anywhere near being a genius. That means that 99 aren't as smart. Comparing yourself to other kids can make you feel inferior. Even dumb. And that's not a comfortable feeling at all. Of course, there are more important things than being smart. Or being strong or rich or athletic. Jeremiah says there is only one thing you should boast about: that you understand and know God (Jeremiah 9:24). Knowing God makes you special in a way that being smarter or stronger than others never could. Knowing God makes you a child of the King, and you're important to him.

Direct Line

¹³When he thunders, the waters in the heavens roar;
　　he makes clouds rise from the ends of the earth.
He sends lightning with the rain
　　and brings out the wind from his storehouses.

¹⁴Everyone is senseless and without knowledge;
　　every goldsmith is shamed by his idols.
His images are a fraud;
　　they have no breath in them.
¹⁵They are worthless, the objects of mockery;
　　when their judgment comes, they will perish.
¹⁶He who is the Portion of Jacob is not like these,
　　for he is the Maker of all things,
including Israel, the tribe of his inheritance—
　　the LORD Almighty is his name.

Coming Destruction

¹⁷Gather up your belongings to leave the land,
　　you who live under siege.
¹⁸For this is what the LORD says:
　　"At this time I will hurl out
　　those who live in this land;
I will bring distress on them
　　so that they may be captured."

¹⁹Woe to me because of my injury!
　　My wound is incurable!
Yet I said to myself,
　　"This is my sickness, and I must endure it."
²⁰My tent is destroyed;
　　all its ropes are snapped.
My sons are gone from me and are no more;
　　no one is left now to pitch my tent
　　or to set up my shelter.
²¹The shepherds are senseless
　　and do not inquire of the LORD;
so they do not prosper
　　and all their flock is scattered.
²²Listen! The report is coming—
　　a great commotion from the land of the north!
It will make the towns of Judah desolate,
　　a haunt of jackals.

Jeremiah's Prayer

²³I know, O LORD, that a man's life is not his own;
　　it is not for man to direct his steps.
²⁴Correct me, LORD, but only with justice—
　　not in your anger,
　　lest you reduce me to nothing.
²⁵Pour out your wrath on the nations
　　that do not acknowledge you,
　　on the peoples who do not call on your name.
For they have devoured Jacob;
　　they have devoured him completely
　　and destroyed his homeland.

11 **The Covenant Is Broken**　This is the word that came to Jeremiah from the LORD: ²"Listen to the terms of this covenant and tell them to the people of Judah and to those who live in Jerusalem. ³Tell them that this is what the LORD, the God of Israel, says: 'Cursed is the man who does not obey the terms of this covenant— [4]the terms I commanded your forefathers when I brought them out of Egypt, out of the iron-smelting furnace.' I said, 'Obey me and do everything I command you, and you will be my people, and I will be your God. [5]Then I will fulfill the oath I swore to your forefathers, to give them a land flowing with milk and honey'—the land you possess today."

I answered, "Amen, LORD."

[6]The LORD said to me, "Proclaim all these words in the towns of Judah and in the streets of Jerusalem: 'Listen to the terms of this covenant and follow them. [7]From the time I brought your forefathers up from Egypt until today, I warned them again and again, saying, "Obey me." [8]But they did not listen or pay attention; instead, they followed the stubbornness of their evil hearts. So I brought on them all the curses of the covenant I had commanded them to follow but that they did not keep.' "

[9]Then the LORD said to me, "There is a conspiracy among the people of Judah and those who live in Jerusalem. [10]They have returned to the sins of their forefathers, who refused to listen to my words. They have followed other gods to serve them. Both the house of Israel and the house of Judah have broken the covenant I made with their forefathers. [11]Therefore this is what the LORD says: 'I will bring on them a disaster they cannot escape. Although they cry out to me, I will not listen to them. [12]The towns of Judah and the people of Jerusalem will go and cry out to the gods to whom they burn incense, but they will not help them at all when disaster strikes. [13]You have as many gods as you have towns, O Judah; and the altars you have set up to burn incense to that shameful god Baal are as many as the streets of Jerusalem.'

[14]"Do not pray for this people nor offer any plea or petition for them, because I will not listen when they call to me in the time of their distress.

[15]"What is my beloved doing in my temple
　　as she works out her evil schemes with many?
　　Can consecrated meat avert ˎyour punishmentˏ?
When you engage in your wickedness,
　　then you rejoice.[a]"

[16]The LORD called you a thriving olive tree
　　with fruit beautiful in form.
But with the roar of a mighty storm
　　he will set it on fire,
　　and its branches will be broken.

[17]The LORD Almighty, who planted you, has decreed disaster for you, because the house of Israel and the house of Judah have done evil and provoked me to anger by burning incense to Baal.

Plot Against Jeremiah　　[18]Because the LORD revealed their plot to me, I knew it, for at that time he showed me what they were doing. [19]I had been like a gentle lamb led to the slaughter; I did not realize that they had plotted against me, saying,

"Let us destroy the tree and its fruit;
　　let us cut him off from the land of the living,
　　that his name be remembered no more."
[20]But, O LORD Almighty, you who judge righteously
　　and test the heart and mind,
let me see your vengeance upon them,
　　for to you I have committed my cause.

---

[a]15 Or *Could consecrated meat avert your punishment? / Then you would rejoice*

²¹"Therefore this is what the Lord says about the men of Anathoth who are seeking your life and saying, 'Do not prophesy in the name of the Lord or you will die by our hands'— ²²therefore this is what the Lord Almighty says: 'I will punish them. Their young men will die by the sword, their sons and daughters by famine. ²³Not even a remnant will be left to them, because I will bring disaster on the men of Anathoth in the year of their punishment.' "

12

Jeremiah's Complaint

You are always righteous, O Lord,
  when I bring a case before you.
Yet I would speak with you about your justice:
  Why does the way of the wicked prosper?
  Why do all the faithless live at ease?
²You have planted them, and they have taken root;
  they grow and bear fruit.
You are always on their lips
  but far from their hearts.
³Yet you know me, O Lord;
  you see me and test my thoughts about you.
Drag them off like sheep to be butchered!
  Set them apart for the day of slaughter!
⁴How long will the land lie parched*a*
  and the grass in every field be withered?
Because those who live in it are wicked,
  the animals and birds have perished.
Moreover, the people are saying,
  "He will not see what happens to us."

God's Answer

⁵"If you have raced with men on foot
  and they have worn you out,
      how can you compete with horses?
  If you stumble in safe country,*b*
      how will you manage in the thickets
          by*c* the Jordan?
⁶Your brothers, your own family—
  even they have betrayed you;
  they have raised a loud cry against
      you.
Do not trust them,
  though they speak well of you.

⁷"I will forsake my house,
  abandon my inheritance;
I will give the one I love
  into the hands of her enemies.
⁸My inheritance has become to me
  like a lion in the forest.
She roars at me;
  therefore I hate her.
⁹Has not my inheritance become to me
  like a speckled bird of prey
  that other birds of prey surround
      and attack?

Direct Line

JEREMIAH 12:1–4

Over and over in the Bible believers get upset and say things like, "Why does the way of the wicked prosper?" (Jeremiah 12:1). You probably know how they feel. It's the guy who lies and gossips about girls who gets the date with the one you like. And how about the girl whose mom types and corrects (rewrites) her term paper? She gets an A while you get a C. Sometimes it's easy to wonder, "Where is God, anyway?" But be sure to remember: nobody gets away with doing wrong in the end. It's just frustrating now. But try not to get discouraged in doing good. God does know. And in the end you'll be the one who wins.

a4 Or land mourn   b5 Or If you put your trust in a land of safety   c5 Or the flooding of

Go and gather all the wild beasts;
    bring them to devour.
¹⁰Many shepherds will ruin my vineyard
    and trample down my field;
they will turn my pleasant field
    into a desolate wasteland.
¹¹It will be made a wasteland,
    parched and desolate before me;
the whole land will be laid waste
    because there is no one who cares.
¹²Over all the barren heights in the desert
    destroyers will swarm,
for the sword of the LORD will devour
    from one end of the land to the other;
    no one will be safe.
¹³They will sow wheat but reap thorns;
    they will wear themselves out but gain nothing.
So bear the shame of your harvest
    because of the LORD's fierce anger."

¹⁴This is what the LORD says: "As for all my wicked neighbors who seize the inheritance I gave my people Israel, I will uproot them from their lands and I will uproot the house of Judah from among them. ¹⁵But after I uproot them, I will again have compassion and will bring each of them back to his own inheritance and his own country. ¹⁶And if they learn well the ways of my people and swear by my name, saying, 'As surely as the LORD lives'—even as they once taught my people to swear by Baal—then they will be established among my people. ¹⁷But if any nation does not listen, I will completely uproot and destroy it," declares the LORD.

A Linen Belt This is what the LORD said to me: "Go and buy a linen belt and put it around your waist, but do not let it touch water." ²So I bought a belt, as the LORD directed, and put it around my waist.

³Then the word of the LORD came to me a second time: ⁴"Take the belt you bought and are wearing around your waist, and go now to Perath*ᵃ* and hide it there in a crevice in the rocks." ⁵So I went and hid it at Perath, as the LORD told me.

⁶Many days later the LORD said to me, "Go now to Perath and get the belt I told you to hide there." ⁷So I went to Perath and dug up the belt and took it from the place where I had hidden it, but now it was ruined and completely useless.

⁸Then the word of the LORD came to me: ⁹"This is what the LORD says: 'In the same way I will ruin the pride of Judah and the great pride of Jerusalem. ¹⁰These wicked people, who refuse to listen to my words, who follow the stubbornness of their hearts and go after other gods to serve and worship them, will be like this belt—completely useless! ¹¹For as a belt is bound around a man's waist, so I bound the whole house of Israel and the whole house of Judah to me,' declares the LORD, 'to be my people for my renown and praise and honor. But they have not listened.'

Wineskins ¹²"Say to them: 'This is what the LORD, the God of Israel, says: Every wineskin should be filled with wine.' And if they say to you, 'Don't we know that every wineskin should be filled with wine?' ¹³then tell them, 'This is what the LORD says: I am going to fill with drunkenness all who live in this land, including the kings who sit on David's throne, the priests, the proph-

ᵃ4 Or possibly the Euphrates; also in verses 5-7

ets and all those living in Jerusalem. ¹⁴I will smash them one against the other, fathers and sons alike, declares the LORD. I will allow no pity or mercy or compassion to keep me from destroying them.' "

Threat of Captivity

¹⁵Hear and pay attention,
  do not be arrogant,
  for the LORD has spoken.
¹⁶Give glory to the LORD your God
  before he brings the darkness,
 before your feet stumble
  on the darkening hills.
You hope for light,
  but he will turn it to thick darkness
  and change it to deep gloom.
¹⁷But if you do not listen,
  I will weep in secret
  because of your pride;
 my eyes will weep bitterly,
  overflowing with tears,
  because the LORD's flock will be taken captive.

¹⁸Say to the king and to the queen mother,
  "Come down from your thrones,
 for your glorious crowns
  will fall from your heads."
¹⁹The cities in the Negev will be shut up,
  and there will be no one to open them.
 All Judah will be carried into exile,
  carried completely away.

²⁰Lift up your eyes and see
  those who are coming from the north.
 Where is the flock that was entrusted to you,
  the sheep of which you boasted?
²¹What will you say when ⸢the LORD⸣ sets over you
  those you cultivated as your special allies?
 Will not pain grip you
  like that of a woman in labor?
²²And if you ask yourself,
  "Why has this happened to me?"—
 it is because of your many sins
  that your skirts have been torn off
  and your body mistreated.
²³Can the Ethiopianᵃ change his skin
  or the leopard its spots?
 Neither can you do good
  who are accustomed to doing evil.

²⁴"I will scatter you like chaff
  driven by the desert wind.
²⁵This is your lot,
  the portion I have decreed for you,"

declares the LORD,

 "because you have forgotten me
  and trusted in false gods.

ᵃ23 Hebrew *Cushite* (probably a person from the upper Nile region)

²⁶I will pull up your skirts over your face
     that your shame may be seen—
²⁷your adulteries and lustful neighings,
     your shameless prostitution!
  I have seen your detestable acts
     on the hills and in the fields.
  Woe to you, O Jerusalem!
     How long will you be unclean?"

14 *Drought, Famine, Sword* This is the word of the LORD to Jeremiah
concerning the drought:

²"Judah mourns,
     her cities languish;
  they wail for the land,
     and a cry goes up from Jerusalem.
³The nobles send their servants for water;
     they go to the cisterns
     but find no water.
  They return with their jars unfilled;
     dismayed and despairing,
     they cover their heads.
⁴The ground is cracked
     because there is no rain in the land;
  the farmers are dismayed
     and cover their heads.
⁵Even the doe in the field
     deserts her newborn fawn
     because there is no grass.
⁶Wild donkeys stand on the barren heights
     and pant like jackals;
  their eyesight fails
     for lack of pasture."

⁷Although our sins testify against us,
     O LORD, do something for the sake of your name.
  For our backsliding is great;
     we have sinned against you.
⁸O Hope of Israel,
     its Savior in times of distress,
  why are you like a stranger in the land,
     like a traveler who stays only a night?
⁹Why are you like a man taken by surprise,
     like a warrior powerless to save?
  You are among us, O LORD,
     and we bear your name;
     do not forsake us!

¹⁰This is what the LORD says about this people:

  "They greatly love to wander;
     they do not restrain their feet.
  So the LORD does not accept them;
     he will now remember their wickedness
     and punish them for their sins."

¹¹Then the LORD said to me, "Do not pray for the well-being of this people.
¹²Although they fast, I will not listen to their cry; though they offer burnt offerings and grain offerings, I will not accept them. Instead, I will destroy
them with the sword, famine and plague."

¹³But I said, "Ah, Sovereign LORD, the prophets keep telling them, 'You will not see the sword or suffer famine. Indeed, I will give you lasting peace in this place.'"

¹⁴Then the LORD said to me, "The prophets are prophesying lies in my name. I have not sent them or appointed them or spoken to them. They are prophesying to you false visions, divinations, idolatries*a* and the delusions of their own minds. ¹⁵Therefore, this is what the LORD says about the prophets who are prophesying in my name: I did not send them, yet they are saying, 'No sword or famine will touch this land.' Those same prophets will perish by sword and famine. ¹⁶And the people they are prophesying to will be thrown out into the streets of Jerusalem because of the famine and sword. There will be no one to bury them or their wives, their sons or their daughters. I will pour out on them the calamity they deserve.

¹⁷"Speak this word to them:

> " 'Let my eyes overflow with tears
>   night and day without ceasing;
> for my virgin daughter—my people—
>   has suffered a grievous wound,
>   a crushing blow.
> ¹⁸If I go into the country,
>   I see those slain by the sword;
> if I go into the city,
>   I see the ravages of famine.
> Both prophet and priest
>   have gone to a land they know not.' "

> ¹⁹Have you rejected Judah completely?
>   Do you despise Zion?
> Why have you afflicted us
>   so that we cannot be healed?
> We hoped for peace
>   but no good has come,
> for a time of healing
>   but there is only terror.
> ²⁰O LORD, we acknowledge our wickedness
>   and the guilt of our fathers;
>   we have indeed sinned against you.
> ²¹For the sake of your name do not despise us;
>   do not dishonor your glorious throne.
> Remember your covenant with us
>   and do not break it.
> ²²Do any of the worthless idols of the nations bring rain?
>   Do the skies themselves send down showers?
> No, it is you, O LORD our God.
>   Therefore our hope is in you,
>   for you are the one who does all this.

Then the LORD said to me: "Even if Moses and Samuel were to stand before me, my heart would not go out to this people. Send them away from my presence! Let them go! ²And if they ask you, 'Where shall we go?' tell them, 'This is what the LORD says:

> " 'Those destined for death, to death;
>   those for the sword, to the sword;

---

a14 Or visions, worthless divinations

those for starvation, to starvation;
those for captivity, to captivity.'

³"I will send four kinds of destroyers against them," declares the LORD, "the sword to kill and the dogs to drag away and the birds of the air and the beasts of the earth to devour and destroy. ⁴I will make them abhorrent to all the kingdoms of the earth because of what Manasseh son of Hezekiah king of Judah did in Jerusalem.

⁵"Who will have pity on you, O Jerusalem?
    Who will mourn for you?
    Who will stop to ask how you are?
⁶You have rejected me," declares the LORD.
    "You keep on backsliding.
  So I will lay hands on you and destroy you;
    I can no longer show compassion.
⁷I will winnow them with a winnowing fork
    at the city gates of the land.
  I will bring bereavement and destruction on my people,
    for they have not changed their ways.
⁸I will make their widows more numerous
    than the sand of the sea.
  At midday I will bring a destroyer
    against the mothers of their young men;
  suddenly I will bring down on them
    anguish and terror.
⁹The mother of seven will grow faint
    and breathe her last.
  Her sun will set while it is still day;
    she will be disgraced and humiliated.
  I will put the survivors to the sword
    before their enemies,"

                                        declares the LORD.

¹⁰Alas, my mother, that you gave me birth,
    a man with whom the whole land strives and contends!
  I have neither lent nor borrowed,
    yet everyone curses me.

¹¹The LORD said,

"Surely I will deliver you for a good purpose;
    surely I will make your enemies plead with you
    in times of disaster and times of distress.

¹²"Can a man break iron—
    iron from the north—or bronze?
¹³Your wealth and your treasures
    I will give as plunder, without charge,
  because of all your sins
    throughout your country.
¹⁴I will enslave you to your enemies
    inᵃ a land you do not know,
  for my anger will kindle a fire
    that will burn against you."

ᵃ14 Some Hebrew manuscripts, Septuagint and Syriac (see also Jer. 17:4); most Hebrew manuscripts *I will cause your enemies to bring you / into*

¹⁵You understand, O LORD;
 remember me and care for me.
 Avenge me on my persecutors.
You are long-suffering—do not take me away;
 think of how I suffer reproach for your sake.
 ¹⁶When your words came, I ate them;
  they were my joy and my heart's delight,
  for I bear your name,
   O LORD God Almighty.
 ¹⁷I never sat in the company of revelers,
  never made merry with them;
 I sat alone because your hand was on me
  and you had filled me with indignation.
 ¹⁸Why is my pain unending
  and my wound grievous and incurable?
Will you be to me like a deceptive brook,
 like a spring that fails?

¹⁹Therefore this is what the LORD says:

"If you repent, I will restore you
 that you may serve me;
if you utter worthy, not worthless, words,
 you will be my spokesman.
Let this people turn to you,
 but you must not turn to them.
 ²⁰I will make you a wall to this people,
 a fortified wall of bronze;
they will fight against you
 but will not overcome you,
for I am with you
 to rescue and save you,"

       declares the LORD.
 ²¹"I will save you from the hands of the wicked
  and redeem you from the grasp of the cruel."

16 *Day of Disaster* Then the word of the LORD came to me: ²"You must not marry and have sons or daughters in this place." ³For this is what the LORD says about the sons and daughters born in this land and about the women who are their mothers and the men who are their fathers: ⁴"They will die of deadly diseases. They will not be mourned or buried but will be like refuse lying on the ground. They will perish by sword and famine, and their dead bodies will become food for the birds of the air and the beasts of the earth."

⁵For this is what the LORD says: "Do not enter a house where there is a funeral meal; do not go to mourn or show sympathy, because I have withdrawn my blessing, my love and my pity from this people," declares the LORD. ⁶"Both high and low will die in this land. They will not be buried or mourned, and no one will cut himself or shave his head for them. ⁷No one will offer food to comfort those who mourn for the dead—not even for a father or a mother—nor will anyone give them a drink to console them.

⁸"And do not enter a house where there is feasting and sit down to eat and drink. ⁹For this is what the LORD Almighty, the God of Israel, says: Before your eyes and in your days I will bring an end to the sounds of joy and gladness and to the voices of bride and bridegroom in this place.

¹⁰"When you tell these people all this and they ask you, 'Why has the LORD decreed such a great disaster against us? What wrong have we done? What sin have we committed against the LORD our God?' ¹¹then say to them, 'It is

> You understand,
> O LORD; remember
> me and care
> for me
> (Jeremiah 15:15).

because your fathers forsook me,' declares the LORD, 'and followed other gods and served and worshiped them. They forsook me and did not keep my law. ¹²But you have behaved more wickedly than your fathers. See how each of you is following the stubbornness of his evil heart instead of obeying me. ¹³So I will throw you out of this land into a land neither you nor your fathers have known, and there you will serve other gods day and night, for I will show you no favor.'

¹⁴"However, the days are coming," declares the LORD, "when men will no longer say, 'As surely as the LORD lives, who brought the Israelites up out of Egypt,' ¹⁵but they will say, 'As surely as the LORD lives, who brought the Israelites up out of the land of the north and out of all the countries where he had banished them.' For I will restore them to the land I gave their forefathers.

¹⁶"But now I will send for many fishermen," declares the LORD, "and they will catch them. After that I will send for many hunters, and they will hunt them down on every mountain and hill and from the crevices of the rocks. ¹⁷My eyes are on all their ways; they are not hidden from me, nor is their sin concealed from my eyes. ¹⁸I will repay them double for their wickedness and their sin, because they have defiled my land with the lifeless forms of their vile images and have filled my inheritance with their detestable idols."

¹⁹O LORD, my strength and my fortress,
     my refuge in time of distress,
  to you the nations will come
     from the ends of the earth and say,
  "Our fathers possessed nothing but false gods,
     worthless idols that did them no good.
²⁰Do men make their own gods?
     Yes, but they are not gods!"

²¹"Therefore I will teach them—
     this time I will teach them
     my power and might.
  Then they will know
     that my name is the LORD.

17 "Judah's sin is engraved with an iron tool,
     inscribed with a flint point,
  on the tablets of their hearts
     and on the horns of their altars.
²Even their children remember
     their altars and Asherah poles*a*
  beside the spreading trees
     and on the high hills.
³My mountain in the land
     and your*b* wealth and all your treasures
  I will give away as plunder,
     together with your high places,
     because of sin throughout your country.
⁴Through your own fault you will lose
     the inheritance I gave you.
  I will enslave you to your enemies
     in a land you do not know,
  for you have kindled my anger,
     and it will burn forever."

---

*a*2 That is, symbols of the goddess Asherah   *b*2,3 Or *hills* / ³*and the mountains of the land.* / *Your*

⁵This is what the Lord says:

"Cursed is the one who trusts in man,
  who depends on flesh for his strength
  and whose heart turns away from the Lord.
⁶He will be like a bush in the wastelands;
  he will not see prosperity when it comes.
He will dwell in the parched places of the desert,
  in a salt land where no one lives.

⁷"But blessed is the man who trusts in the Lord,
  whose confidence is in him.
⁸He will be like a tree planted by the water
  that sends out its roots by the stream.
It does not fear when heat comes;
  its leaves are always green.
It has no worries in a year of drought
  and never fails to bear fruit."

⁹The heart is deceitful above all things
  and beyond cure.
  Who can understand it?

¹⁰"I the Lord search the heart
  and examine the mind,
to reward a man according to his conduct,
  according to what his deeds deserve."

¹¹Like a partridge that hatches eggs it did not lay
  is the man who gains riches by unjust means.
When his life is half gone, they will desert him,
  and in the end he will prove to be a fool.

¹²A glorious throne, exalted from the beginning,
  is the place of our sanctuary.

¹³O Lord, the hope of Israel,
  all who forsake you will be put to
    shame.
Those who turn away from you will be
    written in the dust
  because they have forsaken the
    Lord,
  the spring of living water.

¹⁴Heal me, O Lord, and I will be healed;
  save me and I will be saved,
  for you are the one I praise.
¹⁵They keep saying to me,
  "Where is the word of the Lord?
  Let it now be fulfilled!"
¹⁶I have not run away from being your
    shepherd;
  you know I have not desired the
    day of despair.
  What passes my lips is open before
    you.
¹⁷Do not be a terror to me;
  you are my refuge in the day of
    disaster.
¹⁸Let my persecutors be put to shame,
  but keep me from shame;

Direct Line

JEREMIAH 17:5–9

Even teens brought up in Christian homes will challenge their parents' standards of right and wrong. And they'll question the Bible too. That's OK, because questioning is a first step toward developing personal convictions. The problems begin when you decide to accept the standards of society and ignore God's standards. Jeremiah warns that "the heart is deceitful" (Jeremiah 17:9). People don't decide against God's ways because they've thought things through. People decide against God's ways because they're attracted to sin. Read this passage and begin to think for yourself and depend on God.

let them be terrified,
but keep me from terror.
Bring on them the day of disaster;
destroy them with double destruction.

Keeping the Sabbath Holy   ¹⁹This is what the LORD said to me: "Go and stand at the gate of the people, through which the kings of Judah go in and out; stand also at all the other gates of Jerusalem. ²⁰Say to them, 'Hear the word of the LORD, O kings of Judah and all people of Judah and everyone living in Jerusalem who come through these gates. ²¹This is what the LORD says: Be careful not to carry a load on the Sabbath day or bring it through the gates of Jerusalem. ²²Do not bring a load out of your houses or do any work on the Sabbath, but keep the Sabbath day holy, as I commanded your forefathers. ²³Yet they did not listen or pay attention; they were stiff-necked and would not listen or respond to discipline. ²⁴But if you are careful to obey me, declares the LORD, and bring no load through the gates of this city on the Sabbath, but keep the Sabbath day holy by not doing any work on it, ²⁵then kings who sit on David's throne will come through the gates of this city with their officials. They and their officials will come riding in chariots and on horses, accompanied by the men of Judah and those living in Jerusalem, and this city will be inhabited forever. ²⁶People will come from the towns of Judah and the villages around Jerusalem, from the territory of Benjamin and the western foothills, from the hill country and the Negev, bringing burnt offerings and sacrifices, grain offerings, incense and thank offerings to the house of the LORD. ²⁷But if you do not obey me to keep the Sabbath day holy by not carrying any load as you come through the gates of Jerusalem on the Sabbath day, then I will kindle an unquenchable fire in the gates of Jerusalem that will consume her fortresses.' "

18 *At the Potter's House*   This is the word that came to Jeremiah from the LORD: ²"Go down to the potter's house, and there I will give you my message." ³So I went down to the potter's house, and I saw him working at the wheel. ⁴But the pot he was shaping from the clay was marred in his hands; so the potter formed it into another pot, shaping it as seemed best to him.

⁵Then the word of the LORD came to me: ⁶"O house of Israel, can I not do with you as this potter does?" declares the LORD. "Like clay in the hand of the potter, so are you in my hand, O house of Israel. ⁷If at any time I announce that a nation or kingdom is to be uprooted, torn down and destroyed, ⁸and if that nation I warned repents of its evil, then I will relent and not inflict on it the disaster I had planned. ⁹And if at another time I announce that a nation or kingdom is to be built up and planted, ¹⁰and if it does evil in my sight and does not obey me, then I will reconsider the good I had intended to do for it.

¹¹"Now therefore say to the people of Judah and those living in Jerusalem, 'This is what the LORD says: Look! I am preparing a disaster for you and devising a plan against you. So turn from your evil ways, each one of you, and reform your ways and your actions.' ¹²But they will reply, 'It's no use. We will continue with our own plans; each of us will follow the stubbornness of his evil heart.' "

¹³Therefore this is what the LORD says:

"Inquire among the nations:
Who has ever heard anything like this?
A most horrible thing has been done
by Virgin Israel.
¹⁴Does the snow of Lebanon
ever vanish from its rocky slopes?

Do its cool waters from distant sources
　　ever cease to flow?[a]
15 Yet my people have forgotten me;
　　they burn incense to worthless idols,
which made them stumble in their ways
　　and in the ancient paths.
They made them walk in bypaths
　　and on roads not built up.
16 Their land will be laid waste,
　　an object of lasting scorn;
all who pass by will be appalled
　　and will shake their heads.
17 Like a wind from the east,
　　I will scatter them before their enemies;
I will show them my back and not my face
　　in the day of their disaster."

18 They said, "Come, let's make plans against Jeremiah; for the teaching of the law by the priest will not be lost, nor will counsel from the wise, nor the word from the prophets. So come, let's attack him with our tongues and pay no attention to anything he says."

19 Listen to me, O LORD;
　　hear what my accusers are saying!
20 Should good be repaid with evil?
　　Yet they have dug a pit for me.
Remember that I stood before you
　　and spoke in their behalf
　　to turn your wrath away from them.
21 So give their children over to famine;
　　hand them over to the power of the sword.
Let their wives be made childless and widows;
　　let their men be put to death,
　　their young men slain by the sword in battle.
22 Let a cry be heard from their houses
　　when you suddenly bring invaders against them,
for they have dug a pit to capture me
　　and have hidden snares for my feet.
23 But you know, O LORD,
　　all their plots to kill me.
Do not forgive their crimes
　　or blot out their sins from your sight.
Let them be overthrown before you;
　　deal with them in the time of your anger.

19 This is what the LORD says: "Go and buy a clay jar from a potter. Take along some of the elders of the people and of the priests 2 and go out to the Valley of Ben Hinnom, near the entrance of the Potsherd Gate. There proclaim the words I tell you, 3 and say, 'Hear the word of the LORD, O kings of Judah and people of Jerusalem. This is what the LORD Almighty, the God of Israel, says: Listen! I am going to bring a disaster on this place that will make the ears of everyone who hears of it tingle. 4 For they have forsaken me and made this a place of foreign gods; they have burned sacrifices in it to gods that neither they nor their fathers nor the kings of Judah ever knew, and they have filled this place with the blood of the innocent. 5 They

---

[a]14 The meaning of the Hebrew for this sentence is uncertain.

have built the high places of Baal to burn their sons in the fire as offerings to Baal—something I did not command or mention, nor did it enter my mind. ⁶So beware, the days are coming, declares the LORD, when people will no longer call this place Topheth or the Valley of Ben Hinnom, but the Valley of Slaughter.

⁷" 'In this place I will ruin*a* the plans of Judah and Jerusalem. I will make them fall by the sword before their enemies, at the hands of those who seek their lives, and I will give their carcasses as food to the birds of the air and the beasts of the earth. ⁸I will devastate this city and make it an object of scorn; all who pass by will be appalled and will scoff because of all its wounds. ⁹I will make them eat the flesh of their sons and daughters, and they will eat one another's flesh during the stress of the siege imposed on them by the enemies who seek their lives.'

¹⁰"Then break the jar while those who go with you are watching, ¹¹and say to them, 'This is what the LORD Almighty says: I will smash this nation and this city just as this potter's jar is smashed and cannot be repaired. They will bury the dead in Topheth until there is no more room. ¹²This is what I will do to this place and to those who live here, declares the LORD. I will make this city like Topheth. ¹³The houses in Jerusalem and those of the kings of Judah will be defiled like this place, Topheth—all the houses where they burned incense on the roofs to all the starry hosts and poured out drink offerings to other gods.' "

¹⁴Jeremiah then returned from Topheth, where the LORD had sent him to prophesy, and stood in the court of the LORD's temple and said to all the people, ¹⁵"This is what the LORD Almighty, the God of Israel, says: 'Listen! I am going to bring on this city and the villages around it every disaster I pronounced against them, because they were stiff-necked and would not listen to my words.' "

Jeremiah and Pashhur When the priest Pashhur son of Immer, the chief officer in the temple of the LORD, heard Jeremiah prophesying these things, ²he had Jeremiah the prophet beaten and put in the stocks at the Upper Gate of Benjamin at the LORD's temple. ³The next day, when Pashhur released him from the stocks, Jeremiah said to him, "The LORD's name for you is not Pashhur, but Magor-Missabib.*b* ⁴For this is what the LORD says: 'I will make you a terror to yourself and to all your friends; with your own eyes you will see them fall by the sword of their enemies. I will hand all Judah over to the king of Babylon, who will carry them away to Babylon or put them to the sword. ⁵I will hand over to their enemies all the wealth of this city—all its products, all its valuables and all the treasures of the kings of Judah. They will take it away as plunder and carry it off to Babylon. ⁶And you, Pashhur, and all who live in your house will go into exile to Babylon. There you will die and be buried, you and all your friends to whom you have prophesied lies.' "

Jeremiah's Complaint

⁷O LORD, you deceived*c* me, and I was deceived*c*;
  you overpowered me and prevailed.
I am ridiculed all day long;
  everyone mocks me.
⁸Whenever I speak, I cry out
  proclaiming violence and destruction.
So the word of the LORD has brought me
  insult and reproach all day long.

---

a7 The Hebrew for ruin sounds like the Hebrew for jar (see verses 1 and 10). *b3 Magor-Missabib means terror on every side.* *c7 Or persuaded*

⁹But if I say, "I will not mention him
    or speak any more in his name,"
his word is in my heart like a fire,
    a fire shut up in my bones.
I am weary of holding it in;
    indeed, I cannot.
¹⁰I hear many whispering,
    "Terror on every side!
    Report him! Let's report him!"
All my friends
    are waiting for me to slip, saying,
"Perhaps he will be deceived;
    then we will prevail over him
    and take our revenge on him."

¹¹But the LORD is with me like a mighty warrior;
    so my persecutors will stumble and not prevail.
    They will fail and be thoroughly disgraced;
        their dishonor will never be forgotten.
¹²O LORD Almighty, you who examine the righteous
    and probe the heart and mind,
let me see your vengeance upon them,
    for to you I have committed my cause.

¹³Sing to the LORD!
    Give praise to the LORD!
He rescues the life of the needy
    from the hands of the wicked.

¹⁴Cursed be the day I was born!
    May the day my mother bore me not be blessed!
¹⁵Cursed be the man who brought my father the news,
    who made him very glad, saying,
    "A child is born to you—a son!"
¹⁶May that man be like the towns
    the LORD overthrew without pity.
May he hear wailing in the morning,
    a battle cry at noon.
¹⁷For he did not kill me in the womb,
    with my mother as my grave,
    her womb enlarged forever.
¹⁸Why did I ever come out of the womb
    to see trouble and sorrow
    and to end my days in shame?

> Sing to the LORD!
> Give praise to
> the LORD! He
> rescues the life
> of the needy
> (Jeremiah 20:13).

21 *God Rejects Zedekiah's Request* The word came to Jeremiah from the LORD when King Zedekiah sent to him Pashhur son of Malkijah and the priest Zephaniah son of Maaseiah. They said: ²"Inquire now of the LORD for us because Nebuchadnezzar*ᵃ* king of Babylon is attacking us. Perhaps the LORD will perform wonders for us as in times past so that he will withdraw from us."

³But Jeremiah answered them, "Tell Zedekiah, ⁴'This is what the LORD, the God of Israel, says: I am about to turn against you the weapons of war that are in your hands, which you are using to fight the king of Babylon and the Babylonians*ᵇ* who are outside the wall besieging you. And I will gather them

---

ᵃ2 Hebrew *Nebuchadrezzar,* of which *Nebuchadnezzar* is a variant; here and often in Jeremiah and Ezekiel
ᵇ4 Or *Chaldeans*; also in verse 9

inside this city. ⁵I myself will fight against you with an outstretched hand and a mighty arm in anger and fury and great wrath. ⁶I will strike down those who live in this city—both men and animals—and they will die of a terrible plague. ⁷After that, declares the LORD, I will hand over Zedekiah king of Judah, his officials and the people in this city who survive the plague, sword and famine, to Nebuchadnezzar king of Babylon and to their enemies who seek their lives. He will put them to the sword; he will show them no mercy or pity or compassion.'

⁸"Furthermore, tell the people, 'This is what the LORD says: See, I am setting before you the way of life and the way of death. ⁹Whoever stays in this city will die by the sword, famine or plague. But whoever goes out and surrenders to the Babylonians who are besieging you will live; he will escape with his life. ¹⁰I have determined to do this city harm and not good, declares the LORD. It will be given into the hands of the king of Babylon, and he will destroy it with fire.'

¹¹"Moreover, say to the royal house of Judah, 'Hear the word of the LORD; ¹²O house of David, this is what the LORD says:

" 'Administer justice every morning;
　　rescue from the hand of his oppressor
　　the one who has been robbed,
or my wrath will break out and burn like fire
　　because of the evil you have done—
　　burn with no one to quench it.
¹³I am against you, ˌJerusalem,ˌ
　　you who live above this valley
　　on the rocky plateau,

　　　　　　　　　　　　　　　　declares the LORD—

you who say, "Who can come against us?
　　Who can enter our refuge?"
¹⁴I will punish you as your deeds deserve,

　　　　　　　　　　　　　　　　declares the LORD.

I will kindle a fire in your forests
　　that will consume everything around you.' "

22 *Judgment Against Evil Kings*　This is what the LORD says: "Go down to the palace of the king of Judah and proclaim this message there: ²'Hear the word of the LORD, O king of Judah, you who sit on David's throne—you, your officials and your people who come through these gates. ³This is what the LORD says: Do what is just and right. Rescue from the hand of his oppressor the one who has been robbed. Do no wrong or violence to the alien, the fatherless or the widow, and do not shed innocent blood in this place. ⁴For if you are careful to carry out these commands, then kings who sit on David's throne will come through the gates of this palace, riding in chariots and on horses, accompanied by their officials and their people. ⁵But if you do not obey these commands, declares the LORD, I swear by myself that this palace will become a ruin.' "

⁶For this is what the LORD says about the palace of the king of Judah:

"Though you are like Gilead to me,
　　like the summit of Lebanon,
I will surely make you like a desert,
　　like towns not inhabited.
⁷I will send destroyers against you,
　　each man with his weapons,
and they will cut up your fine cedar beams
　　and throw them into the fire.

⁸"People from many nations will pass by this city and will ask one another, 'Why has the LORD done such a thing to this great city?' ⁹And the answer will be: 'Because they have forsaken the covenant of the LORD their God and have worshiped and served other gods.' "

¹⁰Do not weep for the dead king, or mourn his loss;
    rather, weep bitterly for him who is exiled,
because he will never return
    nor see his native land again.

¹¹For this is what the LORD says about Shallum*a* son of Josiah, who succeeded his father as king of Judah but has gone from this place: "He will never return. ¹²He will die in the place where they have led him captive; he will not see this land again."

¹³"Woe to him who builds his palace by unrighteousness,
    his upper rooms by injustice,
making his countrymen work for nothing,
    not paying them for their labor.
¹⁴He says, 'I will build myself a great palace
    with spacious upper rooms.'
So he makes large windows in it,
    panels it with cedar
    and decorates it in red.

¹⁵"Does it make you a king
    to have more and more cedar?
Did not your father have food and drink?
    He did what was right and just,
    so all went well with him.
¹⁶He defended the cause of the poor and needy,
    and so all went well.
Is that not what it means to know me?"
    declares the LORD.
¹⁷"But your eyes and your heart
    are set only on dishonest gain,

---

a11 Also called *Jehoahaz*

The Bible Says

Care About People

Ever dream about having a sports car? Or a designer wardrobe? Some people feel they have to have such things. They'll do anything to get them.

One king in Jeremiah's day felt that way. Jeremiah warned him that since his eyes and his heart were set only on dishonest gain (Jeremiah 22:13), he would soon die and have the "burial of a donkey" (Jeremiah 22:19). To that king possessions were more important than people. He didn't care if he hurt others as long as he got what he wanted.

It's important to remember that people are more important than possessions. If you set your heart on what is right and just, if you defend the cause of the poor and needy, then you'll know God better, and all will go well with you (Jeremiah 22:15–16).

on shedding innocent blood
and on oppression and extortion."

¹⁸Therefore this is what the LORD says about Jehoiakim son of Josiah king of Judah:

"They will not mourn for him:
  'Alas, my brother! Alas, my sister!'
They will not mourn for him:
  'Alas, my master! Alas, his splendor!'
¹⁹He will have the burial of a donkey—
  dragged away and thrown
  outside the gates of Jerusalem."

²⁰"Go up to Lebanon and cry out,
  let your voice be heard in Bashan,
cry out from Abarim,
  for all your allies are crushed.
²¹I warned you when you felt secure,
  but you said, 'I will not listen!'
This has been your way from your youth;
  you have not obeyed me.
²²The wind will drive all your shepherds away,
  and your allies will go into exile.
Then you will be ashamed and disgraced
  because of all your wickedness.
²³You who live in 'Lebanon,'ᵃ
  who are nestled in cedar buildings,
how you will groan when pangs come upon you,
  pain like that of a woman in labor!

²⁴"As surely as I live," declares the LORD, "even if you, Jehoiachinᵇ son of Jehoiakim king of Judah, were a signet ring on my right hand, I would still pull you off. ²⁵I will hand you over to those who seek your life, those you fear—to Nebuchadnezzar king of Babylon and to the Babylonians.ᶜ ²⁶I will hurl you and the mother who gave you birth into another country, where neither of you was born, and there you both will die. ²⁷You will never come back to the land you long to return to."

²⁸Is this man Jehoiachin a despised, broken pot,
  an object no one wants?
Why will he and his children be hurled out,
  cast into a land they do not know?
²⁹O land, land, land,
  hear the word of the LORD!
³⁰This is what the LORD says:
"Record this man as if childless,
  a man who will not prosper in his lifetime,
for none of his offspring will prosper,
  none will sit on the throne of David
  or rule anymore in Judah."

The Righteous Branch "Woe to the shepherds who are destroying and scattering the sheep of my pasture!" declares the LORD. ²Therefore this is what the LORD, the God of Israel, says to the shepherds who tend my people: "Because you have scattered my flock and driven them

---

ᵃ23 That is, the palace in Jerusalem (see 1 Kings 7:2) ᵇ24 Hebrew *Coniah*, a variant of *Jehoiachin*; also in verse 28 ᶜ25 Or *Chaldeans*

away and have not bestowed care on them, I will bestow punishment on you for the evil you have done," declares the LORD. ³"I myself will gather the remnant of my flock out of all the countries where I have driven them and will bring them back to their pasture, where they will be fruitful and increase in number. ⁴I will place shepherds over them who will tend them, and they will no longer be afraid or terrified, nor will any be missing," declares the LORD.

⁵"The days are coming," declares the LORD,
 "when I will raise up to David*ᵃ* a righteous Branch,
a King who will reign wisely
 and do what is just and right in the land.
⁶In his days Judah will be saved
 and Israel will live in safety.
This is the name by which he will be called:
 The LORD Our Righteousness.

⁷"So then, the days are coming," declares the LORD, "when people will no longer say, 'As surely as the LORD lives, who brought the Israelites up out of Egypt,' ⁸but they will say, 'As surely as the LORD lives, who brought the descendants of Israel up out of the land of the north and out of all the countries where he had banished them.' Then they will live in their own land."

Lying Prophets ⁹Concerning the prophets:

My heart is broken within me;
 all my bones tremble.
I am like a drunken man,
 like a man overcome by wine,
because of the LORD
 and his holy words.
¹⁰The land is full of adulterers;
 because of the curse*ᵇ* the land lies parched*ᶜ*
 and the pastures in the desert are withered.
The ˌprophets˛ follow an evil course
 and use their power unjustly.

¹¹"Both prophet and priest are godless;
 even in my temple I find their wickedness,"
declares the LORD.

¹²"Therefore their path will become slippery;
 they will be banished to darkness
 and there they will fall.
I will bring disaster on them
 in the year they are punished,"
declares the LORD.

¹³"Among the prophets of Samaria
 I saw this repulsive thing:
They prophesied by Baal
 and led my people Israel astray.
¹⁴And among the prophets of Jerusalem
 I have seen something horrible:
They commit adultery and live a lie.
They strengthen the hands of evildoers,
 so that no one turns from his wickedness.
They are all like Sodom to me;
 the people of Jerusalem are like Gomorrah."

ᵃ5 Or *up from David's line* ᵇ10 Or *because of these things* ᶜ10 Or *land mourns*

¹⁵Therefore, this is what the Lord Almighty says concerning the prophets:

> "I will make them eat bitter food
>> and drink poisoned water,
> because from the prophets of Jerusalem
>> ungodliness has spread throughout the land."

¹⁶This is what the Lord Almighty says:

> "Do not listen to what the prophets are prophesying to you;
>> they fill you with false hopes.
> They speak visions from their own minds,
>> not from the mouth of the Lord.
> ¹⁷They keep saying to those who despise me,
>> 'The Lord says: You will have peace.'
> And to all who follow the stubbornness of their hearts
>> they say, 'No harm will come to you.'
> ¹⁸But which of them has stood in the council of the Lord
>> to see or to hear his word?
> Who has listened and heard his word?
> ¹⁹See, the storm of the Lord
>> will burst out in wrath,
> a whirlwind swirling down
>> on the heads of the wicked.
> ²⁰The anger of the Lord will not turn back
>> until he fully accomplishes
>> the purposes of his heart.
> In days to come
>> you will understand it clearly.
> ²¹I did not send these prophets,
>> yet they have run with their message;
> I did not speak to them,
>> yet they have prophesied.
> ²²But if they had stood in my council,
>> they would have proclaimed my words to my people
> and would have turned them from their evil ways
>> and from their evil deeds.

> ²³"Am I only a God nearby,"

>>>> declares the Lord,

>> "and not a God far away?
> ²⁴Can anyone hide in secret places
>> so that I cannot see him?"

>>>> declares the Lord.

>> "Do not I fill heaven and earth?"

>>>> declares the Lord.

²⁵"I have heard what the prophets say who prophesy lies in my name. They say, 'I had a dream! I had a dream!' ²⁶How long will this continue in the hearts of these lying prophets, who prophesy the delusions of their own minds? ²⁷They think the dreams they tell one another will make my people forget my name, just as their fathers forgot my name through Baal worship. ²⁸Let the prophet who has a dream tell his dream, but let the one who has my word speak it faithfully. For what has straw to do with grain?" declares the Lord. ²⁹"Is not my word like fire," declares the Lord, "and like a hammer that breaks a rock in pieces?

³⁰"Therefore," declares the Lord, "I am against the prophets who steal from one another words supposedly from me. ³¹Yes," declares the Lord, "I am against the prophets who wag their own tongues and yet declare, 'The Lord declares.' ³²Indeed, I am against those who prophesy false dreams,"

declares the LORD. "They tell them and lead my people astray with their reckless lies, yet I did not send or appoint them. They do not benefit these people in the least," declares the LORD.

False Oracles and False Prophets [33]"When these people, or a prophet or a priest, ask you, 'What is the oracle[a] of the LORD?' say to them, 'What oracle?[b] I will forsake you, declares the LORD.' [34]If a prophet or a priest or anyone else claims, 'This is the oracle of the LORD,' I will punish that man and his household. [35]This is what each of you keeps on saying to his friend or relative: 'What is the LORD's answer?' or 'What has the LORD spoken?' [36]But you must not mention 'the oracle of the LORD' again, because every man's own word becomes his oracle and so you distort the words of the living God, the LORD Almighty, our God. [37]This is what you keep saying to a prophet: 'What is the LORD's answer to you?' or 'What has the LORD spoken?' [38]Although you claim, 'This is the oracle of the LORD,' this is what the LORD says: You used the words, 'This is the oracle of the LORD,' even though I told you that you must not claim, 'This is the oracle of the LORD.' [39]Therefore, I will surely forget you and cast you out of my presence along with the city I gave to you and your fathers. [40]I will bring upon you everlasting disgrace—everlasting shame that will not be forgotten."

24 ***Two Baskets of Figs*** After Jehoiachin[c] son of Jehoiakim king of Judah and the officials, the craftsmen and the artisans of Judah were carried into exile from Jerusalem to Babylon by Nebuchadnezzar king of Babylon, the LORD showed me two baskets of figs placed in front of the temple of the LORD. [2]One basket had very good figs, like those that ripen early; the other basket had very poor figs, so bad they could not be eaten.

[3]Then the LORD asked me, "What do you see, Jeremiah?"

"Figs," I answered. "The good ones are very good, but the poor ones are so bad they cannot be eaten."

[4]Then the word of the LORD came to me: [5]"This is what the LORD, the God of Israel, says: 'Like these good figs, I regard as good the exiles from Judah, whom I sent away from this place to the land of the Babylonians.[d] [6]My eyes will watch over them for their good, and I will bring them back to this land. I will build them up and not tear them down; I will plant them and not uproot them. [7]I will give them a heart to know me, that I am the LORD. They will be my people, and I will be their God, for they will return to me with all their heart.

> I will give them
> a heart to know
> me . . . They
> will be my people,
> and I will be
> their God
> (Jeremiah 24:7).

[8]" 'But like the poor figs, which are so bad they cannot be eaten,' says the LORD, 'so will I deal with Zedekiah king of Judah, his officials and the survivors from Jerusalem, whether they remain in this land or live in Egypt. [9]I will make them abhorrent and an offense to all the kingdoms of the earth, a reproach and a byword, an object of ridicule and cursing, wherever I banish them. [10]I will send the sword, famine and plague against them until they are destroyed from the land I gave to them and their fathers.' "

25 ***Seventy Years of Captivity*** The word came to Jeremiah concerning all the people of Judah in the fourth year of Jehoiakim son of Josiah king of Judah, which was the first year of Nebuchadnezzar king of Babylon. [2]So Jeremiah the prophet said to all the people of Judah and to all those living in Jerusalem: [3]For twenty-three years—from the thirteenth year

---

[a]33 Or *burden* (see Septuagint and Vulgate) [b]33 Hebrew; Septuagint and Vulgate *'You are the burden.'* (The Hebrew for *oracle* and *burden* is the same.) [c]1 Hebrew *Jeconiah,* a variant of *Jehoiachin* [d]5 Or *Chaldeans*

Addiction (a-dik-shun) n.

psychological or physiological dependence, especially on a drug.

Addiction

Addiction

ALTERNATE DEFINITION
something that's not good for you at all, but that you keep needing and wanting anyway

You probably know drugs give you a high but then drop you into the pits. Once you're hooked you've got to have them. Most burglaries and teenage prostitution are drug related. Druggies don't live very long. You're smart if you keep away from drugs.

"Those who live according to the sinful nature have their minds set on what that nature desires; but those who live in accordance with the Spirit have their minds set on what the Spirit desires...You, however, are controlled not by the sinful nature but by the Spirit, if the Spirit of God lives in you."

ROMANS 8:5,9

Maybe you know too much alcohol kills brain cells and scars your liver. Even one drink lowers your inhibitions and messes up your judgment. That's why alcohol is linked to so many teen pregnancies and to over half of the serious car accidents in the U.S.

Lots of things that aren't as scary as drink or drugs can still get control of your life. They can fill your time and fill your thoughts until you become an addict. Remember Romans 8, and be sure that the only thing in control of your life is the Holy Spirit.

Entertainment (en-ter-tane-ment) n.
a performance or show designed to amuse or divert.

"My parents don't under- stand. They won't let me listen to KBUZ. They won't let me rent this movie I want to see or buy that group's CD. Hey, don't my mom and dad trust me? Besides, just because I watch something doesn't mean I'll go and do it."

Everybody knows this month's top ten. OK, so you don't listen to the words. But one study showed that kids who "don't listen to the words" not only could sing the top ten—they could write the lyrics down.

"Finally, brothers, whatever is true, whatever is noble, whatever is right, whatever is pure, whatever is lovely, whatever is admirable—if anything is excellent or praiseworthy—think about such things."

PHILIPPIANS 4:8

Take movies. Teens in a Florida honors English class wrote reviews on films they liked. The more violent and bloody the films, the higher these 11th graders rated them.

Of course, that's not you. So here's a way to show Mom and Dad you can be trusted. Offer to let them watch that video before you see it. While you're driving together, ask them to turn on KBUZ to check out the disc jockey as well as the songs he or she plays. If you're making good choices, in time, Mom and Dad will learn to trust your judgment and give you more freedom.

of Josiah son of Amon king of Judah until this very day—the word of the LORD has come to me and I have spoken to you again and again, but you have not listened.

⁴And though the LORD has sent all his servants the prophets to you again and again, you have not listened or paid any attention. ⁵They said, "Turn now, each of you, from your evil ways and your evil practices, and you can stay in the land the LORD gave to you and your fathers for ever and ever. ⁶Do not follow other gods to serve and worship them; do not provoke me to anger with what your hands have made. Then I will not harm you."

⁷"But you did not listen to me," declares the LORD, "and you have provoked me with what your hands have made, and you have brought harm to your-selves."

⁸Therefore the LORD Almighty says this: "Because you have not listened to my words, ⁹I will summon all the peoples of the north and my servant Neb-uchadnezzar king of Babylon," declares the LORD, "and I will bring them against this land and its inhabitants and against all the surrounding na-tions. I will completely destroyᵃ them and make them an object of horror and scorn, and an everlasting ruin. ¹⁰I will banish from them the sounds of joy and gladness, the voices of bride and bridegroom, the sound of millstones and the light of the lamp. ¹¹This whole country will become a desolate waste-land, and these nations will serve the king of Babylon seventy years.

¹²"But when the seventy years are fulfilled, I will punish the king of Bab-ylon and his nation, the land of the Babylonians,ᵇ for their guilt," declares the LORD, "and will make it desolate forever. ¹³I will bring upon that land all the things I have spoken against it, all that are written in this book and proph-esied by Jeremiah against all the nations. ¹⁴They themselves will be enslaved by many nations and great kings; I will repay them according to their deeds and the work of their hands."

The Cup of God's Wrath   ¹⁵This is what the LORD, the God of Israel, said to me: "Take from my hand this cup filled with the wine of my wrath and make all the nations to whom I send you drink it. ¹⁶When they drink it, they will stag-ger and go mad because of the sword I will send among them."

¹⁷So I took the cup from the LORD's hand and made all the nations to whom he sent me drink it: ¹⁸Jerusalem and the towns of Judah, its kings and offi-cials, to make them a ruin and an object of horror and scorn and cursing, as they are today; ¹⁹Pharaoh king of Egypt, his attendants, his officials and all his people, ²⁰and all the foreign people there; all the kings of Uz; all the kings of the Philistines (those of Ashkelon, Gaza, Ekron, and the people left at Ashdod); ²¹Edom, Moab and Ammon; ²²all the kings of Tyre and Sidon; the kings of the coastlands across the sea; ²³Dedan, Tema, Buz and all who are in distant placesᶜ; ²⁴all the kings of Arabia and all the kings of the foreign people who live in the desert; ²⁵all the kings of Zimri, Elam and Media; ²⁶and all the kings of the north, near and far, one after the other—all the kingdoms on the face of the earth. And after all of them, the king of Sheshachᵈ will drink it too.

²⁷"Then tell them, 'This is what the LORD Almighty, the God of Israel, says: Drink, get drunk and vomit, and fall to rise no more because of the sword I will send among you.' ²⁸But if they refuse to take the cup from your hand and drink, tell them, 'This is what the LORD Almighty says: You must drink it! ²⁹See, I am beginning to bring disaster on the city that bears my Name, and will you indeed go unpunished? You will not go unpunished, for I am call-ing down a sword upon all who live on the earth, declares the LORD Almighty.'

ᵃ9 The Hebrew term refers to the irrevocable giving over of things or persons to the LORD, often by totally destroying them.   ᵇ12 Or *Chaldeans*   ᶜ23 Or *who clip the hair by their foreheads*   ᵈ26 *Sheshach* is a cryptogram for Babylon.

³⁰"Now prophesy all these words against them and say to them:

" 'The Lord will roar from on high;
  he will thunder from his holy dwelling
  and roar mightily against his land.
He will shout like those who tread the grapes,
  shout against all who live on the earth.
³¹ The tumult will resound to the ends of the earth,
  for the Lord will bring charges against the nations;
he will bring judgment on all mankind
  and put the wicked to the sword,' "

declares the Lord.

³²This is what the Lord Almighty says:

"Look! Disaster is spreading
  from nation to nation;
a mighty storm is rising
  from the ends of the earth."

³³At that time those slain by the Lord will be everywhere—from one end of the earth to the other. They will not be mourned or gathered up or buried, but will be like refuse lying on the ground.

³⁴Weep and wail, you shepherds;
  roll in the dust, you leaders of the flock.
For your time to be slaughtered has come;
  you will fall and be shattered like fine pottery.
³⁵ The shepherds will have nowhere to flee,
  the leaders of the flock no place to escape.
³⁶Hear the cry of the shepherds,
  the wailing of the leaders of the flock,
  for the Lord is destroying their pasture.
³⁷ The peaceful meadows will be laid waste
  because of the fierce anger of the Lord.
³⁸ Like a lion he will leave his lair,
  and their land will become desolate
because of the sword*ᵃ* of the oppressor
  and because of the Lord's fierce anger.

26 *Jeremiah Threatened With Death* Early in the reign of Jehoiakim son of Josiah king of Judah, this word came from the Lord: ²"This is what the Lord says: Stand in the courtyard of the Lord's house and speak to all the people of the towns of Judah who come to worship in the house of the Lord. Tell them everything I command you; do not omit a word. ³Perhaps they will listen and each will turn from his evil way. Then I will relent and not bring on them the disaster I was planning because of the evil they have done. ⁴Say to them, 'This is what the Lord says: If you do not listen to me and follow my law, which I have set before you, ⁵and if you do not listen to the words of my servants the prophets, whom I have sent to you again and again (though you have not listened), ⁶then I will make this house like Shiloh and this city an object of cursing among all the nations of the earth.' "

⁷The priests, the prophets and all the people heard Jeremiah speak these words in the house of the Lord. ⁸But as soon as Jeremiah finished telling all the people everything the Lord had commanded him to say, the priests, the prophets and all the people seized him and said, "You must die! ⁹Why do you

---

ᵃ38 Some Hebrew manuscripts and Septuagint (see also Jer. 46:16 and 50:16); most Hebrew manuscripts *anger*

prophesy in the Lord's name that this house will be like Shiloh and this city will be desolate and deserted?" And all the people crowded around Jeremiah in the house of the Lord.

¹⁰When the officials of Judah heard about these things, they went up from the royal palace to the house of the Lord and took their places at the entrance of the New Gate of the Lord's house. ¹¹Then the priests and the prophets said to the officials and all the people, "This man should be sentenced to death because he has prophesied against this city. You have heard it with your own ears!"

¹²Then Jeremiah said to all the officials and all the people: "The Lord sent me to prophesy against this house and this city all the things you have heard. ¹³Now reform your ways and your actions and obey the Lord your God. Then the Lord will relent and not bring the disaster he has pronounced against you. ¹⁴As for me, I am in your hands; do with me whatever you think is good and right. ¹⁵Be assured, however, that if you put me to death, you will bring the guilt of innocent blood on yourselves and on this city and on those who live in it, for in truth the Lord has sent me to you to speak all these words in your hearing."

¹⁶Then the officials and all the people said to the priests and the prophets, "This man should not be sentenced to death! He has spoken to us in the name of the Lord our God."

¹⁷Some of the elders of the land stepped forward and said to the entire assembly of people, ¹⁸"Micah of Moresheth prophesied in the days of Hezekiah king of Judah. He told all the people of Judah, 'This is what the Lord Almighty says:

> " 'Zion will be plowed like a field,
>   Jerusalem will become a heap of rubble,
>   the temple hill a mound overgrown with thickets.'ᵃ

¹⁹"Did Hezekiah king of Judah or anyone else in Judah put him to death? Did not Hezekiah fear the Lord and seek his favor? And did not the Lord relent, so that he did not bring the disaster he pronounced against them? We are about to bring a terrible disaster on ourselves!"

²⁰(Now Uriah son of Shemaiah from Kiriath Jearim was another man who prophesied in the name of the Lord; he prophesied the same things against this city and this land as Jeremiah did. ²¹When King Jehoiakim and all his officers and officials heard his words, the king sought to put him to death. But Uriah heard of it and fled in fear to Egypt. ²²King Jehoiakim, however, sent Elnathan son of Acbor to Egypt, along with some other men. ²³They brought Uriah out of Egypt and took him to King Jehoiakim, who had him struck down with a sword and his body thrown into the burial place of the common people.)

²⁴Furthermore, Ahikam son of Shaphan supported Jeremiah, and so he was not handed over to the people to be put to death.

ᵃ18 Micah 3:12

JEREMIAH 26:8

Do you have any idea how many people have been killed because they spoke up for God? Acts 7 records the story of the first Christian martyr. Tradition says Peter and Paul were executed for spreading the Christian message. A book called *Foxe's Book of Martyrs* tells about hundreds more. When Jeremiah delivered God's message, he was threatened with death, too. Witnessing has never been easy. At times believers have faced death and still shared God's Word. Compared to that, do you hold back because someone might laugh?

Direct Line

Judah to Serve Nebuchadnezzar Early in the reign of Zedekiah[a] son of Josiah king of Judah, this word came to Jeremiah from the LORD: ²This is what the LORD said to me: "Make a yoke out of straps and crossbars and put it on your neck. ³Then send word to the kings of Edom, Moab, Ammon, Tyre and Sidon through the envoys who have come to Jerusalem to Zedekiah king of Judah. ⁴Give them a message for their masters and say, 'This is what the LORD Almighty, the God of Israel, says: "Tell this to your masters: ⁵With my great power and outstretched arm I made the earth and its people and the animals that are on it, and I give it to anyone I please. ⁶Now I will hand all your countries over to my servant Nebuchadnezzar king of Babylon; I will make even the wild animals subject to him. ⁷All nations will serve him and his son and his grandson until the time for his land comes; then many nations and great kings will subjugate him.

⁸" ' "If, however, any nation or kingdom will not serve Nebuchadnezzar king of Babylon or bow its neck under his yoke, I will punish that nation with the sword, famine and plague, declares the LORD, until I destroy it by his hand. ⁹So do not listen to your prophets, your diviners, your interpreters of dreams, your mediums or your sorcerers who tell you, 'You will not serve the king of Babylon.' ¹⁰They prophesy lies to you that will only serve to remove you far from your lands; I will banish you and you will perish. ¹¹But if any nation will bow its neck under the yoke of the king of Babylon and serve him, I will let that nation remain in its own land to till it and to live there, declares the LORD." ' "

¹²I gave the same message to Zedekiah king of Judah. I said, "Bow your neck under the yoke of the king of Babylon; serve him and his people, and you will live. ¹³Why will you and your people die by the sword, famine and plague with which the LORD has threatened any nation that will not serve the king of Babylon? ¹⁴Do not listen to the words of the prophets who say to you, 'You will not serve the king of Babylon,' for they are prophesying lies to you. ¹⁵'I have not sent them,' declares the LORD. 'They are prophesying lies in my name. Therefore, I will banish you and you will perish, both you and the prophets who prophesy to you.' "

¹⁶Then I said to the priests and all these people, "This is what the LORD says: Do not listen to the prophets who say, 'Very soon now the articles from the LORD's house will be brought back from Babylon.' They are prophesying lies to you. ¹⁷Do not listen to them. Serve the king of Babylon, and you will live. Why should this city become a ruin? ¹⁸If they are prophets and have the word of the LORD, let them plead with the LORD Almighty that the furnishings remaining in the house of the LORD and in the palace of the king of Judah and in Jerusalem not be taken to Babylon. ¹⁹For this is what the LORD Almighty says about the pillars, the Sea, the movable stands and the other furnishings that are left in this city, ²⁰which Nebuchadnezzar king of Babylon did not take away when he carried Jehoiachin[b] son of Jehoiakim king of Judah into exile from Jerusalem to Babylon, along with all the nobles of Judah and Jerusalem— ²¹yes, this is what the LORD Almighty, the God of Israel, says about the things that are left in the house of the LORD and in the palace of the king of Judah and in Jerusalem: ²²'They will be taken to Babylon and there they will remain until the day I come for them,' declares the LORD. 'Then I will bring them back and restore them to this place.' "

The False Prophet Hananiah In the fifth month of that same year, the fourth year, early in the reign of Zedekiah king of Judah, the prophet Hananiah son of Azzur, who was from Gibeon, said to me in the house of the LORD in the presence of the priests and all the people: ²"This is

---

[a]1 A few Hebrew manuscripts and Syriac (see also Jer. 27:3, 12 and 28:1); most Hebrew manuscripts *Jehoiakim* (Most Septuagint manuscripts do not have this verse.)   [b]20 Hebrew *Jeconiah*, a variant of *Jehoiachin*

what the LORD Almighty, the God of Israel, says: 'I will break the yoke of the king of Babylon. ³Within two years I will bring back to this place all the articles of the LORD's house that Nebuchadnezzar king of Babylon removed from here and took to Babylon. ⁴I will also bring back to this place Jehoiachin[a] son of Jehoiakim king of Judah and all the other exiles from Judah who went to Babylon,' declares the LORD, 'for I will break the yoke of the king of Babylon.' "

⁵Then the prophet Jeremiah replied to the prophet Hananiah before the priests and all the people who were standing in the house of the LORD. ⁶He said, "Amen! May the LORD do so! May the LORD fulfill the words you have prophesied by bringing the articles of the LORD's house and all the exiles back to this place from Babylon. ⁷Nevertheless, listen to what I have to say in your hearing and in the hearing of all the people: ⁸From early times the prophets who preceded you and me have prophesied war, disaster and plague against many countries and great kingdoms. ⁹But the prophet who prophesies peace will be recognized as one truly sent by the LORD only if his prediction comes true."

¹⁰Then the prophet Hananiah took the yoke off the neck of the prophet Jeremiah and broke it, ¹¹and he said before all the people, "This is what the LORD says: 'In the same way will I break the yoke of Nebuchadnezzar king of Babylon off the neck of all the nations within two years.' " At this, the prophet Jeremiah went on his way.

¹²Shortly after the prophet Hananiah had broken the yoke off the neck of the prophet Jeremiah, the word of the LORD came to Jeremiah: ¹³"Go and tell Hananiah, 'This is what the LORD says: You have broken a wooden yoke, but in its place you will get a yoke of iron. ¹⁴This is what the LORD Almighty, the God of Israel, says: I will put an iron yoke on the necks of all these nations to make them serve Nebuchadnezzar king of Babylon, and they will serve him. I will even give him control over the wild animals.' "

¹⁵Then the prophet Jeremiah said to Hananiah the prophet, "Listen, Hananiah! The LORD has not sent you, yet you have persuaded this nation to trust in lies. ¹⁶Therefore, this is what the LORD says: 'I am about to remove you from the face of the earth. This very year you are going to die, because you have preached rebellion against the LORD.' "

¹⁷In the seventh month of that same year, Hananiah the prophet died.

29 *A Letter to the Exiles* This is the text of the letter that the prophet Jeremiah sent from Jerusalem to the surviving elders among the exiles and to the priests, the prophets and all the other people Nebuchadnezzar had carried into exile from Jerusalem to Babylon. ²(This was after King Jehoiachin[a] and the queen mother, the court officials and the leaders of Judah and Jerusalem, the craftsmen and the artisans had gone into exile from Jerusalem.) ³He entrusted the letter to Elasah son of Shaphan and to Gemariah son of Hilkiah, whom Zedekiah king of Judah sent to King Nebuchadnezzar in Babylon. It said:

⁴This is what the LORD Almighty, the God of Israel, says to all those I carried into exile from Jerusalem to Babylon: ⁵"Build houses and settle down; plant gardens and eat what they produce. ⁶Marry and have sons and daughters; find wives for your sons and give your daughters in marriage, so that they too may have sons and daughters. Increase in number there; do not decrease. ⁷Also, seek the peace and prosperity of the city

---

JEREMIAH 28

QUIZZER

Q: Hananiah predicted the Jews would return from Babylon in two years (Jeremiah 28:3). Was he right?

BONUS: What did Jeremiah predict would happen to Hananiah?

Answers on page 1021

---

[a] 4,2 Hebrew *Jeconiah*, a variant of *Jehoiachin*

to which I have carried you into exile. Pray to the LORD for it, because if it prospers, you too will prosper." [8]Yes, this is what the LORD Almighty, the God of Israel, says: "Do not let the prophets and diviners among you deceive you. Do not listen to the dreams you encourage them to have. [9]They are prophesying lies to you in my name. I have not sent them," declares the LORD.

[10]This is what the LORD says: "When seventy years are completed for Babylon, I will come to you and fulfill my gracious promise to bring you back to this place. [11]For I know the plans I have for you," declares the LORD, "plans to prosper you and not to harm you, plans to give you hope and a future. [12]Then you will call upon me and come and pray to me, and I will listen to you. [13]You will seek me and find me when you seek me with all your heart. [14]I will be found by you," declares the LORD, "and will bring you back from captivity.[a] I will gather you from all the nations and places where I have banished you," declares the LORD, "and will bring you back to the place from which I carried you into exile."

[15]You may say, "The LORD has raised up prophets for us in Babylon," [16]but this is what the LORD says about the king who sits on David's throne and all the people who remain in this city, your countrymen who did not go with you into exile— [17]yes, this is what the LORD Almighty says: "I will send the sword, famine and plague against them and I will make them like poor figs that are so bad they cannot be eaten. [18]I will pursue them with the sword, famine and plague and will make them abhorrent to all the kingdoms of the earth and an object of cursing and horror, of scorn and reproach, among all the nations where I drive them. [19]For they have not listened to my words," declares the LORD, "words that I sent to them again and again by my servants the prophets. And you exiles have not listened either," declares the LORD.

[20]Therefore, hear the word of the LORD, all you exiles whom I have sent away from Jerusalem to Babylon. [21]This is what the LORD Almighty, the God of Israel, says about Ahab son of Kolaiah and Zedekiah son of Maaseiah, who are prophesying lies to you in my name: "I will hand them over to Nebuchadnezzar king of Babylon, and he will put them to death before your very eyes. [22]Because of them, all the exiles from Judah who are in Babylon will use this curse: 'The LORD treat you like Zedekiah and Ahab, whom the king of Babylon burned in the fire.' [23]For they have done outrageous things in Israel; they have committed adultery with their neighbors' wives and in my name have spoken lies, which I did not tell them to do. I know it and am a witness to it," declares the LORD.

Message to Shemaiah [24]Tell Shemaiah the Nehelamite, [25]"This is what the LORD Almighty, the God of Israel, says: You sent letters in your own name to all the people in Jerusalem, to Zephaniah son of Maaseiah the priest, and to all the other priests. You said to Zephaniah, [26]'The LORD has appointed you priest in place of Jehoiada to be in charge of the house of the LORD; you should put any madman who acts like a prophet into the stocks and neck-irons. [27]So why have you not reprimanded Jeremiah from Anathoth, who poses as a prophet among you? [28]He has sent this message to us in Babylon: It will be a long time. Therefore build houses and settle down; plant gardens and eat what they produce.' "

[29]Zephaniah the priest, however, read the letter to Jeremiah the prophet. [30]Then the word of the LORD came to Jeremiah: [31]"Send this message to all the exiles: 'This is what the LORD says about Shemaiah the Nehelamite: Because Shemaiah has prophesied to you, even though I did not send him, and has

---

[a]14 Or *will restore your fortunes*

Dear Sam,

    I spend most of my free time thinking about killing myself. Nobody loves me, and I never do anything right. I don't want to hurt anyone, but I'm tired of feeling this way. What should I do?

Becky in Bedford

100 Advice Lane, Anywhere, USA

Dear Sam, Inc.

Dear Becky,

    Wanting to kill yourself is a drastic way of escape. You say you don't want to hurt anyone else. If you killed yourself, how do you think your parents, brothers or sisters, other family members, friends and teachers would feel? Absolutely devastated!

    You must get some help. Many times deep depression has a physical cause. Other times emotional problems begin to take over, and people feel overwhelmed by life. Both of these can be overcome by appropriate medication or counseling or both. Talk to one of your parents if you can; otherwise, go to a school psychologist, social worker, counselor or church youth leader. Tell this person what you are feeling and that you need help.

    God has good plans for you, plans that include hope and a future (Jeremiah 29:11-13). Seek him. Get good professional help for your depression. God can bless you in more ways than you can imagine. Give him a chance. And give those around you a chance to help you. Then give yourself a chance to live.

Sam

led you to believe a lie, [32]this is what the Lord says: I will surely punish Shemaiah the Nehelamite and his descendants. He will have no one left among this people, nor will he see the good things I will do for my people, declares the Lord, because he has preached rebellion against me.' "

30 *Restoration of Israel* This is the word that came to Jeremiah from the Lord: [2]"This is what the Lord, the God of Israel, says: 'Write in a book all the words I have spoken to you. [3]The days are coming,' declares the Lord, 'when I will bring my people Israel and Judah back from captivity[a] and restore them to the land I gave their forefathers to possess,' says the Lord."

[4]These are the words the Lord spoke concerning Israel and Judah: [5]"This is what the Lord says:

> " 'Cries of fear are heard—
>   terror, not peace.
> [6]Ask and see:
>   Can a man bear children?
> Then why do I see every strong man
>   with his hands on his stomach like a woman in labor,
>   every face turned deathly pale?
> [7]How awful that day will be!
>   None will be like it.
> It will be a time of trouble for Jacob,
>   but he will be saved out of it.

> [8]" 'In that day,' declares the Lord Almighty,
>   'I will break the yoke off their necks
> and will tear off their bonds;
>   no longer will foreigners enslave them.
> [9]Instead, they will serve the Lord their God
>   and David their king,
>   whom I will raise up for them.

> [10]" 'So do not fear, O Jacob my servant;
>   do not be dismayed, O Israel,'

> declares the Lord.

> 'I will surely save you out of a distant place,
>   your descendants from the land of their exile.
> Jacob will again have peace and security,
>   and no one will make him afraid.
> [11]I am with you and will save you,'
>   declares the Lord.
> 'Though I completely destroy all the nations
>   among which I scatter you,
>   I will not completely destroy you.
> I will discipline you but only with justice;
>   I will not let you go entirely unpunished.'

[12]"This is what the Lord says:

> " 'Your wound is incurable,
>   your injury beyond healing.
> [13]There is no one to plead your cause,
>   no remedy for your sore,
>   no healing for you.
> [14]All your allies have forgotten you;
>   they care nothing for you.

---

[a]3 Or *will restore the fortunes of my people Israel and Judah*

I have struck you as an enemy would
   and punished you as would the cruel,
because your guilt is so great
   and your sins so many.
¹⁵Why do you cry out over your wound,
   your pain that has no cure?
Because of your great guilt and many sins
   I have done these things to you.

¹⁶" 'But all who devour you will be devoured;
   all your enemies will go into exile.
Those who plunder you will be plundered;
   all who make spoil of you I will despoil.
¹⁷But I will restore you to health
   and heal your wounds,'

           declares the LORD,

'because you are called an outcast,
   Zion for whom no one cares.'

¹⁸"This is what the LORD says:

" 'I will restore the fortunes of Jacob's tents
   and have compassion on his dwellings;
the city will be rebuilt on her ruins,
   and the palace will stand in its proper place.
¹⁹From them will come songs of thanksgiving
   and the sound of rejoicing.
I will add to their numbers,
   and they will not be decreased;
I will bring them honor,
   and they will not be disdained.
²⁰Their children will be as in days of old,
   and their community will be established before me;
   I will punish all who oppress them.
²¹Their leader will be one of their own;
   their ruler will arise from among them.
I will bring him near and he will come close to me,
   for who is he who will devote himself
   to be close to me?'

           declares the LORD.

²²" 'So you will be my people,
   and I will be your God.' "

²³See, the storm of the LORD
   will burst out in wrath,
a driving wind swirling down
   on the heads of the wicked.
²⁴The fierce anger of the LORD will not turn back
   until he fully accomplishes
   the purposes of his heart.
In days to come
   you will understand this.

31 "At that time," declares the LORD, "I will be the God of all the clans
of Israel, and they will be my people."
²This is what the LORD says:

"The people who survive the sword
   will find favor in the desert;
I will come to give rest to Israel."

³The Lord appeared to us in the past,ᵃ saying:

"I have loved you with an everlasting love;
        I have drawn you with loving-kindness.
⁴I will build you up again
        and you will be rebuilt, O Virgin Israel.
Again you will take up your tambourines
        and go out to dance with the joyful.
⁵Again you will plant vineyards
        on the hills of Samaria;
the farmers will plant them
        and enjoy their fruit.
⁶There will be a day when watchmen cry out
        on the hills of Ephraim,
'Come, let us go up to Zion,
        to the Lord our God.' "

⁷This is what the Lord says:

"Sing with joy for Jacob;
        shout for the foremost of the nations.
Make your praises heard, and say,
        'O Lord, save your people,
        the remnant of Israel.'
⁸See, I will bring them from the land of the north
        and gather them from the ends of the earth.
Among them will be the blind and the lame,
        expectant mothers and women in labor;
        a great throng will return.
⁹They will come with weeping;
        they will pray as I bring them back.
I will lead them beside streams of water
        on a level path where they will not stumble,
because I am Israel's father,
        and Ephraim is my firstborn son.

¹⁰"Hear the word of the Lord, O nations;
        proclaim it in distant coastlands:
'He who scattered Israel will gather them
        and will watch over his flock like a shepherd.'
¹¹For the Lord will ransom Jacob
        and redeem them from the hand of those stronger than
                they.
¹²They will come and shout for joy on the heights of Zion;
        they will rejoice in the bounty of the Lord—
the grain, the new wine and the oil,
        the young of the flocks and herds.
They will be like a well-watered garden,
        and they will sorrow no more.
¹³Then maidens will dance and be glad,
        young men and old as well.
I will turn their mourning into gladness;
        I will give them comfort and joy instead of sorrow.
¹⁴I will satisfy the priests with abundance,
        and my people will be filled with my bounty,"
                                        declares the Lord.

ᵃ3 Or *Lord has appeared to us from afar*

¹⁵This is what the LORD says:

"A voice is heard in Ramah,
    mourning and great weeping,
Rachel weeping for her children
    and refusing to be comforted,
    because her children are no more."

¹⁶This is what the LORD says:

"Restrain your voice from weeping
    and your eyes from tears,
for your work will be rewarded,"

                    declares the LORD.
    "They will return from the land of the enemy.
¹⁷So there is hope for your future,"

                    declares the LORD.
    "Your children will return to their own land.

¹⁸"I have surely heard Ephraim's moaning:
    'You disciplined me like an unruly calf,
    and I have been disciplined.
Restore me, and I will return,
    because you are the LORD my God.
¹⁹After I strayed,
    I repented;
after I came to understand,
    I beat my breast.
I was ashamed and humiliated
    because I bore the disgrace of my youth.'
²⁰Is not Ephraim my dear son,
    the child in whom I delight?
Though I often speak against him,
    I still remember him.
Therefore my heart yearns
        for him;
    I have great compassion for
        him,"
            declares the LORD.

²¹"Set up road signs;
    put up guideposts.
Take note of the highway,
    the road that you take.
Return, O Virgin Israel,
    return to your towns.
²²How long will you wander,
    O unfaithful daughter?
The LORD will create a new
        thing on earth—
    a woman will surround*ᵃ* a
        man."

²³This is what the LORD Almighty, the God of Israel, says: "When I bring them back from captivity,*ᵇ* the people in the land of Judah and in its towns will once

ᵃ22 Or will go about seeking; or will protect   ᵇ23 Or I restore their fortunes

Now that's a promise I'm looking forward to seeing!

SEE JEREMIAH 31:13

again use these words: 'The Lord bless you, O righteous dwelling, O sacred mountain.' ²⁴People will live together in Judah and all its towns—farmers and those who move about with their flocks. ²⁵I will refresh the weary and satisfy the faint."

²⁶At this I awoke and looked around. My sleep had been pleasant to me.

²⁷"The days are coming," declares the Lord, "when I will plant the house of Israel and the house of Judah with the offspring of men and of animals. ²⁸Just as I watched over them to uproot and tear down, and to overthrow, destroy and bring disaster, so I will watch over them to build and to plant," declares the Lord. ²⁹"In those days people will no longer say,

> 'The fathers have eaten sour grapes,
>   and the children's teeth are set on edge.'

³⁰Instead, everyone will die for his own sin; whoever eats sour grapes—his own teeth will be set on edge.

> ³¹"The time is coming," declares the Lord,
>   "when I will make a new covenant
> with the house of Israel
>   and with the house of Judah.
> ³²It will not be like the covenant
>   I made with their forefathers
> when I took them by the hand
>   to lead them out of Egypt,
> because they broke my covenant,
>   though I was a husband to*ᵃ* them,*ᵇ*"
>   declares the Lord.
> ³³"This is the covenant I will make with the house of Israel
>   after that time," declares the Lord.
> "I will put my law in their minds
>   and write it on their hearts.
> I will be their God,
>   and they will be my people.
> ³⁴No longer will a man teach his neighbor,
>   or a man his brother, saying, 'Know the Lord,'
> because they will all know me,
>   from the least of them to the greatest,"
>   declares the Lord.
> "For I will forgive their wickedness
>   and will remember their sins no more."

³⁵This is what the Lord says,

> he who appoints the sun
>   to shine by day,
> who decrees the moon and stars
>   to shine by night,
> who stirs up the sea
>   so that its waves roar—
>   the Lord Almighty is his name:
> ³⁶"Only if these decrees vanish from my sight,"
>   declares the Lord,
> "will the descendants of Israel ever cease
>   to be a nation before me."

ᵃ32 Hebrew; Septuagint and Syriac / *and I turned away from*   *ᵇ32* Or *was their master*

³⁷This is what the LORD says:

> "Only if the heavens above can be measured
>> and the foundations of the earth below be searched out
> will I reject all the descendants of Israel
>> because of all they have done,"

declares the LORD.

³⁸"The days are coming," declares the LORD, "when this city will be rebuilt for me from the Tower of Hananel to the Corner Gate. ³⁹The measuring line will stretch from there straight to the hill of Gareb and then turn to Goah. ⁴⁰The whole valley where dead bodies and ashes are thrown, and all the terraces out to the Kidron Valley on the east as far as the corner of the Horse Gate, will be holy to the LORD. The city will never again be uprooted or demolished."

Jeremiah Buys a Field This is the word that came to Jeremiah from the LORD in the tenth year of Zedekiah king of Judah, which was the eighteenth year of Nebuchadnezzar. ²The army of the king of Babylon was then besieging Jerusalem, and Jeremiah the prophet was confined in the courtyard of the guard in the royal palace of Judah.

³Now Zedekiah king of Judah had imprisoned him there, saying, "Why do you prophesy as you do? You say, 'This is what the LORD says: I am about to hand this city over to the king of Babylon, and he will capture it. ⁴Zedekiah king of Judah will not escape out of the hands of the Babylonians*ᵃ* but will certainly be handed over to the king of Babylon, and will speak with him face to face and see him with his own eyes. ⁵He will take Zedekiah to Babylon, where he will remain until I deal with him, declares the LORD. If you fight against the Babylonians, you will not succeed.' "

⁶Jeremiah said, "The word of the LORD came to me: ⁷Hanamel son of Shallum your uncle is going to come to you and say, 'Buy my field at Anathoth, because as nearest relative it is your right and duty to buy it.'

⁸"Then, just as the LORD had said, my cousin Hanamel came to me in the courtyard of the guard and said, 'Buy my field at Anathoth in the territory of Benjamin. Since it is your right to redeem it and possess it, buy it for yourself.'

"I knew that this was the word of the LORD; ⁹so I bought the field at Anathoth from my cousin Hanamel and weighed out for him seventeen shekels*ᵇ* of silver. ¹⁰I signed and sealed the deed, had it witnessed, and weighed out the silver on the scales. ¹¹I took the deed of purchase—the sealed copy containing the terms and conditions, as well as the unsealed copy— ¹²and I gave this deed to Baruch son of Neriah, the son of Mahseiah, in the presence of my cousin Hanamel and of the witnesses who had signed the deed and of all the Jews sitting in the courtyard of the guard.

¹³"In their presence I gave Baruch these instructions: ¹⁴This is what the LORD Almighty, the God of Israel, says: Take these documents, both the sealed and unsealed copies of the deed of purchase, and put them in a clay jar so they will last a long time. ¹⁵For this is what the LORD Almighty, the God of Israel, says: Houses, fields and vineyards will again be bought in this land.'

¹⁶"After I had given the deed of purchase to Baruch son of Neriah, I prayed to the LORD:

¹⁷"Ah, Sovereign LORD, you have made the heavens and the earth by your great power and outstretched arm. Nothing is too hard for you. ¹⁸You show love to thousands but bring the punishment for the fathers' sins

---

ᵃ4 Or *Chaldeans;* also in verses 5, 24, 25, 28, 29 and 43   *ᵇ9* That is, about 7 ounces (about 200 grams)

into the laps of their children after them. O great and powerful God, whose name is the LORD Almighty, [19]great are your purposes and mighty are your deeds. Your eyes are open to all the ways of men; you reward everyone according to his conduct and as his deeds deserve. [20]You performed miraculous signs and wonders in Egypt and have continued them to this day, both in Israel and among all mankind, and have gained the renown that is still yours. [21]You brought your people Israel out of Egypt with signs and wonders, by a mighty hand and an outstretched arm and with great terror. [22]You gave them this land you had sworn to give their forefathers, a land flowing with milk and honey. [23]They came in and took possession of it, but they did not obey you or follow your law; they did not do what you commanded them to do. So you brought all this disaster upon them.

[24]"See how the siege ramps are built up to take the city. Because of the sword, famine and plague, the city will be handed over to the Babylonians who are attacking it. What you said has happened, as you now see. [25]And though the city will be handed over to the Babylonians, you, O Sovereign LORD, say to me, 'Buy the field with silver and have the transaction witnessed.' "

[26]Then the word of the LORD came to Jeremiah: [27]"I am the LORD, the God of all mankind. Is anything too hard for me? [28]Therefore, this is what the LORD says: I am about to hand this city over to the Babylonians and to Nebuchadnezzar king of Babylon, who will capture it. [29]The Babylonians who are attacking this city will come in and set it on fire; they will burn it down, along with the houses where the people provoked me to anger by burning incense on the roofs to Baal and by pouring out drink offerings to other gods.

[30]"The people of Israel and Judah have done nothing but evil in my sight from their youth; indeed, the people of Israel have done nothing but provoke me with what their hands have made, declares the LORD. [31]From the day it was built until now, this city has so aroused my anger and wrath that I must remove it from my sight. [32]The people of Israel and Judah have provoked me by all the evil they have done—they, their kings and officials, their priests and prophets, the men of Judah and the people of Jerusalem. [33]They turned their backs to me and not their faces; though I taught them again and again, they would not listen or respond to discipline. [34]They set up their abominable idols in the house that bears my Name and defiled it. [35]They built high places for Baal in the Valley of Ben Hinnom to sacrifice their sons and daughters[a] to Molech, though I never commanded, nor did it enter my mind, that they should do such a detestable thing and so make Judah sin.

> I will make an everlasting covenant with them: I will never stop doing good to them (Jeremiah 32:40).

[36]"You are saying about this city, 'By the sword, famine and plague it will be handed over to the king of Babylon'; but this is what the LORD, the God of Israel, says: [37]I will surely gather them from all the lands where I banish them in my furious anger and great wrath; I will bring them back to this place and let them live in safety. [38]They will be my people, and I will be their God. [39]I will give them singleness of heart and action, so that they will always fear me for their own good and the good of their children after them. [40]I will make an everlasting covenant with them: I will never stop doing good to them, and I will inspire them to fear me, so that they will never turn away from me. [41]I will rejoice in doing them good and will assuredly plant them in this land with all my heart and soul.

[42]"This is what the LORD says: As I have brought all this great calamity on

[a]35 Or *to make their sons and daughters pass through the fire*

this people, so I will give them all the prosperity I have promised them. ⁴³Once more fields will be bought in this land of which you say, 'It is a desolate waste, without men or animals, for it has been handed over to the Babylonians.' ⁴⁴Fields will be bought for silver, and deeds will be signed, sealed and witnessed in the territory of Benjamin, in the villages around Jerusalem, in the towns of Judah and in the towns of the hill country, of the western foothills and of the Negev, because I will restore their fortunes,ᵃ declares the LORD."

33 *Promise of Restoration* While Jeremiah was still confined in the courtyard of the guard, the word of the LORD came to him a second time: ²"This is what the LORD says, he who made the earth, the LORD who formed it and established it—the LORD is his name: ³'Call to me and I will answer you and tell you great and unsearchable things you do not know.' ⁴For this is what the LORD, the God of Israel, says about the houses in this city and the royal palaces of Judah that have been torn down to be used against the siege ramps and the sword ⁵in the fight with the Babyloniansᵇ: 'They will be filled with the dead bodies of the men I will slay in my anger and wrath. I will hide my face from this city because of all its wickedness.

⁶" 'Nevertheless, I will bring health and healing to it; I will heal my people and will let them enjoy abundant peace and security. ⁷I will bring Judah and Israel back from captivityᶜ and will rebuild them as they were before. ⁸I will cleanse them from all the sin they have committed against me and will forgive all their sins of rebellion against me. ⁹Then this city will bring me renown, joy, praise and honor before all nations on earth that hear of all the good things I do for it; and they will be in awe and will tremble at the abundant prosperity and peace I provide for it.'

¹⁰"This is what the LORD says: 'You say about this place, "It is a desolate waste, without men or animals." Yet in the towns of Judah and the streets of Jerusalem that are deserted, inhabited by neither men nor animals, there will be heard once more ¹¹the sounds of joy and gladness, the voices of bride and bridegroom, and the voices of those who bring thank offerings to the house of the LORD, saying,

> "Give thanks to the LORD Almighty,
>   for the LORD is good;
>   his love endures forever."

For I will restore the fortunes of the land as they were before,' says the LORD. ¹²"This is what the LORD Almighty says: 'In this place, desolate and without men or animals—in all its towns there will again be pastures for shepherds to rest their flocks. ¹³In the towns of the hill country, of the western foothills and of the Negev, in the territory of Benjamin, in the villages around Jerusalem and in the towns of Judah, flocks will again pass under the hand of the one who counts them,' says the LORD.

¹⁴" 'The days are coming,' declares the LORD, 'when I will fulfill the gracious promise I made to the house of Israel and to the house of Judah.

> ¹⁵ " 'In those days and at that time
>   I will make a righteous Branch sprout from David's line;
>   he will do what is just and right in the land.
> ¹⁶In those days Judah will be saved
>   and Jerusalem will live in safety.
> This is the name by which itᵈ will be called:
>   The LORD Our Righteousness.'

ᵃ44 Or *will bring them back from captivity*   ᵇ5 Or *Chaldeans*   ᶜ7 Or *will restore the fortunes of Judah and Israel*   ᵈ16 Or *he*

[17]For this is what the LORD says: 'David will never fail to have a man to sit on the throne of the house of Israel, [18]nor will the priests, who are Levites, ever fail to have a man to stand before me continually to offer burnt offerings, to burn grain offerings and to present sacrifices.' "

[19]The word of the LORD came to Jeremiah: [20]"This is what the LORD says: 'If you can break my covenant with the day and my covenant with the night, so that day and night no longer come at their appointed time, [21]then my covenant with David my servant—and my covenant with the Levites who are priests ministering before me—can be broken and David will no longer have a descendant to reign on his throne. [22]I will make the descendants of David my servant and the Levites who minister before me as countless as the stars of the sky and as measureless as the sand on the seashore.' "

[23]The word of the LORD came to Jeremiah: [24]"Have you not noticed that these people are saying, 'The LORD has rejected the two kingdoms[a] he chose'? So they despise my people and no longer regard them as a nation. [25]This is what the LORD says: 'If I have not established my covenant with day and night and the fixed laws of heaven and earth, [26]then I will reject the descendants of Jacob and David my servant and will not choose one of his sons to rule over the descendants of Abraham, Isaac and Jacob. For I will restore their fortunes[b] and have compassion on them.' "

34 *Warning to Zedekiah* While Nebuchadnezzar king of Babylon and all his army and all the kingdoms and peoples in the empire he ruled were fighting against Jerusalem and all its surrounding towns, this word came to Jeremiah from the LORD: [2]"This is what the LORD, the God of Israel, says: Go to Zedekiah king of Judah and tell him, 'This is what the LORD says: I am about to hand this city over to the king of Babylon, and he will burn it down. [3]You will not escape from his grasp but will surely be captured and handed over to him. You will see the king of Babylon with your own eyes, and he will speak with you face to face. And you will go to Babylon.

[4]" 'Yet hear the promise of the LORD, O Zedekiah king of Judah. This is what the LORD says concerning you: You will not die by the sword; [5]you will die peacefully. As people made a funeral fire in honor of your fathers, the former kings who preceded you, so they will make a fire in your honor and lament, "Alas, O master!" I myself make this promise, declares the LORD.' "

[6]Then Jeremiah the prophet told all this to Zedekiah king of Judah, in Jerusalem, [7]while the army of the king of Babylon was fighting against Jerusalem and the other cities of Judah that were still holding out—Lachish and Azekah. These were the only fortified cities left in Judah.

Freedom for Slaves [8]The word came to Jeremiah from the LORD after King Zedekiah had made a covenant with all the people in Jerusalem to proclaim freedom for the slaves. [9]Everyone was to free his Hebrew slaves, both male and female; no one was to hold a fellow Jew in bondage. [10]So all the officials and people who entered into this covenant agreed that they would free their male and female slaves and no longer hold them in bondage. They agreed, and set them free. [11]But afterward they changed their minds and took back the slaves they had freed and enslaved them again.

[12]Then the word of the LORD came to Jeremiah: [13]"This is what the LORD, the God of Israel, says: I made a covenant with your forefathers when I brought them out of Egypt, out of the land of slavery. I said, [14]'Every seventh year each of you must free any fellow Hebrew who has sold himself to you. After he has served you six years, you must let him go free.'[c] Your fathers, however, did not listen to me or pay attention to me. [15]Recently you repented and did what is right in my sight: Each of you proclaimed freedom to his coun-

---

[a]24 Or *families*   [b]26 Or *will bring them back from captivity*   [c]14 Deut. 15:12

trymen. You even made a covenant before me in the house that bears my Name. ¹⁶But now you have turned around and profaned my name; each of you has taken back the male and female slaves you had set free to go where they wished. You have forced them to become your slaves again.

¹⁷"Therefore, this is what the LORD says: You have not obeyed me; you have not proclaimed freedom for your fellow countrymen. So I now proclaim 'freedom' for you, declares the LORD—'freedom' to fall by the sword, plague and famine. I will make you abhorrent to all the kingdoms of the earth. ¹⁸The men who have violated my covenant and have not fulfilled the terms of the covenant they made before me, I will treat like the calf they cut in two and then walked between its pieces. ¹⁹The leaders of Judah and Jerusalem, the court officials, the priests and all the people of the land who walked between the pieces of the calf, ²⁰I will hand over to their enemies who seek their lives. Their dead bodies will become food for the birds of the air and the beasts of the earth.

²¹"I will hand Zedekiah king of Judah and his officials over to their enemies who seek their lives, to the army of the king of Babylon, which has withdrawn from you. ²²I am going to give the order, declares the LORD, and I will bring them back to this city. They will fight against it, take it and burn it down. And I will lay waste the towns of Judah so no one can live there."

35 **The Recabites** This is the word that came to Jeremiah from the LORD during the reign of Jehoiakim son of Josiah king of Judah: ²"Go to the Recabite family and invite them to come to one of the side rooms of the house of the LORD and give them wine to drink."

³So I went to get Jaazaniah son of Jeremiah, the son of Habazziniah, and his brothers and all his sons—the whole family of the Recabites. ⁴I brought them into the house of the LORD, into the room of the sons of Hanan son of Igdaliah the man of God. It was next to the room of the officials, which was over that of Maaseiah son of Shallum the doorkeeper. ⁵Then I set bowls full of wine and some cups before the men of the Recabite family and said to them, "Drink some wine."

⁶But they replied, "We do not drink wine, because our forefather Jonadab son of Recab gave us this command: 'Neither you nor your descendants must ever drink wine. ⁷Also you must never build houses, sow seed or plant vineyards; you must never have any of these things, but must always live in tents. Then you will live a long time in the land where you are nomads.' ⁸We have obeyed everything our forefather Jonadab son of Recab commanded us. Neither we nor our wives nor our sons and daughters have ever drunk wine ⁹or built houses to live in or had vineyards, fields or crops. ¹⁰We have lived in tents and have fully obeyed everything our forefather Jonadab commanded us. ¹¹But when Nebuchadnezzar king of Babylon invaded this land, we said, 'Come, we must go to Jerusalem to escape the Babylonian*ᵃ* and Aramean armies.' So we have remained in Jerusalem."

ᵃ11 Or Chaldean

JEREMIAH 35

Read the end of the story first. The Lord tells the family, "You have obeyed the command of your forefather" (Jeremiah 35:18). As a result, God promised to bless them. When the Bible says honor your parents, it doesn't just mean you should be polite. Part of honoring parents is respecting their beliefs and values and seriously considering making their beliefs and values your own. So don't talk about your parents "forcing you" to go to church. Go, listen actively, and seriously consider the claims of Christ. Mom and Dad can't believe for you, but you can honor them by taking an honest, open look at their faith.

Direct Line

¹²Then the word of the Lord came to Jeremiah, saying: ¹³"This is what the Lord Almighty, the God of Israel, says: Go and tell the men of Judah and the people of Jerusalem, 'Will you not learn a lesson and obey my words?' declares the Lord. ¹⁴Jonadab son of Recab ordered his sons not to drink wine and this command has been kept. To this day they do not drink wine, because they obey their forefather's command. But I have spoken to you again and again, yet you have not obeyed me. ¹⁵Again and again I sent all my servants the prophets to you. They said, "Each of you must turn from your wicked ways and reform your actions; do not follow other gods to serve them. Then you will live in the land I have given to you and your fathers." But you have not paid attention or listened to me. ¹⁶The descendants of Jonadab son of Recab have carried out the command their forefather gave them, but these people have not obeyed me.'

¹⁷"Therefore, this is what the Lord God Almighty, the God of Israel, says: 'Listen! I am going to bring on Judah and on everyone living in Jerusalem every disaster I pronounced against them. I spoke to them, but they did not listen; I called to them, but they did not answer.'"

¹⁸Then Jeremiah said to the family of the Recabites, "This is what the Lord Almighty, the God of Israel, says: 'You have obeyed the command of your forefather Jonadab and have followed all his instructions and have done everything he ordered.' ¹⁹Therefore, this is what the Lord Almighty, the God of Israel, says: 'Jonadab son of Recab will never fail to have a man to serve me.'"

36 *Jehoiakim Burns Jeremiah's Scroll* In the fourth year of Jehoiakim son of Josiah king of Judah, this word came to Jeremiah from the Lord: ²"Take a scroll and write on it all the words I have spoken to you concerning Israel, Judah and all the other nations from the time I began speaking to you in the reign of Josiah till now. ³Perhaps when the people of Judah hear about every disaster I plan to inflict on them, each of them will turn from his wicked way; then I will forgive their wickedness and their sin."

⁴So Jeremiah called Baruch son of Neriah, and while Jeremiah dictated all the words the Lord had spoken to him, Baruch wrote them on the scroll. ⁵Then Jeremiah told Baruch, "I am restricted; I cannot go to the Lord's temple. ⁶So you go to the house of the Lord on a day of fasting and read to the people from the scroll the words of the Lord that you wrote as I dictated. Read them to all the people of Judah who come in from their towns. ⁷Perhaps they will bring their petition before the Lord, and each will turn from his wicked ways, for the anger and wrath pronounced against this people by the Lord are great."

⁸Baruch son of Neriah did everything Jeremiah the prophet told him to do; at the Lord's temple he read the words of the Lord from the scroll. ⁹In the ninth month of the fifth year of Jehoiakim son of Josiah king of Judah, a time of fasting before the Lord was proclaimed for all the people in Jerusalem and those who had come from the towns of Judah. ¹⁰From the room of Gemariah son of Shaphan the secretary, which was in the upper courtyard at the entrance of the New Gate of the temple, Baruch read to all the people at the Lord's temple the words of Jeremiah from the scroll.

¹¹When Micaiah son of Gemariah, the son of Shaphan, heard all the words of the Lord from the scroll, ¹²he went down to the secretary's room in the royal palace, where all the officials were sitting: Elishama the secretary, Delaiah son of Shemaiah, Elnathan son of Acbor, Gemariah son of Shaphan, Zedekiah son of Hananiah, and all the other officials. ¹³After Micaiah told them everything he had heard Baruch read to the people from the scroll, ¹⁴all the officials sent Jehudi son of Nethaniah, the son of Shelemiah, the son of Cushi, to say to Baruch, "Bring the scroll from which you have read to the

people and come." So Baruch son of Neriah went to them with the scroll in his hand. ¹⁵They said to him, "Sit down, please, and read it to us."

So Baruch read it to them. ¹⁶When they heard all these words, they looked at each other in fear and said to Baruch, "We must report all these words to the king." ¹⁷Then they asked Baruch, "Tell us, how did you come to write all this? Did Jeremiah dictate it?"

¹⁸"Yes," Baruch replied, "he dictated all these words to me, and I wrote them in ink on the scroll."

¹⁹Then the officials said to Baruch, "You and Jeremiah, go and hide. Don't let anyone know where you are."

²⁰After they put the scroll in the room of Elishama the secretary, they went to the king in the courtyard and reported everything to him. ²¹The king sent Jehudi to get the scroll, and Jehudi brought it from the room of Elishama the secretary and read it to the king and all the officials standing beside him. ²²It was the ninth month and the king was sitting in the winter apartment, with a fire burning in the firepot in front of him. ²³Whenever Jehudi had read three or four columns of the scroll, the king cut them off with a scribe's knife and threw them into the firepot, until the entire scroll was burned in the fire. ²⁴The king and all his attendants who heard all these words showed no fear, nor did they tear their clothes. ²⁵Even though Elnathan, Delaiah and Gemariah urged the king not to burn the scroll, he would not listen to them. ²⁶Instead, the king commanded Jerahmeel, a son of the king, Seraiah son of Azriel and Shelemiah son of Abdeel to arrest Baruch the scribe and Jeremiah the prophet. But the LORD had hidden them.

²⁷After the king burned the scroll containing the words that Baruch had written at Jeremiah's dictation, the word of the LORD came to Jeremiah: ²⁸"Take another scroll and write on it all the words that were on the first scroll, which Jehoiakim king of Judah burned up. ²⁹Also tell Jehoiakim king of Judah, 'This is what the LORD says: You burned that scroll and said, "Why did you write on it that the king of Babylon would certainly come and destroy this land and cut off both men and animals from it?" ³⁰Therefore, this is what the LORD says about Jehoiakim king of Judah: He will have no one to sit on the throne of David; his body will be thrown out and exposed to the heat by day and the frost by night. ³¹I will punish him and his children and his attendants for their wickedness; I will bring on them and those living in Jerusalem and the people of Judah every disaster I pronounced against them, because they have not listened.' "

³²So Jeremiah took another scroll and gave it to the scribe Baruch son of Neriah, and as Jeremiah dictated, Baruch wrote on it all the words of the scroll that Jehoiakim king of Judah had burned in the fire. And many similar words were added to them.

37 **Jeremiah in Prison** Zedekiah son of Josiah was made king of Judah by Nebuchadnezzar king of Babylon; he reigned in place of Jehoiachinᵃ son of Jehoiakim. ²Neither he nor his attendants nor the people of the land paid any attention to the words the LORD had spoken through Jeremiah the prophet.

³King Zedekiah, however, sent Jehucal son of Shelemiah with the priest Zephaniah son of Maaseiah to Jeremiah the prophet with this message: "Please pray to the LORD our God for us."

⁴Now Jeremiah was free to come and go among the people, for he had not yet been put in prison. ⁵Pharaoh's army had marched out of Egypt, and when

---

JEREMIAH 36

QU*ZZER*

Q: What did King Jehoiakim do with Jeremiah's scroll?

BONUS: How did God react to what King Jehoiakim did?

Answers on page 1032

ᵃ1 Hebrew *Coniah*, a variant of *Jehoiachin*

the Babylonians[a] who were besieging Jerusalem heard the report about them, they withdrew from Jerusalem.

⁶Then the word of the LORD came to Jeremiah the prophet: ⁷"This is what the LORD, the God of Israel, says: Tell the king of Judah, who sent you to inquire of me, 'Pharaoh's army, which has marched out to support you, will go back to its own land, to Egypt. ⁸Then the Babylonians will return and attack this city; they will capture it and burn it down.'

⁹"This is what the LORD says: Do not deceive yourselves, thinking, 'The Babylonians will surely leave us.' They will not! ¹⁰Even if you were to defeat the entire Babylonian[b] army that is attacking you and only wounded men were left in their tents, they would come out and burn this city down."

¹¹After the Babylonian army had withdrawn from Jerusalem because of Pharaoh's army, ¹²Jeremiah started to leave the city to go to the territory of Benjamin to get his share of the property among the people there. ¹³But when he reached the Benjamin Gate, the captain of the guard, whose name was Irijah son of Shelemiah, the son of Hananiah, arrested him and said, "You are deserting to the Babylonians!"

¹⁴"That's not true!" Jeremiah said. "I am not deserting to the Babylonians." But Irijah would not listen to him; instead, he arrested Jeremiah and brought him to the officials. ¹⁵They were angry with Jeremiah and had him beaten and imprisoned in the house of Jonathan the secretary, which they had made into a prison.

¹⁶Jeremiah was put into a vaulted cell in a dungeon, where he remained a long time. ¹⁷Then King Zedekiah sent for him and had him brought to the palace, where he asked him privately, "Is there any word from the LORD?"

"Yes," Jeremiah replied, "you will be handed over to the king of Babylon."

¹⁸Then Jeremiah said to King Zedekiah, "What crime have I committed against you or your officials or this people, that you have put me in prison? ¹⁹Where are your prophets who prophesied to you, 'The king of Babylon will not attack you or this land'? ²⁰But now, my lord the king, please listen. Let me bring my petition before you: Do not send me back to the house of Jonathan the secretary, or I will die there."

²¹King Zedekiah then gave orders for Jeremiah to be placed in the courtyard of the guard and given bread from the street of the bakers each day until all the bread in the city was gone. So Jeremiah remained in the courtyard of the guard.

38 **Jeremiah Thrown Into a Cistern** Shephatiah son of Mattan, Gedaliah son of Pashhur, Jehucal[c] son of Shelemiah, and Pashhur son of Malkijah heard what Jeremiah was telling all the people when he said, ²"This is what the LORD says: 'Whoever stays in this city will die by the sword, famine or plague, but whoever goes over to the Babylonians[d] will live. He will escape with his life; he will live.' ³And this is what the LORD says: 'This city will certainly be handed over to the army of the king of Babylon, who will capture it.' "

⁴Then the officials said to the king, "This man should be put to death. He is discouraging the soldiers who are left in this city, as well as all the people, by the things he is saying to them. This man is not seeking the good of these people but their ruin."

⁵"He is in your hands," King Zedekiah answered. "The king can do nothing to oppose you."

⁶So they took Jeremiah and put him into the cistern of Malkijah, the king's son, which was in the courtyard of the guard. They lowered Jeremiah by

---

[a]5 Or *Chaldeans*; also in verses 8, 9, 13 and 14   [b]10 Or *Chaldean*; also in verse 11   [c]1 Hebrew *Jucal,* a variant of *Jehucal*   [d]2 Or *Chaldeans*; also in verses 18, 19 and 23

ropes into the cistern; it had no water in it, only mud, and Jeremiah sank down into the mud.

[7] But Ebed-Melech, a Cushite,[a] an official[b] in the royal palace, heard that they had put Jeremiah into the cistern. While the king was sitting in the Benjamin Gate, [8] Ebed-Melech went out of the palace and said to him, [9] "My lord the king, these men have acted wickedly in all they have done to Jeremiah the prophet. They have thrown him into a cistern, where he will starve to death when there is no longer any bread in the city."

[10] Then the king commanded Ebed-Melech the Cushite, "Take thirty men from here with you and lift Jeremiah the prophet out of the cistern before he dies."

[11] So Ebed-Melech took the men with him and went to a room under the treasury in the palace. He took some old rags and worn-out clothes from there and let them down with ropes to Jeremiah in the cistern. [12] Ebed-Melech the Cushite said to Jeremiah, "Put these old rags and worn-out clothes under your arms to pad the ropes." Jeremiah did so, [13] and they pulled him up with the ropes and lifted him out of the cistern. And Jeremiah remained in the courtyard of the guard.

Zedekiah Questions Jeremiah Again [14] Then King Zedekiah sent for Jeremiah the prophet and had him brought to the third entrance to the temple of the Lord. "I am going to ask you something," the king said to Jeremiah. "Do not hide anything from me."

[15] Jeremiah said to Zedekiah, "If I give you an answer, will you not kill me? Even if I did give you counsel, you would not listen to me."

[16] But King Zedekiah swore this oath secretly to Jeremiah: "As surely as the Lord lives, who has given us breath, I will neither kill you nor hand you over to those who are seeking your life."

[17] Then Jeremiah said to Zedekiah, "This is what the Lord God Almighty, the God of Israel, says: 'If you surrender to the officers of the king of Babylon, your life will be spared and this city will not be burned down; you and your family will live. [18] But if you will not surrender to the officers of the king of Babylon, this city will be handed over to the Babylonians and they will burn it down; you yourself will not escape from their hands.'"

[19] King Zedekiah said to Jeremiah, "I am afraid of the Jews who have gone over to the Babylonians, for the Babylonians may hand me over to them and they will mistreat me."

[20] "They will not hand you over," Jeremiah replied. "Obey the Lord by doing what I tell you. Then it will go well with you, and your life will be spared. [21] But if you refuse to surrender, this is what the Lord has revealed to me: [22] All the women left in the palace of the king of Judah will be brought out to the officials of the king of Babylon. Those women will say to you:

> " 'They misled you and
> overcame you—
> those trusted friends of
> yours.

First Joseph and now you, Jeremiah! Is this some sort of trend?

SEE JEREMIAH 38:1-13

---

[a] 7 Probably from the upper Nile region   [b] 7 Or *a eunuch*

> Your feet are sunk in the mud;
> your friends have deserted you.'

²³"All your wives and children will be brought out to the Babylonians. You yourself will not escape from their hands but will be captured by the king of Babylon; and this city will*ᵃ* be burned down."

²⁴Then Zedekiah said to Jeremiah, "Do not let anyone know about this conversation, or you may die. ²⁵If the officials hear that I talked with you, and they come to you and say, 'Tell us what you said to the king and what the king said to you; do not hide it from us or we will kill you,' ²⁶then tell them, 'I was pleading with the king not to send me back to Jonathan's house to die there.' "

²⁷All the officials did come to Jeremiah and question him, and he told them everything the king had ordered him to say. So they said no more to him, for no one had heard his conversation with the king.

²⁸And Jeremiah remained in the courtyard of the guard until the day Jerusalem was captured.

The Fall of Jerusalem This is how Jerusalem was taken: ¹In the ninth year of Zedekiah king of Judah, in the tenth month, Nebuchadnezzar king of Babylon marched against Jerusalem with his whole army and laid siege to it. ²And on the ninth day of the fourth month of Zedekiah's eleventh year, the city wall was broken through. ³Then all the officials of the king of Babylon came and took seats in the Middle Gate: Nergal-Sharezer of Samgar, Nebo-Sarsekim*ᵇ* a chief officer, Nergal-Sharezer a high official and all the other officials of the king of Babylon. ⁴When Zedekiah king of Judah and all the soldiers saw them, they fled; they left the city at night by way of the king's garden, through the gate between the two walls, and headed toward the Arabah.*ᶜ*

⁵But the Babylonian*ᵈ* army pursued them and overtook Zedekiah in the plains of Jericho. They captured him and took him to Nebuchadnezzar king of Babylon at Riblah in the land of Hamath, where he pronounced sentence on him. ⁶There at Riblah the king of Babylon slaughtered the sons of Zedekiah before his eyes and also killed all the nobles of Judah. ⁷Then he put out Zedekiah's eyes and bound him with bronze shackles to take him to Babylon.

⁸The Babylonians*ᵉ* set fire to the royal palace and the houses of the people and broke down the walls of Jerusalem. ⁹Nebuzaradan commander of the imperial guard carried into exile to Babylon the people who remained in the city, along with those who had gone over to him, and the rest of the people. ¹⁰But Nebuzaradan the commander of the guard left behind in the land of Judah some of the poor people, who owned nothing; and at that time he gave them vineyards and fields.

¹¹Now Nebuchadnezzar king of Babylon had given these orders about Jeremiah through Nebuzaradan commander of the imperial guard: ¹²"Take him and look after him; don't harm him but do for him whatever he asks." ¹³So Nebuzaradan the commander of the guard, Nebushazban a chief officer, Nergal-Sharezer a high official and all the other officers of the king of Babylon ¹⁴sent and had Jeremiah taken out of the courtyard of the guard. They turned him over to Gedaliah son of Ahikam, the son of Shaphan, to take him back to his home. So he remained among his own people.

¹⁵While Jeremiah had been confined in the courtyard of the guard, the word of the Lord came to him: ¹⁶"Go and tell Ebed-Melech the Cushite, 'This is what the Lord Almighty, the God of Israel, says: I am about to fulfill my words against this city through disaster, not prosperity. At that time they

---

ᵃ23 Or and you will cause this city to ᵇ3 Or Nergal-Sharezer, Samgar-Nebo, Sarsekim ᶜ4 Or the Jordan Valley ᵈ5 Or Chaldean ᵉ8 Or Chaldeans

will be fulfilled before your eyes. [17]But I will rescue you on that day, declares the LORD; you will not be handed over to those you fear. [18]I will save you; you will not fall by the sword but will escape with your life, because you trust in me, declares the LORD.' "

40 *Jeremiah Freed* The word came to Jeremiah from the LORD after Nebuzaradan commander of the imperial guard had released him at Ramah. He had found Jeremiah bound in chains among all the captives from Jerusalem and Judah who were being carried into exile to Babylon. [2]When the commander of the guard found Jeremiah, he said to him, "The LORD your God decreed this disaster for this place. [3]And now the LORD has brought it about; he has done just as he said he would. All this happened because you people sinned against the LORD and did not obey him. [4]But today I am freeing you from the chains on your wrists. Come with me to Babylon, if you like, and I will look after you; but if you do not want to, then don't come. Look, the whole country lies before you; go wherever you please." [5]However, before Jeremiah turned to go,[a] Nebuzaradan added, "Go back to Gedaliah son of Ahikam, the son of Shaphan, whom the king of Babylon has appointed over the towns of Judah, and live with him among the people, or go anywhere else you please."

Then the commander gave him provisions and a present and let him go. [6]So Jeremiah went to Gedaliah son of Ahikam at Mizpah and stayed with him among the people who were left behind in the land.

Gedaliah Assassinated [7]When all the army officers and their men who were still in the open country heard that the king of Babylon had appointed Gedaliah son of Ahikam as governor over the land and had put him in charge of the men, women and children who were the poorest in the land and who had not been carried into exile to Babylon, [8]they came to Gedaliah at Mizpah— Ishmael son of Nethaniah, Johanan and Jonathan the sons of Kareah, Seraiah son of Tanhumeth, the sons of Ephai the Netophathite, and Jaazaniah[b] the son of the Maacathite, and their men. [9]Gedaliah son of Ahikam, the son of Shaphan, took an oath to reassure them and their men. "Do not be afraid to serve the Babylonians,[c]" he said. "Settle down in the land and serve the king of Babylon, and it will go well with you. [10]I myself will stay at Mizpah to represent you before the Babylonians who come to us, but you are to harvest the wine, summer fruit and oil, and put them in your storage jars, and live in the towns you have taken over."

[11]When all the Jews in Moab, Ammon, Edom and all the other countries heard that the king of Babylon had left a remnant in Judah and had appointed Gedaliah son of Ahikam, the son of Shaphan, as governor over them, [12]they all came back to the land of Judah, to Gedaliah at Mizpah, from all the countries where they had been scattered. And they harvested an abundance of wine and summer fruit.

[13]Johanan son of Kareah and all the army officers still in the open country came to Gedaliah at Mizpah [14]and said to him, "Don't you know that Baalis king of the Ammonites has sent Ishmael son of Nethaniah to take your life?" But Gedaliah son of Ahikam did not believe them.

[15]Then Johanan son of Kareah said privately to Gedaliah in Mizpah, "Let me go and kill Ishmael son of Nethaniah, and no one will know it. Why should he take your life and cause all the Jews who are gathered around you to be scattered and the remnant of Judah to perish?"

[16]But Gedaliah son of Ahikam said to Johanan son of Kareah, "Don't do such a thing! What you are saying about Ishmael is not true."

---

[a]5 Or *Jeremiah answered*   [b]8 Hebrew *Jezaniah*, a variant of *Jaazaniah*   [c]9 Or *Chaldeans*; also in verse 10

41 In the seventh month Ishmael son of Nethaniah, the son of Elish-ama, who was of royal blood and had been one of the king's officers, came with ten men to Gedaliah son of Ahikam at Mizpah. While they were eating together there, ²Ishmael son of Nethaniah and the ten men who were with him got up and struck down Gedaliah son of Ahikam, the son of Shaphan, with the sword, killing the one whom the king of Babylon had appointed as governor over the land. ³Ishmael also killed all the Jews who were with Gedaliah at Mizpah, as well as the Babylonian*ᵃ* soldiers who were there.

⁴The day after Gedaliah's assassination, before anyone knew about it, ⁵eighty men who had shaved off their beards, torn their clothes and cut themselves came from Shechem, Shiloh and Samaria, bringing grain offerings and incense with them to the house of the LORD. ⁶Ishmael son of Nethaniah went out from Mizpah to meet them, weeping as he went. When he met them, he said, "Come to Gedaliah son of Ahikam." ⁷When they went into the city, Ishmael son of Nethaniah and the men who were with him slaughtered them and threw them into a cistern. ⁸But ten of them said to Ishmael, "Don't kill us! We have wheat and barley, oil and honey, hidden in a field." So he let them alone and did not kill them with the others. ⁹Now the cistern where he threw all the bodies of the men he had killed along with Gedaliah was the one King Asa had made as part of his defense against Baasha king of Israel. Ishmael son of Nethaniah filled it with the dead.

¹⁰Ishmael made captives of all the rest of the people who were in Mizpah—the king's daughters along with all the others who were left there, over whom Nebuzaradan commander of the imperial guard had appointed Gedaliah son of Ahikam. Ishmael son of Nethaniah took them captive and set out to cross over to the Ammonites.

¹¹When Johanan son of Kareah and all the army officers who were with him heard about all the crimes Ishmael son of Nethaniah had committed, ¹²they took all their men and went to fight Ishmael son of Nethaniah. They caught up with him near the great pool in Gibeon. ¹³When all the people Ishmael had with him saw Johanan son of Kareah and the army officers who were with him, they were glad. ¹⁴All the people Ishmael had taken captive at Mizpah turned and went over to Johanan son of Kareah. ¹⁵But Ishmael son of Nethaniah and eight of his men escaped from Johanan and fled to the Ammonites.

Flight to Egypt ¹⁶Then Johanan son of Kareah and all the army officers who were with him led away all the survivors from Mizpah whom he had recovered from Ishmael son of Nethaniah after he had assassinated Gedaliah son of Ahikam: the soldiers, women, children and court officials he had brought from Gibeon. ¹⁷And they went on, stopping at Geruth Kimham near Bethlehem on their way to Egypt ¹⁸to escape the Babylonians.*ᵇ* They were afraid of them because Ishmael son of Nethaniah had killed Gedaliah son of Ahikam, whom the king of Babylon had appointed as governor over the land.

I thought this was a flight to Egypt!

SEE JEREMIAH 41:16-18   *ᵃ*3 Or *Chaldean*   *ᵇ*18 Or *Chaldeans*

Then all the army officers, including Johanan son of Kareah and Jezaniah*a* son of Hoshaiah, and all the people from the least to the greatest approached ²Jeremiah the prophet and said to him, "Please hear our petition and pray to the Lord your God for this entire remnant. For as you now see, though we were once many, now only a few are left. ³Pray that the Lord your God will tell us where we should go and what we should do."

⁴"I have heard you," replied Jeremiah the prophet. "I will certainly pray to the Lord your God as you have requested; I will tell you everything the Lord says and will keep nothing back from you."

⁵Then they said to Jeremiah, "May the Lord be a true and faithful witness against us if we do not act in accordance with everything the Lord your God sends you to tell us. ⁶Whether it is favorable or unfavorable, we will obey the Lord our God, to whom we are sending you, so that it will go well with us, for we will obey the Lord our God."

⁷Ten days later the word of the Lord came to Jeremiah. ⁸So he called together Johanan son of Kareah and all the army officers who were with him and all the people from the least to the greatest. ⁹He said to them, "This is what the Lord, the God of Israel, to whom you sent me to present your petition, says: ¹⁰'If you stay in this land, I will build you up and not tear you down; I will plant you and not uproot you, for I am grieved over the disaster I have inflicted on you. ¹¹Do not be afraid of the king of Babylon, whom you now fear. Do not be afraid of him, declares the Lord, for I am with you and will save you and deliver you from his hands. ¹²I will show you compassion so that he will have compassion on you and restore you to your land.'

¹³"However, if you say, 'We will not stay in this land,' and so disobey the Lord your God, ¹⁴and if you say, 'No, we will go and live in Egypt, where we will not see war or hear the trumpet or be hungry for bread,' ¹⁵then hear the word of the Lord, O remnant of Judah. This is what the Lord Almighty, the God of Israel, says: 'If you are determined to go to Egypt and you do go to settle there, ¹⁶then the sword you fear will overtake you there, and the famine you dread will follow you into Egypt, and there you will die. ¹⁷Indeed, all who are determined to go to Egypt to settle there will die by the sword, famine and plague; not one of them will survive or escape the disaster I will bring on them.' ¹⁸This is what the Lord Almighty, the God of Israel, says: 'As my anger and wrath have been poured out on those who lived in Jerusalem, so will my wrath be poured out on you when you go to Egypt. You will be an object of cursing and horror, of condemnation and reproach; you will never see this place again.'

¹⁹"O remnant of Judah, the Lord has told you, 'Do not go to Egypt.' Be sure of this: I warn you today ²⁰that you made a fatal mistake*b* when you sent me to the Lord your God and said, 'Pray to the Lord our God for us; tell us everything he says and we will do it.' ²¹I have told you today, but you still have not obeyed the Lord your God in all he sent me to tell you. ²²So now, be sure of this: You will die by the sword, famine and plague in the place where you want to go to settle."

When Jeremiah finished telling the people all the words of the Lord their God—everything the Lord had sent him to tell them— ²Azariah son of Hoshaiah and Johanan son of Kareah and all the arrogant men said to Jeremiah, "You are lying! The Lord our God has not sent you to say, 'You must not go to Egypt to settle there.' ³But Baruch son of Neriah is inciting you against us to hand us over to the Babylonians,*c* so they may kill us or carry us into exile to Babylon."

a1 Hebrew; Septuagint (see also 43:2) Azariah   b20 Or you erred in your hearts   c3 Or Chaldeans

⁴So Johanan son of Kareah and all the army officers and all the people disobeyed the Lord's command to stay in the land of Judah. ⁵Instead, Johanan son of Kareah and all the army officers led away all the remnant of Judah who had come back to live in the land of Judah from all the nations where they had been scattered. ⁶They also led away all the men, women and children and the king's daughters whom Nebuzaradan commander of the imperial guard had left with Gedaliah son of Ahikam, the son of Shaphan, and Jeremiah the prophet and Baruch son of Neriah. ⁷So they entered Egypt in disobedience to the Lord and went as far as Tahpanhes.

⁸In Tahpanhes the word of the Lord came to Jeremiah: ⁹"While the Jews are watching, take some large stones with you and bury them in clay in the brick pavement at the entrance to Pharaoh's palace in Tahpanhes. ¹⁰Then say to them, 'This is what the Lord Almighty, the God of Israel, says: I will send for my servant Nebuchadnezzar king of Babylon, and I will set his throne over these stones I have buried here; he will spread his royal canopy above them. ¹¹He will come and attack Egypt, bringing death to those destined for death, captivity to those destined for captivity, and the sword to those destined for the sword. ¹²Heᵃ will set fire to the temples of the gods of Egypt; he will burn their temples and take their gods captive. As a shepherd wraps his garment around him, so will he wrap Egypt around himself and depart from there unscathed. ¹³There in the temple of the sunᵇ in Egypt he will demolish the sacred pillars and will burn down the temples of the gods of Egypt.' "

44 **Disaster Because of Idolatry** This word came to Jeremiah concerning all the Jews living in Lower Egypt—in Migdol, Tahpanhes and Memphisᶜ—and in Upper Egyptᵈ: ²"This is what the Lord Almighty, the God of Israel, says: You saw the great disaster I brought on Jerusalem and on all the towns of Judah. Today they lie deserted and in ruins ³because of the evil they have done. They provoked me to anger by burning incense and by worshiping other gods that neither they nor you nor your fathers ever knew. ⁴Again and again I sent my servants the prophets, who said, 'Do not do this detestable thing that I hate!' ⁵But they did not listen or pay attention; they did not turn from their wickedness or stop burning incense to other gods. ⁶Therefore, my fierce anger was poured out; it raged against the towns of Judah and the streets of Jerusalem and made them the desolate ruins they are today.

⁷"Now this is what the Lord God Almighty, the God of Israel, says: Why bring such great disaster on yourselves by cutting off from Judah the men and women, the children and infants, and so leave yourselves without a remnant? ⁸Why provoke me to anger with what your hands have made, burning incense to other gods in Egypt, where you have come to live? You will destroy yourselves and make yourselves an object of cursing and reproach among all the nations on earth. ⁹Have you forgotten the wickedness committed by your fathers and by the kings and queens of Judah and the wickedness committed by you and your wives in the land of Judah and the streets of Jerusalem? ¹⁰To this day they have not humbled themselves or shown reverence, nor have they followed my law and the decrees I set before you and your fathers.

¹¹"Therefore, this is what the Lord Almighty, the God of Israel, says: I am determined to bring disaster on you and to destroy all Judah. ¹²I will take away the remnant of Judah who were determined to go to Egypt to settle there. They will all perish in Egypt; they will fall by the sword or die from famine. From the least to the greatest, they will die by sword or famine. They will become an object of cursing and horror, of condemnation and re-

proach. ¹³I will punish those who live in Egypt with the sword, famine and plague, as I punished Jerusalem. ¹⁴None of the remnant of Judah who have gone to live in Egypt will escape or survive to return to the land of Judah, to which they long to return and live; none will return except a few fugitives."

¹⁵Then all the men who knew that their wives were burning incense to other gods, along with all the women who were present—a large assembly— and all the people living in Lower and Upper Egypt,ᵃ said to Jeremiah, ¹⁶"We will not listen to the message you have spoken to us in the name of the LORD! ¹⁷We will certainly do everything we said we would: We will burn incense to the Queen of Heaven and will pour out drink offerings to her just as we and our fathers, our kings and our officials did in the towns of Judah and in the streets of Jerusalem. At that time we had plenty of food and were well off and suffered no harm. ¹⁸But ever since we stopped burning incense to the Queen of Heaven and pouring out drink offerings to her, we have had nothing and have been perishing by sword and famine."

¹⁹The women added, "When we burned incense to the Queen of Heaven and poured out drink offerings to her, did not our husbands know that we were making cakes like her image and pouring out drink offerings to her?"

²⁰Then Jeremiah said to all the people, both men and women, who were answering him, ²¹"Did not the LORD remember and think about the incense burned in the towns of Judah and the streets of Jerusalem by you and your fathers, your kings and your officials and the people of the land? ²²When the LORD could no longer endure your wicked actions and the detestable things you did, your land became an object of cursing and a desolate waste without inhabitants, as it is today. ²³Because you have burned incense and have sinned against the LORD and have not obeyed him or followed his law or his decrees or his stipulations, this disaster has come upon you, as you now see."

²⁴Then Jeremiah said to all the people, including the women, "Hear the word of the LORD, all you people of Judah in Egypt. ²⁵This is what the LORD Almighty, the God of Israel, says: You and your wives have shown by your actions what you promised when you said, 'We will certainly carry out the vows we made to burn incense and pour out drink offerings to the Queen of Heaven.'

"Go ahead then, do what you promised! Keep your vows! ²⁶But hear the word of the LORD, all Jews living in Egypt: 'I swear by my great name,' says the LORD, 'that no one from Judah living anywhere in Egypt will ever again invoke my name or swear, "As surely as the Sovereign LORD lives." ²⁷For I am watching over them for harm, not for good; the Jews in Egypt will perish by sword and famine until they are all destroyed. ²⁸Those who escape the sword and return to the land of Judah from Egypt will be very few. Then the whole remnant of Judah who came to live in Egypt will know whose word will stand—mine or theirs.

²⁹" 'This will be the sign to you that I will punish you in this place,' declares the LORD, 'so that you will know that my threats of harm against you will surely stand.' ³⁰This is what the LORD says: 'I am going to hand Pharaoh Hophra king of Egypt over to his enemies who seek his life, just as I handed Zedekiah king of Judah over to Nebuchadnezzar king of Babylon, the enemy who was seeking his life.' "

45 *A Message to Baruch* This is what Jeremiah the prophet told Baruch son of Neriah in the fourth year of Jehoiakim son of Josiah king of Judah, after Baruch had written on a scroll the words Jeremiah was then dictating: ²"This is what the LORD, the God of Israel, says to you, Bar-

ᵃ15 Hebrew *in Egypt and Pathros*

uch: ³You said, 'Woe to me! The Lord has added sorrow to my pain; I am worn out with groaning and find no rest.' "

⁴ˌThe Lord said,ˌ "Say this to him: 'This is what the Lord says: I will overthrow what I have built and uproot what I have planted, throughout the land. ⁵Should you then seek great things for yourself? Seek them not. For I will bring disaster on all people, declares the Lord, but wherever you go I will let you escape with your life.' "

46 *A Message About Egypt* This is the word of the Lord that came to Jeremiah the prophet concerning the nations:

²Concerning Egypt:

This is the message against the army of Pharaoh Neco king of Egypt, which was defeated at Carchemish on the Euphrates River by Nebuchadnezzar king of Babylon in the fourth year of Jehoiakim son of Josiah king of Judah:

> ³ "Prepare your shields, both large and small,
>   and march out for battle!
> ⁴ Harness the horses,
>   mount the steeds!
> Take your positions
>   with helmets on!
> Polish your spears,
>   put on your armor!
> ⁵ What do I see?
>   They are terrified,
> they are retreating,
>   their warriors are defeated.
> They flee in haste
>   without looking back,
>   and there is terror on every side,"

> declares the Lord.

> ⁶ "The swift cannot flee
>   nor the strong escape.
> In the north by the River Euphrates
>   they stumble and fall.

> ⁷ "Who is this that rises like the Nile,
>   like rivers of surging waters?
> ⁸ Egypt rises like the Nile,
>   like rivers of surging waters.
> She says, 'I will rise and cover the earth;
>   I will destroy cities and their people.'
> ⁹ Charge, O horses!
>   Drive furiously, O charioteers!
> March on, O warriors—
>   men of Cushᵃ and Put who carry shields,
>   men of Lydia who draw the bow.
> ¹⁰ But that day belongs to the Lord, the Lord Almighty—
>   a day of vengeance, for vengeance on his foes.
> The sword will devour till it is satisfied,
>   till it has quenched its thirst with blood.
> For the Lord, the Lord Almighty, will offer sacrifice
>   in the land of the north by the River Euphrates.

ᵃ9 That is, the upper Nile region

[11] "Go up to Gilead and get balm,
   O Virgin Daughter of Egypt.
But you multiply remedies in vain;
   there is no healing for you.
[12] The nations will hear of your shame;
   your cries will fill the earth.
One warrior will stumble over another;
   both will fall down together."

[13] This is the message the LORD spoke to Jeremiah the prophet about the coming of Nebuchadnezzar king of Babylon to attack Egypt:

[14] "Announce this in Egypt, and proclaim it in Migdol;
   proclaim it also in Memphis[a] and Tahpanhes:
'Take your positions and get ready,
   for the sword devours those around you.'
[15] Why will your warriors be laid low?
   They cannot stand, for the LORD will push them down.
[16] They will stumble repeatedly;
   they will fall over each other.
They will say, 'Get up, let us go back
   to our own people and our native lands,
   away from the sword of the oppressor.'
[17] There they will exclaim,
   'Pharaoh king of Egypt is only a loud noise;
   he has missed his opportunity.'

[18] "As surely as I live," declares the King,
   whose name is the LORD Almighty,
"one will come who is like Tabor among the mountains,
   like Carmel by the sea.
[19] Pack your belongings for exile,
   you who live in Egypt,
for Memphis will be laid waste
   and lie in ruins without inhabitant.

[20] "Egypt is a beautiful heifer,
   but a gadfly is coming
   against her from the north.
[21] The mercenaries in her ranks
   are like fattened calves.
They too will turn and flee together,
   they will not stand their ground,
for the day of disaster is coming upon them,
   the time for them to be punished.
[22] Egypt will hiss like a fleeing serpent
   as the enemy advances in force;
they will come against her with axes,
   like men who cut down trees.
[23] They will chop down her forest,"

declares the LORD,

   "dense though it be.
They are more numerous than locusts,
   they cannot be counted.
[24] The Daughter of Egypt will be put to shame,
   handed over to the people of the north."

[a]14 Hebrew *Noph*; also in verse 19

²⁵The LORD Almighty, the God of Israel, says: "I am about to bring punishment on Amon god of Thebes,ᵃ on Pharaoh, on Egypt and her gods and her kings, and on those who rely on Pharaoh. ²⁶I will hand them over to those who seek their lives, to Nebuchadnezzar king of Babylon and his officers. Later, however, Egypt will be inhabited as in times past," declares the LORD.

> ²⁷"Do not fear, O Jacob my servant;
>   do not be dismayed, O Israel.
> I will surely save you out of a distant place,
>   your descendants from the land of their exile.
> Jacob will again have peace and security,
>   and no one will make him afraid.
> ²⁸Do not fear, O Jacob my servant,
>   for I am with you," declares the LORD.
> "Though I completely destroy all the nations
>   among which I scatter you,
>   I will not completely destroy you.
> I will discipline you but only with justice;
>   I will not let you go entirely unpunished."

47 **A Message About the Philistines** This is the word of the LORD that came to Jeremiah the prophet concerning the Philistines before Pharaoh attacked Gaza:

²This is what the LORD says:

> "See how the waters are rising in the north;
>   they will become an overflowing torrent.
> They will overflow the land and everything in it,
>   the towns and those who live in them.
> The people will cry out;
>   all who dwell in the land will wail
> ³at the sound of the hoofs of galloping steeds,
>   at the noise of enemy chariots
>   and the rumble of their wheels.
> Fathers will not turn to help their children;
>   their hands will hang limp.
> ⁴For the day has come
>   to destroy all the Philistines
> and to cut off all survivors
>   who could help Tyre and Sidon.
> The LORD is about to destroy the Philistines,
>   the remnant from the coasts of Caphtor.ᵇ
> ⁵Gaza will shave her head in mourning;
>   Ashkelon will be silenced.
> O remnant on the plain,
>   how long will you cut yourselves?
>
> ⁶" 'Ah, sword of the LORD,' ⸢you cry,⸣
>   'how long till you rest?
> Return to your scabbard;
>   cease and be still.'
> ⁷But how can it rest
>   when the LORD has commanded it,
> when he has ordered it
>   to attack Ashkelon and the coast?"

ᵃ25 Hebrew No   ᵇ4 That is, Crete

48

A Message About Moab   Concerning Moab:

This is what the LORD Almighty, the God of Israel, says:

"Woe to Nebo, for it will be ruined.
    Kiriathaim will be disgraced and captured;
    the stronghold*a* will be disgraced and shattered.
²Moab will be praised no more;
    in Heshbon*b* men will plot her downfall:
    'Come, let us put an end to that nation.'
You too, O Madmen,*c* will be silenced;
    the sword will pursue you.
³Listen to the cries from Horonaim,
    cries of great havoc and destruction.
⁴Moab will be broken;
    her little ones will cry out.*d*
⁵They go up the way to Luhith,
    weeping bitterly as they go;
on the road down to Horonaim
    anguished cries over the destruction are heard.
⁶Flee! Run for your lives;
    become like a bush*e* in the desert.
⁷Since you trust in your deeds and riches,
    you too will be taken captive,
and Chemosh will go into exile,
    together with his priests and officials.
⁸The destroyer will come against every town,
    and not a town will escape.
The valley will be ruined
    and the plateau destroyed,
    because the LORD has spoken.
⁹Put salt on Moab,
    for she will be laid waste*f*;
her towns will become desolate,
    with no one to live in them.

¹⁰"A curse on him who is lax in doing
        the LORD's work!
    A curse on him who keeps his
        sword from bloodshed!

¹¹"Moab has been at rest from youth,
    like wine left on its dregs,
not poured from one jar to
        another—
    she has not gone into exile.
So she tastes as she did,
    and her aroma is unchanged.
¹²But days are coming,"
    declares the LORD,
"when I will send men who pour
        from jars,
    and they will pour her out;

I sure hope no one ever sends *me* a message like one of these!

SEE JEREMIAH 46–51

---

a1 Or / *Misgab*   *b2* The Hebrew for *Heshbon* sounds like the
Hebrew for *plot*.   *c2* The name of the Moabite town Madmen
sounds like the Hebrew for *be silenced*.   *d4* Hebrew; Septuagint
/ *proclaim it to Zoar*   *e6* Or *like Aroer*   *f9* Or *Give wings to Moab,
/ for she will fly away*

they will empty her jars
and smash her jugs.
13 Then Moab will be ashamed of Chemosh,
as the house of Israel was ashamed
when they trusted in Bethel.

14 "How can you say, 'We are warriors,
men valiant in battle'?
15 Moab will be destroyed and her towns invaded;
her finest young men will go down in the slaughter,"
declares the King, whose name is the LORD Almighty.
16 "The fall of Moab is at hand;
her calamity will come quickly.
17 Mourn for her, all who live around her,
all who know her fame;
say, 'How broken is the mighty scepter,
how broken the glorious staff!'

18 "Come down from your glory
and sit on the parched ground,
O inhabitants of the Daughter of Dibon,
for he who destroys Moab
will come up against you
and ruin your fortified cities.
19 Stand by the road and watch,
you who live in Aroer.
Ask the man fleeing and the woman escaping,
ask them, 'What has happened?'
20 Moab is disgraced, for she is shattered.
Wail and cry out!
Announce by the Arnon
that Moab is destroyed.
21 Judgment has come to the plateau—
to Holon, Jahzah and Mephaath,
22   to Dibon, Nebo and Beth Diblathaim,
23   to Kiriathaim, Beth Gamul and Beth Meon,
24   to Kerioth and Bozrah—
to all the towns of Moab, far and near.
25 Moab's horn[a] is cut off;
her arm is broken,"

declares the LORD.

26 "Make her drunk,
for she has defied the LORD.
Let Moab wallow in her vomit;
let her be an object of ridicule.
27 Was not Israel the object of your ridicule?
Was she caught among thieves,
that you shake your head in scorn
whenever you speak of her?
28 Abandon your towns and dwell among the rocks,
you who live in Moab.
Be like a dove that makes its nest
at the mouth of a cave.

29 "We have heard of Moab's pride—

_____

a 25 Horn here symbolizes strength.

her overweening pride and conceit,
  her pride and arrogance
    and the haughtiness of her heart.
³⁰ I know her insolence but it is futile,"

                declares the LORD,

  "and her boasts accomplish nothing.
³¹ Therefore I wail over Moab,
  for all Moab I cry out,
  I moan for the men of Kir Hareseth.
³² I weep for you, as Jazer weeps,
  O vines of Sibmah.
Your branches spread as far as the sea;
  they reached as far as the sea of Jazer.
The destroyer has fallen
  on your ripened fruit and grapes.
³³ Joy and gladness are gone
  from the orchards and fields of Moab.
I have stopped the flow of wine from the presses;
  no one treads them with shouts of joy.
Although there are shouts,
  they are not shouts of joy.

³⁴ "The sound of their cry rises
  from Heshbon to Elealeh and Jahaz,
from Zoar as far as Horonaim and Eglath Shelishiyah,
  for even the waters of Nimrim are dried up.
³⁵ In Moab I will put an end
  to those who make offerings on the high places
  and burn incense to their gods,"

                declares the LORD.

³⁶ "So my heart laments for Moab like a flute;
  it laments like a flute for the men of Kir Hareseth.
  The wealth they acquired is gone.
³⁷ Every head is shaved
  and every beard cut off;
every hand is slashed
  and every waist is covered with sackcloth.
³⁸ On all the roofs in Moab
  and in the public squares
there is nothing but mourning,
  for I have broken Moab
  like a jar that no one wants,"

                declares the LORD.

³⁹ "How shattered she is! How they wail!
  How Moab turns her back in shame!
Moab has become an object of ridicule,
  an object of horror to all those around her."

⁴⁰ This is what the LORD says:

  "Look! An eagle is swooping down,
    spreading its wings over Moab.
⁴¹ Kerioth^a will be captured
  and the strongholds taken.
In that day the hearts of Moab's warriors
  will be like the heart of a woman in labor.

^a41 Or *The cities*

^{42}Moab will be destroyed as a nation
    because she defied the Lord.
^{43}Terror and pit and snare await you,
    O people of Moab,"

declares the Lord.

^{44}"Whoever flees from the terror
    will fall into a pit,
whoever climbs out of the pit
    will be caught in a snare;
for I will bring upon Moab
    the year of her punishment,"

declares the Lord.

^{45}"In the shadow of Heshbon
    the fugitives stand helpless,
for a fire has gone out from Heshbon,
    a blaze from the midst of Sihon;
it burns the foreheads of Moab,
    the skulls of the noisy boasters.
^{46}Woe to you, O Moab!
    The people of Chemosh are destroyed;
your sons are taken into exile
    and your daughters into captivity.

^{47}"Yet I will restore the fortunes of Moab
    in days to come,"

declares the Lord.

Here ends the judgment on Moab.

49 *A Message About Ammon*   Concerning the Ammonites:

This is what the Lord says:

"Has Israel no sons?
    Has she no heirs?
Why then has Molech^a taken possession of Gad?
    Why do his people live in its towns?
^{2}But the days are coming,"
    declares the Lord,
"when I will sound the battle cry
    against Rabbah of the Ammonites;
it will become a mound of ruins,
    and its surrounding villages will be set on fire.
Then Israel will drive out
    those who drove her out,"

says the Lord.

^{3}"Wail, O Heshbon, for Ai is destroyed!
    Cry out, O inhabitants of Rabbah!
Put on sackcloth and mourn;
    rush here and there inside the walls,
for Molech will go into exile,
    together with his priests and officials.
^{4}Why do you boast of your valleys,
    boast of your valleys so fruitful?

$^a1$ Or *their king*; Hebrew *malcam*; also in verse 3

O unfaithful daughter,
    you trust in your riches and say,
    'Who will attack me?'
⁵I will bring terror on you
    from all those around you,"
            declares the Lord, the LORD Almighty.
"Every one of you will be driven away,
    and no one will gather the fugitives.

⁶"Yet afterward, I will restore the fortunes of the Ammonites,"
            declares the LORD.

A Message About Edom   ⁷Concerning Edom:

This is what the LORD Almighty says:

"Is there no longer wisdom in Teman?
    Has counsel perished from the prudent?
    Has their wisdom decayed?
⁸Turn and flee, hide in deep caves,
    you who live in Dedan,
for I will bring disaster on Esau
    at the time I punish him.
⁹If grape pickers came to you,
    would they not leave a few grapes?
If thieves came during the night,
    would they not steal only as much as they wanted?
¹⁰But I will strip Esau bare;
    I will uncover his hiding places,
    so that he cannot conceal himself.
His children, relatives and neighbors will perish,
    and he will be no more.
¹¹Leave your orphans; I will protect their lives.
    Your widows too can trust in me."

¹²This is what the LORD says: "If those who do not deserve to drink the cup must drink it, why should you go unpunished? You will not go unpunished, but must drink it. ¹³I swear by myself," declares the LORD, "that Bozrah will become a ruin and an object of horror, of reproach and of cursing; and all its towns will be in ruins forever."

¹⁴I have heard a message from the LORD:
    An envoy was sent to the nations to say,
"Assemble yourselves to attack it!
    Rise up for battle!"

¹⁵"Now I will make you small among the nations,
    despised among men.
¹⁶The terror you inspire
    and the pride of your heart have deceived you,
you who live in the clefts of the rocks,
    who occupy the heights of the hill.
Though you build your nest as high as the eagle's,
    from there I will bring you down,"
            declares the LORD.

¹⁷"Edom will become an object of horror;
    all who pass by will be appalled and will scoff
    because of all its wounds.
¹⁸As Sodom and Gomorrah were overthrown,
    along with their neighboring towns,"
            says the LORD,

"so no one will live there;
no man will dwell in it.

19 "Like a lion coming up from Jordan's thickets
to a rich pastureland,
I will chase Edom from its land in an instant.
Who is the chosen one I will appoint for this?
Who is like me and who can challenge me?
And what shepherd can stand against me?"

20 Therefore, hear what the LORD has planned against Edom,
what he has purposed against those who live in Teman:
The young of the flock will be dragged away;
he will completely destroy their pasture because of them.

21 At the sound of their fall the earth will tremble;
their cry will resound to the Red Sea.ᵃ

22 Look! An eagle will soar and swoop down,
spreading its wings over Bozrah.
In that day the hearts of Edom's warriors
will be like the heart of a woman in labor.

A Message About Damascus

23 Concerning Damascus:

"Hamath and Arpad are dismayed,
for they have heard bad news.
They are disheartened,
troubled likeᵇ the restless sea.

24 Damascus has become feeble,
she has turned to flee
and panic has gripped her;
anguish and pain have seized her,
pain like that of a woman in labor.

25 Why has the city of renown not been abandoned,
the town in which I delight?

26 Surely, her young men will fall in the streets;
all her soldiers will be silenced in that day,"

declares the LORD Almighty.

27 "I will set fire to the walls of Damascus;
it will consume the fortresses of Ben-Hadad."

A Message About Kedar and Hazor

28 Concerning Kedar and the kingdoms
of Hazor, which Nebuchadnezzar king of Babylon attacked:

This is what the LORD says:

"Arise, and attack Kedar
and destroy the people of the East.

29 Their tents and their flocks will be taken;
their shelters will be carried off
with all their goods and camels.
Men will shout to them,
'Terror on every side!'

30 "Flee quickly away!
Stay in deep caves, you who live in Hazor,"

declares the LORD.

"Nebuchadnezzar king of Babylon has plotted against you;
he has devised a plan against you.

ᵃ21 Hebrew *Yam Suph*, that is, Sea of Reeds   ᵇ23 Hebrew *on* or *by*

31 "Arise and attack a nation at ease,
   which lives in confidence,"

> declares the Lord,

"a nation that has neither gates nor bars;
   its people live alone.
32 Their camels will become plunder,
   and their large herds will be booty.
I will scatter to the winds those who are in distant places[a]
   and will bring disaster on them from every side,"

> declares the Lord.

33 "Hazor will become a haunt of jackals,
   a desolate place forever.
No one will live there;
   no man will dwell in it."

A Message About Elam   34 This is the word of the Lord that came to Jeremiah the prophet concerning Elam, early in the reign of Zedekiah king of Judah:

35 This is what the Lord Almighty says:

"See, I will break the bow of Elam,
   the mainstay of their might.
36 I will bring against Elam the four winds
   from the four quarters of the heavens;
I will scatter them to the four winds,
   and there will not be a nation
   where Elam's exiles do not go.
37 I will shatter Elam before their foes,
   before those who seek their lives;
I will bring disaster upon them,
   even my fierce anger,"

> declares the Lord.

"I will pursue them with the sword
   until I have made an end of them.
38 I will set my throne in Elam
   and destroy her king and officials,"

> declares the Lord.

39 "Yet I will restore the fortunes of Elam
   in days to come,"

> declares the Lord.

50 *A Message About Babylon*   This is the word the Lord spoke through Jeremiah the prophet concerning Babylon and the land of the Babylonians[b]:

2 "Announce and proclaim among the nations,
   lift up a banner and proclaim it;
   keep nothing back, but say,
'Babylon will be captured;
   Bel will be put to shame,
   Marduk filled with terror.
Her images will be put to shame
   and her idols filled with terror.'
3 A nation from the north will attack her
   and lay waste her land.

---

a 32 Or who clip the hair by their foreheads   *b 1 Or Chaldeans; also in verses 8, 25, 35 and 45*

No one will live in it;
    both men and animals will flee away.

4 "In those days, at that time,"
    declares the LORD,
"the people of Israel and the people of Judah together
    will go in tears to seek the LORD their God.
5 They will ask the way to Zion
    and turn their faces toward it.
They will come and bind themselves to the LORD
    in an everlasting covenant
    that will not be forgotten.

6 "My people have been lost sheep;
    their shepherds have led them astray
    and caused them to roam on the mountains.
They wandered over mountain and hill
    and forgot their own resting place.
7 Whoever found them devoured them;
    their enemies said, 'We are not guilty,
for they sinned against the LORD, their true pasture,
    the LORD, the hope of their fathers.'

8 "Flee out of Babylon;
    leave the land of the Babylonians,
    and be like the goats that lead the flock.
9 For I will stir up and bring against Babylon
    an alliance of great nations from the land of the north.
They will take up their positions against her,
    and from the north she will be captured.
Their arrows will be like skilled warriors
    who do not return empty-handed.
10 So Babylonia[a] will be plundered;
    all who plunder her will have their fill,"
                           declares the LORD.

11 "Because you rejoice and are glad,
    you who pillage my inheritance,
because you frolic like a heifer threshing grain
    and neigh like stallions,
12 your mother will be greatly ashamed;
    she who gave you birth will be disgraced.
She will be the least of the nations—
    a wilderness, a dry land, a desert.
13 Because of the LORD's anger she will not be inhabited
    but will be completely desolate.
All who pass Babylon will be horrified and scoff
    because of all her wounds.

14 "Take up your positions around Babylon,
    all you who draw the bow.
Shoot at her! Spare no arrows,
    for she has sinned against the LORD.
15 Shout against her on every side!
    She surrenders, her towers fall,
    her walls are torn down.

a 10 Or Chaldea

Since this is the vengeance of the LORD,
 take vengeance on her;
 do to her as she has done to others.
¹⁶ Cut off from Babylon the sower,
 and the reaper with his sickle at harvest.
Because of the sword of the oppressor
 let everyone return to his own people,
 let everyone flee to his own land.

¹⁷ "Israel is a scattered flock
 that lions have chased away.
The first to devour him
 was the king of Assyria;
the last to crush his bones
 was Nebuchadnezzar king of Babylon."

¹⁸ Therefore this is what the LORD Almighty, the God of Israel, says:

"I will punish the king of Babylon and his land
 as I punished the king of Assyria.
¹⁹ But I will bring Israel back to his own pasture
 and he will graze on Carmel and Bashan;
his appetite will be satisfied
 on the hills of Ephraim and Gilead.
²⁰ In those days, at that time,"
 declares the LORD,
"search will be made for Israel's guilt,
 but there will be none,
and for the sins of Judah,
 but none will be found,
 for I will forgive the remnant I spare.

²¹ "Attack the land of Merathaim
 and those who live in Pekod.
Pursue, kill and completely destroyᵃ them,"

         declares the LORD.

"Do everything I have commanded you.
²² The noise of battle is in the land,
 the noise of great destruction!
²³ How broken and shattered
 is the hammer of the whole earth!
How desolate is Babylon
 among the nations!
²⁴ I set a trap for you, O Babylon,
 and you were caught before you knew it;
you were found and captured
 because you opposed the LORD.
²⁵ The LORD has opened his arsenal
 and brought out the weapons of his wrath,
for the Sovereign LORD Almighty has work to do
 in the land of the Babylonians.
²⁶ Come against her from afar.
 Break open her granaries;
 pile her up like heaps of grain.
Completely destroy her
 and leave her no remnant.

ᵃ21 The Hebrew term refers to the irrevocable giving over of things or persons to the LORD, often by totally destroying them; also in verse 26.

²⁷Kill all her young bulls;
    let them go down to the slaughter!
Woe to them! For their day has come,
    the time for them to be punished.
²⁸Listen to the fugitives and refugees from Babylon
    declaring in Zion
how the LORD our God has taken vengeance,
    vengeance for his temple.

²⁹"Summon archers against Babylon,
    all those who draw the bow.
Encamp all around her;
    let no one escape.
Repay her for her deeds;
    do to her as she has done.
For she has defied the LORD,
    the Holy One of Israel.
³⁰Therefore, her young men will fall in the streets;
    all her soldiers will be silenced in that day,"
                         declares the LORD.
³¹"See, I am against you, O arrogant one,"
    declares the Lord, the LORD Almighty,
"for your day has come,
    the time for you to be punished.
³²The arrogant one will stumble and fall
    and no one will help her up;
I will kindle a fire in her towns
    that will consume all who are around her."

³³This is what the LORD Almighty says:

"The people of Israel are oppressed,
    and the people of Judah as well.
All their captors hold them fast,
    refusing to let them go.
³⁴Yet their Redeemer is strong;
    the LORD Almighty is his name.
He will vigorously defend their cause
    so that he may bring rest to their land,
    but unrest to those who live in Babylon.

³⁵"A sword against the Babylonians!"
    declares the LORD—
"against those who live in Babylon
    and against her officials and wise men!
³⁶A sword against her false prophets!
    They will become fools.
A sword against her warriors!
    They will be filled with terror.
³⁷A sword against her horses and chariots
    and all the foreigners in her ranks!
    They will become women.
A sword against her treasures!
    They will be plundered.
³⁸A drought on*ᵃ* her waters!
    They will dry up.

ᵃ38 Or *A sword against*

For it is a land of idols,
    idols that will go mad with terror.
39 "So desert creatures and hyenas will live there,
    and there the owl will dwell.
  It will never again be inhabited
    or lived in from generation to generation.
40 As God overthrew Sodom and Gomorrah
    along with their neighboring towns,"

                                            declares the LORD,

  "so no one will live there;
    no man will dwell in it.

41 "Look! An army is coming from the north;
    a great nation and many kings
    are being stirred up from the ends of the earth.
42 They are armed with bows and spears;
    they are cruel and without mercy.
  They sound like the roaring sea
    as they ride on their horses;
  they come like men in battle formation
    to attack you, O Daughter of Babylon.
43 The king of Babylon has heard reports about them,
    and his hands hang limp.
  Anguish has gripped him,
    pain like that of a woman in labor.
44 Like a lion coming up from Jordan's thickets
    to a rich pastureland,
  I will chase Babylon from its land in an instant.
    Who is the chosen one I will appoint for this?
  Who is like me and who can challenge me?
    And what shepherd can stand against me?"
45 Therefore, hear what the LORD has planned against
        Babylon,
    what he has purposed against the land of the Babylonians:
  The young of the flock will be dragged away;
    he will completely destroy their pasture because of them.
46 At the sound of Babylon's capture the earth will tremble;
    its cry will resound among the nations.

51 This is what the LORD says:

  "See, I will stir up the spirit of a destroyer
    against Babylon and the people of Leb Kamai.*a*
2 I will send foreigners to Babylon
    to winnow her and to devastate her land;
  they will oppose her on every side
    in the day of her disaster.
3 Let not the archer string his bow,
    nor let him put on his armor.
  Do not spare her young men;
    completely destroy*b* her army.
4 They will fall down slain in Babylon,*c*
    fatally wounded in her streets.

---

a1 Leb Kamai is a cryptogram for Chaldea, that is, Babylonia. *b3* The Hebrew term refers to the
irrevocable giving over of things or persons to the LORD, often by totally destroying them. *c4* Or *Chaldea*

⁵For Israel and Judah have not been forsaken
    by their God, the Lord Almighty,
  though their land*a* is full of guilt
    before the Holy One of Israel.

⁶"Flee from Babylon!
    Run for your lives!
    Do not be destroyed because of her sins.
  It is time for the Lord's vengeance;
    he will pay her what she deserves.
⁷Babylon was a gold cup in the Lord's hand;
    she made the whole earth drunk.
  The nations drank her wine;
    therefore they have now gone mad.
⁸Babylon will suddenly fall and be broken.
    Wail over her!
  Get balm for her pain;
    perhaps she can be healed.

⁹" 'We would have healed Babylon,
    but she cannot be healed;
  let us leave her and each go to his own land,
    for her judgment reaches to the skies,
    it rises as high as the clouds.'

¹⁰" 'The Lord has vindicated us;
    come, let us tell in Zion
    what the Lord our God has done.'

¹¹"Sharpen the arrows,
    take up the shields!
  The Lord has stirred up the kings of the Medes,
    because his purpose is to destroy Babylon.
  The Lord will take vengeance,
    vengeance for his temple.
¹²Lift up a banner against the walls of Babylon!
    Reinforce the guard,
  station the watchmen,
    prepare an ambush!
  The Lord will carry out his purpose,
    his decree against the people of Babylon.
¹³You who live by many waters
    and are rich in treasures,
  your end has come,
    the time for you to be cut off.
¹⁴The Lord Almighty has sworn by himself:
    I will surely fill you with men, as with a swarm of locusts,
    and they will shout in triumph over you.

¹⁵"He made the earth by his power;
    he founded the world by his wisdom
    and stretched out the heavens by his understanding.
¹⁶When he thunders, the waters in the heavens roar;
    he makes clouds rise from the ends of the earth.
  He sends lightning with the rain
    and brings out the wind from his storehouses.

a5 Or / and the land of the Babylonians

¹⁷ "Every man is senseless and without knowledge;
     every goldsmith is shamed by his idols.
  His images are a fraud;
     they have no breath in them.
¹⁸ They are worthless, the objects of mockery;
     when their judgment comes, they will perish.
¹⁹ He who is the Portion of Jacob is not like these,
     for he is the Maker of all things,
  including the tribe of his inheritance—
     the Lᴏʀᴅ Almighty is his name.

²⁰ "You are my war club,
     my weapon for battle—
  with you I shatter nations,
     with you I destroy kingdoms,
²¹ with you I shatter horse and rider,
     with you I shatter chariot and driver,
²² with you I shatter man and woman,
     with you I shatter old man and youth,
     with you I shatter young man and maiden,
²³ with you I shatter shepherd and flock,
     with you I shatter farmer and oxen,
     with you I shatter governors and officials.

²⁴ "Before your eyes I will repay Babylon and all who live in Babyloniaᵃ for
all the wrong they have done in Zion," declares the Lᴏʀᴅ.

²⁵ "I am against you, O destroying mountain,
     you who destroy the whole earth,"
                                        declares the Lᴏʀᴅ.

  "I will stretch out my hand against you,
     roll you off the cliffs,
     and make you a burned-out mountain.
²⁶ No rock will be taken from you for a cornerstone,
     nor any stone for a foundation,
     for you will be desolate forever,"
                                        declares the Lᴏʀᴅ.

²⁷ "Lift up a banner in the land!
     Blow the trumpet among the nations!
  Prepare the nations for battle against her;
     summon against her these kingdoms:
     Ararat, Minni and Ashkenaz.
  Appoint a commander against her;
     send up horses like a swarm of locusts.
²⁸ Prepare the nations for battle against her—
     the kings of the Medes,
  their governors and all their officials,
     and all the countries they rule.
²⁹ The land trembles and writhes,
     for the Lᴏʀᴅ's purposes against Babylon stand—
  to lay waste the land of Babylon
     so that no one will live there.
³⁰ Babylon's warriors have stopped fighting;
     they remain in their strongholds.
  Their strength is exhausted;
     they have become like women.

ᵃ24 Or *Chaldea*; also in verse 35

Her dwellings are set on fire;
  the bars of her gates are broken.
³¹ One courier follows another
  and messenger follows messenger
to announce to the king of Babylon
  that his entire city is captured,
³² the river crossings seized,
  the marshes set on fire,
  and the soldiers terrified."

³³This is what the Lord Almighty, the God of Israel, says:

"The Daughter of Babylon is like a threshing floor
  at the time it is trampled;
  the time to harvest her will soon come."

³⁴ "Nebuchadnezzar king of Babylon has devoured us,
  he has thrown us into confusion,
  he has made us an empty jar.
Like a serpent he has swallowed us
  and filled his stomach with our delicacies,
  and then has spewed us out.
³⁵ May the violence done to our flesh*a* be upon Babylon,"
  say the inhabitants of Zion.
"May our blood be on those who live in Babylonia,"
  says Jerusalem.

³⁶Therefore, this is what the Lord says:

"See, I will defend your cause
  and avenge you;
I will dry up her sea
  and make her springs dry.
³⁷ Babylon will be a heap of ruins,
  a haunt of jackals,
an object of horror and scorn,
  a place where no one lives.
³⁸ Her people all roar like young lions,
  they growl like lion cubs.
³⁹ But while they are aroused,
  I will set out a feast for them
  and make them drunk,
so that they shout with laughter—
  then sleep forever and not awake,"

declares the Lord.

⁴⁰ "I will bring them down
  like lambs to the slaughter,
  like rams and goats.

⁴¹ "How Sheshach*b* will be captured,
  the boast of the whole earth seized!
What a horror Babylon will be
  among the nations!
⁴² The sea will rise over Babylon;
  its roaring waves will cover her.
⁴³ Her towns will be desolate,
  a dry and desert land,

---

a35 Or *done to us and to our children*   *b41 Sheshach* is a cryptogram for Babylon.

a land where no one lives,
  through which no man travels.
⁴⁴I will punish Bel in Babylon
  and make him spew out what he has swallowed.
The nations will no longer stream to him.
  And the wall of Babylon will fall.

⁴⁵"Come out of her, my people!
  Run for your lives!
  Run from the fierce anger of the LORD.
⁴⁶Do not lose heart or be afraid
  when rumors are heard in the land;
one rumor comes this year, another the next,
  rumors of violence in the land
  and of ruler against ruler.
⁴⁷For the time will surely come
  when I will punish the idols of Babylon;
her whole land will be disgraced
  and her slain will all lie fallen within her.
⁴⁸Then heaven and earth and all that is in them
  will shout for joy over Babylon,
for out of the north
  destroyers will attack her,"

declares the LORD.

⁴⁹"Babylon must fall because of Israel's slain,
  just as the slain in all the earth
  have fallen because of Babylon.
⁵⁰You who have escaped the sword,
  leave and do not linger!
Remember the LORD in a distant land,
  and think on Jerusalem."

⁵¹"We are disgraced,
  for we have been insulted
  and shame covers our faces,
because foreigners have entered
  the holy places of the LORD's house."

⁵²"But days are coming," declares the LORD,
  "when I will punish her idols,
and throughout her land
  the wounded will groan.
⁵³Even if Babylon reaches the sky
  and fortifies her lofty stronghold,
  I will send destroyers against her,"

declares the LORD.

⁵⁴"The sound of a cry comes from Babylon,
  the sound of great destruction
  from the land of the Babylonians.^a
⁵⁵The LORD will destroy Babylon;
  he will silence her noisy din.
Waves of enemies will rage like great waters;
  the roar of their voices will resound.
⁵⁶A destroyer will come against Babylon;
  her warriors will be captured,
  and their bows will be broken.

JEREMIAH 51

QUIZZER

Q: What is
the last thing
Jeremiah
did with his
scroll?

BONUS:
What was on
this scroll?

Answers on
page 1059

^a54 Or Chaldeans

For the LORD is a God of retribution;
he will repay in full.
[57] I will make her officials and wise men drunk,
her governors, officers and warriors as well;
they will sleep forever and not awake,"
declares the King, whose name is the LORD Almighty.

[58] This is what the LORD Almighty says:

"Babylon's thick wall will be leveled
and her high gates set on fire;
the peoples exhaust themselves for nothing,
the nations' labor is only fuel for the flames."

[59] This is the message Jeremiah gave to the staff officer Seraiah son of Neriah, the son of Mahseiah, when he went to Babylon with Zedekiah king of Judah in the fourth year of his reign. [60] Jeremiah had written on a scroll about all the disasters that would come upon Babylon—all that had been recorded concerning Babylon. [61] He said to Seraiah, "When you get to Babylon, see that you read all these words aloud. [62] Then say, 'O LORD, you have said you will destroy this place, so that neither man nor animal will live in it; it will be desolate forever.' [63] When you finish reading this scroll, tie a stone to it and throw it into the Euphrates. [64] Then say, 'So will Babylon sink to rise no more because of the disaster I will bring upon her. And her people will fall.' "

The words of Jeremiah end here.

52 The Fall of Jerusalem

Zedekiah was twenty-one years old when he became king, and he reigned in Jerusalem eleven years. His mother's name was Hamutal daughter of Jeremiah; she was from Libnah. [2] He did evil in the eyes of the LORD, just as Jehoiakim had done. [3] It was because of the LORD's anger that all this happened to Jerusalem and Judah, and in the end he thrust them from his presence.

Now Zedekiah rebelled against the king of Babylon.

[4] So in the ninth year of Zedekiah's reign, on the tenth day of the tenth month, Nebuchadnezzar king of Babylon marched against Jerusalem with his whole army. They camped outside the city and built siege works all around it. [5] The city was kept under siege until the eleventh year of King Zedekiah.

[6] By the ninth day of the fourth month the famine in the city had become so severe that there was no food for the people to eat. [7] Then the city wall was broken through, and the whole army fled. They left the city at night through the gate between the two walls near the king's garden, though the Babylonians[a] were surrounding the city. They fled toward the Arabah,[b] [8] but the Babylonian[c] army pursued King Zedekiah and overtook him in the plains of Jericho. All his soldiers were separated from him and scattered, [9] and he was captured.

He was taken to the king of Babylon at Riblah in the land of Hamath, where he pronounced sentence on him. [10] There at Riblah the king of Babylon slaughtered the sons of Zedekiah before his eyes; he also killed all the officials of Judah. [11] Then he put out Zedekiah's eyes, bound him with bronze shackles and took him to Babylon, where he put him in prison till the day of his death.

[12] On the tenth day of the fifth month, in the nineteenth year of Nebuchadnezzar king of Babylon, Nebuzaradan commander of the imperial guard,

---

[a]7 Or *Chaldeans*; also in verse 17   [b]7 Or *the Jordan Valley*   [c]8 Or *Chaldean*; also in verse 14

who served the king of Babylon, came to Jerusalem. ¹³He set fire to the temple of the LORD, the royal palace and all the houses of Jerusalem. Every important building he burned down. ¹⁴The whole Babylonian army under the commander of the imperial guard broke down all the walls around Jerusalem. ¹⁵Nebuzaradan the commander of the guard carried into exile some of the poorest people and those who remained in the city, along with the rest of the craftsmen*a* and those who had gone over to the king of Babylon. ¹⁶But Nebuzaradan left behind the rest of the poorest people of the land to work the vineyards and fields.

¹⁷The Babylonians broke up the bronze pillars, the movable stands and the bronze Sea that were at the temple of the LORD and they carried all the bronze to Babylon. ¹⁸They also took away the pots, shovels, wick trimmers, sprinkling bowls, dishes and all the bronze articles used in the temple service. ¹⁹The commander of the imperial guard took away the basins, censers, sprinkling bowls, pots, lampstands, dishes and bowls used for drink offerings— all that were made of pure gold or silver.

²⁰The bronze from the two pillars, the Sea and the twelve bronze bulls under it, and the movable stands, which King Solomon had made for the temple of the LORD, was more than could be weighed. ²¹Each of the pillars was eighteen cubits high and twelve cubits in circumference*b*; each was four fingers thick, and hollow. ²²The bronze capital on top of the one pillar was five cubits*c* high and was decorated with a network and pomegranates of bronze all around. The other pillar, with its pomegranates, was similar. ²³There were ninety-six pomegranates on the sides; the total number of pomegranates above the surrounding network was a hundred.

²⁴The commander of the guard took as prisoners Seraiah the chief priest, Zephaniah the priest next in rank and the three doorkeepers. ²⁵Of those still in the city, he took the officer in charge of the fighting men, and seven royal advisers. He also took the secretary who was chief officer in charge of conscripting the people of the land and sixty of his men who were found in the city. ²⁶Nebuzaradan the commander took them all and brought them to the king of Babylon at Riblah. ²⁷There at Riblah, in the land of Hamath, the king had them executed.

So Judah went into captivity, away from her land. ²⁸This is the number of the people Nebuchadnezzar carried into exile:

in the seventh year, 3,023 Jews;
²⁹in Nebuchadnezzar's eighteenth year,
     832 people from Jerusalem;
³⁰in his twenty-third year,
     745 Jews taken into exile by Nebuzaradan the commander of the
     imperial guard.
     There were 4,600 people in all.

Jehoiachin Released   ³¹In the thirty-seventh year of the exile of Jehoiachin king of Judah, in the year Evil-Merodach*d* became king of Babylon, he released Jehoiachin king of Judah and freed him from prison on the twenty-fifth day of the twelfth month. ³²He spoke kindly to him and gave him a seat of honor higher than those of the other kings who were with him in Babylon. ³³So Jehoiachin put aside his prison clothes and for the rest of his life ate regularly at the king's table. ³⁴Day by day the king of Babylon gave Jehoiachin a regular allowance as long as he lived, till the day of his death.

Answers
*to Quizzer on
page 1057*

A: He gave Seraiah the scroll and told him to read it, to tie a rock to it and to throw it in the Euphrates River when he arrived in Babylon (Jeremiah 51:59-64).

BONUS: All the disasters that would come to Babylon.

---

*a*15 Or *populace*   *b*21 That is, about 27 feet (about 8.1 meters) high and 18 feet (about 5.4 meters) in circumference   *c*22 That is, about 7 1/2 feet (about 2.3 meters)   *d*31 Also called *Amel-Marduk*

Introduction

to the

book of **Lamentations**

YOU FEEL TERRIBLE!

You lost the big game. You dropped your tray of spaghetti in the cafeteria. You got permanent black marker all over your new jeans. If this kind of thing happened to you every day, you'd feel terrible and you'd be in the right mood for this book.

Lamentations is a book of five poems. They are called "dirges" because they express how awful the Jews felt after the Babylonians destroyed Jerusalem and God's temple. It was terrible for the Jews to look back and realize what happened was their own fault.

Fundamentals

Why is it better to think first rather than later (Lamentations 1:20-22)?

Can you ever sin so bad that there is no longer any hope (Lamentations 3:19-27)?

What can you learn from the painful consequences of doing wrong (Lamentations 3:37-57)?

FAST FACTS

Lamentations means "funeral songs."

Jeremiah probably wrote this book.

Each poem is an acrostic. The first word of each verse begins with a letter of the Hebrew alphabet.

There are 22 letters in the Hebrew alphabet.

1 [a] How deserted lies the city,
  once so full of people!
How like a widow is she,
  who once was great among the nations!
She who was queen among the provinces
  has now become a slave.

2 Bitterly she weeps at night,
  tears are upon her cheeks.
Among all her lovers
  there is none to comfort her.
All her friends have betrayed her;
  they have become her enemies.

3 After affliction and harsh labor,
  Judah has gone into exile.
She dwells among the nations;
  she finds no resting place.
All who pursue her have overtaken her
  in the midst of her distress.

4 The roads to Zion mourn,
  for no one comes to her appointed feasts.
All her gateways are desolate,
  her priests groan,
her maidens grieve,
  and she is in bitter anguish.

5 Her foes have become her masters;
  her enemies are at ease.
The LORD has brought her grief
  because of her many sins.
Her children have gone into exile,
  captive before the foe.

6 All the splendor has departed
  from the Daughter of Zion.
Her princes are like deer
  that find no pasture;
in weakness they have fled
  before the pursuer.

7 In the days of her affliction and wandering
  Jerusalem remembers all the treasures
  that were hers in days of old.
When her people fell into enemy hands,
  there was no one to help her.
Her enemies looked at her
  and laughed at her destruction.

8 Jerusalem has sinned greatly
  and so has become unclean.
All who honored her despise her,
  for they have seen her nakedness;
she herself groans
  and turns away.

9 Her filthiness clung to her skirts;
  she did not consider her future.

[a] This chapter is an acrostic poem, the verses of which begin with the successive letters of the Hebrew alphabet.

Her fall was astounding;
    there was none to comfort her.
"Look, O Lord, on my affliction,
    for the enemy has triumphed."

¹⁰The enemy laid hands
    on all her treasures;
she saw pagan nations
    enter her sanctuary—
those you had forbidden
    to enter your assembly.

¹¹All her people groan
    as they search for bread;
they barter their treasures for food
    to keep themselves alive.
"Look, O Lord, and consider,
    for I am despised."

¹²"Is it nothing to you, all you who pass by?
    Look around and see.
Is any suffering like my suffering
    that was inflicted on me,
that the Lord brought on me
    in the day of his fierce anger?

¹³"From on high he sent fire,
    sent it down into my bones.
He spread a net for my feet
    and turned me back.
He made me desolate,
    faint all the day long.

¹⁴"My sins have been bound into a yoke*;
    by his hands they were woven together.
They have come upon my neck
    and the Lord has sapped my strength.
He has handed me over
    to those I cannot withstand.

¹⁵"The Lord has rejected
    all the warriors in my midst;
he has summoned an army against me
    to* crush my young men.
In his winepress the Lord has trampled
    the Virgin Daughter of Judah.

¹⁶"This is why I weep
    and my eyes overflow with tears.
No one is near to comfort me,
    no one to restore my spirit.
My children are destitute
    because the enemy has prevailed."

¹⁷Zion stretches out her hands,
    but there is no one to comfort her.
The Lord has decreed for Jacob
    that his neighbors become his foes;

*14 Most Hebrew manuscripts; Septuagint *He kept watch over my sins* *15 Or *has set a time for me /
when he will*

Jerusalem has become
an unclean thing among them.

18 "The Lord is righteous,
yet I rebelled against his command.
Listen, all you peoples;
look upon my suffering.
My young men and maidens
have gone into exile.

19 "I called to my allies
but they betrayed me.
My priests and my elders
perished in the city
while they searched for food
to keep themselves alive.

20 "See, O Lord, how distressed I am!
I am in torment within,
and in my heart I am disturbed,
for I have been most rebellious.
Outside, the sword bereaves;
inside, there is only death.

21 "People have heard my groaning,
but there is no one to comfort me.
All my enemies have heard of my distress;
they rejoice at what you have done.
May you bring the day you have announced
so they may become like me.

22 "Let all their wickedness come
before you;
deal with them
as you have dealt with me
because of all my sins.
My groans are many
and my heart is faint."

2 ^a How the Lord has covered the
Daughter of Zion
with the cloud of his anger^b!
He has hurled down the
splendor of Israel
from heaven to earth;
he has not remembered his
footstool
in the day of his anger.

2 Without pity the Lord has
swallowed up
all the dwellings of Jacob;
in his wrath he has torn down
the strongholds of the
Daughter of Judah.

---

^aThis chapter is an acrostic poem, the verses of which
begin with the successive letters of the Hebrew alphabet.
^b1 Or How the Lord in his anger / has treated the
Daughter of Zion with contempt

LAMENTATIONS 1:20–22

Have you ever experienced the
consequences of a poor choice?
Like being grounded because you
skipped a few math assignments
and got a D? Or finding out the
hard way that you can be
arrested for vandalizing a
teacher's car? Lamentations is a
collection of mournful poems
expressing how distressed,
disturbed and tormented the
people of Judah felt in their
captivity. They looked back and
realized how foolish they had
been to go against God's ways.
There's a powerful lesson in
Lamentations for everyone:
Think first. After you've made a
wrong choice, there's often
nothing you can do to avoid
agonizing consequences.

Direct Line

He has brought her kingdom and its princes
    down to the ground in dishonor.

³In fierce anger he has cut off
    every horn^c of Israel.
He has withdrawn his right hand
    at the approach of the enemy.
He has burned in Jacob like a flaming fire
    that consumes everything around it.

⁴Like an enemy he has strung his bow;
    his right hand is ready.
Like a foe he has slain
    all who were pleasing to the eye;
he has poured out his wrath like fire
    on the tent of the Daughter of Zion.

⁵The Lord is like an enemy;
    he has swallowed up Israel.
He has swallowed up all her palaces
    and destroyed her strongholds.
He has multiplied mourning and lamentation
    for the Daughter of Judah.

⁶He has laid waste his dwelling like a garden;
    he has destroyed his place of meeting.
The Lord has made Zion forget
    her appointed feasts and her Sabbaths;
in his fierce anger he has spurned
    both king and priest.

⁷The Lord has rejected his altar
    and abandoned his sanctuary.
He has handed over to the enemy
    the walls of her palaces;
they have raised a shout in the house of the Lord
    as on the day of an appointed feast.

⁸The Lord determined to tear down
    the wall around the Daughter of Zion.
He stretched out a measuring line
    and did not withhold his hand from destroying.
He made ramparts and walls lament;
    together they wasted away.

⁹Her gates have sunk into the ground;
    their bars he has broken and destroyed.
Her king and her princes are exiled among the nations,
    the law is no more,
and her prophets no longer find
    visions from the Lord.

¹⁰The elders of the Daughter of Zion
    sit on the ground in silence;
they have sprinkled dust on their heads
    and put on sackcloth.
The young women of Jerusalem
    have bowed their heads to the ground.

---

^a3 Or / all the strength; or every king; **horn** here symbolizes strength.

¹¹My eyes fail from weeping,
    I am in torment within,
my heart is poured out on the ground
    because my people are destroyed,
because children and infants faint
    in the streets of the city.

¹²They say to their mothers,
    "Where is bread and wine?"
as they faint like wounded men
    in the streets of the city,
as their lives ebb away
    in their mothers' arms.

¹³What can I say for you?
    With what can I compare you,
    O Daughter of Jerusalem?
To what can I liken you,
    that I may comfort you,
    O Virgin Daughter of Zion?
Your wound is as deep as the sea.
    Who can heal you?

¹⁴The visions of your prophets
    were false and worthless;
they did not expose your sin
    to ward off your captivity.
The oracles they gave you
    were false and misleading.

¹⁵All who pass your way
    clap their hands at you;
they scoff and shake their heads
    at the Daughter of Jerusalem:
"Is this the city that was called
    the perfection of beauty,
    the joy of the whole earth?"

¹⁶All your enemies open their mouths
    wide against you;
they scoff and gnash their teeth
    and say, "We have swallowed her up.
This is the day we have waited for;
    we have lived to see it."

¹⁷The Lord has done what he planned;
    he has fulfilled his word,
    which he decreed long ago.
He has overthrown you without pity,
    he has let the enemy gloat over you,
    he has exalted the horn^a of your foes.

¹⁸The hearts of the people
    cry out to the Lord.
O wall of the Daughter of Zion,
    let your tears flow like a river
    day and night;
give yourself no relief,
    your eyes no rest.

^a17 Horn here symbolizes strength.

¹⁹Arise, cry out in the night,
    as the watches of the night begin;
pour out your heart like water
    in the presence of the Lord.
Lift up your hands to him
    for the lives of your children,
who faint from hunger
    at the head of every street.

²⁰"Look, O Lᴏʀᴅ, and consider:
    Whom have you ever treated like this?
Should women eat their offspring,
    the children they have cared for?
Should priest and prophet be killed
    in the sanctuary of the Lord?

²¹"Young and old lie together
    in the dust of the streets;
my young men and maidens
    have fallen by the sword.
You have slain them in the day of your anger;
    you have slaughtered them without pity.

²²"As you summon to a feast day,
    so you summoned against me terrors on every side.
In the day of the Lᴏʀᴅ's anger
    no one escaped or survived;
those I cared for and reared,
    my enemy has destroyed."

3ᵃ   I am the man who has seen affliction
    by the rod of his wrath.
²He has driven me away and made me walk
    in darkness rather than light;
³indeed, he has turned his hand against me
    again and again, all day long.

⁴He has made my skin and my flesh grow old
    and has broken my bones.
⁵He has besieged me and surrounded me
    with bitterness and hardship.
⁶He has made me dwell in darkness
    like those long dead.

⁷He has walled me in so I cannot escape;
    he has weighed me down with chains.
⁸Even when I call out or cry for help,
    he shuts out my prayer.
⁹He has barred my way with blocks of stone;
    he has made my paths crooked.

¹⁰Like a bear lying in wait,
    like a lion in hiding,
¹¹he dragged me from the path and mangled me
    and left me without help.
¹²He drew his bow
    and made me the target for his arrows.

ᵃThis chapter is an acrostic poem; the verses of each stanza begin with the successive letters of the
Hebrew alphabet, and the verses within each stanza begin with the same letter.

¹³He pierced my heart
   with arrows from his quiver.
¹⁴I became the laughingstock of all my people;
   they mock me in song all day long.
¹⁵He has filled me with bitter herbs
   and sated me with gall.

¹⁶He has broken my teeth with gravel;
   he has trampled me in the dust.
¹⁷I have been deprived of peace;
   I have forgotten what prosperity is.
¹⁸So I say, "My splendor is gone
   and all that I had hoped from the Lord."

¹⁹I remember my affliction and my wandering,
   the bitterness and the gall.
²⁰I well remember them,
   and my soul is downcast within me.
²¹Yet this I call to mind
   and therefore I have hope:

²²Because of the Lord's great love we are not consumed,
   for his compassions never fail.
²³They are new every morning;
   great is your faithfulness.
²⁴I say to myself, "The Lord is my portion;
   therefore I will wait for him."

²⁵The Lord is good to those whose hope is in him,
   to the one who seeks him;
²⁶it is good to wait quietly
   for the salvation of the Lord.
²⁷It is good for a man to bear
      the yoke
   while he is young.

²⁸Let him sit alone in silence,
   for the Lord has laid it on
      him.
²⁹Let him bury his face in the
      dust—
   there may yet be hope.
³⁰Let him offer his cheek to one
      who would strike him,
   and let him be filled with
      disgrace.

³¹For men are not cast off
   by the Lord forever.
³²Though he brings grief, he will
      show compassion,
   so great is his unfailing
      love.
³³For he does not willingly bring
      affliction
   or grief to the children of
      men.

³⁴To crush underfoot
   all prisoners in the land,

LAMENTATIONS 3:25–27

The writer of this poem knows that God is punishing him for his sins (Lamentations 3:1). And he wonders: Is there any hope for a person who has done wrong? Will God punish me forever? The answer comes in Lamentations 3:25–27. Even if you've done wrong and are suffering for it, you can still have hope. God "is good to those whose hope is in him" (Lamentations 3:25), and he will forgive you and give you another chance as well. The writer warns that you may have to live through some hard times while you wait for that next chance to come (Lamentations 3:26). But don't give up. Keep on hoping in God, and he will be good to you.

Direct Line

³⁵ to deny a man his rights
before the Most High,
³⁶ to deprive a man of justice—
would not the Lord see such things?

³⁷ Who can speak and have it happen
if the Lord has not decreed it?
³⁸ Is it not from the mouth of the Most High
that both calamities and good things come?
³⁹ Why should any living man complain
when punished for his sins?

⁴⁰ Let us examine our ways and test them,
and let us return to the LORD.
⁴¹ Let us lift up our hearts and our hands
to God in heaven, and say:
⁴² "We have sinned and rebelled
and you have not forgiven.

⁴³ "You have covered yourself with anger and pursued us;
you have slain without pity.
⁴⁴ You have covered yourself with a cloud
so that no prayer can get through.
⁴⁵ You have made us scum and refuse
among the nations.

⁴⁶ "All our enemies have opened their mouths
wide against us.
⁴⁷ We have suffered terror and pitfalls,
ruin and destruction."
⁴⁸ Streams of tears flow from my eyes
because my people are destroyed.

⁴⁹ My eyes will flow unceasingly,
without relief,
⁵⁰ until the LORD looks down
from heaven and sees.
⁵¹ What I see brings grief to my soul
because of all the women of my city.

⁵² Those who were my enemies without cause
hunted me like a bird.
⁵³ They tried to end my life in a pit
and threw stones at me;
⁵⁴ the waters closed over my head,
and I thought I was about to be cut off.

⁵⁵ I called on your name, O LORD,
from the depths of the pit.
⁵⁶ You heard my plea: "Do not close your ears
to my cry for relief."
⁵⁷ You came near when I called you,
and you said, "Do not fear."

⁵⁸ O Lord, you took up my case;
you redeemed my life.
⁵⁹ You have seen, O LORD, the wrong done to me.
Uphold my cause!
⁶⁰ You have seen the depth of their vengeance,
all their plots against me.

⁶¹O Lord, you have heard their insults,
all their plots against me—
⁶²what my enemies whisper and mutter
against me all day long.
⁶³Look at them! Sitting or standing,
they mock me in their songs.

⁶⁴Pay them back what they deserve, O Lord,
for what their hands have done.
⁶⁵Put a veil over their hearts,
and may your curse be on them!
⁶⁶Pursue them in anger and destroy them
from under the heavens of the Lord.

4^a   How the gold has lost its luster,
the fine gold become dull!
The sacred gems are scattered
at the head of every street.

²How the precious sons of Zion,
once worth their weight in gold,
are now considered as pots of clay,
the work of a potter's hands!

³Even jackals offer their breasts
to nurse their young,
but my people have become heartless
like ostriches in the desert.

⁴Because of thirst the infant's tongue
sticks to the roof of its mouth;
the children beg for bread,
but no one gives it to them.

⁵Those who once ate delicacies
are destitute in the streets.
Those nurtured in purple
now lie on ash heaps.

⁶The punishment of my people
is greater than that of Sodom,
which was overthrown in a
moment
without a hand turned to help
her.

⁷Their princes were brighter
than snow
and whiter than milk,
their bodies more ruddy than
rubies,
their appearance like
sapphires.^b

⁸But now they are blacker than
soot;
they are not recognized in the
streets.

Sob!
I need a tissue.

SEE LAMENTATIONS 1–5

^aThis chapter is an acrostic poem, the verses of which begin
with the successive letters of the Hebrew alphabet.   ^b7 Or
lapis lazuli

Their skin has shriveled on their bones;
it has become as dry as a stick.

⁹Those killed by the sword are better off
than those who die of famine;
racked with hunger, they waste away
for lack of food from the field.

¹⁰With their own hands compassionate women
have cooked their own children,
who became their food
when my people were destroyed.

¹¹The LORD has given full vent to his wrath;
he has poured out his fierce anger.
He kindled a fire in Zion
that consumed her foundations.

¹²The kings of the earth did not believe,
nor did any of the world's people,
that enemies and foes could enter
the gates of Jerusalem.

¹³But it happened because of the sins of her prophets
and the iniquities of her priests,
who shed within her
the blood of the righteous.

¹⁴Now they grope through the streets
like men who are blind.
They are so defiled with blood
that no one dares to touch their garments.

¹⁵"Go away! You are unclean!" men cry to them.
"Away! Away! Don't touch us!"
When they flee and wander about,
people among the nations say,
"They can stay here no longer."

¹⁶The LORD himself has scattered them;
he no longer watches over them.
The priests are shown no honor,
the elders no favor.

¹⁷Moreover, our eyes failed,
looking in vain for help;
from our towers we watched
for a nation that could not save us.

¹⁸Men stalked us at every step,
so we could not walk in our streets.
Our end was near, our days were numbered,
for our end had come.

¹⁹Our pursuers were swifter
than eagles in the sky;
they chased us over the mountains
and lay in wait for us in the desert.

²⁰The LORD's anointed, our very life breath,
was caught in their traps.
We thought that under his shadow
we would live among the nations.

²¹ Rejoice and be glad, O Daughter of Edom,
  you who live in the land of Uz.
But to you also the cup will be passed;
  you will be drunk and stripped naked.

²² O Daughter of Zion, your punishment will end;
  he will not prolong your exile.
But, O Daughter of Edom, he will punish your sin
  and expose your wickedness.

5 Remember, O LORD, what has happened to us;
  look, and see our disgrace.
² Our inheritance has been turned over to aliens,
  our homes to foreigners.
³ We have become orphans and fatherless,
  our mothers like widows.
⁴ We must buy the water we drink;
  our wood can be had only at a price.
⁵ Those who pursue us are at our heels;
  we are weary and find no rest.
⁶ We submitted to Egypt and Assyria
  to get enough bread.
⁷ Our fathers sinned and are no more,
  and we bear their punishment.
⁸ Slaves rule over us,
  and there is none to free us from their hands.
⁹ We get our bread at the risk of our lives
  because of the sword in the desert.
¹⁰ Our skin is hot as an oven,
  feverish from hunger.
¹¹ Women have been ravished in Zion,
  and virgins in the towns of Judah.
¹² Princes have been hung up by their hands;
  elders are shown no respect.
¹³ Young men toil at the millstones;
  boys stagger under loads of wood.
¹⁴ The elders are gone from the city gate;
  the young men have stopped their music.
¹⁵ Joy is gone from our hearts;
  our dancing has turned to mourning.
¹⁶ The crown has fallen from our head.
  Woe to us, for we have sinned!
¹⁷ Because of this our hearts are faint,
  because of these things our eyes grow dim
¹⁸ for Mount Zion, which lies desolate,
  with jackals prowling over it.

¹⁹ You, O LORD, reign forever;
  your throne endures from generation to generation.
²⁰ Why do you always forget us?
  Why do you forsake us so long?
²¹ Restore us to yourself, O LORD, that we may return;
  renew our days as of old
²² unless you have utterly rejected us
  and are angry with us beyond measure.

Introduction

to the

book of # Ezekiel

PICTURE IT.

Do you ever wonder what God looks like? Like a dark, angry cloud hurling bolts of lightening? Like an old man with a long white beard? No matter how you use your imagination, it's hard to picture God.

Ezekiel was in Babylon with Jewish captives just before the final invasion of their homeland. He saw God as a fire, about to destroy Jerusalem. God would show his holiness in this terrible judgment. Years after the city was destroyed, Ezekiel preached again. God would now show his love and bring the Jews home to build a new temple.

Fun damentals

Are actions or words better when you're trying to introduce others to God (Ezekiel 4)?

How close can a holy God stay to people who make a practice of sin-ning (Ezekiel 8–11)?

If you try to witness to someone and he or she doesn't listen, is it your fault (Ezekiel 33:1-6)?

The Living Creatures and the Glory of the Lord   In the*ᵃ* thirtieth year, in the fourth month on the fifth day, while I was among the exiles by the Kebar River, the heavens were opened and I saw visions of God.

²On the fifth of the month—it was the fifth year of the exile of King Jehoiachin— ³the word of the Lord came to Ezekiel the priest, the son of Buzi,*ᵇ* by the Kebar River in the land of the Babylonians.*ᶜ* There the hand of the Lord was upon him.

⁴I looked, and I saw a windstorm coming out of the north—an immense cloud with flashing lightning and surrounded by brilliant light. The center of the fire looked like glowing metal, ⁵and in the fire was what looked like four living creatures. In appearance their form was that of a man, ⁶but each of them had four faces and four wings. ⁷Their legs were straight; their feet were like those of a calf and gleamed like burnished bronze. ⁸Under their wings on their four sides they had the hands of a man. All four of them had faces and wings, ⁹and their wings touched one another. Each one went straight ahead; they did not turn as they moved.

¹⁰Their faces looked like this: Each of the four had the face of a man, and on the right side each had the face of a lion, and on the left the face of an ox; each also had the face of an eagle. ¹¹Such were their faces. Their wings were spread out upward; each had two wings, one touching the wing of another creature on either side, and two wings covering its body. ¹²Each one went straight ahead. Wherever the spirit would go, they would go, without turning as they went. ¹³The appearance of the living creatures was like burning coals of fire or like torches. Fire moved back and forth among the creatures; it was bright, and lightning flashed out of it. ¹⁴The creatures sped back and forth like flashes of lightning.

¹⁵As I looked at the living creatures, I saw a wheel on the ground beside each creature with its four faces. ¹⁶This was the appearance and structure of the wheels: They sparkled like chrysolite, and all four looked alike. Each appeared to be made like a wheel intersecting a wheel. ¹⁷As they moved, they would go in any one of the four directions the creatures faced; the wheels did not turn about*ᵈ* as the creatures went. ¹⁸Their rims were high and awesome, and all four rims were full of eyes all around.

¹⁹When the living creatures moved, the wheels beside them moved; and when the living creatures rose from the ground, the wheels also rose. ²⁰Wherever the spirit would go, they would go, and the wheels would rise along with them, because the spirit of the living creatures was in the wheels. ²¹When the creatures moved, they also moved; when the creatures stood still, they also stood still; and when the creatures rose from the ground, the wheels rose along with them, because the spirit of the living creatures was in the wheels.

²²Spread out above the heads of the living creatures was what looked like an expanse, sparkling like ice, and awesome. ²³Under the expanse their wings were stretched out one toward the other, and each had two wings covering its body. ²⁴When the creatures moved, I heard the sound of their wings, like the roar of rushing waters, like the voice of the Almighty,*ᵉ* like the tumult of an army. When they stood still, they lowered their wings.

²⁵Then there came a voice from above the expanse over their heads as they stood with lowered wings. ²⁶Above the expanse over their heads was what looked like a throne of sapphire,*ᶠ* and high above on the throne was a figure like that of a man. ²⁷I saw that from what appeared to be his waist up he looked like glowing metal, as if full of fire, and that from there down he looked like fire; and brilliant light surrounded him. ²⁸Like the ap-

---

ᵃ1 Or my, ᵇ3 Or Ezekiel son of Buzi the priest ᶜ3 Or Chaldeans ᵈ17 Or aside ᵉ24 Hebrew Shaddai ᶠ26 Or lapis lazuli

pearance of a rainbow in the clouds on a rainy day, so was the radiance around him.

This was the appearance of the likeness of the glory of the LORD. When I saw it, I fell facedown, and I heard the voice of one speaking.

Ezekiel's Call He said to me, "Son of man, stand up on your feet and I will speak to you." ²As he spoke, the Spirit came into me and raised me to my feet, and I heard him speaking to me.

³He said: "Son of man, I am sending you to the Israelites, to a rebellious nation that has rebelled against me; they and their fathers have been in revolt against me to this very day. ⁴The people to whom I am sending you are obstinate and stubborn. Say to them, 'This is what the Sovereign LORD says.' ⁵And whether they listen or fail to listen—for they are a rebellious house—they will know that a prophet has been among them. ⁶And you, son of man, do not be afraid of them or their words. Do not be afraid, though briers and thorns are all around you and you live among scorpions. Do not be afraid of what they say or terrified by them, though they are a rebellious house. ⁷You must speak my words to them, whether they listen or fail to listen, for they are rebellious. ⁸But you, son of man, listen to what I say to you. Do not rebel like that rebellious house; open your mouth and eat what I give you."

⁹Then I looked, and I saw a hand stretched out to me. In it was a scroll, ¹⁰which he unrolled before me. On both sides of it were written words of lament and mourning and woe.

And he said to me, "Son of man, eat what is before you, eat this scroll; then go and speak to the house of Israel." ²So I opened my mouth, and he gave me the scroll to eat.

³Then he said to me, "Son of man, eat this scroll I am giving you and fill your stomach with it." So I ate it, and it tasted as sweet as honey in my mouth.

EZEKIEL 2:6–7

Sticks and stones can break my bones, but names will never hurt me." Have you ever heard that old saying? It's not true, you know. If you've ever heard anyone laugh and make a rude remark about your looks, you know words can hurt. If anyone has ever started a rumor about you, you know words can hurt. But words can also heal. A word of encouragement, a simple compliment or an expression of appreciation can make you feel liked and confident. God reminded Ezekiel not to fear the words of his enemies but to "speak my words" to all. Be aware of the words you speak. Be sure they are words that heal rather than hurt.

⁴He then said to me: "Son of man, go now to the house of Israel and speak my words to them. ⁵You are not being sent to a people of obscure speech and difficult language, but to the house of Israel— ⁶not to many peoples of obscure speech and difficult language, whose words you cannot understand. Surely if I had sent you to them, they would have listened to you. ⁷But the house of Israel is not willing to listen to you because they are not willing to listen to me, for the whole house of Israel is hardened and obstinate. ⁸But I will make you as unyielding and hardened as they are. ⁹I will make your forehead like the hardest stone, harder than flint. Do not be afraid of them or terrified by them, though they are a rebellious house."

¹⁰And he said to me, "Son of man, listen carefully and take to heart all the words I speak to you. ¹¹Go now to your countrymen in exile and speak to them. Say to them, 'This is what the Sovereign LORD says,' whether they listen or fail to listen."

¹²Then the Spirit lifted me up, and I heard behind me a loud rumbling

sound—May the glory of the Lord be praised in his dwelling place!— ¹³the sound of the wings of the living creatures brushing against each other and the sound of the wheels beside them, a loud rumbling sound. ¹⁴The Spirit then lifted me up and took me away, and I went in bitterness and in the anger of my spirit, with the strong hand of the Lord upon me. ¹⁵I came to the exiles who lived at Tel Abib near the Kebar River. And there, where they were living, I sat among them for seven days—overwhelmed.

Warning to Israel ¹⁶At the end of seven days the word of the Lord came to me: ¹⁷"Son of man, I have made you a watchman for the house of Israel; so hear the word I speak and give them warning from me. ¹⁸When I say to a wicked man, 'You will surely die,' and you do not warn him or speak out to dissuade him from his evil ways in order to save his life, that wicked man will die for*ᵃ* his sin, and I will hold you accountable for his blood. ¹⁹But if you do warn the wicked man and he does not turn from his wickedness or from his evil ways, he will die for his sin; but you will have saved yourself.

²⁰"Again, when a righteous man turns from his righteousness and does evil, and I put a stumbling block before him, he will die. Since you did not warn him, he will die for his sin. The righteous things he did will not be remembered, and I will hold you accountable for his blood. ²¹But if you do warn the righteous man not to sin and he does not sin, he will surely live because he took warning, and you will have saved yourself."

²²The hand of the Lord was upon me there, and he said to me, "Get up and go out to the plain, and there I will speak to you." ²³So I got up and went out to the plain. And the glory of the Lord was standing there, like the glory I had seen by the Kebar River, and I fell facedown.

²⁴Then the Spirit came into me and raised me to my feet. He spoke to me and said: "Go, shut yourself inside your house. ²⁵And you, son of man, they will tie with ropes; you will be bound so that you cannot go out among the people. ²⁶I will make your tongue stick to the roof of your mouth so that you will be silent and unable to rebuke them, though they are a rebellious house. ²⁷But when I speak to you, I will open your mouth and you shall say to them, 'This is what the Sovereign Lord says.' Whoever will listen let him listen, and whoever will refuse let him refuse; for they are a rebellious house.

EZEKIEL 3

QUIZZER

Q: What strange meal did Ezekiel eat?

BONUS: What would have been the ingredients of the main dish?

Answers on page 1076

Siege of Jerusalem Symbolized "Now, son of man, take a clay tablet, put it in front of you and draw the city of Jerusalem on it. ²Then lay siege to it: Erect siege works against it, build a ramp up to it, set up camps against it and put battering rams around it. ³Then take an iron pan, place it as an iron wall between you and the city and turn your face toward it. It will be under siege, and you shall besiege it. This will be a sign to the house of Israel.

⁴"Then lie on your left side and put the sin of the house of Israel upon yourself.*ᵇ* You are to bear their sin for the number of days you lie on your side. ⁵I have assigned you the same number of days as the years of their sin. So for 390 days you will bear the sin of the house of Israel.

⁶"After you have finished this, lie down again, this time on your right side, and bear the sin of the house of Judah. I have assigned you 40 days, a day for each year. ⁷Turn your face toward the siege of Jerusalem and with bared arm prophesy against her. ⁸I will tie you up with ropes so that you cannot turn from one side to the other until you have finished the days of your siege.

ᵃ18 Or in; also in verses 19 and 20   ᵇ4 Or your side

⁹"Take wheat and barley, beans and lentils, millet and spelt; put them in a storage jar and use them to make bread for yourself. You are to eat it during the 390 days you lie on your side. ¹⁰Weigh out twenty shekels*ᵃ* of food to eat each day and eat it at set times. ¹¹Also measure out a sixth of a hin*ᵇ* of water and drink it at set times. ¹²Eat the food as you would a barley cake; bake it in the sight of the people, using human excrement for fuel." ¹³The LORD said, "In this way the people of Israel will eat defiled food among the nations where I will drive them."

¹⁴Then I said, "Not so, Sovereign LORD! I have never defiled myself. From my youth until now I have never eaten anything found dead or torn by wild animals. No unclean meat has ever entered my mouth."

¹⁵"Very well," he said, "I will let you bake your bread over cow manure instead of human excrement."

¹⁶He then said to me: "Son of man, I will cut off the supply of food in Jerusalem. The people will eat rationed food in anxiety and drink rationed water in despair, ¹⁷for food and water will be scarce. They will be appalled at the sight of each other and will waste away because of*ᶜ* their sin.

"Now, son of man, take a sharp sword and use it as a barber's razor to shave your head and your beard. Then take a set of scales and divide up the hair. ²When the days of your siege come to an end, burn a third of the hair with fire inside the city. Take a third and strike it with the sword all around the city. And scatter a third to the wind. For I will pursue them with drawn sword. ³But take a few strands of hair and tuck them away in the folds of your garment. ⁴Again, take a few of these and throw them into the fire and burn them up. A fire will spread from there to the whole house of Israel.

⁵"This is what the Sovereign LORD says: This is Jerusalem, which I have set in the center of the nations, with countries all around her. ⁶Yet in her wickedness she has rebelled against my laws and decrees more than the nations and countries around her. She has rejected my laws and has not followed my decrees.

⁷"Therefore this is what the Sovereign LORD says: You have been more unruly than the nations around you and have not followed my decrees or kept my laws. You have not even*ᵈ* conformed to the standards of the nations around you.

⁸"Therefore this is what the Sovereign LORD says: I myself am against you, Jerusalem, and I will inflict punishment on you in the sight of the nations. ⁹Because of all your detestable idols, I will do to you what I have never done before and will never do again. ¹⁰Therefore in your midst fathers will eat their children, and children will eat their fathers. I will inflict punishment on you and will scatter all your survivors to the winds. ¹¹Therefore as surely as I live, declares the Sovereign LORD, because you have defiled my sanctuary with all your vile images and detestable practices, I myself will withdraw my favor; I will not look on you with pity or spare you. ¹²A third of your people will die of the plague or perish by famine inside you; a third will fall by the sword outside your walls; and a third I will scatter to the winds and pursue with drawn sword.

¹³"Then my anger will cease and my wrath against them will subside, and I will be avenged. And when I have spent my wrath upon them, they will know that I the LORD have spoken in my zeal.

¹⁴"I will make you a ruin and a reproach among the nations around you, in the sight of all who pass by. ¹⁵You will be a reproach and a taunt, a warning

---

ᵃ10 That is, about 8 ounces (about 0.2 kilogram)   *ᵇ11* That is, about 2/3 quart (about 0.6 liter)   *ᶜ17* Or *away in*   *ᵈ7* Most Hebrew manuscripts; some Hebrew manuscripts and Syriac *You have*

and an object of horror to the nations around you when I inflict punishment on you in anger and in wrath and with stinging rebuke. I the Lord have spoken. ¹⁶When I shoot at you with my deadly and destructive arrows of famine, I will shoot to destroy you. I will bring more and more famine upon you and cut off your supply of food. ¹⁷I will send famine and wild beasts against you, and they will leave you childless. Plague and bloodshed will sweep through you, and I will bring the sword against you. I the Lord have spoken."

6 *A Prophecy Against the Mountains of Israel* The word of the Lord came to me: ²"Son of man, set your face against the mountains of Israel; prophesy against them ³and say: 'O mountains of Israel, hear the word of the Sovereign Lord. This is what the Sovereign Lord says to the mountains and hills, to the ravines and valleys: I am about to bring a sword against you, and I will destroy your high places. ⁴Your altars will be demolished and your incense altars will be smashed; and I will slay your people in front of your idols. ⁵I will lay the dead bodies of the Israelites in front of their idols, and I will scatter your bones around your altars. ⁶Wherever you live, the towns will be laid waste and the high places demolished, so that your altars will be laid waste and devastated, your idols smashed and ruined, your incense altars broken down, and what you have made wiped out. ⁷Your people will fall slain among you, and you will know that I am the Lord.

⁸" 'But I will spare some, for some of you will escape the sword when you are scattered among the lands and nations. ⁹Then in the nations where they have been carried captive, those who escape will remember me—how I have been grieved by their adulterous hearts, which have turned away from me, and by their eyes, which have lusted after their idols. They will loathe themselves for the evil they have done and for all their detestable practices. ¹⁰And they will know that I am the Lord; I did not threaten in vain to bring this calamity on them.

¹¹" 'This is what the Sovereign Lord says: Strike your hands together and stamp your feet and cry out "Alas!" because of all the wicked and detestable practices of the house of Israel, for they will fall by the sword, famine and plague. ¹²He that is far away will die of the plague, and he that is near will fall by the sword, and he that survives and is spared will die of famine. So will I spend my wrath upon them. ¹³And they will know that I am the Lord, when their people lie slain among their idols around their altars, on every high hill and on all the mountaintops, under every spreading tree and every

---

In Ezekiel 6:2–3 God tells Ezekiel to speak to the mountains. Mountains can't hear. Why talk to them?

Like other literature, the Bible uses literary devices. A writer uses literary devices to create a powerful image for the reader. Speaking as if mountains were people is a literary device called "personification." God used this powerful way to tell the people that he knew about the altars they had built on top of the mountains. And he would soon smash those places of pagan worship and destroy the people who worshiped there (Ezekiel 6:3–7).

When the Bible writers used these literary devices, they hoped to create a picture in your mind that would help you better understand God's message to you today.

The Bible Says

Talk to the Hills?

leafy oak—places where they offered fragrant incense to all their idols. ¹⁴And I will stretch out my hand against them and make the land a desolate waste from the desert to Diblah*ᵃ*—wherever they live. Then they will know that I am the LORD.' "

7 *The End Has Come* The word of the LORD came to me: ²"Son of man, this is what the Sovereign LORD says to the land of Israel: The end! The end has come upon the four corners of the land. ³The end is now upon you and I will unleash my anger against you. I will judge you according to your conduct and repay you for all your detestable practices. ⁴I will not look on you with pity or spare you; I will surely repay you for your conduct and the detestable practices among you. Then you will know that I am the LORD.

⁵"This is what the Sovereign LORD says: Disaster! An unheard-ofᵇ disaster is coming. ⁶The end has come! The end has come! It has roused itself against you. It has come! ⁷Doom has come upon you—you who dwell in the land. The time has come, the day is near; there is panic, not joy, upon the mountains. ⁸I am about to pour out my wrath on you and spend my anger against you; I will judge you according to your conduct and repay you for all your detestable practices. ⁹I will not look on you with pity or spare you; I will repay you in accordance with your conduct and the detestable practices among you. Then you will know that it is I the LORD who strikes the blow.

¹⁰"The day is here! It has come! Doom has burst forth, the rod has budded, arrogance has blossomed! ¹¹Violence has grown intoᶜ a rod to punish wickedness; none of the people will be left, none of that crowd—no wealth, nothing of value. ¹²The time has come, the day has arrived. Let not the buyer rejoice nor the seller grieve, for wrath is upon the whole crowd. ¹³The seller will not recover the land he has sold as long as both of them live, for the vision concerning the whole crowd will not be reversed. Because of their sins, not one of them will preserve his life. ¹⁴Though they blow the trumpet and get everything ready, no one will go into battle, for my wrath is upon the whole crowd.

¹⁵"Outside is the sword, inside are plague and famine; those in the country will die by the sword, and those in the city will be devoured by famine and plague. ¹⁶All who survive and escape will be in the mountains, moaning like doves of the valleys, each because of his sins. ¹⁷Every hand will go limp, and every knee will become as weak as water. ¹⁸They will put on sackcloth and be clothed with terror. Their faces will be covered with shame and their heads will be shaved. ¹⁹They will throw their silver into the streets, and their gold will be an unclean thing. Their silver and gold will not be able to save them in the day of the LORD's wrath. They will not satisfy their hunger or fill their stomachs with it, for it has made them stumble into sin. ²⁰They were proud of their beautiful jewelry and used it to make their detestable idols and vile images. Therefore I will turn these into an unclean thing for them. ²¹I will hand it all over as plunder to foreigners and as loot to the wicked of the earth, and they will defile it. ²²I will turn my face away from them, and they will desecrate my treasured place; robbers will enter it and desecrate it.

²³"Prepare chains, because the land is full of bloodshed and the city is full of violence. ²⁴I will bring the most wicked of the nations to take possession of their houses; I will put an end to the pride of the mighty, and their sanctuaries will be desecrated. ²⁵When terror comes, they will seek peace, but there will be none. ²⁶Calamity upon calamity will come, and rumor upon rumor. They will try to get a vision from the prophet; the teaching of the law by the priest will be lost, as will the counsel of the elders. ²⁷The king will

---

ᵃ14 Most Hebrew manuscripts; a few Hebrew manuscripts *Riblah* *ᵇ5* Most Hebrew manuscripts; some Hebrew manuscripts and Syriac *Disaster after* *ᶜ11* Or *The violent one has become*

mourn, the prince will be clothed with despair, and the hands of the people of the land will tremble. I will deal with them according to their conduct, and by their own standards I will judge them. Then they will know that I am the LORD."

8 *Idolatry in the Temple* In the sixth year, in the sixth month on the fifth day, while I was sitting in my house and the elders of Judah were sitting before me, the hand of the Sovereign LORD came upon me there. ²I looked, and I saw a figure like that of a man.*ᵃ* From what appeared to be his waist down he was like fire, and from there up his appearance was as bright as glowing metal. ³He stretched out what looked like a hand and took me by the hair of my head. The Spirit lifted me up between earth and heaven and in visions of God he took me to Jerusalem, to the entrance to the north gate of the inner court, where the idol that provokes to jealousy stood. ⁴And there before me was the glory of the God of Israel, as in the vision I had seen in the plain.

⁵Then he said to me, "Son of man, look toward the north." So I looked, and in the entrance north of the gate of the altar I saw this idol of jealousy.

⁶And he said to me, "Son of man, do you see what they are doing—the utterly detestable things the house of Israel is doing here, things that will drive me far from my sanctuary? But you will see things that are even more detestable."

⁷Then he brought me to the entrance to the court. I looked, and I saw a hole in the wall. ⁸He said to me, "Son of man, now dig into the wall." So I dug into the wall and saw a doorway there.

⁹And he said to me, "Go in and see the wicked and detestable things they are doing here." ¹⁰So I went in and looked, and I saw portrayed all over the walls all kinds of crawling things and detestable animals and all the idols of the house of Israel. ¹¹In front of them stood seventy elders of the house of Israel, and Jaazaniah son of Shaphan was standing among them. Each had a censer in his hand, and a fragrant cloud of incense was rising.

¹²He said to me, "Son of man, have you seen what the elders of the house of Israel are doing in the darkness, each at the shrine of his own idol? They say, 'The LORD does not see us; the LORD has forsaken the land.'" ¹³Again, he said, "You will see them doing things that are even more detestable."

¹⁴Then he brought me to the entrance to the north gate of the house of the LORD, and I saw women sitting there, mourning for Tammuz. ¹⁵He said to me, "Do you see this, son of man? You will see things that are even more detestable than this."

¹⁶He then brought me into the inner court of the house of the LORD, and there at the entrance to the temple, between the portico and the altar, were about twenty-five men. With their backs toward the temple of the LORD and their faces toward the east, they were bowing down to the sun in the east.

¹⁷He said to me, "Have you seen this,

ᵃ2 Or saw a fiery figure

EZEKIEL 8–11

The people in Judah thought they were safe from the Babylonians because God's temple stood in Jerusalem. But in a vision from God Ezekiel saw the "glory of the LORD" (Ezekiel 10:18), God's visible expression, actually leave the temple. Without God the temple was a beautiful but empty heap of stones, and no protection at all. The Babylonian army did sweep down on the little Jewish state. It crushed their defenses, captured the city and destroyed the temple. That terrible defeat is a reminder of an important truth: Just because you belong to the Lord does not mean that he will protect you from the consequences of doing wrong.

Direct Line

son of man? Is it a trivial matter for the house of Judah to do the detestable things they are doing here? Must they also fill the land with violence and continually provoke me to anger? Look at them putting the branch to their nose! [18]Therefore I will deal with them in anger; I will not look on them with pity or spare them. Although they shout in my ears, I will not listen to them."

Idolaters Killed   Then I heard him call out in a loud voice, "Bring the guards of the city here, each with a weapon in his hand." [2]And I saw six men coming from the direction of the upper gate, which faces north, each with a deadly weapon in his hand. With them was a man clothed in linen who had a writing kit at his side. They came in and stood beside the bronze altar.

[3]Now the glory of the God of Israel went up from above the cherubim, where it had been, and moved to the threshold of the temple. Then the LORD called to the man clothed in linen who had the writing kit at his side [4]and said to him, "Go throughout the city of Jerusalem and put a mark on the foreheads of those who grieve and lament over all the detestable things that are done in it."

[5]As I listened, he said to the others, "Follow him through the city and kill, without showing pity or compassion. [6]Slaughter old men, young men and maidens, women and children, but do not touch anyone who has the mark. Begin at my sanctuary." So they began with the elders who were in front of the temple.

[7]Then he said to them, "Defile the temple and fill the courts with the slain. Go!" So they went out and began killing throughout the city. [8]While they were killing and I was left alone, I fell facedown, crying out, "Ah, Sovereign LORD! Are you going to destroy the entire remnant of Israel in this outpouring of your wrath on Jerusalem?"

[9]He answered me, "The sin of the house of Israel and Judah is exceedingly great; the land is full of bloodshed and the city is full of injustice. They say, 'The LORD has forsaken the land; the LORD does not see.' [10]So I will not look on them with pity or spare them, but I will bring down on their own heads what they have done."

[11]Then the man in linen with the writing kit at his side brought back word, saying, "I have done as you commanded."

The Glory Departs From the Temple   I looked, and I saw the likeness of a throne of sapphire[a] above the expanse that was over the heads of the cherubim. [2]The LORD said to the man clothed in linen, "Go in among the wheels beneath the cherubim. Fill your hands with burning coals from among the cherubim and scatter them over the city." And as I watched, he went in.

[3]Now the cherubim were standing on the south side of the temple when the man went in, and a cloud filled the inner court. [4]Then the glory of the LORD rose from above the cherubim and moved to the threshold of the temple. The cloud filled the temple, and the court was full of the radiance of the glory of the LORD. [5]The sound of the wings of the cherubim could be heard as far away as the outer court, like the voice of God Almighty[b] when he speaks.

[6]When the LORD commanded the man in linen, "Take fire from among the wheels, from among the cherubim," the man went in and stood beside a wheel. [7]Then one of the cherubim reached out his hand to the fire that was among them. He took up some of it and put it into the hands of the man in linen, who took it and went out. [8](Under the wings of the cherubim could be seen what looked like the hands of a man.)

a1 Or lapis lazuli   b5 Hebrew El-Shaddai

⁹I looked, and I saw beside the cherubim four wheels, one beside each of the cherubim; the wheels sparkled like chrysolite. ¹⁰As for their appearance, the four of them looked alike; each was like a wheel intersecting a wheel. ¹¹As they moved, they would go in any one of the four directions the cherubim faced; the wheels did not turn about*ᵃ* as the cherubim went. The cherubim went in whatever direction the head faced, without turning as they went. ¹²Their entire bodies, including their backs, their hands and their wings, were completely full of eyes, as were their four wheels. ¹³I heard the wheels being called "the whirling wheels." ¹⁴Each of the cherubim had four faces: One face was that of a cherub, the second the face of a man, the third the face of a lion, and the fourth the face of an eagle.

¹⁵Then the cherubim rose upward. These were the living creatures I had seen by the Kebar River. ¹⁶When the cherubim moved, the wheels beside them moved; and when the cherubim spread their wings to rise from the ground, the wheels did not leave their side. ¹⁷When the cherubim stood still, they also stood still; and when the cherubim rose, they rose with them, because the spirit of the living creatures was in them.

¹⁸Then the glory of the Lᴏʀᴅ departed from over the threshold of the temple and stopped above the cherubim. ¹⁹While I watched, the cherubim spread their wings and rose from the ground, and as they went, the wheels went with them. They stopped at the entrance to the east gate of the Lᴏʀᴅ's house, and the glory of the God of Israel was above them.

²⁰These were the living creatures I had seen beneath the God of Israel by the Kebar River, and I realized that they were cherubim. ²¹Each had four faces and four wings, and under their wings was what looked like the hands of a man. ²²Their faces had the same appearance as those I had seen by the Kebar River. Each one went straight ahead.

11 *Judgment on Israel's Leaders* Then the Spirit lifted me up and brought me to the gate of the house of the Lᴏʀᴅ that faces east. There at the entrance to the gate were twenty-five men, and I saw among them Jaazaniah son of Azzur and Pelatiah son of Benaiah, leaders of the people. ²The Lᴏʀᴅ said to me, "Son of man, these are the men who are plotting evil and giving wicked advice in this city. ³They say, 'Will it not soon be time to build houses?*ᵇ* This city is a cooking pot, and we are the meat.' ⁴Therefore prophesy against them; prophesy, son of man."

⁵Then the Spirit of the Lᴏʀᴅ came upon me, and he told me to say: "This is what the Lᴏʀᴅ says: That is what you are saying, O house of Israel, but I know what is going through your mind. ⁶You have killed many people in this city and filled its streets with the dead.

⁷"Therefore this is what the Sovereign Lᴏʀᴅ says: The bodies you have thrown there are the meat and this city is the pot, but I will drive you out of it. ⁸You fear the sword, and the sword is what I will bring against you, declares the Sovereign Lᴏʀᴅ. ⁹I will drive you out of the city and hand you over to foreigners and inflict punishment on you. ¹⁰You will fall by the sword, and I will execute judgment on you at the borders of Israel. Then you will know that I am the Lᴏʀᴅ. ¹¹This city will not be a pot for you, nor will you be the meat in it; I will execute judgment on you at the borders of Israel. ¹²And you will know that I am the Lᴏʀᴅ, for you have not followed my decrees or kept my laws but have conformed to the standards of the nations around you."

¹³Now as I was prophesying, Pelatiah son of Benaiah died. Then I fell facedown and cried out in a loud voice, "Ah, Sovereign Lᴏʀᴅ! Will you completely destroy the remnant of Israel?"

¹⁴The word of the Lᴏʀᴅ came to me: ¹⁵"Son of man, your brothers—your

---

ᵃ11 Or aside   ᵇ3 Or This is not the time to build houses.

brothers who are your blood relatives*a* and the whole house of Israel—are those of whom the people of Jerusalem have said, 'They are*b* far away from the LORD; this land was given to us as our possession.'

Promised Return of Israel ¹⁶"Therefore say: 'This is what the Sovereign LORD says: Although I sent them far away among the nations and scattered them among the countries, yet for a little while I have been a sanctuary for them in the countries where they have gone.'

¹⁷"Therefore say: 'This is what the Sovereign LORD says: I will gather you from the nations and bring you back from the countries where you have been scattered, and I will give you back the land of Israel again.'

¹⁸"They will return to it and remove all its vile images and detestable idols. ¹⁹I will give them an undivided heart and put a new spirit in them; I will remove from them their heart of stone and give them a heart of flesh. ²⁰Then they will follow my decrees and be careful to keep my laws. They will be my people, and I will be their God. ²¹But as for those whose hearts are devoted to their vile images and detestable idols, I will bring down on their own heads what they have done, declares the Sovereign LORD."

²²Then the cherubim, with the wheels beside them, spread their wings, and the glory of the God of Israel was above them. ²³The glory of the LORD went up from within the city and stopped above the mountain east of it. ²⁴The Spirit lifted me up and brought me to the exiles in Babylonia*c* in the vision given by the Spirit of God.

Then the vision I had seen went up from me, ²⁵and I told the exiles everything the LORD had shown me.

> They will be my people, and I will be their God
> (Ezekiel 11:20).

The Exile Symbolized The word of the LORD came to me: ²"Son of man, you are living among a rebellious people. They have eyes to see but do not see and ears to hear but do not hear, for they are a rebellious people.

³"Therefore, son of man, pack your belongings for exile and in the daytime, as they watch, set out and go from where you are to another place. Perhaps they will understand, though they are a rebellious house. ⁴During the daytime, while they watch, bring out your belongings packed for exile. Then in the evening, while they are watching, go out like those who go into exile. ⁵While they watch, dig through the wall and take your belongings out through it. ⁶Put them on your shoulder as they are watching and carry them out at dusk. Cover your face so that you cannot see the land, for I have made you a sign to the house of Israel."

⁷So I did as I was commanded. During the day I brought out my things packed for exile. Then in the evening I dug through the wall with my hands. I took my belongings out at dusk, carrying them on my shoulders while they watched.

⁸In the morning the word of the LORD came to me: ⁹"Son of man, did not that rebellious house of Israel ask you, 'What are you doing?'

¹⁰"Say to them, 'This is what the Sovereign LORD says: This oracle concerns the prince in Jerusalem and the whole house of Israel who are there.' ¹¹Say to them, 'I am a sign to you.'

"As I have done, so it will be done to them. They will go into exile as captives.

¹²"The prince among them will put his things on his shoulder at dusk and leave, and a hole will be dug in the wall for him to go through. He will cov-

---

*a*15 Or *are in exile with you* (see Septuagint and Syriac) *b*15 Or *those to whom the people of Jerusalem have said, 'Stay* *c*24 Or *Chaldea*

er his face so that he cannot see the land. ¹³I will spread my net for him, and he will be caught in my snare; I will bring him to Babylonia, the land of the Chaldeans, but he will not see it, and there he will die. ¹⁴I will scatter to the winds all those around him—his staff and all his troops—and I will pursue them with drawn sword.

¹⁵"They will know that I am the Lord, when I disperse them among the nations and scatter them through the countries. ¹⁶But I will spare a few of them from the sword, famine and plague, so that in the nations where they go they may acknowledge all their detestable practices. Then they will know that I am the Lord."

¹⁷The word of the Lord came to me: ¹⁸"Son of man, tremble as you eat your food, and shudder in fear as you drink your water. ¹⁹Say to the people of the land: 'This is what the Sovereign Lord says about those living in Jerusalem and in the land of Israel: They will eat their food in anxiety and drink their water in despair, for their land will be stripped of everything in it because of the violence of all who live there. ²⁰The inhabited towns will be laid waste and the land will be desolate. Then you will know that I am the Lord.' "

²¹The word of the Lord came to me: ²²"Son of man, what is this proverb you have in the land of Israel: 'The days go by and every vision comes to nothing'? ²³Say to them, 'This is what the Sovereign Lord says: I am going to put an end to this proverb, and they will no longer quote it in Israel.' Say to them, 'The days are near when every vision will be fulfilled. ²⁴For there will be no more false visions or flattering divinations among the people of Israel. ²⁵But I the Lord will speak what I will, and it shall be fulfilled without delay. For in your days, you rebellious house, I will fulfill whatever I say, declares the Sovereign Lord.' "

²⁶The word of the Lord came to me: ²⁷"Son of man, the house of Israel is saying, 'The vision he sees is for many years from now, and he prophesies about the distant future.'

²⁸"Therefore say to them, 'This is what the Sovereign Lord says: None of my words will be delayed any longer; whatever I say will be fulfilled, declares the Sovereign Lord.' "

13 *False Prophets Condemned* The word of the Lord came to me: ²"Son of man, prophesy against the prophets of Israel who are now prophesying. Say to those who prophesy out of their own imagination: 'Hear the word of the Lord! ³This is what the Sovereign Lord says: Woe to the foolish[a] prophets who follow their own spirit and have seen nothing! ⁴Your prophets, O Israel, are like jackals among ruins. ⁵You have not gone up to the breaks in the wall to repair it for the house of Israel so that it will stand firm in the battle on the day of the Lord. ⁶Their visions are false and their divinations a lie. They say, "The Lord declares," when the Lord has not sent them; yet they expect their words to be fulfilled. ⁷Have you not seen false visions and uttered lying divinations when you say, "The Lord declares," though I have not spoken?

⁸" 'Therefore this is what the Sovereign Lord says: Because of your false words and lying visions, I am against you, declares the Sovereign Lord. ⁹My hand will be against the prophets who see false visions and utter lying divinations. They will not belong to the council of my people or be listed in the records of the house of Israel, nor will they enter the land of Israel. Then you will know that I am the Sovereign Lord.

¹⁰" 'Because they lead my people astray, saying, "Peace," when there is no peace, and because, when a flimsy wall is built, they cover it with whitewash, ¹¹therefore tell those who cover it with whitewash that it is going to fall. Rain

---

a3 Or wicked

will come in torrents, and I will send hailstones hurtling down, and violent winds will burst forth. ¹²When the wall collapses, will people not ask you, "Where is the whitewash you covered it with?"

¹³" 'Therefore this is what the Sovereign LORD says: In my wrath I will unleash a violent wind, and in my anger hailstones and torrents of rain will fall with destructive fury. ¹⁴I will tear down the wall you have covered with whitewash and will level it to the ground so that its foundation will be laid bare. When it*ᵃ* falls, you will be destroyed in it; and you will know that I am the LORD. ¹⁵So I will spend my wrath against the wall and against those who covered it with whitewash. I will say to you, "The wall is gone and so are those who whitewashed it, ¹⁶those prophets of Israel who prophesied to Jerusalem and saw visions of peace for her when there was no peace, declares the Sovereign LORD." '

¹⁷"Now, son of man, set your face against the daughters of your people who prophesy out of their own imagination. Prophesy against them ¹⁸and say, 'This is what the Sovereign LORD says: Woe to the women who sew magic charms on all their wrists and make veils of various lengths for their heads in order to ensnare people. Will you ensnare the lives of my people but preserve your own? ¹⁹You have profaned me among my people for a few handfuls of barley and scraps of bread. By lying to my people, who listen to lies, you have killed those who should not have died and have spared those who should not live.

²⁰" 'Therefore this is what the Sovereign LORD says: I am against your magic charms with which you ensnare people like birds and I will tear them from your arms; I will set free the people that you ensnare like birds. ²¹I will tear off your veils and save my people from your hands, and they will no longer fall prey to your power. Then you will know that I am the LORD. ²²Because you disheartened the righteous with your lies, when I had brought them no grief, and because you encouraged the wicked not to turn from their evil ways and so save their lives, ²³therefore you will no longer see false visions or practice divination. I will save my people from your hands. And then you will know that I am the LORD.' "

14 *Idolaters Condemned* Some of the elders of Israel came to me and sat down in front of me. ²Then the word of the LORD came to me: ³"Son of man, these men have set up idols in their hearts and put wicked stumbling blocks before their faces. Should I let them inquire of me at all? ⁴Therefore speak to them and tell them, 'This is what the Sovereign LORD says: When any Israelite sets up idols in his heart and puts a wicked stumbling block before his face and then goes to a prophet, I the LORD will answer him myself in keeping with his great idolatry. ⁵I will do this to recapture the hearts of the people of Israel, who have all deserted me for their idols.'

⁶"Therefore say to the house of Israel, 'This is what the Sovereign LORD says: Repent! Turn from your idols and renounce all your detestable practices!

⁷" 'When any Israelite or any alien living in Israel separates himself from me and sets up idols in his heart and puts a wicked stumbling block before his face and then goes to a prophet to inquire of me, I the LORD will answer him myself. ⁸I will set my face against that man and make him an example and a byword. I will cut him off from my people. Then you will know that I am the LORD.

⁹" 'And if the prophet is enticed to utter a prophecy, I the LORD have enticed that prophet, and I will stretch out my hand against him and destroy him from among my people Israel. ¹⁰They will bear their guilt—the prophet

ᵃ14 Or the city

will be as guilty as the one who consults him. ¹¹Then the people of Israel will no longer stray from me, nor will they defile themselves anymore with all their sins. They will be my people, and I will be their God, declares the Sovereign LORD.' "

Judgment Inescapable   ¹²The word of the LORD came to me: ¹³"Son of man, if a country sins against me by being unfaithful and I stretch out my hand against it to cut off its food supply and send famine upon it and kill its men and their animals, ¹⁴even if these three men—Noah, Daniel*a* and Job—were in it, they could save only themselves by their righteousness, declares the Sovereign LORD.

¹⁵"Or if I send wild beasts through that country and they leave it childless and it becomes desolate so that no one can pass through it because of the beasts, ¹⁶as surely as I live, declares the Sovereign LORD, even if these three men were in it, they could not save their own sons or daughters. They alone would be saved, but the land would be desolate.

¹⁷"Or if I bring a sword against that country and say, 'Let the sword pass throughout the land,' and I kill its men and their animals, ¹⁸as surely as I live, declares the Sovereign LORD, even if these three men were in it, they could not save their own sons or daughters. They alone would be saved.

¹⁹"Or if I send a plague into that land and pour out my wrath upon it through bloodshed, killing its men and their animals, ²⁰as surely as I live, declares the Sovereign LORD, even if Noah, Daniel and Job were in it, they could save neither son nor daughter. They would save only themselves by their righteousness.

²¹"For this is what the Sovereign LORD says: How much worse will it be when I send against Jerusalem my four dreadful judgments—sword and famine and wild beasts and plague—to kill its men and their animals! ²²Yet there will be some survivors—sons and daughters who will be brought out of it. They will come to you, and when you see their conduct and their actions, you will be consoled regarding the disaster I have brought upon Jerusalem—every disaster I have brought upon it. ²³You will be consoled when you see their conduct and their actions, for you will know that I have done nothing in it without cause, declares the Sovereign LORD."

15 *Jerusalem, A Useless Vine*   The word of the LORD came to me: ²"Son of man, how is the wood of a vine better than that of a branch on any of the trees in the forest? ³Is wood ever taken from it to make anything useful? Do they make pegs from it to hang things on? ⁴And after it is thrown on the fire as fuel and the fire burns both ends and chars the middle, is it then useful for anything? ⁵If it was not useful for anything when it was whole, how much less can it be made into something useful when the fire has burned it and it is charred?

⁶"Therefore this is what the Sovereign LORD says: As I have given the wood of the vine among the trees of the forest as fuel for the fire, so will I treat the people living in Jerusalem. ⁷I will set my face against them. Although they have come out of the fire, the fire will yet consume them. And when I set my face against them, you will know that I am the LORD. ⁸I will make the land desolate because they have been unfaithful, declares the Sovereign LORD."

16 *An Allegory of Unfaithful Jerusalem*   The word of the LORD came to me: ²"Son of man, confront Jerusalem with her detestable practices ³and say, 'This is what the Sovereign LORD says to Jerusalem: Your ancestry and birth were in the land of the Canaanites; your father was an Amorite and your mother a Hittite. ⁴On the day you were born your cord was

---

a14 Or Danel; the Hebrew spelling may suggest a person other than the prophet Daniel; also in verse 20.

not cut, nor were you washed with water to make you clean, nor were you rubbed with salt or wrapped in cloths. [5]No one looked on you with pity or had compassion enough to do any of these things for you. Rather, you were thrown out into the open field, for on the day you were born you were despised.

[6]" 'Then I passed by and saw you kicking about in your blood, and as you lay there in your blood I said to you, "Live!"[a] [7]I made you grow like a plant of the field. You grew up and developed and became the most beautiful of jewels.[b] Your breasts were formed and your hair grew, you who were naked and bare.

[8]" 'Later I passed by, and when I looked at you and saw that you were old enough for love, I spread the corner of my garment over you and covered your nakedness. I gave you my solemn oath and entered into a covenant with you, declares the Sovereign LORD, and you became mine.

[9]" 'I bathed[c] you with water and washed the blood from you and put ointments on you. [10]I clothed you with an embroidered dress and put leather sandals on you. I dressed you in fine linen and covered you with costly garments. [11]I adorned you with jewelry: I put bracelets on your arms and a necklace around your neck, [12]and I put a ring on your nose, earrings on your ears and a beautiful crown on your head. [13]So you were adorned with gold and silver; your clothes were of fine linen and costly fabric and embroidered cloth. Your food was fine flour, honey and olive oil. You became very beautiful and rose to be a queen. [14]And your fame spread among the nations on account of your beauty, because the splendor I had given you made your beauty perfect, declares the Sovereign LORD.

[15]" 'But you trusted in your beauty and used your fame to become a prostitute. You lavished your favors on anyone who passed by and your beauty became his.[d] [16]You took some of your garments to make gaudy high places, where you carried on your prostitution. Such things should not happen, nor should they ever occur. [17]You also took the fine jewelry I gave you, the jewelry made of my gold and silver, and you made for yourself male idols and engaged in prostitution with them. [18]And you took your embroidered clothes to put on them, and you offered my oil and incense before them. [19]Also the food I provided for you—the fine flour, olive oil and honey I gave you to eat—you offered as fragrant incense before them. That is what happened, declares the Sovereign LORD.

[20]" 'And you took your sons and daughters whom you bore to me and sacrificed them as food to the idols. Was your prostitution not enough? [21]You slaughtered my children and sacrificed them[e] to the idols. [22]In all your detestable practices and your prostitution you did not remember the days of your youth, when you were naked and bare, kicking about in your blood.

[23]" 'Woe! Woe to you, declares the Sovereign LORD. In addition to all your other wickedness, [24]you built a mound for yourself and made a lofty shrine in every public square. [25]At the head of every street you built your lofty shrines and degraded your beauty, offering your body with increasing promiscuity to anyone who passed by. [26]You engaged in prostitution with the Egyptians, your lustful neighbors, and provoked me to anger with your increasing promiscuity. [27]So I stretched out my hand against you and reduced your territory; I gave you over to the greed of your enemies, the daughters of the Philistines, who were shocked by your lewd conduct. [28]You engaged in prostitution with the Assyrians too, because you were insatiable; and even after that, you still were not satisfied. [29]Then you increased your promiscu-

---

[a]6 A few Hebrew manuscripts, Septuagint and Syriac; most Hebrew manuscripts *"Live!" And as you lay there in your blood I said to you, "Live!"* [b]7 Or *became mature* [c]9 Or *I had bathed* [d]15 Most Hebrew manuscripts; one Hebrew manuscript (see some Septuagint manuscripts) *by. Such a thing should not happen* [e]21 Or *and made them pass through the fire*

ity to include Babylonia,^{a} a land of merchants, but even with this you were not satisfied.

³⁰ 'How weak-willed you are, declares the Sovereign LORD, when you do all these things, acting like a brazen prostitute! ³¹When you built your mounds at the head of every street and made your lofty shrines in every public square, you were unlike a prostitute, because you scorned payment.

³² 'You adulterous wife! You prefer strangers to your own husband! ³³Every prostitute receives a fee, but you give gifts to all your lovers, bribing them to come to you from everywhere for your illicit favors. ³⁴So in your prostitution you are the opposite of others; no one runs after you for your favors. You are the very opposite, for you give payment and none is given to you.

³⁵ 'Therefore, you prostitute, hear the word of the LORD! ³⁶This is what the Sovereign LORD says: Because you poured out your wealth^b and exposed your nakedness in your promiscuity with your lovers, and because of all your detestable idols, and because you gave them your children's blood, ³⁷therefore I am going to gather all your lovers, with whom you found pleasure, those you loved as well as those you hated. I will gather them against you from all around and will strip you in front of them, and they will see all your nakedness. ³⁸I will sentence you to the punishment of women who commit adultery and who shed blood; I will bring upon you the blood vengeance of my wrath and jealous anger. ³⁹Then I will hand you over to your lovers, and they will tear down your mounds and destroy your lofty shrines. They will strip you of your clothes and take your fine jewelry and leave you naked and bare. ⁴⁰They will bring a mob against you, who will stone you and hack you to pieces with their swords. ⁴¹They will burn down your houses and inflict punishment on you in the sight of many women. I will put a stop to your prostitution, and you will no longer pay your lovers. ⁴²Then my wrath against you will subside and my jealous anger will turn away from you; I will be calm and no longer angry.

⁴³ 'Because you did not remember the days of your youth but enraged me with all these things, I will surely bring down on your head what you have done, declares the Sovereign LORD. Did you not add lewdness to all your other detestable practices?

⁴⁴ 'Everyone who quotes proverbs will quote this proverb about you: "Like mother, like daughter." ⁴⁵You are a true daughter of your mother, who despised her husband and her children; and you are a true sister of your sisters, who despised their husbands and their children. Your mother was a Hittite and your father an Amorite. ⁴⁶Your older sister was Samaria, who lived to the north of you with her daughters; and your younger sister, who lived to the south of you with her daughters, was Sodom. ⁴⁷You not only walked in their ways and copied their detestable practices, but in all your ways you soon became more depraved than they. ⁴⁸As surely as I live, declares the Sovereign LORD, your sister Sodom and her daughters never did what you and your daughters have done.

⁴⁹ 'Now this was the sin of your sister Sodom: She and her daughters were arrogant, overfed and unconcerned; they did not help the poor and needy. ⁵⁰They were haughty and did detestable things before me. Therefore I did away with them as you have seen. ⁵¹Samaria did not commit half the sins you did. You have done more detestable things than they, and have made your sisters seem righteous by all these things you have done. ⁵²Bear your disgrace, for you have furnished some justification for your sisters. Because your sins were more vile than theirs, they appear more righteous than you. So then, be ashamed and bear your disgrace, for you have made your sisters appear righteous.

^{a}29 Or *Chaldea* ^{b}36 Or *lust*

⁵³" 'However, I will restore the fortunes of Sodom and her daughters and of Samaria and her daughters, and your fortunes along with them, ⁵⁴so that you may bear your disgrace and be ashamed of all you have done in giving them comfort. ⁵⁵And your sisters, Sodom with her daughters and Samaria with her daughters, will return to what they were before; and you and your daughters will return to what you were before. ⁵⁶You would not even mention your sister Sodom in the day of your pride, ⁵⁷before your wickedness was uncovered. Even so, you are now scorned by the daughters of Edom*a* and all her neighbors and the daughters of the Philistines—all those around you who despise you. ⁵⁸You will bear the consequences of your lewdness and your detestable practices, declares the Lord.

⁵⁹" 'This is what the Sovereign Lord says: I will deal with you as you deserve, because you have despised my oath by breaking the covenant. ⁶⁰Yet I will remember the covenant I made with you in the days of your youth, and I will establish an everlasting covenant with you. ⁶¹Then you will remember your ways and be ashamed when you receive your sisters, both those who are older than you and those who are younger. I will give them to you as daughters, but not on the basis of my covenant with you. ⁶²So I will establish my covenant with you, and you will know that I am the Lord. ⁶³Then, when I make atonement for you for all you have done, you will remember and be ashamed and never again open your mouth because of your humiliation, declares the Sovereign Lord.' "

Two Eagles and a Vine   The word of the Lord came to me: ²"Son of man, set forth an allegory and tell the house of Israel a parable. ³Say to them, 'This is what the Sovereign Lord says: A great eagle with powerful wings, long feathers and full plumage of varied colors came to Lebanon. Taking hold of the top of a cedar, ⁴he broke off its topmost shoot and carried it away to a land of merchants, where he planted it in a city of traders.

⁵" 'He took some of the seed of your land and put it in fertile soil. He planted it like a willow by abundant water, ⁶and it sprouted and became a low, spreading vine. Its branches turned toward him, but its roots remained under it. So it became a vine and produced branches and put out leafy boughs.

⁷" 'But there was another great eagle with powerful wings and full plumage. The vine now sent out its roots toward him from the plot where it was planted and stretched out its branches to him for water. ⁸It had been planted in good soil by abundant water so that it would produce branches, bear fruit and become a splendid vine.'

⁹"Say to them, 'This is what the Sovereign Lord says: Will it thrive? Will it not be uprooted and stripped of its fruit so that it withers? All its new growth will wither. It will not take a strong arm or many people to pull it up by the roots. ¹⁰Even if it is transplanted, will it thrive? Will it not wither completely when the east wind strikes it—wither away in the plot where it grew?' "

¹¹Then the word of the Lord came to me: ¹²"Say to this rebellious house, 'Do you not know what these things mean?' Say to them: 'The king of Babylon went to Jerusalem and carried off her king and her nobles, bringing them back with him to Babylon. ¹³Then he took a member of the royal family and made a treaty with him, putting him under oath. He also carried away the leading men of the land, ¹⁴so that the kingdom would be brought low, unable to rise again, surviving only by keeping his treaty. ¹⁵But the king rebelled against him by sending his envoys to Egypt to get horses and a large army. Will he succeed? Will he who does such things escape? Will he break the treaty and yet escape?

---

a57 Many Hebrew manuscripts and Syriac; most Hebrew manuscripts, Septuagint and Vulgate *Aram*

16" 'As surely as I live, declares the Sovereign LORD, he shall die in Babylon, in the land of the king who put him on the throne, whose oath he despised and whose treaty he broke. 17Pharaoh with his mighty army and great horde will be of no help to him in war, when ramps are built and siege works erected to destroy many lives. 18He despised the oath by breaking the covenant. Because he had given his hand in pledge and yet did all these things, he shall not escape.

19" 'Therefore this is what the Sovereign LORD says: As surely as I live, I will bring down on his head my oath that he despised and my covenant that he broke. 20I will spread my net for him, and he will be caught in my snare. I will bring him to Babylon and execute judgment upon him there because he was unfaithful to me. 21All his fleeing troops will fall by the sword, and the survivors will be scattered to the winds. Then you will know that I the LORD have spoken.

22" 'This is what the Sovereign LORD says: I myself will take a shoot from the very top of a cedar and plant it; I will break off a tender sprig from its topmost shoots and plant it on a high and lofty mountain. 23On the mountain heights of Israel I will plant it; it will produce branches and bear fruit and become a splendid cedar. Birds of every kind will nest in it; they will find shelter in the shade of its branches. 24All the trees of the field will know that I the LORD bring down the tall tree and make the low tree grow tall. I dry up the green tree and make the dry tree flourish.

" 'I the LORD have spoken, and I will do it.' "

The Soul Who Sins Will Die The word of the LORD came to me: 2"What do you people mean by quoting this proverb about the land of Israel:

" 'The fathers eat sour grapes,
and the children's teeth are set on edge'?

3"As surely as I live, declares the Sovereign LORD, you will no longer quote this proverb in Israel. 4For every living soul belongs to me, the father as well as the son—both alike belong to me. The soul who sins is the one who will die.

5 "Suppose there is a righteous man
who does what is just and right.
6 He does not eat at the mountain shrines
or look to the idols of the house of Israel.
He does not defile his neighbor's wife
or lie with a woman during her period.
7 He does not oppress anyone,
but returns what he took in pledge for a loan.
He does not commit robbery
but gives his food to the hungry
and provides clothing for the naked.
8 He does not lend at usury
or take excessive interest.*
He withholds his hand from doing wrong
and judges fairly between man and man.
9 He follows my decrees
and faithfully keeps my laws.
That man is righteous;
he will surely live,

declares the Sovereign LORD.

*8 Or *take interest*; similarly in verses 13 and 17

[10]"Suppose he has a violent son, who sheds blood or does any of these other things[a] [11](though the father has done none of them):

> "He eats at the mountain shrines.
> He defiles his neighbor's wife.
> [12]He oppresses the poor and needy.
> He commits robbery.
> He does not return what he took in pledge.
> He looks to the idols.
> He does detestable things.
> [13]He lends at usury and takes excessive interest.

Will such a man live? He will not! Because he has done all these detestable things, he will surely be put to death and his blood will be on his own head.

[14]"But suppose this son has a son who sees all the sins his father commits, and though he sees them, he does not do such things:

> [15]"He does not eat at the mountain shrines
>   or look to the idols of the house of Israel.
> He does not defile his neighbor's wife.
> [16]He does not oppress anyone
>   or require a pledge for a loan.
> He does not commit robbery
>   but gives his food to the hungry
>   and provides clothing for the naked.
> [17]He withholds his hand from sin[b]
>   and takes no usury or excessive interest.
> He keeps my laws and follows my decrees.

He will not die for his father's sin; he will surely live. [18]But his father will die for his own sin, because he practiced extortion, robbed his brother and did what was wrong among his people.

[19]"Yet you ask, 'Why does the son not share the guilt of his father?' Since the son has done what is just and right and has been careful to keep all my decrees, he will surely live. [20]The soul who sins is the one who will die. The son will not share the guilt of the father, nor will the father share the guilt of the son. The righteousness of the righteous man will be credited to him, and the wickedness of the wicked will be charged against him.

[21]"But if a wicked man turns away from all the sins he has committed and keeps all my decrees and does what is just and right, he will surely live; he will not die. [22]None of the offenses he has committed will be remembered against him. Because of the righteous things he has done, he will live. [23]Do I take any pleasure in the death of the wicked? declares the Sovereign LORD. Rather, am I not pleased when they turn from their ways and live?

[24]"But if a righteous man turns from his righteousness and commits sin and does the same detestable things the wicked man does, will he live? None of the righteous things he has done will be remembered. Because of the unfaithfulness he is guilty of and because of the sins he has committed, he will die.

[25]"Yet you say, 'The way of the Lord is not just.' Hear, O house of Israel: Is my way unjust? Is it not your ways that are unjust? [26]If a righteous man turns from his righteousness and commits sin, he will die for it; because of the sin he has committed he will die. [27]But if a wicked man turns away from the wickedness he has committed and does what is just and right, he will save his life. [28]Because he considers all the offenses he has committed and turns away from them, he will surely live; he will not die. [29]Yet the house of Israel

---

[a]10 Or *things to a brother*   [b]17 Septuagint (see also verse 8); Hebrew *from the poor*

Dear Sam,

My parents divorced when I was 12. I still feel like it was my fault even though my mom says it wasn't. How can I stop feeling so responsible?

Yolanda in Yonkers

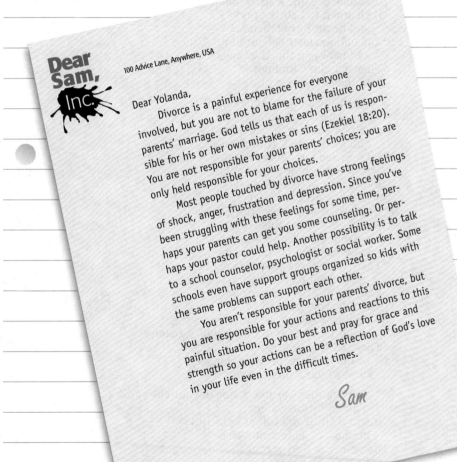

Dear Sam, Inc.

100 Advice Lane, Anywhere, USA

Dear Yolanda,

Divorce is a painful experience for everyone involved, but you are not to blame for the failure of your parents' marriage. God tells us that each of us is responsible for his or her own mistakes or sins (Ezekiel 18:20). You are not responsible for your parents' choices; you are only held responsible for your choices.

Most people touched by divorce have strong feelings of shock, anger, frustration and depression. Since you've been struggling with these feelings for some time, perhaps your parents can get you some counseling. Or perhaps your pastor could help. Another possibility is to talk to a school counselor, psychologist or social worker. Some schools even have support groups organized so kids with the same problems can support each other.

You aren't responsible for your parents' divorce, but you are responsible for your actions and reactions to this painful situation. Do your best and pray for grace and strength so your actions can be a reflection of God's love in your life even in the difficult times.

Sam

says, 'The way of the Lord is not just.' Are my ways unjust, O house of Israel? Is it not your ways that are unjust?

³⁰"Therefore, O house of Israel, I will judge you, each one according to his ways, declares the Sovereign LORD. Repent! Turn away from all your offenses; then sin will not be your downfall. ³¹Rid yourselves of all the offenses you have committed, and get a new heart and a new spirit. Why will you die, O house of Israel? ³²For I take no pleasure in the death of anyone, declares the Sovereign LORD. Repent and live!

19

A Lament for Israel's Princes "Take up a lament concerning the princes of Israel ²and say:

> " 'What a lioness was your mother
>   among the lions!
> She lay down among the young lions
>   and reared her cubs.
> ³She brought up one of her cubs,
>   and he became a strong lion.
> He learned to tear the prey
>   and he devoured men.
> ⁴The nations heard about him,
>   and he was trapped in their pit.
> They led him with hooks
>   to the land of Egypt.
>
> ⁵ 'When she saw her hope unfulfilled,
>   her expectation gone,
> she took another of her cubs
>   and made him a strong lion.
> ⁶He prowled among the lions,
>   for he was now a strong lion.
> He learned to tear the prey
>   and he devoured men.
> ⁷He broke downᵃ their strongholds
>   and devastated their towns.
> The land and all who were in it
>   were terrified by his roaring.
> ⁸Then the nations came against him,
>   those from regions round about.
> They spread their net for him,
>   and he was trapped in their pit.
> ⁹With hooks they pulled him into a cage
>   and brought him to the king of Babylon.
> They put him in prison,
>   so his roar was heard no longer
>   on the mountains of Israel.
>
> ¹⁰ 'Your mother was like a vine in your vineyardᵇ
>   planted by the water;
> it was fruitful and full of branches
>   because of abundant water.
> ¹¹Its branches were strong,
>   fit for a ruler's scepter.
> It towered high
>   above the thick foliage,

ᵃ7 Targum (see Septuagint); Hebrew *He knew*   ᵇ10 Two Hebrew manuscripts; most Hebrew manuscripts *your blood*

> conspicuous for its height
> and for its many branches.
> ¹²But it was uprooted in fury
> and thrown to the ground.
> The east wind made it shrivel,
> it was stripped of its fruit;
> its strong branches withered
> and fire consumed them.
> ¹³Now it is planted in the desert,
> in a dry and thirsty land.
> ¹⁴Fire spread from one of its main^a branches
> and consumed its fruit.
> No strong branch is left on it
> fit for a ruler's scepter.'

This is a lament and is to be used as a lament."

Rebellious Israel In the seventh year, in the fifth month on the tenth day, some of the elders of Israel came to inquire of the LORD, and they sat down in front of me.

²Then the word of the LORD came to me: ³"Son of man, speak to the elders of Israel and say to them, 'This is what the Sovereign LORD says: Have you come to inquire of me? As surely as I live, I will not let you inquire of me, declares the Sovereign LORD.'

⁴"Will you judge them? Will you judge them, son of man? Then confront them with the detestable practices of their fathers ⁵and say to them: 'This is what the Sovereign LORD says: On the day I chose Israel, I swore with uplifted hand to the descendants of the house of Jacob and revealed myself to them in Egypt. With uplifted hand I said to them, "I am the LORD your God." ⁶On that day I swore to them that I would bring them out of Egypt into a land I had searched out for them, a land flowing with milk and honey, the most beautiful of all lands. ⁷And I said to them, "Each of you, get rid of the vile images you have set your eyes on, and do not defile yourselves with the idols of Egypt. I am the LORD your God."

⁸" 'But they rebelled against me and would not listen to me; they did not get rid of the vile images they had set their eyes on, nor did they forsake the idols of Egypt. So I said I would pour out my wrath on them and spend my anger against them in Egypt. ⁹But for the sake of my name I did what would keep it from being profaned in the eyes of the nations they lived among and in whose sight I had revealed myself to the Israelites by bringing them out of Egypt. ¹⁰Therefore I led them out of Egypt and brought them into the desert. ¹¹I gave them my decrees and made known to them my laws, for the man who obeys them will live by them. ¹²Also I gave them my Sabbaths as a sign between us, so they would know that I the LORD made them holy.

¹³" 'Yet the people of Israel rebelled against me in the desert. They did not follow my decrees but rejected my laws—although the man who obeys them will live by them—and they utterly desecrated my Sabbaths. So I said I would pour out my wrath on them and destroy them in the desert. ¹⁴But for the sake of my name I did what would keep it from being profaned in the eyes of the nations in whose sight I had brought them out. ¹⁵Also with uplifted hand I swore to them in the desert that I would not bring them into the land I had given them—a land flowing with milk and honey, most beautiful of all lands— ¹⁶because they rejected my laws and did not follow my decrees and desecrated my Sabbaths. For their hearts were devoted to their idols. ¹⁷Yet I

---

^a14 Or *from under its*

looked on them with pity and did not destroy them or put an end to them in the desert. ¹⁸I said to their children in the desert, "Do not follow the statutes of your fathers or keep their laws or defile yourselves with their idols. ¹⁹I am the LORD your God; follow my decrees and be careful to keep my laws. ²⁰Keep my Sabbaths holy, that they may be a sign between us. Then you will know that I am the LORD your God."

²¹" 'But the children rebelled against me: They did not follow my decrees, they were not careful to keep my laws—although the man who obeys them will live by them—and they desecrated my Sabbaths. So I said I would pour out my wrath on them and spend my anger against them in the desert. ²²But I withheld my hand, and for the sake of my name I did what would keep it from being profaned in the eyes of the nations in whose sight I had brought them out. ²³Also with uplifted hand I swore to them in the desert that I would disperse them among the nations and scatter them through the countries, ²⁴because they had not obeyed my laws but had rejected my decrees and desecrated my Sabbaths, and their eyes lusted after their fathers' idols. ²⁵I also gave them over to statutes that were not good and laws they could not live by; ²⁶I let them become defiled through their gifts—the sacrifice of every firstborn*ᵃ*—that I might fill them with horror so they would know that I am the LORD.'

²⁷"Therefore, son of man, speak to the people of Israel and say to them, 'This is what the Sovereign LORD says: In this also your fathers blasphemed me by forsaking me: ²⁸When I brought them into the land I had sworn to give them and they saw any high hill or any leafy tree, there they offered their sacrifices, made offerings that provoked me to anger, presented their fragrant incense and poured out their drink offerings. ²⁹Then I said to them: What is this high place you go to?' " (It is called Bamah*ᵇ* to this day.)

Judgment and Restoration

³⁰"Therefore say to the house of Israel: 'This is what the Sovereign LORD says: Will you defile yourselves the way your fathers did and lust after their vile images? ³¹When you offer your gifts—the sacrifice of your sons in*ᶜ* the fire—you continue to defile yourselves with all your idols to this day. Am I to let you inquire of me, O house of Israel? As surely as I live, declares the Sovereign LORD, I will not let you inquire of me.

³²" 'You say, "We want to be like the nations, like the peoples of the world, who serve wood and stone." But what you have in mind will never happen. ³³As surely as I live, declares the Sovereign LORD, I will rule over you with a mighty hand and an outstretched arm and with outpoured wrath. ³⁴I will bring you from the nations and gather you from the countries where you have been scattered—with a mighty hand and an outstretched arm and with outpoured wrath. ³⁵I will bring you into the desert of the nations and there, face to face, I will execute judgment upon you. ³⁶As I judged your fathers in the desert of the land of Egypt, so I will judge you, declares the Sovereign LORD. ³⁷I will take note of you as you pass under my rod,

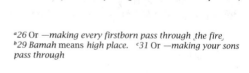

EZEKIEL 20:39

Many of you have family members or friends who don't know the Lord. It hurts when you witness to people you love and they just won't listen. The people of Ezekiel's day didn't listen to God's prophet either. But God gave them a special promise through Ezekiel. "Afterward you will surely listen . . . " A person you love may not listen to you until after he or she suffers the consequences of wrong choices. Sure you'd like your loved ones to avoid being hurt. But some are only willing to listen "afterward." Don't stop praying for your loved ones. And don't give up hope.

Direct Line

ᵃ26 Or *—making every firstborn pass through the fire*
ᵇ29 Bamah means *high place.* *ᶜ31* Or *—making your sons pass through*

and I will bring you into the bond of the covenant. ³⁸I will purge you of those who revolt and rebel against me. Although I will bring them out of the land where they are living, yet they will not enter the land of Israel. Then you will know that I am the Lord.

³⁹" 'As for you, O house of Israel, this is what the Sovereign Lord says: Go and serve your idols, every one of you! But afterward you will surely listen to me and no longer profane my holy name with your gifts and idols. ⁴⁰For on my holy mountain, the high mountain of Israel, declares the Sovereign Lord, there in the land the entire house of Israel will serve me, and there I will accept them. There I will require your offerings and your choice gifts,ᵃ along with all your holy sacrifices. ⁴¹I will accept you as fragrant incense when I bring you out from the nations and gather you from the countries where you have been scattered, and I will show myself holy among you in the sight of the nations. ⁴²Then you will know that I am the Lord, when I bring you into the land of Israel, the land I had sworn with uplifted hand to give to your fathers. ⁴³There you will remember your conduct and all the actions by which you have defiled yourselves, and you will loathe yourselves for all the evil you have done. ⁴⁴You will know that I am the Lord, when I deal with you for my name's sake and not according to your evil ways and your corrupt practices, O house of Israel, declares the Sovereign Lord.' "

Prophecy Against the South ⁴⁵The word of the Lord came to me: ⁴⁶"Son of man, set your face toward the south; preach against the south and prophesy against the forest of the southland. ⁴⁷Say to the southern forest: 'Hear the word of the Lord. This is what the Sovereign Lord says: I am about to set fire to you, and it will consume all your trees, both green and dry. The blazing flame will not be quenched, and every face from south to north will be scorched by it. ⁴⁸Everyone will see that I the Lord have kindled it; it will not be quenched.' "

⁴⁹Then I said, "Ah, Sovereign Lord! They are saying of me, 'Isn't he just telling parables?' "

Babylon, God's Sword of Judgment The word of the Lord came to me: ²"Son of man, set your face against Jerusalem and preach against the sanctuary. Prophesy against the land of Israel ³and say to her: 'This is what the Lord says: I am against you. I will draw my sword from its scabbard and cut off from you both the righteous and the wicked. ⁴Because I am going to cut off the righteous and the wicked, my sword will be unsheathed against everyone from south to north. ⁵Then all people will know that I the Lord have drawn my sword from its scabbard; it will not return again.'

⁶"Therefore groan, son of man! Groan before them with broken heart and bitter grief. ⁷And when they ask you, 'Why are you groaning?' you shall say, 'Because of the news that is coming. Every heart will melt and every hand go limp; every spirit will become faint and every knee become as weak as water.' It is coming! It will surely take place, declares the Sovereign Lord."

⁸The word of the Lord came to me: ⁹"Son of man, prophesy and say, 'This is what the Lord says:

" 'A sword, a sword,
　　sharpened and polished—
¹⁰sharpened for the slaughter,
　　polished to flash like lightning!

" 'Shall we rejoice in the scepter of my son ⸤Judah⸥? The sword despises every such stick.

ᵃ40 Or *and the gifts of your firstfruits*

11" 'The sword is appointed to be polished,
   to be grasped with the hand;
it is sharpened and polished,
   made ready for the hand of the slayer.
12 Cry out and wail, son of man,
   for it is against my people;
   it is against all the princes of Israel.
They are thrown to the sword
   along with my people.
Therefore beat your breast.

13" 'Testing will surely come. And what if the scepter of Judah, which the sword despises, does not continue? declares the Sovereign LORD.'

14 "So then, son of man, prophesy
   and strike your hands together.
Let the sword strike twice,
   even three times.
It is a sword for slaughter—
   a sword for great slaughter,
   closing in on them from every side.
15 So that hearts may melt
   and the fallen be many,
I have stationed the sword for slaughter*a*
   at all their gates.
Oh! It is made to flash like lightning,
   it is grasped for slaughter.
16 O sword, slash to the right,
   then to the left,
   wherever your blade is turned.
17 I too will strike my hands together,
   and my wrath will subside.
I the LORD have spoken."

18 The word of the LORD came to me: 19 "Son of man, mark out two roads for the sword of the king of Babylon to take, both starting from the same country. Make a signpost where the road branches off to the city. 20 Mark out one road for the sword to come against Rabbah of the Ammonites and another against Judah and fortified Jerusalem. 21 For the king of Babylon will stop at the fork in the road, at the junction of the two roads, to seek an omen: He will cast lots with arrows, he will consult his idols, he will examine the liver. 22 Into his right hand will come the lot for Jerusalem, where he is to set up battering rams, to give the command to slaughter, to sound the battle cry, to set battering rams against the gates, to build a ramp and to erect siege works. 23 It will seem like a false omen to those who have sworn allegiance to him, but he will remind them of their guilt and take them captive.

24 "Therefore this is what the Sovereign LORD says: 'Because you people have brought to mind your guilt by your open rebellion, revealing your sins in all that you do—because you have done this, you will be taken captive.

25 " 'O profane and wicked prince of Israel, whose day has come, whose time of punishment has reached its climax, 26 this is what the Sovereign LORD says: Take off the turban, remove the crown. It will not be as it was: The lowly will be exalted and the exalted will be brought low. 27 A ruin! A ruin! I will make it a ruin! It will not be restored until he comes to whom it rightfully belongs; to him I will give it.'

28 "And you, son of man, prophesy and say, 'This is what the Sovereign LORD says about the Ammonites and their insults:

*a*15 Septuagint; the meaning of the Hebrew for this word is uncertain.

> " 'A sword, a sword,
>> drawn for the slaughter,
> polished to consume
>> and to flash like lightning!
> ²⁹Despite false visions concerning you
>> and lying divinations about you,
> it will be laid on the necks
>> of the wicked who are to be slain,
> whose day has come,
>> whose time of punishment has reached its climax.
> ³⁰Return the sword to its scabbard.
>> In the place where you were created,
> in the land of your ancestry,
>> I will judge you.
> ³¹I will pour out my wrath upon you
>> and breathe out my fiery anger against you;
> I will hand you over to brutal men,
>> men skilled in destruction.
> ³²You will be fuel for the fire,
>> your blood will be shed in your land,
> you will be remembered no more;
>> for I the LORD have spoken.' "

22 *Jerusalem's Sins* The word of the LORD came to me: ²"Son of man, will you judge her? Will you judge this city of bloodshed? Then confront her with all her detestable practices ³and say: 'This is what the Sovereign LORD says: O city that brings on herself doom by shedding blood in her midst and defiles herself by making idols, ⁴you have become guilty because of the blood you have shed and have become defiled by the idols you have made. You have brought your days to a close, and the end of your years has come. Therefore I will make you an object of scorn to the nations and a laughingstock to all the countries. ⁵Those who are near and those who are far away will mock you, O infamous city, full of turmoil.

⁶" 'See how each of the princes of Israel who are in you uses his power to shed blood. ⁷In you they have treated father and mother with contempt; in you they have oppressed the alien and mistreated the fatherless and the widow. ⁸You have despised my holy things and desecrated my Sabbaths. ⁹In you are slanderous men bent on shedding blood; in you are those who eat at the mountain shrines and commit lewd acts. ¹⁰In you are those who dishonor their fathers' bed; in you are those who violate women during their period, when they are ceremonially unclean. ¹¹In you one man commits a detestable offense with his neighbor's wife, another shamefully defiles his daughter-in-law, and another violates his sister, his own father's daughter. ¹²In you men accept* bribes to shed blood; you take usury and excessive interest* and make unjust gain from your neighbors by extortion. And you have forgotten me, declares the Sovereign LORD.

¹³" 'I will surely strike my hands together at the unjust gain you have made and at the blood you have shed in your midst. ¹⁴Will your courage endure or your hands be strong in the day I deal with you? I the LORD have spoken, and I will do it. ¹⁵I will disperse you among the nations and scatter you through the countries; and I will put an end to your uncleanness. ¹⁶When you have been defiled* in the eyes of the nations, you will know that I am the LORD.' "

¹⁷Then the word of the LORD came to me: ¹⁸"Son of man, the house of Israel has become dross to me; all of them are the copper, tin, iron and lead left inside a furnace. They are but the dross of silver. ¹⁹Therefore this is what the

*12 Or *usury and interest* *16 Or *When I have allotted you your inheritance*

Sovereign LORD says: 'Because you have all become dross, I will gather you into Jerusalem. ²⁰As men gather silver, copper, iron, lead and tin into a furnace to melt it with a fiery blast, so will I gather you in my anger and my wrath and put you inside the city and melt you. ²¹I will gather you and I will blow on you with my fiery wrath, and you will be melted inside her. ²²As silver is melted in a furnace, so you will be melted inside her, and you will know that I the LORD have poured out my wrath upon you.' "

²³Again the word of the LORD came to me: ²⁴"Son of man, say to the land, 'You are a land that has had no rain or showers*ᵃ* in the day of wrath.' ²⁵There is a conspiracy of her princes*ᵇ* within her like a roaring lion tearing its prey; they devour people, take treasures and precious things and make many widows within her. ²⁶Her priests do violence to my law and profane my holy things; they do not distinguish between the holy and the common; they teach that there is no difference between the unclean and the clean; and they shut their eyes to the keeping of my Sabbaths, so that I am profaned among them. ²⁷Her officials within her are like wolves tearing their prey; they shed blood and kill people to make unjust gain. ²⁸Her prophets whitewash these deeds for them by false visions and lying divinations. They say, 'This is what the Sovereign LORD says'—when the LORD has not spoken. ²⁹The people of the land practice extortion and commit robbery; they oppress the poor and needy and mistreat the alien, denying them justice.

³⁰"I looked for a man among them who would build up the wall and stand before me in the gap on behalf of the land so I would not have to destroy it, but I found none. ³¹So I will pour out my wrath on them and consume them with my fiery anger, bringing down on their own heads all they have done, declares the Sovereign LORD."

23 *Two Adulterous Sisters* The word of the LORD came to me: ²"Son of man, there were two women, daughters of the same mother. ³They became prostitutes in Egypt, engaging in prostitution from their youth. In that land their breasts were fondled and their virgin bosoms caressed. ⁴The older was named Oholah, and her sister was Oholibah. They were mine and gave birth to sons and daughters. Oholah is Samaria, and Oholibah is Jerusalem.

⁵"Oholah engaged in prostitution while she was still mine; and she lusted after her lovers, the Assyrians—warriors ⁶clothed in blue, governors and commanders, all of them handsome young men, and mounted horsemen. ⁷She gave herself as a prostitute to all the elite of the Assyrians and defiled herself with all the idols of everyone she lusted after. ⁸She did not give up the prostitution she began in Egypt, when during her youth men slept with her, caressed her virgin bosom and poured out their lust upon her.

⁹"Therefore I handed her over to her lovers, the Assyrians, for whom she lusted. ¹⁰They stripped her naked, took away her sons and daughters and killed her with the sword. She became a byword among women, and punishment was inflicted on her.

¹¹"Her sister Oholibah saw this, yet in her lust and prostitution she was more depraved than her sister. ¹²She too lusted after the Assyrians—governors and commanders, warriors in full dress, mounted horsemen, all handsome young men. ¹³I saw that she too defiled herself; both of them went the same way.

¹⁴"But she carried her prostitution still further. She saw men portrayed on a wall, figures of Chaldeans*ᶜ* portrayed in red, ¹⁵with belts around their waists and flowing turbans on their heads; all of them looked like Babylonian chariot officers, natives of Chaldea.*ᵈ* ¹⁶As soon as she saw them, she lust-

---

ᵃ24 Septuagint; Hebrew *has not been cleansed or rained on*   *ᵇ25* Septuagint; Hebrew *prophets*   *ᶜ14* Or *Babylonians*   *ᵈ15* Or *Babylonia*; also in verse 16

ed after them and sent messengers to them in Chaldea. ¹⁷Then the Babylonians came to her, to the bed of love, and in their lust they defiled her. After she had been defiled by them, she turned away from them in disgust. ¹⁸When she carried on her prostitution openly and exposed her nakedness, I turned away from her in disgust, just as I had turned away from her sister. ¹⁹Yet she became more and more promiscuous as she recalled the days of her youth, when she was a prostitute in Egypt. ²⁰There she lusted after her lovers, whose genitals were like those of donkeys and whose emission was like that of horses. ²¹So you longed for the lewdness of your youth, when in Egypt your bosom was caressed and your young breasts fondled.ᵃ

²²"Therefore, Oholibah, this is what the Sovereign Lord says: I will stir up your lovers against you, those you turned away from in disgust, and I will bring them against you from every side— ²³the Babylonians and all the Chaldeans, the men of Pekod and Shoa and Koa, and all the Assyrians with them, handsome young men, all of them governors and commanders, chariot officers and men of high rank, all mounted on horses. ²⁴They will come against you with weapons,ᵇ chariots and wagons and with a throng of people; they will take up positions against you on every side with large and small shields and with helmets. I will turn you over to them for punishment, and they will punish you according to their standards. ²⁵I will direct my jealous anger against you, and they will deal with you in fury. They will cut off your noses and your ears, and those of you who are left will fall by the sword. They will take away your sons and daughters, and those of you who are left will be consumed by fire. ²⁶They will also strip you of your clothes and take your fine jewelry. ²⁷So I will put a stop to the lewdness and prostitution you began in Egypt. You will not look on these things with longing or remember Egypt anymore.

²⁸"For this is what the Sovereign Lord says: I am about to hand you over to those you hate, to those you turned away from in disgust. ²⁹They will deal with you in hatred and take away everything you have worked for. They will leave you naked and bare, and the shame of your prostitution will be exposed. Your lewdness and promiscuity ³⁰have brought this upon you, because you lusted after the nations and defiled yourself with their idols. ³¹You have gone the way of your sister; so I will put her cup into your hand.

³²"This is what the Sovereign Lord says:

> "You will drink your sister's cup,
>   a cup large and deep;
> it will bring scorn and derision,
>   for it holds so much.
> ³³You will be filled with drunkenness and sorrow,
>   the cup of ruin and desolation,
>   the cup of your sister Samaria.
> ³⁴You will drink it and drain it dry;
>   you will dash it to pieces
>   and tear your breasts.

I have spoken, declares the Sovereign Lord.

³⁵"Therefore this is what the Sovereign Lord says: Since you have forgotten me and thrust me behind your back, you must bear the consequences of your lewdness and prostitution."

³⁶The Lord said to me: "Son of man, will you judge Oholah and Oholibah? Then confront them with their detestable practices, ³⁷for they have committed adultery and blood is on their hands. They committed adultery with

ᵃ21 Syriac (see also verse 3); Hebrew *caressed because of your young breasts*   ᵇ24 The meaning of the Hebrew for this word is uncertain.

their idols; they even sacrificed their children, whom they bore to me,*a* as food for them. ³⁸They have also done this to me: At that same time they defiled my sanctuary and desecrated my Sabbaths. ³⁹On the very day they sacrificed their children to their idols, they entered my sanctuary and desecrated it. That is what they did in my house.

⁴⁰"They even sent messengers for men who came from far away, and when they arrived you bathed yourself for them, painted your eyes and put on your jewelry. ⁴¹You sat on an elegant couch, with a table spread before it on which you had placed the incense and oil that belonged to me.

⁴²"The noise of a carefree crowd was around her; Sabeans*b* were brought from the desert along with men from the rabble, and they put bracelets on the arms of the woman and her sister and beautiful crowns on their heads. ⁴³Then I said about the one worn out by adultery, 'Now let them use her as a prostitute, for that is all she is.' ⁴⁴And they slept with her. As men sleep with a prostitute, so they slept with those lewd women, Oholah and Oholibah. ⁴⁵But righteous men will sentence them to the punishment of women who commit adultery and shed blood, because they are adulterous and blood is on their hands.

⁴⁶"This is what the Sovereign LORD says: Bring a mob against them and give them over to terror and plunder. ⁴⁷The mob will stone them and cut them down with their swords; they will kill their sons and daughters and burn down their houses.

⁴⁸"So I will put an end to lewdness in the land, that all women may take warning and not imitate you. ⁴⁹You will suffer the penalty for your lewdness and bear the consequences of your sins of idolatry. Then you will know that I am the Sovereign LORD."

24 *The Cooking Pot* In the ninth year, in the tenth month on the tenth day, the word of the LORD came to me: ²"Son of man, record this date, this very date, because the king of Babylon has laid siege to Jerusalem this very day. ³Tell this rebellious house a parable and say to them: 'This is what the Sovereign LORD says:

" 'Put on the cooking pot; put it on
    and pour water into it.
⁴Put into it the pieces of meat,
    all the choice pieces—the leg and the shoulder.
Fill it with the best of these bones;
⁵   take the pick of the flock.
Pile wood beneath it for the bones;
    bring it to a boil
    and cook the bones in it.

⁶" 'For this is what the Sovereign LORD says:

" 'Woe to the city of bloodshed,
    to the pot now encrusted,
    whose deposit will not go away!
Empty it piece by piece
    without casting lots for them.

⁷" 'For the blood she shed is in her midst:
    She poured it on the bare rock;
she did not pour it on the ground,
    where the dust would cover it.
⁸To stir up wrath and take revenge

---

a37 Or even made the children they bore to me pass through the fire, b42 Or drunkards

I put her blood on the bare rock,
so that it would not be covered.

⁹" 'Therefore this is what the Sovereign Lᴏʀᴅ says:

" 'Woe to the city of bloodshed!
I, too, will pile the wood high.
¹⁰ So heap on the wood
and kindle the fire.
Cook the meat well,
mixing in the spices;
and let the bones be charred.
¹¹ Then set the empty pot on the coals
till it becomes hot and its copper glows
so its impurities may be melted
and its deposit burned away.
¹² It has frustrated all efforts;
its heavy deposit has not been removed,
not even by fire.

¹³" 'Now your impurity is lewdness. Because I tried to cleanse you but you would not be cleansed from your impurity, you will not be clean again until my wrath against you has subsided.

¹⁴" 'I the Lᴏʀᴅ have spoken. The time has come for me to act. I will not hold back; I will not have pity, nor will I relent. You will be judged according to your conduct and your actions, declares the Sovereign Lᴏʀᴅ.' "

Ezekiel's Wife Dies ¹⁵The word of the Lᴏʀᴅ came to me: ¹⁶"Son of man, with one blow I am about to take away from you the delight of your eyes. Yet do not lament or weep or shed any tears. ¹⁷Groan quietly; do not mourn for the dead. Keep your turban fastened and your sandals on your feet; do not cover the lower part of your face or eat the customary food ͵of mourners͵."

¹⁸So I spoke to the people in the morning, and in the evening my wife died. The next morning I did as I had been commanded.

¹⁹Then the people asked me, "Won't you tell us what these things have to do with us?"

²⁰So I said to them, "The word of the Lᴏʀᴅ came to me: ²¹Say to the house of Israel, 'This is what the Sovereign Lᴏʀᴅ says: I am about to desecrate my sanctuary—the stronghold in which you take pride, the delight of your eyes, the object of your affection. The sons and daughters you left behind will fall by the sword. ²²And you will do as I have done. You will not cover the lower part of your face or eat the customary food ͵of mourners͵. ²³You will keep your turbans on your heads and your sandals on your feet. You will not mourn or weep but will waste away because of*ᵃ* your sins and groan among yourselves. ²⁴Ezekiel will be a sign to you; you will do just as he has done. When this happens, you will know that I am the Sovereign Lᴏʀᴅ.'

A pocket planner would sure come in handy right about now!

SEE EZEKIEL 24:1

*ᵃ23 Or *away in*

²⁵"And you, son of man, on the day I take away their stronghold, their joy and glory, the delight of their eyes, their heart's desire, and their sons and daughters as well— ²⁶on that day a fugitive will come to tell you the news. ²⁷At that time your mouth will be opened; you will speak with him and will no longer be silent. So you will be a sign to them, and they will know that I am the LORD."

25

A Prophecy Against Ammon   The word of the LORD came to me: ²"Son of man, set your face against the Ammonites and prophesy against them. ³Say to them, 'Hear the word of the Sovereign LORD. This is what the Sovereign LORD says: Because you said "Aha!" over my sanctuary when it was desecrated and over the land of Israel when it was laid waste and over the people of Judah when they went into exile, ⁴therefore I am going to give you to the people of the East as a possession. They will set up their camps and pitch their tents among you; they will eat your fruit and drink your milk. ⁵I will turn Rabbah into a pasture for camels and Ammon into a resting place for sheep. Then you will know that I am the LORD. ⁶For this is what the Sovereign LORD says: Because you have clapped your hands and stamped your feet, rejoicing with all the malice of your heart against the land of Israel, ⁷therefore I will stretch out my hand against you and give you as plunder to the nations. I will cut you off from the nations and exterminate you from the countries. I will destroy you, and you will know that I am the LORD.' "

A Prophecy Against Moab   ⁸"This is what the Sovereign LORD says: 'Because Moab and Seir said, "Look, the house of Judah has become like all the other nations," ⁹therefore I will expose the flank of Moab, beginning at its frontier towns—Beth Jeshimoth, Baal Meon and Kiriathaim—the glory of that land. ¹⁰I will give Moab along with the Ammonites to the people of the East as a possession, so that the Ammonites will not be remembered among the nations; ¹¹and I will inflict punishment on Moab. Then they will know that I am the LORD.' "

A Prophecy Against Edom   ¹²"This is what the Sovereign LORD says: 'Because Edom took revenge on the house of Judah and became very guilty by doing so, ¹³therefore this is what the Sovereign LORD says: I will stretch out my hand against Edom and kill its men and their animals. I will lay it waste, and from Teman to Dedan they will fall by the sword. ¹⁴I will take vengeance on Edom by the hand of my people Israel, and they will deal with Edom in accordance with my anger and my wrath; they will know my vengeance, declares the Sovereign LORD.' "

A Prophecy Against Philistia   ¹⁵"This is what the Sovereign LORD says: 'Because the Philistines acted in vengeance and took revenge with malice in their hearts, and with ancient hostility sought to destroy Judah, ¹⁶therefore this is what the Sovereign LORD says: I am about to stretch out my hand against the Philistines, and I will cut off the Kerethites and destroy those remaining along the coast. ¹⁷I will carry out great vengeance on them and punish them in my wrath. Then they will know that I am the LORD, when I take vengeance on them.' "

26

A Prophecy Against Tyre   In the eleventh year, on the first day of the month, the word of the LORD came to me: ²"Son of man, because Tyre has said of Jerusalem, 'Aha! The gate to the nations is broken, and its doors have swung open to me; now that she lies in ruins I will prosper,' ³therefore this is what the Sovereign LORD says: I am against you, O Tyre, and I will bring many nations against you, like the sea casting up its waves. ⁴They will destroy the walls of Tyre and pull down her towers; I will scrape away her rubble and make her a bare rock. ⁵Out in the sea she will become a place to spread fishnets, for I have spoken, declares the Sovereign LORD. She will become plunder for the nations, ⁶and her settlements on the mainland will be ravaged by the sword. Then they will know that I am the LORD.

⁷"For this is what the Sovereign LORD says: From the north I am going to bring against Tyre Nebuchadnezzarᵃ king of Babylon, king of kings, with horses and chariots, with horsemen and a great army. ⁸He will ravage your settlements on the mainland with the sword; he will set up siege works against you, build a ramp up to your walls and raise his shields against you. ⁹He will direct the blows of his battering rams against your walls and demolish your towers with his weapons. ¹⁰His horses will be so many that they will cover you with dust. Your walls will tremble at the noise of the war horses, wagons and chariots when he enters your gates as men enter a city whose walls have been broken through. ¹¹The hoofs of his horses will trample all your streets; he will kill your people with the sword, and your strong pillars will fall to the ground. ¹²They will plunder your wealth and loot your merchandise; they will break down your walls and demolish your fine houses and throw your stones, timber and rubble into the sea. ¹³I will put an end to your noisy songs, and the music of your harps will be heard no more. ¹⁴I will make you a bare rock, and you will become a place to spread fishnets. You will never be rebuilt, for I the LORD have spoken, declares the Sovereign LORD.

¹⁵"This is what the Sovereign LORD says to Tyre: Will not the coastlands tremble at the sound of your fall, when the wounded groan and the slaughter takes place in you? ¹⁶Then all the princes of the coast will step down from their thrones and lay aside their robes and take off their embroidered garments. Clothed with terror, they will sit on the ground, trembling every moment, appalled at you. ¹⁷Then they will take up a lament concerning you and say to you:

> " 'How you are destroyed, O city of renown,
>   peopled by men of the sea!
> You were a power on the seas,
>   you and your citizens;
> you put your terror
>   on all who lived there.
> ¹⁸Now the coastlands tremble
>   on the day of your fall;
> the islands in the sea
>   are terrified at your collapse.'

¹⁹"This is what the Sovereign LORD says: When I make you a desolate city, like cities no longer inhabited, and when I bring the ocean depths over you and its vast waters cover you, ²⁰then I will bring you down with those who go down to the pit, to the people of long ago. I will make you dwell in the earth below, as in ancient ruins, with those who go down to the pit, and you will not return or take your placeᵇ in the land of the living. ²¹I will bring you to a horrible end and you will be no more. You will be sought, but you will never again be found, declares the Sovereign LORD."

A Lament for Tyre The word of the LORD came to me: ²"Son of man, take up a lament concerning Tyre. ³Say to Tyre, situated at the gateway to the sea, merchant of peoples on many coasts, 'This is what the Sovereign LORD says:

ᵃ7 Hebrew *Nebuchadrezzar*, of which *Nebuchadnezzar* is a variant; here and often in Ezekiel and Jeremiah
ᵇ20 Septuagint; Hebrew *return, and I will give glory*

" 'You say, O Tyre,
  "I am perfect in beauty."
⁴Your domain was on the high seas;
  your builders brought your beauty to perfection.
⁵They made all your timbers
  of pine trees from Senir*ᵃ*;
they took a cedar from Lebanon
  to make a mast for you.
⁶Of oaks from Bashan
  they made your oars;
of cypress wood*ᵇ* from the coasts of Cyprus*ᶜ*
  they made your deck, inlaid with ivory.
⁷Fine embroidered linen from Egypt was your sail
  and served as your banner;
your awnings were of blue and purple
  from the coasts of Elishah.
⁸Men of Sidon and Arvad were your oarsmen;
  your skilled men, O Tyre, were aboard as your seamen.
⁹Veteran craftsmen of Gebal*ᵈ* were on board
  as shipwrights to caulk your seams.
All the ships of the sea and their sailors
  came alongside to trade for your wares.

¹⁰" 'Men of Persia, Lydia and Put
  served as soldiers in your army.
They hung their shields and helmets on your walls,
  bringing you splendor.
¹¹Men of Arvad and Helech
  manned your walls on every side;
men of Gammad
  were in your towers.
They hung their shields around your walls;
  they brought your beauty to perfection.

ᵃ5 That is, Hermon   *ᵇ6* Targum; the Masoretic Text has a different division of the consonants.   *ᶜ6* Hebrew
Kittim   *ᵈ9* That is, Byblos

The Bible Says

Accurate? You Bet!

Every now and then you'll hear someone say that you can't trust the Bible, that it's not historically accurate, that things just didn't happen the way the Old Testament says they did.

Then you come to a passage like Ezekiel 27. Tyre was one of the great trade cities of the ancient world. Its ships traveled all over the Mediterranean. And where do you suppose historians look to learn about trade in those ancient days? They look in Ezekiel 27! They've learned that everything in this chapter is accurate. Archaeological finds have shown that the prophet was right about the trade routes the ships traveled and the goods they carried.

Oh, some people will tell you that you can't trust the Bible. Don't believe them. The Bible is accurate. It's God's Word, and it's not full of mistakes.

¹²" 'Tarshish did business with you because of your great wealth of goods; they exchanged silver, iron, tin and lead for your merchandise.

¹³" 'Greece, Tubal and Meshech traded with you; they exchanged slaves and articles of bronze for your wares.

¹⁴" 'Men of Beth Togarmah exchanged work horses, war horses and mules for your merchandise.

¹⁵" 'The men of Rhodes*ᵃ* traded with you, and many coastlands were your customers; they paid you with ivory tusks and ebony.

¹⁶" 'Aram*ᵇ* did business with you because of your many products; they exchanged turquoise, purple fabric, embroidered work, fine linen, coral and rubies for your merchandise.

¹⁷" 'Judah and Israel traded with you; they exchanged wheat from Minnith and confections,*ᶜ* honey, oil and balm for your wares.

¹⁸" 'Damascus, because of your many products and great wealth of goods, did business with you in wine from Helbon and wool from Zahar.

¹⁹" 'Danites and Greeks from Uzal bought your merchandise; they exchanged wrought iron, cassia and calamus for your wares.

²⁰" 'Dedan traded in saddle blankets with you.

²¹" 'Arabia and all the princes of Kedar were your customers; they did business with you in lambs, rams and goats.

²²" 'The merchants of Sheba and Raamah traded with you; for your merchandise they exchanged the finest of all kinds of spices and precious stones, and gold.

²³" 'Haran, Canneh and Eden and merchants of Sheba, Asshur and Kilmad traded with you. ²⁴In your marketplace they traded with you beautiful garments, blue fabric, embroidered work and multicolored rugs with cords twisted and tightly knotted.

> ²⁵" 'The ships of Tarshish serve
>   as carriers for your wares.
>   You are filled with heavy cargo
>   in the heart of the sea.
> ²⁶Your oarsmen take you
>   out to the high seas.
>   But the east wind will break you to pieces
>   in the heart of the sea.
> ²⁷Your wealth, merchandise and wares,
>   your mariners, seamen and shipwrights,
>   your merchants and all your soldiers,
>   and everyone else on board
>   will sink into the heart of the sea
>   on the day of your shipwreck.
> ²⁸The shorelands will quake
>   when your seamen cry out.
> ²⁹All who handle the oars
>   will abandon their ships;
>   the mariners and all the seamen
>   will stand on the shore.
> ³⁰They will raise their voice
>   and cry bitterly over you;
>   they will sprinkle dust on their heads
>   and roll in ashes.
> ³¹They will shave their heads because of you
>   and will put on sackcloth.

ᵃ15 Septuagint; Hebrew *Dedan*   *ᵇ16* Most Hebrew manuscripts; some Hebrew manuscripts and Syriac *Edom*   *ᶜ17* The meaning of the Hebrew for this word is uncertain.

They will weep over you with anguish of soul
and with bitter mourning.
³² As they wail and mourn over you,
they will take up a lament concerning you:
"Who was ever silenced like Tyre,
surrounded by the sea?"
³³ When your merchandise went out on the seas,
you satisfied many nations;
with your great wealth and your wares
you enriched the kings of the earth.
³⁴ Now you are shattered by the sea
in the depths of the waters;
your wares and all your company
have gone down with you.
³⁵ All who live in the coastlands
are appalled at you;
their kings shudder with horror
and their faces are distorted with fear.
³⁶ The merchants among the nations hiss at you;
you have come to a horrible end
and will be no more.' "

28 *A Prophecy Against the King of Tyre*   The word of the LORD came to me: ²"Son of man, say to the ruler of Tyre, 'This is what the Sovereign LORD says:

" 'In the pride of your heart
you say, "I am a god;
I sit on the throne of a god
in the heart of the seas."
But you are a man and not a god,
though you think you are as wise as a god.
³ Are you wiser than Daniel^a?
Is no secret hidden from you?
⁴ By your wisdom and understanding
you have gained wealth for yourself
and amassed gold and silver
in your treasuries.
⁵ By your great skill in trading
you have increased your wealth,
and because of your wealth
your heart has grown proud.

⁶" 'Therefore this is what the Sovereign LORD says:

" 'Because you think you are wise,
as wise as a god,
⁷ I am going to bring foreigners against you,
the most ruthless of nations;
they will draw their swords against your beauty and wisdom
and pierce your shining splendor.
⁸ They will bring you down to the pit,
and you will die a violent death
in the heart of the seas.
⁹ Will you then say, "I am a god,"
in the presence of those who kill you?

---

a 3 Or *Danel*; the Hebrew spelling may suggest a person other than the prophet Daniel.

You will be but a man, not a god,
    in the hands of those who slay you.
¹⁰You will die the death of the uncircumcised
    at the hands of foreigners.

I have spoken, declares the Sovereign Lord.' "

¹¹The word of the Lord came to me: ¹²"Son of man, take up a lament concerning the king of Tyre and say to him: 'This is what the Sovereign Lord says:

" 'You were the model of perfection,
    full of wisdom and perfect in beauty.
¹³You were in Eden,
    the garden of God;
    every precious stone adorned you:
    ruby, topaz and emerald,
    chrysolite, onyx and jasper,
    sapphire,ᵃ turquoise and beryl.ᵇ
Your settings and mountingsᶜ were made of gold;
    on the day you were created they were prepared.
¹⁴You were anointed as a guardian cherub,
    for so I ordained you.
You were on the holy mount of God;
    you walked among the fiery stones.
¹⁵You were blameless in your ways
    from the day you were created
    till wickedness was found in you.
¹⁶Through your widespread trade
    you were filled with violence,
    and you sinned.
So I drove you in disgrace from the mount of God,
    and I expelled you, O guardian cherub,
    from among the fiery stones.
¹⁷Your heart became proud
    on account of your beauty,
and you corrupted your wisdom
    because of your splendor.
So I threw you to the earth;
    I made a spectacle of you before kings.
¹⁸By your many sins and dishonest trade
    you have desecrated your sanctuaries.
So I made a fire come out from you,
    and it consumed you,
and I reduced you to ashes on the ground
    in the sight of all who were watching.
¹⁹All the nations who knew you
    are appalled at you;
you have come to a horrible end
    and will be no more.' "

A Prophecy Against Sidon ²⁰The word of the Lord came to me: ²¹"Son of man, set your face against Sidon; prophesy against her ²²and say: 'This is what the Sovereign Lord says:

" 'I am against you, O Sidon,
    and I will gain glory within you.

ᵃ13 Or *lapis lazuli* ᵇ13 The precise identification of some of these precious stones is uncertain. ᶜ13 The meaning of the Hebrew for this phrase is uncertain.

They will know that I am the Lord,
　when I inflict punishment on her
　and show myself holy within her.
²³I will send a plague upon her
　and make blood flow in her streets.
The slain will fall within her,
　with the sword against her on every side.
Then they will know that I am the Lord.

²⁴" 'No longer will the people of Israel have malicious neighbors who are painful briers and sharp thorns. Then they will know that I am the Sovereign Lord.

²⁵" 'This is what the Sovereign Lord says: When I gather the people of Israel from the nations where they have been scattered, I will show myself holy among them in the sight of the nations. Then they will live in their own land, which I gave to my servant Jacob. ²⁶They will live there in safety and will build houses and plant vineyards; they will live in safety when I inflict punishment on all their neighbors who maligned them. Then they will know that I am the Lord their God.' "

29 *A Prophecy Against Egypt*　In the tenth year, in the tenth month on the twelfth day, the word of the Lord came to me: ²"Son of man, set your face against Pharaoh king of Egypt and prophesy against him and against all Egypt. ³Speak to him and say: 'This is what the Sovereign Lord says:

" 'I am against you, Pharaoh king of Egypt,
　you great monster lying among your streams.
You say, "The Nile is mine;
　I made it for myself."
⁴But I will put hooks in your jaws
　and make the fish of your streams stick to your scales.
I will pull you out from among your streams,
　with all the fish sticking to your scales.
⁵I will leave you in the desert,
　you and all the fish of your streams.
You will fall on the open field
　and not be gathered or picked up.
I will give you as food
　to the beasts of the earth and the birds of the air.

⁶Then all who live in Egypt will know that I am the Lord.

" 'You have been a staff of reed for the house of Israel. ⁷When they grasped you with their hands, you splintered and you tore open their shoulders; when they leaned on you, you broke and their backs were wrenched.*ᵃ*

⁸" 'Therefore this is what the Sovereign Lord says: I will bring a sword against you and kill your men and their animals. ⁹Egypt will become a desolate wasteland. Then they will know that I am the Lord.

" 'Because you said, "The Nile is mine; I made it," ¹⁰therefore I am against you and against your streams, and I will make the land of Egypt a ruin and a desolate waste from Migdol to Aswan, as far as the border of Cush.*ᵇ* ¹¹No foot of man or animal will pass through it; no one will live there for forty years. ¹²I will make the land of Egypt desolate among devastated lands, and her cities will lie desolate forty years among ruined cities. And I will disperse the Egyptians among the nations and scatter them through the countries.

ᵃ7 Syriac (see also Septuagint and Vulgate); Hebrew *and you caused their backs to stand*　*ᵇ10* That is, the upper Nile region

¹³" 'Yet this is what the Sovereign Lord says: At the end of forty years I will gather the Egyptians from the nations where they were scattered. ¹⁴I will bring them back from captivity and return them to Upper Egypt,ª the land of their ancestry. There they will be a lowly kingdom. ¹⁵It will be the lowliest of kingdoms and will never again exalt itself above the other nations. I will make it so weak that it will never again rule over the nations. ¹⁶Egypt will no longer be a source of confidence for the people of Israel but will be a reminder of their sin in turning to her for help. Then they will know that I am the Sovereign Lord.' "

¹⁷In the twenty-seventh year, in the first month on the first day, the word of the Lord came to me: ¹⁸"Son of man, Nebuchadnezzar king of Babylon drove his army in a hard campaign against Tyre; every head was rubbed bare and every shoulder made raw. Yet he and his army got no reward from the campaign he led against Tyre. ¹⁹Therefore this is what the Sovereign Lord says: I am going to give Egypt to Nebuchadnezzar king of Babylon, and he will carry off its wealth. He will loot and plunder the land as pay for his army. ²⁰I have given him Egypt as a reward for his efforts because he and his army did it for me, declares the Sovereign Lord.

²¹"On that day I will make a hornᵇ grow for the house of Israel, and I will open your mouth among them. Then they will know that I am the Lord."

30

A Lament for Egypt The word of the Lord came to me: ²"Son of man, prophesy and say: 'This is what the Sovereign Lord says:

" 'Wail and say,
   "Alas for that day!"
³For the day is near,
   the day of the Lord is near—
a day of clouds,
   a time of doom for the nations.
⁴A sword will come against Egypt,
   and anguish will come upon Cush.ᶜ
When the slain fall in Egypt,
   her wealth will be carried away
   and her foundations torn down.

⁵Cush and Put, Lydia and all Arabia, Libyaᵈ and the people of the covenant land will fall by the sword along with Egypt.

⁶" 'This is what the Lord says:

" 'The allies of Egypt will fall
   and her proud strength will fail.
From Migdol to Aswan
   they will fall by the sword within her,
                         declares the Sovereign Lord.
⁷" 'They will be desolate
   among desolate lands,
and their cities will lie
   among ruined cities.
⁸Then they will know that I am the Lord,
   when I set fire to Egypt
   and all her helpers are crushed.

⁹" 'On that day messengers will go out from me in ships to frighten Cush out of her complacency. Anguish will take hold of them on the day of Egypt's doom, for it is sure to come.

ª14 Hebrew to Pathros ᵇ21 Horn here symbolizes strength. ᶜ4 That is, the upper Nile region; also in verses 5 and 9 ᵈ5 Hebrew Cub

¹⁰" 'This is what the Sovereign Lord says:

> " 'I will put an end to the hordes of Egypt
>   by the hand of Nebuchadnezzar king of Babylon.
> ¹¹He and his army—the most ruthless of nations—
>   will be brought in to destroy the land.
> They will draw their swords against Egypt
>   and fill the land with the slain.
> ¹²I will dry up the streams of the Nile
>   and sell the land to evil men;
>   by the hand of foreigners
>   I will lay waste the land and everything in it.

I the Lord have spoken.

¹³" 'This is what the Sovereign Lord says:

> " 'I will destroy the idols
>   and put an end to the images in Memphis.ᵃ
> No longer will there be a prince in Egypt,
>   and I will spread fear throughout the land.
> ¹⁴I will lay waste Upper Egypt,ᵇ
>   set fire to Zoan
>   and inflict punishment on Thebes.ᶜ
> ¹⁵I will pour out my wrath on Pelusium,ᵈ
>   the stronghold of Egypt,
>   and cut off the hordes of Thebes.
> ¹⁶I will set fire to Egypt;
>   Pelusium will writhe in agony.
> Thebes will be taken by storm;
>   Memphis will be in constant distress.
> ¹⁷The young men of Heliopolisᵉ and Bubastisᶠ
>   will fall by the sword,
>   and the cities themselves will go into captivity.
> ¹⁸Dark will be the day at Tahpanhes
>   when I break the yoke of Egypt;
>   there her proud strength will come to an end.
> She will be covered with clouds,
>   and her villages will go into captivity.
> ¹⁹So I will inflict punishment on Egypt,
>   and they will know that I am the Lord.' "

²⁰In the eleventh year, in the first month on the seventh day, the word of the Lord came to me: ²¹"Son of man, I have broken the arm of Pharaoh king of Egypt. It has not been bound up for healing or put in a splint so as to become strong enough to hold a sword. ²²Therefore this is what the Sovereign Lord says: I am against Pharaoh king of Egypt. I will break both his arms, the good arm as well as the broken one, and make the sword fall from his hand. ²³I will disperse the Egyptians among the nations and scatter them through the countries. ²⁴I will strengthen the arms of the king of Babylon and put my sword in his hand, but I will break the arms of Pharaoh, and he will groan before him like a mortally wounded man. ²⁵I will strengthen the arms of the king of Babylon, but the arms of Pharaoh will fall limp. Then they will know that I am the Lord, when I put my sword into the hand of the king of Babylon and he brandishes it against Egypt. ²⁶I will disperse the Egyptians among the nations and scatter them through the countries. Then they will know that I am the Lord."

ᵃ13 Hebrew *Noph*; also in verse 16   ᵇ14 Hebrew *waste Pathros*   ᶜ14 Hebrew *No*; also in verses 15 and 16
ᵈ15 Hebrew *Sin*; also in verse 16   ᵉ17 Hebrew *Awen* (or *On*)   ᶠ17 Hebrew *Pi Beseth*

A Cedar in Lebanon   In the eleventh year, in the third month on the first day, the word of the LORD came to me: ²"Son of man, say to Pharaoh king of Egypt and to his hordes:

> " 'Who can be compared with you in majesty?
> ³Consider Assyria, once a cedar in Lebanon,
>   with beautiful branches overshadowing the forest;
> it towered on high,
>   its top above the thick foliage.
> ⁴The waters nourished it,
>   deep springs made it grow tall;
> their streams flowed
>   all around its base
> and sent their channels
>   to all the trees of the field.
> ⁵So it towered higher
>   than all the trees of the field;
> its boughs increased
>   and its branches grew long,
>   spreading because of abundant waters.
> ⁶All the birds of the air
>   nested in its boughs,
> all the beasts of the field
>   gave birth under its branches;
> all the great nations
>   lived in its shade.
> ⁷It was majestic in beauty,
>   with its spreading boughs,
> for its roots went down
>   to abundant waters.
> ⁸The cedars in the garden of God
>   could not rival it,
> nor could the pine trees
>   equal its boughs,
> nor could the plane trees
>   compare with its branches—
> no tree in the garden of God
>   could match its beauty.
> ⁹I made it beautiful
>   with abundant branches,
> the envy of all the trees of Eden
>   in the garden of God.

¹⁰" 'Therefore this is what the Sovereign LORD says: Because it towered on high, lifting its top above the thick foliage, and because it was proud of its height, ¹¹I handed it over to the ruler of the nations, for him to deal with according to its wickedness. I cast it aside, ¹²and the most ruthless of foreign nations cut it down and left it. Its boughs fell on the mountains and in all the valleys; its branches lay broken in all the ravines of the land. All the nations of the earth came out from under its shade and left it. ¹³All the birds of the air settled on the fallen tree, and all the beasts of the field were among its branches. ¹⁴Therefore no other trees by the waters are ever to tower proudly on high, lifting their tops above the thick foliage. No other trees so well-watered are ever to reach such a height; they are all destined for death, for the earth below, among mortal men, with those who go down to the pit.

¹⁵" 'This is what the Sovereign LORD says: On the day it was brought down

to the grave*a* I covered the deep springs with mourning for it; I held back its streams, and its abundant waters were restrained. Because of it I clothed Lebanon with gloom, and all the trees of the field withered away. ¹⁶I made the nations tremble at the sound of its fall when I brought it down to the grave with those who go down to the pit. Then all the trees of Eden, the choicest and best of Lebanon, all the trees that were well-watered, were consoled in the earth below. ¹⁷Those who lived in its shade, its allies among the nations, had also gone down to the grave with it, joining those killed by the sword.

¹⁸" 'Which of the trees of Eden can be compared with you in splendor and majesty? Yet you, too, will be brought down with the trees of Eden to the earth below; you will lie among the uncircumcised, with those killed by the sword.

" 'This is Pharaoh and all his hordes, declares the Sovereign LORD.' "

32 *A Lament for Pharaoh*   In the twelfth year, in the twelfth month on the first day, the word of the LORD came to me: ²"Son of man, take up a lament concerning Pharaoh king of Egypt and say to him:

> " 'You are like a lion among the nations;
>   you are like a monster in the seas
> thrashing about in your streams,
>   churning the water with your feet
>   and muddying the streams.

³" 'This is what the Sovereign LORD says:

> " 'With a great throng of people
>   I will cast my net over you,
>   and they will haul you up in my net.
> ⁴I will throw you on the land
>   and hurl you on the open field.
> I will let all the birds of the air settle on you
>   and all the beasts of the earth gorge themselves on you.
> ⁵I will spread your flesh on the mountains
>   and fill the valleys with your remains.
> ⁶I will drench the land with your flowing blood
>   all the way to the mountains,
>   and the ravines will be filled with your flesh.
> ⁷When I snuff you out, I will cover the heavens
>   and darken their stars;
> I will cover the sun with a cloud,
>   and the moon will not give its light.
> ⁸All the shining lights in the heavens
>   I will darken over you;
>   I will bring darkness over your land,
>   declares the Sovereign LORD.
> ⁹I will trouble the hearts of many peoples
>   when I bring about your destruction among the nations,
>   among*b* lands you have not known.
> ¹⁰I will cause many peoples to be appalled at you,
>   and their kings will shudder with horror because of you
>   when I brandish my sword before them.
> On the day of your downfall
>   each of them will tremble
>   every moment for his life.

---

a15 Hebrew *Sheol*; also in verses 16 and 17   *b9* Hebrew; Septuagint *bring you into captivity among the nations, / to*

¹¹" 'For this is what the Sovereign L<small>ORD</small> says:

" 'The sword of the king of Babylon
    will come against you.
¹²I will cause your hordes to fall
    by the swords of mighty men—
    the most ruthless of all nations.
They will shatter the pride of Egypt,
    and all her hordes will be overthrown.
¹³I will destroy all her cattle
    from beside abundant waters
no longer to be stirred by the foot of man
    or muddied by the hoofs of cattle.
¹⁴Then I will let her waters settle
    and make her streams flow like oil,
                  declares the Sovereign L<small>ORD</small>.
¹⁵When I make Egypt desolate
    and strip the land of everything in it,
when I strike down all who live there,
    then they will know that I am the L<small>ORD</small>.'

¹⁶"This is the lament they will chant for her. The daughters of the nations will chant it; for Egypt and all her hordes they will chant it, declares the Sovereign L<small>ORD</small>."

¹⁷In the twelfth year, on the fifteenth day of the month, the word of the L<small>ORD</small> came to me: ¹⁸"Son of man, wail for the hordes of Egypt and consign to the earth below both her and the daughters of mighty nations, with those who go down to the pit. ¹⁹Say to them, 'Are you more favored than others? Go down and be laid among the uncircumcised.' ²⁰They will fall among those killed by the sword. The sword is drawn; let her be dragged off with all her hordes. ²¹From within the grave^a the mighty leaders will say of Egypt and her allies, 'They have come down and they lie with the uncircumcised, with those killed by the sword.'

²²"Assyria is there with her whole army; she is surrounded by the graves of all her slain, all who have fallen by the sword. ²³Their graves are in the depths of the pit and her army lies around her grave. All who had spread terror in the land of the living are slain, fallen by the sword.

²⁴"Elam is there, with all her hordes around her grave. All of them are slain, fallen by the sword. All who had spread terror in the land of the living went down uncircumcised to the earth below. They bear their shame with those who go down to the pit. ²⁵A bed is made for her among the slain, with all her hordes around her grave. All of them are uncircumcised, killed by the sword. Because their terror had spread in the land of the living, they bear their shame with those who go down to the pit; they are laid among the slain.

²⁶"Meshech and Tubal are there, with all their hordes around their graves. All of them are uncircumcised, killed by the sword because they spread their terror in the land of the living. ²⁷Do they not lie with the other uncircumcised warriors who have fallen, who went down to the grave with their weapons of war, whose swords were placed under their heads? The punishment for their sins rested on their bones, though the terror of these warriors had stalked through the land of the living.

²⁸"You too, O Pharaoh, will be broken and will lie among the uncircumcised, with those killed by the sword.

²⁹"Edom is there, her kings and all her princes; despite their power, they are laid with those killed by the sword. They lie with the uncircumcised, with those who go down to the pit.

^a21 Hebrew *Sheol*; also in verse 27

³⁰"All the princes of the north and all the Sidonians are there; they went down with the slain in disgrace despite the terror caused by their power. They lie uncircumcised with those killed by the sword and bear their shame with those who go down to the pit.

³¹"Pharaoh—he and all his army—will see them and he will be consoled for all his hordes that were killed by the sword, declares the Sovereign LORD. ³²Although I had him spread terror in the land of the living, Pharaoh and all his hordes will be laid among the uncircumcised, with those killed by the sword, declares the Sovereign LORD."

33 *Ezekiel a Watchman* The word of the LORD came to me: ²"Son of man, speak to your countrymen and say to them: 'When I bring the sword against a land, and the people of the land choose one of their men and make him their watchman, ³and he sees the sword coming against the land and blows the trumpet to warn the people, ⁴then if anyone hears the trumpet but does not take warning and the sword comes and takes his life, his blood will be on his own head. ⁵Since he heard the sound of the trumpet but did not take warning, his blood will be on his own head. If he had taken warning, he would have saved himself. ⁶But if the watchman sees the sword coming and does not blow the trumpet to warn the people and the sword comes and takes the life of one of them, that man will be taken away because of his sin, but I will hold the watchman accountable for his blood.'

⁷"Son of man, I have made you a watchman for the house of Israel; so hear the word I speak and give them warning from me. ⁸When I say to the wicked, 'O wicked man, you will surely die,' and you do not speak out to dissuade him from his ways, that wicked man will die for*ᵃ* his sin, and I will hold you accountable for his blood. ⁹But if you do warn the wicked man to turn from his ways and he does not do so, he will die for his sin, but you will have saved yourself.

¹⁰"Son of man, say to the house of Israel, 'This is what you are saying: "Our offenses and sins weigh us down, and we are wasting away because of*ᵇ* them. How then can we live?" ' ¹¹Say to them, 'As surely as I live, declares the Sovereign LORD, I take no pleasure in the death of the wicked, but rather that they turn from their ways and live. Turn! Turn from your evil ways! Why will you die, O house of Israel?'

¹²"Therefore, son of man, say to your countrymen, 'The righteousness of the righteous man will not save him when he disobeys, and the wickedness of the wicked man will not cause him to fall when he turns from it. The righteous man, if he sins, will not be allowed to live because of his former righteousness.' ¹³If I tell the righteous man that he will surely live, but then he trusts in his righteousness and does evil, none of the righteous things he has done will be remembered; he will die for the evil he has done. ¹⁴And if I say to the wicked man, 'You will surely die,' but he then turns away from his sin and does what is just and right— ¹⁵if he gives back what he took in pledge for a loan, returns what he has stolen, follows the decrees that give life, and does no evil, he will surely live; he will not die. ¹⁶None of the sins he has committed will be remembered against him. He has done what is just and right; he will surely live.

¹⁷"Yet your countrymen say, 'The way of the Lord is not just.' But it is their way that is not just. ¹⁸If a righteous man turns from his righteousness and does evil, he will die for it. ¹⁹And if a wicked man turns away from his wickedness and does what is just and right, he will live by doing so. ²⁰Yet, O house of Israel, you say, 'The way of the Lord is not just.' But I will judge each of you according to his own ways."

ᵃ8 Or *in;* also in verse 9   *ᵇ10* Or *away in*

Dear Sam,
        So many of my family and friends have not accepted Christ as their Savior. What's the best way to be a good witness?

William in Watts

100 Advice Lane, Anywhere, USA

Dear William,
        There isn't necessarily a best way to witness. You need to witness in different ways depending on the person and situation. With some people you'll want to talk openly about the way of salvation. With other people, living a happy, Christian life in front of them will be most effective. Your message is the same, but the way you share it is different.

        In Ezekiel 33, Ezekiel was charged by God to be a watchman. He was told to warn people when they did wrong. If he did not give the warning, he was guilty. If he gave the warning but people didn't pay attention, they were responsible.

        When you feel the urge to share your faith but don't, God holds you accountable. If you share the best you can, but the person won't pay attention to you, you have still done your part. And who knows? Perhaps you can plant a seed and later that person will come into God's kingdom.

        Don't get discouraged. God has given you an important job, but you are only responsible for doing that job. You aren't responsible for the results. Share Christ's love and God's grace with a gentle, loving spirit and trust God to do the rest.

                                                Sam

Jerusalem's Fall Explained ²¹In the twelfth year of our exile, in the tenth month on the fifth day, a man who had escaped from Jerusalem came to me and said, "The city has fallen!" ²²Now the evening before the man arrived, the hand of the LORD was upon me, and he opened my mouth before the man came to me in the morning. So my mouth was opened and I was no longer silent.

²³Then the word of the LORD came to me: ²⁴"Son of man, the people living in those ruins in the land of Israel are saying, 'Abraham was only one man, yet he possessed the land. But we are many; surely the land has been given to us as our possession.' ²⁵Therefore say to them, 'This is what the Sovereign LORD says: Since you eat meat with the blood still in it and look to your idols and shed blood, should you then possess the land? ²⁶You rely on your sword, you do detestable things, and each of you defiles his neighbor's wife. Should you then possess the land?'

²⁷"Say this to them: 'This is what the Sovereign LORD says: As surely as I live, those who are left in the ruins will fall by the sword, those out in the country I will give to the wild animals to be devoured, and those in strongholds and caves will die of a plague. ²⁸I will make the land a desolate waste, and her proud strength will come to an end, and the mountains of Israel will become desolate so that no one will cross them. ²⁹Then they will know that I am the LORD, when I have made the land a desolate waste because of all the detestable things they have done.'

³⁰"As for you, son of man, your countrymen are talking together about you by the walls and at the doors of the houses, saying to each other, 'Come and hear the message that has come from the LORD.' ³¹My people come to you, as they usually do, and sit before you to listen to your words, but they do not put them into practice. With their mouths they express devotion, but their hearts are greedy for unjust gain. ³²Indeed, to them you are nothing more than one who sings love songs with a beautiful voice and plays an instrument well, for they hear your words but do not put them into practice.

³³"When all this comes true—and it surely will—then they will know that a prophet has been among them."

34 *Shepherds and Sheep* The word of the LORD came to me: ²"Son of man, prophesy against the shepherds of Israel; prophesy and say to them: 'This is what the Sovereign LORD says: Woe to the shepherds of Israel who only take care of themselves! Should not shepherds take care of the flock? ³You eat the curds, clothe yourselves with the wool and slaughter the choice animals, but you do not take care of the flock. ⁴You have not strengthened the weak or healed the sick or bound up the injured. You have not brought back the strays or searched for the lost. You have ruled them harshly and brutally. ⁵So they were scattered because there was no shepherd, and when they were scattered they became food for all the wild animals. ⁶My sheep wandered over all the mountains and on every high hill. They were scattered over the whole earth, and no one searched or looked for them.

⁷"'Therefore, you shepherds, hear the word of the LORD: ⁸As surely as I live, declares the Sovereign LORD, because my flock lacks a shepherd and so has been plundered and has become food for all the wild animals, and because my shepherds did not search for my flock but cared for themselves rather than for my flock, ⁹therefore, O shepherds, hear the word of the LORD: ¹⁰This is what the Sovereign LORD says: I am against the shepherds and will hold them accountable for my flock. I will remove them from tending the flock so that the shepherds can no longer feed themselves. I will rescue my flock from their mouths, and it will no longer be food for them.

¹¹"'For this is what the Sovereign LORD says: I myself will search for my sheep and look after them. ¹²As a shepherd looks after his scattered flock

when he is with them, so will I look after my sheep. I will rescue them from all the places where they were scattered on a day of clouds and darkness. [13]I will bring them out from the nations and gather them from the countries, and I will bring them into their own land. I will pasture them on the mountains of Israel, in the ravines and in all the settlements in the land. [14]I will tend them in a good pasture, and the mountain heights of Israel will be their grazing land. There they will lie down in good grazing land, and there they will feed in a rich pasture on the mountains of Israel. [15]I myself will tend my sheep and have them lie down, declares the Sovereign Lord. [16]I will search for the lost and bring back the strays. I will bind up the injured and strengthen the weak, but the sleek and the strong I will destroy. I will shepherd the flock with justice.

> As a shepherd looks after his scattered flock . . . so will I look after my sheep (Ezekiel 34:12).

[17]" 'As for you, my flock, this is what the Sovereign Lord says: I will judge between one sheep and another, and between rams and goats. [18]Is it not enough for you to feed on the good pasture? Must you also trample the rest of your pasture with your feet? Is it not enough for you to drink clear water? Must you also muddy the rest with your feet? [19]Must my flock feed on what you have trampled and drink what you have muddied with your feet?

[20]" 'Therefore this is what the Sovereign Lord says to them: See, I myself will judge between the fat sheep and the lean sheep. [21]Because you shove with flank and shoulder, butting all the weak sheep with your horns until you have driven them away, [22]I will save my flock, and they will no longer be plundered. I will judge between one sheep and another. [23]I will place over them one shepherd, my servant David, and he will tend them; he will tend them and be their shepherd. [24]I the Lord will be their God, and my servant David will be prince among them. I the Lord have spoken.

[25]" 'I will make a covenant of peace with them and rid the land of wild beasts so that they may live in the desert and sleep in the forests in safety. [26]I will bless them and the places surrounding my hill.[a] I will send down showers in season; there will be showers of blessing. [27]The trees of the field will yield their fruit and the ground will yield its crops; the people will be secure in their land. They will know that I am the Lord, when I break the bars of their yoke and rescue them from the hands of those who enslaved them. [28]They will no longer be plundered by the nations, nor will wild animals devour them. They will live in safety, and no one will make them afraid. [29]I will provide for them a land renowned for its crops, and they will no longer be victims of famine in the land or bear the scorn of the nations. [30]Then they will know that I, the Lord their God, am with them and that they, the house of Israel, are my people, declares the Sovereign Lord. [31]You my sheep, the sheep of my pasture, are people, and I am your God, declares the Sovereign Lord.' "

35 *A Prophecy Against Edom* The word of the Lord came to me: [2]"Son of man, set your face against Mount Seir; prophesy against it [3]and say: 'This is what the Sovereign Lord says: I am against you, Mount Seir, and I will stretch out my hand against you and make you a desolate waste. [4]I will turn your towns into ruins and you will be desolate. Then you will know that I am the Lord.

[5]" 'Because you harbored an ancient hostility and delivered the Israelites over to the sword at the time of their calamity, the time their punishment reached its climax, [6]therefore as surely as I live, declares the Sovereign Lord,

---

[a]26 Or I will make them and the places surrounding my hill a blessing

I will give you over to bloodshed and it will pursue you. Since you did not hate bloodshed, bloodshed will pursue you. ⁷I will make Mount Seir a desolate waste and cut off from it all who come and go. ⁸I will fill your mountains with the slain; those killed by the sword will fall on your hills and in your valleys and in all your ravines. ⁹I will make you desolate forever; your towns will not be inhabited. Then you will know that I am the Lord.

¹⁰" 'Because you have said, "These two nations and countries will be ours and we will take possession of them," even though I the Lord was there, ¹¹therefore as surely as I live, declares the Sovereign Lord, I will treat you in accordance with the anger and jealousy you showed in your hatred of them and I will make myself known among them when I judge you. ¹²Then you will know that I the Lord have heard all the contemptible things you have said against the mountains of Israel. You said, "They have been laid waste and have been given over to us to devour." ¹³You boasted against me and spoke against me without restraint, and I heard it. ¹⁴This is what the Sovereign Lord says: While the whole earth rejoices, I will make you desolate. ¹⁵Because you rejoiced when the inheritance of the house of Israel became desolate, that is how I will treat you. You will be desolate, O Mount Seir, you and all of Edom. Then they will know that I am the Lord.' "

36 *A Prophecy to the Mountains of Israel* "Son of man, prophesy to the mountains of Israel and say, 'O mountains of Israel, hear the word of the Lord. ²This is what the Sovereign Lord says: The enemy said of you, "Aha! The ancient heights have become our possession." ' ³Therefore prophesy and say, 'This is what the Sovereign Lord says: Because they ravaged and hounded you from every side so that you became the possession of the rest of the nations and the object of people's malicious talk and slander, ⁴therefore, O mountains of Israel, hear the word of the Sovereign Lord: This is what the Sovereign Lord says to the mountains and hills, to the ravines and valleys, to the desolate ruins and the deserted towns that have been plundered and ridiculed by the rest of the nations around you— ⁵this is what the Sovereign Lord says: In my burning zeal I have spoken against the rest of the nations, and against all Edom, for with glee and with malice in their hearts they made my land their own possession so that they might plunder its pastureland.' ⁶Therefore prophesy concerning the land of Israel and say to the mountains and hills, to the ravines and valleys: 'This is what the Sovereign Lord says: I speak in my jealous wrath because you have suffered the scorn of the nations. ⁷Therefore this is what the Sovereign Lord says: I swear with uplifted hand that the nations around you will also suffer scorn.

⁸" 'But you, O mountains of Israel, will produce branches and fruit for my people Israel, for they will soon come home. ⁹I am concerned for you and will look on you with favor; you will be plowed and sown, ¹⁰and I will multiply the number of people upon you, even the whole house of Israel. The towns will be inhabited and the ruins rebuilt. ¹¹I will increase the number of men and animals upon you, and they will be fruitful and become numerous. I will settle people on you as in the past and will make you prosper more than before. Then you will know that I am the Lord. ¹²I will cause people, my people Israel, to walk upon you. They will possess you, and you will be their inheritance; you will never again deprive them of their children.

¹³" 'This is what the Sovereign Lord says: Because people say to you, "You devour men and deprive your nation of its children," ¹⁴therefore you will no longer devour men or make your nation childless, declares the Sovereign Lord. ¹⁵No longer will I make you hear the taunts of the nations, and no longer will you suffer the scorn of the peoples or cause your nation to fall, declares the Sovereign Lord.' "

¹⁶Again the word of the Lord came to me: ¹⁷"Son of man, when the people

of Israel were living in their own land, they defiled it by their conduct and their actions. Their conduct was like a woman's monthly uncleanness in my sight. ¹⁸So I poured out my wrath on them because they had shed blood in the land and because they had defiled it with their idols. ¹⁹I dispersed them among the nations, and they were scattered through the countries; I judged them according to their conduct and their actions. ²⁰And wherever they went among the nations they profaned my holy name, for it was said of them, 'These are the LORD's people, and yet they had to leave his land.' ²¹I had concern for my holy name, which the house of Israel profaned among the nations where they had gone.

²²"Therefore say to the house of Israel, 'This is what the Sovereign LORD says: It is not for your sake, O house of Israel, that I am going to do these things, but for the sake of my holy name, which you have profaned among the nations where you have gone. ²³I will show the holiness of my great name, which has been profaned among the nations, the name you have profaned among them. Then the nations will know that I am the LORD, declares the Sovereign LORD, when I show myself holy through you before their eyes.

²⁴"'For I will take you out of the nations; I will gather you from all the countries and bring you back into your own land. ²⁵I will sprinkle clean water on you, and you will be clean; I will cleanse you from all your impurities and from all your idols. ²⁶I will give you a new heart and put a new spirit in you; I will remove from you your heart of stone and give you a heart of flesh. ²⁷And I will put my Spirit in you and move you to follow my decrees and be careful to keep my laws. ²⁸You will live in the land I gave your forefathers; you will be my people, and I will be your God. ²⁹I will save you from all your uncleanness. I will call for the grain and make it plentiful and will not bring famine upon you. ³⁰I will increase the fruit of the trees and the crops of the field, so that you will no longer suffer disgrace among the nations because of famine. ³¹Then you will remember your evil ways and wicked deeds, and you will loathe yourselves for your sins and detestable practices. ³²I want you to know that I am not doing this for your sake, declares the Sovereign LORD. Be ashamed and disgraced for your conduct, O house of Israel!

³³"'This is what the Sovereign LORD says: On the day I cleanse you from all your sins, I will resettle your towns, and the ruins will be rebuilt. ³⁴The desolate land will be cultivated instead of lying desolate in the sight of all who pass through it. ³⁵They will say, "This land that was laid waste has become like the garden of Eden; the cities that were lying in ruins, desolate and destroyed, are now fortified and inhabited." ³⁶Then the nations around you that remain will know that I the LORD have rebuilt what was destroyed and have replanted what was desolate. I the LORD have spoken, and I will do it.'

³⁷"This is what the Sovereign LORD says: Once again I will yield to the plea of the house of Israel and do this for them: I will make their people as numerous as sheep, ³⁸as numerous as the flocks for offerings at Jerusalem during her appointed feasts. So will the ruined cities be filled with flocks of people. Then they will know that I am the LORD."

37 *The Valley of Dry Bones* The hand of the LORD was upon me, and he brought me out by the Spirit of the LORD and set me in the middle of a valley; it was full of bones. ²He led me back and forth among them, and I saw a great many bones on the floor of the valley, bones that were very dry. ³He asked me, "Son of man, can these bones live?"

I said, "O Sovereign LORD, you alone know."

⁴Then he said to me, "Prophesy to these bones and say to them, 'Dry bones, hear the word of the LORD! ⁵This is what the Sovereign LORD says to

these bones: I will make breath*a* enter you, and you will come to life. ⁶I will attach tendons to you and make flesh come upon you and cover you with skin; I will put breath in you, and you will come to life. Then you will know that I am the Lᴏʀᴅ.' "

⁷So I prophesied as I was commanded. And as I was prophesying, there was a noise, a rattling sound, and the bones came together, bone to bone. ⁸I looked, and tendons and flesh appeared on them and skin covered them, but there was no breath in them.

⁹Then he said to me, "Prophesy to the breath; prophesy, son of man, and say to it, 'This is what the Sovereign Lᴏʀᴅ says: Come from the four winds, O breath, and breathe into these slain, that they may live.' " ¹⁰So I prophesied as he commanded me, and breath entered them; they came to life and stood up on their feet—a vast army.

¹¹Then he said to me: "Son of man, these bones are the whole house of Israel. They say, 'Our bones are dried up and our hope is gone; we are cut off.' ¹²Therefore prophesy and say to them: 'This is what the Sovereign Lᴏʀᴅ says: O my people, I am going to open your graves and bring you up from them; I will bring you back to the land of Israel. ¹³Then you, my people, will know that I am the Lᴏʀᴅ, when I open your graves and bring you up from them. ¹⁴I will put my Spirit in you and you will live, and I will settle you in your own land. Then you will know that I the Lᴏʀᴅ have spoken, and I have done it, declares the Lᴏʀᴅ.' "

One Nation Under One King ¹⁵The word of the Lᴏʀᴅ came to me: ¹⁶"Son of man, take a stick of wood and write on it, 'Belonging to Judah and the Israelites associated with him.' Then take another stick of wood, and write on it, 'Ephraim's stick, belonging to Joseph and all the house of Israel associated with him.' ¹⁷Join them together into one stick so that they will become one in your hand.

¹⁸"When your countrymen ask you, 'Won't you tell us what you mean by this?' ¹⁹say to them, 'This is what the Sovereign Lᴏʀᴅ says: I am going to take the stick of Joseph—which is in Ephraim's hand—and of the Israelite tribes associated with him, and join it to Judah's stick, making them a single stick of wood, and they will become one in my hand.' ²⁰Hold before their eyes the sticks you have written on ²¹and say to them, 'This is what the Sovereign Lᴏʀᴅ says: I will take the Israelites out of the nations where they have gone. I will gather them from all around and bring them back into their own land. ²²I will make them one nation in the land, on the mountains of Israel. There will be one king over all of them and they will never again be two nations or be divided into two kingdoms. ²³They will no longer defile themselves with their idols and vile images or with any of their offenses, for I will save them from all their sinful backsliding,*b* and I will cleanse them. They will be my people, and I will be their God.

²⁴" 'My servant David will be king over them, and they will all have one shepherd. They will follow my laws and be careful to keep my decrees. ²⁵They will live in the land I gave to my servant Jacob, the land where your fathers lived. They and their children and their children's children will live there forever, and David my servant will be their prince forever. ²⁶I will make a covenant of peace with them; it will be an everlasting covenant. I will establish them and increase their numbers, and I will put my sanctuary among them forever. ²⁷My dwelling place will be with them; I will be their God, and they will be my people. ²⁸Then the nations will know that I the Lᴏʀᴅ make Israel holy, when my sanctuary is among them forever.' "

---

a5 The Hebrew for this word can also mean *wind* or *spirit* (see verses 6-14). *b23* Many Hebrew manuscripts (see also Septuagint); most Hebrew manuscripts *all their dwelling places where they sinned*

38 *A Prophecy Against Gog* The word of the LORD came to me: ²"Son of man, set your face against Gog, of the land of Magog, the chief prince of*ᵃ* Meshech and Tubal; prophesy against him ³and say: 'This is what the Sovereign LORD says: I am against you, O Gog, chief prince of*ᵇ* Meshech and Tubal. ⁴I will turn you around, put hooks in your jaws and bring you out with your whole army—your horses, your horsemen fully armed, and a great horde with large and small shields, all of them brandishing their swords. ⁵Persia, Cush*ᶜ* and Put will be with them, all with shields and helmets, ⁶also Gomer with all its troops, and Beth Togarmah from the far north with all its troops—the many nations with you.

⁷" 'Get ready; be prepared, you and all the hordes gathered about you, and take command of them. ⁸After many days you will be called to arms. In future years you will invade a land that has recovered from war, whose people were gathered from many nations to the mountains of Israel, which had long been desolate. They had been brought out from the nations, and now all of them live in safety. ⁹You and all your troops and the many nations with you will go up, advancing like a storm; you will be like a cloud covering the land.

¹⁰" 'This is what the Sovereign LORD says: On that day thoughts will come into your mind and you will devise an evil scheme. ¹¹You will say, "I will invade a land of unwalled villages; I will attack a peaceful and unsuspecting people—all of them living without walls and without gates and bars. ¹²I will plunder and loot and turn my hand against the resettled ruins and the people gathered from the nations, rich in livestock and goods, living at the center of the land." ¹³Sheba and Dedan and the merchants of Tarshish and all her villages*ᵈ* will say to you, "Have you come to plunder? Have you gathered your hordes to loot, to carry off silver and gold, to take away livestock and goods and to seize much plunder?" '

¹⁴"Therefore, son of man, prophesy and say to Gog: 'This is what the Sovereign LORD says: In that day, when my people Israel are living in safety, will you not take notice of it? ¹⁵You will come from your place in the far north, you and many nations with you, all of them riding on horses, a great horde, a mighty army. ¹⁶You will advance against my people Israel like a cloud that covers the land. In days to come, O Gog, I will bring you against my land, so that the nations may know me when I show myself holy through you before their eyes.

¹⁷" 'This is what the Sovereign LORD says: Are you not the one I spoke of in former days by my servants the prophets of Israel? At that time they prophesied for years that I would bring you against them. ¹⁸This is what will happen in that day: When Gog attacks the land of Israel, my hot anger will be aroused, declares the Sovereign LORD. ¹⁹In my zeal and fiery wrath I declare that at that time there shall be a great earthquake in the land of Israel. ²⁰The fish of the sea, the birds of the air, the beasts of the field, every creature that moves along the ground, and all the people on the face of the earth will tremble at my presence. The mountains will be overturned, the cliffs will crumble and every wall will fall to the ground. ²¹I will summon a sword against Gog on all my mountains, declares the Sovereign LORD. Every man's sword will be against his brother. ²²I will execute judgment upon him with plague and bloodshed; I will pour down torrents of rain, hailstones and burning sulfur on him and on his troops and on the many nations with him. ²³And so I will show my greatness and my holiness, and I will make myself known in the sight of many nations. Then they will know that I am the LORD.'

EZEKIEL 38–39

QU*Z*ZER

Q: Where will Israel's final enemy come from?

BONUS: Where are these lands on modern-day maps?

Answers on page 1122

ᵃ2 Or the prince of Rosh, *ᵇ3 Or Gog, prince of Rosh,* *ᶜ5 That is, the upper Nile region* *ᵈ13 Or her strong lions*

"Son of man, prophesy against Gog and say: 'This is what the Sovereign LORD says: I am against you, O Gog, chief prince of[a] Meshech and Tubal. [2]I will turn you around and drag you along. I will bring you from the far north and send you against the mountains of Israel. [3]Then I will strike your bow from your left hand and make your arrows drop from your right hand. [4]On the mountains of Israel you will fall, you and all your troops and the nations with you. I will give you as food to all kinds of carrion birds and to the wild animals. [5]You will fall in the open field, for I have spoken, declares the Sovereign LORD. [6]I will send fire on Magog and on those who live in safety in the coastlands, and they will know that I am the LORD.

[7]" 'I will make known my holy name among my people Israel. I will no longer let my holy name be profaned, and the nations will know that I the LORD am the Holy One in Israel. [8]It is coming! It will surely take place, declares the Sovereign LORD. This is the day I have spoken of.

[9]" 'Then those who live in the towns of Israel will go out and use the weapons for fuel and burn them up—the small and large shields, the bows and arrows, the war clubs and spears. For seven years they will use them for fuel. [10]They will not need to gather wood from the fields or cut it from the forests, because they will use the weapons for fuel. And they will plunder those who plundered them and loot those who looted them, declares the Sovereign LORD.

[11]" 'On that day I will give Gog a burial place in Israel, in the valley of those who travel east toward[b] the Sea.[c] It will block the way of travelers, because Gog and all his hordes will be buried there. So it will be called the Valley of Hamon Gog.[d]

[12]" 'For seven months the house of Israel will be burying them in order to cleanse the land. [13]All the people of the land will bury them, and the day I am glorified will be a memorable day for them, declares the Sovereign LORD.

[14]" 'Men will be regularly employed to cleanse the land. Some will go throughout the land and, in addition to them, others will bury those that remain on the ground. At the end of the seven months they will begin their search. [15]As they go through the land and one of them sees a human bone, he will set up a marker beside it until the gravediggers have buried it in the Valley of Hamon Gog. [16](Also a town called Hamonah[e] will be there.) And so they will cleanse the land.'

[17]"Son of man, this is what the Sovereign LORD says: Call out to every kind of bird and all the wild animals: 'Assemble and come together from all around to the sacrifice I am preparing for you, the great sacrifice on the mountains of Israel. There you will eat flesh and drink blood. [18]You will eat the flesh of mighty men and drink the blood of the princes of the earth as if they were rams and lambs, goats and bulls—all of them fattened animals from Bashan. [19]At the sacrifice I am preparing for you, you will eat fat till you are glutted and drink blood till you are drunk. [20]At my table you will eat your fill of horses and riders, mighty men and soldiers of every kind,' declares the Sovereign LORD.

[21]"I will display my glory among the nations, and all the nations will see the punishment I inflict and the hand I lay upon them. [22]From that day forward the house of Israel will know that I am the LORD their God. [23]And the nations will know that the people of Israel went into exile for their sin, because they were unfaithful to me. So I hid my face from them and handed them over to their enemies, and they all fell by the sword. [24]I dealt with them according to their uncleanness and their offenses, and I hid my face from them.

[25]"Therefore this is what the Sovereign LORD says: I will now bring Jacob back from captivity[f] and will have compassion on all the people of Israel, and

Answers
to Quizzer on page 1121

A: From the north (Ezekiel 38:6).

BONUS: Some think them to be Iraq and parts of what used to be the USSR; others think the answer won't be clear until the prophecy is fulfilled.

[a]1 Or *Gog, prince of Rosh,*   [b]11 Or *of*   [c]11 That is, the Dead Sea   [d]11 *Hamon Gog* means *hordes of Gog.*
[e]16 *Hamonah* means *horde.*   [f]25 Or *now restore the fortunes of Jacob*

I will be zealous for my holy name. ²⁶They will forget their shame and all the unfaithfulness they showed toward me when they lived in safety in their land with no one to make them afraid. ²⁷When I have brought them back from the nations and have gathered them from the countries of their enemies, I will show myself holy through them in the sight of many nations. ²⁸Then they will know that I am the LORD their God, for though I sent them into exile among the nations, I will gather them to their own land, not leaving any behind. ²⁹I will no longer hide my face from them, for I will pour out my Spirit on the house of Israel, declares the Sovereign LORD."

40 *The New Temple Area* In the twenty-fifth year of our exile, at the beginning of the year, on the tenth of the month, in the fourteenth year after the fall of the city—on that very day the hand of the LORD was upon me and he took me there. ²In visions of God he took me to the land of Israel and set me on a very high mountain, on whose south side were some buildings that looked like a city. ³He took me there, and I saw a man whose appearance was like bronze; he was standing in the gateway with a linen cord and a measuring rod in his hand. ⁴The man said to me, "Son of man, look with your eyes and hear with your ears and pay attention to everything I am going to show you, for that is why you have been brought here. Tell the house of Israel everything you see."

The East Gate to the Outer Court ⁵I saw a wall completely surrounding the temple area. The length of the measuring rod in the man's hand was six long cubits, each of which was a cubit*ᵃ* and a handbreadth.*ᵇ* He measured the wall; it was one measuring rod thick and one rod high.

⁶Then he went to the gate facing east. He climbed its steps and measured the threshold of the gate; it was one rod deep.*ᶜ* ⁷The alcoves for the guards were one rod long and one rod wide, and the projecting walls between the alcoves were five cubits thick. And the threshold of the gate next to the portico facing the temple was one rod deep.

⁸Then he measured the portico of the gateway; ⁹it*ᵈ* was eight cubits deep and its jambs were two cubits thick. The portico of the gateway faced the temple.

¹⁰Inside the east gate were three alcoves on each side; the three had the same measurements, and the faces of the projecting walls on each side had the same measurements. ¹¹Then he measured the width of the entrance to the gateway; it was ten cubits and its length was thirteen cubits. ¹²In front of each alcove was a wall one cubit high, and the alcoves were six cubits square. ¹³Then he measured the gateway from the top of the rear wall of one alcove to the top of the opposite one; the distance was twenty-five cubits from one parapet opening to the opposite one. ¹⁴He measured along the faces of the projecting walls all around the inside of the gateway—sixty cubits. The measurement was up to the portico*ᵉ* facing the courtyard.*ᶠ* ¹⁵The distance from the entrance of the gateway to the far end of its portico was fifty cubits. ¹⁶The alcoves and the projecting walls inside the gateway were surmounted by narrow parapet openings all around, as was the portico; the openings all around faced inward. The faces of the projecting walls were decorated with palm trees.

The Outer Court ¹⁷Then he brought me into the outer court. There I saw some rooms and a pavement that had been constructed all around the court; there were thirty rooms along the pavement. ¹⁸It abutted the sides of the

---

ᵃ5 The common cubit was about 1 1/2 feet (about 0.5 meter). *ᵇ5* That is, about 3 inches (about 8 centimeters) *ᶜ6* Septuagint; Hebrew *deep, the first threshold, one rod deep* *ᵈ8,9* Many Hebrew manuscripts, Septuagint, Vulgate and Syriac; most Hebrew manuscripts *gateway facing the temple; it was one rod deep. ⁹Then he measured the portico of the gateway; it* *ᵉ14* Septuagint; Hebrew *projecting wall* *ᶠ14* The meaning of the Hebrew for this verse is uncertain.

gateways and was as wide as they were long; this was the lower pavement.
¹⁹Then he measured the distance from the inside of the lower gateway to the outside of the inner court; it was a hundred cubits on the east side as well as on the north.

The North Gate   ²⁰Then he measured the length and width of the gate facing north, leading into the outer court. ²¹Its alcoves—three on each side—its projecting walls and its portico had the same measurements as those of the first gateway. It was fifty cubits long and twenty-five cubits wide. ²²Its openings, its portico and its palm tree decorations had the same measurements as those of the gate facing east. Seven steps led up to it, with its portico opposite them. ²³There was a gate to the inner court facing the north gate, just as there was on the east. He measured from one gate to the opposite one; it was a hundred cubits.

The South Gate   ²⁴Then he led me to the south side and I saw a gate facing south. He measured its jambs and its portico, and they had the same measurements as the others. ²⁵The gateway and its portico had narrow openings all around, like the openings of the others. It was fifty cubits long and twenty-five cubits wide. ²⁶Seven steps led up to it, with its portico opposite them; it had palm tree decorations on the faces of the projecting walls on each side. ²⁷The inner court also had a gate facing south, and he measured from this gate to the outer gate on the south side; it was a hundred cubits.

Gates to the Inner Court   ²⁸Then he brought me into the inner court through the south gate, and he measured the south gate; it had the same measurements as the others. ²⁹Its alcoves, its projecting walls and its portico had the same measurements as the others. The gateway and its portico had openings all around. It was fifty cubits long and twenty-five cubits wide. ³⁰(The porticoes of the gateways around the inner court were twenty-five cubits wide and five cubits deep.) ³¹Its portico faced the outer court; palm trees decorated its jambs, and eight steps led up to it.

³²Then he brought me to the inner court on the east side, and he measured the gateway; it had the same measurements as the others. ³³Its alcoves, its projecting walls and its portico had the same measurements as the others. The gateway and its portico had openings all around. It was fifty cubits long and twenty-five cubits wide. ³⁴Its portico faced the outer court; palm trees decorated the jambs on either side, and eight steps led up to it.

³⁵Then he brought me to the north gate and measured it. It had the same measurements as the others, ³⁶as did its alcoves, its projecting walls and its portico, and it had openings all around. It was fifty cubits long and twenty-five cubits wide. ³⁷Its portico*ᵃ* faced the outer court; palm trees decorated the jambs on either side, and eight steps led up to it.

The Rooms for Preparing Sacrifices   ³⁸A room with a doorway was by the portico in each of the inner gateways, where the burnt offerings were washed. ³⁹In the portico of the gateway were two tables on each side, on which the burnt offerings, sin offerings and guilt offerings were slaughtered. ⁴⁰By the outside wall of the portico of the gateway, near the steps at the entrance to the north gateway were two tables, and on the other side of the steps were two tables. ⁴¹So there were four tables on one side of the gateway and four on the other—eight tables in all—on which the sacrifices were slaughtered. ⁴²There were also four tables of dressed stone for the burnt offerings, each a cubit and a half long, a cubit and a half wide and a cubit high. On them were placed the utensils for slaughtering the burnt offerings and the other sacrifices. ⁴³And double-pronged hooks, each a handbreadth long, were attached to the wall all around. The tables were for the flesh of the offerings.

ᵃ37 Septuagint (see also verses 31 and 34); Hebrew *jambs*

Rooms for the Priests ⁴⁴Outside the inner gate, within the inner court, were two rooms, oneᵃ at the side of the north gate and facing south, and another at the side of the southᵇ gate and facing north. ⁴⁵He said to me, "The room facing south is for the priests who have charge of the temple, ⁴⁶and the room facing north is for the priests who have charge of the altar. These are the sons of Zadok, who are the only Levites who may draw near to the Lᴏʀᴅ to minister before him."

⁴⁷Then he measured the court: It was square—a hundred cubits long and a hundred cubits wide. And the altar was in front of the temple.

The Temple ⁴⁸He brought me to the portico of the temple and measured the jambs of the portico; they were five cubits wide on either side. The width of the entrance was fourteen cubits and its projecting walls wereᶜ three cubits wide on either side. ⁴⁹The portico was twenty cubits wide, and twelveᵈ cubits from front to back. It was reached by a flight of stairs,ᵉ and there were pillars on each side of the jambs.

41 Then the man brought me to the outer sanctuary and measured the jambs; the width of the jambs was six cubitsᶠ on each side.ᵍ ²The entrance was ten cubits wide, and the projecting walls on each side of it were five cubits wide. He also measured the outer sanctuary; it was forty cubits long and twenty cubits wide.

³Then he went into the inner sanctuary and measured the jambs of the entrance; each was two cubits wide. The entrance was six cubits wide, and the projecting walls on each side of it were seven cubits wide. ⁴And he measured the length of the inner sanctuary; it was twenty cubits, and its width was twenty cubits across the end of the outer sanctuary. He said to me, "This is the Most Holy Place."

⁵Then he measured the wall of the temple; it was six cubits thick, and each side room around the temple was four cubits wide. ⁶The side rooms were on three levels, one above another, thirty on each level. There were ledges all around the wall of the temple to serve as supports for the side rooms, so that the supports were not inserted into the wall of the temple. ⁷The side rooms all around the temple were wider at each successive level. The structure surrounding the temple was built in ascending stages, so that the rooms widened as one went upward. A stairway went up from the lowest floor to the top floor through the middle floor.

⁸I saw that the temple had a raised base all around it, forming the foundation of the side rooms. It was the length of the rod, six long cubits. ⁹The outer wall of the side rooms was five cubits thick. The open area between the side rooms of the temple ¹⁰and the ˌpriests'ˌ rooms was twenty cubits wide all around the temple. ¹¹There were entrances to the side rooms from the open area, one on the north and another on the south; and the base adjoining the open area was five cubits wide all around.

¹²The building facing the temple courtyard on the west side was seventy cubits wide. The wall of the building was five cubits thick all around, and its length was ninety cubits.

¹³Then he measured the temple; it was a hundred cubits long, and the temple courtyard and the building with its walls were also a hundred cubits long. ¹⁴The width of the temple courtyard on the east, including the front of the temple, was a hundred cubits.

¹⁵Then he measured the length of the building facing the courtyard at the

---

ᵃ44 Septuagint; Hebrew *were rooms for singers, which were* ᵇ44 Septuagint; Hebrew *east* ᶜ48 Septuagint; Hebrew *entrance was* ᵈ49 Septuagint *eleven* ᵉ49 Hebrew; Septuagint *Ten steps led up to it* ᶠ1 The common cubit was about 1 1/2 feet (about 0.5 meter). ᵍ1 One Hebrew manuscript and Septuagint; most Hebrew manuscripts *side, the width of the tent*

rear of the temple, including its galleries on each side; it was a hundred cubits.

The outer sanctuary, the inner sanctuary and the portico facing the court, [16]as well as the thresholds and the narrow windows and galleries around the three of them—everything beyond and including the threshold was covered with wood. The floor, the wall up to the windows, and the windows were covered. [17]In the space above the outside of the entrance to the inner sanctuary and on the walls at regular intervals all around the inner and outer sanctuary [18]were carved cherubim and palm trees. Palm trees alternated with cherubim. Each cherub had two faces: [19]the face of a man toward the palm tree on one side and the face of a lion toward the palm tree on the other. They were carved all around the whole temple. [20]From the floor to the area above the entrance, cherubim and palm trees were carved on the wall of the outer sanctuary.

[21]The outer sanctuary had a rectangular doorframe, and the one at the front of the Most Holy Place was similar. [22]There was a wooden altar three cubits high and two cubits square[a]; its corners, its base[b] and its sides were of wood. The man said to me, "This is the table that is before the LORD." [23]Both the outer sanctuary and the Most Holy Place had double doors. [24]Each door had two leaves—two hinged leaves for each door. [25]And on the doors of the outer sanctuary were carved cherubim and palm trees like those carved on the walls, and there was a wooden overhang on the front of the portico. [26]On the sidewalls of the portico were narrow windows with palm trees carved on each side. The side rooms of the temple also had overhangs.

42 **Rooms for the Priests** Then the man led me northward into the outer court and brought me to the rooms opposite the temple courtyard and opposite the outer wall on the north side. [2]The building whose door faced north was a hundred cubits[c] long and fifty cubits wide. [3]Both in the section twenty cubits from the inner court and in the section opposite the pavement of the outer court, gallery faced gallery at the three levels. [4]In front of the rooms was an inner passageway ten cubits wide and a hundred cubits[d] long. Their doors were on the north. [5]Now the upper rooms were narrower, for the galleries took more space from them than from the rooms on the lower and middle floors of the building. [6]The rooms on the third floor had no pillars, as the courts had; so they were smaller in floor space than those on the lower and middle floors. [7]There was an outer wall parallel to the rooms and the outer court; it extended in front of the rooms for fifty cubits. [8]While the row of rooms on the side next to the outer court was fifty cubits long, the row on the side nearest the sanctuary was a hundred cubits long. [9]The lower rooms had an entrance on the east side as one enters them from the outer court.

[10]On the south side[e] along the length of the wall of the outer court, adjoining the temple courtyard and opposite the outer wall, were rooms [11]with a passageway in front of them. These were like the rooms on the north; they had the same length and width, with similar exits and dimensions. Similar to the doorways on the north [12]were the doorways of the rooms on the south. There was a doorway at the beginning of the passageway that was parallel to the corresponding wall extending eastward, by which one enters the rooms.

[13]Then he said to me, "The north and south rooms facing the temple courtyard are the priests' rooms, where the priests who approach the LORD will eat the most holy offerings. There they will put the most holy offerings—the grain offerings, the sin offerings and the guilt offerings—for the place is

---

[a]22 Septuagint; Hebrew *long* [b]22 Septuagint; Hebrew *length* [c]2 The common cubit was about 1 1/2 feet (about 0.5 meter). [d]4 Septuagint and Syriac; Hebrew *and one cubit* [e]10 Septuagint; Hebrew *Eastward*

holy. ¹⁴Once the priests enter the holy precincts, they are not to go into the outer court until they leave behind the garments in which they minister, for these are holy. They are to put on other clothes before they go near the places that are for the people."

¹⁵When he had finished measuring what was inside the temple area, he led me out by the east gate and measured the area all around: ¹⁶He measured the east side with the measuring rod; it was five hundred cubits.ᵃ ¹⁷He measured the north side; it was five hundred cubitsᵇ by the measuring rod. ¹⁸He measured the south side; it was five hundred cubits by the measuring rod. ¹⁹Then he turned to the west side and measured; it was five hundred cubits by the measuring rod. ²⁰So he measured the area on all four sides. It had a wall around it, five hundred cubits long and five hundred cubits wide, to separate the holy from the common.

43 *The Glory Returns to the Temple* Then the man brought me to the gate facing east, ²and I saw the glory of the God of Israel coming from the east. His voice was like the roar of rushing waters, and the land was radiant with his glory. ³The vision I saw was like the vision I had seen when heᶜ came to destroy the city and like the visions I had seen by the Kebar River, and I fell facedown. ⁴The glory of the LORD entered the temple through the gate facing east. ⁵Then the Spirit lifted me up and brought me into the inner court, and the glory of the LORD filled the temple.

⁶While the man was standing beside me, I heard someone speaking to me from inside the temple. ⁷He said: "Son of man, this is the place of my throne and the place for the soles of my feet. This is where I will live among the Israelites forever. The house of Israel will never again defile my holy name—neither they nor their kings—by their prostitutionᵈ and the lifeless idolsᵉ of their kings at their high places. ⁸When they placed their threshold next to my threshold and their doorposts beside my doorposts, with only a wall between me and them, they defiled my holy name by their detestable practices. So I destroyed them in my anger. ⁹Now let them put away from me their prostitution and the lifeless idols of their kings, and I will live among them forever.

¹⁰"Son of man, describe the temple to the people of Israel, that they may be ashamed of their sins. Let them consider the plan, ¹¹and if they are ashamed of all they have done, make known to them the design of the temple—its arrangement, its exits and entrances—its whole design and all its regulationsᶠ and laws. Write these down before them so that they may be faithful to its design and follow all its regulations.

¹²"This is the law of the temple: All

I've got my handy-dandy cubit tape measure here—now for some mental math . . .

SEE EZEKIEL 42:15-20

ᵃ16 See Septuagint of verse 17; Hebrew *rods*; also in verses 18 and 19.   ᵇ17 Septuagint; Hebrew *rods*
ᶜ3 Some Hebrew manuscripts and Vulgate; most Hebrew manuscripts *I*   ᵈ7 Or *their spiritual adultery*; also in verse 9   ᵉ7 Or *the corpses*; also in verse 9
ᶠ11 Some Hebrew manuscripts and Septuagint; most Hebrew manuscripts *regulations and its whole design*

the surrounding area on top of the mountain will be most holy. Such is the law of the temple.

The Altar ¹³"These are the measurements of the altar in long cubits, that cubit being a cubit*a* and a handbreadth*b*: Its gutter is a cubit deep and a cubit wide, with a rim of one span*c* around the edge. And this is the height of the altar: ¹⁴From the gutter on the ground up to the lower ledge it is two cubits high and a cubit wide, and from the smaller ledge up to the larger ledge it is four cubits high and a cubit wide. ¹⁵The altar hearth is four cubits high, and four horns project upward from the hearth. ¹⁶The altar hearth is square, twelve cubits long and twelve cubits wide. ¹⁷The upper ledge also is square, fourteen cubits long and fourteen cubits wide, with a rim of half a cubit and a gutter of a cubit all around. The steps of the altar face east.

¹⁸Then he said to me, "Son of man, this is what the Sovereign LORD says: These will be the regulations for sacrificing burnt offerings and sprinkling blood upon the altar when it is built: ¹⁹You are to give a young bull as a sin offering to the priests, who are Levites, of the family of Zadok, who come near to minister before me, declares the Sovereign LORD. ²⁰You are to take some of its blood and put it on the four horns of the altar and on the four corners of the upper ledge and all around the rim, and so purify the altar and make atonement for it. ²¹You are to take the bull for the sin offering and burn it in the designated part of the temple area outside the sanctuary.

²²"On the second day you are to offer a male goat without defect for a sin offering, and the altar is to be purified as it was purified with the bull. ²³When you have finished purifying it, you are to offer a young bull and a ram from the flock, both without defect. ²⁴You are to offer them before the LORD, and the priests are to sprinkle salt on them and sacrifice them as a burnt offering to the LORD.

²⁵"For seven days you are to provide a male goat daily for a sin offering; you are also to provide a young bull and a ram from the flock, both without defect. ²⁶For seven days they are to make atonement for the altar and cleanse it; thus they will dedicate it. ²⁷At the end of these days, from the eighth day on, the priests are to present your burnt offerings and fellowship offerings*d* on the altar. Then I will accept you, declares the Sovereign LORD."

44 *The Prince, the Levites, the Priests* Then the man brought me back to the outer gate of the sanctuary, the one facing east, and it was shut. ²The LORD said to me, "This gate is to remain shut. It must not be opened; no one may enter through it. It is to remain shut because the LORD, the God of Israel, has entered through it. ³The prince himself is the only one who may sit inside the gateway to eat in the presence of the LORD. He is to enter by way of the portico of the gateway and go out the same way."

⁴Then the man brought me by way of the north gate to the front of the temple. I looked and saw the glory of the LORD filling the temple of the LORD, and I fell facedown.

⁵The LORD said to me, "Son of man, look carefully, listen closely and give attention to everything I tell you concerning all the regulations regarding the temple of the LORD. Give attention to the entrance of the temple and all the exits of the sanctuary. ⁶Say to the rebellious house of Israel, 'This is what the Sovereign LORD says: Enough of your detestable practices, O house of Israel!

EZEKIEL 43

QUIZZER

Q: How many Jewish temples on Mount Zion does the Bible describe?

BONUS: What stands on the temple mount today?

Answers on page 1130

---

a13 The common cubit was about 1 1/2 feet (about 0.5 meter). *b13* That is, about 3 inches (about 8 centimeters) *c13* That is, about 9 inches (about 22 centimeters) *d27* Traditionally *peace offerings*

⁷In addition to all your other detestable practices, you brought foreigners uncircumcised in heart and flesh into my sanctuary, desecrating my temple while you offered me food, fat and blood, and you broke my covenant. ⁸Instead of carrying out your duty in regard to my holy things, you put others in charge of my sanctuary. ⁹This is what the Sovereign LORD says: No foreigner uncircumcised in heart and flesh is to enter my sanctuary, not even the foreigners who live among the Israelites.

¹⁰" 'The Levites who went far from me when Israel went astray and who wandered from me after their idols must bear the consequences of their sin. ¹¹They may serve in my sanctuary, having charge of the gates of the temple and serving in it; they may slaughter the burnt offerings and sacrifices for the people and stand before the people and serve them. ¹²But because they served them in the presence of their idols and made the house of Israel fall into sin, therefore I have sworn with uplifted hand that they must bear the consequences of their sin, declares the Sovereign LORD. ¹³They are not to come near to serve me as priests or come near any of my holy things or my most holy offerings; they must bear the shame of their detestable practices. ¹⁴Yet I will put them in charge of the duties of the temple and all the work that is to be done in it.

¹⁵" 'But the priests, who are Levites and descendants of Zadok and who faithfully carried out the duties of my sanctuary when the Israelites went astray from me, are to come near to minister before me; they are to stand before me to offer sacrifices of fat and blood, declares the Sovereign LORD. ¹⁶They alone are to enter my sanctuary; they alone are to come near my table to minister before me and perform my service.

¹⁷" 'When they enter the gates of the inner court, they are to wear linen clothes; they must not wear any woolen garment while ministering at the gates of the inner court or inside the temple. ¹⁸They are to wear linen turbans on their heads and linen undergarments around their waists. They must not wear anything that makes them perspire. ¹⁹When they go out into the outer court where the people are, they are to take off the clothes they have been ministering in and are to leave them in the sacred rooms, and put on other clothes, so that they do not consecrate the people by means of their garments.

²⁰" 'They must not shave their heads or let their hair grow long, but they are to keep the hair of their heads trimmed. ²¹No priest is to drink wine when he enters the inner court. ²²They must not marry widows or divorced women; they may marry only virgins of Israelite descent or widows of priests. ²³They are to teach my people the difference between the holy and the common and show them how to distinguish between the unclean and the clean.

²⁴" 'In any dispute, the priests are to serve as judges and decide it according to my ordinances. They are to keep my laws and my decrees for all my appointed feasts, and they are to keep my Sabbaths holy.

²⁵" 'A priest must not defile himself by going near a dead person; however, if the dead person was his father or mother, son or daughter, brother or unmarried sister, then he may defile himself. ²⁶After he is cleansed, he must wait seven days. ²⁷On the day he goes into the inner court of the sanctuary to minister in the sanctuary, he is to offer a sin offering for himself, declares the Sovereign LORD.

²⁸" 'I am to be the only inheritance the priests have. You are to give them no possession in Israel; I will be their possession. ²⁹They will eat the grain offerings, the sin offerings and the guilt offerings; and everything in Israel devoted*a* to the LORD will belong to them. ³⁰The best of all the firstfruits and of

---

*a*29 The Hebrew term refers to the irrevocable giving over of things or persons to the LORD.

all your special gifts will belong to the priests. You are to give them the first portion of your ground meal so that a blessing may rest on your household. [31]The priests must not eat anything, bird or animal, found dead or torn by wild animals.

Division of the Land

" 'When you allot the land as an inheritance, you are to present to the LORD a portion of the land as a sacred district, 25,000 cubits long and 20,000[a] wide; the entire area will be holy. [2]Of this, a section 500 cubits square is to be for the sanctuary, with 50 cubits around it for open land. [3]In the sacred district, measure off a section 25,000 cubits[b] long and 10,000 cubits[c] wide. In it will be the sanctuary, the Most Holy Place. [4]It will be the sacred portion of the land for the priests, who minister in the sanctuary and who draw near to minister before the LORD. It will be a place for their houses as well as a holy place for the sanctuary. [5]An area 25,000 cubits long and 10,000 cubits wide will belong to the Levites, who serve in the temple, as their possession for towns to live in.[d]

[6] 'You are to give the city as its property an area 5,000 cubits wide and 25,000 cubits long, adjoining the sacred portion; it will belong to the whole house of Israel.

[7] 'The prince will have the land bordering each side of the area formed by the sacred district and the property of the city. It will extend westward from the west side and eastward from the east side, running lengthwise from the western to the eastern border parallel to one of the tribal portions. [8]This land will be his possession in Israel. And my princes will no longer oppress my people but will allow the house of Israel to possess the land according to their tribes.

[9]" 'This is what the Sovereign LORD says: You have gone far enough, O princes of Israel! Give up your violence and oppression and do what is just and right. Stop dispossessing my people, declares the Sovereign LORD. [10]You are to use accurate scales, an accurate ephah[e] and an accurate bath.[f] [11]The ephah and the bath are to be the same size, the bath containing a tenth of a homer[g] and the ephah a tenth of a homer; the homer is to be the standard measure for both. [12]The shekel[h] is to consist of twenty gerahs. Twenty shekels plus twenty-five shekels plus fifteen shekels equal one mina.[i]

Offerings and Holy Days

[13]" 'This is the special gift you are to offer: a sixth of an ephah from each homer of wheat and a sixth of an ephah from each homer of barley. [14]The prescribed portion of oil, measured by the bath, is a tenth of a bath from each cor (which consists of ten baths or one homer, for ten baths are equivalent to a homer). [15]Also one sheep is to be taken from every flock of two hundred from the well-watered pastures of Israel. These will be used for the grain offerings, burnt offerings and fellowship offerings[j] to make atonement for the people, declares the Sovereign LORD. [16]All the people of the land will participate in this special gift for the use of the prince in Israel. [17]It will be the duty of the prince to provide the burnt offerings, grain offerings and drink offerings at the festivals, the New Moons and the Sabbaths—at all the appointed feasts of the house of Israel. He will provide the sin offerings, grain offerings, burnt offerings and fellowship offerings to make atonement for the house of Israel.

[18]" 'This is what the Sovereign LORD says: In the first month on the first day you are to take a young bull without defect and purify the sanctuary. [19]The

---

[a]1 Septuagint (see also verses 3 and 5 and 48:9); Hebrew *10,000* [b]3 That is, about 7 miles (about 12 kilometers) [c]3 That is, about 3 miles (about 5 kilometers) [d]5 Septuagint; Hebrew *temple; they will have as their possession 20 rooms* [e]10 An ephah was a dry measure. [f]10 A bath was a liquid measure. [g]11 A homer was a dry measure. [h]12 A shekel weighed about 2/5 ounce (about 11.5 grams). [i]12 That is, 60 shekels; the common mina was 50 shekels. [j]15 Traditionally *peace offerings*; also in verse 17

priest is to take some of the blood of the sin offering and put it on the door-posts of the temple, on the four corners of the upper ledge of the altar and on the gateposts of the inner court. ²⁰You are to do the same on the seventh day of the month for anyone who sins unintentionally or through ignorance; so you are to make atonement for the temple.

²¹" 'In the first month on the fourteenth day you are to observe the Passover, a feast lasting seven days, during which you shall eat bread made without yeast. ²²On that day the prince is to provide a bull as a sin offering for himself and for all the people of the land. ²³Every day during the seven days of the Feast he is to provide seven bulls and seven rams without defect as a burnt offering to the Lord, and a male goat for a sin offering. ²⁴He is to provide as a grain offering an ephah for each bull and an ephah for each ram, along with a hin*a* of oil for each ephah.

²⁵" 'During the seven days of the Feast, which begins in the seventh month on the fifteenth day, he is to make the same provision for sin offerings, burnt offerings, grain offerings and oil.

46 " 'This is what the Sovereign Lord says: The gate of the inner court facing east is to be shut on the six working days, but on the Sabbath day and on the day of the New Moon it is to be opened. ²The prince is to enter from the outside through the portico of the gateway and stand by the gatepost. The priests are to sacrifice his burnt offering and his fellowship offerings.*b* He is to worship at the threshold of the gateway and then go out, but the gate will not be shut until evening. ³On the Sabbaths and New Moons the people of the land are to worship in the presence of the Lord at the entrance to that gateway. ⁴The burnt offering the prince brings to the Lord on the Sabbath day is to be six male lambs and a ram, all without defect. ⁵The grain offering given with the ram is to be an ephah,*c* and the grain offering with the lambs is to be as much as he pleases, along with a hin*a* of oil for each ephah. ⁶On the day of the New Moon he is to offer a young bull, six lambs and a ram, all without defect. ⁷He is to provide as a grain offering one ephah with the bull, one ephah with the ram, and with the lambs as much as he wants to give, along with a hin of oil with each ephah. ⁸When the prince enters, he is to go in through the portico of the gateway, and he is to come out the same way.

⁹" 'When the people of the land come before the Lord at the appointed feasts, whoever enters by the north gate to worship is to go out the south gate; and whoever enters by the south gate is to go out the north gate. No one is to return through the gate by which he entered, but each is to go out the opposite gate. ¹⁰The prince is to be among them, going in when they go in and going out when they go out.

¹¹" 'At the festivals and the appointed feasts, the grain offering is to be an ephah with a bull, an ephah with a ram, and with the lambs as much as one pleases, along with a hin of oil for each ephah. ¹²When the prince provides a freewill offering to the Lord—whether a burnt offering or fellowship offerings—the gate facing east is to be opened for him. He shall offer his burnt offering or his fellowship offerings as he does on the Sabbath day. Then he shall go out, and after he has gone out, the gate will be shut.

¹³" 'Every day you are to provide a year-old lamb without defect for a burnt offering to the Lord; morning by morning you shall provide it. ¹⁴You are also to provide with it morning by morning a grain offering, consisting of a sixth of an ephah with a third of a hin of oil to moisten the flour. The presenting of this grain offering to the Lord is a lasting ordinance. ¹⁵So the lamb and the

*a24,5 That is, probably about 4 quarts (about 4 liters)   b2 Traditionally peace offerings; also in verse 12
c5 That is, probably about 3/5 bushel (about 22 liters)*

grain offering and the oil shall be provided morning by morning for a regular burnt offering.

¹⁶" 'This is what the Sovereign LORD says: If the prince makes a gift from his inheritance to one of his sons, it will also belong to his descendants; it is to be their property by inheritance. ¹⁷If, however, he makes a gift from his inheritance to one of his servants, the servant may keep it until the year of freedom; then it will revert to the prince. His inheritance belongs to his sons only; it is theirs. ¹⁸The prince must not take any of the inheritance of the people, driving them off their property. He is to give his sons their inheritance out of his own property, so that none of my people will be separated from his property.' "

¹⁹Then the man brought me through the entrance at the side of the gate to the sacred rooms facing north, which belonged to the priests, and showed me a place at the western end. ²⁰He said to me, "This is the place where the priests will cook the guilt offering and the sin offering and bake the grain offering, to avoid bringing them into the outer court and consecrating the people."

²¹He then brought me to the outer court and led me around to its four corners, and I saw in each corner another court. ²²In the four corners of the outer court were enclosed^a courts, forty cubits long and thirty cubits wide; each of the courts in the four corners was the same size. ²³Around the inside of each of the four courts was a ledge of stone, with places for fire built all around under the ledge. ²⁴He said to me, "These are the kitchens where those who minister at the temple will cook the sacrifices of the people."

47 **The River From the Temple** The man brought me back to the entrance of the temple, and I saw water coming out from under the threshold of the temple toward the east (for the temple faced east). The water was coming down from under the south side of the temple, south of the altar. ²He then brought me out through the north gate and led me around the outside to the outer gate facing east, and the water was flowing from the south side.

³As the man went eastward with a measuring line in his hand, he measured off a thousand cubits^b and then led me through water that was ankle-deep. ⁴He measured off another thousand cubits and led me through water that was knee-deep. He measured off another thousand and led me through water that was up to the waist. ⁵He measured off another thousand, but now it was a river that I could not cross, because the water had risen and was deep enough to swim in—a river that no one could cross. ⁶He asked me, "Son of man, do you see this?"

Then he led me back to the bank of the river. ⁷When I arrived there, I saw a great number of trees on each side of the river. ⁸He said to me, "This water flows toward the eastern region and goes down into the Arabah,^c where it enters the Sea.^d When it empties into the Sea,^d the water there becomes fresh. ⁹Swarms of living creatures will live wherever the river flows. There will be large numbers of fish, because this water flows there and makes the salt water fresh; so where the river flows everything will live. ¹⁰Fishermen will stand along the shore; from En Gedi to En Eglaim there will be places for spreading nets. The fish will be of many kinds—like the fish of the Great Sea.^e ¹¹But the swamps and marshes will not become fresh; they will be left for salt. ¹²Fruit trees of all kinds will grow on both banks of the river. Their leaves will not wither, nor will their fruit fail. Every month they will bear, because the water from the sanctuary flows to them. Their fruit will serve for food and their leaves for healing."

---

^a22 The meaning of the Hebrew for this word is uncertain.   ^b3 That is, about 1,500 feet (about 450 meters)   ^c8 Or *the Jordan Valley*   ^d8 That is, the Dead Sea   ^e10 That is, the Mediterranean; also in verses 15, 19 and 20

The Boundaries of the Land ¹³This is what the Sovereign Lᴏʀᴅ says: "These are the boundaries by which you are to divide the land for an inheritance among the twelve tribes of Israel, with two portions for Joseph. ¹⁴You are to divide it equally among them. Because I swore with uplifted hand to give it to your forefathers, this land will become your inheritance.

¹⁵"This is to be the boundary of the land:

"On the north side it will run from the Great Sea by the Hethlon road past Lebo*ᵃ* Hamath to Zedad, ¹⁶Berothah*ᵇ* and Sibraim (which lies on the border between Damascus and Hamath), as far as Hazer Hatticon, which is on the border of Hauran. ¹⁷The boundary will extend from the sea to Hazar Enan,*ᶜ* along the northern border of Damascus, with the border of Hamath to the north. This will be the north boundary.
¹⁸"On the east side the boundary will run between Hauran and Damascus, along the Jordan between Gilead and the land of Israel, to the eastern sea and as far as Tamar.*ᵈ* This will be the east boundary.
¹⁹"On the south side it will run from Tamar as far as the waters of Meribah Kadesh, then along the Wadi ˌof Egyptˌ to the Great Sea. This will be the south boundary.
²⁰"On the west side, the Great Sea will be the boundary to a point opposite Lebo*ᵉ* Hamath. This will be the west boundary.

²¹"You are to distribute this land among yourselves according to the tribes of Israel. ²²You are to allot it as an inheritance for yourselves and for the aliens who have settled among you and who have children. You are to consider them as native-born Israelites; along with you they are to be allotted an inheritance among the tribes of Israel. ²³In whatever tribe the alien settles, there you are to give him his inheritance," declares the Sovereign Lᴏʀᴅ.

48 *The Division of the Land* "These are the tribes, listed by name: At the northern frontier, Dan will have one portion; it will follow the Hethlon road to Lebo*ᶠ* Hamath; Hazar Enan and the northern border of Damascus next to Hamath will be part of its border from the east side to the west side.
²"Asher will have one portion; it will border the territory of Dan from east to west.
³"Naphtali will have one portion; it will border the territory of Asher from east to west.
⁴"Manasseh will have one portion; it will border the territory of Naphtali from east to west.
⁵"Ephraim will have one portion; it will border the territory of Manasseh from east to west.
⁶"Reuben will have one portion; it will border the territory of Ephraim from east to west.
⁷"Judah will have one portion; it will border the territory of Reuben from east to west.
⁸"Bordering the territory of Judah from east to west will be the portion you are to present as a special gift. It will be 25,000 cubits*ᵍ* wide, and its length from east to west will equal one of the tribal portions; the sanctuary will be in the center of it.
⁹"The special portion you are to offer to the Lᴏʀᴅ will be 25,000 cubits long and 10,000 cubits*ʰ* wide. ¹⁰This will be the sacred portion for the priests. It

---

ᵃ15 Or *past the entrance to* *ᵇ15,16* See Septuagint and Ezekiel 48:1; Hebrew *road to go into Zedad,*
¹⁶Hamath, Berothah *ᶜ17* Hebrew *Enon,* a variant of *Enan* *ᵈ18* Septuagint and Syriac; Hebrew *Israel. You will measure to the eastern sea* *ᵉ20* Or *opposite the entrance to* *ᶠ1* Or *to the entrance to* *ᵍ8* That is, about 7 miles (about 12 kilometers) *ʰ9* That is, about 3 miles (about 5 kilometers)

will be 25,000 cubits long on the north side, 10,000 cubits wide on the west side, 10,000 cubits wide on the east side and 25,000 cubits long on the south side. In the center of it will be the sanctuary of the Lord. ¹¹This will be for the consecrated priests, the Zadokites, who were faithful in serving me and did not go astray as the Levites did when the Israelites went astray. ¹²It will be a special gift to them from the sacred portion of the land, a most holy portion, bordering the territory of the Levites.

¹³"Alongside the territory of the priests, the Levites will have an allotment 25,000 cubits long and 10,000 cubits wide. Its total length will be 25,000 cubits and its width 10,000 cubits. ¹⁴They must not sell or exchange any of it. This is the best of the land and must not pass into other hands, because it is holy to the Lord.

¹⁵"The remaining area, 5,000 cubits wide and 25,000 cubits long, will be for the common use of the city, for houses and for pastureland. The city will be in the center of it ¹⁶and will have these measurements: the north side 4,500 cubits, the south side 4,500 cubits, the east side 4,500 cubits, and the west side 4,500 cubits. ¹⁷The pastureland for the city will be 250 cubits on the north, 250 cubits on the south, 250 cubits on the east, and 250 cubits on the west. ¹⁸What remains of the area, bordering on the sacred portion and running the length of it, will be 10,000 cubits on the east side and 10,000 cubits on the west side. Its produce will supply food for the workers of the city. ¹⁹The workers from the city who farm it will come from all the tribes of Israel. ²⁰The entire portion will be a square, 25,000 cubits on each side. As a special gift you will set aside the sacred portion, along with the property of the city.

²¹"What remains on both sides of the area formed by the sacred portion and the city property will belong to the prince. It will extend eastward from the 25,000 cubits of the sacred portion to the eastern border, and westward from the 25,000 cubits to the western border. Both these areas running the length of the tribal portions will belong to the prince, and the sacred portion with the temple sanctuary will be in the center of them. ²²So the property of the Levites and the property of the city will lie in the center of the area that belongs to the prince. The area belonging to the prince will lie between the border of Judah and the border of Benjamin.

²³"As for the rest of the tribes: Benjamin will have one portion; it will extend from the east side to the west side.

²⁴"Simeon will have one portion; it will border the territory of Benjamin from east to west.

²⁵"Issachar will have one portion; it will border the territory of Simeon from east to west.

²⁶"Zebulun will have one portion; it will border the territory of Issachar from east to west.

²⁷"Gad will have one portion; it will border the territory of Zebulun from east to west.

²⁸"The southern boundary of Gad will run south from Tamar to the waters of Meribah Kadesh, then along the Wadi ˻of Egypt˼ to the Great Sea.[a]

²⁹"This is the land you are to allot as an in-

Where's the gate of Jericho? I thought for sure there'd be one named   after me!

SEE EZEKIEL 48:31

[a]28 That is, the Mediterranean

heritance to the tribes of Israel, and these will be their portions," declares the Sovereign LORD.

The Gates of the City   ³⁰"These will be the exits of the city: Beginning on the north side, which is 4,500 cubits long, ³¹the gates of the city will be named after the tribes of Israel. The three gates on the north side will be the gate of Reuben, the gate of Judah and the gate of Levi.

³²"On the east side, which is 4,500 cubits long, will be three gates: the gate of Joseph, the gate of Benjamin and the gate of Dan.

³³"On the south side, which measures 4,500 cubits, will be three gates: the gate of Simeon, the gate of Issachar and the gate of Zebulun.

³⁴"On the west side, which is 4,500 cubits long, will be three gates: the gate of Gad, the gate of Asher and the gate of Naphtali.

³⁵"The distance all around will be 18,000 cubits.

"And the name of the city from that time on will be:

THE LORD IS THERE."

Introduction
to the
book of Daniel

CONVICTIONS.

What makes it so hard to stand up for them? Do you
find it hard to say, "I don't do that because I'm a
Christian"? Or "I'm going to wait until marriage,
because I know that's right." What other kids think
about you is important, but it isn't *that* important.

Daniel was a teenager, a hostage in Babylon, when
he had to decide: Would he stand up for what he
believed or go along with pagan ways? Because
Daniel decided to be loyal to God, God helped him
become a powerful government official. Even the
emperor came to admire Daniel for his faith.

Fundamentals

*What is the best way to stand up for
your beliefs without alienating others (Daniel 1)?*

*Is there any real risk in being deter-
mined to please God (Daniel 3, 6)?*

*What is one possible outcome if you
stand up for God no matter what the
cost (Daniel 6:24-28)?*

FAST FACTS

*Daniel means "God is my
judge."*

*Daniel was taken to Babylon
in 605 B.C.*

*Daniel was an important official
in two great empires, Babylonia
and Persia.*

*Daniel 10 describes a war
between God's and Satan's
angels.*

1 *Daniel's Training in Babylon* In the third year of the reign of Jehoiakim king of Judah, Nebuchadnezzar king of Babylon came to Jerusalem and besieged it. ²And the Lord delivered Jehoiakim king of Judah into his hand, along with some of the articles from the temple of God. These he carried off to the temple of his god in Babylonia*ᵃ* and put in the treasure house of his god.

³Then the king ordered Ashpenaz, chief of his court officials, to bring in some of the Israelites from the royal family and the nobility— ⁴young men without any physical defect, handsome, showing aptitude for every kind of learning, well informed, quick to understand, and qualified to serve in the king's palace. He was to teach them the language and literature of the Babylonians.*ᵇ* ⁵The king assigned them a daily amount of food and wine from the king's table. They were to be trained for three years, and after that they were to enter the king's service.

⁶Among these were some from Judah: Daniel, Hananiah, Mishael and Azariah. ⁷The chief official gave them new names: to Daniel, the name Belteshazzar; to Hananiah, Shadrach; to Mishael, Meshach; and to Azariah, Abednego.

⁸But Daniel resolved not to defile himself with the royal food and wine, and he asked the chief official for permission not to defile himself this way. ⁹Now God had caused the official to show favor and sympathy to Daniel, ¹⁰but the official told Daniel, "I am afraid of my lord the king, who has assigned your*ᶜ* food and drink. Why should he see you looking worse than the other young men your age? The king would then have my head because of you."

¹¹Daniel then said to the guard whom the chief official had appointed over Daniel, Hananiah, Mishael and Azariah, ¹²"Please test your servants for ten days: Give us nothing but vegetables to eat and water to drink. ¹³Then compare our appearance with that of the young men who eat the royal food, and treat your servants in accordance with what you see." ¹⁴So he agreed to this and tested them for ten days.

¹⁵At the end of the ten days they looked healthier and better nourished than any of the young men who ate the royal food. ¹⁶So the guard took away their choice food and the wine they were to drink and gave them vegetables instead.

¹⁷To these four young men God gave knowledge and understanding of all kinds of literature and learning. And Daniel could understand visions and dreams of all kinds.

¹⁸At the end of the time set by the king to bring them in, the chief official presented them to Nebuchadnezzar. ¹⁹The king talked with them, and he found none equal to Daniel, Hananiah, Mishael and Azariah; so they entered the king's service. ²⁰In every matter of wisdom and understanding about which the king questioned them, he found them ten times better than all the magicians and enchanters in his whole kingdom.

²¹And Daniel remained there until the first year of King Cyrus.

2 *Nebuchadnezzar's Dream* In the second year of his reign, Nebuchadnezzar had dreams; his mind was troubled and he could not sleep. ²So the king summoned the magicians, enchanters, sorcerers and astrologers*ᵈ* to tell him what he had dreamed. When they came in and stood before the king, ³he said to them, "I have had a dream that troubles me and I want to know what it means.*ᵉ*"

⁴Then the astrologers answered the king in Aramaic,*ᶠ* "O king, live forever! Tell your servants the dream, and we will interpret it."

ᵃ2 Hebrew *Shinar*   *ᵇ4* Or *Chaldeans*   *ᶜ10* The Hebrew for *your* and *you* in this verse is plural.   *ᵈ2* Or *Chaldeans*; also in verses 4, 5 and 10   *ᵉ3* Or *was*   *ᶠ4* The text from here through chapter 7 is in Aramaic.

Dear Sam,

Are Christian values as important as my mother says? My friends don't share most of them, so I feel a little weird.

Phillip in Philadelphia

100 Advice Lane, Anywhere, USA

Dear Phillip,

No one wants to feel weird. But who decides what is weird and what isn't?

Daniel was a young man who was taken from his native land of Judah. Nebuchadnezzar had just conquered Judah and had ordered an official to bring some "hand-some, well informed" young men of nobility to serve in the king's palace (Daniel 1:3-4). The young captives were given food and drink from the king's table. But Daniel did not want to eat foods God had called unclean, so he went to an official and asked for vegetables and water for himself and three other young men from Judah. That must have sounded like a weird request! Daniel asked for a ten-day trial period. If after ten days they didn't look as healthy as the other young men, they would eat as the others did. But after the ten days, "they looked healthier and better nourished than any of the young men who ate the royal food . . . . To these four young men God gave knowledge and understanding . . . . And Daniel could understand visions and dreams of all kinds" (Daniel 1:15,17).

You may feel a little weird, but when you honor God with your obedience, he honors you with blessing.

Sam

⁵The king replied to the astrologers, "This is what I have firmly decided: If you do not tell me what my dream was and interpret it, I will have you cut into pieces and your houses turned into piles of rubble. ⁶But if you tell me the dream and explain it, you will receive from me gifts and rewards and great honor. So tell me the dream and interpret it for me."

⁷Once more they replied, "Let the king tell his servants the dream, and we will interpret it."

⁸Then the king answered, "I am certain that you are trying to gain time, because you realize that this is what I have firmly decided: ⁹If you do not tell me the dream, there is just one penalty for you. You have conspired to tell me misleading and wicked things, hoping the situation will change. So then, tell me the dream, and I will know that you can interpret it for me."

¹⁰The astrologers answered the king, "There is not a man on earth who can do what the king asks! No king, however great and mighty, has ever asked such a thing of any magician or enchanter or astrologer. ¹¹What the king asks is too difficult. No one can reveal it to the king except the gods, and they do not live among men."

¹²This made the king so angry and furious that he ordered the execution of all the wise men of Babylon. ¹³So the decree was issued to put the wise men to death, and men were sent to look for Daniel and his friends to put them to death.

¹⁴When Arioch, the commander of the king's guard, had gone out to put to death the wise men of Babylon, Daniel spoke to him with wisdom and tact. ¹⁵He asked the king's officer, "Why did the king issue such a harsh decree?" Arioch then explained the matter to Daniel. ¹⁶At this, Daniel went in to the king and asked for time, so that he might interpret the dream for him.

¹⁷Then Daniel returned to his house and explained the matter to his friends Hananiah, Mishael and Azariah. ¹⁸He urged them to plead for mercy from the God of heaven concerning this mystery, so that he and his friends might not be executed with the rest of the wise men of Babylon. ¹⁹During the night the mystery was revealed to Daniel in a vision. Then Daniel praised the God of heaven ²⁰and said:

> "Praise be to the name of God for ever and ever;
>   wisdom and power are his.
> ²¹He changes times and seasons;
>   he sets up kings and deposes them.
> He gives wisdom to the wise
>   and knowledge to the discerning.
> ²²He reveals deep and hidden things;
>   he knows what lies in darkness,
>   and light dwells with him.
> ²³I thank and praise you, O God of my fathers:
>   You have given me wisdom and power,
> you have made known to me what we asked of you,
>   you have made known to us the dream of the king."

Daniel Interprets the Dream   ²⁴Then Daniel went to Arioch, whom the king had appointed to execute the wise men of Babylon, and said to him, "Do not execute the wise men of Babylon. Take me to the king, and I will interpret his dream for him."

²⁵Arioch took Daniel to the king at once and said, "I have found a man among the exiles from Judah who can tell the king what his dream means."

²⁶The king asked Daniel (also called Belteshazzar), "Are you able to tell me what I saw in my dream and interpret it?"

²⁷Daniel replied, "No wise man, enchanter, magician or diviner can explain to the king the mystery he has asked about, ²⁸but there is a God in heaven who reveals mysteries. He has shown King Nebuchadnezzar what will hap-

pen in days to come. Your dream and the visions that passed through your mind as you lay on your bed are these:

²⁹"As you were lying there, O king, your mind turned to things to come, and the revealer of mysteries showed you what is going to happen. ³⁰As for me, this mystery has been revealed to me, not because I have greater wisdom than other living men, but so that you, O king, may know the interpretation and that you may understand what went through your mind.

³¹"You looked, O king, and there before you stood a large statue—an enormous, dazzling statue, awesome in appearance. ³²The head of the statue was made of pure gold, its chest and arms of silver, its belly and thighs of bronze, ³³its legs of iron, its feet partly of iron and partly of baked clay. ³⁴While you were watching, a rock was cut out, but not by human hands. It struck the statue on its feet of iron and clay and smashed them. ³⁵Then the iron, the clay, the bronze, the silver and the gold were broken to pieces at the same time and became like chaff on a threshing floor in the summer. The wind swept them away without leaving a trace. But the rock that struck the statue became a huge mountain and filled the whole earth.

³⁶"This was the dream, and now we will interpret it to the king. ³⁷You, O king, are the king of kings. The God of heaven has given you dominion and power and might and glory; ³⁸in your hands he has placed mankind and the beasts of the field and the birds of the air. Wherever they live, he has made you ruler over them all. You are that head of gold.

³⁹"After you, another kingdom will rise, inferior to yours. Next, a third kingdom, one of bronze, will rule over the whole earth. ⁴⁰Finally, there will be a fourth kingdom, strong as iron—for iron breaks and smashes everything—and as iron breaks things to pieces, so it will crush and break all the others. ⁴¹Just as you saw that the feet and toes were partly of baked clay and partly of iron, so this will be a divided kingdom; yet it will have some of the strength of iron in it, even as you saw iron mixed with clay. ⁴²As the toes were partly iron and partly clay, so this kingdom will be partly strong and partly brittle. ⁴³And just as you saw the iron mixed with baked clay, so the people will be a mixture and will not remain united, any more than iron mixes with clay.

⁴⁴"In the time of those kings, the God of heaven will set up a kingdom that will never be destroyed, nor will it be left to another people. It will crush all those kingdoms and bring them to an end, but it will itself endure forever. ⁴⁵This is the meaning of the vision of the rock cut out of a mountain, but not by human hands—a rock that broke the iron, the bronze, the clay, the silver and the gold to pieces.

"The great God has shown the king what will take place in the future. The dream is true and the interpretation is trustworthy."

⁴⁶Then King Nebuchadnezzar fell prostrate before Daniel and paid him honor and ordered that an offering and incense be presented to him. ⁴⁷The king said to Daniel, "Surely your God is the God of gods and the Lord of kings and a revealer of mysteries, for you were able to reveal this mystery."

⁴⁸Then the king placed Daniel in a high position and lavished many gifts on him. He made him ruler over the entire province of Babylon and placed him in charge of all its wise men. ⁴⁹Moreover, at Daniel's request the king appointed Shadrach, Meshach and Abednego administrators over the province of Babylon, while Daniel himself remained at the royal court.

The Image of Gold and the Fiery Furnace King Nebuchadnezzar made an image of gold, ninety feet high and nine feet*ᵃ* wide, and set it up on the plain of Dura in the province of Babylon. ²He then summoned the satraps, prefects, governors, advisers, treasurers, judges, magistrates and all

ᵃ1 Aramaic *sixty cubits high and six cubits wide* (about 27 meters high and 2.7 meters wide)

the other provincial officials to come to the dedication of the image he had set up. ³So the satraps, prefects, governors, advisers, treasurers, judges, magistrates and all the other provincial officials assembled for the dedication of the image that King Nebuchadnezzar had set up, and they stood before it.

⁴Then the herald loudly proclaimed, "This is what you are commanded to do, O peoples, nations and men of every language: ⁵As soon as you hear the sound of the horn, flute, zither, lyre, harp, pipes and all kinds of music, you must fall down and worship the image of gold that King Nebuchadnezzar has set up. ⁶Whoever does not fall down and worship will immediately be thrown into a blazing furnace."

⁷Therefore, as soon as they heard the sound of the horn, flute, zither, lyre, harp and all kinds of music, all the peoples, nations and men of every language fell down and worshiped the image of gold that King Nebuchadnezzar had set up.

⁸At this time some astrologers*a* came forward and denounced the Jews. ⁹They said to King Nebuchadnezzar, "O king, live forever! ¹⁰You have issued a decree, O king, that everyone who hears the sound of the horn, flute, zither, lyre, harp, pipes and all kinds of music must fall down and worship the image of gold, ¹¹and that whoever does not fall down and worship will be thrown into a blazing furnace. ¹²But there are some Jews whom you have set over the affairs of the province of Babylon—Shadrach, Meshach and Abednego—who pay no attention to you, O king. They neither serve your gods nor worship the image of gold you have set up."

¹³Furious with rage, Nebuchadnezzar summoned Shadrach, Meshach and Abednego. So these men were brought before the king, ¹⁴and Nebuchadnezzar said to them, "Is it true, Shadrach, Meshach and Abednego, that you do not serve my gods or worship the image of gold I have set up? ¹⁵Now when you hear the sound of the horn, flute, zither, lyre, harp, pipes and all kinds of music, if you are ready to fall down and worship the image I made, very good. But if you do not worship it, you will be thrown immediately into a blazing furnace. Then what god will be able to rescue you from my hand?"

¹⁶Shadrach, Meshach and Abednego replied to the king, "O Nebuchadnezzar, we do not need to defend ourselves before you in this matter. ¹⁷If we are thrown into the blazing furnace, the God we serve is able to save us from it, and he will rescue us from your hand, O king. ¹⁸But even if he does not, we want you to know, O king, that we will not serve your gods or worship the image of gold you have set up."

¹⁹Then Nebuchadnezzar was furious with Shadrach, Meshach and Abednego, and his attitude toward them changed. He ordered the furnace heated seven times hotter than usual ²⁰and commanded some of the strongest soldiers in his army to tie up Shadrach, Meshach and Abednego and throw them into the blazing furnace. ²¹So these men, wear-

DANIEL 3:17–18

Your convictions can be a hard thing to stick to at times. You can witness, but you can't tell whether the person you speak to will listen or laugh. You can say no when friends urge you to do something wrong, but you don't know whether they'll respect you or ridicule you. When threatened with death Daniel's three friends said, "The God we serve is able to save us . . . But even if he does not . . . we will not serve your gods." When you face a tough decision, you know that God is able to make things turn out right, but you never know for sure that he will. That's what faith is all about: being determined to do what is right, no matter what.

*a*8 Or *Chaldeans*

ing their robes, trousers, turbans and other clothes, were bound and thrown into the blazing furnace. ²²The king's command was so urgent and the furnace so hot that the flames of the fire killed the soldiers who took up Shadrach, Meshach and Abednego, ²³and these three men, firmly tied, fell into the blazing furnace.

²⁴Then King Nebuchadnezzar leaped to his feet in amazement and asked his advisers, "Weren't there three men that we tied up and threw into the fire?"

They replied, "Certainly, O king."

²⁵He said, "Look! I see four men walking around in the fire, unbound and unharmed, and the fourth looks like a son of the gods."

²⁶Nebuchadnezzar then approached the opening of the blazing furnace and shouted, "Shadrach, Meshach and Abednego, servants of the Most High God, come out! Come here!"

So Shadrach, Meshach and Abednego came out of the fire, ²⁷and the satraps, prefects, governors and royal advisers crowded around them. They saw that the fire had not harmed their bodies, nor was a hair of their heads singed; their robes were not scorched, and there was no smell of fire on them.

²⁸Then Nebuchadnezzar said, "Praise be to the God of Shadrach, Meshach and Abednego, who has sent his angel and rescued his servants! They trusted in him and defied the king's command and were willing to give up their lives rather than serve or worship any god except their own God. ²⁹Therefore I decree that the people of any nation or language who say anything against the God of Shadrach, Meshach and Abednego be cut into pieces and their houses be turned into piles of rubble, for no other god can save in this way."

³⁰Then the king promoted Shadrach, Meshach and Abednego in the province of Babylon.

Nebuchadnezzar's Dream of a Tree

King Nebuchadnezzar,

To the peoples, nations and men of every language, who live in all the world:

May you prosper greatly!

²It is my pleasure to tell you about the miraculous signs and wonders that the Most High God has performed for me.

³How great are his signs,
  how mighty his wonders!
His kingdom is an eternal kingdom;
  his dominion endures from generation to generation.

⁴I, Nebuchadnezzar, was at home in my palace, contented and prosperous. ⁵I had a dream that made me afraid. As I was lying in my bed, the images and visions that passed through my mind terrified me. ⁶So I commanded that all the wise men of Babylon be brought before me to interpret the dream for me. ⁷When the magicians, enchanters, astrologersᵃ and diviners came, I told them the dream, but they could not interpret it for me. ⁸Finally, Daniel came into my presence and I told him the dream. (He is called Belteshazzar, after the name of my god, and the spirit of the holy gods is in him.)

⁹I said, "Belteshazzar, chief of the magicians, I know that the spirit of the holy gods is in you, and no mystery is too difficult for you. Here is my dream; interpret it for me. ¹⁰These are the visions I saw while lying

ᵃ7 Or *Chaldeans*

in my bed: I looked, and there before me stood a tree in the middle of the land. Its height was enormous. ¹¹The tree grew large and strong and its top touched the sky; it was visible to the ends of the earth. ¹²Its leaves were beautiful, its fruit abundant, and on it was food for all. Under it the beasts of the field found shelter, and the birds of the air lived in its branches; from it every creature was fed.

¹³"In the visions I saw while lying in my bed, I looked, and there before me was a messenger,*ᵃ* a holy one, coming down from heaven. ¹⁴He called in a loud voice: 'Cut down the tree and trim off its branches; strip off its leaves and scatter its fruit. Let the animals flee from under it and the birds from its branches. ¹⁵But let the stump and its roots, bound with iron and bronze, remain in the ground, in the grass of the field.

" 'Let him be drenched with the dew of heaven, and let him live with the animals among the plants of the earth. ¹⁶Let his mind be changed from that of a man and let him be given the mind of an animal, till seven times*ᵇ* pass by for him.

¹⁷" 'The decision is announced by messengers, the holy ones declare the verdict, so that the living may know that the Most High is sovereign over the kingdoms of men and gives them to anyone he wishes and sets over them the lowliest of men.'

¹⁸"This is the dream that I, King Nebuchadnezzar, had. Now, Belteshazzar, tell me what it means, for none of the wise men in my kingdom can interpret it for me. But you can, because the spirit of the holy gods is in you."

Daniel Interprets the Dream ¹⁹Then Daniel (also called Belteshazzar) was greatly perplexed for a time, and his thoughts terrified him. So the king said, "Belteshazzar, do not let the dream or its meaning alarm you."

Belteshazzar answered, "My lord, if only the dream applied to your enemies and its meaning to your adversaries! ²⁰The tree you saw, which grew large and strong, with its top touching the sky, visible to the whole earth, ²¹with beautiful leaves and abundant fruit, providing food for all, giving shelter to the beasts of the field, and having nesting places in its branches for the birds of the air— ²²you, O king, are that tree! You have become great and strong; your greatness has grown until it reaches the sky, and your dominion extends to distant parts of the earth.

²³"You, O king, saw a messenger, a holy one, coming down from heaven and saying, 'Cut down the tree and destroy it, but leave the stump, bound with iron and bronze, in the grass of the field, while its roots remain in the ground. Let him be drenched with the dew of heaven; let him live like the wild animals, until seven times pass by for him.'

²⁴"This is the interpretation, O king, and this is the decree the Most High has issued against my lord the king: ²⁵You will be driven away from people and will live with the wild animals; you will eat grass like cattle and be drenched with the dew of heaven. Seven times will pass by for you until you acknowledge that the Most High is sovereign over the kingdoms of men and gives them to anyone he wishes. ²⁶The command to leave the stump of the tree with its roots means that your kingdom will be restored to you when you acknowledge that Heaven rules. ²⁷Therefore, O king, be pleased to accept my advice: Renounce your sins by doing what is right, and your wickedness by being kind to the oppressed. It may be that then your prosperity will continue."

The Dream Is Fulfilled ²⁸All this happened to King Nebuchadnezzar. ²⁹Twelve months later, as the king was walking on the roof of the royal

---

ᵃ13 Or *watchman;* also in verses 17 and 23   *ᵇ16* Or *years;* also in verses 23, 25 and 32 palace of Babylon, ³⁰he said, "Is not this the great Babylon I have built as the royal residence, by my mighty power and for the glory of my majesty?"

³¹The words were still on his lips when a voice came from heaven, "This is what is decreed for you, King Nebuchadnezzar: Your royal authority has been taken from you. ³²You will be driven away from people and will live with the wild animals; you will eat grass like cattle. Seven times will pass by for you until you acknowledge that the Most High is sovereign over the kingdoms of men and gives them to anyone he wishes."

³³Immediately what had been said about Nebuchadnezzar was fulfilled. He was driven away from people and ate grass like cattle. His body was drenched with the dew of heaven until his hair grew like the feathers of an eagle and his nails like the claws of a bird.

³⁴At the end of that time, I, Nebuchadnezzar, raised my eyes toward heaven, and my sanity was restored. Then I praised the Most High; I honored and glorified him who lives forever.

> His dominion is an eternal dominion;
>> his kingdom endures from generation to generation.
> ³⁵All the peoples of the earth
>> are regarded as nothing.
> He does as he pleases
>> with the powers of heaven
>> and the peoples of the earth.
> No one can hold back his hand
>> or say to him: "What have you done?"

³⁶At the same time that my sanity was restored, my honor and splendor were returned to me for the glory of my kingdom. My advisers and nobles sought me out, and I was restored to my throne and became even greater than before. ³⁷Now I, Nebuchadnezzar, praise and exalt and glorify the King of heaven, because everything he does is right and all his ways are just. And those who walk in pride he is able to humble.

DANIEL 4:33–37

Pick a candidate for the person you know who's "least likely to become a Christian." Got him or her in mind? Then compare that person with Nebuchadnezzar of Babylon. That ruler was master of his world, an emperor whose word was law throughout the Middle East. He didn't believe in God. And he didn't feel any need for God. But read these verses, and you discover that Nebuchadnezzar did come to know and worship the Lord through Daniel's faithful witness and a personal tragedy. Don't give up, even on that person "least likely to become a Christian." You and God together may reach him or her after all!

Direct Line

The Writing on the Wall King Belshazzar gave a great banquet for a thousand of his nobles and drank wine with them. ²While Belshazzar was drinking his wine, he gave orders to bring in the gold and silver goblets that Nebuchadnezzar his father*a* had taken from the temple in Jerusalem, so that the king and his nobles, his wives and his concubines might drink from them. ³So they brought in the gold goblets that had been taken from the temple of God in Jerusalem, and the king and his nobles, his wives and his concubines drank from them. ⁴As they drank the wine, they praised the gods of gold and silver, of bronze, iron, wood and stone.

⁵Suddenly the fingers of a human hand appeared and wrote on the plaster of the

---

*a*2 Or *ancestor*; or *predecessor*; also in verses 11, 13 and 18 wall, near the lampstand in the royal palace. The king watched the hand as it wrote. ⁶His face turned pale and he was so frightened that his knees knocked together and his legs gave way.

⁷The king called out for the enchanters, astrologers*a* and diviners to be brought and said to these wise men of Babylon, "Whoever reads this writing and tells me what it means will be clothed in purple and have a gold chain placed around his neck, and he will be made the third highest ruler in the kingdom."

⁸Then all the king's wise men came in, but they could not read the writing or tell the king what it meant. ⁹So King Belshazzar became even more terrified and his face grew more pale. His nobles were baffled.

¹⁰The queen,*b* hearing the voices of the king and his nobles, came into the banquet hall. "O king, live forever!" she said. "Don't be alarmed! Don't look so pale! ¹¹There is a man in your kingdom who has the spirit of the holy gods in him. In the time of your father he was found to have insight and intelligence and wisdom like that of the gods. King Nebuchadnezzar your father—your father the king, I say—appointed him chief of the magicians, enchanters, astrologers and diviners. ¹²This man Daniel, whom the king called Belteshazzar, was found to have a keen mind and knowledge and understanding, and also the ability to interpret dreams, explain riddles and solve difficult problems. Call for Daniel, and he will tell you what the writing means."

¹³So Daniel was brought before the king, and the king said to him, "Are you Daniel, one of the exiles my father the king brought from Judah? ¹⁴I have heard that the spirit of the gods is in you and that you have insight, intelligence and outstanding wisdom. ¹⁵The wise men and enchanters were brought before me to read this writing and tell me what it means, but they could not explain it. ¹⁶Now I have heard that you are able to give interpretations and to solve difficult problems. If you can read this writing and tell me what it means, you will be clothed in purple and have a gold chain placed around your neck, and you will be made the third highest ruler in the kingdom."

¹⁷Then Daniel answered the king, "You may keep your gifts for yourself and give your rewards to someone else. Nevertheless, I will read the writing for the king and tell him what it means.

¹⁸"O king, the Most High God gave your father Nebuchadnezzar sovereignty and greatness and glory and splendor. ¹⁹Because of the high position he gave him, all the peoples and nations and men of every language dreaded and feared him. Those the king wanted to put to death, he put to death; those he wanted to spare, he spared; those he wanted to promote, he promoted; and those he wanted to humble, he humbled. ²⁰But when his heart became arrogant and hardened with pride, he was deposed from his royal throne and stripped of his glory. ²¹He was driven away from people and given the mind of an animal; he lived with the wild donkeys and ate grass like cattle; and his body was drenched with the dew of heaven, until he acknowledged that the Most High God is sovereign over the kingdoms of men and sets over them anyone he wishes.

²²"But you his son,*c* O Belshazzar, have not humbled yourself, though you knew all this. ²³Instead, you have set yourself up against the Lord of heaven. You had the goblets from his temple brought to you, and you and your nobles, your wives and your concubines drank wine from them. You praised the gods of silver and gold, of bronze, iron, wood and stone, which cannot see or hear or understand. But you did not honor the God who holds in his hand your life

---

*a*7 Or *Chaldeans*; also in verse 11   *b*10 Or *queen mother*   *c*22 Or *descendant*; or *successor*

and all your ways. ²⁴Therefore he sent the hand that wrote the inscription. ²⁵"This is the inscription that was written:

MENE, MENE, TEKEL, PARSIN*ᵃ*

²⁶"This is what these words mean:

*Mene*ᵇ: God has numbered the days of your reign and brought it to an end.

²⁷ *Tekel*ᶜ: You have been weighed on the scales and found wanting.

²⁸ *Peres*ᵈ: Your kingdom is divided and given to the Medes and Persians."

²⁹Then at Belshazzar's command, Daniel was clothed in purple, a gold chain was placed around his neck, and he was proclaimed the third highest ruler in the kingdom.

³⁰That very night Belshazzar, king of the Babylonians,ᵉ was slain, ³¹and Darius the Mede took over the kingdom, at the age of sixty-two.

6 *Daniel in the Den of Lions* It pleased Darius to appoint 120 satraps to rule throughout the kingdom, ²with three administrators over them, one of whom was Daniel. The satraps were made accountable to them so that the king might not suffer loss. ³Now Daniel so distinguished himself among the administrators and the satraps by his exceptional qualities that the king planned to set him over the whole kingdom. ⁴At this, the administrators and the satraps tried to find grounds for charges against Daniel in his conduct of government affairs, but they were unable to do so. They could find no corruption in him, because he was trustworthy and neither corrupt nor negligent. ⁵Finally these men said, "We will never find any basis for charges against this man Daniel unless it has something to do with the law of his God."

Answers
to Quizzer on
page 1145

A: He wrote on
the wall with
"the fingers of
a human hand"
(Daniel 5:5).

BONUS: The
Bible says, "His
face turned pale
and he was
so frightened
that his knees
knocked together
and his legs
gave way"
(Daniel 5:6).

⁶So the administrators and the satraps went as a group to the king and said: "O King Darius, live forever! ⁷The royal administrators, prefects, satraps, advisers and governors have all agreed that the king should issue an edict and enforce the decree that anyone who prays to any god or man during the next thirty days, except to you, O king, shall be thrown into the lions' den. ⁸Now, O king, issue the decree and put it in writing so that it cannot be altered—in accordance with the laws of the Medes and Persians, which cannot be repealed." ⁹So King Darius put the decree in writing.

¹⁰Now when Daniel learned that the decree had been published, he went home to his upstairs room where the windows opened toward Jerusalem. Three times a day he got down on his knees and prayed, giving thanks to his God, just as he had done before. ¹¹Then these men went as a group and found Daniel praying and asking God for help. ¹²So they went to the king and spoke to him about his royal decree: "Did you not publish a decree that during the next thirty days anyone who prays to any god or man except to you, O king, would be thrown into the lions' den?"

The king answered, "The decree stands—in accordance with the laws of the Medes and Persians, which cannot be repealed."

¹³Then they said to the king, "Daniel, who is one of the exiles from Judah, pays no attention to you, O king, or to the decree you put in writing. He still prays three times a day." ¹⁴When the king heard this, he was greatly distressed; he was determined to rescue Daniel and made every effort until sundown to save him.

¹⁵Then the men went as a group to the king and said to him, "Remember, O king, that according to the law of the Medes and Persians no decree or edict that the king issues can be changed."

ᵃ25 Aramaic *UPARSIN* (that is, *AND PARSIN*) ᵇ26 *Mene* can mean *numbered* or *mina* (a unit of money).
ᶜ27 *Tekel* can mean *weighed* or *shekel.*   ᵈ28 *Peres* (the singular of *Parsin*) can mean *divided* or *Persia* or *a half mina* or *a half shekel.* ᵉ30 Or *Chaldeans*

¹⁶So the king gave the order, and they brought Daniel and threw him into the lions' den. The king said to Daniel, "May your God, whom you serve continually, rescue you!"

¹⁷A stone was brought and placed over the mouth of the den, and the king sealed it with his own signet ring and with the rings of his nobles, so that Daniel's situation might not be changed. ¹⁸Then the king returned to his palace and spent the night without eating and without any entertainment being brought to him. And he could not sleep.

¹⁹At the first light of dawn, the king got up and hurried to the lions' den. ²⁰When he came near the den, he called to Daniel in an anguished voice, "Daniel, servant of the living God, has your God, whom you serve continually, been able to rescue you from the lions?"

²¹Daniel answered, "O king, live forever! ²²My God sent his angel, and he shut the mouths of the lions. They have not hurt me, because I was found innocent in his sight. Nor have I ever done any wrong before you, O king."

²³The king was overjoyed and gave orders to lift Daniel out of the den. And when Daniel was lifted from the den, no wound was found on him, because he had trusted in his God.

²⁴At the king's command, the men who had falsely accused Daniel were brought in and thrown into the lions' den, along with their wives and children. And before they reached the floor of the den, the lions overpowered them and crushed all their bones.

²⁵Then King Darius wrote to all the peoples, nations and men of every language throughout the land:

"May you prosper greatly!

²⁶"I issue a decree that in every part of my kingdom people must fear and reverence the God of Daniel.

> "For he is the living God
>   and he endures forever;
> his kingdom will not be destroyed,
>   his dominion will never end.
> ²⁷He rescues and he saves;
>   he performs signs and wonders
>   in the heavens and on the earth.
> He has rescued Daniel
>   from the power of the lions."

²⁸So Daniel prospered during the reign of Darius and the reign of Cyrus*a* the Persian.

Daniel's Dream of Four Beasts In the first year of Belshazzar king of Babylon, Daniel had a dream, and visions passed through his mind as he was lying on his bed. He wrote down the substance of his dream.

²Daniel said: "In my vision at night I looked, and there before me were the four winds of heaven churning up the great sea. ³Four great beasts, each different from the others, came up out of the sea.

⁴"The first was like a lion, and it had the wings of an eagle. I watched until its wings were torn off and it was lifted from the ground so that it stood on two feet like a man, and the heart of a man was given to it.

⁵"And there before me was a second beast, which looked like a bear. It was raised up on one of its sides, and it had three ribs in its mouth between its teeth. It was told, 'Get up and eat your fill of flesh!'

⁶"After that, I looked, and there before me was another beast, one that looked like a leopard. And on its back it had four wings like those of a bird. This beast had four heads, and it was given authority to rule.

---

a28 Or Darius, that is, the reign of Cyrus

⁷"After that, in my vision at night I looked, and there before me was a fourth beast—terrifying and frightening and very powerful. It had large iron teeth; it crushed and devoured its victims and trampled underfoot whatever was left. It was different from all the former beasts, and it had ten horns.

⁸"While I was thinking about the horns, there before me was another horn, a little one, which came up among them; and three of the first horns were uprooted before it. This horn had eyes like the eyes of a man and a mouth that spoke boastfully.

⁹"As I looked,

"thrones were set in place,
    and the Ancient of Days took his seat.
His clothing was as white as snow;
    the hair of his head was white like wool.
His throne was flaming with fire,
    and its wheels were all ablaze.
¹⁰A river of fire was flowing,
    coming out from before him.
Thousands upon thousands attended him;
    ten thousand times ten thousand stood before him.
The court was seated,
    and the books were opened.

¹¹"Then I continued to watch because of the boastful words the horn was speaking. I kept looking until the beast was slain and its body destroyed and thrown into the blazing fire. ¹²(The other beasts had been stripped of their authority, but were allowed to live for a period of time.)

¹³"In my vision at night I looked, and there before me was one like a son of man, coming with the clouds of heaven. He approached the Ancient of Days and was led into his presence. ¹⁴He was given authority, glory and sovereign power; all peoples, nations and men of every language worshiped him. His dominion is an everlasting dominion that will not pass away, and his kingdom is one that will never be destroyed.

This is more like a nightmare than a dream!

DANIEL 7-8

The Interpretation of the Dream ¹⁵"I, Daniel, was troubled in spirit, and the visions that passed through my mind disturbed me. ¹⁶I approached one of those standing there and asked him the true meaning of all this.

"So he told me and gave me the interpretation of these things: ¹⁷'The four great beasts are four kingdoms that will rise from the earth. ¹⁸But the saints of the Most High will receive the kingdom and will possess it forever—yes, for ever and ever.'

¹⁹"Then I wanted to know the true meaning of the fourth beast, which was different from all the others and most terrifying, with its iron teeth and bronze claws—the beast that crushed and devoured its victims and trampled underfoot whatever was left. ²⁰I also wanted to know about the ten horns on its head and about the other horn that came up, before which three of them fell—the horn that looked more imposing than the others and that had eyes and a mouth that spoke boastfully. ²¹As I watched, this horn was waging war against the saints and

defeating them, [22]until the Ancient of Days came and pronounced judgment in favor of the saints of the Most High, and the time came when they possessed the kingdom.

[23]"He gave me this explanation: 'The fourth beast is a fourth kingdom that will appear on earth. It will be different from all the other kingdoms and will devour the whole earth, trampling it down and crushing it. [24]The ten horns are ten kings who will come from this kingdom. After them another king will arise, different from the earlier ones; he will subdue three kings. [25]He will speak against the Most High and oppress his saints and try to change the set times and the laws. The saints will be handed over to him for a time, times and half a time.[a]

[26]" 'But the court will sit, and his power will be taken away and completely destroyed forever. [27]Then the sovereignty, power and greatness of the kingdoms under the whole heaven will be handed over to the saints, the people of the Most High. His kingdom will be an everlasting kingdom, and all rulers will worship and obey him.'

[28]"This is the end of the matter. I, Daniel, was deeply troubled by my thoughts, and my face turned pale, but I kept the matter to myself."

8 *Daniel's Vision of a Ram and a Goat* In the third year of King Belshazzar's reign, I, Daniel, had a vision, after the one that had already appeared to me. [2]In my vision I saw myself in the citadel of Susa in the province of Elam; in the vision I was beside the Ulai Canal. [3]I looked up, and there before me was a ram with two horns, standing beside the canal, and the horns were long. One of the horns was longer than the other but grew up later. [4]I watched the ram as he charged toward the west and the north and the south. No animal could stand against him, and none could rescue from his power. He did as he pleased and became great.

[5]As I was thinking about this, suddenly a goat with a prominent horn between his eyes came from the west, crossing the whole earth without touching the ground. [6]He came toward the two-horned ram I had seen standing beside the canal and charged at him in great rage. [7]I saw him attack the ram furiously, striking the ram and shattering his two horns. The ram was powerless to stand against him; the goat knocked him to the ground and trampled on him, and none could rescue the ram from his power. [8]The goat became very great, but at the height of his power his large horn was broken off, and in its place four prominent horns grew up toward the four winds of heaven.

[9]Out of one of them came another horn, which started small but grew in power to the south and to the east and toward the Beautiful Land. [10]It grew until it reached the host of the heavens, and it threw some of the starry host down to the earth and trampled on them. [11]It set itself up to be as great as the Prince of the host; it took away the daily sacrifice from him, and the place of his sanctuary was brought low. [12]Because of rebellion, the host of the saints,[b] and the daily sacrifice were given over to it. It prospered in everything it did, and truth was thrown to the ground.

[13]Then I heard a holy one speaking, and another holy one said to him, "How long will it take for the vision to be fulfilled—the vision concerning the daily sacrifice, the rebellion that causes desolation, and the surrender of the sanctuary and of the host that will be trampled underfoot?"

[14]He said to me, "It will take 2,300 evenings and mornings; then the sanctuary will be reconsecrated."

The Interpretation of the Vision [15]While I, Daniel, was watching the vision and trying to understand it, there before me stood one who looked like a

---

[a]25 Or *for a year, two years and half a year*   [b]12 Or *rebellion, the armies*

man. ¹⁶And I heard a man's voice from the Ulai calling, "Gabriel, tell this man the meaning of the vision."

¹⁷As he came near the place where I was standing, I was terrified and fell prostrate. "Son of man," he said to me, "understand that the vision concerns the time of the end."

¹⁸While he was speaking to me, I was in a deep sleep, with my face to the ground. Then he touched me and raised me to my feet.

¹⁹He said: "I am going to tell you what will happen later in the time of wrath, because the vision concerns the appointed time of the end.ᵃ ²⁰The two-horned ram that you saw represents the kings of Media and Persia. ²¹The shaggy goat is the king of Greece, and the large horn between his eyes is the first king. ²²The four horns that replaced the one that was broken off represent four kingdoms that will emerge from his nation but will not have the same power.

²³"In the latter part of their reign, when rebels have become completely wicked, a stern-faced king, a master of intrigue, will arise. ²⁴He will become very strong, but not by his own power. He will cause astounding devastation and will succeed in whatever he does. He will destroy the mighty men and the holy people. ²⁵He will cause deceit to prosper, and he will consider himself superior. When they feel secure, he will destroy many and take his stand against the Prince of princes. Yet he will be destroyed, but not by human power.

²⁶"The vision of the evenings and mornings that has been given you is true, but seal up the vision, for it concerns the distant future."

²⁷I, Daniel, was exhausted and lay ill for several days. Then I got up and went about the king's business. I was appalled by the vision; it was beyond understanding.

Daniel's Prayer In the first year of Darius son of Xerxesᵇ (a Mede by descent), who was made ruler over the Babylonianᶜ kingdom— ²in the first year of his reign, I, Daniel, understood from the Scriptures, according to the word of the LORD given to Jeremiah the prophet, that the desolation of Jerusalem would last seventy years. ³So I turned to the Lord God and pleaded with him in prayer and petition, in fasting, and in sackcloth and ashes.

⁴I prayed to the LORD my God and confessed:

"O Lord, the great and awesome God, who keeps his covenant of love with all who love him and obey his commands, ⁵we have sinned and done wrong. We have been wicked and have rebelled; we have turned away from your commands and laws. ⁶We have not listened to your servants the prophets, who spoke in your name to our kings, our princes and our fathers, and to all the people of the land.

⁷"Lord, you are righteous, but this day we are covered with shame— the men of Judah and people of Jerusalem and all Israel, both near and far, in all the countries where you have scattered us because of our unfaithfulness to you. ⁸O LORD, we and our kings, our princes and our fathers are covered with shame because we have sinned against you. ⁹The Lord our God is merciful and forgiving, even though we have rebelled against him; ¹⁰we have not obeyed the LORD our God or kept the laws he gave us through his servants the prophets. ¹¹All Israel has transgressed your law and turned away, refusing to obey you.

"Therefore the curses and sworn judgments written in the Law of Moses, the servant of God, have been poured out on us, because we have sinned against you. ¹²You have fulfilled the words spoken against us and against our rulers by bringing upon us great disaster. Under the whole

---

ᵃ19 Or because the end will be at the appointed time *ᵇ1 Hebrew Ahasuerus* *ᶜ1 Or Chaldean*

heaven nothing has ever been done like what has been done to Jerusalem. [13]Just as it is written in the Law of Moses, all this disaster has come upon us, yet we have not sought the favor of the LORD our God by turning from our sins and giving attention to your truth. [14]The LORD did not hesitate to bring the disaster upon us, for the LORD our God is righteous in everything he does; yet we have not obeyed him.

[15]"Now, O Lord our God, who brought your people out of Egypt with a mighty hand and who made for yourself a name that endures to this day, we have sinned, we have done wrong. [16]O Lord, in keeping with all your righteous acts, turn away your anger and your wrath from Jerusalem, your city, your holy hill. Our sins and the iniquities of our fathers have made Jerusalem and your people an object of scorn to all those around us.

[17]"Now, our God, hear the prayers and petitions of your servant. For your sake, O Lord, look with favor on your desolate sanctuary. [18]Give ear, O God, and hear; open your eyes and see the desolation of the city that bears your Name. We do not make requests of you because we are righteous, but because of your great mercy. [19]O Lord, listen! O Lord, forgive! O Lord, hear and act! For your sake, O my God, do not delay, because your city and your people bear your Name."

The Seventy "Sevens"   [20]While I was speaking and praying, confessing my sin and the sin of my people Israel and making my request to the LORD my God for his holy hill— [21]while I was still in prayer, Gabriel, the man I had seen in the earlier vision, came to me in swift flight about the time of the evening sacrifice. [22]He instructed me and said to me, "Daniel, I have now come to give you insight and understanding. [23]As soon as you began to pray, an answer was given, which I have come to tell you, for you are highly esteemed. Therefore, consider the message and understand the vision:

[24]"Seventy 'sevens'[a] are decreed for your people and your holy city to finish[b] transgression, to put an end to sin, to atone for wickedness, to bring in everlasting righteousness, to seal up vision and prophecy and to anoint the most holy.[c]

[25]"Know and understand this: From the issuing of the decree[d] to restore and rebuild Jerusalem until the Anointed One,[e] the ruler, comes, there will be seven 'sevens,' and sixty-two 'sevens.' It will be rebuilt with streets and a trench, but in times of trouble. [26]After the sixty-two 'sevens,' the Anointed One will be cut off and will have nothing.[f] The people of the ruler who will come will destroy the city and the sanctuary. The end will come like a flood: War will continue until the end, and desolations have been decreed. [27]He will confirm a covenant with many for one 'seven.'[g] In the middle of the 'seven'[g] he will put an end to sacrifice and offering. And on a wing of the temple he will set up an abomination that causes desolation, until the end that is decreed is poured out on him.[h],[i]

10   *Daniel's Vision of a Man*   In the third year of Cyrus king of Persia, a revelation was given to Daniel (who was called Belteshazzar). Its message was true and it concerned a great war.[j] The understanding of the message came to him in a vision.

[2]At that time I, Daniel, mourned for three weeks. [3]I ate no choice food; no meat or wine touched my lips; and I used no lotions at all until the three weeks were over.

---

[a]24 Or 'weeks'; also in verses 25 and 26   [b]24 Or restrain   [c]24 Or Most Holy Place; or most holy One   [d]25 Or word   [e]25 Or an anointed one; also in verse 26   [f]26 Or off and will have no one; or off, but not for himself   [g]27 Or 'week'   [h]27 Or it   [i]27 Or And one who causes desolation will come upon the pinnacle of the abominable temple, until the end that is decreed is poured out on the desolated city   [j]1 Or true and burdensome

⁴On the twenty-fourth day of the first month, as I was standing on the bank of the great river, the Tigris, ⁵I looked up and there before me was a man dressed in linen, with a belt of the finest gold around his waist. ⁶His body was like chrysolite, his face like lightning, his eyes like flaming torches, his arms and legs like the gleam of burnished bronze, and his voice like the sound of a multitude.

⁷I, Daniel, was the only one who saw the vision; the men with me did not see it, but such terror overwhelmed them that they fled and hid themselves. ⁸So I was left alone, gazing at this great vision; I had no strength left, my face turned deathly pale and I was helpless. ⁹Then I heard him speaking, and as I listened to him, I fell into a deep sleep, my face to the ground.

¹⁰A hand touched me and set me trembling on my hands and knees. ¹¹He said, "Daniel, you who are highly esteemed, consider carefully the words I am about to speak to you, and stand up, for I have now been sent to you." And when he said this to me, I stood up trembling.

¹²Then he continued, "Do not be afraid, Daniel. Since the first day that you set your mind to gain understanding and to humble yourself before your God, your words were heard, and I have come in response to them. ¹³But the prince of the Persian kingdom resisted me twenty-one days. Then Michael, one of the chief princes, came to help me, because I was detained there with the king of Persia. ¹⁴Now I have come to explain to you what will happen to your people in the future, for the vision concerns a time yet to come."

¹⁵While he was saying this to me, I bowed with my face toward the ground and was speechless. ¹⁶Then one who looked like a man[a] touched my lips, and I opened my mouth and began to speak. I said to the one standing before me, "I am overcome with anguish because of the vision, my lord, and I am helpless. ¹⁷How can I, your servant, talk with you, my lord? My strength is gone and I can hardly breathe."

¹⁸Again the one who looked like a man touched me and gave me strength. ¹⁹"Do not be afraid, O man highly esteemed," he said. "Peace! Be strong now; be strong."

When he spoke to me, I was strengthened and said, "Speak, my lord, since you have given me strength."

a16 Most manuscripts of the Masoretic Text; one manuscript of the Masoretic Text, Dead Sea Scrolls and Septuagint Then something that looked like a man's hand

The Bible Says

Angel Armies Struggle

The Bible doesn't say a lot about angels. But read Daniel 10:1–14, and notice these fascinating things about angels:

* The angels of God and the angels of Satan battle each other in an invisible war.
* Angels seem to have rank. Daniel's "major" angel was stopped by an enemy "colonel" angel, until "general" Michael appeared.
* Satan assigns angels to nations. The angel assigned to Persia is called "the prince of the Persian kingdom."

Most people are curious about angels and would like to know more. But the Bible focuses on things that are more important for human beings, like how to trust God and live in ways that please him. You'll learn all you need to know about angels when you get to heaven.

²⁰So he said, "Do you know why I have come to you? Soon I will return to fight against the prince of Persia, and when I go, the prince of Greece will come; ²¹but first I will tell you what is written in the Book of Truth. (No one

11 supports me against them except Michael, your prince. ¹And in the first year of Darius the Mede, I took my stand to support and protect him.)

The Kings of the South and the North ²"Now then, I tell you the truth: Three more kings will appear in Persia, and then a fourth, who will be far richer than all the others. When he has gained power by his wealth, he will stir up everyone against the kingdom of Greece. ³Then a mighty king will appear, who will rule with great power and do as he pleases. ⁴After he has appeared, his empire will be broken up and parceled out toward the four winds of heaven. It will not go to his descendants, nor will it have the power he exercised, because his empire will be uprooted and given to others.

⁵"The king of the South will become strong, but one of his commanders will become even stronger than he and will rule his own kingdom with great power. ⁶After some years, they will become allies. The daughter of the king of the South will go to the king of the North to make an alliance, but she will not retain her power, and he and his power*ᵃ* will not last. In those days she will be handed over, together with her royal escort and her father*ᵇ* and the one who supported her.

⁷"One from her family line will arise to take her place. He will attack the forces of the king of the North and enter his fortress; he will fight against them and be victorious. ⁸He will also seize their gods, their metal images and their valuable articles of silver and gold and carry them off to Egypt. For some years he will leave the king of the North alone. ⁹Then the king of the North will invade the realm of the king of the South but will retreat to his own country. ¹⁰His sons will prepare for war and assemble a great army, which will sweep on like an irresistible flood and carry the battle as far as his fortress.

¹¹"Then the king of the South will march out in a rage and fight against the king of the North, who will raise a large army, but it will be defeated. ¹²When the army is carried off, the king of the South will be filled with pride and will slaughter many thousands, yet he will not remain triumphant. ¹³For the king of the North will muster another army, larger than the first; and after several years, he will advance with a huge army fully equipped.

¹⁴"In those times many will rise against the king of the South. The violent men among your own people will rebel in fulfillment of the vision, but without success. ¹⁵Then the king of the North will come and build up siege ramps and will capture a fortified city. The forces of the South will be powerless to resist; even their best troops will not have the strength to stand. ¹⁶The invader will do as he pleases; no one will be able to stand against him. He will establish himself in the Beautiful Land and will have the power to destroy it. ¹⁷He will determine to come with the might of his entire kingdom and will make an alliance with the king of the South. And he will give him a daughter in marriage in order to overthrow the kingdom, but his plans*ᶜ* will not succeed or help him. ¹⁸Then he will turn his attention to the coastlands and will take many of them, but a commander will put an end to his insolence and will turn his insolence back upon him. ¹⁹After this, he will turn back toward the fortresses of his own country but will stumble and fall, to be seen no more.

²⁰"His successor will send out a tax collector to maintain the royal splendor. In a few years, however, he will be destroyed, yet not in anger or in battle.

²¹"He will be succeeded by a contemptible person who has not been given the honor of royalty. He will invade the kingdom when its people feel secure,

ᵃ6 Or offspring ᵇ6 Or child (see Vulgate and Syriac) ᶜ17 Or but she

and he will seize it through intrigue. ²²Then an overwhelming army will be swept away before him; both it and a prince of the covenant will be destroyed. ²³After coming to an agreement with him, he will act deceitfully, and with only a few people he will rise to power. ²⁴When the richest provinces feel secure, he will invade them and will achieve what neither his fathers nor his forefathers did. He will distribute plunder, loot and wealth among his followers. He will plot the overthrow of fortresses—but only for a time.

²⁵"With a large army he will stir up his strength and courage against the king of the South. The king of the South will wage war with a large and very powerful army, but he will not be able to stand because of the plots devised against him. ²⁶Those who eat from the king's provisions will try to destroy him; his army will be swept away, and many will fall in battle. ²⁷The two kings, with their hearts bent on evil, will sit at the same table and lie to each other, but to no avail, because an end will still come at the appointed time. ²⁸The king of the North will return to his own country with great wealth, but his heart will be set against the holy covenant. He will take action against it and then return to his own country.

²⁹"At the appointed time he will invade the South again, but this time the outcome will be different from what it was before. ³⁰Ships of the western coastlands*a* will oppose him, and he will lose heart. Then he will turn back and vent his fury against the holy covenant. He will return and show favor to those who forsake the holy covenant.

³¹"His armed forces will rise up to desecrate the temple fortress and will abolish the daily sacrifice. Then they will set up the abomination that causes desolation. ³²With flattery he will corrupt those who have violated the covenant, but the people who know their God will firmly resist him.

³³"Those who are wise will instruct many, though for a time they will fall by the sword or be burned or captured or plundered. ³⁴When they fall, they will receive a little help, and many who are not sincere will join them. ³⁵Some of the wise will stumble, so that they may be refined, purified and made spotless until the time of the end, for it will still come at the appointed time.

The King Who Exalts Himself ³⁶"The king will do as he pleases. He will exalt and magnify himself above every god and will say unheard-of things against

a30 Hebrew *of Kittim*

The Bible Says

Will We Live Again?

The New Testament teaches a resurrection, but what about the Old Testament? Did people then know that they would live again? They did if they believed the Scriptures:

* God will "swallow up death forever" (Isaiah 25:8).
* "Your dead will live; their bodies will rise" (Isaiah 26:19).
* "Multitudes who sleep in the dust of the earth will awake: some to everlasting life, others to shame and everlasting contempt" (Daniel 12:2).

Old Testament passages don't speak about a resurrection as much as the New Testament—but the entire Bible tells about one God, who has always loved human beings and who has always planned that people who live by faith will live forever with him.

the God of gods. He will be successful until the time of wrath is completed, for what has been determined must take place. ³⁷He will show no regard for the gods of his fathers or for the one desired by women, nor will he regard any god, but will exalt himself above them all. ³⁸Instead of them, he will honor a god of fortresses; a god unknown to his fathers he will honor with gold and silver, with precious stones and costly gifts. ³⁹He will attack the mightiest fortresses with the help of a foreign god and will greatly honor those who acknowledge him. He will make them rulers over many people and will distribute the land at a price.*

⁴⁰"At the time of the end the king of the South will engage him in battle, and the king of the North will storm out against him with chariots and cavalry and a great fleet of ships. He will invade many countries and sweep through them like a flood. ⁴¹He will also invade the Beautiful Land. Many countries will fall, but Edom, Moab and the leaders of Ammon will be delivered from his hand. ⁴²He will extend his power over many countries; Egypt will not escape. ⁴³He will gain control of the treasures of gold and silver and all the riches of Egypt, with the Libyans and Nubians in submission. ⁴⁴But reports from the east and the north will alarm him, and he will set out in a great rage to destroy and annihilate many. ⁴⁵He will pitch his royal tents between the seas at* the beautiful holy mountain. Yet he will come to his end, and no one will help him.

12 *The End Times* "At that time Michael, the great prince who protects your people, will arise. There will be a time of distress such as has not happened from the beginning of nations until then. But at that time your people—everyone whose name is found written in the book—will be delivered. ²Multitudes who sleep in the dust of the earth will awake: some to everlasting life, others to shame and everlasting contempt. ³Those who are wise* will shine like the brightness of the heavens, and those who lead many to righteousness, like the stars for ever and ever. ⁴But you, Daniel, close up and seal the words of the scroll until the time of the end. Many will go here and there to increase knowledge."

⁵Then I, Daniel, looked, and there before me stood two others, one on this bank of the river and one on the opposite bank. ⁶One of them said to the man clothed in linen, who was above the waters of the river, "How long will it be before these astonishing things are fulfilled?"

⁷The man clothed in linen, who was above the waters of the river, lifted his right hand and his left hand toward heaven, and I heard him swear by him who lives forever, saying, "It will be for a time, times and half a time.* When the power of the holy people has been finally broken, all these things will be completed."

⁸I heard, but I did not understand. So I asked, "My lord, what will the outcome of all this be?"

⁹He replied, "Go your way, Daniel, because the words are closed up and sealed until the time of the end. ¹⁰Many will be purified, made spotless and refined, but the wicked will continue to be wicked. None of the wicked will understand, but those who are wise will understand.

¹¹"From the time that the daily sacrifice is abolished and the abomination that causes desolation is set up, there will be 1,290 days. ¹²Blessed is the one who waits for and reaches the end of the 1,335 days.

¹³"As for you, go your way till the end. You will rest, and then at the end of the days you will rise to receive your allotted inheritance."

---

*39 Or *land for a reward*   *45 Or *the sea and*   *3 Or *who impart wisdom*   *7 Or *a year, two years and half a year*

Introduction

to the

book of # Hosea

BETRAYAL.

Have you ever written a very personal note to a friend and then had that friend turn around and show the note to everyone? Or told your mom something confidential and later found out she told your grandma and two aunts? You probably felt betrayed.

The prophet Hosea must have felt the same way about his unfaithful wife. But God told Hosea to keep on loving her even though she hurt him. Why? Because Hosea was to be like God, who keeps on loving his people even when they're unfaithful to him. What you do can hurt the Lord. But even then he keeps on loving you.

Fundamentals

How will God respond if his people turn back to him (Hosea 2:21-23)?

What do God's people do that hurts the Lord (Hosea 4)?

Will God stay angry with you if you come back to him after you've sinned (Hosea 14)?

FAST FACTS

Hosea means "salvation."

Hosea prophesied in Israel around the middle of the eighth century B.C.

Hosea's wife was a prostitute, but he continued to love her and later brought her home.

Commitment is loving people even when they hurt you.

The word of the LORD that came to Hosea son of Beeri during the reigns of Uzziah, Jotham, Ahaz and Hezekiah, kings of Judah, and during the reign of Jeroboam son of Jehoash[a] king of Israel:

Hosea's Wife and Children ²When the LORD began to speak through Hosea, the LORD said to him, "Go, take to yourself an adulterous wife and children of unfaithfulness, because the land is guilty of the vilest adultery in departing from the LORD." ³So he married Gomer daughter of Diblaim, and she conceived and bore him a son.

⁴Then the LORD said to Hosea, "Call him Jezreel, because I will soon punish the house of Jehu for the massacre at Jezreel, and I will put an end to the kingdom of Israel. ⁵In that day I will break Israel's bow in the Valley of Jezreel."

⁶Gomer conceived again and gave birth to a daughter. Then the LORD said to Hosea, "Call her Lo-Ruhamah,[b] for I will no longer show love to the house of Israel, that I should at all forgive them. ⁷Yet I will show love to the house of Judah; and I will save them—not by bow, sword or battle, or by horses and horsemen, but by the LORD their God."

⁸After she had weaned Lo-Ruhamah, Gomer had another son. ⁹Then the LORD said, "Call him Lo-Ammi,[c] for you are not my people, and I am not your God.

¹⁰"Yet the Israelites will be like the sand on the seashore, which cannot be measured or counted. In the place where it was said to them, 'You are not my people,' they will be called 'sons of the living God.' ¹¹The people of Judah and the people of Israel will be reunited, and they will appoint one leader and will come up out of the land, for great will be the day of Jezreel.

"Say of your brothers, 'My people,' and of your sisters, 'My loved one.'

Israel Punished and Restored

² "Rebuke your mother, rebuke her,
　　for she is not my wife,
　　and I am not her husband.
　Let her remove the adulterous look from her face
　　and the unfaithfulness from between her breasts.
³ Otherwise I will strip her naked
　　and make her as bare as on the day she was born;
　I will make her like a desert,
　　turn her into a parched land,
　　and slay her with thirst.
⁴ I will not show my love to her children,
　　because they are the children of adultery.
⁵ Their mother has been unfaithful
　　and has conceived them in disgrace.
　She said, 'I will go after my lovers,
　　who give me my food and my water,
　　my wool and my linen, my oil and my drink.'
⁶ Therefore I will block her path with thornbushes;
　　I will wall her in so that she cannot find her way.
⁷ She will chase after her lovers but not catch them;
　　she will look for them but not find them.
　Then she will say,
　　'I will go back to my husband as at first,
　　for then I was better off than now.'

---

a1 Hebrew Joash, a variant of *Jehoash* *b6 Lo-Ruhamah* means *not loved.* *c9 Lo-Ammi* means *not my people.*

⁸She has not acknowledged that I was the one
who gave her the grain, the new wine and oil,
who lavished on her the silver and gold—
which they used for Baal.

⁹"Therefore I will take away my grain when it ripens,
and my new wine when it is ready.
I will take back my wool and my linen,
intended to cover her nakedness.
¹⁰So now I will expose her lewdness
before the eyes of her lovers;
no one will take her out of my hands.
¹¹I will stop all her celebrations:
her yearly festivals, her New Moons,
her Sabbath days—all her appointed feasts.
¹²I will ruin her vines and her fig trees,
which she said were her pay from her lovers;
I will make them a thicket,
and wild animals will devour them.
¹³I will punish her for the days
she burned incense to the Baals;
she decked herself with rings and jewelry,
and went after her lovers,
but me she forgot,"

declares the LORD.

¹⁴"Therefore I am now going to allure her;
I will lead her into the desert
and speak tenderly to her.
¹⁵There I will give her back her vineyards,
and will make the Valley of Achor*a* a door of hope.
There she will sing*b* as in the days of her youth,
as in the day she came up out of Egypt.

¹⁶"In that day," declares the LORD,
"you will call me 'my husband';
you will no longer call me 'my master.'*c*

a15 Achor means *trouble.*   *b15 Or respond*   *c16 Hebrew baal*

The Bible Says

God Is Jealous

Jealousy is a powerful emotion. When you feel jealous, you usually feel hateful and angry. So when the Bible says God is jealous (Exodus 20:5), does that mean he feels hateful and angry too?

Actually, the Bible doesn't say that God is jealous *against* anyone. Instead God is jealous *for* someone—his people. God cares so much that he becomes upset when the way you live keeps you from experiencing his very best.

Hosea 2 shows how God's jealousy works. God's people were unfaithful. No matter how good God was to them, they still worshiped idols. But God continued to love his people, knowing that without him they were lost! So he took away their good things—not to destroy them, but to bring them to their senses—so that once again they would turn to him and receive his blessing.

¹⁷I will remove the names of the Baals from her lips;
  no longer will their names be invoked.
¹⁸In that day I will make a covenant for them
  with the beasts of the field and the birds of the air
  and the creatures that move along the ground.
 Bow and sword and battle
  I will abolish from the land,
  so that all may lie down in safety.
¹⁹I will betroth you to me forever;
  I will betroth you in*ᵃ* righteousness and justice,
  in*ᵇ* love and compassion.
²⁰I will betroth you in faithfulness,
  and you will acknowledge the Lᴏʀᴅ.

²¹"In that day I will respond,"
  declares the Lᴏʀᴅ—
 "I will respond to the skies,
  and they will respond to the earth;
²²and the earth will respond to the grain,
  the new wine and oil,
  and they will respond to Jezreel.*ᶜ*
²³I will plant her for myself in the land;
  I will show my love to the one I called 'Not my loved one.'*ᵈ*
 I will say to those called 'Not my people,'*ᵉ* 'You are my people';
  and they will say, 'You are my God.' "

Hosea's Reconciliation With His Wife The Lᴏʀᴅ said to me, "Go, show your love to your wife again, though she is loved by another and is an adulteress. Love her as the Lᴏʀᴅ loves the Israelites, though they turn to other gods and love the sacred raisin cakes."

²So I bought her for fifteen shekels*ᶠ* of silver and about a homer and a lethek*ᵍ* of barley. ³Then I told her, "You are to live with*ʰ* me many days; you must not be a prostitute or be intimate with any man, and I will live with*ʰ* you."

⁴For the Israelites will live many days without king or prince, without sacrifice or sacred stones, without ephod or idol. ⁵Afterward the Israelites will return and seek the Lᴏʀᴅ their God and David their king. They will come trembling to the Lᴏʀᴅ and to his blessings in the last days.

The Charge Against Israel
 Hear the word of the Lᴏʀᴅ, you Israelites,
  because the Lᴏʀᴅ has a charge to bring
  against you who live in the land:
 "There is no faithfulness, no love,
  no acknowledgment of God in the land.
²There is only cursing,*ⁱ* lying and murder,
  stealing and adultery;
 they break all bounds,
  and bloodshed follows bloodshed.
³Because of this the land mourns,*ʲ*
  and all who live in it waste away;
 the beasts of the field and the birds of the air
  and the fish of the sea are dying.

ᵃ19 Or with; also in verse 20   *ᵇ19 Or with*   *ᶜ22 Jezreel* means *God plants.*   *ᵈ23 Hebrew Lo-Ruhamah*
ᵉ23 Hebrew Lo-Ammi   *ᶠ2 That is,* about 6 ounces (about 170 grams)   *ᵍ2 That is,* probably about 10
bushels (about 330 liters)   *ʰ3 Or wait for*   *ⁱ2 That is,* to pronounce a curse upon   *ʲ3 Or dries up*

⁴"But let no man bring a charge,
  let no man accuse another,
for your people are like those
  who bring charges against a priest.
⁵You stumble day and night,
  and the prophets stumble with you.
So I will destroy your mother—
⁶   my people are destroyed from lack of knowledge.

"Because you have rejected knowledge,
  I also reject you as my priests;
because you have ignored the law of your God,
  I also will ignore your children.
⁷The more the priests increased,
  the more they sinned against me;
they exchanged*a* their*b* Glory for something disgraceful.
⁸They feed on the sins of my people
  and relish their wickedness.
⁹And it will be: Like people, like priests.
  I will punish both of them for their ways
  and repay them for their deeds.

¹⁰"They will eat but not have enough;
  they will engage in prostitution but not increase,
because they have deserted the LORD
  to give themselves ¹¹to prostitution,
to old wine and new,
  which take away the understanding ¹²of my people.
They consult a wooden idol
  and are answered by a stick of wood.
A spirit of prostitution leads them astray;
  they are unfaithful to their God.
¹³They sacrifice on the mountaintops
  and burn offerings on the hills,
under oak, poplar and terebinth,
  where the shade is pleasant.
Therefore your daughters turn to prostitution
  and your daughters-in-law to adultery.

¹⁴"I will not punish your daughters
  when they turn to prostitution,
nor your daughters-in-law
  when they commit adultery,
because the men themselves consort with harlots
  and sacrifice with shrine prostitutes—
  a people without understanding will come to ruin!

¹⁵"Though you commit adultery, O Israel,
  let not Judah become guilty.

"Do not go to Gilgal;
  do not go up to Beth Aven.*c*
  And do not swear, 'As surely as the LORD lives!'
¹⁶The Israelites are stubborn,
  like a stubborn heifer.

---

*a*7 Syriac and an ancient Hebrew scribal tradition; Masoretic Text *I will exchange*   *b*7 Masoretic Text; an ancient Hebrew scribal tradition *my*   *c*15 *Beth Aven* means *house of wickedness* (a name for Bethel, which means *house of God*).

How then can the LORD pasture them
    like lambs in a meadow?
¹⁷Ephraim is joined to idols;
    leave him alone!
¹⁸Even when their drinks are gone,
    they continue their prostitution;
    their rulers dearly love shameful ways.
¹⁹A whirlwind will sweep them away,
    and their sacrifices will bring them
      shame.

5 Judgment Against Israel

"Hear this, you priests!
    Pay attention, you Israelites!
Listen, O royal house!
    This judgment is against you:
You have been a snare at Mizpah,
    a net spread out on Tabor.
²The rebels are deep in slaughter.
    I will discipline all of them.
³I know all about Ephraim;
    Israel is not hidden from me.
Ephraim, you have now turned to
      prostitution;
    Israel is corrupt.

⁴"Their deeds do not permit them
    to return to their God.
A spirit of prostitution is in their heart;
    they do not acknowledge the LORD.
⁵Israel's arrogance testifies against them;
    the Israelites, even Ephraim, stumble in
      their sin;
    Judah also stumbles with them.
⁶When they go with their flocks and herds
    to seek the LORD,
they will not find him;
    he has withdrawn himself
      from them.
⁷They are unfaithful to the
      LORD;
    they give birth to illegitimate
      children.
Now their New Moon festivals
    will devour them and their
      fields.

⁸"Sound the trumpet in
      Gibeah,
    the horn in Ramah.
Raise the battle cry in Beth
      Aven*;
    lead on,
      O Benjamin.

---

*8 Beth Aven means *house of wickedness* (a name for
Bethel, which means *house of God*).

HOSEA 4:16

Sometimes it can be interesting
to put your name in the place of
a word or name in a Bible verse.
Like this verse: "The Israelites are
stubborn, like a stubborn heifer.
How then can the LORD pasture
them like lambs in a meadow?"
Now take "Israelites" out of this
verse and put your name in.
Pretty interesting, hey? "_____ is
stubborn. How then can the Lord
bless _____?" Of course, you're
not stubborn, are you? And you
don't intend to be, right? Why
would you want to pass up God's
blessing?

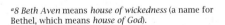

Direct Line

Dear Sam,

My friend says I'm two-faced because I act like a Christian at church, but at school I swear and tell a dirty joke now and then. Is that wrong?

Kelly in Kankakee

100 Advice Lane, Anywhere, USA

Dear Sam, Inc.

Dear Kelly,

You have a good friend who cares enough about you to confront you on an important issue. It might be easier to just ignore that person, but maybe it would be a good idea to listen.

Most teens are a little freer at school than at church, and it's easy to get carried away when you spend a lot of time with non-Christian friends. But are you letting your desire to fit in get in the way of the values God wants you to live by? No one is perfect; God understands that. But he still expects you to be responsible for your actions. If you don't live consistently by God's values, soon your life may spin so out of control that it becomes nearly impossible to stay close to God (Hosea 5:4). Remember how Daniel remained faithful to God along with his three friends (Daniel 1)? Perhaps you need to seek out a few good friends who will help you stay on the right path. And don't forget to pray for God's help.

Sam

⁹Ephraim will be laid waste
 on the day of reckoning.
Among the tribes of Israel
 I proclaim what is certain.
¹⁰Judah's leaders are like those
 who move boundary stones.
I will pour out my wrath on them
 like a flood of water.
¹¹Ephraim is oppressed,
 trampled in judgment,
 intent on pursuing idols.ᵃ
¹²I am like a moth to Ephraim,
 like rot to the people of Judah.

¹³"When Ephraim saw his sickness,
 and Judah his sores,
then Ephraim turned to Assyria,
 and sent to the great king for help.
But he is not able to cure you,
 not able to heal your sores.
¹⁴For I will be like a lion to Ephraim,
 like a great lion to Judah.
I will tear them to pieces and go away;
 I will carry them off, with no one to rescue them.
¹⁵Then I will go back to my place
 until they admit their guilt.
And they will seek my face;
 in their misery they will earnestly seek me."

Israel Unrepentant

6 "Come, let us return to the Lord.
He has torn us to pieces
 but he will heal us;
he has injured us
 but he will bind up our wounds.
²After two days he will revive us;
 on the third day he will restore us,
 that we may live in his presence.
³Let us acknowledge the Lord;
 let us press on to acknowledge him.
As surely as the sun rises,
 he will appear;
he will come to us like the winter rains,
 like the spring rains that water the earth."

⁴"What can I do with you, Ephraim?
 What can I do with you, Judah?
Your love is like the morning mist,
 like the early dew that disappears.
⁵Therefore I cut you in pieces with my prophets,
 I killed you with the words of my mouth;
 my judgments flashed like lightning upon you.
⁶For I desire mercy, not sacrifice,
 and acknowledgment of God rather than burnt
  offerings.

ᵃ11 The meaning of the Hebrew for this word is uncertain.

⁷Like Adam,ᵃ they have broken the covenant—
  they were unfaithful to me there.
⁸Gilead is a city of wicked men,
  stained with footprints of blood.
⁹As marauders lie in ambush for a man,
  so do bands of priests;
 they murder on the road to Shechem,
  committing shameful crimes.
¹⁰I have seen a horrible thing
  in the house of Israel.
 There Ephraim is given to prostitution
  and Israel is defiled.

¹¹"Also for you, Judah,
  a harvest is appointed.

7

"Whenever I would restore the fortunes of my people,
¹   whenever I would heal Israel,
 the sins of Ephraim are exposed
  and the crimes of Samaria revealed.
 They practice deceit,
   thieves break into houses,
   bandits rob in the streets;
²but they do not realize
   that I remember all their evil deeds.
 Their sins engulf them;
   they are always before me.

³"They delight the king with their wickedness,
   the princes with their lies.
⁴They are all adulterers,
   burning like an oven
 whose fire the baker need not stir
   from the kneading of the dough till it rises.
⁵On the day of the festival of our king
   the princes become inflamed with wine,
   and he joins hands with the mockers.
⁶Their hearts are like an oven;
   they approach him with intrigue.
 Their passion smolders all night;
   in the morning it blazes like a flaming fire.
⁷All of them are hot as an oven;
   they devour their rulers.
 All their kings fall,
   and none of them calls on me.

⁸"Ephraim mixes with the nations;
   Ephraim is a flat cake not turned over.
⁹Foreigners sap his strength,
   but he does not realize it.
 His hair is sprinkled with gray,
   but he does not notice.
¹⁰Israel's arrogance testifies against him,
   but despite all this
 he does not return to the Lᴏʀᴅ his God
   or search for him.

ᵃ7 Or *As at Adam;* or *Like men*

¹¹"Ephraim is like a dove,
    easily deceived and senseless—
  now calling to Egypt,
    now turning to Assyria.
¹²When they go, I will throw my net over them;
    I will pull them down like birds of the air.
  When I hear them flocking together,
    I will catch them.
¹³Woe to them,
    because they have strayed from me!
  Destruction to them,
    because they have rebelled against me!
  I long to redeem them
    but they speak lies against me.
¹⁴They do not cry out to me from their hearts
    but wail upon their beds.
  They gather together[a] for grain and new wine
    but turn away from me.
¹⁵I trained them and strengthened them,
    but they plot evil against me.
¹⁶They do not turn to the Most High;
    they are like a faulty bow.
  Their leaders will fall by the sword
    because of their insolent words.
  For this they will be ridiculed
    in the land of Egypt.

Israel to Reap the Whirlwind

8 "Put the trumpet to your lips!
    An eagle is over the house of the LORD
  because the people have broken my covenant
    and rebelled against my law.
²Israel cries out to me,
    'O our God, we acknowledge you!'
³But Israel has rejected what is good;
    an enemy will pursue him.
⁴They set up kings without my consent;
    they choose princes without my approval.
  With their silver and gold
    they make idols for themselves
    to their own destruction.
⁵Throw out your calf-idol, O Samaria!
    My anger burns against them.
  How long will they be incapable of purity?
⁶ They are from Israel!
  This calf—a craftsman has made it;
    it is not God.
  It will be broken in pieces,
    that calf of Samaria.

⁷"They sow the wind
    and reap the whirlwind.
  The stalk has no head;
    it will produce no flour.

---

[a]14 Most Hebrew manuscripts; some Hebrew manuscripts and Septuagint *They slash themselves*

Were it to yield grain,
   foreigners would swallow it up.
⁸Israel is swallowed up;
   now she is among the nations
   like a worthless thing.
⁹For they have gone up to Assyria
   like a wild donkey wandering alone.
   Ephraim has sold herself to lovers.
¹⁰Although they have sold themselves among the nations,
   I will now gather them together.
They will begin to waste away
   under the oppression of the mighty king.

¹¹"Though Ephraim built many altars for sin offerings,
   these have become altars for sinning.
¹²I wrote for them the many things of my law,
   but they regarded them as something alien.
¹³They offer sacrifices given to me
   and they eat the meat,
   but the LORD is not pleased with them.
Now he will remember their wickedness
   and punish their sins:
   They will return to Egypt.
¹⁴Israel has forgotten his Maker
   and built palaces;
   Judah has fortified many towns.
But I will send fire upon their cities
   that will consume their fortresses."

Punishment for Israel

Do not rejoice, O Israel;
   do not be jubilant like the other nations.
For you have been unfaithful to your God;
   you love the wages of a prostitute
   at every threshing floor.
²Threshing floors and winepresses will not feed the
      people;
   the new wine will fail them.
³They will not remain in the LORD's land;
   Ephraim will return to Egypt
   and eat unclean*ᵃ* food in Assyria.
⁴They will not pour out wine offerings to the LORD,
   nor will their sacrifices please him.
Such sacrifices will be to them like the bread of mourners;
   all who eat them will be unclean.
This food will be for themselves;
   it will not come into the temple of the LORD.

⁵What will you do on the day of your appointed feasts,
   on the festival days of the LORD?
⁶Even if they escape from destruction,
   Egypt will gather them,
   and Memphis will bury them.
Their treasures of silver will be taken over by briers,
   and thorns will overrun their tents.

ᵃ3 That is, ceremonially unclean

⁷The days of punishment are coming,
    the days of reckoning are at hand.
    Let Israel know this.
Because your sins are so many
    and your hostility so great,
the prophet is considered a fool,
    the inspired man a maniac.
⁸The prophet, along with my God,
    is the watchman over Ephraim,^a
yet snares await him on all his paths,
    and hostility in the house of his God.
⁹They have sunk deep into corruption,
    as in the days of Gibeah.
God will remember their wickedness
    and punish them for their sins.

¹⁰"When I found Israel,
    it was like finding grapes in the desert;
when I saw your fathers,
    it was like seeing the early fruit on the fig tree.
But when they came to Baal Peor,
    they consecrated themselves to that shameful idol
    and became as vile as the thing they loved.
¹¹Ephraim's glory will fly away like a bird—
    no birth, no pregnancy, no conception.
¹²Even if they rear children,
    I will bereave them of every one.
Woe to them
    when I turn away from them!
¹³I have seen Ephraim, like Tyre,
    planted in a pleasant place.
But Ephraim will bring out
    their children to the slayer."

¹⁴Give them, O Lord—
    what will you give them?
Give them wombs that miscarry
    and breasts that are dry.

¹⁵"Because of all their wickedness in Gilgal,
    I hated them there.
Because of their sinful deeds,
    I will drive them out of my house.
I will no longer love them;
    all their leaders are rebellious.
¹⁶Ephraim is blighted,
    their root is withered,
    they yield no fruit.
Even if they bear children,
    I will slay their cherished offspring."

¹⁷My God will reject them
    because they have not obeyed him;
    they will be wanderers among the nations.

^a8 Or The prophet is the watchman over Ephraim, / the people of my God

10 Israel was a spreading vine;
　　he brought forth fruit for himself.
As his fruit increased,
　　he built more altars;
as his land prospered,
　　he adorned his sacred stones.
2 Their heart is deceitful,
　　and now they must bear their guilt.
The LORD will demolish their altars
　　and destroy their sacred stones.

3 Then they will say, "We have no king
　　because we did not revere the LORD.
But even if we had a king,
　　what could he do for us?"
4 They make many promises,
　　take false oaths
　　and make agreements;
therefore lawsuits spring up
　　like poisonous weeds in a plowed field.
5 The people who live in Samaria fear
　　for the calf-idol of Beth Aven.*a*
Its people will mourn over it,
　　and so will its idolatrous priests,
those who had rejoiced over its splendor,
　　because it is taken from them into exile.
6 It will be carried to Assyria
　　as tribute for the great king.
Ephraim will be disgraced;
　　Israel will be ashamed of its wooden idols.*b*
7 Samaria and its king will float away
　　like a twig on the surface of the waters.
8 The high places of wickedness*c* will be destroyed—
　　it is the sin of Israel.
Thorns and thistles will grow up
　　and cover their altars.
Then they will say to the mountains, "Cover us!"
　　and to the hills, "Fall on us!"

9 "Since the days of Gibeah, you have sinned, O Israel,
　　and there you have remained.*d*
Did not war overtake
　　the evildoers in Gibeah?
10 When I please, I will punish them;
　　nations will be gathered against them
　　to put them in bonds for their double sin.
11 Ephraim is a trained heifer
　　that loves to thresh;
so I will put a yoke
　　on her fair neck.
I will drive Ephraim,
　　Judah must plow,
　　and Jacob must break up the ground.
12 Sow for yourselves righteousness,
　　reap the fruit of unfailing love,

---

a5 Beth Aven means *house of wickedness* (a name for Bethel, which means *house of God*).　*b6 Or its counsel*
c8 Hebrew aven, a reference to Beth Aven (a derogatory name for Bethel)　*d9 Or there a stand was taken*

and break up your unplowed ground;
    for it is time to seek the LORD,
until he comes
    and showers righteousness on you.
[13] But you have planted wickedness,
    you have reaped evil,
    you have eaten the fruit of deception.
Because you have depended on your own strength
    and on your many warriors,
[14] the roar of battle will rise against your people,
    so that all your fortresses will be devastated—
as Shalman devastated Beth Arbel on the day of battle,
    when mothers were dashed to the ground with their
        children.
[15] Thus will it happen to you, O Bethel,
    because your wickedness is great.
When that day dawns,
    the king of Israel will be completely destroyed.

11

God's Love for Israel

"When Israel was a child, I loved him,
    and out of Egypt I called my son.
[2] But the more I[a] called Israel,
    the further they went from me.[b]
They sacrificed to the Baals
    and they burned incense to images.
[3] It was I who taught Ephraim to walk,
    taking them by the arms;
but they did not realize
    it was I who healed them.
[4] I led them with cords of human kindness,
    with ties of love;
I lifted the yoke from their neck
    and bent down to feed them.

[5] "Will they not return to Egypt
    and will not Assyria rule over them
    because they refuse to repent?
[6] Swords will flash in their cities,
    will destroy the bars of their gates
    and put an end to their plans.
[7] My people are determined to turn from me.
    Even if they call to the Most High,
    he will by no means exalt them.

[8] "How can I give you up, Ephraim?
    How can I hand you over, Israel?
How can I treat you like Admah?
    How can I make you like Zeboiim?
My heart is changed within me;
    all my compassion is aroused.
[9] I will not carry out my fierce anger,
    nor will I turn and devastate Ephraim.
For I am God, and not man—

---

[a] 2 Some Septuagint manuscripts; Hebrew *they* [b] 2 Septuagint; Hebrew *them*

the Holy One among you.
I will not come in wrath.*

¹⁰They will follow the LORD;
he will roar like a lion.
When he roars,
his children will come trembling from the west.
¹¹They will come trembling
like birds from Egypt,
like doves from Assyria.
I will settle them in their homes,"
declares the LORD.

Israel's Sin

¹²Ephraim has surrounded me with lies,
the house of Israel with deceit.
And Judah is unruly against God,
even against the faithful Holy One.
¹Ephraim feeds on the wind;
he pursues the east wind all day
and multiplies lies and violence.
He makes a treaty with Assyria
and sends olive oil to Egypt.
²The LORD has a charge to bring against Judah;
he will punish Jacob*ᵇ* according to his ways
and repay him according to his deeds.
³In the womb he grasped his brother's heel;
as a man he struggled with God.
⁴He struggled with the angel and overcame him;
he wept and begged for his favor.
He found him at Bethel
and talked with him there—
⁵the LORD God Almighty,
the LORD is his name of renown!
⁶But you must return to your God;
maintain love and justice,
and wait for your God always.

⁷The merchant uses dishonest scales;
he loves to defraud.
⁸Ephraim boasts,
"I am very rich; I have become wealthy.
With all my wealth they will not find in me
any iniquity or sin."

⁹"I am the LORD your God,
who brought you out of*ᶜ* Egypt;
I will make you live in tents again,
as in the days of your appointed feasts.
¹⁰I spoke to the prophets,
gave them many visions
and told parables through them."

¹¹Is Gilead wicked?
Its people are worthless!
Do they sacrifice bulls in Gilgal?

ᵃ9 Or come against any city   *ᵇ2 Jacob means he grasps the heel (figuratively, he deceives).*   *ᶜ9 Or God /*
ever since you were in

Their altars will be like piles of stones
    on a plowed field.
¹²Jacob fled to the country of Aram*ᵃ*;
    Israel served to get a wife,
    and to pay for her he tended sheep.
¹³The Lᴏʀᴅ used a prophet to bring Israel up from Egypt,
    by a prophet he cared for him.
¹⁴But Ephraim has bitterly provoked him to anger;
    his Lord will leave upon him the guilt of his bloodshed
    and will repay him for his contempt.

The Lᴏʀᴅ's Anger Against Israel

When Ephraim spoke, men trembled;
    he was exalted in Israel.
    But he became guilty of Baal worship and died.
²Now they sin more and more;
    they make idols for themselves from their silver,
  cleverly fashioned images,
    all of them the work of craftsmen.
  It is said of these people,
    "They offer human sacrifice
    and kissᵇ the calf-idols."
³Therefore they will be like the morning mist,
    like the early dew that disappears,
    like chaff swirling from a threshing floor,
    like smoke escaping through a window.

⁴"But I am the Lᴏʀᴅ your God,
    ‿who brought you‿ out ofᶜ Egypt.
  You shall acknowledge no God but me,
    no Savior except me.
⁵I cared for you in the desert,
    in the land of burning heat.
⁶When I fed them, they were satisfied;
    when they were satisfied, they became proud;
    then they forgot me.
⁷So I will come upon them like a lion,
    like a leopard I will lurk by the path.
⁸Like a bear robbed of her cubs,
    I will attack them and rip them open.
  Like a lion I will devour them;
    a wild animal will tear them apart.

⁹"You are destroyed, O Israel,
    because you are against me, against your helper.
¹⁰Where is your king, that he may save you?
    Where are your rulers in all your towns,
  of whom you said,
    'Give me a king and princes'?
¹¹So in my anger I gave you a king,
    and in my wrath I took him away.
¹²The guilt of Ephraim is stored up,
    his sins are kept on record.
¹³Pains as of a woman in childbirth come to him,
    but he is a child without wisdom;

ᵃ12 That is, Northwest Mesopotamia *ᵇ2* Or *"Men who sacrifice / kiss* *ᶜ4* Or *God / ever since you were in*

when the time arrives,
    he does not come to the opening of the womb.

¹⁴"I will ransom them from the power of the grave^a;
    I will redeem them from death.
Where, O death, are your plagues?
    Where, O grave,^a is your destruction?

"I will have no compassion,
¹⁵   even though he thrives among his
        brothers.
An east wind from the LORD will come,
    blowing in from the desert;
his spring will fail
    and his well dry up.
His storehouse will be plundered
    of all its treasures.
¹⁶The people of Samaria must bear their guilt,
    because they have rebelled against their God.
They will fall by the sword;
    their little ones will be dashed to the ground,
    their pregnant women ripped open."

> I will ransom them from the power of the grave; I will redeem them from death (Hosea 13:14).

14

Repentance to Bring Blessing

Return, O Israel, to the LORD your God.
    Your sins have been your downfall!
²Take words with you
    and return to the LORD.
Say to him:
    "Forgive all our sins
and receive us graciously,
    that we may offer the fruit of our lips.^b
³Assyria cannot save us;
    we will not mount war-horses.
We will never again say 'Our gods'
    to what our own hands have made,
    for in you the fatherless find compassion."

⁴"I will heal their waywardness
    and love them freely,
    for my anger has turned away from them.
⁵I will be like the dew to Israel;
    he will blossom like a lily.
Like a cedar of Lebanon
    he will send down his roots;
⁶   his young shoots will grow.
His splendor will be like an olive tree,
    his fragrance like a cedar of Lebanon.
⁷Men will dwell again in his shade.
    He will flourish like the grain.
He will blossom like a vine,
    and his fame will be like the wine from Lebanon.
⁸O Ephraim, what more have I^c to do with idols?
    I will answer him and care for him.
I am like a green pine tree;
    your fruitfulness comes from me."

---

^a14 Hebrew *Sheol*   ^b2 Or *offer our lips as sacrifices of bulls*   ^c8 Or *What more has Ephraim*

[9] Who is wise? He will realize these things.
    Who is discerning? He will understand them.
The ways of the LORD are right;
    the righteous walk in them,
    but the rebellious stumble in them.

Introduction
to the
book of Joel

DIVINE JUDGMENT.

Is a California earthquake a judgment from God? Is AIDS a divine warning? When something bad happens to you, is God shouting in your ear?

A terrible cloud of locusts destroyed all the vegetation in Palestine. Animals and people were threatened with starvation. Joel saw this as a divine judgment. In the second half of his little book, Joel predicts that at history's end God will send a human army just as great to swarm into Palestine and punish his sinning people. God does punish sin. But in the end God saves.

Fundamentals

What would you do if you knew what happened to you was punishment for sin (Joel 1:13)?

Will it make any difference if you turn to God after doing wrong (Joel 2:18-27)?

FAST FACTS

Locust swarms could be so great they blotted out the sun for hours.

Locusts ate every growing thing, and their larvae ate new plants.

How did Joel know the locusts were God's judgment (Deuteronomy 28:42)?

The day of the Lord usually refers to history's end and terrible judgments (Joel 1:15; 2:1,11,31; 3:14).

1

The word of the LORD that came to Joel son of Pethuel.

An Invasion of Locusts

² Hear this, you elders;
  listen, all who live in the land.
 Has anything like this ever happened in your days
  or in the days of your forefathers?
³ Tell it to your children,
  and let your children tell it to their children,
  and their children to the next generation.
⁴ What the locust swarm has left
  the great locusts have eaten;
 what the great locusts have left
  the young locusts have eaten;
 what the young locusts have left
  other locusts*ᵃ* have eaten.

⁵ Wake up, you drunkards, and weep!
  Wail, all you drinkers of wine;
 wail because of the new wine,
  for it has been snatched from your lips.
⁶ A nation has invaded my land,
  powerful and without number;
 it has the teeth of a lion,
  the fangs of a lioness.
⁷ It has laid waste my vines
  and ruined my fig trees.
 It has stripped off their bark
  and thrown it away,
  leaving their branches white.

⁸ Mourn like a virginᵇ in
   sackcloth
  grieving for the husbandᶜ of
   her youth.
⁹ Grain offerings and drink
   offerings
  are cut off from the house
   of the LORD.
 The priests are in mourning,
  those who minister before
   the LORD.
¹⁰ The fields are ruined,
  the ground is dried upᵈ;
 the grain is destroyed,
  the new wine is dried up,
  the oil fails.
¹¹ Despair, you farmers,
  wail, you vine growers;
 grieve for the wheat and the
   barley,
  because the harvest of the
   field is destroyed.

ᵃ4 The precise meaning of the four Hebrew words used here for locusts is uncertain. ᵇ8 Or *young woman* ᶜ8 Or *betrothed* ᵈ10 Or *ground mourns*

JOEL 1:5–12

Have you ever gotten to a class and been totally surprised that you were having a test that day? Somehow you didn't hear any announcement—five of them, the teacher says!—about a test. When you read the Old Testament prophets you can get sort of tired of hearing the same warnings again and again. If you wonder why there's so much repetition, the answer is simple. These people listened to God's prophets about as carefully as some teens listen to their teachers! Not listening to teachers can mean a bad grade. But Joel 1:5–11 is a reminder that not listening to God means weeping, wailing, mourning, grief and despair.

Direct Line

¹²The vine is dried up
   and the fig tree is withered;
the pomegranate, the palm and the apple tree—
   all the trees of the field—are dried up.
Surely the joy of mankind
   is withered away.

A Call to Repentance

¹³Put on sackcloth, O priests, and mourn;
   wail, you who minister before the altar.
Come, spend the night in sackcloth,
   you who minister before my God;
for the grain offerings and drink offerings
   are withheld from the house of your God.
¹⁴Declare a holy fast;
   call a sacred assembly.
Summon the elders
   and all who live in the land
to the house of the LORD your God,
   and cry out to the LORD.

¹⁵Alas for that day!
   For the day of the LORD is near;
   it will come like destruction from the Almighty.ᵃ

¹⁶Has not the food been cut off
   before our very eyes—
joy and gladness
   from the house of our God?
¹⁷The seeds are shriveled
   beneath the clods.ᵇ
The storehouses are in ruins,
   the granaries have been broken down,
   for the grain has dried up.
¹⁸How the cattle moan!
   The herds mill about
because they have no pasture;
   even the flocks of sheep are suffering.

¹⁹To you, O LORD, I call,
   for fire has devoured the open pastures
   and flames have burned up all the trees of the field.
²⁰Even the wild animals pant for you;
   the streams of water have dried up
   and fire has devoured the open pastures.

An Army of Locusts

2 Blow the trumpet in Zion;
   sound the alarm on my holy hill.
Let all who live in the land tremble,
   for the day of the LORD is coming.
It is close at hand—
²   a day of darkness and gloom,
   a day of clouds and blackness.

ᵃ15 Hebrew *Shaddai*   ᵇ17 The meaning of the Hebrew for this word is uncertain.

Like dawn spreading across the mountains
    a large and mighty army comes,
such as never was of old
    nor ever will be in ages to come.

³Before them fire devours,
    behind them a flame blazes.
Before them the land is like the garden of Eden,
    behind them, a desert waste—
    nothing escapes them.
⁴They have the appearance of horses;
    they gallop along like cavalry.
⁵With a noise like that of chariots
    they leap over the mountaintops,
like a crackling fire consuming stubble,
    like a mighty army drawn up for battle.

⁶At the sight of them, nations are in anguish;
    every face turns pale.
⁷They charge like warriors;
    they scale walls like soldiers.
They all march in line,
    not swerving from their course.
⁸They do not jostle each other;
    each marches straight ahead.
They plunge through defenses
    without breaking ranks.
⁹They rush upon the city;
    they run along the wall.
They climb into the houses;
    like thieves they enter through the windows.

¹⁰Before them the earth shakes,
    the sky trembles,
the sun and moon are
      darkened,
    and the stars no longer
      shine.
¹¹The LORD thunders
    at the head of his army;
his forces are beyond number,
    and mighty are those who
      obey his command.
The day of the LORD is great;
    it is dreadful.
    Who can endure it?

Rend Your Heart

¹²"Even now," declares the LORD,
    "return to me with all your
      heart,
    with fasting and weeping
      and mourning."

¹³Rend your heart
    and not your garments.
Return to the LORD your God,
    for he is gracious and
      compassionate,

JOEL 2:12–27

Sometimes life just doesn't seem like it's worth living. One national survey indicated that about 24 percent of teenage girls consider suicide in any given year. Many attempt suicide. And some succeed. Joel describes some terrors that will drive many in Judah to despair. But he also gives them God's wonderful promise: "Return to me with all your heart . . . I will repay you for the years the locusts have eaten" (Joel 2:12,25). One day you too are likely to be so hurt or disappointed you feel life isn't worth living. But really, it is. Turn to God, and know that he will more than repay your pain with good things in your future.

Direct Line

slow to anger and abounding in love,
   and he relents from sending calamity.
[14]Who knows? He may turn and have pity
   and leave behind a blessing—
grain offerings and drink offerings
   for the LORD your God.

[15]Blow the trumpet in Zion,
   declare a holy fast,
   call a sacred assembly.
[16]Gather the people,
   consecrate the assembly;
bring together the elders,
   gather the children,
   those nursing at the breast.
Let the bridegroom leave his room
   and the bride her chamber.
[17]Let the priests, who minister before the LORD,
   weep between the temple porch and the altar.
Let them say, "Spare your people, O LORD.
   Do not make your inheritance an object of scorn,
   a byword among the nations.
Why should they say among the peoples,
   'Where is their God?' "

The LORD's Answer

[18]Then the LORD will be jealous for his land
   and take pity on his people.

[19]The LORD will reply[a] to them:

"I am sending you grain, new wine and oil,
   enough to satisfy you fully;
never again will I make you
   an object of scorn to the nations.

[20]"I will drive the northern army far from you,
   pushing it into a parched and barren land,
with its front columns going into the eastern sea[b]
   and those in the rear into the western sea.[c]
And its stench will go up;
   its smell will rise."

Surely he has done great things.[d]
[21]   Be not afraid, O land;
   be glad and rejoice.
Surely the LORD has done great things.
[22]   Be not afraid, O wild animals,
   for the open pastures are becoming green.
The trees are bearing their fruit;
   the fig tree and the vine yield their riches.
[23]Be glad, O people of Zion,
   rejoice in the LORD your God,
for he has given you
   the autumn rains in righteousness.[e]

---

[a]18,19 Or LORD was jealous . . . / and took pity . . . / [19]The LORD replied   [b]20 That is, the Dead Sea
[c]20 That is, the Mediterranean   [d]20 Or rise. / Surely it has done great things."   [e]23 Or / the teacher for
righteousness:

He sends you abundant showers,
both autumn and spring rains, as before.
²⁴The threshing floors will be filled with grain;
the vats will overflow with new wine and oil.

²⁵"I will repay you for the years the locusts have eaten—
the great locust and the young locust,
the other locusts and the locust swarm*—
my great army that I sent among you.
²⁶You will have plenty to eat, until you are full,
and you will praise the name of the LORD your God,
who has worked wonders for you;
never again will my people be shamed.
²⁷Then you will know that I am in Israel,
that I am the LORD your God,
and that there is no other;
never again will my people be shamed.

The Day of the LORD

²⁸"And afterward,
I will pour out my Spirit on all people.
Your sons and daughters will prophesy,
your old men will dream dreams,
your young men will see visions.
²⁹Even on my servants, both men and women,
I will pour out my Spirit in those days.
³⁰I will show wonders in the heavens
and on the earth,
blood and fire and billows of smoke.
³¹The sun will be turned to darkness
and the moon to blood
before the coming of the great and dreadful day
of the LORD.
³²And everyone who calls
on the name of the LORD will be saved;
for on Mount Zion and in Jerusalem
there will be deliverance,
as the LORD has said,
among the survivors
whom the LORD calls.

The Nations Judged

3 "In those days and at that time,
when I restore the fortunes of Judah and Jerusalem,
²I will gather all nations
and bring them down to the Valley of Jehoshaphat.*
There I will enter into judgment against them
concerning my inheritance, my people Israel,
for they scattered my people among the nations
and divided up my land.
³They cast lots for my people
and traded boys for prostitutes;
they sold girls for wine
that they might drink.

---

*25 The precise meaning of the four Hebrew words used here for locusts is uncertain.   *2 Jehoshaphat
means *the LORD judges*; also in verse 12.

⁴"Now what have you against me, O Tyre and Sidon and all you regions of Philistia? Are you repaying me for something I have done? If you are paying me back, I will swiftly and speedily return on your own heads what you have done. ⁵For you took my silver and my gold and carried off my finest treasures to your temples. ⁶You sold the people of Judah and Jerusalem to the Greeks, that you might send them far from their homeland.

⁷"See, I am going to rouse them out of the places to which you sold them, and I will return on your own heads what you have done. ⁸I will sell your sons and daughters to the people of Judah, and they will sell them to the Sabeans, a nation far away." The Lord has spoken.

> ⁹Proclaim this among the nations:
> Prepare for war!
> Rouse the warriors!
> Let all the fighting men draw near and attack.
> ¹⁰Beat your plowshares into swords
> and your pruning hooks into spears.
> Let the weakling say,
> "I am strong!"
> ¹¹Come quickly, all you nations from every side,
> and assemble there.
>
> Bring down your warriors, O Lord!
>
> ¹²"Let the nations be roused;
> let them advance into the Valley of Jehoshaphat,
> for there I will sit
> to judge all the nations on every side.
> ¹³Swing the sickle,
> for the harvest is ripe.
> Come, trample the grapes,
> for the winepress is full
> and the vats overflow—
> so great is their wickedness!"
>
> ¹⁴Multitudes, multitudes
> in the valley of decision!
> For the day of the Lord is near
> in the valley of decision.
> ¹⁵The sun and moon will be darkened,
> and the stars no longer shine.
> ¹⁶The Lord will roar from Zion
> and thunder from Jerusalem;
> the earth and the sky will tremble.
> But the Lord will be a refuge for his people,
> a stronghold for the people of Israel.

Blessings for God's People

> ¹⁷"Then you will know that I, the Lord your God,
> dwell in Zion, my holy hill.
> Jerusalem will be holy;
> never again will foreigners invade her.
>
> ¹⁸"In that day the mountains will drip new wine,
> and the hills will flow with milk;
> all the ravines of Judah will run with water.
> A fountain will flow out of the Lord's house
> and will water the valley of acacias.ᵃ

ᵃ18 Or Valley of Shittim

¹⁹But Egypt will be desolate,
    Edom a desert waste,
  because of violence done to the people of Judah,
    in whose land they shed innocent blood.
²⁰Judah will be inhabited forever
    and Jerusalem through all generations.
²¹Their bloodguilt, which I have not pardoned,
    I will pardon."

The Lord dwells in Zion!

TIRED?

Do you get tired of food drives at school and at church? Do you sometimes wish those people would stop complaining about being poor? Why don't they go out and get a job? But isn't that kind of a selfish attitude? If you've got it so good, why shouldn't you share with those who don't?

The prophet Amos lived in Israel in a time of prosperity. Yet the rich cared more about their luxuries than about people. Amos warned that any society that isn't fair to poor people will be judged. Christians should be generous and should fight for justice for the poor and for opportunities for the poor to get an education and a job.

Fundamentals

Can you find anything like this in today's newspapers (Amos 2:6-8)?

If God loves you, will he ever let bad things happen to you (Amos 4:6-12)?

Are you looking forward to Jesus' return? Who do you suppose isn't (Amos 5:18-27)?

FAST FACTS

Amos means "burden bearer."

Israel was rich and powerful in Amos's day.

Amos 5:14-15 is this book's key passage.

Religion was popular with the rich. Many had second homes at the worship centers in Bethel and Dan.

When doesn't God accept worship (Amos 5:23-24)?

1 The words of Amos, one of the shepherds of Tekoa—what he saw concerning Israel two years before the earthquake, when Uzziah was king of Judah and Jeroboam son of Jehoash*a* was king of Israel. ²He said:

> "The LORD roars from Zion
> and thunders from Jerusalem;
> the pastures of the shepherds dry up,*b*
> and the top of Carmel withers."

Judgment on Israel's Neighbors ³This is what the LORD says:

> "For three sins of Damascus,
> even for four, I will not turn back ͺmy wrathͺ.
> Because she threshed Gilead
> with sledges having iron teeth,
> ⁴I will send fire upon the house of Hazael
> that will consume the fortresses of Ben-Hadad.
> ⁵I will break down the gate of Damascus;
> I will destroy the king who is in*c* the Valley of Aven*d*
> and the one who holds the scepter in Beth Eden.
> The people of Aram will go into exile to Kir,"
>
> > says the LORD.

⁶This is what the LORD says:

> "For three sins of Gaza,
> even for four, I will not turn back ͺmy wrathͺ.
> Because she took captive whole communities
> and sold them to Edom,
> ⁷I will send fire upon the walls of Gaza
> that will consume her fortresses.
> ⁸I will destroy the king*e* of Ashdod
> and the one who holds the scepter in Ashkelon.
> I will turn my hand against Ekron,
> till the last of the Philistines is dead,"
>
> > says the Sovereign LORD.

⁹This is what the LORD says:

> "For three sins of Tyre,
> even for four, I will not turn back ͺmy wrathͺ.
> Because she sold whole communities of captives to Edom,
> disregarding a treaty of brotherhood,
> ¹⁰I will send fire upon the walls of Tyre
> that will consume her fortresses."

¹¹This is what the LORD says:

> "For three sins of Edom,
> even for four, I will not turn back ͺmy wrathͺ.
> Because he pursued his brother with a sword,
> stifling all compassion,*f*
> because his anger raged continually
> and his fury flamed unchecked,
> ¹²I will send fire upon Teman
> that will consume the fortresses of Bozrah."

---

a1 Hebrew *Joash*, a variant of *Jehoash* *b2* Or *shepherds mourn* *c5* Or *the inhabitants of* *d5 Aven* means *wickedness.* *e8* Or *inhabitants* *f11* Or *sword / and destroyed his allies*

¹³This is what the Lord says:

"For three sins of Ammon,
        even for four, I will not turn back ˎmy wrathˎ.
Because he ripped open the pregnant women of Gilead
        in order to extend his borders,
¹⁴I will set fire to the walls of Rabbah
        that will consume her fortresses
amid war cries on the day of battle,
        amid violent winds on a stormy day.
¹⁵Her king*ᵃ* will go into exile,
        he and his officials together,"

says the Lord.

This is what the Lord says:

"For three sins of Moab,
        even for four, I will not turn back ˎmy wrathˎ.
Because he burned, as if to lime,
        the bones of Edom's king,
²I will send fire upon Moab
        that will consume the fortresses of Kerioth.*ᵇ*
Moab will go down in great tumult
        amid war cries and the blast of the trumpet.
³I will destroy her ruler
        and kill all her officials with him,"

says the Lord.

⁴This is what the Lord says:

"For three sins of Judah,
        even for four, I will not turn back ˎmy wrathˎ.
Because they have rejected the law of the Lord
        and have not kept his decrees,
because they have been led astray by false gods,*ᶜ*
        the gods*ᵈ* their ancestors followed,

ᵃ15 Or / Molech; Hebrew malcam   ᵇ2 Or of her cities   ᶜ4 Or by lies   ᵈ4 Or lies

The Bible Says

Change

Were Bible times so different from today? Here's one way to check. Read today's newspaper, then read Amos 2:6–8. Were the events of Amos's day anything like the events recorded in today's newspapers?

Every generation thinks things are different for them. It's true that your world is different from the world in which your parents grew up. But one thing never changes—the fact that you must make a choice. You can choose to live God's way, even though it may be hard sometimes. Or you can choose to be greedy and sinful, to hurt rather than help others. Oh, and remember: God hasn't changed either. He loves you—but he will surely punish those who choose to do wrong.

⁵I will send fire upon Judah
    that will consume the fortresses of Jerusalem."

Judgment on Israel ⁶This is what the LORD says:

"For three sins of Israel,
    even for four, I will not turn back ؛my wrath؛.
They sell the righteous for silver,
    and the needy for a pair of sandals.
⁷They trample on the heads of the poor
    as upon the dust of the ground
    and deny justice to the oppressed.
Father and son use the same girl
    and so profane my holy name.
⁸They lie down beside every altar
    on garments taken in pledge.
In the house of their god
    they drink wine taken as fines.

⁹"I destroyed the Amorite before them,
    though he was tall as the cedars
    and strong as the oaks.
I destroyed his fruit above
    and his roots below.

¹⁰"I brought you up out of Egypt,
    and I led you forty years in the desert
    to give you the land of the Amorites.
¹¹I also raised up prophets from among your sons
    and Nazirites from among your young men.
Is this not true, people of Israel?"
                          declares the LORD.
¹²"But you made the Nazirites drink wine
    and commanded the prophets not to prophesy.

¹³"Now then, I will crush you
    as a cart crushes when loaded with grain.
¹⁴The swift will not escape,
    the strong will not muster their strength,
    and the warrior will not save his life.
¹⁵The archer will not stand his ground,
    the fleet-footed soldier will not get away,
    and the horseman will not save his life.
¹⁶Even the bravest warriors
    will flee naked on that day,"
                          declares the LORD.

3 *Witnesses Summoned Against Israel* Hear this word the LORD has spoken against you, O people of Israel—against the whole family I brought up out of Egypt:

²"You only have I chosen
    of all the families of the earth;
therefore I will punish you
    for all your sins."

³Do two walk together
    unless they have agreed to do so?
⁴Does a lion roar in the thicket
    when he has no prey?

Does he growl in his den
  when he has caught nothing?
⁵Does a bird fall into a trap on the ground
  where no snare has been set?
Does a trap spring up from the earth
  when there is nothing to catch?
⁶When a trumpet sounds in a city,
  do not the people tremble?
When disaster comes to a city,
  has not the LORD caused it?

⁷Surely the Sovereign LORD does nothing
  without revealing his plan
  to his servants the prophets.

⁸The lion has roared—
  who will not fear?
The Sovereign LORD has spoken—
  who can but prophesy?

⁹Proclaim to the fortresses of Ashdod
  and to the fortresses of Egypt:
"Assemble yourselves on the mountains of Samaria;
  see the great unrest within her
  and the oppression among her people."

¹⁰"They do not know how to do right," declares the LORD,
  "who hoard plunder and loot in their fortresses."

¹¹Therefore this is what the Sovereign LORD says:

"An enemy will overrun the land;
  he will pull down your strongholds
  and plunder your fortresses."

¹²This is what the LORD says:

"As a shepherd saves from the lion's mouth
  only two leg bones or a piece of an ear,
  so will the Israelites be saved,
those who sit in Samaria
  on the edge of their beds
  and in Damascus on their couches.ᵃ"

¹³"Hear this and testify against the house of Jacob," declares the Lord, the LORD God Almighty.

¹⁴"On the day I punish Israel for her sins,
  I will destroy the altars of Bethel;
the horns of the altar will be cut off
  and fall to the ground.
¹⁵I will tear down the winter house
  along with the summer house;
the houses adorned with ivory will be destroyed
  and the mansions will be demolished,"
                                  declares the LORD.

Israel Has Not Returned to God

Hear this word, you cows of Bashan on Mount Samaria,
  you women who oppress the poor and crush the needy
  and say to your husbands, "Bring us some drinks!"

ᵃ12 The meaning of the Hebrew for this line is uncertain.

² The Sovereign Lᴏʀᴅ has sworn by his holiness:
  "The time will surely come
 when you will be taken away with hooks,
  the last of you with fishhooks.
³ You will each go straight out
  through breaks in the wall,
  and you will be cast out toward Harmon,ᵃ"
                    declares the Lᴏʀᴅ.

⁴ "Go to Bethel and sin;
  go to Gilgal and sin yet more.
 Bring your sacrifices every morning,
  your tithes every three years.ᵇ
⁵ Burn leavened bread as a thank offering
  and brag about your freewill offerings—
 boast about them, you Israelites,
  for this is what you love to do,"
               declares the Sovereign Lᴏʀᴅ.

⁶ "I gave you empty stomachsᶜ in every city
  and lack of bread in every town,
  yet you have not returned to me,"
                    declares the Lᴏʀᴅ.

AMOS 4

**Q: What did
Amos call
some of the
women of
Israel?**

*BONUS: Why
did he call
them this?*

**Answers on
page 1188**

⁷ "I also withheld rain from you
  when the harvest was still three
    months away.
 I sent rain on one town,
  but withheld it from another.
 One field had rain;
  another had none and dried up.
⁸ People staggered from town to town for water
  but did not get enough to drink,
  yet you have not returned to me,"
                    declares the Lᴏʀᴅ.

⁹ "Many times I struck your gardens and vineyards,
  I struck them with blight and mildew.
 Locusts devoured your fig and olive trees,
  yet you have not returned to me,"
                    declares the Lᴏʀᴅ.

¹⁰ "I sent plagues among you
  as I did to Egypt.
 I killed your young men with the sword,
  along with your captured horses.
 I filled your nostrils with the stench of your camps,
  yet you have not returned to me,"
                    declares the Lᴏʀᴅ.

¹¹ "I overthrew some of you
  as Iᵈ overthrew Sodom and Gomorrah.
 You were like a burning stick snatched from the fire,
  yet you have not returned to me,"
                    declares the Lᴏʀᴅ.

¹² "Therefore this is what I will do to you, Israel,
  and because I will do this to you,
  prepare to meet your God, O Israel."

---

*ᵃ3 Masoretic Text; with a different word division of the Hebrew (see Septuagint) out, O mountain of
oppression   ᵇ4 Or tithes on the third day   ᶜ6 Hebrew you cleanness of teeth   ᵈ11 Hebrew God*

¹³He who forms the mountains,
 creates the wind,
 and reveals his thoughts to man,
he who turns dawn to darkness,
 and treads the high places of the earth—
 the Lord God Almighty is his name.

5 *A Lament and Call to Repentance*   Hear this word, O house of Israel,
this lament I take up concerning you:

² "Fallen is Virgin Israel,
 never to rise again,
deserted in her own land,
 with no one to lift her up."

³This is what the Sovereign Lord says:

"The city that marches out a thousand strong for Israel
 will have only a hundred left;
the town that marches out a hundred strong
 will have only ten left."

⁴This is what the Lord says to the house of Israel:

"Seek me and live;
⁵   do not seek Bethel,
do not go to Gilgal,
 do not journey to Beersheba.
For Gilgal will surely go into exile,
 and Bethel will be reduced to nothing.ᵃ"
⁶Seek the Lord and live,
 or he will sweep through the house of Joseph like a fire;
it will devour,
 and Bethel will have no one to quench it.

⁷You who turn justice into bitterness
 and cast righteousness to the ground
⁸(he who made the Pleiades and Orion,
 who turns blackness into dawn
 and darkens day into night,
who calls for the waters of the sea
 and pours them out over the face of the land—
 the Lord is his name—
⁹he flashes destruction on the stronghold
 and brings the fortified city to ruin),
¹⁰you hate the one who reproves in court
 and despise him who tells the truth.

¹¹You trample on the poor
 and force him to give you grain.
Therefore, though you have built stone mansions,
 you will not live in them;
though you have planted lush vineyards,
 you will not drink their wine.
¹²For I know how many are your offenses
 and how great your sins.

You oppress the righteous and take bribes
 and you deprive the poor of justice in the courts.

Answers

*to Quizzer on
page 1187*

A: Cows
(Amos 4:1)!

**BONUS: Because
they were selfish
and pampered,
and they wanted
their husbands to
take advantage
of the poor in
order to support
their own lavish
lifestyles.**

ᵃ5 Or *grief;* or *wickedness;* Hebrew *aven,* a reference to Beth Aven (a derogatory name for Bethel)

¹³Therefore the prudent man keeps quiet in such times,
    for the times are evil.

¹⁴Seek good, not evil,
    that you may live.
Then the Lᴏʀᴅ God Almighty will be with you,
    just as you say he is.
¹⁵Hate evil, love good;
    maintain justice in the courts.
Perhaps the Lᴏʀᴅ God Almighty will have mercy
    on the remnant of Joseph.

¹⁶Therefore this is what the Lord, the Lᴏʀᴅ God Almighty, says:

"There will be wailing in all the streets
    and cries of anguish in every public square.
The farmers will be summoned to weep
    and the mourners to wail.
¹⁷There will be wailing in all the vineyards,
    for I will pass through your midst,"
                                says the Lᴏʀᴅ.

The Day of the Lᴏʀᴅ

¹⁸Woe to you who long
    for the day of the Lᴏʀᴅ!
Why do you long for the day of the Lᴏʀᴅ?
    That day will be darkness, not light.
¹⁹It will be as though a man fled from a lion
    only to meet a bear,
as though he entered his house
    and rested his hand on the wall
    only to have a snake bite him.
²⁰Will not the day of the Lᴏʀᴅ be darkness, not light—
    pitch-dark, without a ray of brightness?

²¹"I hate, I despise your religious feasts;
    I cannot stand your assemblies.
²²Even though you bring me burnt offerings and grain offerings,
    I will not accept them.
Though you bring choice fellowship offerings,ᵃ
    I will have no regard for them.
²³Away with the noise of your songs!
    I will not listen to the music of your harps.
²⁴But let justice roll on like a river,
    righteousness like a never-failing stream!

²⁵"Did you bring me sacrifices and offerings
    forty years in the desert, O house of Israel?
²⁶You have lifted up the shrine of your king,
    the pedestal of your idols,
    the star of your godᵇ—
    which you made for yourselves.
²⁷Therefore I will send you into exile beyond Damascus,"
    says the Lᴏʀᴅ, whose name is God Almighty.

Woe to the Complacent

6 Woe to you who are complacent in Zion,
    and to you who feel secure on Mount Samaria,

ᵃ22 Traditionally *peace offerings* ᵇ26 Or *lifted up Sakkuth your king / and Kaiwan your idols, / your star-gods*; Septuagint *lifted up the shrine of Molech / and the star of your god Rephan, / their idols*

you notable men of the foremost nation,
to whom the people of Israel come!
²Go to Calneh and look at it;
go from there to great Hamath,
and then go down to Gath in Philistia.
Are they better off than your two kingdoms?
Is their land larger than yours?
³You put off the evil day
and bring near a reign of terror.
⁴You lie on beds inlaid with ivory
and lounge on your couches.
You dine on choice lambs
and fattened calves.
⁵You strum away on your harps like David
and improvise on musical instruments.
⁶You drink wine by the bowlful
and use the finest lotions,
but you do not grieve over the ruin of Joseph.
⁷Therefore you will be among the first to go into exile;
your feasting and lounging will end.

The LORD Abhors the Pride of Israel   ⁸The Sovereign LORD has sworn by himself—the LORD God Almighty declares:

"I abhor the pride of Jacob
and detest his fortresses;
I will deliver up the city
and everything in it."

⁹If ten men are left in one house, they too will die. ¹⁰And if a relative who is to burn the bodies comes to carry them out of the house and asks anyone still hiding there, "Is anyone with you?" and he says, "No," then he will say, "Hush! We must not mention the name of the LORD."

¹¹For the LORD has given the command,
and he will smash the great house into pieces
and the small house into bits.

¹²Do horses run on the rocky crags?
Does one plow there with oxen?
But you have turned justice into poison
and the fruit of righteousness into bitterness—
¹³you who rejoice in the conquest of Lo Debar*ᵃ*
and say, "Did we not take Karnaim*ᵇ* by our own strength?"

¹⁴For the LORD God Almighty declares,
"I will stir up a nation against you, O house of Israel,
that will oppress you all the way
from Lebo*ᶜ* Hamath to the valley of the Arabah."

Locusts, Fire and a Plumb Line   This is what the Sovereign LORD showed me: He was preparing swarms of locusts after the king's share had been harvested and just as the second crop was coming up. ²When they had stripped the land clean, I cried out, "Sovereign LORD, forgive! How can Jacob survive? He is so small!"

³So the LORD relented.

"This will not happen," the LORD said.

⁴This is what the Sovereign LORD showed me: The Sovereign LORD was call-

---

ᵃ13 Lo Debar means nothing.   ᵇ13 Karnaim means horns; horn here symbolizes strength.   ᶜ14 Or from the entrance to

ing for judgment by fire; it dried up the great deep and devoured the land. ⁵Then I cried out, "Sovereign LORD, I beg you, stop! How can Jacob survive? He is so small!"

⁶So the LORD relented.

"This will not happen either," the Sovereign LORD said.

⁷This is what he showed me: The Lord was standing by a wall that had been built true to plumb, with a plumb line in his hand. ⁸And the LORD asked me, "What do you see, Amos?"

"A plumb line," I replied.

Then the Lord said, "Look, I am setting a plumb line among my people Israel; I will spare them no longer.

⁹"The high places of Isaac will be destroyed
　　and the sanctuaries of Israel will be ruined;
　　with my sword I will rise against the house of Jeroboam."

Amos and Amaziah　¹⁰Then Amaziah the priest of Bethel sent a message to Jeroboam king of Israel: "Amos is raising a conspiracy against you in the very heart of Israel. The land cannot bear all his words. ¹¹For this is what Amos is saying:

" 'Jeroboam will die by the sword,
　　and Israel will surely go into exile,
　　away from their native land.' "

¹²Then Amaziah said to Amos, "Get out, you seer! Go back to the land of Judah. Earn your bread there and do your prophesying there. ¹³Don't prophesy anymore at Bethel, because this is the king's sanctuary and the temple of the kingdom."

¹⁴Amos answered Amaziah, "I was neither a prophet nor a prophet's son, but I was a shepherd, and I also took care of sycamore-fig trees. ¹⁵But the LORD took me from tending the flock and said to me, 'Go, prophesy to my people Israel.' ¹⁶Now then, hear the word of the LORD. You say,

" 'Do not prophesy against Israel,
　　and stop preaching against
　　　the house of Isaac.'

¹⁷"Therefore this is what the LORD says:

" 'Your wife will become a
　　　prostitute in the city,
　　and your sons and daughters
　　　will fall by the sword.
Your land will be measured and
　　　divided up,
　　and you yourself will die in a
　　　pagan*ᵃ* country.
And Israel will certainly go into
　　　exile,
　　away from their native land.' "

A Basket of Ripe Fruit　This is what the Sovereign LORD showed me: a basket of ripe fruit. ²"What do you see, Amos?" he asked.

"A basket of ripe fruit," I answered.

Then the LORD said to me, "The time is ripe for my people Israel; I will spare them no longer.

ᵃ17 Hebrew an unclean

Doesn't matter how dark it gets. I won't be seen without my shades.

SEE AMOS 8:9

³"In that day," declares the Sovereign Lord, "the songs in the temple will turn to wailing.ᵃ Many, many bodies—flung everywhere! Silence!"

⁴Hear this, you who trample the needy
and do away with the poor of the land,

⁵saying,

"When will the New Moon be over
that we may sell grain,
and the Sabbath be ended
that we may market wheat?"—
skimping the measure,
boosting the price
and cheating with dishonest scales,
⁶buying the poor with silver
and the needy for a pair of sandals,
selling even the sweepings with the wheat.

⁷The Lord has sworn by the Pride of Jacob: "I will never forget anything they have done.

⁸"Will not the land tremble for this,
and all who live in it mourn?
The whole land will rise like the Nile;
it will be stirred up and then sink
like the river of Egypt.

⁹"In that day," declares the Sovereign Lord,

"I will make the sun go down at noon
and darken the earth in broad daylight.
¹⁰I will turn your religious feasts into mourning
and all your singing into weeping.
I will make all of you wear sackcloth
and shave your heads.
I will make that time like mourning for an only son
and the end of it like a bitter day.

¹¹"The days are coming," declares the Sovereign Lord,
"when I will send a famine through the land—
not a famine of food or a thirst for water,
but a famine of hearing the words of the Lord.
¹²Men will stagger from sea to sea
and wander from north to east,
searching for the word of the Lord,
but they will not find it.

¹³"In that day

"the lovely young women and strong young men
will faint because of thirst.
¹⁴They who swear by the shameᵇ of Samaria,
or say, 'As surely as your god lives, O Dan,'
or, 'As surely as the godᶜ of Beersheba lives'—
they will fall,
never to rise again."

ᵃ3 Or "the temple singers will wail   ᵇ14 Or by Ashima; or by the idol   ᶜ14 Or power

9 *Israel to Be Destroyed* I saw the Lord standing by the altar, and he said:

> "Strike the tops of the pillars
>   so that the thresholds shake.
> Bring them down on the heads of all the people;
>   those who are left I will kill with the sword.
> Not one will get away,
>   none will escape.
> ² Though they dig down to the depths of the grave,ᵃ
>   from there my hand will take them.
> Though they climb up to the heavens,
>   from there I will bring them down.
> ³ Though they hide themselves on the top of Carmel,
>   there I will hunt them down and seize them.
> Though they hide from me at the bottom of the sea,
>   there I will command the serpent to bite them.
> ⁴ Though they are driven into exile by their enemies,
>   there I will command the sword to slay them.
> I will fix my eyes upon them
>   for evil and not for good."

> ⁵ The Lord, the Lᴏʀᴅ Almighty,
>   he who touches the earth and it melts,
>   and all who live in it mourn—
> the whole land rises like the Nile,
>   then sinks like the river of Egypt—
> ⁶ he who builds his lofty palaceᵇ in the heavens
>   and sets its foundationᶜ on the earth,
> who calls for the waters of the sea
>   and pours them out over the face of the land—
>   the Lᴏʀᴅ is his name.

> ⁷ "Are not you Israelites
>   the same to me as the Cushitesᵈ?"

declares the Lᴏʀᴅ.

> "Did I not bring Israel up from Egypt,
>   the Philistines from Caphtorᵉ
>   and the Arameans from Kir?

> ⁸ "Surely the eyes of the Sovereign Lᴏʀᴅ
>   are on the sinful kingdom.
> I will destroy it
>   from the face of the earth—
> yet I will not totally destroy
>   the house of Jacob,"

declares the Lᴏʀᴅ.

> ⁹ "For I will give the command,
>   and I will shake the house of Israel
>   among all the nations
> as grain is shaken in a sieve,
>   and not a pebble will reach the ground.
> ¹⁰ All the sinners among my people
>   will die by the sword,
> all those who say,
>   'Disaster will not overtake or meet us.'

ᵃ*2* Hebrew *to Sheol*   ᵇ*6* The meaning of the Hebrew for this phrase is uncertain.   ᶜ*6* The meaning of the Hebrew for this word is uncertain.   ᵈ*7* That is, people from the upper Nile region   ᵉ*7* That is, Crete

Israel's Restoration

¹¹"In that day I will restore
David's fallen tent.
I will repair its broken places,
restore its ruins,
and build it as it used to be,
¹²so that they may possess the remnant of Edom
and all the nations that bear my name,^a"
declares the Lord, who will do these things.

¹³"The days are coming," declares the Lord,

"when the reaper will be overtaken by the plowman
and the planter by the one treading grapes.
New wine will drip from the mountains
and flow from all the hills.
¹⁴I will bring back my exiled^b people Israel;
they will rebuild the ruined cities and live in them.
They will plant vineyards and drink their wine;
they will make gardens and eat their fruit.
¹⁵I will plant Israel in their own land,
never again to be uprooted
from the land I have given them,"

says the Lord your God.

---

^a12 Hebrew; Septuagint *so that the remnant of men / and all the nations that bear my name may seek the Lord;*   ^b14 Or *will restore the fortunes of my*

GETTING EVEN.

Have you ever wanted to get even with someone who has hurt you? Is it kind of fun to plot revenge—like trashing his locker or stealing her sweater? You have to do something or that person will get away with what he or she did, right?

Obadiah's one-chapter prophecy expresses God's anger with Edom, an enemy of his people. Obadiah promises that the Edomites will be punished by God. You don't have to worry about revenge. God is the judge of his universe, and he'll handle those who hurt his people.

Fundamentals

Are you responsible if you stand by and let someone else be hurt (Obadiah 10–11)?

Do people get away with doing harm to others (Obadiah 15)?

FAST FACTS

Obadiah means "servant of the Lord."

No one knows when this book was written.

The Edomites took part in at least three attacks on Jerusalem.

The Edomites disappeared as a people after A.D. 70.

King Herod the Great, who tried to kill Jesus, was an Idumean (Edomite).

¹The vision of Obadiah.

This is what the Sovereign Lord says about Edom—

> We have heard a message from the Lord:
> An envoy was sent to the nations to say,
> "Rise, and let us go against her for battle"—

² "See, I will make you small among the nations;
   you will be utterly despised.
³ The pride of your heart has deceived you,
   you who live in the clefts of the rocks*ᵃ*
   and make your home on the heights,
 you who say to yourself,
   'Who can bring me down to the ground?'
⁴ Though you soar like the eagle
   and make your nest among the stars,
   from there I will bring you down,"

declares the Lord.

⁵ "If thieves came to you,
   if robbers in the night—
 Oh, what a disaster awaits you—
   would they not steal only as much as they wanted?
 If grape pickers came to you,
   would they not leave a few grapes?
⁶ But how Esau will be ransacked,
   his hidden treasures pillaged!
⁷ All your allies will force you to the border;
   your friends will deceive and overpower you;
 those who eat your bread will set a trap for you,*ᵇ*
   but you will not detect it.

⁸ "In that day," declares the Lord,
   "will I not destroy the wise men of Edom,
   men of understanding in the mountains of Esau?
⁹ Your warriors, O Teman, will be terrified,
   and everyone in Esau's mountains
   will be cut down in the slaughter.
¹⁰ Because of the violence against your brother Jacob,
   you will be covered with shame;
   you will be destroyed forever.
¹¹ On the day you stood aloof
   while strangers carried off his wealth
 and foreigners entered his gates
   and cast lots for Jerusalem,
   you were like one of them.
¹² You should not look down on your brother
   in the day of his misfortune,
 nor rejoice over the people of Judah
   in the day of their destruction,
 nor boast so much
   in the day of their trouble.
¹³ You should not march through the gates of my people
   in the day of their disaster,
 nor look down on them in their calamity
   in the day of their disaster,

ᵃ3 Or of Sela ᵇ7 The meaning of the Hebrew for this clause is uncertain.

nor seize their wealth
   in the day of their disaster.
¹⁴You should not wait at the crossroads
   to cut down their fugitives,
nor hand over their survivors
   in the day of their trouble.

¹⁵"The day of the Lord is near
   for all nations.
As you have done, it will be done to you;
   your deeds will return upon your own head.
¹⁶Just as you drank on my holy hill,
   so all the nations will drink continually;
they will drink and drink
   and be as if they had never been.
¹⁷But on Mount Zion will be deliverance;
   it will be holy,
and the house of Jacob
   will possess its inheritance.
¹⁸The house of Jacob will be a fire
   and the house of Joseph a flame;
the house of Esau will be stubble,
   and they will set it on fire and consume it.
There will be no survivors
   from the house of Esau."

                                The Lord has spoken.

¹⁹People from the Negev will occupy
   the mountains of Esau,
and people from the foothills will possess
   the land of the Philistines.
They will occupy the fields of Ephraim and Samaria,
   and Benjamin will possess Gilead.
²⁰This company of Israelite exiles who are in Canaan
   will possess the land as far as Zarephath;
the exiles from Jerusalem who are in Sepharad
   will possess the towns of the Negev.
²¹Deliverers will go up on*ᵃ* Mount Zion
   to govern the mountains of Esau.
   And the kingdom will be the Lord's.

ᵃ21 Or from

MISTAKES.

We all make them. But does one mistake mean your life is ruined? Or does God give you another chance? Some bad decisions have lifelong consequences. Someone who drinks, drives and has an accident may well end up crippled. But God forgives and often gives another chance.

Jonah made a bad decision. When God told him to go north to Nineveh, Jonah took a ship going south and ended up in the stomach of a great fish! But did you notice that instead of punishing his prophet, God gave Jonah another chance to obey? This time Jonah did obey, and the people of Nineveh listened to God's warning.

Fun
damentals

Can you be a good influence on others when you're out of step with God (Jonah 1)?

What's the best thing to do when God gives you another chance (Jonah 2)?

Have you ever been upset because God has been good to someone else (Jonah 4)?

FAST FACTS

Nineveh was the capital of Assyria, Israel's enemy.

Jonah was sent to Nineveh about 785 B.C.

In 720 B.C. Assyria invaded and crushed Israel.

Jonah 4:2 is this book's key verse.

1 *Jonah Flees From the Lord* The word of the Lord came to Jonah son of Amittai: ²"Go to the great city of Nineveh and preach against it, because its wickedness has come up before me."

³But Jonah ran away from the Lord and headed for Tarshish. He went down to Joppa, where he found a ship bound for that port. After paying the fare, he went aboard and sailed for Tarshish to flee from the Lord.

⁴Then the Lord sent a great wind on the sea, and such a violent storm arose that the ship threatened to break up. ⁵All the sailors were afraid and each cried out to his own god. And they threw the cargo into the sea to lighten the ship.

But Jonah had gone below deck, where he lay down and fell into a deep sleep. ⁶The captain went to him and said, "How can you sleep? Get up and call on your god! Maybe he will take notice of us, and we will not perish."

⁷Then the sailors said to each other, "Come, let us cast lots to find out who is responsible for this calamity." They cast lots and the lot fell on Jonah.

⁸So they asked him, "Tell us, who is responsible for making all this trouble for us? What do you do? Where do you come from? What is your country? From what people are you?"

⁹He answered, "I am a Hebrew and I worship the Lord, the God of heaven, who made the sea and the land."

¹⁰This terrified them and they asked, "What have you done?" (They knew he was running away from the Lord, because he had already told them so.)

¹¹The sea was getting rougher and rougher. So they asked him, "What should we do to you to make the sea calm down for us?"

¹²"Pick me up and throw me into the sea," he replied, "and it will become calm. I know that it is my fault that this great storm has come upon you."

¹³Instead, the men did their best to row back to land. But they could not, for the sea grew even wilder than before. ¹⁴Then they cried to the Lord, "O Lord, please do not let us die for taking this man's life. Do not hold us accountable for killing an innocent man, for you, O Lord, have done as you pleased." ¹⁵Then they took Jonah and threw him overboard, and the raging sea grew calm. ¹⁶At this the men greatly feared the Lord, and they offered a sacrifice to the Lord and made vows to him.

¹⁷But the Lord provided a great fish to swallow Jonah, and Jonah was inside the fish three days and three nights.

2 *Jonah's Prayer* From inside the fish Jonah prayed to the Lord his God. ²He said:

"In my distress I called to the
  Lord,
  and he answered me.
From the depths of the grave*a* I
    called for help,
  and you listened to my cry.
³You hurled me into the deep,
  into the very heart of the
    seas,
  and the currents swirled
    about me;
all your waves and breakers
    swept over me.
⁴I said, 'I have been banished
    from your sight;

a2 Hebrew Sheol

JONAH 1:16

Have you ever felt like you have so many faults yourself you just can't talk to anyone else about God? Take a look at Jonah. He ran away, deliberately disobeying God's command to go preach in Nineveh. When God sent a great storm, Jonah said it was his fault, because he was running away. As a result of Jonah's words and the great storm, all the sailors believed in the Lord and began to worship him. You don't have to be perfect to reach others for the Lord. God can even use people like Jonah, who are running away from him.

Direct Line

yet I will look again
  toward your holy temple.'
⁵The engulfing waters threatened me,ᵃ
  the deep surrounded me;
  seaweed was wrapped around my head.
⁶To the roots of the mountains I sank down;
  the earth beneath barred me in forever.
But you brought my life up from the pit,
  O Lᴏʀᴅ my God.

⁷"When my life was ebbing away,
  I remembered you, Lᴏʀᴅ,
and my prayer rose to you,
  to your holy temple.

⁸"Those who cling to worthless idols
  forfeit the grace that could be theirs.
⁹But I, with a song of thanksgiving,
  will sacrifice to you.
What I have vowed I will make good.
  Salvation comes from the Lᴏʀᴅ."

¹⁰And the Lᴏʀᴅ commanded the fish, and it vomited Jonah onto dry land.

Jonah Goes to Nineveh Then the word of the Lᴏʀᴅ came to Jonah a second time: ²"Go to the great city of Nineveh and proclaim to it the message I give you."

³Jonah obeyed the word of the Lᴏʀᴅ and went to Nineveh. Now Nineveh was a very important city—a visit required three days. ⁴On the first day, Jonah started into the city. He proclaimed: "Forty more days and Nineveh will be overturned." ⁵The Ninevites believed God. They declared a fast, and all of them, from the greatest to the least, put on sackcloth.

⁶When the news reached the king of Nineveh, he rose from his throne, took off his royal robes, covered himself with sackcloth and sat down in the dust. ⁷Then he issued a proclamation in Nineveh:

"By the decree of the king and his nobles:

Do not let any man or beast, herd or flock, taste anything; do not let them eat or drink. ⁸But let man and beast be covered with sackcloth. Let everyone call urgently on God. Let them give up their evil ways and their violence. ⁹Who knows? God may yet relent and with compassion turn from his fierce anger so that we will not perish."

¹⁰When God saw what they did and how they turned from their evil ways, he had compassion and did not bring upon them the destruction he had threatened.

Jonah's Anger at the Lᴏʀᴅ's Compassion But Jonah was greatly displeased and became angry. ²He prayed to the Lᴏʀᴅ, "O Lᴏʀᴅ, is this not what I said when I was still at home? That is why I was so quick to flee to Tarshish. I knew that you are a gracious and compassionate God, slow to anger and abounding in love, a God who relents from sending calamity. ³Now, O Lᴏʀᴅ, take away my life, for it is better for me to die than to live."

⁴But the Lᴏʀᴅ replied, "Have you any right to be angry?"

⁵Jonah went out and sat down at a place east of the city. There he made himself a shelter, sat in its shade and waited to see what would happen to

ᵃ5 Or *waters were at my throat*

Dear Sam,

I lost control of myself on a date and went all the way. I feel so guilty and dirty. I'm so ashamed I almost wish I were dead.

Barb in Brownsville

100 Advice Lane, Anywhere, USA

Dear Barb,

There are several things you need to consider, but the most important is that when you confess your sin, God forgives you and remembers your sin no more. Now you must forgive yourself. God still loves you!

Sometimes, even though you have been forgiven, there are consequences for your actions. If you are pregnant or if you get an STD (sexually transmitted disease), you will have to tell someone and get help and support.

Read the four short chapters of Jonah to see how God often gives his people a second chance. Jonah got a second chance and so did the people of Nineveh.

In any event, don't feel that since you've gone all the way once, it doesn't matter anymore. It does. When Jesus forgave the woman who had been caught in adultery he told her, "Go now and leave your life of sin" (John 8:11). Your God is a great and compassionate God. You've made a mistake, but he forgives you and gives you another chance. Go and sin no more.

Sam

the city. ⁶Then the LORD God provided a vine and made it grow up over Jonah to give shade for his head to ease his discomfort, and Jonah was very happy about the vine. ⁷But at dawn the next day God provided a worm, which chewed the vine so that it withered. ⁸When the sun rose, God provided a scorching east wind, and the sun blazed on Jonah's head so that he grew faint. He wanted to die, and said, "It would be better for me to die than to live."

⁹But God said to Jonah, "Do you have a right to be angry about the vine?"

"I do," he said. "I am angry enough to die."

¹⁰But the LORD said, "You have been concerned about this vine, though you did not tend it or make it grow. It sprang up overnight and died overnight. ¹¹But Nineveh has more than a hundred and twenty thousand people who cannot tell their right hand from their left, and many cattle as well. Should I not be concerned about that great city?"

SURPRISE!

Is God ever surprised? You make plans and then you have to change them. You get a summer job, and the store you were going to work in burns down. You get a ticket to the World Series, and, boom, there's an earthquake. You can plan, but you can't be sure what will happen.

God is never surprised. The prophet Micah warned Israel and Judah that because of their sins they would be conquered by enemy nations. Micah also saw ahead 700 years and predicted the town where the Savior would be born! Nothing in your future can surprise God. And nothing can shake his love for you.

Fun damentals

What kind of plans does God have for wicked people (Micah 2:1-3)?

Is it really hard to please God? What do you have to do (Micah 6:7-8)?

What destiny does God plan for his own people (Micah 7:18-20)?

FAST FACTS

Micah prophesied from 750-686 B.C., while Assyria destroyed Israel and threatened Judah.

Micah means "Who is like the Lord?"

To see what God is like, check Micah 7:18.

God intends to bring world peace (Micah 4:1-5).

The Bible says God spoke through Micah (Jeremiah 26:18).

The word of the LORD that came to Micah of Moresheth during the reigns of Jotham, Ahaz and Hezekiah, kings of Judah—the vision he saw concerning Samaria and Jerusalem.

²Hear, O peoples, all of you,
 listen, O earth and all who are in it,
that the Sovereign LORD may witness against you,
 the Lord from his holy temple.

Judgment Against Samaria and Jerusalem

³Look! The LORD is coming from his dwelling place;
 he comes down and treads the high places of the earth.
⁴The mountains melt beneath him
 and the valleys split apart,
like wax before the fire,
 like water rushing down a slope.
⁵All this is because of Jacob's transgression,
 because of the sins of the house of Israel.
What is Jacob's transgression?
 Is it not Samaria?
What is Judah's high place?
 Is it not Jerusalem?

⁶"Therefore I will make Samaria a heap of rubble,
 a place for planting vineyards.
I will pour her stones into the valley
 and lay bare her foundations.
⁷All her idols will be broken to pieces;
 all her temple gifts will be burned with fire;
 I will destroy all her images.
Since she gathered her gifts from the wages of prostitutes,
 as the wages of prostitutes they will again be used."

Weeping and Mourning

⁸Because of this I will weep and wail;
 I will go about barefoot and naked.
I will howl like a jackal
 and moan like an owl.
⁹For her wound is incurable;
 it has come to Judah.
It^a has reached the very gate of my people,
 even to Jerusalem itself.
¹⁰Tell it not in Gath^b;
 weep not at all.^c
In Beth Ophrah^d
 roll in the dust.
¹¹Pass on in nakedness and shame,
 you who live in Shaphir.^e
Those who live in Zaanan^f
 will not come out.
Beth Ezel is in mourning;
 its protection is taken from you.
¹²Those who live in Maroth^g writhe in pain,
 waiting for relief,

---

^a9 Or He ^b10 Gath sounds like the Hebrew for tell. ^c10 Hebrew; Septuagint may suggest not in Acco. The Hebrew for in Acco sounds like the Hebrew for weep. ^d10 Beth Ophrah means house of dust. ^e11 Shaphir means pleasant. ^f11 Zaanan sounds like the Hebrew for come out. ^g12 Maroth sounds like the Hebrew for bitter.

because disaster has come from the LORD,
even to the gate of Jerusalem.
¹³You who live in Lachish,ᵃ
harness the team to the chariot.
You were the beginning of sin
to the Daughter of Zion,
for the transgressions of Israel
were found in you.
¹⁴Therefore you will give parting gifts
to Moresheth Gath.
The town of Aczibᵇ will prove deceptive
to the kings of Israel.
¹⁵I will bring a conqueror against you
who live in Mareshah.ᶜ
He who is the glory of Israel
will come to Adullam.
¹⁶Shave your heads in mourning
for the children in whom you delight;
make yourselves as bald as the vulture,
for they will go from you into exile.

Man's Plans and God's

Woe to those who plan iniquity,
to those who plot evil on their beds!
At morning's light they carry it out
because it is in their power to do it.
²They covet fields and seize them,
and houses, and take them.
They defraud a man of his home,
a fellowman of his inheritance.

³Therefore, the LORD says:

"I am planning disaster against this people,
from which you cannot save yourselves.
You will no longer walk proudly,
for it will be a time of calamity.
⁴In that day men will ridicule you;
they will taunt you with this mournful song:
'We are utterly ruined;
my people's possession is divided up.
He takes it from me!
He assigns our fields to traitors.'"

⁵Therefore you will have no one in the assembly of the LORD
to divide the land by lot.

False Prophets

⁶"Do not prophesy," their prophets say.
"Do not prophesy about these things;
disgrace will not overtake us."
⁷Should it be said, O house of Jacob:
"Is the Spirit of the LORD angry?
Does he do such things?"

ᵃ13 Lachish sounds like the Hebrew for *team*.   ᵇ14 Aczib means *deception*.   ᶜ15 Mareshah sounds like the Hebrew for *conqueror*.

"Do not my words do good
　　to him whose ways are upright?
[8]Lately my people have risen up
　　like an enemy.
You strip off the rich robe
　　from those who pass by without a care,
　　like men returning from battle.
[9]You drive the women of my people
　　from their pleasant homes.
You take away my blessing
　　from their children forever.
[10]Get up, go away!
　　For this is not your resting place,
　because it is defiled,
　　it is ruined, beyond all remedy.
[11]If a liar and deceiver comes and says,
　　'I will prophesy for you plenty of wine and beer,'
　　he would be just the prophet for this people!

Deliverance Promised

[12]"I will surely gather all of you, O Jacob;
　　I will surely bring together the remnant of Israel.
I will bring them together like sheep in a pen,
　　like a flock in its pasture;
　　the place will throng with people.
[13]One who breaks open the way will go up before them;
　　they will break through the gate and go out.
Their king will pass through before them,
　　the LORD at their head."

3 Leaders and Prophets Rebuked   Then I said,

"Listen, you leaders of Jacob,
　　you rulers of the house of Israel.
Should you not know justice,
[2]　you who hate good and love evil;
who tear the skin from my people
　　and the flesh from their bones;
[3]who eat my people's flesh,
　　strip off their skin
　　and break their bones in pieces;
who chop them up like meat for the pan,
　　like flesh for the pot?"

[4]Then they will cry out to the LORD,
　　but he will not answer them.
At that time he will hide his face from them
　　because of the evil they have done.

[5]This is what the LORD says:

"As for the prophets
　　who lead my people astray,
if one feeds them,
　　they proclaim 'peace';
if he does not,
　　they prepare to wage war against him.
[6]Therefore night will come over you, without visions,
　　and darkness, without divination.

The sun will set for the prophets,
    and the day will go dark for them.
⁷The seers will be ashamed
    and the diviners disgraced.
They will all cover their faces
    because there is no answer from God."

⁸But as for me, I am filled with power,
    with the Spirit of the LORD,
    and with justice and might,
to declare to Jacob his transgression,
    to Israel his sin.
⁹Hear this, you leaders of the house of Jacob,
    you rulers of the house of Israel,
who despise justice
    and distort all that is right;
¹⁰who build Zion with bloodshed,
    and Jerusalem with wickedness.
¹¹Her leaders judge for a bribe,
    her priests teach for a price,
    and her prophets tell fortunes for money.
Yet they lean upon the LORD and say,
    "Is not the LORD among us?
    No disaster will come upon us."
¹²Therefore because of you,
    Zion will be plowed like a field,
Jerusalem will become a heap of rubble,
    the temple hill a mound overgrown with thickets.

4 *The Mountain of the LORD*   In the last days

the mountain of the LORD's temple will be established
    as chief among the mountains;
it will be raised above the hills,
    and peoples will stream to it.

²Many nations will come and say,

"Come, let us go up to the mountain of the
        LORD,
    to the house of the God of Jacob.
He will teach us his ways,
    so that we may walk in his paths."
The law will go out from Zion,
    the word of the LORD from Jerusalem.
³He will judge between many peoples
    and will settle disputes for strong nations far
        and wide.
They will beat their swords into plowshares
    and their spears into pruning hooks.
Nation will not take up sword against nation,
    nor will they train for war anymore.
⁴Every man will sit under his own vine
    and under his own fig tree,
and no one will make them afraid,
    for the LORD Almighty has spoken.
⁵All the nations may walk
    in the name of their gods;

> Let us go up to the mountain of the LORD . . . He will teach us his ways (Micah 4:2).

we will walk in the name of the LORD
our God for ever and ever.

The LORD's Plan   ⁶"In that day," declares the LORD,

"I will gather the lame;
   I will assemble the exiles
   and those I have brought to grief.
⁷I will make the lame a remnant,
   those driven away a strong nation.
The LORD will rule over them in Mount Zion
   from that day and forever.
⁸As for you, O watchtower of the flock,
   O stronghold*ᵃ* of the Daughter of Zion,
the former dominion will be restored to you;
   kingship will come to the Daughter of Jerusalem."

⁹Why do you now cry aloud—
   have you no king?
Has your counselor perished,
   that pain seizes you like that of a woman in labor?
¹⁰Writhe in agony, O Daughter of Zion,
   like a woman in labor,
for now you must leave the city
   to camp in the open field.
You will go to Babylon;
   there you will be rescued.
There the LORD will redeem you
   out of the hand of your enemies.

¹¹But now many nations
   are gathered against you.
They say, "Let her be defiled,
   let our eyes gloat over Zion!"
¹²But they do not know
   the thoughts of the LORD;
they do not understand his plan,
   he who gathers them like sheaves to the threshing floor.

¹³"Rise and thresh, O Daughter of Zion,
   for I will give you horns of iron;
I will give you hoofs of bronze
   and you will break to pieces many nations."

You will devote their ill-gotten gains to the LORD,
   their wealth to the Lord of all the earth.

A Promised Ruler From Bethlehem

5 Marshal your troops, O city of troops,*ᵇ*
   for a siege is laid against us.
They will strike Israel's ruler
   on the cheek with a rod.

²"But you, Bethlehem Ephrathah,
   though you are small among the clans*ᶜ* of Judah,
out of you will come for me
   one who will be ruler over Israel,
whose origins*ᵈ* are from of old,
   from ancient times.*ᵉ*"

ᵃ8 Or hill   ᵇ1 Or Strengthen your walls, O walled city   ᶜ2 Or rulers   ᵈ2 Hebrew goings out   ᵉ2 Or from days of eternity

³Therefore Israel will be abandoned
    until the time when she who is in labor gives birth
and the rest of his brothers return
    to join the Israelites.

⁴He will stand and shepherd his flock
    in the strength of the LORD,
    in the majesty of the name of the LORD his God.
And they will live securely, for then his greatness
    will reach to the ends of the earth.
⁵   And he will be their peace.

Deliverance and Destruction

When the Assyrian invades our land
    and marches through our fortresses,
we will raise against him seven shepherds,
    even eight leaders of men.
⁶They will rule*a* the land of Assyria with
    the sword,
    the land of Nimrod with drawn
        sword.*b*
He will deliver us from the Assyrian
    when he invades our land
    and marches into our borders.

MICAH 5

Q: When did
Micah predict
Jesus' birth-
place?

BONUS:
How many
prophecies
about Jesus
are there in
the Old
Testament?

Answers on
page 1211

⁷The remnant of Jacob will be
    in the midst of many peoples
like dew from the LORD,
    like showers on the grass,
which do not wait for man
    or linger for mankind.
⁸The remnant of Jacob will be among the nations,
    in the midst of many peoples,
like a lion among the beasts of the forest,
    like a young lion among flocks of sheep,
which mauls and mangles as it goes,
    and no one can rescue.
⁹Your hand will be lifted up in triumph over your
        enemies,
    and all your foes will be destroyed.

¹⁰"In that day," declares the LORD,

"I will destroy your horses from among you
    and demolish your chariots.
¹¹I will destroy the cities of your land
    and tear down all your strongholds.
¹²I will destroy your witchcraft
    and you will no longer cast spells.
¹³I will destroy your carved images
    and your sacred stones from among you;
you will no longer bow down
    to the work of your hands.
¹⁴I will uproot from among you your Asherah poles*c*
    and demolish your cities.
¹⁵I will take vengeance in anger and wrath
    upon the nations that have not obeyed me."

a6 Or crush   *b6 Or Nimrod in its gates*   *c14 That is, symbols of the goddess Asherah*

6 *The Lord's Case Against Israel* Listen to what the Lord says:

"Stand up, plead your case before the mountains;
   let the hills hear what you have to say.
²Hear, O mountains, the Lord's accusation;
   listen, you everlasting foundations of the earth.
For the Lord has a case against his people;
   he is lodging a charge against Israel.

³"My people, what have I done to you?
   How have I burdened you? Answer me.
⁴I brought you up out of Egypt
   and redeemed you from the land of slavery.
I sent Moses to lead you,
   also Aaron and Miriam.
⁵My people, remember
   what Balak king of Moab counseled
   and what Balaam son of Beor answered.
Remember ⸤your journey⸥ from Shittim to Gilgal,
   that you may know the righteous acts of the
      Lord."

⁶With what shall I come before the Lord
   and bow down before the exalted God?
Shall I come before him with burnt offerings,
   with calves a year old?
⁷Will the Lord be pleased with thousands of rams,
   with ten thousand rivers of oil?
Shall I offer my firstborn for my transgression,
   the fruit of my body for the sin of my soul?
⁸He has showed you, O man, what is
      good.
   And what does the Lord require of
      you?
To act justly and to love mercy
   and to walk humbly with your God.

Israel's Guilt and Punishment
⁹Listen! The Lord is calling to the city—
   and to fear your name is wisdom—
   "Heed the rod and the One who
      appointed it.ᵃ
¹⁰Am I still to forget, O wicked house,
   your ill-gotten treasures
   and the short ephah,ᵇ which is
      accursed?
¹¹Shall I acquit a man with dishonest
      scales,
   with a bag of false weights?
¹²Her rich men are violent;
   her people are liars
   and their tongues speak
      deceitfully.

ᵃ9 The meaning of the Hebrew for this line is uncertain.
ᵇ10 An ephah was a dry measure.

Direct Line

MICAH 6:8

You probably feel at least some pressure to live up to others' expectations. You want to please your coach. You want Mom and Dad to be proud of you. You want to fit in with the other kids. It can be kind of confusing at times, trying to be the way all those different people expect and want you to be. The most important thing, of course, is to be the person God wants you to be. Micah 6:8 is a special verse because it describes what God expects of his followers. And there's a bonus involved: If you set your heart on being God's kind of person, just about everyone you care about will like and respect you too.

¹³ Therefore, I have begun to destroy you,
  to ruin you because of your sins.
¹⁴ You will eat but not be satisfied;
  your stomach will still be empty.ᵃ
 You will store up but save nothing,
  because what you save I will give to the sword.
¹⁵ You will plant but not harvest;
  you will press olives but not use the oil on yourselves,
  you will crush grapes but not drink the wine.
¹⁶ You have observed the statutes of Omri
   and all the practices of Ahab's house,
   and you have followed their traditions.
 Therefore I will give you over to ruin
   and your people to derision;
   you will bear the scorn of the nations.ᵇ"

7 *Israel's Misery*
  What misery is mine!
  I am like one who gathers summer fruit
   at the gleaning of the vineyard;
  there is no cluster of grapes to eat,
   none of the early figs that I crave.
² The godly have been swept from the land;
   not one upright man remains.
 All men lie in wait to shed blood;
   each hunts his brother with a net.
³ Both hands are skilled in doing evil;
   the ruler demands gifts,
  the judge accepts bribes,
   the powerful dictate what they desire—
  they all conspire together.
⁴ The best of them is like a brier,
   the most upright worse than a thorn hedge.
 The day of your watchmen has come,
   the day God visits you.
  Now is the time of their confusion.
⁵ Do not trust a neighbor;
   put no confidence in a friend.
 Even with her who lies in your embrace
   be careful of your words.
⁶ For a son dishonors his father,
   a daughter rises up against her mother,
  a daughter-in-law against her mother-in-law—
   a man's enemies are the members of his own
     household.

⁷ But as for me, I watch in hope for the LORD,
   I wait for God my Savior;
   my God will hear me.

Israel Will Rise
⁸ Do not gloat over me, my enemy!
   Though I have fallen, I will rise.
 Though I sit in darkness,
   the LORD will be my light.

ᵃ14 The meaning of the Hebrew for this word is uncertain.   ᵇ16 Septuagint; Hebrew *scorn due my people*

⁹Because I have sinned against him,
    I will bear the LORD's wrath,
until he pleads my case
    and establishes my right.
He will bring me out into the light;
    I will see his righteousness.
¹⁰Then my enemy will see it
    and will be covered with shame,
she who said to me,
    "Where is the LORD your God?"
My eyes will see her downfall;
    even now she will be trampled underfoot
    like mire in the streets.

¹¹The day for building your walls will come,
    the day for extending your boundaries.
¹²In that day people will come to you
    from Assyria and the cities of Egypt,
even from Egypt to the Euphrates
    and from sea to sea
    and from mountain to mountain.
¹³The earth will become desolate because of its
        inhabitants,
    as the result of their deeds.

Prayer and Praise

¹⁴Shepherd your people with your staff,
    the flock of your inheritance,
which lives by itself in a forest,
    in fertile pasturelands.ᵃ
Let them feed in Bashan and Gilead
    as in days long ago.

¹⁵"As in the days when you came out of
        Egypt,
    I will show them my wonders."

¹⁶Nations will see and be ashamed,
    deprived of all their power.
They will lay their hands on their mouths
    and their ears will become deaf.
¹⁷They will lick dust like a snake,
    like creatures that crawl on the ground.
They will come trembling out of their dens;
    they will turn in fear to the LORD our God
    and will be afraid of you.
¹⁸Who is a God like you,
    who pardons sin and forgives the transgression
    of the remnant of his inheritance?
You do not stay angry forever
    but delight to show mercy.
¹⁹You will again have compassion on us;
    you will tread our sins underfoot
    and hurl all our iniquities into the depths of
        the sea.

> Who is a God like you, who pardons sin . . . ? You do not stay angry forever but delight to show mercy (Micah 7:18).

ᵃ14 Or *in the middle of Carmel*

²⁰You will be true to Jacob,
 and show mercy to Abraham,
as you pledged on oath to our fathers
 in days long ago.

to the

book of **Nahum**

JUDGMENT.

When something bad happens to another person, it's not right to feel good about it. But what if that person has abused you for years or hurt you seriously? You just might cheer when he or she is judged and must pay for the harm done.

Nahum sees God as a judge, pronouncing sentence on Nineveh. Nineveh was the capital of Assyria, a nation that invaded Israel and carried 200,000 of her people into captivity. The prophet describes how the Assyrians will suffer when their own capital is attacked. After decades of terror, it was right for Judah to rejoice. It was Assyria's time to be judged.

Fundamentals

Is it OK for God to take vengeance if you aren't supposed to (Nahum 1:1-8)?

Is it sometimes natural to be happy over an enemy's trouble (Nahum 3:19)?

FAST FACTS

Nahum prophesied between 663 and 612 B.C.

It was Assyrian policy to be cruel to enemies.

Nineveh was enclosed by an eight mile, 50-foot-high wall.

Four chariots could ride next to each other on top of the wall.

Nineveh fell to the Babylonians just as Nahum described.

1 An oracle concerning Nineveh. The book of the vision of Nahum the Elkoshite.

The LORD's Anger Against Nineveh

² The LORD is a jealous and avenging God;
 the LORD takes vengeance and is filled with wrath.
The LORD takes vengeance on his foes
 and maintains his wrath against his enemies.
³ The LORD is slow to anger and great in power;
 the LORD will not leave the guilty unpunished.
His way is in the whirlwind and the storm,
 and clouds are the dust of his feet.
⁴ He rebukes the sea and dries it up;
 he makes all the rivers run dry.
Bashan and Carmel wither
 and the blossoms of Lebanon fade.
⁵ The mountains quake before him
 and the hills melt away.
The earth trembles at his presence,
 the world and all who live in it.
⁶ Who can withstand his indignation?
 Who can endure his fierce anger?
His wrath is poured out like fire;
 the rocks are shattered before him.

⁷ The LORD is good,
 a refuge in times of trouble.
He cares for those who trust in him,
⁸ but with an overwhelming flood
he will make an end of ⌞Nineveh⌟;
 he will pursue his foes into darkness.

⁹ Whatever they plot against the LORD
 he*a* will bring to an end;
 trouble will not come a second time.
¹⁰ They will be entangled among thorns
 and drunk from their wine;
 they will be consumed like dry stubble.*b*
¹¹ From you, ⌞O Nineveh,⌟ has one come forth
 who plots evil against the LORD
 and counsels wickedness.

¹²This is what the LORD says:

"Although they have allies and are numerous,
 they will be cut off and pass away.
Although I have afflicted you, ⌞O Judah,⌟
 I will afflict you no more.
¹³ Now I will break their yoke from your neck
 and tear your shackles away."

¹⁴ The LORD has given a command concerning you, ⌞Nineveh⌟:
 "You will have no descendants to bear your name.
I will destroy the carved images and cast idols
 that are in the temple of your gods.
I will prepare your grave,
 for you are vile."

> The LORD is good,
> a refuge in times
> of trouble. He
> cares for those
> who trust in him
> (Nahum 1:7).

---

*a*9 Or *What do you foes plot against the* LORD*? / He* *b*10 The meaning of the Hebrew for this verse is uncertain.

¹⁵Look, there on the mountains,
  the feet of one who brings good news,
  who proclaims peace!
Celebrate your festivals, O Judah,
  and fulfill your vows.
No more will the wicked invade you;
  they will be completely destroyed.

Nineveh to Fall

An attacker advances against you, ˏNinevehˎ.
  Guard the fortress,
  watch the road,
  brace yourselves,
  marshal all your strength!

²The LORD will restore the splendor of Jacob
  like the splendor of Israel,
though destroyers have laid them waste
  and have ruined their vines.

³The shields of his soldiers are red;
  the warriors are clad in scarlet.
The metal on the chariots flashes
  on the day they are made ready;
  the spears of pine are brandished.ᵃ
⁴The chariots storm through the streets,
  rushing back and forth through the squares.
They look like flaming torches;
  they dart about like lightning.

⁵He summons his picked troops,
  yet they stumble on their way.
They dash to the city wall;
  the protective shield is put in place.
⁶The river gates are thrown open
  and the palace collapses.
⁷It is decreedᵇ that ˏthe cityˎ
  be exiled and carried away.
Its slave girls moan like doves
  and beat upon their breasts.
⁸Nineveh is like a pool,
  and its water is draining away.
"Stop! Stop!" they cry,
  but no one turns back.
⁹Plunder the silver!
  Plunder the gold!
The supply is endless,
  the wealth from all its treasures!
¹⁰She is pillaged, plundered, stripped!
  Hearts melt, knees give way,
  bodies tremble, every face grows pale.

¹¹Where now is the lions' den,
  the place where they fed their young,

ᵃ3 Hebrew; Septuagint and Syriac / *the horsemen rush to and fro*   ᵇ7 The meaning of the Hebrew for this word is uncertain.

where the lion and lioness went,
and the cubs, with nothing to fear?
¹²The lion killed enough for his cubs
and strangled the prey for his mate,
filling his lairs with the kill
and his dens with the prey.

¹³"I am against you,"
declares the LORD Almighty.
"I will burn up your chariots in smoke,
and the sword will devour your young lions.
I will leave you no prey on the earth.
The voices of your messengers
will no longer be heard."

Woe to Nineveh

3 Woe to the city of blood,
full of lies,
full of plunder,
never without victims!
²The crack of whips,
the clatter of wheels,
galloping horses
and jolting chariots!
³Charging cavalry,
flashing swords
and glittering spears!
Many casualties,
piles of dead,
bodies without number,
people stumbling over the corpses—
⁴all because of the wanton lust of a harlot,
alluring, the mistress of sorceries,
who enslaved nations by her prostitution
and peoples by her witchcraft.

⁵"I am against you," declares the LORD Almighty.
"I will lift your skirts over your face.
I will show the nations your nakedness
and the kingdoms your shame.
⁶I will pelt you with filth,
I will treat you with contempt
and make you a spectacle.
⁷All who see you will flee from you and say,
'Nineveh is in ruins—who will mourn for her?'
Where can I find anyone to comfort you?"
⁸Are you better than Thebes,ᵃ
situated on the Nile,
with water around her?
The river was her defense,
the waters her wall.
⁹Cushᵇ and Egypt were her boundless strength;
Put and Libya were among her allies.
¹⁰Yet she was taken captive
and went into exile.

ᵃ8 Hebrew *No Amon*   ᵇ9 That is, the upper Nile region

Her infants were dashed to pieces
at the head of every street.
Lots were cast for her nobles,
and all her great men were put in chains.
¹¹You too will become drunk;
you will go into hiding
and seek refuge from the enemy.

¹²All your fortresses are like fig trees
with their first ripe fruit;
when they are shaken,
the figs fall into the mouth of the eater.
¹³Look at your troops—
they are all women!
The gates of your land
are wide open to your enemies;
fire has consumed their bars.

¹⁴Draw water for the siege,
strengthen your defenses!
Work the clay,
tread the mortar,
repair the brickwork!
¹⁵There the fire will devour you;
the sword will cut you down
and, like grasshoppers, consume you.
Multiply like grasshoppers,
multiply like locusts!
¹⁶You have increased the number of your merchants
till they are more than the stars of the sky,
but like locusts they strip the land
and then fly away.
¹⁷Your guards are like locusts,
your officials like swarms of locusts
that settle in the walls on a cold day—
but when the sun appears they fly away,
and no one knows where.

¹⁸O king of Assyria, your shepherdsᵃ slumber;
your nobles lie down to rest.
Your people are scattered on the mountains
with no one to gather them.
¹⁹Nothing can heal your wound;
your injury is fatal.
Everyone who hears the news about you
claps his hands at your fall,
for who has not felt
your endless cruelty?

"Multiply like grasshoppers, multiply like locusts!" Multiply like me! Oops, nope. I don't know how to multiply!

SEE NAHUM 3:15

ᵃ18 Or *rulers*

Introduction

to the

book of # Habakkuk

LIFE ISN'T FAIR.

Someone writes you a note, and you're the one who gets in trouble. Someone starts a fight with you, and you're the one who gets sent to the principal's office. The crooks have the big house and lots of money, and your family has hardly enough to live on.

Habakkuk didn't think life was fair either. He was upset because it looked to him like the bad guys were winning. Why wasn't God doing something about it? God had an answer. Sinners would be punished. In the meantime success wouldn't make them happy. Think about it. Wouldn't you rather have little and be happy and right with God than have millions and always feel unsatisfied?

Fundamentals

Are there people today about whom Habakkuk 1:11 is true?

Why aren't people who "succeed" by doing wrong ever happy (Habakkuk 2:4-5)?

What kinds of idols do people worship today (Habakkuk 2:18)?

FAST FACTS

Habakkuk lived in the time of godly King Hezekiah.

Habakkuk probably led worship at the temple.

The book is dialogue: Habakkuk speaks, and God answers.

The book explains five ways God judges the wicked.

The oracle that Habakkuk the prophet received.

Habakkuk's Complaint

²How long, O LORD, must I call for help,
    but you do not listen?
Or cry out to you, "Violence!"
    but you do not save?
³Why do you make me look at injustice?
    Why do you tolerate wrong?
Destruction and violence are before me;
    there is strife, and conflict abounds.
⁴Therefore the law is paralyzed,
    and justice never prevails.
The wicked hem in the righteous,
    so that justice is perverted.

The LORD's Answer

⁵"Look at the nations and watch—
    and be utterly amazed.
For I am going to do something in your days
    that you would not believe,
    even if you were told.
⁶I am raising up the Babylonians,ᵃ
    that ruthless and impetuous people,
who sweep across the whole earth
    to seize dwelling places not their own.
⁷They are a feared and dreaded people;
    they are a law to themselves
    and promote their own honor.
⁸Their horses are swifter than leopards,
    fiercer than wolves at dusk.
Their cavalry gallops headlong;
    their horsemen come from afar.
They fly like a vulture swooping to devour;
⁹   they all come bent on violence.
Their hordesᵇ advance like a desert wind
    and gather prisoners like sand.
¹⁰They deride kings
    and scoff at rulers.
They laugh at all fortified cities;
    they build earthen ramps and capture them.
¹¹Then they sweep past like the wind and go on—
    guilty men, whose own strength is their god."

Habakkuk's Second Complaint

¹²O LORD, are you not from everlasting?
    My God, my Holy One, we will not die.
O LORD, you have appointed them to execute judgment;
    O Rock, you have ordained them to punish.
¹³Your eyes are too pure to look on evil;
    you cannot tolerate wrong.
Why then do you tolerate the treacherous?
    Why are you silent while the wicked
    swallow up those more righteous than themselves?
¹⁴You have made men like fish in the sea,
    like sea creatures that have no ruler.

ᵃ6 Or *Chaldeans* ᵇ9 The meaning of the Hebrew for this word is uncertain.

¹⁵The wicked foe pulls all of them up with hooks,
   he catches them in his net,
 he gathers them up in his dragnet;
   and so he rejoices and is glad.
¹⁶Therefore he sacrifices to his net
   and burns incense to his dragnet,
 for by his net he lives in luxury
   and enjoys the choicest food.
¹⁷Is he to keep on emptying his net,
   destroying nations without mercy?

2 I will stand at my watch
   and station myself on the ramparts;
 I will look to see what he will say to me,
   and what answer I am to give to this
      complaint.*a*

The Lord's Answer ²Then the Lord replied:

 "Write down the revelation
   and make it plain on tablets
   so that a herald*b* may run with it.
³For the revelation awaits an appointed time;
   it speaks of the end
   and will not prove false.
 Though it linger, wait for it;
   it*c* will certainly come and will not delay.

⁴"See, he is puffed up;
   his desires are not upright—
   but the righteous will live by his faith*d*—
⁵indeed, wine betrays him;
   he is arrogant and never at rest.
 Because he is as greedy as the grave*e*
   and like death is never satisfied,
 he gathers to himself all the nations
   and takes captive all the peoples.

⁶"Will not all of them taunt him with ridicule and scorn, saying,

 " 'Woe to him who piles up stolen goods
   and makes himself wealthy by extortion!
   How long must this go on?'
⁷Will not your debtors*f* suddenly arise?
   Will they not wake up and make you tremble?
   Then you will become their victim.
⁸Because you have plundered many nations,
   the peoples who are left will plunder you.
 For you have shed man's blood;
   you have destroyed lands and cities and everyone in them.

⁹"Woe to him who builds his realm by unjust gain
   to set his nest on high,
   to escape the clutches of ruin!
¹⁰You have plotted the ruin of many peoples,
   shaming your own house and forfeiting your life.

HABAKKUK 1

QUIZZER

Q: What
doesn't God
look at?

*BONUS:
What doesn't
God listen to?*

**Answers on
page 1223**

---

*a1 Or and what to answer when I am rebuked   b2 Or so that whoever reads it   c3 Or Though he linger,
wait for him; / he   d4 Or faithfulness   e5 Hebrew Sheol   f7 Or creditors*

Dear Sam,

The most popular guy in school wants me to give him answers during our math tests. Is it really so wrong to cheat?

Scott in Scarsdale

100 Advice Lane, Anywhere, USA

Dear Scott,

The fact that you're worried about this tells me that you know it's not right to help someone do wrong. Succeeding in doing something wrong doesn't bring a sense of satisfaction but rather a perverse desire to try again (Habakkuk 2:5). Those who help others cheat or who drink, lie or have sex just to be popular won't find any happiness.

If being friends with this guy is really so important, why not offer to tutor him? Tell him he'll be better off in the long run. If he insists he only wants to cheat, do you really want him as your friend? Maybe you shouldn't place so much importance on being part of that crowd. Instead, find a good friend or two who share your values. Getting ahead by doing what is wrong did not help people in Habakkuk's time, and it will not help you either!

Sam

¹¹The stones of the wall will cry out,
    and the beams of the woodwork will echo it.

¹²"Woe to him who builds a city with bloodshed
    and establishes a town by crime!
¹³Has not the LORD Almighty determined
    that the people's labor is only fuel for the fire,
    that the nations exhaust themselves for nothing?
¹⁴For the earth will be filled with the knowledge of the glory of
      the LORD,
    as the waters cover the sea.

¹⁵"Woe to him who gives drink to his neighbors,
    pouring it from the wineskin till they are drunk,
    so that he can gaze on their naked bodies.
¹⁶You will be filled with shame instead of glory.
    Now it is your turn! Drink and be exposed^a!
The cup from the LORD's right hand is coming around to you,
    and disgrace will cover your glory.
¹⁷The violence you have done to Lebanon will overwhelm
      you,
    and your destruction of animals will terrify you.
For you have shed man's blood;
    you have destroyed lands and cities and everyone in them.

¹⁸"Of what value is an idol, since a man has carved it?
    Or an image that teaches lies?
For he who makes it trusts in his own creation;
    he makes idols that cannot speak.
¹⁹Woe to him who says to wood, 'Come to life!'
    Or to lifeless stone, 'Wake up!'
Can it give guidance?
    It is covered with gold and silver;
    there is no breath in it.
²⁰But the LORD is in his holy temple;
    let all the earth be silent before him."

Answers
to Quizzer on
page 1221

**A: Evil. Because
his "eyes are
too pure to
look on" it
(Habakkuk 1:13).**

**BONUS: God can
hear everything,
but he does not
listen to those
who won't listen
to him (Jeremiah
11:10-11).**

Habakkuk's Prayer A prayer of Habakkuk the prophet. On *shigio-noth.*^b

²LORD, I have heard of your fame;
    I stand in awe of your deeds, O LORD.
Renew them in our day,
    in our time make them known;
    in wrath remember mercy.

³God came from Teman,
    the Holy One from Mount Paran.   *Selah*^c
His glory covered the heavens
    and his praise filled the earth.
⁴His splendor was like the sunrise;
    rays flashed from his hand,
    where his power was hidden.
⁵Plague went before him;
    pestilence followed his steps.
⁶He stood, and shook the earth;
    he looked, and made the nations tremble.

---

^a16 Masoretic Text; Dead Sea Scrolls, Aquila, Vulgate and Syriac (see also Septuagint) *and stagger*
^b1 Probably a literary or musical term   ^c3 A word of uncertain meaning; possibly a musical term; also in
verses 9 and 13

The ancient mountains crumbled
and the age-old hills collapsed.
His ways are eternal.
⁷I saw the tents of Cushan in distress,
the dwellings of Midian in anguish.

⁸Were you angry with the rivers, O LORD?
Was your wrath against the streams?
Did you rage against the sea
when you rode with your horses
and your victorious chariots?
⁹You uncovered your bow,
you called for many arrows.   *Selah*
You split the earth with rivers;
¹⁰ the mountains saw you and writhed.
Torrents of water swept by;
the deep roared
and lifted its waves on high.

¹¹Sun and moon stood still in the heavens
at the glint of your flying arrows,
at the lightning of your flashing spear.
¹²In wrath you strode through the earth
and in anger you threshed the nations.
¹³You came out to deliver your people,
to save your anointed one.
You crushed the leader of the land of wickedness,
you stripped him from head to foot.   *Selah*
¹⁴With his own spear you pierced his head
when his warriors stormed out to scatter us,
gloating as though about to devour
the wretched who were in hiding.
¹⁵You trampled the sea with your
horses,
churning the great waters.

¹⁶I heard and my heart pounded,
my lips quivered at the sound;
decay crept into my bones,
and my legs trembled.
Yet I will wait patiently for the day of
calamity
to come on the nation invading us.
¹⁷Though the fig tree does not bud
and there are no grapes on the
vines,
though the olive crop fails
and the fields produce no food,
though there are no sheep in the pen
and no cattle in the stalls,
¹⁸yet I will rejoice in the LORD,
I will be joyful in God my Savior.

¹⁹The Sovereign LORD is my strength;
he makes my feet like the feet of a
deer,
he enables me to go on the heights.

For the director of music. On my
stringed instruments.

HABAKKUK 3:16–19

For most people, family means security. Parents supply food and clothing and housing as well as love and support. But what happens if Dad loses his job? Or if Mom and Dad divorce? Or if a parent dies? Suddenly your whole future is in doubt. Look what happened to Habakkuk. God warned him that a terrible judgment was about to strike his homeland. Habakkuk was frightened (Habakkuk 3:16). But he came to realize that it isn't peace or prosperity that provides security: it's the Lord (Habakkuk 3:18–19). No matter how uncertain your future is, God can be your strength, today and tomorrow.

Direct Line

book of Zephaniah

DO SOMETHING!

Does it ever bother you when there's a problem and no one does anything about it? The authorities complain about drunk driving but don't take action. Tough kids bug you on the school bus, but no one makes them stop. Why doesn't someone do something?

In Zephaniah's day the wicked grinned and thought, "The LORD will do nothing, either good or bad" (Zephaniah 1:12). But the prophet had a surprise for them. God was about to act and punish not only Judah, but also nearby nations. Zephaniah reminds you that God really does judge. God says that in his own time, "[He] will deal with all who oppressed you" (Zephaniah 3:19).

FAST FACTS

Zephaniah means "the Lord protects."

Zephaniah preached in King Josiah's time before Josiah's religious revival.

Within ten years of Josiah's death in 609 B.C., the Babylonians fulfilled Zephaniah's prophecies.

God has a very good reason for not judging right now (Romans 2:4).

Fundamentals

Do you think God cares what you do (Zephaniah 1)?

Isn't being humble kind of wimpy (Zephaniah 2:1-3)?

What would life be like if everyone respected God (Zephaniah 3:9-13)?

The word of the LORD that came to Zephaniah son of Cushi, the son of Gedaliah, the son of Amariah, the son of Hezekiah, during the reign of Josiah son of Amon king of Judah:

Warning of Coming Destruction

2 "I will sweep away everything
   from the face of the earth,"

declares the LORD.

3 "I will sweep away both men and animals;
   I will sweep away the birds of the air
   and the fish of the sea.
The wicked will have only heaps of rubble[a]
   when I cut off man from the face of the earth,"

declares the LORD.

Against Judah

4 "I will stretch out my hand against Judah
   and against all who live in Jerusalem.
I will cut off from this place every remnant of Baal,
   the names of the pagan and the idolatrous priests—
5 those who bow down on the roofs
   to worship the starry host,
those who bow down and swear by the LORD
   and who also swear by Molech,[b]
6 those who turn back from following the LORD
   and neither seek the LORD nor inquire of him.
7 Be silent before the Sovereign LORD,
   for the day of the LORD is near.
The LORD has prepared a sacrifice;
   he has consecrated those he has invited.
8 On the day of the LORD's sacrifice
   I will punish the princes
   and the king's sons

---

[a]3 The meaning of the Hebrew for this line is uncertain.   [b]5 Hebrew *Malcam*, that is, Milcom

---

The Bible Says

No "Do Nothing" God

In Zephaniah's day most of the people of Judah supposed they had a "do nothing" God. They thought they could do anything they wanted, and God would just sit there, frustrated, doing nothing at all.

Were they wrong! God brought enemy armies against his people, crushing their defenses. The people of Judah went off to captivity in Babylon. Do nothing? Hah!

It's good to remember that you don't have a "do nothing" God. Read Zephaniah to learn some of the things God says he will do:

* God will punish those who abandon him (Zephaniah 1:4–6).
* God will shelter those who do what he commands (Zephaniah 2:3).
* God will bless those who trust in his name (Zephaniah 3:12–13).
* God will deal with those who oppress his own (Zephaniah 3:19).

and all those clad
   in foreign clothes.
⁹On that day I will punish
   all who avoid stepping on the threshold,ᵃ
who fill the temple of their gods
   with violence and deceit.

¹⁰"On that day," declares the Lᴏʀᴅ,
   "a cry will go up from the Fish Gate,
wailing from the New Quarter,
   and a loud crash from the hills.
¹¹Wail, you who live in the market districtᵇ;
   all your merchants will be wiped out,
   all who trade withᶜ silver will be ruined.
¹²At that time I will search Jerusalem with lamps
   and punish those who are complacent,
   who are like wine left on its dregs,
who think, 'The Lᴏʀᴅ will do nothing,
   either good or bad.'
¹³Their wealth will be plundered,
   their houses demolished.
They will build houses
   but not live in them;
they will plant vineyards
   but not drink the wine.

The Great Day of the Lᴏʀᴅ

¹⁴"The great day of the Lᴏʀᴅ is near—
   near and coming quickly.
Listen! The cry on the day of the Lᴏʀᴅ will be bitter,
   the shouting of the warrior there.
¹⁵That day will be a day of wrath,
   a day of distress and anguish,
a day of trouble and ruin,
   a day of darkness and gloom,
   a day of clouds and blackness,
¹⁶a day of trumpet and battle cry
   against the fortified cities
   and against the corner towers.
¹⁷I will bring distress on the people
   and they will walk like blind men,
   because they have sinned against the Lᴏʀᴅ.
Their blood will be poured out like dust
   and their entrails like filth.
¹⁸Neither their silver nor their gold
   will be able to save them
   on the day of the Lᴏʀᴅ's wrath.
In the fire of his jealousy
   the whole world will be consumed,
for he will make a sudden end
   of all who live in the earth."

2 Gather together, gather together,
   O shameful nation,
²before the appointed time arrives
   and that day sweeps on like chaff,

ᵃ9 See 1 Samuel 5:5. ᵇ11 Or *the Mortar* ᶜ11 Or *in*

before the fierce anger of the LORD comes upon you,
before the day of the LORD's wrath comes upon you.
³Seek the LORD, all you humble of the land,
you who do what he commands.
Seek righteousness, seek humility;
perhaps you will be sheltered
on the day of the LORD's anger.

Against Philistia

⁴Gaza will be abandoned
and Ashkelon left in ruins.
At midday Ashdod will be emptied
and Ekron uprooted.
⁵Woe to you who live by the sea,
O Kerethite people;
the word of the LORD is against you,
O Canaan, land of the Philistines.

"I will destroy you,
and none will be left."

⁶The land by the sea, where the Kerethites*ª* dwell,
will be a place for shepherds and sheep pens.
⁷It will belong to the remnant of the house of Judah;
there they will find pasture.
In the evening they will lie down
in the houses of Ashkelon.
The LORD their God will care for them;
he will restore their fortunes.*ᵇ*

Against Moab and Ammon

⁸"I have heard the insults of Moab
and the taunts of the Ammonites,
who insulted my people
and made threats against their land.
⁹Therefore, as surely as I live,"
declares the LORD Almighty, the God of Israel,
"surely Moab will become like Sodom,
the Ammonites like Gomorrah—
a place of weeds and salt pits,
a wasteland forever.
The remnant of my people will plunder them;
the survivors of my nation will inherit their land."

¹⁰This is what they will get in return for their pride,
for insulting and mocking the people of the LORD Almighty.
¹¹The LORD will be awesome to them
when he destroys all the gods of the land.
The nations on every shore will worship him,
every one in its own land.

Against Cush

¹²"You too, O Cushites,*ᶜ*
will be slain by my sword."

Against Assyria

¹³He will stretch out his hand against the north
and destroy Assyria,

ª6 The meaning of the Hebrew for this word is uncertain.   *ᵇ7* Or *will bring back their captives*   *ᶜ12* That is, people from the upper Nile region

leaving Nineveh utterly desolate
and dry as the desert.
¹⁴Flocks and herds will lie down there,
creatures of every kind.
The desert owl and the screech owl
will roost on her columns.
Their calls will echo through the windows,
rubble will be in the doorways,
the beams of cedar will be exposed.
¹⁵This is the carefree city
that lived in safety.
She said to herself,
"I am, and there is none besides me."
What a ruin she has become,
a lair for wild beasts!
All who pass by her scoff
and shake their fists.

3 The Future of Jerusalem

Woe to the city of oppressors,
rebellious and defiled!
²She obeys no one,
she accepts no correction.
She does not trust in the Lord,
she does not draw near to her God.
³Her officials are roaring lions,
her rulers are evening wolves,
who leave nothing for the morning.
⁴Her prophets are arrogant;
they are treacherous men.
Her priests profane the sanctuary
and do violence to the law.
⁵The Lord within her is righteous;
he does no wrong.
Morning by morning he
dispenses his justice,
and every new day he does
not fail,
yet the unrighteous know no
shame.

⁶"I have cut off nations;
their strongholds are
demolished.
I have left their streets
deserted,
with no one passing
through.
Their cities are destroyed;
no one will be left—no one
at all.
⁷I said to the city,
'Surely you will fear me
and accept correction!'
Then her dwelling would not
be cut off,

ZEPHANIAH 3:9–13

You're just one person. How can you make the world a better place? Should you get behind a political candidate? Start a "Save the Acorn" foundation? Pass out "Bikes Don't Pollute" bumper stickers? Zephaniah 3:12–13 has a better idea. If you want to make the world better, the place to start is with you personally. Be meek and humble. Trust in the Lord. Don't do wrong. Don't tell lies. Live like this every day, and that little bit of the world in which you live will be better for you being there.

Direct Line

nor all my punishments come upon
her.
But they were still eager
to act corruptly in all they did.
[8]"Therefore wait for me," declares the LORD,
"for the day I will stand up to testify.[a]
I have decided to assemble the nations,
to gather the kingdoms
and to pour out my wrath on them—
all my fierce anger.
The whole world will be consumed
by the fire of my jealous anger.

[9]"Then will I purify the lips of the peoples,
that all of them may call on the name of the LORD
and serve him shoulder to shoulder.
[10]From beyond the rivers of Cush[b]
my worshipers, my scattered people,
will bring me offerings.
[11]On that day you will not be put to shame
for all the wrongs you have done to me,
because I will remove from this city
those who rejoice in their pride.
Never again will you be haughty
on my holy hill.
[12]But I will leave within you
the meek and humble,
who trust in the name of the LORD.
[13]The remnant of Israel will do no wrong;
they will speak no lies,
nor will deceit be found in their mouths.
They will eat and lie down
and no one will make them afraid."

[14]Sing, O Daughter of Zion;
shout aloud, O Israel!
Be glad and rejoice with all your heart,
O Daughter of Jerusalem!
[15]The LORD has taken away your punishment,
he has turned back your enemy.
The LORD, the King of Israel, is with you;
never again will you fear any harm.
[16]On that day they will say to Jerusalem,
"Do not fear, O Zion;
do not let your hands hang limp.
[17]The LORD your God is with you,
he is mighty to save.
He will take great delight in you,
he will quiet you with his love,
he will rejoice over you with singing."

[18]"The sorrows for the appointed feasts
I will remove from you;
they are a burden and a reproach to you.[c]
[19]At that time I will deal
with all who oppressed you;

I will rescue the lame
    and gather those who have been scattered.
I will give them praise and honor
    in every land where they were put to shame.
²⁰ At that time I will gather you;
    at that time I will bring you home.
I will give you honor and praise
    among all the peoples of the earth
when I restore your fortunes[a]
    before your very eyes,"

                    says the LORD.

[a]20 Or *I bring back your captives*

Introduction

to the

book of # Haggai

WRITE IT DOWN.

When you listen to a sermon at church, do you take notes? Do you plan how you can put God's Word into practice right away? One problem most Old Testament prophets had was that people would listen, but they wouldn't respond to God's Word. They kept on living the same old way.

Haggai's preaching was different. He encouraged the people who had returned from captivity in Babylon to finish the temple they'd begun 18 years earlier. He preached one brief sermon, and the people immediately went to work! Because the people obeyed, God said, "From this day on I will bless you" (Haggai 2:19).

Fundamentals

If you follow God, what does he promise you (Haggai 1:13)?

What is the use of obeying God (Haggai 2)?

FAST FACTS

Haggai means "festival."

Haggai's sermons were preached August 29, October 17, and December 18 in 520 B.C.

The temple the exiles built was half the size of Solomon's temple.

This temple would have more glory (Haggai 2:9) because Jesus himself would preach in it.

1 *A Call to Build the House of the Lᴏʀᴅ* In the second year of King Darius, on the first day of the sixth month, the word of the Lᴏʀᴅ came through the prophet Haggai to Zerubbabel son of Shealtiel, governor of Judah, and to Joshua*ᵃ* son of Jehozadak, the high priest:

²This is what the Lᴏʀᴅ Almighty says: "These people say, 'The time has not yet come for the Lᴏʀᴅ's house to be built.' "

³Then the word of the Lᴏʀᴅ came through the prophet Haggai: ⁴"Is it a time for you yourselves to be living in your paneled houses, while this house remains a ruin?"

⁵Now this is what the Lᴏʀᴅ Almighty says: "Give careful thought to your ways. ⁶You have planted much, but have harvested little. You eat, but never have enough. You drink, but never have your fill. You put on clothes, but are not warm. You earn wages, only to put them in a purse with holes in it."

⁷This is what the Lᴏʀᴅ Almighty says: "Give careful thought to your ways. ⁸Go up into the mountains and bring down timber and build the house, so that I may take pleasure in it and be honored," says the Lᴏʀᴅ. ⁹"You expected much, but see, it turned out to be little. What you brought home, I blew away. Why?" declares the Lᴏʀᴅ Almighty. "Because of my house, which remains a ruin, while each of you is busy with his own house. ¹⁰Therefore, because of you the heavens have withheld their dew and the earth its crops. ¹¹I called for a drought on the fields and the mountains, on the grain, the new wine, the oil and whatever the ground produces, on men and cattle, and on the labor of your hands."

¹²Then Zerubbabel son of Shealtiel, Joshua son of Jehozadak, the high priest, and the whole remnant of the people obeyed the voice of the Lᴏʀᴅ their God and the message of the prophet Haggai, because the Lᴏʀᴅ their God had sent him. And the people feared the Lᴏʀᴅ.

¹³Then Haggai, the Lᴏʀᴅ's messenger, gave this message of the Lᴏʀᴅ to the people: "I am with you," declares the Lᴏʀᴅ. ¹⁴So the Lᴏʀᴅ stirred up the spirit of Zerubbabel son of Shealtiel, governor of Judah, and the spirit of Joshua son of Jehozadak, the high priest, and the spirit of the whole remnant of the people. They came and began to work on the house of the Lᴏʀᴅ Almighty, their God, ¹⁵on the twenty-fourth day of the sixth month in the second year of King Darius.

2 *The Promised Glory of the New House* On the twenty-first day of the seventh month, the word of the Lᴏʀᴅ came through the prophet Haggai: ²"Speak to Zerubbabel son of Shealtiel, governor of Judah, to Joshua son of Jehozadak, the high priest, and to the remnant of the people. Ask them, ³'Who of you is left who saw this house in its former glory? How does it look to you now? Does it not seem to you like nothing? ⁴But now be strong, O Zerubbabel,' declares the Lᴏʀᴅ. 'Be strong, O Joshua son of Jehozadak, the high priest. Be strong, all you people of the land,' declares the Lᴏʀᴅ, 'and work. For I am with

ᵃ1 A variant of *Jeshua*; here and elsewhere in Haggai

HAGGAI 2:18–19

Wouldn't it be great to hear God say to you, "From this day on I will bless you"? That's what God said to the people of Haggai's day. These people responded to Haggai's message and immediately set about finishing God's temple. Now, there's no guarantee that if you make a habit of responding to what God says all your problems will go away. Or that your family will suddenly be very rich. Or that you'll start getting all A's without studying. But there is one thing you can count on. If you put God's Word into practice, you put yourself in the place where God can bless you. And he will!

Direct Line

Dear Sam,

My friends and I all find the sermons at church so boring. How can we get anything out of a message when we can't even keep our minds on it?

Heather in Hollywood

100 Advice Lane, Anywhere, USA

Dear Heather,

You aren't the only one who is bored during sermons. Many adults are too. Yet listening to messages from God's Word is extremely important.

In Haggai's time the people were trying to build houses and grow crops, but the results were very poor (Haggai 1:6). Haggai told them these things were happening because they weren't paying attention to God's message. They were supposed to finish rebuilding the temple, but instead they had been thinking only of themselves and their own homes and needs. When the people listened to Haggai and obeyed God's message, they received blessings for hearing and doing God's Word.

If your mind wanders during the sermon, try writing down one or two important points. Doing this keeps you tuned in. (You may want to try this in school if your mind wanders off there as well.) Later in the service or later in the day, jot down how you can act on these points during the week. Remember that hearing and acting on God's Word will bring blessing.

Sam

you,' declares the LORD Almighty. ⁵'This is what I covenanted with you when you came out of Egypt. And my Spirit remains among you. Do not fear.'

⁶"This is what the LORD Almighty says: 'In a little while I will once more shake the heavens and the earth, the sea and the dry land. ⁷I will shake all nations, and the desired of all nations will come, and I will fill this house with glory,' says the LORD Almighty. ⁸'The silver is mine and the gold is mine,' declares the LORD Almighty. ⁹'The glory of this present house will be greater than the glory of the former house,' says the LORD Almighty. 'And in this place I will grant peace,' declares the LORD Almighty."

Blessings for a Defiled People ¹⁰On the twenty-fourth day of the ninth month, in the second year of Darius, the word of the LORD came to the prophet Haggai: ¹¹"This is what the LORD Almighty says: 'Ask the priests what the law says: ¹²If a person carries consecrated meat in the fold of his garment, and that fold touches some bread or stew, some wine, oil or other food, does it become consecrated?' "

The priests answered, "No."

¹³Then Haggai said, "If a person defiled by contact with a dead body touches one of these things, does it become defiled?"

"Yes," the priests replied, "it becomes defiled."

¹⁴Then Haggai said, " 'So it is with this people and this nation in my sight,' declares the LORD. 'Whatever they do and whatever they offer there is defiled.

¹⁵" 'Now give careful thought to this from this day on*ᵃ*—consider how things were before one stone was laid on another in the LORD's temple. ¹⁶When anyone came to a heap of twenty measures, there were only ten. When anyone went to a wine vat to draw fifty measures, there were only twenty. ¹⁷I struck all the work of your hands with blight, mildew and hail, yet you did not turn to me,' declares the LORD. ¹⁸'From this day on, from this twenty-fourth day of the ninth month, give careful thought to the day when the foundation of the LORD's temple was laid. Give careful thought: ¹⁹Is there yet any seed left in the barn? Until now, the vine and the fig tree, the pomegranate and the olive tree have not borne fruit.

" 'From this day on I will bless you.' "

Zerubbabel the LORD's Signet Ring ²⁰The word of the LORD came to Haggai a second time on the twenty-fourth day of the month: ²¹"Tell Zerubbabel governor of Judah that I will shake the heavens and the earth. ²²I will overturn royal thrones and shatter the power of the foreign kingdoms. I will overthrow chariots and their drivers; horses and their riders will fall, each by the sword of his brother.

²³" 'On that day,' declares the LORD Almighty, 'I will take you, my servant Zerubbabel son of Shealtiel,' declares the LORD, 'and I will make you like my signet ring, for I have chosen you,' declares the LORD Almighty."

ᵃ15 Or to the days past

WHAT'S AHEAD FOR THE WORLD?

Will there be a nuclear war? Will there be another Great Depression? Will pollution or drugs destroy our cities? No one can answer these questions, because the Bible doesn't mention North America. But you can understand why people would like to know.

Haggai, who preached at the same time as Zechariah, said the Savior would enter the temple the returned exiles were rebuilding. Zechariah answers the questions "When?" and "What will happen when he comes?" Centuries would pass before God acted, but the time of God's intervention surely would come.

FAST FACTS

Zechariah preached from 520 to 518 B.C.

Zechariah predicted Jesus' Palm Sunday visit to Jerusalem (Zechariah 9:9; Matthew 21).

Zechariah predicted Jesus' disciples would run away (Zechariah 13:7; Matthew 26:31).

Zechariah predicted Judas would betray Jesus for 30 silver coins (Zechariah 11:12; Matthew 26:14-16).

Fundamentals

Is there anything you can do while you wait for God to act (Zechariah 7:9-10)?

The beautiful promise from God in Zechariah 13:9 is as true for you today as it was for the exiles.

1 *A Call to Return to the Lord* In the eighth month of the second year of Darius, the word of the Lord came to the prophet Zechariah son of Berekiah, the son of Iddo:

²"The Lord was very angry with your forefathers. ³Therefore tell the people: This is what the Lord Almighty says: 'Return to me,' declares the Lord Almighty, 'and I will return to you,' says the Lord Almighty. ⁴Do not be like your forefathers, to whom the earlier prophets proclaimed: This is what the Lord Almighty says: 'Turn from your evil ways and your evil practices.' But they would not listen or pay attention to me, declares the Lord. ⁵Where are your forefathers now? And the prophets, do they live forever? ⁶But did not my words and my decrees, which I commanded my servants the prophets, overtake your forefathers?

"Then they repented and said, 'The Lord Almighty has done to us what our ways and practices deserve, just as he determined to do.' "

The Man Among the Myrtle Trees ⁷On the twenty-fourth day of the eleventh month, the month of Shebat, in the second year of Darius, the word of the Lord came to the prophet Zechariah son of Berekiah, the son of Iddo.

⁸During the night I had a vision—and there before me was a man riding a red horse! He was standing among the myrtle trees in a ravine. Behind him were red, brown and white horses.

⁹I asked, "What are these, my lord?"

The angel who was talking with me answered, "I will show you what they are."

¹⁰Then the man standing among the myrtle trees explained, "They are the ones the Lord has sent to go throughout the earth."

¹¹And they reported to the angel of the Lord, who was standing among the myrtle trees, "We have gone throughout the earth and found the whole world at rest and in peace."

¹²Then the angel of the Lord said, "Lord Almighty, how long will you withhold mercy from Jerusalem and from the towns of Judah, which you have been angry with these seventy years?" ¹³So the Lord spoke kind and comforting words to the angel who talked with me.

¹⁴Then the angel who was speaking to me said, "Proclaim this word: This is what the Lord Almighty says: 'I am very jealous for Jerusalem and Zion, ¹⁵but I am very angry with the nations that feel secure. I was only a little angry, but they added to the calamity.'

¹⁶"Therefore, this is what the Lord says: 'I will return to Jerusalem with mercy, and there my house will be rebuilt. And the measuring line will be stretched out over Jerusalem,' declares the Lord Almighty.

¹⁷"Proclaim further: This is what the Lord Almighty says: 'My towns will again overflow with prosperity, and the Lord will again comfort Zion and choose Jerusalem.' "

Four Horns and Four Craftsmen ¹⁸Then I looked up—and there before me were four horns! ¹⁹I asked the angel who was speaking to me, "What are these?"

He answered me, "These are the horns that scattered Judah, Israel and Jerusalem."

²⁰Then the Lord showed me four craftsmen. ²¹I asked, "What are these coming to do?"

He answered, "These are the horns that scattered Judah so that no one could raise his head, but the craftsmen have come to terrify them and throw down these horns of the nations who lifted up their horns against the land of Judah to scatter its people."

2 *A Man With a Measuring Line* Then I looked up—and there before me was a man with a measuring line in his hand! ²I asked, "Where are you going?"

He answered me, "To measure Jerusalem, to find out how wide and how long it is."

³Then the angel who was speaking to me left, and another angel came to meet him ⁴and said to him: "Run, tell that young man, 'Jerusalem will be a city without walls because of the great number of men and livestock in it. ⁵And I myself will be a wall of fire around it,' declares the LORD, 'and I will be its glory within.'

⁶"Come! Come! Flee from the land of the north," declares the LORD, "for I have scattered you to the four winds of heaven," declares the LORD.

⁷"Come, O Zion! Escape, you who live in the Daughter of Babylon!" ⁸For this is what the LORD Almighty says: "After he has honored me and has sent me against the nations that have plundered you—for whoever touches you touches the apple of his eye— ⁹I will surely raise my hand against them so that their slaves will plunder them.ᵃ Then you will know that the LORD Almighty has sent me.

¹⁰"Shout and be glad, O Daughter of Zion. For I am coming, and I will live among you," declares the LORD. ¹¹"Many nations will be joined with the LORD in that day and will become my people. I will live among you and you will know that the LORD Almighty has sent me to you. ¹²The LORD will inherit Judah as his portion in the holy land and will again choose Jerusalem. ¹³Be still before the LORD, all mankind, because he has roused himself from his holy dwelling."

> "I am coming, and I will live among you," declares the LORD (Zechariah 2:10).

Clean Garments for the High Priest Then he showed me Joshuaᵇ the high priest standing before the angel of the LORD, and Satanᶜ standing at his right side to accuse him. ²The LORD said to Satan, "The LORD rebuke you, Satan! The LORD, who has chosen Jerusalem, rebuke you! Is not this man a burning stick snatched from the fire?"

³Now Joshua was dressed in filthy clothes as he stood before the angel. ⁴The angel said to those who were standing before him, "Take off his filthy clothes."

Then he said to Joshua, "See, I have taken away your sin, and I will put rich garments on you."

⁵Then I said, "Put a clean turban on his head." So they put a clean turban on his head and clothed him, while the angel of the LORD stood by.

⁶The angel of the LORD gave this charge to Joshua: ⁷"This is what the LORD Almighty says: 'If you will walk in my ways and keep my requirements, then you will govern my house and have charge of my courts, and I will give you a place among these standing here.

⁸"'Listen, O high priest Joshua and your associates seated before you, who are men symbolic of things to come: I am going to bring my servant, the Branch. ⁹See, the stone I have set in front of Joshua! There are seven eyesᵈ on that one stone, and I will engrave an inscription on it,' says the LORD Almighty, 'and I will remove the sin of this land in a single day.

¹⁰"'In that day each of you will invite his neighbor to sit under his vine and fig tree,' declares the LORD Almighty."

The Gold Lampstand and the Two Olive Trees Then the angel who talked with me returned and wakened me, as a man is wakened from his sleep. ²He asked me, "What do you see?"

I answered, "I see a solid gold lampstand with a bowl at the top and seven lights on it, with seven channels to the lights. ³Also there are two olive trees by it, one on the right of the bowl and the other on its left."

ᵃ8,9 Or says after . . . eye: ⁹"I . . . plunder them."   ᵇ1 A variant of Jeshua; here and elsewhere in Zechariah   ᶜ1 Satan means accuser.   ᵈ9 Or facets

⁴I asked the angel who talked with me, "What are these, my lord?"
⁵He answered, "Do you not know what these are?"

"No, my lord," I replied.

⁶So he said to me, "This is the word of the LORD to Zerubbabel: 'Not by might nor by power, but by my Spirit,' says the LORD Almighty.

⁷"What*a* are you, O mighty mountain? Before Zerubbabel you will become level ground. Then he will bring out the capstone to shouts of 'God bless it! God bless it!' "

⁸Then the word of the LORD came to me: ⁹"The hands of Zerubbabel have laid the foundation of this temple; his hands will also complete it. Then you will know that the LORD Almighty has sent me to you.

¹⁰"Who despises the day of small things? Men will rejoice when they see the plumb line in the hand of Zerubbabel.

"(These seven are the eyes of the LORD, which range throughout the earth.)"

¹¹Then I asked the angel, "What are these two olive trees on the right and the left of the lampstand?"

¹²Again I asked him, "What are these two olive branches beside the two gold pipes that pour out golden oil?"

¹³He replied, "Do you not know what these are?"

"No, my lord," I said.

¹⁴So he said, "These are the two who are anointed to*b* serve the Lord of all the earth."

5 **The Flying Scroll** I looked again—and there before me was a flying scroll!
²He asked me, "What do you see?"

I answered, "I see a flying scroll, thirty feet long and fifteen feet wide.*c*"

³And he said to me, "This is the curse that is going out over the whole land; for according to what it says on one side, every thief will be banished, and according to what it says on the other, everyone who swears falsely will be banished. ⁴The LORD Almighty declares, 'I will send it out, and it will enter the house of the thief and the house of him who swears falsely by my name. It will remain in his house and destroy it, both its timbers and its stones.' "

The Woman in a Basket ⁵Then the angel who was speaking to me came forward and said to me, "Look up and see what this is that is appearing."

⁶I asked, "What is it?"

He replied, "It is a measuring basket.*d*" And he added, "This is the iniquity*e* of the people throughout the land."

⁷Then the cover of lead was raised, and there in the basket sat a woman!
⁸He said, "This is wickedness," and he pushed her back into the basket and pushed the lead cover down over its mouth.

⁹Then I looked up—and there before me were two women, with the wind in their wings! They had wings like those of a stork, and they lifted up the basket between heaven and earth.

¹⁰"Where are they taking the basket?" I asked the angel who was speaking to me.

¹¹He replied, "To the country of Babylonia*f* to build a house for it. When it is ready, the basket will be set there in its place."

6 **Four Chariots** I looked up again—and there before me were four chariots coming out from between two mountains—mountains of bronze!
²The first chariot had red horses, the second black, ³the third white, and the

ZECHARIAH 5

QUIZZER

Q: What did Zechariah see a scroll doing?

BONUS: When Zechariah lifted the lid on a basket, what did he find?

Answers on page 1240

---

*a*7 Or *Who*   *b*14 Or *two who bring oil and*   *c*2 Hebrew *twenty cubits long and ten cubits wide* (about 9 meters long and 4.5 meters wide)   *d*6 Hebrew *an ephah*; also in verses 7-11   *e*6 Or *appearance*
*f*11 Hebrew *Shinar*

fourth dappled—all of them powerful. ⁴I asked the angel who was speaking to me, "What are these, my lord?"

⁵The angel answered me, "These are the four spirits*a* of heaven, going out from standing in the presence of the Lord of the whole world. ⁶The one with the black horses is going toward the north country, the one with the white horses toward the west,*b* and the one with the dappled horses toward the south."

⁷When the powerful horses went out, they were straining to go throughout the earth. And he said, "Go throughout the earth!" So they went throughout the earth.

⁸Then he called to me, "Look, those going toward the north country have given my Spirit*c* rest in the land of the north."

nswers
to Quizzer on
page 1239

A Crown for Joshua ⁹The word of the LORD came to me: ¹⁰"Take silver and gold from the exiles Heldai, Tobijah and Jedaiah, who have arrived from Babylon. Go the same day to the house of Josiah son of Zephaniah. ¹¹Take the silver and gold and make a crown, and set it on the head of the high priest, Joshua son of Jehozadak. ¹²Tell him this is what the LORD Almighty says: 'Here is the man whose name is the Branch, and he will branch out from his place and build the temple of the LORD. ¹³It is he who will build the temple of the LORD, and he will be clothed with majesty and will sit and rule on his throne. And he will be a priest on his throne. And there will be harmony between the two.' ¹⁴The crown will be given to Heldai,*d* Tobijah, Jedaiah and Hen*e* son of Zephaniah as a memorial in the temple of the LORD. ¹⁵Those who are far away will come and help to build the temple of the LORD, and you will know that the LORD Almighty has sent me to you. This will happen if you diligently obey the LORD your God."

Justice and Mercy, Not Fasting In the fourth year of King Darius, the word of the LORD came to Zechariah on the fourth day of the ninth month, the month of Kislev. ²The people of Bethel had sent Sharezer and Regem-Melech, together with their men, to entreat the LORD ³by asking the priests of the house of the LORD Almighty and the prophets, "Should I mourn and fast in the fifth month, as I have done for so many years?"

⁴Then the word of the LORD Almighty came to me: ⁵"Ask all the people of the land and the priests, 'When you fasted and mourned in the fifth and seventh months for the past seventy years, was it really for me that you fasted? ⁶And when you were eating and drinking, were you not just feasting for yourselves? ⁷Are these not the words the LORD proclaimed through the earlier prophets when Jerusalem and its surrounding towns were at rest and prosperous, and the Negev and the western foothills were settled?' "

⁸And the word of the LORD came again to Zechariah: ⁹"This is what the LORD Almighty says: 'Administer true justice; show mercy and compassion to one another. ¹⁰Do not oppress the widow or the fatherless, the alien or the poor. In your hearts do not think evil of each other.'

¹¹"But they refused to pay attention; stubbornly they turned their backs and stopped up their ears. ¹²They made their hearts as hard as flint and would not listen to the law or to the words that the LORD Almighty had sent by his Spirit through the earlier prophets. So the LORD Almighty was very angry.

¹³" 'When I called, they did not listen; so when they called, I would not listen,' says the LORD Almighty. ¹⁴'I scattered them with a whirlwind among all the nations, where they were strangers. The land was left so desolate behind them that no one could come or go. This is how they made the pleasant land desolate.' "

a5 Or *winds* *b6* Or *horses after them* *c8* Or *spirit* *d14* Syriac; Hebrew *Helem* *e14* Or *and the gracious one, the*

8 *The Lord Promises to Bless Jerusalem* Again the word of the Lord Almighty came to me. ²This is what the Lord Almighty says: "I am very jealous for Zion; I am burning with jealousy for her."

³This is what the Lord says: "I will return to Zion and dwell in Jerusalem. Then Jerusalem will be called the City of Truth, and the mountain of the Lord Almighty will be called the Holy Mountain."

⁴This is what the Lord Almighty says: "Once again men and women of ripe old age will sit in the streets of Jerusalem, each with cane in hand because of his age. ⁵The city streets will be filled with boys and girls playing there."

⁶This is what the Lord Almighty says: "It may seem marvelous to the remnant of this people at that time, but will it seem marvelous to me?" declares the Lord Almighty.

⁷This is what the Lord Almighty says: "I will save my people from the countries of the east and the west. ⁸I will bring them back to live in Jerusalem; they will be my people, and I will be faithful and righteous to them as their God."

⁹This is what the Lord Almighty says: "You who now hear these words spoken by the prophets who were there when the foundation was laid for the house of the Lord Almighty, let your hands be strong so that the temple may be built. ¹⁰Before that time there were no wages for man or beast. No one could go about his business safely because of his enemy, for I had turned every man against his neighbor. ¹¹But now I will not deal with the remnant of this people as I did in the past," declares the Lord Almighty.

¹²"The seed will grow well, the vine will yield its fruit, the ground will produce its crops, and the heavens will drop their dew. I will give all these things as an inheritance to the remnant of this people. ¹³As you have been an object of cursing among the nations, O Judah and Israel, so will I save you, and you will be a blessing. Do not be afraid, but let your hands be strong."

¹⁴This is what the Lord Almighty says: "Just as I had determined to bring disaster upon you and showed no pity when your fathers angered me," says the Lord Almighty, ¹⁵"so now I have determined to do good again to Jerusalem and Judah. Do not be afraid. ¹⁶These are the things you are to do: Speak the truth to each other, and render true and sound judgment in your courts; ¹⁷do not plot evil against your neighbor, and do not love to swear falsely. I hate all this," declares the Lord.

¹⁸Again the word of the Lord Almighty came to me. ¹⁹This is what the Lord Almighty says: "The fasts of the fourth, fifth, seventh and tenth months will become joyful and glad occasions and happy festivals for Judah. Therefore love truth and peace."

²⁰This is what the Lord Almighty says: "Many peoples and the inhabitants of many cities will yet come, ²¹and the inhabitants of one city will go to another and say, 'Let us go at once to entreat the Lord and seek the Lord Almighty. I myself am going.' ²²And many peoples and powerful nations will come to Jerusalem to seek the Lord Almighty and to entreat him."

²³This is what the Lord Almighty says: "In those days ten men from all languages and nations will take firm hold of one Jew by the hem of his robe and say, 'Let us go with you, because we have heard that God is with you.' "

9 *Judgment on Israel's Enemies*

An Oracle

The word of the Lord is against the land of Hadrach
  and will rest upon Damascus—
for the eyes of men and all the tribes of Israel
  are on the Lord—*ᵃ*

ᵃ1 Or *Damascus. / For the eye of the* Lord *is on all mankind, / as well as on the tribes of Israel,*

²and upon Hamath too, which borders on it,
  and upon Tyre and Sidon, though they are very skillful.
³Tyre has built herself a stronghold;
  she has heaped up silver like dust,
  and gold like the dirt of the streets.
⁴But the Lord will take away her possessions
  and destroy her power on the sea,
  and she will be consumed by fire.
⁵Ashkelon will see it and fear;
  Gaza will writhe in agony,
  and Ekron too, for her hope will wither.
Gaza will lose her king
  and Ashkelon will be deserted.
⁶Foreigners will occupy Ashdod,
  and I will cut off the pride of the Philistines.
⁷I will take the blood from their mouths,
  the forbidden food from between their teeth.
Those who are left will belong to our God
  and become leaders in Judah,
  and Ekron will be like the Jebusites.
⁸But I will defend my house
  against marauding forces.
Never again will an oppressor overrun my people,
  for now I am keeping watch.

The Coming of Zion's King

⁹Rejoice greatly, O Daughter of Zion!
  Shout, Daughter of Jerusalem!
See, your king*a* comes to you,
  righteous and having salvation,
          gentle and riding on a donkey,
          on a colt, the foal of a donkey.
¹⁰I will take away the chariots from
          Ephraim
  and the war-horses from Jerusalem,
  and the battle bow will be broken.
He will proclaim peace to the nations.
  His rule will extend from sea to sea
  and from the River*b* to the ends of
          the earth.*c*
¹¹As for you, because of the blood of my
          covenant with you,
  I will free your prisoners from the
          waterless pit.
¹²Return to your fortress, O prisoners of
          hope;
  even now I announce that I will
          restore twice as much to you.
¹³I will bend Judah as I bend my bow
  and fill it with Ephraim.
I will rouse your sons, O Zion,
  against your sons, O Greece,
  and make you like a warrior's
          sword.

Direct Line

ZECHARIAH 9:9

This verse is a prophecy Jesus fulfilled on Palm Sunday (see Matthew 21:1–11). Do you know why riding a donkey was significant? When kings in the ancient world went to war, they rode horses. When they visited a city in peace, they rode donkeys. King Jesus rode a donkey into Jerusalem to show he threatened no one, even though religious leaders in that city treated him as an enemy. Why not follow Jesus' example? Be sure others realize you're no threat to them. You're not out to put them down or to win theological arguments. You're there to be like Jesus: loving, caring and eager to help others whether or not they know the Lord.

---

*a*9 Or *King*   *b*10 That is, the Euphrates   *c*10 Or *the end of the land*

The Lord Will Appear

¹⁴Then the Lord will appear over them;
 his arrow will flash like lightning.
The Sovereign Lord will sound the trumpet;
 he will march in the storms of the south,
¹⁵ and the Lord Almighty will shield them.
They will destroy
 and overcome with slingstones.
They will drink and roar as with wine;
 they will be full like a bowl
 used for sprinkling*a* the corners of the altar.
¹⁶The Lord their God will save them on that day
 as the flock of his people.
They will sparkle in his land
 like jewels in a crown.
¹⁷How attractive and beautiful they will be!
 Grain will make the young men thrive,
 and new wine the young women.

10

The Lord Will Care for Judah

Ask the Lord for rain in the springtime;
 it is the Lord who makes the storm clouds.
He gives showers of rain to men,
 and plants of the field to everyone.
²The idols speak deceit,
 diviners see visions that lie;
they tell dreams that are false,
 they give comfort in vain.
Therefore the people wander like sheep
 oppressed for lack of a shepherd.

³"My anger burns against the shepherds,
 and I will punish the leaders;
for the Lord Almighty will care
 for his flock, the house of Judah,
 and make them like a proud horse in battle.
⁴From Judah will come the cornerstone,
 from him the tent peg,
 from him the battle bow,
 from him every ruler.
⁵Together they*b* will be like mighty men
 trampling the muddy streets in battle.
Because the Lord is with them,
 they will fight and overthrow the horsemen.

⁶"I will strengthen the house of Judah
 and save the house of Joseph.
I will restore them
 because I have compassion on them.
They will be as though
 I had not rejected them,
for I am the Lord their God
 and I will answer them.
⁷The Ephraimites will become like mighty men,
 and their hearts will be glad as with wine.

a15 Or bowl, / like b4,5 Or ruler, all of them together. / 5They

Their children will see it and be joyful;
　　their hearts will rejoice in the LORD.
⁸I will signal for them
　　and gather them in.
Surely I will redeem them;
　　they will be as numerous as before.
⁹Though I scatter them among the peoples,
　　yet in distant lands they will remember me.
They and their children will survive,
　　and they will return.
¹⁰I will bring them back from Egypt
　　and gather them from Assyria.
I will bring them to Gilead and Lebanon,
　　and there will not be room enough for them.
¹¹They will pass through the sea of trouble;
　　the surging sea will be subdued
　　and all the depths of the Nile will dry up.
Assyria's pride will be brought down
　　and Egypt's scepter will pass away.
¹²I will strengthen them in the LORD
　　and in his name they will walk,"

　　　　　　　　　　　　　　　　declares the LORD.

11 Open your doors, O Lebanon,
　　so that fire may devour your cedars!
²Wail, O pine tree, for the cedar has fallen;
　　the stately trees are ruined!
Wail, oaks of Bashan;
　　the dense forest has been cut down!
³Listen to the wail of the shepherds;
　　their rich pastures are destroyed!
Listen to the roar of the lions;
　　the lush thicket of the Jordan is ruined!

Two Shepherds ⁴This is what the LORD my God says: "Pasture the flock marked for slaughter. ⁵Their buyers slaughter them and go unpunished. Those who sell them say, 'Praise the LORD, I am rich!' Their own shepherds do not spare them. ⁶For I will no longer have pity on the people of the land," declares the LORD. "I will hand everyone over to his neighbor and his king. They will oppress the land, and I will not rescue them from their hands."

⁷So I pastured the flock marked for slaughter, particularly the oppressed of the flock. Then I took two staffs and called one Favor and the other Union, and I pastured the flock. ⁸In one month I got rid of the three shepherds.

The flock detested me, and I grew weary of them ⁹and said, "I will not be your shepherd. Let the dying die, and the perishing perish. Let those who are left eat one another's flesh."

¹⁰Then I took my staff called Favor and broke it, revoking the covenant I had made with all the nations. ¹¹It was revoked on that day, and so the afflicted of the flock who were watching me knew it was the word of the LORD.

¹²I told them, "If you think it best, give me my pay; but if not, keep it." So they paid me thirty pieces of silver.

¹³And the LORD said to me, "Throw it to the potter"—the handsome price at which they priced me! So I took the thirty pieces of silver and threw them into the house of the LORD to the potter.

¹⁴Then I broke my second staff called Union, breaking the brotherhood between Judah and Israel.

¹⁵Then the LORD said to me, "Take again the equipment of a foolish shepherd. ¹⁶For I am going to raise up a shepherd over the land who will not care for the lost, or seek the young, or heal the injured, or feed the healthy, but will eat the meat of the choice sheep, tearing off their hoofs.

> ¹⁷"Woe to the worthless shepherd,
>   who deserts the flock!
>   May the sword strike his arm and his right eye!
>   May his arm be completely withered,
>   his right eye totally blinded!"

Jerusalem's Enemies to Be Destroyed

An Oracle

This is the word of the LORD concerning Israel. The LORD, who stretches out the heavens, who lays the foundation of the earth, and who forms the spirit of man within him, declares: ²"I am going to make Jerusalem a cup that sends all the surrounding peoples reeling. Judah will be besieged as well as Jerusalem. ³On that day, when all the nations of the earth are gathered against her, I will make Jerusalem an immovable rock for all the nations. All who try to move it will injure themselves. ⁴On that day I will strike every horse with panic and its rider with madness," declares the LORD. "I will keep a watchful eye over the house of Judah, but I will blind all the horses of the nations. ⁵Then the leaders of Judah will say in their hearts, 'The people of Jerusalem are strong, because the LORD Almighty is their God.'

⁶"On that day I will make the leaders of Judah like a firepot in a woodpile, like a flaming torch among sheaves. They will consume right and left all the surrounding peoples, but Jerusalem will remain intact in her place.

⁷"The LORD will save the dwellings of Judah first, so that the honor of the house of David and of Jerusalem's inhabitants may not be greater than that of Judah. ⁸On that day the LORD will shield those who live in Jerusalem, so that the feeblest among them will be like David, and the house of David will be like God, like the Angel of the LORD going before them. ⁹On that day I will set out to destroy all the nations that attack Jerusalem.

Mourning for the One They Pierced   ¹⁰"And I will pour out on the house of David and the inhabitants of Jerusalem a spirit[a] of grace and supplication. They will look on[b] me, the one they have pierced, and they will mourn for him as one mourns for an only child, and grieve bitterly for him as one grieves for a firstborn son. ¹¹On that day the weeping in Jerusalem will be great, like the weeping of Hadad Rimmon in the plain of Megiddo. ¹²The land will mourn, each clan by itself, with their wives by themselves: the clan of the house of David and their wives, the clan of the house of Nathan and their wives, ¹³the clan of the house of Levi and their wives, the clan of Shimei and their wives, ¹⁴and all the rest of the clans and their wives.

Cleansing From Sin   "On that day a fountain will be opened to the house of David and the inhabitants of Jerusalem, to cleanse them from sin and impurity.

²"On that day, I will banish the names of the idols from the land, and they will be remembered no more," declares the LORD Almighty. "I will remove

ZECHARIAH 11

QUIZZER

Q: When Zechariah predicted Jesus' betrayal, how much did he say the betrayer would be paid?

BONUS:
Was that amount a lot of money?

Answers on page 1246

---

a10 Or the Spirit   *b10 Or to*

both the prophets and the spirit of impurity from the land. ³And if anyone still prophesies, his father and mother, to whom he was born, will say to him, 'You must die, because you have told lies in the LORD's name.' When he prophesies, his own parents will stab him.

⁴"On that day every prophet will be ashamed of his prophetic vision. He will not put on a prophet's garment of hair in order to deceive. ⁵He will say, 'I am not a prophet. I am a farmer; the land has been my livelihood since my youth.ᵃ' ⁶If someone asks him, 'What are these wounds on your bodyᵇ?' he will answer, 'The wounds I was given at the house of my friends.'

The Shepherd Struck, the Sheep Scattered

⁷"Awake, O sword, against my shepherd,
    against the man who is close to me!"
    declares the LORD Almighty.
"Strike the shepherd,
    and the sheep will be scattered,
    and I will turn my hand against the little ones.
⁸In the whole land," declares the LORD,
    "two-thirds will be struck down and perish;
    yet one-third will be left in it.
⁹This third I will bring into the fire;
    I will refine them like silver
    and test them like gold.
They will call on my name
    and I will answer them;
I will say, 'They are my people,'
    and they will say, 'The LORD is our God.' "

The LORD Comes and Reigns   A day of the LORD is coming when your plunder will be divided among you.

²I will gather all the nations to Jerusalem to fight against it; the city will be captured, the houses ransacked, and the women raped. Half of the city will go into exile, but the rest of the people will not be taken from the city.

³Then the LORD will go out and fight against those nations, as he fights in the day of battle. ⁴On that day his feet will stand on the Mount of Olives, east of Jerusalem, and the Mount of Olives will be split in two from east to west, forming a great valley, with half of the mountain moving north and half moving south. ⁵You will flee by my mountain valley, for it will extend to Azel. You will flee as you fled from the earthquakeᶜ in the days of Uzziah king of Judah. Then the LORD my God will come, and all the holy ones with him.

⁶On that day there will be no light, no cold or frost. ⁷It will be a unique day, without daytime or nighttime—a day known to the LORD. When evening comes, there will be light.

⁸On that day living water will flow out from Jerusalem, half to the eastern seaᵈ and half to the western sea,ᵉ in summer and in winter.

⁹The LORD will be king over the whole earth. On that day there will be one LORD, and his name the only name.

¹⁰The whole land, from Geba to Rimmon, south of Jerusalem, will become like the Arabah. But Jerusalem will be raised up and remain in its place, from the Benjamin Gate to the site of the First Gate, to the Corner Gate, and from the Tower of Hananel to the royal winepresses. ¹¹It will be inhabited; never again will it be destroyed. Jerusalem will be secure.

ᵃ5 Or *farmer; a man sold me in my youth*   ᵇ6 Or *wounds between your hands*   ᶜ5 Or ⁵*My mountain valley will be blocked and will extend to Azel. It will be blocked as it was blocked because of the earthquake*   ᵈ8 That is, the Dead Sea   ᵉ8 That is, the Mediterranean

¹²This is the plague with which the Lord will strike all the nations that fought against Jerusalem: Their flesh will rot while they are still standing on their feet, their eyes will rot in their sockets, and their tongues will rot in their mouths. ¹³On that day men will be stricken by the Lord with great panic. Each man will seize the hand of another, and they will attack each other. ¹⁴Judah too will fight at Jerusalem. The wealth of all the surrounding nations will be collected—great quantities of gold and silver and clothing. ¹⁵A similar plague will strike the horses and mules, the camels and donkeys, and all the animals in those camps.

¹⁶Then the survivors from all the nations that have attacked Jerusalem will go up year after year to worship the King, the Lord Almighty, and to celebrate the Feast of Tabernacles. ¹⁷If any of the peoples of the earth do not go up to Jerusalem to worship the King, the Lord Almighty, they will have no rain. ¹⁸If the Egyptian people do not go up and take part, they will have no rain. The Lord*ᵃ* will bring on them the plague he inflicts on the nations that do not go up to celebrate the Feast of Tabernacles. ¹⁹This will be the punishment of Egypt and the punishment of all the nations that do not go up to celebrate the Feast of Tabernacles.

²⁰On that day HOLY TO THE LORD will be inscribed on the bells of the horses, and the cooking pots in the Lord's house will be like the sacred bowls in front of the altar. ²¹Every pot in Jerusalem and Judah will be holy to the Lord Almighty, and all who come to sacrifice will take some of the pots and cook in them. And on that day there will no longer be a Canaanite*ᵇ* in the house of the Lord Almighty.

ᵃ18 Or part, then the Lord   ᵇ21 Or merchant

Introduction

to the
book of Malachi

WHO, ME?

Have you ever seen someone play innocent? They do wrong, but they aren't going to admit it! It's almost funny. But it's frustrating too. What can you do with someone who won't admit anything, even when caught in the act?

In Malachi's day the "Who, me?" people were descendants of the captives who returned to Judah from Babylon. They'd become indifferent to God, and their lives showed it. No matter how they pretended, though, they couldn't fool the Lord. You might fool other people, but no one can fool God.

Fundamentals

Can someone really rob or steal from God (Malachi 3:6-9)?

What does God promise to those who give him what he's due (Malachi 3:10-12)?

Whose "treasured possession" are you (Malachi 3:17-18)?

FAST FACTS

Malachi means "my messenger."

Malachi preached about 430 B.C.

Only 50,000 lived in Judah at this time.

After Malachi, God didn't speak through the prophets for more than 400 years.

An oracle: The word of the LORD to Israel through Malachi.[a]

Jacob Loved, Esau Hated

[2]"I have loved you," says the LORD.

"But you ask, 'How have you loved us?'"

"Was not Esau Jacob's brother?" the LORD says. "Yet I have loved Jacob, [3]but Esau I have hated, and I have turned his mountains into a wasteland and left his inheritance to the desert jackals."

[4]Edom may say, "Though we have been crushed, we will rebuild the ruins."

But this is what the LORD Almighty says: "They may build, but I will demolish. They will be called the Wicked Land, a people always under the wrath of the LORD. [5]You will see it with your own eyes and say, 'Great is the LORD—even beyond the borders of Israel!'

Blemished Sacrifices

[6]"A son honors his father, and a servant his master. If I am a father, where is the honor due me? If I am a master, where is the respect due me?" says the LORD Almighty. "It is you, O priests, who show contempt for my name.

"But you ask, 'How have we shown contempt for your name?'"

[7]"You place defiled food on my altar.

"But you ask, 'How have we defiled you?'"

"By saying that the LORD's table is contemptible. [8]When you bring blind animals for sacrifice, is that not wrong? When you sacrifice crippled or diseased animals, is that not wrong? Try offering them to your governor! Would he be pleased with you? Would he accept you?" says the LORD Almighty.

[9]"Now implore God to be gracious to us. With such offerings from your hands, will he accept you?"—says the LORD Almighty.

[10]"Oh, that one of you would shut the temple doors, so that you would not light useless fires on my altar! I am not pleased with you," says the LORD Almighty, "and I will accept no offering from your hands. [11]My name will be great among the nations, from the rising to the setting of the sun. In every place incense and pure offerings will be brought to my name, because my name will be great among the nations," says the LORD Almighty.

[12]"But you profane it by saying of the Lord's table, 'It is defiled,' and of its food, 'It is contemptible.' [13]And you say, 'What a burden!' and you sniff at it contemptuously," says the LORD Almighty.

"When you bring injured, crippled or diseased animals and offer them as sacrifices, should I accept them from your hands?" says the LORD. [14]"Cursed is the cheat who has an acceptable male in his flock and vows to give it, but then sacrifices a blemished animal to the Lord. For I am a great king," says the LORD Almighty, "and my name is to be feared among the nations.

Admonition for the Priests

"And now this admonition is for you, O priests. [2]If you do not listen, and if you do not set your heart to honor my name," says the LORD Almighty, "I will send a

---

[a]1 Malachi means my messenger.

MALACHI 1:1-2

Take a quick look at the first two verses in Malachi. Notice anything significant? The very first thing that God wanted to be sure his people knew was that *he loved them.* God had a lot of negative things to say to these people. He had a lot of scolding to do. But first he said, "I love you." In your relationships, especially with your family, is it easier to concentrate on what bugs you about them? What drives you nuts? Or just the fact that down deep you really love them? Keeping love at the front of your mind will have a tremendous impact on how you treat others. Try to remember that when you're at home today.

Direct Line

curse upon you, and I will curse your blessings. Yes, I have already cursed them, because you have not set your heart to honor me.

³"Because of you I will rebuke[a] your descendants[b]; I will spread on your faces the offal from your festival sacrifices, and you will be carried off with it. ⁴And you will know that I have sent you this admonition so that my covenant with Levi may continue," says the LORD Almighty. ⁵"My covenant was with him, a covenant of life and peace, and I gave them to him; this called for reverence and he revered me and stood in awe of my name. ⁶True instruction was in his mouth and nothing false was found on his lips. He walked with me in peace and uprightness, and turned many from sin.

⁷"For the lips of a priest ought to preserve knowledge, and from his mouth men should seek instruction—because he is the messenger of the LORD Almighty. ⁸But you have turned from the way and by your teaching have caused many to stumble; you have violated the covenant with Levi," says the LORD Almighty. ⁹"So I have caused you to be despised and humiliated before all the people, because you have not followed my ways but have shown partiality in matters of the law."

Judah Unfaithful ¹⁰Have we not all one Father[c]? Did not one God create us? Why do we profane the covenant of our fathers by breaking faith with one another?

¹¹Judah has broken faith. A detestable thing has been committed in Israel and in Jerusalem: Judah has desecrated the sanctuary the LORD loves, by marrying the daughter of a foreign god. ¹²As for the man who does this, whoever he may be, may the LORD cut him off from the tents of Jacob[d]—even though he brings offerings to the LORD Almighty.

¹³Another thing you do: You flood the LORD's altar with tears. You weep and wail because he no longer pays attention to your offerings or accepts them with pleasure from your hands. ¹⁴You ask, "Why?" It is because the LORD is acting as the witness between you and the wife of your youth, because you have broken faith with her, though she is your partner, the wife of your marriage covenant.

¹⁵Has not the LORD made them one? In flesh and spirit they are his. And why one? Because he was seeking godly offspring.[e] So guard yourself in your spirit, and do not break faith with the wife of your youth.

¹⁶"I hate divorce," says the LORD God of Israel, "and I hate a man's covering himself[f] with violence as well as with his garment," says the LORD Almighty.

So guard yourself in your spirit, and do not break faith.

The Day of Judgment ¹⁷You have wearied the LORD with your words.

"How have we wearied him?" you ask.

By saying, "All who do evil are good in the eyes of the LORD, and he is pleased with them" or "Where is the God of justice?"

3 "See, I will send my messenger, who will prepare the way before me. Then suddenly the Lord you are seeking will come to his temple; the messenger of the covenant, whom you desire, will come," says the LORD Almighty.

²But who can endure the day of his coming? Who can stand when he appears? For he will be like a refiner's fire or a launderer's soap. ³He will sit as a refiner and purifier of silver; he will purify the Levites and refine them like gold and silver. Then the LORD will have men who will bring offerings in

---

[a]3 Or *cut off* (see Septuagint) [b]3 Or *will blight your grain* [c]10 Or *father* [d]12 Or ¹²*May the LORD cut off from the tents of Jacob anyone who gives testimony in behalf of the man who does this* [e]15 Or ¹⁵*But the one who is our father, did not do this, not as long as life remained in him. And what was he seeking? An offspring from God* [f]16 Or *his wife*

Dear Sam,

The girls at school who are sexually active seem to be very popular. I want to stay a virgin, but is it really worth being mocked and lonely?

Erin in Erie

100 Advice Lane, Anywhere, USA

Dear Erin,

It makes me sad to think that you should be mocked for doing what is so right and good in the eyes of God! You should receive great encouragement from reading Malachi 3:14-18. The people in that day were upset, just as you are, that those who were doing wrong were the ones who were getting all the breaks. But God reminded them, and you, that if you love God and obey him, he writes your name on his "scroll of remembrance," his "honor roll." And he calls you his "treasured possession."

Being popular by defiling your body, risking pregnancy and disease, isn't as desirable as keeping yourself pure for a special love and for making it on God's honor roll! Keep yourself as you are. Find Christian friends who will encourage you to be faithful to God. And let the others reap what they sow—you'll have a better harvest!

Sam

righteousness, [4]and the offerings of Judah and Jerusalem will be acceptable to the LORD, as in days gone by, as in former years.

[5]"So I will come near to you for judgment. I will be quick to testify against sorcerers, adulterers and perjurers, against those who defraud laborers of their wages, who oppress the widows and the fatherless, and deprive aliens of justice, but do not fear me," says the LORD Almighty.

Robbing God [6]"I the LORD do not change. So you, O descendants of Jacob, are not destroyed. [7]Ever since the time of your forefathers you have turned away from my decrees and have not kept them. Return to me, and I will return to you," says the LORD Almighty.

"But you ask, 'How are we to return?'

[8]"Will a man rob God? Yet you rob me.

"But you ask, 'How do we rob you?'

"In tithes and offerings. [9]You are under a curse—the whole nation of you—because you are robbing me. [10]Bring the whole tithe into the storehouse, that there may be food in my house. Test me in this," says the LORD Almighty, "and see if I will not throw open the floodgates of heaven and pour out so much blessing that you will not have room enough for it. [11]I will prevent pests from devouring your crops, and the vines in your fields will not cast their fruit," says the LORD Almighty. [12]"Then all the nations will call you blessed, for yours will be a delightful land," says the LORD Almighty.

[13]"You have said harsh things against me," says the LORD.

"Yet you ask, 'What have we said against you?'

[14]"You have said, 'It is futile to serve God. What did we gain by carrying out his requirements and going about like mourners before the LORD Almighty? [15]But now we call the arrogant blessed. Certainly the evildoers prosper, and even those who challenge God escape.' "

[16]Then those who feared the LORD talked with each other, and the LORD listened and heard. A scroll of remembrance was written in his presence concerning those who feared the LORD and honored his name.

[17]"They will be mine," says the LORD Almighty, "in the day when I make up my treasured possession.[a] I will spare them, just as in compassion a man spares his son who serves him. [18]And you will again see the distinction between the righteous and the wicked, between those who serve God and those who do not.

The Day of the LORD "Surely the day is coming; it will burn like a furnace. All the arrogant and every evildoer will be stubble, and that day that is coming will set them on fire," says the LORD Almighty. "Not a root or a branch will be left to them. [2]But for you who revere my name, the sun of righteousness will rise with healing in its wings. And you will go out and leap like calves released from the stall. [3]Then you will trample down the wicked; they will be ashes under the soles of your feet on the day when I do these things," says the LORD Almighty.

[4]"Remember the law of my servant Moses, the decrees and laws I gave him at Horeb for all Israel.

[5]"See, I will send you the prophet Elijah before that great and dreadful day of the LORD comes. [6]He will turn the hearts of the fathers to their children, and the hearts of the children to their fathers; or else I will come and strike the land with a curse."

> "They will be mine," says the LORD Almighty, "in the day when I make up my treasured possession" (Malachi 3:17).

---

[a]17 Or Almighty, "my treasured possession, in the day when I act

The *New* Testament

LOOKS.

Have you ever had someone describe a person to you? You get a mental picture of how that person looks. Then you meet him or her. Can that be the person? He or she sure doesn't look anything like you expected.

First-century Jews expected the promised Savior to be a conqueror. Jesus was a teacher. Instead of raising an army to defeat the Romans, he urged the people to trust him as God's Son. Matthew wrote to prove that Jesus really did fulfill the prophecies from the Old Testament and is the promised Savior. What Jesus conquered was sin. And the kingdom he rules today is in your heart.

Fun damentals

How can you keep from giving in to temptation (Matthew 4:1-11)?

How are you supposed to give help to others (Matthew 6:1-4)?

Are the do's and don'ts some churches have important (Matthew 12:3-8)?

FAST FACTS

Matthew was one of Jesus' 12 disciples.

Matthew quotes the Old Testament 53 times to show Jesus is the Messiah.

Messiah means the "anointed one."

Matthew was a hated tax collector before becoming Jesus' follower (Matthew 9:9-13).

The Genealogy of Jesus   A record of the genealogy of Jesus Christ the son of David, the son of Abraham:

2 Abraham was the father of Isaac,
  Isaac the father of Jacob,
  Jacob the father of Judah and his brothers,
3 Judah the father of Perez and Zerah, whose mother was Tamar,
  Perez the father of Hezron,
  Hezron the father of Ram,
4 Ram the father of Amminadab,
  Amminadab the father of Nahshon,
  Nahshon the father of Salmon,
5 Salmon the father of Boaz, whose mother was Rahab,
  Boaz the father of Obed, whose mother was Ruth,
  Obed the father of Jesse,
6 and Jesse the father of King David.

David was the father of Solomon, whose mother had been Uriah's wife,
7 Solomon the father of Rehoboam,
  Rehoboam the father of Abijah,
  Abijah the father of Asa,
8 Asa the father of Jehoshaphat,
  Jehoshaphat the father of Jehoram,
  Jehoram the father of Uzziah,
9 Uzziah the father of Jotham,
  Jotham the father of Ahaz,
  Ahaz the father of Hezekiah,
10 Hezekiah the father of Manasseh,
  Manasseh the father of Amon,
  Amon the father of Josiah,
11 and Josiah the father of Jeconiah[a] and his brothers at the time of the exile to Babylon.

12 After the exile to Babylon:
  Jeconiah was the father of Shealtiel,
  Shealtiel the father of Zerubbabel,
13 Zerubbabel the father of Abiud,
  Abiud the father of Eliakim,
  Eliakim the father of Azor,
14 Azor the father of Zadok,
  Zadok the father of Akim,
  Akim the father of Eliud,
15 Eliud the father of Eleazar,
  Eleazar the father of Matthan,
  Matthan the father of Jacob,
16 and Jacob the father of Joseph, the husband of Mary, of whom was born Jesus, who is called Christ.

17 Thus there were fourteen generations in all from Abraham to David, fourteen from David to the exile to Babylon, and fourteen from the exile to the Christ.[b]

The Birth of Jesus Christ   18 This is how the birth of Jesus Christ came about: His mother Mary was pledged to be married to Joseph, but before they came together, she was found to be with child through the Holy Spirit. 19 Because Joseph her husband was a righteous man and did not want to expose her to public disgrace, he had in mind to divorce her quietly.

---

[a]11 That is, Jehoiachin; also in verse 12   [b]17 Or *Messiah.* "The Christ" (Greek) and "the Messiah" (Hebrew) both mean "the Anointed One."

²⁰But after he had considered this, an angel of the Lord appeared to him in a dream and said, "Joseph son of David, do not be afraid to take Mary home as your wife, because what is conceived in her is from the Holy Spirit. ²¹She will give birth to a son, and you are to give him the name Jesus,ᵃ because he will save his people from their sins."

²²All this took place to fulfill what the Lord had said through the prophet: ²³"The virgin will be with child and will give birth to a son, and they will call him Immanuel"ᵇ—which means, "God with us."

²⁴When Joseph woke up, he did what the angel of the Lord had commanded him and took Mary home as his wife. ²⁵But he had no union with her until she gave birth to a son. And he gave him the name Jesus.

The Visit of the Magi After Jesus was born in Bethlehem in Judea, during the time of King Herod, Magiᶜ from the east came to Jerusalem ²and asked, "Where is the one who has been born king of the Jews? We saw his star in the eastᵈ and have come to worship him."

³When King Herod heard this he was disturbed, and all Jerusalem with him. ⁴When he had called together all the people's chief priests and teachers of the law, he asked them where the Christᵉ was to be born. ⁵"In Bethlehem in Judea," they replied, "for this is what the prophet has written:

⁶" 'But you, Bethlehem, in the land of
    Judah,
are by no means least among the rulers
    of Judah;
for out of you will come a ruler
    who will be the shepherd of my people Israel.'ᶠ "

⁷Then Herod called the Magi secretly and found out from them the exact time the star had appeared. ⁸He sent them to Bethlehem and said, "Go and make a careful search for the child. As soon as you find him, report to me, so that I too may go and worship him."

⁹After they had heard the king, they went on their way, and the star they had seen in the eastᵍ went ahead of them until it stopped over the place where the child was. ¹⁰When they saw the star, they were overjoyed. ¹¹On coming to the house, they saw the child with his mother Mary, and they bowed down and worshiped him. Then they opened their treasures and presented him with gifts of gold and of incense and of myrrh. ¹²And having been warned in a dream not to go back to Herod, they returned to their country by another route.

The Escape to Egypt ¹³When they had gone, an angel of the Lord appeared to Joseph in a dream. "Get up," he said, "take the child and his mother and escape to Egypt. Stay there until I tell you, for Herod is going to search for the child to kill him."

¹⁴So he got up, took the child and his mother during the night and left for Egypt, ¹⁵where he stayed until the death of Herod. And so was fulfilled what the Lord had said through the prophet: "Out of Egypt I called my son."ʰ

¹⁶When Herod realized that he had been outwitted by the Magi, he was furious, and he gave orders to kill all the boys in Bethlehem and its vicinity who were two years old and under, in accordance with the time he had learned from the Magi. ¹⁷Then what was said through the prophet Jeremiah was fulfilled:

MATTHEW 2

QUIZZER

Q: How many wise men, or Magi, came to see Jesus?

BONUS: Where did they come from and how did they know about the star?

Answers on page 1258

ᵃ21 *Jesus* is the Greek form of *Joshua,* which means *the Lord saves.*   ᵇ23 Isaiah 7:14   ᶜ1 Traditionally *Wise Men*   ᵈ2 Or *star when it rose*   ᵉ4 Or *Messiah*   ᶠ6 Micah 5:2   ᵍ9 Or *seen when it rose*   ʰ15 Hosea 11:1

> [18]"A voice is heard in Ramah,
> weeping and great mourning,
> Rachel weeping for her children
> and refusing to be comforted,
> because they are no more."[a]

The Return to Nazareth [19]After Herod died, an angel of the Lord appeared in a dream to Joseph in Egypt [20]and said, "Get up, take the child and his mother and go to the land of Israel, for those who were trying to take the child's life are dead."

[21]So he got up, took the child and his mother and went to the land of Israel. [22]But when he heard that Archelaus was reigning in Judea in place of his father Herod, he was afraid to go there. Having been warned in a dream, he withdrew to the district of Galilee, [23]and he went and lived in a town called Nazareth. So was fulfilled what was said through the prophets: "He will be called a Nazarene."

Answers
to Quizzer on
page 1257

A: No one knows, because the Bible doesn't say!

BONUS: "Magi" (Matthew 2:1–2) were scholars in ancient Persia. Most think the Magi had studied the Jewish Scriptures and connected the star with Numbers 24:17.

John the Baptist Prepares the Way In those days John the Baptist came, preaching in the Desert of Judea [2]and saying, "Repent, for the kingdom of heaven is near." [3]This is he who was spoken of through the prophet Isaiah:

> "A voice of one calling in the desert,
> 'Prepare the way for the Lord,
> make straight paths for him.' "[b]

[4]John's clothes were made of camel's hair, and he had a leather belt around his waist. His food was locusts and wild honey. [5]People went out to him from Jerusalem and all Judea and the whole region of the Jordan. [6]Confessing their sins, they were baptized by him in the Jordan River.

[7]But when he saw many of the Pharisees and Sadducees coming to where he was baptizing, he said to them: "You brood of vipers! Who warned you to flee from the coming wrath? [8]Produce fruit in keeping with repentance. [9]And do not think you can say to yourselves, 'We have Abraham as our father.' I tell you that out of these stones God can raise up children for Abraham. [10]The ax is already at the root of the trees, and every tree that does not produce good fruit will be cut down and thrown into the fire.

[11]"I baptize you with[c] water for repentance. But after me will come one who is more powerful than I, whose sandals I am not fit to carry. He will baptize you with the Holy Spirit and with fire. [12]His winnowing fork is in his hand, and he will clear his threshing floor, gathering his wheat into the barn and burning up the chaff with unquenchable fire."

The Baptism of Jesus [13]Then Jesus came from Galilee to the Jordan to be baptized by John. [14]But John tried to deter him, saying, "I need to be baptized by you, and do you come to me?"

[15]Jesus replied, "Let it be so now; it is proper for us to do this to fulfill all righteousness." Then John consented.

[16]As soon as Jesus was baptized, he went up out of the water. At that moment heaven was opened, and he saw the Spirit of God descending like a dove and lighting on him. [17]And a voice from heaven said, "This is my Son, whom I love; with him I am well pleased."

The Temptation of Jesus Then Jesus was led by the Spirit into the desert to be tempted by the devil. [2]After fasting forty days and forty nights, he was hungry. [3]The tempter came to him and said, "If you are the Son of God, tell these stones to become bread."

[a]18 Jer. 31:15 [b]3 Isaiah 40:3 [c]11 Or in

[4]Jesus answered, "It is written: 'Man does not live on bread alone, but on every word that comes from the mouth of God.'[a]"

[5]Then the devil took him to the holy city and had him stand on the highest point of the temple. [6]"If you are the Son of God," he said, "throw yourself down. For it is written:

> " 'He will command his angels concerning you,
> and they will lift you up in their hands,
> so that you will not strike your foot against a stone.'[b]"

[7]Jesus answered him, "It is also written: 'Do not put the Lord your God to the test.'[c]"

[8]Again, the devil took him to a very high mountain and showed him all the kingdoms of the world and their splendor. [9]"All this I will give you," he said, "if you will bow down and worship me."

[10]Jesus said to him, "Away from me, Satan! For it is written: 'Worship the Lord your God, and serve him only.'[d]"

[11]Then the devil left him, and angels came and attended him.

Jesus Begins to Preach [12]When Jesus heard that John had been put in prison, he returned to Galilee. [13]Leaving Nazareth, he went and lived in Capernaum, which was by the lake in the area of Zebulun and Naphtali— [14]to fulfill what was said through the prophet Isaiah:

> [15]"Land of Zebulun and land of Naphtali,
> the way to the sea, along the Jordan,
> Galilee of the Gentiles—
> [16]the people living in darkness
> have seen a great light;
> on those living in the land of the shadow of death
> a light has dawned."[e]

[17]From that time on Jesus began to preach, "Repent, for the kingdom of heaven is near."

The Calling of the First Disciples [18]As Jesus was walking beside the Sea of Galilee, he saw two brothers, Simon called Peter and his brother Andrew. They were casting a net into the lake, for they were fishermen. [19]"Come, follow me," Jesus said, "and I will make you fishers of men." [20]At once they left their nets and followed him.

[21]Going on from there, he saw two other brothers, James son of Zebedee and his brother John. They were in a boat with their father Zebedee, preparing their nets. Jesus called them, [22]and immediately they left the boat and their father and followed him.

Jesus Heals the Sick [23]Jesus went throughout Galilee, teaching in their synagogues, preaching the good news of the kingdom, and healing every disease and sickness among the people. [24]News about him spread all over Syria, and people brought

---

MATTHEW 4:1–11

Did you hear about the preacher who asked his congregation, "Do you ever have trouble with giving in to temptation?" A voice from the choir answered, "Never. I can give in to temptation any time!" No doubt. But can you be tempted without giving in? Yes, if you follow Jesus' example. When Satan tempted him, Jesus looked to Scripture for guidance. Jesus knew that God's Word would show him what was right in each situation, and he put it into practice right then and there. If you trust God's Word as your guide to right and wrong, and if you choose to act on God's Word when you're tempted, you'll overcome your temptations too.

---

[a]4 Deut. 8:3 [b]6 Psalm 91:11,12 [c]7 Deut. 6:16 [d]10 Deut. 6:13 [e]16 Isaiah 9:1,2

to him all who were ill with various diseases, those suffering severe pain, the demon-possessed, those having seizures, and the paralyzed, and he healed them. [25]Large crowds from Galilee, the Decapolis,[a] Jerusalem, Judea and the region across the Jordan followed him.

The Beatitudes Now when he saw the crowds, he went up on a mountainside and sat down. His disciples came to him, [2]and he began to teach them, saying:

[3]"Blessed are the poor in spirit,
for theirs is the kingdom of heaven.
[4]Blessed are those who mourn,
for they will be comforted.
[5]Blessed are the meek,
for they will inherit the earth.
[6]Blessed are those who hunger and thirst for righteousness,
for they will be filled.
[7]Blessed are the merciful,
for they will be shown mercy.
[8]Blessed are the pure in heart,
for they will see God.
[9]Blessed are the peacemakers,
for they will be called sons of God.
[10]Blessed are those who are persecuted because of righteousness,
for theirs is the kingdom of heaven.

[11]"Blessed are you when people insult you, persecute you and falsely say all kinds of evil against you because of me. [12]Rejoice and be glad, because great is your reward in heaven, for in the same way they persecuted the prophets who were before you.

> Blessed are the pure in heart, for they will see God (Matthew 5:8).

Salt and Light [13]"You are the salt of the earth. But if the salt loses its saltiness, how can it be made salty again? It is no longer good for anything, except to be thrown out and trampled by men.

[14]"You are the light of the world. A city on a hill cannot be hidden. [15]Neither do people light a lamp and put it under a bowl. Instead they put it on its stand, and it gives light to everyone in the house. [16]In the same way, let your light shine before men, that they may see your good deeds and praise your Father in heaven.

The Fulfillment of the Law [17]"Do not think that I have come to abolish the Law or the Prophets; I have not come to abolish them but to fulfill them. [18]I tell you the truth, until heaven and earth disappear, not the smallest letter, not the least stroke of a pen, will by any means disappear from the Law until everything is accomplished. [19]Anyone who breaks one of the least of these commandments and teaches others to do the same will be called least in the kingdom of heaven, but whoever practices and teaches these commands will be called great in the kingdom of heaven. [20]For I tell you that unless your righteousness surpasses that of the Pharisees and the teachers of the law, you will certainly not enter the kingdom of heaven.

Murder [21]"You have heard that it was said to the people long ago, 'Do not murder,[b] and anyone who murders will be subject to judgment.' [22]But I tell you that anyone who is angry with his brother[c] will be subject to judgment.

[a]25 That is, the Ten Cities [b]21 Exodus 20:13 [c]22 Some manuscripts *brother without cause*

Again, anyone who says to his brother, 'Raca,'*a* is answerable to the Sanhedrin. But anyone who says, 'You fool!' will be in danger of the fire of hell.

²³"Therefore, if you are offering your gift at the altar and there remember that your brother has something against you, ²⁴leave your gift there in front of the altar. First go and be reconciled to your brother; then come and offer your gift.

²⁵"Settle matters quickly with your adversary who is taking you to court. Do it while you are still with him on the way, or he may hand you over to the judge, and the judge may hand you over to the officer, and you may be thrown into prison. ²⁶I tell you the truth, you will not get out until you have paid the last penny.*b*

Adultery   ²⁷"You have heard that it was said, 'Do not commit adultery.'*c* ²⁸But I tell you that anyone who looks at a woman lustfully has already committed adultery with her in his heart. ²⁹If your right eye causes you to sin, gouge it out and throw it away. It is better for you to lose one part of your body than for your whole body to be thrown into hell. ³⁰And if your right hand causes you to sin, cut it off and throw it away. It is better for you to lose one part of your body than for your whole body to go into hell.

Divorce   ³¹"It has been said, 'Anyone who divorces his wife must give her a certificate of divorce.'*d* ³²But I tell you that anyone who divorces his wife, except for marital unfaithfulness, causes her to become an adulteress, and anyone who marries the divorced woman commits adultery.

Oaths   ³³"Again, you have heard that it was said to the people long ago, 'Do not break your oath, but keep the oaths you have made to the Lord.' ³⁴But I tell you, Do not swear at all: either by heaven, for it is God's throne; ³⁵or by the earth, for it is his footstool; or by Jerusalem, for it is the city of the Great King. ³⁶And do not swear by your head, for you cannot make even one hair white or black. ³⁷Simply let your 'Yes' be 'Yes,' and your 'No,' 'No'; anything beyond this comes from the evil one.

An Eye for an Eye   ³⁸"You have heard that it was said, 'Eye for eye, and tooth for tooth.'*e* ³⁹But I tell you, Do not resist an evil person. If someone strikes you on the right cheek, turn to him the other also. ⁴⁰And if someone wants to sue you and take your tunic, let him have your cloak as well. ⁴¹If someone forces you to go one mile, go with him two miles. ⁴²Give to the one who asks you, and do not turn away from the one who wants to borrow from you.

Love for Enemies   ⁴³"You have heard that it was said, 'Love your neighbor*f* and hate your enemy.' ⁴⁴But I tell you: Love your enemies*g* and pray for those who persecute you, ⁴⁵that you may be sons of your Father in heaven. He causes his sun to rise on the evil and the good, and sends rain on the righteous and the unrighteous. ⁴⁶If you love those who love you, what reward will you get? Are not even the tax collectors doing that? ⁴⁷And if you greet only your brothers, what are you doing more than others? Do not even pagans do that? ⁴⁸Be perfect, therefore, as your heavenly Father is perfect.

Giving to the Needy   "Be careful not to do your 'acts of righteousness' before men, to be seen by them. If you do, you will have no reward from your Father in heaven.

²"So when you give to the needy, do not announce it with trumpets, as the hypocrites do in the synagogues and on the streets, to be honored by men. I tell you the truth, they have received their reward in full. ³But when you give to the needy, do not let your left hand know what your right hand is doing,

a22 An Aramaic term of contempt   *b26* Greek *kodrantes*   *c27* Exodus 20:14   *d31* Deut. 24:1   *e38* Exodus 21:24; Lev. 24:20; Deut. 19:21   *f43* Lev. 19:18   *g44* Some late manuscripts *enemies, bless those who curse you, do good to those who hate you*

[4]so that your giving may be in secret. Then your Father, who sees what is done in secret, will reward you.

Prayer [5]"And when you pray, do not be like the hypocrites, for they love to pray standing in the synagogues and on the street corners to be seen by men. I tell you the truth, they have received their reward in full. [6]But when you pray, go into your room, close the door and pray to your Father, who is unseen. Then your Father, who sees what is done in secret, will reward you. [7]And when you pray, do not keep on babbling like pagans, for they think they will be heard because of their many words. [8]Do not be like them, for your Father knows what you need before you ask him.

[9]"This, then, is how you should pray:

> " 'Our Father in heaven,
>   hallowed be your name,
> [10]your kingdom come,
>   your will be done
>   on earth as it is in heaven.
> [11]Give us today our daily bread.
> [12]Forgive us our debts,
>   as we also have forgiven our debtors.
> [13]And lead us not into temptation,
>   but deliver us from the evil one.[a]'

[14]For if you forgive men when they sin against you, your heavenly Father will also forgive you. [15]But if you do not forgive men their sins, your Father will not forgive your sins.

Fasting [16]"When you fast, do not look somber as the hypocrites do, for they disfigure their faces to show men they are fasting. I tell you the truth, they have received their reward in full. [17]But when you fast, put oil on your head and wash your face, [18]so that it will not be obvious to men that you are fasting, but only to your Father, who is unseen; and your Father, who sees what is done in secret, will reward you.

Treasures in Heaven [19]"Do not store up for yourselves treasures on earth, where moth and rust destroy, and where thieves break in and steal. [20]But store up for yourselves treasures in heaven, where moth and rust do not destroy, and where thieves do not break in and steal. [21]For where your treasure is, there your heart will be also.

[22]"The eye is the lamp of the body. If your eyes are good, your whole body will be full of light. [23]But if your eyes are bad, your whole body will be full of darkness. If then the light within you is darkness, how great is that darkness!

[24]"No one can serve two masters. Either he will hate the one and love the other, or he will be devoted to the one and despise the other. You cannot serve both God and Money.

Do Not Worry [25]"Therefore I tell you, do not worry about your life, what you will eat

---

Direct Line

MATTHEW 6:1–8

No one likes the word *hypocrite*. Do you wonder sometimes if it applies to you? Does wanting to fit in with the other kids at school or wanting to be popular make you a hypocrite? No. It's natural to want to be accepted. Besides, how could you share your faith with others if everyone looked at you as an outsider? In the Bible a hypocrite is someone who is pretending, who is playing a role to impress others rather than being real. As long as you live by your convictions and don't pretend in order to fit in, you're no hypocrite. Not at all.

---

[a]13 Or *from evil*; some late manuscripts *one, / for yours is the kingdom and the power and the glory forever. Amen.*

Dear Sam,

If my prayers aren't answered,
I feel like it's my fault for having too
little faith. How should I pray?

Paul in St. Paul

100 Advice Lane, Anywhere, USA

Dear Paul,

Sometimes when Jesus addressed God he called him Abba, which we might translate as "Daddy," an affectionate, informal term for his Father. If you think of your Father in heaven as Daddy, you immediately change the distant feeling into a feeling of closeness.

When Christ's disciples asked him how they should pray, he told them not to babble on and on the way people do when they're trying to talk someone into doing something (Matthew 6:6-7). Instead he taught them a very brief prayer, which we now call the Lord's Prayer. You can use it as a model for your prayers.

When you pray, remember to be thankful for what God has already done for you. Remember to praise his greatness each time you look at the beauty of the universe he's created. Take your needs and your pain to him. Ask for what you want, but don't forget to add, "if this is your best for me." Remember that not getting something five minutes after you pray for it doesn't mean God hasn't answered your prayer. Just like your mom and dad, God may sometimes say no. Or not yet. But you can trust him. He hears your prayers, and he'll answer them.

Sam

or drink; or about your body, what you will wear. Is not life more important than food, and the body more important than clothes? ²⁶Look at the birds of the air; they do not sow or reap or store away in barns, and yet your heavenly Father feeds them. Are you not much more valuable than they? ²⁷Who of you by worrying can add a single hour to his life*?

²⁸"And why do you worry about clothes? See how the lilies of the field grow. They do not labor or spin. ²⁹Yet I tell you that not even Solomon in all his splendor was dressed like one of these. ³⁰If that is how God clothes the grass of the field, which is here today and tomorrow is thrown into the fire, will he not much more clothe you, O you of little faith? ³¹So do not worry, saying, 'What shall we eat?' or 'What shall we drink?' or 'What shall we wear?' ³²For the pagans run after all these things, and your heavenly Father knows that you need them. ³³But seek first his kingdom and his righteousness, and all these things will be given to you as well. ³⁴Therefore do not worry about tomorrow, for tomorrow will worry about itself. Each day has enough trouble of its own.

Judging Others   "Do not judge, or you too will be judged. ²For in the same way you judge others, you will be judged, and with the measure you use, it will be measured to you.

³"Why do you look at the speck of sawdust in your brother's eye and pay no attention to the plank in your own eye? ⁴How can you say to your brother, 'Let me take the speck out of your eye,' when all the time there is a plank in your own eye? ⁵You hypocrite, first take the plank out of your own eye, and then you will see clearly to remove the speck from your brother's eye.

⁶"Do not give dogs what is sacred; do not throw your pearls to pigs. If you do, they may trample them under their feet, and then turn and tear you to pieces.

Ask, Seek, Knock   ⁷"Ask and it will be given to you; seek and you will find; knock and the door will be opened to you. ⁸For everyone who asks receives; he who seeks finds; and to him who knocks, the door will be opened.

⁹"Which of you, if his son asks for bread, will give him a stone? ¹⁰Or if he asks for a fish, will give him a snake? ¹¹If you, then, though you are evil, know how to give good gifts to your children, how much more will your Father in heaven give good gifts to those who ask him! ¹²So in everything, do to others what you would have them do to you, for this sums up the Law and the Prophets.

> Ask and it will be given to you; seek and you will find; knock and the door will be opened to you
> (Matthew 7:7).

The Narrow and Wide Gates   ¹³"Enter through the narrow gate. For wide is the gate and broad is the road that leads to destruction, and many enter through it. ¹⁴But small is the gate and narrow the road that leads to life, and only a few find it.

A Tree and Its Fruit   ¹⁵"Watch out for false prophets. They come to you in sheep's clothing, but inwardly they are ferocious wolves. ¹⁶By their fruit you will recognize them. Do people pick grapes from thornbushes, or figs from thistles? ¹⁷Likewise every good tree bears good fruit, but a bad tree bears bad fruit. ¹⁸A good tree cannot bear bad fruit, and a bad tree cannot bear good fruit. ¹⁹Every tree that does not bear good fruit is cut down and thrown into the fire. ²⁰Thus, by their fruit you will recognize them.

²¹"Not everyone who says to me, 'Lord, Lord,' will enter the kingdom of heaven, but only he who does the will of my Father who is in heaven. ²²Many will say to me on that day, 'Lord, Lord, did we not prophesy in your name,

27 Or single cubit to his height

and in your name drive out demons and perform many miracles?' ²³Then I will tell them plainly, 'I never knew you. Away from me, you evildoers!'

The Wise and Foolish Builders ²⁴"Therefore everyone who hears these words of mine and puts them into practice is like a wise man who built his house on the rock. ²⁵The rain came down, the streams rose, and the winds blew and beat against that house; yet it did not fall, because it had its foundation on the rock. ²⁶But everyone who hears these words of mine and does not put them into practice is like a foolish man who built his house on sand. ²⁷The rain came down, the streams rose, and the winds blew and beat against that house, and it fell with a great crash."

²⁸When Jesus had finished saying these things, the crowds were amazed at his teaching, ²⁹because he taught as one who had authority, and not as their teachers of the law.

8 *The Man With Leprosy* When he came down from the mountainside, large crowds followed him. ²A man with leprosy*ᵃ* came and knelt before him and said, "Lord, if you are willing, you can make me clean."

³Jesus reached out his hand and touched the man. "I am willing," he said. "Be clean!" Immediately he was cured*ᵇ* of his leprosy. ⁴Then Jesus said to him, "See that you don't tell anyone. But go, show yourself to the priest and offer the gift Moses commanded, as a testimony to them."

The Faith of the Centurion ⁵When Jesus had entered Capernaum, a centurion came to him, asking for help. ⁶"Lord," he said, "my servant lies at home paralyzed and in terrible suffering."

⁷Jesus said to him, "I will go and heal him."

⁸The centurion replied, "Lord, I do not deserve to have you come under my roof. But just say the word, and my servant will be healed. ⁹For I myself am a man under authority, with soldiers under me. I tell this one, 'Go,' and he goes; and that one, 'Come,' and he comes. I say to my servant, 'Do this,' and he does it."

¹⁰When Jesus heard this, he was astonished and said to those following him, "I tell you the truth, I have not found anyone in Israel with such great faith. ¹¹I say to you that many will come from the east and the west, and will take their places at the feast with Abraham, Isaac and Jacob in the kingdom of heaven. ¹²But the subjects of the kingdom will be thrown outside, into the darkness, where there will be weeping and gnashing of teeth."

¹³Then Jesus said to the centurion, "Go! It will be done just as you believed it would." And his servant was healed at that very hour.

Jesus Heals Many ¹⁴When Jesus came into Peter's house, he saw Peter's mother-in-law lying in bed with a fever. ¹⁵He touched her hand and the fever left her, and she got up and began to wait on him.

¹⁶When evening came, many who were demon-possessed were brought to him, and he drove out the spirits with a word and healed all the sick. ¹⁷This was to fulfill what was spoken through the prophet Isaiah:

> "He took up our infirmities
> and carried our diseases."*ᶜ*

The Cost of Following Jesus ¹⁸When Jesus saw the crowd around him, he gave orders to cross to the other side of the lake. ¹⁹Then a teacher of the law came to him and said, "Teacher, I will follow you wherever you go."

²⁰Jesus replied, "Foxes have holes and birds of the air have nests, but the Son of Man has no place to lay his head."

ᵃ2 The Greek word was used for various diseases affecting the skin—not necessarily leprosy.   *ᵇ3* Greek *made clean*   *ᶜ17* Isaiah 53:4

[21]Another disciple said to him, "Lord, first let me go and bury my father." [22]But Jesus told him, "Follow me, and let the dead bury their own dead."

Jesus Calms the Storm   [23]Then he got into the boat and his disciples followed him. [24]Without warning, a furious storm came up on the lake, so that the waves swept over the boat. But Jesus was sleeping. [25]The disciples went and woke him, saying, "Lord, save us! We're going to drown!"

[26]He replied, "You of little faith, why are you so afraid?" Then he got up and rebuked the winds and the waves, and it was completely calm.

[27]The men were amazed and asked, "What kind of man is this? Even the winds and the waves obey him!"

The Healing of Two Demon-possessed Men   [28]When he arrived at the other side in the region of the Gadarenes,[a] two demon-possessed men coming from the tombs met him. They were so violent that no one could pass that way. [29]"What do you want with us, Son of God?" they shouted. "Have you come here to torture us before the appointed time?"

[30]Some distance from them a large herd of pigs was feeding. [31]The demons begged Jesus, "If you drive us out, send us into the herd of pigs."

[32]He said to them, "Go!" So they came out and went into the pigs, and the whole herd rushed down the steep bank into the lake and died in the water. [33]Those tending the pigs ran off, went into the town and reported all this, including what had happened to the demon-possessed men. [34]Then the whole town went out to meet Jesus. And when they saw him, they pleaded with him to leave their region.

Jesus Heals a Paralytic   Jesus stepped into a boat, crossed over and came to his own town. [2]Some men brought to him a paralytic, lying on a mat. When Jesus saw their faith, he said to the paralytic, "Take heart, son; your sins are forgiven."

[3]At this, some of the teachers of the law said to themselves, "This fellow is blaspheming!"

[4]Knowing their thoughts, Jesus said, "Why do you entertain evil thoughts in your hearts? [5]Which is easier: to say, 'Your sins are forgiven,' or to say,

---

[a]28 Some manuscripts *Gergesenes*; others *Gerasenes*

The Bible Says

Demons Are Real

In the New Testament evil beings are called demons, or evil spirits (Matthew 8:28–34). Most believe that demons are angels who followed Satan in his rebellion against God. Those who practice witchcraft worship demons, not God or his angels (1 Corinthians 10:20).

It is important to remember that demons are the enemies of God and of human beings.

* Demons are violent and malicious (Matthew 8:28).
* Demons cause sickness (Matthew 4:24; 12:22; 17:15–18).
* Demons corrupt morals (1 Timothy 4:1–3).
* Demons aim their arsenal at believers (Ephesians 6:12).

Don't be tempted to toy with the occult. Remember to rely on Jesus. After all, Jesus easily overpowered every demon he met.

'Get up and walk'? ⁶But so that you may know that the Son of Man has authority on earth to forgive sins . . ." Then he said to the paralytic, "Get up,
take your mat and go home." ⁷And the man got up and went home. ⁸When
the crowd saw this, they were filled with awe; and they praised God, who had
given such authority to men.

The Calling of Matthew   ⁹As Jesus went on from there, he saw a man named
Matthew sitting at the tax collector's booth. "Follow me," he told him, and
Matthew got up and followed him.

¹⁰While Jesus was having dinner at Matthew's house, many tax collectors
and "sinners" came and ate with him and his disciples. ¹¹When the Pharisees
saw this, they asked his disciples, "Why does your teacher eat with tax collectors and 'sinners'?"

¹²On hearing this, Jesus said, "It is not the healthy who need a doctor, but
the sick. ¹³But go and learn what this means: 'I desire mercy, not sacrifice.'ᵃ
For I have not come to call the righteous, but sinners."

Jesus Questioned About Fasting   ¹⁴Then John's disciples came and asked
him, "How is it that we and the Pharisees fast, but your disciples do not
fast?"

¹⁵Jesus answered, "How can the guests of the bridegroom mourn while he
is with them? The time will come when the bridegroom will be taken from
them; then they will fast.

¹⁶"No one sews a patch of unshrunk cloth on an old garment, for the patch
will pull away from the garment, making the tear worse. ¹⁷Neither do men
pour new wine into old wineskins. If they do, the skins will burst, the wine
will run out and the wineskins will be ruined. No, they pour new wine into
new wineskins, and both are preserved."

A Dead Girl and a Sick Woman   ¹⁸While he was saying this, a ruler came and
knelt before him and said, "My daughter has just died. But come and put
your hand on her, and she will live." ¹⁹Jesus got up and went with him, and
so did his disciples.

²⁰Just then a woman who had been subject to bleeding for twelve years
came up behind him and touched the edge of his cloak. ²¹She said to herself,
"If I only touch his cloak, I will be healed."

²²Jesus turned and saw her. "Take heart, daughter," he said, "your faith has
healed you." And the woman was healed from that moment.

²³When Jesus entered the ruler's house and saw the flute players and the
noisy crowd, ²⁴he said, "Go away. The girl is not dead but asleep." But they
laughed at him. ²⁵After the crowd had been put outside, he went in and took
the girl by the hand, and she got up. ²⁶News of this spread through all that
region.

Jesus Heals the Blind and Mute   ²⁷As Jesus went on from there, two blind
men followed him, calling out, "Have mercy on us, Son of David!"

²⁸When he had gone indoors, the blind men came to him, and he asked
them, "Do you believe that I am able to do this?"

"Yes, Lord," they replied.

²⁹Then he touched their eyes and said, "According to your faith will it be
done to you"; ³⁰and their sight was restored. Jesus warned them sternly,
"See that no one knows about this." ³¹But they went out and spread the news
about him all over that region.

³²While they were going out, a man who was demon-possessed and could
not talk was brought to Jesus. ³³And when the demon was driven out, the
man who had been mute spoke. The crowd was amazed and said, "Nothing
like this has ever been seen in Israel."

ᵃ*13* Hosea 6:6

³⁴But the Pharisees said, "It is by the prince of demons that he drives out demons."

The Workers Are Few ³⁵Jesus went through all the towns and villages, teaching in their synagogues, preaching the good news of the kingdom and healing every disease and sickness. ³⁶When he saw the crowds, he had compassion on them, because they were harassed and helpless, like sheep without a shepherd. ³⁷Then he said to his disciples, "The harvest is plentiful but the workers are few. ³⁸Ask the Lord of the harvest, therefore, to send out workers into his harvest field."

10 ***Jesus Sends Out the Twelve*** He called his twelve disciples to him and gave them authority to drive out evil*ᵃ* spirits and to heal every disease and sickness.

²These are the names of the twelve apostles: first, Simon (who is called Peter) and his brother Andrew; James son of Zebedee, and his brother John; ³Philip and Bartholomew; Thomas and Matthew the tax collector; James son of Alphaeus, and Thaddaeus; ⁴Simon the Zealot and Judas Iscariot, who betrayed him.

⁵These twelve Jesus sent out with the following instructions: "Do not go among the Gentiles or enter any town of the Samaritans. ⁶Go rather to the lost sheep of Israel. ⁷As you go, preach this message: 'The kingdom of heaven is near.' ⁸Heal the sick, raise the dead, cleanse those who have leprosy,*ᵇ* drive out demons. Freely you have received, freely give. ⁹Do not take along any gold or silver or copper in your belts; ¹⁰take no bag for the journey, or extra tunic, or sandals or a staff; for the worker is worth his keep.

¹¹"Whatever town or village you enter, search for some worthy person there and stay at his house until you leave. ¹²As you enter the home, give it your greeting. ¹³If the home is deserving, let your peace rest on it; if it is not, let your peace return to you. ¹⁴If anyone will not welcome you or listen to your words, shake the dust off your feet when you leave that home or town. ¹⁵I tell you the truth, it will be more bearable for Sodom and Gomorrah on the day of judgment than for that town. ¹⁶I am sending you out like sheep among wolves. Therefore be as shrewd as snakes and as innocent as doves.

¹⁷"Be on your guard against men; they will hand you over to the local councils and flog you in their synagogues. ¹⁸On my account you will be brought before governors and kings as witnesses to them and to the Gentiles. ¹⁹But when they arrest you, do not worry about what to say or how to say it. At that time you will be given what to say, ²⁰for it will not be you speaking, but the Spirit of your Father speaking through you.

²¹"Brother will betray brother to death, and a father his child; children will rebel against their parents and have them put to death. ²²All men will hate you because of me, but he who stands firm to the end will be saved. ²³When you are persecuted in one place, flee to another. I tell you the truth, you will not finish going through the cities of Israel before the Son of Man comes.

²⁴"A student is not above his teacher, nor a servant above his master. ²⁵It is enough for the student to be like his teacher, and the servant like his master. If the head of the house has been called Beelzebub,*ᶜ* how much more the members of his household!

²⁶"So do not be afraid of them. There is nothing concealed that will not be disclosed, or hidden that will not be made known. ²⁷What I tell you in the dark, speak in the daylight; what is whispered in your ear, proclaim from the roofs. ²⁸Do not be afraid of those who kill the body but cannot kill the soul. Rather, be afraid of the One who can destroy both soul and body in hell. ²⁹Are not two

---

ᵃ1 Greek *unclean* *ᵇ8* The Greek word was used for various diseases affecting the skin—not necessarily leprosy. *ᶜ25* Greek *Beezeboul* or *Beelzeboul*

Prayer (prar) n.
the act of talking with God in word or thought.

Prayer

"This, then, is how you should pray: 'Our Father...'"
MATTHEW 6:9

Prayer is remembering that God is your Father.
He likes it when you stop to talk with him.
He wants to hear how you feel and what you're
thinking. And he's never upset when you talk
to him about something you want.

Does God listen? Why not start
a prayer journal? Jot down the
things you talk to God about.
Make a note when a prayer is
answered. After a few months
look back and find out for
yourself that God
does answer prayer.

There's no guarantee God
will say yes when you pray.
If he says no, it won't be
because you didn't have
enough faith. It will be
because what you asked for
wasn't the best for you and
others. Like a good and wise
father, God only gives
what's best for you.

Is God listening
when I pray? Does he
get mad if I ask for
something I don't
need? If I believe
hard enough, does
God have to give me
what I ask for? Isn't
there some promise
in the Bible that
says if I ask in Jesus'
name, I'll get what I
ask for? What do I
have to do to get my
prayers answered?

"Do not be anxious about anything, but in everything, by prayer and petition, with thanksgiving, present your requests to God. And the peace of God...will guard your hearts and your minds in Christ Jesus."
PHILIPPIANS 4:6-7

Wit-ness-ing (wit-nes-ing) n.
to see or hear or experience something and to testify to its occurrence.

ALTERNATE DEFINITION
telling your friends about God and sometimes having them laugh at you

"How do I lead my friends to Christ without them getting mad at me? Why is it so hard? How can I witness to my friends? How do I talk to them about God without being too nosy? What if they laugh at me?"

What did you say?
Keep the focus on Jesus. He's the one who died to win your forgiveness. He's the one who brings you to God. He's the one to whom you want to introduce your friends.

"How can they believe in the one of whom they have not heard?"
ROMANS 10:14

Witnessing isn't:
—grabbing a friend's shirt and yelling, "You're going to hell!"
—letting kids with bad reputations know you think they're scum.
—carrying a great big Bible on top of your school books.

"Do not worry about what to say or how to say it. At that time you will be given what to say, for it will not be you speaking, but the Spirit of your Father speaking through you."
MATTHEW 10:19-20

You can earn the right to witness by being real. By taking an honest interest in others. By being friendly. By stating what you believe without attacking others or putting them down. When you earn respect some may still laugh, but they'll listen to what you say.

sparrows sold for a penny^a? Yet not one of them will fall to the ground apart from the will of your Father. ³⁰And even the very hairs of your head are all numbered. ³¹So don't be afraid; you are worth more than many sparrows.

³²"Whoever acknowledges me before men, I will also acknowledge him before my Father in heaven. ³³But whoever disowns me before men, I will disown him before my Father in heaven.

³⁴"Do not suppose that I have come to bring peace to the earth. I did not come to bring peace, but a sword. ³⁵For I have come to turn

> " 'a man against his father,
>   a daughter against her mother,
>   a daughter-in-law against her mother-in-law—
> ³⁶   a man's enemies will be the members of his own
>   household.'^{b}

³⁷"Anyone who loves his father or mother more than me is not worthy of me; anyone who loves his son or daughter more than me is not worthy of me; ³⁸and anyone who does not take his cross and follow me is not worthy of me. ³⁹Whoever finds his life will lose it, and whoever loses his life for my sake will find it.

⁴⁰"He who receives you receives me, and he who receives me receives the one who sent me. ⁴¹Anyone who receives a prophet because he is a prophet will receive a prophet's reward, and anyone who receives a righteous man because he is a righteous man will receive a righteous man's reward. ⁴²And if anyone gives even a cup of cold water to one of these little ones because he is my disciple, I tell you the truth, he will certainly not lose his reward."

Jesus and John the Baptist   After Jesus had finished instructing his twelve disciples, he went on from there to teach and preach in the towns of Galilee.^{c}

²When John heard in prison what Christ was doing, he sent his disciples ³to ask him, "Are you the one who was to come, or should we expect someone else?"

⁴Jesus replied, "Go back and report to John what you hear and see: ⁵The blind receive sight, the lame walk, those who have leprosy^d are cured, the deaf hear, the dead are raised, and the good news is preached to the poor. ⁶Blessed is the man who does not fall away on account of me."

⁷As John's disciples were leaving, Jesus began to speak to the crowd about John: "What did you go out into the desert to see? A reed swayed by the wind? ⁸If not, what did you go out to see? A man dressed in fine clothes? No, those who wear fine clothes are in kings' palaces. ⁹Then what did you go out to see? A prophet? Yes, I tell you, and more than a prophet. ¹⁰This is the one about whom it is written:

> " 'I will send my messenger
>   ahead of you,
>   who will prepare your way
>   before you.'^{e}

^{a}29 Greek *an assarion* ^{b}36 Micah 7:6 ^{c}1 Greek *in their towns* ^{d}5 The Greek word was used for various diseases affecting the skin—not necessarily leprosy. ^{e}10 Mal. 3:1

MATTHEW 10:34–38

This is one of the hardest sayings in the New Testament. And it describes a hard experience. For some teens becoming a Christian creates real conflict in the family. Some parents will forbid a teen to go to a youth group or church of his or her choice. So what do you do? You're supposed to obey your parents. But you want to be with your Christian friends too. Usually it's best to honor your parents' wishes, read your Bible, and try to meet with one or two friends to talk and pray. That way you can be faithful to the Lord and to your parents too. Only in the most unusual case will loving Christ mean a serious break with those at home.

Direct Line

[11]I tell you the truth: Among those born of women there has not risen anyone greater than John the Baptist; yet he who is least in the kingdom of heaven is greater than he. [12]From the days of John the Baptist until now, the kingdom of heaven has been forcefully advancing, and forceful men lay hold of it. [13]For all the Prophets and the Law prophesied until John. [14]And if you are willing to accept it, he is the Elijah who was to come. [15]He who has ears, let him hear.

[16]"To what can I compare this generation? They are like children sitting in the marketplaces and calling out to others:

[17]" 'We played the flute for you,
  and you did not dance;
we sang a dirge,
  and you did not mourn.'

[18]For John came neither eating nor drinking, and they say, 'He has a demon.' [19]The Son of Man came eating and drinking, and they say, 'Here is a glutton and a drunkard, a friend of tax collectors and "sinners." ' But wisdom is proved right by her actions."

> Come to me, all you who are weary and burdened, and I will give you rest (Matthew 11:28).

Woe on Unrepentant Cities [20]Then Jesus began to denounce the cities in which most of his miracles had been performed, because they did not repent. [21]"Woe to you, Korazin! Woe to you, Bethsaida! If the miracles that were performed in you had been performed in Tyre and Sidon, they would have repented long ago in sackcloth and ashes. [22]But I tell you, it will be more bearable for Tyre and Sidon on the day of judgment than for you. [23]And you, Capernaum, will you be lifted up to the skies? No, you will go down to the depths.[a] If the miracles that were performed in you had been performed in Sodom, it would have remained to this day. [24]But I tell you that it will be more bearable for Sodom on the day of judgment than for you."

Rest for the Weary [25]At that time Jesus said, "I praise you, Father, Lord of heaven and earth, because you have hidden these things from the wise and learned, and revealed them to little children. [26]Yes, Father, for this was your good pleasure.

[27]"All things have been committed to me by my Father. No one knows the Son except the Father, and no one knows the Father except the Son and those to whom the Son chooses to reveal him.

[28]"Come to me, all you who are weary and burdened, and I will give you rest. [29]Take my yoke upon you and learn from me, for I am gentle and humble in heart, and you will find rest for your souls. [30]For my yoke is easy and my burden is light."

Lord of the Sabbath At that time Jesus went through the grainfields on the Sabbath. His disciples were hungry and began to pick some heads of grain and eat them. [2]When the Pharisees saw this, they said to him, "Look! Your disciples are doing what is unlawful on the Sabbath."

[3]He answered, "Haven't you read what David did when he and his companions were hungry? [4]He entered the house of God, and he and his companions ate the consecrated bread—which was not lawful for them to do, but only for the priests. [5]Or haven't you read in the Law that on the Sabbath the priests in the temple desecrate the day and yet are innocent? [6]I tell you that one[b] greater than the temple is here. [7]If you had known what these words mean, 'I desire mercy, not sacrifice,'[c] you would not have condemned the innocent. [8]For the Son of Man is Lord of the Sabbath."

---

[a]23 Greek *Hades* [b]6 Or *something*; also in verses 41 and 42 [c]7 Hosea 6:6

⁹Going on from that place, he went into their synagogue, ¹⁰and a man with a shriveled hand was there. Looking for a reason to accuse Jesus, they asked him, "Is it lawful to heal on the Sabbath?"

¹¹He said to them, "If any of you has a sheep and it falls into a pit on the Sabbath, will you not take hold of it and lift it out? ¹²How much more valuable is a man than a sheep! Therefore it is lawful to do good on the Sabbath."

¹³Then he said to the man, "Stretch out your hand." So he stretched it out and it was completely restored, just as sound as the other. ¹⁴But the Pharisees went out and plotted how they might kill Jesus.

God's Chosen Servant   ¹⁵Aware of this, Jesus withdrew from that place. Many followed him, and he healed all their sick, ¹⁶warning them not to tell who he was. ¹⁷This was to fulfill what was spoken through the prophet Isaiah:

> ¹⁸"Here is my servant whom I have chosen,
>> the one I love, in whom I delight;
> I will put my Spirit on him,
>> and he will proclaim justice to the nations.
> ¹⁹He will not quarrel or cry out;
>> no one will hear his voice in the streets.
> ²⁰A bruised reed he will not break,
>> and a smoldering wick he will not snuff out,
>> till he leads justice to victory.
> ²¹   In his name the nations will put their hope."*ᵃ*

Jesus and Beelzebub   ²²Then they brought him a demon-possessed man who was blind and mute, and Jesus healed him, so that he could both talk and see. ²³All the people were astonished and said, "Could this be the Son of David?"

²⁴But when the Pharisees heard this, they said, "It is only by Beelzebub,*ᵇ* the prince of demons, that this fellow drives out demons."

²⁵Jesus knew their thoughts and said to them, "Every kingdom divided against itself will be ruined, and every city or household divided against itself will not stand. ²⁶If Satan drives out Satan, he is divided against himself. How then can his kingdom stand? ²⁷And if I drive out demons by Beelzebub, by whom do your people drive them out? So then, they will be your judges. ²⁸But if I drive out demons by the Spirit of God, then the kingdom of God has come upon you.

²⁹"Or again, how can anyone enter a strong man's house and carry off his possessions unless he first ties up the strong man? Then he can rob his house.

³⁰"He who is not with me is against me, and he who does not gather with me scatters. ³¹And so I tell you, every sin and blasphemy will be forgiven men, but the blasphemy against the Spirit will not be forgiven. ³²Anyone who speaks a word against the Son of Man will be forgiven, but anyone who speaks against the Holy Spirit will not be forgiven, either in this age or in the age to come.

³³"Make a tree good and its fruit will be good, or make a tree bad and its fruit will be bad, for a tree is recognized by its fruit. ³⁴You brood of vipers, how can you who are evil say anything good? For out of the overflow of the heart the mouth speaks. ³⁵The good man brings good things out of the good stored up in him, and the evil man brings evil things out of the evil stored up in him. ³⁶But I tell you that men will have to give account on the day of judgment for every careless word they have spoken. ³⁷For by your words you will be acquitted, and by your words you will be condemned."

ᵃ21 Isaiah 42:1-4   *ᵇ24* Greek *Beezeboul* or *Beelzeboul;* also in verse 27

The Sign of Jonah   ³⁸Then some of the Pharisees and teachers of the law said to him, "Teacher, we want to see a miraculous sign from you."

³⁹He answered, "A wicked and adulterous generation asks for a miraculous sign! But none will be given it except the sign of the prophet Jonah. ⁴⁰For as Jonah was three days and three nights in the belly of a huge fish, so the Son of Man will be three days and three nights in the heart of the earth. ⁴¹The men of Nineveh will stand up at the judgment with this generation and condemn it; for they repented at the preaching of Jonah, and now one*ª* greater than Jonah is here. ⁴²The Queen of the South will rise at the judgment with this generation and condemn it; for she came from the ends of the earth to listen to Solomon's wisdom, and now one greater than Solomon is here.

⁴³"When an evil*ᵇ* spirit comes out of a man, it goes through arid places seeking rest and does not find it. ⁴⁴Then it says, 'I will return to the house I left.' When it arrives, it finds the house unoccupied, swept clean and put in order. ⁴⁵Then it goes and takes with it seven other spirits more wicked than itself, and they go in and live there. And the final condition of that man is worse than the first. That is how it will be with this wicked generation."

Jesus' Mother and Brothers   ⁴⁶While Jesus was still talking to the crowd, his mother and brothers stood outside, wanting to speak to him. ⁴⁷Someone told him, "Your mother and brothers are standing outside, wanting to speak to you."*ᶜ*

⁴⁸He replied to him, "Who is my mother, and who are my brothers?" ⁴⁹Pointing to his disciples, he said, "Here are my mother and my brothers. ⁵⁰For whoever does the will of my Father in heaven is my brother and sister and mother."

The Parable of the Sower   That same day Jesus went out of the house and sat by the lake. ²Such large crowds gathered around him that he got into a boat and sat in it, while all the people stood on the shore. ³Then he told them many things in parables, saying: "A farmer went out to sow his seed. ⁴As he was scattering the seed, some fell along the path, and the birds came and ate it up. ⁵Some fell on rocky places, where it did not have much soil. It sprang up quickly, because the soil was shallow. ⁶But when the sun came up, the plants were scorched, and they withered because they had no root. ⁷Other seed fell among thorns, which grew up and choked the plants. ⁸Still other seed fell on good soil, where it produced a crop—a hundred, sixty or thirty times what was sown. ⁹He who has ears, let him hear."

¹⁰The disciples came to him and asked, "Why do you speak to the people in parables?"

¹¹He replied, "The knowledge of the secrets of the kingdom of heaven has been given to you, but not to them. ¹²Whoever has will be given more, and he will have an abundance. Whoever does not have, even what he has will be taken from him. ¹³This is why I speak to them in parables:

"Though seeing, they do not see;
    though hearing, they do not hear or
        understand.

¹⁴In them is fulfilled the prophecy of Isaiah:

" 'You will be ever hearing but never
        understanding;

I think I have ears under here somewhere!

SEE MATTHEW 13:9

*ª41 Or *something*; also in verse 42   *ᵇ43 Greek *unclean*   *ᶜ47 Some manuscripts do not have verse 47.

you will be ever seeing but never
    perceiving.
¹⁵For this people's heart has become calloused;
    they hardly hear with their ears,
    and they have closed their eyes.
Otherwise they might see with their eyes,
    hear with their ears,
    understand with their hearts
and turn, and I would heal them.'ᵃ

¹⁶But blessed are your eyes because they see, and your ears because they hear. ¹⁷For I tell you the truth, many prophets and righteous men longed to see what you see but did not see it, and to hear what you hear but did not hear it.

¹⁸"Listen then to what the parable of the sower means: ¹⁹When anyone hears the message about the kingdom and does not understand it, the evil one comes and snatches away what was sown in his heart. This is the seed sown along the path. ²⁰The one who received the seed that fell on rocky places is the man who hears the word and at once receives it with joy. ²¹But since he has no root, he lasts only a short time. When trouble or persecution comes because of the word, he quickly falls away. ²²The one who received the seed that fell among the thorns is the man who hears the word, but the worries of this life and the deceitfulness of wealth choke it, making it unfruitful. ²³But the one who received the seed that fell on good soil is the man who hears the word and understands it. He produces a crop, yielding a hundred, sixty or thirty times what was sown."

The Parable of the Weeds   ²⁴Jesus told them another parable: "The kingdom of heaven is like a man who sowed good seed in his field. ²⁵But while everyone was sleeping, his enemy came and sowed weeds among the wheat, and went away. ²⁶When the wheat sprouted and formed heads, then the weeds also appeared.

²⁷"The owner's servants came to him and said, 'Sir, didn't you sow good seed in your field? Where then did the weeds come from?'

²⁸" 'An enemy did this,' he replied.

"The servants asked him, 'Do you want us to go and pull them up?'

²⁹" 'No,' he answered, 'because while you are pulling the weeds, you may root up the wheat with them. ³⁰Let both grow together until the harvest. At that time I will tell the harvesters: First collect the weeds and tie them in bundles to be burned; then gather the wheat and bring it into my barn.' "

The Parables of the Mustard Seed and the Yeast   ³¹He told them another parable: "The kingdom of heaven is like a mustard seed, which a man took and planted in his field. ³²Though it is the smallest of all your seeds, yet when it grows, it is the largest of garden plants and becomes a tree, so that the birds of the air come and perch in its branches."

³³He told them still another parable: "The kingdom of heaven is like yeast that a woman took and mixed into a large amountᵇ of flour until it worked all through the dough."

³⁴Jesus spoke all these things to the crowd in parables; he did not say anything to them without using a parable. ³⁵So was fulfilled what was spoken through the prophet:

    "I will open my mouth in parables,
      I will utter things hidden since the creation of the world."ᶜ

ᵃ15 Isaiah 6:9,10 ᵇ33 Greek *three satas* (probably about 1/2 bushel or 22 liters) ᶜ35 Psalm 78:2

The Parable of the Weeds Explained ³⁶Then he left the crowd and went into the house. His disciples came to him and said, "Explain to us the parable of the weeds in the field."

³⁷He answered, "The one who sowed the good seed is the Son of Man. ³⁸The field is the world, and the good seed stands for the sons of the kingdom. The weeds are the sons of the evil one, ³⁹and the enemy who sows them is the devil. The harvest is the end of the age, and the harvesters are angels.

⁴⁰"As the weeds are pulled up and burned in the fire, so it will be at the end of the age. ⁴¹The Son of Man will send out his angels, and they will weed out of his kingdom everything that causes sin and all who do evil. ⁴²They will throw them into the fiery furnace, where there will be weeping and gnashing of teeth. ⁴³Then the righteous will shine like the sun in the kingdom of their Father. He who has ears, let him hear.

The Parables of the Hidden Treasure and the Pearl ⁴⁴"The kingdom of heaven is like treasure hidden in a field. When a man found it, he hid it again, and then in his joy went and sold all he had and bought that field.

⁴⁵"Again, the kingdom of heaven is like a merchant looking for fine pearls. ⁴⁶When he found one of great value, he went away and sold everything he had and bought it.

The Parable of the Net ⁴⁷"Once again, the kingdom of heaven is like a net that was let down into the lake and caught all kinds of fish. ⁴⁸When it was full, the fishermen pulled it up on the shore. Then they sat down and collected the good fish in baskets, but threw the bad away. ⁴⁹This is how it will be at the end of the age. The angels will come and separate the wicked from the righteous ⁵⁰and throw them into the fiery furnace, where there will be weeping and gnashing of teeth.

⁵¹"Have you understood all these things?" Jesus asked.

"Yes," they replied.

⁵²He said to them, "Therefore every teacher of the law who has been instructed about the kingdom of heaven is like the owner of a house who brings out of his storeroom new treasures as well as old."

A Prophet Without Honor ⁵³When Jesus had finished these parables, he moved on from there. ⁵⁴Coming to his hometown, he began teaching the people in their synagogue, and they were amazed. "Where did this man get this wisdom and these miraculous powers?" they asked. ⁵⁵"Isn't this the carpenter's son? Isn't his mother's name Mary, and aren't his brothers James, Joseph, Simon and Judas? ⁵⁶Aren't all his sisters with us? Where then did this man get all these things?" ⁵⁷And they took offense at him.

But Jesus said to them, "Only in his hometown and in his own house is a prophet without honor."

⁵⁸And he did not do many miracles there because of their lack of faith.

John the Baptist Beheaded At that time Herod the tetrarch heard the reports about Jesus, ²and he said to his attendants, "This is John the Baptist; he has risen from the dead! That is why miraculous powers are at work in him."

³Now Herod had arrested John and bound him and put him in prison because of Herodias, his brother Philip's wife, ⁴for John had been saying to him: "It is not lawful for you to have her." ⁵Herod wanted to kill John, but he was afraid of the people, because they considered him a prophet.

⁶On Herod's birthday the daughter of Herodias danced for them and pleased Herod so much ⁷that he promised with an oath to give her whatever she asked. ⁸Prompted by her mother, she said, "Give me here on a platter the head of John the Baptist." ⁹The king was distressed, but because of his oaths and his dinner guests, he ordered that her request be granted ¹⁰and

Dear Sam,

I see girls cry all the time, and nobody thinks they're wimps. What's a guy supposed to do with his feelings?

John in Juneau

100 Advice Lane, Anywhere, USA

Dear John,

God gave everyone emotions, and everyone deals with them differently. The Bible has stories about many emotional men. King David was certainly one. He danced in joy and mourned deeply in grief, yet he definitely was not a wimp, as he proved by his valor and leadership many, many times.

Christ was another man who was in touch with his feelings. When he heard of his cousin's death, he wanted to be by himself (Matthew 14:1-13). However, when the crowds wouldn't leave him alone, he looked closely at them and felt sorry for them (Matthew 14:14). When the temple was used as a marketplace, he reacted with righteous anger (John 2:14-16). After the death of his good friend Lazarus, Jesus cried very real tears (John 11:33-35).

There is a time for laughter and a time for tears (Ecclesiastes 3:4). It is normal to have feelings, and you are not a wimp if you express them. God made you a human being with very real emotions, and you have the ability and the right to express them.

Sam

had John beheaded in the prison. ¹¹His head was brought in on a platter and given to the girl, who carried it to her mother. ¹²John's disciples came and took his body and buried it. Then they went and told Jesus.

Jesus Feeds the Five Thousand   ¹³When Jesus heard what had happened, he withdrew by boat privately to a solitary place. Hearing of this, the crowds followed him on foot from the towns. ¹⁴When Jesus landed and saw a large crowd, he had compassion on them and healed their sick.

¹⁵As evening approached, the disciples came to him and said, "This is a remote place, and it's already getting late. Send the crowds away, so they can go to the villages and buy themselves some food."

¹⁶Jesus replied, "They do not need to go away. You give them something to eat."

¹⁷"We have here only five loaves of bread and two fish," they answered.

¹⁸"Bring them here to me," he said. ¹⁹And he directed the people to sit down on the grass. Taking the five loaves and the two fish and looking up to heaven, he gave thanks and broke the loaves. Then he gave them to the disciples, and the disciples gave them to the people. ²⁰They all ate and were satisfied, and the disciples picked up twelve basketfuls of broken pieces that were left over. ²¹The number of those who ate was about five thousand men, besides women and children.

Jesus Walks on the Water   ²²Immediately Jesus made the disciples get into the boat and go on ahead of him to the other side, while he dismissed the crowd. ²³After he had dismissed them, he went up on a mountainside by himself to pray. When evening came, he was there alone, ²⁴but the boat was already a considerable distance*a* from land, buffeted by the waves because the wind was against it.

²⁵During the fourth watch of the night Jesus went out to them, walking on the lake. ²⁶When the disciples saw him walking on the lake, they were terrified. "It's a ghost," they said, and cried out in fear.

²⁷But Jesus immediately said to them: "Take courage! It is I. Don't be afraid."

²⁸"Lord, if it's you," Peter replied, "tell me to come to you on the water."

²⁹"Come," he said.

Then Peter got down out of the boat, walked on the water and came toward Jesus. ³⁰But when he saw the wind, he was afraid and, beginning to sink, cried out, "Lord, save me!"

³¹Immediately Jesus reached out his hand and caught him. "You of little faith," he said, "why did you doubt?"

³²And when they climbed into the boat, the wind died down. ³³Then those who were in the boat worshiped him, saying, "Truly you are the Son of God."

³⁴When they had crossed over, they landed at Gennesaret. ³⁵And when the men of that place recognized Jesus, they sent word to all the surrounding country. People brought all their sick to him ³⁶and begged him to let the sick just touch the edge of his cloak, and all who touched him were healed.

a24 Greek many stadia

MATTHEW 14:22–36

It's scary to feel uncertain about your faith. But everybody wonders at times. Can I really believe the Bible? Am I truly saved? Is salvation for real? Am I fooling myself when I say I believe? Doubt is scary. But this Bible story helps. Peter believed in Jesus enough to get out of the boat and walk on water. But once out there, even Peter began to doubt. And to sink! What's important is that Jesus "immediately" caught him. Peter doubted, but Jesus was there anyway. Doubts don't drive Jesus away. He's there even when the doubts come. And you are much too important for Jesus to let you sink.

Direct Line

Clean and Unclean Then some Pharisees and teachers of the law came to Jesus from Jerusalem and asked, [2]"Why do your disciples break the tradition of the elders? They don't wash their hands before they eat!"

[3]Jesus replied, "And why do you break the command of God for the sake of your tradition? [4]For God said, 'Honor your father and mother'[a] and 'Anyone who curses his father or mother must be put to death.'[b] [5]But you say that if a man says to his father or mother, 'Whatever help you might otherwise have received from me is a gift devoted to God,' [6]he is not to 'honor his father'[c] with it. Thus you nullify the word of God for the sake of your tradition. [7]You hypocrites! Isaiah was right when he prophesied about you:

[8]" 'These people honor me with their lips,
　　but their hearts are far from me.
[9]They worship me in vain;
　　their teachings are but rules taught by men.'[d]"

[10]Jesus called the crowd to him and said, "Listen and understand. [11]What goes into a man's mouth does not make him 'unclean,' but what comes out of his mouth, that is what makes him 'unclean.' "

[12]Then the disciples came to him and asked, "Do you know that the Pharisees were offended when they heard this?"

[13]He replied, "Every plant that my heavenly Father has not planted will be pulled up by the roots. [14]Leave them; they are blind guides.[e] If a blind man leads a blind man, both will fall into a pit."

[15]Peter said, "Explain the parable to us."

[16]"Are you still so dull?" Jesus asked them. [17]"Don't you see that whatever enters the mouth goes into the stomach and then out of the body? [18]But the things that come out of the mouth come from the heart, and these make a man 'unclean.' [19]For out of the heart come evil thoughts, murder, adultery, sexual immorality, theft, false testimony, slander. [20]These are what make a man 'unclean'; but eating with unwashed hands does not make him 'unclean.' "

The Faith of the Canaanite Woman [21]Leaving that place, Jesus withdrew to the region of Tyre and Sidon. [22]A Canaanite woman from that vicinity came to him, crying out, "Lord, Son of David, have mercy on me! My daughter is suffering terribly from demon-possession."

[23]Jesus did not answer a word. So his disciples came to him and urged him, "Send her away, for she keeps crying out after us."

[24]He answered, "I was sent only to the lost sheep of Israel."

[25]The woman came and knelt before him. "Lord, help me!" she said.

[26]He replied, "It is not right to take the children's bread and toss it to their dogs."

[27]"Yes, Lord," she said, "but even the dogs eat the crumbs that fall from their masters' table."

[28]Then Jesus answered, "Woman, you have great faith! Your request is granted." And her daughter was healed from that very hour.

Jesus Feeds the Four Thousand [29]Jesus left there and went along the Sea of Galilee. Then he went up on a mountainside and sat down. [30]Great crowds came to him, bringing the lame, the blind, the crippled, the mute and many others, and laid them at his feet; and he healed them. [31]The people were amazed when they saw the mute speaking, the crippled made well, the lame walking and the blind seeing. And they praised the God of Israel.

[32]Jesus called his disciples to him and said, "I have compassion for these

---

[a]4 Exodus 20:12; Deut. 5:16　[b]4 Exodus 21:17; Lev. 20:9　[c]6 Some manuscripts *father or his mother*
[d]9 Isaiah 29:13　[e]14 Some manuscripts *guides of the blind*

people; they have already been with me three days and have nothing to eat. I do not want to send them away hungry, or they may collapse on the way."

³³His disciples answered, "Where could we get enough bread in this remote place to feed such a crowd?"

³⁴"How many loaves do you have?" Jesus asked.

"Seven," they replied, "and a few small fish."

³⁵He told the crowd to sit down on the ground. ³⁶Then he took the seven loaves and the fish, and when he had given thanks, he broke them and gave them to the disciples, and they in turn to the people. ³⁷They all ate and were satisfied. Afterward the disciples picked up seven basketfuls of broken pieces that were left over. ³⁸The number of those who ate was four thousand, besides women and children. ³⁹After Jesus had sent the crowd away, he got into the boat and went to the vicinity of Magadan.

16 *The Demand for a Sign* The Pharisees and Sadducees came to Jesus and tested him by asking him to show them a sign from heaven.

²He replied,ᵃ "When evening comes, you say, 'It will be fair weather, for the sky is red,' ³and in the morning, 'Today it will be stormy, for the sky is red and overcast.' You know how to interpret the appearance of the sky, but you cannot interpret the signs of the times. ⁴A wicked and adulterous generation looks for a miraculous sign, but none will be given it except the sign of Jonah." Jesus then left them and went away.

The Yeast of the Pharisees and Sadducees ⁵When they went across the lake, the disciples forgot to take bread. ⁶"Be careful," Jesus said to them. "Be on your guard against the yeast of the Pharisees and Sadducees."

⁷They discussed this among themselves and said, "It is because we didn't bring any bread."

⁸Aware of their discussion, Jesus asked, "You of little faith, why are you talking among yourselves about having no bread? ⁹Do you still not understand? Don't you remember the five loaves for the five thousand, and how many basketfuls you gathered? ¹⁰Or the seven loaves for the four thousand, and how many basketfuls you gathered? ¹¹How is it you don't understand that I was not talking to you about bread? But be on your guard against the yeast of the Pharisees and Sadducees." ¹²Then they understood that he was not telling them to guard against the yeast used in bread, but against the teaching of the Pharisees and Sadducees.

Peter's Confession of Christ ¹³When Jesus came to the region of Caesarea Philippi, he asked his disciples, "Who do people say the Son of Man is?"

¹⁴They replied, "Some say John the Baptist; others say Elijah; and still others, Jeremiah or one of the prophets."

¹⁵"But what about you?" he asked. "Who do you say I am?"

¹⁶Simon Peter answered, "You are the Christ,ᵇ the Son of the living God."

¹⁷Jesus replied, "Blessed are you, Simon son of Jonah, for this was not revealed to you by man, but by my Father in heaven. ¹⁸And I tell you that you are Peter,ᶜ and on this rock I will build my church, and the gates of Hadesᵈ will not overcome it.ᵉ ¹⁹I will give you the keys of the kingdom of heaven; whatever you bind on earth will beᶠ bound in heaven, and whatever you loose on earth will beᶠ loosed in heaven." ²⁰Then he warned his disciples not to tell anyone that he was the Christ.

Jesus Predicts His Death ²¹From that time on Jesus began to explain to his disciples that he must go to Jerusalem and suffer many things at the hands

---

ᵃ*2* Some early manuscripts do not have the rest of verse 2 and all of verse 3. ᵇ*16* Or *Messiah*; also in verse 20 ᶜ*18 Peter* means *rock.* ᵈ*18* Or *hell* ᵉ*18* Or *not prove stronger than it* ᶠ*19* Or *have been*

of the elders, chief priests and teachers of the law, and that he must be killed and on the third day be raised to life.

²²Peter took him aside and began to rebuke him. "Never, Lord!" he said. "This shall never happen to you!"

²³Jesus turned and said to Peter, "Get behind me, Satan! You are a stumbling block to me; you do not have in mind the things of God, but the things of men."

²⁴Then Jesus said to his disciples, "If anyone would come after me, he must deny himself and take up his cross and follow me. ²⁵For whoever wants to save his life*ᵃ* will lose it, but whoever loses his life for me will find it. ²⁶What good will it be for a man if he gains the whole world, yet forfeits his soul? Or what can a man give in exchange for his soul? ²⁷For the Son of Man is going to come in his Father's glory with his angels, and then he will reward each person according to what he has done. ²⁸I tell you the truth, some who are standing here will not taste death before they see the Son of Man coming in his kingdom."

The Transfiguration   After six days Jesus took with him Peter, James and John the brother of James, and led them up a high mountain by themselves. ²There he was transfigured before them. His face shone like the sun, and his clothes became as white as the light. ³Just then there appeared before them Moses and Elijah, talking with Jesus.

⁴Peter said to Jesus, "Lord, it is good for us to be here. If you wish, I will put up three shelters—one for you, one for Moses and one for Elijah."

⁵While he was still speaking, a bright cloud enveloped them, and a voice from the cloud said, "This is my Son, whom I love; with him I am well pleased. Listen to him!"

⁶When the disciples heard this, they fell facedown to the ground, terrified. ⁷But Jesus came and touched them. "Get up," he said. "Don't be afraid." ⁸When they looked up, they saw no one except Jesus.

⁹As they were coming down the mountain, Jesus instructed them, "Don't tell anyone what you have seen, until the Son of Man has been raised from the dead."

¹⁰The disciples asked him, "Why then do the teachers of the law say that Elijah must come first?"

¹¹Jesus replied, "To be sure, Elijah comes and will restore all things. ¹²But I tell you, Elijah has already come, and they did not recognize him, but have done to him everything they wished. In the same way the Son of Man is going to suffer at their hands." ¹³Then the disciples understood that he was talking to them about John the Baptist.

The Healing of a Boy With a Demon   ¹⁴When they came to the crowd, a man approached Jesus and knelt before him. ¹⁵"Lord, have mercy on my son," he said. "He has seizures and is suffering greatly. He often falls into the fire or into the water. ¹⁶I brought him to your disciples, but they could not heal him."

¹⁷"O unbelieving and perverse generation," Jesus replied, "how long shall I stay with you? How long shall I put up with you? Bring the boy here to me." ¹⁸Jesus rebuked the demon, and it came out of the boy, and he was healed from that moment.

¹⁹Then the disciples came to Jesus in private and asked, "Why couldn't we drive it out?"

MATTHEW 16

QUIZZER

Q: Who was given the keys of the kingdom of heaven?

_BONUS:
What are
those keys?_

Answers on
page 1280

---

*ᵃ25 The Greek word means either _life_ or _soul_; also in verse 26.

[20]He replied, "Because you have so little faith. I tell you the truth, if you have faith as small as a mustard seed, you can say to this mountain, 'Move from here to there' and it will move. Nothing will be impossible for you.[a]"

[22]When they came together in Galilee, he said to them, "The Son of Man is going to be betrayed into the hands of men. [23]They will kill him, and on the third day he will be raised to life." And the disciples were filled with grief.

The Temple Tax [24]After Jesus and his disciples arrived in Capernaum, the collectors of the two-drachma tax came to Peter and asked, "Doesn't your teacher pay the temple tax[b]?"

[25]"Yes, he does," he replied.

When Peter came into the house, Jesus was the first to speak. "What do you think, Simon?" he asked. "From whom do the kings of the earth collect duty and taxes—from their own sons or from others?"

[26]"From others," Peter answered.

"Then the sons are exempt," Jesus said to him. [27]"But so that we may not offend them, go to the lake and throw out your line. Take the first fish you catch; open its mouth and you will find a four-drachma coin. Take it and give it to them for my tax and yours."

The Greatest in the Kingdom of Heaven At that time the disciples came to Jesus and asked, "Who is the greatest in the kingdom of heaven?"

[2]He called a little child and had him stand among them. [3]And he said: "I tell you the truth, unless you change and become like little children, you will never enter the kingdom of heaven. [4]Therefore, whoever humbles himself like this child is the greatest in the kingdom of heaven.

[5]"And whoever welcomes a little child like this in my name welcomes me. [6]But if anyone causes one of these little ones who believe in me to sin, it would be better for him to have a large millstone hung around his neck and to be drowned in the depths of the sea.

[7]"Woe to the world because of the things that cause people to sin! Such things must come, but woe to the man through whom they come! [8]If your hand or your foot causes you to sin, cut it off and throw it away. It is better for you to enter life maimed or crippled than to have two hands or two feet and be thrown into eternal fire. [9]And if your eye causes you to sin, gouge it out and throw it away. It is better for you to enter life with one eye than to have two eyes and be thrown into the fire of hell.

The Parable of the Lost Sheep [10]"See that you do not look down on one of these little ones. For I tell you that their angels in heaven always see the face of my Father in heaven.[c]

[12]"What do you think? If a man owns a hundred sheep, and one of them wanders away, will he not leave the ninety-nine on the hills and go to look for the one that wandered off? [13]And if he finds it, I tell you the truth, he is happier about that one sheep than about the ninety-nine that did not wander off. [14]In the same way your Father in heaven is not willing that any of these little ones should be lost.

A Brother Who Sins Against You [15]"If your brother sins against you,[d] go and show him his fault, just between the two of you. If he listens to you, you have won your brother over. [16]But if he will not listen, take one or two others along, so that 'every matter may be established by the testimony of two or three witnesses.'[e] [17]If he refuses to listen to them, tell it to the church; and

---

[a]20 Some manuscripts *you.* [21]*But this kind does not go out except by prayer and fasting.* [b]24 Greek *the two drachmas* [c]10 Some manuscripts *heaven.* [11]*The Son of Man came to save what was lost.* [d]15 Some manuscripts do not have *against you.* [e]16 Deut. 19:15

Dear Sam,

My best friend did something behind my back that was really unthinkable. I don't think I'll ever be able to forgive him. Should I quit speaking to him and ignore him?

Ryan in Ripon

100 Advice Lane, Anywhere, USA

Dear Sam, Inc.

Dear Ryan,

In Matthew 18 Christ tells you exactly how he wants you to handle a painful situation like this one. First, go talk to your friend alone and explain how you feel. If he won't listen, bring another friend to help you straighten the situation out. If he still won't listen, perhaps you could ask your youth pastor to help. Only if he rejects all your efforts to restore the friendship may you ignore him (Matthew 18:15-17).

The best way to patch up differences is by direct confrontation. It is then the responsibility of the person who wronged you to admit it and apologize. Then you can forgive him. Forgiveness always takes two people—one to extend forgiveness, and one to receive it. You do your part by going to the person who has wronged you. Then he has to do his part. Pray about it, and then take the first step.

Sam

if he refuses to listen even to the church, treat him as you would a pagan or a tax collector.

¹⁸"I tell you the truth, whatever you bind on earth will be*a* bound in heaven, and whatever you loose on earth will be*a* loosed in heaven.

¹⁹"Again, I tell you that if two of you on earth agree about anything you ask for, it will be done for you by my Father in heaven. ²⁰For where two or three come together in my name, there am I with them."

The Parable of the Unmerciful Servant ²¹Then Peter came to Jesus and asked, "Lord, how many times shall I forgive my brother when he sins against me? Up to seven times?"

²²Jesus answered, "I tell you, not seven times, but seventy-seven times.*b*

²³"Therefore, the kingdom of heaven is like a king who wanted to settle accounts with his servants. ²⁴As he began the settlement, a man who owed him ten thousand talents*c* was brought to him. ²⁵Since he was not able to pay, the master ordered that he and his wife and his children and all that he had be sold to repay the debt.

²⁶"The servant fell on his knees before him. 'Be patient with me,' he begged, 'and I will pay back everything.' ²⁷The servant's master took pity on him, canceled the debt and let him go.

²⁸"But when that servant went out, he found one of his fellow servants who owed him a hundred denarii.*d* He grabbed him and began to choke him. 'Pay back what you owe me!' he demanded.

²⁹"His fellow servant fell to his knees and begged him, 'Be patient with me, and I will pay you back.'

³⁰"But he refused. Instead, he went off and had the man thrown into prison until he could pay the debt. ³¹When the other servants saw what had happened, they were greatly distressed and went and told their master everything that had happened.

³²"Then the master called the servant in. 'You wicked servant,' he said, 'I canceled all that debt of yours because you begged me to. ³³Shouldn't you have had mercy on your fellow servant just as I had on you?' ³⁴In anger his master turned him over to the jailers to be tortured, until he should pay back all he owed.

³⁵"This is how my heavenly Father will treat each of you unless you forgive your brother from your heart."

Divorce When Jesus had finished saying these things, he left Galilee and went into the region of Judea to the other side of the Jordan. ²Large crowds followed him, and he healed them there.

³Some Pharisees came to him to test him. They asked, "Is it lawful for a man to divorce his wife for any and every reason?"

⁴"Haven't you read," he replied, "that at the beginning the Creator 'made them male and female,'*e* ⁵and said, 'For this reason a man will leave his father and mother and be united to his wife, and the two will become one flesh'*f*? ⁶So they are no longer two, but one. Therefore what God has joined together, let man not separate."

⁷"Why then," they asked, "did Moses command that a man give his wife a certificate of divorce and send her away?"

⁸Jesus replied, "Moses permitted you to divorce your wives because your hearts were hard. But it was not this way from the beginning. ⁹I tell you that anyone who divorces his wife, except for marital unfaithfulness, and marries another woman commits adultery."

¹⁰The disciples said to him, "If this is the situation between a husband and wife, it is better not to marry."

---

a18 Or *have been* *b22* Or *seventy times seven* *c24* That is, millions of dollars *d28* That is, a few dollars *e4* Gen. 1:27 *f5* Gen. 2:24

[11]Jesus replied, "Not everyone can accept this word, but only those to whom it has been given. [12]For some are eunuchs because they were born that way; others were made that way by men; and others have renounced marriage[a] because of the kingdom of heaven. The one who can accept this should accept it."

The Little Children and Jesus   [13]Then little children were brought to Jesus for him to place his hands on them and pray for them. But the disciples rebuked those who brought them. [14]Jesus said, "Let the little children come to me, and do not hinder them, for the kingdom of heaven belongs to such as these." [15]When he had placed his hands on them, he went on from there.

The Rich Young Man   [16]Now a man came up to Jesus and asked, "Teacher, what good thing must I do to get eternal life?"

[17]"Why do you ask me about what is good?" Jesus replied. "There is only One who is good. If you want to enter life, obey the commandments."

[18]"Which ones?" the man inquired.

Jesus replied, " 'Do not murder, do not commit adultery, do not steal, do not give false testimony, [19]honor your father and mother,'[b] and 'love your neighbor as yourself.'[c]"

[20]"All these I have kept," the young man said. "What do I still lack?"

[21]Jesus answered, "If you want to be perfect, go, sell your possessions and give to the poor, and you will have treasure in heaven. Then come, follow me."

[22]When the young man heard this, he went away sad, because he had great wealth.

[23]Then Jesus said to his disciples, "I tell you the truth, it is hard for a rich man to enter the kingdom of heaven. [24]Again I tell you, it is easier for a camel to go through the eye of a needle than for a rich man to enter the kingdom of God."

[25]When the disciples heard this, they were greatly astonished and asked, "Who then can be saved?"

---

[a]12 Or *have made themselves eunuchs*   [b]19 Exodus 20:12-16; Deut. 5:16-20   [c]19 Lev. 19:18

Some Christians feel believers can never get a divorce. Others feel it's OK for certain reasons. One thing is for sure. You want to take your time and pray about the person you choose as a life partner! Divorce hurts. It's painful for everyone involved.

In Matthew 19:1–12 Jesus said a few things about divorce:

✳ God's ideal is a lifetime union (Matthew 19:4–6).
✳ God never permits divorce just because a person wants to marry someone else. That's definitely wrong (Matthew 19:9).

The Bible Says

Divorce, Yes or No?

If you're a victim of your parents' divorce, you know how much it can hurt. Do your best not to get involved in who's to blame. And don't think the divorce is your fault. Instead read the story that follows Jesus' teaching on divorce (Matthew 19:13–15), and remember Jesus places his hands on you and prays for you right now.

²⁶Jesus looked at them and said, "With man this is impossible, but with God all things are possible."

²⁷Peter answered him, "We have left everything to follow you! What then will there be for us?"

²⁸Jesus said to them, "I tell you the truth, at the renewal of all things, when the Son of Man sits on his glorious throne, you who have followed me will also sit on twelve thrones, judging the twelve tribes of Israel. ²⁹And everyone who has left houses or brothers or sisters or father or mother*ᵃ* or children or fields for my sake will receive a hundred times as much and will inherit eternal life. ³⁰But many who are first will be last, and many who are last will be first.

The Parable of the Workers in the Vineyard "For the kingdom of heaven is like a landowner who went out early in the morning to hire men to work in his vineyard. ²He agreed to pay them a denarius for the day and sent them into his vineyard.

³"About the third hour he went out and saw others standing in the marketplace doing nothing. ⁴He told them, 'You also go and work in my vineyard, and I will pay you whatever is right.' ⁵So they went.

"He went out again about the sixth hour and the ninth hour and did the same thing. ⁶About the eleventh hour he went out and found still others standing around. He asked them, 'Why have you been standing here all day long doing nothing?'

⁷"'Because no one has hired us,' they answered.

"He said to them, 'You also go and work in my vineyard.'

⁸"When evening came, the owner of the vineyard said to his foreman, 'Call the workers and pay them their wages, beginning with the last ones hired and going on to the first.'

⁹"The workers who were hired about the eleventh hour came and each received a denarius. ¹⁰So when those came who were hired first, they expected to receive more. But each one of them also received a denarius. ¹¹When they received it, they began to grumble against the landowner. ¹²'These men who were hired last worked only one hour,' they said, 'and you have made them equal to us who have borne the burden of the work and the heat of the day.'

¹³"But he answered one of them, 'Friend, I am not being unfair to you. Didn't you agree to work for a denarius? ¹⁴Take your pay and go. I want to give the man who was hired last the same as I gave you. ¹⁵Don't I have the right to do what I want with my own money? Or are you envious because I am generous?'

¹⁶"So the last will be first, and the first will be last."

Jesus Again Predicts His Death ¹⁷Now as Jesus was going up to Jerusalem, he took the twelve disciples aside and said to them, ¹⁸"We are going up to Jerusalem, and the Son of Man will be betrayed to the chief priests and the teachers of the law. They will condemn him to death ¹⁹and will turn him over to the Gentiles to be mocked and flogged and crucified. On the third day he will be raised to life!"

A Mother's Request ²⁰Then the mother of Zebedee's sons came to Jesus with her sons and, kneeling down, asked a favor of him.

²¹"What is it you want?" he asked.

She said, "Grant that one of these two sons of mine may sit at your right and the other at your left in your kingdom."

²²"You don't know what you are asking," Jesus said to them. "Can you drink the cup I am going to drink?"

ᵃ29 Some manuscripts *mother or wife*

"We can," they answered.

²³Jesus said to them, "You will indeed drink from my cup, but to sit at my right or left is not for me to grant. These places belong to those for whom they have been prepared by my Father."

²⁴When the ten heard about this, they were indignant with the two brothers. ²⁵Jesus called them together and said, "You know that the rulers of the Gentiles lord it over them, and their high officials exercise authority over them. ²⁶Not so with you. Instead, whoever wants to become great among you must be your servant, ²⁷and whoever wants to be first must be your slave— ²⁸just as the Son of Man did not come to be served, but to serve, and to give his life as a ransom for many."

Two Blind Men Receive Sight ²⁹As Jesus and his disciples were leaving Jericho, a large crowd followed him. ³⁰Two blind men were sitting by the roadside, and when they heard that Jesus was going by, they shouted, "Lord, Son of David, have mercy on us!"

³¹The crowd rebuked them and told them to be quiet, but they shouted all the louder, "Lord, Son of David, have mercy on us!"

³²Jesus stopped and called them. "What do you want me to do for you?" he asked.

³³"Lord," they answered, "we want our sight."

³⁴Jesus had compassion on them and touched their eyes. Immediately they received their sight and followed him.

The Triumphal Entry As they approached Jerusalem and came to Bethphage on the Mount of Olives, Jesus sent two disciples, ²saying to them, "Go to the village ahead of you, and at once you will find a donkey tied there, with her colt by her. Untie them and bring them to me. ³If anyone says anything to you, tell him that the Lord needs them, and he will send them right away."

⁴This took place to fulfill what was spoken through the prophet:

> ⁵"Say to the Daughter of Zion,
> 'See, your king comes to you,
> gentle and riding on a donkey,
> on a colt, the foal of a donkey.' "ᵃ

⁶The disciples went and did as Jesus had instructed them. ⁷They brought the donkey and the colt, placed their cloaks on them, and Jesus sat on them. ⁸A very large crowd spread their cloaks on the road, while others cut branches from the trees and spread them on the road. ⁹The crowds that went ahead of him and those that followed shouted,

> "Hosannaᵇ to the Son of David!"

> "Blessed is he who comes in the name of the Lord!"ᶜ

> "Hosannaᵇ in the highest!"

¹⁰When Jesus entered Jerusalem, the whole city was stirred and asked, "Who is this?"

¹¹The crowds answered, "This is Jesus, the prophet from Nazareth in Galilee."

Jesus at the Temple ¹²Jesus entered the temple area and drove out all who were buying and selling there. He overturned the tables of the money changers and the benches of those selling doves. ¹³"It is written," he said to them, " 'My house will be called a house of prayer,'ᵈ but you are making it a 'den of robbers.'ᵉ"

ᵃ5 Zech. 9:9   ᵇ9 A Hebrew expression meaning "Save!" which became an exclamation of praise; also in verse 15   ᶜ9 Psalm 118:26   ᵈ13 Isaiah 56:7   ᵉ13 Jer. 7:11

¹⁴The blind and the lame came to him at the temple, and he healed them. ¹⁵But when the chief priests and the teachers of the law saw the wonderful things he did and the children shouting in the temple area, "Hosanna to the Son of David," they were indignant.

¹⁶"Do you hear what these children are saying?" they asked him.

"Yes," replied Jesus, "have you never read,

> " 'From the lips of children and infants
> you have ordained praise'ᵃ?"

¹⁷And he left them and went out of the city to Bethany, where he spent the night.

The Fig Tree Withers   ¹⁸Early in the morning, as he was on his way back to the city, he was hungry. ¹⁹Seeing a fig tree by the road, he went up to it but found nothing on it except leaves. Then he said to it, "May you never bear fruit again!" Immediately the tree withered.

²⁰When the disciples saw this, they were amazed. "How did the fig tree wither so quickly?" they asked.

²¹Jesus replied, "I tell you the truth, if you have faith and do not doubt, not only can you do what was done to the fig tree, but also you can say to this mountain, 'Go, throw yourself into the sea,' and it will be done. ²²If you believe, you will receive whatever you ask for in prayer."

The Authority of Jesus Questioned   ²³Jesus entered the temple courts, and, while he was teaching, the chief priests and the elders of the people came to him. "By what authority are you doing these things?" they asked. "And who gave you this authority?"

²⁴Jesus replied, "I will also ask you one question. If you answer me, I will tell you by what authority I am doing these things. ²⁵John's baptism—where did it come from? Was it from heaven, or from men?"

They discussed it among themselves and said, "If we say, 'From heaven,' he will ask, 'Then why didn't you believe him?' ²⁶But if we say, 'From men'—we are afraid of the people, for they all hold that John was a prophet."

²⁷So they answered Jesus, "We don't know."

Then he said, "Neither will I tell you by what authority I am doing these things.

The Parable of the Two Sons   ²⁸"What do you think? There was a man who had two sons. He went to the first and said, 'Son, go and work today in the vineyard.'

²⁹" 'I will not,' he answered, but later he changed his mind and went.

³⁰"Then the father went to the other son and said the same thing. He answered, 'I will, sir,' but he did not go.

³¹"Which of the two did what his father wanted?"

"The first," they answered.

Jesus said to them, "I tell you the truth, the tax collectors and the prostitutes are entering the kingdom of God ahead of you. ³²For John came to you to show you the way of righteousness, and you did not believe him, but the tax collectors and the prostitutes did. And even after you saw this, you did not repent and believe him.

The Parable of the Tenants   ³³"Listen to another parable: There was a landowner who planted a vineyard. He put a wall around it, dug a winepress in it and built a watchtower. Then he rented the vineyard to some farmers and went away on a journey. ³⁴When the harvest time approached, he sent his servants to the tenants to collect his fruit.

³⁵"The tenants seized his servants; they beat one, killed another, and

ᵃ*16* Psalm 8:2

stoned a third. ³⁶Then he sent other servants to them, more than the first time, and the tenants treated them the same way. ³⁷Last of all, he sent his son to them. 'They will respect my son,' he said.

³⁸"But when the tenants saw the son, they said to each other, 'This is the heir. Come, let's kill him and take his inheritance.' ³⁹So they took him and threw him out of the vineyard and killed him.

⁴⁰"Therefore, when the owner of the vineyard comes, what will he do to those tenants?"

⁴¹"He will bring those wretches to a wretched end," they replied, "and he will rent the vineyard to other tenants, who will give him his share of the crop at harvest time."

⁴²Jesus said to them, "Have you never read in the Scriptures:

" 'The stone the builders rejected
    has become the capstone*;
the Lord has done this,
    and it is marvelous in our eyes'*ᵇ?

⁴³"Therefore I tell you that the kingdom of God will be taken away from you and given to a people who will produce its fruit. ⁴⁴He who falls on this stone will be broken to pieces, but he on whom it falls will be crushed."ᶜ

⁴⁵When the chief priests and the Pharisees heard Jesus' parables, they knew he was talking about them. ⁴⁶They looked for a way to arrest him, but they were afraid of the crowd because the people held that he was a prophet.

The Parable of the Wedding Banquet Jesus spoke to them again in parables, saying: ²"The kingdom of heaven is like a king who prepared a wedding banquet for his son. ³He sent his servants to those who had been invited to the banquet to tell them to come, but they refused to come.

⁴"Then he sent some more servants and said, 'Tell those who have been invited that I have prepared my dinner: My oxen and fattened cattle have been butchered, and everything is ready. Come to the wedding banquet.'

⁵"But they paid no attention and went off—one to his field, another to his business. ⁶The rest seized his servants, mistreated them and killed them. ⁷The king was enraged. He sent his army and destroyed those murderers and burned their city.

⁸"Then he said to his servants, 'The wedding banquet is ready, but those I invited did not deserve to come. ⁹Go to the street corners and invite to the banquet anyone you find.' ¹⁰So the servants went out into the streets and gathered all the people they could find, both good and bad, and the wedding hall was filled with guests.

¹¹"But when the king came in to see the guests, he noticed a man there who was

ᵃ42 Or *cornerstone* ᵇ42 Psalm 118:22,23 ᶜ44 Some manuscripts do not have verse 44.

MATTHEW 22:1–14

Suppose a king invited you to a banquet. Would you be excited? You bet! You'd have to get a new dress or suit. And fix your hair. You'd want to look your absolute best! But the people in Jesus' parable acted bored. "Sorry, King [yawn]." Some of them were even angry. "Get out of here. Don't bug me!" It's a weird parable because no one would act this way if invited to a king's banquet. Yet people do act this way when God invites them to the biggest party the world will ever know. A party that will last forever. How about you? Too busy? Or upset that God keeps bugging you to accept his invitation and believe? Well, why?

Direct Line

not wearing wedding clothes. [12]'Friend,' he asked, 'how did you get in here without wedding clothes?' The man was speechless.

[13]"Then the king told the attendants, 'Tie him hand and foot, and throw him outside, into the darkness, where there will be weeping and gnashing of teeth.'

[14]"For many are invited, but few are chosen."

Paying Taxes to Caesar [15]Then the Pharisees went out and laid plans to trap him in his words. [16]They sent their disciples to him along with the Herodians. "Teacher," they said, "we know you are a man of integrity and that you teach the way of God in accordance with the truth. You aren't swayed by men, because you pay no attention to who they are. [17]Tell us then, what is your opinion? Is it right to pay taxes to Caesar or not?"

[18]But Jesus, knowing their evil intent, said, "You hypocrites, why are you trying to trap me? [19]Show me the coin used for paying the tax." They brought him a denarius, [20]and he asked them, "Whose portrait is this? And whose inscription?"

[21]"Caesar's," they replied.

Then he said to them, "Give to Caesar what is Caesar's, and to God what is God's."

[22]When they heard this, they were amazed. So they left him and went away.

Marriage at the Resurrection [23]That same day the Sadducees, who say there is no resurrection, came to him with a question. [24]"Teacher," they said, "Moses told us that if a man dies without having children, his brother must marry the widow and have children for him. [25]Now there were seven brothers among us. The first one married and died, and since he had no children, he left his wife to his brother. [26]The same thing happened to the second and third brother, right on down to the seventh. [27]Finally, the woman died. [28]Now then, at the resurrection, whose wife will she be of the seven, since all of them were married to her?"

[29]Jesus replied, "You are in error because you do not know the Scriptures or the power of God. [30]At the resurrection people will neither marry nor be given in marriage; they will be like the angels in heaven. [31]But about the resurrection of the dead—have you not read what God said to you, [32]'I am the God of Abraham, the God of Isaac, and the God of Jacob'[a]? He is not the God of the dead but of the living."

[33]When the crowds heard this, they were astonished at his teaching.

The Greatest Commandment [34]Hearing that Jesus had silenced the Sadducees, the Pharisees got together. [35]One of them, an expert in the law, tested him with this question: [36]"Teacher, which is the greatest commandment in the Law?"

[37]Jesus replied: " 'Love the Lord your God with all your heart and with all your soul and with all your mind.'[b] [38]This is the first and greatest commandment. [39]And the second is like it: 'Love your neighbor as yourself.'[c] [40]All the Law and the Prophets hang on these two commandments."

Whose Son Is the Christ? [41]While the Pharisees were gathered together, Jesus asked them, [42]"What do you think about the Christ[d]? Whose son is he?"

"The son of David," they replied.

[43]He said to them, "How is it then that David, speaking by the Spirit, calls him 'Lord'? For he says,

> [44]" 'The Lord said to my Lord:
> "Sit at my right hand
> until I put your enemies
> under your feet." '[e]

---

[a]32 Exodus 3:6   [b]37 Deut. 6:5   [c]39 Lev. 19:18   [d]42 Or *Messiah*   [e]44 Psalm 110:1

⁴⁵If then David calls him 'Lord,' how can he be his son?" ⁴⁶No one could say a word in reply, and from that day on no one dared to ask him any more questions.

Seven Woes Then Jesus said to the crowds and to his disciples: ²"The teachers of the law and the Pharisees sit in Moses' seat. ³So you must obey them and do everything they tell you. But do not do what they do, for they do not practice what they preach. ⁴They tie up heavy loads and put them on men's shoulders, but they themselves are not willing to lift a finger to move them.

⁵"Everything they do is done for men to see: They make their phylacteries*ᵃ* wide and the tassels on their garments long; ⁶they love the place of honor at banquets and the most important seats in the synagogues; ⁷they love to be greeted in the marketplaces and to have men call them 'Rabbi.'

⁸"But you are not to be called 'Rabbi,' for you have only one Master and you are all brothers. ⁹And do not call anyone on earth 'father,' for you have one Father, and he is in heaven. ¹⁰Nor are you to be called 'teacher,' for you have one Teacher, the Christ.*ᵇ* ¹¹The greatest among you will be your servant. ¹²For whoever exalts himself will be humbled, and whoever humbles himself will be exalted.

¹³"Woe to you, teachers of the law and Pharisees, you hypocrites! You shut the kingdom of heaven in men's faces. You yourselves do not enter, nor will you let those enter who are trying to.*ᶜ*

¹⁵"Woe to you, teachers of the law and Pharisees, you hypocrites! You travel over land and sea to win a single convert, and when he becomes one, you make him twice as much a son of hell as you are.

¹⁶"Woe to you, blind guides! You say, 'If anyone swears by the temple, it means nothing; but if anyone swears by the gold of the temple, he is bound by his oath.' ¹⁷You blind fools! Which is greater: the gold, or the temple that makes the gold sacred? ¹⁸You also say, 'If anyone swears by the altar, it means nothing; but if anyone swears by the gift on it, he is bound by his oath.' ¹⁹You blind men! Which is greater: the gift, or the altar that makes the gift sacred? ²⁰Therefore, he who swears by the altar swears by it and by everything on it. ²¹And he who swears by the temple swears by it and by the one who dwells in it. ²²And he who swears by heaven swears by God's throne and by the one who sits on it.

²³"Woe to you, teachers of the law and Pharisees, you hypocrites! You give a tenth of your spices—mint, dill and cummin. But you have neglected the more important matters of the law—justice, mercy and faithfulness. You should have practiced the latter, without neglecting the former. ²⁴You blind guides! You strain out a gnat but swallow a camel.

²⁵"Woe to you, teachers of the law and Pharisees, you hypocrites! You clean the outside of the cup and dish, but inside they are full of greed and self-indulgence. ²⁶Blind Pharisee! First clean the inside of the cup and dish, and then the outside also will be clean.

²⁷"Woe to you, teachers of the law and Pharisees, you hypocrites! You are like whitewashed tombs, which look beautiful on the outside but on the inside are full of dead men's bones and everything unclean. ²⁸In the same way, on the outside you appear to people as righteous but on the inside you are full of hypocrisy and wickedness.

²⁹"Woe to you, teachers of the law and Pharisees, you hypocrites! You build tombs for the prophets and decorate the graves of the righteous. ³⁰And you say, 'If we had lived in the days of our forefathers, we would not have taken

---

ᵃ5 That is, boxes containing Scripture verses, worn on forehead and arm   *ᵇ10* Or *Messiah*   *ᶜ13* Some manuscripts *to.* *¹⁴Woe to you, teachers of the law and Pharisees, you hypocrites! You devour widows' houses and for a show make lengthy prayers. Therefore you will be punished more severely.*

part with them in shedding the blood of the prophets.' ³¹So you testify against yourselves that you are the descendants of those who murdered the prophets. ³²Fill up, then, the measure of the sin of your forefathers!

³³"You snakes! You brood of vipers! How will you escape being condemned to hell? ³⁴Therefore I am sending you prophets and wise men and teachers. Some of them you will kill and crucify; others you will flog in your synagogues and pursue from town to town. ³⁵And so upon you will come all the righteous blood that has been shed on earth, from the blood of righteous Abel to the blood of Zechariah son of Berekiah, whom you murdered between the temple and the altar. ³⁶I tell you the truth, all this will come upon this generation.

³⁷"O Jerusalem, Jerusalem, you who kill the prophets and stone those sent to you, how often I have longed to gather your children together, as a hen gathers her chicks under her wings, but you were not willing. ³⁸Look, your house is left to you desolate. ³⁹For I tell you, you will not see me again until you say, 'Blessed is he who comes in the name of the Lord.'*ᵃ*"

Signs of the End of the Age   Jesus left the temple and was walking away when his disciples came up to him to call his attention to its buildings. ²"Do you see all these things?" he asked. "I tell you the truth, not one stone here will be left on another; every one will be thrown down."

³As Jesus was sitting on the Mount of Olives, the disciples came to him privately. "Tell us," they said, "when will this happen, and what will be the sign of your coming and of the end of the age?"

⁴Jesus answered: "Watch out that no one deceives you. ⁵For many will come in my name, claiming, 'I am the Christ,*ᵇ*' and will deceive many. ⁶You will hear of wars and rumors of wars, but see to it that you are not alarmed. Such things must happen, but the end is still to come. ⁷Nation will rise against nation, and kingdom against kingdom. There will be famines and earthquakes in various places. ⁸All these are the beginning of birth pains.

⁹"Then you will be handed over to be persecuted and put to death, and you will be hated by all nations because of me. ¹⁰At that time many will turn away from the faith and will betray and hate each other, ¹¹and many false prophets will appear and deceive many people. ¹²Because of the increase of wickedness, the love of most will grow cold, ¹³but he who stands firm to the end will be saved. ¹⁴And this gospel of the kingdom will be preached in the whole world as a testimony to all nations, and then the end will come.

¹⁵"So when you see standing in the holy place 'the abomination that causes desolation,'*ᶜ* spoken of through the prophet Daniel—let the reader understand— ¹⁶then let those who are in Judea flee to the mountains. ¹⁷Let no one on the roof of his house go down to take anything out of the house. ¹⁸Let no one in the field go back to get his cloak. ¹⁹How dreadful it will be in those days for pregnant women and nursing mothers! ²⁰Pray that your flight will not take place in winter or on the Sabbath. ²¹For then there will be great distress, unequaled from the beginning of the world until now—and never to be equaled again. ²²If those days had not been cut short, no one would survive, but for the sake of the elect those days will be shortened. ²³At that time if anyone says to you, 'Look, here is the Christ!' or, 'There he is!' do not believe it. ²⁴For false Christs and false prophets will appear and perform great signs and miracles to deceive even the elect—if that were possible. ²⁵See, I have told you ahead of time.

²⁶"So if anyone tells you, 'There he is, out in the desert,' do not go out; or, 'Here he is, in the inner rooms,' do not believe it. ²⁷For as lightning that

---

ᵃ39 Psalm 118:26   *ᵇ5* Or *Messiah*; also in verse 23   *ᶜ15* Daniel 9:27; 11:31; 12:11

comes from the east is visible even in the west, so will be the coming of the Son of Man. ²⁸Wherever there is a carcass, there the vultures will gather.

²⁹"Immediately after the distress of those days

> " 'the sun will be darkened,
>   and the moon will not give its light;
> the stars will fall from the sky,
>   and the heavenly bodies will be shaken.'ᵃ

³⁰"At that time the sign of the Son of Man will appear in the sky, and all the nations of the earth will mourn. They will see the Son of Man coming on the clouds of the sky, with power and great glory. ³¹And he will send his angels with a loud trumpet call, and they will gather his elect from the four winds, from one end of the heavens to the other.

³²"Now learn this lesson from the fig tree: As soon as its twigs get tender and its leaves come out, you know that summer is near. ³³Even so, when you see all these things, you know that itᵇ is near, right at the door. ³⁴I tell you the truth, this generationᶜ will certainly not pass away until all these things have happened. ³⁵Heaven and earth will pass away, but my words will never pass away.

The Day and Hour Unknown ³⁶"No one knows about that day or hour, not even the angels in heaven, nor the Son,ᵈ but only the Father. ³⁷As it was in the days of Noah, so it will be at the coming of the Son of Man. ³⁸For in the days before the flood, people were eating and drinking, marrying and giving in marriage, up to the day Noah entered the ark; ³⁹and they knew nothing about what would happen until the flood came and took them all away. That is how it will be at the coming of the Son of Man. ⁴⁰Two men will be in the field; one will be taken and the other left. ⁴¹Two women will be grinding with a hand mill; one will be taken and the other left.

⁴²"Therefore keep watch, because you do not know on what day your Lord will come. ⁴³But understand this: If the owner of the house had known at what time of night the thief was coming, he would have kept watch and would not have let his house be broken into. ⁴⁴So you also must be ready, because the Son of Man will come at an hour when you do not expect him.

⁴⁵"Who then is the faithful and wise servant, whom the master has put in charge of the servants in his household to give them their food at the proper time? ⁴⁶It will be good for that servant whose master finds him doing so when he returns. ⁴⁷I tell you the truth, he will put him in charge of all his possessions. ⁴⁸But suppose that servant is wicked and says to himself, 'My master is staying away a long time,' ⁴⁹and he then begins to beat his fellow servants and to eat and drink with drunkards. ⁵⁰The master of that servant will come on a day when he does not expect him and at an hour he is not aware of. ⁵¹He will cut him to pieces and assign him a place with the hypocrites, where there will be weeping and gnashing of teeth.

The Parable of the Ten Virgins "At that time the kingdom of heaven will be like ten virgins who took their lamps and went out to meet the bridegroom. ²Five of them were foolish and five were wise. ³The foolish ones took their lamps but did not take any oil with them. ⁴The wise, however, took oil in jars along with their lamps. ⁵The bridegroom was a long time in coming, and they all became drowsy and fell asleep.

⁶"At midnight the cry rang out: 'Here's the bridegroom! Come out to meet him!'

⁷"Then all the virgins woke up and trimmed their lamps. ⁸The foolish ones said to the wise, 'Give us some of your oil; our lamps are going out.'

ᵃ29 Isaiah 13:10; 34:4   ᵇ33 Or *he*   ᶜ34 Or *race*   ᵈ36 Some manuscripts do not have *nor the Son.*

⁹" 'No,' they replied, 'there may not be enough for both us and you. Instead, go to those who sell oil and buy some for yourselves.'

¹⁰"But while they were on their way to buy the oil, the bridegroom arrived. The virgins who were ready went in with him to the wedding banquet. And the door was shut.

¹¹"Later the others also came. 'Sir! Sir!' they said. 'Open the door for us!'

¹²"But he replied, 'I tell you the truth, I don't know you.'

¹³"Therefore keep watch, because you do not know the day or the hour.

The Parable of the Talents ¹⁴"Again, it will be like a man going on a journey, who called his servants and entrusted his property to them. ¹⁵To one he gave five talents*ᵃ* of money, to another two talents, and to another one talent, each according to his ability. Then he went on his journey. ¹⁶The man who had received the five talents went at once and put his money to work and gained five more. ¹⁷So also, the one with the two talents gained two more. ¹⁸But the man who had received the one talent went off, dug a hole in the ground and hid his master's money.

¹⁹"After a long time the master of those servants returned and settled accounts with them. ²⁰The man who had received the five talents brought the other five. 'Master,' he said, 'you entrusted me with five talents. See, I have gained five more.'

²¹"His master replied, 'Well done, good and faithful servant! You have been faithful with a few things; I will put you in charge of many things. Come and share your master's happiness!'

²²"The man with the two talents also came. 'Master,' he said, 'you entrusted me with two talents; see, I have gained two more.'

²³"His master replied, 'Well done, good and faithful servant! You have been faithful with a few things; I will put you in charge of many things. Come and share your master's happiness!'

This guy had no talent for finance.

SEE MATTHEW 25:18

²⁴"Then the man who had received the one talent came. 'Master,' he said, 'I knew that you are a hard man, harvesting where you have not sown and gathering where you have not scattered seed. ²⁵So I was afraid and went out and hid your talent in the ground. See, here is what belongs to you.'

²⁶"His master replied, 'You wicked, lazy servant! So you knew that I harvest where I have not sown and gather where I have not scattered seed? ²⁷Well then, you should have put my money on deposit with the bankers, so that when I returned I would have received it back with interest.

²⁸" 'Take the talent from him and give it to the one who has the ten talents. ²⁹For everyone who has will be given more, and he will have an abundance. Whoever does not have, even what he has will be taken from him. ³⁰And throw that worthless servant outside, into the darkness, where there will be weeping and gnashing of teeth.'

The Sheep and the Goats ³¹"When the Son of Man comes in his glory, and all the angels with him, he will sit on his throne in heavenly glory.

ᵃ15 A talent was worth more than a thousand dollars.

³²All the nations will be gathered before him, and he will separate the people one from another as a shepherd separates the sheep from the goats. ³³He will put the sheep on his right and the goats on his left.

³⁴"Then the King will say to those on his right, 'Come, you who are blessed by my Father; take your inheritance, the kingdom prepared for you since the creation of the world. ³⁵For I was hungry and you gave me something to eat, I was thirsty and you gave me something to drink, I was a stranger and you invited me in, ³⁶I needed clothes and you clothed me, I was sick and you looked after me, I was in prison and you came to visit me.'

³⁷"Then the righteous will answer him, 'Lord, when did we see you hungry and feed you, or thirsty and give you something to drink? ³⁸When did we see you a stranger and invite you in, or needing clothes and clothe you? ³⁹When did we see you sick or in prison and go to visit you?'

⁴⁰"The King will reply, 'I tell you the truth, whatever you did for one of the least of these brothers of mine, you did for me.'

⁴¹"Then he will say to those on his left, 'Depart from me, you who are cursed, into the eternal fire prepared for the devil and his angels. ⁴²For I was hungry and you gave me nothing to eat, I was thirsty and you gave me nothing to drink, ⁴³I was a stranger and you did not invite me in, I needed clothes and you did not clothe me, I was sick and in prison and you did not look after me.'

⁴⁴"They also will answer, 'Lord, when did we see you hungry or thirsty or a stranger or needing clothes or sick or in prison, and did not help you?'

⁴⁵"He will reply, 'I tell you the truth, whatever you did not do for one of the least of these, you did not do for me.'

⁴⁶"Then they will go away to eternal punishment, but the righteous to eternal life."

26 *The Plot Against Jesus* When Jesus had finished saying all these things, he said to his disciples, ²"As you know, the Passover is two days away—and the Son of Man will be handed over to be crucified."

³Then the chief priests and the elders of the people assembled in the palace of the high priest, whose name was Caiaphas, ⁴and they plotted to arrest Jesus in some sly way and kill him. ⁵"But not during the Feast," they said, "or there may be a riot among the people."

Jesus Anointed at Bethany ⁶While Jesus was in Bethany in the home of a man known as Simon the Leper, ⁷a woman came to him with an alabaster jar

---

Jesus told his listeners in no uncertain terms that hell is for real. He talked about "the fire of hell" (Matthew 5:22), and he described someone's "whole body [going] into hell" (Matthew 5:30). He also told a story about a man who was "in agony in this fire" (Luke 16:19–31).

The Bible mentions three things about hell:

✳ It is permanent (Matthew 25:46).
✳ It is a punishment for sin and disbelief (2 Thessalonians 1:8).
✳ It is separation from God (2 Thessalonians 1:9).

The Bible also says that God doesn't want anyone to perish in hell (2 Peter 3:9). God was willing to send his Son to die in order to save everyone who believes from punishment in hell.

The Bible Says

Hell Is for Real!

of very expensive perfume, which she poured on his head as he was reclining at the table.

⁸When the disciples saw this, they were indignant. "Why this waste?" they asked. ⁹"This perfume could have been sold at a high price and the money given to the poor."

¹⁰Aware of this, Jesus said to them, "Why are you bothering this woman? She has done a beautiful thing to me. ¹¹The poor you will always have with you, but you will not always have me. ¹²When she poured this perfume on my body, she did it to prepare me for burial. ¹³I tell you the truth, wherever this gospel is preached throughout the world, what she has done will also be told, in memory of her."

Judas Agrees to Betray Jesus ¹⁴Then one of the Twelve—the one called Judas Iscariot—went to the chief priests ¹⁵and asked, "What are you willing to give me if I hand him over to you?" So they counted out for him thirty silver coins. ¹⁶From then on Judas watched for an opportunity to hand him over.

The Lord's Supper ¹⁷On the first day of the Feast of Unleavened Bread, the disciples came to Jesus and asked, "Where do you want us to make preparations for you to eat the Passover?"

¹⁸He replied, "Go into the city to a certain man and tell him, 'The Teacher says: My appointed time is near. I am going to celebrate the Passover with my disciples at your house.'" ¹⁹So the disciples did as Jesus had directed them and prepared the Passover.

²⁰When evening came, Jesus was reclining at the table with the Twelve. ²¹And while they were eating, he said, "I tell you the truth, one of you will betray me."

²²They were very sad and began to say to him one after the other, "Surely not I, Lord?"

²³Jesus replied, "The one who has dipped his hand into the bowl with me will betray me. ²⁴The Son of Man will go just as it is written about him. But woe to that man who betrays the Son of Man! It would be better for him if he had not been born."

²⁵Then Judas, the one who would betray him, said, "Surely not I, Rabbi?" Jesus answered, "Yes, it is you."*ᵃ*

²⁶While they were eating, Jesus took bread, gave thanks and broke it, and gave it to his disciples, saying, "Take and eat; this is my body."

²⁷Then he took the cup, gave thanks and offered it to them, saying, "Drink from it, all of you. ²⁸This is my blood of the*ᵇ* covenant, which is poured out for many for the forgiveness of sins. ²⁹I tell you, I will not drink of this fruit of the vine from now on until that day when I drink it anew with you in my Father's kingdom."

³⁰When they had sung a hymn, they went out to the Mount of Olives.

Jesus Predicts Peter's Denial ³¹Then Jesus told them, "This very night you will all fall away on account of me, for it is written:

> " 'I will strike the shepherd,
>   and the sheep of the flock will be scattered.'*ᶜ*

³²But after I have risen, I will go ahead of you into Galilee."

³³Peter replied, "Even if all fall away on account of you, I never will."

³⁴"I tell you the truth," Jesus answered, "this very night, before the rooster crows, you will disown me three times."

³⁵But Peter declared, "Even if I have to die with you, I will never disown you." And all the other disciples said the same.

ᵃ25 Or "You yourself have said it" *ᵇ28 Some manuscripts the new* *ᶜ31 Zech. 13:7*

Gethsemane ³⁶Then Jesus went with his disciples to a place called Gethsemane, and he said to them, "Sit here while I go over there and pray." ³⁷He took Peter and the two sons of Zebedee along with him, and he began to be sorrowful and troubled. ³⁸Then he said to them, "My soul is overwhelmed with sorrow to the point of death. Stay here and keep watch with me."

³⁹Going a little farther, he fell with his face to the ground and prayed, "My Father, if it is possible, may this cup be taken from me. Yet not as I will, but as you will."

⁴⁰Then he returned to his disciples and found them sleeping. "Could you men not keep watch with me for one hour?" he asked Peter. ⁴¹"Watch and pray so that you will not fall into temptation. The spirit is willing, but the body is weak."

⁴²He went away a second time and prayed, "My Father, if it is not possible for this cup to be taken away unless I drink it, may your will be done."

⁴³When he came back, he again found them sleeping, because their eyes were heavy. ⁴⁴So he left them and went away once more and prayed the third time, saying the same thing.

⁴⁵Then he returned to the disciples and said to them, "Are you still sleeping and resting? Look, the hour is near, and the Son of Man is betrayed into the hands of sinners. ⁴⁶Rise, let us go! Here comes my betrayer!"

Jesus Arrested ⁴⁷While he was still speaking, Judas, one of the Twelve, arrived. With him was a large crowd armed with swords and clubs, sent from the chief priests and the elders of the people. ⁴⁸Now the betrayer had arranged a signal with them: "The one I kiss is the man; arrest him." ⁴⁹Going at once to Jesus, Judas said, "Greetings, Rabbi!" and kissed him.

⁵⁰Jesus replied, "Friend, do what you came for."*ᵃ*

Then the men stepped forward, seized Jesus and arrested him. ⁵¹With that, one of Jesus' companions reached for his sword, drew it out and struck the servant of the high priest, cutting off his ear.

⁵²"Put your sword back in its place," Jesus said to him, "for all who draw the sword will die by the sword. ⁵³Do you think I cannot call on my Father, and he will at once put at my disposal more than twelve legions of angels? ⁵⁴But how then would the Scriptures be fulfilled that say it must happen in this way?"

⁵⁵At that time Jesus said to the crowd, "Am I leading a rebellion, that you have come out with swords and clubs to capture me? Every day I sat in the temple courts teaching, and you did not arrest me. ⁵⁶But this has all taken place that the writings of the prophets might be fulfilled." Then all the disciples deserted him and fled.

Before the Sanhedrin ⁵⁷Those who had arrested Jesus took him to Caiaphas, the high priest, where the teachers of the law and the elders had assembled. ⁵⁸But Peter followed him at a distance, right up to the courtyard of the high priest. He entered and sat down with the guards to see the outcome.

⁵⁹The chief priests and the whole Sanhedrin were looking for false evidence against Jesus so that they could put him to death. ⁶⁰But they did not find any, though many false witnesses came forward.

Finally two came forward ⁶¹and declared, "This fellow said, 'I am able to destroy the temple of God and rebuild it in three days.' "

⁶²Then the high priest stood up and said to Jesus, "Are you not going to answer? What is this testimony that these men are bringing against you?" ⁶³But Jesus remained silent.

The high priest said to him, "I charge you under oath by the living God: Tell us if you are the Christ,*ᵇ* the Son of God."

ᵃ50 Or *"Friend, why have you come?"* *ᵇ63* Or *Messiah*; also in verse 68

Dear Sam,

I try so hard, but I still fail at almost everything, even when I pray for the strength to follow through. What can I do?

Amy in Atlanta

100 Advice Lane, Anywhere, USA

Dear Amy,

It's painful to try so hard and then feel as if you've failed. You might be surprised, however, to find out that you're in very good company.

Take a look at Peter's track record. Peter walked on water with Jesus but began to sink because of his lack of faith (Matthew 14:28-31). Yet later, Jesus praised Peter for his faith (Matthew 16:13-20). When Jesus predicted that Peter would disown him, Peter denied it hotly. Peter's resolve was firm. He loved Jesus so much that he would die with him before disowning him. But later that night his resolve was forgotten, and he swore three times that he didn't know Jesus. When he heard the rooster crow, he remembered Jesus' words and "wept bitterly" (Matthew 26:69-75).

Quite a roller coaster, wouldn't you say? Up one moment, down the next. Did Christ tell Peter he was a failure? No. He knew what was in Peter's heart. Christ knows your heart too. He knows how you feel when you fall short. Trust his love, and don't give up.

Sam

[64]"Yes, it is as you say," Jesus replied. "But I say to all of you: In the future you will see the Son of Man sitting at the right hand of the Mighty One and coming on the clouds of heaven."

[65]Then the high priest tore his clothes and said, "He has spoken blasphemy! Why do we need any more witnesses? Look, now you have heard the blasphemy. [66]What do you think?"

"He is worthy of death," they answered.

[67]Then they spit in his face and struck him with their fists. Others slapped him [68]and said, "Prophesy to us, Christ. Who hit you?"

Peter Disowns Jesus [69]Now Peter was sitting out in the courtyard, and a servant girl came to him. "You also were with Jesus of Galilee," she said.

[70]But he denied it before them all. "I don't know what you're talking about," he said.

[71]Then he went out to the gateway, where another girl saw him and said to the people there, "This fellow was with Jesus of Nazareth."

[72]He denied it again, with an oath: "I don't know the man!"

[73]After a little while, those standing there went up to Peter and said, "Surely you are one of them, for your accent gives you away."

[74]Then he began to call down curses on himself and he swore to them, "I don't know the man!"

Immediately a rooster crowed. [75]Then Peter remembered the word Jesus had spoken: "Before the rooster crows, you will disown me three times." And he went outside and wept bitterly.

Judas Hangs Himself Early in the morning, all the chief priests and the elders of the people came to the decision to put Jesus to death. [2]They bound him, led him away and handed him over to Pilate, the governor.

[3]When Judas, who had betrayed him, saw that Jesus was condemned, he was seized with remorse and returned the thirty silver coins to the chief priests and the elders. [4]"I have sinned," he said, "for I have betrayed innocent blood."

"What is that to us?" they replied. "That's your responsibility."

[5]So Judas threw the money into the temple and left. Then he went away and hanged himself.

[6]The chief priests picked up the coins and said, "It is against the law to put this into the treasury, since it is blood money." [7]So they decided to use the money to buy the potter's field as a burial place for foreigners. [8]That is why it has been called the Field of Blood to this day. [9]Then what was spoken by Jeremiah the prophet was fulfilled: "They took the thirty silver coins, the price set on him by the people of Israel, [10]and they used them to buy the potter's field, as the Lord commanded me."[a]

Jesus Before Pilate [11]Meanwhile Jesus stood before the governor, and the governor asked him, "Are you the king of the Jews?"

"Yes, it is as you say," Jesus replied.

[12]When he was accused by the chief priests and the elders, he gave no answer. [13]Then Pilate asked him, "Don't you hear the testimony they are bringing against you?" [14]But Jesus made no reply, not even to a single charge—to the great amazement of the governor.

[15]Now it was the governor's custom at the Feast to release a prisoner chosen by the crowd. [16]At that time they had a notorious prisoner, called Barabbas. [17]So when the crowd had gathered, Pilate asked them, "Which one do you want me to release to you: Barabbas, or Jesus who is called Christ?" [18]For he knew it was out of envy that they had handed Jesus over to him.

[a]10 See Zech. 11:12,13; Jer. 19:1-13; 32:6-9.

[19]While Pilate was sitting on the judge's seat, his wife sent him this message: "Don't have anything to do with that innocent man, for I have suffered a great deal today in a dream because of him."

[20]But the chief priests and the elders persuaded the crowd to ask for Barabbas and to have Jesus executed.

[21]"Which of the two do you want me to release to you?" asked the governor.

"Barabbas," they answered.

[22]"What shall I do, then, with Jesus who is called Christ?" Pilate asked.

They all answered, "Crucify him!"

[23]"Why? What crime has he committed?" asked Pilate.

But they shouted all the louder, "Crucify him!"

[24]When Pilate saw that he was getting nowhere, but that instead an uproar was starting, he took water and washed his hands in front of the crowd. "I am innocent of this man's blood," he said. "It is your responsibility!"

[25]All the people answered, "Let his blood be on us and on our children!"

[26]Then he released Barabbas to them. But he had Jesus flogged, and handed him over to be crucified.

The Soldiers Mock Jesus [27]Then the governor's soldiers took Jesus into the Praetorium and gathered the whole company of soldiers around him. [28]They stripped him and put a scarlet robe on him, [29]and then twisted together a crown of thorns and set it on his head. They put a staff in his right hand and knelt in front of him and mocked him. "Hail, king of the Jews!" they said. [30]They spit on him, and took the staff and struck him on the head again and again. [31]After they had mocked him, they took off the robe and put his own clothes on him. Then they led him away to crucify him.

The Crucifixion [32]As they were going out, they met a man from Cyrene, named Simon, and they forced him to carry the cross. [33]They came to a place called Golgotha (which means The Place of the Skull). [34]There they offered Jesus wine to drink, mixed with gall; but after tasting it, he refused to drink it. [35]When they had crucified him, they divided up his clothes by casting lots.[a] [36]And sitting down, they kept watch over him there. [37]Above his head they placed the written charge against him: THIS IS JESUS, THE KING OF THE JEWS. [38]Two robbers were crucified with him, one on his right and one on his left. [39]Those who passed by hurled insults at him, shaking their heads [40]and saying, "You who are going to destroy the temple and build it in three days, save yourself! Come down from the cross, if you are the Son of God!"

[41]In the same way the chief priests, the teachers of the law and the elders mocked him. [42]"He saved others," they said, "but he can't save himself! He's the King of Israel! Let him come down now from the cross, and we will believe in him. [43]He trusts in God. Let God rescue him now if he wants him, for he said, 'I am the Son of

---

MATTHEW 27:45–50

It's an awful, empty feeling. Suddenly you feel totally alone. Your mom says she and your dad are going to divorce. Or your grandma dies. Or your closest friend ignores you. It's surprising how many things can make you feel completely alone. When Jesus hung on the cross, carrying our sins, God the Father himself looked away. Jesus knows what it feels like to be forsaken. To be left alone. But Jesus *volunteered* to be forsaken. He went to the cross knowing what it would mean. Why? So that even when you feel most alone, you won't be. No matter what happens, Christ will never forsake you or let you down.

Direct Line

---

[a]*35* A few late manuscripts *lots that the word spoken by the prophet might be fulfilled: "They divided my garments among themselves and cast lots for my clothing"* (Psalm 22:18)

God.' " ⁴⁴In the same way the robbers who were crucified with him also heaped insults on him.

The Death of Jesus ⁴⁵From the sixth hour until the ninth hour darkness came over all the land. ⁴⁶About the ninth hour Jesus cried out in a loud voice, *"Eloi, Eloi,ᵃ* lama *sabachthani?"* —which means, "My God, my God, why have you forsaken me?"ᵇ

⁴⁷When some of those standing there heard this, they said, "He's calling Elijah."

⁴⁸Immediately one of them ran and got a sponge. He filled it with wine vinegar, put it on a stick, and offered it to Jesus to drink. ⁴⁹The rest said, "Now leave him alone. Let's see if Elijah comes to save him."

⁵⁰And when Jesus had cried out again in a loud voice, he gave up his spirit.

⁵¹At that moment the curtain of the temple was torn in two from top to bottom. The earth shook and the rocks split. ⁵²The tombs broke open and the bodies of many holy people who had died were raised to life. ⁵³They came out of the tombs, and after Jesus' resurrection they went into the holy city and appeared to many people.

⁵⁴When the centurion and those with him who were guarding Jesus saw the earthquake and all that had happened, they were terrified, and exclaimed, "Surely he was the Sonᶜ of God!"

⁵⁵Many women were there, watching from a distance. They had followed Jesus from Galilee to care for his needs. ⁵⁶Among them were Mary Magdalene, Mary the mother of James and Joses, and the mother of Zebedee's sons.

The Burial of Jesus ⁵⁷As evening approached, there came a rich man from Arimathea, named Joseph, who had himself become a disciple of Jesus. ⁵⁸Going to Pilate, he asked for Jesus' body, and Pilate ordered that it be given to him. ⁵⁹Joseph took the body, wrapped it in a clean linen cloth, ⁶⁰and placed it in his own new tomb that he had cut out of the rock. He rolled a big stone in front of the entrance to the tomb and went away. ⁶¹Mary Magdalene and the other Mary were sitting there opposite the tomb.

The Guard at the Tomb ⁶²The next day, the one after Preparation Day, the chief priests and the Pharisees went to Pilate. ⁶³"Sir," they said, "we remember that while he was still alive that deceiver said, 'After three days I will rise again.' ⁶⁴So give the order for the tomb to be made secure until the third day. Otherwise, his disciples may come and steal the body and tell the people that he has been raised from the dead. This last deception will be worse than the first."

⁶⁵"Take a guard," Pilate answered. "Go, make the tomb as secure as you know how." ⁶⁶So they went and made the tomb secure by putting a seal on the stone and posting the guard.

The Resurrection After the Sabbath, at dawn on the first day of the week, Mary Magdalene and the other Mary went to look at the tomb.

²There was a violent earthquake, for an angel of the Lord came down from heaven and, going to the tomb, rolled back the stone and sat on it. ³His appearance was like lightning, and his clothes were white as snow. ⁴The guards were so afraid of him that they shook and became like dead men.

⁵The angel said to the women, "Do not be afraid, for I know that you are looking for Jesus, who was crucified. ⁶He is not here; he has risen, just as he said. Come and see the place where he lay. ⁷Then go quickly and tell his disciples: 'He has risen from the dead and is going ahead of you into Galilee. There you will see him.' Now I have told you."

ᵃ46 Some manuscripts *Eli, Eli* ᵇ46 Psalm 22:1 ᶜ54 Or *a son*

⁸So the women hurried away from the tomb, afraid yet filled with joy, and ran to tell his disciples. ⁹Suddenly Jesus met them. "Greetings," he said. They came to him, clasped his feet and worshiped him. ¹⁰Then Jesus said to them, "Do not be afraid. Go and tell my brothers to go to Galilee; there they will see me."

The Guards' Report ¹¹While the women were on their way, some of the guards went into the city and reported to the chief priests everything that had happened. ¹²When the chief priests had met with the elders and devised a plan, they gave the soldiers a large sum of money, ¹³telling them, "You are to say, 'His disciples came during the night and stole him away while we were asleep.' ¹⁴If this report gets to the governor, we will satisfy him and keep you out of trouble." ¹⁵So the soldiers took the money and did as they were instructed. And this story has been widely circulated among the Jews to this very day.

> Surely I am with
> you always,
> to the very end
> of the age
> (Matthew 28:20).

The Great Commission ¹⁶Then the eleven disciples went to Galilee, to the mountain where Jesus had told them to go. ¹⁷When they saw him, they worshiped him; but some doubted. ¹⁸Then Jesus came to them and said, "All authority in heaven and on earth has been given to me. ¹⁹Therefore go and make disciples of all nations, baptizing them in*ᵃ* the name of the Father and of the Son and of the Holy Spirit, ²⁰and teaching them to obey everything I have commanded you. And surely I am with you always, to the very end of the age."

ᵃ19 Or into; see Acts 8:16; 19:5; Romans 6:3; 1 Cor. 1:13; 10:2 and Gal. 3:27.

WHO?

What kind of people do you like? The guys who play sports? The girls who are popular? Kids who study? Who are good-looking? Who dress in style? Or do you look for someone kind and friendly?

Mark wrote his Gospel to show that Jesus was the kind of person that the Romans in the empire would appreciate. Mark shows Jesus as a man of action, a man with authority. Jesus came to earth with a mission, and he didn't rest until he finished what he came here to do.

Fundamentals

Do demons or evil spirits have a chance against the power of Jesus (Mark 1:21-28)?

What is the "unforgivable sin" (Mark 3:20-29)?

Is it wrong for Christians to want to be rich (Mark 10:17-31)?

Have you ever been afraid to speak up when a teacher mocked Christians (Mark 14:66-72)?

FAST FACTS

Mark was not one of Jesus' 12 disciples.

Mark recorded Peter's stories about Jesus.

A key word in Mark is "immediately."

The apostle Paul once refused to take Mark on a missionary trip (Acts 15:36-41).

John the Baptist Prepares the Way The beginning of the gospel about Jesus Christ, the Son of God.[a]

[2]It is written in Isaiah the prophet:
"I will send my messenger ahead of you,
who will prepare your way"[b]—
[3]"a voice of one calling in the desert,
'Prepare the way for the Lord,
make straight paths for him.' "[c]

[4]And so John came, baptizing in the desert region and preaching a baptism of repentance for the forgiveness of sins. [5]The whole Judean countryside and all the people of Jerusalem went out to him. Confessing their sins, they were baptized by him in the Jordan River. [6]John wore clothing made of camel's hair, with a leather belt around his waist, and he ate locusts and wild honey. [7]And this was his message: "After me will come one more powerful than I, the thongs of whose sandals I am not worthy to stoop down and untie. [8]I baptize you with[d] water, but he will baptize you with the Holy Spirit."

The Baptism and Temptation of Jesus [9]At that time Jesus came from Nazareth in Galilee and was baptized by John in the Jordan. [10]As Jesus was coming up out of the water, he saw heaven being torn open and the Spirit descending on him like a dove. [11]And a voice came from heaven: "You are my Son, whom I love; with you I am well pleased."

[12]At once the Spirit sent him out into the desert, [13]and he was in the desert forty days, being tempted by Satan. He was with the wild animals, and angels attended him.

The Calling of the First Disciples [14]After John was put in prison, Jesus went into Galilee, proclaiming the good news of God. [15]"The time has come," he said. "The kingdom of God is near. Repent and believe the good news!"

[16]As Jesus walked beside the Sea of Galilee, he saw Simon and his brother Andrew casting a net into the lake, for they were fishermen. [17]"Come, follow me," Jesus said, "and I will make you fishers of men." [18]At once they left their nets and followed him.

[19]When he had gone a little farther, he saw James son of Zebedee and his brother John in a boat, preparing their nets. [20]Without delay he called them, and they left their father Zebedee in the boat with the hired men and followed him.

Jesus Drives Out an Evil Spirit [21]They went to Capernaum, and when the Sabbath came, Jesus went into the synagogue and began to teach. [22]The people were amazed at his teaching, because he taught them as one who had authority, not as the teachers of the law. [23]Just then a man in their synagogue who was possessed by an evil[e] spirit cried out, [24]"What do you want with us, Jesus of Nazareth? Have you come to destroy us? I know who you are—the Holy One of God!"

Direct Line

MARK 1:35-37

You know that prayer is important. Everyone knows that. But it's not easy to find the time. Jesus was so busy it was hard for him to find time too. Mark says that Jesus' solution was to get up "very early in the morning, while it was still dark" and slip away to a "solitary place" where he could pray in private (Mark 1:35). Maybe you're not a "morning person." But setting your alarm just five or ten minutes early would give you time to start the day off right. And if you can't find a private place to pray, try the bathroom. You never know. You might find that getting up early for prayer can be important for you too.

[a]1 Some manuscripts do not have *the Son of God.*
[b]2 Mal. 3:1 [c]3 Isaiah 40:3 [d]8 Or *in* [e]23 Greek *unclean*; also in verses 26 and 27

²⁵"Be quiet!" said Jesus sternly. "Come out of him!" ²⁶The evil spirit shook the man violently and came out of him with a shriek.

²⁷The people were all so amazed that they asked each other, "What is this? A new teaching—and with authority! He even gives orders to evil spirits and they obey him." ²⁸News about him spread quickly over the whole region of Galilee.

Jesus Heals Many   ²⁹As soon as they left the synagogue, they went with James and John to the home of Simon and Andrew. ³⁰Simon's mother-in-law was in bed with a fever, and they told Jesus about her. ³¹So he went to her, took her hand and helped her up. The fever left her and she began to wait on them.

³²That evening after sunset the people brought to Jesus all the sick and demon-possessed. ³³The whole town gathered at the door, ³⁴and Jesus healed many who had various diseases. He also drove out many demons, but he would not let the demons speak because they knew who he was.

Jesus Prays in a Solitary Place   ³⁵Very early in the morning, while it was still dark, Jesus got up, left the house and went off to a solitary place, where he prayed. ³⁶Simon and his companions went to look for him, ³⁷and when they found him, they exclaimed: "Everyone is looking for you!"

³⁸Jesus replied, "Let us go somewhere else—to the nearby villages—so I can preach there also. That is why I have come." ³⁹So he traveled throughout Galilee, preaching in their synagogues and driving out demons.

A Man With Leprosy   ⁴⁰A man with leprosy*ᵃ* came to him and begged him on his knees, "If you are willing, you can make me clean."

⁴¹Filled with compassion, Jesus reached out his hand and touched the man. "I am willing," he said. "Be clean!" ⁴²Immediately the leprosy left him and he was cured.

⁴³Jesus sent him away at once with a strong warning: ⁴⁴"See that you don't tell this to anyone. But go, show yourself to the priest and offer the sacrifices that Moses commanded for your cleansing, as a testimony to them." ⁴⁵Instead he went out and began to talk freely, spreading the news. As a result, Jesus could no longer enter a town openly but stayed outside in lonely places. Yet the people still came to him from everywhere.

Jesus Heals a Paralytic   A few days later, when Jesus again entered Capernaum, the people heard that he had come home. ²So many gathered that there was no room left, not even outside the door, and he preached the word to them. ³Some men came, bringing to him a paralytic, carried by four of them. ⁴Since they could not get him to Jesus because of the crowd, they made an opening in the roof above Jesus and, after digging through it, lowered the mat the paralyzed man was lying on. ⁵When Jesus saw their faith, he said to the paralytic, "Son, your sins are forgiven."

⁶Now some teachers of the law were sitting there, thinking to themselves, ⁷"Why does this fellow talk like that? He's blaspheming! Who can forgive sins but God alone?"

⁸Immediately Jesus knew in his spirit that this was what they were thinking in their hearts, and he said to them, "Why are you thinking these things? ⁹Which is easier: to say to the paralytic, 'Your sins are forgiven,' or to say, 'Get up, take your mat and walk'? ¹⁰But that you may know that the Son of Man has authority on earth to forgive sins . . ." He said to the paralytic, ¹¹"I

MARK 1

QU?ZZER

Q: What disease is mentioned most in the Bible?

BONUS: Why was this disease so terrible?

Answers on page 1305

ᵃ40 The Greek word was used for various diseases affecting the skin—not necessarily leprosy.

tell you, get up, take your mat and go home." ¹²He got up, took his mat and walked out in full view of them all. This amazed everyone and they praised God, saying, "We have never seen anything like this!"

The Calling of Levi ¹³Once again Jesus went out beside the lake. A large crowd came to him, and he began to teach them. ¹⁴As he walked along, he saw Levi son of Alphaeus sitting at the tax collector's booth. "Follow me," Jesus told him, and Levi got up and followed him.

¹⁵While Jesus was having dinner at Levi's house, many tax collectors and "sinners" were eating with him and his disciples, for there were many who followed him. ¹⁶When the teachers of the law who were Pharisees saw him eating with the "sinners" and tax collectors, they asked his disciples: "Why does he eat with tax collectors and 'sinners'?"

¹⁷On hearing this, Jesus said to them, "It is not the healthy who need a doctor, but the sick. I have not come to call the righteous, but sinners."

Jesus Questioned About Fasting ¹⁸Now John's disciples and the Pharisees were fasting. Some people came and asked Jesus, "How is it that John's disciples and the disciples of the Pharisees are fasting, but yours are not?"

¹⁹Jesus answered, "How can the guests of the bridegroom fast while he is with them? They cannot, so long as they have him with them. ²⁰But the time will come when the bridegroom will be taken from them, and on that day they will fast.

²¹"No one sews a patch of unshrunk cloth on an old garment. If he does, the new piece will pull away from the old, making the tear worse. ²²And no one pours new wine into old wineskins. If he does, the wine will burst the skins, and both the wine and the wineskins will be ruined. No, he pours new wine into new wineskins."

Lord of the Sabbath ²³One Sabbath Jesus was going through the grainfields, and as his disciples walked along, they began to pick some heads of grain. ²⁴The Pharisees said to him, "Look, why are they doing what is unlawful on the Sabbath?"

²⁵He answered, "Have you never read what David did when he and his companions were hungry and in need? ²⁶In the days of Abiathar the high priest, he entered the house of God and ate the consecrated bread, which is lawful only for priests to eat. And he also gave some to his companions."

²⁷Then he said to them, "The Sabbath was made for man, not man for the Sabbath. ²⁸So the Son of Man is Lord even of the Sabbath."

Another time he went into the synagogue, and a man with a shriveled hand was there. ²Some of them were looking for a reason to accuse Jesus, so they watched him closely to see if he would heal him on the Sabbath. ³Jesus said to the man with the shriveled hand, "Stand up in front of everyone."

⁴Then Jesus asked them, "Which is lawful on the Sabbath: to do good or to do evil, to save life or to kill?" But they remained silent.

⁵He looked around at them in anger and, deeply distressed at their stubborn hearts, said to the man, "Stretch out your hand." He stretched it out, and his hand was completely restored. ⁶Then the Pharisees went out and began to plot with the Herodians how they might kill Jesus.

Crowds Follow Jesus ⁷Jesus withdrew with his disciples to the lake, and a large crowd from Galilee followed. ⁸When they heard all he was doing, many people came to him from Judea, Jerusalem, Idumea, and the regions across the Jordan and around Tyre and Sidon. ⁹Because of the crowd he told his disciples to have a small boat ready for him, to keep the people from crowding him. ¹⁰For he had healed many, so that those with diseases were pushing forward to touch him. ¹¹Whenever the evil*ᵃ* spirits saw him, they fell down before him and cried out, "You are the Son of God." ¹²But he gave them strict orders not to tell who he was.

The Appointing of the Twelve Apostles   ¹³Jesus went up on a mountainside and called to him those he wanted, and they came to him. ¹⁴He appointed twelve—designating them apostles*ᵇ*—that they might be with him and that he might send them out to preach ¹⁵and to have authority to drive out demons. ¹⁶These are the twelve he appointed: Simon (to whom he gave the name Peter); ¹⁷James son of Zebedee and his brother John (to them he gave the name Boanerges, which means Sons of Thunder); ¹⁸Andrew, Philip, Bartholomew, Matthew, Thomas, James son of Alphaeus, Thaddaeus, Simon the Zealot ¹⁹and Judas Iscariot, who betrayed him.

Jesus and Beelzebub   ²⁰Then Jesus entered a house, and again a crowd gathered, so that he and his disciples were not even able to eat. ²¹When his family heard about this, they went to take charge of him, for they said, "He is out of his mind."

²²And the teachers of the law who came down from Jerusalem said, "He is possessed by Beelzebub*ᶜ*! By the prince of demons he is driving out demons."

²³So Jesus called them and spoke to them in parables: "How can Satan drive out Satan? ²⁴If a kingdom is divided against itself, that kingdom cannot stand. ²⁵If a house is divided against itself, that house cannot stand. ²⁶And if Satan opposes himself and is divided, he cannot stand; his end has come. ²⁷In fact, no one can enter a strong man's house and carry off his possessions unless he first ties up the strong man. Then he can rob his house. ²⁸I tell you the truth, all the sins and blasphemies of men will be forgiven them. ²⁹But whoever blasphemes against the Holy Spirit will never be forgiven; he is guilty of an eternal sin."

³⁰He said this because they were saying, "He has an evil spirit."

Jesus' Mother and Brothers   ³¹Then Jesus' mother and brothers arrived. Standing outside, they sent someone in to call him. ³²A crowd was sitting around him, and they told him, "Your mother and brothers are outside looking for you."

³³"Who are my mother and my brothers?" he asked.

³⁴Then he looked at those seated in a circle around him and said, "Here are my mother and my brothers! ³⁵Whoever does God's will is my brother and sister and mother."

The Parable of the Sower   Again Jesus began to teach by the lake. The crowd that gathered around him was so large that he got into a boat and sat in it out on the lake, while all the people were along the shore at the water's edge. ²He taught them many things by parables, and in his teaching said: ³"Listen! A farmer went out to sow his seed. ⁴As he was scattering the seed, some fell along the path, and the birds came and ate it up. ⁵Some fell on rocky places, where it did not have much soil. It sprang up quickly, because the soil was shallow. ⁶But when the sun came up, the plants were scorched, and they withered because they had no root. ⁷Other seed fell among thorns, which grew up and choked the plants, so that they did not bear grain. ⁸Still other seed fell on good soil. It came up, grew and produced a crop, multiplying thirty, sixty, or even a hundred times."

⁹Then Jesus said, "He who has ears to hear, let him hear."

¹⁰When he was alone, the Twelve and the others around him asked him

Answers
to Quizzer on
page 1303

A: Leprosy (Mark 1:40), also called an "infectious skin disease" (Leviticus 13).

BONUS: Victims were completely isolated; they couldn't worship or live with uninfected people. They couldn't even touch them.

ᵃ11 Greek *unclean*; also in verse 30   *ᵇ14* Some manuscripts do not have *designating them apostles*.
ᶜ22 Greek *Beezeboul* or *Beelzeboul*

Dear Sam,

My friend told me that not all sins can be forgiven. She gave me a list of sins, with those that can't be forgiven at the end. Can't all sins that are confessed be forgiven?

Elise in Evergreen

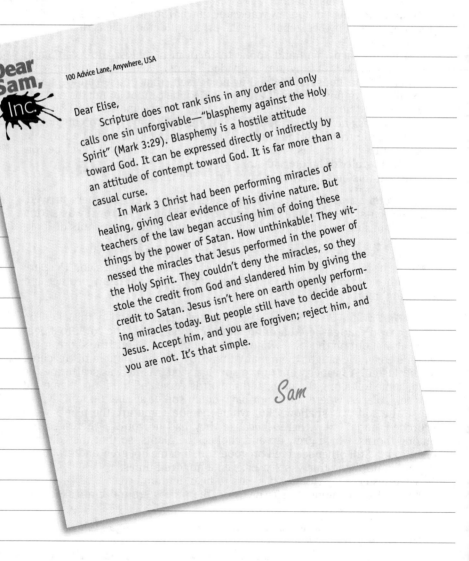

100 Advice Lane, Anywhere, USA

Dear Elise,

Scripture does not rank sins in any order and only calls one sin unforgivable—"blasphemy against the Holy Spirit" (Mark 3:29). Blasphemy is a hostile attitude toward God. It can be expressed directly or indirectly by an attitude of contempt toward God. It is far more than a casual curse.

In Mark 3 Christ had been performing miracles of healing, giving clear evidence of his divine nature. But teachers of the law began accusing him of doing these things by the power of Satan. How unthinkable! They witnessed the miracles that Jesus performed in the power of the Holy Spirit. They couldn't deny the miracles, so they stole the credit from God and slandered him by giving the credit to Satan. Jesus isn't here on earth openly performing miracles today. But people still have to decide about Jesus. Accept him, and you are forgiven; reject him, and you are not. It's that simple.

Sam

about the parables. ¹¹He told them, "The secret of the kingdom of God has been given to you. But to those on the outside everything is said in parables ¹²so that,

> " 'they may be ever seeing but never perceiving,
>   and ever hearing but never understanding;
> otherwise they might turn and be forgiven!'ᵃ"

¹³Then Jesus said to them, "Don't you understand this parable? How then will you understand any parable? ¹⁴The farmer sows the word. ¹⁵Some people are like seed along the path, where the word is sown. As soon as they hear it, Satan comes and takes away the word that was sown in them. ¹⁶Others, like seed sown on rocky places, hear the word and at once receive it with joy. ¹⁷But since they have no root, they last only a short time. When trouble or persecution comes because of the word, they quickly fall away. ¹⁸Still others, like seed sown among thorns, hear the word; ¹⁹but the worries of this life, the deceitfulness of wealth and the desires for other things come in and choke the word, making it unfruitful. ²⁰Others, like seed sown on good soil, hear the word, accept it, and produce a crop—thirty, sixty or even a hundred times what was sown."

A Lamp on a Stand   ²¹He said to them, "Do you bring in a lamp to put it under a bowl or a bed? Instead, don't you put it on its stand? ²²For whatever is hidden is meant to be disclosed, and whatever is concealed is meant to be brought out into the open. ²³If anyone has ears to hear, let him hear."

²⁴"Consider carefully what you hear," he continued. "With the measure you use, it will be measured to you—and even more. ²⁵Whoever has will be given more; whoever does not have, even what he has will be taken from him."

The Parable of the Growing Seed   ²⁶He also said, "This is what the kingdom of God is like. A man scatters seed on the ground. ²⁷Night and day, whether he sleeps or gets up, the seed sprouts and grows, though he does not know how. ²⁸All by itself the soil produces grain—first the stalk, then the head, then the full kernel in the head. ²⁹As soon as the grain is ripe, he puts the sickle to it, because the harvest has come."

The Parable of the Mustard Seed   ³⁰Again he said, "What shall we say the kingdom of God is like, or what parable shall we use to describe it? ³¹It is like a mustard seed, which is the smallest seed you plant in the ground. ³²Yet when planted, it grows and becomes the largest of all garden plants, with such big branches that the birds of the air can perch in its shade."

³³With many similar parables Jesus spoke the word to them, as much as they could understand. ³⁴He did not say anything to them without using a parable. But when he was alone with his own disciples, he explained everything.

Jesus Calms the Storm   ³⁵That day when evening came, he said to his disciples, "Let us go over to the other side." ³⁶Leaving the crowd behind, they took

ᵃ*12* Isaiah 6:9,10

MARK 4:21–23

Do your friends know you're a Christian? Or hasn't the subject ever come up? Some teens (and adults too) hesitate to stand up for their faith. But as a Christian you really *are* different. When you try to hide what you are, it just isn't right. When people in Bible times lit a lamp, they didn't hide it. They put it on a stand so everyone could see. Jesus didn't come into your life to be hidden. He came into your life so you could be his light, so you could hold him up for others to see the way to eternal life.

Direct Line

him along, just as he was, in the boat. There were also other boats with him. [37]A furious squall came up, and the waves broke over the boat, so that it was nearly swamped. [38]Jesus was in the stern, sleeping on a cushion. The disciples woke him and said to him, "Teacher, don't you care if we drown?"

[39]He got up, rebuked the wind and said to the waves, "Quiet! Be still!" Then the wind died down and it was completely calm.

[40]He said to his disciples, "Why are you so afraid? Do you still have no faith?"

[41]They were terrified and asked each other, "Who is this? Even the wind and the waves obey him!"

The Healing of a Demon-possessed Man   They went across the lake to the region of the Gerasenes.[a] [2]When Jesus got out of the boat, a man with an evil[b] spirit came from the tombs to meet him. [3]This man lived in the tombs, and no one could bind him any more, not even with a chain. [4]For he had often been chained hand and foot, but he tore the chains apart and broke the irons on his feet. No one was strong enough to subdue him. [5]Night and day among the tombs and in the hills he would cry out and cut himself with stones.

[6]When he saw Jesus from a distance, he ran and fell on his knees in front of him. [7]He shouted at the top of his voice, "What do you want with me, Jesus, Son of the Most High God? Swear to God that you won't torture me!" [8]For Jesus had said to him, "Come out of this man, you evil spirit!"

[9]Then Jesus asked him, "What is your name?"

"My name is Legion," he replied, "for we are many." [10]And he begged Jesus again and again not to send them out of the area.

[11]A large herd of pigs was feeding on the nearby hillside. [12]The demons begged Jesus, "Send us among the pigs; allow us to go into them." [13]He gave them permission, and the evil spirits came out and went into the pigs. The herd, about two thousand in number, rushed down the steep bank into the lake and were drowned.

[14]Those tending the pigs ran off and reported this in the town and countryside, and the people went out to see what had happened. [15]When they came to Jesus, they saw the man who had been possessed by the legion of demons, sitting there, dressed and in his right mind; and they were afraid. [16]Those who had seen it told the people what had happened to the demon-possessed man—and told about the pigs as well. [17]Then the people began to plead with Jesus to leave their region.

[18]As Jesus was getting into the boat, the man who had been demon-possessed begged to go with him. [19]Jesus did not let him, but said, "Go home to your family and tell them how much the Lord has done for you, and how he has had mercy on you." [20]So the man went away and began to tell in the Decapolis[c] how much Jesus had done for him. And all the people were amazed.

A Dead Girl and a Sick Woman   [21]When Jesus had again crossed over by boat to the other side of the lake, a large crowd gathered around him while he was by the lake. [22]Then one of the synagogue rulers, named Jairus, came there. Seeing Jesus, he fell at his feet [23]and pleaded earnestly with him, "My little daughter is dying. Please come and put your hands on her so that she will be healed and live." [24]So Jesus went with him.

A large crowd followed and pressed around him. [25]And a woman was there who had been subject to bleeding for twelve years. [26]She had suffered a great deal under the care of many doctors and had spent all she had, yet instead

---

[a]*1* Some manuscripts *Gadarenes*; other manuscripts *Gergesenes*   [b]*2* Greek *unclean*; also in verses 8 and 13   [c]*20* That is, the Ten Cities

of getting better she grew worse. ²⁷When she heard about Jesus, she came up behind him in the crowd and touched his cloak, ²⁸because she thought, "If I just touch his clothes, I will be healed." ²⁹Immediately her bleeding stopped and she felt in her body that she was freed from her suffering.

³⁰At once Jesus realized that power had gone out from him. He turned around in the crowd and asked, "Who touched my clothes?"

³¹"You see the people crowding against you," his disciples answered, "and yet you can ask, 'Who touched me?' "

³²But Jesus kept looking around to see who had done it. ³³Then the woman, knowing what had happened to her, came and fell at his feet and, trembling with fear, told him the whole truth. ³⁴He said to her, "Daughter, your faith has healed you. Go in peace and be freed from your suffering."

³⁵While Jesus was still speaking, some men came from the house of Jairus, the synagogue ruler. "Your daughter is dead," they said. "Why bother the teacher any more?"

³⁶Ignoring what they said, Jesus told the synagogue ruler, "Don't be afraid; just believe."

³⁷He did not let anyone follow him except Peter, James and John the brother of James. ³⁸When they came to the home of the synagogue ruler, Jesus saw a commotion, with people crying and wailing loudly. ³⁹He went in and said to them, "Why all this commotion and wailing? The child is not dead but asleep." ⁴⁰But they laughed at him.

After he put them all out, he took the child's father and mother and the disciples who were with him, and went in where the child was. ⁴¹He took her by the hand and said to her, *"Talitha koum!"* (which means, "Little girl, I say to you, get up!"). ⁴²Immediately the girl stood up and walked around (she was twelve years old). At this they were completely astonished. ⁴³He gave strict orders not to let anyone know about this, and told them to give her something to eat.

A Prophet Without Honor   Jesus left there and went to his hometown, accompanied by his disciples. ²When the Sabbath came, he began to teach in the synagogue, and many who heard him were amazed.

"Where did this man get these things?" they asked. "What's this wisdom that has been given him, that he even does miracles! ³Isn't this the carpenter? Isn't this Mary's son and the brother of James, Joseph,ᵃ Judas and Simon? Aren't his sisters here with us?" And they took offense at him.

⁴Jesus said to them, "Only in his hometown, among his relatives and in his own house is a prophet without honor." ⁵He could not do any miracles there, except lay his hands on a few sick people and heal them. ⁶And he was amazed at their lack of faith.

Jesus Sends Out the Twelve   Then Jesus went around teaching from village to village. ⁷Calling the Twelve to him, he sent them out two by two and gave them authority over evilᵇ spirits.

⁸These were his instructions: "Take nothing for the journey except a staff—no bread, no bag, no money in your belts. ⁹Wear sandals but not an extra tunic. ¹⁰Whenever you enter a house, stay there until you leave that town. ¹¹And if any place will not welcome you or listen to you, shake the dust off your feet when you leave, as a testimony against them."

¹²They went out and preached that people should repent. ¹³They drove out many demons and anointed many sick people with oil and healed them.

John the Baptist Beheaded   ¹⁴King Herod heard about this, for Jesus' name had become well known. Some were saying,ᶜ "John the Baptist has been raised from the dead, and that is why miraculous powers are at work in him."

ᵃ3 Greek *Joses*, a variant of *Joseph*   ᵇ7 Greek *unclean*.   ᶜ14 Some early manuscripts *He was saying*

[15]Others said, "He is Elijah."

And still others claimed, "He is a prophet, like one of the prophets of long ago."

[16]But when Herod heard this, he said, "John, the man I beheaded, has been raised from the dead!"

[17]For Herod himself had given orders to have John arrested, and he had him bound and put in prison. He did this because of Herodias, his brother Philip's wife, whom he had married. [18]For John had been saying to Herod, "It is not lawful for you to have your brother's wife." [19]So Herodias nursed a grudge against John and wanted to kill him. But she was not able to, [20]because Herod feared John and protected him, knowing him to be a righteous and holy man. When Herod heard John, he was greatly puzzled[a]; yet he liked to listen to him.

[21]Finally the opportune time came. On his birthday Herod gave a banquet for his high officials and military commanders and the leading men of Galilee. [22]When the daughter of Herodias came in and danced, she pleased Herod and his dinner guests.

The king said to the girl, "Ask me for anything you want, and I'll give it to you." [23]And he promised her with an oath, "Whatever you ask I will give you, up to half my kingdom."

[24]She went out and said to her mother, "What shall I ask for?"

"The head of John the Baptist," she answered.

[25]At once the girl hurried in to the king with the request: "I want you to give me right now the head of John the Baptist on a platter."

[26]The king was greatly distressed, but because of his oaths and his dinner guests, he did not want to refuse her. [27]So he immediately sent an executioner with orders to bring John's head. The man went, beheaded John in the prison, [28]and brought back his head on a platter. He presented it to the girl, and she gave it to her mother. [29]On hearing of this, John's disciples came and took his body and laid it in a tomb.

MARK 6:14–29

Have you ever tried to rewrite the end of a Bible story? Try this one. Herodias's daughter wanted the head of John the Baptist. If the king hadn't been so worried about what his guests would think, what could he have said? Perhaps, "I said half my kingdom. I didn't say I'd kill someone for you." Or, "That's against God's law, my dear." Or, "What a terrible thing to ask. Guards, get her out of my sight!" There's always something you can do besides give in to peer pressure. Remember the last time you gave in? Try rewriting the end of that story. Now the next time you're under pressure, try out one of those "different endings."

Direct Line

Jesus Feeds the Five Thousand [30]The apostles gathered around Jesus and reported to him all they had done and taught. [31]Then, because so many people were coming and going that they did not even have a chance to eat, he said to them, "Come with me by yourselves to a quiet place and get some rest."

[32]So they went away by themselves in a boat to a solitary place. [33]But many who saw them leaving recognized them and ran on foot from all the towns and got there ahead of them. [34]When Jesus landed and saw a large crowd, he had compassion on them, because they were like sheep without a shepherd. So he began teaching them many things.

[35]By this time it was late in the day, so his disciples came to him. "This is a remote place," they said, "and it's already very late. [36]Send the people away so they can go to the surrounding countryside and villages and buy themselves something to eat."

[a]20 Some early manuscripts *he did many things*

³⁷But he answered, "You give them something to eat."

They said to him, "That would take eight months of a man's wages*a*! Are we to go and spend that much on bread and give it to them to eat?"

³⁸"How many loaves do you have?" he asked. "Go and see."

When they found out, they said, "Five—and two fish."

³⁹Then Jesus directed them to have all the people sit down in groups on the green grass. ⁴⁰So they sat down in groups of hundreds and fifties. ⁴¹Taking the five loaves and the two fish and looking up to heaven, he gave thanks and broke the loaves. Then he gave them to his disciples to set before the people. He also divided the two fish among them all. ⁴²They all ate and were satisfied, ⁴³and the disciples picked up twelve basketfuls of broken pieces of bread and fish. ⁴⁴The number of the men who had eaten was five thousand.

Jesus Walks on the Water ⁴⁵Immediately Jesus made his disciples get into the boat and go on ahead of him to Bethsaida, while he dismissed the crowd. ⁴⁶After leaving them, he went up on a mountainside to pray.

⁴⁷When evening came, the boat was in the middle of the lake, and he was alone on land. ⁴⁸He saw the disciples straining at the oars, because the wind was against them. About the fourth watch of the night he went out to them, walking on the lake. He was about to pass by them, ⁴⁹but when they saw him walking on the lake, they thought he was a ghost. They cried out, ⁵⁰because they all saw him and were terrified.

Immediately he spoke to them and said, "Take courage! It is I. Don't be afraid." ⁵¹Then he climbed into the boat with them, and the wind died down. They were completely amazed, ⁵²for they had not understood about the loaves; their hearts were hardened.

⁵³When they had crossed over, they landed at Gennesaret and anchored there. ⁵⁴As soon as they got out of the boat, people recognized Jesus. ⁵⁵They ran throughout that whole region and carried the sick on mats to wherever they heard he was. ⁵⁶And wherever he went—into villages, towns or countryside—they placed the sick in the marketplaces. They begged him to let them touch even the edge of his cloak, and all who touched him were healed.

7 *Clean and Unclean* The Pharisees and some of the teachers of the law who had come from Jerusalem gathered around Jesus and ²saw some of his disciples eating food with hands that were "unclean," that is, unwashed. ³(The Pharisees and all the Jews do not eat unless they give their hands a ceremonial washing, holding to the tradition of the elders. ⁴When they come from the marketplace they do not eat unless they wash. And they observe many other traditions, such as the washing of cups, pitchers and kettles.*b*)

⁵So the Pharisees and teachers of the law asked Jesus, "Why don't your disciples live according to the tradition of the elders instead of eating their food with 'unclean' hands?"

Leftovers! Let's see—fish sandwiches, fish casserole, fish pudding, fish gumbo . . .

SEE MARK 6:42-43

*a*37 Greek *take two hundred denarii* *b*4 Some early manuscripts *pitchers, kettles and dining couches*

[6]He replied, "Isaiah was right when he prophesied about you hypocrites; as it is written:

> " 'These people honor me with their lips,
>   but their hearts are far from me.
> [7]They worship me in vain;
>   their teachings are but rules taught by men.'[a]

[8]You have let go of the commands of God and are holding on to the traditions of men."

[9]And he said to them: "You have a fine way of setting aside the commands of God in order to observe[b] your own traditions! [10]For Moses said, 'Honor your father and your mother,'[c] and, 'Anyone who curses his father or mother must be put to death.'[d] [11]But you say that if a man says to his father or mother: 'Whatever help you might otherwise have received from me is Corban' (that is, a gift devoted to God), [12]then you no longer let him do anything for his father or mother. [13]Thus you nullify the word of God by your tradition that you have handed down. And you do many things like that."

[14]Again Jesus called the crowd to him and said, "Listen to me, everyone, and understand this. [15]Nothing outside a man can make him 'unclean' by going into him. Rather, it is what comes out of a man that makes him 'unclean.'[e]"

[17]After he had left the crowd and entered the house, his disciples asked him about this parable. [18]"Are you so dull?" he asked. "Don't you see that nothing that enters a man from the outside can make him 'unclean'? [19]For it doesn't go into his heart but into his stomach, and then out of his body." (In saying this, Jesus declared all foods "clean.")

[20]He went on: "What comes out of a man is what makes him 'unclean.' [21]For from within, out of men's hearts, come evil thoughts, sexual immorality, theft, murder, adultery, [22]greed, malice, deceit, lewdness, envy, slander, arrogance and folly. [23]All these evils come from inside and make a man 'unclean.' "

The Faith of a Syrophoenician Woman   [24]Jesus left that place and went to the vicinity of Tyre.[f] He entered a house and did not want anyone to know it; yet he could not keep his presence secret. [25]In fact, as soon as she heard about him, a woman whose little daughter was possessed by an evil[g] spirit came and fell at his feet. [26]The woman was a Greek, born in Syrian Phoenicia. She begged Jesus to drive the demon out of her daughter.

[27]"First let the children eat all they want," he told her, "for it is not right to take the children's bread and toss it to their dogs."

[28]"Yes, Lord," she replied, "but even the dogs under the table eat the children's crumbs."

[29]Then he told her, "For such a reply, you may go; the demon has left your daughter."

[30]She went home and found her child lying on the bed, and the demon gone.

The Healing of a Deaf and Mute Man   [31]Then Jesus left the vicinity of Tyre and went through Sidon, down to the Sea of Galilee and into the region of the Decapolis.[h] [32]There some people brought to him a man who was deaf and could hardly talk, and they begged him to place his hand on the man.

[33]After he took him aside, away from the crowd, Jesus put his fingers into the man's ears. Then he spit and touched the man's tongue. [34]He looked

---

[a]*6,7* Isaiah 29:13   [b]*9* Some manuscripts *set up*   [c]*10* Exodus 20:12; Deut. 5:16   [d]*10* Exodus 21:17; Lev. 20:9   [e]*15* Some early manuscripts *'unclean.'* *16If anyone has ears to hear, let him hear.*   [f]*24* Many early manuscripts *Tyre and Sidon*   [g]*25* Greek *unclean*   [h]*31* That is, the Ten Cities

up to heaven and with a deep sigh said to him, *"Ephphatha!"* (which means, "Be opened!"). ³⁵At this, the man's ears were opened, his tongue was loosened and he began to speak plainly.

³⁶Jesus commanded them not to tell anyone. But the more he did so, the more they kept talking about it. ³⁷People were overwhelmed with amazement. "He has done everything well," they said. "He even makes the deaf hear and the mute speak."

Jesus Feeds the Four Thousand During those days another large crowd gathered. Since they had nothing to eat, Jesus called his disciples to him and said, ²"I have compassion for these people; they have already been with me three days and have nothing to eat. ³If I send them home hungry, they will collapse on the way, because some of them have come a long distance."

⁴His disciples answered, "But where in this remote place can anyone get enough bread to feed them?"

⁵"How many loaves do you have?" Jesus asked.

"Seven," they replied.

⁶He told the crowd to sit down on the ground. When he had taken the seven loaves and given thanks, he broke them and gave them to his disciples to set before the people, and they did so. ⁷They had a few small fish as well; he gave thanks for them also and told the disciples to distribute them. ⁸The people ate and were satisfied. Afterward the disciples picked up seven basketfuls of broken pieces that were left over. ⁹About four thousand men were present. And having sent them away, ¹⁰he got into the boat with his disciples and went to the region of Dalmanutha.

¹¹The Pharisees came and began to question Jesus. To test him, they asked him for a sign from heaven. ¹²He sighed deeply and said, "Why does this generation ask for a miraculous sign? I tell you the truth, no sign will be given to it." ¹³Then he left them, got back into the boat and crossed to the other side.

The Yeast of the Pharisees and Herod ¹⁴The disciples had forgotten to bring bread, except for one loaf they had with them in the boat. ¹⁵"Be careful," Jesus warned them. "Watch out for the yeast of the Pharisees and that of Herod."

¹⁶They discussed this with one another and said, "It is because we have no bread."

¹⁷Aware of their discussion, Jesus asked them: "Why are you talking about having no bread? Do you still not see or understand? Are your hearts hardened? ¹⁸Do you have eyes but fail to see, and ears but fail to hear? And don't you remember? ¹⁹When I broke the five loaves for the five thousand, how many basketfuls of pieces did you pick up?"

"Twelve," they replied.

²⁰"And when I broke the seven loaves for the four thousand, how many basketfuls of pieces did you pick up?"

They answered, "Seven."

²¹He said to them, "Do you still not understand?"

The Healing of a Blind Man at Bethsaida ²²They came to Bethsaida, and some people brought a blind man and begged Jesus to touch him. ²³He took the blind man by the hand and led him outside the village. When he had spit on the man's eyes and put his hands on him, Jesus asked, "Do you see anything?"

²⁴He looked up and said, "I see people; they look like trees walking around."

²⁵Once more Jesus put his hands on the man's eyes. Then his eyes were

opened, his sight was restored, and he saw everything clearly. ²⁶Jesus sent him home, saying, "Don't go into the village.ᵃ"

Peter's Confession of Christ ²⁷Jesus and his disciples went on to the villages around Caesarea Philippi. On the way he asked them, "Who do people say I am?"

²⁸They replied, "Some say John the Baptist; others say Elijah; and still others, one of the prophets."

²⁹"But what about you?" he asked. "Who do you say I am?"

Peter answered, "You are the Christ.ᵇ"

³⁰Jesus warned them not to tell anyone about him.

Jesus Predicts His Death ³¹He then began to teach them that the Son of Man must suffer many things and be rejected by the elders, chief priests and teachers of the law, and that he must be killed and after three days rise again. ³²He spoke plainly about this, and Peter took him aside and began to rebuke him.

³³But when Jesus turned and looked at his disciples, he rebuked Peter. "Get behind me, Satan!" he said. "You do not have in mind the things of God, but the things of men."

³⁴Then he called the crowd to him along with his disciples and said: "If anyone would come after me, he must deny himself and take up his cross and follow me. ³⁵For whoever wants to save his lifeᶜ will lose it, but whoever loses his life for me and for the gospel will save it. ³⁶What good is it for a man to gain the whole world, yet forfeit his soul? ³⁷Or what can a man give in exchange for his soul? ³⁸If anyone is ashamed of me and my words in this adulterous and sinful generation, the Son of Man will be ashamed of him when he comes in his Father's glory with the holy angels."

9 And he said to them, "I tell you the truth, some who are standing here will not taste death before they see the kingdom of God come with power."

The Transfiguration ²After six days Jesus took Peter, James and John with him and led them up a high mountain, where they were all alone. There he

---

ᵃ26 Some manuscripts *Don't go and tell anyone in the village* ᵇ29 Or *Messiah.* "The Christ" (Greek) and "the Messiah" (Hebrew) both mean "the Anointed One." ᶜ35 The Greek word means either *life* or *soul;* also in verse 36.

The Bible Says

Our Cross Is Different

Jesus said anyone who wants to follow him must "deny himself and take up his cross" (Mark 8:34). The cross meant suffering and death for Jesus. Does that mean you'll have to suffer too?

The cross is more than a place where Jesus died. It is a symbol of our salvation and a symbol of God's will. The cross was God's will for Jesus. But your cross, God's will for your life, is different. What is Jesus telling you?

* Deny yourself. Choose what God wants, not what you want.
* Take up your cross. Do God's will each day.
* Keep on following Jesus.

Following Jesus will make a difference. The old you will be left behind, and you will become a new and beautiful person in Jesus.

was transfigured before them. ³His clothes became dazzling white, whiter than anyone in the world could bleach them. ⁴And there appeared before them Elijah and Moses, who were talking with Jesus.

⁵Peter said to Jesus, "Rabbi, it is good for us to be here. Let us put up three shelters—one for you, one for Moses and one for Elijah." ⁶(He did not know what to say, they were so frightened.)

⁷Then a cloud appeared and enveloped them, and a voice came from the cloud: "This is my Son, whom I love. Listen to him!"

⁸Suddenly, when they looked around, they no longer saw anyone with them except Jesus.

⁹As they were coming down the mountain, Jesus gave them orders not to tell anyone what they had seen until the Son of Man had risen from the dead. ¹⁰They kept the matter to themselves, discussing what "rising from the dead" meant.

¹¹And they asked him, "Why do the teachers of the law say that Elijah must come first?"

¹²Jesus replied, "To be sure, Elijah does come first, and restores all things. Why then is it written that the Son of Man must suffer much and be rejected? ¹³But I tell you, Elijah has come, and they have done to him everything they wished, just as it is written about him."

The Healing of a Boy With an Evil Spirit   ¹⁴When they came to the other disciples, they saw a large crowd around them and the teachers of the law arguing with them. ¹⁵As soon as all the people saw Jesus, they were overwhelmed with wonder and ran to greet him.

¹⁶"What are you arguing with them about?" he asked.

¹⁷A man in the crowd answered, "Teacher, I brought you my son, who is possessed by a spirit that has robbed him of speech. ¹⁸Whenever it seizes him, it throws him to the ground. He foams at the mouth, gnashes his teeth and becomes rigid. I asked your disciples to drive out the spirit, but they could not."

¹⁹"O unbelieving generation," Jesus replied, "how long shall I stay with you? How long shall I put up with you? Bring the boy to me."

²⁰So they brought him. When the spirit saw Jesus, it immediately threw the boy into a convulsion. He fell to the ground and rolled around, foaming at the mouth.

²¹Jesus asked the boy's father, "How long has he been like this?"

"From childhood," he answered. ²²"It has often thrown him into fire or water to kill him. But if you can do anything, take pity on us and help us."

²³" 'If you can'?" said Jesus. "Everything is possible for him who believes."

²⁴Immediately the boy's father exclaimed, "I do believe; help me overcome my unbelief!"

²⁵When Jesus saw that a crowd was running to the scene, he rebuked the evil*ᵃ* spirit. "You deaf and mute spirit," he said, "I command you, come out of him and never enter him again."

²⁶The spirit shrieked, convulsed him violently and came out. The boy looked so much like a corpse that many said, "He's dead." ²⁷But Jesus took him by the hand and lifted him to his feet, and he stood up.

²⁸After Jesus had gone indoors, his disciples asked him privately, "Why couldn't we drive it out?"

²⁹He replied, "This kind can come out only by prayer.*ᵇ*"

³⁰They left that place and passed through Galilee. Jesus did not want anyone to know where they were, ³¹because he was teaching his disciples. He said to them, "The Son of Man is going to be betrayed into the hands of men. They will kill him, and after three days he will rise." ³²But they did not understand what he meant and were afraid to ask him about it.

ᵃ25 Greek *unclean*   *ᵇ29* Some manuscripts *prayer and fasting*

Who Is the Greatest? ³³They came to Capernaum. When he was in the house, he asked them, "What were you arguing about on the road?" ³⁴But they kept quiet because on the way they had argued about who was the greatest.

³⁵Sitting down, Jesus called the Twelve and said, "If anyone wants to be first, he must be the very last, and the servant of all."

³⁶He took a little child and had him stand among them. Taking him in his arms, he said to them, ³⁷"Whoever welcomes one of these little children in my name welcomes me; and whoever welcomes me does not welcome me but the one who sent me."

Whoever Is Not Against Us Is for Us ³⁸"Teacher," said John, "we saw a man driving out demons in your name and we told him to stop, because he was not one of us."

³⁹"Do not stop him," Jesus said. "No one who does a miracle in my name can in the next moment say anything bad about me, ⁴⁰for whoever is not against us is for us. ⁴¹I tell you the truth, anyone who gives you a cup of water in my name because you belong to Christ will certainly not lose his reward.

Causing to Sin ⁴²"And if anyone causes one of these little ones who believe in me to sin, it would be better for him to be thrown into the sea with a large millstone tied around his neck. ⁴³If your hand causes you to sin, cut it off. It is better for you to enter life maimed than with two hands to go into hell, where the fire never goes out.*ᵃ* ⁴⁵And if your foot causes you to sin, cut it off. It is better for you to enter life crippled than to have two feet and be thrown into hell.*ᵇ* ⁴⁷And if your eye causes you to sin, pluck it out. It is better for you to enter the kingdom of God with one eye than to have two eyes and be thrown into hell, ⁴⁸where

> " 'their worm does not die,
>   and the fire is not quenched.'*ᶜ*

⁴⁹Everyone will be salted with fire.

⁵⁰"Salt is good, but if it loses its saltiness, how can you make it salty again? Have salt in yourselves, and be at peace with each other."

10 *Divorce* Jesus then left that place and went into the region of Judea and across the Jordan. Again crowds of people came to him, and as was his custom, he taught them.

²Some Pharisees came and tested him by asking, "Is it lawful for a man to divorce his wife?"

³"What did Moses command you?" he replied.

⁴They said, "Moses permitted a man to write a certificate of divorce and send her away."

⁵"It was because your hearts were hard that Moses wrote you this law," Jesus replied. ⁶"But at the beginning of creation

---

Direct Line

MARK 9:38–41

Some teens feel uncomfortable with kids from other churches or denominations. They're uncertain about how big a difference their differences make. Even Christ's disciples were uncomfortable when they saw a man driving out demons in Jesus' name. He wasn't one of them. Jesus corrected them and said, "Whoever is not against us is for us." Christians don't agree on every belief. But all who trust Jesus as Savior become members of God's family. If you refuse to emphasize differences and instead emphasize commitment to Christ, you'll feel a lot more comfortable with Christian teens from other groups.

ᵃ43 Some manuscripts out, ⁴⁴where / " 'their worm does not die, / and the fire is not quenched.' ᵇ45 Some manuscripts hell, ⁴⁶where / " 'their worm does not die, / and the fire is not quenched.' ᶜ48 Isaiah 66:24

God 'made them male and female.'*a* *7*'For this reason a man will leave his father and mother and be united to his wife,*b* *8*and the two will become one flesh.'*c* So they are no longer two, but one. *9*Therefore what God has joined together, let man not separate."

*10*When they were in the house again, the disciples asked Jesus about this. *11*He answered, "Anyone who divorces his wife and marries another woman commits adultery against her. *12*And if she divorces her husband and marries another man, she commits adultery."

The Little Children and Jesus *13*People were bringing little children to Jesus to have him touch them, but the disciples rebuked them. *14*When Jesus saw this, he was indignant. He said to them, "Let the little children come to me, and do not hinder them, for the kingdom of God belongs to such as these. *15*I tell you the truth, anyone who will not receive the kingdom of God like a little child will never enter it." *16*And he took the children in his arms, put his hands on them and blessed them.

The Rich Young Man *17*As Jesus started on his way, a man ran up to him and fell on his knees before him. "Good teacher," he asked, "what must I do to inherit eternal life?"

18"Why do you call me good?" Jesus answered. "No one is good—except God alone. *19*You know the commandments: 'Do not murder, do not commit adultery, do not steal, do not give false testimony, do not defraud, honor your father and mother.'*d*"

20"Teacher," he declared, "all these I have kept since I was a boy."

*21*Jesus looked at him and loved him. "One thing you lack," he said. "Go, sell everything you have and give to the poor, and you will have treasure in heaven. Then come, follow me."

*22*At this the man's face fell. He went away sad, because he had great wealth.

*23*Jesus looked around and said to his disciples, "How hard it is for the rich to enter the kingdom of God!"

*24*The disciples were amazed at his words. But Jesus said again, "Children, how hard it is*e* to enter the kingdom of God! *25*It is easier for a camel to go through the eye of a needle than for a rich man to enter the kingdom of God."

*26*The disciples were even more amazed, and said to each other, "Who then can be saved?"

*27*Jesus looked at them and said, "With man this is impossible, but not with God; all things are possible with God."

*28*Peter said to him, "We have left everything to follow you!"

29"I tell you the truth," Jesus replied, "no one who has left home or brothers or sisters or mother or father or children or fields for me and the gospel *30*will fail to receive a hundred times as much in this present age (homes, brothers, sisters, mothers, children and fields—

a6 Gen. 1:27 *b7* Some early manuscripts do not have *and be united to his wife.* *c8* Gen. 2:24 *d19* Exodus 20:12-16; Deut. 5:16-20 *e24* Some manuscripts *is for those who trust in riches*

MARK 10:17–31

Do you ever envy that rich girl in your class? The one whose Dad bought her a new convertible for her 16th birthday? Do you feel cheated? In Bible times most people thought wealth was a sign of God's favor. So Jesus shocked his disciples when he said that it's hard for a rich person to "enter the kingdom of God" (Mark 10:23). What Jesus meant is that a rich person is likely to depend on possessions instead of on God. And a rich person is likely to value possessions more than pleasing God. It's not wrong to be rich. But this would be an appropriate label on all your possessions: "May be hazardous to your [spiritual] health."

Direct Line

and with them, persecutions) and in the age to come, eternal life. ³¹But many who are first will be last, and the last first."

Jesus Again Predicts His Death ³²They were on their way up to Jerusalem, with Jesus leading the way, and the disciples were astonished, while those who followed were afraid. Again he took the Twelve aside and told them what was going to happen to him. ³³"We are going up to Jerusalem," he said, "and the Son of Man will be betrayed to the chief priests and teachers of the law. They will condemn him to death and will hand him over to the Gentiles, ³⁴who will mock him and spit on him, flog him and kill him. Three days later he will rise."

The Request of James and John ³⁵Then James and John, the sons of Zebedee, came to him. "Teacher," they said, "we want you to do for us whatever we ask."

³⁶"What do you want me to do for you?" he asked.

³⁷They replied, "Let one of us sit at your right and the other at your left in your glory."

³⁸"You don't know what you are asking," Jesus said. "Can you drink the cup I drink or be baptized with the baptism I am baptized with?"

³⁹"We can," they answered.

Jesus said to them, "You will drink the cup I drink and be baptized with the baptism I am baptized with, ⁴⁰but to sit at my right or left is not for me to grant. These places belong to those for whom they have been prepared."

⁴¹When the ten heard about this, they became indignant with James and John. ⁴²Jesus called them together and said, "You know that those who are regarded as rulers of the Gentiles lord it over them, and their high officials exercise authority over them. ⁴³Not so with you. Instead, whoever wants to become great among you must be your servant, ⁴⁴and whoever wants to be first must be slave of all. ⁴⁵For even the Son of Man did not come to be served, but to serve, and to give his life as a ransom for many."

Blind Bartimaeus Receives His Sight ⁴⁶Then they came to Jericho. As Jesus and his disciples, together with a large crowd, were leaving the city, a blind man, Bartimaeus (that is, the Son of Timaeus), was sitting by the roadside begging. ⁴⁷When he heard that it was Jesus of Nazareth, he began to shout, "Jesus, Son of David, have mercy on me!"

⁴⁸Many rebuked him and told him to be quiet, but he shouted all the more, "Son of David, have mercy on me!"

⁴⁹Jesus stopped and said, "Call him."

So they called to the blind man, "Cheer up! On your feet! He's calling you." ⁵⁰Throwing his cloak aside, he jumped to his feet and came to Jesus.

⁵¹"What do you want me to do for you?" Jesus asked him.

The blind man said, "Rabbi, I want to see."

⁵²"Go," said Jesus, "your faith has healed you." Immediately he received his sight and followed Jesus along the road.

The Triumphal Entry As they approached Jerusalem and came to Bethphage and Bethany at the Mount of Olives, Jesus sent two of his disciples, ²saying to them, "Go to the village ahead of you, and just as you enter it, you will find a colt tied there, which no one has ever ridden. Untie it and bring it here. ³If anyone asks you, 'Why are you doing this?' tell him, 'The Lord needs it and will send it back here shortly.' "

⁴They went and found a colt outside in the street, tied at a doorway. As they untied it, ⁵some people standing there asked, "What are you doing, untying that colt?" ⁶They answered as Jesus had told them to, and the people let them go. ⁷When they brought the colt to Jesus and threw their cloaks over it, he sat on it. ⁸Many people spread their cloaks on the road, while others

spread branches they had cut in the fields. ⁹Those who went ahead and those who followed shouted,

"Hosanna!ᵃ"

"Blessed is he who comes in the name of the Lord!"ᵇ

¹⁰"Blessed is the coming kingdom of our father David!"

"Hosanna in the highest!"

¹¹Jesus entered Jerusalem and went to the temple. He looked around at everything, but since it was already late, he went out to Bethany with the Twelve.

Jesus Clears the Temple   ¹²The next day as they were leaving Bethany, Jesus was hungry. ¹³Seeing in the distance a fig tree in leaf, he went to find out if it had any fruit. When he reached it, he found nothing but leaves, because it was not the season for figs. ¹⁴Then he said to the tree, "May no one ever eat fruit from you again." And his disciples heard him say it.

¹⁵On reaching Jerusalem, Jesus entered the temple area and began driving out those who were buying and selling there. He overturned the tables of the money changers and the benches of those selling doves, ¹⁶and would not allow anyone to carry merchandise through the temple courts. ¹⁷And as he taught them, he said, "Is it not written:

" 'My house will be called
a house of prayer for all nations'ᶜ?

But you have made it 'a den of robbers.'ᵈ"

¹⁸The chief priests and the teachers of the law heard this and began looking for a way to kill him, for they feared him, because the whole crowd was amazed at his teaching.

¹⁹When evening came, theyᵉ went out of the city.

The Withered Fig Tree   ²⁰In the morning, as they went along, they saw the fig tree withered from the roots. ²¹Peter remembered and said to Jesus, "Rabbi, look! The fig tree you cursed has withered!"

²²"Haveᶠ faith in God," Jesus answered. ²³"I tell you the truth, if anyone says to this mountain, 'Go, throw yourself into the sea,' and does not doubt in his heart but believes that what he says will happen, it will be done for him. ²⁴Therefore I tell you, whatever you ask for in prayer, believe that you have received it, and it will be yours. ²⁵And when you stand praying, if you hold anything against anyone, forgive him, so that your Father in heaven may forgive you your sins.ᵍ"

The Authority of Jesus Questioned   ²⁷They arrived again in Jerusalem, and while Jesus was walking in the temple courts, the chief priests, the teachers of the law and the elders came to him. ²⁸"By what authority are you doing these things?" they asked. "And who gave you authority to do this?"

²⁹Jesus replied, "I will ask you one question. Answer me, and I will tell you by what authority I am doing these things. ³⁰John's baptism—was it from heaven, or from men? Tell me!"

³¹They discussed it among themselves and said, "If we say, 'From heaven,' he will ask, 'Then why didn't you believe him?' ³²But if we say, 'From men' . . . ." (They feared the people, for everyone held that John really was a prophet.)

³³So they answered Jesus, "We don't know."

Jesus said, "Neither will I tell you by what authority I am doing these things."

ᵃ9 A Hebrew expression meaning "Save!" which became an exclamation of praise; also in verse 10 ᵇ9 Psalm 118:25,26 ᶜ17 Isaiah 56:7 ᵈ17 Jer. 7:11 ᵉ19 Some early manuscripts *he* ᶠ22 Some early manuscripts *If you have* ᵍ25 Some manuscripts *sins. 26But if you do not forgive, neither will your Father who is in heaven forgive your sins.*

Dear Sam,

My friend went forward to accept Christ at a teen rally. But now he laughs at what he calls a bunch of hocus-pocus. What happened?

Pam in Panama City

100 Advice Lane, Anywhere, USA

Dear Pam,

On the first Palm Sunday, the crowds were praising Christ as he entered Jerusalem (Mark 11:1-11). Yet just a few days later some of those same people were shouting angrily to crucify him. Obviously, their enthusiasm for Jesus had no staying power.

Faith isn't just going forward at a revival meeting. It's committing yourself to Jesus and trusting him enough to follow him. In Matthew 13 Christ told a parable about a farmer sowing seeds. The birds ate the seed that fell on the path. Seed that fell on rocky places sprang up quickly but soon withered. Other seed fell among thorns that choked the young plants. But some seed fell on good soil, where it flourished and grew.

Your friend is like the poor soil. The seed (the news of Christ) did not take root in him. It withered and died because at this time he had no nourishment for faith. It had no staying power. Perhaps the seed will lie dormant and one day take root again and grow. Perhaps not. The choice is his. Keep praying for him.

Sam

The Parable of the Tenants He then began to speak to them in parables: "A man planted a vineyard. He put a wall around it, dug a pit for the winepress and built a watchtower. Then he rented the vineyard to some farmers and went away on a journey. ²At harvest time he sent a servant to the tenants to collect from them some of the fruit of the vineyard. ³But they seized him, beat him and sent him away empty-handed. ⁴Then he sent another servant to them; they struck this man on the head and treated him shamefully. ⁵He sent still another, and that one they killed. He sent many others; some of them they beat, others they killed.

⁶"He had one left to send, a son, whom he loved. He sent him last of all, saying, 'They will respect my son.'

⁷"But the tenants said to one another, 'This is the heir. Come, let's kill him, and the inheritance will be ours.' ⁸So they took him and killed him, and threw him out of the vineyard.

⁹"What then will the owner of the vineyard do? He will come and kill those tenants and give the vineyard to others. ¹⁰Haven't you read this scripture:

> " 'The stone the builders rejected
>   has become the capstone[a];
> ¹¹ the Lord has done this,
>   and it is marvelous in our eyes'[b]?"

¹²Then they looked for a way to arrest him because they knew he had spoken the parable against them. But they were afraid of the crowd; so they left him and went away.

Paying Taxes to Caesar ¹³Later they sent some of the Pharisees and Herodians to Jesus to catch him in his words. ¹⁴They came to him and said, "Teacher, we know you are a man of integrity. You aren't swayed by men, because you pay no attention to who they are; but you teach the way of God in accordance with the truth. Is it right to pay taxes to Caesar or not? ¹⁵Should we pay or shouldn't we?"

But Jesus knew their hypocrisy. "Why are you trying to trap me?" he asked. "Bring me a denarius and let me look at it." ¹⁶They brought the coin, and he asked them, "Whose portrait is this? And whose inscription?"

"Caesar's," they replied.

¹⁷Then Jesus said to them, "Give to Caesar what is Caesar's and to God what is God's."

And they were amazed at him.

Marriage at the Resurrection ¹⁸Then the Sadducees, who say there is no resurrection, came to him with a question. ¹⁹"Teacher," they said, "Moses wrote for us that if a man's brother dies and leaves a wife but no children, the man must marry the widow and have children for his brother. ²⁰Now there were seven brothers. The first one married and died without leaving any children. ²¹The second one married the widow, but he also died, leaving no child. It was the same with the third. ²²In fact, none of the seven left any children. Last of all, the woman died too. ²³At the resurrection[c] whose wife will she be, since the seven were married to her?"

²⁴Jesus replied, "Are you not in error because you do not know the Scriptures or the power of God? ²⁵When the dead rise, they will neither marry nor be given in marriage; they will be like the angels in heaven. ²⁶Now about the dead rising—have you not read in the book of Moses, in the account of the bush, how God said to him, 'I am the God of Abraham, the God of Isaac, and the God of Jacob'[d]? ²⁷He is not the God of the dead, but of the living. You are badly mistaken!"

---

[a]10 Or *cornerstone* [b]11 Psalm 118:22,23 [c]23 Some manuscripts *resurrection, when men rise from the dead,* [d]26 Exodus 3:6

The Greatest Commandment ²⁸One of the teachers of the law came and heard them debating. Noticing that Jesus had given them a good answer, he asked him, "Of all the commandments, which is the most important?"

²⁹"The most important one," answered Jesus, "is this: 'Hear, O Israel, the Lord our God, the Lord is one.ᵃ ³⁰Love the Lord your God with all your heart and with all your soul and with all your mind and with all your strength.'ᵇ ³¹The second is this: 'Love your neighbor as yourself.'ᶜ There is no commandment greater than these."

³²"Well said, teacher," the man replied. "You are right in saying that God is one and there is no other but him. ³³To love him with all your heart, with all your understanding and with all your strength, and to love your neighbor as yourself is more important than all burnt offerings and sacrifices."

³⁴When Jesus saw that he had answered wisely, he said to him, "You are not far from the kingdom of God." And from then on no one dared ask him any more questions.

Whose Son Is the Christ? ³⁵While Jesus was teaching in the temple courts, he asked, "How is it that the teachers of the law say that the Christᵈ is the son of David? ³⁶David himself, speaking by the Holy Spirit, declared:

> " 'The Lord said to my Lord:
> "Sit at my right hand
> until I put your enemies
> under your feet." 'ᵉ

³⁷David himself calls him 'Lord.' How then can he be his son?"

The large crowd listened to him with delight.

³⁸As he taught, Jesus said, "Watch out for the teachers of the law. They like to walk around in flowing robes and be greeted in the marketplaces, ³⁹and have the most important seats in the synagogues and the places of honor at banquets. ⁴⁰They devour widows' houses and for a show make lengthy prayers. Such men will be punished most severely."

The Widow's Offering ⁴¹Jesus sat down opposite the place where the offerings were put and watched the crowd putting their money into the temple treasury. Many rich people threw in large amounts. ⁴²But a poor widow came and put in two very small copper coins,ᶠ worth only a fraction of a penny.ᵍ

⁴³Calling his disciples to him, Jesus said, "I tell you the truth, this poor widow has put more into the treasury than all the others. ⁴⁴They all gave out of their wealth; but she, out of her poverty, put in everything—all she had to live on."

Signs of the End of the Age As he was leaving the temple, one of his disciples said to him, "Look, Teacher! What massive stones! What magnificent buildings!"

²"Do you see all these great buildings?" replied Jesus. "Not one stone here will be left on another; every one will be thrown down."

³As Jesus was sitting on the Mount of

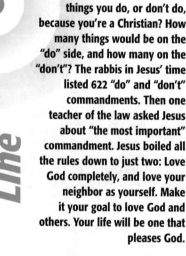

MARK 12:28–34

Did you ever try to list the things you do, or don't do, because you're a Christian? How many things would be on the "do" side, and how many on the "don't"? The rabbis in Jesus' time listed 622 "do" and "don't" commandments. Then one teacher of the law asked Jesus about "the most important" commandment. Jesus boiled all the rules down to just two: Love God completely, and love your neighbor as yourself. Make it your goal to love God and others. Your life will be one that pleases God.

Direct Line

ᵃ29 Or *the Lord our God is one Lord*   ᵇ30 Deut. 6:4,5
ᶜ31 Lev. 19:18   ᵈ35 Or *Messiah*   ᵉ36 Psalm 110:1
ᶠ42 Greek *two lepta*   ᵍ42 Greek *kodrantes*

Olives opposite the temple, Peter, James, John and Andrew asked him privately, [4]"Tell us, when will these things happen? And what will be the sign that they are all about to be fulfilled?"

[5]Jesus said to them: "Watch out that no one deceives you. [6]Many will come in my name, claiming, 'I am he,' and will deceive many. [7]When you hear of wars and rumors of wars, do not be alarmed. Such things must happen, but the end is still to come. [8]Nation will rise against nation, and kingdom against kingdom. There will be earthquakes in various places, and famines. These are the beginning of birth pains.

[9]"You must be on your guard. You will be handed over to the local councils and flogged in the synagogues. On account of me you will stand before governors and kings as witnesses to them. [10]And the gospel must first be preached to all nations. [11]Whenever you are arrested and brought to trial, do not worry beforehand about what to say. Just say whatever is given you at the time, for it is not you speaking, but the Holy Spirit.

[12]"Brother will betray brother to death, and a father his child. Children will rebel against their parents and have them put to death. [13]All men will hate you because of me, but he who stands firm to the end will be saved.

[14]"When you see 'the abomination that causes desolation'[a] standing where it[b] does not belong—let the reader understand—then let those who are in Judea flee to the mountains. [15]Let no one on the roof of his house go down or enter the house to take anything out. [16]Let no one in the field go back to get his cloak. [17]How dreadful it will be in those days for pregnant women and nursing mothers! [18]Pray that this will not take place in winter, [19]because those will be days of distress unequaled from the beginning, when God created the world, until now—and never to be equaled again. [20]If the Lord had not cut short those days, no one would survive. But for the sake of the elect, whom he has chosen, he has shortened them. [21]At that time if anyone says to you, 'Look, here is the Christ[c]!' or, 'Look, there he is!' do not believe it. [22]For false Christs and false prophets will appear and perform signs and miracles to deceive the elect—if that were possible. [23]So be on your guard; I have told you everything ahead of time.

[24]"But in those days, following that distress,

" 'the sun will be darkened,
   and the moon will not give its light;
[25] the stars will fall from the sky,
   and the heavenly bodies will be shaken.'[d]

[26]"At that time men will see the Son of Man coming in clouds with great power and glory. [27]And he will send his angels and gather his elect from the four winds, from the ends of the earth to the ends of the heavens.

[28]"Now learn this lesson from the fig tree: As soon as its twigs get tender and its leaves come out, you know that summer is near. [29]Even so, when you see these things happening, you know that it is near, right at the door. [30]I tell you the truth, this generation[e] will certainly not pass away until all these things have happened. [31]Heaven and earth will pass away, but my words will never pass away.

The Day and Hour Unknown [32]"No one knows about that day or hour, not even the angels in heaven, nor the Son, but only the Father. [33]Be on guard! Be alert[f]! You do not know when that time will come. [34]It's like a man going away: He leaves his house and puts his servants in charge, each with his assigned task, and tells the one at the door to keep watch.

[35]"Therefore keep watch because you do not know when the owner of the

[a]14 Daniel 9:27; 11:31; 12:11 [b]14 Or he; also in verse 29 [c]21 Or Messiah [d]25 Isaiah 13:10; 34:4
[e]30 Or race [f]33 Some manuscripts alert and pray

house will come back—whether in the evening, or at midnight, or when the rooster crows, or at dawn. ³⁶If he comes suddenly, do not let him find you sleeping. ³⁷What I say to you, I say to everyone: 'Watch!' "

14 *Jesus Anointed at Bethany* Now the Passover and the Feast of Unleavened Bread were only two days away, and the chief priests and the teachers of the law were looking for some sly way to arrest Jesus and kill him. ²"But not during the Feast," they said, "or the people may riot."

³While he was in Bethany, reclining at the table in the home of a man known as Simon the Leper, a woman came with an alabaster jar of very expensive perfume, made of pure nard. She broke the jar and poured the perfume on his head.

⁴Some of those present were saying indignantly to one another, "Why this waste of perfume? ⁵It could have been sold for more than a year's wages*ᵃ* and the money given to the poor." And they rebuked her harshly.

⁶"Leave her alone," said Jesus. "Why are you bothering her? She has done a beautiful thing to me. ⁷The poor you will always have with you, and you can help them any time you want. But you will not always have me. ⁸She did what she could. She poured perfume on my body beforehand to prepare for my burial. ⁹I tell you the truth, wherever the gospel is preached throughout the world, what she has done will also be told, in memory of her."

¹⁰Then Judas Iscariot, one of the Twelve, went to the chief priests to betray Jesus to them. ¹¹They were delighted to hear this and promised to give him money. So he watched for an opportunity to hand him over.

The Lord's Supper ¹²On the first day of the Feast of Unleavened Bread, when it was customary to sacrifice the Passover lamb, Jesus' disciples asked him, "Where do you want us to go and make preparations for you to eat the Passover?"

¹³So he sent two of his disciples, telling them, "Go into the city, and a man carrying a jar of water will meet you. Follow him. ¹⁴Say to the owner of the house he enters, 'The Teacher asks: Where is my guest room, where I may eat the Passover with my disciples?' ¹⁵He will show you a large upper room, furnished and ready. Make preparations for us there."

ᵃ5 Greek than three hundred denarii

The Bible Says

Jesus Is Coming

The Bible says that Jesus will return to earth. What do you know about his coming? Here are some things you can be sure about:

* Jesus will come in power and glory (Mark 13:26).
* Jesus will come back in person (Acts 1:11).
* Christians will rise from the dead (1 Thessalonians 4:13–18).
* Jesus will punish those who do not know God (2 Thessalonians 1:8–9).

No one knows just when Jesus will return. Some people think they'll change the way they live next week or next year. But Jesus warned that he might return at any time! Jesus urges you to "Be alert!" (Mark 13:32). If you expect Jesus to return at any moment, you'll be careful at all times to do the things that please him.

¹⁶The disciples left, went into the city and found things just as Jesus had told them. So they prepared the Passover.

¹⁷When evening came, Jesus arrived with the Twelve. ¹⁸While they were reclining at the table eating, he said, "I tell you the truth, one of you will betray me—one who is eating with me."

¹⁹They were saddened, and one by one they said to him, "Surely not I?"

²⁰"It is one of the Twelve," he replied, "one who dips bread into the bowl with me. ²¹The Son of Man will go just as it is written about him. But woe to that man who betrays the Son of Man! It would be better for him if he had not been born."

²²While they were eating, Jesus took bread, gave thanks and broke it, and gave it to his disciples, saying, "Take it; this is my body."

²³Then he took the cup, gave thanks and offered it to them, and they all drank from it.

²⁴"This is my blood of the*ᵃ* covenant, which is poured out for many," he said to them. ²⁵"I tell you the truth, I will not drink again of the fruit of the vine until that day when I drink it anew in the kingdom of God."

²⁶When they had sung a hymn, they went out to the Mount of Olives.

Jesus Predicts Peter's Denial   ²⁷"You will all fall away," Jesus told them, "for it is written:

> " 'I will strike the shepherd,
>   and the sheep will be scattered.'ᵇ

²⁸But after I have risen, I will go ahead of you into Galilee."

²⁹Peter declared, "Even if all fall away, I will not."

³⁰"I tell you the truth," Jesus answered, "today—yes, tonight—before the rooster crows twiceᶜ you yourself will disown me three times."

³¹But Peter insisted emphatically, "Even if I have to die with you, I will never disown you." And all the others said the same.

Gethsemane   ³²They went to a place called Gethsemane, and Jesus said to his disciples, "Sit here while I pray." ³³He took Peter, James and John along with him, and he began to be deeply distressed and troubled. ³⁴"My soul is overwhelmed with sorrow to the point of death," he said to them. "Stay here and keep watch."

³⁵Going a little farther, he fell to the ground and prayed that if possible the hour might pass from him. ³⁶"*Abba,*ᵈ Father," he said, "everything is possible for you. Take this cup from me. Yet not what I will, but what you will."

³⁷Then he returned to his disciples and found them sleeping. "Simon," he said to Peter, "are you asleep? Could you not keep watch for one hour? ³⁸Watch and pray so that you will not fall into temptation. The spirit is willing, but the body is weak."

³⁹Once more he went away and prayed the same thing. ⁴⁰When he came back, he again found them sleeping, because their eyes were heavy. They did not know what to say to him.

⁴¹Returning the third time, he said to them, "Are you still sleeping and resting? Enough! The hour has come. Look, the Son of Man is betrayed into the hands of sinners. ⁴²Rise! Let us go! Here comes my betrayer!"

Jesus Arrested   ⁴³Just as he was speaking, Judas, one of the Twelve, appeared. With him was a crowd armed with swords and clubs, sent from the chief priests, the teachers of the law, and the elders.

⁴⁴Now the betrayer had arranged a signal with them: "The one I kiss is the man; arrest him and lead him away under guard." ⁴⁵Going at once to Jesus, Judas said, "Rabbi!" and kissed him. ⁴⁶The men seized Jesus and arrested

---

ᵃ24 Some manuscripts *the new* *ᵇ27* Zech. 13:7 *ᶜ30* Some early manuscripts do not have *twice.*
ᵈ36 Aramaic for *Father*

him. ⁴⁷Then one of those standing near drew his sword and struck the servant of the high priest, cutting off his ear.

⁴⁸"Am I leading a rebellion," said Jesus, "that you have come out with swords and clubs to capture me? ⁴⁹Every day I was with you, teaching in the temple courts, and you did not arrest me. But the Scriptures must be fulfilled." ⁵⁰Then everyone deserted him and fled.

⁵¹A young man, wearing nothing but a linen garment, was following Jesus. When they seized him, ⁵²he fled naked, leaving his garment behind.

Before the Sanhedrin ⁵³They took Jesus to the high priest, and all the chief priests, elders and teachers of the law came together. ⁵⁴Peter followed him at a distance, right into the courtyard of the high priest. There he sat with the guards and warmed himself at the fire.

⁵⁵The chief priests and the whole Sanhedrin were looking for evidence against Jesus so that they could put him to death, but they did not find any. ⁵⁶Many testified falsely against him, but their statements did not agree.

⁵⁷Then some stood up and gave this false testimony against him: ⁵⁸"We heard him say, 'I will destroy this man-made temple and in three days will build another, not made by man.' " ⁵⁹Yet even then their testimony did not agree.

⁶⁰Then the high priest stood up before them and asked Jesus, "Are you not going to answer? What is this testimony that these men are bringing against you?" ⁶¹But Jesus remained silent and gave no answer.

Again the high priest asked him, "Are you the Christ,ᵃ the Son of the Blessed One?"

⁶²"I am," said Jesus. "And you will see the Son of Man sitting at the right hand of the Mighty One and coming on the clouds of heaven."

⁶³The high priest tore his clothes. "Why do we need any more witnesses?" he asked. ⁶⁴"You have heard the blasphemy. What do you think?"

They all condemned him as worthy of death. ⁶⁵Then some began to spit at him; they blindfolded him, struck him with their fists, and said, "Prophesy!" And the guards took him and beat him.

Peter Disowns Jesus ⁶⁶While Peter was below in the courtyard, one of the servant girls of the high priest came by. ⁶⁷When she saw Peter warming himself, she looked closely at him.

"You also were with that Nazarene, Jesus," she said.

⁶⁸But he denied it. "I don't know or understand what you're talking about," he said, and went out into the entryway.ᵇ

⁶⁹When the servant girl saw him there, she said again to those standing around, "This fellow is one of them." ⁷⁰Again he denied it.

After a little while, those standing near said to Peter, "Surely you are one of them, for you are a Galilean."

⁷¹He began to call down curses on himself, and he swore to them, "I don't know this man you're talking about."

⁷²Immediately the rooster crowed the second time.ᶜ Then Peter remembered the word Jesus had spoken to him: "Before the rooster crows twiceᵈ you will disown me three times." And he broke down and wept.

15 **Jesus Before Pilate** Very early in the morning, the chief priests, with the elders, the teachers of the law and the whole Sanhedrin, reached a decision. They bound Jesus, led him away and handed him over to Pilate.

²"Are you the king of the Jews?" asked Pilate.

"Yes, it is as you say," Jesus replied.

ᵃ61 Or *Messiah* ᵇ68 Some early manuscripts *entryway and the rooster crowed* ᶜ72 Some early manuscripts do not have *the second time.* ᵈ72 Some early manuscripts do not have *twice.*

³The chief priests accused him of many things. ⁴So again Pilate asked him, "Aren't you going to answer? See how many things they are accusing you of."

⁵But Jesus still made no reply, and Pilate was amazed.

⁶Now it was the custom at the Feast to release a prisoner whom the people requested. ⁷A man called Barabbas was in prison with the insurrectionists who had committed murder in the uprising. ⁸The crowd came up and asked Pilate to do for them what he usually did.

⁹"Do you want me to release to you the king of the Jews?" asked Pilate, ¹⁰knowing it was out of envy that the chief priests had handed Jesus over to him. ¹¹But the chief priests stirred up the crowd to have Pilate release Barabbas instead.

¹²"What shall I do, then, with the one you call the king of the Jews?" Pilate asked them.

¹³"Crucify him!" they shouted.

¹⁴"Why? What crime has he committed?" asked Pilate.

But they shouted all the louder, "Crucify him!"

¹⁵Wanting to satisfy the crowd, Pilate released Barabbas to them. He had Jesus flogged, and handed him over to be crucified.

The Soldiers Mock Jesus ¹⁶The soldiers led Jesus away into the palace (that is, the Praetorium) and called together the whole company of soldiers. ¹⁷They put a purple robe on him, then twisted together a crown of thorns and set it on him. ¹⁸And they began to call out to him, "Hail, king of the Jews!" ¹⁹Again and again they struck him on the head with a staff and spit on him. Falling on their knees, they paid homage to him. ²⁰And when they had mocked him, they took off the purple robe and put his own clothes on him. Then they led him out to crucify him.

The Crucifixion ²¹A certain man from Cyrene, Simon, the father of Alexander and Rufus, was passing by on his way in from the country, and they forced him to carry the cross. ²²They brought Jesus to the place called Golgotha (which means The Place of the Skull). ²³Then they offered him wine mixed with myrrh, but he did not take it. ²⁴And they crucified him. Dividing up his clothes, they cast lots to see what each would get.

²⁵It was the third hour when they crucified him. ²⁶The written notice of the charge against him read: THE KING OF THE JEWS. ²⁷They crucified two robbers with him, one on his right and one on his left.*ᵃ* ²⁹Those who passed by hurled insults at him, shaking their heads and saying, "So! You who are going to destroy the temple and build it in three days, ³⁰come down from the cross and save yourself!"

³¹In the same way the chief priests and the teachers of the law mocked him among themselves. "He saved others," they said, "but he can't save himself! ³²Let this Christ,*ᵇ* this King of Israel, come down now from the cross, that we may see and believe." Those crucified with him also heaped insults on him.

ᵃ27 Some manuscripts left, ²⁸and the scripture was fulfilled which says, "He was counted with the lawless ones" (Isaiah 53:12) ᵇ32 Or Messiah

MARK 15:29–32

Many who watched Jesus on the cross ridiculed and insulted him. Probably none of them understood that Christ's death was self-sacrifice. He was giving his life for them, and for you. Self-sacrifice is usually misunderstood. You give up good times to help take care of your little brothers and sisters. And the kids your age say you're a loner and think you don't like them. You get a job to help out because your dad can't work. And some teachers get on you because you fall asleep in class. Please don't get discouraged. Yes, the sacrifices you make for others may be misunderstood. But you're following a perfect example: Jesus.

Direct Line

The Death of Jesus ³³At the sixth hour darkness came over the whole land until the ninth hour. ³⁴And at the ninth hour Jesus cried out in a loud voice, *"Eloi, Eloi, lama sabachthani?"* —which means, "My God, my God, why have you forsaken me?"ᵃ

³⁵When some of those standing near heard this, they said, "Listen, he's calling Elijah."

³⁶One man ran, filled a sponge with wine vinegar, put it on a stick, and offered it to Jesus to drink. "Now leave him alone. Let's see if Elijah comes to take him down," he said.

³⁷With a loud cry, Jesus breathed his last.

³⁸The curtain of the temple was torn in two from top to bottom. ³⁹And when the centurion, who stood there in front of Jesus, heard his cry andᵇ saw how he died, he said, "Surely this man was the Sonᶜ of God!"

⁴⁰Some women were watching from a distance. Among them were Mary Magdalene, Mary the mother of James the younger and of Joses, and Salome. ⁴¹In Galilee these women had followed him and cared for his needs. Many other women who had come up with him to Jerusalem were also there.

The Burial of Jesus ⁴²It was Preparation Day (that is, the day before the Sabbath). So as evening approached, ⁴³Joseph of Arimathea, a prominent member of the Council, who was himself waiting for the kingdom of God, went boldly to Pilate and asked for Jesus' body. ⁴⁴Pilate was surprised to hear that he was already dead. Summoning the centurion, he asked him if Jesus had already died. ⁴⁵When he learned from the centurion that it was so, he gave the body to Joseph. ⁴⁶So Joseph bought some linen cloth, took down the body, wrapped it in the linen, and placed it in a tomb cut out of rock. Then he rolled a stone against the entrance of the tomb. ⁴⁷Mary Magdalene and Mary the mother of Joses saw where he was laid.

16 ***The Resurrection*** When the Sabbath was over, Mary Magdalene, Mary the mother of James, and Salome bought spices so that they might go to anoint Jesus' body. ²Very early on the first day of the week, just after sunrise, they were on their way to the tomb ³and they asked each other, "Who will roll the stone away from the entrance of the tomb?"

⁴But when they looked up, they saw that the stone, which was very large, had been rolled away. ⁵As they entered the tomb, they saw a young man dressed in a white robe sitting on the right side, and they were alarmed.

⁶"Don't be alarmed," he said. "You are looking for Jesus the Nazarene, who was crucified. He has risen! He is not here. See the place where they laid him. ⁷But go, tell his disciples and Peter, 'He is going ahead of you into Galilee. There you will see him, just as he told you.' "

⁸Trembling and bewildered, the women went out and fled from the tomb. They said nothing to anyone, because they were afraid.

They told me gospel meant "good news." This is it, people!

SEE MARK 16

ᵃ34 Psalm 22:1 ᵇ39 Some manuscripts do not have *heard his cry and* ᶜ39 Or *a son*

[The earliest manuscripts and some other ancient witnesses do not have Mark 16:9-20.]

⁹When Jesus rose early on the first day of the week, he appeared first to Mary Magdalene, out of whom he had driven seven demons. ¹⁰She went and told those who had been with him and who were mourning and weeping. ¹¹When they heard that Jesus was alive and that she had seen him, they did not believe it.

¹²Afterward Jesus appeared in a different form to two of them while they were walking in the country. ¹³These returned and reported it to the rest; but they did not believe them either.

¹⁴Later Jesus appeared to the Eleven as they were eating; he rebuked them for their lack of faith and their stubborn refusal to believe those who had seen him after he had risen.

¹⁵He said to them, "Go into all the world and preach the good news to all creation. ¹⁶Whoever believes and is baptized will be saved, but whoever does not believe will be condemned. ¹⁷And these signs will accompany those who believe: In my name they will drive out demons; they will speak in new tongues; ¹⁸they will pick up snakes with their hands; and when they drink deadly poison, it will not hurt them at all; they will place their hands on sick people, and they will get well."

¹⁹After the Lord Jesus had spoken to them, he was taken up into heaven and he sat at the right hand of God. ²⁰Then the disciples went out and preached everywhere, and the Lord worked with them and confirmed his word by the signs that accompanied it.

IGNORED.

It's no fun to be ignored. A teacher ignores your raised hand and doesn't answer your question. A parent butts in and ignores what you were trying to say. A friend walks away when you're talking.

Luke wants you to know Jesus wasn't like that. Jesus showed a loving interest in all kinds of people. He had time for children. He often spoke about caring for the poor and oppressed. And Luke was careful to mention by name the women Jesus met and spoke to. Luke will help you realize that, whoever you are, Jesus has time for you.

Fundamentals

This girl had courage (Luke 1:26-38)!

What would people think if you were nice to a girl with a bad reputation (Luke 7:36-50)?

Should you bother Jesus with your troubles (Luke 13:10-17)?

Why don't some people want Jesus as Savior and Lord (Luke 20:9-19)?

FAST FACTS

Luke was a medical doctor.

Luke wrote to Gentiles to show Jesus as an ideal human being.

Luke mentions ten different times when Jesus prayed.

Six miracles and 19 parables are reported only by Luke.

1 *Introduction* Many have undertaken to draw up an account of the things that have been fulfilled*ᵃ* among us, ²just as they were handed down to us by those who from the first were eyewitnesses and servants of the word. ³Therefore, since I myself have carefully investigated everything from the beginning, it seemed good also to me to write an orderly account for you, most excellent Theophilus, ⁴so that you may know the certainty of the things you have been taught.

The Birth of John the Baptist Foretold ⁵In the time of Herod king of Judea there was a priest named Zechariah, who belonged to the priestly division of Abijah; his wife Elizabeth was also a descendant of Aaron. ⁶Both of them were upright in the sight of God, observing all the Lord's commandments and regulations blamelessly. ⁷But they had no children, because Elizabeth was barren; and they were both well along in years.

⁸Once when Zechariah's division was on duty and he was serving as priest before God, ⁹he was chosen by lot, according to the custom of the priesthood, to go into the temple of the Lord and burn incense. ¹⁰And when the time for the burning of incense came, all the assembled worshipers were praying outside.

¹¹Then an angel of the Lord appeared to him, standing at the right side of the altar of incense. ¹²When Zechariah saw him, he was startled and was gripped with fear. ¹³But the angel said to him: "Do not be afraid, Zechariah; your prayer has been heard. Your wife Elizabeth will bear you a son, and you are to give him the name John. ¹⁴He will be a joy and delight to you, and many will rejoice because of his birth, ¹⁵for he will be great in the sight of the Lord. He is never to take wine or other fermented drink, and he will be filled with the Holy Spirit even from birth.*ᵇ* ¹⁶Many of the people of Israel will he bring back to the Lord their God. ¹⁷And he will go on before the Lord, in the spirit and power of Elijah, to turn the hearts of the fathers to their children and the disobedient to the wisdom of the righteous—to make ready a people prepared for the Lord."

¹⁸Zechariah asked the angel, "How can I be sure of this? I am an old man and my wife is well along in years."

¹⁹The angel answered, "I am Gabriel. I stand in the presence of God, and I have been sent to speak to you and to tell you this good news. ²⁰And now you will be silent and not able to speak until the day this happens, because you did not believe my words, which will come true at their proper time."

²¹Meanwhile, the people were waiting for Zechariah and wondering why he stayed so long in the temple. ²²When he came out, he could not speak to them. They realized he had seen a vision in the temple, for he kept making signs to them but remained unable to speak.

²³When his time of service was completed, he returned home. ²⁴After this his wife Elizabeth became pregnant and for five months remained in seclusion. ²⁵"The

ᵃ1 Or been surely believed ᵇ15 Or from his mother's womb

LUKE 1:26–38

When you think of real heroes and heroines, you have to put a teenager named Mary at the top of the list. When this young virgin said she was willing to bear Jesus, she knew what it meant. She was engaged; her husband-to-be would think she was unfaithful. Everyone, even her parents, would think she'd had sex before marriage. It took a tremendous amount of courage to say, "I am the Lord's servant." There are still teenage heroes around. They're the ones who say no even when they're laughed at and called prudes. They're the ones who resist all the pressures to do wrong and instead echo Mary's words: "I am the Lord's servant. I choose to do God's will."

Direct Line

Lord has done this for me," she said. "In these days he has shown his favor and taken away my disgrace among the people."

The Birth of Jesus Foretold ²⁶In the sixth month, God sent the angel Gabriel to Nazareth, a town in Galilee, ²⁷to a virgin pledged to be married to a man named Joseph, a descendant of David. The virgin's name was Mary. ²⁸The angel went to her and said, "Greetings, you who are highly favored! The Lord is with you."

²⁹Mary was greatly troubled at his words and wondered what kind of greeting this might be. ³⁰But the angel said to her, "Do not be afraid, Mary, you have found favor with God. ³¹You will be with child and give birth to a son, and you are to give him the name Jesus. ³²He will be great and will be called the Son of the Most High. The Lord God will give him the throne of his father David, ³³and he will reign over the house of Jacob forever; his kingdom will never end."

³⁴"How will this be," Mary asked the angel, "since I am a virgin?"

³⁵The angel answered, "The Holy Spirit will come upon you, and the power of the Most High will overshadow you. So the holy one to be born will be called*ᵃ* the Son of God. ³⁶Even Elizabeth your relative is going to have a child in her old age, and she who was said to be barren is in her sixth month. ³⁷For nothing is impossible with God."

³⁸"I am the Lord's servant," Mary answered. "May it be to me as you have said." Then the angel left her.

Mary Visits Elizabeth ³⁹At that time Mary got ready and hurried to a town in the hill country of Judea, ⁴⁰where she entered Zechariah's home and greeted Elizabeth. ⁴¹When Elizabeth heard Mary's greeting, the baby leaped in her womb, and Elizabeth was filled with the Holy Spirit. ⁴²In a loud voice she exclaimed: "Blessed are you among women, and blessed is the child you will bear! ⁴³But why am I so favored, that the mother of my Lord should come to me? ⁴⁴As soon as the sound of your greeting reached my ears, the baby in my womb leaped for joy. ⁴⁵Blessed is she who has believed that what the Lord has said to her will be accomplished!"

Mary's Song ⁴⁶And Mary said:

> "My soul glorifies the Lord
> ⁴⁷ and my spirit rejoices in God my Savior,
> ⁴⁸for he has been mindful
>   of the humble state of his servant.
> From now on all generations will call me blessed,
> ⁴⁹ for the Mighty One has done great things for me—
>   holy is his name.
> ⁵⁰His mercy extends to those who fear him,
>   from generation to generation.
> ⁵¹He has performed mighty deeds with his arm;
>   he has scattered those who are proud in their inmost
>   thoughts.
> ⁵²He has brought down rulers from their thrones
>   but has lifted up the humble.
> ⁵³He has filled the hungry with good things
>   but has sent the rich away empty.
> ⁵⁴He has helped his servant Israel,
>   remembering to be merciful
> ⁵⁵to Abraham and his descendants forever,
>   even as he said to our fathers."

ᵃ35 Or So the child to be born will be called holy,

⁵⁶Mary stayed with Elizabeth for about three months and then returned home.

The Birth of John the Baptist ⁵⁷When it was time for Elizabeth to have her baby, she gave birth to a son. ⁵⁸Her neighbors and relatives heard that the Lord had shown her great mercy, and they shared her joy.

⁵⁹On the eighth day they came to circumcise the child, and they were going to name him after his father Zechariah, ⁶⁰but his mother spoke up and said, "No! He is to be called John."

⁶¹They said to her, "There is no one among your relatives who has that name."

⁶²Then they made signs to his father, to find out what he would like to name the child. ⁶³He asked for a writing tablet, and to everyone's astonishment he wrote, "His name is John." ⁶⁴Immediately his mouth was opened and his tongue was loosed, and he began to speak, praising God. ⁶⁵The neighbors were all filled with awe, and throughout the hill country of Judea people were talking about all these things. ⁶⁶Everyone who heard this wondered about it, asking, "What then is this child going to be?" For the Lord's hand was with him.

Zechariah's Song ⁶⁷His father Zechariah was filled with the Holy Spirit and prophesied:

> ⁶⁸"Praise be to the Lord, the God of Israel,
>   because he has come and has redeemed his people.
> ⁶⁹He has raised up a horn*ᵃ* of salvation for us
>   in the house of his servant David
> ⁷⁰(as he said through his holy prophets of long ago),
> ⁷¹salvation from our enemies
>   and from the hand of all who hate us—
> ⁷²to show mercy to our fathers
>   and to remember his holy covenant,
> ⁷³   the oath he swore to our father Abraham:
> ⁷⁴to rescue us from the hand of our enemies,
>   and to enable us to serve him without fear
> ⁷⁵   in holiness and righteousness before him all our days.
>
> ⁷⁶And you, my child, will be called a prophet of the Most High;
>   for you will go on before the Lord to prepare the way for
>   him,
> ⁷⁷to give his people the knowledge of salvation
>   through the forgiveness of their sins,
> ⁷⁸because of the tender mercy of our God,
>   by which the rising sun will come to us from heaven
> ⁷⁹to shine on those living in darkness
>   and in the shadow of death,
> to guide our feet into the path of peace."

⁸⁰And the child grew and became strong in spirit; and he lived in the desert until he appeared publicly to Israel.

2 **The Birth of Jesus** In those days Caesar Augustus issued a decree that a census should be taken of the entire Roman world. ²(This was the first census that took place while Quirinius was governor of Syria.) ³And everyone went to his own town to register.

⁴So Joseph also went up from the town of Nazareth in Galilee to Judea, to Bethlehem the town of David, because he belonged to the house and line of

---

ᵃ69 Horn here symbolizes strength.

David. ⁵He went there to register with Mary, who was pledged to be married to him and was expecting a child. ⁶While they were there, the time came for the baby to be born, ⁷and she gave birth to her firstborn, a son. She wrapped him in cloths and placed him in a manger, because there was no room for them in the inn.

The Shepherds and the Angels ⁸And there were shepherds living out in the fields nearby, keeping watch over their flocks at night. ⁹An angel of the Lord appeared to them, and the glory of the Lord shone around them, and they were terrified. ¹⁰But the angel said to them, "Do not be afraid. I bring you good news of great joy that will be for all the people. ¹¹Today in the town of David a Savior has been born to you; he is Christ[a] the Lord. ¹²This will be a sign to you: You will find a baby wrapped in cloths and lying in a manger."

¹³Suddenly a great company of the heavenly host appeared with the angel, praising God and saying,

> ¹⁴"Glory to God in the highest,
>   and on earth peace to men on whom his favor rests."

¹⁵When the angels had left them and gone into heaven, the shepherds said to one another, "Let's go to Bethlehem and see this thing that has happened, which the Lord has told us about."

¹⁶So they hurried off and found Mary and Joseph, and the baby, who was lying in the manger. ¹⁷When they had seen him, they spread the word concerning what had been told them about this child, ¹⁸and all who heard it were amazed at what the shepherds said to them. ¹⁹But Mary treasured up all these things and pondered them in her heart. ²⁰The shepherds returned, glorifying and praising God for all the things they had heard and seen, which were just as they had been told.

Jesus Presented in the Temple ²¹On the eighth day, when it was time to circumcise him, he was named Jesus, the name the angel had given him before he had been conceived.

²²When the time of their purification according to the Law of Moses had been completed, Joseph and Mary took him to Jerusalem to present him to the Lord ²³(as it is written in the Law of the Lord, "Every firstborn male is to be consecrated to the Lord"[b]), ²⁴and to offer a sacrifice in keeping with what is said in the Law of the Lord: "a pair of doves or two young pigeons."[c]

²⁵Now there was a man in Jerusalem called Simeon, who was righteous and devout. He was waiting for the consolation of Israel, and the Holy Spirit was upon him. ²⁶It had been revealed to him by the Holy Spirit that he would not die before he had seen the Lord's Christ. ²⁷Moved by the Spirit, he went into the temple courts. When the parents brought in the child Jesus to do for him what the custom of the Law required, ²⁸Simeon took him in his arms and praised God, saying:

> ²⁹"Sovereign Lord, as you have promised,
>   you now dismiss[d] your servant in peace.
> ³⁰For my eyes have seen your salvation,
> ³¹   which you have prepared in the sight of all people,
> ³²a light for revelation to the Gentiles
>   and for glory to your people Israel."

³³The child's father and mother marveled at what was said about him. ³⁴Then Simeon blessed them and said to Mary, his mother: "This child is destined to cause the falling and rising of many in Israel, and to be a sign that will be spoken against, ³⁵so that the thoughts of many hearts will be revealed. And a sword will pierce your own soul too."

---

[a]*11* Or *Messiah.* "The Christ" (Greek) and "the Messiah" (Hebrew) both mean "the Anointed One"; also in verse 26. [b]*23* Exodus 13:2,12 [c]*24* Lev. 12:8 [d]*29* Or *promised, / now dismiss*

³⁶There was also a prophetess, Anna, the daughter of Phanuel, of the tribe of Asher. She was very old; she had lived with her husband seven years after her marriage, ³⁷and then was a widow until she was eighty-four.ª She never left the temple but worshiped night and day, fasting and praying. ³⁸Coming up to them at that very moment, she gave thanks to God and spoke about the child to all who were looking forward to the redemption of Jerusalem.

³⁹When Joseph and Mary had done everything required by the Law of the Lord, they returned to Galilee to their own town of Nazareth. ⁴⁰And the child grew and became strong; he was filled with wisdom, and the grace of God was upon him.

The Boy Jesus at the Temple ⁴¹Every year his parents went to Jerusalem for the Feast of the Passover. ⁴²When he was twelve years old, they went up to the Feast, according to the custom. ⁴³After the Feast was over, while his parents were returning home, the boy Jesus stayed behind in Jerusalem, but they were unaware of it. ⁴⁴Thinking he was in their company, they traveled on for a day. Then they began looking for him among their relatives and friends. ⁴⁵When they did not find him, they went back to Jerusalem to look for him. ⁴⁶After three days they found him in the temple courts, sitting among the teachers, listening to them and asking them questions. ⁴⁷Everyone who heard him was amazed at his understanding and his answers. ⁴⁸When his parents saw him, they were astonished. His mother said to him, "Son, why have you treated us like this? Your father and I have been anxiously searching for you."

⁴⁹"Why were you searching for me?" he asked. "Didn't you know I had to be in my Father's house?" ⁵⁰But they did not understand what he was saying to them.

⁵¹Then he went down to Nazareth with them and was obedient to them. But his mother treasured all these things in her heart. ⁵²And Jesus grew in wisdom and stature, and in favor with God and men.

John the Baptist Prepares the Way In the fifteenth year of the reign of Tiberius Caesar—when Pontius Pilate was governor of Judea, Herod tetrarch of Galilee, his brother Philip tetrarch of Iturea and Traconitis, and Lysanias tetrarch of Abilene— ²during the high priesthood of Annas and Caiaphas, the word of God came to John son of Zechariah in the desert. ³He went into all the country around the Jordan, preaching a baptism of repentance for the forgiveness of sins. ⁴As is written in the book of the words of Isaiah the prophet:

> "A voice of one calling in the desert,
> 'Prepare the way for the Lord,
>   make straight paths for him.
> ⁵ Every valley shall be filled in,
>   every mountain and hill made low.
> The crooked roads shall become straight,
>   the rough ways smooth.
> ⁶ And all mankind will see God's salvation.' "ᵇ

⁷John said to the crowds coming out to be baptized by him, "You brood of vipers! Who warned you to flee from the coming wrath? ⁸Produce fruit in keeping with repentance. And do not begin to say to yourselves, 'We have Abraham as our father.' For I tell you that out of these stones God can raise up children for Abraham. ⁹The ax is already at the root of the trees, and every tree that does not produce good fruit will be cut down and thrown into the fire."

ª37 Or *widow for eighty-four years* ᵇ6 Isaiah 40:3-5

¹⁰"What should we do then?" the crowd asked.

¹¹John answered, "The man with two tunics should share with him who has none, and the one who has food should do the same."

¹²Tax collectors also came to be baptized. "Teacher," they asked, "what should we do?"

¹³"Don't collect any more than you are required to," he told them.

¹⁴Then some soldiers asked him, "And what should we do?"

He replied, "Don't extort money and don't accuse people falsely—be content with your pay."

¹⁵The people were waiting expectantly and were all wondering in their hearts if John might possibly be the Christ.ᵃ ¹⁶John answered them all, "I baptize you withᵇ water. But one more powerful than I will come, the thongs of whose sandals I am not worthy to untie. He will baptize you with the Holy Spirit and with fire. ¹⁷His winnowing fork is in his hand to clear his threshing floor and to gather the wheat into his barn, but he will burn up the chaff with unquenchable fire." ¹⁸And with many other words John exhorted the people and preached the good news to them.

¹⁹But when John rebuked Herod the tetrarch because of Herodias, his brother's wife, and all the other evil things he had done, ²⁰Herod added this to them all: He locked John up in prison.

The Baptism and Genealogy of Jesus ²¹When all the people were being baptized, Jesus was baptized too. And as he was praying, heaven was opened ²²and the Holy Spirit descended on him in bodily form like a dove. And a voice came from heaven: "You are my Son, whom I love; with you I am well pleased."

²³Now Jesus himself was about thirty years old when he began his ministry. He was the son, so it was thought, of Joseph,

the son of Heli, ²⁴the son of Matthat,
the son of Levi, the son of Melki,
the son of Jannai, the son of Joseph,
²⁵the son of Mattathias, the son of Amos,
the son of Nahum, the son of Esli,
the son of Naggai, ²⁶the son of Maath,
the son of Mattathias, the son of Semein,
the son of Josech, the son of Joda,
²⁷the son of Joanan, the son of Rhesa,
the son of Zerubbabel, the son of Shealtiel,
the son of Neri, ²⁸the son of Melki,
the son of Addi, the son of Cosam,
the son of Elmadam, the son of Er,
²⁹the son of Joshua, the son of Eliezer,
the son of Jorim, the son of Matthat,
the son of Levi, ³⁰the son of Simeon,
the son of Judah, the son of Joseph,
the son of Jonam, the son of Eliakim,
³¹the son of Melea, the son of Menna,
the son of Mattatha, the son of Nathan,
the son of David, ³²the son of Jesse,
the son of Obed, the son of Boaz,
the son of Salmon,ᶜ the son of Nahshon,

LUKE 3:7–9

So you've been brought up in a Christian home. Mom and Dad take you to church every week. You pray at every meal, and Mom and Dad even talk about God around the house. That makes you a Christian. Right? Wrong. Going to church doesn't make you a Christian any more than going into a barn once a week would make you a cow. You have to be born a calf to be a cow. And you have to be born again to be a Christian. That's what John told the religious people who came to hear him. Don't talk about your parents. Only your own personal faith in Christ counts. Why not trust him now?

Direct Line

ᵃ15 Or *Messiah* ᵇ16 Or *in* ᶜ32 Some early manuscripts *Sala*

³³the son of Amminadab, the son of Ram,ᵃ
  the son of Hezron, the son of Perez,
  the son of Judah, ³⁴the son of Jacob,
  the son of Isaac, the son of Abraham,
  the son of Terah, the son of Nahor,
³⁵the son of Serug, the son of Reu,
  the son of Peleg, the son of Eber,
  the son of Shelah, ³⁶the son of Cainan,
  the son of Arphaxad, the son of Shem,
  the son of Noah, the son of Lamech,
³⁷the son of Methuselah, the son of Enoch,
  the son of Jared, the son of Mahalalel,
  the son of Kenan, ³⁸the son of Enosh,
  the son of Seth, the son of Adam,
  the son of God.

The Temptation of Jesus Jesus, full of the Holy Spirit, returned from the Jordan and was led by the Spirit in the desert, ²where for forty days he was tempted by the devil. He ate nothing during those days, and at the end of them he was hungry.

³The devil said to him, "If you are the Son of God, tell this stone to become bread."

⁴Jesus answered, "It is written: 'Man does not live on bread alone.'ᵇ"

⁵The devil led him up to a high place and showed him in an instant all the kingdoms of the world. ⁶And he said to him, "I will give you all their authority and splendor, for it has been given to me, and I can give it to anyone I want to. ⁷So if you worship me, it will all be yours."

⁸Jesus answered, "It is written: 'Worship the Lord your God and serve him only.'ᶜ"

⁹The devil led him to Jerusalem and had him stand on the highest point of the temple. "If you are the Son of God," he said, "throw yourself down from here. ¹⁰For it is written:

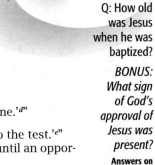

LUKE 3

QUIZZER

Q: How old was Jesus when he was baptized?

BONUS: What sign of God's approval of Jesus was present?

Answers on page 1338

" 'He will command his angels concerning you
    to guard you carefully;
¹¹they will lift you up in their hands,
    so that you will not strike your foot against a stone.'ᵈ"

¹²Jesus answered, "It says: 'Do not put the Lord your God to the test.'ᵉ"

¹³When the devil had finished all this tempting, he left him until an opportune time.

Jesus Rejected at Nazareth ¹⁴Jesus returned to Galilee in the power of the Spirit, and news about him spread through the whole countryside. ¹⁵He taught in their synagogues, and everyone praised him.

¹⁶He went to Nazareth, where he had been brought up, and on the Sabbath day he went into the synagogue, as was his custom. And he stood up to read. ¹⁷The scroll of the prophet Isaiah was handed to him. Unrolling it, he found the place where it is written:

¹⁸"The Spirit of the Lord is on me,
    because he has anointed me
    to preach good news to the poor.

ᵃ33 Some manuscripts *Amminadab, the son of Admin, the son of Arni;* other manuscripts vary widely.
ᵇ4 Deut. 8:3 ᶜ8 Deut. 6:13 ᵈ11 Psalm 91:11,12 ᵉ12 Deut. 6:16

He has sent me to proclaim freedom for the prisoners
    and recovery of sight for the blind,
to release the oppressed,
    [19] to proclaim the year of the Lord's favor."[a]

[20]Then he rolled up the scroll, gave it back to the attendant and sat down. The eyes of everyone in the synagogue were fastened on him, [21]and he began by saying to them, "Today this scripture is fulfilled in your hearing."

[22]All spoke well of him and were amazed at the gracious words that came from his lips. "Isn't this Joseph's son?" they asked.

[23]Jesus said to them, "Surely you will quote this proverb to me: 'Physician, heal yourself! Do here in your hometown what we have heard that you did in Capernaum.' "

[24]"I tell you the truth," he continued, "no prophet is accepted in his hometown. [25]I assure you that there were many widows in Israel in Elijah's time, when the sky was shut for three and a half years and there was a severe famine throughout the land. [26]Yet Elijah was not sent to any of them, but to a widow in Zarephath in the region of Sidon. [27]And there were many in Israel with leprosy[b] in the time of Elisha the prophet, yet not one of them was cleansed—only Naaman the Syrian."

[28]All the people in the synagogue were furious when they heard this. [29]They got up, drove him out of the town, and took him to the brow of the hill on which the town was built, in order to throw him down the cliff. [30]But he walked right through the crowd and went on his way.

Jesus Drives Out an Evil Spirit   [31]Then he went down to Capernaum, a town in Galilee, and on the Sabbath began to teach the people. [32]They were amazed at his teaching, because his message had authority.

[33]In the synagogue there was a man possessed by a demon, an evil[c] spirit. He cried out at the top of his voice, [34]"Ha! What do you want with us, Jesus of Nazareth? Have you come to destroy us? I know who you are—the Holy One of God!"

[35]"Be quiet!" Jesus said sternly. "Come out of him!" Then the demon threw the man down before them all and came out without injuring him.

[36]All the people were amazed and said to each other, "What is this teaching? With authority and power he gives orders to evil spirits and they come out!" [37]And the news about him spread throughout the surrounding area.

Jesus Heals Many   [38]Jesus left the synagogue and went to the home of Simon. Now Simon's mother-in-law was suffering from a high fever, and they asked Jesus to help her. [39]So he bent over her and rebuked the fever, and it left her. She got up at once and began to wait on them.

[40]When the sun was setting, the people brought to Jesus all who had various kinds of sickness, and laying his hands on each one, he healed them. [41]Moreover, demons came out of many people, shouting, "You are the Son of God!" But he rebuked them and would not allow them to speak, because they knew he was the Christ.[d]

[42]At daybreak Jesus went out to a solitary place. The people were looking for him and when they came to where he was, they tried to keep him from leaving them. [43]But he said, "I must preach the good news of the kingdom of God to the other towns also, because that is why I was sent." [44]And he kept on preaching in the synagogues of Judea.[e]

A**nswers**
to Quizzer on
page 1337

A: About 30 years old (Luke 3:23).

BONUS: A dove came and rested on Jesus, and a voice came from heaven and said God was pleased with Jesus his Son (Luke 3:22).

[a]19 Isaiah 61:1,2 [b]27 The Greek word was used for various diseases affecting the skin—not necessarily leprosy. [c]33 Greek *unclean*; also in verse 36 [d]41 Or *Messiah* [e]44 Or *the land of the Jews*; some manuscripts *Galilee*

5 *The Calling of the First Disciples* One day as Jesus was standing by the Lake of Gennesaret,*ᵃ* with the people crowding around him and listening to the word of God, ²he saw at the water's edge two boats, left there by the fishermen, who were washing their nets. ³He got into one of the boats, the one belonging to Simon, and asked him to put out a little from shore. Then he sat down and taught the people from the boat.

⁴When he had finished speaking, he said to Simon, "Put out into deep water, and let down*ᵇ* the nets for a catch."

⁵Simon answered, "Master, we've worked hard all night and haven't caught anything. But because you say so, I will let down the nets."

⁶When they had done so, they caught such a large number of fish that their nets began to break. ⁷So they signaled their partners in the other boat to come and help them, and they came and filled both boats so full that they began to sink.

⁸When Simon Peter saw this, he fell at Jesus' knees and said, "Go away from me, Lord; I am a sinful man!" ⁹For he and all his companions were astonished at the catch of fish they had taken, ¹⁰and so were James and John, the sons of Zebedee, Simon's partners.

Then Jesus said to Simon, "Don't be afraid; from now on you will catch men." ¹¹So they pulled their boats up on shore, left everything and followed him.

The Man With Leprosy ¹²While Jesus was in one of the towns, a man came along who was covered with leprosy.*ᶜ* When he saw Jesus, he fell with his face to the ground and begged him, "Lord, if you are willing, you can make me clean."

¹³Jesus reached out his hand and touched the man. "I am willing," he said. "Be clean!" And immediately the leprosy left him.

¹⁴Then Jesus ordered him, "Don't tell anyone, but go, show yourself to the priest and offer the sacrifices that Moses commanded for your cleansing, as a testimony to them."

¹⁵Yet the news about him spread all the more, so that crowds of people came to hear him and to be healed of their sicknesses. ¹⁶But Jesus often withdrew to lonely places and prayed.

Jesus Heals a Paralytic ¹⁷One day as he was teaching, Pharisees and teachers of the law, who had come from every village of Galilee and from Judea and Jerusalem, were sitting there. And the power of the Lord was present for him to heal the sick. ¹⁸Some men came carrying a paralytic on a mat and tried to take him into the house to lay him before Jesus. ¹⁹When they could not find a way to do this because of the crowd, they went up on the roof and lowered him on his mat through the tiles into the middle of the crowd, right in front of Jesus.

²⁰When Jesus saw their faith, he said, "Friend, your sins are forgiven."

²¹The Pharisees and the teachers of the

ᵃ1 That is, Sea of Galilee   ᵇ4 The Greek verb is plural.
ᶜ12 The Greek word was used for various diseases affecting the skin—not necessarily leprosy.

LUKE 5:1–11

You've probably heard all the stories about Jesus' miracles and his kindness to hurting people. That's good, but that isn't all, nor is it enough. The first time Peter met Jesus, he not only realized he was special but that he was powerful. After not catching any fish all night, at Jesus' command Peter and his friends filled their boats with a huge catch. The Bible says Peter was "astonished" (Luke 5:9). So much so that he fell on his knees and called Jesus "Lord!" That's something each person needs to experience. You have to go from knowing that Jesus is someone special, to "Lord," confessing Jesus to be God.

Direct Line

law began thinking to themselves, "Who is this fellow who speaks blasphemy? Who can forgive sins but God alone?"

²²Jesus knew what they were thinking and asked, "Why are you thinking these things in your hearts? ²³Which is easier: to say, 'Your sins are forgiven,' or to say, 'Get up and walk'? ²⁴But that you may know that the Son of Man has authority on earth to forgive sins . . ." He said to the paralyzed man, "I tell you, get up, take your mat and go home." ²⁵Immediately he stood up in front of them, took what he had been lying on and went home praising God. ²⁶Everyone was amazed and gave praise to God. They were filled with awe and said, "We have seen remarkable things today."

The Calling of Levi   ²⁷After this, Jesus went out and saw a tax collector by the name of Levi sitting at his tax booth. "Follow me," Jesus said to him, ²⁸and Levi got up, left everything and followed him.

²⁹Then Levi held a great banquet for Jesus at his house, and a large crowd of tax collectors and others were eating with them. ³⁰But the Pharisees and the teachers of the law who belonged to their sect complained to his disciples, "Why do you eat and drink with tax collectors and 'sinners'?"

³¹Jesus answered them, "It is not the healthy who need a doctor, but the sick. ³²I have not come to call the righteous, but sinners to repentance."

Jesus Questioned About Fasting   ³³They said to him, "John's disciples often fast and pray, and so do the disciples of the Pharisees, but yours go on eating and drinking."

³⁴Jesus answered, "Can you make the guests of the bridegroom fast while he is with them? ³⁵But the time will come when the bridegroom will be taken from them; in those days they will fast."

³⁶He told them this parable: "No one tears a patch from a new garment and sews it on an old one. If he does, he will have torn the new garment, and the patch from the new will not match the old. ³⁷And no one pours new wine into old wineskins. If he does, the new wine will burst the skins, the wine will run out and the wineskins will be ruined. ³⁸No, new wine must be poured into new wineskins. ³⁹And no one after drinking old wine wants the new, for he says, 'The old is better.' "

Lord of the Sabbath   One Sabbath Jesus was going through the grainfields, and his disciples began to pick some heads of grain, rub them in their hands and eat the kernels. ²Some of the Pharisees asked, "Why are you doing what is unlawful on the Sabbath?"

³Jesus answered them, "Have you never read what David did when he and his companions were hungry? ⁴He entered the house of God, and taking the consecrated bread, he ate what is lawful only for priests to eat. And he also gave some to his companions." ⁵Then Jesus said to them, "The Son of Man is Lord of the Sabbath."

⁶On another Sabbath he went into the synagogue and was teaching, and a man was there whose right hand was shriveled. ⁷The Pharisees and the teachers of the law were looking for a reason to accuse Jesus, so they watched him closely to see if he would heal on the Sabbath. ⁸But Jesus knew what they were thinking and said to the man with the shriveled hand, "Get up and stand in front of everyone." So he got up and stood there.

⁹Then Jesus said to them, "I ask you, which is lawful on the Sabbath: to do good or to do evil, to save life or to destroy it?"

¹⁰He looked around at them all, and then said to the man, "Stretch out your hand." He did so, and his hand was completely restored. ¹¹But they were furious and began to discuss with one another what they might do to Jesus.

The Twelve Apostles   ¹²One of those days Jesus went out to a mountainside to pray, and spent the night praying to God. ¹³When morning came, he called his disciples to him and chose twelve of them, whom he also designated apostles: ¹⁴Simon (whom he named Peter), his brother Andrew, James, John, Philip, Bartholomew, ¹⁵Matthew, Thomas, James son of Alphaeus, Simon who was called the Zealot, ¹⁶Judas son of James, and Judas Iscariot, who became a traitor.

Blessings and Woes ¹⁷He went down with them and stood on a level place. A large crowd of his disciples was there and a great number of people from all over Judea, from Jerusalem, and from the coast of Tyre and Sidon, ¹⁸who had come to hear him and to be healed of their diseases. Those troubled by evil*ᵃ* spirits were cured, ¹⁹and the people all tried to touch him, because power was coming from him and healing them all.

²⁰Looking at his disciples, he said:

"Blessed are you who are poor,
for yours is the kingdom of God.
²¹ Blessed are you who hunger now,
for you will be satisfied.
Blessed are you who weep now,
for you will laugh.
²² Blessed are you when men hate you,
when they exclude you and insult you
and reject your name as evil,
because of the Son of Man.

²³"Rejoice in that day and leap for joy, because great is your reward in heaven. For that is how their fathers treated the prophets.

²⁴ "But woe to you who are rich,
for you have already received your comfort.
²⁵ Woe to you who are well fed now,
for you will go hungry.
Woe to you who laugh now,
for you will mourn and weep.
²⁶ Woe to you when all men speak well of you,
for that is how their fathers treated the false prophets.

Love for Enemies ²⁷"But I tell you who hear me: Love your enemies, do good to those who hate you, ²⁸bless those who curse you, pray for those who mistreat you. ²⁹If someone strikes you on one cheek, turn to him the other also. If someone takes your cloak, do not stop him from taking your tunic. ³⁰Give to everyone who asks you, and if anyone takes what belongs to you, do not demand it back. ³¹Do to others as you would have them do to you.

³²"If you love those who love you, what credit is that to you? Even 'sinners' love those who love them. ³³And if you do good to those who are good to you, what credit is that to you? Even 'sinners' do that. ³⁴And if you lend to those from whom you expect repayment, what credit is that to you? Even 'sinners' lend to 'sinners,' expecting to be repaid in full. ³⁵But love your enemies, do good to them, and lend to them without expecting to get anything back. Then your reward will be great, and you will be sons of the Most High, because he is kind to the ungrateful and wicked. ³⁶Be merciful, just as your Father is merciful.

Judging Others ³⁷"Do not judge, and you will not be judged. Do not condemn, and you will not be condemned. Forgive, and you will be forgiven. ³⁸Give, and it will be given to you. A good measure, pressed down, shaken together and running over, will be poured into your lap. For with the measure you use, it will be measured to you."

ᵃ18 Greek unclean

Dear Sam,

How can I keep from killing my brother and sister? We're always having huge fights. I hate them most of the time!

Seth in South Bend

100 Advice Lane, Anywhere, USA

Dear Seth,

You probably won't like my answer, but don't put on your gloves and come looking for me! From your letter it's hard to tell what exactly is happening. If there is constant violence and hostility in your home, perhaps your parents should consider some family meetings to talk things over. If things are too out of control, professional counseling may be needed. Maybe you could be the one to suggest to your family that things are getting out of control and something needs to be done.

In the meantime, remember the words of Jesus, "But I tell you who hear me: Love your enemies, do good to those who hate you, bless those who curse you, pray for those who mistreat you . . . Do to others as you would have them do to you" (Luke 6:27-28,31). Someone has to break the pattern of anger and getting even. You're elected!

Sam

[39]He also told them this parable: "Can a blind man lead a blind man? Will they not both fall into a pit? [40]A student is not above his teacher, but everyone who is fully trained will be like his teacher.

[41]"Why do you look at the speck of sawdust in your brother's eye and pay no attention to the plank in your own eye? [42]How can you say to your brother, 'Brother, let me take the speck out of your eye,' when you yourself fail to see the plank in your own eye? You hypocrite, first take the plank out of your eye, and then you will see clearly to remove the speck from your brother's eye.

A Tree and Its Fruit   [43]"No good tree bears bad fruit, nor does a bad tree bear good fruit. [44]Each tree is recognized by its own fruit. People do not pick figs from thornbushes, or grapes from briers. [45]The good man brings good things out of the good stored up in his heart, and the evil man brings evil things out of the evil stored up in his heart. For out of the overflow of his heart his mouth speaks.

The Wise and Foolish Builders   [46]"Why do you call me, 'Lord, Lord,' and do not do what I say? [47]I will show you what he is like who comes to me and hears my words and puts them into practice. [48]He is like a man building a house, who dug down deep and laid the foundation on rock. When a flood came, the torrent struck that house but could not shake it, because it was well built. [49]But the one who hears my words and does not put them into practice is like a man who built a house on the ground without a foundation. The moment the torrent struck that house, it collapsed and its destruction was complete."

The Faith of the Centurion   When Jesus had finished saying all this in the hearing of the people, he entered Capernaum. [2]There a centurion's servant, whom his master valued highly, was sick and about to die. [3]The centurion heard of Jesus and sent some elders of the Jews to him, asking him to come and heal his servant. [4]When they came to Jesus, they pleaded earnestly with him, "This man deserves to have you do this, [5]because he loves our nation and has built our synagogue." [6]So Jesus went with them.

He was not far from the house when the centurion sent friends to say to him: "Lord, don't trouble yourself, for I do not deserve to have you come under my roof. [7]That is why I did not even consider myself worthy to come to you. But say the word, and my servant will be healed. [8]For I myself am a

Some people are uncomfortable at the thought that God is everywhere. It means he sees everything they do! Certainly that's what the Bible says.

* God "observes the sons of men" (Psalm 11:4).
* "The eyes of the Lord are on the righteous" (Psalm 34:15).
* You can never run from God. He is everywhere (Psalm 139:7–8).

Of course, knowing God is everywhere doesn't make you uncomfortable unless you're making bad choices. In Luke 7:1–10 a Roman soldier asked Jesus to heal his servant. The soldier didn't insist Jesus go where the servant was. He just said, "Say the word, and my servant will be healed."

God can see you! He's right here with you—and he'll help you any time you ask.

The
Bible
Says

God Sees You!

man under authority, with soldiers under me. I tell this one, 'Go,' and he goes; and that one, 'Come,' and he comes. I say to my servant, 'Do this,' and he does it."

⁹When Jesus heard this, he was amazed at him, and turning to the crowd following him, he said, "I tell you, I have not found such great faith even in Israel." ¹⁰Then the men who had been sent returned to the house and found the servant well.

Jesus Raises a Widow's Son   ¹¹Soon afterward, Jesus went to a town called Nain, and his disciples and a large crowd went along with him. ¹²As he approached the town gate, a dead person was being carried out—the only son of his mother, and she was a widow. And a large crowd from the town was with her. ¹³When the Lord saw her, his heart went out to her and he said, "Don't cry."

¹⁴Then he went up and touched the coffin, and those carrying it stood still. He said, "Young man, I say to you, get up!" ¹⁵The dead man sat up and began to talk, and Jesus gave him back to his mother.

¹⁶They were all filled with awe and praised God. "A great prophet has appeared among us," they said. "God has come to help his people." ¹⁷This news about Jesus spread throughout Judea*a* and the surrounding country.

Jesus and John the Baptist   ¹⁸John's disciples told him about all these things. Calling two of them, ¹⁹he sent them to the Lord to ask, "Are you the one who was to come, or should we expect someone else?"

²⁰When the men came to Jesus, they said, "John the Baptist sent us to you to ask, 'Are you the one who was to come, or should we expect someone else?'"

²¹At that very time Jesus cured many who had diseases, sicknesses and evil spirits, and gave sight to many who were blind. ²²So he replied to the messengers, "Go back and report to John what you have seen and heard: The blind receive sight, the lame walk, those who have leprosy*b* are cured, the deaf hear, the dead are raised, and the good news is preached to the poor. ²³Blessed is the man who does not fall away on account of me."

²⁴After John's messengers left, Jesus began to speak to the crowd about John: "What did you go out into the desert to see? A reed swayed by the wind? ²⁵If not, what did you go out to see? A man dressed in fine clothes? No, those who wear expensive clothes and indulge in luxury are in palaces. ²⁶But what did you go out to see? A prophet? Yes, I tell you, and more than a prophet. ²⁷This is the one about whom it is written:

> " 'I will send my messenger ahead of you,
>   who will prepare your way before you.'*c*

²⁸I tell you, among those born of women there is no one greater than John; yet the one who is least in the kingdom of God is greater than he."

²⁹(All the people, even the tax collectors, when they heard Jesus' words, acknowledged that God's way was right, because they had been baptized by John. ³⁰But the Pharisees and experts in the law rejected God's purpose for themselves, because they had not been baptized by John.)

³¹"To what, then, can I compare the people of this generation? What are they like? ³²They are like children sitting in the marketplace and calling out to each other:

> " 'We played the flute for you,
>   and you did not dance;
>   we sang a dirge,
>   and you did not cry.'

---

a17 Or *the land of the Jews*   *b22* The Greek word was used for various diseases affecting the skin—not necessarily leprosy.   *c27* Mal. 3:1

33For John the Baptist came neither eating bread nor drinking wine, and you say, 'He has a demon.' 34The Son of Man came eating and drinking, and you say, 'Here is a glutton and a drunkard, a friend of tax collectors and "sinners." ' 35But wisdom is proved right by all her children."

Jesus Anointed by a Sinful Woman 36Now one of the Pharisees invited Jesus to have dinner with him, so he went to the Pharisee's house and reclined at the table. 37When a woman who had lived a sinful life in that town learned that Jesus was eating at the Pharisee's house, she brought an alabaster jar of perfume, 38and as she stood behind him at his feet weeping, she began to wet his feet with her tears. Then she wiped them with her hair, kissed them and poured perfume on them.

39When the Pharisee who had invited him saw this, he said to himself, "If this man were a prophet, he would know who is touching him and what kind of woman she is—that she is a sinner."

40Jesus answered him, "Simon, I have something to tell you."

"Tell me, teacher," he said.

41"Two men owed money to a certain moneylender. One owed him five hundred denarii,*a* and the other fifty. 42Neither of them had the money to pay him back, so he canceled the debts of both. Now which of them will love him more?"

43Simon replied, "I suppose the one who had the bigger debt canceled."

"You have judged correctly," Jesus said.

44Then he turned toward the woman and said to Simon, "Do you see this woman? I came into your house. You did not give me any water for my feet, but she wet my feet with her tears and wiped them with her hair. 45You did not give me a kiss, but this woman, from the time I entered, has not stopped kissing my feet. 46You did not put oil on my head, but she has poured perfume on my feet. 47Therefore, I tell you, her many sins have been forgiven— for she loved much. But he who has been forgiven little loves little."

48Then Jesus said to her, "Your sins are forgiven."

49The other guests began to say among themselves, "Who is this who even forgives sins?"

50Jesus said to the woman, "Your faith has saved you; go in peace."

The Parable of the Sower After this, Jesus traveled about from one town and village to another, proclaiming the good news of the kingdom of God. The Twelve were with him, 2and also some women who had been cured of evil spirits and diseases: Mary (called Magdalene) from whom seven demons had come out; 3Joanna the wife of Cuza, the manager of Herod's household; Susanna; and many others. These women were helping to support them out of their own means.

4While a large crowd was gathering and people were coming to Jesus from town after town, he told this parable: 5"A farmer went out to sow his seed. As he was scattering the seed, some fell along the path; it was trampled on, and the birds of

a41 A denarius was a coin worth about a day's wages.

LUKE 7:36–50

Can you think of anyone—some "bad" person—you'd be shocked to see with someone from your church youth group? Someone who would make you say, "I never thought I'd see Jim with her." Then you understand why the Pharisee was so shocked when a known prostitute slipped into his house and wept at Jesus' feet. It's hard. You're told to keep away from the wrong kind of people. But you're also told to love everyone and witness for Jesus. How can you do both? Begin by praying every day for at least one of those "bad" teenagers. Then if God opens up the door to be a friend to him or her, give it a try.

Direct Line

the air ate it up. ⁶Some fell on rock, and when it came up, the plants withered because they had no moisture. ⁷Other seed fell among thorns, which grew up with it and choked the plants. ⁸Still other seed fell on good soil. It came up and yielded a crop, a hundred times more than was sown."

When he said this, he called out, "He who has ears to hear, let him hear."

⁹His disciples asked him what this parable meant. ¹⁰He said, "The knowledge of the secrets of the kingdom of God has been given to you, but to others I speak in parables, so that,

"'though seeing, they may not see;
though hearing, they may not understand.'ᵃ

¹¹"This is the meaning of the parable: The seed is the word of God. ¹²Those along the path are the ones who hear, and then the devil comes and takes away the word from their hearts, so that they may not believe and be saved. ¹³Those on the rock are the ones who receive the word with joy when they hear it, but they have no root. They believe for a while, but in the time of testing they fall away. ¹⁴The seed that fell among thorns stands for those who hear, but as they go on their way they are choked by life's worries, riches and pleasures, and they do not mature. ¹⁵But the seed on good soil stands for those with a noble and good heart, who hear the word, retain it, and by persevering produce a crop.

A Lamp on a Stand ¹⁶"No one lights a lamp and hides it in a jar or puts it under a bed. Instead, he puts it on a stand, so that those who come in can see the light. ¹⁷For there is nothing hidden that will not be disclosed, and nothing concealed that will not be known or brought out into the open. ¹⁸Therefore consider carefully how you listen. Whoever has will be given more; whoever does not have, even what he thinks he has will be taken from him."

Jesus' Mother and Brothers ¹⁹Now Jesus' mother and brothers came to see him, but they were not able to get near him because of the crowd. ²⁰Someone told him, "Your mother and brothers are standing outside, wanting to see you."

²¹He replied, "My mother and brothers are those who hear God's word and put it into practice."

Jesus Calms the Storm ²²One day Jesus said to his disciples, "Let's go over to the other side of the lake." So they got into a boat and set out. ²³As they sailed, he fell asleep. A squall came down on the lake, so that the boat was being swamped, and they were in great danger.

²⁴The disciples went and woke him, saying, "Master, Master, we're going to drown!"

He got up and rebuked the wind and the raging waters; the storm subsided, and all was calm. ²⁵"Where is your faith?" he asked his disciples.

In fear and amazement they asked one another, "Who is this? He commands even the winds and the water, and they obey him."

The Healing of a Demon-possessed Man ²⁶They sailed to the region of the Gerasenes,ᵇ which is across the lake from Galilee. ²⁷When Jesus stepped ashore, he was met by a demon-possessed man from the town. For a long time this man had not worn clothes or lived in a house, but had lived in the tombs. ²⁸When he saw Jesus, he cried out and fell at his feet, shouting at the top of his voice, "What do you want with me, Jesus, Son of the Most High God? I beg you, don't torture me!" ²⁹For Jesus had commanded the evilᶜ spirit to come out of the man. Many times it had seized him, and though he was

---

ᵃ*10* Isaiah 6:9 ᵇ*26* Some manuscripts *Gadarenes*; other manuscripts *Gergesenes*; also in verse 37
ᶜ*29* Greek *unclean*

chained hand and foot and kept under guard, he had broken his chains and had been driven by the demon into solitary places.

³⁰Jesus asked him, "What is your name?"

"Legion," he replied, because many demons had gone into him. ³¹And they begged him repeatedly not to order them to go into the Abyss.

³²A large herd of pigs was feeding there on the hillside. The demons begged Jesus to let them go into them, and he gave them permission. ³³When the demons came out of the man, they went into the pigs, and the herd rushed down the steep bank into the lake and was drowned.

³⁴When those tending the pigs saw what had happened, they ran off and reported this in the town and countryside, ³⁵and the people went out to see what had happened. When they came to Jesus, they found the man from whom the demons had gone out, sitting at Jesus' feet, dressed and in his right mind; and they were afraid. ³⁶Those who had seen it told the people how the demon-possessed man had been cured. ³⁷Then all the people of the region of the Gerasenes asked Jesus to leave them, because they were overcome with fear. So he got into the boat and left.

³⁸The man from whom the demons had gone out begged to go with him, but Jesus sent him away, saying, ³⁹"Return home and tell how much God has done for you." So the man went away and told all over town how much Jesus had done for him.

A Dead Girl and a Sick Woman   ⁴⁰Now when Jesus returned, a crowd welcomed him, for they were all expecting him. ⁴¹Then a man named Jairus, a ruler of the synagogue, came and fell at Jesus' feet, pleading with him to come to his house ⁴²because his only daughter, a girl of about twelve, was dying.

As Jesus was on his way, the crowds almost crushed him. ⁴³And a woman was there who had been subject to bleeding for twelve years,ᵃ but no one could heal her. ⁴⁴She came up behind him and touched the edge of his cloak, and immediately her bleeding stopped.

⁴⁵"Who touched me?" Jesus asked.

When they all denied it, Peter said, "Master, the people are crowding and pressing against you."

⁴⁶But Jesus said, "Someone touched me; I know that power has gone out from me."

⁴⁷Then the woman, seeing that she could not go unnoticed, came trembling and fell at his feet. In the presence of all the people, she told why she had touched him and how she had been instantly healed. ⁴⁸Then he said to her, "Daughter, your faith has healed you. Go in peace."

⁴⁹While Jesus was still speaking, someone came from the house of Jairus, the synagogue ruler. "Your daughter is dead," he said. "Don't bother the teacher any more."

⁵⁰Hearing this, Jesus said to Jairus, "Don't be afraid; just believe, and she will be healed."

⁵¹When he arrived at the house of Jairus, he did not let anyone go in with him except Peter, John and James, and the child's father and mother. ⁵²Meanwhile, all the people were wailing and mourning for her. "Stop wailing," Jesus said. "She is not dead but asleep."

⁵³They laughed at him, knowing that she was dead. ⁵⁴But he took her by the hand and said, "My child, get up!" ⁵⁵Her spirit returned, and at once she stood up. Then Jesus told them to give her something to eat. ⁵⁶Her parents were astonished, but he ordered them not to tell anyone what had happened.

ᵃ43 Many manuscripts *years, and she had spent all she had on doctors*

9 *Jesus Sends Out the Twelve* When Jesus had called the Twelve together, he gave them power and authority to drive out all demons and
to cure diseases, ²and he sent them out to preach the kingdom of God and
to heal the sick. ³He told them: "Take nothing for the journey—no staff, no
bag, no bread, no money, no extra tunic. ⁴Whatever house you enter, stay
there until you leave that town. ⁵If people do not welcome you, shake the
dust off your feet when you leave their town, as a testimony against them."
⁶So they set out and went from village to village, preaching the gospel and
healing people everywhere.

⁷Now Herod the tetrarch heard about all that was going on. And he was
perplexed, because some were saying that John had been raised from the
dead, ⁸others that Elijah had appeared, and still others that one of the prophets of long ago had come back to life. ⁹But Herod said, "I beheaded John.
Who, then, is this I hear such things about?" And he tried to see him.

Jesus Feeds the Five Thousand ¹⁰When the apostles returned, they reported
to Jesus what they had done. Then he took them with him and they withdrew
by themselves to a town called Bethsaida, ¹¹but the crowds learned about it
and followed him. He welcomed them and spoke to them about the kingdom
of God, and healed those who needed healing.

¹²Late in the afternoon the Twelve came to him and said, "Send the crowd
away so they can go to the surrounding villages and countryside and find
food and lodging, because we are in a remote place here."

¹³He replied, "You give them something to eat."

They answered, "We have only five loaves of bread and two fish—unless
we go and buy food for all this crowd." ¹⁴(About five thousand men were
there.)

But he said to his disciples, "Have them sit down in groups of about fifty
each." ¹⁵The disciples did so, and everybody sat down. ¹⁶Taking the five
loaves and the two fish and looking up to heaven, he gave thanks and broke
them. Then he gave them to the disciples to set before the people. ¹⁷They all
ate and were satisfied, and the disciples picked up twelve basketfuls of
broken pieces that were left over.

Peter's Confession of Christ ¹⁸Once when Jesus was praying in private and
his disciples were with him, he asked them, "Who do the crowds say I am?"

¹⁹They replied, "Some say John the Baptist; others say Elijah; and still others, that one of the prophets of long ago has come back to life."

²⁰"But what about you?" he asked. "Who do you say I am?"

Peter answered, "The Christᵃ of God."

²¹Jesus strictly warned them not to tell this to anyone. ²²And he said, "The
Son of Man must suffer many things and be rejected by the elders, chief
priests and teachers of the law, and he must be killed and on the third day
be raised to life."

²³Then he said to them all: "If anyone would come after me, he must deny
himself and take up his cross daily and follow me. ²⁴For whoever wants to
save his life will lose it, but whoever loses his life for me will save it. ²⁵What
good is it for a man to gain the whole world, and yet lose or forfeit his very
self? ²⁶If anyone is ashamed of me and my words, the Son of Man will be
ashamed of him when he comes in his glory and in the glory of the Father
and of the holy angels. ²⁷I tell you the truth, some who are standing here will
not taste death before they see the kingdom of God."

The Transfiguration ²⁸About eight days after Jesus said this, he took Peter,
John and James with him and went up onto a mountain to pray. ²⁹As he was
praying, the appearance of his face changed, and his clothes became as

ᵃ*20 Or Messiah*

bright as a flash of lightning. ³⁰Two men, Moses and Elijah, ³¹appeared in glorious splendor, talking with Jesus. They spoke about his departure, which he was about to bring to fulfillment at Jerusalem. ³²Peter and his companions were very sleepy, but when they became fully awake, they saw his glory and the two men standing with him. ³³As the men were leaving Jesus, Peter said to him, "Master, it is good for us to be here. Let us put up three shelters—one for you, one for Moses and one for Elijah." (He did not know what he was saying.)

³⁴While he was speaking, a cloud appeared and enveloped them, and they were afraid as they entered the cloud. ³⁵A voice came from the cloud, saying, "This is my Son, whom I have chosen; listen to him." ³⁶When the voice had spoken, they found that Jesus was alone. The disciples kept this to themselves, and told no one at that time what they had seen.

The Healing of a Boy With an Evil Spirit   ³⁷The next day, when they came down from the mountain, a large crowd met him. ³⁸A man in the crowd called out, "Teacher, I beg you to look at my son, for he is my only child. ³⁹A spirit seizes him and he suddenly screams; it throws him into convulsions so that he foams at the mouth. It scarcely ever leaves him and is destroying him. ⁴⁰I begged your disciples to drive it out, but they could not."

⁴¹"O unbelieving and perverse generation," Jesus replied, "how long shall I stay with you and put up with you? Bring your son here."

⁴²Even while the boy was coming, the demon threw him to the ground in a convulsion. But Jesus rebuked the evil*ᵃ* spirit, healed the boy and gave him back to his father. ⁴³And they were all amazed at the greatness of God.

While everyone was marveling at all that Jesus did, he said to his disciples, ⁴⁴"Listen carefully to what I am about to tell you: The Son of Man is going to be betrayed into the hands of men." ⁴⁵But they did not understand what this meant. It was hidden from them, so that they did not grasp it, and they were afraid to ask him about it.

Who Will Be the Greatest?   ⁴⁶An argument started among the disciples as to which of them would be the greatest. ⁴⁷Jesus, knowing their thoughts, took a little child and had him stand beside him. ⁴⁸Then he said to them, "Whoever welcomes this little child in my name welcomes me; and whoever welcomes me welcomes the one who sent me. For he who is least among you all—he is the greatest."

⁴⁹"Master," said John, "we saw a man driving out demons in your name and we tried to stop him, because he is not one of us."

⁵⁰"Do not stop him," Jesus said, "for whoever is not against you is for you."

Samaritan Opposition   ⁵¹As the time approached for him to be taken up to heaven, Jesus resolutely set out for Jerusalem. ⁵²And he sent messengers on ahead, who went into a Samaritan village to get things ready for him; ⁵³but the people there did not welcome him, because he

What are these guys arguing about? I thought everyone knew Jesus is the greatest.

SEE LUKE 9:46

was heading for Jerusalem. ⁵⁴When the disciples James and John saw this, they asked, "Lord, do you want us to call fire down from heaven to destroy them*?" ⁵⁵But Jesus turned and rebuked them, ⁵⁶and* they went to another village.

The Cost of Following Jesus

⁵⁷As they were walking along the road, a man said to him, "I will follow you wherever you go."

⁵⁸Jesus replied, "Foxes have holes and birds of the air have nests, but the Son of Man has no place to lay his head."

⁵⁹He said to another man, "Follow me."

But the man replied, "Lord, first let me go and bury my father."

⁶⁰Jesus said to him, "Let the dead bury their own dead, but you go and proclaim the kingdom of God."

⁶¹Still another said, "I will follow you, Lord; but first let me go back and say good-by to my family."

⁶²Jesus replied, "No one who puts his hand to the plow and looks back is fit for service in the kingdom of God."

Jesus Sends Out the Seventy-two

After this the Lord appointed seventy-two* others and sent them two by two ahead of him to every town and place where he was about to go. ²He told them, "The harvest is plentiful, but the workers are few. Ask the Lord of the harvest, therefore, to send out workers into his harvest field. ³Go! I am sending you out like lambs among wolves. ⁴Do not take a purse or bag or sandals; and do not greet anyone on the road.

⁵"When you enter a house, first say, 'Peace to this house.' ⁶If a man of peace is there, your peace will rest on him; if not, it will return to you. ⁷Stay in that house, eating and drinking whatever they give you, for the worker deserves his wages. Do not move around from house to house.

⁸"When you enter a town and are welcomed, eat what is set before you. ⁹Heal the sick who are there and tell them, 'The kingdom of God is near you.' ¹⁰But when you enter a town and are not welcomed, go into its streets and say, ¹¹'Even the dust of your town that sticks to our feet we wipe off against you. Yet be sure of this: The kingdom of God is near.' ¹²I tell you, it will be more bearable on that day for Sodom than for that town.

¹³"Woe to you, Korazin! Woe to you, Bethsaida! For if the miracles that were performed in you had been performed in Tyre and Sidon, they would have repented long ago, sitting in sackcloth and ashes. ¹⁴But it will be more bearable for Tyre and Sidon at the judgment than for you. ¹⁵And you, Capernaum, will you be lifted up to the skies? No, you will go down to the depths.*

¹⁶"He who listens to you listens to me; he who rejects you rejects me; but he who rejects me rejects him who sent me."

¹⁷The seventy-two returned with joy and said, "Lord, even the demons submit to us in your name."

¹⁸He replied, "I saw Satan fall like lightning from heaven. ¹⁹I have given you authority to trample on snakes and scorpions and to overcome all the power of the enemy; nothing will harm you. ²⁰However, do not rejoice that the spirits submit to you, but rejoice that your names are written in heaven."

²¹At that time Jesus, full of joy through the Holy Spirit, said, "I praise you, Father, Lord of heaven and earth, because you have hidden these things from the wise and learned, and revealed them to little children. Yes, Father, for this was your good pleasure.

²²"All things have been committed to me by my Father. No one knows who

*54 Some manuscripts them, even as Elijah did *55,56 Some manuscripts them. And he said, "You do not know what kind of spirit you are of, for the Son of Man did not come to destroy men's lives, but to save them." *56And *1 Some manuscripts seventy; also in verse 17 *15 Greek Hades

the Son is except the Father, and no one knows who the Father is except the Son and those to whom the Son chooses to reveal him."

²³Then he turned to his disciples and said privately, "Blessed are the eyes that see what you see. ²⁴For I tell you that many prophets and kings wanted to see what you see but did not see it, and to hear what you hear but did not hear it."

The Parable of the Good Samaritan ²⁵On one occasion an expert in the law stood up to test Jesus. "Teacher," he asked, "what must I do to inherit eternal life?"

²⁶"What is written in the Law?" he replied. "How do you read it?"

²⁷He answered: " 'Love the Lord your God with all your heart and with all your soul and with all your strength and with all your mind'*ᵃ*; and, 'Love your neighbor as yourself.'*ᵇ*"

²⁸"You have answered correctly," Jesus replied. "Do this and you will live."

²⁹But he wanted to justify himself, so he asked Jesus, "And who is my neighbor?"

³⁰In reply Jesus said: "A man was going down from Jerusalem to Jericho, when he fell into the hands of robbers. They stripped him of his clothes, beat him and went away, leaving him half dead. ³¹A priest happened to be going down the same road, and when he saw the man, he passed by on the other side. ³²So too, a Levite, when he came to the place and saw him, passed by on the other side. ³³But a Samaritan, as he traveled, came where the man was; and when he saw him, he took pity on him. ³⁴He went to him and bandaged his wounds, pouring on oil and wine. Then he put the man on his own donkey, took him to an inn and took care of him. ³⁵The next day he took out two silver coins*ᶜ* and gave them to the innkeeper. 'Look after him,' he said, 'and when I return, I will reimburse you for any extra expense you may have.'

³⁶"Which of these three do you think was a neighbor to the man who fell into the hands of robbers?"

³⁷The expert in the law replied, "The one who had mercy on him."

Jesus told him, "Go and do likewise."

At the Home of Martha and Mary ³⁸As Jesus and his disciples were on their way, he came to a village where a woman named Martha opened her home to him. ³⁹She had a sister called Mary, who sat at the Lord's feet listening to what he said. ⁴⁰But Martha was distracted by all the preparations that had to

ᵃ27 Deut. 6:5   *ᵇ27* Lev. 19:18   *ᶜ35* Greek *two denarii*

The story of the Good Samaritan (Luke 10:25–37) teaches that being a neighbor is more than being friendly or being nice. Being a neighbor means being sensitive to others' problems and being willing to help. Anyone who passes by a person in need is not being a neighbor. You may not feel safe stopping on a lonely highway to help change a tire. But you surely can go to a phone and let the police know there's someone who needs help.

It's even more personal with friends. Do you know anyone who is hurting or has problems? Then right now that person is your neighbor. You can be a Good Samaritan to him or her, as you "love your neighbor as yourself" (Leviticus 19:18).

The Bible Says

Love Your Neighbor

be made. She came to him and asked, "Lord, don't you care that my sister has left me to do the work by myself? Tell her to help me!"

⁴¹"Martha, Martha," the Lord answered, "you are worried and upset about many things, ⁴²but only one thing is needed.ᵃ Mary has chosen what is better, and it will not be taken away from her."

11 **Jesus' Teaching on Prayer** One day Jesus was praying in a certain place. When he finished, one of his disciples said to him, "Lord, teach us to pray, just as John taught his disciples."

²He said to them, "When you pray, say:

> " 'Father,ᵇ
> hallowed be your name,
> your kingdom come.ᶜ
> ³Give us each day our daily bread.
> ⁴Forgive us our sins,
>   for we also forgive everyone who sins against us.ᵈ
> And lead us not into temptation.ᵉ' "

⁵Then he said to them, "Suppose one of you has a friend, and he goes to him at midnight and says, 'Friend, lend me three loaves of bread, ⁶because a friend of mine on a journey has come to me, and I have nothing to set before him.'

⁷"Then the one inside answers, 'Don't bother me. The door is already locked, and my children are with me in bed. I can't get up and give you anything.' ⁸I tell you, though he will not get up and give him the bread because he is his friend, yet because of the man's boldnessᶠ he will get up and give him as much as he needs.

⁹"So I say to you: Ask and it will be given to you; seek and you will find; knock and the door will be opened to you. ¹⁰For everyone who asks receives; he who seeks finds; and to him who knocks, the door will be opened.

¹¹"Which of you fathers, if your son asks forᵍ a fish, will give him a snake instead? ¹²Or if he asks for an egg, will give him a scorpion? ¹³If you then, though you are evil, know how to give good gifts to your children, how much more will your Father in heaven give the Holy Spirit to those who ask him!"

Jesus and Beelzebub ¹⁴Jesus was driving out a demon that was mute. When the demon left, the man who had been mute spoke, and the crowd was amazed. ¹⁵But some of them said, "By Beelzebub,ʰ the prince of demons, he is driving out demons." ¹⁶Others tested him by asking for a sign from heaven.

¹⁷Jesus knew their thoughts and said to them: "Any kingdom divided against itself will be ruined, and a house divided against itself will fall. ¹⁸If Satan is divided

Direct Line

LUKE 11:5-13

Does God hear your prayers? How can you know? Even if you get what you asked for, how can you know if it's an answer to prayer or if it would have happened anyway? This passage gives Jesus' answer. He asks you to think about what God is like. Is God a neighbor, who only gives you what you want to get rid of you (Luke 11:5-8)? No, God is a good Father, who gives good gifts to his children. He has already given those who pray to him the best gift—his Holy Spirit (Luke 11:9-13). Surely he will also answer all your prayers. Don't expect a yes to every request. Like every good father, there are times the Lord says no.

ᵃ42 Some manuscripts *but few things are needed—or only one* ᵇ2 Some manuscripts *Our Father in heaven* ᶜ2 Some manuscripts *come. May your will be done on earth as it is in heaven.* ᵈ4 Greek *everyone who is indebted to us* ᵉ4 Some manuscripts *temptation but deliver us from the evil one* ᶠ8 Or *persistence* ᵍ11 Some manuscripts *for bread, will give him a stone; or if he asks for* ʰ15 Greek *Beezeboul* or *Beelzeboul*; also in verses 18 and 19

against himself, how can his kingdom stand? I say this because you claim that I drive out demons by Beelzebub. ¹⁹Now if I drive out demons by Beelzebub, by whom do your followers drive them out? So then, they will be your judges. ²⁰But if I drive out demons by the finger of God, then the kingdom of God has come to you.

²¹"When a strong man, fully armed, guards his own house, his possessions are safe. ²²But when someone stronger attacks and overpowers him, he takes away the armor in which the man trusted and divides up the spoils.

²³"He who is not with me is against me, and he who does not gather with me, scatters.

²⁴"When an evil*a* spirit comes out of a man, it goes through arid places seeking rest and does not find it. Then it says, 'I will return to the house I left.' ²⁵When it arrives, it finds the house swept clean and put in order. ²⁶Then it goes and takes seven other spirits more wicked than itself, and they go in and live there. And the final condition of that man is worse than the first."

²⁷As Jesus was saying these things, a woman in the crowd called out, "Blessed is the mother who gave you birth and nursed you."

²⁸He replied, "Blessed rather are those who hear the word of God and obey it."

The Sign of Jonah ²⁹As the crowds increased, Jesus said, "This is a wicked generation. It asks for a miraculous sign, but none will be given it except the sign of Jonah. ³⁰For as Jonah was a sign to the Ninevites, so also will the Son of Man be to this generation. ³¹The Queen of the South will rise at the judgment with the men of this generation and condemn them; for she came from the ends of the earth to listen to Solomon's wisdom, and now one*b* greater than Solomon is here. ³²The men of Nineveh will stand up at the judgment with this generation and condemn it; for they repented at the preaching of Jonah, and now one greater than Jonah is here.

The Lamp of the Body ³³"No one lights a lamp and puts it in a place where it will be hidden, or under a bowl. Instead he puts it on its stand, so that those who come in may see the light. ³⁴Your eye is the lamp of your body. When your eyes are good, your whole body also is full of light. But when they are bad, your body also is full of darkness. ³⁵See to it, then, that the light within you is not darkness. ³⁶Therefore, if your whole body is full of light, and no part of it dark, it will be completely lighted, as when the light of a lamp shines on you."

Six Woes ³⁷When Jesus had finished speaking, a Pharisee invited him to eat with him; so he went in and reclined at the table. ³⁸But the Pharisee, noticing that Jesus did not first wash before the meal, was surprised.

³⁹Then the Lord said to him, "Now then, you Pharisees clean the outside of the cup and dish, but inside you are full of greed and wickedness. ⁴⁰You foolish people! Did not the one who made the outside make the inside also? ⁴¹But give what is inside the dish*c* to the poor, and everything will be clean for you.

⁴²"Woe to you Pharisees, because you give God a tenth of your mint, rue and all other kinds of garden herbs, but you neglect justice and the love of God. You should have practiced the latter without leaving the former undone.

⁴³"Woe to you Pharisees, because you love the most important seats in the synagogues and greetings in the marketplaces.

⁴⁴"Woe to you, because you are like unmarked graves, which men walk over without knowing it."

⁴⁵One of the experts in the law answered him, "Teacher, when you say these things, you insult us also."

---

a24 Greek *unclean*   *b31* Or *something;* also in verse 32   *c41* Or *what you have*

⁴⁶Jesus replied, "And you experts in the law, woe to you, because you load people down with burdens they can hardly carry, and you yourselves will not lift one finger to help them.

⁴⁷"Woe to you, because you build tombs for the prophets, and it was your forefathers who killed them. ⁴⁸So you testify that you approve of what your forefathers did; they killed the prophets, and you build their tombs. ⁴⁹Because of this, God in his wisdom said, 'I will send them prophets and apostles, some of whom they will kill and others they will persecute.' ⁵⁰Therefore this generation will be held responsible for the blood of all the prophets that has been shed since the beginning of the world, ⁵¹from the blood of Abel to the blood of Zechariah, who was killed between the altar and the sanctuary. Yes, I tell you, this generation will be held responsible for it all.

⁵²"Woe to you experts in the law, because you have taken away the key to knowledge. You yourselves have not entered, and you have hindered those who were entering."

⁵³When Jesus left there, the Pharisees and the teachers of the law began to oppose him fiercely and to besiege him with questions, ⁵⁴waiting to catch him in something he might say.

12 *Warnings and Encouragements* Meanwhile, when a crowd of many thousands had gathered, so that they were trampling on one another, Jesus began to speak first to his disciples, saying: "Be on your guard against the yeast of the Pharisees, which is hypocrisy. ²There is nothing concealed that will not be disclosed, or hidden that will not be made known. ³What you have said in the dark will be heard in the daylight, and what you have whispered in the ear in the inner rooms will be proclaimed from the roofs.

⁴"I tell you, my friends, do not be afraid of those who kill the body and after that can do no more. ⁵But I will show you whom you should fear: Fear him who, after the killing of the body, has power to throw you into hell. Yes, I tell you, fear him. ⁶Are not five sparrows sold for two pennies*? Yet not one of them is forgotten by God. ⁷Indeed, the very hairs of your head are all numbered. Don't be afraid; you are worth more than many sparrows.

⁸"I tell you, whoever acknowledges me before men, the Son of Man will also acknowledge him before the angels of God. ⁹But he who disowns me before men will be disowned before the angels of God. ¹⁰And everyone who speaks a word against the Son of Man will be forgiven, but anyone who blasphemes against the Holy Spirit will not be forgiven.

¹¹"When you are brought before synagogues, rulers and authorities, do not worry about how you will defend yourselves or what you will say, ¹²for the Holy Spirit will teach you at that time what you should say."

The Parable of the Rich Fool ¹³Someone in the crowd said to him, "Teacher, tell my brother to divide the inheritance with me."

¹⁴Jesus replied, "Man, who appointed me a judge or an arbiter between you?" ¹⁵Then he said to them, "Watch out! Be on your guard against all kinds of greed; a man's life does not consist in the abundance of his possessions."

¹⁶And he told them this parable: "The ground of

Only God knows how much hair I have.

SEE LUKE 12:7   *6 Greek *two assaria*

a certain rich man produced a good crop. ¹⁷He thought to himself, 'What shall I do? I have no place to store my crops.'

¹⁸"Then he said, 'This is what I'll do. I will tear down my barns and build bigger ones, and there I will store all my grain and my goods. ¹⁹And I'll say to myself, "You have plenty of good things laid up for many years. Take life easy; eat, drink and be merry." '

²⁰"But God said to him, 'You fool! This very night your life will be demanded from you. Then who will get what you have prepared for yourself?'

²¹"This is how it will be with anyone who stores up things for himself but is not rich toward God."

Do Not Worry ²²Then Jesus said to his disciples: "Therefore I tell you, do not worry about your life, what you will eat; or about your body, what you will wear. ²³Life is more than food, and the body more than clothes. ²⁴Consider the ravens: They do not sow or reap, they have no storeroom or barn; yet God feeds them. And how much more valuable you are than birds! ²⁵Who of you by worrying can add a single hour to his life*a*? ²⁶Since you cannot do this very little thing, why do you worry about the rest?

²⁷"Consider how the lilies grow. They do not labor or spin. Yet I tell you, not even Solomon in all his splendor was dressed like one of these. ²⁸If that is how God clothes the grass of the field, which is here today, and tomorrow is thrown into the fire, how much more will he clothe you, O you of little faith! ²⁹And do not set your heart on what you will eat or drink; do not worry about it. ³⁰For the pagan world runs after all such things, and your Father knows that you need them. ³¹But seek his kingdom, and these things will be given to you as well.

³²"Do not be afraid, little flock, for your Father has been pleased to give you the kingdom. ³³Sell your possessions and give to the poor. Provide purses for yourselves that will not wear out, a treasure in heaven that will not be exhausted, where no thief comes near and no moth destroys. ³⁴For where your treasure is, there your heart will be also.

Watchfulness ³⁵"Be dressed ready for service and keep your lamps burning, ³⁶like men waiting for their master to return from a wedding banquet, so that when he comes and knocks they can immediately open the door for him. ³⁷It will be good for those servants whose master finds them watching when he comes. I tell you the truth, he will dress himself to serve, will have them recline at the table and will come and wait on them. ³⁸It will be good for those servants whose master finds them ready, even if he comes in the second or third watch of the night. ³⁹But understand this: If the owner of the house had known at what hour the thief was coming, he would not have let his house be broken into. ⁴⁰You also must be ready, because the Son of Man will come at an hour when you do not expect him."

⁴¹Peter asked, "Lord, are you telling this parable to us, or to everyone?"

⁴²The Lord answered, "Who then is the faithful and wise manager, whom the master puts in charge of his servants to give them their food allowance at the proper time? ⁴³It will be good for that servant whom the master finds doing so when he returns. ⁴⁴I tell you the truth, he will put him in charge of all his possessions. ⁴⁵But suppose the servant says to himself, 'My master is taking a long time in coming,' and he then begins to beat the menservants and maidservants and to eat and drink and get drunk. ⁴⁶The master of that servant will come on a day when he does not expect him and at an hour he is not aware of. He will cut him to pieces and assign him a place with the unbelievers.

⁴⁷"That servant who knows his master's will and does not get ready or does not do what his master wants will be beaten with many blows. ⁴⁸But the one

a25 Or single cubit to his height

who does not know and does things deserving punishment will be beaten with few blows. From everyone who has been given much, much will be demanded; and from the one who has been entrusted with much, much more will be asked.

Not Peace but Division ⁴⁹"I have come to bring fire on the earth, and how I wish it were already kindled! ⁵⁰But I have a baptism to undergo, and how distressed I am until it is completed! ⁵¹Do you think I came to bring peace on earth? No, I tell you, but division. ⁵²From now on there will be five in one family divided against each other, three against two and two against three. ⁵³They will be divided, father against son and son against father, mother against daughter and daughter against mother, mother-in-law against daughter-in-law and daughter-in-law against mother-in-law."

Interpreting the Times ⁵⁴He said to the crowd: "When you see a cloud rising in the west, immediately you say, 'It's going to rain,' and it does. ⁵⁵And when the south wind blows, you say, 'It's going to be hot,' and it is. ⁵⁶Hypocrites! You know how to interpret the appearance of the earth and the sky. How is it that you don't know how to interpret this present time?

⁵⁷"Why don't you judge for yourselves what is right? ⁵⁸As you are going with your adversary to the magistrate, try hard to be reconciled to him on the way, or he may drag you off to the judge, and the judge turn you over to the officer, and the officer throw you into prison. ⁵⁹I tell you, you will not get out until you have paid the last penny.*"*

13 *Repent or Perish* Now there were some present at that time who told Jesus about the Galileans whose blood Pilate had mixed with their sacrifices. ²Jesus answered, "Do you think that these Galileans were worse sinners than all the other Galileans because they suffered this way? ³I tell you, no! But unless you repent, you too will all perish. ⁴Or those eighteen who died when the tower in Siloam fell on them—do you think they were more guilty than all the others living in Jerusalem? ⁵I tell you, no! But unless you repent, you too will all perish."

⁶Then he told this parable: "A man had a fig tree, planted in his vineyard, and he went to look for fruit on it, but did not find any. ⁷So he said to the man who took care of the vineyard, 'For three years now I've been coming to look for fruit on this fig tree and haven't found any. Cut it down! Why should it use up the soil?'

⁸"'Sir,' the man replied, 'leave it alone for one more year, and I'll dig around it and fertilize it. ⁹If it bears fruit next year, fine! If not, then cut it down.'"

A Crippled Woman Healed on the Sabbath ¹⁰On a Sabbath Jesus was teaching in one of the synagogues, ¹¹and a woman was there who had been crippled by a spirit for eighteen years. She was bent over and could not straighten up at all. ¹²When Jesus saw her, he called her forward and said to her, "Woman, you are set free from your infirmity." ¹³Then he put his hands on her, and immediately she straightened up and praised God.

¹⁴Indignant because Jesus had healed on the Sabbath, the synagogue ruler said to the people, "There are six days for work. So come and be healed on those days, not on the Sabbath."

¹⁵The Lord answered him, "You hypocrites! Doesn't each of you on the Sabbath untie his ox or donkey from the stall and lead it out to give it water? ¹⁶Then should not this woman, a daughter of Abraham, whom Satan has kept bound for eighteen long years, be set free on the Sabbath day from what bound her?"

⁵⁹ Greek lepton

¹⁷When he said this, all his opponents were humiliated, but the people were delighted with all the wonderful things he was doing.

The Parables of the Mustard Seed and the Yeast ¹⁸Then Jesus asked, "What is the kingdom of God like? What shall I compare it to? ¹⁹It is like a mustard seed, which a man took and planted in his garden. It grew and became a tree, and the birds of the air perched in its branches."

²⁰Again he asked, "What shall I compare the kingdom of God to? ²¹It is like yeast that a woman took and mixed into a large amount*ᵃ* of flour until it worked all through the dough."

The Narrow Door ²²Then Jesus went through the towns and villages, teaching as he made his way to Jerusalem. ²³Someone asked him, "Lord, are only a few people going to be saved?"

He said to them, ²⁴"Make every effort to enter through the narrow door, because many, I tell you, will try to enter and will not be able to. ²⁵Once the owner of the house gets up and closes the door, you will stand outside knocking and pleading, 'Sir, open the door for us.'

"But he will answer, 'I don't know you or where you come from.'

²⁶"Then you will say, 'We ate and drank with you, and you taught in our streets.'

²⁷"But he will reply, 'I don't know you or where you come from. Away from me, all you evildoers!'

²⁸"There will be weeping there, and gnashing of teeth, when you see Abraham, Isaac and Jacob and all the prophets in the kingdom of God, but you yourselves thrown out. ²⁹People will come from east and west and north and south, and will take their places at the feast in the kingdom of God. ³⁰Indeed there are those who are last who will be first, and first who will be last."

Jesus' Sorrow for Jerusalem ³¹At that time some Pharisees came to Jesus and said to him, "Leave this place and go somewhere else. Herod wants to kill you."

³²He replied, "Go tell that fox, 'I will drive out demons and heal people today and tomorrow, and on the third day I will reach my goal.' ³³In any case, I must keep going today and tomorrow and the next day—for surely no prophet can die outside Jerusalem!

³⁴"O Jerusalem, Jerusalem, you who kill the prophets and stone those sent to you, how often I have longed to gather your children together, as a hen gathers her chicks under her wings, but you were not willing! ³⁵Look, your house is left to you desolate. I tell you, you will not see me again until you say, 'Blessed is he who comes in the name of the Lord.'*ᵇ*"

14 *Jesus at a Pharisee's House* One Sabbath, when Jesus went to eat in the house of a prominent Pharisee, he was being carefully watched. ²There in front of him was a man suffering from dropsy. ³Jesus asked the Pharisees and experts in the law, "Is it lawful to heal on the Sabbath or not?" ⁴But they remained silent. So taking hold of the man, he healed him and sent him away.

⁵Then he asked them, "If one of you has a son*ᶜ* or an ox that falls into a well on the Sabbath day, will you not immediately pull him out?" ⁶And they had nothing to say.

⁷When he noticed how the guests picked the places of honor at the table, he told them this parable: ⁸"When someone invites you to a wedding feast, do not take the place of honor, for a person more distinguished than you may have been invited. ⁹If so, the host who invited both of you will come and

ᵃ21 Greek three satas (probably about 1/2 bushel or 22 liters) ᵇ35 Psalm 118:26 ᶜ5 Some manuscripts donkey say to you, 'Give this man your seat.' Then, humiliated, you will have to take the least important place. [10]But when you are invited, take the lowest place, so that when your host comes, he will say to you, 'Friend, move up to a better place.' Then you will be honored in the presence of all your fellow guests. [11]For everyone who exalts himself will be humbled, and he who humbles himself will be exalted."

[12]Then Jesus said to his host, "When you give a luncheon or dinner, do not invite your friends, your brothers or relatives, or your rich neighbors; if you do, they may invite you back and so you will be repaid. [13]But when you give a banquet, invite the poor, the crippled, the lame, the blind, [14]and you will be blessed. Although they cannot repay you, you will be repaid at the resurrection of the righteous."

The Parable of the Great Banquet   [15]When one of those at the table with him heard this, he said to Jesus, "Blessed is the man who will eat at the feast in the kingdom of God."

[16]Jesus replied: "A certain man was preparing a great banquet and invited many guests. [17]At the time of the banquet he sent his servant to tell those who had been invited, 'Come, for everything is now ready.'

[18]"But they all alike began to make excuses. The first said, 'I have just bought a field, and I must go and see it. Please excuse me.'

[19]"Another said, 'I have just bought five yoke of oxen, and I'm on my way to try them out. Please excuse me.'

[20]"Still another said, 'I just got married, so I can't come.'

[21]"The servant came back and reported this to his master. Then the owner of the house became angry and ordered his servant, 'Go out quickly into the streets and alleys of the town and bring in the poor, the crippled, the blind and the lame.'

[22]" 'Sir,' the servant said, 'what you ordered has been done, but there is still room.'

[23]"Then the master told his servant, 'Go out to the roads and country lanes and make them come in, so that my house will be full. [24]I tell you, not one of those men who were invited will get a taste of my banquet.' "

The Cost of Being a Disciple   [25]Large crowds were traveling with Jesus, and turning to them he said: [26]"If anyone comes to me and does not hate his father and mother, his wife and children, his brothers and sisters—yes, even his own life—he cannot be my disciple. [27]And anyone who does not carry his cross and follow me cannot be my disciple.

[28]"Suppose one of you wants to build a tower. Will he not first sit down and estimate the cost to see if he has enough money to complete it? [29]For if he lays the foundation and is not able to finish it, everyone who sees it will ridicule him, [30]saying, 'This fellow began to build and was not able to finish.'

[31]"Or suppose a king is about to go to war against another king. Will he not first sit down and consider whether he is able with ten thousand men to oppose the one coming against him with twenty thousand? [32]If he is not able, he will send a

LUKE 14:12–14

Have you ever helped someone in math who later "didn't have time" when you needed help in history? Situations like that can upset you; they aren't fair. Most friendships are based, at least in part, on payback. You help each other out. You pick each other for teams. You call each other to check on school assignments. Adults do the same thing. They invite a couple over for dinner and expect to be invited back. But should all your relationships be based on payback? Jesus says no. You should try to do good things for people who can't pay you back. When you do, the payback you get will come from God!

Direct Line

delegation while the other is still a long way off and will ask for terms of peace. ³³In the same way, any of you who does not give up everything he has cannot be my disciple.

³⁴"Salt is good, but if it loses its saltiness, how can it be made salty again? ³⁵It is fit neither for the soil nor for the manure pile; it is thrown out.

"He who has ears to hear, let him hear."

The Parable of the Lost Sheep Now the tax collectors and "sinners" were all gathering around to hear him. ²But the Pharisees and the teachers of the law muttered, "This man welcomes sinners and eats with them."

³Then Jesus told them this parable: ⁴"Suppose one of you has a hundred sheep and loses one of them. Does he not leave the ninety-nine in the open country and go after the lost sheep until he finds it? ⁵And when he finds it, he joyfully puts it on his shoulders ⁶and goes home. Then he calls his friends and neighbors together and says, 'Rejoice with me; I have found my lost sheep.' ⁷I tell you that in the same way there will be more rejoicing in heaven over one sinner who repents than over ninety-nine righteous persons who do not need to repent.

The Parable of the Lost Coin ⁸"Or suppose a woman has ten silver coins*ᵃ* and loses one. Does she not light a lamp, sweep the house and search carefully until she finds it? ⁹And when she finds it, she calls her friends and neighbors together and says, 'Rejoice with me; I have found my lost coin.' ¹⁰In the same way, I tell you, there is rejoicing in the presence of the angels of God over one sinner who repents."

The Parable of the Lost Son ¹¹Jesus continued: "There was a man who had two sons. ¹²The younger one said to his father, 'Father, give me my share of the estate.' So he divided his property between them.

¹³"Not long after that, the younger son got together all he had, set off for a distant country and there squandered his wealth in wild living. ¹⁴After he had spent everything, there was a severe famine in that whole country, and he began to be in need. ¹⁵So he went and hired himself out to a citizen of that country, who sent him to his fields to feed pigs. ¹⁶He longed to fill his stomach with the pods that the pigs were eating, but no one gave him anything.

¹⁷"When he came to his senses, he said, 'How many of my father's hired men have food to spare, and here I am starving to death! ¹⁸I will set out and go back to my father and say to him: Father, I have sinned against heaven and against you. ¹⁹I am no longer worthy to be called your son; make me like one of your hired men.' ²⁰So he got up and went to his father.

"But while he was still a long way off, his father saw him and was filled with compassion for him; he ran to his son, threw his arms around him and kissed him.

²¹"The son said to him, 'Father, I have

LUKE 15:8–10

Some people think women didn't count in Bible times. They say the husband paid a "bride price" to the father to "buy" his wife. She was just property! But brides weren't bought and sold. The bride price compensated the father for the loss of his precious daughter. And then the father gave his daughter a dowry, so she wouldn't enter the marriage as a pauper, but as a partner. In Jesus' day the dowry was often made up of coins, with a hole drilled in the center so they could be strung like beads. The woman in this story was probably upset because she had lost a dowry coin. In Bible times, as today, women truly are important.

Direct Line

ᵃ8 Greek ten drachmas, each worth about a day's wages

sinned against heaven and against you. I am no longer worthy to be called your son.*'

22"But the father said to his servants, 'Quick! Bring the best robe and put it on him. Put a ring on his finger and sandals on his feet. 23Bring the fattened calf and kill it. Let's have a feast and celebrate. 24For this son of mine was dead and is alive again; he was lost and is found.' So they began to celebrate.

25"Meanwhile, the older son was in the field. When he came near the house, he heard music and dancing. 26So he called one of the servants and asked him what was going on. 27'Your brother has come,' he replied, 'and your father has killed the fattened calf because he has him back safe and sound.'

28"The older brother became angry and refused to go in. So his father went out and pleaded with him. 29But he answered his father, 'Look! All these years I've been slaving for you and never disobeyed your orders. Yet you never gave me even a young goat so I could celebrate with my friends. 30But when this son of yours who has squandered your property with prostitutes comes home, you kill the fattened calf for him!'

31" 'My son,' the father said, 'you are always with me, and everything I have is yours. 32But we had to celebrate and be glad, because this brother of yours was dead and is alive again; he was lost and is found.' "

The Parable of the Shrewd Manager

Jesus told his disciples: "There was a rich man whose manager was accused of wasting his possessions. 2So he called him in and asked him, 'What is this I hear about you? Give an account of your management, because you cannot be manager any longer.'

3"The manager said to himself, 'What shall I do now? My master is taking away my job. I'm not strong enough to dig, and I'm ashamed to beg— 4I know what I'll do so that, when I lose my job here, people will welcome me into their houses.'

5"So he called in each one of his master's debtors. He asked the first, 'How much do you owe my master?'

6" 'Eight hundred gallons*b* of olive oil,' he replied.

"The manager told him, 'Take your bill, sit down quickly, and make it four hundred.'

7"Then he asked the second, 'And how much do you owe?'

" 'A thousand bushels*c* of wheat,' he replied.

"He told him, 'Take your bill and make it eight hundred.'

8"The master commended the dishonest manager because he had acted shrewdly. For the people of this world are more shrewd in dealing with their own kind than are the people of the light. 9I tell you, use worldly wealth to gain friends for yourselves, so that when it is gone, you will be welcomed into eternal dwellings.

10"Whoever can be trusted with very little can also be trusted with much, and whoever is dishonest with very little will also be dishonest with much. 11So if you have not been trustworthy in handling worldly wealth, who will trust you with true riches? 12And if you have not been trustworthy with someone else's property, who will give you property of your own?

13"No servant can serve two masters. Either he will hate the one and love the other, or he will be devoted to the one and despise the other. You cannot serve both God and Money."

14The Pharisees, who loved money, heard all this and were sneering at Jesus. 15He said to them, "You are the ones who justify yourselves in the eyes of men, but God knows your hearts. What is highly valued among men is detestable in God's sight.

---

a21 Some early manuscripts son. Make me like one of your hired men. *b6 Greek one hundred batous* (probably about 3 kiloliters) *c7 Greek one hundred korous* (probably about 35 kiloliters)

Additional Teachings   ¹⁶"The Law and the Prophets were proclaimed until John. Since that time, the good news of the kingdom of God is being preached, and everyone is forcing his way into it. ¹⁷It is easier for heaven and earth to disappear than for the least stroke of a pen to drop out of the Law.

¹⁸"Anyone who divorces his wife and marries another woman commits adultery, and the man who marries a divorced woman commits adultery.

The Rich Man and Lazarus   ¹⁹"There was a rich man who was dressed in purple and fine linen and lived in luxury every day. ²⁰At his gate was laid a beggar named Lazarus, covered with sores ²¹and longing to eat what fell from the rich man's table. Even the dogs came and licked his sores.

²²"The time came when the beggar died and the angels carried him to Abraham's side. The rich man also died and was buried. ²³In hell,ᵃ where he was in torment, he looked up and saw Abraham far away, with Lazarus by his side. ²⁴So he called to him, 'Father Abraham, have pity on me and send Lazarus to dip the tip of his finger in water and cool my tongue, because I am in agony in this fire.'

²⁵"But Abraham replied, 'Son, remember that in your lifetime you received your good things, while Lazarus received bad things, but now he is comforted here and you are in agony. ²⁶And besides all this, between us and you a great chasm has been fixed, so that those who want to go from here to you cannot, nor can anyone cross over from there to us.'

²⁷"He answered, 'Then I beg you, father, send Lazarus to my father's house, ²⁸for I have five brothers. Let him warn them, so that they will not also come to this place of torment.'

²⁹"Abraham replied, 'They have Moses and the Prophets; let them listen to them.'

³⁰" 'No, father Abraham,' he said, 'but if someone from the dead goes to them, they will repent.'

³¹"He said to him, 'If they do not listen to Moses and the Prophets, they will not be convinced even if someone rises from the dead.' "

17 *Sin, Faith, Duty*   Jesus said to his disciples: "Things that cause people to sin are bound to come, but woe to that person through whom they come. ²It would be better for him to be thrown into the sea with

---

ᵃ23 Greek *Hades*

Some people think that when a person dies, that's the end. The dead are just gone. Forever. But they're wrong.

Jesus made it very clear that death is not the end. He told a story about what happened after death to a rich man and a beggar (Luke 16:19–31). This story gives the clearest picture in the Bible of what happens to a person after death.

✳ People remain conscious after their bodies die (Luke 16:25).
✳ People have some kind of body after they die (Luke 16:24).
✳ People can feel pleasure or pain after they die (Luke 16:25).

There really is no end for any human being. You will either live forever with God or live forever separated from him.

The Bible Says

Death Isn't the End

a millstone tied around his neck than for him to cause one of these little ones to sin. ³So watch yourselves.

"If your brother sins, rebuke him, and if he repents, forgive him. ⁴If he sins against you seven times in a day, and seven times comes back to you and says, 'I repent,' forgive him."

⁵The apostles said to the Lord, "Increase our faith!"

⁶He replied, "If you have faith as small as a mustard seed, you can say to this mulberry tree, 'Be uprooted and planted in the sea,' and it will obey you.

⁷"Suppose one of you had a servant plowing or looking after the sheep. Would he say to the servant when he comes in from the field, 'Come along now and sit down to eat'? ⁸Would he not rather say, 'Prepare my supper, get yourself ready and wait on me while I eat and drink; after that you may eat and drink'? ⁹Would he thank the servant because he did what he was told to do? ¹⁰So you also, when you have done everything you were told to do, should say, 'We are unworthy servants; we have only done our duty.' "

Ten Healed of Leprosy ¹¹Now on his way to Jerusalem, Jesus traveled along the border between Samaria and Galilee. ¹²As he was going into a village, ten men who had leprosy*ᵃ* met him. They stood at a distance ¹³and called out in a loud voice, "Jesus, Master, have pity on us!"

¹⁴When he saw them, he said, "Go, show yourselves to the priests." And as they went, they were cleansed.

¹⁵One of them, when he saw he was healed, came back, praising God in a loud voice. ¹⁶He threw himself at Jesus' feet and thanked him—and he was a Samaritan.

¹⁷Jesus asked, "Were not all ten cleansed? Where are the other nine? ¹⁸Was no one found to return and give praise to God except this foreigner?" ¹⁹Then he said to him, "Rise and go; your faith has made you well."

The Coming of the Kingdom of God ²⁰Once, having been asked by the Pharisees when the kingdom of God would come, Jesus replied, "The kingdom of God does not come with your careful observation, ²¹nor will people say, 'Here it is,' or 'There it is,' because the kingdom of God is within*ᵇ* you."

²²Then he said to his disciples, "The time is coming when you will long to see one of the days of the Son of Man, but you will not see it. ²³Men will tell you, 'There he is!' or 'Here he is!' Do not go running off after them. ²⁴For the Son of Man in his day*ᶜ* will be like the lightning, which flashes and lights up the sky from one end to the other. ²⁵But first he must suffer many things and be rejected by this generation.

²⁶"Just as it was in the days of Noah, so also will it be in the days of the Son of Man. ²⁷People were eating, drinking, marrying and being given in marriage up to the day Noah entered the ark. Then the flood came and destroyed them all.

²⁸"It was the same in the days of Lot. People were eating and drinking, buying

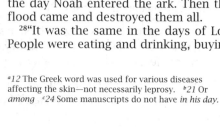

ᵃ12 The Greek word was used for various diseases affecting the skin—not necessarily leprosy. *ᵇ21* Or *among* *ᶜ24* Some manuscripts do not have *in his day.*

Direct Line

LUKE 17:24–30

Most of your days are pretty routine. School, homework, food, friends, family. And you expect the next day to be pretty much the same—unless you take Jesus' promised return seriously. Then you might wake up and wonder if today is the day Jesus will come back. Or you might go to bed and wonder if Jesus will give you your wake-up call instead of Mom. Most people are so busy with their own affairs they ignore the fact that Jesus is coming again. People who expect Jesus are a lot more careful about the choices they make. They know he's coming back soon and that everything they do matters.

and selling, planting and building. ²⁹But the day Lot left Sodom, fire and sulfur rained down from heaven and destroyed them all.

³⁰"It will be just like this on the day the Son of Man is revealed. ³¹On that day no one who is on the roof of his house, with his goods inside, should go down to get them. Likewise, no one in the field should go back for anything. ³²Remember Lot's wife! ³³Whoever tries to keep his life will lose it, and whoever loses his life will preserve it. ³⁴I tell you, on that night two people will be in one bed; one will be taken and the other left. ³⁵Two women will be grinding grain together; one will be taken and the other left.ᵃ"

³⁷"Where, Lord?" they asked.

He replied, "Where there is a dead body, there the vultures will gather."

The Parable of the Persistent Widow Then Jesus told his disciples a parable to show them that they should always pray and not give up. ²He said: "In a certain town there was a judge who neither feared God nor cared about men. ³And there was a widow in that town who kept coming to him with the plea, 'Grant me justice against my adversary.'

⁴"For some time he refused. But finally he said to himself, 'Even though I don't fear God or care about men, ⁵yet because this widow keeps bothering me, I will see that she gets justice, so that she won't eventually wear me out with her coming!' "

⁶And the Lord said, "Listen to what the unjust judge says. ⁷And will not God bring about justice for his chosen ones, who cry out to him day and night? Will he keep putting them off? ⁸I tell you, he will see that they get justice, and quickly. However, when the Son of Man comes, will he find faith on the earth?"

The Parable of the Pharisee and the Tax Collector ⁹To some who were confident of their own righteousness and looked down on everybody else, Jesus told this parable: ¹⁰"Two men went up to the temple to pray, one a Pharisee and the other a tax collector. ¹¹The Pharisee stood up and prayed aboutᵇ himself: 'God, I thank you that I am not like other men—robbers, evildoers, adulterers—or even like this tax collector. ¹²I fast twice a week and give a tenth of all I get.'

¹³"But the tax collector stood at a distance. He would not even look up to heaven, but beat his breast and said, 'God, have mercy on me, a sinner.'

¹⁴"I tell you that this man, rather than the other, went home justified before God. For everyone who exalts himself will be humbled, and he who humbles himself will be exalted."

The Little Children and Jesus ¹⁵People were also bringing babies to Jesus to have him touch them. When the disciples saw this, they rebuked them. ¹⁶But Jesus called the children to him and said, "Let the little children come to me, and do not hinder them, for the kingdom of God belongs to such as these. ¹⁷I tell you the truth, anyone who will not receive the kingdom of God like a little child will never enter it."

The Rich Ruler ¹⁸A certain ruler asked him, "Good teacher, what must I do to inherit eternal life?"

¹⁹"Why do you call me good?" Jesus answered. "No one is good—except God alone. ²⁰You know the commandments: 'Do not commit adultery, do not murder, do not steal, do not give false testimony, honor your father and mother.'ᶜ"

²¹"All these I have kept since I was a boy," he said.

²²When Jesus heard this, he said to him, "You still lack one thing. Sell ev-

---

ᵃ35 Some manuscripts *left.* ³⁶*Two men will be in the field; one will be taken and the other left.* ᵇ11 Or *to*
ᶜ20 Exodus 20:12-16; Deut. 5:16-20

erything you have and give to the poor, and you will have treasure in heaven. Then come, follow me."

²³When he heard this, he became very sad, because he was a man of great wealth. ²⁴Jesus looked at him and said, "How hard it is for the rich to enter the kingdom of God! ²⁵Indeed, it is easier for a camel to go through the eye of a needle than for a rich man to enter the kingdom of God."

²⁶Those who heard this asked, "Who then can be saved?"

²⁷Jesus replied, "What is impossible with men is possible with God."

²⁸Peter said to him, "We have left all we had to follow you!"

²⁹"I tell you the truth," Jesus said to them, "no one who has left home or wife or brothers or parents or children for the sake of the kingdom of God ³⁰will fail to receive many times as much in this age and, in the age to come, eternal life."

Jesus Again Predicts His Death ³¹Jesus took the Twelve aside and told them, "We are going up to Jerusalem, and everything that is written by the prophets about the Son of Man will be fulfilled. ³²He will be handed over to the Gentiles. They will mock him, insult him, spit on him, flog him and kill him. ³³On the third day he will rise again."

³⁴The disciples did not understand any of this. Its meaning was hidden from them, and they did not know what he was talking about.

A Blind Beggar Receives His Sight ³⁵As Jesus approached Jericho, a blind man was sitting by the roadside begging. ³⁶When he heard the crowd going by, he asked what was happening. ³⁷They told him, "Jesus of Nazareth is passing by."

³⁸He called out, "Jesus, Son of David, have mercy on me!"

³⁹Those who led the way rebuked him and told him to be quiet, but he shouted all the more, "Son of David, have mercy on me!"

⁴⁰Jesus stopped and ordered the man to be brought to him. When he came near, Jesus asked him, ⁴¹"What do you want me to do for you?"

"Lord, I want to see," he replied.

⁴²Jesus said to him, "Receive your sight; your faith has healed you." ⁴³Immediately he received his sight and followed Jesus, praising God. When all the people saw it, they also praised God.

Direct Line

LUKE 18:22

Are you ready to haul out your TV, bike, CD player and baseball card collection for a garage sale? No? Then how do you get around Luke 18:22? To understand a verse you need to see *who* the verse is directed to, *what* the context is and *how* the verse applies. Who: Jesus was speaking to a rich man. What: The rich man thought he could get to heaven by doing good. How: Deep down the rich man put money first, not God. You don't have to get rid of all your stuff, but even so, this verse is saying something important to you. Don't let anything you own or anything you want become more important to you than pleasing the Lord.

19 *Zacchaeus the Tax Collector*

Jesus entered Jericho and was passing through. ²A man was there by the name of Zacchaeus; he was a chief tax collector and was wealthy. ³He wanted to see who Jesus was, but being a short man he could not, because of the crowd. ⁴So he ran ahead and climbed a sycamore-fig tree to see him, since Jesus was coming that way.

⁵When Jesus reached the spot, he looked up and said to him, "Zacchaeus, come down immediately. I must stay at your house today." ⁶So he came down at once and welcomed him gladly.

⁷All the people saw this and began to mutter, "He has gone to be the guest of a 'sinner.' "

⁸But Zacchaeus stood up and said to the Lord, "Look, Lord! Here and now I give

half of my possessions to the poor, and if I have cheated anybody out of anything, I will pay back four times the amount."

⁹Jesus said to him, "Today salvation has come to this house, because this man, too, is a son of Abraham. ¹⁰For the Son of Man came to seek and to save what was lost."

The Parable of the Ten Minas   ¹¹While they were listening to this, he went on to tell them a parable, because he was near Jerusalem and the people thought that the kingdom of God was going to appear at once. ¹²He said: "A man of noble birth went to a distant country to have himself appointed king and then to return. ¹³So he called ten of his servants and gave them ten minas.ᵃ 'Put this money to work,' he said, 'until I come back.'

¹⁴"But his subjects hated him and sent a delegation after him to say, 'We don't want this man to be our king.'

¹⁵"He was made king, however, and returned home. Then he sent for the servants to whom he had given the money, in order to find out what they had gained with it.

¹⁶"The first one came and said, 'Sir, your mina has earned ten more.'

¹⁷" 'Well done, my good servant!' his master replied. 'Because you have been trustworthy in a very small matter, take charge of ten cities.'

¹⁸"The second came and said, 'Sir, your mina has earned five more.'

¹⁹"His master answered, 'You take charge of five cities.'

²⁰"Then another servant came and said, 'Sir, here is your mina; I have kept it laid away in a piece of cloth. ²¹I was afraid of you, because you are a hard man. You take out what you did not put in and reap what you did not sow.'

²²"His master replied, 'I will judge you by your own words, you wicked servant! You knew, did you, that I am a hard man, taking out what I did not put in, and reaping what I did not sow? ²³Why then didn't you put my money on deposit, so that when I came back, I could have collected it with interest?'

²⁴"Then he said to those standing by, 'Take his mina away from him and give it to the one who has ten minas.'

²⁵" 'Sir,' they said, 'he already has ten!'

²⁶"He replied, 'I tell you that to everyone who has, more will be given, but as for the one who has nothing, even what he has will be taken away. ²⁷But those enemies of mine who did not want me to be king over them—bring them here and kill them in front of me.' "

The Triumphal Entry   ²⁸After Jesus had said this, he went on ahead, going up to Jerusalem. ²⁹As he approached Bethphage and Bethany at the hill called the Mount of Olives, he sent two of his disciples, saying to them, ³⁰"Go to the village ahead of you, and as you enter it, you will find a colt tied there, which no one has ever ridden. Untie it and bring it here. ³¹If anyone asks you, 'Why are you untying it?' tell him, 'The Lord needs it.' "

³²Those who were sent ahead went and found it just as he had told them. ³³As they were untying the colt, its owners asked them, "Why are you untying the colt?"

³⁴They replied, "The Lord needs it."

³⁵They brought it to Jesus, threw their cloaks on the colt and put Jesus on it. ³⁶As he went along, people spread their cloaks on the road.

³⁷When he came near the place where the road goes down the Mount of Olives, the whole crowd of disciples began joyfully to praise God in loud voices for all the miracles they had seen:

> ³⁸"Blessed is the king who comes in the name of the Lord!"ᵇ
>
> "Peace in heaven and glory in the highest!"

ᵃ*13* A mina was about three months' wages.   ᵇ*38* Psalm 118:26

³⁹Some of the Pharisees in the crowd said to Jesus, "Teacher, rebuke your disciples!"

⁴⁰"I tell you," he replied, "if they keep quiet, the stones will cry out."

⁴¹As he approached Jerusalem and saw the city, he wept over it ⁴²and said, "If you, even you, had only known on this day what would bring you peace— but now it is hidden from your eyes. ⁴³The days will come upon you when your enemies will build an embankment against you and encircle you and hem you in on every side. ⁴⁴They will dash you to the ground, you and the children within your walls. They will not leave one stone on another, because you did not recognize the time of God's coming to you."

Jesus at the Temple   ⁴⁵Then he entered the temple area and began driving out those who were selling. ⁴⁶"It is written," he said to them, " 'My house will be a house of prayer'ᵃ; but you have made it 'a den of robbers.'ᵇ"

⁴⁷Every day he was teaching at the temple. But the chief priests, the teachers of the law and the leaders among the people were trying to kill him. ⁴⁸Yet they could not find any way to do it, because all the people hung on his words.

20 **The Authority of Jesus Questioned**   One day as he was teaching the people in the temple courts and preaching the gospel, the chief priests and the teachers of the law, together with the elders, came up to him. ²"Tell us by what authority you are doing these things," they said. "Who gave you this authority?"

³He replied, "I will also ask you a question. Tell me, ⁴John's baptism—was it from heaven, or from men?"

⁵They discussed it among themselves and said, "If we say, 'From heaven,' he will ask, 'Why didn't you believe him?' ⁶But if we say, 'From men,' all the people will stone us, because they are persuaded that John was a prophet."

⁷So they answered, "We don't know where it was from."

⁸Jesus said, "Neither will I tell you by what authority I am doing these things."

The Parable of the Tenants   ⁹He went on to tell the people this parable: "A man planted a vineyard, rented it to some farmers and went away for a long time. ¹⁰At harvest time he sent a servant to the tenants so they would give him some of the fruit of the vineyard. But the tenants beat him and sent him away empty-handed. ¹¹He sent another servant, but that one also they beat and treated shamefully and sent away empty-handed. ¹²He sent still a third, and they wounded him and threw him out.

¹³"Then the owner of the vineyard said, 'What shall I do? I will send my son, whom I love; perhaps they will respect him.'

¹⁴"But when the tenants saw him, they talked the matter over. 'This is the heir,' they said. 'Let's kill him, and the inheritance will be ours.' ¹⁵So they threw him out of the vineyard and killed him.

LUKE 20:9–19

Do you ever wonder why everyone doesn't believe in Jesus? Where else can you get eternal life as a free gift? One answer is found in this parable. When the owner of the vineyard sends his son, the tenants kill him. They just aren't willing to submit. They want to be their own god. Down deep people know that if they accept Christ as Savior, they no longer belong to themselves. They belong to the Lord. And they don't like the thought of not being their own boss. They want control. They want final say. But one thing they don't understand: giving control to Jesus frees people to be much more than they could ever be on their own.

Direct Line

ᵃ46 Isaiah 56:7   ᵇ46 Jer. 7:11

"What then will the owner of the vineyard do to them? [16]He will come and kill those tenants and give the vineyard to others."

When the people heard this, they said, "May this never be!"

[17]Jesus looked directly at them and asked, "Then what is the meaning of that which is written:

> " 'The stone the builders rejected
> has become the capstone[a][b]?

[18]Everyone who falls on that stone will be broken to pieces, but he on whom it falls will be crushed."

[19]The teachers of the law and the chief priests looked for a way to arrest him immediately, because they knew he had spoken this parable against them. But they were afraid of the people.

Paying Taxes to Caesar [20]Keeping a close watch on him, they sent spies, who pretended to be honest. They hoped to catch Jesus in something he said so that they might hand him over to the power and authority of the governor. [21]So the spies questioned him: "Teacher, we know that you speak and teach what is right, and that you do not show partiality but teach the way of God in accordance with the truth. [22]Is it right for us to pay taxes to Caesar or not?"

[23]He saw through their duplicity and said to them, [24]"Show me a denarius. Whose portrait and inscription are on it?"

[25]"Caesar's," they replied.

He said to them, "Then give to Caesar what is Caesar's, and to God what is God's."

[26]They were unable to trap him in what he had said there in public. And astonished by his answer, they became silent.

The Resurrection and Marriage [27]Some of the Sadducees, who say there is no resurrection, came to Jesus with a question. [28]"Teacher," they said, "Moses wrote for us that if a man's brother dies and leaves a wife but no children, the man must marry the widow and have children for his brother. [29]Now there were seven brothers. The first one married a woman and died childless. [30]The second [31]and then the third married her, and in the same way the seven died, leaving no children. [32]Finally, the woman died too. [33]Now then, at the resurrection whose wife will she be, since the seven were married to her?"

[34]Jesus replied, "The people of this age marry and are given in marriage. [35]But those who are considered worthy of taking part in that age and in the resurrection from the dead will neither marry nor be given in marriage, [36]and they can no longer die; for they are like the angels. They are God's children, since they are children of the resurrection. [37]But in the account of the bush, even Moses showed that the dead rise, for he calls the Lord 'the God of Abraham, and the God of Isaac, and the God of Jacob.'[c] [38]He is not the God of the dead, but of the living, for to him all are alive."

[39]Some of the teachers of the law responded, "Well said, teacher!" [40]And no one dared to ask him any more questions.

Whose Son Is the Christ? [41]Then Jesus said to them, "How is it that they say the Christ[d] is the Son of David? [42]David himself declares in the Book of Psalms:

> " 'The Lord said to my Lord:
> "Sit at my right hand
> [43]until I make your enemies
> a footstool for your feet." '[e]

[44]David calls him 'Lord.' How then can he be his son?"

---

[a]17 Or *cornerstone*   [b]17 Psalm 118:22   [c]37 Exodus 3:6   [d]41 Or *Messiah*   [e]43 Psalm 110:1

⁴⁵While all the people were listening, Jesus said to his disciples, ⁴⁶"Beware of the teachers of the law. They like to walk around in flowing robes and love to be greeted in the marketplaces and have the most important seats in the synagogues and the places of honor at banquets. ⁴⁷They devour widows' houses and for a show make lengthy prayers. Such men will be punished most severely."

21 *The Widow's Offering* As he looked up, Jesus saw the rich putting their gifts into the temple treasury. ²He also saw a poor widow put in two very small copper coins.ᵃ ³"I tell you the truth," he said, "this poor widow has put in more than all the others. ⁴All these people gave their gifts out of their wealth; but she out of her poverty put in all she had to live on."

Signs of the End of the Age ⁵Some of his disciples were remarking about how the temple was adorned with beautiful stones and with gifts dedicated to God. But Jesus said, ⁶"As for what you see here, the time will come when not one stone will be left on another; every one of them will be thrown down."

⁷"Teacher," they asked, "when will these things happen? And what will be the sign that they are about to take place?"

⁸He replied: "Watch out that you are not deceived. For many will come in my name, claiming, 'I am he,' and, 'The time is near.' Do not follow them. ⁹When you hear of wars and revolutions, do not be frightened. These things must happen first, but the end will not come right away."

¹⁰Then he said to them: "Nation will rise against nation, and kingdom against kingdom. ¹¹There will be great earthquakes, famines and pestilences in various places, and fearful events and great signs from heaven.

¹²"But before all this, they will lay hands on you and persecute you. They will deliver you to synagogues and prisons, and you will be brought before kings and governors, and all on account of my name. ¹³This will result in your being witnesses to them. ¹⁴But make up your mind not to worry beforehand how you will defend yourselves. ¹⁵For I will give you words and wisdom that none of your adversaries will be able to resist or contradict. ¹⁶You will

---

ᵃ2 Greek *two lepta*

The Bible Says

Dark Before Dawn

Three Gospels report Jesus' teachings about the future (Matthew 24—25; Mark 13; Luke 21)—that it holds wars, revolutions, famines and earthquakes. The Gospel writers also warn that at times Christians will be persecuted for their faith. But in the end Jesus will return with "power and great glory" (Luke 21:27).

How are you to live through the dark times before Jesus comes and brings the dawn?

* Don't be frightened of terrible events (Luke 21:9).
* Don't worry about how to defend yourself when persecuted (Luke 21:14).
* Be careful to stay faithful to the Lord (Luke 21:34).

God doesn't promise you an easy life here, but he does promise to be with you and to take you to be with him forever.

be betrayed even by parents, brothers, relatives and friends, and they will put some of you to death. ¹⁷All men will hate you because of me. ¹⁸But not a hair of your head will perish. ¹⁹By standing firm you will gain life.

²⁰"When you see Jerusalem being surrounded by armies, you will know that its desolation is near. ²¹Then let those who are in Judea flee to the mountains, let those in the city get out, and let those in the country not enter the city. ²²For this is the time of punishment in fulfillment of all that has been written. ²³How dreadful it will be in those days for pregnant women and nursing mothers! There will be great distress in the land and wrath against this people. ²⁴They will fall by the sword and will be taken as prisoners to all the nations. Jerusalem will be trampled on by the Gentiles until the times of the Gentiles are fulfilled.

²⁵"There will be signs in the sun, moon and stars. On the earth, nations will be in anguish and perplexity at the roaring and tossing of the sea. ²⁶Men will faint from terror, apprehensive of what is coming on the world, for the heavenly bodies will be shaken. ²⁷At that time they will see the Son of Man coming in a cloud with power and great glory. ²⁸When these things begin to take place, stand up and lift up your heads, because your redemption is drawing near."

> I will give you words and wisdom that none of your adversaries will be able to resist or contradict (Luke 21:15).

²⁹He told them this parable: "Look at the fig tree and all the trees. ³⁰When they sprout leaves, you can see for yourselves and know that summer is near. ³¹Even so, when you see these things happening, you know that the kingdom of God is near.

³²"I tell you the truth, this generation^a will certainly not pass away until all these things have happened. ³³Heaven and earth will pass away, but my words will never pass away.

³⁴"Be careful, or your hearts will be weighed down with dissipation, drunkenness and the anxieties of life, and that day will close on you unexpectedly like a trap. ³⁵For it will come upon all those who live on the face of the whole earth. ³⁶Be always on the watch, and pray that you may be able to escape all that is about to happen, and that you may be able to stand before the Son of Man."

³⁷Each day Jesus was teaching at the temple, and each evening he went out to spend the night on the hill called the Mount of Olives, ³⁸and all the people came early in the morning to hear him at the temple.

22 *Judas Agrees to Betray Jesus* Now the Feast of Unleavened Bread, called the Passover, was approaching, ²and the chief priests and the teachers of the law were looking for some way to get rid of Jesus, for they were afraid of the people. ³Then Satan entered Judas, called Iscariot, one of the Twelve. ⁴And Judas went to the chief priests and the officers of the temple guard and discussed with them how he might betray Jesus. ⁵They were delighted and agreed to give him money. ⁶He consented, and watched for an opportunity to hand Jesus over to them when no crowd was present.

The Last Supper ⁷Then came the day of Unleavened Bread on which the Passover lamb had to be sacrificed. ⁸Jesus sent Peter and John, saying, "Go and make preparations for us to eat the Passover."

⁹"Where do you want us to prepare for it?" they asked.

¹⁰He replied, "As you enter the city, a man carrying a jar of water will meet you. Follow him to the house that he enters, ¹¹and say to the owner of the house, 'The Teacher asks: Where is the guest room, where I may eat the Passover with my disciples?' ¹²He will show you a large upper room, all furnished. Make preparations there."

^a32 Or *race*

[13]They left and found things just as Jesus had told them. So they prepared the Passover.

[14]When the hour came, Jesus and his apostles reclined at the table. [15]And he said to them, "I have eagerly desired to eat this Passover with you before I suffer. [16]For I tell you, I will not eat it again until it finds fulfillment in the kingdom of God."

[17]After taking the cup, he gave thanks and said, "Take this and divide it among you. [18]For I tell you I will not drink again of the fruit of the vine until the kingdom of God comes."

[19]And he took bread, gave thanks and broke it, and gave it to them, saying, "This is my body given for you; do this in remembrance of me."

[20]In the same way, after the supper he took the cup, saying, "This cup is the new covenant in my blood, which is poured out for you. [21]But the hand of him who is going to betray me is with mine on the table. [22]The Son of Man will go as it has been decreed, but woe to that man who betrays him." [23]They began to question among themselves which of them it might be who would do this.

[24]Also a dispute arose among them as to which of them was considered to be greatest. [25]Jesus said to them, "The kings of the Gentiles lord it over them; and those who exercise authority over them call themselves Benefactors. [26]But you are not to be like that. Instead, the greatest among you should be like the youngest, and the one who rules like the one who serves. [27]For who is greater, the one who is at the table or the one who serves? Is it not the one who is at the table? But I am among you as one who serves. [28]You are those who have stood by me in my trials. [29]And I confer on you a kingdom, just as my Father conferred one on me, [30]so that you may eat and drink at my table in my kingdom and sit on thrones, judging the twelve tribes of Israel.

[31]"Simon, Simon, Satan has asked to sift you[a] as wheat. [32]But I have prayed for you, Simon, that your faith may not fail. And when you have turned back, strengthen your brothers."

[33]But he replied, "Lord, I am ready to go with you to prison and to death."

[34]Jesus answered, "I tell you, Peter, before the rooster crows today, you will deny three times that you know me."

[35]Then Jesus asked them, "When I sent you without purse, bag or sandals, did you lack anything?"

"Nothing," they answered.

[36]He said to them, "But now if you have a purse, take it, and also a bag; and if you don't have a sword, sell your cloak and buy one. [37]It is written: 'And he was numbered with the transgressors'[b]; and I tell you that this must be fulfilled in me. Yes, what is written about me is reaching its fulfillment."

[38]The disciples said, "See, Lord, here are two swords."

"That is enough," he replied.

Jesus Prays on the Mount of Olives

[39]Jesus went out as usual to the Mount of Olives, and his disciples followed him. [40]On reaching the place, he said to them, "Pray that you will not fall into temptation." [41]He withdrew about a stone's throw beyond them, knelt down and prayed, [42]"Father, if you are willing, take this cup from me; yet not my will, but yours be done." [43]An angel from heaven appeared to him and strengthened him. [44]And being in anguish, he prayed more earnestly, and his sweat was like drops of blood falling to the ground.[c]

QUIZZER

LUKE 22

Q: How did Judas identify Jesus when he betrayed him?

BONUS:
What did one of Jesus' followers do to a servant who was present?

Answers on page 1372

---

[a]31 The Greek is plural.　[b]37 Isaiah 53:12　[c]44 Some early manuscripts do not have verses 43 and 44.

⁴⁵When he rose from prayer and went back to the disciples, he found them asleep, exhausted from sorrow. ⁴⁶"Why are you sleeping?" he asked them. "Get up and pray so that you will not fall into temptation."

Jesus Arrested   ⁴⁷While he was still speaking a crowd came up, and the man who was called Judas, one of the Twelve, was leading them. He approached Jesus to kiss him, ⁴⁸but Jesus asked him, "Judas, are you betraying the Son of Man with a kiss?"

⁴⁹When Jesus' followers saw what was going to happen, they said, "Lord, should we strike with our swords?" ⁵⁰And one of them struck the servant of the high priest, cutting off his right ear.

⁵¹But Jesus answered, "No more of this!" And he touched the man's ear and healed him.

⁵²Then Jesus said to the chief priests, the officers of the temple guard, and the elders, who had come for him, "Am I leading a rebellion, that you have come with swords and clubs? ⁵³Every day I was with you in the temple courts, and you did not lay a hand on me. But this is your hour—when darkness reigns."

Peter Disowns Jesus   ⁵⁴Then seizing him, they led him away and took him into the house of the high priest. Peter followed at a distance. ⁵⁵But when they had kindled a fire in the middle of the courtyard and had sat down together, Peter sat down with them. ⁵⁶A servant girl saw him seated there in the firelight. She looked closely at him and said, "This man was with him."

⁵⁷But he denied it. "Woman, I don't know him," he said.

⁵⁸A little later someone else saw him and said, "You also are one of them." "Man, I am not!" Peter replied.

⁵⁹About an hour later another asserted, "Certainly this fellow was with him, for he is a Galilean."

⁶⁰Peter replied, "Man, I don't know what you're talking about!" Just as he was speaking, the rooster crowed. ⁶¹The Lord turned and looked straight at Peter. Then Peter remembered the word the Lord had spoken to him: "Before the rooster crows today, you will disown me three times." ⁶²And he went outside and wept bitterly.

The Guards Mock Jesus   ⁶³The men who were guarding Jesus began mocking and beating him. ⁶⁴They blindfolded him and demanded, "Prophesy! Who hit you?" ⁶⁵And they said many other insulting things to him.

Jesus Before Pilate and Herod   ⁶⁶At daybreak the council of the elders of the people, both the chief priests and teachers of the law, met together, and Jesus was led before them. ⁶⁷"If you are the Christ,*ᵃ*" they said, "tell us."

Jesus answered, "If I tell you, you will not believe me, ⁶⁸and if I asked you, you would not answer. ⁶⁹But from now on, the Son of Man will be seated at the right hand of the mighty God."

⁷⁰They all asked, "Are you then the Son of God?"

He replied, "You are right in saying I am."

⁷¹Then they said, "Why do we need any more testimony? We have heard it from his own lips."

23 Then the whole assembly rose and led him off to Pilate. ²And they began to accuse him, saying, "We have found this man subverting our nation. He opposes payment of taxes to Caesar and claims to be Christ,*ᵇ* a king."

³So Pilate asked Jesus, "Are you the king of the Jews?"

"Yes, it is as you say," Jesus replied.

ᵃ67 Or *Messiah*   *ᵇ2* Or *Messiah*; also in verses 35 and 39

⁴Then Pilate announced to the chief priests and the crowd, "I find no basis for a charge against this man."

⁵But they insisted, "He stirs up the people all over Judea^a by his teaching. He started in Galilee and has come all the way here."

⁶On hearing this, Pilate asked if the man was a Galilean. ⁷When he learned that Jesus was under Herod's jurisdiction, he sent him to Herod, who was also in Jerusalem at that time.

⁸When Herod saw Jesus, he was greatly pleased, because for a long time he had been wanting to see him. From what he had heard about him, he hoped to see him perform some miracle. ⁹He plied him with many questions, but Jesus gave him no answer. ¹⁰The chief priests and the teachers of the law were standing there, vehemently accusing him. ¹¹Then Herod and his soldiers ridiculed and mocked him. Dressing him in an elegant robe, they sent him back to Pilate. ¹²That day Herod and Pilate became friends—before this they had been enemies.

¹³Pilate called together the chief priests, the rulers and the people, ¹⁴and said to them, "You brought me this man as one who was inciting the people to rebellion. I have examined him in your presence and have found no basis for your charges against him. ¹⁵Neither has Herod, for he sent him back to us; as you can see, he has done nothing to deserve death. ¹⁶Therefore, I will punish him and then release him.^b"

¹⁸With one voice they cried out, "Away with this man! Release Barabbas to us!" ¹⁹(Barabbas had been thrown into prison for an insurrection in the city, and for murder.)

²⁰Wanting to release Jesus, Pilate appealed to them again. ²¹But they kept shouting, "Crucify him! Crucify him!"

²²For the third time he spoke to them: "Why? What crime has this man committed? I have found in him no grounds for the death penalty. Therefore I will have him punished and then release him."

²³But with loud shouts they insistently demanded that he be crucified, and their shouts prevailed. ²⁴So Pilate decided to grant their demand. ²⁵He released the man who had been thrown into prison for insurrection and murder, the one they asked for, and surrendered Jesus to their will.

The Crucifixion ²⁶As they led him away, they seized Simon from Cyrene, who was on his way in from the country, and put the cross on him and made him carry it behind Jesus. ²⁷A large number of people followed him, including women who mourned and wailed for him. ²⁸Jesus turned and said to them, "Daughters of Jerusalem, do not weep for me; weep for yourselves and for your children. ²⁹For the time will come when you will say, 'Blessed are the barren women, the wombs that never bore and the breasts that never nursed!' ³⁰Then

> " 'they will say to the mountains, "Fall on us!"
> and to the hills, "Cover us!" '^c

³¹For if men do these things when the tree is green, what will happen when it is dry?"

³²Two other men, both criminals, were also led out with him to be executed. ³³When they came to the place called the Skull, there they crucified him, along with the criminals—one on his right, the other on his left. ³⁴Jesus said, "Father, forgive them, for they do not know what they are doing."^d And they divided up his clothes by casting lots.

³⁵The people stood watching, and the rulers even sneered at him. They said, "He saved others; let him save himself if he is the Christ of God, the Chosen One."

Answers

*to Quizzer on
page 1370*

**A: He kissed him
(Luke 22:47-48).**

**BONUS: He cut
off his ear
(Luke 22:50).**

---

^a5 Or *over the land of the Jews* ^b16 Some manuscripts *him." ¹⁷Now he was obliged to release one man to them at the Feast.* ^c30 Hosea 10:8 ^d34 Some early manuscripts do not have this sentence.

³⁶The soldiers also came up and mocked him. They offered him wine vinegar ³⁷and said, "If you are the king of the Jews, save yourself."

³⁸There was a written notice above him, which read: THIS IS THE KING OF THE JEWS.

³⁹One of the criminals who hung there hurled insults at him: "Aren't you the Christ? Save yourself and us!"

⁴⁰But the other criminal rebuked him. "Don't you fear God," he said, "since you are under the same sentence? ⁴¹We are punished justly, for we are getting what our deeds deserve. But this man has done nothing wrong."

⁴²Then he said, "Jesus, remember me when you come into your kingdom.ᵃ"

⁴³Jesus answered him, "I tell you the truth, today you will be with me in paradise."

Jesus' Death   ⁴⁴It was now about the sixth hour, and darkness came over the whole land until the ninth hour, ⁴⁵for the sun stopped shining. And the curtain of the temple was torn in two. ⁴⁶Jesus called out with a loud voice, "Father, into your hands I commit my spirit." When he had said this, he breathed his last.

⁴⁷The centurion, seeing what had happened, praised God and said, "Surely this was a righteous man." ⁴⁸When all the people who had gathered to witness this sight saw what took place, they beat their breasts and went away. ⁴⁹But all those who knew him, including the women who had followed him from Galilee, stood at a distance, watching these things.

Jesus' Burial   ⁵⁰Now there was a man named Joseph, a member of the Council, a good and upright man, ⁵¹who had not consented to their decision and action. He came from the Judean town of Arimathea and he was waiting for the kingdom of God. ⁵²Going to Pilate, he asked for Jesus' body. ⁵³Then he took it down, wrapped it in linen cloth and placed it in a tomb cut in the rock, one in which no one had yet been laid. ⁵⁴It was Preparation Day, and the Sabbath was about to begin.

⁵⁵The women who had come with Jesus from Galilee followed Joseph and saw the tomb and how his body was laid in it. ⁵⁶Then they went home and prepared spices and perfumes. But they rested on the Sabbath in obedience to the commandment.

The Resurrection   On the first day of the week, very early in the morning, the women took the spices they had prepared and went to the tomb. ²They found the stone rolled away from the tomb, ³but when they entered, they did not find the body of the Lord Jesus. ⁴While they were wondering about this, suddenly two men in clothes that gleamed like lightning stood beside them. ⁵In their fright the women bowed down with their faces to the ground, but the men said to them, "Why do you look for the living among the dead? ⁶He is not here; he has risen! Remember how he told you, while he was still with you in Galilee: ⁷'The Son of Man must be delivered into the hands of sinful men, be crucified and on the third day be raised again.' " ⁸Then they remembered his words.

⁹When they came back from the tomb, they told all these things to the Eleven and to all the others. ¹⁰It was Mary Magdalene, Joanna, Mary the mother of James, and the others with them who told this to the apostles. ¹¹But they did not believe the women, because their words seemed to them like nonsense. ¹²Peter, however, got up and ran to the tomb. Bending over, he saw the strips of linen lying by themselves, and he went away, wondering to himself what had happened.

On the Road to Emmaus   ¹³Now that same day two of them were going to a village called Emmaus, about seven milesᵇ from Jerusalem. ¹⁴They were talk-

---

ᵃ42 Some manuscripts *come with your kingly power*   ᵇ13 Greek *sixty stadia* (about 11 kilometers)

ing with each other about everything that had happened. ¹⁵As they talked and discussed these things with each other, Jesus himself came up and walked along with them; ¹⁶but they were kept from recognizing him.

¹⁷He asked them, "What are you discussing together as you walk along?"

They stood still, their faces downcast. ¹⁸One of them, named Cleopas, asked him, "Are you only a visitor to Jerusalem and do not know the things that have happened there in these days?"

¹⁹"What things?" he asked.

"About Jesus of Nazareth," they replied. "He was a prophet, powerful in word and deed before God and all the people. ²⁰The chief priests and our rulers handed him over to be sentenced to death, and they crucified him; ²¹but we had hoped that he was the one who was going to redeem Israel. And what is more, it is the third day since all this took place. ²²In addition, some of our women amazed us. They went to the tomb early this morning ²³but didn't find his body. They came and told us that they had seen a vision of angels, who said he was alive. ²⁴Then some of our companions went to the tomb and found it just as the women had said, but him they did not see."

²⁵He said to them, "How foolish you are, and how slow of heart to believe all that the prophets have spoken! ²⁶Did not the Christ*a* have to suffer these things and then enter his glory?" ²⁷And beginning with Moses and all the Prophets, he explained to them what was said in all the Scriptures concerning himself.

²⁸As they approached the village to which they were going, Jesus acted as if he were going farther. ²⁹But they urged him strongly, "Stay with us, for it is nearly evening; the day is almost over." So he went in to stay with them.

³⁰When he was at the table with them, he took bread, gave thanks, broke it and began to give it to them. ³¹Then their eyes were opened and they recognized him, and he disappeared from their sight. ³²They asked each other, "Were not our hearts burning within us while he talked with us on the road and opened the Scriptures to us?"

³³They got up and returned at once to Jerusalem. There they found the

a26 Or Messiah; also in verse 46

The Bible Says

Jesus Is Alive

How do you know that Jesus rose from the dead? The resurrection of Jesus is one of the clearest teachings of the Bible. Many people witnessed it:

* Two disciples (Luke 24:13–31)
* The apostles (Luke 24:36–45; John 20—21)
* Several women (Matthew 28:8–10)
* Mary Magdalene (John 20:11–18)
* Paul (Acts 9:3–6)
* Stephen (Acts 7:55)
* Some 500 in Galilee (1 Corinthians 15:6)
* James (1 Corinthians 15:7)
* John (Revelation 1:10–18)

Jesus was seen alive again by many people. Because he rose from the dead, you can be sure that you will be resurrected too.

Eleven and those with them, assembled together ³⁴and saying, "It is true! The Lord has risen and has appeared to Simon." ³⁵Then the two told what had happened on the way, and how Jesus was recognized by them when he broke the bread.

Jesus Appears to the Disciples   ³⁶While they were still talking about this, Jesus himself stood among them and said to them, "Peace be with you."

³⁷They were startled and frightened, thinking they saw a ghost. ³⁸He said to them, "Why are you troubled, and why do doubts rise in your minds? ³⁹Look at my hands and my feet. It is I myself! Touch me and see; a ghost does not have flesh and bones, as you see I have."

⁴⁰When he had said this, he showed them his hands and feet. ⁴¹And while they still did not believe it because of joy and amazement, he asked them, "Do you have anything here to eat?" ⁴²They gave him a piece of broiled fish, ⁴³and he took it and ate it in their presence.

⁴⁴He said to them, "This is what I told you while I was still with you: Everything must be fulfilled that is written about me in the Law of Moses, the Prophets and the Psalms."

⁴⁵Then he opened their minds so they could understand the Scriptures. ⁴⁶He told them, "This is what is written: The Christ will suffer and rise from the dead on the third day, ⁴⁷and repentance and forgiveness of sins will be preached in his name to all nations, beginning at Jerusalem. ⁴⁸You are witnesses of these things. ⁴⁹I am going to send you what my Father has promised; but stay in the city until you have been clothed with power from on high."

The Ascension   ⁵⁰When he had led them out to the vicinity of Bethany, he lifted up his hands and blessed them. ⁵¹While he was blessing them, he left them and was taken up into heaven. ⁵²Then they worshiped him and returned to Jerusalem with great joy. ⁵³And they stayed continually at the temple, praising God.

GOD?

Is Jesus really God? Some religions teach that Jesus is special but not that he is God the Son, who existed from all eternity and who created the universe and died to save you.

John makes sure you won't be confused. All the Gospels tell you that Jesus is the Son of God. But John emphasizes that Jesus is the God of the Old Testament, the God who loved you enough to come to earth to be with you and to save you from your sins.

Fundamentals

Why did God's Son come to earth (John 3:16)?

If Jesus is the Son, does that mean God the Father is greater (John 5:16-30)?

Did Jesus ever say he was God (John 8:48-59)?

How can Jesus be real to you every day (John 14:15-27)?

FAST FACTS

John the disciple, not John the Baptist, wrote this Gospel.

John earned his living as a fisherman.

This Gospel was the last to be written.

John's nickname was once "Son of Thunder."

John changed. "Love" is the key word in this Gospel and in the three letters of John.

1 *The Word Became Flesh* In the beginning was the Word, and the Word was with God, and the Word was God. ²He was with God in the beginning.

³Through him all things were made; without him nothing was made that has been made. ⁴In him was life, and that life was the light of men. ⁵The light shines in the darkness, but the darkness has not understood*ᵃ* it.

⁶There came a man who was sent from God; his name was John. ⁷He came as a witness to testify concerning that light, so that through him all men might believe. ⁸He himself was not the light; he came only as a witness to the light. ⁹The true light that gives light to every man was coming into the world.*ᵇ*

¹⁰He was in the world, and though the world was made through him, the world did not recognize him. ¹¹He came to that which was his own, but his own did not receive him. ¹²Yet to all who received him, to those who believed in his name, he gave the right to become children of God— ¹³children born not of natural descent,*ᶜ* nor of human decision or a husband's will, but born of God.

¹⁴The Word became flesh and made his dwelling among us. We have seen his glory, the glory of the One and Only,*ᵈ* who came from the Father, full of grace and truth.

¹⁵John testifies concerning him. He cries out, saying, "This was he of whom I said, 'He who comes after me has surpassed me because he was before me.' " ¹⁶From the fullness of his grace we have all received one blessing after another. ¹⁷For the law was given through Moses; grace and truth came through Jesus Christ. ¹⁸No one has ever seen God, but God the One and Only,*ᵈ,ᵉ* who is at the Father's side, has made him known.

John the Baptist Denies Being the Christ ¹⁹Now this was John's testimony when the Jews of Jerusalem sent priests and Levites to ask him who he was. ²⁰He did not fail to confess, but confessed freely, "I am not the Christ.*ᶠ*"

²¹They asked him, "Then who are you? Are you Elijah?"

ᵃ5 Or *darkness, and the darkness has not overcome* *ᵇ9* Or *This was the true light that gives light to every man who comes into the world* *ᶜ13* Greek *of bloods* *ᵈ14,18* Or *the Only Begotten* *ᵉ18* Some manuscripts *but the only* (or *only begotten*) *Son* *ᶠ20* Or *Messiah.* "The Christ" (Greek) and "the Messiah" (Hebrew) both mean "the Anointed One"; also in verse 25.

John 1 is just one of many Bible passages that tell you Jesus is God, not an ordinary human being. Here John calls Jesus the "Word." Just as you communicate by words, God communicates through the Word, Jesus:

The Bible Says

Jesus Is God

* The Word was God from the very beginning (John 1:1).
* The Word created all things (John 1:3).
* The Word is the source of life (John 1:4).
* The Word became a human being (John 1:14).

Why is it important that Jesus is God and not just a special human being? Jesus came to give those who believe in him "the right to become children of God" (John 1:12–13). No mere human being could accomplish that.

He said, "I am not."

"Are you the Prophet?"

He answered, "No."

[22]Finally they said, "Who are you? Give us an answer to take back to those who sent us. What do you say about yourself?"

[23]John replied in the words of Isaiah the prophet, "I am the voice of one calling in the desert, 'Make straight the way for the Lord.' "[a]

[24]Now some Pharisees who had been sent [25]questioned him, "Why then do you baptize if you are not the Christ, nor Elijah, nor the Prophet?"

[26]"I baptize with[b] water," John replied, "but among you stands one you do not know. [27]He is the one who comes after me, the thongs of whose sandals I am not worthy to untie."

[28]This all happened at Bethany on the other side of the Jordan, where John was baptizing.

Jesus the Lamb of God   [29]The next day John saw Jesus coming toward him and said, "Look, the Lamb of God, who takes away the sin of the world! [30]This is the one I meant when I said, 'A man who comes after me has surpassed me because he was before me.' [31]I myself did not know him, but the reason I came baptizing with water was that he might be revealed to Israel."

[32]Then John gave this testimony: "I saw the Spirit come down from heaven as a dove and remain on him. [33]I would not have known him, except that the one who sent me to baptize with water told me, 'The man on whom you see the Spirit come down and remain is he who will baptize with the Holy Spirit.' [34]I have seen and I testify that this is the Son of God."

Jesus' First Disciples   [35]The next day John was there again with two of his disciples. [36]When he saw Jesus passing by, he said, "Look, the Lamb of God!"

[37]When the two disciples heard him say this, they followed Jesus. [38]Turning around, Jesus saw them following and asked, "What do you want?"

They said, "Rabbi" (which means Teacher), "where are you staying?"

[39]"Come," he replied, "and you will see."

So they went and saw where he was staying, and spent that day with him. It was about the tenth hour.

[40]Andrew, Simon Peter's brother, was one of the two who heard what John had said and who had followed Jesus. [41]The first thing Andrew did was to find his brother Simon and tell him, "We have found the Messiah" (that is, the Christ). [42]And he brought him to Jesus.

Jesus looked at him and said, "You are Simon son of John. You will be called Cephas" (which, when translated, is Peter[c]).

Jesus Calls Philip and Nathanael   [43]The next day Jesus decided to leave for Galilee. Finding Philip, he said to him, "Follow me."

[44]Philip, like Andrew and Peter, was from the town of Bethsaida. [45]Philip found Nathanael and told him, "We have found the one Moses wrote about in the Law, and about whom the prophets also wrote—Jesus of Nazareth, the son of Joseph."

Direct Line

JOHN 1:40-42

Maybe the hardest thing a teen can do is witness to family. Especially if it's to unsaved parents. What can make family witness easier? Look how Andrew witnessed. He met Jesus personally. Then he said to his brother, "We have found the Messiah" (John 1:41). He didn't argue about the Bible or try to get his brother to go to church.

He simply shared his own experience of having met Jesus. You don't have to convince your family of anything. Just follow Jesus yourself and talk naturally about what he means to you. God the Holy Spirit will do the rest.

---

[a]23 Isaiah 40:3   [b]26 Or in; also in verses 31 and 33
[c]42 Both Cephas (Aramaic) and Peter (Greek) mean rock.

⁴⁶"Nazareth! Can anything good come from there?" Nathanael asked.
"Come and see," said Philip.

⁴⁷When Jesus saw Nathanael approaching, he said of him, "Here is a true Israelite, in whom there is nothing false."

⁴⁸"How do you know me?" Nathanael asked.

Jesus answered, "I saw you while you were still under the fig tree before Philip called you."

⁴⁹Then Nathanael declared, "Rabbi, you are the Son of God; you are the King of Israel."

⁵⁰Jesus said, "You believeᵃ because I told you I saw you under the fig tree. You shall see greater things than that." ⁵¹He then added, "I tell youᵇ the truth, youᵇ shall see heaven open, and the angels of God ascending and descending on the Son of Man."

Jesus Changes Water to Wine   On the third day a wedding took place at Cana in Galilee. Jesus' mother was there, ²and Jesus and his disciples had also been invited to the wedding. ³When the wine was gone, Jesus' mother said to him, "They have no more wine."

⁴"Dear woman, why do you involve me?" Jesus replied. "My time has not yet come."

⁵His mother said to the servants, "Do whatever he tells you."

⁶Nearby stood six stone water jars, the kind used by the Jews for ceremonial washing, each holding from twenty to thirty gallons.ᶜ

⁷Jesus said to the servants, "Fill the jars with water"; so they filled them to the brim.

⁸Then he told them, "Now draw some out and take it to the master of the banquet."

They did so, ⁹and the master of the banquet tasted the water that had been turned into wine. He did not realize where it had come from, though the servants who had drawn the water knew. Then he called the bridegroom aside ¹⁰and said, "Everyone brings out the choice wine first and then the cheaper wine after the guests have had too much to drink; but you have saved the best till now."

¹¹This, the first of his miraculous signs, Jesus performed at Cana in Galilee. He thus revealed his glory, and his disciples put their faith in him.

Jesus Clears the Temple   ¹²After this he went down to Capernaum with his mother and brothers and his disciples. There they stayed for a few days.

¹³When it was almost time for the Jewish Passover, Jesus went up to Jerusalem. ¹⁴In the temple courts he found men selling cattle, sheep and doves, and others sitting at tables exchanging money. ¹⁵So he made a whip out of cords, and drove all from the temple area, both sheep and cattle; he scattered the coins of the money changers and overturned their tables. ¹⁶To those who sold doves he said, "Get these out of here! How dare you turn my Father's house into a market!"

¹⁷His disciples remembered that it is written: "Zeal for your house will consume me."ᵈ

¹⁸Then the Jews demanded of him, "What miraculous sign can you show us to prove your authority to do all this?"

¹⁹Jesus answered them, "Destroy this temple, and I will raise it again in three days."

²⁰The Jews replied, "It has taken forty-six years to build this temple, and you are going to raise it in three days?" ²¹But the temple he had spoken of was his body. ²²After he was raised from the dead, his disciples recalled

---

ᵃ50 Or *Do you believe . . . ?*   ᵇ51 The Greek is plural.   ᶜ6 Greek *two to three metretes* (probably about 75 to 115 liters)   ᵈ17 Psalm 69:9

what he had said. Then they believed the Scripture and the words that Jesus had spoken.

²³Now while he was in Jerusalem at the Passover Feast, many people saw the miraculous signs he was doing and believed in his name.^a ²⁴But Jesus would not entrust himself to them, for he knew all men. ²⁵He did not need man's testimony about man, for he knew what was in a man.

Jesus Teaches Nicodemus Now there was a man of the Pharisees named Nicodemus, a member of the Jewish ruling council. ²He came to Jesus at night and said, "Rabbi, we know you are a teacher who has come from God. For no one could perform the miraculous signs you are doing if God were not with him."

³In reply Jesus declared, "I tell you the truth, no one can see the kingdom of God unless he is born again.^b"

⁴"How can a man be born when he is old?" Nicodemus asked. "Surely he cannot enter a second time into his mother's womb to be born!"

⁵Jesus answered, "I tell you the truth, no one can enter the kingdom of God unless he is born of water and the Spirit. ⁶Flesh gives birth to flesh, but the Spirit^c gives birth to spirit. ⁷You should not be surprised at my saying, 'You^d must be born again.' ⁸The wind blows wherever it pleases. You hear its sound, but you cannot tell where it comes from or where it is going. So it is with everyone born of the Spirit."

⁹"How can this be?" Nicodemus asked.

¹⁰"You are Israel's teacher," said Jesus, "and do you not understand these things? ¹¹I tell you the truth, we speak of what we know, and we testify to what we have seen, but still you people do not accept our testimony. ¹²I have spoken to you of earthly things and you do not believe; how then will you believe if I speak of heavenly things? ¹³No one has ever gone into heaven except the one who came from heaven—the Son of Man.^e ¹⁴Just as Moses lifted up the snake in the desert, so the Son of Man must be lifted up, ¹⁵that everyone who believes in him may have eternal life.^f

¹⁶"For God so loved the world that he gave his one and only Son,^g that whoever believes in him shall not perish but have eternal life. ¹⁷For God did

---

^a23 Or *and believed in him*   ^b3 Or *born from above*; also in verse 7   ^c6 Or *but spirit*   ^d7 The Greek is plural.   ^e13 Some manuscripts *Man, who is in heaven*   ^f15 Or *believes may have eternal life in him*   ^g16 Or *his only begotten Son*

The Bible Says

You Can Know

If someone asked you if you're saved, what would you say? Some people say, "I hope I'll be saved." Some people say, "I think I'm saved." And then other people say, "I know I'm saved!"

A verse that is probably the most famous one in the Bible tells you that you can know. Take a minute to read John 3:16. Now read verse 17 also. It's pretty clear. God sent his Son to give everlasting life to whoever believes in him. And whoever believes in him is not condemned.

Try something. Take out that "whoever," and put your own name there. Read the verse again with your name in it, and think about it. You believe in Jesus? Then you have God's own word that you are saved. For sure!

not send his Son into the world to condemn the world, but to save the world through him. ¹⁸Whoever believes in him is not condemned, but whoever does not believe stands condemned already because he has not believed in the name of God's one and only Son.ᵃ ¹⁹This is the verdict: Light has come into the world, but men loved darkness instead of light because their deeds were evil. ²⁰Everyone who does evil hates the light, and will not come into the light for fear that his deeds will be exposed. ²¹But whoever lives by the truth comes into the light, so that it may be seen plainly that what he has done has been done through God."ᵇ

John the Baptist's Testimony About Jesus   ²²After this, Jesus and his disciples went out into the Judean countryside, where he spent some time with them, and baptized. ²³Now John also was baptizing at Aenon near Salim, because there was plenty of water, and people were constantly coming to be baptized. ²⁴(This was before John was put in prison.) ²⁵An argument developed between some of John's disciples and a certain Jewᶜ over the matter of ceremonial washing. ²⁶They came to John and said to him, "Rabbi, that man who was with you on the other side of the Jordan—the one you testified about— well, he is baptizing, and everyone is going to him."

²⁷To this John replied, "A man can receive only what is given him from heaven. ²⁸You yourselves can testify that I said, 'I am not the Christᵈ but am sent ahead of him.' ²⁹The bride belongs to the bridegroom. The friend who attends the bridegroom waits and listens for him, and is full of joy when he hears the bridegroom's voice. That joy is mine, and it is now complete. ³⁰He must become greater; I must become less.

³¹"The one who comes from above is above all; the one who is from the earth belongs to the earth, and speaks as one from the earth. The one who comes from heaven is above all. ³²He testifies to what he has seen and heard, but no one accepts his testimony. ³³The man who has accepted it has certified that God is truthful. ³⁴For the one whom God has sent speaks the words of God, for Godᵉ gives the Spirit without limit. ³⁵The Father loves the Son and has placed everything in his hands. ³⁶Whoever believes in the Son has eternal life, but whoever rejects the Son will not see life, for God's wrath remains on him."ᶠ

Jesus Talks With a Samaritan Woman   The Pharisees heard that Jesus was gaining and baptizing more disciples than John, ²although in fact it was not Jesus who baptized, but his disciples. ³When the Lord learned of this, he left Judea and went back once more to Galilee.

⁴Now he had to go through Samaria. ⁵So he came to a town in Samaria called Sychar, near the plot of ground Jacob had given to his son Joseph. ⁶Jacob's well was there, and Jesus, tired as he was from the journey, sat down by the well. It was about the sixth hour.

⁷When a Samaritan woman came to draw water, Jesus said to her, "Will you give me a drink?" ⁸(His disciples had gone into the town to buy food.)

⁹The Samaritan woman said to him, "You are a Jew and I am a Samaritan woman. How can you ask me for a drink?" (For Jews do not associate with Samaritans.ᵍ)

¹⁰Jesus answered her, "If you knew the gift of God and who it is that asks you for a drink, you would have asked him and he would have given you living water."

¹¹"Sir," the woman said, "you have nothing to draw with and the well is deep. Where can you get this living water? ¹²Are you greater than our father

---

ᵃ18 Or *God's only begotten Son*   ᵇ21 Some interpreters end the quotation after verse 15.   ᶜ25 Some manuscripts *and certain Jews*   ᵈ28 Or *Messiah*   ᵉ34 Greek *he*   ᶠ36 Some interpreters end the quotation after verse 30.   ᵍ9 Or *do not use dishes Samaritans have used*

Jacob, who gave us the well and drank from it himself, as did also his sons and his flocks and herds?"

¹³Jesus answered, "Everyone who drinks this water will be thirsty again, ¹⁴but whoever drinks the water I give him will never thirst. Indeed, the water I give him will become in him a spring of water welling up to eternal life."

¹⁵The woman said to him, "Sir, give me this water so that I won't get thirsty and have to keep coming here to draw water."

¹⁶He told her, "Go, call your husband and come back."

¹⁷"I have no husband," she replied.

Jesus said to her, "You are right when you say you have no husband. ¹⁸The fact is, you have had five husbands, and the man you now have is not your husband. What you have just said is quite true."

¹⁹"Sir," the woman said, "I can see that you are a prophet. ²⁰Our fathers worshiped on this mountain, but you Jews claim that the place where we must worship is in Jerusalem."

²¹Jesus declared, "Believe me, woman, a time is coming when you will worship the Father neither on this mountain nor in Jerusalem. ²²You Samaritans worship what you do not know; we worship what we do know, for salvation is from the Jews. ²³Yet a time is coming and has now come when the true worshipers will worship the Father in spirit and truth, for they are the kind of worshipers the Father seeks. ²⁴God is spirit, and his worshipers must worship in spirit and in truth."

²⁵The woman said, "I know that Messiah" (called Christ) "is coming. When he comes, he will explain everything to us."

²⁶Then Jesus declared, "I who speak to you am he."

The Disciples Rejoin Jesus ²⁷Just then his disciples returned and were surprised to find him talking with a woman. But no one asked, "What do you want?" or "Why are you talking with her?"

²⁸Then, leaving her water jar, the woman went back to the town and said to the people, ²⁹"Come, see a man who told me everything I ever did. Could this be the Christᵃ?" ³⁰They came out of the town and made their way toward him.

³¹Meanwhile his disciples urged him, "Rabbi, eat something."

³²But he said to them, "I have food to eat that you know nothing about."

³³Then his disciples said to each other, "Could someone have brought him food?"

³⁴"My food," said Jesus, "is to do the will of him who sent me and to finish his work. ³⁵Do you not say, 'Four months more and then the harvest'? I tell you, open your eyes and look at the fields! They are ripe for harvest. ³⁶Even now the reaper draws his wages, even now he harvests the crop for eternal life, so that the sower and the reaper may be glad together. ³⁷Thus the saying 'One sows and another reaps' is true. ³⁸I sent you to reap what you have not worked for. Others have done the hard work, and you have reaped the benefits of their labor."

Many Samaritans Believe ³⁹Many of the Samaritans from that town believed in him because of the woman's testimony, "He told me everything I ever did." ⁴⁰So when the Samaritans came to him, they urged him to stay with them, and he stayed two days. ⁴¹And because of his words many more became believers.

⁴²They said to the woman, "We no longer believe just because of what you said; now we have heard for ourselves, and we know that this man really is the Savior of the world."

Jesus Heals the Official's Son ⁴³After the two days he left for Galilee. ⁴⁴(Now Jesus himself had pointed out that a prophet has no honor in his own coun-

ᵃ29 Or *Messiah*

try.) ⁴⁵When he arrived in Galilee, the Galileans welcomed him. They had seen all that he had done in Jerusalem at the Passover Feast, for they also had been there.

⁴⁶Once more he visited Cana in Galilee, where he had turned the water into wine. And there was a certain royal official whose son lay sick at Capernaum. ⁴⁷When this man heard that Jesus had arrived in Galilee from Judea, he went to him and begged him to come and heal his son, who was close to death.

⁴⁸"Unless you people see miraculous signs and wonders," Jesus told him, "you will never believe."

⁴⁹The royal official said, "Sir, come down before my child dies."

⁵⁰Jesus replied, "You may go. Your son will live."

The man took Jesus at his word and departed. ⁵¹While he was still on the way, his servants met him with the news that his boy was living. ⁵²When he inquired as to the time when his son got better, they said to him, "The fever left him yesterday at the seventh hour."

⁵³Then the father realized that this was the exact time at which Jesus had said to him, "Your son will live." So he and all his household believed.

⁵⁴This was the second miraculous sign that Jesus performed, having come from Judea to Galilee.

5 *The Healing at the Pool* Some time later, Jesus went up to Jerusalem for a feast of the Jews. ²Now there is in Jerusalem near the Sheep Gate a pool, which in Aramaic is called Bethesda*ᵃ* and which is surrounded by five covered colonnades. ³Here a great number of disabled people used to lie— the blind, the lame, the paralyzed.*ᵇ* ⁵One who was there had been an invalid for thirty-eight years. ⁶When Jesus saw him lying there and learned that he had been in this condition for a long time, he asked him, "Do you want to get well?"

⁷"Sir," the invalid replied, "I have no one to help me into the pool when the water is stirred. While I am trying to get in, someone else goes down ahead of me."

⁸Then Jesus said to him, "Get up! Pick up your mat and walk." ⁹At once the man was cured; he picked up his mat and walked.

The day on which this took place was a Sabbath, ¹⁰and so the Jews said to the man who had been healed, "It is the Sabbath; the law forbids you to carry your mat."

¹¹But he replied, "The man who made me well said to me, 'Pick up your mat and walk.' "

¹²So they asked him, "Who is this fellow who told you to pick it up and walk?"

¹³The man who was healed had no idea who it was, for Jesus had slipped away into the crowd that was there.

¹⁴Later Jesus found him at the temple and said to him, "See, you are well again. Stop sinning or something worse may

---

ᵃ2 Some manuscripts Bethzatha; other manuscripts *Bethsaida ᵇ3 Some less important manuscripts paralyzed—and they waited for the moving of the waters. ⁴From time to time an angel of the Lord would come down and stir up the waters. The first one into the pool after each such disturbance would be cured of whatever disease he had.*

JOHN 5:1–13

Do you want to get well?" (John 5:6). That's the question Jesus asked a man who was paralyzed for 38 years. Why that question? Maybe because he didn't want to get well. For 38 years he lived by begging. Healed, he'd have to go to work and support himself. How about your prayers? God can answer them. Did you ask God to help you pass that test? If so, you'll have to study. Did you tell God you want to witness? Then you'll have to speak up. God can answer your prayers, but you'll have to do your part too.

Direct Line

happen to you." ¹⁵The man went away and told the Jews that it was Jesus who had made him well.

Life Through the Son   ¹⁶So, because Jesus was doing these things on the Sabbath, the Jews persecuted him. ¹⁷Jesus said to them, "My Father is always at his work to this very day, and I, too, am working." ¹⁸For this reason the Jews tried all the harder to kill him; not only was he breaking the Sabbath, but he was even calling God his own Father, making himself equal with God.

¹⁹Jesus gave them this answer: "I tell you the truth, the Son can do nothing by himself; he can do only what he sees his Father doing, because whatever the Father does the Son also does. ²⁰For the Father loves the Son and shows him all he does. Yes, to your amazement he will show him even greater things than these. ²¹For just as the Father raises the dead and gives them life, even so the Son gives life to whom he is pleased to give it. ²²Moreover, the Father judges no one, but has entrusted all judgment to the Son, ²³that all may honor the Son just as they honor the Father. He who does not honor the Son does not honor the Father, who sent him.

²⁴"I tell you the truth, whoever hears my word and believes him who sent me has eternal life and will not be condemned; he has crossed over from death to life. ²⁵I tell you the truth, a time is coming and has now come when the dead will hear the voice of the Son of God and those who hear will live. ²⁶For as the Father has life in himself, so he has granted the Son to have life in himself. ²⁷And he has given him authority to judge because he is the Son of Man.

²⁸"Do not be amazed at this, for a time is coming when all who are in their graves will hear his voice ²⁹and come out—those who have done good will rise to live, and those who have done evil will rise to be condemned. ³⁰By myself I can do nothing; I judge only as I hear, and my judgment is just, for I seek not to please myself but him who sent me.

Testimonies About Jesus   ³¹"If I testify about myself, my testimony is not valid. ³²There is another who testifies in my favor, and I know that his testimony about me is valid.

³³"You have sent to John and he has testified to the truth. ³⁴Not that I accept human testimony; but I mention it that you may be saved. ³⁵John was a lamp that burned and gave light, and you chose for a time to enjoy his light.

³⁶"I have testimony weightier than that of John. For the very work that the Father has given me to finish, and which I am doing, testifies that the Father has sent me. ³⁷And the Father who sent me has himself testified concerning me. You have never heard his voice nor seen his form, ³⁸nor does his word dwell in you, for you do not believe the one he sent. ³⁹You diligently study*a* the Scriptures because you think that by them you possess eternal life. These are the Scriptures that testify about me, ⁴⁰yet you refuse to come to me to have life.

⁴¹"I do not accept praise from men, ⁴²but I know you. I know that you do not have the love of God in your hearts. ⁴³I have come in my Father's name, and you do not accept me; but if someone else comes in his own name, you will accept him. ⁴⁴How can you believe if you accept praise from one another, yet make no effort to obtain the praise that comes from the only God*b*?

⁴⁵"But do not think I will accuse you before the Father. Your accuser is Moses, on whom your hopes are set. ⁴⁶If you believed Moses, you would believe me, for he wrote about me. ⁴⁷But since you do not believe what he wrote, how are you going to believe what I say?"

---

a39 Or *Study diligently* (the imperative)   *b44* Some early manuscripts *the Only One*

6 *Jesus Feeds the Five Thousand*   Some time after this, Jesus crossed to the far shore of the Sea of Galilee (that is, the Sea of Tiberias), ²and a great crowd of people followed him because they saw the miraculous signs he had performed on the sick. ³Then Jesus went up on a mountainside and sat down with his disciples. ⁴The Jewish Passover Feast was near.

⁵When Jesus looked up and saw a great crowd coming toward him, he said to Philip, "Where shall we buy bread for these people to eat?" ⁶He asked this only to test him, for he already had in mind what he was going to do.

⁷Philip answered him, "Eight months' wages*a* would not buy enough bread for each one to have a bite!"

⁸Another of his disciples, Andrew, Simon Peter's brother, spoke up, ⁹"Here is a boy with five small barley loaves and two small fish, but how far will they go among so many?"

¹⁰Jesus said, "Have the people sit down." There was plenty of grass in that place, and the men sat down, about five thousand of them. ¹¹Jesus then took the loaves, gave thanks, and distributed to those who were seated as much as they wanted. He did the same with the fish.

¹²When they had all had enough to eat, he said to his disciples, "Gather the pieces that are left over. Let nothing be wasted." ¹³So they gathered them and filled twelve baskets with the pieces of the five barley loaves left over by those who had eaten.

¹⁴After the people saw the miraculous sign that Jesus did, they began to say, "Surely this is the Prophet who is to come into the world." ¹⁵Jesus, knowing that they intended to come and make him king by force, withdrew again to a mountain by himself.

Jesus Walks on the Water   ¹⁶When evening came, his disciples went down to the lake, ¹⁷where they got into a boat and set off across the lake for Capernaum. By now it was dark, and Jesus had not yet joined them. ¹⁸A strong wind was blowing and the waters grew rough. ¹⁹When they had rowed three or three and a half miles,*b* they saw Jesus approaching the boat, walking on the water; and they were terrified. ²⁰But he said to them, "It is I; don't be afraid." ²¹Then they were willing to take him into the boat, and immediately the boat reached the shore where they were heading.

²²The next day the crowd that had stayed on the opposite shore of the lake realized that only one boat had been there, and that Jesus had not entered it with his disciples, but that they had gone away alone. ²³Then some boats from Tiberias landed near the place where the people had eaten the bread after the Lord had given thanks. ²⁴Once the crowd realized that neither Jesus nor his disciples were there, they got into the boats and went to Capernaum in search of Jesus.

Jesus the Bread of Life   ²⁵When they found him on the other side of the lake, they asked him, "Rabbi, when did you get here?"

²⁶Jesus answered, "I tell you the truth, you are looking for me, not because you saw miraculous signs but because you ate the loaves and had your fill. ²⁷Do not work for food that spoils, but for food that endures to eternal life, which the Son of Man will give you. On him God the Father has placed his seal of approval."

²⁸Then they asked him, "What must we do to do the works God requires?"

²⁹Jesus answered, "The work of God is this: to believe in the one he has sent."

³⁰So they asked him, "What miraculous sign then will you give that we may see it and believe you? What will you do? ³¹Our forefathers ate the manna in the desert; as it is written: 'He gave them bread from heaven to eat.'*c*"

---

a7 Greek *two hundred denarii*   *b19* Greek *rowed twenty-five or thirty stadia* (about 5 or 6 kilometers)
c31 Exodus 16:4; Neh. 9:15; Psalm 78:24,25

³²Jesus said to them, "I tell you the truth, it is not Moses who has given you the bread from heaven, but it is my Father who gives you the true bread from heaven. ³³For the bread of God is he who comes down from heaven and gives life to the world."

³⁴"Sir," they said, "from now on give us this bread."

³⁵Then Jesus declared, "I am the bread of life. He who comes to me will never go hungry, and he who believes in me will never be thirsty. ³⁶But as I told you, you have seen me and still you do not believe. ³⁷All that the Father gives me will come to me, and whoever comes to me I will never drive away. ³⁸For I have come down from heaven not to do my will but to do the will of him who sent me. ³⁹And this is the will of him who sent me, that I shall lose none of all that he has given me, but raise them up at the last day. ⁴⁰For my Father's will is that everyone who looks to the Son and believes in him shall have eternal life, and I will raise him up at the last day."

⁴¹At this the Jews began to grumble about him because he said, "I am the bread that came down from heaven." ⁴²They said, "Is this not Jesus, the son of Joseph, whose father and mother we know? How can he now say, 'I came down from heaven'?"

⁴³"Stop grumbling among yourselves," Jesus answered. ⁴⁴"No one can come to me unless the Father who sent me draws him, and I will raise him up at the last day. ⁴⁵It is written in the Prophets: 'They will all be taught by God.'ᵃ Everyone who listens to the Father and learns from him comes to me. ⁴⁶No one has seen the Father except the one who is from God; only he has seen the Father. ⁴⁷I tell you the truth, he who believes has everlasting life. ⁴⁸I am the bread of life. ⁴⁹Your forefathers ate the manna in the desert, yet they died. ⁵⁰But here is the bread that comes down from heaven, which a man may eat and not die. ⁵¹I am the living bread that came down from heaven. If anyone eats of this bread, he will live forever. This bread is my flesh, which I will give for the life of the world."

⁵²Then the Jews began to argue sharply among themselves, "How can this man give us his flesh to eat?"

⁵³Jesus said to them, "I tell you the truth, unless you eat the flesh of the Son of Man and drink his blood, you have no life in you. ⁵⁴Whoever eats my flesh and drinks my blood has eternal life, and I will raise him up at the last day. ⁵⁵For my flesh is real food and my blood is real drink. ⁵⁶Whoever eats my flesh and drinks my blood remains in me, and I in him. ⁵⁷Just as the living Father sent me and I live because of the Father, so the one who feeds on me will live because of me. ⁵⁸This is the bread that came down from heaven. Your forefathers ate manna and died, but he who feeds on this bread will live forever." ⁵⁹He said this while teaching in the synagogue in Capernaum.

Many Disciples Desert Jesus   ⁶⁰On hearing it, many of his disciples said, "This is a hard teaching. Who can accept it?"

⁶¹Aware that his disciples were grumbling about this, Jesus said to them, "Does this offend you? ⁶²What if you see the Son of Man ascend to where he was before! ⁶³The Spirit gives life; the flesh counts for nothing. The words I have spoken to you are spiritᵇ and they are life. ⁶⁴Yet there are some of you who do not believe." For Jesus had known from the beginning which of them did not believe and who would betray him. ⁶⁵He went on to say, "This is why I told you that no one can come to me unless the Father has enabled him."

⁶⁶From this time many of his disciples turned back and no longer followed him.

> My Father's will is that everyone who looks to the Son and believes in him shall have eternal life (John 6:40).

ᵃ45 Isaiah 54:13   ᵇ63 Or *Spirit*

⁶⁷"You do not want to leave too, do you?" Jesus asked the Twelve.

⁶⁸Simon Peter answered him, "Lord, to whom shall we go? You have the words of eternal life. ⁶⁹We believe and know that you are the Holy One of God."

⁷⁰Then Jesus replied, "Have I not chosen you, the Twelve? Yet one of you is a devil!" ⁷¹(He meant Judas, the son of Simon Iscariot, who, though one of the Twelve, was later to betray him.)

Jesus Goes to the Feast of Tabernacles   After this, Jesus went around in Galilee, purposely staying away from Judea because the Jews there were waiting to take his life. ²But when the Jewish Feast of Tabernacles was near, ³Jesus' brothers said to him, "You ought to leave here and go to Judea, so that your disciples may see the miracles you do. ⁴No one who wants to become a public figure acts in secret. Since you are doing these things, show yourself to the world." ⁵For even his own brothers did not believe in him.

⁶Therefore Jesus told them, "The right time for me has not yet come; for you any time is right. ⁷The world cannot hate you, but it hates me because I testify that what it does is evil. ⁸You go to the Feast. I am not yet*a* going up to this Feast, because for me the right time has not yet come." ⁹Having said this, he stayed in Galilee.

¹⁰However, after his brothers had left for the Feast, he went also, not publicly, but in secret. ¹¹Now at the Feast the Jews were watching for him and asking, "Where is that man?"

¹²Among the crowds there was widespread whispering about him. Some said, "He is a good man."

Others replied, "No, he deceives the people." ¹³But no one would say anything publicly about him for fear of the Jews.

Jesus Teaches at the Feast   ¹⁴Not until halfway through the Feast did Jesus go up to the temple courts and begin to teach. ¹⁵The Jews were amazed and asked, "How did this man get such learning without having studied?"

¹⁶Jesus answered, "My teaching is not my own. It comes from him who sent me. ¹⁷If anyone chooses to do God's will, he will find out whether my teaching comes from God or whether I speak on my own. ¹⁸He who speaks on his own does so to gain honor for himself, but he who works for the honor of the one who sent him is a man of truth; there is nothing false about him. ¹⁹Has not Moses given you the law? Yet not one of you keeps the law. Why are you trying to kill me?"

²⁰"You are demon-possessed," the crowd answered. "Who is trying to kill you?"

²¹Jesus said to them, "I did one miracle, and you are all astonished. ²²Yet, because Moses gave you circumcision (though actually it did not come from Moses, but from the patriarchs), you circumcise a child on the Sabbath. ²³Now if a child can be circumcised on the Sabbath so that the law of Moses may not be broken, why are you angry with me for healing the whole man on the Sabbath? ²⁴Stop judging by mere appearances, and make a right judgment."

a8 Some early manuscripts do not have yet.

JOHN 6:60–69

Where did God come from? Why doesn't the Bible say anything about dinosaurs? How could Jesus be born without a human father? There are no easy answers to questions like these. No one created God; he always existed. We don't know where dinosaurs fit in. And Mary was a virgin when Jesus was conceived. We can't explain everything we believe. So what do we do when we don't understand some teaching of the Bible? Stop following Jesus, like the disciples in this story? No way! Like the Twelve we say, "We believe and know that you are the Holy One of God" (John 6:69). Our hard questions will be answered when Jesus comes again.

Direct Line

Is Jesus the Christ? ²⁵At that point some of the people of Jerusalem began to ask, "Isn't this the man they are trying to kill? ²⁶Here he is, speaking publicly, and they are not saying a word to him. Have the authorities really concluded that he is the Christ^a? ²⁷But we know where this man is from; when the Christ comes, no one will know where he is from."

²⁸Then Jesus, still teaching in the temple courts, cried out, "Yes, you know me, and you know where I am from. I am not here on my own, but he who sent me is true. You do not know him, ²⁹but I know him because I am from him and he sent me."

³⁰At this they tried to seize him, but no one laid a hand on him, because his time had not yet come. ³¹Still, many in the crowd put their faith in him. They said, "When the Christ comes, will he do more miraculous signs than this man?"

³²The Pharisees heard the crowd whispering such things about him. Then the chief priests and the Pharisees sent temple guards to arrest him.

³³Jesus said, "I am with you for only a short time, and then I go to the one who sent me. ³⁴You will look for me, but you will not find me; and where I am, you cannot come."

³⁵The Jews said to one another, "Where does this man intend to go that we cannot find him? Will he go where our people live scattered among the Greeks, and teach the Greeks? ³⁶What did he mean when he said, 'You will look for me, but you will not find me,' and 'Where I am, you cannot come'?"

³⁷On the last and greatest day of the Feast, Jesus stood and said in a loud voice, "If anyone is thirsty, let him come to me and drink. ³⁸Whoever believes in me, as^b the Scripture has said, streams of living water will flow from within him." ³⁹By this he meant the Spirit, whom those who believed in him were later to receive. Up to that time the Spirit had not been given, since Jesus had not yet been glorified.

⁴⁰On hearing his words, some of the people said, "Surely this man is the Prophet."

⁴¹Others said, "He is the Christ."

Still others asked, "How can the Christ come from Galilee? ⁴²Does not the Scripture say that the Christ will come from David's family^c and from Bethlehem, the town where David lived?" ⁴³Thus the people were divided because of Jesus. ⁴⁴Some wanted to seize him, but no one laid a hand on him.

Unbelief of the Leaders ⁴⁵Finally the temple guards went back to the chief priests and Pharisees, who asked them, "Why didn't you bring him in?"

⁴⁶"No one ever spoke the way this man does," the guards declared.

⁴⁷"You mean he has deceived you also?" the Pharisees retorted. ⁴⁸"Has any of the rulers or of the Pharisees believed in him? ⁴⁹No! But this mob that knows nothing of the law—there is a curse on them."

⁵⁰Nicodemus, who had gone to Jesus earlier and who was one of their own number, asked, ⁵¹"Does our law condemn anyone without first hearing him to find out what he is doing?"

⁵²They replied, "Are you from Galilee, too? Look into it, and you will find that a prophet^d does not come out of Galilee."

[The earliest manuscripts and many other ancient witnesses do not have John 7:53–8:11.]

⁵³Then each went to his own home.

---

^a26 Or *Messiah*; also in verses 27, 31, 41 and 42   ^b37,38 Or / *If anyone is thirsty, let him come to me. / And let him drink,* ³⁸*who believes in me. / As*   ^c42 Greek *seed*   ^d52 Two early manuscripts *the Prophet*

But Jesus went to the Mount of Olives. [2]At dawn he appeared again in the temple courts, where all the people gathered around him, and he sat down to teach them. [3]The teachers of the law and the Pharisees brought in a woman caught in adultery. They made her stand before the group [4]and said to Jesus, "Teacher, this woman was caught in the act of adultery. [5]In the Law Moses commanded us to stone such women. Now what do you say?" [6]They were using this question as a trap, in order to have a basis for accusing him.

But Jesus bent down and started to write on the ground with his finger. [7]When they kept on questioning him, he straightened up and said to them, "If any one of you is without sin, let him be the first to throw a stone at her." [8]Again he stooped down and wrote on the ground.

[9]At this, those who heard began to go away one at a time, the older ones first, until only Jesus was left, with the woman still standing there. [10]Jesus straightened up and asked her, "Woman, where are they? Has no one condemned you?"

[11]"No one, sir," she said.

"Then neither do I condemn you," Jesus declared. "Go now and leave your life of sin."

The Validity of Jesus' Testimony   [12]When Jesus spoke again to the people, he said, "I am the light of the world. Whoever follows me will never walk in darkness, but will have the light of life."

[13]The Pharisees challenged him, "Here you are, appearing as your own witness; your testimony is not valid."

[14]Jesus answered, "Even if I testify on my own behalf, my testimony is valid, for I know where I came from and where I am going. But you have no idea where I come from or where I am going. [15]You judge by human standards; I pass judgment on no one. [16]But if I do judge, my decisions are right, because I am not alone. I stand with the Father, who sent me. [17]In your own Law it is written that the testimony of two men is valid. [18]I am one who testifies for myself; my other witness is the Father, who sent me."

[19]Then they asked him, "Where is your father?"

"You do not know me or my Father," Jesus replied. "If you knew me, you would know my Father also." [20]He spoke these words while teaching in the temple area near the place where the offerings were put. Yet no one seized him, because his time had not yet come.

[21]Once more Jesus said to them, "I am going away, and you will look for me, and you will die in your sin. Where I go, you cannot come."

[22]This made the Jews ask, "Will he kill himself? Is that why he says, 'Where I go, you cannot come'?"

[23]But he continued, "You are from below; I am from above. You are of this world; I am not of this world. [24]I told you that you would die in your sins; if you do not believe that I am the one I claim to be,[a] you will indeed die in your sins."

[25]"Who are you?" they asked.

"Just what I have been claiming all along," Jesus replied. [26]"I have much to say in judg-

Too bad I can't read Aramaic!

[a]24 Or *I am he*; also in verse 28

SEE JOHN 8:8

ment of you. But he who sent me is reliable, and what I have heard from him I tell the world."

²⁷They did not understand that he was telling them about his Father. ²⁸So Jesus said, "When you have lifted up the Son of Man, then you will know that I am the one I claim to be, and that I do nothing on my own but speak just what the Father has taught me. ²⁹The one who sent me is with me; he has not left me alone, for I always do what pleases him." ³⁰Even as he spoke, many put their faith in him.

The Children of Abraham ³¹To the Jews who had believed him, Jesus said, "If you hold to my teaching, you are really my disciples. ³²Then you will know the truth, and the truth will set you free."

³³They answered him, "We are Abraham's descendants*a* and have never been slaves of anyone. How can you say that we shall be set free?"

³⁴Jesus replied, "I tell you the truth, everyone who sins is a slave to sin. ³⁵Now a slave has no permanent place in the family, but a son belongs to it forever. ³⁶So if the Son sets you free, you will be free indeed. ³⁷I know you are Abraham's descendants. Yet you are ready to kill me, because you have no room for my word. ³⁸I am telling you what I have seen in the Father's presence, and you do what you have heard from your father.*b*"

³⁹"Abraham is our father," they answered.

"If you were Abraham's children," said Jesus, "then you would*c* do the things Abraham did. ⁴⁰As it is, you are determined to kill me, a man who has told you the truth that I heard from God. Abraham did not do such things. ⁴¹You are doing the things your own father does."

"We are not illegitimate children," they protested. "The only Father we have is God himself."

The Children of the Devil ⁴²Jesus said to them, "If God were your Father, you would love me, for I came from God and now am here. I have not come on my own; but he sent me. ⁴³Why is my language not clear to you? Because you are unable to hear what I say. ⁴⁴You belong to your father, the devil, and you want to carry out your father's desire. He was a murderer from the beginning, not holding to the truth, for there is no truth in him. When he lies, he speaks his native language, for he is a liar and the father of lies. ⁴⁵Yet because I tell the truth, you do not believe me! ⁴⁶Can any of you prove me guilty of sin? If I am telling the truth, why don't you believe me? ⁴⁷He who belongs to God hears what God says. The reason you do not hear is that you do not belong to God."

The Claims of Jesus About Himself ⁴⁸The Jews answered him, "Aren't we right in saying that you are a Samaritan and demon-possessed?"

⁴⁹"I am not possessed by a demon," said Jesus, "but I honor my Father and you dishonor me. ⁵⁰I am not seeking glory for myself; but there is one who seeks it, and he is the judge. ⁵¹I tell you the truth, if anyone keeps my word, he will never see death."

⁵²At this the Jews exclaimed, "Now we know that you are demon-possessed! Abraham died and so did the prophets, yet you say that if anyone keeps your word, he will never taste death. ⁵³Are you greater than our father Abraham? He died, and so did the prophets. Who do you think you are?"

⁵⁴Jesus replied, "If I glorify myself, my glory means nothing. My Father, whom you claim as your God, is the one who glorifies me. ⁵⁵Though you do not know him, I know him. If I said I did not, I would be a liar like you, but I do know him and keep his word. ⁵⁶Your father Abraham rejoiced at the thought of seeing my day; he saw it and was glad."

---

a33 Greek seed; also in verse 37   b38 Or presence. Therefore do what you have heard from the Father.
c39 Some early manuscripts "If you are Abraham's children," said Jesus, "then

⁵⁷"You are not yet fifty years old," the Jews said to him, "and you have seen Abraham!"

⁵⁸"I tell you the truth," Jesus answered, "before Abraham was born, I am!" ⁵⁹At this, they picked up stones to stone him, but Jesus hid himself, slipping away from the temple grounds.

Jesus Heals a Man Born Blind As he went along, he saw a man blind from birth. ²His disciples asked him, "Rabbi, who sinned, this man or his parents, that he was born blind?"

³"Neither this man nor his parents sinned," said Jesus, "but this happened so that the work of God might be displayed in his life. ⁴As long as it is day, we must do the work of him who sent me. Night is coming, when no one can work. ⁵While I am in the world, I am the light of the world."

⁶Having said this, he spit on the ground, made some mud with the saliva, and put it on the man's eyes. ⁷"Go," he told him, "wash in the Pool of Siloam" (this word means Sent). So the man went and washed, and came home seeing.

⁸His neighbors and those who had formerly seen him begging asked, "Isn't this the same man who used to sit and beg?" ⁹Some claimed that he was.

Others said, "No, he only looks like him."

But he himself insisted, "I am the man."

¹⁰"How then were your eyes opened?" they demanded.

¹¹He replied, "The man they call Jesus made some mud and put it on my eyes. He told me to go to Siloam and wash. So I went and washed, and then I could see."

¹²"Where is this man?" they asked him.

"I don't know," he said.

The Pharisees Investigate the Healing ¹³They brought to the Pharisees the man who had been blind. ¹⁴Now the day on which Jesus had made the mud and opened the man's eyes was a Sabbath. ¹⁵Therefore the Pharisees also asked him how he had received his sight. "He put mud on my eyes," the man replied, "and I washed, and now I see."

¹⁶Some of the Pharisees said, "This man is not from God, for he does not keep the Sabbath."

But others asked, "How can a sinner do such miraculous signs?" So they were divided.

¹⁷Finally they turned again to the blind man, "What have you to say about him? It was your eyes he opened."

The man replied, "He is a prophet."

¹⁸The Jews still did not believe that he had been blind and had received his sight until they sent for the man's parents. ¹⁹"Is this your son?" they asked. "Is this the one you say was born blind? How is it that now he can see?"

²⁰"We know he is our son," the parents answered, "and we know he was born blind. ²¹But how he can see now, or who opened his eyes, we don't know. Ask him. He is of age; he will speak for himself." ²²His parents said this because they were afraid of the Jews, for already the Jews had decided that anyone who acknowledged that Jesus was the Christ*ᵃ* would be put out of the synagogue. ²³That was why his parents said, "He is of age; ask him."

²⁴A second time they summoned the man who had been blind. "Give glory to God,*ᵇ*" they said. "We know this man is a sinner."

²⁵He replied, "Whether he is a sinner or not, I don't know. One thing I do know. I was blind but now I see!"

²⁶Then they asked him, "What did he do to you? How did he open your eyes?"

²⁷He answered, "I have told you already and you did not listen. Why do you want to hear it again? Do you want to become his disciples, too?"

---

*ᵃ22 Or Messiah ᵇ24 A solemn charge to tell the truth (see Joshua 7:19)

²⁸Then they hurled insults at him and said, "You are this fellow's disciple! We are disciples of Moses! ²⁹We know that God spoke to Moses, but as for this fellow, we don't even know where he comes from."

³⁰The man answered, "Now that is remarkable! You don't know where he comes from, yet he opened my eyes. ³¹We know that God does not listen to sinners. He listens to the godly man who does his will. ³²Nobody has ever heard of opening the eyes of a man born blind. ³³If this man were not from God, he could do nothing."

³⁴To this they replied, "You were steeped in sin at birth; how dare you lecture us!" And they threw him out.

Spiritual Blindness ³⁵Jesus heard that they had thrown him out, and when he found him, he said, "Do you believe in the Son of Man?"

³⁶"Who is he, sir?" the man asked. "Tell me so that I may believe in him."

³⁷Jesus said, "You have now seen him; in fact, he is the one speaking with you."

³⁸Then the man said, "Lord, I believe," and he worshiped him.

³⁹Jesus said, "For judgment I have come into this world, so that the blind will see and those who see will become blind."

⁴⁰Some Pharisees who were with him heard him say this and asked, "What? Are we blind too?"

⁴¹Jesus said, "If you were blind, you would not be guilty of sin; but now that you claim you can see, your guilt remains."

10 ***The Shepherd and His Flock*** "I tell you the truth, the man who does not enter the sheep pen by the gate, but climbs in by some other way, is a thief and a robber. ²The man who enters by the gate is the shepherd of his sheep. ³The watchman opens the gate for him, and the sheep listen to his voice. He calls his own sheep by name and leads them out. ⁴When he has brought out all his own, he goes on ahead of them, and his sheep follow him because they know his voice. ⁵But they will never follow a stranger; in fact, they will run away from him because they do not recognize a stranger's voice." ⁶Jesus used this figure of speech, but they did not understand what he was telling them.

⁷Therefore Jesus said again, "I tell you the truth, I am the gate for the sheep. ⁸All who ever came before me were thieves and robbers, but the sheep did not listen to them. ⁹I am the gate; whoever enters through me will be saved.ᵃ He will come in and go out, and find pasture. ¹⁰The thief comes only to steal and kill and destroy; I have come that they may have life, and have it to the full.

¹¹"I am the good shepherd. The good shepherd lays down his life for the sheep. ¹²The hired hand is not the shepherd who owns the sheep. So when he sees the wolf coming, he abandons the sheep and runs away. Then the wolf attacks the flock and scatters it. ¹³The man runs away because he is a hired hand and cares nothing for the sheep.

¹⁴"I am the good shepherd; I know my

Direct Line

JOHN 10:1–21

Oops. Here it is again. Another one of those stories for little kids. Sheep? And shepherds? How cute, right? Wrong. Little kids see sheep as furry, cuddly things. But in Jesus' day people saw sheep as wealth. A shepherd often risked his life to protect the sheep under his care. Think about this passage that way, and sheep and shepherds aren't for little kids at all. They're for teens and adults. When Jesus says, "I am the good shepherd," he's telling you how valuable you are to God. And he proved that claim by dying for you. Check this passage out. What else do you see that tells you you're really important to the Lord?

ᵃ9 Or *kept safe*

sheep and my sheep know me— ¹⁵just as the Father knows me and I know the Father—and I lay down my life for the sheep. ¹⁶I have other sheep that are not of this sheep pen. I must bring them also. They too will listen to my voice, and there shall be one flock and one shepherd. ¹⁷The reason my Father loves me is that I lay down my life—only to take it up again. ¹⁸No one takes it from me, but I lay it down of my own accord. I have authority to lay it down and authority to take it up again. This command I received from my Father."

¹⁹At these words the Jews were again divided. ²⁰Many of them said, "He is demon-possessed and raving mad. Why listen to him?"

²¹But others said, "These are not the sayings of a man possessed by a demon. Can a demon open the eyes of the blind?"

The Unbelief of People ²²Then came the Feast of Dedication*ᵃ* at Jerusalem. It was winter, ²³and Jesus was in the temple area walking in Solomon's Colonnade. ²⁴The Jews gathered around him, saying, "How long will you keep us in suspense? If you are the Christ,*ᵇ* tell us plainly."

²⁵Jesus answered, "I did tell you, but you do not believe. The miracles I do in my Father's name speak for me, ²⁶but you do not believe because you are not my sheep. ²⁷My sheep listen to my voice; I know them, and they follow me. ²⁸I give them eternal life, and they shall never perish; no one can snatch them out of my hand. ²⁹My Father, who has given them to me, is greater than all*ᶜ*; no one can snatch them out of my Father's hand. ³⁰I and the Father are one."

³¹Again the Jews picked up stones to stone him, ³²but Jesus said to them, "I have shown you many great miracles from the Father. For which of these do you stone me?"

³³"We are not stoning you for any of these," replied the Jews, "but for blasphemy, because you, a mere man, claim to be God."

³⁴Jesus answered them, "Is it not written in your Law, 'I have said you are gods'*ᵈ*? ³⁵If he called them 'gods,' to whom the word of God came—and the Scripture cannot be broken— ³⁶what about the one whom the Father set apart as his very own and sent into the world? Why then do you accuse me of blasphemy because I said, 'I am God's Son'? ³⁷Do not believe me unless I do what my Father does. ³⁸But if I do it, even though you do not believe me, believe the miracles, that you may know and understand that the Father is in me, and I in the Father." ³⁹Again they tried to seize him, but he escaped their grasp.

⁴⁰Then Jesus went back across the Jordan to the place where John had been baptizing in the early days. Here he stayed ⁴¹and many people came to him. They said, "Though John never performed a miraculous sign, all that John said about this man was true." ⁴²And in that place many believed in Jesus.

The Death of Lazarus Now a man named Lazarus was sick. He was from Bethany, the village of Mary and her sister Martha. ²This Mary, whose brother Lazarus now lay sick, was the same one who poured perfume on the Lord and wiped his feet with her hair. ³So the sisters sent word to Jesus, "Lord, the one you love is sick."

⁴When he heard this, Jesus said, "This sickness will not end in death. No, it is for God's glory so that God's Son may be glorified through it." ⁵Jesus loved Martha and her sister and Lazarus. ⁶Yet when he heard that Lazarus was sick, he stayed where he was two more days.

⁷Then he said to his disciples, "Let us go back to Judea."

ᵃ22 That is, Hanukkah ᵇ24 Or Messiah ᶜ29 Many early manuscripts What my Father has given me is greater than all ᵈ34 Psalm 82:6

⁸"But Rabbi," they said, "a short while ago the Jews tried to stone you, and yet you are going back there?"

⁹Jesus answered, "Are there not twelve hours of daylight? A man who walks by day will not stumble, for he sees by this world's light. ¹⁰It is when he walks by night that he stumbles, for he has no light."

¹¹After he had said this, he went on to tell them, "Our friend Lazarus has fallen asleep; but I am going there to wake him up."

¹²His disciples replied, "Lord, if he sleeps, he will get better." ¹³Jesus had been speaking of his death, but his disciples thought he meant natural sleep.

¹⁴So then he told them plainly, "Lazarus is dead, ¹⁵and for your sake I am glad I was not there, so that you may believe. But let us go to him."

¹⁶Then Thomas (called Didymus) said to the rest of the disciples, "Let us also go, that we may die with him."

Jesus Comforts the Sisters ¹⁷On his arrival, Jesus found that Lazarus had already been in the tomb for four days. ¹⁸Bethany was less than two miles* from Jerusalem, ¹⁹and many Jews had come to Martha and Mary to comfort them in the loss of their brother. ²⁰When Martha heard that Jesus was coming, she went out to meet him, but Mary stayed at home.

²¹"Lord," Martha said to Jesus, "if you had been here, my brother would not have died. ²²But I know that even now God will give you whatever you ask."

²³Jesus said to her, "Your brother will rise again."

²⁴Martha answered, "I know he will rise again in the resurrection at the last day."

²⁵Jesus said to her, "I am the resurrection and the life. He who believes in me will live, even though he dies; ²⁶and whoever lives and believes in me will never die. Do you believe this?"

²⁷"Yes, Lord," she told him, "I believe that you are the Christ,* the Son of God, who was to come into the world."

²⁸And after she had said this, she went back and called her sister Mary aside. "The Teacher is here," she said, "and is asking for you." ²⁹When Mary heard this, she got up quickly and went to him. ³⁰Now Jesus had not yet entered the village, but was still at the place where Martha had met him. ³¹When the Jews who had been with Mary in the house, comforting her, noticed how quickly she got up and went out, they followed her, supposing she was going to the tomb to mourn there.

³²When Mary reached the place where Jesus was and saw him, she fell at his feet and said, "Lord, if you had been here, my brother would not have died."

³³When Jesus saw her weeping, and the Jews who had come along with her also weeping, he was deeply moved in spirit and troubled. ³⁴"Where have you laid him?" he asked.

"Come and see, Lord," they replied.

³⁵Jesus wept.

³⁶Then the Jews said, "See how he loved him!"

³⁷But some of them said, "Could not he who opened the eyes of the blind man have kept this man from dying?"

Jesus Raises Lazarus From the Dead   ³⁸Jesus, once more deeply moved, came to the tomb. It was a cave with a stone laid across the entrance. ³⁹"Take away the stone," he said.

"But, Lord," said Martha, the sister of the dead man, "by this time there is a bad odor, for he has been there four days."

ª18 Greek fifteen stadia (about 3 kilometers) ᵇ27 Or Messiah

⁴⁰Then Jesus said, "Did I not tell you that if you believed, you would see the glory of God?"

⁴¹So they took away the stone. Then Jesus looked up and said, "Father, I thank you that you have heard me. ⁴²I knew that you always hear me, but I said this for the benefit of the people standing here, that they may believe that you sent me."

⁴³When he had said this, Jesus called in a loud voice, "Lazarus, come out!" ⁴⁴The dead man came out, his hands and feet wrapped with strips of linen, and a cloth around his face.

Jesus said to them, "Take off the grave clothes and let him go."

The Plot to Kill Jesus   ⁴⁵Therefore many of the Jews who had come to visit Mary, and had seen what Jesus did, put their faith in him. ⁴⁶But some of them went to the Pharisees and told them what Jesus had done. ⁴⁷Then the chief priests and the Pharisees called a meeting of the Sanhedrin.

"What are we accomplishing?" they asked. "Here is this man performing many miraculous signs. ⁴⁸If we let him go on like this, everyone will believe in him, and then the Romans will come and take away both our place*ᵃ* and our nation."

⁴⁹Then one of them, named Caiaphas, who was high priest that year, spoke up, "You know nothing at all! ⁵⁰You do not realize that it is better for you that one man die for the people than that the whole nation perish."

⁵¹He did not say this on his own, but as high priest that year he prophesied that Jesus would die for the Jewish nation, ⁵²and not only for that nation but also for the scattered children of God, to bring them together and make them one. ⁵³So from that day on they plotted to take his life.

⁵⁴Therefore Jesus no longer moved about publicly among the Jews. Instead he withdrew to a region near the desert, to a village called Ephraim, where he stayed with his disciples.

⁵⁵When it was almost time for the Jewish Passover, many went up from the country to Jerusalem for their ceremonial cleansing before the Passover. ⁵⁶They kept looking for Jesus, and as they stood in the temple area they asked one another, "What do you think? Isn't he coming to the Feast at all?" ⁵⁷But the chief priests and Pharisees had given orders that if anyone found out where Jesus was, he should report it so that they might arrest him.

nswers

to Quizzer on page 1394

A: Three: Lazarus (John 11:44), a young girl (Matthew 9:25) and a widow's son (Luke 7:15).

BONUS: Lazarus was raised three days after his burial, so everyone was sure he was really dead.

Jesus Anointed at Bethany   Six days before the Passover, Jesus arrived at Bethany, where Lazarus lived, whom Jesus had raised from the dead. ²Here a dinner was given in Jesus' honor. Martha served, while Lazarus was among those reclining at the table with him. ³Then Mary took about a pint*ᵇ* of pure nard, an expensive perfume; she poured it on Jesus' feet and wiped his feet with her hair. And the house was filled with the fragrance of the perfume.

⁴But one of his disciples, Judas Iscariot, who was later to betray him, objected, ⁵"Why wasn't this perfume sold and the money given to the poor? It was worth a year's wages.*ᶜ*" ⁶He did not say this because he cared about the poor but because he was a thief; as keeper of the money bag, he used to help himself to what was put into it.

⁷"Leave her alone," Jesus replied. "It was intended that she should save this perfume for the day of my burial. ⁸You will always have the poor among you, but you will not always have me."

⁹Meanwhile a large crowd of Jews found out that Jesus was there and came, not only because of him but also to see Lazarus, whom he had raised from the dead. ¹⁰So the chief priests made plans to kill Lazarus as well, ¹¹for

---

ᵃ48 Or temple   ᵇ3 Greek a litra (probably about 0.5 liter)   ᶜ5 Greek three hundred denarii

on account of him many of the Jews were going over to Jesus and putting their faith in him.

The Triumphal Entry [12]The next day the great crowd that had come for the Feast heard that Jesus was on his way to Jerusalem. [13]They took palm branches and went out to meet him, shouting,

> "Hosanna![a]"
>
> "Blessed is he who comes in the name of the Lord!"[b]
>
> "Blessed is the King of Israel!"

[14]Jesus found a young donkey and sat upon it, as it is written,

> [15]"Do not be afraid, O Daughter of Zion;
> see, your king is coming,
> seated on a donkey's colt."[c]

[16]At first his disciples did not understand all this. Only after Jesus was glorified did they realize that these things had been written about him and that they had done these things to him.

[17]Now the crowd that was with him when he called Lazarus from the tomb and raised him from the dead continued to spread the word. [18]Many people, because they had heard that he had given this miraculous sign, went out to meet him. [19]So the Pharisees said to one another, "See, this is getting us nowhere. Look how the whole world has gone after him!"

Jesus Predicts His Death [20]Now there were some Greeks among those who went up to worship at the Feast. [21]They came to Philip, who was from Bethsaida in Galilee, with a request. "Sir," they said, "we would like to see Jesus." [22]Philip went to tell Andrew; Andrew and Philip in turn told Jesus.

[23]Jesus replied, "The hour has come for the Son of Man to be glorified. [24]I tell you the truth, unless a kernel of wheat falls to the ground and dies, it remains only a single seed. But if it dies, it produces many seeds. [25]The man who loves his life will lose it, while the man who hates his life in this world will keep it for eternal life. [26]Whoever serves me must follow me; and where I am, my servant also will be. My Father will honor the one who serves me.

[27]"Now my heart is troubled, and what shall I say? 'Father, save me from this hour'? No, it was for this very reason I came to this hour. [28]Father, glorify your name!"

Then a voice came from heaven, "I have glorified it, and will glorify it again." [29]The crowd that was there and heard it said it had thundered; others said an angel had spoken to him.

[30]Jesus said, "This voice was for your benefit, not mine. [31]Now is the time for judgment on this world; now the prince of this world will be driven out. [32]But I, when I am lifted up from the earth, will draw all men to myself." [33]He said this to show the kind of death he was going to die.

Direct Line

JOHN 12:37–44

These verses identify three groups of people. Some would not believe even after Jesus did "all these miraculous signs in their presence" (John 12:37). Some believed but didn't want to tell anyone. Some, like the disciples, believed and were eager to say they were followers of Jesus. Which group do you fit into? 1. Unbeliever. 2. Secret believer. 3. Open believer. In a way, both unbelievers and open believers are being honest. The secret believer, who doesn't want anyone to know he or she is a Christian, isn't being honest. Isn't it great to be an open believer, who cares more about what God thinks than about what people think?

---

[a]13 A Hebrew expression meaning "Save!" which became an exclamation of praise [b]13 Psalm 118:25, 26 [c]15 Zech. 9:9

³⁴The crowd spoke up, "We have heard from the Law that the Christ*a* will remain forever, so how can you say, 'The Son of Man must be lifted up'? Who is this 'Son of Man'?"

³⁵Then Jesus told them, "You are going to have the light just a little while longer. Walk while you have the light, before darkness overtakes you. The man who walks in the dark does not know where he is going. ³⁶Put your trust in the light while you have it, so that you may become sons of light." When he had finished speaking, Jesus left and hid himself from them.

The People Continue in Their Unbelief   ³⁷Even after Jesus had done all these miraculous signs in their presence, they still would not believe in him. ³⁸This was to fulfill the word of Isaiah the prophet:

> "Lord, who has believed our message
>   and to whom has the arm of the Lord been revealed?"*b*

³⁹For this reason they could not believe, because, as Isaiah says elsewhere:

> ⁴⁰"He has blinded their eyes
>   and deadened their hearts,
> so they can neither see with their eyes,
>   nor understand with their hearts,
>   nor turn—and I would heal them."*c*

⁴¹Isaiah said this because he saw Jesus' glory and spoke about him.

⁴²Yet at the same time many even among the leaders believed in him. But because of the Pharisees they would not confess their faith for fear they would be put out of the synagogue; ⁴³for they loved praise from men more than praise from God.

⁴⁴Then Jesus cried out, "When a man believes in me, he does not believe in me only, but in the one who sent me. ⁴⁵When he looks at me, he sees the one who sent me. ⁴⁶I have come into the world as a light, so that no one who believes in me should stay in darkness.

⁴⁷"As for the person who hears my words but does not keep them, I do not judge him. For I did not come to judge the world, but to save it. ⁴⁸There is a judge for the one who rejects me and does not accept my words; that very word which I spoke will condemn him at the last day. ⁴⁹For I did not speak of my own accord, but the Father who sent me commanded me what to say and how to say it. ⁵⁰I know that his command leads to eternal life. So whatever I say is just what the Father has told me to say."

Jesus Washes His Disciples' Feet   It was just before the Passover **13** Feast. Jesus knew that the time had come for him to leave this world and go to the Father. Having loved his own who were in the world, he now showed them the full extent of his love.*d*

²The evening meal was being served, and the devil had already prompted Judas Iscariot, son of Simon, to betray Jesus. ³Jesus knew that the Father had put all things under his power, and that he had come from God and was returning to God; ⁴so he got up from the meal, took off his outer clothing, and wrapped a towel around his waist. ⁵After that, he poured water into a basin and began to wash his disciples' feet, drying them with the towel that was wrapped around him.

⁶He came to Simon Peter, who said to him, "Lord, are you going to wash my feet?"

⁷Jesus replied, "You do not realize now what I am doing, but later you will understand."

⁸"No," said Peter, "you shall never wash my feet."

a34 Or Messiah   b38 Isaiah 53:1   c40 Isaiah 6:10   d1 Or he loved them to the last

Jesus answered, "Unless I wash you, you have no part with me."

[9]"Then, Lord," Simon Peter replied, "not just my feet but my hands and my head as well!"

[10]Jesus answered, "A person who has had a bath needs only to wash his feet; his whole body is clean. And you are clean, though not every one of you." [11]For he knew who was going to betray him, and that was why he said not every one was clean.

[12]When he had finished washing their feet, he put on his clothes and returned to his place. "Do you understand what I have done for you?" he asked them. [13]"You call me 'Teacher' and 'Lord,' and rightly so, for that is what I am. [14]Now that I, your Lord and Teacher, have washed your feet, you also should wash one another's feet. [15]I have set you an example that you should do as I have done for you. [16]I tell you the truth, no servant is greater than his master, nor is a messenger greater than the one who sent him. [17]Now that you know these things, you will be blessed if you do them.

Jesus Predicts His Betrayal   [18]"I am not referring to all of you; I know those I have chosen. But this is to fulfill the scripture: 'He who shares my bread has lifted up his heel against me.'[a]

[19]"I am telling you now before it happens, so that when it does happen you will believe that I am He. [20]I tell you the truth, whoever accepts anyone I send accepts me; and whoever accepts me accepts the one who sent me."

[21]After he had said this, Jesus was troubled in spirit and testified, "I tell you the truth, one of you is going to betray me."

[22]His disciples stared at one another, at a loss to know which of them he meant. [23]One of them, the disciple whom Jesus loved, was reclining next to him. [24]Simon Peter motioned to this disciple and said, "Ask him which one he means."

[25]Leaning back against Jesus, he asked him, "Lord, who is it?"

[26]Jesus answered, "It is the one to whom I will give this piece of bread when I have dipped it in the dish." Then, dipping the piece of bread, he gave it to Judas Iscariot, son of Simon. [27]As soon as Judas took the bread, Satan entered into him.

"What you are about to do, do quickly," Jesus told him, [28]but no one at the

[a]18 Psalm 41:9

The Bible Says

Love One Another

The night before he was crucified, Jesus issued a "new command" that his disciples love one another (John 13:34).

The call to love others isn't new (Leviticus 19:18,34). What then is "new" about this commandment?

✳ A new relationship—Christians are family, not just neighbors.
✳ A new standard—Christians love as Jesus loved.
✳ A new outcome—when Christians love each other, people who are not yet believers realize these are Jesus' followers.

Love isn't optional for Christians. They are to be people who love. When they love each other in the self-sacrificing way that Jesus loves, non-Christians see how real Jesus is by the difference he makes in their lives.

meal understood why Jesus said this to him. [29]Since Judas had charge of the money, some thought Jesus was telling him to buy what was needed for the Feast, or to give something to the poor. [30]As soon as Judas had taken the bread, he went out. And it was night.

Jesus Predicts Peter's Denial [31]When he was gone, Jesus said, "Now is the Son of Man glorified and God is glorified in him. [32]If God is glorified in him,[a] God will glorify the Son in himself, and will glorify him at once.

[33]"My children, I will be with you only a little longer. You will look for me, and just as I told the Jews, so I tell you now: Where I am going, you cannot come.

[34]"A new command I give you: Love one another. As I have loved you, so you must love one another. [35]By this all men will know that you are my disciples, if you love one another."

[36]Simon Peter asked him, "Lord, where are you going?"

Jesus replied, "Where I am going, you cannot follow now, but you will follow later."

[37]Peter asked, "Lord, why can't I follow you now? I will lay down my life for you."

[38]Then Jesus answered, "Will you really lay down your life for me? I tell you the truth, before the rooster crows, you will disown me three times!

14 *Jesus Comforts His Disciples* "Do not let your hearts be troubled. Trust in God[b]; trust also in me. [2]In my Father's house are many rooms; if it were not so, I would have told you. I am going there to prepare a place for you. [3]And if I go and prepare a place for you, I will come back and take you to be with me that you also may be where I am. [4]You know the way to the place where I am going."

Jesus the Way to the Father [5]Thomas said to him, "Lord, we don't know where you are going, so how can we know the way?"

[6]Jesus answered, "I am the way and the truth and the life. No one comes to the Father except through me. [7]If you really knew me, you would know[c] my Father as well. From now on, you do know him and have seen him."

[8]Philip said, "Lord, show us the Father and that will be enough for us."

[9]Jesus answered: "Don't you know me, Philip, even after I have been among you such a long time? Anyone who has seen me has seen the Father. How can you say, 'Show us the Father'? [10]Don't you believe that I am in the Father, and that the Father is in me? The words I say to you are not just my own. Rather, it is the Father, living in me, who is doing his work. [11]Believe me when I say that I am in the Father and the Father is in me; or at least believe on the evidence of the miracles themselves. [12]I tell you the truth, anyone who has faith in me will do what I have been doing. He will do even greater things than these, because I am going to the Father. [13]And I will do whatever you ask in my name, so that the Son may bring glory to the Father. [14]You may ask me for anything in my name, and I will do it.

Jesus Promises the Holy Spirit [15]"If you love me, you will obey what I command. [16]And I will ask the Father, and he will give you another Counselor to be with you forever— [17]the Spirit of truth. The world cannot accept him, because it neither sees him nor knows him. But you know him, for he lives with you and will be[d] in you. [18]I will not leave you as orphans; I will come to you. [19]Before long, the world will not see me anymore, but you will see me. Because I live, you also will live. [20]On that day you will realize that I am in my Father, and you are in me, and I am in you. [21]Whoever has my commands and

---

[a]32 Many early manuscripts do not have *If God is glorified in him.* [b]1 Or *You trust in God* [c]7 Some early manuscripts *If you really have known me, you will know* [d]17 Some early manuscripts *and is*

obeys them, he is the one who loves me. He who loves me will be loved by my Father, and I too will love him and show myself to him."

[22]Then Judas (not Judas Iscariot) said, "But, Lord, why do you intend to show yourself to us and not to the world?"

[23]Jesus replied, "If anyone loves me, he will obey my teaching. My Father will love him, and we will come to him and make our home with him. [24]He who does not love me will not obey my teaching. These words you hear are not my own; they belong to the Father who sent me.

[25]"All this I have spoken while still with you. [26]But the Counselor, the Holy Spirit, whom the Father will send in my name, will teach you all things and will remind you of everything I have said to you. [27]Peace I leave with you; my peace I give you. I do not give to you as the world gives. Do not let your hearts be troubled and do not be afraid.

[28]"You heard me say, 'I am going away and I am coming back to you.' If you loved me, you would be glad that I am going to the Father, for the Father is greater than I. [29]I have told you now before it happens, so that when it does happen you will believe. [30]I will not speak with you much longer, for the prince of this world is coming. He has no hold on me, [31]but the world must learn that I love the Father and that I do exactly what my Father has commanded me.

"Come now; let us leave."

15 *The Vine and the Branches* "I am the true vine, and my Father is the gardener. [2]He cuts off every branch in me that bears no fruit, while every branch that does bear fruit he prunes[a] so that it will be even more fruitful. [3]You are already clean because of the word I have spoken to you. [4]Remain in me, and I will remain in you. No branch can bear fruit by itself; it must remain in the vine. Neither can you bear fruit unless you remain in me.

[5]"I am the vine; you are the branches. If a man remains in me and I in him, he will bear much fruit; apart from me you can do nothing. [6]If anyone does not remain in me, he is like a branch that is thrown away and withers; such branches are picked up, thrown into the fire and burned. [7]If you remain in me and my words remain in you, ask whatever you wish, and it will be given you. [8]This is to my Father's glory, that you bear much fruit, showing yourselves to be my disciples.

[9]"As the Father has loved me, so have I loved you. Now remain in my love. [10]If you obey my commands, you will remain in my love, just as I have obeyed my Father's commands and remain in his love. [11]I have told you this so that my joy may be in you and that your joy may be complete. [12]My command is this: Love each other as I have loved you. [13]Greater love has no one than this, that he lay down his life for his friends. [14]You are my friends if you do what I command. [15]I no longer call you servants, because a servant does not know his master's business. Instead, I have called you friends, for everything that I learned from my Father I have made known to you. [16]You did not choose me, but I chose you and appointed you to go and bear fruit—fruit that will last. Then the Father will give you whatever you ask in my name. [17]This is my command: Love each other.

The World Hates the Disciples [18]"If the world hates you, keep in mind that it hated me first. [19]If you belonged to the world, it would love you as its own. As it is, you do not belong to the world, but I have chosen you out of the world. That is why the world hates you. [20]Remember the words I spoke to you: 'No servant is greater than his master.'[b] If they persecuted me, they will persecute you also. If they obeyed my teaching, they will obey yours also.

---

[a]2 The Greek for *prunes* also means *cleans.* [b]20 John 13:16

Dear Sam,

I excel at just about everything I do, so I feel good about myself. How can I explain this to my friends who think I'm conceited?

Cori in Centerville

Dear Sam, Inc.

100 Advice Lane, Anywhere, USA

Dear Cori,

You can explain your success as well as your positive attitude by explaining how you received your abilities. Give the credit to God, not to yourself. You have a lot of gifts from God. You didn't pay for your abilities or choose your talents. It is because you have been given these abilities that you do so well. So you have nothing to be stuck-up about.

You are who you are because you belong to Jesus; you are a branch on his vine (John 15:1-8). He has given you certain gifts, and he expects you to use those gifts to serve him and others. He has given you many good things, and he has given you the responsibility of using these gifts for his glory, not your own.

It may be hard for your friends to understand exactly why you feel good about yourself, especially if they don't feel good about themselves. But you will go a long way toward explaining yourself if you give credit to the right person: God.

Sam

²¹They will treat you this way because of my name, for they do not know the One who sent me. ²²If I had not come and spoken to them, they would not be guilty of sin. Now, however, they have no excuse for their sin. ²³He who hates me hates my Father as well. ²⁴If I had not done among them what no one else did, they would not be guilty of sin. But now they have seen these miracles, and yet they have hated both me and my Father. ²⁵But this is to fulfill what is written in their Law: 'They hated me without reason.'ᵃ

²⁶"When the Counselor comes, whom I will send to you from the Father, the Spirit of truth who goes out from the Father, he will testify about me. ²⁷And you also must testify, for you have been with me from the beginning.

16 "All this I have told you so that you will not go astray. ²They will put you out of the synagogue; in fact, a time is coming when anyone who kills you will think he is offering a service to God. ³They will do such things because they have not known the Father or me. ⁴I have told you this, so that when the time comes you will remember that I warned you. I did not tell you this at first because I was with you.

The Work of the Holy Spirit ⁵"Now I am going to him who sent me, yet none of you asks me, 'Where are you going?' ⁶Because I have said these things, you are filled with grief. ⁷But I tell you the truth: It is for your good that I am going away. Unless I go away, the Counselor will not come to you; but if I go, I will send him to you. ⁸When he comes, he will convict the world of guiltᵇ in regard to sin and righteousness and judgment: ⁹in regard to sin, because men do not believe in me; ¹⁰in regard to righteousness, because I am going to the Father, where you can see me no longer; ¹¹and in regard to judgment, because the prince of this world now stands condemned.

¹²"I have much more to say to you, more than you can now bear. ¹³But when he, the Spirit of truth, comes, he will guide you into all truth. He will not speak on his own; he will speak only what he hears, and he will tell you what is yet to come. ¹⁴He will bring glory to me by taking from what is mine and making it known to you. ¹⁵All that belongs to the Father is mine. That is why I said the Spirit will take from what is mine and make it known to you.

¹⁶"In a little while you will see me no more, and then after a little while you will see me."

The Disciples' Grief Will Turn to Joy ¹⁷Some of his disciples said to one another, "What does he mean by saying, 'In a little while you will see me no more, and then after a little while you will see me,' and 'Because I am going to the Father'?" ¹⁸They kept asking, "What does he mean by 'a little while'? We don't understand what he is saying."

¹⁹Jesus saw that they wanted to ask him about this, so he said to them, "Are you asking one another what I meant when I said, 'In a little while you will see me no more, and then after a little while you will see me'? ²⁰I tell you the truth, you will weep and mourn while the world rejoices. You will grieve, but your grief will turn to joy. ²¹A woman giving birth to a child has pain because her time has come; but when

---

Direct Line

JOHN 16:23–24

Is Jesus' promise in John 16:23, "My Father will give you whatever you ask in my name," sort of like a blank check? You get whatever you want? What will you ask for? First you need to understand the "in my name" part. In Bible times a name wasn't just a label. Names reflected character. Asking "in Jesus' name" doesn't mean tacking those words on at the end of your prayers. It means asking for the kind of thing Jesus himself would ask for. Jesus' promise means that when you want to glorify God as he did and serve others as he served them, God will gladly answer those prayers!

ᵃ*25 Psalms 35:19; 69:4 ᵇ8 Or *will expose the guilt of the world*

her baby is born she forgets the anguish because of her joy that a child is born into the world. ²²So with you: Now is your time of grief, but I will see you again and you will rejoice, and no one will take away your joy. ²³In that day you will no longer ask me anything. I tell you the truth, my Father will give you whatever you ask in my name. ²⁴Until now you have not asked for anything in my name. Ask and you will receive, and your joy will be complete.

²⁵"Though I have been speaking figuratively, a time is coming when I will no longer use this kind of language but will tell you plainly about my Father. ²⁶In that day you will ask in my name. I am not saying that I will ask the Father on your behalf. ²⁷No, the Father himself loves you because you have loved me and have believed that I came from God. ²⁸I came from the Father and entered the world; now I am leaving the world and going back to the Father."

²⁹Then Jesus' disciples said, "Now you are speaking clearly and without figures of speech. ³⁰Now we can see that you know all things and that you do not even need to have anyone ask you questions. This makes us believe that you came from God."

³¹"You believe at last!"ᵃ Jesus answered. ³²"But a time is coming, and has come, when you will be scattered, each to his own home. You will leave me all alone. Yet I am not alone, for my Father is with me.

³³"I have told you these things, so that in me you may have peace. In this world you will have trouble. But take heart! I have overcome the world."

17 ***Jesus Prays for Himself*** After Jesus said this, he looked toward heaven and prayed:

"Father, the time has come. Glorify your Son, that your Son may glorify you. ²For you granted him authority over all people that he might give eternal life to all those you have given him. ³Now this is eternal life: that they may know you, the only true God, and Jesus Christ, whom you have sent. ⁴I have brought you glory on earth by completing the work you gave me to do. ⁵And now, Father, glorify me in your presence with the glory I had with you before the world began.

Jesus Prays for His Disciples ⁶"I have revealed youᵇ to those whom you gave me out of the world. They were yours; you gave them to me and they have obeyed your word. ⁷Now they know that everything you have given me comes from you. ⁸For I gave them the words you gave me and they accepted them. They knew with certainty that I came from you, and they believed that you sent me. ⁹I pray for them. I am not praying for the world, but for those you have given me, for they are yours. ¹⁰All I have is yours, and all you have is mine. And glory has come to me through them. ¹¹I will remain in the world no longer, but they are still in the world, and I am coming to you. Holy Father, protect them by the power of your name—the name you gave me—so that they may be one as we are one. ¹²While I was with them, I protected them and kept them safe by that name you gave me. None has been lost except the one doomed to destruction so that Scripture would be fulfilled.

¹³"I am coming to you now, but I say these things while I am still in the world, so that they may have the full measure of my joy within them. ¹⁴I have given them your word and the world has hated them, for they are not of the world any more than I am of the world. ¹⁵My prayer is not that you take them out of the world but that you protect them from the evil

ᵃ31 Or *"Do you now believe?"* *ᵇ6* Greek *your name*; also in verse 26 one. [16]They are not of the world, even as I am not of it. [17]Sanctify[a] them by the truth; your word is truth. [18]As you sent me into the world, I have sent them into the world. [19]For them I sanctify myself, that they too may be truly sanctified.

Jesus Prays for All Believers [20]"My prayer is not for them alone. I pray also for those who will believe in me through their message, [21]that all of them may be one, Father, just as you are in me and I am in you. May they also be in us so that the world may believe that you have sent me. [22]I have given them the glory that you gave me, that they may be one as we are one: [23]I in them and you in me. May they be brought to complete unity to let the world know that you sent me and have loved them even as you have loved me.

[24]"Father, I want those you have given me to be with me where I am, and to see my glory, the glory you have given me because you loved me before the creation of the world.

[25]"Righteous Father, though the world does not know you, I know you, and they know that you have sent me. [26]I have made you known to them, and will continue to make you known in order that the love you have for me may be in them and that I myself may be in them."

18 *Jesus Arrested* When he had finished praying, Jesus left with his disciples and crossed the Kidron Valley. On the other side there was an olive grove, and he and his disciples went into it.

[2]Now Judas, who betrayed him, knew the place, because Jesus had often met there with his disciples. [3]So Judas came to the grove, guiding a detachment of soldiers and some officials from the chief priests and Pharisees. They were carrying torches, lanterns and weapons.

[4]Jesus, knowing all that was going to happen to him, went out and asked them, "Who is it you want?"

[5]"Jesus of Nazareth," they replied.

"I am he," Jesus said. (And Judas the traitor was standing there with them.) [6]When Jesus said, "I am he," they drew back and fell to the ground.

[7]Again he asked them, "Who is it you want?"

And they said, "Jesus of Nazareth."

[8]"I told you that I am he," Jesus answered. "If you are looking for me, then let these men go." [9]This happened so that the words he had spoken would be fulfilled: "I have not lost one of those you gave me."[b]

[10]Then Simon Peter, who had a sword, drew it and struck the high priest's servant, cutting off his right ear. (The servant's name was Malchus.)

[11]Jesus commanded Peter, "Put your sword away! Shall I not drink the cup the Father has given me?"

Jesus Taken to Annas [12]Then the detachment of soldiers with its commander and the Jewish officials arrested Jesus. They bound him [13]and brought him first to Annas, who was the father-in-law of Caiaphas, the high priest that year. [14]Caiaphas

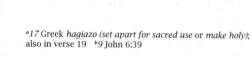

JOHN 17:20–23

Jesus prayed that believers would "be one" and "be brought to complete unity." Ha! That's one prayer that wasn't answered! Right? Look at all the different denominations! But read carefully. What Jesus asked was that believers be one with him, be united to him and the Father. This isn't about denominations at all. And this prayer has been answered: Every Christian is united to Jesus when he or she believes (see Romans 6:1–14).

---

[a]17 Greek *hagiazo (set apart for sacred use* or *make holy)*; also in verse 19   [b]9 John 6:39

was the one who had advised the Jews that it would be good if one man died for the people.

Peter's First Denial ¹⁵Simon Peter and another disciple were following Jesus. Because this disciple was known to the high priest, he went with Jesus into the high priest's courtyard, ¹⁶but Peter had to wait outside at the door. The other disciple, who was known to the high priest, came back, spoke to the girl on duty there and brought Peter in.

¹⁷"You are not one of his disciples, are you?" the girl at the door asked Peter.

He replied, "I am not."

¹⁸It was cold, and the servants and officials stood around a fire they had made to keep warm. Peter also was standing with them, warming himself.

The High Priest Questions Jesus ¹⁹Meanwhile, the high priest questioned Jesus about his disciples and his teaching.

²⁰"I have spoken openly to the world," Jesus replied. "I always taught in synagogues or at the temple, where all the Jews come together. I said nothing in secret. ²¹Why question me? Ask those who heard me. Surely they know what I said."

²²When Jesus said this, one of the officials nearby struck him in the face. "Is this the way you answer the high priest?" he demanded.

²³"If I said something wrong," Jesus replied, "testify as to what is wrong. But if I spoke the truth, why did you strike me?" ²⁴Then Annas sent him, still bound, to Caiaphas the high priest.*ᵃ*

Peter's Second and Third Denials ²⁵As Simon Peter stood warming himself, he was asked, "You are not one of his disciples, are you?"

He denied it, saying, "I am not."

²⁶One of the high priest's servants, a relative of the man whose ear Peter had cut off, challenged him, "Didn't I see you with him in the olive grove?" ²⁷Again Peter denied it, and at that moment a rooster began to crow.

Jesus Before Pilate ²⁸Then the Jews led Jesus from Caiaphas to the palace of the Roman governor. By now it was early morning, and to avoid ceremonial uncleanness the Jews did not enter the palace; they wanted to be able to eat the Passover. ²⁹So Pilate came out to them and asked, "What charges are you bringing against this man?"

³⁰"If he were not a criminal," they replied, "we would not have handed him over to you."

³¹Pilate said, "Take him yourselves and judge him by your own law."

"But we have no right to execute anyone," the Jews objected. ³²This happened so that the words Jesus had spoken indicating the kind of death he was going to die would be fulfilled.

³³Pilate then went back inside the palace, summoned Jesus and asked him, "Are you the king of the Jews?"

³⁴"Is that your own idea," Jesus asked, "or did others talk to you about me?"

³⁵"Am I a Jew?" Pilate replied. "It was your people and your chief priests who handed you over to me. What is it you have done?"

³⁶Jesus said, "My kingdom is not of this world. If it were, my servants would fight to prevent my arrest by the Jews. But now my kingdom is from another place."

³⁷"You are a king, then!" said Pilate.

Jesus answered, "You are right in saying I am a king. In fact, for this reason I was born, and for this I came into the world, to testify to the truth. Everyone on the side of truth listens to me."

³⁸"What is truth?" Pilate asked. With this he went out again to the Jews and

ᵃ24 Or (Now Annas had sent him, still bound, to Caiaphas the high priest.)

said, "I find no basis for a charge against him. ³⁹But it is your custom for me to release to you one prisoner at the time of the Passover. Do you want me to release 'the king of the Jews'?"

⁴⁰They shouted back, "No, not him! Give us Barabbas!" Now Barabbas had taken part in a rebellion.

19 *Jesus Sentenced to be Crucified*   Then Pilate took Jesus and had him flogged. ²The soldiers twisted together a crown of thorns and put it on his head. They clothed him in a purple robe ³and went up to him again and again, saying, "Hail, king of the Jews!" And they struck him in the face.

⁴Once more Pilate came out and said to the Jews, "Look, I am bringing him out to you to let you know that I find no basis for a charge against him." ⁵When Jesus came out wearing the crown of thorns and the purple robe, Pilate said to them, "Here is the man!"

⁶As soon as the chief priests and their officials saw him, they shouted, "Crucify! Crucify!"

But Pilate answered, "You take him and crucify him. As for me, I find no basis for a charge against him."

⁷The Jews insisted, "We have a law, and according to that law he must die, because he claimed to be the Son of God."

⁸When Pilate heard this, he was even more afraid, ⁹and he went back inside the palace. "Where do you come from?" he asked Jesus, but Jesus gave him no answer. ¹⁰"Do you refuse to speak to me?" Pilate said. "Don't you realize I have power either to free you or to crucify you?"

¹¹Jesus answered, "You would have no power over me if it were not given to you from above. Therefore the one who handed me over to you is guilty of a greater sin."

¹²From then on, Pilate tried to set Jesus free, but the Jews kept shouting, "If you let this man go, you are no friend of Caesar. Anyone who claims to be a king opposes Caesar."

¹³When Pilate heard this, he brought Jesus out and sat down on the judge's seat at a place known as the Stone Pavement (which in Aramaic is Gabbatha). ¹⁴It was the day of Preparation of Passover Week, about the sixth hour.

"Here is your king," Pilate said to the Jews.

¹⁵But they shouted, "Take him away! Take him away! Crucify him!"

"Shall I crucify your king?" Pilate asked.

"We have no king but Caesar," the chief priests answered.

¹⁶Finally Pilate handed him over to them to be crucified.

The Crucifixion   So the soldiers took charge of Jesus. ¹⁷Carrying his own cross, he went out to the place of the Skull (which in Aramaic is called Golgotha). ¹⁸Here they crucified him, and with him two others—one on each side and Jesus in the middle.

¹⁹Pilate had a notice prepared and fastened to the cross. It read: JESUS OF NAZARETH, THE KING OF THE JEWS. ²⁰Many of the Jews read this sign, for the place where Jesus was crucified was near the city, and the sign was written in Aramaic, Latin and Greek. ²¹The chief priests of the Jews protested to Pilate, "Do not write 'The King of the Jews,' but that this man claimed to be king of the Jews."

²²Pilate answered, "What I have written, I have written."

²³When the soldiers crucified Jesus, they took his clothes, dividing them into four shares, one for each of them, with the undergarment remaining. This garment was seamless, woven in one piece from top to bottom.

²⁴"Let's not tear it," they said to one another. "Let's decide by lot who will get it."

This happened that the scripture might be fulfilled which said,

"They divided my garments among them
and cast lots for my clothing."[a]

So this is what the soldiers did.

[25]Near the cross of Jesus stood his mother, his mother's sister, Mary the wife of Clopas, and Mary Magdalene. [26]When Jesus saw his mother there, and the disciple whom he loved standing nearby, he said to his mother, "Dear woman, here is your son," [27]and to the disciple, "Here is your mother." From that time on, this disciple took her into his home.

The Death of Jesus [28]Later, knowing that all was now completed, and so that the Scripture would be fulfilled, Jesus said, "I am thirsty." [29]A jar of wine vinegar was there, so they soaked a sponge in it, put the sponge on a stalk of the hyssop plant, and lifted it to Jesus' lips. [30]When he had received the drink, Jesus said, "It is finished." With that, he bowed his head and gave up his spirit.

[31]Now it was the day of Preparation, and the next day was to be a special Sabbath. Because the Jews did not want the bodies left on the crosses during the Sabbath, they asked Pilate to have the legs broken and the bodies taken down. [32]The soldiers therefore came and broke the legs of the first man who had been crucified with Jesus, and then those of the other. [33]But when they came to Jesus and found that he was already dead, they did not break his legs. [34]Instead, one of the soldiers pierced Jesus' side with a spear, bringing a sudden flow of blood and water. [35]The man who saw it has given testimony, and his testimony is true. He knows that he tells the truth, and he testifies so that you also may believe. [36]These things happened so that the scripture would be fulfilled: "Not one of his bones will be broken,"[b] [37]and, as another scripture says, "They will look on the one they have pierced."[c]

The Burial of Jesus [38]Later, Joseph of Arimathea asked Pilate for the body of Jesus. Now Joseph was a disciple of Jesus, but secretly because he feared the Jews. With Pilate's permission, he came and took the body away. [39]He was accompanied by Nicodemus, the man who earlier had visited Jesus at night. Nicodemus brought a mixture of myrrh and aloes, about seventy-five pounds.[d] [40]Taking Jesus' body, the two of them wrapped it, with the spices, in strips of linen. This was in accordance with Jewish burial customs. [41]At the place where Jesus was crucified, there was a garden, and in the garden a new tomb, in which no one had ever been laid. [42]Because it was the Jewish day of Preparation and since the tomb was nearby, they laid Jesus there.

The Empty Tomb Early on the first day of the week, while it was still dark, Mary Magdalene went to the tomb and saw that the stone had been removed from the entrance. [2]So she came running to Simon Peter and the other disciple, the one Jesus loved, and said, "They have taken the Lord out of the tomb, and we don't know where they have put him!"

[3]So Peter and the other disciple started for the tomb. [4]Both were running, but the other disciple outran Peter and reached the tomb first. [5]He bent over and looked in at the strips of linen lying there but did not go in. [6]Then Simon Peter, who was behind him, arrived and went into the tomb. He saw the strips of linen lying there, [7]as well as the burial cloth that had been around Jesus' head. The cloth was folded up by itself, separate from the linen. [8]Finally the other disciple, who had reached the tomb first, also went inside. He

JOHN 19

QUIZZER

Q: What two men went to get Jesus' body after the crucifixion?

BONUS: What was unusual about these men?

Answers on page 1408

[a]24 Psalm 22:18 [b]36 Exodus 12:46; Num. 9:12; Psalm 34:20 [c]37 Zech. 12:10 [d]39 Greek *a hundred litrai* (about 34 kilograms)

saw and believed. ⁹(They still did not understand from Scripture that Jesus had to rise from the dead.)

Jesus Appears to Mary Magdalene   ¹⁰Then the disciples went back to their homes, ¹¹but Mary stood outside the tomb crying. As she wept, she bent over to look into the tomb ¹²and saw two angels in white, seated where Jesus' body had been, one at the head and the other at the foot.

Answers

to Quizzer on
page 1407

A: Joseph of Arimathea and Nicodemus (John 19:38-40).

BONUS: Both had been secret followers of Jesus, and Joseph was a rich man, which fulfilled the prophecy of Isaiah 53:9.

¹³They asked her, "Woman, why are you crying?"

"They have taken my Lord away," she said, "and I don't know where they have put him." ¹⁴At this, she turned around and saw Jesus standing there, but she did not realize that it was Jesus.

¹⁵"Woman," he said, "why are you crying? Who is it you are looking for?"

Thinking he was the gardener, she said, "Sir, if you have carried him away, tell me where you have put him, and I will get him."

¹⁶Jesus said to her, "Mary."

She turned toward him and cried out in Aramaic, "Rabboni!" (which means Teacher).

¹⁷Jesus said, "Do not hold on to me, for I have not yet returned to the Father. Go instead to my brothers and tell them, 'I am returning to my Father and your Father, to my God and your God.' "

¹⁸Mary Magdalene went to the disciples with the news: "I have seen the Lord!" And she told them that he had said these things to her.

Jesus Appears to His Disciples   ¹⁹On the evening of that first day of the week, when the disciples were together, with the doors locked for fear of the Jews, Jesus came and stood among them and said, "Peace be with you!" ²⁰After he said this, he showed them his hands and side. The disciples were overjoyed when they saw the Lord.

²¹Again Jesus said, "Peace be with you! As the Father has sent me, I am sending you." ²²And with that he breathed on them and said, "Receive the Holy Spirit. ²³If you forgive anyone his sins, they are forgiven; if you do not forgive them, they are not forgiven."

Jesus Appears to Thomas   ²⁴Now Thomas (called Didymus), one of the Twelve, was not with the disciples when Jesus came. ²⁵So the other disciples told him, "We have seen the Lord!"

But he said to them, "Unless I see the nail marks in his hands and put my finger where the nails were, and put my hand into his side, I will not believe it."

²⁶A week later his disciples were in the house again, and Thomas was with them. Though the doors were locked, Jesus came and stood among them and said, "Peace be with you!" ²⁷Then he said to Thomas, "Put your finger here; see my hands. Reach out your hand and put it into my side. Stop doubting and believe."

²⁸Thomas said to him, "My Lord and my God!"

²⁹Then Jesus told him, "Because you have seen me, you have believed; blessed are those who have not seen and yet have believed."

³⁰Jesus did many other miraculous signs in the presence of his disciples, which are not recorded in this book. ³¹But these are written that you may*ᵃ* believe that Jesus is the Christ, the Son of God, and that by believing you may have life in his name.

Jesus and the Miraculous Catch of Fish   Afterward Jesus appeared **21** again to his disciples, by the Sea of Tiberias.*ᵇ* It happened this way: ²Simon Peter, Thomas (called Didymus), Nathanael from Cana in Galilee, the sons of Zebedee, and two other disciples were together. ³"I'm going

---

ᵃ31 Some manuscripts *may continue to*   ᵇ1 That is, Sea of Galilee

out to fish," Simon Peter told them, and they said, "We'll go with you." So they went out and got into the boat, but that night they caught nothing.

⁴Early in the morning, Jesus stood on the shore, but the disciples did not realize that it was Jesus.

⁵He called out to them, "Friends, haven't you any fish?"

"No," they answered.

⁶He said, "Throw your net on the right side of the boat and you will find some." When they did, they were unable to haul the net in because of the large number of fish.

⁷Then the disciple whom Jesus loved said to Peter, "It is the Lord!" As soon as Simon Peter heard him say, "It is the Lord," he wrapped his outer garment around him (for he had taken it off) and jumped into the water. ⁸The other disciples followed in the boat, towing the net full of fish, for they were not far from shore, about a hundred yards.ᵃ ⁹When they landed, they saw a fire of burning coals there with fish on it, and some bread.

¹⁰Jesus said to them, "Bring some of the fish you have just caught."

¹¹Simon Peter climbed aboard and dragged the net ashore. It was full of large fish, 153, but even with so many the net was not torn. ¹²Jesus said to them, "Come and have breakfast." None of the disciples dared ask him, "Who are you?" They knew it was the Lord. ¹³Jesus came, took the bread and gave it to them, and did the same with the fish. ¹⁴This was now the third time Jesus appeared to his disciples after he was raised from the dead.

Jesus Reinstates Peter ¹⁵When they had finished eating, Jesus said to Simon Peter, "Simon son of John, do you truly love me more than these?"

"Yes, Lord," he said, "you know that I love you."

Jesus said, "Feed my lambs."

¹⁶Again Jesus said, "Simon son of John, do you truly love me?"

He answered, "Yes, Lord, you know that I love you."

Jesus said, "Take care of my sheep."

¹⁷The third time he said to him, "Simon son of John, do you love me?"

Peter was hurt because Jesus asked him the third time, "Do you love me?" He said, "Lord, you know all things; you know that I love you."

Jesus said, "Feed my sheep. ¹⁸I tell you the truth, when you were younger you dressed yourself and went where you wanted; but when you are old you will stretch out your hands, and someone else will dress you and lead you where you do not want to go." ¹⁹Jesus said this to indicate the kind of death by which Peter would glorify God. Then he said to him, "Follow me!"

²⁰Peter turned and saw that the disciple whom Jesus loved was following them. (This was the one who had leaned back against Jesus at the supper and had said, "Lord, who is going to betray you?") ²¹When Peter saw him, he asked, "Lord, what about him?"

²²Jesus answered, "If I want him to remain alive until I return, what is that to

ᵃ8 Greek *about two hundred cubits* (about 90 meters)

JOHN 21:15-19

Have you ever made a bad choice and felt like you let your parents and God down? Something like Peter's choice to deny that he knew Jesus (John 18:15-27)? When you make that kind of choice, it's natural to wonder if the Lord still loves you. The next time Jesus saw Peter he asked him, "Do you truly love me?" (John 21:15). Peter felt embarrassed and ashamed, but he answered, "Yes, Lord, you know that I love you" (John 21:15). A mistake, even a terribly wrong choice, doesn't mean that the bond of love you have with Jesus has been broken. If you should make one of those bad choices, picture Christ asking you, "Do you truly love me?" Then answer yes.

Direct Line

you? You must follow me." ²³Because of this, the rumor spread among the brothers that this disciple would not die. But Jesus did not say that he would not die; he only said, "If I want him to remain alive until I return, what is that to you?"

²⁴This is the disciple who testifies to these things and who wrote them down. We know that his testimony is true.

²⁵Jesus did many other things as well. If every one of them were written down, I suppose that even the whole world would not have room for the books that would be written.

Introduction

to the

book of Acts

YOU BELONG.

You are a member of a very special group: the church of Jesus Christ. The people in this group care about you. They will support you when you're down and help you when doing right seems hard. They love you, and you love them. You're family.

The book of Acts tells how this family began and grew. Some people think "church" is just a building where people go to worship. In fact, for nearly 300 years there were no church buildings! In the book of Acts you'll learn the truth. The church is people, people who love Jesus and care about each other.

Fundamentals

What brings people close to each other (Acts 2:42-47)?

How can others help when you're facing a tough decision (Acts 4:23-31)?

Have you ever prayed for something and then been surprised by the answer you got (Acts 12:1-19)?

Have you ever fallen asleep during a long sermon (Acts 20:7-12)?

FAST FACTS

Luke, the author of the Gospel of Luke, wrote this book.

Luke traveled with Paul on his missionary trips.

Peter and Paul are the book's main characters.

People throughout the Roman empire spoke the same language, Greek.

Jews made up ten percent of the people in the Roman empire.

1

Jesus Taken Up Into Heaven In my former book, Theophilus, I wrote about all that Jesus began to do and to teach ²until the day he was taken up to heaven, after giving instructions through the Holy Spirit to the apostles he had chosen. ³After his suffering, he showed himself to these men and gave many convincing proofs that he was alive. He appeared to them over a period of forty days and spoke about the kingdom of God. ⁴On one occasion, while he was eating with them, he gave them this command: "Do not leave Jerusalem, but wait for the gift my Father promised, which you have heard me speak about. ⁵For John baptized with*ᵃ* water, but in a few days you will be baptized with the Holy Spirit."

⁶So when they met together, they asked him, "Lord, are you at this time going to restore the kingdom to Israel?"

⁷He said to them: "It is not for you to know the times or dates the Father has set by his own authority. ⁸But you will receive power when the Holy Spirit comes on you; and you will be my witnesses in Jerusalem, and in all Judea and Samaria, and to the ends of the earth."

⁹After he said this, he was taken up before their very eyes, and a cloud hid him from their sight.

¹⁰They were looking intently up into the sky as he was going, when suddenly two men dressed in white stood beside them. ¹¹"Men of Galilee," they said, "why do you stand here looking into the sky? This same Jesus, who has been taken from you into heaven, will come back in the same way you have seen him go into heaven."

> You will receive power when the Holy Spirit comes on you; and you will be my witnesses (Acts 1:8).

Matthias Chosen to Replace Judas ¹²Then they returned to Jerusalem from the hill called the Mount of Olives, a Sabbath day's walk*ᵇ* from the city. ¹³When they arrived, they went upstairs to the room where they were staying. Those present were Peter, John, James and Andrew; Philip and Thomas, Bartholomew and Matthew; James son of Alphaeus and Simon the Zealot, and Judas son of James. ¹⁴They all joined together constantly in prayer, along with the women and Mary the mother of Jesus, and with his brothers.

¹⁵In those days Peter stood up among the believers*ᶜ* (a group numbering about a hundred and twenty) ¹⁶and said, "Brothers, the Scripture had to be fulfilled which the Holy Spirit spoke long ago through the mouth of David concerning Judas, who served as guide for those who arrested Jesus— ¹⁷he was one of our number and shared in this ministry."

¹⁸(With the reward he got for his wickedness, Judas bought a field; there he fell headlong, his body burst open and all his intestines spilled out. ¹⁹Everyone in Jerusalem heard about this, so they called that field in their language Akeldama, that is, Field of Blood.)

²⁰"For," said Peter, "it is written in the book of Psalms,

> " 'May his place be deserted;
> let there be no one to dwell in it,'*ᵈ*

and,

> " 'May another take his place of leadership.'*ᵉ*

²¹Therefore it is necessary to choose one of the men who have been with us the whole time the Lord Jesus went in and out among us, ²²beginning from John's baptism to the time when Jesus was taken up from us. For one of these must become a witness with us of his resurrection."

²³So they proposed two men: Joseph called Barsabbas (also known as Jus-

---

ᵃ5 Or in ᵇ12 That is, about 3/4 mile (about 1,100 meters) ᶜ15 Greek brothers ᵈ20 Psalm 69:25
ᵉ20 Psalm 109:8

tus) and Matthias. 24Then they prayed, "Lord, you know everyone's heart. Show us which of these two you have chosen 25to take over this apostolic ministry, which Judas left to go where he belongs." 26Then they cast lots, and the lot fell to Matthias; so he was added to the eleven apostles.

The Holy Spirit Comes at Pentecost When the day of Pentecost came, they were all together in one place. 2Suddenly a sound like the blowing of a violent wind came from heaven and filled the whole house where they were sitting. 3They saw what seemed to be tongues of fire that separated and came to rest on each of them. 4All of them were filled with the Holy Spirit and began to speak in other tongues*a* as the Spirit enabled them.

5Now there were staying in Jerusalem God-fearing Jews from every nation under heaven. 6When they heard this sound, a crowd came together in bewilderment, because each one heard them speaking in his own language. 7Utterly amazed, they asked: "Are not all these men who are speaking Galileans? 8Then how is it that each of us hears them in his own native language? 9Parthians, Medes and Elamites; residents of Mesopotamia, Judea and Cappadocia, Pontus and Asia, 10Phrygia and Pamphylia, Egypt and the parts of Libya near Cyrene; visitors from Rome 11(both Jews and converts to Judaism); Cretans and Arabs—we hear them declaring the wonders of God in our own tongues!" 12Amazed and perplexed, they asked one another, "What does this mean?"

13Some, however, made fun of them and said, "They have had too much wine.*b*"

Peter Addresses the Crowd 14Then Peter stood up with the Eleven, raised his voice and addressed the crowd: "Fellow Jews and all of you who live in Jerusalem, let me explain this to you; listen carefully to what I say. 15These men are not drunk, as you suppose. It's only nine in the morning! 16No, this is what was spoken by the prophet Joel:

> 17" 'In the last days, God says,
> I will pour out my Spirit on all people.
> Your sons and daughters will prophesy,
> your young men will see visions,
> your old men will dream dreams.

a4 Or languages; also in verse 11   *b13 Or sweet wine*

One of history's most exciting days came just 50 days after the resurrection of Jesus. That day was a regular Jewish holiday called the day of Pentecost, when the Jewish people brought harvest gifts to the temple. But on this Pentecost, God gave believers a special harvest gift: the Holy Spirit!

Three things happened that Pentecost day to mark it as special:

* There was a sound like a violent wind (Acts 2:2).
* Tongues of fire rested on each believer (Acts 2:3).
* The believers spoke "in other tongues" (Acts 2:4).

The three signs that together marked the coming of the Spirit have never happened together again. They don't have to. The Spirit has come and now lives in every Christian (Romans 8:9).

The Bible Says

The Spirit Is Here!

¹⁸Even on my servants, both men and women,
> I will pour out my Spirit in those days,
> and they will prophesy.
¹⁹I will show wonders in the heaven above
> and signs on the earth below,
> blood and fire and billows of smoke.
²⁰The sun will be turned to darkness
> and the moon to blood
> before the coming of the great and glorious day of the Lord.
²¹And everyone who calls
> on the name of the Lord will be saved.'^a

²²"Men of Israel, listen to this: Jesus of Nazareth was a man accredited by God to you by miracles, wonders and signs, which God did among you through him, as you yourselves know. ²³This man was handed over to you by God's set purpose and foreknowledge; and you, with the help of wicked men,^b put him to death by nailing him to the cross. ²⁴But God raised him from the dead, freeing him from the agony of death, because it was impossible for death to keep its hold on him. ²⁵David said about him:

> " 'I saw the Lord always before me.
> Because he is at my right hand,
> I will not be shaken.
²⁶Therefore my heart is glad and my tongue rejoices;
> my body also will live in hope,
²⁷because you will not abandon me to the grave,
> nor will you let your Holy One see decay.
²⁸You have made known to me the paths of life;
> you will fill me with joy in your presence.'^c

²⁹"Brothers, I can tell you confidently that the patriarch David died and was buried, and his tomb is here to this day. ³⁰But he was a prophet and knew that God had promised him on oath that he would place one of his descendants on his throne. ³¹Seeing what was ahead, he spoke of the resurrection of the Christ,^d that he was not abandoned to the grave, nor did his body see decay. ³²God has raised this Jesus to life, and we are all witnesses of the fact. ³³Exalted to the right hand of God, he has received from the Father the promised Holy Spirit and has poured out what you now see and hear. ³⁴For David did not ascend to heaven, and yet he said,

> " 'The Lord said to my Lord:
> "Sit at my right hand
³⁵until I make your enemies
> a footstool for your feet." '^e

³⁶"Therefore let all Israel be assured of this: God has made this Jesus, whom you crucified, both Lord and Christ."

³⁷When the people heard this, they were cut to the heart and said to Peter and the other apostles, "Brothers, what shall we do?"

³⁸Peter replied, "Repent and be baptized, every one of you, in the name of Jesus Christ for the forgiveness of your sins. And you will receive the gift of the Holy Spirit. ³⁹The promise is for you and your children and for all who are far off—for all whom the Lord our God will call."

⁴⁰With many other words he warned them; and he pleaded with them, "Save yourselves from this corrupt generation." ⁴¹Those who accepted his

---

^a21 Joel 2:28-32 ^b23 Or *of those not having the law* (that is, Gentiles) ^c28 Psalm 16:8-11 ^d31 Or *Messiah.*
"The Christ" (Greek) and "the Messiah" (Hebrew) both mean "the Anointed One"; also in verse 36.
^e35 Psalm 110:1

message were baptized, and about three thousand were added to their number that day.

The Fellowship of the Believers ⁴²They devoted themselves to the apostles' teaching and to the fellowship, to the breaking of bread and to prayer. ⁴³Everyone was filled with awe, and many wonders and miraculous signs were done by the apostles. ⁴⁴All the believers were together and had everything in common. ⁴⁵Selling their possessions and goods, they gave to anyone as he had need. ⁴⁶Every day they continued to meet together in the temple courts. They broke bread in their homes and ate together with glad and sincere hearts, ⁴⁷praising God and enjoying the favor of all the people. And the Lord added to their number daily those who were being saved.

3 *Peter Heals the Crippled Beggar* One day Peter and John were going up to the temple at the time of prayer—at three in the afternoon. ²Now a man crippled from birth was being carried to the temple gate called Beautiful, where he was put every day to beg from those going into the temple courts. ³When he saw Peter and John about to enter, he asked them for money. ⁴Peter looked straight at him, as did John. Then Peter said, "Look at us!" ⁵So the man gave them his attention, expecting to get something from them.

⁶Then Peter said, "Silver or gold I do not have, but what I have I give you. In the name of Jesus Christ of Nazareth, walk." ⁷Taking him by the right hand, he helped him up, and instantly the man's feet and ankles became strong. ⁸He jumped to his feet and began to walk. Then he went with them into the temple courts, walking and jumping, and praising God. ⁹When all the people saw him walking and praising God, ¹⁰they recognized him as the same man who used to sit begging at the temple gate called Beautiful, and they were filled with wonder and amazement at what had happened to him.

Peter Speaks to the Onlookers ¹¹While the beggar held on to Peter and John, all the people were astonished and came running to them in the place called Solomon's Colonnade. ¹²When Peter saw this, he said to them: "Men of Israel, why does this surprise you? Why do you stare at us as if by our own power or godliness we had made this man walk? ¹³The God of Abraham, Isaac and Jacob, the God of our fathers, has glorified his servant Jesus. You handed him over to be killed, and you disowned him before Pilate, though he had decided to let him go. ¹⁴You disowned the Holy and Righteous One and asked that a murderer be released to you. ¹⁵You killed the author of life, but God raised him from the dead. We are witnesses of this. ¹⁶By faith in the name of Jesus, this man whom you see and know was made strong. It is Jesus' name and the faith that comes through him that has given this complete healing to him, as you can all see.

¹⁷"Now, brothers, I know that you acted in ignorance, as did your leaders. ¹⁸But this is how God fulfilled what he had foretold through all the prophets, saying that his Christ^a would suffer. ¹⁹Repent, then, and turn to God, so that your sins may be wiped out, that times of refreshing may come from the Lord, ²⁰and that he may send the Christ, who has been appointed for you—even Jesus. ²¹He must remain in heaven until the time comes for God to restore everything, as he promised long ago through his holy prophets. ²²For Moses said, 'The Lord your God will raise up for you a prophet like me from among your own people; you must listen to everything he tells you. ²³Anyone who does not listen to him will be completely cut off from among his people.'^b

²⁴"Indeed, all the prophets from Samuel on, as many as have spoken, have foretold these days. ²⁵And you are heirs of the prophets and of the covenant God made with your fathers. He said to Abraham, 'Through your offspring all

---

a18 Or Messiah; also in verse 20   b23 Deut. 18:15,18,19

peoples on earth will be blessed.'ᵃ ²⁶When God raised up his servant, he sent him first to you to bless you by turning each of you from your wicked ways."

Peter and John Before the Sanhedrin The priests and the captain of the temple guard and the Sadducees came up to Peter and John while they were speaking to the people. ²They were greatly disturbed because the apostles were teaching the people and proclaiming in Jesus the resurrection of the dead. ³They seized Peter and John, and because it was evening, they put them in jail until the next day. ⁴But many who heard the message believed, and the number of men grew to about five thousand.

⁵The next day the rulers, elders and teachers of the law met in Jerusalem. ⁶Annas the high priest was there, and so were Caiaphas, John, Alexander and the other men of the high priest's family. ⁷They had Peter and John brought before them and began to question them: "By what power or what name did you do this?"

⁸Then Peter, filled with the Holy Spirit, said to them: "Rulers and elders of the people! ⁹If we are being called to account today for an act of kindness shown to a cripple and are asked how he was healed, ¹⁰then know this, you and all the people of Israel: It is by the name of Jesus Christ of Nazareth, whom you crucified but whom God raised from the dead, that this man stands before you healed. ¹¹He is

> " 'the stone you builders rejected,
> which has become the capstone.ᵇ'ᶜ

¹²Salvation is found in no one else, for there is no other name under heaven given to men by which we must be saved."

¹³When they saw the courage of Peter and John and realized that they were unschooled, ordinary men, they were astonished and they took note that these men had been with Jesus. ¹⁴But since they could see the man who had been healed standing there with them, there was nothing they could say. ¹⁵So they ordered them to withdraw from the Sanhedrin and then conferred together. ¹⁶"What are we going to do with these men?" they asked. "Everybody living in Jerusalem knows they have done an outstanding miracle, and we cannot deny it. ¹⁷But to stop this thing from spreading any further among the people, we must warn these men to speak no longer to anyone in this name."

¹⁸Then they called them in again and commanded them not to speak or teach at all in the name of Jesus. ¹⁹But Peter and John replied, "Judge for yourselves whether it is right in God's sight to obey you rather than God. ²⁰For we cannot help speaking about what we have seen and heard."

²¹After further threats they let them go. They could not decide how to punish them, because all the people were praising God for what had happened. ²²For the man who was miraculously healed was over forty years old.

The Believers' Prayer ²³On their release, Peter and John went back to their own people and reported all that the chief priests and elders had said to them. ²⁴When they heard this, they raised their voices together in prayer to God. "Sovereign Lord," they said, "you made the heaven and the earth and the sea, and everything in them. ²⁵You spoke by the Holy Spirit through the mouth of your servant, our father David:

> " 'Why do the nations rage
> and the peoples plot in vain?
> ²⁶The kings of the earth take their stand
> and the rulers gather together
> against the Lord
> and against his Anointed One.ᵈ'ᵉ

ᵃ25 Gen. 22:18; 26:4   ᵇ11 Or *cornerstone*   ᶜ11 Psalm 118:22   ᵈ26 That is, Christ or Messiah   ᵉ26 Psalm 2:1,2

²⁷Indeed Herod and Pontius Pilate met together with the Gentiles and the people*ᵃ* of Israel in this city to conspire against your holy servant Jesus, whom you anointed. ²⁸They did what your power and will had decided beforehand should happen. ²⁹Now, Lord, consider their threats and enable your servants to speak your word with great boldness. ³⁰Stretch out your hand to heal and perform miraculous signs and wonders through the name of your holy servant Jesus."

³¹After they prayed, the place where they were meeting was shaken. And they were all filled with the Holy Spirit and spoke the word of God boldly.

The Believers Share Their Possessions　　³²All the believers were one in heart and mind. No one claimed that any of his possessions was his own, but they shared everything they had. ³³With great power the apostles continued to testify to the resurrection of the Lord Jesus, and much grace was upon them all. ³⁴There were no needy persons among them. For from time to time those who owned lands or houses sold them, brought the money from the sales ³⁵and put it at the apostles' feet, and it was distributed to anyone as he had need.

³⁶Joseph, a Levite from Cyprus, whom the apostles called Barnabas (which means Son of Encouragement), ³⁷sold a field he owned and brought the money and put it at the apostles' feet.

5 *Ananias and Sapphira*　　Now a man named Ananias, together with his wife Sapphira, also sold a piece of property. ²With his wife's full knowledge he kept back part of the money for himself, but brought the rest and put it at the apostles' feet.

³Then Peter said, "Ananias, how is it that Satan has so filled your heart that you have lied to the Holy Spirit and have kept for yourself some of the money you received for the land? ⁴Didn't it belong to you before it was sold? And after it was sold, wasn't the money at your disposal? What made you think of doing such a thing? You have not lied to men but to God."

⁵When Ananias heard this, he fell down and died. And great fear seized all who heard what had happened. ⁶Then the young men came forward, wrapped up his body, and carried him out and buried him.

⁷About three hours later his wife came in, not knowing what had happened. ⁸Peter asked her, "Tell me, is this the price you and Ananias got for the land?"

"Yes," she said, "that is the price."

⁹Peter said to her, "How could you agree to test the Spirit of the Lord? Look! The feet of the men who buried your husband are at the door, and they will carry you out also."

¹⁰At that moment she fell down at his feet and died. Then the young men came in and, finding her dead, carried her out and buried her beside her husband. ¹¹Great fear seized the whole church and all who heard about these events.

The Apostles Heal Many　　¹²The apostles performed many miraculous signs and wonders among the people. And all the be-

---

ACTS 5:1–11

How much does God care about your money? Actually, not much. He can get along without the dollars or cents you put in the offering plate. He could get along without the money of Ananias and Sapphira too. So why did he strike them dead when they held back some of the money? Because they lied, not just before other people, but before God. They acted as if God wasn't real and didn't know what they were doing. As Peter said, the property belonged to them before it was sold, and the money was theirs to use as they saw fit. Giving is a privilege for Christians, not a duty. What's important is to remember that God is real. Don't behave as if he isn't.

Direct Line

ᵃ27 The Greek is plural.

Dear Sam,

I have a very difficult decision to make. Should I pray and try to do it on my own, or should I get advice from my friends? I want to do what's best, but I'm having a hard time.

Dee in Detroit

Dear Sam, Inc.

100 Advice Lane, Anywhere, USA

Dear Dee,

Your question shows a desire for God's will and how to know it. That's great! Some decisions are very tough, and sometimes choosing an option isn't as clear as we'd like.

Shortly after Christ's death, Peter and John were persecuted, beaten and imprisoned. In the Jewish religious court, they were told to stop preaching about Christ. As soon as they were released, Peter and John "went back to their own people" to tell them what had happened. Their prayer would be a good model for you. First the disciples praised God for his greatness, they told God about their problem, and then they asked for special strength to be true to him despite the difficulties (Acts 4:23-30). And God answered that prayer and gave them the strength they needed.

Sometimes it's hard to know what to do. Talking with your friends can help you think things through. But then you definitely need to talk with God and ask him to make his will plain and to give you the strength to do what is best and right.

Sam

lievers used to meet together in Solomon's Colonnade. [13]No one else dared join them, even though they were highly regarded by the people. [14]Nevertheless, more and more men and women believed in the Lord and were added to their number. [15]As a result, people brought the sick into the streets and laid them on beds and mats so that at least Peter's shadow might fall on some of them as he passed by. [16]Crowds gathered also from the towns around Jerusalem, bringing their sick and those tormented by evil[a] spirits, and all of them were healed.

The Apostles Persecuted [17]Then the high priest and all his associates, who were members of the party of the Sadducees, were filled with jealousy. [18]They arrested the apostles and put them in the public jail. [19]But during the night an angel of the Lord opened the doors of the jail and brought them out. [20]"Go, stand in the temple courts," he said, "and tell the people the full message of this new life."

[21]At daybreak they entered the temple courts, as they had been told, and began to teach the people.

When the high priest and his associates arrived, they called together the Sanhedrin—the full assembly of the elders of Israel—and sent to the jail for the apostles. [22]But on arriving at the jail, the officers did not find them there. So they went back and reported, [23]"We found the jail securely locked, with the guards standing at the doors; but when we opened them, we found no one inside." [24]On hearing this report, the captain of the temple guard and the chief priests were puzzled, wondering what would come of this.

[25]Then someone came and said, "Look! The men you put in jail are standing in the temple courts teaching the people." [26]At that, the captain went with his officers and brought the apostles. They did not use force, because they feared that the people would stone them.

[27]Having brought the apostles, they made them appear before the Sanhedrin to be questioned by the high priest. [28]"We gave you strict orders not to teach in this name," he said. "Yet you have filled Jerusalem with your teaching and are determined to make us guilty of this man's blood."

[29]Peter and the other apostles replied: "We must obey God rather than men! [30]The God of our fathers raised Jesus from the dead—whom you had killed by hanging him on a tree. [31]God exalted him to his own right hand as Prince and Savior that he might give repentance and forgiveness of sins to Israel. [32]We are witnesses of these things, and so is the Holy Spirit, whom God has given to those who obey him."

[33]When they heard this, they were furious and wanted to put them to death. [34]But a Pharisee named Gamaliel, a teacher of the law, who was honored by all the people, stood up in the Sanhedrin and ordered that the men be put outside for a little while. [35]Then he addressed them: "Men of Israel, consider carefully what you intend to do to these men. [36]Some time ago Theudas appeared, claiming to be somebody, and about four hundred men rallied to him. He was killed, all his followers were dispersed, and it all came to nothing. [37]After him, Judas the Galilean appeared in the days of the census and led a band of people in revolt. He too was killed, and all his followers were scattered. [38]Therefore, in the present case I advise you: Leave these men alone! Let them go! For if their purpose or activity is of human origin, it will fail. [39]But if it is from God, you will not be able to stop these men; you will only find yourselves fighting against God."

[40]His speech persuaded them. They called the apostles in and had them flogged. Then they ordered them not to speak in the name of Jesus, and let them go.

[41]The apostles left the Sanhedrin, rejoicing because they had been count-

[a]16 Greek *unclean*

ed worthy of suffering disgrace for the Name. ⁴²Day after day, in the temple courts and from house to house, they never stopped teaching and proclaiming the good news that Jesus is the Christ.ᵃ

The Choosing of the Seven In those days when the number of disciples was increasing, the Grecian Jews among them complained against the Hebraic Jews because their widows were being overlooked in the daily distribution of food. ²So the Twelve gathered all the disciples together and said, "It would not be right for us to neglect the ministry of the word of God in order to wait on tables. ³Brothers, choose seven men from among you who are known to be full of the Spirit and wisdom. We will turn this responsibility over to them ⁴and will give our attention to prayer and the ministry of the word."

⁵This proposal pleased the whole group. They chose Stephen, a man full of faith and of the Holy Spirit; also Philip, Procorus, Nicanor, Timon, Parmenas, and Nicolas from Antioch, a convert to Judaism. ⁶They presented these men to the apostles, who prayed and laid their hands on them.

⁷So the word of God spread. The number of disciples in Jerusalem increased rapidly, and a large number of priests became obedient to the faith.

Stephen Seized ⁸Now Stephen, a man full of God's grace and power, did great wonders and miraculous signs among the people. ⁹Opposition arose, however, from members of the Synagogue of the Freedmen (as it was called)—Jews of Cyrene and Alexandria as well as the provinces of Cilicia and Asia. These men began to argue with Stephen, ¹⁰but they could not stand up against his wisdom or the Spirit by whom he spoke.

¹¹Then they secretly persuaded some men to say, "We have heard Stephen speak words of blasphemy against Moses and against God."

¹²So they stirred up the people and the elders and the teachers of the law. They seized Stephen and brought him before the Sanhedrin. ¹³They produced false witnesses, who testified, "This fellow never stops speaking against this holy place and against the law. ¹⁴For we have heard him say that this Jesus of Nazareth will destroy this place and change the customs Moses handed down to us."

¹⁵All who were sitting in the Sanhedrin looked intently at Stephen, and they saw that his face was like the face of an angel.

OT 101. Stephen sure knew his Old Testament history.

SEE ACTS 7

Stephen's Speech to the Sanhedrin Then the high priest asked him, "Are these charges true?"

²To this he replied: "Brothers and fathers, listen to me! The God of glory appeared to our father Abraham while he was still in Mesopotamia, before he lived in Haran. ³'Leave your country and your people,' God said, 'and go to the land I will show you.'ᵇ

⁴"So he left the land of the Chaldeans and settled in Haran. After the death of his father, God sent him to this land where you are now living. ⁵He gave him no inheritance here, not even a foot of ground. But God promised him that he and his descendants after him would possess the land, even though at that time Abraham had no child. ⁶God spoke to him in this way: 'Your descendants will be strangers in a country not

ᵃ42 Or Messiah ᵇ3 Gen. 12:1

their own, and they will be enslaved and mistreated four hundred years. [7]But I will punish the nation they serve as slaves,' God said, 'and afterward they will come out of that country and worship me in this place.'[a] [8]Then he gave Abraham the covenant of circumcision. And Abraham became the father of Isaac and circumcised him eight days after his birth. Later Isaac became the father of Jacob, and Jacob became the father of the twelve patriarchs.

[9]"Because the patriarchs were jealous of Joseph, they sold him as a slave into Egypt. But God was with him [10]and rescued him from all his troubles. He gave Joseph wisdom and enabled him to gain the goodwill of Pharaoh king of Egypt; so he made him ruler over Egypt and all his palace.

[11]"Then a famine struck all Egypt and Canaan, bringing great suffering, and our fathers could not find food. [12]When Jacob heard that there was grain in Egypt, he sent our fathers on their first visit. [13]On their second visit, Joseph told his brothers who he was, and Pharaoh learned about Joseph's family. [14]After this, Joseph sent for his father Jacob and his whole family, seventy-five in all. [15]Then Jacob went down to Egypt, where he and our fathers died. [16]Their bodies were brought back to Shechem and placed in the tomb that Abraham had bought from the sons of Hamor at Shechem for a certain sum of money.

[17]"As the time drew near for God to fulfill his promise to Abraham, the number of our people in Egypt greatly increased. [18]Then another king, who knew nothing about Joseph, became ruler of Egypt. [19]He dealt treacherously with our people and oppressed our forefathers by forcing them to throw out their newborn babies so that they would die.

[20]"At that time Moses was born, and he was no ordinary child.[b] For three months he was cared for in his father's house. [21]When he was placed outside, Pharaoh's daughter took him and brought him up as her own son. [22]Moses was educated in all the wisdom of the Egyptians and was powerful in speech and action.

[23]"When Moses was forty years old, he decided to visit his fellow Israelites. [24]He saw one of them being mistreated by an Egyptian, so he went to his defense and avenged him by killing the Egyptian. [25]Moses thought that his own people would realize that God was using him to rescue them, but they did not. [26]The next day Moses came upon two Israelites who were fighting. He tried to reconcile them by saying, 'Men, you are brothers; why do you want to hurt each other?'

[27]"But the man who was mistreating the other pushed Moses aside and said, 'Who made you ruler and judge over us? [28]Do you want to kill me as you killed the Egyptian yesterday?'[c] [29]When Moses heard this, he fled to Midian, where he settled as a foreigner and had two sons.

[30]"After forty years had passed, an angel appeared to Moses in the flames of a burning bush in the desert near Mount Sinai. [31]When he saw this, he was amazed at the sight. As he went over to look more closely, he heard the Lord's voice: [32]'I am the God of your fathers, the God of Abraham, Isaac and Jacob.'[d] Moses trembled with fear and did not dare to look.

[33]"Then the Lord said to him, 'Take off your sandals; the place where you are standing is holy ground. [34]I have indeed seen the oppression of my people in Egypt. I have heard their groaning and have come down to set them free. Now come, I will send you back to Egypt.'[e]

[35]"This is the same Moses whom they had rejected with the words, 'Who made you ruler and judge?' He was sent to be their ruler and deliverer by God himself, through the angel who appeared to him in the bush. [36]He led them out of Egypt and did wonders and miraculous signs in Egypt, at the Red Sea[e] and for forty years in the desert.

---

[a]7 Gen. 15:13,14   [b]20 Or was fair in the sight of God   [c]28 Exodus 2:14   [d]32 Exodus 3:6   [e]34 Exodus 3:5,7,8,10   [e]36 That is, Sea of Reeds

[37]"This is that Moses who told the Israelites, 'God will send you a prophet like me from your own people.'[a] [38]He was in the assembly in the desert, with the angel who spoke to him on Mount Sinai, and with our fathers; and he received living words to pass on to us.

[39]"But our fathers refused to obey him. Instead, they rejected him and in their hearts turned back to Egypt. [40]They told Aaron, 'Make us gods who will go before us. As for this fellow Moses who led us out of Egypt—we don't know what has happened to him!'[b] [41]That was the time they made an idol in the form of a calf. They brought sacrifices to it and held a celebration in honor of what their hands had made. [42]But God turned away and gave them over to the worship of the heavenly bodies. This agrees with what is written in the book of the prophets:

" 'Did you bring me sacrifices and offerings
    forty years in the desert, O house of Israel?
[43]You have lifted up the shrine of Molech
    and the star of your god Rephan,
    the idols you made to worship.
Therefore I will send you into exile'[c] beyond Babylon.

[44]"Our forefathers had the tabernacle of the Testimony with them in the desert. It had been made as God directed Moses, according to the pattern he had seen. [45]Having received the tabernacle, our fathers under Joshua brought it with them when they took the land from the nations God drove out before them. It remained in the land until the time of David, [46]who enjoyed God's favor and asked that he might provide a dwelling place for the God of Jacob.[d] [47]But it was Solomon who built the house for him.

[48]"However, the Most High does not live in houses made by men. As the prophet says:

[49]" 'Heaven is my throne,
    and the earth is my footstool.
What kind of house will you build for me?
                       says the Lord.
Or where will my resting place be?
[50]Has not my hand made all these things?'[e]

[51]"You stiff-necked people, with uncircumcised hearts and ears! You are just like your fathers: You always resist the Holy Spirit! [52]Was there ever a prophet your fathers did not persecute? They even killed those who predicted the coming of the Righteous One. And now you have betrayed and murdered him— [53]you who have received the law that was put into effect through angels but have not obeyed it."

The Stoning of Stephen [54]When they heard this, they were furious and gnashed their teeth at him. [55]But Stephen, full of the Holy Spirit, looked up to heaven and saw the glory of God, and Jesus standing at the right hand of God. [56]"Look," he said, "I see heaven open and the Son of Man standing at the right hand of God."

[57]At this they covered their ears and, yelling at the top of their voices, they all rushed at him, [58]dragged him out of the city and began to stone him. Meanwhile, the witnesses laid their clothes at the feet of a young man named Saul.

[59]While they were stoning him, Stephen prayed, "Lord Jesus, receive my spirit." [60]Then he fell on his knees and cried out, "Lord, do not hold this sin against them." When he had said this, he fell asleep.

---

[a]37 Deut. 18:15 [b]40 Exodus 32:1 [c]43 Amos 5:25-27 [d]46 Some early manuscripts *the house of Jacob*
[e]50 Isaiah 66:1,2

And Saul was there, giving approval to his death.

The Church Persecuted and Scattered On that day a great persecution broke out against the church at Jerusalem, and all except the apostles were scattered throughout Judea and Samaria. ²Godly men buried Stephen and mourned deeply for him. ³But Saul began to destroy the church. Going from house to house, he dragged off men and women and put them in prison.

Philip in Samaria ⁴Those who had been scattered preached the word wherever they went. ⁵Philip went down to a city in Samaria and proclaimed the Christ*ᵃ* there. ⁶When the crowds heard Philip and saw the miraculous signs he did, they all paid close attention to what he said. ⁷With shrieks, evil*ᵇ* spirits came out of many, and many paralytics and cripples were healed. ⁸So there was great joy in that city.

Simon the Sorcerer ⁹Now for some time a man named Simon had practiced sorcery in the city and amazed all the people of Samaria. He boasted that he was someone great, ¹⁰and all the people, both high and low, gave him their attention and exclaimed, "This man is the divine power known as the Great Power." ¹¹They followed him because he had amazed them for a long time with his magic. ¹²But when they believed Philip as he preached the good news of the kingdom of God and the name of Jesus Christ, they were baptized, both men and women. ¹³Simon himself believed and was baptized. And he followed Philip everywhere, astonished by the great signs and miracles he saw.

¹⁴When the apostles in Jerusalem heard that Samaria had accepted the word of God, they sent Peter and John to them. ¹⁵When they arrived, they prayed for them that they might receive the Holy Spirit, ¹⁶because the Holy Spirit had not yet come upon any of them; they had simply been baptized into*ᶜ* the name of the Lord Jesus. ¹⁷Then Peter and John placed their hands on them, and they received the Holy Spirit.

¹⁸When Simon saw that the Spirit was given at the laying on of the apostles' hands, he offered them money ¹⁹and said, "Give me also this ability so that everyone on whom I lay my hands may receive the Holy Spirit."

²⁰Peter answered: "May your money perish with you, because you thought you could buy the gift of God with money! ²¹You have no part or share in this ministry, because your heart is not right before God. ²²Repent of this wickedness and pray to the Lord. Perhaps he will forgive you for having such a thought in your heart. ²³For I see that you are full of bitterness and captive to sin."

²⁴Then Simon answered, "Pray to the Lord for me so that nothing you have said may happen to me."

²⁵When they had testified and proclaimed the word of the Lord, Peter and John returned to Jerusalem, preaching the gospel in many Samaritan villages.

Philip and the Ethiopian ²⁶Now an angel of the Lord said to Philip, "Go south to the road—the desert road—that goes down from Jerusalem to Gaza." ²⁷So he started out, and on his way he met an Ethiopian*ᵈ* eunuch, an important official in charge of all the treasury of Candace, queen of the Ethiopians. This man had gone to Jerusalem to worship, ²⁸and on his way home was sitting in his chariot reading the book of Isaiah the prophet. ²⁹The Spirit told Philip, "Go to that chariot and stay near it."

³⁰Then Philip ran up to the chariot and heard the man reading Isaiah the prophet. "Do you understand what you are reading?" Philip asked.

ᵃ5 Or *Messiah* *ᵇ7* Greek *unclean* *ᶜ16* Or *in* *ᵈ27* That is, from the upper Nile region

³¹"How can I," he said, "unless someone explains it to me?" So he invited Philip to come up and sit with him.

³²The eunuch was reading this passage of Scripture:

> "He was led like a sheep to the slaughter,
>   and as a lamb before the shearer is silent,
>   so he did not open his mouth.
> ³³In his humiliation he was deprived of justice.
>   Who can speak of his descendants?
>   For his life was taken from the earth."ᵃ

³⁴The eunuch asked Philip, "Tell me, please, who is the prophet talking about, himself or someone else?" ³⁵Then Philip began with that very passage of Scripture and told him the good news about Jesus.

³⁶As they traveled along the road, they came to some water and the eunuch said, "Look, here is water. Why shouldn't I be baptized?"ᵇ ³⁸And he gave orders to stop the chariot. Then both Philip and the eunuch went down into the water and Philip baptized him. ³⁹When they came up out of the water, the Spirit of the Lord suddenly took Philip away, and the eunuch did not see him again, but went on his way rejoicing. ⁴⁰Philip, however, appeared at Azotus and traveled about, preaching the gospel in all the towns until he reached Caesarea.

9 **Saul's Conversion** Meanwhile, Saul was still breathing out murderous threats against the Lord's disciples. He went to the high priest ²and asked him for letters to the synagogues in Damascus, so that if he found any there who belonged to the Way, whether men or women, he might take them as prisoners to Jerusalem. ³As he neared Damascus on his journey, suddenly a light from heaven flashed around him. ⁴He fell to the ground and heard a voice say to him, "Saul, Saul, why do you persecute me?"

⁵"Who are you, Lord?" Saul asked.

"I am Jesus, whom you are persecuting," he replied. ⁶"Now get up and go into the city, and you will be told what you must do."

⁷The men traveling with Saul stood there speechless; they heard the sound but did not see anyone. ⁸Saul got up from the ground, but when he opened his eyes he could see nothing. So they led him by the hand into Damascus. ⁹For three days he was blind, and did not eat or drink anything.

¹⁰In Damascus there was a disciple named Ananias. The Lord called to him in a vision, "Ananias!"

"Yes, Lord," he answered.

¹¹The Lord told him, "Go to the house of Judas on Straight Street and ask for a man from Tarsus named Saul, for he is praying. ¹²In a vision he has seen a man named Ananias come and place his hands on him to restore his sight."

¹³"Lord," Ananias answered, "I have

ACTS 8:26–40

Does the thought of giving an oral report in school terrify you? Would you rather give up your stereo than sing a solo in church? Lots of people feel that way. Everyone has a "comfort level" when it comes to speaking up with others around. Some are comfortable with a thousand. Some are OK if a group isn't over twenty. For some the comfort level is two or three, or even one. And that's all right. In fact, God took Philip away from a ministry to crowds (Acts 8:6) to send him to just one person. If your comfort level is one or two, don't be down on yourself. That's you. And God can use you the way you are.

Direct Line

ᵃ33 Isaiah 53:7,8   ᵇ36 Some late manuscripts *baptized?"* ³⁷*Philip said, "If you believe with all your heart, you may." The eunuch answered, "I believe that Jesus Christ is the Son of God."*

heard many reports about this man and all the harm he has done to your saints in Jerusalem. [14]And he has come here with authority from the chief priests to arrest all who call on your name."

[15]But the Lord said to Ananias, "Go! This man is my chosen instrument to carry my name before the Gentiles and their kings and before the people of Israel. [16]I will show him how much he must suffer for my name."

[17]Then Ananias went to the house and entered it. Placing his hands on Saul, he said, "Brother Saul, the Lord—Jesus, who appeared to you on the road as you were coming here—has sent me so that you may see again and be filled with the Holy Spirit." [18]Immediately, something like scales fell from Saul's eyes, and he could see again. He got up and was baptized, [19]and after taking some food, he regained his strength.

Saul in Damascus and Jerusalem   Saul spent several days with the disciples in Damascus. [20]At once he began to preach in the synagogues that Jesus is the Son of God. [21]All those who heard him were astonished and asked, "Isn't he the man who raised havoc in Jerusalem among those who call on this name? And hasn't he come here to take them as prisoners to the chief priests?" [22]Yet Saul grew more and more powerful and baffled the Jews living in Damascus by proving that Jesus is the Christ.[a]

[23]After many days had gone by, the Jews conspired to kill him, [24]but Saul learned of their plan. Day and night they kept close watch on the city gates in order to kill him. [25]But his followers took him by night and lowered him in a basket through an opening in the wall.

[26]When he came to Jerusalem, he tried to join the disciples, but they were all afraid of him, not believing that he really was a disciple. [27]But Barnabas took him and brought him to the apostles. He told them how Saul on his journey had seen the Lord and that the Lord had spoken to him, and how in Damascus he had preached fearlessly in the name of Jesus. [28]So Saul stayed with them and moved about freely in Jerusalem, speaking boldly in the name of the Lord. [29]He talked and debated with the Grecian Jews, but they tried to kill him. [30]When the brothers learned of this, they took him down to Caesarea and sent him off to Tarsus.

[31]Then the church throughout Judea, Galilee and Samaria enjoyed a time of peace. It was strengthened; and encouraged by the Holy Spirit, it grew in numbers, living in the fear of the Lord.

Aeneas and Dorcas   [32]As Peter traveled about the country, he went to visit the saints in Lydda. [33]There he found a man named Aeneas, a paralytic who had been bedridden for eight years. [34]"Aeneas," Peter said to him, "Jesus Christ heals you. Get up and take care of your mat." Immediately Aeneas got up. [35]All those who lived in Lydda and Sharon saw him and turned to the Lord.

[36]In Joppa there was a disciple named Tabitha (which, when translated, is Dorcas[b]), who was always doing good and helping the poor. [37]About that time she became sick and died, and her body was washed and placed in an upstairs room.

---

[a]22 Or *Messiah*   [b]36 Both *Tabitha* (Aramaic) and *Dorcas* (Greek) mean *gazelle.*

ACTS 9:26–30

When Paul came to Jerusalem he was more than an outsider. He'd been an enemy, and everyone was suspicious of him. Only Barnabas was willing to risk acting like a friend to Paul, bringing this outsider in. You can read the rest of the story. It's especially important for Christians to reach out and welcome others. Introduce yourself to the newcomer. Invite him or her to the next youth group activity. You'll not only do a good deed. You may help start someone out on an exciting spiritual journey.

Direct Line

³⁸Lydda was near Joppa; so when the disciples heard that Peter was in Lydda, they sent two men to him and urged him, "Please come at once!"

³⁹Peter went with them, and when he arrived he was taken upstairs to the room. All the widows stood around him, crying and showing him the robes and other clothing that Dorcas had made while she was still with them.

⁴⁰Peter sent them all out of the room; then he got down on his knees and prayed. Turning toward the dead woman, he said, "Tabitha, get up." She opened her eyes, and seeing Peter she sat up. ⁴¹He took her by the hand and helped her to her feet. Then he called the believers and the widows and presented her to them alive. ⁴²This became known all over Joppa, and many people believed in the Lord. ⁴³Peter stayed in Joppa for some time with a tanner named Simon.

10 *Cornelius Calls for Peter* At Caesarea there was a man named Cornelius, a centurion in what was known as the Italian Regiment. ²He and all his family were devout and God-fearing; he gave generously to those in need and prayed to God regularly. ³One day at about three in the afternoon he had a vision. He distinctly saw an angel of God, who came to him and said, "Cornelius!"

⁴Cornelius stared at him in fear. "What is it, Lord?" he asked.

The angel answered, "Your prayers and gifts to the poor have come up as a memorial offering before God. ⁵Now send men to Joppa to bring back a man named Simon who is called Peter. ⁶He is staying with Simon the tanner, whose house is by the sea."

⁷When the angel who spoke to him had gone, Cornelius called two of his servants and a devout soldier who was one of his attendants. ⁸He told them everything that had happened and sent them to Joppa.

Peter's Vision ⁹About noon the following day as they were on their journey and approaching the city, Peter went up on the roof to pray. ¹⁰He became hungry and wanted something to eat, and while the meal was being prepared, he fell into a trance. ¹¹He saw heaven opened and something like a large sheet being let down to earth by its four corners. ¹²It contained all kinds of four-footed animals, as well as reptiles of the earth and birds of the air. ¹³Then a voice told him, "Get up, Peter. Kill and eat."

¹⁴"Surely not, Lord!" Peter replied. "I have never eaten anything impure or unclean."

¹⁵The voice spoke to him a second time, "Do not call anything impure that God has made clean."

¹⁶This happened three times, and immediately the sheet was taken back to heaven.

¹⁷While Peter was wondering about the meaning of the vision, the men sent by Cornelius found out where Simon's house was and stopped at the gate. ¹⁸They called out, asking if Simon who was known as Peter was staying there.

¹⁹While Peter was still thinking about the vision, the Spirit said to him, "Simon, three*ᵃ* men are looking for you. ²⁰So get up and go downstairs. Do not hesitate to go with them, for I have sent them."

²¹Peter went down and said to the men, "I'm the one you're looking for. Why have you come?"

²²The men replied, "We have come from Cornelius the centurion. He is a righteous and God-fearing man, who is respected by all the Jewish people. A holy angel told him to have you come to his house so that he could hear what you have to say." ²³Then Peter invited the men into the house to be his guests.

ᵃ19 One early manuscript *two*; other manuscripts do not have the number.

Peter at Cornelius' House The next day Peter started out with them, and some of the brothers from Joppa went along. ²⁴The following day he arrived in Caesarea. Cornelius was expecting them and had called together his relatives and close friends. ²⁵As Peter entered the house, Cornelius met him and fell at his feet in reverence. ²⁶But Peter made him get up. "Stand up," he said, "I am only a man myself."

²⁷Talking with him, Peter went inside and found a large gathering of people. ²⁸He said to them: "You are well aware that it is against our law for a Jew to associate with a Gentile or visit him. But God has shown me that I should not call any man impure or unclean. ²⁹So when I was sent for, I came without raising any objection. May I ask why you sent for me?"

³⁰Cornelius answered: "Four days ago I was in my house praying at this hour, at three in the afternoon. Suddenly a man in shining clothes stood before me ³¹and said, 'Cornelius, God has heard your prayer and remembered your gifts to the poor. ³²Send to Joppa for Simon who is called Peter. He is a guest in the home of Simon the tanner, who lives by the sea.' ³³So I sent for you immediately, and it was good of you to come. Now we are all here in the presence of God to listen to everything the Lord has commanded you to tell us."

³⁴Then Peter began to speak: "I now realize how true it is that God does not show favoritism ³⁵but accepts men from every nation who fear him and do what is right. ³⁶You know the message God sent to the people of Israel, telling the good news of peace through Jesus Christ, who is Lord of all. ³⁷You know what has happened throughout Judea, beginning in Galilee after the baptism that John preached— ³⁸how God anointed Jesus of Nazareth with the Holy Spirit and power, and how he went around doing good and healing all who were under the power of the devil, because God was with him.

³⁹"We are witnesses of everything he did in the country of the Jews and in Jerusalem. They killed him by hanging him on a tree, ⁴⁰but God raised him from the dead on the third day and caused him to be seen. ⁴¹He was not seen by all the people, but by witnesses whom God had already chosen—by us who ate and drank with him after he rose from the dead. ⁴²He commanded us to preach to the people and to testify that he is the one whom God appointed as judge of the living and the dead. ⁴³All the prophets testify about him that everyone who believes in him receives forgiveness of sins through his name."

⁴⁴While Peter was still speaking these words, the Holy Spirit came on all who heard the message. ⁴⁵The circumcised believers who had come with Peter were astonished that the gift of the Holy Spirit had been poured out even on the Gentiles. ⁴⁶For they heard them speaking in tongues*a* and praising God.

Then Peter said, ⁴⁷"Can anyone keep these people from being baptized with water? They have received the Holy Spirit just as we have." ⁴⁸So he ordered that they be baptized in the name of Jesus Christ. Then they asked Peter to stay with them for a few days.

Peter Explains His Actions The apostles and the brothers throughout Judea heard that the Gentiles also had received the word of God. ²So when Peter went up to Jerusalem, the circumcised believers criticized him ³and said, "You went into the house of uncircumcised men and ate with them."

⁴Peter began and explained everything to them precisely as it had happened: ⁵"I was in the city of Joppa praying, and in a trance I saw a vision. I saw something like a large sheet being let down from heaven by its four corners, and it came down to where I was. ⁶I looked into it and saw four-footed animals of the earth, wild beasts, reptiles, and birds of the air. ⁷Then I heard a voice telling me, 'Get up, Peter. Kill and eat.'

a46 Or other languages

8"I replied, 'Surely not, Lord! Nothing impure or unclean has ever entered my mouth.'

9"The voice spoke from heaven a second time, 'Do not call anything impure that God has made clean.' 10This happened three times, and then it was all pulled up to heaven again.

11"Right then three men who had been sent to me from Caesarea stopped at the house where I was staying. 12The Spirit told me to have no hesitation about going with them. These six brothers also went with me, and we entered the man's house. 13He told us how he had seen an angel appear in his house and say, 'Send to Joppa for Simon who is called Peter. 14He will bring you a message through which you and all your household will be saved.'

15"As I began to speak, the Holy Spirit came on them as he had come on us at the beginning. 16Then I remembered what the Lord had said: 'John baptized with*a* water, but you will be baptized with the Holy Spirit.' 17So if God gave them the same gift as he gave us, who believed in the Lord Jesus Christ, who was I to think that I could oppose God?"

18When they heard this, they had no further objections and praised God, saying, "So then, God has granted even the Gentiles repentance unto life."

The Church in Antioch   19Now those who had been scattered by the persecution in connection with Stephen traveled as far as Phoenicia, Cyprus and Antioch, telling the message only to Jews. 20Some of them, however, men from Cyprus and Cyrene, went to Antioch and began to speak to Greeks also, telling them the good news about the Lord Jesus. 21The Lord's hand was with them, and a great number of people believed and turned to the Lord.

22News of this reached the ears of the church at Jerusalem, and they sent Barnabas to Antioch. 23When he arrived and saw the evidence of the grace of God, he was glad and encouraged them all to remain true to the Lord with all their hearts. 24He was a good man, full of the Holy Spirit and faith, and a great number of people were brought to the Lord.

25Then Barnabas went to Tarsus to look for Saul, 26and when he found him, he brought him to Antioch. So for a whole year Barnabas and Saul met with the church and taught great numbers of people. The disciples were called Christians first at Antioch.

27During this time some prophets came down from Jerusalem to Antioch. 28One of them, named Agabus, stood up and through the Spirit predicted that a severe famine would spread over the entire Roman world. (This happened during the reign of Claudius.) 29The disciples, each according to his ability, decided to provide help for the brothers living in Judea. 30This they did, sending their gift to the elders by Barnabas and Saul.

Peter's Miraculous Escape From Prison   It was about this time that King Herod arrested some who belonged to the church, intending to persecute them. 2He had James, the brother of John, put to death with the sword. 3When he saw that this pleased the Jews, he proceeded to seize Peter also. This happened during the Feast of Unleavened Bread. 4After arresting him, he put him in prison, handing him over to be guarded by four squads of four soldiers each. Herod intended to bring him out for public trial after the Passover.

5So Peter was kept in prison, but the church was earnestly praying to God for him.

a16 Or in

⁶The night before Herod was to bring him to trial, Peter was sleeping between two soldiers, bound with two chains, and sentries stood guard at the entrance. ⁷Suddenly an angel of the Lord appeared and a light shone in the cell. He struck Peter on the side and woke him up. "Quick, get up!" he said, and the chains fell off Peter's wrists.

⁸Then the angel said to him, "Put on your clothes and sandals." And Peter did so. "Wrap your cloak around you and follow me," the angel told him. ⁹Peter followed him out of the prison, but he had no idea that what the angel was doing was really happening; he thought he was seeing a vision. ¹⁰They passed the first and second guards and came to the iron gate leading to the city. It opened for them by itself, and they went through it. When they had walked the length of one street, suddenly the angel left him.

¹¹Then Peter came to himself and said, "Now I know without a doubt that the Lord sent his angel and rescued me from Herod's clutches and from everything the Jewish people were anticipating."

¹²When this had dawned on him, he went to the house of Mary the mother of John, also called Mark, where many people had gathered and were praying. ¹³Peter knocked at the outer entrance, and a servant girl named Rhoda came to answer the door. ¹⁴When she recognized Peter's voice, she was so overjoyed she ran back without opening it and exclaimed, "Peter is at the door!"

¹⁵"You're out of your mind," they told her. When she kept insisting that it was so, they said, "It must be his angel."

¹⁶But Peter kept on knocking, and when they opened the door and saw him, they were astonished. ¹⁷Peter motioned with his hand for them to be quiet and described how the Lord had brought him out of prison. "Tell James and the brothers about this," he said, and then he left for another place.

¹⁸In the morning, there was no small commotion among the soldiers as to what had become of Peter. ¹⁹After Herod had a thorough search made for him and did not find him, he cross-examined the guards and ordered that they be executed.

Herod's Death   Then Herod went from Judea to Caesarea and stayed there a while. ²⁰He had been quarreling with the people of Tyre and Sidon; they now joined together and sought an audience with him. Having secured the support of Blastus, a trusted personal servant of the king, they asked for peace, because they depended on the king's country for their food supply.

²¹On the appointed day Herod, wearing his royal robes, sat on his throne and delivered a public address to the people. ²²They shouted, "This is the voice of a god, not of a man." ²³Immediately, because Herod did not give praise to God, an angel of the Lord struck him down, and he was eaten by worms and died.

²⁴But the word of God continued to increase and spread.

²⁵When Barnabas and Saul had finished their mission, they returned from*ᵃ* Jerusalem, taking with them John, also called Mark.

13 *Barnabas and Saul Sent Off*   In the church at Antioch there were prophets and teachers: Barnabas, Simeon called Niger, Lucius of Cyrene, Manaen (who had been brought up with Herod the tetrarch) and Saul. ²While they were worshiping the Lord and fasting, the Holy Spirit said, "Set apart for me Barnabas and Saul for the work to which I have called them." ³So after they had fasted and prayed, they placed their hands on them and sent them off.

On Cyprus   ⁴The two of them, sent on their way by the Holy Spirit, went down to Seleucia and sailed from there to Cyprus. ⁵When they arrived at Sal-

Answers
to Quizzer on page 1428

A: Believers were first called "Christians" in the city of Antioch (Acts 11:26).

BONUS: *It means "belonging to Christ."*

ᵃ25 Some manuscripts *to*

amis, they proclaimed the word of God in the Jewish synagogues. John was with them as their helper.

[6]They traveled through the whole island until they came to Paphos. There they met a Jewish sorcerer and false prophet named Bar-Jesus, [7]who was an attendant of the proconsul, Sergius Paulus. The proconsul, an intelligent man, sent for Barnabas and Saul because he wanted to hear the word of God. [8]But Elymas the sorcerer (for that is what his name means) opposed them and tried to turn the proconsul from the faith. [9]Then Saul, who was also called Paul, filled with the Holy Spirit, looked straight at Elymas and said, [10]"You are a child of the devil and an enemy of everything that is right! You are full of all kinds of deceit and trickery. Will you never stop perverting the right ways of the Lord? [11]Now the hand of the Lord is against you. You are going to be blind, and for a time you will be unable to see the light of the sun."

Immediately mist and darkness came over him, and he groped about, seeking someone to lead him by the hand. [12]When the proconsul saw what had happened, he believed, for he was amazed at the teaching about the Lord.

In Pisidian Antioch   [13]From Paphos, Paul and his companions sailed to Perga in Pamphylia, where John left them to return to Jerusalem. [14]From Perga they went on to Pisidian Antioch. On the Sabbath they entered the synagogue and sat down. [15]After the reading from the Law and the Prophets, the synagogue rulers sent word to them, saying, "Brothers, if you have a message of encouragement for the people, please speak."

[16]Standing up, Paul motioned with his hand and said: "Men of Israel and you Gentiles who worship God, listen to me! [17]The God of the people of Israel chose our fathers; he made the people prosper during their stay in Egypt, with mighty power he led them out of that country, [18]he endured their conduct[a] for about forty years in the desert, [19]he overthrew seven nations in Canaan and gave their land to his people as their inheritance. [20]All this took about 450 years.

"After this, God gave them judges until the time of Samuel the prophet. [21]Then the people asked for a king, and he gave them Saul son of Kish, of the tribe of Benjamin, who ruled forty years. [22]After removing Saul, he made David their king. He testified concerning him: 'I have found David son of Jesse a man after my own heart; he will do everything I want him to do.'

[23]"From this man's descendants God has brought to Israel the Savior Jesus, as he promised. [24]Before the coming of Jesus, John preached repentance and baptism to all the people of Israel. [25]As John was completing his work, he said: 'Who do you think I am? I am not that one. No, but he is coming after me, whose sandals I am not worthy to untie.'

[26]"Brothers, children of Abraham, and you God-fearing Gentiles, it is to us that this message of salvation has been sent. [27]The people of Jerusalem and their rulers did not recognize Jesus, yet in condemning him they fulfilled the words of the prophets that are read every Sabbath. [28]Though they found no proper ground for a death sentence, they asked Pilate to have him executed. [29]When they had carried out all that was written about him, they took him down from the tree and laid him in a tomb. [30]But God raised him from the dead, [31]and for many days he was seen by those who had traveled with him from Galilee to Jerusalem. They are now his witnesses to our people.

[32]"We tell you the good news: What God promised our fathers [33]he has fulfilled for us, their children, by raising up Jesus. As it is written in the second Psalm:

> " 'You are my Son;
>   today I have become your Father.'[b][c]

---

[a]18 Some manuscripts *and cared for them*   [b]33 Or *have begotten you*   [c]33 Psalm 2:7

³⁴The fact that God raised him from the dead, never to decay, is stated in these words:

> " 'I will give you the holy and sure blessings promised to David.'ᵃ

³⁵So it is stated elsewhere:

> " 'You will not let your Holy One see decay.'ᵇ

³⁶"For when David had served God's purpose in his own generation, he fell asleep; he was buried with his fathers and his body decayed. ³⁷But the one whom God raised from the dead did not see decay.

³⁸"Therefore, my brothers, I want you to know that through Jesus the forgiveness of sins is proclaimed to you. ³⁹Through him everyone who believes is justified from everything you could not be justified from by the law of Moses. ⁴⁰Take care that what the prophets have said does not happen to you:

> ⁴¹" 'Look, you scoffers,
>   wonder and perish,
> for I am going to do something in your days
>   that you would never believe,
>   even if someone told you.'ᶜ"

⁴²As Paul and Barnabas were leaving the synagogue, the people invited them to speak further about these things on the next Sabbath. ⁴³When the congregation was dismissed, many of the Jews and devout converts to Judaism followed Paul and Barnabas, who talked with them and urged them to continue in the grace of God.

⁴⁴On the next Sabbath almost the whole city gathered to hear the word of the Lord. ⁴⁵When the Jews saw the crowds, they were filled with jealousy and talked abusively against what Paul was saying.

⁴⁶Then Paul and Barnabas answered them boldly: "We had to speak the word of God to you first. Since you reject it and do not consider yourselves worthy of eternal life, we now turn to the Gentiles. ⁴⁷For this is what the Lord has commanded us:

> " 'I have made youᵈ a light for
>   the Gentiles,
>   that youᵈ may bring
>   salvation to the ends of
>   the earth.'ᵉ"

⁴⁸When the Gentiles heard this, they were glad and honored the word of the Lord; and all who were appointed for eternal life believed.

⁴⁹The word of the Lord spread through the whole region. ⁵⁰But the Jews incited the God-fearing women of high standing and the leading men of the city. They stirred up persecution against Paul and Barnabas, and expelled them from their region. ⁵¹So they shook the dust from their feet in protest against them and went to Iconium. ⁵²And the disciples were filled with joy and with the Holy Spirit.

ᵃ34 Isaiah 55:3   ᵇ35 Psalm 16:10   ᶜ41 Hab. 1:5   ᵈ47 The Greek is singular.   ᵉ47 Isaiah 49:6

ACTS 13:46–52

The devil doesn't bother to bother some Christians. Like believers who go along with the crowd or who keep quiet about their relationship with Jesus. The person who doesn't go along with the crowd and who shares his or her faith is the one who gets persecuted. It happened in Acts. Persecution was stirred up when "the word of the Lord spread" (Acts 13:49). So if you start a morning prayer group or if a couple of kids become Christians through your witness, don't be surprised if you face opposition. It's not much fun, but if persecution does come, it tells you that you're getting to Satan and becoming a spiritual success!

Direct Line

14 *In Iconium* At Iconium Paul and Barnabas went as usual into the Jewish synagogue. There they spoke so effectively that a great number of Jews and Gentiles believed. ²But the Jews who refused to believe stirred up the Gentiles and poisoned their minds against the brothers. ³So Paul and Barnabas spent considerable time there, speaking boldly for the Lord, who confirmed the message of his grace by enabling them to do miraculous signs and wonders. ⁴The people of the city were divided; some sided with the Jews, others with the apostles. ⁵There was a plot afoot among the Gentiles and Jews, together with their leaders, to mistreat them and stone them. ⁶But they found out about it and fled to the Lycaonian cities of Lystra and Derbe and to the surrounding country, ⁷where they continued to preach the good news.

ACTS 14

QUIZZER

Q: Who did the people of Lystra think Paul and Barnabas were?

BONUS: Why did they think this?

Answers on page 1433

In Lystra and Derbe ⁸In Lystra there sat a man crippled in his feet, who was lame from birth and had never walked. ⁹He listened to Paul as he was speaking. Paul looked directly at him, saw that he had faith to be healed ¹⁰and called out, "Stand up on your feet!" At that, the man jumped up and began to walk.

¹¹When the crowd saw what Paul had done, they shouted in the Lycaonian language, "The gods have come down to us in human form!" ¹²Barnabas they called Zeus, and Paul they called Hermes because he was the chief speaker. ¹³The priest of Zeus, whose temple was just outside the city, brought bulls and wreaths to the city gates because he and the crowd wanted to offer sacrifices to them.

¹⁴But when the apostles Barnabas and Paul heard of this, they tore their clothes and rushed out into the crowd, shouting: ¹⁵"Men, why are you doing this? We too are only men, human like you. We are bringing you good news, telling you to turn from these worthless things to the living God, who made heaven and earth and sea and everything in them. ¹⁶In the past, he let all nations go their own way. ¹⁷Yet he has not left himself without testimony: He has shown kindness by giving you rain from heaven and crops in their seasons; he provides you with plenty of food and fills your hearts with joy." ¹⁸Even with these words, they had difficulty keeping the crowd from sacrificing to them.

¹⁹Then some Jews came from Antioch and Iconium and won the crowd over. They stoned Paul and dragged him outside the city, thinking he was dead. ²⁰But after the disciples had gathered around him, he got up and went back into the city. The next day he and Barnabas left for Derbe.

The Return to Antioch in Syria ²¹They preached the good news in that city and won a large number of disciples. Then they returned to Lystra, Iconium and Antioch, ²²strengthening the disciples and encouraging them to remain true to the faith. "We must go through many hardships to enter the kingdom of God," they said. ²³Paul and Barnabas appointed elders*ª* for them in each church and, with prayer and fasting, committed them to the Lord, in whom they had put their trust. ²⁴After going through Pisidia, they came into Pamphylia, ²⁵and when they had preached the word in Perga, they went down to Attalia.

²⁶From Attalia they sailed back to Antioch, where they had been committed to the grace of God for the work they had now completed. ²⁷On arriving there, they gathered the church together and reported all that God had done through them and how he had opened the door of faith to the Gentiles. ²⁸And they stayed there a long time with the disciples.

ª23 Or Barnabas ordained elders; or Barnabas had elders elected

15 **The Council at Jerusalem** Some men came down from Judea to Antioch and were teaching the brothers: "Unless you are circumcised, according to the custom taught by Moses, you cannot be saved." ²This brought Paul and Barnabas into sharp dispute and debate with them. So Paul and Barnabas were appointed, along with some other believers, to go up to Jerusalem to see the apostles and elders about this question. ³The church sent them on their way, and as they traveled through Phoenicia and Samaria, they told how the Gentiles had been converted. This news made all the brothers very glad. ⁴When they came to Jerusalem, they were welcomed by the church and the apostles and elders, to whom they reported everything God had done through them.

⁵Then some of the believers who belonged to the party of the Pharisees stood up and said, "The Gentiles must be circumcised and required to obey the law of Moses."

⁶The apostles and elders met to consider this question. ⁷After much discussion, Peter got up and addressed them: "Brothers, you know that some time ago God made a choice among you that the Gentiles might hear from my lips the message of the gospel and believe. ⁸God, who knows the heart, showed that he accepted them by giving the Holy Spirit to them, just as he did to us. ⁹He made no distinction between us and them, for he purified their hearts by faith. ¹⁰Now then, why do you try to test God by putting on the necks of the disciples a yoke that neither we nor our fathers have been able to bear? ¹¹No! We believe it is through the grace of our Lord Jesus that we are saved, just as they are."

¹²The whole assembly became silent as they listened to Barnabas and Paul telling about the miraculous signs and wonders God had done among the Gentiles through them. ¹³When they finished, James spoke up: "Brothers, listen to me. ¹⁴Simon*ᵃ* has described to us how God at first showed his concern by taking from the Gentiles a people for himself. ¹⁵The words of the prophets are in agreement with this, as it is written:

> ¹⁶" 'After this I will return
>   and rebuild David's fallen tent.
>   Its ruins I will rebuild,
>   and I will restore it,
> ¹⁷that the remnant of men may seek the Lord,
>   and all the Gentiles who bear my name,
>   says the Lord, who does these things'ᵇ
> ¹⁸   that have been known for ages.ᶜ

¹⁹"It is my judgment, therefore, that we should not make it difficult for the Gentiles who are turning to God. ²⁰Instead we should write to them, telling them to abstain from food polluted by idols, from sexual immorality, from the meat of strangled animals and from blood. ²¹For Moses has been preached in every city from the earliest times and is read in the synagogues on every Sabbath."

The Council's Letter to Gentile Believers ²²Then the apostles and elders, with the whole church, decided to choose some of their own men and send them to Antioch with Paul and Barnabas. They chose Judas (called Barsabbas) and Silas, two men who were leaders among the brothers. ²³With them they sent the following letter:

The apostles and elders, your brothers,

To the Gentile believers in Antioch, Syria and Cilicia:

Greetings.

ᵃ14 Greek *Simeon,* a variant of *Simon;* that is, Peter   *ᵇ17* Amos 9:11,12   *ᶜ17,18* Some manuscripts *things'— /* *¹⁸known to the Lord for ages is his work*

²⁴We have heard that some went out from us without our authorization and disturbed you, troubling your minds by what they said. ²⁵So we all agreed to choose some men and send them to you with our dear friends Barnabas and Paul— ²⁶men who have risked their lives for the name of our Lord Jesus Christ. ²⁷Therefore we are sending Judas and Silas to confirm by word of mouth what we are writing. ²⁸It seemed good to the Holy Spirit and to us not to burden you with anything beyond the following requirements: ²⁹You are to abstain from food sacrificed to idols, from blood, from the meat of strangled animals and from sexual immorality. You will do well to avoid these things.

Farewell.

³⁰The men were sent off and went down to Antioch, where they gathered the church together and delivered the letter. ³¹The people read it and were glad for its encouraging message. ³²Judas and Silas, who themselves were prophets, said much to encourage and strengthen the brothers. ³³After spending some time there, they were sent off by the brothers with the blessing of peace to return to those who had sent them.ᵃ ³⁵But Paul and Barnabas remained in Antioch, where they and many others taught and preached the word of the Lord.

Disagreement Between Paul and Barnabas ³⁶Some time later Paul said to Barnabas, "Let us go back and visit the brothers in all the towns where we preached the word of the Lord and see how they are doing." ³⁷Barnabas wanted to take John, also called Mark, with them, ³⁸but Paul did not think it wise to take him, because he had deserted them in Pamphylia and had not continued with them in the work. ³⁹They had such a sharp disagreement that they parted company. Barnabas took Mark and sailed for Cyprus, ⁴⁰but Paul chose Silas and left, commended by the brothers to the grace of the Lord. ⁴¹He went through Syria and Cilicia, strengthening the churches.

Timothy Joins Paul and Silas He came to Derbe and then to Lystra, where a disciple named Timothy lived, whose mother was a Jewess and a believer, but whose father was a Greek. ²The brothers at Lystra and Iconium spoke well of him. ³Paul wanted to take him along on the journey, so he circumcised him because of the Jews who lived in that area, for they all knew that his father was a Greek. ⁴As they traveled from town to town, they delivered the decisions reached by the apostles and elders in Jerusalem for the people to obey. ⁵So the churches were strengthened in the faith and grew daily in numbers.

Paul's Vision of the Man of Macedonia ⁶Paul and his companions traveled throughout the region of Phrygia and Galatia, having been kept by the Holy Spirit from preaching the word in the province of Asia. ⁷When they came to the border of Mysia, they tried to enter Bithynia, but the Spirit of Jesus would not allow them to. ⁸So they passed by Mysia

---

Direct Line

ACTS 15:36–40

It would be nice if all arguments could be quickly settled. On TV maybe it happens. But in real life? Hey, even in Christian families hostility can develop between brothers and sisters and husbands and wives. Take Paul and Barnabas. They'd been friends and partners, and both were dedicated Christians. But they had a "sharp disagreement" that drove them apart. The beauty is that the split caused each to go his own way, providing for two missionary endeavors instead of one. Proof positive that God can use even our disagreements to accomplish his good!

ᵃ33 Some manuscripts *them,* ³⁴*but Silas decided to remain there* and went down to Troas. [9]During the night Paul had a vision of a man of Macedonia standing and begging him, "Come over to Macedonia and help us." [10]After Paul had seen the vision, we got ready at once to leave for Macedonia, concluding that God had called us to preach the gospel to them.

Lydia's Conversion in Philippi [11]From Troas we put out to sea and sailed straight for Samothrace, and the next day on to Neapolis. [12]From there we traveled to Philippi, a Roman colony and the leading city of that district of Macedonia. And we stayed there several days.

[13]On the Sabbath we went outside the city gate to the river, where we expected to find a place of prayer. We sat down and began to speak to the women who had gathered there. [14]One of those listening was a woman named Lydia, a dealer in purple cloth from the city of Thyatira, who was a worshiper of God. The Lord opened her heart to respond to Paul's message. [15]When she and the members of her household were baptized, she invited us to her home. "If you consider me a believer in the Lord," she said, "come and stay at my house." And she persuaded us.

Paul and Silas in Prison [16]Once when we were going to the place of prayer, we were met by a slave girl who had a spirit by which she predicted the future. She earned a great deal of money for her owners by fortune-telling. [17]This girl followed Paul and the rest of us, shouting, "These men are servants of the Most High God, who are telling you the way to be saved." [18]She kept this up for many days. Finally Paul became so troubled that he turned around and said to the spirit, "In the name of Jesus Christ I command you to come out of her!" At that moment the spirit left her.

[19]When the owners of the slave girl realized that their hope of making money was gone, they seized Paul and Silas and dragged them into the marketplace to face the authorities. [20]They brought them before the magistrates and said, "These men are Jews, and are throwing our city into an uproar [21]by advocating customs unlawful for us Romans to accept or practice."

[22]The crowd joined in the attack against Paul and Silas, and the magistrates ordered them to be stripped and beaten. [23]After they had been severely flogged, they were thrown into prison, and the jailer was commanded to guard them carefully. [24]Upon receiving such orders, he put them in the inner cell and fastened their feet in the stocks.

[25]About midnight Paul and Silas were praying and singing hymns to God, and the other prisoners were listening to them. [26]Suddenly there was such a violent earthquake that the foundations of the prison were shaken. At once all the prison doors flew open, and everybody's chains came loose. [27]The jailer woke up, and when he saw the prison doors open, he drew his sword and was about to kill himself because he thought the prisoners had escaped. [28]But Paul shouted, "Don't harm yourself! We are all here!"

[29]The jailer called for lights, rushed in and fell trembling before Paul and Silas. [30]He then brought them out and asked, "Sirs, what must I do to be saved?"

[31]They replied, "Believe in the Lord Jesus, and you will be saved—you and your household." [32]Then they spoke the word of the Lord to him and to all the others in his house. [33]At that hour of the night the jailer took them and washed their wounds; then immediately he and all his family were baptized. [34]The jailer brought them into his house and set a meal before them; he was filled with joy because he had come to believe in God—he and his whole family.

[35]When it was daylight, the magistrates sent their officers to the jailer with the order: "Release those men." [36]The jailer told Paul, "The magistrates have ordered that you and Silas be released. Now you can leave. Go in peace."

ACTS 16

QU*I*ZZER

Q: What did Paul and Silas do while they were in prison in Philippi?

BONUS: What exciting events happened that night?

Answers on page 1437

37But Paul said to the officers: "They beat us publicly without a trial, even though we are Roman citizens, and threw us into prison. And now do they want to get rid of us quietly? No! Let them come themselves and escort us out."

38The officers reported this to the magistrates, and when they heard that Paul and Silas were Roman citizens, they were alarmed. 39They came to appease them and escorted them from the prison, requesting them to leave the city. 40After Paul and Silas came out of the prison, they went to Lydia's house, where they met with the brothers and encouraged them. Then they left.

In Thessalonica When they had passed through Amphipolis and Apollonia, they came to Thessalonica, where there was a Jewish synagogue. 2As his custom was, Paul went into the synagogue, and on three Sabbath days he reasoned with them from the Scriptures, 3explaining and proving that the Christ*a* had to suffer and rise from the dead. "This Jesus I am proclaiming to you is the Christ,*a*" he said. 4Some of the Jews were persuaded and joined Paul and Silas, as did a large number of God-fearing Greeks and not a few prominent women.

5But the Jews were jealous; so they rounded up some bad characters from the marketplace, formed a mob and started a riot in the city. They rushed to Jason's house in search of Paul and Silas in order to bring them out to the crowd.*b* 6But when they did not find them, they dragged Jason and some other brothers before the city officials, shouting: "These men who have caused trouble all over the world have now come here, 7and Jason has welcomed them into his house. They are all defying Caesar's decrees, saying that there is another king, one called Jesus." 8When they heard this, the crowd and the city officials were thrown into turmoil. 9Then they made Jason and the others post bond and let them go.

In Berea 10As soon as it was night, the brothers sent Paul and Silas away to Berea. On arriving there, they went to the Jewish synagogue. 11Now the Bereans were of more noble character than the Thessalonians, for they received the message with great eagerness and examined the Scriptures every day to see if what Paul said was true. 12Many of the Jews believed, as did also a number of prominent Greek women and many Greek men.

13When the Jews in Thessalonica learned that Paul was preaching the word of God at Berea, they went there too, agitating the crowds and stirring them up. 14The brothers immediately sent Paul to the coast, but Silas and Timothy stayed at Berea. 15The men who escorted Paul brought him to Athens and then left with instructions for Silas and Timothy to join him as soon as possible.

In Athens 16While Paul was waiting for them in Athens, he was greatly distressed to see that the city was full of idols. 17So he reasoned in the synagogue with the Jews and the God-fearing Greeks, as well as in the marketplace day by day with those who happened to be there. 18A group of Epicurean and Stoic philosophers began to dispute with him. Some of them asked, "What is this babbler trying to say?" Others remarked, "He seems to be advocating foreign gods." They said this because Paul was preaching the good news about Jesus and the resurrection. 19Then they took him and brought him to a meeting of the Areopagus, where they said to him, "May we know what this new teaching is that you are presenting? 20You are bringing some strange ideas to our ears, and we want to know what they mean." 21(All the Athenians and the foreigners who lived there spent their time doing nothing but talking about and listening to the latest ideas.)

---

*a*3 Or *Messiah* *b*5 Or *the assembly of the people*

²²Paul then stood up in the meeting of the Areopagus and said: "Men of Athens! I see that in every way you are very religious. ²³For as I walked around and looked carefully at your objects of worship, I even found an altar with this inscription: TO AN UNKNOWN GOD. Now what you worship as something unknown I am going to proclaim to you.

²⁴"The God who made the world and everything in it is the Lord of heaven and earth and does not live in temples built by hands. ²⁵And he is not served by human hands, as if he needed anything, because he himself gives all men life and breath and everything else. ²⁶From one man he made every nation of men, that they should inhabit the whole earth; and he determined the times set for them and the exact places where they should live. ²⁷God did this so that men would seek him and perhaps reach out for him and find him, though he is not far from each one of us. ²⁸'For in him we live and move and have our being.' As some of your own poets have said, 'We are his offspring.'

²⁹"Therefore since we are God's offspring, we should not think that the divine being is like gold or silver or stone—an image made by man's design and skill. ³⁰In the past God overlooked such ignorance, but now he commands all people everywhere to repent. ³¹For he has set a day when he will judge the world with justice by the man he has appointed. He has given proof of this to all men by raising him from the dead."

³²When they heard about the resurrection of the dead, some of them sneered, but others said, "We want to hear you again on this subject." ³³At that, Paul left the Council. ³⁴A few men became followers of Paul and believed. Among them was Dionysius, a member of the Areopagus, also a woman named Damaris, and a number of others.

Answers
to Quizzer on page 1435

A: They sang hymns to God (Acts 16:25).

BONUS: There was a violent earthquake, all of the prison doors fell open, and the jailer became a believer in Jesus (Acts 16:26-34).

18 *In Corinth* After this, Paul left Athens and went to Corinth. ²There he met a Jew named Aquila, a native of Pontus, who had recently come from Italy with his wife Priscilla, because Claudius had ordered all the Jews to leave Rome. Paul went to see them, ³and because he was a tentmaker as they were, he stayed and worked with them. ⁴Every Sabbath he reasoned in the synagogue, trying to persuade Jews and Greeks.

⁵When Silas and Timothy came from Macedonia, Paul devoted himself exclusively to preaching, testifying to the Jews that Jesus was the Christ.ᵃ ⁶But when the Jews opposed Paul and became abusive, he shook out his clothes in protest and said to them, "Your blood be on your own heads! I am clear of my responsibility. From now on I will go to the Gentiles."

⁷Then Paul left the synagogue and went next door to the house of Titius Justus, a worshiper of God. ⁸Crispus, the synagogue ruler, and his entire household believed in the Lord; and many of the Corinthians who heard him believed and were baptized.

⁹One night the Lord spoke to Paul in a vision: "Do not be afraid; keep on speaking, do not be silent. ¹⁰For I am with you, and no one is going to attack and harm you, because I have many people in this city." ¹¹So Paul stayed for a year and a half, teaching them the word of God.

¹²While Gallio was proconsul of Achaia, the Jews made a united attack on Paul and brought him into court. ¹³"This man," they charged, "is persuading the people to worship God in ways contrary to the law."

¹⁴Just as Paul was about to speak, Gallio said to the Jews, "If you Jews were making a complaint about some misdemeanor or serious crime, it would be reasonable for me to listen to you. ¹⁵But since it involves questions about words and names and your own law—settle the matter yourselves. I will not be a judge of such things." ¹⁶So he had them ejected from the court. ¹⁷Then

ᵃ5 Or *Messiah;* also in verse 28

they all turned on Sosthenes the synagogue ruler and beat him in front of the court. But Gallio showed no concern whatever.

Priscilla, Aquila and Apollos ¹⁸Paul stayed on in Corinth for some time. Then he left the brothers and sailed for Syria, accompanied by Priscilla and Aquila. Before he sailed, he had his hair cut off at Cenchrea because of a vow he had taken. ¹⁹They arrived at Ephesus, where Paul left Priscilla and Aquila. He himself went into the synagogue and reasoned with the Jews. ²⁰When they asked him to spend more time with them, he declined. ²¹But as he left, he promised, "I will come back if it is God's will." Then he set sail from Ephesus. ²²When he landed at Caesarea, he went up and greeted the church and then went down to Antioch.

²³After spending some time in Antioch, Paul set out from there and traveled from place to place throughout the region of Galatia and Phrygia, strengthening all the disciples.

²⁴Meanwhile a Jew named Apollos, a native of Alexandria, came to Ephesus. He was a learned man, with a thorough knowledge of the Scriptures. ²⁵He had been instructed in the way of the Lord, and he spoke with great fervor*ᵃ* and taught about Jesus accurately, though he knew only the baptism of John. ²⁶He began to speak boldly in the synagogue. When Priscilla and Aquila heard him, they invited him to their home and explained to him the way of God more adequately.

²⁷When Apollos wanted to go to Achaia, the brothers encouraged him and wrote to the disciples there to welcome him. On arriving, he was a great help to those who by grace had believed. ²⁸For he vigorously refuted the Jews in public debate, proving from the Scriptures that Jesus was the Christ.

19 ***Paul in Ephesus*** While Apollos was at Corinth, Paul took the road through the interior and arrived at Ephesus. There he found some disciples ²and asked them, "Did you receive the Holy Spirit when*ᵇ* you believed?"

They answered, "No, we have not even heard that there is a Holy Spirit."

³So Paul asked, "Then what baptism did you receive?"

"John's baptism," they replied.

⁴Paul said, "John's baptism was a baptism of repentance. He told the people to believe in the one coming after him, that is, in Jesus." ⁵On hearing this, they were baptized into*ᶜ* the name of the Lord Jesus. ⁶When Paul placed his hands on them, the Holy Spirit came on them, and they spoke in tongues*ᵈ* and prophesied. ⁷There were about twelve men in all.

⁸Paul entered the synagogue and spoke boldly there for three months, arguing persuasively about the kingdom of God. ⁹But some of them became obstinate; they refused to believe and publicly maligned the Way. So Paul left them. He took the disciples with him and had discussions daily in the lecture hall of Tyrannus. ¹⁰This went on for two years, so that all the Jews and Greeks who lived in the province of Asia heard the word of the Lord.

¹¹God did extraordinary miracles through Paul, ¹²so that even handkerchiefs and aprons that had touched him were taken to the sick, and their illnesses were cured and the evil spirits left them.

¹³Some Jews who went around driving out evil spirits tried to invoke the name of the Lord Jesus over those who were demon-possessed. They would say, "In the name of Jesus, whom Paul preaches, I command you to come out." ¹⁴Seven sons of Sceva, a Jewish chief priest, were doing this. ¹⁵One day the evil spirit answered them, "Jesus I know, and I know about Paul, but who are you?" ¹⁶Then the man who had the evil spirit jumped on them and overpowered them all. He gave them such a beating that they ran out of the house naked and bleeding.

ᵃ25 Or with fervor in the Spirit   ᵇ2 Or after   ᶜ5 Or in   ᵈ6 Or other languages

¹⁷When this became known to the Jews and Greeks living in Ephesus, they were all seized with fear, and the name of the Lord Jesus was held in high honor. ¹⁸Many of those who believed now came and openly confessed their evil deeds. ¹⁹A number who had practiced sorcery brought their scrolls together and burned them publicly. When they calculated the value of the scrolls, the total came to fifty thousand drachmas.[a] ²⁰In this way the word of the Lord spread widely and grew in power.

²¹After all this had happened, Paul decided to go to Jerusalem, passing through Macedonia and Achaia. "After I have been there," he said, "I must visit Rome also." ²²He sent two of his helpers, Timothy and Erastus, to Macedonia, while he stayed in the province of Asia a little longer.

The Riot in Ephesus ²³About that time there arose a great disturbance about the Way. ²⁴A silversmith named Demetrius, who made silver shrines of Artemis, brought in no little business for the craftsmen. ²⁵He called them together, along with the workmen in related trades, and said: "Men, you know we receive a good income from this business. ²⁶And you see and hear how this fellow Paul has convinced and led astray large numbers of people here in Ephesus and in practically the whole province of Asia. He says that man-made gods are no gods at all. ²⁷There is danger not only that our trade will lose its good name, but also that the temple of the great goddess Artemis will be discredited, and the goddess herself, who is worshiped throughout the province of Asia and the world, will be robbed of her divine majesty."

²⁸When they heard this, they were furious and began shouting: "Great is Artemis of the Ephesians!" ²⁹Soon the whole city was in an uproar. The people seized Gaius and Aristarchus, Paul's traveling companions from Macedonia, and rushed as one man into the theater. ³⁰Paul wanted to appear before the crowd, but the disciples would not let him. ³¹Even some of the officials of the province, friends of Paul, sent him a message begging him not to venture into the theater.

³²The assembly was in confusion: Some were shouting one thing, some another. Most of the people did not even know why they were there. ³³The Jews pushed Alexander to the front, and some of the crowd shouted in-

---

[a]19 A drachma was a silver coin worth about a day's wages.

Today's magicians pull rabbits out of hats and do other tricks to make people or even elephants seem to disappear. But that's not real magic. Real magic involves the use of charms, spells or rituals to influence people or events. Much magic in Bible times was an attempt to control demons and other supernatural beings. To some extent, all occult practices involve the use of real magic.

People often turn to magic because they want more control over what happens to them. They're afraid, and they don't trust God's control of the events of their lives.

When many people in Ephesus became Christians, they realized the evil in real magic. They burned their books of magic (Acts 19:18–20). People who know that God loves them don't have to be afraid of the future. God is in control, and he will take care of them always.

The
Bible
Says

Magic, No

structions to him. He motioned for silence in order to make a defense before the people. ³⁴But when they realized he was a Jew, they all shouted in unison for about two hours: "Great is Artemis of the Ephesians!"

³⁵The city clerk quieted the crowd and said: "Men of Ephesus, doesn't all the world know that the city of Ephesus is the guardian of the temple of the great Artemis and of her image, which fell from heaven? ³⁶Therefore, since these facts are undeniable, you ought to be quiet and not do anything rash. ³⁷You have brought these men here, though they have neither robbed temples nor blasphemed our goddess. ³⁸If, then, Demetrius and his fellow craftsmen have a grievance against anybody, the courts are open and there are proconsuls. They can press charges. ³⁹If there is anything further you want to bring up, it must be settled in a legal assembly. ⁴⁰As it is, we are in danger of being charged with rioting because of today's events. In that case we would not be able to account for this commotion, since there is no reason for it." ⁴¹After he had said this, he dismissed the assembly.

20 *Through Macedonia and Greece* When the uproar had ended, Paul sent for the disciples and, after encouraging them, said good-by and set out for Macedonia. ²He traveled through that area, speaking many words of encouragement to the people, and finally arrived in Greece, ³where he stayed three months. Because the Jews made a plot against him just as he was about to sail for Syria, he decided to go back through Macedonia. ⁴He was accompanied by Sopater son of Pyrrhus from Berea, Aristarchus and Secundus from Thessalonica, Gaius from Derbe, Timothy also, and Tychicus and Trophimus from the province of Asia. ⁵These men went on ahead and waited for us at Troas. ⁶But we sailed from Philippi after the Feast of Unleavened Bread, and five days later joined the others at Troas, where we stayed seven days.

Eutychus Raised From the Dead at Troas ⁷On the first day of the week we came together to break bread. Paul spoke to the people and, because he intended to leave the next day, kept on talking until midnight. ⁸There were many lamps in the upstairs room where we were meeting. ⁹Seated in a window was a young man named Eutychus, who was sinking into a deep sleep as Paul talked on and on. When he was sound asleep, he fell to the ground from the third story and was picked up dead. ¹⁰Paul went down, threw himself on the young man and put his arms around him. "Don't be alarmed," he said. "He's alive!" ¹¹Then he went upstairs again and broke bread and ate. After talking until daylight, he left. ¹²The people took the young man home alive and were greatly comforted.

Paul's Farewell to the Ephesian Elders ¹³We went on ahead to the ship and sailed for Assos, where we were going to take Paul aboard. He had made this arrangement because he was going there on foot. ¹⁴When he met us at Assos, we took him aboard and went on to Mitylene. ¹⁵The next day we set sail from there and arrived off Kios. The day after that we crossed over to Samos, and on the following day arrived at Miletus. ¹⁶Paul had decided to sail past Ephesus to avoid spending time in the province of Asia, for he was in a hurry to reach Jerusalem, if possible, by the day of Pentecost.

¹⁷From Miletus, Paul sent to Ephesus for the elders of the church. ¹⁸When they arrived, he said to them: "You know how I lived the whole time I was with you, from the first day I came into the province of Asia. ¹⁹I served the Lord with great humility and with tears, although I was severely tested by the plots of the Jews. ²⁰You know that I have not hesitated to preach anything that would be helpful to you but have taught you publicly and from house to house. ²¹I have declared to both Jews and Greeks that they must turn to God in repentance and have faith in our Lord Jesus.

²²"And now, compelled by the Spirit, I am going to Jerusalem, not know-

ing what will happen to me there. ²³I only know that in every city the Holy Spirit warns me that prison and hardships are facing me. ²⁴However, I consider my life worth nothing to me, if only I may finish the race and complete the task the Lord Jesus has given me—the task of testifying to the gospel of God's grace.

²⁵"Now I know that none of you among whom I have gone about preaching the kingdom will ever see me again. ²⁶Therefore, I declare to you today that I am innocent of the blood of all men. ²⁷For I have not hesitated to proclaim to you the whole will of God. ²⁸Keep watch over yourselves and all the flock of which the Holy Spirit has made you overseers.ᵃ Be shepherds of the church of God,ᵇ which he bought with his own blood. ²⁹I know that after I leave, savage wolves will come in among you and will not spare the flock. ³⁰Even from your own number men will arise and distort the truth in order to draw away disciples after them. ³¹So be on your guard! Remember that for three years I never stopped warning each of you night and day with tears.

³²"Now I commit you to God and to the word of his grace, which can build you up and give you an inheritance among all those who are sanctified. ³³I have not coveted anyone's silver or gold or clothing. ³⁴You yourselves know that these hands of mine have supplied my own needs and the needs of my companions. ³⁵In everything I did, I showed you that by this kind of hard work we must help the weak, remembering the words the Lord Jesus himself said: 'It is more blessed to give than to receive.'"

³⁶When he had said this, he knelt down with all of them and prayed. ³⁷They all wept as they embraced him and kissed him. ³⁸What grieved them most was his statement that they would never see his face again. Then they accompanied him to the ship.

21 *On to Jerusalem* After we had torn ourselves away from them, we put out to sea and sailed straight to Cos. The next day we went to Rhodes and from there to Patara. ²We found a ship crossing over to Phoenicia, went on board and set sail. ³After sighting Cyprus and passing to the south of it, we sailed on to Syria. We landed at Tyre, where our ship was to unload its cargo. ⁴Finding the disciples there, we stayed with them seven days. Through the Spirit they urged Paul not to go on to Jerusalem. ⁵But when our time was up, we left and continued on our way. All the disciples and their wives and children accompanied us out of the city, and there on the beach we knelt to pray. ⁶After saying good-by to each other, we went aboard the ship, and they returned home.

⁷We continued our voyage from Tyre and landed at Ptolemais, where we greeted the brothers and stayed with them for a day. ⁸Leaving the next day, we reached Caesarea and stayed at the house of Philip the evangelist, one of the Seven. ⁹He had four unmarried daughters who prophesied.

¹⁰After we had been there a number of days, a prophet named Agabus came down from Judea. ¹¹Coming over to us, he took Paul's belt, tied his own hands and

ᵃ28 Traditionally *bishops* ᵇ28 Many manuscripts *of the Lord*

ACTS 20:22-24

Want to build a good self-image? Take on a tough task and see it through. Don't go out for football and quit after the first set of sweaty calisthenics. Don't drop calculus the first week. Don't decide to read your Bible every morning and then hit the snooze button when your alarm goes off. Take a look at Paul. He was warned that he faced prison and hardship in Jerusalem. But he said, "I am going" (Acts 20:22). Paul had confidence, not only that God was sending him, but also that he'd be able to see hard times through. There's only one way to develop that kind of confidence in yourself. Don't quit.

Direct Line

feet with it and said, "The Holy Spirit says, 'In this way the Jews of Jerusalem will bind the owner of this belt and will hand him over to the Gentiles.' "

[12]When we heard this, we and the people there pleaded with Paul not to go up to Jerusalem. [13]Then Paul answered, "Why are you weeping and breaking my heart? I am ready not only to be bound, but also to die in Jerusalem for the name of the Lord Jesus." [14]When he would not be dissuaded, we gave up and said, "The Lord's will be done."

[15]After this, we got ready and went up to Jerusalem. [16]Some of the disciples from Caesarea accompanied us and brought us to the home of Mnason, where we were to stay. He was a man from Cyprus and one of the early disciples.

Paul's Arrival at Jerusalem [17]When we arrived at Jerusalem, the brothers received us warmly. [18]The next day Paul and the rest of us went to see James, and all the elders were present. [19]Paul greeted them and reported in detail what God had done among the Gentiles through his ministry.

[20]When they heard this, they praised God. Then they said to Paul: "You see, brother, how many thousands of Jews have believed, and all of them are zealous for the law. [21]They have been informed that you teach all the Jews who live among the Gentiles to turn away from Moses, telling them not to circumcise their children or live according to our customs. [22]What shall we do? They will certainly hear that you have come, [23]so do what we tell you. There are four men with us who have made a vow. [24]Take these men, join in their purification rites and pay their expenses, so that they can have their heads shaved. Then everybody will know there is no truth in these reports about you, but that you yourself are living in obedience to the law. [25]As for the Gentile believers, we have written to them our decision that they should abstain from food sacrificed to idols, from blood, from the meat of strangled animals and from sexual immorality."

[26]The next day Paul took the men and purified himself along with them. Then he went to the temple to give notice of the date when the days of purification would end and the offering would be made for each of them.

Paul Arrested [27]When the seven days were nearly over, some Jews from the province of Asia saw Paul at the temple. They stirred up the whole crowd and seized him, [28]shouting, "Men of Israel, help us! This is the man who teaches all men everywhere against our people and our law and this place. And besides, he has brought Greeks into the temple area and defiled this holy place." [29](They had previously seen Trophimus the Ephesian in the city with Paul and assumed that Paul had brought him into the temple area.)

[30]The whole city was aroused, and the people came running from all directions. Seizing Paul, they dragged him from the temple, and immediately the gates were shut. [31]While they were trying to kill him, news reached the commander of the Roman troops that the whole city of Jerusalem was in an uproar. [32]He at once took some officers and soldiers and ran down

---

Direct Line

ACTS 21:17–26

Lots of teens wonder why they have to dress up for church. The answer? You don't. But picture yourself getting ready for a special date. Do you wear your oldest, dirtiest sweats? Of course not. Church is pretty much the same thing. You dress appropriately. When Paul went to Jerusalem, he followed some rules that he didn't think were necessary. He didn't have to, but he was sensitive to the convictions of others. You should be too. Maybe dressing appropriately for church falls into this category. It shows those around you that you are sensitive to their opinions and that you love and respect the God you both serve.

to the crowd. When the rioters saw the commander and his soldiers, they stopped beating Paul.

³³The commander came up and arrested him and ordered him to be bound with two chains. Then he asked who he was and what he had done. ³⁴Some in the crowd shouted one thing and some another, and since the commander could not get at the truth because of the uproar, he ordered that Paul be taken into the barracks. ³⁵When Paul reached the steps, the violence of the mob was so great he had to be carried by the soldiers. ³⁶The crowd that followed kept shouting, "Away with him!"

Paul Speaks to the Crowd ³⁷As the soldiers were about to take Paul into the barracks, he asked the commander, "May I say something to you?"

"Do you speak Greek?" he replied. ³⁸"Aren't you the Egyptian who started a revolt and led four thousand terrorists out into the desert some time ago?"

³⁹Paul answered, "I am a Jew, from Tarsus in Cilicia, a citizen of no ordinary city. Please let me speak to the people."

⁴⁰Having received the commander's permission, Paul stood on the steps and motioned to the crowd. When they were all silent, he said to them in Aramaic*ᵃ*: ¹"Brothers and fathers, listen now to my defense."

²When they heard him speak to them in Aramaic, they became very quiet.

Then Paul said: ³"I am a Jew, born in Tarsus of Cilicia, but brought up in this city. Under Gamaliel I was thoroughly trained in the law of our fathers and was just as zealous for God as any of you are today. ⁴I persecuted the followers of this Way to their death, arresting both men and women and throwing them into prison, ⁵as also the high priest and all the Council can testify. I even obtained letters from them to their brothers in Damascus, and went there to bring these people as prisoners to Jerusalem to be punished.

⁶"About noon as I came near Damascus, suddenly a bright light from heaven flashed around me. ⁷I fell to the ground and heard a voice say to me, 'Saul! Saul! Why do you persecute me?'

⁸" 'Who are you, Lord?' I asked.

" 'I am Jesus of Nazareth, whom you are persecuting,' he replied. ⁹My companions saw the light, but they did not understand the voice of him who was speaking to me.

¹⁰" 'What shall I do, Lord?' I asked.

" 'Get up,' the Lord said, 'and go into Damascus. There you will be told all that you have been assigned to do.' ¹¹My companions led me by the hand into Damascus, because the brilliance of the light had blinded me.

¹²"A man named Ananias came to see me. He was a devout observer of the law and highly respected by all the Jews living there. ¹³He stood beside me and said, 'Brother Saul, receive your sight!' And at that very moment I was able to see him.

¹⁴"Then he said: 'The God of our fathers has chosen you to know his will and to see the Righteous One and to hear words from his mouth. ¹⁵You will be his witness to all men of what you have seen and heard. ¹⁶And now what are you waiting for? Get up, be baptized and wash your sins away, calling on his name.'

¹⁷"When I returned to Jerusalem and was praying at the temple, I fell into a trance ¹⁸and saw the Lord speaking. 'Quick!' he said to me. 'Leave Jerusalem immediately, because they will not accept your testimony about me.'

¹⁹" 'Lord,' I replied, 'these men know that I went from one synagogue to another to imprison and beat those who believe in you. ²⁰And when the blood of your martyr*ᵇ* Stephen was shed, I stood there giving my approval and guarding the clothes of those who were killing him.'

ᵃ40 Or possibly Hebrew; also in 22:2   ᵇ20 Or witness

²¹"Then the Lord said to me, 'Go; I will send you far away to the Gentiles.' "

Paul the Roman Citizen   ²²The crowd listened to Paul until he said this. Then they raised their voices and shouted, "Rid the earth of him! He's not fit to live!"

²³As they were shouting and throwing off their cloaks and flinging dust into the air, ²⁴the commander ordered Paul to be taken into the barracks. He directed that he be flogged and questioned in order to find out why the people were shouting at him like this. ²⁵As they stretched him out to flog him, Paul said to the centurion standing there, "Is it legal for you to flog a Roman citizen who hasn't even been found guilty?"

²⁶When the centurion heard this, he went to the commander and reported it. "What are you going to do?" he asked. "This man is a Roman citizen."

²⁷The commander went to Paul and asked, "Tell me, are you a Roman citizen?"

"Yes, I am," he answered.

²⁸Then the commander said, "I had to pay a big price for my citizenship."

"But I was born a citizen," Paul replied.

²⁹Those who were about to question him withdrew immediately. The commander himself was alarmed when he realized that he had put Paul, a Roman citizen, in chains.

Before the Sanhedrin   ³⁰The next day, since the commander wanted to find out exactly why Paul was being accused by the Jews, he released him and ordered the chief priests and all the Sanhedrin to assemble. Then he brought Paul and had him stand before them.

23 Paul looked straight at the Sanhedrin and said, "My brothers, I have fulfilled my duty to God in all good conscience to this day." ²At this the high priest Ananias ordered those standing near Paul to strike him on the mouth. ³Then Paul said to him, "God will strike you, you whitewashed wall! You sit there to judge me according to the law, yet you yourself violate the law by commanding that I be struck!"

⁴Those who were standing near Paul said, "You dare to insult God's high priest?"

⁵Paul replied, "Brothers, I did not realize that he was the high priest; for it is written: 'Do not speak evil about the ruler of your people.'ᵃ"

⁶Then Paul, knowing that some of them were Sadducees and the others Pharisees, called out in the Sanhedrin, "My brothers, I am a Pharisee, the son of a Pharisee. I stand on trial because of my hope in the resurrection of the dead." ⁷When he said this, a dispute broke out between the Pharisees and the Sadducees, and the assembly was divided. ⁸(The Sadducees say that there is no resurrection, and that there are neither angels nor spirits, but the Pharisees acknowledge them all.)

⁹There was a great uproar, and some of the teachers of the law who were Pharisees stood up and argued vigorously. "We find nothing wrong with this man," they said. "What if a spirit or an angel has spoken to him?" ¹⁰The dispute became so violent that the commander was afraid Paul would be torn to pieces by them. He ordered the troops to go down and take him away from them by force and bring him into the barracks.

¹¹The following night the Lord stood near Paul and said, "Take courage! As you have testified about me in Jerusalem, so you must also testify in Rome."

The Plot to Kill Paul   ¹²The next morning the Jews formed a conspiracy and bound themselves with an oath not to eat or drink until they had killed Paul.

ᵃ5 Exodus 22:28

¹³More than forty men were involved in this plot. ¹⁴They went to the chief priests and elders and said, "We have taken a solemn oath not to eat anything until we have killed Paul. ¹⁵Now then, you and the Sanhedrin petition the commander to bring him before you on the pretext of wanting more accurate information about his case. We are ready to kill him before he gets here."

¹⁶But when the son of Paul's sister heard of this plot, he went into the barracks and told Paul.

¹⁷Then Paul called one of the centurions and said, "Take this young man to the commander; he has something to tell him." ¹⁸So he took him to the commander.

The centurion said, "Paul, the prisoner, sent for me and asked me to bring this young man to you because he has something to tell you."

¹⁹The commander took the young man by the hand, drew him aside and asked, "What is it you want to tell me?"

²⁰He said: "The Jews have agreed to ask you to bring Paul before the Sanhedrin tomorrow on the pretext of wanting more accurate information about him. ²¹Don't give in to them, because more than forty of them are waiting in ambush for him. They have taken an oath not to eat or drink until they have killed him. They are ready now, waiting for your consent to their request."

²²The commander dismissed the young man and cautioned him, "Don't tell anyone that you have reported this to me."

Paul Transferred to Caesarea ²³Then he called two of his centurions and ordered them, "Get ready a detachment of two hundred soldiers, seventy horsemen and two hundred spearmen*ᵃ* to go to Caesarea at nine tonight. ²⁴Provide mounts for Paul so that he may be taken safely to Governor Felix."

²⁵He wrote a letter as follows:

²⁶Claudius Lysias,

To His Excellency, Governor Felix:

Greetings.

²⁷This man was seized by the Jews and they were about to kill him, but I came with my troops and rescued him, for I had learned that he is a Roman citizen. ²⁸I wanted to know why they were accusing him, so I brought him to their Sanhedrin. ²⁹I found that the accusation had to do with questions about their law, but there was no charge against him that deserved death or imprisonment. ³⁰When I was informed of a plot to be carried out against the man, I sent him to you at once. I also ordered his accusers to present to you their case against him.

³¹So the soldiers, carrying out their orders, took Paul with them during the night and brought him as far as Antipatris. ³²The next day they let the cavalry go on with him, while they returned to the barracks. ³³When the cavalry arrived in Caesarea, they delivered the letter to the governor and handed Paul over to him. ³⁴The governor read the letter and asked what province he was from. Learning that he was from Cilicia, ³⁵he said, "I will hear your case when your accusers get here." Then he ordered that Paul be kept under guard in Herod's palace.

24 *The Trial Before Felix* Five days later the high priest Ananias went down to Caesarea with some of the elders and a lawyer named Tertullus, and they brought their charges against Paul before the governor.

ᵃ23 The meaning of the Greek for this word is uncertain.

²When Paul was called in, Tertullus presented his case before Felix: "We have enjoyed a long period of peace under you, and your foresight has brought about reforms in this nation. ³Everywhere and in every way, most excellent Felix, we acknowledge this with profound gratitude. ⁴But in order not to weary you further, I would request that you be kind enough to hear us briefly.

⁵"We have found this man to be a troublemaker, stirring up riots among the Jews all over the world. He is a ringleader of the Nazarene sect ⁶and even tried to desecrate the temple; so we seized him. ⁸By*ᵃ* examining him yourself you will be able to learn the truth about all these charges we are bringing against him."

⁹The Jews joined in the accusation, asserting that these things were true.

¹⁰When the governor motioned for him to speak, Paul replied: "I know that for a number of years you have been a judge over this nation; so I gladly make my defense. ¹¹You can easily verify that no more than twelve days ago I went up to Jerusalem to worship. ¹²My accusers did not find me arguing with anyone at the temple, or stirring up a crowd in the synagogues or anywhere else in the city. ¹³And they cannot prove to you the charges they are now making against me. ¹⁴However, I admit that I worship the God of our fathers as a follower of the Way, which they call a sect. I believe everything that agrees with the Law and that is written in the Prophets, ¹⁵and I have the same hope in God as these men, that there will be a resurrection of both the righteous and the wicked. ¹⁶So I strive always to keep my conscience clear before God and man.

¹⁷"After an absence of several years, I came to Jerusalem to bring my people gifts for the poor and to present offerings. ¹⁸I was ceremonially clean when they found me in the temple courts doing this. There was no crowd with me, nor was I involved in any disturbance. ¹⁹But there are some Jews from the province of Asia, who ought to be here before you and bring charges if they have anything against me. ²⁰Or these who are here should state what crime they found in me when I stood before the Sanhedrin— ²¹unless it was this one thing I shouted as I stood in their presence: 'It is concerning the resurrection of the dead that I am on trial before you today.' "

²²Then Felix, who was well acquainted with the Way, adjourned the proceedings. "When Lysias the commander comes," he said, "I will decide your

---

ᵃ6-8 Some manuscripts *him and wanted to judge him according to our law. ⁷But the commander, Lysias, came and with the use of much force snatched him from our hands ⁸and ordered his accusers to come before you. By*

The Bible Says

Guilty?

Your conscience is that inner voice that tells you when you've done something wrong or warns you that what you want to do isn't right. Here are some things the Bible says about the conscience:

* The conscience can be weak (1 Corinthians 8:12).
* The conscience can be corrupted (Titus 1:15).
* The conscience can be cleansed (Hebrews 10:22).

It's wonderful to know that God forgives you and will cleanse your conscience. But it's even better to keep your conscience clear. Paul said, "I strive always to keep my conscience clear before God and man" (Acts 24:16). Live the way God wants you to live, and your conscience won't nag at you about what you've done wrong.

case." ²³He ordered the centurion to keep Paul under guard but to give him some freedom and permit his friends to take care of his needs.

²⁴Several days later Felix came with his wife Drusilla, who was a Jewess. He sent for Paul and listened to him as he spoke about faith in Christ Jesus. ²⁵As Paul discoursed on righteousness, self-control and the judgment to come, Felix was afraid and said, "That's enough for now! You may leave. When I find it convenient, I will send for you." ²⁶At the same time he was hoping that Paul would offer him a bribe, so he sent for him frequently and talked with him.

²⁷When two years had passed, Felix was succeeded by Porcius Festus, but because Felix wanted to grant a favor to the Jews, he left Paul in prison.

25 *The Trial Before Festus* Three days after arriving in the province, Festus went up from Caesarea to Jerusalem, ²where the chief priests and Jewish leaders appeared before him and presented the charges against Paul. ³They urgently requested Festus, as a favor to them, to have Paul transferred to Jerusalem, for they were preparing an ambush to kill him along the way. ⁴Festus answered, "Paul is being held at Caesarea, and I myself am going there soon. ⁵Let some of your leaders come with me and press charges against the man there, if he has done anything wrong."

⁶After spending eight or ten days with them, he went down to Caesarea, and the next day he convened the court and ordered that Paul be brought before him. ⁷When Paul appeared, the Jews who had come down from Jerusalem stood around him, bringing many serious charges against him, which they could not prove.

⁸Then Paul made his defense: "I have done nothing wrong against the law of the Jews or against the temple or against Caesar."

⁹Festus, wishing to do the Jews a favor, said to Paul, "Are you willing to go up to Jerusalem and stand trial before me there on these charges?"

¹⁰Paul answered: "I am now standing before Caesar's court, where I ought to be tried. I have not done any wrong to the Jews, as you yourself know very well. ¹¹If, however, I am guilty of doing anything deserving death, I do not refuse to die. But if the charges brought against me by these Jews are not true, no one has the right to hand me over to them. I appeal to Caesar!"

¹²After Festus had conferred with his council, he declared: "You have appealed to Caesar. To Caesar you will go!"

Festus Consults King Agrippa ¹³A few days later King Agrippa and Bernice arrived at Caesarea to pay their respects to Festus. ¹⁴Since they were spending many days there, Festus discussed Paul's case with the king. He said: "There is a man here whom Felix left as a prisoner. ¹⁵When I went to Jerusalem, the chief priests and elders of the Jews brought charges against him and asked that he be condemned.

¹⁶"I told them that it is not the Roman custom to hand over any man before he has faced his accusers and has had an opportunity to defend himself against their charges. ¹⁷When they came here with me, I did not delay the case, but convened the court the next day and ordered the man to be brought in. ¹⁸When his accusers got up to speak, they did not charge him with any of the crimes I had expected. ¹⁹Instead, they had some points of dispute with him about their own religion and about a dead man named Jesus who Paul claimed was alive. ²⁰I was at a loss how to investigate such matters; so I asked if he would be willing to go to Jerusalem and stand trial there on these charges. ²¹When Paul made his appeal to be held over for the Emperor's decision, I ordered him held until I could send him to Caesar."

²²Then Agrippa said to Festus, "I would like to hear this man myself."

He replied, "Tomorrow you will hear him."

Paul Before Agrippa ²³The next day Agrippa and Bernice came with great pomp and entered the audience room with the high ranking officers and the leading men of the city. At the command of Festus, Paul was brought in. ²⁴Festus said: "King Agrippa, and all who are present with us, you see this man! The whole Jewish community has petitioned me about him in Jerusalem and here in Caesarea, shouting that he ought not to live any longer. ²⁵I found he had done nothing deserving of death, but because he made his appeal to the Emperor I decided to send him to Rome. ²⁶But I have nothing definite to write to His Majesty about him. Therefore I have brought him before all of you, and especially before you, King Agrippa, so that as a result of this investigation I may have something to write. ²⁷For I think it is unreasonable to send on a prisoner without specifying the charges against him."

26 Then Agrippa said to Paul, "You have permission to speak for yourself."

So Paul motioned with his hand and began his defense: ²"King Agrippa, I consider myself fortunate to stand before you today as I make my defense against all the accusations of the Jews, ³and especially so because you are well acquainted with all the Jewish customs and controversies. Therefore, I beg you to listen to me patiently.

⁴"The Jews all know the way I have lived ever since I was a child, from the beginning of my life in my own country, and also in Jerusalem. ⁵They have known me for a long time and can testify, if they are willing, that according to the strictest sect of our religion, I lived as a Pharisee. ⁶And now it is because of my hope in what God has promised our fathers that I am on trial today. ⁷This is the promise our twelve tribes are hoping to see fulfilled as they earnestly serve God day and night. O king, it is because of this hope that the Jews are accusing me. ⁸Why should any of you consider it incredible that God raises the dead?

⁹"I too was convinced that I ought to do all that was possible to oppose the name of Jesus of Nazareth. ¹⁰And that is just what I did in Jerusalem. On the authority of the chief priests I put many of the saints in prison, and when they were put to death, I cast my vote against them. ¹¹Many a time I went from one synagogue to another to have them punished, and I tried to force them to blaspheme. In my obsession against them, I even went to foreign cities to persecute them.

¹²"On one of these journeys I was going to Damascus with the authority and commission of the chief priests. ¹³About noon, O king, as I was on the road, I saw a light from heaven, brighter than the sun, blazing around me and my companions. ¹⁴We all fell to the ground, and I heard a voice saying to me in Aramaic,ᵃ 'Saul, Saul, why do you persecute me? It is hard for you to kick against the goads.'

¹⁵"Then I asked, 'Who are you, Lord?'

" 'I am Jesus, whom you are persecuting,' the Lord replied. ¹⁶'Now get up and stand on your feet. I have appeared to you to appoint you as a servant and as a witness of what you have seen of me and what I will show you. ¹⁷I will rescue you from your own people and from the Gentiles. I am sending you to them ¹⁸to open their eyes and turn them from darkness to light, and from the power of Satan to God, so that they may receive forgiveness of sins and a place among those who are sanctified by faith in me.'

¹⁹"So then, King Agrippa, I was not disobedient to the vision from heaven. ²⁰First to those in Damascus, then to those in Jerusalem and in all Judea, and to the Gentiles also, I preached that they should repent and turn to God and prove their repentance by their deeds. ²¹That is why the Jews seized me in the temple courts and tried to kill me. ²²But I have had God's help to this very day, and so I stand here and testify to small and great alike. I am saying nothing beyond what the prophets and Moses said would happen— ²³that the

ᵃ14 Or Hebrew

Christ[a] would suffer and, as the first to rise from the dead, would proclaim light to his own people and to the Gentiles."

²⁴At this point Festus interrupted Paul's defense. "You are out of your mind, Paul!" he shouted. "Your great learning is driving you insane." ²⁵"I am not insane, most excellent Festus," Paul replied. "What I am saying is true and reasonable. ²⁶The king is familiar with these things, and I can speak freely to him. I am convinced that none of this has escaped his notice, because it was not done in a corner. ²⁷King Agrippa, do you believe the prophets? I know you do."

²⁸Then Agrippa said to Paul, "Do you think that in such a short time you can persuade me to be a Christian?"

²⁹Paul replied, "Short time or long—I pray God that not only you but all who are listening to me today may become what I am, except for these chains."

³⁰The king rose, and with him the governor and Bernice and those sitting with them. ³¹They left the room, and while talking with one another, they said, "This man is not doing anything that deserves death or imprisonment." ³²Agrippa said to Festus, "This man could have been set free if he had not appealed to Caesar."

27 *Paul Sails for Rome* When it was decided that we would sail for Italy, Paul and some other prisoners were handed over to a centurion named Julius, who belonged to the Imperial Regiment. ²We boarded a ship from Adramyttium about to sail for ports along the coast of the province of Asia, and we put out to sea. Aristarchus, a Macedonian from Thessalonica, was with us.

³The next day we landed at Sidon; and Julius, in kindness to Paul, allowed him to go to his friends so they might provide for his needs. ⁴From there we put out to sea again and passed to the lee of Cyprus because the winds were against us. ⁵When we had sailed across the open sea off the coast of Cilicia and Pamphylia, we landed at Myra in Lycia. ⁶There the centurion found an Alexandrian ship sailing for Italy and put us on board. ⁷We made slow headway for many days and had difficulty arriving off Cnidus. When the wind did not allow us to hold our course, we sailed to the lee of Crete, opposite Salmone. ⁸We moved along the coast with difficulty and came to a place called Fair Havens, near the town of Lasea.

⁹Much time had been lost, and sailing had already become dangerous because by now it was after the Fast.[b] So Paul warned them, ¹⁰"Men, I can see that our voyage is going to be disastrous and bring great loss to ship and cargo, and to our own lives also." ¹¹But the centurion, instead of listening to what Paul said, followed the advice of the pilot and of the owner of the ship. ¹²Since the harbor was unsuitable to winter in, the majority decided that we should sail on, hoping to reach Phoenix and winter there. This was a harbor in Crete, facing both southwest and northwest.

[a]23 Or *Messiah* [b]9 That is, the Day of Atonement (Yom Kippur)

ACTS 26:24–25

It may be hard to believe, but a lot of teens know next to nothing about Christianity. Only one student in a certain junior class knew what Good Friday and Easter celebrate. Others had never heard that Jesus had no human father but was the Son of God. Often the people who give you the hardest time about your beliefs don't have any idea what the Bible teaches! So if someone pulls a Festus and says, "You are out of your mind" (Acts 26:24), don't back down. Give him Paul's answer: "What I am saying is true and reasonable" (Acts 26:25). And be ready to tell how Jesus has changed your life.

Direct Line

The Storm ¹³When a gentle south wind began to blow, they thought they had obtained what they wanted; so they weighed anchor and sailed along the shore of Crete. ¹⁴Before very long, a wind of hurricane force, called the "northeaster," swept down from the island. ¹⁵The ship was caught by the storm and could not head into the wind; so we gave way to it and were driven along. ¹⁶As we passed to the lee of a small island called Cauda, we were hardly able to make the lifeboat secure. ¹⁷When the men had hoisted it aboard, they passed ropes under the ship itself to hold it together. Fearing that they would run aground on the sandbars of Syrtis, they lowered the sea anchor and let the ship be driven along. ¹⁸We took such a violent battering from the storm that the next day they began to throw the cargo overboard. ¹⁹On the third day, they threw the ship's tackle overboard with their own hands. ²⁰When neither sun nor stars appeared for many days and the storm continued raging, we finally gave up all hope of being saved.

²¹After the men had gone a long time without food, Paul stood up before them and said: "Men, you should have taken my advice not to sail from Crete; then you would have spared yourselves this damage and loss. ²²But now I urge you to keep up your courage, because not one of you will be lost; only the ship will be destroyed. ²³Last night an angel of the God whose I am and whom I serve stood beside me ²⁴and said, 'Do not be afraid, Paul. You must stand trial before Caesar; and God has graciously given you the lives of all who sail with you.' ²⁵So keep up your courage, men, for I have faith in God that it will happen just as he told me. ²⁶Nevertheless, we must run aground on some island."

The Shipwreck ²⁷On the fourteenth night we were still being driven across the Adriatic[a] Sea, when about midnight the sailors sensed they were approaching land. ²⁸They took soundings and found that the water was a hundred and twenty feet[b] deep. A short time later they took soundings again and found it was ninety feet[c] deep. ²⁹Fearing that we would be dashed against the rocks, they dropped four anchors from the stern and prayed for daylight. ³⁰In an attempt to escape from the ship, the sailors let the lifeboat down into the sea, pretending they were going to lower some anchors from the bow. ³¹Then Paul said to the centurion and the soldiers, "Unless these men stay with the ship, you cannot be saved." ³²So the soldiers cut the ropes that held the lifeboat and let it fall away.

³³Just before dawn Paul urged them all to eat. "For the last fourteen days," he said, "you have been in constant suspense and have gone without food—you haven't eaten anything. ³⁴Now I urge you to take some food. You need it to survive. Not one of you will lose a single hair from his head." ³⁵After he said this, he took some bread and gave thanks to God in front of them all. Then he broke it and began to eat. ³⁶They were all encouraged and ate some food themselves. ³⁷Altogether there were 276 of us on board. ³⁸When they had eaten as much as they wanted, they lightened the ship by throwing the grain into the sea.

³⁹When daylight came, they did not recognize the land, but they saw a bay with a sandy beach, where they decided to run the ship aground if they could. ⁴⁰Cutting loose the anchors, they left them in the sea and at the same time untied the ropes that held the rudders. Then they hoisted the foresail to the wind and made for the beach. ⁴¹But the ship struck a sandbar and ran

ACTS 27

QUIZZER

Q: How did Paul get to Rome from Caesarea?

BONUS: What made travel safer at that time?

Answers on page 1451

---

a27 In ancient times the name referred to an area extending well south of Italy. *b28* Greek *twenty orguias* (about 37 meters) *c28* Greek *fifteen orguias* (about 27 meters)

aground. The bow stuck fast and would not move, and the stern was broken to pieces by the pounding of the surf. ⁴²The soldiers planned to kill the prisoners to prevent any of them from swimming away and escaping. ⁴³But the centurion wanted to spare Paul's life and kept them from carrying out their plan. He ordered those who could swim to jump overboard first and get to land. ⁴⁴The rest were to get there on planks or on pieces of the ship. In this way everyone reached land in safety.

28 *Ashore on Malta*   Once safely on shore, we found out that the island was called Malta. ²The islanders showed us unusual kindness. They built a fire and welcomed us all because it was raining and cold. ³Paul gathered a pile of brushwood and, as he put it on the fire, a viper, driven out by the heat, fastened itself on his hand. ⁴When the islanders saw the snake hanging from his hand, they said to each other, "This man must be a murderer; for though he escaped from the sea, Justice has not allowed him to live." ⁵But Paul shook the snake off into the fire and suffered no ill effects. ⁶The people expected him to swell up or suddenly fall dead, but after waiting a long time and seeing nothing unusual happen to him, they changed their minds and said he was a god.

⁷There was an estate nearby that belonged to Publius, the chief official of the island. He welcomed us to his home and for three days entertained us hospitably. ⁸His father was sick in bed, suffering from fever and dysentery. Paul went in to see him and, after prayer, placed his hands on him and healed him. ⁹When this had happened, the rest of the sick on the island came and were cured. ¹⁰They honored us in many ways and when we were ready to sail, they furnished us with the supplies we needed.

Arrival at Rome   ¹¹After three months we put out to sea in a ship that had wintered in the island. It was an Alexandrian ship with the figurehead of the twin gods Castor and Pollux. ¹²We put in at Syracuse and stayed there three days. ¹³From there we set sail and arrived at Rhegium. The next day the south wind came up, and on the following day we reached Puteoli. ¹⁴There we found some brothers who invited us to spend a week with them. And so we came to Rome. ¹⁵The brothers there had heard that we were coming, and they traveled as far as the Forum of Appius and the Three Taverns to meet us. At the sight of these men Paul thanked God and was encouraged. ¹⁶When we got to Rome, Paul was allowed to live by himself, with a soldier to guard him.

Paul Preaches at Rome Under Guard   ¹⁷Three days later he called together the leaders of the Jews. When they had assembled, Paul said to them: "My brothers, although I have done nothing against our people or against the customs of our ancestors, I was arrested in Jerusalem and handed over to the Romans. ¹⁸They examined me and wanted to release me, because I was not guilty of any crime deserving death. ¹⁹But when the Jews objected, I was compelled to appeal to Caesar—not that I had any charge to bring against my own people. ²⁰For this reason I have asked to see you and talk with you. It is because of the hope of Israel that I am bound with this chain."

²¹They replied, "We have not received any letters from Judea concerning you, and none of the brothers who have come from there has reported or said anything bad about you. ²²But we want to hear what your views are, for we know that people everywhere are talking against this sect."

²³They arranged to meet Paul on a certain day, and came in even larger numbers to the place where he was staying. From morning till evening he explained and declared to them the kingdom of God and tried to convince them about Jesus from the Law of Moses and from the Prophets. ²⁴Some were convinced by what he said, but others would not believe. ²⁵They disagreed

Answers
to Quizzer on page 1450

A: By ship (Acts 27:2).

BONUS: Travel was made safe by Roman forces who defeated pirates and chased robbers. However, the ships were still at the mercy of the weather (Acts 27:13-44).

among themselves and began to leave after Paul had made this final statement: "The Holy Spirit spoke the truth to your forefathers when he said through Isaiah the prophet:

26 " 'Go to this people and say,
  "You will be ever hearing but never understanding;
   you will be ever seeing but never perceiving."
27 For this people's heart has become calloused;
   they hardly hear with their ears,
   and they have closed their eyes.
  Otherwise they might see with their eyes,
   hear with their ears,
   understand with their hearts
   and turn, and I would heal them.'a

28 "Therefore I want you to know that God's salvation has been sent to the Gentiles, and they will listen!"b

30 For two whole years Paul stayed there in his own rented house and welcomed all who came to see him. 31 Boldly and without hindrance he preached the kingdom of God and taught about the Lord Jesus Christ.

PAUL'S TRIP TO ROME

SEE ACTS 27-28

---

a27 Isaiah 6:9,10   b28 Some manuscripts *listen!*" 29*After he said this, the Jews left, arguing vigorously among themselves.*

A GOOD PERSON.

That's what most of you probably want to be. But everyone falls short. Oh, maybe you do better than many others. Compared to some, you may be doing great. But compared to God or compared to what you know you ought to be, well, you know you just don't quite measure up.

Romans tells you what God has done for "not quite good enough" people. Instead of insisting that you be perfect, God invites you to trust in him. Then he gives you the Holy Spirit so you can live a holy life. God doesn't want you to fail. He intends to help you be all you can be.

Fun damentals

Are people who never heard of Jesus lost (Romans 2:12-16)?

What is "faith" anyway? Don't most people believe there's a God (Romans 4:13-25)?

Why do you do wrong when you don't want to (Romans 7:7-25)?

Rules. Rules. Rules. Are they so important (Romans 14:1-12)?

FAST FACTS

Rome was the capital of the Roman empire.

One million of the empire's 54 million people lived in Rome.

Both Peter and Paul were later executed in Rome.

Paul had not yet visited Rome when he wrote this letter.

Many Roman emperors were worshiped as gods.

Paul, a servant of Christ Jesus, called to be an apostle and set apart for the gospel of God— [2]the gospel he promised beforehand through his prophets in the Holy Scriptures [3]regarding his Son, who as to his human nature was a descendant of David, [4]and who through the Spirit[a] of holiness was declared with power to be the Son of God[b] by his resurrection from the dead: Jesus Christ our Lord. [5]Through him and for his name's sake, we received grace and apostleship to call people from among all the Gentiles to the obedience that comes from faith. [6]And you also are among those who are called to belong to Jesus Christ.

[7]To all in Rome who are loved by God and called to be saints:

Grace and peace to you from God our Father and from the Lord Jesus Christ.

Paul's Longing to Visit Rome   [8]First, I thank my God through Jesus Christ for all of you, because your faith is being reported all over the world. [9]God, whom I serve with my whole heart in preaching the gospel of his Son, is my witness how constantly I remember you [10]in my prayers at all times; and I pray that now at last by God's will the way may be opened for me to come to you.

[11]I long to see you so that I may impart to you some spiritual gift to make you strong— [12]that is, that you and I may be mutually encouraged by each other's faith. [13]I do not want you to be unaware, brothers, that I planned many times to come to you (but have been prevented from doing so until now) in order that I might have a harvest among you, just as I have had among the other Gentiles.

[14]I am obligated both to Greeks and non-Greeks, both to the wise and the foolish. [15]That is why I am so eager to preach the gospel also to you who are at Rome.

[16]I am not ashamed of the gospel, because it is the power of God for the salvation of everyone who believes: first for the Jew, then for the Gentile. [17]For in the gospel a righteousness from God is revealed, a righteousness that is by faith from first to last,[c] just as it is written: "The righteous will live by faith."[d]

God's Wrath Against Mankind   [18]The wrath of God is being revealed from heaven against all the godlessness and wickedness of men who suppress the truth by their wickedness, [19]since what may be known about God is plain to them, because God has made it plain to them. [20]For since the creation of the world God's invisible qualities—his eternal power and divine nature—have been clearly seen, being understood from what has been made, so that men are without excuse.

[21]For although they knew God, they neither glorified him as God nor gave thanks to him, but their thinking became futile and their foolish hearts were darkened. [22]Although they claimed to be wise, they became fools [23]and exchanged the glory of the immortal God for images made to look like mortal man and birds and animals and reptiles.

[24]Therefore God gave them over in the sinful desires of their hearts to sexual impurity for the degrading of their bodies with one another. [25]They exchanged the truth of God for a lie, and worshiped and served created things rather than the Creator—who is forever praised. Amen.

[26]Because of this, God gave them over to shameful lusts. Even their women exchanged natural relations for unnatural ones. [27]In the same way the men also abandoned natural relations with women and were inflamed with lust for one another. Men committed indecent acts with other men, and received in themselves the due penalty for their perversion.

[a]4 Or *who as to his spirit*   [b]4 Or *was appointed to be the Son of God with power*   [c]17 Or *is from faith to faith*   [d]17 Hab. 2:4

²⁸Furthermore, since they did not think it worthwhile to retain the knowledge of God, he gave them over to a depraved mind, to do what ought not to be done. ²⁹They have become filled with every kind of wickedness, evil, greed and depravity. They are full of envy, murder, strife, deceit and malice. They are gossips, ³⁰slanderers, God-haters, insolent, arrogant and boastful; they invent ways of doing evil; they disobey their parents; ³¹they are senseless, faithless, heartless, ruthless. ³²Although they know God's righteous decree that those who do such things deserve death, they not only continue to do these very things but also approve of those who practice them.

God's Righteous Judgment   You, therefore, have no excuse, you who pass judgment on someone else, for at whatever point you judge the other, you are condemning yourself, because you who pass judgment do the same things. ²Now we know that God's judgment against those who do such things is based on truth. ³So when you, a mere man, pass judgment on them and yet do the same things, do you think you will escape God's judgment? ⁴Or do you show contempt for the riches of his kindness, tolerance and patience, not realizing that God's kindness leads you toward repentance?

⁵But because of your stubbornness and your unrepentant heart, you are storing up wrath against yourself for the day of God's wrath, when his righteous judgment will be revealed. ⁶God "will give to each person according to what he has done."*ᵃ* ⁷To those who by persistence in doing good seek glory, honor and immortality, he will give eternal life. ⁸But for those who are self-seeking and who reject the truth and follow evil, there will be wrath and anger. ⁹There will be trouble and distress for every human being who does evil: first for the Jew, then for the Gentile; ¹⁰but glory, honor and peace for everyone who does good: first for the Jew, then for the Gentile. ¹¹For God does not show favoritism.

¹²All who sin apart from the law will also perish apart from the law, and all who sin under the law will be judged by the law. ¹³For it is not those who hear the law who are righteous in God's sight, but it is those who obey the law who will be declared righteous. ¹⁴(Indeed, when Gentiles, who do not have the law, do by nature things required by the law, they are a law for themselves, even though they do not have the law, ¹⁵since they show that the

ᵃ6 Psalm 62:12; Prov. 24:12

Creation is like God's radio station, sending out the message that God exists and that he is all-powerful. When the Bible says, "What may be known about God is plain" (Romans 1:19), it means that God has created human beings with an internal radio, tuned to his station. The message that God exists is sent and received!

Does that mean everyone will be saved? Not at all. Though people have no excuse for not worshiping God or being thankful (Romans 1:21), instead of responding to God, they turn away from him.

Just knowing that God exists isn't enough. Having faith in him, loving him, accepting his love for you—that is what makes the difference.

The Bible Says

All Know God Exists

requirements of the law are written on their hearts, their consciences also bearing witness, and their thoughts now accusing, now even defending them.) [16]This will take place on the day when God will judge men's secrets through Jesus Christ, as my gospel declares.

The Jews and the Law [17]Now you, if you call yourself a Jew; if you rely on the law and brag about your relationship to God; [18]if you know his will and approve of what is superior because you are instructed by the law; [19]if you are convinced that you are a guide for the blind, a light for those who are in the dark, [20]an instructor of the foolish, a teacher of infants, because you have in the law the embodiment of knowledge and truth— [21]you, then, who teach others, do you not teach yourself? You who preach against stealing, do you steal? [22]You who say that people should not commit adultery, do you commit adultery? You who abhor idols, do you rob temples? [23]You who brag about the law, do you dishonor God by breaking the law? [24]As it is written: "God's name is blasphemed among the Gentiles because of you."[a]

[25]Circumcision has value if you observe the law, but if you break the law, you have become as though you had not been circumcised. [26]If those who are not circumcised keep the law's requirements, will they not be regarded as though they were circumcised? [27]The one who is not circumcised physically and yet obeys the law will condemn you who, even though you have the[b] written code and circumcision, are a lawbreaker.

[28]A man is not a Jew if he is only one outwardly, nor is circumcision merely outward and physical. [29]No, a man is a Jew if he is one inwardly; and circumcision is circumcision of the heart, by the Spirit, not by the written code. Such a man's praise is not from men, but from God.

God's Faithfulness What advantage, then, is there in being a Jew, or what value is there in circumcision? [2]Much in every way! First of all, they have been entrusted with the very words of God.

[3]What if some did not have faith? Will their lack of faith nullify God's faithfulness? [4]Not at all! Let God be true, and every man a liar. As it is written:

> "So that you may be proved right when you speak
> and prevail when you judge."[c]

[5]But if our unrighteousness brings out God's righteousness more clearly, what shall we say? That God is unjust in bringing his wrath on us? (I am using a human argument.) [6]Certainly not! If that were so, how could God judge the world? [7]Someone might argue, "If my falsehood enhances God's truthfulness and so increases his glory, why am I still condemned as a sinner?" [8]Why not say—as we are being slanderously reported as saying and as some claim that we say—"Let us do evil that good may result"? Their condemnation is deserved.

No One Is Righteous [9]What shall we conclude then? Are we any better[d]? Not at all! We have already made the charge that Jews and Gentiles alike are all under sin. [10]As it is written:

> "There is no one righteous, not even one;
> [11]   there is no one who understands,
>   no one who seeks God.
> [12]All have turned away,
>   they have together become worthless;
>   there is no one who does good,
>   not even one."[e]

---

[a]*24* Isaiah 52:5; Ezek. 36:22 [b]*27* Or *who, by means of a* [c]*4* Psalm 51:4 [d]*9* Or *worse* [e]*12* Psalms 14:1-3; 53:1-3; Eccles. 7:20

13 "Their throats are open graves;
  their tongues practice deceit."[a]
"The poison of vipers is on their lips."[b]
14   "Their mouths are full of cursing and bitterness."[c]
15 "Their feet are swift to shed blood;
16   ruin and misery mark their ways,
17 and the way of peace they do not know."[d]
18   "There is no fear of God before their eyes."[e]

19 Now we know that whatever the law says, it says to those who are under the law, so that every mouth may be silenced and the whole world held accountable to God. 20 Therefore no one will be declared righteous in his sight by observing the law; rather, through the law we become conscious of sin.

Righteousness Through Faith 21 But now a righteousness from God, apart from law, has been made known, to which the Law and the Prophets testify. 22 This righteousness from God comes through faith in Jesus Christ to all who believe. There is no difference, 23 for all have sinned and fall short of the glory of God, 24 and are justified freely by his grace through the redemption that came by Christ Jesus. 25 God presented him as a sacrifice of atonement,[f] through faith in his blood. He did this to demonstrate his justice, because in his forbearance he had left the sins committed beforehand unpunished— 26 he did it to demonstrate his justice at the present time, so as to be just and the one who justifies those who have faith in Jesus.

27 Where, then, is boasting? It is excluded. On what principle? On that of observing the law? No, but on that of faith. 28 For we maintain that a man is justified by faith apart from observing the law. 29 Is God the God of Jews only? Is he not the God of Gentiles too? Yes, of Gentiles too, 30 since there is only one God, who will justify the circumcised by faith and the uncircumcised through that same faith. 31 Do we, then, nullify the law by this faith? Not at all! Rather, we uphold the law.

Abraham Justified by Faith What then shall we say that Abraham, our forefather, discovered in this matter? 2 If, in fact, Abraham was justified by works, he had something to boast about—but not before God. 3 What does the Scripture say? "Abraham believed God, and it was credited to him as righteousness."[g]

4 Now when a man works, his wages are not credited to him as a gift, but as an obligation. 5 However, to the man who does not work but trusts God who justifies the wicked, his faith is credited as righteousness. 6 David says the same thing when he speaks of the blessedness of the man to whom God credits righteousness apart from works:

7 "Blessed are they
  whose transgressions are
    forgiven,
  whose sins are covered.
8 Blessed is the man
  whose sin the Lord will never
    count against him."[h]

ROMANS 4:1-8

How can Abraham be praised for his faith even though he lied twice and said his wife Sarah was his sister? Or how can David be praised even though he sinned with Bathsheba? For that matter, how can you be on your way to heaven? You haven't been perfect either. This passage explains: God didn't just say, "Oh forget it. Sin isn't all that bad." Instead God said, "Sin is so terrible it must be punished." And Jesus took that punishment for you so that God could do the right thing—punish sin—and still forgive.

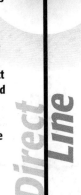

a 13 Psalm 5:9   b 13 Psalm 140:3   c 14 Psalm 10:7
d 17 Isaiah 59:7,8   e 18 Psalm 36:1   f 25 Or as the one who
would turn aside his wrath, taking away sin   g 3 Gen. 15:6;
also in verse 22   h 8 Psalm 32:1,2

⁹Is this blessedness only for the circumcised, or also for the uncircumcised? We have been saying that Abraham's faith was credited to him as righteousness. ¹⁰Under what circumstances was it credited? Was it after he was circumcised, or before? It was not after, but before! ¹¹And he received the sign of circumcision, a seal of the righteousness that he had by faith while he was still uncircumcised. So then, he is the father of all who believe but have not been circumcised, in order that righteousness might be credited to them. ¹²And he is also the father of the circumcised who not only are circumcised but who also walk in the footsteps of the faith that our father Abraham had before he was circumcised.

¹³It was not through law that Abraham and his offspring received the promise that he would be heir of the world, but through the righteousness that comes by faith. ¹⁴For if those who live by law are heirs, faith has no value and the promise is worthless, ¹⁵because law brings wrath. And where there is no law there is no transgression.

¹⁶Therefore, the promise comes by faith, so that it may be by grace and may be guaranteed to all Abraham's offspring—not only to those who are of the law but also to those who are of the faith of Abraham. He is the father of us all. ¹⁷As it is written: "I have made you a father of many nations."[a] He is our father in the sight of God, in whom he believed—the God who gives life to the dead and calls things that are not as though they were.

¹⁸Against all hope, Abraham in hope believed and so became the father of many nations, just as it had been said to him, "So shall your offspring be."[b] ¹⁹Without weakening in his faith, he faced the fact that his body was as good as dead—since he was about a hundred years old—and that Sarah's womb was also dead. ²⁰Yet he did not waver through unbelief regarding the promise of God, but was strengthened in his faith and gave glory to God, ²¹being fully persuaded that God had power to do what he had promised. ²²This is why "it was credited to him as righteousness." ²³The words "it was credited to him" were written not for him alone, ²⁴but also for us, to whom God will credit righteousness—for us who believe in him who raised Jesus our Lord from the dead. ²⁵He was delivered over to death for our sins and was raised to life for our justification.

5 *Peace and Joy* Therefore, since we have been justified through faith, we[c] have peace with God through our Lord Jesus Christ, ²through whom we have gained access by faith into this grace in which we now stand. And we[c] rejoice in the hope of the glory of God. ³Not only so, but we[c] also rejoice in our sufferings, because we know that suffering produces perseverance; ⁴perseverance, character; and character, hope. ⁵And hope does not disappoint us, because God has poured out his love into our hearts by the Holy Spirit, whom he has given us.

⁶You see, at just the right time, when we were still powerless, Christ died for the ungodly. ⁷Very rarely will anyone die for a righteous man, though for a good

Direct Line

ROMANS 4:18-25

What's the difference between wishful thinking and faith? Wishful thinking says, "Maybe we'll win a sweepstakes so I can go to college." Faith says, "If I don't get a scholarship, I'll work to put myself through." Wishful thinking is unrealistic. Faith looks at things honestly and squarely, and believes. That's what Abraham did. He knew he and Sarah were too old to have children. But when God said they would have a son, Abraham chose to believe. Some people think faith is wishful thinking. It isn't. The wishful thinker is kidding himself or herself. The person with faith sees the difficulties but also clearly sees God.

[a]17 Gen. 17:5 [b]18 Gen. 15:5 [c]1,2,3 Or *let us*

man someone might possibly dare to die. [8]But God demonstrates his own love for us in this: While we were still sinners, Christ died for us.

[9]Since we have now been justified by his blood, how much more shall we be saved from God's wrath through him! [10]For if, when we were God's enemies, we were reconciled to him through the death of his Son, how much more, having been reconciled, shall we be saved through his life! [11]Not only is this so, but we also rejoice in God through our Lord Jesus Christ, through whom we have now received reconciliation.

Death Through Adam, Life Through Christ [12]Therefore, just as sin entered the world through one man, and death through sin, and in this way death came to all men, because all sinned— [13]for before the law was given, sin was in the world. But sin is not taken into account when there is no law. [14]Nevertheless, death reigned from the time of Adam to the time of Moses, even over those who did not sin by breaking a command, as did Adam, who was a pattern of the one to come.

[15]But the gift is not like the trespass. For if the many died by the trespass of the one man, how much more did God's grace and the gift that came by the grace of the one man, Jesus Christ, overflow to the many! [16]Again, the gift of God is not like the result of the one man's sin: The judgment followed one sin and brought condemnation, but the gift followed many trespasses and brought justification. [17]For if, by the trespass of the one man, death reigned through that one man, how much more will those who receive God's abundant provision of grace and of the gift of righteousness reign in life through the one man, Jesus Christ.

[18]Consequently, just as the result of one trespass was condemnation for all men, so also the result of one act of righteousness was justification that brings life for all men. [19]For just as through the disobedience of the one man the many were made sinners, so also through the obedience of the one man the many will be made righteous.

[20]The law was added so that the trespass might increase. But where sin increased, grace increased all the more, [21]so that, just as sin reigned in death, so also grace might reign through righteousness to bring eternal life through Jesus Christ our Lord.

6 *Dead to Sin, Alive in Christ* What shall we say, then? Shall we go on sinning so that grace may increase? [2]By no means! We died to sin; how can we live in it any longer? [3]Or don't you know that all of us who were baptized into Christ Jesus were baptized into his death? [4]We were therefore buried with him through baptism into death in order that, just as Christ was raised from the dead through the glory of the Father, we too may live a new life.

[5]If we have been united with him like this in his death, we will certainly also be united with him in his resurrection. [6]For we know that our old self was crucified with him so that the body of sin might be done away with,[a] that we should no longer be slaves to sin— [7]because anyone who has died has been freed from sin.

> Now if we died with Christ, we believe that we will also live with him
> (Romans 6:8).

[8]Now if we died with Christ, we believe that we will also live with him. [9]For we know that since Christ was raised from the dead, he cannot die again; death no longer has mastery over him. [10]The death he died, he died to sin once for all; but the life he lives, he lives to God.

[11]In the same way, count yourselves dead to sin but alive to God in Christ Jesus. [12]Therefore do not let sin reign in your mortal body so that you obey its evil desires. [13]Do not offer the parts of your body to sin, as instruments

---

[a]6 Or *be rendered powerless*

of wickedness, but rather offer yourselves to God, as those who have been brought from death to life; and offer the parts of your body to him as instruments of righteousness. ¹⁴For sin shall not be your master, because you are not under law, but under grace.

Slaves to Righteousness ¹⁵What then? Shall we sin because we are not under law but under grace? By no means! ¹⁶Don't you know that when you offer yourselves to someone to obey him as slaves, you are slaves to the one whom you obey—whether you are slaves to sin, which leads to death, or to obedience, which leads to righteousness? ¹⁷But thanks be to God that, though you used to be slaves to sin, you wholeheartedly obeyed the form of teaching to which you were entrusted. ¹⁸You have been set free from sin and have become slaves to righteousness.

¹⁹I put this in human terms because you are weak in your natural selves. Just as you used to offer the parts of your body in slavery to impurity and to ever-increasing wickedness, so now offer them in slavery to righteousness leading to holiness. ²⁰When you were slaves to sin, you were free from the control of righteousness. ²¹What benefit did you reap at that time from the things you are now ashamed of? Those things result in death! ²²But now that you have been set free from sin and have become slaves to God, the benefit you reap leads to holiness, and the result is eternal life. ²³For the wages of sin is death, but the gift of God is eternal life in*ᵃ* Christ Jesus our Lord.

7 *An Illustration From Marriage* Do you not know, brothers—for I am speaking to men who know the law—that the law has authority over a man only as long as he lives? ²For example, by law a married woman is bound to her husband as long as he is alive, but if her husband dies, she is released from the law of marriage. ³So then, if she marries another man while her husband is still alive, she is called an adulteress. But if her husband dies, she is released from that law and is not an adulteress, even though she marries another man.

⁴So, my brothers, you also died to the law through the body of Christ, that you might belong to another, to him who was raised from the dead, in order that we might bear fruit to God. ⁵For when we were controlled by the sinful nature,*ᵇ* the sinful passions aroused by the law were at work in our bodies, so that we bore fruit for death. ⁶But now, by dying to what once bound us, we have been released from the law so that we serve in the new way of the Spirit, and not in the old way of the written code.

Struggling With Sin ⁷What shall we say, then? Is the law sin? Certainly not! Indeed I would not have known what sin was except through the law. For I would not have known what coveting really was if the law had not said, "Do not covet."*ᶜ* ⁸But sin, seizing the opportunity afforded by the commandment, produced in me every kind of covetous desire. For apart from law, sin is dead. ⁹Once I was alive apart from law; but when the commandment came, sin sprang to life and I died. ¹⁰I found that the very commandment that

ROMANS 7:7-25

God's rules tell you what is wrong and what is right. And you agree. But that doesn't help! You want to do right, but you want to do what's wrong too. It's like you're two different people: one who wants to do right but another who wants to do wrong. Then even when you do what's right, you feel that evil "I" right there inside you, starting to feel proud, and you know pride is a sin. Paul said he just couldn't seem to get rid of the parts of him that were at war within. The chapter ends here. But Paul doesn't stop. Look at Romans 8!

Direct Line

---

*ᵃ23 Or through ᵇ5 Or the flesh; also in verse 25
ᶜ7 Exodus 20:17; Deut. 5:21*

was intended to bring life actually brought death. ¹¹For sin, seizing the opportunity afforded by the commandment, deceived me, and through the commandment put me to death. ¹²So then, the law is holy, and the commandment is holy, righteous and good.

¹³Did that which is good, then, become death to me? By no means! But in order that sin might be recognized as sin, it produced death in me through what was good, so that through the commandment sin might become utterly sinful.

¹⁴We know that the law is spiritual; but I am unspiritual, sold as a slave to sin. ¹⁵I do not understand what I do. For what I want to do I do not do, but what I hate I do. ¹⁶And if I do what I do not want to do, I agree that the law is good. ¹⁷As it is, it is no longer I myself who do it, but it is sin living in me. ¹⁸I know that nothing good lives in me, that is, in my sinful nature.ᵃ For I have the desire to do what is good, but I cannot carry it out. ¹⁹For what I do is not the good I want to do; no, the evil I do not want to do—this I keep on doing. ²⁰Now if I do what I do not want to do, it is no longer I who do it, but it is sin living in me that does it.

²¹So I find this law at work: When I want to do good, evil is right there with me. ²²For in my inner being I delight in God's law; ²³but I see another law at work in the members of my body, waging war against the law of my mind and making me a prisoner of the law of sin at work within my members. ²⁴What a wretched man I am! Who will rescue me from this body of death? ²⁵Thanks be to God—through Jesus Christ our Lord!

So then, I myself in my mind am a slave to God's law, but in the sinful nature a slave to the law of sin.

8 *Life Through the Spirit*   Therefore, there is now no condemnation for those who are in Christ Jesus,ᵇ ²because through Christ Jesus the law of the Spirit of life set me free from the law of sin and death. ³For what the law was powerless to do in that it was weakened by the sinful nature,ᶜ God did by sending his own Son in the likeness of sinful man to be a sin offering.ᵈ And so he condemned sin in sinful man,ᵉ ⁴in order that the righteous requirements of the law might be fully met in us, who do not live according to the sinful nature but according to the Spirit.

⁵Those who live according to the sinful nature have their minds set on what that nature desires; but those who live in accordance with the Spirit have their minds set on what the Spirit desires. ⁶The mind of sinful manᶠ is death, but the mind controlled by the Spirit is life and peace; ⁷the sinful mindᵍ is hostile to God. It does not submit to God's law, nor can it do so. ⁸Those controlled by the sinful nature cannot please God.

⁹You, however, are controlled not by the sinful nature but by the Spirit, if the Spirit of God lives in you. And if anyone does not have the Spirit of Christ, he does

ᵃ18 Or *my flesh*   ᵇ1 Some later manuscripts *Jesus, who do not live according to the sinful nature but according to the Spirit,*   ᶜ3 Or *the flesh;* also in verses 4, 5, 8, 9, 12 and 13   ᵈ3 Or *man, for sin*   ᵉ3 Or *In the flesh*   ᶠ6 Or *mind set on the flesh*   ᵍ7 Or *the mind set on the flesh*

ROMANS 8:1–11

Paul is explaining in this passage that because of Jesus you're not condemned to keep on sinning. Jesus died so you would be able to live a good life—the good life that law describes but can't help anyone achieve. What's the secret? The Holy Spirit. Through the Holy Spirit Jesus himself lives in you. The Spirit's power is here right now to help you do what's right in spite of the pull that sin still has on you (see Romans 7:7–25). How do you do it? You don't. You just fix your thoughts on what the Spirit desires, choose to respond and let God's Spirit give you the strength to obey.

Direct Line

not belong to Christ. ¹⁰But if Christ is in you, your body is dead because of sin, yet your spirit is alive because of righteousness. ¹¹And if the Spirit of him who raised Jesus from the dead is living in you, he who raised Christ from the dead will also give life to your mortal bodies through his Spirit, who lives in you.

¹²Therefore, brothers, we have an obligation—but it is not to the sinful nature, to live according to it. ¹³For if you live according to the sinful nature, you will die; but if by the Spirit you put to death the misdeeds of the body, you will live, ¹⁴because those who are led by the Spirit of God are sons of God. ¹⁵For you did not receive a spirit that makes you a slave again to fear, but you received the Spirit of sonship.*ᵃ* And by him we cry, *"Abba,*ᵇ* Father."* ¹⁶The Spirit himself testifies with our spirit that we are God's children. ¹⁷Now if we are children, then we are heirs—heirs of God and co-heirs with Christ, if indeed we share in his sufferings in order that we may also share in his glory.

Future Glory   ¹⁸I consider that our present sufferings are not worth comparing with the glory that will be revealed in us. ¹⁹The creation waits in eager expectation for the sons of God to be revealed. ²⁰For the creation was subjected to frustration, not by its own choice, but by the will of the one who subjected it, in hope ²¹thatᶜ the creation itself will be liberated from its bondage to decay and brought into the glorious freedom of the children of God.

²²We know that the whole creation has been groaning as in the pains of childbirth right up to the present time. ²³Not only so, but we ourselves, who have the firstfruits of the Spirit, groan inwardly as we wait eagerly for our adoption as sons, the redemption of our bodies. ²⁴For in this hope we were saved. But hope that is seen is no hope at all. Who hopes for what he already has? ²⁵But if we hope for what we do not yet have, we wait for it patiently.

²⁶In the same way, the Spirit helps us in our weakness. We do not know what we ought to pray for, but the Spirit himself intercedes for us with groans that words cannot express. ²⁷And he who searches our hearts knows the mind of the Spirit, because the Spirit intercedes for the saints in accordance with God's will.

More Than Conquerors   ²⁸And we know that in all things God works for the good of those who love him,ᵈ whoᵉ have been called according to his purpose. ²⁹For those God foreknew he also predestined to be conformed to the likeness of his Son, that he might be the firstborn among many brothers. ³⁰And those he predestined, he also called; those he called, he also justified; those he justified, he also glorified.

³¹What, then, shall we say in response to this? If God is for us, who can be against us? ³²He who did not spare his own Son, but gave him up for us all—how will he not also, along with him, graciously give us all things? ³³Who will bring any charge against those whom God has chosen? It is God who justifies. ³⁴Who is he that condemns? Christ Jesus, who died—more than that, who was raised to life—is at the right hand of God and is also interceding for us. ³⁵Who shall separate us from the love of Christ? Shall trouble or hardship or persecution or famine or nakedness or danger or sword? ³⁶As it is written:

"For your sake we face death all day long;
　we are considered as sheep to be slaughtered."ᶠ

³⁷No, in all these things we are more than conquerors through him who loved us. ³⁸For I am convinced that neither death nor life, neither angels nor demons,ᵍ neither the present nor the future, nor any powers, ³⁹neither height

---

ᵃ15 Or *adoption* ᵇ15 Aramaic for *Father* ᶜ20,21 Or *subjected it in hope.* ²¹*For* ᵈ28 Some manuscripts *And we know that all things work together for good to those who love God* ᵉ28 Or *works together with those who love him to bring about what is good—with those who* ᶠ36 Psalm 44:22 ᵍ38 Or *nor heavenly rulers*

nor depth, nor anything else in all creation, will be able to separate us from the love of God that is in Christ Jesus our Lord.

God's Sovereign Choice I speak the truth in Christ—I am not lying, my conscience confirms it in the Holy Spirit— [2]I have great sorrow and unceasing anguish in my heart. [3]For I could wish that I myself were cursed and cut off from Christ for the sake of my brothers, those of my own race, [4]the people of Israel. Theirs is the adoption as sons; theirs the divine glory, the covenants, the receiving of the law, the temple worship and the promises. [5]Theirs are the patriarchs, and from them is traced the human ancestry of Christ, who is God over all, forever praised![a] Amen.

[6]It is not as though God's word had failed. For not all who are descended from Israel are Israel. [7]Nor because they are his descendants are they all Abraham's children. On the contrary, "It is through Isaac that your offspring will be reckoned."[b] [8]In other words, it is not the natural children who are God's children, but it is the children of the promise who are regarded as Abraham's offspring. [9]For this was how the promise was stated: "At the appointed time I will return, and Sarah will have a son."[c]

[10]Not only that, but Rebekah's children had one and the same father, our father Isaac. [11]Yet, before the twins were born or had done anything good or bad—in order that God's purpose in election might stand: [12]not by works but by him who calls—she was told, "The older will serve the younger."[d] [13]Just as it is written: "Jacob I loved, but Esau I hated."[e]

[14]What then shall we say? Is God unjust? Not at all! [15]For he says to Moses,

> "I will have mercy on whom I have mercy,
> and I will have compassion on whom I have compassion."[f]

[16]It does not, therefore, depend on man's desire or effort, but on God's mercy. [17]For the Scripture says to Pharaoh: "I raised you up for this very purpose, that I might display my power in you and that my name might be proclaimed in all the earth."[g] [18]Therefore God has mercy on whom he wants to have mercy, and he hardens whom he wants to harden.

---

[a]5 Or *Christ, who is over all. God be forever praised!* Or *Christ. God who is over all be forever praised!* [b]7 Gen. 21:12 [c]9 Gen. 18:10,14 [d]12 Gen. 25:23 [e]13 Mal. 1:2,3 [f]15 Exodus 33:19 [g]17 Exodus 9:16

Did you ever think that if you did something good, God would *have* to reward you? Like, if you gave all your money to starving children, God would have to make sure you got that new outfit? In Romans 9 Paul shows from Bible history that people can't "make" God do anything. God is free to choose.

✸ God chose Isaac, not Ishmael (Romans 9:7–9).
✸ God chose Jacob rather than Esau (Romans 9:10–13).
✸ God let Pharaoh follow his own heart (Romans 9:14–18).

The Bible Says

God Chooses

Paul isn't saying that God chooses to send some people to hell. He is saying that God doesn't "depend on man's desire or effort" (Romans 9:16). He depends on his own free choice to have mercy. No one deserves any reward from God. Everyone deserves to be punished. It's a good thing that God is free to choose—because God chooses to have mercy.

¹⁹One of you will say to me: "Then why does God still blame us? For who resists his will?" ²⁰But who are you, O man, to talk back to God? "Shall what is formed say to him who formed it, 'Why did you make me like this?' "ᵃ ²¹Does not the potter have the right to make out of the same lump of clay some pottery for noble purposes and some for common use?

²²What if God, choosing to show his wrath and make his power known, bore with great patience the objects of his wrath—prepared for destruction? ²³What if he did this to make the riches of his glory known to the objects of his mercy, whom he prepared in advance for glory— ²⁴even us, whom he also called, not only from the Jews but also from the Gentiles? ²⁵As he says in Hosea:

> "I will call them 'my people' who are not my people;
>> and I will call her 'my loved one' who is not my loved one,"ᵇ

²⁶and,

> "It will happen that in the very place where it was said to them,
>> 'You are not my people,'
> they will be called 'sons of the living God.' "ᶜ

²⁷Isaiah cries out concerning Israel:

> "Though the number of the Israelites be like the sand by the sea,
>> only the remnant will be saved.
> ²⁸For the Lord will carry out
>> his sentence on earth with speed and finality."ᵈ

²⁹It is just as Isaiah said previously:

> "Unless the Lord Almighty
>> had left us descendants,
> we would have become like Sodom,
>> we would have been like Gomorrah."ᵉ

Israel's Unbelief ³⁰What then shall we say? That the Gentiles, who did not pursue righteousness, have obtained it, a righteousness that is by faith; ³¹but Israel, who pursued a law of righteousness, has not attained it. ³²Why not? Because they pursued it not by faith but as if it were by works. They stumbled over the "stumbling stone." ³³As it is written:

> "See, I lay in Zion a stone that causes men to stumble
>> and a rock that makes them fall,
> and the one who trusts in him will never be put to
>> shame."ᶠ

10 Brothers, my heart's desire and prayer to God for the Israelites is that they may be saved. ²For I can testify about them that they are zealous for God, but their zeal is not based on knowledge. ³Since they did not know the righteousness that comes from God and sought to establish their own, they did not submit to God's righteousness. ⁴Christ is the end of the law so that there may be righteousness for everyone who believes.

⁵Moses describes in this way the righteousness that is by the law: "The man who does these things will live by them."ᵍ ⁶But the righteousness that is by faith says: "Do not say in your heart, 'Who will ascend into heaven?'ʰ" (that is, to bring Christ down) ⁷"or 'Who will descend into the deep?'ⁱ" (that is, to bring Christ up from the dead). ⁸But what does it say? "The word is near you; it is in your mouth and in your heart,"ʲ that is, the word of faith we are

---

ᵃ*20* Isaiah 29:16; 45:9 ᵇ*25* Hosea 2:23 ᶜ*26* Hosea 1:10 ᵈ*28* Isaiah 10:22,23 ᵉ*29* Isaiah 1:9 ᶠ*33* Isaiah 8:14; 28:16 ᵍ*5* Lev. 18:5 ʰ*6* Deut. 30:12 ⁱ*7* Deut. 30:13 ʲ*8* Deut. 30:14

proclaiming: ⁹That if you confess with your mouth, "Jesus is Lord," and believe in your heart that God raised him from the dead, you will be saved. ¹⁰For it is with your heart that you believe and are justified, and it is with your mouth that you confess and are saved. ¹¹As the Scripture says, "Anyone who trusts in him will never be put to shame."ᵃ ¹²For there is no difference between Jew and Gentile—the same Lord is Lord of all and richly blesses all who call on him, ¹³for, "Everyone who calls on the name of the Lord will be saved."ᵇ

¹⁴How, then, can they call on the one they have not believed in? And how can they believe in the one of whom they have not heard? And how can they hear without someone preaching to them? ¹⁵And how can they preach unless they are sent? As it is written, "How beautiful are the feet of those who bring good news!"ᶜ

¹⁶But not all the Israelites accepted the good news. For Isaiah says, "Lord, who has believed our message?"ᵈ ¹⁷Consequently, faith comes from hearing the message, and the message is heard through the word of Christ. ¹⁸But I ask: Did they not hear? Of course they did:

> "Their voice has gone out into all the earth,
>   their words to the ends of the world."ᵉ

¹⁹Again I ask: Did Israel not understand? First, Moses says,

> "I will make you envious by those who are not a
>   nation;
> I will make you angry by a nation that has no
>   understanding."ᶠ

²⁰And Isaiah boldly says,

> "I was found by those who did not seek me;
>   I revealed myself to those who did not ask for me."ᵍ

²¹But concerning Israel he says,

> "All day long I have held out
>   my hands
>   to a disobedient and
>   obstinate people."ʰ

The Remnant of Israel I ask then: Did God reject his people? By no means! I am an Israelite myself, a descendant of Abraham, from the tribe of Benjamin. ²God did not reject his people, whom he foreknew. Don't you know what the Scripture says in the passage about Elijah—how he appealed to God against Israel: ³"Lord, they have killed your prophets and torn down your altars; I am the only one left, and they are trying to kill me"ⁱ? ⁴And what was God's answer to him? "I have reserved for myself seven thousand who have not bowed the knee to Baal."ʲ ⁵So too, at the present time there is a

ᵃ11 Isaiah 28:16   ᵇ13 Joel 2:32   ᶜ15 Isaiah 52:7   ᵈ16 Isaiah 53:1   ᵉ18 Psalm 19:4   ᶠ19 Deut. 32:21   ᵍ20 Isaiah 65:1   ʰ21 Isaiah 65:2   ⁱ3 1 Kings 19:10,14   ʲ4 1 Kings 19:18

ROMANS 10:12–15

The best-looking feet don't belong to a famous model or a basketball superstar. The really beautiful feet belong to people who bring others the Good News. These verses raise questions every Christian needs to ask. How can unbelievers call on Jesus if they don't believe? And how can they believe if they've never heard of him? And how can they hear if no one tells them? When some people use "Jesus" as a swear word, it doesn't mean they know about him. In fact, it shows they don't know enough! They can't believe until they hear. And they can't hear unless someone (you?) tells them. Check out your feet. Beautiful? You bet!

Direct Line

remnant chosen by grace. [6]And if by grace, then it is no longer by works; if it were, grace would no longer be grace.[a]

[7]What then? What Israel sought so earnestly it did not obtain, but the elect did. The others were hardened, [8]as it is written:

> "God gave them a spirit of stupor,
>   eyes so that they could not see
>   and ears so that they could not hear,
> to this very day."[b]

[9]And David says:

> "May their table become a snare and a trap,
>   a stumbling block and a retribution for them.
> [10]May their eyes be darkened so they cannot see,
>   and their backs be bent forever."[c]

Ingrafted Branches [11]Again I ask: Did they stumble so as to fall beyond recovery? Not at all! Rather, because of their transgression, salvation has come to the Gentiles to make Israel envious. [12]But if their transgression means riches for the world, and their loss means riches for the Gentiles, how much greater riches will their fullness bring!

[13]I am talking to you Gentiles. Inasmuch as I am the apostle to the Gentiles, I make much of my ministry [14]in the hope that I may somehow arouse my own people to envy and save some of them. [15]For if their rejection is the reconciliation of the world, what will their acceptance be but life from the dead? [16]If the part of the dough offered as firstfruits is holy, then the whole batch is holy; if the root is holy, so are the branches.

[17]If some of the branches have been broken off, and you, though a wild olive shoot, have been grafted in among the others and now share in the nourishing sap from the olive root, [18]do not boast over those branches. If you do, consider this: You do not support the root, but the root supports you. [19]You will say then, "Branches were broken off so that I could be grafted in." [20]Granted. But they were broken off because of unbelief, and you stand by faith. Do not be arrogant, but be afraid. [21]For if God did not spare the natural branches, he will not spare you either.

[22]Consider therefore the kindness and sternness of God: sternness to those who fell, but kindness to you, provided that you continue in his kindness. Otherwise, you also will be cut off. [23]And if they do not persist in unbelief, they will be grafted in, for God is able to graft them in again. [24]After all, if you were cut out of an olive tree that is wild by nature, and contrary to nature were grafted into a cultivated olive tree, how much more readily will these, the natural branches, be grafted into their own olive tree!

All Israel Will Be Saved [25]I do not want you to be ignorant of this mystery, brothers, so that you may not be conceited: Israel has experienced a hardening in part until the full number of the Gentiles has come in. [26]And so all Israel will be saved, as it is written:

> "The deliverer will come from Zion;
>   he will turn godlessness away from Jacob.
> [27]And this is[d] my covenant with them
>   when I take away their sins."[e]

[28]As far as the gospel is concerned, they are enemies on your account; but as far as election is concerned, they are loved on account of the patriarchs, [29]for God's gifts and his call are irrevocable. [30]Just as you who were at one time disobedient to God have now received mercy as a result of their disobe-

---

[a]6 Some manuscripts *by grace. But if by works, then it is no longer grace; if it were, work would no longer be work.* [b]8 Deut. 29:4; Isaiah 29:10 [c]10 Psalm 69:22,23 [d]27 Or *will be* [e]27 Isaiah 59:20,21; 27:9; Jer. 31:33,34

dience, ³¹so they too have now become disobedient in order that they too may now*a* receive mercy as a result of God's mercy to you. ³²For God has bound all men over to disobedience so that he may have mercy on them all.

Doxology

³³Oh, the depth of the riches of the wisdom and*b* knowledge
of God!
How unsearchable his judgments,
and his paths beyond tracing out!
³⁴"Who has known the mind of the Lord?
Or who has been his counselor?"*c*
³⁵"Who has ever given to God,
that God should repay him?"*d*
³⁶For from him and through him and to him are all things.
To him be the glory forever! Amen.

12 *Living Sacrifices* Therefore, I urge you, brothers, in view of God's mercy, to offer your bodies as living sacrifices, holy and pleasing to God—this is your spiritual*e* act of worship. ²Do not conform any longer to the pattern of this world, but be transformed by the renewing of your mind. Then you will be able to test and approve what God's will is—his good, pleasing and perfect will.

³For by the grace given me I say to every one of you: Do not think of yourself more highly than you ought, but rather think of yourself with sober judgment, in accordance with the measure of faith God has given you. ⁴Just as each of us has one body with many members, and these members do not all have the same function, ⁵so in Christ we who are many form one body, and each member belongs to all the others. ⁶We have different gifts, according-

ing to the grace given us. If a man's gift is prophesying, let him use it in proportion to his*f* faith. ⁷If it is serving, let him serve; if it is teaching, let him teach; ⁸if it is encouraging, let him encourage; if it is contributing to the needs of others, let him give generously; if it is leadership, let him govern diligently; if it is showing mercy, let him do it cheerfully.

Love ⁹Love must be sincere. Hate what is evil; cling to what is good. ¹⁰Be devoted to one another in brotherly love. Honor one another above yourselves. ¹¹Never be lacking in zeal, but keep your spiritual fervor, serving the Lord. ¹²Be joyful in hope, patient in affliction, faithful in prayer. ¹³Share with God's people who are in need. Practice hospitality.

¹⁴Bless those who persecute you; bless and do not curse. ¹⁵Rejoice with those who rejoice; mourn with those who mourn. ¹⁶Live in harmony with one another. Do not be proud, but be willing to associate with people of low position.*g* Do not be conceited.

SEE ROMANS 12:13

a31 Some manuscripts do not have *now.* *b33* Or *riches and the wisdom and the* *c34* Isaiah 40:13 *d35* Job 41:11 *e1* Or *reasonable* *f6* Or *in agreement with the* *g16* Or *willing to do menial work*

Dear Sam,

There are so many things I want to do that my parents and my youth pastor don't think Christians should do. I want to do what's right, but I also want to have fun. Help!

Shawna in Selma

Dear Sam, Inc

100 Advice Lane, Anywhere, USA

Dear Shawna,

Hey! What you're feeling is natural. You want to strike out on your own, make your own choices, have fun in life. That's natural. But what is also natural is our human nature's desire to sin. Now I'm not saying that everything you want to do is sinful. But some of it may be dangerous or just plain not good for you.

Take a look at Romans 12:2. God wants you to be "transformed by the renewing of your mind." That's allowing God to work in you and make you the best you can be. He also doesn't want you to conform "to the pattern of this world." That means different things to different Christians. But I think the key here is that it is better to stay as far away as possible from the "fires" of the world, rather than to see how close you can walk to them without getting burned.

Talk things over very frankly with your parents. You must obey them, but perhaps you can negotiate about some of the activities you think you would enjoy.

Sam

[17]Do not repay anyone evil for evil. Be careful to do what is right in the eyes of everybody. [18]If it is possible, as far as it depends on you, live at peace with everyone. [19]Do not take revenge, my friends, but leave room for God's wrath, for it is written: "It is mine to avenge; I will repay,"[a] says the Lord. [20]On the contrary:

> "If your enemy is hungry, feed him;
>   if he is thirsty, give him something to drink.
> In doing this, you will heap burning coals on his head."[b]

[21]Do not be overcome by evil, but overcome evil with good.

Submission to the Authorities Everyone must submit himself to the governing authorities, for there is no authority except that which God has established. The authorities that exist have been established by God. [2]Consequently, he who rebels against the authority is rebelling against what God has instituted, and those who do so will bring judgment on themselves. [3]For rulers hold no terror for those who do right, but for those who do wrong. Do you want to be free from fear of the one in authority? Then do what is right and he will commend you. [4]For he is God's servant to do you good. But if you do wrong, be afraid, for he does not bear the sword for nothing. He is God's servant, an agent of wrath to bring punishment on the wrongdoer. [5]Therefore, it is necessary to submit to the authorities, not only because of possible punishment but also because of conscience.

[6]This is also why you pay taxes, for the authorities are God's servants, who give their full time to governing. [7]Give everyone what you owe him: If you owe taxes, pay taxes; if revenue, then revenue; if respect, then respect; if honor, then honor.

Love, for the Day Is Near [8]Let no debt remain outstanding, except the continuing debt to love one another, for he who loves his fellowman has fulfilled the law. [9]The commandments, "Do not commit adultery," "Do not murder," "Do not steal," "Do not covet,"[c] and whatever other commandment there may be, are summed up in this one rule: "Love your neighbor as yourself."[d] [10]Love does no harm to its neighbor. Therefore love is the fulfillment of the law.

[11]And do this, understanding the present time. The hour has come for you to wake up from your slumber, because our salvation is nearer now than when we first believed. [12]The night is nearly over; the day is almost here. So let us put aside the deeds of darkness and put on the armor of light. [13]Let us behave decently, as in the daytime, not in orgies and drunkenness, not in sexual immorality and debauchery, not in dissension and jealousy. [14]Rather, clothe yourselves with the Lord Jesus Christ, and do not think about how to gratify the desires of the sinful nature.[e]

The Weak and the Strong Accept him whose faith is weak, without passing judgment on disputable matters. [2]One man's faith allows him to eat everything, but another man, whose faith is weak, eats only vegetables. [3]The man who eats everything must not look down on him who does not, and the man who does not eat everything must not condemn the man who does, for God has accepted him. [4]Who are you to judge someone else's servant? To his own master he stands or falls. And he will stand, for the Lord is able to make him stand.

[5]One man considers one day more sacred than another; another man con-

---

[a]19 Deut. 32:35   [b]20 Prov. 25:21,22   [c]9 Exodus 20:13-15,17; Deut. 5:17-19,21   [d]9 Lev. 19:18   [e]14 Or the flesh

siders every day alike. Each one should be fully convinced in his own mind. [6]He who regards one day as special, does so to the Lord. He who eats meat, eats to the Lord, for he gives thanks to God; and he who abstains, does so to the Lord and gives thanks to God. [7]For none of us lives to himself alone and none of us dies to himself alone. [8]If we live, we live to the Lord; and if we die, we die to the Lord. So, whether we live or die, we belong to the Lord.

[9]For this very reason, Christ died and returned to life so that he might be the Lord of both the dead and the living. [10]You, then, why do you judge your brother? Or why do you look down on your brother? For we will all stand before God's judgment seat. [11]It is written:

> " 'As surely as I live,' says the Lord,
> 'every knee will bow before me;
> every tongue will confess to God.' "[a]

[12]So then, each of us will give an account of himself to God.

[13]Therefore let us stop passing judgment on one another. Instead, make up your mind not to put any stumbling block or obstacle in your brother's way. [14]As one who is in the Lord Jesus, I am fully convinced that no food[b] is unclean in itself. But if anyone regards something as unclean, then for him it is unclean. [15]If your brother is distressed because of what you eat, you are no longer acting in love. Do not by your eating destroy your brother for whom Christ died. [16]Do not allow what you consider good to be spoken of as evil. [17]For the kingdom of God is not a matter of eating and drinking, but of righteousness, peace and joy in the Holy Spirit, [18]because anyone who serves Christ in this way is pleasing to God and approved by men.

[19]Let us therefore make every effort to do what leads to peace and to mutual edification. [20]Do not destroy the work of God for the sake of food. All food is clean, but it is wrong for a man to eat anything that causes someone else to stumble. [21]It is better not to eat meat or drink wine or to do anything else that will cause your brother to fall.

[22]So whatever you believe about these things keep between yourself and God. Blessed is the man who does not condemn himself by what he approves. [23]But the man who has doubts is condemned if he eats, because his eating is not from faith; and everything that does not come from faith is sin.

15 We who are strong ought to bear with the failings of the weak and not to please ourselves. [2]Each of us should please his neighbor for his good, to build him up. [3]For even Christ did not please himself but, as it is written: "The insults of those who insult you have fallen on me."[c] [4]For everything that was written in the past was written to teach us, so that through endurance and the encouragement of the Scriptures we might have hope.

[5]May the God who gives endurance and encouragement give you a spirit of unity among yourselves as you follow Christ Jesus, [6]so that with one heart and mouth you may glorify the God and Father of our Lord Jesus Christ.

[7]Accept one another, then, just as Christ accepted you, in order to bring praise to God. [8]For I tell you that Christ has become a servant of the Jews[d] on behalf of God's truth, to confirm the promises made to the patriarchs [9]so that the Gentiles may glorify God for his mercy, as it is written:

> "Therefore I will praise you among the Gentiles;
> I will sing hymns to your name."[e]

Accept one another, then, just as Christ accepted you, in order to bring praise to God (Romans 15:7).

---

[a]11 Isaiah 45:23   [b]14 Or *that nothing*   [c]3 Psalm 69:9   [d]8 Greek *circumcision*   [e]9 2 Samuel 22:50; Psalm 18:49

[10]Again, it says,

> "Rejoice, O Gentiles, with his people."[a]

[11]And again,

> "Praise the Lord, all you Gentiles,
>   and sing praises to him, all you peoples."[b]

[12]And again, Isaiah says,

> "The Root of Jesse will spring up,
>   one who will arise to rule over the nations;
> the Gentiles will hope in him."[c]

[13]May the God of hope fill you with all joy and peace as you trust in him, so that you may overflow with hope by the power of the Holy Spirit.

Paul the Minister to the Gentiles   [14]I myself am convinced, my brothers, that you yourselves are full of goodness, complete in knowledge and competent to instruct one another. [15]I have written you quite boldly on some points, as if to remind you of them again, because of the grace God gave me [16]to be a minister of Christ Jesus to the Gentiles with the priestly duty of proclaiming the gospel of God, so that the Gentiles might become an offering acceptable to God, sanctified by the Holy Spirit.

[17]Therefore I glory in Christ Jesus in my service to God. [18]I will not venture to speak of anything except what Christ has accomplished through me in leading the Gentiles to obey God by what I have said and done— [19]by the power of signs and miracles, through the power of the Spirit. So from Jerusalem all the way around to Illyricum, I have fully proclaimed the gospel of Christ. [20]It has always been my ambition to preach the gospel where Christ was not known, so that I would not be building on someone else's foundation. [21]Rather, as it is written:

> "Those who were not told about him will see,
>   and those who have not heard will understand."[d]

[22]This is why I have often been hindered from coming to you.

Paul's Plan to Visit Rome   [23]But now that there is no more place for me to work in these regions, and since I have been longing for many years to see you, [24]I plan to do so when I go to Spain. I hope to visit you while passing through and to have you assist me on my journey there, after I have enjoyed your company for a while. [25]Now, however, I am on my way to Jerusalem in the service of the saints there. [26]For Macedonia and Achaia were pleased to make a contribution for the poor among the saints in Jerusalem. [27]They were pleased to do it, and indeed they owe it to them. For if the Gentiles have shared in the Jews' spiritual blessings, they owe it to the Jews to share with them their material blessings. [28]So after I have completed this task and have made sure that they have received this fruit, I will go to Spain and visit you on the way. [29]I know that when I come to you, I will come in the full measure of the blessing of Christ.

[30]I urge you, brothers, by our Lord Jesus Christ and by the love of the Spirit, to join me in my struggle by praying to God for me. [31]Pray that I may be rescued from the unbelievers in Judea and that my service in Jerusalem may be acceptable to the saints there, [32]so that by God's will I may come to you with joy and together with you be refreshed. [33]The God of peace be with you all. Amen.

---

a10 Deut. 32:43   *b11* Psalm 117:1   *c12* Isaiah 11:10   *d21* Isaiah 52:15

16 *Personal Greetings* I commend to you our sister Phoebe, a servant*a* of the church in Cenchrea. ²I ask you to receive her in the Lord in a way worthy of the saints and to give her any help she may need from you, for she has been a great help to many people, including me.

³Greet Priscilla*b* and Aquila, my fellow workers in Christ Jesus. ⁴They risked their lives for me. Not only I but all the churches of the Gentiles are grateful to them.

⁵Greet also the church that meets at their house.

Greet my dear friend Epenetus, who was the first convert to Christ in the province of Asia.

⁶Greet Mary, who worked very hard for you.

⁷Greet Andronicus and Junias, my relatives who have been in prison with me. They are outstanding among the apostles, and they were in Christ before I was.

⁸Greet Ampliatus, whom I love in the Lord.

⁹Greet Urbanus, our fellow worker in Christ, and my dear friend Stachys.

¹⁰Greet Apelles, tested and approved in Christ.

Greet those who belong to the household of Aristobulus.

¹¹Greet Herodion, my relative.

Greet those in the household of Narcissus who are in the Lord.

¹²Greet Tryphena and Tryphosa, those women who work hard in the Lord.

Greet my dear friend Persis, another woman who has worked very hard in the Lord.

¹³Greet Rufus, chosen in the Lord, and his mother, who has been a mother to me, too.

¹⁴Greet Asyncritus, Phlegon, Hermes, Patrobas, Hermas and the brothers with them.

¹⁵Greet Philologus, Julia, Nereus and his sister, and Olympas and all the saints with them.

¹⁶Greet one another with a holy kiss.

All the churches of Christ send greetings.

ROMANS 16:1-18

In Rome all sorts of people belonged to the church. Romans 16 points up some of the variety. Some names here are Roman and some are Greek. Women are mentioned often and are praised as dedicated Christian workers. The mention of Aristobulus's "household" (Romans 16:10) is a reminder that some early Christians were rich while others were slaves. But they all knew Jesus and that made them members of God's family. The differences didn't count. They don't count at your church or youth group either. Since every Christian belongs to God's family, make sure all believers are welcome in your group.

Direct Line

¹⁷I urge you, brothers, to watch out for those who cause divisions and put obstacles in your way that are contrary to the teaching you have learned. Keep away from them. ¹⁸For such people are not serving our Lord Christ, but their own appetites. By smooth talk and flattery they deceive the minds of naive people. ¹⁹Everyone has heard about your obedience, so I am full of joy over you; but I want you to be wise about what is good, and innocent about what is evil.

²⁰The God of peace will soon crush Satan under your feet.

The grace of our Lord Jesus be with you.

²¹Timothy, my fellow worker, sends his greetings to you, as do Lucius, Jason and Sosipater, my relatives.

²²I, Tertius, who wrote down this letter, greet you in the Lord.

²³Gaius, whose hospitality I and the whole church here enjoy, sends you his greetings.

*a1 Or deaconess *b3 Greek *Prisca*, a variant of *Priscilla*

Erastus, who is the city's director of public works, and our brother Quartus send you their greetings.*

²⁵Now to him who is able to establish you by my gospel and the proclamation of Jesus Christ, according to the revelation of the mystery hidden for long ages past, ²⁶but now revealed and made known through the prophetic writings by the command of the eternal God, so that all nations might believe and obey him— ²⁷to the only wise God be glory forever through Jesus Christ! Amen.

---

*23 Some manuscripts *their greetings.* ²⁴*May the grace of our Lord Jesus Christ be with all of you. Amen.*

Introduction

to the

book of 1 Corinthians

PROBLEMS.

Who helps you with your problems? Good friends with whom you talk things over. A mom and dad who listen and give good advice. A youth leader at church. Everyone needs help sometimes to think through difficult issues.

When the church at Corinth had problems, Paul helped. What if little groups of close friends won't let outsiders in? What do you do about a Christian friend who's living an immoral life? How come some people have such strict convictions? Paul answers these and many other practical questions in this practical New Testament book.

Fundamentals

One of your friends is having sex. What should you do (1 Corinthians 5)?

Your mom isn't a Christian. Should your dad divorce her (1 Corinthians 7)?

Do you ever wonder if you're worth anything at all (1 Corinthians 12:7)?

FAST FACTS

The apostle Paul wrote 1 Corinthians about A.D. 55.

Paul had planted the church in Corinth several years earlier.

Corinth was a wealthy seaport in Paul's time.

First Corinthians 11 and 14 cover the role of women in the church.

First Corinthians 13 tells what real love is like.

1 Paul, called to be an apostle of Christ Jesus by the will of God, and our brother Sosthenes,

²To the church of God in Corinth, to those sanctified in Christ Jesus and called to be holy, together with all those everywhere who call on the name of our Lord Jesus Christ—their Lord and ours:

³Grace and peace to you from God our Father and the Lord Jesus Christ.

Thanksgiving ⁴I always thank God for you because of his grace given you in Christ Jesus. ⁵For in him you have been enriched in every way—in all your speaking and in all your knowledge— ⁶because our testimony about Christ was confirmed in you. ⁷Therefore you do not lack any spiritual gift as you eagerly wait for our Lord Jesus Christ to be revealed. ⁸He will keep you strong to the end, so that you will be blameless on the day of our Lord Jesus Christ. ⁹God, who has called you into fellowship with his Son Jesus Christ our Lord, is faithful.

Divisions in the Church ¹⁰I appeal to you, brothers, in the name of our Lord Jesus Christ, that all of you agree with one another so that there may be no divisions among you and that you may be perfectly united in mind and thought. ¹¹My brothers, some from Chloe's household have informed me that there are quarrels among you. ¹²What I mean is this: One of you says, "I follow Paul"; another, "I follow Apollos"; another, "I follow Cephas*ᵃ*"; still another, "I follow Christ."

¹³Is Christ divided? Was Paul crucified for you? Were you baptized into*ᵇ* the name of Paul? ¹⁴I am thankful that I did not baptize any of you except Crispus and Gaius, ¹⁵so no one can say that you were baptized into my name. ¹⁶(Yes, I also baptized the household of Stephanas; beyond that, I don't remember if I baptized anyone else.) ¹⁷For Christ did not send me to baptize, but to preach the gospel—not with words of human wisdom, lest the cross of Christ be emptied of its power.

Christ the Wisdom and Power of God ¹⁸For the message of the cross is foolishness to those who are perishing, but to us who are being saved it is the power of God. ¹⁹For it is written:

"I will destroy the wisdom of the wise;
    the intelligence of the intelligent I will frustrate."*ᶜ*

²⁰Where is the wise man? Where is the scholar? Where is the philosopher of this age? Has not God made foolish the wisdom of the world? ²¹For since in the wisdom of God the world through its wisdom did not know him, God was pleased through the foolishness of what was preached to save those who believe. ²²Jews demand miraculous signs and Greeks look for wisdom, ²³but we preach Christ crucified: a stumbling block to Jews and foolishness to Gentiles, ²⁴but to those whom God has called, both Jews and Greeks, Christ the power of God and the wisdom of God. ²⁵For the foolishness of God is wiser than man's wisdom, and the weakness of God is stronger than man's strength.

²⁶Brothers, think of what you were when you were called. Not many of you were wise by human standards; not many were influential; not many were of noble birth. ²⁷But God chose the foolish things of the world to shame the wise; God chose the weak things of the world to shame the strong. ²⁸He chose the lowly things of this world and the despised things—and the things that are not—to nullify the things that are, ²⁹so that no one may boast before him. ³⁰It is because of him that you are in Christ Jesus, who has become for us wisdom from God—that is, our righteousness, holiness and redemption. ³¹Therefore, as it is written: "Let him who boasts boast in the Lord."*ᵈ*

ᵃ12 That is, Peter *ᵇ13* Or *in;* also in verse 15 *ᶜ19* Isaiah 29:14 *ᵈ31* Jer. 9:24

When I came to you, brothers, I did not come with eloquence or superior wisdom as I proclaimed to you the testimony about God.[a] [2]For I resolved to know nothing while I was with you except Jesus Christ and him crucified. [3]I came to you in weakness and fear, and with much trembling. [4]My message and my preaching were not with wise and persuasive words, but with a demonstration of the Spirit's power, [5]so that your faith might not rest on men's wisdom, but on God's power.

Wisdom From the Spirit [6]We do, however, speak a message of wisdom among the mature, but not the wisdom of this age or of the rulers of this age, who are coming to nothing. [7]No, we speak of God's secret wisdom, a wisdom that has been hidden and that God destined for our glory before time began. [8]None of the rulers of this age understood it, for if they had, they would not have crucified the Lord of glory. [9]However, as it is written:

> "No eye has seen,
>   no ear has heard,
> no mind has conceived
>   what God has prepared for those who love him"[b]—

[10]but God has revealed it to us by his Spirit.

The Spirit searches all things, even the deep things of God. [11]For who among men knows the thoughts of a man except the man's spirit within him? In the same way no one knows the thoughts of God except the Spirit of God. [12]We have not received the spirit of the world but the Spirit who is from God, that we may understand what God has freely given us. [13]This is what we speak, not in words taught us by human wisdom but in words taught by the Spirit, expressing spiritual truths in spiritual words.[c] [14]The man without the Spirit does not accept the things that come from the Spirit of God, for they are foolishness to him, and he cannot understand them, because they are spiritually discerned. [15]The spiritual man makes judgments about all things, but he himself is not subject to any man's judgment:

[16]"For who has known the mind of
    the Lord
  that he may instruct him?"[d]

But we have the mind of Christ.

On Divisions in the Church Brothers, I could not address you as spiritual but as worldly—mere infants in Christ. [2]I gave you milk, not solid food, for you were not yet ready for it. Indeed, you are still not ready. [3]You are still worldly. For since there is jealousy and quarreling among you, are you not worldly? Are you not acting like mere men? [4]For when one says, "I follow Paul," and another, "I follow Apollos," are you not mere men?

[5]What, after all, is Apollos? And what is Paul? Only servants, through whom you came to believe—as the Lord has assigned to each his task. [6]I planted the seed, Apollos watered it, but God made it grow. [7]So neither he who plants nor he who waters

---

Direct Line

1 CORINTHIANS 2:2–5

You want to speak up when your biology teacher jokes about the creation theory. Or when the class brain says he can prove God doesn't exist. But you don't know enough biology to argue. And you're not half as smart as the class brain. So what do you do? You might do what the apostle Paul did. Paul was an educated man. But instead of relying on his superior knowledge, Paul "resolved to know nothing while I was with you except Jesus Christ and him crucified." Witnessing isn't trying to persuade others. It's telling them about Jesus and counting on the Holy Spirit's power to bring the message home.

---

[a]1 Some manuscripts *as I proclaimed to you God's mystery* [b]9 Isaiah 64:4 [c]13 Or *Spirit, interpreting spiritual truths to spiritual men* [d]16 Isaiah 40:13

is anything, but only God, who makes things grow. [8]The man who plants and the man who waters have one purpose, and each will be rewarded according to his own labor. [9]For we are God's fellow workers; you are God's field, God's building.

[10]By the grace God has given me, I laid a foundation as an expert builder, and someone else is building on it. But each one should be careful how he builds. [11]For no one can lay any foundation other than the one already laid, which is Jesus Christ. [12]If any man builds on this foundation using gold, silver, costly stones, wood, hay or straw, [13]his work will be shown for what it is, because the Day will bring it to light. It will be revealed with fire, and the fire will test the quality of each man's work. [14]If what he has built survives, he will receive his reward. [15]If it is burned up, he will suffer loss; he himself will be saved, but only as one escaping through the flames.

[16]Don't you know that you yourselves are God's temple and that God's Spirit lives in you? [17]If anyone destroys God's temple, God will destroy him; for God's temple is sacred, and you are that temple.

[18]Do not deceive yourselves. If any one of you thinks he is wise by the standards of this age, he should become a "fool" so that he may become wise. [19]For the wisdom of this world is foolishness in God's sight. As it is written: "He catches the wise in their craftiness"[a]; [20]and again, "The Lord knows that the thoughts of the wise are futile."[b] [21]So then, no more boasting about men! All things are yours, [22]whether Paul or Apollos or Cephas[c] or the world or life or death or the present or the future—all are yours, [23]and you are of Christ, and Christ is of God.

Apostles of Christ So then, men ought to regard us as servants of Christ and as those entrusted with the secret things of God. [2]Now it is required that those who have been given a trust must prove faithful. [3]I care very little if I am judged by you or by any human court; indeed, I do not even judge myself. [4]My conscience is clear, but that does not make me innocent. It is the Lord who judges me. [5]Therefore judge nothing before the appointed time; wait till the Lord comes. He will bring to light what is hidden in darkness and will expose the motives of men's hearts. At that time each will receive his praise from God.

[6]Now, brothers, I have applied these things to myself and Apollos for your benefit, so that you may learn from us the meaning of the saying, "Do not go beyond what is written." Then you will not take pride in one man over against another. [7]For who makes you different from anyone else? What do you have that you did not receive? And if you did receive it, why do you boast as though you did not?

[8]Already you have all you want! Already you have become rich! You have become kings—and that without us! How I wish that you really had become kings so that we might be kings with you! [9]For it seems to me that God has put us apostles on display at the end of the procession, like men condemned to die in the arena. We have been made a spectacle to the whole universe, to angels as well as to men. [10]We

[a]19 Job 5:13 [b]20 Psalm 94:11 [c]22 That is, Peter

---

1 CORINTHIANS 3:10–15

Do you ever feel like you just can't do anything totally right? You get four A's and Dad zeroes in on the one B. You clean the basement, and Mom finds two cobwebs you missed. These verses in 1 Corinthians may sound like God is going to do the same thing: examine the bad you've done and ignore the good. But take a look at verse 14. It speaks of reward. God won't ignore the A's or the parts of the basement you did clean. It can be tough not to be appreciated when you try so hard. But remember: God appreciates what you do and who you are. From him you'll get praise and a reward.

Direct Line

are fools for Christ, but you are so wise in Christ! We are weak, but you are strong! You are honored, we are dishonored! ¹¹To this very hour we go hungry and thirsty, we are in rags, we are brutally treated, we are homeless. ¹²We work hard with our own hands. When we are cursed, we bless; when we are persecuted, we endure it; ¹³when we are slandered, we answer kindly. Up to this moment we have become the scum of the earth, the refuse of the world.

¹⁴I am not writing this to shame you, but to warn you, as my dear children. ¹⁵Even though you have ten thousand guardians in Christ, you do not have many fathers, for in Christ Jesus I became your father through the gospel. ¹⁶Therefore I urge you to imitate me. ¹⁷For this reason I am sending to you Timothy, my son whom I love, who is faithful in the Lord. He will remind you of my way of life in Christ Jesus, which agrees with what I teach everywhere in every church.

¹⁸Some of you have become arrogant, as if I were not coming to you. ¹⁹But I will come to you very soon, if the Lord is willing, and then I will find out not only how these arrogant people are talking, but what power they have. ²⁰For the kingdom of God is not a matter of talk but of power. ²¹What do you prefer? Shall I come to you with a whip, or in love and with a gentle spirit?

5 *Expel the Immoral Brother!* It is actually reported that there is sexual immorality among you, and of a kind that does not occur even among pagans: A man has his father's wife. ²And you are proud! Shouldn't you rather have been filled with grief and have put out of your fellowship the man who did this? ³Even though I am not physically present, I am with you in spirit. And I have already passed judgment on the one who did this, just as if I were present. ⁴When you are assembled in the name of our Lord Jesus and I am with you in spirit, and the power of our Lord Jesus is present, ⁵hand this man over to Satan, so that the sinful nature*a* may be destroyed and his spirit saved on the day of the Lord.

⁶Your boasting is not good. Don't you know that a little yeast works through the whole batch of dough? ⁷Get rid of the old yeast that you may be a new batch without yeast—as you really are. For Christ, our Passover lamb,

a5 Or that his body; or *that the flesh*

The Bible Says

Don't Judge

Sometimes it's confusing. Paul tells you not to judge (Romans 14:1); he says he doesn't "even judge" himself (1 Corinthians 4:3). And then he says he has "already passed judgment" and tells the church to expel a sinning believer (1 Corinthians 5:3–5)! Actually, it's not so confusing if you look carefully at each Bible passage:

✴ Don't judge others' motives or service (1 Corinthians 4:3).
✴ Don't judge others' personal convictions (Romans 14:1–8).
✴ Do judge others who do what the Bible says is sin (1 Corinthians 5).

When a fellow Christian makes a habit of doing something God says is sin, you can agree with God and say, "That's wrong!" Don't criticize others or gossip about them. But if a friend makes a habit of sinning, urge him or her to stop.

has been sacrificed. [8]Therefore let us keep the Festival, not with the old yeast, the yeast of malice and wickedness, but with bread without yeast, the bread of sincerity and truth.

[9]I have written you in my letter not to associate with sexually immoral people— [10]not at all meaning the people of this world who are immoral, or the greedy and swindlers, or idolaters. In that case you would have to leave this world. [11]But now I am writing you that you must not associate with anyone who calls himself a brother but is sexually immoral or greedy, an idolater or a slanderer, a drunkard or a swindler. With such a man do not even eat.

[12]What business is it of mine to judge those outside the church? Are you not to judge those inside? [13]God will judge those outside. "Expel the wicked man from among you."[a]

Lawsuits Among Believers If any of you has a dispute with another, dare he take it before the ungodly for judgment instead of before the saints? [2]Do you not know that the saints will judge the world? And if you are to judge the world, are you not competent to judge trivial cases? [3]Do you not know that we will judge angels? How much more the things of this life! [4]Therefore, if you have disputes about such matters, appoint as judges even men of little account in the church![b] [5]I say this to shame you. Is it possible that there is nobody among you wise enough to judge a dispute between believers? [6]But instead, one brother goes to law against another—and this in front of unbelievers!

[7]The very fact that you have lawsuits among you means you have been completely defeated already. Why not rather be wronged? Why not rather be cheated? [8]Instead, you yourselves cheat and do wrong, and you do this to your brothers.

[9]Do you not know that the wicked will not inherit the kingdom of God? Do not be deceived: Neither the sexually immoral nor idolaters nor adulterers nor male prostitutes nor homosexual offenders [10]nor thieves nor the greedy nor drunkards nor slanderers nor swindlers will inherit the kingdom of God. [11]And that is what some of you were. But you were washed, you were sanctified, you were justified in the name of the Lord Jesus Christ and by the Spirit of our God.

Sexual Immorality [12]"Everything is permissible for me"—but not everything is beneficial. "Everything is permissible for me"—but I will not be mastered by anything. [13]"Food for the stomach and the stomach for food"—but God will destroy them both. The body is not meant for sexual immorality, but for the Lord, and the Lord for the body. [14]By his power God raised the Lord from the dead, and he will raise us also. [15]Do you not know that your bodies are members of Christ himself? Shall I then take the members of Christ and unite them with a prostitute? Never! [16]Do you not know that he who unites himself with a prostitute is one with her in body? For it is said, "The two will become one flesh."[c] [17]But he who unites himself with the Lord is one with him in spirit.

> Your body is a temple of the Holy Spirit, who is in you, whom you have received from God (1 Corinthians 6:19).

[18]Flee from sexual immorality. All other sins a man commits are outside his body, but he who sins sexually sins against his own body. [19]Do you not know that your body is a temple of the Holy Spirit, who is in you, whom you have received from God? You are not your own; [20]you were bought at a price. Therefore honor God with your body.

---

[a]13 Deut. 17:7; 19:19; 21:21; 22:21,24; 24:7 [b]4 Or *matters, do you appoint as judges men of little account in the church?* [c]16 Gen. 2:24

Marriage Now for the matters you wrote about: It is good for a man not to marry.*ª* ²But since there is so much immorality, each man should have his own wife, and each woman her own husband. ³The husband should fulfill his marital duty to his wife, and likewise the wife to her husband. ⁴The wife's body does not belong to her alone but also to her husband. In the same way, the husband's body does not belong to him alone but also to his wife. ⁵Do not deprive each other except by mutual consent and for a time, so that you may devote yourselves to prayer. Then come together again so that Satan will not tempt you because of your lack of self-control. ⁶I say this as a concession, not as a command. ⁷I wish that all men were as I am. But each man has his own gift from God; one has this gift, another has that.

⁸Now to the unmarried and the widows I say: It is good for them to stay unmarried, as I am. ⁹But if they cannot control themselves, they should marry, for it is better to marry than to burn with passion.

¹⁰To the married I give this command (not I, but the Lord): A wife must not separate from her husband. ¹¹But if she does, she must remain unmarried or else be reconciled to her husband. And a husband must not divorce his wife.

¹²To the rest I say this (I, not the Lord): If any brother has a wife who is not a believer and she is willing to live with him, he must not divorce her. ¹³And if a woman has a husband who is not a believer and he is willing to live with her, she must not divorce him. ¹⁴For the unbelieving husband has been sanctified through his wife, and the unbelieving wife has been sanctified through her believing husband. Otherwise your children would be unclean, but as it is, they are holy.

¹⁵But if the unbeliever leaves, let him do so. A believing man or woman is not bound in such circumstances; God has called us to live in peace. ¹⁶How do you know, wife, whether you will save your husband? Or, how do you know, husband, whether you will save your wife?

¹⁷Nevertheless, each one should retain the place in life that the Lord assigned to him and to which God has called him. This is the rule I lay down in all the churches. ¹⁸Was a man already circumcised when he was called? He should not become uncircumcised. Was a man uncircumcised when he was called? He should not be circumcised. ¹⁹Circumcision is nothing and uncircumcision is nothing. Keeping God's commands is what counts. ²⁰Each one should remain in the situation which he was in when God called him. ²¹Were you a slave when you were called? Don't let it trouble you—although if you can gain your freedom, do so. ²²For he who was a slave when he was called by the Lord is the Lord's freedman; similarly, he who was a free man when he was called is Christ's slave. ²³You were bought at a price; do not become slaves of men. ²⁴Brothers, each man, as responsible to God, should remain in the situation God called him to.

²⁵Now about virgins: I have no command from the Lord, but I give a judgment as one who by the Lord's mercy is trustworthy. ²⁶Because of the present crisis, I think that it is good for you to re-

Direct Line

1 CORINTHIANS 7:19–24

More than likely there are things about yourself you would like to change. Maybe it's your looks or your financial situation or the color of your skin. Whatever, it's not easy to hear Paul's words, "Don't let it trouble you" (1 Corinthians 7:21). And Paul said this to slaves. Seems like it was probably easy for Paul to say—he wasn't a slave. He had full Roman citizenship. But what Paul is saying here is that you are important to God. Your identity as a child of God doesn't depend on being handsome or beautiful or smart or a particular color. The you inside is important. And Paul's "Don't let it trouble you" makes a lot of sense.

ª1 Or "It is good for a man not to have sexual relations with a woman."

main as you are. [27]Are you married? Do not seek a divorce. Are you unmarried? Do not look for a wife. [28]But if you do marry, you have not sinned; and if a virgin marries, she has not sinned. But those who marry will face many troubles in this life, and I want to spare you this.

[29]What I mean, brothers, is that the time is short. From now on those who have wives should live as if they had none; [30]those who mourn, as if they did not; those who are happy, as if they were not; those who buy something, as if it were not theirs to keep; [31]those who use the things of the world, as if not engrossed in them. For this world in its present form is passing away.

[32]I would like you to be free from concern. An unmarried man is concerned about the Lord's affairs—how he can please the Lord. [33]But a married man is concerned about the affairs of this world—how he can please his wife— [34]and his interests are divided. An unmarried woman or virgin is concerned about the Lord's affairs: Her aim is to be devoted to the Lord in both body and spirit. But a married woman is concerned about the affairs of this world—how she can please her husband. [35]I am saying this for your own good, not to restrict you, but that you may live in a right way in undivided devotion to the Lord.

[36]If anyone thinks he is acting improperly toward the virgin he is engaged to, and if she is getting along in years and he feels he ought to marry, he should do as he wants. He is not sinning. They should get married. [37]But the man who has settled the matter in his own mind, who is under no compulsion but has control over his own will, and who has made up his mind not to marry the virgin—this man also does the right thing. [38]So then, he who marries the virgin does right, but he who does not marry her does even better.[a]

[39]A woman is bound to her husband as long as he lives. But if her husband dies, she is free to marry anyone she wishes, but he must belong to the Lord. [40]In my judgment, she is happier if she stays as she is—and I think that I too have the Spirit of God.

8 ***Food Sacrificed to Idols*** Now about food sacrificed to idols: We know that we all possess knowledge.[b] Knowledge puffs up, but love builds up. [2]The man who thinks he knows something does not yet know as he ought to know. [3]But the man who loves God is known by God.

[4]So then, about eating food sacrificed to idols: We know that an idol is nothing at all in the world and that there is no God but one. [5]For even if there are so-called gods, whether in heaven or on earth (as indeed there are many "gods" and many "lords"), [6]yet for us there is but one God, the Father, from whom all things came and for whom we live; and there is but one Lord, Jesus Christ, through whom all things came and through whom we live.

[7]But not everyone knows this. Some people are still so accustomed to idols that when they eat such food they think of it as having been sacrificed to an idol, and since their conscience is weak, it is defiled. [8]But food does not bring us near to God; we are no worse if we do not eat, and no better if we do.

[9]Be careful, however, that the exercise of your freedom does not become a stumbling block to the weak. [10]For if anyone with a weak conscience sees you who have this knowledge eating in an idol's temple, won't he be emboldened to eat what has been sacrificed to idols? [11]So this weak brother, for whom Christ died, is destroyed by your knowledge. [12]When you sin against

---

[a]36-38 Or [36]*If anyone thinks he is not treating his daughter properly, and if she is getting along in years, and he feels she ought to marry, he should do as he wants. He is not sinning. He should let her get married.* [37]*But the man who has settled the matter in his own mind, who is under no compulsion but has control over his own will, and who has made up his mind to keep the virgin unmarried—this man also does the right thing.* [38]*So then, he who gives his virgin in marriage does right, but he who does not give her in marriage does even better.* [b]1 Or *"We all possess knowledge," as you say*

your brothers in this way and wound their weak conscience, you sin against Christ. [13]Therefore, if what I eat causes my brother to fall into sin, I will never eat meat again, so that I will not cause him to fall.

The Rights of an Apostle Am I not free? Am I not an apostle? Have I not seen Jesus our Lord? Are you not the result of my work in the Lord? [2]Even though I may not be an apostle to others, surely I am to you! For you are the seal of my apostleship in the Lord.

[3]This is my defense to those who sit in judgment on me. [4]Don't we have the right to food and drink? [5]Don't we have the right to take a believing wife along with us, as do the other apostles and the Lord's brothers and Cephas[a]? [6]Or is it only I and Barnabas who must work for a living?

[7]Who serves as a soldier at his own expense? Who plants a vineyard and does not eat of its grapes? Who tends a flock and does not drink of the milk? [8]Do I say this merely from a human point of view? Doesn't the Law say the same thing? [9]For it is written in the Law of Moses: "Do not muzzle an ox while it is treading out the grain."[b] Is it about oxen that God is concerned? [10]Surely he says this for us, doesn't he? Yes, this was written for us, because when the plowman plows and the thresher threshes, they ought to do so in the hope of sharing in the harvest. [11]If we have sown spiritual seed among you, is it too much if we reap a material harvest from you? [12]If others have this right of support from you, shouldn't we have it all the more?

But we did not use this right. On the contrary, we put up with anything rather than hinder the gospel of Christ. [13]Don't you know that those who work in the temple get their food from the temple, and those who serve at the altar share in what is offered on the altar? [14]In the same way, the Lord has commanded that those who preach the gospel should receive their living from the gospel.

[15]But I have not used any of these rights. And I am not writing this in the hope that you will do such things for me. I would rather die than have anyone deprive me of this boast. [16]Yet when I preach the gospel, I cannot boast, for I am compelled to preach. Woe to me if I do not preach the gospel! [17]If I preach voluntarily, I have a reward; if not voluntarily, I am simply discharging the trust committed to me. [18]What then is my reward? Just this: that in preaching the gospel I may offer it free of charge, and so not make use of my rights in preaching it.

[19]Though I am free and belong to no man, I make myself a slave to everyone, to win as many as possible. [20]To the Jews I became like a Jew, to win the Jews. To those under the law I became like one under the law (though I myself am not under the law), so as to win those under the law. [21]To those not having the law I became like one not having the law (though I am not free from God's law but am under Christ's law), so as to win those not having the law. [22]To the weak I became weak, to win the weak. I have become all things to all men so that by all

Direct Line

1 CORINTHIANS 9:19–23

How different is a Christian supposed to be? Should you carry a big Bible with your books? Or preach in the street near your school? If you want to be persecuted, maybe. But if you're serious about sharing Christ, you'd do a lot better trying to fit in. That's what Paul says here. Instead of emphasizing his differences from the people he was with, Paul made a real effort to fit in with them. Of course, Paul didn't take part in any of their sins, but he knew if he was accepted, they would be much more likely to listen to him. So go out and get involved. And don't be afraid to make friends with those who aren't Christians.

[a]5 That is, Peter   [b]9 Deut. 25:4

possible means I might save some. ²³I do all this for the sake of the gospel, that I may share in its blessings.

²⁴Do you not know that in a race all the runners run, but only one gets the prize? Run in such a way as to get the prize. ²⁵Everyone who competes in the games goes into strict training. They do it to get a crown that will not last; but we do it to get a crown that will last forever. ²⁶Therefore I do not run like a man running aimlessly; I do not fight like a man beating the air. ²⁷No, I beat my body and make it my slave so that after I have preached to others, I myself will not be disqualified for the prize.

10

Warnings From Israel's History For I do not want you to be ignorant of the fact, brothers, that our forefathers were all under the cloud and that they all passed through the sea. ²They were all baptized into Moses in the cloud and in the sea. ³They all ate the same spiritual food ⁴and drank the same spiritual drink; for they drank from the spiritual rock that accompanied them, and that rock was Christ. ⁵Nevertheless, God was not pleased with most of them; their bodies were scattered over the desert.

⁶Now these things occurred as examples*ᵃ* to keep us from setting our hearts on evil things as they did. ⁷Do not be idolaters, as some of them were; as it is written: "The people sat down to eat and drink and got up to indulge in pagan revelry."*ᵇ* ⁸We should not commit sexual immorality, as some of them did—and in one day twenty-three thousand of them died. ⁹We should not test the Lord, as some of them did—and were killed by snakes. ¹⁰And do not grumble, as some of them did—and were killed by the destroying angel.

¹¹These things happened to them as examples and were written down as warnings for us, on whom the fulfillment of the ages has come. ¹²So, if you think you are standing firm, be careful that you don't fall! ¹³No temptation has seized you except what is common to man. And God is faithful; he will not let you be tempted beyond what you can bear. But when you are tempted, he will also provide a way out so that you can stand up under it.

Idol Feasts and the Lord's Supper ¹⁴Therefore, my dear friends, flee from idolatry. ¹⁵I speak to sensible people; judge for yourselves what I say. ¹⁶Is not the cup of thanksgiving for which we give thanks a participation in the blood of Christ? And is not the bread that we break a participation in the body of Christ? ¹⁷Because there is one loaf, we, who are many, are one body, for we all partake of the one loaf.

¹⁸Consider the people of Israel: Do not those who eat the sacrifices participate in the altar? ¹⁹Do I mean then that a sacrifice offered to an idol is anything, or that an idol is anything? ²⁰No, but the sacrifices of pagans are offered to demons, not to God, and I do not want you to be participants with demons. ²¹You cannot drink the cup of the Lord and the cup of demons too; you cannot have a part in both the Lord's table and the table of demons. ²²Are we trying to arouse the Lord's jealousy? Are we stronger than he?

ᵃ6 Or types; also in verse 11   *ᵇ7 Exodus 32:6*

1 CORINTHIANS 10:13

Would you like a simple way to overcome temptation? One that always works? It's laid out right here in this verse. With every temptation, God provides "a way out." Now think about those words: "a way out." Let's say that some friends are gossiping about a person you know, and you have something juicy to add. What a temptation. So you get up and leave! Or some guys are poring over a girlie magazine. You just turn around and leave. The best way out of temptation is to get out of situations where you feel tempted. And stay out!

Direct Line

The Believer's Freedom ²³"Everything is permissible"—but not everything is beneficial. "Everything is permissible"—but not everything is constructive. ²⁴Nobody should seek his own good, but the good of others.

²⁵Eat anything sold in the meat market without raising questions of conscience, ²⁶for, "The earth is the Lord's, and everything in it."^a

²⁷If some unbeliever invites you to a meal and you want to go, eat whatever is put before you without raising questions of conscience. ²⁸But if anyone says to you, "This has been offered in sacrifice," then do not eat it, both for the sake of the man who told you and for conscience' sake^b— ²⁹the other man's conscience, I mean, not yours. For why should my freedom be judged by another's conscience? ³⁰If I take part in the meal with thankfulness, why am I denounced because of something I thank God for?

³¹So whether you eat or drink or whatever you do, do it all for the glory of God. ³²Do not cause anyone to stumble, whether Jews, Greeks or the church of God— ³³even as I try to please everybody in every way. For I am not seeking my own good but the good of many, so that they may be saved. ¹Follow my example, as I follow the example of Christ.

11

Propriety in Worship ²I praise you for remembering me in everything and for holding to the teachings,^c just as I passed them on to you.

³Now I want you to realize that the head of every man is Christ, and the head of the woman is man, and the head of Christ is God. ⁴Every man who prays or prophesies with his head covered dishonors his head. ⁵And every woman who prays or prophesies with her head uncovered dishonors her head—it is just as though her head were shaved. ⁶If a woman does not cover her head, she should have her hair cut off; and if it is a disgrace for a woman to have her hair cut or shaved off, she should cover her head. ⁷A man ought not to cover his head,^d since he is the image and glory of God; but the woman is the glory of man. ⁸For man did not come from woman, but woman from man; ⁹neither was man created for woman, but woman for man. ¹⁰For this reason, and because of the angels, the woman ought to have a sign of authority on her head.

¹¹In the Lord, however, woman is not independent of man, nor is man independent of woman. ¹²For as woman came from man, so also man is born of woman. But everything comes from God. ¹³Judge for yourselves: Is it proper for a woman to pray to God with her head uncovered? ¹⁴Does not the very nature of things teach you that if a man has long hair, it is a disgrace to him, ¹⁵but that if a woman has long hair, it is her glory? For long hair is given to her as a covering. ¹⁶If anyone wants to be contentious about this, we have no other practice—nor do the churches of God.

The Lord's Supper ¹⁷In the following directives I have no praise for you, for your meetings do more harm than good. ¹⁸In the first place, I hear that when you come together as a church, there are divisions among you, and to some extent I believe it. ¹⁹No doubt there have to be differences among you to show which of you have God's approval. ²⁰When you come together, it is not the Lord's Supper you eat, ²¹for as you eat, each of you goes ahead without waiting for anybody else. One remains hungry, another gets drunk. ²²Don't you have homes to eat and drink in? Or do you despise the church of God and humiliate those who have nothing? What shall I say to you? Shall I praise you for this? Certainly not!

---

^a26 Psalm 24:1 ^b28 Some manuscripts *conscience' sake, for "the earth is the Lord's and everything in it"*
^c2 Or *traditions* ^d4-7 Or ⁴*Every man who prays or prophesies with long hair dishonors his head.* ⁵*And every woman who prays or prophesies with no covering of hair on her head dishonors her head—she is just like one of the "shorn women."* ⁶*If a woman has no covering, let her be for now with short hair, but since it is a disgrace for a woman to have her hair shorn or shaved, she should grow it again.* ⁷*A man ought not to have long hair*

²³For I received from the Lord what I also passed on to you: The Lord Jesus, on the night he was betrayed, took bread, ²⁴and when he had given thanks, he broke it and said, "This is my body, which is for you; do this in remembrance of me." ²⁵In the same way, after supper he took the cup, saying, "This cup is the new covenant in my blood; do this, whenever you drink it, in remembrance of me." ²⁶For whenever you eat this bread and drink this cup, you proclaim the Lord's death until he comes.

²⁷Therefore, whoever eats the bread or drinks the cup of the Lord in an unworthy manner will be guilty of sinning against the body and blood of the Lord. ²⁸A man ought to examine himself before he eats of the bread and drinks of the cup. ²⁹For anyone who eats and drinks without recognizing the body of the Lord eats and drinks judgment on himself. ³⁰That is why many among you are weak and sick, and a number of you have fallen asleep. ³¹But if we judged ourselves, we would not come under judgment. ³²When we are judged by the Lord, we are being disciplined so that we will not be condemned with the world.

³³So then, my brothers, when you come together to eat, wait for each other. ³⁴If anyone is hungry, he should eat at home, so that when you meet together it may not result in judgment.

And when I come I will give further directions.

12 *Spiritual Gifts* Now about spiritual gifts, brothers, I do not want you to be ignorant. ²You know that when you were pagans, somehow or other you were influenced and led astray to mute idols. ³Therefore I tell you that no one who is speaking by the Spirit of God says, "Jesus be cursed," and no one can say, "Jesus is Lord," except by the Holy Spirit.

⁴There are different kinds of gifts, but the same Spirit. ⁵There are different kinds of service, but the same Lord. ⁶There are different kinds of working, but the same God works all of them in all men.

⁷Now to each one the manifestation of the Spirit is given for the common good. ⁸To one there is given through the Spirit the message of wisdom, to another the message of knowledge by means of the same Spirit, ⁹to another faith by the same Spirit, to another gifts of healing by that one Spirit, ¹⁰to another miraculous powers, to another prophecy, to another distinguishing

---

You may never become president. Or a famous movie star. But as one of Jesus' followers, you are definitely a VIP.

The church is like a body, and each member is like a body part (1 Corinthians 12). What's more, God has given you a "spiritual gift," a special way the Holy Spirit will work through you to help others grow in the Lord. How do you find your gift and use it?

The Bible Says

You Count

✱ Remember there are many different kinds of gifts (1 Corinthians 12:4–6).

✱ Remember all gifts are intended to help others (1 Corinthians 12:7).

Get involved with other Christian young people and look for ways to help. God will use you, and as he does, you'll discover what your spiritual gift is.

between spirits, to another speaking in different kinds of tongues,*a* and to still another the interpretation of tongues.*a* ¹¹All these are the work of one and the same Spirit, and he gives them to each one, just as he determines.

One Body, Many Parts ¹²The body is a unit, though it is made up of many parts; and though all its parts are many, they form one body. So it is with Christ. ¹³For we were all baptized by*b* one Spirit into one body—whether Jews or Greeks, slave or free—and we were all given the one Spirit to drink.

¹⁴Now the body is not made up of one part but of many. ¹⁵If the foot should say, "Because I am not a hand, I do not belong to the body," it would not for that reason cease to be part of the body. ¹⁶And if the ear should say, "Because I am not an eye, I do not belong to the body," it would not for that reason cease to be part of the body. ¹⁷If the whole body were an eye, where would the sense of hearing be? If the whole body were an ear, where would the sense of smell be? ¹⁸But in fact God has arranged the parts in the body, every one of them, just as he wanted them to be. ¹⁹If they were all one part, where would the body be? ²⁰As it is, there are many parts, but one body.

²¹The eye cannot say to the hand, "I don't need you!" And the head cannot say to the feet, "I don't need you!" ²²On the contrary, those parts of the body that seem to be weaker are indispensable, ²³and the parts that we think are less honorable we treat with special honor. And the parts that are unpresentable are treated with special modesty, ²⁴while our presentable parts need no special treatment. But God has combined the members of the body and has given greater honor to the parts that lacked it, ²⁵so that there should be no division in the body, but that its parts should have equal concern for each other. ²⁶If one part suffers, every part suffers with it; if one part is honored, every part rejoices with it.

²⁷Now you are the body of Christ, and each one of you is a part of it. ²⁸And in the church God has appointed first of all apostles, second prophets, third teachers, then workers of miracles, also those having gifts of healing, those able to help others, those with gifts of administration, and those speaking in different kinds of tongues. ²⁹Are all apostles? Are all prophets? Are all teachers? Do all work miracles? ³⁰Do all have gifts of healing? Do all speak in tongues*c*? Do all interpret? ³¹But eagerly desire*d* the greater gifts.

Love And now I will show you the most excellent way.

If I speak in the tongues*e* of men and of angels, but have not love, I am only a resounding gong or a clanging cymbal. ²If I have the gift of prophecy and can fathom all mysteries and all knowledge, and if I have a faith that can move mountains, but have not love, I am nothing. ³If I give all I possess to the poor and surrender my body to the flames,*f* but have not love, I gain nothing.

⁴Love is patient, love is kind. It does not envy, it does not boast, it is not proud. ⁵It is not rude, it is not self-seeking, it is not easily angered, it keeps no record of wrongs. ⁶Love does not delight in evil but rejoices with the truth. ⁷It always protects, always trusts, always hopes, always perseveres.

⁸Love never fails. But where there are prophecies, they will cease; where there are tongues, they will be stilled; where there is knowledge, it will pass away. ⁹For we know in part and we prophesy in part, ¹⁰but when perfection comes, the imperfect disappears. ¹¹When I was a child, I talked like a child, I thought like a child, I reasoned like a child. When I became a man, I put childish ways behind me. ¹²Now we see but a poor reflection as in a mirror; then we shall see face to face. Now I know in part; then I shall know fully, even as I am fully known.

---

*a*10 Or *languages*; also in verse 28   *b*13 Or *with*; or *in*   *c*30 Or *other languages*   *d*31 Or *But you are eagerly desiring*   *e*1 Or *languages*   *f*3 Some early manuscripts *body that I may boast*

Dear Sam,

My friend gets all A's and doesn't even have to study. I work hard in school and get C's. It's not fair! Should I quit school?

Doug in Dover

100 Advice Lane, Anywhere, USA

Dear Doug,

It would be nice if everyone could get all A's in school, but that's not the reality of our existence. Each person has different abilities, talents and interests. If everyone became rocket scientists, who would fix the plumbing? If everyone sold vacuum cleaners, who would design clothes? If everyone built cars, who would take care of the sick?

God has given different gifts (abilities) to different people (1 Corinthians 12:14-26). This passage is directed to gifts that are used in the church, but the truth applies to careers also. Each gift or ability is important and contributes to the goodness of life for everyone.

God knew when he created you that there were many kinds of jobs to be done. So your gift isn't getting easy A's. Sure, getting good grades is important. But it's not the only thing. Discover what it is that you are good at, and then use that gift to the best of your ability. Stay in school, learn as much as you can, do the best you can at whatever you do. Whatever you do, it is important. And so are you.

Sam

Dear Sam,

My parents and I fight constantly over the way I keep my room. But I like my room that way! Can't I have a little "space"?

Karen in Kalamazoo

100 Advice Lane, Anywhere, USA

Dear Karen,

The bedroom battleground between parents and teens has been going on for longer than I've been around! And there's no simple answer to satisfy everyone.

I agree that as you grow older, it's nice to feel you have your own space. I also know damp bath towels thrown in with heaps of clothes can grow mold and mildew. Library books get lost and accumulate fines. Food left on plates in dark corners draws bugs or turns fuzzy.

Being a teenager is tough because you're not really ready to put aside all of your childish ways; yet you're not satisfied to be treated as a child either (1 Corinthians 13:11). Perhaps you can do some negotiating with your parents.

Are you allowed to put up posters? May you change the color of paint on your walls? Are you allowed to have the furniture arranged the way you want it? How often do your parents want your room picked up? Sit down and negotiate. When you reach an agreement, be sure to live up to its terms, or they won't want to negotiate with you again. I wish you the best!

Sam

¹³And now these three remain: faith, hope and love. But the greatest of these is love.

14 **Gifts of Prophecy and Tongues** Follow the way of love and eagerly desire spiritual gifts, especially the gift of prophecy. ²For anyone who speaks in a tongue*ᵃ* does not speak to men but to God. Indeed, no one understands him; he utters mysteries with his spirit.*ᵇ* ³But everyone who prophesies speaks to men for their strengthening, encouragement and comfort. ⁴He who speaks in a tongue edifies himself, but he who prophesies edifies the church. ⁵I would like every one of you to speak in tongues,*ᶜ* but I would rather have you prophesy. He who prophesies is greater than one who speaks in tongues,*ᶜ* unless he interprets, so that the church may be edified.

⁶Now, brothers, if I come to you and speak in tongues, what good will I be to you, unless I bring you some revelation or knowledge or prophecy or word of instruction? ⁷Even in the case of lifeless things that make sounds, such as the flute or harp, how will anyone know what tune is being played unless there is a distinction in the notes? ⁸Again, if the trumpet does not sound a clear call, who will get ready for battle? ⁹So it is with you. Unless you speak intelligible words with your tongue, how will anyone know what you are saying? You will just be speaking into the air. ¹⁰Undoubtedly there are all sorts of languages in the world, yet none of them is without meaning. ¹¹If then I do not grasp the meaning of what someone is saying, I am a foreigner to the speaker, and he is a foreigner to me. ¹²So it is with you. Since you are eager to have spiritual gifts, try to excel in gifts that build up the church.

¹³For this reason anyone who speaks in a tongue should pray that he may interpret what he says. ¹⁴For if I pray in a tongue, my spirit prays, but my mind is unfruitful. ¹⁵So what shall I do? I will pray with my spirit, but I will also pray with my mind; I will sing with my spirit, but I will also sing with my mind. ¹⁶If you are praising God with your spirit, how can one who finds himself among those who do not understand*ᵈ* say "Amen" to your thanksgiving, since he does not know what you are saying? ¹⁷You may be giving thanks well enough, but the other man is not edified.

¹⁸I thank God that I speak in tongues more than all of you. ¹⁹But in the church I would rather speak five intelligible words to instruct others than ten thousand words in a tongue.

²⁰Brothers, stop thinking like children. In regard to evil be infants, but in your thinking be adults. ²¹In the Law it is written:

> "Through men of strange tongues
> and through the lips of foreigners
> I will speak to this people,
> but even then they will not listen to me,"*ᵉ*

says the Lord.

²²Tongues, then, are a sign, not for believers but for unbelievers; prophecy, however, is for believers, not for unbelievers. ²³So if the whole church comes together and everyone speaks in tongues, and some who do not understand*ᶠ* or some unbelievers come in, will they not say that you are out of your mind? ²⁴But if an unbeliever or someone who does not understand*ᵍ* comes in while everybody is prophesying, he will be convinced by all that he is a sinner and will be judged by all, ²⁵and the secrets of his heart will be laid bare. So he will fall down and worship God, exclaiming, "God is really among you!"

---

*ᵃ*2 Or *another language*; also in verses 4, 13, 14, 19, 26 and 27   *ᵇ*2 Or *by the Spirit*   *ᶜ*5 Or *other languages*; also in verses 6, 18, 22, 23 and 39   *ᵈ*16 Or *among the inquirers*   *ᵉ*21 Isaiah 28:11,12   *ᶠ*23 Or *some inquirers*   *ᵍ*24 Or *or some inquirer*

Orderly Worship ²⁶What then shall we say, brothers? When you come together, everyone has a hymn, or a word of instruction, a revelation, a tongue or an interpretation. All of these must be done for the strengthening of the church. ²⁷If anyone speaks in a tongue, two—or at the most three—should speak, one at a time, and someone must interpret. ²⁸If there is no interpreter, the speaker should keep quiet in the church and speak to himself and God.

²⁹Two or three prophets should speak, and the others should weigh carefully what is said. ³⁰And if a revelation comes to someone who is sitting down, the first speaker should stop. ³¹For you can all prophesy in turn so that everyone may be instructed and encouraged. ³²The spirits of prophets are subject to the control of prophets. ³³For God is not a God of disorder but of peace.

As in all the congregations of the saints, ³⁴women should remain silent in the churches. They are not allowed to speak, but must be in submission, as the Law says. ³⁵If they want to inquire about something, they should ask their own husbands at home; for it is disgraceful for a woman to speak in the church.

³⁶Did the word of God originate with you? Or are you the only people it has reached? ³⁷If anybody thinks he is a prophet or spiritually gifted, let him acknowledge that what I am writing to you is the Lord's command. ³⁸If he ignores this, he himself will be ignored.ᵃ

³⁹Therefore, my brothers, be eager to prophesy, and do not forbid speaking in tongues. ⁴⁰But everything should be done in a fitting and orderly way.

The Resurrection of Christ Now, brothers, I want to remind you of the gospel I preached to you, which you received and on which you have taken your stand. ²By this gospel you are saved, if you hold firmly to the word I preached to you. Otherwise, you have believed in vain.

³For what I received I passed on to you as of first importanceᵇ: that Christ died for our sins according to the Scriptures, ⁴that he was buried, that he was raised on the third day according to the Scriptures, ⁵and that he appeared to Peter,ᶜ and then to the Twelve. ⁶After that, he appeared to more than five hundred of the brothers at the same time, most of whom are still living, though some have fallen asleep. ⁷Then he appeared to James, then to all the apostles, ⁸and last of all he appeared to me also, as to one abnormally born.

⁹For I am the least of the apostles and do not even deserve to be called an apostle, because I persecuted the church of God. ¹⁰But by the grace of God I am what I am, and his grace to me was not without effect. No, I worked harder than all of them—yet not I, but the grace of God that was with me. ¹¹Whether, then, it was I or they, this is what we preach, and this is what you believed.

The Resurrection of the Dead ¹²But if it is preached that Christ has been raised from the dead, how can some of you say that there is no resurrection of the dead? ¹³If there is no resurrection of the dead, then not even Christ has been raised. ¹⁴And if Christ has not been raised, our preaching is useless and so is your faith. ¹⁵More than that, we are then found to be false witnesses about God, for we have testified about God that he raised Christ from the dead. But he did not raise him if in fact the dead are not raised. ¹⁶For if the dead are not raised, then Christ has not been raised either. ¹⁷And if Christ has not been raised, your faith is futile; you are still in your sins. ¹⁸Then those also who have fallen asleep in Christ are lost. ¹⁹If only for this life we have hope in Christ, we are to be pitied more than all men.

²⁰But Christ has indeed been raised from the dead, the firstfruits of those

---

ᵃ38 Some manuscripts *If he is ignorant of this, let him be ignorant*   ᵇ3 Or *you at the first*   ᶜ5 Greek *Cephas* who have fallen asleep. ²¹For since death came through a man, the resurrection of the dead comes also through a man. ²²For as in Adam all die, so in Christ all will be made alive. ²³But each in his own turn: Christ, the firstfruits; then, when he comes, those who belong to him. ²⁴Then the end will come, when he hands over the kingdom to God the Father after he has destroyed all dominion, authority and power. ²⁵For he must reign until he has put all his enemies under his feet. ²⁶The last enemy to be destroyed is death. ²⁷For he "has put everything under his feet."ᵃ Now when it says that "everything" has been put under him, it is clear that this does not include God himself, who put everything under Christ. ²⁸When he has done this, then the Son himself will be made subject to him who put everything under him, so that God may be all in all.

²⁹Now if there is no resurrection, what will those do who are baptized for the dead? If the dead are not raised at all, why are people baptized for them? ³⁰And as for us, why do we endanger ourselves every hour? ³¹I die every day—I mean that, brothers—just as surely as I glory over you in Christ Jesus our Lord. ³²If I fought wild beasts in Ephesus for merely human reasons, what have I gained? If the dead are not raised,

> "Let us eat and drink,
>   for tomorrow we die."ᵇ

³³Do not be misled: "Bad company corrupts good character." ³⁴Come back to your senses as you ought, and stop sinning; for there are some who are ignorant of God—I say this to your shame.

The Resurrection Body   ³⁵But someone may ask, "How are the dead raised? With what kind of body will they come?" ³⁶How foolish! What you sow does not come to life unless it dies. ³⁷When you sow, you do not plant the body that will be, but just a seed, perhaps of wheat or of something else. ³⁸But God gives it a body as he has determined, and to each kind of seed he gives its own body. ³⁹All flesh is not the same: Men have one kind of flesh, animals have another, birds another and fish another. ⁴⁰There are also heavenly bodies and there are earthly bodies; but the splendor of the heavenly bodies is one kind, and the splendor of the earthly bodies is another. ⁴¹The sun has one kind of splendor, the moon another and the stars another; and star differs from star in splendor.

⁴²So will it be with the resurrection of the dead. The body that is sown is perishable, it is raised imperishable; ⁴³it is sown in dishonor, it is raised in glory; it is sown in weakness, it is raised in power; ⁴⁴it is sown a natural body, it is raised a spiritual body.

If there is a natural body, there is also a spiritual body. ⁴⁵So it is written: "The first man Adam became a living being"ᶜ; the last Adam, a life-giving spirit. ⁴⁶The spiritual did not come first, but the natural, and after that the spiritual. ⁴⁷The first man was of the dust of the earth, the second man from heaven. ⁴⁸As was the earthly man, so are those who are of the

---

ᵃ*27* Psalm 8:6   ᵇ*32* Isaiah 22:13   ᶜ*45* Gen. 2:7

1 CORINTHIANS 15:35–49

Death isn't scary for Christians. Yes, it hurts if a loved one dies. But for you, personally, what lies beyond can be downright exciting. Like this new body you'll have. First John 3:2 says that when Jesus comes you'll be like him. After his resurrection Jesus could pass through walls and enter a locked room (John 20:19). There's no telling just what your resurrection life will be like. But from hints in the Bible, you can be sure it's going to be great! Yes, God wants you to enjoy a long and active life here. But he also wants to be sure you don't fear dying. You have good years ahead of you. And after that, a great eternity.

earth; and as is the man from heaven, so also are those who are of heaven. [49]And just as we have borne the likeness of the earthly man, so shall we[a] bear the likeness of the man from heaven.

[50]I declare to you, brothers, that flesh and blood cannot inherit the kingdom of God, nor does the perishable inherit the imperishable. [51]Listen, I tell you a mystery: We will not all sleep, but we will all be changed— [52]in a flash, in the twinkling of an eye, at the last trumpet. For the trumpet will sound, the dead will be raised imperishable, and we will be changed. [53]For the perishable must clothe itself with the imperishable, and the mortal with immortality. [54]When the perishable has been clothed with the imperishable, and the mortal with immortality, then the saying that is written will come true: "Death has been swallowed up in victory."[b]

> We will not all sleep, but we will all be changed . . . For the trumpet will sound, [and] the dead will be raised
>
> (1 Corinthians 15:51-52).

[55] "Where, O death, is your victory?
  Where, O death, is your sting?"[c]

[56]The sting of death is sin, and the power of sin is the law. [57]But thanks be to God! He gives us the victory through our Lord Jesus Christ.

[58]Therefore, my dear brothers, stand firm. Let nothing move you. Always give yourselves fully to the work of the Lord, because you know that your labor in the Lord is not in vain.

16

The Collection for God's People Now about the collection for God's people: Do what I told the Galatian churches to do. [2]On the first day of every week, each one of you should set aside a sum of money in keeping with his income, saving it up, so that when I come no collections will have to be made. [3]Then, when I arrive, I will give letters of introduction to the men you approve and send them with your gift to Jerusalem. [4]If it seems advisable for me to go also, they will accompany me.

Personal Requests [5]After I go through Macedonia, I will come to you—for I will be going through Macedonia. [6]Perhaps I will stay with you awhile, or even spend the winter, so that you can help me on my journey, wherever I go. [7]I do not want to see you now and make only a passing visit; I hope to spend some time with you, if the Lord permits. [8]But I will stay on at Ephesus until Pentecost, [9]because a great door for effective work has opened to me, and there are many who oppose me.

[10]If Timothy comes, see to it that he has nothing to fear while he is with you, for he is carrying on the work of the Lord, just as I am. [11]No one, then, should refuse to accept him. Send him on his way in peace so that he may return to me. I am expecting him along with the brothers.

[12]Now about our brother Apollos: I strongly urged him to go to you with the

Direct Line

1 CORINTHIANS 16:13

You're tired of being a 98-pound weakling? Then you should eat healthy foods, lift weights and exercise. You'll do it because you don't want to stay a 98-pound weakling all your life. How do you rate yourself spiritually? Are you strong? Or are you the spiritual equivalent of that 98-pound weakling? You can become strong spiritually the same way you become strong physically: by exercising your faith! How? Be on your guard (against evil). Stand firm (in your convictions). Be a person of courage (speak out for what's right). Be strong (don't quit under pressure). Exercise your faith in these ways, and watch yourself grow!

[a]49 Some early manuscripts *so let us* [b]54 Isaiah 25:8 [c]55 Hosea 13:14

brothers. He was quite unwilling to go now, but he will go when he has the opportunity.

¹³Be on your guard; stand firm in the faith; be men of courage; be strong. ¹⁴Do everything in love.

¹⁵You know that the household of Stephanas were the first converts in Achaia, and they have devoted themselves to the service of the saints. I urge you, brothers, ¹⁶to submit to such as these and to everyone who joins in the work, and labors at it. ¹⁷I was glad when Stephanas, Fortunatus and Achaicus arrived, because they have supplied what was lacking from you. ¹⁸For they refreshed my spirit and yours also. Such men deserve recognition.

Final Greetings   ¹⁹The churches in the province of Asia send you greetings. Aquila and Priscilla*ᵃ* greet you warmly in the Lord, and so does the church that meets at their house. ²⁰All the brothers here send you greetings. Greet one another with a holy kiss.

²¹I, Paul, write this greeting in my own hand.

²²If anyone does not love the Lord—a curse be on him. Come, O Lord*ᵇ*!

²³The grace of the Lord Jesus be with you.

²⁴My love to all of you in Christ Jesus. Amen.*ᶜ*

ᵃ19 Greek *Prisca*, a variant of *Priscilla*   *ᵇ22* In Aramaic the expression *Come, O Lord* is *Marana tha*.
ᶜ24 Some manuscripts do not have *Amen.*

2 Corinthians

LOVE THEM?

Why should you? Why should you love those "friends" who are now saying they don't like you? They're trying to turn others against you? What can you do? Tell them off? Start talking about them like they're talking about you? What can a person do, anyway?

Most people in Corinth followed the advice Paul gave in his first letter. But some kept talking against Paul. Instead of getting mad, Paul wrote this letter. In it he shares how he feels and tells why he acts as he does. Paul loves the Corinthians. If you care about others, people who criticize or lie about you won't get very far.

Fundamentals

Why do bad things sometimes happen to Christians (2 Corinthians 1:9)?

Do you ever feel useless? Like you'll never measure up? What can you do (2 Corinthians 4)?

You don't have much money. Do you still have to give to the church (2 Corinthians 9:6-7)?

What chance do you have if you're not smart or good-looking (2 Corinthians 12:7-10)?

FAST FACTS

The apostle Paul wrote this letter.

The letter is about how to minister to others.

The best way to encourage others is to keep on believing God will help them change.

Repentance means being sorry enough to change your ways.

God doesn't always say yes when you pray for healing (2 Corinthians 12:7-8).

1 Paul, an apostle of Christ Jesus by the will of God, and Timothy our brother,

To the church of God in Corinth, together with all the saints throughout Achaia:

²Grace and peace to you from God our Father and the Lord Jesus Christ.

The God of All Comfort ³Praise be to the God and Father of our Lord Jesus Christ, the Father of compassion and the God of all comfort, ⁴who comforts us in all our troubles, so that we can comfort those in any trouble with the comfort we ourselves have received from God. ⁵For just as the sufferings of Christ flow over into our lives, so also through Christ our comfort overflows. ⁶If we are distressed, it is for your comfort and salvation; if we are comforted, it is for your comfort, which produces in you patient endurance of the same sufferings we suffer. ⁷And our hope for you is firm, because we know that just as you share in our sufferings, so also you share in our comfort.

⁸We do not want you to be uninformed, brothers, about the hardships we suffered in the province of Asia. We were under great pressure, far beyond our ability to endure, so that we despaired even of life. ⁹Indeed, in our hearts we felt the sentence of death. But this happened that we might not rely on ourselves but on God, who raises the dead. ¹⁰He has delivered us from such a deadly peril, and he will deliver us. On him we have set our hope that he will continue to deliver us, ¹¹as you help us by your prayers. Then many will give thanks on our*ᵃ* behalf for the gracious favor granted us in answer to the prayers of many.

Paul's Change of Plans ¹²Now this is our boast: Our conscience testifies that we have conducted ourselves in the world, and especially in our relations with you, in the holiness and sincerity that are from God. We have done so not according to worldly wisdom but according to God's grace. ¹³For we do not write you anything you cannot read or understand. And I hope that, ¹⁴as you have understood us in part, you will come to understand fully that you can boast of us just as we will boast of you in the day of the Lord Jesus.

¹⁵Because I was confident of this, I planned to visit you first so that you might benefit twice. ¹⁶I planned to visit you on my way to Macedonia and to come back to you from Macedonia, and then to have you send me on my way to Judea. ¹⁷When I planned this, did I do it lightly? Or do I make my plans in a worldly manner so that in the same breath I say, "Yes, yes" and "No, no"?

¹⁸But as surely as God is faithful, our message to you is not "Yes" and "No." ¹⁹For the Son of God, Jesus Christ, who was preached among you by me and Si-las*ᵇ* and Timothy, was not "Yes" and "No," but in him it has always been "Yes."

ᵃ11 Many manuscripts your   ᵇ19 Greek Silvanus, a variant of Silas

---

2 CORINTHIANS 1:15–21

Mike asks you to the movies and then says he can't go. Mom says she'll take you to the mall and then decides she has to go to Grandma's instead. Do you have a right to be angry and call them both liars? The apostle Paul was accused of going back on a promise to visit the Corinthian church. Paul explained that when he told them his plan to visit, he didn't do it "lightly" (2 Corinthians 1:17). He meant what he said. But at times things beyond people's control cause them to change their plans. Of course, if someone lets you down again and again, he or she probably does promise "lightly." But as for others? Hey, give them a break.

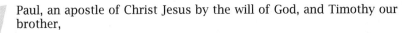

Dear Sam,

I never see my dad. My mother is an alcoholic, and I don't see much of her either. I'm sort of raising myself. The problem is I feel so lonely.

Cherie in Chicago

100 Advice Lane, Anywhere, USA

Dear Cherie,

I sense a lot of strength and maturity for someone your age. It's no wonder you feel lonely. It sounds like you're doing a very good job under very bad circumstances.

There's a passage in the Bible that I think will help. It's 2 Corinthians 1:3-4, where Paul is praising God for being "the God of all comfort." Isn't that a great phrase? God doesn't just offer comfort some of the time. He doesn't give just a little comfort. He doesn't ignore your pain. God sees what you are going through and offers you all comfort. God the Holy Spirit dwells in you. When you feel alone, remember that the Holy Spirit is right there, filling you and keeping you company.

But when you need a flesh-and-blood hug, maybe a nearby grandparent could be there for you. Or perhaps a parent of a good friend could be a help. God loves you and will supply all your needs and give you comfort. If you need someone in the flesh, pray and keep your eyes open. You are loved!

Sam

²⁰For no matter how many promises God has made, they are "Yes" in Christ. And so through him the "Amen" is spoken by us to the glory of God. ²¹Now it is God who makes both us and you stand firm in Christ. He anointed us, ²²set his seal of ownership on us, and put his Spirit in our hearts as a deposit, guaranteeing what is to come.

, ²³I call God as my witness that it was in order to spare you that I did not return to Corinth. ²⁴Not that we lord it over your faith, but we work with you for your joy, because it is by faith you stand firm. ¹So I made up my mind that I would not make another painful visit to you. ²For if I grieve you, who is left to make me glad but you whom I have grieved? ³I wrote as I did so that when I came I should not be distressed by those who ought to make me rejoice. I had confidence in all of you, that you would all share my joy. ⁴For I wrote you out of great distress and anguish of heart and with many tears, not to grieve you but to let you know the depth of my love for you.

Forgiveness for the Sinner ⁵If anyone has caused grief, he has not so much grieved me as he has grieved all of you, to some extent—not to put it too severely. ⁶The punishment inflicted on him by the majority is sufficient for him. ⁷Now instead, you ought to forgive and comfort him, so that he will not be overwhelmed by excessive sorrow. ⁸I urge you, therefore, to reaffirm your love for him. ⁹The reason I wrote you was to see if you would stand the test and be obedient in everything. ¹⁰If you forgive anyone, I also forgive him. And what I have forgiven—if there was anything to forgive—I have forgiven in the sight of Christ for your sake, ¹¹in order that Satan might not outwit us. For we are not unaware of his schemes.

Ministers of the New Covenant ¹²Now when I went to Troas to preach the gospel of Christ and found that the Lord had opened a door for me, ¹³I still had no peace of mind, because I did not find my brother Titus there. So I said good-by to them and went on to Macedonia.

¹⁴But thanks be to God, who always leads us in triumphal procession in Christ and through us spreads everywhere the fragrance of the knowledge of him. ¹⁵For we are to God the aroma of Christ among those who are being saved and those who are perishing. ¹⁶To the one we are the smell of death; to the other, the fragrance of life. And who is equal to such a task? ¹⁷Unlike so many, we do not peddle the word of God for profit. On the contrary, in Christ we speak before God with sincerity, like men sent from God.

Are we beginning to commend ourselves again? Or do we need, like some people, letters of recommendation to you or from you? ²You yourselves are our letter, written on our hearts, known and read by everybody. ³You show that you are a letter from Christ, the result of our ministry, written not with ink but with the Spirit of the living God, not on tablets of stone but on tablets of human hearts.

⁴Such confidence as this is ours through Christ before God. ⁵Not that we are competent in ourselves to claim anything for ourselves, but our competence comes from God. ⁶He has made us competent as ministers of a new covenant—not of the letter but of the Spirit; for the letter kills, but the Spirit gives life.

The Glory of the New Covenant ⁷Now if the ministry that brought death, which was engraved in letters on stone, came with glory, so that the Israelites could not look steadily at the face of Moses because of its glory, fading though it was, ⁸will not the ministry of the Spirit be even more glorious? ⁹If the ministry that condemns men is glorious, how much more glorious is the ministry that brings righteousness! ¹⁰For what was glorious has no glory now in comparison with the surpassing glory. ¹¹And if what was fading away came with glory, how much greater is the glory of that which lasts!

¹²Therefore, since we have such a hope, we are very bold. ¹³We are not like Moses, who would put a veil over his face to keep the Israelites from gazing at it while the radiance was fading away. ¹⁴But their minds were made dull, for to this day the same veil remains when the old covenant is read. It has not been removed, because only in Christ is it taken away. ¹⁵Even to this day when Moses is read, a veil covers their hearts. ¹⁶But whenever anyone turns to the Lord, the veil is taken away. ¹⁷Now the Lord is the Spirit, and where the Spirit of the Lord is, there is freedom. ¹⁸And we, who with unveiled faces all reflect*ᵃ* the Lord's glory, are being transformed into his likeness with ever-increasing glory, which comes from the Lord, who is the Spirit.

> Where the Spirit of the Lord is, there is freedom (2 Corinthians 3:17).

4 *Treasures in Jars of Clay* Therefore, since through God's mercy we have this ministry, we do not lose heart. ²Rather, we have renounced secret and shameful ways; we do not use deception, nor do we distort the word of God. On the contrary, by setting forth the truth plainly we commend ourselves to every man's conscience in the sight of God. ³And even if our gospel is veiled, it is veiled to those who are perishing. ⁴The god of this age has blinded the minds of unbelievers, so that they cannot see the light of the gospel of the glory of Christ, who is the image of God. ⁵For we do not preach ourselves, but Jesus Christ as Lord, and ourselves as your servants for Jesus' sake. ⁶For God, who said, "Let light shine out of darkness,"*ᵇ* made his light shine in our hearts to give us the light of the knowledge of the glory of God in the face of Christ.

⁷But we have this treasure in jars of clay to show that this all-surpassing power is from God and not from us. ⁸We are hard pressed on every side, but not crushed; perplexed, but not in despair; ⁹persecuted, but not abandoned; struck down, but not destroyed. ¹⁰We always carry around in our body the death of Jesus, so that the life of Jesus may also be revealed in our body. ¹¹For we who are alive are always being given over to death for Jesus' sake, so that his life may be revealed in our mortal body. ¹²So then, death is at work in us, but life is at work in you.

¹³It is written: "I believed; therefore I have spoken."*ᶜ* With that same spirit of faith we also believe and therefore speak, ¹⁴because we know that the one who raised the Lord Jesus from the dead will also raise us with Jesus and present us with you in his presence. ¹⁵All this is for your benefit, so that the grace that is reaching more and more people may cause thanksgiving to overflow to the glory of God.

¹⁶Therefore we do not lose heart. Though outwardly we are wasting away, yet inwardly we are being renewed day by day. ¹⁷For our light and momentary troubles are achieving for us an eternal glory that far outweighs them all. ¹⁸So we fix our eyes not on what is seen, but on what is unseen. For what is seen is temporary, but what is unseen is eternal.

5 *Our Heavenly Dwelling* Now we know that if the earthly tent we live in is destroyed, we have a building from God, an eternal house in heaven, not built by human hands. ²Meanwhile we groan, longing to be clothed with our heavenly dwelling, ³because when we are clothed, we will not be found naked. ⁴For while we are in this tent, we groan and are burdened, because we do not wish to be unclothed but to be clothed with our heavenly dwelling, so that what is mortal may be swallowed up by life. ⁵Now it is God who has made us for this very purpose and has given us the Spirit as a deposit, guaranteeing what is to come.

ᵃ18 Or *contemplate* *ᵇ6* Gen. 1:3 *ᶜ13* Psalm 116:10

⁶Therefore we are always confident and know that as long as we are at home in the body we are away from the Lord. ⁷We live by faith, not by sight. ⁸We are confident, I say, and would prefer to be away from the body and at home with the Lord. ⁹So we make it our goal to please him, whether we are at home in the body or away from it. ¹⁰For we must all appear before the judgment seat of Christ, that each one may receive what is due him for the things done while in the body, whether good or bad.

The Ministry of Reconciliation ¹¹Since, then, we know what it is to fear the Lord, we try to persuade men. What we are is plain to God, and I hope it is also plain to your conscience. ¹²We are not trying to commend ourselves to you again, but are giving you an opportunity to take pride in us, so that you can answer those who take pride in what is seen rather than in what is in the heart. ¹³If we are out of our mind, it is for the sake of God; if we are in our right mind, it is for you. ¹⁴For Christ's love compels us, because we are convinced that one died for all, and therefore all died. ¹⁵And he died for all, that those who live should no longer live for themselves but for him who died for them and was raised again.

¹⁶So from now on we regard no one from a worldly point of view. Though we once regarded Christ in this way, we do so no longer. ¹⁷Therefore, if anyone is in Christ, he is a new creation; the old has gone, the new has come! ¹⁸All this is from God, who reconciled us to himself through Christ and gave us the ministry of reconciliation: ¹⁹that God was reconciling the world to himself in Christ, not counting men's sins against them. And he has committed to us the message of reconciliation. ²⁰We are therefore Christ's ambassadors, as though God were making his appeal through us. We implore you on Christ's behalf: Be reconciled to God. ²¹God made him who had no sin to be sin*ᵃ* for us, so that in him we might become the righteousness of God.

6 As God's fellow workers we urge you not to receive God's grace in vain. ²For he says,

> "In the time of my favor I heard you,
> and in the day of salvation I helped you."*ᵇ*

I tell you, now is the time of God's favor, now is the day of salvation.

Paul's Hardships ³We put no stumbling block in anyone's path, so that our ministry will not be discredited. ⁴Rather, as servants of God we commend ourselves in every way: in great endurance; in troubles, hardships and distresses; ⁵in beatings, imprisonments and riots; in hard work, sleepless nights and hunger; ⁶in purity, understanding, patience and kindness; in the Holy Spirit and in sincere love; ⁷in truthful speech and in the power of God; with weapons of righteousness in the right hand and in the left; ⁸through glory and dishonor, bad report and good report; genuine, yet regarded as impostors; ⁹known, yet regarded as unknown; dying, and yet we live on; beaten, and yet not killed; ¹⁰sorrow-

Paul's motto must have been, "When the going gets tough, the tough   rely on God."

SEE 2 CORINTHIANS 6:3-10

ᵃ21 Or be a sin offering ᵇ2 Isaiah 49:8

ful, yet always rejoicing; poor, yet making many rich; having nothing, and yet possessing everything.

¹¹We have spoken freely to you, Corinthians, and opened wide our hearts to you. ¹²We are not withholding our affection from you, but you are withholding yours from us. ¹³As a fair exchange—I speak as to my children—open wide your hearts also.

Do Not Be Yoked With Unbelievers

¹⁴Do not be yoked together with unbelievers. For what do righteousness and wickedness have in common? Or what fellowship can light have with darkness? ¹⁵What harmony is there between Christ and Belial*ᵃ*? What does a believer have in common with an unbeliever? ¹⁶What agreement is there between the temple of God and idols? For we are the temple of the living God. As God has said: "I will live with them and walk among them, and I will be their God, and they will be my people."*ᵇ*

¹⁷"Therefore come out from them
   and be separate,
                                                              says the Lord.
   Touch no unclean thing,
      and I will receive you."*ᶜ*
¹⁸"I will be a Father to you,
   and you will be my sons and daughters,
                                      says the Lord Almighty."*ᵈ*

Since we have these promises, dear friends, let us purify ourselves from everything that contaminates body and spirit, perfecting holiness out of reverence for God.

Paul's Joy

²Make room for us in your hearts. We have wronged no one, we have corrupted no one, we have exploited no one. ³I do not say this to condemn you; I have said before that you have such a place in our hearts that we would live or die with you. ⁴I have great confidence in you; I take great pride in you. I am greatly encouraged; in all our troubles my joy knows no bounds.

⁵For when we came into Macedonia, this body of ours had no rest, but we were harassed at every turn—conflicts on the outside, fears within. ⁶But God, who comforts the downcast, comforted us by the coming of Titus, ⁷and not only by his coming but also by the comfort you had given him. He told us about your longing for me, your deep sorrow, your ardent concern for me, so that my joy was greater than ever.

⁸Even if I caused you sorrow by my letter, I do not regret it. Though I did regret it—I see that my letter hurt you, but only for a little while— ⁹yet now I am happy, not because you were made sorry, but because your sorrow led you to repentance. For you became sorrowful as God intend-

Direct Line

2 CORINTHIANS 6:14–18

Is it good or bad to be friends with non-Christians? Should a Christian date a non-Christian? Many just say, "Do not be yoked together with unbelievers." But what does that mean? Does it mean that you must not be friends with non-Christians? But how will they hear about Jesus if Christians don't befriend them? The best thing is to understand "yoked" as a partnership, a relationship involving commitment. Don't be partners with non-Christians because when it comes to values and commitments you have nothing in common. Marry a non-Christian? Definitely no. Date or hang around? You decide whether any commitment is involved.

ᵃ15 Greek *Beliar*, a variant of *Belial* *ᵇ16* Lev. 26:12; Jer. 32:38; Ezek. 37:27 *ᶜ17* Isaiah 52:11; Ezek. 20:34,41 *ᵈ18* 2 Samuel 7:14; 7:8

ed and so were not harmed in any way by us. ¹⁰Godly sorrow brings repentance that leads to salvation and leaves no regret, but worldly sorrow brings death. ¹¹See what this godly sorrow has produced in you: what earnestness, what eagerness to clear yourselves, what indignation, what alarm, what longing, what concern, what readiness to see justice done. At every point you have proved yourselves to be innocent in this matter. ¹²So even though I wrote to you, it was not on account of the one who did the wrong or of the injured party, but rather that before God you could see for yourselves how devoted to us you are. ¹³By all this we are encouraged.

In addition to our own encouragement, we were especially delighted to see how happy Titus was, because his spirit has been refreshed by all of you. ¹⁴I had boasted to him about you, and you have not embarrassed me. But just as everything we said to you was true, so our boasting about you to Titus has proved to be true as well. ¹⁵And his affection for you is all the greater when he remembers that you were all obedient, receiving him with fear and trembling. ¹⁶I am glad I can have complete confidence in you.

8 *Generosity Encouraged* And now, brothers, we want you to know about the grace that God has given the Macedonian churches. ²Out of the most severe trial, their overflowing joy and their extreme poverty welled up in rich generosity. ³For I testify that they gave as much as they were able, and even beyond their ability. Entirely on their own, ⁴they urgently pleaded with us for the privilege of sharing in this service to the saints. ⁵And they did not do as we expected, but they gave themselves first to the Lord and then to us in keeping with God's will. ⁶So we urged Titus, since he had earlier made a beginning, to bring also to completion this act of grace on your part. ⁷But just as you excel in everything—in faith, in speech, in knowledge, in complete earnestness and in your love for us*ᵃ*—see that you also excel in this grace of giving.

⁸I am not commanding you, but I want to test the sincerity of your love by comparing it with the earnestness of others. ⁹For you know the grace of our Lord Jesus Christ, that though he was rich, yet for your sakes he became poor, so that you through his poverty might become rich.

---

*ᵃ7 Some manuscripts *in our love for you*

The Israelites were commanded to tithe, to give 10 percent of their income to God. The New Testament doesn't repeat that command, but it does teach these principles:

* Giving is a privilege (2 Corinthians 8:4).
* Jesus set an excellent example of giving (2 Corinthians 8:9).
* Give generously, and you will reap generously (2 Corinthians 9:6).
* You are free to decide how much to give (2 Corinthians 9:7).
* Give cheerfully (2 Corinthians 9:7).
* Trust God to supply your needs (2 Corinthians 9:11).

Now is a good time to get into the habit of giving. Don't think, "I don't have much now, but I'll give when I get a job." God measures your giving by what you have, not by what you don't have (2 Corinthians 8:12).

The Bible Says

Give Until It Feels Good

[10]And here is my advice about what is best for you in this matter: Last year you were the first not only to give but also to have the desire to do so. [11]Now finish the work, so that your eager willingness to do it may be matched by your completion of it, according to your means. [12]For if the willingness is there, the gift is acceptable according to what one has, not according to what he does not have.

[13]Our desire is not that others might be relieved while you are hard pressed, but that there might be equality. [14]At the present time your plenty will supply what they need, so that in turn their plenty will supply what you need. Then there will be equality, [15]as it is written: "He who gathered much did not have too much, and he who gathered little did not have too little."[a]

Titus Sent to Corinth   [16]I thank God, who put into the heart of Titus the same concern I have for you. [17]For Titus not only welcomed our appeal, but he is coming to you with much enthusiasm and on his own initiative. [18]And we are sending along with him the brother who is praised by all the churches for his service to the gospel. [19]What is more, he was chosen by the churches to accompany us as we carry the offering, which we administer in order to honor the Lord himself and to show our eagerness to help. [20]We want to avoid any criticism of the way we administer this liberal gift. [21]For we are taking pains to do what is right, not only in the eyes of the Lord but also in the eyes of men.

[22]In addition, we are sending with them our brother who has often proved to us in many ways that he is zealous, and now even more so because of his great confidence in you. [23]As for Titus, he is my partner and fellow worker among you; as for our brothers, they are representatives of the churches and an honor to Christ. [24]Therefore show these men the proof of your love and the reason for our pride in you, so that the churches can see it.

9 There is no need for me to write to you about this service to the saints. [2]For I know your eagerness to help, and I have been boasting about it to the Macedonians, telling them that since last year you in Achaia were ready to give; and your enthusiasm has stirred most of them to action. [3]But I am sending the brothers in order that our boasting about you in this matter should not prove hollow, but that you may be ready, as I said you would be. [4]For if any Macedonians come with me and find you unprepared, we—not to say anything about you—would be ashamed of having been so confident. [5]So I thought it necessary to urge the brothers to visit you in advance and finish the arrangements for the generous gift you had promised. Then it will be ready as a generous gift, not as one grudgingly given.

Sowing Generously   [6]Remember this: Whoever sows sparingly will also reap sparingly, and whoever sows generously will also reap generously. [7]Each man should give what he has decided in his heart to give, not reluctantly or under compulsion, for God loves a cheerful giver. [8]And God is able to make all grace abound to you, so that in all things at all times, having all that you need, you will abound in every good work. [9]As it is written:

"He has scattered abroad his gifts to the poor;
    his righteousness endures forever."[b]

[10]Now he who supplies seed to the sower and bread for food will also supply and increase your store of seed and will enlarge the harvest of your righteousness. [11]You will be made rich in every way so that you can be generous on every occasion, and through us your generosity will result in thanksgiving to God.

[12]This service that you perform is not only supplying the needs of God's people but is also overflowing in many expressions of thanks to God. [13]Be-

[a]15 Exodus 16:18   [b]9 Psalm 112:9

cause of the service by which you have proved yourselves, men will praise God for the obedience that accompanies your confession of the gospel of Christ, and for your generosity in sharing with them and with everyone else. [14]And in their prayers for you their hearts will go out to you, because of the surpassing grace God has given you. [15]Thanks be to God for his indescribable gift!

10 *Paul's Defense of His Ministry* By the meekness and gentleness of Christ, I appeal to you—I, Paul, who am "timid" when face to face with you, but "bold" when away! [2]I beg you that when I come I may not have to be as bold as I expect to be toward some people who think that we live by the standards of this world. [3]For though we live in the world, we do not wage war as the world does. [4]The weapons we fight with are not the weapons of the world. On the contrary, they have divine power to demolish strongholds. [5]We demolish arguments and every pretension that sets itself up against the knowledge of God, and we take captive every thought to make it obedient to Christ. [6]And we will be ready to punish every act of disobedience, once your obedience is complete.

[7]You are looking only on the surface of things.[a] If anyone is confident that he belongs to Christ, he should consider again that we belong to Christ just as much as he. [8]For even if I boast somewhat freely about the authority the Lord gave us for building you up rather than pulling you down, I will not be ashamed of it. [9]I do not want to seem to be trying to frighten you with my letters. [10]For some say, "His letters are weighty and forceful, but in person he is unimpressive and his speaking amounts to nothing." [11]Such people should realize that what we are in our letters when we are absent, we will be in our actions when we are present.

[12]We do not dare to classify or compare ourselves with some who commend themselves. When they measure themselves by themselves and compare themselves with themselves, they are not wise. [13]We, however, will not boast beyond proper limits, but will confine our boasting to the field God has assigned to us, a field that reaches even to you. [14]We are not going too far in our boasting, as would be the case if we had not come to you, for we did get as far as you with the gospel of Christ. [15]Neither do we go beyond our limits by boasting of work done by others.[b] Our hope is that, as your faith continues to grow, our area of activity among you will greatly expand, [16]so that we can preach the gospel in the regions beyond you. For we do not want to boast about work already done in another man's territory. [17]But, "Let him who boasts boast in the Lord."[c] [18]For it is not the one who commends himself who is approved, but the one whom the Lord commends.

11 *Paul and the False Apostles* I hope you will put up with a little of my foolishness; but you are already

[a]7 Or *Look at the obvious facts* [b]13-15 Or [13]*We, however, will not boast about things that cannot be measured, but we will boast according to the standard of measurement that the God of measure has assigned us—a measurement that relates even to you.* [14] . . . . [15]*Neither do we boast about things that cannot be measured in regard to the work done by others.* [c]17 Jer. 9:24

2 CORINTHIANS 10:12

Carol has nicer clothes. Jason is smarter. Carl can dunk a basketball. Karen has thick, wavy hair. Danny makes friends easily. And there you are. Discount store clothes. Mostly C's. Straight hair. And shy. To measure yourself by others, as Paul says, is "not wise." So to whom do you compare yourself? No one. You learn to see yourself as God made you, with your own strengths and weaknesses. And you work hard to develop your strengths and overcome your weaknesses. When you become the best "you" that you can be, you'll be a success. Really.

Direct Line

doing that. ²I am jealous for you with a godly jealousy. I promised you to one husband, to Christ, so that I might present you as a pure virgin to him. ³But I am afraid that just as Eve was deceived by the serpent's cunning, your minds may somehow be led astray from your sincere and pure devotion to Christ. ⁴For if someone comes to you and preaches a Jesus other than the Jesus we preached, or if you receive a different spirit from the one you received, or a different gospel from the one you accepted, you put up with it easily enough. ⁵But I do not think I am in the least inferior to those "super-apostles." ⁶I may not be a trained speaker, but I do have knowledge. We have made this perfectly clear to you in every way.

⁷Was it a sin for me to lower myself in order to elevate you by preaching the gospel of God to you free of charge? ⁸I robbed other churches by receiving support from them so as to serve you. ⁹And when I was with you and needed something, I was not a burden to anyone, for the brothers who came from Macedonia supplied what I needed. I have kept myself from being a burden to you in any way, and will continue to do so. ¹⁰As surely as the truth of Christ is in me, nobody in the regions of Achaia will stop this boasting of mine. ¹¹Why? Because I do not love you? God knows I do! ¹²And I will keep on doing what I am doing in order to cut the ground from under those who want an opportunity to be considered equal with us in the things they boast about.

¹³For such men are false apostles, deceitful workmen, masquerading as apostles of Christ. ¹⁴And no wonder, for Satan himself masquerades as an angel of light. ¹⁵It is not surprising, then, if his servants masquerade as servants of righteousness. Their end will be what their actions deserve.

Paul Boasts About His Sufferings   ¹⁶I repeat: Let no one take me for a fool. But if you do, then receive me just as you would a fool, so that I may do a little boasting. ¹⁷In this self-confident boasting I am not talking as the Lord would, but as a fool. ¹⁸Since many are boasting in the way the world does, I too will boast. ¹⁹You gladly put up with fools since you are so wise! ²⁰In fact, you even put up with anyone who enslaves you or exploits you or takes advantage of you or pushes himself forward or slaps you in the face. ²¹To my shame I admit that we were too weak for that!

What anyone else dares to boast about—I am speaking as a fool—I also dare to boast about. ²²Are they Hebrews? So am I. Are they Israelites? So am I. Are they Abraham's descendants? So am I. ²³Are they servants of Christ? (I am out of my mind to talk like this.) I am more. I have worked much harder, been in prison more frequently, been flogged more severely, and been exposed to death again and again. ²⁴Five times I received from the Jews the forty lashes minus one. ²⁵Three times I was beaten with rods, once I was stoned, three times I was shipwrecked, I spent a night and a day in the open sea, ²⁶I have been constantly on the move. I have been in danger from rivers, in danger from bandits, in danger from my own countrymen, in danger from Gentiles; in danger in the city, in danger in the country, in danger at sea; and in danger from false brothers. ²⁷I have labored and toiled and have often gone without sleep; I have known hunger and thirst and have often gone without food; I have been cold and naked. ²⁸Besides everything else, I face daily the pressure of my concern for all the churches. ²⁹Who is weak, and I do not feel weak? Who is led into sin, and I do not inwardly burn?

³⁰If I must boast, I will boast of the things that show my weakness. ³¹The God and Father of the Lord Jesus, who is to be praised forever, knows that I am not lying. ³²In Damascus the governor under King Aretas had the city of the Damascenes guarded in order to arrest me. ³³But I was lowered in a basket from a window in the wall and slipped through his hands.

12 *Paul's Vision and His Thorn* I must go on boasting. Although there is nothing to be gained, I will go on to visions and revelations from the Lord. ²I know a man in Christ who fourteen years ago was caught up to the third heaven. Whether it was in the body or out of the body I do not know—God knows. ³And I know that this man—whether in the body or apart from the body I do not know, but God knows— ⁴was caught up to paradise. He heard inexpressible things, things that man is not permitted to tell. ⁵I will boast about a man like that, but I will not boast about myself, except about my weaknesses. ⁶Even if I should choose to boast, I would not be a fool, because I would be speaking the truth. But I refrain, so no one will think more of me than is warranted by what I do or say.

⁷To keep me from becoming conceited because of these surpassingly great revelations, there was given me a thorn in my flesh, a messenger of Satan, to torment me. ⁸Three times I pleaded with the Lord to take it away from me. ⁹But he said to me, "My grace is sufficient for you, for my power is made perfect in weakness." Therefore I will boast all the more gladly about my weaknesses, so that Christ's power may rest on me. ¹⁰That is why, for Christ's sake, I delight in weaknesses, in insults, in hardships, in persecutions, in difficulties. For when I am weak, then I am strong.

Paul's Concern for the Corinthians ¹¹I have made a fool of myself, but you drove me to it. I ought to have been commended by you, for I am not in the least inferior to the "super-apostles," even though I am nothing. ¹²The things that mark an apostle—signs, wonders and miracles—were done among you with great perseverance. ¹³How were you inferior to the other churches, except that I was never a burden to you? Forgive me this wrong!

¹⁴Now I am ready to visit you for the third time, and I will not be a burden to you, because what I want is not your possessions but you. After all, children should not have to save up for their parents, but parents for their children. ¹⁵So I will very gladly spend for you everything I have and expend myself as well. If I love you more, will you love me less? ¹⁶Be that as it may, I have not been a burden to you. Yet, crafty fellow that I am, I caught you by trickery! ¹⁷Did I exploit you through any of the men I sent you? ¹⁸I urged Titus to go to you and I sent our brother with him. Titus did not exploit you, did he? Did we not act in the same spirit and follow the same course?

¹⁹Have you been thinking all along that we have been defending ourselves to you? We have been speaking in the sight of God as those in Christ; and everything we do, dear friends, is for your strengthening. ²⁰For I am afraid that when I come I may not find you as I want you to be, and you may not find me as you want me to be. I fear that there may be quarreling, jealousy, outbursts of anger, factions, slander, gossip, arrogance and disorder. ²¹I am afraid that when I come again my God will humble me before you, and I will be grieved over many who have sinned ear-

ᵃ1 Deut. 19:15

2 CORINTHIANS 13:1–4

Stay out too late? You get grounded. Get in a fight at school? Suspended! Someone is always there to punish you when you mess up. However, your parents can't follow you around all the time. You know very well there are lots of things you could do that Mom and Dad would probably never find out about! So why not go ahead? Some Corinthians figured that since Paul wasn't around they could do whatever they wanted. Paul didn't threaten, but he did warn them: "Christ . . . is not weak in dealing with you" (2 Corinthians 13:3). Remember that God will know what you've done, and he doesn't let Christians get away with practicing sin.

Direct Line

Dear Sam,

I recently lost the vision in my left eye. I have prayed for healing, but the doctor says it won't happen. Why won't God listen?

Blair in Boulder

100 Advice Lane, Anywhere, USA

Dear Blair,

What a difficult situation for you! I'm sure that it's been hard to adjust. But are you sure that God didn't listen or answer your prayer? When you were little and asked for a candy bar, did your mom ever say, "Not now"? She knew it wasn't best for you at that time. Maybe you thought she was mean. But just because you were too little to understand doesn't mean she didn't understand or listen or care. Perhaps God is telling you not yet or maybe even no. But that doesn't mean he didn't listen or that he doesn't care. Even the apostle Paul didn't always get the answer he wanted to his prayers (2 Corinthians 12:7-9).

God's wisdom is perfect. It is our understanding that is imperfect. God may just want you to find strength in him instead of in yourself. Maybe in the future there will be a cure for you. Or maybe you'll have to learn to live with it, just as Paul learned to live with his "thorn" in the flesh. You may never fully understand all the things that happen in your life. But you can be sure that God will use even the worst situations for his glory and your weaknesses as his strengths.

Sam

lier and have not repented of the impurity, sexual sin and debauchery in which they have indulged.

13 *Final Warnings* This will be my third visit to you. "Every matter must be established by the testimony of two or three witnesses."[a] [2]I already gave you a warning when I was with you the second time. I now repeat it while absent: On my return I will not spare those who sinned earlier or any of the others, [3]since you are demanding proof that Christ is speaking through me. He is not weak in dealing with you, but is powerful among you. [4]For to be sure, he was crucified in weakness, yet he lives by God's power. Likewise, we are weak in him, yet by God's power we will live with him to serve you.

[5]Examine yourselves to see whether you are in the faith; test yourselves. Do you not realize that Christ Jesus is in you—unless, of course, you fail the test? [6]And I trust that you will discover that we have not failed the test. [7]Now we pray to God that you will not do anything wrong. Not that people will see that we have stood the test but that you will do what is right even though we may seem to have failed. [8]For we cannot do anything against the truth, but only for the truth. [9]We are glad whenever we are weak but you are strong; and our prayer is for your perfection. [10]This is why I write these things when I am absent, that when I come I may not have to be harsh in my use of authority—the authority the Lord gave me for building you up, not for tearing you down.

Final Greetings [11]Finally, brothers, good-by. Aim for perfection, listen to my appeal, be of one mind, live in peace. And the God of love and peace will be with you.

[12]Greet one another with a holy kiss. [13]All the saints send their greetings.

[14]May the grace of the Lord Jesus Christ, and the love of God, and the fellowship of the Holy Spirit be with you all.

THOSE RULES AGAIN.

Do you ever feel like it's hard to be a Christian? That Christians have to obey all sort of rules other people ignore? Not that you don't want to be a good Christian, it's just hard sometimes.

In New Testament times false teachers visited some of the churches founded by Paul. They told the new Christians they had to follow all the Old Testament rules. In this letter to the Galatians Paul explains that being a Christian means trusting Jesus completely and letting the Holy Spirit change you as a person from within. It's not trying to change by keeping somebody's rules.

Fundamentals

Why don't you follow Old Testament rules? They're in the Bible (Galatians 3:11-25).

What does the Bible mean when it says you're "free." Free to do what (Galatians 5:1-12)?

If you don't have to live by God's laws, what will keep you from sinning (Galatians 5:13-26)?

FAST FACTS

Galatia was a Roman province.

Paul wrote Galatians to all the churches he founded in Galatia on his first missionary journey.

Men who said Christians must keep Moses' Law are called "Judaizers."

A church council held in Jerusalem (Acts 15) agreed that Christians are not required to follow Old Testament laws.

1 Paul, an apostle—sent not from men nor by man, but by Jesus Christ and God the Father, who raised him from the dead— ²and all the brothers with me,

To the churches in Galatia:

³Grace and peace to you from God our Father and the Lord Jesus Christ, ⁴who gave himself for our sins to rescue us from the present evil age, according to the will of our God and Father, ⁵to whom be glory for ever and ever. Amen.

No Other Gospel ⁶I am astonished that you are so quickly deserting the one who called you by the grace of Christ and are turning to a different gospel— ⁷which is really no gospel at all. Evidently some people are throwing you into confusion and are trying to pervert the gospel of Christ. ⁸But even if we or an angel from heaven should preach a gospel other than the one we preached to you, let him be eternally condemned! ⁹As we have already said, so now I say again: If anybody is preaching to you a gospel other than what you accepted, let him be eternally condemned!

¹⁰Am I now trying to win the approval of men, or of God? Or am I trying to please men? If I were still trying to please men, I would not be a servant of Christ.

> The Lord Jesus Christ . . . gave himself for our sins to rescue us from the present evil age (Galatians 1:3-4).

Paul Called by God ¹¹I want you to know, brothers, that the gospel I preached is not something that man made up. ¹²I did not receive it from any man, nor was I taught it; rather, I received it by revelation from Jesus Christ.

¹³For you have heard of my previous way of life in Judaism, how intensely I persecuted the church of God and tried to destroy it. ¹⁴I was advancing in Judaism beyond many Jews of my own age and was extremely zealous for the traditions of my fathers. ¹⁵But when God, who set me apart from birth*a* and called me by his grace, was pleased ¹⁶to reveal his Son in me so that I might preach him among the Gentiles, I did not consult any man, ¹⁷nor did I go up to Jerusalem to see those who were apostles before I was, but I went immediately into Arabia and later returned to Damascus.

¹⁸Then after three years, I went up to Jerusalem to get acquainted with Peter*b* and stayed with him fifteen days. ¹⁹I saw none of the other apostles— only James, the Lord's brother. ²⁰I assure you before God that what I am writing you is no lie. ²¹Later I went to Syria and Cilicia. ²²I was personally unknown to the churches of Judea that are in Christ. ²³They only heard the report: "The man who formerly persecuted us is now preaching the faith he once tried to destroy." ²⁴And they praised God because of me.

2 *Paul Accepted by the Apostles* Fourteen years later I went up again to Jerusalem, this time with Barnabas. I took Titus along also. ²I went in response to a revelation and set before them the gospel that I preach among the Gentiles. But I did this privately to those who seemed to be leaders, for fear that I was running or had run my race in vain. ³Yet not even Titus, who was with me, was compelled to be circumcised, even though he was a Greek. ⁴This matter arose because some false brothers had infiltrated our ranks to spy on the freedom we have in Christ Jesus and to make us slaves. ⁵We did not give in to them for a moment, so that the truth of the gospel might remain with you.

⁶As for those who seemed to be important—whatever they were makes no difference to me; God does not judge by external appearance—those men

---

*a*15 Or *from my mother's womb*   *b*18 Greek *Cephas*

added nothing to my message. ⁷On the contrary, they saw that I had been entrusted with the task of preaching the gospel to the Gentiles,ᵃ just as Peter had been to the Jews.ᵇ ⁸For God, who was at work in the ministry of Peter as an apostle to the Jews, was also at work in my ministry as an apostle to the Gentiles. ⁹James, Peterᶜ and John, those reputed to be pillars, gave me and Barnabas the right hand of fellowship when they recognized the grace given to me. They agreed that we should go to the Gentiles, and they to the Jews. ¹⁰All they asked was that we should continue to remember the poor, the very thing I was eager to do.

Paul Opposes Peter ¹¹When Peter came to Antioch, I opposed him to his face, because he was clearly in the wrong. ¹²Before certain men came from James, he used to eat with the Gentiles. But when they arrived, he began to draw back and separate himself from the Gentiles because he was afraid of those who belonged to the circumcision group. ¹³The other Jews joined him in his hypocrisy, so that by their hypocrisy even Barnabas was led astray.

¹⁴When I saw that they were not acting in line with the truth of the gospel, I said to Peter in front of them all, "You are a Jew, yet you live like a Gentile and not like a Jew. How is it, then, that you force Gentiles to follow Jewish customs?

¹⁵"We who are Jews by birth and not 'Gentile sinners' ¹⁶know that a man is not justified by observing the law, but by faith in Jesus Christ. So we, too, have put our faith in Christ Jesus that we may be justified by faith in Christ and not by observing the law, because by observing the law no one will be justified.

¹⁷"If, while we seek to be justified in Christ, it becomes evident that we ourselves are sinners, does that mean that Christ promotes sin? Absolutely not! ¹⁸If I rebuild what I destroyed, I prove that I am a lawbreaker. ¹⁹For through the law I died to the law so that I might live for God. ²⁰I have been crucified with Christ and I no longer live, but Christ lives in me. The life I live in the body, I live by faith in the Son of God, who loved me and gave himself for me. ²¹I do not set aside the grace of God, for if righteousness could be gained through the law, Christ died for nothing!"ᵈ

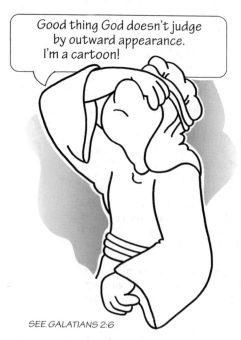

Good thing God doesn't judge by outward appearance. I'm a cartoon!

SEE GALATIANS 2:6

Faith or Observance of the Law You foolish Galatians! Who has bewitched you? Before your very eyes Jesus Christ was clearly portrayed as crucified. ²I would like to learn just one thing from you: Did you receive the Spirit by observing the law, or by believing what you heard? ³Are you so foolish? After beginning with the Spirit, are you now trying to attain your goal by human effort? ⁴Have you suffered so much for nothing—if it really was for nothing? ⁵Does God give you his Spirit and work miracles among you because you observe the law, or because you believe what you heard?

⁶Consider Abraham: "He believed God, and it was credited to him as righteousness."ᵉ ⁷Understand, then, that those who believe are children of Abraham. ⁸The Scripture foresaw that God would justify the

---

ᵃ7 Greek *uncircumcised* ᵇ7 Greek *circumcised*; also in verses 8 and 9 ᶜ9 Greek *Cephas*; also in verses 11 and 14 ᵈ21 Some interpreters end the quotation after verse 14. ᵉ6 Gen. 15:6

Gentiles by faith, and announced the gospel in advance to Abraham: "All nations will be blessed through you."*a* 9So those who have faith are blessed along with Abraham, the man of faith.

10All who rely on observing the law are under a curse, for it is written: "Cursed is everyone who does not continue to do everything written in the Book of the Law."*b* 11Clearly no one is justified before God by the law, because, "The righteous will live by faith."*c* 12The law is not based on faith; on the contrary, "The man who does these things will live by them."*d* 13Christ redeemed us from the curse of the law by becoming a curse for us, for it is written: "Cursed is everyone who is hung on a tree."*e* 14He redeemed us in order that the blessing given to Abraham might come to the Gentiles through Christ Jesus, so that by faith we might receive the promise of the Spirit.

The Law and the Promise   15Brothers, let me take an example from everyday life. Just as no one can set aside or add to a human covenant that has been duly established, so it is in this case. 16The promises were spoken to Abraham and to his seed. The Scripture does not say "and to seeds," meaning many people, but "and to your seed,"*f* meaning one person, who is Christ. 17What I mean is this: The law, introduced 430 years later, does not set aside the covenant previously established by God and thus do away with the promise. 18For if the inheritance depends on the law, then it no longer depends on a promise; but God in his grace gave it to Abraham through a promise.

19What, then, was the purpose of the law? It was added because of transgressions until the Seed to whom the promise referred had come. The law was put into effect through angels by a mediator. 20A mediator, however, does not represent just one party; but God is one.

21Is the law, therefore, opposed to the promises of God? Absolutely not! For if a law had been given that could impart life, then righteousness would certainly have come by the law. 22But the Scripture declares that the whole world is a prisoner of sin, so that what was promised, being given through faith in Jesus Christ, might be given to those who believe.

23Before this faith came, we were held prisoners by the law, locked up until faith should be revealed. 24So the law was put in charge to lead us to Christ*g* that we might be justified by faith. 25Now that faith has come, we are no longer under the supervision of the law.

---

a8 Gen. 12:3; 18:18; 22:18   *b10* Deut. 27:26   *c11* Hab. 2:4   *d12* Lev. 18:5   *e13* Deut. 21:23   *f16* Gen. 12:7; 13:15; 24:7   *g24* Or *charge until Christ came*

The Bible Says

Don't Try— Rely

Try as hard as you can, you can't earn heaven and you can't become a stronger Christian by trying to keep God's law. The important word here is *try*. To try is to attempt to do something on your own. You've done that, and you know how easy it is to fail. Try harder, and you still fail. In fact, that's what the law is best at: showing you how you fail no matter how hard you try (Galatians 3:19–22).

The Bible says to rely, not try. Your relationship with God is based on faith, not on trying to keep his law (Galatians 3:6–9). That means you trust God so much you step out and do what's right. Not by extra effort. Not by depending on yourself. But by relying on the Lord and discovering that he really will help you succeed, not fail.

Sons of God [26]You are all sons of God through faith in Christ Jesus, [27]for all of you who were baptized into Christ have clothed yourselves with Christ. [28]There is neither Jew nor Greek, slave nor free, male nor female, for you are all one in Christ Jesus. [29]If you belong to Christ, then you are Abraham's seed, and heirs according to the promise.

4 What I am saying is that as long as the heir is a child, he is no different from a slave, although he owns the whole estate. [2]He is subject to guardians and trustees until the time set by his father. [3]So also, when we were children, we were in slavery under the basic principles of the world. [4]But when the time had fully come, God sent his Son, born of a woman, born under law, [5]to redeem those under law, that we might receive the full rights of sons. [6]Because you are sons, God sent the Spirit of his Son into our hearts, the Spirit who calls out, *"Abba,*[a] Father." [7]So you are no longer a slave, but a son; and since you are a son, God has made you also an heir.

Paul's Concern for the Galatians [8]Formerly, when you did not know God, you were slaves to those who by nature are not gods. [9]But now that you know God—or rather are known by God—how is it that you are turning back to those weak and miserable principles? Do you wish to be enslaved by them all over again? [10]You are observing special days and months and seasons and years! [11]I fear for you, that somehow I have wasted my efforts on you.

[12]I plead with you, brothers, become like me, for I became like you. You have done me no wrong. [13]As you know, it was because of an illness that I first preached the gospel to you. [14]Even though my illness was a trial to you, you did not treat me with contempt or scorn. Instead, you welcomed me as if I were an angel of God, as if I were Christ Jesus himself. [15]What has happened to all your joy? I can testify that, if you could have done so, you would have torn out your eyes and given them to me. [16]Have I now become your enemy by telling you the truth?

[17]Those people are zealous to win you over, but for no good. What they want is to alienate you ⌊from us⌋, so that you may be zealous for them. [18]It is fine to be zealous, provided the purpose is good, and to be so always and not just when I am with you. [19]My dear children, for whom I am again in the pains of childbirth until Christ is formed in you, [20]how I wish I could be with you now and change my tone, because I am perplexed about you!

Hagar and Sarah [21]Tell me, you who want to be under the law, are you not aware of what the law says? [22]For it is written that Abraham had two sons, one by the slave woman and the other by the free woman. [23]His son by the slave woman was born in the ordinary way; but his son by the free woman was born as the result of a promise.

[24]These things may be taken figuratively, for the women represent two covenants. One covenant is from Mount Sinai and bears children who are to be slaves: This is Hagar. [25]Now Hagar stands for Mount Sinai in Arabia and corresponds to the present city of Jerusalem, because she is in slavery with her children. [26]But the Jerusalem that is above is free, and she is our mother. [27]For it is written:

> "Be glad, O barren woman,
>   who bears no children;
> break forth and cry aloud,
>   you who have no labor pains;
> because more are the children of the desolate woman
>   than of her who has a husband."[b]

[a]6 Aramaic for *Father* [b]27 Isaiah 54:1

²⁸Now you, brothers, like Isaac, are children of promise. ²⁹At that time the son born in the ordinary way persecuted the son born by the power of the Spirit. It is the same now. ³⁰But what does the Scripture say? "Get rid of the slave woman and her son, for the slave woman's son will never share in the inheritance with the free woman's son."ᵃ ³¹Therefore, brothers, we are not children of the slave woman, but of the free woman.

5 *Freedom in Christ* It is for freedom that Christ has set us free. Stand firm, then, and do not let yourselves be burdened again by a yoke of slavery.

²Mark my words! I, Paul, tell you that if you let yourselves be circumcised, Christ will be of no value to you at all. ³Again I declare to every man who lets himself be circumcised that he is obligated to obey the whole law. ⁴You who are trying to be justified by law have been alienated from Christ; you have fallen away from grace. ⁵But by faith we eagerly await through the Spirit the righteousness for which we hope. ⁶For in Christ Jesus neither circumcision nor uncircumcision has any value. The only thing that counts is faith expressing itself through love.

⁷You were running a good race. Who cut in on you and kept you from obeying the truth? ⁸That kind of persuasion does not come from the one who calls you. ⁹"A little yeast works through the whole batch of dough." ¹⁰I am confident in the Lord that you will take no other view. The one who is throwing you into confusion will pay the penalty, whoever he may be. ¹¹Brothers, if I am still preaching circumcision, why am I still being persecuted? In that case the offense of the cross has been abolished. ¹²As for those agitators, I wish they would go the whole way and emasculate themselves!

¹³You, my brothers, were called to be free. But do not use your freedom to indulge the sinful natureᵇ; rather, serve one another in love. ¹⁴The entire law is summed up in a single command: "Love your neighbor as yourself."ᶜ ¹⁵If you keep on biting and devouring each other, watch out or you will be destroyed by each other.

Life by the Spirit ¹⁶So I say, live by the Spirit, and you will not gratify the desires of the sinful nature. ¹⁷For the sinful nature desires what is contrary to the Spirit, and the Spirit what is contrary to the sinful nature. They are in conflict with each other, so that you do not do what you want. ¹⁸But if you are led by the Spirit, you are not under law.

¹⁹The acts of the sinful nature are obvious: sexual immorality, impurity and debauchery; ²⁰idolatry and witchcraft; hatred, discord, jealousy, fits of rage, selfish ambition, dissensions, factions ²¹and envy; drunkenness, orgies, and the like. I warn you, as I did before, that those who live like this will not inherit the kingdom of God.

²²But the fruit of the Spirit is love, joy, peace, patience, kindness, goodness, faithfulness, ²³gentleness and self-control.

ᵃ*30* Gen. 21:10   ᵇ*13* Or *the flesh*; also in verses 16, 17, 19 and 24   ᶜ*14* Lev. 19:18

GALATIANS 5:22–25

What does God want from you? Does he want you to pass out tracts in school? Or pray five hours a day? Or be a missionary? Or a preacher? Maybe. But there is something he wants for sure. And not from you. *For* you. What God wants for you is a life filled with love, joy, peace, patience, kindness, goodness, faithfulness, gentleness and self-control. To make sure you have that kind of life, he has given you the Holy Spirit. Sure, you can choose to follow your sinful impulses (Galatians 5:16–21). Or you can choose to follow those good impulses that the Holy Spirit gives you. Why not concentrate on what God wants for you? And enjoy!

Direct Line

Against such things there is no law. ²⁴Those who belong to Christ Jesus have crucified the sinful nature with its passions and desires. ²⁵Since we live by the Spirit, let us keep in step with the Spirit. ²⁶Let us not become conceited, provoking and envying each other.

6 *Doing Good to All* Brothers, if someone is caught in a sin, you who are spiritual should restore him gently. But watch yourself, or you also may be tempted. ²Carry each other's burdens, and in this way you will fulfill the law of Christ. ³If anyone thinks he is something when he is nothing, he deceives himself. ⁴Each one should test his own actions. Then he can take pride in himself, without comparing himself to somebody else, ⁵for each one should carry his own load.

⁶Anyone who receives instruction in the word must share all good things with his instructor.

⁷Do not be deceived: God cannot be mocked. A man reaps what he sows. ⁸The one who sows to please his sinful nature, from that nature^a will reap destruction; the one who sows to please the Spirit, from the Spirit will reap eternal life. ⁹Let us not become weary in doing good, for at the proper time we will reap a harvest if we do not give up. ¹⁰Therefore, as we have opportunity, let us do good to all people, especially to those who belong to the family of believers.

Not Circumcision but a New Creation ¹¹See what large letters I use as I write to you with my own hand!

¹²Those who want to make a good impression outwardly are trying to compel you to be circumcised. The only reason they do this is to avoid being persecuted for the cross of Christ. ¹³Not even those who are circumcised obey the law, yet they want you to be circumcised that they may boast about your flesh. ¹⁴May I never boast except in the cross of our Lord Jesus Christ, through which^b the world has been crucified to me, and I to the world. ¹⁵Neither circumcision nor uncircumcision means anything; what counts is a new creation. ¹⁶Peace and mercy to all who follow this rule, even to the Israel of God.

¹⁷Finally, let no one cause me trouble, for I bear on my body the marks of Jesus.

¹⁸The grace of our Lord Jesus Christ be with your spirit, brothers. Amen.

^a8 Or his flesh, from the flesh *^b14 Or whom*

Dear Sam,

Some Christians say AIDS is a punishment for immoral behavior. If someone gets AIDS from a blood transfusion, is God punishing that person?

Alex in Abilene

Dear Sam, Inc.

100 Advice Lane, Anywhere, USA

Dear Alex,

For many people AIDS is a natural consequence of their sinful behavior. Scripture speaks clearly about the homosexual lifestyle. Though many will tell you that homosexuality is a normal alternative lifestyle, God tells you it's a perversion. What people sow they will reap (Galatians 6:7-8).

If you stick your hand in a fire and it gets burned, is God punishing you? Or are you simply experiencing the natural consequences of your actions? Statistics show that those who engage in homosexual activities or do drugs with dirty needles or participate in promiscuous sex are at a very high risk for getting AIDS. They've knowingly put their hand in the fire. And they'll probably get burned.

But some people, like the person you mention, contract AIDS through no fault of their own. Sometimes terrible things happen to innocent people just because there is sin in the world. Since Adam and Eve sinned in the Garden of Eden, everyone has suffered due to circumstances beyond his or her control. Anyone can get burned accidentally. But when someone plays with fire, getting burned is that person's own fault.

Sam

Introduction

to the

book of **Ephesians**

LONELY.

Most of you will feel lonely at some time or other. You will have times when you're sure no one cares about you. And most of you realize you aren't strong enough to make it on your own. That's why God invented the church—not the building, but people who are family for you.

That's what Ephesians is all about. Before you were born, God knew you would be a member of his church. He gave you new life and made a place for you in his family. Ephesians shows you how to combat loneliness and how to find love and support in the family of God.

Fundamentals

You say you don't feel very special (Ephesians 1:1-14)?

Prejudiced? No, you're just not comfortable with people who are "different" (Ephesians 2:11-22).

Can your youth group be "family" (Ephesians 4:17–5:2)?

What do you do if your parents aren't fair? Obey them anyway (Ephesians 6:1-4)?

FAST FACTS

Ephesus was the fourth largest city in the Roman empire.

The temple of Artemis in Ephesus was one of the seven wonders of the ancient world.

The temple of Artemis was longer than a football field. Thousands of pilgrims came to worship in Ephesus each year.

Jesus' church is not a marble building. It's people who love. That's the real wonder of the world!

1 Paul, an apostle of Christ Jesus by the will of God,

To the saints in Ephesus,*a* the faithful*b* in Christ Jesus:

²Grace and peace to you from God our Father and the Lord Jesus Christ.

Spiritual Blessings in Christ ³Praise be to the God and Father of our Lord Jesus Christ, who has blessed us in the heavenly realms with every spiritual blessing in Christ. ⁴For he chose us in him before the creation of the world to be holy and blameless in his sight. In love ⁵he*c* predestined us to be adopted as his sons through Jesus Christ, in accordance with his pleasure and will— ⁶to the praise of his glorious grace, which he has freely given us in the One he loves. ⁷In him we have redemption through his blood, the forgiveness of sins, in accordance with the riches of God's grace ⁸that he lavished on us with all wisdom and understanding. ⁹And he*d* made known to us the mystery of his will according to his good pleasure, which he purposed in Christ, ¹⁰to be put into effect when the times will have reached their fulfillment—to bring all things in heaven and on earth together under one head, even Christ.

¹¹In him we were also chosen,*e* having been predestined according to the plan of him who works out everything in conformity with the purpose of his will, ¹²in order that we, who were the first to hope in Christ, might be for the praise of his glory. ¹³And you also were included in Christ when you heard the word of truth, the gospel of your salvation. Having believed, you were marked in him with a seal, the promised Holy Spirit, ¹⁴who is a deposit guaranteeing our inheritance until the redemption of those who are God's possession—to the praise of his glory.

Thanksgiving and Prayer ¹⁵For this reason, ever since I heard about your faith in the Lord Jesus and your love for all the saints, ¹⁶I have not stopped giving thanks for you, remembering you in my prayers. ¹⁷I keep asking that the God of our Lord Jesus Christ, the glorious Father, may give you the Spirit*f* of wisdom and revelation, so that you may know him better. ¹⁸I pray also that the eyes of your heart may be enlightened in order that you may know the hope to which he has called you, the riches of his glorious inheritance in the saints, ¹⁹and his incomparably great power for us who believe. That power is like the working of his mighty strength, ²⁰which he exerted in Christ when he raised him from the dead and seated him at his right hand in the heavenly realms, ²¹far above all rule and authority, power and dominion, and every title that can be given, not only in the present age but also in the one to come. ²²And God placed all things under his feet and appointed him to be head over everything for the church, ²³which is his body, the fullness of him who fills everything in every way.

2 *Made Alive in Christ* As for you, you were dead in your transgressions and sins, ²in which you used to live when you followed the ways of this world and of the ruler of the kingdom of the air, the spirit who is now at work in those who are disobedient. ³All of us also lived among them at one time, gratifying the cravings of our sinful nature*g* and following its desires and thoughts. Like the rest, we were by nature objects of wrath. ⁴But because of his great love for us, God, who is rich in mercy, ⁵made us alive with Christ even when we were dead in transgressions—it is by grace you have been saved. ⁶And God raised us up with Christ and seated us with him in the heavenly realms in Christ Jesus, ⁷in order that in the coming ages he might

---

a1 Some early manuscripts do not have in Ephesus. b1 Or believers who are c4,5 Or sight in love. 5He d8,9 Or us. With all wisdom and understanding, 9he e11 Or were made heirs f17 Or a spirit g3 Or our flesh

show the incomparable riches of his grace, expressed in his kindness to us in Christ Jesus. [8]For it is by grace you have been saved, through faith—and this not from yourselves, it is the gift of God— [9]not by works, so that no one can boast. [10]For we are God's workmanship, created in Christ Jesus to do good works, which God prepared in advance for us to do.

One in Christ [11]Therefore, remember that formerly you who are Gentiles by birth and called "uncircumcised" by those who call themselves "the circumcision" (that done in the body by the hands of men)— [12]remember that at that time you were separate from Christ, excluded from citizenship in Israel and foreigners to the covenants of the promise, without hope and without God in the world. [13]But now in Christ Jesus you who once were far away have been brought near through the blood of Christ.

[14]For he himself is our peace, who has made the two one and has destroyed the barrier, the dividing wall of hostility, [15]by abolishing in his flesh the law with its commandments and regulations. His purpose was to create in himself one new man out of the two, thus making peace, [16]and in this one body to reconcile both of them to God through the cross, by which he put to death their hostility. [17]He came and preached peace to you who were far away and peace to those who were near. [18]For through him we both have access to the Father by one Spirit.

[19]Consequently, you are no longer foreigners and aliens, but fellow citizens with God's people and members of God's household, [20]built on the foundation of the apostles and prophets, with Christ Jesus himself as the chief cornerstone. [21]In him the whole building is joined together and rises to become a holy temple in the Lord. [22]And in him you too are being built together to become a dwelling in which God lives by his Spirit.

3 *Paul the Preacher to the Gentiles* For this reason I, Paul, the prisoner of Christ Jesus for the sake of you Gentiles—

[2]Surely you have heard about the administration of God's grace that was given to me for you, [3]that is, the mystery made known to me by revelation, as I have already written briefly. [4]In reading this, then, you will be able to understand my insight into the mystery of Christ, [5]which was not made known to men in other generations as it has now been revealed by the Spirit to God's holy apostles and prophets. [6]This mystery is that through the gospel the Gentiles are heirs together with Israel, members together of one body, and sharers together in the promise in Christ Jesus.

[7]I became a servant of this gospel by the gift of God's grace given me through the working of his power. [8]Although I am less than the least of all God's people, this grace was given me: to preach to the Gentiles the unsearchable riches of Christ, [9]and to make plain to everyone the administration of this mystery, which for ages past was kept hidden in God, who created all things. [10]His intent was that now, through the church, the manifold wisdom of God should be made known to the rulers and authorities in the heavenly

Direct Line

EPHESIANS 2:11–22

You say, "I'm not prejudiced," but you also say, "I don't feel comfortable with people who are 'different.'" That was a real problem in the first century. Jews and Gentiles didn't feel comfortable with each other. In fact, history records riots between Jews and Gentiles in many cities of the Roman Empire during this period. The Bible says what counts now is "Christian"– not white, not poor, not black, not educated, not Methodist, not Catholic. It's hard to feel comfortable with others if you emphasize differences. But, if instead you focus on your mutual love for Jesus, the differences don't matter that much after all.

realms, ¹¹according to his eternal purpose which he accomplished in Christ Jesus our Lord. ¹²In him and through faith in him we may approach God with freedom and confidence. ¹³I ask you, therefore, not to be discouraged because of my sufferings for you, which are your glory.

A Prayer for the Ephesians   ¹⁴For this reason I kneel before the Father, ¹⁵from whom his whole family*ᵃ* in heaven and on earth derives its name. ¹⁶I pray that out of his glorious riches he may strengthen you with power through his Spirit in your inner being, ¹⁷so that Christ may dwell in your hearts through faith. And I pray that you, being rooted and established in love, ¹⁸may have power, together with all the saints, to grasp how wide and long and high and deep is the love of Christ, ¹⁹and to know this love that surpasses knowledge— that you may be filled to the measure of all the fullness of God.

²⁰Now to him who is able to do immeasurably more than all we ask or imagine, according to his power that is at work within us, ²¹to him be glory in the church and in Christ Jesus throughout all generations, for ever and ever! Amen.

> I pray that out of his glorious riches he may strengthen you with power through his Spirit (Ephesians 3:16).

Unity in the Body of Christ   As a prisoner for the Lord, then, I urge you to live a life worthy of the calling you have received. ²Be completely humble and gentle; be patient, bearing with one another in love. ³Make every effort to keep the unity of the Spirit through the bond of peace. ⁴There is one body and one Spirit— just as you were called to one hope when you were called— ⁵one Lord, one faith, one baptism; ⁶one God and Father of all, who is over all and through all and in all.

⁷But to each one of us grace has been given as Christ apportioned it. ⁸This is why it*ᵇ* says:

> "When he ascended on high,
>   he led captives in his train
>   and gave gifts to men."*ᶜ*

⁹(What does "he ascended" mean except that he also descended to the lower, earthly regions*ᵈ*? ¹⁰He who descended is the very one who ascended higher than all the heavens, in order to fill the whole universe.) ¹¹It was he who gave some to be apostles, some to be prophets, some to be evangelists, and some to be pastors and teachers, ¹²to prepare God's people for works of service, so that the body of Christ may be built up ¹³until we all reach unity in the faith and in the knowledge of the Son of God and become mature, attaining to the whole measure of the fullness of Christ.

¹⁴Then we will no longer be infants, tossed back and forth by the waves, and blown here and there by every wind of teaching and by the cunning and craftiness of men in their deceitful scheming. ¹⁵Instead, speaking the truth in love, we will in all things grow up into him who is the Head, that is, Christ. ¹⁶From him the whole body, joined and held together by every supporting ligament, grows and builds itself up in love, as each part does its work.

Living as Children of Light   ¹⁷So I tell you this, and insist on it in the Lord, that you must no longer live as the Gentiles do, in the futility of their thinking. ¹⁸They are darkened in their understanding and separated from the life of God because of the ignorance that is in them due to the hardening of their hearts. ¹⁹Having lost all sensitivity, they have given themselves over to sensuality so as to indulge in every kind of impurity, with a continual lust for more.

ᵃ15 Or *whom all fatherhood* *ᵇ8* Or *God* *ᶜ8* Psalm 68:18 *ᵈ9* Or *the depths of the earth*

Dear Sam,

Is it important to have close Christian fellowship?

Betsy in Belmont

100 Advice Lane, Anywhere, USA

Dear Betsy,

One of the great benefits of knowing and getting together with believers who love you is that they teach you who God is and how he loves you. The relationships you have with them will draw you closer to God and his love (Ephesians 3:14-19).

God and his love are reflected to you from those who are one with you in the Spirit. Whatever the circumstances in your life, you can experience encouragement through the love of fellow believers (Hebrews 10:25). When you get together with other believers, the fellowship you have can be a comfort to them and to you (2 Corinthians 1:3-5).

But none of this will happen if you don't get together.

Sam

²⁰You, however, did not come to know Christ that way. ²¹Surely you heard of him and were taught in him in accordance with the truth that is in Jesus. ²²You were taught, with regard to your former way of life, to put off your old self, which is being corrupted by its deceitful desires; ²³to be made new in the attitude of your minds; ²⁴and to put on the new self, created to be like God in true righteousness and holiness.

²⁵Therefore each of you must put off falsehood and speak truthfully to his neighbor, for we are all members of one body. ²⁶"In your anger do not sin"ᵃ: Do not let the sun go down while you are still angry, ²⁷and do not give the devil a foothold. ²⁸He who has been stealing must steal no longer, but must work, doing something useful with his own hands, that he may have something to share with those in need.

²⁹Do not let any unwholesome talk come out of your mouths, but only what is helpful for building others up according to their needs, that it may benefit those who listen. ³⁰And do not grieve the Holy Spirit of God, with whom you were sealed for the day of redemption. ³¹Get rid of all bitterness, rage and anger, brawling and slander, along with every form of malice. ³²Be kind and compassionate to one another, forgiving each other, just as in Christ God forgave you.

5 Be imitators of God, therefore, as dearly loved children ²and live a life of love, just as Christ loved us and gave himself up for us as a fragrant offering and sacrifice to God.

³But among you there must not be even a hint of sexual immorality, or of any kind of impurity, or of greed, because these are improper for God's holy people. ⁴Nor should there be obscenity, foolish talk or coarse joking, which are out of place, but rather thanksgiving. ⁵For of this you can be sure: No immoral, impure or greedy person—such a man is an idolater—has any inheritance in the kingdom of Christ and of God.ᵇ ⁶Let no one deceive you with empty words, for because of such things God's wrath comes on those who are disobedient. ⁷Therefore do not be partners with them.

⁸For you were once darkness, but now you are light in the Lord. Live as children of light ⁹(for the fruit of the light consists in all goodness, righteousness and truth) ¹⁰and find out what pleases the Lord. ¹¹Have nothing to do with the fruitless deeds of darkness, but rather expose them. ¹²For it is shameful even to mention what the disobedient do in secret. ¹³But everything exposed by the light becomes visible, ¹⁴for it is light that makes everything visible. This is why it is said:

> "Wake up, O sleeper,
>   rise from the dead,
>   and Christ will shine on you."

¹⁵Be very careful, then, how you live—not as unwise but as wise, ¹⁶making the most of every opportunity, because the days are evil. ¹⁷Therefore do not be foolish, but understand what the Lord's will is. ¹⁸Do not get drunk on wine, which leads to debauchery. Instead, be filled with the Spirit. ¹⁹Speak to one another with psalms, hymns and spiritual songs. Sing and make music in your heart to the Lord, ²⁰always giving thanks to God the Father for everything, in the name of our Lord Jesus Christ.

²¹Submit to one another out of reverence for Christ.

Wives and Husbands   ²²Wives, submit to your husbands as to the Lord. ²³For the husband is the head of the wife as Christ is the head of the church, his body, of which he is the Savior. ²⁴Now as the church submits to Christ, so also wives should submit to their husbands in everything.

ᵃ26 Psalm 4:4   ᵇ5 Or *kingdom of the Christ and God*

²⁵Husbands, love your wives, just as Christ loved the church and gave himself up for her ²⁶to make her holy, cleansing*a* her by the washing with water through the word, ²⁷and to present her to himself as a radiant church, without stain or wrinkle or any other blemish, but holy and blameless. ²⁸In this same way, husbands ought to love their wives as their own bodies. He who loves his wife loves himself. ²⁹After all, no one ever hated his own body, but he feeds and cares for it, just as Christ does the church— ³⁰for we are members of his body. ³¹"For this reason a man will leave his father and mother and be united to his wife, and the two will become one flesh."*b* ³²This is a profound mystery—but I am talking about Christ and the church. ³³However, each one of you also must love his wife as he loves himself, and the wife must respect her husband.

Children and Parents   Children, obey your parents in the Lord, for this is right. ²"Honor your father and mother"—which is the first commandment with a promise— ³"that it may go well with you and that you may enjoy long life on the earth."*c*

⁴Fathers, do not exasperate your children; instead, bring them up in the training and instruction of the Lord.

Slaves and Masters   ⁵Slaves, obey your earthly masters with respect and fear, and with sincerity of heart, just as you would obey Christ. ⁶Obey them not only to win their favor when their eye is on you, but like slaves of Christ, doing the will of God from your heart. ⁷Serve wholeheartedly, as if you were serving the Lord, not men, ⁸because you know that the Lord will reward everyone for whatever good he does, whether he is slave or free.

⁹And masters, treat your slaves in the same way. Do not threaten them, since you know that he who is both their Master and yours is in heaven, and there is no favoritism with him.

The Armor of God   ¹⁰Finally, be strong in the Lord and in his mighty power. ¹¹Put on the full armor of God so that you can take your stand against the devil's schemes. ¹²For our struggle is not against flesh and blood, but against the rulers, against the authorities, against the powers of this dark world and against the spiritual forces of evil in the heavenly realms. ¹³Therefore put on the full armor of God, so that when the day of evil comes, you may be able to stand your ground, and after you have done everything, to stand. ¹⁴Stand firm then, with the belt of truth buckled around your waist, with the breastplate of righteousness in place, ¹⁵and with your feet fitted with the readiness that comes from the gospel of peace. ¹⁶In addition to all this, take up the shield of faith, with which you can extinguish all the flaming arrows of the evil one. ¹⁷Take the helmet of salvation and the sword of the Spirit, which is the word of God. ¹⁸And pray in the Spirit on all occasions with all kinds of prayers and requests. With this in mind, be alert and always keep on praying for all the saints.

¹⁹Pray also for me, that whenever I open my mouth, words may be given me so

---

Direct Line

EPHESIANS 5:17–20

Debauchery. The sound of the word is almost as disgusting as its meaning: "orgies; extreme involvement in sensuality or sexual immorality." The Bible uses it only five times, four times in relation to sexual immorality and once, in this verse, in relation to drunkenness. Paul wants the Ephesian Christians to be filled with the Holy Spirit instead of wine. Sounds like good advice for today too. Drinking alcohol loosens inhibitions and leads to acts that you'd never consider when sober. Think about it. Is it worth the risk? No.

---

a26 Or having cleansed b31 Gen. 2:24 c3 Deut. 5:16

that I will fearlessly make known the mystery of the gospel, [20]for which I am an ambassador in chains. Pray that I may declare it fearlessly, as I should.

Final Greetings   [21]Tychicus, the dear brother and faithful servant in the Lord, will tell you everything, so that you also may know how I am and what I am doing. [22]I am sending him to you for this very purpose, that you may know how we are, and that he may encourage you.

[23]Peace to the brothers, and love with faith from God the Father and the Lord Jesus Christ. [24]Grace to all who love our Lord Jesus Christ with an undying love.

Philippians

BE HAPPY!

Most people want to have fun and be happy. The trouble is all those emotional ups and downs. You feel happy, and then something goes wrong and you're in the pits.

In Philippians the key words are joy and rejoice. Paul was in prison when he wrote this letter. He didn't have any of the things people today think will make them happy. But Paul knew the secret of an inner joy that won't quit when things go wrong. That's a secret worth knowing!

Fundamentals

Working together to serve Jesus is one source of joy (Philippians 1:3-11).

What does it mean to "be like Jesus" (Philippians 2:1-11)?

What is a good way to pick your friends (Philippians 3:17-21)?

Does the Bible say anything about books or movies or music (Philippians 4:8-9)?

FAST FACTS

Paul started the church in Philippi about A.D. 50 and wrote this letter in A.D. 61.

Many retired Roman soldiers lived in Philippi, and the city had special privileges as a Roman colony.

On his first visit to Philippi Paul was beaten and put in prison.

The words joy and rejoice are used 14 times in this short letter.